D0984586

The Holy Bible

INDULGENCES

Pope Leo XIII granted to the faithful who shall read for at least a quarter of an hour the books of the Sacred Scripture with the veneration due to the Divine Word and as spiritual reading, an indulgence of 300 days.

Preces et Pia Opera, 645.

The Holy Bible

Translated from the Latin Vulgate and diligently compared with the Hebrew, Greek and other editions in divers languages (The Old Testament was first published by the English College at Douay, A.D. 1609 and The New Testament was first published by the English College at Rheims, A.D. 1582.)

With notes by Bishop Challoner and also The Encyclical Letter "On the Study of the Holy Scriptures."

by

Pope Leo Xlll

and a Preface by

Rev. William H. McClellan, S.J.

Woodstock College, Md.

Also an Appendix containing an Historical and Chronological Index, a Table of References, Maps and other helpful matter.

Loreto Publications

Fitzwilliam, New Hampshire

2002

Nihil Obstat

Arthur J. Scanlan, S.T.D.
  Censor Librorum

Imprimatur

✠ Francis J. Spellman, D.D.
  Archbishop of New York

New York, February 3, 1941

ISBN:1-930278-24-1

PREFACE

THE Bible is a library within a single cover, and a library whose contents have no equal. Even if we did not know it as the Word of God, and judged it only by appearances, no other writing awakens keener interest, nor compares with it in influence for good. Although its earliest and its latest book were written fifteen centuries apart, a perfect harmony of thought and purpose unites the whole collection. Yet many different styles of writing serve this single cause. Popular narrative, solid reasoning, stirring oratory, joyous praise, homely piety, intimate and fervent prayer, are all to be found in the biblical writings, and clothed in poetry as well as prose. The Bible's subjects, too, are as varied as its literary forms. Commonplace history; dramatic stories of adventure, endurance and high achievement; words of true belief in things eternal, and rules of right conduct for this mortal life; practical prudence and spiritual counsel; stern reproof of vice, and inspiriting praise of virtue; hope and consolation surpassing all affliction; pictures of great characters, and, above all, the record of the only perfect life that history has ever known,—all these are in the matchless pages of the Bible.

The Old Testament preserves a divine revelation, given step by step through ages past, to prepare the world for its deliverance from error and sin. The New Testament records the fact of that deliverance through Jesus Christ our Lord, and the substance of the full and final revelation that is His. Thus the common aim of the Bible's writers has been to give their readers the true religion, not arranged in systematic order, but recorded in the setting of its earthly history.

The fact that the sacred writers have done this with such unrivalled power is not alone enough to prove the Bible's inspiration. This divine property, which no other writing shares, is not a mere effect of natural genius. In Catholic belief, biblical inspiration is nothing less than divine authorship, directly due to a special control of the Holy Spirit over the purpose and the understanding of every biblical writer. Such influence is a supernatural action of

God, of which no one but Himself could assure us. He has done so through the perpetual teaching of His Church. That the Scriptures are indeed inspired by God (2 Tim. 3, 16) is an article of Catholic Faith, given to the Church by Christ's Apostles as having been received from Him. It is to her divine tradition of Christ's revelation that the Church appeals, in her formal Councils and in her common teaching, as the source of her untarnished faith in the divine authority and perfect truth of Holy Scripture.

It is because of this belief that the Church warns her members away from the writings of men who have lost, even partly, the Christian truth and spirit. Bibles and biblical commentaries, to be lawful for Catholic readers, must bear the approval of a Bishop of the Church. But, owing again to the same belief, this caution against erring guides lives side by side with a constant purpose that the true and uncorrupted Scriptures should be known to all the faithful.

Hence the tireless industry of the Church's learned men in translating the Bible from tongue to tongue. The New Testament, first written in Greek, had been done into Latin within the second Christian century. So too had the Old Testament, taken from a Greek version made by pre-Christian Jews for their own use, and accepted by the early Church in eastern lands. The Latin of both Testaments was soon carefully revised, and became in turn the source from which translations continued to be made into the later languages of Catholic Europe. All of this took place long before the invention of printing, and involved the tedious labor of writing every word with pen and ink. Yet the work of translating and copying went steadily on through the Christian centuries, fulfilling the Church's steadfast purpose that her children of every nation should receive the message of the Bible in their own familiar speech.

Latin, the common medium of the learned world, had become the language of the Church's worship and doctrine. When the Council of Trent reaffirmed the Faith and revived the discipline of the Church amid the confusion of that age, its earliest sessions (in 1546) repeated the list of the Bible's books and the truth of their sacred authority. At the time there were different Latin versions known in Europe. To fix upon one of them as an authoritative standard, the Council gave its approbation to "the Vulgate," prepared late in the fourth century by Saint Jerome, the greatest biblical scholar of antiquity. The Council well knew that the Hebrew text of the Old Testament, and the Greek of the New, were older and nearer to the original writings than even the oldest Latin translations. It had no intention to make the Vulgate supersede the older manuscripts for purposes of study. But the Church's liturgy, her use of the pulpit, her theological writings and discussions were filled with biblical passages in Latin, and these must be kept to one form in which all could agree. It was with this aim that the Council fixed upon the Vulgate as the standard Latin Bible for purposes of common reference.

Hence it is that Catholic versions of the Scriptures in modern tongues are commonly taken from the Vulgate, and must be so if destined to any public use. For example, the English version of the Gospel which is read at every Sunday's Mass must be translated from the Vulgate, and not directly from the Greek. The same was true, in fact, of the first complete English Bible produced for Catholics after the invention of printing. Though intended quite as much for private as for public reading, it was taken direct from the Latin of the Vulgate. This was known as the Rheims-Douay Version, edited entire in 1610. It was succeeded in 1750 by the version of Bishop Challoner, which also went back to the same source. Although published as a revision of the Rheims-Douay, this version was really "little short of a new translation," as Cardinal Wiseman has publicly affirmed.

Most modern Catholics have never seen a copy of the Rheims-Douay Version. It is chiefly Challoner's revision that is still the model for our familiar Catholic Bibles in English. Such is the case with the issue herewith presented to American readers. One of the greatest values of Challoner's work has always lain in its footnotes, designed to clarify texts which may be somewhat obscure, or to explain those which have often been misinterpreted by religious prejudice. These notes are intended as a guide to private reading, and are actually of much assistance to the layman in studying his Bible in English.

Recent times have seen fresh emphasis laid upon the Church's encouragement of all her members to acquaint themselves with Holy Scripture. In 1898 Pope Leo XIII announced a grant of three hundred days' indulgence to all who devoutly read the Gospels for at least fifteen minutes, and a plenary indulgence for doing so every day for a month besides fulfilling the usual conditions of such an indulgence. In 1920 Pope Benedict XV, in his encyclical letter *Spiritus Paraclitus,* expressed the same attitude towards the reading of the Scriptures generally, though without any additional grant of indulgences. "Our one desire for all the Church's children," he writes in conclusion, "is that, being saturated with the Bible, they may arrive at the all-surpassing knowledge of Jesus Christ."

A marked response to these holy aspirations of the Supreme Pontiffs already shows itself among the faithful throughout America. It has even been felt that present conditions warrant the publication of an entirely new English translation of Holy Scripture. In the mean time, however, we face a large and ever growing demand for well printed copies of the entire Bible in the version already familiar to us. Every effort should clearly be made to meet this demand, and it is hoped that the edition here offered to American Catholics may assist in supplying it.

W. H. McClellan, S.J.

January 13, 1941.

ENCYCLICAL LETTER

(*PROVIDENTISSIMUS DEUS*)

OF OUR HOLY FATHER BY DIVINE PROVIDENCE

Pope Leo XIII

ON THE STUDY OF HOLY SCRIPTURE

TO OUR VENERABLE BRETHREN, ALL PATRI-ARCHS, PRIMATES, ARCHBISHOPS, AND BISHOPS OF THE CATHOLIC WORLD, IN GRACE AND COMMUNION WITH THE APOSTOLIC SEE.

Pope Leo XIII

VENERABLE BRETHREN, HEALTH AND APOSTOLIC BENEDICTION.

THE God of all Providence, Who in the adorable designs of His love at first elevated the human race to the participation of the Divine nature, and afterwards delivered it from universal guilt and ruin, restoring it to its primitive dignity, has in consequence bestowed upon man a splendid gift and safeguard—making known to him, by supernatural means, the hidden mysteries of His Divinity, His wisdom and His mercy. For although in Divine revelation there are contained some things which are not beyond the reach of unassisted reason, and which are made the objects of such revelation in order "that all may come to know them with facility, certainty, and safety from error, yet not on this account can supernatural Revelation be said to be absolutely necessary; it is only necessary because God has ordinated man to a supernatural end."[1] This supernatural revelation, according to the belief of the universal Church, is contained both in unwritten Tradition, and in written Books, which are therefore called sacred and canonical because, "being written under the inspiration of the Holy Ghost, they have God for their author and as such have been delivered to the Church."[2] This belief has been perpetually held and professed by the Church in regard to the Books of both Testaments; and there are well-known documents of the gravest kind, coming down to us from the earliest times, which proclaim that God, Who spoke first by the Prophets, then by His own mouth, and lastly by the Apostles, composed also the Canonical Scriptures,[3] and that these are His own oracles and words[4]—a Letter, written by our heavenly Father, and transmitted by the sacred writers to the human race in its pilgrimage so far from its heavenly country.[5] If, then, such and so great is the excellence and the dignity of the Scriptures, that God Himself has composed them, and that they treat of God's marvellous mysteries, counsels and works, it follows that the branch of sacred Theology which is concerned with the defence and elucidation of these divine Books must be excellent and useful in the highest degree.

Now We, who by the help of God, and not without fruit, have by frequent Letters and exhortation endeavoured to promote other branches of study which seemed capable of advancing the glory of God and contributing to the salvation of souls, have for a long time cherished the desire to give an impulse to the noble science of Holy Scripture, and to impart to Scripture study a direction suitable to the needs of the present day. The solicitude of the Apostolic office naturally urges, and even compels us, not only to desire that this grand source of Catholic revelation should be made safely and abundantly accessible to the flock of Jesus Christ, but also not to suffer any attempt to defile or corrupt it, either on the part of those who impiously and openly assail the Scriptures, or of those who are led astray into fallacious and imprudent novelties. We are not ignorant, indeed, Venerable Brethren, that there are not a few Catholics, men of talent and learning, who do devote themselves with ardour to the defence of the sacred writings and to making them better known and understood. But whilst giving to these the commendation they deserve, We cannot but earnestly exhort others also, from whose skill and piety and learning we have a right to expect good results, to give themselves to the same most praiseworthy work. It is Our wish and fervent desire to see an increase in the number of the approved and persevering labourers in the cause of Holy Scripture; and more especially that those whom Divine Grace has called to Holy Orders, should, day-by-day, as their state demands, display greater diligence and industry in reading, meditating, and explaining it.

Holy Scripture Most Profitable To Doctrine and Morality

Among the reasons for which the Holy Scripture is so worthy of commendation—in addition to its own excellence and to the homage which we owe to God's Word—the chief of all is, the innumerable benefits of which it is the source; according to the infallible testimony of the Holy Ghost Himself, who says: "All Scripture, inspired of God, is profitable to teach, to reprove, to correct, to instruct in justice, that the man of God may be perfect, furnished to every good work."[6] That such was the purpose of God in giving the Scripture to men is shown by the example of Christ our Lord and of His Apostles. For He Himself Who "obtained authority by miracles, merited belief by authority, and by belief drew to Himself the multitude"[7] was accustomed in the exercise of His Divine Mission, to appeal to the Scriptures. He uses them at times to prove that He is sent by God, and is God Himself. From them He cites instructions for His disciples and confirmation of His doctrine. He vindicates them from the calumnies of objectors; he quotes them against Sadducees and Pharisees, and retorts from them upon Satan himself when he dares to tempt Him. At the close of His life His utterances are from Holy Scripture, and it is the Scripture that He expounds to His disciples after His resurrection, until He ascends to the glory of His Father. Faithful to His precepts, the Apostles, although He Himself granted "signs and wonders to be done by their hands"[8] nevertheless used with the greatest effect the sacred writings, in order to persuade the nations everywhere of the wisdom of Christianity, to conquer the obstinacy of the Jews, and to suppress the outbreak of heresy. This is plainly seen in their discourses, especially in those of St. Peter: these were often little less than a series of citations from the Old Testament supporting in the strongest manner the new dispensation. We find the same thing in the Gospels of St. Matthew and St. John and in the Catholic Epistles; and most remarkably of all in the words of him who "boasts that he learned the law at the feet of Gamaliel, in order that, being armed with spiritual weapons, he might afterwards say with confidence, 'The arms of our warfare are not carnal but mighty unto God.'"[9] Let all, therefore, especially the novices of the ecclesiastical army, understand how deeply the sacred Books should be esteemed, and with what eagerness and reverence they should approach this great arsenal of heavenly arms. For those whose duty it is to handle Catholic doctrine before the learned or the unlearned will nowhere find more ample matter or more abundant exhortation, whether on the subject of God, the supreme Good and the all-perfect Being, or of the works which display His Glory and His love. Nowhere is there anything more full or more express on the subject of the Saviour of the world than is to be found in the whole range of the Bible. As St. Jerome says, "To be ignorant of the Scripture is not to know Christ."[10] In its pages His image stands out, living and breathing; diffusing everywhere around consolation in trouble, encouragement to virtue and attraction to the love of God. And as to the Church, her institutions, her nature, her office, and her gifts, we find in Holy Scripture so many references and so many ready and convincing arguments, that as St. Jerome again most truly says: "A man who is well grounded in the testimonies of the Scripture is the bulwark of the Church."[11] And if we come to morality and discipline, an apostolic man finds in the sacred writings abundant and excellent assistance; most holy precepts, gentle and strong exhortation, splendid examples of every virtue, and finally the promise of eternal reward and the threat of eternal punishment, uttered in terms of solemn import, in God's name and in God's own words.

And it is this peculiar and singular power of Holy Scripture, arising from the inspiration of the Holy Ghost, which gives authority to the sacred orator, fills him with apostolic liberty of speech, and communicates force and power to his eloquence. For those who infuse into their efforts the spirit and strength of the Word of God, speak "not in word only but in power also, and in the Holy Ghost, and in much fulness."[12] Hence those preachers are foolish and improvident who, in speaking of religion and proclaiming the things of God, use no words but those of human science and human prudence, trusting to their own reasonings rather than to those of God. Their discourses may be brilliant and fine, but they must be feeble and they must be cold, for they are without the fire of the utterance of God[13] and they must fall far short of that mighty power which the speech of God possesses: "for the Word of God is living and effectual, and more piercing than any two-edged sword; and reaching unto the division of the soul and the spirit."[14] But, indeed, all those who have a right to speak are agreed that there is in the Holy Scripture an eloquence that is wonderfully varied and rich, and worthy of great themes. This St. Augustine thoroughly understood and has abundantly set forth.[15] This also is confirmed by the best preachers of all ages, who have gratefully acknowledged that they owed their repute chiefly to the assiduous use of the Bible, and to devout meditation on its pages.

The Holy Fathers well knew all this by practical experience, and they never cease to extol the sacred Scripture and its fruits. In innumerable passages of their writings we find them applying to it such phrases as "an inexhaustible treasury of heavenly doctrine,"[16] or "an overflowing fountain of salvation,"[17] or putting it before us as fertile pastures and beautiful gardens in which the flock of the Lord is marvellously refreshed and delighted.[18] Let us listen to the words of St. Jerome, in his Epistle to Nepotian: "Often read the divine Scriptures; yea, let holy reading be always in thy hand; study that which thou thyself must preach. . . Let the speech of the priest be ever seasoned with Scriptural reading."[19] St. Gregory the Great, than whom no one has more admirably described the pastoral office, writes in the same sense: "Those," he says, "who are zealous in the work of preaching must never cease the study of the written word of God."[20] St. Augustine, however, warns us that "vainly does the preacher utter the Word of God exteriorly unless he listens to it interiorly;"[21] and St. Gregory instructs sacred orators "first to find in Holy Scripture the knowledge of themselves, and then to carry it to others, lest in reproving others they forget themselves."[22] Admonitions such as these had, indeed, been uttered long before by the Apostolic voice which had learnt its lesson from Christ Himself, Who "began to do and teach." It was not to Timothy alone, but to the whole order of the clergy, that the command was addressed: "Take heed to thyself and to doctrine; be earnest in them. For in doing this thou shall both save thyself and them that hear thee."[23] For the saving and for the perfection of ourselves and of others there is at hand the very best of help in the Holy Scriptures, as the Book of Psalms, among others, so constantly insists; but those only will find it who bring to this divine reading not only docility and attention, but also piety and an innocent life. For the Sacred Scripture is not like other books. Dictated by the Holy Ghost, it contains things of the deepest importance, which in many instances are most difficult and obscure. To understand and explain such things there is always required the "coming"[24] of the same Holy Spirit; that is to say, His light and His grace; and these, as the Royal Psalmist so frequently insists, are to be sought by humble prayer and guarded by holiness of life.

What the Bible Owes to the Catholic Church

It is in this that the watchful care of the Church shines forth conspicuously. By admirable laws and regulations, she has always shown herself solicitous that "the celestial treasure of the Sacred Books, so bountifully bestowed upon man by the Holy Spirit, should not lie neglected."[25] She has prescribed that a considerable portion of them shall be read and piously reflected upon by all her ministers in the daily office of the sacred psalmody. She has ordered that in Cathedral Churches, in monasteries, and in other convents in which study can conveniently be pursued, they shall be expounded and interpreted by capable men; and she has strictly commanded that her children shall be fed with the saving words of the Gospel at least on Sundays and solemn feasts.[26] Moreover, it is owing to the wisdom and exertions of the Church that there has always been continued from century to century that cultivation of Holy Scripture which has been so remarkable and has borne such ample fruit.

And here, in order to strengthen Our teaching and Our exhortations, it is well to recall how, from the beginning of Christianity, all who have been renowned for holiness of life and sacred learning have given their deep and constant attention to Holy Scripture. If we consider the immediate disciples of the Apostles, St. Clement of Rome, St. Ignatius of Antioch, St. Polycarp—or the apologists, such as St. Justin and St. Irenaeus, we find that in their letters and their books, whether in defence of the Catholic Faith or in its commendation, they draw faith, strength, and unction from the Word of God. When there arose, in various Sees, Catechetical and Theological schools, of which the most celebrated were those of Alexandria and of Antioch, there was little taught in those schools but what was contained in the reading, the interpretation and the defence of the divine written word. From them came forth numbers of Fathers and writers whose laborious studies and admirable writings have justly merited for the three following centuries the appellation of the golden age of biblical exegesis. In the Eastern Church, the greatest name of all is Origen—a man remarkable alike for penetration of genius and for persevering labour; from whose numerous works and his great *Hexapla* almost all have drawn that came after him. Others who have widened the field of this science may also be named, as especially eminent; thus, Alexandria could boast of St. Clement and St. Cyril; Palestine, of Eusebius and the other St. Cyril; Cappadocia, of St. Basil the Great and the two St. Gregories, of Nazianzus and Nyssa; Antioch, of St. John Chrysostom, in whom the science of Scripture was rivalled by the splendour of his eloquence. In the Western Church there were many names as great: Tertullian, St. Cyprian, St. Hilary, St. Ambrose, St. Leo the Great, St. Gregory the Great; most famous of all, St. Augustine and St. Jerome, of whom the former was so marvellously acute in penetrating the sense of God's Word and so fertile in the use that he made of it for the promotion of the Catholic truth, and the latter has received from the Church, by reason of his pre-eminent knowledge of Scripture and his labours in promoting its use, the name of the "great Doctor."[27] From this period down to the eleventh century, although Biblical studies did not flourish with the same vigour and the same fruitfulness as before, yet they did flourish, and principally by the instrumentality of the clergy. It was their care and solicitude that selected the best and most useful things that the ancients had left, arranged them in order, and published them with additions of their own—as did St. Isidore of Seville, Venerable Bede, and Alcuin, among the most prominent; it was they who illustrated the sacred pages with "glosses" or short commentaries, as we see in Walafrid Strabo and St. Anselm of Laon, or expended fresh labour in securing their integrity, as did St. Peter Damian and Blessed Lanfranc. In the twelfth century many took up with great success the allegorical exposition of Scripture. In this kind, St. Bernard is pre-eminent; and his writings, it may be said, are Scripture all through. With the age of the scholastics came fresh and welcome progress in the study of the Bible. That the scholastics were solicitous about the genuineness of the Latin version is evident from the *Correctoria Biblica,* or lists of emendations, which they have left. But they expended their labours and industry chiefly on interpretation and explanation. To them we owe the accurate and clear distinction, such as had not been given before, of the various senses of the sacred words; the assignment of the value of each "sense" in theology; the division of books into parts, and the summaries of the various parts; the investigation of the objects of the writers; the demonstration of the connection of sentence with sentence, and clause with clause; all of which is calculated to throw much light on the more obscure passages of the sacred volume. The valuable work of the scholastics in Holy Scripture is seen in their theological treatises and in their Scripture commentaries; and in this respect the greatest name among them all is St. Thomas of Aquin.

When our predecessor, Clement V., established chairs of Oriental literature in the Roman College and in the principal Universities of Europe, Catholics began to make more accurate investigation into the original text of the Bible, as well as of the Latin version. The revival amongst us of Greek learning, and, much more, the happy invention of the art of printing, gave a strong impetus to Biblical studies. In a brief space of time, innumerable editions, especially of the Vulgate, poured from the press and were diffused throughout the Catholic world; so honoured and loved was Holy Scripture during that very period against which the enemies of the Church direct their calumnies. Nor must we forget how many learned men there were, chiefly among the religious orders, who did excellent work for the Bible between the Council of Vienne and that of Trent; men who, by the employment of modern means and appliances, and by the tribute of their own genius and learning, not only added to the rich stores of ancient times, but prepared the way for the succeeding century, the century which followed the Council of Trent, when it almost seemed that the great age of the Fathers had returned. For it is well known, and We recall it with pleasure, that Our predecessors from Pius IV. to Clement VIII. caused to be prepared the celebrated editions of the Vulgate and the Septuagint, which, having been published by the command and authority of Sixtus V. and of the same Clement, are now in common use. At this time, moreover, were carefully brought out various other ancient versions of the Bible, and the Polyglots of Antwerp and of Paris, most important for the investigation of the true meaning of the text; nor is there any one Book of either Testament which did not find more than one expositor, nor any grave question which did not profitably exercise the ability of many inquirers, among whom there are not a few—more especially of those who made most use of the Fathers—who have acquired great reputation. From that time downwards the labour and solicitude of Catholics has never been wanting; for, as time went on, eminent scholars have carried on Biblical study with success, and have defended Holy Scripture against *rationalism* with the same weapons of philology and kindred sciences with which it had been attacked. The calm and fair consideration of what has been said will clearly show that the Church has never failed in taking due measures to bring the Scriptures within reach of her children, and that she has ever held fast and exercised profitably that guardianship conferred upon her by Almighty God for the protection and glory of His Holy Word; so that she has never required, nor does she now require, any stimulation from without.

How to Study Holy Scripture

We must now, Venerable Brethren, as our purpose demands, impart to you such counsels as seem best suited for carrying on successfully the study of Biblical science. But first it must be clearly understood whom we have to oppose and contend against, and what are their tactics and their arms. In earlier times the contest was chiefly with those who, relying on private judgment and repudiating the divine traditions and teaching office of the Church, held the Scriptures to be the one source of revelation and the final appeal in matters of Faith. Now, we have to meet the Rationalists, true children and inheritors of the older heretics, who, trusting in their turn to their own way of thinking, have rejected even the scraps and remnants of Christian belief which had been handed down to them. They deny that there is any such thing as revelation or inspiration, or Holy Scripture at all; they see, instead, only the forgeries and the falsehoods of men; they set down the Scripture narratives as stupid fables and lying stories: the prophecies and the oracles of God are to them either predictions made up after the event or forecasts formed by the light of nature; the miracles and the wonders of God's power are not what they are said to be, but the startling effects of natural law, or else mere tricks and myths; and the Apostolic Gospels and writings are not the work of the Apostles at all. These detestable errors, whereby they think they destroy the truth of the divine Books, are obtruded on the world as the peremptory pronouncements of a certain newly-invented "free science;" a science, however, which is so far from final that they are perpetually modifying and supplementing it. And there are some of them who, notwithstanding their impious opinions and utterances about God, and Christ, the Gospels and the rest of Holy Scripture, would fain be considered both theologians and Christians and men of the Gospel, and who attempt to disguise by such honourable names their rashness and their pride. To them we must add not a few professors of other sciences who approve their views and give them assistance, and are urged to attack the Bible by a similar intolerance of revelation. And it is deplorable to see these attacks growing every day more numerous and more severe. It is sometimes men of learning and judgment who are assailed; but these have little difficulty in defending themselves from evil consequences. The efforts and the arts of the enemy are chiefly directed against the more ignorant masses of the people. They diffuse their deadly poison by means of books, pamphlets, and newspapers; they spread it by addresses and by conversation; they are found everywhere; and *they are in possession of numerous schools, taken by violence from the Church,* in which, by ridicule and scurrilous jesting, they pervert the credulous and unformed minds of the young to the contempt of Holy Scripture. Should not these things, Venerable Brethren, stir up and set on fire the heart of every Pastor, so that to this "knowledge, falsely so called,"[28] may be opposed the ancient and true science which the Church, through the Apostles, has received from Christ, and that Holy Scripture may find the champions that are needed in so momentous a battle?

Let our first care, then be to see that in Seminaries and Academical institutions the study of Holy Scripture be placed on such a footing as its own importance and the circumstances of the time demand. With this view, the first thing which requires attention is the wise choice of Professors. Teachers of Sacred Scripture are not to be appointed at hap-hazard out of the crowd; but they must be men whose character and fitness are proved by their love of, and their long familiarity with, the Bible, and by suitable learning and study.

It is a matter of equal importance to provide in time for a continuous succession of such teachers; and it will be well, wherever this can be done, to select young men of good promise who have successfully accomplished their theological course, and to set them apart exclusively for Holy Scripture, affording them facilities for full and complete studies. Professors thus chosen and thus prepared may enter with confidence on the task that is appointed for them; and that they may carry out their work well and profitably, let them take heed to the instructions We now proceed to give.

At the commencement of a course of Holy Scripture let the Professor strive earnestly to form the judgment of the young beginners so as to train them equally to defend the sacred writings and to penetrate their meaning. This is the object of the treatise which is called "Introduction." Here the student is taught how to prove the integrity and authority of the Bible, how to investigate and ascertain its true sense, and how to meet and refute objections. It is needless to insist upon the importance of making these preliminary studies in an orderly and thorough fashion, with the accompaniment and assistance of Theology; for the whole subsequent course must rest on the foundation thus laid and make use of the light thus acquired. Next, the teacher will turn his earnest attention to that more fruitful division of Scripture science which has to do with Interpretation; wherein is imparted the method of using the word of God for the advantage of religion and piety. We recognize without hesitation that neither the extent of the matter nor the time at disposal allows each single Book of the Bible to be separately gone through. But the teaching should result in a definite and ascertained method of interpretation—and therefore the Professor should equally avoid the mistake of giving a mere taste of every Book, and of dwelling at too great length on a part of one Book. If most schools cannot do what is done in the large institutions—that is, take the students through the whole of one or two Books continuously and with a certain development—yet at least those parts which are selected should be treated with suitable fulness; in such a way that the students may learn from the sample that is thus put before them to love and use the remainder of the sacred Book during the whole of their lives. The Professor, following the tradition of antiquity, will make use of the Vulgate as his text; for the Council of Trent decreed that "in public lectures, disputations, preaching, and exposition,"[29] the Vulgate is the "authentic" version; and this is the existing custom of the Church. At the same time, the other versions which Christian antiquity has approved, should not be neglected, more especially the more ancient MSS. For although the meaning of the Hebrew and Greek is substantially rendered by the Vulgate, nevertheless wherever there may be ambiguity or want of clearness, the "examination of older tongues,"[30] to quote St. Augustine, will be useful and advantageous. But in this matter we need hardly say that the greatest prudence is required, for the "office of a commentator," as St. Jerome says, "is to set forth not what he himself would prefer, but what his author says."[31] The question of "readings" having been, when necessary, carefully discussed, the next thing is to investigate and expound the meaning. And the first counsel to be given is this: That the more our adversaries contend to the contrary, so much the more solicitously should we adhere to the received and approved canons of interpretation. Hence, whilst weighing the meanings of words, the connection of ideas, the parallelism of passages, and the like, we should by all means make use of such illustrations as can be drawn from apposite erudition of an external sort; but this should be done with caution, so as not to bestow on questions of this kind more labour and time than are spent on the Sacred Books themselves, and not to overload the minds of the students with a mass of information that will be rather a hindrance than a help.

Holy Scripture and Theology; Interpretation; the Fathers

The Professor may now safely pass on to the use of Scripture in matters of Theology. On this head it must be observed that in addition to the usual reasons which make ancient writings more or less difficult to understand, there are some which are peculiar to the Bible. For the language of the Bible is employed to express, under the inspiration of the Holy Ghost, many things which are beyond the power and scope of the reason of man—that is to say, divine mysteries and all that is related to them. There is sometimes in such passages a fulness and a hidden depth of meaning which the letter hardly expresses and which the laws of interpretation hardly warrant. Moreover, the literal sense itself frequently admits other senses, adapted to illustrate dogma or to confirm morality. Wherefore it must be recognized that the sacred writings are wrapt in a certain religious obscurity, and that no one can enter into their interior without a guide;[32] God so disposing, as the Holy Fathers commonly teach, in order that men may investigate them with greater ardour and earnestness, and that what is attained with difficulty may sink more deeply into the mind and heart; and, most of all, that they may understand that God has delivered the Holy Scriptures to the Church, and that in reading and making use of His Word, they must follow the Church as their guide and their teacher. St. Irenaeus long since laid down, that where the charismata of God were, there the truth was to be learnt, and that Holy Scripture was safely interpreted by those who had the Apostolic succession.[33] His teaching, and that of other Holy Fathers, is taken up by the Council of the Vatican, which, in renewing the decree of Trent declares its "mind" to be this—that "in things of faith and morals, belonging to the building up of Christian doctrine, that is to be considered the true sense of Holy Scripture which has been held and is held by our Holy Mother the Church, whose place it is to judge of the true sense and interpretation of the Scriptures; and therefore that it is permitted to no one to interpret Holy Scripture against such sense or also against the unanimous agreement of the Fathers."[34] By this most wise decree the Church by no means prevents or restrains the pursuit of Biblical science, but rather protects it from error, and largely assists its real progress. A wide field is still left open to the private student, in which his hermeneutical skill may display itself with signal effect and to the advantage of the Church. On the one hand, in those passages of Holy Scripture which have not as yet received a certain and definitive interpretation, such labours may, in the benignant providence of God, prepare for and bring to maturity the judgment of the Church; on the other, in passages already defined, the private student may do work equally valuable, either by setting them forth more clearly to the flock and more skillfully to scholars, or by defending them more powerfully from hostile attack. Wherefore the first and dearest object of the Catholic commentator should be to interpret those passages which have received an authentic interpretation either from the sacred writers themselves, under the inspiration of the Holy Ghost (as in many places of the New Testament), or from the Church, under the assistance of the same Holy Spirit, whether by her solemn judgment or her ordinary and universal magisterium[35]—to interpret these passages in that identical sense, and to prove, by all the resources of science, that sound hermeneutical laws admit of no other interpretation. In the other passages, the analogy of faith should be followed, and Catholic doctrine, as authoritatively proposed by the Church, should be held as the supreme law; for, seeing that the same God is the author both of the Sacred Books and of the doctrine committed to the Church, it is clearly impossible that any teaching can by legitimate means be extracted from the former, which shall in any respect be at variance with the latter. Hence it follows that all interpretation is foolish and false which either makes the sacred writers disagree one with another, or is opposed to the doctrine of the Church. The Professor of Holy Scripture, therefore, amongst other recommendations, must be well acquainted with the whole circle of Theology and deeply read in the commentaries of the Holy Fathers and Doctors, and other interpreters of mark.[36] This is inculcated by St. Jerome, and still more frequently by St. Augustine, who thus justly complains: "If there is no branch of teaching, however humble and easy to learn, which does not require a master, what can be a greater sign of rashness and pride than to refuse to study the Books of the divine mysteries by the help of those who have interpreted them?"[37] The other Fathers have said the same, and have confirmed it by their example, for they "endeavoured to acquire the understanding of the Holy Scriptures not by their own lights and ideas, but from the writings and authority of the ancients, who in their turn, as we know, received the rule of interpretation in direct line from the Apostles."[38] The Holy Fathers "to whom, after the Apostles, the Church owes its growth—who have planted, watered, built, governed, and cherished it,"[39] the Holy Fathers, We say, are of supreme authority, whenever they all interpret in one and the same manner any text of the Bible, as pertaining to the doctrine of faith or morals; for their unanimity clearly evinces that such interpretation has come down from the Apostles as a matter of Catholic faith. The opinion of the Fathers is also of very great weight when they treat of these matters in their capacity of doctors, unofficially; not only because they excel in their knowledge of revealed doctrine and in their acquaintance with many things which are useful in understanding the apostolic Books, but because they are men of eminent sanctity and of ardent zeal for the truth, on whom God has bestowed a more ample measure of His light. Wherefore the expositor should make it his duty to follow their footsteps with all reverence, and to use their labours with intelligent appreciation.

But he must not on that account consider that it is forbidden, when just cause exists, to push inquiry and exposition beyond what the Fathers have done; provided he carefully observes the rule so wisely laid down by St. Augustine—not to depart from the literal and obvious sense, except only where reason makes it untenable or necessity requires;[40] a rule to which it is the more necessary to adhere strictly in these times, when the thirst for novelty and unrestrained freedom of thought make the danger of error most real and proximate. Neither should those passages be neglected which the Fathers have understood in an allegorical or figurative sense, more especially when such interpretation is justified by the literal, and when it rests on the authority of many. For this method of interpretation has been received by the Church from the Apostles, and has been approved by her own practice, as the holy Liturgy attests; although it is true that the holy Fathers did not thereby pretend directly to demonstrate dogmas of faith, but used it as a means of promoting virtue and piety, such as, by their own experience, they knew to be most valuable. The authority of other Catholic interpreters is not so great; but the study of Scripture has always continued to advance in the Church, and, therefore, these commentaries also have their own honourable place, and are serviceable in many ways for the refutation of assailants and the explanation of difficulties. But it is most unbecoming to pass by, in ignorance or contempt, the excellent work which Catholics have left in abundance, and to have recourse to the works of non-Catholics—and to seek in them, to the detriment of sound doctrine and often to the peril of faith, the explanation of passages on which Catholics long ago have successfully employed their talent and their labour. For although the studies of non-Catholics, used with prudence, may sometimes be of use to the Catholic student, he should, nevertheless, bear well in mind—as the Fathers also teach in numerous passages[41]—that the sense of Holy Scripture can nowhere be found incorrupt outside of the Church, and cannot be expected to be found in writers who, being without the true faith, only gnaw the bark of the Sacred Scripture, and never attain its pith.

Most desirable is it, and most essential, that the whole teaching of Theology should be pervaded and animated by the use of the divine Word of God. This is what the Fathers and the greatest theologians of all ages have desired and reduced to practice. It was chiefly out of the Sacred Writings that they endeavoured to proclaim and establish the Articles of Faith and the truths therewith connected, and it was in them, together with divine Tradition, that they found the refutation of heretical error, and the reasonableness, the true meaning, and the mutual relation of the truths of Catholicism. Nor will any one wonder at this who considers that the Sacred Books hold such an eminent position among the sources of revelation that without their assiduous study and use, Theology cannot be placed on its true footing, or treated as its dignity demands. For although it is right and proper that students in academies and schools should be chiefly exercised in acquiring a scientific knowledge of dogma, by means of reasoning from the Articles of Faith to their consequences, according to the rules of approved and sound philosophy—nevertheless the judicious and instructed theologian will by no means pass by that method of doctrinal demonstration which draws its proof from the authority of the Bible; "for (Theology) does not receive her first principles from any other science, but immediately from God by revelation. And, therefore, she does not receive of other sciences as from a superior, but uses them as her inferiors or handmaids."[42] It is this view of doctrinal teaching which is laid down and recommended by the prince of theologians, St. Thomas of Aquin;[43] who, moreover, shows—such being the essential character of Christian Theology—how she can defend her own principles against attack: "If the adversary," he says, "do but grant any portion of the divine revelation, we have an argument against him; thus, against a heretic we can employ Scripture authority, and against those who deny one article, we can use another. But if our opponent reject divine revelation entirely, there is then no way left to prove the Article of Faith by reasoning; we can only solve the difficulties which are raised against them."[44] Care must be taken, then, that beginners approach the study of the Bible well prepared and furnished; otherwise, just hopes will be frustrated, or, perchance, what is worse, they will unthinkingly risk the danger of error, falling an easy prey to the sophisms and laboured erudition of the Rationalists. The best preparation will be a conscientious application to philosophy and theology under the guidance of St. Thomas of Aquin, and a thorough training therein—as We ourselves have elsewhere pointed out and directed. By this means, both in Biblical studies and in that part of Theology which is called *positive*, they will pursue the right path and make satisfactory progress.

The Authority of Holy Scripture; Modern Criticism; Physical Science

To prove, to expound, to illustrate Catholic Doctrine by the legitimate and skilful interpretation of the Bible, is much; but there is a second part of the subject of equal importance and equal difficulty—the maintenance in the strongest possible way of its full authority. This cannot be done completely or satisfactorily except by means of the living and proper *magisterium* of the Church. The Church, "by reason of her wonderful propagation, her distinguished sanctity and inexhaustible fecundity in good, her Catholic unity, and her unshaken stability, is herself a great and perpetual motive of credibility, and an unassailable testimony to her own Divine mission."[45] But since the divine and infallible *magisterium* of the Church rests also on the authority of Holy Scripture, the first thing to be done is to vindicate the trustworthiness of the sacred records at least as human documents, from which can be clearly proved, as from primitive and authentic testimony, the Divinity and the mission of Christ our Lord, the institution of a hierarchical Church and the primacy of Peter and his successors. It is most desirable, therefore, that there should be numerous members of the clergy well prepared to enter upon a contest of this nature, and to repulse hostile assaults, chiefly trusting in that armour of God recommended by the Apostle,[46] but also not unaccustomed to modern methods of attack. This is beautifully alluded to by St. John Chrysostom, when describing the duties of priests: "We must use every endeavour that the `Word of God may dwell in us abundantly'[47] and not merely for one kind of fight must we be prepared—for the contest is many-sided and the enemy is of every sort; and they do not all use the same weapons nor make their onset in the same way. Wherefore it is needful that the man who has to contend against all should be acquainted with the engines and the arts of all—that he should be at once archer and slinger, commandant and officer, general and private soldier, foot-soldier and horseman, skilled in sea-fight and in siege; for unless he knows every trick and turn of war, the devil is well able, if only a single door be left open, to get in his fierce bands and carry off the sheep."[48] The sophisms of the enemy and his manifold arts of attack we have already touched upon. Let us now say a word of advice on the means of defence. The first means is the study of the Oriental languages and of the art of criticism. These two acquirements are in these days held in high estimation, and therefore the clergy, by making themselves more or less fully acquainted with them as time and place may demand, will the better be able to discharge their office with becoming credit; for they must make themselves "all to all,"[49] always "ready to satisfy every one that asketh them a reason for the hope that is in them."[50] Hence it is most proper that Professors of Sacred Scripture and theologians should master those tongues in which the sacred Books were originally written; and it would be well that Church students also should cultivate them, more especially those who aspire to academic degrees. And endeavours should be made to establish in all academic institutions—as has already been laudably done in many—chairs of the other ancient languages, especially the Semitic, and of subjects connected therewith, for the benefit principally of those who are intended to profess sacred literature. These latter, with a similar object in view, should make themselves well and thoroughly acquainted with the art of true criticism. There has arisen, to the great detriment of religion, an inept method, dignified by the name of the "higher criticism," which pretends to judge of the origin, integrity and authority of each Book from internal indications alone. It is clear, on the other hand, that in historical questions, such as the origin and the handing down of writings, the witness of history is of primary importance, and that historical investigation should be made with the utmost care; and that in this matter internal evidence is seldom of great value, except as confirmation. To look upon it in any other light will be to open the door to many evil consequences. It will make the enemies of religion much more bold and confident in attacking and mangling the Sacred Books; and this vaunted "higher criticism" will resolve itself into the reflection of the bias and the prejudice of the critics. It will not throw on the Scripture the light which is sought, or prove of any advantage to doctrine; it will only give rise to disagreement and dissension, those sure notes of error, which the critics in question so plentifully exhibit in their own persons; and seeing that most of them are tainted with false philosophy and rationalism, it must lead to the elimination from the sacred writings of all prophecy and miracle, and of everything else that is outside the natural order.

In the second place, we have to contend against those who, making an evil use of physical science, minutely scrutinize the Sacred Book in order to detect the writers in a mistake, and to take occasion to vilify its contents. Attacks of this kind, bearing as they do on matters of sensible experience, are peculiarly dangerous to the masses, and also to the young who are beginning their literary studies; for the young, if they lose their reverence for the Holy Scripture on one or more points, are easily led to give up believing in it altogether. It need not be pointed out how the nature of science, just as it is so admirably adapted to show forth the glory of the Great Creator, provided it be taught as it should be, so if it be perversely imparted to the youthful intelligence, it may prove most fatal in destroying the principles of true philosophy and in the corruption of morality. Hence to the Professor of Sacred Scripture a knowledge of natural science will be of very great assistance in detecting such attacks on the Sacred Books, and in refuting them. There can never, indeed, be any real discrepancy between the theologian and the physicist, as long as each confines himself within his own lines, and both are careful, as St. Augustine warns us, "not to make rash assertions, or to assert what is not known as known."[51] If dissension should arise between them, here is the rule also laid down by St. Augustine, for the theologian: "Whatever they can really demonstrate to be true of physical nature, we must show to be capable of reconciliation with our Scriptures; and whatever they assert in their treatises which is contrary to these Scriptures of ours, that is to Catholic faith, we must either prove it as well as we can to be entirely false, or at all events we must, without the smallest hesitation, believe it to be so."[52] To understand how just is the rule here formulated we must remember, first, that the sacred writers, or to speak more accurately, the Holy Ghost "Who spoke by them, did not intend to teach men these things (that is to say, the essential nature of the things of the visible universe), things in no way profitable unto salvation."[53] Hence they did not seek to penetrate the secrets of nature, but rather described and dealt with things in more or less figurative language, or in terms which were commonly used at the time, and which in many instances are in daily use at this day, even by the most eminent men of science. Ordinary speech primarily and properly describes what comes under the senses; and somewhat in the same way the sacred writers—as the Angelic Doctor also reminds us—"went by what sensibly appeared,"[54] or put down what God, speaking to men, signified, in the way men could understand and were accustomed to.

The unshrinking defence of the Holy Scripture, however, does not require that we should equally uphold all the opinions which each of the Fathers or the more recent interpreters have put forth in explaining it; for it may be that, in commenting on passages where physical matters occur, they have sometimes expressed the ideas of their own times, and thus made statements which in these days have been abandoned as incorrect. Hence, in their interpretations, we must carefully note what they lay down as belonging to faith, or as intimately connected with faith—what they are unanimous in. For "in those things which do not come under the obligation of faith, the Saints were at liberty to hold divergent opinions, just as we ourselves are,"[55] according to the saying of St. Thomas. And in another place he says most admirably: "When philosophers are agreed upon a point, and it is not contrary to our faith, it is safer, in my opinion, neither to lay down such a point as a dogma of faith, even though it is perhaps so presented by the philosophers, nor to reject it as against faith, lest we thus give to the wise of this world an occasion of despising our faith."[56] The Catholic interpreter, although he should show that those facts of natural science which investigators affirm to be now quite certain are not contrary to the Scripture rightly explained, must nevertheless always bear in mind, that much which has been held and proved as certain has afterwards been called in question and rejected. And if writers on physics travel outside the boundaries of their own branch, and carry their erroneous teaching into the domain of philosophy, let them be handed over to philosophers for refutation.

Inspiration Incompatible with Error

The principles here laid down will apply to cognate sciences, and especially to history. It is a lamentable fact that there are many who with great labour carry out and publish investigations on the monuments of antiquity, the manners and institutions of nations and other illustrative subjects, and whose chief purpose in all this is too often to find mistakes in the sacred writings and so to shake and weaken their authority. Some of these writers display not only extreme hostility, but the greatest unfairness; in their eyes a profane book or ancient document is accepted without hesitation, whilst the Scripture, if they only find in it a suspicion of error, is set down with the slightest possible discussion as quite untrustworthy. It is true, no doubt, that copyists have made mistakes in the text of the Bible; this question, when it arises, should be carefully considered on its merits, and the fact not too easily admitted, but only in those passages where the proof is clear. It may also happen that the sense of a passage remains ambiguous, and in this case good hermeneutical methods will greatly assist in clearing up the obscurity. But it is absolutely wrong and forbidden, either to narrow inspiration to certain parts only of Holy Scripture, or to admit that the sacred writer has erred. For the system of those who, in order to rid themselves of these difficulties, do not hesitate to concede that divine inspiration regards the things of faith and morals, and nothing beyond, because (as they wrongly think) in a question of the truth or falsehood of a passage, we should consider not so much what God has said as the reason and purpose which He had in mind in saying it—this system cannot be tolerated. For all the books which the Church receives as sacred and canonical, are written wholly and entirely, with all their parts, at the dictation of the Holy Ghost; and so far is it from being possible that any error can co-exist with inspiration, that inspiration not only is essentially incompatible with error, but excludes and rejects it as absolutely and necessarily as it is impossible that God Himself, the supreme Truth, can utter that which is not true. This is the ancient and unchanging faith of the Church, solemnly defined in the Councils of Florence and of Trent, and finally confirmed and more expressly formulated by the Council of the Vatican. These are the words of the last:

"The Books of the Old and New Testament, whole and entire, with all their parts, as enumerated in the decree of the same Council (Trent) and in the ancient Latin Vulgate, are to be received as sacred and canonical. And the Church holds them as sacred and canonical, not because, having been composed by human industry, they were afterwards approved by her authority; nor only because they contain revelation without error; but because, having been written under the inspiration of the Holy Ghost, they have God for their author."[57] Hence, because the Holy Ghost employed men as His instruments, we cannot therefore say that it was these inspired instruments who, perchance, have fallen into error, and not the primary author. For, by supernatural power, He so moved and impelled them to write—He was so present to them—that the things which He ordered, and those only, they, first, rightly understood, then willed faithfully to write down, and finally expressed in apt words and with infallible truth. Otherwise, it could not be said that He was the Author of the entire Scripture. Such has always been the persuasion of the Fathers. "Therefore," says St. Augustine, "since they wrote the things which He showed and uttered to them, it cannot be pretended that He is not the writer; for His members executed what their Head dictated."[58] And St. Gregory the Great thus pronounces: "Most superfluous it is to inquire who wrote these things—we loyally believe the Holy Ghost to be the Author of the book. He wrote it Who dictated it for writing; He wrote it Who inspired its execution."[59]

It follows that those who maintain that an error is possible in any genuine passage of the sacred writings, either pervert the Catholic notion of inspiration, or make God the author of such error. And so emphatically were all the Fathers and Doctors agreed that the divine writings, as left by the hagiographers, are free from all error, that they laboured earnestly, with no less skill than reverence, to reconcile with each other those numerous passages which seem at variance—the very passages which in great measure have been taken up by the "higher criticism;" for they were unanimous in laying it down, that those writings, in their entirety and in all their parts were equally from the *afflatus* of Almighty God, and that God, speaking by the sacred writers, could not set down anything but what was true. The words of St. Augustine to St. Jerome may sum up what they taught: "On my part I confess to your charity that it is only to those Books of Scripture which are now called canonical that I have learned to pay such honour and reverence as to believe most firmly that none of their writers has fallen into any error. And if in these Books I meet anything which seems contrary to truth, I shall not hesitate to conclude either that the text is faulty, or that the translator has not expressed the meaning of the passage, or that I myself do not understand."[60]

But to undertake fully and perfectly, and with all the weapons of the best science, the defence of the Holy Bible is far more than can be looked for from the exertions of commentators and theologians alone. It is an enterprise in which we have a right to expect the co-operation of all those Catholics who have acquired reputation in any branch of learning whatever. As in the past, so at the present time, the Church is never without the graceful support of her accomplished children; may their services to the Faith grow and increase! For there is nothing which We believe to be more needful than that truth should find defenders more powerful and more numerous than the enemies it has to face; nor is there anything which is better calculated to impress the masses with respect for truth than to see it boldly proclaimed by learned and distinguished men. Moreover, the bitter tongues of objectors will be silenced, or at least they will not dare to insist so shamelessly that faith is the enemy of science, when they see that scientific men of eminence in their profession show towards faith the most marked honour and respect. Seeing, then, that those can do so much for the advantage of religion on whom the goodness of Almighty God has bestowed, together with the grace of the faith, great natural talent, let such men, in this bitter conflict of which the Holy Scripture is the object, select each of them the branch of study most suitable to his circumstances, and endeavour to excel therein, and thus be prepared to repulse with credit and distinction the assaults on the Word of God. And it is Our pleasing duty to give deserved praise to a work which certain Catholics have taken up—that is to say, the formation of societies and the contribution of considerable sums of money, for the purpose of supplying studious and learned men with every kind of help and assistance in carrying out complete studies. Truly an excellent fashion of investing money, and well-suited to the times in which we live! The less hope of public patronage there is for Catholic study, the more ready and the more abundant should be the liberality of private persons—those to whom God has given riches thus willingly making use of their means to safeguard the treasure of His revealed doctrine.

Summary

In order that all these endeavours and exertions may really prove advantageous to the cause of the Bible, let scholars keep steadfastly to the principles which We have in this Letter laid down. Let them loyally hold that God, the Creator and Ruler of all things, is also the Author of the Scriptures—and that therefore nothing can be proved either by physical science or archaeology which can really contradict the Scriptures. If, then, apparent contradiction be met with, every effort should be made to remove it. Judicious theologians and commentators should be consulted as to what is the true or most probable meaning of the passage in discussion, and the hostile arguments should be carefully weighed. Even if the difficulty is after all not cleared up and the discrepancy seems to remain, the contest must not be abandoned; truth cannot contradict truth, and we may be sure that some mistake has been made either in the interpretation of the sacred words, or in the polemical discussion itself; and if no such mistake can be detected, we must then suspend judgment for the time being. There have been objections without number perseveringly directed against the Scripture for many a long year, which have been proved to be futile and are now never heard of; and not unfrequently interpretations have been placed on certain passages of Scripture (not belonging to the rule of faith or morals) which have been rectified by more careful investigations. As time goes on, mistaken views die and disappear; but "truth remaineth and groweth stronger for ever and ever."[61] Wherefore, as no one should be so presumptuous as to think that he understands the whole of the

Scripture, in which St. Augustine himself confessed that there was more that he did not know, than that he knew,[62] so, if he should come upon anything that seems incapable of solution, he must take to heart the cautious rule of the same holy Doctor: "It is better even to be oppressed by unknown but useful signs, than to interpret them uselessly and thus to throw off the yoke only to be caught in the trap of error."[63]

As to those who pursue the subsidiary studies of which We have spoken, if they honestly and modestly follow the counsels we have given—if by their pen and their voice they make their studies profitable against the enemies of the truth, and useful in saving the young from the loss of their faith—they may justly congratulate themselves on their worthy service of the Sacred Writings, and on affording to Catholicism that assistance which the Church has a right to expect from the piety and learning of her children.

Such, Venerable Brethren, are the admonitions and the instructions which, by the help of God, We have thought it well, at the present moment, to offer to you on the study of Holy Scripture. It will now be your province to see that what we have said be observed and put in practice with all due reverence and exactness; that so, we may prove our gratitude to God for the communication to man of the Words of his Wisdom, and that all the good results so much to be desired may be realized, especially as they affect the training of the students of the Church, which is our own great solicitude and the Church's hope. Exert yourselves with willing alacrity, and use your authority and your persuasion in order that these studies may be held in just regard and may flourish, in Seminaries and in the educational Institutions which are under your jurisdiction. Let them flourish in completeness and in happy success, under the direction of the Church, in accordance with the salutary teaching and example of the Holy Fathers and the laudable traditions of antiquity; and, as time goes on, let them be widened and extended as the interests and glory of truth may require—the interest of that Catholic Truth which comes from above, the never-failing source of man's salvation. Finally, We admonish with paternal love all students and ministers of the Church always to approach the Sacred Writings with reverence and piety; for it is impossible to attain to the profitable understanding thereof unless the arrogance of "earthly" science be laid aside, and there be excited in the heart the holy desire for that wisdom "which is from above." In this way the intelligence which is once admitted to these sacred studies, and thereby illuminated and strengthened, will acquire a marvellous facility in detecting and avoiding the fallacies of human science, and in gathering and using for eternal salvation all that is valuable and precious; whilst at the same time the heart will grow warm, and will strive with ardent longing to advance in virtue and in divine love. "Blessed are they who examine His testimonies; they shall seek Him with their whole heart."[64]

And now, filled with hope in the divine assistance, and trusting to your pastoral solicitude—as a pledge of heavenly grace and a sign of Our special goodwill—to you all, and to the Clergy and the whole flock entrusted to you, We lovingly impart in Our Lord the Apostolic Benediction.

Given at St. Peter's, at Rome, the 18th day of November, 1893, the eighteenth year of Our Pontificate.

1. Conc. Vac. sess. iii. cap. ii. de revel.
2. Ibid.
3. S. Aug. *de civ.* dei xi., 3.
4. S. Clem. Rom. I ad. Cor. 45; S. Polycarp. *ad Phil.* 7; S. Iren. *c haer.* ii. 28, 2.
5. S. Chrys. in Gen. hom. 2, 2; S. Aug. *in Ps.* xxx., *serm.*, 2, I; S. Greg. M. *ad Theod. ep.* iv., 31.
6. 2 *Tim.* iii., 16-17.
7. S. Aug. *de util. cred.* xiv. 32.
8. *Act* xiv., 3.
9. St. Hieron. *de stud. Script. ad. Paulin.* ep. liii. 3.
10. *In Isiam Prol.*
11. *In Isaiam* liv., 12.
12. *Thess.* i., 5.
13. *Jerem.* xxiii., 29.
14. *Hebr.* iv., 12.
15. *De doctr. Chr.* iv., 6, 7.
16. S. Chrys. *in Gen.* Hom. xxi., 2; Hom. lx., 3; S. Aug. *de Disc. Chrisc.*, ii.
17. S. Athan. *ep. fest.* xxxix.
18. S. Aug. *serm.* xxvi., 24; S. Ambr. in Ps. cxviii., *serm.* xix, 2.
19. S. Hier. *de vita cleric.* ad Nepot.
20. S. Greg. M., *Regul.* past. ii., II (al. 22); *Moral.* xviii., 26 (a1.14).
21. S. Aug. *serm.* clxxix., I.
22. S. Greg. M. *Regul. past.*, iii., 24 (al. 48).
23. i *Tim.* iv., 16.
24. S. Hier. *in Mic.* i., 10.
25. Conc. Trid. sess. v. *decret. de reform*, I.
26. *Ibid.* 1-2.
27. See the Collect on his feast, September 30.
28. I *Tim.* vi., 20.
29. Sess. iv., decr. *de edit. et usu sacr. libror.*
30. *De door. chr.* iii., 4.
31. *Ad Pammachium.*
32. S. Hier. *ad Paulin. de studio Script.* ep. liii., 4.
33. *C. haer.* iv., 26, 5.
34. *Sess. iii., cap. ii., de revel.; cf.* Conc. Trid, *sess. iv. decret de edit. et usu sacr. libror.*
35. Conc. Vat. *sess. iii., cap. ii., de fide.*
36. *Ibid.* 6, 7.
37. *Ad Honorat. de util. cred.* xvii., 35.
38. Rufinus *His2 eccl.* ii., 9.
39. S. Aug. *c. Julian.* ii, 10, 37.
40. *De Gen. ad lift.* I, viii., c. 7, 13.
41. Cfr. Clem. Alex. *Strom.* vii., 16; Orig. *de print.* iv., 8; in *Levit. hom.* 4, 8; Tertull. *de praescr.* 15, *seqq.; S. Hilar.* Pict. *in Matth.* 13, I.
42. S. Greg. M. Moral xx., 9 (al. II).
43. *Summ. theol.* p. i., q. i., a. 5 ad 2.
44. *Ibid.* a. 8.
45. Conc. Vat. *sess. iii., c. iii. de fide.*
46. Eph. vi., 13, seqq.
47. Cfr., *Coloss.* iii., 16.
48. *De sacerdotio* iv., 4.
49. I *Cor.* ix., 22.
50. I *Peter* iii., 15.
51. *In Gen. op. imperf.* ix., 30.
52. *De Gen. ad lift.* i. 21, 41.
53. S. Aug. *ib.* ii., 9, 20.
54. *Summa theol.* p. I, q. lxx., a. I, ad 3.
55. *In Sent. ii., Dist. q.* i., a. 3.
56. *Opusc.* x.
57. *Sess. iii., c. ii., de Rev.*
58. *De consensu Evangel.* 1. I, c. 35.
59. *Praef. in Job, n.* 2.
60. *Ep.* lxxxii., i. *et crebrius alibi.*
61. 3 *Esdr.* iv., 38.
62. *ad Ianuar.* ep. lv., 21.
63. *De Doctr.* chr. iii., 9, 18.
64. *Ps.* xviii., 2.

CONTENTS

THE NAMES OF THE BOOKS OF THE OLD AND NEW TESTAMENTS ARRANGED IN THEIR ORDER WITH NUMBER OF CHAPTERS AND PAGE REFERENCES

The Old Testament

The New Testament

A List of the Books of
The Old and New Testaments
In Alphabetical Order With Page References

The Old Testament

The New Testament

ABBREVIATIONS OF THE NAMES OF
THE BOOKS OF THE BIBLE USED IN THIS EDITION

The Old Testament

ABDIAS, *Abd.*
AGGEUS, *Agg.*
AMOS, *Amos*
BARUCH, *Bar.*
CANTICLE OF CANTICLES, *Cant.*
DANIEL, *Dan.*
DEUTERONOMY, *Deut.*
ECCLESIASTES, *Eccles.*
ECCLESIASTICUS, *Ecclus.*
ESDRAS, *1 Esd., 2 Esd.*
ESTHER, *Esth.*
EXODUS, *Exod.*
EZECHIEL, *Ezech.*
GENESIS, *Gen.*
HABACUC, *Hab.*
ISAIAS, *Isai.*
JEREMIAS, *Jer.*
JOB, *Job*
JOEL, *Joel*
JONAS, *Jonas*

JOSUE, *Jos.*
JUDGES, *Judges*
JUDITH, *Judith*
KINGS, *1, 2, 3, 4 Kings*
LAMENTATIONS, *Lam.*
LEVITICUS, *Lev.*
MACHABEES, *1 Mach., 2 Mach.*
MALACHIAS, *Mal.*
MICHEAS, *Mich.*
NAHUM, *Nah.*
NUMBERS, *Num.*
OSEE, *Osee*
PARALIPOMENON, *1 Par., 2 Par.*
PROVERBS, *Prov.*
PSALMS, *Ps.*
RUTH, *Ruth*
SOPHONIAS, *Soph.*
TOBIAS, *Tob.*
WISDOM, *Wisd.*
ZACHARIAS, *Zach.*

The New Testament

ACTS OF THE APOSTLES, THE, *Acts*
APOCALYPSE, *Apoc.*
COLOSSIANS, *Col.*
CORINTHIANS, *1 Cor., 2 Cor.*
EPHESIANS, *Eph.*
GALATIANS, *Gal.*
HEBREWS, *Heb.*
JAMES, ST., *Jas.*
JOHN, ST., *John; 1, 2, 3 John*
JUDE, ST., *Jude*

LUKE, ST., *Luke*
MARK, ST., *Mark*
MATTHEW, ST., *Matt.*
PETER, ST., *1, 2 Pet.*
PHILEMON, *Philemon*
PHILIPPIANS, *Phil.*
ROMANS, *Rom.*
THESSALONIANS, *1, 2 Thess.*
TIMOTHY, *1, 2 Tim.*
TITUS, *Tit.*

The Old Testament

Prayers

PRAYER BEFORE READING THE HOLY SCRIPTURES.

O KING of Glory, Lord of Hosts, Who didst triumphantly ascend the heavens, leave us not as orphans, but send us the Promised of the Father, the Spirit of Truth. We implore Thee, O Lord, that the Consoler, Who proceedeth from Thee, will enlighten our souls and infuse into them all truth, as Thy Son hath promised.

O God, Father of our Lord Jesus Christ, vouchsafe to grant us, according to the riches of Thy glory that Christ by faith may dwell in our hearts, which rooted and grounded in charity, may acknowledge the love of Christ, surpassing all knowledge. Through the same Christ our Lord. Amen.

(Ephes. III., 14, 17, 19.)

PRAYER AFTER READING THE HOLY SCRIPTURES.

(Prayer of St. Bede the Venerable. Died 735)

LET me not, O Lord, be puffed up with worldly wisdom, which passes away, but grant me that love which never abates, that I may not choose to know anything among men, but Jesus, and Him crucified.

(I Cor. XIII., 8; II., 2).

I beg Thee, dear Jesus, that he upon whom Thou hast graciously bestowed the sweet savor of the words of Thy Knowledge, may also possess Thee, Fount of all Wisdom, and shine forever before Thy countenance. Amen.

THE OLD TESTAMENT

THE BOOK OF

GENESIS

This book is so called from its treating of the GENERATION, *that is, of the creation and the beginning of the world. The Hebrews call it* BERESITH, *from the Word with which it begins. It contains not only the history of the Creation of the world; but also an account of its progress until the death of* Joseph.

CHAPTER 1

God createth Heaven and Earth, and all things therein, in six days.

IN the beginning God created ¹ heaven, and earth.

2 And the earth was void and empty, and darkness was upon the face of the deep. And the spirit of God moved over the waters.

3 And God said: ² Be light made. And light was made.

4 And God saw the light that it was good; and he divided the light from the darkness.

5 And he called the light Day, and the darkness Night. And there was evening and morning one day.

6 And God said: Let there be a firmament made amidst the waters: and let it divide the waters from the waters.

7 And ³ God made a firmament, and divided the waters that were under the firmament, from those that were above the firmament. And it was so.

8 And God called the firmament Heaven. And the evening and morning were the second day.

9 God also said: Let the waters that are under the heaven, be gathered together into one place, and let the dry land appear. And it was so done.

10 And God called the dry land ⁴ Earth; and the gathering together of

¹ Ps. 32, 6; 135, 5; Ecclus. 18, 1; Acts. 14, 14; 17, 24. ² Heb. 11, 3. ³ Ps. 135, 5; 148, 4; Jer. 10, 12; 51, 15. ⁴ Job. 38, 4; Ps. 32, 7; 88, 12; 135, 6. ⁵ Ps. 135, 7.

CHAP. 1. Ver. 6. *A firmament.* By this name is here understood the whole space between the earth, and the highest stars, the lower part of which divideth the waters that are upon the earth from those that are above in the clouds.

Ver. 16. *Two great lights.* God created on the first day, *light,* which being moved from east to west, by its rising and setting, made morning and evening. But on the fourth day he ordered and distributed this light, and made the sun, moon, and stars. The moon, though much less than the stars, is here called a *great light,* from its giving a far greater light to the earth than any of them.

the waters, he called Seas. And God saw that it was good.

11 And he said: Let the earth bring forth the green herb, and such as may yield seed, and the fruit tree yielding fruit after its kind, which may have seed in itself upon the earth. And it was so done.

12 And the earth brought forth the green herb, and such as yieldeth seed according to its kind, and the tree that beareth fruit, having seed each one according to its kind. And God saw that it was good.

13 And the evening and the morning were the third day.

14 And God said: Let there be lights made in the firmament of heaven, to divide the day and the night, ⁵ and let them be for signs, and for seasons, and for days and years:

15 To shine in the firmament of heaven, and to give light upon the earth. And it was so done.

16 And God made two great lights: a greater light to rule the day: and a lesser light to rule the night: and the stars.

17 And he set them in the firmament of heaven to shine upon the earth.

18 And to rule the day and the night, and to divide the light and the darkness. And God saw that it was good.

19 And the evening and morning were the fourth day.

20 God also said: Let the waters bring forth the creeping creature having life, and the fowl that may fly over the earth under the firmament of heaven.

21 And God created the great whales, and every living and moving creature, which the waters brought forth, according to their kinds, and every winged fowl according to its kind. And God saw that it was good.

22 And he blessed them, saying: Increase and multiply, and fill the waters of the sea; and let the birds be multiplied upon the earth.

23 And the evening and the morning were the fifth day.

24 And God said: Let the earth bring forth the living creature in its kind, cattle and creeping things, and beasts of the earth, according to their kinds. And it was so done.

25 And God made the beasts of the earth according to their kinds, and cattle, and every thing that creepeth on the earth after its kind. And God saw that it was good.

26 And he said: ⁶Let us make man to our image and likeness; and let him have dominion over the fishes of the sea, and the fowls of the air, and the beasts, and the whole earth, and every creeping creature that moveth upon the earth.

27 And God created man to his own image; ⁷to the image of God he created him. Male and female he created them.⁸

28 And God blessed them, saying: ⁹Increase and multiply, and fill the earth, and subdue it, and rule over the fishes of the sea, and the fowls of the air, and all living creatures that move upon the earth.

29 And God said: Behold I have given you every herb bearing seed upon the earth, and all trees that have in themselves seed of their own kind, to be your meat: ¹⁰

30 And to all beasts of the earth, and to every fowl of the air, and to all that move upon the earth, and wherein there is life, that they may have to feed upon. And it was so done.

31 ¹¹ And God saw all the things that he had made, and they were very good. And the evening and morning were the sixth day.

CHAPTER 2

God resteth on the seventh day and blesseth it. The earthly paradise, in which God placeth man. He commandeth him not to eat of the tree of knowledge. And formeth a woman of his rib.

SO the heavens and the earth were finished, and all the furniture of them.

2 And on the seventh day God ended his work which he had made: ¹and he rested on the seventh day from all his work which he had done.

3 And he blessed the seventh day, and sanctified it: because in it he had rested from all his work which God created and made.

4 These are the generations of the heaven and the earth, when they were created, in the day that the Lord God made the heaven and the earth:

5 And every plant of the field before it sprung up in the earth, and every herb of the ground before it grew: for the Lord God had not rained upon the earth and there was not a man to till the earth.

6 But a spring rose out of the earth, watering all the surface of the earth.

7 And the Lord God formed man of the slime of the earth, and breathed into his face the breath of life; and man became a living soul.²

8 And the Lord God had planted a paradise of pleasure from the beginning: wherein he placed man whom he had formed.

9 And the Lord God brought forth of the ground all manner of trees, fair to behold, and pleasant to eat of: the tree of life also in the midst of paradise: and the tree of knowledge of good and evil.

10 And a river went out of the place of pleasure to water paradise, which from thence is divided into four heads.

11 ³ The name of the one is Phison: that is it which compasseth all the land of Hevilath, where gold groweth.

12 And the gold of that land is very good: there is found bdellium, and the onyx stone.

13 And the name of the second river is Gehon: the same is it that compasseth all the land of Ethiopia.

14 And the name of the third river is Tigris: the same passeth along by the Assyrians. And the fourth river is Euphrates.

15 And the Lord God took man, and put him into the paradise of pleasure, to dress it, and to keep it.

16 And he commanded him, saying: Of every tree of paradise thou shalt eat:

17 But of the tree of knowledge of good and evil, thou shalt not eat. For

⁶ Gen. 5, 1; 9, 6; 1 Cor. 11, 7; Col. 3, 10. ⁷ Wisd. 2, 23; Ecclus. 17, 1. ⁸ Matt. 19, 4. ⁹ Gen. 8, 17; 9, 1. ¹⁰ Gen. 9, 3. ¹¹ Ecclus. 39, 21; Mark, 7, 37. CHAP. 2, ¹ Exod. 20, 11; 31, 17; Deut. 5, 14; Heb. 4, 4. ² 1 Cor. 15, 45. ³ Ecclus. 24, 35.

Ver. 26. *Let us make man to our image.* This *image* of God in man, is not in the body, but in the soul; which is a *spiritual* substance, endued with understanding and free will. God speaketh here in the plural number, to insinuate the plurality of *persons* in the Deity.

Ver. 28. *Increase and multiply.* This is not a precept, as some Protestant controvertists would have it, but a blessing, rendering them fruitful; for God had said the same words to the *fishes,* and *birds,* (ver. 22) who were incapable of receiving a precept.

CHAP. 2. Ver. 2. *He rested.* That is, he ceased to make or create any new kinds of things. Though, as our Lord tells us (John 5, 17), *He still worketh,* viz., by conserving and governing all things, and creating souls.

Ver. 9. *The tree of life.* So called because it had that quality, that by eating of the fruit of it, man would have been preserved in a constant state of health, vigour, and strength, and would not have died at all. *The tree of knowledge.* To which the deceitful serpent falsely attributed the power of imparting a superior kind of knowledge, beyond that which God was pleased to give.

in what day soever thou shalt eat of it, thou shalt die the death.

18 And the Lord God said: It is not good for man to be alone; let us make him a help like unto himself.

19 And the Lord God having formed out of the ground all the beasts of the earth, and all the fowls of the air, brought them to Adam to see what he would call them [1]: for whatsoever Adam called any living creature the same is its name.

20 And Adam called all the beasts by their names, and all the fowls of the air, and all the cattle of the field: but for Adam there was not found a helper like himself.

21 Then the Lord God cast a deep sleep upon Adam: and when he was fast asleep, he took one of his ribs, and filled up flesh for it.

22 And the Lord God built the rib which he took from Adam into a woman: and brought her to Adam.

23 And Adam said: [5] This now is bone of my bones, and flesh of my flesh; she shall be called woman, because she was taken out of man.

24 [6] Wherefore a man shall leave father and mother, and shall cleave to his wife: [7] and they shall be two in one flesh.

25 And they were both naked, to wit, Adam and his wife: and were not ashamed.

CHAPTER 3

The serpent's craft. The fall of our first parents. Their punishment. The promise of a Redeemer.

NOW the serpent was more subtle than any of the beasts of the earth which the Lord God had made. And he said to the woman: Why hath God commanded you, that you should not eat of every tree of paradise?

2 And the woman answered him, *saying:* Of the fruit of the trees that are in paradise we do eat:

[4] Ps. 146, 4. [5] 1 Cor. 11, 9; Eph. 5, 31. [6] Matt. 19, 5; Mark 10, 7. [7] 1 Cor. 6, 16. CHAP. 3. [1] 2 Cor. 11, 3. [2] Ecclus. 25, 33; 1 Tim. 2, 14. [3] Isai. 49, 23; 65, 25; Mich. 7, 17; Ps. 72, 9. [4] Apoc. 12, 1; Gen. 49, 17; 1 Cor. 14, 34.

CHAP. 3. Ver. 7. *Were opened.* Not that they were blind before, (for *the woman saw that the tree was fair to the eyes,* ver. 6) nor yet that their eyes were opened to any more perfect knowledge of good; but only to the unhappy experience of having lost the *good* of original grace and innocence, and incurred the dreadful *evil* of sin. From whence followed a shame of their being naked; which they minded not before; because being now stript of original grace, they quickly began to be subject to the shameful rebellions of the flesh.

Ver. 15. *She shall crush. Ipsa,* the woman; so divers of the fathers read this place, conformably to the Latin: others read it *ipsum,* that is, the seed. The sense is the same: for it is by her seed, *Jesus Christ,* that the woman crushes the serpent's head.

3 But of the fruit of the tree which is in the midst of paradise, God hath commanded us that we should not eat; and that we should not touch it, lest perhaps we die.

4 And the serpent said to the woman: [1] No, you shall not die the death.

5 For God doth know that in what day soever you shall eat thereof, your eyes shall be opened: and you shall be as Gods, knowing good and evil.

6 And the woman saw that the tree was good to eat, and fair to the eyes, and delightful to behold: [2] and she took of the fruit thereof, and did eat, and gave to her husband who did eat.

7 And the eyes of them both were opened: and when they perceived themselves to be naked, they sewed together fig leaves, and made themselves aprons.

8 And when they heard the voice of the Lord God walking in paradise at the afternoon air, Adam and his wife hid themselves from the face of the Lord God, amidst the trees of paradise.

9 And the Lord God called Adam, and said to him: Where art thou?

10 And he said: I heard thy voice in paradise and I was afraid, because I was naked, and I hid myself.

11 And he said to him: And who hath told thee that thou wast naked, but that thou hast eaten of the tree whereof I commanded thee that thou shouldst not eat?

12 And Adam said: The woman, whom thou gavest me to be my companion, gave me of the tree, and I did eat.

13 And the Lord God said to the woman: Why hast thou done this? And she answered: The serpent deceived me, and I did eat.

14 And the Lord God said to the serpent: Because thou hast done this thing, thou art cursed among all cattle, and beasts of the earth. Upon thy breast shalt thou go,[3] and earth shalt thou eat all the days of thy life.

15 I will put enmities between thee and the woman, and thy seed and her seed: she shall crush thy head, and thou shalt lie in wait for her heel.[4]

16 To the woman also he said: I will multiply thy sorrows, and thy conceptions. In sorrow shalt thou bring forth children, and thou shalt be under thy husband's power, and he shall have dominion over thee.

17 And to Adam he said: Because thou hast hearkened to the voice of thy wife, and hast eaten of the tree, whereof I commanded thee that thou shouldst not eat, cursed is the earth in thy work; with labour and toil shalt thou eat thereof all the days of thy life.

18 Thorns and thistles shall it bring

forth to thee; and thou shalt eat the herbs of the earth.

19 In the sweat of thy face shalt thou eat bread till thou return to the earth, out of which thou wast taken: for dust thou art, and into dust thou shalt return.[5]

20 And Adam called the name of his wife Eve: because she was the mother of all the living.

21 And the Lord God made for Adam and his wife garments of skins, and clothed them.

22 And he said: Behold Adam is become as one of us, knowing good and evil: now, therefore, lest perhaps he put forth his hand, and take also of the tree of life, and eat, and live for ever.

23 And the Lord God sent him out of the paradise of pleasure, to till the earth from which he was taken.

24 And he cast out Adam; and placed before the paradise of pleasure Cherubims, and a flaming sword, turning every way, to keep the way of the tree of life.

CHAPTER 4

The history of Cain and Abel.

AND Adam knew Eve his wife: who conceived and brought forth Cain, saying: I have gotten a man through God.

2 And again she brought forth his brother Abel. And Abel was a shepherd, and Cain a husbandman.

3 And it came to pass after many days, that Cain offered, of the fruits of the earth, gifts to the Lord.

4 [1] Abel also offered of the firstlings of his flock, and of their fat: and the Lord had respect to Abel, and to his offerings.

5 But to Cain and his offerings he had no respect: and Cain was exceedingly angry, and his countenance fell.

6 And the Lord said to him: Why art thou angry? And why is thy countenance fallen?

7 If thou do well, shalt thou not receive? But if ill, shall not sin forthwith be present at the door? But the lust thereof shall be under thee, and thou shalt have dominion over it.

8 And Cain said to Abel his brother: Let us go forth abroad. And when they were in the field, Cain rose up against his brother Abel, and slew him.[2]

9 And the Lord said to Cain: Where is thy brother Abel? And he answered: I know not. Am I my brother's keeper?

10 And he said to him: What hast thou done? The voice of thy brother's blood crieth to me from the earth.

11 Now, therefore, cursed shalt thou be upon the earth, which hath opened her mouth, and received the blood of thy brother at thy hand.

12 When thou shalt till it, it shall not yield to thee its fruit: a fugitive and a vagabond shalt thou be upon the earth.

13 And Cain said to the Lord: My iniquity is greater than that I may deserve pardon.

14 Behold thou dost cast me out this day from the face of the earth, and I shall be hidden from thy face, and I shall be a vagabond and a fugitive on the earth: every one, therefore, that findeth me, shall kill me.

15 And the Lord said to him: No, it shall not be so: but whosoever shall kill Cain, shall be punished sevenfold. And the Lord set a mark upon Cain, that whosoever found him should not kill him.

16 And Cain went out from the face of the Lord, and dwelt as a fugitive on the earth, at the east side of Eden.

17 And Cain knew his wife, and she conceived, and brought forth Henoch: and he built a city, and called the name thereof by the name of his son Henoch.

18 And Henoch begot Irad; and Irad begot Maviael, and Maviael begot Mathusael; and Mathusael begot Lamech.

19 Who took two wives: the name of the one was Ada, and the name of the other Sella.

20 And Ada brought forth Jabel: who was the father of such as dwell in tents, and of herdsmen.

5 Gen. 18, 27; Ps. 102, 14; 22, 6; Ecclus. 7, 12. Chap. 4. 1 Heb. 11, 4. 2 Wisd. 10, 3; Matt. 23, 35; 1 John, 3, 12; Jude, 5, 11.

Ver. 22. *Behold Adam.* This was spoken by way of reproaching him with his pride, in affecting a knowledge that might make him like to God.

Chap. 4. Ver. 4. *Had respect.* That is, shewed his acceptance of his sacrifice (as coming from a heart full of devotion); and that, as we may suppose, by some visible token, such as sending fire from heaven upon his offerings.

Ver. 14. *Every one that findeth me shall kill me.* His guilty conscience made him fear his own brothers and nephews; of whom, by this time, there might be a good number upon the earth; which had now endured near one hundred and thirty years; as may be gathered from Gen. 5, 3, compared with Gen. 4, 25, though in the compendious account given in the scriptures, only Cain and Abel are mentioned.

Ver. 15. *Set a mark.* The more common opinion of the interpreters of holy writ supposes this mark to have been a trembling of the body; or a horror and consternation in his countenance.

Ver. 17. *His wife.* She was a daughter of Adam, and Cain's own sister; God dispensing with such marriages in the beginning of the world, as mankind could not otherwise be propagated. He *built a city,* viz., In process of time, when his race was multiplied, so as to be numerous enough to people it. For in the many hundred years he lived, his race might be multiplied even to millions.

21 And his brother's name was Jubal; he was the father of them that play upon the harp and the organs.

22 Sella also brought forth Tubalcain, who was a hammerer and artificer in every work of brass and iron. And the sister of Tubalcain was Noema.

23 And Lamech said to his wives, Ada and Sella: Hear my voice, ye wives of Lamech, hearken to my speech: for I have slain a man to the wounding of myself, and a stripling to my own bruising.

24 Sevenfold vengeance shall be taken for Cain: but for Lamech seventy times sevenfold.[3]

25 Adam also knew his wife again; and she brought forth a son, and called his name Seth, saying: God hath given me another seed, for Abel whom Cain slew.

26 But to Seth also was born a son, whom he called Enos: this man began to call upon the name of the Lord.

CHAPTER 5

The genealogy, age, and death of the Patriarchs, from Adam to Noe. The translation of Henoch.

THIS is the book of the generation of Adam. In the day that God created man, [1] he made him to the likeness of God.

2 He created them male and female; and blessed them; and called their name Adam, in the day when they were created.

3 [1] And Adam lived a hundred and thirty years, and begot a son to his own image and likeness, and called his name Seth.

4 And the days of Adam, after he begot Seth, were eight hundred years: and he begot sons and daughters.

5 And all the time that Adam lived came to nine hundred and thirty years: and he died.

6 Seth also lived a hundred and five years, and begot Enos.[2]

7 And Seth lived after he begot Enos, eight hundred and seven years, and begot sons and daughters.

8 And all the days of Seth were nine hundred and twelve years: and he died.

9 And Enos lived ninety years, and begot Cainan.

10 After whose birth he lived eight hundred and fifteen years, and begot sons and daughters.

11 And all the days of Enos were nine hundred and five years: and he died.

12 And Cainan lived seventy years, and begot Malaleel.

13 And Cainan lived after he begot Malaleel, eight hundred and forty years, and begot sons and daughters.

14 And all the days of Cainan were nine hundred and ten years: and he died.

15 And Malaleel lived sixty-five years, and begot Jared.

16 And Malaleel lived after he begot Jared, eight hundred and thirty years, and begot sons and daughters.

17 And all the days of Malaleel were eight hundred and ninety-five years: and he died.

18 And Jared lived a hundred and sixty-two years, and begot Henoch.

19 And Jared lived after he begot Henoch, eight hundred years, and begot sons and daughters.

20 And all the days of Jared were nine hundred and sixty-two years: and he died.

21 And Henoch lived sixty-five years, and begot Mathusala.

22 And Henoch walked with God: and lived after he begot Mathusala, three hundred years, and begot sons and daughters.

23 And all the days of Henoch were three hundred and sixty-five years.

24 And he walked with God, and was seen no more: because God took him.

25 And Mathusala lived a hundred and eighty-seven years, and begot Lamech.

26 And Mathusala lived after he begot Lamech, seven hundred and eighty-two years, and begot sons and daughters.

27 And all the days of Mathusala were nine hundred and sixty-nine years: and he died.

28 And Lamech lived a hundred and eighty-two years, and begot a son.

29 And he called his name Noe, saying: This same shall comfort us from the works and labours of our hands on the earth, which the Lord hath cursed.

30 And Lamech lived after he begot Noe, five hundred and ninety-five years, and begot sons and daughters.

31 And all the days of Lamech came to seven hundred and seventy-seven years: and he died. And Noe, when he was five hundred years old begot Sem, Cham, and Japheth.

---

[0] Matt. 18, 22. CHAP. 5. [1] Wisd. 2, 23; Ecclus. 17, 1; Gen. 9, 6. [2] 1 Par. 1.

Ver. 23. *I have slain a man.* It is the tradition of the Hebrews, that Lamech in hunting slew Cain, mistaking him for a wild beast; and that having discovered what he had done, he beat so unmercifully the youth, by whom he was led into that mistake, that he died of the blows.

Ver. 26. *Began to call upon.* Not that Adam and Seth had not called upon God, before the birth of Enos; but that Enos used more solemnity in the worship and invocation of God.

CHAPTER 6

Man's sin is the cause of the deluge. Noe is commanded to build the ark.

AND after that men began to be multiplied upon the earth, and daughters were born to them,

2 The sons of God seeing the daughters of men, that they were fair, took to themselves wives of all which they chose.

3 And God said: My spirit shall not remain in man for ever, because he is flesh; and his days shall be a hundred and twenty years.

4 Now giants were upon the earth in those days. For after the sons of God went in to the daughters of men, and they brought forth children, these are the mighty men of old, men of renown.[1]

5 And God seeing that the wickedness of men was great on the earth, and that all the thought of their heart was bent upon evil at all times.[2]

6 It repented him that he had made man on the earth. And being touched inwardly with sorrow of heart,

7 He said: I will destroy man, whom I have created, from the face of the earth, from man even to beasts, from the creeping thing even to the fowls of the air; for it repenteth me that I have made them.

8 But Noe found grace before the Lord.

9 These are the generations of Noe.[3] Noe was a just and perfect man in his generations; he walked with God.

10 And he begot three sons, Sem, Cham, and Japheth.

11 And the earth was corrupted before God, and was filled with iniquity.

12 And when God had seen that the earth was corrupted (for all flesh had corrupted its way upon the earth),

13 He said to Noe: The end of all flesh is come before me; the earth is filled with iniquity through them; and I will destroy them with the earth.[4]

14 Make thee an ark of timber planks: thou shalt make little rooms in the ark, and thou shalt pitch it within and without.

15 And thus shalt thou make it: The length of the ark shall be three hundred cubits; the breadth of it fifty cubits; and the height of it thirty cubits.

16 Thou shalt make a window in the ark, and in a cubit shalt thou finish the top of it; and the door of the ark thou shalt set in the side; with lower, middle chambers, and third stories shalt thou make it.

17 Behold I will bring the waters of a great flood upon the earth, to destroy all flesh, wherein is the breath of life, under heaven. All things that are in the earth shall be consumed.

18 And I will establish my covenant with thee, and thou shalt enter into the ark: thou and thy sons, and thy wife, and the wives of thy sons with thee.

19 And of every living creature of all flesh, thou shalt bring two of a sort into the ark, that they may live with thee: of the male sex, and the female.

20 Of fowls according to their kind, and of beasts in their kind, and of every thing that creepeth on the earth according to its kind; two of every sort shall go in with thee, that they may live.

21 Thou shalt take unto thee of all food that may be eaten, and thou shalt lay it up with thee: and it shall be food for thee and them.

22 And Noe did all things which God commanded him.

CHAPTER 7

Noe with his family go into the ark. The deluge overflows the earth.

AND the Lord said to him: Go in thou and all thy house into the

CHAP. 6. [1] Bar. 3, 26; Amos. 2, 9; Wisd. 14, 6; Ecclus. 16, 8. [2] Gen. 8, 21; Matt. 15, 19. [3] Ecclus. 44, 17. [4] 1 Peter, 3, 20; 2 Peter, 2, 5.

CHAP. 6. Ver. 2. *The sons of God.* The descendants of Seth and Enos are here called *sons of God* from their religion and piety: whereas the ungodly race of Cain, who by their carnal affections lay grovelling upon the earth, are called the children of men. The unhappy consequence of the former marrying with the latter, ought to be a warning to Christians to be very circumspect in their marriages; and not to suffer themselves to be determined in their choice by their carnal passion, to the prejudice of virtue or religion.

Ver. 3. *His days shall be.* The meaning is, that man's days, which before the flood were usually nine hundred years, should now be reduced to one hundred and twenty years. Or rather, that God would allow men this term of one hundred and twenty years, for their repentance and conversion, before he would send the deluge.

Ver. 4. *Giants.* It is likely the generality of men before the flood were of a gigantic stature in comparison with what men now are. But these here spoken of are called *giants*, as being not only tall in stature, but violent and savage in their dispositions, and mere monsters of cruelty and lust.

Ver. 6. *It repented him.* God, who is unchangeable, is not capable of repentance, grief, or any other passion. But these expressions are used to declare the enormity of the sins of men, which was so provoking as to determine their Creator to destroy these his creatures, whom before he had so much favoured.

Ver. 15. *Three hundred cubits.* The ark, according to the dimensions here set down, contained four hundred and fifty thousand square cubits; which was more than enough to contain all the kinds of living creatures, with all necessary provisions: even supposing the cubits here spoken of to have been only a foot and a half each, which was the least kind of cubits.

ark; for thee I have seen just before me in this generation.[1]

2 Of all clean beasts take seven and seven, the male and the female.

3 But of the beasts that are unclean two and two, the male and the female. Of the fowls also of the air seven and seven, the male and the female: that seed may be saved upon the face of the whole earth.

4 For yet a while, and after seven days, I will rain upon the earth forty days and forty nights; and I will destroy every substance that I have made, from the face of the earth.

5 And Noe did all things which the Lord had commanded him.

6 And he was six hundred years old, when the waters of the flood overflowed the earth.

7 [2] And Noe went in, and his sons, his wife and the wives of his sons with him, into the ark, because of the waters of the flood.

8 And of beasts clean and unclean, and of fowls, and of every thing that moveth upon the earth,

9 Two and two went in to Noe into the ark, male and female: as the Lord had commanded Noe.

10 And after the seven days were passed, the waters of the flood overflowed the earth.

11 In the six hundredth year of the life of Noe, in the second month, in the seventeenth day of the month, all the fountains of the great deep were broken up, and the flood gates of heaven were opened:

12 And the rain fell upon the earth forty days and forty nights.

13 In the selfsame day, Noe, and Sem, and Cham, and Japheth his sons: his wife, and the three wives of his sons with them, went into the ark:

14 They and every beast according to its kind, and all the cattle in their kind, and every thing that moveth upon the earth according to its kind, and every fowl according to its kind, all birds, and all that fly,

15 Went in to Noe into the ark, two and two, of all flesh wherein was the breath of life.

16 And they that went in, went in male and female of all flesh, as God had

commanded him: and the Lord shut him in on the outside.

17 And the flood was forty days upon the earth, and the waters increased, and lifted up the ark on high from the earth.

18 For they overflowed exceedingly: and filled all on the face of the earth: and the ark was carried upon the waters.

19 And the waters prevailed beyond measure upon the earth: and all the high mountains under the whole heaven were covered.

20 The water was fifteen cubits higher than the mountains which it covered.

21 [3] And all flesh was destroyed that moved upon the earth, both of fowl, and of cattle, and of beasts, and of all creeping things that creep upon the earth: and all men.

22 And all things wherein there is the breath of life on the earth, died.

23 And he destroyed all the substance that was upon the earth, from man even to beast, and the creeping things and fowls of the air; and they were destroyed from the earth. And Noe only remained, and they that were with him in the ark.

24 And the waters prevailed upon the earth a hundred and fifty days.

CHAPTER 8

The deluge ceaseth. Noe goeth out of the ark, and offereth a sacrifice. God's covenant to him.

AND God remembered Noe, and all the living creatures, and all the cattle which were with him in the ark: and brought a wind upon the earth, and the waters were abated.

2 The fountains also of the deep, and the flood gates of heaven were shut up: and the rain from heaven was restrained.

3 And the waters returned from off the earth going and coming: and they began to be abated after a hundred and fifty days.

4 And the ark rested in the seventh month, the seven and twentieth day of the month, upon the mountains of Armenia.

5 And the waters were going and decreasing until the tenth month: for in the tenth month, the first day of the month, the tops of the mountains appeared.

6 And after that forty days were passed, Noe, opening the window of the ark which he had made, sent forth a raven:

7 Which went forth and did not return, till the waters were dried up upon the earth.

8 He sent forth also a dove after him,

CHAP. 7. [1] Heb. 11, 7; 2 Peter. 2, 5. [2] Matt. 24, 37; Luke, 17, 26; 1 Peter. 3, 20. [3] Wisd. 10, 4; Ecclus. 29, 28; 1 Peter, 3, 20.

CHAP. 7. Ver. 2. *Of all clean.* The distinction of clean and unclean beasts appears to have been made before the law of Moses.

CHAP. 8. Ver. 7. *Did not return.* The raven did not return into the ark; but (as it may be gathered from the Hebrew) *went to and fro;* sometimes going to the mountains, where it found carcasses to feed on; and other times returning, to rest upon the top of the ark.

to see if the waters had now ceased upon the face of the earth.

9 But she, not finding where her foot might rest, returned to him into the ark: for the waters were upon the whole earth: and he put forth his hand, and caught her, and brought her into the ark.

10 And having waited yet seven other days, he again sent forth the dove out of the ark.

11 And she came to him in the evening, carrying a bough of an olive tree with green leaves, in her mouth. Noe therefore understood that the waters were ceased upon the earth.

12 And he stayed yet other seven days: and he sent forth the dove, which returned not any more unto him.

13 Therefore in the six hundredth and first year, the first month, the first day of the month, the waters were lessened upon the earth. And Noe opening the covering of the ark, looked, and saw that the face of the earth was dried.

14 In the second month, the seven and twentieth day of the month, the earth was dried.

15 And God spoke to Noe, saying:

16 Go out of the ark, thou and thy wife, thy sons, and the wives of thy sons with thee.

17 All living things that are with thee of all flesh, as well in fowls as in beasts, and all creeping things that creep upon the earth, bring out with thee, and go ye upon the earth: ¹ increase and multiply upon it.

18 So Noe went out, he and his sons: his wife, and the wives of his sons with him.

19 And all living things, and cattle, and creeping things that creep upon the earth, according to their kinds, went out of the ark.

20 And Noe built an altar unto the Lord: and taking of all cattle and fowls that were clean, offered holocausts upon the altar.

21 And the Lord smelled a sweet savour, and said: I will no more curse the earth for the sake of man: ² for the imagination and thought of man's heart are prone to evil from his youth: therefore I will no more destroy every living soul as I have done.

22 All the days of the earth, seed-time and harvest, cold and heat, summer and winter, night and day, shall not cease.

CHAPTER 9

God blesseth Noe: forbiddeth blood, and promiseth never more to destroy the world by water. The blessing of Sem and Japheth.

AND God blessed Noe and his sons. And he said to them: ¹ Increase and multiply, and fill the earth.

2 And let the fear and dread of you be upon all the beasts of the earth, and upon all the fowls of the air, and all that move upon the earth: all the fishes of the sea are delivered into your hand.

3 And every thing that moveth and liveth shall be meat for you: even as the green herbs have I delivered them all to you: ²

4 Saving that flesh with blood you shall not eat.³

5 For I will require the blood of your lives at the hand of every beast, and at the hand of man. At the hand of every man, and of his brother, will I require the life of man.

6 ⁴ Whosoever shall shed man's blood, his blood shall be shed: for man was made to the image of God.⁵

7 ⁶ But increase you and multiply: and go upon the earth, and fill it.

8 Thus also said God to Noe, and to his sons with him:

9 Behold, I will establish my covenant with you, and with your seed after you.

10 And with every living soul that is with you, as well in all birds as in cattle and beasts of the earth, that are come forth out of the ark: and in all the beasts of the earth.

11 ⁷ I will establish my covenant with you: and all flesh shall be no more destroyed with the waters of a flood: neither shall there be from henceforth a flood to waste the earth.

12 And God said: This is the sign of the covenant which I give between me and you, and to every living soul that is with you, for perpetual generations.

13 I will set my bow in the clouds, and it shall be the sign of a covenant between me, and between the earth.

14 ⁸ And when I shall cover the sky with clouds, my bow shall appear in the clouds:

15 And I will remember my covenant with you, and with every living soul that beareth flesh: and there shall no more be waters of a flood to destroy all flesh.

16 And the bow shall be in the clouds, and I shall see it, and shall remember the everlasting covenant, that was

CHAP. 8. ¹ Gen. 1, 28; 9, 1. ² Gen. 6, 5; Matt. 15, 19. CHAP. 9. ¹ Gen. 1, 22; 8, 17. ² Gen. 1, 29. ³ Lev. 17, 14; Acts, 15, 29. ⁴ Matt. 26, 52; Apoc. 13, 10. ⁵ Gen. 1, 27. ⁶ Gen. 1, 28; 8, 17. ⁷ Isai. 54, 9. ⁸ Ecclus. 43, 12.

Ver. 20. *Holocausts.* Whole burnt offerings: those in which the whole victim was consumed by fire upon God's altar, and no part was reserved for the use of priest or people.

Ver. 21. *Smelled.* A figurative expression, denoting that God was well pleased with the sacrifices which his servant offered.

made between God and every living soul of all flesh which is upon the earth.

17 And God said to Noe: This shall be the sign of the covenant which I have established between me and all flesh upon the earth.

18 And the sons of Noe who came out of the ark, were Sem, Cham, and Japheth: and Cham is the father of Chanaan.

19 These three are the sons of Noe: and from these was all mankind spread over the whole earth.

20 And Noe, a husbandman, began to till the ground, and planted a vineyard,

21 And drinking of the wine was made drunk, and was uncovered in his tent.

22 Which when Cham the father of Chanaan had seen, to wit, that his father's nakedness was uncovered, he told it to his two brethren without.

23 But Sem and Japheth put a cloak upon their shoulders, and going backward covered the nakedness of their father: and their faces were turned away, and they saw not their father's nakedness.

24 And Noe awakening from the wine, when he had learned what his younger son had done to him,

25 He said: Cursed be Chanaan; a servant of servants shall he be unto his brethren.

26 And he said: Blessed be the Lord God of Sem; be Chanaan his servant.

27 May God enlarge Japheth, and may he dwell in the tents of Sem; and Chanaan be his servant.

28 And Noe lived after the flood three hundred and fifty years.

CHAP. 10. ¹ 1 Par. 4.

CHAP. 9. Ver. 21. *Drunk.* Noe by the judgment of the fathers was not guilty of sin, in being overcome by wine: because he knew not the strength of it.

Ver. 23. *Covered the nakedness.* Thus, as St. Gregory takes notice in the Third Book of his Morals (Ch. XXII.), we ought to cover the nakedness, that is, the sins, of our spiritual parents and superiors.

Ver. 25. *Cursed by Chanaan.* The *curses*, as well as the *blessings,* of the patriarchs, were *prophetical.* And this in particular is here recorded by Moses, for the children of Israel, who were to possess the land of Chanaan. But why should Chanaan be cursed for his father's faults? The Hebrews answer, that he being then a boy, was the first that saw his grandfather's nakedness, and told his father Cham of it; and joined with him in laughing at it: which drew upon him, rather than upon the rest of the children of Cham, this prophetical curse.

CHAP. 10. Ver. 5. *The islands.* So the Hebrews called all the remote countries, to which they went by ships from Judea, to Greece, Italy, Spain, &c.

Ver. 9. *A stout hunter.* Not of beasts but of men: whom by violence and tyranny he brought under his dominion. And such he was, not only in the opinion of men, but *before the Lord,* that is, in his sight who cannot be deceived.

29 And all his days were in the whole nine hundred and fifty years: and he died.

CHAPTER 10

The genealogy of the children of Noe, by whom the world was peopled after the flood.

THESE are the generations of the sons of Noe: Sem, Cham, and Japheth. And unto them sons were born after the flood.¹

2 The sons of Japheth: Gomer, and Magog, and Madai, and Javan, and Thubal and Mosoch, and Thiras.

3 And the sons of Gomer: Ascenez and Riphath and Thogorma.

4 And the sons of Javan: Elisa and Tharsis, Cetthim and Dodanim.

5 By these were divided the islands of the Gentiles in their lands: every one according to his tongue and their families in their nations.

6 And the sons of Cham: Chus, and Mesraim, and Phuth, and Chanaan.

7 And the sons of Chus: Saba, and Hevila, and Sabatha, and Regma, and Sabatacha. The sons of Regma: Saba and Dadan.

8 Now Chus begot Nemrod: he began to be mighty on the earth.

9 And he was a stout hunter before the Lord. Hence came a proverb: Even as Nemrod the stout hunter before the Lord.

10 And the beginning of his kingdom was Babylon, and Arach, and Achad, and Chalanne in the land of Sennaar.

11 Out of that land came forth Assur, and built Ninive, and the streets of the city, and Chale.

12 Resen also between Ninive and Chale: this is the great city.

13 And Mesraim begot Ludim, and Anamim, and Laabim, Nepthuim,

14 And Phetrusim, and Chasluim: of whom came forth the Philistines, and the Capthorim.

15 And Chanaan begot Sidon, his first-born, the Hethite,

16 And the Jebusite, and the Amorrhite, and the Gergesite,

17 The Hevite and the Aracite: the Sinite,

18 And the Aradian, the Samarite, and the Hamathite: and afterwards the families of the Chanaanites were spread abroad.

19 And the limits of Chanaan were from Sidon as one comes to Gerara even to Gaza, until thou enter Sodom and Gomorrha, and Adama, and Seboim even to Lesa.

20 These are the children of Cham in their kindreds, and tongues, and generations, and lands, and nations.

21 Of Sem also, the father of all the children of Heber, the elder brother of Japheth, sons were born.

22 The sons of Sem: ² Elam and Assur, and Arphaxad, and Lud, and Aram.

23 The sons of Aram: Us and Hull, and Gether, and Mess.

24 But Arphaxad begot Sale, of whom was born Heber.

25 And to Heber were born two sons: the name of the one was Phaleg, because in his days the earth was divided: and his brother's name Jectan.

26 Which Jectan begot Elmodad, and Saleph, and Asarmoth; Jare,

27 And Aduram, and Uzal, and Decla,

28 And Ebal, and Abimael: Saba,

29 And Ophir, and Hevila, and Jobab. All these were the sons of Jectan.

30 And their dwelling was from Messa, as we go on as far as Sephar, a mountain in the east.

31 These are the children of Sem, according to their kindreds and tongues, and countries, in their nations.

32 These are the families of Noe, according to their peoples and nations. By these were the nations divided on the earth after the flood.

CHAPTER 11

The tower of Babel. The confusion of tongues. The genealogy of Sem down to Abram.

AND the earth was of one tongue, ¹ and of the same speech.

2 And when they removed from the east, they found a plain in the land of Sennaar, and dwelt in it.

3 And each one said to his neighbour: Come, let us make brick, and bake them with fire. And they had brick instead of stones, and slime instead of mortar.

4 And they said: Come, let us make a city and a tower, the top whereof may reach to heaven: and let us make our name famous, before we be scattered abroad into all lands.

5 And the Lord came down to see the city and the tower, which the children of Adam were building.

6 And he said: Behold, it is one people, and all have one tongue; and they have begun to do this, neither will they leave off from their designs, till they accomplish them in deed.

7 Come ye, therefore, let us go down, and there confound their tongue, that they may not understand one another's speech.

8 And so the Lord scattered them from that place into all lands, and they ceased to build the city.

9 And therefore the name thereof was called Babel, because there the language of the whole earth was confounded: and from thence the Lord scattered them abroad upon the face of all countries.

10 These are the generations of Sem.² Sem was a hundred years old when he begot Arphaxad, two years after the flood.

11 And Sem lived after he begot Arphaxad, five hundred years; and begot sons and daughters.

12 And Arphaxad lived thirty-five years, and begot Sale.

13 And Arphaxad lived after he begot Sale, three hundred and three years: and begot sons and daughters.

14 Sale also lived thirty years and begot Heber.

15 And Sale lived after he begot Heber, four hundred and three years; and begot sons and daughters.

16 And Heber lived thirty-four years, and begot Phaleg.

17 And Heber lived after he begot Phaleg, four hundred and thirty years; and begot sons and daughters.

18 Phaleg also lived thirty years, and begot Reu.

19 ³ And Phaleg lived after he begot Reu, two hundred and nine years; and begot sons and daughters.

20 And Reu lived thirty-two years, and begot Sarug.

21 And Reu lived after he begot Sarug, two hundred and seven years; and begot sons and daughters.

22 And Sarug lived thirty years, and begot Nachor.

23 And Sarug lived after he begot Nachor, two hundred years: and begot sons and daughters.

24 And Nachor lived nine and twenty years, and begot Thare.

25 ⁴ And Nachor lived after he begot Thare, a hundred and nineteen years; and begot sons and daughters.

26 ⁵ And Thare lived seventy years, and begot Abram, and Nachor, and Aran.

27 And these are the generations of Thare: Thare begot Abram, Nachor, and Aran. And Aran begot Lot.

28 And Aran died before Thare his father, in the land of his nativity in Ur of the Chaldees.

29 And Abram and Nachor married wives. The name of Abram's wife was Sarai: and the name of Nachor's wife, Melcha, the daughter of Aran.

CHAP. 11. Ver. 9. *Babel.* That is, *confusion.*

father of Melcha, and father of Jescha.

30 And Sarai was barren, and had no children.

31 And Thare took Abram, his son, and Lot the son of Aran, his son's son, and Sarai his daughter in law, the wife of Abram his son; and brought them out of Ur of the Chaldees, to go into the land of Chanaan. And they came as far as Haran, and dwelt there.

32 And the days of Thare were two hundred and five years: and he died in Haran.

CHAPTER 12

The call of Abram, and the promise made to him. He sojourneth in Chanaan, and then by occasion of a famine, goeth down to Egypt.

AND the Lord said to Abram: [1] Go forth out of thy country, and from thy kindred, and out of thy father's house, and come into the land which I shall shew thee.

2 And I will make of thee a great nation, and I will bless thee, and magnify thy name: and thou shalt be blessed.

3 I will bless them that bless thee, and curse them that curse thee; and [2] IN THEE shall all the kindred of the earth be blessed.

4 So Abram went out as the Lord had commanded him; and Lot went with him. Abram was seventy-five years old when he went forth from Haran.

5 And he took Sarai his wife, and Lot his brother's son, and all the substance which they had gathered, and the souls which they had gotten in Haran: and they went out to go into the land of Chanaan. And when they were come into it,

6 Abram passed through the country into the place of Sichem, as far as the noble vale. Now the Chanaanite was at that time in the land.

7 And the Lord appeared to Abram, and said to him: [3] To thy seed will I give this land. And he built there an altar to the Lord, who had appeared to him.

8 And passing on from thence to a mountain, that was on the east side of Bethel, he there pitched his tent, having Bethel on the west, and Hai on the east. He built there also an altar to the Lord, and called upon his name.

9 And Abram went forward, going and proceeding on to the south.

⁰ Judith, 5, 7; Acts, 7, 2. CHAP. 12. ¹ Acts, 7, 3.
² Gen. 18, 18; 22, 18; 26, 4; Gal. 3, 8; Heb. 11, 8.
³ Gal. 3, 17; Gen. 13, 14; 15, 18; 26, 2; Deut. 34,
4. ⁴ Gen. 20, 12. CHAP. 13. ¹ Gen. 12, 7. ² Gen.
36, 7.

CHAP. 12. Ver. 13. *My sister.* This was no lie: because she was his niece, being daughter to his brother Aran, and therefore, in the style of the Hebrews, she might truly be called his *sister,* as Lot is called Abram's *brother,* (Gen. 14, 14). See Gen. 20, 12.

10 And there came a famine in the country. And Abram went down into Egypt, to sojourn there; for the famine was very grievous in the land.

11 And when he was near to enter into Egypt, he said to Sarai his wife: I know that thou art a beautiful woman:

12 And that when the Egyptians shall see thee, they will say: She is his wife. And they will kill me, and keep thee.

13 [4] Say, therefore, I pray thee, that thou art my sister: that I may be well used for thee, and that my soul may live for thy sake.

14 And when Abram was come into Egypt, the Egyptians saw the woman that she was very beautiful.

15 And the princes told Pharao, and praised her before him: and the woman was taken into the house of Pharao.

16 And they used Abram well for her sake. And he had sheep and oxen, and he-asses, and men-servants and maid-servants, and she-asses, and camels.

17 But the Lord scourged Pharao and his house with most grievous stripes for Sarai, Abram's wife.

18 And Pharao called Abram, and said to him: What is this that thou hast done to me? Why didst thou not tell me that she was thy wife?

19 For what cause didst thou say, she was thy sister, that I might take her to my wife? Now, therefore, there is thy wife, take her, and go thy way.

20 And Pharao gave *his* men orders concerning Abram: and they led him away, and his wife, and all that he had.

CHAPTER 13

Abram and Lot part from each other. God's promise to Abram.

AND Abram went up out of Egypt: he and his wife, and all that he had, and Lot with him, into the south.

2 And he was very rich in possession of gold and silver.

3 And he returned by the way that he came, from the south to Bethel, to the place where before he had pitched his tent between Bethel and Hai:

4 [1] In the place of the altar which he had made before. And there he called upon the name of the Lord.

5 But Lot also, who was with Abram, had flocks of sheep, and herds of beasts, and tents.

6 Neither was the land able to bear them, that they might dwell together: [2] for their substance was great, and they could not dwell together.

7 Whereupon also there arose a strife between the herdsmen of Abram and of

Lot. And at that time the Chanaanite and the Pherezite dwelled in that country.

8 Abram therefore said to Lot: Let there be no quarrel, I beseech thee, between me and thee, and between my herdsmen and thy herdsmen: for we are brethren.

9 Behold the whole land is before thee: depart from me I pray thee. If thou wilt go to the left hand, I will take the right: if thou choose the right hand, I will pass to the left.

10 And Lot, lifting up his eyes, saw all the country about the Jordan, which was watered throughout, before the Lord destroyed Sodom and Gomorrha, as the paradise of the Lord, and like Egypt as one comes to Segor.

11 And Lot chose to himself the country about the Jordan, and he departed from the east: and they were separated one brother from the other.

12 Abram dwelt in the land of Chanaan; and Lot abode in the towns that were about the Jordan, and dwelt in Sodom.

13 And the men of Sodom were very wicked, and sinners before the face of the Lord, beyond measure.

14 And the Lord said to Abram, after Lot was separated from him: [3] Lift up thy eyes, and look from the place wherein thou now art, to the north and to the south, to the east and to the west.

15 All the land which thou seest, I will give to thee, and to thy seed for ever.

16 And I will make thy seed as the dust of the earth: if any man be able to number the dust of the earth, he shall be able to number thy seed also.

17 Arise and walk through the land in the length, and in the breadth thereof: for I will give it to thee.

18 So Abram removing his tent came and dwelt by the vale of Mambre, which is in Hebron: and he built there an altar to the Lord.

CHAPTER 14

The expedition of the four kings. The victory of Abram. He is blessed by Melchisedech.

AND it came to pass at that time, that Amraphel king of Sennaar, and Arioch king of Pontus, and Chodorlahomor king of the Elamites, and Thadal king of nations.

2 Made war against Bara king of Sodom, and against Bersa king of Gomorrha and against Sennaab king of Adama, and against Semeber king of Seboim, and against the king of Bala, which is Segor.

3 All these came together into the woodland vale, which now is the salt sea.[1]

4 For they had served Chodorlahomor twelve years, and in the thirteenth year they revolted from him.

5 And in the fourteenth year came Chodorlahomor, and the kings that were with him: and they smote the Raphaim in Astarothcarnaim, and the Zuzim with them, and the Emim in Save of Cariathaim.

6 And the Chorreans in the mountains of Seir, even to the plains of Pharan, which is in the wilderness.

7 And they returned, and came to the fountain of Misphat, the same is Cades: and they smote all the country of the Amalecites, and the Amorrhean that dwelt in Asasonthamar.

8 And the king of Sodom, and the king of Gomorrha, and the king of Adama, and the king of Seboim, and the king of Bala, which is Segar, went out. And they set themselves against them in battle array in the woodland vale:

9 To wit, against Chodorlahomor king of the Elamites, and Thadal king of nations, and Amraphel king of Sennaar, and Arioch king of Pontus: four kings against five.

10 Now the woodland vale had many pits of slime. And the king of Sodom, and the king of Gomorrha turned their backs and were overthrown there: and they that remained fled to the mountain.

11 And they took all the substance of the Sodomites, and Gomorrhites, and all their victuals; and went their way.

12 And Lot also, the son of Abram's brother, who dwelt in Sodom, and his substance.

13 And behold one that had escaped told Abram the Hebrew, who dwelt in the vale of Mambre the Amorrhite, the brother of Escol, and the brother of Aner: for these had made league with Abram.

14 Which when Abram had heard, to wit, that his brother Lot was taken, he numbered of the servants born in his house, three hundred and eighteen well appointed: and pursued them to Dan.

15 And dividing his company, rushed upon them in the night: and defeated them, and pursued them as far as Hoba, which is on the left hand of Damascus.

16 And he brought back all the substance, and Lot his brother, with his

[3] Gen. 12, 7; 15, 18; 26, 4; Deut. 34, 4. CHAP. 14.
[1] Gen. 19, 24.

CHAP. 14. Ver. 10. *Of slime. Bituminis.* This was a kind of pitch, which served for mortar in the building of Babel, (Gen. 11, 3), and was used by Noe in pitching the ark.

substance, the women also and the people.

17 And the king of Sodom went out to meet him, after he returned from the slaughter of Chodorlahomor, and of the kings that were with him in the vale of Save, which is the king's vale.

18 ² But Melchisedech the king of Salem, bringing forth bread and wine, for he was the priest of the most high God,

19 Blessed him, and said: Blessed be Abram by the most high God, who created heaven and earth.

20 And blessed be the most high God, by whose protection the enemies are in thy hands. And he gave him the tithes of all.

21 And the king of Sodom said to Abram: Give me the persons, and the rest take to thyself.

22 And he answered him: I lift up my hand to the Lord God the most high, the possessor of heaven and earth,

23 That from the very woof thread unto the shoe latchet, I will not take of any things that are thine, lest thou say: I have enriched Abram.

24 Except such things as the young men have eaten, and the shares of the men that came with me, Aner, Escol, and Mambre: these shall take their shares.

CHAPTER 15

God promiseth seed to Abram. His faith, sacrifice and vision.

NOW when these things were done, the word of the Lord came to Abram by a vision, saying: Fear not, Abram, I am thy protector, and thy reward exceeding great.

2 And Abram said: Lord God, what wilt thou give me? I shall go without children: and the son of the steward of my house is this Damascus Eliezer.

3 And Abram added: But to me thou hast not given seed: and lo, my servant, born in my house, shall be my heir.

4 And immediately the word of the Lord came to him, saying: He shall not be thy heir: but he that shall come out of thy bowels, him shalt thou have for thy heir.

5 And he brought him forth abroad, and said to him: ¹ Look up to heaven, and number the stars, if thou canst. And he said to him: So shall thy seed be.

² Heb. 7, 1. Chap. 15. ¹ Rom. 4, 18. ² Rom. 4, 3; Gal. 3, 6; James, 2, 23. ³ Jer. 34, 18. ⁴ Acts, 7, 6. ⁵ Gen. 12, 7; 13, 15; 26, 4; Deut. 34, 4; 2 Par. 9, 26; 3 Kings, 4, 20; 3 Kings, 4, 21.

Chap. 16. Ver. 3. *To wife.* Plurality of wives, though contrary to the primitive institution of marriage, (Gen. 2, 24), was by divine dispensation allowed to the patriarchs: which allowance seems to have continued during the time of the law of Moses. But Christ our Lord reduced marriage to its primitive institution (Matt. 19).

6 ² Abram believed God, and it was reputed to him unto justice.

7 And he said to him: I am the Lord who brought thee out from Ur of the Chaldees, to give thee this land, and that thou mightest possess it.

8 But he said: Lord God, whereby may I know that I shall possess it?

9 And the Lord answered, and said: Take me a cow of three years old, and a she-goat of three years, and a ram of three years, a turtle also, and a pigeon.

10 ³ And he took all these, and divided them in the midst, and laid the two pieces of each one against the other; but the birds he divided not.

11 And the fowls came down upon the carcasses: and Abram drove them away.

12 And when the sun was setting, a deep sleep fell upon Abram: and a great and darksome horror seized upon him.

13 And it was said unto him: ' Know thou beforehand that thy seed shall be a stranger in a land not their own, and they shall bring them under bondage, and afflict them, four hundred years.

14 But I will judge the nation which they shall serve, and after this they shall come out with great substance.

15 And thou shalt go to thy fathers in peace, and be buried in a good old age.

16 But in the fourth generation they shall return hither: for as yet the iniquities of the Amorrhites are not at the full, until this present time.

17 And when the sun was set, there arose a dark mist; and there appeared a smoking furnace, and a lamp of fire passing between those divisions.

18 ⁵ That day God made a covenant with Abram, saying: To thy seed will I give this land, from the river of Egypt even to the great river Euphrates.

19 The Cineans and Cenezites, the Cedmonites,

20 And the Hethites, and the Pherezites, the Raphaim also,

21 And the Amorrhites, and the Chanaanites, and the Gergesites, and the Jebusites.

CHAPTER 16

Abram marrieth Agar, who bringeth forth Ismael.

NOW Sarai, the wife of Abram, had brought forth no children; but having a handmaid, an Egyptian, named Agar,

2 She said to her husband: Behold, the Lord hath restrained me from bearing. Go in unto my handmaid; it may be I may have children of her at least. And when he agreed to her request,

3 She took Agar the Egyptian, her

handmaid, ten years after they first dwelt in the land of Chanaan: and gave her to her husband to wife.

4 And he went in to her. But she, perceiving that she was with child, despised her mistress.

5 And Sarai said to Abram: Thou dost unjustly with me; I gave my handmaid into thy bosom, and she, perceiving herself to be with child, despiseth me. The Lord judge between me and thee.

6 And Abram made answer, and said to her: Behold thy handmaid is in thy own hand; use her as it pleaseth thee. And when Sarai afflicted her, she ran away.

7 And the angel of the Lord having found her, by a fountain of water in the wilderness, which is in the way to Sur in the desert,

8 He said to her: Agar, handmaid of Sarai, whence comest thou? And whither goest thou? And she answered: I flee from the face of Sarai, my mistress.

9 And the angel of the Lord said to her: Return to thy mistress, and humble thyself under her hand.

10 And again he said: I will multiply thy seed exceedingly, and it shall not be numbered for multitude.

11 And again: Behold, said he, thou art with child, and thou shalt bring forth a son, and thou shalt call his name Ismael: because the Lord hath heard thy affliction.

12 He shall be a wild man. His hand will be against all men, and all men's hands against him: and he shall pitch his tents over against all his brethren.

13 And she called the name of the Lord that spoke unto her: Thou, the God who hast seen me. For she said: Verily here have I seen the hinder parts of him that seeth me.[1]

14 Therefore she called that well: The well of him that liveth and seeth me. The same is between Cades and Barad.

15 And Agar brought forth a son to Abram: who called his name Ismael.

16 Abram was fourscore and six years old when Agar brought him forth Ismael.

CHAPTER 17

The Covenant of circumcision.

AND after he began to be ninety and nine years old, the Lord appeared to him: and said unto him: I am the Almighty God; walk before me, and be perfect.

2 And I will make my covenant between me and thee: and I will multiply thee exceedingly.

3 Abram fell flat on his face.

4 And God said to him: I AM. And my covenant is with thee; [1] and thou shalt be a father of many nations.

5 Neither shall thy name be called any more Abram. But thou shalt be called Abraham: because I have made thee a father of many nations.

6 And I will make thee increase, exceedingly: and I will make nations of thee; and kings shall come out of thee.

7 And I will establish my covenant between me and thee, and between thy seed after thee in their generations, by a perpetual covenant: to be a God to thee, and to thy seed after thee.

8 And I will give to thee, and to thy seed, the land of thy sojournment, all the land of Chanaan for a perpetual possession: and I will be their God.

9 Again God said to Abraham: [2] And thou therefore shalt keep my covenant, and thy seed after thee in their generations.

10 This is my covenant which you shall observe, between me and you, and thy seed after thee: All the male kind of you shall be circumcised.

11 And you shall circumcise the flesh of your foreskin: that it may be for a [3] sign of the covenant between me and you.

12 An infant of eight days old shall be circumcised among you, every man child in your generations. He that is born in the house, as well as the bought servant shall be circumcised, and whosoever is not of your stock.

13 And my covenant shall be in your flesh, for a perpetual covenant.

14 The male, whose flesh of his foreskin shall not be circumcised, that soul shall be destroyed out of his people: because he hath broken my covenant.

15 God said also to Abraham: Sarai, thy wife, thou shalt not call Sarai, but Sara.

16 And I will bless her, and of her I will give thee a son, whom I will bless: and he shall become nations, and kings of people shall spring from him.

17 Abraham fell upon his face, and laughed, saying in his heart: Shall a son, thinkest thou, be born to him that is a hundred years old? And shall Sara that is ninety years old bring forth?

18 And he said to God: O that Ismael may live before thee.

19 And God said to Abraham: [4] Sara, thy wife, shall bear thee a son; and thou shalt call his name Isaac. And I

CHAP. 16. [1] Gen. 24, 62. CHAP. 17. [1] Ecclus. 44, 20; Rom. 4, 17. [2] Acts, 7, 8. [3] Lev. 12, 3; Luke, 2, 21; Rom. 4, 11. [4] Gen. 18, 10; 21, 2.

CHAP. 17. Ver. 5. *Abram,* in the Hebrew, signifies *a high father:* but *Abraham,* the *father of the multitude. Sarai* signifies *my Lady,* but *Sara* absolutely *Lady.*

will establish my covenant with him for a perpetual covenant, and with his seed after him.

20 And as for Ismael I have also heard thee. Behold, I will bless him, and increase, and multiply him exceedingly: he shall beget twelve chiefs, and I will make him a great nation.

21 But my covenant I will establish with Isaac, whom Sara shall bring forth to thee at this time in the next year.

22 And when he had left off speaking with him, God went up from Abraham.

23 And Abraham took Ismael his son, and all that were born in his house; and all whom he had bought, every male among the men of his house. And he circumcised the flesh of their foreskin forthwith, the very same day, as God had commanded him.

24 Abraham was ninety and nine years old, when he circumcised the flesh of his foreskin.

25 And Ismael his son was full thirteen years old at the time of his circumcision.

26 The selfsame day was Abraham circumcised, and Ismael his son.

27 And all the men of his house, as well they that were born in his house, as the bought servants and strangers were circumcised with him.

CHAPTER 18

Angels are entertained by Abraham. They foretell the birth of Isaac. Abraham's prayer for the men of Sodom.

AND [1] the Lord appeared to him in the vale of Mambre as he was sitting at the door of his tent, in the very heat of the day.

2 And when he had lifted up his eyes, there appeared to him three men standing near him: and as soon as he saw them he ran to meet them from the door of his tent, and adored down to the ground.

3 And he said: Lord, if I have found favour in thy sight, pass not away from thy servant:

4 But I will fetch a little water; and wash ye your feet, and rest ye under the tree.

5 And I will set a morsel of bread, and strengthen ye your heart; afterwards you shall pass on: for therefore are you come aside to your servant. And they said: Do as thou hast spoken.

CHAP. 18. [1] Heb. 13, 2. [2] Gen. 17, 19; 21, 1; Rom. 9, 9. [3] Luke, 1, 18. [4] 1Peter, 3, 6. [5] Gen. 12, 3; 22, 18.

CHAP. 18. Ver. 21. *I will go down.* The Lord here accommodates his discourse to the way of speaking and acting amongst men; for he knoweth all things, and needeth not to go anywhere for information. Note here, that two of the three angels went away immediately for Sodom; whilst the third, who represented the Lord, remained with Abraham.

6 Abraham made haste into the tent to Sara, and said to her: Make haste, temper together three measures of flour, and make cakes upon the hearth.

7 And he himself ran to the herd, and took from thence a calf very tender and very good: and gave it to a young man, who made haste and boiled it.

8 He took also butter and milk, and the calf which he had boiled; and set before them. But he stood by them under the tree.

9 And when they had eaten, they said to him: Where is Sara thy wife? He answered: Lo, she is in the tent.

10 And he said to him: [2] I will return and come to thee at this time, life accompanying; and Sara thy wife shall have a son. Which when Sara heard, she laughed behind the door of the tent.

11 [3] Now they were both old, and far advanced in years, and it had ceased to be with Sara after the manner of women.

12 And she laughed secretly, saying: After I am grown old, [4] and my lord is an old man, shall I give myself to pleasure?

13 And the Lord said to Abraham: Why did Sara laugh, saying: Shall I who am an old woman bear a child indeed?

14 Is there any thing hard to God? According to appointment, I will return to thee at this same time, life accompanying; and Sara shall have a son.

15 Sara denied, saying: I did not laugh. For she was afraid. But the Lord said: Nay; But thou didst laugh:

16 And when the men rose up from thence, they turned their eyes towards Sodom: and Abraham walked with with them, bringing them on the way.

17 And the Lord said: Can I hide from Abraham what I am about to do:

18 [5] Seeing he shall become a great and mighty nation, and in him all the nations of the earth shall be blessed?

19 For I know that he will command his children, and his household after him to keep the way of the Lord, and do judgment and justice: that for Abraham's sake the Lord may bring to effect all the things he hath spoken unto him.

20 And the Lord said: The cry of Sodom and Gomorrha is multiplied, and their sin is become exceedingly grievous

21 I will go down and see whether they have done according to the cry that is come to me: or whether it be not so, that I may know.

22 And they turned themselves from thence, and went their way to Sodom:

but Abraham as yet stood before the Lord.

23 And drawing nigh, he said: Wilt thou destroy the just with the wicked?

24 If there be fifty just men in the city, shall they perish withal? And wilt thou not spare that place for the sake of the fifty just, if they be therein?

25 Far be it from thee to do this thing, and to slay the just with the wicked, and for the just to be in like case as the wicked. This is not beseeming thee: thou, who judgest all the earth, wilt not make this judgment.

26 And the Lord said to him: If I find in Sodom fifty just within the city, I will spare the whole place for their sake.

27 And Abraham answered, and said: Seeing I have once begun, I will speak to my Lord, whereas I am dust and ashes.

28 What if there be five less than fifty just persons? Wilt thou for five and forty destroy the whole city? And he said: I will not destroy it, if I find five and forty.

29 And again he said to him: But if forty be found there, what wilt thou do? He said: I will not destroy it for the sake of forty.

30 Lord, saith he, be not angry, I beseech thee, if I speak: What if thirty shall be found there? He answered: I will not do it, if I find thirty there.

31 Seeing, saith he, I have once begun, I will speak to my Lord. What if twenty be found there? He said: I will not destroy it for the sake of twenty.

32 I beseech thee, saith he, be not angry, Lord, if I speak yet once more: What if ten should be found there? And he said: I will not destroy it for the sake of ten.

33 And the Lord departed, after he had left speaking to Abraham: and Abraham returned to his place.

CHAPTER 19

Lot, entertaining Angels in his house, is delivered from Sodom, which is destroyed. His wife for looking back is turned into a statue of salt.

AND [1] the two angels came to Sodom in the evening, and Lot was sitting in the gate of the city. And seeing them, he rose up and went to meet them: and worshipped prostrate to the ground,

2 And said: I beseech you, my lords turn in to the house of your servant and lodge there; wash your feet, and in the morning you shall go on your way. And they said: No, but we will abide in the street.

3 He pressed them very much to turn

in unto him: and when they were come in to his house, he made them a feast, and baked unleavened bread; and they ate:

4 But before they went to bed, the men of the city beset the house both young and old, all the people together.

5 And they called Lot, and said to him: Where are the men that came in to thee at night? Bring them out hither that we may know them.

6 Lot went out to them, and shut the door after him, and said.

7 Do not so, I beseech you, my brethren; do not commit this evil.

8 I have two daughters who as yet have not known man: I will bring them out to you, and abuse you them as it shall please you, so that you do no evil to these men, because they are come in under the shadow of my roof.

9 But they said: Get thee back thither. And again: Thou camest in, said they, as a stranger, was it to be a judge? Therefore we will afflict thee more than them. [2] And they pressed very violently upon Lot: and they were even at the point of breaking open the doors.

10 And behold the men put out their hand, and drew in Lot unto them, and shut the door.

11 And them that were without, [3] they struck with blindness from the least to the greatest, so that they could not find the door.

12 And they said to Lot: Hast thou here any of thine? Son-in-law, or sons, or daughters, all that are thine, bring them out of this city.

13 For we will destroy this place; because their cry is grown loud before the Lord, who hath sent us to destroy them.

14 So Lot went out, and spoke to his sons-in-law that were to have his daughters, and said: Arise: get you out of this place, because the Lord will destroy this city. And he seemed to them to speak as it were in jest.

15 And when it was morning, the angels pressed him, saying: Arise, take thy wife, and the two daughters which thou hast; lest thou also perish in the wickedness of the city.

16 And as he lingered, they took his hand, and the hand of his wife, and of his two daughters; because the Lord spared him.

17 [4] And they brought him forth, and set him without the city. And there they spoke to him, saying: Save thy life: look not back, neither stay thou in all the country about: but save thyself

CHAP. 19. [1] Heb. 13, 2. [2] Peter, 2, 8. [3] Wisd. 19, 16; 2 Kings, 18, 6. [4] Wisd. 10, 6.

in the mountain, lest thou be also consumed.

18 And Lot said to them: I beseech thee, my Lord,

19 Because thy servant hath found grace before thee, and thou hast magnified thy mercy, which thou hast shewn to me, in saving my life, and I cannot escape to the mountain, lest some evil seize me, and I die:

20 There is this city here at hand, to which I may flee. It is a little one, and I shall be saved in it. Is it not a little one, and my soul shall live?

21 And he said to him: Behold, also in this, I have heard thy prayers, not to destroy the city for which thou hast spoken.

22 ⁵Make haste and be saved there, because I cannot do any thing till thou go in thither. Therefore the name of that city was called Segor.

23 The sun was risen upon the earth; and Lot entered into Segor.

24 ⁶And the Lord rained upon Sodom and Gomorrha brimstone and fire from the Lord out of heaven.

25 And he destroyed these cities, and all the country about: all the inhabitants of the cities, and all things that spring from the earth.

26 ⁷And his wife looking behind her, was turned into a statue of salt.

27 And Abraham got up early in the morning: and in the place where he had stood before with the Lord,⁸

28 He looked towards Sodom and Gomorrha, and the whole land of that country: and he saw the ashes rise up from the earth as the smoke of a furnace.

29 Now when God destroyed the cities of that country, remembering Abraham, he delivered Lot out of the destruction of the cities wherein he had dwelt.

30 And Lot went up out of Segor, and abode in the mountain, and his two daughters with him (for he was afraid to stay in Segor): and he dwelt in a cave, he and his two daughters with him.

31 And the elder said to the younger: Our father is old, and there is no man left on the earth, to come in unto us after the manner of the whole earth.

32 Come, let us make him drunk with wine, and let us lie with him, that we may preserve seed of our father.

33 And they made their father drink wine that night: and the elder went in and lay with her father: but he perceived not neither when his daughter lay down, nor when she rose up.

34 And the next day the elder said to the younger: Behold I lay last night with my father; let us make him drink wine also to-night, and thou shalt lie with him, that we may save seed of our father.

35 They made their father drink wine that night also, and the younger daughter went in, and lay with him: and neither then did he perceive when she lay down, nor when she rose up.

36 So the two daughters of Lot were with child by their father.

37 And the elder bore a son, and she called his name Moab: he is the father of the Moabites unto this day.

38 The younger also bore a son, and she called his name Ammon, that is, the son of my people: he is the father of the Ammonites unto this day.

CHAPTER 20

Abraham sojourned in Gerara: Sara is taken into king Abimelech's house, but by God's commandment is restored untouched.

ABRAHAM removed from thence, to the south country, and dwelt between Cades and Sur, and sojourned in Gerara.

2 And he said of Sara his wife: She is my sister. So Abimelech the king of Gerara sent, and took her.

3 And God came to Abimelech in a dream by night, and he said to him: Lo, thou shalt die for the woman thou hast taken; for she hath a husband.

4 Now Abimelech had not touched her, and he said: Lord, wilt thou slay a nation, that is ignorant and just?

5 Did not he say to me: She is my sister; and she say: He is my brother? In the simplicity of my heart, and cleanness of my hands, have I done this.

6 And God said to him: And I know that thou didst it with a sincere heart: and therefore I withheld thee from sinning against me, and I suffered thee not to touch her.

7 Now therefore restore the man his wife; for he is a prophet. And he shall pray for thee, and thou shalt live: but if thou wilt not restore her, know that thou shalt surely die, thou and all that are thine.

8 And Abimelech forthwith rising up in the night, called all his servants: and spoke all these words in their hearing. And all the men were exceedingly afraid.

9 And Abimelech called also for Abraham, and said to him: What hast thou done to us? What have we offended thee in, that thou hast brought upon me and upon my kingdom a great sin?

---

⁵ Wisd. 10, 6. ⁶ Deut. 29, 23; Isai. 13, 19; Jer. 50, 40; Ezech. 16, 49; Osee, 11, 8; Amos. 4, 11; Luke, 17, 29; Jude, 7. ⁷ Luke, 17, 32. ⁸ Gen. 18, 1.

CHAP. 19. Ver. 22. *Segor*. That is, *a little one.*
Ver. 26. *And his wife.* As a standing memorial to the servants of God to proceed in virtue, and not to look back to vice or its allurements.

Thou hast done to us what thou oughtest not to do.

10 And again he expostulated with him, and said: What sawest thou, that thou hast done this?

11 Abraham answered: I thought with myself, saying: Perhaps there is not the fear of God in this place; and they will kill me for the sake of my wife.

12 Howbeit, otherwise also she is truly my sister, [1] the daughter of my father, and not the daughter of my mother, and I took her to wife.

13 And after God brought me out of my father's house, I said to her: [2] Thou shalt do me this kindness: In every place, to which we shall come, thou shalt say that I am thy brother.

14 And Abimelech took sheep and oxen, and servants and handmaids, and gave to Abraham: and restored to him Sara, his wife.

15 And said: The land is before you; dwell wheresoever it shall please thee.

16 And to Sara he said: Behold I have given thy brother a thousand pieces of silver. This shall serve thee for a covering of thy eyes to all that are with thee, and whithersoever thou shalt go: and remember thou wast taken.

17 And when Abraham prayed, God healed Abimelech and his wife, and his handmaids: and they bore children.

18 For the Lord had closed up every womb of the house of Abimelech, on account of Sara, Abraham's wife.

CHAPTER 21
Isaac is born. Agar and Ismael are cast forth.

AND the Lord visited [1] Sara, as he had promised: and fulfilled what he had spoken.

2 [2] And she conceived and bore a son in her old age, at the time that God had foretold her.

3 And Abraham called the name of his son, whom Sara bore him, Isaac.

4 And he circumcised him the eighth day, [3] as God had commanded him,

5 When he was a hundred years old: for at this age of his father was Isaac born.

6 And Sara said: God hath made a laughter for me. Whosoever shall hear of it will laugh with me.

7 And again she said: Who would believe that Abraham should hear that Sara gave suck to a son, whom she bore to him in his old age?

8 And the child grew and was weaned: and Abraham made a great feast on the day of his weaning.

9 And when Sara had seen the son of Agar the Egyptian playing with Isaac her son, she said to Abraham:

10 Cast out this bondwoman, and her son; for the son of the bondwoman shall not be heir with my son Isaac.

11 Abraham took this grievously for his son.

12 And God said to him: Let it not seem grievous to thee for the boy, and for thy bondwoman. In all that Sara hath said to thee, hearken to her voice: [1] for in Isaac shall thy seed be called.

13 But I will make the son also of the bondwoman a great nation: because he is thy seed.

14 So Abraham rose up in the morning, and taking bread and a bottle of water, put it upon her shoulder, and delivered the boy, and sent her away. And she departed, and wandered in the wilderness of Bersabee.

15 And when the water in the bottle was spent, she cast the boy under one of the trees that were there.

16 And she went her way, and sat over against him a great way off as far as a bow can carry. For she said: I will not see the boy die. And sitting over against, she lifted up her voice and wept.

17 And God heard the voice of the boy. And an angel of God called to Agar from heaven, saying: What art thou doing, Agar? Fear not: for God hath heard the voice of the boy, from the place wherein he is.

18 Arise, take up the boy, and hold him by the hand: for I will make him a great nation.

19 And God opened her eyes: and she saw a well of water, and went and filled the bottle, and gave the boy to drink.

20 And *God* was with him: and he grew, and dwelt in the wilderness, and became a young man, an archer.

21 And he dwelt in the wilderness of Pharan: and his mother took a wife for him out of the land of Egypt.

22 At the same time, Abimelech, and Phicol the general of his army said to Abraham: God is with thee in all that thou dost.

23 Swear therefore by God, that thou wilt not hurt me, nor my posterity, nor my stock: but according to the kindness [5] that I have done to thee, thou shalt do to me, and to the land wherein thou hast lived a stranger.

CHAP. 20. [1] Gen. 12, 13; 11, 29. [2] Gen. 21, 23. CHAP. 21. [1] Gen. 17, 19; 18, 10. [2] Gal. 4, 23; Heb. 11, 11. [3] Gen. 17, 10; Matt. 1, 2. [4] Rom. 9, 7; Heb. 11, 18. [5] Gen. 20, 13.

CHAP. 21. Ver. 3. *Isaac.* This word signifies *laughter.*

24 And Abraham said: I will swear.

25 And he reproved Abimelech for a well of water, which his servants had taken away by force.

26 And Abimelech answered: I knew not who did this thing; and thou didst not tell me, and I heard not of it till to day.

27 And Abraham took sheep and oxen, and gave them to Abimelech: and both of them made a league.

28 And Abraham set apart seven ewe lambs of the flock.

29 And Abimelech said to him: What mean these seven ewe lambs which thou hast set apart?

30 But he said: Thou shalt take seven ewe lambs at my hand: that they may be a testimony for me, that I dug this well.

31 Therefore that place was called Bersabee: because there both of them did swear.

32 And they made a league for the well of oath.

33 And Abimelech, and Phicol the general of his army, arose and returned to the land of the Palestines. But Abraham planted a grove in Bersabee, and there called upon the name of the Lord God eternal.

34 And he was a sojourner in the land of the Palestines many days.

CHAPTER 22

The faith and obedience of Abraham is proved in his readiness to sacrifice his son Isaac. He is stayed from the act by an angel. Former promises are renewed to him. His brother Nachor's issue.

AFTER these things, [1] God tempted Abraham, and said to him: Abraham, Abraham. And he answered: Here I am.

2 He said to him: Take thy only begotten son Isaac, whom thou lovest, and go into the land of vision: and there thou shalt offer him for an holocaust upon one of the mountains which I will shew thee.

3 So Abraham rising up in the night, saddled his ass: and took with him two young men, and Isaac his son. And when he had cut wood for the holocaust, he went his way to the place which God had commanded him.

4 And on the third day, lifting up his eyes, he saw the place afar off.

5 And he said to his young men: Stay you here with the ass. I and the boy will go with speed as far as yonder, and after we have worshipped, will return to you.

6 And he took the wood for the holocaust, and laid it upon Isaac his son: and he himself carried in his hands fire and a sword. And as they two went on together,

7 Isaac said to his father: My father. And he answered: What wilt thou, son? Behold, saith he, fire and wood; where is the victim for the holocaust?

8 And Abraham said: God will provide himself a victim for an holocaust, my son. So they went on together.

9 And they came to the place which God had shewn him, where he built an altar, and laid the wood in order upon it. And when he had bound Isaac his son, he laid him on the altar upon the pile of wood.

10 [2] And he put forth his hand and took the sword, to sacrifice his son.

11 And behold an angel of the Lord from heaven called to him, saying: Abraham, Abraham. And he answered: Here I am.

12 And he said to him: Lay not thy hand upon the boy, neither do thou any thing to him. Now I know that thou fearest God, and hast not spared thy only begotten son for my sake.

13 Abraham lifted up his eyes, and saw behind his back a ram amongst the briers sticking fast by the horns: which he took and offered for a holocaust instead of his son.

14 And he called the name of that place: The Lord seeth. Whereupon even to this day it is said: In the mountain, The Lord will see.

15 And the angel of the Lord called to Abraham a second time from heaven, saying:

16 [3] By my own self have I sworn, saith the Lord: Because thou hast done this thing, and hast not spared thy only begotten son for my sake:

17 I will bless thee, and I will multiply thy seed as the stars of heaven, and as the sand that is by the sea shore. Thy seed shall possess the gates of their enemies.

18 [4] And in thy seed shall all the nations of the earth be blessed; because thou hast obeyed my voice.

19 Abraham returned to his young men, and they went to Bersabee together. And he dwelt there.

20 After these things, it was told Abraham that Melcha also had borne children to Nachor, his brother.

21 Hus the firstborn, and Buz his

[5] Gen. 20, 13. CHAP. 22. [1]Judith, 8, 22; Heb. 11, 17. [2] James, 2, 21. [3] Ps. 104, 9; Ecclus, 44, 21; 1 Mach, 2, 52; Luke, 1, 73; Heb. 6, 13, 17. [4] Gen. 12, 3; 18, 18; 26, 4; Ecclus, 44, 25; Acts 3, 25.

Ver. 31. *Bersabee.* That is, *the well of oath.*

CHAP. 22. Ver. 1. *God tempted Abraham.* God *tempteth no man to evil* (James, 1, 13); *but by trial and experiment maketh known to the world, and to ourselves, what we are, as here by this trial the singular faith and obedience of Abraham was made manifest.*

brother, and Camuel the father of the Syrians.

22 And Cased, and Azau, and Pheldas, and Jedlaph,

23 And Bathuel, of whom was born Rebecca: These eight did Melcha bear to Nachor Abraham's brother.

24 And his concubine, named Roma, bore Tabee, and Gaham, and Tahas, and Maacha.

CHAPTER 23

Sara's death and burial in the field bought of Ephron.

AND Sara lived a hundred and twenty-seven years.

2 And she died in the city of Arbee which is Hebron, in the land of Chanaan: and Abraham came to mourn and weep for her.

3 And after he rose up from the funeral obsequies, he spoke to the children of Heth, saying:

4 I am a stranger and sojourner among you: give me the right of a buryingplace with you, that I may bury my dead.

5 The children of Heth answered, saying:

6 My Lord, hear us: Thou art a prince of God among us. Bury thy dead in our principal sepulchres: and no man shall have power to hinder thee from burying thy dead in his sepulchre.

7 Abraham rose up, and bowed down to the people of the land, to wit the children of Heth:

8 And said to them: If it please your soul that I should bury my dead, hear me, and intercede for me to Ephron the son of Seor.

9 That he may give me the double cave, which he hath in the end of his field. For as much money as it is worth he shall give it me before you, for a possession of a buryingplace.

10 Now Ephron dwelt in the midst of the children of Heth. And Ephron made answer to Abraham in the hearing of all that went in at the gate of the city, saying:

11 Let it not be so, my lord, but do thou rather hearken to what I say: The field I deliver to thee, and the cave that is therein, in the presence of the children of my people, to bury thy dead.

12 Abraham bowed down before the people of the land,

13 And he spoke to Ephron, in the presence of the people: I beseech thee to hear me. I will give money for the field. Take it, and so I will bury my dead in it.

14 And Ephron answered:

15 My lord, hear me. The ground which thou desirest, is worth four hundred sicles of silver. This is the price between me and thee. But what is this? Bury thy dead.

16 And when Abraham had heard this, he weighed out the money that Ephron had asked, in the hearing of the children of Heth, four hundred sicles of silver of common current money.

17 And the field that before was Ephron's, wherein was the double cave, looking towards Mambre, both it and the cave, and all the trees thereof in all its limits round about,

18 Was made sure to Abraham for a possession, in the sight of the children of Heth, and of all that went in at the gate of his city.

19 And so Abraham buried Sara his wife, in a double cave of the field, that looked towards [1]Mambre. This is Hebron in the land of Chanaan.

20 And the field was made sure to Abraham, and the cave that was in it, for a possession to bury in, by the children of Heth.

CHAPTER 24

Abraham's servant, sent by him into Mesopotamia, bringeth from thence Rebecca, who is married to Isaac.

NOW Abraham was old, and advanced in age: and the Lord had blessed him in all things.

2 And he said to the elder servant of his house, who was ruler over all he had: [1]Put thy hand under my thigh,

3 That I may make thee swear, by the Lord the God of heaven and earth, that thou take not a wife for my son of the daughters of the Chanaanites, among whom I dwell:

4 But that thou go to my own country and kindred, and take a wife from thence for my son Isaac.

5 The servant answered: If the woman will not come with me into this land, must I bring thy son back again to the place, from whence thou camest out?

6 And Abraham said: Beware, thou never bring my son back again thither.

7 The Lord God of heaven, who took me out of my father's house, and out of my native country, who spoke to me,

---

Chap. 23. [1] Gen. 35, 27. Chap. 24. [1] Gen. 47, 29.

Chap. 23. Ver. 7. *Bowed down to the people. Adoravit,* literally *adored.* But this word here, as well as in many other places in the Latin scriptures, is used to signify only an inferior honour and reverence paid to men, expressed by a bowing down of the body.

Chap. 24. Ver. 7. *He will send his angel before thee.* This shows that the Hebrews believed that God gave them guardian angels for their protection.

and swore to me, saying: [2] To thy seed will I give this land; he will send his angel before thee, and thou shalt take from thence a wife for my son. [3]

8 But if the woman will not follow thee, thou shalt not be bound by the oath; only bring not my son back thither again.

9 The servant therefore put his hand under the thigh of Abraham, his lord, and swore to him upon this word.

10 And he took ten camels of his master's herd, and departed, carrying something of all his goods with him: and he set forward and went on to Mesopotamia to the city of Nachor.

11 And when he had made the camels lie down without the town near a well of water in the evening, at the time when women are wont to come out to draw water, he said:

12 O Lord the God of my master Abraham, meet me to day, I beseech thee, and shew kindness to my master Abraham.

13 Behold I stand nigh the spring of water, and the daughters of the inhabitants of this city will come out to draw water.

14 Now, therefore, the maid to whom I shall say: Let down thy pitcher that I may drink: and she shall answer, Drink, and I will give thy camels drink also: Let it be the same whom thou hast provided for thy servant Isaac. And by this I shall understand, that thou hast shewn kindness to my master.

15 He had not yet ended these words within himself, and behold Rebecca came out, the daughter of Bathuel, son of Melcha, wife to Nachor the brother of Abraham, having a pitcher on her shoulder. [4]

16 An exceeding comely maid, and a most beautiful virgin, and not known to man: and she went down to the spring, and filled her pitcher and was coming back.

17 And the servant ran to meet her, and said: Give me a little water to drink of thy pitcher.

18 And she answered: Drink, my lord. And quickly she let down the pitcher upon her arm, and gave him drink.

19 And when he had drunk, she said: I will draw water for thy camels also, till they all drink.

20 And pouring out the pitcher into the troughs, she ran back to the well to draw water: and having drawn she gave to all the camels.

21 But he, musing, beheld her with silence, desirous to know whether the

[2] Gen. 12, 7; 13, 15; 15, 8.   [3] Gen. 26, 2.   [4] Exod. 11, 16; Gen. 29, 8.

Lord had made his journey prosperous or not.

22 And after that the camels had drunk, the man took out golden earrings, weighing two sicles: and as many bracelets of ten sicles weight.

23 And he said to her: Whose daughter art thou? Tell me: Is there any place in thy father's house to lodge?

24 And she answered: I am the daughter of Bathuel, the son of Melcha, whom she bore to Nachor.

25 And she said moreover to him: We have good store of both straw and hay, and a large place to lodge in.

26 The man bowed himself down, and adored the Lord,

27 Saying: Blessed be the Lord God of my master Abraham, who hath not taken away his mercy and truth from my master, and hath brought me the straight way into the house of my master's brother.

28 Then the maid ran, and told in her mother's house, all that she had heard.

29 And Rebecca had a brother named Laban, who went out in haste to the man, to the well.

30 And when he had seen the earrings and bracelets in his sister's hands, and had heard all that she related, saying: Thus and thus, the man spoke to me; He came to the man who stood by the camels, and near to the spring of water,

31 And said to him: Come in, thou blessed of the Lord: Why standest thou without? I have prepared the house, and a place for the camels.

32 And he brought him in into his lodging: and he unharnessed the camels; and gave straw and hay, and water to wash his feet, and the feet of the men that were come with him.

33 And bread was set before him. But he said: I will not eat, till I tell my message. He answered him: Speak.

34 And he said: I am the servant of Abraham.

35 And the Lord hath blessed my master wonderfully, and he is become great: and he hath given him sheep and oxen, silver and gold, men-servants and women-servants, camels and asses.

36 And Sara, my master's wife, hath borne my master a son in her old age: and he hath given him all that he had.

37 And my master made me swear, saying: Thou shalt not take a wife for my son of the Chanaanites, in whose land I dwell.

38 But thou shalt go to my father's house, and shalt take a wife of my own kindred for my son.

39 But I answered my master: What if the woman will not come with me?

40 The Lord, said he, in whose sight I walk, will send his angel with thee, and will direct thy way. And thou shalt take a wife for my son of my own kindred, and of my father's house.

41 But thou shalt be clear from my curse, when thou shalt come to my kindred, if they will not give thee one.

42 And I came to day to the well of water, and said: O Lord God of my master Abraham, if thou hast prospered my way, wherein I now walk,

43 Behold I stand by the well of water, and the virgin, that shall come out to draw water, who shall hear me say: Give me a little water to drink of thy pitcher:

44 And shall say to me: Both drink thou, and I will also draw for thy camels: Let the same be the woman, whom the Lord hath prepared for my master's son.

45 And whilst I pondered these things secretly with myself, Rebecca appeared, coming with a pitcher, which she carried on her shoulder: and she went down to the well and drew water. And I said to her: Give me a little to drink.

46 And she speedily let down the pitcher from her shoulder, and said to me: Both drink thou, and to thy camels I will give drink. I drank, and she watered the camels.

47 And I asked her, and said: Whose daughter art thou? And she answered: I am the daughter of Bathuel, the son of Nachor, whom Melcha bore to him. So I put earrings on her to adorn her face, and I put bracelets on her hands.

48 And falling down, I adored the Lord, blessing the Lord God of my master Abraham, who hath brought me the straight way to take the daughter of my master's brother for his son.

49 Wherefore, if you do according to mercy and truth with my master, tell me: but if it please you otherwise, tell me that also, that I may go to the right hand, or to the left.

50 And Laban and Bathuel answered: The word hath proceeded from the Lord; we cannot speak any other thing to thee but his pleasure.

51 Behold Rebecca is before thee: Take her and go thy way, and let her be the wife of thy master's son, as the Lord hath spoken.

52 Which when Abraham's servant heard, falling down to the ground, he adored the Lord.

53 And bringing forth vessels of silver and gold, and garments, he gave them to Rebecca for a present. He offered gifts also to her brothers, and to her mother.

54 And a banquet was made, and they ate and drank together, and lodged there. And in the morning, the servant arose, and said: Let me depart, that I may go to my master.

55 And her brother and mother answered: Let the maid stay at least ten days with us, and afterwards she shall depart.

56 Stay me not, said he, because the Lord hath prospered my way: send me away, that I may go to my master.

57 And they said: Let us call the maid, and ask her will.

58 And they called her, and when she was come, they asked: Wilt thou go with this man? She said: I will go.

59 So they sent her away, and her nurse, and Abraham's servant, and his company,

60 Wishing prosperity to their sister, and saying: Thou art our sister: Mayst thou increase to thousands of thousands, and may thy seed possess the gates of their enemies.

61 So Rebecca and her maids, being set upon camels, followed the man who with speed returned to his master.

62 At the same time Isaac was walking along the way to the well,[1] which is called, Of the Living and the Seeing: for he dwelt in the south country.

63 And he was gone forth to meditate in the field, the day being now well spent: and when he had lifted up his eyes, he saw camels coming afar off.

64 Rebecca also, when she saw Isaac, lighted off the camel.

65 And said to the servant: Who is that man who cometh towards us along the field? And he said to her: That man is my master. But she quickly took *her* cloak, and covered herself.

66 And the servant told Isaac all that he had done.

67 Who brought her into the tent of Sara his mother, and took her to wife. And he loved her so much, that it moderated the sorrow which was occasioned by his mother's death.

CHAPTER 25

Abraham's children, by Cetura. His death and that of Ismael. Isaac hath Esau and Jacob twins. Esau selleth his first birth-right to Jacob.

AND Abraham married another wife named Cetura:[1]

2 Who bore him Zamran, and Jecsan, and Madan, and Madian, and Jesboc, and Sue.

3 Jecsan, also begot Saba and Dadan.

---

[1] Gen. 16, 14. CHAP. 25. [1] Par. 1, 32.

Ver. 57. *Let us call the maid, and ask her will.* Not as to her marriage, as she had already consented, but of her quitting her parents and going to her husband.

The children of Dadan were Assurim, and Latusim and Loomin.

4 But of Madian was born Epha, and Opher, and Henoch, and Abida, and Eldaa. All these were the children of Cetura.

5 And Abraham gave all his possessions to Isaac.

6 And to the children of the concubines he gave gifts, and separated them from Isaac his son, while he yet lived, to the east country.

7 And the days of Abraham's life were a hundred and seventy-five years.

8 And decaying he died in a good old age, having lived a long time, and being full of days: and was gathered to his people.

9 And Isaac and Ismael, his sons, buried him in the double cave, which was situated in the field of Ephron, the son of Seor the Hethite, over against Mambre;

10 Which he had bought of the children of Heth. There was he buried, and Sara his wife.

11 And after his death, God blessed Isaac his son, who dwelt by the well named, Of the Living and Seeing.

12 These are the generations of Ismael the son of Abraham, whom Agar the Egyptian, Sara's servant, bore unto him:

13 And these are the names of his children according to their calling and generations. [2] The firstborn of Ismael was Nabajoth, then Cedar, and Adbeel, and Mabsam.

14 And Masma, and Duma, and Massa,

15 Hadar, and Thema, and Jethur, and Naphis, and Cedma.

16 These are the sons of Ismael: and these are their names by their castles and towns, twelve princes of their tribes.

17 And the years of Ismael's life were a hundred and thirty-seven: and decaying he died, and was gathered unto his people.

18 And he dwelt from Hevila as far as Sur, which looketh towards Egypt, to them that go towards the Assyrians. He died in the presence of all his brethren.

19 These also are the generations of Isaac the son of Abraham: Abraham begot Isaac.

20 Who when he was forty years old took to wife Rebecca the daughter of Bathuel the Syrian, of Mesopotamia, sister to Laban.

21 And Isaac besought the Lord for his wife, because she was barren; and he heard him, and made Rebecca to conceive.

22 But the children struggled in her womb; and she said: If it were to be so with me, what need was there to conceive? And she went to consult the Lord.

23 And he answering said: [3] Two nations are in thy womb, and two peoples shall be divided out of thy womb. And one people shall overcome the other; and the elder shall serve the younger.

24 And when her time was come to be delivered, behold twins were found in her womb.

25 [4] He that came forth first was red, and hairy like a skin: and his name was called Esau. [5] Immediately the other coming forth, held his brother's foot in his hand, and therefore he was called Jacob.

26 Isaac was threescore years old when the children were born unto him.

27 And when they were grown up, Esau became a skilful hunter, and a husbandman: but Jacob a plain man dwelt in tents.

28 Isaac loved Esau, because he ate of his hunting: and Rebecca loved Jacob.

29 And Jacob boiled pottage: to whom Esau, coming faint out of the field,

30 Said: Give me of this red pottage, for I am exceeding faint. For which reason his name was called Edom.[6]

31 And Jacob said to him: Sell me thy first birthright.

32 He answered: Lo, I die. What will the first birthright avail me?

33 Jacob said: Swear therefore to me. Esau swore to him, and sold his first birthright.

34 And so, taking bread and the pottage of lentils, he ate, and drank, and went his way; making little account of having sold his first birthright.

CHAPTER 26

Isaac sojourneth in Gerara, where God reneweth to him the promise made to Abraham. King Abimelech maketh league with him.

AND when a famine came in the land, after that barrenness which had happened in the days of Abraham, Isaac went to Abimelech, King of the Palestines, to Gerara.

2 And the Lord appeared to him and said: Go not down into Egypt, but stay in the land that I shall tell thee.

3 And sojourn in it, and I will be with thee, and will bless thee: for to thee and to thy seed I will give all these

---

[2] 1 Par. 1, 29. [3] Rom. 9, 10. [4] Osee, 12, 3. [5] Matt. 1, 2. [6] Abd. 1, 1; Heb. 12, 16.

CHAP. 25. Ver. 6. *Concubines.* Agar and Cetura are here called *concubines,* (though they were lawful wives, and in other places are so called,) because they were of an inferior degree, and such in scripture are usually called concubines.

countries, [1] to fulfil the oath which I swore to Abraham thy father.

4 And I will multiply thy seed like the stars of heaven: and I will give to thy posterity all these countries. And in thy seed shall all the nations of the earth be blessed.[2]

5 Because Abraham obeyed my voice, and kept my precepts and commandments, and observed my ceremonies and laws.

6 So Isaac abode in Gerara.

7 And when he was asked by the men of that place, concerning his wife, he answered: She is my sister.[3] For he was afraid to confess that she was his wife, thinking lest perhaps they would kill him because of her beauty.

8 And when very many days were passed, and he abode there, Abimelech king of the Palestines, looking out through a window, saw him playing with Rebecca his wife.

9 And calling for him, he said: It is evident she is thy wife. Why didst thou feign her to be thy sister? He answered: I feared lest I should die for her sake.

10 And Abimelech said: Why hast thou deceived us? Some man of the people might have lain with thy wife, and thou hadst brought upon us a great sin. And he commanded all the people, saying:

11 He that shall touch this man's wife, shall surely be put to death.

12 And Isaac sowed in that land, and he found that same year a hundredfold: and the Lord blessed him.

13 And the man was enriched, and he went on prospering and increasing, till he became exceeding great.

14 And he had possessions of sheep and of herds, and a very great family. Wherefore the Palestines, envying him,

15 Stopped up at that time all the wells, that the servants of his father Abraham had digged, filling them up with earth:

16 Insomuch that Abimelech himself said to Isaac: Depart from us, for thou art become much mightier than we.

17 So he departed, and came to the torrent of Gerara, to dwell there.

18 And he digged again other wells, which the servants of his father Abraham had digged, and which, after his death, the Palestines had of old stopped up. And he called them by the same names by which his father before had called them.

19 And they digged in the torrent, and found living water.

20 But there also the herdsmen of Gerara strove against the herdsmen of Isaac, saying: It is our water. Where-

fore he called the name of the well, on occasion of that which had happened, Calumny.

21 And they digged also another; and for that they quarrelled likewise, and he called the name of it, Enmity.

22 Going forward from thence, he digged another well, for which they contended not: therefore he called the name thereof, Latitude, saying: Now hath the Lord given us room, and made us to increase upon the earth.[4]

23 And he went up from that place to Bersabee,

24 Where the Lord appeared to him that same night, saying: I am the God of Abraham thy father: Do not fear, for I am with thee. I will bless thee, and multiply thy seed, for my servant Abraham's sake.

25 And he built there an altar: and called upon the name of the Lord, and pitched his tent. And he commanded his servants to dig a well.

26 To which place when Abimelech, and Ochozath his friend, and Phicol chief captain of his soldiers, came from Gerara,

27 Isaac said to them: Why are ye come to me, a man whom you hate, and have thrust out from you?

28 And they answered: We saw that the Lord is with thee, and therefore we said: Let there be an oath between us, and let us make a covenant,

29 That thou do us no harm, as we on our part have touched nothing of thine, nor have done any thing to hurt thee: but with peace have sent thee away, increased with the blessing of the Lord.

30 And he made them a feast, and after they had eaten and drunk:

31 Arising in the morning, they swore one to another: and Isaac sent them away peaceably to their own home.

32 And behold the same day the servants of Isaac came, telling him of a well which they had digged, and saying: We have found water.

33 Whereupon he called it, Abundance: and the name of the city was called Bersabee, even to this day.

34 And Esau being forty years old, married wives, Judith, the daughter of Beeri the Hethite, and Basemath, the daughter of Elon, of the same place.

35 [5]And they both offended the mind of Isaac and Rebecca.

CHAP. 26. [1] Gen. 12, 7; 15, 18. [2] Gen. 12, 3; 18, 18; 22, 18; 28, 14. [3] Gen. 20, 11. [4] Ps. 4, 1. [5] Gen. 27, 46.

CHAP. 26. Ver. 19. *Torrent.* That is, a channel where sometimes a torrent or violent stream had run.

Ver. 22. *Latitude.* That is, wideness, or room.

CHAPTER 27

Jacob, by his mother's counsel, obtaineth his father's blessing instead of Esau. And by her is advised to fly to his uncle Laban.

NOW Isaac was old, and his eyes were dim, and he could not see: and he called Esau, his elder son, and said to him: My son? And he answered: Here I am.

2 And his father said to him: Thou seest that I am old, and know not the day of my death.

3 Take thy arms, thy quiver, and bow, and go abroad: and when thou hast taken some thing by hunting,

4 Make me savoury meat thereof, as thou knowest I like, and bring it, that I may eat: and my soul may bless thee before I die.

5 And when Rebecca had heard this; and he was gone into the field to fulfil his father's commandment,

6 She said to her son Jacob: I heard thy father talking with Esau thy brother, and saying to him:

7 Bring me of thy hunting, and make me meats that I may eat, and bless thee in the sight of the Lord, before I die.

8 Now, therefore, my son, follow my counsel:

9 And go thy way to the flock; bring me two kids of the best, that I may make of them meat for thy father, such as he gladly eateth.

10 Which when thou hast brought in, and he hath eaten, he may bless thee before he die.

11 And he answered her: Thou knowest that Esau my brother is a hairy man, and I am smooth.

12 If my father shall feel me, and perceive it, I fear lest he will think I would have mocked him: and I shall bring upon me a curse instead of a blessing.

13 And his mother said to him: Upon me be this curse, my son: Only hear thou my voice, and go, fetch me the things which I have said.

14 He went, and brought, and gave them to his mother. She dressed meats, such as she knew his father liked.

15 And she put on him very good garments of Esau, which she had at home with her.

16 And the little skins of the kids she

put about his hands, and covered the bare of his neck.

17 And she gave him the savoury meat, and delivered him bread that she had baked.

18 Which when he had carried in, he said: My father? But he answered: I hear. Who art thou, my son?

19 And Jacob said: I am Esau thy firstborn: I have done as thou didst command me. Arise, sit, and eat of my venison, that thy soul may bless me.

20 And Isaac said to his son: How couldst thou find it so quickly, my son? He answered: It was the will of God that what I sought came quickly in my way.

21 And Isaac said: Come hither, that I may feel thee, my son, and may prove whether thou be my son Esau, or not.

22 He came near to his father, and when he had felt him, Isaac said: The voice indeed is the voice of Jacob; but the hands are the hands of Esau.

23 And he knew him not, because his hairy hands made him like to the elder. Then blessing him,

24 He said: Art thou my son Esau? He answered: I am.

25 Then he said: Bring me the meats of thy hunting, my son, that my soul may bless thee. And when they were brought, and he had eaten, he offered him wine also. Which after he had drunk,

26 He said to him: Come near me, and give me a kiss, my son.

27 He came near, and kissed him. And immediately as he smelled the fragrant smell of his garments, blessing him, he said: Behold the smell of my son is as the smell of a plentiful field, which the Lord hath blessed.

28 God give thee the dew of heaven, and of the fatness of the earth, abundance of corn and wine.

29 And let peoples serve thee, and tribes worship thee. Be thou lord of thy brethren, and let thy mother's children bow down before thee. Cursed be he that curseth thee: and let him that blesseth thee be filled with blessings.

30 Isaac had scarce ended his words, when Jacob being now gone out abroad, Esau came,

31 And brought in to his father meats made of what he had taken in hunting, saying: Arise, my father, and eat of thy son's venison; that thy soul may bless me.

32 And Isaac said to him: Why? Who art thou? He answered: I am thy firstborn son Esau.

33 Isaac was struck with fear, and astonished exceedingly: and wondering beyond what can be believed, said: Who is he then that even now brought me

venison that he had taken, and I ate of all before thou camest? And I have blessed him; and he shall be blessed.

34 Esau having heard his father's words, roared out with a great cry: and being in a great consternation, said: Bless me also, my father.

35 And he said: Thy brother came deceitfully and got thy blessing.

36 But he said again: Rightly is his name called Jacob; for he hath supplanted me, lo, this second time. [1] My first birthright he took away before, and now this second time he hath stolen away my blessing. And again he said to his father: Hast thou not reserved me also a blessing?

37 Isaac answered: I have appointed him thy lord, and have made all his brethren his servants. I have established him with corn and wine, and after this, what shall I do more for thee, my son?

38 And Esau said to him: Hast thou only one blessing, father? I beseech thee, bless me also. And when he wept with a loud cry,[2]

39 Isaac being moved, said to him: In the fat of the earth, and in the dew of heaven from above,

40 Shall thy blessing be. Thou shalt live by the sword and shalt serve thy brother. And the time shall come, when thou shalt shake off and loose his yoke from thy neck.

41 Esau therefore always hated Jacob for the blessing wherewith his father had blessed him: and he said in his heart: [3] The days will come of the mourning of my father, and I will kill my brother Jacob.

42 These things were told to Rebecca. And she sent and called Jacob her son, and said to him: Behold Esau thy brother threateneth to kill thee.

43 Now therefore, my son, hear my voice: Arise and flee to Laban, my brother, to Haran:

44 And thou shalt dwell with him a few days, till the wrath of thy brother be assuaged,

45 And his indignation cease, and he forget the things thou hast done to him. Afterwards I will send, and bring thee from thence hither. Why shall I be deprived of both my sons in one day?

46 And Rebecca said to Isaac: [4] I am weary of my life because of the daughters of Heth. If Jacob take a wife of the stock of this land, I choose not to live.

CHAPTER 28

Jacob's journey to Mesopotamia. His vision and vow.

AND Isaac called Jacob, and blessed him, and charged him, saying: Take not a wife of the stock of Chanaan:

2 But go, and take a journey to Mesopotamia of Syria, to the house of Bathuel, thy mother's father: and take thee a wife thence of the daughters of Laban thy uncle.

3 And God almighty bless thee, and make thee to increase, and multiply thee: that thou mayst be a multitude of people.

4 And give the blessings of Abraham to thee, and to thy seed after thee: that thou mayst possess the land of thy sojournment, which he promised to thy grandfather.

5 [1] And when Isaac had sent him away, he took his journey and went to Mesopotamia of Syria to Laban the son of Bathuel the Syrian, brother to Rebecca his mother.

6 And Esau, seeing that his father had blessed Jacob, and had sent him into Mesopotamia of Syria, to marry a wife thence; and that after the blessing he had charged him, saying: Thou shalt not take a wife of the daughters of Chanaan:

7 And that Jacob obeying his parents was gone into Syria:

8 Experiencing also that his father was not well pleased with the daughters of Chanaan:

9 He went to Ismael, and took to wife, besides them he had before, Maheleth the daughter of Ismael, Abraham's son, the sister of Nabajoth.

10 But Jacob, being departed from Bersabee, went on to Haran.

11 And when he was come to a certain place, and would rest in it after sunset, he took of the stones that lay there, and putting under his head, slept in the same place.

12 And he saw in his sleep a ladder standing upon the earth, and the top thereof touching heaven; the angels also of God ascending and descending by it;

13 And the Lord, leaning upon the ladder, saying to him: [2] I am the Lord God of Abraham thy father, and the God of Isaac. The land, wherein thou sleepest, I will give to thee and to thy seed.

14 And thy seed shall be as the dust of the earth: [3] Thou shalt spread abroad to the west, and to the east, and to the north, and to the south. AND IN THEE AND THY SEED ALL THE TRIBES OF THE EARTH SHALL BE BLESSED.

15 And I will be thy keeper whither-

CHAP. 27. [1] Gen. 25, 34. [2] Heb. 11, 20. [0] Abd. 1, 10. [4] Gen. 26, 35. CHAP. 28. [1] Osee. 12, 12. [2] John, 1, 51; Gen. 35, 1; 48, 3. [3] Deut. 12, 20; 19, 8; Gen. 26, 4.
Ver. 36. *Jacob.* That is, a *supplanter.*

soever thou goest, and will bring thee back into this land: neither will I leave thee, till I shall have accomplished all that I have said.

16 And when Jacob awaked out of sleep, he said: Indeed the Lord is in this place, and I knew it not.

17 And trembling he said: How terrible is this place! This is no other but the house of God, and the gate of heaven.

18 And Jacob, arising in the morning, took the stone, which he had laid under his head, and set it up for a title, pouring oil upon the top of it.[4]

19 And he called the name of the city, Bethel, which before was called Luza.

20 And he made a vow, saying: If God shall be with me, and shall keep me in the way by which I walk, and shall give me bread to eat, and raiment to put on,

21 And I shall return prosperously to my father's house: the Lord shall be my God:

22 And this stone, which I have set up for a title, shall be called the house of God: and of all things that thou shalt give me, I will offer tithes to thee.

CHAPTER 29

Jacob serveth Laban seven years for Rachel: but is deceived with Lia. He afterwards marrieth Rachel. Lia bears him four sons.

THEN Jacob went on in his journey, and came into the east country.

2 And he saw a well in the field, and three flocks of sheep lying by it: for the beasts were watered out of it, and the mouth thereof was closed with a great stone.

3 And the custom was, when all the sheep were gathered together, to roll away the stone, and after the sheep were watered, to put it on the mouth of the well again.

4 And he said to the shepherds: Brethren, whence are you? They answered: Of Haran.

5 And he asked them, saying: Know you Laban the son of Nachor? They said: We know him.

6 He said: Is he in health? He is in health, say they: and behold Rachel his daughter cometh with his flock.

7 And Jacob said: There is yet much day remaining, neither is it time to bring the flocks into the folds again First give the sheep drink, and so lead them back to feed.

8 They answered: We cannot, till all the cattle be gathered together, and

we remove the stone from the well's mouth, that we may water the flocks.

9 They were yet speaking, and behold Rachel came with her father's sheep: for she fed the flock.

10 And when Jacob saw her, and knew her to be his cousin-german, and that they were the sheep of Laban, his uncle: he removed the stone wherewith the well was closed.

11 And having watered the flock, he kissed her: and lifting up his voice, wept.

12 And he told her that he was her father's brother, and the son of Rebecca. But she went in haste and told her father.

13 Who, when he heard that Jacob his sister's son was come, ran forth to meet him; and embracing him, and heartily kissing him, brought him into his house. And when he had heard the causes of his journey,

14 He answered: Thou art my bone and my flesh. And after the days of one month were expired,

15 He said to him: Because thou art my brother, shalt thou serve me without wages? Tell me what wages thou wilt have.

16 Now he had two daughters, the name of the elder was Lia: and the younger was called Rachel.

17 But Lia was blear eyed: Rachel was well favoured, and of a beautiful countenance.

18 And Jacob being in love with her, said: I will serve thee seven years for Rachel thy younger daughter.

19 Laban answered: It is better that I give her to thee than to another man; stay with me.

20 So Jacob served seven years for Rachel: and they seemed but a few days, because of the greatness of his love.

21 And he said to Laban: Give me my wife; for now the time is fulfilled, that I may go in unto her.

22 And he, having invited a great number of his friends to the feast, made the marriage.

23 And at night he brought in Lia, his daughter, to him,

24 Giving his daughter a handmaid, named Zelpha. Now when Jacob had gone in to her according to custom, when morning was come he saw it was Lia:

25 And he said to his father-in-law: What is it that thou didst mean to do? Did not I serve thee for Rachel? Why hast thou deceived me?

26 Laban answered: It is not the cus-

---

[4] Gen. 31, 13.

CHAP. 28. Ver. 19. *Bethel*. This name signifies the house of God.

tom in this place to give the younger in marriage first.

27 Make up the week of days of this match: and I will give thee her also, for the service that thou shalt render me other seven years.

28 He yielded to his pleasure: and after the week was past, he married Rachel.

29 To whom her father gave Bala for her servant.

30 And having at length obtained the marriage he wished for, he preferred the love of the latter before the former, and served with him other seven years.

31 And the Lord seeing that he despised Lia, opened her womb, but her sister remained barren.

32 And she conceived and bore a son, and called his name Ruben, saying: The Lord saw my affliction. Now my husband will love me.

33 And again she conceived and bore a son, and said: Because the Lord heard that I was despised, he hath given this also to me. And she called his name Simeon.

34 And she conceived the third time, and bore another son, and said: Now also my husband will be joined to me, because I have borne him three sons. And therefore she called his name Levi.

35 The fourth time she conceived and bore a son, and said: Now will I praise the Lord. And for this she called him Juda.[1] And she left bearing.

CHAPTER 30

Rachel, being barren, delivereth her handmaid to Jacob. She beareth two sons. Lia ceasing to bear, giveth also her handmaid, and she beareth two more. Then Lia beareth other two sons and one daughter. Rachel beareth Joseph. Jacob desirous to return home, is hired to stay for a certain part of the flock's increase, whereby he becometh exceeding rich.

AND Rachel, seeing herself without children, envied her sister, and said to her husband: Give me children, otherwise I shall die.

2 And Jacob being angry with her, answered: Am I as God, who hath deprived thee of the fruit of thy womb?

3 But she said: I have here my servant Bala. Go in unto her, that she may bear upon my knees, and I may have children by her.

4 And she gave him Bala in marriage: who,

5 When her husband had gone in unto her, conceived and bore a son.

6 And Rachel said: The Lord hath judged for me, and hath heard my

voice, giving me a son. And therefore she called his name Dan.

7 And again Bala conceived and bore another.

8 For whom Rachel said: God hath compared me with my sister, and I have prevailed. And she called him Nephtali.

9 Lia, perceiving that she had left off bearing, gave Zelpha her handmaid to her husband.

10 And when she had conceived and brought forth a son,

11 She said: Happily. And therefore called his name Gad.

12 Zelpha also bore another.

13 And Lia said: This is for my happiness: for women will call me blessed. Therefore she called him Aser.

14 And Ruben, going out in the time of the wheat harvest into the field, found mandrakes: which he brought to his mother Lia. And Rachel said: Give me part of thy son's mandrakes.

15 She answered: Dost thou think it a small matter, that thou hast taken my husband from me, unless thou take also my son's mandrakes? Rachel said: He shall sleep with thee this night, for thy son's mandrakes.

16 And when Jacob returned at even from the field, Lia went out to meet him, and said: Thou shalt come in unto me, because I have hired thee for my son's mandrakes. And he slept with her that night.

17 And God heard her prayers: and she conceived and bore the fifth son.

18 And said: God hath given me a reward, because I gave my handmaid to my husband. And she called his name Issachar.

19 And Lia conceived again, and bore the sixth son,

20 And said: God hath endowed me with a good dowry: this turn also my husband will be with me, because I have borne him six sons. And therefore she called his name Zabulon.

21 After whom she bore a daughter, named Dina.

22 The Lord also remembering Rachel, heard her, and opened her womb,

23 And she conceived, and bore a son, saying: God hath taken away my reproach.

24 And she called his name Joseph, saying: The Lord give me also another son.

25 And when Joseph was born, Jacob said to his father-in-law: Send me away that I may return into my country, and to my land.

26 Give me my wives, and my chil-

dren, for whom I have served thee, that I may depart: thou knowest the service that I have rendered thee.

27 Laban said to him: Let me find favour in thy sight: I have learned by experience, that God hath blessed me for thy sake:

28 Appoint thy wages which I shall give thee.

29 But he answered: Thou knowest how I have served thee, and how great thy possession hath been in my hands.

30 Thou hadst but little before I came to thee, and now thou art become rich: and the Lord hath blessed thee at my coming. It is reasonable therefore that I should now provide also for my own house.

31 And Laban said: What shall I give thee? But he said: I require nothing. But if thou wilt do what I demand, I will feed, and keep thy sheep again.

32 Go round through all thy flocks, and separate all the sheep of divers colours, and speckled: and all that is brown and spotted, and of divers colours, as well among the sheep, as among the goats, shall be my wages.

33 And my justice shall answer for me to morrow before thee when the time of the bargain shall come: and all that is not of divers colours, and spotted, and brown, as well among the sheep as among the goats, shall accuse me of theft.

34 And Laban said: I like well what thou demandest.

35 And he separated the same day the she-goats, and the sheep, and the he-goats, and the rams of divers colours, and spotted: and all the flock of one colour, that is, of white and black fleece, he delivered into the hands of his sons.

36 And he set the space of three days' journey betwixt himself and his son-in-law, who fed the rest of his flock.

37 And Jacob took green rods of poplar, and of almond, and of plane trees, and pilled them in part: so when the bark was taken off, in the parts that were pilled, there appeared whiteness: but the parts that were whole remained green. And by this means the colour was divers.

38 And he put them in the troughs, where the water was poured out: that when the flocks should come to drink, they might have the rods before their eyes, and in the sight of them might conceive.

39 And it came to pass that in the very heat of coition, the sheep beheld the rods, and brought forth spotted, and of divers colours, and speckled.

40 And Jacob separated the flock, and put the rods in the troughs before the eyes of the rams. And all the white and the black were Laban's: and the rest were Jacob's, when the flocks were separated one from the other.

41 So when the ewes went first to ram, Jacob put the rods in the troughs of water before the eyes of the rams, and of the ewes, that they might conceive while they were looking upon them.

42 But when the latter coming was, and the last conceiving, he did not put them. And those that were lateward, became Laban's: and they of the first time, Jacob's.

43 And the man was enriched exceedingly: and he had many flocks, maidservants and men-servants, camels and asses.

CHAPTER 31

Jacob's departure. He is pursued and overtaken by Laban. They make a covenant.

BUT after that he heard the words of the sons of Laban, saying: Jacob hath taken away all that was our father's, and being enriched by his substance is become great.

2 And perceiving also that Laban's countenance was not towards him as yesterday and the other day,

3 Especially the Lord saying to him: Return into the land of thy fathers, and to thy kindred, and I will be with thee.

4 He sent, and called Rachel and Lia into the field, where he fed the flocks.

5 And said to them: I see your father's countenance is not towards me as yesterday and the other day: but the God of my father hath been with me.

6 And you know that I have served your father to the uttermost of my power.

7 Yea, your father also hath overreached me, and hath changed my wages ten times: and yet God hath not suffered him to hurt me.

8 If at any time he said: The speckled shall be thy wages: All the sheep brought forth speckled. But when he said on the contrary: Thou shalt take all the white ones for thy wages: All the flocks brought forth white ones.

9 And God hath taken your father's substance, and given it to me.

10 For after that time came of the ewes conceiving, I lifted up my eyes, and saw in my sleep *that* the males which leaped upon the females *were* of divers colours, and spotted, and speckled.

11 And the angel of God said to me

in my sleep: Jacob? And I answered: Here I am.

12 And he said: Lift up thy eyes, and see *that* all the males leaping upon the females, *are* of divers colours, spotted, and speckled. For I have seen all that Laban hath done to thee.

13 I am the God of Bethel, [1] where thou didst anoint the stone, and make a vow to me. Now therefore arise, and go out of this land, and return into thy native country.

14 And Rachel and Lia answered: Have we any thing left among the goods and inheritance of our father's house?

15 Hath he not counted us as strangers and sold us, and eaten up the price of us?

16 But God hath taken our father's riches, and delivered them to us, and to our children: wherefore do all that God hath commanded thee.

17 Then Jacob rose up, and having set his children and wives upon camels, went his way.

18 And he took all his substance, and flocks, and whatsoever he had gotten in Mesopotamia: and went forward to Isaac his father to the land of Chanaan.

19 At that time Laban was gone to shear his sheep, and Rachel stole away her father's idols.

20 And Jacob would not confess to his father-in-law that he was flying away.

21 And when he was gone, together with all that belonged to him, and, having passed the river, was going on towards mount Galaad,

22 It was told Laban on the third day that Jacob fled.

23 And he took his brethren with him, and pursued after him seven days; and overtook him in the mount of Galaad.

24 And he saw in a dream God saying to him: Take heed thou speak not any thing harshly against Jacob.

25 Now Jacob had pitched his tent in the mountain: and when he with his brethren had overtaken him, he pitched his tent in the same mount of Galaad.

26 And he said to Jacob: Why hast thou done thus, to carry away, without my knowledge, my daughters, as captives taken with the sword?

27 Why wouldst thou run away privately and not acquaint me, that I might have brought thee on the way with joy, and with songs, and with timbrels, and with harps?

28 Thou hast not suffered me to kiss my sons and daughters: and now, indeed,

29 It is in my power to return thee evil: but the God of your father said to me yesterday: [2] Take heed thou speak not any thing harshly against Jacob.

30 Suppose thou didst desire to go to thy friends, and hadst a longing after thy father's house: why hast thou stolen away my gods?

31 Jacob answered: That I departed unknown to thee, it *was* for fear lest thou wouldst take away thy daughters by force.

32 But whereas thou chargest me with theft: with whomsoever thou shalt find thy gods, let him be slain before our brethren. Search, and if thou find any of thy things with me, take them away. Now when he said this, he knew not that Rachel had stolen the idols.

33 So Laban went into the tent of Jacob, and of Lia, and of both the handmaids, and found them not. And when he was entered into Rachel's tent,

34 She in haste hid the idols under the camel's furniture, and sat upon them: and when he had searched all the tent, and found nothing,

35 She said: Let not my lord be angry that I cannot rise up before thee, because it has now happened to me, according to the custom of women. So his careful search was in vain.

36 And Jacob being angry, said in a chiding manner: For what fault of mine, and for what offence on my part hast thou so hotly pursued me,

37 And searched all my household stuff? What hast thou found of all the substance of thy house? Lay it here before my brethren, and thy brethren, and let them judge between me and thee.

38 Have I therefore been with thee twenty years? Thy ewes and goats were not barren, the rams of thy flocks I did not eat.

39 Neither did I shew thee that which the beast had torn. I made good all the damage: [3] whatsoever was lost by theft, thou didst exact it of me.

40 Day and night was I parched with heat, and with frost; and sleep departed from my eyes.

41 And in this manner have I served thee in thy house twenty years; fourteen for thy daughters, and six for thy flocks: thou hast changed also my wages ten times.

42 Unless the God of my father Abraham, and the fear of Isaac had stood by me, peradventure now thou

CHAP. 31. [1] Gen. 28, 18. [2] Gen. 48, 16. [3] Exod. 22, 12.

CHAP. 31. Ver. 19. *Her father's idols.* By this it appears that Laban was an idolater; and some of the fathers are of opinion that Rachel stole away these idols to withdraw him from idolatry, removing the occasion of his sin.

hadst sent me away naked: God beheld my affliction and the labour of my hands, and rebuked thee yesterday.

43 Laban answered him: The daughters are mine and the children, and thy flocks, and all things that thou seest are mine: what can I do to my children, and grandchildren?

44 Come therefore, let us enter into a league: that it may be for a testimony between me and thee.

45 And Jacob took a stone, and set it up for a title.

46 And he said to his brethren: Bring hither stones. And they gathering stones together, made a heap, and they ate upon it.

47 And Laban called it, The witness heap: and Jacob, The hillock of testimony: each of them according to the propriety of his language.

48 And Laban said: This heap shall be a witness between me and thee this day; and therefore the name thereof was called Galaad, that is, The witness heap.

49 The Lord behold and judge between us when we shall be gone one from the other,

50 If thou afflict my daughters, and if thou bring in other wives over them. None is witness of our speech but God, who is present and beholdeth.

51 And he said again to Jacob: Behold this heap, and the stone which I have set up between me and thee,

52 Shall be a witness: this heap, I say, and the stone, be they for a testimony, if either I shall pass beyond it going towards thee, or thou shalt pass beyond it, thinking harm to me.

53 The God of Abraham, and the God of Nachor, the God of their father, judge between us. And Jacob swore by the fear of his father Isaac.

54 And after he had offered sacrifices in the mountain, he called his brethren to eat bread. And when they had eaten, they lodged there:

55 But Laban arose in the night, and kissed his sons, and daughters, and blessed them: and returned to his place.

CHAPTER 32

Jacob's vision of angels. His message and presents to Esau. His wrestling with an angel.

JACOB [1] also went on the journey he had begun: and the angels of God met him.

2 And when he saw them, he said: These are the camps of God. And he called the name of that place Mahanaim, that is, Camps.

3 And he sent messengers before him

to Esau his brother to the land of Seir to the country of Edom.

4 And he commanded them, saying: Thus shall ye speak to my lord Esau: Thus saith thy brother Jacob: I have sojourned with Laban, and have been with him until this day.

5 I have oxen, and asses, and sheep, and men-servants, and women-servants: and now I send a message to my lord, that I may find favour in thy sight.

6 And the messengers returned to Jacob, saying: We came to Esau thy brother; and behold he cometh with speed to meet thee with four hundred men.

7 Then Jacob was greatly afraid; and in his fear divided the people that was with him, and the flocks, and the sheep, and the oxen, and the camels, into two companies.

8 Saying: If Esau come to one company and destroy it, the other company that is left shall escape.

9 And Jacob said: O God of my father Abraham, and God of my father Isaac, O Lord, who saidst to me: Return to thy land and to the place of thy birth, and I will do well for thee,

10 I am not worthy of the least of all thy mercies, and of thy truth which thou hast fulfilled to thy servant. With my staff I passed over this Jordan, and now I return with two companies.

11 Deliver me from the hand of my brother Esau, for I am greatly afraid of him: lest perhaps he come, and kill the mother with the children.

12 Thou didst say that thou wouldst do well by me, and multiply my seed like the sand of the sea, which cannot be numbered for multitude.

13 And when he had slept there that night, he set apart, of the things which he had, presents for his brother Esau.

14 Two hundred she-goats, twenty he-goats, two hundred ewes, and twenty rams,

15 Thirty milch camels with their colts, forty kine, and twenty bulls, twenty she-asses, and ten of their foals.

16 And he sent them by the hands of his servants, every drove by itself, and he said to his servants: Go before me, and let there be a space between drove and drove.

17 And he commanded the first, saying: If thou meet my brother Esau, and he ask thee: Whose art thou? Or, Whither goest thou? Or, Whose are these before thee?

18 Thou shalt answer: Thy servant Jacob's: he hath sent them as a present to my lord Esau: and he cometh after us.

19 In like manner he commanded the

second and the third, and all that followed the droves, saying: Speak ye the
same words to Esau, when ye find him.

20 And ye shall add: Thy servant
Jacob himself also followeth after us.
For he said: I will appease him with
the presents that go before, and afterwards I will see him. Perhaps he will be
gracious to me.

21 So the presents went before him;
but himself lodged that night in the
camp.

22 And rising early he took his two
wives, and his two handmaids, with his
eleven sons, and passed over the ford
of Jaboc.

23 And when all things were brought
over that belonged to him,

24 He remained alone: and behold a
man wrestled with him till morning.

25 And when he saw that he could
not overcome him, he touched the sinew
of his thigh, and forthwith it shrank.

26 And he said to him: Let me go,
for it is break of day. He answered: I
will not let thee go except thou bless me.

27 And he said: What is thy name?
He answered: Jacob.

28 But he said: Thy name shall not
be called Jacob but Israel: for if thou
hast been strong against God, how
much more shalt thou prevail against
men?

29 Jacob asked him, Tell me by what
name art thou called? He answered:
Why dost thou ask my name? And he
blessed him in the same place.

30 And Jacob called the name of the
place Phanuel, saying: I have seen God
face to face, and my soul has been
saved.

31 And immediately the sun rose upon him, after he was past Phanuel; but
he halted on his foot.

32 Therefore the children of Israel,
unto this day, eat not the sinew, that
shrank in Jacob's thigh: because he
touched the sinew of his thigh and it
shrank.

CHAPTER 33

Jacob and Esau meet. Jacob goeth to Salem, where he raiseth an altar.

AND Jacob lifting up his eyes, saw
Esau coming, and with him four
hundred men; and he divided the children of Lia, and of Rachel, and of the
two handmaids:

2 And he put both the handmaids
and their children foremost: and Lia
and her children in the second place:
and Rachel and Joseph last.

3 And he went forward and bowed
down with his face to the ground seven
times, until his brother came near.

4 Then Esau ran to meet his brother,

and embraced him: and clasping him
fast about the neck, and kissing him,
wept.

5 And lifting up his eyes, he saw the
women and their children, and said:
What mean these? And do they belong
to thee? He answered: They are the
children which God hath given to me
thy servant.

6 Then the handmaids and their children came near. and bowed themselves.

7 Lia also with her children came
near, and bowed down in like manner:
and last of all Joseph and Rachel bowed
down.

8 And Esau said: What are the droves
that I met? He answered: That I might
find favour before my lord.

9 But he said: I have plenty, my
brother; keep what is thine for
thyself.

10 And Jacob said: Do not so I beseech thee, but if I have found favour
in thy eyes, receive a little present at
my hands: for I have seen thy face, as
if I should have seen the countenance
of God. Be gracious to me,

11 And take the blessing, which I
have brought thee, and which God hath
given me, who giveth all things. He
took it with much ado at his brother's
earnest pressing him,

12 And said: Let us go on together,
and I will accompany thee in thy journey.

13 And Jacob said: My lord, thou
knowest that I have with me tender
children, and sheep, and kine with
young: which, if I should cause to be
overdriven, in one day all the flocks
will die.

14 May it please my lord to go before
his servant: and I will follow softly after
him, as I shall see my children to be
able, until I come to my lord in Seir.

15 Esau answered: I beseech thee,
that some of the people at least. who
are with me, may stay to accompany
thee in the way. And he said: There is
no necessity; I want nothing else but
only to find favour, my lord, in thy sight.

16 So Esau returned, that day, the
way that he came, to Seir.

17 And Jacob came to Socoth: where
having built a house, and pitched tents,

he called the name of the place Socoth, that is, Tents.

18 And he passed over to Salem, a city of the Sichemites, which is in the land of Chanaan, after he returned from Mesopotamia of Syria: and he dwelt by the town.

19 And he bought that part of the field, in which he pitched his tents, of the children of Hemor, the father of Sichem, for a hundred lambs.

20 And raising an altar there, he invoked upon it the most mighty God of Israel.

CHAPTER 34

Dina is ravished, for which the Sichemites are destroyed.

AND Dina the daughter of Lia went out to see the women of that country.

2 And when Sichem, the son of Hemor the Hevite, the prince of that land, saw her, he was in love with her: and took her away, and lay with her, ravishing the virgin.

3 And his soul was fast knit unto her: and, whereas she was sad, he comforted her with sweet words.

4 And going to Hemor his father, he said: Get me this damsel to wife.

5 But when Jacob had heard this, his sons being absent, and employed in feeding the cattle, he held his peace till they came back.

6 And when Hemor, the father of Sichem, was come out to speak to Jacob,

7 Behold his sons came from the field: and hearing what had passed, they were exceeding angry, because he had done a foul thing in Israel, and committed an unlawful act, in ravishing Jacob's daughter.

8 And Hemor spoke to them: The soul of my son Sichem has a longing for your daughter; give her him to wife:

9 And let us contract marriages one with another: give us your daughters, and take you our daughters,

10 And dwell with us: the land is at your command, till, trade, and possess it.

11 Sichem also said to her father and to her brethren: Let me find favour in your sight; and whatsoever you shall appoint I will give.

12 Raise the dowry, and ask gifts, and I will gladly give what you shall demand: only give me this damsel to wife.

13 The sons of Jacob answered Sichem and his father deceitfully, being enraged at the deflowering of their sister:

14 We cannot do what you demand, nor give our sister to one that is un-circumcised, which with us is unlawful and abominable.

15 But in this we may be allied with you, if you will be like us, and all the male sex among you be circumcised:

16 Then will we mutually give and take your daughters, and ours: and we will dwell with you, and will be one people:

17 But if you will not be circumcised, we will take our daughter and depart.

18 Their offer pleased Hemor, and Sichem his son.

19 And the young man made no delay, but forthwith fulfilled what was required: for he loved the damsel exceedingly, and he was the greatest man in all his father's house.

20 And, going into the gate of the city, they spoke to the people.

21 These men are peaceable and willing to dwell with us: let them trade in the land, and till it, which being large and wide wanteth men to till it. We shall take their daughters for wives, and we will give them ours.

22 One thing there is for which so great a good is deferred: We must circumcise every male among us, following the manner of the nation.

23 And their substance, and cattle, and all that they possess, shall be ours: only in this let us condescend, and by dwelling together, we shall make one people.

24 And they all agreed, and circumcised all the males.

25 And behold the third day, when the pain of the wound was greatest, two of the sons of Jacob, Simeon and Levi, the brothers of Dina, taking their swords, entered boldly into the city, and slew all the men:[1]

26 And they killed also Hemor and Sichem, and took away their sister Dina, out of Sichem's house.

27 And when they were gone out, the other sons of Jacob came upon the slain; and plundered the city in revenge of the rape.

28 And they took their sheep and their herds and their asses, wasting all they had in their houses and in the fields.

29 And their children and wives they took captive.

30 And when they had boldly perpetrated these things, Jacob said to Simeon and Levi: You have troubled me and made me hateful to the Chanaanites and Pherezites, the inhabitants of

CHAP. 34. [1] Gen. 49. 6.

CHAP. 34. Ver. 13. *Deceitfully.* The sons of Jacob, on this occasion, were guilty of a grievous sin, as well by falsely pretending religion, as by excess of revenge: though otherwise their zeal against so foul a crime was commendable.

this land. We are few: they will gather themselves together and kill me; and both I, and my house, shall be destroyed.

31 They answered: Should they abuse our sister as a strumpet?

CHAPTER 35

Jacob purgeth his family from idols. Goeth by God's commanament to Bethel, and there buildeth an altar. God appearing again to Jacob blesseth him, and changeth his name into Israel. Rachel dieth in childbirth. Isaac also dieth.

IN the mean time, God said to Jacob: Arise, and go up to Bethel, and dwell there, and make there an altar to God, [1] who appeared to thee when thou didst flee from Esau thy brother.

2 And Jacob having called together all his household, said: Cast away the strange gods that are among you, and be cleansed and change your garments.

3 Arise, and let us go up to Bethel, that we may make there an altar to God: who heard me in the day of my affliction, and accompanied me in my journey.

4 So they gave him all the strange gods they had, and the earrings which were in their ears: and he buried them under the turpentine tree, that is behind the city of Sichem.

5 And when they were departed, the terror of God fell upon all the cities round about, and they durst not pursue after them as they went away.

6 And Jacob came to Luza, which is in the land of Chanaan, surnamed Bethel: he and all the people that were with him.

7 And he built there an altar, and called the name of that place, The house of God: [2] for there God appeared to him when he fled from his brother.

8 At the same time Debora, the nurse of Rebecca, died, and was buried at the foot of Bethel under an oak: and the name of that place was called, The oak of weeping.

9 And God appeared again to Jacob, after he returned from Mesopotamia of Syria, and he blessed him,

10 Saying: [3] Thou shalt not be called any more Jacob, but Israel shall be thy name. And he called him Israel.

11 And said to him: I am God Almighty. Increase thou and be multiplied. Nations and peoples of nations shall be from thee, and kings shall come out of thy loins.

12 And the land which I gave to Abraham and Isaac, I will give to thee, and to thy seed after thee.

13 And he departed from him.

14 But he set up a monument of stone, in the place where God had spoken to him: pouring drink offerings upon it, and pouring oil thereon:

15 And calling the name of that place Bethel.

16 And going forth from thence, he came in the springtime to the land which leadeth to Ephrata: wherein when Rachel was in travail,

17 By reason of her hard labour, she began to be in danger, and the midwife said to her: Fear not, for thou shalt have this son also.

18 And when her soul was departing for pain, and death was now at hand she called the name of her son Benoni, that is, The son of my pain: but his father called him Benjamin, that is, The son of the right hand.

19 So Rachel died, and was buried in the highway that leadeth to Ephrata. This is Bethlehem.

20 And Jacob erected a pillar over her sepulchre. [4] This is the pillar of Rachel's monument, to this day.

21 Departing thence, he pitched his tent beyond the Flock tower.

22 [5] And when he dwelt in that country, Ruben went, and slept with Bala, the concubine of his father: which he was not ignorant of. Now the sons of Jacob were twelve.

23 The sons of Lia: Ruben the firstborn, and Simeon, and Levi, and Juda, and Issachar, and Zabulon.

24 The sons of Rachel: Joseph and Benjamin.

25 The sons of Bala, Rachel's handmaid: Dan and Nephtali.

26 The sons of Zelpha, Lia's handmaid: Gad and Aser. These are the sons of Jacob, that were born to him in Mesopotamia of Syria.

27 And he came to Isaac his father in Mambre,[6] the city of Arbee. This is Hebron, wherein Abraham and Isaac sojourned.

28 And the days of Isaac were a hundred and eighty years.

29 And being spent with age he died, and was gathered to his people, being old and full of days: and his sons Esau and Jacob buried him.

CHAPTER 36

Esau with his wives and children parteth from Jacob. An account of his descendants, and of the first kings of Edom.

AND these are the generations of Esau: the same is Edom.

2 Esau took wives of the daughters

CHAP. 35. [1] Gen. 28, 13. [2] Gen. 28, 18. [3] Gen. 32, 28. [4] Gen. 48, 7. [5] Gen. 49, 4. [6] Gen. 23, 10.
CHAP. 35. Ver. 10. *Israel.* This name signifieth one that prevaileth with God.
Ver. 22. *The concubine.* She was his lawful wife; but, according to the style of the Hebrews, is called *concubine*, because of her servile extraction.

of Chanaan: Ada the daughter of Elon the Hethite, and Oolibama the daughter of Ana, the daughter of Sebeon the Hevite:

3 [1] And Basemath the daughter of Ismael, sister of Nabajoth.

4 [2] And Ada bore Eliphaz: Basemath bore Rahuel:

5 Oolibama bore Jehus and Ihelon and Core. These *are* the sons of Esau, that were born to him in the land of Chanaan.

6 And Esau took his wives and his sons and daughters, and every soul of his house, and his substance, and cattle, and all that he was able to acquire in the land of Chanaan: and went into another country, and departed from his brother Jacob.

7 [3] For they were exceeding rich, and could not dwell together: neither was the land in which they sojourned able to bear them, for the multitude of *their* flocks.

8 [4] And Esau dwelt in mount Seir: he is Edom.

9 And these are the generations of Esau the father of Edom in mount Seir.

10 And these the names of his sons: [5] Eliphaz the son of Ada the wife of Esau: and Rahuel the son of Basemath his wife.

11 And Eliphaz had sons: Theman, Omar, Sepho, and Gatham, and Cenez.

12 And Thamna was the concubine of Eliphaz the son of Esau: and she bore him Amalech. These are the sons of Ada the wife of Esau.

13 And the sons of Rahuel *were* Nahath and Zara, Samma and Meza. These *were* the sons of Basemath the wife of Esau.

14 And these were the sons of Oolibama, the daughter of Ana, the daughter of Sebeon, the wife of Esau, whom she bore to him, Jehus, and Ihelon, and Core.

15 These *were* dukes of the sons of Esau: the sons of Eliphaz the firstborn of Esau: duke Theman, duke Omar, duke Sepho, duke Cenez,

16 Duke Core, duke Gatham, duke Amalech: these are the sons of Eliphaz in the land of Edom, and these the sons of Ada.

17 And these *were* the sons of Rahuel the son of Esau: duke Nahath, duke Zara, duke Samma, duke Meza. And these *are* the dukes of Rahuel, in the land of Edom: these the sons of Basemath the wife of Esau.

18 And these the sons of Oolibama the wife of Esau: duke Jehus, duke Ihelon, duke Core. These are the dukes of Oolibama, the daughter of Ana, and wife of Esau.

19 These are the sons of Esau, and these the dukes of them: the same is Edom.

20 [6] These are the sons of Seir the Horrite, the inhabitants of the land: Lotan, and Sobal, and Sebeon, and Ana,

21 And Dison, and Eser, and Disan. These *are* dukes of the Horrites, the sons of Seir in the land of Edom.

22 And Lotan had sons: Hori and Heman. And the sister of Lotan was Thamna.

23 And these the sons of Sobal: Alvan and Manahat, and Ebal, and Sepho, and Oman.

24 And these the sons of Sebeon: Aia and Ana. This is Ana that found the hot waters in the wilderness, when he fed the asses of Sebeon his father:

25 And he had a son Dison, and a daughter Oolibama.

26 And these *were* the sons of Dison: Hamdan, and Eseban, and Jethram, and Charan.

27 These also *were* the sons of Eser: Balaan, and Zavan, and Acan.

28 And Disan had sons: Hus, and Aram.

29 These *were* dukes of the Horrites: duke Lotan, duke Sobal, duke Sebeon, duke Ana,

30 Duke Dison, duke Eser, duke Disan: these *were* dukes of the Horrites that ruled in the land of Seir.

31 And the kings that ruled in the land of Edom, before the children of Israel had a king, were these:

32 Bela, the son of Beor, and the name of his city Denaba.

33 And Bela died, and Jobab the son of Zara of Bosra reigned in his stead.

34 And when Jobab was dead, Husam of the land of the Themanites reigned in his stead.

35 And after his death, Adad the son of Badad reigned in his stead, who defeated the Madianites in the country of Moab: and the name of his city was Avith.

36 And when Adad was dead, there reigned in his stead, Semla of Masreca.

37 And he being dead, Saul of the river Rohoboth, reigned in his stead.

38 And when he also was dead Balanan the son of Achobor succeeded to the kingdom.

39 This man also being dead, Adar reigned in his place, and the name of

CHAP. 36. Ver. 2. *Ada.* These wives of Esau are called by other names, Gen. 26. But it was very common amongst the ancients for the same persons to have two names, as Esau himself was also called Edom.

his city was Phau: and his wife was called Meetabel, the daughter of Matred, daughter of Mezaab.

40 And these *are* the names of the dukes of Esau in their kindreds, and places, and callings: duke Thamna, duke Alva, duke Jetheth,

41 Duke Oolibama, duke Ela, duke Phinon,

42 Duke Cenez, duke Theman, duke Mabsar,

43 Duke Magdiel, duke Hiram. These *are* the dukes of Edom dwelling in the land of their government; the same is Esau the father of the Edomites.

CHAPTER 37

Joseph's dreams. He is sold by his brethren, and carried into Egypt.

AND Jacob dwelt in the land of Chanaan wherein his father sojourned.

2 And these are his generations. Joseph, when he was sixteen years old, was feeding the flock with his brethren, being *but* a boy. And he was with the sons of Bala and of Zelpha his father's wives. And he accused his brethren to his father of a most wicked crime.

3 Now Israel loved Joseph above all his sons, because he had him in his old age: and he made him a coat of divers colours.

4 And his brethren seeing that he was loved by his father, more than all his sons, hated him, and could not speak peaceably to him.

5 Now it fell out also that he told his brethren a dream, that he had dreamed: which occasioned them to hate him the more.

6 And he said to them: Hear my dream which I dreamed.

7 I thought we were binding sheaves in the field: and my sheaf arose as it were, and stood, and your sheaves standing about, bowed down before my sheaf.

8 His brethren answered: Shalt thou be our king? Or shall we be subject to thy dominion? Therefore this matter of his dreams and words ministered nourishment to *their* envy and hatred.

9 He dreamed also another dream, which he told his brethren, saying: I saw in a dream, as it were the sun, and the moon, and eleven stars worshipping me.

10 And when he had told this to his father and brethren, his father rebuked him, and said: What mcaneth this dream that thou hast dreamed? Shall I and thy mother, and thy brethren worship thee upon the earth?

11 His brethren therefore envied

him: but his father considered the thing with himself.

12 And when his brethren abode in Sichem feeding their father's flocks,

13 Israel said to him: Thy brethren feed the sheep in Sichem: come, I will send thee to them. And when he answered:

14 I am ready; he said to him: Go, and see if all things be well with thy brethren, and the cattle; and bring me word again what is doing. So being sent from the vale of Hebron, he came to Sichem.

15 And a man found him there wandering in the field, and asked what he sought.

16 But he answered: I seek my brethren; tell me where they feed the flocks,

17 And the man said to him: They are departed from this place; for I heard them say: Let us go to Dothain. And Joseph went forward after his brethren, and found them in Dothain.

18 And when they saw him afar off, before he came nigh them, they thought to kill him.

19 And said one to another: Behold the dreamer cometh.

20 Come, let us kill him, and cast him into some old pit; and we will say: Some evil beast hath devoured him: and then it shall appear what his dreams avail him:

21 [1]And Ruben hearing this, endeavoured to deliver him out of their hands, and said:

22 Do not take away his life, nor shed *his* blood: [2] but cast him into this pit, that is in the wilderness, and keep your hands harmless. Now he said this, being desirous to deliver him out of their hands and to restore him to his father.

23 And as soon as he came to his brethren, they forthwith stript him of his outside coat, that was of divers colours:

24 And cast him into an old pit, where there was no water.

25 And sitting down to eat bread, they saw some Ismaelites on their way coming from Galaad, with their camels, carrying spices, and balm, and myrrh to Egypt.

---

[1] Gen. 9, 6; 42, 22. [2] Gen. 9, 6.

CHAP. 37. Ver. 5. *A dream.* These dreams of Joseph were *prophetical*, and sent from God; as were also those which he interpreted, Gen. 40 and 41; otherwise generally speaking, the observing of dreams is condemned in the Scripture, as superstitious and sinful. See Deut. 18, 10: Ecclus. 34, 2, 3.

Ver. 10. *Worship.* This word is not used here to signify *divine worship*, but an *inferior veneration*, expressed by the bowing of the body, and that, according to the manner of the eastern nations, down to the ground.

26 And Juda said to his brethren: What will it profit us to kill our brother, and conceal his blood?

27 It is better that he be sold to the Ismaelites, and that our hands be not defiled: for he is our brother and our flesh. His brethren agreed to his words.

28 [3]And when the Madianite merchants passed by, they drew him out of the pit, and sold him to the Ismaelites, for twenty pieces of silver: and they led him into Egypt.

29 And Ruben, returning to the pit, found not the boy:

30 And rending his garments he went to his brethren, and said: The boy doth not appear, and whither shall I go?

31 And they took his coat, and dipped it in the blood of a kid, which they had killed.

32 Sending some to carry it to their father, and to say: This we have found; see whether it be thy son's coat, or not.

33 And the father acknowledging it, said: It is my son's coat; an evil wild beast hath eaten him; a beast hath devoured Joseph.

34 And tearing his garments, he put on sackcloth, mourning for his son a long time.

35 And all his children being gathered together to comfort their father in his sorrow, he would not receive comfort, but said: I will go down to my son into hell, mourning. And whilst he continued weeping,

36 The Madianites sold Joseph in Egypt to Putiphar, an eunuch to Pharao, captain of the soldiers.

CHAPTER 38

The sons of Juda. The death of Her and Onan. The birth of Phares and Zara.

AT that time Juda went down from his brethren, and turned in to a certain Odollamite, named Hiras.

2 [1]And he saw there the daughter of a man of Chanaan, called Sue: and taking her to wife, he went in unto her.

3 And she conceived, and bore a son, and called his name Her.

4 [2]And conceiving again, she bore a son, and called him Onan.

[3] Wisd. 10, 13. CHAP. 38. [1]Par. 2, 3 [2]Num. 20, 13. [6]Num. 26, 19.

Ver. 35. *Into hell.* That is, into *limbo*, the place where the souls of the just were received before the death of our Redeemer. For allowing that the word *hell* sometimes is taken for the *grave*, it cannot be so taken in this place; since Jacob did not believe his son to be in the *grave*, (whom he supposed could not mean to go down to him thither: but certainly meant the place of rest where he believed his soul to be.

Ver. 36. *An eunuch.* This word sometimes signifies a *chamberlain, courtier,* or *officer of the* king: and so it is taken in this place.

5 She bore also a third: whom she called Sela. After whose birth, she ceased to bear any more.

6 And Juda took a wife for Her his firstborn, whose name was Thamar.

7 [3]And Her, the firstborn of Juda, was wicked in the sight of the Lord: and was slain by him.

8 Juda therefore said to Onan his son: Go in to thy brother's wife and marry her, that thou mayst raise seed to thy brother.

9 He knowing that the children should not be his, when he went in to his brother's wife, spilled *his* seed upon the ground, lest children should be born in his brother's name.

10 And therefore the Lord slew him, because he did a detestable thing.

11 Wherefore Juda said to Thamar his daughter-in-law: Remain a widow in thy father's house, till Sela my son grow up. For he was afraid lest he also might die, as his brethren did. She went her way and dwelt in her father's house.

12 And after many days were past, the daughter of Sue the wife of Juda died: and when he had taken comfort after his mourning he went up to Thamnas, to the shearers of his sheep, he and Hiras the Odollamite the shepherd of *his* flock.

13 And it was told Thamar that her father-in-law was come up to Thamnas, to shear his sheep.

14 And she put off the garments of her widowhood, and took a veil, and changing her dress, sat in the cross way, that leadeth to Thamnas; because Sela was grown up, and she had not been married to him.

15 When Juda saw her, he thought she was a harlot: for she had covered her face, lest she should be known.

16 And going to her, he said: Suffer me to lie with thee; for he knew her not to be his daughter-in-law. And she answered: What wilt thou give me to enjoy my company?

17 He said: I will send thee a kid out of the flock. And when she said again: I will suffer what thou wilt, if thou give a pledge, till thou send what thou promisest.

18 Juda said: What wilt thou have for a pledge? She answered: Thy ring and bracelet, and the staff which thou holdest in thy hand. The woman therefore at one copulation conceived.

19 And she arose and went her way: and putting off the apparel which she had taken, put on the garments of her widowhood.

20 And Juda sent a kid by his shepherd, the Odollamite, that he might receive the pledge again, which he had

given to the woman: but he, not finding her,

21 Asked the men of that place: Where is the woman that sat in the cross way? And when they all made answer: There was no harlot in this place,

22 He returned to Juda, and said to him: I have not found her; moreover the men of that place said to me, that there never sat a harlot there.

23 Juda said: Let her take it to herself; surely she cannot charge us with a lie. I sent the kid which I promised: and thou didst not find her.

24 And behold after three months they told Juda, saying: Thamar, thy daughter-in-law hath played the harlot, and she appeareth to have a big belly. And Juda said: Bring her out that she may be burnt.

25 But when she was led to execution she sent to her father-in-law, saying: By the man, to whom these things belong, I am with child. See whose ring and bracelet, and staff this is.

26 But he acknowledging the gifts said: She is juster than I; because I did not give her to Sela my son. However, he knew her no more.

27 'And when she was ready to be brought to bed, there appeared twins in her womb: and in the very delivery of the infants, one put forth a hand whereon the midwife tied a scarlet thread, saying:

28 This shall come forth the first.

29 But he drawing back his hand, the other came forth. And the woman said: Why is the partition divided for thee? And therefore called his name Phares.

30 ⁵Afterwards his brother came out, on whose hand was the scarlet thread: and she called him Zara.

CHAPTER 39

Joseph hath charge of his master's house. Rejecteth his mistress's solicitations. Is falsely accused by her, and cast into prison, where he hath the charge of all the prisoners.

AND Joseph was brought into Egypt; and Putiphar an eunuch of Pharao, chief captain of the army, an Egyptian, bought him of the Ismaelites, by whom he was brought.

2 And the Lord was with him, and he was a prosperous man in all things: and he dwelt in his master's house.

3 Who knew very well that the Lord was with him, and made all that he did to prosper in his hand.

4 And Joseph found favour in the sight of his master, and ministered to him: and being set over all by him, he governed the house committed to him,

and all things that were delivered to him:

5 And the Lord blessed the house of the Egyptian for Joseph's sake: and multiplied all his substance, both at home, and in the fields.

6 Neither knew he any other thing, but the bread which he ate. And Joseph was of a beautiful countenance, and comely to behold.

7 And after many days his mistress cast her eyes on Joseph, and said: Lie with me.

8 But he, in no wise consenting to *that* wicked act, said to her: Behold, my master hath delivered all things to me, and knoweth not what he hath in his own house.

9 Neither is there any thing which is not in my power, or that he hath not delivered to me, but thee, who art his wife: How then can I do this wicked thing, and sin against my God?

10 With such words as these, day by day, both the woman was importunate with the young man, and he refused the adultery.

11 Now it happened on a certain day, that Joseph went into the house, and was doing some business without any man with him;

12 And she catching the skirt of his garment, said: Lie with me. But he leaving the garment in her hand, fled, and went out.

13 And when the woman saw the garment in her hands, and herself disregarded,

14 She called to her the men of her house, and said to them: See, he hath brought in a Hebrew, to abuse us. He came in to me, to lie with me: and when I cried out,

15 And he heard my voice, he left the garment that I held, and got him out.

16 For a proof therefore of her fidelity, she kept the garment, and shewed it to her husband when he returned home:

17 And said: The Hebrew servant, whom that hast brought, came to me to abuse me.

18 And when he heard me cry, he left the garment which I held, and fled out.

19 His master hearing these things, and giving too much credit to his wife's words, was very angry:

20 ¹And cast Joseph into the prison, where the king's prisoners were kept. And he was there shut up.

21 But the Lord was with Joseph, and

---

⁴ Matt. 1, 3.   ⁵ 1 Par. 2, 4.   CHAP. 39.   ¹ Ps. 104, 18.

CHAP. 38. Ver. 29. *Phares.* That is, a breach or division.
CHAP. 39. Ver. 16. *A proof of her fidelity,* or *on argument to gain credit (argumentum fidei).*

having mercy upon him gave him favour in the sight of the chief keeper of the prison.

22 Who delivered into his hand all the prisoners that were kept in custody: and whatsoever was done was under him.

23 Neither did he himself know any thing, having committed all things to him; for the Lord was with him, and made all that he did to prosper.

CHAPTER 40

Joseph interpreteth the dreams of two of Pharao's servants in prison. The event declareth the interpretations to be true, but Joseph is forgotten.

AFTER this, it came to pass that two eunuchs, the butler and the baker of the king of Egypt, offended their lord.

2 And Pharao being angry with them (now the one was chief butler, the other chief baker),

3 He sent them to the prison of the commander of the soldiers, in which Joseph also was prisoner,

4 But the keeper of the prison delivered them to Joseph, and he served them. Some little time passed, and they were kept in custody.

5 And they both dreamed a dream the same night, according to the interpretation agreeing to themselves.

6 And when Joseph was come in to them in the morning, and saw them sad,

7 He asked them, saying: Why is your countenance sadder to-day than usual?

8 They answered: We have dreamed a dream, and there is nobody to interpret it to us. And Joseph said to them: Doth not interpretation belong to God? Tell me what you have dreamed.

9 The chief butler first told his dream: I saw before me a vine,

10 On which were three branches which by little and little sent out buds and after the blossoms brought forth ripe grapes.

11 And the cup of Pharao was in my hand: and I took the grapes, and

pressed them into the cup which I held, and I gave the cup to Pharao.

12 Joseph answered: This is the interpretation of the dream. The three branches are yet three days:

13 After which Pharao will remember thy service, and will restore thee to thy former place. And thou shalt present him the cup according to thy office, as before thou wast wont to do.

14 Only remember me, when it shall be well with thee: and do me this kindness to put Pharao in mind to take me out of this prison.

15 For I was stolen away out of the land of the Hebrews, and here without any fault was cast into the dungeon.

16 The chief baker seeing that he had wisely interpreted the dream, said: I also dreamed a dream, that I had three baskets of meal upon my head;

17 And that in one basket which was uppermost, I carried all meats that are made by the art of baking, and that the birds ate out of it.

18 Joseph answered: This is the interpretation of the dream. The three baskets are yet three days:

19 After which Pharao will take thy head from thee, and hang thee on a cross; and the birds shall tear thy flesh.

20 The third day after this was the birthday of Pharao: and he made a great feast for his servants, and at the banquet remembered the chief butler, and the chief baker.

21 And he restored the one to his place to present him the cup:

22 The other he hanged on a gibbet, that the truth of the interpreter might be shewn.

23 But the chief butler, when things prospered with him, forgot his interpreter.

CHAPTER 41

Joseph interpreteth the two dreams of Pharao. He is made ruler over all Egypt.

AFTER two years Pharao had a dream. He thought he stood by the river.

2 Out of which came up seven kine, very beautiful and fat: and they fed in marshy places.

3 Other seven also came up out of the river, ill favoured, and lean-fleshed: and they fed on the very bank of the river, in green places.

4 And they devoured them, whose bodies were very beautiful and well conditioned. So Pharao awoke.

5 He slept again, and dreamed another dream: Seven ears of corn came up upon one stalk full and fair.

CHAP. 40. Ver. 8. *Doth not interpretation belong to God?* When dreams are from God, as these were, the interpretation of them is a gift of God. But the generality of dreams are not of this sort; but either proceed from the natural complexions and dispositions of persons, or the roving of their imaginations in the day on such objects as they are much affected with, or from their mind being disturbed with cares and troubles, or oppressed with bodily infirmities, or they are suggested by evil spirits, to flatter, or to terrify weak minds, in order to gain belief, and so draw them into error or superstition; or at least to trouble them in their sleep, whom they cannot move when they are awake: so that the general rule, with regard to dreams, is not to observe them, nor to give any credit to them.

6 Then seven other ears sprung up thin and blasted,

7 And devoured all the beauty of the former. Pharao awaked after his rest.

8 And when morning was come, being struck with fear, he sent to all the interpreters of Egypt, and to all the wise men. And they being called for, he told them his dream; and there was not any one that could interpret it.

9 Then at length the chief butler remembering, said: I confess my sin.

10 The king being angry with his servants, commanded me and the chief baker to be cast into the prison of the captain of the soldiers;

11 Where in one night both of us dreamed a dream foreboding things to come.

12 There was there a young man, a Hebrew, servant to the same captain of the soldiers: to whom we told our dreams.

13 And we heard what afterwards the event of the thing proved to be so. For I was restored to my office: and he was hanged upon a gibbet.

14 Forthwith at the king's command, Joseph was brought out of the prison: and they shaved him, and changing his apparel, brought him in to him.

15 And he said to him: I have dreamed dreams, and there is no one that can expound them. Now I have heard that thou art very wise at interpreting them.

16 Joseph answered: Without me, [1] God shall give Pharao a prosperous answer.

17 So Pharao told what he had dreamed: Methought I stood upon the bank of the river:

18 And seven kine came up out of the river exceeding beautiful and full of flesh. And they grazed on green places in a marshy pasture.

19 And behold, there followed these other seven kine, so very ill favoured and lean, that I never saw the like in the land of Egypt.

20 And they devoured and consumed the former,

21 And yet gave no mark of their being full: but were as lean and ill favoured as before. I awoke, *and then* fell asleep again,

22 And dreamed a dream: Seven ears of corn grew upon one stalk, full and very fair.

23 Other seven also, thin and blasted, sprung of the stock.

24 And they devoured the beauty of the former. I told *this* dream to the conjecturers, and there is no man that can expound it.

25 Joseph answered: The king's dream is one. God hath shewn to Pharao what he is about to do.

26 The seven beautiful kine, and the seven full ears, are seven years of plenty: and *both* contain the same meaning of the dream.

27 And the seven lean and thin kine that came up after them, and the seven thin ears that were blasted with the burning wind, are seven years of famine to come.

28 Which shall be fulfilled in this order:

29 Behold, there shall come seven years of great plenty in the whole land of Egypt:

30 After which shall follow other seven years of so great scarcity, that all the abundance before shall be forgotten. For the famine shall consume all the land,

31 And the greatness of the scarcity shall destroy the greatness of the plenty.

32 And for that thou didst see the second time a dream pertaining to the same thing: it is a token of the certainty, and that the word of God cometh to pass, and is fulfilled speedily.

33 Now therefore let the king provide a wise and industrious man, and make him ruler over the land of Egypt,

34 That he may appoint overseers over all the countries; and gather into barns the fifth part of the fruits, during the seven fruitful years,

35 That shall now presently ensue. And let all the corn be laid up under Pharao's hands, and be reserved in the cities.

36 And let it be in readiness, against the famine of seven years to come, which shall oppress Egypt. And the land shall not be consumed with scarcity.

37 The counsel pleased Pharao and all his servants.

38 And he said to them: Can we find such another man, that is full of the spirit of God?

39 He said therefore to Joseph: Seeing God hath shewn thee all that thou hast said, can I find one wiser and one like unto thee?

40 [2] Thou shalt be over my house, and at the commandment of thy mouth all the people shall obey: only in the kingly throne will I be above thee.

41 And again Pharao said to Joseph: Behold, I have appointed thee over the whole land of Egypt.

42 And he took his ring from his own hand, and gave it into his hand: and he

---

1 Matt. 10, 20. 2 Ps. 104, 21; 1 Mach. 2, 53; Acts, 7, 10.

put upon him a robe of silk, and put a chain of gold about his neck.

43 And he made him go up into his second chariot, the crier proclaiming that all should bow their knee before him, and that they should know he was made governor over the whole land of Egypt.

44 And the king said to Joseph: I am Pharao; without thy commandment no man shall move hand or foot in all the land of Egypt.

45 And he turned his name, and called him in the Egyptian tongue, The saviour of the world. And he gave him to wife Aseneth, the daughter of Putiphare, priest of Heliopolis. Then Joseph went out to the land of Egypt:

46 (Now he was thirty years old when he stood before king Pharao): and he went round all the countries of Egypt.

47 And the fruitfulness of the seven years came: and the corn being bound up into sheaves was gathered together into the barns of Egypt.

48 And all the abundance of grain was laid up in every city.

49 And there was so great abundance of wheat, that it was equal to the sand of the sea: and the plenty exceeded measure.

50 ³ And before the famine came, Joseph had two sons born: whom Aseneth, the daughter of Putiphare, priest of Heliopolis, bore unto him.

51 And he called the name of the firstborn Manasses, saying: God hath made me to forget all my labours, and my father's house.

52 And he named the second Ephraim, saying: God hath made me to grow in the land of my poverty.

53 Now when the seven years of the plenty that had been in Egypt were past,

54 The seven years of scarcity which Joseph had foretold, began to come: and the famine prevailed in the whole world. But there was bread in all the land of Egypt.

55 And when there also they began to be famished, the people cried to Pharao for food. And he said to them: Go to Joseph; and do all that he shall say to you.

56 And the famine increased daily in all the land. And Joseph opened

³ Gen. 46, 20; 48, 5.

CHAP. 41. Ver. 45. *The saviour of the world.* Zaphnah paaneah.
Ver. 51. *Manasses.* That is, *oblivion,* or *forgetting.*
Ver. 52. *Ephraim.* That is, *fruitful,* or *growing.*
CHAP. 42. Ver. 9. *You are spies.* This he said by way of examining them, to see what they would answer.

all the barns, and sold to the Egyptians: for the famine had oppressed them also.

57 And all provinces came into Egypt, to buy food, and to seek some relief of their want.

CHAPTER 42

Jacob sendeth his ten sons to buy corn in Egypt. Their treatment by Joseph.

AND Jacob hearing that food was sold in Egypt, said to his sons: Why are ye careless?

2 I have heard that wheat is sold in Egypt. Go ye down, and buy us necessaries, that we may live, and not be consumed with want.

3 So the ten brethren of Joseph went down, to buy corn in Egypt.

4 Whilst Benjamin was kept at home by Jacob, who said to his brethren: Lest perhaps he take any harm in the journey.

5 And they entered into the land of Egypt with others that went to buy. For the famine was in the land of Chanaan.

6 And Joseph was governor in the land of Egypt, and corn was sold by his direction to the people. And when his brethren had bowed down to him,

7 And he knew them, he spoke as it were to strangers somewhat roughly, asking them: Whence came you? They answered: From the land of Chanaan, to buy necessaries of life.

8 And though he knew his brethren, he was not known by them.

9 And remembering the dreams, which formerly he had dreamed, he said to them: You are spies. You are come to view the weaker parts of the land.

10 But they said: It is not so, my lord; but thy servants are come to buy food.

11 We are all the sons of one man: we are come as peaceable men; neither do thy servants go about any evil.

12 And he answered them: It is otherwise: you are come to consider the unfenced parts of this land.

13 But they said: We thy servants are twelve brethren, the sons of one man in the land of Chanaan. The youngest is with our father, the other is not living.

14 He saith: This is it that I said: You are spies.

15 I shall now presently try what you are. By the health of Pharao, you shall not depart hence, until your youngest brother come.

16 Send one of you to fetch him: and

you shall be in prison, till what you have said be proved, whether it be true or false: or else by the health of Pharao you are spies.

17 So he put them in prison three days.

18 And the third day he brought them out of prison, and said: Do as 1 have said, and you shall live; for I fear God.

19 If you be peaceable men, let one of your brethren be bound in prison: and go ye your ways and carry the corn that you have bought, unto your houses.

20 [1]And bring your youngest brother to me, that I may find your words to be true, and you may not die. And they did as he had said.

21 And they talked one to another: We deserve to suffer these things, because we have sinned against our brother, seeing the anguish of his soul, when he besought us, and we would not hear. Therefore is this affliction come upon us.

22 And Ruben, one of them, said: Did not I say to you: [2] Do not sin against the boy; and you would not hear me? Behold his blood is required.

23 And they knew not that Joseph understood; because he spoke to them by an interpreter.

24 And he turned himself away a little while, and wept: and returning he spoke to them.

25 And taking Simeon, and binding him in their presence, he commanded his servants to fill their sacks with wheat, and to put every man's money again in their sacks, and to give them besides provisions for the way. And they did so.

26 But they having loaded their asses with the corn, went their way.

27 And one of them opening his sack, to give his beast provender in the inn, saw the money in the sacks' mouth;

28 And said to his brethren: My money is given me again; behold, it is in the sack. And they were astonished, and troubled, and said to one another: What is this that God hath done unto us?

29 And they came to Jacob their father in the land of Chanaan; and they told him all things that had befallen them, saying:

30 The lord of the land spoke roughly to us, and took us to be spies of the country.

31 And we answered him: We are peaceable men, and we mean no plot.

32 We are twelve brethren born of one father. One is not living; the youngest is with our father in the land of Chanaan.

33 And he said to us: Hereby shall I know that you are peaceable men; Leave one of your brethren with me, and take ye necessary provision for your houses, and go your ways.

34 And bring your youngest brother to me, that I may know you are not spies: and you may receive this man again, that is kept in prison: and afterwards may have leave to buy what you will.

35 When they had told this, they poured out their corn, and every man found his money tied in the mouth of his sack. And all being astonished together,

36 Their father Jacob said: You have made me to be without children: Joseph is not living, Simeon is kept in bonds, and Benjamin you will take away. All these evils are fallen upon me.

37 And Ruben answered him: Kill my two sons, if I bring him not again to thee. Deliver him into my hand, and I will restore him to thee.

38 But he said: My son shall not go down with you. His brother is dead, and he is left alone: if any mischief befall him in the land to which you go, you will bring down my gray hairs with sorrow to hell.

CHAPTER 43

The sons of Jacob go again into Egypt with Benjamin. They are entertained by Joseph.

IN the mean time the famine was heavy upon all the land.

2 And when they had eaten up all the corn, which they had brought out of Egypt, Jacob said to his sons: Go again and buy us a little food.

3 Juda answered: The man declared unto us with the attestation of an oath, saying: You shall not see my face, unless you bring your youngest brother with you.

4 If therefore thou wilt send him with us, we will set out together, and will buy necessaries for thee.

5 But if thou wilt not, we will not go: for the man, as we have often said, declared unto us, saying: [1]You shall not see my face without your youngest brother.

6 Israel said to them: You have done

CHAP. 42. [1] Gen. 43, 5. [2] Gen. 37, 21. CHAP. 43. [1] Gen. 42, 20.

Ver. 16. *Or else by the health of Pharao you are spies.* That is, if these things you say be proved false, you are *to be held for spies* for your lying, and shall be treated as such. Joseph dealt in this manner with his brethren, to bring them by the means of affliction to a sense of their former sin, and a sincere repentance for it.

Ver. 38. *To hell.* That is, to that place, where the souls of the just then remained, as above, chapter 37, ver. 35.

this for my misery in that you told him you had also another brother.

7 But they answered: The man asked us in order concerning our kindred: if our father lived: if we had a brother: and we answered him regularly, according to what he demanded. Could we know that he would say: Bring hither your brother with you?

8 And Juda said to his father: Send the boy with me, that we, may set forward, and may live; lest both we and our children perish.

9 [2] I take the boy upon me; require him at my hand. Unless I bring him again, and restore him to thee, I will be guilty of sin against thee for ever.

10 If delay had not been made, we had been here again the second time.

11 Then Israel said to them: If it must needs be so, do what you will. Take of the best fruits of the land in your vessels, and carry down presents to the man, a little balm, and honey, and storax, myrrh, turpentine, and almonds.

12 And take with you double money; and carry back what you found in your sacks, lest perhaps it was done by mistake.

13 And take also your brother, and go to the man.

14 And may my almighty God make him favourable to you; and send back with you your brother, whom he keepeth, and this Benjamin. And as for me I shall be desolate without children.

15 So the men took the presents, and double money, and Benjamin: and went down into Egypt, and stood before Joseph.

16 And when he had seen them, and Benjamin with them, he commanded the steward of his house, saying: Bring in the men into the house, and kill victims, and prepare a feast; because they shall eat with me at noon.

17 He did as he was commanded, and brought the men into the house.

18 And they being much afraid, said there one to another: Because of the money, which we carried back the first time in our sacks, we are brought in: that he may bring upon use a false accusation, and by violence make slaves of us and our asses.

19 Wherefore going up to the steward of the house, at the door.

20 They said: Sir, we desire thee to hear us: [3] We came down once before to buy food.

21 And when we had bought, and come to the inn, we opened our sacks

[2] Gen. 44. 32. [3] Gen. 42, 3.

CHAP. 43. Ver. 11. *Balm.* Literally *rosin*, *resinæ*; but here by that name is meant *balm.*

and found our money in the mouths of the sacks: which we have now brought again in the same weight.

22 And we have brought other money besides, to buy what we want: we cannot tell who put it in our bags.

23 But he answered: Peace be with you, fear not: your God, and the God of your father hath given you treasure in your sacks. For the money, which you gave me, I have for good. And he brought Simeon out to them.

24 And having brought them into the house, he fetched water; and they washed their feet, and he gave provender to their asses.

25 But they made ready the presents, against Joseph came at noon: for they had heard that they should eat bread there.

26 Then Joseph came into his house, and they offered him the presents holding them in their hands: and they bowed down with their face to the ground.

27 But he, courteously saluting them again, asked them, saying: Is the old man your father in health, of whom you told me? Is he yet living?

28 And they answered: Thy servant, our father, is in health; he is yet living. And bowing themselves they made obeisance to him.

29 And Joseph, lifting up his eyes, saw Benjamin his brother, by the same mother, and said: Is this your young brother, of whom you told me? And he said: God be gracious to thee, my son.

30 And he made haste because his heart was moved upon his brother, and tears gushed out. And going into his chamber he wept.

31 And when he had washed his face, coming out again, he refrained himself, and said: Set bread on the table.

32 And when it was set on, for Joseph apart, and for his brethren apart, for the Egyptians also that ate with him, apart (for it is unlawful for the Egyptians to eat with the Hebrews, and they think such a feast profane),

33 They sat before him, the firstborn according to his birthright, and the youngest according to his age. And they wondered very much.

34 Taking the messes which they received of him. And the greater mess came to Benjamin, so that it exceeded by five parts. And they drank, and were merry with him.

CHAPTER 44

Joseph's contrivance to stop his brethren. The humble supplication of Juda.

AND Joseph commanded the steward of his house, saying: Fill

their sacks with corn, as much as they can hold; and put the money of every one in the top of his sack.

2 And in the mouth of the younger's sack put my silver cup, and the price which he gave for the wheat. And it was so done.

3 And when the morning arose, they were sent away with their asses.

4 And when they were now departed out of the city, and had gone forward a little way, Joseph sending for the steward of his house, said: Arise, and pursue after the men. And when thou hast overtaken them, say to them: Why have you returned evil for good?

5 The cup which you have stolen is that in which my lord drinketh, and in which he is wont to divine: you have done a very evil thing.

6 He did as he had commanded him. And having overtaken them, he spoke to them the same words.

7 And they answered: Why doth our lord speak so, as though thy servants had committed so heinous a fact?

8 The money, that we found in the top of our sacks, we brought back to thee from the land of Chanaan: How then should it be that we should steal out of thy lord's house, gold or silver?

9 With whomsoever of thy servants shall be found that which thou seekest, let him die, and we will be the bondmen of my lord.

10 And he said to them: Let it be according to your sentence. With whomsoever it shall be found, let him be my servant, and you shall be blameless.

11 Then they speedily took down their sacks to the ground, and every man opened his sack.

12 Which when he had searched, beginning at the eldest, and ending at the youngest, he found the cup in Benjamin's sack.

13 Then they rent their garments, and loading their asses again, returned into the town.

14 And Juda at the head of his brethren went in to Joseph (for he was not yet gone out of the place): and they altogether fell down before him on the ground.

15 And he said to them: Why would you do so? Know you not that there is no one like me in the science of divining.

16 And Juda said to him: What shall we answer my lord? Or what shall we say, or be able justly to allege? God hath found out the iniquity of thy servants: Behold, we are all bondmen to my lord, both we, and he with whom the cup was found.

17 Joseph answered: God forbid that I should do so. He that stole the cup, he shall be my bondman. And go you away free to your father.

18 Then Juda coming nearer, said boldly: I beseech thee, my lord, let thy servant speak a word in thy ears, and be not angry with thy servant; for after Pharao thou art

19 My lord. [1] Thou didst ask thy servants the first time: Have you a father or a brother?

20 And we, answered thee, my lord: We have a father an old man, and a young boy, that was born in his old age, whose brother by the mother is dead: and he alone is left of his mother, and his father loveth him tenderly.

21 And thou saidst to thy servants: Bring him hither to me, and I will set my eyes on him.

22 We suggested to my lord: The boy cannot leave his father; for if he leave him, he will die.

23 [2] And thou saidst to thy servants: Except your youngest brother come with you, you shall see my face no more.

24 Therefore when we were gone up to thy servant our father, we told him all that my lord had said.

25 And our father said: Go again, and buy us a little wheat.

26 And we said to him: We cannot go. If our youngest brother go down with us, we will set out together; otherwise, without him we dare not see the man's face.

27 Whereunto he answered: You know that my wife bore me two.

28 One went out, and you said: [3] A beast devoured him. And hitherto he appeareth not.

29 If you take this also, and any thing befall him in the way, you will bring down my gray hairs with sorrow unto hell.

30 Therefore if I shall go to thy servant our father, and the boy be wanting (whereas his life dependeth upon the life of him):

31 And he shall see that he is not with us, he will die, and thy servants shall bring down his gray hairs with sorrow unto hell.

32 Let me be thy proper servant. who took him into my trust, and promised, saying: [4] If I bring him not again, I will

CHAP. 44. [1] Gen. 42, 13. [2] Gen. 43, 3, 4, 5. [3] Gen. 37, 20-33. [4] Gen. 43, 9.

CHAP. 44. Ver. 15. *The science of divining.* He speaks of himself according to what he was esteemed in that kingdom. And indeed, he being truly a prophet, knew more without comparison than any of the Egyptian sorcerers.

Ver. 31. *His gray hairs.* That is, his person, now far advanced in years.—*With sorrow unto hell.* The Hebrew word for *hell* is here *sheol*, the Greek *hades:* it is not taken for the *hell* of the damned; but for that place of souls below where the servants of God were kept before the coming of Christ. Which place, both in the Scripture and in the creed, is named *hell.*

be guilty of sin against my father for ever.

33 Therefore I thy servant will stay instead of the boy in the service of my lord, and let the boy go up with his brethren.

34 For I cannot return to my father without the boy, lest I be a witness of the calamity that will oppress my father.

CHAPTER 45

Joseph maketh himself known to his brethren. And sendeth for his father.

JOSEPH could no longer refrain himself before many that stood by: whereupon he commanded that all should go out, and no stranger be present at their knowing one another.

2 And he lifted up his voice with weeping, which the Egyptians and all the house of Pharao heard.

3 And he said to his brethren: I am Joseph. Is my father yet living? His brethren could not answer him, being struck with exceeding great fear.

4 And he said mildly to them: Come nearer to me. And when they were come near him, he said: [1] I am Joseph, your brother, whom you sold into Egypt.

5 Be not afraid, and let it not seem to you a hard case that you sold me into these countries: [2] for God sent me before you into Egypt for your preservation.

6 For it is two years since the famine began to be upon the land, and five years more remain, wherein there can be neither ploughing nor reaping.

7 And God sent me before, that you may be preserved upon the earth, and may have food to live.

8 Not by your counsel was I sent hither, but by the will of God: who hath made me as it were a father to Pharao, and lord of his whole house, and governor in all the land of Egypt.

9 Make haste, and go ye up to my father, and say to him: Thus saith thy son Joseph: God hath made me lord of the whole land of Egypt. Come down to me, linger not.

10 And thou shalt dwell in the land of Gessen: and thou shalt be near me, thou and thy sons, and thy sons' sons, thy sheep, and thy herds, and all things that thou hast.

11 And there I will feed thee (for there are yet five years of famine remaining): lest both thou perish, and thy house, and all things that thou hast.

12 Behold: your eyes, and the eyes of my brother Benjamin see that it is my mouth that speaketh to you.

13 You shall tell my father of all my

CHAP. 45. [1] Acts, 7, 13. [2] Gen. 50, 20.

glory, and all things that you have seen in Egypt: make haste and bring him to me.

14 And falling upon the neck of his brother Benjamin, he embraced him and wept: and Benjamin in like manner wept also on his neck.

15 And Joseph kissed all his brethren, and wept upon every one of them: after which they were emboldened to speak to him.

16 And it was heard, and the fame was abroad in the king's court: The brethren of Joseph are come. And Pharao with all his family was glad.

17 And he spoke to Joseph that he should give orders to his brethren, saying: Load your beasts, *and* go into the land of Chanaan.

18 And bring away from thence your father and kindred, and come to me: and I will give you all the good things of Egypt, that you may eat the marrow of the land.

19 Give orders also that they take wagons out of the land of Egypt, for the carriage of their children and their wives. And say: Take up your father, and make haste to come with all speed.

20 And leave nothing of your household stuff: for all the riches of Egypt shall be yours.

21 And the sons of Israel did as they were bid. And Joseph gave them wagons according to Pharao's commandment: and provisions for the way.

22 He ordered also to be brought out for every one of them two robes: but to Benjamin he gave three hundred pieces of silver with five robes of the best.

23 Sending to his father as much money and raiment, adding besides ten he-asses to carry off all the riches of Egypt, and as many she-asses, carrying wheat and bread for the journey.

24 So he sent away his brethren, and at their departing said to them: Be not angry in the way.

25 And they went up out of Egypt: and came into the land of Chanaan to their father Jacob.

26 And they told him, saying: Joseph thy son is living; and he is ruler in all the land of Egypt. Which when Jacob heard, he awaked as it were out of a deep sleep, yet did not believe them.

27 They, on the other side, told the whole order of the thing. And when he saw the wagons and all that he had sent, his spirit revived.

28 And he said: It is enough for me, if Joseph my son be yet living: I will go and see him before I die.

CHAPTER 46

Israel, warranted by a vision from God, goeth down into Egypt with all his family.

AND Israel taking his journey, with all that he had, came to the well of the oath, and killing victims there to the God of his father Isaac,

2 He heard him by a vision in the night calling him, and saying to him: Jacob, Jacob. And he answered him: Lo, here I am.

3 God said to him: I am the most mighty God of thy father. Fear not, go down into Egypt, for I will make a great nation of thee there.

4 I will go down with thee thither, and will bring thee back again from thence: Joseph also shall put his hands upon thy eyes.

5 And Jacob rose up from the well of the oath: [1] and his sons took him up with their children and wives in the wagons, which Pharao had sent to carry the old man,

6 And all that he had in the land of Chanaan. And he came into Egypt with all his seed: [2]

7 His sons, and grandsons, daughters, and all his offspring together.

8 And these are the names of the children of Israel, that entered into Egypt, he and his children. [3] His firstborn Ruben.

9 The sons of Ruben: Henoch and Phallu, and Hesron and Charmi.

10 [4] The sons of Simeon: Jamuel and Jamin and Ahod, and Jachin and Sohar, and Saul the son of a woman of Chanaan.

11 [5] The sons of Levi: Gerson and Caath and Merari.

12 [6] The sons of Juda: Her and Onan and Sela and Phares and Zara. And Her and Onan died in the land of Chanaan. And sons were born to Phares: Hesron and Hamul.

13 [7] The sons of Issachar: Thola and Phua and Job and Semron.

14 The sons of Zabulon: Sared and Elon and Jahelel.

15 These are the sons of Lia, whom she bore in Mesopotamia of Syria, with Dina his daughter. All the souls of her sons and daughters, thirty-three.

16 The sons of Gad: Sephian and Haggi and Suni and Esebon and Heri and Arodi and Areli.

17 [8] The sons of Aser: Jamne and Jesua and Jessuri and Beria, and Sara their sister. The sons of Beria: Heber and Melchiel.

18 These are the sons of Zelpha whom Laban gave to Lia his daughter. And these she bore to Jacob, sixteen souls.

19 The sons of Rachel, Jacob's wife: Joseph and Benjamin.

20 [9] And sons were born to Joseph, in the land of Egypt, whom Aseneth the daughter of Putiphare priest of Heliopolis bore him: Manasses and Ephraim.

21 The sons of Benjamin: [10] Bela and Bechor and Asbel and Gera and Naaman and Echi and Ros and Mophim and Ophim and Ared.

22 These are the sons of Rachel, whom she bore to Jacob. All the souls, fourteen.

23 The sons of Dan: Husim.

24 The sons of Nephtali: Jaziel and Guni and Jeser and Sallem.

25 These are the sons of Bala, whom Laban gave to Rachel his daughter: and these she bore to Jacob. All the souls, seven.

26 All the souls that went with Jacob into Egypt, and that came out of his thigh, besides his sons' wives, sixty-six.

27 And the sons of Joseph, that were born to him in the land of Egypt, two souls. [11] All the souls of the house of Jacob, that entered into Egypt, were seventy.

28 And he sent Juda before him to Joseph, to tell him; and that he should meet him in Gessen.

29 And when he was come thither, Joseph made ready his chariot, and went up to meet his father, in the same place: and seeing him, he fell upon his neck, and embracing him wept.

30 And the father said to Joseph: Now shall I die with joy, because I have seen thy face, and leave thee alive.

31 And Joseph said to his brethren, and to all his father's house: I will go up, and will tell Pharao, and will say to him: My brethren and my father's house, that were in the land of Chanaan, are come to me.

32 And the men are shepherds, and their occupation is to feed cattle: their flocks and herds, and all they have, they have brought with them.

33 And when he shall call you, and shall say: What is your occupation?

34 You shall answer: We thy servants are shepherds, from our infancy until now, both we and our fathers. And this you shall say, that you may dwell in the land of Gessen, because the Egyptians have all shepherds in abomination.

CHAPTER 47

Jacob and his sons are presented before Pharao. He giveth them the land of Gessen. The famine forceth the Egyptians to sell all their possessions to the king.

CHAP. 46. [1] Acts, 7, 15. [2] Jos. 24, 4; Ps. 104, 23; Isai. 52, 4. [3] Exod. 1, 2; 6, 14; Num. 26, 5; 1 Par. 5, 1-3. [4] Exod. 6, 15; 1 Par. 4, 24. [5] 1 Par. 6, 1. [6] 1 Par. 2, 3; 4, 21. [7] 1 Par. 7, 1. [8] 1 Par. 7, 30. [9] Gen. 41, 50. [10] 1 Par. 7, 0; 8, 1. [11] Deut. 10, 22.

CHAP. 46. Ver. 1. *The well of the oath.* Bersabee.

THEN Joseph went in and told Pharao, saying: My father and brethren, their sheep and their herds, and all that they possess, are come out of the land of Chanaan; and behold they stay in the land of Gessen.

2 Five men also the last of his brethren, he presented before the king.

3 And he asked them: What is your occupation? They answered: We thy servants are shepherds, both we, and our fathers.

4 We are come to sojourn in thy land, because there is no grass for the flocks of thy servants, the famine being very grievous in the land of Chanaan: and we pray thee to give orders that we thy servants may be in the land of Gessen.

5 The king therefore said to Joseph: Thy father and thy brethren are come to thee.

6 The land of Egypt is before thee: make them dwell in the best place, and give them the land of Gessen. And if thou knowest that there are industrious men among them, make them rulers over my cattle.

7 After this Joseph brought in his father to the king, and presented him before him. And he blessed him.

8 And being asked by him: How many are the days of the years of thy life?

9 He answered: The days of my pilgrimage are a hundred and thirty years, few, and evil. And they are not come up to the days of the pilgrimage of my fathers.

10 And blessing the king, he went out.

11 But Joseph gave a possession to his father and his brethren in Egypt, in the best place of the land, in Ramesses, as Pharao had commanded.

12 And he nourished them, and all his father's house, allowing food to every one.

13 For in the whole world there was want of bread, and a famine had oppressed the land: more especially of Egypt and Chanaan.

14 Out of which he gathered up all the money for the corn which they bought: and brought it into the king's treasure.

15 And when the buyers wanted money, all Egypt came to Joseph, saying: Give us bread. Why should we die in thy presence, having now no money?

16 And he answered them: Bring me

CHAP. 47. Ver. 2. The last. Extremos. Some interpret this word of the chiefest, and most rightly; but Joseph seems rather to have chosen out such as had the meanest appearance, that Pharao might not think of employing them at court, with danger of their morals and religion.

your cattle, and for them I will give you food, if you have no money.

17 And when they had brought them, he gave them food in exchange for their horses, and sheep, and oxen, and asses: and he maintained them that year for the exchange of their cattle.

18 And they came the second year, and said to him: We will not hide from our lord, how that our money is spent, and our cattle also are gone. Neither art thou ignorant that we have nothing now left but our bodies and our lands.

19 Why therefore shall we die before thy eyes? We will be thine, both we and our lands. Buy us to be the king's servants, and give us seed, lest for want of tillers the land be turned into wilderness.

20 So Joseph bought all the land of Egypt, every man selling his possessions, because of the greatness of the famine. And he brought it into Pharao's hands:

21 And all its people from one end of the borders of Egypt, even to the other end thereof,

22 Except the land of the priests, which had been given them by the king: to whom also a certain allowance of food was given out of the public stores. And therefore they were not forced to sell their possessions.

23 Then Joseph said to the people: Behold as you see, both you and your lands belong to Pharao. Take seed and sow the fields,

24 That you may have corn. The fifth part you shall give to the king: the other four you shall have for seed, and for food for your families and children.

25 And they answered: Our life is in thy hand. Only let my lord look favourably upon us, and we will gladly serve the king.

26 From that time unto this day, in the whole land of Egypt, the fifth part is paid to the king: and it is become as a law, except the land of the priests, which was free from this covenant.

27 So Israel dwelt in Egypt, that is, in the land of Gessen, and possessed it: and grew, and was multiplied exceedingly.

28 And he lived in it seventeen years: and all the days of his life came to a hundred and forty-seven years.

29 And when he saw that the day of his death drew nigh, he called his son Joseph, and said to him: If I have found favour in thy sight, [1] put thy hand under my thigh, and thou shalt shew me this kindness and truth, not to bury me in Egypt.

30 But I will sleep with my fathers; and thou shalt take me away out of this land, and bury me in the burying place of my ancestors. ² And Joseph answered him: I will do what thou hast commanded.

31 And he said: Swear then to me. And as he was swearing, Israel adored God, turning to the bed's head.

CHAPTER 48

Joseph visiteth his father in his sickness, who adopteth his two sons Manasses and Ephraim, and blesseth them, preferring the younger before the elder.

AFTER these things, it was told Joseph that his father was sick: and he set out to go to him, taking his two sons Manasses and Ephraim.

2 And it was told the old man: Behold thy son Joseph cometh to thee. And being strengthened he sat on his bed.

3 And when Joseph was come in to him, he said: ¹ God Almighty appeared to me at Luza, which is in the land of Chanaan, and he blessed me.

4 And he said: I will cause thee to increase and multiply, and I will make of thee a multitude of people. And I will give this land to thee, and to thy seed after thee for an everlasting possession.

5 ² So thy two sons who were born to thee in the land of Egypt before I came hither to thee, shall be mine: ³ Ephraim and Manasses shall be reputed to me as Ruben and Simeon.

6 But the rest whom thou shalt have after them, shall be thine, and shall be called by the name of their brethren in their possessions.

7 For, when I came out of Mesopotamia, ⁴ Rachel died from me in the land of Chanaan in the very journey. And it was springtime, and I was going to Ephrata: and I buried her near the way of Ephrata, which by another name is called Bethlehem:

8 Then seeing his sons, he said to him: Who are these?

9 He answered: They are my sons whom God hath given me in this place. And he said: Bring them to me that I may bless them.

10 For Israel's eyes were dim by reason of his great age, and he could not see clearly. And when they were brought to him, he kissed and embraced them.

11 And said to his son: I am not deprived of seeing thee. Moreover God hath shewed me thy seed.

12 And when Joseph had taken them from his father's lap, he bowed down with his face to the ground.

13 And he set Ephraim on his right hand, that is, towards the left hand of Israel; but Manasses on his left hand, to wit, towards his father's right hand: and brought them near to him.

14 But he stretching forth his right hand, put it upon the head of Ephraim the younger brother; and the left upon the head of Manasses who was the elder, changing his hands.

15 ⁵ And Jacob blessed the sons of Joseph, and said: God, in whose sight my fathers Abraham and Isaac walked, God that feedeth me from my youth until this day:

16 ⁶ The angel that delivereth me from all evils, bless these boys: and let my name be called upon them, and the names of my fathers Abraham, and Isaac: and may they grow into a multitude upon the earth.

17 And Joseph seeing that his father had put his right hand upon the head of Ephraim, was much displeased: and taking his father's hand he tried to lift it from Ephraim's head, and to remove it to the head of Manasses.

18 And he said to his father: It should not be so, my father: for this is the firstborn, put thy right hand upon his head.

19 But he refusing, said: I know, my son, I know. And this also shall become peoples, and shall be multiplied: but this younger brother shall be greater than he: and his seed shall grow into nations.

20 And be blessed them at that time, saying: In thee shall Israel be blessed. And it shall be said: God do to thee as to Ephraim, and as to Manasses. And he set Ephraim before Manasses.

21 And he said to Joseph his son: Behold I die, and God will be with you, and will bring you back into the land of your fathers.

22 ⁷ I give thee a portion above thy brethren, which I took out of the hand of the Amorrhite ⁸ with my sword and bow.

CHAPTER 49

Jacob's prophetical blessing of his twelve sons. His death.

CHAP. 47. ¹ Gen. 24, 2. ² Gen. 23, 17. CHAP. 48. ¹ Gen. 28, 13. ² Gen. 41, 50. ³ Jos. 13, 7, 29 ⁴ Gen. 35, 19. ⁵ Heb. 11, 21. ⁶ Gen. 31, 29; Matt. 18, 10. ⁷ Jos. 26, 1; 15, 7. ⁸ Jos. 24, 8.

Ver. 31. *To the bed's head.* St. Paul (Heb. 11, 21), following the Greek translation of the Septuagint, reads *adored the top of his rod.* Where note, that the same word in the Hebrew, according to the different pointing of it, signifies both a *bed* and a *rod.* And to verify both these sentences, we must understand that Jacob leaning on Joseph's rod adored, turning towards the head of his bed: which adoration, inasmuch as it was referred to God, was an absolute and sovereign worship: but inasmuch as it was referred to the rod of Joseph, as a figure of the sceptre, that is, of the royal dignity of Christ, was only an inferior and relative honour.

AND Jacob called his sons, and said to them: Gather yourselves together that I may tell you the things that shall befall you in the last days.

2 Gather yourselves together, and hear, O ye sons of Jacob: hearken to Israel your father.

3 Ruben, my firstborn, thou art my strength, and the beginning of my sorrow: excelling in gifts, greater in command.

4 Thou art poured out as water, grow thou not: [1] because thou wentest up to thy father's bed, and didst defile his couch.

5 Simeon and Levi brethren: vessels of iniquity, waging war.

6 Let not my soul go into their counsel, nor my glory be in their assembly: [2] because in their fury they slew a man, and in their self-will they undermined a wall.

CHAP. 49. [1] Gen. 35, 22; 1 Par. 5, 1. [2] Gen. 34, 25. [3] Jos. 19, 1. [4] 1 Par. 5, 2. [5] Matt. 2, 6; John, 1, 45. [6] 1 Par. 5, 1.

CHAP. 49. Ver. 3. *My strength*. He calls him his *strength*, as being born whilst his father was in his full strength and vigour: he calls him *the beginning of his sorrow*, because *cares* and *sorrows* usually come on·with the birth of children. *Excelling in gifts*, because the firstborn had a title to a *double portion*, and to have the command over his brethren, which Ruben forfeited by his sin; being *poured out as water*, that is, spilt and lost.

Ver. 4. *Grow thou not*. This was not meant by·way of a curse or imprecation; but by way of a prophecy foretelling that the tribe of Ruben should not inherit the pre-eminences usually annexed to the first birthright, namely, the double portion, the being prince or lord over the other brethren, and the priesthood: of which the double portion was given to Joseph, the princely office to Juda, and the priesthood to Levi.

Ver. 6. *Slew a man*. Sichem the son of Hemor, with all his people (Gen. 34). Mystically and prophetically it alludes to Christ, whom their posterity, the priests and the scribes, put to death.

Ver. 9. *A lion's whelp*. This blessing of Juda foretelleth the strength of his tribe, the fertility of his inheritance; and principally that the sceptre and legislative power should not be utterly taken away from his race till about the time of the coming of Christ: as in effect it never was. Which is a demonstration against the modern Jews, that the Messiah is long since come: for the sceptre has long since been utterly taken away from Juda.

Ver. 16. *Dan shall judge*. This was verified in Samson, who was of the tribe of Dan, and began to deliver Israel (Judges 13, 5). But as this delivering was but temporal and very imperfect, the holy patriarch (ver. 18) aspires after another kind of deliverer, saying: *I will look for thy salvation, O Lord*.

Ver 19. *Gad being girded*. It seems to allude to the tribe of Gad; when after they had received for their lot the land of Galaad, they marched in arms before the rest of the Israelites, to the conquest of the land of Chanaan: from whence they afterwards returned loaded with spoils. See Jos. 4 and 12.

Ver. 22. *Run to and fro*. To behold his beauty; whilst his envious brethren turned their darts against him.

Ver. 24. *His brow rested upon the strong*. That is, upon God, who was his strength: who also *loosed his bands*, and brought him out of prison to be the *pastor*, that is, the feeder and ruler of Egypt, and the *stone*, that is, the rock and support of Israel.

7 Cursed be their fury, because it was stubborn: and their wrath because it was cruel. [3] I will divide them in Jacob, and will scatter them in Israel.

8 Juda, thee shall thy brethren praise. Thy hands shall be on the necks of thy enemies: the sons of thy father shall bow down to thee.

9 [4] Juda *is* a lion's whelp: to the prey my son, thou art gone up. Resting thou hast couched as a lion, and as a lioness. Who shall rouse him?

10 [5] The sceptre shall not be taken away from Juda, nor a ruler from his thigh, till he come that is to be sent: and he shall be the expectation of nations.

11 Tying his foal to the vineyard, and his ass, O my son, to the vine. He shall wash his robe in wine, and his garment in the blood of the grape.

12 His eyes are more beautiful than wine: and his teeth whiter than milk.

13 Zabulon shall dwell on the sea shore, and in the road of ships, reaching as far as Sidon.

14 Issachar shall be a strong ass lying down between the borders.

15 He saw rest that it was good: and the land that it was excellent. And he bowed his shoulder to carry, and became a servant under tribute.

16 Dan shall judge his people like another tribe in Israel.

17 Let Dan be a snake in the way, a serpent in the path, that biteth the horse's heels that his rider may fall backward.

18 I will look for thy salvation, O Lord.

19 Gad, being girded, shall fight before him: and he himself shall be girded backward.

20 Aser: his bread shall be fat, and he shall yield dainties to kings.

21 Nephtali: a hart let loose, and giving words of beauty.

22 [6] Joseph is a growing son, a growing son and comely to behold: the daughters run to and fro upon the wall.

23 But they that held darts provoked him, and quarrelled with him, and envied him.

24 His bow rested upon the strong, and the bands of his arms and his hands were loosed, by the hands of the mighty one of Jacob: thence he came forth a pastor, the stone of Israel.

25 The God of thy father shall be thy helper, and the Almighty shall bless thee with the blessings of heaven above, with the blessings of the deep that lieth beneath, with the blessings of the breasts and of the womb.

26 The blessings of thy father are

strengthened with the blessings of his fathers: until the desire of the everlasting hills should come. May they be upon the head of Joseph, and upon the crown of the Nazarite among his brethren.

27 Benjamin a ravenous wolf, in the morning shall eat the prey, and in the evening shall divide the spoil.

28 All these are the twelve tribes of Israel: these things their father spoke to them, and he blessed every one, with their proper blessings.

29 And he charged them, saying: I am now going to be gathered to my people: bury me with my fathers in the double cave, which is in the field of Ephron the Hethite,

30 Over against Mambre in the land of Chanaan, [7] which Abraham bought together with the field of Ephron the Hethite for a possession to bury in.

31 There they buried him, and Sara his wife. There was Isaac buried with Rebecca his wife. There also Lia doth lie buried.

32 And when he had ended the commandments, wherewith he instructed his sons, he drew up his feet upon the bed, and died. And he was gathered to his people.

CHAPTER 50

The mourning for Jacob, and his interment. Joseph's kindness towards his brethren. His death.

AND when Joseph saw this, he fell upon his father's face weeping and kissing him.

2 And he commanded his servants the physicians to embalm his father.

3 And while they were fulfilling his commands, there passed forty days: for this was the manner with bodies that were embalmed. And Egypt mourned for him seventy days.

4 And the time of the mourning being expired, Joseph spoke to the family of Pharao: If I have found favour in your sight, speak in the ears of Pharao.

5 For my father made me swear to him, saying: Behold I die; thou shalt bury me in my sepulchre [1] which I have digged for myself in the land of Chanaan. So I will go up and bury my father, and return.

6 And Pharao said to him: Go up and bury thy father according as he made thee swear.

7 So he went up, and there went with him all the ancients of Pharao's house, and all the elders of the land of Egypt.

8 And the house of Joseph with his brethren, except their children, and their flocks and herds, which they left in the land of Gessen.

9 He had also in his train chariots and horsemen: and it was a great company.

10 And they came to the threshingfloor of Atad, which is situated beyond the Jordan: where celebrating the exequies with a great and vehement lamentation, they spent full seven days.

11 And when the inhabitants of Chanaan saw this they said: This is a great mourning to the Egyptians. And therefore the name of that place was called: The mourning of Egypt.

12 So the sons of Jacob did as he had commanded them.

13 And carrying him into the land of Chanaan, [2] they buried him in the double cave which Abraham had bought, together with the field for a possession of a buryingplace, of Ephron the Hethite over against Mambre.

14 And Joseph returned into Egypt with his brethren, and all that were in his company, after he had buried his father.

15 Now he being dead, his brethren were afraid, and talked one with another: Lest perhaps he should remember the wrong he suffered, and requite us all the evil that we did to him.

16 And they sent a message to him, saying: Thy father commanded us before he died,

17 That we should say thus much to thee from him: I beseech thee to forget the wickedness of thy brethren, and the sin and malice they practised against thee. We also pray thee, to forgive the servants of the God of thy father this wickedness. And when Joseph heard this, he wept.

18 And his brethren came to him: and worshipping prostrate on the ground they said: We are thy servants.

19 And he answered them: Fear not. Can we resist the will of God?

20 [3] You thought evil against me: but God turned it into good, that he

7 Gen. 23, 17. CHAP. 50. 1 Gen. 47, 29. 2 Acts 7, 16; Gen. 23, 17. 3 Gen. 45, 5.

Ver. 26. *The blessings of thy father.* That is, thy father's blessings are made more prevalent and effectual in thy regard, by the additional strength they receive from his inheriting the blessings of his progenitors Abraham and Isaac. *The desire of the everlasting hills.* These blessings all looked forward towards Christ, called *the desire of the everlasting hills,* as being longed for, as it were, by the whole creation. Mystically, the patriarchs and prophets are called the *everlasting hills,* by reason of the eminence of their wisdom and holiness. *The Nazarite.* This word signifies one *separated;* and agrees to Joseph, as being separated from, and more eminent than, his brethren. As the ancient *Nazarites* were so called from their being set aside for God, and vowed to him.

Ver. 29. *To be gathered to my people.* That is, I am going to die, and so to follow my ancestors that are gone before me, and to join their company in another world.

might exalt me, as at present you see, and might save many people.

21 ⁴Fear not: I will feed you and your children. And he comforted them, and spoke gently and mildly.

22 And he dwelt in Egypt with all his father's house: and lived a hundred and ten years. And he saw the children of Ephraim to the third generation. ⁵The children also of Machir the son of Manasses were born on Joseph's knees.

23 After which he told his brethren: ⁶God will visit you after my death, and will make you go up out of this land, to the land which he swore to Abraham, Isaac, and Jacob.

24 And he made them swear to him, saying: God will visit you. ⁷Carry my bones with you out of this place.

25 And he died being a hundred and ten years old. And being embalmed he was laid in a coffin in Egypt.

THE BOOK OF

EXODUS

The Second Book of MOSES *is called* EXODUS, *from the Greek word* EXODOS, *which signifies* going out: *because it contains the history of the going out of the children of Israel out of Egypt. The Hebrews, from the words with which it begins, call it* VEELLE SEMOTH. *These are the names. It contains transactions for one hundred and forty-five years; that is, from the death of Joseph to the erecting of the tabernacle.*

CHAPTER 1

The Israelites are multiplied in Egypt. They are oppressed by a new king, who commandeth all their male children to be killed.

THESE are the names of the children of Israel, that went into Egypt with Jacob: they went in, every man with his household.¹

2 Ruben, Simeon, Levi, Juda,

3 Issachar, Zabulon, and Benjamin,

4 Dan, and Nepthtali, Gad and Aser.

5 And all the souls that came out of Jacob's thigh, were seventy: ²but Joseph was in Egypt.

6 After he was dead, and all his brethren, and all that generation,

7 ³The children of Israel increased. and sprung up into multitudes. And growing exceedingly strong they filled the land.

8 In the mean time there arose a new king over Egypt, that knew not Joseph.

9 And he said to his people: Behold the people of the children of Israel are numerous and stronger than we.

10 Come, let us wisely oppress them. lest they multiply: and if any war shall rise against us, join with our enemies. and having overcome us, depart out of the land.

11 Therefore he set over them masters of the works, to afflict them with burdens. And they built for Pharao cities of tabernacles, Phithom and Ramesses.

12 But the more they oppressed them, the more they were multiplied, and increased.

13 And the Egyptians hated the children of Israel: and afflicted them and mocked them.

14 And they made their life bitter with hard works in clay, and brick, and with all manner of service, wherewith they were overcharged in the works of the earth.

15 And the king of Egypt spoke to the midwives of the Hebrews, of whom one was called Sephora, the other Phua,

16 Commanding them: When you shall do the office of midwives to the Hebrew women, and the time of delivery is come: if it be a man child, kill it; if a woman, keep it alive.

17 But the midwives feared God, and did not do as the king of Egypt had commanded; but saved the men children.

18 And the king called for them and said: What is that you meant to do, that you would save the men children?

19 They answered: The Hebrew women are not as the Egyptian women. For they themselves are skilful in the office of a midwife; and they are delivered before we come to them.

---

⁴ Gen. 47, 12.   ⁵ Num. 32, 39.   ⁶ Heb. 11, 22.   ⁷ Exod. 13, 19; Jos. 24, 32.   CHAP. 1.   ¹ Gen. 46, 8.   ² Gen. 46, 27.   ³ Acts, 7, 17.

CHAP. 1. Ver. 11. *Of tabernacles.* That is, of storehouses.

20 Therefore God dealt well with the midwives: and the people multiplied and grew exceedingly strong.

21 And because the midwives feared God, he built them houses.

22 Pharao therefore charged all his people, saying: Whatsoever shall be born of the male sex, ye shall cast into the river: whatsoever of the female, ye shall save alive.

CHAPTER 2

Moses is born and exposed on the bank of the river. He is taken up by the daughter of Pharao, and adopted for her son. He killeth an Egyptian, and fleeth into Madian. He marrieth a wife.

AFTER this there went a man of the house of Levi; [1] and took a wife of his own kindred.

2 And she conceived, and bore a son: [2] and seeing him a goodly *child*, hid him three months.

3 And when she could hide *him* no longer, she took a basket made of bulrushes, and daubed it with slime and pitch: and put the little babe therein, and laid him in the sedges by the river's brink,

4 His sister standing afar off, and taking notice what would be done.

5 And behold the daughter of Pharao came down to wash herself in the river: and her maids walked by the river's brink. And when she saw the basket in the sedges, she sent one of her maids for it. And when it was brought,

6 She opened it and seeing within it an infant crying, having compassion on it she said: This is one of the babes of the Hebrews.

7 And the child's sister said to her: Shall I go and call to thee a Hebrew woman, to nurse the babe?

8 She answered: Go. The maid went and called her mother.

9 And Pharao's daughter said to her: Take this child and nurse him for me. I will give thee thy wages. The woman took, and nursed the child: and when he was grown up, she delivered him to Pharao's daughter.

10 And she adopted him for a son, and called him Moses, saying: Because I took him out of the water.

11 In those days after Moses was grown up, [3] he went out to his brethren, and saw their affliction, and an Egyptian striking one of the Hebrews his brethren.

12 And when he had looked about this way and that way, and saw no one there, he slew the Egyptian and hid him in the sand.

13 And going out the next day, he saw two Hebrews quarrelling. And he said to him that did the wrong: Why strikest thou thy neighbour?

14 But he answered: Who hath appointed thee prince and judge over us: wilt thou kill me, as thou didst yesterday kill the Egyptian? Moses feared, and said: How is this come to be known?

15 And Pharao heard of this word and sought to kill Moses. But he fled from his sight, and abode in the land of Madian: and he sat down by a well.

16 And the priest of Madian had seven daughters, who came to draw water: and when the troughs were filled, desired to water their father's flocks.

17 And the shepherds came and drove them away: and Moses arose, and defending the maids, watered their sheep.

18 And when they returned to Raguel their father, he said to them: Why are ye come sooner than usual?

19 They answered: A man of Egypt delivered us from the hands of the shepherds; and he drew water also with us, and gave the sheep to drink.

20 But he said: Where is he? Why have you let the man go? Call him that he may eat bread.

21 And Moses swore that he would dwell with him. [4] And he took Sephora his daughter to wife.

22 And she bore him a son, whom he called Gersam, saying: I have been a stranger in a foreign country. And she bore another, whom he called Eliezer, saying: For the God of my father, my helper, hath delivered me out of the hand of Pharao.

23 Now after a long time the king of Egypt died. And the children of Israel groaning, cried out because of the

CHAP. 2. [1] Exod. 6, 20. [2] Heb. 11, 23. [3] Heb. 11, 24. [4] Exod. 18, 2; 1 Par. 23, 15.

Ver. 21. *Because the midwives feared God.* The midwives were rewarded, not for their lie, which was a venial sin; but for their fear of God, and their humanity: but this reward was only temporal, in *building them houses*, that is, in establishing and enriching their families.

CHAP. 2. Ver. 10. *Moses* or *Moyses.* In the Egyptian tongue, this word signifies one *taken or saved out of the water.*

Ver. 12. *He slew the Egyptian.* This he did by a particular inspiration of God; as a prelude to his delivering the people from their oppression and bondage. *He thought,* says St. Stephen (Acts, 7, 25), *that his brethren understood that God by his hand would save them.* But such particular and extraordinary examples are not to be imitated.

Ver. 15. *Madian.* A city and country of Arabia, which took its name from Madian the son of Abraham, by Cetura, and was peopled by his posterity.

Ver. 18. *Raguel.* He had two names, being also called *Jethro,* as appears from the first verse of the following chapter.

Ver. 22. *Gersam,* or *Gershom.* This name signifies *a stranger there:* as *Eliezer* signifies *the help of God.*

works: and their cry went up unto God from the works.

24 And he heard their groaning: and remembered the covenant which he made with Abraham, Isaac, and Jacob.

25 And the Lord looked upon the children of Israel: and he knew them.

CHAPTER 3

God appeareth to Moses in a bush, and sendeth him to deliver Israel.

NOW Moses fed the sheep of Jethro his father-in-law, the priest of Madian: and he drove the flock to the inner parts of the desert, and came to the mountain of God, Horeb.

2 ¹ And the Lord appeared to him in a flame of fire out of the midst of a bush: and he saw that the bush was on fire and was not burnt.

3 And Moses said: I will go and see this great sight, why the bush is not burnt.

4 And when the Lord saw that he went forward to see, he called to him out of the midst of the bush, and said: Moses, Moses. And he answered: Here I am.

5 And he said: Come not nigh hither. Put off the shoes from thy feet: for the place whereon thou standest is holy ground.

6 And he said: ² I am the God of thy father, the God of Abraham, the God of Isaac, and the God of Jacob. Moses hid his face: for he durst not look at God.

7 And the Lord said to him: I have seen the affliction of my people in Egypt, and I have heard their cry; because of the rigour of them that are over the works.

8 And knowing their sorrow, I am come down to deliver them out of the hands of the Egyptians: and to bring them out of that land into a good and spacious land, into a land that floweth with milk and honey, to the places of the Chanaanite, and Hethite, and Amorrhite, and Pherezite, and Hevite, and Jebusite.

9 For the cry of the children of Israel is come unto me: and I have seen their affliction, wherewith they are oppressed by the Egyptians.

10 But come, and I will send thee to Pharao, that thou mayst bring forth my people, the children of Israel out of Egypt.

11 And Moses said to God: Who am I that I should go to Pharao, and should bring forth the children of Israel out of Egypt?

12 And he said to him: I will be with thee. And this thou shalt have for a sign that I have sent thee: When thou shalt have brought my people out of Egypt, thou shalt offer sacrifice to God upon this mountain.

13 Moses said to God: Lo, I shall go to the children of Israel, and say to them: The God of your fathers hath sent me to you. If they should say to me: What is his name? What shall I say to them?

14 God said to Moses: I AM WHO AM. He said: Thus shalt thou say to the children of Israel: HE WHO IS, hath sent me to you.

15 And God said again to Moses: Thus shalt thou say to the children of Israel: The Lord God of your fathers, the God of Abraham, the God of Isaac, and the God of Jacob, hath sent me to you. This is my name for ever, and this is my memorial unto all generations.

16 Go, gather together the ancients of Israel, and thou shalt say to them: The Lord God of your fathers, the God of Abraham, the God of Isaac, and the God of Jacob, hath appeared to me, saying: Visiting I have visited you, and I have seen all that hath befallen you in Egypt.

17 And I have said the word to bring you forth out of the affliction of Egypt into the land of the Chanaanite, the Hethite, and the Amorrhite, and Pherezite, and Hevite, and Jebusite, to a land that floweth with milk and honey.

18 And they shall hear thy voice. And thou shalt go in, thou and the ancients of Israel, to the king of Egypt, and thou shalt say to him: The Lord God of the Hebrews hath called us. We will go three days' journey into the wilderness, to sacrifice unto the Lord our God.

19 But I know that the king of Egypt will not let you go, but by a mighty hand.

20 For I will stretch forth my hand, and will strike Egypt with all my wonders which I will do in the midst of them. After these he will let you go.

21 And I will give favour to this people, in the sight of the Egyptians: ³ and when you go forth, you shall not depart empty.

22 But every woman shall ask of her neighbour, and of her that is in her house, vessels of silver and of gold, and

CHAP. 3. ¹ Acts, 7, 30. ² Matt. 22, 32; Mark, 12, 26; Luke, 20, 37. ³ Exod. 11, 2; 12, 35.

Ver. 25. *Knew them.* That is, he had respect to them, he cast a merciful eye upon them.

CHAP. 3. Ver. 2. *The Lord appeared.* That is, an angel representing God, and speaking in his name.

Ver. 14. *I am who am.* That is, I am *being* itself, eternal, self-existent, independent, infinite; without beginning, end, or change; and the source of all other beings.

raiment: and you shall put them on your sons and daughters and shall spoil Egypt.

CHAPTER 4

Moses is empowered to confirm his mission with miracles. His brother Aaron is appointed to assist him.

MOSES answered and said: They will not believe me, nor hear my voice. But they will say: The Lord hath not appeared to thee.

2 Then he said to him: What is that thou holdest in thy hand? He answered: A rod.

3 And the Lord said: Cast it down upon the ground. He cast it down, and it was turned into a serpent: so that Moses fled from it.

4 And the Lord said: Put out thy hand and take it by the tail. He put forth his hand, and took hold of it; and it was turned into a rod.

5 That they may believe, saith he, that the Lord God of their fathers, the God of Abraham, the God of Isaac, and the God of Jacob, hath appeared to thee.

6 And the Lord said again: Put thy hand into thy bosom. And when he had put it into *his* bosom, he brought it forth leprous as snow.

7 And he said: Put back thy hand into thy bosom. He put it back, and brought it out again, and it was like the other flesh.

8 If they will not believe thee, saith he, nor hear the voice of the former sign, they will believe the word of the latter sign.

9 But if they will not even believe these two signs, nor hear thy voice: take of the river water, and pour it out upon the dry land, and whatsoever thou drawest out of the river shall be turned into blood.

10 Moses said: I beseech thee, Lord, I am not eloquent from yesterday and the day before; and since thou hast spoken to thy servant, I have more impediment and slowness of tongue.

11 The Lord said to him: Who made man's mouth? Or who made the dumb and the deaf, the seeing and the blind? Did not I?

12 Go therefore, ¹ and I will be in thy mouth: and I will teach thee what thou shalt speak.

13 But he said: I beseech thee, Lord send whom thou wilt send.

14 The Lord being angry at Moses said: Aaron the Levite is thy brother I know that he is eloquent: behold, he cometh forth to meet thee, and seeing thee shall be glad at heart.

15 Speak to him, and put my words

in his mouth: and I will be in thy mouth, and in his mouth, ² and will shew you what you must do.

16 He shall speak in thy stead to the people, and shall be thy mouth: but thou shalt be to him in those things that pertain to God.

17 And take this rod in thy hand, wherewith thou shalt do the signs.

18 Moses went his way, and returned to Jethro his father-in-law and said to him: I will go and return to my brethren into Egypt, that I may see if they be yet alive. And Jethro said to him: Go in peace.

19 And the Lord said to Moses, in Madian: Go, and return into Egypt; for they are all dead that sought thy life.

20 Moses therefore took his wife, and his sons, and set them upon an ass: and returned into Egypt, carrying the rod of God in his hand.

21 And the Lord said to him, as he was returning into Egypt: See that thou do all the wonders before Pharao, which I have put in thy hand. I shall harden his heart, and he will not let the people go.

22 And thou shalt say to him: Thus saith the Lord: Israel is my son, my firstborn.

23 I have said to thee: Let my son go, that he may serve me: and thou wouldst not let him go. Behold, I will kill thy son, thy firstborn.

24 And when he was in his journey, in the inn, the Lord met him, and would have killed him.

25 Immediately Sephora took a very sharp stone, and circumcised the foreskin of her son, and touched his feet, and said: A bloody spouse art thou to me.

26 And he let him go after she had said: A bloody spouse art thou to me; because of the circumcision.

27 And the Lord said to Aaron: Go into the desert to meet Moses. And he went forth to meet him in the mountain of God and kissed him.

CHAP. 4. ¹ Matt. 10, 20. ² Exod. 7, 2.

Ver. 22. *Shall spoil Egypt.* That is, you shall strip, and take away the goods of the Egyptians. This was not authorizing theft or injustice; but was a just disposal made by Him, who is the great lord and master of all things, in order to pay the children of Israel some part of what was due to them from the Egyptians for their labours.

CHAP. 4. Ver 21. *I shall harden his heart.* Not by being the efficient cause of his sin: but by withdrawing from him, for his just punishment, the dew of grace that might have softened his heart; and so suffering him to grow harder and harder.

Ver. 24. *The Lord met him, and would have killed him.* This was an angel representing the Lord, who treated Moses in this manner, for having neglected the circumcision of his younger son; which his wife understanding, circumcised her child upon the spot, upon which the angel let Moses go.

28 And Moses told Aaron all the words of the Lord, by which he had sent him, and the signs that he had commanded.

29 And they came together: and they assembled all the ancients of the children of Israel.

30 And Aaron spoke all the words which the Lord had said to Moses: and he wrought the signs before the people.

31 And the people believed. And they heard that the Lord had visited the children of Israel: and that he had looked upon their affliction. And falling down they adored.

CHAPTER 5

Pharao refuseth to let the people go. They are more oppressed.

AFTER these things Moses and Aaron went in, and said to Pharao: Thus saith the Lord God of Israel: Let my people go that they may sacrifice to me in the desert.

2 But he answered: Who is the Lord, that I should hear his voice, and let Israel go? I know not the Lord, neither will I let Israel go.

3 And they said: The God of the Hebrews hath called us, to go three days' journey into the wilderness and to sacrifice to the Lord our God; lest a pestilence or the sword fall upon us.

4 The king of Egypt said to them: Why do you, Moses and Aaron, draw off the people from their works? Get you gone to your burdens.

5 And Pharao said: The people of the land is numerous. You see that the multitude is increased: How much more if you give them rest from their works?

6 Therefore he commanded the same day the overseers of the works, and the taskmasters of the people, saying:

7 You shall give straw no more to the people to make brick, as before: but let them go and gather straw.

8 And you shall lay upon them the task of bricks, which they did before, neither shall you diminish anything thereof. For they are idle, and therefore they cry, saying: Let us go and sacrifice to our God.

9 Let them be oppressed with works, and let them fulfil them: that they may not regard lying words.

10 And the overseers of the works and the taskmasters went out and said to the people: Thus saith Pharao, I allow you no straw.

11 Go, and gather it where you can find it: neither shall any thing of your work be diminished.

12 And the people was scattered through all the land of Egypt to gather straw.

13 And the overseers of the works pressed them, saying: Fulfil your work every day as before you were wont to do when straw was given you.

14 And they that were over the works of the children of Israel were scourged by Pharao's taskmasters, saying: Why have you not made up the task of bricks both yesterday and to-day as before?

15 And the officers of the children of Israel came, and cried out to Pharao, saying: Why dealest thou so with thy servants?

16 Straw is not given us, and bricks are required of us as before. Behold, we thy servants are beaten with whips; and thy people is unjustly dealt withal.

17 And he said: You are idle, and therefore you say: Let us go and sacrifice to the Lord.

18 Go therefore, and work. Straw shall not be given you; and you shall deliver the accustomed number of bricks.

19 And the officers of the children of Israel saw that they were in evil case, because it was said to them: There shall not a whit be diminished of the bricks for every day.

20 And they met Moses and Aaron, who stood over against them as they came out from Pharao.

21 And they said to them: The Lord see and judge, because you have made our saviour to stink before Pharao and his servants; and you have given him a sword to kill us.

22 And Moses returned to the Lord, and said: Lord, why hast thou afflicted this people? Wherefore hast thou sent me?

23 For since the time that I went in to Pharao to speak in thy name, he hath afflicted thy people: and thou hast not delivered them.

CHAPTER 6

God reneweth his promise. The genealogies of Ruben, Simeon and Levi, down to Moses and Aaron.

AND the Lord said to Moses: Now thou shalt see what I will do to Pharao. For by a mighty hand shall he let them go, and with a strong hand shall he cast them out of his land.

2 And the Lord spoke to Moses, saying: I am the Lord,

3 That appeared to Abraham, to Isaac, and to Jacob, by the name of God Almighty: and my name ADONAI I did not shew them.

4 And I made a covenant with them, to give them the land of Chanaan, the land of their pilgrimage wherein they were strangers.

5 I have heard the groaning of the children of Israel, wherewith the Egyptians have oppressed them: and I have remembered my covenant.

6 Therefore say to the children of Israel: I am the Lord who will bring you out from the work prison of the Egyptians; and will deliver you from bondage, and redeem you with a high arm, and great judgments.

7 And I will take you to myself for my people. I will be your God: and you shall know that I am the Lord your God, who brought you out from the work prison of the Egyptians.

8 And brought you into the land, concerning which I lifted up my hand to give it to Abraham, Isaac, and Jacob. And I will give it you to possess, I am the Lord.

9 And Moses told all this to the children of Israel; but they did not hearken to him, for anguish of spirit, and most painful work.

10 And the Lord spoke to Moses, saying:

11 Go in, and speak to Pharao king of Egypt, that he let the children of Israel go out of his land.

12 Moses answered before the Lord: Behold the children of Israel do not hearken to me; and how will Pharao hear me, especially as I am of uncircumcised lips?

13 And the Lord spoke to Moses and Aaron, and he gave them a charge unto the children of Israel, and unto Pharao the king of Egypt, that they should bring forth the children of Israel out of the land of Egypt.

14 [1] These are the heads of their houses by their families. The sons of Ruben the firstborn of Israel: Henoch and Phallu, Hesron and Charmi.

15 These are the kindreds of Ruben. [2] The sons of Simeon: Jamuel and Jamin, and Ahod, and Jachin, and Soar and Saul the son of a Chanaanitess. These are the families of Simeon.

16 And these are the names of the sons of Levi by their kindreds: Gerson and Caath, and Merari. And the years of the life of Levi were a hundred and thirty-seven.

17 [3] The sons of Gerson: Lobni and Semei, by their kindreds.

18 [4] The sons of Caath: Amram, and Isaar, and Hebron, and Oziel. And the years of Caath's life were a hundred and thirty-three.

19 The sons of Merari: Moholi and Musi. These are the kindreds of Levi by their families.

20 And Amram took to wife Jochabed his aunt by the father's side: and she bore him Aaron and Moses. And the years of Amram's life were a hundred and thirty-seven.

21 The sons also of Isaar: Core, and Nepheg, and Zechri.

22 The sons also of Oziel: Mizael, and Elizaphan, and Sethri.

23 And Aaron took to wife Elizabeth the daughter of Aminadab, sister of Nahason, who bore him Nabad, and Abiu, and Eleazer, and Ithamar.

24 The sons also of Core: Aser, and Elcana, and Abiasaph. These are the kindreds of the Corites.

25 But Eleazer the son of Aaron took a wife of the daughters of Phutiel: and she bore him Phinees. These are the heads of the Levitical families by their kindreds.

26 These are Aaron and Moses, whom the Lord commanded to bring forth the children of Israel out of the land of Egypt by their companies.

27 These are they that speak to Pharao king of Egypt, in order to bring out the children of Israel from Egypt. These are that Moses and Aaron.

28 In the day when the Lord spoke to Moses in the land of Egypt.

29 And the Lord spoke to Moses, saying: I am the Lord: Speak thou to Pharao king of Egypt all that I say to thee.

30 And Moses said before the Lord: Lo, I am of uncircumcised lips. How will Pharao hear me?

CHAPTER 7

Moses and Aaron go in to Pharao. They turn the rod into a serpent; and the waters of Egypt into blood, which was the first plague. The magicians do the like, and Pharao's heart is hardened.

AND the Lord said to Moses: Behold I have appointed thee the

[1] Gen. 46, 9; Num. 26, 5; 1 Par. 5, 1. [2] 1 Par. 4, 24. [3] 1 Par. 6, 1; 23, 5. [4] Num. 3, 9; 26, 57; 1 Par. 6, 2; 23, 12.

CHAP. 6. Ver. 3. *My name Adonai.* The name, which is in the Hebrew text, is that most proper name of God, which signifieth his *eternal, self-existing being,* (Exod. 3, 14,) which the Jews out of reverence never pronounce; but, instead of it, whenever it occurs in the Bible, they read *Adonai,* which signifies *the Lord;* and, therefore, they put the points or vowels, which belong to the name *Adonai,* to the four letters of that other ineffable name, Jod, He, Vau, He. Hence some moderns have framed the name of *Jehovah,* unknown to all the ancients, whether Jews or Christians; for the true pronunciation of the name, which is in the Hebrew text, by long disuse is now quite lost.

Ver. 12. *Uncircumcised lips.* So he calls the defect he had in his words, or utterance.

God of Pharao: and Aaron thy brother shall be thy prophet.

2 [1] Thou shalt speak to him all that I command thee; and he shall speak to Pharao, that he let the children of Israel go out of his land.

3 But I shall harden his heart, and shall multiply my signs and wonders in the land of Egypt.

4 And he will not hear you: and I will lay my hand upon Egypt, and will bring forth my army and my people the children of Israel out of the land of Egypt, by very great judgments.

5 And the Egyptians shall know that I am the Lord, who have stretched forth my hand upon Egypt; and have brought forth the children of Israel out of the midst of them.

6 And Moses and Aaron did as the Lord had commanded: so did they.

7 And Moses was eighty years old, and Aaron eighty-three, when they spoke to Pharao.

8 And the Lord said to Moses and Aaron:

9 When Pharao shall say to you: Shew signs; Thou shalt say to Aaron: Take thy rod, and cast it down before Pharao, and it shall be turned into a serpent.

10 So Moses and Aaron went in unto Pharao, and did as the Lord had commanded. And Aaron took the rod before Pharao, and his servants, and it was turned into a serpent.

11 [2] And Pharao called the wise men and the magicians: and they also by Egyptian enchantments and certain secrets did in like manner.

12 And they every one cast down their rods; and they were turned into serpents. But Aaron's rod devoured their rods.

13 And Pharao's heart was hardened, and he did not hearken to them, as the Lord had commanded.

14 And the Lord said to Moses: Pharao's heart is hardened; he will not let the people go.

15 Go to him in the morning. Behold, he will go out to the waters: and thou shalt stand to meet him on the bank of the river. And thou shalt take in thy hand the rod that was turned into a serpent.

16 And thou shalt say to him: The Lord God of the Hebrews sent me to thee, saying: Let my people go to sacrifice to me in the desert. And hitherto thou wouldst not hear.

17 Thus therefore saith the Lord: In this thou shalt know that I am the Lord. Behold, I will strike with the rod, that is in my hand, the water of the river: and it shall be turned into blood.

18 And the fishes that are in the river shall die, and the waters shall be corrupted: and the Egyptians shall be afflicted when they drink the water of the river.

19 The Lord also said to Moses: Say to Aaron: Take thy rod, and stretch forth thy hand upon the waters of Egypt, and upon their rivers, and streams and pools, and all the ponds of waters, that they may be turned into blood. And let blood be in all the land of Egypt, both in vessels of wood and of stone.

20 And Moses and Aaron did as the Lord had commanded: [3] and lifting up the rod he struck the water of the river before Pharao and his servants: and it was turned into blood.

21 And the fishes that were in the river died: and the river corrupted, and the Egyptians could not drink the water of the river, and there was blood in all the land of Egypt.

22 [4] And the magicians of the Egyptians with their enchantments did in like manner. And Pharao's heart was hardened: neither did he hear them, as the Lord had commanded.

23 And he turned himself away and went into his house: neither did he set his heart to it this time also.

24 And all the Egyptians dug round about the river for water to drink: for they could not drink of the water of the river.

25 And seven days were fully ended, after that the Lord struck the river.

CHAPTER 8

The second plague is of frogs. Pharao promiseth to let the Israelites go, but breaketh his promise. The third plague is of sciniphs. The fourth is of flies. Pharao again promiseth to dismiss the people, but doth it not.

AND the Lord said to Moses: Go in to Pharao, and thou shalt say to him: Thus saith the Lord: Let my people go to sacrifice to me.

2 But if thou wilt not let them go, behold, I will strike all thy coasts with frogs.

3 And the river shall bring forth an abundance of frogs: which shall come up, and enter into thy house, and thy bedchamber, and upon thy bed, and

CHAP. 7. [1] Exod. 4, 15. [2] Tim. 3, 8. [3] Exod. 17, 5; Ps. 77, 44. [4] Wisd. 17, 7.

CHAP. 7. Ver. 1. *The God of Pharao.* That is, to be his *judge;* and to exercise a *divine power,* as God's instrument, over him and his people.

Ver. 3. *I shall harden his heart.* Not by being the efficient cause of his hardness of heart, but by permitting it; and by withdrawing grace from him, in punishment of his malice; which alone was the proper cause of his being hardened.

Ver. 11. *Magicians. Jannes,* and *Mambres,* or *Jambres* (2 Tim. 3, 8).

into the houses of thy servants, and to thy people, and into thy ovens, and into the remains of thy meats.

4 And the frogs shall come in to thee, and to thy people, and to all thy servants.

5 And the Lord said to Moses: Say to Aaron: Stretch forth thy hand upon the streams and upon the rivers and the pools; and bring forth frogs upon the land of Egypt.

6 And Aaron stretched forth his hand upon the waters of Egypt: and the frogs came up, and covered the land of Egypt.

7 And the magicians also by their enchantments did in like manner: and they brought forth frogs upon the land of Egypt.

8 But Pharao called Moses and Aaron, and said to them: Pray ye to the Lord to take away the frogs from me and my people; and I will let the people go to sacrifice to the Lord.

9 And Moses said to Pharao: Set me a time when I shall pray for thee, and for thy servants, and for thy people that the frogs may be driven away from thee and from thy house, and from thy servants, and from thy people; and may remain only in the river.

10 And he answered: To-morrow. But he said: I will do according to thy word; that thou mayst know that there is none like to the Lord our God.

11 And the frogs shall depart from thee, and from thy house, and from thy servants, and from thy people: and shall remain only in the river.

12 And Moses and Aaron went forth from Pharao: and Moses cried to the Lord for the promise, which he had made to Pharao concerning the frogs.

13 And the Lord did according to the word of Moses: and the frogs died out of the houses, and out of the villages, and out of the fields:

14 And they gathered them together into immense heaps, and the land was corrupted.

15 And Pharao seeing that rest was given, hardened his own heart, and did not hear them, as the Lord had commanded.

16 And the Lord said to Moses: Say to Aaron, Stretch forth thy rod, and strike the dust of the earth. And may there be sciniphs in all the land of Egypt.

17 And they did so. And Aaron stretched forth his hand, holding the rod: and he struck the dust of the earth, and there came sciniphs on men and on beasts. All the dust of the earth was turned into sciniphs, through all the land of Egypt.

18 And the magicians with their enchantments practised in like manner to bring forth sciniphs, and they could not: and there were sciniphs as well on men as on beasts.

19 And the magicians said to Pharao: This is the finger of God. And Pharao's heart was hardened: and he hearkened not unto them, as the Lord had commanded.

20 The Lord also said to Moses: Arise early, and stand before Pharao; for he will go forth to the waters. And thou shalt say to him: Thus saith the Lord: Let my people go to sacrifice to me.

21 But if thou wilt not let them go, behold I will send in upon thee, and upon thy servants, and upon thy houses all kinds of flies: and the houses of the Egyptians shall be filled with flies of divers kinds, and the whole land whereinto they shall be.

22 And I will make the land of Gessen wherein my people is, wonderful in that day, so that flies shall not be there: and thou shalt know that I am the Lord in the midst of the earth.

23 And I will put a division between my people and thy people. To-morrow shall this sign be.

24 And the Lord did so. [1] And there came a very grievous swarm of flies into the houses of Pharao and of his servants, and into all the land of Egypt: and the land was corrupted by this kind of flies.

25 And Pharao called Moses and Aaron, and said to them: Go, and sacrifice to your God in this land.

26 And Moses said: It cannot be so: for we shall sacrifice the abominations of the Egyptians to the Lord our God. Now if we kill those things which the Egyptians worship, in their presence, they will stone us.

27 We will go three days' journey into the wilderness: and will sacrifice to the Lord our God, [2] as he hath commanded us.

CHAP. 8. [1] Wisd. 16, 9. [2] Exod. 3, 18.

CHAP. 8. Ver. 8. *Pray ye to the Lord.* By this it appears, that though the magicians, by the help of the devil, could bring frogs, yet they could not take them away: God being pleased to abridge in this the power of Satan. So we see they could not afterwards produce the lesser insects; and in this restraint of the power of the devil, were forced to acknowledge *the finger of God.*

Ver. 15. *Pharao hardened his own heart.* By this we see that Pharao was himself the efficient cause of his heart being hardened, and not God.— See the same repeated in ver. 32. *Pharao hardened his heart at this time also:* likewise chap. 9, 7, 85, and chap. 13, 15.

Ver. 16. *Sciniphs.* Or *Cinifs* (Hebrew *Chinnim*), small flying insects, very troublesome both to men and beasts.

Ver. 26. *The abominations of the Egyptians.* That is, the things they worship for Gods: oxen, rams, &c. It is the usual style of the scriptures to call all idols and false gods, *abominations*, to signify how much the people of God ought to detest and abhor them.

28 And Pharao said: I will let you go to sacrifice to the Lord your God in the wilderness. But go no farther: pray for me.

29 And Moses said: I will go out from thee, and will pray to the Lord. And the flies shall depart from Pharao, and from his servants, and from his people to-morrow: but do not deceive any more, in not letting the people go to sacrifice to the Lord.

30 So Moses went out from Pharao, and prayed to the Lord.

31 And he did according to his word: and he took away the flies from Pharao, and from his servants, and from his people. There was not left so much as one.

32 And Pharao's heart was hardened, so that neither this time would he let the people go.

CHAPTER 9

The fifth plague is a murrain among the cattle. The sixth, of boils in men and beasts. The seventh, of hail. Pharao promiseth again to let the people go, and breaketh his word.

AND the Lord said to Moses: Go in to Pharao, and speak to him: Thus saith the Lord God of the Hebrews: Let my people go to sacrifice to me.

2 But if thou refuse, and withhold them still:

3 Behold my hand shall be upon thy fields: and a very grievous murrain upon thy horses, and asses, and camels, and oxen, and sheep.

4 And the Lord will make a wonderful difference between the possessions of Israel and the possessions of the Egyptians: that nothing at all shall die of those things that belong to the children of Israel.

5 And the Lord appointed a time, saying: To-morrow will the Lord do this thing in the land.

6 The Lord therefore did this thing the next day. And all the beasts of the Egyptians died: but of the beasts of the children of Israel there died not one.

7 And Pharao sent to see: and there was not any thing dead of that which Israel possessed. And Pharao's heart was hardened, and he did not let the people go.

8 And the Lord said to Moses and Aaron: Take to you handfuls of ashes out of the chimney, and let Moses sprinkle it in the air in the presence of Pharao.

CHAP. 9. ¹ Rom. 9, 7. ² Wisd. 16, 16; 19, 19.
CHAP. 9. Ver. 6. *All the beasts.* That is, many of *all* kinds.
Ver. 12. *Hardened Pharao's heart.* See the annotations above (4, 21; 7, 3: 8. 15).

9 And be there dust upon all the land of Egypt: for there shall be boils and swelling blains both in men and beasts, in the whole land of Egypt.

10 And they took ashes out of the chimney, and stood before Pharao. And Moses sprinkled it in the air: and there came boils with swelling blains in men and beasts.

11 Neither could the magicians stand before Moses, for the boils that were upon them, and in all the land of Egypt.

12 And the Lord hardened Pharao's heart: and he hearkened not unto them, as the Lord had spoken to Moses.

13 And the Lord said to Moses: Arise in the morning, and stand before Pharao. And thou shalt say to him: Thus saith the Lord the God of the Hebrews: Let my people go to sacrifice to me.

14 For I will at this time send all my plagues upon thy heart, and upon thy servants, and upon thy people: that thou mayst know there is none like me in all the earth.

15 For now I will stretch out my hand to strike thee, and thy people with pestilence: and thou shalt perish from the earth.

16 ¹And therefore have I raised thee, that I may shew my power in thee: and my name may be spoken of throughout all the earth.

17 Dost thou yet hold back my people: and wilt thou not let them go?

18 Behold I will cause it to rain to-morrow at this same hour, an exceeding great hail: such as hath not been in Egypt, from the day that it was founded, until this present time.

19 Send therefore now presently, and gather together thy cattle, and all that thou hast in the field: for men and beasts, and all things that shall be found abroad, and not gathered together out of the fields, which the hail shall fall upon, shall die.

20 He that feared the word of the Lord among Pharao's servants, made his servants and his cattle flee into houses.

21 But he that regarded not the word of the Lord, left his servants and his cattle in the fields.

22 And the Lord said to Moses: Stretch forth thy hand towards heaven, that there may be hail in the whole land of Egypt, upon men, and upon beasts, and upon every herb of the field in the land of Egypt.

23 ²And Moses stretched forth his rod towards heaven: and the Lord sent thunder and hail, and lightning running along the ground. And the Lord rained hail upon the land of Egypt.

24 And the hail and fire mixed with

it drove on together: and it was of so great bigness, as never before was seen in the whole land of Egypt since that nation was founded.

25 And the hail destroyed through all the land of Egypt all things that were in the fields, both man and beast: and the hail smote every herb of the field; and it broke every tree of the country.

26 Only in the land of Gessen, where the children of Israel were, the hail fell not.

27 And Pharao sent and called Moses and Aaron, saying to them: I have sinned this time also. The Lord is just: I and my people are wicked.

28 Pray ye to the Lord, that the thunderings of God and the hail may cease: that I may let you go, and that you may stay here no longer.

29 Moses said: As soon as I am gone out of the city, I will stretch forth my hands to the Lord; and the thunders shall cease, and the hail shall be no more: that thou mayst know that the earth is the Lord's.

30 But I know that neither thou, nor thy servants do yet fear the Lord God.

31 The flax therefore and the barley were hurt: because the barley was green, and the flax was now bolled.

32 But the wheat, and other winter corn were not hurt: because they were lateward.

33 And when Moses was gone from Pharao out of the city, he stretched forth his hands to the Lord: and the thunders and the hail ceased. Neither did there drop any more rain upon the earth.

34 And Pharao seeing that the rain and the hail, and the thunders were ceased, increased his sin.

35 And his heart was hardened, and the heart of his servants: and it was made exceeding hard. Neither did he let the children of Israel go, as the Lord had commanded by the hand of Moses.

CHAPTER 10

The eighth plague of the locusts. The ninth, of darkness: Pharao is still hardened.

AND the Lord said to Moses: Go in to Pharao. For I have hardened his heart, and the heart of his servants: that I may work these my signs in him.

2 And thou mayest tell in the ears of thy sons, and of thy grandsons, how often I have plagued the Egyptians, and wrought my signs amongst them: and you may know that I am the Lord.

3 Therefore Moses and Aaron went in to Pharao, and said to him: Thus saith the Lord God of the Hebrews: How long refusest thou to submit to me? Let my people go to sacrifice to me.

4 [1] But if thou resist, and wilt not let them go: Behold, I will bring in to-morrow the locust into thy coasts:

5 To cover the face of the earth that nothing thereof may appear, but that which the hail hath left may be eaten: for they shall feed upon all the trees that spring in the fields.

6 And they shall fill thy houses, and the houses of thy servants, and of all the Egyptians: such a number as thy fathers have not seen, nor thy grandfathers, from the time they were first upon the earth, until this present day. And he turned himself away, and went forth from Pharao.

7 And Pharao's servants said to him: How long shall we endure this scandal? Let the men go to sacrifice to the Lord their God. Dost thou not see that Egypt is undone?

8 And they called back Moses and Aaron to Pharao. And he said to them: Go, sacrifice to the Lord your God. Who are they that shall go?

9 Moses said: We will go with our young and old, with our sons and daughters, with our sheep and herds: for it is the solemnity of the Lord our God.

10 And Pharao answered: So be the Lord with you, as I shall let you and your children go. Who can doubt but that you intend some great evil?

11 It shall not be so: but go ye men only, and sacrifice to the Lord; for this yourselves also desired. And immediately they were cast out from Pharao's presence.

12 And the Lord said to Moses: Stretch forth thy hand upon the land of Egypt, unto the locust, that it come upon it, and devour every herb that is left after the hail.

13 And Moses stretched forth his rod upon the land of Egypt: and the Lord brought a burning wind all that day, and night. And when it was morning, the burning wind raised the locusts:

14 And they came up over the whole land of Egypt: and rested in all the coasts of the Egyptians innumerable, the like as had not been before that time, nor shall be hereafter.

15 And they covered the whole face of the earth, wasting all things. And the grass of the earth was devoured, and what fruits soever were on the trees, which the hail had left. And there remained not any thing that was

---

CHAP. 10. [1] Wisd. 16, 9.

green on the trees, or in the herbs of the earth in all Egypt.

16 Wherefore Pharao in haste called Moses and Aaron, and said to them: I have sinned against the Lord your God, and against you.

17 But now forgive me my sin this time also: and pray to the Lord your God, that he take away from me this death.

18 And Moses going forth from the presence of Pharao, prayed to the Lord.

19 And he made a very strong wind to blow from the west: and it took the locusts and cast them into the Red Sea. There remained not so much as one in all the coasts of Egypt.

20 And the Lord hardened Pharao's heart: neither did he let the children of Israel go.

21 And the Lord said to Moses: Stretch out thy hand towards heaven: and may there be darkness upon the land of Egypt, so thick that it may be felt.

22 And Moses stretched forth his hand towards heaven: and there came horrible darkness in all the land of Egypt for three days.

23 ²No man saw his brother, nor moved himself out of the place where he was: ³but wheresoever the children of Israel dwelt there was light.

24 And Pharao called Moses and Aaron, and said to them: Go sacrifice to the Lord. Let your sheep only, and herds remain; let your children go with you.

25 Moses said: Thou shalt give us also sacrifices and burnt offerings, to the Lord our God.

26 All the flocks shall go with us. There shall not a hoof remain of them: for they are necessary for the service of the Lord our God; especially as we know not what must be offered, till we come to the very place.

27 And the Lord hardened Pharao's heart: and he would not let them go.

28 And Pharao said to Moses: Get thee from me, and beware thou see not my face any more. In what day soever thou shalt come in my sight, thou shalt die.

29 Moses answered: So shall it be as thou hast spoken. I will not see thy face any more.

² Wisd. 17, 2. ³ Wisd. 18, 1. CHAP. 11.. ¹ Exod. 3, 22; 12, 35. ² Ecclus. 45, 1.

CHAP. 10. Ver. 21. *Darkness upon the land of Egypt, so thick that it may be felt.* By means of the gross exhalations, which were to cause and accompany the darkness.

CHAP. 11. Ver. 10. *The Lord hardened Pharao's heart.* See the annotations above (4, 21; 7, 3).

CHAPTER 11

Pharao and his people are threatened with the death of their firstborn.

AND the Lord said to Moses: Yet one plague more will I bring upon Pharao and Egypt; and after that he shall let you go, and thrust you out.

2 ¹Therefore thou shalt tell all the people that every man ask of his friend, and every woman of her neighbour, vessels of silver, and of gold.

3 And the Lord will give favour to his people in the sight of the Egyptians. And ²Moses was a very great man in the land of Egypt, in the sight of Pharao's servants, and of all the people.

4 And he said: Thus saith the Lord: At midnight I will enter into Egypt:

5 And every firstborn in the land of the Egyptians shall die, from the firstborn of Pharao, who sitteth on his throne, even to the firstborn of the handmaid, that is at the mill, and all the firstborn of beasts.

6 And there shall be a great cry in all the land of Egypt, such as neither hath been before, nor shall be hereafter.

7 But with all the children of Israel there shall not a dog make the least noise, from man even to beast: that you may know how wonderful a difference the Lord maketh between the Egyptians and Israel.

8 And all these thy servants shall come down to me, and shall worship me, saying: Go forth thou, and all the people that is under thee. After that we will go out.

9 And he went out from Pharao exceeding angry. But the Lord said to Moses: Pharao will not hear you, that many signs may be done in the land of Egypt.

10 And Moses and Aaron did all the wonders that are written, before Pharao. And the Lord hardened Pharao's heart: neither did he let the children of Israel go out of his land.

CHAPTER 12

The manner of preparing, and eating the paschal lamb. The firstborn of Egypt are all slain. The Israelites depart.

AND the Lord said to Moses and Aaron in the land of Egypt:

2 This month shall be to you the beginning of months: it shall be the first in the months of the year.

3 Speak ye to the whole assembly of the children of Israel, and say to them: On the tenth day of this month let every man take a lamb by their families and houses.

4 But if the number be less than may suffice to eat the lamb, he shall take

unto him his neighbour that joineth to his house, according to the number of souls which may be enough to eat the lamb.

5 And it shall be a lamb without blemish, a male, of one year: according to which rite also you shall take a kid.

6 And you shall keep it until the fourteenth day of this month: and the whole multitude of the children of Israel shall sacrifice it in the evening.

7 And they shall take of the blood thereof, and put it upon both the side posts, and on the upper door posts of the houses, wherein they shall eat it.

8 And they shall eat the flesh that night roasted at the fire: and unleavened bread with wild lettuce.

9 You shall not eat thereof any thing raw, nor boiled in water, but only roasted at the fire. You shall eat the head with the feet and entrails thereof.

10 Neither shall there remain any thing of it until morning. [1] If there be any thing left, you shall burn it with fire.

11 And thus you shall eat it: You shall gird your reins, and you shall have shoes on your feet, holding staves in your hands, and you shall eat in haste; for it is the Phase (that is the Passage) of the Lord.

12 And I will pass through the land of Egypt that night, and will kill every firstborn in the land of Egypt both man and beast: and against all the gods of Egypt I will execute judgments. I *am* the Lord.

13 And the blood shall be unto you for a sign in the houses where you shall be: and I shall see the blood, and shall pass over you. And the plague shall not be upon you to destroy you, when I shall strike the land of Egypt.

14 And this day shall be for a memorial to you: and you shall keep it a feast to the Lord in your generations with an everlasting observance.

15 Seven days shall you eat unleavened bread. In the first day there shall be no leaven in your houses: whosoever shall eat any thing leavened, from the first day until the seventh day, that soul shall perish out of Israel.

16 The first day shall be holy and solemn, and the seventh day shall be kept with the like solemnity: you shall do no work in them, except those things that belong to eating.

17 And you shall observe *the feast of* the unleavened bread: for in this same day I will bring forth your army out of the land of Egypt; and you shall keep this day in your generations by a perpetual observance.

18 [2] The first month, the fourteenth day of the month in the evening, you shall eat unleavened bread, until the one and twentieth day of the same month in the evening.

19 Seven days there shall not be found any leaven in your houses: he that shall eat leavened bread, his soul shall perish out of the assembly of Israel, whether he be a stranger or born in the land.

20 You shall not eat any thing leavened: in all your habitations you shall eat unleavened bread.

21 And Moses called all the ancients of the children of Israel, and said to them: Go take a lamb by your families, and sacrifice the Phase.

22 [3] And dip a bunch of hyssop in the blood that is at the door, and sprinkle the transom of the door therewith, and both the door cheeks. Let none of you go out of the door of his house till morning.

23 For the Lord will pass through striking the Egyptians: and when he shall see the blood on the transom, and on both the posts, he will pass over the door of the house, and not suffer the destroyer to come into your houses and to hurt *you*.

24 Thou shalt keep this thing as a law for thee and thy children for ever.

25 And when you have entered into the land which the Lord will give you as he hath promised, you shall observe these ceremonies.

26 And when your children shall say to you: What is the meaning of this service?

27 You shall say to them: It is the victim of the passage of the Lord, when he passed over the houses of the children of Israel in Egypt, striking the Egyptians, and saving our houses. And the people bowing themselves, adored.

28 And the children of Israel going forth did as the Lord had commanded Moses and Aaron.

29 And it came to pass at midnight, [4] the Lord slew every firstborn in the land of Egypt, from the firstborn of Pharao, who sat on his throne, [5] unto the firstborn of the captive woman that was in the prison, and all the firstborn of cattle.

Chap. 12. [1] Lev. 7, 15. [2] Lev. 23, 5; Num. 28, 16. [3] Heb. 11, 28. [4] Exod. 11, 5. [5] Wisd. 18, 5.

Chap. 12. Ver. 5. *A kid.* The *phase* might be performed, either with a lamb or with a kid: and all the same rites and ceremonies were to be used with the one as with the other.

Ver. 18. *Unleavened bread.* By this it appears that our Saviour made use of unleavened bread, in the institution of the blessed sacrament, which was on the evening of the paschal solemnity, at which time there was no leavened bread to be found in Israel.

Ver. 22. *Sprinkle.* This sprinkling the doors of the Israelites with the blood of the paschal lamb, in order to their being delivered from the sword of the destroying angel, was a lively figure of our redemption by the blood of Christ.

30 And Pharao arose in the night, and all his servants, and all Egypt: and there arose a great cry in Egypt; for there was not a house wherein there lay not one dead.

31 And Pharao, calling Moses and Aaron, in the night, said: Arise and go forth from among my people, you and the children of Israel. Go, sacrifice to the Lord as you say.

32 Your sheep and herds take along with you, as you demanded: and departing, bless me.

33 And the Egyptians pressed the people to go forth out of the land speedily, saying: We shall all die.

34 The people therefore took dough before it was leavened: and tying it in *their* cloaks, put it on their shoulders.

35 ⁶And the children of Israel did as Moses had commanded: and they asked of the Egyptians vessels of silver and gold, and very much raiment.

36 And the Lord gave favour to the people in the sight of the Egyptians, so that they lent unto them. And they stripped the Egyptians.

37 And the children of Israel set forward from Ramesse to Socoth, being about six hundred thousand men on foot, beside children.

38 And a mixed multitude without number went up also with them: sheep and herds and beasts of divers kinds, exceeding many.

39 And they baked the meal which a little before they had brought out of Egypt, in dough. And they made earth cakes unleavened: for it could not be leavened, the Egyptians pressing them to depart, and not suffering them to make any stay: neither did they think of preparing any meat.

40 And the abode of the children of Israel that they made in Egypt, was four hundred and thirty years.

41 Which being expired, the same day all the army of the Lord went forth out of the land of Egypt.

42 This is the observable night of the Lord, when he brought them forth out of the land of Egypt: this night all the children of Israel must observe in their generations.

43 And the Lord said to Moses and Aaron: This is the service of the Phase. No foreigner shall eat of it.

44 But every bought servant shall be circumcised, and so shall eat.

45 The stranger and the hireling shall not eat thereof.

46 ⁷In one house shall it be eaten: neither shall you carry forth of the flesh thereof out of the house: neither shall you break a bone thereof.

47 All the assembly of the children of Israel shall keep it.

48 And if any stranger be willing to dwell among you, and to keep the Phase of the Lord, all his males shall first be circumcised: and then shall he celebrate it according to the manner. And he shall be as he that is born in the land: but if any man be uncircumcised, he shall not eat thereof.

49 The same law shall be to him that is born in the land, and to the proselyte that sojourneth with you.

50 And all the children of Israel did as the Lord had commanded Moses and Aaron.

51 And the same day the Lord brought forth the children of Israel out of the land of Egypt by their companies.

CHAPTER 13

The paschal solemnity is to be observed, and the firstborn are to be consecrated to God. The people are conducted through the desert by a pillar of fire in the night, and a cloud in the day.

AND the Lord spoke to Moses, saying:

2 ¹Sanctify unto me every firstborn that openeth the womb among the children of Israel, as well of men as of beasts: for they are all mine.

3 And Moses said to the people: Remember this day in which you came forth out of Egypt, and out of the house of bondage, for with a strong hand hath the Lord brought you forth out of this place: that you eat no leavened bread.

4 This day you go forth in the month of new corn.

5 And when the Lord shall have brought thee into the land of the Chanaanite, and the Hethite, and the Amorrhite, and the Hevite, and the Jebusite, which he swore to thy fathers that he would give thee, a land that floweth with milk and honey: thou shalt celebrate this manner of sacred rites in this month.

6 Seven days shalt thou eat unleavened bread: and on the seventh day shall be the solemnity of the Lord.

7 Unleavened bread shall you eat seven days: there shall not be seen any thing leavened with thee, nor in all thy coasts.

8 And thou shalt tell thy son in that day, saying: This is what the Lord did to me when I came forth out of Egypt.

9 And it shall be as a sign in thy

⁶ Exod. 3, 22; 11, 2. ⁷ Num. 9, 12; John. 19, 36. CHAP. 13. ¹ Exod. 34, 19; Lev. 27, 26; Num. 8, 16; Luke, 2, 23.

CHAP. 13. Ver. 2. *Sanctify unto me every firstborn.* Sanctification in this place means that the firstborn males of the Hebrews should be deputed to the ministry in the divine worship; and the firstborn of beasts to be given for a sacrifice.

hand, and as a memorial before thy eyes: and that the law of the Lord be always in thy mouth; for with a strong hand the Lord hath brought thee out of the land of Egypt.

10 Thou shalt keep this observance at the set time from days to days.

11 And when the Lord shall have brought thee into the land of the Chanaanite, as he swore to thee and thy fathers, and shall give it thee:

12 [2]Thou shalt set apart all that openeth the womb for the Lord, and all that is first brought forth of thy cattle. Whatsoever thou shalt have of the male sex, thou shalt consecrate to the Lord.

13 The firstborn of an ass thou shalt change for a sheep: and if thou do not redeem it, thou shalt kill it. And every firstborn of men thou shalt redeem with a price.

14 And when thy son shall ask thee to-morrow, saying: What is this? Thou shalt answer him: With a strong hand did the Lord bring us forth out of the land of Egypt, out of the house of bondage.

15 For when Pharao was hardened, and would not let us go, the Lord slew every firstborn in the land of Egypt, from the firstborn of man to the firstborn of beasts: therefore I sacrifice to the Lord all that openeth the womb of the male sex, and all the firstborn of my sons I redeem.

16 [3]And it shall be as a sign in thy hand, and as a thing hung between thy eyes, for a remembrance: because the Lord hath brought us forth out of Egypt by a strong hand.

17 And when Pharao had sent out the people, the Lord led them not by the way of the land of the Philistines which is near: thinking lest perhaps they would repent, if they should see wars arise against them, and would return into Egypt.

18 But he led them about by the way of the desert, which is by the Red Sea: and the children of Israel went up armed out of the land of Egypt.

19 And Moses took Joseph's bones with him; because he had adjured the children of Israel, saying: [4]God shall visit you. Carry out my bones from hence with you.

20 And marching from Socoth, they encamped in Etham, in the utmost coasts of the wilderness.

21 [5]And the Lord went before them to shew the way by day in a pillar of a cloud, and by night in a pillar of fire: that he might be the guide of their journey at both times.

22 There never failed the pillar of the cloud by day, nor the pillar of fire by night, before the people.

CHAPTER 14

Pharao pursueth the children of Israel. They murmur against Moses, but are encouraged by him, and pass through the Red Sea. Pharao and his army following them are drowned.

AND the Lord spoke to Moses, saying:

2 Speak to the children of Israel: Let them turn and encamp over against Phihahiroth, which is between Magdal and the sea, over against Beelsephon. You shall encamp before it upon the sea.

3 And Pharao will say of the children of Israel: They are straitened in the land; the desert hath shut them in.

4 And I shall harden his heart, and he will pursue you; and I shall be glorified in Pharao, and in all his army: and the Egyptians shall know that I am the Lord. And they did so.

5 And it was told the king of the Egyptians that the people was fled. And the heart of Pharao and of his servants was changed with regard to the people, and they said: What meant we to do, that we let Israel go from serving us?

6 So he made ready his chariot, and took all his people with him.

7 And he took six hundred chosen chariots, and all the chariots that were in Egypt: and the captains of the whole army.

8 And the Lord hardened the heart of Pharao king of Egypt, and he pursued the children of Israel: but they were gone forth in a mighty hand.

9 [1]And when the Egyptians followed the steps of them who were gone before, they found them encamped at the sea side. All Pharao's horse and chariots, and the whole army were in Phihahiroth before Beelsephon.

10 And when Pharao drew near, the children of Israel, lifting up their eyes, saw the Egyptians behind them: and they feared exceedingly, and cried to the Lord.

11 And they said to Moses: Perhaps there were no graves in Egypt: therefore thou hast brought us to die in the wilderness. Why wouldst thou do this, to lead us out of Egypt?

12 Is not this the word that we spoke to thee in Egypt, saying: Depart from us that we may serve the Egyptians? For it was much better to serve them, than to die in the wilderness.

13 And Moses said to the people: Fear not. Stand and see the great wonders of the Lord, which he will do this

[2] Exod. 22, 29; 34, 19; Ezech. 44, 30. [3] Deut. 6, 8. [4] Gen. 50, 24. [5] Num. 14, 14; 2 Esd. 9, 12; 1 Cor. 10, 1. Chap. 14. [1] Jos. 24, 6; 1 Mach. 4, 9.

day: for the Egyptians, whom you see now, you shall see no more for ever.

14 The Lord will fight for you: and you shall hold your peace.

15 And the Lord said to Moses: Why criest thou to me? Speak to the children of Israel to go forward.

16 But lift thou up thy rod, and stretch forth thy hand over the sea, and divide it: that the children of Israel may go through the midst of the sea on dry ground.

17 And I will harden the heart of the Egyptians to pursue you: and I will be glorified in Pharao, and in all his hosts, and in his chariots, and in his horsemen.

18 And the Egyptians shall know that I am the Lord: when I shall be glorified in Pharao, and in his chariots and in his horsemen.

19 And the angel of God, who went before the camp of Israel, removing went behind them: and together with him the pillar of the cloud, leaving the forepart,

20 Stood behind, between the Egyptians' camp and the camp of Israel. And it was a dark cloud, and enlightening the night, so that they could not come at one another all the night.

21 ²And when Moses had stretched forth his hand over the sea, the Lord took it away by a strong and burning wind blowing all the night; and turned it into dry ground: and the water was divided.

22 And the children of Israel went in through the midst of the sea dried up: for the water was as a wall on their right hand and on their left.

23 And the Egyptians pursuing went in after them: and all Pharao's horses his chariots and horsemen through the midst of the sea,

24 And now the morning watch was come, ³ and, behold, the Lord, looking upon the Egyptian army through the pillar of fire and of the cloud, slew their host.

25 And overthrew the wheels of the chariots, and they were carried into the deep. And the Egyptians said: Let us flee from Israel; for the Lord fighteth for them against us.

26 And the Lord said to Moses: Stretch forth thy hand over the sea that the waters may come again upon the Egyptians, upon their chariots and horsemen.

27 And when Moses had stretched forth his hand towards the sea, it returned at the first break of day to the former place: and as the Egyptians were fleeing away, the waters came upon them, and the Lord shut them up in the middle of the waves.

28 And the waters returned, and covered the chariots and the horsemen of all the army of Pharao, who had come into the sea after them: neither did there so much as one of them remain.

29 But the children of Israel marched through the midst of the sea upon dry land: and the waters were to them as a wall on the right hand and on the left.

30 And the Lord delivered Israel on that day out of the hands of the Egyptians.

31 And they saw the Egyptians dead upon the sea shore, and the mighty hand that the Lord had used against them. And the people feared the Lord, and they believed the Lord, and Moses his servant.

CHAPTER 15

The canticle of Moses. The bitter waters of Mara are made sweet.

THEN ¹ Moses and the children of Israel sung this canticle to the Lord, and said: Let us sing to the Lord, for he is gloriously magnified: the horse and the rider he hath thrown into the sea.

2 ² The Lord *is* my strength and my praise: and he is become salvation to me. He *is* my God and I will glorify him: the God of my father, and I will exalt him.

3 The Lord *is* as a man of war: Almighty *is* his name.

4 Pharao's chariots and his army he hath cast into the sea: his chosen captains are drowned in the Red Sea.

5 The depths have covered them: they are sunk to the bottom like a stone.

6 Thy right hand, O Lord, is magnified in strength: thy right hand, O Lord, hath slain the enemy.

7 And in the multitude of thy glory thou hast put down thy adversaries: thou hast sent thy wrath, which hath devoured them like stubble.

8 And with the blast of thy anger the waters were gathered together. The flowing water stood: the depths were gathered together in the midst of the sea.

9 The enemy said: I will pursue and overtake: I will divide the spoils, my soul shall have its fill. I will draw my sword; my hand shall slay them.

10 Thy wind blew and the sea covered them: they sunk as lead in the mighty waters.

² Ps. 77, 13; 104, 37; 113, 3; Heb. 11, 29. ³ Wisd. 18, 15. CHAP. 15. ¹ Wisd. 10, 20. ² Ps. 117, 14; Isai. 12, 2.

CHAP. 14. Ver. 20. *A dark cloud, and enlightening the night.* It was a *dark cloud* to the Egyptians; but enlightend the night to the Israelites, by giving them a great light.

11 Who is like to thee, among the strong, O Lord? Who is like to thee, glorious in holiness, terrible and praiseworthy, doing wonders?

12 Thou stretchedst forth thy hand: and the earth swallowed them.

13 In thy mercy thou hast been a leader to the people which thou hast redeemed: and in thy strength thou hast carried them to thy holy habitation.

14 Nations rose up, and were angry: sorrows took hold on the inhabitants of Philisthiim.

15 Then were the princes of Edom troubled, trembling seized on the stout men of Moab: all the inhabitants of Chanaan became stiff.

16 Let fear and dread fall upon them, in the greatness of thy arm; let them become unmoveable as a stone, until thy people, O Lord, pass by: until this thy people pass by, which thou hast possessed.

17 Thou shalt bring them in, and plant them in the mountain of thy inheritance, in thy most firm habitation which thou hast made, O Lord: thy sanctuary, O Lord, which thy hands have established.

18 The Lord shall reign for ever and ever.

19 For Pharao went in on horseback with his chariots and horsemen into the sea: and the Lord brought back upon them the waters of the sea. But the children of Israel walked on dry ground in the midst thereof.

20 So Mary the prophetess, the sister of Aaron, took a timbrel in her hand: and all the women went forth after her with timbrels and with dances:

21 And she began the song to them saying: Let us sing to the Lord, for he is gloriously magnified: the horse and his rider he hath thrown into the sea.

22 And Moses brought Israel from the Red Sea, and they went forth into the wilderness of Sur: and they marched three days through the wilderness, and found no water.

23 And they came into Mara, and they could not drink the waters of Mara, because they were bitter: whereupon he gave a name also agreeable to the place, calling it Mara, that is, bitterness.

24 And the people murmured against Moses, saying: What shall we drink?

25 But he cried to the Lord, and he shewed him a tree, [3] which when he had cast into the waters, they were turned into sweetness. There he appointed him ordinances, and judgments, and there he proved him.

26 Saying: If thou wilt hear the voice of the Lord thy God, and do what is

right before him, and obey his commandments, and keep all his precepts, none of the evils that I laid upon Egypt, will I bring upon thee: for I am the Lord thy healer.

27 And the children of Israel came into Elim, where there were twelve fountains of water, and seventy palm trees: and they encamped by the waters.

CHAPTER 16

The people murmur for want of meat. God giveth them quails and manna.

AND they set forward from Elim, and all the multitude of the children of Israel came into the desert of Sin, which is between Elim and Sinai: [1] the fifteenth day of the second month, after they came out of the land of Egypt.

2 And all the congregation of the children of Israel murmured against Moses and Aaron in the wilderness.

3 And the children of Israel said to them: Would to God we had died by the hand of the Lord in the land of Egypt, when we sat over the flesh pots, and ate bread to the full. Why have you brought us into this desert, that you might destroy all the multitude with famine?

4 And the Lord said to Moses: Behold I will rain bread from heaven for you. Let the people go forth, and gather what is sufficient for every day: that I may prove them whether they will walk in my law, or not.

5 But the sixth day, let them provide for to bring in: and let it be double to that they were wont to gather every day.

6 And Moses and Aaron said to the children of Israel: In the evening you shall know that the Lord hath brought you forth out of the land of Egypt:

7 And in the morning you shall see the glory of the Lord. For he hath heard your murmurings against the Lord: but as for us, what are we, that you mutter against us?

8 And Moses said: In the evening the Lord will give you flesh to eat, and in the morning bread to the full; for he hath heard your murmurings, with which you have murmured against him. For what are we? Your murmuring is not against us, but against the Lord.

9 Moses also said to Aaron: Say to the whole congregation of the children of Israel: Come before the Lord, for he hath heard your murmuring.

10 And when Aaron spoke to all the assembly of the children of Israel, they looked towards the wilderness: [2] and,

[3] Judith, 5, 15; Ecclus.38, 5.   [4] Num. 33, 9.   **Chap.** 16.   [1] Wisd. 11, 2.   [2] Ecclus. 45, 3.

behold, the glory of the Lord appeared in a cloud.

11 And the Lord spoke to Moses, saying:

12 I have heard the murmuring of the children of Israel. Say to them: In the evening you shall eat flesh, and in the morning you shall have your fill of bread. And you shall know that I am the Lord your God.

13 So it came to pass in the evening [3] that quails coming up, covered the camp: and in the morning a dew lay round about the camp.

14 And when it had covered the face of the earth, [4] it appeared in the wilderness small, and as it were beaten with a pestle, like unto the hoar frost on the ground.

15 And when the children of Israel saw it, they said one to another: Manhu! which signifieth: What is this! For they knew not what it was. And Moses said to them: [5] This is the bread, which the Lord hath given you to eat.

16 This is the word, that the Lord hath commanded: Let every one gather of it as much as is enough to eat. A gomor for every man, according to the number of your souls that dwell in a tent, so shall you take of it.

17 And the children of Israel did so: and they gathered, one more, another less.

18 And they measured by the measure of a gomor. [6] Neither had he more that had gathered more; nor did he find less that had provided less: but every one had gathered, according to what they were able to eat.

19 And Moses said to them: Let no man leave thereof till the morning.

20 And they hearkened not to him, but some of them left until the morning: and it began to be full of worms, and it putrefied, and Moses was angry with them.

21 Now every one of them gathered in the morning, as much as might suffice to eat: and after the sun grew hot, it melted.

22 But on the sixth day they gathered twice as much, that is, two gomors every man: and all the rulers of the multitude came, and told Moses.

23 And he said to them: This is what the Lord hath spoken: To-morrow is the rest of the sabbath sanctified to the Lord. Whatsoever work is to be done do it: and the meats that are to be dressed, dress them. And whatsoever shall remain, lay it up until the morning.

24 And they did so as Moses had

commanded, and it did not putrefy: neither was there worm found in it.

25 And Moses said: Eat it to-day, because it is the sabbath of the Lord: to-day it shall not be found in the field.

26 Gather it six days. But on the seventh day is the sabbath of the Lord: therefore it shall not be found.

27 And the seventh day came: and some of the people going forth to gather, found none.

28 And the Lord said to Moses: How long will you refuse to keep my commandments, and my law?

29 See that the Lord hath given you the sabbath, and for this reason on the sixth day he giveth you a double provision: let each man stay at home, and let none go forth out of his place the seventh day.

30 And the people kept the sabbath on the seventh day.

31 And the house of Israel called the name thereof Manna: and it was like coriander seed white, and the taste thereof like to flour with honey.

32 And Moses said: This is the word, which the Lord hath commanded: Fill a gomor of it, and let it be kept unto generations to come hereafter: that they may know the bread, wherewith I fed you in the wilderness, when you were brought forth out of the land of Egypt.

33 And Moses said to Aaron: Take a vessel, and put manna into it, as much as a gomor can hold: and lay it up before the Lord to keep unto your generations,

34 As the Lord commanded Moses. And Aaron put it in the tabernacle to be kept.

35 [7] And the children of Israel ate manna forty years, till they came to a habitable land: with this meat were they fed, until they reached the borders of the land of Chanaan.

36 Now a gomor is the tenth part of an ephi.

CHAPTER 17

The people murmur again for want of drink. The Lord giveth them water out of a rock. Moses lifting up his hand in prayer, Amalec is overcome.

THEN all the multitude of the children of Israel setting forward from the desert of Sin, by their mansions, according to the word of the Lord, encamped in Raphidim, where there was no water for the people to drink.

2 [1] And they chode with Moses, and said: Give us water, that we may drink. And Moses answered them: Why chide you with me? Wherefore do you tempt the Lord?

[3] Num. 11, 31. [4] Exod. 16, 20; Num. 11, 7; Ps. 77, 24; John, 6, 31. [5] 1 Cor. 10, 3. [6] 2 Cor. 8, 15. [7] Esd. 11, 21; Judith, 5, 15. CHAP. 17. [1] Num. 20, 4.

3 So the people were thirsty there for want of water, and murmured against Moses, saying: Why didst thou make us go forth out of Egypt, to kill us and our children, and our beasts with thirst?

4 And Moses cried to the Lord, saying: What shall I do to this people? Yet a little more and they will stone me.

5 And the Lord said to Moses: Go before the people, and take with thee of the ancients of Israel. And take in thy hand the rod wherewith thou didst strike the river,[2] and go.

6 Behold I will stand there before thee, upon the rock Horeb: and thou shalt strike the rock, and water shall come out of it that the people may drink. Moses did so before the ancients of Israel:

7 And he called the name of that place Temptation, because of the chiding of the children of Israel; and for that they tempted the Lord, saying: Is the Lord amongst us or not?

8 [3]And Amalec came, and fought against Israel in Raphidim.

9 And Moses said to Josue: Choose out men: and go out and fight against Amalec. To-morrow I will stand on the top of the hill having the rod of God in my hand.

10 Josue did as Moses had spoken, and he fought against Amalec: but Moses, and Aaron, and Hur went up upon the top of the hill.

11 And when Moses lifted up his hands, Israel overcame: but if he let them down a little, Amalec overcame.

12 And Moses' hands were heavy; so they took a stone, and put under him, and he sat on it: and Aaron and Hur stayed up his hands on both sides. And it came to pass that his hands were not weary until sunset.

13 And Josue put Amalec and his people to flight, by the edge of the sword.

14 And the Lord said to Moses: Write this for a memorial in a book, and deliver it to the ears of Josue; for I will destroy the memory of Amalec from under heaven.

15 And Moses built an altar: and called the name thereof, The Lord my exaltation, saying:

16 Because the hand of the throne of the Lord, and the war of the Lord shall be against Amalec, from generation to generation.

CHAPTER 18

Jethro bringeth to Moses his wife and children. His counsel.

AND when Jethro the priest of Madian, the kinsman of Moses, had heard all the things that God had done to Moses, and to Israel his people, and that the Lord had brought forth Israel out of Egypt,

2 He took Sephora the wife of Moses whom he had sent back.

3 And her two sons, of whom one was called Gersam, his father saying: [1]I have been a stranger in a foreign country.

4 And the other, Eliezer: For the God of my father, said he, is my helper, and hath delivered me from the sword of Pharao.

5 And Jethro, the kinsman of Moses, came with his sons and his wife, to Moses into the desert, where he was camped by the mountain of God.

6 And he sent word to Moses, saying: I Jethro thy kinsman come to thee, and thy wife, and thy two sons with her.

7 And he went out to meet his kinsman, and worshipped and kissed him: and they saluted one another with words of peace. And when he was come into the tent,

8 Moses told his kinsman all that the Lord had done to Pharao, and the Egyptians, in favour of Israel: and all the labour which had befallen them in the journey; and that the Lord had delivered them.

9 And Jethro rejoiced for all the good things that the Lord had done to Israel: because he had delivered them out of the hands of the Egyptians.

10 And he said: Blessed is the Lord, who hath delivered you out of the hand of Pharao, and out of the hand of the Egyptians; who hath delivered his people out of the hand of Egypt.

11 Now I know that the Lord is great above all gods: [2]because they dealt proudly against them.

12 So Jethro, the kinsman of Moses offered holocausts and sacrifices to God: and Aaron and all the ancients of Israel came, to eat bread with them before God.

13 And the next day Moses sat, to judge the people, who stood by Moses from morning until night.

14 And when his kinsman had seen all things that he did among the people, he said: What is it that thou dost among the people? Why sittest thou alone, and all the people wait from morning till night?

15 And Moses answered him: The people come to me to seek the judgment of God.

16 And when any controversy falleth out among them, they come to me to judge between them, and to shew the precepts of God, and his laws.

[2] Exod. 14, 21; Ps. 77, 15; 1 Cor. 10, 4. [3] Deut. 25, 17; Judith, 4, 13; Wisd. 11, 3. CHAP. 18. [1] Exod. 2, 22. [2] Exod. 1, 14; 5, 7; 10, 10; 14, 8.

17 But he said: The thing thou dost is not good.

18 Thou art spent with foolish labour, both thou and this people that is with thee: the business is above thy strength. [3] Thou alone canst not bear it.

19 But hear my words and counsels, and God shall be with thee. Be thou to the people in those things that pertain to God, to bring their words to him:

20 And to shew the people the ceremonies and the manner of worshipping, and the way wherein they ought to walk, and the work that they ought to do.

21 And provide out of all the people able men, such as fear God, in whom there is truth, and that hate avarice: and appoint of them rulers of thousands, and of hundreds, and of fifties, and of tens,

22 Who may judge the people at all times. And when any great matter soever shall fall out, let them refer it to thee, and let them judge the lesser matters only: that so it may be lighter for thee, the burden being shared out unto others.

23 If thou dost this, thou shalt fulfil the commandment of God, and shalt be able to bear his precepts: and all this people shall return to their places with peace.

24 And when Moses heard this, he did all things that he had suggested unto him.

25 And choosing able men out of all Israel, he appointed them rulers of the people, rulers over thousands, and over hundreds, and over fifties, and over tens.

26 And they judged the people at all times: and whatsoever was of greater difficulty they referred to him; and they judged the easier cases only.

27 And he let his kinsman depart: and he returned, and went into his own country.[4]

CHAPTER 19

They come to Sinai. The people are commanded to be sanctified. The Lord, coming in thunder and lightning, speaketh with Moses.

IN the third month of the departure of Israel [1] out of the land of Egypt, on this day, they came into the wilderness of Sinai:

2 For departing out of Raphidim, and coming to the desert of Sinai, they camped in the same place: and there

Israel pitched their tents over against the mountain.

3 [2]And Moses went up to God. And the Lord called unto him from the mountain, and said: Thus shalt thou say to the house of Jacob, and tell the children of Israel:

4 [3] You have seen what I have done to the Egyptians, how I have carried you upon the wings of eagles, and have taken you to myself.

5 If therefore you will hear my voice, and keep my covenant, you shall be my peculiar possession above all people: [4] for all the earth is mine.

6 [5]And you shall be to me a priestly kingdom, and a holy nation. These are the words thou shalt speak to the children of Israel.

7 Moses came, and calling together the elders of the people, he declared all the words which the Lord had commanded.

8 And all the people answered together: All that the Lord hath spoken, we will do. And when Moses had related the people's words to the Lord,

9 The Lord said to him: Lo, now will I come to thee in the darkness of a cloud, that the people may hear me speaking to thee, and may believe thee for ever. And Moses told the words of the people to the Lord.

10 And he said to him: Go to the people, and sanctify them to-day, and to-morrow; and let them wash their garments.

11 And let them be ready against the third day: for on the third day the Lord will come down in the sight of all the people upon mount Sinai.

12 And thou shalt appoint certain limits to the people round about, and thou shalt say to them: [6] Take heed you go not up into the mount, and that ye touch not the borders thereof. Every one that toucheth the mount dying he shall die.

13 No hands shall touch him, but he shall be stoned to death, or shall be shot through with arrows: whether it be beast, or man, he shall not live. When the trumpet shall begin to sound, then let them go up into the mount.

14 And Moses came down from the mount to the people, and sanctified them. And when they had washed their garments,

15 He said to them: Be ready against the third day, and come not near your wives.

16 And now the third day was come, and the morning appeared: and behold thunders began to be heard, and lightning to flash, and a very thick cloud to cover the mount. And the noise of the

[3] Deut. 1, 12. [4] Num. 20, 29. CHAP. 19. [1] Num. 33, 15. [2] Acts, 7, 38. [3] Deut. 19, 2. [4] Ps. 23, 1. [5] 1 Peter, 2, 9. [6] Heb. 12, 18.

CHAP. 19. Ver. 3. *And Moses went up to God.* Moses went up to mount Sinai, where God spoke to him.

trumpet sounded exceeding loud, and the people that was in the camp, feared.

17 And when Moses had brought them forth to meet God from the place of the camp, they stood at the bottom of the mount.

18 [7]And all mount Sinai was on a smoke: because the Lord was come down upon it in fire, and the smoke arose from it as out of a furnace. And all the mount was terrible.

19 And the sound of the trumpet grew by degrees louder and louder, and was drawn out to a greater length: Moses spoke, and God answered him.

20 And the Lord came down upon mount Sinai, in the very top of the mount: and he called Moses unto the top thereof. And when he was gone up thither,

21 He said unto him: Go down, and charge the people; lest they should have a mind to pass the limits to see the Lord, and a very great multitude of them should perish.

22 The priests also that come to the Lord, let them be sanctified; lest he strike them.

23 And Moses said to the Lord: The people cannot come up to mount Sinai: for thou didst charge, and command, saying: Set limits about the mount, and sanctify it.

24 And the Lord said to him: Go, get thee down. And thou shalt come up thou and Aaron with thee: but let not the priests and the people pass the limits, nor come up to the Lord, lest he kill them.

25 And Moses went down to the people and told them all.

CHAPTER 20

The ten commandments.

AND the Lord spoke all these words:[1]

2 I am the Lord thy God, who brought thee out of the land of Egypt, out of the house of bondage.

3 Thou shalt not have strange gods before me.

4 [2]Thou shalt not make to thyself a graven thing, nor the likeness of any thing that is in heaven above, or in the earth beneath, nor of those things that are in the waters under the earth.

5 Thou shalt not adore them, nor serve them. I am the Lord thy God, mighty, jealous, visiting the iniquity of the fathers upon the children, unto the third and fourth generation of them that hate me:

6 And shewing mercy unto thousands to them that love me, and keep my commandments.

7 [3]Thou shalt not take the name of the Lord thy God in vain: for the Lord will not hold him guiltless that shall take the name of the Lord his God in vain.

8 [4]Remember that thou keep holy the sabbath day.

9 Six days shalt thou labour, and shalt do all thy works.

10 But on the seventh day is the sabbath of the Lord thy God: thou shalt do no work on it, thou nor thy son, nor thy daughter, nor thy man-servant, nor thy maid-servant, nor thy beast, nor the stranger that is within thy gates.

11 [5]For in six days the Lord made heaven and earth, and the sea, and all things that are in them, and rested on the seventh day: therefore the Lord blessed the seventh day, and sanctified it.

12 [6]Honour thy father and thy mother, that thou mayest be long-lived upon the land which the Lord thy God will give thee.

13 [7]Thou shalt not kill.

14 Thou shalt not commit adultery.

15 Thou shalt not steal.

16 Thou shalt not bear false witness against thy neighbour.

17 [8]Thou shalt not covet thy neighbour's house: neither shalt thou desire his wife, nor his servant, nor his handmaid, nor his ox, nor his ass, nor any thing that is his.

18 And all the people saw the voices and the flames, and the sound of the trumpet, and the mount smoking: and being terrified and struck with fear, they stood afar off,

19 Saying to Moses: Speak thou to us, and we will hear. Let not the Lord speak to us, lest we die.

20 And Moses said to the people: Fear not: for God is come to prove you, and that the dread of him might be in you, and that you should not sin.

21 And the people stood afar off. [9]But Moses went to the dark cloud wherein God was.

[7]Deut. 4, 11. CHAP. 20. [1]Deut. 5, 6; Ps. 80, 11.
[2]Lev. 26, 1; Deut. 4, 15; Jos. 24, 14; Ps. 96, 7.
[3]Lev. 19, 12; Deut. 5, 11; Matt. 5, 33. [4]Exod. 31, 13; Deut. 5, 14; Ezech. 20, 12. [5]Gen. 2, 2.
[6]Deut. 5, 16; Matt. 15, 4; Eph. 6, 2. [7]Matt. 5, 21. [8]Rom. 7, 7; 13, 9. [9]Deut. 18, 16; Heb. 12, 18.

CHAP. 20. Ver. 4. *A graven thing, nor the likeness of anything that is in heaven above.* All such images, or likenesses are forbidden by this commandment, as are made to be adored and served; according to that which immediately follows, *thou shalt not adore them, nor serve them.* That is, all such as are designed for *idols* or *image-gods,* and are worshipped with *divine honour.* But otherwise images, pictures, or representations, even in the house of God, and in the very sanctuary, so far from being forbidden, are expressly authorized by the word of God (Exod. 25, 15; 38, 7; Num. 21, 8, 9; 1 Par. 28, 18; 2 Par. 3, 10).

22 And the Lord said to Moses: Thus shalt thou say to the children of Israel: You have seen that I have spoken to you from heaven.

23 You shall not make gods of silver: nor shall you make to yourselves gods of gold.

24 [10] You shall make an altar of earth unto me: and you shall offer upon it your holocausts and peace offerings, your sheep and oxen, in every place where the memory of my name shall be. I will come to thee, and will bless thee.

25 [11]And if thou make an altar of stone unto me, thou shalt not build it of hewn stones: for if thou lift up a tool upon it, it shall be defiled.

26 Thou shalt not go up by steps unto my altar, lest thy nakedness be discovered.

CHAPTER 21
Laws relating to Justice.

THESE are the judgments which thou shalt set before them.

2 [1] If thou buy a Hebrew servant, six years shall he serve thee: in the seventh he shall go out free for nothing.

3 With what raiment he came in, with the like let him go out: if having a wife, his wife also shall go out with him.

4 But if his master gave him a wife, and she hath borne sons and daughters: the woman and her children shall be her master's. But he himself shall go out with his raiment.

5 And if the servant shall say: I love my master and my wife and children, I will not go out free:

6 His master shall bring him to the gods: and he shall be set to the door and the posts, and he shall bore his ear through with an awl. And he shall be his servant for ever.

7 If any man sell his daughter to be a servant, she shall not go out as bondwomen are wont to go out.

8 If she displease the eyes of her master to whom she was delivered, he shall let her go: but he shall have no power to sell her to a foreign nation, if he despise her.

9 But if he have betrothed her to his son, he shall deal with her after the manner of daughters.

10 And if he take another wife for him, he shall provide her a marriage, and raiment; neither shall he refuse the price of her chastity.

[10] Exod. 27, 8; 38, 7. [11] Deut. 27, 5; Jos. 8, 31. Chap. 21. [1] Deut. 15, 12; Jer. 34, 14. [2] Lev. 24, 17. [3] Deut. 19, 2. [4] Lev. 20, 9; Prov. 20, 20; Matt. 15, 4; Mark, 7, 10. [5] Lev. 24, 20; Deut. 19, 21; Matt. 5, 38.

Chap. 21. Ver. 6. *To the gods:* Elohim. That is, to the judges, or magistrates, authorized by God.

11 If he do not these three things, she shall go out free without money.

12 [2] He that striketh a man with a will to kill him, shall be put to death.

13 But he that did not lie in wait for him, but God delivered him into his hands: [3] I will appoint thee a place to which he must flee.

14 If a man kill his neighbour on set purpose, and by lying in wait for him: thou shalt take him away from my altar, that he may die.

15 He that striketh his father or mother, shall be put to death.

16 He that shall steal a man, and sell him, being convicted of the guilt, shall be put to death.

17 [4] He that curseth his father, or mother, shall die the death.

18 If men quarrel, and the one strike his neighbour with a stone or with his fist, and he die not, but keepeth his bed:

19 If he rise again and walk abroad upon his staff, he that struck him shall be quit: yet so that he make restitution for his work, and for his expenses upon the physicians.

20 He that striketh his bondman or bondwoman with a rod, and they die under his hands, shall be guilty of the crime.

21 But if the party remain alive a day or two, he shall not be subject to the punishment, because it is his money.

22 If men quarrel, and one strike a woman with child, and she miscarry indeed, but live herself: he shall be answerable for so much damage as the woman's husband shall require, and as arbiters shall award.

23 But if her death ensue thereupon, he shall render life for life.

24 [5] Eye for eye, tooth for tooth, hand for hand, foot for foot,

25 Burning for burning, wound for wound, stripe for stripe.

26 If any man strike the eye of his man-servant or maid-servant, and leave them but one eye, he shall let them go free for the eye which he put out.

27 Also if he strike out a tooth of his man-servant or maid-servant, he shall in like manner make them free.

28 If an ox gore a man or a woman, and they die, he shall be stoned: and his flesh shall not be eaten, but the owner of the ox shall be quit.

29 But if the ox was wont to push with his horn yesterday and the day before, and they warned his master, and he did not shut him up, and he shall kill a man or a woman: then the ox shall be stoned, and his owner also shall be put to death.

30 And if they set a price upon him,

he shall give for his life whatsoever is laid upon him.

31 If he have gored a son, or a daughter, he shall fall under the like sentence.

32 If he assault a bondman or a bondwoman, he shall give thirty sicles of silver to their master, and the ox shall be stoned.

33 If a man open a pit, and dig one, and cover it not, and an ox or an ass fall into it,

34 The owner of the pit shall pay the price of the beasts: and that which is dead shall be his own.

35 If one man's ox gore another man's ox, and he die: they shall sell the live ox, and shall divide the price, and the carcass of that which died they shall part between them.

36 But if he knew that his ox was wont to push yesterday and the day before, and his master did not keep him in: he shall pay ox for ox, and shall take the whole carcass.

CHAPTER 22

The punishment of theft, and other trespasses. The law of lending without usury, of taking pledges, of reverences to superiors, and of paying tithes.

IF any man steal an ox or a sheep and kill or sell it: he shall restore five oxen for one ox, [1] and four sheep for one sheep.

2 If a thief be found breaking open a house or undermining it, and be wounded so as to die: he that slew him shall not be guilty of blood.

3 But if he did this when the sun is risen, he hath committed murder, and he shall die. If he have not wherewith to make restitution for the theft, he shall be sold.

4 If that which he stole be found with him, alive, either ox, or ass, or sheep: he shall restore double.

5 If any man hurt a field or a vineyard, and put in his beast to feed upon that which is other men's: he shall restore the best of whatsoever he hath in his own field, or in his vineyard, according to the estimation of the damage.

6 If a fire breaking out light upon thorns, and catch stacks of corn, or corn standing in the fields, he that kindled the fire shall make good the loss.

7 If a man deliver money, or any vessel unto his friend to keep, and they be stolen away from him that received them: if the thief be found he shall restore double.

8 If the thief be not known, the master of the house shall be brought to the gods: and shall swear that he did not lay his hand upon his neighbour's goods,

9 To do any fraud, either in ox, or in ass, or sheep, or raiment, or any thing that may bring damage. The cause of both parties shall come to the gods: and if they give judgment, he shall restore double to his neighbour.

10 If a man deliver ass, ox, sheep, or any beast, to his neighbour's custody, and it die, or be hurt, or be taken by enemies, and no man saw it:

11 There shall be an oath between them, that he did not put forth his hand to his neighbour's goods. And the owner shall accept of the oath: and he shall not be compelled to make restitution.

12 [2] But if it were taken away by stealth: he shall make the loss good to the owner.

13 If it were eaten by a beast: let him bring to him that which was slain, and he shall not make restitution.

14 If a man borrow of his neighbour any of these things, and it be hurt or die, the owner not being present: he shall be obliged to make restitution.

15 But if the owner be present, he shall not make restitution: especially if it were hired and came for the hire of his work.

16 [3] If a man seduce a virgin not yet espoused, and lie with her: he shall endow her, and have her to wife.

17 If the maid's father will not give her to him: he shall give money according to the dowry, which virgins are wont to receive.

18 Wizards thou shalt not suffer to live.

19 Whosoever copulateth with a beast shall be put to death.

20 [4] He that sacrificeth to gods, shall be put to death, save only to the Lord.

21 Thou shalt not molest a stranger, nor afflict him: for yourselves also were strangers in the land of Egypt.

22 [5] You shall not hurt a widow or an orphan.

23 If you hurt them they will cry out to me, and I will hear their cry:

24 And my rage shall be enkindled, and I will strike you with the sword; and your wives shall be widows, and your children fatherless.

25 If thou lend money to any of my people that is poor, that dwelleth with thee: thou shalt not be hard upon them as an extortioner, nor oppress them with usuries.

26 [6] If thou take of thy neighbour's garment in pledge: thou shalt give it him again before sunset.

27 For that same is the only thing wherewith he is covered, the clothing

CHAP. 22. [1] Kings, 12, 6. [2] Gen. 31, 39. [3] Deut. 22, 28. [4] Lev. 19, 4. [5] Zach. 7, 10. [6] Deut. 24, 13.

of his body: neither hath he any other to sleep in. If he cry to me, I will hear him, because I am compassionate.

28 Thou shalt not speak ill of the gods: and [7] the prince of thy people thou shalt not curse.

29 Thou shalt not delay to pay thy tithes and thy firstfruits. [8] Thou shalt give the firstborn of thy sons to me.

30 Thou shalt do the same with the firstborn of thy oxen also and sheep: seven days let it be with its dam, the eighth day thou shalt give it to me.

31 You shall be holy men to me: [9] the flesh that beasts have tasted of before, you shall not eat, but shall cast it to the dogs.

CHAPTER 23

Laws for judges. The rest of the seventh year, and day. Three principal feasts to be solemnized every year. The promise of an angel, to conduct and protect them. Idols are to be destroyed.

THOU shalt not receive the voice of a lie: neither shalt thou join thy hand to bear false witness for a wicked person.

2 Thou shalt not follow the multitude to do evil: neither shalt thou yield in judgment, to the opinion of the most part, to stray from the truth.

3 Neither shalt thou favour a poor man in judgment.

4 [1] If thou meet thy enemy's ox or ass going astray, bring it back to him.

5 If thou see the ass of him that hateth thee lie underneath his burden, thou shalt not pass by, but shall lift him up with him.

6 Thou shalt not go aside in the poor man's judgment.

7 Thou shalt fly lying. [2] The innocent and just person thou shalt not put to death: because I abhor the wicked.

8 [3] Neither shalt thou take bribes, which even blind the wise, and pervert the words of the just.

9 Thou shalt not molest a stranger, for you know the hearts of strangers: [4] for you also were strangers in the land of Egypt.

10 Six years thou shalt sow thy ground, and shalt gather the corn thereof.

11 [5] But the seventh year thou shalt let it alone, and suffer it to rest, that the poor of thy people may eat: and whatsoever shall be left, let the beasts of the field eat it. So shalt thou do with thy vineyard and thy oliveyard.

12 Six days thou shalt work: the seventh day thou shalt cease; that thy ox and thy ass may rest, and the son of thy handmaid and the stranger may be refreshed.

13 Keep all things that I have said to you. And by the name of strange gods you shall not swear, neither shall it be heard out of your mouth.

14 Three times every year you shall celebrate feasts to me.

15 Thou shalt keep the feast of unleavened bread. [6] Seven days shalt thou eat unleavened bread, as I commanded thee, in the time of the month of new corn, when thou didst come forth out of Egypt. [7] Thou shalt not appear empty before me.

16 And the feast of the harvest of the firstfruits of thy work, whatsoever thou hast sown in the field. The feast also in the end of the year, when thou hast gathered in all thy corn out of the field.

17 [8] Thrice a year shall all thy males appear before the Lord thy God.

18 Thou shalt not sacrifice the blood of my victim upon leaven: neither shall the fat of my solemnity remain until the morning.

19 [9] Thou shalt carry the firstfruits of the corn of thy ground to the house of the Lord thy God. [10] Thou shalt not boil a kid in the milk of his dam.

20 Behold I will send my angel, who shall go before thee, and keep thee in thy journey: and bring thee into the place that I have prepared.

21 Take notice of him, and hear his voice, and do not think him one to be contemned: for he will not forgive when thou hast sinned, and my name is in him.

22 [11] But if thou wilt hear his voice, and do all that I speak: I will be an enemy to thy enemies, and will afflict them that afflict thee.

23 [12] And my angel shall go before thee, and shall bring thee in unto the Amorrhite, and the Hethite, and the Pherezite, and the Chanaanite, and the Hevite, and the Jebusite, whom I will destroy.

24 Thou shalt not adore their gods, nor serve them. Thou shalt not do their works: but shalt destroy them, and break their statues.

25 And you shall serve the Lord your God, that I may bless your bread and *your* waters: and may take away sickness from the midst of thee.

26 There shall not be one fruitless nor barren in thy land. I will fill the number of thy days.

27 I will send my fear before thee, and will destroy all the people to whom

[7] Acts, 23, 5. [8] Exod. 13, 2; 34, 19; Ezech. 44, 30. [9] Lev. 22, 8. CHAP. 23. [1] Deut. 21, 1. [2] Dan. 13, 53. [3] Deut. 16, 19; Ecclus. 20, 31. [4] Gen. 46, 6. [5] Lev. 25, 4. [6] Exod. 13, 3; 34, 22. [7] Deut. 16, 16; Ecclus. 35, 6. [8] Exod. 34, 23; Deut. 16, 16. [9] Exod. 34, 26. [10] Deut. 14, 21. [11] Deut. 7, 11. [12] Exod. 33, 2; Jos. 24, 11; Deut. 7, 22.

thou shalt come: and will turn the backs of all thy enemies before thee.

28 [13] Sending out hornets before, that shall drive away the Hevite, and the Chanaanite, and the Hethite, before thou come in.

29 I will not cast them out from thy face in one year: lest the land be brought into a wilderness, and the beasts multiply against thee.

30 By little and little I will drive them out from before thee: till thou be increased, and dost possess the land.

31 And I will set thy bounds from the Red Sea to the sea of the Palestines: and from the desert to the river. I will deliver the inhabitants of the land into your hands: and will drive them out from before you.

32 [14] Thou shalt not enter into league with them, nor with their gods.

33 Let them not dwell in thy land, lest perhaps they make thee sin against me, if thou serve their gods: which undoubtedly will be a scandal to thee.

CHAPTER 24

Moses writeth his law. After offering sacrifices, sprinkleth the blood of the testament upon the people. Goeth up the mountain which God covereth with a fiery cloud.

AND he said to Moses: Come up to the Lord, thou, and Aaron, Nadab, and Abiu, and seventy of the ancients of Israel. And you shall adore afar off.

2 And Moses alone shall come up to the Lord; but they shall not come nigh: neither shall the people come up with him.

3 So Moses came and told the people all the words of the Lord, and all the judgments. And all the people answered with one voice: We will do all the words of the Lord, which he hath spoken.

4 And Moses wrote all the words of the Lord: and rising in the morning he built an altar at the foot of the mount and twelve titles according to the twelve tribes of Israel.

5 And he sent young men of the children of Israel: and they offered holocausts, and sacrificed pacific victims of calves to the Lord.

6 Then Moses took half of the blood and put it into bowls: and the rest he poured upon the altar.

7 And taking the book of the covenant, he read it in the hearing of the people: and they said: All things that the Lord hath spoken we will do. We will be obedient.

8 And he took the blood and sprinkled it upon the people, and he said: [1] This is the blood of the covenant which the

Lord hath made with you concerning all these words.

9 Then Moses and Aaron, Nadab and Abiu, and seventy of the ancients of Israel went up.

10 And they saw the God of Israel: and under his feet as it were a work of sapphire stone, and as the heaven, when clear.

11 Neither did he lay his hand upon those of the children of Israel, that retired afar off. And they saw God, and they did eat and drink.

12 And the Lord said to Moses: Come up to me into the mount, and be there. And I will give thee tables of stone, and the law, and the commandments which I have written: that thou mayst teach them.

13 Moses rose up, and his minister Josue: and Moses going up into the mount of God,

14 Said to the ancients: Wait ye here till we return to you. You have Aaron and Hur with you: if any question shall arise, you shall refer it to them.

15 And when Moses was gone up, a cloud covered the mount.

16 And the glory of the Lord dwelt upon Sinai, covering it with a cloud six days: and the seventh day he called him out of the midst of the cloud.

17 And the sight of the glory of the Lord was like a burning fire upon the top of the mount, in the eyes of the children of Israel.

18 And Moses, entering into the midst of the cloud, went up into the mountain: [2] and he was there forty days, and forty nights.

CHAPTER 25

Offerings prescribed for making the tabernacle, the ark, the candlestick, etc.

AND the Lord spoke to Moses, saying:

2 Speak to the children of Israel, [1] that they bring firstfruits to me: of every man that offereth of his own accord, you shall take them.

3 And these are the things you must take: gold, and silver, and brass,

4 Violet and purple, and scarlet twice dyed, and fine linen, and goats' hair,

5 And rams' skins dyed red, and violet skins, and setim wood:

[13] Deut. 7, 20. [14] Exod. 34, 15; Deut. 7, 2. CHAP. 24. [1] Heb. 9, 20. [2] Deut. 9, 9. CHAP. 25. [1] Exod. 35, 5.

CHAP. 24. Ver. 4. *Titles.* That is, pillars.
Ver. 5. *Holocausts.* Whole burnt offerings, in which the whole sacrifice was consumed with fire upon the altar.
CHAP. 25. Ver. 2. *Firstfruits.* Offerings of some of the best and choicest of their goods.
Ver. 5. *Setim wood.* The wood of a tree that grows in the wilderness, which is said to be incorruptible.

6 Oil to make lights: spices for ointment, and for sweet-smelling incense:

7 Onyx stones, and precious stones to adorn the ephod and the rational.

8 And they shall make me a sanctuary: and I will dwell in the midst of them.

9 [2] According to all the likeness of the tabernacle which I will shew thee, and of all the vessels for the service thereof: and thus you shall make it.

10 Frame an ark of setim wood, the length whereof shall be of two cubits and a half: the breadth, a cubit and a half: the height, likewise, a cubit and a half.

11 And thou shalt overlay it with the purest gold within and without: and over it thou shalt make a golden crown round about.

12 And four golden rings, which thou shalt put at the four corners of the ark. Let two rings be on the one side, and two on the other.

13 Thou shalt make bars also of setim wood: and shalt overlay them with gold.

14 And thou shalt put them in through the rings that are in the sides of the ark, that it may be carried on them.

15 And they shall be always in the rings: neither shall they at any time be drawn out of them.

16 And thou shalt put in the ark the testimony which I will give thee.

17 Thou shalt make also a propitiatory of the purest gold: the length thereof shall be two cubits and a half, and the breadth a cubit and a half.

18 Thou shalt make also two cherubims of beaten gold, on the two sides of the oracle.

19 Let one cherub be on the one side, and the other on the other.

20 Let them cover both sides of the

propitiatory, spreading their wings, and covering the oracle: and let them look one towards the other, their faces being turned towards the propitiatory wherewith the ark is to be covered.

21 In which thou shalt put the testimony that I will give thee.

22 Thence will I give orders, and will speak to thee over the propitiatory, and from the midst of the two cherubims, which shall be upon the ark of the testimony, all things which I will command the children of Israel by thee.

23 Thou shalt make a table also of setim wood, of two cubits in length, and a cubit in breadth, and a cubit and a half in height.

24 And thou shalt overlay it with the purest gold: and thou shalt make to it a golden ledge round about.

25 And to the ledge itself a polished crown, four inches high: and over the same another little golden crown.

26 Thou shalt prepare also four golden rings, and shalt put them in the four corners of the same table over each foot.

27 Under the crown shall the golden rings be: that the bars may be put through them, and the table may be carried.

28 The bars also themselves thou shalt make of setim wood: and shalt overlay them with gold to bear up the table.

29 Thou shalt prepare also dishes and bowls, censers, and cups, wherein the libations are to be offered: of the purest gold.

30 And thou shalt set upon the table loaves of proposition, in my sight always.

31 Thou shalt make also a candlestick of beaten work of the finest gold: the shaft thereof, and the branches, the cups, and the bowls and the lilies going forth from it.

32 Six branches shall come out of the sides: three out of the one side, and three out of the other.

33 Three cups as it were nuts to every branch, and a bowl withal, and a lily; and three cups, likewise of the fashion of nuts in the other branch, and a bowl withal, and a lily. Such shall be the work of the six branches, that are to come out from the shaft.

34 And in the candlestick itself shall be four cups in the manner of a nut: and at every one, bowls and lilies.

35 Bowls under two branches in three places, which together make six coming forth out of one shaft.

36 And both the bowls and the branches shall be of the same beaten work of the purest gold.

---

[2] Heb. 9, 2.

Ver. 7. *The ephod and the rational.* The *ephod* was the high priest's upper vestment; and the *rational* his breastplate, in which were twelve gems, &c.

Ver. 17. *A propitiatory.* A covering for the ark: called a *propitiatory*, or *mercy seat*, because the Lord, who was supposed to sit there upon the wings of the cherubims, with the ark for his footstool, from thence shewed mercy. It is also called the *oracle*, ver. 18 and 20; because from thence God gave his orders and his answers.

Ver. 23. *A table.* On which were to be placed the twelve *loaves of proposition*: or, as they are called in the Hebrew, the *face bread*, because they were always to stand before the *face* of the Lord in his temple: as a figure of the eucharistic sacrifice and sacrament, in the church of Christ.

Ver. 29. *Libations.* That is, drink offerings.

Ver. 31. *A candlestick.* This candlestick, with its seven lamps, which was always to give light in the house of God, was a figure of the light of the Holy Ghost, and his sevenfold grace, in the sanctuary of the church of Christ.

37 Thou shalt make also seven lamps: and shalt set them upon the candlestick, to give light over against.

38 The snuffers also and where the snuffings shall be put out, shall be made of the purest gold.

39 The whole weight of the candlestick with all the furniture thereof shall be a talent of the purest gold.

40 [3] Look and make it according to the pattern, that was shewn thee in the mount.

CHAPTER 26

The form of the tabernacle with its appurtenances.

AND thou shalt make the tabernacle in this manner: Thou shalt make ten curtains of fine twisted linen and violet and purple, and scarlet twice dyed, diversified with embroidery.

2 The length of one curtain shall be twenty-eight cubits, the breadth shall be four cubits. All the curtains shall be of one measure.

3 Five curtains shall be joined one to another, and the other five shall be coupled together in like manner.

4 Thou shalt make loops of violet in the sides and tops of the curtains, that they may be joined one to another.

5 Every curtain shall have fifty loops on both sides; so set on, that one loop may be against another loop, and one may be fitted to the other.

6 Thou shalt make also fifty rings of gold wherewith the veils of the curtains are to be joined, that it may be made one tabernacle.

7 Thou shalt make also eleven curtains of goats' hair, to cover the top of the tabernacle.

8 The length of one hair curtain shall be thirty cubits: and the breadth four. The measure of all the curtains shall be equal.

9 Five of which thou shalt couple by themselves, and the six others thou shalt couple one to another: so as to double the sixth curtain in the front of the roof.

10 Thou shalt make also fifty loops in the edge of one curtain, that it may be joined with the other: and fifty loops in the edge of the other curtain, that it may be coupled with its fellow.

11 Thou shalt make also fifty buckles of brass, wherewith the loops may be joined: that of all there may be made one covering.

12 And that which shall remain of the curtains, that are prepared for the roof, to wit: one curtain that is over and above. With the half thereof thou shalt cover the back parts of the tabernacle.

13 And there shall hang down a cubit on the one side, and another on the other side, which is over and above in the length of the curtains; fencing both sides of the tabernacle.

14 Thou shalt make also another cover to the roof, of rams' skins dyed red: and over that again another cover of violet coloured skins.

15 Thou shalt make also the boards of the tabernacle standing upright of setim wood.

16 Let every one of them be ten cubits in length, and in breadth one cubit and a half.

17 In the sides of the boards shall be made two mortises, whereby one board may be joined to another board: and after this manner shall all the boards be prepared.

18 Of which twenty shall be in the south side southward.

19 For which thou shalt cast forty sockets of silver, that under every board may be put two sockets at the two corners.

20 In the second side also, the tabernacle that looketh to the north, there shall be twenty boards,

21 Having forty sockets of silver. Two sockets shall be put under each board.

22 But on the west side of the tabernacle thou shalt make six boards.

23 And again other two which shall be erected in the corners at the back of the tabernacle.

24 And they shall be joined together from beneath unto the top; and one joint shall hold them all. The like joining shall be observed for the two boards also that are to be put in the corners.

25 And they shall be in all eight boards: and their silver sockets sixteen, reckoning two sockets for each board.

26 Thou shalt make also five bars of setim wood, to hold together the boards on one side of the tabernacle.

27 And five others on the other side: and as many at the west side:

28 And they shall be put along by the midst of the boards from one end to the other.

29 The boards also themselves thou shalt overlay with gold, and shalt cast rings of gold to be set upon them, for places for the bars to hold together the board-work: which *bars* thou shalt cover with plates of gold.

30 And thou shalt rear up the tabernacle according to the pattern that was [1] shewn thee in the mount.

31 Thou shalt make also a veil of violet and purple, and scarlet twice dyed, and fine twisted linen, wrought

[3] Heb. 8, 5; Acts, 7, 44. Chap. 26. [1] Exod. 25, 40.

with embroidered work, and goodly variety.

32 And thou shalt hang it up before four pillars of setim wood, which themselves also shall be overlaid with gold, and shall have heads of gold, but sockets of silver.

33 And the veils shall be hanged or with rings: and within it thou shalt put the ark of the testimony. And the sanctuary, and the holy of holies shall be divided with it.

34 And thou shalt set the propitiatory upon the ark of the testimony in the holy of holies.

35 And the table without the veil. And over against the table, the candlestick in the south side of the tabernacle: for the table shall stand in the north side.

36 Thou shalt make also a hanging in the entrance of the tabernacle of violet and purple, and scarlet twice dyed, and fine twisted linen with embroidered work.

37 And thou shalt overlay with gold five pillars of setim wood, before which the hanging shall be drawn: their heads shall be of gold, and the sockets of brass.

CHAPTER 27

The altar. The court of the tabernacle with its hangings and pillars. Provision of oil for lamps.

THOU shalt make also an altar of setim wood, which shall be five cubits long and as many broad: that is, foursquare, and three cubits high.[1]

2 And there shall be horns at the four corners of the same: and thou shalt cover it with brass.

3 And thou shalt make for the uses thereof pans to receive the ashes, and tongs and fleshhooks, and firepans: all its vessels thou shalt make of brass.

4 And a grate of brass in manner of a net: at the four corners of which shall be four rings of brass,

5 Which thou shalt put under the hearth of the altar: and the grate shall be even to the midst of the altar.

6 Thou shalt make also two bars for the altar of setim wood, which thou shalt cover with plates of brass.

7 And thou shalt draw them through rings: and they shall be on both sides of the altar to carry it.

8 Thou shalt not make it solid, but

CHAP. 27. [1] Exod. 38, 6. [2] Exod. 20, 24.

CHAP. 26. Ver. 33. *The sanctuary.* That part of the tabernacle, which was without the veil, into which the priests daily entered, is here called *the sanctuary,* or holy place; that part which was within the veil, into which no one but the high priest ever went, and he but once a year, is called *the holy of holies,* (literally, *the sanctuary of the sanctuaries,*) as being the most holy of all holy places.

empty and hollow in the inside: as it was shewn thee in the mount.

9 Thou shalt make also the court of the tabernacle: in the south side whereof southward there shall be hangings of fine twisted linen of a hundred cubits long for one side.

10 And twenty pillars with as many sockets of brass, the heads of which with their engraving shall be of silver.

11 In like manner also on the north side there shall be hangings of a hundred cubits long, twenty pillars: and as many sockets of brass, and their heads with their engraving of silver.

12 But in the breadth of the court, that looketh to the west, there shall be hangings of fifty cubits, and ten pillars, and as many sockets.

13 In that breadth also of the court, which looketh to the east, there shall be fifty cubits.

14 In which there shall be for one side hangings of fifteen cubits, and three pillars and as many sockets.

15 And in the other side there shall be hangings of fifteen cubits, with three pillars and as many sockets.

16 And in the entrance of the court there shall be made a hanging of twenty cubits of violet and purple, and scarlet twice dyed, and fine twisted linen, with embroidered work. It shall have four pillars with as many sockets.

17 All the pillars of the court round about shall be garnished with plates of silver, silver heads, and sockets of brass.

18 In length the court shall take up a hundred cubits, in breadth fifty. The height shall be of five cubits; and it shall be made of fine twisted linen, and shall have sockets of brass.

19 All the vessels of the tabernacle for all uses and ceremonies, and the pins both of it, and of the court, thou shalt make of brass.

20 Command the children of Israel that they bring thee the purest oil of the olives, and beaten with a pestle: that a lamp may burn always.

21 In the tabernacle of the testimony, without the veil that hangs before the testimony. And Aaron and his sons shall order it, that it may give light before the Lord until the morning. It shall be a perpetual observance throughout their successions among the children of Israel.

CHAPTER 28

The holy vestments for Aaron and his sons.

TAKE unto thee also Aaron thy brother with his sons, from among the children of Israel, that they may minister to me in the priest's office:

Aaron, Nadab, and Abiu, Eleazar, and Ithamar.

2 And thou shalt make a holy vesture for Aaron thy brother: for glory and for beauty.

3 And thou shalt speak to all the wise of heart, whom I have filled with the spirit of wisdom: that they may make Aaron's vestments, in which he being consecrated may minister to me.

4 And these shall be the vestments that they shall make: A rational and and an ephod, a tunick and a strait linen garment, a mitre and a girdle. They shall make the holy vestments for thy brother Aaron and his sons: that they may do the office of priesthood unto me.

5 And they shall take gold, and violet, and purple, and scarlet twice dyed, and fine linen.

6 And they shall make the ephod of gold, and violet, and purple, and scarlet twice dyed, and fine twisted linen, embroidered with divers colours.

7 It shall have the two edges joined in the top on both sides, that they may be closed together.

8 The very workmanship also and all the variety of the work shall be of gold, and violet, and purple, and scarlet twice dyed, and fine twisted linen.

9 And thou shalt take two onyx stones: and shalt grave on them the names of the children of Israel:

10 Six names on one stone, and the other six on the other: according to the order of their birth.

11 With the work of an engraver and the graving of a jeweller, thou shalt engrave them with the names of the children of Israel, set in gold and compassed about.

12 And thou shalt put them in both sides of the ephod: a memorial for the children of Israel. And Aaron shall bear their names before the Lord upon both shoulders, for a remembrance.

13 Thou shalt make also hooks of gold.

14 And two little chains of the purest gold linked one to another, which thou shalt put into the hooks.

15 And thou shalt make the rational of judgment with embroidered work of divers colours, according to the workmanship of the ephod: of gold, violet, and purple, and scarlet twice dyed, and fine twisted linen.

16 It shall be foursquare and doubled: it shall be the measure of a span both in length and in breadth.

17 And thou shalt set in it four rows of stones: in the first row shall be a sardius stone, and a topaz, and an emerald:

18 In the second a carbuncle, a sapphire and a jasper.

19 In the third a ligurius, an agate, and an amethyst:

20 In the fourth a chrysolite, an onyx, and a beryl. They shall be set in gold by their rows.

21 And they shall have the names of the children of Israel: with twelve names shall they be engraved, each stone with the name of one according to the twelve tribes.

22 And thou shalt make on the rational chains linked one to another of the purest gold:

23 And two rings of gold, which thou shalt put in the two ends at the top of the rational.

24 And the golden chains thou shalt join to the rings, that are in the ends thereof.

25 And the ends of the chains themselves thou shalt join together with two hooks on both sides of the ephod, which is towards the rational.

26 Thou shalt make also two rings of gold which thou shalt put in the top parts of the rational, in the borders that are over against the ephod, and look towards the back parts thereof.

27 Moreover also other two rings of gold, which are to be set on each side of the ephod beneath, that looketh towards the nether joining: that the rational may be fitted with the ephod,

28 And may be fastened by the rings thereof unto the rings of the ephod with a violet fillet: that the joining artificially wrought may continue, and the rational and the ephod may not be loosed one from the other.

29 And Aaron shall bear the names of the children of Israel in the rational of judgment upon his breast, when he shall enter into the sanctuary: a memorial before the Lord for ever.

30 And thou shalt put in the rational of judgment, doctrine and truth, which shall be on Aaron's breast, when he shall go in before the Lord: and he shall bear the judgment of the children of Israel on his breast, in the sight of the Lord always.

31 And thou shalt make the tunick of the ephod all of violet.

CHAP. 28. Ver. 15. *The rational of judgment.* This part of the priest's attire, which he wore at his breast, was called *the rational of judgment;* partly because it admonished both priest and people of their duty to God, by carrying the names of all their tribes in his presence; and by the *Urim* and *Thummim,* that is, *doctrine* and *truth,* which were written upon it; and partly because it gave divine answers and oracles, as if it were *rational* and endowed with judgment.

Ver. 30. *Doctrine and truth.* Hebrew, *Urim* and *Thummim: illuminations and perfections.* These words, written on the *rational,* seem to signify the light of doctrine and the integrity of life, with which the priests of God ought to approach to him.

32 In the midst whereof above shall be a hole for the head, and a border round about it woven, as is wont to be made in the outmost parts of garments: that it may not easily be broken.

33 And beneath at the feet of the same tunick round about, thou shalt make as it were pomegranates, of violet, and purple, and scarlet twice dyed, with little bells set between:

34 So that there shall be a golden bell and a pomegranate: and again another golden bell and a pomegranate.

35 [1] And Aaron shall be vested with it in the office of his ministry: that the sound may be heard, when he goeth in and cometh out of the sanctuary, in the sight of the Lord; and that he may not die.

36 Thou shalt make also a plate of the purest gold: wherein thou shalt grave with engraver's work: HOLY TO THE LORD.

37 And thou shalt tie it with a violet fillet; and it shall be upon the mitre,

38 Hanging over the forehead of the high priest. And Aaron shall bear the iniquities of those things, which the children of Israel have offered and sanctified, in all their gifts and offerings. And the plate shall be always on his forehead, that the Lord may be well pleased with them.

39 And thou shalt gird the tunick with fine linen: and thou shalt make a fine linen mitre, and a girdle of embroidered work.

40 Moreover for the sons of Aaron thou shalt prepare linen tunicks, and girdles and mitres for glory and beauty.

41 And with all these things thou shalt vest Aaron thy brother, and his sons with him. And thou shalt consecrate the hands of them all, and shalt sanctify them: that they may do the office of priesthood unto me.

42 Thou shalt make also linen breeches, to cover the flesh of their nakedness from the reins to the thighs.

43 And Aaron and his sons shall use them when they shall go into the tabernacle of the testimony, or when they approach to the altar to minister in the sanctuary: lest being guilty of iniquity they die. It shall be a law for ever to Aaron, and to his seed after him.

CHAPTER 29

The manner of consecrating Aaron and other priests. The institution of the daily sacrifice of two lambs, one in the morning, the other at evening.

AND thou shalt also do this, that they may be consecrated to me

in priesthood. [1] Take a calf from the herd, and two rams without blemish,

2 And unleavened bread, and a cake without leaven, tempered with oil: wafers also unleavened, anointed with oil. Thou shalt make them all of wheaten flour.

3 And thou shalt put them in a basket and offer *them*: and the calf and the two rams.

4 And thou shalt bring Aaron and his sons to the door of the tabernacle of the testimony. And when thou hast washed the father and his sons with water,

5 Thou shalt clothe Aaron with his vestments: that is, with the linen garment and the tunick, and the ephod and the rational, which thou shalt gird with the girdle.

6 And thou shalt put the mitre upon his head, and the holy plate upon the mitre,

7 And thou shalt pour the oil of unction upon his head: and by this rite shall he be consecrated.

8 Thou shalt bring his sons also: and shalt put on them the linen tunicks, and gird them with a girdle.

9 To wit, Aaron and his children: and thou shalt put mitres upon them. And they shall be priests to me by a perpetual ordinance. After thou shalt have consecrated their hands,

10 [2] Thou shalt present also the calf before the tabernacle of the testimony. And Aaron and his sons shall lay their hands upon his head,

11 And thou shalt kill him in the sight of the Lord, beside the door of the tabernacle of the testimony.

12 And taking some of the blood of the calf, thou shalt put *it* upon the horns of the altar with thy finger: and the rest of the blood thou shalt pour at the bottom thereof.

13 [3] Thou shalt take also all the fat that covereth the entrails, and the caul of the liver, and the two kidneys, and the fat that is upon them: and shalt offer a burnt offering upon the altar.

14 But the flesh of the calf and the hide and the dung, thou shalt burn abroad, without the camp, because it is for sin.

15 Thou shalt take also one ram, upon the head whereof Aaron and his sons shall lay their hands.

16 And when thou hast killed him, thou shalt take of the blood thereof, and pour round about the altar.

17 And thou shalt cut the ram in pieces, and having washed his entrails and feet, thou shalt put them upon the flesh that is cut in pieces, and upon his head.

18 And thou shalt offer the whole

ram for a burnt offering upon the altar. It is an oblation to the Lord: a most sweet savour of the victim of the Lord.

19 Thou shalt take also the other ram, upon whose head Aaron and his sons shall lay their hands.

20 And when thou hast sacrificed him, thou shalt take of his blood, and put upon the tip of the right ear of Aaron and of his sons, and upon the thumbs and great toes of their right hand and foot: and thou shalt pour the blood upon the altar round about.

21 And when thou hast taken of the blood, that is upon the altar, and of the oil of unction, thou shalt sprinkle Aaron and his vesture, his sons and their vestments. And after they and their vestments are consecrated,

22 Thou shalt take the fat of the ram, and the rump, and the fat that covereth the lungs, and the caul of the liver, and the two kidneys, and the fat that is upon them, and the right shoulder: because it is the ram of consecration.

23 And one roll of bread, a cake tempered with oil, a wafer out of the basket of unleavened bread, which is set in the sight of the Lord.

24 And thou shalt put all upon the hands of Aaron and of his sons: and shalt sanctify them, elevating before the Lord.

25 And thou shalt take all from their hands, and shalt burn them upon the altar for a holocaust: a most sweet savour in the sight of the Lord, because it is his oblation.

26 Thou shalt take also the breast of the ram, wherewith Aaron was consecrated, and elevating it thou shalt sanctify it before the Lord: and it shall fall to thy share.

27 And thou shalt sanctify both the consecrated breast, and the shoulder that thou didst separate of the ram,

28 Wherewith Aaron was consecrated and his sons; and they shall fall to Aaron's share and his sons' by a perpetual right from the children of Israel: because they are the choicest and the beginnings of their peace victims which they offer to the Lord.

29 And the holy vesture, which Aaron shall use, his sons shall have after him: that they may be anointed, and their hands consecrated in it.

30 He of his sons that shall be appointed high priest in his stead, and that shall enter into the tabernacle of the testimony to minister in the sanctuary, shall wear it seven days.

31 And thou shalt take the ram of the consecration: and shalt boil the flesh thereof in the holy place:

32 And Aaron and his sons shall eat it. ⁴ The loaves also, that are in the basket, they shall eat in the entry of the tabernacle of the testimony,

33 That it may be an atoning sacrifice, and the hands of the offerers may be sanctified. A stranger shall not eat of them, because they are holy.

34 And if there remain of the consecrated flesh, or of the bread till the morning, thou shalt burn the remainder with fire. They shall not be eaten, because they are sanctified.

35 All that I have commanded thee, thou shalt do unto Aaron and his sons. Seven days shalt thou consecrate their hands:

36 And thou shalt offer a calf for sin every day for expiation. And thou shalt cleanse the altar when thou hast offered the victim of expiation: and shalt anoint it to sanctify it.

37 Seven days shalt thou expiate the altar and sanctify it: and it shall be most holy. Every one that shall touch it shall be holy.

38 This is what thou shalt sacrifice upon the altar: Two lambs of a year old, every day continually.

39 One lamb in the morning and another in the evening.

40 With one lamb a tenth part of flour tempered with beaten oil, of the fourth part of a hin: and wine for libation of the same measure.

41 And the other lamb thou shalt offer in the evening, according to the rite of the morning oblation, and according to what we have said: for a savour of sweetness.

42 It is a sacrifice to the Lord, by perpetual oblation unto your generations, at the door of the tabernacle of the testimony before the Lord, where I will appoint to speak unto thee.

43 And there will I command the children of Israel: and the altar shall be sanctified by my glory.

44 I will sanctify also the tabernacle of the testimony with the altar, and Aaron with his sons, to do the office of priesthood unto me.

45 And I will dwell in the midst of the children of Israel, and will be their God:

46 And they shall know that I am the Lord their God, who have brought them out of the land of Egypt, that I might abide among them: I the Lord their God.

CHAPTER 30

The altar of incense. Money to be gathered for the use of the tabernacle. The brazen laver. The holy oil of unction, and the composition of the perfume.

---

⁴ Lev. 8, 31; 24, 9; Matt. 12, 4.

Chap. 30. Ver. 1. *An altar to burn incense.* This burning of incense was an emblem of prayer, ascending to God from an inflamed heart (Ps. 140, 2; Apoc. 5, 8, and 8, 4).

THOU shalt make also an altar to burn incense, of setim wood.

2 It shall be a cubit in length, and another in breadth, that is, foursquare: and two in height. Horns shall go out of the same.

3 And thou shalt overlay it with the purest gold, as well as the grate thereof, as the walls round about and the horns. And thou shalt make to it a crown of gold round about.

4 And two golden rings under the crown on either side: that the bars may be put into them, and the altar be carried.

5 And thou shalt make the bars also of setim wood, and shalt overlay them with gold.

6 And thou shalt set the altar over against the veil, that hangeth before the ark of the testimony before the propitiatory wherewith the testimony is covered, where I will speak to thee.

7 And Aaron shall burn sweet-smelling incense upon it in the morning. When he shall dress the lamps, he shall burn it.

8 And when he shall place them in the evening, he shall burn an everlasting incense before the Lord throughout your generations.

9 You shall not offer upon it incense of another composition nor oblation, and victim: neither shall you offer libations.

10 And Aaron shall pray upon the horns thereof once a year, with the blood of that which was offered for sin: and shall make atonement upon it in your generations. It shall be most holy to the Lord.

11 And the Lord spoke to Moses, saying:

12 [1] When thou shalt take the sum of the children of Israel according to their number, every one of them shall give a price for their souls to the Lord: and there shall be no scourge among them, when they shall be reckoned.

13 And this shall every one give that passeth at the naming, half a sicle according to the standard of the temple. [2] A sicle hath twenty obols. Half a sicle shall be offered to the Lord.

14 He that is counted in the number from twenty years and upwards, shall give the price.

15 The rich man shall not add to half a sicle: and the poor man shall diminish nothing.

CHAP. 30. [1] Num. 1, 2. [2] Lev. 27, 25; Num. 3, 47; Ezech. 45, 12.

Ver. 13. *Half a sicle.* A *sicle* or *shekel* of silver, (which was also called a *stater,*) according to the standard or weight of the sanctuary, which was the most just and exact, was half an ounce of silver, that is about half a crown of English money. The *obol,* or *gerah,* was about three halfpence.

16 And the money received which was contributed by the children of Israel, thou shalt deliver unto the uses of the tabernacle of the testimony: that it may be a memorial of them before the Lord, and he may be merciful to their souls.

17 And the Lord spoke to Moses, saying:

18 Thou shalt make also a brazen laver with its foot, to wash in: and thou shalt set it between the tabernacle of the testimony and the altar. And water being put into it,

19 Aaron and his sons shall wash their hands and feet in it:

20 When they are going into the tabernacle of the testimony, and when they are to come to the altar, to offer on it incense to the Lord:

21 Lest perhaps they die. It shall be an everlasting law to him, and to his seed by successions.

22 And the Lord spoke to Moses,

23 Saying: Take spices, of principal and chosen myrrh five hundred sicles; and of cinnamon half so much, that is, two hundred and fifty sicles; of calamus in like manner two hundred and fifty.

24 And of cassia five hundred sicles by the weight of the sanctuary; of oil of olives the measure hin.

25 And thou shalt make the holy oil of unction: an ointment compounded after the art of the perfumer,

26 And therewith thou shalt anoint the tabernacle of the testimony, and the ark of the testament:

27 And the table with the vessels thereof; the candlestick and furniture thereof; the altars of incense,

28 And of holocaust; and all the furniture that belongeth to the service of them.

29 And thou shalt sanctify all: and they shall be most holy. He that shall touch them shall be sanctified.

30 Thou shalt anoint Aaron and his sons, and shalt sanctify them: that they may do the office of priesthood unto me.

31 And thou shalt say to the children of Israel: This oil of unction shall be holy unto me throughout your generations.

32 The flesh of man shall not be anointed therewith: and you shall make none other of the same composition; because it is sanctified, and shall be holy unto you.

33 What man soever shall compound such, and shall give thereof to a stranger, he shall be cut off from his people.

34 And the Lord said to Moses: Take unto thee spices, stacte, and onycha, galbanum of sweet savour, and the

clearest frankincense. All shall be of equal weight.

35 And thou shalt make incense compounded by the work of the perfumer; well tempered together, and pure, and most worthy of sanctification.

36 And when thou hast beaten all into very small powder, thou shalt set of it before the tabernacle of the testimony, in the place where I will appear to thee. Most holy shall this incense be unto you.

37 You shall not make such a composition for your own uses, because it is holy to the Lord.

38 What man soever shall make the like, to enjoy the smell thereof, he shall perish out of his people.

CHAPTER 31

Beseleel and Ooliab are appointed by the Lord to make the tabernacle, and the things belonging thereto. The observation of the sabbath day is again commanded. And the Lord delivereth to Moses two tables written with the finger of God.

AND the Lord spoke to Moses, saying:

2 Behold, I have called by name Beseleel, the son of Uri, the son of Hur, of the tribe of Juda,

3 And I have filled him with the spirit of God, with wisdom and understanding, and knowledge in all manner of work.

4 To devise whatsoever may be artificially made of gold, and silver, and brass,

5 Of marble, and precious stones, and variety of wood.

6 And I have given him for his companion, Ooliab, the son of Achisamech, of the tribe of Dan. And I have put wisdom in the heart of every skilful man, that they may make all things which I have commanded thee:

7 The tabernacle of the covenant, and the ark of the testimony, and the propitiatory that is over it, and all the vessels of the tabernacle:

8 And the table and the vessels thereof, the most pure candlestick with the vessels thereof, and the altars of incense:

9 And of holocaust, and all their vessels, the laver with its foot:

10 The holy vestments in the ministry, for Aaron the priest, and for his sons, that they may execute their office about the sacred things:

11 The oil of unction, and the incense of spices in the sanctuary. All things which I have commanded thee, shall they make.

12 And the Lord spoke to Moses, saying:

13 Speak to the children of Israel, and thou shalt say to them: [1] See that thou keep my sabbath; because it is a sign between me and you in your generations; that you may know that I am the Lord, who sanctify you.

14 Keep you my sabbath: for it is holy unto you. He that shall profane it, shall be put to death: he that shall do any work in it, his soul shall perish out of the midst of his people.

15 Six days shall you do work: in the seventh day is the sabbath, the rest holy to the Lord. Every one that shall do any work on this day, shall die.

16 Let the children of Israel keep the sabbath, and celebrate it in their generations. It is an everlasting covenant

17 Between me and the children of Israel, and a perpetual sign. [2] For in six days the Lord made heaven and earth: and in the seventh he ceased from work.

18 And the Lord, when he had ended these words in mount Sinai, [3] gave to Moses two stone tables of testimony, written with the finger of God.

CHAPTER 32

The people fall into idolatry. Moses prayeth for them. He breaketh the tables, destroyeth the idol, blameth Aaron, and causeth many of the idolaters to be slain.

AND the people seeing that Moses delayed to come down from the mount, gathering together against Aaron, said [1] Arise, make us gods, that may go before us; for as to this Moses, the man that brought us out of the land of Egypt, we know not what has befallen him.

2 And Aaron said to them: Take the golden earrings from the ears of your wives, and your sons and daughters, and bring them to me.

3 And the people did what he had commanded, bringing the earrings to Aaron.

4 [2] And when he had received them, he fashioned them by founders' work, and made of them a molten calf. And they said: These are thy gods, O Israel, that have brought thee out of the land of Egypt.

5 And when Aaron saw this, he built an altar before it, and made proclamation by a crier's voice, saying: To-morrow is the solemnity of the Lord.

6 And rising in the morning, they offered holocausts, and peace victims: [3] and the people sat down to eat, and drink, and they rose up to play.

7 And the Lord spoke to Moses, saying: [4] Go, get thee down: thy people, which thou hast brought out of the land of Egypt, hath sinned.

CHAP. 31. [1] Exod. 20, 8; Ezech. 20, 12. [2] Gen. 1, 31; 2, 2. [3] Deut. 9, 10. CHAP. 32. [1] Acts, 7, 40. [2] Ps. 105, 19. [3] 1 Cor. 10, 7. [4] Deut. 9, 12.

8 They have quickly strayed from the way which thou didst shew them: and they have made to themselves a molten calf, and have adored it, and sacrificing victims to it, have said: [5] These are thy gods, O Israel, that have brought thee out of the land of Egypt.

9 And again the Lord said to Moses: [6] See that this people is stiffnecked.

10 Let me alone, that my wrath may be kindled against them, and that I may destroy them: and I will make of thee a great nation.

11 But Moses besought the Lord his God, saying: [7] Why, O Lord, is thy indignation enkindled against thy people, whom thou hast brought out of the land of Egypt, with great power, and with a mighty hand?

12 Let not the Egyptians say, I beseech thee: He craftily brought them out, that he might kill them in the mountains, and destroy them from the earth. Let thy anger cease, and be appeased upon the wickedness of thy people.

13 Remember Abraham, Isaac, and Israel, thy servants, to whom thou sworest by thy own self, saying: [8] I will multiply your seed as the stars of heaven: and this whole land that I have spoken of, I will give to your seed; and you shall possess it for ever.

14 And the Lord was appeased from doing the evil which he had spoken against his people.

15 And Moses returned from the mount, carrying the two tables of the testimony in his hand, written on both sides,

16 And made by the work of God. The writing also of God was graven in the tables.

17 And Josue hearing the noise of the people shouting, said to Moses: The noise of battle is heard in the camp.

18 But he answered: It is not the cry of men encouraging to fight, nor the shout of men compelling to flee. But I hear the voice of singers.

19 And when he came nigh to the camp, he saw the calf, and the dances: and being very angry, he threw the tables out of his hand, and broke them at the foot of the mount.

20 And laying hold of the calf which they had made, he burnt it, [9] and beat it to powder, which he strowed into water,

and gave thereof to the children of Israel to drink.

21 And he said to Aaron: What has this people done to thee, that thou shouldst bring upon them a most heinous sin?

22 And he answered him: Let not my lord be offended; for thou knowest this people, [10] that they are prone to evil.

23 They said to me: Make us gods, that may go before us; for as to this Moses, who brought us forth out of the land of Egypt, we know not what is befallen him.

24 And I said to them: Which of you hath any gold? And they took and brought it to me: and I cast it into the fire, and this calf came out.

25 And when Moses saw that the people were naked, (for Aaron had stripped them by occasion of the shame of the filth, and had set them naked among their enemies,)

26 Then standing in the gate of the camp, he said: If any man be on the Lord's side let him join with me. And all the sons of Levi gathered themselves together unto him.

27 And he said to them: Thus saith the Lord God of Israel: Put every man his sword upon his thigh. Go, and return from gate to gate through the midst of the camp, and let every man kill his brother, [11] and friend, and neighbour.

28 And the sons of Levi did according to the words of Moses: and there were slain that day about three and twenty thousand men.

29 And Moses said: You have consecrated your hands this day to the Lord: every man in his son and in his brother, that a blessing may be given to you.

30 And when the next day was come, Moses spoke to the people: You have sinned a very great sin. I will go up to the Lord, if by any means I may be able to entreat him for your crime.

31 And returning to the Lord, he said: I beseech thee: this people hath sinned a heinous sin, and they have made to themselves gods of gold. Either forgive them this trespass,

32 Or if thou do not, strike me out of the book that thou hast written.

33 And the Lord answered him: He that hath sinned against me, him will I strike out of my book:

34 But go thou, and lead this people whither I have told thee. My angel shall go before thee. And I in the day of revenge will visit this sin also of theirs.

35 The Lord therefore struck the people for the guilt on occasion of the calf which Aaron had made,

[5] 3 Kings, 12, 28. [6] Exod. 33, 3; Deut. 9, 13. [7] Num. 14, 13; Ps. 105, 23. [8] Gen. 12, 7; 15, 7; 48, 16. [9] Deut. 9, 21. [10] 1 John, 5, 12. [11] Deut. 33, 9.

CHAP. 32. Ver. 25. *Naked.* Having lost not only their gold, and their honour, but what was worst of all, being stripped also of the grace of God, and having lost him.—*The shame of the filth.* That is, of the idol, which they had taken for their god. It is the usual phrase of the Scripture to call idols *filth* and *abominations.*

CHAPTER 33

The people mourn for their sin. Moses pitcheth the tabernacle without the camp. He converseth familiarly with God. Desireth to see His glory.

AND the Lord spoke to Moses, saying: Go, get thee up from this place, thou and thy people which thou hast brought out of the land of Egypt, into the land concerning which I swore to Abraham, Isaac, and Jacob, saying: ¹ To thy seed I will give it.

2 ² And I will send an angel before thee, that I may cast out the ³ Chanaanite, and the Amorrhite, and the Hethite, and the Pherezite, and the Hevite, and the Jebusite.

3 That thou mayst enter into the land that floweth with milk and honey. For I will not go up with thee, ¹ because thou art a stiffnecked people: lest I destroy thee in the way.

4 And the people hearing these very bad tidings, mourned: and no man put on his ornaments according to custom.

5 And the Lord said to Moses: Say to the children of Israel: Thou art a stiffnecked people; once I shall come up in the midst of thee, and shall destroy thee. Now presently lay aside thy ornaments, that I may know what to do to thee.

6 So the children of Israel laid aside their ornaments by mount Horeb.

7 Moses also, taking the tabernacle, pitched it without the camp afar off, and called the name thereof, The tabernacle of the covenant. And all the people that had any question, went forth to the tabernacle of the covenant, without the camp.

8 And when Moses went forth to the tabernacle, all the people rose up, and every one stood in the door of his pavilion: and they beheld the back of Moses, till he went into the tabernacle.

9 And when he was gone into the tabernacle of the covenant, the pillar of the cloud came down, and stood at the door: and he spoke with Moses.

10 And all saw that the pillar of the cloud stood at the door of the tabernacle. And they stood, and worshipped at the doors of their tents.

11 And the Lord spoke to Moses face to face, as a man is wont to speak to his friend. And when he returned into the camp, his servant Josue the son of Nun, a young man, departed not from the tabernacle.

12 And Moses said to the Lord: Thou commandest me to lead forth this people. And thou dost not let me know whom thou wilt send with me, especially whereas thou hast said: I know thee by name, and thou hast found favour in my sight.

13 If therefore I have found favour in thy sight, shew me thy face, that I may know thee, and may find grace before thy eyes. Look upon thy people this nation.

14 And the Lord said: My face shall go before thee, and I will give thee rest.

15 And Moses said: If thou thyself dost not go before, bring us not out of this place.

16 For how shall we be able to know, I and thy people, that we have found grace in thy sight, unless thou walk with us: that we may be glorified by all people that dwell upon the earth?

17 And the Lord said to Moses: This word also, which thou hast spoken, will I do. For thou hast found grace before me: and thee I have known by name.

18 And he said: Shew me thy glory.

19 He answered: I will shew thee all good, and I will proclaim in the name of the Lord before thee: ⁵ And I will have mercy on whom I will: and I will be merciful to whom it shall please me.

20 And again he said: Thou canst not see my face: for man shall not see me and live.

21 And again he said: Behold there is a place with me, and thou shalt stand upon the rock.

22 And when my glory shall pass, I will set thee in a hole of the rock, and protect thee with my right hand, till I pass.

23 And I will take away my hand, and thou shalt see my back parts: but my face thou canst not see.

CHAPTER 34

The tables are renewed. All society with the Chanaanites is forbid. Some precepts concerning the firstborn, the sabbath, and other feasts. After forty days' fast, Moses returneth to the people with the commandments, and his face appearing horned with rays of light, he covereth it, whensoever he speaketh to the people.

AND after this he said: ¹ Hew thee two tables of stone like unto the

CHAP. 33. ¹ Gen. 12, 7. ² Exod. 32, 34. ³ Deut. 7, 22; Jos. 24, 11. ⁴ Exod. 32, 9; Deut. 9, 13. ⁵ Rom. 9, 15. CHAP. 34. ¹ Deut. 10, 1.

CHAP. 33. Ver. 11. *Face to face.* That is, in a most familiar manner. Though as we learn from this very chapter, Moses could not see the *face* of the Lord.
Ver. 12. *I know thee by name.* In the language of the scriptures, God is said to *know* such as he approves and loves: and to *know by name*, those whom he favours in a most singular manner, as he did his servant Moses.
Ver. 23. *See my back parts.* The Lord by his angel, usually spoke to Moses in the pillar of the cloud, so that he could not see the glory of him that spoke familiarly with him. In the vision here mentioned he was allowed to see something of him, in an assumed corporeal form: not in the face, the rays of which were too bright for mortal eye to bear, but to view him as it were behind, when his face was turned from him.

former: and I will write upon them the words which were in the tables, which thou brokest.

2 Be ready in the morning, that thou mayst forthwith go up into mount Sinai: and thou shalt stand with me upon the top of the mount.

3 Let no man go up with thee: and let not any man be seen throughout all the mount. Neither let the oxen nor the sheep feed over against it.

4 Then he cut out two tables of stone, such as had been before: and rising very early he went up into the mount Sinai, as the Lord had commanded him, carrying with him the tables.

5 And when the Lord was come down in a cloud, Moses stood with him, calling upon the name of the Lord.

6 And when he passed before him, he said: O the Lord, the Lord God, merciful and gracious, patient and of much compassion, and true,

7 [2] Who keepest mercy unto thousands: who takest away iniquity, and wickedness, and sin, [3] and no man of himself is innocent before thee. [4] Who renderest the iniquity of the fathers to the children, and to the grandchildren, unto the third and fourth generation.

8 And Moses making haste, bowed down prostrate unto the earth, and adoring,

9 Said: If I have found grace in thy sight, O Lord, I beseech thee, that thou wilt go with us, (for it is a stiffnecked people,) and take away our iniquities and sin, and possess us.

10 The Lord answered: [5] I will make a covenant in the sight of all. I will do signs such as were never seen upon the earth, nor in any nations: that this people, in the midst of whom thou art may see the terrible work of the Lord which I will do.

11 Observe all things which this day I command thee. I myself will drive out before thy face the Amorrhite, and the Chanaanite, and the Hethite, and the Pherezite, and the Hevite, and the Jebusite.

12 Beware thou never join in friendship with the inhabitants of that land, which may be thy ruin.

13 But destroy their altars, break their statues, and cut down their groves.

14 Adore not any strange god. The Lord his name is Jealous: he is a jealous God.

15 [6] Make no covenant with the men of those countries: lest, when they have committed fornication with their gods, and have adored their idols, some one call thee to eat of the things sacrificed.

16 [7] Neither shalt thou take of their daughters a wife for thy son: lest after they themselves have committed fornication, they make thy sons also to commit fornication with their gods.

17 Thou shalt not make to thyself any molten gods.

18 Thou shalt keep the feast of the unleavened bread. Seven days shalt thou eat unleavened bread, as I commanded thee in the time of the month of the new corn: for in the month of the springtime thou camest out from Egypt.

19 [8] All of the male kind, that openeth the womb, shall be mine. Of all beasts, both of oxen and of sheep, it shall be mine.

20 The firstling of an ass thou shalt redeem with a sheep: but if thou wilt not give a price for it, it shall be slain. The firstborn of thy sons thou shalt redeem: neither shalt thou appear before me empty.

21 Six days shalt thou work: the seventh day thou shalt cease to plough, and to reap.

22 [9] Thou shalt keep the feast of weeks with the firstfruits of the corn of thy wheat harvest: and the feast when the time of the year returneth that all things are laid in.

23 [10] Three times in the year all thy males shall appear in the sight of the Almighty Lord, the God of Israel.

24 For when I shall have taken away the nations from thy face, and shall have enlarged thy borders, no man shall lie in wait against thy land when thou shalt go up and appear in the sight of the Lord thy God, thrice in a year.

25 [11] Thou shalt not offer the blood of my sacrifice upon leaven: neither shall there remain in the morning any thing of the victim of the solemnity of the Phase.

26 The first of the fruits of thy ground thou shalt offer in the house of the Lord thy God. [12] Thou shalt not boil a kid in the milk of his dam.

27 And the Lord said to Moses: Write thee these words by which I have made a covenant both with thee and with Israel.

28 And he was there with the Lord [13] forty days and forty nights: He neither ate bread nor drank water: and he wrote upon the tables [14] the ten words of the covenant.

29 And when Moses came down from the mount Sinai, he held the two tables of the testimony: and he knew not that

[2] Deut. 5, 10; Jer. 32, 18. [3] Ps. 142, 2. [4] Deut. 5, 9; Jer. 32, 18. [5] Deut. 5, 2; Jer. 32, 40. [6] Exod. 23, 32; Deut. 7, 2. [7] 3 Kings, 11, 2; Deut. 7, 3. [8] Exod. 13, 2; 22, 29. [9] Exod. 23, 15. [10] Exod. 23, 17; Deut. 16, 16; [11] Exod. 23, 18. [12] Exod. 23, 19; Deut. 14, 21. [13] Exod. 24, 18; Deut. 9, 9. [14] Deut. 4, 13.

CHAP. 34. Ver. 29. Horned. That is, shining, and sending forth rays of light like horns.

his face was horned from the conversation of the Lord.

30 And Aaron and the children of Israel seeing the face of Moses horned, were afraid to come near.

31 And being called by him, they returned, both Aaron and the rulers of the congregation. And after that he spoke to them.

32 And all the children of Israel came to him: and he gave them in commandment all that he had heard of the Lord in mount Sinai.

33 And having done speaking, [15] he put a veil upon his face.

34 But when he went in to the Lord, and spoke with him, he took it away until he came forth: and then he spoke to the children of Israel all things that had been commanded him.

35 And they saw that the face of Moses when he came out was horned: but he covered his face again, if at any time he spoke to them.

CHAPTER 35

The sabbath. Offerings for making the tabernacle. Beseleel and Ooliab are called to the work.

AND all the multitude of the children of Israel being gathered together, he said to them: These are the things which the Lord hath commanded to be done.

2 Six days you shall do work: the seventh day shall be holy unto you, the sabbath, and the rest of the Lord. He that shall do any work on it, shall be put to death.

3 You shall kindle no fire in any of your habitations on the sabbath day.

4 And Moses said to all the assembly of the children of Israel: This is the word the Lord hath commanded, saying:

5 Set aside with your firstfruits to the Lord. [1] Let every one that is willing and hath a ready heart, offer them to the Lord: gold, and silver, and brass:

6 Violet and purple, and scarlet twice dyed, and fine linen, goat's hair:

7 And rams' skins dyed red, and violet coloured skins, setim wood:

8 And oil to maintain lights, and to make ointment, and most sweet incense:

9 Onyx stones, and precious stones, for the adorning of the ephod and the rational.

10 Whosoever of you is wise, let him come, and make that which the Lord hath commanded:

11 To wit, the tabernacle and the roof thereof, and the cover, the rings, and the board work with the oars, the pillars, and the sockets:

12 The ark and the staves, the propitiatory, and the veil that is drawn before it:

13 The table with the bars and the vessels, and the loaves of proposition:

14 The candlestick to bear up the lights, the vessels thereof and the lamps, and the oil for the nourishing of fires:

15 The altar of incense, and the bars, and the oil of unction and the incense of spices: the hanging at the door of the tabernacle:

16 The altar of holocaust, and its grate of brass, with the bars and vessels thereof: the laver and its foot:

17 The curtains of the court with the pillars and the sockets: the hanging in the doors of the entry:

18 The pins of the tabernacle and of the court with their little cords:

19 The vestments that are to be used in the ministry of the sanctuary: the vesture of Aaron the high priest, and of his sons, to do the office of priesthood to me.

20 And all the multitude of the children of Israel going out from the presence of Moses,

21 Offered firstfruits to the Lord with a most ready and devout mind, to make the work of the tabernacle of the testimony. Whatsoever was necessary to the service, and to the holy vestments,

22 Both men and women gave bracelets and earrings, rings and tablets: every vessel of gold was set aside to be offered to the Lord.

23 If any man had violet, and purple, and scarlet twice dyed, fine linen and goats' hair, rams' skins dyed red, and violet coloured skins,

24 Metal of silver and brass: they offered it to the Lord, and setim wood for divers uses.

25 The skilful women also gave such things as they had spun: violet, purple, and scarlet, and fine linen,

26 And goats' hair, giving all of their own accord.

27 But the princes offered onyx stones, and precious stones, for the ephod and the rational:

28 And spices and oil for the lights, and for the preparing of ointment, and to make the incense of most sweet savour.

29 All both men and women with devout mind offered gifts, that the works might be done which the Lord had commanded by the hand of Moses. All the children of Israel dedicated voluntary offerings to the Lord.

30 And Moses said to the children of Israel: [2] Behold the Lord hath called

by name Beseleel, the son of Uri, the son of Hur, of the tribe of Juda.

31 And hath filled him with the spirit of God: with wisdom and understanding and knowledge and all learning,

32 To devise and to work in gold and silver and brass,

33 And in engraving stones, and in carpenters' work. Whatsoever can be devised artificially,

34 He hath given in his heart. Ooliab also, the son of Achisamech, of the tribe of Dan.

35 Both of them hath he instructed with wisdom, to do carpenters' work, *and* tapestry, *and* embroidery in blue and purple, and scarlet twice dyed, and fine linen; and to weave all things, and to invent all new things.

CHAPTER 36

The offerings are delivered to the workmen. The curtains, coverings, boards, bars, veil, pillars, and hanging are made.

BESELEEL, therefore, and Ooliab and every wise man, to whom the Lord gave wisdom and understanding, to know how to work artificially, made ¹ the things that are necessary for the uses of the sanctuary, and which the Lord commanded.

2 ² And when Moses had called them, and every skilful man, to whom the Lord had given wisdom, and such as of their own accord had offered themselves to the making of the work,

3 He delivered all the offerings of the children of Israel unto them. And while they were earnest about the work, the people daily in the morning offered their vows.

4 Whereupon the workmen being constrained to come,

5 Said to Moses: The people offereth more than is necessary.

6 Moses therefore commanded proclamation to be made by the crier's voice: Let neither man nor woman offer any more for the work of the sanctuary. And so they ceased from offering gifts,

7 Because the things that were offered did suffice, and were too much.

8 And all the men that were wise of heart, to accomplish the work of the tabernacle, made ten curtains of twisted fine linen, and violet, and purple, and scarlet twice dyed, with varied work, and the art of embroidering.

9 The length of one curtain was twenty-eight cubits, and the breadth four: all the curtains were of the same size.

10 And he joined five curtains one to another: and the other five he coupled one to another.

11 He made also loops of violet in the edge of one curtain on both sides, and in the edge of the other curtain in like manner:

12 That the loops might meet one against another, and might be joined each with the other.

13 Whereupon also he cast fifty rings of gold, that might catch the loops of the curtains, and they might be made one tabernacle.

14 He made also eleven curtains of goats' hair, to cover the roof of the tabernacle.

15 One curtain was thirty cubits long and four cubits broad: all the curtains were of one measure.

16 Five of which he joined apart, and the other six apart.

17 And he made fifty loops in the edge of one curtain, and fifty in the edge of another curtain, that they might be joined one to another.

18 And fifty buckles of brass wherewith the roof might be knit together: that of all the curtains there might be made one covering.

19 He made also a cover for the tabernacle of rams' skins dyed red: and another cover over that of violet skins.

20 He made also the boards of the tabernacle of setim wood standing.

21 The length of one board was ten cubits: and the breadth was one cubit and a half.

22 There were two mortises throughout every board, that one might be joined to the other. And in this manner he made for all the boards of the tabernacle.

23 Of which twenty were at the south side southward,

24 With forty sockets of silver. Two sockets were put under one board on the two sides of the corners, where the mortises of the sides end in the corners.

25 At that side also of the tabernacle, that looketh toward the north, he made twenty boards,

26 With forty sockets of silver, two sockets for every board.

27 But against the west, to wit, at that side of the tabernacle, which looketh to the sea, he made six boards.

28 And two others at each corner of the tabernacle behind:

29 Which were also joined from beneath unto the top, and went together into one joint. Thus he did on both sides at the corners.

30 So there were in all eight boards: and they had sixteen sockets of silver, to wit, two sockets under every board.

31 He made also bars of setim wood:

CHAP. 36. ¹ Exod. 26, 1. ² 1 Par. 21, 29.

five to hold together the boards of one side of the tabernacle:

32 And five others to join together the boards of the other side: and besides these, five other bars at the west side of the tabernacle towards the sea.

33 He made also another bar, that might come by the midst of the boards from corner to corner.

34 And the board works themselves he overlaid with gold, casting for them sockets of silver. And their rings he made of gold, through which the bars might be drawn: and he covered the *bars* themselves with plates of gold.

35 He made also a veil of violet, and purple, scarlet, and fine twisted linen, varied and distinguished with embroidery:

36 And four pillars of setim wood, which with their heads he overlaid with gold, casting for them sockets of silver.

37 He made also a hanging in the entry of the tabernacle of violet, purple, scarlet, and fine twisted linen, with the work of an embroiderer.

38 And five pillars with their heads, which he covered with gold, and their sockets he cast of brass.

CHAPTER 37

Beseleel maketh the ark, the propitiatory, and cherubims, the table, the candlestick, the lamps, and the altar of incense, and compoundeth the incense.

AND Beseleel made also the ark of setim wood. It was two cubits and a half in length, and a cubit and a half in breadth, and the height was of one cubit and a half: and he overlaid it with the purest gold within and without.

2 And he made to it a crown of gold round about,

3 Casting four rings of gold at the four corners thereof: two rings in one side, and two in the other.

4 And he made bars of setim wood, which he overlaid with gold,

5 And he put them into the rings that were at the sides of the ark to carry it.

6 He made also the propitiatory, that is, the oracle, of the purest gold: two cubits and a half in length, and a cubit and a half in breadth.

7 Two cherubims also of beaten gold, which he set on the two sides of the propitiatory.

8 One cherub in the top of one side, and the other cherub in the top of the other side: two cherubims at the two ends of the propitiatory.

9 Spreading their wings, and covering the propitiatory, and looking one towards the other, and towards it.

10 He made also the table of setim wood, in length two cubits, and in breadth one cubit: and in height it was a cubit and a half.

11 And he overlaid it with the finest gold: and he made to it a golden ledge round about.

12 And to the ledge itself he made a polished crown of gold, of four fingers' breadth, and upon the same another golden crown.

13 And he cast four rings of gold, which he put in the four corners at each foot of the table,

14 Over against the crown. And he put the bars into them, that the table might be carried.

15 And the bars also themselves he made of setim wood: and overlaid them with gold.

16 And the vessels for the divers uses of the table, dishes, bowls, and cups, and censers of pure gold, wherein the libations are to be offered.

17 He made also the candlestick of beaten work of the finest gold. From the shaft whereof *its* branches, its cups, and bowls, and lilies came out:

18 Six on the two sides; three branches on one side, and three on the other.

19 Three cups in manner of a nut on each branch, and bowls withal and lilies; and three cups of the fashion of a nut in another branch, and bowls withal and lilies. The work of the six branches that went out from the shaft of the candlestick was equal.

20 And in the shaft itself were four cups after the manner of a nut: and bowls withal at every one, and lilies.

21 And bowls under two branches in three places, which together make six branches going out from one shaft.

22 So both the bowls, and the branches were of the same, all beaten work of the purest gold.

23 He made also the seven lamps with their snuffers, and the vessels where the snuffings were to be put out, of the purest gold.

24 The candlestick with all the vessels thereof weighed a talent of gold.

25 He made also the altar of incense of setim wood, being a cubit on every side foursquare, and in height two *cubits:* from the corners of which went out horns.

26 And he overlaid it with the purest gold, with *its* grate and the sides, and the horns.

27 And he made to it a crown of gold round about, and two golden rings under the crown at each side: that the bars might be put into them, and the altar be carried.

28 And the bars themselves he made, also of setim wood: and overlaid them with plates of gold.

29 He compounded also the oil for the ointment of sanctification, and incense of the purest spices, according to the work of a perfumer.

CHAPTER 38

He maketh the altar of holocaust. The brazen laver. The court with its pillars and hangings. The sum of what the people offered.

HE made also the altar [1] of holocaust of setim wood, five cubits square, and three in height.

2 The horns whereof went out from the corners: and he overlaid it with plates of brass.

3 And for the uses thereof, he prepared divers vessels of brass: cauldrons, tongs, fleshhooks, pothooks, and firepans.

4 And he made the grate thereof of brass, in manner of a net: and under it in the midst of the altar a hearth.

5 Casting four rings at the four ends of the net at the top, to put in bars to carry it.

6 And he made the bars of setim wood: and overlaid them with plates of brass:

7 And he drew them through the rings that stood out in the sides of the altar. [2] And the altar itself was not solid, but hollow, of boards, and empty within.

8 He made also the laver of brass, with the foot thereof, of the mirrors of the women that watched at the door of the tabernacle.

9 He made also the court, in the south side whereof were hangings of fine twisted linen, of a hundred cubits,

10 Twenty pillars of brass with their sockets: the heads of the pillars, and the whole graving of the work, of silver.

11 In like manner at the north side the hangings, the pillars, and the sockets and heads of the pillars were of the same measure, and work and metal.

12 But on that side that looketh to the west, there were hangings of fifty cubits, ten pillars of brass with their sockets: and the heads of the pillars, and all the graving of the work, of silver.

13 Moreover towards the east, he prepared hangings of fifty cubits:

14 Fifteen cubits of which were on one side with three pillars, and their sockets.

15 And on the other side (for between the two he made the entry of the tabernacle) there were hangings equal-

ly of fifteen cubits, and three pillars, and as many sockets.

16 All the hangings of the court were woven with twisted linen.

17 The sockets of the pillars were of brass, and their heads with all their gravings of silver: and he overlaid the pillars of the court also with silver.

18 And he made in the entry thereof an embroidered hanging of violet, purple, scarlet, and fine twisted linen, that was twenty cubits long, and five cubits high according to the measure of all the hangings of the court.

19 And the pillars in the entry were four with sockets of brass, and their heads and gravings of silver.

20 The pins also of the tabernacle and of the court round about, he made of brass.

21 These are the instruments of the tabernacle of the testimony, which were counted according to the commandment of Moses, in the ceremonies of the Levites, by the hand of Ithamar son of Aaron, the priest:

22 Which Beseleel, the son of Uri, the son of Hur, of the tribe of Juda, had made as the Lord commanded by Moses,

23 Having for his companion Ooliab, the son of Achisamech, of the tribe of Dan: who also was an excellent artificer in wood, and worker in tapestry and embroidery, in violet, purple, scarlet, and fine linen.

24 All the gold that was spent in the work of the sanctuary, and that was offered in gifts was nine and twenty talents, and seven hundred and thirty sicles according to the standard of the sanctuary.

25 And it was offered by them that went to be numbered, from twenty years old and upwards, of six hundred and three thousand, five hundred and fifty men able to bear arms.

26 There were moreover a hundred talents of silver, whereof were cast the sockets of the sanctuary, and of the entry where the veil hangeth.

27 A hundred sockets were made of a hundred talents: one talent being reckoned for every socket.

28 And of the thousand seven hundred and seventy-five, he made the heads of the pillars, which also he overlaid with silver.

29 And there were offered of brass also seventy-two thousand talents, and four hundred sicles besides.

30 Of which were cast the sockets in the entry of the tabernacle of the testimony, and the altar of brass with the grate thereof, and all the vessels that belong to the use thereof.

31 And the sockets of the court as well round about as in the entry thereof,

CHAP. 38. [1] 2 Par. 1, 5. [2] Exod. 27, 8.

and the pins of the tabernacle and of the court round about.

CHAPTER 39

All the ornaments of Aaron and his sons are made. And the whole work of the tabernacle is finished.

AND he made, [1] of violet and purple, scarlet and fine linen, the vestments for Aaron to wear when he ministered in the holy places, as the Lord commanded Moses.

2 So he made an ephod of gold, violet, and purple, and scarlet twice dyed, and fine twisted linen,

3 With embroidered work. And he cut thin plates of gold: and drew them small into threads, that they might be twisted with the woof of the aforesaid colours,

4 And two borders coupled one to the other in the top on either side.

5 And a girdle of the same colours, as the Lord had commanded Moses.

6 He prepared also two onyx stones, fast set and closed in gold, and graven by the art of a lapidary, with the names of the children of Israel:

7 And he set them in the sides of the ephod, for a memorial of the children of Israel, as the Lord had commanded Moses.

8 He made also a rational with embroidered work, according to the work of the ephod, of gold, violet, purple, and scarlet twice dyed, and fine twisted linen:

9 Foursquare, double, of the measure of a span.

10 And he set four rows of precious stones in it. In the first row was a sardius, a topaz, an emerald.

11 In the second, a carbuncle, a sapphire, and a jasper.

12 In the third, a ligurius, an agate, and an amethyst.

13 In the fourth, a chrysolite, an onyx, and a beryl, set and enclosed in gold by their rows.

14 And the twelve stones were engraved with the names of the twelve tribes of Israel, each one with its several name.

15 They made also in the rational little chains, linked one to another, of the purest gold,

16 And two hooks, and as many rings of gold. And they set the rings on either side of the rational.

17 On which rings the two golden chains should hang, which they put into the hooks that stood out in the corners of the ephod.

18 These both before and behind so answered one another, that the ephod

and the rational were bound together,

19 Being fastened to the girdle and strongly coupled with rings, which a violet fillet joined: lest they should flag loose, and be moved one from the other, as the Lord commanded Moses.

20 They made also the tunick of the ephod all of violet,

21 And a hole for the head in the upper part at the middle, and a woven border round about the hole:

22 And beneath at the feet pomegranates of violet, purple, scarlet, and fine twisted linen:

23 And little bells of the purest gold, which they put between the pomegranates at the bottom of the tunick round about:

24 To wit, a bell of gold, and a pomegranate, wherewith the high priest went adorned, when he discharged his ministry, as the Lord had commanded Moses.

25 They made also fine linen tunicks, with woven work, for Aaron and his sons.

26 And mitres with their little crowns of fine linen.

27 And linen breeches of fine linen.

28 And a girdle of fine twisted linen: violet, purple, and scarlet twice dyed, of embroidery work, as the Lord had commanded Moses.

29 They made also the plate of sacred veneration of the purest gold: and they wrote on it with the engraving of a lapidary, THE HOLY OF THE LORD.

30 And they fastened it to the mitre with a violet fillet, as the Lord had commanded Moses.

31 So all the work of the tabernacle and of the roof of the testimony was finished: and the children of Israel did all things which the Lord had commanded Moses.

32 And they offered the tabernacle and the roof and the whole furniture, the rings, the boards, the bars, the pillars, and their sockets:

33 The cover of rams' skins dyed red, and the other cover of violet skins:

34 The veil, the ark, the bars, the propitiatory:

35 The table, with the vessels thereof, and the loaves of proposition:

36 The candlestick, the lamps, and the furniture of them with the oil:

37 The altar of gold, and the ointment, and the incense of spices:

38 And the hanging in the entry of the tabernacle:

39 The altar of brass, the grate, the bars, and all the vessels thereof: the laver with the foot thereof: the hang-

CHAP. 39. [1] Exod. 28, 6.

ings of the court, and the pillars with their sockets:

40 The hanging in the entry of the court, and the little cords, and the pins thereof. Nothing was wanting of the vessels, that were commanded to be made for the ministry of the tabernacle, and for the roof of the covenant.

41 The vestments also, which the priests, to wit, Aaron and his sons, used in the sanctuary,

42 The children of Israel offered as the Lord had commanded.

43 And when Moses saw all things finished, he blessed them.

CHAPTER 40

The tabernacle is commanded to be set up and anointed. God filleth it with his majesty.

AND the Lord spoke to Moses, saying:

2 The first month, the first day of the month, thou shalt set up the tabernacle of the testimony:

3 And shalt put the ark in it, and shalt let down the veil before it.

4 And thou shalt bring in the table, and set upon it the things that are commanded according to the rite. The candlestick shall stand with its lamps:

5 And the altar of gold whereon the incense is burnt, before the ark of the testimony. Thou shalt put the hanging in the entry of the tabernacle:

6 And before it the altar of holocaust.

7 The laver between the altar and the tabernacle: and thou shalt fill it with water.

8 And thou shalt encompass the court with hangings, and the entry thereof.

9 And thou shalt take the oil of unction and anoint the tabernacle with its vessels, that they may be sanctified.

10 The altar of holocaust and all its vessels.

11 The laver with its foot. Thou shalt consecrate all with the oil of unction, that they may be most holy.

12 And thou shalt bring Aaron and his sons to the door of the tabernacle of the testimony, and having washed them with water,

13 ¹ Thou shalt put on them the holy vestments, that they may minister to me: and that the unction of them may prosper to an everlasing priesthood.

14 And Moses did all that the Lord had commanded.

15 So in the first month of the second year, the first day of the month, the tabernacle was set up.

16 ² And Moses reared it up, and placed the boards and the sockets and the bars, and set up the pillars.

17 And spread the roof over the tabernacle, putting over it a cover, as the Lord had commanded.

18 And he put the testimony in the ark, thrusting bars underneath, and the oracle above.

19 And when he had brought the ark into the tabernacle, he drew the veil before it, to fulfil the commandment of the Lord.

20 And he set the table in the tabernacle of the testimony at the north side, without the veil:

21 Setting there in order the loaves of proposition, as the Lord had commanded Moses.

22 He set the candlestick also in the tabernacle of the testimony over against the table on the south side:

23 Placing the lamps in order, according to the precept of the Lord.

24 He set also the altar of gold under the roof of the testimony over against the veil:

25 And burnt upon it the incense of spices, as the Lord had commanded Moses.

26 And he put also the hanging in the entry of the tabernacle of the testimony.

27 And the altar of holocaust of the entry of the testimony, offering the holocaust, and the sacrifices upon it, as the Lord had commanded.

28 And he set the laver between the tabernacle of the testimony and the altar, filling it with water.

29 And Moses and Aaron, and his sons washed their hands and feet,

30 When they went into the tabernacle of the covenant, and went to the altar, as the Lord had commanded Moses.

31 He set up also the court round about the tabernacle and the altar, drawing the hanging in the entry thereof. After all things were perfected,

32 ³ The cloud covered the tabernacle of the testimony, and the glory of the Lord filled it.

33 Neither could Moses go into the tabernacle of the covenant, the cloud covering all things and the majesty of the Lord shining: for the cloud had covered all.

34 If at any time the cloud removed from the tabernacle, the children of Israel went forward by their troops.

35 If it hung over, they remained in the same place.

CHAP. 40. ¹ Exod. 28, 35; Lev. 8, 2. ² Num. 7, 1. ³ Num. 9, 15; 3 Kings, 8, 10.

36 For the cloud of the Lord hung over the tabernacle by day, and a fire by night, in the sight of all the children of Israel throughout all their mansions.

THE BOOK OF
LEVITICUS

This Book is called LEVITICUS, *because it treats of the Offices, Ministries, Rites and Ceremonies of the Priests and Levites. The Hebrews call it* VAICRA, *from the word with which it begins.*

CHAPTER 1

Of holocausts or burnt offerings.

AND the Lord called Moses, and spoke to him from the tabernacle of the testimony, saying:

2 Speak to the children of Israel, and thou shalt say to them: The man among you that shall offer to the Lord a sacrifice of the cattle, that is, offering victims of oxen and sheep:

3 ¹ If his offering be a holocaust, and of the herd, he shall offer a male without blemish, at the door of the testimony, to make the Lord favourable to him.

4 And he shall put his hand upon the head of the victim: and it shall be acceptable, and help to its expiation.

5 And he shall immolate the calf before the Lord: and the priests the sons of Aaron shall offer the blood thereof, pouring it round about the altar, which is before the door of the tabernacle.

6 And when they have flayed the victim, they shall cut the joints into pieces:

7 And shall put fire on the altar, having before laid in order a pile of wood.

8 And they shall lay the parts that are cut out in order thereupon: to wit, the head, and all things that cleave to the liver;

9 The entrails and feet being washed with water. And the priest shall burn them upon the altar for a holocaust, and a sweet savour to the Lord.

10 And if the offering be of the flocks, a holocaust of sheep or of goats, he shall offer a male without blemish.

11 And he shall immolate it at the side of the altar that looketh to the north, before the Lord: but the sons of Aaron shall pour the blood thereof upon the altar round about.

12 And they shall divide the joints, the head, and all that cleave to the liver: and shall lay them upon the wood under which the fire is to be put.

13 But the entrails and the feet they shall wash with water. And the priest shall offer it all and burn it all upon the altar for a holocaust, and most sweet savour to the Lord.

14 But if the oblation of a holocaust to the Lord be of birds, of turtles, or of young pigeons:

15 The priest shall offer it at the altar: and twisting back the neck, and breaking the place of the wound, he shall make the blood run down upon the brim of the altar.

16 But the crop of the throat, and the feathers he shall cast beside the altar at the east side, in the place where the ashes are wont to be poured out.

17 And he shall break the pinions thereof, and shall not cut, nor divide it with a knife: and shall burn it upon the altar, putting fire under the wood. It is a holocaust and oblation of most sweet savour to the Lord.

CHAPTER 2

Of offerings of flour, and firstfruits.

WHEN any one shall offer an oblation of sacrifice to the Lord, his offering shall be of fine flour: and he shall pour oil upon it, and put frankincense,

2 And shall bring it to the sons of

CHAP. 1. ¹ Exod. 29, 10.

CHAP. 1. Ver. 3. *A holocaust.* That is, a whole burnt offering (*olokauston*), so called, because the whole victim was consumed with fire; and given in such manner to God as wholly to evaporate, as it were, for his *honour and glory:* without having any part of it reserved for the use of man. The other sacrifices of the Old Testament were either *offerings for sin,* or *peace offerings:* and these latter again were either offered in *thanksgiving* for blessings received; or by way of *prayer* for new favours or graces. So that sacrifices were then offered to God for four different ends or intentions, answerable to the different obligations which man has to God: 1. By way of adoration, homage, praise and glory due to his divine majesty. 2. By way of thanksgiving for all benefits received from him. 3. By way of confessing and craving pardon for sins. 4. By way of prayer and petition for grace and relief in all necessities. In the New Law we have but one sacrifice, viz., that of the body and blood of Christ: but this one sacrifice of the New Testament perfectly answers all these four ends: and both priest and people, as often as it is celebrated, ought to join in offering it up for these four ends.

Aaron the priests. And one of them shall take a handful of the flour and oil, and all the frankincense; and shall put it a memorial upon the altar for a most sweet savour to the Lord.

3 [1] And the remnant of the sacrifice shall be Aaron's, and his sons': holy of holies of the offerings of the Lord.

4 But when thou offerest a sacrifice baked in the oven of flour, to wit, loaves without leaven, tempered with oil, and unleavened wafers, anointed with oil:

5 If thy oblation be from the frying-pan, of flour tempered with oil, and without leaven:

6 Thou shalt divide it into little pieces, and shalt pour oil upon it.

7 And if the sacrifice be from the gridiron, in like manner the flour shall be tempered with oil.

8 And when thou offerest it to the Lord, thou shalt deliver it to the hands of the priest.

9 And when he hath offered it, he shall take a memorial out of the sacrifice, and burn it upon the altar for a sweet savour to the Lord.

10 And whatsoever is left, shall be Aaron's, and his sons': holy of holies of the offerings of the Lord.

11 Every oblation that is offered to the Lord shall be made without leaven: neither shall any leaven or honey be burnt in the sacrifice to the Lord.

12 You shall offer only the firstfruits of them and gifts: but they shall not be put upon the altar, for a savour of sweetness.

13 Whatsoever sacrifice thou offerest, [2] thou shalt season it with salt: neither shalt thou take away the salt of the covenant of thy God from thy sacrifice. In all thy oblations thou shalt offer salt.

14 But if thou offer a gift of the first-fruits of thy corn to the Lord, of the ears yet green, thou shalt dry it at the fire, and break it small like meal; and

CHAP. 2. [1] Ecclus. 7, 34. [2] Mark, 9, 48. CHAP. 3. [1] Exod. 29, 13.

CHAP. 2. Ver. 3. *Holy of holies.* That is, *most holy,* as being dedicated to God, and set aside by his ordinance for the use of his priests.
Ver. 11. *Without leaven, or honey.* No *leaven* nor *honey* was to be used in the sacrifice offered to God: to signify that we are to exclude from the pure worship of the gospel, all double dealing and affection to carnal pleasures.
Ver. 13. *Salt.* In every sacrifice salt was to be used, which is an emblem of *wisdom* and *discretion,* without which none of our performances are agreeable to God.
CHAP. 3. Ver. 1. *Peace offerings. Peace,* in the scripture language, signifies happiness, welfare or prosperity; in a word, all kind of blessings.—Such sacrifices, therefore, as were offered either on occasion of blessings received, or to obtain new favours, were called *pacific* or *peace offerings.* In these, some part of the victim was consumed with fire on the altar of God: other parts were eaten by the priests and by the persons for whom the sacrifice was offered.

so shalt thou offer thy firstfruits to the Lord:

15 Pouring oil upon it and putting on frankincense, because it is the oblation of the Lord.

16 Whereof the priest shall burn for a memorial of the gift, part of the corn broken small and of the oil, and all the frankincense.

CHAPTER 3
Of peace offerings.

AND if his oblation be a sacrifice of peace offerings, and he will offer of the herd, whether male or female: he shall offer them without blemish before the Lord.

2 And he shall lay his hand upon the head of his victim, which shall be slain in the entry of the tabernacle of the testimony: and the sons of Aaron the priests shall pour the blood round about upon the altar.

3 And they shall offer of the sacrifice of peace offerings, for an oblation to the Lord: [1] the fat that covereth the entrails, and all the fat that is within.

4 The two kidneys with the fat wherewith the flanks are covered, and the caul of the liver with the two little kidneys.

5 And they shall burn them upon the altar, for a holocaust, putting fire under the wood: for an oblation of most sweet savour to the Lord.

6 But if his oblation and the sacrifice of peace offering be of the flock, whether he offer male or female, they shall be without blemish.

7 If he offer a lamb before the Lord:

8 He shall put his hand upon the head of the victim. And it shall be slain in the entry of the tabernacle of the testimony: and the sons of Aaron shall pour the blood thereof round about upon the altar.

9 And they shall offer of the victim of peace offerings, a sacrifice to the Lord: the fat and the whole rump,

10 With the kidneys, and the fat that covereth the belly and all the vitals and both the little kidneys, with the fat that is about the flanks, and the caul of the liver with the little kidneys.

11 And the priest shall burn them upon the altar, for the food of the fire, and of the oblation of the Lord.

12 If his offering be a goat, and he offer it to the Lord:

13 He shall put his hand upon the head thereof: and shall immolate it in the entry of the tabernacle of the testimony. And the sons of Aaron shall pour the blood thereof round about upon the altar.

14 And they shall take of it for the food of the Lord's fire, the fat that covereth the belly, and that covereth all the vital parts:

15 The two little kidneys with the caul that is upon them which is by the flanks, and the fat of the liver with the little kidneys.

16 And the priest shall burn them upon the altar, for the food of the fire, and of a most sweet savour. All the fat shall be the Lord's.

17 By a perpetual law for your generations, and in all your habitations: neither blood nor fat shall you eat at all.

CHAPTER 4

Of offerings for sins of ignorance.

AND the Lord spoke to Moses, saying:

2 Say to the children of Israel: The soul that sinneth through ignorance, and doth any thing concerning any of the commandments of the Lord, which he commanded not to be done:

3 If the priest that is anointed shall sin, making the people to offend, he shall offer to the Lord for his sin a calf without blemish.

4 And he shall bring it to the door of the testimony before the Lord: and shall put his hand upon the head thereof, and shall sacrifice it to the Lord.

5 He shall take also of the blood of the calf: and carry it into the tabernacle of the testimony.

6 And having dipped his finger in the blood, he shall sprinkle with it seven times before the Lord, before the veil of the sanctuary.

7 And he shall put some of the same blood upon the horns of the altar of the sweet incense most acceptable to the Lord, which is in the tabernacle of the testimony. And he shall pour all the rest of the blood at the foot of the altar of holocaust in the entry of the tabernacle.

8 And he shall take off the fat of the calf for the sin offering, as well that which covereth the entrails, as all the inwards:

9 The two little kidneys, and the caul that is upon them, which is by the flanks, and the fat of the liver with the little kidneys:

10 As it is taken off from the calf of the sacrifice of peace offerings. And he shall burn them upon the altar of holocaust.

11 But the skin and all the flesh with the head and the feet and the bowels and the dung:

12 And the rest of the body, he shall carry forth without the camp into a clean place where the ashes are wont to be poured out; and he shall burn them upon a pile of wood. They shall be burnt in the place where the ashes are poured out.

13 And if all the multitude of Israel shall be ignorant, and through ignorance shall do that which is against the commandment of the Lord,

14 And afterwards shall understand their sin: they shall offer for their sin a calf, and shall bring it to the door of the tabernacle.

15 And the ancients of the people shall put their hands upon the head thereof before the Lord. And the calf being immolated in the sight of the Lord:

16 The priest that is anointed shall carry of the blood into the tabernacle of the testimony.

17 And shall dip his finger in it and sprinkle it seven times before the veil.

18 And he shall put of the same blood on the horns of the altar that is before the Lord, in the tabernacle of the testimony. And the rest of the blood he shall pour at the foot of the altar of holocaust, which is at the door of the tabernacle of the testimony.

19 And all the fat thereof he shall take off, and shall burn it upon the altar:

20 Doing so with this calf, as he did also with that before. And the priest praying for them, the Lord will be merciful unto them.

21 But the calf itself he shall carry forth without the camp, and shall burn it as he did the former calf: because it is for the sin of the multitude.

22 If a prince shall sin, and through ignorance do any one of the things that the law of the Lord forbiddeth,

23 And afterwards shall come to know his sin: he shall offer a buckgoat without blemish, a sacrifice to the Lord.

24 And he shall put his hand upon the head thereof: and when he hath immolated it in the place where the holocaust is wont to be slain before the Lord, because it is for sin,

25 The priest shall dip his finger in the blood of the victim for sin, touching therewith the horns of the altar of holocaust, and pouring out the rest at the foot thereof.

Ver. 17. *Fat.* It is meant of the fat, which by the prescription of the law was to be offered on God's altar; not of the fat of meat, such as we commonly eat.

CHAP. 4. Ver. 2. *Ignorance.* To be ignorant of what we are bound to know is sinful; and for such culpable ignorance, these sacrifices, prescribed in this and the following chapter, were appointed.

Ver. 5. *The blood.* As the figure of the *blood* of Christ shed for the remission of our sins, and carried by him into the sanctuary of heaven.

26 But the fat he shall burn upon it, as is wont to be done with the victims of peace offerings. And the priest shall pray for him, and for his sin: and it shall be forgiven him.

27 And if any one of the people of the land shall sin through ignorance, doing any of those things that by the law of the Lord are forbidden, and offending,

28 And shall come to know his sin: he shall offer a she-goat without blemish.

29 And he shall put his hand upon the head of the victim that is for sin: and shall immolate it in the place of the holocaust.

30 And the priest shall take of the blood with his finger, and shall touch the horns of the altar of holocaust: and shall pour out the rest at the foot thereof.

31 But taking off all the fat, as is wont to be taken away of the victims of peace offerings, he shall burn it upon the altar, for a sweet savour to the Lord: and he shall pray for him, and it shall be forgiven him.

32 But if he offer of the flock a victim for his sin, to wit, an ewe without blemish:

33 He shall put his hand upon the head thereof, and shall immolate it in the place where the victims of holocausts are wont to be slain.

34 And the priest shall take of the blood thereof with his finger, and shall touch the horns of the altar of holocaust: and the rest he shall pour out at the foot thereof.

35 All the fat also he shall take off, as the fat of the ram that is offered for peace offerings is wont to be taken away: and shall burn it upon the altar, for a burnt sacrifice of the Lord. And he shall pray for him and his sin, and it shall be forgiven him.

CHAPTER 5

Of other sacrifices for sins.

IF any one sin, and hear the voice of one swearing, and is a witness either because he himself hath seen, or is privy to it: if he do not utter it, he shall bear his iniquity.

2 Whosoever toucheth any unclean thing, either that which hath been killed by a beast, or died of itself, or any other creeping thing: and forgetteth his uncleanness, he is guilty, and hath offended.

3 And if he touch any thing of the uncleanness of man, according to any uncleanness wherewith he is wont to be defiled: and having forgotten it, come

CHAP. 5. [1] Lev. 12, 8; Luke, 2, 24.

afterwards to know it, he shall be guilty of an offence.

4 The person that sweareth, and uttereth with his lips, that he would do either evil or good, and bindeth the same with an oath, and his word: and having forgotten it afterwards understandeth his offence,

5 Let him do penance for his sin:

6 And offer of the flocks an ewe lamb, or a she-goat, and the priest shall pray for him and for his sin.

7 But if he be not able to offer a beast, let him offer two turtles, [1] or two young pigeons to the Lord, one for sin, and the other for a holocaust,

8 And he shall give them to the priest: who shall offer the first for sin, and twist back the head of it to the little pinions, so that it stick to the neck, and be not altogether broken off.

9 And of its blood he shall sprinkle the side of the altar: and whatsoever is left, he shall let it drop at the bottom thereof, because it is for sin.

10 And the other he shall burn for a holocaust, as is wont to be done. And the priest shall pray for him, and for his sin, and it shall be forgiven him.

11 And if his hand be not able to offer two turtles, or two young pigeons, he shall offer for his sin the tenth part of an ephi of flour. He shall not put oil upon it, nor put any frankincense thereon, because it is for sin.

12 And he shall deliver it to the priest, who shall take a handful thereof, and shall burn it upon the altar for a memorial of him that offered it:

13 Praying for him and making atonement. But the part that is left, he himself shall have for a gift.

14 And the Lord spoke to Moses, saying:

15 If any one shall sin through mistake, transgressing the ceremonies in those things that are sacrificed to the Lord, he shall offer for his offence a ram without blemish out of the flocks, that may be bought for two sicles, according to the weight of the sanctuary.

16 And he shall make good the damage itself which he hath done, and shall add the fifth part besides, delivering it to the priest, who shall pray for him, offering the ram: and it shall be forgiven him.

17 If any one sin through ignorance, and do one of those things which by the law of the Lord are forbidden, and being guilty of sin, understand his iniquity:

18 He shall offer of the flocks a ram without blemish to the priest, according to the measure and estimation of the sin. And *the priest* shall pray for

him, because he did it ignorantly: and it shall be forgiven him,

19 Because by mistake he trespassed against the Lord.

CHAPTER 6

Oblation for sins of injustice. Ordinances concerning the holocausts and the perpetual fire. The sacrifices of the priests, and the sin offerings.

THE Lord spoke to Moses, saying:
2 Whosoever shall sin, and despising the Lord, shall deny to his neighbour the thing delivered to his keeping, which was committed to his trust; or shall by force extort any thing, or commit oppression;

3 Or shall find a thing lost, and denying it, shall also swear falsely, or shall do any other of the many things, wherein men are wont to sin:

4 Being convicted of the offence, he shall restore

5 All that he would have gotten by fraud, in the principal, [1] and the fifth part besides to the owner, whom he wronged.

6 Moreover for his sin he shall offer a ram without blemish out of the flock: and shall give it to the priest, according to the estimation and measure of the offence.

7 And he shall pray for him before the Lord: and he shall have forgiveness for every thing in doing of which he hath sinned.

8 And the Lord spoke to Moses, saying:

9 Command Aaron and his sons: This is the law of a holocaust. It shall be burnt upon the altar, all night until morning: the fire shall be of the same altar.

10 The priest shall be vested with the tunick and the linen breeches; and he shall take up the ashes of that which the devouring fire hath burnt: and putting them beside the altar,

11 Shall put off his former vestments, and being clothed with others, shall carry them forth without the camp, and shall cause them to be consumed to dust in a very clean place.

12 And the fire on the altar shall always burn, and the priest shall feed it, putting wood on it every day in the morning: and laying on the holocaust, shall burn thereupon the fat of the peace offerings.

13 This is the perpetual fire which shall never go out on the altar.

14 This is the law of the sacrifice and libations, which the children of Aaron shall offer before the Lord, and before the altar.

15 The priest shall take a handful of the flour that is tempered with oil, and all the frankincense that is put upon the flour: and he shall burn it on the altar for a memorial of most sweet odour to the Lord.

16 And the part of the flour that is left, Aaron and his sons shall eat, without leaven: and he shall eat it in the holy place of the court of the tabernacle.

17 And therefore it shall not be leavened, because part thereof is offered for the burnt sacrifice of the Lord. It shall be most holy, as that which is offered for sin and for trespass.

18 The males only of the race of Aaron shall eat it. It shall be an ordinance everlasting in your generations concerning the sacrifices of the Lord: Every one that toucheth them shall be sanctified.

19 And the Lord spoke to Moses, saying:

20 This is the oblation of Aaron, and of his sons, which they must offer to the Lord, in the day of their anointing. They shall offer the tenth part of an ephi of flour for a perpetual sacrifice, half of it in the morning, and half of it in the evening.

21 It shall be tempered with oil, and shall be fried in a fryingpan.

22 And the priest that rightfully succeedeth his father, shall offer it hot, for a most sweet odour to the Lord: and it shall be wholly burnt on the altar.

23 For every sacrifice of the priest shall be consumed with fire: neither shall any man eat thereof.

24 And the Lord spoke to Moses, saying:

25 Say to Aaron and his sons: This is the law of the victim for sin. In the place where the holocaust is offered, it shall be immolated before the Lord. It is holy of holies.

26 The priest that offereth it, shall eat it in a holy place, in the court of the tabernacle.

27 Whatsoever shall touch the flesh thereof, shall be sanctified. If a garment be sprinkled with the blood thereof, it shall be washed in a holy place.

28 And the earthen vessel, wherein it was sodden, shall be broken: but if the vessel be of brass, it shall be scoured, and washed with water.

29 Every male of the priestly race shall eat of the flesh thereof, because it is holy of holies.

30 For the victim that is slain for sin,

CHAP. 6. [1] Num. 5, 7.

CHAP. 6. Ver. 13. *The perpetual fire.* This fire came from heaven, (Lev. chap. 9, 24,) and was always kept burning on the altar, as a figure of the heavenly fire of divine love, which ought to be always burning in the heart of a Christian.

² the blood of which is carried into the tabernacle of the testimony to make atonement in the sanctuary, shall not be eaten, but shall be burnt with fire.

CHAPTER 7

Of sacrifices for trespasses and thanks offerings. No fat nor blood is to be eaten.

THIS also is the law of the sacrifice for a trespass: it is most holy.

2 Therefore where the holocaust is immolated, the victim also for a trespass shall be slain: the blood thereof shall be poured round about the altar.

3 They shall offer thereof the rump and the fat that covereth the entrails:

4 The two little kidneys, and the fat which is by the flanks, and the caul of the liver with the little kidneys.

5 And the priest shall burn them upon the altar: it is the burnt sacrifice of the Lord for a trespass.

6 Every male of the priestly race, shall eat this flesh in a holy place, because it is most holy.

7 As the sacrifice for sin is offered, so is also that for a trespass: the same shall be the law of both these sacrifices. It shall belong to the priest that offereth it.

8 The priest that offereth the victim of holocaust, shall have the skin thereof.

9 And every sacrifice of flour that is baked in the oven, and whatsoever is dressed on the gridiron, or in the frying-pan, shall be the priest's that offereth it.

10 Whether they be tempered with oil, or dry, all the sons of Aaron shall have one as much as another.

11 This is the law of the sacrifice of peace offerings that is offered to the Lord.

12 If the oblation be for thanksgiving, they shall offer loaves without leaven tempered with oil, and unleavened wafers anointed with oil, and fine flour fried, and cakes tempered and mingled with oil.

13 Moreover loaves of leavened bread with the sacrifice of thanks, which is offered for peace offerings:

14 Of which one shall be offered to the Lord for firstfruits, and shall be the priest's that shall pour out the blood of the victim.

15 And the flesh of it shall be eaten the same day: neither shall any of it remain until the morning.

16 If any man by vow, or of his own

accord offer a sacrifice, it shall in like manner be eaten the same day. And if any of it remain until the morrow, it is lawful to eat it.

17 But whatsoever shall be found on the third day shall be consumed with fire.

18 If any man eat of the flesh of the victim of peace offerings on the third day, the oblation shall be of no effect: neither shall it profit the offerer. Yea rather, whatsoever soul shall defile itself with such meat, shall be guilty of transgression.

19 The flesh that hath touched any unclean thing, shall not be eaten; but shall be burnt with fire. He that is clean shall eat of it.

20 If any one that is defiled shall eat of the flesh of the sacrifice of peace offerings, which is offered to the Lord, he shall be cut off from his people.

21 And he that hath touched the uncleanness of man, or of beast, or of any thing that can defile, and shall eat of such kind of flesh: shall be cut off from his people.

22 And the Lord spoke to Moses, saying:

23 Say to the children of Israel: The fat of a sheep, and of an ox, and of a goat you shall not eat.

24 The fat of a carcass that hath died of itself, and of a beast that was caught by another beast, you shall have for divers uses.

25 If any man eat the fat that should be offered for the burnt sacrifice of the Lord, he shall perish out of his people.

26 Moreover you shall not eat the blood of any creature whatsoever, whether of birds or beasts.

27 Every one that eateth blood, shall perish from among the people.

28 And the Lord spoke to Moses, saying:

29 Speak to the children of Israel, saying: He that offereth a victim of peace offerings to the Lord, let him offer therewith a sacrifice also, that is, the libations thereof.

30 He shall hold in his hands the fat of the victim, and the breast. And when he hath offered and consecrated both to the Lord, he shall deliver *them* to the priest,

31 Who shall burn the fat upon the altar. But the breast shall be Aaron's and his sons'.

32 The right shoulder also of the victims of peace offerings shall fall to the priest for firstfruits.

33 He among the sons of Aaron, that offereth the blood, and the fat: he shall have the right shoulder also for his portion.

---

² Lev. 4, 5; Heb. 13, 11.

CHAP. 7. Ver. 1. *Trespass.* Trespasses, for which these offerings were to be made, were lesser offences than those for which the sin offerings were appointed.

34 For the breast that is elevated and the shoulder that is separated I have taken of the children of Israel, from off their victims of peace offerings: and have given them/to Aaron the priest, and to his sons, by a law for ever, from all the people of Israel.

35 This is the anointing of Aaron and his sons, in the ceremonies of the Lord, in the day when Moses offered them, that they might do the office of priesthood.

36 And the things that the Lord commanded to be given them by the children of Israel, by a perpetual observance in their generations.

37 This is the law of holocaust, and of the sacrifice for sin, and for trespass, and for consecration, and the victims of peace offerings:

38 Which the Lord appointed to Moses in mount Sinai, when he commanded the children of Israel, that they should offer their oblations to the Lord in the desert of Sinai.

CHAPTER 8

Moses consecrateth Aaron and his sons.

AND the Lord spoke to Moses, saying:

2 [1] Take Aaron with his sons, their vestments, and the oil of unction: a calf for sin, two rams, a basket with unleavened bread.

3 And thou shalt gather together all the congregation to the door of the tabernacle.

4 And Moses did as the Lord had commanded. And all the multitude being gathered together before the door of the tabernacle:

5 He said: This is the word that the Lord hath commanded to be done.

6 And immediately he offered Aaron and his sons. And when he had washed them,

7 He vested the high priest with the strait linen garment, girding him with the girdle, and putting on him the violet tunick: and over it he put the ephod.

8 And binding it with the girdle, he fitted it to the rational, on which was Doctrine and Truth.

9 He put also the mitre upon his head: and upon the mitre over the forehead, he put the plate of gold, consecrated with sanctification, as the Lord had commanded him.

10 He took also the oil of unction, with which he anointed the tabernacle, with all the furniture thereof.

11 And when he had sanctified and sprinkled the altar seven times, he anointed it, and all the vessels thereof: and the laver with the foot thereof, he sanctified with the oil.

12 [2] And he poured it upon Aaron's head: and he anointed and consecrated him.

13 And after he had offered his sons, he vested them with linen tunicks, and girded them with girdles: and put mitres on them as the Lord had commanded.

14 He offered also the calf for sin: and when Aaron and his sons had put their hands upon the head thereof,

15 He immolated it: and took the blood, and dipping his finger in it, he touched the horns of the altar round about. Which being expiated, and sanctified, he poured the rest of the blood at the bottom thereof.

16 But the fat that was upon the entrails, and the caul of the liver, and the two little kidneys, with their fat, he burnt upon the altar.

17 And the calf with the skin, and the flesh and the dung, he burnt without the camp, as the Lord had commanded.

18 He offered also a ram for holocaust. And when Aaron and his sons had put their hands upon its head:

19 He immolated it, and poured the blood thereof round about the altar.

20 And cutting the ram into pieces, the head thereof, and the joints, and the fat he burnt in the fire.

21 Having first washed the entrails, and the feet, and the whole ram together he burnt upon the altar: because it was a holocaust of most sweet odour to the Lord, as he had commanded him.

22 He offered also the second ram, in the consecration of priests: and Aaron, and his sons put their hands upon the head thereof.

23 And when Moses had immolated it, he took of the blood thereof, and touched the tip of Aaron's right ear, and the thumb of his right hand, and in like manner also the great toe of his right foot.

24 He offered also the sons of Aaron: and when with the blood of the ram that was immolated, he had touched the tip of the right ear of every one of them, and the thumbs of their right hands, and the great toes of their right feet, the rest he poured on the altar round about.

25 But the fat, and the rump, and all the fat that covereth the entrails, and the caul of the liver, and the two kidneys with their fat, and with the right shoulder, he separated.

26 And taking out of the basket of unleavened bread, which was before the Lord, a loaf without leaven, and a cake tempered with oil and a wafer, he

CHAP. 8. [1] Exod. 29, 35; 40, 13. [2] Ecclus. 45, 18.

put *them* upon the fat, and the right shoulder:

27 Delivering all to Aaron, and to his sons. Who having lifted them up before the Lord,

28 He took them again from their hands, and burnt them upon the altar of holocaust: because it was the oblation of consecration, for a sweet odour of sacrifice to the Lord.

29 And he took of the ram of consecration, the breast for his portion, elevating it before the Lord, as the Lord had commanded him.

30 And taking the ointment, and the blood that was upon the altar, he sprinkled Aaron, and his sons, and their vestments, and his sons, and their vestments with it.

31 And when he had sanctified them in their vestments, he commanded them, saying: Boil the flesh before the door of the tabernacle, and there eat it. Eat ye also the loaves of consecration, that are laid in the basket, as the Lord commanded me, saying: ³ Aaron and his sons shall eat them.

32 And whatsoever shall be left of the flesh and the loaves, shall be consumed with fire.

33 And you shall not go out of the door of the tabernacle for seven days, until the day wherein the time of your consecration shall be expired. For in seven days the consecration is finished:

34 As at this present it hath been done, that the rite of the sacrifice might be accomplished.

35 Day and night shall you remain in the tabernacle observing the watches of the Lord, lest you die. For so it hath been commanded me.

36 And Aaron and his sons did all things which the Lord spoke by the hand of Moses.

CHAPTER 9

Aaron offereth sacrifice for himself and the people. Fire cometh from the Lord upon the altar.

AND when the eighth day was come, Moses called Aaron and his sons, and the ancients of Israel, and said to Aaron: ¹

2 Take of the herd a calf for sin, and a ram for a holocaust, both without blemish, and offer them before the Lord.

3 And to the children of Israel thou shalt say: Take ye a he-goat for sin, and a calf, and a lamb, both of a year old, and without blemish for a holocaust.

³ Exod. 22, 32; 30, 22; 40, 9; Lev. 25, 9. CHAP. 9. ¹ Exod. 29, 1.

4 Also a bullock and a ram for peace offerings. And immolate them before the Lord, offering for the sacrifice of every one of them flour tempered with oil: for to-day the Lord will appear to you.

5 They brought therefore all things that Moses had commanded before the door of the tabernacle: where when all the multitude stood,

6 Moses said: This is the word, which the Lord hath commanded. Do *it*, and his glory will appear to you.

7 And he said tc Aaron: Approach to the altar, and offer sacrifice for thy sin. Offer the holocaust, and pray for thyself and for the people: and when thou hast slain the people's victim, pray for them, as the Lord hath commanded.

8 And forthwith Aaron, approaching to the altar, immolated the calf for his sin.

9 And his sons brought him the blood of it: and he dipped his finger therein, and touched the horns of the altar, and poured the rest at the foot thereof.

10 And the fat, and the little kidneys, and the caul of the liver, which are for sin, he burnt upon the altar, as the Lord had commanded Moses.

11 But the flesh and skins thereof he burnt with fire without the camp.

12 He immolated also the victim of holocaust: and his sons brought him the blood thereof, which he poured round about on the altar.

13 And the victim being cut into pieces, they brought to him the head and all the members: all which he burnt with fire upon the altar.

14 Having first washed the entrails and the feet with water.

15 Then offering for the sin of the people, he slew the he-goat: and expiating the altar,

16 He offered the holocaust.

17 Adding in the sacrifice the libations, which are offered withal, and burning them upon the altar, besides the ceremonies of the morning holocaust.

18 He immolated also the bullock and the ram, and peace offerings of the people: and his sons brought him the blood, which he poured upon the altar round about.

19 The fat also of the bullock, and the rump of the ram, and the two little kidneys with their fat, and the caul of the liver,

20 They put upon the breasts. And after the fat was burnt upon the altar,

21 Aaron separated their breasts, and the right shoulders, elevating them before the Lord, as Moses had commanded.

22 And stretching forth his hands to the people, he blessed them. And so the victims for sin, and the holocausts, and the peace offerings being finished, he came down.

23 And Moses and Aaron went into the tabernacle of the testimony, and afterwards came forth and blessed the people. ² And the glory of the Lord appeared to all the multitude.

24 And, behold, a fire, coming forth from the Lord, devoured the holocaust and the fat that was upon the altar: which when the multitude saw, they praised the Lord, falling on their faces.

CHAPTER 10

Nadab and Abiu for offering strange fire, are burnt by fire. Priests are forbidden to drink wine, when they enter into the tabernacle. The law of eating the holy things.

AND Nadab and Abiu, the sons of Aaron, taking *their* censers, put fire therein, and incense on it, offering before the Lord strange fire: which was not commanded them. ¹

2 And fire coming out from the Lord destroyed them: and they died before the Lord.

3 And Moses said to Aaron: This is what the Lord hath spoken. I will be sanctified in them that approach to me: and I will be glorified in the sight of all the people. And when Aaron heard this, he held his peace.

4 And Moses called Misael and Elisaphan, the sons of Oziel, the uncle of Aaron, and said to them: Go and take away your brethren from before the sanctuary, and carry them without the camp.

5 And they went forthwith and took them as they lay, vested with linen tunicks, and cast them forth, as had been commanded them.

6 And Moses said to Aaron, and to Eleazar and Ithamar, his sons: Uncover not your heads, and rend not your garments, lest perhaps you die, and indignation come upon all the congregation. Let your brethren, and all the house of Israel, bewail the burning which the Lord hath kindled.

7 But you shall not go out of the door of the tabernacle: otherwise you shall perish, for the oil of the holy unction is on you. And they did all things according to the precept of Moses.

8 The Lord also said to Aaron:

9 You shall not drink wine nor any thing that may make drunk, thou nor thy sons, when you enter into the tabernacle of the testimony, lest you die. Because it is an everlasting precept through your generations:

10 And that you may have knowledge to discern between holy and unholy, between unclean and clean:

11 And may teach the children of Israel all my ordinances which the Lord hath spoken to them by the hand of Moses.

12 And Moses spoke to Aaron, and to Eleazar and Ithamar, his sons that were left: Take the sacrifice that is remaining of the oblation of the Lord, and eat it without leaven beside the altar, because it is holy of holies.

13 And you shall eat it in a holy place: which is given to thee and thy sons of the oblations of the Lord, as it hath been commanded me.

14 The breast also that is offered, and the shoulder that is separated, you shall eat in a most clean place, thou and thy sons, and thy daughters with thee. For they are set aside for thee and thy children, of the victims of peace offerings of the children of Israel.

15 Because they have elevated before the Lord the shoulder and the breast, and the fat that is burnt on the altar: and they belong to thee and to thy sons by a perpetual law, as the Lord hath commanded.

16 ² While these things were a doing, when Moses sought for the buck-goat, that had been offered for sin, he found it burnt. And being angry with Eleazar and Ithamar, the sons of Aaron that were left, he said:

17 Why did you not eat in the holy place the sacrifice for sin, which is most holy, and given to you, that you may bear the iniquity of the people, and may pray for them in the sight of the Lord.

18 Especially, whereas none of the blood thereof hath been carried within the holy places: and you ought to have eaten it in the sanctuary, as was commanded me?

19 Aaron answered: This day hath been offered the victim for sin, and the holocaust before the Lord: and to me what thou seest has happened. How could I eat it, or please the Lord in the ceremonies, having a sorrowful heart?

20 Which when Moses had heard he was satisfied.

CHAPTER 11

The distinction of clean and unclean animals.

AND the Lord spoke to Moses and Aaron, saying:

2 Say to the children of Israel ¹ These are the animals which you are to eat of all the living things of the earth.

² 2 Mach. 2, 10. CHAP. 10. ¹ Num. 3, 4; 1 Par. 24, 2. ² Mach. 2, 11. CHAP. 11. ¹ Deut. 14, 3.

3 Whatsoever hath the hoof divided, and cheweth the cud among the beasts, you shall eat.

4 But whatsoever cheweth indeed the cud, and hath a hoof, but divideth it not, as the camel, and others: that you shall not eat, but shall reckon it among the unclean.

5 The cherogrillus which cheweth the cud, but divideth not the hoof, is unclean.

6 The hare also: for that too cheweth the cud, but divideth not the hoof.

7 [2] And the swine, which, though it divideth the hoof, cheweth not the cud.

8 The flesh of these you shall not eat, nor shall you touch their carcasses, because they are unclean to you.

9 These are the things that breed in the waters, and which it is lawful to eat. All that hath fins, and scales, as well in the sea, as in the rivers, and the pools, you shall eat.

10 But whatsoever hath not fins and scales, of those things that move and live in the waters, shall be an abomination to you,

11 And detestable. Their flesh you shall not eat: and their carcasses you shall avoid.

12 All that have not fins and scales, in the waters, shall be unclean.

13 Of birds these are they which you must not eat, and which are to be avoided by you: The eagle, and the griffon, and the osprey.

14 And the kite, and the vulture, according to their kind.

15 And all that is of the raven kind, according to their likeness.

[2] 2 Mach. 6, 18.

CHAP. 11. Ver. 2. *Animals which you are to eat.* The prohibition of so many kinds of beasts, birds, and fishes, in the law, was ordered, 1st, to exercise the people in obedience, and temperance; 2ndly, to restrain them from the vices of which these animals were symbols; 3rdly, because the things here forbidden were for the most part unwholesome, and not proper to be eaten; 4thly, that the people of God, by being obliged to abstain from things *corporally unclean*, might be trained up to seek a *spiritual cleanness.*

Ver. 3. *Hoof divided, and cheweth the cud.* The dividing of the hoof and chewing of the cud, signify discretion between good and evil, and meditating on the law of God; and where either of these is wanting a man is unclean. In like manner fishes were reputed unclean that had not fins and scales: that is, souls that did not raise themselves up by prayer and cover themselves with the scales of virtues.

Ver. 5. *The cherogrillus.* Some suppose it to be the *rabbit*, others the *hedgehog.* St. Jerome intimates that it is another kind of animal common in Palestine, which lives in the holes of rocks or in the earth. We choose here, as also in the names of several other creatures that follow, (which are little known in this part of the world,) to keep the Greek or Latin names.

Ver. 13. *The griffon.* Not the monster which the painters represent, which hath no being upon earth; but a bird of the eagle kind, larger than the common.

16 The ostrich, and the owl, and the larus, and the hawk according to its kind.

17 The screech owl, and the cormorant, and the ibis.

18 And the swan, and the bittern, and the porphyrion.

19 The heron, and the charadrion according to its kind: the houp also, and the bat.

20 Of things that fly, whatsoever goeth upon four feet, shall be abominable to you.

21 But whatsoever walketh upon four feet, but hath the legs behind longer, wherewith it hoppeth upon the earth.

22 That you shall eat: as the bruchus in its kind, the attacus, and ophimachus, and the locust, every one according to their kind.

23 But of flying things whatsoever hath four feet only, shall be an abomination to you.

24 And whosoever shall touch the carcasses of them, shall be defiled: and shall be unclean until the evening:

25 And if it be necessary that he carry any of these things when they are dead: he shall wash his clothes, and shall be unclean until the sun set.

26 Every beast that hath a hoof, but divideth it not, nor cheweth the cud shall be unclean: and he that toucheth it, shall be defiled.

27 That which walketh upon hands of all animals which go on all four, shall be unclean: he that shall touch their carcasses shall be defiled until evening.

28 And he that shall carry such carcasses, shall wash his clothes, and shall be unclean until evening: because all these things are unclean to you.

29 These also shall be reckoned among unclean things, of all that move upon the earth. The weasel, and the mouse, and the crocodile, every one according to their kind:

30 The shrew, and the chameleon, and the stellio, and the lizard, and the mole.

31 All these are unclean. He that toucheth their carcasses shall be unclean until the evening.

32 And upon what thing soever any of their carcasses shall fall, it shall be defiled, whether it be a vessel of wood, or a garment, or skins or haircloths; or any thing in which work is done. They shall be dipped in water, and shall be unclean until the evening, and so afterwards shall be clean.

33 But an earthen vessel, into which any of these shall fall, shall be defiled: and therefore is to be broken.

34 Any meat which you eat, if water *from such a vessel* be poured upon it, shall be unclean; and every liquor that is drunk out of any *such* vessel, shall be unclean.

35 And upon whatsoever thing any of these dead beasts shall fall, it shall be unclean. Whether it be oven, or pots with feet, they shall be destroyed, and shall be unclean.

36 But fountains and cisterns, and all gatherings together of waters shall be clean. He that toucheth their carcasses shall be defiled.

37 If it fall upon seed corn, it shall not defile it.

38 But if any man pour water upon the seed, and afterwards it be touched by the carcasses, it shall be forthwith defiled.

39 If any beast die, of which it is lawful for you to eat, he that toucheth the carcass thereof, shall be unclean until the evening.

40 And he that eateth or carrieth any thing thereof, shall wash his clothes, and shall be unclean until the evening.

41 All that creepeth upon the earth shall be abominable: neither shall it be taken for meat.

42 Whatsoever goeth upon the breast on four feet, or hath many feet, or traileth on the earth, you shall not eat, because it is abominable.

43 Do not defile your souls, nor touch aught thereof, lest you be unclean.

44 For I am the Lord your God. [3] Be holy because I am holy. Defile not your souls by any creeping thing, that moveth upon the earth.

45 For I am the Lord, who brought you out of the land of Egypt, that I might be your God.

46 You shall be holy, because I am holy. This is the law of beasts and fowls, and of every living creature that moveth in the waters, and creepeth on the earth:

47 That you may know the differences of the clean, and unclean, and know what you ought to eat, and what to refuse.

CHAPTER 12

The purification of women after childbirth.

AND the Lord spoke to Moses, saying:

2 Speak to the children of Israel, and thou shalt say to them: [1] If a woman having received seed shall bear a man child, she shall be unclean seven days, according to the days of separation of her flowers.

3 [2] And on the eighth day the infant shall be circumcised:

4 But she shall remain three and thirty days in the blood of her purification. She shall touch no holy thing: neither shall she enter into the sanctuary, until the days of her purification be fulfilled.

5 But if she shall bear a maid child, she shall be unclean two weeks, according to the custom of her monthly courses. And she shall remain in the blood of her purification sixty-six days.

6 And when the days of her purification are expired, for a son, or for a daughter, she shall bring to the door of the tabernacle of the testimony, a lamb of a year old for a holocaust, and a young pigeon or a turtle for sin: and shall deliver them to the priest.

7 Who shall offer them before the Lord, and shall pray for her: and so she shall be cleansed from the issue of her blood. This is the law for her that beareth a man child or a maid child.

8 And if her hand find not sufficiency, and she is not able to offer a lamb, she shall take two turtles, [3] or two young pigeons, one for a holocaust, and another for sin: and the priest shall pray for her, and so she shall be cleansed.

CHAPTER 13

The law concerning leprosy in men, and in garments.

AND the Lord spoke to Moses and Aaron, saying:

2 The man in whose skin or flesh shall arise a different colour or a blister, or as it were something shining, that is, the stroke of the leprosy, shall be brought to Aaron the priest, or any one of his sons.

3 And if he see the leprosy in his skin, and the hair turned white and the place where the leprosy appears lower than the skin and the rest of the flesh: it is the stroke of the leprosy, and upon his judgment he shall be separated.

4 But if there be a shining whiteness in the skin, and not lower than the other flesh, and the hair be of the former colour, the priest shall shut him up seven days.

5 And the seventh day he shall look on him: and if the leprosy be grown no farther, and hath not spread itself in the skin, he shall shut him up again other seven days.

6 And on the seventh day, he shall look on him. If the leprosy be somewhat obscure, and not spread in the skin, he shall declare him clean, because it is *but* a scab: and the man shall wash his clothes, and shall be clean.

7 But if the leprosy grow again, after

---

[3] 1 Peter, 1, 16. CHAP. 12. [1] Luke, 2, 22. [2] John, 7, 22. [3] Lev. 5, 7; Luke, 2, 24.

he was seen by the priest and restored to cleanness, he shall be brought to him:

8 And shall be condemned of uncleanness.

9 If the stroke of the leprosy be in a man, he shall be brought to the priest:

10 And he shall view him. And when there shall be a white colour in the skin, and it shall have changed the look of the hair, and the living flesh itself shall appear:

11 It shall be judged an inveterate leprosy, and grown into the skin. The priest therefore shall declare him unclean: and shall not shut him up, because he is evidently unclean.

12 But if the leprosy spring out running about in the skin, and cover all the skin from the head to the feet, whatsoever falleth under the sight of the eyes:

13 The priest shall view him, and shall judge that the leprosy which he has is very clean: because it is all turned into whiteness, and therefore the man shall be clean.

14 But when the live flesh shall appear in him:

15 Then by the judgment of the priest he shall be defiled, and shall be reckoned among the unclean. For live flesh, if it be spotted with leprosy, is unclean.

16 And if again it be turned into whiteness, and cover all the man:

17 The priest shall view him, and shall judge him to be clean.

18 When also there has been an ulcer in the flesh and the skin, and it has been healed:

19 And in the place of the ulcer, there appeareth a white scar, or somewhat red, the man shall be brought to the priest.

20 And when he shall see the place of the leprosy lower than the other flesh, and the hair turned white: he shall declare him unclean, for the plague of leprosy is broken out in the ulcer.

21 But if the hair be of the former colour, and the scar somewhat obscure, and be not lower than the flesh that is near it: he shall shut him up seven days.

22 And if it spread, he shall judge him to have the leprosy:

23 But if it stay in its place, it is *but* the scar of an ulcer: and the man shall be clean.

24 The flesh also and skin that hath been burnt, and after it is healed hath a white or a red scar:

25 The priest shall view it, and if he see it turned white, and the place thereof is lower than the other skin: he shall declare him unclean, because the evil of leprosy is broken out in the scar.

26 But if the colour of the hair be not changed, nor the blemish lower than the other flesh, and the appearance of the leprosy be somewhat obscure: he shall shut him up seven days,

27 And on the seventh day he shall view him. If the leprosy be grown farther in the skin, he shall declare him unclean.

28 But if the whiteness stay in its place, and be not very clear, it is the sore of a burning: and therefore he shall be cleansed, because it is *only* the scar of a burning.

29 If the leprosy break out in the head or the beard of a man or woman, the priest shall see them,

30 And if the place be lower than the other flesh, and the hair yellow, and thinner than usual: he shall declare them unclean, because it is the leprosy of the head and the beard;

31 But if he perceive the place of the spot is equal with the flesh that is near it, and the hair black: he shall shut him up seven days,

32 And on the seventh day he shall look upon it. If the spot be not grown, and the hair keep its colour, and the place of the blemish be even with the other flesh:

33 The man shall be shaven all but the place of the spot: and he shall be shut up other seven days.

34 If on the seventh day the evil seem to have stayed in its place, and not lower than the other flesh, he shall cleanse him: and his clothes being washed he shall be clean.

35 But if after his cleansing the spot spread again in the skin:

36 He shall seek no more whether the hair be turned yellow, because he is evidently unclean.

37 But if the spot be stayed, and the hair be black, let him know that the man is healed: and let him confidently pronounce him clean.

38 If a whiteness appear in the skin of a man or a woman,

39 The priest shall view them. If he find that a darkish whiteness shineth in the skin, let him know that it is not the leprosy, but a white blemish, and that the man is clean.

40 The man whose hair falleth off from his head, he is bald and clean:

41 And if the hair fall from his forehead, he is bald before and clean.

42 But if in the bald head or in the bald forehead there be risen a white or reddish colour:

43 And the priest perceive this, he shall condemn him undoubtedly of leprosy which is risen in the bald part.

44 Now whosoever shall be defiled with the leprosy, and is separated by the judgment of the priest:

45 Shall have his clothes hanging loose, his head bare, his mouth covered with a cloth: and he shall cry out that he is defiled and unclean.

46 All the time that he is a leper and unclean he shall dwell alone without the camp.

47 A woollen or linen garment that shall have the leprosy

48 In the warp, and the woof: or a skin, or whatsoever is made of a skin:

49 If it be infected with a white or red spot, it shall be accounted the leprosy, and shall be shewn to the priest.

50 And he shall look upon it and shall shut it up seven days.

51 And on the seventh day when he looketh on it again, if he find that it is grown, it is a fixed leprosy. He shall judge the garment unclean, and every thing wherein it shall be found.

52 And therefore it shall be burnt with fire.

53 But if he see that it is not grown,

54 He shall give orders, and they shall wash that part wherein the leprosy is: and he shall shut it up other seven days.

55 And when he shall see that the former colour is not returned, nor yet the leprosy spread, he shall judge it unclean: and shall burn it with fire, for the leprosy has taken hold of the outside of the garment, or through the whole.

56 But if the place of the leprosy be somewhat dark, after the garment is washed, he shall tear it off, and divide it from that which is sound.

57 And if after this there appear in those places that before were without spot, a flying and wandering leprosy: it must be burnt with fire.

58 If it cease, he shall wash with water the parts that are pure, the second time: and they shall be clean.

59 This is the law touching the leprosy of any woollen or linen garment, either in the warp or woof, or any thing of skins: how it ought to be cleansed, or pronounced unclean.

CHAPTER 14

The rites of sacrifices in cleansing the leprosy. Leprosy in houses.

AND the Lord spoke to Moses, saying:

2 This is the rite of a leper, when he is to be cleansed. He shall be brought to the priest:

3 [1] Who going out of the camp, when he shall find that the leprosy is cleansed,

4 [2] Shall command him that is to be purified, to offer for himself two living sparrows, which it is lawful to eat, and cedar wood, and scarlet, and hyssop.

5 And he shall command one of the sparrows to be immolated in an earthen vessel over living waters.

6 But the other that is alive, he shall dip, with the cedar wood, and the scarlet and the hyssop, in the blood of the sparrow that is immolated:

7 Wherewith he shall sprinkle him that is to be cleansed seven times, that he may be rightly purified. And he shall let go the living sparrow, that it may fly into the field.

8 And when the man hath washed his clothes, he shall shave all the hair of his body, and shall be washed with water: and being purified he shall enter into the camp, yet so that he tarry without his own tent seven days.

9 And on the seventh day he shall shave the hair of his head, and his beard and his eyebrows, and the hair of all his body. And having washed again his clothes, and his body,

10 On the eighth day, he shall take two lambs without blemish, and an ewe of a year old without blemish, and three tenths of flour tempered with oil for a sacrifice, and a sextary of oil apart.

11 And when the priest that purifieth the man, hath presented him, and all these things before the Lord, at the door of the tabernacle of the testimony:

12 He shall take a lamb, and offer it for a trespass offering with the sextary of oil. And having offered all before the Lord,

13 He shall immolate the lamb, where the victim for sin is wont to be immolated, and the holocaust, that is, in the holy place. For as that which is for sin, so also the victim for a trespass offering pertaineth to the priest: it is holy of holies.

14 And the priest taking of the blood of the victim that was immolated for trespass, shall put it upon the tip of the right ear of him that is cleansed, and upon the thumb of his right hand and the great toe of his right foot.

CHAP. 14. [1] Matt. 8, 4. [2] Mark, 1, 44; Luke, 5, 14.

CHAP. 14. Ver. 5. *Living waters.* That is, waters taken from a spring, brook, or river.

Ver. 10. *A sextary,* Heb. *log:* a measure of liquids, which was the twelfth part of a *hin;* and held about as much as six eggs.

Ver. 14. *Taking of the blood.* These ceremonies used in the cleansing of a leper, were mysterious

15 And he shall pour of the sextary of oil into his own left hand,

16 And shall dip his right finger in it, and sprinkle it before the Lord seven times.

17 And the rest of the oil in his left hand, he shall pour upon the tip of the right ear of him that is cleansed, and upon the thumb of his right hand and the great toe of his right foot, and upon the blood that was shed for trespass:

18 And upon his head.

19 And he shall pray for him before the Lord, and shall offer the sacrifice for sin. Then shall he immolate the holocaust,

20 And put it on the altar with the libations thereof: and the man shall be rightly cleansed.

21 But if he be poor, and his hand cannot find the things aforesaid: he shall take a lamb for an offering for trespass, that the priest may pray for him, and a tenth part of flour tempered with oil for a sacrifice, and a sextary of oil:

22 ³ And two turtles or two young pigeons, of which one may be for sin, and the other for a holocaust.

23 And he shall offer them on the eighth day of his purification to the priest, at the door of the tabernacle of the testimony before the Lord.

24 And the *priest* receiving the lamb for trespass, and the sextary of oil, shall elevate them together.

25 And the lamb being immolated, he shall put of the blood thereof upon the tip of the right ear of him that is cleansed, and upon the thumb of his right hand, and the great toe of his right foot.

³ Lev. 5, 7; 12, 8; Luke, 2, 24.

26 But he shall pour part of the oil into his own left hand,

27 And dipping the finger of his right hand in it, he shall sprinkle it seven times before the Lord.

28 And he shall touch the tip of the right ear of him that is cleansed, and the thumb of his right hand and the great toe of his right foot, in the place of the blood that was shed for trespass.

29 And the other part of the oil that is in his left hand, he shall pour upon the head of the purified person, that he may appease the Lord for him.

30 And he shall offer a turtle, or young pigeon,

31 One for trespass, and the other for a holocaust, with their libations.

32 This is the sacrifice of a leper, that is not able to have all things that appertain to his cleansing.

33 And the Lord spoke to Moses and Aaron, saying:

34 When you shall come into the land of Chanaan, which I will give you for a possession, if there be the plague of leprosy in a house:

35 He whose house it is, shall go and tell the priest, saying: It seemeth to me, that there is the plague of leprosy in my house,

36 And he shall command, that they carry forth all things out of the house, before he go into it, and see whether it have the leprosy, lest all things become unclean that are in the house. And afterwards he shall go in to view the leprosy of the house.

37 And if he see in the walls thereof as it were little dints, disfigured with paleness or redness, and lower than all the rest:

38 He shall go out of the door of the house, and forthwith shut it up seven days,

39 And returning on the seventh day, he shall look upon it. If he find that the leprosy is spread,

40 He shall command, that the stones wherein the leprosy is, be taken out, and cast without the city into an unclean place:

41 And that the house be scraped on the inside round about, and the dust of the scraping be scattered without the city into an unclean place:

42 And that other stones be laid in the place of them that were taken away, and the house be plastered with other mortar.

43 But if, after the stones be taken out, and the dust scraped off, and it be plastered with other earth,

44 The priest going in perceive that the leprosy is returned, and the walls

and very significative. The sprinkling seven times with the blood of the little bird, the washing himself and his clothes, the shaving his hair and his beard, signify the means which are to be used in the reconciliation of a sinner, and the steps by which he is to return to God, viz., by the repeated application of the blood of Christ: the washing his conscience with the waters of compunction: and retrenching all vanities and superfluities, by employing all that is over and above what is necessary in alms deeds. The sin offering, and the holocaust or burnt offering, which he was to offer at his cleansing, signify the sacrifice of a contrite and humble heart, and that of adoration in spirit and truth, with gratitude and thankfulness, for the forgiveness of sins, with which we are ever to appear before the Almighty. The touching the right ear, the thumb of the right hand, and the great toe of the right foot, first with the blood of the victim, and then with the remainder of the oil, which had been sprinkled seven times before the Lord, signify the application of the blood of Christ, and the unction of the sevenfold grace of the Holy Ghost; to the sinner's right ear, that he may duly hearken to and obey the law of God; and to his right hand and foot, that the works of his hands, and all the steps or affections of his soul, signified by the feet, may be rightly directed to God.

full of spots, it is a lasting leprosy, and the house is unclean.

45 And they shall destroy it forthwith, and shall cast the stones and timber thereof, and all the dust without the town into an unclean place.

46 He that entereth into the house when it is shut, shall be unclean until evening.

47 And he that sleepeth in it, and eateth any thing, shall wash his clothes.

48 But if the priest going in perceive that the leprosy is not spread in the house, after it was plastered again, he shall purify it, it being cured.

49 And for the purification thereof he shall take two sparrows, and cedar wood, and scarlet, and hyssop.

50 And having immolated one sparrow in an earthen vessel, over living waters,

51 He shall take the cedar wood, and the hyssop, and the scarlet, and the living sparrow, and shall dip all in the blood of the sparrow that is immolated, and in the living water: and he shall sprinkle the house seven times.

52 And shall purify it as well with the blood of the sparrow, as with the living water, and with the living sparrow, and with the cedar wood, and the hyssop, and the scarlet.

53 And when he hath let go the sparrow to fly freely away into the field, he shall pray for the house: and it shall be rightly cleansed.

54 This is the law of every kind of leprosy and stroke.

55 Of the leprosy of garments and houses,

56 Of a scar and of blisters breaking out, of a shining spot, and when the colours are diversely changed:

57 That it may be known when a thing is clean or unclean.

CHAPTER 15

Other legal uncleannesses.

AND the Lord spoke to Moses and Aaron, saying:

2 Speak to the children of Israel, and say to them: The man that hath an issue of seed, shall be unclean.

3 And then shall he be judged subject to this evil, when a filthy humour, at every moment, cleaveth to his flesh, and gathereth there.

4 Every bed on which he sleepeth, shall be unclean, and every place on which he sitteth.

5 If any man touch his bed, he shall wash his clothes: and being washed with water, he shall be unclean until the evening.

6 If a man sit where that man hath sitten, he also shall wash his clothes: and being washed with water, shall be unclean until the evening.

7 He that toucheth his flesh, shall wash his clothes: and being himself washed with water shall be unclean until the evening.

8 If such a man cast his spittle upon him that is clean, he shall wash his clothes: and being washed with water, he shall be unclean until the evening.

9 The saddle on which he hath sitten shall be unclean.

10 And whatsoever has been under him that hath the issue of seed, shall be unclean until the evening. He that carrieth any of these things, shall wash his clothes: and being washed with water, he shall be unclean until the evening.

11 Every person whom such a one shall touch, not having washed his hands before, shall wash his clothes: and being washed with water, shall be unclean until the evening.

12 If he touch a vessel of earth, it shall be broken: but if a vessel of wood, it shall be washed with water.

13 If he who suffereth this disease be healed, he shall number seven days after his cleansing: and having washed his clothes, and all his body in living water, he shall be clean.

14 And on the eighth day he shall take two turtles, or two young pigeons, and he shall come before the Lord, to the door of the tabernacle of the testimony, and shall give them to the priest.

15 Who shall offer one for sin, and the other for a holocaust: and he shall pray for him before the Lord, that he may be cleansed of the issue of his seed.

16 The man from whom the seed of copulation goeth out, shall wash all his body with water: and he shall be unclean until the evening.

17 The garment or skin that he weareth, he shall wash with water: and it shall be unclean until the evening.

18 The woman, with whom he copulateth, shall be washed with water: and shall be unclean until the evening.

19 The woman, who at the return of the month, hath her issue of blood, shall be separated seven days.

20 Every one that toucheth her, shall be unclean until the evening.

21 And every thing that she sleepeth on, or that she sitteth on in the days of her separation, shall be defiled.

22 He that toucheth her bed shall wash his clothes: and being himself

washed with water, shall be unclean until the evening.

23 Whosoever shall touch any vessel on which she sitteth, shall wash his clothes: and himself being washed with water, shall be defiled until the evening.

24 If a man copulateth with her in the time of her flowers, he shall be unclean seven days: and every bed on which he shall sleep, shall be defiled.

25 The woman that hath an issue of blood many days out of her ordinary time, or that ceaseth not to flow after the monthly courses, as long as she is subject to this disease, shall be unclean, in the same manner as if she were in her flowers.

26 Every bed on which she sleepeth, and every vessel on which she sitteth, shall be defiled.

27 Whosoever toucheth them shall wash his clothes: and himself being washed with water, shall be unclean until the evening.

28 If the blood stop and cease to run, she shall count seven days of her purification:

29 And on the eighth day she shall offer for herself to the priest, two turtles, or two young pigeons, at the door of the tabernacle of the testimony:

30 And he shall offer one for sin, and the other for a holocaust, and he shall pray for her before the Lord, and for the issue of her uncleanness.

31 You shall teach therefore the children of Israel to take heed of uncleanness, that they may not die in their filth, when they shall have defiled my tabernacle that is among them.

32 This is the law of him that hath the issue of seed, and that is defiled by copulation.

33 And of the woman that is separated in her monthly times, or that hath a continual issue of blood, and of the man that sleepeth with her.

CHAPTER 16

When and how the high priest must enter into the sanctuary. The feast of expiation.

AND the Lord spoke to Moses, after the death of the two sons of Aaron, when they were slain upon their offering strange fire: [1]

2 And he commanded him, saying: Speak to Aaron thy brother, [2] that he enter not at all into the sanctuary, which is within the veil before the pro-

pitiatory, with which the ark is covered, lest he die, (for I will appear in a cloud over the oracle),

3 Unless he first do these things. He shall offer a calf for sin, and a ram for a holocaust.

4 He shall be vested with a linen tunick: he shall cover his nakedness with linen breeches: he shall be girded with a linen girdle, and he shall put a linen mitre upon his head. For these are holy vestments: all which he shall put on, after he is washed.

5 And he shall receive from the whole multitude of the children of Israel two buck-goats for sin, and one ram for a holocaust.

6 And when he hath offered the calf and prayed for himself and for his own house:

7 He shall make the two buck-goats to stand before the Lord in the door of the tabernacle of the testimony.

8 And casting lots upon them both, one to be offered to the Lord, and the other to be the emissary goat:

9 That whose lot fell to be offered to the Lord, he shall offer for sin.

10 But that whose lot was to be the emissary goat, he shall present alive before the Lord, that he may pour our prayers upon him, and let him go into the wilderness.

11 After these things are duly celebrated, he shall offer the calf: and praying for himself and for his own house, he shall immolate it.

12 And taking the censer, which he hath filled with the burning coals of the altar, and taking up with his hand the compounded perfume for incense, he shall go in within the veil into the holy place:

13 That when the perfumes are put upon the fire, the cloud and vapour thereof may cover the oracle, which is over the testimony, and he may not die.

14 He shall take also of the blood of the calf, and sprinkle with his finger seven times towards the propitiatory to the east.

15 And when he hath killed the buck-goat for the sin of the people, he shall carry in the blood thereof within the veil, as he was commanded to do with the blood of the calf, that he may sprinkle it over against the oracle:

16 And may expiate the sanctuary from the uncleanness of the children of Israel, and from their transgressions, and all their sins. According to this rite shall he do to the tabernacle of the testimony, which is fixed among them in the midst of the filth of their habitation.

CHAP. 16. [1] Lev. 10, 1. [2] Exod. 30, 10; Heb. 9, 7.

CHAP. 16. Ver. 2. *Enter not.* No one but the high priest, and he once a year, could enter into the sanctuary; to signify that no one could enter into the sanctuary of heaven, till Christ our high priest opened it by his passion (Heb. 10. 8).

17 [3] Let no man be in the tabernacle when the high priest goeth into the sanctuary, to pray for himself and his house, and for the whole congregation of Israel, until he come out.

18 And when he is come out to the altar that is before the Lord, let him pray for himself: and taking the blood of the calf, and of the buck-goat, let him pour it upon the horns thereof round about.

19 And sprinkling with his finger seven times, let him expiate, and sanctify it from the uncleanness of the children of Israel.

20 After he hath cleansed the sanctuary, and the tabernacle, and the altar, then let him offer the living goat.

21 And putting both hands upon his head, let him confess all the iniquities of the children of Israel, and all their offences and sins. And praying that they may light on his head, he shall turn him out by a man ready for it, into the desert.

22 And when the goat hath carried all their iniquities into an uninhabited land, and shall be let go into the desert:

23 Aaron shall return into the tabernacle of the testimony, and putting off the vestments, which he had on him before when he entered into the sanctuary, and leaving them there,

24 He shall wash his flesh in the holy place, and shall put on his own garments. And after that he has come out and hath offered his own holocaust, and that of the people, he shall pray both for himself, and for the people.

25 And the fat that is offered for sins, he shall burn on the altar.

26 But he that hath let go the emissary goat, shall wash his clothes, and his body with water, and so shall enter into the camp.

27 But the calf and the buck-goat, that were sacrificed for sin, and whose blood was carried into the sanctuary, to accomplish the atonement, they shall carry forth without the camp, [4] and shall burn with fire: their skins and their flesh, and their dung.

28 And whosoever burneth them shall wash his clothes, and flesh with water: and so shall enter into the camp.

29 And this shall be to you an everlasting ordinance. [5] The seventh month, the tenth day of the month, you shall afflict your souls, and shall do no work, whether it be one of your own country, or a stranger that sojourneth among you.

30 Upon this day shall be the expiation for you, and the cleansing from all your sins. You shall be cleansed before the Lord.

31 For it is a sabbath of rest: and you shall afflict your souls by a perpetual religion.

32 And the priest that is anointed, and whose hands are consecrated to do the office of the priesthood in his father's stead, shall make atonement. And he shall be vested with the linen robe and the holy vestments.

33 And he shall expiate the sanctuary and the tabernacle of the testimony and the altar: the priest also and all the people.

34 And this shall be an ordinance for ever, that you pray for the children of Israel, and for all their sins once in a year. He did therefore as the Lord had commanded Moses.

CHAPTER 17

No sacrifices to be offered but at the door of the tabernacle. A prohibition of blood.

AND the Lord spoke to Moses, saying:

2 Speak to Aaron and his sons, and to all the children of Israel, saying to them: This is the word, which the Lord hath commanded, saying:

3 Any man whosoever of the house of Israel, if he kill an ox, or a sheep, or a goat in the camp, or without the camp,

4 And offer it not at the door of the tabernacle an oblation to the Lord, shall be guilty of blood. As if he had shed blood, so shall he perish from the midst of his people.

5 Therefore the children of Israel shall bring to the priest their victims, which they kill in the field, that they may be sanctified to the Lord before the door of the tabernacle of the testimony: and they may sacrifice them for peace offerings to the Lord.

6 And the priest shall pour the blood upon the altar of the Lord, at the door of the tabernacle of the testimony: and shall burn the fat for a sweet odour to the Lord.

7 And they shall no more sacrifice their victims to devils, with whom they have committed fornication. It shall be an ordinance for ever to them and to their posterity.

8 And thou shalt say to them: The man of the house of Israel, and of the strangers who sojourn among you, that offereth a holocaust or a victim,

9 And bringeth it not to the door of the tabernacle of the testimony, that

---

[3] Luke, 1, 10. [4] Heb. 13, 11. [5] Lev. 23, 27.

CHAP. 17. Ver. 3. *If he kill.* That is, in order to sacrifice. The law of God forbids sacrifices to be offered in any other place but at the tabernacle or temple of the Lord; to signify that no sacrifice would be acceptable to God, out of his true temple, the one, holy, catholic, apostolic church.

it may be offered to the Lord, shall perish from among his people.

10 If any man whosoever of the house of Israel, and of the strangers that sojourn among them, eat blood, I will set my face against his soul, and will cut him off from among his people.

11 Because the life of the flesh is in the blood: and I have given it to you, that you may make atonement with it upon the altar for your souls, and the blood may be for an expiation of the soul.

12 Therefore I have said to the children of Israel: No soul of you, nor of the strangers that sojourn among you, shall eat blood.

13 Any man whosoever of the children of Israel, and of the strangers that sojourn among you, if by hunting or fowling, he take a wild beast or a bird, which is lawful to eat, let him pour out its blood, and cover it with earth.

14 [1] For the life of all flesh is in the blood. Therefore I said to the children of Israel: You shall not eat the blood of any flesh at all, because the life of the flesh is in the blood, and whosoever eateth it, shall be cut off.

15 The soul that eateth that which died of itself, or has been caught by a beast, whether he be one of your own country or a stranger, shall wash his clothes' and himself with water, and shall be defiled until the evening: and in this manner he shall be made clean.

16 But if he do not wash his clothes, and his body, he shall bear his iniquity.

CHAPTER 18

Marriage is prohibited in certain degrees of kindred. And all unnatural lusts.

AND the Lord spoke to Moses, saying:

2 Speak to the children of Israel, and thou shalt say to them: I am the Lord your God.

3 You shall not do according to the custom of the land of Egypt, in which you dwelt: neither shall you act according to the manner of the country of Chanaan, into which I will bring you. Nor shall you walk in their ordinances.

4 You shall do my judgments, and shall observe my precepts, and shall walk in them. I am the Lord your God.

5 [1] Keep my laws and my judgments: which if a man do, he shall live in them. I am the Lord.

CHAP. 17. [1] Gen. 9, 4; Lev. 7, 26. CHAP. 18. [1] Ezech. 20, 11; Rom. 10, 5; Gal. 3, 12. [2] Lev. 20, 2.

Ver. 10. *Eat blood.* To eat *blood* was forbidden in the law; partly, because God reserved it to himself, to be offered in sacrifices on the altar, as to the Lord of life and death; and as a figure of the blood of Christ; and partly, to give man a horror of shedding *blood.* Gen. 9, 4, 5, 6.

6 No man shall approach to her that is near of kin to him, to uncover her nakedness. I am the Lord.

7 Thou shalt not uncover the nakedness of thy father, or the nakedness of thy mother: she is thy mother, thou shalt not uncover her nakedness.

8 Thou shalt not uncover the nakedness of thy father's wife: for it is the nakedness of thy father.

9 Thou shalt not uncover the nakedness of thy sister by father or by mother: whether born at home or abroad.

10 Thou shalt not uncover the nakedness of thy son's daughter, or thy daughter's daughter: because it is thy own nakedness.

11 Thou shalt not uncover the nakedness of thy father's wife's daughter, whom she bore to thy father: and who is thy sister.

12 Thou shalt not uncover the nakedness of thy father's sister: because she is the flesh of thy father.

13 Thou shalt not uncover the nakedness of thy mother's sister: because she is thy mother's flesh.

14 Thou shalt not uncover the nakedness of thy father's brother: neither shalt thou approach to his wife, who is joined to thee by affinity.

15 Thou shalt not uncover the nakedness of thy daughter-in-law: because she is thy son's wife, neither shalt thou discover her shame.

16 Thou shalt not uncover the nakedness of thy brother's wife: because it is the nakedness of thy brother.

17 Thou shalt not uncover the nakedness of thy wife and her daughter. Thou shalt not take her son's daughter or her daughter's daughter, to discover her shame: because they are her flesh, and such copulation is incest.

18 Thou shalt not take thy wife's sister for a harlot, to rival her: neither shalt thou discover her nakedness, while she is yet living.

19 Thou shalt not approach to a woman having her flowers: neither shalt thou uncover her nakedness.

20 Thou shalt not lie with thy neighbour's wife: nor be defiled with mingling of seed.

21 [2] Thou shalt not give any of thy seed to be consecrated to the idol Moloch, nor defile the name of thy God. I am the Lord.

22 Thou shalt not lie with mankind as with womankind: because it is an abomination.

23 Thou shalt not copulate with any beast: neither shalt thou be defiled with it. [3] A woman shall not lie down to a

beast, nor copulate with it: because it is a *heinous* crime.

24 Defile not yourselves with any of these things with which all the nations have been defiled, which I will cast out before you,

25 And with which the land is defiled: the abominations of which I will visit, that it may vomit out its inhabitants.

26 Keep ye my ordinances and my judgments: and do not any of these abominations. Neither any of your own nation, nor any stranger that sojourneth among you.

27 For all these detestable things the inhabitants of the land have done, that were before you, and have defiled it.

28 Beware then, lest in like manner, it vomit you also out, if you do the like things: as it vomited out the nation that was before you.

29 Every soul that shall commit any of these abominations, shall perish from the midst of his people.

30 Keep my commandments. Do not the things which they have done, that have been before you: and be not defiled therein. I am the Lord your God.

CHAPTER 19
Divers ordinances, partly moral, partly ceremonial or judicial.

THE Lord spoke to Moses, saying: 2 Speak to all the congregation of the children of Israel. And thou shalt say to them: [1] Be ye holy, because I the Lord your God am holy.

3 Let every one fear his father, and his mother. Keep my sabbaths. I am the Lord your God.

4 Turn ye not to idols: nor make to yourselves molten gods. I am the Lord your God.

5 If ye offer in sacrifice a peace offering to the Lord, that he may be favourable:

6 You shall eat it on the same day it was offered, and the next day. And whatsoever shall be left until the third day, you shall burn with fire.

7 If after two days any man eat thereof, he shall be profane and guilty of impiety:

8 And shall bear his iniquity, because he hath defiled the holy thing of the Lord. And that soul shall perish from among his people.

9 [2] When thou reapest the corn of thy land, thou shalt not cut down *all that is* on the face of the earth to the very ground: nor shalt thou gather the ears that remain.

10 Neither shalt thou gather the bunches and grapes that fall down in thy vineyard: but shalt leave them to the poor and the strangers to take. I am the Lord your God.

11 You shall not steal. You shall not lie: neither shall any man deceive his neighbour.

12 [3] Thou shalt not swear falsely by my name, nor profane the name of thy God. I am the Lord.

13 [4] Thou shalt not calumniate thy neighbour, nor oppress him by violence. [5] The wages of him that hath been hired by thee shall not abide with thee until the morning.

14 Thou shalt not speak evil of the deaf, nor put a stumbling block before the blind: but thou shalt fear the Lord thy God, because I am the Lord.

15 Thou shalt not do that which is unjust, nor judge unjustly. [6] Respect not the person of the poor: nor honour the countenance of the mighty. *But* judge thy neighbour according to justice.

16 Thou shalt not be a detractor nor a whisperer among the people. Thou shalt not stand against the blood of thy neighbour. I am the Lord.

17 [7] Thou shalt not hate thy brother in thy heart: [8] but reprove him openly, lest thou incur sin through him.

18 Seek not revenge, nor be mindful of the injury of thy citizens. [9] Thou shalt love thy friend as thyself. I am the Lord.

19 Keep ye my laws. Thou shalt not make thy cattle to gender with beasts of any other kind. Thou shalt not sow thy field with different seeds. Thou shalt not wear a garment that is woven of two sorts.

20 If a man carnally lie with a woman that is a bondservant and marriageable, and yet not redeemed with a price, nor made free: they both shall be scourged; and they shall not be put to death, because she was not a free woman.

21 And for his trespass he shall offer a ram to the Lord, at the door of the tabernacle of the testimony.

22 And the priest shall pray for him and for his sin before the Lord: and he

[3] Lev. 20, 16. CHAP. 19. [1] Lev. 11, 44; 1 Peter, 1, 16. [2] Lev. 23, 22. [3] Exod. 20, 7. [4] Ecclus. 10, 6. [5] Deut. 24, 14; Job. 4, 15. [6] Deut. 1, 17; 16, 19; Prov. 24, 23; Ecclus. 42, 1; James, 2, 2. [7] 1 John, 2, 11; 3, 14. [8] Ecclus. 19, 13; Matt. 18, 15; Luke, 17, 8. [9] Matt. 5, 43; 22, 39; Luke, 6, 27; Rom. 13, 9.

CHAP. 18. Ver. 23. *Because it is a* heinous *crime.* In Hebrew, this word *heinous crime* is expressed by the word *confusion,* signifying the shamefulness and baseness of this abominable sin.

CHAP. 19. Ver. 19. *Different seeds.* This law tends to recommend simplicity and plain dealing in all things, and to teach the people not to join any false worship or heresy with the worship of the true God.

shall have mercy on him, and the sin shall be forgiven.

23 When you shall be come into the land, and shall have planted in it fruit trees, you shall take away the firstfruits of them. The fruit that comes forth shall be unclean to you: neither shall you eat of them.

24 But in the fourth year, all their fruit shall be sanctified, to the praise of the Lord.

25 And in the fifth year you shall eat the fruits thereof, gathering the increase thereof. I am the Lord your God.

26 You shall not eat with blood. You shall not divine nor observe dreams.

27 Nor shall you cut *your* hair roundwise: nor shave *your* beard.

28 You shall not make any cuttings in your flesh, for the dead: neither shall you make in yourselves any figures or marks. I am the Lord.

29 Make not thy daughter a common strumpet, lest the land be defiled, and filled with wickedness.

30 Keep ye my sabbaths, and reverence my sanctuary. I am the Lord.

31 Go not aside after wizards: neither ask any thing of soothsayers, to be defiled by them. I am the Lord your God.

32 Rise up before the hoary head, and honour the person of the aged man: and fear the Lord thy God. I am the Lord.

33 [10] If a stranger dwell in your land, and abide among you, do not upbraid him:

34 But let him be among you as one of the same country. And you shall love him as yourselves: for you were strangers in the land of Egypt. I am the Lord your God.

35 Do not any unjust thing in judgment, in rule, in weight, or in measure.

36 Let the balance be just and the weights equal, the bushel just, and the sextary equal. I am the Lord your God, that brought you out of the land of Egypt.

37 Keep all my precepts, and all my judgments: and do them. I am the Lord.

---

[10] Exod. 22, 21. Chap. 20. [1] Lev. 18, 21. [2] 1 Peter, 1, 16. [2] Exod. 21, 17; Prov. 20, 20; Matt. 15, 4; Mark, 7, 10. [4] Deut. 22, 22; John, 8, 5.

Ver. 23. *The firstfruits. Praeputia*, literally, their foreskins; it alludes to circumcision, and signifies that for the first three years the trees were to be as uncircumcised, and their fruit unclean: till in the fourth year their increase was sanctified and given to the Lord, that is, to the priests.

Chap. 20. Ver. 15. *The beast also ye shall kill.* The killing of the beast was for the greater horror of the crime, and to prevent the remembrance of such abomination.

CHAPTER 20

Divers crimes to be punished with death.

AND the Lord spoke to Moses, saying:

2 Thus shalt thou say to the children of Israel: [1] If any man of the children of Israel, or of the strangers that dwell in Israel, give of his seed to the idol Moloch, dying let him die. The people of the land shall stone him.

3 And I will set my face against him: and I will cut him off from the midst of his people, because he hath given of his seed to Moloch, and hath defiled my sanctuary, and profaned my holy name.

4 And if the people of the land neglecting, and as it were little regarding my commandment, let alone the man that hath given of his seed to Moloch, and will not kill him:

5 I will set my face against that man, and his kindred, and will cut off both him and all that consented with him, to commit fornication with Moloch, out of the midst of their people.

6 The soul that shall go aside after magicians, and soothsayers, and shall commit fornication with them: I will set my face against that soul, and destroy it out of the midst of its people.

7 [2] Sanctify yourselves, and be ye holy: because I am the Lord your God.

8 Keep my precepts, and do them. I am the Lord that sanctify you.

9 [3] He that curseth his father, or mother, dying let him die. He hath cursed his father, and mother: let his blood be upon him.

10 [4] If any man commit adultery with the wife of another, and defile his neighbour's wife: let them be put to death, both the adulterer and the adulteress.

11 If a man lie with his stepmother, and discover the nakedness of his father, let them both be put to death: their blood be upon them.

12 If any man lie with his daughter-in-law: let both die, because they have done a heinous crime. Their blood be upon them.

13 If any one lie with a man as with a woman, both have committed an abomination: let them be put to death. Their blood be upon them.

14 If any man after marrying the daughter, marry her mother, he hath done a heinous crime. He shall be burnt alive with them: neither shall so great an abomination remain in the midst of you.

15 He that shall copulate with any beast or cattle, dying let him die: the beast also ye shall kill.

16 ⁵ The woman that shall lie under any beast, shall be killed together with the same. Their blood be upon them.

17 If any man take his sister, the daughter of his father, or the daughter of his mother, and see her nakedness, and she behold her brother's shame: they have committed a crime. They shall be slain, in the sight of their people, because they have discovered one another's nakedness. And they shall bear their iniquity.

18 If any man lie with a woman in her flowers, and uncover her nakedness, and she open the fountain of her blood: both shall be destroyed out of the midst of their people.

19 Thou shalt not uncover the nakedness of thy aunt by thy mother, and of thy aunt by thy father. He that doth this, hath uncovered the shame of his own flesh: both shall bear their iniquity.

20 If any man lie with the wife of his uncle by the father, or of his uncle by the mother, and uncover the shame of his near akin, both shall bear their sin. They shall die without children.

21 He that marrieth his brother's wife, doth an unlawful thing: he hath uncovered his brother's nakedness. They shall be without children.

22 Keep my laws and my judgments, and do them: lest the land into which you are to enter to dwell therein, vomit you also out.

23 Walk not after the laws of the nations, which I will cast out before you. For they have done all these things: and therefore I abhorred them.

24 But to you I say: Possess their land which I will give you for an inheritance, a land flowing with milk and honey. I am the Lord your God, who have separated you from other people.

25 Therefore do you also separate the clean beast from the unclean, and the clean fowl from the unclean. Defile not your souls with beasts, or birds, or any things that move on the earth, and which I have shewn you to be unclean.

26 ⁶ You shall be holy unto me, because I the Lord am holy: and I have separated you from other people, that you should be mine.

27 ⁷ A man, or woman, in whom there is a pythonical or divining spirit, dying let them die. They shall stone them. Their blood be upon them.

CHAPTER 21

Ordinances relating to the priests.

THE Lord said also to Moses: Speak to the priests the sons of Aaron, and thou shalt say to them: Let not a priest incur an uncleanness at the death of his citizens.

2 But only for his kin, such as are near in blood: that is to say, for his father and for his mother, and for his son, and for his daughter, for his brother also:

3 And for a maiden sister, who hath had no husband.

4 But not even for the prince of his people shall he do any thing that may make him unclean.

5 ¹ Neither shall they shave their head, nor their beard, nor make incisions in their flesh.

6 They shall be holy to their God, and shall not profane his name. For they offer the burnt offering of the Lord, and the bread of their God: and therefore they shall be holy.

7 ² They shall not take to wife a harlot or a vile prostitute, nor one that has been put away from her husband: because they are consecrated to their God,

8 And offer the loaves of proposition. Let them therefore be holy because I also am holy: the Lord, who sanctify them.

9 If the daughter of a priest be taken in whoredom, and dishonour the name of her father, she shall be burnt with fire.

10 The high priest, that is to say; the priest who is the greatest among his brethren, upon whose head the oil of unction hath been poured; and whose hands have been consecrated for the priesthood; and who hath been vested with the holy vestments. He shall not uncover his head: he shall not rend his garments.

11 Nor shall he go in at all to any dead person: not even for his father, or his mother, shall he be defiled.

12 Neither shall he go out of the holy places, lest he defile the sanctuary of the Lord: because the oil of the holy unction of his God is upon him. I am the Lord.

13 ³ He shall take a virgin unto his wife.

14 But a widow or one that is divorced, or defiled, or a harlot, he shall not take: but a maid of his own people.

15 He shall not mingle the stock of his kindred with the common people of his nation: for I am the Lord who sanctify him.

16 And the Lord spoke to Moses, saying:

17 Say to Aaron: Whosoever of thy seed throughout their families, hath a

⁵ Lev. 18, 23. ⁶ 1 Peter, 1, 16. ⁷ Deut. 18, 11; 1 Kings, 28, 7. Chap. 21. ¹ Lev. 19, 27; Ezech. 44, 20. ² Lev. 19, 29. ³ Ezech. 44, 22.

Chap. 21. Ver. 1. *An uncleanness,* such as was contracted in laying out the dead body, or touching it; or in going into the home, or assisting at the funeral, and so forth.

blemish, he shall not offer bread to his God.

18 Neither shall he approach to minister to him: If he be blind; if he be lame; if he have a little, or a great, or a crooked nose;

19 If his foot, or if his hand be broken;

20 If he be crookbacked; or blear eyed; or have a pearl in his eye, or a continual scab, or a dry scurf in his body, or a rupture.

21 Whosoever of the seed of Aaron the priest hath a blemish: he shall not approach to offer sacrifices to the Lord, nor bread to his God.

22 He shall eat nevertheless of the loaves, that are offered in the sanctuary.

23 Yet so that he enter not within the veil, nor approach to the altar: because he hath a blemish, and he must not defile my sanctuary. I am the Lord who sanctify them.

24 Moses, therefore spoke to Aaron, and to his sons and to all Israel, all the things that had been commanded him.

CHAPTER 22

Who may eat the holy things, and what things may be offered.

AND the Lord spoke to Moses, saying:

2 Speak to Aaron and to his sons, that they beware of those things that are consecrated of the children of Israel: and defile not the name of the things sanctified to me, which they offer. I am the Lord.

3 Say to them and to their posterity: Every man of your race, that approacheth to those things that are consecrated, and which the children of Israel have offered to the Lord, in whom there is uncleanness, shall perish before the Lord. I am the Lord.

4 The man of the seed of Aaron, that is a leper, or that suffereth a running of the seed, shall not eat of those things that are sanctified to me, until he be healed. He that toucheth any thing unclean by occasion of the dead: and he whose seed goeth from him as in generation:

5 And he that toucheth a creeping thing, or any unclean thing, the touching of which is defiling:

6 Shall be unclean until the evening, and shall not eat those things that are sanctified. But when he hath washed his flesh with water,

CHAP. 22. ¹ Lev. 17, 15; Exod. 22, 31; Deut. 14, 21; Ezech. 44, 31. ² Deut. 15, 21; Ecclus. 35, 14.

CHAP. 22. Ver. 3. *Approacheth.* This is to give us to understand with what purity of soul we are to approach to the Blessed Sacrament of which these meats that had been offered in sacrifice were a figure.

7 And the sun is down, then being purified, he shall eat of the sanctified things, because it is his meat.

8 ¹ That which dieth of itself, and that which was taken by a beast, they shall not eat, nor be defiled therewith. I am the Lord.

9 Let them keep my precepts, that they may not fall into sin, and die in the sanctuary, when they shall have defiled it. I am the Lord who sanctify them.

10 No stranger shall eat of the sanctified things: a sojourner of the priests, or a hired servant, shall not eat of them.

11 But he whom the priest hath bought, and he that is his servant, born in his house, these shall eat of them.

12 If the daughter of a priest be married to any of the people, she shall not eat of those things that are sanctified, nor of the firstfruits.

13 But if she be a widow, or divorced, and having no children return to her father's house, she shall eat of her father's meats, as she was wont to do when she was a maid. No stanger hath leave to eat of them.

14 He that eateth of the sanctified things through ignorance, shall add the fifth part with that which he ate, and shall give it to the priest into the sanctuary.

15 And they shall not profane the sanctified things of the children of Israel, which they offer to the Lord:

16 Lest perhaps they bear the iniquity of their trespass, when they shall have eaten the sanctified things. I am the Lord who sanctify them.

17 And the Lord spoke to Moses, saying:

18 Speak to Aaron, and to his sons, and to all the children of Israel, and thou shalt say to them: The man of the house of Israel, and of the strangers who dwell with you, that offereth his oblation, either paying his vows, or offering of his own accord, whatsoever it be which he presenteth for a holocaust of the Lord,

19 To be offered by you: it shall be a male without blemish of the beeves, or of the sheep, or of the goats.

20 If it have a blemish you shall not offer it: neither shall it be acceptable.

21 ² The man that offereth a victim of peace offerings to the Lord, either paying his vows, or offering of his own accord, whether of beeves or of sheep, shall offer it without blemish, that it may be acceptable. There shall be no blemish in it.

22 If it be blind, or broken, or have a scar or blisters, or a scab, or a dry scurf: you shall not offer them to the

Lord, nor burn any thing of them upon the Lord's altar.

23 An ox or a sheep, that hath the ear and the tail cut off, thou mayst offer voluntarily: but a vow may not be paid with them.

24 You shall not offer to the Lord any beast that hath the testicles bruised, or crushed, or cut and taken away: neither shall you do any such thing in your land.

25 You shall not offer bread to your God, from the hand of a stranger, nor any other thing that he would give: because they are all corrupted, and defiled. You shall not receive them.

26 And the Lord spoke to Moses, saying:

27 When a bullock, or a sheep, or a goat, is brought forth, they shall be seven days under the udder of their dam: but the eighth day, and thenceforth, they may be offered to the Lord.

28 Whether it be a cow, or a sheep, they shall not be sacrificed the same day with their young ones.

29 If you immolate a victim for thanksgiving to the Lord, that he may be favourable,

30 You shall eat it the same day. There shall not any of it remain until the morning of the next day. I am the Lord.

31 Keep my commandments, and do them. I am the Lord.

32 Profane not my holy name, that I may be sanctified in the midst of the children of Israel. I am the Lord who sanctify you:

33 And who brought you out of the land of Egypt, that I might be your God. I am the Lord.

CHAPTER 23

Holy days to be kept.

AND the Lord spoke to Moses, saying:

2 Speak to the children of Israel, and thou shalt say to them: These are the feasts of the Lord, which you shall call holy.

3 Six days shall ye do work: the seventh day, because it is the rest of the sabbath, shall be called holy. You shall do no work on that day: it is the sabbath of the Lord in all your habitations.

4 These also are the holy days of the Lord, which you must celebrate in their seasons.

5 [1] The first month, the fourteenth day of the month at evening, is the phase of the Lord.

6 And the fifteenth day of the same month is the solemnity of the un-

leavened bread of the Lord. Seven days shall you eat unleavened bread.

7 The first day shall be most solemn unto you, and holy: you shall do no servile work therein.

8 But you shall offer sacrifice in fire to the Lord seven days. And the seventh day shall be more solemn, and more holy: and you shall do no servile work therein.

9 And the Lord spoke to Moses, saying:

10 Speak to the children of Israel, and thou shalt say to them: When you shall have entered into the land which I will give you, and shall reap your corn, you shall bring sheaves of ears, the firstfruits of your harvest to the priest.

11 Who shall lift up the sheaf before the Lord, the next day after the sabbath, that it may be acceptable for you, and shall sanctify it.

12 And on the same day that the sheaf is consecrated, a lamb without blemish of the first year shall be killed for a holocaust of the Lord.

13 And the libations shall be offered with it: two tenths of flour tempered with oil, for a burnt offering of the Lord, and a most sweet odour. Libations also of wine, the fourth part of a hin.

14 You shall not eat either bread, or parched corn, or frumenty of the harvest, until the day that you shall offer thereof to your God. It is a precept for ever throughout your generations, and all your dwellings.

15 [2] You shall count therefore from the morrow after the sabbath, wherein you offered the sheaf of firstfruits, seven full weeks:

16 Even unto the morrow after the seventh week be expired, that is to say, fifty days: and so you shall offer a new sacrifice to the Lord.

17 Out of all your dwellings, two loaves of the firstfruits, of two tenths of flour leavened, which you shall bake for the firstfruits of the Lord.

18 And you shall offer with the loaves seven lambs without blemish of the first year, and one calf from the herd, and two rams: and they shall be for a holocaust with their libations for a most sweet odour to the Lord.

19 You shall offer also a buck-goat for sin, and two lambs of the first year for sacrifices of peace offerings.

20 And when the priest hath lifted them up with the loaves of the firstfruits before the Lord, they shall fall to his use.

21 And you shall call this day most

CHAP. 23. [1] Exod. 12, 18; Num. 28, 16. [2] Deut. 16, 9.

solemn, and most holy. You shall do no servile work therein. It shall be an everlasting ordinance in all your dwellings and generations.

22 And when you reap the corn of your land, you shall not cut it to the very ground: neither shall you gather the ears that remain. But you shall leave them for the poor and for the strangers. I am the Lord your God.

23 And the Lord spoke to Moses, saying:

24 'Say to the children of Israel: The seventh month, on the first day of the month, you shall keep a sabbath, a memorial, with the sound of trumpets, and it shall be called holy.

25 You shall do no servile work therein, and you shall offer a holocaust to the Lord.

26 And the Lord spoke to Moses, saying:

27 [5] Upon the tenth day of this seventh month shall be the day of atonement. It shall be most solemn, and shall be called holy: and you shall afflict your souls on that day, and shall offer a holocaust to the Lord.

28 You shall do no servile work in the time of this day: because it is a day of propitiation, that the Lord your God may be merciful unto you.

29 Every soul that is not afflicted on this day, shall perish from among his people.

30 And every soul that shall do any work, the same will I destroy from among his people.

31 You shall do no work therefore on that day: it shall be an everlasting ordinance unto you in all your generations, and dwellings.

32 It is a sabbath of rest, and you shall afflict your souls beginning on the ninth day of the month. From evening until evening you shall celebrate your sabbaths.

33 And the Lord spoke to Moses, saying:

34 Say to the children of Israel: From the fifteenth day of this same seventh month, shall be kept the feast of tabernacles, seven days to the Lord.

35 The first day shall be called most solemn and most holy: you shall do no servile work therein. And seven days you shall offer holocausts to the Lord.

36 The eighth day also shall be most solemn and most holy: and you shall offer holocausts to the Lord. For it is the day of assembly and congregation. You shall do no servile work therein.

37 These are the feasts of the Lord which you shall call most solemn and most holy, and shall offer on them obla-tions to the Lord: holocausts and libations according to the rite of every day.

38 Besides the sabbaths of the Lord, and your gifts, and those things that you offer by vow, or which you shall give to the Lord voluntarily.

39 So from the fifteenth day of the seventh month, when you shall have gathered in all the fruits of your land, you shall celebrate the feast of the Lord seven days. On the first day and the eighth shall be a sabbath: that is a day of rest.

40 And you shall take to you on the first day the fruits of the fairest tree, and branches of palm trees, and boughs of thick trees, and willows of the brook: and you shall rejoice before the Lord your God.

41 And you shall keep the solemnity thereof seven days in the year. It shall be an everlasting ordinance in your generations. In the seventh month shall you celebrate this feast.

42 And you shall dwell in bowers seven days. Every one that is of the race of Israel, shall dwell in tabernacles:

43 That your posterity may know, that I made the children of Israel to dwell in tabernacles, when I brought them out of the land of Egypt. I am the Lord your God.

44 And Moses spoke concerning the feasts of the Lord to the children of Israel.

CHAPTER 24

The oil for the lamps. The loaves of proposition. The punishment of blasphemy.

AND the Lord spoke to Moses, saying:

2 Command the children of Israel, that they bring unto thee the finest and clearest oil of olives, to furnish the lamps continually,

3 Without the veil of the testimony in the tabernacle of the covenant. And Aaron shall set them from evening until morning before the Lord, by a perpetual service and rite in your generations.

4 They shall be set upon the most pure candlestick before the Lord continually.

5 Thou shalt take also fine flour, and shalt bake twelve loaves thereof, two tenths shall be in every loaf.

6 And thou shalt set them six and six, one against another, upon the most clean table before the Lord.

7 And thou shalt put upon them the clearest frankincense, that the bread may be for a memorial of the oblation of the Lord.

8 Every sabbath they shall be changed before the Lord: being re-

ceived of the children of Israel by an everlasting covenant.

9 And they shall be Aaron's and his sons', that they may eat them in the holy place: because it is most holy of the sacrifices of the Lord by a perpetual right.

10 And behold there went out the son of a woman of Israel, whom she had of an Egyptian, among the children of Israel: and fell at words in the camp with a man of Israel.

11 And when he had blasphemed the name, and had cursed it, he was brought to Moses. (Now his mother was called Salumith, the daughter of Dabri, of the tribe of Dan.)

12 And they put him into prison, till they might know what the Lord would command.

13 And the Lord spoke to Moses,

14 Saying: Bring forth the blasphemer without the camp: and let them that heard him, put their hands upon his head: and let all the people stone him.

15 And thou shalt speak to the children of Israel: The man that curseth his God, shall bear his sin:

16 And he that blasphemeth the name of the Lord, dying let him die. All the multitude shall stone him, whether he be a native or a stranger. He that blasphemeth the name of the Lord, dying let him die.

17 [1] He that striketh and killeth a man: dying let him die.

18 He that killeth a beast, shall make it good: that is to say, shall give beast for beast.

19 He that giveth a blemish to any of his neighbours: as he hath done, so shall it be done to him:

20 [2] Breach for breach, eye for eye, tooth for tooth, shall he restore. What blemish he gave, the like shall he be compelled to suffer.

21 He that striketh a beast, shall render another. He that striketh a man shall be punished.

22 Let there be equal judgment among you, whether he be a stranger, or a native that offends: because I am the Lord your God.

23 And Moses spoke to the children of Israel. And they brought forth him that had blasphemed, without the camp: and they stoned him. And the children of Israel did as the Lord had commanded Moses.

CHAPTER 25

The law of the seventh and of the fiftieth year of jubilee.

AND the Lord spoke to Moses in mount Sinai, saying:

2 Speak to the children of Israel, and thou shalt say to them: When you shall have entered into the land which I will give you, observe the rest of the sabbath of the Lord.

3 [1] Six years thou shalt sow thy field and six years thou shalt prune thy vineyard, and shalt gather the fruits thereof.

4 But in the seventh year there shall be a sabbath to the land, of the resting of the Lord. Thou shalt not sow thy field, nor prune thy vineyard.

5 What the ground shall bring forth of itself, thou shalt not reap: neither shalt thou gather the grapes of the firstfruits as a vintage. For it is a year of rest to the land.

6 But they shall be unto you for meat, to thee and to thy man-servant, to thy maid-servant and thy hireling, and to the strangers that sojourn with thee.

7 All things that grow shall be meat to thy beasts and to thy cattle.

8 Thou shalt also number to thee seven weeks of years: that is to say, seven times seven, which together make forty-nine years.

9 And thou shalt sound the trumpet in the seventh month, the tenth day of the month, in the time of the expiation in all your land.

10 And thou shalt sanctify the fiftieth year, and shalt proclaim remission to all the inhabitants of thy land: for it is the year of jubilee. Every man shall return to his possession, and every one shall go back to his former family:

11 Because it is the jubilee and the fiftieth year. You shall not sow, nor reap the things that grow in the field of their own accord, neither shall you gather the firstfruits of the vines,

12 Because of the sanctification of the jubilee. But as they grow you shall presently eat them.

13 In the year of the jubilee all shall return to their possessions.

14 When thou shalt sell any thing to thy neighbour, or shalt buy of him: grieve not thy brother. But thou shalt buy of him according to the number of years from the jubilee.

15 And he shall sell to thee according to the computation of the fruits.

16 The more years remain after the jubilee, the more shall the price increase: and the less time is counted, so much the less shall the purchase cost. For he shall sell to thee the time of the fruits.

Chap. 24. [1] Exod. 21, 12. [2] Exod. 21, 24; Deut. 19, 21; Matt. 5, 38. Chap. 25. [1] Exod. 23, 10.

Chap. 25. Ver. 10. *Remission.* That is, a general release and discharge from debts and bondage, and a reinstating of every man in his former possessions.

17 Do not afflict your countrymen: but let every one fear his God. Because I am the Lord your God.

18 Do my precepts, and keep my judgments, and fulfil them: that you may dwell in the land without any fear.

19 And the ground may yield you its fruits, of which you may eat your fill, fearing no man's invasion.

20 But if you say: What shall we eat the seventh year, if we sow not, nor gather our fruits?

21 I will give you my blessing the sixth year: and it shall yield the fruits of three years.

22 And the eighth year you shall sow, and shall eat of the old fruits, until the ninth year: till new grow up, you shall eat the old store.

23 The land also shall not be sold for ever: because it is mine, and you are strangers and sojourners with me.

24 For which cause all the country of your possession shall be under the condition of redemption.

25 If thy brother being impoverished sell his little possession, and his kinsman will: he may redeem what he had sold.

26 But if he have no kinsman, and he himself can find the price to redeem it:

27 The value of the fruits shall be counted from that time when he sold it. And the overplus he shall restore to the buyer, and so shall receive his possession again.

28 But if his hands find not the means to repay the price, the buyer shall have what he bought, until the year of the jubilee. For in that year all that is sold shall return to the owner, and to the ancient possessor.

29 He that selleth a house within the walls of a city, shall have the liberty to redeem it, until one year be expired.

30 If he redeem it not, and the whole year be fully out, the buyer shall possess it, and his posterity for ever, and it cannot be redeemed, not even in the jubilee.

31 But if the house be in a village, that hath no walls, it shall be sold according to the same law as the fields. If it be not redeemed before, in the jubilee it shall return to the owner.

32 The houses of Levites, which are in cities, may always be redeemed.

33 If they be not redeemed, in the jubilee they shall all return to the owners: because the houses of the cities of the Levites are for their possessions among the children of Israel.

34 But let not their suburbs be sold, because it is a perpetual possession.

35 If thy brother be impoverished and weak of hand, and thou receive him

as a stranger and sojourner, and he live with thee:

36 Take not usury of him nor more than thou gavest. Fear thy God, that thy brother may live with thee.

37 Thou shalt not give him thy money upon usury: nor exact of him any increase of fruits.

38 I am the Lord your God, who brought you out of the land of Egypt, that I might give you the land of Chanaan, and might be your God.

39 If thy brother constrained by poverty, sell himself to thee: thou shalt not oppress him with the service of bondservants.

40 But he shall be as a hireling, and a sojourner: he shall work with thee until the year of the jubilee.

41 And afterwards he shall go out with his children: and shall return to his kindred and to the possession of his fathers.

42 For they are my servants, and I brought them out of the land of Egypt: let them not be sold as bondmen.

43 Afflict him not by might: but fear thy God.

44 Let your bondmen, and your bondwomen, be of the nations that are round about you:

45 And of the strangers that sojourn among you, or that were born of them in your land. These you shall have for servants:

46 And by right of inheritance shall leave them to your posterity, and shall possess them for ever. But oppress not your brethren the children of Israel by might.

47 If the hand of a stranger or a sojourner grow strong among you, and thy brother being impoverished sell himself to him, or to any of his race:

48 After the sale he may be redeemed. He that will of his brethren shall redeem him:

49 Either his uncle, or his uncle's son, or his kinsman, by blood, or by affinity. But if he himself be able also, he shall redeem himself.

50 Counting only the years from the time of his selling unto the year of the jubilee: and counting the money that he was sold for, according to the number of the years and the reckoning of a hired servant.

51 If there be many years that remain until the jubilee, according to them shall he also repay the price.

52 If few, he shall make the reckoning with him according to the number of the years: and shall repay to the buyer of what remaineth of the years.

53 His wages being allowed for which

he served before: he shall not afflict him violently in thy sight.

54 And if by these means he cannot be redeemed, in the year of the jubilee he shall go out with his children.

55 For the children of Israel are my servants, whom I brought forth out of the land of Egypt.

CHAPTER 26

God's promises to them that keep his commandments. And the many punishments with which he threatens transgressors.

I AM the Lord your God. [1] You shall not make to yourselves any idol or graven thing: neither shall you erect pillars, nor set up a remarkable stone in your land, to adore it. For I am the Lord your God.

2 Keep my sabbaths, and reverence my sanctuary. I am the Lord.

3 [2] If you walk in my precepts, and keep my commandments, and do them, I will give you rain in due seasons.

4 And the ground shall bring forth its increase: and the trees shall be filled with fruit.

5 The threshing of your harvest shall reach unto the vintage, and the vintage shall reach unto the sowing time: and you shall eat your bread to the full, and dwell in your land without fear.

6 I will give peace in your coasts: you shall sleep, and there shall be none to make you afraid. I will take away evil beasts: and the sword shall not pass through your quarters.

7 You shall pursue your enemies: and they shall fall before you.

8 Five of yours shall pursue a hundred others: and a hundred of you ten thousand. Your enemies shall fall before you by the sword.

9 I will look on you, and make you increase: you shall be multiplied, and I will establish my covenant with you.

10 You shall eat the oldest of the old store: and, new coming on, you shall cast away the old.

11 I will set my tabernacle in the midst of you: and my soul shall not cast you off.

12 [3] I will walk among you, and will be your God: and you shall be my people.

13 I *am* the Lord your God: who have brought you out of the land of the Egyptians, that you should not serve them; and who have broken the chains of your necks, that you might go upright.

14 [4] But if you will not hear me, nor do all my commandments:

15 If you despise my laws, and contemn my judgments so as not to do

those things which are appointed by me, and to make void my covenant:

16 I also will do these things to you. I will quickly visit you with poverty, and burning heat, which shall waste your eyes, and consume your lives. You shall sow your seed in vain, which shall be devoured by your enemies.

17 I will set my face against you, and you shall fall down before your enemies: and shall be made subject to them that hate you. You shall flee when no man pursueth you.

18 But if you will not yet for all this obey me: I will chastise you seven times more for your sins.

19 And I will break the pride of your stubbornness: and I will make to you the heaven above as iron, and the earth as brass.

20 Your labour shall be spent in vain: the ground shall not bring forth her increase: nor the trees yield their fruit.

21 If you walk contrary to me, and will not hearken to me, I will bring seven times more plagues upon you for your sins.

22 And I will send in upon you the beasts of the field, to destroy you and your cattle, and make you few in number: and that your highways may be desolate.

23 And if even so you will not amend, but will walk contrary to me:

24 I also will walk contrary to you, and will strike you seven times for your sins.

25 And I will bring in upon you the sword that shall avenge my covenant. And when you shall flee into the cities, I will send the pestilence in the midst of you. And you shall be delivered into the hands of your enemies,

26 After I shall have broken the staff of your bread: so that ten women shall bake your bread in one oven, and give it out by weight: and you shall eat, and shall not be filled.

27 But if you will not for all this hearken to me, but will walk against me

28 I will also go against you with opposite fury: and I will chastise you with seven plagues for your sins.

29 So that you shall eat the flesh of your sons and of your daughters.

30 I will destroy your high places, and break your idols. You shall fall among the ruins of your idols, and my soul shall abhor you.

31 Insomuch that I will bring your cities to be a wilderness: and I will make your sanctuaries desolate: and will receive no more your sweet odours.

CHAP. 26. [1] Exod. 20, 4; Deut. 5, 8; Ps. 96, 7. [2] Deut. 28, 1. [3] 2 Cor. 6, 16. [4] Deut. 28, 15; Mal. 2, 2.

32 And I will destroy your land: and your enemies shall be astonished at it, when they shall be the inhabitants thereof.

33 And I will scatter you among the Gentiles: and I will draw out the sword after you. And your land shall be desert, and your cities destroyed.

34 Then shall the land enjoy her sabbaths all the days of her desolation. When you shall be

35 In the enemy's land, she shall keep a sabbath, and rest in the sabbaths of her desolation: because she did not rest in your sabbaths when you dwelt therein.

36 And as to them that shall remain of you I will send fear in their hearts in the countries of their enemies. The sound of a flying leaf shall terrify them: and they shall flee as it were from the sword. They shall fall, when no man pursueth them.

37 And they shall every one fall upon their brethren as fleeing from wars: none of you shall dare to resist your enemies.

38 You shall perish among the Gentiles: and an enemy's land shall consume you.

39 And if of them also some remain, they shall pine away in their iniquities, in the land of their enemies: and they shall be afflicted for the sins of their fathers, and their own.

40 Until they confess their iniquities, and the iniquities of their ancestors, whereby they have transgressed against me, and walked contrary unto me.

41 Therefore I also will walk against them, and bring them into their enemies' land until their uncircumcised mind be ashamed. Then shall they pray for their sins.

42 And I will remember my covenant, that I made with Jacob, and Isaac, and Abraham. I will remember also the land:

43 Which when she shall be left by them, shall enjoy her sabbaths, being desolate for them. But they shall pray for their sins, because they rejected my judgments, and despised my laws.

44 And yet for all that when they were in the land of their enemies, I did not cast them off altogether. Neither did I so despise them that they should be quite consumed: and I should make void my covenant with them. For I am the Lord their God.

45 And I will remember my former covenant, when I brought them out of the land of Egypt, in the sight of the Gentiles, to be their God. I *am* the Lord. These are the judgments, and precepts, and laws, which the Lord gave

between him and the children of Israel, in mount Sinai, by the hand of Moses.

CHAPTER 27

Of vows and tithes.

AND the Lord spoke to Moses, saying:

2 Speak to the children of Israel, and thou shalt say to them: The man that shall have made a vow, and promised his soul to God, shall give the price according to estimation.

3 If it be a man from twenty years old unto sixty years old, he shall give fifty sicles of silver, after the weight of the sanctuary:

4 If a woman, thirty.

5 But from the fifth year until the twentieth, a man shall give twenty sicles: a woman ten.

6 From one month until the fifth year, for a male shall be given five sicles: for a female three.

7 A man that is sixty years old or upward, shall give fifteen sicles: a woman ten.

8 If he be poor, and not able to pay the estimation, he shall stand before the priest: and as much as he shall value him at, and see him able to pay, so much shall he give.

9 But a beast that may be sacrificed to the Lord, if any one shall vow, shall be holy,

10 And cannot be changed: that is to say, neither a better for a worse, nor a worse for a better. And if he shall change it: both that which was changed, and that for which it was changed, shall be consecrated to the Lord.

11 An unclean beast, which cannot be sacrificed to the Lord, if any man shall vow, shall be brought before the priest:

12 Who judging whether it be good or bad, shall set the price.

13 Which, if he that offereth it will give, he shall add above the estimation the fifth part.

14 If a man shall vow his house, and sanctify it to the Lord, the priest shall consider it, whether it be good or bad: and it shall be sold according to the price, which he shall appoint.

15 But if he that vowed, will redeem it, he shall give the fifth part of the estimation over and above: and shall have the house.

16 And if he vow the field of his possession, and consecrate it to the Lord, the price shall be rated according to the measure of the seed. If the ground be sown with thirty bushels of barley, let it be sold for fifty sicles of silver.

17 If he vow his field immediately from the year of jubilee that is beginning: as much as it may be worth, at so much it shall be rated.

18 But if some time after, the priest shall reckon the money according to the number of years that remain until the jubilee, and the price shall be abated.

19 And if he that had vowed, will redeem his field, he shall add the fifth part of the money of the estimation, and shall possess it.

20 And if he will not redeem it, but it be sold to any other man, he that vowed it, may not redeem it any more.

21 For when the day of jubilee cometh, it shall be sanctified to the Lord, and *as* a possession consecrated, pertaineth to the right of the priests.

22 If a field that was bought, and not of a man's ancestors' possession, be sanctified to the Lord:

23 The priest shall reckon the price according to the number of years, unto the jubilee. And he that had vowed, shall give that to the Lord.

24 But in the jubilee, it shall return to the former owner, who had sold it, and had it in the lot of his possession.

25 All estimation shall be made according to the sicle of the sanctuary. [1] A sicle hath twenty obols.

26 The firstborn, which belong to the Lord, no man may sanctify and vow: whether it be bullock, or sheep, they are the Lord's.

27 And if it be an unclean beast, he that offereth it shall redeem it, according to thy estimation, and shall add the fifth part of the price. If he will not redeem it, it shall be sold to another for how much soever it was estimated by thee.

28 [2] Any thing that is devoted to the Lord, whether it be man, or beast, or field, shall not be sold: neither may it be redeemed. Whatsoever is once consecrated shall be holy of holies to the Lord.

29 And any consecration that is offered by man, shall not be redeemed, but dying shall die.

30 All tithes of the land, whether of corn, or of the fruits of trees, are the Lord's, and are sanctified to him.

31 And if any man will redeem his tithes, he shall add the fifth part of them.

32 Of all the tithes of oxen, and sheep, and goats, that pass under the shepherd's rod, every tenth that cometh shall be sanctified to the Lord.

33 It shall not be chosen neither good nor bad, neither shall it be changed for another. If any man change it: both that which was changed, and that for which it was changed, shall be sanctified to the Lord, and shall not be redeemed.

34 These are the precepts which the Lord commanded Moses for the children of Israel in mount Sinai.

THE BOOK OF
NUMBERS

This fourth Book of Moses is called NUMBERS, *because it begins with the numbering of the people. The Hebrews, from its first words, call it* VAIEDABBER. *It contains the transactions of the Israelites from the second month of the second year after their going out of Egypt, until the beginning of the eleventh month of the fortieth year; that is, a history almost of thirty-nine years.*

CHAPTER 1

The children of Israel are numbered. The Levites are designed to serve the tabernacle.

AND the Lord spoke to Moses in the desert of Sinai in the tabernacle of the covenant, the first day of the second month, the second year of their going out of Egypt, saying:

2 [1] Take the sum of all the congregation of the children of Israel by their families, and houses: and the names of every one, as many as are of the male sex,

3 From twenty years old and upwards, of all the men of Israel fit for war. And you shall number them by their troops, thou and Aaron.

4 And there shall be with you the princes of the tribes, and of the houses in their kindreds.

5 Whose names are these: Of Ruben, Elisur the son of Sedeur.

6 Of Simeon, Salamiel the son of Surisaddai.

7 Of Juda, Nahasson the son of Aminadab.

CHAP. 27. [1] Exod. 30, 13; Num. 3, 47; Ezech. 45, 12. [2] Jos. 6, 19. CHAP. 1. [1] Exod. 30, 12.

8 Of Issachar, Nathanael the son of Suar.

9 Of Zabulon, Eliab the son of Helon.

10 And of the sons of Joseph: of Ephraim, Elisama the son of Ammiud: of Manasses, Gamaliel the son of Phadassur.

11 Of Benjamin, Abidan the son of Gedeon.

12 Of Dan, Ahiezer the son of Ammisaddai.

13 Of Aser, Phegiel the son of Ochran.

14 Of Gad, Eliasaph the son of Duel.

15 Of Nephtali, Ahira the son of Enan.

16 These are the most noble princes of the multitude by their tribes and kindreds, and the chiefs of the army of Israel,

17 Whom Moses and Aaron took with all the multitude of the common people:

18 And assembled them on the first day of the second month, reckoning them up by the kindreds, and houses, and families, and heads, and names of every one from twenty years old and upward:

19 As the Lord had commanded Moses. And they were numbered in the desert of Sinai.

20 Of Ruben, the eldest son of Israel, by their generations and families and houses and names of every head, all that were of the male sex, from twenty years old and upward, that were able to go forth to war,

21 Were forty-six thousand five hundred.

22 Of the sons of Simeon by their generations and families, and houses of their kindreds, were reckoned up by the names and heads of every one, all that were of the male sex, from twenty years old and upward, that were able to go forth to war,

23 Fifty-nine thousand three hundred.

24 Of the sons of Gad, by their generations and families and houses of their kindreds were reckoned up by the names of every one from twenty years old and upward, all that were able to go forth to war,

25 Forty-five thousand six hundred and fifty.

26 Of the sons of Juda, by their generations and families and houses of their kindreds, by the names of every one from twenty years old and upward, all that were able to go forth to war,

27 Were reckoned up seventy-four thousand six hundred.

28 Of the sons of Issachar, by their generations and families and houses of their kindreds, by the names of every one from twenty years old and upward, all that could go forth to war,

29 Were reckoned up fifty-four thousand four hundred.

30 Of the sons of Zabulon, by the generations and families and houses of their kindreds, were reckoned up by the names of every one from twenty years old and upward, all that were able to go forth to war,

31 Fifty-seven thousand four hundred.

32 Of the sons of Joseph, namely, of the sons of Ephraim, by the generations and families and houses of their kindreds, were reckoned up by the names of every one, from twenty years old and upward, all that were able to go forth to war,

33 Forty thousand five hundred.

34 Moreover of the sons of Manasses, by the generations and families and houses of their kindreds, were reckoned up by the names of every one from twenty years old and upward, all that could go forth to war,

35 Thirty-two thousand two hundred.

36 Of the sons of Benjamin, by their generations and families and houses of their kindreds, were reckoned up by the names of every one from twenty years old and upward, all that were able to go forth to war,

37 Thirty-five thousand four hundred.

38 Of the sons of Dan, by their generations and families and houses of their kindreds, were reckoned up by the names of every one from twenty years old and upward, all that were able to go forth to war,

39 Sixty-two thousand seven hundred.

40 Of the sons of Aser, by their generations and families and houses of their kindreds, were reckoned up by the names of every one from twenty years old and upward, all that were able to go forth to war,

41 Forty-one thousand and five hundred.

42 Of the sons of Nephtali, by their generations and families and houses of their kindreds, were reckoned up by the names of every one from twenty years old and upward, all that were able to go forth to war,

43 Fifty-three thousand four hundred.

44 These are they who were numbered by Moses and Aaron, and the twelve princes of Israel, every one by the houses of their kindreds.

45 And the whole number of the chil-

dren of Israel by their houses and families, from twenty years old and upward, that were able to go to war,

46 Were six hundred and three thousands five hundred and fifty men.

47 But the Levites in the tribes of their families were not numbered with them.

48 And the Lord spoke to Moses, saying:

49 Number not the tribe of Levi, neither shalt thou put down the sum of them with the children of Israel:

50 But appoint them over the tabernacle of the testimony, and all the vessels thereof, and whatsoever pertaineth to the ceremonies. They shall carry the tabernacle and all the furniture thereof: and they shall minister, and shall camp round about the tabernacle.

51 When you are to go forward, the Levites shall take down the tabernacle: when you are to camp, they shall set it up. What stranger soever cometh to it, shall be slain.

52 And the children of Israel shall camp every man by his troops and bands and army.

53 But the Levites shall pitch their tents round about the tabernacle, lest there come indignation upon the multitude of the children of Israel: and they shall keep watch, and guard the tabernacle of the testimony.

54 And the children of Israel did according to all things which the Lord had commanded Moses.

CHAPTER 2

The order of the tribes in their camp.

AND the Lord spoke to Moses and Aaron, saying:

2 All the children of Israel shall camp by their troops, ensigns, and standards, and the houses of their kindreds, round about the tabernacle of the covenant.

3 On the east Juda shall pitch his tents by the bands of his army: and the prince of his sons shall be Nahasson the son of Aminadab.

4 And the whole sum of the fighting men of his stock, were seventy-four thousand six hundred.

5 Next unto him they of the tribe of Issachar encamped: whose prince was Nathanael, the son of Suar.

6 And the whole number of his fighting men were fifty-four thousand four hundred.

7 In the tribe of Zabulon the prince was Eliab the son of Helon.

8 And all the army of fighting men of his stock, were fifty-seven thousand four hundred.

9 All that were numbered in the camp of Juda, were a hundred and eighty-six thousand four hundred: and they by their troops shall march first.

10 In the camp of the sons of Ruben, on the south side, the prince shall be Elisur the son of Sedeur.

11 And the whole army of his fighting men, that were numbered, were forty-six thousand five hundred.

12 Beside him camped they of the tribe of Simeon: whose prince was Salamiel the son of Surisaddai.

13 And the whole army of his fighting men, that were numbered, were fifty-nine thousand three hundred.

14 In the tribe of Gad the prince was Eliasaph the son of Duel.

15 And the whole army of his fighting men that were numbered, were forty-five thousand six hundred and fifty.

16 All that were reckoned up in the camp of Ruben, were a hundred and fifty-one thousand four hundred and fifty, by their troops: they shall march in the second place.

17 And the tabernacle of the testimony shall be carried by the officers of the Levites and their troops. As it shall be set up, so shall it be taken down. Every one shall march according to their places, and ranks.

18 On the west side shall be the camp of the sons of Ephraim, whose prince was Elisama the son of Ammiud.

19 The whole army of his fighting men, that were numbered, were forty thousand five hundred.

20 And with them the tribe of the sons of Manasses, whose prince was Gamaliel the son of Phadassur.

21 And the whole army of his fighting men, that were numbered, were thirty-two thousand two hundred.

22 In the tribe of the sons of Benjamin the prince was Abidan the son of Gedeon.

23 And the whole army of his fighting men, that were reckoned up, were thirty-five thousand four hundred.

24 All that were numbered in the camp of Ephraim, were a hundred and eight thousand one hundred by their troops: they shall march in the third place.

25 On the north side camped the sons of Dan: whose prince was Ahiezer the son of Ammisaddai.

26 And the whole army of his fighting men, that were numbered, were sixty-two thousand seven hundred.

27 Beside him they of the tribe of Aser pitched their tents: whose prince was Phegiel the son of Ochran.

28 The whole army of his fighting

men, that were numbered, were forty-one thousand five hundred.

29 Of the tribe of the sons of Nephtali the prince was Ahira the son of Enan.

30 The whole army of his fighting men, were fifty-three thousand four hundred.

31 All that were numbered in the camp of Dan, were a hundred and fifty-seven thousand six hundred: and they shall march last.

32 This is the number of the children of Israel, of *their* army divided according to the houses of their kindreds and their troops: six hundred and three thousand five hundred and fifty.

33 And the Levites were not numbered among the children of Israel: for so the Lord had commanded Moses.

34 And the children of Israel did according to all things that the Lord had commanded. They camped by their troops, and marched by the families and houses of their fathers.

CHAPTER 3

The Levites are numbered and their offices distinguished. They are taken in the place of the firstborn of the children of Israel.

THESE are the generations of Aaron and Moses in the day that the Lord spoke to Moses in mount Sinai.

2 ¹ And these the names of the sons of Aaron: his firstborn Nadab, then Abiu, and Eleazar, and Ithamar.

3 These the names of the sons of Aaron the priest that were anointed, and whose hands were filled and consecrated, to do the functions of priesthood.

4 ² Now Nadab and Abiu died, without children, when they offered strange fire before the Lord, in the desert of Sinai: and Eleazar and Ithamar performed the priestly office in the presence of Aaron their father.

5 And the Lord spoke to Moses, saying:

6 Bring the tribe of Levi, and make them stand in the sight of Aaron the priest to minister to him. And let them watch,

7 And observe whatsoever appertaineth to the service of the multitude before the tabernacle of the testimony.

8 And let them keep the vessels of the tabernacle, serving in the ministry thereof.

9 And thou shalt give the Levites for a gift,

10 To Aaron and to his sons, to whom they are delivered by the children of Israel. But thou shalt appoint Aaron and his sons over the service of priest-hood. The stranger that approacheth to minister, shall be put to death.

11 And the Lord spoke to Moses, saying:

12 I have taken the Levites from the children of Israel, for every firstborn that openeth the womb among the children of Israel: and the Levites shall be mine.

13 ³ For every firstborn is mine. Since I struck the firstborn in the land of Egypt, I have sanctified to myself whatsoever is firstborn in Israel both of man and beast. They are mine. I *am* the Lord.

14 And the Lord spoke to Moses in the desert of Sinai, saying:

15 Number the sons of Levi by the houses of their fathers and their families, every male from one month and upward.

16 Moses numbered them as the Lord had commanded.

17 ⁴ And there were found sons of Levi by their names, Gerson and Caath and Merari.

18 The sons of Gerson: Lebni and Semei.

19 The sons of Caath: Amram, and Jessar, Hebron and Oziel.

20 The sons of Merari: Moholi and Musi.

21 Of Gerson were two families, the Lebnites, and the Semeites:

22 Of which were numbered, people of the male sex from one month and upward, seven thousand five hundred.

23 These shall pitch behind the tabernacle on the west,

24 Under their prince Eliasaph the son of Lael.

25 And their charge shall be in the tabernacle of the covenant:

26 The tabernacle itself and the cover thereof; the hanging that is drawn before the doors of the tabernacle of the covenant, and the curtains of the court; the hanging also that is hanged in the entry of the court of the tabernacle, and whatsoever belongeth to the rite of the altar; the cords of the tabernacle, and all the furniture thereof.

27 Of the kindred of Caath come the families of the Amramites and Jesaarites and Hebronites and Ozielites. These are the families of the Caathites reckoned up by their names:

28 All of the male sex from one month and upward, eight thousand six hundred. They shall have the guard of the sanctuary,

29 And shall camp on the south side.

30 And their prince shall be Elisaphan the son of Oziel.

CHAP. 3. ¹ Exod. 6, 23. ² Lev. 10, 1; 1 Par. 24, 2. ³ Exod. 13, 2; Num. 8, 16. ⁴ Exod. 6, 10.

31 And they shall keep the ark, and the table and the candlestick, the altars, and the vessels of the sanctuary, wherewith they minister; and the veil, and all the furniture of this kind.

32 And the prince of the princes of the Levites, Eleazar, the son of Aaron the priest, shall be over them that watch for the guard of the sanctuary.

33 And of Merari are the families of the Moholites, and Musites, reckoned up by their names:

34 All of the male kind from one month and upward, six thousand two hundred.

35 Their prince Suriel the son of Abihaiel. They shall camp on the north side.

36 Under their custody shall be the boards of the tabernacle, and the bars, and the pillars and their sockets, and all things that pertain to this kind of service:

37 And the pillars of the court round about with their sockets, and the pins with their cords.

38 Before the tabernacle of the covenant, that is to say on the east side, shall Moses and Aaron camp, with their sons: having the custody of the sanctuary, in the midst of the children of Israel. What stranger soever cometh unto it, shall be put to death.

39 All the Levites, that Moses and Aaron numbered according to the precept of the Lord, by their families, of the male kind from one month and upward, were twenty-two thousand.

40 And the Lord said to Moses: Number the firstborn of the male sex of the children of Israel, from one month and upward: and thou shalt take the sum of them.

41 And thou shalt take the Levites to me for all the firstborn of the children of Israel. I am the Lord. And their cattle for all the firstborn of the cattle of the children of Israel.

42 Moses reckoned up, as the Lord had commanded, the firstborn of the children of Israel.

43 And the males by their names, from one month and upward, were twenty-two thousand two hundred and seventy-three.

44 And the Lord spoke to Moses, saying:

45 Take the Levites for the firstborn of the children of Israel, and the cattle of the Levites for their cattle: and the Levites shall be mine. I am the Lord.

46 But for the price of the two hundred and seventy-three, of the firstborn of the children of Israel, that exceed the number of the Levites:

47 Thou shalt take five sicles for every head, according to the weight of the sanctuary. [5] A sicle hath twenty obols.

48 And thou shalt give the money to Aaron and his sons: the price of them that are above.

49 Moses therefore took the money of them that were above, and whom they had redeemed from the Levites,

50 For the firstborn of the children of Israel, one thousand three hundred and sixty-five sicles, according to the weight of the sanctuary:

51 And gave it to Aaron and his sons, according to the word that the Lord had commanded him.

CHAPTER 4

*The age and time of the Levites' service.
Their offices and burdens.*

AND the Lord spoke to Moses, and Aaron, saying:

2 Take the sum of the sons of Caath from the midst of the Levites, by their houses and families.

3 From thirty years old and upward, to fifty years old; of all that go in to stand and to minister in the tabernacle of the covenant.

4 This is the service of the sons of Caath.

5 When the camp is to set forward, Aaron and his sons shall go into the tabernacle of the covenant, and the holy of holies, and shall take down the veil that hangeth before the door, and shall wrap up the ark of the testimony in it,

6 And shall cover it again with a cover of violet skins, and shall spread over it a cloth all of violet, and shall put in the bars.

7 They shall wrap up also the table of proposition in a cloth of violet, and shall put with it the censers and little mortars, the cups and bowls to pour out the libations. The loaves shall be always on it.

8 And they shall spread over it a cloth of scarlet, which again they shall cover with a covering of violet skins, and shall put in the bars.

9 They shall take also a cloth of violet wherewith they shall cover the candlestick with the lamps and tongs thereof: and the snuffers and all the oil vessels, which are necessary for the dressing of the lamps.

10 And over all they shall put a cover of violet skins and put in the bars.

11 And they shall wrap up the golden altar also in a cloth of violet: and shall

spread over it a cover of violet skins, and put in the bars.

12 All the vessels wherewith they minister in the sanctuary, they shall wrap up in a cloth of violet: and shall spread over it a cover of violet skins, and put in the bars.

13 They shall cleanse the altar also from the ashes: and shall wrap it up in a purple cloth,

14 And shall put it with all the vessels that they use in the ministry thereof: that is to say, firepans, fleshhooks and forks, pothooks and shovels. They shall cover all the vessels of the altar together with a covering of violet skins: and shall put in the bars.

15 And when Aaron and his sons have wrapped up the sanctuary and the vessels thereof at the removing of the camp, then shall the [1] sons of Caath enter in to carry the things wrapped up. And they shall not touch the vessels of the sanctuary, lest they die. These are the burdens of the sons of Caath in the tabernacle of the covenant.

16 And over them shall be Eleazar the son of Aaron the priest, to whose charge pertaineth the oil to dress the lamps, and the sweet incense, and the sacrifice, that is always offered, and the oil of unction: and whatsoever pertaineth to the service of the tabernacle, and of all the vessels that are in the sanctuary.

17 And the Lord spoke to Moses and Aaron, saying:

18 Destroy not the people of Caath from the midst of the Levites.

19 But do this to them, that they may live, and not die, by touching the holies of holies. Aaron and his sons shall go in, and they shall appoint every man his work: and shall divide the burdens that every man is to carry.

20 Let not others by any curiosity see the things that are in the sanctuary before they be wrapped up. Otherwise they shall die.

21 And the Lord spoke to Moses, saying:

22 Take the sum of the sons of Gerson also by their houses and families and kindreds.

23 From thirty years old and upward, unto fifty years old. Number them all that go in and minister in the tabernacle of the covenant.

24 This is the office of the family of the Gersonites.

25 To carry the curtains of the tabernacle and the roof of the covenant, the other covering, and the violet covering over all, and the hanging that hangeth

in the entry of the tabernacle of the covenant:

26 The curtains of the court, and the veil in the entry that is before the tabernacle. All things that pertain to the altar, the cords and the vessels of the ministry,

27 The sons of Gerson shall carry, by the commandment of Aaron and his sons. And each man shall know to what burden he must be assigned.

28 This is the service of the family of the Gersonites in the tabernacle of the covenant: and they shall be under the hand of Ithamar the son of Aaron the priest.

29 Thou shalt reckon up the sons of Merari also by the families and houses of their fathers,

30 From thirty years old and upward, unto fifty years old, all that go in to the office of their ministry, and to the service of the covenant of the testimony.

31 These are their burdens. They shall carry the boards of the tabernacle and the bars thereof, the pillars and their sockets:

32 The pillars also of the court round about, with their sockets and pins and cords. They shall receive by account all the vessels and furniture: and so shall carry them.

33 This is the office of the family of the Merarites, and their ministry in the tabernacle of the covenant: and they shall be under the hand of Ithamar the son of Aaron the priest.

34 So Moses and Aaron and the princes of the synagogue reckoned up the sons of Caath, by their kindreds and the houses of their fathers,

35 From thirty years old and upward, unto fifty years old, all that go in to the ministry of the tabernacle of the covenant.

36 And they were found two thousand seven hundred and fifty.

37 This is the number of the people of Caath that go in to the tabernacle of the covenant: these did Moses and Aaron number according to the word of the Lord by the hand of Moses.

38 The sons of Gerson also were numbered by the kindreds and houses of their fathers,

39 From thirty years old and upward, unto fifty years old, all that go in to minister in the tabernacle of the covenant.

40 And they were found two thousand six hundred and thirty.

41 This is the people of the Gersonites, whom Moses and Aaron numbered according to the word of the Lord.

42 The sons of Merari also were num-

bered by the kindreds and houses of their fathers.

43 From thirty years old and upward, unto fifty years old, all that go in to fulfil the rites of the tabernacle of the covenant.

44 And they were found three thousand two hundred.

45 This is the number of the sons of Merari, whom Moses and Aaron reckoned up according to the commandment of the Lord by the hand of Moses.

46 All that were reckoned up of the Levites, and whom Moses and Aaron and the princes of Israel took by name, by the kindreds and houses of their fathers,

47 From thirty years old and upward, until fifty years old, that go into the ministry of the tabernacle, and to carry the burdens,

48 Were in all eight thousand five hundred and eighty.

49 Moses reckoned them up according to the word of the Lord, every one according to their office and burdens, as the Lord had commanded him.

CHAPTER 5

The unclean are removed out of the camp. Confession of sins, and satisfaction. Firstfruits and oblations belonging to the priests. Trial of jealousy.

AND the Lord spoke to Moses, saying:

2 Command the children of Israel, that they cast out of the camp every leper, and whosoever hath an issue of seed, or is defiled by the dead.

3 Whether it be man or woman, cast ye them out of the camp: lest they defile it when I shall dwell with you.

4 And the children of Israel did so: and they cast them forth without the camp, as the Lord had spoken to Moses.

5 And the Lord spoke to Moses, saying:

6 Say to the children of Israel: When a man or woman shall have committed any of all the sins that men are wont to commit, and by negligence shall have transgressed the commandment of the Lord, and offended:

7 They shall confess their sin, and restore the principal itself, and the fifth part over and above, to him against whom they have sinned.

8 But if there be no one to receive it, they shall give it to the Lord, and it shall be the priest's: besides the ram that is offered for expiation, to be an atoning sacrifice.

9 All the firstfruits also, which the children of Israel offer, belong to the priest.

10 And whatsoever is offered into the sanctuary by every one, and is delivered into the hands of the priest, it shall be his.

11 And the Lord spoke to Moses, saying:

12 Speak to the children of Israel, and thou shalt say to them: The man whose wife shall have gone astray, and contemning her husband,

13 Shall have slept with another man, and her husband cannot discover it, but the adultery is secret, and cannot be proved by witnesses, because she was not found in the adultery:

14 If the spirit of jealousy stir up the husband against his wife, who either is defiled, or is charged with false suspicion:

15 He shall bring her to the priest, and shall offer an oblation for her, the tenth part of a measure of barley meal. He shall not pour oil thereon, nor put frankincense upon it: because it is a sacrifice of jealousy, and an oblation searching out adultery.

16 The priest therefore shall offer it, and set it before the Lord.

17 And he shall take holy water in an earthen vessel: and he shall cast a little earth of the pavement of the tabernacle into it.

18 And when the woman shall stand before the Lord, he shall uncover her head: and shall put on her hands the sacrifice of remembrance, and the oblation of jealousy. And he himself shall hold the most bitter waters, whereon he hath heaped curses with execration.

19 And he shall adjure her, and shall say: If another man hath not slept with thee, and if thou be not defiled by forsaking thy husband's bed, these most bitter waters, on which I have heaped curses, shall not hurt thee.

20 But if thou hast gone aside from thy husband, and art defiled, and hast lain with another man:

21 These curses shall light upon thee. The Lord make thee a curse, and an example for all among his people. May he make thy thigh to rot: and may thy belly swell and burst asunder.

22 Let the cursed waters enter into thy belly: and may thy womb swell and thy thigh rot. And the woman shall answer: Amen, amen.

23 And the priest shall write these curses in a book, and shall wash them out with the most bitter waters, upon which he hath heaped the curses.

CHAP. 5. Ver. 7. *Shall confess.* This confession and satisfaction, ordained in the Old Law, was a figure of the sacrament of penance.
Ver. 14. *The spirit of jealousy.* This ordinance was designed to clear the innocent, and to prevent jealous husbands from doing mischief to their wives; as likewise to give all a horror of adultery, by punishing it in so remarkable a manner.

24 And he shall give them her to drink. And when she hath drunk them up,

25 The priest shall take from her hand the sacrifice of jealousy: and shall elevate it before the Lord, and shall put it upon the altar. Yet so as first,

26 To take a handful of the sacrifice of that which is offered, and burn it upon the altar: and so give the most bitter waters to the woman to drink.

27 And when she hath drunk them, if she be defiled, and having despised her husband be guilty of adultery, the malediction shall go through her: and *her* belly swelling, *her* thigh shall rot. And the woman shall be a curse, and an example to all the people.

28 But if she be not defiled, she shall not be hurt, and shall bear children.

29 This is the law of jealousy. If a woman hath gone aside from her husband, and be defiled,

30 And the husband stirred up by the spirit of jealousy bring her before the Lord, and the priest do to her according to all things that are *here* written,

31 The husband shall be blameless, and she shall bear her iniquity.

CHAPTER 6

The law of the Nazarites: the form of blessing the people.

AND the Lord spoke to Moses, saying:

2 Speak to the children of Israel, and thou shalt say to them: When a man, or woman, shall make a vow to be sanctified, and will consecrate themselves to the Lord:

3 They shall abstain from wine, and from every thing that may make a man drunk. They shall not drink vinegar of wine, or of any other drink: nor any thing that is pressed out of the grape. Nor shall they eat grapes either fresh or dried.

4 All the days that they are consecrated to the Lord by vow, they shall eat nothing that cometh of the vineyard, from the raisin even to the kernel.

5 All the time of his separation [1] no razor shall pass over his head, until the day be fulfilled of his consecration to the Lord. He shall be holy, and shall let the hair of his head grow.

6 All the time of his consecration he shall not go into any dead.

7 Neither shall he make himself unclean, even for his father, or for his mother, or for his brother, or for his sister, when they die: because the consecration of his God is upon his head.

8 All the days of his separation he shall be holy to the Lord.

CHAP. 6. [1] Judges, 13, 5. [2] Acts, 21, 24.

9 But if any man die suddenly before him, the head of his consecration shall be defiled. And he shall shave it forthwith on the same day of his purification: and again on the seventh day.

10 And on the eighth day he shall bring two turtles, or two young pigeons to the priest in the entry of the covenant of the testimony.

11 And the priest shall offer one for sin, and the other for a holocaust: and shall pray for him, for that he hath sinned by the dead. And he shall sanctify his head that day.

12 And shall consecrate to the Lord the days of his separation, offering a lamb of one year for sin: yet so that the former days be made void, because his sanctification was profaned.

13 This is the law of consecration. When the days which he had determined by vow shall be expired, he shall bring him to the door of the tabernacle of the covenant:

14 And shall offer his oblation to the Lord: one he-lamb of a year old without blemish for a holocaust, and one ewe lamb of a year old without blemish for a sin offering, and one ram without blemish for a victim of peace offering:

15 A basket also of unleavened bread, tempered with oil, and wafers without leaven anointed with oil, and the libations of each.

16 And the priest shall present them before the Lord: and shall offer both the sin offering and the holocaust.

17 But the ram he shall immolate for a sacrifice of peace offering to the Lord: offering at the same time the basket of unleavened bread, and the libations that are due by custom.

18 [2] Then shall the hair of the consecration of the Nazarite, be shaved off before the door of the tabernacle of the covenant. And he shall take his hair, and lay it upon the fire, which is under the sacrifice of the peace offerings.

19 And shall take the boiled shoulder of the ram, and one unleavened cake out of the basket, and one unleavened wafer: and he shall deliver them into the hands of the Nazarite, after his head is shaven.

20 And receiving them again from him, he shall elevate them in the sight of the Lord. And they being sanctified shall belong to the priest, as the breast, which was commanded to be separated, and the shoulder. After this the Nazarite may drink wine.

21 This is the law of the Nazarite, when he hath vowed his oblation to the Lord in the time of his consecration. Besides those things which his hand shall find, according to that which he

had vowed in his mind, so shall he do for the fulfilling of his sanctification.

22 And the Lord spoke to Moses, saying:

23 Say to Aaron and his sons: Thus shall you bless the children of Israel, and you shall say to them:

24 ³ The Lord bless thee, and keep thee.

25 The Lord shew his face to thee, and have mercy on thee.

26 The Lord turn his countenance to thee, and give thee peace.

27 And they shall invoke my name upon the children of Israel: and I will bless them.

CHAPTER 7

The offerings of the princes at the dedication of the tabernacle. God speaketh to Moses from the propitiatory.

AND it came to pass in the day that Moses had finished the tabernacle, ¹ and set it up, and had anointed and sanctified *it* with all its vessels, the altar likewise and all the vessels thereof:

2 The princes of Israel and the heads of the families, in every tribe, who were the rulers of them who had been numbered, offered

3 Their gifts before the Lord: six wagons covered, and twelve oxen. Two princes offered one wagon, and each one an ox: and they offered them before the tabernacle.

4 And the Lord said to Moses:

5 Receive them from them to serve in the ministry of the tabernacle: and thou shalt deliver them to the Levites according to the order of their ministry.

6 Moses therefore receiving the wagons and the oxen, delivered them to the Levites.

7 Two wagons and four oxen he gave to the sons of Gerson, according to their necessity.

8 The other four wagons, and eight oxen he gave to the sons of Merari, according to their offices and service, under the hand of Ithamar the son of Aaron the priest.

9 But to the sons of Caath he gave no wagons or oxen: because they serve in the sanctuary and carry their burdens upon their own shoulders.

10 And the princes offered for the dedication of the altar on the day when it was anointed, their oblation before the altar.

11 And the Lord said to Moses: Let each of the princes one day after another offer their gifts for the dedication of the altar.

12 The first day Nahasson the son of Aminadab of the tribe of Juda offered his offering.

13 And his offering was a silver dish weighing one hundred and thirty sicles: a silver bowl of seventy sicles according to the weight of the sanctuary, both full of flour tempered with oil for a sacrifice:

14 A little mortar of ten sicles of gold full of incense:

15 An ox of the herd, and a ram, and a lamb of a year old for a holocaust:

16 And a buck-goat for sin:

17 And for the sacrifice of peace offerings, two oxen, five rams, five he-goats, five lambs of a year old. This was the offering of Nahasson the son of Aminadab.

18 The second day Nathanael the son of Suar, prince of the tribe of Issachar, made his offering.

19 A silver dish weighing one hundred and thirty sicles: a silver bowl of seventy sicles, according to the weight of the sanctuary, both full of flour tempered with oil for a sacrifice:

20 A little mortar of gold weighing ten sicles full of incense:

21 An ox of the herd, and a ram, and a lamb of a year old for a holocaust:

22 And a buck-goat for sin:

23 And for the sacrifice of peace offerings, two oxen, five rams, five buck-goats, five lambs of a year old. This was the offering of Nathanael the son of Suar.

24 The third day the prince of the sons of Zabulon, Eliab the son of Helon,

25 Offered a silver dish weighing one hundred and thirty sicles: a silver bowl of seventy sicles by the weight of the sanctuary, both full of flour tempered with oil for a sacrifice:

26 A little mortar of gold weighing ten sicles full of incense:

27 An ox of the herd, and a ram, and a lamb of a year old for a holocaust:

28 And a buck-goat for sin:

29 And for the sacrifice of peace offerings, two oxen, five rams, five buck-goats, five lambs of a year old. This is the oblation of Eliab the son of Helon.

30 The fourth day the prince of the sons of Ruben, Elisur the son of Sedeur,

31 Offered a silver dish weighing one hundred and thirty sicles: a silver bowl of seventy sicles according to the weight of the sanctuary, both full of flour tempered with oil for a sacrifice:

32 A little mortar of gold weighing ten sicles full of incense:

33 An ox of the herd, and a ram, and a lamb of a year old, for a holocaust:

³ Ecclus. 36, 19. Chap. 7. ¹ Exod. 40, 16.

34 And a buck-goat for sin:

35 And for victims of peace offerings two oxen, five rams, five buck-goats, five lambs of a year old. This was the offering of Elisur the son of Sedeur.

36 The fifth day the prince of the sons of Simeon, Salamiel the son of Surisaddai,

37 Offered a silver dish weighing one hundred and thirty sicles: a silver bowl of seventy sicles after the weight of the sanctuary, both full of flour tempered with oil for a sacrifice:

38 A little mortar of gold weighing ten sicles full of incense:

39 An ox of the herd, and a ram, and a lamb of a year old for a holocaust:

40 And a buck-goat for sin:

41 And for sacrifices of peace offerings, two oxen, five rams, five buck-goats, five lambs of a year old. This was the offering of Salamiel the son of Surisaddai.

42 The sixth day the prince of the sons of Gad, Eliasaph the son of Duel,

43 Offered a silver dish weighing a hundred and thirty sicles: a silver bowl of seventy sicles by the weight of the sanctuary, both full of flour tempered with oil for a sacrifice:

44 A little mortar of gold weighing ten sicles full of incense:

45 An ox of the herd, and a ram, and a lamb of a year old for a holocaust:

46 And a buck-goat for sin:

47 And for sacrifices of peace offerings, two oxen, five rams, five buck-goats, five lambs of a year old. This was the offering of Eliasaph the son of Duel.

48 The seventh day the prince of the sons of Ephraim, Elisama the son of Ammiud,

49 Offered a silver dish weighing a hundred and thirty sicles: a silver bowl of seventy sicles according to the weight of the sanctuary, both full of flour tempered with oil for a sacrifice:

50 A little mortar of gold weighing ten sicles full of incense:

51 An ox of the herd, and a ram, and a lamb of a year old for a holocaust:

52 And a buck-goat for sin:

53 And for sacrifices of peace offerings, two oxen, five rams, five buck-goats, five lambs of a year old. This was the offering of Elisama the son of Ammiud.

54 The eighth day the prince of the sons of Manasses, Gamaliel the son of Phadassur,

55 Offered a silver dish weighing a hundred and thirty sicles: a silver bowl of seventy sicles, according to the weight of the sanctuary, both full of flour tempered with oil for a sacrifice:

56 A little mortar of gold weighing ten sicles full of incense:

57 An ox of the herd, and a ram, and a lamb of a year old for a holocaust:

58 And a buck-goat for sin:

59 And for sacrifices of peace offerings, two oxen, five rams, five buck-goats, five lambs of a year old. This was the offering of Gamaliel the son of Phadassur.

60 The ninth day the prince of the sons of Benjamin, Abidan the son of Gedeon,

61 Offered a silver dish weighing a hundred and thirty sicles: a silver bowl of seventy sicles by the weight of the sanctuary, both full of flour tempered with oil for a sacrifice:

62 A little mortar of gold weighing ten sicles full of incense:

63 An ox of the herd, and a ram, and a lamb of a year old for a holocaust:

64 And a buck-goat for sin:

65 And for sacrifices of peace offerings, two oxen, five rams, five buck-goats, five lambs of a year old. This was the offering of Abidan the son of Gedeon.

66 The tenth day the prince of the sons of Dan, Ahiezer the son of Ammisaddai,

67 Offered a silver dish weighing a hundred and thirty sicles: a silver bowl of seventy sicles, according to the weight of the sanctuary, both full of flour tempered with oil for a sacrifice:

68 A little mortar of gold weighing ten sicles full of incense:

69 An ox of the herd, and a ram, and a lamb of a year old, for a holocaust:

70 And a buck-goat for sin:

71 And for sacrifices of peace offerings, two oxen, five rams, five buck-goats, five lambs of a year old. This was the offering of Ahiezer the son of Ammisaddai.

72 The eleventh day the prince of the sons of Aser, Phegiel the son of Ochran,

73 Offered a silver dish weighing a hundred and thirty sicles: a silver bowl of seventy sicles, according to the weight of the sanctuary, both full of flour tempered with oil for a sacrifice:

74 A little mortar of gold weighing ten sicles full of incense:

75 An ox of the herd, and a ram, and a lamb of a year old for a holocaust:

76 And a buck-goat for sin:

77 And for sacrifices of peace offerings, two oxen, five rams, five buck-goats, five lambs of a year old. This was the offering of Phegiel the son of Ochran.

78 The twelfth day the prince of the sons of Nephtali, Ahira the son of Enan,

79 Offered a silver dish weighing a hundred and thirty sicles: a silver bowl of seventy sicles, according to the weight of the sanctuary, both full of flour tempered with oil for a sacrifice:

80 A little mortar of gold weighing ten sicles full of incense:

81 An ox of the herd, and a ram, and a lamb of a year old for a holocaust:

82 And a buck-goat for sin:

83 And for sacrifices of peace offerings, two oxen, five rams, five buck-goats, five lambs of a year old. This was the offering of Ahira the son of Enan.

84 These were the offerings made by the princes of Israel in the dedication of the altar, in the day wherein it was consecrated. Twelve dishes of silver: twelve silver bowls: twelve little mortars of gold:

85 Each dish weighing a hundred and thirty sicles of silver, and each bowl seventy sicles: that is, putting all the vessels of silver together, two thousand four hundred sicles, by the weight of the sanctuary.

86 Twelve little mortars of gold full of incense, weighing ten sicles apiece, by the weight of the sanctuary: that is, in all a hundred and twenty sicles of gold.

87 Twelve oxen out of the herd for a holocaust, twelve rams, twelve lambs of a year old, and their libations: twelve buck-goats for sin.

88 And for sacrifices of peace offerings, oxen twenty-four, rams sixty, buck-goats sixty, lambs of a year old sixty. These things were offered in the dedication of the altar, when it was anointed.

89 And when Moses entered into the tabernacle of the covenant, to consult the oracle, he heard the voice of one speaking to him from the propitiatory, that was over the ark between the two cherubims: and from this place he spoke to him.

CHAPTER 8

The seven lamps are placed on the golden candlestick, to shine towards the loaves of proposition. The ordination of the Levites. And to what age they shall serve in the tabernacle.

AND the Lord spoke to Moses, saying:

2 Speak to Aaron, and thou shalt say to him: When thou shalt place the seven lamps, let the candlestick be set up on the south side. Give orders therefore that the lamps look over against the north, towards the table of the loaves of proposition. Over against

that part shall they give light, towards which the candlestick looketh.

3 And Aaron did so: and he put the lamps upon the candlestick, as the Lord had commanded Moses.

4 Now this was the work of the candlestick. It was of beaten gold, both the shaft in the middle, and all that came out of both sides of the branches. According to the pattern which the Lord had shewn to Moses, so he made the candlestick.

5 And the Lord spoke to Moses, saying:

6 Take the Levites out of the midst of the children of Israel: and thou shalt purify them,

7 According to this rite. Let them be sprinkled with the water of purification, and let them shave all the hairs of their flesh. And when they shall have washed their garments, and are cleansed,

8 They shall take an ox of the herd, and for the offering thereof fine flour tempered with oil. And thou shalt take another ox of the herd for a sin offering.

9 And thou shalt bring the Levites before the tabernacle of the covenant, calling together all the multitude of the children of Israel.

10 And when the Levites are before the Lord, the children of Israel shall put their hands upon them.

11 And Aaron shall offer the Levites, as a gift in the sight of the Lord from the children of Israel, that they may serve in his ministry.

12 The Levites also shall put their hands upon the heads of the oxen: of which thou shalt sacrifice one for sin, and the other for a holocaust to the Lord, to pray for them.

13 And thou shalt set the Levites in the sight of Aaron and of his sons: and shalt consecrate them being offered to the Lord.

14 And shalt separate them from the midst of the children of Israel, to be mine.

15 And afterwards they shall enter into the tabernacle of the covenant, to serve me. And thus shalt thou purify and consecrate them for an oblation of the Lord: for as a gift they were given me by the children of Israel.

16 [1] I have taken them instead of the firstborn that open every womb in Israel.

17 For all the firstborn of the children of Israel, both of men and of

---

CHAP. 8. [1] Exod. 13, 2; Num. 3, 13; Luke, 2, 23.

CHAP. 8. Ver. 7. *Let them be sprinkled with the water of purification.* That was the holy water mixed with the ashes of the red cow (Num. 19), appointed for purifying all that were unclean. It was a figure of the blood of Christ, applied to our souls by his holy sacraments.

beasts, are mine. From the day that I slew every firstborn in the land of Egypt, have I sanctified them to myself.

18 And I have taken the Levites for all the firstborn of the children of Israel:

19 And have delivered them for a gift to Aaron and his sons out of the midst of the people, to serve me for Israel in the tabernacle of the covenant, and to pray for them, lest there should be a plague among the people, if they should presume to approach unto my sanctuary.

20 And Moses and Aaron and all the multitude of the children of Israel did with the Levites all that the Lord had commanded Moses.

21 And they were purified, and washed ,their garments. And Aaron lifted them up in the sight of the Lord, and prayed for them,

22 That being purified they might go into the tabernacle of the covenant to do their services before Aaron and his sons. As the Lord had commanded Moses touching the Levites, so was it done.

23 And the Lord spoke to Moses, saying:

24 This is the law of the Levites: From twenty-five years old and upwards, they shall go in to minister in the tabernacle of the covenant.

25 And when they shall have accomplished the fiftieth year of their age, they shall cease to serve.

26 And they shall be the ministers of their brethren in the tabernacle of the covenant, to keep the things that are committed to their care: but not to do the works. Thus shalt thou order the Levites touching their charge.

CHAPTER 9

The precept of the pasch is renewed. The unclean and travellers are to observe it the second month. The camp is guided by the pillar of the cloud.

THE Lord spoke to Moses in the desert of Sinai, the second year after they were come out of the land of Egypt, in the first month, saying:

2 [1] Let the children of Israel make the phase in its due time,

3 The fourteenth day of this month in the evening, according to all the ceremonies and justifications thereof.

4 And Moses commanded the chil-

CHAP. 9. [1] Exod. 12, 3. [2] Exod. 12, 46; John, 19, 36. [3] Exod. 40, 16; Num. 7, 1. [4] 1 Cor. 10, 1.

CHAP. 9. Ver. 2. *Make the phase.* That is, keep the paschal solemnity, and eat the paschal lamb.

Ver. 6. *Behold some who were unclean by occasion of the soul of a man.* That is, by having touched or come near a dead body, out of which the soul was departed.

dren of Israel that they should make the phase.

5 And they made it in its proper time: the fourteenth day of the month at evening, in mount Sinai. The children of Israel did according to all things that the Lord had commanded Moses.

6 But, behold, some who were unclean by occasion of the soul of a man, who could not make the phase on that day, coming to Moses and Aaron,

7 Said to them: We are unclean by occasion of the soul of a man. Why are we kept back that we may not offer in its season the offering to the Lord among the children of Israel?

8 And Moses answered them: Stay that I may consult the Lord what he will ordain concerning you.

9 And the Lord spoke to Moses, saying:

10 Say to the children of Israel: The man that shall be unclean by occasion of one that is dead, or shall be in a journey afar off in your nation, let him make the phase to the Lord.

11 In the second month, on the fourteenth day of the month in the evening, they shall eat it with unleavened bread and wild lettuce.

12 They shall not leave any thing thereof until morning, [2] nor break a bone thereof: they shall observe all the ceremonies of the phase.

13 But if any man is clean, and was not on a journey, and did not make the phase, that soul shall be cut off from among his people. Because he offered not sacrifice to the Lord in due season, he shall bear his sin.

14 The sojourner also and the stranger if they be among you, shall make the phase to the Lord according to the ceremonies and justifications thereof. The same ordinance shall be with you both for the stranger, and for him that was born in the land.

15 [3] Now on the day that the tabernacle was reared up, a cloud covered it. But from the evening there was over the tabernacle, as it were, the appearance of fire until the morning.

16 So it was always: by day the cloud covered it, and by night, as it were, the appearance of fire.

17 And when the cloud that covered the tabernacle was taken up, then the children of Israel marched forward: and in the place where the cloud stood still, there they camped.

18 At the commandment of the Lord they marched, and at his commandment they pitched the tabernacle. [4] All the days that the cloud abode over the tabernacle, they remained in the same place.

19 And if it was so that it continued over it a long time: the children of Israel kept the watches of the Lord, and marched not,

20 For as many days soever as the cloud stayed over the tabernacle. At the commandment of the Lord they pitched their tents: and at his commandment they took them down.

21 If the cloud tarried from evening until morning, and immediately at break of day left the tabernacle, they marched forward. And if it departed after a day and a night, they took down their tents.

22 But if it remained over the tabernacle for two days or a month or a longer time, the children of Israel remained in the same place, and marched not. But immediately as soon as it departed, they removed the camp.

23 By the word of the Lord they pitched their tents, and by his word they marched: and kept the watches of the Lord according to his commandment by the hand of Moses.

CHAPTER 10

The silver trumpets and their use. They march from Sinai.

AND the Lord spoke to Moses, saying:

2 Make thee two trumpets of beaten silver, wherewith thou mayest call together the multitude when the camp is to be removed.

3 And when thou shalt sound the trumpets, all the multitude shall gather unto thee to the door of the tabernacle of the covenant.

4 If thou sound but once, the princes and the heads of the multitude of Israel shall come to thee.

5 But if the sound of the trumpets be longer, and with interruptions, they that are on the east side, shall first go forward.

6 And at the second sounding and like noise of the trumpet, they who lie on the south side shall take up their tents. And after this manner shall the rest do, when the trumpets shall sound for a march.

7 But when the people is to be gathered together, the sound of the trumpets shall be plain: and they shall not make a broken sound.

8 And the sons of Aaron the priest shall sound the trumpets: and this shall be an ordinance for ever in your generations.

9 If you go forth to war out of your land against the enemies that fight against you, you shall sound aloud with the trumpets: and there shall be a remembrance of you before the Lord your God, that you may be delivered out of the hands of your enemies.

10 If at any time you shall have a banquet, and on your festival days, and on the first days of your months, you shall sound the trumpets over the holocausts, and the sacrifices of peace offerings, that they may be to you for a remembrance of your God. I am the Lord your God.

11 The second year, in the second month, the twentieth day of the month, the cloud was taken up from the tabernacle of the covenant.

12 And the children of Israel marched by their troops from the desert of Sinai: and the cloud rested in the wilderness of Pharan.

13 And the first went forward according to the commandment of the Lord by the hand of Moses.

14 [1] The sons of Juda by their troops: whose prince was Nahasson the son of Aminadab.

15 In the tribe of the sons of Issachar, the prince was Nathanael the son of Suar.

16 In the tribe of Zabulon, the prince was Eliab the son of Helon.

17 And the tabernacle was taken down: and the sons of Gerson and Merari set forward, bearing it.

18 And the sons of Ruben also marched, by their troops and ranks: whose prince was Helisur the son of Sedeur.

19 And in the tribe of Simeon, the prince was Salamiel the son of Surisaddai.

20 And in the tribe of Gad, the prince was Eliasaph the son of Duel.

21 Then the Caathites also marched carrying the sanctuary. So long was the tabernacle carried, till they came to the place of setting it up.

22 The sons of Ephraim also moved their camp by their troops: in whose army the prince was Elisama the son of Ammiud.

23 And in the tribe of the sons of Manasses, the prince was Gamaliel the son of Phadassur.

24 And in the tribe of Benjamin, the prince was Abidan the son of Gedeon.

25 The last of all the camp marched the sons of Dan by their troops: in whose army the prince was Ahiezer the son of Ammisaddai.

26 And in the tribe of the sons of Aser, the prince was Phegiel the son of Ochran.

27 And in the tribe of the sons of Nephtali, the prince was Ahira the son of Enan.

28 This was the order of the camps,

CHAP. 10. [1] Num. 1, 7.

and marches of the children of Israel by their troops, when they set forward.

29 And Moses said to Hobab the son of Raguel the Madianite, his kinsman: We are going towards the place which the Lord will give us. Come with us, that we may do thee good: for the Lord hath promised good things to Israel.

30 But he answered him: I will not go with thee, but I will return to my ³country, wherein I was born.

31 And he said: Do not leave us: for thou knowest in what places we should encamp in the wilderness, and thou shalt be our guide.

32 And if thou comest with us, we will give thee what is the best of the riches which the Lord shall deliver to us.

33 So they marched from the mount of the Lord three days' journey: and the ark of the covenant of the Lord went before them, for three days providing a place for the camp.

34 The cloud also of the Lord was over them by day when they marched.

35 And when the ark was lifted up Moses said: ³Arise, O Lord, and let thine enemies be scattered: and let them that hate thee, flee from before thy face.

36 And when it was set down, he said: Return, O Lord, to the multitude of the host of Israel.

CHAPTER 11

The people murmur, and are punished with fire. God appointeth seventy ancients for assistants to Moses. They prophesy. The people have their fill of flesh, but forthwith many die of the plague.

IN the mean time there arose a ¹murmuring of the people against the Lord, as it were repining at their fatigue. And when the Lord heard it, he was angry. ²And the fire of the Lord being kindled against them, devoured them that were at the uttermost part of the camp.

2 And when the people cried to Moses, Moses prayed to the Lord, and the fire was swallowed up.

³Exod. 18, 27. ³Ps. 47, 2. CHAP. 11. ¹Num. 33, 16; Ps. 77, 19; 1 Cor. 10, 10. ²Ps. 77, 21. ³1 Cor. 10, 3. ⁴Exod. 16, 14; Ps. 77, 24; Wisd. 16, 20; John, 6, 31.

CHAP. 11. Ver. 3. *The burning.* Hebrew, *Taberah.*
Ver. 3. *A mixt multitude.* These were people that came with them out of Egypt, who were not of the race of Israel; who, by their murmuring, drew also the children of Israel to murmur. This should teach us the danger of associating ourselves with the children of Egypt, that is, with the lovers and admirers of this wicked world.
Ver. 7. *Bdellium. Bdellium,* according to Pliny, was of the colour of a man's nail, white and bright.
Ver. 16. *Seventy men.* This was the first institution of the council or senate, called the *Sanhedrim,* consisting of seventy or seventy-two senators or counsellors.

3 And he called the name of that place, The burning: for that the fire of the Lord had been kindled against them.

4 For a mixt multitude of people, that came up with them, burned with desire, sitting and weeping, (the children of Israel also being joined with them,) and said: ³Who shall give us flesh to eat?

5 We remember the fish that we ate in Egypt free cost. The cucumbers come into our mind, and the melons, and the leeks, and the onions, and the garlic.

6 Our soul is dry: our eyes behold nothing else but manna.

7 ⁴Now the manna was like coriander seed, of the colour of bdellium.

8 And the people went about, and gathering it, ground it in a mill, or beat it in a mortar, and boiled it in a pot: and made cakes thereof of the taste of bread tempered with oil.

9 And when the dew fell in the night upon the camp, the manna also fell with it.

10 Now Moses heard the people weeping by their families, every one at the door of his tent. And the wrath of the Lord was exceedingly enkindled. To Moses also the thing seemed insupportable.

11 And he said to the Lord: Why hast thou afflicted thy servant? Wherefore do I not find favour before thee? And why hast thou laid the weight of all this people upon me?

12 Have I conceived all this multitude, or begotten them, that thou shouldst say to me: Carry them in thy bosom, as the nurse is wont to carry the little infant: and bear them into the land, for which thou hast sworn to their fathers?

13 Whence should I have flesh to give to so great a multitude? They weep against me, saying: Give us flesh that we may eat.

14 I am not able alone to bear all this people, because it is too heavy for me.

15 But if it seem unto thee otherwise, I beseech thee to kill me: and let me find grace in thy eyes, that I be not afflicted with so great evils.

16 And the Lord said to Moses: Gather unto me seventy men of the ancients of Israel, whom thou knowest to be ancients and masters of the people. And thou shalt bring them to the door of the tabernacle of the covenant: and shalt make them stand there with thee,

17 That I may come down and speak

with thee. And I will take of thy spirit, and will give to them, that they may bear with thee the burden of the people: and thou mayest not be burthened alone.

18 And thou shalt say to the people: Be ye sanctified: to-morrow you shall eat flesh. For I have heard you say: Who will give us flesh to eat? It was well with us in Egypt. That the Lord may give you flesh, and you may eat:

19 Not for one day, nor two, nor five, nor ten, no nor for twenty.

20 But even for a month of days, till it come out at your nostrils, and become loathsome to you. Because you have cast off the Lord, who is in the midst of you, and have wept before him, saying: Why came we out of Egypt?

21 And Moses said: There are six hundred thousand footmen of this people, and sayest thou: I will give them flesh to eat a whole month?

22 ⁵ Shall then a multitude of sheep and oxen be killed, that it may suffice for their food? Or shall the fishes of the sea be gathered together to fill them?

23 And the Lord answered him: ⁶ Is the hand of the Lord unable? Thou shalt presently see whether my word shall come to pass or no.

24 Moses therefore came, and told the people the words of the Lord, and assembled seventy men of the ancients of Israel, and made them to stand about the tabernacle.

25 And the Lord came down in a cloud, and spoke to him, taking away of the spirit that was in Moses, and giving to the seventy men. And when the spirit had rested on them they prophesied, nor did they cease afterwards.

26 Now there remained in the camp two of the men, of whom one was called Eldad, and the other Medad, upon whom the spirit rested; for they also had been enrolled, but were not gone forth to the tabernacle.

27 And when they prophesied in the camp, there ran a young man, and told Moses, saying: Eldad and Medad prophesy in the camp.

28 Forthwith Josue the son of Nun, the minister of Moses, and chosen out of many, said: My lord Moses, forbid them.

29 But he said: Why hast thou emulation for me? O that all the people might prophesy, and that the Lord would give them his spirit!

30 And Moses returned, with the ancients of Israel, into the camp.

31 ⁷ And a wind going out from the Lord, taking quails up beyond the sea, brought them, and cast them into the camp for the space of one day's journey, on every side of the camp round about: and they flew in the air two cubits high above the ground.

32 The people therefore rising up all that day, and night, and the next day, gathered together of quails, he that did least, ten cores: and they dried them round about the camp.

33 ⁸ As yet the flesh was between their teeth, neither had that kind of meat failed: when, behold, the wrath of the Lord being provoked against the people, struck them with an exceeding great plague.

34 And that place was called, The graves of lust: for there they buried the people that had lusted. And departing from the graves of lust, they came unto Haseroth, and abode there.

CHAPTER 12

Mary and Aaron murmur against Moses, whom God praiseth above other prophets. Mary being struck with leprosy, Aaron confesseth his fault. Moses prayeth for her, and after seven days' separation from the camp, she is restored.

AND Mary and Aaron spoke against Moses, because of his wife the Ethiopian,

2 And they said: Hath the Lord spoken by Moses only? Hath he not also spoken to us in like manner? And when the Lord heard this,

3 (For Moses was a man exceeding meek above all men that dwelt upon earth)

4 Immediately he spoke to him, and to Aaron and Mary: Come out you three only to the tabernacle of the covenant. And when they were come out,

5 The Lord came down in a pillar of the cloud, and stood in the entry of the tabernacle calling to Aaron and Mary. And when they were come,

6 He said to them: Hear my words: If there be among you a prophet of the Lord, I will appear to him in a vision, or I will speak to him in a dream.

7 But it is not so with my servant

⁵ John. 6, 10. ⁶ Isai. 59, 1. ⁷ Ps. 77, 26, 27. ⁸ Ps. 77, 30.

Ver. 34. *The graves of lust.* Or, the sepulchres of concupiscence; so called from their irregular desire of flesh. In Hebrew, *Kibroth, Hattaavah.*

CHAP. 12. Ver. 1. Ethiopian. Sephora the wife of Moses was of Madian, which bordered upon the land of Chus or Ethiopia: and therefore she is called an Ethiopian: where note, that the Ethiopia here spoken of is not that of Africa, but that of Arabia.

Ver. 3. *Exceeding meek.* Moses being the meekest of men, would not contend for himself. Therefore, God inspired him to write here his own defence, and the Holy Spirit, whose dictate he wrote, obliged him to declare the truth, though it was so much to his own praise.

Moses [1] who is most faithful in all my house.

8 [2] For I speak to him mouth to mouth, and plainly: and not by riddles and figures doth he see the Lord. Why then were you not afraid to speak ill of my servant Moses?

9 And being angry with them he went away.

10 The cloud also that was over the tabernacle departed. [3] And, behold, Mary appeared white as snow with a leprosy. And when Aaron had looked on her, and saw her all covered with leprosy,

11 He said to Moses: I beseech thee, my lord, lay not upon us this sin, which we have foolishly committed.

12 Let her not be as one dead, and as an abortive, that is cast forth from the mother's womb. Lo, now one half of her flesh is consumed with the leprosy.

13 And Moses cried to the Lord, saying: O God, I beseech *thee* heal her.

14 And the Lord answered him: If her father had spitten upon her face, ought she not to have been ashamed for seven days at least? Let her be separated seven days without the camp, and afterwards she shall be called again.

15 Mary therefore was put out of the camp seven days: and the people moved not from that place until Mary was called again.

CHAPTER 13

The twelve spies are sent to view the land. The relation they make of it.

AND the people marched from Haseroth, and pitched their tents in the desert of Pharan.

2 And there the Lord spoke to Moses, saying:

3 Send men to view the land of Chanaan, which I will give to the children of Israel: one of every tribe, of the rulers.

4 Moses did what the Lord had commanded, sending from the desert of Pharan, principal men, whose names are these:

5 Of the tribe of Ruben, Sammua the son of Zechur.

6 Of the tribe of Simeon, Saphat the son of Huri.

7 Of the tribe of Juda, Caleb the son of Jephone.

8 Of the tribe of Issachar, Igal the son of Joseph.

9 Of the tribe of Ephraim, Osee the son of Nun.

10 Of the tribe of Benjamin, Phalti the son of Raphu.

CHAP. 12. [1] Heb. 3, 2. [2] Exod. 33, 11. [3] Deut. 24, 9. CHAP. 13. [1] Acts, 7, 45; Heb. 4, 8. [2] Jos. 15, 14. [3] Deut. 1, 24.

11 Of the tribe of Zabulon, Geddiel the son of Sodi.

12 Of the tribe of Joseph, of the sceptre of Manasses, Gaddi the son of Susi.

13 Of the tribe of Dan, Ammiel the son of Gemalli.

14 Of the tribe of Aser, Sthur the son of Michael.

15 Of the tribe of Nephtali, Nahabi the son of Vapsi.

16 Of the tribe of Gad, Guel the son of Machi.

17 These are the names of the men, whom Moses sent to view the land: and he called Osee the son of Nun, Josue. [1]

18 And Moses sent them to view the land of Chanaan, and said to them: Go you up by the south side. And when you shall come to the mountains,

19 View the land, of what sort it is: and the people that are the inhabitants thereof, whether they be strong or weak: few in number or many:

20 The land itself, whether it be good or bad: what manner of cities, walled or without walls:

21 The ground, fat or barren, woody or without trees. Be of good courage, and bring us of the fruits of the land. Now it was the time when the first ripe grapes are fit to be eaten.

22 And when they were gone up, they viewed the land, from the desert of Sin, unto Rohob, as you enter into Emath.

23 And they went up at the south side, and came to Hebron, where were [2] Achiman and Sisai and Tholmai, the sons of Enac. For Hebron was built seven years before Tanis the city of Egypt.

24 [3] And going forward as far as the torrent of the cluster of grapes, they cut off a branch with its cluster of grapes, which two men carried upon a lever. They took also of the pomegranates and of the figs of that place:

25 Which was called Nehelescol, that is to say, the torrent of the cluster of grapes, because from thence the children of Israel had carried a cluster of grapes.

26 And they that went to spy out the land returned after forty days, having gone round all the country:

27 And came to Moses and Aaron and to all the assembly of the children of Israel to the desert of Pharan, which is in Cades. And speaking to them and to all the multitude, they shewed them the fruits of the land.

28 And they related and said: We came into the land to which thou sentest us, which in very deed floweth with milk and honey as may be known by these fruits.

29 But it hath very strong inhabitants: and the cities are great and walled. We saw there the race of Enac.

30 Amalec dwelleth in the south, the Hethite and the Jebusite and the Amorrhite in the mountains: but the Chanaanite abideth by the sea and near the streams of the Jordan.

31 In the mean time Caleb, to still the murmuring of the people that rose against Moses, said: Let us go up and possess the land, for we shall be able to conquer it.

32 But the others, that had been with him, said: No, we are not able to go up to this people, because they are stronger than we.

33 And they spoke ill of the land, which they had viewed, before the children of Israel, saying: The land which we have viewed, devoureth its inhabitants. The people, that we beheld, are of a tall stature.

34 There we saw certain monsters of the sons of Enac, of the giant kind: in comparison of whom, we seemed like locusts.

CHAPTER 14

The people murmur. God threateneth to destroy them. He is appeased by Moses, yet so as to exclude the murmurers from entering the promised land. The authors of the sedition are struck dead. The rest going to fight against the will of God are beaten.

THEREFORE the whole multitude crying wept that night.

2 And all the children of Israel murmured against Moses and Aaron, saying:

3 Would God that we had died in Egypt! And would God we may die in this vast wilderness, and that the Lord may not bring us into this land: lest we fall by the sword, and our wives and children be led away captives. Is it not better to return into Egypt?

4 And they said one to another: Let us appoint a captain, and let us return into Egypt.

5 And when Moses and Aaron heard this, they fell down flat upon the ground before the multitude of the children of Israel.

6 [1] But Josue the son of Nun, and Caleb the son of Jephone, who themselves also had viewed the land, rent their garments,

7 And said to all the multitude of the children of Israel: The land which we have gone round is very good.

8 If the Lord be favourable, he will bring us into it: and give us a land flowing with milk and honey.

9 Be not rebellious against the Lord. And fear ye not the people of this land:

for we are able to eat them up as bread. All aid is gone from them. The Lord is with us: fear ye not.

10 And when all the multitude cried out, and would have stoned them, the glory of the Lord appeared over the tabernacle of the covenant to all the children of Israel.

11 And the Lord said to Moses: How long will this people detract me? How long will they not believe me for all the signs that I have wrought before them?

12 I will strike them therefore with pestilence, and will consume them: but thee I will make a ruler over a great nation, and a mightier than this is.

13 And Moses said to the Lord: That the Eygptians, from the midst of whom thou hast brought forth this people,

14 And the inhabitants of this land, (who have heard that thou, O Lord, art among this people, and art seen face to face, [2] and thy cloud protecteth them, and thou goest before them in a pillar of a cloud by day, and in a pillar of fire by night,)

15 May hear that thou hast killed so great a multitude as it were one man and may say:

16 He could not bring the people into the land for which he had sworn. [3] Therefore did he kill them in the wilderness.

17 Let then the strength of the Lord be magnified, as thou hast sworn, saying:

18 [4] The Lord is patient and full of mercy, [5] taking away iniquity and wickedness, and leaving no man clear. [6] Who visitest the sins of the fathers upon the children unto the third and fourth generation:

19 Forgive, I beseech thee, the sins of this people, according to the greatness of thy mercy, as thou hast been merciful to them from their going out of Egypt unto this place.

20 And the Lord said: I have forgiven according to thy word.

21 As I live: and the whole earth shall be filled with the glory of the Lord.

22 But yet all the men that have seen my majesty, and the signs that I have done in Egypt, and in the wilderness, and have tempted me now ten times, and have not obeyed my voice,

CHAP. 14. [1] Ecclus. 46, 9; 1 Mach. 2, 55. [2] Exod. 13, 21. [3] Exod. 32, 28. [4] Ps. 102, 8. [5] Exod. 34, 7. [6] Exod. 20, 5.

CHAP. 13. Ver. 33. *Spoke ill.* These men, who by their misrepresentations of the land of promise, discouraged the Israelites from attempting the conquest of it, were a figure of worldlings, who, by decrying or misrepresenting true devotion, discourage Christians from seeking in earnest and acquiring so great a good, and thereby securing to themselves a happy eternity.

CHAP. 14. Ver. 18. *Clear.* Who deserves punishment.

23 [7] Shall not see the land for which I swore to their fathers, neither shall any one of them that hath detracted me behold it.

24 [8] My servant Caleb, who being full of another spirit hath followed me, I will bring into this land which he hath gone round. And his seed shall possess it.

25 For the Amalecite and the Chanaanite dwell in the valleys. To-morrow, remove the camp: and return into the wilderness by the way of the Red Sea.

26 And the Lord spoke to Moses and Aaron, saying:

27 How long doth this wicked multitude murmur against me? I have heard the murmurings of the children of Israel.

28 Say therefore to them: As I live, saith the Lord: According as you have spoken in my hearing, so will I do to you.

29 [9] In the wilderness shall your carcasses lie. All you that were numbered from twenty years old and upward, and have murmured against me,

30 [10] Shall not enter into the land, over which I lifted up my hand to make you dwell therein: except Caleb the son of Jephone, and Josue the son of Nun.

31 But your children, of whom you said, that they should be a prey to the enemies, will I bring in: that they may see the land which you have despised.

32 Your carcasses shall lie in the wilderness.

33 Your children shall wander in the desert forty years, and shall bear your fornication, until the carcasses of their fathers be consumed in the desert.

34 According to the number of the forty days, wherein you viewed the land: [11] a year shall be counted for a day. [12] And forty years you shall receive your iniquities, and shall know my revenge.

35 For as I have spoken, so will I do to all this wicked multitude, that hath risen up together against me: in this wilderness shall it faint away and die.

36 [13] Therefore all the men, whom Moses had sent to view the land, and who at their return had made the whole multitude to murmur against him, speaking ill of the land that it was naught,

37 Died and were struck in the sight of the Lord.

38 But Josue the son of Nun, and Caleb the son of Jephone lived, of all them that had gone to view the land.

39 And Moses spoke all these words to all the children of Israel: and the people mourned exceedingly.

40 And, behold, rising up very early in the morning, they went up to the top of the mountain, and said: We are ready to go up to the place, of which the Lord hath spoken. For we have sinned.

41 And Moses said to them: Why transgress you the word of the Lord, which shall not succeed prosperously with you?

42 [11] Go not up, for the Lord is not with you: lest you fall before your enemies.

43 The Amalecite and the Chanaanite are before you: and by their sword you shall fall, because you would not consent to the Lord, neither will the Lord be with you.

44 But they being blinded went up to the top of the mountain. But the ark of the testament of the Lord and Moses departed not from the camp.

45 And the Amalecite came down, and the Chanaanite that dwelt in the mountain: and smiting and slaying them pursued them as far as Horma.

CHAPTER 15

Certain laws concerning sacrifices. Sabbath breaking is punished with death. The law of fringes on their garments.

AND the Lord spoke to Moses, saying:

2 Speak to the children of Israel, and thou shalt say to them: When you shall be come into the land of your habitation, which I will give you,

3 And shall make an offering to the Lord, for a holocaust, or a victim, paying your vows, or voluntarily offering gifts, or in your solemnities burning a sweet savour unto the Lord, of oxen or of sheep:

4 Whosoever immolateth the victim, shall offer a sacrifice of fine flour, the tenth part of an ephi, tempered with the fourth part of a hin of oil.

5 And he shall give the same measure of wine to pour out in libations for the holocaust or for the victim. For every lamb,

6 And for every ram there shall be a sacrifice of flour of two tenths, which shall be tempered with the third part of a hin of oil.

7 And he shall offer the third part of the same measure of wine for the libation, for a sweet savour to the Lord.

8 But when thou offerest a holocaust or sacrifice of oxen, to fulfil *thy* vow or for victims of peace offerings,

9 Thou shalt give for every ox three tenths of flour tempered with half a hin of oil:

---

[7] Deut. 1, 35. [8] Jos. 14, 6. [9] Ps. 105, 26. [10] Deut. 1, 35. [11] Ezech. 4, 6. [12] Ps. 94, 10. [13] Judith, 8, 24; 1 Cor. 10, 10; Heb. 3, 17; Jude. 5. [14] Deut. 1, 42.

Ver. 33. *Shall bear your fornication.* That is, shall bear the punishment of your disloyalty to God, which in the scripture language is here called a *fornication*, in a spiritual sense.

10 And wine for libations of the same measure, for an offering of most sweet savour to the Lord.

11 Thus shalt thou do.

12 For every ox and ram and lamb and kid.

13 Both they that are born in the land, and the strangers.

14 Shall offer sacrifices after the same rite.

15 There shall be all one law and judgment both for you and for them who are strangers in the land.

16 And the Lord spoke to Moses, saying:

17 Speak to the children of Israel, and thou shalt say to them:

18 When you are come into the land which I will give you,

19 And shall eat of the bread of that country, you shall separate firstfruits to the Lord,

20 Of the things you eat. As you separate firstfruits of your barnfloors.

21 So also shall you give firstfruits of your dough to the Lord.

22 And if through ignorance you omit any of these things, which the Lord hath spoken to Moses,

23 And by him hath commanded you, from the day that he began to command and thenceforward,

24 And the multitude have forgotten to do it: they shall offer a calf out of the herd, a holocaust for a most sweet savour to the Lord, and the sacrifice and libations thereof, as the ceremonies require, and a buck-goat for sin.

25 And the priest shall pray for all the multitude of the children of Israel: and it shall be forgiven them, because they sinned ignorantly, offering notwithstanding a burnt offering to the Lord for themselves and for their sin and their ignorance.

26 And it shall be forgiven all the people of the children of Israel: and the strangers that sojourn among them: because it is the fault of all the people through ignorance.

27 But if one soul shall sin ignorantly, he shall offer a she-goat of a year old for his sin.

28 And the priest shall pray for him, because he sinned ignorantly before the Lord: and he shall obtain his pardon, and it shall be forgiven him.

29 The same law shall be for all that sin by ignorance, whether they be natives or strangers.

30 But the soul that committeth any thing through pride, whether he be born in the land or a stranger (because he hath been rebellious against the Lord) shall be cut off from among his people.

31 For he hath contemned the word of the Lord, and made void his precept: therefore shall he be destroyed, and shall bear his iniquity.

32 And it came to pass, when the children of Israel were in the wilderness, and had found a man gathering sticks on the sabbath day,

33 That they brought him to Moses and Aaron and the whole multitude.

34 And they put him into prison, not knowing what they should do with him.

35 And the Lord said to Moses: Let that man die. Let all the multitude stone him without the camp.

36 And when they had brought him out, they stoned him: and he died as the Lord had commanded.

37 The Lord also said to Moses:

38 Speak to the children of Israel, and thou shalt tell them [1] to make to themselves fringes in the corners of their garments, putting in them ribands of blue.

39 That when they shall see them, they may remember all the commandments of the Lord, and not follow their own thoughts and eyes going astray after divers things.

40 But rather being mindful of the precepts of the Lord, may do them: and be holy to their God.

41 I am the Lord your God, who brought you out of the land of Egypt, that I might be your God.

CHAPTER 16

The schism of Core and his adherents. Their punishment.

AND behold Core the son of Isaar, the son of Caath, the son of Levi, and Dathan and Abiron the sons of Eliab, and Hon the son of Pheleth of the children of Ruben:

2 Rose up against Moses: and *with them* two hundred and fifty others of the children of Israel, leading men of the synagogue, and who in the time of assembly were called by name.

3 [1] And when they had stood up against Moses and Aaron, they said: Let it be enough for you, that all the multitude consisteth of holy ones, and the

CHAP. 15. [1] Deut. 22, 12; Matt. 23, 5. CHAP. 16. [1] Ecclus. 45, 22; 1 Cor. 10, 10; Jude, 11.

CHAP. 15. Ver. 38. *Fringes.* The Pharisees enlarged these fringes through hypocrisy (Matt. 23, 5), to appear more serious than other men for the law of God.

CHAP. 16. Ver. 2. *Rose up.* The crime of these men, which was punished in so remarkable a manner, was that of schism, and of rebellion against the authority established by God in the church; and their pretending to the priesthood without being lawfully called and sent. The same is the case of all modern sectaries.

Lord is among them. Why lift you up yourselves above the people of the Lord?

4 When Moses heard this, he fell flat on his face.

5 And speaking to Core and all the multitude, he said: In the morning the Lord will make known who belong to him, and the holy he will join to himself. And whom he shall choose, they shall approach to him.

6 Do this therefore: Take every man of you your censers: thou Core, and all thy company.

7 And putting fire *in them* to-morrow, put incense upon it before the Lord. And whomsoever he shall choose, the same shall be holy. You take too much upon you, ye sons of Levi.

8 And he said again to Core: Hear ye sons of Levi.

9 Is it a small thing unto you, that the God of Israel hath spared you from all the people, and joined you to himself, that you should serve him in the service of the tabernacle, and should stand before the congregation of the people, and should minister to him?

10 Did he therefore make thee and all thy brethren, the sons of Levi, to approach unto him, that you should challenge to yourselves the priesthood also?

11 And that all thy company should stand against the Lord? For what is Aaron that you murmur against him?

12 Then Moses sent to call Dathan and Abiron, the sons of Eliab. But they answered: We will not come.

13 Is it a small matter to thee, that thou hast brought us out of a land that flowed with milk and honey, to kill us in the desert, except thou rule also like a lord over us?

14 Thou hast brought us indeed into a land that floweth with rivers of milk and honey, and hast given us possessions of fields and vineyards. Wilt thou also pull out our eyes? We will not come.

15 Moses therefore being very angry, said to the Lord: Respect not their sacrifices. Thou knowest that I have not taken of them so much as a young ass at any time: nor have injured any of them.

16 And he said to Core: Do thou and thy congregation stand apart before the Lord to-morrow, and Aaron apart.

17 Take every one of you censers, and put incense upon them, offering to the Lord two hundred and fifty censers. Let Aaron also hold his censer.

² Deut. 11, 6; Ps. 105, 17.

Ver. 15. *Very angry.* This anger was a zeal against sin; and an indignation at the affront offered to God; like that which the same holy prophet conceived upon the sight of the golden calf (Exod. 32, 19).

18 When they had done this, Moses and Aaron standing,

19 And had drawn up all the multitude against them to the door of the tabernacle: the glory of the Lord appeared to them all.

20 And the Lord speaking to Moses and Aaron, said:

21 Separate yourselves from among this congregation, that I may presently destroy them.

22 They fell flat on their faces, and said: O most mighty, the God of the spirits of all flesh, for one man's sin shall thy wrath rage against all?

23 And the Lord said to Moses:

24 Command the whole people to separate themselves from the tents of Core and Dathan and Abiron.

25 And Moses arose, and went to Dathan and Abiron: and the ancients of Israel following him,

26 He said to the multitude: Depart from the tents of these wicked men, and touch nothing of theirs, lest you be involved in their sins.

27 And when they were departed from their tents round about, Dathan and Abiron, coming out stood in the entry of their pavilions with their wives and children, and all the people.

28 And Moses said: By this you shall know that the Lord hath sent me to do all things that you see, and that I have not forged them of my own head.

29 If these men die the common death of men, and if they be visited with a plague, wherewith others also are wont to be visited, the Lord did not send me.

30 But if the Lord do a new thing, and the earth opening her mouth swallow them down, and all things that belong to them, and they go down alive into hell, you shall know that they have blasphemed the Lord.

31 ² And immediately as he had made an end of speaking, the earth broke asunder under their feet.

32 And, opening her mouth, devoured them with their tents and all their substance.

33 And they went down alive into hell, the ground closing upon them: and they perished from among the people.

34 But all Israel, that was standing round about, fled at the cry of them that were perishing; saying: Lest perhaps the earth swallow us up also.

35 And a fire coming out from the Lord, destroyed the two hundred and fifty men that offered the incense.

36 And the Lord spoke to Moses, saying:

37 Command Eleazar, the son of

Aaron the priest, to take up the censers that lie in the burning, and to scatter the fire of one side and the other: because they are sanctified

38 In the deaths of the sinners. And let him beat them into plates, and fasten them to the altar, because incense hath been offered in them to the Lord, and they are sanctified: that the children of Israel may see them for a sign and a memorial.

39 Then Eleazar the priest took the brazen censers, wherein they had offered, whom the burning fire had devoured: and beat them into plates, fastening them to the altar.

40 That the children of Israel might have for the time to come wherewith they should be admonished, that no stranger or any one that is not of the seed of Aaron should come near to offer incense to the Lord: lest he should suffer as Core suffered, and all his congregation: according as the Lord spoke to Moses.

41 The following day all the multitude of the children of Israel murmured against Moses and Aaron, saying: You have killed the people of the Lord.

42 And when there arose a sedition, and the tumult increased,

43 Moses and Aaron fled to the tabernacle of the covenant. And when they were gone into it, the cloud covered it, and the glory of the Lord appeared.

44 And the Lord said to Moses:

45 Get you out from the midst of this multitude. This moment will I destroy them. And as they were lying on the ground,

46 Moses said to Aaron: Take the censer, and putting fire in it from the altar, put incense upon it: and go quickly to the people to pray for them. For already wrath is gone out from the Lord, and the plague rageth.

47 When Aaron had done this, and had run to the midst of the multitude which the burning fire was now destroying, he offered the incense.

48 And standing between the dead and the living, he prayed for the people: and the plague ceased.

49 And the number of them that were slain was fourteen thousand and seven hundred men, besides them that had perished in the sedition of Core.

50 And Aaron returned to Moses to the door of the tabernacle of the covenant after the destruction was over.

CHAPTER 17

The priesthood is confirmed to Aaron by the miracle of the blooming of his rod, which is kept for a monument in the tabernacle.

AND the Lord spoke to Moses, saying:

2 Speak to the children of Israel, and take of every one of them a rod by their kindreds, of all the princes of the tribes, twelve rods: and write the name of every man upon his rod.

3 And the name of Aaron shall be for the tribe of Levi: and one rod shall contain all their families.

4 And thou shalt lay them up in the tabernacle of the covenant before the testimony, where I will speak to thee.

5 Whomsoever of these I shall choose, his rod shall blossom. And I will make to cease from me the murmurings of the children of Israel, wherewith they murmur against you.

6 And Moses spoke to the children of Israel: and all the princes gave him rods one for every tribe. And there were twelve rods besides the rod of Aaron.

7 And when Moses had laid them up before the Lord in the tabernacle of the testimony:

8 He returned on the following day, and found that the rod of Aaron for the house of Levi, was budded: and that the buds swelling it had bloomed blossoms, which spreading the leaves, were formed into almonds.

9 Moses therefore brought out all the rods from before the Lord to all the children of Israel. And they saw: and every one received their rods.

10 And the Lord said to Moses: Carry back the rod of Aaron into the tabernacle of the testimony, [1] that it may be kept there for a token of the rebellious children of Israel: and that their complaints may cease from me, lest they die.

11 And Moses did as the Lord had commanded.

12 And the children of Israel said to Moses: Behold we are consumed, we all perish.

13 Whosoever approacheth to the tabernacle of the Lord, he dieth. Are we all to a man to be utterly destroyed?

CHAPTER 18

The charge of the priests and of the Levites, and their portion.

AND the Lord said to Aaron: Thou, and thy sons, and thy father's house with thee shall bear the iniquity of the sanctuary. And thou and thy sons with thee shall bear the sins of your priesthood.

CHAP. 17. [1] Heb. 9, 4.

CHAP. 17. Ver. 8. *The rod of Aaron for the house of Levi, was budded.* This rod of Aaron which thus miraculously brought forth fruit, was a figure of the blessed Virgin conceiving and bringing forth her Son without any prejudice to her virginity.

CHAP. 18. Ver. 1. *Thou, and thy father's house with thee, shall bear the iniquity of the sanc-*

2 And take with thee thy brethren also of the tribe of Levi, and the sceptre of thy father: and let them be ready in hand, and minister to thee. But thou and thy sons shall minister in the tabernacle of the testimony.

3 And the Levites shall watch to do thy commands, and about all the works of the tabernacle. Only they shall not come nigh the vessels of the sanctuary nor the altar: lest both they die, and you also perish with them.

4 But let them be with thee, and watch in the charge of the tabernacle, and in all the ceremonies thereof. A stranger shall not join himself with you.

5 Watch ye in the charge of the sanctuary, and in the ministry of the altar: lest indignation rise upon the children of Israel.

6 I have given you your brethren, the Levites, from among the children of Israel, and have delivered them for a gift to the Lord, to serve in the ministries of the tabernacle.

7 But thou and thy sons look ye to the priesthood. And all things that pertain to the service of the altar, and that are within the veil, shall be executed by the priests. If any stranger shall approach, he shall be slain.

8 And the Lord said to Aaron: Behold I have given thee the charge of my firstfruits. All things that are sanctified by the children of Israel, I have delivered to thee and to thy sons for the priestly office, by everlasting ordinances.

9 These therefore shalt thou take of the things that are sanctified, and are offered to the Lord. Every offering, and sacrifice, and whatsoever is rendered to me for sin and for trespass, and becometh holy of holies, shall be for thee and thy sons.

10 Thou shalt eat it in the sanctuary: the males only shall eat thereof, because it is a consecrated thing to thee.

11 But the firstfruits, which the children of Israel shall vow and offer, I have given to thee, and to thy sons, and to thy daughters, by a perpetual law. He that is clean in thy house, shall eat them.

12 All the best of the oil, and of the wine, and of the corn, whatsoever firstfruits they offer to the Lord, I have given them to thee.

Chap. 18. ¹ Exod. 30, 13; Lev. 27, 25; Num. 3, 47; Ezech. 45, 12. ² Deut. 18, 1.

tuary. That is, you shall be punished if, through negligence or want of due attention, you err in the discharge of the sacred functions for which you were ordained.
Ver. 19. A covenant of salt. It is a proverbial expression, signifying a covenant not to be altered or corrupted; as salt is used to keep things from corruption; a covenant perpetual, like that by which it was appointed, that salt should be used in every sacrifice (Lev. 2).
Ver. 22. Deadly sin. That is, sin which will bring death after it.

13 All the first ripe of the fruits, that the ground bringeth forth, and which are brought to the Lord, shall be for thy use. He that is clean in thy house, shall eat them.

14 Every thing that the children of Israel shall give by vow, shall be thine.

15 Whatsoever is firstborn of all flesh, which they offer to the Lord, whether it be of men, or of beasts, shall belong to thee. Only for the firstborn of man thou shalt take a price: and every beast that is unclean thou shalt cause to be redeemed,

16 And the redemption of it shall be after one month, for five sicles of silver, by the weight of the sanctuary. ¹A sicle hath twenty obols.

17 But the firstling of a cow and of a sheep and of a goat thou shalt not cause to be redeemed, because they are sanctified to the Lord. Their blood only thou shalt pour upon the attar: and their fat thou shalt burn for a most sweet odour to the Lord.

18 But the flesh shall fall to thy use, as the consecrated breast, and the right shoulder shall be thine.

19 All the firstfruits of the sanctuary which the children of Israel offer to the Lord, I have given to thee and to thy sons and daughters, by a perpetual ordinance. It is a covenant of salt for ever before the Lord, to thee and to thy sons.

20 And the Lord said to Aaron: You shall possess nothing in their land. neither shall you have a portion among them. I am thy portion and inheritance in the midst of the children of Israel.

21 And I have given to the sons of Levi all the tithes of Israel for a possession, for the ministry wherewith they serve me in the tabernacle of the covenant:

22 That the children of Israel may not approach any more to the tabernacle, nor commit deadly sin,

23 But only the sons of Levi may serve me in the tabernacle, and bear the sins of the people. It shall be an everlasting ordinance in your generations. ² They shall not possess any other thing:

24 But be content with the oblation or tithes, which I have separated for their uses and necessities.

25 And the Lord spoke to Moses, saying:

26 Command the Levites, and declare unto them: When you shall receive of the children of Israel the tithes, which I have given you, offer the firstfruits of them to the Lord, that is to say, the tenth part of the tenth.

27 That it may be reckoned to you

as an oblation of firstfruits, as well of the barnfloors as of the winepresses.

28 And of all the things of which you receive tithes, offer the firstfruits to the Lord: and give them to Aaron the priest.

29 All the things that you shall offer of the tithes, and shall separate for the gifts of the Lord, shall be the best and choicest things.

30 And thou shalt say to them: If you offer all the goodly and the better things of the tithes, it shall be reckoned to you as if you had given the firstfruits of the barnfloor and the winepress.

31 And you shall eat them in all your places, both you and your families: because it is your reward for the ministry, wherewith you serve in the tabernacle of the testimony.

32 And you shall not sin in this point, by reserving the choicest and fat things to yourselves: lest you profane the oblations of the children of Israel, and die.

CHAPTER 19

The law of the sacrifice of the red cow, and the water of expiation.

AND the Lord spoke to Moses and Aaron, saying:

2 This is the observance of the victim, which the Lord hath ordained. Command the children of Israel, that they bring unto thee a red cow of full age, in which there is no blemish, and which hath not carried the yoke.

3 And you shall deliver her to Eleazar the priest, [1] who shall bring her forth without the camp, and shall immolate her in the sight of all.

4 And dipping his finger in her blood, shall sprinkle it over against the door of the tabernacle seven times.

5 And shall burn her in the sight of all: delivering up to the fire her skin, and her flesh, and her blood, and her dung.

6 The priest shall also take cedar wood, and hyssop, and scarlet twice dyed: and cast it into the flame, with which the cow is consumed.

7 And then after washing his garments, and body, he shall enter into the camp: and shall be unclean until the evening.

8 He also that hath burned her, shall wash his garments, and his body: and shall be unclean until the evening.

9 And a man that is clean shall gather up the ashes of the cow, and shall pour them forth without the camp in a most clean place: that they may be reserved for the multitude of the children of Israel, and for a water of aspersion: because the cow was burnt for sin.

10 And when he that carried the ashes of the cow, hath washed his garments, he shall be unclean until the evening. The children of Israel, and the strangers that dwell among them, shall observe this for a holy thing by a perpetual ordinance.

11 He that toucheth the corpse of a man, and is therefore unclean seven days,

12 Shall be sprinkled with this water on the third day, and on the seventh, and so shall be cleansed. If he were not sprinkled on the third day, he cannot be cleansed on the seventh.

13 Every one that toucheth the corpse of a man, and is not sprinkled with this mixture, shall profane the tabernacle of the Lord, and shall perish out of Israel. Because he was not sprinkled with the water of expiation, he shall be unclean; and his uncleanness shall remain upon him.

14 This is the law of a man that dieth in a tent: All that go into his tent and all the vessels that are there, shall be unclean seven days.

15 The vessel that hath no cover, nor binding over it, shall be unclean.

16 If any man in the field touch the corpse of a man that was slain, or that died of himself, or his bone, or his grave, he shall be unclean seven days.

17 And they shall take of the ashes of the burning and of the sin offering: and shall pour living waters upon them into a vessel.

18 And a man that is clean shall dip hyssop in them, and shall sprinkle therewith all the tent, and all the furniture, and the men that are defiled with touching any such thing.

19 And in this manner he that is clean shall purify the unclean on the third and on the seventh day. And being expiated the seventh day, he shall wash both himself and his garments, and be unclean until the evening.

20 If any man be not expiated after this rite, his soul shall perish out of the midst of the church: because he hath profaned the sanctuary of the Lord, and was not sprinkled with the water of purification.

21 This precept shall be an ordinance for ever. He also that sprinkled the water, shall wash his garments. Every one that shall touch the waters of expiation, shall be unclean until the evening.

CHAP. 19. [1] Heb. 13, 11.

CHAP. 19. Ver. 2. *A red cow.* This red cow, offered in sacrifice for sin, and consumed with fire without the camp, with the ashes of which, mingled with water, the unclean were to be expiated and purified; was a figure of the passion of Christ, by whose precious blood applied to our souls in the holy sacraments, we are cleansed from our sins.

22 Whatsoever a person toucheth who is unclean, he shall make it unclean: and the person that toucheth any of these things, shall be unclean until the evening.

CHAPTER 20

The death of Mary the sister of Moses. The people murmur for want of water. God giveth it them from the rock. The death of Aaron.

AND the children of Israel, and all the multitude came into the desert of Sin, in the first month: and the people abode in Cades. And Mary died there, and was buried in the same place.

2 And the people wanting water. came together against Moses and Aaron.

3 And making a sedition, they said: Would God we had perished among our brethren before the Lord.

4 [1] Why have you brought out the church of the Lord into the wilderness that both we and our cattle should die?

5 Why have you made us come up out of Egypt, and have brought us into this wretched place which cannot be sowed: nor bringeth forth figs, nor vines, nor pomegranates: neither is there any water to drink?

6 And Moses and Aaron leaving the multitude, went into the tabernacle of the covenant, and fell flat upon the ground, and cried to the Lord, and said: O Lord God, hear the cry of this people and open to them thy treasure, a fountain of living water, that being satisfied they may cease to murmur. And the glory of the Lord appeared over them.

7 And the Lord spoke to Moses, saying:

8 Take the rod, and assemble the people together, thou and Aaron thy brother: and speak to the rock before them, and it shall yield waters. And when thou hast brought forth water out of the rock, all the multitude and their cattle shall drink.

9 [2] Moses therefore took the rod which was before the Lord, as he had commanded him,

10 And having gathered together the multitude before the rock, he said to

CHAP. 20. [1] Exod. 17, 3. [2] Exod. 17, 5; Wisd. 11, 4. [3] Ps. 77, 15; 1 Cor. 10, 4. [4] Deut. 1, 37.

CHAP. 20. Ver. 11. *The rock.* This rock was a figure of Christ, and the water that issued out from the rock, of his Precious Blood, the source of all our good.
Ver. 12. *You have not believed.* The fault of Moses and Aaron, on this occasion, was a certain diffidence and weakness of faith; not doubting of God's power or veracity; but apprehending the unworthiness of that rebellious and incredulous people, and therefore speaking with some ambiguity.
Ver. 13. *The Water of contradiction or strife.* Hebrew, *Meribah.*

them: Hear, ye rebellious and incredulous: [3] Can we bring you forth water out of this rock?

11 And when Moses had lifted up his hand, and struck the rock twice with the rod, there came forth water in great abundance, so that the people and their cattle drank,

12 And the Lord said to Moses and Aaron: [4] Because you have not believed me, to sanctify me before the children of Israel, you shall not bring these people into the land, which I will give them.

13 This is the Water of contradiction, where the children of Israel strove with words against the Lord: and he was sanctified in them.

14 In the mean time Moses sent messengers from Cades to the king of Edom, to say: Thus saith thy brother Israel: Thou knowest all the labour that hath come upon us:

15 In what manner our fathers went down into Egypt, and there we dwelt a long time, and the Egyptians afflicted us and our fathers.

16 And how we cried to the Lord, and he heard us, and sent an angel, who hath brought us out of Egypt. Lo, we are now in the city of Cades, which is in the uttermost of thy borders:

17 And we beseech thee that we may have leave to pass through thy country. We will not go through the fields, nor through the vineyards: we will not drink the waters of thy wells: but we will go by the common highway, neither turning aside to the right hand, nor to the left, till we are past thy borders.

18 And Edom answered them: Thou shalt not pass by me. If thou dost I will come out armed against thee.

19 And the children of Israel said: We will go by the beaten way: and if we and our cattle drink of thy waters, we will give thee what is just. There shall be no difficulty in the price; only let us pass speedily.

20 But he answered: Thou shalt not pass. And immediately he came forth to meet them with an infinite multitude, and a strong hand,

21 Neither would he condescend to their desire to grant them passage through his borders. Wherefore Israel turned another way from him.

22 And when they had removed the camp from Cades, they came to mount Hor, which is in the borders of the land of Edom.

23 Where the Lord spoke to Moses:

24 Let Aaron, saith he, go to his people: for he shall not go into the land which I have given the children of Israel, because he was incredulous to

my words, at the waters of contradiction.

25 ⁵ Take Aaron and his son with him, and bring them up into mount Hor.

26 And when thou hast stripped the father of his vesture, thou shalt vest therewith Eleazar his son. Aaron shall be gathered *to his people,* and die there.

27 Moses did as the Lord had commanded: and they went up into mount Hor before all the multitude.

28 And when he had stripped Aaron of his vestments, he vested Eleazar his son with them.

29 And Aaron being dead in the top of the mountain, he came down with Eleazar.

30 And all the multitude seeing that Aaron was dead, mourned for him thirty days throughout all their families.

CHAPTER 21

King Arad is overcome. The people murmur and are punished with fiery serpents. They are healed by the brazen serpent. They conquer the kings Sehon and Og.

AND when king Arad the Chanaanite, who dwelt towards the south, had heard this: to wit, that Israel was come by the way of the spies, he fought against them, and overcoming them carried off their spoils.

2 But Israel, binding himself by vow to the Lord, ¹ said: If thou wilt deliver this people into my hand, I will utterly destroy their cities.

3 And the Lord heard the prayers of Israel, and delivered up the Chanaanite: and they cut them off and destroyed their cities. And they called the name of that place Horma, that is to say, Anathema.

4 And they marched from mount Hor, by the way that leadeth to the Red Sea, to compass the land of Edom. And the people began to be weary of their journey and labour.

5 And speaking against God and Moses, they said: Why didst thou bring us out of Egypt, to die in the wilderness? There is no bread, nor have we any waters: our soul now loatheth this very light food.

6 ² Wherefore the Lord sent among the people fiery serpents, which bit them and killed many of them.

7 Upon which they came to Moses, and said: We have sinned, because we have spoken against the Lord and thee. Pray that he may take away these serpents from us. And Moses prayed for the people.

8 And the Lord said to him: Make a brazen serpent, and set it up for a sign. Whosoever being struck shall look on it shall live.

9 ³ Moses therefore made a brazen serpent, and set it up for a sign: which when they that were bitten looked upon, they were healed.

10 And the children of Israel setting forwards camped in Oboth.

11 And departing thence they pitched their tents in Jeabarim, in the wilderness, that faceth Moab toward the east.

12 And removing from thence, they came to the torrent Zared:

13 ⁴ Which they left and encamped over against Arnon, which is in the desert and standeth out on the borders of the Amorrhite. ⁵ For Arnon is the border of Moab, dividing the Moabites and the Amorrhites.

14 Wherefore it is said in the book of the wars of the Lord: As he did in the Red Sea, so will he do in the streams of Arnon.

15 The rocks of the torrents were bowed down that they might rest in Ar: and lie down in the borders of the Moabites.

16 *When they went* from that place, the well appeared whereof the Lord said to Moses: Gather the people together, and I will give them water.

17 Then Israel sung this song: Let the well spring up. They sung thereto:

18 The well, which the princes dug, and the chiefs of the people prepared by *the direction* of the lawgiver, and with their staves. *And they marched* from the wilderness to Mathana.

19 From Mathana unto Nahaliel: from Nahaliel unto Bamoth.

20 From Bamoth, is a valley in the country of Moab, to the top of Phasga, which looked towards the desert.

21 ⁶ And Israel sent messengers to Sehon king of the Amorrhites, saying:

22 I beseech thee that I may have leave to pass through thy land. We will not go aside into the fields or the vineyards, we will not drink waters of the wells, we will go the king's highway, till we be past thy borders.

23 And he would not grant that Israel should pass by his borders: but

---

⁵ Num. 33, 38; Deut. 32, 50. CHAP. 21. ¹ Num. 33, 40. ² Judith, 8, 25; Wisd. 16, 5; 1 Cor. 10, 9. ³ John, 3, 14. ⁴ Deut. 2, 13. ⁵ Judges, 11, 18; Deut. 2, 24. ⁶ Deut. 2, 26; Judges, 11, 19.

CHAP. 21. Ver. 3. *Anathema.* That is, a thing devoted to utter destruction.

Ver. 5. *Very light food.* So they call the heavenly manna: thus worldlings loathe the things of heaven, for which they have no relish.

Ver. 6. *Fiery serpents.* They are so called, because they that were bitten by them were burnt with a violent heat.

Ver. 9. *A brazen serpent.* This was a figure of Christ crucified, and of the efficacy of a lively faith in him, against the bites of the hellish serpent (John, 3, 14).

Ver. 14. *The book of the wars.* An ancient book, which, like several others quoted in scripture, has been lost.

rather gathering an army, went forth to meet them in the desert, and came to Jasa, and fought against them.

24 ⁷ And he was slain by them with the edge of the sword: and they possessed his land from the Arnon unto the Jeboc, and to the confines of the children of Ammon. For the borders of the Ammonites, were kept with a strong garrison.

25 So Israel took all his cities, and dwelt in the cities of the Amorrhite: to wit, in Hesebon, and in the villages thereof.

26 Hesebon was the city of Sehon the king of the Amorrhites, who fought against the king of Moab: and took all the land, that had been of his dominions, as far as the Arnon.

27 Therefore it is said in the proverb: Come into Hesebon. Let the city of Sehon be built and set up.

28 A fire is gone out of Hesebon, a flame from the city of Sehon, and hath consumed Ar of the Moabites, and the inhabitants of the high places of the Arnon.

29 ⁸ Woe to thee Moab: thou art undone, O people of Chamos. He hath given his sons to flight, and his daughters into captivity to Sehon the king of the Amorrhites.

30 Their yoke is perished from Hesebon unto Dibon. They came weary to Nophe, and unto Medaba.

31 So Israel dwelt in the land of the Amorrhite.

32 And Moses sent some to take a view of Jazer. And they took the villages of it, and conquered the inhabitants.

33 ⁹ And they turned themselves, and went up by the way of Basan: and Og the king of Basan came against them with all his people, to fight in Edrai.

34 And the Lord said to Moses: Fear him not, for I have delivered him and all his people, and his country into thy hand. And thou shalt do to him as thou didst to Sehon the king of the Amorrhites, the inhabitant of Hesebon.

35 So they slew him also with his sons, and all his people, not letting any one escape: and they possessed his land.

CHAPTER 22

Balac, king of Moab, sendeth twice for Balaam to curse Israel. In his way Balaam is rebuked by an angel.

AND they went forward: and encamped in the plains of Moab, *over against* where Jericho is situate beyond the Jordan.

⁷ Ps. 134, 11; Amos. 2, 9. ⁸ Judges, 11, 24; 3 Kings, 11, 7. ⁹ Deut. 3, 3; 29, 7. Chap. 22. ¹ Jos. 24, 9. ² Num. 24, 13.

Chap. 22. Ver. 19. *To stay.* His desiring them to stay, after he had been fully informed already that it was not God's will he should go, came

2 And Balac the son of Sephor, seeing all that Israel had done to the Amorrhite:

3 And that the Moabites were in great fear of him, and were not able to sustain his assault:

4 He said to the elders of Madian: So will this people destroy all that dwell in our borders, as the ox is wont to eat the grass to the very roots. Now he was at that time king of Moab.

5 ¹ He sent therefore messengers to Balaam, the son of Beor, a soothsayer, who dwelt by the river of the land of the children of Ammon, to call him, and to say: Behold, a people is come out of Egypt, that hath covered the face of the earth, sitting over against me.

6 Come therefore, and curse this people, because it is mightier than I, if by any means I may beat them and drive them out of my land. For I know that he whom thou shalt bless is blessed, and he whom thou shalt curse is cursed.

7 And the ancients of Moab, and the elders of Madian, went with the price of divination in their hands. And when they were come to Balaam, and had told him all the words of Balac:

8 He answered: Tarry here this night, and I will answer whatsoever the Lord shall say to me. And while they stayed with Balaam, God came and said to him:

9 What mean these men that are with thee?

10 He answered: Balac, the son of Sephor, king of the Moabites, hath sent to me,

11 Saying: Behold a people that is come out of Egypt, hath covered the face of the land. Come and curse them, if by any means I may fight with them and drive them away.

12 And God said to Balaam: Thou shalt not go with them, nor shalt thou curse the people: because it is blessed.

13 And he rose in the morning and said to the princes: Go into your country, because the Lord hath forbid me to come with you.

14 The princes returning, said to Balac: Balaam would not come with us.

15 Then he sent many more and more noble than he had sent before.

16 Who, when they were come to Balaam, said: Thus saith Balac the son of Sephor: Delay not to come to me.

17 For I am ready to honour thee, and will give thee whatsoever thou wilt. Come and curse this people.

18 Balaam answered: ² If Balac would give me his house full of silver and gold, I cannot alter the word of the Lord my God, to speak either more or less.

19 I pray you to stay here this night

also, that I may know what the Lord will answer me once more.

20 God therefore came to Balaam in the night, and said to him: If these men be come to call thee, arise and go with them. Yet so, that thou do what I shall command thee.

21 Balaam arose in the morning, and saddling his ass went with them.

22 ³ And God was angry. And an angel of the Lord stood in the way against Balaam, who sat on the ass, and had two servants with him.

23 The ass seeing the angel standing in the way, with a drawn sword, turned herself out of the way, and went into the field. And when Balaam beat her, and had a mind to bring her again to the way,

24 The angel stood in a narrow place between two walls, wherewith the vineyards were enclosed.

25 And the ass seeing him, thrust herself close to the wall, and bruised the foot of the rider. But he beat her again.

26 And nevertheless, the angel going on to a narrow place, where there was no way to turn aside either to the right hand or to the left, stood to meet him.

27 And when the ass saw the angel standing, she fell under the feet of the rider: who being angry beat her sides more vehemently with a staff.

28 And the Lord opened the mouth of the ass, and she said: What have I done to thee? Why strikest thou me, lo, now this third time?

29 Balaam answered: Because thou hast deserved it, and hast served me ill. I would I had a sword that I might kill thee.

30 The ass said: Am not I thy beast, on which thou hast been always accustomed to ride until this present day? Tell me if I ever did the like thing to thee. But he said: Never.

31 Forthwith the Lord opened the eyes of Balaam, and he saw the angel standing in the way with a drawn sword: and he worshipped him falling flat on the ground.

32 And the angel said to him: Why beatest thou thy ass these three times? I am come to withstand thee, because thy way is perverse, and contrary to me.

33 And unless the ass had turned out of the way, giving place to me who stood against thee, I had slain thee, and she should have lived.

34 Balaam said: I have sinned, not knowing that thou didst stand against me. And now if it displease thee that I go, I will return.

35 The angel said: Go with these men, and see thou speak no other thing

than what I shall command thee. He went therefore with the princes.

36 And when Balac heard it, he came forth to meet him in a town of the Moabites, that is situate in the uttermost borders of Arnon.

37 And he said to Balaam: I sent messengers to call thee. Why didst thou not come immediately to me? Was it because I am not able to reward thy coming?

38 He answered him: Lo, here I am: Shall I have power to speak any other thing but that which God shall put in my mouth?

39 So they went on together, and came into a city, that was in the uttermost borders of his kingdom.

40 And when Balac had killed oxen and sheep, he sent presents to Balaam, and to the princes that were with him.

41 And when morning was come, he brought him to the high places of Baal: and he beheld the uttermost part of the people.

CHAPTER 23

Balaam, instead of cursing Israel, is obliged to bless them, and prophesy good things of them.

AND Balaam said to Balac: Build me here seven altars: and prepare as many calves, and the same number of rams.

2 And when he had done according to the word of Balaam, they laid together a calf and a ram upon *every* altar.

3 And Balaam said to Balac: Stand a while by thy burnt offering, until I go, *to see* if perhaps the Lord will meet me: and whatsoever he shall command, I will speak to thee.

4 And when he was gone with speed, God met him. And Balaam speaking to him, said: I have erected seven altars, and have laid on *every* one a calf and a ram.

5 And the Lord put the word in his mouth, and said: Return to Balac, and thus shalt thou speak.

6 Returning, he found Balac standing by his burnt offering, with all the princes of the Moabites.

---

³ 2 Peter, 2, 15.

from the inclination he had to gratify Balac, for the sake of worldly gain. And this perverse disposition God punished by permitting him to go (though not to curse the people as he would willingly have done), and suffering him to fall still deeper into sin, till he came at last to give that abominable counsel against the people of God, which ended in his own destruction. So sad a thing it is to indulge a passion for money.

Ver. 28. *Opened the mouth.* The angel moved the tongue of the ass, to utter these speeches, to rebuke, by the mouth of a brute beast, the brutal fury and folly of Balaam.

Ver. 32. *Perverse* Because thy inclinations are wicked in being willing for the sake of gain to curse the people of whom I am the guardian.

7 And taking up his parable, he said: Balac king of the Moabites hath brought me from Aram, from the mountains of the east: Come, said he, and curse Jacob: Make haste and detest Israel.

8 How shall I curse *him*, whom God hath not cursed? By what means should I detest *him*, whom the Lord detesteth not?

9 I shall see him from the tops of the rocks, and shall consider him from the hills. *This* people shall dwell alone, and shall not be reckoned among the nations.

10 Who can count the dust of Jacob, and know the number of the stock of Israel? Let my soul die the death of the just; and my last end be like to them.

11 And Balac said to Balaam: What is this that thou dost? I sent for thee to curse my enemies: and thou contrariwise blessest them.

12 He answered him: Can I speak any thing else but what the Lord commandeth?

13 Balac therefore said: Come with me to another place from whence thou mayest see part of Israel, and canst not see them all. Curse them from thence.

14 And when he had brought him to a high place, upon the top of mount Phasga, Balaam built seven altars, and laying on *every one* a calf and a ram.

15 He said to Balac: Stand here by thy burnt offering while I go to meet *him*.

16 And when the Lord had met him, and had put the word in his mouth, he said: Return to Balac, and thus shalt thou say to him.

17 Returning he found him standing by his burnt sacrifice, and the princes of the Moabites with him. And Balac said to him. What hath the Lord spoken?

18 But he taking up his parable, said: Stand, O Balac, and give ear: hear, thou son of Sephor.

19 God is not a man, that he should lie: nor as the son of man, that he should be changed. Hath he said then, and will he not do? Hath he spoken, and will he not fulfil?

20 I was brought to bless: the blessing I am not able to hinder.

21 There is no idol in Jacob, neither is there an image-god to be seen in Israel. The Lord his God is with him: and the sound of the victory of the king in him.

22 [1] God hath brought him out of Egypt, whose strength is like to the rhinoceros.

23 There is no soothsaying in Jacob, nor divination in Israel. In their times it shall be told to Jacob and to Israel what God hath wrought.

24 Behold the people shall rise up as a lioness: and shall lift itself up as a lion. It shall not lie down till it devour the prey, and drink the blood of the slain.

25 And Balac said to Balaam: Neither curse, nor bless him.

26 And he said: Did I not tell thee, that whatsoever God should command me, that I would do?

27 And Balac said to him: Come and I will bring thee to another place. If peradventure it please God that thou mayest curse them from thence.

28 And when he had brought him upon the top of mount Phogor, which looketh towards the wilderness,

29 Balaam said to him: Build me here seven altars, and prepare as many calves, and the same number of rams.

30 Balac did as Balaam had said: and he laid on every altar, a calf and a ram.

CHAPTER 24
Balaam still continues to prophesy good things in favour of Israel.

AND when Balaam saw that it pleased the Lord that he should bless Israel, he went not as he had gone before, to seek divination: but setting his face towards the desert,

2 And lifting up his eyes, he saw Israel abiding in their tents by their tribes. And the spirit of God rushing upon him,

3 He took up his parable and said: Balaam the son of Beor hath said: The man hath said, whose eye is stopped up:

4 The hearer of the words of God hath said: He that hath beheld the vision of the Almighty: He that falleth, and so his eyes are opened:

5 How beautiful are thy tabernacles, O Jacob, and thy tents, O Israel!

6 As woody valleys: as watered gardens near the rivers: as tabernacles which the Lord hath pitched: as cedars by the waterside.

7 Water shall flow out of his bucket: and his seed shall be in many waters. For Agag his king shall be removed: and his kingdom shall be taken away.

8 God hath brought him out of Egypt, [1] whose strength is like to the rhinoceros. They shall devour the nations *that are* his enemies, and break their bones, and pierce them with arrows.

9 Lying down he hath slept as a lion, and as a lioness, whom none shall dare

to rouse. He that blesseth thee, shall also himself be blessed. He that curseth thee shall be reckoned accursed.

10 And Balac being angry against Balaam, clapped his hands together and said: I called thee to curse my enemies: and thou on the contrary hast blessed them three times.

11 Return to thy place. I had determined indeed greatly to honour thee: but the Lord hath deprived thee of the honour designed for thee.

12 Balaam made answer to Balac: Did I not say to thy messengers, whom thou sentest to me:

13 [2] If Balac would give me his house full of silver and gold, I cannot go beyond the word of the Lord my God, to utter any thing of my own head either good or evil: but whatsoever the Lord shall say, that I will speak?

14 But yet going to my people, I will give thee counsel, what this people shall do to thy people in the latter days.

15 Therefore taking up his parable, again he said: Balaam, the son of Beor, hath said: The man whose eye is stopped up, hath said:

16 The hearer of the words of God hath said, who knoweth the doctrine of the Highest, and seeth the visions of the Almighty, who falling hath his eyes opened:

17 I shall see him: but not now. I shall behold him, but not near. [3] A STAR SHALL RISE out of Jacob, and a sceptre shall spring up from Israel: and shall strike the chiefs of Moab, and shall waste all the children of Seth.

18 And he shall possess Idumea. The inheritance of Seir shall come to their enemies: but Israel shall do manfully.

19 Out of Jacob shall he come that shall rule, and shall destroy the remains of the city.

20 And when he saw Amalec, he took up his parable, and said: Amalec, the beginning of nations, whose latter ends shall be destroyed.

21 He saw also the Cinite, and took up his parable, and said: Thy habitation indeed is strong: but though thou build thy nest in a rock,

22 And thou be chosen of the stock of Cin, how long shalt thou be able to continue? For Assur shall take thee captive.

23 And taking up his parable, again he said: Alas, who shall live when God shall do these things?

24 [4] They shall come in galleys from Italy: they shall overcome the Assyrians, and shall waste the Hebrews: and at the last they themselves also shall perish.

25 And Balaam rose, and returned to his place. Balac also returned the way that he came.

CHAPTER 25

The people fall into fornication and idolatry; for which twenty-four thousand are slain. The zeal of Phinees.

AND Israel at that time [1] abode in Settim: and the people committed fornication with the daughters of Moab.

2 Who called them to their sacrifices: and they ate *of them,* and adored their gods.

3 [2] And Israel was initiated to Beelphegor. Upon which the Lord being angry.

4 Said to Moses: [3] Take all the princes of the people, and hang them up on gibbets against the sun: that my fury may be turned away from Israel.

5 And Moses said to the judges of Israel: [4] Let every man kill his neighbours, that have been initiated to Beelphegor.

6 And, behold, one of the children of Israel went in before his brethren to a harlot of Madian, in the sight of Moses, and of all the children of Israel, who were weeping before the door of the tabernacle.

7 [5] And when Phinees, the son of Eleazar, the son of Aaron the priest, saw it, he rose up from the midst of the multitude, and taking a dagger,

8 Went in after the Israelite into the brothel house, and thrust both of them through together: to wit, the man and the woman in the genital parts. And the scourge ceased from the children of Israel.

9 And there were slain four and twenty thousand men.

10 And the Lord said to Moses:

11 Phinees, the son of Eleazar, the son of Aaron the priest, hath turned away my wrath from the children of Israel: because he was moved with my zeal against them, that I myself might not destroy the children of Israel in my zeal.

12 Therefore say to him: [6] Behold I give him the peace of my covenant.

13 And the covenant of the priesthood for ever shall be both to him and his seed, because he hath been zealous for his God, and hath made atonement for the wickedness of the children of Israel.

14 And the name of the Israelite, that

[2] Num. 22, 18. [3] Matt. 2, 2. [4] Dan. 11, 30. CHAP. 25. [1] Jos. 3, 1. [2] Jos. 22, 17. [3] Deut. 4, 3. [4] Exod. 32, 27. [5] Ps. 105, 30; 1 Mach. 2, 26; 1 Cor. 10, 8. [6] Eclus. 45, 30; 1 Mach. 2, 54.

CHAP. 25. Ver. 3. *Initiated to Beelphegor.* That is, they took to the worship of Beelphegor, an obscene idol of the Moabites, and were consecrated, as it were, to him.

was slain with the woman of Madian, was Zambri, the son of Salu, a prince of the kindred and tribe of Simeon.

15 And the Madianite woman, that was slain with him, was called Cozbi, the daughter of Sur, a most noble prince among the Madianites.

16 And the Lord spoke to Moses, saying:

17 [7] Let the Madianites find you their enemies, and slay you them:

18 Because they also have acted like enemies against you, and have guilefully deceived you by the idol Phogor, and Cozbi their sister, a daughter of a prince of Madian, who was slain in the day of the plague for the sacrilege of Phogor.

CHAPTER 26

The people are again numbered by their tribes and families.

AFTER the blood of the guilty was shed, the Lord said to Moses and to Eleazar, the son of Aaron, the priest:

2 [1] Number the whole sum of the children of Israel from twenty years old and upward, by their houses and kindreds, all that are able to go forth to war.

3 Moses therefore and Eleazar the priest, *being* in the plains of Moab upon the Jordan over against Jericho, spoke to them that were

4 From twenty years old and upward, as the Lord had commanded. And this is the number of them:

5 Ruben the firstborn of Israel. [2] His sons *were* Henoch, of whom *is* the family of the Henochites: and Phallu, of whom *is* the family of the Phalluites:

6 And Hesron, of whom *is* the family of the Hesronites: and Charmi, of whom *is* the family of the Charmites.

7 These are the families of the stock of Ruben: whose number was found to be forty-three thousand seven hundred and thirty.

8 The son of Phallu *was* Eliab.

9 His sons, *were* Namuel and Dathan and Abiron. These are Dathan and Abiron the princes of the people, [3] that rose against Moses and Aaron in the sedition of Core, when they rebelled against the Lord.

10 And the earth opening her mouth swallowed up Core, many *others* dying: when the fire burned two hundred and fifty men. And there was a great miracle wrought,

11 That when Core perished, his sons did not perish.

12 The sons of Simeon by their

kindreds: Namuel, of him is the family of the Namuelites: Jamin, of him is the family of the Jaminites: Jachim, of him is the family of the Jachimites:

13 Zare, of him is the family of the Zarites: Saul, of him is the family of the Saulites.

14 These are the families of the stock of Simeon, of which the whole number was twenty-two thousand two hundred.

15 The sons of Gad by their kindreds: Sephon, of him is the family of the Sephonites: Aggi, of him is the family of the Aggites: Suni, of him is the family of the Sunites:

16 Ozni, of him is the family of the Oznites: Her, of him is the family of the Herites:

17 Arod, of him is the family of the Arodites: Ariel, of him is the family of the Arielites.

18 These are the families of Gad, of which the whole number was forty thousand five hundred.

19 [4] The sons of Juda: Her and Onan, who both died in the land of Chanaan.

20 And the sons of Juda by their kindreds were: Sela, of whom is the family of the Selaites: Phares, of whom is the family of the Pharesites: Zare, of whom is the family of the Zarites.

21 Moreover the sons of Phares *were:* Hesron, of whom is the family of the Hesronites: and Hamul, of whom is the family of the Hamulites.

22 These are the families of Juda, of which the whole number was seventy-six thousand five fundred.

23 The sons of Issachar, by their kindreds: Thola, of whom is the family of the Tholaites: Phua, of whom is the family of the Phuaites:

24 Jasub, of whom is the family of the Jasubites: Semran, of whom is the family of the Semranites.

25 These are the kindreds of Issachar, whose number was sixty-four thousand three hundred.

26 The sons of Zabulon by their kindreds: Sared, of whom is the family of the Saredites: Elon, of whom is the family of the Elonites: Jalel, of whom is the family of the Jalelites.

27 These are the kindreds of Zabulon, whose number was sixty thousand five hundred.

28 The sons of Joseph by their kindred, Manasses and Ephraim.

29 Of Manasses was born Machir, of whom is the family of the Machirites: [5] Machir begot Galaad, of whom is the family of the Galaadites.

30 Galaad had sons: Jezer, of whom is the family of the Jezerites: and Helec, of whom is the family of the Helecites:

31 And Asriel, of whom is the family

[7] Num. 31, 2. Chap. 26. [1] Num. 1, 2. [2] Gen. 46, 9; Exod. 6, 14; 1 Par. 5, 8. [3] Num. 16, 1. [4] Gen. 38, 3. [5] Jos. 17. 1.

of the Asrielites: and Sechem, of whom is the family of the Sechemites:

32 And Semida, of whom is the family of the Semidaites: [6] and Hepher, of whom is the family of the Hepherites.

33 And Hepher was the father of Salphaad, who had no sons, but only daughters, whose names are these [7] Maala, and Noa, and Hegla, and Melcha, and Thersa.

34 These are the families of Manasses, and the number of them fifty-two thousand seven hundred.

35 And the sons of Ephraim by their kindreds were these: Suthala, of whom is the family of the Suthalaites: Becher, of whom is the family of the Becherites: Thehen, of whom is the family of the Thehenites.

36 Now the son of Suthala was Heran, of whom is the family of the Heranites.

37 These are the kindreds of the sons of Ephraim: whose number was thirty-two thousand five hundred.

38 These are the sons of Joseph by their families. The sons of Benjamin in their kindreds: Bela, of whom is the family of the Belaites: Asbel, of whom is the family of the Asbelites: Ahiram, of whom is the family of the Ahiramites:

39 Supham, of whom is the family of the Suphamites: Hupham, of whom is the family of the Huphamites.

40 The sons of Bela: Hered, and Noeman. Of Hered, is the family of the Heredites: of Noeman, the family of the Noemanites.

41 These are the sons of Benjamin by their kindreds, whose number was forty-five thousand six hundred.

42 The sons of Dan by their kindreds: Suham, of whom is the family of the Suhamites. These are the kindreds of Dan by their families.

43 All were Suhamites, whose number was sixty-four thousand four hundred.

44 The sons of Aser by their kindreds: Jemna, of whom is the family of the Jemnaites: Jessui, of whom is the family of the Jessuites: Brie, of whom is the family of the Brieites.

45 The sons of Brie: Heber, of whom is the family of the Heberites: and Melchiel, of whom is the family of the Melchielites.

46 And the name of the daughter of Aser was Sara.

47 These are the kindreds of the sons of Aser, and their number fifty-three thousand four hundred.

48 The sons of Nephtali by their kindreds: Jesiel, of whom is the family of the Jesielites: Guni, of whom is the family of the Gunites:

49 Jeser, of whom is the family of the Jeserites: Sellem, of whom is the family of the Sellemites.

50 These are the kindreds of the sons of Nephtali by their families: whose number was forty-five thousand four hundred.

51 This is the sum of the children of Israel, that were reckoned up: six hundred and one thousand seven hundred and thirty.

52 And the Lord spoke to Moses, saying:

53 To these shall the land be divided for their possessions according to the number of names.

54 To the greater number thou shalt give a greater portion, and to the fewer a less. To every one, as they have now been reckoned up, shall a possession be delivered:

55 Yet so that by lot the land be divided to the tribe and families.

56 Whatsoever shall fall by lot, that shall be taken by the more, or the fewer.

57 [8] This also is the number of the sons of Levi by their families: Gerson, of whom is the family of the Gersonites: Caath, of whom is the family of the Caathites: Merari, of whom is the family of the Merarites.

58 These are the families of Levi: The family of Lobni, the family of Hebroni, the family of Moholi, the family of Musi, the family of Core. Now Caath begot Amram

59 Who had to wife Jochabed the daughter of Levi, who was born to him in Egypt. She bore to her husband Amram sons, Aaron and Moses, and Mary their sister.

60 Of Aaron were born Nadab and Abiu, and Eleazar and Ithamar:

61 [9] Of whom Nadab and Abiu died, when they had offered the strange fire before the Lord.

62 And all that were numbered, were twenty-three thousand males from one month old and upward. For they were not reckoned up among the children of Israel, neither was a possession given to them with the rest.

63 This is the number of the children of Israel, that were enrolled by Moses and Eleazar the priest, in the plains of Moab upon the Jordan, over against Jericho.

64 [10] Among whom there was not one of them that were numbered before by Moses and Aaron in the desert of Sinai.

65 [11] For the Lord had foretold that they should die in the wilderness. And none remained of them, but Caleb the

son of Jephone, and Josue the son of Nun.

CHAPTER 27

The law of inheritance. Josue is appointed to succeed Moses.

THEN [1] came the daughters of Salphaad, the son of Hepher, the son of Galaad, the son of Machir, the son of Manasses, who was the son of Joseph: and their names are Maala, and Noa, and Hegla, and Melcha, and Thersa.

2 And they stood before Moses and Eleazar the priest, and all the princes of the people at the door of the tabernacle of the covenant, and said:

3 Our father died in the desert, and was not in the sedition, [2] that was raised against the Lord under Core: but he died in his own sin. *And* he had no male children. Why is his name taken away out of his family, because he had no son? Give us a possession among the kinsmen of our father.

4 And Moses referred their cause to the judgment of the Lord.

5 And *the Lord* said to him:

6 The daughters of Salphaad demand a just thing: Give them a possession among their father's kindred, and let them succeed him in his inheritance.

7 And to the children of Israel thou shalt speak these things:

8 When a man dieth without a son, his inheritance shall pass to his daughter.

9 If he have no daughter, his brethren shall succeed him.

10 And if he have no brethren, you shall give the inheritance to his father's brethren.

11 But if he have no uncles by the father, the inheritance shall be given to them that are the next akin. And this shall be to the children of Israel sacred, by a perpetual law, as the Lord hath commanded Moses.

12 The Lord also said to Moses: [3] Go up into this mountain Abarim: and view from thence the land which I will give to the children of Israel.

13 And when thou shalt have seen it, thou also shalt go to thy people, as thy brother Aaron is gone.

14 [4] Because you offended me in the desert of Sin in the contradiction of the multitude: neither would you sanctify me before them at the waters. These are the waters of contradiction in Cades of the desert of Sin.

15 And Moses answered him:

16 May the Lord the God of the

spirits of all flesh provide a man, that may be over this multitude:

17 And may go out and in before them: and may lead them out, or bring them in: lest the people of the Lord be as sheep without a shepherd.

18 And the Lord said to him: [5] Take Josue, the son of Nun, a man in whom is the Spirit, and put thy hand upon him.

19 And he shall stand before Eleazar the priest and all the multitude.

20 And thou shalt give him precepts in the sight of all, and part of thy glory, that all the congregation of the children of Israel may hear him.

21 If any thing be to be done, Eleazar the priest shall consult the Lord for him. He and all the children of Israel with him, and the rest of the multitude, shall go out and go in at his word.

22 Moses did as the Lord had commanded. And when he had taken Josue, he set him before Eleazar the priest, and all the assembly of the people.

23 And laying his hands on his head, he repeated all things that the Lord had commanded.

CHAPTER 28

Sacrifices are appointed as well for every day as for sabbaths, and other festivals.

THE Lord also said to Moses:
2 Command the children of Israel, and thou shalt say to them: Offer ye my oblation and my bread, and burnt sacrifice of most sweet odour, in their due seasons.

3 These are the sacrifices which you shall offer. [1] Two lambs of a year old without blemish every day for the perpetual holocaust.

4 One you shall offer in the morning, and the other in the evening.

5 *And* the tenth part of an ephi of flour, which shall be tempered with the purest oil: of the measure of the fourth part of a hin.

6 It is the continual holocaust which you offered in mount Sinai for a most sweet odour of a sacrifice by fire to the Lord.

7 And for a libation you shall offer of wine the fourth part of a hin for every lamb in the sanctuary of the Lord.

8 And you shall offer the other lamb in like manner in the evening according to all the rites of the morning sacrifice, and of the libations thereof: an oblation of most sweet odour to the Lord.

9 [2] And on the sabbath day you shall offer two lambs of a year old without blemish: and two tenths of flour tempered with oil in sacrifice: and the libations,

10 Which regularly are poured out

<hr>

CHAP. 27. [1] Num. 26, 32; 36, 1; Jos. 17, 1. [2] Num. 16, 1. [3] Deut. 32, 49. [4] Num. 20, 12; Deut. 32, 51. [5] Deut. 3, 21. CHAP. 28. [1] Exod. 29, 38. [2] Matt. 12, .5.

every sabbath for the perpetual holocaust.

11 And on the first day of the month you shall offer a holocaust to the Lord, two calves of the herd, one ram, and seven lambs of a year old, without blemish.

12 And three tenths of flour tempered with oil in sacrifice for every calf: and two tenths of flour tempered with oil for every ram:

13 And the tenth of a tenth of flour *tempered* with oil in sacrifice for every lamb. It is a holocaust of most sweet odour and an offering by fire to the Lord.

14 And these shall be the libations of wine that are to be poured out for every victim. Half a hin for every calf, a third for a ram, *and* a fourth for a lamb. This shall be the holocaust for every month, as they succeed one another in the course of the year.

15 A buck-goat also shall be offered to the Lord for a sin offering over and above the perpetual holocaust with its libations.

16 [3] And in the first month, on the fourteenth day of the month, shall be the phase of the Lord.

17 And on the fifteenth day the solemn feast. Seven days shall they eat unleavened bread.

18 And the first day of them shall be venerable and holy: you shall not do any servile work therein.

19 And you shall offer a burnt sacrifice a holocaust to the Lord: two calves of the herd, one ram, seven lambs of a year old, without blemish.

20 And for the sacrifices of every one, three tenths of flour which shall be tempered with oil to every calf, and two tenths to every ram.

21 And the tenth of a tenth, to every lamb, that is to say, to all the seven lambs.

22 And one buck-goat for sin, to make atonement for you:

23 Besides the morning holocaust which you shall always offer.

24 So shall you do every day of the seven days for the food of the fire, and for a most sweet odour to the Lord, which shall rise from the holocaust, and from the libations of each.

25 The seventh day also shall be most solemn and holy unto you: you shall do no servile work therein.

26 The day also of firstfruits, when after the weeks are accomplished, you shall offer new fruits to the Lord, shall be venerable and holy: you shall do no servile work therein.

27 And you shall offer a holocaust for a most sweet odour to the Lord: two

calves of the herd, one ram, and seven lambs of a year old, without blemish.

28 And in the sacrifices of them three tenths of flour tempered with oil to every calf, two to every ram:

29 The tenth of a tenth to every lamb, which in all are seven lambs: a buck-goat also,

30 Which is slain for expiation: besides the perpetual holocaust and the libations thereof.

31 You shall offer them all without blemish with their libations.

CHAPTER 29
Sacrifices for the festivals of the seventh month.

THE first day also of the seventh month shall be venerable and holy unto you; you shall do no servile work therein, because it is the day of the sounding and of trumpets.

2 And you shall offer a holocaust for a most sweet odour to the Lord: one calf of the herd, one ram and seven lambs of a year old, without blemish.

3 And for their sacrifices, three tenths of flour tempered with oil to every calf, two tenths to a ram:

4 One tenth to a lamb, which in all are seven lambs:

5 And a buck-goat for sin, which is offered for the expiation of the people:

6 Besides the holocaust of the first day of the month with the sacrifices thereof, and the perpetual holocaust with the accustomed libations. With the same ceremonies you shall offer a burnt sacrifice for a most sweet odour to the Lord.

7 [1] The tenth day also of this seventh month shall be holy and venerable unto you: and you shall afflict your souls. You shall do no servile work therein.

8 And you shall offer a holocaust to the Lord for a most sweet odour: one calf of the herd, one ram, and seven lambs of a year old, without blemish:

9 And for their sacrifices, three tenths of flour tempered with oil to every calf, two tenths to a ram:

10 The tenth of a tenth to every lamb, which are in all seven lambs:

11 And a buck-goat for sin: besides the things that are wont to be offered for sin, for expiation, and for the perpetual holocaust with their sacrifice and libations.

12 And on the fifteenth day of the seventh month, which shall be unto you holy and venerable, you shall do no servile work, but shall celebrate a solemnity to the Lord seven days.

13 And you shall offer a holocaust for

3 Exod. 12, 18; Lev. 23, 5. CHAP. 29. 1 Lev. 16, 29; 23, 24.

a most sweet odour to the Lord: thirteen calves of the herd, two rams, *and* fourteen lambs of a year old, without blemish.

14 And for their libations three tenths of flour tempered with oil to every calf, being in all thirteen calves: and two tenths to each ram, being two rams:

15 And the tenth of a tenth to every lamb, being in all fourteen lambs:

16 And a buck-goat for sin: besides the perpetual holocaust, and the sacrifice and the libation thereof.

17 On the second day you shall offer twelve calves of the herd, two rams and fourteen lambs of a year old, without blemish.

18 And the sacrifices and the libations for every one, for the calves and for the rams, and for the lambs, you shall duly celebrate:

19 And a buck-goat for a sin offering: besides the perpetual holocaust, and the sacrifice and the libation thereof.

20 The third day you shall offer eleven calves, two rams, and fourteen lambs of a year old, without blemish.

21 And the sacrifices and the libations of every one for the calves and for the rams and for the lambs you shall offer according to the rite:

22 And a buck-goat for sin: besides the perpetual bolocaust, and the sacrifice and the libation thereof.

23 The fourth day you shall offer ten calves, two rams, and fourteen lambs of a year old, without blemish.

24 And the sacrifices and the libations of every one for the calves and for the rams and for the lambs you shall celebrate in right manner:

25 And a buck-goat for sin: besides the perpetual holocaust, and the sacrifice and the libation thereof.

26 The fifth day you shall offer nine calves, two rams, and fourteen lambs of a year old, without blemish.

27 And the sacrifices and the libations of every one for the calves and for the rams and for the lambs you shall celebrate according to the rite:

28 And a buck-goat for sin: besides the perpetual holocaust, and the sacrifice and the libation thereof.

29 The sixth day you shall offer eight calves, two rams, and fourteen lambs of a year old, without blemish.

30 And the sacrifices and the libations of every one for the calves and for the rams and for the lambs you shall celebrate according to the rite:

31 And a buck-goat for sin: besides the perpetual holocaust, and the sacrifice and the libation thereof.

32 The seventh day you shall offer seven calves and two rams, and fourteen lambs of a year old, without blemish.

33 And the sacrifices and the libations of every one for the calves and for the rams and for the lambs you shall celebrate according to the rite:

34 And a buck-goat for sin: besides the perpetual holocaust, and the sacrifice and the libation thereof.

35 On the eighth day, which is most solemn, you shall do no servile work.

36 But you shall offer a holocaust for a most sweet odour to the Lord, one calf, one ram, and seven lambs of a year old, without blemish.

37 And the sacrifices and the libations of every one for the calves and for the rams and for the lambs you shall celebrate according to the rite:

38 And a buck-goat for sin: besides the perpetual holocaust, and the sacrifice and the libation thereof.

39 These things shall you offer to the Lord in your solemnities: besides your vows and voluntary oblations for holocaust, for sacrifice, for libation, and for victims of peace offerings.

CHAPTER 30

Of vows and oaths, and their obligation.

AND Moses told the children of Israel all that the Lord had commanded him.

2 And he said to the princes of the tribes of the children of Israel: This is the word that the Lord hath commanded.

3 If any man make a vow to the Lord, or bind himself by an oath: he shall not make his word void but shall fulfil all that he promised.

4 If a woman vow any thing, and bind herself by an oath, being in her father's house, and but yet a girl in age: if her father knew the vow that she hath promised, and the oath wherewith she hath bound her soul, and held his peace, she shall be bound by the vow.

5 Whatsoever she promised and swore, she shall fulfil in deed.

6 But if her father, immediately as soon as he heard it, gainsaid it, both her vows and her oaths shall be void: neither shall she be bound to what she promised, because her father hath gainsaid it.

7 If she have a husband, and shall vow any thing, and the word once going out of her mouth shall bind her soul by an oath:

8 The day that her husband shall hear it, and not gainsay it, she shall be bound to the vow, and shall give whatsoever she promised.

9 But if, as soon as he heareth, he gainsay it, and make her promises and the words wherewith she had bound her soul of no effect: the Lord will forgive her.

10 The widow, and she that is divorced, shall fulfil whatsoever they vow.

11 If the wife in the house of her husband, hath bound herhelf by vow and by oath:

12 If her husband hear, and hold his peace, and doth not disallow the promise, she shall accomplish whatsoever she had promised.

13 But if forthwith he gainsay it, she shall not be bound by the promise: because her husband gainsaid it, and the Lord will be merciful to her.

14 If she vow and bind herself by oath, to afflict her soul by fasting, or abstinence from other things, it shall depend on the will of her husband, whether she shall do it, or not do it.

15 But if the husband hearing it hold his peace, and defer the declaring his mind till another day: whatsoever she had vowed and promised, she shall fulfil: because immediately as he heard it, he held his peace.

16 But if he gainsay it after that he knew it, he shall bear her iniquity.

17 These are the laws which the Lord appointed to Moses between the husband and the wife, between the father and the daughter that is as yet but a girl in age, or that abideth in her father's house.

CHAPTER 31

The Madianites are slain for having drawn the people of Israel into sin. The dividing of the booty.

AND the Lord spoke to Moses, saying:

2 Revenge first the children of Israel on the Madianites: and so thou shalt be gathered to thy people.

3 And Moses forthwith said: [1] Arm of you men to fight, who may take the revenge of the Lord on the Madianites.

4 Let a thousand men be chosen out of every tribe of Israel to be sent to the war.

5 And they gave a thousand of every tribe: that is to say, twelve thousand men well appointed for battle.

6 And Moses sent them with Phinees the son of Eleazar the priest: and he delivered to him the holy vessels, and the trumpets to sound.

7 And when they had fought against the Madianites and had overcome them, they slew all the men.

8 [2] And their kings, Evi, and Recem, and Sur, and Hur, and Rebe, five princes of the nation. Balaam also, the son of Beor, they killed with the sword.

9 And they took their women, and their children captives, and all their cattle, and all their goods: and all their possessions they plundered.

10 And all their cities, and their villages, and castles, they burned.

11 And they carried away the booty, and all that they had taken both of men and of beasts.

12 And they brought them to Moses, and Eleazar the priest, and to all the multitude of the children of Israel. But the rest of the things for use they carried to the camp on the plains of Moab, beside the Jordan over against Jericho.

13 And Moses and Eleazar the priest and all the princes of the synagogue went forth to meet them without the camp.

14 And Moses being angry with the chief officers of the army, the tribunes, and the centurions that were come from the battle,

15 Said: Why have you saved the women?

16 [3] Are not these they, that deceived the children of Israel, by the counsel of Balaam, and made you transgress against the Lord by the sin of Phogor, for which also the people was punished?

17 [4] Therefore kill all that are of the male sex, even of the children: and put to death the women that have carnally known men.

18 But the girls, and all the women that are virgins save for yourselves.

19 And stay without the camp seven days. He that hath killed a man, or touched one that is killed, shall be purified the third day and the seventh day.

20 And of all the spoil, every garment, or vessel, or any thing made for use, of the skins, or hair of goats, or of wood, shall be purified.

21 Eleazar also the priest spoke to the men of the army, that had fought, in this manner: This is the ordinance of the law, [5] which the Lord hath commanded Moses.

22 Gold, and silver, and brass, and iron, and lead, and tin:

23 And all that may pass through the fire, shall be purified by fire, but whatsoever cannot abide the fire, shall be sanctified with the water of expiation.

CHAP. 31. [1] Num. 25, 17. [2] Js. 13, 21. [3] Num. 25, 18. [4] Judges, 21, 11. [5] Lev. 6, 28; 11, 33; 15, 11.

CHAP. 31. Ver. 16. *The sin of Phogor.* The sin committed in the worship of *Beelphegor.*
Ver. 17. *Of children.* Women and children, ordinarily speaking, were not to be killed in war (Deut. 20, 14). But the great Lord of life and death was pleased to order it otherwise in the present case, in detestation of the wickedness of this people, who by the counsel of Balaam, had sent their women among the Israelites on purpose to draw them from God.

24 And you shall wash your garments the seventh day, and being purified, you shall afterwards enter into the camp.

25 And the Lord said to Moses:

26 Take the sum of the things that were taken both of man and beast, thou and Eleazar the priest and the princes of the multitude.

27 And thou shalt divide the spoil equally, between them that fought and went out to the war, and between the rest of the multitude.

28 And thou shalt separate a portion to the Lord from them that fought and were in the battle: one soul of five hundred as well of persons as of oxen and asses and sheep.

29 And thou shalt give it to Eleazar the priest, because they are the first-fruits of the Lord.

30 Out of the moiety also of the children of Israel thou shalt take the fiftieth head of persons, and of oxen, and asses, and sheep, and of all beasts: and thou shalt give them to the Levites that watch in the charge of the tabernacle of the Lord.

31 And Moses and Eleazar did as the Lord had commanded.

32 And the spoil which the army had taken, was six hundred seventy-five thousand sheep.

33 Seventy-two thousand oxen:

34 Sixty-one thousand asses:

35 And thirty-two thousand persons of the female sex, that had not known men.

36 And one half was given to them that had been in the battle: to wit three hundred thirty-seven thousand five hundred sheep.

37 Out of which, for the portion of the Lord, were reckoned six hundred seventy-five sheep.

38 And out of the thirty-six thousand oxen, seventy-two oxen.

39 Out of the thirty thousand five hundred asses, sixty-one asses.

40 Out of the sixteen thousand persons, there fell to the portion of the Lord, thirty-two souls.

41 And Moses delivered the number of the firstfruits of the Lord to Eleazar the priest, as had been commanded him.

42 Out of the half of the children of Israel, which he had separated for them that had been in the battle.

43 But out of the half that fell to the rest of the multitude: that is to say, out of the three hundred thirty-seven thousand five hundred sheep.

44 And out of the thirty-six thousand oxen,

45 And out of the thirty thousand five hundred asses,

46 And out of the sixteen thousand persons,

47 Moses took the fiftieth head: and gave it to the Levites that watched in the tabernacle of the Lord, as the Lord had commanded.

48 And when the commanders of the army, and the tribunes and centurions were come to Moses, they said:

49 We, thy servants, have reckoned up the number of the fighting men, whom we had under our hand, and not so much as one was wanting.

50 Therefore we offer as gifts to the Lord what gold every one of us could find in the booty: in garters and tablets, rings and bracelets, and chains, that thou mayst pray to the Lord for us.

51 And Moses and Eleazar the priest received all the gold in divers kinds,

52 In weight sixteen thousand seven hundred and fifty sicles, from the tribunes and from the centurions.

53 For that which every one had taken in the booty was his own.

54 And that which was received they brought into the tabernacle of the testimony, for a memorial of the children of Israel before the Lord.

CHAPTER 32

The tribes of Ruben and Gad, and half of the tribe of Manasses, receive their inheritance on the east side of Jordan, upon conditions approved of by Moses.

AND [1] the sons of Ruben and Gad had many flocks of cattle: and their substance in beasts was infinite. And when they saw the lands of Jazer and Galaad fit for feeding cattle:

2 They came to Moses and Eleazar the priest, and the princes of the multitude, and said:

3 Ataroth, and Dibon, and Jazer, and Nemra, Hesebon, and Eleale, and Saban, and Nebo, and Beon:

4 The land, which the Lord hath conquered in the sight of the children of Israel, is a very fertile soil for the feeding of beasts: and we thy servants have very much cattle,

5 And we pray thee, if we have found favour in thy sight, that thou give it to us thy servants in possession, and make us not pass over the Jordan.

6 And Moses answered them: What, shall your brethren go to fight, and will you sit here?

7 Why do ye overturn the minds of the children of Israel, that they may not dare to pass into the place which the Lord hath given them?

8 Was it not thus your fathers did, when I sent from Cadesbarne to view the land?

9 [2] And when they were come as far

CHAP. 32. [1] Deut. 3, 12. [2] Num. 13. 24

as the valley of the cluster, having viewed all the country, they overturned the hearts of the children of Israel, that they should not enter into the coasts, which the Lord gave them.

10 [3] And he swore in his anger, saying:

11 If these men, that came up out of Egypt, from twenty years old and upward, shall see the land, which I promised with an oath to Abraham, Isaac, and Jacob, because they would not follow me:

12 Except Caleb the son of Jephone the Cenezite, and Josue the son of Nun. These have fulfilled my will.

13 And the Lord being angry against Israel, led them about through the desert forty years, until the old generation, that had done evil in his sight was consumed.

14 And, behold, said he, you are risen up instead of your fathers, the increase and offspring of sinful men, to augment the fury of the Lord against Israel.

15 For if you will not follow him, he will leave the people in the wilderness: and you shall be the cause of the destruction of all.

16 But they coming near, said: We will make sheepfolds, and stalls for our cattle, and strong cities for our children.

17 And we ourselves will go armed and ready for battle before the children of Israel, until we bring them in unto their places. Our little ones, and all we have, shall be in walled cities, for fear of the ambushes of the inhabitants.

18 We will not return into our houses until the children of Israel possess their inheritance.

19 Neither will we seek anything beyond the Jordan, because we have already our possession on the east side thereof.

20 And Moses said to them: [4] If you do what you promise, go on well appointed for war before the Lord.

21 And let every fighting man pass over the Jordan, until the Lord overthrow his enemies:

22 And all the land be brought under him. Then shall you be blameless before the Lord and before Israel: and you shall obtain the countries that you desire, before the Lord.

23 But if you do not what you say, no man can doubt but you sin against God. And know ye, that your sin shall overtake you.

24 Build therefore cities for your children, and folds and stalls for your sheep and beasts: and accomplish what you have promised.

25 [5] And the children of Gad and Ruben said to Moses: We are thy serv-

ants, we will do what my lord commandeth.

26 We will leave our children, and our wives and sheep and cattle, in the cities of Galaad.

27 And we thy servants all well appointed will march on to the war, as thou, my lord, speakest.

28 Moses therefore commanded Eleazar the priest, and Josue the son of Nun, and the princes of the families of all the tribes of Israel, and said to them:

29 [6] If the children of Gad, and the children of Ruben pass with you over the Jordan, all armed for war before the Lord, and the land be made subject to you: give them Galaad in possession.

30 But if they will not pass armed with you into the land of Chanaan: let them receive places to dwell in among you.

31 And the children of Gad, and the children of Ruben answered: As the Lord hath spoken to his servants, so will we do.

32 We will go armed before the Lord into the land of Chanaan: and we confess that we have already received our possession beyond the Jordan.

33 Moses therefore gave to the children of Gad and of Ruben, and to the half tribe of Manasses, the son of Joseph, the kingdom of Sehon king of the Amorrhites, and the kingdom of Og king of Basan, and their land and the cities thereof round about.

34 And the sons of Gad built Dibon, and Ataroth, and Aroer,

35 And Etroth, and Sopham, and Jazer, and Jegbaa,

36 And Bethnemra, and Betharan: fenced cities, and folds for their cattle.

37 But the children of Ruben built Hesebon, and Eleale, and Cariathaim.

38 And Nabo, and Baalmeon (their names being changed) and Sabama: giving names to the cities which they had built.

39 [7] Moreover the children of Machir, the son of Manasses, went into Galaad, and wasted it, cutting off the Amorrhites, the inhabitants thereof.

40 And Moses gave the land of Galaad to Machir the son of Manasses: and he dwelt in it.

41 And Jair the son of Manasses went, and took the villages thereof: and he called them Havoth Jair, that is to say, the villages of Jair.

42 Nobe also went, and took Canath with the villages thereof: and he called it by his own name, Nobe.

---

[3] Num. 14, 29. [4] Jos. 1, 14. [5] Jos. 4, 12. [6] Deut. 3, 12; Jos. 13, 8; 22, 4. [7] Gen. 1, 22.

CHAPTER 33

The mansions or journeys of the children of Israel towards the land of promise.

THESE are the mansions of the children of Israel, who went out of Egypt by their troops under the conduct of Moses and Aaron,

2 Which Moses wrote down according to the places of their encamping, which they changed by the commandment of the Lord.

3 Now the children of Israel departed from Ramesses the first month, on the fifteenth day of the first month, the day after the phase, with a mighty hand, in the sight of all the Egyptians,

4 [1] Who were burying their firstborn, whom the Lord had slain (upon their gods also he had executed vengeance),

5 And they camped in Soccoth.

6 And from Soccoth they came into Etham, which is in the uttermost borders of the wilderness.

7 [2] Departing from thence they came over against Phihahiroth, which looketh towards Beelsephon, and they camped before Magdalum.

8 And departing from Phihahiroth, they passed through the midst of the sea into the wilderness. [3] And having marched three days through the desert of Etham, they camped in Mara.

9 [4] And departing from Mara, they came into Elim, where there were twelve fountains of waters, and seventy palm trees: and there they camped.

10 But departing from thence also, they pitched their tents by the Red Sea. And departing from the Red Sea,

11 They camped in the desert of Sin.

12 And they removed from thence, and came to Daphca.

13 And departing from Daphca, they camped in Alus.

14 And departing from Alus, they pitched their tents in Raphidim. [5] where the people wanted water to drink.

15 And departing from Raphidim they camped in the desert of Sinai.

16 But departing also from the desert [6] of Sinai, they came to the graves of lust.

17 And departing from the graves of lust, they camped in Haseroth.

18 [7] And from Haseroth they came to Rethma.

19 And departing from Rethma, they camped in Remmomphares.

20 And they departed from thence and came to Lebna.

21 Removing from Lebna they camped in Ressa.

22 And departing from Ressa, they came to Ceelatha.

23 And they removed from thence and camped in the mountain Sepher.

24 Departing from the mountain Sepher, they came to Arada.

25 From thence they went and camped in Maceloth.

26 And departing from Maceloth, they came to Thahath.

27 Removing from Thahath they camped in Thare.

28 And they departed from thence, and pitched their tents in Methca.

29 And removing from Methca, they camped in Hesmona.

30 And departing from Hesmona they came to Moseroth.

31 And *removing* from Moseroth, they camped in Benejaacan.

32 [8] And departing from Benejaacan, they came to mount Gadgad.

33 From thence they went and camped in Jetebatha.

34 And from Jetebatha they came to Hebrona.

35 And departing from Hebrona, they camped in Asiongaber.

36 [9] They removed from thence and came into the desert of Sin, which is Cades.

37 And departing from Cades, they camped in mount Hor, in the uttermost borders of the land of Edom.

38 [10] And Aaron the priest went up into mount Hor at the commandment of the Lord: and there he died in the fortieth year of the coming forth of the children of Israel out of Egypt, the fifth month, the first day of the month,

39 When he was a hundred and twenty-three years old.

40 And king Arad the Chanaanite, who dwelt towards the south, heard that the children of Israel were come to the land of Chanaan.

41 And they departed from mount Hor, and camped in Salmona.

42 From whence they removed and came to Phunon.

43 And departing from Phunon, they camped in Oboth.

44 And from Oboth they came to Ijeabarim, which is in the borders of the Moabites.

45 And departing from Ijeabarim they pitched their tents in Dibongab.

CHAP. 33. [1] Exod. 12, 12. [2] Exod. 14, 2. [3] Exod. 15, 22. [4] Exod. 15, 27. [5] Exod. 17, 1. [6] Exod. 19, 2; Num. 11, 34. [7] Num. 13, 1. [8] Deut. 10, 7. [9] Num. 20, 21. [10] Num. 20, 25; Deut. 32, 50.

CHAP. 33. Ver. 1. *The mansions.* These mansions or journeys of the children of Israel from Egypt to the land of promise, were figures, according to the fathers, of the steps and degrees by which Christians leaving sin are to advance from virtue to virtue, till they come to the heavenly mansions, after this life, to see and enjoy God.

46 From thence they went and camped in Helmondeblathaim.

47 And departing from Helmondeblathaim, they came to the mountains of Abarim over against Nabo.

48 And departing from the mountains of Abarim, they passed to the plains of Moab, by the Jordan, over against Jericho.

49 And there they camped from Bethsimoth even to Ablesatim in the plains of the Moabites,

50 Where the Lord said to Moses:

51 Command the children of Israel, and say to them: When you shall have passed over the Jordan, entering into the land of Chanaan,

52 Destroy all the inhabitants of that land. [11] Beat down their pillars, and break in pieces their statues, and waste all their high places,

53 Cleansing the land, and dwelling in it. For I have given it to you for a possession.

54 And you shall divide it among you by lot. To the more you shall give a larger part, and to the fewer a lesser. To every one as the lot shall fall, so shall the inheritance be given. The possession shall be divided by the tribes and the families.

55 But if you will not kill the inhabitants of the land: they that remain, shall be unto you as nails in *your* eyes and spears in *your* sides. And they shall be your adversaries in the land of your habitation.

56 And whatsoever I had thought to do to them, I will do to you.

CHAPTER 34

The limits of Chanaan, with the names of the men that make the division of it.

AND the Lord spoke to Moses, saying:

2 Command the children of Israel, and thou shalt say to them: When you are entered into the land of Chanaan, and it shall be fallen into your possession by lot, it shall be bounded by these limits.

3 [1] The south side shall begin from the wilderness of Sin, which is by Edom, and shall have the most salt sea for its furthest limits eastward.

4 Which limits shall go round on the south side by the ascent of the Scorpion and so into Senna, and reach toward the south as far as Cadesbarne: from whence the frontiers shall go out to the town called Adar, and shall reach as far as Asemona.

5 And the limits shall fetch a compass from Asemona to the torrent of Egypt, and shall end in the shore of the great sea.

6 And the west side shall begin from the great sea: and the same shall be the end thereof.

7 But toward the north side the borders shall begin from the great sea, reaching to the most high mountain:

8 From which they shall come to Emath, as far as the borders of Sedada.

9 And the limits shall go as far as Zephrona, and the village of Enan. These shall be the borders on the north side.

10 From thence they shall mark out the bounds towards the east side from the village of Enan unto Sephama.

11 And from Sephama the bounds shall go down to Rebla over against the fountain of Daphnis. From thence they shall come eastward to the sea of Cenereth:

12 And shall reach as far as the Jordan: and at the last shall be closed in by the most salt sea. This shall be your land with its borders round about.

13 And Moses commanded the children of Israel, saying: This shall be the land which you shall possess by lot, and which the Lord hath commanded to be given to the nine tribes, and to the half tribe.

14 For the tribe of the children of Ruben by their families, and the tribe of the children of Gad according to the number of their kindreds, and half of the tribe of Manasses,

15 (That is, two tribes and a half) have received their portion beyond the Jordan, over against Jericho, at the east side.

16 And the Lord said to Moses:

17 [2] These are the names of the men, that shall divide the land unto you. Eleazar the priest, and Josue the son of Nun,

18 And one prince of every tribe:

19 Whose names are these: Of the tribe of Juda, Caleb the son of Jephone.

20 Of the tribe of Simeon, Samuel the son of Ammiud.

21 Of the tribe of Benjamin, Elidad the son of Chaselon.

22 Of the tribe of the children of Dan, Bocci the son of Jogli.

23 Of the children of Joseph, of the tribe of Manasses, Hanniel the son of Ephod.

24 Of the tribe of Ephraim, Camuel the son of Sephtan.

---

[11] Deut. 7, 5; Judges, 2, 2. **Chap. 34.** [1] Jos. 15, 1. [2] Jos. 14, 1.

Chap. 34. Ver. 3. *The most salt sea.* The lake of Sodom, otherwise called the Dead Sea.

Ver. 4. *The Scorpion.* A mountain so called from having a great number of scorpions.

Ver. 5. *The great sea.* The Mediterranean.

Ver. 7. *The most high mountain.* Libanus.

Ver. 11. *Sea of Cenereth.* This is the sea of Galilee, illustrated by the miracles of our Lord.

25 Of the tribe of Zabulon, Elisaphan the son of Pharnach.

26 Of the tribe of Issachar, Phaltiel the prince, the son of Ozan.

27 Of the tribe of Aser, Ahiud the son of Salomi.

28 Of the tribe of Nephtali, Phedael the son of Ammiud.

29 These are they whom the Lord hath commanded to divide the land of Chanaan to the children of Israel.

CHAPTER 35

Cities are appointed for the Levites. Of which six are to be the cities of refuge.

AND the Lord spoke these things also to Moses in the plains of Moab by the Jordan, over against Jericho:

2 [1] Command the children of Israel that they give to the Levites out of their possessions,

3 Cities to dwell in, and their suburbs round about: that they may abide in the towns, and the suburbs may be for their cattle and beasts.

4 Which suburbs shall reach from the walls of the cities outward, a thousand paces on every side.

5 Toward the east shall be two thousand cubits: and toward the south in like manner shall be two thousand cubits: toward the sea also, which looketh to the west, shall be the same extent: and the north side shall be bounded with the like limits. And the cities shall be in the midst, and the suburbs without.

6 [2] And among the cities, which you shall give to the Levites, six shall be separated for refuge to fugitives, that he who hath shed blood may flee to them. And besides these there shall be other forty-two cities:

7 That is, in all forty-eight with their suburbs.

8 And of these cities which shall be given out of the possessions of the children of Israel, from them that have more, more shall be taken: and *from them* that have less, fewer. Each shall give towns to the Levites according to the extent of their inheritance.

9 The Lord said to Moses:

10 Speak to the children of Israel. and thou shalt say to them: When you shall have passed over the Jordan into the land of Chanaan,

11 Determine what cities shall be for the refuge of fugitives, who have shed blood against their will.

CHAP. 35. [1] Jos. 21, 2. [2] Deut. 19, 2; Jos. 20, 2. [3] Deut. 4, 41; Jos. 20, 7. [4] Deut. 19, 11.

CHAP. 35. Ver. 25. *Until the death.* This mystically signified that our deliverance was to be effected by the death of Christ, the high priest and the anointed of God.

12 And when the fugitive shall be in them, the kinsman of him that is slain may not have power to kill him, until he stand before the multitude, and his cause be judged.

13 [3] And of those cities, that are separated for the refuge of fugitives,

14 Three shall be beyond the Jordan, and three in the land of Chanaan.

15 As well for the children of Israel as for strangers and sojourners, that he may flee to them, who hath shed blood against his will.

16 If any man strike with iron, and he die that was struck: he shall be guilty of murder, and he himself shall die.

17 If he throw a stone, and he that is struck die: he shall be punished in the same manner.

18 If he that is struck with wood die: he shall be revenged by the blood of him that struck him.

19 The kinsman of him that was slain, shall kill the murderer: as soon as he apprehendeth him, he shall kill him.

20 [4] If through hatred any one push a man; or fling any thing at him with ill design:

21 Or being his enemy, strike him with his hand, and he die: the striker shall be guilty of murder. The kinsman of him that was slain, as soon as he findeth him, shall kill him.

22 But if by chance medley, and without hatred,

23 And enmity, he do any of these things:

24 And this be proved in the hearing of the people, and the cause be debated between him that struck, and the next of kin:

25 The innocent shall be delivered from the hand of the revenger, and shall be brought back by sentence into the city, to which he had fled: and he shall abide there until the death of the high priest, that is anointed with the holy oil.

26 If the murderer be found without the limits of the cities that are appointed for the banished,

27 And be struck by him that is the avenger of blood: he shall not be guilty that killed him.

28 For the fugitive ought to have stayed in the city until the death of the high priest. And after he is dead, then shall the manslayer return to his own country.

29 These things shall be perpetual, and for an ordinance in all your dwellings.

30 The murderer shall be punished

by witnesses: none shall be condemned upon the evidence of one man.

31 You shall not take money of him that is guilty of blood: *but* he shall die forthwith.

32 The banished and fugitives before the death of the high priest may by no means return into their own cities.

33 Defile not the land of your habitation, which is stained with the blood of the innocent. Neither can it otherwise be expiated, but by his blood that hath shed the blood of another.

34 And thus shall your possession be cleansed, myself abiding with you. For I am the Lord that dwell among the children of Israel.

CHAPTER 36

That the inheritances may not be alienated from one tribe to another, all are to marry within their own tribes.

AND the princes of the families of Galaad, the son of Machir, the son of Manasses, of the stock of the children of Joseph, came and spoke to Moses before the princes of Israel, and said: [1]

2 The Lord hath commanded thee, my lord, that thou shouldst divide the land by lot to the children of Israel, and that thou shouldst give to the daughters of Salphaad our brother the possession due to their father.

3 Now if men of another tribe take them to wives, their possession will follow them: and being transferred to another tribe, will be a diminishing of our inheritance.

4 And so it shall come to pass, that when the jubilee, that is, the fiftieth year of remission, is come, the distribution made by the lots shall be confounded: and the possession of the one shall pass to the others.

5 Moses answered the children of Israel, and said by the command of the Lord: The tribe of the children of Joseph hath spoken rightly.

6 And this is the law promulgated by the Lord touching the daughters of Salphaad: [2] Let them marry to whom they will, only so that it be to men of their own tribe.

7 Lest the possession of the children of Israel be mingled from tribe to tribe. For all men shall marry wives of their own tribe and kindred.

8 And all women shall take husbands of the same tribe: that the inheritance may remain in the families,

9 And that the tribes be not mingled one with another, but remain so

10 As they were separated by the Lord. And the daughters of Salphaad did as was commanded.

11 And Maala, and Thersa, and Hegla, and Melcha, and Noa were married to the sons of their uncle by their father.

12 Of the family of Manasses, who was the son of Joseph. And the possession that had been alotted to them, remained in the tribe and family of their father.

13 These are the commandments and judgments, which the Lord commanded by the hand of Moses to the children of Israel, in the plains of Moab upon the Jordan over against Jericho.

THE BOOK OF
DEUTERONOMY

This Book is called DEUTERONOMY, *which signifies a* SECOND LAW, *because it repeats and inculcates the ordinances formerly given on mount Sinai, with other precepts not expressed before. The Hebrews, from the first words in the book, call it* ELLE HADDEBARIM.

CHAPTER 1

A repetition of what passed at Sinai and Cadesbarne, and of the people's murmuring and their punishment.

THESE are the words, which Moses spoke to all Israel beyond the Jordan, in the plain wilderness, over against the Red Sea, between Pharan and Thophel and Laban and Haseroth, where there is very much gold:

2 Eleven days' journey from Horeb by the way of mount Seir to Cadesbarne.

3 In the fortieth year, the eleventh month, the first day of the month, Moses spoke to the children of Israel all that the Lord had commanded him to say to them.

4 [1] After that he had slain Sehon king of the Amorrhites, who dwelt in Hesebon: and Og king of Basan who abode in Astaroth, and in Edrai,

5 Beyond the Jordan in the land of Moab. And Moses began to expound the law, and to say:

CHAP. 36. [1] Num. 27, 1. [2] Tob. 7, 14. CHAP. 1. [1] Num. 21, 24.

6 The Lord our God spoke to us in Horeb, saying: You have stayed long enough in this mountain.

7 Turn you, and come to the mountain of the Amorrhites, and to the other places that are next to it: the plains and the hills and the vales towards the south, and by the sea shore: the land of the Chanaanites, and of Libanus, as far as the great river Euphrates.

8 Behold, said he, I have delivered it to you: go in and possess it, concerning which the Lord swore to your fathers Abraham, Isaac, and Jacob, that he would give it to them, and to their seed after them.

9 And I said to you at that time:

10 ²I alone am not able to bear you: for the Lord your God hath multiplied you, and you are this day as the stars of heaven for multitude.

11 (The Lord God of your fathers add to this number many thousands, and bless you as he hath spoken.)

12 I alone am not able to bear your business, and the charge of you and your differences.

13 Let me have from among you wise and understanding men, and such whose conversation is approved among your tribes, that I may appoint them your rulers.

14 Then you answered me: The thing is good which thou meanest to do.

15 And I took out of your tribes men wise and honourable, and appointed them rulers, tribunes, and centurions, and officers over fifties, and over tens, who might teach you all things.

16 And I commanded them, saying: Hear them, and judge that which is just, ³whether he be one of your country, or a stranger.

17 ⁴There shall be no difference of persons. You shall hear the little as well as the great. Neither shall you respect any man's person, because it is the judgment of God. And if any thing seem hard to you, refer it to me, and I will hear it.

18 And I commanded you all things that you were to do.

19 And departing from Horeb, we passed through the terrible and vast wilderness, which you saw, by the way of the mountain of the Amorrhite, as the Lord our God had commanded us. And when we were come into Cadesbarne,

20 I said to you: You are come to

---

¹Exod. 18, 18. ²John, 7, 24. ⁴Lev. 19, 15; Deut. 16, 19; Prov. 24, 23; Ecclus. 42, 1; James, 2, 1. ⁵Num. 13; 32, 8. ⁶Exod. 13, 21; Num. 14, 14. ⁷Num. 14, 23; Ps. 94, 11.

CHAP. 1. Ver. 28. *Walled up to the sky.* A figurative expression, signifying the walls to be very high.

---

the mountain of the Amorrhite, which the Lord our God will give to us.

21 See the land which the Lord thy God giveth thee: go up and possess it, as the Lord our God hath spoken to thy fathers. Fear not; nor be any way discouraged.

22 ⁵And you came all to me, and said: Let us send men who may view the land, and bring us word what way we shall go up, and to what cities we shall go.

23 And because the saying pleased me, I sent of you twelve men, one of every tribe,

24 Who, when they had set forward and had gone up to the mountains, came as far as the valley of the cluster: and having viewed the land,

25 Taking of the fruits thereof, to shew its fertility, they brought them to us, and said: The land is good, which the Lord our God will give us.

26 And you would not go up, but being incredulous to the word of the Lord our God,

27 You murmured in your tents, and said: The Lord hateth us, and therefore he hath brought us out of the land of Egypt, that he might deliver us into the hand of the Amorrhite, and destroy us.

28 Whither shall we go up? The messengers have terrified our hearts, saying: The multitude is very great, and taller than we. The cities are great, and walled up to the sky. We have seen the sons of the Enacims there.

29 And I said to you: Fear not, neither be ye afraid of them.

30 The Lord God, who is your leader, himself will fight for you, as he did in Egypt in the sight of all.

31 And in the wilderness (as thou hast seen) the Lord thy God hath carried thee, as a man is wont to carry his little son, all the way that you have come, until you came to this place.

32 And yet for all this you did not believe the Lord your God,

33 ⁶Who went before you in the way, and marked out the place, wherein you should pitch your tents: in the night shewing you the way by fire, and in the day by the pillar of a cloud.

34 And when the Lord had heard the voice of your words, he was angry and swore, and said:

35 ⁷Not one of the men of this wicked generation shall see the good land, which I promised with an oath to your fathers.

36 Except Caleb the son of Jephone: for he shall see it, and to him I will give the land that he hath trodden

upon, and to his children, because he hath followed the Lord.

37 Neither is his indignation against the people to be wondered at, since the Lord was angry with me also on your account, and said: Neither shalt thou go in thither.

38 But Josue the son of Nun, thy minister, he shall go in for thee. Exhort and encourage him, and he shall divide the land by lot to Israel.

39 Your children, of whom you said that they should be led away captives, and your sons who know not this day the difference of good and evil, they shall go in. And to them I will give the land: and they shall possess it.

40 But return you and go into the wilderness by the way of the Red Sea.

41 [8] And you answered me: We have sinned against the Lord: we will go up and fight, as the Lord our God hath commanded. And when you went ready armed unto the mountain.

42 The Lord said to me: Say to them: [9] Go not up, and fight not, for I am not with you: lest you fall before your enemies.

43 I spoke, and you hearkened not: but resisting the commandment of the Lord, and swelling with pride, you went up into the mountain.

44 And the Amorrhite that dwelt in the mountains coming out, and meeting you, chased you, as bees do: and made slaughter of you from Seir as far as Horma.

45 And when you returned and wept before the Lord, he heard you not, neither would he yield to your voice.

46 So you abode in Cadesbarne a long time.

CHAPTER 2

They are forbid to fight against the Edomites, Moabites, and Ammonites. Their victory over Sehan king of Hesebon.

AND departing from thence we came into the wilderness that leadeth to the Red Sea, as the Lord had spoken to me: and we compassed mount Seir a long time.

2 And the Lord said to me:

3 You have compassed this mountain long enough. Go toward the north.

4 And command thou the people, saying: You shall pass by the borders of your brethren the children of Esau, who dwell in Seir, and they will be afraid of you.

5 Take ye then good heed that you stir not against them. For I will not give you of their land so much as the step of one foot can tread upon, because I have given mount Seir to Esau, for a possession.

6 You shall buy meats of them for money and shall eat: you shall draw waters for money, and shall drink.

7 The Lord thy God hath blessed thee in every work of thy hands. The Lord thy God dwelling with thee, knoweth thy journey: how thou hast passed through this great wilderness, for forty years, and thou hast wanted nothing.

8 And when we had passed by our brethren the children of Esau, that dwelt in Seir, by the way of the plain from Elath and from Asiongaber, we came to the way that leadeth to the desert of Moab.

9 And the Lord said to me: [1] Fight not againt the Moabites, neither go to battle against them. For I will not give thee any of their land, because I have given Ar to the children of Lot in possession.

10 The Emims first were the inhabitants thereof: a people great, and strong, and so tall, that like the race of the Enacims.

11 They were esteemed as giants, and were like the sons of the Enacims. But the Moabites call them Emims.

12 The Horrhites also formerly dwelt in Seir. Who being driven out and destroyed, the children of Esau dwelt there, as Israel did in the land of his possession, which the Lord gave him.

13 Then rising up to pass the torrent Zared, we came to it.

14 And the time that we journeyed from Cadesbarne till we passed over the torrent Zared, was thirty-eight years: until all the generation of the men that were fit for war was consumed out of the camp, as the Lord had sworn.

15 *For* his hand was against them, that they should perish from the midst of the camp.

16 And after all the fighting men were dead,

17 The Lord spoke to me, saying:

18 Thou shalt pass this day the borders of Moab, the city named Ar.

19 And when thou comest nigh the frontiers of the children of Ammon, take heed thou fight not against them, nor once move to battle. For I will not give thee of the land of the children of Ammon, because I have given it to the children of Lot for a possession.

20 It was accounted a land of giants: and giants formerly dwelt in it, whom the Ammonites call Zomzommims:

21 A people great and many, and of tall stature, like the Enacims whom the Lord destroyed before their face. And he made them to dwell in their stead,

22 As he had done in favour of the children of Esau, that dwell in Seir,

[8] Num. 14, 40.   [9] Num. 14, 42.   Chap. 2.   [1] Num. 21, 15.

destroying the Horrhites, and delivering their land to them, which they possess to this day.

23 The Hevites also, that dwelt in Haserim as far as Gaza, were expelled by the Cappadocians: who came out of Cappadocia, and destroyed them, and dwelt in their stead.

24 Arise ye, and pass the torrent Arnon: Behold I have delivered into thy hand Sehon king of Hesebon the Amorrhite. And begin thou to possess his land and make war against him.

25 This day will I begin to send the dread and fear of thee upon the nations that dwell under the whole heaven: that when they hear thy name they may fear and tremble, and be in pain like women in travail.

26 ² So I sent messengers from the wilderness of Cademoth to Sehon the king of Hesebon with peaceable words, saying:

27 We will pass through thy land: we will go along by the highway: we will not turn aside neither to the right hand nor to the left.

28 Sell us meat for money, that we may eat. Give us water for money and so we will drink. We only ask that thou wilt let us pass through,

29 As the children of Esau have done, that dwell in Seir, and the Moabites, that abide in Ar: until we come to the Jordan, and pass to the land which the Lord our God will give us.

30 And Sehon the king of Hesebon would not let us pass: because the Lord thy God had hardened his spirit, and fixed his heart, that he might be delivered into thy hands, as now thou seest.

31 And the Lord said to me: ³ Behold I have begun to deliver unto thee Sehon and his land. Begin to possess it.

32 And Sehon came out to meet us with all his people to fight at Jasa.

33 And the Lord our God delivered him to us: and we slew him with his sons and all his people.

34 And we took all his cities at that time, killing the inhabitants of them, men and women and children. We left nothing of them:

35 Except the cattle which came to the share of them that took them: and the spoils of the cities, which we took:

36 From Aroer, which is upon the bank of the torrent Arnon, a town that is situate in a valley, as far as Galaad. There was not a village or city, that

escaped our hands: the Lord our God delivered all unto us:

37 Except the land of the children of Ammon, to which we approached not: and all that border upon the torrent Jeboc: and the cities in the mountains: and all the places which the Lord our God forbade us.

CHAPTER 3

The victory over Og king of Basan. Ruben, Gad, and half the tribe of Manasses receive their possession on the other side of Jordan.

THEN we turned and went by the way of Basan: ¹ and Og the king of Basan came out to meet us with his people to fight in Edrai.

2 And the Lord said to me: Fear him not: because he is delivered into thy hand, with all his people and his land. And thou shalt do to him as thou hast done to Sehon king of the Amorrhites, that dwelt in Hesebon.

3 ² So the Lord our God delivered into our hands, Og also the king of Basan, and all his people. And we utterly destroyed them:

4 Wasting all his cities at one time. There was not a town that escaped us: sixty cities, all the country of Argob, the kingdom of Og in Basan.

5 All the cities were fenced with very high walls, and with gates and bars: besides innumerable towns that had no walls.

6 And we utterly destroyed them, as we had done to Sehon the king of Hesebon: destroying every city, men and women and children.

7 But the cattle and the spoils of the cities we took for our prey.

8 And we took at that time the land out of the hand of the two kings of the Amorrhites, that were beyond the Jordan. From the torrent Arnon unto the the mount Hermon

9 (Which the Sidonians call Sarion, and the Amorrhites Sanir) ³.

10 All the cities that are situate in the plain: and all the land of Galaad and Basan as far as Selcha and Edrai, cities of the kingdom of Og in Basan.

11 For only Og king of Basan remained of the race of the giants. His bed of iron is shewn, which is in Rabbath of the children of Ammon, being nine cubits long, and four broad after the measure of the cubit of a man's hand.

12 And we possessed the land at that time from Aroer, which is upon the bank of the torrent Arnon, unto the half of mount Galaad. ⁴ And I gave the cities thereof to Ruben and Gad.

13 And I delivered the other part of

---

³ Num. 21, 21. ³ Amos, 2, 9. CHAP. 3. ¹ Num. 21, 34. ² Num. 21, 35. ³ Deut. 4, 48. ⁴ Num. 32, 29.

CHAP. 2. Ver. 30. *Hardened.* That is, in punishment of his past sins he left him to his own stubborn and perverse disposition, which drew him to his ruin. See the note on Exod. 7, 3.

Galaad, and all Basan the kingdom of Og to the half tribe of Manasses: all the country of Argob. And all Basan is called the Land of giants.

14 Jair the son of Manasses possessed all the country of [5] Argob unto the borders of Gessuri, and Machati. And he called Basan by his own name, Havoth Jair: that is to say, the towns of Jair, until this present day.

15 To Machir also I gave Galaad.

16 And to the tribes of Ruben and Gad I gave of the land of Galaad as far as the torrent Arnon; half the torrent; and the confines even unto the torrent Jeboc, which is the border of the children of Ammon.

17 And the plain of the wilderness: and the Jordan: and the borders of Cenereth unto the sea of the desert, which is the most salt sea, to the foot of mount Phasga eastward.

18 And I commanded you at that time, saying: The Lord your God giveth you this land for in inheritance. Go ye well appointed before your brethren the children of Israel, all the strong men of you,

19 Leaving your wives and children and cattle. For I know you have much cattle: and they must remain in the cities, which I have delivered to you.

20 Until the Lord give rest to your brethren, as he hath given to you: and they also possess the land, which he will give them beyond the Jordan. Then shall every man return to his possession, which I have given you.

21 [6] I commanded Josue also at that time, saying: Thy eyes have seen what the Lord your God hath done to these two kings. So will he do to all the kingdoms to which thou shalt pass.

22 Fear them not: for the Lord your God will fight for you.

23 And I besought the Lord at that time, saying:

24 Lord God, thou hast begun to shew unto thy servant thy greatness, and most mighty hand: for there is no other God either in heaven or earth, that is able to do thy works, or to be compared to thy strength.

25 I will pass over therefore, and will see this excellent land beyond the Jordan, and this goodly mountain, and Libanus.

26 And the Lord was angry with me on your account and heard me not, but said to me: It is enough. Speak no more to me of this matter.

27 Go up to the top of Phasga, and cast thy eyes round about to the west, and to the north, and to the south, and to the east, and behold it. [7] For thou shalt not pass this Jordan.

28 Command Josue, and encourage and strengthen him. For he shall go before this people: and shall divide unto them the land which thou shalt see.

29 And we abode in the valley over against the temple of Phogor.

CHAPTER 4

Moses exhorteth the people to keep God's commandments: particularly to fly idolatry. Appointeth three cities of refuge, on that side of the Jordan.

AND now, O Israel, hear the commandments and judgments which I teach thee that doing them, thou mayst live, and entering in mayst possess the land which the Lord the God of your fathers will give you.

2 You shall not add to the word that I speak to you: neither shall you take away from it. Keep the commandments of the Lord your God which I command you.

3 [1] Your eyes have seen all that the Lord hath done against Beelphegor: how he hath destroyed all his worshippers from among you.

4 But you that adhere to the Lord your God, are all alive until this present day.

5 You know that I have taught you statutes and justices, as the Lord my God hath commanded me: so shall you do them in the land which you shall possess.

6 And you shall observe, and fulfil them in practice. For this is your wisdom, and understanding in the sight of nations, that hearing all these precepts, they may say: Behold a wise and understanding people, a great nation.

7 Neither is there any other nation so great, that hath gods so nigh them, as our God is present to all our petitions.

8 For what other nation is there so renowned that hath ceremonies, and just judgments, and all the law, which I will set forth this day before your eyes?

9 Keep thyself therefore, and thy soul carefully. Forget not the words that thy eyes have seen: and let them not go out of thy heart all the days of thy life. Thou shalt teach them to thy sons and to thy grandsons.

10 From the day in which thou didst stand before the Lord thy God in Horeb, when the Lord spoke to me, saying: Call together the people unto me, that they may hear my words, and may learn to fear me all the time that they live on the earth, and may teach their children.

11 [2] And you came to the foot of the mount, which burned even unto heaven: and there was darkness, and a cloud and obscurity in it.

[5] Num. 21, 34.   [6] Num. 27, 18.   [7] Deut. 31, 2; 34, 4. CHAP. 4.   [1] Num. 25, 4; Jos. 22, 17.   [2] Exod. 19, 18.

12 And the Lord spoke to you from the midst of the fire. You heard the voice of his words, but you saw not any form at all.

13 And he shewed you his covenant, which he commanded you to do, and the [3] ten words that he wrote in two tables of stone.

14 And he commanded me at that time that I should teach you the ceremonies and judgments which you shall do in the land, that you shall possess.

15 Keep therefore your souls carefully. [4] You saw not any similitude in the day that the Lord God spoke to you in Horeb from the midst of the fire:

16 Lest perhaps being deceived you might make you a graven similitude, or image of male or female,

17 The similitude of any beasts, that are upon the earth, or of birds, that fly under heaven,

18 Or of creeping things, that move on the earth, or of fishes, that abide in the waters under the earth:

19 Lest perhaps lifting up thy eyes to heaven, thou see the sun and the moon, and all the stars of heaven, and being deceived by error thou adore and serve them, which the Lord thy God created for the service of all the nations, that are under heaven.

20 But the Lord hath taken you and brought you out of the iron furnace of Egypt, to make you his people of inheritance, as it is this present day.

21 [5] And the Lord was angry with me for your words: and he swore that I should not pass over the Jordan, nor enter into the excellent land, which he will give you.

22 Behold I die in this land: I shall not pass over the Jordan. You shall pass, and possess the goodly land.

23 Beware lest thou ever forget the covenant of the Lord thy God, which he hath made with thee: and make to thyself a graven likeness of those things which the Lord hath forbid to be made.

24 [6] Because the Lord thy God is a consuming fire, a jealous God.

25 If you shall beget sons and grandsons, and abide in the land, and being deceived, make to yourselves any similitude, committing evil before the Lord your God, to provoke him to wrath:

26 I call this day heaven and earth to witness, that you shall quickly perish out of the land, which, when you have passed over the Jordan, you shall possess. You shall not dwell therein long, but the Lord will destroy you:

27 And scatter you among all nations: and you shall remain a few among the nations, to which the Lord shall lead you.

28 And there you shall serve gods, that were framed with men's hands: wood and stone, that neither see, nor hear, nor eat, nor smell.

29 And when thou shalt seek there the Lord thy God, thou shalt find him: yet so, if thou seek him with all thy heart, and all the affliction of thy soul.

30 After all the things aforesaid shall find thee: in the latter time thou shalt return to the Lord thy God, and shalt hear his voice.

31 Because the Lord thy God is a merciful God. He will not leave thee: nor altogether destroy thee: nor forget the covenant, by which he swore to thy fathers.

32 Ask of the days of old, that have been before thy time from the day that God created man upon the earth, from one end of heaven to the other end thereof, if ever there was done the like thing, or it hath been known at any time:

33 That a people should hear the voice of God speaking out of the midst of fire, as thou hast heard, and lived.

34 If God *ever* did so as to go, and take to himself a nation out of the midst of nations by temptations, signs, and wonders, by fight, and a strong hand, and stretched out arm, and horrible visions, according to all the things that the Lord your God did for you in Egypt, before thy eyes.

35 That thou mightest know that the Lord he is God: and there is no other besides him.

36 From heaven he made thee to hear his voice, that he might teach thee. And upon earth he shewed thee his exceeding great fire: and thou didst hear his words out of the midst of the fire,

37 Because he loved thy fathers, and chose their seed after them. [7] And he brought thee out of Egypt, going before thee with his great power.

38 To destroy at thy coming very great nations, and stronger than thou *art:* and to bring thee in: and give thee their land for a possession, as thou seest at this present day.

39 Know therefore this day: and think in thy heart that the Lord he is God in heaven above, and in the earth beneath, and there is no other.

40 Keep his precepts and commandments, which I command thee. That it may be well with thee, and thy children after thee: and thou mayst remain a long time upon the land, which the Lord thy God will give thee.

41 [8] Then Moses set aside three cities beyond the Jordan at the east side.

[3] Exod. 20, 21, 22, 23. [4] Exod. 24, 10. [5] Deut. 1, 37. [6] Heb. 12, 9. [7] Exod. 13, 21. [8] Num. 35, 14.

42 That any one might flee to them who should kill his neighbour unwillingly, and was not his enemy a day or two before: and that he might escape to some one of these cities:

43 ⁹ Bosor in the wilderness, which is situate in the plains of the tribe of Ruben: and Ramoth in Galaad, which is in the tribe of Gad: and Golan in Basan, which is in the tribe of Manasses.

44 This is the law, that Moses set before the children of Israel.

45 And these are the testimonies and ceremonies and judgments, which he spoke to the children of Israel, when they came out of Egypt:

46 Beyond the Jordan in the valley over against the temple of Phogor, in the land of Sehon king of the Amorrhites, that dwelt in Hesebon, whom Moses slew. And the children of Israel coming out of Egypt,

47 Possessed his land, and the land of Og king of Basan: of the two kings of the Amorrhites, who were beyond the Jordan towards the rising of the sun.

48 From Aroer, which is situate upon the bank of the torrent Arnon, unto mount Sion, which is also called Hermon.

49 All the plain beyond the Jordan at the east side, unto the sea of the wilderness, and unto the foot of mount Phasga.

CHAPTER 5

The ten commandments are repeated and explained.

AND Moses called all Israel, and said to them: Hear, O Israel, the ceremonies and judgments, which I speak in your ears this day. Learn them, and fulfil them in work.

2 The Lord our God made a covenant with us in Horeb.

3 He made not the covenant with our fathers: but with us, who are now present and living.

4 He spoke to us face to face in the mount out of the midst of fire.

5 I was the mediator and stood between the Lord and you at that time, to shew you his words. For you feared the fire, and went not up into the mountain. And he said:

6 ¹ I am the Lord thy God, who brought thee out of the land of Egypt, out of the house of bondage.

7 ² Thou shalt not have strange gods in my sight.

8 ³ Thou shalt not make to thyself a graven thing, nor the likeness of any things, that are in heaven above, or that *are* in the earth beneath, or that abide in the waters under the earth.

9 ⁴ Thou shalt not adore them: and

thou shalt not serve *them.* For I am the Lord thy God, a jealous God, visiting the iniquity of the fathers upon their children unto the third and fourth generation, to them that hate me:

10 And shewing mercy unto many thousands, to them that love me, and keep my commandments.

11 ⁵ Thou shalt not take the name of the Lord thy God in vain: for he shall not be unpunished that taketh his name upon a vain thing.

12 Observe the day of the sabbath, to sanctify it, as the Lord thy God hath commanded thee.

13 Six days shalt thou labour, and shalt do all thy works.

14 ⁶ The seventh is the day of the sabbath, that is, the rest of the Lord thy God. Thou shalt not do any work therein: thou nor thy son nor thy daughter, nor thy man-servant nor thy maid-servant, nor thy ox, nor thy ass, nor any of thy beasts, nor the stranger that is within thy gates: that thy man-servant and thy maid-servant may rest, even as thyself.

15 Remember that thou also didst serve in Egypt, and the Lord thy God brought thee out from thence with a strong hand, and a stretched out arm. Therefore hath he commanded thee that thou shouldst observe the sabbath day.

16 ⁷ Honour thy father and mother, as the Lord thy God hath commanded thee: that thou mayst live a long time, and it may be well with thee in the land, which the Lord thy God will give thee.

17 Thou shalt not kill.

18 Neither shalt thou commit adultery.

19 And thou shalt not steal.

20 Neither shalt thou bear false witness against thy neighbour.

21 ⁸ Thou shalt not covet thy neighbour's wife: nor *his* house, nor his field, nor his man-servant, nor his maid-servant, nor his ox, nor his ass, nor any thing that is his.

22 These words the Lord spoke to all the multitude of you in the mountain, out of the midst of the fire, and the cloud, and the darkness, with a loud voice, adding nothing more. And he wrote them in two tables of stone, which he delivered unto me.

23 But you, after you heard the voice out of the midst of the darkness, and saw the mountain burn, came to me, all the princes of the tribes and the elders. And you said:

⁹ Jos. 20, 3. **CHAP. 5.** ¹ Exod. 20, 2; Lev. 26, 1; Ps. 80, 11. ² Exod. 20, 3; Ps. 80, 10. ³ Exod. 20, 4; Lev. 26, 1; Ps. 96, 7. ⁴ Exod. 34, 14. ⁵ Exod. 20, 7; Lev. 19, 12; Matt. 5, 33. ⁶ Gen. 2, 2; Exod. 20, 10; Heb. 4, 4. ⁷ Exod. 20, 12; Ecclus. 3, 9; Matt. 15, 4; Mark, 7, 10; Eph. 6, 2. ⁸ Matt. 5, 28; Rom. 7, 7.

24 Behold the Lord our God hath shewn us his majesty and his greatness: we have heard his voice out of the midst of the fire, and have proved this day that God speaking with man, man hath lived.

25 Why shall we die therefore, and why shall this exceeding great fire consume us: for if we hear the voice of the Lord our God any more, we shall die.

26 What is all flesh, that it should hear the voice of the living God, who speaketh out of the midst of the fire, as we have heard, and be able to live?

27 Approach thou rather: and hear all things that the Lord our God shall say to thee, and thou shalt speak to us, and we will hear and will do them.

28 And when the Lord had heard this, he said to me: I have heard the voice of the words of this people, which they spoke to thee. They have spoken all things well.

29 Who shall give them to have such a mind, to fear me, and to keep all my commandments at all times, that it may be well with them and with their children for ever?

30 Go and say to them: Return into your tents.

31 But stand thou here with me: and I will speak to thee all my commandments, and ceremonies and judgments. Which thou shalt teach them, that they may do them in the land, which I will give them for a possession.

32 Keep therefore and do the things which the Lord God hath commanded you. You shall not go aside neither to the right hand, nor to the left.

33 But you shall walk in the way that the Lord your God hath commanded, that you may live, and it may be well with you, and *your* days may be long in the land of your possession.

CHAPTER 6

An exhortation to the love of God, and obedience to his law.

THESE are the precepts, and ceremonies, and judgments, which the Lord your God commanded that I should teach you: and that you should do them in the land into which you pass over to possess it.

2 That thou mayst fear the Lord thy God, and keep all his commandments and precepts, which I command thee, and thy sons, and thy grandsons, all the days of thy life, that thy days may be prolonged.

3 Hear, O Israel, and observe to do the things which the Lord hath commanded thee, that it may be well with

CHAP. 6. [1] Deut. 11, 13; Matt. 22, 37; Mark, 12, 30; Luke, 10, 27. [2] Deut. 10, 20; Matt. 4, 10; Luke, 4, 8. [3] Matt. 4, 7; Luke, 4, 12.

thee, and thou mayst be greatly multiplied: as the Lord the God of thy fathers hath promised thee a land flowing with milk and honey.

4 Hear, O Israel: the Lord our God is one Lord.

5 [1] Thou shalt love the Lord thy God with thy whole heart, and with thy whole soul, and with thy whole strength.

6 And these words which I command thee this day, shall be in thy heart.

7 And thou shalt tell them to thy children: and thou shalt meditate upon them sitting in thy house, and walking on thy journey, sleeping and rising.

8 And thou shalt bind them as a sign on thy hand: and they shall be and shall move between thy eyes.

9 And thou shalt write them in the entry, and on the doors of thy house.

10 And when the Lord thy God shall have brought thee into the land, for which he swore to thy fathers Abraham, Isaac, and Jacob: and shall have given thee great and goodly cities, which thou didst not build,

11 Houses full of riches, which thou didst not set up, cisterns which thou didst not dig, vineyards and oliveyards, which thou didst not plant:

12 And thou shalt have eaten and be full:

13 Take heed diligently lest thou forget the Lord, who brought thee out of the land of Egypt, out of the house of bondage. [2] Thou shalt fear the Lord thy God, and shalt serve him only: and thou shalt swear by his name.

14 You shall not go after the strange gods of all the nations, that are round about you:

15 Because the Lord thy God is a jealous God in the midst of thee: lest at any time the wrath of the Lord thy God be kindled against thee, and take thee away from the face of the earth.

16 [3] Thou shalt not tempt the Lord thy God, as thou temptedst him in the place of temptation.

17 Keep the precepts of the Lord thy God, and the testimonies and ceremonies which he hath commanded thee.

18 And do that which is pleasing and good in the sight of the Lord: that it may be well with thee: and going in thou mayst possess the goodly land, concerning which the Lord swore to thy fathers,

19 That he would destroy all thy enemies before thee, as he hath spoken.

20 And when thy son shall ask thee to-morrow, saying: What mean these testimonies, and ceremonies and judgments, which the Lord our God hath commanded us?

21 Thou shalt say to him: We were

bondmen of Pharao in Egypt, and the Lord brought us out of Egypt with a strong hand.

22 And he wrought signs and wonders great and very grievous in Egypt against Pharao, and all his house, in our sight.

23 And he brought us out from thence, that he might bring us in and give us the land, concerning which he swore to our fathers.

24 And the Lord commanded that we should do all these ordinances, and should fear the Lord our God: that it might be well with us all the days of our life, as it is at this day.

25 And he will be merciful to us, if we keep and do all his precepts before the Lord our God, as he hath commanded us.

CHAPTER 7

No league nor fellowship to be made with the Chanaanites. God promiseth his people his blessing and assistance, if they keep his commandments.

WHEN the Lord thy God shall have brought thee into the land, which thou art going in to possess, and shall have destroyed many nations before thee: ¹ the Hethite, and the Gergezite, and the Amorrhite, and the Chanaanite, and the Pherezite, and the Hevite, and the Jebusite: seven nations much more numerous than thou art, and stronger than thou:

2 And the Lord thy God shall have delivered them to thee: thou shalt utterly destroy them. ² Thou shalt make no league with them, nor shew mercy to them.

3 Neither shalt thou make marriages with them. Thou shalt not give thy daughter to his son, nor take his daughter for thy son.

4 For she will turn away thy son from following me, that he may rather serve strange gods: and the wrath of the Lord will be kindled, and will quickly destroy thee.

5 But thus rather shall you deal with them: ³ Destroy their altars, and break their statues, and cut down their groves, and burn their graven things.

6 ⁴ Because thou art a holy people to the Lord thy God. ⁵ The Lord thy God hath chosen thee, to be his peculiar people of all peoples that are upon the earth.

7 Not because you surpass all nations in number, is the Lord joined unto you, and hath chosen you: for you are the fewest of any people.

8 But because the Lord hath loved you, and hath kept his oath, which he swore to your fathers: and hath brought you out with a strong hand, and redeemed you from the house of bondage,

out of the hand of Pharao the king of Egypt.

9 And thou shalt know that the Lord thy God, he is a strong and faithful God, keeping his covenant and mercy to them that love him, and to them that keep his commandments, unto a thousand generations:

10 And repaying forthwith them that hate him, so as to destroy them without further delay immediately rendering to them what they deserve.

11 Keep therefore the precepts and ceremonies and judgments, which I command thee this day to do.

12 If after thou hast heard these judgments, thou keep and do them, the Lord thy God will also keep his covenant to thee, and the mercy which he swore to thy fathers.

13 And he will love thee and multiply thee, and will bless the fruit of thy womb, and the fruit of thy land, thy corn, and thy vintage, thy oil, and thy herds, *and* the flocks of thy sheep upon the land, for which he swore to thy fathers that he would give it thee.

14 Blessed shalt thou be among all people. ⁶ No one shall be barren among you of either sex, neither of men nor cattle.

15 The Lord will take away from thee all sickness: and the grievous infirmities of Egypt, which thou knowest, he will not bring upon thee, but upon thy enemies.

16 Thou shalt consume all the people, which the Lord thy God will deliver to thee. Thy eye shall not spare them: neither shalt thou serve their gods, lest they be thy ruin.

17 If thou say in thy heart: These nations are more than I, how shall I be able to destroy them?

18 Fear not: but remember what the Lord thy God did to Pharao and to all the Egyptians,

19 The exceeding great plagues, which thy eyes saw, and the signs and wonders, and the strong hand, and the stretched out arm, with which the Lord thy God brought thee out. So will he do to all the people, whom thou fearest.

20 ⁷ Moreover the Lord thy God will send also hornets among them, until he destroy and consume all that have escaped thee, and could hide themselves.

21 Thou shalt not fear them, because the Lord thy God is in the midst of thee, a God mighty and terrible.

22 He will consume these nations in thy sight by little and little and by de-

CHAP. 7. ¹ Exod. 23, 23; 33, 2. ² Exod. 23, 32; 34, 15. ³ Exod. 23, 24; Deut. 2, 3; 16, 22. ⁴ Deut. 14, 2. ⁵ Deut. 26, 18. ⁶ Exod. 23, 26. ⁷ Exod. 23, 28; Jos. 24, 12.

grees. Thou wilt not be able to destroy them altogether: lest perhaps the beasts of the earth should increase upon thee.

23 But the Lord thy God shall deliver them in thy sight: and shall slay them until they be utterly destroyed.

24 And he shall deliver their kings into thy hands, and thou shalt destroy their names from under Heaven. No man shall be able to resist thee, until thou destroy them.

25 [8] Their graven things thou shalt burn with fire. Thou shalt not covet the silver and gold of which they are made: neither shalt thou take to thee any thing thereof, lest thou offend, because it is an abomination to the Lord thy God.

26 Neither shalt thou bring any thing of the idol into thy house, lest thou become an anathema, like it. Thou shalt detest it as dung: and shalt utterly abhor it as uncleanness and filth, because it is an anathema.

CHAPTER 8

The people is put in mind of God's dealings with them, to the end that they may love him and serve him.

ALL the commandments, that I command thee this day, take great care to observe: that you may live, and be multiplied, and going in may possess the land, for which the Lord swore to your fathers.

2 And thou shalt remember all the way through which the Lord thy God hath brought thee for forty years through the desert, to afflict thee and to prove thee: and that the things that were in thy heart might be made known, whether thou wouldst keep his commandments or no.

3 He afflicted thee with want, and gave the manna for *thy* food, which neither thou nor thy fathers knew: to shew that [1] not in bread alone doth man live, but in every word that proceedeth from the mouth of God.

4 Thy raiment, with which thou wast covered, hath not decayed for age, and thy foot is not worn: lo, this is the fortieth year:

5 That thou mayst consider in thy heart, that as a man traineth up his

son, so the Lord thy God hath trained thee up.

6 That thou shouldst keep the commandments of the Lord thy God, and walk in his ways, and fear him.

7 For the Lord thy God will bring thee into a good land, of brooks and of waters, and of fountains: in the plains of which and the hills deep rivers break out.

8 A land of wheat, and barley, and vineyards, wherein fig trees and pomegranates, and olive yards grow: a land of oil and honey.

9 Where without any want thou shalt eat thy bread, and enjoy abundance of all things: where the stones are iron, and out of its hills are dug mines of brass.

10 That when thou hast eaten, and art full, thou mayst bless the Lord thy God for the excellent land which he hath given thee.

11 Take heed, and beware lest at any time thou forget the Lord thy God, and neglect his commandments and judgments and ceremonies, which I command thee this day.

12 Lest after thou hast eaten and art filled, hast built goodly houses, and dwelt in them,

13 And shalt have herds of oxen and flocks of sheep, and plenty of gold and of silver, and of all things:

14 Thy heart be lifted up, and thou remember not the Lord thy God, who brought thee out of the land of Egypt, out of the house of bondage,

15 Who was thy leader in the great and terrible wilderness, [2] wherein there was the serpent burning with his breath, and the scorpion and the dipsas, and no waters at all. [3] Who brought forth streams out of the hardest rock:

16 [4] And fed thee in the wilderness with manna which thy fathers knew not. And after he had afflicted and proved thee, at the last he had mercy on thee:

17 Lest thou shouldst say in thy heart: My own might, and the strength of my own hand have achieved all these things for me.

18 But remember the Lord thy God, that he hath given thee strength, that he might fulfil his covenant, concerning which he swore to thy fathers, as this present day sheweth.

19 But if thou forget the Lord thy God, and follow strange gods, and serve and adore them: behold now I foretell thee that thou shalt utterly perish.

20 As the nations, which the Lord destroyed at thy entrance, so shall you also perish, if you be disobedient to the voice of the Lord your God.

[8] 2 Mach. 12, 40. CHAP. 8. [1] Matt. 4, 4; Luke, 4, 4. [2] Num. 20, 9; 21, 6. [3] Exod. 17, 6. [4] Exod. 16, 14.

CHAP. 7. Ver. 25. *Graven things.* Idols, so called by contempt.
Ver. 26. *An anathema.* That is, a thing devoted to destruction; and which carries along with it a curse.
CHAP. 8. Ver. 3. *Not in bread alone.* That is, that God is able to make food of what he pleases for the support of man.
Ver. 15. *The Dipsas.* A serpent whose bite causeth a violent thirst; from whence it has its name, for in Greek *dipsa* (δίψα) signifies *thirst.*

CHAPTER 9

Lest they should impute their victories to their own merits, they are put in mind of their manifold rebellions and other sins, for which they should have been destroyed, but God spared them for his promise made to Abraham, Isaac, and Jacob.

HEAR, O Israel. Thou shalt go over the Jordan this day, to possess nations very great, and stronger than thyself, cities great, and walled up to the sky:

2 A people great and tall, the sons of the Enacims, whom thou hast seen, and heard of, against whom no man is able to stand.

3 Thou shalt know therefore this day that the Lord thy God himself will pass over before thee, a devouring and consuming fire, to destroy and extirpate and bring them to nothing before thy face quickly, as he hath spoken to thee.

4 Say not in thy heart, when the Lord thy God shall have destroyed them in thy sight: For my justice hath the Lord brought me in to possess this land, whereas these nations are destroyed for their wickedness.

5 For it is not for thy justices, and the uprightness of thy heart that thou shalt go in to possess their lands. But because they have done wickedly, they are destroyed at thy coming in: and that the Lord might accomplish his word, which he promised by oath to thy fathers Abraham, Isaac and Jacob.

6 Know therefore that the Lord thy God giveth thee not this excellent land in possession for thy justices: for thou art a very stiffnecked people.

7 Remember, and forget not how thou provokedst the Lord thy God to wrath in the wilderness. From the day that thou camest out of Egypt unto this place, thou hast always strove against the Lord.

8 [1] For in Horeb also thou didst provoke him: and he was angry, and would have destroyed thee,

9 [2] When I went up into the mount to receive the tables of stone, the tables of the covenant which the Lord made with you. And I continued in the mount forty days and nights, neither eating bread, nor drinking water.

10 [3] And the Lord gave me two tables of stone written with the finger of God, and containing all the words that he spoke to you in the mount from the midst of the fire, when the people were assembled together.

11 And when forty days were passed and as many nights, the Lord gave me the two tables of stone, the tables of the covenant.

12 And said to me: [4] Arise, and go down from hence quickly: for thy people, which thou hast brought out of Egypt, have quickly forsaken the way that thou hast shewn them, and have made to themselves a molten *idol.*

13 And again the Lord said to me: I see that this people is stiffnecked.

14 Let me alone that I may destroy them, and abolish their name from under heaven, and set thee over a nation, that is greater and stronger than this.

15 And when I came down from the burning mount, and held the two tables of the covenant with both hands:

16 And saw that you had sinned against the Lord your God, and had made to yourselves a molten calf, and had quickly forsaken his way, which he had shewn you:

17 I cast the tables out of my hands, and broke them in your sight.

18 And I fell down before the Lord as before, forty days and nights neither eating bread, nor drinking water, for all your sins, which you had committed against the Lord, and had provoked him to wrath.

19 For I feared his indignation and anger, wherewith being moved against you, he would have destroyed you. And the Lord heard me this time also.

20 And he was exceeding angry against Aaron also, and would have destroyed him: and I prayed in like manner for him.

21 And your sin that you had committed, that is, the calf, I took, and burned it with fire: and breaking it into pieces, until it was as small as dust, I threw it into the torrent, which cometh down from the mountain.

22 [5] At the burning also, and at the place of temptation, and at the graves of lust you provoked the Lord.

23 And when he sent you from Cadesbarne, saying: Go up, and possess the land that I have given you: and you slighted the commandment of the Lord your God, and did not believe him. Neither would you hearken to his voice:

24 But were always rebellious from the day that I began to know you.

25 And I lay prostrate before the Lord forty days and nights, in which I humbly besought him, that he would not destroy you as he had threatened.

26 And praying, I said: O Lord God, destroy not thy people, and thy inheritance, which thou hast redeemed in thy greatness, whom thou hast brought out of Egypt with a strong hand.

27 Remember thy servants Abraham, Isaac, and Jacob: look not on the stub-

CHAP. 9. [1] Exod. 17, 6; 19, 3. [2] Exod. 24, 18. [3] Exod. 31, 18; 32, 15. [4] Exod. 32, 7; Deut. 9, 12. [5] Num. 11, 1; 16, 35; 21, 6.

bornness of this people, nor on their wickedness and sin.

28 Lest perhaps the inhabitants of the land, out of which thou hast brought us, say: The Lord could not bring them into the land that he promised them, and he hated them. Therefore he brought them out, that he might kill them in the wilderness.

29 Who are thy people and thy inheritance, whom thou hast brought out by thy great strength, and in thy stretched out arm.

CHAPTER 10

God giveth the second tables of the law. A further exhortation to fear and serve the Lord.

AT that time the Lord said to me: [1] Hew thee two tables of stone like the former, and come up to me into the mount. And thou shalt make an ark of wood.

2 And I will write on the tables the words that were in them, which thou brokest before; and thou shalt put them in the ark.

3 And I made an ark of setim wood. And when I had hewn two tables of stone like the former, I went up into the mount, having them in my hands.

4 And he wrote in the tables, according as he had written before, the ten words, which the Lord spoke to you in the mount from the midst of the fire, when the people were assembled. And he gave them to me.

5 And returning from the mount, I came down, and put the tables into the ark, that I had made: and they are there till this present, as the Lord commanded me.

6 [2] And the children of Israel removed their camp from Beroth of the children of Jacan into Mosera: where [3] Aaron died and was buried, and Eleazar his son succeeded him in the priestly office.

7 From thence they came to Gadgad; from which place they departed, and camped in Jetebatha, in a land of waters and torrents.

8 At that time he separated the tribe of Levi: to carry the ark of the covenant of the Lord, and to stand before him in the ministry, and to bless in his name until this present day.

9 Wherefore Levi hath no part nor possession with his brethren: because

the Lord himself is his possession, as the Lord thy God promised him.

10 And I stood in the mount, as before, forty days and nights: and the Lord heard me this time also, and would not destroy thee.

11 And he said to me: Go, and walk before the people, that they may enter, and possess the land, which I swore to their fathers that I would give them.

12 And now, Israel, what doth the Lord thy God require of thee: but that thou fear the Lord thy God, and walk in his ways, and love him, and serve the Lord thy God, with all thy heart, and with all thy soul:

13 And keep the commandments of the Lord, and his ceremonies, which I command thee this day, that it may be well with thee?

14 Behold heaven is the Lord's thy God, and the heaven of heaven, the earth and all things that are therein.

15 And yet the Lord hath been closely joined to thy fathers, and loved them and chose their seed after them: that is to say, you, out of all nations, as this day it is proved.

16 Circumcise therefore the foreskin of your heart; and stiffen your neck no more.

17 Because the Lord your God he is the God of gods, and the Lord of lords, a great God and mighty and terrible, [4] who accepteth no person nor taketh bribes.

18 He doth judgment to the fatherless and the widow, loveth the stranger, and giveth him food and raiment.

19 And do you therefore love strangers: because you also were strangers in the land of Egypt.

20 [5] Thou shalt fear the Lord thy God, and serve him only. To him thou shalt adhere; and shalt swear by his name.

21 He is thy praise, and thy God, that hath done for thee these great and terrible things, which thy eyes have seen.

22 In seventy souls thy fathers went down into Egypt: and behold now the Lord thy God hath multiplied thee as the stars of heaven.

CHAPTER 11

The love and service of God are still inculcated, with a blessing to them that serve him, and threats of punishment if they forsake his law.

THEREFORE, love the Lord thy God and observe his precepts and ceremonies, his judgments and commandments at all times.

2 Know this day the things that your children know now, who saw not the chastisement of the Lord your God: his great doings and strong hand, and stretched out arm:

Chap. 10. [1] Exod. 34, 1. [2] Num. 33, 31. [3] Num. 20, 28. [4] Par. 19, 7; Job. 34, 19; Wisd. 6, 8; Ecclus. 35, 15; Acts, 10, 34; Rom. 2, 11; Gal. 2, 6. [5] Deut. 6, 13; Matt. 4, 10; Luke, 4, 8.

Chap. 10. Ver. 6. *Mosera.* By mount Hor, for there Aaron died (Num. 20). This and the following verses seem to be inserted by way of parenthesis.

3 The signs and works which he did in the midst of Egypt to king Pharao, and to all his land:

4 And to all the host of the Egyptians, and to their horses and chariots. How the waters of the Red Sea covered them, when they pursued you: and how the Lord destroyed them until this present day.

5 And what he hath done to you in the wilderness, till you came to this place:

6 ¹And to Dathan and Abiron the sons of Eliab, who was the son of Ruben.² Whom the earth, opening her mouth, swallowed up with their households and tents, and all their substance, which they had in the midst of Israel.

7 Your eyes have seen all the great works of the Lord, that he hath done.

8 That you may keep all his commandments, which I command you this day: and may go in, and possess the land, to which you are entering.

9 And may live in it a long time. Which the Lord promised by oath to your fathers, and to their seed: *a land* which floweth with milk and honey.

10 For the land, which thou goest to possess, is not like the land of Egypt, from whence thou camest out: where, when the seed is sown, waters are brought in to water it after the manner of gardens.

11 But it is a land of hills and plains expecting rain from heaven.

12 And the Lord thy God doth always visit it: and his eyes are on it from the beginning of the year unto the end thereof.

13 ³If then you obey my commandments, which I command you this day that you love the Lord your God, and serve him with all your heart, and with all your soul:

14 He will give to your land the early rain and the latter rain, that you may gather in your corn, and your wine, and your oil,

15 And your hay out of the fields to feed your cattle: and that you may eat and be filled.

16 Beware lest perhaps your heart be deceived: and you depart from the Lord, and serve strange gods, and adore them.

17 And the Lord being angry shut up heaven, that the rain come not down, nor the earth yield her fruit: and you perish quickly from the excellent land, which the Lord will give you.

18 ⁴Lay up these my words in your hearts and minds: and hang them for a sign on your hands, and place them between your eyes.

19 Teach your children that they meditate on them, when thou sittest in thy house, and when thou walkest on the way, and when thou liest down and risest up.

20 Thou shalt write them upon the posts and the doors of thy house:

21 That thy days may be multiplied, and the days of thy children in the land which the Lord swore to thy fathers, that he would give them as long as the heaven hangeth over the earth.

22 For if you keep the commandments which I command you, and do them; to love the Lord your God, and walk in all his ways, cleaving unto him:

23 The Lord will destroy all these nations before your face, and you shall possess them, which are greater and stronger than you.

24 ⁵Every place, that your foot shall tread upon, shall be yours. From the desert, and from Libanus, from the great river Euphrates unto the western sea shall be your borders.

25 None shall stand against you. The Lord your God shall lay the dread and fear of you upon all the land that you shall tread upon, as he hath spoken to you.

26 Behold I set forth in your sight this day a blessing and a curse.

27 A blessing if you obey the commandments of the Lord your God, which I command you this day.

28 A curse, if you obey not the commandments of the Lord your God, but revolt from the way which now I shew you, and walk after strange gods which you know not.

29 And when the Lord thy God shall have brought thee into the land, whither thou goest to dwell, thou shalt put the blessing upon mount Garizim, the curse upon mount Hebal:

30 Which are beyond the Jordan, behind the way that goeth to the setting of the sun, in the land of the Chanaanite who dwelleth in the plain country over against Galgala, which is near the valley that reacheth and entereth far.

31 For you shall pass over the Jordan, to possess the land, which the Lord your God will give you, that you may have it and possess it.

32 See therefore that you fulfil the ceremonies and judgments, which I shall set this day before you.

CHAPTER 12

All idolatry must be extirpated. Sacrifices, tithes, and firstfruits must be offered in one only place. All eating of blood is prohibited.

Chap. 11. ¹Num. 16, 1. ²Num. 16, 32. ³Deut. 10, 12. ⁴Deut. 6, 6. ⁵Jos. 1, 3.

Chap. 11. Ver. 29. *Put the blessing.* See Deut. 27, 12, &c., and Josue, 8, 33, &c.

HESE are the precepts and judgments, that you must do in the land, which the Lord the God of thy fathers will give thee, to possess it all the days that thou shalt walk upon the earth.

2 Destroy all the places in which the nations, that you shall possess, worshipped their gods upon high mountains, and hills, and under every shady tree.

3 ¹ Overthrow their altars, and break down their statues: burn their groves with fire, and break their idols in pieces. Destroy their names out of those places.

4 You shall not do so to the Lord your God.

5 But you shall come to the place, which the Lord your God shall choose out of all your tribes, to put his name there, and to dwell in it.

6 And you shall offer in that place your holocausts and victims, the tithes and firstfruits of your hands and your vows and gifts, the firstborn of your herds and your sheep.

7 And you shall eat there in the sight of the Lord your God: and you shall rejoice in all things, whereunto you shall put your hand, you and your houses wherein the Lord your God hath blessed you.

8 You shall not do there the things we do here this day: every man that which seemeth good to himself.

9 For until this present time you are not come to rest, and to the possession, which the Lord your God will give you.

10 You shall pass over the Jordan, and shall dwell in the land which the Lord your God will give you, that you may have rest from all enemies round about: and may dwell without any fear,

11 In the place, which the Lord your God shall choose, that his name may be therein. Thither shall you bring all the things that I command you: holocausts, and victims, and tithes, and the firstfruits of your hands, and whatsoever is the choicest in the gifts which you shall vow to the Lord.

12 There shall you feast before the Lord your God, you and your sons and your daughters, your men-servants and maid-servants, and the Levite that dwelleth in your cities. For he hath no other part and possession among you.

13 Beware lest thou offer thy holocausts in every place that thou shalt see.

14 But in the place which the Lord shall choose in one of thy tribes shalt thou offer sacrifices, and shalt do all that I command thee.

15 But if thou desirest to eat, and the eating of flesh delight thee, kill, and

eat according to the blessing of the Lord thy God, which he hath given thee, in thy cities. Whether it be unclean (that is to say, having blemish or defect) : or clean (that is to say, sound and without blemish), such as may be offered, as the roe and the hart, shalt thou eat it.

16 Only the blood thou shalt not eat: but thou shalt pour it out upon the earth as water.

17 Thou mayst not eat in thy towns the tithes of thy corn, and thy wine, and thy oil, the firstborn of thy herds and thy cattle, nor any thing that thou vowest, and that thou wilt offer voluntarily, and the firstfruits of thy hands.

18 But thou shalt eat them before the Lord thy God in the place which the Lord thy God shall choose, thou and thy son and thy daughter, and thy man-servant, and maid-servant, and the Levite that dwelleth in thy cities. And thou shalt rejoice and be refreshed before the Lord thy God in all things, whereunto thou shalt put thy hand.

19 Take heed thou forsake not the Levite all the time that thou livest in the land.

20 ² When the Lord thy God shall have enlarged thy borders, as he hath spoken to thee, and thou wilt eat the flesh that thy soul desireth:

21 And if the place which the Lord thy God shall choose, that his name should be there, be far off: thou shalt kill of thy herds and of thy flocks, as I have commanded thee, and shalt eat in thy towns, as it pleaseth thee.

22 Even as the roe and the hart is eaten, so shalt thou eat them: both the clean and unclean shall eat of them alike.

23 Only beware of this, that thou eat not the blood: for the blood is for the soul. And therefore thou must not eat the soul with the flesh:

24 But thou shalt pour it upon the earth as water,

25 That it may be well with thee and thy children after thee, when thou shalt do that which is pleasing in the sight of the Lord.

26 But the things which thou hast sanctified and vowed to the Lord, thou shalt take, and shalt come to the place which the Lord shall choose:

27 And shalt offer thy oblations the flesh and the blood upon the altar of the Lord thy God. The blood of thy victims thou shalt pour on the altar: and the flesh thou thyself shalt eat.

28 Observe and hear all the things that I command thee, that it may be well with thee and thy children after thee for ever, when thou shalt do what is good and pleasing in the sight of the Lord thy God.

CHAP. 12. ¹ Deut. 7, 25; 2 Mach. 12, 40. ² Gen. 28, 14; Exod. 34, 24; Deut. 19, 8.

29 [3] When the Lord thy God shall have destroyed before thy face the nations, which thou shalt go in to possess, and *when* thou shalt possess them, and dwell in their land:

30 Beware lest thou imitate them, after they are destroyed at thy coming in, and lest thou seek after their ceremonies, saying: As these nations have worshipped their gods, so will I also worship.

31 Thou shalt not do in like manner to the Lord thy God. For they have done to their gods all the abominations which the Lord abhorreth, offering their sons and daughters, and burning them with fire.

32 What I command thee, that only do thou to the Lord: neither add any thing, nor diminish.

CHAPTER 13

False prophets must be slain, and idolatrous cities destroyed.

IF there rise in the midst of thee a prophet or one that saith he hath dreamed a dream, and he foretell a sign and a wonder:

2 And that come to pass which he spoke, and he say to thee: Let us go and follow strange gods, which thou knowest not, and let us serve them.

3 Thou shalt not hear the words of that prophet or dreamer. For the Lord your God trieth you, that it may appear whether you love him with all your heart, and with all your soul, or not.

4 Follow the Lord your God, and fear him, and keep his commandments, and hear his voice. Him you shall serve, and to him you shall cleave.

5 And that prophet or forger of dreams shall be slain: because he spoke to draw you away from the Lord your God, who brought you out of the land of Egypt, and redeemed you from the house of bondage: to make thee go out of the way, which the Lord thy God commanded thee. And thou shalt take away the evil out of the midst of thee.

6 If thy brother the son of thy mother, or thy son, or daughter, or thy wife that is in thy bosom, or thy friend, whom thou lovest as thy own soul, would persuade thee secretly, saying: Let us go, and serve strange gods, which thou knowest not, nor thy fathers,

7 Of all the nations round about, that are near or afar off, from one end of the earth to the other.

8 Consent not to him, hear him not: neither let thy eye spare him to pity and conceal him.

9 But thou shalt presently put him to death. [1] Let thy hand be first upon him: and afterwards the hands of all the people.

10 With stones shall he be stoned to death. Because he would have withdrawn thee from the Lord thy God, who brought thee out of the land of Egypt, from the house of bondage.

11 That all Israel hearing may fear, and may do no more any thing like this.

12 If in one of thy cities, which the Lord thy God shall give thee to dwell in, thou hear some say:

13 Children of Belial are gone out of the midst of thee, and have withdrawn the inhabitants of their city, and have said: Let us go, and serve strange gods which you know not.

14 Inquire carefully and diligently, the truth of the thing by looking well into it: and if thou find that which is said to be certain, and that this abomination hath been really committed,

15 Thou shalt forthwith kill the inhabitants of that city with the edge of the sword, and shalt destroy it and all things that are in it, even the cattle.

16 And all the household goods that are there, thou shalt gather together in the midst of the streets thereof, and shalt burn them with the city itself, so as to consume all for the Lord thy God, and that it be a heap for ever. It shall be built no more.

17 And there shall nothing of that anathema stick to thy hand: that the Lord may turn from the wrath of his fury, and may have mercy on thee, and multiply thee as he swore to thy fathers:

18 When thou shalt hear the voice of the Lord thy God, keeping all his precepts, which I commanded thee this day, that thou mayst do what is pleasing in the sight of the Lord thy God.

CHAPTER 14

In mourning for the dead they are not to follow the ways of the Gentiles. The distinction of clean and unclean meats. Ordinances concerning tithes, and first-fruits.

BE ye children of the Lord your God. You shall not cut yourselves, nor make any baldness for the dead;

2 [1] Because thou art a holy people to the Lord thy God: and he chose thee

---

[3] Deut. 19, 1. CHAP. 13. [1] Deut. 17, 7. CHAP. 14. [1] Deut. 7, 6; 28, 18.

CHAP. 12. Ver. 32. *That only do thou.* They are forbid here to follow the ceremonies of the heathens; or to make any alterations in the divine ordinances.

CHAP. 13. Ver. 9. *Presently put him to death.* Not by killing him by private authority, but by informing the magistrate, and proceeding by order of justice.

Ver. 13. *Belial.* That is, *without yoke.* Hence the wicked, who refuse to be subject to the divine law, are called in scripture the children of Belial.

to be his peculiar people of all nations that are upon the earth.

3 ² Eat not the things that are unclean.

4 These are the beasts that you shall eat: the ox, and the sheep, and the goat,

5 The hart and the roe, the buffle, the chamois, the pygarg, the wild goat, the camelopardalus.

6 Every beast that divideth the hoof in two parts, and cheweth the cud, you shall eat.

7 But of them that chew the cud, but divide not the hoof, you shall not eat, such as the camel, the hare, and the cherogril. Because they chew the cud, but divide not the hoof, they shall be unclean to you.

8 The swine also, because it divideth the hoof, but cheweth not the cud, shall be unclean: their flesh you shall not eat, and their carcasses you shall not touch.

9 These shall you eat of all that abide in the waters: All that have fins and scales, you shall eat.

10 Such as are without fins and scales, you shall not eat, because they are unclean.

11 All birds that are clean you shall eat.

12 The unclean eat not: to wit, the eagle, and the grype, and the osprey,

13 The ringtail, and the vulture, and the kite according to their kind:

14 And all of the raven's kind:

15 And the ostrich, and the owl, and the larus, and the hawk according to its kind:

16 The heron, and the swan, and the stork,

17 And the cormorant, the porphirion, and the night crow,

18 The bittern, and the charadrion, every one in their kind: the hoop also and the bat.

19 Every thing that creepeth, and hath little wings, shall be unclean, and shall not be eaten.

20 All that is clean, you shall eat.

21 But whatsoever is dead of itself, eat not thereof. Give it to the stranger, that is within thy gates, to eat; or sell it to him: because thou art the holy people of the Lord thy ³ God. Thou shalt not boil a kid in the milk of his dam.

² Lev. 11, 4. ³ Exod. 23, 19; 34, 26.

CHAP. 14. Ver. 3. *Unclean.* See the annotations on Lev. 9.

CHAP. 15. Ver. 4. *There shall be no poor.* It is not to be understood as *a promise*, that there should be no poor in Israel, as appears from ver. 11, where we learn that God's people would never be at a loss to find objects for their charity: but it is an ordinance that all should do their best endeavours to prevent any of their brethren from suffering the hardships of poverty and want.

22 Every year thou shalt set aside the tithes of all thy fruits that the earth bringeth forth.

23 And thou shalt eat before the Lord thy God in the place which he shall choose, that his name may be called upon therein, the tithe of thy corn, and thy wine, and thy oil, and the firstborn of thy herds and thy sheep: that thou mayest learn to fear the Lord thy God at all times.

24 But when the way and the place which the Lord thy God shall choose, are far off, and he hath blessed thee, and thou canst not carry all these things thither,

25 Thou shalt sell them all, and turn them into money, and shalt carry it in thy hand, and shalt go to the place which the Lord shall choose

26 And thou shalt buy with the same money whatsoever pleaseth thee, either of the herds or of sheep, wine also and strong drink, and all that thy soul desireth: and thou shalt eat before the Lord thy God, and shalt feast, thou and thy house.

27 And the Levite that is within thy gates, beware thou forsake him not, because he hath no other part in thy possession.

28 The third year thou shalt separate another tithe of all things that grow to thee at that time, and shalt lay it up within thy gates.

29 And the Levite that hath no other part nor possession with thee, and the stranger and the fatherless and the widow, that are within thy gates, shall come and shall eat and be filled: that the Lord thy God may bless thee in all the works of thy hands that thou shalt do.

CHAPTER 15

The law of the seventh year of remission. The firstlings of cattle are to be sanctified to the Lord.

IN the seventh year thou shalt make a remission,

2 Which shall be celebrated in this order. He to whom any thing is owing from his friend or neighbour or brother, cannot demand it again: because it is the year of remission of the Lord.

3 Of the foreigner or stranger thou mayst exact *it.* Of thy countryman and neighbour thou shalt not have power to demand it again.

4 And there shall be no poor nor beggar among you: that the Lord thy God may bless thee in the land which he will give thee in possession.

5 Yet so, if thou hear the voice of the Lord thy God, and keep all things that he hath ordained, and which I com-

mand thee this day, he will bless thee, as he hath promised.

6 Thou shalt lend to many nations, and thou shalt borrow of no man. Thou shalt have dominion over very many nations: and no one shall have dominion over thee.

7 If one of thy brethren that dwelleth within the gates of thy city in the land which the Lord thy God will give thee, come to poverty: thou shalt not harden thy heart, nor close thy hand,

8 But shalt open it to the poor man. [1] Thou shalt lend him, that which thou perceivest he hath need of.

9 Beware lest perhaps a wicked thought steal in upon thee, and thou say in thy heart: [2] The seventh year of remission draweth nigh. And thou turn away thy eyes from thy poor brother, denying to lend him that which he asketh: lest he cry against thee to the Lord, and it become a sin unto thee.

10 But thou shalt give to him. Neither shalt thou do any thing craftily in relieving his necessities: that the Lord thy God may bless thee at all times, and in all things to which thou shalt put thy hand.

11 [3] There will not be wanting poor in the land of my habitation: therefore I command thee to open thy hand to thy needy and poor brother, that liveth in the land.

12 [4] When thy brother, a Hebrew man, or Hebrew woman, is sold to thee, and hath served thee six years, in the seventh year thou shalt let him go free.

13 And when thou sendest him out free, thou shalt not let him go away empty.

14 But shalt give him for his way: out of thy flocks, and out of thy barn-floor, and thy winepress, wherewith the Lord thy God shall bless thee.

15 Remember that thou also wast a bondservant in the land of Egypt, and the Lord thy God made thee free: and therefore I now command thee this.

16 But if he say: I will not depart; because he loveth thee, and thy house, and findeth that he is well with thee.

17 Thou shalt take an awl, and bore through his ear in the door of thy house, and he shall serve thee for ever. Thou shalt do in like manner to thy woman-servant also.

18 Turn not away thy eyes from them when thou makest them free: because he hath served thee six years according to the wages of a hireling. That the Lord thy God may bless thee in all the works that thou dost.

19 Of the firstlings, that come of thy herds and thy sheep, thou shalt sanctify to the Lord thy God whatsoever is of the male sex. Thou shalt not work with the firstling of a bullock: and thou shalt not shear the firstlings of thy sheep.

20 In the sight of the Lord thy God shalt thou eat them every year, in the place that the Lord shall choose, thou and thy house.

21 [5] But if it have a blemish, or be lame, or blind, or in any part disfigured or feeble, it shall not be sacrificed to the Lord thy God.

22 But thou shalt eat it within the gates of thy city: the clean and the unclean shall eat them alike, as the roe and as the hart.

23 Only thou shalt take heed not to eat their blood, but pour it out on the earth as water.

CHAPTER 16

The three principal solemnities to be observed. Just judges to be appointed in every city. All occasions of idolatry to be avoided.

OBSERVE the month of new corn, which is the first of the spring, that thou mayst celebrate the phase to the Lord thy God: because in this month the Lord thy God brought thee out of Egypt by night.

2 And thou shalt sacrifice the phase to the Lord thy God, of sheep, and of oxen, in the place which the Lord thy God shall choose, that his name may dwell there.

3 Thou shalt not eat with it leavened bread: seven days shalt thou eat without leaven, the bread of affliction, because thou camest out of Egypt in fear. That thou mayst remember the day of thy coming out of Egypt, all the days of thy life.

4 No leaven shall be seen in all thy coasts for seven days: neither shall any of the flesh of that which was sacrificed the first day in the evening remain until morning.

5 Thou mayst not immolate the phase in any one of thy cities, which the Lord thy God will give thee

6 But in the place which the Lord thy God shall choose, that his name may dwell there. Thou shalt immolate the phase in the evening, at the going down of the sun, at which time thou camest out of Egypt.

7 And thou shalt dress, and eat it in the place which the Lord thy God shall choose: and in the morning rising up thou shalt go into thy dwellings.

8 Six days shalt thou eat unleavened bread: and on the seventh day, because it is the assembly of the Lord thy God, thou shalt do no work.

CHAP. 15. [1] Matt. 5, 42; Luke, 6, 34. [2] Exod. 23, 11; Lev. 25, 2. [3] Matt. 26, 11. [4] Exod. 21, 2; Jer. 34, 14. [5] Lev. 22, 20; Ecclus. 35, 14.

9 Thou shalt number unto thee seven weeks from that day, wherein thou didst put the sickle to the corn.

10 And thou shalt celebrate the festival of weeks to the Lord thy God: a voluntary oblation of thy hand, which thou shalt offer according to the blessing of the Lord thy God.

11 And thou shalt feast before the Lord thy God, thou, and thy son, and thy daughter, and thy man-servant, and thy maid-servant, and the Levite that is within thy gates, and the stranger and the fatherless, and the widow, who abide with you: in the place which the Lord thy God shall choose, that his name may dwell there.

12 And thou shalt remember that thou wast a servant in Egypt: and thou shalt keep and do the things that are commanded.

13 Thou shalt celebrate the solemnity also of tabernacles seven days, when thou hast gathered in thy fruit of the barnfloor and of the winepress.

14 And thou shalt make merry in thy festival time, thou, thy son, and thy daughter, thy man-servant, and thy maid-servant: the Levite also and the stranger, and the fatherless and the widow that are within thy gates.

15 Seven days shalt thou celebrate feasts to the Lord thy God in the place which the Lord shall choose. And the Lord thy God will bless thee in all thy fruits, and in every work of thy hands, and thou shalt be in joy.

16 Three times in a year shall all thy males appear before the Lord thy God in the place which he shall choose: in the feast of unleavened bread, in the feast of weeks, and in the feast of tabernacles. [1] No one shall appear with his hands empty before the Lord.

17 But every one shall offer according to what he hath, according to the blessings of the Lord his God, which he shall give him.

18 Thou shalt appoint judges and magistrates in all thy gates, which the Lord thy God shall give thee, in all thy tribes. That they may judge the people with just judgment,

19 And not go aside to either part. [2] Thou shalt not accept person nor gifts: for gifts blind the eyes of the wise, and change the words of the just.

20 Thou shalt follow justly after that which is just: that thou mayst live and possess the land, which the Lord thy God shall give thee.

21 Thou shalt plant no grove, nor any tree near the altar of the Lord thy God.

22 Neither shalt thou make nor set up to thyself a statue: which things the Lord thy God hateth.

CHAPTER 17

Victims must be without blemish. Idolaters are to be slain. Controversies are to be decided by the high priest and council, whose sentences must be obeyed under pain of death. The duty of a king, who is to receive the law of God at the priest's hands.

THOU shalt not sacrifice to the Lord thy God a sheep, or an ox, wherein there is blemish, or any fault: for that is an abomination to the Lord thy God.

2 When there shall be found among you within any of thy gates, which the Lord thy God shall give thee, man or woman that do evil in the sight of the Lord thy God, and transgress his covenant:

3 So as to go and serve strange gods, and adore them, the sun and the moon, and all the host of heaven, which I have not commanded:

4 And this is told thee, and hearing it thou hast inquired diligently, and found it to be true, and that the abomination is committed in Israel:

5 Thou shalt bring forth the man or the woman, who have committed that most wicked thing, to the gates of thy city, and they shall be stoned.

6 [1] By the mouth of two or three witnesses shall he die that is to be slain. Let no man be put to death, when only one beareth witness against him.

7 The hands of the witnesses shall be first upon him to kill him: [2] and afterwards the hands of the rest of the people. That thou mayst take away the evil out of the midst of thee.

8 If thou perceive that there be among you a hard and doubtful *matter* in judgment between blood and blood, cause and cause, leprosy and leprosy: and thou see that the words of the judges within thy gates do vary: arise, and go up to the place, which the Lord thy God shall choose.

9 [3] And thou shalt come to the priests of the Levitical race, and to the judge, that shall be at that time. And thou shalt ask of them. And they shall shew thee the truth of the judgment.

10 And thou shalt do whatsoever they shall say, that preside in the place, which the Lord shall choose, and what they shall teach thee,

CHAP. 16. [1] Exod. 23, 15; 34, 20; Ecclus. 35, 6. [2] Exod. 23, 8; Lev. 19, 15; Deut. 1, 17; Ecclus. 20, 31. CHAP. 17. [1] Deut. 19, 15; Matt. 18, 16; 2 Cor. 13, 1. [2] Deut. 13, 9. [3] 2 Par. 19, 8.

CHAP. 17. Ver. **3.** *The host of heaven.* That is, the stars.

Ver. 8. *If thou perceive. Here* we see what authority God was pleased to give to the church guides of the Old Testament, in deciding without appeal, all controversies relating to the law, promising that they should not err therein; and surely he has not done less for the church guides of the New Testament.

11 According to his law. And thou shalt follow their sentence: neither shalt thou decline to the right hand nor to the left hand.

12 But he that will be proud, and refuse to obey the commandment of the priest, who ministereth at that time to the Lord thy God, and the decree of the judge: that man shall die, and thou shalt take away the evil from Israel.

13 And all the people hearing it shall fear, that no one afterwards swell with pride.

14 When thou art come into the land, which the Lord thy God will give thee, and possessest it, and shalt say: I will set a king over me, as all nations have that are round about,

15 Thou shalt set him whom the Lord thy God shall choose out of the number of thy brethren. Thou mayst not make a man of another nation king, that is not thy brother.

16 And when he is made *king*, he shall not multiply horses to himself, nor lead back the people into Egypt, being lifted up with the number of his horsemen: especially since the Lord hath commanded you to return no more the same way.

17 He shall not have many wives, that may allure his mind, nor immense sums of silver and gold.

18 But after he is raised to the throne of his kingdom, he shall copy out to himself the Deuteronomy of this law in a volume, taking the copy of the priests of the Levitical tribe.

19 And he shall have it with him, and shall read it all the days of his life: that he may learn to fear the Lord his God, and keep his words and ceremonies, that are commanded in the law:

20 And that his heart be not lifted up with pride over his brethren, nor decline to the right or to the left: that he and his sons may reign a long time over Israel.

CHAPTER 18

The Lord is the inheritance of the priests and Levites. Heathenish abominations are to be avoided. The great PROPHET CHRIST *is promised. False prophets must be slain.*

THE priests and Levites, [1] and all that are of the same tribe, shall have no part nor inheritance with the rest of Israel: because they shall eat the sacrifices of the Lord, and his oblation.

2 And they shall receive nothing else of the possession of their brethren: for the Lord himself is their inheritance, as he hath said to them.

3 This shall be the priest's due from the people, and from them that offer victims. Whether they sacrifice an ox, or a sheep, they shall give to the priest the shoulder and the breast:

4 [2] The firstfruits *also* of corn, of wine, and of oil, and a part of the wool from the shearing of their sheep.

5 For the Lord thy God hath chosen him of all thy tribes, to stand and to minister to the name of the Lord: him and his sons for ever.

6 If a Levite go out of any one of the cities throughout all Israel, in which he dwelleth, and have a longing mind to come to the place which the Lord shall choose:

7 He shall minister in the name of the Lord his God, as all his brethren the Levites *do*, that shall stand at that time before the Lord.

8 He shall receive the same portion of food that the rest do: besides that which is due to him in his own city, by succession from his fathers.

9 When thou art come into the land which the Lord thy God shall give thee, beware lest thou have a mind to imitate the abominations of those nations.

10 [3] Neither let there be found among you any one that shall expiate his son or daughter, making them to pass through the fire: or that consulteth soothsayers, or observeth dreams and omens. Neither let there be any wizard,

11 Nor charmer, nor any one that consulteth pythonic spirits, or fortune tellers: [4] or that seeketh the truth from the dead.

12 For the Lord abhorreth all these things: and for these abominations he will destroy them at thy coming.

13 Thou shalt be perfect: and without spot before the Lord thy God.

14 These nations, whose land thou shalt possess, hearken to soothsayers and diviners: but thou art otherwise instructed by the Lord thy God.

15 [5] The Lord thy God will raise up to thee a PROPHET of thy nation and of thy brethren like unto me. Him thou shalt hear.

16 As thou desiredst of the Lord thy God in [6] Horeb, when the assembly was gathered together, and saidst: Let me not hear any more the voice of the Lord my God, neither let me see any more this exceeding great fire, lest I die.

17 And the Lord said to me: They have spoken all things well.

18 [7] I will raise them up a prophet out of the midst of their brethren like to thee. And I will put my words in his mouth: and he shall speak to them all that I shall command him.

19 And he that will not hear his

CHAP. 18. [1] Num. 18, 20; Deut. 10, 9; 1 Cor. 9, 13. [2] Num. 18, 21. [3] Lev. 20, 27. [4] 1 Kings, 28, 7. [5] John, 1, 45; Acts, 3, 22. [6] Exod. 20, 21. [7] John, 1, 45.

words, which he shall speak in my name, I will be the revenger.

20 But the prophet, who being corrupted with pride, shall speak in my name things that I did not command him to say, or in the name of strange gods, shall be slain.

21 And if in silent thought thou answer: How shall I know the word that the Lord hath not spoken?

22 Thou shalt have this sign: Whatsoever that same prophet foretelleth in the name of the Lord, and it cometh not to pass: that thing the Lord hath not spoken, but the prophet hath forged it by the pride of his mind. And therefore thou shalt not fear him.

CHAPTER 19

The cities of refuge. Wilful murder, and false witnesses must be punished.

WHEN the Lord thy God hath destroyed the nations, whose land he will deliver to thee, and thou shalt possess it, and shalt dwell in the cities and houses thereof.

2 [1] Thou shalt separate to thee three cities in the midst of the land, which the Lord will give thee in possession,

3 Paving diligently the way. And thou shalt divide the whole province of thy land equally into three parts: that he who is forced to flee for manslaughter, may have near at hand whither to escape.

4 This shall be the law of the slayer that fleeth, whose life is to be saved. He that killeth his neighbour ignorantly, and who is proved to have had no hatred against him yesterday and the day before:

5 But to have gone with him to the wood to hew wood, and in cutting down the tree the axe slipped out of his hand, and the iron slipping from the handle struck his friend, and killed him: he shall flee to one of the cities aforesaid, and live.

6 Lest perhaps the next kinsman of him whose blood was shed, pushed on by his grief should pursue, and apprehend him, if the way be too long: and take away the life of him who is not guilty of death, because he is proved to have had no hatred before against him that was slain.

7 Therefore I command thee, that thou separate three cities at equal distance one from another.

8 [2] And when the Lord thy God shall have enlarged thy borders, as he swore to thy fathers, and shall give thee all the land that he promised them:

9 (Yet so, if thou keep his commandments, and do the things which I command thee this day, that thou love the Lord thy God, and walk in his ways at all times) thou shalt add to thee other three cities, and shalt double the number of the three cities aforesaid.

10 That innocent blood may not be shed in the midst of the land which the Lord thy God will give thee to possess: lest thou be guilty of blood.

11 [3] But if any man hating his neighbour, lie in wait for his life, and rise and strike him, and he die; and he flee to one of the cities aforesaid:

12 The ancients of his city shall send, and take him out of the place of refuge: and shall deliver him into the hand of the kinsman of him whose blood was shed. And he shall die.

13 Thou shalt not pity him, and thou shalt take away the *guilt of* innocent blood out of Israel, that it may be well with thee.

14 Thou shalt not take nor remove thy neighbour's landmark, which *thy* predecessors have set in thy possession, which the Lord thy God will give thee in the land that thou shalt receive to possess.

15 [4] One witness shall not rise up against any man, whatsoever the sin or wickedness be. But in the mouth of two or three witnesses every word shall stand.

16 If a lying witness stand against a man, accusing him of transgression:

17 Both of them, between whom the controversy is, shall stand before the Lord in the sight of the priests and the judges that shall be in those days.

18 [5] And when after most diligent inquisition, they shall find that the false witness hath told a lie against his brother:

19 They shall render to him as he meant to do to his brother; and thou shalt take away the evil out of the midst of thee.

20 That others hearing may fear, and may not dare to do such things.

21 Thou shalt not pity him: [6] but shalt require life for life, eye for eye, tooth for tooth, hand for hand, foot for foot.

CHAPTER 20

Laws relating to war.

IF thou go out to war against thy enemies, and see horsemen and chariots, and the numbers of the enemy's army greater than thine, thou shalt not fear them: because the Lord thy God is with thee, who brought thee out of the land of Egypt.

2 And when the battle is now at hand, the priest shall stand before the

CHAP. 19. [1] Num. 35, 11; Jos. 20, 2. [2] Gen. 28, 14; Exod. 34, 24; Deut. 12, 20. [3] Num. 35, 20. [4] Deut. 17, 6; Matt. 18, 16; 2 Cor. 13, 1. [5] Dan. 13, 62. [6] Exod. 21, 23; Lev. 24, 20; Matt. 5, 38.

army, and shall speak to the people in this manner:

3 Hear, O Israel. You join battle this day against your enemies: let not your heart be dismayed, be not afraid, do not give back, fear ye them not.

4 Because the Lord your God is in the midst of you, and will fight for you against your enemies, to deliver you from danger.

5 And the captains shall proclaim through every band in the hearing of the army: [1] What man is there, that hath built a new house, and hath not dedicated it? Let him go and return to his house, lest he die in the battle, and another man dedicate it.

6 What man is there, that hath planted a vineyard, and hath not as yet made it to be common, whereof all men may eat? Let him go, and return to his house, lest he die in the battle, and another man execute his office.

7 What man is there, that hath espoused a wife, and not taken her? Let him go, and return to his house, lest he die in the war, and another man take her.

8 After these things are declared they shall add the rest, and shall speak to the people: [2] What man is there that is fearful, and faint hearted? Let him go, and return to his house, lest he make the hearts of his brethren to fear, as he himself is possessed with fear.

9 And when the captains of the army shall hold their peace, and have made an end of speaking, every man shall prepare their bands to fight.

10 If at any time thou come to fight against a city, thou shalt first offer it peace.

11 If they receive it, and open the gates to thee, all the people that are therein, shall be saved, and shall serve thee paying tribute.

12 But if they will not make peace, and shall begin war against thee, thou shalt besiege it.

13 And when the Lord thy God shall deliver it into thy hands, thou shalt slay all that are therein of the male sex, with the edge of the sword:

14 Excepting women and children, cattle and other things, that are in the city. And thou shalt divide all the prey to the army: and thou shalt eat the spoils of thy enemies, which the Lord thy God shall give thee.

15 So shalt thou do to all cities that are at a great distance from thee, and are not of these cities which thou shalt receive in possession.

16 But of those cities that shall be given thee, thou shalt suffer none at all to live.

17 But shalt kill them with the edge of the sword: to wit, the Hethite, and the Amorrhite, and the Chanaanite, the Pherezite, and the Hevite, and the Jebusite, as the Lord thy God hath commanded thee.

18 Lest they teach you to do all the abominations which they have done to their gods: and you should sin against the Lord your God.

19 When thou hast besieged a city a long time, and hath compassed it with bulwarks to take it, thou shalt not cut down the trees that may be eaten of: neither shalt thou spoil the country round about with axes. For it is a tree, and not a man: neither can it increase the number of them that fight against thee.

20 But if there be any trees that are not fruitful, but wild, and fit for other uses: cut them down, and make engines, until thou take the city, which fighteth against thee.

CHAPTER 21

The expiation of a secret murder. The marrying a captive. The eldest son must not be deprived of his birthright for hatred of his mother. A stubborn son is to be stoned to death. When one is hanged on a gibbet, he must be taken down the same day and buried.

WHEN there shall be found in the land, which the Lord thy God will give thee, the corpse of a man slain, and it is not known who is guilty of the murder:

2 Thy ancients and judges shall go out, and shall measure from the place where the body lieth the distance of every city round about.

3 And the ancients of that city which they shall perceive to be nearer than the rest, shall take a heifer of the herd, that hath not drawn in the yoke, nor ploughed the ground.

4 And they shall bring her into a rough and stony valley, that never was ploughed, nor sown. And there they shall strike off the head of the heifer.

5 And the priests the sons of Levi shall come, whom the Lord thy God hath chosen to minister to him, and to bless in his name, and that by their word every matter *should be decided*, and whatsoever is clean or unclean should be judged.

6 And the ancients of that city shall come to the person slain, and shall wash their hands over the heifer that was killed in the valley:

7 And shall say: Our hands did not shed this blood, nor did *our* eyes see it.

8 Be merciful to thy people Israel, whom thou hast redeemed, O Lord, and lay not innocent blood to their charge, in the midst of thy people Israel. And

CHAP. 20. [1] 1 Mach. 3, 6. [2] Judges, 7, 3.

the guilt of blood shall be taken from them.

9 And thou shalt be free from the innocent's blood, that was shed, when thou shalt have done what the Lord hath commanded thee.

10 If thou go out to fight against thy enemies, and the Lord thy God deliver them into thy hand, and thou lead them away captives:

11 And seest in the number of the captives a beautiful woman, and lovest her, and wilt have her to wife:

12 Thou shalt bring her into thy house. And she shall shave her hair, and pare her nails:

13 And shall put off the raiment, wherein she was taken: and shall remain in thy house, and mourn for her father and mother one month. And after that thou shalt go in unto her and shall sleep with her: and she shall be thy wife.

14 But if afterwards she please thee not, thou shalt let her go free: but thou mayst not sell her for money nor oppress her by might; because thou hast humbled her.

15 If a man have two wives, one beloved, and the other hated, and they have had children by him, and the son of the hated be the firstborn:

16 And he meaneth to divide his substance among his sons: he may not make the son of the beloved the firstborn, and prefer him before the son of the hated.

17 [1] But he shall acknowledge the son of the hated for the firstborn: and shall give him a double portion of all he hath. For this is the first of his children: and to him are due the first birthrights.

18 If a man have a stubborn and unruly son, who will not hear the commandments of his father or mother, and being corrected, slighteth obedience:

19 They shall take him and bring him to the ancients of his city, and to the gate of judgment:

20 And shall say to them: This our son is rebellious and stubborn; he slighteth hearing our admonitions; he giveth himself to revelling, and to debauchery and banquetings.

21 The people of the city shall stone him: and he shall die, that you may

take away the evil out of the midst of you, and all Israel hearing it may be afraid.

22 When a man hath committed a crime for which he is to be punished with death, and being condemned to die is hanged on a gibbet:

23 His body shall not remain upon the tree, but shall be buried the same day. [2] For he is accursed of God that hangeth on a tree: and thou shalt not defile thy land, which the Lord thy God shall give thee in possession.

CHAPTER 22

Humanity towards neighbours. Neither sex may use the apparel of the other. Cruelty to be avoided even to birds. Battlements about the roof of a house. Things of divers kinds not be be mixed. The punishment of him that slandereth his wife, as also of adultery and rape.

THOU shalt not pass by if thou seest thy brother's ox, [1] or his sheep go astray: but thou shalt bring them back to thy brother.

2 And if thy brother be not nigh, or thou know him not: thou shalt bring *them* to thy house, and they shall be with thee until thy brother seek them, and receive them.

3 Thou shalt do in like manner with his ass, and with his raiment, and with every thing that is thy brother's, which is lost. If thou find it, neglect it not as pertaining to another.

4 If thou see thy brother's ass or his ox to be fallen down in the way, thou shalt not slight it, but shalt lift it up with him.

5 A woman shall not be clothed with man's apparel: neither shall a man use woman's apparel. For he that doeth these things is abominable before God.

6 If thou find as thou walkest by the way, a bird's nest in a tree, or on the ground, and the dam sitting upon the young or upon the eggs: thou shalt not take her with her young.

7 But shalt let her go, keeping the young which thou hast caught: that it may be well with thee, and thou mayst live a long time.

8 When thou buildest a new house, thou shalt make a battlement to the roof round about: lest blood be shed in thy house, and thou be guilty, if any one slip, and fall down headlong.

9 Thou shalt not sow thy vineyard with divers seeds: lest both the seed which thou hast sown, and the fruit of the vineyard, be sanctified together.

10 Thou shalt not plough with an ox and an ass together.

11 Thou shalt not wear a garment that is woven of woollen and linen together.

CHAP. 21. [1] Par. 5, 1. [2] Gal. 3, 13. CHAP. 22. [1] Exod. 23, 4.

CHAP. 22. Ver. 6. *Thou shalt not take.* This was to shew them to exercise a certain mercy even to irrational creatures; and by that means to train them up to a horror of cruelty; and to the exercise of humanity and mutual charity one to another.

Ver. 8. *Battlement.* This precaution was necessary, because all thir houses had flat tops, and it was usual to walk and to converse together upon them.

12 [2] Thou shalt make strings in the hem at the four corners of thy cloak, wherewith thou shalt be covered.

13 If a man marry a wife, and afterwards hate her,

14 And seek occasions to put her away, laying to her charge a very ill name, and say: I took this woman to wife, and going in to her, I found her not a virgin.

15 Her faher and mother shall take her, and shall bring with them the tokens of her virginity to the ancients of the city that are in the gate.

16 And the father shall say. I gave my daughter unto this man to wife. And because he hateth her,

17 He layeth to her charge a very ill name, so as to say: I found not thy daughter a virgin. And behold these are the tokens of my daughter's virginity. And they shall spread the cloth before the ancients of the city.

18 And the ancients of that city shall take that man, and beat him,

19 Condemning him besides in a hundred sicles of silver, which he shall give to the damsel's father, because he hath defamed by a very ill name a virgin of Israel. And he shall have her to wife, and may not put her away all the days of his life.

20 But if what he charged her with be true, and virginity be not found in the damsel:

21 They shall cast her out of the doors of her father's house: and the men of the city shall stone her to death, and she shall die. Because she hath done a wicked thing in Israel, to play the whore in her father's house: and thou shalt take away the evil out of the midst of thee.

22 [3] If a man lie with another man's wife, they shall both die, that is to say, the adulterer and the adulteress: and thou shalt take away the evil out of Israel.

23 If a man have espoused a damsel that is a virgin, and some one find her in the city, and lie with her,

24 Thou shalt bring them both out to the gate of that city, and they shall be stoned: the damsel, because she cried not out, being in the city: the man, because he hath humbled his neighbour's wife. And thou shalt take away the evil from the midst of thee.

25 But if a man find a damsel that is betrothed, in the field, and taking hold of her, lie with her, he alone shall die.

26 The damsel shall suffer nothing. neither is she guilty of death. For as a robber riseth against his brother, and taketh away his life, so also did the damsel suffer:

27 She was alone in the field: she cried, and there was no man to help her.

28 If a man find a damsel that is a virgin, who is not espoused, and taking her, lie with her, and the matter come to judgment:

29 [4] He that lay with her shall give to the father of the maid fifty sicles of silver, and shall have her to wife, because he hath humbled her. He may not put her away all the days of his life.

30 No man shall take his father's wife, nor remove his covering.

CHAPTER 23

Who may and who may not enter into the church. Uncleanness to be avoided. Other precepts concerning fugitives, fornication, usury, vows, and eating other men's grapes and corn.

AN eunuch, whose testicles are broken or cut away, or yard cut off, shall not enter into the church of the Lord.

2 A mamzer, that is to say, one born of a prostitute, shall not enter into the church of the Lord, until the tenth generation.

3 [1] The Ammonite and the Moabite, even after the tenth generation, shall not enter into the church of the Lord for ever:

4 Because they would not meet you with bread and water in the way, when you came out of Egypt: [2] and because they hired against thee Balaam, the son of Beor, from Mesopotamia in Syria, to curse thee.

5 And the Lord thy God would not hear Balaam: and he turned his cursing into thy blessing, because he loved thee.

6 Thou shalt not make peace with them: neither shalt thou seek their prosperity all the days of thy life for ever.

7 Thou shalt not abhor the Edomite, because he is thy brother: nor the Egyptian, because thou wast a stranger in his land.

8 They that are born of them, in the third generation shall enter into the church of the Lord.

9 When thou goest out to war against thy enemies, thou shalt keep thyself from every evil thing.

10 If there be among you any man, that is defiled in a dream by night, he shall go forth out of the camp.

11 And shall not return, before he be washed with water in the evening: and

[2] Num. 15, 38. [3] Lev. 20, 10. [4] Exod. 22, 16. CHAP. 23. [1] 2 Esd. 13, 1. [2] Num. 22, 5; Jos. 24, 9.
CHAP. 23. Ver. 1. *Eunuch.* By these are meant, in the spiritual sense, such as are barren in good works. *Into the church.* That is, into the assembly or congregation of Israel, so as to have the privilege of an Israelite, or to be capable of any place or office among the people of God.

after sunset he shall return into the camp.

12 Thou shalt have a place without the camp, to which thou mayst go for the necessities of nature,

13 Carrying a paddle at thy girdle. And when thou sittest down, thou shalt dig round about, and with the earth that is dug up thou shalt cover

14 That which thou art eased of (for the Lord thy God walketh in the midst of thy camp, to deliver thee, and to give up thy enemies to thee). And let thy camp be holy, and let no uncleanness appear therein, lest he go away from thee.

15 Thou shalt not deliver to his master the servant that is fled to thee.

16 He shall dwell with thee in the place that shall please him, and shall rest in one of thy cities. Give him no trouble.

17 There shall be no whore among the daughters of Israel, nor whoremonger among the sons of Israel.

18 Thou shalt not offer the hire of a strumpet, nor the price of a dog, in the house of the Lord thy God, whatsoever it be that thou hast vowed: because both these are an abomination to the Lord thy God.

19 Thou shalt not lend to thy brother money to usury, nor corn, nor any other thing:

20 But to the stranger. To thy brother thou shalt lend that which he wanteth, without usury: that the Lord thy God may bless thee in all thy works in the land, which thou shalt go in to possess.

21 When thou hast made a vow to the Lord thy God, thou shalt not delay to pay it: because the Lord thy God will require it. And if thou delay, it shall be imputed to thee for a sin.

22 If thou wilt not promise, thou shalt be without sin.

23 But that which is once gone out of thy lips, thou shalt observe: and shalt do as thou hast promised to the Lord thy God, and hast spoken with thy own will and with thy own mouth.

24 Going into thy neighbour's vineyard, thou mayst eat as many grapes as thou pleasest: but must carry none out with thee.

CHAP. 24. [1]Matt. 5, 31; 19, 7; Mark, 10, 4. [2]Num. 12, 10. [3]Lev. 19, 13; Tob. 4, 15.

Ver. 14. *No uncleanness.* This caution against suffering any filth in the camp, was to teach them to fly the filth of sin, which driveth God away from the soul.

Ver. 20. *To the stranger.* This was a dispensation granted by God to his people, who being the Lord of all things, can give a right and title to one upon the goods of another. Otherwise the scripture everywhere condemns usury, as contrary to the law of God, and a crying sin. (See Exod. 22. 25; Lev. 25, 36; 2 Esd. 5, 7; Ps. 14, 5; Ezech. 18, 8, &c.)

25 If thou go into thy friend's corn, thou mayst break the ears, and rub them in thy hand: but not reap them with a sickle.

CHAPTER 24

Divorce permitted to avoid greater evil. The newly married must not go to war. Of men stealers, of leprosy, of pledges, of labourers' hire, of justice, and of charity to the poor.

IF a man take a wife, [1]and have her, and she find not favour in his eyes, for some uncleanness: he shall write a bill of divorce, and shall give it in her hand, and send her out of his house.

2 And when she is departed, and marrieth another husband:

3 And he also hateth her, and hath given her a bill of divorce, and hath sent her out of his house, or is dead:

4 The former husband cannot take her again to wife: because she is defiled, and is become abominable before the Lord: lest thou cause thy land to sin, which the Lord thy God shall give thee to possess.

5 When a man hath lately taken a wife, he shall not go out to war, neither shall any public business be enjoined him: but he shall be free at home without fault, that for one year he may rejoice with his wife.

6 Thou shalt not take the nether, nor the upper millstone to pledge: for he hath pledged his life to thee.

7 If any man be found soliciting his brother of the children of Israel, and selling him shall take a price, he shall be put to death; and thou shalt take away the evil from the midst of thee.

8 Observe diligently that thou incur not the stroke of the leprosy: but thou shalt do whatever the priests of the Levitical race shall teach thee, according to what I have commanded them. And fulfil thou it carefully.

9 [2]Remember what the Lord your God did to Mary, in the way when you came out of Egypt.

10 When thou shalt demand of thy neighbour any thing that he oweth thee, thou shalt not go into his house to take away a pledge.

11 But thou shalt stand without: and he shall bring out to thee what he hath.

12 But if he be poor, the pledge shall not lodge with thee that night,

13 But thou shalt restore it to him presently before the going down of the sun: that he may sleep in his own raiment and bless thee, and thou mayst have justice before the Lord thy God.

14 [3]Thou shalt not refuse the hire of the needy, and the poor, whether he be thy brother, or a stranger that

dwelleth with thee in the land, and is within thy gates.

15 But thou shalt pay him the price of his labour the same day, before the going down of the sun, because he is poor, and with it maintaineth his life: lest he cry against thee to the Lord, and it be reputed to thee for a sin.

16 ⁴ The fathers shall not be put to death for the children, nor the children for the fathers: but every one shall die for his own sin.

17 Thou shalt not pervert the judgment of the stranger nor of the fatherless: neither shalt thou take away the widow's raiment for a pledge.

18 Remember that thou wast a slave in Egypt, and the Lord thy God delivered thee from thence. Therefore I command thee to do this thing.

19 When thou hast reaped the corn in thy field, and hast forgot and left a sheaf, thou shalt not return to take it away: but thou shalt suffer the stranger, and the fatherless and the widow to take it away: that the Lord thy God may bless thee in all the works of thy hands.

20 If thou have gathered the fruit of thy olive trees, thou shalt not return to gather whatsoever remaineth on the trees: but shalt leave it for the stranger, for the fatherless, and the widow.

21 If thou make the vintage of thy vineyard, thou shalt not gather the clusters that remain: but they shall be for the stranger, the fatherless, and the widow.

22 Remember that thou also wast a bondman in Egypt: and therefore I command thee to do this thing.

CHAPTER 25

Stripes must not exceed forty. The ox is not to be muzzled. Of raising seed to the brother. Of the immodest woman. Of unjust weight. Of destroying the Amalecites.

IF there be a controversy between men, and they call upon the judges: they shall give the prize of justice to him whom they perceive to be just. And him whom they find to be wicked, they shall condemn of wickedness.

2 And if they see that the offender be worthy of stripes: they shall lay him down, and shall cause him to be beaten before them. According to the measure of the sin shall be the measure also of the stripes be.

3 Yet so, ¹ that they exceed not the number of forty: lest thy brother depart shamefully torn before thy eyes.

4 ² Thou shalt not muzzle the ox that treadeth out thy corn on the floor.

5 ³ When brethren dwell together, and one of them dieth without children, the wife of the deceased shall not marry to another: but his brother shall take her, and raise up seed for his brother.

6 And the first son he shall have of her he shall call by his name: that his name be not abolished out of Israel.

7 But if he will not take his brother's wife, who by law belongeth to him, the woman shall go to the gate of the city, and call upon the ancients, and say: ⁴ My husband's brother refuseth to raise up his brother's name in Israel: and will not take me to wife.

8 And they shall cause him to be sent for forthwith, and shall ask him. If he answer: I will not take her to wife:

9 The woman shall come to him before the ancients, and shall take off his shoe from his foot, and spit in his face, and say: So shall it be done to the man that will not build up his brother's house.

10 And his name shall be called in Israel, the house of the unshod.

11 If two men have words together, and one begin to fight against the other, and the other's wife willing to deliver her husband out of the hand of the stronger, shall put forth her hand, and take him by the secrets,

12 Thou shalt cut off her hand, neither shalt thou be moved with any pity in her regard.

13 Thou shalt not have divers weights in thy bag, a greater and a less.

14 Neither shall there be in thy house a greater bushel and a less.

15 Thou shalt have a just and a true weight: and thy bushel shall be equal and true. That thou mayst live a long time upon the land which the Lord thy God shall give thee.

16 For the Lord thy God abhorreth him that doth these things: and he hateth all injustice.

17 ⁵ Remember what Amalec did to thee in the way when thou camest out of Egypt:

18 How he met thee: and slew the hindmost of the army, who sat down, being weary, when thou wast spent with hunger and labour, and he feared not God.

19 Therefore when the Lord thy God shall give thee rest, and shall have sub-

---

⁴ 4 Kings, 14, 6; 2 Par. 25, 4; Ezech. 18, 20. CHAP. 25. ¹ 2 Cor. 11, 24. ² 1 Cor. 9, 9; 1 Tim. 5, 18. ³ Matt. 23, 24; Mark, 12, 19; Luke, 20, 28. ⁴ Ruth, 4, 5. ⁵ Exod. 17, 8.

CHAP. 25. Ver. 4. *Not muzzle.* St. Paul understands this of the spiritual labourer in the church of God, who is not to be denied his maintenance (1 Cor. 9, 8, 9, 10).

Ver. 17. *Amalec.* This order for destroying the Amalecites, in the mystical sense, sheweth how hateful they are to God, and what punishments they are to look for from his justice, who attack and discourage his servants when they are but just come out, as it were, of the Egypt of this wicked world, and being yet weak and faint hearted, are but beginning their journey to the land of promise.

dued all the nations round about in the land which he hath promised thee: thou shalt blot out his name from under heaven. See thou forget it not.

CHAPTER 26

The form of words with which the first-fruits and tithes are to be offered. God's covenant.

AND when thou art come into the land which the Lord thy God will give thee to possess, and hast conquered it, and dwellest in it:

2 Thou shalt take the first of all thy fruits, and put them in a basket, and shalt go to the place which the Lord thy God shall choose, that his name may be invocated there.

3 And thou shalt go to the priest that shall be in those days, and say to him: I profess this day before the Lord thy God, that I am come into the land, for which he swore to our fathers, that he would give it us.

4 And the priest taking the basket at thy hand, shall set it before the altar of the Lord thy God.

5 And thou shalt speak thus in the sight of the Lord thy God: The Syrian pursued my father, who went down into Egypt, and sojourned there in a very small number, and grew into a nation great and strong and of an infinite multitude.

6 And the Egyptians afflicted us, and persecuted us, laying on us most grievous burdens.

7 And we cried to the Lord God of our fathers: who heard us, and looked down upon our affliction, and labour, and distress.

8 And brought us out of Egypt with a strong hand, and a stretched out arm, with great terror, with signs and wonders.

9 And brought us into this place, and gave us this land flowing with milk and honey.

10 And therefore now I offer the firstfruits of the land which the Lord hath given me. And thou shalt leave them in the sight of the Lord thy God, adoring the Lord thy God.

11 And thou shalt feast in all the good things which the Lord thy God hath given thee, and thy house; thou and the Levite, and the stranger that is with thee.

12 When thou hast made an end of tithing all thy fruits, in the third year of tithes thou shalt give it to the Levite, and to the stranger, and to the fatherless, and to the widow, that they may eat within thy gates, and be filled.

CHAP. 26. [1] Deut. 14, 29. [2] Isai. 63, 15; Bar. 2, 16. [3] Deut. 7, 6.

CHAP. 26. Ver. 5. *The Syrian.* Laban. See Gen. 27.

13 And thou shalt speak *thus* in the sight of the Lord thy God: [1] I have taken that which was sanctified out of my house, and I have given it to the Levite, and to the stranger, and to the fatherless, and to the widow, as thou hast commanded me. I have not transgressed thy commandments nor forgotten thy precepts.

14 I have not eaten of them in my mourning, nor separated them for any uncleanness, nor spent any thing of them in funerals. I have obeyed the voice of the Lord my God, and have done all things as thou hast commanded me.

15 [2] Look from thy sanctuary, and thy high habitation of heaven, and bless thy people Israel, and the land which thou hast given us, as thou didst swear to our fathers, a land flowing with milk and honey.

16 This day the Lord thy God hath commanded thee to do these commandments and judgments: and to keep and fulfil them with all thy heart, and with all thy soul.

17 Thou hast chosen the Lord this day to be thy God, and to walk in his ways and keep his ceremonies, and precepts, and judgments, and obey his command.

18 [3] And the Lord hath chosen thee this day, to be his peculiar people, as he hath spoken to thee and to keep all his commandments.

19 And to make thee higher than all nations which he hath created, to his own praise, and name, and glory. That thou mayst be a holy people of the Lord thy God, as he hath spoken.

CHAPTER 27

The commandments must be written on stones, and an altar erected, and sacrifices offered. The observers of the commandments are to be blessed, and the transgressors cursed.

AND Moses with the ancients of Israel commanded the people, saying: Keep every commandment that I command you this day.

2 And when you are passed over the Jordan into the land which the Lord thy God will give thee, thou shalt set up great stones, and shalt plaster them over with plaster:

3 That thou mayst write on them all the words of this law, when thou art passed over the Jordan; that thou mayst enter into the land which the Lord thy God will give thee, a land flowing with milk and honey, as he swore to thy fathers.

4 Therefore when you are passed over the Jordan, set up the stones which I command you this day, in mount

Hebal: and thou shalt plaster them with plaster.

5 And thou shalt build there an altar to the Lord thy God, [1] of stones which iron hath not touched,

6 And of stones not fashioned nor polished. And thou shalt offer upon it holocausts to the Lord thy God.

7 And shalt immolate peace victims, and eat there, and feast before the Lord thy God.

8 And thou shalt write upon the stones all the words of this law plainly and clearly.

9 And Moses and the priests of the race of Levi said to all Israel: Attend, and hear, O Israel. This day thou art made the people of the Lord thy God.

10 Thou shalt hear his voice, and do the commandments and justices which I command thee.

11 And Moses commanded the people in the day, saying:

12 These shall stand upon mount Garizim to bless the people, when you are passed the Jordan: Simeon, Levi, Juda, Issachar, Joseph and Benjamin.

13 And over against them shall stand on mount Hebal to curse: Ruben, Gad, and Aser, and Zabulon, Dan, and Nephtali.

14 [2] And the Levites shall pronounce, and say to all the men of Israel with a loud voice:

15 Cursed be the man that maketh a graven and molten thing, the abomination of the Lord, the work of the hands of artificers, and shall put it in a secret place. And all the people shall answer and say: Amen.

16 Cursed be he that honoureth not his father and mother. And all the people shall say: Amen.

17 Cursed be he that removeth his neighbour's landmarks. And all the people shall say: Amen.

18 Cursed be he that maketh the blind to wander out of his way. And all the people shall say: Amen.

19 Cursed be he that perverteth the judgment of the stranger, of the fatherless and the widow. And all the people shall say: Amen.

20 Cursed be he that lieth with his father's wife, and uncovereth his bed. And all the people shall say: Amen.

21 Cursed be he that lieth with any beast. And all the people shall say: Amen.

22 Cursed be he that lieth with his sister, the daughter of his father, or of his mother. And all the people shall say: Amen.

23 Cursed be he that lieth with his mother-in-law. And all the people shall say: Amen.

24 Cursed be he that secretly killeth his neighbour. And all the people shall say: Amen.

25 Cursed be he that taketh gifts, to slay an innocent person. And all the people shall say: Amen.

26 Cursed be he that abideth not in the words of this law, and fulfilleth them not in work. And all the people shall say: Amen.

CHAPTER 28

Many blessings are promised to the observers of God's commandments, and curses threatened to transgressors.

NOW if thou wilt hear the voice of the Lord thy God, to do and keep all his commandments, which I command thee this day, the Lord thy God will make thee higher than all the nations that are on the earth.

2 And all these blessings shall come upon thee and overtake thee: yet so if thou hear his precepts.

3 Blessed shalt thou be in the city, and blessed in the field.

4 Blessed shall be the fruit of thy womb, and the fruit of thy ground, and the fruit of thy cattle, the droves of thy herds, and the folds of thy sheep.

5 Blessed shall be thy barns and blessed thy stores.

6 Blessed shalt thou be coming in and going out.

7 The Lord shall cause thy enemies, that rise up against thee, to fall down before thy face. One way shall they come out against thee, and seven ways shall they flee before thee.

8 The Lord will send forth a blessing upon thy storehouses, and upon all the works of thy hands: and will bless thee in the land that thou shalt receive.

9 The Lord will raise thee up to be a holy people to himself. As he swore to thee: If thou keep the commandments of the Lord thy God, and walk in his ways.

10 And all the people of the earth shall see that the name of the Lord is invocated upon thee: and they shall fear thee.

11 The Lord will make thee abound with all goods, with the fruit of thy womb, and the fruit of thy cattle, with the fruit of thy land, which the Lord swore to thy fathers that he would give thee.

12 The Lord will open his excellent

CHAP. 27. [1] Exod. 20, 25; Jos. 8, 31. [2] Dan. 9, 11.

CHAP. 28. Ver. 2. *All these blessings.* In the Old Testament, God promised *temporal* blessings to the keepers of his law, heaven not being opened as yet; and that gross and sensual people being more moved with present and sensible things. But in the New Testament the goods that are promised us are spiritual and eternal; and temporal evils are turned into blessings.

treasure, the heaven, that it may give rain in due season: and he will bless all the works of thy hands. And thou shalt lend to many nations, and shalt not borrow of any one.

13 And the Lord shall make thee the head and not the tail: and thou shalt be always above, and not beneath. Yet so if thou wilt hear the commandments of the Lord thy God which I command thee this day, and keep and do them:

14 And turn not away from them neither to the right hand, nor to the left, nor follow strange gods, nor worship them.

15 But if thou wilt not hear the voice of the Lord thy God, to keep and to do all his commandments and ceremonies, which I command thee this day, [1] all these curses shall come upon thee, and overtake thee.

16 Cursed shalt thou be in the city: cursed in the field.

17 Cursed *shall* be thy barn: and cursed thy stores.

18 Cursed shall be the fruit of thy womb, and the fruit of thy ground: the herds of thy oxen, and the flocks of thy sheep.

19 Cursed shalt thou be coming in: and cursed going out.

20 The Lord shall send upon thee famine and hunger, and a rebuke upon all the works which thou shalt do. Until he consume and destroy thee quickly, for thy most wicked inventions, by which thou hast forsaken me.

21 May the Lord set the pestilence upon thee: until he consume thee out of the land, which thou shalt go in to possess.

22 May the Lord afflict thee with miserable want, with the fever and with cold, with burning air and with heat, and with corrupted air and with blasting: and pursue thee till thou perish.

23 Be the heaven, that is over thee, of brass: and the ground thou treadest on, of iron.

24 The Lord give thee dust for rain upon thy land: and let ashes come down from heaven upon thee, till thou be consumed.

25 The Lord make thee to fall down before thy enemies. One way mayst thou go out against them, and flee seven *ways:* and be scattered throughout all the kingdoms of the earth.

26 And be thy carcass meat for all the fowls of the air, and the beasts of

the earth: and be there none to drive them away.

27 The Lord strike thee with the ulcer of Egypt, and the part of thy body, by which the dung is cast out, with the scab and with the itch: so that thou canst not be healed.

28 The Lord strike thee with madness and blindness and fury of mind.

29 And mayst thou grope at midday as the blind is wont to grope in the dark, and not make straight thy ways. And mayst thou at all times suffer wrong, and be oppressed with violence: and mayst thou have no one to deliver thee.

30 Mayst thou take a wife, and another sleep with her. Mayst thou build a house, and not dwell therein. Mayst thou plant a vineyard and not gather the vintage thereof.

31 May thy ox be slain before thee, and thou not eat thereof. May thy ass be taken away in thy sight, and not restored to thee. May thy sheep be given to thy enemies: and may there be none to help thee.

32 May thy sons and thy daughters be given to another people, thy eyes looking on, and languishing at the sight of them all the day: and may there be no strength in thy hand.

33 May a people which thou knowest not, eat the fruits of thy land, and all thy labours: and mayst thou always suffer oppression, and be crushed at all times.

34 And be astonished at the terror of those things which thy eyes shall see.

35 May the Lord strike thee with a very sore ulcer in the knees and in the legs: and be thou incurable from the sole of the foot to the top of the head.

36 The Lord shall bring thee, and thy king, whom thou shalt have appointed over thee, into a nation which thou and thy fathers know not: and there thou shalt serve strange gods, wood and stone.

37 And thou shalt be lost, as a proverb and a byword to all people, among whom the Lord shall bring thee in.

38 [2] Thou shalt cast much seed into the ground, and gather little: because the locusts shall consume all.

39 Thou shalt plant a vineyard, and dig it, and shalt not drink the wine, nor gather any thing thereof: because it shall be wasted with worms.

40 Thou shalt have olive trees in all thy borders, and shalt not be anointed with the oil: for the olives shall fall off and perish.

41 Thou shalt beget sons and daughters, and shalt not enjoy them: because they shall be led into captivity.

CHAP. 28. [1] Lev. 26, 14; Lament. 2, 17; Bar. 1, 20; Mal. 2, 2. [2] Mich. 6, 15; Agg. 1, 6.

Ver. 15. *All these curses.* Thus God dealt with the transgressors of his law in the Old Testament: but now he often suffers sinners to prosper in this world, rewarding them for some little good they have done, and reserving their punishment for the other world.

42 The blast shall consume all the trees and the fruits of thy ground.

43 The stranger that liveth with thee in the land, shall rise up over thee, and shall be higher: and thou shalt go down, and be lower.

44 He shall lend to thee, and thou shalt not lend to him. He shall be as the head, and thou shalt be the tail.

45 And all these curses shall come upon thee, and shall pursue and overtake thee, till thou perish: because thou heardst not the voice of the Lord thy God, and didst not keep his commandments and ceremonies which he commanded thee.

46 And they shall be as signs and wonders on thee, and on thy seed for ever.

47 Because thou didst not serve the Lord thy God with joy and gladness of heart, for the abundance of all things:

48 Thou shalt serve thy enemy whom the Lord will send upon thee, in hunger, and thirst, and nakedness, and in want of all things. And he shall put an iron yoke upon thy neck, till he consume thee.

49 The Lord will bring upon thee a nation from afar, and from the uttermost ends of the earth, like an eagle that flieth swiftly, whose tongue thou canst not understand:

50 A most insolent nation, that will shew no regard to the ancients, nor have pity on the infant:

51 And will devour the fruit of thy cattle, and the fruits of thy land: until thou be destroyed. And will leave thee no wheat, nor wine, nor oil, nor herds of oxen, nor flocks of sheep: until he destroy thee,

52 And consume thee in all thy cities: and thy strong and high walls be brought down, wherein thou trustedst in all thy land. Thou shalt be besieged within thy gates in all thy land which the Lord thy God will give thee.

53 [3] And thou shalt eat the fruit of thy womb, and the flesh of thy sons and of thy daughters, which the Lord thy God shall give thee, in the distress and extremity wherewith thy enemy shall oppress thee.

54 The man that is nice among you, and very delicate, shall envy his own brother, and his wife, that lieth in his bosom,

55 So that he will not give them of the flesh of his children, which he shall eat. Because he hath nothing else in the siege and the want, wherewith thy enemies shall distress thee within all thy gates.

56 The tender and delicate woman, that could not go upon the ground, nor set down her foot for over much niceness and tenderness, will envy her husband who lieth in her bosom, the flesh of her son, and of her daughter,

57 And the filth of the afterbirths, that come forth from between her thighs, and the children that are born the same hour. For they shall eat them secretly for the want of all things, in the siege and distress, wherewith thy enemy shall oppress thee within thy gates.

58 If thou wilt not keep, and fulfil all the words of this law, that are written in this volume, and fear his glorious and terrible name: that is, The Lord thy God.

59 The Lord shall increase thy plagues, and the plagues of thy seed, plagues great and lasting, infirmities grievous and perpetual.

60 And he shall bring back on thee all the afflictions of Egypt, which thou wast afraid of: and they shall stick fast to thee.

61 Moreover the Lord will bring upon thee all the diseases, and plagues, that are not written in the volume of this law till he consume thee.

62 And you shall remain few in number, who before were as the stars of heaven for multitude: because thou heardst not the voice of the Lord thy God.

63 And as the Lord rejoiced upon you before doing good to you, and multiplying you: so he shall rejoice destroying and bringing you to nought, so that you shall be taken away from the land which thou shalt go in to possess.

64 The Lord shall scatter thee among all people, from the farthest parts of the earth to the ends thereof. And there thou shalt serve strange gods, which both thou art ignorant of and thy fathers, wood and stone.

65 Neither shalt thou be quiet, even in those nations, nor shall there be any rest for the sole of thy foot. For the Lord will give thee a fearful heart, and languishing eyes, and a soul consumed with pensiveness.

66 And thy life shall be as it were hanging before thee. Thou shalt fear night and day: neither shalt thou trust thy life.

67 In the morning thou shalt say: Who will grant me evening? And at evening: Who will grant me morning? For the fearfulness of thy heart, wherewith thou shalt be terrified, and for those things which thou shalt see with thy eyes.

68 The Lord shall bring thee again with ships into Egypt, by the way

[3] Lament. 4, 10; Bar. 2, 2.

whereof he said to thee that thou shouldst see it no more. There shalt thou be set to sale to thy enemies for bondmen and bondwomen: and no man shall buy you.

CHAPTER 29

The covenant is solemnly confirmed between God and his people. Threats against those that shall break it.

THESE are the words of the covenant which the Lord commanded Moses to make with the children of Israel in the land of Moab: beside that covenant which he made with them in Horeb.

2 And Moses called all Israel, and said to them: ¹ You have seen all the things that the Lord did before you in the land of Egypt to Pharao, and to all his servants, and to his whole land.

3 The great temptations, which thy eyes have seen, those mighty signs and wonders.

4 And the Lord hath not given you a heart to understand, and eyes to see, and ears that may hear, unto this present day.

5 ² He hath brought you forty years through the desert. Your garments are not worn out, neither are the shoes of your feet consumed with age.

6 You have not eaten bread, nor have you drunk wine or strong drink: that you might know that I am the Lord your God.

7 And you came to this place. ³ And Sehon king of Hesebon, and Og king of Basan, came out against us to fight. And we slew them.

8 And took their land, and delivered it for a possession to ⁴ Ruben and Gad, and the half tribe of Manasses.

9 Keep therefore the words of this covenant, and fulfil them: that you may understand all that you do.

10 You all stand this day before the Lord your God, your princes, and tribes, and ancients, and doctors, all the people of Israel:

11 Your children and your wives, and the stranger that abideth with thee in the camp: besides the hewers of wood, and them that bring water.

12 That thou mayst pass in the cove-

nant of the Lord thy God, and in the oath which this day the Lord thy God maketh with thee.

13 That he may raise thee up a people to himself, and he may be thy God: as he hath spoken to thee, and as he swore to thy fathers Abraham, Isaac, and Jacob.

14 Neither with you only do I make this covenant, and confirm these oaths:

15 But with all that are present and that are absent.

16 For you know how we dwelt in the land of Egypt: and how we have passed through the midst of nations. And passing through them,

17 You have seen their abominations and filth: that is to say, their idols, wood and stone, silver and gold, which they worshipped.

18 Lest perhaps there should be among you a man or a woman, a family or a tribe, whose heart is turned away this day from the Lord our God, to go and serve the gods of those nations: and there should be among you a root bringing forth gall and bitterness.

19 And when he shall hear the words of this oath, he should bless himself in his heart, saying: I shall have peace, and will walk on in the naughtiness of my heart; and the drunken may consume the thirsty.

20 And the Lord shall not forgive him: but his wrath and jealousy against that man should be exceedingly enkindled at that time. And all the curses that are written in this volume should light upon him: and the Lord should blot out his name from under heaven,

21 And utterly destroy him out of all the tribes of Israel, according to the curses that are contained in the book of this law and covenant.

22 And the following generation shall say, and the children that shall be born hereafter, and the strangers that shall come from afar: seeing the plagues of that land and the evils wherewith the Lord hath afflicted it,

23 Burning it with brimstone, and the heat of salt, so that it cannot be sown any more, ⁵ nor any green thing grown therein, after the example of the destruction of Sodom and Gomorrha, Adama and Seboim, which the Lord destroyed in his wrath and indignation:

24 And all the nations shall say: ⁶ Why hath the Lord done thus to this land? What meaneth this exceeding great heat of his wrath!

25 And they shall answer: Because they forsook the covenant of the Lord, which he made with their fathers, when he brought them out of the land of Egypt.

26 And they have served strange

CHAP. 29. ¹ Exod. 19, 4. ² Deut. 8, 2. ³ Deut. 3, 1. ⁴ Deut. 3, 1; Deut. 3, 16; Num. 32, 19; Jos. 13, 8; 22, 4. ⁵ Gen. 19, 24. ⁶ 3 Kings, 9, 8; Jer. 28, 8.

CHAP. 29. Ver. 4. *Hath not given you.* Through your own fault and because you resisted his grace.

Ver. 19. *The drunken. Absumat ebria sitientem.* It is a proverbial expression, which may either be understood, as spoken by the sinner, *blessing*, that is, flattering himself in his sins with the imagination of peace, and so great an abundance as may satisfy, and as it were, *consume* all *thirst* and want: or it may be referred to the *root of bitterness*, spoken of before, which being *drunken* with sin may attract, and by that means *consume*, such as *thirst* after the like evils.

gods, and adored them, whom they knew not, and for whom they had not been assigned.

27 Therefore the wrath of the Lord was kindled against this land, to bring upon it all the curses that are written in this volume:

28 And he hath cast them out of their land, in anger and in wrath, and in very great indignation: and hath thrown them into a strange land, as it is seen this day.

29 Secret things to the Lord our God: *things* that are manifest, to us and to our children for ever, that we may do all the words of this law.

CHAPTER 30

Great mercies are promised to the penitent. God's commandment is feasible. Life and death are set before them.

NOW when all these things shall be come upon thee, the blessing or the curse, which I have set forth before thee: and thou shalt be touched with repentance of thy heart among all the nations, into which the Lord thy God shall have scattered thee:

2 And shalt return to him, and obey his commandments, as I command thee this day, thou and thy children, with all thy heart, and with all thy soul:

3 The Lord thy God will bring back again thy captivity, and will have mercy on thee, and gather thee again out of all the nations, into which he scattered thee before.

4 If thou be driven as far as the poles of heaven, the Lord thy God will fetch thee back from thence.

5 [1] And will take thee to himself, and bring thee into the land which thy fathers possessed: and thou shalt possess it. And blessing thee, he will make thee more numerous than were thy fathers.

6 The Lord thy God will circumcise thy heart, and the heart of thy seed: that thou mayst love the Lord thy God with all thy heart and with all thy soul, that thou mayst live.

7 And he will turn all these curses upon thy enemies, and upon them that hate and persecute thee.

8 But thou shalt return, and hear the voice of the Lord thy God: and shalt do all the commandments which I command thee this day.

9 And the Lord thy God will make thee abound in all the works of thy hands, in the fruit of thy womb, and in the fruit of thy cattle, in the fruitfulness of thy land, and in the plenty of all things. For the Lord will return to rejoice over thee in all good things, as he rejoiced in thy fathers.

10 Yet so if thou hear the voice of the Lord thy God, and keep his precepts and ceremonies, which are written in this law: and return to the Lord thy God with all thy heart, and with all thy soul.

11 This commandment, that I command thee this day is not above thee, nor far off from thee.

12 Nor is it in heaven, that thou shouldst say: Which of us can go up to heaven to bring it unto us, and we may hear and fulfil it in work?

13 Nor is it beyond the sea: that thou mayst excuse thyself, and say: [2] Which of us can cross the sea, and bring it unto us: that we may hear, and do that which is commanded?

14 But the word is very nigh unto thee, in thy mouth and in thy heart, that thou mayst do it.

15 Consider that I have set before thee this day life and good, and on the other hand death and evil.

16 That thou mayst love the Lord thy God, and walk in his ways, and keep his commandments and ceremonies and judgments: and thou mayst live, and he may multiply thee, and bless thee in the land, which thou shalt go in to possess.

17 But if thy heart be turned away, so that thou wilt not hear, and being deceived with error thou adore strange gods, and serve them:

18 I foretell thee this day that thou shalt perish, and shalt remain but a short time in the land, to which thou shalt pass over the Jordan, and shalt go in to possess it.

19 I call heaven and earth to witness this day, that I have set before you life and death, blessing and cursing. Choose therefore life, that both thou and thy seed may live.

20 And that thou mayst love the Lord thy God, and obey his voice, and adhere to him (for he is thy life, and the length of thy days): that thou mayst dwell in the land, for which the Lord swore to thy fathers Abraham, Isaac, and Jacob that he would give it them.

CHAPTER 31

Moses encourageth the people, and Josue, who is appointed to succeed him. He delivereth the law to the priests. God foretelleth that the people will often forsake him, and that he will punish them. He commandeth Moses to write a canticle, as a constant remembrancer of the law.

AND Moses went, and spoke all these words to all Israel.

CHAP. 30. [1] 2 Mach. 1, 29. [2] Rom. 10, 6.
Ver. 29. *Secret things.* As much as to say, secret things belong to, and are known to, God alone; our business must be to observe what he has *revealed* and *manifested* to us, and to direct our lives accordingly.

2 And he said to them: I am this day a hundred and twenty years old. I can no longer go out and come in, especially as the Lord also hath said to me: [1] Thou shalt not pass over this Jordan.

3 The Lord thy God then will pass over before thee: he will destroy all these nations in thy sight, and thou shalt possess them. And this Josue shall go before thee, as the Lord hath spoken.

4 And the Lord shall do to them [2] as he did to Sehon and Og the kings of the Amorrhites, and to their land: and shall destroy them.

5 Therefore when the Lord shall have delivered these also to you, [3] you shall do in like manner to them as I have commanded you.

6 Do manfully and be of good heart: fear not, nor be ye dismayed at their sight. For the Lord thy God he himself is thy leader, and will not leave thee nor forsake thee.

7 And Moses called Josue, and said to him before all Israel: [4] Take courage, and be valiant. For thou shalt bring this people into the land which the Lord swore he would give to their fathers, and thou shalt divide it by lot.

8 And the Lord who is your leader, he himself will be with thee: he will not leave thee, nor forsake thee. Fear not, neither be dismayed.

9 And Moses wrote this law, and delivered it to the priests the sons of Levi who carried the ark of the covenant of the Lord, and to all the ancients of Israel.

10 And he commanded them, saying: After seven years, in the year of remission, in the feast of tabernacles,

11 When all Israel come together, to appear in the sight of the Lord thy God in the place which the Lord shall choose, thou shalt read the words of this law before all Israel, in their hearing.

12 And the people being all assembled together, both men and women, children and strangers, that are within thy gates: that hearing they may learn, and fear the Lord your God, and keep, and fulfil all the words of this law:

13 That their children also, who now are ignorant, may hear, and fear the Lord their God, all the days that they live in the land whither you are going over the Jordan to possess it.

14 And the Lord said to Moses: Do hold the days of thy death are nigh: call Josue, and stand ye in the tabernacle of the testimony, that I may give him a charge. So Moses and Josue went

and stood in the tabernacle of the testimony.

15 And the Lord appeared there in the pillar of a cloud, which stood in the entry of the tabernacle.

16 And the Lord said to Moses: Behold thou shalt sleep with thy fathers, and this people rising up will go a fornicating after strange gods in the land, to which it goeth in to dwell. There will they forsake me, and will make void the covenant, which I have made with them,

17 And my wrath shall be kindled against them in that day: and I will forsake them, and will hide my face from them: and they shall be devoured. All evils and afflictions shall find them, so that they shall say in that day: In truth it is because God is not with me, that these evils have found me.

18 But I will hide, and cover my face in that day, for all the evils which they have done, because they have followed strange gods.

19 Now therefore write you this canticle, and teach the children of Israel: that they may know it by heart, and sing it by mouth, and this song may be unto me for a testimony among the children of Israel.

20 For I will bring them into the land, for which I swore to their fathers, that floweth with milk and honey. And when they have eaten, and are full and fat, they will turn away after strange gods, and will serve them: and will despise me, and make void my covenant.

21 And after many evils and afflictions shall have come upon them, this canticle shall answer them for a testimony, which no oblivion shall take away out of the mouth of their seed. For I know their thoughts, and what they are about to do this day, before that I bring them into the land which I have promised them.

22 Moses therefore wrote the canticle: and taught it to the children of Israel.

23 And the Lord commanded Josue the son of Nun, and said: Take courage, and be valiant: for thou shalt bring the children of Israel into the land which I have promised, and I will be with thee.

24 Therefore after Moses had wrote the words of this law in a volume, and finished it:

25 He commanded the Levites, who carried the ark of the covenant of the Lord, saying:

26 Take this book, and put it in the side of the ark of the covenant of the Lord your God: that it may be there for a testimony against thee.

CHAP. 31. [1] Deut. 3, 27; Num. 27, 13. [2] Num. 21, 24. [3] Deut. 7, 2. [4] Jos. 1, 6; 3 Kings, 2, 2.

27 For I know thy obstinacy, and thy most stiff neck. While I am yet living, and going in with you, you have always been rebellious against the Lord. How much more when I shall be dead?

28 Gather unto me all the ancients of your tribes, and your doctors, and I will speak these words in their hearing: and will call heaven and earth to witness against them.

29 For I know that, after my death, you will do wickedly, and will quickly turn aside from the way that I have commanded you: and evils shall come upon you in the latter times, when you shall do evil in the sight of the Lord, to provoke him by the works of your hands.

30 Moses therefore spoke, in the hearing of the whole assembly of Israel, the words of this canticle, and finished it even to the end.

CHAPTER 32

A canticle for the remembrance of the law. Moses is commanded to go up into a mountain, from whence he shall see the promised land but not enter into it.

HEAR, O ye heavens, the things I speak: let the earth give ear to the words of my mouth.

2 Let my doctrine gather as the rain, let my speech distil as the dew: as a shower upon the herb, and as drops upon the grass.

3 Because I will invoke the name of the Lord: give ye magnificence to our God.

4 The works of God are perfect, and all his ways are judgments: God is faithful and without any iniquity; he is just and right.

5 They have sinned against him, and are none of his children in *their* filth: *they are* a wicked and perverse generation.

6 Is this the return thou makest to the Lord, O foolish and senseless people? Is not he thy father, that hath possessed thee, and made thee, and created thee?

7 [1] Remember the days of old: think upon every generation. Ask thy father, and he will declare to thee: thy elders and they will tell thee.

8 When the Most High divided the nations, when he separated the sons of Adam: he appointed the bounds of people according to the number of the children of Israel.

9 But the Lord's portion is his people: Jacob the lot of his inheritance.

10 He found him in a desert land, in a place of horror, and of vast wilderness. He led him about, and taught him: and he kept him as the apple of his eye.

11 As the eagle enticing her young to fly, and hovering over them, he spread his wings: and hath taken him and carried him on his shoulders.

12 The Lord alone was his leader: and there was no strange god with him,

13 He set him upon high land: that he might eat the fruits of the fields, that he might suck honey out of the rock, and oil out of the hardest stone,

14 Butter of the herd, and milk of the sheep with the fat of lambs, and of the rams of the breed of Basan. And goats with the marrow of wheat: and might drink the purest blood of the grape.

15 The beloved grew fat, and kicked: he grew fat, and thick and gross. He forsook God who made him: and departed from God his saviour.

16 They provoked him by strange gods: and stirred him up to anger, with *their* abominations.

17 They sacrificed to devils and not to God: to gods whom they knew not: that were newly come up, whom their fathers worshipped not.

18 Thou hast forsaken the God that begot thee: and hast forgotten the Lord that created thee.

19 The Lord saw, and was moved to wrath: because his own sons and daughters provoked him.

20 And he said: I will hide my face from them, and will consider what their last end shall be. For it is a perverse generation, and unfaithful children.

21 They have provoked me with that which was no god, and have angered me with their vanities. [2] And I will provoke them with that which is no people, and will vex them with a foolish nation.

22 A fire is kindled in my wrath, and shall burn even to the lowest hell: and shall devour the earth with her increase, and shall burn the foundations of the mountains.

23 I will heap evils upon them: and will spend my arrows among them.

24 They shall be consumed with famine, and birds shall devour them with a most bitter bite. I will send the teeth of beasts upon them, with the fury of creatures that trail upon the ground, and of serpents.

25 Without, the sword shall lay them waste, and terror within: both the young man and the virgin, the sucking child with the man in years.

26 I said: Where are they? I will make the memory of them to cease from among men.

27 But for the wrath of the enemies I have deferred it: lest perhaps their enemies might be proud, and should

CHAP. 32. [1] Job, 8, 8. [2] Jer. 15, 14; Rom. 10, 19.

say: Our mighty hand and not the Lord, hath done all these things.

28 They are a nation without counsel, and without wisdom.

29 [3] O that they would be wise and would understand, and would provide for their last end!

30 How should one pursue after a thousand, and two chase ten thousand? Was it not, because their God had sold them, and the Lord had shut them up?

31 For our God is not as their gods: our enemies themselves are judges.

32 Their vines are of the vineyard of Sodom, and of the suburbs of Gomorrha: their grapes are grapes of gall, and their clusters most bitter.

33 Their wine is the gall of dragons, and the venom of asps, which is incurable.

34 Are not these things stored up with me, and sealed up in my treasures?

35 [4] Revenge is mine, and I will repay them in *due* time, that their foot may slide. The day of destruction is at hand, and the time makes haste to come.

36 The Lord will judge his people, [5] and will have mercy on his servants. He shall see that *their* hand is weakened, and that they who were shut up have also failed, and they that remained are consumed.

37 And he shall say: [6] Where are their gods, in whom they trusted?

38 Of whose victims they ate the fat, and drank the wine of their drink offerings. Let them arise and help you, and protect you in your distress.

39 See ye that I alone am, and there is no other God besides me: [7] I will kill and I will make to live. I will strike, and I will heal; [8] and there is none that can deliver out of my hand.

40 I will lift up my hand to heaven; and I will say: I live for ever.

41 If I shall whet my sword as the lightning, and my hand take hold on judgment: I will render vengeance to my enemies, and repay them that hate me.

42 I will make my arrows drunk with blood, and my sword shall devour flesh, of the blood of the slain and of the captivity, of the bare head of the enemies.

43 [9] Praise his people, ye nations; for he will revenge the blood of his servants, and will render vengeance to their enemies: and he will be merciful to the land of his people.

44 So Moses came and spoke all the words of this canticle in the ears of the people, and Josue the son of Nun.

45 And he ended all these words, speaking to all Israel.

46 And he said to them: Set your hearts on all the words, which I testify to you this day: which you shall command your children to observe and to do, and to fulfil all that is written in this law.

47 For they are not commanded you in vain, but that every one should live in them: and that doing them you may continue a long time in the land whither you are going over the Jordan to possess it.

48 And the Lord spoke to Moses the same day, saying:

49 Go up into this mountain Abarim (that is to say, of passages), unto mount Nebo, which is in the land of Moab over against Jericho. And see the land of Chanaan, which I will deliver to the children of Israel to possess. And die thou in the mountain.

50 When thou art gone up into it thou shalt be gathered to thy people, [10] as Aaron thy brother died in mount Hor, and was gathered to his people:

51 [11] Because you trespassed against me in the midst of the children of Israel, at the waters of contradiction in Cades of the desert of Sin: and you did not sanctify me among the children of Israel.

52 Thou shalt see the land before thee, which I will give to the children of Israel: but thou shalt not enter into it.

CHAPTER 33

Moses before his death blesseth the tribes of Israel.

THIS is the blessing, wherewith the man of God Moses blessed the children of Israel, before his death.

2 And he said: The Lord came from Sinai, and from Seir he rose up to us. He hath appeared from mount Pharan, and with him thousands of saints. In his right hand a fiery law.

3 He hath loved the people: [1] all the saints are in his hand. And they that approach to his feet, shall receive of his doctrine.

4 Moses commanded us a law, the inheritance of the multitude of Jacob.

5 He shall be king with the most right: the princes of the people being assembled with the tribes of Israel.

6 Let Ruben live, and not die: and be small in number.

7 This is the blessing of Juda. Hear, O Lord, the voice of Juda, and bring him in unto his people. His hands shall fight for him, and he shall be his helper against his enemies.

[3] Jer. 9, 12. [4] Ecclus. 28, 1; Rom. 12, 19; Heb. 10, 30. [5] 2 Mach. 7, 6. [6] Jer. 2, 28. [7] 1 Kings, 2, 6; Tob. 13, 2; Wisd. 16, 13. [8] Job. 10, 7; Wisd. 16, 15. [9] 2 Mach. 7, 6. [10] Num. 20, 26; 27, 13. [11] Num. 20, 12; 27, 24. CHAP. 33. [1] Wisd. 3, 1; 5, 5.

8 To Levi also he said: Thy perfection, and thy doctrine *be* to thy holy man, whom thou hast proved in the temptation, and judged at the waters of contradiction.

9 [2]Who hath said to his father, and to his mother: I do not know you. And to his brethren: I know you not: and their own children they have not known. These have kept thy word, and observed thy covenant,

10 Thy judgments, O Jacob, and thy law, O Israel: they shall put incense in thy wrath and holocaust upon thy altar.

11 Bless, O Lord, his strength, and receive the works of his hands. Strike the backs of his enemies, and let not them that hate him rise.

12 And to Benjamin he said: The best beloved of the Lord shall dwell confidently in him. As in a bride chamber shall he abide all the day long: and between his shoulders shall be rest.

13 To Joseph also he said: Of the blessing of the Lord be his land, of the fruits of heaven, and of the dew, and of the deep that lieth beneath.

14 Of the fruits brought forth by the sun and by the moon.

15 Of the tops of the ancient mountains, of the fruits of the everlasting hills.

16 And of the fruits of the earth, and of the fulness thereof. The blessing of him [3] that appeared in the bush, come upon the head of Joseph, and upon the crown of the Nazarite among his brethren.

17 His beauty as of the firstling of a bullock, his horns *as* the horns of a rhinoceros: with them shall he push the nations even to the ends of the earth. These are the multitudes of Ephraim; and these the thousands of Manasses.

18 And to Zabulon he said: Rejoice, O Zabulon, in thy going out; and Issachar in thy tabernacles.

19 They shall call the people to the mountain: there shall they sacrifice the victims of justice. Who shall suck as milk the abundance of the sea, and the hidden treasures of the sands.

20 And to Gad he said: Blessed *be* Gad in *his* breadth: he hath rested as a lion, and hath seized upon the arm and the top of the head.

21 And he saw his pre-eminence, that in his portion the teacher was laid up. Who was with the princes of the people: and did the justices of the Lord, and his judgment with Israel.

22 To Dan also he said: Dan is a young lion: he shall flow plentifully from Basan.

23 And to Nephtali he said: Nephtali shall enjoy abundance, and shall be full of the blessings of the Lord. He shall possess the sea and the south.

24 To Aser also he said: Let Aser be blessed with children, let him be acceptable to his brethren, and let him dip his foot in oil.

25 His shoe shall be iron and brass. As the days of thy youth, so also shall the old age be.

26 There is no other God like the God of the rightest: he that is mounted upon the heaven is thy helper. By his magnificence the clouds run hither and thither.

27 His dwelling is above, and underneath are the everlasting arms. He shall cast out the enemy from before thee, and shall say: Be thou brought to nought.

28 Israel shall dwell in safety, and alone. The eye of Jacob in a land of corn and wine, and the heavens shall be misty with dew.

29 Blessed art thou, Israel: Who is like to thee, O people, that art saved by the Lord? The shield of thy help, and the sword of thy glory. Thy enemies shall deny thee, and thou shalt tread upon their necks.

CHAPTER 34

Moses seeth the promised land, but is not suffered to go into it. He dieth at the age of 120 years. God burieth his body secretly, and all Israel mourn for him thirty days. Josue, replenished (by imposition of Mose's hands) with the spirit of God, succeedeth. But Moses, for his special familiarity with God, and for most wonderful miracles, is commended above all other prophets.

THEN Moses [1] went up from the plains of Moab upon mount Nebo, to the top of Phasga over against Jericho. And the Lord shewed him all the land of Galaad as far as Dan.

2 And all Nephtali: and the land of Ephraim and Manasses: and all the land of Juda unto the furthermost sea.

[2] Exod. 32, 27; Lev. 10, 5. [3] Exod. 3, 2. CHAP. 34. [1] Deut. 3, 27; 32, 49; 2 Mach. 2, 4.

CHAP. 33. Ver. 8. *Holy man.* Aaron and his successors in the priesthood.

Ver. 9. *Who hath said.* It is the duty of the priestly tribe to prefer God's honour and service before all considerations of flesh and blood: in such manner as to behave as strangers to their nearest akin, when these would withdraw them from the business of their calling.

Ver. 12. *Shall dwell.* This seems to allude to the temple being built in the confines of the tribe of Benjamin.

Ver. 16. *The Nazarite.* See the note on Gen. 49, 26.

Ver. 21. *He saw.* The pre-eminence of the tribe of Gad, to which this alludeth, was their having the lawgiver Moses buried in their borders; though the particular place was not known.

Ver. 23. *The sea.* The lake of Genesareth.

Ver. 27. *Underneath are the everlasting arms.* Though the dwelling of God be above in heaven, his arms are always stretched out to help us here below.

3 And the south part, and the breadth of the plain of Jericho, the city of palm trees, as far as Segor.

4 And the Lord said to him: [2] This is the land, for which I swore to Abraham, Isaac, and Jacob, saying: I will give it to thy seed. Thou hast seen it with thy eyes, and shalt not pass over to it.

5 And Moses the servant of the Lord died there, in the land of Moab, by the commandment of the Lord.

6 And he buried him in the valley of the land of Moab over against Phogor: and no man hath known of his sepulchre until this present day.

7 Moses was a hundred and twenty years old when he died: his eye was not dim, neither were his teeth moved.

8 And the children of Israel mourned for him in the plains of Moab thirty days. And the days of their mourning in which they mourned for Moses were ended.

9 And Josue the son of Nun was filled with the spirit of wisdom, because Moses had laid his hands upon him. And the children of Israel obeyed him, and did as the Lord commanded Moses.

10 And there arose no more a prophet in Israel like unto Moses, whom the Lord knew face to face:

11 In all the signs and wonders which he sent by him, to do in the land of Egypt to Pharao, and to all his servants, and to his whole land:

12 And all the mighty hand, and great miracles, which Moses did before all Israel.

THE BOOK OF
JOSUE

This Book is called Josue, *because it contains the history of what passed under him, and according to the common opinion was written by him. The Greeks call him Jesus: for Josue and Jesus in the Hebrew, are the same name, and have the same signification, viz., a Saviour. And it was not without a mystery that he who was to bring the people into the land of promise should have his name changed from* Osee *(for so he was called before,* Num. 13, 17) *to* Josue *or* Jesus, *to give us to understand, that Moses by his law could only bring the people within sight of the promised inheritance, but that our Saviour* Jesus *was to bring us into it.*

CHAPTER 1

Josue, encouraged by the Lord, admonisheth the people to prepare themselves to pass over the Jordan.

NOW it came to pass after the death of Moses the servant of the Lord, that the Lord spoke to Josue the son of Nun, the minister of Moses, and said to him:

2 Moses my servant is dead. Arise, and pass over this Jordan, thou and thy people with thee, into the land which I will give to the children of Israel.

3 [1] I will deliver to you every place that the sole of your foot shall tread upon, as I have said to Moses.

4 From the desert and from Libanus

unto the great river Euphrates: all the land of the Hethites unto the great sea toward the going down of the sun, shall be your border.

5 No man shall be able to resist you all the days of thy life. [2] As I have been with Moses, so will I be with thee: I will not leave thee, nor forsake thee.

6 [3] Take courage, and be strong: for thou shalt divide by lot to this people the land, for which I swore to their fathers, that I would deliver it to them.

7 Take courage therefore, and be very valiant: that thou mayst observe and do all the law, which Moses my servant hath commanded thee. Turn not from it to the right hand or to the left, that thou mayst understand all things which thou dost.

8 Let not the book of this law depart from thy mouth: but thou shalt meditate on it day and night, that thou mayst observe and do all things that are written in it. Then shalt thou direct thy way, and understand it.

9 Behold I command thee, take

---

[2] Gen. 12, 7; 15, 18. Chap. 1. [1] Deut. 11, 24. [2] Jos. 3, 7; Heb. 13, 5. [3] Deut. 31, 7; 3 Kings, 2, 2.

Chap. 34. Ver. 5. *Died there. This last chapter of Deuteronomy, in which the death of Moses is related, was written by Josue, or by some of the prophets.

Ver. 6. *He buried him.* By the ministry of angels, and would have the place of his burial to be unknown, lest the Israelites, who were so prone to idolatry, might worship him with divine honours.

courage, and be strong. Fear not and be not dismayed: because the Lord thy God is with thee in all things whatsoever thou shalt go to.

10 And Josue commanded the princes of the people, saying: Pass through the midst of the camp, and command the people, and say:

11 Prepare you victuals: for after the third day you shall pass over the Jordan and shall go in to possess the land, which the Lord your God will give you.

12 And he said to the Rubenites, and the Gadites, and the half tribe of Manasses:

13 Remember the word, which Moses the servant of the Lord commanded you, saying: The Lord your God hath given you rest, and all this land.

14 **'** Your wives, and children, and cattle shall remain in the land which Moses gave you on this side of the Jordan. But pass you over armed before your brethren, all of you that are strong of hand, and fight for them:

15 Until the Lord give rest to your brethren as he hath given you, and they also possess the land which the Lord your God will give them. And so you shall return into the land of your possession, and you shall dwell in it, which Moses the servant of the Lord gave you beyond the Jordan, toward the rising of the sun.

16 And they made answer to Josue, and said: All that thou hast commanded us we will do; and whithersoever thou shalt send us, we will go.

17 As we obeyed Moses in all things, so will we obey thee also: only be the Lord thy God with thee, as he was with Moses.

18 He that shall gainsay thy mouth, and not obey all thy words, that thou shalt command him, let him die: only take thou courage, and do manfully.

CHAPTER 2

Two spies are sent to Jericho, who are received and concealed by Rahab.

AND Josue the son of Nun sent from Setim two men, to spy secretly: and said to them: Go, and view the land and the city of Jericho. **¹** They went and entered into the house of a woman that was a harlot named Rahab, and lodged with her.

2 And it was told the king of Jericho, and was said: Behold there are men come in hither, by night, of the children of Israel, to spy the land.

3 And the king of Jericho sent to Rahab, saying: Bring forth the men that came to thee, and are entered into thy house: for they are spies, and are come to view all the land.

4 **²** And the woman taking the men, hid them, and said: I confess they came to me, but I knew not whence they were:

5 And at the time of shutting the gate in the dark, they also went out together. I know not whither they are gone. Pursue after them quickly, and you will overtake them.

6 But she made the men go up to the top of her house, and covered them with the stalks of flax, which was there.

7 Now they that were sent, pursued after them, by the way that leadeth to the fords of the Jordan: and as soon as they were gone out, the gate was presently shut.

8 The men that were hidden were not yet asleep, when behold the woman went up to them, and said:

9 I know that the Lord hath given this land to you: for the dread of you is fallen upon us, and all the inhabitants of the land have lost all strength.

10 We have heard that **³** the Lord dried up the water of the Red Sea at your going in, when you came out of Egypt: **⁴** and what things you did to the two kings of the Amorrhites, that were beyond the Jordan: Sehon and Og whom you slew.

11 And hearing these things we were affrighted, and our heart fainted away: neither did there remain any spirit in us at your coming in. For the Lord your God he is God in heaven above, and in the earth beneath.

12 **⁵** Now therefore swear ye to me by the Lord, that as I have shewn mercy to you, so you also will shew mercy to my father's house. And give me a true token,

13 That you will save my father and mother, my brethren and sisters, and all things that are theirs, and deliver our souls from death.

14 They answered her: Be our lives for you unto death, only if thou betray us not. And when the Lord shall have delivered us the land, we will shew thee mercy and truth.

15 Then she let them down with a cord out of a window: for her house joined close to the wall.

16 And she said to them: Get ye up to the mountains, lest perhaps they meet you as they return; and there lie ye hid three days, till they come back. And so you shall go on your way.

17 And they said to her: We shall be blameless of this oath, which thou hast made us swear,

18 If when we come into the land this scarlet cord be a sign, and thou tie it in the window, by which thou hast

---

⁴ Num. 32, 26. CHAP. 2. **¹** Heb. 11, 31; James, 2, 25. **²** Jos. 6, 17. **³** Exod. 14, 21. **⁴** Num. 21, 24. **⁵** Jos. 6, 22.

let us down: and gather together thy father and mother, and brethren and all thy kindred into thy house.

19 Whosoever shall go out of the door of thy house, his blood shall be upon his own head, and we shall be quit. But the blood of all that shall be with thee in the house, shall light upon our head, if any man touch them.

20 But if thou wilt betray us, and utter this word abroad, we shall be quit of this oath which thou hast made us swear.

21 And she answered: As you have spoken, so be it done. And sending them on their way, she hung the scarlet cord in the window.

22 But they went and came to the mountains, and stayed there three days till they that pursued them were returned. For having sought them through all the way, they found them not.

23 And when they were gone back into the city, the spies returned, and came down from the mountain: and passing over the Jordan, they came to Josue the son of Nun, and told him all that befel them.

24 And said: The Lord hath delivered all this land into our hands, and all the inhabitants thereof are overthrown with fear.

CHAPTER 3

The river Jordan is miraculously dried up for the passage of the children of Israel.

AND Josue rose before daylight, and removed the camp: and they departed from Setim, and came to the Jordan: he, and all the children of Israel; and they abode there for three days.

2 After which, the heralds went through the midst of the camp.

3 And began to proclaim: When you shall see the ark of the covenant of the Lord your God, and the priests of the race of Levi carrying it, rise you up also, and follow them as they go before.

4 And let there be between you and the ark the space of two thousand cubits: that you may see it afar off, and know which way you must go: for you have not gone this way before. And take care you come not near the ark.

5 And Josue said to the people: Be ye sanctified: for to-morrow the Lord will do wonders among you.

6 And he said to the priests: Take up the ark of the covenant, and go before the people. And they obeyed his commands, and took it up and walked before them.

7 And the Lord said to Josue: This

day will I begin to exalt thee before Israel: that they may know that as I was with [1] Moses, so I am with thee also.

8 And do thou command the priests that carry the ark of the covenant, and say to them: When you shall have entered into part of the water of the Jordan, stand in it.

9 And Josue said to the children of Israel: Come hither and hear the word of the Lord your God.

10 And again he said: By this you shall know that the Lord the living God is in the midst of you, and that he shall destroy before your sight the Chanaanite and the Hethite, the Hevite and the Pherezite, the Gergesite also and the Jebusite, and the Amorrhite.

11 [2] Behold the ark of the covenant of the Lord of all the earth shall go before you into the Jordan.

12 Prepare ye twelve men of the tribes of Israel, one of every tribe.

13 And when the priests, that carry the ark of the Lord, the God of the whole earth, shall set the soles of their feet in the waters of the Jordan, the waters that are beneath shall run down and go off: and those that come from above, shall stand together upon a heap.

14 So the people went out of their tents, to pass over the Jordan: and the priests that carried the ark of the covenent, went on before them.

15 And as soon as they came into the Jordan, and their feet were dipped in part of the water (now the Jordan, [3] it being harvest time, had filled the banks of its channel),

16 The waters that came down from above stood in one place, and swelling up like a mountain, were seen afar off from the city that is called Adom, to the place of Sarthan: but those that were beneath, ran down into the sea of the wilderness (which now is called the Dead Sea) until they wholly failed.

17 And the people marched over against Jericho: and the priests that carried the ark of the covenant of the Lord, stood girded upon the dry ground in the midst of the Jordan. And all the people passed over through the channel that was dried up.

CHAPTER 4

Twelve stones are taken out of the river to be set up for a monument of the miracle. Other twelve are placed in the midst of the river.

AND when they were passed over, the Lord said to Josue:

2 Choose twelve men, one of every tribe:

3 And command them to take out of the midst of the Jordan, where the feet

CHAP. 3. [1] Jos. 1, 5. [2] Acts, 7, 45. [3] Ecclus. 24, 36.

of the priests stood, twelve very hard stones, which you shall set in the place of the camp, where you shall pitch your tents this night.

4 And Josue called twelve men, whom he had chosen out of the children of Israel, one out of every tribe.

5 And he said to them: Go before the ark of the Lord your God to the midst of the Jordan, and carry from thence every man a stone on your shoulders, according to the number of the children of Israel.

6 That it may be a sign among you: and when your children shall ask you to-morrow saying: What mean these stones?

7 You shall answer them: The waters of the Jordan ran off before the ark of the covenant of the Lord, when it passed over the same. Therefore were these stones set for a monument of the children of Israel for ever.

8 The children of Israel therefore did as Josue commanded them, carrying out of the channel of the Jordan twelve stones, as the Lord had commanded him, according to the number of the children of Israel, unto the place wherein they camped: and there they set them.

9 And Josue put other twelve stones in the midst of the channel of the Jordan, where the priests stood that carried the ark of the covenant: and they are there until this present day.

10 Now the priests that carried the ark, stood in the midst of the Jordan till all things were accomplished which the Lord had commanded Josue to speak to the people, and Moses had said to him. And the people made haste and passed over.

11 And when they had all passed over, the ark also of the Lord passed over: and the priests went before the people.

12 The children of Ruben also and Gad, and half the tribe of Manasses, went armed before the children of Israel, [1] as Moses had commanded them.

13 And forty thousand fighting men by their troops, and bands, marched through the plains and fields of the city of Jericho.

14 In that day the Lord magnified Josue in the sight of all Israel, that they should fear him, as they had feared Moses, while he lived.

15 And he said to him:

16 Command the priests, that carry the ark of the covenant, to come up out of the Jordan.

17 And he commanded them, saying: Come ye up out of the Jordan.

18 And when they that carried the

ark of the covenant of the Lord, were come up, and began to tread on the dry ground, the waters returned into the channel, and ran as they were wont before.

19 And the people came up out of the Jordan, the tenth day of the first month, and camped in Galgal, over against the east side of the city of Jericho.

20 And the twelve stones which they had taken out of the channel of the Jordan, Josue pitched in Galgal:

21 And said to the children of Israel: When your children shall ask their fathers, to-morrow, and shall say to them: What mean these stones?

22 You shall teach them and say: Israel passed over this Jordan through the dry channel.

23 The Lord your God drying up the waters thereof in your sight, until you passed over:

24 [2] As he had done before in the Red Sea, which he dried up till we passed through.

25 That all the people of the earth may learn the most mighty hand of the Lord: that you also may fear the Lord your God for ever.

CHAPTER 5

The people are circumcised. They keep the pasch. The manna ceaseth. An angel appeareth to Josue.

NOW when all the kings of the Amorrhites who dwelt beyond the Jordan westward, and all the kings of Chanaan, who possessed the places near the great sea, had heard that the Lord had dried up the waters of the Jordan before the children of Israel, till they passed over, their heart failed them and there remained no spirit in them, fearing the coming in of the children of Israel.

2 At that time the Lord said to Josue: Make thee knives of stone, and circumcise the second time the children of Israel.

3 He did what the Lord had commanded: and he circumcised the children of Israel in the hill of the foreskins.

4 Now this is the cause of the second circumcision: All the people that came out of Egypt that were males, all the men fit for war, died in the desert, dur-

---

CHAP. 4. [1] Num. 32, 28. [2] Exod. 14, 21.

CHAP. 5. Ver. 2. *The second time.* Not that such as had been circumcised before were to be circumcised again; but that they were now to renew, and take up again the practice of circumcision; which had been omitted during their forty years' sojourning in the wilderness; by reason of their being always uncertain when they should be obliged to march.

ing the time of the long going about in the way.

5 Now these were all circumcised. But the people that were born in the desert,

6 During the forty years of the journey in the wide wilderness, were uncircumcised: till all they were consumed that had not heard the voice of the Lord, and to whom he had sworn before, that he would not shew them the land flowing with milk and honey.

7 The children of these succeeded in the place of their fathers, and were circumcised by Josue: for they were uncircumcised even as they were born, and no one had circumcised them in the way.

8 Now after they were all circumcised, they remained in the same place of the camp, until they were healed.

9 And the Lord said to Josue: This day have I taken away from you the reproach of Egypt. And the name of that place was called Galgal, until this present day.

10 And the children of Israel abode in Galgal, and they kept the phase on the fourteenth day of the month, at evening, in the plains of Jericho.

11 And they ate on the next day unleavened bread of the corn of the land, and frumenty of the same year.

12 And the manna ceased after they ate of the corn of the land, neither did the children of Israel use that food any more: but they ate of the corn of the present year of the land of Chanaan.

13 And when Josue was in the field of the city of Jericho, he lifted up his eyes, and saw a man standing over against him, holding a drawn sword. And he went to him, and said: Art thou one of ours, or of our adversaries?

14 And he answered: No: but I am prince of the host of the Lord, and now I am come.

15 Josue fell on his face to the ground. And worshipping, said: What saith my lord to his servant?

16 [1] Loose, saith he, thy shoes from off thy feet: for the place whereon thou standest is holy. And Josue did as was commanded him.

CHAPTER 6

After seven days' processions, the priests sounding the trumpets, the walls of Jericho fall down. The city is taken and destroyed.

CHAP. 5. [1] Exod. 3, 5; Acts, 7, 33.

Ver. 14. *Prince of the host of the Lord.* St. Michael, who is called prince of the people of Israel, Dan. 10, 21.

Ver. 15. *Worshipping.* Not with divine honour but with a religious veneration of an inferior kind, suitable to the dignity of his person.

NOW Jericho was close shut up and fenced, for fear of the children of Israel, and no man durst go out or come in.

2 And the Lord said to Josue: Behold I have given into thy hands Jericho, and the king thereof, and all the valiant men.

3 Go round about the city, all ye fighting men, once a day: so shall ye do for six days.

4 And on the seventh day the priests shall take the seven trumpets, which are used in the jubilee, and shall go before the ark of the covenant: and you shall go about the city seven times, and the priests shall sound the trumpets.

5 And when the voice of the trumpet shall give a longer and broken tune, and shall sound in your ears, all the people shall shout together with a very great shout: and the walls of the city shall fall to the gound. And they shall enter in every one at the place against which they shall stand.

6 Then Josue the son of Nun called the priests, and said to them: Take the ark of the covenant: and let seven other priests take the seven trumpets of the jubilee, and march before the ark of the Lord.

7 And he said to the people: Go, and compass the city, armed, marching before the ark of the Lord.

8 And when Josue had ended his words, and the seven priests blew the seven trumpets before the ark of the covenant of the Lord,

9 And all the armed men went before: the rest of the common people followed the ark. And the sound of the trumpets was heard on all sides.

10 But Josue had commanded the people, saying: You shall not shout, nor shall your voice be heard, nor any word go out of your mouth: until the day come wherein I shall say to you: Cry and shout.

11 So the ark of the Lord went about the city once a day, and returning into the camp, abode there.

12 And Josue rising before day, the priests took the ark of the Lord,

13 And seven of them seven trumpets, which are used in the jubilee. And they went before the ark of the Lord walking and sounding the trumpets: and the armed men went before them, and the rest of the common people followed the ark. And they blew the trumpets.

14 And they went round about the city the second day once, and returned into the camp. So they did six days.

15 But the seventh day, rising up early, they went about the city, as it was ordered, seven times.

16 And when in the seventh going about the priests sounded with the trumpets, Josue said to all Israel: Shout: for the Lord hath delivered the city to you.

17 And let this city be an anathema, and all things that are in it, to the Lord. Let only Rahab the harlot live, with all that are with her in the house: [1] for she hid the messengers whom we sent.

18 But beware ye lest you touch aught of those things that are forbidden, and you be guilty of transgression: and all the camp of Israel be under sin, and be troubled.

19 But whatsoever gold or silver there shall be, or vessels of brass and iron, let it be consecrated to the Lord, laid up in his treasures.

20 [2] So all the people making a shout, and the trumpets sounding when the voice and the sound thundered in the ears of the multitude, the walls forthwith fell down. And every man went up by the place that was over against him. [3] And they took the city,

21 And killed all that were in it, man and woman, young and old. The oxen also and the sheep, and the asses, they slew with the edge of the sword.

22 [4] But Josue said to the two men that had been sent for spies: Go into the harlot's house, and bring her out, and all things that are hers, as you assured her by oath.

23 [5] And the young men went in and brought out Rahab, and her parents: her brethren also and all her goods and her kindred, and made them to stay without the camp.

24 [6] But they burned the city, and all things that were therein: except the gold and silver, and vessels of brass and iron, which they consecrated into the treasury of the Lord.

25 But Josue saved Rahab the harlot and her father's house, and all she had, and they dwelt in the midst of Israel until this present day: because she hid the messengers whom he had sent to spy out Jericho. At that time, Josue made an imprecation, saying:

26 [7] Cursed be the man before the Lord, that shall raise up and build the city of Jericho. In his firstborn may he lay the foundation thereof, and in the last of his children set up its gates.

27 And the Lord was with Josue, and his name was noised throughout all the land.

CHAPTER 7

For the sin of Achan, the Israelites are defeated at Hai. The offender is found out, and stoned to death and God's wrath is turned from them.

BUT the children of Israel [1] transgressed the commandment, and took to their own use of the anathema. [2] For Achan the son of Charmi, the son of Zabdi, the son of Zare of the tribe of Juda, took something of the anathema. And the Lord was angry against the children of Israel.

2 And when Josue sent men from Jericho against Hai, which is beside Bethaven, on the east side of the town of Bethel, he said to them: Go up, and view the country. And they fulfilled his command, and viewed Hai.

3 And returning they said to him: Let not all the people go up, but let two or three thousand men go and destroy the city. Why should all the people be troubled in vain against enemies that are very few?

4 There went up therefore three thousand fighting men: who immediately turned their backs,

5 And were defeated by the men of the city of Hai. And there fell of them six and thirty men: and the enemies pursued them from the gate as far as Sabarim. And they slew them as they fled by the descent: and the heart of the people was struck with fear, and melted like water.

6 But Josue rent his garments, and fell flat on the ground before the ark of the Lord until the evening, both he and all the ancients of Israel: and they put dust upon their heads.

7 And Josue said: Alas, O Lord God, why wouldst thou bring this people over the river Jordan, to deliver us into the hand of the Amorrhite, and to destroy us? Would God, we had stayed beyond the Jordan as we began!

8 My Lord God, what shall I say, seeing Israel turning their backs to their enemies?

9 The Chanaanites, and all the inhabitants of the land will hear of it, and being gathered together will surround us and cut off our name from the earth. And what wilt thou do to thy great name?

10 And the Lord said to Josue: Arise, Why liest thou flat on the ground?

11 Israel hath sinned, and transgressed my covenant: and they have taken of the anathema, and have stolen and lied, and have hidden it among their goods.

CHAP. 6. [1] Jos. 2, 4; Heb. 11, 31. [2] Heb. 11, 30. [3] 2 Mach. 12, 15. [4] Jos. 2, 1. [5] Heb. 11, 31. [6] Jos. 8, 2. [7] 3 Kings, 16, 34. CHAP. 7. [1] Jos. 22, 20. [2] 1 Par. 2, 7.

CHAP. 6. Ver. 26. *Cursed.* Jericho, in the mystical sense, signifies *iniquity*: the sounding of the trumpets by the priests, the preaching of the word of God; by which the walls of Jericho are thrown down, when sinners are converted; and a dreadful curse will light on them who build them up again.

12 Neither can Israel stand before his enemies, but he shall flee from them: because he is defiled with the anathema. I will be no more with you, till you destroy him that is guilty of this wickedness.

13 Arise, [3] sanctify the people, and say to them: Be ye sanctified against to-morrow. For thus saith the Lord God of Israel: The anathema is in the midst of thee, O Israel: thou canst not stand before thy enemies, till he be destroyed out of thee that is defiled with this wickedness.

14 And you shall come in the morning every one by your tribes: and what tribe soever the lot shall find, it shall come by its kindreds and the kindred by its houses, and the house by the men.

15 And whosoever he be that shall be found guilty of this fact, he shall be burnt with fire with all his substance: because he hath transgressed the covenant of the Lord, and hath done wickedness in Israel.

16 Josue, therefore, when he rose in the morning, made Israel to come by their tribes: and the tribe of Juda was found.

17 Which being brought by its families, it was found to be the family of Zare. Bringing that also by the houses, he found it *to be* Zabdi.

18 And bringing his house man by man, he found Achan the son of Charmi, the son of Zabdi, the son of Zare of the tribe of Juda.

19 And Josue said to Achan: My son, give glory to the Lord God of Israel, and confess, and tell me what thou hast done. Hide it not.

20 And Achan answered Josue, and said to him: Indeed I have sinned against the Lord the God of Israel, and thus and thus have I done.

21 For I saw among the spoils a scarlet garment exceeding good, and two hundred sicles of silver, and a golden rule of fifty sicles. And I coveted them, and I took them away, and hid them in the ground in the midst of my tent: and the silver I covered with the earth that I dug up.

22 Josue therefore sent ministers: who running to his tent, found all hidden in the same place, together with the silver.

23 And taking them away out of the tent, they brought them to Josue, and to all the children of Israel, and threw them down before the Lord.

24 Then Josue and all Israel with him took Achan the son of Zare, and the silver and the garments, and the golden rule, his sons also and his daughters, his oxen and asses and sheep, the tent also, and all the goods, and brought them to the valley of Achor.

25 Where Josue said: Because thou hast troubled us, the Lord trouble thee this day. And all Israel stoned him: and all things that were his, were consumed with fire.

26 [4] And they gathered together upon him a great heap of stones, which remaineth until this present day. And the wrath of the Lord was turned away from them. And the name of that place was called the Valley of Achor, until this day.

CHAPTER 8

Hai is taken and burnt, and all the inhabitants slain. An altar is built, and sacrifices offered. The law is written on stones, and the blessings and cursings are read before all the people.

AND the Lord said to Josue: Fear not, nor be thou dismayed. Take with thee all the multitude of fighting men: arise and go up to the town of Hai. Behold I have delivered into thy hand the king thereof, and the people, and the city, and the land.

2 And thou shalt do to the city of Hai, and to the king thereof, [1] as thou hast done to Jericho, and to the king thereof: but the spoils and all the cattle you shall take for a prey to yourselves. Lay an ambush for the city behind it.

3 And Josue arose, and all the army of the fighting men with him, to go up against Hai. And he sent thirty thousand chosen valiant men in the night,

4 And commanded them, saying: Lay an ambush behind the city: and go not very far from it: and be ye all ready.

5 But I and the rest of the multitude which is with me, will approach on the contrary side against the city. And when they shall come out against us, [2] we will flee, and turn our backs, as we did before:

6 Till they pursuing us be drawn farther from the city. For they will think that we flee as before.

7 And whilst we are fleeing, and they pursuing, you shall arise out of the ambush, and shall destroy the city. And the Lord your God will deliver it into our hands.

8 And when you shall have taken it, set it on fire; and you shall do all things so as I have commanded.

9 And he sent them away, and they went on to the place of the ambush, and abode between Bethel and Hai, on the west side of the city of Hai. But Josue stayed that night in the midst of the people.

3 Lev. 20, 7; Num. 11, 18; Jos. 3, 5; 1 Kings, 16, 5. 4 Kings, 18, 17. CHAP. 8. 1 Jos. 6, 24. 2 Jos. 7, 4.

CHAP. 7. Ver. 24. *His sons.* Probably conscious to, or accomplices of, the crime of their father.

10 And rising early in the morning, he mustered his soldiers, and went up with the ancients in the front of the army environed with the aid of the fighting men.

11 And when they were come, and were gone up over against the city, they stood on the north side of the city, between which and them there was a valley in the midst.

12 And he had chosen five thousand men: and set them to lie in ambush between Bethel and Hai, on the west side of the same city.

13 But all the rest of the army went in battle array on the north side, so that the last of that multitude reached to the west side of the city. So Josue went that night, and stood in the midst of the valley.

14 And when the king of Hai saw this, he made haste in the morning, and went out with all the army of the city, and set it in battle array toward the desert, not knowing that there lay an ambush behind his back.

15 But Josue, and all Israel gave back, making as if they were afraid, and fleeing by the way of the wilderness.

16 But they shouting together, and encouraging one another, pursued them. And when they were come from the city,

17 And not one remained in the city of Hai and of Bethel, that did not pursue after Israel, leaving the towns open as they had rushed out.

18 The Lord said to Josue: Lift up the shield that is in thy hand, towards the city of Hai, for I will deliver it to thee.

19 And when he had lifted up his shield toward the city, the ambush that lay hid, rose up immediately: and going to the city, took it and set it on fire.

20 And the men of the city, that pursued after Josue, looking back and seeing the smoke of the city rise up to heaven, had no more power to flee this way or that way: especially as they that had counterfeited flight, and were going toward the wilderness, turned back most valiantly against them that pursued.

21 So Josue and all Israel seeing that the city was taken, and that the smoke of the city rose up, returned and slew the men of Hai.

22 And they also that had taken and set the city on fire, issuing out of the city to meet their own men, began to cut off the enemies who were surrounded by them. So that the enemies being cut off on both sides, not one of so great a multitude was saved.

23 And they took the king of the city of Hai alive, and brought him to Josue.

24 So all being slain that had pursued after Israel in his flight to the wilderness, and falling by the sword in the same place, the children of Israel returned and laid waste the city.

25 And the number of them that fell that day, both of men and women, was twelve thousand persons all of the city of Hai.

26 But Josue drew not back his hand, which he had stretched out on high, holding the shield, till all the inhabitants of Hai were slain.

27 And the children of Israel divided among them the cattle and the prey of the city, as the Lord had commanded Josue.

28 And he burned the city, and made it a heap for ever.

29 And he hung the king thereof on a gibbet until the evening and the going down of the sun. Then Josue commanded, and they took down his carcass from the gibbet: and threw it in the very entrance of the city, heaping upon it a great heap of stones, which remaineth until this present day.

30 Then Josue built an altar to the Lord the God of Israel in mount Hebal,

31 [3] As Moses the servant of the Lord had commanded the children of Israel, and it is written in the book of the law of Moses: an altar of unhewn stones which iron had not touched. And he offered upon it holocausts to the Lord, and immolated victims of peace offerings.

32 And he wrote upon stones the Deuteronomy of the law of Moses, which he had ordered before the children of Israel.

33 And all the people, and the ancients, and the princes and judges stood on both sides of the ark, before the priests that carried the ark of the covenant of the Lord, (both the stranger and he that was born among them,) half of them by mount Garizim, and half by mount Hebal, as Moses the servant of the Lord had commanded. And first he blessed the people of Israel.

34 After this he read all the words of the blessing and the cursing, and all things that were written in the book of the law.

35 He left out nothing of those things which Moses had commanded: but he repeated all before all the people of Israel with the women and children and strangers that dwelt among them.

[3] Exod. 20, 25; Deut. 27, 5.

CHAP. 8. Ver. 12. *Five thousand*. These were part of the thirty thousand mentioned above, ver. 3.

CHAPTER 9

Josue is deceived by the Gabaonites, who being detected are condemned to be perpetual servants.

NOW when these things were heard of, all the kings beyond the Jordan, that dwelt in the mountains and in the plains, in the places near the sea, and on the coasts of the great sea; they also that dwell by Libanus, the Hethite and the Amorrhite, the Chanaanite, the Pherezite, and the Hevite, and the Jebusite,

2 Gathered themselves together, to fight against Josue and Israel with one mind, and one resolution.

3 But they that dwelt in Gabaon, hearing all that Josue had done to Jericho and Hai:

4 Cunningly devising, took for themselves provisions, laying old sacks upon their asses, and wine bottles rent and sewed up again,

5 And very old shoes, which for a show of age were clouted with patches, and old garments upon them. The loaves also, which they carried for provisions by the way, were hard, and broken into pieces.

6 And they went to Josue, who then abode in the camp at Galgal, and said to him, and to all Israel with him: We are come from a far country, desiring to make peace with you. And the children of Israel answered them, and said:

7 Perhaps you dwell in the land which falls to our lot: if so, we can make no league with you.

8 But they said to Josue: We are thy servants. Josue said to them: Who are you? And whence came you?

9 They answered: From a very far country thy servants are come in the name of the Lord thy God. For we have heard the fame of his power, all the things that he did in Egypt.

10 ¹ And to the two kings of the Amorrhites that were beyond the Jordan, Sehon king of Hesebon, and Og king of Basan, that was in Astaroth.

11 And our ancients, and all the inhabitants of our country said to us: Take with you victuals for a long way, and go meet them, and say: We are your servants, make ye a league with us.

12 Behold, these loaves we took hot when we set out from our houses to come to you: now they are become dry, and broken in pieces, by being exceeding old.

13 These bottles of wine when we filled them were new: now they are rent and burst. These garments we have on, and the shoes we have on our feet, by

CHAP. 9. ¹ Num. 21, 13. ² Kings, 21, 2.

reason of the very long journey are worn out, and almost consumed.

14 They took therefore of their victuals, and consulted not the mouth of the Lord.

15 ² And Josue made peace with them, and entering into a league promised that they should not be slain: the princes also of the multitude swore to them.

16 Now three days after the league was made, they heard that they dwelt nigh, and they should be among them.

17 And the children of Israel removed the camp, and came into their cities on the third day: the names of which are Gabaon, and Caphira, and Beroth, and Cariathiarim.

18 And they slew them not, because the princes of the multitude had sworn in the name of the Lord the God of Israel. Then all the common people murmured against the princes.

19 And they answered them: We have sworn to them in the name of the Lord the God of Israel, and therefore we may not touch them.

20 But this we will do to them: Let their lives be saved, lest the wrath of the Lord be stirred up against us, if we should be forsworn.

21 But so let them live, as to serve the whole multitude in hewing wood, and bringing in water. As they were speaking these things,

22 Josue called the Gabaonites and said to them: Why would you impose upon us, saying: We dwell far off from you, whereas you are in the midst of us?

23 Therefore you shall be under a curse, and your race shall always be hewers of wood, and carriers of water unto the house of my God.

24 They answered: It was told us thy servants, that the Lord thy God had promised his servant Moses to give you all the land, and to destroy all the inhabitants thereof. Therefore we feared exceedingly and provided for our lives, compelled by the dread we had of you, and we took this counsel.

25 And now we are in thy hand: deal with us as it seemeth good and right unto thee.

26 So Josue did as he had said, and delivered them from the hand of the children of Israel, that they should not be slain.

27 And he gave orders in that day that they should be in the service of all the people, and of the altar of the Lord, hewing wood and carrying water, until this present time, in the place which the Lord hath chosen.

CHAPTER 10

Five kings war against Gabaon. Josue defeateth them. Many are slain with hailstones. At the prayer of Josue the sun and moon stand still the space of one day. The five kings are hanged. Divers cities are taken.

WHEN Adonisedec, king of Jerusalem, had heard these things, to wit, that Josue had taken Hai, and had destroyed it, (for as he had done to Jericho and the king thereof, so did he to Hai, and its king,) and that the Gabaonites were gone over to Israel, and were their confederates,

2 He was exceedingly afraid. For Gabaon was a great city, and one of the royal cities, and greater than the town of Hai: and all its fighting men were most valiant.

3 Therefore Adonisedec, king of Jerusalem, sent to Oham, king of Hebron, and to Pharam, king of Jerimoth, and to Japhia, king of Lachis, and to Dabir, king of Eglon, saying:

4 Come up to me, and bring help, that we may take Gabaon, because it hath gone over to Josue, and to the children of Israel.

5 So the five kings of the Amorrhites being assembled together went up: the king of Jerusalem, the king of Hebron, the king of Jerimoth, the king of Lachis, the king of Eglon: they and their armies, and camped about Gabaon, laying siege to it.

6 But the inhabitants of the city of Gabaon which was besieged, sent to Josue; who then abode in the camp at Galgal, and said to him: Withdraw not thy hands from helping thy servants: come up quickly and save us, and bring us succour. For all the kings of the Amorrhites, who dwell in the mountains, are gathered together against us.

7 And Josue went up from Galgal, and all the army of the warriors with him, most valiant men.

8 And the Lord said to Josue: Fear them not: for I have delivered them into thy hands. None of them shall be able to stand against thee.

9 So Josue going up from Galgal all the night, came upon them suddenly.

10 ¹ And the Lord troubled them at the sight of Israel: and he slew them with a great slaughter in Gabaon, and pursued them by the way of the ascent to Beth-horon, and cut them off all the way to Azeca and Maceda.

11 And when they were fleeing from the children of Israel, and were in the descent of Beth-horon, the Lord cast down upon them great stones from heaven as far as Azeca. And many more were killed with the hailstones than

were slain by the swords of the children of Israel.

12 Then Josue spoke to the Lord, in the day that he delivered the Amorrhite in the sight of the children of Israel, and he said before them: Move not, O sun, toward Gabaon, nor thou, O moon, toward the valley of Ajalon.

13 And the ² sun and the moon stood still, till the people revenged themselves of their enemies. Is not this written in the book of the just? So the sun stood still in the midst of heaven, and hasted not to go down the space of one day.

14 There was not before nor after so long a day, the Lord obeying the voice of a man, and fighting for Israel.

15 And Josue returned with all Israel into the camp of Galgal.

16 For the five kings were fled, and had hidden themselves in a cave of the city of Maceda.

17 And it was told Josue that the five kings were found hidden in a cave of the city of Maceda.

18 And he commanded them that were with him, saying: Roll great stones to the mouth of the cave and set careful men, to keep them shut up.

19 And stay you not, but pursue after the enemies: and kill all the hindermost of them as they flee, and do not suffer them whom the Lord God hath delivered into your hands to shelter themselves in their cities.

20 So the enemies being slain with a great slaughter, and almost utterly consumed, they that were able to escape from Israel, entered into fenced cities.

21 And all the army returned to Josue in Maceda, where the camp then was, in good health and without the loss of any one. And no man durst move his tongue against the children of Israel.

22 And Josue gave orders, saying: Open the mouth of the cave, and bring forth to me the five kings that lie hid therein.

23 And the ministers did as they were commanded. And they brought out to him the five kings out of the cave: the king of Jerusalem, the king of Hebron, the king of Jerimoth, the king of Lachis, the king of Eglon.

24 And when they were brought out to him, he called all the men of Israel, and said to the chiefs of the army that were with him: Go, and set your feet on the necks of these kings. And when they had gone, and put their feet upon the necks of them lying under them,

25 He said again to them: Fear not:

CHAP. 10. ¹ Kings, 7, 10. ² Ecclus. 46, 5; Isai. 28, 21.

CHAP. 10. Ver. 13. *The book of the just.* In Hebrew *Jasher:* an ancient book long since lost.

neither be ye dismayed. Take courage and be strong. For so will the Lord do to all your enemies, against whom you fight.

26 And Josue struck, and slew them, and hanged them upon five gibbets: and they hung until the evening.

27 ³ And when the sun was down, he commanded the soldiers to take them down from the gibbets. And after they were taken down, they cast them into the cave where they had lain hid, and put great stones at the mouth thereof, which remain until this day.

28 The same day Josue took Maceda and destroyed it, with the edge of the sword: and killed the king and all the inhabitants thereof. He left not in it the least remains. And he did to the king of Maceda, as he had done to the king of Jericho.

29 And he passed from Maceda with all Israel to Lebna, and fought against it.

30 And the Lord delivered it with the king thereof into the hands of Israel. And they destroyed the city with the edge of the sword, and all the inhabitants thereof. They left not in it any remains. And they did to the king of Lebna, ⁴ as they had done to the king of Jericho.

31 From Lebna he passed unto Lachis, with all Israel: and investing it with his army, besieged it.

32 And the Lord delivered Lachis into the hands of Israel: and he took it the following day, and put it to the sword, and every soul that was in it, as he had done to Lebna.

33 At that time Horam, king of Gazer, came up to succour Lachis: and Josue slew him with all his people, so as to leave none alive.

34 And he passed from Lachis to Eglon, and surrounded it.

35 And he took it the same day: and put to the sword all the souls that were in it, according to all that he had done to Lachis.

36 He went up also with all Israel from Eglon to Hebron, and fought against it:

37 Took it, and destroyed it with the edge of the sword: the king also thereof, and all the towns of that country, and all the souls that dwelt in it. He

left not therein any remains: as he had done to Eglon, so did he also to Hebron, putting to the sword all that he found in it.

38 Returning from thence to Dabir,

39 He took it and destroyed it: the king also thereof and all the towns round about he destroyed with the edge of the sword. He left not in it any remains: as he had done to Hebron and Lebna and to their kings, so did he to Dabir and to the king thereof.

40 So Josue conquered all the country of the hills and of the south and of the plain, and of Asedoth, with their kings. He left not any remains therein, but slew all that breathed, as the Lord the God of Israel had commanded him,

41 From Cadesbarne even to Gaza, All the land of Gosen even to Gabaon,

42 And all their kings, and their lands he took and wasted at one onset: for the Lord the God of Israel fought for him.

43 And he returned with all Israel to the place of the camp in Galgal.

CHAPTER 11

The kings of the north are overthrown. The whole country is taken.

AND when Jabin, king of Asor had heard these things, he sent to Jobab, king of Madon, and to the king of Semeron, and to the king of Achsaph:

2 And to the kings of the north, that dwelt in the mountains and in the plains over against the south side of Ceneroth, and in the levels and in the countries of Dor by the sea side:

3 To the Chanaanites also on the east and on the west, and the Amorrhite, and the Hethite, and the Pherezite, and the Jebusite in the mountains: to the Hevite also who dwelt at the foot of Hermon in the land of Maspha.

4 And they all came out with their troops, a people exceeding numerous as the sand that is on the sea shore: their horses also and chariots a very great multitude.

5 And all these kings assembled together at the waters of Merom, to fight against Israel.

6 And the Lord said to Josue: Fear them not: for to-morrow at this same hour I will deliver all these to be slain in the sight of Israel. Thou shalt hamstring their horses, and thou shalt burn their chariots with fire.

7 And Josue came, and all the army with him, against them to the waters of Merom on a sudden, and fell upon them.

8 And the Lord delivered them into the hands of Israel. And they defeated them, and chased them as far as the

---

³ Deut. 21, 23.   ⁴ Jos. 6, 2.

Ver. 37. *The king.* The new king, who succeeded him that was slain, ver. 26.

Ver. 40. *Any remains therein, but slew.* God ordered these people to be utterly destroyed, in punishment of their manifold abominations; and that they might not draw the Israelites into the like sins.

CHAP. 11. Ver. 6. *Hamstring their horses, and burn their chariots with fire.* God so ordained, that his people might not trust in chariots and horses, but in him.

great Sidon, and the waters of Maserophot, and the field of Masphe, which is on the east side thereof. He slew them all, so as to leave no remains of them.

9 And he did as the Lord had commanded him: he hamstringed their horses and burned their chariots.

10 And presently turning back he took Asor: and slew the king thereof with the sword. Now Asor of old was the head of all these kingdoms.

11 And he cut off all the souls that abode there: he left not in it any remains, but utterly destroyed all, and burned the city itself with fire.

12 And he took and put to the sword and destroyed all the cities round about, and their kings, [1] as Moses the servant of God had commanded him.

13 Except the cities that were on hills and high places, the rest Israel burned: only Asor that was very strong he consumed with fire.

14 And the children of Israel divided among themselves all the spoil of these cities and the cattle, killing all the men.

15 [2] As the Lord had commanded Moses his servant, so did Moses command Josue, and he accomplished all. He left not one thing undone of all the commandments which the Lord had commanded Moses.

16 So Josue took all the country of the hills, and of the south, and the land of Gosen, and the plains and the west country, and the mountain of Israel, and the plains thereof:

17 And part of the mountain that goeth up to Seir as far as Baalgad, by the plain of Libanus under mount Hermon. All their kings he took, smote and slew.

18 Josue made war a long time against these kings.

19 There was not a city that delivered itself to the children of Israel, except the Hevite, who dwelt in Gabaon: for he took all by fight.

20 For it was the sentence of the Lord, that their hearts should be hardened, and they should fight against Israel, and fall, and should not deserve any clemency, and should be destroyed as the Lord had commanded Moses.

21 At that time Josue came and cut off the Enacims from the mountains, from Hebron, and Dabir, and Anab, and from all the mountain of Juda and Israel, and destroyed their cities.

22 He left not any of the stock of the Enacims, in the land of the children of Israel: except the cities of Gaza, and Geth, and Azotus, in which alone they were left.

23 So Josue took all the land, as the

Lord spoke to Moses, and delivered it in possession to the children of Israel, according to their divisions and tribes. [3] And the land rested from wars.

CHAPTER 12

A list of the kings slain by Moses and Josue.

THESE are the kings, whom the children of Israel slew and possessed their land. Beyond the Jordan towards the rising of the sun, from the torrent Arnon unto mount Hermon, and all the east country that looketh towards the wilderness:

2 Sehon king of the Amorrhites, who dwelt in Hesebon, *and* had dominion from Aroer, which is seated upon the bank of the torrent Arnon, and of the middle part in the valley, and of half Galaad, as far as the torrent Jaboc, which is the border of the children of Ammon.

3 And from the wilderness, to the sea of Ceneroth towards the east, and to the sea of the wilderness, which is the most salt sea, on the east side by the way that leadeth to Bethsimoth: and on the south side that lieth under Asedoth, Phasga.

4 The border of Og the king of Basan, of the remnant of the Raphaims who dwelt in Astaroth, and in Edrai, and had dominion in mount Hermon, and in Salecha, and in all Basan unto the borders

5 Of Gessuri and Machati, and of half Galaad: the borders of Sehon the king of Hesebon.

6 Moses the servant of the Lord, and the children of Israel slew them: and Moses delivered their land in possession to the Rubenites, and Gadites, and the half tribe of Manasses.

7 These are the kings of the land, whom Josue and the children of Israel slew. Beyond the Jordan on the west side from Baalgad in the field of Libanus, unto the mount, part of which goeth up into Seir. And Josue delivered it in possession to the tribes of Israel, to every one their divisions,

8 As well in the mountains as in the plains and the champaign countries. In Asedoth, and in the wilderness, and in the south was the Hethite and the Amorrhite, the Chanaanite and the Pherezite, the Hevite and the Jebusite.

9 The king of Jericho one: the king of Hai, which is on the side of Bethel, one:

CHAP. 11. [1] Deut. 7, 1. [2] Exod. 34, 11; Deut. 7, 1. [3] Jos. 14, 15.

Ver. 18. *A long time.* Seven years, as appears from chap. 14, 10.
Ver. 20. *Hardened.* This hardening of their hearts, was their having no thought of yielding or submitting: which was a sentence or judgment of God upon them in punishment of their enormous crimes.

10 The king of Jerusalem one, the king of Hebron one,

11 The king of Jerimoth one, the king of Lachis one,

12 The king of Eglon one, the king of Gazer one,

13 The king of Dabir one, the king of Gader one,

14 The king of Herma one, the king of Hered one,

15 The king of Lebna one, the king of Odullam one,

16 The king of Maceda one, the king of Bethel one,

17 The king of Taphua one, the king of Opher one,

18 The king of Aphec one, the king of Saron one,

19 The king of Madon one, the king of Asor one,

20 The king of Semeron one, the king of Achsaph one,

21 The king of Thenac one, the king of Mageddo one,

22 The king of Cades one, the king of Jachanan of Carmel one,

23 The king of Dor, and of the province of Dor one, the king of the nations of Galgal one,

24 The king of Thersa one: all the kings thirty and one.

CHAPTER 13

God commandeth Josue to divide the land. The possessions of Ruben, Gad, and half the tribe of Manasses, beyond the Jordan.

JOSUE was old, and far advanced in years, and the Lord said to him: Thou art grown old, and advanced in age, and there is a very large country left, which is not yet divided by lot:

2 To wit, all Galilee, Philistia, and all Gessuri.

3 From the troubled river, that watereth Egypt, unto the borders of Accaron northward: the land of Chanaan, which is divided among the lords of the Philistines, the Gazites, the Azotians, the Ascalonites, the Gethites, and the Accronites.

4 And on the south side are the Hevites, all the land of Chanaan, and Maara of the Sidonians as far as Apheca, and the borders of the Amorrhite,

5 And his confines. The country also

of Libanus towards the east from Baalgad under mount Hermon to the entering into Emath.

6 Of all that dwell in the mountains from Libanus, to the waters of Maserephoth, and all the Sidonians. I am he that will cut them off from before the face of the children of Israel. So let their land come in as a part of the inheritance of Israel, as I have commanded thee.

7 And now divide the land in possession to the nine tribes, and to the half tribe of Manasses,

8 With whom Ruben and Gad have possessed the land, [1] which Moses the servant of the Lord delivered to them beyond the river Jordan, on the east side.

9 From Aroer, which is upon the bank of the torrent Arnon, and in the midst of the valley and all the plains of Medaba, as far as Dibon.

10 And all the cities of Sehon, king of the Amorrhites, who reigned in Hesebon, unto the borders of the children of Ammon.

11 And Galaad, and the borders of Gessuri and Machati, and all mount Hermon, and all Basan as far as Salecha.

12 All the kingdom of Og in Basan, who reigned in Astaroth and Edrai. He was of the remains of the Raphaims: and Moses overthrew and destroyed them.

13 And the children of Israel would not destroy Gessuri and Machati: and they have dwelt in the midst of Israel, until this present day.

14 [2] But to the tribe of Levi he gave no possession: but the sacrifices and victims of the Lord God of Israel, are his inheritance, as he spoke to him.

15 And Moses gave a possession to the children of Ruben according to their kindreds.

16 And their border was from Aroer, which is on the bank of the torrent Arnon, and in the midst of the valley of the same torrent: all the plain, that leadeth to Medaba.

17 And Hesebon, and all their villages, which are in the plains. Dibon also, and Bamothbaal, and the town of Baalmaon:

18 And Jassa, and Cidimoth, and Mephaath:

19 And Cariathaim, and Sabama, and Sarathasar in the mountain of the valley.

20 Bethphogor and Asedoth, Phasga and Bethiesimoth:

21 And all the cities of the plain. And all the kingdoms of Sehon king of the Amorrhites, that reigned in Hesebon, [3] whom Moses slew with the princes of

CHAP. 13. [1] Num. 32, 33. [2] Num. 18, 20. [3] Num. 31, 8.

CHAP. 13. Ver. 1. *Josue was old, and far advanced in years.* He was then about one hundred and one years old.—*And there is a very large country left, which is not yet divided by lot.* Not yet possessed by the children of Israel.

Ver. 8. *With whom.* That is, with the other half of that same tribe.

Ver. 21. *The princes of Madian.* It appears from hence that these were subjects of king Sehon: they are said to have been *slain with him*, that is, about the same time, but not in the same battle.

Madian: Hevi, and Recem, and Sur and Hur, and Rebe, dukes of Sehon inhabitants of the land.

22 Balaam also the son of Beor, the soothsayer, the children of Israel slew with the sword among the rest that were slain.

23 And the river Jordan was the border of the children of Ruben. This is the possession of the Rubenites, by their kindreds, of cities and villages.

24 And Moses gave to the tribe of Gad and to his children by their kindreds a possession of which this is the division.

25 The border of Jaser, and all the cities of Galaad, and half the land of the children of Ammon: as far as Aroer which is over against Rabba.

26 And from Hesebon unto Ramoth, Masphe and Betonim: and from Manaim unto the borders of Dabir.

27 And in the valley Betharan and Bethnemra, and Socoth, and Saphon, the other part of the kingdom of Sehon king of Hesebon. The limit of this also is the Jordan, as far as the uttermost part of the sea of Cenereth beyond the Jordan on the east side.

28 This is the possession of the children of Gad by their families, their cities, and villages.

29 He gave also to the half tribe of Manasses and his children possession according to their kindreds.

30 The beginning whereof is this: from Manaim all Basan, and all the kingdoms of Og king of Basan, and all the villages of Jair, which are in Basan, threescore towns.

31 And half Galaad, and Astaroth, and Edrai, cities of the kingdom of Og in Basan: to the children of Machir, the son of Manasses, to one half of the children of Machir according to their kindreds.

32 This possession Moses divided in the plains of Moab, beyond the Jordan, over against Jericho on the east side.

33 ⁴ But to the tribe of Levi he gave no possession: because the Lord the God of Israel himself is their possession, as he spoke to them.

CHAPTER 14

Caleb's petition. Hebron is given to him and to his seed.

THIS is what the children of Israel possessed in the land of Chanaan, which Eleazar the priest, and Josue the son of Nun, and the princes of the families by the tribes of Israel gave to them:

2 Dividing all by lot, ¹ as the Lord had commanded by the hand of Moses, to the nine tribes, and the half tribe.

3 For to two tribes and a half Moses had given possession beyond the Jordan: besides the Levites, who received no land among their brethren.

4 But in their place succeeded the children of Joseph divided into two tribes, of Manasses and Ephraim. Neither did the Levites receive other portion of land, but cities to dwell in, and their suburbs to feed their beasts and flocks.

5 As the Lord had commanded Moses, so did the children of Israel: and they divided the land.

6 Then the children of Juda came to Josue in Galgal, and Caleb the son of Jephone the Cenezite spoke to him: ² Thou knowest what the Lord spoke to Moses the man of God concerning me and thee in Cadesbarne.

7 I was forty years old when Moses the servant of the Lord sent me ³ from Cadesbarne, to view the land: and I brought him word again as to me seemed true.

8 But my brethren, that had gone up with me, discouraged the heart of the people: and I nevertheless followed the Lord my God.

9 And Moses swore in that day, saying: The land which thy foot hath trodden upon shall be thy possession, and thy children's for ever, because thou hast followed the Lord my God.

10 The Lord therefore hath granted me life, as he promised until this present day. It is forty and five years since the Lord spoke this word to Moses, when Israel journeyed through the wilderness: this day I am eighty-five years old,

11 As strong as I was at that time when I was sent to view *the land:* ⁴ the strength of that time continueth in me until this day, as well to fight as to march.

12 Give me therefore this mountain, which the Lord promised, in thy hearing also, wherein are the Enacims, and cities great and strong: if so be the Lord *will* be with me, and I shall be able to destroy them, as he promised me.

13 And Josue blessed him, and gave him Hebron in possession.

14 And from that time Hebron belonged to Caleb the son of Jephone the Cenezite, until this present day: because he followed the Lord the God of Israel.

15 The name of Hebron before was called Cariath-Arbe: Adam the great-

⁴ Num. 18, 20. CHAP. 14. ¹ Num. 34, 13. ² Num. 14, 24. ³ Deut. 2, 14. ⁴ Ecclus. 46, 11.

CHAP. 14. Ver. 14. *Hebron belonged.* All the country thereabouts, depending on Hebron, was given to Caleb; but the city itself with the suburbs, was one of those that were given to the priests to dwell in.

est among the Enacims was laid there.
5 And the land rested from wars.

CHAPTER 15

The borders of the lot of Juda. Caleb's portion and conquest. The cities of Juda.

NOW the lot of the children of Juda by their kindreds was this: 1 From the frontier of Edom, to the desert of Sin southward, and to the uttermost part of the south coast.

2 Its beginning *was* from the top of the most salt sea, and from the bay thereof, that looketh to the south.

3 And it goeth out towards the ascent of the Scorpion, and passeth on to Sina: and ascendeth into Cadesbarne, and reacheth into Esron, going up to Addar, and compassing Carcaa:

4 And from thence passing along into Asemona, and reaching the torrent of Egypt. And the bounds thereof shall be the great sea. This shall be the limit of the south coast.

5 But on the east side the beginning shall be the most salt sea even to the end of the Jordan: and towards the north, from the bay of the sea unto the same river Jordan.

6 And the border goeth up into Beth-Hagla, and passeth by the north into Beth-Araba: going up to the stone of Boen the son of Ruben.

7 And reaching as far as the borders of Debara from the valley of Achor, and so northward looking towards Galgal, which is opposite to the ascent of Adommin, on the south side of the torrent. And *the border passeth* the waters that are called the fountain of the sun: and goings out thereof shall be at the fountain Rogel.

8 And it goeth up by the valley of the son of Ennom on the side of the Jebusite towards the south (the same is Jerusalem): and thence ascending to the top of the mountain, which is over against Geennom to the west in the end of the valley of Raphaim, northward.

9 And it passeth on from the top of the mountain to the fountain of the water of Nephtoa: and reacheth to the towns of mount Ephron. And it bendeth towards Baala, which is Cariathiarim, that is to say, the city of the woods.

10 And it compasseth from Baala westward unto mount Seir: and passeth by the side of mount Jarim to the north into Cheslon: and goeth down into Bethsames, and passeth into Thamna.

11 And it reacheth northward to a part of Accaron at the side: and bendeth to Sechrona, and passeth mount Baala: and cometh into Jebneel, and is bounded westward with the great sea.

5 Jos. 11, 23. CHAP. 15. 1 Num. 34, 3. 2 Judges, 1. 20: Num. 13, 23.

12 These are the borders round about of the children of Juda in their kindreds.

13 But to Caleb the son of Jephone he gave a portion in the midst of the children of Juda, as the Lord had commanded him: Cariath-Arbe, the father of Enac, which is Hebron.

14 2 And Caleb destroyed out of it the three sons of Enac, Sesai and Ahiman, and Tholmai of the race of Enac.

15 And going up from thence, he came to the inhabitants of Dabir, which before was called Cariath-Sepher, that is to say, the city of letters.

16 And Caleb said: He that shall smite Cariath-Sepher, and take it, I will give him Axa my daughter to wife.

17 And Othoniel the son of Cenez, the younger brother of Caleb, took it: and he gave him Axa his daughter to wife.

18 And as they were going together, she was moved by her husband to ask a field of her father, and she sighed as she sat on her ass. And Caleb said to her: What aileth thee?

19 But she answered: Give me a blessing. Thou hast given me a southern and dry land, give me also a *land* that is watered. And Caleb gave her the upper and the nether watery ground.

20 This is the possession of the tribe of the children of Juda by their kindreds.

21 And the cities, from the uttermost parts of the children of Juda by the borders of Edom to the south, were Cabseel and Eder and Jagur,

22 And Cina and Dimona and Adada,

23 And Cades and Asor and Jethnam,

24 Ziph and Telem and Baloth,

25 New Asor and Carioth, Hesron, which is Asor.

26 Amam, Sama and Molada,

27 And Asergadda and Hassemon and Bethphelet,

28 And Hasersual and Bersabee and Baziothia,

29 And Baala and Jim and Esem,

30 And Eltholad and Cesil and Harma,

31 And Siceleg and Medemena and Sensenna,

32 Lebaoth and Selim and Aen and Remmon: all the cities twenty-nine, and their villages.

33 But in the plains: Estaol and Sarea and Asena,

34 And Zanoe and Engannim and Taphua and Enaim,

35 And Jerimoth and Adullam, Socho and Azeca,

36 And Saraim and Adithaim and

Gedera and Gederothaim: fourteen cities, and their villages.

37 Sanan and Hadassa and Magdalgad,

38 Delean and Masepha and Jecthel,

39 Lachis and Bascath and Eglon,

40 Chebbon and Leheman and Cethlis,

41 And Gideroth and Bethdagon and Naama and Maceda: sixteen cities, and their villages.

42 Labana and Ether and Asan,

43 Jephtha and Esna and Nesib,

44 And Ceila and Achzib and Maresa: nine cities, and their villages.

45 Accaron with the towns and villages thereof.

46 From Accaron even to the sea: all places that lie towards Azotus and the villages thereof.

47 Azotus with its towns and villages, Gaza with its towns and villages, even to the torrent of Egypt, and the great sea that is the border thereof.

48 And in the mountain Samir and Jether and Socoth,

49 And Danna and Cariath-senna, this is Dabir:

50 Anab and Istemo and Anim,

51 Gosen and Olon and Gilo: eleven cities and their villages.

52 Arab and Ruma and Esaan,

53 And Janum and Beththaphua and Apheca,

54 Athmatha and Cariath-Arbe, this is Hebron and Sior: nine cities and their villages.

55 Maon and Carmel and Ziph and Jota,

56 Jezrael and Jucadam and Zanoe,

57 Accain, Gabaa and Thamna: ten cities and their villages.

58 Halhul, and Bessur, and Gedor,

59 Mareth and Bethanoth, and Eltecon: six cities and their villages.

60 Cariathbaal, the same is Cariathiarim, the city of woods, and Arebba: two cities and their villages.

61 In the desert Betharaba, Meddin and Sachacha,

62 And Nebsan, and the city of salt, and Engaddi: six cities and their villages.

63 But the children of Juda could not destroy the Jebusite that dwelt in Jerusalem. And the Jebusite dwelt with the children of Juda in Jerusalem until this present day.

CHAPTER 16

The lot of the sons of Joseph. The borders of the tribe of Ephraim.

AND the lot of the sons of Joseph fell from the Jordan over against Jericho and the waters thereof, on the east: the wilderness which goeth up from Jericho to the mountain of Bethel:

2 And goeth out from Bethel to Luza: and passeth the border of Archi, to Ataroth:

3 And goeth down westward, by the border of Jephleti, unto the borders of Beth-horon the nether, and to Gazer. And the countries of it are ended by the great sea.

4 And Manasses and Ephraim the children of Joseph possessed it.

5 And the border of the children of Ephraim was according to their kindreds: and their possession towards the east was Ataroth-addar unto Bethhoron the upper.

6 And the confines go out unto the sea. But Machmethath looketh to the north: and it goeth round the borders eastward into Thanath-selo: and passeth along on the east side to Janoe.

7 And it goeth down from Janoe into Ataroth and Naaratha: and it cometh to Jericho: and goeth out to the Jordan.

8 From Taphua it passeth on towards the sea into the valley of reeds, and the goings out thereof are at the most salt sea. This is the possession of the tribe of the children of Ephraim by their families.

9 And there were cities with their villages separated for the children of Ephraim in the midst of the possession of the children of Manasses.

10 And the children of Ephraim slew not the Chanaanite, who dwelt in Gazer: and the Chanaanite dwelt in the midst of Ephraim until this day, paying tribute.

CHAPTER 17

The lot of the half tribe of Manasses.

AND this lot fell to the tribe of Manasses (for he is the firstborn of Joseph), to Machir the firstborn of Manasses, the father of Galaad, who was a warlike man, and had for possession Galaad and Basan.

2 ¹ And to the rest of the children of Manasses according to their families: to the children of Abiezer, and to the children of Helec, and to the children of Esriel, and to the children of Sechem, and to the children of Hepher, and to the children of Semida. These are the male children of Manasses the son of Joseph, by their kindreds.

3 ² But Salphaad, the son of Hepher, the son of Galaad, the son of Machir,

CHAP. 17. ¹ Num. 26, 30. ² Num. 27, 1; 36, 11.

CHAP. 16. Ver. 6. *Looketh to the north.* The meaning is, that the border went towards the north, by *Machmethath*, and then turned eastward to *Thanath-selo.*

the son of Manasses, had no sons, but only daughters: whose names are these, Maala and Noa and Hegla and Melcha and Thersa.

4 And they came in the presence of Eleazar the priest and of Josue the son of Nun, and of the princes, saying: The Lord commanded by the hand of Moses, that a possession should be given us in the midst of our brethren. And he gave them according to the commandment of the Lord a possession amongst the brethren of their father.

5 And there fell ten portions to Manasses, beside the land of Galaad and Basan beyond the Jordan.

6 For the daughters of Manasses possessed inheritance in the midst of his sons. And the land of Galaad fell to the lot of the rest of the children of Manasses.

7 And the border of Manasses was from Aser, Machmethath which looketh towards Sichem: and it goeth out on the right hand by the inhabitants of the fountain of Taphua.

8 For the lot of Manasses took in the land of Taphua, which is on the borders of Manasses, and belongs to the children of Ephraim.

9 And the border goeth down to the valley of the reeds, to the south of the torrent of the cities of Ephraim, which are in the midst of the cities of Manasses. The border of Manassas is on the north side of the torrent, and the outgoings of it are at the sea.

10 So that the possession of Ephraim is on the south, and on the north that of Manasses. And the sea is the border of both: and they are joined together in the tribe of Aser on the north, and in the tribe of Issachar on the east.

11 And the inheritance of Manasses in Issachar and in Aser, was Bethsan and its villages, and Jeblaam with its villages, and the inhabitants of Dor, with the towns thereof: the inhabitants also of Endor with the villages thereof: and in like manner the inhabitants of Thenac with the villages thereof: and the inhabitants of Mageddo with their villages, and the third part of the city of Nopheth.

12 Neither could the children of Manasses overthrow these cities: but the Chanaanite began to dwell in his land.

13 But after that the children of Israel were grown strong, they subdued the Chanaanites, and made them their tributaries: and they did not kill them.

14 And the children of Joseph spoke to Josue, and said: Why hast thou given

me but one lot and one portion to possess, whereas I am of so great a multitude, and the Lord hath blessed me?

15 And Josue said to them: If thou be a great people, go up into the woodland, and cut down room for thyself in the land of the Pherezite and the Raphaims: because the possession of Mount Ephraim is too narrow for thee.

16 And the children of Joseph answered him: We cannot go up to the mountains, for the Chanaanites that dwell in the low lands, wherein are situate Bethsan with its towns, and Jezrael in the midst of the valley, have chariots of iron.

17 And Josue said to the house of Joseph, to Ephraim and Manasses: Thou art a great people, and of great strength: thou shalt not have one lot only.

18 But thou shalt pass to the mountain, and shall cut down the wood, and make thyself room to dwell in: and mayst proceed farther, when thou hast destroyed the Chanaanites, who, as thou sayest have iron chariots, and are very strong.

CHAPTER 18

Surveyors are sent to divide the rest of the land into seven tribes. The lot of Benjamin.

AND all the children of Israel assembled together in Silo. And there they set up the tabernacle of the testimony: and the land was subdued before them.

2 But there remained seven tribes of the children of Israel, which as yet had not received their possessions.

3 And Josue said to them: How long are you indolent and slack, and go not in to possess the land which the Lord the God of your fathers hath given you?

4 Choose of every tribe three men, that I may send them, and they may go and compass the land, and mark it out according to the number of each multitude: and bring back to me what they have marked out.

5 Divide to yourselves the land into seven parts. Let Juda be in his bounds on the south side, and the house of Joseph on the north.

6 The land in the midst between these mark ye out into seven parts. And you shall come hither to me, that I may cast lots for you before the Lord your God.

7 For the Levites have no part among you, but the priesthood of the Lord is their inheritance. And Gad and Ruben, and the half tribe of Manasses have already received their possessions beyond the Jordan eastward: which Moses the servant of the Lord gave them.

CHAP. 18. Ver. 6. *The land in the midst between these mark ye out in seven parts. That is to say, the rest of the land, which is not already assigned to Juda or Joseph.*

8 And when the men were risen up, to go to mark out the land, Josue commanded them, saying: Go round the land and mark it out, and return to me: that I may cast lots for you before the Lord in Silo.

9 So they went: and surveying it divided it into seven parts, writing them down in a book. And they returned to Josue, to the camp in Silo.

10 And he cast lots before the Lord in Silo, and divided the land to the children of Israel into seven parts.

11 And first came up the lot of the children of Benjamin by their families, to possess the land between the children of Juda and the children of Joseph.

12 And their border northward was from the Jordan: going along by the side of Jericho on the north side, and thence going up westward to the mountains, and reaching to the wilderness of Bethaven:

13 And passing along southward by ¹ Luza (the same is Bethel): and it goeth down into Ataroth-addar to the mountain that is on the south of the nether Beth-horon.

14 And it bendeth *thence* going round towards the sea, south of the mountain that looketh towards Bethhoron to the southwest: and the outgoings thereof are into Cariathbaal, which is called also Cariathiarim, a city of the children of Juda. This is their coast towards the sea, westward.

15 But on the south side the border goeth out from part of Cariathiarim towards the sea, and cometh to the fountain of the waters of Nephtoa.

16 And it goeth down to that part of the mountain that looketh on the valley of the children of Ennom: and is over against the north quarter in the furthermost part of the valley of Raphaim. And it goeth down into Geenom (that is the valley of Ennom) by the side of the Jebusite to the south: and cometh to the fountain of Rogel:

17 Passing *thence* to the north, and going out to Ensemes, that is to say, the fountain of the sun.

18 And it passeth along to the hills that are over against the ascent of Adommim: and it goeth down to Abenboen, that is, the stone of Boen the son of Ruben: and it passeth on the north side to the champaign countries; and goeth down into the plain.

19 And it passeth by Bethhagla northward: and the outgoings thereof are towards the north of the most salt sea at the south end of the Jordan:

20 Which is the border of it on the east side. This is the possession of the children of Benjamin by their borders round about, and their families.

21 And their cities were: Jericho and Bethhagla and Vale-Casis,

22 Betharaba and Samaraim and Bethel,

23 And Avim and Aphara and Ophera,

24 The town Emona and Ophni and Gabee: twelve cities, and their villages.

25 Gabam and Rama and Beroth,

26 And Mesphe, and Caphara, and Amosa,

27 And Recem, Jarephel and Tharcla,

28 And Sela, Eleph and Jebus, which is Jerusalem, Gabaath and Cariath: fourteen cities, and their villages. This is the possession of the children of Benjamin by their families.

CHAPTER 19

The lots of the tribes of Simeon, Zabulon, Issachar, Aser, Nephtali and Dan. A city is given to Josue.

AND the second lot came forth for the children of Simeon by their kindreds. And their inheritance was

2 In the midst of the possession of the children of Juda: Bersabee and Sabee and Molada,

3 And Hasersual, Bala and Asem,

4 And Eltholad, Bethul and Harma,

5 And Siceleg and Bethmarchaboth and Hasersusa,

6 And Bethlebaoth and Sarohen: thirteen cities, and their villages.

7 Ain and Remmon and Athor and Asan: four cities, and their villages.

8 And all the villages round about these cities to Baalath Beer Ramath to the south quarter. This is the inheritance of the children of Simeon according to their kindreds,

9 In the possession and lot of the children of Juda: because it was too great. And therefore the children of Simeon had their possession in the midst of their inheritance.

10 And the third lot fell to the children of Zabulon by their kindreds. And the border of their possession was unto Sarid.

11 And it went up from the sea and from Merala, and came to Debbaseth: as far as the torrent, which is over against Jeconam.

12 And it returneth from Sarid eastward to the borders of Ceseleththabor: and it goeth out to Dabereth, and ascendeth towards Japhie.

13 And it passeth along from thence to the east side of Gethhepher and Thacasin: and goeth out to Remmon, Amthar and Noa.

14 And it turneth about to the north

CHAP. 18. ¹ Gen. 28, 19.

of Hanathon: and the outgoings thereof are the valley of Jephtahel,

15 And Cateth and Naalol and Semeron and Jedala and Bethlehem: twelve cities and their villages.

16 This is the inheritance of the tribe of the children of Zabulon by their kindreds, the cities and their villages.

17 The fourth lot came out to Issachar by their kindreds.

18 And his inheritance was Jezrael and Casaloth and Sunem,

19 And Hapharaim and Seon and Anaharath,

20 And Rabboth and Cesion, Abes,

21 And Rameth and Engannim and Enhadda and Bethpheses.

22 And the border thereof cometh to Thabor and Sehesima and Bethsames: and the outgoings thereof shall be at the Jordan: sixteen cities, and their villages.

23 This is the possession of the sons of Issachar by their kindreds, the cities and their villages.

24 And the fifth lot fell to the tribe of the children of Aser by their kindreds.

25 And their border was Halcath and Chali and Beten and Axaph,

26 And Elmelech and Amaad and Messal: and it reacheth to Carmel by the sea and Sihor and Labanath.

27 And it returneth towards the east to Bethdagon and passeth along to Zabulon and to the valley of Jephthael towards the north to Bethemec and Nehiel. And it goeth out to the left side of Cabul:

28 And to Abaran and Rohob and Hamon and Cana, as far as the great Sidon.

29 And it returneth to Horma to the strong city of Tyre, and to Hosa: and the outgoings thereof shall be at the sea from the portion of Achziba.

30 And Amma and Aphec and Rohob: twenty-two cities, and their villages.

31 This is the possession of the children of Aser by their kindreds, and the cities and their villages.

32 The sixth lot came out to the sons of Nephtali by their families.

33 And the border began from Heleph and Elon to Saananim, and Adami, which is Neceb, and Jebnael even to Lecum: and their outgoings unto the Jordan.

34 And the border returneth westward to Azanotthabor, and goeth out from thence to Hucuca, and passeth along to Zebulon southward, and to Aser westward, and to Juda upon the Jordan towards the rising of the sun.

CHAP. 20. 1 Num. 35, 10; Deut. 19, 2.

35 And the strong cities are Assedim, Ser, and Emath, and Reccath and Cenereth,

36 And Edema and Arama, Asor,

37 And Cedes and Edri, Enhasor,

38 And Jeron and Magdalel, Horem, and Bethanath and Bethsames: nineteen cities, and their villages.

39 This is the possession of the tribe of the children of Nephtali by their kindreds, the cities and their villages.

40 The seventh lot came out to the tribe of the children of Dan by their families.

41 And the border of their possession was Saraa and Esthaol, and Hirsemes, that is, the city of the sun.

42 Selebin and Aialon and Jethela,

43 Elon and Themma and Acron,

44 Elthece, Gebbethon and Balaath:

45 And Jud and Bane and Barach and Gethremmon:

46 And Mejarcon and Arecon, with the border that looketh towards Joppe,

47 And is terminated there. And the children of Dan went up and fought against Lesem, and took it. And they put it to the sword, and possessed it, and dwelt in it, calling the name of it Lesem Dan, by the name of Dan their father.

48 This is the possession of the tribe of the sons of Dan, by their kindreds, the cities and their villages.

49 And when he had made an end of dividing the land by lot to each one by their tribes, the children of Israel gave a possession to Josue the son of Nun in the midst of them,

50 According to the commandment of the Lord, the city which he asked for, Thamnath Saraa, in mount Ephraim. And he built up the city, and dwelt in it.

51 These are the possessions which Eleazar the priest, and Josue the son of Nun, and the princes of the families, and of the tribes of the children of Israel, distributed by lot in Silo, before the Lord at the door of the tabernacle of the testimony. And they divided the land.

CHAPTER 20

The cities of refuge are appointed for casual manslaughter.

AND the Lord spoke to Josue, saying: Speak to the children of Israel and say to them:

2 Appoint cities of refuge, 1 of which I spoke to you by the hand of Moses.

3 That whosoever shall kill a person unawares may flee to them: and may escape the wrath of the kinsman, who is the avenger of blood.

4 And when he shall flee to one of these cities, he shall stand before the

gate of the city, and shall speak to the ancients of that city, such things as prove him innocent. And so shall they receive him, and give him a place to dwell in.

5 And when the avenger of blood shall pursue him, they shall not deliver him into his hands, because he slew his neighbour unawares, and is not proved to have been his enemy two or three days before.

6 And he shall dwell in that city, till he stand before judgment to give an account of his fact, and till the death of the high priest, who shall be at that time. Then shall the manslayer return, and go into his own city and house from whence he fled.

7 And they appointed Cedes in Galilee of mount Nephtali, and Sichem in mount Ephraim, and Cariath-Arbe, the same is Hebron in the mountain of Juda.

8 And beyond the Jordan to the east of Jericho, [2] they appointed Bosor, which is upon the plain of the wilderness of the tribe of Ruben, and Ramoth in Galaad of the tribe of Gad, and Gaulon in Basan of the tribe of Manasses.

9 These cities were appointed for all the children of Israel, and for the strangers, that dwelt among them: that whosoever had killed a person unawares might flee to them, and not die by the hand of the kinsman, coveting to revenge the blood that was shed, until he should stand before the people to lay open his cause.

CHAPTER 21

Cities with their suburbs are assigned for the priests and Levites.

THEN the princes of the families of Levi came to Eleazar the priest, and to Josue the son of Nun, and to the princes of the kindreds of all the tribes of the children of Israel.

2 And they spoke to them in Silo in the land of Chanaan, and said: [1] The Lord commanded by the hand of Moses, that cities should be given us to dwell in, and their suburbs to feed our cattle.

3 And the children of Israel gave out of their possessions according to the commandment of the Lord, cities and their suburbs.

4 And the lot came out for the family of Caath of the children of Aaron the priest, out of the tribes of Juda, and of Simeon, and of Benjamin, thirteen cities.

5 And to the rest of the children of Caath, that is, to the Levites who remained, out of the tribes of Ephraim, and of Dan, and the half tribe of Manasses, ten cities.

6 And the lot came out to the children of Gerson, that they should take of the tribes of Issachar and of Aser and of Nephtali, and of the half tribe of Manasses in Basan, thirteen cities.

7 And to the sons of Merari by their kindreds, of the tribes of Ruben and of Gad and of Zabulon, twelve cities.

8 And the children of Israel gave to the Levites the cities and their suburbs, as the Lord commanded by the hand of Moses, giving to every one by lot.

9 Of the tribes of the children of Juda and of Simeon Josue gave cities, [2] whose names are these:

10 To the sons of Aaron, of the families of Caath of the race of Levi (for the first lot came out for them),

11 The city of Arbe the father of Enac, which is called Hebron, in the mountain of Juda, and the suburbs thereof round about.

12 [3] But the fields and the villages thereof he had given to Caleb the son of Jephone for his possession.

13 He gave therefore to the children of Aaron the priest, Hebron, a city of refuge, and the suburbs thereof: and Lobna with the suburbs thereof,

14 And Jether and Estemo,

15 And Holon, and Dabir,

16 And Ain, and Jeta, and Bethsames, with their suburbs: nine cities out of the two tribes, as hath been said.

17 And out of the tribe of the children of Benjamin, Gabaon, and Gabae.

18 And Anathoth and Almon, with their suburbs: four cities.

19 All the cities together of the children of Aaron the priest, were thirteen, with their suburbs.

20 And to the rest of the families of the children of Caath of the race of Levi was given this possession.

21 Of the tribe of Ephraim, Sichem one of the cities of refuge, with suburbs thereof in mount Ephraim, and Gazer,

22 And Cibsaim, and Beth-horon, with their suburbs, four cities.

23 And of the tribe of Dan, Eltheco and Gabathon,

24 And Aialon and Gethremmon, with their suburbs, four cities.

25 And of the half tribe of Manasses, Thanac and Gethremmon, with their suburbs, two cities.

26 All the cities were ten, with their suburbs, which were given to the children of Caath, of the inferior degree.

27 To the children of Gerson also of the race of Levi, out of the half tribe of Manasses, Gaulon in Basan, *one* of the

[2] Deut. 4, 43. CHAP. 21, [1] Num. 35, 2. [2] 1 Par. 6, 2. [3] Jos. 14, 14; 1 Par. 6, 56.

cities of refuge, and Bosra, with their suburbs, two cities.

28 And of the tribe of Issachar, Cesion, and Dabereth,

29 And Jaramoth, and Engannim, with their suburbs, four cities.

30 And of the tribe of Aser, Masal and Abdon,

31 And Helcath, and Rohob, with their suburbs, four cities.

32 Of the tribe also of Nephtali, Cedes in Galilee, one of the cities of refuge: and Hammoth Dor, and Carthan, with their suburbs, three cities.

33 All the cities of the families of Gerson, were thirteen, with their suburbs.

34 And to the children of Merari, Levites of the inferior degree, by their families were given of the tribe of Zabulon, Jecnam and Cartha,

35 And Damna and Naalol, four cities with their suburbs.

36 Of the tribe of Ruben beyond the Jordan over against Jericho, Bosor in the wilderness, one of the cities of refuge, Misor and Jaser and Jethson and Mephaath, four cities with their suburbs.

37 Of the tribe of Gad, Ramoth in Galaad, one of the cities of refuge, and Manaim and Hesebon and Jaser, four cities with their suburbs.

38 All the cities of the children of Merari by their families and kindreds, were twelve.

39 So all the cities of the Levites within the possession of the children of Israel were forty-eight,

40 With their suburbs, each distributed by the families.

41 And the Lord God gave to Israel all the land that he had sworn to give to their fathers. And they possessed it and dwelt in it.

42 And he gave them peace from all nations round about. And none of their enemies durst stand against them: but were brought under their dominion.

43 Not so much as one word, which he had promised to perform unto them, was made void: but all came to pass.

CHAPTER 22

The tribes of Ruben and Gad, and half the tribe of Manasses return to their possessions. They build an altar by the side of the Jordan, which alarms the other tribes. An embassage is sent to them, to which they give a satisfactory answer.

AT the same time Josue called the Rubenites, and the Gadites, and the half tribe of Manasses,

CHAP. 22. [1] Num. 32, 33; Jos. 1, 13; 13, 8.

CHAP. 21. Ver. 36. *Four cities.* There are no more, though there be five names: for *Misor* is the same city as *Bosor*, which is to be observed in some other places, where the number of names exceeds the number of cities.

2 And said to them: You have done all that Moses the servant of the Lord commanded you: you have also obeyed me in all things.

3 Neither have you left your brethren this long time, until this present day, keeping the commandment of the Lord your God.

4 Therefore, as the Lord your God hath given your brethren rest and peace, as he promised, return, and go to your dwellings, and to the land of your possession, [1] which Moses the servant of the Lord gave you beyond the Jordan.

5 Yet so that you observe attentively, and in work fulfil the commandment and the law which Moses the servant of the Lord commanded you. That you love the Lord your God, and walk in all his ways, and keep all his commandments, and cleave to him, and serve him with all your heart, and with all your soul.

6 And Josue blessed them, and sent them away: and they returned to their dwellings.

7 Now to half the tribe of Manasses, Moses had given a possession in Basan: and therefore to the half that remained, Josue gave a lot among the rest of their brethren beyond the Jordan to the west. And when he sent them away to their dwellings and had blessed them,

8 He said to them: With much substance and riches, you return to your settlements: with silver and gold, brass and iron, and variety of raiment. Divide the prey of your enemies with your brethren.

9 So the children of Ruben, and the children of Gad, and the half tribe of Manasses returned, and parted from the children of Israel in Silo, which is in Chanaan, to go into Galaad, the land of their possession, which they had obtained according to the commandment of the Lord by the hand of Moses.

10 And when they were come to the banks of the Jordan, in the land of Chanaan, they built an altar immensely great near the Jordan.

11 And when the children of Israel had heard of it, and certain messengers had brought them an account that the children of Ruben, and of Gad, and the half tribe of Manasses had built an altar in the land of Chanaan, upon the banks of the Jordan, over against the children of Israel,

12 They all assembled in Silo, to go up and fight against them.

13 And in the mean time they sent to them into the land of Galaad, Phinees the son of Eleazar the priest:

14 And ten princes with him, one of every tribe.

15 Who came to the children of Ruben, and of Gad, and the half tribe of Manasses, into the land of Galaad, and said to them:

16 Thus saith all the people of the Lord: What meaneth this transgression? Why have you forsaken the Lord the God of Israel, building a sacrilegious altar, and revolting from the worship of him?

17 Is it a small thing to you [2] that you sinned with Beelphegor, and the stain of that crime remaineth in us to this day? And many of the people perished.

18 And you have forsaken the Lord to-day, and to-morrow his wrath will rage against all Israel.

19 But if you think the land of your possession to be unclean, pass over to the land wherein is the tabernacle of the Lord, and dwell among us. Only depart not from the Lord, and from our society, by building an altar beside the altar of the Lord our God.

20 [3] Did not Achan the son of Zare transgress the commandment of the Lord, and his wrath lay upon all the people of Israel? And he was *but* one man: and would to God he alone had perished in his wickedness!

21 And the children of Ruben, and of Gad, and of the half tribe of Manasses answered the princes of the embassage of Israel:

22 The Lord, the most mighty God, the Lord, the most mighty God, he knoweth, and Israel also shall understand: If with the design of transgression we have set up this altar, let him not save us, but punish us immediately.

23 And if we did it with that mind, that we might lay upon it holocausts, and sacrifice, and victims of peace offerings, let him require and judge.

24 And not rather with this thought and design, that we should say: To-morrow your children will say to our children: What have you to do with the Lord the God of Israel?

25 The Lord hath put the river Jordan for a border between us and you, O ye children of Ruben, and ye children of Gad: and therefore you have no part in the Lord. And by this occasion your children shall turn away our children from the fear of the Lord. We therefore thought it best,

26 And said: Let us build us an altar, not for holocausts, nor to offer victims,

27 But for a testimony between us and you, and our posterity and yours, that we may serve the Lord, and that we may have a right to offer both holocausts, and victims and sacrifices of peace offerings. And that your children to-morrow may not say to our children: You have no part in the Lord.

28 And if they will say so, they shall answer them: Behold the altar of the Lord, which our fathers made, not for holocausts, nor for sacrifice, but for a testimony between us and you.

29 God keep us from any such wickedness that we should revolt from the Lord, and leave off following his steps, by building an altar to offer holocausts, and sacrifices, and victims, beside the altar of the Lord our God, which is erected before his tabernacle.

30 And when Phinees the priest, and the princes of the embassage, who were with him, had heard this, they were satisfied: and they admitted most willingly the words of the children of Ruben, and Gad and of the half tribe of Manasses.

31 And Phinees the priest the son of Eleazar said to them: Now we know that the Lord is with us, because you are not guilty of this revolt, and you have delivered the children of Israel from the hand of the Lord.

32 And he returned with the princes from the children of Ruben and Gad, out of the land of Galaad, into the land of Chanaan, to the children of Israel, and brought them word again.

33 And the saying pleased all that heard it. And the children of Israel praised God, and they no longer said that they would go up against them, and fight, and destroy the land of their possession.

34 And the children of Ruben, and the children of Gad called the altar which they had built, Our testimony, that the Lord is God.

CHAPTER 23

Josue being old admonisheth the people to keep God's commandments, and to avoid marriages and all society with the Gentiles for fear of being brought to idolatry.

AND when a long time was passed, after that the Lord had given peace to Israel, all the nations round about being subdued, and Josue being now old, and far advanced in years:

2 Josue called for all Israel, and for the elders, and for the princes, and for the judges, and for the masters, and said to them: I am old, and far advanced in years.

3 And you see all that the Lord your God hath done to all the nations round about: how he himself hath fought for you.

4 And now since he hath divided to you by lot all the land, from the east of the Jordan unto the great sea, and many nations yet remain:

5 The Lord your God will destroy them, and take them away from before

[2] Num. 25, 3; Deut. 4, 3.   [3] Jos. 7, 1.

your face: and you shall possess the land as he hath promised you.

6 Only take courage, and be careful to observe all things that are written in the book of the law of Moses. And turn not aside from them neither to the right hand nor to the left:

7 Lest after that you are come in among the Gentiles, who will remain among you, you should swear by the name of their gods, and serve them, and adore them.

8 But cleave ye unto the Lord your God: as you have done until this day.

9 And then the Lord God will take away before your eyes nations that are great and very strong: and no man shall be able to resist you.

10 One of you shall chase a thousand men of the enemies: because the Lord your God himself will fight for you, as he hath promised.

11 This only take care of with all diligence, that you love the Lord your God.

12 But if you will embrace the errors of these nations that dwell among you, and make marriages with them, and join friendships:

13 Know ye for a certainty that the Lord your God will not destroy them before your face: but they shall be a pit and a snare in your way, and a stumbling-block at your side, and stakes in your eyes, till he take you away and destroy you from off this excellent land, which he hath given you.

14 ¹ Behold, this day I am going into the way of all the earth: and you shall know with all your mind that of all the words which the Lord promised to perform for you, not one hath failed.

15 Therefore as he hath fulfilled in deed, what he promised, and all things prosperous have come: so will he bring upon you all the evils he hath threatened, till he take you away and destroy you from off this excellent land, which he hath given you,

16 When you shall have transgressed the covenant of the Lord your God, which he hath made with you, and shall have served strange gods, and adored them. Then shall the indignation of the Lord rise up quickly and speedily against you: and you shall be taken away from this excellent land, which he hath delivered to you.

CHAPTER 24

Josue assembleth the people, and reneweth the covenant between them and God. His death and burial.

Chap. 23. ¹ 3 Kings, 2, 2. ²ibid. 14. ¹Gen. 11,
10. ²Gen. 11, 31. ³Gen. 21, 2. ⁴Gen. 25, 26.
⁵Gen. 36, 8. ⁶Gen. 46, 6. ⁷Exod. 3, 10. ⁸Exod.
12, 37. ⁹Exod. 14, 9. ¹⁰Num. 21, 24. ¹¹Num. 22,
5. ¹²Jos. 3, 14; 6, 1; 11, 3. ¹³Exod. 23, 28; Deut.
7, 20: Jos. 11, 20.
Chap. 24. Ver. 2. *Of the river.* The Euphrates.

AND Josue gathered together all the tribes of Israel in Sichem: and called for the ancients, and the princes, and the judges, and the masters. And they stood in the sight of the Lord.

2 And he spoke thus to the people: Thus saith the Lord the God of Israel: Your fathers dwelt of old on the other side of the river: ¹ Thare the father of Abraham, and Nachor. And they served strange gods.

3 ² And I took your father Abraham from the borders of Mesopotamia: and brought him into the land of Chanaan: and I multiplied his seed:

4 ³ And gave him Isaac. ⁴ And to him again I gave Jacob and Esau. ⁵ And I gave to Esau mount Seir for his possession: ⁶ but Jacob and his children went down into Egypt.

5 ⁷ And I sent Moses and Aaron: and I struck Egypt with many signs and wonders.

6 ⁸ And I brought you and your fathers out of Egypt: and you came to the sea: ⁹ and the Egyptians pursued your fathers with chariots and horsemen, as far as the Red Sea.

7 And the children of Israel cried to the Lord. And he put darkness between you and the Egyptians, and brought the sea upon them, and covered them. Your eyes saw all that I did in Egypt: and you dwelt in the wilderness a long time:

8 And I brought you into the land of the Amorrhite, who dwelt beyond the Jordan.¹⁰ And when they fought against you, I delivered them into your hands: and you possessed their land, and slew them.

9 And Balac son of Sephor king of Moab arose and fought against Israel. ¹¹ And he sent and called for Balaam son of Beor, to curse you.

10 And I would not hear him: but on the contrary I blessed you by him, and I delivered you out of his hand.

11 ¹² And you passed over the Jordan, and you came to Jericho. And the men of that city fought against you, the Amorrhite, and the Pherezite, and the Chanaanite, and the Hethite, and the Gergesite, and the Hevite, and the Jebusite: and I delivered them into your hands.

12 ¹³ And I sent before you hornets: and I drove them out from their places, the two kings of the Amorrhites, not with thy sword nor with thy bow.

13 And I gave you a land, in which you had not laboured, and cities to dwell in which you built not, vineyards and oliveyards, which you planted not.

14 ¹⁴ Now therefore fear the Lord, and serve him with a perfect and most sincere heart. And put away the gods which your fathers served in Mesopotamia and in Egypt, and serve the Lord.

15 But if it seem evil to you to serve the Lord, you have your choice: choose this day that which pleaseth you, whom you would rather serve, whether the gods which your fathers served in Mesopotamia, or the gods of the Amorrhites, in whose land you dwell. But as for me and my house we will serve the Lord.

16 And the people answered, and said: God forbid we should leave the Lord, and serve strange gods.

17 The Lord our God he brought us and our fathers out of the land of Egypt, out of the house of bondage: and did very great signs in our sight, and preserved us in all the way by which we journeyed, and among all the people through whom we passed.

18 And he hath cast out all the nations, the Amorrhite, the inhabitant of the land into which we are come. Therefore we will serve the Lord, for he is our God.

19 And Josue said to the people: You will not be able to serve the Lord. For he is a holy God, and mighty and jealous, and will not forgive your wickedness and sins.

20 If you leave the Lord, and serve strange gods, he will turn, and will afflict you, and will destroy you after all the good he hath done you.

21 And the people said to Josue: No. It shall not be so as thou sayest, but we will serve the Lord.

22 And Josue said to the people: You are witnesses, that you yourselves have chosen you the Lord to serve him. And they answered: *We are* witnesses.

23 Now therefore, said he, put away strange gods from among you: and incline your hearts to the Lord the God of Israel.

24 And the people said to Josue: We will serve the Lord our God: and we will be obedient to his commandments.

25 Josue therefore on that day made a covenant, and set before the people commandments and judgments in Sichem.

26 And he wrote all these things in the volume of the law of the Lord. And he took a great stone, and set it under the oak that was in the sanctuary of the Lord.

27 And he said to all the people: Behold, this stone shall be a testimony unto you, that it hath heard all the words of the Lord, which he hath spoken to you: lest perhaps hereafter you will deny it, and lie to the Lord your God.

28 And he sent the people away, every one to their own possession.

29 And after these things Josue the son of Nun the servant of the Lord died, being a hundred and ten years old.

30 And they buried him in the border of his possession in Thamnathsare, which is situate in mount Ephraim, on the north side of mount Gaas.

31 And Israel served the Lord all the days of Josue, and of the ancients that lived a long time after Josue, and that had known all the works of the Lord which he had done in Israel.

32 ¹⁵ And the bones of Joseph which the children of Israel had taken out of Egypt, they buried in Sichem, in that part of the field ¹⁶ which Jacob had bought of the sons of Hemor the father of Sichem, for a hundred young ewes: and it was in the possession of the sons of Joseph.

33 Eleazar also the son of Aaron died. And they buried him in Gabaath, *that belongeth* to Phinees his son, which was given him in mount Ephraim.

---

¹⁴ 1 Kings, 7, 3; Tob. 14, 10. ¹⁵ Gen. 50, 24; Exod. 13, 19. ¹⁶ Gen. 33, 19.

Ver. 19. *You will not be able to serve the Lord.* This was not said by way of discouraging them; but rather to make them more earnest and resolute, by setting before them the greatness of the undertaking, and the courage and constancy necessary to go through with it.

Ver. 27. *It hath heard.* This is a figure of speech, by which sensation is attributed to inanimate things; and they are called upon, as it were, to bear witness in favour of the great Creator, whom they on their part constantly obey.

Ver. 29. *And after,* &c. If Josue wrote this book, as is commonly believed, these last verses were added by Samuel, or some other prophet.

THE BOOK OF

JUDGES

This Book is called JUDGES, because it contains the history of what passed under the government of the judges, who ruled Israel before they had kings. The writer of it, according to the more general opinion, was the prophet Samuel.

CHAPTER 1

The expedition and victory of Juda against the Chanaanites. They are tolerated in many places.

AFTER the death of Josue, the children of Israel consulted the Lord, saying: Who shall go up before us against the Chanaanite, and shall be the leader of the war?

2 And the Lord said: Juda shall go up. Behold, I have delivered the land into his hands.

3 And Juda said to Simeon his brother: Come up with me into my lot, and fight against the Chanaanite, that I also may go along with thee into thy lot. And Simeon went with him.

4 And Juda went up, and the Lord delivered the Chanaanite, and the Pherezite into their hands: and they slew *of them* in Bezec ten thousand men.

5 And they found Adonibezec in Bezec, and fought against him: and they defeated the Chanaanite, and the Pherezite.

6 And Adonibezec fled: and they pursued after him and took him, and cut off his fingers and toes.

7 And Adonibezec said: Seventy

CHAP. 1. [1] Jos. 15, 14.

CHAP. 1. Ver. 8. *Jerusalem*. This city was divided into two: one part was called *Jebus*, the other *Salem*. The one was in the tribe of Juda, the other in the tribe of Benjamin. After it was taken and burnt by the men of Juda, it was quickly rebuilt again by the Jebusites, as we may gather from ver. 21; and continued in their possession till it was taken by king David.
Ver. 10. *Hebron*. This expedition against Hebron is the same as is related, Jos. 15, 24. It is here repeated, to give the reader at once a short sketch of all the achievements of the tribe of Juda against the Chanaanites.
Ver. 11. *The city of letters*. Perhaps so called from some famous school, or library, kept there.
Ver. 16. *The Cinite*. Jethro the father-in-law of Moses was called *Cinæus*, or the Cinite: and his children who came along with the children of Israel settled themselves among them in the land of Chanaan, embracing their worship and religion. From these the Rechabites sprung, of whom see Jer. 35. *The city of palms*. Jericho, so called from the abundance of palm trees.
Ver. 18. *Gaza*. These were three of the principal cities of the Philistines, famous both in sacred and profane history. They were taken at this time by the Israelites: but as they took no care to put garrisons in them, the Philistines soon recovered them again.

kings having their fingers and toes cut off, gathered up the leavings of the meat under my table. As I have done, so hath God requited me. And they brought him to Jerusalem, and he died there.

8 And the children of Juda besieging Jerusalem, took it, and put it to the sword, and set the whole city on fire.

9 And afterwards they went down and fought against the Chanaanite, who dwelt in the mountains, and in the south, and in the plains.

10 [1] And Juda going forward against the Chanaanite, that dwelt in Hebron (the name whereof was in former times Cariath-Arbe) slew Sesai, and Ahiman, and Tholmai:

11 And departing from thence he went to the inhabitants of Dabir, the ancient name of which was Cariath-Sepher, that is, the city of letters.

12 And Caleb said: He that shall take Cariath-Sepher, and lay it waste, to him will I give my daughter Axa to wife.

13 And Othoniel the son of Cenez, the younger brother of Caleb, having taken it, he gave him Axa his daughter to wife.

14 And as she was going on her way her husband admonished her to ask a field of her father. And as she sighed sitting on her ass, Caleb said to her: What aileth thee?

15 But she answered: Give me a blessing, for thou hast given me a dry land: give me also a watery *land*. So Caleb gave her the upper and the nether watery ground.

16 And the children of the Cinite, the kinsman of Moses, went up from the city of palms, with the children of Juda into the wilderness of his lot, which is at the south side of Arad, and they dwelt with him.

17 And Juda went with Simeon his brother, and they together defeated the Chanaanites that dwelt in Sephaath, and slew them. And the name of the city was called Horma, that is, Anathema.

18 And Juda took Gaza with its confines, and Ascalon and Accaron with their confines.

19 And the Lord was with Juda, and he possessed the hill country: but was not able to destroy the inhabitants of the valley, because they had many chariots armed with scythes.

20 And they gave Hebron to Caleb, [2] as Moses had said: who destroyed out of it the three sons of Enac.

21 But the sons of Benjamin did not destroy the Jebusites that inhabited Jerusalem: and the Jebusite hath dwelt with the sons of Benjamin in Jerusalem until this present day.

22 The house of Joseph also went up against Bethel: and the Lord was with them.

23 For when they were besieging the city, which before was called Luza,

24 They saw a man coming out of the city, and they said to him: Shew us the entrance into the city, and we will shew thee mercy.

25 And when he had shewn them, they smote the city with the edge of the sword: but that man and all his kindred they let go.

26 Who being sent away, went into the land of Hethim, and built there a city, and called it Luza: which is so called until this day.

27 Manasses also did not destroy Bethsan, and Thanac with their villages, nor the inhabitants of Dor, and Jeblaam, and Mageddo with their villages. And the Chanaanite began to dwell with them.

28 But after Israel was grown strong he made them tributaries, and would not destroy them.

29 Ephraim also did not slay the Chanaanite that dwelt in Gazer, but dwelt with him.

30 Zabulon destroyed not the inhabitants of Cetron, and Naalol: but the Chanaanite dwelt among them, and became their tributaries.

31 Aser also destroyed not the inhabitants of Accho, and of Sidon, of Ahalab, and of Achazib, and of Helba, and of Aphec, and of Rohob.

32 And he dwelt in the midst of the Chanaanites the inhabitants of that land, and did not slay them.

33 Nephtali also destroyed not the inhabitants of Bethsames, and of Bethanath. And he dwelt in the midst of the Chanaanites the inhabitants of the land, and the Bethsamites and Bethanites were tributaries to him.

34 And the Amorrhite straitened the children of Dan in the mountain, and gave them not place to go down to the plain.

35 And he dwelt in the mountain Hares, that is, of potsherds, in Aialon and Salebim. And the hand of the house of Joseph was heavy *upon him*, and he became tributary to him.

36 And the border of the Amorrhite was from the ascent of the scorpion, the rock, and the higher places.

CHAPTER 2

An angel reproveth Israel. They weep for their sins. After the death of Josue, they often fall, and repenting are delivered from their afflictions, but still fall worse and worse.

AND an angel of the Lord went up from Galgal to the place of weepers, and said: I made you go out of Egypt, and have brought you into the land for which I swore to your fathers. And I promised that I would not make void my covenant with you for ever:

2 On condition that you should not make a league with the inhabitants of this land, but should throw down their altars. And you would not hear my voice. Why have you done this?

3 Wherefore I would not destroy them from before your face: that you may have enemies, and their gods may be your ruin.

4 And when the angel of the Lord spoke these words to all the children of Israel, they lifted up their voice, and wept.

5 And the name of that place was called, The place of weepers, or of tears: and there they offered sacrifices to the Lord.

6 [1] And Josue sent away the people: and the children of Israel went every one to his own possession to hold it.

7 And they served the Lord all his days, and the days of the ancients, that lived a long time after him, and who knew all the works of the Lord, which he had done for Israel.

8 And Josue the son of Nun, the servant of the Lord, died, being a hundred and ten years old,

9 And they buried him in the borders of his possessions in Thamnathsare in mount Ephraim, on the north side of mount Gaas.

10 And all that generation was gathered to their fathers: and there arose others that knew not the Lord, and the works which he had done for Israel.

11 And the children of Israel did evil in the sight of the Lord, and they served Baalim.

[2] Num. 14, 24; Jos. 15, 14. CHAP. 2. [1] Jos. 24, 28.

Ver. 19. *Was not able.* Through a cowardly fear of their chariots armed with hooks and scythes, and for want of confidence in God.
Ver. 35. *He dwelt.* That is, the Amorrhite.
CHAP. 2. Ver. 1. *An angel.* Taking the shape of a man.
Ver. 6. *And Josue.* This is here inserted out of Jos. 24 by way of recapitulation of what had happened before, and by way of an introduction to that which follows.

12 And they left the Lord the God of their fathers, who had brought them out of the land of Egypt: and they followed strange gods, and the gods of the people that dwelt round about them, and they adored them. And they provoked the Lord to anger:

13 Forsaking him, and serving Baal and Astaroth.

14 And the Lord being angry against Israel, delivered them into the hands of plunderers: who took them and sold them to their enemies, that dwelt round about. Neither could they stand against their enemies:

15 But whithersoever they meant to go, the hand of the Lord was upon them as he had said, and as he had sworn to them. And they were greatly distressed.

16 And the Lord raised up judges, to deliver them from the hands of those that oppressed them: but they would not hearken to them,

17 Committing fornication with strange gods, and adoring them. They quickly forsook the way, in which their fathers had walked: and hearing the commandments of the Lord, they did all things contrary.

18 And when the Lord raised them up judges, in their days he was moved to mercy, and heard the groanings of the afflicted, and delivered them from the slaughter of the oppressors.

19 But after the judge was dead, they returned, and did much worse things than their fathers had done, following strange gods, serving them and adoring them. They left not their own inventions, and the stubborn way, by which they were accustomed to walk.

20 And the wrath of the Lord was kindled against Israel, and he said: Behold this nation hath made void my covenant, which I had made with their fathers, and hath despised to hearken to my voice.

21 I also will not destroy the nations which Josue left, when he died:

22 That through them I may try Israel, whether they will keep the way of the Lord, and walk in it, as their fathers kept it, or not.

23 The Lord therefore left all these nations, and would not quickly destroy

them: neither did he deliver them into the hands of Josue.

CHAPTER 3

The people falling into idolatry are oppressed by their enemies. Repenting are delivered by Othoniel, Aod, and Samger.

THESE are the nations which the Lord left, that by them he might instruct Israel, and all that had not known the wars of the Chanaanites:

2 That afterwards their children might learn to fight with their enemies, and to be trained up to war.

3 The five princes of the Philistines, and all the Chanaanites, and the Sidonians, and the Hevites that dwelt in mount Libanus, from mount Baal Hermon to the entering into Emath.

4 And he left them, that he might try Israel by them, whether they would hear the commandments of the Lord, which he had commanded their fathers by the hand of Moses, or not.

5 So the children of Israel dwelt in the midst of the Chanaanite, and the Hethite, and the Amorrhite, and the Pherezite, and the Hevite, and the Jebusite.

6 And they took their daughters to wives, and they gave their own daughters to their sons, and they served their gods.

7 And they did evil in the sight of the Lord: and they forgot their God, and served Baalim and Astaroth.

8 And the Lord being angry with Israel, delivered them into the hands of Chusan Rasathaim king of Mesopotamia: and they served him eight years.

9 And they cried to the Lord, who raised them up a saviour, and delivered them: to wit, Othoniel the son of Cenez, the younger brother of Caleb.

10 And the spirit of the Lord was in him, and he judged Israel. And he went out to fight, and the Lord delivered into his hands Chusan Rasathaim king of Syria. And he overthrew him.

11 And the land rested forty years: and Othoniel the son of Cenez died.

12 And the children of Israel did evil again in the sight of the Lord. Who strengthened against them Eglon king of Moab: because they did evil in his sight.

13 And he joined to him the children of Ammon, and Amelec: and he went and overthrew Israel, and possessed the city of palm trees.

14 And the children of Israel served Eglon king of Moab eighteen years.

15 And afterwards they cried to the Lord, who raised them up a saviour called Aod, the son of Gera, the son of Jemini, who used the left hand as well

Ver. 12. *They followed strange gods.* What is here said of the children of Israel, as to their falling so often into idolatry, is to be understood of a great part of them; but not so universally, as if the true worship of God was ever quite abolished among them. For the succession of the true church and religion was kept up all this time by the priests and Levites, at least in the house of God in Silo.

CHAP. 3. Ver. 3. *Mesopotamia.* In Hebrew *Aramnaharim. Syria of the two rivers:* so called because it lies between the Euphrates and the Tigris. It is absolutely called Syria, ver. 10.

as the right. And the children of Israel sent presents to Eglon king of Moab by him.

16 And he made himself a two-edged sword, with a haft in the midst of the length of the palm of the hand: and was girded therewith under his garment on the right thigh.

17 And he presented the gifts to Eglon king of Moab. Now Eglon was exceeding fat.

18 And when he had presented the gifts unto him, he followed his companions that came along with him.

19 Then returning from Galgal, where the idols were, he said to the king: I have a secret message to thee, O king. And he commanded silence: and all being gone out that were about him,

20 Aod went in to him. Now he was sitting in a summer parlour alone, and he said: I have a word from God to thee. And he forthwith rose up from his throne,

21 And Aod put forth his left hand, and took the dagger from his right thigh, and thrust it into his belly,

22 With such force that the haft went in after the blade into the wound, and was closed up with the abundance of fat. So that he did not draw out the dagger, but left it in his body as he had struck it in. And forthwith by the secret parts of nature the excrements of the belly came out.

23 But Aod carefully shutting the doors of the parlour and locking them,

24 Went out by a postern door. And the king's servants going in, saw the doors of the parlour shut: and they said: Perhaps he is easing nature in his summer parlour.

25 And waiting a long time till they were ashamed, and seeing that no man opened the door, they took a key: and opening, they found their lord lying dead on the ground.

26 But Aod, while they were in confusion, escaped, and passed by the place of the idols, from whence he had returned. And he came to Seirath.

27 And forthwith he sounded the trumpet in mount Ephraim and the children of Israel went down with him, he himself going in the front.

28 And he said to them: Follow me: for the Lord hath delivered our enemies the Moabites into our hands. And they went down after him, and seized upon the fords of the Jordan, which are in the way to Moab: and they suffered no man to pass over.

29 But they slew of the Moabites at that time, about ten thousand, all strong and valiant men: none of them could escape.

30 And Moab was humbled that day under the hand of Israel. And the land rested eighty years.

31 After him was Samgar the son of Anath, who slew of the Philistines six hundred men with a ploughshare. And he also defended Israel.

CHAPTER 4

Debbora and Barac deliver Israel from Jabin and Sisara. Jahel killeth Sisara.

AND the children of Israel again did evil in the sight of the Lord after the death of Aod.

2 [1] And the Lord delivered them up into the hands of Jaban king of Chanaan, who reigned in Asor. And he had a general of his army named Sisara: and he dwelt in Haroseth of the Gentiles.

3 And the children of Israel cried to the Lord: for he had nine hundred chariots set with scythes, and for twenty years had grievously oppressed them.

4 And there was at that time Debbora a prophetess the wife of Lapidoth, who judged the people.

5 And she sat under a palm tree, which was called by her name, between Rama and Bethel in mount Ephraim: and the children of Israel came up to her for all judgment.

6 And she sent and called Barac the son of Abinoem out of Cedes in Nephtali. And she said to him: The Lord God of Israel hath commanded thee: Go, and lead an army to mount Thabor and thou shalt take with thee ten thousand fighting men of the children of Nephtali, and of the children of Zabulon.

7 And I will bring unto thee in the place of the torrent Cison, Sisara the general of Jabin's army, and his chariots, and all his multitude, and will deliver them into thy hand.

8 And Barac said to her: If thou wilt come with me, I will go: if thou wilt not come with me, I will not go.

9 She said to him: I will go indeed with thee, but at this time the victory shall not be attributed to thee, because Sisara shall be delivered into the hand of a woman. Debbora therefore arose, and went with Barac to Cedes.

10 And he called unto him Zabulon and Nephtali, and went up with ten thousand fighting men, having Debbora in his company.

11 Now Haber the Cinite had some time before departed from the rest of

CHAP. 4. [1] 1 Kings, 12, 9.

Ver. 20. *A word from God.* What Aod, who was judge and chief magistrate of Israel, did on this occasion, was by a special inspiration of God: but such things are not to be imitated by private men.

the Cinites his brethren the sons of Hobab, the kinsman of Moses: and had pitched his tents unto the valley which is called Sennim, and was near Cedes.

12 And it was told Sisara, that Barac the son of Abinoem was gone up to mount Thabor.

13 And he gathered together his nine hundred chariots armed with scythes, and all his army from Haroseth of the Gentiles to the torrent Cison.

14 And Debbora said to Barac: Arise, for this is the day wherein the Lord hath delivered Sisara into thy hands: Behold, he is thy leader. And Barac went down from mount Thabor, and ten thousand fighting men with him.

15 * And the Lord struck a terror into Sisara, and all his chariots, and all his multitudes, with the edge of the sword, at the sight of Barac, insomuch that Sisara leaping down from off his chariot, fled away on foot.

16 And Barac pursued after the fleeing chariots and the army unto Haroseth of the Gentiles: and all the multitude of the enemies was utterly destroyed.

17 But Sisara fleeing came to the tent of Jahel the wife of Haber the Cinite: for there was peace between Jabin the king of Asor, and the house of Haber the Cinite.

18 And Jahel went forth to meet Sisara, and said to him: Come in to me, my lord, come in, fear not. He went in to her tent, and being covered by her with a cloak,

19 Said to her: Give me, I beseech thee, a little water, for I am very thirsty. She opened a bottle of milk, and gave him to drink, and covered him.

20 And Sisara said to her: Stand before the door of the tent, and when any shall come and inquire of thee, saying: Is there any man here? Thou shalt say: There is none

21 So Jahel, Haber's wife, took a nail of the tent, and taking also a hammer, and going in softly, and with silence, she put the nail upon the temples of his head, and striking it with the hammer, drove it through his brain fast into the ground. And so passing from deep sleep to death, he fainted away and died.

---

² Ps. 82, 10.

CHAP. 5. Ver. 6. *The paths rested.* The ways to the sanctuary of God were unfrequented: and men walked in the by-ways of error and sin.

Ver. 14. *Out of Ephraim.* The enemies straggling in their flight were destroyed, as they were running through the land of Ephraim, and of Benjamin, which lies after, that is beyond Ephraim: and so on to the very confines of Amalec. Or, it alludes to former victories of the people of God, particularly that which was freshest in memory, when the men of Ephraim and Benjamin, with Aod at their head, overthrew their enemies the Moabites with the Amalecites their allies (see chap. 3). *Machir.* The tribe of Manasses, whose eldest son was Machir.

22 And behold Barac came pursuing after Sisara. And Jahel went out to meet him, and said to him: Come, and I will shew thee the man whom thou seekest. And when he came into her tent, he saw Sisara lying dead, and the nail fastened in his temples.

23 So God that day humbled Jabin the king of Chanaan before the children of Israel:

24 Who grew daily stronger, and with a mighty hand overpowered Jabin king of Chanaan, till they quite destroyed him.

CHAPTER 5

The canticle of Debbora and Barac after their victory.

IN that day Debbora and Barac, son of Abinoem, sung, and said:

2 O you of Israel, that have willingly offered your lives to danger, bless the Lord.

3 Hear, O ye kings, give ear, ye princes: It is I, it is I, that will sing to the Lord. I will sing to the Lord the God of Israel.

4 O Lord, when thou wentest out of Seir, and passedst by the regions of Edom: the earth trembled, and the heavens dropped water.

5 The mountains melted before the face of the Lord, and Sinai before the face of the Lord the God of Israel.

6 In the days of Samgar the son of Anath, in the days of Jahel the paths rested: and they that went by them, walked through by-ways.

7 The valiant men ceased, and rested in Israel until Debbora arose: a mother arose in Israel.

8 The Lord chose new wars, and he himself overthrew the gates of the enemies: a shield and spear was not seen among forty thousand of Israel.

9 My heart loveth the princes of Israel. O you that of your own good will offered yourselves to danger, bless the Lord.

10 Speak, you that ride upon fair asses, and you that sit in judgment, and walk in the way.

11 Where the chariots were dashed together, and the army of the enemies was choked, there let the justices of the Lord be rehearsed, and his clemency towards the brave men of Israel. Then the people of the Lord went down to the gates, and obtained the sovereignty.

12 Arise, arise, O Debbora, arise, arise, and utter a canticle. Arise, Barac, and take hold of thy captives, O son of Abinoem.

13 The remnants of the people are saved: the Lord hath fought among the valiant ones.

14 Out of Ephraim he destroyed

them into Amalec, and after him out of Benjamin into thy people, O Amalec. Out of Machir there came down princes: and out of Zabulon they that led the army to fight.

15 The captives of Issachar were with Debbora, and followed the steps of Barac, who exposed himself to danger, as one going headlong, and into a pit. Ruben being divided against himself, there was found a strife of courageous men.

16 Why dwellest thou between two borders, that thou mayest hear the bleatings of the flocks? Ruben being divided against himself, there was found a strife of courageous men.

17 Galaad rested beyond the Jordan, and Dan applied himself to ships. Aser dwelt on the sea shore, and abode in the havens.

18 But Zabulon and Nephtali offered their lives to death in the region of Merome.

19 The kings came and fought, the kings of Chanaan fought in Thanach by the waters of Mageddo: and yet they took no spoils.

20 War from heaven was made against them: the stars remaining in their order and courses fought against Sisara.

21 The torrent of Cison dragged their carcasses, the torrent of Cadumim, the torrent of Cison. Tread thou, my soul, upon the strong ones.

22 The hoofs of the horses were broken whilst the stoutest of the enemies fled amain, and fell headlong down.

23 Curse ye the land of Meroz, said the angel of the Lord: curse the inhabitants thereof, because they came not to the help of the Lord, to help his most valiant men.

24 Blessed among women be Jahel the wife of Haber the Cinite: and blessed be she in her tent.

25 He asked her water: and she gave him milk, and offered him butter in a dish *fit* for princes.

26 She put her left hand to the nail, and her right hand to the workman's hammer: and she struck Sisara, seeking in his head a place for the wound, and strongly piercing through his temples.

27 At her feet he fell: he fainted, and he died. He rolled before her feet, and he lay lifeless and wretched.

28 His mother looked out at a window, and howled. And she spoke from the dining room: Why is his chariot so long in coming back? Why are the feet of his horses so slow?

29 One that was wiser than the rest of his wives, returned this answer to her mother-in-law:

30 Perhaps he is now dividing the spoils, and the fairest of the women is chosen out for him. Garments of divers colours are given to Sisara for his prey, and furniture of different kinds is heaped together to adorn the necks.

31 So let all thy enemies perish, O Lord: but let them that love thee shine, as the sun shineth in his rising.

32 And the land rested for forty years.

CHAPTER 6

The people for their sins, are oppressed by the Madianites. Gedeon is called to deliver them.

AND the children of Israel again did evil in the sight of the Lord: and he delivered them into the hand of Madian seven years.

2 And they were grievously oppressed by them. And they made themselves dens and caves in the mountains, and strong holds to resist.

3 And when Israel had sown, Madian and Amalec, and the rest of the eastern nations came up.

4 And pitching their tents among them, wasted all things as they were in the blade even to the entrance of Gaza. And they left nothing at all in Israel for sustenance of life, nor sheep, nor oxen, nor asses.

5 For they and all their flocks came with their tents, and like locusts filled all places: an innumerable multitude of men, and of camels, wasting whatsoever they touched.

6 And Israel was humbled exceedingly in the sight of Madian.

7 And he cried to the Lord desiring help against the Madianites.

8 And he sent unto them a prophet, and he spoke: Thus saith the Lord the God of Israel: I made you to come up out of Egypt, and brought you out of the house of bondage:

9 And delivered you out of the hands of the Egyptians, and of all the enemies that afflicted you. And I cast them out at your coming in, and gave you their land.

10 And I said: I *am* the Lord your God: Fear not the gods of the Amorrhites, in whose land you dwell. And you would not hear my voice.

11 And an angel of the Lord came,

Ver. 15. *Divided against himself.* By this it seems that the valiant men of the tribe of Ruben were divided in their sentiments, with relation to this war; which division kept them at home within their own borders, to hear the bleating of their flocks.

Ver. 23. *Meroz.* Where this land of Meroz was, which is here laid under a curse, we cannot find; nor is there mention of it anywhere else in holy writ. In the spiritual sense, they are cursed who refuse to assist the people of God in their warfare against their spiritual enemies.

and sat under an oak, that was in Ephra, and belonged to Joas the father of the family of Ezri. And when Gedeon his son was threshing and cleansing wheat by the winepress, to flee from Madian,

12 The angel of the Lord appeared to him, and said: The Lord is with thee, O most valiant of men.

13 And Gedeon said to him: I beseech thee, my lord, if the Lord be with us, why have these evils fallen upon us? Where are his miracles, which our fathers have told us of, saying: The Lord brought us out of Egypt? But now the Lord hath forsaken us, and delivered us into the hands of Madian.

14 And the Lord looked upon him, and said: [1] Go in this thy strength: and thou shalt deliver Israel out of the hand of Madian. Know that I have sent thee.

15 He answered and said: I beseech thee, my lord, wherewith shall I deliver Israel? Behold my family is the meanest in Manasses, and I am the least in my father's house.

16 And the Lord said to him: I will be with thee: and thou shalt cut off Madian as one man.

17 And he said: If I have found grace before thee, give me a sign that it is thou that speakest to me:

18 And depart not hence, till I return to thee, and bring a sacrifice, and offer it to thee. And he answered: I will wait thy coming.

19 So Gedeon went in, and boiled a kid, and made unleavened loaves of a measure of flour: and putting the flesh in a basket, and the broth of the flesh into a pot, he carried all under the oak, and presented to him.

20 And the angel of the Lord said to him: Take the flesh and the unleavened loaves, and lay them upon that rock, and pour out the broth thereon. And when he had done so,

21 The angel of the Lord put forth the tip of the rod, which he held in his hand, and touched the flesh and the unleavened loaves. And there arose a fire from the rocks, and consumed the flesh and the unleavened loaves: and the angel of the Lord vanished out of his sight.

22 And Gedeon seeing that it was the angel of the Lord, said: Alas, my Lord God: for I have seen the angel of the Lord face to face

23 And the Lord said to him: Peace be with thee. Fear not, thou shalt not die.

24 And Gedeon built there an altar to the Lord, and called it the Lord's peace, until this present day. And when he was yet in Ephra, which is of the family of Ezri,

25 That night the Lord said to him: Take a bullock of thy father's, and another bullock of seven years. And thou shalt destroy the altar of Baal, which is thy father's: and cut down the grove that is about the altar.

26 And thou shalt build an altar to the Lord thy God in the top of this rock, whereupon thou didst lay the sacrifice before. And thou shalt take the second bullock, and shalt offer a holocaust upon a pile of the wood, which thou shalt cut down out of the grove.

27 Then Gedeon taking ten men of his servants, did as the Lord had commanded him. But fearing his father's house, and the men of that city, he would not do it by day, but did all by night.

28 And when the men of that town were risen in the morning, they saw the altar of Baal destroyed, and the grove cut down, and the second bullock laid upon the altar, which then was built.

29 And they said one to another: Who hath done this? And when they inquired for the author of the fact, it was said: Gedeon the son of Joas did all this.

30 And they said to Joas: Bring out thy son hither, that he may die; because he hath destroyed the altar of Baal, and hath cut down his grove.

31 He answered them: Are you the avengers of Baal, that you fight for him? He that is his adversary, let him die before to-morrow light appear. If he be a god, let him revenge himself on him that hath cast down his altar.

32 From that day Gedeon was called Jerobaal, because Joas had said: Let Baal revenge himself on him that hath cast down his altar.

33 Now all Madian, and Amalec, and the eastern people were gathered together: and passing over the Jordan, camped in the valley of Jezrael.

34 But the spirit of the Lord came upon Gedeon: and he sounded the trumpet and called together the house of Abiezer, to follow him.

35 And he sent messengers into all Manasses, and they also followed him: and other messengers into Aser and Zabulon and Nephtali, and they came to meet him.

36 And Gedeon said to God: If thou wilt save Israel by my hand, as thou hast said,

37 I will put this fleece of wool on the floor. If there be dew on the fleece only, and it be dry on all the ground beside,

---

CHAP. 6.   [1] 1 Kings, 12, 11.

CHAP. 6.   Ver. 15. *The meanest in Manasses.* Mark how the Lord chooseth the humble (who are mean and little in their own eyes) for the greatest enterprises.

I shall know that by my hand, as thou hast said thou wilt deliver Israel.

38 And it was so. And rising before day wringing the fleece, he filled a vessel with the dew.

39 And he said again to God: Let not thy wrath be kindled against me if I try once more, seeking a sign in the fleece. I pray that the fleece only may be dry, and all the ground wet with dew.

40 And God did that night as he had requested. And it was dry on the fleece only, and there was dew on all the ground.

CHAPTER 7

Gedeon, with three hundred men, by stratagem defeateth the Madianites.

THEN Jerobaal, who is the same as Gedeon, rising up early and all the people with him, came to the fountain that is called Harad. Now the camp of Madian was in the valley on the north side of the high hill.

2 And the Lord said to Gedeon: The people that are with thee are many, and Madian shall not be delivered into their hands. Lest Israel should glory against me, and say: I was delivered by my own strength.

3 Speak to the people, and proclaim in the hearing of all: [1] Whosoever is fearful and timorous, let him return. So two and twenty thousand men went away from mount Galaad and returned home; and only ten thousand remained.

4 And the Lord said to Gedeon: The people are still too many; bring them to the waters, and there I will try them. And of whom I shall say to thee: This shall go with thee, let him go. Whom I shall forbid to go, let him return.

5 And when the people were come down to the waters, the Lord said to Gedeon: They that shall lap the water with their tongues, as dogs are wont to lap, thou shalt set apart by themselves. But they that shall drink bowing down their knees, shall be on the other side.

6 And the number of them that had lapped water, casting it with the hand to their mouth, was three hundred men: and all the rest of the multitude had drunk kneeling.

7 And the Lord said to Gedeon: By the three hundred men, that lapped water, I will save you, and deliver Madian into thy hand. But let all the rest of the people return to their place.

8 So taking victuals and trumpets according to their number, he ordered all the rest of the multitude to depart to their tents: and he with the three hundred gave himself to the battle. Now the camp of Madian was beneath him in the valley.

9 The same night the Lord said to him: Arise, and go down into the camp; because I have delivered them into thy hand.

10 But if thou be afraid to go alone, let Phara thy servant go down with thee.

11 And when thou shalt hear what they are saying, then shall thy hands be strengthened, and thou shalt go down more secure to the enemies' camp. And he went down with Phara his servant into part of the camp, where was the watch of men in arms.

12 But Madian and Amalec, and all the eastern people lay scattered in the valley, as a multitude of locusts. Their camels also were innumerable as the sand that lieth on the sea shore.

13 And when Gedeon was come, one told his neighbour a dream: and in this manner related what he had seen: I dreamt a dream, and it seemed to me as if a hearth cake of barley bread rolled and came down into the camp of Madian. And when it was come to a tent it struck it, and beat it down flat to the ground.

14 He to whom he spoke, answered: This is nothing else but the sword of Gedeon the son of Joas a man of Israel. For the Lord hath delivered Madian, and all their camp into his hand.

15 And when Gedeon had heard the dream, and the interpretation thereof, he adored: and returned to the camp of Israel, and said: Arise, for the Lord hath delivered the camp of Madian into our hands.

16 And he divided the three hundred men into three parts, and gave them trumpets in their hands, and empty pitchers, and lamps within the pitchers.

17 And he said to them: What you shall see me do, do you the same. I will go into one part of the camp: and do you as I shall do.

18 When the trumpet shall sound in my hand, do you also blow the trumpets on every side of the camp.

CHAP. 7. [1] Deut. 20, 8; 1 Mach. 3, 56.

CHAP. 7. Ver. 2. *Lest Israel.* By this we see that God will not choose for his instruments in great achievements, which depend purely on his grace, such as, through pride and self-conceit, will take the glory to themselves.

Ver. 7. *That lapped water.* These were preferred that took the water up in their hands, and so lapped it, before them who laid themselves quite down to the waters to drink: which argued a more eager and sensual disposition.

Ver. 13. *A dream.* Observation of dreams is commonly superstitious, and as such is condemned in the word of God: but in some extraordinary cases, as we here see, God is pleased by dreams to foretell what he is about to do.

Ver. 19. *Their trumpets.* In a mystical sense, the preachers of the gospel, in order to spiritual conquests, must not only sound with the trumpet of the word of God, but must also break their earthen pitchers, by the mortification of the flesh and its passions, and carry lamps in their hands by the light of their virtues.

19 And Gedeon, and the three hundred men that were with him, went into part of the camp, at the beginning of the midnight watch: and the watchmen being alarmed, they began to sound their trumpets, and to clap their pitchers one against another.

20 And when they sounded their trumpets in three places round about the camp, and had broken their pitchers, they held their lamps in their left hands, and with their right hands the trumpets which they blew: and they cried out: The sword of the Lord and of Gedeon:

21 Standing every man in his place round about the enemies' camp. So all the camp was troubled: and crying out and howling they fled away.

22 And the three hundred men nevertheless persisted sounding the trumpets. [2] And the Lord sent the sword into all the camp, and they killed one another,

23 Fleeing as far as Bethsetta, and the border of Abelmahula in Tebbath. But the men of Israel shouting from Nephtali and Aser, and from all Manasses pursued after Madian.

24 And Gedeon sent messengers into all mount Ephraim, saying: Come down to meet Madian, and take the waters before them to Bethbera and the Jordan. And all Ephraim shouted, and took the waters before them and the Jordan as far as Bethbera.

25 [3] And having taken two men of Madian, Oreb and Zeb: Oreb they slew in the rock of Oreb, and Zeb in the winepress of Zeb. And they pursued Madian, carrying the heads of Oreb and Zeb to Gedeon beyond the waters of Jordan.

CHAPTER 8

Gedeon appeaseth the Ephraimites. Taketh Zebee and Salmana. Destroyeth Soccoth and Phanuel. Refuseth to be king. Maketh an ephod of the gold of the prey. And dieth in a good old age. The people return to idolatry.

AND the men of Ephraim said to him: What is this that thou meanest to do, that thou wouldst not call us when thou wentest to fight against Madian? And they chid him sharply and almost offered violence.

2 And he answered them: What could I have done like to that which you have done? Is not one bunch of grapes of Ephraim better than the vintages of Abiezer?

[2 Ps. 90, 10.   3 Ps. 88, 13. Isai. 10, 26.   CHAP. 8.]
[1 Osee. 10, 14.]

Ver. 25. *Two men.* That is, two of their chiefs.
CHAP. 8. Ver. 2. *What could I have done.* A meek and humble answer appeased them; who otherwise might have come to extremities. So great is the power of humility both with God and man.

3 The Lord hath delivered into your hands the princes of Madian, Oreb and Zeb. What could I have done like to what you have done? And when he had said this, their spirit was appeased, with which they swelled against him.

4 And when Gedeon was come to the Jordan, he passed over it with the three hundred men, that were with him: who were so weary that they could not pursue after them that fled.

5 And he said to the men of Soccoth: Give, I beseech you, bread to the people that is with me, for they are faint: that we may pursue Zebee, and Salmana the kings of Madian.

6 The princes of Soccoth answered: Peradventure the palms of the hands of Zebee and Salmana are in thy hand, and therefore thou demandest that we should give bread to thy army.

7 And he said to them: When the Lord therefore shall have delivered Zebee and Salmana into my hands, I will thresh your flesh with the thorns and briers of the desert.

8 And going up from thence, he came to Phanuel: and he spoke the like things to the men of that place. And they also answered him, as the men of Soccoth had answered.

9 He said therefore to them also: When I shall return a conqueror in peace, I will destroy this tower.

10 But Zebee and Salmana were resting with all their army. For fifteen thousand men were left of all the troops of the eastern people, and one hundred and twenty thousand warriors that drew the sword, were slain.

11 [1] And Gedeon went up by the way of them that dwelt in tents, on the east of Nobe and Jegbaa: and smote the camp of the enemies, who were secure, and suspected no hurt.

12 And Zebee and Salmana fled: and Gedeon pursued and took them, all their host being put in confusion.

13 And returning from the battle before the sun rising,

14 He took a boy of the men of Soccoth: and he asked him the names of the princes and ancients of Soccoth. And he described unto him seventy-seven men.

15 And he came to Soccoth and said to them: Behold Zebee and Salmana, concerning whom you upbraided me, saying: Peradventure the hands of Zebee and Salmana, are in thy hands, and therefore thou demandest that we should give bread to the men that are weary and faint.

16 So he took the ancients of the city, and thorns and briers of the desert: and tore them with the same, and cut in pieces the men of Soccoth.

17 And he demolished the tower of Phanuel, and slew the men of the city.

18 And he said to Zebee and Salmana: What manner of men were they whom you slew in Thabor? They answered: They were like thee, and one of them as the son of a king.

19 He answered them: They were my brethren, the sons of my mother. *As* the Lord liveth, if you had saved them, I would not kill you.

20 And he said to Jether his eldest son: Arise, and slay them. But he drew not his sword: for he was afraid, being but yet a boy.

21 And Zebee and Salmana said: Do thou rise, and run upon us: because the strength of a man is according to his age. ² Gedeon rose up and slew Zebee and Salmana: and he took the ornaments and bosses, with which the necks of the camels of kings are wont to be adorned.

22 And all the men of Israel said to Gedeon: Rule thou over us, and thy son, and thy son's son: because thou hast delivered us from the hand of Madian.

23 And he said to them: I will not rule over you, neither shall my son rule over you: but the Lord shall rule over you.

24 And he said to them: I desire one request of you. Give me the earlets of your spoils. For the Ismaelites were accustomed to wear golden earlets.

25 They answered: We will give them most willingly. And spreading a mantle on the ground, they cast upon it the earlets of the spoils.

26 And the weight of the earlets that he requested, was a thousand seven hundred sicles of gold, besides the ornaments, and jewels, and purple raiment which the kings of Madian were wont to use, and besides the golden chains that were about the camels' necks.

27 And Gedeon made an ephod thereof, and put it in his city Ephra. And all Israel committed fornication with it: and it became a ruin to Gedeon and to all his house.

28 But Madian was humbled before the children of Israel, neither could they any more lift up their heads. But the land rested for forty years, while Gedeon presided.

29 So Jerobaal the son of Joas went, and dwelt in his own house.

30 And he had seventy sons, who came out of his thigh: for he had many wives.

31 And his concubine, that he had in Sichem, bore him a son, whose name was Abimelech.

32 And Gedeon, the son of Joas, died in a good old age, and was buried in the sepulchre of his father in Ephra of the family of Ezri.

33 But after Gedeon was dead, the children of Israel turned again, and committed fornication with Baalim. And they made a covenant with Baal, that he should be their god.

34 And they remembered not the Lord their God, who delivered them out of the hands of all their enemies round about.

35 Neither did they shew mercy to the house of Jerobaal Gedeon, according to all the good things he had done to Israel.

CHAPTER 9

Abimelech killeth his brethren. Joatham's parable. Gaal conspireth with the Sichemites against Abimelech, but is overcome. Abimelech destroyeth Sichem: but is killed at Thebes.

AND Abimelech, the son of Jerobaal, went to Sichem, to his mother's brethren, and spoke to them, and to all the kindred of his mother's father, saying:

2 Speak to all the men of Sichem: Whether is better for you that seventy men all the sons of Jerobaal should rule over you, or that one man should rule over you? And withal consider that I am your bone, and your flesh.

3 And his mother's brethren spoke of him to all the men of Sichem, all these words: and they inclined their hearts after Abimelech, saying: He is our brother.

4 And they gave him seventy weight of silver out of the temple of Baalberith: wherewith he hired to himself men that were needy, and vagabonds, and they followed him.

5 And he came to his father's house in Ephra, and slew his brethren the sons of Jerobaal, seventy men, upon one stone. And there remained *only* Joatham the youngest son of Jerobaal, who was hidden.

6 And all the men of Sichem were gathered together, and all the families of the city of Mello. And they went and made Abimelech king, by the oak that stood in Sichem.

7 This being told to Joatham, he went and stood on the top of mount

---

² Ps. 82, 12.

Ver. 27. *An ephod.* A priestly garment which Gedeon made with a good design; but the Israelites, after his death, abused it by making it an instrument of their idolatrous worship.

Ver. 31. *His concubine.* She was his servant, but not his harlot: and is called his concubine, as wives of an inferior degree are commonly called in the Old Testament, though otherwise lawfully married.

Chap. 9. Ver. 4. *Baalberith.* This is, Baal of the *covenant*, so called from the covenant they had made with Baal (8, 33).

Garizim. And lifting up his voice, he cried, and said: Hear me, ye men of Sichem, so may God hear you.

8 The trees went to anoint a king over them. And they said to the olive tree: Reign thou over us.

9 And it answered: Can I leave my fatness, which both gods and men make use of, to come to be promoted among the trees?

10 And the trees said to the fig tree: Come thou and reign over us.

11 And it answered them: Can I leave my sweetness, and my delicious fruits, and go to be promoted among the other trees?

12 And the trees said to the vine: Come thou and reign over us.

13 And it answered them: Can I forsake my wine, that cheereth God and men, and be promoted among the other trees?

14 And all the trees said to the bramble: Come thou and reign over us.

15 And it answered them: If indeed you mean to make me king, come ye and rest under my shadow. But if you mean it not, let fire come out from the bramble, and devour the cedars of Libanus.

16 Now therefore if you have done well, and without sin in appointing Abimelech king over you, and have dealt well with Jerobaal, and with his house, and have made a suitable return for the benefits of him, who fought for you,

17 And exposed his life to dangers, to deliver you from the hands of Madian:

18 And you are now risen up against my father's house, and have killed his sons seventy men upon one stone, and have made Abimelech the son of his handmaid king over the inhabitants of Sichem, because he is your brother:

19 If therefore you have dealt well, and without fault with Jerobaal, and his house, rejoice ye this day in Abimelech: and may he rejoice in you.

20 But if unjustly: Let fire come out from him, and consume the inhabitants of Sichem, and the town of Mello: and let fire come out from the men of Sichem, and from the town of Mello, and devour Abimelech.

21 And when he had said thus he fled, and went into Bera: and dwelt there for fear of Abimelech his brother.

Ver. 9. *Both gods and men make use of.* The olive tree is introduced, speaking in this manner, because oil was used both in the worship of the true God, and in that of the false gods, whom the Sichemites served.

Ver. 13. *Cheereth God and men.* Wine is here represented as agreeable to God, because he had appointed it to be offered up with his sacrifices. But we are not obliged to take these words, spoken by the trees, in Joatham's parable, according to the strict literal sense: but only in a sense accommodated to the design of the parable expressed in the conclusion of it.

22 So Abimelech reigned over Israel for three years.

23 And the Lord sent a very evil spirit between Abimelech and the inhabitants of Sichem: who began to detest him,

24 And to leave the crime of the murder of the seventy sons of Jerobaal, and the shedding of their blood upon Abimelech their brother, and upon the rest of the princes of the Sichemites, who aided him.

25 And they set an ambush against him on the top of the mountains: and while they waited for his coming, they committed robberies, taking spoils of all that passed by. And it was told Abimelech.

26 And Gaal the son of Obed came with his brethren, and went over to Sichem. And the inhabitants of Sichem taking courage at his coming,

27 Went out into the fields, wasting the vineyards, and treading down the grapes. And singing and dancing they went into the temple of their god, and in their banquets and cups they cursed Abimelech.

28 And Gaal the son of Obed cried: Who is Abimelech, and what is Sichem, that we should serve him? Is he not the son of Jerobaal, and hath made Zebul his servant ruler over the men of Emor the father of Sichem? Why then shall we serve him?

29 Would to God that some man would put this people under my hand, that I might remove Abimelech out of the way! And it was said to Abimelech: Gather together the multitude of an army, and come.

30 For Zebul, the ruler of the city, hearing the words of Gaal, the son of Obed, was very angry,

31 And sent messengers privately to Abimelech, saying: Behold Gaal the son of Obed is come into Sichem with his brethren, and endeavoureth to set the city against thee.

32 Arise therefore in the night with the people that is with thee and lie hid in the field.

33 And betimes in the morning at sun rising set upon the city. And when he shall come out against thee with his people, do to him what thou shalt be able.

34 Abimelech therefore arose with all his army by night, and laid ambushes near Sichem in four places.

35 And Gaal the son of Obed went out, and stood in the entrance of the gate of the city. And Abimelech rose up, and all his army with him from the places of the ambushes.

36 And when Gaal saw the people, he said to Zebul: Behold a multitude cometh down from the mountains. And he

answered him: Thou seest the shadows of the mountains as if they were the heads of men, and this is thy mistake.

37 Again Gaal said: Behold there cometh people down from the middle of the land, and one troop cometh by the way that looketh towards the oak.

38 And Zebul said to him: Where is now thy mouth wherewith thou saidst? Who is Abimelech that we should serve him? Is not this the people which thou didst despise? Go out, and fight against him.

39 So Gaal went out in the sight of the people of Sichem, and fought against Abimelech:

40 Who chased and put him to flight, and drove him to the city. And many were slain of his people, even to the gate of the city.

41 And Abimelech sat down in Ruma: but Zebul drove Gaal, and his companions out of the city, and would not suffer them to abide in it.

42 So the day following the people went out into the field. And it was told Abimelech.

43 And he took his army, and divided it into three companies, and laid ambushes in the fields. And seeing that the people came out of the city, he arose and set upon them,

44 With his own company, assaulting and besieging the city: whilst the two other companies chased the enemies that were scattered about the field.

45 And Abimelech assaulted the city all that day: and took it, and killed the inhabitants thereof: and demolished it, so that he sowed salt in it.

46 And when they who dwelt in the tower of Sichem had heard this, they went into the temple of their god Berith: where they had made a covenant with him, and from thence the place had taken its name. And it was exceeding strong.

47 Abimelech also hearing that the men of the tower of Sichem were gathered together,

48 Went up into mount Selmon he and all his people with him. And taking an axe, he cut down the bough of a tree, and laying it on his shoulder and carrying it, he said to his companions: What you see me do, do you out of hand.

49 So they cut down boughs from the trees, every man as fast as he could. and followed their leader. And surrounding the fort they set it on fire. And so it came to pass that with the smoke and with the fire a thousand persons were killed, men and women together, of the inhabitants of the tower of Sichem.

50 Then Abimelech departing from thence came to the town of Thebes, which he surrounded and besieged with his army.

51 And there was in the midst of the city a high tower, to which both the men and the women were fled together, and all the princes of the city. And having shut and strongly barred the gate, they stood upon the battlements of the tower to defend themselves.

52 And Abimelech coming near the tower, fought stoutly: and approaching to the gate, endeavoured to set fire to it.

53 [1] And behold a certain woman casting a piece of a millstone from above, dashed it against the head of Abimelech, and broke his skull.

54 [2] And he called hastily to his armourbearer, and said to him: Draw thy sword, and kill me: lest it should be said that I was slain by a woman. He did as he was commanded, and slew him.

55 And when he was dead, all the men of Israel that were with him, returned to their homes.

56 And God repaid the evil, that Abimelech had done against his father, killing his seventy brethren.

57 The Sichemites also were rewarded for what they had done: and the curse of Joatham the son of Jerobaal came upon them.

CHAPTER 10

Thola ruleth Israel twenty-three years, and Jair twenty-two. The people fall again into idolatry, and are afflicted by the Philistines and Ammonites. They cry to God for help, who upon their repentance hath compassion on them.

AFTER Abimelech there arose a ruler in Israel, Thola son of Phua the uncle of Abimelech, a man of Issachar, who dwelt in Samir of mount Ephraim.

2 And he judged Israel three and twenty years, and he died: and was buried in Samir.

3 To him succeeded Jair the Galaadite, who judged Israel for two and twenty years:

4 Having thirty sons that rode on thirty ass colts, and were princes of thirty cities, which from his name were called Havoth Jair, that is, the towns of Jair, until this present day in the land of Galaad.

5 And Jair died, and was buried in the place which was called Camon.

CHAP. 9. [1] 2 Kings, 11, 21. [2] 1 Kings, 31, 4; 1 Par. 10, 4.

Ver. 45. *Sowed salt.* To make the ground barren, and fit for nothing.

CHAP. 10. Ver. 1. *Uncle of Abimelech.* That is, half brother to Gedeon, as being born of the same mother, but by a different father, and of a different tribe.

Ver. 4. *Havoth Jair.* This name was now confirmed to these towns, which they had formerly received from another Jair (Num. 32, 41).

6 But the children of Israel, adding new sins to their old ones, did evil in the sight of the Lord, and served idols, Baalim and Astaroth, and the gods of Syria and of Sidon and of Moab and of the children of Ammon and of the Philistines. And they left the Lord, and did not serve him.

7 And the Lord being angry with them, delivered them into the hands of the Philistines and of the children of Ammon.

8 And they were afflicted, and grievously oppressed for eighteen years, all they that dwelt beyond Jordan in the land of the Amorrhite, who is in Galaad:

9 Insomuch that the children of Ammon passing over the Jordan, wasted Juda and Benjamin and Ephraim. And Israel was distressed exceedingly.

10 And they cried to the Lord, and said: We have sinned against thee, because we have forsaken the Lord our God, and have served Baalim.

11 And the Lord said to them: Did not the Egyptians and the Amorrhites, and the children of Ammon and the Philistines.

12 The Sidonians also and Amalec and Chanaan oppress you, and you cried to me, and I delivered you out of their hand?

13 And yet you have forsaken me, and have worshipped strange gods: therefore I will deliver you no more.

14 Go and call upon the gods which you have chosen. Let them deliver you in the time of distress.

15 And the children of Israel said to the Lord: We have sinned: do thou unto us whatsoever pleaseth thee. Only deliver us this time.

16 And saying these things, they cast away out of their coasts all the idols of strange gods and served the Lord their God. And he was touched with their miseries.

17 And the children of Ammon shouting together, pitched their tents in Galaad: against whom the children of Israel assembled themselves together and camped in Maspha.

18 And the princes of Galaad said one to another: Whosoever of us shall first begin to fight against the children of Ammon, he shall be the leader of the people of Galaad.

CHAPTER 11

Jephte is made ruler of the people of Galaad. Pleads their cause against the Ammonites. Making a vow obtains a signal victory. Performs his vow.

CHAP. 11. [1] Gen. 26, 27. [2] Num. 21, 24.

THERE was at that time Jephte the Galaadite, a most valiant man and a warrior, the son of a woman that was a harlot: and his father was Galaad.

2 Now Galaad had a wife of whom he had sons. Who after they were grown up, thrust out Jephte, saying: Thou canst not inherit in the house of our father, because thou art born of another mother.

3 Then he fled and avoided them and dwelt in the land of Tob. And there were gathered to him needy men, and robbers: and they followed him as their prince.

4 In those days the children of Ammon made war against Israel.

5 And as they pressed hard upon them, the ancients of Galaad went to fetch Jephte out of the land of Tob to help them.

6 And they said to him: Come thou and be our prince, and fight against the children of Ammon.

7 And he answered them: [1] Are not you the men that hated me, and cast me out of my father's house, and now you are come to me constrained by necessity?

8 And the princes of Galaad said to Jephte: For this cause we are now come to thee, that thou mayst go with us, and fight against the children of Ammon, and be head over all the inhabitants of Galaad.

9 Jephte also said to them: If you be come to me sincerely, that I should fight for you against the children of Ammon: and the Lord shall deliver them into my hand, shall I be your prince?

10 They answered him: The Lord who heareth these things, he himself is mediator and witness that we will do as we have promised.

11 Jephte therefore went with the princes of Galaad; and all the people made him their prince. And Jephte spoke all his words before the Lord in Maspha.

12 And he sent messengers to the king of the children of Ammon, to say in his name: What hast thou to do with me, that thou art come against me, to waste my land?

13 And he answered them: [2] Because Israel took away my land when he came up out of Egypt, from the confines of the Arnon unto the Jaboc and the Jordan. Now therefore restore the same peaceably to me.

14 And Jephte again sent word by them, and commanded them to say to the king of Ammon:

15 Thus saith Jephte: Israel did not

take away the land of Moab, nor the land of the children of Ammon.

16 But when they came up out of Egypt, he walked through the desert to the Red Sea, and came into Cades.

17 ³ And he sent messengers to the king of Edom, saying: Suffer me to pass through thy land. But he would not condescend to his request. He sent also to the king of Moab, who likewise refused to give him passage. He abode therefore in Cades:

18 And went round the land of Edom at the side, and the land of Moab: and came over against the east coast of the land of Moab: and camped on the other side of the Arnon. ⁴ And he would not enter the bounds of Moab.

19 So Israel sent messengers to Sehon king of the Amorrhites, who dwelt in Hesebon, and they said to him: Suffer me to pass through thy land to the river.

20 But he also despising the words of Israel, suffered him not to pass through his borders. But gathering an infinite multitude, went out against him to Jasa, and made strong opposition.

21 And the Lord delivered him with all his army into the hands of Israel. And he slew him, and possessed all the land of the Amorrhite the inhabitant of that country,

22 And all the coasts thereof from the Arnon to the Jaboc, and from the wilderness to the Jordan.

23 So the Lord the God of Israel destroyed the Amorrhite, his people of Israel fighting against him. And wilt thou now possess this land?

24 Are not those things which thy god Chamos possesseth, due to thee by right? But what the Lord our God hath obtained by conquest, shall be our possession.

25 ⁵ Unless perhaps thou art better than Balac the son of Sephor king of Moab: or canst shew that he strove against Israel and fought against him,

26 Whereas he hath dwelt in Hesebon, and the villages thereof, and in Aroer, and its villages, and in all the cities near the Jordan, for three hundred years. Why have you for so long a time attempted nothing about this claim?

27 Therefore I do not trespass against thee, but thou wrongest me by declaring an unjust war against me. The Lord be judge and decide this day between Israel and the children of Ammon.

28 And the king of the children of Ammon would not hearken to the words of Jephte, which he sent him by the messengers.

29 Therefore the spirit of the Lord came upon Jephte, and going round Galaad, and Manasses, and Maspha of Galaad, and passing over from thence to the children of Ammon,

30 He made a vow to the Lord, saying: If thou wilt deliver the children of Ammon into my hands,

31 Whosoever shall first come forth out of the doors of my house, and shall meet me when I return in peace from the children of Ammon, the same will I offer a holocaust to the Lord.

32 And Jephte passed over to the children of Ammon, to fight against them: and the Lord delivered them into his hands.

33 And he smote *them* from Aroer till you come to Mennith, twenty cities, and as far as Abel, which is set with vineyards, with a very great slaughter. And the children of Ammon were humbled by the children of Israel.

34 And when Jephte returned into Maspha to his house, his only daughter met him with timbrels and with dances: for he had no other children.

35 And when he saw her, he rent his garments, and said: Alas! my daughter, thou hast deceived me, and thou thyself art deceived: for I have opened my mouth to the Lord, and I can do no other thing.

36 And she answered him: My father, if thou hast opened thy mouth to the Lord, do unto me whatsoever thou hast promised, since the victory hath been granted to thee, and revenge of thy enemies.

37 And she said to her father: Grant me only this which I desire: Let me go, that I may go about the mountains for

---

³ Num. 20, 14.   ⁴ Num. 21, 13.   ⁵ Num. 22, 2.

CHAP. 11. Ver. 24. *Chamos.* The idol of the Moabites and Ammonites. He argues from their opinion, who thought they had a just title to the countries which they imagined they had conquered by the help of their gods: how much more then had Israel an indisputable title to the countries which God, by visible miracles, had conquered for them.

Ver. 31. *Whosoever.* Some are of opinion, that the meaning of this vow of Jephte, was to consecrate to God whatsoever should first meet him, according to the condition of the thing; so as to offer it up as a holocaust, if it were such a thing as might be so offered by the law; or to devote it otherwise to God, if it were not such as the law allowed to be offered in sacrifice. And therefore they think the daughter of Jephte was not slain by her father, but only consecrated to perpetual virginity. But the common opinion followed by the generality of the holy fathers and divines is, that she was offered as a holocaust, in consequence of her father's vow: and that Jephte did not sin, at least not mortally, neither in making, nor in keeping, his vow: since he is no ways blamed for it in scripture; and was even inspired by God himself to make the vow (as appears from ver. 29, 30) in consequence of which he obtained the victory; and therefore he reasonably concluded that God, who is the master of life and death, was pleased on this occasion to dispense with his own law; and that it was the divine will he should fulfil his vow.

two months, and may bewail my virginity with my companions.

38 And he answered her: Go. And he sent her away for two months. And when she was gone with her comrades and companions, she mourned her virginity in the mountains.

38 And the two months being expired, she returned to her father, and he did to her as he had vowed, and she knew no man. From thence came a fashion in Israel and a custom has been kept:

40 That from year to year the daughters of Israel assemble together, and lament the daughter of Jephte the Galaadite for four days.

CHAPTER 12

The Ephraimites quarrel with Jephte. Forty-two thousand of them are slain. Abesan, Ahialon, and Abdon, are judges.

BUT behold there arose a sedition in Ephraim. And passing towards the north, they said to Jephte: When thou wentest to fight against the children of Ammon, why wouldst thou not call us, that we might go with thee? Therefore we will burn thy house.

2 And he answered them: I and my people were at great strife with the children of Ammon. And I called you to assist me: and you would not do it.

3 And when I saw this, I put my life in my own hands, and passed over against the children of Ammon, and the Lord delivered them into my hands. What have I deserved, that you should rise up to fight against me?

4 Then calling to him all the men of Galaad, he fought against Ephraim. And the men of Galaad defeated Ephraim, because he had said: Galaad is a fugitive of Ephraim, and dwelleth in the midst of Ephraim and Manasses.

5 And the Galaadites secured the fords of the Jordan, by which Ephraim was to return. And when any one of the number of Ephraim came thither in the flight, and said: I beseech you let me pass; the Galaadites said to him: Art thou not an Ephraimite? If he said: I am not;

6 They asked him: Say then, Scibboleth, which is interpreted, An ear of corn. But he answered, Sibboleth, not being able to express an ear of corn by the same letter. Then presently they took him and killed him in the very passage of the Jordan. And there fell at that time of Ephraim two and forty thousand.

7 And Jephte the Galaadite judged Israel six years. And he died, and was buried in his city of Galaad.

8 After him Abesan of Bethlehem judged Israel.

9 He had thirty sons, and as many daughters, whom he sent abroad, and gave to husbands, and took wives for his sons of the same number, bringing them into his house. And he judged Israel seven years.

10 And he died, and was buried in Bethlehem.

11 To him succeeded Ahialon a Zabulonite: and he judged Israel ten years.

12 And he died, and was buried in Zabulon.

13 After him Abdon, the son of Illel, a Pharathonite, judged Israel.

14 And he had forty sons, and of them thirty grandsons, mounted upon seventy ass colts: and he judged Israel eight years.

15 And he died, and was buried in Pharathon in the land of Ephraim, in the mount of Amalech.

CHAPTER 13

The people fall again into idolatry and are afflicted by the Philistines. An angel foretelleth the birth of Samson.

AND [1] the children of Israel did evil again in the sight of the Lord: and he delivered them into the hands of the Philistines forty years.

2 Now there was a certain man of Saraa, and of the race of Dan, whose name was Manue, and his wife was barren.

3. And an angel of the Lord appeared to her, and said: Thou art barren and without children; [2] but thou shalt conceive and bear a son.

4 [3] Now therefore beware and drink no wine nor strong drink, and eat not any unclean thing.

5 Because thou shalt conceive and bear a son, and no razor shall touch his head. For he shall be a Nazarite of God, from his infancy, and from his mother's womb: and he shall begin to deliver Israel from the hands of the Philistines.

6 And when she was come to her husband she said to him: A man of God came to me, having the countenance of an angel, very awful. And when I asked him who he was, and whence he came, and by what name he was called, he would not tell me.

7 But he answered thus: Behold thou shalt conceive and bear a son: beware thou drink no wine, nor strong drink, nor eat any unclean thing. For the child shall be a Nazarite of God from his infancy, from his mother's womb until the day of his death.

Chap. 10. [1] Judges, 10, 6. [2] Gen. 16, 11; 1 Kings, 1, 20; Luke, 1, 31. [3] Num. 6, 4.

Ver. 37. *Bewail my virginity.* The bearing of children was much coveted under the Old Testament, when women might hope that from some child of theirs, the Saviour of the world might one day spring. But under the New Testament virginity is preferred (1 Cor. 7, 35).

8 Then Manue prayed to the Lord, and said: I beseech thee, O Lord, that the man of God, whom thou didst send, may come again, and teach us what we ought to do concerning the child that shall be born.

9 And the Lord heard the prayer of Manue, and the angel of the Lord appeared again to his wife as she was sitting in the field. But Manue her husband was not with her. And when she saw the angel,

10 She made haste and ran to her husband; and told him saying: Behold the man hath appeared to me whom I saw before.

11 He rose up and followed his wife: and coming to the man, said to him: Art thou he that spoke to the woman? And he answered: I am.

12 And Manue said to him: When thy word shall come to pass, what wilt thou that the child should do? Or from what shall he keep himself?

13 And the angel of the Lord said to Manue: From all the things I have spoken of to thy wife, let her refrain herself.

14 And let her eat nothing that cometh of the vine: neither let her drink wine or strong drink, nor eat any unclean thing. And whatsoever I have commanded her, let her fulfil and observe.

15 And Manue said to the angel of the Lord: I beseech thee to consent to my request, and let us dress a kid for thee.

16 And the angel answered him: If thou press me, I will not eat of thy bread; but if thou wilt offer a holocaust, offer it to the Lord. And Manue knew not it was the angel of the Lord.

17 And he said to him: What is thy name, that, if thy word shall come to pass, we may honour thee?

18 And he answered him: 'Why askest thou my name, which is wonderful?

19 Then Manue took a kid of the flocks, and the libations, and put them upon a rock, offering to the Lord, who doth wonderful things: and he and his wife looked on.

20 And when the flame from the altar went up towards heaven, the angel of the Lord ascended also in the flame. And when Manue and his wife saw this, they fell flat on the ground.

21 And the angel of the Lord appeared to them no more. And forthwith Manue understood that it was an angel of the Lord,

22 And he said to his wife: We shall certainly die, because we have seen God.

23 And his wife answered him: If the Lord had a mind to kill us, he would not

have received a holocaust and libations at our hands. Neither would he have shewed us all these things, nor have told us the things that are to come.

24 And she bore a son, and called his name Samson. And the child grew, and the Lord blessed him.

25 And the spirit of the Lord began to be with him in the camp of Dan, between Saraa and Esthaol.

CHAPTER 14

Samson desireth a wife of the Philistines. He killeth a lion: in whose mouth he afterwards findeth honey. His marriage feast, and riddle, which is discovered by his wife. He killeth, and strippeth thirty Philistines. His wife taketh another man.

THEN Samson went down to Thamnatha, and seeing there a woman of the daughters of the Philistines,

2 He came up, and told his father and his mother, saying: I saw a woman in Thamnatha of the daughters of the Philistines: I beseech you, take her for me to wife.

3 And his father and mother said to him: Is there no woman among the daughters of thy brethren, or among all my people, that thou wilt take a wife of the Philistines, who are uncircumcised? And Samson said to his father: Take this woman for me, for she hath pleased my eyes.

4 Now his parents knew not that the thing was done by the Lord, and that he sought an occasion against the Philistines: for at that time the Philistines had dominion over Israel.

5 Then Samson went down with his father and mother to Thamnatha. And when they were come to the vineyards of the town, behold a young lion met him raging and roaring.

6 And the spirit of the Lord came upon Samson, and he tore the lion as he would have torn a kid in pieces, having

---

4 Gen. 32, 29.

CHAP. 13. Ver. 13. *Let her refrain.* By the Latin text it is not clear whether this abstinence was prescribed to the mother, or to the child; but the Hebrew (in which the verbs relating thereto are of the feminine gender) determineth it to the mother. But then the child also was to refrain from the like things, because he was to be from his infancy a *Nazarite of God* (ver. 5), that is, one set aside, in a particular manner, and consecrated to God: now the Nazarites by the law were to abstain from all these things.

Ver. 22. *Seen God.* Not in his own person, but in the person of his messenger. The Israelites, in those days, imagined they should die if they saw an angel, taking occasion perhaps from those words spoken by the Lord to Moses (Exod. 33, 20), *No man shall see me and live.* But the event demonstrated that it was but a groundless imagination.

CHAP. 14. Ver. 3. *Is there no woman among the daughters of thy brethren.* This shews his parents were at first against his marriage with a Gentile, it being prohibited (Deut. 7, 3); but afterwards they consented, knowing it to be by the dispensation of God; which otherwise would have been sinful in acting contrary to the law.

nothing at all in his hand: and he would not tell this to his father and mother.

7 And he went down and spoke to the woman that had pleased his eyes.

8 And after some days returning to take her, he went aside to see the carcass of the lion, and behold there was a swarm of bees in the mouth of the lion and a honeycomb.

9 And when he had taken it in his hands, he went on eating: and coming to his father and mother, he gave them of it, and they ate. But he would not tell them, that he had taken the honey from the body of the lion.

10 So his father went down to the woman, and made a feast for his son Samson: for so the young men used to do.

11 And when the citizens of that place saw him, they brought him thirty companions to be with him.

12 And Samson said to them: I will propose to you a riddle, which if you declare unto me within the seven days of the feast, I will give you thirty shirts, and as many coats.

13 But if you shall not be able to declare it, you shall give me thirty shirts and the same number of coats. They answered him: Put forth the riddle that we may hear it.

14 And he said to them: Out of the eater came forth meat, and out of the strong came forth sweetness. And they could not in three days expound the riddle.

15 And when the seventh day came, they said to the wife of Samson: Soothe thy husband, and persuade him to tell thee what the riddle meaneth. But if thou wilt not do it, we will burn thee, and thy father's house. Have you called us to the wedding on purpose to strip us?

16 So she wept before Samson and complained, saying: Thou hatest me, and dost not love me; therefore thou wilt not expound to me the riddle which thou hast proposed to the sons of my people. But he answered: I would not tell it to my father and mother, and how can I tell it to thee?

17 So she wept before him the seven days of the feast: and at length on the seventh day as she was troublesome to him, he expounded it. And she immediately told her countrymen.

18 And they on the seventh day before the sun went down said to him: What is sweeter than honey? And what is stronger than a lion? And he said

CHAP. 15. Ver. 4. *Foxes.* Being judge of the people he might have many to assist him to catch with nets or otherwise a number of these animals; of which there were great numbers in that country.

to them: If you had not ploughed with my heifer, you had not found out my riddle.

19 And the spirit of the Lord came upon him, and he went down to Ascalon, and slew there thirty men, whose garments he took away and gave to them that had declared the riddle. And being exceeding angry he went up to his father's house.

20 But his wife took one of his friends and bridal companions for her husband.

CHAPTER 15

Samson is denied his wife. He burns the corn of the Philistines, and kills many of them.

AND a while after, when the days of the wheat harvest were at hand, Samson came, meaning to visit his wife, and he brought her a kid of the flock. And when he would have gone into her chamber as usual, her father would not suffer him, saying:

2 I thought thou hadst hated her, and therefore I gave her to thy friend. But she hath a sister, who is younger and fairer than she: take her to wife instead of her.

3 And Samson answered him: From this day I shall be blameless *in what I do* against the Philistines; for I will do you evils.

4 And he went and caught three hundred foxes, and coupled them tail to tail, and fastened torches between the tails.

5 And setting them on fire he let the foxes go, that they might run about hither and thither. And they presently went into the standing corn of the Philistines. Which being set on fire, both the corn that was already carried together, and that which was yet standing, was all burnt, insomuch, that the flame consumed also the vineyards and the oliveyards.

6 Then the Philistines said: Who hath done this thing? And it was answered: Samson, the son-in-law of the Thamnathite, because he took away his wife, and gave her to another, hath done these things. And the Philistines went up and burnt both the woman and her father.

7 But Samson said to them: Although you have done this, yet will I be revenged of you, and then I will be quiet.

8 And he made a great slaughter of them, so that in astonishment they laid the calf of the leg upon the thigh. And going down he dwelt in a cavern of the rock Etam.

9 Then the Philistines, going up into the land of Juda, camped in the place which afterwards was called Lechi, that

is, the Jawbone, where their army was spread.

10 And the men of the tribe of Juda said to them: Why are you come up against us? They answered: We are come to bind Samson, and to pay him for what he hath done against us.

11 Wherefore three thousand men of Juda, went down to the cave of the rock Etam, and said to Samson: Knowest thou not that the Philistines rule over us? Why wouldst thou do thus? And he said to them: As they did to me, so have I done to them.

12 And they said to him, We are come to bind thee and to deliver thee into the hands of the Philistines. And Samson said to them: Swear to me, and promise me, that you will not kill me.

13 They said: We will not kill thee; but we will deliver thee up bound. And they bound him with two new cords, and brought him from the rock Etam.

14 Now when he was come to the place of the Jawbone, and the Philistines shouting went to meet him, the spirit of the Lord came strongly upon him: and as the flax is wont to be consumed at the approach of fire, so the bands with which he was bound were broken and loosed.

15 And finding a jawbone, even the jawbone of an ass which lay there, catching it up, he slew therewith a thousand men.

16 And he said: With the jawbone of an ass, with the jaw of the colt of asses, I have destroyed them, and have slain a thousand men.

17 And when he had ended these words singing, he threw the jawbone out of his hand, and called the name of that place Ramathlechi, which is interpreted, The lifting up of the jawbone.

18 And being very thirsty, he cried to the Lord, and said: Thou hast given this very great deliverance and victory into the hand of thy servant; and behold I die for thirst, and shall fall into the hands of the uncircumcised.

19 Then the Lord opened a great tooth in the jaw of the ass, and waters issued out of it. And when he had drank them he refreshed his spirit, and recovered his strength. Therefore the name of that place was called, The Spring of him that invoked from the jawbone, until this present day.

20 And he judged Israel in the days of the Philistines twenty years.[1]

CHAPTER 16

Samson is deluded by Dalila, and falls into the hands of the Philistines. His death.

ᕼE went also into Gaza, and saw there a woman a harlot, and went in unto her.

2 And when the Philistines had heard this, and it was noised about among them, that Samson was come into the city, they surrounded him, setting guards at the gate of the city, and watching there all the night in silence, that in the morning they might kill him as he went out.

3 But Samson slept till midnight: and then rising he took both the doors of the gate, with the posts thereof, and the bolt, and laying them on his shoulders, carried them up to the top of the hill, which looketh towards Hebron.

4 After this he loved a woman, who dwelt in the valley of Sorec: and she was called Dalila.

5 And the princes of the Philistines came to her, and said: Deceive him, and learn of him wherein his great strength lieth, and how we may be able to overcome him, to bind and afflict him. Which if thou shalt do, we will give thee every one of us eleven hundred pieces of silver.

6 And Dalila said to Samson: Tell me, I beseech thee, wherein thy greatest strength lieth, and what it is wherewith, if thou wert bound, thou couldst not break loose.

7 And Samson answered her: If I shall be bound with seven cords made of sinews not yet dry, but still moist, I shall be weak like other men.

8 And the princes of the Philistines brought unto her seven cords, such as he spoke of, with which she bound him;

9 Men lying privately in wait with her, and in the chamber expecting the event of the thing. And she cried out to him: The Philistines are upon thee, Samson. And he broke the bands, as a man would break a thread of tow twined with spittle, when it smelleth the fire. So it was not known wherein his strength lay.

10 And Dalila said to him: Behold thou hast mocked me, and hast told me a false thing: but now at least tell me wherewith thou mayest be bound.

11 And he answered her: If I shall be bound with new ropes, that were never in work, I shall be weak and like other men.

12 And Dalila bound him again with these, and cried out: The Philistines are upon thee, Samson, there being an ambush prepared for him in the chamber. But he broke the bands like threads of webs.

CHAP. 15. [1] Judges, 16, 31.

CHAP. 16. Ver. 4. *Dalila.* Some are of opinion she was married to Samson; others that she was his harlot. If the latter opinion be true, we cannot wonder that, in punishment of his lust, the Lord delivered him up, by her means, into the hands of his enemies. However if he was guilty, it is not to be doubted but that under his afflictions he heartily repented and returned to God, and so obtained forgiveness of his sins.

13 And Dalila said to him again: How long dost thou deceive me, and tell me lies? Shew me wherewith thou mayest be bound. And Samson answered her: If thou plattest the seven locks of my head with a lace, and tying them round about a nail fastenest it in the ground, I shall be weak.

14 And when Dalila had done this she said to him: The Philistines are upon thee, Samson. And awaking out of his sleep, he drew out the nail with the hairs and the lace.

15 And Dalila said to him: How dost thou say thou lovest me, when thy mind is not with me? Thou hast told me lies these three times, and wouldst not tell me wherein thy strength lieth.

16 And when she pressed him much, and continually hung upon him for many days giving him no time to rest, his soul fainted away, and was wearied even until death.

17 Then opening the truth of the thing, he said to her: The razor hath never come upon my head; for I am a Nazarite, that is to say, consecrated to God from my mother's womb. If my head be shaven, my strength shall depart from me, and I shall become weak, and shall be like other men.

18 Then seeing that he had discovered to her all his mind, she sent to the princes of the Philistines, saying: Come up this once more, for now he hath opened his heart to me. And they went up taking with them the money which they had promised.

19 But she made him sleep upon her knees, and lay his head in her bosom. And she called a barber, and shaved his seven locks, and began to drive him away, and thrust him from her: for immediately his strength departed from him.

20 And she said: The Philistines are upon thee, Samson. And awaking from sleep, he said in his mind: I will go out as I did before, and shake my self, not knowing that the Lord was departed from him.

21 Then the Philistines seized upon him, and forthwith pulled out his eyes; and led him bound in chains to Gaza; and shutting him up in prison made him grind.

22 And now his hair began to grow again.

23 And the princes of the Philistines assembled together, to offer great sacrifices to Dagon their god, and to make merry, saying: Our god hath delivered our enemy Samson into our hands.

24 And the people also seeing this, praised their god, and said the same: Our god hath delivered our adversary into our hands, him that destroyed our country and killed very many.

25 And rejoicing in their feasts, when they had now taken their good cheer, they commanded that Samson should be called, and should play before them. And being brought out of prison, he played before them, and they made him stand between two pillars.

26 And he said to the lad that guided his steps: Suffer me to touch the pillars which support the whole house; and let me lean upon them, and rest a little.

27 Now the house was full of men and women, and all the princes of the Philistines were there. Moreover about three thousand persons of both sexes from the roof and the higher part of the house, were beholding Samson's play.

28 But he called upon the Lord, saying: O Lord God, remember me, and restore to me now my former strength, O my God, that I may revenge myself on my enemies, and for the loss of my two eyes I may take one revenge.

29 And laying hold on both the pillars on which the house rested, and holding the one with his right hand, and the other with his left,

30 He said: Let me die with the Philistines. And when he had strongly shook the pillars, the house fell upon all the princes, and the rest of the multitude that was there. And he killed many more at his death, than he had killed before in his life.

31 And his brethren and all his kindred, going down took his body, and buried it between Saraa and Esthaol in the buryingplace of his father Manue. And he judged Israel twenty years.

CHAPTER 17

The history of the idol of Michas, and the young Levite.

THERE was at that time a man of mount Ephraim whose name was Michas.

2 Who said to his mother: The eleven hundred pieces of silver, which thou hadst put aside for thyself, and concerning which thou didst swear in my hearing, behold I have, and they are with me. And she said to him: Blessed be my son by the Lord.

3 So he restored them to his mother,

Ver. 28. *Revenge myself.* This desire of revenge was out of zeal for justice against the enemies of God and his people; and not out of private rancour and malice of heart.

Ver. 30. *Let me die.* Literally, *let my soul die.* Samson did not sin in this occasion, though he was indirectly the cause of his own death. Because he was moved to what he did, by a particular inspiration of God, who also concurred with him by a miracle, in restoring his strength upon the spot, in consequence of his prayer. Samson, by dying in this manner, was a figure of Christ, who by his death overcame all his enemies.

who said to him: I have consecrated and vowed this silver to the Lord, that my son may receive it at my hand, and make a graven and a molten *god*. So now I deliver it to thee.

4 And he restored them to his mother. And she took two hundred pieces of silver and gave them to the silversmith, to make of them a graven and a molten *god*, which was in the house of Michas.

5 And he separated also therein a little temple for the god, and made an ephod, and theraphim, that is to say, a priestly garment, and idols. And he filled the hand of one of his sons, and he became his priest.

6 In those days there was no king in Israel; but every one did that which seemed right to himself.

7 There was also another young man of Bethlehem Juda, of the kindred thereof: and he was a Levite, and dwelt there.

8 Now he went out from the city of Bethlehem, and desired to sojourn wheresoever he should find it convenient for him. And when he was come to mount Ephraim, as he was on his journey, and had turned aside a little into the house of Michas,

9 He was asked by him whence he came. And he answered: I am a Levite of Bethlehem Juda, and I am going to dwell where I can, and where I shall find a place to my advantage.

10 And Michas said: Stay with me, and be unto me a father and a priest; and I will give thee every year ten pieces of silver, and a double suit of apparel, and thy victuals.

11 He was content, and abode with the man, and was unto him as one of his sons.

12 And Michas filled his hand, and had the young man with him, for his priest, saying:

13 Now I know God will do me good, since I have a priest of the race of the Levites.

CHAPTER 18

The expedition of the men of Dan against Lais. In their way they rob Michas of his priest and his gods.

IN those days there was no king in Israel, and the tribe of Dan sought them an inheritance to dwell in: for unto that day they had not received their lot among the other tribes.

2 So the children of Dan sent five most valiant men of their stock and family from Saraa and Esthaol, to spy out the land, and to view it diligently. And they said to them: Go, and view the land. They went on their way, and when they came to mount Ephraim,

they went into the house of Michas, and rested there.

3 And knowing the voice of the young man the Levite, and lodging with him, they said to him: Who brought thee hither? What dost thou here? Why wouldst thou come hither?

4 He answered them: Michas hath done such and such things for me, and hath hired me to be his priest.

5 Then they desired him to consult the Lord, that they might know whether their journey should be prosperous, and the thing should have effect.

6 He answered them: Go in peace. The Lord looketh on your way, and the journey that you go.

7 So the five men going on came to Lais. And they saw how the people dwelt therein without any fear, according to the custom of the Sidonians, secure and easy, having no man at all to oppose them, being very rich, and living separated, at a distance from Sidon and from all men.

8 And they returned to their brethren in Saraa and Esthaol, who asked them what they had done? To whom they answered:

9 Arise, and let us go up to them; for we have seen the land *which* is exceeding rich and fruitful. Neglect not; lose no time: let us go and possess it. There will be no difficulty.

10 We shall come to a people that is secure, into a spacious country; and the Lord will deliver the place to us, in which there is no want of anything that groweth on the earth.

11 There went therefore of the kindred of Dan, to wit, from Saraa, and Esthaol, six hundred men, furnished with arms for war.

12 And going up they lodged in Cariathiarim of Juda: which place from that time is called the camp of Dan, and is behind Cariathiarim.

13 From thence they passed into mount Ephraim. And when they were come to the house of Michas,

14 The five men, that before had been sent to view the land of Lais, said to the rest of their brethren: You know that in these houses there is an ephod, and theraphim, and a graven, and a molten *god*. See what you are pleased to do.

15 And when they had turned a little aside, they went into the house of the young man the Levite, who was in the

CHAP. 17. Ver. 5. *Filled the hand.* That is, appointed and consecrated him to the priestly office.

CHAP. 18. Ver. 1. *Not received.* They had their portions assigned them (Jos. 19, 40). But, through their own sloth, possessed as yet but a small part of it (Judges, 1, 34).

house of Michas: and they saluted him with words of peace.

16 And the six hundred men stood before the door, appointed with their arms.

17 But they that were gone into the house of the young man, went about to take away the graven *god*, and the ephod, and the theraphim, and the molten *god*. And the priest stood before the door, the six hundred valiant men waiting not far off.

18 So they that were gone in took away the graven thing, the ephod, and the idols, and the molten *god*. And the priest said to them: What are you doing?

19 And they said to him: Hold thy peace and put thy finger on thy mouth and come with us, that we may have thee for a father, and a priest. Whether is better for thee, to be a priest in the house of one man, or in a tribe and family in Israel?

20 When he had heard this, he agreed to their words, and took the ephod, and the idols, and the graven *god*, and departed with them.

21 And when they were going forward, and had put before them the children and the cattle and all that was valuable.

22 And were now at a distance from the house of Michas, the men that dwelt in the houses of Michas gathering together followed them;

23 And began to shout out after them. They looked back, and said to Michas: What aileth thee? Why dost thou cry?

24 And he answered: You have taken away my gods which I have made me and the priest, and all that I have, and do you say: What aileth thee?

25 And the children of Dan said to him: See thou say no more to us, lest men enraged come upon thee, and thou perish with all thy house.

26 And so they went on the journey they had begun. But Michas seeing that they were stronger than he, returned to his house.

27 And the six hundred men took the priest, and the things we spoke of before, and came to Lais to a people that was quiet and secure, and smote them with the edge of the sword. And the city was burnt with fire,

28 There being no man at all who brought them any succour, because they dwelt far from Sidon, and had no society or business with any man. And the city was in the land of Rohob: and they rebuilt it and dwelt therein.

29 Calling the name of the city Dan after the name of their father, who was the son of Israel, which before was called Lais.

30 And they set up to themselves the graven idol: and Jonathan the son of Gersam the son of Moses, he and his sons *were* priests in the tribe of Dan, until the day of their captivity.

31 And the idol of Michas remained with them all the time that the house of God was in Silo. In those days there was no king in Israel.

CHAPTER 19

A Levite bringing home his wife, is lodged by an old man at Gabaa in the tribe of Benjamin. His wife is there abused by wicked men, and in the morning found dead. Her husband cutteth her body in pieces, and sendeth to every tribe of Israel, requiring them to revenge the wicked fact.

THERE was a certain Levite, who dwelt on the side of mount Ephraim, who took a wife of Bethlehem Juda.

2 And she left him and returned to her father's house in Bethlehem, and abode with him four months.

3 And her husband followed her, willing to be reconciled with her, and to speak kindly to her, and to bring her back with him, having with him a servant and two asses: and she received him, and brought him into her father's house. And when his father-in-law had heard this, and had seen him, he met him with joy:

4 And embraced the man. And the son-in-law tarried in the house of his father-in-law three days, eating with him and drinking familiarly.

5 But on the fourth day arising early in the morning he desired to depart. But his father-in-law kept him, and said to him: Taste first a little bread, and strengthen thy stomach, and so thou shalt depart.

6 And they sat down together, and ate and drank. And the father of the young woman said to his son-in-law: I beseech thee to stay here to-day, and let us make merry together.

7 But he rising up began to be for departing. And nevertheless his father-in-law earnestly pressed him, and made him stay with him.

8 But when morning was come, the Levite prepared to go on his journey. And his father-in-law said to him again: I beseech thee to take a little meat; and strengthening thyself, till the day be farther advanced, afterwards thou mayest depart. And they ate together.

9 And the young man arose to set forward with his wife and servant. And his father-in-law spoke to him

again: Consider that the day is declining, and draweth toward evening. Tarry with me to-day also, and spend the day in mirth; and to-morrow thou shalt depart, that thou mayest go into thy house.

10 His son-in-law would not consent to his words: but forthwith went forward and came over against Jebus, which by another name is called Jerusalem, leading with him two asses laden, and his concubine.

11 And now they were come near Jebus, and the day was far spent. And the servant said to his master: Come, I beseech thee, let us turn into the city of the Jebusites, and lodge there.

12 His master answered him: I will not go into the town of another nation, who are not of the children of Israel, but I will pass over to Gabaa.

13 And when I shall come thither, we will lodge there, or at least in the city of Rama.

14 So they passed by Jebus, and went on their journey, and the sun went down upon them when they were by Gabaa, which is in the tribe of Benjamin:

15 And they turned into it, to lodge there. And when they were come in, they sat in the street of the city, for no man would receive them to lodge.

16 And behold they saw an old man, returning out of the field and from his work in the evening; and he also was of mount Ephraim, and dwelt as a stranger in Gabaa. But the men of that country were the children of Jemini.

17 And the old man lifting up his eyes, saw the man sitting with his bundles in the street of the city, and said to him: Whence comest thou? And whither goest thou?

18 He answered him: We came out from Bethlehem Juda, and we are going to our home, which is on the side of mount Ephraim, from whence we went to Bethlehem. And now we go to the house of God, and none will receive us under his roof.

19 We have straw and hay for provender of the asses, and bread and wine for the use of myself and of thy handmaid, and of the servant that is with me: we want nothing but lodging.

20 And the old man answered him: Peace be with thee: I will furnish all things that are necessary. Only I beseech thee, stay not in the street.

21 And he brought him into his house, and gave provender to his asses: and after they had washed their feet, he entertained them with a feast.

22 While they were making merry and refreshing their bodies with meat and drink, after the labour of the journey, the men of that city, sons of Belial, (that is, without yoke,) came and beset the old man's house, and began to knock at the door, calling to the master of the house, and saying: [1] Bring forth the man that came into thy house, that we may abuse him.

23 And the old man went out to them, and said: Do not so, my brethren, do not so wickedly, because this man is come into my lodging: and cease I pray you from this folly.

24 I have a maiden daughter, and this man hath a concubine. I will bring them out to you, and you may humble them, and satisfy your lust. Only, I beseech you, commit not this crime against nature on the man.

25 [2] They would not be satisfied with his words; which the man seeing, brought out his concubine to them, and abandoned her to their wickedness. And when they had abused her all the night, they let her go in the morning.

26 But the woman, at the dawning of the day, came to the door of the house where her lord lodged, and there fell down.

27 And in the morning the man arose, and opened the door that he might end the journey he had begun. And, behold, his concubine lay before the door with her hands spread on the threshold.

28 He thinking she was taking her rest, said to her: Arise, and let us be going. But as she made no answer, perceiving she was dead, he took her up, and laid her upon his ass, and returned to his house.

29 And when he was come home he took a sword, and divided the dead body of his wife and her bones into twelve parts: and sent the pieces into all the borders of Israel.

30 And when every one had seen this, they all cried out: There was never such a thing done in Israel from the day that our fathers came up out of Egypt, until this day. Give sentence, and decree in common what ought to be done.

CHAPTER 20

The Israelites warring against Benjamin are twice defeated; but in the third battle the Benjamites are all slain, saving six hundred men.

THEN all the children of Israel went out and gathered together as one man from Dan to Bersabee, with the land of Galaad, to the Lord in Maspha.

2 And all the chiefs of the people, and all the tribes of Israel, met together in

CHAP. 19. [1] Gen. 19, 5. [2] Osee, 9, 9.

CHAP. 19. Ver. 10. *Concubine.* She was his lawful wife, but even lawful wives are frequently in scripture called concubines. See above, chap. 8, ver. 31.
Ver. 16. *Jemini.* That is, Benjamin.

the assembly of the people of God, four hundred thousand footmen fit for war.

3 (Nor were the children of Benjamin ignorant that the children of Israel were come up to Maspha.) And the Levite the husband of the woman that was killed, being asked, how so great a wickedness had been committed,

4 Answered: I came into Gabaa of Benjamin with my wife, and there I lodged.

5 And behold the men of that city in the night beset the house wherein I was, intending to kill me, and abused my wife with an incredible fury of lust, so that at last she died.

6 And I took her and cut her in pieces, and sent the parts into all the borders of your possession: because there never was so heinous a crime, and so great an abomination committed in Israel.

7 You are all here, O children of Israel: determine what you ought to do.

8 And all the people standing, answered as by the voice of one man: We will not return to our tents, neither shall any one of us go into his own house:

9 But this we will do in common against Gabaa.

10 We will take ten men of a hundred out of all the tribes of Israel, and a hundred out of a thousand, and a thousand out of ten thousand, to bring victuals for the army, that we might fight against Gabaa of Benjamin, and render to it for its wickedness, what it deserveth.

11 And all Israel were gathered together against the city, as one man, with one mind, and one counsel.

12 And they sent messengers to all the tribe of Benjamin to say to them: Why hath so great an abomination been found among you?

13 Deliver up the men of Gabaa, that have committed this heinous crime, that they may die, and the evil may be taken away out of Israel. But they would not hearken to the proposition of their brethren the children of Israel.

14 But out of all the cities which were of their lot, they gathered themselves together into Gabaa, to aid them, and to fight against the whole people of Israel.

15 And there were found of Benjamin five and twenty thousand men that drew the sword, besides the inhabitants of Gabaa,

16 Who were seven hundred most valiant men, fighting with the left hand as well as with the right: and slinging stones so sure that they could hit even a hair, and not miss by the stone's going on either side.

17 Of the men of Israel also, beside the children of Benjamin, were found four hundred thousand that drew swords, and were prepared to fight.

18 And they arose and came to the house of God, that is, to Silo. And they consulted God, and said: Who shall be in our army the first to go to the battle against the children of Benjamin? And the Lord answered them: Let Juda be your leader.

19 And forthwith the children of Israel rising in the morning, camped by Gabaa.

20 And going out from thence to fight against Benjamin, began to assault the city.

21 And the children of Benjamin coming out of Gabaa, slew of the children of Israel that day two and twenty thousand men.

22 Again Israel trusting in their strength and their number, set their army in array in the same place, where they had fought before.

23 Yet so that they first went up and wept before the Lord until night, and consulted him, and said: Shall I go out any more to fight against the children of Benjamin my brethren, or not? And he answered them: Go up against them, and join battle.

24 And when the children of Israel went out the next day to fight against the children of Benjamin,

25 The children of Benjamin sallied forth out of the gates of Gabaa: and meeting them made so great a slaughter of them, as to kill eighteen thousand men that drew the sword.

26 Wherefore all the children of Israel came to the house of God, and sat and wept before the Lord . And they fasted that day till the evening, and offered to him holocausts, and victims of peace offerings:

27 And inquired of him concerning their state. At that time the ark of the covenant of the Lord was there.

28 And Phinees the son of Eleazar the son of Aaron was over the house . So they consulted the Lord and said: Shall we go out any more to fight against the children of Benjamin our brethren, or shall we cease? And the Lord said to them: Go up, for tomorrow I will deliver them into your hands.

Chap. 20. Ver. 22. *Trusting in their strength.* The Lord suffered them to be overthrown and many of them to be slain, though their cause was just; partly in punishment of the idolatry which they exercised or tolerated in the tribe of Dan, and elsewhere; and partly because they trusted in their own strength; and therefore, though he bid them fight, he would not give them the victory, till they were thoroughly humbled and had learned to trust in him alone.

29 And the children of Israel set ambushes round about the city of Gabaa.

30 And they drew up their army against Benjamin the third time, as they had done the first and second.

31 And the children of Benjamin boldly issued out of the city, and seeing their enemies flee, pursued them a long way, so as to wound and kill some of them, as they had done the first and second day, whilst they fled by two highways, whereof one goeth up to Bethel, and the other to Gabaa, and they slew about thirty men:

32 For they thought to cut them off, as they did before. But they artfully feigning a flight, designed to draw them away from the city, and by their seeming to flee to bring them to the highways aforesaid.

33 Then all the children of Israel rising up out of the places where they were, set their army in battle array, in the place which is called Baalthamar. The ambushes also which were about the city, began by little and little to come forth.

34 And to march from the west side of the city. And other ten thousand men chosen out of all Israel attacked the inhabitants of the city. And the battle grew hot against the children of Benjamin: and they understood not that present death threatened them on every side.

35 And the Lord defeated them before the children of Israel: and they slew of them in that day five and twenty thousand, and one hundred, all fighting men and that drew the sword.

36 But the children of Benjamin when they saw themselves to be too weak, began to flee. Which the children of Israel seeing, gave them place to flee, that they might come to the ambushes that were prepared, which they had set near the city.

37 And they that were in ambush arose on a sudden out of their coverts, and whilst Benjamin turned their backs to the slayers, went into the city, and smote it with the edge of the sword.

38 Now the children of Israel had given a sign to them, whom they had laid in ambushes, that after they had taken the city, they should make a fire: that by the smoke rising on high, they might shew that the city was taken.

39 And when the children of Israel saw this in the battle (for the children of Benjamin thought they fled and pursued them vigorously, killing thirty men of their army):

40 And perceived as it were a pillar of smoke rise up from the city; and Benjamin looking back, saw that the city was taken, and that the flames ascended on high:

41 They that before had made as if they fled, turning their faces stood bravely against them. Which the children of Benjamin seeing, turned their backs,

42 And began to go towards the way of the desert, the enemy pursuing them thither also. And they that fired the city came also out to meet them.

43 And so it was, that they were slain on both sides by the enemies, and there was no rest of their men dying. They fell and were beaten down on the east side of the city Gabaa.

44 And they that were slain in the same place were eighteen thousand men, all most valiant soldiers.

45 And when they that remained of Benjamin saw this, they fled into the wilderness and made towards the rock that is called Remmon. In that flight, also as they were straggling and going different ways, they slew of them five thousand men. And as they went farther, they still pursued them, and slew also other two thousand.

46 And so it came to pass, that all that were slain of Benjamin in divers places, were five and twenty thousand fighting men, most valiant for war.

47 And there remained of all the number of Benjamin only six hundred men that were able to escape, and flee to the wilderness. And they abode in the rock of Remmon four months.

48 But the children of Israel returning, put all the remains of the city to the sword, both men and beasts: and all the cities and villages of Benjamin were consumed with devouring flames.

CHAPTER 21

The tribe of Benjamin is saved from being utterly extinct, by providing wives for the six hundred that remained.

NOW the children of Israel had also sworn in Maspha, saying: None of us shall give of his daughters to the children of Benjamin to wife.

2 And they all came to the house of God in Silo; and abiding before him till the evening, lifted up their voices, and began to lament and weep, saying:

3 O Lord God of Israel, why is so great an evil come to pass in thy people, that this day one tribe should be taken away from among us?

4 And rising early the next day, they built an altar: and offered there holocausts, and victims of peace. And they said:

5 Who is there among all the tribes of Israel that came not up with the army of the Lord? For they had bound themselves with a great oath, when they

were in Maspha, that whosoever were wanting should be slain.

6 And the children of Israel being moved with repentance for their brother Benjamin, began to say: One tribe is taken away from Israel.

7 Whence shall they take wives? For we have all in general sworn, not to give our daughters to them.

8 Therefore they said: Who is there of all the tribes of Israel, that came not up to the Lord to Maspha? And behold the inhabitants of Jabes Galaad were found not to have been in that army.

9 (At that time also when they were in Silo, no one of them was found there.)

10 So they sent ten thousand of the most valiant men, and commanded them, saying: Go and put the inhabitants of Jabes Galaad to the sword, with their wives and their children.

11 And this is what you shall observe: [1] Every male, and all women that have known men, you shall kill, but the virgins you shall save.

12 And there were found of Jabes Galaad four hundred virgins, that had not known the bed of a man: and they brought them to the camp in Silo, into the land of Chanaan.

13 And they sent messengers to the children of Benjamin, that were in the rock Remmon, and commanded them to receive them in peace.

14 And the children of Benjamin came at that time, and wives were given them of the daughters of Jabes Galaad: but they found no others, whom they might give in like manner.

15 And all Israel was very sorry, and repented for the destroying of one tribe out of Israel.

16 And the ancients said: What shall we do with the rest, that have not received wives? For all the women in Benjamin are dead.

17 And we must use all care, and provide with great diligence, that one tribe be not destroyed out of Israel.

18 For as to our own daughters we cannot give them, being bound with an oath and a curse, whereby we said: Cursed be he that shall give Benjamin any of his daughters to wife.

19 So they took counsel, and said: Behold there is a yearly solemnity of the Lord in Silo, which is situate on the north of the city of Bethel, and on the east side of the way, that goeth from Bethel to Sichem, and on the south of the town of Lebona.

20 And they commanded the children of Benjamin, and said: Go, and lie hid in the vineyards,

21 And when you shall see the daughters of Silo come out, as the custom is, to dance, come ye on a sudden out of the vineyards; and catch you every man his wife among them: and go into the land of Benjamin.

22 And when their fathers and their brethren shall come, and shall begin to complain against you, and to chide, we will say to them: Have pity on them; for they took them not away as by the right of war or conquest, but when they asked to have them, you gave them not, and the fault was committed on your part.

23 And the children of Benjamin did, as they had been commanded: and according to their number, they carried off for themselves every man his wife of them that were dancing. And they went into their possession and built up their cities, and dwelt in them.

24 The children of Israel also returned by their tribes, and families, to their dwellings. In those days there was no king in Israel: but every one did that which seemed right to himself.

THE BOOK OF

RUTH

This Book is called RUTH, *from the name of the person whose history is here recorded: who, being a Gentile, became a convert to the true faith, and marrying Booz, the great-grandfather of David, was one of those from whom Christ sprung according to the flesh, and an illustrious figure of the Gentile. church. It is thought this book was written by the prophet Samuel.*

CHAPTER 1

Elimelech of Bethlehem going with his wife Noemi, and two sons, into the land of Moab, dieth there. His sons marry wives of that country and die without issue. Noemi returneth home with her daughter-in-law Ruth, who refuseth to part with her.

IN the days of one of the judges, when the judges ruled, there came a famine in the land. And a certain man of Bethlehem Juda, went to sojourn in the land of Moab with his wife and his two sons.

2 He was named Elimelech, and his wife, Noemi: and his two sons, the one Mahalon, and the other Chelion, Ephrathites of Bethlehem Juda. And entering into the country of Moab, they abode there.

3 And Elimelech the husband of Noemi died: and she remained with her sons.

4 And they took wives of the women of Moab, of which one was called Orpha, and the other Ruth. And they dwelt there ten years.

5 And they both died, to wit, Mahalon and Chelion: and the woman was left alone, having lost both her sons and her husband.

6 And she arose to go from the land of Moab to her own country with both her · daughters-in-law: for she had heard that the Lord had looked upon his people, and had given them food.

7 Wherefore she went forth out of the place of her sojournment, with both her daughters-in-law: and being now in the way to return into the land of Juda,

8 She said to them: Go ye home to your mothers. The Lord deal mercifully with you, as you have dealt with the dead and with me.

9 May he grant you to find rest in the houses of the husbands which you shall take. And she kissed them. And they lifted up their voice and began to weep,

10 And to say: We will go on with thee to thy people.

11 But she answered them: Return, my daughters. Why come ye with me? Have I any more sons in my womb, that you may hope for husbands of me?

12 Return again, my daughters, and go your ways: for I am now spent with age, and not fit for wedlock. Although I might conceive this night, and bear children,

13 If you would wait till they were grown up, and come to man's estate, you would be old women before you marry. Do not so, my daughters, I beseech you: for I am grieved the more for your distress, and the hand of the Lord is gone out against me.

14 And they lifted up their voice, and began to weep again. Orpha kissed her mother-in-law and returned: Ruth stuck close to her mother-in-law.

15 And Noemi said to her: Behold thy kinswoman is returned to her people, and to her gods, go thou with her.

16 She answered: Be not against me, to desire that I should leave thee and depart. For whithersoever thou shalt go, I will go: and where thou shalt dwell, I also will dwell. Thy people *shall be* my people, and thy God my God.

17 The land that shall receive thee dying, in the same will I die: and there will I be buried. The Lord do so and so to me, and add more also, if aught but death part me and thee.

18 Then Noemi, seeing that Ruth was steadfastly determined to go with her, would not be against it, nor persuade her any more to return to her friends.

19 So they went together and came

CHAP. 1. Ver. 15. *To her gods.* Noemi did not mean to persuade Ruth to return to the false gods she had formerly worshipped: but by this manner of speech, insinuated to her, that if she would go with her, she must renounce her false gods and return to the Lord the God of Israel.
Ver. 17. *The Lord do so and so.* A form of swearing usual in the history of the Old Testament, by which the person wished such and such evils to fall upon them, if they did not do what they said.

to Bethlehem. And when they were come into the city, the report was quickly spread among all; and the women said: This is that Noemi.

20 But she said to them: Call me not Noemi (that is, beautiful), but call me Mara (that is, bitter), for the Almighty hath quite filled me with bitterness.

21 I went out full, and the Lord hath brought me back empty. Why then do you call me Noemi, whom the Lord hath humbled and the Almighty hath afflicted?

22 So Noemi came with Ruth the Moabitess her daughter-in-law, from the land of her sojournment: and returned into Bethlehem in the beginning of the barley harvest.

CHAPTER 2

Ruth gleaneth in the field of Booz, who sheweth her favour.

NOW her husband Elimelech had a kinsman, a powerful man, and very rich, whose name was Booz.

2 And Ruth the Moabitess said to her mother-inlaw: If thou wilt, I will go into the field, and glean the ears of corn that escape the hands of the reapers, wheresoever I shall find grace with a householder that will be favorable to me. And she answered her: Go, my daughter

3 She went therefore and gleaned the ears of corn after the reapers. And it happened that the owner of that field was Booz, who was of the kindred of Elimelech.

4 And, behold, he came out of Bethlehem, and said to the reapers: The Lord be with you. And they answered him: The Lord bless thee.

5 And Booz said to the young man that was set over the reapers: Whose maid is this?

6 And he answered him: This is the Moabitess who came with Noemi, from the land of Moab:

7 And she desired leave to glean the ears of corn that remain, following the steps of the reapers: and she hath been in the field from morning till now, and hath not gone home for one moment.

8 And Booz said to Ruth: Hear me, daughter, do not go to glean in any other field: and do not depart from this place: but keep with my maids:

9 And follow where they reap. For I have charged my young men, not to molest thee. And if thou art thirsty, go to the vessels, and drink of the waters whereof the servants drink.

10 She fell on her face and worshipping upon the ground, said to him: Whence cometh this to me, that I should find grace before thy eyes, and

that thou shouldst vouchsafe to take notice of me a woman of another country?

11 And he answered her: All hath been told me, that thou hast done to thy mother-in-law after the death of thy husband; and how thou hast left thy parents, and the land wherein thou wast born, and art come to a people which thou knewest not heretofore,

12 The Lord render unto thee for thy work: and mayest thou receive a full reward of the Lord the God of Israel, to whom thou art come, and under whose wings thou art fled.

13 And she said: I have found grace in thy eyes, my lord, who hast comforted me and hast spoken to the heart of thy handmaid, who am not like to one of thy maids.

14 And Booz said to her: At mealtime come thou hither, and eat of the bread, and dip thy morsel in the vinegar. So she sat at the side of the reapers, and she heaped to herself frumenty, and ate and was filled, and took the leavings.

15 And she arose from thence, to glean the ears of corn as before. And Booz commanded his servants, saying: If she would even reap with you, hinder her not.

16 And let fall some of your handfuls of purpose, and leave them, that she may gather them without shame: and let no man rebuke her when she gathereth them.

17 She gleaned therefore in the field till evening. And beating out with a rod and threshing what she had gleaned, she found about the measure of an ephi of barley, that is, three bushels:

18 Which she took up and returned into the city, and shewed it to her mother-in-law. Moreover she brought out, and gave her of the remains of her meat, wherewith she had been filled.

19 And her mother-in-law said to her: Where hast thou gleaned to-day, and where hast thou wrought? Blessed be he that hath had pity on thee. And she told her with whom she had wrought. And she told the man's name, that he was called Booz.

20 And Noemi answered her: Blessed be he of the Lord, because the same kindness which he shewed to the living, he hath kept also to the dead. And again she said: The man is our kinsman.

21 And Ruth said: He also charged me, that I should keep close to his reapers, till all the corn should be reaped.

22 And her mother-in-law said to her: It is better for thee, my daughter, to go out to reap with his maids, lest

in another man's field some one may resist thee.

23 So she kept close to the maids of Booz: and continued to glean with them, till all the barley and the wheat were laid up in the barns.

CHAPTER 3

Ruth instructed by her mother-in-law lieth at Booz's feet, claiming him for her husband by the law of affinity. She receiveth a good answer, and six measures of barley.

AFTER she was returned to her mother-in-law, Noemi said to her: My daughter, I will seek rest for thee, and will provide that it may be well with thee.

2 This Booz, with whose maids thou wast joined in the field, is our near kinsman: and, behold, this night he winnoweth barley in the threshingfloor.

3 Wash thyself therefore and anoint thee, and put on thy best garments, and go down to the barnfloor: but let not the man see thee, till he shall have done eating and drinking

4 And when he shall go to sleep, mark the place wherein he sleepeth. And thou shalt go in, and lift up the clothes wherewith he is covered towards his feet. And shalt lay thyself down there: and he will tell thee what thou must do.

5 She answered: Whatsoever thou shalt command, I will do.

6 And she went down to the barnfloor, and did all that her mother-in-law had bid her.

7 And when Booz had eaten, and drunk, and was merry, he went to sleep by the heap of sheaves: and she came softly and uncovering his feet, laid herself down.

8 And behold, when it was now midnight the man was afraid, and troubled: and he saw a woman lying at his feet,

9 And he said to her: Who art thou? And she answered: I am Ruth thy handmaid. Spread thy coverlet over thy servant, for thou art a near kinsman.

10 And he said: Blessed art thou of the Lord, my daughter, and thy latter kindness has surpassed the former: because thou hast not followed young men either poor or rich.

11 Fear not therefore, but whatsoever thou shalt say to me I will do to thee. For all the people that dwell within the gates of my city, know that thou art a virtuous woman.

12 Neither do I deny myself to be near of kin, but there is another nearer than I.

13 Rest thou this night: and when morning is come, if he will take thee by the right of kindred, all is well. But if he will not, I will undoubtedly take thee, *as* the Lord liveth. Sleep till the morning.

14 So she slept at his feet till the night was going off. And she arose before men could know one another, and Booz said: Beware lest any man know that thou camest hither.

15 And again he said: Spread thy mantle, wherewith thou art covered, and hold it with both hands. And when she spread it and held it, he measured six measures of barley, and laid it upon her. And she carried it and went into the city,

16 And came to her mother-in-law; who said to her: What hast thou done, daughter: And she told her all that the man had done to her.

17 And she said: Behold he hath given me six measures of barley; for he said: I will not have thee return empty to thy mother-in-law.

18 And Noemi said: Wait my daughter, till we see what end the thing will have. For the man will not rest until he have accomplished what he hath said.

CHAPTER 4

Upon the refusal of the nearer kinsman, Booz marrieth Ruth, who bringeth forth Obed, the grandfather of David.

THEN Booz went up to the gate, and sat there. And when he had seen the kinsman going by, of whom he had spoken before, he said to him, calling him by his name: Turn aside for a little while, and sit down here. He turned aside, and sat down.

2 And Booz taking ten men of the ancients of the city, said to them: Sit ye down here.

3 They sat down, and he spoke to the kinsman: Noemi, who is returned from the country of Moab, will sell a parcel of land that belonged to our brother Elimelech.

4 I would have thee to understand this, and would tell thee before all that sit *here,* and before the ancients of my people. If thou wilt take possession of it by the right of kindred: buy it and possess it. But if it please thee not, tell me so, that I may know what I have to do. For there is no near kinsman besides thee, who art first, and me, who am second. But he answered: I will buy the field.

5 [1] And Booz said to him: When thou shalt buy the field at the woman's hand, thou must take also Ruth the Moabitess, who was the wife of the deceased: to

---

CHAP. 4. [1] Deut. 25, 7.

CHAP. 3. Ver. 10. *Thy latter kindness,* that is, to thy husband deceased in seeking to keep up his name and family by marrying his relation according to the law, and not following after young men. For Booz, it seems, was then in years.

raise up the name of thy kinsman in his inheritance.

6 He answered: I yield up my right of next akin; for I must not cut off the posterity of my own family. Do thou make use of my privilege, which I profess I do willingly forego.

7 Now this in former times was the manner in Israel between kinsmen, that if at any time one yielded his right to another: that the grant might be sure, the man put off his shoe, and gave it to his neighbour. This was a testimony of cession of right in Israel.

8 So Booz said to his kinsman: Put off thy shoe. And immediately he took it off from his foot.

9 And he said to the ancients and to all the people: You are witnesses this day, that I have bought all that was Elimelech's, and Chelion's, and Mahalon's, of the hand of Noemi.

10 And have taken to wife Ruth the Moabitess, the wife of Mahalon, to raise up the name of the deceased in his inheritance lest his name be cut off, from among his family and his brethren and his people. You, I say, are witnesses of this thing.

11 Then all the people that were in the gate, and the ancients answered: We are witnesses. The Lord make this woman who cometh into thy house, like Rachel, and Lia, who built up the house of Israel: that she may be an example of virtue in Ephrata, and may have a famous name in Bethlehem.

12 And that thy house may be, as the house of Phares, [2] whom Thamar bore unto Juda, of the seed which the Lord shall give thee of this young woman.

13 Booz therefore took Ruth, and married her and went in unto her: and the Lord gave her to conceive and bear a son.

14 And the women said to Noemi: Blessed be the Lord, who hath not suffered thy family to want a successor, that his name should be preserved in Israel.

15 And thou shouldst have one to comfort thy soul, and cherish thy old age. For he is born of thy daughter-in-law: who loveth thee: and is much better to thee, than if thou hadst seven sons.

16 And Noemi taking the child laid it in her bosom, and she carried it, and was a nurse unto it.

17 And the women her neighbours, congratulating with her and saying: There is a son born to Noemi: and they have called his name Obed. He is the father of Isai, the father of David.

18 These are the generations of Phares: [3] Phares begot Esron,

19 Esron begot Aram, Aram begot Aminadab,

20 Aminadab begot Nahasson, Nahasson begot Salmon,

21 Salmon begot Booz, Booz begot Obed,

22 Obed begot Isai, Isai begot David.

THE FIRST BOOK OF

SAMUEL

OTHERWISE CALLED THE

FIRST BOOK OF KINGS

This and the following Book are called by the Hebrews the books of Samuel, because they contain the history of Samuel, and of the two kings, Saul and David, whom he anointed. They are more commonly named by the Fathers, the First and Second book of Kings. As to the writer of them, it is common opinion that Samuel composed the first book, as far as the twenty-fifth chapter; and that the prophets Nathan and Gad finished the first, and wrote the second book. See 1 Paralipomenon, otherwise 1 Chronicles, 23, 29.

CHAPTER 1

Anna the wife of Elcana being barren, by vow and prayer obtaineth a son, whom she calleth Samuel. She presenteth him

[1] Gen. 38, 29. [3] 1 Par. 2, 5; 4, 1; Matt. 1, 3.

CHAP. 4. Ver. 11. *Ephrata.* Another name for Bethlehem.

CHAP. 1. Ver. 1. *An Ephraimite.* He was of the tribe of Levi (1 Par. 6, 34), but is called an Ephraimite from dwelling in mount Ephraim.

to the service of God in Silo, according to her vow.

THERE was a man of Ramathaimso-phim, of mount Ephraim, and his name was Elcana, the son of Jeroham, the son of Eliu, the son of Thohu, the son of Suph, an Ephraimite.

2 And he had two wives, the name of one was Anna, and the name of the

other Phenenna. Phenenna had children: but Anna had no children.

3 And this man went up out of his city upon the appointed days, to adore and to offer sacrifice to the Lord of hosts in Silo. And the two sons of Heli, Ophni and Phinees, were there priests of the Lord.

4 Now the day came, and Elcana offered sacrifice, and gave to Phenenna his wife, and to all her sons and daughters, portions.

5 But to Anna he gave one portion with sorrow, because he loved Anna. And the Lord had shut up her womb.

6 Her rival also afflicted her, and troubled her exceedingly, insomuch that she upbraided her, that the Lord had shut up her womb.

7 And thus she did every year, when the time returned that they went up to the temple of the Lord; and thus she provoked her. But Anna wept, and did not eat.

8 Then Elcana her husband said to her: Anna, why weepest thou? And why dost thou not eat? And why dost thou afflict thy heart? Am not I better to thee than ten children?

9 So Anna arose after she had eaten and drunk in Silo. And, Heli the priest sitting upon a stool before the door of the temple of the Lord,

10 As Anna had her heart full of grief, she prayed to the Lord, shedding many tears.

11 And she made a vow, saying: O Lord of hosts, if thou wilt look down on the affliction of thy servant, and wilt be mindful of me, and not forget thy handmaid, and wilt give to thy servant a man child: I will give him to the Lord all the days of his life, and no razor shall come upon his head.

12 And it came to pass, as she multiplied prayers before the Lord, that Heli observed her mouth.

13 Now Anna spoke in her heart, and only her lips moved: but her voice was not heard at all. Heli therefore thought her to be drunk,

14 And said to her: How long wilt thou be drunk? Digest a little the wine, of which thou hast taken too much.

15 Anna answering, said: Not so, my lord: for I am an exceeding unhappy woman, and have drunk neither wine nor any strong drink, but I have poured out my soul before the Lord.

16 Count not thy handmaid for one of the daughters of Belial: for out of the abundance of my sorrow and grief have I spoken till now.

17 Then Heli said to her: Go in peace: and the God of Israel grant thee thy petition, which thou hast asked of him.

18 And she said: Would to God thy handmaid may find grace in thy eyes. So the woman went on her way, and ate, and her countenance was no more changed.

19 And they rose in the morning, and worshipped before the Lord: and they returned, and came into their house at Ramatha. And Elcana knew Anna his wife: and the Lord remembered her.

20 And it came to pass when the time was come about, Anna conceived and bore a son, and called his name Samuel: because she had asked him of the Lord.

21 And Elcana her husband went up, and all his house, to offer to the Lord the solemn sacrifice, and his vow.

22 But Anna went not up. For she said to her husband: I will not go till the child be weaned, and till I may carry him, that he may appear before the Lord, and may abide always there.

23 And Elcana her husband said to her: Do what seemeth good to thee, and stay till thou wean him; and I pray that the Lord may fulfil his word. So the woman stayed at home, and gave her son suck, till she weaned him.

24 And after she had weaned him, she carried him with her, with three calves, and three bushels of flour, and a bottle of wine, and she brought him to the house of the Lord in Silo. Now the child was as yet very young.

25 And they immolated a calf, and offered the child to Heli.

26 And Anna said: I beseech thee, my lord, as thy soul liveth, my lord: I am that woman who stood before thee here praying to the Lord.

27 For this child did I pray, and the Lord hath granted me my petition, which I asked of him.

28 Therefore I also have lent him to the Lord. All the days of his life he shall be lent to the Lord. And they adored the Lord there. And Anna prayed, and said:

CHAPTER 2

The canticle of Anna. The wickedness of the sons of Heli; for which they are not duly corrected by their father. A prophesy against the house of Heli.

Ⓜ Y heart hath rejoiced in the Lord, and my horn is exalted in my God: my mouth is enlarged over my enemies, because I have joyed in thy salvation.

2 There is none holy as the Lord is:

Ver. 20. *Samuel.* This name imports, *asked of God.*

Chap. 2. Ver 1. *My horn.* The *horn* in the scriptures signifies strength, power, and glory; so the horn is said to be exalted, when a person receives an increase of strength or glory.

for there is no other beside thee, and there is none strong like our God.

3 Do not multiply to speak lofty things, boasting: let old matters depart from your mouth. For the Lord is a God of all knowledge, and to him are thoughts prepared.

4 The bow of the mighty is overcome: and the weak are girt with strength.

5 They that were full before have hired out themselves for bread: and the hungry are filled; so that the barren hath borne many: and she that had many children is weakened.

6 [1] The Lord killeth and maketh alive: he bringth down to hell and bringeth back again.

7 The Lord maketh poor and maketh rich: he humbleth and he exalteth.

8 He raiseth up the needy from the dust, and lifteth up the poor from the dunghill: that he may sit with princes, and hold the throne of glory. For the poles of the earth are the Lord's, and upon them he hath set the world.

9 He will keep the feet of his saints, and the wicked shall be silent in darkness: because no man shall prevail by his own strength.

10 The adversaries of the Lord shall fear him: and upon them shall he thunder in the heavens. The Lord shall judge the ends of the earth; and he shall give empire to his king, and shall exalt the horn of his Christ.

11 And Elcana went to Ramatha, to his house: but the child ministered in the sight of the Lord before the face of Heli the priest.

12 Now the sons of Heli were children of Belial, not knowing the Lord,

13 Nor the office of the priests to the people: but whosoever had offered a sacrifice, the servant of the priest came, while the flesh was in boiling, with a fleshhook of three teeth in his hand;

14 And thrust it into the kettle, or into the caldron, or into the pot, or into the pan: and all that the fleshhook brought up, the priest took to himself. Thus did they to all Israel that came to Silo.

15 Also before they burnt the fat, the servant of the priest came, and said to

CHAP. 2. [1] Deut. 32, 39; Tob. 13, 2; Wisd. 16, 13.

Ver. 25. *Who shall pray for him.* By these words Heli would have his sons understand, that by their wicked abuse of sacred things, and of the very sacrifices which were appointed to appease the Lord, they deprived themselves of the ordinary means of reconciliation with God; which was by sacrifices. The more, because as they were the *chief priests* whose business it was to intercede for all others, they had no other to offer sacrifices and to make atonement for them. —*Because the Lord would slay them.* In consequence of their manifold sacrileges, he would not soften their hearts with his efficacious grace, but was determined to destroy them.

the man that sacrificed: Give me flesh to boil for the priest: for I will not take of thee sodden flesh, but raw.

16 And he that sacrificed said to him: Let the fat first be burnt to-day according to the custom, and then take as much as thy soul desireth. But he answered and said to him: Not so; but thou shalt give it me now, or else I will take it by force.

17 Wherefore the sin of the young men was exceeding great before the Lord: because they withdrew men from the sacrifice of the Lord.

18 But Samuel ministered before the face of the Lord: being a child girded with a linen ephod.

19 And his mother made him a little coat, which she brought to him on the appointed days, when she went up with her husband, to offer the solemn sacrifice.

20 And Heli blessed Elcana and his wife. And he said to him: The Lord give thee seed of this woman, for the loan thou hast lent to the Lord. And they went to their own home.

21 And the Lord visited Anna: and she conceived, and bore three sons and two daughters. And the child Samuel became great before the Lord.

22 Now Heli was very old, and he heard all that his sons did to all Israel: and how they lay with the women that waited at the door of the tabernacle.

23 And he said to them: Why do ye these kinds of things, which I hear, very wicked things, from all the people?

24 Do not so, my sons: for it is no good report that I hear, that you make the people of the Lord to transgress.

25 If one man shall sin against another, God may be appeased in his behalf: but if a man shall sin against the Lord, who shall pray for him? And they hearkened not to the voice of their father, because the Lord would slay them.

26 But the child Samuel advanced, and grew on, and pleased both the Lord and men.

27 And there came a man of God to Heli, and said to him: Thus saith the Lord: Did I not plainly appear to thy father's house, when they were in Egypt in the house of Pharao?

28 And I chose him out of all the tribes of Israel to be my priest, to go up to my altar, and burn incense to me, and to wear the ephod before me: and I gave to thy father's house of all the sacrifices of the children of Israel.

29 Why have you kicked away my victims, and my gifts which I commanded to be offered in the temple: and thou hast rather honoured thy sons

than me, to eat the firstfruits of every sacrifice of my people Israel?

30 Wherefore thus saith the Lord the God of Israel: [2] I said indeed that thy house, and the house of thy father should minister in my sight, for ever. But now saith the Lord: Far be this from me. But whosoever shall glorify me, him will I glorify; but they that despise me, shall be despised.

31 Behold the days come: and I will cut off thy arm, and the arm of thy father's house, that there shall not be an old man in thy house.

32 And thou shalt see thy rival in the temple, in all the prosperity of Israel, and there shall not be an old man in thy house for ever.

33 However I will not altogether take away a man of thee from my altar: but that thy eyes may faint and thy soul be spent. And a great part of thy house shall die when they come to man's estate.

34 And this shall be a sign to thee, that shall come upon thy two sons, Ophni and Phinees: In one day they shall both of them die.

35 And I will raise me up a faithful priest, who shall do according to my heart, and my soul; and I will build him a faithful house; and he shall walk all days before my anointed.

36 And it shall come to pass, that whosoever shall remain in thy house, shall come that he may be prayed for; and shall offer a piece of silver, and a roll of bread; and shall say: Put me, I beseech thee, to somewhat of the priestly office, that I may eat a morsel of bread.

CHAPTER 3

Samuel is four times called by the Lord: who revealeth to him the evil that shall fall on Heli, and his house.

NOW the child Samuel ministered to the Lord before Heli. And the word of the Lord was precious in those days: there was no manifest vision.

2 And it came to pass one day when Heli lay in his place, and his eyes were grown dim, that he could not see:

3 Before the lamp of God went out, Samuel slept in the temple of the Lord, where the ark of God was.

4 And the Lord called Samuel. And he answered: Here am I.

5 And he ran to Heli and said: Here am I; for thou didst call me. He said: I did not call. Go back and sleep. And he went and slept.

6 And the Lord called Samuel again. And Samuel arose and went to Heli, and said: Here am I; for thou calledst me. He answered: I did not call thee, my son. Return and sleep.

7 Now Samuel did not yet know the Lord; neither had the word of the Lord been revealed to him.

8 And the Lord called Samuel again the third time. And he arose up and went to Heli.

9 And said: Here am I; for thou didst call me. Then Heli understood that the Lord called the child, and he said to Samuel: Go, and sleep. And if he shall call thee any more, thou shalt say: Speak, Lord, for thy servant heareth. So Samuel went and slept in his place.

10 And the Lord came and stood. And he called, as he had called the other times: Samuel, Samuel. And Samuel said: Speak, Lord, for thy servant heareth.

11 And the Lord said to Samuel: Behold I do a thing in Israel: and whosoever shall hear it, both his ears shall tingle.

12 In that day I will raise up against Heli all the things I have spoken concerning his house: I will begin, and I will make an end.

13 For I have foretold unto him, that I will judge his house for ever, for iniquity; because he knew that his sons did wickedly, and did not chastise them.

14 Therefore have I sworn to the house of Heli, that the iniquity of his house shall not be expiated with victims nor offerings for ever.

15 And Samuel slept till morning, and opened the doors of the house of the Lord. And Samuel feared to tell the vision to Heli.

16 Then Heli called Samuel, and said: Samuel, my son. And he answered: Here am I.

17 And he asked him: What is the word that the Lord hath spoken to thee? I beseech thee hide it not from me. May God do so and so to thee, and add so and so, if thou hide from me one word of all that were said to thee.

18 So Samuel told him all the words, and did not hide them from him. And he answered: It is the Lord. Let him do what is good in his sight.

19 And Samuel grew, and the Lord was with him: and not one of his words fell to the ground.

20 And all Israel from Dan to Bersabee, knew that Samuel was a faithful prophet of the Lord.

21 And the Lord again appeared in

[2] 3 Kings, 2, 27.

Ver. 32. *Thy rival.* A priest of another race. This was partly fulfilled, when Abiathar, of the race of Heli, was removed from the priesthood, and *Sadoc*, who was of another line, was substituted in his place. But it was more fully accomplished in the New Testament, when the priesthood of Aaron gave place to that of Christ. CHAP. 3. Ver. 1. *Precious.* That is, rare.

Silo; for the Lord revealed himself to Samuel in Silo, according to the word of the Lord. And the word of Samuel came to pass to all Israel.

CHAPTER 4

The Israelites being overcome by the Philistines, send for the ark of God: but they are beaten again. The sons of Heli are killed, and the ark taken. Upon the hearing of the news, Heli falleth backward and dieth.

AND it came to pass in those days, that the Philistines gathered themselves together to fight: and Israel went out to war against the Philistines, and camped by the Stone of Help. And the Philistines came to Aphec,

2 And put their army in array against Israel. And when they had joined battle, Israel turned their backs to the Philistines. And there was slain in that fight here and there in the fields about four thousand men.

3 And the people returned to the camp: and the ancients of Israel said: Why hath the Lord defeated us to-day before the Philistines? Let us fetch unto us the ark of the covenant of the Lord from Silo: and let it come in the midst of us, that it may save us from the hand of our enemies.

4 So the people sent to Silo; and they brought from thence the ark of the covenant of the Lord of hosts sitting upon the cherubims. And the two sons of Heli, Ophni and Phinees, were with the ark of the covenant of God.

5 And when the ark of the covenant of the Lord was come into the camp, all Israel shouted with a great shout, and the earth rang again.

6 And the Philistines heard the noise of the shout, and they said: What is this noise of a great shout in the camp of the Hebrews? And they understood that the ark of the Lord was come into the camp.

7 And the Philistines were afraid, saying: God is come into the camp. And sighing, they said:

8 Woe to us: for there was no such great joy yesterday and the day before. Woe to us. Who shall deliver us from the hand of these high gods? These are

the gods that struck Egypt with all the plagues in the desert.

9 Take courage and behave like men, ye Philistines: lest you come to be servants to the Hebrews, as they have served you. Take courage and fight.

10 So the Philistines fought; and Israel was overthrown; and every man fled to his own dwelling. And there was an exceeding great slaughter; for there fell of Israel thirty thousand footmen.

11 And the ark of God was taken: and the two sons of Heli, Ophni and Phinees, were slain.

12 And there ran a man of Benjamin out of the army, and came to Silo the same day, with his clothes rent, and his head strewed with dust.

13 And when he was come, Heli sat upon a stool over against the way watching. For his heart was fearful for the ark of God. And when the man was come into the city, he told it: and all the city cried out.

14 And Heli heard the noise of the cry, and he said: What meaneth the noise of this uproar? But he made haste, and came, and told Heli.

15 Now Heli was ninety and eight years old; and his eyes were dim, and he could not see.

16 And he said to Heli: I am he that came from the battle, and have fled out of the field this day. And he said to him: What is there done, my son?

17 And he that brought the news answered, and said: Israel has fled before the Philistines; and there has been a great slaughter of the people. Moreover thy two sons, Ophni and Phinees, are dead. And the ark of God is taken.

18 And when he had named the ark of God, he fell from his stool backwards by the door, and broke his neck, and died. For he was an old man, and far advanced in years. And he judged Israel forty years.

19 And his daughter-in-law the wife of Phinees, was big with child, and near her time. And hearing the news that the ark of God was taken, and her father-in-law, and her husband, were dead, she bowed herself and fell in labour: for her pains came upon her on a sudden.

20 And when she was upon the point of death, they that stood about her said to her: Fear not, for thou hast borne a son. She answered them not, nor gave heed to them.

21 And she called the child Ichabod, saying: The glory is gone from Israel, because the ark of God was taken, and for her father-in-law, and her husband.

22 And she said: The glory is departed from Israel, because the ark of God was taken.

CHAP. 4. Ver. 1. *The Stone of Help.* In Hebrew *Eben-ezer;* so called from the *help* which the Lord was pleased afterwards to give to his people Israel in that place by the prayers of Samuel (1 Kings, 7, 12).

Ver. 18. *Named the ark of God.* There is great reason, by all these circumstances, to hope that Heli died in a state of grace; and by his temporal punishments escaped the eternal.

Ver. 21. *Ichabod.* That is, *Where is the glory?* or, *There is no glory.* We see how much the Israelites lamented the loss of the ark, which was but the symbol of God's presence amongst them. How much more ought Christians to lament the loss of God himself, when by sin they have driven him out of their souls?

CHAPTER 5

*Dagon twice falleth down before the ark.
The Philistines are grievously afflicted,
wherever the ark cometh.*

AND the Philistines took the ark of God, and carried it from the Stone of Help into Azotus.

2 And the Philistines took the ark of God, and brought it into the temple of Dagon, and set it by Dagon.

3 And when the Azotians arose early the next day, behold Dagon lay upon his face on the ground before the ark of the Lord. And they took Dagon, and set him again in his place.

4 And the next day again, when they rose in the morning, they found Dagon lying upon his face on the earth before the ark of the Lord. And the head of Dagon, and both the palms of his hands were cut off upon the threshold:

5 And only the stump of Dagon remained in its place. For this cause neither the priests of Dagon, nor any that go into the temple tread on the threshold of Dagon in Azotus unto this day.

6 And the hand of the Lord was heavy upon the Azotians, and he destroyed them, and ¹ afflicted Azotus and the coasts thereof with emerods. And in the villages and fields in the midst of that country, there came forth a multitude of mice; and there was the confusion of a great mortality in the city.

7 And the men of Azotus seeing this kind of plague, said: The ark of the God of Israel shall not stay with us; for his hand is heavy upon us, and upon Dagon our god.

8 And sending, they gathered together all the lords of the Philistines to them, and said: What shall we do with the ark of the God of Israel? And the Gethrites answered: Let the ark of the God of Israel be carried about. And they carried the ark of the God of Israel about.

9 And while they were carrying it about, the hand of the Lord came upon every city with an exceeding great slaughter. And he smote the men of every city, both small and great, and they had emerods in their secret parts. And the Gethrites consulted together, and made themselves seats of skins.

10 Therefore they sent the ark of God into Accaron. And when the ark of God was come into Accaron, the Accaronites cried out, saying: They have brought the ark of the God of Israel to us, to kill us and our people.

11 They sent therefore and gathered together all the lords of the Philistines: and they said: Send away the ark of the God of Israel; and let it return into its own place, and not kill us and our people.

12 For there was the fear of death in every city; and the hand of God was exceeding heavy. The men also that did not die, were afflicted with the emerods: and the cry of every city went up to heaven.

CHAPTER 6

The ark is sent back to Bethsames: where many are slain for looking through curiosity into it.

NOW the ark of God was in the land of the Philistines seven months.

2 And the Philistines called for the priests and the diviners, saying: What shall we do with the ark of the Lord? Tell us how we are to send it back to its place? And they said:

3 If you send back the ark of the God of Israel, send it not away empty; but render unto him what you owe for sin. And then you shall be healed; and you shall know why his hand departeth not from you.

4 They answered: What is it we ought to render unto him for sin? And they answered:

5 According to the number of the provinces of the Philistines you shall make five golden emerods, and five golden mice; for the same plague hath been upon you all, and upon your lords. And you shall make the likeness of your emerods, and the likeness of the mice that have destroyed the land; and you shall give glory to the God of Israel, to see if he will take off his hand from you, and from your gods, and from your land.

6 Why do you harden your hearts, as Egypt and Pharao hardened their hearts? ¹ Did not he, after he was struck, then let them go, and they departed?

7 Now therefore take and make a new cart. And two kine that have calved, on which there hath come no yoke, tie to the cart; and shut up their calves at home.

8 And you shall take the ark of the Lord, and lay it on the cart. And the vessels of gold, which you have paid him for sin, you shall put into a little box, at the side thereof. And send it away that it may go.

9 And you shall look: and if it go up by the way of his own coasts towards Bethsames, then he hath done us this great evil. But if not, we shall know that it is not his hand hath touched us, but it hath happened by chance.

10 They did therefore in this manner: and taking two kine, that had

CHAP. 5. ¹ Ps. 77, 66. CHAP. 6. ¹ Exod. 12, 31.

suckling calves, they yoked them to the cart, and shut up their calves at home.

11 And they laid the ark of God upon the cart, and the little box that had in it the golden mice and the likeness of the emerods.

12 And the kine took the straight way that leadeth to Bethsames; and they went along the way, lowing as they went; and turned not aside neither to the right hand nor to the left. And the lords of the Philistines followed them as far as the borders of Bethsames.

13 Now the Bethsamites were reaping wheat in the valley: and lifting up their eyes they saw the ark, and rejoiced to see it.

14 And the cart came into the field of Josue a Bethsamite, and stood there. And there was a great stone; and they cut in pieces the wood of the cart, and laid the kine upon it, a holocaust to the Lord.

15 And the Levites took down the ark of God, and the little box that was at the side of it, wherein were the vessels of gold; and they put them upon the great stone. The men also of Bethsames offered holocausts and sacrificed victims that day to the Lord.

16 And the five princes of the Philistines saw: and they returned to Accaron the same day.

17 And these are the golden emerods, which the Philistines returned for sin to the Lord: For Azotus one, for Gaza one, for Ascalon one, for Geth one, for Accaron one:

18 And the golden mice according to the number of the cities of the Philistines, of the five provinces, from the fenced city to the village that was without wall, and to the great Abel (*the stone*) whereon they set down the ark of the Lord, which was till that day in the field of Josue the Bethsamite.

19 But he slew of the men of Bethsames, because they had seen the ark of the Lord: and he slew of the people seventy men, and fifty thousand of the common people. And the people lamented, because the Lord had smitten the people with a great slaughter.

20 And the men of Bethsames said: Who shall be able to stand before the Lord this holy God? And to whom shall he go up from us?

21 And they sent messengers to the inhabitants of Cariathiarim, saying: The Philistines have brought back the ark of the Lord. Come ye down and fetch it up to you.

CHAP. 7. ¹ Deut. 6, 13; Matt. 4, 10. ² Ecclus. 46, 21.

CHAP. 6. Ver. 19. *Seen.* Curiously looked into. It is likely this plague reached to all the neighbouring country, as well as the city of Bethsames.

CHAP. 7. Ver. 1. *In Gabaa.* That is, on the hill; for Gabaa signifieth a hill.

CHAPTER 7

The ark is brought to Cariathiarim. By Samuel's exhortation, the people cast away their idols and serve God alone. The Lord defeateth the Philistines, while Samuel offereth sacrifice.

AND the men of Cariathiarim came and fetched up the ark of the Lord and carried it into the house of Abinadab in Gabaa. And they sanctified Eleazar his son, to keep the ark of the Lord.

2 And it came to pass, that from the day the ark of the Lord abode in Cariathiarim days were multiplied (for it was now the twentieth year), and all the house of Israel rested following the Lord.

3 And Samuel spoke to all the house of Israel, saying: ¹ If you turn to the Lord with all your heart, put away the strange gods from among you, Baalim and Astaroth. And prepare your hearts unto the Lord, and serve him only; and he will deliver you out of the hand of the Philistines.

4 Then the children of Israel put away Baalim and Astaroth, and served the Lord only.

5 And Samuel said: Gather all Israel to Masphath, that I may pray to the Lord for you.

6 And they gathered together to Masphath. And they drew water, and poured it out before the Lord; and they fasted on that day, and they said there: We have sinned against the Lord. And Samuel judged the children of Israel in Masphath.

7 And the Philistines heard that the children of Israel were gathered together to Masphath; and the lords of the Philistines went up against Israel. And when the children of Israel heard this, they were afraid of the Philistines.

8 And they said to Samuel: Cease not to cry to the Lord our God for us, that he may save us out of the hand of the Philistines.

9 And Samuel took a sucking lamb, and offered it whole for a holocaust to the Lord: and Samuel cried to the Lord for Israel. And the Lord heard him.

10 And it came to pass, when Samuel was offering the holocaust, the Philistines began the battle against Israel: ² but the Lord thundered with a great thunder on that day upon the Philistines, and terrified them; and they were overthrown before the face of Israel.

11 And the men of Israel going out of Masphath pursued after the Philistines, and made slaughter of them till they came under Bethchar.

12 And Samuel took a stone, and laid

it between Masphath and Sen: and he called the place, the Stone of Help. And he said: Thus far the Lord hath helped us.

13 And the Philistines were humbled, and they did not come any more into the borders of Israel. And the hand of the Lord was against the Philistines, all the days of Samuel.

14 And the cities, which the Philistines had taken from Israel, were restored to Israel, from Accaron to Geth, and their borders. And he delivered Israel from the hand of the Philistines; and there was peace between Israel and the Amorrhites.

15 And Samuel judged Israel all the days of his life.

16 And he went every year about to Bethel and to Galgal and to Masphath; and he judged Israel in the aforesaid places.

17 And he returned to Ramatha: for there was his house, and there he judged Israel. He built also there an altar to the Lord.

CHAPTER 8

Samuel growing old, and his sons not walking in his ways, the people desire a king.

AND it came to pass when Samuel was old, that he appointed his sons to be judges over Israel.

2 Now the name of his firstborn son was Joel: and the name of the second was Abia, judges in Bersabee.

3 And his sons walked not in his ways: but they turned aside after lucre, and took bribes, and perverted judgment.

4 Then all the ancients of Israel being assembled, came to Samuel to Ramatha.

5 And they said to him: Behold thou art old, and thy sons walk not in thy ways. [1] Make us a king, to judge us, as all nations have.

6 And the word was displeasing in the eyes of Samuel, that they should say: Give us a king, to judge us. And Samuel prayed to the Lord.

7 And the Lord said to Samuel: Hearken to the voice of the people in all that they say to thee. For they have not rejected thee, but me, that I should not reign over them.

8 According to all their works, they have done from the day that I brought them out of Egypt until this day: as they have forsaken me, and served strange gods, so do they also unto thee.

9 Now therefore hearken to their voice: but yet testify to them, and foretell them the right of the king, that shall reign over them.

10 Then Samuel told all the words of the Lord to the people that had desired a king of him,

11 And said: This will be the right of the king, that shall reign over you. He will take your sons, and put them in his chariots, and will make them his horsemen, and his running footmen to run before his chariots.

12 And he will appoint of them to be his tribunes, and centurions, and to plough his fields, and to reap his corn, and to make him arms and chariots.

13 Your daughters also he will take to make him ointments, and to be his cooks, and bakers.

14 And he will take your fields, and your vineyards, and your best oliveyards, and give them to his servants.

15 Moreover he will take the tenth of your corn, and of the revenues of your vineyards, to give his eunuchs and servants.

16 Your servants also and handmaids, and your goodliest young men, and your asses he will take away, and put them to his work.

17 Your flocks also he will tithe, and you shall be his servants.

18 And you shall cry out in that day from the face of the king, whom you have chosen to yourselves: and the Lord will not hear you in that day, because you desired unto yourselves a king.

19 But the people would not hear the voice of Samuel, and they said: Nay: but there shall be a king over us.

20 And we also will be like all nations: and our king shall judge us, and go out before us, and fight our battles for us.

21 And Samuel heard all the words of the people, and rehearsed them in the ears of the Lord.

22 And the Lord said to Samuel: Hearken to their voice, and make them a king. And Samuel said to the men of Israel: Let every man go to his city.

CHAPTER 9

Saul seeking his father's asses, cometh to Samuel, by whom he is entertained.

NOW there was a man of Benjamin whose name was Cis, the son of Abiel, the son of Seror, the son of Bechorath, the son of Aphia, the son of a man of Jemini, valiant and strong.

2 And he had a son whose name was

CHAP. 8. [1] Osee, 13, 10; Acts, 13, 21.

CHAP. 8. Ver. 7. *They have not rejected thee, but me.* The government of Israel hitherto had been a theocracy; in which God himself immediately ruled, by laws which he had enacted, and by judges extraordinarily raised up by himself; and therefore he complains that his people rejected him, in desiring a change of government.

Ver. 9. *The right.* That is, the *manner* (misphat) after which he shall proceed, having no one to control him, when he has the power in his hand.

Saul, a choice and goodly man. And there was not among the children of Israel a goodlier person than he: from his shoulders and upward he appeared above all the people.

3 And the asses of Cis, Saul's father, were lost. And Cis said to his son Saul: Take one of the servants with thee; and arise. Go, and seek the asses. And when they had passed through mount Ephraim,

4 And through the land of Salisa, and had not found them, they passed also through the land of Salim; and they were not there: and through the land of Jemini, and found them not.

5 And when they were come to the land of Suph, Saul said to the servant that was with him: Come, let us return, lest perhaps my father forget the asses, and be concerned for us.

6 And he said to him: Behold there is a man of God in this city, a famous man: all that he saith, cometh certainly to pass. Now therefore let us go thither; perhaps he may tell us of our way, for which we are come.

7 And Saul said to his servant: Behold, we will go: *but* what shall we carry to the man of God? The bread is spent in our bags: and we have no present to make to the man of God, nor any thing at all.

8 The servant answered Saul again, and said: Behold there is found in my hand the fourth part of a sicle of silver. Let us give it to the man of God, that he may tell us our way.

9 Now in time past, in Israel when a man went to consult God he spoke thus: Come, let us go to the seer. For he that is now called a Prophet, in time past was called a Seer.

10 And Saul said to his servant: Thy word is very good. Come, let us go. And

CHAP. 9. [1] Acts 13, 21.

CHAP. 9. Ver. 9. *A seer.* Because of his *seeing* by divine light hidden things and things to come.

Ver. 12. *A sacrifice.* The law did not allow of sacrifices in any other place, but at the tabernacle or temple, in which the ark of the covenant was kept; but Samuel, by divine dispensation, offered sacrifices in other places. For which dispensation this reason may be alleged, that the house of God in Silo, having lost the ark, was now cast off; as a figure of the reprobation of the Jews (Ps. 77, 60, 67). And in Cariathiarim where the ark was, there was neither tabernacle, nor altar.—*The high place* (*Excelsum*). The *excelsa*, or *high places*, so often mentioned in scripture, were places of worship, in which were altars for sacrifice. These were sometimes employed in the service of the true God, as in the present case: but more frequently in the service of idols; and were called (which is commonly (though perhaps not so accurately) rendered *high places*; not because they were always upon hills, for the very worst of all, which was that of *Topheth* or *Geennom* (Jer. 19)), was in a valley; but because of the *high altars*, and *pillars*, or *monuments*, erected there, on which were set up the idols, or images of their deities.

they went into the city, where the man of God was.

11 And when they went up the ascent to the city, they found maids coming out to draw water, and they said to them: Is the seer here?

12 They answered and said to them: He is. Behold he is before you; make haste now. For he came to-day into the city; for there is a sacrifice of the people to-day in the high place.

13 As soon as you come into the city, you shall immediately find him, before he go up to the high place to eat. For the people will not eat till he come: because he blesseth the victim; and afterwards they eat that are invited. Now therefore go up, for to-day you shall find him.

14 And they went up into the city. And when they were walking in the midst of the city, behold Samuel was coming out over against them, to go up to the high place.

15 [1] Now the Lord had revealed to the ear of Samuel the day before Saul came, saying:

16 To-morrow about this same hour I will send thee a man of the land of Benjamin. And thou shalt anoint him to be ruler over my people Israel; and he shall save my people out of the hand of the Philistines: for I have looked down upon my people, because their cry is come to me.

17 And when Samuel saw Saul, the Lord said to him: Behold the man, of whom I spoke to thee. This man shall reign over my people.

18 And Saul came to Samuel in the midst of the gate and said: Tell me, I pray thee, where is the house of the seer?

19 And Samuel answered Saul, saying: I am the seer. Go up before me to the high place, that you may eat with me to-day; and I will let thee go in the morning. And tell thee all that is in thy heart.

20 And as for the asses, which were lost three days ago, be not solicitous, because they are found. And for whom shall be all the best things of Israel? Shall they not be for thee and for all thy father's house?

21 And Saul answering said: Am not I a son of Jemini of the least tribe of Israel, and my kindred the last among all the families of the tribe of Benjamin? Why then hast thou spoken this word to me?

22 Then Samuel taking Saul and his servant, brought them into the parlour, and gave them a place at the head of them that were invited. For there were about thirty men.

23 And Samuel said to the cook: Bring the portion, which I gave thee, and commanded thee to set it apart by thee.

24 And the cook took up the shoulder, and set it before Saul. And Samuel said: Behold what is left. Set it before thee, and eat: because it was kept of purpose for thee, when I invited the people. And Saul ate with Samuel that day.

25 And they went down from the high place into the town. And he spoke with Saul upon the top of the house: and he prepared a bed for Saul on the top of the house; and he slept.

26 And when they were risen in the morning, and it began now to be light, Samuel called Saul on the top of the house, saying: Arise, that I may let thee go. And Saul arose. And they went out both of them: to wit, he and Samuel.

27 And as they were going down in the end of the city, Samuel said to Saul: Speak to the servant to go before us, and pass on. But stand thou still a while, that I may tell thee the word of the Lord.

CHAPTER 10

Saul is anointed. He prophesieth, and is changed into another man. Samuel calleth the people together, to make a king. The lot falleth on Saul.

AND [1] Samuel took a little vial of oil, and poured it upon his head; and kissed him; and said: Behold, the Lord hath anointed thee to be prince over his inheritance: and thou shalt deliver his people out of the hands of their enemies, that are round about them. And this shall be a sign unto thee, that God hath anointed thee to be prince.

2 When thou shalt depart from me this day, thou shalt find two men by the sepulchre of Rachel in the borders of Benjamin to the south. And they shall say to thee: The asses are found which thou wentest to seek; and thy father thinking no more of the asses is concerned for you, and saith: What shall I do for my son?

3 And when thou shalt depart from thence, and go farther on, and shalt come to the oak of Thabor, there shall meet thee three men going up to God to Bethel, one carrying three kids, and another three loaves of bread, and another carrying a bottle of wine.

4 And they will salute thee, and will give thee two loaves. And thou shalt take them at their hand.

5 After that thou shalt come to the hill of God, where the garrison of the Philistines is. And when thou shalt be come there into the city, thou shalt meet a company of prophets coming down from the high place, with a psaltery and a timbrel, and a pipe, and a harp before them; and they shall be prophesying.

6 And the spirit of the Lord shall come upon thee. And thou shalt prophesy with them, and shalt be changed into another man.

7 When therefore these signs shall happen to thee, do whatsoever thy hand shall find, for the Lord is with thee.

8 And thou shalt go down before me to Galgal (for I will come down to thee), that thou mayest offer an oblation, and sacrifice, victims of peace. Seven days shalt thou wait, [2] till I come to thee: and I will shew thee what thou art to do.

9 So when he had turned his back to go from Samuel, God gave unto him another heart: and all these things came to pass that day.

10 And they came to the foresaid hill, and behold a company of prophets met him. And the spirit of the Lord came upon him, and he prophesied in the midst of them.

11 And all that had known him yesterday and the day before, seeing that he was with the prophets, and prophesied, said to each other: What is this that hath happened to the son of Cis? *Is* Saul also among the prophets?

12 And one answered another, saying: And who is their father? Therefore it became a proverb: [3] Is Saul also among the prophets?

13 And when he had made an end of prophesying, he came to the high place.

14 And Saul's uncle said to him, and to his servant: Whither went you? They answered: To seek the asses: and not finding them we went to Samuel.

15 And his uncle said to him: Tell me what Samuel said to thee.

16 And Saul said to his uncle: He told us that the asses were found. But of the matter of the kingdom of which Samuel had spoken to him, he told him not.

CHAP. 10. [1] Acts 13, 21. [2] 1 Kings, 13, 8. [3] 1 Kings, 19, 24.

CHAP. 10. Ver. 3. *Bethel.* Where there was at that time an altar of God; it being one of the places where Samuel judged Israel.
Ver. 5. *The hill of God.* Gabaa, in which there was also at that time, a *high place* or *altar.*—*Prophets.* These were men whose office it was to sing hymns and praises to God; for such in holy writ are called *prophets,* and their singing praises to God is called *prophesying* (1 Par., or 1 Chron. 15, 22; 25, 1). Now there were in those days colleges, or schools for training up these prophets; and it seems there was one of these schools at this *hill of God;* and another at Najoth in Ramatha (1 Kings, 19, 20, 21).
Ver. 8. *Galgal.* Here also by dispensation was an altar of God.
Ver. 12. *Their father.* That is, their teacher or superior. As much as to say, Who could bring such a wonderful change as to make Saul a prophet?

17 And Samuel called together the people to the Lord in Maspha.

18 And he said to the children of Israel: Thus saith the Lord the God of Israel: I brought up Israel out of Egypt, and delivered you from the hand of the Egyptians, and from the hand of all the kings who afflicted you.

19 But you this day have rejected your God, who only hath saved you out of all your evils and your tribulations; and you have said: ⁴ Nay: but set a king over us. Now therefore stand before the Lord by your tribes, and by your families.

20 And Samuel brought to him all the tribes of Israel, and the lot fell on the tribe of Benjamin.

21 And he brought the tribe of Benjamin and the kindreds thereof. and the lot fell upon the kindred of Metri: and it came to Saul the son of Cis. They sought him therefore and he was not found.

22 And after this they consulted the Lord whether he would come thither. And the Lord answered: Behold he is hidden at home.

23 And they ran and fetched him thence. And he stood in the midst of the people; and he was higher than any of the people from the shoulders and upward.

24 And Samuel said to all the people: Surely you see him whom the Lord hath chosen, that there is none like him among all the people. And all the people cried and said: God save the king.

25 And Samuel told the people the law of the kingdom, and wrote it in a book, and laid it up before the Lord: and Samuel sent away all the people, every one to his own house.

26 Saul also departed to his own house in Gabaa: and there went with him a part of the army, whose hearts God had touched.

27 But the children of Belial said: Shall this fellow be able to save us? And they despised him, and brought him no presents. But he dissembled as though he heard not.

CHAPTER 11

Saul defeateth the Ammonites, and delivereth Jabes Galaad.

AND it came to pass about a month after this that Naas, the Ammonite came up, and began to fight against Jabes Galaad. And all the men of Jabes said to Naas: Make a covenant with us; and we will serve thee.

2 And Naas the Ammonite answered them: On this condition will I make a covenant with you, that I may pluck out all your right eyes, and make you a reproach in all Israel.

3 And the ancients of Jabes said to him: Allow us seven days, that we may send messengers to all the coasts of Israel, and if there be no one to defend us, we will come out to thee.

4 The messengers therefore came to Gabaa of Saul: and they spoke these words in the hearing of the people. And all the people lifted up their voices, and wept.

5 And behold Saul came, following oxen out of the field, and he said: What aileth the people that they weep? And they told him the words of the men of Jabes.

6 And the spirit of the Lord came upon Saul, when he had heard these words; and his anger was exceedingly kindled.

7 And taking both the oxen, he cut them in pieces, and sent them into all the coasts of Israel by messengers, saying: Whosoever shall not come forth, and follow Saul and Samuel, so shall it be done to his oxen. And the fear of the Lord fell upon the people, and they went out as one man.

8 And he numbered them in Bezec. And there were of the children of Israel three hundred thousand: and of the men of Juda thirty thousand.

9 And they said to the messengers that came: Thus shall you say to the men of Jabes Galaad: To-morrow, when the sun shall be hot, you shall have relief. The messengers therefore came, and told the men of Jabes; and they were glad.

10 And they said: In the morning we will come out to you; and you shall do what you please with us.

11 And it came to pass, when the morrow was come that Saul put the people in three companies. And he came into the midst of the camp in the morning watch; and he slew the Ammonites until the day grew hot. And the rest were scattered, so that two of them were not left together.

12 And the people said to Samuel: ¹ Who is he that said: Shall Saul reign over us? Bring the men and we will kill them.

13 And Saul said: No man shall be killed this day, because the Lord this day hath wrought salvation in Israel.

14 And Samuel said to the people: Come and let us to go Galgal, and let us renew the kingdom there.

15 And all the people went to Galgal. And there they made Saul king before the Lord in Galgal; and they sacrificed there victims of peace before the Lord. And there Saul and all the men of Israel rejoiced exceedingly.

⁴ 1 Kings, 8, 19. Chap. 11. ¹ Kings, 10, 27.

CHAPTER 12

Samuel's integrity is acknowledged. God sheweth by a sign from heaven that they had done ill in asking for a king.

AND Samuel said to all Israel: Behold I have hearkened to your voice in all that you said to me, and have made a king over you.

2 And now the king goeth before you. But I am old and greyheaded: and my sons are with you. Having then conversed with you from my youth unto this day, behold here I am.

3 ¹ Speak of me before the Lord, and before his anointed, whether I have taken any man's ox, or ass: If I have wronged any man: If I have oppressed any man: If I have taken a bribe at any man's hand. And I will despise it this day, and will restore it to you.

4 And they said: Thou hast not wronged us, nor oppressed us, nor taken ought at any man's hand.

5 And he said to them: The Lord is witness against you; and his anointed is witness this day, that you have not found any thing in my hand. And they said: He is witness.

6 And Samuel said to the people: *It is* the Lord, who made Moses and Aaron, and brought our fathers out of the land of Egypt.

7 Now therefore stand up, that I may plead in judgment against you before the Lord, concerning all the kindness of the Lord, which he hath shewn to you, and to your fathers:

8 ² How Jacob went into Egypt, and your fathers cried to the Lord: and the Lord sent Moses and Aaron, and brought your fathers out of Egypt; and made them dwell in this place.

9 And they forgot the Lord their God: ³ and he delivered them into the hands of Sisera, captain of the army of Hasor, and into the hands of the Philistines, and into the hand of the king of Moab: and they fought against them.

10 But afterwards they cried to the Lord, and said: We have sinned, because we have forsaken the Lord, and have served Baalim and Astaroth. But now deliver us from the hand of our enemies, and we will serve thee.

11 ⁴ And the Lord sent Jerobaal, and Badan, and Jephte, and Samuel, and delivered you from the hand of your enemies round about: and you dwelt securely.

12 But seeing that Naas king of the children of Ammon was come against you, you said to me: ⁵ Nay, but a king shall reign over us: whereas the Lord your God was your king.

13 Now therefore your king is here, whom you have chosen and desired: Behold the Lord hath given you a king.

14 If you will fear the Lord, and serve him, and hearken to his voice, and not provoke the mouth of the Lord: then shall both you, and the king who reigneth over you, be followers of the Lord your God.

15 But if you will not hearken to the voice of the Lord, but will rebel against his words, the hand of the Lord shall be upon you, and upon your fathers.

16 Now then stand, and see this great thing which the Lord will do in your sight.

17 Is it not wheat harvest to-day? I will call upon the Lord, and he shall send thunder and rain. And you shall know and see that you yourselves have done a great evil in the sight of the Lord, in desiring a king over you.

18 And Samuel cried unto the Lord: and the Lord sent thunder and rain that day.

19 And all the people greatly feared the Lord and Samuel. And all the people said to Samuel: Pray for thy servants to the Lord thy God, that we may not die; for we have added to all our sins this evil, to ask for a king.

20 And Samuel said to the people: Fear not. You have done all this evil: but yet depart not from following the Lord; but serve the Lord with all your heart.

21 And turn not aside after vain things which shall never profit you, nor deliver you, because they are vain.

22 And the Lord will not forsake his people for his great name's sake: because the Lord hath sworn to make you his people.

23 And far from me be this sin against the Lord, that I should cease to pray for you. And I will teach you the good and right way.

24 Therefore fear the Lord, and serve him in truth and with your whole heart; for you have seen the great works which he hath done among you.

25 But if you will still do wickedly: both you and your king shall perish together.

CHAPTER 13

The war between Saul and the Philistines. The distress of the Israelites. Saul offereth sacrifice before the coming of Samuel; for which he is reproved.

CHAP. 12. ¹ Ecclus. 46, 22. ² Gen. 46, 5. ³ Judges, 4, 2. ⁴ Judges, 6, 14. ⁵ 1 Kings, 8, 19; 10, 19.

CHAP. 12. Ver. 11. *Jerobaal and Badan.* That is, Gedeon and Samson, called here Badan or Bedan, because he was of Dan.

Ver. 17. *Wheat harvest.* At which time of the year, it never thunders or rains in those countries.

SAUL was a child of one year when he began to reign, and he reigned two years over Israel.

2 And Saul chose him three thousand men of Israel. And two thousand were with Saul in Machmas, and in mount Bethel: and a thousand with Jonathan in Gabaa of Benjamin. And the rest of the people he sent back every man to their dwellings.

3 And Jonathan smote the garrison of the Philistines which was in Gabaa. And when the Philistines had heard of it, Saul sounded the trumpet over all the land, saying: Let the Hebrews hear.

4 And all Israel heard this report: Saul hath smitten the garrison of the Philistines. And Israel took courage against the Philistines. And the people were called together after Saul to Galgal.

5 The Philistines also were assembled to fight against Israel: thirty thousand chariots, and six thousand horsemen, and a multitude of people besides, like the sand on the sea shore for number. And going up they camped in Machmas at the east of Bethaven.

6 And when the men of Israel saw that they were straitened (for the people were distressed), they hid themselves in caves, and in thickets, and in rocks, and in dens, and in pits.

7 And *some of* the Hebrews passed over the Jordan into the land of Gad and Galaad. And when Saul was yet in Galgal, all the people that followed him were greatly afraid.

8 And he waited seven days according to the appointment of Samuel; [1] and Samuel came not to Galgal. And the people slipt away from him.

9 Then Saul said: Bring me the holocaust, and the peace offerings. And he offered the holocaust.

10 And when he had made an end of offering the holocaust, behold Samuel came: and Saul went forth to meet him and salute him.

11 And Samuel said to him: What hast thou done? Saul answered: Because I saw that the people slipt from me, and thou wast not come according to the days appointed, and the Philistines were gathered together in Machmas.

12 I said: Now will the Philistines come down upon me to Galgal; and I have not appeased the face of the Lord. Forced by necessity, I offered the holocaust.

13 And Samuel said to Saul: Thou hast done foolishly, and hast not kept the commandments of the Lord thy God, which he commanded thee. And if thou hadst not done thus, the Lord would now have established thy kingdom over Israel for ever.

14 But thy kingdom shall not continue. [2] The Lord hath sought him a man according to his own heart: and him hath the Lord commanded to be prince over his people, because thou hast not observed that which the Lord commanded.

15 And Samuel arose and went up from Galgal to Gabaa of Benjamin. And the rest of the people went up after Saul, to meet the people who fought against them, going from Galgal to Gabaa in the hill of Benjamin. And Saul numbered the people, that were found with him, about six hundred men.

16 And Saul and Jonathan his son, and the people that were present with them, were in Gabaa of Benjamin: but the Philistines encamped in Machmas.

17 And there went out of the camp of the Philistines three companies to plunder. One company went towards the way of Ephra to the land of Sual,

18 And another went by the way of Beth-horon; and the third turned to the way of the border, above the valley of Seboim towards the desert.

19 Now there was no smith to be found in all the land of Israel; for the Philistines had taken this precaution, lest the Hebrews should make them swords or spears.

20 So all Israel went down to the Philistines, to sharpen every man his ploughshare, and his spade, and his axe, and his rake.

21 So that their shares, and their spades, and their forks, and their axes were blunt, even to the goad, which was to be mended.

22 And when the day of battle was come, there was neither sword nor spear found in the hand of any of the people that were with Saul and Jonathan, except Saul and Jonathan his son.

23 And the army of the Philistines went out in order to advance further in Machmas.

CHAPTER 14

Jonathan attacketh the Philistines. A miraculous victory. Saul's unadvised oath, by which Jonathan is put in danger of his life, but is delivered by the people.

NOW it came to pass one day that Jonathan the son of Saul said to the young man that bore his armour: Come, and let us go over to the garrison of the Philistines, which is on the other side of yonder place. But he told not this to his father

---

CHAP. 13. [1] Kings, 10, 8. [2] Acts, 13, 22. CHAP. 14. [1] Kings, 4, 21.

CHAP. 13. Ver. 1. *Of one year.* That is, he was good and like an innocent child, and for two years continued in that innocency.

2 And Saul abode in the uttermost part of Gabaa under the pomegranate tree, which was in Magron: and the people with him were about six hundred men.

3 And Achias the son of Achitob brother to Ichabod the son of Phinees, [1] the son of Heli the priest of the Lord in Silo, wore the ephod. And the people knew not whither Jonathan was gone.

4 Now there were between the ascents, by which Jonathan sought to go over to the garrison of the Philistines, rocks standing up on both sides, and steep cliffs like teeth on the one side, and on the other. The name of the one was Boses, and the name of the other was Sene.

5 One rock stood out towards the north over against Machmas; and the other to the south over against Gabaa.

6 And Jonathan said to the young man that bore his armour: Come, let us go over to the garrison of these uncircumcised. It may be the Lord will do for us, because it is easy for the Lord to save either by many, or by few.

7 And his armourbearer said to him: Do all that pleaseth thy mind. Go whither thou wilt, and I will be with thee wheresoever thou hast a mind.

8 And Jonathan said: Behold we will go over to these men. And when we shall be seen by them,

9 If they shall speak thus to us: Stay till we come to you: Let us stand still in our place, and not go up to them.

10 But if they shall say: Come up to us; Let us go up, because the Lord hath delivered them into our hands. This shall be a sign unto us.

11 So both of them discovered themselves to the garrison of the Philistines. And the Philistines said: Behold the Hebrews come forth out of the holes wherein they were hid.

12 And the men of the garrison spoke to Jonathan, and to his armourbearer, and said: Come up to us, and we will shew you a thing. And Jonathan said to his armourbearer: Let us go up. Follow me; [2] for the Lord hath delivered them into the hands of Israel.

13 And Jonathan went up creeping on his hands and feet; and his armourbearer after him. And some fell before Jonathan: others his armourbearer slew as he followed him.

14 And the first slaughter which Jonathan and his armourbearer made, was of about twenty men, within half an acre of land, which a yoke of oxen is wont to plough in a day.

15 And there was a miracle in the camp, through the fields: yea and all the people of their garrison, who had gone out to plunder, were amazed. And the earth trembled: and it happened as a miracle from God.

16 And the watchmen of Saul, who were in Gabaa of Benjamin looked. And behold a multitude overthrown, and fleeing this way and that.

17 And Saul said to the people that were with him: Look, and see who is gone from us. And when they had sought, it was found that Jonathan and his armourbearer were not there.

18 And Saul said to Achias: Bring the ark of the Lord. (For the ark of God was there that day with the children of Israel.)

19 And while Saul spoke to the priest, there arose a great uproar in the camp of the Philistines: and it increased by degrees, and was heard more clearly. And Saul said to the priest: Draw in thy hand.

20 Then Saul and all the people that were with him, shouted together, and they came to the place of the fight. And behold every man's sword was turned upon his neighbour; and there was a very great slaughter.

21 Moreover the Hebrews that had been with the Philistines yesterday and the day before, and went up with them into the camp, returned to be with the Israelites, who were with Saul and Jonathan.

22 And all the Israelites that had hid themselves in Mount Ephraim, hearing that the Philistines fled, joined themselves with their countrymen in the fight. And there were with Saul about ten thousand men.

23 And the Lord saved Israel that day. And the fight went on as far as Bethaven.

24 And the men of Israel were joined together that day; and Saul adjured the people, saying: Cursed be the man that shall eat food till evening, till I be revenged of my enemies. So none of the people tasted any food.

25 And all the common people came into a forest, in which there was honey upon the ground.

26 And when the people came into the forest, behold the honey dropped, but no man put his hand to his mouth. For the people feared the oath.

27 But Jonathan had not heard when his father adjured the people: and he put forth the end of the rod, which he had in his hand, and dipt it in a honey-

---

[2] 1 Mach. 4, 30.

CHAP. 14. Ver. 10. *This shall be a sign.* It is likely Jonathan was instructed by divine inspiration to make choice of this sign: otherwise the observation of *omens* is superstitious and sinful.

comb. And he carried his hand to his mouth; and his eyes were enlightened.

28 And one of the people answering, said: Thy father hath bound the people with an oath, saying: Cursed be the man that shall eat any food this day. (And the people were faint.)

29 And Jonathan said: My father hath troubled the land. You have seen yourselves that my eyes are enlightened, because I tasted a little of this honey:

30 How much more if the people had eaten of the prey of their enemies, which they found? Had there not been made a greater slaughter among the Philistines?

31 So they smote that day the Philistines from Machmas to Ailon. And the people were wearied exceedingly.

32 And falling upon the spoils, they took sheep, and oxen, and calves, and slew them on the ground. And the people ate them with the blood.

33 And they told Saul that the people had sinned against the Lord, eating with the blood. And he said: You have transgressed. Roll here to me now a great stone.

34 And Saul said: Disperse yourselves among the people; and tell them to bring me every man his ox and his ram, and slay them upon this stone, and eat. And you shall not sin against the Lord in eating with the blood. So all the people brought every man his ox with him till the night: and slew them there.

35 And Saul built an altar to the Lord: and he then first began to build an altar to the Lord.

36 And Saul said: Let us fall upon the Philistines by night, and destroy them till the morning light, and let us not leave a man of them. And the people said: Do all that seemeth good in thy eyes. And the priest said: Let us draw near hither unto God.

37 And Saul consulted the Lord: Shall I pursue after the Philistines? Wilt thou deliver them into the hands of Israel? And he answered him not that day.

38 And Saul said: Bring hither all the corners of the people; and know, and see by whom this sin hath happened to-day.

39 As the Lord liveth who is the saviour of Israel, if it was done by Jonathan my son, he shall surely die. In this none of the people gainsaid him.

40 And he said to all Israel: Be you on one side, and I with Jonathan my son will be on the other side. And the people answered Saul: Do what seemeth good in thy eyes.

41 And Saul said to the Lord: O Lord God of Israel, give a sign, by *which we may know*, what the meaning is, that thou answerest not thy servant to-day. If this iniquity be in me, or in my son Jonathan, give a proof: or if this iniquity be in thy people, give holiness. And Jonathan and Saul were taken, and the people escaped.

42 And Saul said: Cast lots between me, and Jonathan my son. And Jonathan was taken.

43 And Saul said to Jonathan: Tell me what thou hast done. And Jonathan told him, and said: I did but taste a little honey with the end of the rod, which was in my hand; and behold I *must* die.

44 And Saul said: May God do so and so to me, and add still more: for dying thou shalt die, O Jonathan.

45 And the people said to Saul: Shall Jonathan then die, who hath wrought this great salvation in Israel? This must not be. As the Lord liveth, there shall not one hair of his head fall to the ground: for he hath wrought with God this day. So the people delivered Jonathan, that he should not die.

46 And Saul went back, and did not pursue after the Philistines: and the Philistines went to their own places.

47 And Saul having his kingdom established over Israel, fought against all his enemies round about, against Moab, and against the children of Ammon, and Edom, and the kings of Soba, and the Philistines; and whithersoever he turned himself, he overcame.

48 And gathering together an army, he defeated Amalec, and delivered Israel from the hand of them that spoiled them.

49 And the sons of Saul, were Jonathan, and Jessui, and Melchisua. And the names of his two daughters: the name of the firstborn *was* Merob, and the name of the younger Michol.

50 And the name of Saul's wife, was Achinoam the daughter of Achimaas. And the name of the captain of his army was Abner, the son of Ner, the cousin german of Saul.

51 For Cis was the father of Saul and Ner the father of Abner, was son of Abiel.

52 And there was a great war against the Philistines all the days of Saul. For whomsoever Saul saw to be a valiant man, and fit for war, he took him to himself.

Ver. 42. *Jonathan was taken*. Though Jonathan was excused from sin, through ignorance of the prohibition, yet God was pleased on this occasion to let the lot fall upon him, to shew unto all the great obligation of obedience to princes and parents.

CHAPTER 15

Saul is sent to destroy Amalec. He spareth their king and the best of their cattle: for which disobedience he is cast off by the Lord.

AND Samuel said to Saul: The Lord sent me to anoint thee king over his people Israel: now therefore hearken thou unto the voice of the Lord.

2 Thus saith the Lord of hosts: I have reckoned up all that Amalec hath done to Israel: [1] How he opposed them in the way when they came up out of Egypt.

3 Now therefore go, and smite Amalec, and utterly destroy all that he hath. Spare him not, nor covet any thing that is his: but slay both man and woman, child and suckling, ox and sheep, camel and ass.

4 So Saul commanded the people, and numbered them as lambs: two hundred thousand footmen, and ten thousand of the men of Juda.

5 And when Saul was come to the city of Amalec, he laid ambushes in the torrent.

6 And Saul said to the Cinite: Go, depart and get ye down from Amalec; lest I destroy thee with him. For thou hast shewn kindness to all the children of Israel, when they came up out of Egypt. And the Cinite departed from the midst of Amalec.

7 And Saul smote Amalec from Hevila, until thou comest to Sur, which is over against Egypt.

8 And he took Agag the king of Amalec alive: but all the common people he slew with the edge of the sword.

9 And Saul and the people spared Agag and the best of the flocks of sheep and of the herds, and the garments and the rams, and all that was beautiful, and would not destroy them: but every thing that was vile and good for nothing, that they destroyed.

10 And the word of the Lord came to Samuel, saying:

11 It repenteth me that I have made Saul king: for he hath forsaken me, and hath not executed my commandments. And Samuel was grieved, and he cried unto the Lord all night.

12 And when Samuel rose early, to go to Saul in the morning, it was told Samuel, that Saul was come to Carmel, and had erected for himself a triumphant arch: and returning had passed on, and gone down to Galga And Samuel came to Saul; and Saul was offering a holocaust to the Lord out of the choicest of the spoils which he had brought from Amalec.

13 And when Samuel was come to Saul, Saul said to him: Blessed be thou of the Lord. I have fulfilled the word of the Lord.

14 And Samuel said: What meaneth then this bleating of the flocks, which soundeth in my ears, and the lowing of the herds, which I hear?

15 And Saul said: They have brought them from Amalec. For the people spared the best of the sheep and of the herds that they might be sacrificed to the Lord thy God; but the rest we have slain.

16 And Samuel said to Saul: Suffer me, and I will tell thee what the Lord hath said to me this night. And he said to him: Speak.

17 And Samuel said: When thou wast a little one in thy own eyes, wast thou not made the head of the tribes of Israel? And the Lord anointed thee to be king over Israel.

18 And the Lord sent thee on the way, and said: Go, and kill the sinners of Amalec; and thou shalt fight against them until thou hast utterly destroyed them.

19 Why then didst thou not hearken to the voice of the Lord: but hast turned to the prey, and hast done evil in the eyes of the Lord?

20 And Saul said to Samuel: Yea, I have hearkened to the voice of the Lord, and have walked in the way by which the Lord sent me, and have brought Agag the king of Amalec, and Amalec I have slain.

21 But the people took of the spoils sheep and oxen, as the firstfruits of those things that were slain, to offer sacrifice to the Lord their God in Galgal.

22 And Samuel said: [2] Doth the Lord desire holocausts and victims, and not rather that the voice of the Lord should be obeyed? For obedience is better than sacrifices: and to hearken rather than to offer the fat of rams.

23 Because it is like the sin of witchcraft, to rebel: and like the crime of idolatry, to refuse to obey. Forasmuch therefore as thou hast rejected the word of the Lord, the Lord hath *also* rejected thee from being king.

24 And Saul said to Samuel: I have sinned because I have transgressed the commandment of the Lord, and thy words, fearing the people, and obeying their voice.

CHAP. 15. [1] Exod. 17, 8. [2] Ecclus. 4, 17; Osee, 6, 6; Matt. 9, 13; 12, 7.

CHAP. 15. Ver. 3. *Child.* The great Master of life and death (who cuts off one half of all mankind whilst they are children) has been pleased sometimes to ordain that children should be put to the sword, in detestation of the crimes of their parents, and that they might not live to follow the same wicked ways. But without such ordinance of God it is not allowable, in any wars, how just soever, to kill children.

25 But now bear, I beseech thee, my sin: and return with me, that I may adore the Lord.

26 And Samuel said to Saul: I will not return with thee, because thou hast rejected the word of the Lord, and the Lord hath rejected thee from being king over Israel.

27 And Samuel turned about to go away: but he laid hold upon the skirt of his mantle, and it rent.

28 And Samuel said to him: ³The Lord hath rent the kingdom of Israel from thee this day, and hath given it to thy neighbour who is better than thee.

29 But the triumpher in Israel will not spare, and will not be moved to repentance: for he is not a man that he should repent.

30 Then he said: I have sinned. Yet honour me now before the ancients of my people, and before Israel, and return with me, that I may adore the Lord thy God.

31 So Samuel turned again after Saul: and Saul adored the Lord.

32 And Samuel said: Bring hither to me Agag the king of Amalec. And Agag was presented to him, very fat, and trembling. And Agag said: Doth bitter death separate in this manner?

33 And Samuel said: As thy sword hath made women childless, so shall thy mother be childless among women. And Samuel hewed him in pieces before the Lord in Galgal.

34 And Samuel departed to Ramatha: but Saul went up to his house in Gabaa.

35 And Samuel saw Saul no more till the day of his death: nevertheless Samuel mourned for Saul, because the Lord repented that he had made him king over Israel.

CHAPTER 16

Samuel is sent to Bethlehem, where he anointeth David: who is taken into Saul's family.

AND the Lord said to Samuel: How long wilt thou mourn for Saul whom I have rejected from reigning over Israel? Fill thy horn with oil, and come, that I may send thee to Isai the Bethlehemite: for I have provided me a king among his sons.

2 And Samuel said: How shall I go, for Saul will hear of it, and he will kill me? And the Lord said: Thou shalt take with thee a calf of the herd, and thou shalt say: I am come to sacrifice to the Lord.

3 And thou shalt call Isai to the sacrifice, and I will shew thee what thou art to do: and thou shalt anoint him whom I shall shew to thee.

4 Then Samuel did as the Lord had said to him. And he came to Bethlehem, and the ancients of the city wondered, and meeting him, they said: Is thy coming hither peaceable?

5 And he said: *It is* peaceable. I am come to offer sacrifice to the Lord: be ye sanctified, and come with me to the sacrifice. And he sanctified Isai and his sons, and called them to the sacrifice.

6 And when they were come in, he saw Eliab, and said: Is the Lord's anointed before him?

7 And the Lord said to Samuel: Look not on his countenance, nor on the height of his stature: because I have rejected him. Nor do I judge according to the look of man: for man seeth those things that appear; ¹but the Lord beholdeth the heart.

8 And Isai called Abinadab, and brought him before Samuel. And he said: Neither hath the Lord chosen this.

9 And Isai brought Samma, and he said of him: Neither hath the Lord chosen this.

10 Isai therefore brought his seven sons before Samuel. And Samuel said to Isai: The Lord hath not chosen any one of these.

11 And Samuel said to Isai: Are here all thy sons? He answered: There remaineth yet a young one, who keepeth the sheep. And Samuel said to Isai: Send, and fetch him, for we will not sit down till he come hither.

12 He sent therefore and brought him. Now he was ruddy and beautiful to behold, and of a comely face. And the Lord said: Arise, and anoint him, for this is he.

13 Then Samuel took the horn of oil, ²and anointed him in the midst of his brethren. And the spirit of the Lord came upon David from that day forward: and Samuel rose up, and went to Ramatha.

14 But the spirit of the Lord departed from Saul: and an evil spirit from the Lord troubled him.

15 And the servants of Saul said to him: Behold *now* an evil spirit from God troubleth thee.

16 Let our lord give orders, and thy servants who are before thee will seek out a man skilful in playing on the harp, that when the evil spirit from the Lord is upon thee, he may play with his hand, and thou mayest bear it more easily.

---

⁵ 1 Kings, 28, 17. CHAP. 16. ¹ Ps. 7, 10. ² 2 Kings, 7, 8; Ps. 77, 70; 88, 21; Acts, 7, 46; 13, 90.
Ver. 35. *Saw Saul no more till the day of his death.* That is, he went no more to see him: he visited him no more.
CHAP. 16. Ver. 14. *From the Lord.* An evil spirit, by divine permission, and for his punishment, either possessed or obsessed him.

17 And Saul said to his servants: Provide me then some man that can play well, and bring him to me.

18 And one of the servants answering, said: Behold I have seen a son of Isai the Bethlehemite, a skilful player, and one of great strength, and a man fit for war, and prudent in his words, and a comely person. And the Lord is with him.

19 Then Saul sent messengers to Isai, saying: Send me David thy son, who is in the pastures.

20 And Isai took an ass laden with bread, and a bottle of wine, and a kid of the flock, and sent them by the hand of David his son to Saul.

21 And David came to Saul, and stood before him: and he loved him exceedingly, and made him his armourbearer.

22 And Saul sent to Isai, saying: Let David stand before me; for he hath found favour in my sight.

23 So whensoever the evil spirit from the Lord was upon Saul, David took his harp, and played with his hand: and Saul was refreshed, and was better, for the evil spirit departed from him.

CHAPTER 17

War with the Philistines, Goliath challengeth Israel. He is slain by David.

NOW the Philistines gathering together their troops to battle, assembled at Socho of Juda, and camped between Socho and Azeca in the borders of Dommim.

2 And Saul and the children of Israel being gathered together came to the valley of Terebinth: and they set the army in array to fight against the Philistines.

3 And the Philistines stood on a mountain on the one side, and Israel stood on a mountain on the other side. And there was a valley between them.

4 And there went out a man baseborn from the camp of the Philistines named Goliath, of Geth, whose height was six cubits and a span.

5 And he had a helmet of brass upon his head; and he was clothed with a coat of mail with scales. And the weight of his coat of mail was five thousand sicles of brass.

6 And he had greaves of brass on his legs; and a buckler of brass covered his shoulders.

7 And the staff of his spear was like a weaver's beam, and the head of his spear weighed six hundred sicles of iron. And his armourbearer went before him.

8 And standing he cried out to the bands of Israel, and said to them: Why

are you come out prepared to fight? Am not I a Philistine, and you the servants of Saul? Choose out a man of you; and let him come down and fight hand to hand.

9 If he be able to fight with me, and kill me, we will be servants to you: but if I prevail against him, and kill him, you shall be servants, and shall serve us.

10 And the Philistine said: I have defied the bands of Israel this day. Give me a man, and let him fight with me hand to hand.

11 And Saul and all the Israelites hearing these words of the Philistine were dismayed, and greatly afraid.

12 ¹ Now David was the son of that Ephrathite of Bethlehem Juda before mentioned, whose name was Isai, who had eight sons, and was an old man in the days of Saul, and of great age among men.

13 And his three eldest sons followed Saul to the battle: and the names of his three sons that went to the battle, were Eliab the firstborn, and the second Abinadab, and the third Samma.

14 But David was the youngest. So the three eldest having followed Saul,

15 David went, and returned from Saul, to feed his father's flock at Bethlehem.

16 Now the Philistine came out morning and evening, and presented himself forty days.

17 And Isai said to David his son: Take for thy brethren an ephi of frumenty, and these ten loaves; and run to the camp to thy brethren.

18 And carry these ten little cheeses to the tribune. And go see thy brethren, if they are well: and learn with whom they are placed.

19 But Saul, and they, and all the children of Israel were in the valley of Terebinth fighting against the Philistines.

20 David therefore arose in the morning, and gave the charge of the flock to the keeper: and went away loaded as Isai had commanded him. And he came to the place of Magala, and to the army, which was going out to fight, and shouted for the battle.

21 For Israel had put themselves in array: and the Philistines who stood against them were prepared.

22 And David leaving the vessels which he had brought, under the care of the keeper of the baggage, ran to the place of the battle and asked if all things went well with his brethren.

23 And as he talked with them, that

CHAP. 17. ¹ 1 Kings, 6, 1.

Ver. 23. *Departed from him.* Chased away by David's devotion.

baseborn man whose name was Goliath, the Philistine, of Geth, shewed himself coming up from the camp of the Philistines. And he spoke according to the same words; *and* David heard *them*.

24 And all the Israelites when they saw the man, fled from his face, fearing him exceedingly.

25 And some one of Israel said: Have you seen this man that is come up, for he is come up to defy Israel? And the man that shall slay him, the king will enrich with great riches, and will give him his daughter, and will make his father's house free from tribute in Israel.

26 And David spoke to the men that stood by him, saying: What shall be given to the man that shall kill this Philistine, and shall take away the reproach from Israel? For who is this uncircumcised Philistine, that he should defy the armies of the living God?

27 And the people answered him the same words saying: These things shall be given to the man that shall slay him.

28 Now when Eliab his eldest brother heard this, when he was speaking with others, he was angry with David, and said: Why camest thou hither? And why didst thou leave those few sheep in the desert? I know thy pride, and the wickedness of thy heart: that thou art come down to see the battle.

29 And David said: What have I done? Is there not cause to speak?

30 And he turned a little aside from him to another: and said the same word. And the people answered him as before.

31 And the words which David spoke were heard, and were rehearsed before Saul.

32 And when he was brought to him, he said to him: Let not any man's heart be dismayed in him. I thy servant will go, and will fight against the Philistine.

33 And Saul said to David: Thou art not able to withstand this Philistine, nor to fight against him; for thou art *but* a boy, but he is a warrior from his youth.

34 And David said to Saul: [2] Thy servant kept his father's sheep, and there came a lion, [3] or a bear, and took a ram out of the midst of the flock.

35 And I pursued after them, and struck them, and delivered it out of their mouth. And they rose up against me; and I caught them by the throat; and I strangled and killed them.

36 For I thy servant have killed both a lion and a bear: and this uncircumcised Philistine shall be also as one of them. I will go now, and take away the

reproach of the people. For who is this uncircumcised Philistine, who hath dared to curse the army of the living God?

37 And David said: The Lord who delivered me out of the paw of the lion, and out of the paw of the bear, he will deliver me out of the hand of this Philistine. And Saul said to David: Go, and the Lord be with thee.

38 And Saul clothed David with his garments, and put a helmet of brass upon his head, and armed him with a coat of mail.

39 And David having girded his sword upon his armour, began to try if he would walk in armour: for he was not accustomed to it. And David said to Saul: I cannot go thus, for I am not used to it. And he laid them off,

40 And he took his staff, which he had always in his hands: and chose him five smooth stones out of the brook, and put them into the shepherd's scrip, which he had with him. And he took a sling in his hand, and went forth against the Philistine.

41 And the Philistine came on, and drew nigh against David, and his armourbearer before him.

42 And when the Philistine looked, and beheld David, he despised him. For he was a young man, ruddy, and of a comely countenance.

43 And the Philistine said to David: Am I a dog, that thou comest to me with a staff? And the Philistine cursed David by his gods.

44 And he said to David: Come to me, and I will give thy flesh to the birds of the air, and to the beasts of the earth.

45 And David said to the Philistine: Thou comest to me with a sword, and with a spear, and with a shield: but I come to thee in the name of the Lord of hosts, the God of the armies of Israel, which thou hast defied.

46 This day, and the Lord will deliver thee into my hand, and I will slay thee, and take away thy head from thee. And I will give the carcasses of the army of the Philistines this day to the birds of the air, and to the beasts of the earth: that all the earth may know that there is a God in Israel.

47 And all this assembly shall know, that the Lord saveth not with sword and spear: for it is his battle; and he will deliver you into our hands.

48 And when the Philistine arose and was coming, and drew nigh to meet David, David made haste, and ran to the fight to meet the Philistine.

49 And he put his hand into his scrip, and took a stone, and cast it with the sling, and fetching it about struck the

[2] Ecclus. 47, 3. [3] *Or* for *and*. [4] Ecclus. 47, 4; 1 Mach. 4, 30.

Philistine in the forehead. And the stone was fixed in his forehead: and he fell on his face upon the earth.

50 *And David prevailed over the Philistine, with a sling and a stone: and he struck, and slew the Philistine. And as David had no sword in his hand,

51 He ran, and stood over the Philistine, and took his sword, and drew it out of the sheath, and slew him, and cut off his head. And the Philistines seeing that their champion was dead, fled away.

52 And the men of Israel and Juda rising up shouted, and pursued after the Philistines till they came to the valley and to the gates of Accaron. And there fell *many* wounded of the Philistines in the way of Saraim, and as far as Geth, and as far as Accaron.

53 And the children of Israel returning, after they had pursued the Philistines, fell upon their camp.

54 And David taking the head of the Philistine brought it to Jerusalem: but his armour he put in his tent.

55 Now at the time that Saul saw David going out against the Philistines, he said to Abner the captain of the army: Of what family is this young man descended, Abner? And Abner said: As thy soul liveth, O king, I know not.

56 And the king said: Inquire thou, whose son this man is.

57 And when David was returned, after the Philistine was slain, Abner took him, and brought him in before Saul, with the head of the Philistine in his hand.

58 And Saul said to him: Young man, of what family art thou? And David said: I am the son of thy servant Isai the Bethlehemite.

CHAPTER 18

The friendship of Jonathan and David. The envy of Saul, and his design upon David's life. He marrieth him to his daughter Michol.

AND it came to pass, when he had made an end of speaking to Saul, the soul of Jonathan was knit with the soul of David, and Jonathan loved him as his own soul.

2 And Saul took him that day, and would not let him return to his father's house.

3 And David and Jonathan made a covenant: for he loved him as his own soul.

4 And Jonathan stripped himself of the coat with which he was clothed, and gave it to David, and the rest of his garments, even to his sword, and to his bow, and to his girdle.

5 And David went out to whatsoever

business Saul sent him, and he behaved himself prudently. And Saul set him over the soldiers; and he was acceptable in the eyes of all the people, and especially in the eyes of Saul's servants.

6 Now when David returned, after he slew the Philistine, the women came out of all the cities of Israel, singing and dancing, to meet king Saul, with timbrels of joy, and cornets.

7 And the women sung as they played. And they said: ¹ Saul slew his thousands, and David his ten thousands.

8 And Saul was exceeding angry, and this word was displeasing in his eyes, and he said: They have given David ten thousands, and to me they have given *but* a thousand. What can he have more but the kingdom?

9 And Saul did not look on David with a good eye from that day and forward

10 And the day after, the evil spirit from God came upon Saul, and he prophesied in the midst of his house. And David played with his hand as at other times. And Saul held a spear in his hand,

11 And threw it, thinking to nail David to the wall: and David stept aside out of his presence twice.

12 And Saul feared David, because the Lord was with him, and was departed from himself.

13 Therefore Saul removed him from him, and made him a captain over a thousand men: and he went out and came in before the people.

14 And David behaved wisely in all his ways: ² and the Lord was with him.

15 And Saul saw that he was exceeding prudent, and began to beware of him.

16 But all Israel and Juda loved David, for he came in and went out before them.

17 And Saul said to David: Behold my elder daughter Merob: her will I give thee to wife. Only be a valiant man, ³ and fight the battles of the Lord. Now Saul said within himself: Let not my hand be upon him; but let the hands of the Philistines be upon him.

18 And David said to Saul: Who am I, or what is my life, or my father's family in Israel, that I should be son-in-law of the king?

19 And it came to pass at the time when Merob the daughter of Saul should have been given to David, that she was given to Hadriel the Molathite to wife.

20 But Michol the other daughter of

CHAP. 18. ¹ 1 Kings, 21, 11; Ecclus. 47, 7. ² Kings, 16, 13. ³ 1 Kings, 25, 28.

CHAP. 18. Ver. 10. *Prophesied.* Acted the prophet in a mad manner.

Saul loved David. And it was told Saul, and it pleased him.

21 And Saul said: I will give her to him, that she may be a stumblingblock to him, and that the hand of the Philistines may be upon him. And Saul said to David: In two things thou shalt be my son-in-law this day.

22 And Saul commanded his servants to speak to David privately, saying: Behold thou pleasest the king; and all his servants love thee. Now therefore be the king's son-in-law.

23 And the servants of Saul spoke all these words in the ears of David. And David said: Doth it seem to you a small matter to be the king's son-in-law? But I am a poor man, and of small ability.

24 And the servants of Saul told him, saying: Such words as these hath David spoken.

25 And Saul said: Speak thus to David: The king desireth not any dowry, but only a hundred foreskins of the Philistines, to be avenged of the king's enemies. Now Saul thought to deliver David into the hands of the Philistines.

26 And when his servants had told David the words that Saul had said, the word was pleasing in the eyes of David to be the king's son-in-law.

27 And after a few days David rose up, and went with the men that were under him. And he slew of the Philistines two hundred men, and brought their foreskins and numbered them out to the king, that he might be his son-in-law. Saul therefore gave him Michol his daughter to wife.

28 And Saul saw, and understood that the Lord was with David. And Michol the daughter of Saul loved him.

29 And Saul began to fear David more: and Saul became David's enemy continually.

30 And the princes of the Philistines went forth: and from the beginning of their going forth, David behaved himself more wisely than all the servants of Saul. And his name became very famous.

CHAPTER 19

Other attempts of Saul upon David's life. He cometh to Samuel. Saul's messengers and Saul himself prophesy.

AND Saul spoke to Jonathan his son and to all his servants, that they should kill David. But Jonathan the son of Saul loved David exceedingly.

2 And Jonathan told David, saying: Saul my father seeketh to kill thee. Wherefore look to thyself, I beseech thee, in the morning; and thou shalt abide in a secret place and shalt be hid.

3 And I will go out and stand beside my father in the field where thou art. And I will speak of thee to my father: and whatsoever I shall see, I will tell thee.

4 And Jonathan spoke good things of David to Saul his father; and said to him: Sin not, O king, against thy servant, David, because he hath not sinned against thee; and his works are very good towards thee.

5 And he put his life in his hand, and slew the Philistine; and the Lord wrought great salvation for all Israel. Thou sawest it and didst rejoice. Why therefore wilt thou sin against innocent blood by killing David, who is without fault?

6 And when Saul heard this he was appeased with the words of Jonathan, and swore: As the Lord liveth he shall not be slain.

7 Then Jonathan called David and told him all these words. And Jonathan brought in David to Saul: and he was before him, as he had been yesterday and the day before.

8 And the war began again. And David went out and fought against the Philistines, and defeated them with a great slaughter: and they fled from his face.

9 And the evil spirit from the Lord came upon Saul: and he sat in his house, and held a spear in his hand. And David played with his hand.

10 And Saul endeavoured to nail David to the wall with his spear. And David slipt away out of the presence of Saul: and the spear missed him, and was fastened in the wall. And David fled and escaped that night.

11 Saul therefore sent his guards to David's house to watch him, that he might be killed in the morning. And when Michol David's wife had told him this, saying: Unless thou save thyself this night, to-morrow thou wilt die.

12 She let him down through a window. And he went and fled away and escaped.

13 And Michol took an image and laid it on the bed: and put a goat's skin with the hair at the head of it, and covered it with clothes.

14 And Saul sent officers to seize David: and it was answered that he was sick.

15 And again Saul sent to see David, saying: Bring him to me in the bed, that he may be slain.

16 And when the messengers were come in, they found an image upon the bed, and a goat's skin at its head.

17 And Saul said to Michol: Why hast thou deceived me so, and let my enemy go and flee away? And Michol

answered Saul: Because he said to me: Let me go, or else I will kill thee.

18 But David fled and escaped, and came to Samuel in Ramatha, and told him all that Saul had done to him. And he and Samuel went and dwelt in Najoth.

19 And it was told Saul by some, saying: Behold David is in Najoth in Ramatha.

20 So Saul sent officers to take David: and when they saw a company of prophets prophesying, and Samuel presiding over them, the spirit of the Lord came also upon them, and they likewise began to prophesy.

21 And when this was told Saul, he sent other messengers: but they also prophesied. And again Saul sent messengers the third time: and they prophesied also. And Saul being exceedingly angry,

22 Went also himself to Ramatha, and came as far as the great cistern, which is in Socho, and he asked, and said: In what place are Samuel and David? And it was told him: Behold they are in Najoth in Ramatha.

23 And he went to Najoth in Ramatha. And the spirit of the Lord came upon him also; and he went on, and prophesied till he came to Najoth in Ramatha.

24 And he stripped himself also of his garments, and prophesied with the rest before Samuel, and lay down naked all that day and night. This gave occasion to a proverb: [1] What! Is Saul too among the prophets?

CHAPTER 20

Saul being obstinately bent upon killing David, he is sent away by Jonathan.

BUT David fled from Najoth, which is in Ramatha, and came and said to Jonathan: What have I done? What is my iniquity, and what *is* my sin against thy father, that he seeketh my life?

2 And he said to him: God forbid, thou shalt not die: for my father will do nothing great or little, without first telling me. Hath then my father hid this word only from me? No: this shall not be.

3 And he swore again to David. And David said: Thy father certainly knoweth that I have found grace in thy sight; and he will say: Let not Jonathan know this, lest he be grieved. But truly as the Lord liveth, and thy soul liveth, there is but one step (as I may say) between me and death.

4 And Jonathan said to David: Whatsoever thy soul shall say to me, I will do for thee.

5 And David said to Jonathan: Behold to-morrow is the new moon, and I according to custom am wont to sit beside the king to eat. Let me go then that I may be hid in the field till the evening of the third day.

6 If thy father look and inquire for me, thou shalt answer him: David asked me that he might run to Bethlehem [1] his own city: because there are solemn sacrifices there for all his tribe.

7 If he shall say: *It is well:* thy servant shall have peace. But if he be angry, know that his malice is come to its height.

8 Deal mercifully then with thy servant: for thou hast brought me thy servant into a covenant of the Lord with thee. But if there be any iniquity in me, do thou kill me, and bring me not in to thy father.

9 And Jonathan said: Far be this from thee: for, if I should certainly know that evil is determined by my father against thee, I could do no otherwise than tell thee.

10 And David answered Jonathan: Who shall bring me word, if thy father should answer thee harshly concerning me?

11 And Jonathan said to David: Come and let us go out into the field. And when they were both of them gone out into the field,

12 Jonathan said to David: O Lord God of Israel, if I shall discover my father's mind, to-morrow or the day after, and there be any thing good for David, and I send not immediately to thee, and make it known to thee,

13 May the Lord do so and so to Jonathan, and add still more. But if my father shall continue in malice against thee, I will discover it to thy ear; and will send thee away, that thou mayest go in peace, and the Lord be with thee, as he hath been with my father.

14 And if I live, thou shalt shew me the kindness of the Lord: but if I die,

15 Thou shalt not take away thy kindness from my house for ever, when

CHAP. 19. [1] Kings, 10, 12. CHAP. 20. [1] Luke, 2, 4.

CHAP. 19. Ver. 18. *Najoth.* It was probably a school or college of prophets, in or near Ramatha under the direction of Samuel.

Ver. 20. *Prophesying.* That is, singing praises to God by a divine impulse. God was pleased on this occasion that both Saul's messengers and himself should experience the like impulse, that he might understand, by this instance of the divine power, how vain are the designs of man against him whom God protects.

CHAP. 20. Ver. 5. *To-morrow is the new moon.* The *neomenia,* or first day of the moon, kept according to the law, as a festival. Therefore Saul feasted on that day, and expected the attendance of his family.

Ver. 15. *May he take away Jonathan.* It is a curse upon himself, if he should not be faithful to his promise.—*Require it.* That is, revenge it upon David's enemies, and upon me, if I should fail of my word given to him.

the Lord shall have rooted out the enemies of David, every one of them from the earth. May he take away Jonathan from his house: and may the Lord require it at the hands of David's enemies.

16 Jonathan therefore made a covenant with the house of David: and the Lord required it at the hands of David's enemies.

17 And Jonathan swore again to David, because he loved him: for he loved him as his own soul.

18 And Jonathan said to him: To-morrow is the new moon, and thou wilt be missed:

19 For thy seat will be empty till after to-morrow. So thou shalt go down quickly, and come to the place, where thou must be hid on the day when it is lawful to work; and thou shalt remain beside the stone, which is called Ezel.

20 And I will shoot three arrows near it, and will shoot as if I were exercising myself at a mark.

21 And I will send a boy, saying to him: Go and fetch me the arrows.

22 If I shall say to the boy: Behold the arrows are on this side of thee, take them up: come thou to me, because there is peace to thee, and there is no evil, as the Lord liveth. But if I shall speak thus to the boy: Behold the arrows are beyond thee: go in peace, for the Lord hath sent thee away.

23 And concerning the word which I and thou have spoken, the Lord be between thee and me for ever.

24 So David was hid in the field. And the new moon came: and the king sat down to eat bread.

25 And when the king sat down upon his chair (according to custom) which was beside the wall, Jonathan arose; and Abner sat by Saul's side; and David's place appeared empty.

26 And Saul said nothing that day: for he thought it might have happened to him, that he was not clean, nor purified.

27 And when the second day after the new moon was come, David's place appeared empty again. And Saul said to Jonathan his son: Why cometh not the son of Isai to meat neither yesterday nor to-day?

28 And Jonathan answered Saul: He asked leave of me earnestly to go to Bethlehem.

29 And he said: Let me go, for there is a solemn sacrifice in the city. One of my brethren hath sent for me; and now if I have found favour in thy eyes, I will go quickly, and see my brethren. For this cause he came not to the king's table.

30 Then Saul being angry against Jonathan said to him: Thou son of a woman that is the ravisher of a man, do I not know that thou lovest the son of Isai to thy own confusion and to the confusion of thy shameless mother?

31 For as long as the son of Isai liveth upon earth, thou shalt not be established, nor thy kingdom. Therefore now presently send, and fetch him to me: for he is the son of death.

32 And Jonathan answering Saul his father, said: Why shall he die? What hath he done?

33 And Saul caught up a spear to strike him. And Jonathan understood that it was determined by his father to kill David.

34 So Jonathan rose from the table in great anger, and did not eat bread on the second day after the new moon. For he was grieved for David, because his father had put him to confusion.

35 And when the morning came, Jonathan went into the field, according to the appointment with David and a little boy with him.

36 And he said to his boy: Go, and fetch me the arrows which I shoot. And when the boy ran, he shot another arrow beyond the boy.

37 The boy therefore came to the place of the arrow which Jonathan had shot: and Jonathan cried after the boy, and said: Behold the arrow is there further beyond thee.

38 And Jonathan cried again after the boy, saying: Make haste speedily. Stand not. And Jonathan's boy gathered up the arrows, and brought them to his master.

39 And he knew not at all what was doing: for only Jonathan and David knew the matter.

40 Jonathan therefore gave his arms to the boy, and said to him: Go, and carry them into the city.

41 And when the boy was gone, David rose out of his place, which was towards the south; and falling on his face to the ground, adored thrice. And kissing one another, they wept together, but David more.

42 And Jonathan said to David: Go in peace. And let all stand that we have sworn both of us in the name of the Lord, saying: The Lord be between me and thee, and between my seed and thy seed for ever.

43 And David arose, and departed: and Jonathan went into the city.

CHAPTER 21

David receiveth holy bread of Achimelech the priest: and feigneth himself mad before Achis king of Geth.

Ver. 31. *The son of death.* That is, one that deserveth death, and shall surely be put to death.

AND David came to Nobe to Achimelech the priest: and Achimelech was astonished at David's coming. And he said to him: Why art thou alone, and no man with thee?

2 And David said to Achimelech the priest: The king hath commanded me a business, and said: Let no man know the thing for which thou art sent by me, and what manner of commands I have given thee. And I have appointed my servants to such and such a place.

3 Now therefore if thou have any thing at hand, though it were but five loaves, give me, or whatsoever thou canst find.

4 And the priest answered David, saying: I have no common bread at hand, but only holy bread, if the young men be clean, especially from women?

5 And David answered the priest, and said to him: Truly, as to what concerneth women, we have refrained ourselves from yesterday and the day before, when we came out, and the vessels of the young men were holy. Now this way is defiled: but it shall also be sanctified this day in the vessels.

6 [1] The priest therefore gave him hallowed bread: for there was no bread there, but only the loaves of proposition, which had been taken away from before the face of the Lord, that hot loaves might be set up.

7 Now a certain man of the servants of Saul was there that day, within the tabernacle of the Lord: and his name was Doeg, an Edomite, the chiefest of Saul's herdsmen.

8 And David said to Achimelech: Hast thou here at hand a spear, or a sword? For I brought not my own sword, nor my own weapons with me, for the king's business required haste.

9 And the priest said: Lo, here is the sword of Goliath the Philistine whom thou slewest in the valley of Terebinth, wrapped up in a cloth behind the ephod. If thou wilt take this, take it: for here is no other but this. And David said: There is none like that. Give it me.

10 And David arose and fled that day from the face of Saul: and came to Achis the king of Geth.

11 And the servants of Achis, when they saw David, said to him: Is not this David the king of the land? Did they not sing to him in their dances, saying: [2] Saul hath slain his thousands, and David his ten thousands?

12 But David laid up these words in his heart, and was exceedingly afraid at the face of Achis the king of Geth.

13 And he changed his countenance before them, and slipt down between their hands. And he stumbled against the doors of the gate; and his spittle ran down upon his beard.

14 And Achis said to his servants: You saw the man *was* mad. Why have you brought him to me?

15 Have we need of madmen, that you have brought in this fellow, to play the madman in my presence? Shall this fellow come into my house?

CHAPTER 22

Many resort to David. Doeg accuseth Achimelech to Saul. He ordereth him and all the other priests of Nobe to be slain. Abiathar escapeth.

DAVID therefore went from thence and fled to the cave of Odollam. And when his brethren, and all his father's house had heard of it, they went down to him thither.

2 And all that were in distress and oppressed with debt, and under affliction of mind gathered themselves unto him. And he became their prince. And there were with him about four hundred men.

3 And David departed from thence into Maspha of Moab. And he said to the king of Moab: let my father and my mother tarry with you, I beseech thee, till I know what God will do for me.

4 And he left them under the eyes of the king of Moab: and they abode with him all the days that David was in the hold.

5 And Gad the prophet said to David: Abide not in the hold. Depart, and go into the land of Juda. And David departed, and came into the forest of Haret.

6 And Saul heard that David was seen, and the men that were with him. Now, whilst Saul abode in Gabaa, and was in the wood, which is by Rama, having his spear in his hand, and all his servants were standing about him,

7 He said to his servants that stood about him: Hear me now, ye sons of

CHAP. 21. [1] Matt. 12, 3, 4. [2] 1 Kings, 18, 7; Ecclus. 47, 7.

CHAP. 21. Ver. 1. *Nobe.* A city in the tribe of Benjamin, to which the tabernacle of the Lord had been translated from Silo.

Ver. 4. *If the young men be clean.* If this cleanness was required of them that were to eat that bread, which was but a figure of the bread of life which we receive in the blessed sacrament; how clean ought Christians to be when they approach to our tremendous mysteries. And how much reason hath the church of God to admit none to be her ministers to consecrate and daily receive this most pure sacrament, but such as devote themselves to a life of perpetual purity.

Ver. 5. *The vessels,* that is, their bodies, have been *holy,* have been kept from impurity.—*Is defiled.* Is liable to expose us to dangers of uncleanness.—*Be sanctified.* That is, we shall take care, notwithstanding these dangerous circumstances, to keep our *vessels holy,* that is, to keep our bodies from every thing that may defile us.

CHAP. 22. Ver. 4. *The hold.* The strong hold, or fortress of Maspha.

Jemini: Will the son of Isai give every one of you fields, and vineyards, and make you all tribunes, and centurions:

8 That all of you have conspired against me, and there is no one to inform me, especially when even my son hath entered into league with the son of Isai? There is not one of you that pitieth my case, nor that giveth me any information: because my son hath raised up my servant against me, plotting against me to this day.

9 And Doeg the Edomite who stood by, and was the chief among the servants of Saul, answering, said: I saw the son of Isai, in Nobe, with Achimelech the son of Achitob the priest.

10 And he consulted the Lord for him, and gave him victuals, and gave him the sword of Goliath the Philistine.

11 Then the king sent to call for Achimelech the priest the son of Achitob, and all his father's house, the priests that were in Nobe; and they came all of them to the king.

12 And Saul said to Achimelech: Hear, thou son of Achitob. He answered: Here I am, my lord.

13 And Saul said to him: Why have you conspired against me, thou, and the son of Isai? And thou hast given him bread and a sword, and hast consulted the Lord for him, that he should rise up against me, continuing a traitor to this day.

14 And Achimelech answering the king, said: And who amongst all thy servants is so faithful as David, who is the king's son-in-law, and goeth forth at thy bidding, and is honourable in thy house?

15 Did I begin to-day to consult the Lord for him? Far be this from me. Let not the king suspect such a thing against his servant, or any one in all my father's house: for thy servant knew nothing of this matter, either little or great.

16 And the king said: Dying thou shalt die, Achimelech. Thou and all thy father's house.

17 And the king said to the messengers that stood about him: Turn, and kill the priests of the Lord. For their hand is with David: because they knew that he was fled; and they told it not to me. And the king's servants would not put forth their hands against the priests of the Lord.

18 And the king said to Doeg: Turn thou, and fall upon the priests. And Doeg the Edomite turned, and fell upon the priests, and slew in that day eighty-five men that wore the linen ephod.

CHAP. 23. Ver. 6. An ephod, or the ephod. That is, the vestment of the high priest, with the urim and thummim, by which the Lord gave his oracles.

19 And Nobe the city of the priests he smote with the edge of his sword, both men and women, children, and sucklings, and ox and ass, and sheep, with the edge of the sword.

20 But one of the sons of Achimelech the son of Achitob, whose name was Abiathar, escaped, and fled to David,

21 And told him that Saul had slain the priests of the Lord.

22 And David said to Abiathar: I knew that day when Doeg the Edomite was there, that without doubt he would tell Saul. I have been the occasion of the death of all the souls of thy father's house.

23 Abide thou with me. Fear not: for he that seeketh my life, seeketh thy life also; and with me thou shalt be saved.

CHAPTER 23

David relieveth Ceila, besieged by the Philistines. He fleeth into the desert of Ziph. Jonathan and he confirm their former covenant. The Ziphites discover him to Saul, who pursuing close after him, is called away by an invasion from the Philistines.

AND they told David, saying: Behold the Philistines fight against Ceila; and they rob the barns.

2 Therefore David consulted the Lord, saying: Shall I go and smite these Philistines? And the Lord said to David: Go. And thou shalt smite the Philistines, and shalt save Ceila.

3 And the men that were with David, said to him: Behold we are in fear here in Judea. How much more if we go to Ceila against the bands of the Philistines?

4 Therefore David consulted the Lord again. And he answered and said to him: Arise, and go to Ceila: for I will deliver the Philistines into thy hand.

5 David therefore, and his men, went to Ceila, and fought against the Philistines; and brought away their cattle; and made a great slaughter of them. And David saved the inhabitants of Ceila.

6 Now at that time, when Abiathar the son of Achimelech fled to David to Ceila, he came down having an ephod with him.

7 And it was told Saul that David was come to Ceila. And Saul said: The Lord hath delivered him into my hands; and he is shut up, being come into a city, that hath gates and bars.

8 And Saul commanded all the people to go down to fight against Ceila, and to besiege David, and his men.

9 Now when David understood, that Saul secretly prepared evil against him,

he said to Abiathar the priest: Bring hither the ephod.

10 And David said: O Lord God of Israel, thy servant hath heard a report, that Saul designeth to come to Ceila, to destroy the city for my sake.

11 Will the men of Ceila deliver me into his hands? And will Saul come down, as thy servant hath heard? O Lord God of Israel, tell thy servant. And the Lord said: He will come down.

12 And David said: Will the men of Ceila deliver me, and my men, into the hands of Saul? And the Lord said: They will deliver thee up.

13 Then David and his men, who were about six hundred, arose, and departing from Ceila, wandered up and down uncertain where they should stay. And it was told Saul that David was fled from Ceila, and had escaped: wherefore he forbore to go out.

14 But David abode in the desert in strong holds; and he remained in a mountain of the desert of Ziph, in a woody hill. And Saul sought him always: but the Lord delivered him not into his hands.

15 And David saw that Saul was come out to seek his life. And David was in the desert of Ziph, in a wood.

16 And Jonathan the son of Saul arose, and went to David into the wood, and strengthened his hands in God. And he said to him:

17 Fear not. For the hand of my father Saul shall not find thee: and thou shalt reign over Israel: and I shall be next to thee. Yea, and my father knoweth this.

18 And the two made a covenant before the Lord. And David abode in the wood: but Jonathan returned to his house.

19 ¹ And the Ziphites went up to Saul in Gabaa, saying: Lo, Doth not David lie hid with us in the strong holds of the wood, in mount Hachila, which is on the right hand of the desert?

20 Now therefore come down, as thy soul hath desired to come down: and it shall be our business to deliver him into the king's hands.

21 And Saul said: Blessed be ye of the Lord; for you have pitied my case.

22 Go therefore, I pray you, and use all diligence, and curiously inquire, and consider the place where his foot is, and who hath seen him there. For he thinketh of me, that I lie craftily in wait for him.

23 Consider and see all his lurking holes, wherein he is hid; and return to me with the certainty of the thing, that I may go with you. And if he should even go down into the earth to hide

himself, I will search him out in all the thousands of Juda.

24 And they arose and went to Ziph before Saul. And David and his men were in the desert of Maon, in the plain at the right hand of Jesimon.

25 Then Saul and his men went to seek him. And it was told David: and forthwith he went down to the rock, and abode in the wilderness of Maon. And when Saul had heard of it he pursued after David in the wilderness of Maon.

26 And Saul went on this side of the mountain: and David and his men were on the other side of the mountain. And David despaired of being able to escape from the face of Saul. And Saul and his men encompassed David and his men round about to take them.

27 And a messenger came to Saul, saying: Make haste to come, for the Philistines have poured in themselves upon the land.

28 Wherefore Saul returned, leaving the pursuit of David, and went to meet the Philistines. For this cause they called that place, the Rock of Division.

CHAPTER 24

Saul seeketh David in the wilderness of Engaddi. He goeth into a cave where David hath him in his power.

THEN David went up from thence, and dwelt in strong holds of Engaddi.

2 And when Saul was returned from following the Philistines, they told him, saying: Behold, David is in the desert of Engaddi.

3 Saul therefore took three thousand chosen men out of all Israel, and went out to seek after David, and his men, even upon the most craggy rocks, which are accessible only to wild goats.

4 And he came to the sheepcotes, which were in his way. And there was a cave, into which Saul went, to ease nature. Now David and his men lay hid in the inner part of the cave.

5 And the servants of David said to him: Behold the day, of which the Lord said to thee: I will deliver thy enemy unto thee, that thou mayest do to him as it shall seem good in thy eyes. Then David arose, and secretly cut off the hem of Saul's robe.

6 After which David's heart struck him, because he had cut off the hem of Saul's robe.

7 And he said to his men: The Lord be merciful unto me, that I may do no such thing to my master the Lord's

CHAP. 23. ¹ 1 Kings, 26, 1.
CHAP. 24. Ver. 6. *David's heart struck him.* Thus is, with remorse, as fearing he had done amiss.

anointed, as to lay my hand upon him, because he is the Lord's anointed.

8 And David stopped his men with his words, and suffered them not to rise against Saul. But Saul rising up out of the cave, went on his way.

9 And David also rose up after him: and going out of the cave cried after Saul, saying: My lord the king. And Saul looked behind him: and David bowing himself down to the ground, worshipped,

10 And said to Saul: Why dost thou hear the words of men that say, David seeketh thy hurt?

11 Behold this day thy eyes have seen, that the Lord hath delivered thee into my hand, in the cave, and I had a thought to kill thee, but my eye hath spared thee. For I said: I will not put out my hand against my lord, because he is the Lord's anointed.

12 Moreover see and know, O my father, the hem of thy robe in my hand, that when I cut off the hem of thy robe, I would not put out my hand against thee. Reflect, and see, that there is no evil in my hand, nor iniquity; neither have I sinned against thee: but thou liest in wait for my life, to take it away.

13 The Lord judge between me and thee; and the Lord revenge me of thee: But my hand shall not be upon thee.

14 As also it is said in the old proverb: *From the wicked shall wickedness come forth.* Therefore my hand shall not be upon thee. After whom dost thou come out, O king of Israel?

15 After whom dost thou pursue? After a dead dog? After a flea?

16 Be the Lord judge; and judge between me and thee; and see, and judge my cause; and deliver me out of thy hand.

17 And when David had made an end of speaking these words to Saul, Saul said: Is this thy voice, my son David? And Saul lifted up his voice, and wept.

18 And he said to David: Thou art more just than I. For thou hast done good to me; and I have rewarded thee with evil.

19 And thou hast shewn this day what good things thou hast done to

me: how the Lord delivered me into thy hand; and thou hast not killed me.

20 For who when he hath found his enemy, will let him go well away? But the Lord reward thee for this good turn, for what thou hast done to me this day.

21 And now as I know that thou shalt surely be king, and have the kingdom of Israel in thy hand:

22 Swear to me by the Lord, that thou wilt not destroy my seed after me, nor take away my name from the house of my father.

23 And David swore to Saul. So Saul went home: and David and his men went up into safer places.

CHAPTER 25

The death of Samuel. David, provoked by Nabal, threateneth to destroy him. Is appeased by Abigail.

AND Samuel died. [1] And all Israel was gathered together; and they mourned for him, and buried him in his house in Ramatha. And David rose and went down into the wilderness of Pharan.

2 Now there was a certain man in the wilderness of Maon, and his possessions were in Carmel. And the man was very great: and he had three thousand sheep, and a thousand goats. And it happened that he was shearing his sheep in Carmel.

3 Now the name of the man was Nabal: and the name of his wife was Abigail. And she was a prudent and very comely woman; but her husband was churlish, and very bad and ill natured. And he was of the house of Caleb.

4 And when David heard in the wilderness that Nabal was shearing his sheep,

5 He sent ten young men, and said to them: Go up to Carmel, and go to Nabal, and salute him in my name with peace.

6 And you shall say: Peace be to my brethren, and to thee, and peace to thy house, and peace to all that thou hast.

7 I heard that thy shepherds that were with us in the desert were shearing. We never molested them: neither was there aught missing to them of the flock at any time, all the while they were with us in Carmel.

8 Ask thy servants, and they will tell thee. Now therefore let thy servants find favour in thy eyes: for we are come in a good day. Whatsoever thy hand shall find give to thy servants, and to thy son David.

9 And when David's servants came, they spoke to Nabal all these words in

---

CHAP. 25. [1] 1 Kings, 28, 3; Ecclus, 46, 23.

Ver. 11. *A thought to kill thee.* That is, a suggestion, to which I did not consent.

Ver. 13. *Revenge me of thee,* or (as it is in the hebrew), will revenge me. The meaning is, that he refers his whole cause to God, to judge and punish according to his justice: yet so as to keep himself in the mean time, from all personal hatred to Saul, or desire of gratifying his own passion, by seeking revenge. So far from it, that when Saul was afterwards slain, we find, that instead of rejoicing at his death, he mourned most bitterly for him.

David's name: and then held their peace.

10 But Nabal answering the servants of David, said: Who is David? And what is the son of Isai? Servants are multiplied now a days who flee from their masters.

11 Shall I then take my bread, and my water, and the flesh of my cattle, which I have killed for my shearers, and give to men whom I know not whence they are?

12 So the servants of David went back their way: and returning came and told him all the words that he said.

13 Then David said to his young men: Let every man gird on his sword. And they girded on every man his sword. And David also girded on his sword: and there followed David about four hundred men. And two hundred remained with the baggage.

14 But one of the servants told Abigail the wife of Nabal, saying: Behold David sent messengers out of the wilderness, to salute our master; and he rejected them.

15 These men were very good to us, and gave us no trouble: neither did we ever lose any thing all the time that we conversed with them in the desert.

16 They were a wall unto us both by night and day, all the while we were with them keeping the sheep.

17 Wherefore consider, and think what thou hast to do: for evil is determined against thy husband, and against thy house. And he is a son of Belial, so that no man can speak to him.

18 Then Abigail made haste and took two hundred loaves, and two vessels of wine, and five sheep ready dressed, and five measures of parched corn, and a hundred clusters of raisins, and two hundred cakes of dry figs, and laid them upon asses.

19 And she said to her servants: Go before me. Behold I will follow after you. But she told not her husband Nabal.

20 And when she had gotten upon an ass, and was coming down to the foot of the mountain, David and his men came down over against her, and she met them.

21 And David said: Truly in vain have I kept all that belonged to this man in the wilderness, and nothing was lost of all that pertained unto him: and he hath returned me evil for good.

22 May God do so and so, and add more to the foes of David, if I leave of all that belong to him till the morning, any that pisseth against the wall.

23 And when Abigail saw David she made haste and lighted off the ass, and

fell before David, on her face, and adored upon the ground.

24 And she fell at his feet, and said: Upon me let this iniquity be, my lord. Let thy handmaid speak, I beseech thee, in thy ears: and hear the words of thy servant.

25 Let not my lord the king, I pray, regard this naughty man Nabal: for according to his name, he is a fool, and folly is with him. But I thy handmaid did not see thy servants, my lord, whom thou sentest.

26 Now therefore, my lord, the Lord liveth, and thy soul liveth, who hath withholden thee from coming to blood, and hath saved thy hand to thee: and now let thy enemies be as Nabal, and all they that seek evil to my lord.

27 Wherefore receive this blessing, which thy handmaid hath brought to thee, my lord: and give it to the young men that follow thee, my lord.

28 Forgive the iniquity of thy handmaid: for the Lord will surely make for my lord a faithful house, [2] because thou, my lord, fightest the battles of the Lord. Let not evil therefore be found in thee all the days of thy life.

29 For if a man at any time shall rise, and persecute thee, and seek thy life, the soul of my lord shall be kept, as in the bundle of the living, with the Lord thy God. But the souls of thy enemies shall be whirled, as with the violence and whirling of a sling.

30 And when the Lord shall have done to thee, my lord, all the good that he hath spoken concerning thee, and shall have made thee prince over Israel,

31 This shall not be an occasion of grief to thee, and a scruple of heart to my lord, that thou hast shed innocent blood, or hast revenged thyself: and when the Lord shall have done well by my Lord, thou shalt remember thy handmaid.

32 And David said to Abigail: Blessed be the Lord the God of Israel, who sent thee this day to meet me, and blessed be thy speech.

33 And blessed be thou, who hast kept me to-day, from coming to blood, and revenging me with my own hand.

34 Otherwise, as the Lord liveth the God of Israel, who hath withholden me from doing thee any evil: if thou hadst not quickly come to meet me, there had

---

[2] 1 Kings, 16, 18; 17, 40.

CHAP. 25. Ver. 22. *If I leave of all that belong to him.* David certainly sinned in his designs against Nabal and his family, as he himself was afterwards sensible, when he blessed God for hindering him from executing the revenge he had proposed.

Ver. 25. *His name. Nabal,* in Hebrew, signifies *a fool.*

not been left to Nabal by the morning light any that pisseth against the wall.

35 And David received at her hand all that she had brought him, and said to her: Go in peace into thy house. Behold I have heard thy voice, and have honoured thy face.

36 And Abigail came to Nabal. And behold he had a feast in his house, like the feast of a king; and Nabal's heart was merry: for he was very drunk. And she told him nothing less or more until morning.

37 But early in the morning when Nabal had digested his wine, his wife told him these words: and his heart died within him, and he became as a stone.

38 And after ten days had passed, the Lord struck Nabal, and he died.

39 And when David had heard that Nabal was dead, he said: Blessed be the Lord, who hath judged the cause of my reproach at the hand of Nabal, and hath kept his servant from evil; and the Lord hath returned the wickedness of Nabal upon his head. Then David sent and treated with Abigail, that he might take her to himself for a wife.

40 And David's servants came to Abigail to Carmel, and spoke to her, saying: David hath sent us to thee, to take thee to himself for a wife.

41 And she arose and bowed herself down with her face to the earth, and said: Behold, let thy servant be a handmaid, to wash the feet of the servants of my lord.

42 And Abigail arose, and made haste, and got upon an ass: and five damsels went with her, her waiting maids; and she followed the messengers of David, and became his wife.

43 Moreover David took also Achinoam of Jezrahel. And they were both of them his wives.

44 But Saul gave Michol his daughter, David's wife, to Phalti, the son of Lais, who was of Gallium.

CHAPTER 26

Saul goeth out again after David who cometh by night where Saul and his men are asleep, but suffereth him not to be touched. Saul again confesseth his fault, and promiseth peace.

AND the men of Ziph came to Saul in Gabaa, saying: [1] Behold David is hid in the hill of Hachila, which is over against the wilderness.

Chap. 26. [1] Kings, 23, 19.

Ver. 39. *Blessed be the Lord.* David praiseth God, on this occasion, not out of joy for the death of Nabal (which would have argued a rancour of heart), but because he saw that God had so visibly taken his cause in hand, in punishing the injury done to him; whilst by a merciful providence he kept him from revenging himself.

2 And Saul arose, and went down to the wilderness of Ziph, having with him three thousand chosen men of Israel, to seek David in the wilderness of Ziph.

3 And Saul encamped in Gabaa Hachila, which was over against the wilderness in the way: and David abode in the wilderness. And seeing that Saul was come after him into the wilderness,

4 He sent spies, and learned that he was most certainly come thither.

5 And David arose secretly, and came to the place where Saul was. And when he had beheld the place, wherein Saul slept, and Abner the son of Ner, the captain of his army, and Saul sleeping in a tent, and the rest of the multitude round about him.

6 David spoke to Achimelech the Hethite, and Abisai the son of Sarvia the brother of Joab, saying: Who will go down with me to Saul into the camp? And Abisai said: I will go with thee.

7 So David and Abisai came to the people by night, and found Saul lying and sleeping in the tent, and his spear fixed in the ground at his head: and Abner and the people sleeping round about him.

8 And Abisai said to David: God hath shut up thy enemy this day into thy hands. Now then I will run him through with my spear even to the earth at once; and there shall be no need of a second time.

9 And David said to Abisai: Kill him not. For who shall put forth his hand against the Lord's anointed, and shall be guiltless?

10 And David said: As the Lord liveth, unless the Lord shall strike him: or his day shall come to die: or he shall go down to battle and perish.

11 The Lord be merciful unto me, that I extend not my hand upon the Lord's anointed. But now take the spear, which is at his head, and the cup of water, and let us go.

12 So David took the spear, and the cup of water which was at Saul's head, and they went away. And no man saw it, or knew it, or awaked; but they were all asleep, for a deep sleep from the Lord was fallen upon them.

13 And when David was gone over to the other side, and stood on the top of the hill afar off, and a good space was between them,

14 David cried to the people, and to Abner the son of Ner, saying: Wilt thou not answer, Abner? And Abner answering, said: Who art thou, that criest and disturbest the king?

15 And David said to Abner: Art not thou a man? And who is like thee in Israel? Why then hast thou not kept

thy lord the king? For there came one of the people in to kill the king thy lord.

16 This thing is not good, that thou hast done. As the Lord liveth, you are the sons of death, who have not kept your master, the Lord's anointed. And now where is the king's spear, and the cup of water, which was at his head?

17 And Saul knew David's voice, and said: Is this thy voice, my son David? And David said: It is my voice, my lord the king.

18 And he said: Wherefore doth my lord persecute his servant? What have I done? Or what evil is there in my hand?

19 Now therefore hear, I pray thee, my lord the king, the words of thy servant: If the Lord stir thee up against me, let him accept of sacrifice. But if the sons of men, they are cursed in the sight of the Lord, who have cast me out this day, that I should not dwell in the inheritance of the Lord, saying: Go, serve strange gods.

20 And now let not my blood be shed upon the earth before the Lord: for the king of Israel is come out to seek a flea, as the partridge is hunted in the mountains.

21 And Saul said: I have sinned. Return, my son, David, for I will no more do thee harm, because my life hath been precious in thy eyes this day: for it appeareth that I have done foolishly, and have been ignorant in very many things.

22 And David answering, said: Behold the king's spear. Let one of the king's servants come over and fetch it.

23 And the Lord will reward every one according to his justice, and his faithfulness: for the Lord hath delivered thee this day into my hand, and I would not put forth my hand against the Lord's anointed.

24 And as thy life hath been much set by this day in my eyes, so let my life be much set by in the eyes of the Lord: and let him deliver me from all distress.

25 Then Saul said to David: Blessed art thou, my son David: and truly doing thou shalt do, and prevailing thou shalt prevail. And David went on his way, and Saul returned to his place.

CHAPTER 27

David goeth again to Achis king of Geth, and obtaineth of him the city of Siceleg.

AND David said in his heart: I shall one day or other fall into the hands of Saul. Is it not better for me to flee, and to be saved in the land of the Philistines, that Saul may despair

of me, and cease to seek me in all the coasts of Israel? I will flee then out of his hands.

2 And David arose and went away, both he and the six hundred men that were with him, to Achis the son of Maoch, king of Geth.

3 And David dwelt with Achis at Geth, he and his men: every man with his household, and David with his two wives, Achinoam the Jezrahelitess, and Abigail the wife of Nabal of Carmel.

4 And it was told Saul that David was fled to Geth: and he sought no more after him.

5 And David said to Achis: If I have found favour in thy sight, let a place be given me in one of the cities of this country, that I may dwell there. For why should thy servant dwell in the royal city with thee?

6 Then Achis gave him Siceleg that day: for which reason Siceleg belongeth to the kings of Juda unto this day.

7 And the time that David dwelt in the country of the Philistines was four months.

8 And David and his men went up, and pillaged Gessuri, and Gerzi, and the Amalecites: for these were of old the inhabitants of the countries, as men go to Sur, even to the land of Egypt.

9 And David wasted all the land, and left neither man nor woman alive: and took away the sheep and the oxen, and the asses, and the camels, and the apparel, and returned and came to Achis.

10 And Achis said to him: Whom hast thou gone against to-day? David answered: Against the south of Juda, and against the south of Jerameel, and against the south of Ceni.

11 And David saved neither man nor woman, neither brought he any of them to Geth, saying: Lest they should speak against us. So did David, and such was his proceeding all the days that he dwelt in the country of the Philistines.

12 And Achis believed David, saying: He hath done much harm to his people Israel; therefore he shall be my servant for ever.

CHAPTER 28

The Philistines go out to war against Israel. Saul being forsaken by God, hath recourse to a witch. Samuel appeareth to him.

AND it came to pass in those days, that the Philistines gathered to-

CHAP. 27. Ver. 8. *Pillaged Gessuri.* These probably were enemies of the people of God: and some, if not all of them, were of the number of those whom God had ordered to be destroyed: which justifies David's proceedings in their regard. Though it is to be observed here, that we are not under an obligation of justifying every thing that he did: for the scripture, in relating what was done, doth not say that it was well done. And even such as are true servants of God, are not to be imitated in all they do.

gether their armies to be prepared for war against Israel. And Achis said to David: Know thou now assuredly, that thou shalt go out with me to the war, thou, and thy men.

2 And David said to Achis: Now thou shalt know what thy servant will do. And Achis said to David: And I will appoint thee to guard my life for ever.

3 [1] Now Samuel was dead, and all Israel mourned for him, and buried him in Ramatha his city. And Saul had put away all the magicians and soothsayers out of the land.

4 And the Philistines were gathered together, and came and camped in Sunam. And Saul also gathered together all Israel, and came to Gelboe.

5 And Saul saw the army of the Philistines, and was afraid: and his heart was very much dismayed.

6 And he consulted the Lord, and he answered him not; neither by dreams, nor by priests, nor by prophets.

7 And Saul said to his servants: Seek me a woman that hath a [2] divining spirit; and I will go to her, and inquire by her. And his servants said to him: There is a woman that hath a divining spirit at Endor.

8 Then he disguised himself and put on other clothes. And he went, and two men with him, and they came to the woman by night. And he said to her: Divine to me by thy divining spirit, and bring me up him whom I shall tell thee.

9 And the woman said to him: Behold thou knowest all that Saul hath done, and how he hath rooted out the magicians and soothsayers from the land. Why then dost thou lay a snare for my life, to cause me to be put to death?

10 And Saul swore unto her by the Lord, saying: As the Lord liveth there shall be no evil happen to thee for this thing.

11 And the woman said to him: Whom shall I bring up to thee? And he said, Bring me up Samuel.

12 And when the woman saw Samuel, she cried out with a loud voice, and said to Saul: Why hast thou deceived me? For thou art Saul.

13 And the king said to her: Fear

not. What hast thou seen? And the woman said to Saul: I saw gods ascending out of the earth.

14 And he said to her: What form is he of? And she said: An old man cometh up; and he is covered with a mantle. And Saul understood that it was Samuel, and he bowed himself with his face to the ground, and adored.

15 And Samuel said to Saul: [3] Why hast thou disturbed my rest, that I should be brought up? And Saul said: I am in great distress; for the Philistines fight against me; and God is departed from me; and would not hear me, neither by the hand of prophets, nor by dreams. Therefore I have called thee, that thou mayest shew me what I shall do.

16 And Samuel said: Why askest thou me, seeing the Lord has departed from thee, and is gone over to thy rival?

17 For the Lord will do to thee as he spoke by me, and he will rend thy kingdom out of thy hand, and will give it to thy neighbour David.

18 Because thou didst not obey the voice of the Lord, neither didst thou execute the wrath of his indignation upon Amalec. Therefore hath the Lord done to thee what thou sufferest this day.

19 And the Lord also will deliver Israel with thee into the hands of the Philistines. And to-morrow thou and thy sons shall be with me. And the Lord will also deliver the army of Israel into the hands of the Philistines.

20 And forthwith Saul fell all along on the ground, for he was frightened with the words of Samuel: and there was no strength in him, for he had eaten no bread all that day.

21 And the woman came to Saul (for he was very much troubled) and said to him: Behold thy handmaid hath obeyed thy voice; and I have put my life in my hand; and I hearkened unto the words which thou spokest to me.

22 Now therefore hear thou also the voice of thy handmaid: and let me set before thee a morsel of bread, that thou mayest eat and recover strength, and be able to go on thy journey.

23 But he refused, and said: I will not eat. But his servants and the woman forced him; and at length hearkening to their voice, he arose from the ground and sat upon the bed.

24 Now the woman had a fatted calf in the house, and she made haste and killed it: and taking meal kneaded it, and baked some unleavened bread,

25 And set it before Saul, and before his servants. And when they had eaten they rose up, and walked all that night.

CHAP. 28. [1] 1 Kings, 25, 1; Ecclus. 46, 23. [2] Lev. 20, 27; Deut. 18, 11; Acts 16, 16. [3] Ecclus. 46, 23.

CHAP. 28. Ver. 14. *Understood that it was Samuel.* It is the more common opinion of the holy fathers, and interpreters, that the soul of Samuel appeared indeed; and not, as some have imagined, an evil spirit in his shape. Not that the power of her magic could bring him thither: but that God was pleased for the punishment of Saul, that Samuel himself should denounce unto him the evils that were falling upon him (Ecclus. 46, 23)

Ver. 19. *With me.* That is, in the state of the dead, and in another world, though not in the same place.

CHAPTER 29

David going with the Philistines is sent back by their princes.

NOW all the troops of the Philistines were gathered together to Aphec: and Israel also camped by the fountain which is in Jezrahel.

2 And the lords of the Philistines marched with their hundreds and their thousands. But David and his men were in the rear with Achis.

3 And the princes of the Philistines said to Achis: What mean these Hebrews? And Achis said to the princes of the Philistines: Do you not know David, who was the servant of Saul the king of Israel, and hath been with me many days, or years; and I have found no fault in him, since the day that he fled over to me until this day?

4 ¹ But the princes of the Philistines were angry with him; and they said to him: Let this man return, and abide in his place, which thou hast appointed him. And let him not go down with us to battle, lest he be an adversary to us, when we shall begin to fight: for how can he otherwise appease his master, but with our heads?

5 Is not this David, to whom they sung in their dances, saying: Saul slew his thousands, and David his ten thousands?

6 Then Achis called David, and said to him: As the Lord liveth, thou art upright and good in my sight; and so is thy going out, and thy coming in with me in the army. And I have not found any evil in thee, since the day that thou camest to me unto this day: but thou pleasest not the lords.

7 Return therefore, and go in peace and offend not the eyes of the princes of the Philistines.

8 And David said to Achis: But what have I done, and what hast thou found in me thy servant, from the day that I have been in thy sight until this day, that I may not go and fight against the enemies of my lord the king?

9 And Achis answering said to David: I know that thou art good in my sight, ² as an angel of God; but the princes of the Philistines have said: He shall not go up with us to the battle.

10 Therefore arise in the morning, thou, and the servants of thy lord, who came with thee; and when you are up before day, and it shall begin to be light, go on your way.

11 So David and his men arose in the night, that they might set forward in the morning, and returned to the land of the Philistines. And the Philistines went up to Jezrahel.

CHAPTER 30

The Amalecites burn Siceleg, and carry off the prey. David pursueth after them, and recovereth all out of their hands.

NOW when David and his men were come to Siceleg on the third day, ¹ the Amalecites had made an invasion on the south side upon Siceleg, and had smitten Siceleg, and burnt it with fire.

2 And had taken the women captives that were in it, both little and great: and they had not killed any person, but had carried them with them, and went on their way.

3 So when David and his men came to the city, and found it burnt with fire, and that their wives and their sons, and their daughters were taken captives,

4 David and the people that were with him, lifted up their voices, and wept till they had no more tears.

5 For the two wives also of David were taken captives, Achinoam the Jezrahelitess, and Abigail the wife of Nabal of Carmel.

6 And David was greatly afflicted. For the people had a mind to stone him; for the soul of every man was bitterly grieved for his sons, and daughters. But David took courage in the Lord his God.

7 And he said to Abiathar the priest the son of Achimelech: Bring me hither the ephod. And Abiathar brought the ephod to David.

8 And David consulted the Lord, saying: Shall I pursue after these robbers, and shall I overtake them, or not? And the Lord said to him: Pursue after them. For thou shalt·surely overtake them and recover the prey.

9 So David went, he and the six hundred men that were with him. And they came to the torrent Besor: and some being weary stayed there.

10 But David pursued, he and four hundred men: for two hundred stayed, who being weary could not go over the torrent Besor.

11 And they found an Egyptian in the field, and brought him to David: and they gave him bread to eat, and water to drink,

12 As also a piece of a cake of figs, and two bunches of raisins. And when he had eaten them his spirit returned, and he was refreshed: for he had not eaten bread, nor drunk water three days, and three nights.

13 And David said to him: To whom dost thou belong? Or whence dost thou come? And whither art thou going?

CHAP. 29. ¹ 1 Par. 12, 19. ² 2 Kings, 14, 17, 20; 19, 37. CHAP. 30. ¹ 1 Par. 12. 20

He said: I am a young man of Egypt, the servant of an Amalecite; and my master left me, because I began to be sick three days ago.

14 For we made an invasion on the south side of Cerethi, and upon Juda, and upon the south of Caleb, and we burnt Siceleg with fire.

15 And David said to him: Canst thou bring me to this company? And he said: Swear to me by God, that thou wilt not kill me, nor deliver me into the hands of my master, and I will bring thee to this company. And David swore to him.

16 And when he had brought him, behold they were lying spread upon all the ground, eating and drinking, and as it were keeping a festival day, for all the prey, and the spoils which they had taken out of the land of the Philistines, and out of the land of Juda.

17 And David slew them from the evening unto the evening of the next day: and there escaped not a man of them, but four hundred young men, who had gotten upon camels, and fled.

18 So David recovered all that the Amalecites had taken; and he rescued his two wives.

19 And there was nothing missing small or great, neither of their sons or their daughters, nor of the spoils: and whatsoever they had taken David recovered all.

20 And he took all the flocks and the herds, and made them go before him. And they said: This is the prey of David.

21 And David came to the two hundred men, who being weary had stayed, and were not able to follow David, and he had ordered them to abide at the torrent Besor. And they came out to meet David, and the people that were with him. And David coming to the people saluted them peaceably.

22 Then all the wicked and unjust men that had gone with David answering, said: Because they came not with us, we will not give them any thing of the prey which we have recovered. But let every man take his wife and children, and be contented with them, and go his way.

23 But David said: You shall not do so, my brethren, with these things which the Lord hath given us, who hath kept us, and hath delivered the robbers that invaded us into our hands.

24 And no man shall hearken to you in this matter. But equal shall be the portion of him that went down to battle and of him that abode at the baggage; and they shall divide alike.

25 And this hath been done from that day forward, and since was made a

statute, and an ordinance, and as a law in Israel.

26 Then David came to Siceleg, and sent presents of the prey to the ancients of Juda his neighbours, saying: Receive a blessing of the prey of the enemies of the Lord.

27 To them that were in Bethel, and that were in Ramoth to the south, and to them that were in Jether,

28 And to them that were in Aroer and that were in Sephamoth, and that were in Esthamo,

29 And that were in Rachal, and that were in the cities of Jerameel, and that were in the cities of Ceni,

30 And that were in Arama, and that were in the lake Asan, and that were in Athach,

31 And that were in Hebron, and to the rest that were in those places, in which David had abode with his men.

CHAPTER 31

Israel is defeated by the Philistines. Saul and his sons are slain.

AND the Philistines fought against Israel: and the men of Israel fled from before the Philistines, and fell down slain in mount Gelboe.

2 [1] And the Philistines fell upon Saul, and upon his sons: and they slew Jonathan, and Abinadab and Melchisua the sons of Saul.

3 And the whole weight of the battle was turned upon Saul: and the archers overtook him. And he was grievously wounded by the archers.

4 [2] Then Saul said to his armourbearer: Draw thy sword, and kill me: lest these uncircumcised come, and slay me, and mock at me. And his armourbearer would not: for he was struck with exceeding great fear. Then Saul took his sword, and fell upon it.

5 And when his armourbearer saw this, to wit, that Saul was dead, he also fell upon his sword and died with him.

6 So Saul died, and his three sons, and his armourbearer, and all his men that same day together.

7 And the men of Israel, that were beyond the valley, and beyond the Jordan, seeing that the Israelites were fled, and that Saul was dead, and his sons, forsook their cities, and fled: and the Philistines came, and dwelt there.

8 And on the morrow the Philistines came to strip the slain: and they found Saul and his three sons lying in mount Gelboe.

9 And they cut off Saul's head, and stripped him of his armour, and sent into the land of the Philistines round about, to publish it in the temples of their idols, and among their people.

10 And they put his armour in the temple of Astaroth: but his body they hung on the wall of Bethsan.

11 ⁸ Now when the inhabitants of Jabes Galaad had heard all that the Philistines had done to Saul,

12 All the most valiant men arose,

and walked all the night, and took the body of Saul, and the bodies of his sons, from the wall of Bethsam And they came to Jabes Galaad, and burnt them there.

13 And they took their bones and buried them in the wood of Jabes: and fasted seven days.

THE SECOND BOOK OF

SAMUEL

OTHERWISE CALLED THE

SECOND BOOK OF KINGS

This Book relates the transactions from the death of Saul until the end of David's reign, being a history for the space of about forty-six years.

CHAPTER 1

David mourneth for the death of Saul and Jonathan. He ordereth the man to be slain who pretended he had killed Saul.

NOW it came to pass, after Saul was dead, that David returned from the slaughter of the Amalecites, and abode two days in Siceleg.

2 And on the third day, there appeared a man who came out of Saul's camp, with his garments rent, and dust strewed on his head: and when he came to David, he fell upon his face, and adored.

3 And David said to him: From whence comest thou? And he said to him: I am fled out of the camp of Israel.

4 And David said unto him: What is the matter that is come to pass? Tell me. He said: The people are fled from the battle: and many of the people are fallen and dead. Moreover Saul and Jonathan his son are slain.

5 And David said to the young man that told him: How knowest thou that Saul and Jonathan his son, are dead?

6 And the young man that told him, said: I came by chance upon mount Gelboe, and Saul leaned upon his spear: and the chariots and horsemen drew nigh unto him.

7 And looking behind him, and seeing me, he called me. And I answered: Here am I.

8 And he said to me: Who art thou? And I said to him: I am an Amalecite.

9 And he said to me: Stand over me,

and kill me. For anguish is come upon me; and as yet my whole life is in me.

10 So standing over him, I killed him: for I knew that he could not live after the fall. And I took the diadem that was on his head, and the bracelet that was on his arm, and have brought *them* hither to thee, my lord.

11 Then David took hold of his garments and rent them; and likewise all the men that were with him.

12 And they mourned, and wept, and fasted until evening for Saul, and for Jonathan his son, and for the people of the Lord, and for the house of Israel: because they were fallen by the sword.

13 And David said to the young man that told him: Whence art thou? He answered: I am the son of a stranger of Amalec.

14 And David said to him: ¹ Why didst thou not fear to put out thy hand to kill the Lord's anointed?

15 And David calling one of his servants, said: Go near and fall upon him. And he struck him so that he died.

16 And David said to him: Thy blood be upon thy own head. For thy own mouth hath spoken against thee, saying: I have slain the Lord's anointed.

17 And David made this kind of lamentation over Saul, and over Jonathan his son.

³ 2 Kings, 2, 4. CHAP. 1. ¹ Ps. 104, 15.

CHAP. 1. Ver. 10. *I killed him.* This story of the young Amalecite was not true, as may easily be proved by comparing it with the last chapter of the foregoing book.

18 (Also he commanded that they should teach the children of Juda the use of the bow, as it is written in the book of the just.) And he said: Consider, O Israel, for them that are dead, wounded on thy high places.

19 The illustrious of Israel are slain upon thy mountains: How are the valiant fallen!

20 Tell it not in Geth, publish it not in the streets of Ascalon: lest the daughters of the Philistines rejoice, lest the daughters of the uncircumcised triumph.

21 Ye mountains of Gelboe, let neither dew, nor rain come upon you: neither be they fields of firstfruits. For there was cast away the shield of the valiant, the shield of Saul as though he had not been anointed with oil.

22 From the blood of the slain, from the fat of the valiant, the arrow of Jonathan never turned back; and the sword of Saul did not return empty.

23 Saul and Jonathan, lovely, and comely in their life, even in death they were not divided: they were swifter than eagles, stronger than lions.

24 Ye daughters of Israel, weep over Saul, who clothed you with scarlet in delights, who gave ornaments of gold for your attire.

25 How are the valiant fallen in battle? Jonathan slain in the high places?

26 I grieve for thee, my brother Jonathan: exceedingly beautiful and amiable to *me* above the love of women. As the mother loveth her only son, so did I love thee.

27 How are the valiant fallen, and the weapons of war perished?

CHAPTER 2

David is received and anointed king of Juda. Isboseth the son of Saul reigneth over the rest of Israel. A battle between Abner and Joab.

AND after these things David consulted the Lord, saying: Shall I go up into one of the cities of Juda? And the Lord said to him: Go up. And David said: Whither shall I go up? And he answered him: Into Hebron.

2 So David went up, and his two wives, Achinoam the Jezrahelitess, and Abigail the wife of Nabal of Carmel.

3 And the men also that were with him, David brought up every man with his household: and they abode in the towns of Hebron.

4 ¹ And the men of Juda came, and anointed David there, to be king over

CHAP. 2. ¹ 1 Mach. 2, 57; 2 Kings, 5, 3.

CHAP. 2. Ver. 10. *He reigned two years.* That is, before he began visibly to decline: but in all he reigned seven years and six months; for so long David reigned in Hebron.

the house of Juda. And it was told David that the men of Jabes Galaad had buried Saul.

5 David therefore sent messengers to the men of Jabes Galaad, and said to them: Blessed be you to the Lord, who have shewn this mercy to your master Saul, and have buried him.

6 And now the Lord surely will render you mercy and truth; and I also will requite you for this good turn, because you have done this thing.

7 Let your hands be strengthened; and be ye men of valour: for although your master Saul be dead, yet the house of Juda hath anointed me to be their king.

8 But Abner the son of Ner, general of Saul's army, took Isboseth the son of Saul, and led him about through the camp.

9 And made him king over Galaad, and over Gessuri, and over Jezrahel, and over Ephraim, and over Benjamin, and over all Israel.

10 Isboseth the son of Saul was forty years old when he began to reign over Israel. And he reigned two years; and only the house of Juda followed David.

11 And the number of the days that David abode, reigning in Hebron over the house of Juda, was seven years and six months.

12 And Abner the son of Ner, and the servants of Isboseth the son of Saul, went out from the camp to Gabaon.

13 And Joab the son of Sarvia, and the servants of David went out, and met them by the pool of Gabaon. And when they were come together, they sat down over against one another: the one on the one side of the pool, and the other on the other side.

14 And Abner said to Joab: Let the young men rise, and play before us. And Joab answered: Let them rise.

15 Then there arose and went over twelve in number of Benjamin, of the part of Isboseth the son of Saul, and twelve of the servants of David.

16 And every one catching his fellow by the head, thrust his sword into the side of his adversary: and they fell down together. And the name of the place was called: The field of the valiant, in Gabaon.

17 And there was a very fierce battle that day: and Abner was put to flight, with the men of Israel, by the servants of David.

18 And there were the three sons of Sarvia there, Joab, and Abisai, and Asael. Now Asael was a most swift runner, like one of the roes that abide in the woods.

19 And Asael pursued after Abner,

and turned not to the right hand nor to the left from following Abner.

20 And Abner looked behind him, and said: Art thou Asael? And he answered: I am.

21 And Abner said to him: Go to the right hand or to the left, and lay hold on one of the young men and take thee his spoils. But Asael would not leave off following him close.

22 And again Abner said to Asael: Go off, and do not follow me, lest I be obliged to stab thee to the ground; and I shall not be able to hold up my face to Joab thy brother.

23 But he refused to hearken to him, and would not turn aside. Wherefore Abner struck him with his spear with a back stroke in the groin, and thrust him through. And he died upon the spot: and all that came to the place where Asael fell down and died, stood still.

24 Now while Joab and Abisai pursued after Abner, the sun went down. And they came as far as the hill of the aqueduct, that lieth over against the valley by the way of the wilderness in Gabaon.

25 And the children of Benjamin gathered themselves together to Abner: and being joined in one body, they stood on the top of a hill.

26 And Abner cried out to Joab, and said: Shall thy sword rage unto utter destruction? Knowest thou not that it is dangerous to drive people to despair? How long dost thou defer to bid the people cease from pursuing after their brethren?

27 And Joab said: As the Lord liveth, if thou hadst spoke sooner, *even* in the morning the people should have retired from pursuing after their brethren.

28 Then Joab sounded the trumpet, and all the army stood still, and did not pursue after Israel any farther, nor fight any more.

29 And Abner and his men walked all that night through the plains. And they passed the Jordan: and having gone through all Beth-horon, came to the camp.

30 And Joab returning, after he had left Abner, assembled all the people: and there were wanting of David's servants nineteen men, beside Asael.

31 But the servants of David had killed of Benjamin, and of the men that were with Abner, three hundred and sixty, who all died.

32 And they took Asael, and buried him in the sepulchre of his father in Bethlehem. And Joab, and the men that were with him, marched all the night, and they came to Hebron at break of day.

CHAPTER 3

David groweth daily stronger. Abner cometh over to him. He is treacherously slain by Joab.

NOW there was a long war between the house of Saul and the house of David: David prospering and growing always stronger and stronger, but the house of Saul decaying daily.

2 [1] And sons were born to David in Hebron. And his firstborn was Amnon of Achinoam the Jezrahelitess:

3 And his second Cheleab of Abigail the wife of Nabal of Carmel: and the third Absalom the son of Maacha the daughter of Tholmai king of Gessur:

4 And the fourth Adonias, the son of Haggith: and the fifth Saphathia the son of Abital:

5 And the sixth Jethraam of Egla the wife of David. These were born to David in Hebron.

6 Now while there was war between the house of Saul and the house of David, Abner the son of Ner ruled the house of Saul.

7 And Saul had a concubine named Respha, the daughter of Aia. And Isboseth said to Abner:

8 Why didst thou go in to my father's concubine? And he was exceedingly angry for the words of Isboseth, and said: Am I a dog's head against Juda this day, who have shewn mercy to the house of Saul thy father, and to his brethren and friends, and have not delivered thee into the hands of David; and hast thou sought this day against me to charge me with a matter concerning a woman?

9 So do God to Abner, and more also, unless as the Lord hath sworn to David, so I do to him,

10 That the kingdom be translated from the house of Saul, and the throne of David be set up over Israel, and over Juda from Dan to Bersabee.

11 And he could not answer him a word, because he feared him.

12 Abner therefore sent messengers to David for himself, saying: Whose is the land? And that they should say: Make a league with me, and my hand shall be with thee: and I will bring all Israel to thee.

13 And he said: Very well. I will make a league with thee; but one thing I require of thee, saying: Thou shalt not see my face before thou bring Michol the daughter of Saul. And so thou shalt come, and see me.

14 And David sent messengers to

CHAP. 3. [1] Par. 3, 1.
CHAP. 3. Ver. 1. *There was a long war.* Rather a strife or emulation than a war with arms; it lasted five years and a half.

Isboseth the son of Saul, saying: ²Restore my wife Michol, whom I espoused to me for a hundred foreskins of the Philistines.

15 And Isboseth sent, and took her from her husband Phaltiel, the son of Lais.

16 And her husband followed her, weeping as far as Bahurim. And Abner said to him: Go and return. And he returned.

17 Abner also spoke to the ancients of Israel, saying: Both yesterday and the day before you sought for David that he might reign over you.

18 Now then do it; because the Lord hath spoken to David, saying: By the hand of my servant David I will save my people Israel from the hands of the Philistines, and of all their enemies.

19 And Abner spoke also to Benjamin. And he went to speak to David in Hebron all that seemed good to Israel, and to all Benjamin.

20 And he came to David in Hebron with twenty men. And David made a feast for Abner, and his men that came with him.

21 And Abner said to David: I will rise, that I may gather all Israel unto thee my lord the king, and may enter into a league with thee, and that thou mayst reign over all, as thy soul desireth. Now when David had brought Abner on his way, and he was gone in peace,

22 Immediately David's servants and Joab came, after having slain the robbers, with an exceeding great booty. And Abner was not with David in Hebron; for he had now sent him away, and he was gone in peace.

23 And Joab and all the army that was with him, came afterwards. And it was told Joab, that Abner the son of Ner came to the king, and he hath sent him away, and he is gone in peace.

24 And Joab went in to the king, and said: What hast thou done? Behold Abner came to thee: Why didst thou send him away? And he is gone and departed.

25 Knowest thou not Abner the son of Ner, that to this end he came to thee, that he might deceive thee, and to know thy going out, and thy coming in, and to know all thou dost?

26 Then Joab going out from David, sent messengers after Abner, and brought him back from the cistern of Sira, David knowing nothing of it.

27 And when ³Abner was returned to Hebron, Joab took him aside to the middle of the gate, to speak to him treacherously. And he stabbed him

¹ 1 Kings, 18, 27.   ³ 3 Kings, 2, 5.

there in the groin: and he died, in revenge of the blood of Asael his brother.

28 And when David heard of it, after the thing was now done, he said: I, and my kingdom are innocent before the Lord for ever of the blood of Abner the son of Ner.

29 And may it come upon the head of Joab, and upon all his father's house: and let there not fail from the house of Joab one that hath an issue of seed, or that is a leper, or that holdeth the distaff, or that falleth by the sword, or that wanteth bread.

30 So Joab and Abisai his brother slew Abner, because he had killed their brother Asael at Gabaon in the battle.

31 And David said to Joab, and to all the people that were with him: Rend your garments, and gird yourselves with sackcloths, and mourn before the funeral of Abner. And king David himself followed the bier.

32 And when they had buried Abner in Hebron, king David lifted up his voice, and wept at the grave of Abner: and all the people also wept.

33 And the king mourning and lamenting over Abner, said: Not as cowards are wont to die, hath Abner died.

34 Thy hands were not bound, nor thy feet laden with fetters: but as men fall before the children of iniquity, so didst thou fall. And all the people repeating it wept over him.

35 And when all the people came to take meat with David, while it was yet broad day, David swore, saying: So do God to me, and more also, if I taste bread or anything else before sunset.

36 And all the people heard: and they were pleased. And all that the king did seemed good in the sight of all the people.

37 And all the people, and all Israel understood that day that it was not the king's doing, that Abner the son of Ner was slain.

38 The king also said to his servants: Do you not know that a prince and a great man is slain this day in Israel?

39 But I as yet am tender, *though* anointed king: and these men the sons of Sarvia are too hard for me. The Lord reward him that doth evil according to his wickedness.

CHAPTER 4

Isboseth is murdered by two of his servants,
David punisheth the murderers.

AND Isboseth the son of Saul heard that Abner was slain in Hebron: and his hands were weakened: And all Israel was troubled.

2 Now the son of Saul had two men

captains of his bands. The name of the one was Baana, and the name of the other Rechab, the sons of Remmon a Berothite of the children of Benjamin: for Beroth also was reckoned in Benjamin.

3 And the Berothites fled into Gethaim, and were sojourners there until that time.

4 And Jonathan the son of Saul had a son that was lame of his feet: for he was five years old when the tidings came of Saul and Jonathan from Jezrahel. And his nurse took him up and fled: and as she made haste to flee, he fell and became lame. And his name was Miphiboseth.

5 And the sons of Remmon the Berothite, Rechab and Baana, coming, went into the house of Isboseth in the heat of the day: and he was sleeping upon his bed at noon. And the doorkeeper of the house, who was cleansing wheat, was fallen asleep.

6 And they entered into the house secretly taking ears of corn: and Rechab and Baana his brother stabbed him in the groin, and fled away.

7 For when they came into the house, he was sleeping upon his bed in a parlour: and they struck him and killed him. And taking away his head they went off by the way of the wilderness, *walking* all night.

8 And they brought the head of Isboseth to David to Hebron; and they said to the king: Behold the head of Isboseth the son of Saul thy enemy who sought thy life. And the Lord hath revenged my lord the king this day of Saul, and of his seed.

9 But David answered Rechab and Baana his brother, the sons of Remmon the Berothite, and said to them: As the Lord liveth, who hath delivered my soul out of all distress,

10 ¹ The man that told me, and said: Saul is dead, who thought he brought good tidings, I apprehended, and slew him in Siceleg, who should have been rewarded for his news.

11 How much more now when wicked men have slain an innocent man in his own house, upon his bed, shall I not require his blood at your hand, and take you away from the earth?

12 And David commanded his servants: and they slew them, and cutting off their hands and feet, hanged them up over the pool in Hebron. But the head of Isboseth they took and buried in the sepulchre of Abner in Hebron.

CHAPTER 5

David is anointed king of all Israel. He taketh Jerusalem, and dwelleth there. He defeateth the Philistines.

THEN all the tribes of Israel came to David in Hebron, saying: ¹ Behold we are thy bone and flesh.

2 Moreover yesterday also and the day before, when Saul was king over us, thou wast he that did lead out and bring in Israel. And the Lord said to thee: Thou shalt feed my people Israel, and thou shalt be prince over Israel.

3 The ancients also of Israel came to the king to Hebron, and king David made a league with them in Hebron before the Lord. ² And they anointed David to be king over Israel.

4 David was thirty years old when he began to reign, ³ and he reigned forty years.

5 In Hebron he reigned over Juda seven years and six months: and in Jerusalem he reigned three and thirty years over all Israel and Juda.

6 And the king and all the men that were with him went to Jerusalem to the Jebusites the inhabitants of the land. And they said to David: Thou shalt not come in hither unless thou take away the blind and the lame that say: David shall not come in hither.

7 But David took the castle of Sion. The same is the city of David.

8 For David had offered that day a reward to whosoever should strike the Jebusites and get up to the gutters of the tops of the houses, and take away the blind and the lame that hated the soul of David. Therefore it is said in the proverb: The blind and the lame shall not come into the temple.

9 ⁴ And David dwelt in the castle, and called it, The city of David: and built round about from Mello and inwards.

10 And he went on prospering and growing up: and the Lord God of hosts was with him.

11 ⁵ And·Hiram the king of Tyre sent messengers to David, and cedar trees, and carpenters, and masons for walls. And they built a house for David.

12 And David knew that the Lord had confirmed him king over Israel, and that he had exalted his kingdom over his people Israel.

13 ⁶ And David took more concubines and wives of Jerusalem, after he was come from Hebron: and there were born to David other sons also and daughters.

14 And these are the names of them, that were born to him in Jerusalem:

CHAP. 4. 1 2 Kings, 1, 14. CHAP. 5. 1 1 Par. 11, 1. 2 2 Kings, 2, 4. 3 3 Kings, 2, 11. 4 1 Par. 11, 8. 5 1 Par. 14, 1. 6 1 Par. 3, 1, 2.

CHAP. 5. Ver. 13. *David took more concubines and wives of Jerusalem.* Not harlots, but wives of an inferior condition; for such, in scripture, are styled *concubines.*

Samua, and Sobab, and Nathan, and Solomon,

15 And Jebahar, and Elisua, and Nepheg,

16 And Japhia, and Elisama, and Elioda, and Eliphaleth.

17 And the Philistines heard that they had anointed David to be king over Israel. And they all came to seek David: and when David heard of it, he went down to a strong hold.

18 ⁷And the Philistines coming spread themselves in the valley of Raphaim.

19 And David consulted the Lord, saying: Shall I go up to the Philistines? And wilt thou deliver them into my hand? And the Lord said to David: Go up, for I will surely deliver the Philistines into thy hand.

20 ⁸And David came to Baal Pharisim: and defeated them there. And he said: The Lord hath divided my enemies before me, as waters are divided. ⁹Therefore the name of the place was called Baal Pharisim.

21 And they left there their idols: which David and his men took away.

22 And the Philistines came up again; and spread themselves in the valley of Raphaim.

23 And David consulted the Lord: Shall I go up against the Philistines, and wilt thou deliver them into my hands? He answered: Go not up against them, but fetch a compass behind them; and thou shalt come upon them over against the pear trees.

24 And when thou shalt hear the sound of one going in the tops of the pear trees, then shalt thou join battle. For then will the Lord go out before thy face to strike the army of the Philistines.

25 And David did as the Lord had commanded him: and he smote the Philistines from Gabaa until thou come to Gezer.

CHAPTER 6

David fetcheth the ark from Cariathiarim. Oza is struck dead for touching it. It is deposited in the house of Obededom: and from thence carried to David's house.

AND David again gathered together all the chosen men of Israel, thirty thousand.

2 ¹And David arose and went, with all the people that were with him of the men of Juda to fetch the ark of God, upon which the name of the Lord

of hosts is invoked, who sitteth over it upon the cherubims.

3 And they laid the ark of God upon a new cart; and took it out of the house of Abinadab, who was in Gabaa. And Oza, and Ahio, the sons of Abinadab, drove the new cart.

4 ²And when they had taken it out of the house of Abinadab, who was in Gabaa, Ahio having care of the ark of God went before the ark.

5 But David and all Israel played before the Lord on all manner of instruments made of wood: on harps and lutes and timbrels and cornets and cymbals.

6 And when they came to the floor of Nachon, Oza put forth his hand to the ark of God, and took hold of it: because the oxen kicked and made it lean aside.

7 And the indignation of the Lord was enkindled against Oza: and he struck him for his rashness. And he died there before the ark of God.

8 ³And David was grieved because the Lord had struck Oza; and the name of that place was called: The striking of Oza, to this day.

9 And David was afraid of the Lord that day, saying: How shall the ark of the Lord come to me?

10 And he would not have the ark of the Lord brought in to himself into the city of David: but he caused it to be carried into the house of Obededom the Gethite.

11 And the ark of the Lord abode in the house of Obededom the Gethite three months: and the Lord blessed Obededom, and all his household.

12 ⁴And it was told king David, that the Lord had blessed Obededom, and all that he had, because of the ark of God. So David went, and brought away the ark of God out of the house of Obededom into the city of David with joy. And there were with David seven choirs and calves for victims.

13 ⁵And when they that carried the ark of the Lord had gone six paces, he sacrificed an ox and a ram.

14 And David danced with all his might before the Lord. And David was girded with a linen ephod.

15 And David and all the house of Israel brought the ark of the covenant of the Lord with joyful shouting, and with sound of trumpet.

16 And when the ark of the Lord was come into the city of David, Michol the daughter of Saul, looking out through a window, saw king David leaping and dancing before the Lord: and she despised him in her heart.

17 And they brought the ark of the

---

⁷ 1 Par. 14, 9. ⁸ Isai. 28, 21. ⁹ 1 Par. 14, 11. Chap. 6. ¹ 1 Par. 13, 5. ² 1 Kings, 7, 1. ³ 1 Par. 13, 11. ⁴ 1 Par. 15, 25. ⁵ 1 Par. 15, 26.

Chap. 6. Ver. 3. *Gabaa*. The hill of Cariathiarim, where the ark had been in the house of Abinadab, from the time of its being restored back by the Philistines.

Ver. 12. *Choirs*. Or companies of musicians.

Lord, and set it in its place in the midst of the tabernacle, which David had pitched for it. And David offered holocausts, and peace offerings before the Lord.

18 And when he had made an end of offering holocausts and peace offerings, he blessed the people in the name of the Lord of hosts.

19 And he distributed to all the multitude of Israel, both men and women, to every one, a cake of bread, and a piece of roasted beef, and fine flour fried with oil. And all the people departed every one to his house.

20 And David returned to bless his own house. And Michol the daughter of Saul coming out to meet David, said: How glorious was the king of Israel today, uncovering himself before the handmaids of his servants, and was naked as if one of the buffoons should be naked.

21 And David said to Michol: Before the Lord, who chose me rather than thy father, and than all his house, and commanded me to be ruler over the people of the Lord in Israel,

22 I will both play and make myself meaner than I have done. And I will be little in my own eyes: and with the handmaids of whom thou speakest, I shall appear more glorious.

23 Therefore Michol the daughter of Saul had no child to the day of her death.

CHAPTER 7

David's purpose to build a temple is rewarded with the promise of great blessings in his seed. His prayer and thanksgiving.

AND it came to pass when the king sat in his house, and the Lord had given him rest on every side from all his enemies,

2 He said to Nathan the prophet: [1] Dost thou see that I dwell in a house of cedar, and the ark of God is lodged within skins?

3 And Nathan said to the king: Go, do all that is in thy heart; because the Lord is with thee.

4 But it came to pass that night, that the word of the Lord came to Nathan, saying:

5 Go, and say to my servant David: Thus saith the Lord: Shalt thou build me a house to dwell in?

6 Whereas I have not dwelt in a house from the day that I brought the children of Israel out of the land of Egypt even to this day: but have walked in a tabernacle, and in a tent.

7 In all the places that I have gone through with all the children of Israel, did ever I speak a word to any one of the tribes of Israel, whom I commanded to feed my people Israel, saying: Why have you not built me a house of cedar?

8 And now thus shalt thou speak to my servant David: Thus saith the Lord of hosts: [2] I took thee out of the pastures from following the sheep to be ruler over my people Israel.

9 And I have been with thee wheresoever thou hast walked, and have slain all thy enemies from before thy face. And I have made thee a great man, like unto the name of the great ones that are on the earth.

10 And I will appoint a place for my people Israel; and I will plant them; and they shall dwell therein, and shall be disturbed no more. Neither shall the children of iniquity afflict them any more as they did before,

11 From the day that I appointed judges over my people Israel. And I will give thee rest from all thy enemies. And the Lord foretelleth to thee, that the Lord will make thee a house.

12 [3] And when thy days shall be fulfilled, and thou shalt sleep with thy fathers, I will raise up thy seed after thee, which shall proceed out of thy bowels: and I will establish his kingdom.

13 [4] He shall build a house to my name: and I will establish the throne of his kingdom for ever.

14 [5] I will be to him a father: and he shall be to me a son. And if he commit any iniquity, I will correct him with the rod of men, and with the stripes of the children of men.

15 [6] But my mercy I will not take away from him, as I took it from Saul, whom I removed from before my face.

16 And thy house shall be faithful, and thy kingdom for ever before thy face: [7] and thy throne shall be firm for ever.

17 According to all these words and according to all this vision, so did Nathan speak to David.

18 And David went in, and sat before the Lord, and said: Who am I, O Lord God, and what is my house, that thou hast brought me thus far?

19 But yet this hath seemed little in thy sight, O Lord God, unless thou didst also speak of the house of thy servant for a long time to come: for this is the law of Adam, O Lord God.

20 And what can David say more

CHAP. 7. [1] 1 Par. 17, 1. [2] 1 Kings, 16, 13; Ps. 70, 17. [3] 3 Kings, 8, 19. [4] 3 Kings, 5, 5. [5] 1 Par. 22, 10; Heb. 1, 5. [6] Ps. 88, 4, 47. [7] Heb. 1, 8.

CHAP. 7. Ver. 12. *I will establish his kingdom.* This prophecy partly relateth to Solomon: but much more to Christ, who is called the son of David in scripture, and who is the builder of the true temple, which is the church, his everlasting kingdom, which shall never fail.

unto thee? For thou knowest thy servant, O Lord God.

21 For thy word's sake, and according to thy own heart thou hast done all these great things, so that thou wouldst make it known to thy servant.

22 Therefore thou art magnified, O Lord God, because there is none like to thee: neither is there any God besides thee, in all the things that we have heard with our ears.

23 And what nation is there upon earth, as thy people Israel, whom God went to redeem for a people to himself, and to make him a name, and to do for them great and terrible things, upon the earth, before the face of thy people, whom thou redeemest to thyself out of Egypt, from the nations and their gods?

24 For thou hast confirmed to thyself thy people Israel to be an everlasting people: and thou, O Lord God, art become their God.

25 And now, O Lord God, raise up for ever the word that thou hast spoken, concerning thy servant and concerning his house: and do as thou hast spoken,

26 That thy name may be magnified for ever, and it may be said: The Lord of hosts is God over Israel. And the house of thy servant David shall be established before the Lord.

27 Because thou, O Lord of hosts, God of Israel, hast revealed to the ear of thy servant, saying: I will build thee a house. Therefore hath thy servant found in his heart to pray this prayer to thee.

28 And now, O Lord God, thou art God, and thy words shall be true: for thou hast spoken to thy servant these good things.

29 And now begin, and bless the house of thy servant, that it may endure for ever before thee: because thou, O Lord God, hast spoken it, and with thy blessing let the house of thy servant be blessed for ever.

CHAPTER 8

David's victories, and his chief officers.

AND it came to pass after this that David defeated the Philistines, and brought them down. [1] And David took the bridle of tribute out of the hand of the Philistines.

2 And he defeated Moab, and measured them with a line, casting them down to the earth. And he measured

with two lines, one to put to death, and one to save alive: and Moab was made to serve David under tribute.

3 David defeated also Adarezer the son of Rohob king of Soba, when he went to extend his dominion over the river [2] Euphrates.

4 And David took from him a thousand and seven hundred horsemen, and twenty thousand footmen, and houghed all the chariot horses: and only reserved of them for one hundred chariots.

5 And the Syrians of Damascus came to succour Adarezer the king of Soba: and David slew of the Syrians two and twenty thousand men.

6 And David put garrisons in Syria of Damascus: and Syria served David under tribute. And the Lord preserved David in all his enterprises, whithersoever he went.

7 And David took the arms of gold, which the servants of Adarezer wore, and brought them to Jerusalem.

8 And out of Bete, and out of Beroth, cities of Adarezer, king David took an exceeding great quantity of brass.

9 And Thou the king of Emath heard that David had defeated all the forces of Adarezer.

10 And Thou sent Joram his son to king David, to salute him, and to congratulate with him, and to return him thanks: because he had fought against Adarezer, and had defeated him. For Thou was an enemy to Adarezer: and in his hand were vessels of gold, and vessels of silver, and vessels of brass.

11 And king David dedicated them to the Lord, together with the silver and gold that he had dedicated of all the nations, which he had subdued:

12 Of Syria, and of Moab, and of the children of Ammon, and of the Philistines, and of Amalec, and of the spoils of Adarezer the son of Rohob king of Soba.

13 David also made himself a name, when he returned after taking Syria in the valley of the saltpits, killing eighteen thousand:

14 And he put guards in Edom, and placed *there* a garrison: and all Edom was made to serve David. And the Lord preserved David in all enterprises he went about.

15 And David reigned over all Israel: and David did judgment and justice to all his people.

16 And Joab the son of Sarvia was over the army: and Josaphat the son of Ahilud was recorder:

17 And Sadoc the son of Achitob, and Achimelech the son of Abiathar, were the priests: and Saraias was the scribe:

18 And Banaias the son of Joiada was

CHAP. 8. [1] 1 Par. 18, 1.   [2] 1 Par. 18, 3.

CHAP. 8. Ver. 16. *Recorder.* Chancellor.
Ver. 17. *Scribe.* Secretary.
Ver. 18. *The Cerethi and Phelethi.* The king's guards.—*Princes.* Literally *priests.* (Cohen.) So called, by a title of honour, and not from exercising the priestly functions.

over the Cerethi and Phelethi: and the sons of David were the princes.

CHAPTER 9

David's kindness to Miphiboseth for the sake of his father Jonathan.

AND David said: Is there any one, think you, left of the house of Saul, that I may shew kindness to him for Jonathan's sake?

2 Now there was of the house of Saul, a servant named Siba. And when the king had called him to him, he said to him: Art thou Siba? And he answered: I am Siba thy servant.

3 And the king said: Is there any one left of the house of Saul, that I may shew the mercy of God unto him? And Siba said to the king: There is a son of Jonathan left, who is lame of his feet.

4 Where is he? said he. And Siba said to the king: Behold he is in the house of Machir the son of Ammiel in Lodabar.

5 Then king David sent, and brought him out of the house of Machir the son Ammiel of Lodabar.

6 And when Miphiboseth the son of Jonathan the son of Saul was come to David, he fell on his face and worshipped. And David said: Miphiboseth? And he answered: Behold thy servant.

7 And David said to him: Fear not, for I will surely shew thee mercy for Jonathan thy father's sake; and I will restore the lands of Saul thy father; and thou shalt eat bread at my table always.

8 He bowed down to him, and said: Who am I thy servant, that thou shouldst look upon such a dead dog as I am?

9 Then the king called Siba, the servant of Saul, and said to him: All that belonged to Saul, and all his house, I have given to thy master's son.

10 Thou therefore and thy sons and thy servants shall till the land for him: and thou shalt bring in food for thy master's son, that he may be maintained: and Miphiboseth the son of thy master shall always' eat bread at my table. And Siba had fifteen sons and twenty servants.

11 And Siba said to the king: As thou my lord the king hast commanded thy servant, so will thy servant do: and Miphiboseth shall eat at my table, as one of the sons of the king.

12 And Miphiboseth had a young son whose name was Micha: and all the kindred of the house of Siba served Miphiboseth.

13 But Miphiboseth dwelt in Jerusalem: because he ate always of the king's table. And he was lame of both feet.

CHAPTER 10

The Ammonites shamefully abuse the ambassadors of David. They hire the Syrians to their assistance: but are overthrown with their allies.

AND it came to pass after this, that the king of the children of Ammon died, and Hanon his son reigned in his stead.

2 And David said: [1] I will shew kindness to Hanon the son of Daas, as his father shewed kindness to me. So David sent his servants to comfort him for the death of his father. But when the servants of David were come into the land of the children of Ammon,

3 The princes of the children of Ammon said to Hanon their lord. Thinkest thou that for the honour of thy father, David hath sent comforters to thee; and hath not David rather sent his servants to thee to search, and spy into the city, and overthrow it?

4 Wherefore Hanon took the servants of David, and shaved off the one half of their beards, and cut away half of their garments even to the buttocks, and sent them away.

5 When this was told David, he sent to meet them. For the men were sadly put to confusion, and David commanded them, *saying:* Stay at Jericho, till your beards be grown, and then return.

6 And the children of Ammon seeing that they had done an injury to David, sent and hired the Syrians of Rohob, and the Syrians of Soba, twenty thousand footmen, and of the king of Maacha a thousand men, and of Istob twelve thousand men.

7 And when David heard this, he sent Joab and the whole army of warriors.

8 And the children of Ammon came out, and set their men in array at the entering in of the gate: but the Syrians of Soba, and of Rohob, and of Istob, and of Maacha were by themselves in the field.

9 Then Joab seeing that the battle was prepared against him, both before and behind, chose of all the choice men of Israel, and put them in array against the Syrians.

10 And the rest of the people he delivered to Abisai his brother, who set them in array against the children of Ammon.

11 And Joab said: If the Syrians are too strong for me, then thou shalt help me. But if the children of Ammon are too strong for thee, then I will help thee.

CHAP. 10. [1] 1 Par. 19, 2.

12 Be of good courage, and let us fight for our people, and for the city of our God: and the Lord will do what is good in his sight.

13 And Joab and the people that were with him, began to fight against the Syrians: and they immediately fled before him.

14 And the children of Ammon seeing that the Syrians were fled, they fled also before Abisai, and entered into the city. And Joab returned from the children of Ammon, and came to Jerusalem.

15 Then the Syrians seeing that they had fallen before Israel, gathered themselves together.

16 And Adarezer sent and fetched the Syrians, that were beyond the river, and brought *over* their army. And Sobach, the captain of the host of Adarezer, was their general.

17 And when this was told David, he gathered all Israel together, and passed over the Jordan, and came to Helam. And the Syrians set themselves in array against David; and fought against him.

18 And the Syrians fled before Israel. And David slew of the Syrians *the men* of seven hundred chariots, and forty thousand horsemen: and smote Sobach the captain of the army, who presently died.

19 And all the kings that were auxiliaries of Adarezer, seeing themselves overcome by Israel, were afraid and fled away, eight and fifty thousand men before Israel. And they made peace with Israel: and served them; and all the Syrians were afraid to help the children of Ammon any more.

CHAPTER 11

David falleth into the crime of adultery with Bethsabee: and not finding other means to conceal it, causeth her husband Urias to be slain. Then marrieth her, who beareth him a son.

AND it came to pass at the return of the year, [1] at the time when kings go forth to war, that David sent Joab and his servants with him, and all Israel. And they spoiled the children of Ammon, and besieged Rabba: but David remained in Jerusalem.

2 In the mean time it happened that David arose from his bed after noon, and walked upon the roof of the king's house. And he saw from the roof of his house a woman washing herself, over against him: and the woman was very beautiful.

3 And the king sent, and inquired who the woman was. And it was told him, that she was Bethsabee the daughter of Eliam, the wife of Urias the Hethite.

4 And David sent messengers, and took her, and she came in to him, and he slept with her: [2] and presently she was purified from her uncleanness.

5 And she returned to her house having conceived. And she sent and told David, and said: I have conceived.

6 And David sent to Joab, saying: Send me Urias the Hethite. And Joab sent Urias to David.

7 And Urias came to David. And David asked how Joab did, and the people, and how the war was carried on.

8 And David said to Urias: Go into thy house, and wash thy feet. And Urias went out from the king's house; and there went out after him a mess of meat from the king.

9 But Urias slept before the gate of the king's house, with the other servants of his lord; and went not down to his own house.

10 And it was told David by some that said: Urias went not to his house. And David said to Urias: Didst thou not come from thy journey? Why didst thou not go down to thy house?

11 And Urias said to David: The ark of God and Israel and Juda dwell in tents, and my lord Joab and the servants of my lord abide upon the face of the earth. And shall I go into my house, to eat and to drink, and to sleep with my wife? By thy welfare and by the welfare of thy soul I will not do this thing.

12 Then David said to Urias: Tarry here to-day; and to-morrow I will send thee away. Urias tarried in Jerusalem that day and the next.

13 And David called him to eat and to drink before him, and he made him drunk. And he went out in the evening, and slept on his couch with the servants of his lord; and went not down into his house.

14 And when the morning was come, David wrote a letter to Joab: and sent it by the hand of Urias.

15 Writing in the letter: Set ye Urias in the front of the battle, where the fight is strongest: and leave ye him, that he may be wounded and die.

16 Wherefore as Joab was besieging the city, he put Urias in the place where he knew the bravest men were.

17 And the men coming out of the city, fought against Joab. and there fell some of the people of the servants of David. And Urias the Hethite was killed also.

18 Then Joab sent, and told David all things concerning the battle.

19 And he charged the messenger,

CHAP. 11. [1] Par. 20, 1. [2] Lev. 15, 18.

saying: When thou hast told all the words of the battle to the king,

20 If thou see him to be angry, and he shall say: Why did you approach so near to the wall to fight? Knew you not that many darts are thrown from above off the wall?

21 Who killed Abimelech the son of Jerobaal? [3] Did not a woman cast a piece of a millstone upon him from the wall, and slew him in Thebes? Why did you go near the wall? Thou shalt say: Thy servant Urias the Hethite is also slain.

22 So the messenger departed; and came and told David all that Joab had commanded him.

23 And the messenger said to David: The men prevailed against us; and they came out to us into the field: and we vigorously charged and pursued them even to the gate of the city.

24 And the archers shot their arrows at thy servants from off the wall above. And some of the king's servants are slain: and thy servant Urias the Hethite is also dead.

25 And David said to the messenger: Thus shalt thou say to Joab: Let not this thing discourage thee; for various is the event of war. And sometimes one, sometimes another is consumed by the sword. Encourage thy warriors against the city: and exhort them that thou mayest overthrow it.

26 And the wife of Urias heard that Urias her husband was dead: and she mourned for him.

27 And the mourning being over, David sent and brought her into his house. And she became his wife; and she bore him a son. And this thing which David had done, was displeasing to the Lord.

CHAPTER 12

Nathan's parable. David confesseth his sin, and is forgiven: yet so as to be sentenced to most severe temporal punishments. The death of the child. The birth of Solomon. The taking of Rabbath.

AND the Lord sent Nathan to David. And when he was come to him, he said to him: There were two men in one city, the one rich, and the other poor.

2 The rich man had exceeding many sheep and oxen.

3 But the poor man had nothing at all but one little ewe lamb, which he had bought and nourished up, and which had grown up in his house together with his children, eating of his bread, and drinking of his cup, and sleeping in his bosom: and it was unto him as a daughter.

4 And when a certain stranger was come to the rich man, he spared to take of his own sheep and oxen, to make a feast for that stranger, who was come to him: but took the poor man's ewe, and dressed it for the man that was come to him.

5 And David's anger being exceedingly kindled against that man, he said to Nathan: As the Lord liveth, the man that hath done this is a child of death.

6 [1] He shall restore the ewe fourfold: because he did this thing, and had no pity.

7 And Nathan said to David: Thou art the man. Thus saith the Lord the God of Israel: I anointed thee king over Israel; and I delivered thee from the hand of Saul,

8 And gave thee thy master's house and thy master's wives into thy bosom, and gave thee the house of Israel and Juda. And if these things be little, I shall add far greater things unto thee.

9 Why therefore hast thou despised the word of the Lord, to do evil in my sight? Thou hast killed Urias the Hethite with the sword; and hast taken his wife to be thy wife; and hast slain him with the sword of the children of Ammon.

10 Therefore the sword shall never depart from thy house: because thou hast despised me, and hast taken the wife of Urias the Hethite to be thy wife.

11 Thus saith the Lord: Behold, I will raise up evil against thee out of thy own house; and I will take thy wives before thy eyes [3] and give them to thy neighbour: and he shall lie with thy wives in the sight of this sun.

12 For thou didst it secretly: but I will do this thing in the sight of all Israel, and in the sight of the sun.

13 And David said to Nathan: I have sinned against the Lord. And Nathan said to David: [3] The Lord also hath taken away thy sin. Thou shalt not die.

14 Nevertheless, because thou' hast given ocassion to the enemies of the Lord to blaspheme, for this thing, the child that is born to thee, shall surely die.

15 And Nathan returned to his house. The Lord also struck the child which the wife of Urias had borne to David; and his life was despaired of.

16 And David besought the Lord for the child: and David kept a fast, and going in by himself lay upon the ground.

[3] Judges, 9, 53. CHAP. 12. [1] Exod. 22, 1. [2] 2 Kings, 16, 22. [3] Ecclus. 47, 13.

CHAP. 12. Ver. 11. *I will raise up evil.* All these evils, inasmuch as they were *punishments,* came upon David by a just judgment of God, for his sin. And therefore God says, *I will raise up evil;* but inasmuch as they were *sins,* on the part of Absalom and his associates, God was not the author of them, but only permitted them.

17 And the ancients of his house came, to make him rise from the ground: but he would not, neither did he eat meat with them.

18 And it came to pass on the seventh day that the child died. And the servants of David feared to tell him, that the child was dead. For they said: Behold when the child was yet alive, we spoke to him, and he would not hearken to our voice. How much more will he afflict himself if we tell him that the child is dead?

19 But when David saw his servants whispering, he understood that the child was dead. And he said to his servants: Is the child dead? They answered him: He is dead.

20 And David arose from the ground, and washed and anointed himself. And when he had changed his apparel, he went into the house of the Lord: and worshipped. And then he came into his own house; and he called for bread, and ate.

21 And his servants said to him: What thing is this that thou hast done? Thou didst fast and weep for the child, while it was alive; but when the child was dead, thou didst rise up, and eat bread.

22 And he said: While the child was yet alive, I fasted and wept for him. For I said: Who knoweth whether the Lord may not give him to me, and the child may live?

23 But now that he is dead, why should I fast? Shall I be able to bring him back any more? I shall go to him rather: but he shall not return to me.

24 And David comforted Bethsabee his wife, and went in unto her, and slept with her. And she bore a son; and he called his name Solomon; and the Lord loved him.

25 And he sent by the hand of Nathan the prophet, and called his name: Amiable to the Lord; because the Lord loved him.

26 ‘ And Joab fought against Rabbath of the children of Ammon, and laid close siege to the royal city.

27 And Joab sent messengers to David, saying: I have fought against Rabbath; and the city of waters is about to be taken.

28 Now therefore gather thou the rest of the people together, and besiege the city and take it: lest when the city

shall be wasted by me, the victory be ascribed to my name.

29 Then David gathered all the people together, and went out against Rabbath: and after fighting, he took it.

30 And he took the crown of their king from his head, the weight of which was a talent of gold, set with most precious stones: and it was put upon David's head. And the spoils of the city which were very great he carried away.

31 And bringing forth the people thereof, he sawed them, and drove over them chariots armed with iron: and divided them with knives, and made them pass through brick-kilns. So did he to all the cities of the children of Ammon. And David returned, with all the army to Jerusalem.

CHAPTER 13

Amnon ravisheth Thamar. For which Absalom killeth him, and flieth to Gessur.

AND it came to pass after this, that Amnon the son of David loved the sister of Absalom the son of David, who was very beautiful: and her name was Thamar.

2 And he was exceedingly fond of her, so that he fell sick for the love of her: for, as she was a virgin, he thought it hard to do any thing dishonestly with her.

3 Now Amnon had a friend named Jonadab the son of Semmaa the brother of David, a very wise man.

4 And he said to him: Why dost thou grow so lean from day to day, O son of the king? Why dost thou not tell me the reason of it? And Amnon said to him: I am in love with Thamar the sister of my brother Absalom.

5 And Jonadab said to him: Lie down upon thy bed, and feign thyself sick; and when thy father shall come to visit thee say to him: Let my sister Thamar, I pray thee, come to me, to give me to eat, and to make me a mess, that I may eat it at her hand.

6 So Amnon lay down, and made as if he were sick: and when the king came to visit him, Amnon said to the king: I pray thee let my sister Thamar come, and make in my sight two little messes, that I may eat at her hand.

7 Then David sent home to Thamar, saying: Come to the house of thy brother Amnon, and make him a mess.

8 And Thamar came to the house of Amnon her brother: but he was laid down. And she took meal and tempered it: and dissolving it in his sight she made little messes.

9 And taking what she had boiled, she poured it out, and set it before him: but he would not eat. And Amnon said:

<hr/>

¶ I Par. 20, 1.

Ver. 25. *Amiable to the Lord.* Or, beloved of the Lord. In Hebrew, *Jedidiah.*
Ver. 27. *The city of waters.* Rabbath the royal city of the Ammonites, was called *the city of waters,* from being encompassed with waters.
Chap. 13. Ver. 3. *A very wise man.* That is, a crafty and subtle man: for the counsel he gave on this occasion shews that his wisdom was but carnal and worldly.

Put out all persons from me. And when they had put all persons out,

10 Amnon said to Thamar: Bring the mess into the chamber, that I may eat at thy hand. And Thamar took the little messes which she had made, and brought them in to her brother Amnon in the chamber.

11 And when she had presented him the meat, he took hold of her, and said: Come lie with me, my sister.

12 She answered him: Do not so, my brother, do not force me: for no such thing must be done in Israel. Do not thou this folly.

13 For I shall not be able to bear my shame; and thou shalt be as one of the fools in Israel. But rather speak to the king; and he will not deny me to thee.

14 But he would not hearken to her prayers; but being stronger overpowered her and lay with her.

15 Then Amnon hated her with an exceeding great hatred: so that the hatred wherewith he hated her was greater than the love with which he had loved her before. And Amnon said to her: Arise, and get thee gone.

16 She answered him: This evil which now thou didst against me, in driving me away, is greater than that which thou didst before. And he would not hearken to her.

17 But calling the servants that ministered to him, he said: Thrust this woman out from me, and shut the door after her.

18 And she was clothed with a long robe: for the king's daughters that were virgins, used such kind of garments. Then his servant thrust her out, and shut the door after her.

19 And she put ashes on her head, and rent her long robe, and laid her hands upon her head, and went on crying.

20 And Absalom her brother said to her: Hath thy brother Amnon lain with thee? But now, sister, hold thy peace, he is thy brother: and afflict not thy heart for this thing. So Thamar remained pining away in the house of Absalom her brother.

21 And when king David heard of these things he was exceedingly grieved: and he would not afflict the spirit of his son Amnon, for he loved him, because he was his firstborn.

22 But Absalom spoke not to Amnon neither good nor evil: for Absalom hated Amnon because he had ravished his sister Thamar.

23 And it came to pass after two years, that the sheep of Absalom were shorn in Baalhasor, which is near Ephraim: and Absalom invited all the king's sons.

24 And he came to the king, and said to him: Behold thy servant's sheep are shorn. Let the king, I pray, with his servants come to his servant.

25 And the king said to Absalom: Nay, my son, do not ask that we should all come, and be chargeable to thee. And when he pressed him, and he would not go, he blessed him.

26 And Absalom said: If thou wilt not come, at least let my brother Amnon, I beseech thee, come with us. And the king said to him: It is not necessary that he should go with thee.

27 But Absalom pressed him, so that he let Amnon and all the king's sons go with him. And Absalom made a feast as it were the feast of a king.

28 And Absalom had commanded his servants, saying: Take notice when Amnon shall be drunk with wine, and when I shall say to you: Strike him, and kill him; fear not for it is I that command you. Take courage, and be valiant men.

29 And the servants of Absalom did to Amnon as Absalom had commanded them. And all the king's sons arose and got up every man upon his mule, and fled.

30 And while they were yet in the way, a rumour came to David, saying: Absalom hath slain all the king's sons; and there is not one of them left.

31 Then the king rose up, and rent his garments: and fell upon the ground. And all his servants, that stood about him, rent their garments.

32 But Jonadab the son of Semmaa David's brother answering, said: Let not my lord the king think that all the king's sons are slain: Amnon only is dead, for he was appointed by the mouth of Absalom from the day that he ravished his sister Thamar.

33 Now therefore let not my lord the king take this thing into his heart, saying: All the king's sons are slain; for Amnon only is dead.

34 But Absalom fled away. And the young man that kept the watch, lifted up his eyes and looked: and behold there came much people by a byeway on the side of the mountain.

35 And Jonadab said to the king: Behold the king's sons are come: as thy servant said, so it is.

36 And when he made an end of speaking, the king's sons also appeared. And coming in they lifted up their voice, and wept: and the king also and all his servants wept very much.

37 But Absalom fled, and went to Tholomai the son of Ammiud the king of Gessur. And David mourned for his son every day.

38 And Absalom after he was fled, and come into Gessur, was there three years. And king David ceased to pursue after Absalom, because he was comforted concerning the death of Amnon.

CHAPTER 14

Joab procureth Absalom's return, and his admittance to the king's presence.

AND Joab the son of Sarvia, understanding that the king's heart was turned to Absalom.

2 Sent to Thecua, and fetched from thence a wise woman: and said to her: Feign thyself to be a mourner, and put on mourning apparel, and be not anointed with oil, that thou mayest be as a woman that had a long time been mourning for one dead.

3 And thou shalt go in to the king, and shalt speak to him in this manner. And Joab put the words in her mouth.

4 And when the woman of Thecua was come in to the king, she fell before him upon the ground, and worshipped, and said: Save me, O king.

5 And the king said to her: What is the matter with thee? She answered: Alas, I am a widow woman; for my husband is dead.

6 And thy handmaid had two sons: and they quarrelled with each other in the field, and there was none to part them. And the one struck the other, and slew him.

7 And behold the whole kindred rising against thy handmaid, saith: Deliver him that hath slain his brother, that we may kill him for the life of his brother, whom he slew, and that we may destroy the heir. And they seek to quench my spark which is left, and will leave my husband no name, nor remainder upon the earth.

8 And the king said to the woman: Go to thy house; and I will give charge concerning thee.

9 And the woman of Thecua said to the king: Upon me, my lord, be the iniquity, and upon the house of my father; but may the king and his throne be guiltless.

10 And the king said: If any one shall say aught against thee, bring him to me; and he shall not touch thee any more.

11 And she said: Let the king remember the Lord his God, that the next of kin be not multiplied to take revenge, and that they may not kill my son. And he said: As the Lord liveth, there shall not one hair of thy son fall to the earth.

12 Then the woman said: Let thy handmaid speak one word to my lord the king. And he said: Speak.

13 And the woman said: Why hast thou thought such a thing against the people of God, and why hath the king spoken this word, to sin, and not bring home again his own exile?

14 We all die, and like waters that return no more, we fall down into the earth. [1] Neither will God have a soul to perish, but recalleth; meaning that he that is cast off should not altogether perish.

15 Now therefore I am come, to speak this word to my lord the king before the people. And thy handmaid said: I will speak to the king. It may be the king will perform the request of his handmaid.

16 And the king hath hearkened to me to deliver his handmaid out of the hand of all that would destroy me and my son together, out of the inheritance of God.

17 Then let thy handmaid say, that the word of the lord the king be made as a sacrifice. [2] For even as an angel of God, so is my lord the king, that he is neither moved with blessing nor cursing. Wherefore the Lord thy God is also with thee.

18 And the king answering, said to the woman: Hide not from me the thing that I ask thee. And the woman said to him: Speak, my lord the king.

19 And the king said: Is not the hand of Joab with thee in all this? The woman answered, and said: By the health of thy soul, my lord, O king, it is neither on the left hand, nor on the right, in all these things which my lord the king hath spoken. For thy servant Joab, he commanded me, and he put all these words into the mouth of thy handmaid.

20 That I should come about with this form of speech, thy servant Joab commanded this: but thou, my lord, O king, art wise, according to the wisdom of an angel of God, to understand all things upon earth.

21 And the king said to Joab: Behold I am appeased and have granted thy request. Go therefore and fetch back the boy Absalom.

22 And Joab falling down to the ground upon his face, adored, and blessed the king. And Joab said: This day thy servant hath understood, that I have found grace in thy sight, my lord, O king, for thou hast fulfilled the request of thy servant.

23 Then Joab arose and went to Gessur, and brought Absalom to Jerusalem.

24 But the king said: Let him return into his house, and let him not see my

CHAP. 14. [1] Ezech. 18, 32; 33, 11. [2] 1 Kings, 29, 9.

CHAP. 14. Ver. 22. *Blessed.* That is, and gave thanks to the king.

face. So Absalom returned into his house, and saw not the king's face.

25 But in all Israel there was not a man so comely, and so exceedingly beautiful as Absalom: from the sole of the foot to the crown of his head there was no blemish in him.

26 And when he polled his hair (now he was polled once a year, because his hair was burdensome to him) he weighed the hair of his head at two hundred sicles, according to the common weight.

27 And there were born to Absalom three sons, and one daughter, whose name was Thamar; and she was very beautiful.

28 And Absalom dwelt two years in Jerusalem, and saw not the king's face.

29 He sent therefore to Joab, to send him to the king: but he would not come to him. And when he had sent the second time, and he would not come to him.

30 He said to his servants: You know the field of Joab near my field, that hath a crop of barley. Go now and set it on fire. So the servants of Absalom set the corn on fire. And Joab's servants coming with their garments rent said: The servants of Absalom have set part of the field on fire.

31 Then Joab arose, and came to Absalom to his house, and said: Why have thy servants set my corn on fire?

32 And Absalom answered Joab: I sent to thee beseeching thee to come to me, that I might send thee to the king, to say to him: Wherefore am I come from Gessur? It had been better for me to be there. I beseech thee therefore that I may see the face of the king: and if he be mindful of my iniquity, let him kill me.

33 So Joab going in to the king, told him all; and Absalom was called for. And he went in to the king, and prostrated himself on the ground before him: and the king kissed Absalom.

CHAPTER 15

Absalom's policy and conspiracy. David is obliged to flee.

NOW after these things Absalom made himself chariots, and horsemen, and fifty men to run before him.

2 And Absalom rising up early stood by the entrance of the gate; and when any man had business to come to the king's judgment, Absalom called him to him, and said: Of what city art thou? He answered, and said: Thy servant is of such a tribe of Israel.

3 And Absalom answered him: Thy words seem to me good and just. But there is no man appointed by the king to hear thee. And Absalom said:

4 O that they would make me judge over the land, that all that have business might come to me, that I might do them justice.

5 Moreover when any man came to him to salute him, he put forth his hand, and took him, and kissed him.

6 And this he did to all Israel that came for judgment, to be heard by the king: and he enticed the hearts of the men of Israel.

7 And after forty years, Absalom said to king David: Let me go, and pay my vows which I have vowed to the Lord in Hebron.

8 For thy servant made a vow, when he was in Gessur of Syria, saying: If the Lord shall bring me again into Jerusalem, I will offer sacrifice to the Lord.

9 And king David said to him: Go in peace. And he arose, and went to Hebron.

10 And Absalom sent spies into all the tribes of Israel, saying: As soon as you shall hear the sound of the trumpet, say ye: Absalom reigneth in Hebron.

11 Now there went with Absalom two hundred men out of Jerusalem that were called, going with simplicity of heart, and knowing nothing of the design.

12 Absalom also sent for Achitophel the Gilonite, David's counsellor, from his city Gilo. And while he was offering sacrifices, there was a strong conspiracy: and the people running together increased with Absalom.

13 And there came a messenger to David, saying: All Israel with their whole heart followeth Absalom.

14 And David said to his servants, that were with him in Jerusalem: Arise and let us flee; for we shall not escape else from the face of Absalom. Make haste to go out, lest he come and overtake us, and bring ruin upon us, and smite the city with the edge of the sword.

15 And the king's servants said to him: Whatsoever our lord the king shall command, we thy servants will willingly execute.

16 And the king went forth, and all his household on foot. And the king left ten women his concubines to keep the house.

17 And the king going forth and all Israel on foot, stood afar off from the house.

18 And all his servants walked by him: and the bands of the Cerethi, and the Phelethi, and all the Gethites, valiant warriors, six hundred men who

CHAP. 15. Ver. 16. *Concubines.* That is, wives of an inferior degree.

had followed him from Geth on foot, went before the king.

19 And the king said to Ethai the Gethite: Why comest thou with us? Return and dwell with the king, for thou art a stranger, and art come out of thy own place.

20 Yesterday thou camest, and to-day shalt thou be forced to go forth with us? But, I shall go whither I am going: return thou, and take back thy brethren with thee. And the Lord will shew thee mercy, and truth, because thou hast shewn grace and fidelity.

21 And Ethai answered the king, saying: As the Lord liveth, and as my lord the king liveth: in what place soever thou shalt be, my lord, O king, either in death, or in life, there will thy servant be.

22 And David said to Ethai: Come, and pass over. And Ethai the Gethite passed; and all the men that were with him, and the rest of the people.

23 And they all wept with a loud voice, and all the people passed over. The king also himself went over the brook Cedron: and all the people marched towards the way that looketh to the desert.

24 And Sadoc the priest also came, and all the Levites with him carrying the ark of the covenant of God: and they set down the ark of God. And Abiathar went up, till all the people that was come out of the city had done passing.

25 And the king said to Sadoc: Carry back the ark of God into the city. If I shall find grace in the sight of the Lord, he will bring me again: and he will shew me it, and his tabernacle.

26 But if he shall say to me: Thou pleasest me not: I am ready. Let him do that which is good before him.

27 And the king said to Sadoc the priest: O seer, return into the city in peace; and let Achimaas thy son, and Jonathan the son of Abiathar, your two sons, be with you.

28 Behold I will lie hid in the plains of the wilderness, till there come word from you to certify me.

29 So Sadoc and Abiathar carried back the ark of God into Jerusalem: and they tarried there.

30 But David went up by the ascent of mount Olivet, going up and weeping, walking barefoot, and with his head covered: and all the people that were with them, went up with their heads covered weeping.

31 And it was told David that Achi-

CHAP. 16. 1 2 Kings, 19, 27.

Ver. 30. *Weeping.* David on this occasion wept for his sins, which he knew were the cause of all his sufferings.

tophel also was in the conspiracy with Absalom. And David said: Infatuate, O Lord, I beseech thee, the counsel of Achitophel.

32 And when David was come to the top of the mountain, where he was about to adore the Lord, behold Chusai the Arachite, came to meet him with his garment rent and his head covered with earth.

33 And David said to him: If thou come with me, thou wilt be a burden to me.

34 But if thou return into the city, and wilt say to Absalom: I am thy servant, O king. As I have been thy father's servant, so I will be thy servant: thou shalt defeat the counsel of Achitophel.

35 And thou hast with thee Sadoc and Abiathar, the priests: and what thing soever thou shalt hear out of the king's house, thou shalt tell it to Sadoc and Abiathar, the priests.

36 And there are with them their two sons Achimaas the son of Sadoc, and Jonathan the son of Abiathar: and you shall send by them to me every thing that you shall hear.

37 Then Chusai the friend of David went into the city: and Absalom came into Jerusalem.

CHAPTER 16

Siba bringeth provisions to David. Semei curseth him. Absalom defileth his father's wives.

AND when David was a little past the top of the hill, behold Siba the servant of Miphiboseth came to meet him with two asses, laden with two hundred loaves of bread, and a hundred bunches of raisins, a hundred cakes of figs, and a vessel of wine.

2 And the king said to Siba: What mean these things? And Siba answered: The asses *are* for the king's household to sit on: and the loaves and the figs for thy servants to eat: and the wine to drink if any man be faint in the desert.

3 And the king said: Where is thy master's son? [1] And Siba answered the king: He remained in Jerusalem, saying: To-day will the house of Israel restore me the kingdom of my father.

4 And the king said to Siba: I give thee all that belonged to Miphiboseth. And Siba said: I beseech thee let me find grace before thee, my lord, O king.

5 And king David came as far as Bahurim: and behold there came out from thence a man of the kindred of the house of Saul named Semei, the son of Gera. And coming out [2] he cursed as he went on.

6 And he threw stones at David, and

at all the servants of king David: and all the people, and all the warriors walked on the right, and on the left side of the king.

7 And thus said Semei when he cursed the king: Come out, come out, thou man of blood, and thou man of Belial.

8 The Lord hath repaid thee for all the blood of the house of Saul: because thou hast usurped the kingdom in his stead. And the Lord hath given the kingdom into the hand of Absalom thy son: and behold thy evils press upon thee, because thou art a man of blood.

9 And Abisai the son of Sarvia said to the king: Why should this dead dog curse my lord the king? I will go, and cut off his head.

10 And the king said: What have I to do with you, ye sons of Sarvia? Let him alone and let him curse: for the Lord hath bid him curse David. And who is he that shall dare say, Why hath he done so?

11 And the king said to Abisai, and to all his servants: Behold my son, who came forth from my bowels, seeketh my life. How much more now a son of Jemini? Let him alone that he may curse as the Lord hath bidden him.

12 Perhaps the Lord may look upon my affliction, and the Lord may render me good for the cursing of this day.

13 And David and his men with him went by the way. And Semei by the hill's side went over against him, cursing, and casting stones at him, and scattering earth.

14 And the king and all the people with him came weary, and refreshed themselves there.

15 But Absalom and all his people came into Jerusalem; and Achitophel was with him.

16 And when Chusai the Arachite, David's friend, was come to Absalom, he said to him: God save thee, O king; God save thee, O king.

17 And Absalom said to him: Is this thy kindness to thy friend? Why wentest thou not with thy friend?

18 And Chusai answered Absalom: Nay: for I will be his, whom the Lord hath chosen, and all this people, and all Israel; and with him will I abide.

19 Besides this, whom shall I serve? Is it not the king's son? As I have served thy father, so will I serve thee also.

20 And Absalom said to Achitophel: Consult what we are to do.

21 And Achitophel said to Absalom: Go in to the concubines of thy father, whom he hath left to keep the house: that when all Israel shall hear that thou hast disgraced thy father, their hands may be strengthened with thee.

22 [3] So they spread a tent for Absalom on the top of the house: and he went in to his father's concubines before all Israel.

23 Now the counsel of Achitophel, which he gave in those days, *was* as if a man should consult God. So was all the counsel of Achitophel, both when he was with David, and when he was with Absalom.

CHAPTER 17

Achitophel's counsel is defeated by Chusai: who sendeth intelligence to David. Achitophel hangeth himself.

AND Achitophel said to Absalom: I will choose me twelve thousand men; and I will arise and pursue after David this night.

2 And coming upon him (for he is now weary and weak handed) I will defeat him: and when all the people is put to flight that is with him, I will kill the king who will be left alone.

3 And I will bring back all the people, as if they were but one man; for thou seekest *but* one man. And all the people shall be in peace.

4 And his saying pleased Absalom, and all the ancients of Israel.

5 But Absalom said: Call Chusai the Arachite; and let us hear what he also saith.

6 And when Chusai was come to Absalom, Absalom said to him: Achitophel hath spoken after this manner. Shall we do it or not? What counsel dost thou give?

7 And Chusai said to Absalom: The counsel that Achitophel hath given this time is not good.

8 And again Chusai said: Thou knowest thy father, and the men that are with him, that they are very valiant, and bitter in their mind, as a bear raging in the wood when her whelps are taken away. And thy father is a warrior, and will not lodge with the people.

9 Perhaps he now lieth hid in pits, or in some other place where he list. And when any one shall fall at the first, every one that heareth it shall say: There is a slaughter among the people that followed Absalom.

<hr/>

[2] 3 Kings, 2, 8.   [3] 2 Kings, 12, 11.

CHAP. 16. Ver. 10 and 11. *Hath bid him curse.* Not that the Lord was the author of Semei's sin, which proceeded purely from his own malice, and the abuse of his free will. But that knowing, and suffering his malicious disposition to break out on this occasion, he made use of him as his instrument to punish David for his sins.

Ver. 21. *Their hands may be strengthened.* The people might apprehend lest Absalom should be reconciled to his father, and therefore they followed him with some fear of being left in the lurch, till they saw such a crime committed as seemed to make a reconciliation impossible.

10 And the most valiant man whose heart is as the heart of a lion, shall melt for fear: for all the people of Israel know thy father to be a valiant man, and that all who are with him are valiant.

11 But this seemeth to me to be good counsel: Let all Israel be gathered to thee, from Dan to Bersabee, as the sand of the sea which cannot be numbered. And thou shalt be in the midst of them.

12 And we shall come upon him in what place soever he shall be found: and we shall cover him, as the *dew falleth upon the ground: and we shall not leave of the men that are with him, not so much as one.

13 And if he shall enter into any city, all Israel shall cast ropes round about that city: and we will draw it into the river, so that there shall not be found so much as one small stone thereof.

14 And Absalom, and all the men of Israel said: The counsel of Chusai the Arachite is better than the counsel of Achitophel. And by the will of the Lord the profitable counsel of Achitophel was defeated, that the Lord might bring evil upon Absalom.

15 And Chusai said to Sadoc and Abiathar the priests: Thus and thus did Achitophel counsel Absalom, and the ancients of Israel; and thus and thus did I counsel them.

16 Now therefore send quickly and tell David, saying: Tarry not this night in the plains of the wilderness, but without delay pass over: lest the king be swallowed up, and all the people that is with him.

17 And Jonathan and Achimaas stayed by the fountain Rogel: and there went a maid and told them. And they went forward, to carry the message to king David, for they might not be seen, nor enter into the city.

18 But a certain boy saw them, and told Absalom. But they making haste went into the house of a certain man in Bahurim, who had a well in his court; and they went down into it.

19 And a woman took, and spread a covering over the mouth of the well, as it were to dry sodden barley: and so the thing was not known.

20 And when Absalom's servants were come into the house, they said to the woman: Where is Achimaas and Jonathan? And the woman answered them: They passed on in haste, after they had tasted a little water. But they that sought them, when they found them not, returned into Jerusalem.

Chap. 17. Ver. 24. *To the camp.* The city of Mahanaim, the name of which, in Hebrew, signifies *The camp.* It was a city of note at that time, as appears from its having been chosen by Isboseth for the place of his residence.

21 And when they were gone, they came up out of the well; and going on told king David, and said: Arise, and pass quickly over the river; for this manner of counsel has Achitophel given against you.

22 So David arose, and all the people that were with him, and they passed over the Jordan, until it grew light, and not one of them was left that was not gone over the river.

23 But Achitophel seeing that his counsel was not followed, saddled his ass, and arose and went home to his house and to his city. And putting his house in order, he hanged himself, and was buried in the sepulchre of his father.

24 But David came to the camp: and Absalom passed over the Jordan, he and all the men of Israel with him.

25 Now Absalom appointed Amasa in Joab's stead over the army. And Amasa was the son of a man who was called Jethra of Jezrael, who went in to Abigail the daughter of Naas, the sister of Sarvia who was the mother of Joab.

26 And Israel camped with Absalom in the land of Galaad.

27 And when David was come to the camp, Sobi the son of Naas of Rabbath of the children of Ammon, and Machir the son of Ammihel of Lodabar, and Berzellai the Galaadite of Rogelim,

28 Brought him beds, and tapestry, and earthen vessels, and wheat, and barley, and meal, and parched corn, and beans, and lentils, and fried pulse,

29 And honey, and butter, and sheep, and fat calves. And they gave to David and the people that were with him, to eat: for they suspected that the people were faint with hunger and thirst in the wilderness.

CHAPTER 18

Absalom is defeated, and slain by Joab. David mourneth for him.

AND David having reviewed his people, appointed over them captains of thousands and of hundreds.

2 And sent forth a third part of the people under the hand of Joab, and a third part under the hand of Abisai the son of Sarvia, Joab's brother, and a third part under the hand of Ethai, who was of Geth. And the king said to the people: I also will go forth with you.

3 And the people answered: Thou shalt not go forth; for if we flee away, they will not much mind us. Or if half of us should fall, they will not greatly care: for thou alone art accounted for ten thousand. It is better therefore that thou shouldst be in the city to succour us.

4 And the king said to them: What seemeth good to you, that will I do. And the king stood by the gate: and all the people went forth by their troops, by hundreds and by thousands.

5 And the king commanded Joab, and Abisai, and Ethai, saying: Save me the boy Absalom. And all the people heard the king giving charge to all the princes concerning Absalom.

6 So the people went out into the field against Israel: and the battle was fought in the forest of Ephraim.

7 And the people of Israel were defeated there by David's army: and a great slaughter was made that day of twenty thousand men.

8 And the battle there was scattered over the face of all the country: and there were many more of the people whom the forest consumed, than whom the sword devoured that day.

9 And it happened that Absalom met the servants of David, riding on a mule. And as the mule went under a thick and large oak, his head stuck in the oak: and while he hung between the heaven and the earth, the mule on which he rode passed on.

10 And one saw this and told Joab, saying: I saw Absalom hanging upon an oak.

11 And Joab said to the man that told him: If thou sawest him, why didst thou not stab him to the ground, and I would have given thee ten sicles of silver, and a belt?

12 And he said to Joab: If thou wouldst have paid down in my hands a thousand pieces of silver, I would not lay my hands upon the king's son. For in our hearing the king charged thee, and Abisai, and Ethai, saying: Save me the boy Absalom.

13 Yea, and if I should have acted boldly against my own life, this could not have been hid from the king. And wouldst thou have stood by me?

14 And Joab said: Not as thou wilt, but I will set upon him in thy sight. So he took three lances in his hand, and thrust them into the heart of Absalom. And whilst he yet panted for life, sticking on the oak.

15 Ten young men, armourbearers of Joab, ran up, and striking him slew him.

16 And Joab sounded the trumpet, and kept back the people from pursuing after Israel in their flight, being willing to spare the multitude.

17 And they took Absalom, and cast him into a great pit in the forest: and they laid an exceeding great heap of stones upon him. But all Israel fled to their own dwellings.

18 Now Absalom had reared up for himself, in his lifetime, a pillar, which is in the king's valley. For he said: I have no son; and this shall be the monument of my name. And he called the pillar by his own name, and it is called the hand of Absalom, to this day.

19 And Achimaas the son of Sadoc said: I will run and tell the king, that the Lord hath done judgment for him from the hand of his enemies.

20 And Joab said to him: Thou shalt not be the messenger this day, but shalt bear tidings another day. This day I will not have thee bear tidings, because the king's son is dead.

21 And Joab said to Chusai: Go, and tell the king what thou hast seen. Chusai bowed down to Joab, and ran.

22 Then Achimaas the son of Sadoc said to Joab again: Why might not I also run after Chusai? And Joab said to him: Why wilt thou run, my son? Thou wilt not be the bearer of good tidings.

23 He answered: But what if I run? And he said to him: Run. Then Achimaas running by a nearer way passed Chusai.

24 And David sat between the two gates: and the watchman that was on the top of the gate upon the wall, lifting up his eyes, saw a man running alone.

25 And crying out he told the king. And the king said: If he be alone, there are good tidings in his mouth. And as he was coming apace, and drawing nearer,

26 The watchman saw another man running; and crying aloud from above, he said: I see another man running alone. And the king said: He also is a good messenger.

27 And the watchman said: The running of the foremost seemeth to me like the running of Achimaas the son of Sadoc. And the king said: He is a good man; and cometh with good news.

28 And Achimaas crying out said to the king: God save thee, O king. And falling down before the king with his face to the ground, he said: Blessed be the Lord thy God, who hath shut up the men that have lifted up their hands against the lord my king.

29 And the king said: Is the young man Absalom safe? And Achimaas said: I saw a great tumult, O king, when thy servant Joab sent me thy servant. I know nothing else.

30 And the king said to him: Pass, and stand here.

Chap. 18. Ver. 8. *Consumed*, that is, by pits and precipices.

Ver. 18. *No sign*. The sons mentioned above (14, 27) were dead when this pillar was erected: unless we suppose he raised this pillar before they were born.

31 And when he had passed, and stood still, Chusai appeared. And coming up he said: I bring good tidings, my lord, the king; for the Lord hath judged for thee this day from the hand of all that have risen up against thee.

32 And the king said to Chusai: Is the young man Absalom safe? And Chusai answering him, said: Let the enemies of my lord, the king, and all that rise against him unto evil, be as the young man is.

33 The king therefore being much moved, went up to the high chamber over the gate, and wept. And as he went he spoke in this manner: [1] My son Absalom, Absalom my son! Would to God that I might die for thee, Absalom my son, my son Absalom!

CHAPTER 19

David, at the remonstances of Joab, ceaseth his mourning. He is invited back and met by Semei and Miphiboseth. A strife between the men of Juda and the men of Israel.

AND it was told Joab, that the king wept and mourned for his son.

2 And the victory that day was turned into mourning unto all the people. For the people heard say that day: The king grieveth for his son.

3 And the people shunned the going into the city that day as a people would do that hath turned their backs, and fled away from the battle.

4 And the king covered his head, and cried with a loud voice: O my son Absalom, O Absalom my son, O my son!

5 Then Joab going into the house to the king, said: Thou hast shamed this day the faces of all thy servants, that have saved thy life, and the lives of thy sons, and of thy daughters, and the lives of thy wives, and the lives of thy concubines.

6 Thou lovest them that hate thee, and thou hatest them that love thee. And thou hast shewn this day that thou carest not for thy nobles, nor for thy servants. And I now plainly perceive that if Absalom had lived, and all we had been slain, then it would have pleased thee.

7 Now therefore arise, and go out, and speak to the satisfaction of thy servants: for I swear to thee by the Lord, that if thou wilt not go forth, there will not tarry with thee so much

Ver. 33. *Would to God.* David lamented the death of Absalom, because of the wretched state in which he died: and therefore would have been glad to have saved his life, even by dying for him. In which he was a figure of Christ weeping, praying and dying for his rebellious children, and even for them that crucified him.

as one this night. And that will be worse to thee, than all the evils that have befallen thee from thy youth until now.

8 Then the king arose and sat in the gate: and it was told to all the people that the king sat in the gate. And all the people came before the king: but Israel fled to their own dwellings.

9 And all the people were at strife in all the tribes of Israel, saying: The king delivered us out of the hand of our enemies, and he saved us out of the hand of the Philistines; and now he is fled out of the land for Absalom.

10 But Absalom, whom we anointed over us, is dead in the battle. How long are you silent, and bring not back the king?

11 And king David sent to Sadoc and Abiathar, the priests, saying: Speak to the ancients of Juda, saying: Why are you the last to bring the king back to his house? (For the talk of all Israel was come to the king in his house.)

12 You are my brethren; you are my bone, and my flesh: Why are you the last to bring back the king?

13 And say ye to Amasa: Art not thou my bone, and my flesh? So do God to me and add more, if thou be not the chief captain of the army before me always in the place of Joab.

14 And he inclined the heart of all the men of Juda, as it were of one man. And they sent to the king, saying: Return thou, and all thy servants.

15 And the king returned and came as far as the Jordan: and all Juda came as far as Galgal to meet the king, and to bring him over the Jordan.

16 [1] And Semei the son of Gera the son of Jemini of Bahurim, made haste and went down with the men of Juda to meet king David,

17 With a thousand men of Benjamin, and Siba the servant of the house of Saul. And his fifteen sons, and twenty servants were with him. And going over the Jordan,

18 They passed the fords before the king, that they might help over the king's household, and do according to his commandment. And Semei the son of Gera falling down before the king, when he was come over the Jordan,

19 Said to him: Impute not to me, my lord, the iniquity, nor remember the injuries of thy servant on the day that thou, my lord, the king, wentest out of Jerusalem, nor lay it up in thy heart, O king.

20 For I thy servant acknowledge my sin: and therefore I am come this day the first of all the house of Joseph, and am come down to meet my lord the king.

21 But Abisai the son of Sarvia answering, said: Shall Semei for these words not be put to death, because he cursed the Lord's anointed?

22 And David said: What have I to do with you, ye sons of Sarvia? Why are you a satan this day to me? Shall there any man be killed this day in Israel? Do not I know that this day I am made king over Israel?

23 And the king said to Semei: Thou shalt not die. And he swore unto him.

24 And Miphiboseth the son of Saul came down to meet the king: and he had neither washed his feet, nor trimmed his beard, nor washed his garments from the day that the king went out, until the day of his return in peace.

25 And when he met the king at Jerusalem, the king said to him: Why camest thou not with me, Miphiboseth?

26 And he answering, said: My lord, O king, my servant despised me. For I thy servant spoke to him to saddle me an ass, that I might get on and go with the king: for I thy servant am lame.

27 [2] Moreover he hath also accused me thy servant to thee, my lord the king: but [3] thou, my lord the king, art as an angel of God. Do what pleaseth thee.

28 For all of my father's house were no better than worthy of death before my lord the king; and thou hast set me thy servant among the guests of thy table. What just complaint therefore have I? Or what right to cry any more to the king?

29 Then the king said to him: Why speakest thou any more? What I have said is determined: thou and Siba divide the possessions.

30 And Miphiboseth answered the king: Yea, let him take all; forasmuch as my lord the king is returned peaceably into his house.

31 Berzellai also the Galaadite coming down from Rogelim, brought the king over the Jordan, being ready also to wait on him beyond the river.

32 [4] Now Berzellai the Galaadite was of a great age, that is to say, fourscore years old: and he provided the king with sustenance when he abode in the camp; for he was a man exceeding rich.

33 And the king said to Berzellai: Come with me that thou mayest rest secure with me in Jerusalem.

34 And Berzellai said to the king: How many are the days of the years of my life, that I should go up with the king to Jerusalem?

35 [5] I am this day fourscore years old. Are my senses quick to discern sweet and bitter? Or can meat or drink delight thy servant? Or can I hear any more the voice of singing men and singing women? Why should thy servant be a burden to my lord, the king?

36 I thy servant will go on a little way from the Jordan with thee. I need not this recompense.

37 But I beseech thee let thy servant return, and die in my own city, and be buried by the sepulchre of my father and of my mother. But there is thy servant Chamaam, let him go with thee, my lord, the king, and do to him whatsoever seemeth good to thee.

38 Then the king said to him: Let Chamaam go over with me, and I will do for him whatsoever shall please thee; and all that thou shalt ask of me, thou shalt obtain.

39 And when all the people and the king had passed over the Jordan, the king kissed Berzellai, and blessed him. And he returned to his own place.

40 So the king went on to Galgal, and Chamaam with him. Now all the people of Juda had brought the king over, and only half of the people of Israel were there.

41 Therefore all the men of Israel running together to the king, said to him: Why have our brethren the men of Juda stolen thee away, and have brought the king and his household over the Jordan, and all the men of David with him?

42 And all the men of Juda answered the men of Israel: Because the king is nearer to me. Why art thou angry for this matter? Have we eaten any thing of the king's, or have any gifts been given us?

43 And the men of Israel answered the men of Juda, and said: I have ten parts in the king more than thou; and David belongeth to me more than to thee. Why hast thou done me a wrong, and why was it not told me first, that I might bring back my king? And the men of Juda answered more harshly than the men of Israel.

CHAPTER 20

Seba's rebellion. Amasa is slain by Joab. Abela is besieged, but upon the citizens casting over the wall the head of Seba, Joab departeth with his army.

AND there happened to be there a man of Belial, whose name was Seba, the son of Bochri, a man of Jemini. And he sounded the trumpet, and said: We have no part in David, nor inheritance in the son of Isai. Return to thy dwellings, O Israel.

2 And all Israel departed from David, and followed Seba the son of Bochri: but the men of Juda stuck to

their king from the Jordan unto Jerusalem.

3 And when the king was come into his house at Jerusalem, he took the ten women his concubines, whom he had left to keep the house, and put them in ward, allowing them provisions. And he went not in unto them; but they were shut up unto the day of their death living in widowhood.

4 And the king said to Amasa: Assemble to me all the men of Juda against the third day. And be thou here present.

5 So Amasa went to assemble the men of Juda; but he tarried beyond the set time which the king had appointed him.

6 And David said to Abisai: Now will Seba the son of Bochri do us more harm than did Absalom. Take thou therefore the servants of thy lord, and pursue after him, lest he find fenced cities, and escape us.

7 So Joab's men went out with him, and the Cerethi and the Phelethi: and all the valiant men went out of Jerusalem to pursue after Seba the son of Bochri.

8 And when they were at the great stone which is in Gabaon, Amasa coming met them. And Joab had on a close coat of equal length with his habit; and over it was girded with a sword hanging down to his flank, in a scabbard, made in such manner as to come out with the least motion and strike.

9 And Joab said to Amasa: God save thee, my brother. [1] And he took Amasa by the chin with his right hand to kiss him.

10 But Amasa, did not take notice of the sword, which Joab had: and he struck him in the side, and shed out his bowels to the ground, and gave him not a second wound. And he died. And Joab, and Abisai his brother pursued after Seba the son of Bochri.

11 In the mean time some men of Joab's company stopping at the dead body of Amasa, said: Behold he that would have been in Joab's stead the companion of David.

12 And Amasa, imbrued with blood, lay in the midst of the way. A certain man saw this that all the people stood still to look upon him. So he removed Amasa out of the highway into the field, and covered him with a garment, that they who passed might not stop on his account.

13 And when he was removed out of the way, all the people went on follow-

ing Joab to pursue after Seba the son of Bochri.

14 Now he had passed through all the tribes of Israel unto Abela and Bethmaacha: and all the chosen men were gathered together unto him.

15 And they came, and besieged him in Abela and in Bethmaacha, and they cast up works round the city, and the city was besieged. And all the people that were with Joab, laboured to throw down the walls.

16 And a wise woman cried out from the city: Hear, hear, and say to Joab: Come near hither, and I will speak with thee.

17 And when he was come near to her, she said to him: Art thou Joab? And he answered: I am. And she spoke thus to him: Hear the words of thy handmaid. He answered: I do hear.

18 And she again said: A saying was used in the old proverb: They that inquire, let them inquire in Abela: and so they made an end.

19 Am not I she that answers truth in Israel? And thou seekest to destroy the city, and to overthrow a mother in Israel? Why wilt thou throw down the inheritance of the Lord?

20 And Joab answering said: God forbid, God forbid that I should. I do not throw down nor destroy.

21 The matter is not so, but a man of mount Ephraim, Seba the son of Bochri by name, hath lifted up his hand against king David: deliver him only, and we will depart from the city. And the woman said to Joab: Behold his head shall be thrown to thee from the wall.

22 So she went to all the people, and spoke to them wisely. And they cut off the head of Seba the son of Bochri, and cast it out to Joab. And he sounded the trumpet: and they departed from the city, every one to their home. And Joab returned to Jerusalem to the king.

23 [2] So Joab was over all the army of Israel: and Banaias the son of Joiada was over the Cerethites and Phelethites.

24 But Aduram over the tributes: and Josaphat the son of Ahilud was recorder.

25 And Siva *was* scribe: and Sadoc and Abiathar, priests.

26 And Ira the Jairite was the priest of David.

CHAPTER 21

A famine of three years, for the sin of Saul against the Gabaonites, at whose desire seven of Saul's race are crucified. War again with the Philistines.

AND there was a famine in the days of David for thee years suc-

CHAP. 20. [1] 3 Kings, 2, 5. [2] 2 Kings, 8, 16.

CHAP. 20. Ver. 14. *Abela and Bethmaacha.* Cities of the tribe of Nephtali.

cessively: and David consulted the oracle of the Lord. And the Lord said: *It is* for Saul, and his bloody house, because he slew the Gabaonites.

2 Then the king, calling for the Gabaonites, said to them: (Now the Gabaonites were not of the children of Israel, but the remains of the Amorrhites: ¹ and the children of Israel had sworn to them, and Saul sought to slay them out of zeal, as it were for the children of Israel and Juda:)

3 David therefore said to the Gabaonites: What shall I do for you? And what shall be the atonement for you that you may bless the inheritance of the Lord?

4 And the Gabaonites said to him: We have no contest about silver and gold, but against Saul and against his house. Neither do we desire that any man be slain of Israel. And the king said to them: What will you then that I should do for you?

5 And they said to the king: The man that crushed us and oppressed us unjustly, we must destroy in such manner that there be not so much as one left of his stock in all the coasts of Israel.

6 Let seven men of his children be delivered unto us, that we may crucify them to the Lord in Gabaa of Saul, once the chosen of the Lord. And the king said: I will give them.

7 ² And the king spared Miphiboseth the son of Jonathan the son of Saul, because of the oath of the Lord, that had been between David and Jonathan the son of Saul.

8 So the king took the two sons of Respha the daughter of Aia, whom she bore to Saul, Armoni, and Miphiboseth: and the five sons of Michol the daughter of Saul, whom she bore to Hadriel the son of Berzellai, that was of Molathi:

9 And gave them into the hands of the Gabaonites. And they crucified them on a hill before the Lord: and these seven died together in the first days of the harvest, when the barley began to be reaped.

10 And Respha the daughter of Aia took haircloth, and spread it under her upon the rock, from the beginning of the harvest, till water dropped upon them out of heaven: and suffered neither the birds to tear them by day, nor the beasts by night.

11 And it was told David, what Respha the daughter of Aia, the concubine of Saul, had done.

12 And David went, and took the bones of Saul, and the bones of Jonathan his son from the men of Jabes

Galaad, ³ who had stolen them from the street of Bethsan, where the Philistines had hanged them when they had slain Saul in Gelboe.

13 And he brought from thence the bones of Saul, and the bones of Jonathan his son: and they gathered up the bones of them that were crucified,

14 And they buried them with the bones of Saul, and of Jonathan his son in the land of Benjamin, in the side, in the sepulchre of Cis his father. And they did all that the king had commanded: and God shewed mercy again to the land after these things.

15 And the Philistines made war again against Israel, and David went down, and his servants with him, and fought against the Philistines. And David growing faint,

16 Jesbibenob, who was of the race of Arapha, ⁴ the iron of whose spear weighed three hundred ounces, being girded with a new sword, attempted to kill David.

17 And Abisai the son of Sarvia rescued him, and striking the Philistine killed him. Then David's men swore unto him, saying: Thou shalt go no more out with us to battle, lest thou put out the lamp of Israel.

18 ⁵ There was also a second battle in Gob against the Philistines: then Sobochai of Husathi slew Saph of the race of Arapha of the family of the giants.

19 And there was a third battle in Gob against the Philistines, in which Adeodatus the son of the Forrest an embroiderer of Bethlehem slew Goliath the Gethite, the shaft of whose spear was like a weaver's beam.

20 A fourth battle was in Geth: where there was a man of great stature, that had six fingers on each hand, and six toes on each foot, four and twenty in all. And he was of the race of Arapha.

21 And he reproached Israel: and Jonathan the son of Samaa the brother of David slew him.

22 These four were born of Arapha in Geth: and they fell by the hand of David and of his servants.

CHAPTER 22

King David's psalm of thanksgiving for his deliverance from all his enemies.

Chap. 21. ¹ Jos. 9, 15. ² 1 Kings, 18, 3. ³ 1 Kings, 31, 12. ⁴ 1 Kings, 17, 7. ⁵ 1 Par. 20, 4.

Chap. 21. Ver. 8. *Of Michol.* They were the sons of Merob, who was married to Hadriel: but they are here called the sons of Michol, because she adopted them, and brought them up as her own.

Ver. 19. *Adeodatus the son of the Forrest.* So it is rendered in the Latin Vulgate, by giving the interpretation of the Hebrew names, which are Elhanan the son of Jaare.

ND David spoke to the Lord the words of this canticle, in the day that the Lord delivered him out of the hand of all his enemies, and out of the hand of Saul,

2 And he said: [1] The Lord is my rock, and my strength, and my saviour.

3 God is my strong one, in him will I trust: my shield, and the horn of my salvation. He lifteth me up, and *is* my refuge: my saviour, thou wilt deliver me from iniquity.

4 [2] I will call on the Lord who is worthy to be praised: and I shall be saved from my enemies.

5 For the pangs of death have surrounded me: the floods of Belial have made me afraid.

6 The cords of hell compassed me: the snares of death prevented me.

7 In my distress I will call upon the Lord, and I will cry to my God: and he will hear my voice out of his temple, and my cry shall come to his ears.

8 The earth shook and trembled, the foundations of the mountains were moved, and shaken: because he was angry with them.

9 A smoke went up from his nostrils, and a devouring fire out of his mouth: coals were kindled by it.

10 He bowed the heavens, and came down: and darkness *was* under his feet.

11 And he rode upon the cherubims, and flew: and slid upon the wings of the wind.

12 He made darkness a covering round about him: dropping waters out of the clouds of the heavens.

13 By the brightness before him, the coals of fire were kindled.

14 The Lord shall thunder from heaven: and the Most High shall give forth his voice.

15 He shot arrows and scattered them: lightning, and consumed them.

16 And the overflowings of the sea appeared, and the foundations of the world were laid open at the rebuke of the Lord: at the blast of the spirit of his wrath.

17 He sent from on high, and took me: and drew me out of many waters.

18 He delivered me from my most mighty enemy, and from them that hated me: for they were too strong for me.

19 He prevented me in the day of my affliction: and the Lord became my stay.

20 And he brought me forth into a large place: he delivered me, because I pleased him.

21 The Lord will reward me according to my justice: and according to the cleanness of my hands he will render to me.

22 Because I have kept the ways of the Lord: and have not wickedly departed from my God.

23 For all his judgments are in my sight: and his precepts I have not removed from me.

24 And I shall be perfect with him: and shall keep myself from my iniquity.

25 And the Lord will recompense me according to my justice: and according to the cleanness of my hands in the sight of his eyes.

26 With the holy one thou wilt be holy: and with the valiant perfect.

27 With the elect thou wilt be elect: and with the perverse thou wilt be perverted.

28 And the poor people thou wilt save: and with thy eyes thou wilt humble the haughty.

29 For thou art my lamp, O Lord: and thou, O Lord, wilt enlighten my darkness.

30 For in thee I will run girded: in my God I will leap over the wall.

31 God, his way *is* immaculate, the word of the Lord is tried by fire: he is the shield of all that trust in him.

32 Who is God but the Lord: and who is strong but our God?

33 God who hath girded me with strength, and made my way perfect.

34 [3] Making my feet like the feet of harts: and setting me upon my high places.

35 He teacheth my hands to war: and maketh my arms like a bow of brass.

36 Thou hast given me the shield of my salvation: and thy mildness hath multiplied me.

37 Thou shalt enlarge my steps under me: and my ankles shall not fail.

38 I will pursue after my enemies, and crush them: and will not return again till I consume them.

39 I will consume them and break them in pieces, so that they shall not rise: they shall fall under my feet.

40 Thou hast girded me with strength to battle: thou hast made them that resisted me to bow under me.

41 My enemies thou hast made to turn their back to me: them that hated me, and I shall destroy them.

42 They shall cry, and there shall be none to save: to the Lord, and he shall not hear them.

43 I shall beat them as small as the dust of the earth: I shall crush them and spread them abroad like the mire of the streets.

44 Thou wilt save me from the contradictions of my people; thou wilt keep

CHAP. 22. [1] Ps. 17, 3. [2] Ps. 17, 4. [3] Ps. 143, 1.

me to be the head of the Gentiles: the people which I know not, shall serve me,

45 The sons of the stranger will resist me: at the hearing of the ear they will obey me.

46 The strangers are melted away: and shall be straitened in their distresses.

47 The Lord liveth, and my God is blessed: and the strong God of my salvation shall be exalted.

48 God who givest me revenge, and bringest down people under me:

49 Who bringest me forth from my enemies, and liftest me up from them that resist me. ⁴ From the wicked man thou shalt deliver me.

50 ⁵ Therefore will I give thanks to thee, O Lord, among the Gentiles: and will sing to thy name.

51 Giving great salvation to his king: and shewing mercy to David his anointed, and to his seed for ever.

CHAPTER 23

The last words of David. A catalogue of his valiant men.

NOW these are David's last words. David the son of Isai said: The man to whom it was appointed concerning the Christ of the God of Jacob, ¹ the excellent psalmist of Israel, said:

2 The spirit of the Lord hath spoken by me: and his word by my tongue.

3 The God of Israel said to me, the strong one of Israel spoke, the ruler of men, the just ruler in the fear of God.

4 As the light of the morning, when the sun riseth, shineth in the morning without clouds; and as the grass springeth out of the earth by rain.

5 Neither is my house so great with God, that he should make with me an eternal covenant, firm in all things and assured. For *he is* all my salvation, and all my will: neither is there aught thereof that springeth not up.

6 But transgressors shall all of them be plucked up as thorns: which are not taken away with hands.

7 And if a man will touch them, he must be armed with iron and with the staff of a lance: but they shall be set on fire and burnt to nothing.

8 ² These are the names of the valiant men of David. *Jesbaham* sitting in the chair *was* the wisest chief among the three: he was like the most tender little worm of the wood. Who killed eight hundred men at one onset.

9 After him was Eleazar the son of Dodo the Ahohite, one of the three valiant men that were with David when they defied the Philistines, and they were there gathered together to battle.

10 And when the men of Israel were gone away, he stood and smote the Philistines till his hand was weary, and grew stiff with the sword. And the Lord wrought a great victory that day: and the people that were fled away, returned to take spoils of them that were slain.

11 And after him was Semma the son of Age of Arari. And the Philistines were gathered together in a troop: for there was a field full of lentils. And when the people were fled from the face of the Philistines,

12 He stood in the midst of the field, and defended it, and defeated the Philistines. And the Lord gave a great victory.

13 Moreover also before this the three who were princes ³ among the thirty, went down and came to David in the harvest time into the cave of Odollam: and the camp of the Philistines was in the valley of the giants.

14 And David was then in a hold: and there was a garrison of the Philistines then in Bethlehem.

15 And David longed, and said: O that some man would get me a drink of the water out of the cistern, that is in Bethlehem, by the gate!

16 And the three valiant men broke through the camp of the Philistines, and drew water out of the cistern of Bethlehem, that was by the gate, and brought it to David. But he would not drink, but offered it to the Lord,

17 Saying: The Lord be merciful to me, that I may not do this. Shall I drink the blood of these men that went, and the peril of their lives? Therefore he would not drink. These things did these three mighty men.

18 Abisai also the brother of Joab, the son of Sarvia, was chief among three. And he lifted up his spear against three hundred whom he slew. And he was renowned among the three,

19 And the noblest of three, and was

---

⁴ Ps. 17, 49. ⁵ Rom. 15, 9. CHAP. 23. ¹ Acts, 2, 30. ² 1 Par. 11, 10. ³ 1 Par. 11, 15.

CHAP. 23. Ver. 4. *As the light of the morning.* So shall be the kingdom of Christ.

Ver. 5. *Neither is my house so great.* As if he should say: This everlasting covenant was not due to my house: but purely owing to his bounty; who is all my salvation, and my will: that is, who hath always saved me, and granted me what I beseeched of him; so that I and my house, through his blessing, have sprung up, and succeeded in all things.

Ver. 8. *Jesbaham,* the son of Hachamoni. For this was the name of this hero, as appears from 1 Par. 11.—*Most tender.* He appeared like one tender and weak, but was indeed most valiant and strong. It seems the Latin has here given the interpretation of the Hebrew name of the hero, to whom *Jesbaham* was like, instead of the name itself, which was *Adino the Eznite,* one much renowned of old for his valour.

Ver. 9. *Dodo.* In Latin, *Patrui ejus,* which is the interpretation of the Hebrew name *Dodo.* The same occurs in ver 24.

their chief: but to the three first he attained not.

20 And Banaias the son of Joiada a most valiant man, of great deeds, of Cabseel. He slew the two lions of Moab: and he went down, and slew a lion in the midst of a pit, in the time of snow.

21 He also slew an Egyptian, a man worthy to be a sight, having a spear in his hand: but he went down to him with a rod, and forced the spear out of the hand of the Egyptian, and slew him with his own spear.

22 These things did Banaias the son of Joiada.

23 And he *was* renowned among the three valiant men, who were the most honourable among the thirty: but he attained not to the first three. And David made him of his privy council.

24 Asael the brother of Joab was one of the thirty, Elehanan the son of Dodo of Bethlehem,

25 Semma of Harodi, Elica of Harodi,

26 Heles of Phalti, Hira the son of Acces of Thecua,

27 Abiezer of Anathoth, Mobonnai of Husati,

28 Selmon the Ahohite, Maharai the Netophathite,

29 Heled the son of Baana, also a Netophathite, Ithai the son of Ribai of Gabaath of the children of Benjamin,

30 Banaia the Pharathonite, Heddai of the torrent Gaas,

31 Abialbon the Arbathite, Azmaveth of Beromi,

32 Eliaba of Salaboni, the sons of Jassen, Jonathan,

33 Semma of Orori, Aliam the son of Sarar the Arorite,

34 Eliphelet the son of Aasbai the son of Machati, Eliam the son of Achitophel the Gelonite,

35 Hesrai of Carmel, Pharai of Arbi,

36 Igaal the son of Nathan of Soba, Bonni of Gadi,

37 Selec of Ammoni, Naharai the Berothite, armourbearer of Joab the son of Sarvia,

38 Ira the Jethrite, Gareb also a Jethrite,

39 Urias the Hethite: thirty and seven in all.

CHAPTER 24

David numbereth the people. God sendeth a pestilence, which is stopt by David's prayer and sacrifice.

CHAP. 24. [1] 1 Par. 21, 1. [2] 1 Kings, 24, 6.

Char. 24. Ver. 1. *Stirred up.* This stirring up was not the doing of God, but of Satan; as it is expressly declared (1 Par. 21, 1).

Ver. 10. *David's heart struck him, after the people were numbered.* That is he was touched with a great remorse for the vanity and pride which had put him upon numbering the people.

AND the anger of the Lord [1] was again kindled against Israel, and stirred up David among them, saying: Go, number Israel and Juda.

2 And the king said to Joab the general of his army: Go through all the tribes of Israel from Dan to Bersabee, and number ye the people that I may know the number of them.

3 And Joab said to the king: The Lord thy God increase thy people, and make them as many more as they are now, and again multiply them a hundredfold in the sight of my lord the king. But what meaneth my lord the king by this kind of thing?

4 But the king's words prevailed over the words of Joab, and of the captains of the army. And Joab, and the captains of the soldiers went out from the presence of the king, to number the people of Israel.

5 And when they had passed the Jordan, they came to Aroer to the right side of the city, which is in the vale of Gad.

6 And by Jazer they passed into Galaad, and to the lower land of Hodsi: and they came into the woodlands of Dan. And going about by Sidon,

7 They passed near the walls of Tyre, and all the land of the Hevite, and the Chanaanite: and they came to the south of Juda into Bersabee.

8 And having gone through the whole land, after nine months and twenty days, they came to Jerusalem.

9 And Joab gave up the sum of the number of the people to the king, and there were found of Israel eight hundred thousand valiant men that drew the sword: and of Juda five hundred thousand fighting men.

10 [2] But David's heart struck him, after the people were numbered. And David said to the Lord: I have sinned very much in what I have done; but I pray thee, O Lord, to take away the iniquity of thy servant, because I have done exceeding foolishly.

11 And David arose in the morning; and the word of the Lord came to Gad the prophet and the seer of David, saying:

12 Go, and say to David: Thus saith the Lord: I give thee thy choice of three things. Choose one of them which thou wilt, that I may do it to thee.

13 And when Gad was come to David, he told him, saying: Either seven years of famine shall come to thee in thy land: or thou shalt flee three months before thy adversaries, and they shall pursue thee: or for three days there shall be a pestilence in thy land. Now therefore deliberate, and see what answer I shall return to him that sent me.

14 And David said to Gad: I am in a great strait; [3] but it is better that I should fall into the hands of the Lord (for his mercies are many) than into the hands of men.

15 And the Lord sent a pestilence upon Israel, from the morning unto the time appointed. And there died of the people from Dan to Bersabee seventy thousand men.

16 And when the angel of the Lord had stretched out his hand over Jerusalem to destroy it, the Lord had pity on the affliction, and said to the angel that slew the people: It is enough. Now hold thy hand. And the angel of the Lord was by the thrashingfloor of Areuna the Jebusite.

17 And David said to the Lord, when he saw the angel striking the people: It is I. I am he that have sinned: I have done wickedly. These that are the sheep, what have they done? Let thy hand, I beseech thee, be turned against me, and against my father's house.

18 And Gad came to David that day, and said: Go up, and build an altar to the Lord in the thrashingfloor of Areuna the Jebusite.

19 And David went up according to the word of Gad which the Lord had commanded him.

20 And Areuna looked, and saw the king and his servants coming towards him.

21 And going out he worshipped the king, bowing with his face to the earth, and said: Wherefore is my lord the king come to his servant? And David said to him: To buy the thrashingfloor of thee, and build an altar to the Lord, that the plague, which rageth among the people, may cease.

22 And Areuna said to David: Let my Lord the king take, and offer, as it seemeth good to him. Thou hast here oxen for a holocaust, and the wain, and the yokes of the oxen for wood.

23 All these things Areuna as a king gave to the king. And Areuna said to the king: The Lord thy God receive thy vow.

24 And the king answered him, and said: Nay, but I will buy it of thee at a price, and I will not offer to the Lord my God holocausts free cost. So David bought the floor, and the oxen, for fifty sicles of silver.

25 And David built there an altar to the Lord, and offered holocausts and peace offerings. And the Lord became merciful to the land: and the plague was stayed from Israel.

THE THIRD BOOK OF
KINGS

This and the following Book are called by the holy fathers the third and fourth book of Kings; but by the Hebrews, the first and second. They contain the history of the kingdoms of Israel and Juda, from the beginning of the reign of Solomon, to the captivity. As to the writer of these books, it seems most probable they were not written by one man; but as there was all along a succession of prophets in Israel, who recorded, by divine inspiration, the most remarkable things that happened in their days, these books seem to have been written by these prophets. See 2. Paralip. (otherwise 2 Chron.) 9, 29; 12, 15; 13, 22; 20, 34; 26, 22; 32, 32.

CHAPTER 1

King David growing old, Abisag a Sunamitess is brought to him. Adonias pretending to reign, Nathan and Bethsabee obtain that Solomon should be declared and anointed king.

NOW king David was old, and advanced in years: and when he was covered with clothes, he was not warm.

2 His servants therefore said to him: Let us seek for our lord the king, a young virgin, and let her stand before the king, and cherish him, and sleep in his bosom, and warm our lord the king.

3 So they sought a beautiful young woman in all the coasts of Israel: and they found Abisag a Sunamitess, and brought her to the king.

4 And the damsel was exceeding beautiful; and she slept with the king, and served him: but the king did not know her.

5 And Adonias the son of Haggith exalted himself, saying: I will be king. And he made himself chariots and horsemen, and fifty men to run before him.

[3] Dan. 13, 23. CHAP. 1. [1] 1 Kings, 2, 29; 2 Kings, 13, 21; 5, 1.

6 ¹ Neither did his father rebuke him at any time, saying: Why hast thou done this? And he also was very beautiful, the next in birth after Absalom.

7 And he conferred with Joab the son of Sarvia, and with Abiathar the priest, who furthered Adonias's side.

8 But Sadoc the priest, and Banaias the son of Joiada, and Nathan the prophet, and Semei, and Rei, and the strength of David's army, was not with Adonias.

9 And Adonias, having slain rams and calves and all fat cattle by the stone of Zoheleth, which was near the fountain Rogel, invited all his brethren, the king's sons, and all the men of Juda, the king's servants:

10 But Nathan the prophet, and Banaias, and all the valiant men, and Solomon his brother, he invited not.

11 And Nathan said to Bethsabee the mother of Solomon: Hast thou not heard that Adonias the son of Haggith reigneth, and our lord David knoweth it not?

12 Now then come, take my counsel and save thy life, and the life of thy son Solomon.

13 Go, and get thee in to king David, and say to him: Didst not thou, my lord O king, swear to me thy handmaid, saying: Solomon thy son shall reign after me, and he shall sit on my throne? Why then doth Adonias reign?

14 And while thou art yet speaking there with the king, I will come in after thee, and will fill up thy words.

15 So Bethsabee went in to the king into the chamber. Now the king was very old, and Abisag the Sunamitess ministered to him.

16 Bethsabee bowed herself, and worshipped the king. And the king said to her: What is thy will?

17 She answered and said: My lord, thou didst swear to thy handmaid by the Lord thy God, saying: Solomon thy son shall reign after me, and he shall sit on my throne.

18 And behold now Adonias reigneth: and thou, my lord the king, knowest nothing of it.

19 He hath killed oxen, and all fat cattle, and many rams, and invited all the king's sons, and Abiathar the priest, and Joab the general of the army: but Solomon thy servant he invited not.

20 And now, my lord O king, the eyes of all Israel are upon thee, that thou shouldst tell them who shall sit on thy throne, my lord the king, after thee.

21 Otherwise it shall come to pass, when my lord the king sleepeth with his fathers, that I and my son Solomon shall be counted offenders.

22 As she was yet speaking with the king, Nathan the prophet came.

23 And they told the king, saying: Nathan the prophet is here. And when he was come in before the king, and had worshipped, bowing down to the ground,

24 Nathan said: My lord O king, hast thou said: Let Adonias reign after me, and let him sit upon my throne?

25 Because he is gone down to-day, and hath killed oxen, and fatlings, and many rams, and invited all the king's sons, and the captains of the army, and Abiathar the priest. And they are eating and drinking before him, and saying: God save king Adonias.

26 But me thy servant, and Sadoc the priest, and Banaias the son of Joiada, and Solomon thy servant he hath not invited.

27 Is this word come out from my lord the king, and hast thou not told me thy servant who should sit on the throne of my lord the king after him?

28 And king David answered and said: Call to me Bethsabee. And when she was come in to the king, and stood before him,

29 The king swore and said: As the Lord liveth, who hath delivered my soul out of all distress,

30 Even as I swore to thee by the Lord the God of Israel, saying: Solomon thy son shall reign after me; and he shall sit upon my throne in my stead, so will I do this day.

31 And Bethsabee bowing with her face to the earth worshipped the king, saying: May my lord David live for ever.

32 King David also said: Call me Sadoc the priest, and Nathan the prophet, and Banaias the son of Joiada. And when they were come in before the king,

33 He said to them: Take with you the servants of your lord, and set my son Solomon upon my mule, and bring him to Gihon.

34 And let Sadoc the priest, and Nathan the prophet anoint him there king over Israel. And you shall sound the trumpet, and shall say: God save king Solomon.

35 And you shall come up after him: and he shall come, and shall sit upon my throne. And he shall reign in my stead: and I will appoint him to be ruler over Israel, and over Juda.

36 And Banaias the son of Joiada answered the king, saying: Amen. So say the Lord the God of my lord the king!

37 As the Lord hath been with my lord the king, so be he with Solomon, and make his throne higher than the throne of my lord king David.

38 So Sadoc the priest, and Nathan the prophet went down, and Banaias the son of Joiada, and the Cerethi, and Phelethi: and they set Solomon upon the mule of king David, and brought him to Gihon.

39 And Sadoc the priest took a horn of oil out of the tabernacle, and anointed Solomon. And they sounded the trumpet; and all the people said: God save king Solomon.

40 And all the multitude went up after him, and the people played with pipes, and rejoiced with a great joy: and the earth rang with the noise of their cry.

41 And Adonias, and all that were invited by him, heard it, and now the feast was at an end. Joab also hearing the sound of the trumpet, said: What meaneth this noise of the city in an uproar?

42 While he yet spoke, Jonathan the son of Abiathar the priest came. And Adonias said to him: Come in, because thou art a valiant man, and bringest good news.

43 And Jonathan answered Adonias: Not so: for our lord king David hath appointed Solomon king.

44 And hath sent with him Sadoc the priest, and Nathan the prophet, and Banaias the son of Joiada, and the Cerethi, and Phelethi: and they have set him upon the king's mule.

45 And Sadoc the priest, and Nathan the prophet have anointed him king in Gihon: and they are gone up from thence rejoicing, so that the city rang again. This is the noise that you have heard.

46 Moreover Solomon sitteth upon the throne of the kingdom,

47 And the king's servants going in have blessed our lord king David, saying: May God make the name of Solomon greater than thy name, and make his throne greater than thy throne. And the king adored in his bed.

48 And he said: Blessed be the Lord the God of Israel, who hath given this day one to sit on my throne, my eyes seeing it.

49 Then all the guests of Adonias were afraid: and they all arose and every man went his way.

50 And Adonias fearing Solomon, arose, and went, and took hold on the horn of the altar.

51 And they told Solomon, saying: Behold Adonias, fearing king Solomon, hath taken hold of the horn of the altar, saying: Let king Solomon swear to me this day, that he will not kill his servant with the sword.

52 And Solomon said: If he be a good man, there shall not so much as one hair of his head fall to the ground; but if evil be found in him, he shall die.

53 Then king Solomon sent, and brought him out from the altar. And going in he worshipped king Solomon: and Solomon said to him: Go to thy house.

CHAPTER 2

David, after giving his last charge to Solomon, dieth. Adonias is put to death. Abiathar is banished. Joab and Semei are slain.

AND the days of David drew nigh that he should die, and he charged his son Solomon, saying:

2 I am going the way of all flesh. Take thou courage, and shew thyself a man.

3 And keep the charge of the Lord thy God, to walk in his ways, and observe his ceremonies, and his precepts, and judgments, and testimonies, [1] as it is written in the law of Moses: that thou mayest understand all thou dost, and whithersoever thou shalt turn thyself.

4 That the Lord may confirm his words, which he hath spoken of me, saying: If thy children shall take heed to their ways, and shall walk before me in truth, with all their heart, and with all their soul, there shall not be taken away from thee a man on the throne of Israel.

5 Thou knowest also what Joab the son of Sarvia hath done to me, what he did to the two captains of the army of Israel, [2] to Abner the son of Ner, and [3] to Amasa the son of Jether: whom he slew, and shed the blood of war in peace, and put the blood of war on his girdle that was about his loins, and in his shoes that were on his feet.

6 Do therefore according to thy wisdom: and let not his hoary head go down to hell in peace.

7 But shew kindness to the sons of Berzellai the Galaadite, and let them eat at thy table: [4] for they met me when I fled from the face of Absalom thy brother.

8 [5] Thou hast also with thee Semei the son of Gera, the son of Jemini of Bahurim, who cursed me with a grievous curse, when I went to the camp; but because he came down to meet me when I passed over the Jordan, and I swore to

CHAP. 2. [1] Deut. 17, 19. [2] 2 Kings, 3, 27. [3] 2 Kings, 20, 10. [4] 2 Kings, 19, 31. [5] 2 Kings, 16, 5; 19, 19.

CHAP. 2. Ver. 5. *Joab.* These instructions given by David to his son, with relation to Joab and Semei, proceeded not from any rancour of heart, or private pique; but from a zeal for justice, that crimes so public and heinous might not pass unpunished.

Ver. 6. *To hell.* This word hell doth not here signify the place or state of damnation; but the place and state of the dead.

him by the Lord, saying: I will not kill thee with a sword.

9 Do not thou hold him guiltless. But thou art a wise man, and knowest what to do with him: and thou shalt bring down his grey hairs with blood to hell.

10 [6] So David slept with his fathers, and was buried in the city of David.

11 [7] And the days that David reigned in Israel, were forty years. In Hebron he reigned seven years; in Jerusalem thirty-three.

12 And Solomon sat upon the throne of his father David: and his kingdom was strengthened exceedingly.

13 And Adonias the son of Haggith came to Bethsabee the mother of Solomon. And she said to him: Is thy coming peaceable? He answered: Peaceable.

14 And he added: I have a word to speak with thee. She said to him: Speak. And he said:

15 Thou knowest that the kingdom was mine, and all Israel had preferred me to be their king: but the kingdom is transferred, and is become my brother's; for it was appointed him by the Lord.

16 Now therefore I ask one petition of thee: turn not away my face. And she said to him: Say on.

17 And he said: I pray thee speak to king Solomon (for he cannot deny thee any thing) to give me Abisag the Sunamitess to wife.

18 And Bethsabee said: Well, I will speak for thee to the king.

19 Then Bethsabee came to king Solomon, to speak to him for Adonias: and the king arose to meet her, and bowed to her, and sat down upon his throne. And a throne was set for the king's mother: and she sat on his right hand.

20 And she said to him: I desire one small petition of thee; do not put me to confusion. And the king said to her: My mother, ask; for I must not turn away thy face.

21 And she said: Let Abisag the Sunamitess be given to Adonias thy brother to wife.

22 And king Solomon answered, and said to his mother: Why dost thou ask Abisag the Sunamitess for Adonias? Ask for him also the kingdom: for he is my elder brother, and hath Abiathar the priest and Joab the son of Sarvia.

23 Then king Solomon swore by the Lord, saying: So and so may God do to me, and add more, if Adonias hath not spoken this word against his own life.

24 And now, as the Lord liveth, who hath established me, and placed me upon the throne of David my father,

[6] Acts, 2, 29. [7] 1 Par. 29, 27. [8] 1 Kings, 2, 31. [9] 2 Kings, 3, 27; 20, 10.

and who hath made me a house, as he promised, Adonias shall be put to death this day.

25 And king Solomon sent by the hand of Banaias the son of Joiada, who slew him: and he died.

26 And the king said also to Abiathar the priest: Go to Anathoth to thy lands, for indeed thou art worthy of death. But I will not at this time put thee to death, because thou didst carry the ark of the Lord God before David my father, and hast endured trouble in all the troubles my father endured.

27 So Solomon cast out Abiathar, from being the priest of the Lord, [8] that the word of the Lord might be fulfilled, which he spoke concerning the house of Heli in Silo.

28 And the news came to Joab, because Joab had turned after Adonias, and had not turned after Solomon. And Joab fled into the tabernacle of the Lord and laid hold on the horn of the altar.

29 And it was told king Solomon, that Joab was fled into the tabernacle of the Lord, and was by the altar. And Solomon sent Banaias the son of Joiada, saying: Go, kill him.

30 And Banaias came to the tabernacle of the Lord, and said to him: Thus saith the king: Come forth. And he said: I will not come forth, but here I will die. Banaias brought word back to the king, saying: Thus saith Joab, and thus he answered me.

31 And the King said to him: Do as he hath said: and kill him, and bury him. And thou shalt remove the innocent blood which hath been shed by Joab, from me, and from the house of my father.

32 And the Lord shall return his blood upon his own head, because he murdered two men, just and better than himself; and slew them with the sword, my father David not knowing it: [9] Abner the son of Ner, general of the army of Israel, and Amasa the son of Jether, general of the army of Juda.

33 And their blood shall return upon the head of Joab, and upon the head of his seed for ever. But to David and his seed and his house, and to his throne be peace for ever from the Lord.

34 So Banaias the son of Joiada went up, and setting upon him slew him: and he was buried in his house in the desert.

35 And the king appointed Banaias the son of Joiada in his room over the army: and Sadoc the priest he put in the place of Abiathar.

36 The king also sent, and called for Semei, and said to him: Build thee a house in Jerusalem, and dwell there; and go not out from thence any whither.

37 For on what day soever thou shalt go out and shalt pass over the brook Cedron, know that thou shalt be put to death. Thy blood shall be upon thy own head.

38 And Semei said to the king: The saying is good. As my lord the king hath said, so will thy servant do. And Semei dwelt in Jerusalem, many days.

39 And it came to pass after three years, that the servants of Semei ran away to Achis the son of Maacha the king of Geth: and it was told Semei that his servants were gone to Geth.

40 And Semei arose, and saddled his ass, and went to Achis to Geth to seek his servants: and he brought them out of Geth.

41 And it was told Solomon that Semei had gone from Jerusalem to Geth, and was come back.

42 And sending he called for him, and said to him: Did I not protest to thee by the Lord, and tell thee before: On what day soever thou shalt go out and walk abroad any whither, know that thou shalt die? And thou answeredst me: The word that I have heard is good.

43 Why then hast thou not kept the oath of the Lord, and the commandment that I laid upon thee?

44 And the king said to Semei: Thou knowest all the evil, of which thy heart is conscious, which thou didst to David my father. The Lord hath returned thy wickedness upon thy own head.

45 And king Solomon shall be blessed: and the throne of David shall be established before the Lord for ever.

46 So the king commanded Banaias the son of Joiada. And he went out and struck him: and he died.

CHAPTER 3

Solomon marrieth Pharao's daughter. He sacrificeth in Gabaon. In the choice which God gave him he preferreth wisdom. His wise judgment between the two harlots.

AND the kingdom was established ¹ in the land of Solomon, and he made affinity with Pharao the king of Egypt: for he took his daughter, and brought her into the city of David, ² until he had made an end of building his own house, and the house of the Lord, and the wall of Jerusalem round about.

2 But yet the people sacrificed in the high places: for there was no temple built to the name of the Lord until that day.

3 And Solomon loved the Lord, walking in the precepts of David his father. Only he sacrificed in the high places, and burnt incense.

4 He went therefore to Gabaon, to sacrifice there: for that was the great high place. A thousand victims for holocausts did Solomon offer upon that altar in Gabaon.

5 And the Lord appeared to Solomon in a dream by night, saying: Ask what thou wilt that I should give thee.

6 And Solomon said: Thou hast shewn great mercy to thy servant David my father, even as he walked before thee in truth, and justice, and an upright heart with thee; and thou hast kept thy great mercy for him, and hast given him a son to sit on his throne, as it is this day.

7 And now, O Lord God, thou hast made thy servant king instead of David my father. And I am but a child, and know not how to go out and come in.

8 And thy servant is in the midst of the people which thou hast chosen, an immense people, which cannot be numbered nor counted for multitude.

9 ³ Give therefore to thy servant an understanding heart, to judge thy people, and discern between good and evil. For who shall be able to judge this people, thy people which is so numerous?

10 And the word was pleasing to the Lord that Solomon had asked such a thing.

11 And the Lord said to Solomon: Because thou hast asked this thing, and hast not asked for thyself long life or riches, nor the lives of thy enemies, but hast asked for thyself wisdom to discern judgment.

12 Behold I have done for thee according to thy words, and have given thee a wise and understanding heart; insomuch that there hath been no one like thee before thee, nor shall arise after thee.

13 ⁴ Yea and the things also which thou didst not ask, I have given thee: to wit, riches and glory, so that no one hath been like thee among the kings in all days heretofore.

14 And if thou wilt walk in my ways, and keep my precepts, and my commandments, as thy father walked, I will lengthen thy days.

15 And Solomon awaked, and perceived that it was a dream. And when he was come to Jerusalem, he stood before the ark of the covenant of the Lord,

CHAP. 3. ¹ 2 Par. 1, 1. ² 2 Par. 8, 11. ³ 2 Par. 1, 10. ⁴ Wisd. 7, 11; Matt. 6, 29.

CHAP. 3. Ver. 2. *High places.* That is, altars where they worshipped the Lord, but not according to the ordinance of the law; which allowed of no other places for sacrifice but the temple of God. Among these high places that of Gabaon was the chiefest, because there was the tabernacle of the testimony, which had been removed from Silo to Nobe and from Nobe to Gabaon.

and offered holocausts, and sacrificed victims of peace offerings, and made a great feast for all his servants.

16 Then there came two women that were harlots, to the king, and stood before him:

17 And one of them said: I beseech thee, my lord, I and this woman dwelt in one house, and I was delivered of a child with her in the chamber.

18 And the third day, after that I was delivered, she also was delivered: and we were together, and no other person with us in the house, only we two.

19 And this woman's child died in the night: for in her sleep she overlaid him.

20 And rising in the dead time of the night, she took my child from my side, while I thy handmaid was asleep, and laid it in her bosom: and laid her dead child in my bosom.

21 And when I rose in the morning to give my child suck, behold it was dead: but considering him more diligently when it was clear day, I found that it was not mine which I bore.

22 And the other woman answered: It is not so as thou sayest, but thy child is dead, and mine is alive. On the contrary she said: Thou liest; for my child liveth, and thy child is dead. And in this manner they strove before the king.

23 Then said the king: The one saith: My child is alive, and thy child is dead. And the other answereth: Nay, but thy child is dead, and mine liveth.

24 The king therefore said: Bring me a sword. And when they had brought a sword before the king,

25 Divide, said he, the living child in two, and give half to the one, and half to the other.

26 But the woman whose child was alive, said to the king (for her bowels were moved upon her child): I beseech thee, my lord, give her the child alive, and do not kill it. But the other said: Let it be neither mine nor thine, but divide it.

27 The king answered, and said: Give the living child to this woman, and let it not be killed; for she is the mother thereof.

28 And all Israel heard the judgment which the king had judged: and they feared the king, seeing that the wisdom of God was in him to do judgment.

CHAPTER 4

Solomon's chief officers. His riches and wisdom.

CHAP. 4. [1] Ecclus. 47, 15.

CHAP. 4. Ver. 4. *Abiathar.* By this it appears that Abiathar was not altogether deposed from the high priesthood; but only banished to his country house, and by that means excluded from the exercise of his functions.
Ver. 21. *The river.* Euphrates.

AND king Solomon reigned over all Israel:

2 And these were the princes which he had: Azarias the son of Sadoc, the priest:

3 Elihoreph, and Ahia, the sons of Sisa, scribes: Josaphat the son of Ahilud, recorder:

4 Banaias the son of Joiada, over the army: and Sadoc and Abiathar, priests:

5 Azarias the son of Nathan, over them that were about the king: Zabud, the son of Nathan the priest, the king's friend:

6 And Ahisar, governor of the house: and Adoniram the son of Abda, over the tribute.

7 And Solomon had twelve governors over all Israel, who provided victuals for the king and for his household: for every one provided necessaries, each man his month in the year.

8 And these are their names: Benhur, in mount Ephraim.

9 Bendecar, in Macces, and in Salebim, and in Bethsames, and in Elon, and in Bethanan.

10 Benhesed, in Aruboth: his was Socho, and all the land of Epher.

11 Benabinadab, to whom belonged all Nephath-Dor: he had Tapheth the daughter of Solomon to wife.

12 Bana the son of Ahilud, who governed Thanac and Mageddo, and all Bethsan, which is by Sarthana beneath Jezrael, from Bethsan unto Abelmehula over against Jecmaan.

13 Bengaber, in Ramoth Galaad: he had the towns of Jair the son of Manasses in Galaad: he was chief in all the country of Argob, which is in Basan, threescore great cities with walls, and brazen bolts.

14 Abinadab the son of Addo was chief in Manaim.

15 Achimaas in Nephtali: he also had Basemath the daughter of Solomon to wife.

16 Baana the son of Husi, in Aser and in Baloth.

17 Josaphat the son of Pharus, in Issachar.

18 Semei the son of Ela, in Benjamin.

19 Gaber the son of Uri, in the land of Galaad, in the land of Sehon the king of the Amorrhites and of Og the king of Basan: over all that were in that land.

20 Juda and Israel *were* innumerable, as the sand of the sea in multitude: eating and drinking, and rejoicing.

21 [1] And Solomon had under him all the kingdoms from the river to the land of the Philistines, even to the border of Egypt: and they brought him presents, and served him, all the days of his life.

22 And the provision of Solomon for each day, was thirty measures of fine flour, and threescore measures of meal;

23 Ten fat oxen and twenty out of the pastures, and a hundred rams, besides venison of harts, roes, and buffles, and fatted fowls.

24 For he had all the country which was beyond the river, from Thaphsa to Gazan, and all the kings of those countries. And he had peace on every side round about.

25 And Juda and Israel dwelt without any fear, every one under his vine, and under his fig tree, from Dan to Bersabee, all the days of Solomon.

26 ² And Solomon had forty thousand stalls of chariot horses, and twelve thousand for the saddle.

27 And the foresaid governors of the king fed them: and they furnished the necessaries also for king Solomon's table, with great care in their time.

28 They brought barley also and straw for the horses and beasts, to the place where the king was, according as it was appointed them.

29 And God gave to Solomon wisdom and understanding exceeding much, and largeness of heart as the sand that is on the shore.

30 And the wisdom of Solomon surpassed the wisdom of all the Orientals and of the Egyptians,

31 ³ And he was wiser than all men: wiser than Ethan the Ezrahite, and Heman, and Chalcol, and Dorda the son of Mahol. And he was renowned in all nations round about.

32 Solomon also spoke three thousand parables: and his poems were a thousand and five.

33 And he treated about trees from the cedar that is in Libanus, unto the hyssop, that cometh out of the wall: and he discoursed of beasts, and of fowls, and of creeping things, and of fishes.

34 And they came from all nations to hear the wisdom of Solomon and from all the kings of the earth who heard of his wisdom.

CHAPTER 5

Hiram king of Tyre agreeth to furnish timber and workmen for building the temple. The number of workmen and overseers.

AND Hiram king of Tyre sent his servants to Solomon: for he heard that they had anointed him king in the room of his father. For Hiram had always been David's friend.

2 And Solomon sent to Hiram, saying:

3 Thou knowest the will of David my father, and that he could not build a house to the name of the Lord his God, because of the wars that were round about him, until the Lord put them under the soles of his feet.

4 But now the Lord my God hath given me rest round about: and there is no adversary nor evil occurrence.

5 Wherefore I purpose to build a temple to the name of the Lord my God, as the Lord spoke to David my father, saying: ¹ Thy son, whom I will set upon the throne in thy place, he shall build a house to my name.

6 Give orders therefore that thy servants cut me down cedar trees out of Libanus: and let my servants be with thy servants. And I will give thee the hire of thy servants whatsoever thou wilt ask: for thou knowest how there is not among my people a man that has skill to hew wood like to the Sidonians.

7 Now when Hiram had heard the words of Solomon, he rejoiced exceedingly, and said: Blessed be the Lord God this day, who hath given to David a very wise son over this numerous people.

8 And Hiram sent to Solomon, saying: I have heard all thou hast desired of me; and I will do all thy desire concerning cedar trees and fir trees.

9 My servants shall bring them down from Libanus to the sea. And I will put them together in floats in the sea, and convey them to the place, which thou shalt signify to me; and will land them there. And thou shalt receive them: and thou shalt allow me necessaries, to furnish food for my household.

10 So Hiram gave Solomon cedar trees, and fir trees, according to all his desire.

11 And Solomon allowed Hiram twenty thousand measures of wheat, for provision for his house, and twenty measures of the purest oil. Thus gave Solomon to Hiram every year.

12 ² And the Lord gave wisdom to Solomon, as he promised him: and there was peace between Hiram and Solomon, and they two made a league together.

13 And king Solomon chose workmen out of all Israel: and the levy was of thirty thousand men.

14 And he sent them to Libanus, ten thousand every month by turns, so that two months they were at home. And Adoniram was over this levy.

²² Par. 9, 25. ³ Ecclus. 47, 10. CHAP. 5. ¹² Kings, 7, 13; 1 Par. 22, 10. ² 3 Kings, 3, 12.

Ver. 32. *Three thousand parables.* These works are all lost, excepting some part of the parables extant in the book of Proverbs; and his chief poem called the Canticle of Canticles.

15 And Solomon had seventy thousand to carry burdens, and eighty thousand to hew stones in the mountain:

16 Besides the overseers who were over every work, in number three thousand: and three hundred that ruled over the people, and them that did the work.

17 And the king commanded, that they should bring great stones, costly stones, for the foundation of the temple, and should square them.

18 And the masons of Solomon, and the masons of Hiram hewed them: and the Giblians prepared timber and stones to build the house.

CHAPTER 6

The building of Solomon's temple.

AND it came to pass [1] in the four hundred and eightieth year after the children of Israel came out of the land of Egypt, in the fourth year of the reign of Solomon over Israel, in the month Zio (the same is the second month), he began to build a house to the Lord.

2 And the house, which king Solomon built to the Lord, was three-score cubits in length, and twenty cubits in breadth, and thirty cubits in height.

3 And there was a porch before the temple of twenty cubits in length, according to the measure of the breadth of the temple: and it was ten cubits in breadth before the face of the temple.

4 And he made in the temple oblique windows.

5 And upon the wall of the temple he built floors round about, in the walls of the house round about the temple and the oracle: and he made sides round about.

6 The floor that was underneath, was five cubits in breadth; and the middle floor was six cubits in breadth; and the third floor was seven cubits in breadth. And he put beams in the house round about on the outside, that they might not be fastened in the walls of the temple.

7 And the house, when it was in building, was built of stones hewed and made ready: so that there was neither

CHAP. 6. [1] 2 Par. 3, 1. [2] 2 Kings, 7, 16. [3] 1 Par. 22, 9.

CHAP. 6. Ver. 5. *Upon the wall.* That is, joining to the wall.—*He built floors round about.* Chambers or cells adjoining to the temple, for the use of the temple and of the priests, so contrived as to be between the inward and outward wall of the temple, in three stories, one above another.—*The oracle.* The inner temple or Holy of Holies, where God gave his oracles.

Ver. 7. *Made ready.* So the stones for the building of God's eternal temple in the heavenly Jerusalem, (who are the faithful,) must first be hewn and polished here by many trials and sufferings, before they can be admitted to have a place in that celestial structure.

hammer nor axe nor any tool of iron heard in the house when it was in building.

8 The door for the middle side was on the right hand of the house: and by winding stairs they went up to the middle room, and from the middle to the third.

9 So he built the house, and finished it. And he covered the house with roofs of cedar.

10 And he built a floor over all the house five cubits in height: and he covered the house with timber of cedar.

11 And the word of the Lord came to Solomon, saying:

12 This house, which thou buildest, if thou wilt walk in my statutes, and execute my judgments, and keep all my commandments, walking in them, I will fulfil my word to thee [2] which I spoke to David thy father.

13 [3] And I will dwell in the midst of the children of Israel, and will not forsake my people Israel.

14 So Solomon built the house and finished it.

15 And he built the walls of the house on the inside, with boards of cedar, from the floor of the house to the top of the walls, and to the roofs. He covered it with boards of cedar on the inside: and he covered the floor of the house with planks of fir.

16 And he built up twenty cubits with boards of cedar at the hinder part of the temple, from the floor to the top: and made the inner house of the oracle to be the Holy of Holies.

17 And the temple itself before the doors of the oracle was forty cubits long.

18 And all the house was covered within with cedar, having the turnings, and the joints thereof artfully wrought and carvings projecting out. All was covered with boards of cedar: and no stone could be seen in the wall at all.

19 And he made the oracle in the midst of the house, in the inner part, to set there the ark of the covenant of the Lord.

20 Now the oracle was twenty cubits in length, and twenty cubits in breadth, and twenty cubits in height. And he covered and overlaid it with most pure gold. And the altar also he covered with cedar.

21 And the house before the oracle he overlaid with most pure gold, and fastened on the plates with nails of gold.

22 And there was nothing in the temple that was not covered with gold: the whole altar of the oracle he covered also with gold.

23 And he made in the oracle two cherubims of olive tree, of ten cubits in height.

24 One wing of the cherub was five cubits, and the other wing of the cherub was five cubits: that is, in all ten cubits, from the extremity of one wing to the extremity of the other wing.

25 The second cherub also was ten cubits. And the measure, and the work, was the same in both the cherubims:

26 That is to say, one cherub was ten cubits high, and in like manner the other cherub.

27 And he set the cherubims in the midst of the inner temple: and the cherubims stretched forth their wings. And the wing of the one touched one wall, and the wing of the other cherub touched the other wall: and the other wings in the midst of the temple touched one another.

28 And he overlaid the cherubims with gold.

29 And all the walls of the temple round about he carved with divers figures and carvings: and he made in them cherubims and palm trees, and divers representations, as it were, standing out, and coming forth from the wall.

30 And the floor of the house he also overlaid with gold within and without.

31 And in the entrance of the oracle he made little doors of olive tree, and posts of five corners:

32 And two doors of olive tree. And he carved upon them figures of cherubims, and figures of palm trees, and carvings very much projecting: and he overlaid them with gold. And he covered both the cherubims and the palm trees, and the other things with gold.

33 And he made in the entrance of the temple posts of olive tree foursquare:

34 And two doors of fir tree, one of each side. And each door was double, and so opened with folding leaves.

35 And he carved cherubims, and palm trees, and carved work standing very much out: and he overlaid all with golden plates in square work by rule.

36 And he built the inner court with three rows of polished stones, and one row of beams of cedar.

37 In the fourth year was the house of the Lord founded in the month Zio.

38 And in the eleventh year in the month Bul (which is the eight month) the house was finished in all the works thereof, and in all the appurtenances thereof. And he was seven years in building it.

CHAPTER 7

Solomon's palace, his house in the forest, and the queen's house. The work of the two pillars. The sea (or laver) and other vessels.

AND Solomon built his own house in ¹ thirteen years, and brought it to perfection.

2 He built also the house of the forest of Libanus. The length of it was a hundred cubits, and the breadth fifty cubits, and the height thirty cubits: and four galleries between pillars of cedar: for he had cut cedar trees into pillars.

3 And he covered the whole vault with boards of cedar, and it was held up with five and forty pillars. And one row had fifteen pillars,

4 Set one against another:

5 And looking one upon another, with equal space between the pillars, and over the pillars were square beams in all things equal.

6 And he made a porch of pillars of fifty cubits in length, and thirty cubits in breadth: and another porch before the greater porch; and pillars, and chapiters upon the pillars.

7 He made also the porch of the throne, wherein is the seat of judgment: and covered it with cedar wood from the floor to the top.

8 And in the midst of the porch, was a small house where he sat in judgment, of the like work. He made also a house for the daughter of Pharao (² whom Solomon had taken to wife) of the same work, as this porch,

9 All of costly stones: which were sawed by a certain rule and measure both within and without, from the foundation to the top of the walls, and without unto the great court.

10 And the foundations were of costly stones, great stones of ten cubits or eight cubits.

11 And above there were costly stones, of equal measure, hewed; and, in like manner, planks of cedar.

12 And the greater court *was made* round with three rows of hewed stones, and one row of planks of cedar: moreover also in the inner court of the house of the Lord, and in the porch of the house.

13 And king Solomon sent, and brought Hiram from Tyre,

14 The son of a widow woman of the tribe of Nephtali, whose father was a Tyrian, an artificer in brass, and full of wisdom, and understanding, and skill to work all work in brass. And when he was come to king Solomon, he wrought all his work.

15 And he cast two pillars in brass. Each pillar was eighteen cubits high: ³ and a line of twelve cubits compassed both the pillars.

16 He made also two chapiters of

CHAP. 7. ¹ 3 Kings, 6, 38; 9, 10. ² 3 Kings, 3, 1. ³ Jer. 52, 21.

molten brass, to be set upon the tops of the pillars (the height of one chapiter was five cubits, and the height of the other chapiter was five cubits),

17 And a kind of network, and chain work wreathed together with wonderful art. Both the chapiters of the pillars were cast: seven rows of nets were on one chapter, and seven nets on the other chapiter.

18 And he made the pillars, and two rows round about each network to cover the chapiters, that were upon the top, with pomegranates: and in like manner did he to the other chapiter.

19 And the chapiters that were upon the top of the pillars were of lily work in the porch, of four cubits.

20 And again other chapiters in the top of the pillars above, according to the measure of the pillar over against the network. And of pomegranates there were two hundred in rows round about the other chapiter.

21 And he set up the two pillars in the porch of the temple. And when he had set up the pillar on the right hand, he called the name thereof Jachin: in like manner he set up the second pillar, and called the name thereof Booz.

22 And upon the tops of the pillars he made lily work. So the work of the pillars was finished.

23 ' He made also a molten sea of ten cubits from brim to brim, round all about; the height of it was five cubits, and a line of thirty cubits compassed it round about.

24 And a graven work under the brim of it compassed it, for ten cubits going about the sea. There were two rows cast of chamfered sculptures.

25 And it stood upon twelve oxen, of which three looked towards the north, and three towards the west, and three towards the south, and three towards the east: and the sea was above upon them, and their hinder parts were all hid within.

26 And the laver was a hand-breadth thick: and the brim thereof was like the brim of a cup, or the leaf of a crisped lily. It contained two thousand bates.

27 And he made ten bases of brass: every base was four cubits in length,

⁴ 2 Par. 4, 2.

CHAP. 7. Ver. 21. *Jachin.* That is, *firmly estab-lished.*—*Booz.* That is, *in its strength.* By record-ing these names in holy writ, the Spirit of God would have us understand the invincible firmness and strength of the pillars on which the true temple of God, which is the church, is estab-lished.

Ver. 26. *Two thousand bates.* That is, about ten thousand gallons. This was the quantity of water which was usually put into it: but it was capable, if brimful, of holding three thousand. See 2 Par. 4. 5.

and four cubits in breadth, and three cubits high.

28 And the work itself of the bases, was intergraven: and there were gravings between the joinings.

29 And between the little crowns and the ledges were lions, and oxen, and cherubims: and in the joinings likewise above: and under the lions and oxen, as it were bands of brass hanging down.

30 And every base had four wheels, and axletrees of brass: and at the four sides were undersetters under the laver molten, looking one against another.

31 The mouth also of the laver with-in, was in the top of the chapiter. And that which appeared without, was of one cubit all round: and together it was one cubit and a half. And in the corners of the pillars were divers engravings: and the spaces between the pillars were square, not round.

32 And the four wheels, which were at the four corners of the base, were joined one to another under the base: the height of a wheel was a cubit and a half.

33 And they were such wheels as are used to be made in a chariot: and their axletrees, and spokes, and strakes, and naves, were all cast.

34 And the four undersetters that were at every corner of each base were of the base itself cast and joined together.

35 And in the top of the base there was a round compass of half a cubit, so wrought that the laver might be set thereon, having its gravings, and divers sculptures of itself.

36 He engraved also in those plates, which were of brass, and in the corners, cherubims, and lions, and palm trees, in likeness of a man standing: so that they seemed not to be engraven, but added round about.

37 After this manner he made ten bases: of one casting and measure, and the like graving.

38 He made also ten lavers of brass. One laver contained four bases, and was of four cubits: and upon every base, in all ten, he put as many lavers.

39 And he set the ten bases, five on the right side of the temple, and five on the left: and the sea he put on the right side of the temple over against the east southward.

40 And Hiram made caldrons, and shovels, and basins, and finished all the work of king Solomon in the temple of the Lord.

41 The two pillars and the two cords of the chapiters, upon the chapiters of the pillars: and the two networks, to cover the two cords, that were upon the top of the pillars.

42 And four hundred pomegranates for the two networks: two rows of pomegranates for each network, to cover the cords of the chapiters, which were upon the tops of the pillars.

43 And the ten bases, and the ten lavers on the bases.

44 And one sea, and twelve oxen under the sea.

45 And the caldrons, and the shovels, and the basins. All the vessels that Hiram made for king Solomon for the house of the Lord were of fine brass.

46 In the plains of the Jordan did the king cast them, in a clay ground, between Socoth and Sartham.

47 And Solomon placed all the vessels: but for exceeding great multitude the brass could not be weighed.

48 And Solomon made all the vessels for the house of the Lord: the altar of gold: and the table of gold, upon which the loaves of proposition should be set:

49 And the golden candlesticks, five on the right hand, and five on the left, over against the oracle, of pure gold: and the flowers like lilies: and the lamps over them of gold: and golden snuffers.

50 And pots, and fleshhooks, and bowls, and mortars, and censers, of most pure gold. And the hinges for the doors of the inner house of the Holy of Holies, and for the doors of the house of the temple were of gold.

51 [5] And Solomon finished all the work that he made in the house of the Lord: and brought in the things that David his father had dedicated, the silver and the gold, and the vessels; and laid them up in the treasures of the house of the Lord.

CHAPTER 8

The dedication of the temple. Solomon's prayer and sacrifices.

THEN all the ancients of Israel [1] with the princes of the tribes, and the heads of the families of the children of Israel were assembled to king Solomon in Jerusalem: that they might carry the ark of the covenant of the Lord out of the city of David, that is, out of Sion.

2 And all Israel assembled themselves to king Solomon on the festival day in the month of Ethanim: the same is the seventh month.

3 And all the ancients of Israel came: and the priests took up the ark,

4 And carried the ark of the Lord, and the tabernacle of the covenant, and all the vessels of the sanctuary, that were in the tabernacle. And the priests and the Levites carried them.

5 And king Solomon, and all the mul-

titude of Israel, that were assembled unto him went with him before the ark. And they sacrificed sheep and oxen that could not be counted or numbered.

6 And the priests brought in the ark of the covenant of the Lord into its place, into the oracle of the temple into the Holy of Holies under the wings of the cherubims.

7 For the cherubims spread forth their wings over the place of the ark, and covered the ark, and the staves thereof above.

8 And whereas the staves stood out, the ends of them were seen without in the sanctuary before the oracle, but were not seen farther out: and there they have been unto this day.

9 Now in the ark there was nothing else [2] but the two tables of stone, which Moses put there at Horeb, when the Lord made a covenant with the children of Israel, when they came out of the land of Egypt.

10 And it came to pass, when the priests were come out of the sanctuary, that a cloud filled the house of the Lord.

11 And the priests could not stand to minister because of the cloud: for the glory of the Lord had filled the house of the Lord.

12 Then Solomon said: [3] The Lord said that he would dwell in a cloud.

13 Building I have built a house for thy dwelling, to be thy most firm throne for ever.

14 And the king turned his face, and blessed all the assembly of Israel: for all the assembly of Israel stood.

15 And Solomon said: Blessed be the Lord the God of Israel, who spoke with his mouth to David my father, and with his own hands hath accomplished it, saying:

16 Since the day that I brought my people Israel out of Egypt, I chose no city out of all the tribes of Israel, for a house to be built, that my name might be there; but I chose David to be over my people Israel.

17 [4] And David my father would have built a house to the name of the Lord the God of Israel.

18 And the Lord said to David my father: Whereas thou hast thought in thy heart to build a house to my name, thou hast done well in having this same thing in thy mind.

19 Nevertheless thou shalt not build me a house: but thy son, that shall come

---

[5] 2 Par. 5, 1. CHAP. 8. [1] 2 Par. 5, 2. [2] Exod. 34, 27; Heb. 9, 4. [3] 2 Par. 6, 1. [4] 2 Kings, 7, 5.

CHAP. 8. Ver. 9. *Nothing else.* There was nothing else but the tables of the law *within* the ark: but on the outside of the ark, or near the ark were also the rod of Aaron, and a golden urn with manna (Heb. 9, 4).

forth out of thy loins, he shall build a house to my name.

20 The Lord hath performed his word which he spoke. And I stand in the room of David my father: and sit upon the throne of Israel, as the Lord promised: and have built a house to the name of the Lord, the God of Israel.

21 And I have set there a place for the ark, wherein is the covenant of the Lord, which he made with our fathers, when they came out of the land of Egypt.

22 And Solomon stood before the altar of the Lord in the sight of the assembly of Israel, and spread forth his hands towards heaven.

23 And said: Lord God of Israel, there is no God like thee in heaven above, or on earth beneath: who keepest covenant and mercy with thy servants that have walked before thee with all their heart.

24 Who hast kept with thy servant David my father what thou hast promised him. With thy mouth thou didst speak, and with thy hands thou hast performed, as this day proveth.

25 Now therefore, O Lord God of Israel, keep with thy servant David my father what thou hast spoken to him: saying: [5] There shall not be taken away of thee a man in my sight, to sit on the throne of Israel; yet so that thy children take heed to their way, that they walk before me as thou hast walked in my sight.

26 And now, Lord God of Israel, let thy words be established, which thou hast spoken to thy servant David my father.

27 Is it then to be thought that God should indeed dwell upon earth? For if heaven, and the heavens of heavens cannot contain thee, how much less this house which I have built?

28 But have regard to the prayer of thy servant, and to his supplications, O Lord my God. Hear the hymn and the prayer, which thy servant prayeth before thee this day:

29 That thy eyes may be open upon this house night and day; upon the house of which thou hast said: [6] My name shall be there. That thou mayest hearken to the prayer, which thy servant prayeth in this place to thee.

30 That thou mayest hearken to the supplication of thy servant and of thy people Israel, whatsoever they shall pray for in this place: and hear them in the place of thy dwelling in heaven: and when thou hearest, shew them mercy.

31 If any man trespass against his neighbour, and have an oath upon him, wherewith he is bound: and come because of the oath before thy altar to thy house,

32 Then hear thou in heaven. And do, and judge thy servants, condemning the wicked, and bringing his way upon his own head; and justifying the just, and rewarding him according to his justice.

33 If thy people Israel shall fly before their enemies (because they will sin against thee), and doing penance, and confessing to thy name, shall come, and pray, and make supplications to thee in this house:

34 Then hear thou in heaven, and forgive the sin of thy people Israel, and bring them back to the land which thou gavest to their fathers.

35 If heaven shall be shut up, and there shall be no rain, because of their sins, and they, praying in this place, shall do penance to thy name, and shall be converted from their sins, by occasion of their afflictions:

36 Then hear thou them in heaven, and forgive the sins of thy servants, and of thy people Israel; and shew them the good way wherein they should walk; and give rain upon thy land, which thou hast given to thy people in possession.

37 If a famine arise in the land, or a pestilence, or corrupt air, or blasting, or locust, or mildew; if their enemy afflict them besieging the gates, whatsoever plague, whatsoever infirmity:

38 Whatsoever curse or imprecation shall happen to any man of thy people Israel: when a man shall know the wound of his own heart, and shall spread forth his hands in this house:

39 Then hear thou in heaven, in the place of thy dwelling, and forgive, and do so as to give to every one according to his ways, as thou shalt see his heart (for thou only knowest the heart of all the children of men).

40 That they may fear thee all the days that they live upon the face of the land, which thou hast given to our fathers.

41 Moreover also the stranger, who is not of thy people Israel, when he shall come out of a far country for thy name's sake, (for they shall hear every where of thy great name and thy mighty hand,

42 And thy stretched out arm,) so when he shall come, and shall pray in this place:

43 Then hear thou in heaven, in the firmament of thy dwelling place, and do all those things, for whch that stranger shall call upon thee. That all the people of the earth may learn to

[5] 2 Kings, 7, 12. [6] Deut. 12, 11.

fear thy name, as do thy people Israel, and may prove that thy name is called upon on this house, which I have built.

44 If thy people go out to war against their enemies, by what way soever thou shalt send them, they shall pray to thee towards the way of the city, which thou hast chosen, and towards the house, which I have built to thy name.

45 And then hear thou in heaven their prayers, and their supplications: and do judgment for them.

46 But if they sin against thee (⁷ for there is no man who sinneth not) and thou being angry deliver them up to their enemies, so that they be led away captives into the land of their enemies far or near:

47 Then if they do penance in their heart in the place of captivity, and being converted make supplication to thee in their captivity, saying: We have sinned, we have done unjustly, we have committed wickedness:

48 And return to thee with all their heart, and all their soul, in the land of their enemies, to which they had been led captives: and pray to thee towards the way of their land, which thou gavest to their fathers, and of the city which thou hast chosen, and of the temple which I have built to thy name:

49 Then hear thou in heaven, in the firmament of thy throne, their prayers, and their supplications, and do judgment for them.

50 And forgive thy people, that have sinned against thee, and all their iniquities, by which they have transgressed against thee. And give them mercy before them that have made them captives, that they may have compassion on them.

51 For they are thy people, and thy inheritance, whom thou hast brought out of the land of Egypt, from the midst of the furnace of iron.

52 That thy eyes may be open to the supplication of thy servant, and of thy people Israel, to hear them in all things for which they shall call upon thee.

53 For thou hast separated them to thyself for an inheritance from among all the people of the earth, as thou hast spoken by Moses thy servant, when thou broughtest our fathers out of Egypt, O Lord God.

54 And it came to pass, when Solomon had made an end of praying all this prayer and supplication to the Lord, that he rose from before the altar of the Lord: for he had fixed both knees on the ground, and had spread his hands towards heaven.

55 And he stood and blessed all the assembly of Israel with a loud voice, saying:

56 Blessed be the Lord, who hath given rest to his people Israel, according to all that he promised. There hath not failed so much as one word of all the good things that he promised by his servant Moses.

57 The Lord our God be with us, as he was with our fathers, and not leave us, nor cast us off.

58 But may he incline our hearts to himself, that we may walk in all his ways, and keep his commandments, and his ceremonies, and all his judgments which he commanded our fathers.

59 And let these my words, wherewith I have prayed before the Lord, be nigh unto the Lord our God day and night: that he may do judgment for his servant, and for his people Israel day by day:

60 That all the people of the earth may know, that the Lord he is God, and there is no other besides him.

61 Let our hearts also be perfect with the Lord our God, that we may walk in his statutes, and keep his commandments, as at this day.

62 And the king, and all Israel with him, offered victims before the Lord.

63 And Solomon slew victims of peace offerings, which he sacrificed to the Lord, two and twenty thousand oxen, and a hundred and twenty thousand sheep. So the king, and the children of Israel dedicated the temple of the Lord.

64 In that day the king sanctified the middle of the court that was before the house of the Lord. For there he offered the holocaust and sacrifice and fat of the peace offerings: because the brazen altar that was before the Lord, was too little to receive the holocaust and sacrifice and fat of the peace offerings.

65 And Solomon made at the same time a solemn feast, and all Israel with him: a great multitude, from the entrance of Emath to the river of Egypt, before the Lord our God, seven days and seven days, that is, fourteen days.

66 And on the eighth day he sent away the people. And they blessed the king, and went to their dwellings rejoicing and glad in heart for all the good things that the Lord had done for David his servant, and for Israel his people.

CHAPTER 9

The Lord appeareth again to Solomon. He buildeth cities. He sendeth a fleet to Ophir.

AND it came to pass when Solomon had finished the building of the house of the Lord, and the king's house,

⁷ 2 Par. 6, 36; Ecclus. 7, 21; 1 John, 1, 8.

and all that he desired, and was pleased to do,

2 That the Lord appeared to him the second time, [1] as he had appeared to him in Gabaon.

3 And the Lord said to him: I have heard thy prayer and thy supplication, which thou hast made before me. I have sanctified this house, which thou hast built, to put my name there for ever: and my eyes and my heart shall be there always.

4 And if thou wilt walk before me, as thy father walked, in simplicity of heart, and in uprightness: and wilt do all that I have commanded thee: and wilt keep my ordinances and my judgments,

5 [2] I will establish the throne of thy kingdom over Israel for ever, as I promised David thy father, saying: There shall not fail a man of thy race upon the throne of Israel.

6 But if you and your children revolting shall turn away from following me, and will not keep my commandments, and my ceremonies, which I have set before you, but will go and worship strange gods, and adore them:

7 I will take away Israel from the face of the land which I have given them. And the temple which I have sanctified to my name, I will cast out of my sight. And Israel shall be a proverb, and a byword among all people.

8 And this house shall be made an example of. Every one that shall pass by it shall be astonished, and shall hiss, and say: [3] Why hath the Lord done thus to this land, and to this house?

9 And they shall answer: Because they forsook the Lord their God, who brought their fathers out of the land of Egypt, and followed strange gods, and adored them, and worshipped them. Therefore hath the Lord brought upon them all this evil.

10 [4] And when twenty years were ended after Solomon had built the two houses, that is, the house of the Lord, and the house of the king,

11 (Hiram the king of Tyre furnishing Solomon with cedar trees and fir trees and gold, according to all he had need of): then Solomon gave Hiram twenty cities in the land of Galilee.

12 And Hiram came out of Tyre to see the towns which Solomon had given him, and they pleased him not.

13 And he said: Are these the cities

CHAP. 9. [1] 3 Kings, 3, 5; 2 Par. 7, 12. [2] 2 Kings, 7, 12, 16. [3] Deut. 29, 24; Jer. 22, 8. [4] 2 Par. 8, 1. [5] 2 Par. 8, 11.

CHAP. 9. Ver. 4. As thy father walked, in simplicity of heart. That is, in the sincerity and integrity of a single heart, as opposite to all double dealing and deceit.
Ver. 13. Chabul. That is, dirty or displeasing.

which thou hast given me, brother? And he called them the land of Chabul, unto this day.

14 And Hiram sent to king Solomon a hundred and twenty talents of gold.

15 This is the sum of the expenses, which king Solomon offered to build the house of the Lord, and his own house, and Mello, and the wall of Jerusalem, and Heser, and Mageddo, and Gazer.

16 Pharao the king of Egypt came up and took Gazer, and burnt it with fire: and slew the Chanaanite that dwelt in the city: and gave it for a dowry to his daughter, Solomon's wife.

17 So Solomon built Gazer, and Bethhoron the nether,

18 And Baalath, and Palmira in the land of the wilderness.

19 And all the towns that belonged to himself and were not walled, he fortified: the cities also of the chariots, and the cities of the horsemen, and whatsoever he had a mind to build in Jerusalem, and in Libanus, and in all the land of his dominion.

20 All the people that were left of the Amorrhites, and Hethites, and Pherezites, and Hevites, and Jebusites, that are not of the children of Israel:

21 Their children, that were left in the land, to wit, such as the children of Israel had not been able to destroy, Solomon made tributary unto this day.

22 But of the children of Israel Solomon made not any to be bondmen: but they were men of war, and his servants, and his princes, and captains, and overseers of the chariots and horses.

23 And there were five hundred and fifty chief officers set over all the works of Solomon: and they had people under them, and had charge over the appointed works.

24 [5] And the daughter of Pharao came up out of the city of David to her house, which Solomon had built for her. Then did he build Mello.

25 Solomon also offered three times every year holocausts, and victims of peace offerings upon the altar which he had built to the Lord: and he burnt incense before the Lord. And the temple was finished.

26 And king Solomon made a fleet in Asiongaber, which is by Ailath, on the shore of the Red Sea in the land of Edom.

27 And Hiram sent his servants in the fleet, sailors that had knowledge of the sea, with the servants of Solomon.

28 And they came to Ophir: and they brought from thence to king Solomon four hundred and twenty talents of gold.

CHAPTER 10

The queen of Saba cometh to king Solomon.
His riches and glory.

AND [1] the queen of Saba, having heard of the fame of Solomon in the name of the Lord, came to try him with hard questions.

2 And entering into Jerusalem with a great train, and riches, and camels that carried spices, and an immense quantity of gold, and precious stones, she came to king Solomon, and spoke to him all that she had in her heart.

3 And Solomon informed her of all the things she proposed to him. There was not any word the king was ignorant of, and which he could not answer her.

4 And when the queen of Saba saw all the wisdom of Solomon, and the house which he had built,

5 And the meat of his table, and the apartments of his servants, and the order of his ministers, and their apparel, and the cupbearers, and the holocausts, which he offered in the house of the Lord: she had no longer any spirit in her.

6 And she said to the king: The report is true, which I heard in my own country,

7 Concerning thy words, and concerning thy wisdom. And I did not believe them that told me, till I came myself and saw with my own eyes, and have found that the half hath not been told me. Thy wisdom and thy works, exceed the fame which I heard.

8 Blessed are thy men, and blessed are thy servants, who stand before thee always, and hear thy wisdom.

9 Blessed be the Lord thy God, whom thou hast pleased, and who hath set thee upon the throne of Israel: because the Lord hath loved Israel for ever, and hath appointed thee king, to do judgment and justice.

10 [3] And she gave the king a hundred and twenty talents of gold, and of spices a very great store, and precious stones. There was brought no more such abundance of spices as these which the queen of Saba gave to king Solomon.

11 ([3] The navy also of Hiram, which brought gold from Ophir, brought from Ophir great plenty of thyine trees and precious stones.

12 And the king made of the thyine trees the rails of the house of the Lord and of the king's house, and citterns and harps for singers: there were no such thyine trees as these brought, nor seen unto this day.)

13 And king Solomon gave the queen of Saba all that she desired, and asked of him: besides what he offered her of himself of his royal bounty. And she returned, and went to her own country with her servants.

14 And the weight of the gold that was brought to Solomon every year was six hundred and sixty-six talents of gold.

15 Besides that which the men brought him that were over the tributes, and the merchants, and they that sold by retail, and all the kings of Arabia, and the governors of the country.

16 And Solomon made two hundred shields of the purest gold: he allowed six hundred sicles of gold for the plates of one shield.

17 And three hundred targets of fine gold: three hundred pounds of gold covered one target. And the king put them in the house of the forest of Libanus.

18 King Solomon also made a great throne of ivory: and overlaid it with the finest gold.

19 It had six steps: and the top of the throne was round behind. And there were two hands on either side holding the seat: and two lions stood, one at each hand.

20 And twelve little lions stood upon the six steps on the one side and on the other. There was no such work made in any kingdom.

21 Moreover all the vessels, out of which king Solomon drank, were of gold: and all the furniture of the house of the forest of Libanus was of most pure gold. There was no silver, nor was any account made of it in the days of Solomon.

22 For the king's navy, once in three years, went with the navy of Hiram by sea to Tharsis; and brought from thence gold, and silver, and elephants' teeth, and apes, and peacocks.

23 And king Solomon exceeded all the kings of the earth in riches, and wisdom.

24 And all the earth desired to see Solomon's face, to hear his wisdom, which God had given in his heart.

25 And every one brought him presents: vessels of silver and of gold, garments and armour, and spices, and horses and mules every year.

26 [4] And Solomon gathered together chariots and horsemen: and he had a thousand four hundred chariots, and twelve thousand horsemen. And he bestowed them in fenced cities, and with the king in Jerusalem.

27 And he made silver to be as plentiful in Jerusalem as stones: and cedars to be as common as sycamores which grow in the plains.

28 And horses were brought for Solo-

mon out of Egypt, and Coa: for the king's merchants brought them out of Coa, and bought them at a set price.

29 And a chariot of four horses came out of Egypt, for six hundred sicles of silver, and a horse, for a hundred and fifty. And after this manner did all the kings of the Hethites and of Syria sell horses.

CHAPTER 11

Solomon by means of his wives falleth into idolatry. God raiseth him adversaries, Abad, Razon, and Jeroboam. Solomon dieth.

AND king Solomon ¹ loved many strange women besides the daughter of Pharao. And women of Moab, and of Ammon, and of Edom, and of Sidon, and of the Hethites:

2 Of the nations concerning which the Lord said to the children of Israel: ² You shall not go in unto them, neither shall any of them come in to yours; for they will most certainly turn away your heart to follow their gods. And to these was Solomon joined with a most ardent love.

3 And he had seven hundred wives as queens, and three hundred concubines. And the women turned away his heart.

4 And when he was now old, his heart was turned away by women to follow strange gods: and his heart was not perfect with the Lord his God, as was the heart of David his father.

5 But Solomon worshipped Astarthe, the goddess of the Sidonians, and Moloch, the idol of the Ammonites.

6 And Solomon did that which was not pleasing before the Lord: and did not fully follow the Lord, as David his father.

7 Then Solomon built a temple for Chamos, the idol of Moab, on the hill that is over against Jerusalem: and for Moloch, the idol of the children of Ammon.

8 And he did in this manner for all his wives that were strangers, who burnt incense, and offered sacrifice to their gods.

9 And the Lord was angry with Solomon, because his mind was turned away from the Lord the God of Israel, ³ who had appeared to him twice,

10 And had commanded him concerning this thing, that he should not follow strange gods. But he kept not the things which the Lord commanded him.

11 The Lord therefore said to Solomon. Because thou hast done this, and

hast not kept my covenant, and my precepts, which I have commanded thee, I will divide and rend thy kingdom, and will give it to thy servant.

12 ⁴ Nevertheless in thy days I will not do it, for David thy father's sake: but I will rend it out of the hand of thy son.

13 Neither will I take away the whole kingdom: but I will give one tribe to thy son for the sake of David my servant, and Jerusalem which I have chosen.

14 And the Lord raised up an adversary to Solomon, Adad the Edomite of the king's seed, in Edom.

15 ⁵ For when David was in Edom, and Joab the general of the army was gone up to bury them that were slain, and had killed every male in Edom

16 (For Joab remained there six months with all Israel, till he had slain every male in Edom),

17 Then Adad fled, he and certain Edomites of his father's servants with him, to go into Egypt: and Adad was *then* a little boy.

18 And they arose out of Madian, and came into Pharan. And they took men with them from Pharan, and went into Egypt to Pharao the king of Egypt: who gave him a house, and appointed him victuals, and assigned him land.

19 And Adad found great favour before Pharao, insomuch that he gave him to wife, the own sister of his wife Taphnes, the queen.

20 And the sister of Taphnes bore him his son Genubath: and Taphnes brought him up in the house of Pharao. And Genubath dwelt with Pharao among his children.

21 And when Adad heard in Egypt that David slept with his fathers, and that Joab the general of the army was dead, he said to Pharao: Let me depart, that I may go to my own country.

22 And Pharao said to him: Why, what is wanting to thee with me, that thou seekest to go to thy own country? But he answered: Nothing: yet I beseech thee to let me go.

23 God also raised up against him an adversary, Razon the son of Eliada, ⁶ who had fled from his master Adarezer the king of Soba.

24 And he gathered men against him, and he became a captain of robbers, when David slew them *of Soba*. And they went to Damascus, and dwelt there: and they made him king in Damascus.

25 And he was an adversary to Israel, all the days of Solomon. And this is the evil of Adad, and his hatred against Israel: and he reigned in Syria.

26 ⁷ Jeroboam also the son of Nabat,

CHAP. 11. ¹ Deut. 17, 17; Ecclus. 47, 21. ² Exod. 34, 16. ³ 3 Kings, 9, 2. ⁴ 3 Kings, 12, 15. ⁵ 2 Kings, 8, 14. ⁶ 2 Kings, 8, 6; 1 Par. 18, 6, 13, 6. ⁷ 2 Par. 6.

CHAP. 11. Ver. 13. *One tribe.* Besides that of Juda, his own native tribe.

an Ephrathite of Sareda, a servant of Solomon, whose mother was named Sarua, a widow woman, lifted up his hand against the king.

27 And this is the cause of his rebellion against him, for Solomon built Mello, and filled up the breach of the city of David his father.

28 And Jeroboam was a valiant and mighty man: and Solomon seeing him a young man ingenious and industrious, made him chief over the tributes of all the house of Joseph.

29 [8] So it came to pass at that time, that Jeroboam went out of Jerusalem, and the prophet Ahias the Silonite, clad with a new garment, found him in the way: and they two were alone in the field.

30 And Ahias taking his new garment, wherewith he was clad, divided it into twelve parts.

31 And he said to Jeroboam: Take to thee ten pieces. For thus saith the Lord the God of Israel: Behold I will rend the kingdom out of the hand of Solomon, and will give thee ten tribes.

32 But one tribe shall remain to him for the sake of my servant David; and Jerusalem, the city which I have chosen out of all the tribes of Israel:

33 Because he hath forsaken me, and hath adored Astarthe the goddess of the Sidonians, and Chamos the god of Moab, and Moloch the god of the children of Ammon: and hath not walked in my ways, to do justice before me, and to keep my precepts, and judgments as did David his father.

34 Yet I will not take away all the kingdom out of his hand: but I will make him prince all the days of his life, for David my servant's sake, whom I chose, who kept my commandments and my precepts.

35 But I will take away the kingdom out of his son's hand and will give thee ten tribes.

36 And to his son I will give one tribe, that there may remain a lamp for my servant David before me always in Jerusalem, the city which I have chosen, that my name might be there.

37 And I will take thee: and thou shalt reign over all that thy soul desireth, and thou shalt be king over Israel.

38 If then thou wilt hearken to all that I shall command thee, and wilt walk in my ways, and do what is right before me, keeping my commandments and my precepts, as David my servant did: I will be with thee, and will build thee up a faithful house, as I built a house for David; and I will deliver Israel to thee.

39 And I will for this afflict the seed of David, but yet not for ever.

40 Solomon therefore sought to kill Jeroboam: but he arose, and fled into Egypt to Sesac the king of Egypt, and was in Egypt till the death of Solomon.

41 And the rest of the words of Solomon, and all that he did, and his wisdom: behold they are all written in the book of the words of the days of Solomon.

42 And the days that Solomon reigned in Jerusalem over all Israel, were forty years.

43 And Solomon slept with his fathers, and was buried in the city of David his father. And Roboam his son reigned in his stead.

CHAPTER 12

Roboam following the counsel of young men alienateth from him the minds of the people. They make Jeroboam king over ten tribes. He setteth up idolatry.

AND Roboam went to Sichem: [1] for thither were all Israel come together to make him king.

2 But Jeroboam the son of Nabat who was yet in Egypt, a fugitive from the face of king Solomon, hearing of his death, returned out of Egypt.

3 And they sent and called him. And Jeroboam came, and all the multitude of Israel; and they spoke to Roboam, saying:

4 Thy father laid a grievous yoke upon us. Now therefore do thou take off a little of the grievous service of thy father, and of his most heavy yoke, which he put upon us: and we will serve thee.

5 And he said to them: Go till the third day, and come to me again. And when the people was gone,

6 King Roboam took counsel with the old men, that stood before Solomon his father while he yet lived. And he said: What counsel do you give me, that I may answer this people?

7 They said to him: If thou wilt yield to this people to-day, and condescend to them, and grant their petition, and wilt speak gentle words to them, they will be thy servants always.

8 But he left the counsel of the old men, which they had given him, and consulted with the young men, that had been brought up with him, and stood before him.

9 And he said to them: What counsel

[8] 2 Par. 10, 15. CHAP. 12. [1] 2 Par. 10, 1.

Ver. 41. *The book of the words.* This book is lost, with divers others mentioned in holy writ.
Ver. 43. *Solomon slept.* That is, died. He was then about fifty-eight years of age, having reigned forty years.

do you give me, that I may answer this people, who have said to me: Make the yoke which thy father put upon us lighter?

10 And the young men that had been brought up with him, said: Thus shalt thou speak to this people, who have spoken to thee, saying: Thy father made our yoke heavy, do thou ease us. Thou shalt say to them: My little finger is thicker than the back of my father.

11 And now my father put a heavy yoke upon you: but I will add to your yoke. My father beat you with whips: but I will beat you with scorpions.

12 So Jeroboam and all the people came to Roboam the third day, as the king had appointed, saying: Come to me again the third day.

13 And the king answered the people roughly, leaving the counsel of the old men, which they had given him.

14 And he spoke to them according to the counsel of the young men, saying: My father made your yoke heavy; but I will add to your yoke. My father beat you with whips: but I will beat you with scorpions.

15 And the king condescended not to the people: for the Lord was turned away from him, to make good his word, ² which he had spoken in the hand of Ahias the Silonite, to Jeroboam the son of Nabat.

16 Then the people seeing that the king would not hearken to them, answered him, saying: What portion have we in David? Or what inheritance in the son of Isai? Go home to thy dwellings, O Israel. Now, David, look to thy own house. So Israel departed to their dwellings.

17 But as for all the children of Israel that dwelt in the cities of Juda, Roboam reigned over them.

18 Then king Roboam sent Aduram, who was over the tribute: and all Israel stoned him: and he died. Wherefore king Roboam made haste to get him up into his chariot, and he fled to Jerusalem.

19 And Israel revolted from the house of David, unto this day.

20 And it came to pass when all Israel heard that Jeroboam was come again, that they gathered an assembly, and sent and called him, and made him king over all Israel. And there was none that followed the house of David but the tribe of Juda only.

21 And Roboam came to Jerusalem, and gathered together all the house of Juda, and the tribe of Benjamin, a hundred fourscore thousand chosen men for war, to fight against the house of Israel, and to bring the kingdom again under Roboam the son of Solomon.

22 ³ But the word of the Lord came to Semeias, the man of God, saying:

23 Speak to Roboam the son of Solomon, the king of Juda, and to all the house of Juda, and Benjamin, and the rest of the people, saying:

24 Thus saith the Lord: You shall not go up nor fight against your brethren the children of Israel. Let every man return to his house, for this thing is from me. They hearkened to the word of the Lord, and returned from their journey, as the Lord had commanded them.

25 And Jeroboam built Sichem in mount Ephraim, and dwelt there: and going out from thence he built Phanuel.

26 And Jeroboam said in his heart: Now shall the kingdom return to the house of David,

27 If this people go up to offer sacrifices in the house of the Lord at Jerusalem. And the heart of this people will turn to their lord Roboam the king of Juda: and they will kill me, and return to him.

28 ⁴ And finding out a device he made two golden calves, and said to them: Go ye up no more to Jerusalem: ⁵ Behold thy gods, O Israel, who brought thee out of the land of Egypt.

29 And he set the one in Bethel, and the other in Dan.

30 And this thing became an occasion of sin: for the people went to adore the calf as far as Dan.

31 And he made temples in the high places, ⁶ and priests of the lowest of the people, who were not of the sons of Levi.

32 And he appointed a feast in the eighth month, on the fifteenth day of the month, after the manner of the feast that was celebrated in Juda. And going up to the altar, he did in like manner in Bethel, to sacrifice to the calves, which he had made. And he placed in Bethel priests of the high places, which he had made.

33 And he went up to the altar, which he had built in Bethel, on the fifteenth day of the eighth month, which he had devised of his own heart. And he ordained a feast to the children of Israel:

---

² 3 Kings, 11, 31.   ³ 2 Par. 11, 2.   ⁴ Tob. 1, 5.   ⁵ Exod. 32, 8.   ⁶ 2 Par. 11, 15.

CHAP. 12. Ver. 20. *Juda only.* Benjamin was a small tribe, and so intermixed with the tribe of Juda, (the very city of Jerusalem being partly in Juda, partly in Benjamin,) that they are here counted but as one tribe.

Ver. 28. *Golden calves.* It is likely, by making his gods in this form, he mimicked the Egyptians, among whom he had sojourned, who worshipped their Apis and their Osiris under the form of a bullock.

Ver. 29. *Bethel and Dan.* Bethel was a city of the tribe of Ephraim in the southern part of the dominions of Jeroboam, about six leagues from Jerusalem; Dan was in the extremity of his dominions to the north in the confines of Syria.

and went upon the altar to burn incense.

CHAPTER 13

*A prophet sent from Juda to Bethel fore-
telleth the birth of Josias, and the destruction of Jeroboam's altar. Jeroboam's
hand offering violence to the prophet
withereth, but is restored by the
prophet's prayer. The same prophet is
deceived by another prophet, and slain
by a lion.*

AND behold there came a man of
God out of Juda, by the word of
the Lord to Bethel, when Jeroboam was
standing upon the altar, and burning
incense.

2 And he cried out against the altar
in the word of the Lord, and said: O
Altar, Altar, thus saith the Lord: [1] Behold a child shall be born to the house
of David, Josias by name. And he shall
immolate upon these the priests of the
high places, who now burn incense
upon thee: and he shall burn men's
bones upon thee.

3 And he gave a sign the same day,
saying: This shall be the sign, that the
Lord hath spoken: Behold the altar
shall be rent: and the ashes that are
upon it shall be poured out.

4 And when the king had heard the
word of the man of God, which he had
cried out against the altar in Bethel,
he stretched forth his hand from the
altar, saying: Lay hold on him. And
his hand which he stretched forth
against him withered: and he was not
able to draw it back again to him.

5 The altar also was rent: and the
ashes were poured out from the altar:
according to the sign which the man
of God had given before in the word
of the Lord.

6 And the king said to the man of
God: Entreat the face of the Lord thy
God, and pray for me, that my hand
may be restored to me. And the man
of God besought the face of the Lord:
and the king's hand was restored to
him; and it became as it was before.

7 And the king said to the man of
God: Come home with me to dine, and
I will make thee presents.

8 And the man of God answered the
king: If thou wouldst give me half thy
house I will not go with thee, nor eat
bread, nor drink water in this place:

9 For so it was enjoined me by the
word of the Lord commanding me:
Thou shalt not eat bread nor drink
water, nor return by the same way that
thou camest.

10 So he departed by another way,
and returned not by the way that he
came into Bethel.

11 Now a certain old prophet dwelt

in Bethel: and his sons came to him
and told him all the works that the
man of God had done that day in
Bethel. And they told their father the
words which he had spoken to the king.

12 And their father said to them:
What way went he? His sons shewed
him the way by which the man of God
went, who came out of Juda.

13 And he said to his sons: Saddle
me the ass. And when they had saddled
him, he got up,

14 And went after the man of God,
and found him sitting under a turpentine tree. And he said to him: Art thou
the man of God that camest from Juda?
He answered: I am.

15 And he said to him: Come home
with me, to eat bread.

16 But he said: I must not return,
nor go with thee; neither will I eat
bread, nor drink water in this place,

17 Because the Lord spoke to me in
the word of the Lord, saying: Thou
shalt not eat bread, and thou shalt
not drink water there, nor return by
the way thou wentest.

18 He said to him: I also am a
prophet like unto thee. And an angel
spoke to me in the word of the Lord,
saying: Bring him back with thee into
thy house, that he may eat bread, and
drink water. He deceived him.

19 And brought him back with him.
So he ate bread and drank water in his
house.

20 And as they sat at table, the word
of the Lord came to the prophet that
brought him back.

21 And he cried out to the man of
God who came out of Juda, saying:
Thus saith the Lord: Because thou hast
not been obedient to the Lord, and hast
not kept the commandment which the
Lord thy God commanded thee,

22 And hast returned and eaten
bread, and drunk water in the place
wherein he commanded thee that thou
shouldst not eat bread, nor drink
water, thy dead body shall not be
brought into the sepulchre of thy
fathers.

23 And when he had eaten and
drunk, he saddled his ass for the
prophet, whom he had brought back.

24 And when he was gone, a lion
found him in the way, and killed him.
And his body was cast in the way; and
the ass stood by him; and the lion stood
by the dead body.

25 And behold, men passing by saw

CHAP. 13. [1] 4 Kings, 23, 16.

CHAP. 13. Ver. 18. *An angel spoke to me.* This
old man of Bethel was indeed a prophet, but he
sinned in thus deceiving the man of God; the
more because he pretended a revelation for what
he did.

the dead body cast in the way, and the lion standing by the body. And they came and told it in the city, wherein that old prophet dwelt.

26 And when that prophet, who had brought him back out of the way, heard of it, he said: It is the man of God, that was disobedient to the mouth of the Lord; and the Lord hath delivered him to the lion; and he hath torn him, and killed him according to the word of the Lord, which he spoke to him.

27 And he said to his sons: Saddle me an ass. And when they had saddled it,

28 And he was gone, he found the dead body cast in the way, and the ass and the lion standing by the carcass. The lion had not eaten of the dead body, nor hurt the ass.

29 And the prophet took up the body of the man of God, and laid it upon the ass: and going back brought it into the city of the old prophet, to mourn for him.

30 And he laid his dead body in his own sepulchre: and they mourned over him, *saying:* Alas! alas! my brother.

31 And when they had mourned over him, he said to his sons: When I am dead, bury me in the sepulchre wherein the man of God is buried. Lay my bones beside his bones.

32 For assuredly the word shall come to pass which he hath foretold in the word of the Lord against the altar that is in Bethel: and against all the temples of the high places, that are in the cities of Samaria.

33 After these words Jeroboam came not back from his wicked way: but on the contrary he made of the meanest of the people priests of the high places. Whosoever would, he filled his hand: and he was made a priest of the high places.

34 And for this cause did the house of Jeroboam sin: and was cut off and destroyed from the face of the earth.

CHAPTER 14

Ahias prophesieth the destruction of the family of Jeroboam. He dieth and is succeeded by his son Nadab. The king of Egypt taketh and pillageth Jerusalem. Roboam dieth and his son Abiam succeedeth.

AT that time Abia the son of Jeroboam fell sick.

2 And Jeroboam said to his wife: Arise, and change thy dress, that thou be not known to be the wife of Jero-

CHAP. 14. ¹ 3 Kings, 11, 31. ² 3 Kings, 15, 29.
Ver. 24. *Killed him.* Thus the Lord often punishes his servants here, that he may spare them hereafter. For the generality of divines are of opinion, that the sin of this prophet, considered with all its circumstances, was not mortal.

boam. And go to Silo, where Ahias the prophet is, ¹ who told me, that I should reign over this people.

3 Take also with thee ten loaves, and cracknels, and a pot of honey; and go to him: for he will tell thee what shall become of this child.

4 Jeroboam's wife did as he told her: and rising up went to Silo, and came to the house of Ahias: but he could not see, for his eyes were dim by reason of his age.

5 And the Lord said to Ahias: Behold the wife of Jeroboam cometh in, to consult thee concerning her son that is sick. Thus and thus shalt thou speak to her. So when she was coming in, and made as if she were another woman,

6 Ahias heard the sound of her feet coming in at the door, and said: Come in, thou wife of Jeroboam. Why dost thou feign thyself to be another? But I am sent to thee with heavy tidings.

7 Go, and tell Jeroboam: Thus saith the Lord the God of Israel: Forasmuch as I exalted thee from among the people, and made thee prince over my people Israel:

8 And rent the kingdom away from the house of David, and gave it to thee: and thou hast not been as my servant David, who kept my commandments, and followed me with all his heart, doing that which was well pleasing in my sight:

9 But hast done evil above all that were before thee, and hast made thee strange gods and molten gods, to provoke me to anger, and hast cast me behind thy back:

10 Therefore behold I will bring evils upon the house of Jeroboam, and ² will cut off from Jeroboam him that pisseth against the wall, and him that is shut up, and the last in Israel. And I will sweep away the remnant of the house of Jeroboam, as dung is swept away till all be clean.

11 Them that shall die of Jeroboam in the city, the dogs shall eat: and them that shall die in the field, the birds of the air shall devour: for the Lord hath spoken *it.*

12 Arise thou therefore, and go to thy house. And when thy feet shall be entering into the city, the child shall die.

13 And all Israel shall mourn for him, and shall bury him: for he only of Jeroboam shall be laid in a sepulchre, because in his regard there is found a good word from the Lord the God of Israel, in the house of Jeroboam.

14 And the Lord hath appointed himself a king over Israel, who shall cut

off the house of Jeroboam in this day, and in this time.

15 And the Lord God shall strike Israel as a reed is shaken in the water. And he shall root up Israel out of this good land, which he gave to their fathers, and shall scatter them beyond the river: because they have made to themselves groves, to provoke the Lord.

16 And the Lord shall give up Israel for the sins of Jeroboam, who hath sinned, and made Israel to sin.

17 And the wife of Jeroboam arose, and departed, and came to Thersa. And when she was coming in to the threshold of the house, the child died.

18 And they buried him. And all Israel mourned for him according to the word of the Lord, which he spoke by the hand of his servant Ahias the prophet.

19 And the rest of the acts of Jeroboam, how he fought, and how he reigned, behold they are written in the book of the words of the days of the kings of Israel.

20 And the days that Jeroboam reigned, were two and twenty years. And he slept with his fathers: and Nadab his son reigned in his stead.

21 [3] And Roboam the son of Solomon reigned in Juda. Roboam was one and forty years old when he began to reign: and he reigned seventeen years in Jerusalem the city, which the Lord chose out of all the tribes of Juda to put his name there. And his mother's name was Naama an Ammonitess.

22 And Juda did evil in the sight of the Lord, and provoked him above all that their fathers had done, in their sins which they committed.

23 For they also built them altars, and statues, and groves upon every high hill and under every green tree.

24 There were also the effeminate in the land: and they did according to all the abominations of the people whom the Lord had destroyed before the face of the children of Israel.

25 And in the fifth year of the reign of Roboam, Sesac king of Egypt came up against Jerusalem.

26 And he took away the treasures of the house of the Lord, and the king's treasures, and carried all off: as also the shields of gold which [4] Solomon had made.

27 And Roboam made shields of brass instead of them, and delivered them into the hand of the captains of the shieldbearers, and of them that kept watch before the gate of the king's house.

28 And when the king went into the house of the Lord, they whose office it was to go before him, carried them: and afterwards they brought them back to the armoury of the shieldbearers.

29 Now the rest of the acts of Roboam, and all that he did, behold they are written in the book of the words of the days of the kings of Juda.

30 And there was war between Roboam and Jeroboam always.

31 And Roboam slept with his fathers, and was buried with them in the city of David: and his mother's name was Naama an Ammonitess. And Abiam his son reigned in his stead.

CHAPTER 15

The acts of Abiam and of Asa kings of Juda. And of Nadab and Baasa kings of Israel.

NOW in the eighteenth year of the reign of Jeroboam the son of Nabat, Abiam reigned over Juda.

2 He reigned three years in Jerusalem. [1] The name of his mother was Maacha the daughter of Abessalom.

3 And he walked in all the sins of his father, which he had done before him: and his heart was not perfect with the Lord his God, as was the heart of David his father.

4 But for David's sake the Lord his God gave him a lamp in Jerusalem, to set up his son after him, and to establish Jerusalem:

5 Because David had done that which was right in the eyes of the Lord, and had not turned aside from any thing that he commanded him, all the days of his life, [2] except the matter of Urias the Hethite.

6 But there was war between Roboam and Jeroboam all the time of his life.

7 And the rest of the words of Abiam, and all that he did, are they not written in the book of the words of the days of the kings of Juda? [3] And there was war between Abiam and Jeroboam.

8 And Abiam slept with his fathers, and they buried him in the city of David. [4] And Asa his son reigned in his stead.

9 So in the twentieth year of Jeroboam king of Israel, reigned Asa king of Juda.

---

[3] 2 Par. 12, 13. [4] 3 Kings, 10, 16. Chap. 15. [1] 2 Par. 13, 2. [2] 2 Kings, 11, 14. [3] 2 Par. 13, 3. [4] 2 Par. 14, 1.

Chap. 14. Ver. 19. *The book of the words of the days of the kings of Israel.* This book, which is often mentioned in the Book of Kings, is long since lost. For as to the books of Paralipomenon, or Chronicles, (which the Hebrews call *the words of the days,*) they were certainly written after the Book of Kings, since they frequently refer to them.

Ver. 24. *The effeminate.* Catamites, or men addicted to unnatural lust.

Chap. 15. Ver. 2. *Maacha.* She is called elsewhere Michaia, daughter of Uriel; but it was common in those days for the same person to have two names.

10 And he reigned one and forty years in Jerusalem. His mother's name was Maacha, the daughter of Abessalom.

11 And Asa did that which was right in the sight of the Lord, as did David his father.

12 And he took away the effeminate out of the land: and he removed all the filth of the idols, which his fathers had made.

13 Moreover he also removed his mother Maacha, from being the princess in the sacrifices of Priapus, and in the grove which she had consecrated to him. And he destroyed her den, and broke in pieces the filthy idol, and burnt it by the torrent Cedron.

14 But the high places he did not take away. Nevertheless the heart of Asa was perfect with the Lord all his days.

15 And he brought in the things which his father had dedicated, and he had vowed, into the house of the Lord: silver and gold, and vessels.

16 And there was war between Asa, and Baasa king of Israel all their days.

17 ⁵ And Baasa king of Israel went up against Juda, and built Rama; that no man might go out or come in, of the side of Asa king of Juda.

18 Then Asa took all the silver and gold that remained in the treasures of the house of the Lord, and in the treasures of the king's house, and delivered it into the hands of his servants. And sent them to Benadad son of Tabremon the son of Hezion, king of Syria, who dwelt in Damascus, saying:

19 There is a league between me and thee, and between my father and thy father. Therefore I have sent thee presents of silver and gold: and I desire thee to come, and break thy league with Baasa king of Israel, that he may depart from me.

20 Benadad hearkening to king Asa, sent the captains of his army against the cities of Israel: and they smote Ahion, and Dan, and Abeldomum Maacha, and all Ceneroth, that is all the land of Nephtali.

21 And when Baasa had heard this, he left off building Rama, and returned into Thersa.

⁵ 2 Par. 16, 1. ⁶ 2 Par. 17, 1. ⁷ 3 Kings, 21, 22.
⁸ 3 Kings, 14, 10.

Ver. 10. *His mother.* That is, his grandmother; unless we suppose, which is not improbable, that the Maacha here named is different from the Maacha mentioned, ver. 2.

Ver. 14. *The high places.* There were *excelsa* or *high places* of two different kinds. Some were set up, and dedicated to the worship of idols, or strange gods; and these Asa removed (2 Par. 14, 2); others were only altars of the true God, but were erected contrary to the law, which allowed of no sacrifices but in the temple; and these were not removed by Asa.—*Perfect with the Lord.* Asa had his faults; but never forsook the worship of the Lord.

22 But king Asa sent word into all Juda, saying: Let no man be excused. And they took away the stones from Rama and the timber thereof, wherewith Baasa had been building: and with them king Asa built Gabaa of Benjamin, and Maspha.

23 But the rest of all the acts of Asa, and all his strength, and all that he did, and the cities that he built, are they not written in the book of the words of the days of the kings of Juda? But in the time of his old age he was diseased in his feet.

24 And he slept with his fathers: and was buried with them in the city of David his father. ⁶ And Josaphat his son reigned in his place.

25 But Nadab the son of Jeroboam reigned over Israel the second year of Asa king of Juda: and he reigned over Israel two years.

26 And he did evil in the sight of the Lord, and walked in the ways of his father, and in his sins, wherewith he made Israel to sin.

27 And Baasa the son of Ahias of the house of Issachar, conspired against him, and slew him in Gebbethon, which is a city of the Philistines: for Nadab and all Israel besieged Gebbethon.

28 So Baasa slew him in the third year of Asa king of Juda; and reigned in his place.

29 ⁷ And when he was king he cut off all the house of Jeroboam. He left not so much as one soul of his seed, till he had utterly destroyed him, according to the word of the Lord, ⁸ which he had spoken in the hand of Ahias the Silonite:

30 Because of the sin of Jeroboam, which he had sinned, and wherewith he had made Israel to sin, and for the offence, wherewith he provoked the Lord the God of Israel.

31 But the rest of the acts of Nadab, and all that he did, are they not written in the book of the words of the days of the kings of Israel?

32 And there was war between Asa and Baasa, the king of Israel, all their days.

33 In the third year of Asa, king of Juda, Baasa the son of Ahias reigned over all Israel, in Thersa, four and twenty years.

34 And he did evil before the Lord, and walked in the ways of Jeroboam, and in his sins, wherewith he made Israel to sin.

CHAPTER 16

Jehu prophesieth against Baasa. His son Ela is slain and all his family destroyed by Zambri. Of the reign of Amri father of Achab.

HEN the word of the Lord came to Jehu the son of Hanani against Baasa, saying:

2 Forasmuch as I have exalted thee out of the dust, and made thee prince over my people Israel, and thou hast walked in the way of Jeroboam, and hast made my people Israel to sin, to provoke me to anger with their sins:

3 Behold, I will cut down the posterity of Baasa, and the posterity of his house: and I will make thy house as the house of Jeroboam the son of Nabat.

4 ¹ Him that dieth of Baasa in the city, the dogs shall eat: and him that dieth of his in the country, the fowls of the air shall devour.

5 ² But the rest of the acts of Baasa and all that he did, and his battles, are they not written in the book of the words of the days of the kings of Israel?

6 So Baasa slept with his fathers, and was buried in Thersa: and Ela his son reigned in his stead.

7 And when the word of the Lord came in the hand of Jehu the son of Hanani the prophet, against Baasa, and against his house, and against all the evil that he had done before the Lord, to provoke him to anger by the works of his hands, to become as the house of Jeroboam: for this cause he slew him, that is to say, Jehu the son of Hanani, the prophet.

8 In the six and twentieth year of Asa king of Juda, Ela the son of Baasa reigned over Israel in Thersa two years.

9 And his servant Zambri, who was captain of half the horsemen, rebelled against him. Now Ela was drinking in Thersa: and drunk in the house of Arsa the governor of Thersa.

10 ³ And Zambri rushing in, struck him and slew him in the seven and twentieth year of Asa king of Juda: and he reigned in his stead.

11 And when he was king and sat upon his throne, he slew all the house of Baasa: and he left not one thereof to piss against a wall, and all his kinsfolks and friends.

12 And Zambri destroyed all the house of Baasa, according to the word of the Lord, that he had spoken to Baasa, in the hand of Jehu the prophet:

13 For all the sins of Baasa, and the sins of Ela his son, who sinned, and made Israel to sin, provoking the Lord, the God of Israel, with their vanities.

14 But the rest of the acts of Ela, and all that he did, are they not written in the book of the words of the days of the kings of Israel?

15 In the seven and twentieth year of Asa, king of Juda, Zambri reigned seven days in Thersa. Now the army was besieging Gebbethon, a city of the Philistines.

16 And when they heard that Zambri had rebelled, and slain the king, all Israel made Amri their king, who was general over Israel in the camp that day.

17 And Amri went up, and all Israel with him from Gebbethon: and they besieged Thersa.

18 And Zambri seeing that the city was about to be taken, went into the palace and burnt himself with the king's house. And he died

19 In his sins, which he had sinned, doing evil before the Lord, and walking in the way of Jeroboam, and in his sin, wherewith he made Israel to sin.

20 But the rest of the acts of Zambri, and of his conspiracy and tyranny, are they not written in the book of the words of the days of the kings of Israel?

21 Then were the people of Israel divided into two parts. One half of the people followed Thebni the son of Gineth, to make him king: and one half followed Amri.

22 But the people that were with Amri, prevailed over the people that followed Thebni the son of Gineth: and Thebni died, and Amri reigned.

23 In the one and thirtieth year of Asa, king of Juda, Amri reigned over Israel twelve years. In Thersa he reigned six years.

24 And he bought the hill of Samaria of Semer for two talents of silver. And he built upon it, and he called the city which he built Samaria, after the name of Semer, the owner of the hill.

25 And Amri did evil in the sight of the Lord, and acted wickedly above all that were before him.

26 And he walked in all the way of Jeroboam the son of Nabat, and in his sins wherewith he made Israel to sin: to provoke the Lord the God of Israel to anger with their vanities.

27 Now the rest of the acts of Amri, and the battles he fought, are they not written in the book of the words of the days of the kings of Israel?

28 And Amri slept with his fathers: and was buried in Samaria. And Achab his son reigned in his stead.

29 Now Achab the son of Amri reigned over Israel in the eight and

CHAP. 16. ¹ 3 Kings, 14, 11. ² 2 Par. 16, 1. ³ 4 Kings, 9, 31.

CHAP. 16. Ver. 23. *In the one and thirtieth year.* Amri began to reign in the seven and twentieth year of Asa; but had not quiet possession of the kingdom till the death of his competitor Thebni, which was in the one and thirtieth year of Asa's reign.

Ver. 26. *With their vanities.* That is, their idols, their golden calves, vain, false, deceitful things.

thirtieth year of Asa king of Juda. And Achab the son of Amri reigned over Israel in Samaria two and twenty years.

30 And Achab the son of Amri did evil in the sight of the Lord above all that were before him.

31 Nor was it enough for him to walk in the sins of Jeroboam the son of Nabat: but he also took to wife Jezabel daughter of Ethbaal king of the Sidonians. And he went, and served Baal, and adored him.

32 And he set up an altar for Baal in the temple of Baal, which he had built in Samaria:

33 And he planted a grove. And Achab did more to provoke the Lord, the God of Israel, than all the kings of Israel that were before him.

34 In his days Hiel of Bethel built Jericho: in Abiram his firstborn he laid its foundations: and in his youngest *son* Segub he set up the gates thereof: according to the word of the Lord, which he spoke in the hand of Josue the son of ⁴Nun.

CHAPTER 17

Elias shutteth up the heaven from raining. He is fed by ravens and afterwards by a widow of Sarephta. He raiseth the widow's son to life.

AND Elias the Thesbite¹ of the inhabitants of Galaad said to Achab: As the Lord liveth, the God of Israel, in whose sight I stand, there shall not be dew nor rain these years, but according to the words of my mouth.

2 And the word of the Lord came to him, saying:

3 Get thee hence, and go towards the east, and hide thyself by the torrent of Carith, which is over against the Jordan.

4 And there thou shalt drink of the torrent: and I have commanded the ravens to feed thee there.

5 So he went, and did according to the word of the Lord. And going, he dwelt by the torrent, Carith, which is over against the Jordan.

6 And the ravens brought him bread and flesh in the morning, and bread and flesh in the evening: and he drank of the torrent.

7 But after some time the torrent was dried up, for it had not rained upon the earth.

8 Then the word of the Lord came to him, saying:

9 Arise, and go to Sarephta of the Sidonians, and dwell there: for I have commanded a widow woman there to feed thee.

10 ²He arose, and went to Sarephta. And when he was come to the gate of the city, he saw the widow woman gathering sticks; and he called her, and said to her: Give me a little water in a vessel, that I may drink.

11 And when she was going to fetch it he called after her, saying: Bring me also, I beseech thee, a morsel of bread in thy hand.

12 And she answered: As the Lord thy God liveth, I have no bread, but only a handful of meal in a pot, and a little oil in a cruse. Behold I am gathering two sticks that I may go in and dress it, for me and for my son, that we may eat it, and die.

13 And Elias said to her: Fear not, but go, and do as thou hast said. But first make for me of the same meal a little hearth cake, and bring it to me; and after make for thyself and thy son.

14 For thus saith the Lord the God of Israel: The pot of meal shall not waste, nor the cruse of oil be diminished, until the day wherein the Lord will give rain upon the face of the earth.

15 She went and did according to the word of Elias. And he ate, and she, and her house: and from that day

16 The pot of meal wasted not, and the cruse of oil was not diminished, according to the word of the Lord, which he spoke in the hand of Elias.

17 And it came to pass after this that the son of the woman, the mistress of the house, fell sick. And the sickness was very grievous, so that there was no breath left in him.

18 And she said to Elias: What have I to do with thee, thou man of God? Art thou come to me that my iniquities should be remembered, and that thou shouldst kill my son?

19 And Elias said to her: Give me thy son. And he took him out of her bosom, and carried him into the upper chamber where he abode, and laid him upon his own bed.

20 And he cried to the Lord, and said: O Lord my God, hast thou afflicted also the widow, with whom I am after a sort maintained, so as to kill her son?

21 And he stretched, and measured himself upon the child three times, and cried to the Lord, and said: O Lord my God, let the soul of this child, I beseech thee, return into his body.

22 And the Lord heard the voice of Elias: and the soul of the child returned into him; and he revived.

23 And Elias took the child, and brought him down from the upper chamber to the house below, and delivered him to his mother, and said to her: Behold thy son liveth.

⁴ Jos. 6, 26. CHAP. 17. ¹ Ecclus. 48, 1; James, 5, 17. ² Luke, 4, 26.

CHAP. 17. Ver. 9. *Sarephta of the Sidonians.* That is, a city of the Sidonians.

24 And the woman said to Elias: Now, by this I know that thou art a man of God; and the word of the Lord in thy mouth is true.

CHAPTER 18

Elias cometh before Achab. He convinceth the false prophets by bringing fire from heaven. He obtaineth rain by his prayer.

AFTER many days the word of the Lord came to Elias, in the third year, saying: Go and shew thyself to Achab, that I may give rain upon the face of the earth.

2 And Elias went to shew himself to Achab: and there was a grievous famine in Samaria.

3 And Achab called Abdias, the governor of his house. Now Abdias feared the Lord very much.

4 For when Jezabel killed the prophets of the Lord, he took a hundred prophets and hid them by fifty and fifty in caves, and fed them with bread and water.

5 And Achab said to Abdias: Go into the land unto all fountains of waters, and into all valleys, to see if we can find grass, and save the horses and mules, that the beasts may not utterly perish.

6 And they divided the countries between them, that they might go round about them: Achab went one way, and Abdias another way by himself.

7 And as Abdias was in the way Elias met him. And he knew him, and fell on his face, and said: Art thou my lord Elias?

8 And he answered: I am. Go, and tell thy master: Elias is here.

9 And he said: What have I sinned, that thou wouldst deliver me thy servant into the hand of Achab, that he should kill me?

10 As the Lord my God liveth, there is no nation or kingdom, whither my Lord hath not sent to seek thee. And when all answered: He is not here, he took an oath of every kingdom and nation, because thou wast not found.

11 And now thou sayest to me: Go, and tell thy master: Elias is here.

12 And when I am gone from thee, the spirits of the Lord will carry thee into a place that I know not: and I shall go in and tell Achab, and he not finding thee, will kill me. But thy servant feareth the Lord from his infancy.

13 Hath it not been told thee, my lord, what I did when Jezabel killed the prophets of the Lord, how I hid a hundred men of the prophets of the Lord by fifty and fifty in caves, and fed them with bread and water?

14 And now thou sayest to me: Go, and tell thy master: Elias is here; that he may kill me.

15 And Elias said: As the Lord of hosts liveth, before whose face I stand, this day I will shew myself unto him.

16 Abdias therefore went to meet Achab, and told him: and Achab came to meet Elias.

17 And when he had seen him, he said: Art thou he that troublest Israel?

18 And he said: I have not troubled Israel, but thou and thy father's house, who have forsaken the commandments of the Lord, and have followed Baalim.

19 Nevertheless send now, and gather unto me all Israel, unto mount Carmel: and the prophets of Baal, four hundred and fifty: and the prophets of the groves four hundred, who eat at Jezabel's table.

20 Achab sent to all the children of Israel, and gathered together the prophets unto mount Carmel.

21 And Elias coming to all the people, said: How long do you halt between two sides? If the Lord be God, follow him: but if Baal, then follow him. And the people did not answer him a word.

22 And Elias said again to the people: I only remain, a prophet of the Lord: but the prophets of Baal are four hundred and fifty men.

23 Let two bullocks be given us, and let them choose one bullock for themselves, and cut it in pieces and lay it upon wood, but put no fire under: and I will dress the other bullock, and lay it on wood, and put no fire under it.

24 Call ye on the names of your gods, and I will call on the name of my Lord: and the God that shall answer by fire, let him be God. And all the people answering said: A very good proposal.

25 Then Elias said to the prophets of Baal: Choose you one bullock, and dress it first, because you are many: and call on the names of your gods, but put no fire under.

26 And they took the bullock which he gave them, and dressed it. And they called on the name of Baal from morning even till noon, saying: O Baal, hear us. But there was no voice, nor any that answered: and they leaped over the altar that they had made.

27 And when it was now noon, Elias jested at them, saying: Cry with a louder voice; for he is a God, and perhaps he is talking, or is in an inn, or on a journey; or perhaps he is asleep, and must be awaked.

28 So they cried with a loud voice, and cut themselves after their manner with knives and lancets, till they were all covered with blood.

29 And after midday was past, and while they were prophesying, the time was come of offering sacrifice: and

there was no voice heard, nor did any one answer, nor regard them as they prayed.

30 Elias said to all the people: Come ye unto me. And the people coming near unto him, he repaired the altar of the Lord, that was broken down.

31 And he took twelve stones according to the number of the tribes of the sons of Jacob, to whom the word of the Lord came, saying: [1] Israel shall be thy name.

32 And he built with the stones an altar to the name of the Lord: and he made a trench for water, of the breadth of two furrows round about the altar.

33 And he laid the wood in order, and cut the bullock in pieces, and laid it upon the wood.

34 And he said: Fill four buckets with water, and pour it upon the burnt offering, and upon the wood. And again he said: Do the same the second time. And when they had done it the second time, he said: Do the same also the third time. And they did so the third time.

35 And the water ran round about the altar: and the trench was filled with water.

36 And when it was now time to offer the holocaust, Elias the prophet came near and said: O Lord God of Abraham, and Isaac, and Israel, shew this day that thou art the God of Israel, and I thy servant, and that according to thy commandment I have done all these things.

37 Hear me, O Lord, hear me: that this people may learn, that thou art the Lord God, and that thou hast turned their heart again.

38 Then the fire of the Lord fell, and consumed the holocaust, and the wood, and the stones, and the dust, and licked up the water that was in the trench.

39 And when all the people saw this, they fell on their faces. And they said: The Lord he is God; the Lord he is God.

40 And Elias said to them: Take the prophets of Baal, and let not one of them escape. And when they had taken them, Elias brought them down to the torrent Cison, and killed them there.

41 And Elias said to Achab: Go up,

CHAP. 18. [1] Gen. 32, 28.

CHAP. 19. Ver. 4. *That he might die.* Elias requested to die, not out of impatience or pusillanimity, but out of zeal against sin; and that he might no longer be witness of the miseries of his people; and the war they were waging against God and his servants. See ver. 10.
Ver. 8. *In the strength of that food.* This bread, with which Elias was fed in the wilderness, was a figure of the bread of life which we receive in the Blessed Sacrament; by the strength of which we are to be supported in our journey through the wilderness of this world till we come to the true mountain of God, and his vision in a happy eternity.

eat, and drink; for there is a sound of abundance of rain.

42 Achab went up to eat and drink. And Elias went up to the top of Carmel, and casting himself down upon the earth put his face between his knees.

43 And he said to his servant: Go up, and look toward the sea. And he went up, and looked, and said: There is nothing. And again he said to him: Return seven times.

44 And at the seventh time, behold, a little cloud arose out of the sea like a man's foot. And he said: Go up and say to Achab: Prepare thy chariot and go down, lest the rain prevent thee.

45 And while he turned himself this way and that way, behold the heavens grew dark, with clouds, and wind: and there fell a great rain. And Achab getting up went away to Jezrahel.

46 And the hand of the Lord was upon Elias: and he girded up his loins and ran before Achab, till he came to Jezrahel.

CHAPTER 19

Elias, fleeing from Jezabel, is fed by an angel in the desert; and by the strength of that food walketh forty days, till he cometh to Horeb, where he hath a vision of God.

AND Achab told Jezabel all that Elias had done, and how he had slain all the prophets with the sword.

2 And Jezabel sent a messenger to Elias, saying: Such and such things may the gods do to me, and add still more, if by this hour to-morrow I make not thy life as the life of one of them.

3 Then Elias was afraid, and rising up he went whithersoever he had a mind. And he came to Bersabee of Juda, and left his servant there.

4 And he went forward, one day's journey into the desert. And when he was there, and sat under a juniper tree, he requested for his soul that he might die, and said: It is enough for me. Lord, take away my soul; for I am no better than my fathers.

5 And he cast himself down, and slept in the shadow of the juniper tree. And behold an angel of the Lord touched him, and said to him: Arise and eat.

6 He looked, and behold there was at his head a hearth cake, and a vessel of water. And he ate and drank; and he fell asleep again.

7 And the angel of the Lord came again the second time, and touched him, and said to him: Arise, eat; for thou hast yet a great way to go.

8 And he arose, and ate, and drank, and walked in the strength of that food forty days and forty nights, unto the mount of God, Horeb.

9 And when he was come thither, he abode in a cave. And behold the word of the Lord *came* unto him, and he said to him: What dost thou here, Elias?

10 And he answered: With zeal have I been zealous for the Lord God of hosts: for the children of Israel have forsaken thy covenant. They have thrown down thy altars, they have slain thy prophets with the sword, and I alone am left: and they seek my life to take it away.

11 And he said to him: Go forth, and stand upon the mount before the Lord. And behold the Lord passeth. And a great and strong wind before the Lord overthrowing the mountains, and breaking the rocks in pieces: the Lord is not in the wind. And after the wind an earthquake: the Lord is not in the earthquake.

12 And after the earthquake a fire: the Lord is not in the fire. And after the fire a whistling of a gentle air.

13 And when Elias heard it, he covered his face with his mantle, and coming forth stood in the entering in of the cave. And behold a voice unto him, saying: What dost thou here, Elias? And he answered:

14 With zeal have I been zealous for the Lord God of hosts; [1] because the children of Israel have forsaken thy covenant. They have destroyed thy altars; they have slain thy prophets with the sword. And I alone am left: and they seek my life to take it away.

15 And the Lord said to him: Go, and return on thy way through the desert to Damascus. And when thou art come thither, thou shalt anoint Hazael to be king over Syria.

16 [2] And thou shalt anoint Jehu the son of Namsi to be king over Israel. And Eliseus the son of Saphat, of Abelmeula, thou shalt anoint to be prophet in thy room.

17 And it shall come to pass, that whosoever shall escape the sword of Hazael, shall be slain by Jehu: and whosoever shall escape the sword of Jehu, shall be slain by Eliseus.

18 [3] And I will leave me seven thousand men in Israel, whose knees have not been bowed before Baal, and every mouth that hath not worshipped him kissing the hands.

19 And Elias departing from thence, found Eliseus the son of Saphat, ploughing with twelve yoke of oxen. And he was one of them that were ploughing with twelve yoke of oxen. And when Elias came up to him, he cast his mantle upon him.

20 And he forthwith left the oxen and ran after Elias, and said: Let me, I pray thee, kiss my father and my mother, and then I will follow thee. And he said to him: Go, and return back; for that which was my part, I have done to thee.

21 And returning back from him, he took a yoke of oxen, and killed them, and boiled the flesh with the plough of the oxen, and gave to the people, and they ate. And rising up, he went away, and followed Elias, and ministered to him.

CHAPTER 20

The Syrians besiege Samaria. They are twice defeated by Achab. Achab is reprehended by a prophet for letting Benadad go.

AND Benadad, king of Syria, gathered together all his host. And there were two and thirty kings with him, and horses, and chariots: and going up, he fought against Samaria, and besieged it.

2 And, sending messengers to Achab king of Israel into the city,

3 He said: Thus saith Benadad: Thy silver, and thy gold is mine: and thy wives, and thy goodliest children are mine.

4 And the king of Israel answered: According to thy word, my lord, O king, I am thine, and all that I have.

5 And the messengers came again, and said: Thus saith Benadad, who sent us unto thee: Thy silver, and thy gold, and thy wives, and thy children, thou shalt deliver up to me.

6 To-morrow therefore at this same hour I will send my servants to thee: and they shall search thy house, and the houses of thy servants: and all that pleaseth them, they shall put in their hands, and take away.

7 And the king of Israel called all the ancients of the land, and said: Mark, and see that he layeth snares for us. For he sent to me for my wives, and for my children, and for my silver and gold: and I said not nay.

8 And all the ancients, and all the people said to him: Hearken not to him, nor consent to him.

CHAP. 19. [1] Rom. 11, 3. [2] 4 Kings, 9, 2. [3] Rom. 11, 4.

Ver. 10. *I alone am left.* That is, of the prophets in the kingdom of Israel, or of the ten tribes; for in the kingdom of Juda religion was at that time in a very flourishing condition under the kings Asa and Josaphat. And even in Israel there remained several prophets, though not then known to Elias. See 20, 13; 28, 35.

Ver. 17. *Shall be slain by Eliseus.* Eliseus did not kill any of the idolaters with the material sword: but he is here joined with Hazael and Jehu, the great instruments of God in punishing the idolatry of Israel, because he foretold to the former his exaltation to the kingdom of Syria, and the vengeance he would execute against Israel, and anointed the latter by one of his disciples to be king of Israel, with commission to extirpate the house of Achab.

9 Wherefore he answered the messengers of Benadad: Tell my lord the king: All that thou didst send for to me thy servant at first, I will do: but this thing I cannot do.

10 And the messengers returning brought him word. And he sent again and said: Such and such things may the gods do to me, and more may they add, if the dust of Samaria shall suffice for handfuls for all the people that follow me.

11 And the king of Israel answering, said: Tell him: Let not the girded boast himself as the ungirded.

12 And it came to pass, when Benadad heard this word, that he and the kings were drinking in pavilions, and he said to his servants: Beset the city. And they beset it.

13 And behold a prophet coming to Achab king of Israel, said to him: Thus saith the Lord: Hast thou seen all this exceeding great multitude? Behold I will deliver them into thy hand this day: that thou mayest know that I am the Lord.

14 And Achab said: By whom? And he said to him: Thus saith the Lord: By the servants of the princes of the provinces. And he said: Who shall begin to fight? And he said: Thou.

15 So he mustered the servants of the princes of the provinces: and he found the number of two hundred and thirty-two. And he mustered after them the people, all the children of Israel, seven thousand.

16 And they went out at noon. But Benadad was drinking himself drunk in his pavilion, and the two and thirty kings with him, who were come to help him.

17 And the servants of the princes of the provinces went out first. And Benadad sent. And they told him, saying: There are men come out of Samaria.

18 And he said: Whether they come for peace, take them alive: or whether *they come* to fight, take them alive.

19 So the servants of the princes of the provinces went out, and the rest of the army followed.

20 And every one slew the man that came against him. And the Syrians fled: and Israel pursued after them. And Benadad king of Syria fled away on horseback with his horsemen.

21 But the king of Israel going out overthrew the horses and chariots, and slew the Syrians with a great slaughter.

22 (And a prophet coming to the king of Israel, said to him: Go, and strengthen thyself, and know, and see what

CHAP. 20. Ver. 11. *Let not the girded boast.* Let him not boast before the victory: it will then be time to glory when he putteth off his armour, having overcome his adversary.

thou dost: for the next year the king of Syria will come up against thee.)

23 But the servants of the king of Syria said to him: Their gods are gods of the hills; therefore they have overcome us. But it is better that we should fight against them in the plains; and we shall overcome them.

24 Do thou therefore this thing: Remove all the kings from thy army, and put captains in their stead.

25 And make up the number of soldiers that have been slain of thine, and horses according to the former horses, and chariots according to the chariots which thou hadst before. And we will fight against them in the plains: and thou shalt see that we shall overcome them. He believed their counsel and did so.

26 Wherefore, at the return of the year, Benadad mustered the Syrians, and went up to Aphec, to fight against Israel.

27 And the children of Israel were mustered; and taking victuals went out on the other side, and camped over against them, like two little flocks of goats. But the Syrians filled the land.

28 (And a man of God coming, said to the king of Israel: Thus saith the Lord: Because the Syrians have said: The Lord is God of the hills, but is not God of the valleys: I will deliver all this great multitude into thy hand; and you shall know that I am the Lord.)

29 And both sides set their armies in array one against the other, seven days. And on the seventh day the battle was fought: and the children of Israel slew of the Syrians a hundred thousand footmen in one day.

30 And they that remained fled to Aphec, into the city: and the wall fell upon seven and twenty thousand men that were left. And Benadad fleeing went into the city, into a chamber that was within a chamber.

31 And his servants said to him: Behold, we have heard that the kings of the house of Israel are merciful. So let us put sackcloth on our loins, and ropes on our heads, and go out to the king of Israel: perhaps he will save our lives.

32 So they girded sackcloth on their loins, and put ropes on their heads, and came to the king of Israel, and said to him: Thy servant Benadad saith: I beseech thee let me have my life. And he said: If he be yet alive he is my brother.

33 The men took this for a sign: and in haste caught the word out of his mouth, and said: Thy brother Benadad. And he said to them: Go, and bring him to me. Then Benadad came out to him: and he lifted him up into his chariot.

34 And he said to him: The cities

which my father took from thy father, I will restore. And do thou make thee streets in Damascus, as my father made in Samaria: and having made a league, I will depart from thee. So he made a league with him, and let him go.

35 Then a certain man of the sons of the prophets said to his companion in the word of the Lord: Strike me. But he would not strike.

36 Then he said to him: Because thou wouldst not hearken to the word of the Lord, behold thou shalt depart from me, and a lion shall slay thee. And when he was gone a little from him, a lion found him, and slew him.

37 Then he found another man, and said to him: Strike me. And he struck him, and wounded him.

38 So the prophet went, and met the king in the way, and disguised himself by sprinkling dust on his face and his eyes.

39 And as the king passed by, he cried to the king, and said: Thy servant went out to fight hand to hand. And when a certain man was run away, one brought him to me, and said: Keep this man; and if he shall slip away, thy life shall be for his life, or thou shalt pay a talent of silver.

40 And whilst I in a hurry turned this way and that, on a sudden he was not to be seen. And the king of Israel said to him: This is thy judgment, which thyself hast decreed.

41 But he forthwith wiped off the dust from his face: and the king of Israel knew him, that he was one of the prophets.

42 And he said to him: Thus saith the Lord: Because thou hast let go out of thy hand a man worthy of death, thy life shall be for his life, and thy people for his people.

43 And the king of Israel returned to his house, slighting to hear: and raging came into Samaria.

CHAPTER 21

Naboth, for denying his vineyard to king Achab, is by Jezabel's commandment, falsely accused and stoned to death. For which crime Elias denounceth to Achab the judgments of God. Upon his humbling himself the sentence is mitigated.

AND after these things, Naboth the Jezrahelite, who was in Jezrahel, had at that time a vineyard near the palace of Achab king of Samaria.

2 And Achab spoke to Naboth, saying: Give me thy vineyard, that I may make me a garden of herbs, because it is nigh, and adjoining to my house: and I will give thee for it a better vineyard. Or if thou think it more convenient for thee, I will give thee the worth of it in money.

3 Naboth answered him: The Lord be merciful to me, and not let me give thee the inheritance of my fathers.

4 And Achab came into his house angry and fretting, because of the word that Naboth the Jezrahelite had spoken to him, saying: I will not give thee the inheritance of my fathers. And casting himself upon his bed, he turned away his face to the wall, and would eat no bread.

5 And Jezabel his wife went in to him, and said to him: What is the matter that thy soul is so grieved? And why eatest thou no bread?

6 And he answered her: I spoke to Naboth the Jezrahelite, and said to him: Give me thy vineyard, and take money for it; or if it please thee, I will give thee a better vineyard for it. And he said: I will not give thee my vineyard.

7 Then Jezabel his wife said to him: Thou art of great authority indeed, and governest well the kingdom of Israel. Arise, and eat bread, and be of good cheer. I will give thee the vineyard of Naboth the Jezrahelite.

8 So she wrote letters in Achab's name, and sealed them with his ring, and sent them to the ancients, and the chief men that were in his city, and that dwelt with Naboth.

9 And this was the tenor of the letters: Proclaim a fast, and make Naboth sit among the chief of the people.

10 And suborn two men, sons of Belial, against him: and let them bear false witness that he hath blasphemed God and the king: and then carry him out, and stone him and so let him die.

11 And the men of his city, the ancients and nobles that dwelt with him in the city, did as Jezabel had commanded them, and as it was written in the letters which she had sent to them.

12 They proclaimed a fast, and made Naboth sit among the chief of the people.

13 And bringing two men, sons of the devil, they made thm sit against him. And they, like men of the devil, bore witness against him before the people, saying: Naboth hath blasphemed God and the king. Wherefore they brought him forth without the city, and stoned him to death.

14 And they sent to Jezabel, saying: Naboth is stoned, and is dead.

15 And it came to pass when Jezabel heard that Naboth was stoned and dead, that she said to Achab: Arise and take possession of the vineyard of Naboth the Jezrahelite, who would not agree with thee, and give it thee for money. For Naboth is not alive, but dead.

16 And when Achab heard this, to wit, that Naboth was dead, he arose and went down to the vineyard of Naboth the Jezrahelite, to take possession of it.

17 And the word of the Lord came to Elias the Thesbite, saying:

18 Arise, and go down to meet Achab king of Israel, who is in Samaria: behold he is going down to the vineyard of Naboth, to take possession of it.

19 And thou shalt speak to him, saying: Thus saith the Lord: Thou hast slain. Moreover also thou hast taken possession. And after these words thou shalt add: Thus saith the Lord: [1] In this place, wherein the dogs have licked the blood of Naboth, they shall lick thy blood also.

20 And Achab said to Elias: Hast thou found me thy enemy? He said: I have found thee, because thou art sold, to do evil in the sight of the Lord.

21 [2] Behold I will bring evil upon thee, and I will cut down thy posterity, and I will kill of Achab him that pisseth against the wall, and him that is shut up, and the last in Israel.

22 And I will make thy house like [3] the house of Jeroboam the son of Nabat, and like the house of [4] Baasa the son of Ahias: for what thou hast done, to provoke me to anger, and for making Israel to sin.

23 [5] And to Jezabel also the Lord spoke, saying: The dogs shall eat Jezabel in the field of Jezrahel.

24 If Achab die in the city, the dogs shall eat him: but if he die in the field, the birds of the air shall eat him.

25 Now there was not such another as Achab, who was sold to do evil in the sight of the Lord: for his wife Jezabel set him on.

26 And he became abominable, insomuch that he followed the idols which the Amorrhites had made, whom the Lord destroyed before the face of the children of Israel.

27 And when Achab had heard these words, he rent his garments, and put haircloth upon his flesh, and fasted and slept in sackcloth, and walked with his head cast down.

28 And the word of the Lord came to Elias the Thesbite, saying:

29 Hast thou not seen Achab humbled before me? Therefore, because he hath humbled himself for my sake, I will not bring the evil in his days: [6] but in his son's days will I bring the evil upon his house.

CHAPTER 22

Achab, believing his false prophets rather than Micheas, is slain in Ramoth Galaad. Ochozias succeedeth him. Good king Josaphat dieth, and his son Joram succeedeth him.

AND [1] there passed three years without war between Syria and Israel.

2 And in the third year, Josaphat king of Juda came down to the king of Israel.

3 (And the king of Israel said to his servants: Know ye not that Ramoth Galaad is ours, and we neglect to take it out of the hand of the king of Syria?)

4 And he said to Josaphat: Wilt thou come with me to battle to Ramoth Galaad?

5 And Josaphat said to the king of Israel: As I am, so art thou. My people and thy people are one: and my horsemen, thy horsemen. And Josaphat said to the king of Israel: Inquire, I beseech thee, this day, the word of the Lord.

6 Then the king of Israel assembled the prophets, about four hundred men, and he said to them: Shall I go to Ramoth Galaad to fight, or shall I forbear? They answered: Go up, and the Lord will deliver it into the hand of the king.

7 And Josaphat said: Is there not here some prophet of the Lord, that we may inquire by him?

8 And the king of Israel said to Josaphat: There is one man left, by whom we may inquire of the Lord, Micheas the son of Jemla; but I hate him, for he doth not prophesy good to me, but evil. And Josaphat said: Speak not so, O king.

9 Then the king of Israel called an eunuch, and said to him: Make haste, and bring hither Micheas the son of Jemla.

10 Then the king of Israel, and Josaphat king of Juda, sat each on his throne clothed with royal robes, in a court by the entrance of the gate of Samaria: and all the prophets prophesied before them.

11 And Sedecias the son of Chanaana made himself horns of iron, and said: Thus saith the Lord: With these shalt thou push Syria, till thou destroy it.

12 And all the prophets prophesied in like manner, saying: Go up to Ramoth Galaad, and prosper; for the Lord will deliver it into the king's hands.

13 And the messenger, that went to call Micheas, spoke to him, saying: Behold the words of the prophets with one

CHAP. 21. [1] 3 Kings, 22, 38. [2] 4 Kings, 9, 8. [3] 3 Kings, 15, 29. [4] 3 Kings, 16, 3. [5] 4 Kings, 9, 36. [6] 4 Kings, 9, 26. CHAP. 22. [1] 2 Par. 18, 1.

CHAP. 21. Ver. 20. *Sold, to do evil in the sight of the Lord.* That is, so addicted to evil, as if thou hadst sold thyself to the devil, to be his slave to work all kinds of evil.

mouth declare good things to the king. Let thy word therefore be like to theirs, and speak that which is good.

14 But Micheas said to him: As the Lord liveth, whatsoever the Lord shall say to me, that will I speak.

15 So he came to the king, and the king said to him: Micheas, shall we go to Ramoth Galaad to battle, or shall we forbear? He answered him: Go up, and prosper, and the Lord shall deliver it into the king's hands.

16 But the king said to him: I adjure thee again and again, that thou tell me nothing but that which is true in the name of the Lord.

17 And he said: I saw all Israel scattered upon the hills, like sheep that have no shepherd. [2] And the Lord said: These have no master: let every man of them return to his house in peace.

18 (Then the king of Israel said to Josaphat: Did I not tell thee, that he prophesieth no good to me, but always evil?)

19 And he added and said: Hear thou therefore the word of the Lord: I saw the Lord sitting on his throne, and all the army of heaven standing [3] by him on the right hand and on the left.

20 And the Lord said: Who shall deceive Achab king of Israel, that he may go up, and fall at Ramoth Galaad? And one spoke words of this manner, and another· otherwise.

21 And there came forth a spirit, and stood before the Lord, and said: I will deceive him. And the Lord said to him: By what means?

22 And he said: I will go forth, and be a lying spirit in the mouth of all his prophets. And the Lord said: Thou shalt deceive *him,* and shalt prevail. [4] Go forth, and do so.

23 Now therefore behold the Lord hath given a lying spirit in the mouth of all thy prophets that are here: and the Lord hath spoken evil against thee.

24 And Sedecias the son of Chanaana came, and struck Micheas on the cheek, and said: Hath then the spirit of the Lord left me and spoken to thee?

25 And Micheas said: Thou shalt see in the day when thou shalt go into a chamber within a chamber to hide thyself.

26 And the king of Israel said: Take Micheas, and let him abide with Ammon the governor of the city, and with Joas the son of Amalech.

27 And tell them: Thus saith the king: Put this man in prison, and feed him with bread of affliction, and water of distress, till I return in peace.

28 And Micheas said: If thou return in peace, the Lord hath not spoken to me. And he said: Hear, all ye people.

29 So the king of Israel, and Josaphat king of Juda went up to Ramoth Galaad.

30 And the king of Israel said to Josaphat: Take armour, and go into the battle, and put on thy own garments. But the king of Israel changed his dress, and went into the battle.

31 And the king of Syria had commanded the two and thirty captains of the chariots, saying: You shall not fight against any, small or great, but against the king of Israel only.

32 So when the captains of the chariots saw Josaphat, they suspected that he was the king of Israel: and making a violent assault they fought against him. And Josaphat cried out.

33 And the captains of the chariots perceived that he was not the king of Israel: and they turned away from him.

34 And a certain man bent his bow, shooting at a venture, and chanced to strike the king of Israel between the lungs and the stomach. But he said to the driver of his chariot: Turn thy hand, and carry me out of the army, for I am grievously wounded.

35 And the battle was fought that day, and the king of Israel stood in his chariot against the Syrians. And he died in the evening: and the blood ran out of the wound into the midst of the chariot.

36 And the herald proclaimed through all the army before the sun set, saying: Let every man return to his own city, and to his own country.

37 And the king died, and was carried into Samaria: and they buried the king in Samaria.

38 [5] And they washed his chariot in the pool of Samaria: and the dogs licked

[2] Num. 27, 17; Matt. 9, 36. [3] Joel, 1, 6. [4] Matt. 8, 32; Apoc. 20, 3. [5] 3 Kings, 21, 19.

Chap. 22. Ver. 15. *Go up, and prosper.* This was spoken ironically, and by way of jesting at the flattering speeches of the false prophets: and so the king understood it, as appears by his adjuring Micheas, in the following verse, to tell him the truth in the name of the Lord.

Ver. 20. *The Lord said.* God standeth not in need of any counsellor; nor are we to suppose that things pass in heaven in the manner here described: but this representation was made to the prophet, to be delivered by him in a manner adapted to the common ways and notions of men.

Ver. 22. *Go forth, and do so.* This was not a command, but a permission: for God never ordaineth lies; though he often permitteth the lying spirit to deceive those who love not the truth (2 Thess. 2, 10). And in this sense it is said in the following verse, *The Lord hath given a lying spirit in the mouth of all thy prophets.*

Ver. 25. *Go into a chamber.* This happened when he heard the king was slain, and justly apprehended that he should be punished for his false prophecy.

up his blood. And they washed the reins, according to the word of the Lord which he had spoken.

39 But the rest of the acts of Achab and all that he did, and the house of ivory that he made, and all the cities that he built, are they not written in the book of the words of the days of the kings of Israel?

40 So Achab slept with his fathers, and Ochozias his son reigned in his stead.

41 But Josaphat the son of Asa began to reign over Juda in the fourth year of Achab king of Israel.

42 He was five and thirty years old when he began to reign, and he reigned five and twenty years in Jerusalem. The name of his mother was Azuba the daughter of Salai.

43 And he walked in all the way of Asa his father, and he declined not from it: and he did that which was right in the sight of the Lord.

44 Nevertheless he took not away the high places: for as yet the people offered sacrifices and burnt incense in the high places.

45 And Josaphat had peace with the king of Israel.

46 But the rest of the acts of Josaphat, and his works which he did, and his battles, are they not written in the book of the words of the days of the kings of Juda?

47 And the remnant also of the effeminate, who remained in the days of Asa his father, he took out of the land.

48 And there was then no king appointed in Edom.

49 But king Josaphat made navies on the sea, to sail into Ophir for gold: but they could not go, [6]for the ships were broken in Asiongaber.

50 Then Ochozias the son of Achab said to Josaphat: Let my servants go with thy servants in the ships. And Josaphat would not.

51 And Josaphat slept with his fathers, and was buried with them in in the city of David his father. And Joram his son reigned in his stead.

52 And Ochozias the son of Achab began to reign over Israel in Samaria, in the seventeenth year of Josaphat king of Juda. And he reigned over Israel two years.

53 And he did evil in the sight of the Lord, and walked in the way of his father and his mother, and in the way of Jeroboam the son of Nabat, who made Israel to sin.

54 He served also Baal, and worshipped him, and provoked the Lord the God of Israel according to all that his father had done.

THE FOURTH BOOK OF

KINGS

CHAPTER 1

Ochozias sendeth to consult Beelzebub. Elias foretelleth his death. He causeth fire to come down from heaven, upon two captains and their companies.

AND Moab rebelled against Israel, after the death of Achab.

2 And Ochozias fell through the lattices of his upper chamber which he had in Samaria, and was sick. And he sent messengers, saying to them: Go, consult Beelzebub, the god of Accaron, whether I shall recover of this my illness.

3 And an angel of the Lord spoke to Elias the Thesbite, saying: Arise, and go up to meet the messengers of the king of Samaria, and say to them: Is there not a God in Israel, that ye go to consult Beelzebub the god of Accaron?

4 Wherefore thus saith the Lord: From the bed, on which thou art gone up, thou shalt not come down; but thou shalt surely die. And Elias went away.

5 And the messengers turned back to Ochozias. And he said to them: Why are you come back?

6 But they answered him: A man met us, and said to us: Go, and return to the king, that sent you, and you shall say to him: Thus saith the Lord: Is it because there was no God in Israel that thou sendest to Beelzebub the god of Accaron? Therefore thou shalt not come down from the bed, on which thou art gone up; but thou shalt surely die.

7 And he said to them: What manner of man was he who met you, and spoke these words?

8 But they said: A hairy man with a

[6] 2 Par. 20, 36.

Ver. 44. *He took not away the high places.* He left some of the high places, namely, those in which they worshipped the true God: but took away all others (2 Par. 17, 6; 3 Kings, 15, 14 *note*).

Ver. 50. *Would not.* He had been reprehended before for admitting such a partner: and therefore would have no more to do with him.

girdle of leather about his loins. And he said: It is Elias the Thesbite.

9 And he sent to him a captain of fifty, and the fifty men that were under him. And he went up to him, and as he was sitting on the top of a hill, said to him: Man of God, the king hath commanded that thou come down.

10 And Elias answering, said to the captain of fifty: If I be a man of God, let fire come down from heaven, and consume thee, and thy fifty. And there came down fire from heaven, and consumed him, and the fifty that were with him.

11 And again he sent to him another captain of fifty men, and his fifty with him. And he said to him: Man of God, thus saith the king: Make haste and come down.

12 Elias answering, said: If I be a man of God, let fire come down from heaven, and consume thee and thy fifty. And fire came down from heaven, and consumed him and his fifty.

13 Again he sent a third captain of fifty men, and the fifty that were with him. And when he was come, he fell upon his knees, before Elias, and besought him, and said: Man of God, despise not my life, and the lives of thy servants that are with me.

14 Behold fire came down from heaven, and consumed the two first captains of fifty men, and the fifties that were with them: but now I beseech thee to spare my life.

15 And the angel of the Lord spoke to Elias, saying: Go down with him. Fear not. He arose therefore, and went down with him to the king.

16 And he said to him: Thus saith the Lord: Because thou hast sent messengers to consult Beelzebub the god of Accaron, as though there were not a God in Israel, of whom thou mightest inquire the word; therefore from the bed on which thou art gone up, thou shalt not come down, but thou shalt surely die.

17 So he died according to the word of the Lord which Elias spoke. And Joram his brother reigned in his stead, in the second year of Joram the son of Josaphat king of Juda: because he had no son.

18 But the rest of the acts of Ochozias which he did, are they not written in the book of the words of the days of the kings of Israel?

CHAPTER 2

Eliseus will not part from Elias. The water of the Jordan is divided by Elias's cloak. Elias is taken up in a fiery chariot, and his double spirit is given to Eliseus. Eliseus healeth the waters by casting in salt. Boys are torn by bears for mocking Eliseus.

AND it came to pass, when the Lord would take up Elias into heaven by a whirlwind, that Elias and Eliseus were going from Galgal.

2 And Elias said to Eliseus: Stay thou here, because the Lord hath sent me as far as Bethel. And Eliseus said to him: As the Lord liveth, and as thy soul liveth, I will not leave thee. And when they were come down to Bethel,

3 The sons of the prophets, that were at Bethel, came forth to Eliseus, and said to him: Dost thou know that this day the Lord will take away thy master from thee? And he answered: I also know it. Hold your peace.

4 And Elias said to Eliseus: Stay here because the Lord hath sent me to Jericho. And he said: As the Lord liveth, and as thy soul liveth, I will not leave thee. And when they were come to Jericho,

5 The sons of the prophets that were at Jericho, came to Eliseus, and said to him: Dost thou know that this day the Lord will take away thy master from thee? And he said: I also know it. Hold your peace.

6 And Elias said to him: Stay here, because the Lord hath sent me as far as the Jordan. And he said: As the Lord liveth, and as thy soul liveth, I will not leave thee. And they two went on together,

7 And fifty men of the sons of the prophets followed them, and stood in sight at a distance. But they two stood by the Jordan.

8 And Elias took his mantle, and folded it together, and struck the waters: and they were divided hither and thither. And they both passed over on dry ground.

9 And when they were gone over, Elias said to Eliseus: Ask what thou wilt have me to do for thee, before I be taken away from thee. And Eliseus said: I beseech thee that in me may be thy double spirit.

10 And he answered: Thou hast

CHAP. 1. Ver. 10. *Let fire come down from heaven.* Elias was inspired to call for fire from heaven upon these captains, who came to apprehend him; not out of a desire to gratify any private passion; but to punish the insult offered to religion, to confirm his mission, and to shew how vain are the efforts of men against God, and his servants, whom he willeth to protect.

Ver. 17. *The second year of Joram.* Counted from the time that he was associated to the throne by his father Josaphat.

CHAP. 2. Ver. 1. *Heaven.* By *heaven* here is meant the air, the lowest of the heavenly regions.

Ver. 3. *The sons of the prophets.* That is, the disciples of the prophets: who seem to have had their schools, like colleges or communities, in Bethel, Jericho, and other places in the days of Elias and Eliseus.

Ver. 9. *Double spirit.* A *double* portion of thy *spirit*, as thy eldest son and heir: or thy *spirit* which is *double* in comparison of that which God usually imparteth to his prophets.

asked a hard thing. Nevertheless if thou see me when I am taken from thee, thou shalt have what thou hast asked: but if thou see me not, thou shalt not have it.

11 And as they went on, walking and talking together, behold a fiery chariot, and fiery horses parted them both asunder: [1] and Elias went up by a whirlwind into heaven.

12 And Eliseus saw him, and cried: My father, my father, the chariot of Israel, and the driver thereof. And he saw him no more. And he took hold of his own garments, and rent them in two pieces.

13 And he took up the mantle of Elias, that fell from him: and going back, he stood upon the bank of the Jordan,

14 And he struck the waters with the mantle of Elias, that had fallen from him, and they were not divided. And he said: Where is now the God of Elias? And he struck the waters, and they were divided, hither and thither: and Eliseus passed over.

15 And the sons of the prophets at Jericho, who were over against him, seeing it said: The spirit of Elias hath rested upon Eliseus. And coming to meet him, they worshipped him, falling to the ground;

16 And they said to him: Behold, there are with thy servants fifty strong men, that can go, and seek thy master: lest perhaps the spirit of the Lord hath taken him up and cast him upon some mountain or into some valley. And he said: Do not send.

17 But they pressed him, till he consented, and said: Send. And they sent fifty men: and they sought three days but found him not.

18 And they came back to him: for he abode at Jericho. And he said to them: Did I not say to you: Do not send?

19 And the men of the city said to Eliseus: Behold the situation of this city is very good, as thou, my lord, seest; but the waters are very bad, and the ground barren.

20 And he said: Bring me a new vessel, and put salt into it. And when they had brought it,

21 He went out to the spring of the waters, and cast the salt into it, and said: Thus saith the Lord: I have healed these waters, and there shall be no more in them death or barrenness.

22 And the waters were healed unto this day, according to the word of Eliseus, which he spoke.

23 And he went up from thence to Bethel. And as he was going up by the way, little boys came out of the city and mocked him, saying: Go up, thou bald head. Go up, thou bald head.

24 And looking back, he saw them, and cursed them in the name of the Lord: and there came forth two bears out of the forest, and tore of them two and forty boys.

25 And from thence he went to mount Carmel: and from thence he returned to Samaria.

CHAPTER 3

The kings of Israel, Juda and Edom, fight against the king of Moab. They want water, which Eliseus procureth without rain: and prophesieth victory. The king of Moab is overthrown, his city is besieged. He sacrificeth his firstborn son. The Israelites raise the siege.

AND Joram the son of Achab reigned over Israel in Samaria in the eighteenth year of Josaphat king of Juda. And he reigned twelve years.

2 And he did evil before the Lord, but not like his father and his mother: for he took away the statues of Baal, which his father had made.

3 Nevertheless he stuck to the sins of Jeroboam the son of Nabat, who made Israel to sin, nor did he depart from them.

4 Now Mesa, king of Moab, nourished many sheep: and he paid to the king of Israel a hundred thousand lambs, and a hundred thousand rams with their fleeces.

5 And when Achab was dead, he broke the league which he had made with the king of Israel.

6 And king Joram went out that day from Samaria, and mustered all Israel.

7 And he sent to Josaphat king of Juda, saying: The king of Moab is revolted from me; come with me against him to battle. And he answered: I will come up. He that is mine, is thine: my people, thy people: and my horses, thy horses.

8 And he said: Which way shall we go up? But he answered: By the desert of Edom.

9 So the king of Israel, and the king of Juda, and the king of Edom went: and they fetched a compass of seven days' journey. And there was no water for the army, and for the beasts, that followed them.

CHAP. 2. [1] Ecclus. 48, 13; 1 Mach. 2, 58.

Ver. 15. *They worshipped him,* namely, with an inferior, yet religious veneration, not for any temporal, but spiritual excellency.

Ver. 24. *Cursed them.* This curse, which was followed by so visible a judgment of God, was not the effect of passion, or of a desire of revenging himself; but of zeal for religion, which was insulted by these boys, in the person of the prophet; and of a divine inspiration: God punishing in this manner the inhabitants of Bethel, (the chief seat of the calf worship,) who had trained up their children in a prejudice against the true religion and its ministers.

10 And the king of Israel said: Alas, alas, alas, the Lord hath gathered us three kings together, to deliver us into the hands of Moab!

11 And Josaphat said: Is there not here a prophet of the Lord, that we may beseech the Lord by him? And one of the servants of the king of Israel answered: Here is Eliseus the son of Saphat, who poured water on the hands of Elias.

12 And Josaphat said: The word of the Lord is with him. And the king of Israel, and Josaphat king of Juda, and the king of Edom went down to him.

13 And Eliseus said to the king of Israel: What have I to do with thee? Go to the prophets of thy father, and thy mother. And the king of Israel said to him: Why hath the Lord gathered together these three kings, to deliver them into the hands of Moab?

14 And Eliseus said to him: As the Lord of hosts liveth, in whose sight I stand, if I did not reverence the face of Josaphat king of Juda, I would not have hearkened to thee, nor looked on thee.

15 But now bring me hither a minstrel. And when the minstrel played, the hand of the Lord came upon him, and he said:

16 Thus saith the Lord: Make the channel of this torrent full of ditches.

17 For thus saith the Lord: You shall not see wind, nor rain: and yet this channel shall be filled with waters. And you shall drink, you and your families, and your beasts.

18 And this is a small thing in the sight of the Lord. Moreover he will deliver also Moab into your hands.

19 And you shall destroy every fenced city; and every choice city, and shall cut down every fruitful tree, and shall stop up all the springs of waters: and every goodly field you shall cover with stones.

20 And it came to pass in the morning, when the sacrifices used to be offered, that, behold, water came by the way of Edom: and the country was filled with water.

And all the Moabites hearing that the kings were come up to fight against them, gathered together all that were girded with a belt upon them, and stood in the borders.

22 And they rose early in the morning, and the sun being now up, and shining upon the waters, the Moabites saw the waters over against them red, like blood,

23 And they said: It is the blood of the sword: the kings have fought among themselves, and they have killed one another. Go now, Moab, to the spoils.

24 And they went into the camp of Israel: but Israel rising up defeated Moab, who fled before them. And they being conquerors, went and smote Moab.

25 And they destroyed the cities: and they filled every goodly field, every man casting his stone. And they stopt up all the springs of waters: and cut down all the trees that bore fruit, so that brick walls only remained. And the city was beset by the slingers, and a great part thereof destroyed.

26 And when the king of Moab saw this, to wit, that the enemies had prevailed, he took with him seven hundred men that drew the sword, to break in upon the king of Edom. But they could not.

27 Then he took his eldest son that should have reigned in his stead, and offered him for a burnt offering upon the wall. And there was great indignation in Israel; and presently they departed from him, and returned into their own country.

CHAPTER 4

Miracles of Eliseus. He raiseth a dead child to life.

NOW a certain woman of the wives of the prophets cried to Eliseus, saying: Thy servant my husband is dead. And thou knowest that thy servant was one that feared God: and behold the creditor is come to take away my two sons to serve him.

2 And Eliseus said to her: What wilt thou have me to do for thee? Tell me, what hast thou in thy house? And she answered: I thy handmaid have nothing in my house but a little oil, to anoint me.

3 And he said to her: Go, borrow of all thy neighbours empty vessels not a few.

4 And go in, and shut thy door, when thou art within, and thy sons: and pour out thereof into all those vessels: and when they are full take them away.

5 So the woman went, and shut the door upon her, and upon her sons. They brought her the vessels, and she poured in.

6 And when the vessels were full, she said to her son: Bring me yet a vessel. And he answered: I have no more. And the oil stood.

7 And she came, and told the man of God. And he said: Go, sell the oil, and pay thy creditor; and thou and thy sons live of the rest.

8 And there was a day when Eliseus passed by Sunam. Now there was a

CHAP. 3. Ver. 25. *Brick walls only remained.* It was the proper name of the capital city of the Moabites. In Hebrew, *Kir-Haraseth.*

great woman there, who detained him to eat bread; and as he passed often that way, he turned into her house to eat bread.

9 And she said to her husband: I perceive that this is a holy man of God, who often passeth by us.

10 Let us therefore make him a little chamber, and put a little bed in it for him, and a table, and a stool, and a candlestick, that when he cometh to us, he may abide there.

11 Now there was a certain day when he came and turned in to the chamber, and rested there.

12 And he said to Giezi his servant: Call this Sunamitess. And when he had called her, and she stood before him,

13 He said to his servant: Say to her: Behold thou hast diligently served us in all things, what wilt thou have me to do for thee? Hast thou any business, and wilt thou that I speak to the king, or to the general of the army? And she answered: I dwell in the midst of my own people.

14 And he said: What will she then that I do for her? And Giezi said: Do not ask; for she hath no son, and her husband is old.

15 Then he bid him call her. And when she was called, and stood before the door,

16 He said to her: At this time, and this same hour, if life accompany, thou shalt have a son in thy womb. But she answered: Do not, I beseech thee, my lord, thou man of God, do not lie to thy handmaid.

17 And the woman conceived, and brought forth a son in the time, and at the same hour, that Eliseus had said.

18 And the child grew. And on a certain day, when he went out to his father to the reapers,

19 He said to his father: My head acheth, my head acheth. But he said to his servant: Take him, and carry him to his mother.

20 And when he had taken him, and brought him to his mother, she set him on her knees until noon: and then he died.

CHAP. 4. Ver. 29. *Salute him not.* He that is sent to raise to life the sinner spiritually dead, must not suffer himself to be called off, or diverted from his enterprise, by the salutations or ceremonies of the world.

Ver. 31. St. Augustine considers a great mystery in this miracle wrought by the prophet Eliseus, thus: By the staff sent by his servant is figured the rod of Moses, or the Old Law, which was not sufficient to bring mankind to life then dead in sin. It was necessary that Christ himself should come, and by taking on human nature, become flesh of our flesh, and restore us to life. In this Eliseus was a figure of Christ, as it was necessary that he should come himself to bring the dead child to life and restore him to his mother, who is here, in a mystical sense, a figure of the Church.

21 And she went up and laid him upon the bed of the man of God, and shut the door. And going out,

22 She called her husband, and said: Send with me, I beseech thee, one of thy servants, and an ass that I may run to the man of God, and come again.

23 And he said to her: Why dost thou go to him? To-day is neither new moon nor sabbath. She answered: I will go.

24 And she saddled an ass, and commanded her servant: Drive, and make haste. Make no stay in going. And do that which I bid thee.

25 So she went forward, and came to the man of God to mount Carmel. And when the man of God saw her coming towards, he said to Giezi his servant: Behold that Sunamitess.

26 Go therefore to meet her, and say to her: Is it well with thee, and with thy husband, and with thy son? And she answered: Well.

27 And when she came to the man of God to the mount, she caught hold on his feet. And Giezi came to remove her. And the man of God said: Let her alone for her soul is in anguish, and the Lord hath hid it from me, and hath not told me.

28 And she said to him: Did I ask a son of my lord? Did I not say to thee: Do not deceive me?

29 Then he said to Giezi: Gird up thy loins, and take my staff in thy hand, and go. If any man meet thee, salute him not: and if any man salute thee, answer him not: and lay my staff upon the face of the child.

30 But the mother of the child said: As the Lord liveth, and as thy soul liveth, I will not leave thee. He arose, therefore, and followed her.

31 But Giezi was gone before them and laid the staff upon the face of the child: and there was no voice nor sense. And he returned to meet him, and told him, saying: The child is not risen.

32 Eliseus therefore went into the house: and behold the child lay dead on his bed.

33 And going in he shut the door upon him, and upon the child, and prayed to the Lord.

34 And he went up, and lay upon the child: and he put his mouth upon his mouth, and his eyes upon his eyes, and his hands upon his hands: and he bowed himself upon him. And the child's flesh grew warm.

35 Then he returned and walked in the house, once to and fro. And he went up, and lay upon him: and the child gaped seven times, and opened his eyes.

36 And he called Giezi, and said to

him: Call this Sunamitess. And she being called, went in to him. And he said: Take up thy son.

37 She came and fell at his feet, and worshipped upon the ground: and took up her son, and went out.

38 And Eliseus returned to Galgal. And there was a famine in the land; and the sons of the prophets dwelt before him. And he said to one of his servants: Set on the great pot, and boil pottage for the sons of the prophets.

39 And one went out into the field to gather wild herbs: and he found something like a wild vine, and gathered of it wild gourds of the field, and filled his mantle. And coming back, he shred them into the pot of pottage, for he knew not what it was.

40 And they poured it out for their companions to eat: and when they had tasted of the pottage, they cried out, saying: Death is in the pot, O man of God. And they could not eat thereof.

41 But he said: Bring some meal. And when they had brought it, he cast it into the pot, and said: Pour out for the people, that they may eat. And there was now no bitterness in the pot.

42 And a certain man came from Baalsalisa bringing to the man of God bread of the firstfruits, twenty loaves of barley, and new corn in his scrip. And he said: Give to the people, that they may eat.

43 And his servant answered him: How much is this, that I should set it before a hundred men? He said again: Give to the people, that they may eat. For thus saith the Lord: They shall eat, and there shall be left.

44 So he set it before them: and they ate. And there was left according to the word of the Lord.

CHAPTER 5

Naaman the Syrian is cleansed of his leprosy. He professeth his belief in one God, promising to serve him. Giezi taketh gifts of Naaman, and is struck with leprosy.

NAAMAN, general of the army of the king of Syria, was a great man with his master, and honourable: for by him the Lord gave deliverance to Syria. And he was a valiant man and rich, but a leper.

2 Now there had gone out robbers from Syria, and had led away captive out of the land of Israel a little maid: and she waited upon Naaman's wife.

3 And she said to her mistress: I wish my master had been with the prophet, that is in Samaria. He would certainly have healed him of the leprosy which he hath.

4 Then Naaman went in to his lord, and told him, saying: Thus and thus said the girl from the land of Israel.

5 And the king of Syria said to him: Go, and I will send a letter to the king of Israel. And he departed, and took with him ten talents of silver, and six thousand pieces of gold, and ten changes of raiment.

6 And brought the letter to the king of Israel, in these words: When thou shalt receive this letter, know that I have sent to thee Naaman my servant, that thou mayest heal him of his leprosy.

7 And when the king of Israel had read the letter, he rent his garments, and said: Am I God, to be able to kill and give life, that this man hath sent to me, to heal a man of his leprosy? Mark, and see how he seeketh occasions against me.

8 And when Eliseus the man of God had heard this, to wit, that the king of Israel had rent his garments, he sent to him, saying: Why hast thou rent thy garments? Let him come to me; and let him know that there is a prophet in Israel.

9 So Naaman came with his horses and chariots, and stood at the door of the house of Eliseus.

10 And Eliseus sent a messenger to him, saying: Go, and wash seven times in the Jordan; and thy flesh shall recover health; and thou shalt be clean.

11 Naaman was angry and went away, saying: I thought he would have come out to me, and standing would have invoked the name of the Lord his God, and touched with his hand the place of the leprosy, and healed me.

12 Are not the Abana, and the Pharphar, rivers of Damascus, better than all the waters of Israel, that I may wash in them, and be made clean? So, as he turned and was going away with indignation,

13 His servants came to him, and said to him: Father, if the prophet had bid thee do some great thing, surely thou shouldst have done it. How much rather what he now hath said to thee: Wash, and thou shalt be clean?

14 [1] Then he went down, and washed in the Jordan seven times: according to the word of the man of God. And his flesh was restored, like the flesh of a little child: and he was made clean.

15 And returning to the man of God with all his train, he came, and stood before him, and said: In truth, I know there is no other God in all the earth,

Chap. 5. [1] Luke, 4, 27.

Ver. 39. *Wild gourds of the field. Colocynthidas.* They are extremely bitter, and therefore are called the *gall of the earth;* and are poisonous if taken in a great quantity.

Chap. 5. Ver. 15. *A blessing.* A present.

but only in Israel. I beseech thee therefore take a blessing of thy servant.

16 But he answered: As the Lord liveth, before whom I stand, I will receive none. And when he pressed him, he still refused.

17 And Naaman said: As thou wilt; but I beseech thee, grant to me thy servant, to take from hence two mules' burden of earth. For thy servant will not henceforth offer holocaust, or victim, to other gods, but to the Lord.

18 But there is only this, for which thou shalt entreat the Lord for thy servant. When my master goeth into the temple of Remmon, to worship, and he leaneth upon my hand: if I bow down in the temple of Remmon, when he boweth down in the same place, that the Lord pardon me thy servant for this thing.

19 And he said to him: Go in peace. So he departed from him in the springtime of the earth.

20 But Giezi the servant of the man of God said: My master hath spared Naaman this Syrian, in not receiving of him that which he brought. As the Lord liveth, I will run after him, and take some thing of him.

21 And Giezi followed after Naaman: and when he saw him running after him, he leapt down from his chariot to meet him, and said: Is all well?

22 And he said: Well: My master hath sent me to thee, saying: Just now there are come to me from mount Ephraim, two young men of the sons of the prophets. Give them a talent of silver, and two changes of garments.

23 And Naaman said: It is better that thou take two talents. And he forced him, and bound two talents of silver in two bags, and two changes of garments, and laid them upon two of his servants; and they carried them before him.

24 And when he was come, and now it was the evening, he took them from their hands, and laid them up in the house, and sent the men away. And they departed.

25 But he went in, and stood before his master. And Eliseus said: Whence comest thou, Giezi? He answered: Thy servant went no whither.

26 But he said: Was not my heart

Ver. 19. *Go in peace.* What the prophet here allowed, was not an outward conformity to an idolatrous worship; but only a service which by his office he owed to his master, who on all public occasions leaned on him: so that his bowing down when his master bowed himself down was not in effect adoring the idols: nor was it so understood by the standers by, since he publicly professed himself a worshipper of the only true and living God, but it was no more than doing a civil office to the king his master, whose leaning upon him obliged him to bow at the same time that he bowed.

present, when the man turned back from his chariot to meet thee? So now thou hast received money, and received garments, to buy oliveyards, and vineyards, and sheep, and oxen, and menservants, and maid-servants.

27 But the leprosy of Naaman shall also stick to thee, and to thy seed for ever. And he went out from him a leper as white as snow.

CHAPTER 6

Eliseus maketh iron to swim upon the water. He leadeth the Syrians that were sent to apprehend him into Samaria, where their eyes being opened, they are courteously entertained. The Syrians besiege Samaria. The famine there causeth a woman to eat her own child. Upon this the king commandeth Eliseus to be put to death.

AND the sons of the prophets said to Eliseus: Behold the place where we dwell with thee is too strait for us.

2 Let us go as far as the Jordan and take out of the wood every man a piece of timber, that we may build us there a place to dwell in. And he said: Go.

3 And one of them said: But come thou also with thy servants. He answered: I will come.

4 So he went with them. And when they were come to the Jordan they cut down wood.

5 And it happened, as one was felling some timber, that the head of the axe fell into the water. And he cried out, and said: Alas, alas, alas, my lord, for this same was borrowed.

6 And the man of God said: Where did it fall? And he shewed him the place. Then he cut off a piece of wood, and cast it in thither: and the iron swam.

7 And he said: Take it up. And he put out his hand and took it.

8 And the king of Syria warred against Israel, and took counsel with his servants, saying: In such and such a place let us lay ambushes.

9 And the man of God sent to the king of Israel, saying: Beware that thou pass not to such a place; for the Syrians are there in ambush.

10 And the king of Israel sent to the place which the man of God had told him, and prevented him, and looked well to himself there, not once nor twice.

11 And the heart of the king of Syria was troubled for this thing. And calling together his servants, he said: Why do you not tell me who it is that betrays me to the king of Israel?

12 And one of his servants said: No one, my lord O king. But Eliseus the

prophet, that is in Israel, telleth the king of Israel all the words, that thou speakest in thy privy chamber.

13 And he said to them: Go, and see where he is, that I may send, and take him. And they told him, saying: Behold he is in Dothan.

14 Therefore he sent thither horses and chariots, and the strength of an army. And they came by night, and beset the city.

15 And the servant of the man of God rising early, went out, and saw an army round about the city, and horses and chariots. And he told him, saying: Alas, alas, alas, my lord, what shall we do?

16 But he answered: Fear not; for there are more with us than with them.

17 And Eliseus prayed, and said: Lord, open his eyes, that he may see. And the Lord opened the eyes of the servant, and he saw. And behold the mountain *was* full of horses, and chariots of fire round about Eliseus.

18 And the enemies came down to him, but Eliseus prayed to the Lord, saying: Strike, I beseech thee, this people with blindness. And the Lord struck them with blindness, according to the word of Eliseus.

19 And Eliseus said to them: This is not the way, neither is this the city. Follow me; and I will shew you the man whom you seek. So he led them into Samaria.

20 And when they were come into Samaria, Eliseus said: Lord, open the eyes of these men, that they may see. And the Lord opened their eyes: and they saw themselves to be in the midst of Samaria.

21 And the king of Israel said to Eliseus, when he saw them: My father, shall I kill them?

22 And he said: Thou shalt not kill them; for thou didst not take them with thy sword, or thy bow, that thou mayest kill them. But set bread and water before them, that they may eat and drink, and go to their master.

23 And a great provision of meats was set before them, and they ate and drank. And he let them go: and they went away to their master. And the robbers of Syria came no more into the land of Israel.

24 And it came to pass after these things, that Benadad king of Syria gathered together all his army, and went up, and besieged Samaria.

25 And there was a great famine in Samaria: and so long did the siege continue, till the head of an ass was sold for fourscore pieces of silver, and the fourth part of a cabe of pigeons' dung, for five pieces of silver.

26 And as the king of Israel was passing by the wall, a certain woman cried out to him, saying: Save me, my lord O king.

27 And he said: If the Lord doth not save thee, how can I save thee? Out of the barnfloor, or out of the winepress? And the king said to her: What aileth thee? And she answered:

28 This woman said to me: Give thy son, that we may eat him to-day, and we will eat my son to-morrow.

29 So we boiled my son, and ate him. And I said to her on the next day: Give thy son that we may eat him. And she hath hid her son.

30 When the king heard this, he rent his garments, and passed by upon the wall. And all the people saw the haircloth which he wore within next to his flesh.

31 And the king said: May God do so and so to me, and may he add more, if the head of Eliseus the son of Saphat shall stand on him this day.

32 But Eliseus sat in his house, and the ancients sat with him. So he sent a man before. And before that messenger came, he said to the ancients: Do you know that this son of a murderer hath sent to cut off my head? Look then, when the messenger shall come, shut the door, and suffer him not to come in: for behold the sound of his master's feet is behind him.

33 While he was yet speaking to them, the messenger appeared who was coming to him. And he said: Behold, so great an evil is from the Lord. What shall I look for more from the Lord?

CHAPTER 7

Eliseus prophesieth a great plenty, which presently ensueth upon the sudden flight of the Syrians; of which four lepers bring the news to the city. The incredulous nobleman is trod to death.

AND Eliseus said: Hear ye the word of the Lord: Thus saith the Lord: To-morrow about this time a bushel of fine flour shall be sold for a stater, and two bushels of barley for a stater, in the gate of Samaria.

2 Then one of the lords, upon whose hand the king leaned, answering the man of God, said: If the Lord should make flood-gates in heaven, can that

CHAP. 6. Ver. 18. *Blindness.* The blindness here spoken of was of a particular kind, which hindered them from seeing the objects that were really before them; and represented other different objects to their imagination: so that they no longer perceived the city of Dothan, nor were able to know the person of Eliseus; but were easily led by him, whom they took to be another man, to Samaria. So that he truly told them: *this is not the way, neither is this the city,* because he spoke with relation to the *way* and to *the city,* which was represented to them.

CHAP. 7. Ver. 1. *A stater.* It is the same as a sicle or shekel.

possibly be which thou sayest? And he said: Thou shalt see it with thy eyes, but shalt not eat thereof.

3 Now there were four lepers, at the entering in of the gate. And they said one to another: What mean we to stay here till we die?

4 If we will enter into the city, we shall die with the famine: and if we will remain here, we must also die. Come, therefore, and let us run over to the camp of the Syrians. If they spare us, we shall live: but if they kill us, we shall but die.

5 So they arose in the evening, to go to the Syrian camp. And when they were come to the first part of the camp of the Syrians, they found no man there.

6 For the Lord had made them hear, in the camp of Syria the noise of chariots, and of horses, and of a very great army. And they said one to another: Behold the king of Israel hath hired against us the kings of the Bethites, and of the Egyptians; and they are come upon us.

7 Wherefore they arose, and fled away in the dark, and left their tents, and their horses and asses in the camp, and fled, desiring to save their lives.

8 So when these lepers were come to the beginning of the camp, they went into one tent, and ate and drank. And they took from thence silver, and gold, and raiment, and went, and hid it: and they came again, and went into another tent, and carried from thence in like manner. and hid it.

9 Then they said one to another: We do not well; for this is a day of good tidings. If we hold our peace, and do not tell it till the morning, we shall be charged with a crime. Come, let us go and tell it in the king's court.

10 So they came to the gate of the city, and told them, saying: We went to the camp of the Syrians, and we found no man there, but horses, and asses, tied, and the tents standing.

11 Then the guards of the gate went, and told it within the king's palace.

12 And he arose in the night and said to his servants: I tell you what the Syrians have done to us. They know that we suffer great famine, and therefore they are gone out of the camp, and lie hid in the fields, saying: When they come out of the city we shall take them alive, and then we may get into the city.

13 And one of his servants answered: Let us take the five horses that are remaining in the city (because there are no more in the whole multitude of Israel, for the rest are consumed), and let us send and see.

14 They brought therefore two horses; and the king sent into the camp of the Syrians, saying: Go, and see.

15 And they went after them as far as the Jordan. And behold all the way was full of garments, and vessels, which the Syrians had cast away in their fright. And the messengers returned and told the king.

16 And the people going out pillaged the camp of the Syrians: and a bushel of fine flour was sold for a stater, and two bushels of barley for a stater, according to the word of the Lord.

17 And the king appointed that lord on whose hand he leaned, to stand at the gate. And the people trod upon him in the entrance of the gate; and he died, as the man of God had said, when the king came down to him.

18 And it came to pass according to the word of the man of God, which he spoke to the king, when he said: Two bushels of barley shall be for a stater, and a bushel of fine flour for a stater, at this very time to-morrow ¹n the gate of Samaria.

19 When that lord answered the man of God, and said: Although the Lord should make flood-gates in heaven, could this come to pass which thou sayest? And he said to him: Thou shalt see with thy eyes, and shalt not eat thereof.

20 And so it fell out to him as it was foretold: and the people trod upon him in the gate, and he died.

CHAPTER 8

After seven years' famine foretold by Eliseus, the Sunamitess returning home, recovereth her lands, and revenues. Eliseus foresheweth the death of Benadad, king of Syria, and the reign of Hazael. Joram's wicked reign in Juda. He dieth, and his son Ochozias succeedeth.

AND Eliseus spoke to the woman, ¹ whose son he had restored to life, saying: Arise, and go thou and thy household, and sojourn wheresoever thou canst find. For the Lord hath called a famine, and it shall come upon the land seven years.

2 And she arose, and did according to the word of the man of God. And going with her household, she sojourned in the land of the Philistines many days.

3 And when the seven years were ended, the woman returned out of the land of the Philistines: and she went forth to speak to the king for her house, and for her lands.

4 And the king talked with Giezi, the servant of the man of God, saying: Tell me all the great things that Eliseus hath done.

5 And when he was telling the king

how he had raised one dead to life, the woman appeared, whose son he had restored to life, crying to the king for her house, and her lands. And Giezi said: My lord O king, this is the woman, and this is her son, whom Eliseus raised to life.

6 And the king asked the woman: and she told him. And the king appointed her an eunuch, saying: Restore her all that is hers, and all the revenues of the lands, from the day that she left the land, to this present.

7 Eliseus also came to Damascus; and Benadad king of Syria was sick. And they told him, saying: The man of God is come hither.

8 And the king said to Hazael: Take with thee presents, and go to meet the man of God, and consult the Lord by him, saying: Can I recover of this my illness?

9 And Hazael went to meet him, taking with him presents, and all the good things of Damascus, the burdens of forty camels. And when he stood before him, he said: Thy son Benadad the king of Syria hath sent me to thee, saying: Can I recover of this my illness?

10 And Eliseus said to him: Go tell him: Thou shalt recover. But the Lord hath shewn me that he shall surely die.

11 And he stood with him, and was troubled so far as to blush: and the man of God wept.

12 And Hazael said to him: Why doth my lord weep? And he said: Because I know the evil that thou wilt do to the children of Israel. [2] Their strong cities thou wilt burn with fire, and their young men thou wilt kill with the sword: and thou wilt dash their children, and rip up their pregnant women.

13 And Hazael said: But what am I thy servant a dog, that I should do this great thing? And Eliseus said: The Lord hath shewn me that thou shalt be king of Syria.

14 And when he was departed from Eliseus, he came to his master, who said to him: What saith Eliseus to thee? And he answered: He told me: Thou shalt recover.

15 And on the next day he took a blanket, and poured water on it, and spread it upon his face. And he died: and Hazael reigned in his stead.

16 In the fifth year of Joram son of Achab king of Israel, and of Josaphat king of Juda, reigned Joram son of Josaphat king of Juda.

17 [3] He was two and thirty years old when he began to reign: and he reigned eight years in Jerusalem.

18 And he walked in the ways of the kings of Israel, as the house of Achab had walked (for the daughter of Achab was his wife): and he did that which was evil in the sight of the Lord.

19 [4] But the Lord would not destroy Juda, for David his servant's sake: as he had promised him, to give him a light, and to his children always.

20 [5] In his days Edom revolted, from being under Juda, and made themselves a king.

21 And Joram came to Seira, and all the chariots with him. And he arose in the night, and defeated the Edomites that had surrounded him, and the captains of the chariots: but the people fled into their tents.

22 So Edom revolted from being under Juda, unto this day. Then Lobna also revolted at the same time.

23 But the rest of the acts of Joram, and all that he did, are they not written in the book of the words of the days of the kings of Juda?

24 And Joram slept with his fathers, and was buried with them in the city of David: and Ochozias his son reigned in his stead.

25 [6] In the twelfth year of Joram son of Achab king of Israel, reigned Ochozias son of Joram king of Juda.

26 Ochozias was two and twenty years old when he began to reign: and he reigned one year in Jerusalem. The name of his mother was Athalia the daughter of Amri king of Israel.

27 And he walked in the ways of the house of Achab: and he did evil before the Lord, as did the house of Achab; for he was the son-in-law of the house of Achab.

28 He went also with Joram son of Achab, to fight against Hazael king of Syria in Ramoth Galaad: and the Syrians wounded Joram.

29 And he went back to be healed, in Jezrahel: because the Syrians had wounded him in Ramoth when he fought against Hazael king of Syria. And Ochozias the son of Joram king of Juda, went down to visit Joram the son of Achab in Jezrahel: because he was sick there.

[2] 4 Kings, 13, 7. [3] 2 Par. 21, 5. [4] 2 Kings, 7, 16. [5] Gen. 27, 40; 2 Par. 21, 8. [6] 2 Par. 22, 1.

CHAP. 8. Ver. 10. *Tell him: Thou shalt recover.* By these words the prophet signified that the king's disease was not mortal: and that he would recover if no violence were used. Or he might only express himself in this manner, by way of giving Hazael to understand that he knew both what he would say and do; that he would indeed tell the king he should recover; but would be himself the instrument of his death.

Ver. 16. *Josaphat.* That is, Josaphat being yet alive, who some time before his death made his son Joram king, as David had done before by his son Solomon.

Ver. 26. *Daughter.* That is, granddaughter; for she was daughter of Achab son of Amri (ver. 18).

CHAPTER 9

Jehu is anointed king of Israel, to destroy the house of Achab and Jezabel. He killeth Joram king of Israel, and Ochozias king of Juda, Jezabel is eaten by dogs.

AND Eliseus the prophet called one of the sons of the prophets and said to him: Gird up thy loins, and take this little bottle of oil in thy hand, and go to Ramoth Galaad.

2 ¹ And when thou art come thither, thou shalt see Jehu the son of Josaphat the son of Namsi. And going in thou shalt make him rise up from amongst his brethren, and carry him into an inner chamber.

3 Then taking the little bottle of oil, thou shalt pour it on his head, and shalt say: Thus saith the Lord: I have anointed thee king over Israel. And thou shalt open the door and flee, and shalt not stay there.

4 So the young man, the servant of the prophet, went away to Ramoth Galaad,

5 And went in thither. And behold the captains of the army were sitting; and he said: I have a word to thee, O prince. And Jehu said: Unto whom of us all? And he said: To thee, O prince.

6 And he arose, and went into the chamber. And he poured the oil upon his head, and said: Thus saith the Lord God of Israel: I have anointed thee king over Israel, the people of the Lord.

7 And thou shalt cut off the house of Achab thy master: and I will revenge the blood of my servants the prophets, and the blood of all the servants of the Lord at the hand of Jezabel,

8 ² And I will destroy all the house of Achab, and I will cut off from Achab him that pisseth against the wall, and him that is shut up, and the meanest in Israel.

9 And I will make the house of Achab like ³ the house of Jeroboam the son of Nabat, and like the house of ⁴ Baasa the son of Ahias.

10 And the dogs shall eat Jezabel in the field of Jezrahel: and there shall be no one to bury her. And he opened the door and fled.

11 Then Jehu went forth to the servants of his lord. And they said to him: Are all things well? Why came this mad man to thee? And he said to them: You know the man, and what he said.

12 But they answered: It is false; but rather do thou tell us. And he said to them: Thus and thus did he speak to me. And he said: Thus saith the Lord: I have anointed thee king over Israel.

13 Then they made haste and taking

Chap. 9. ¹ 3 Kings, 19, 16. ² 3 Kings, 21, 21. ³ 3 Kings, 15, 29. ⁴ 3 Kings, 16, 3. ⁵ 4 Kings, 8, 28.

every man his garment laid it under his feet, after the manner of a judgment seat. And they sounded the trumpet, and said: Jehu is king.

14 So Jehu the son of Josaphat the son of Namsi conspired against Joram. ⁵ Now Joram had besieged Ramoth Galaad, he and all Israel, fighting with Hazael king of Syria:

15 And was returned to be healed in Jezrahel of his wounds, for the Syrians had wounded him, when he fought with Hazael king of Syria. And Jehu said: If it please you, let no man go forth or flee out of the city, lest he go, and tell in Jezrahel.

16 And he got up, and went into Jezrahel: for Joram was sick there, and Ochozias king of Juda was come down to visit Joram.

17 The watchmen therefore, that stood upon the tower of Jezrahel, saw the troop of Jehu coming, and said: I see a troop. And Joram said: Take a chariot, and send to meet them, and let him that goeth say: Is all well?

18 So there went one in a chariot to meet him, and said: Thus saith the king: Are all things peaceable? And Jehu said: What hast thou to do with peace? Go behind and follow me. And the watchman told, saying: The messenger came to them; but he returneth not.

19 And he sent a second chariot of horses. And he came to them, and said: Thus saith the king: Is there peace? And Jehu said: What hast thou to do with peace? Pass, and follow me.

20 And the watchman told, saying: He came even to them, but returneth not. And the driving is like the driving of Jehu the son of Namsi, for he drives furiously.

21 And Joram said: Make ready the chariot. And they made ready his chariot. And Joram king of Israel, and Ochozias king of Juda went out, each in his own chariot. And they went out to meet Jehu: and met him in the field of Naboth the Jezrahelite.

22 And when Joram saw Jehu, he said: Is there peace, Jehu? And, he answered: What peace? So long as the fornications of Jezabel thy mother, and her many sorceries are in their vigour.

23 And Joram turned his hand, and fleeing said to Ochozias: There is treachery, Ochozias.

24 But Jehu bent his bow with his hand, and shot Joram between the shoulders. And the arrow went out through his heart: and immediately he fell in his chariot.

25 And Jehu said to Badacer his captain: Take him, and cast him into the

field of Naboth the Jezrahelite. For I remember when I and thou sitting in a chariot followed Achab this man's father, that the Lord laid this burden upon him, saying:

26 ⁶ If I do not requite thee in this field, saith the Lord, for the blood of Naboth, and for the blood of his children, which I saw yesterday, saith the Lord. So now take him, and cast him into the field, according to the word of the Lord.

27 But Ochozias king of Juda seeing this, fled by the way of the garden house. And Jehu pursued him, and said: Strike him also in his chariot. And they struck him in the going up to Gaver, which is by Jeblaam. And he fled into Mageddo, and died there.

28 And his servants laid him upon his chariot, and carried him to Jerusalem: and they buried him in his sepulchre with his fathers in the city of David.

29 In the eleventh year of Joram the son of Achab, Ochozias reigned over Juda.

30 And Jehu came into Jezrahel; but Jezabel hearing of his coming in, painted her face with stibic stone, and adorned her head, and looked out of a window

31 At Jehu coming in at the gate, and said: ⁷ Can there be peace for Zambri, that hath killed his master?

32 And Jehu lifted up his face to the window, and said: Who is this? And two or three eunuchs bowed down to him.

33 And he said to them: Throw her down headlong. And they threw her down. And the wall was sprinkled with her blood: and the hoofs of the horses trod upon her.

34 And when he was come in, to eat, and to drink, he said: Go, and see after that cursed woman, and bury her; because she is a king's daughter.

35 And when they went to bury her, they found nothing but the skull, and the feet, and the extremities of her hands.

36 And coming back they told him. And Jehu said: ⁸ It is the word of the Lord, which he spoke by his servant Elias the Thesbite, saying: In the field of Jezrahel the dogs shall eat the flesh of Jezabel;

37 And the flesh of Jezabel shall be as dung upon the face of the earth in the field of Jezrahel, so that they who pass by shall say: Is this that same Jezabel?

CHAPTER 10

Jehu destroyeth the house of Achab. He abolisheth the worship of Baal, and killeth the worshippers: but sticketh to the calves of Jeroboam. Israel is afflicteth by the Syrians.

AND Achab had seventy sons in Samaria. So Jehu wrote letters, and sent to Samaria, to the chief men of the city, and to the ancients, and to them that brought up Achab's children, saying:

2 As soon as you receive these letters, ye that have your master's sons, and chariots, and horses, and fenced cities, and armour,

3 Choose the best, and him that shall please you most of your master's sons: and set him on his father's throne, and fight for the house of your master.

4 But they were exceedingly afraid, and said: Behold two kings could not stand before him, and how shall we be able to resist?

5 Therefore the overseers of the house, and the rulers of the city, and the ancients, and the tutors sent to Jehu, saying: We are thy servants: whatsoever thou shalt command us we will do; neither will we make us a king. Do thou all that pleaseth thee.

6 And he wrote letters the second time to them, saying: If you be mine, and will obey me, take the heads of the sons of your master, and come to me to Jezrahel by to-morrow this time. Now the king's sons, being seventy men, were brought up with the chief men of the city.

7 And when the letters came to them, they took the king's sons, and slew seventy persons, and put their heads in baskets, and sent them to him to Jezrahel.

8 And a messenger came, and told him, saying: They have brought the heads of the king's sons. And he said: Lay ye them in two heaps by the entering in of the gate until the morning.

9 And when it was light, he went out, and standing said to all the people: You are just. If I conspired against my master, and slew him, who hath slain all these?

10 ¹ See therefore now that there hath not fallen to the ground any of the words of the Lord, which the Lord spoke concerning the house of Achab: and the Lord hath done that which he spoke in the hand of his servant Elias.

11 So Jehu slew all that were left of the house of Achab in Jezrahel, and all his chief men, and his friends, and his priests, till there were no remains left of him.

12 And he arose, and went to Samaria. And when he was come to the shepherds' cabin in the way,

13 He met with the brethren of Ochozias king of Juda, and he said to them: Who are you? And they answered: We are the brethren of Ochozias, and are

⁶ 3 Kings, 21, 22.　⁷ 3 Kings, 15, 10.　⁸ 3 Kings, 21, 23.　CHAP. 10.　¹ 3 Kings, 21, 29.

come down to salute the sons of the
king, and the sons of the queen.

14 And he said: Take them alive.
And they took them alive, and killed
them at the pit by the cabin, two and
forty men: and he left not any of them.

15 And when he was departed thence,
he found Jonadab the son of Rechab
coming to meet him, and he blessed him.
And he said to him: Is thy heart right
as my heart is with thy heart? And
Jonadab said: It is. If it be, said he,
give me thy hand. He gave him his
hand. And he lifted him up to him into
the chariot,

16 And he said to him: Come with
me, and see my zeal for the Lord. So he
made him ride in his chariot,

17 And brought him into Samaria.
And he slew all that were left of Achab
in Samaria, to a man, according to the
word of the Lord, which he spoke by
Elias.

18 And Jehu gathered together all
the people, and said to them: ² Achab
worshipped Baal a little; but I will worship him more.

19 Now therefore call to me all the
prophets of Baal, and all his servants,
and all his priests. Let none be wanting,
for I have a great sacrifice to offer to
Baal. Whosoever shall be wanting shall
not live. Now Jehu did this craftily,
that he might destroy the worshippers
of Baal.

20 And he said: Proclaim a festival
for Baal. And he called,

21 And he sent into all the borders
of Israel: and all the servants of Baal
came. There was not one left that did
not come. And they went into the temple of Baal: and the house of Baal was
filled, from one end to the other.

22 And he said to them that were
over the wardrobe: Bring forth garments for all the servants of Baal. And
they brought them forth garments.

23 And Jehu and Jonadab the son of
Rechab went to the temple of Baal, and
said to the worshippers of Baal: Search,
and see that there be not any with you
of the servants of the Lord, but that
there be the servants of Baal only.

24 And they went in to offer sacrifices and burnt offerings. But Jehu
had prepared him fourscore men without, and said to them: If any of the
men escape, whom I have brought into
your hands, he that letteth go shall
answer life for life.

25 And it came to pass, when the

² 3 Kings, 16, 31. ³ 4 Kings, 15, 12. CHAP. 11.
¹ 2 Par. 22, 10.

CHAP. 10. Ver. 18. I will worship him more.
Jehu sinned in thus pretending to worship Baal,
and causing sacrifice to be offered to him: because evil is not to be done, that good may come
of it (Rom. 3, 8).

burnt offering was ended, that Jehu
commanded his soldiers and captains,
saying: Go in, and kill them. Let none
escape. And the soldiers and captains
slew them with the edge of the sword,
and cast them out. And they went into
the city of the temple of Baal,

26 And brought the statue out of
Baal's temple, and burnt it,

27 And broke it in pieces. They destroyed also the temple of Baal, and
made a jakes in its place unto this day.

28 So Jehu destroyed Baal out of
Israel.

29 But yet he departed not from the
sins of Jeroboam the son of Nabat, who
made Israel to sin: nor did he forsake
the golden calves that were in Bethel
and Dan.

30 And the Lord said to Jehu: Because thou hast diligently executed that
which was right and pleasing in my
eyes, and hast done to the house of
Achab according to all that was in my
heart, ³ thy children shall sit upon the
throne of Israel to the fourth generation.

31 But Jehu took no heed to walk
in the law of the Lord the God of Israel
with all his heart: for he departed not
from the sins of Jeroboam, who had
made Israel to sin.

32 In those days the Lord began to
be weary of Israel: and Hazael ravaged
them in all the coasts of Israel.

33 From the Jordan eastward, all the
land of Galaad, and Gad, and Ruben,
and Manasses, from Aroer, which is
upon the torrent Arnon, and Galaad,
and Basan.

34 But the rest of the acts of Jehu,
and all that he did, and his strength,
are they not written in the book of the
words of the days of the kings of Israel?

35 And Jehu slept with his fathers,
and they buried him in Samaria: and
Joachaz his son reigned in his stead.

36 And the time that Jehu reigned
over Israel, in Samaria, was eight and
twenty years.

CHAPTER 11

*Athalia's usurpation and tyranny. Joas is
made king. Athalia is slain.*

AND ¹ Athalia the mother of
Ochozias, seeing that her son
was dead, arose, and slew all the royal
seed.

2 But Josaba the daughter of king
Joram, sister of Ochozias, took Joas the
son of Ochozias: and stole him from
among the king's sons that were slain,
out of the bedchamber with his nurse:
and hid him from the face of Athalia,
so that he was not slain.

3 And he was with her six years, hid

in the house of the Lord, And Athalia reigned over the land.

4 ² And in the seventh year Joiada sent, and taking the centurions and the soldiers, brought them in to him into the temple of the Lord, and made a covenant with them. And taking an oath of them in the house of the Lord, he shewed them the king's son.

5 And he commanded them, saying: This is the thing that you must do.

6 Let a third part of you go in on the sabbath, and keep the watch of the king's house. And let a third part be at the gate of Sur. And let a third part be at the gate behind the dwelling of the shieldbearers. And you all shall keep the watch of the house of Messa.

7 But let two parts of you, all that go forth on the sabbath, keep the watch of the house of the Lord about the king.

8 And you shall compass him round about, having weapons in your hands. And if any man shall enter the precinct of the temple, let him be slain: and you shall be with the king, coming in and going out.

9 And the centurions did according to all things that Joiada the priest had commanded them: and taking every one their men, that went in on the sabbath, with them that went out on the sabbath, came to Joiada the priest.

10 And he gave them the spears, and the arms of king David, which were in the house of the Lord.

11 And they stood, having every one their weapons in their hands, from the right side of the temple, unto the left side of the altar, and of the temple, about the king.

12 And he brought forth the king's son, and put the diadem upon him, and the testimony. And they made him king, and anointed him. And clapping their hands, they said: God save the king.

13 And Athalia heard the noise of the people running. And going in to the people into the temple of the Lord,

14 She saw the king standing upon a tribunal, as the manner was, and the singers, and the trumpets near him, and all the people of the land rejoicing, and sounding the trumpets. And she rent her garments, and cried: A conspiracy, a conspiracy!

15 But Joiada commanded the centurions that were over the army, and said to them: Have her forth without the precinct of the temple; and whosoever shall follow her, let him be slain with the sword. For the priest had said: Let her not be slain in the temple of the Lord.

16 And they laid hands on her: and

thrust her out by the way by which the horses go in, by the palace. And she was slain there.

17 And Joiada made a covenant between the Lord, and the king, and the people, that they should be the people of the Lord, and between the king and the people.

18 And all the people of the land went into the temple of Baal, and broke down his altars: and his images they broke in pieces thoroughly. They slew also Mathan the priest of Baal before the altar. And the priest set guards in the house of the Lord.

19 And he took the centurions, and the bands of the Cerethi and the Phelethi, and all the people of the land: and they brought the king from the house of the Lord. And they came by the way of the gate of the shieldbearers into the palace: and he sat on the throne of the kings.

20 And all the people of the land rejoiced, and the city was quiet: but Athalia was slain with the sword in king's house.

21 Now Joas was seven years old, when he began to reign.

CHAPTER 12

The temple is repaired. Hazael is bought off from attacking Jerusalem. Joas is slain.

IN the seventh year of Jehu, Joas began to reign: and he reigned forty years in Jerusalem. The name of his mother was Sebia of Bersabee.

2 And Joas did that which was right before the Lord all the days that Joiada the priest taught him.

3 But yet he took not away the high places: for the people still sacrificed and burnt incense in the high places.

4 And Joas said to the priests: All the money of the sanctified things, which is brought into the temple of the Lord by those that pass, which is offered for the price of a soul, and which of their own accord, and of their own free heart they bring into the temple of the Lord:

5 Let the priests take it according to their order, and repair the house wheresoever they shall see any thing that wanteth repairing.

6 Now till the three and twentieth year of king Joas, the priests did not make the repairs of the temple.

7 And king Joas called Joiada the

² 2 Par. 23, 1.

CHAP. 11. Ver. 12. *The testimony.* The book of the law.
Ver. 14. *A tribunal.* A tribune, or a place elevated above the rest.
CHAP. 12. Ver. 4. *Sanctified.* That is, dedicated to God's service.—*The price of a soul.* That is, the ordinary oblation, which every soul was to offer by the law (Exod. 30).

high priest and the priests, saying to them: Why do you not repair the temple? Take you therefore money no more according to your order; but restore it for the repairing of the temple.

8 And the priests were forbidden to take any more money of the people, and to make the repairs of the house.

9 And Joiada the high priest took a chest and bored a hole in the top, and set it by the altar at the right hand of them that came into the house of the Lord: and the priests that kept the doors put therein all the money that was brought to the temple of the Lord.

10 And when they saw that there was very much money in the chest, the king's scribe and the high priest came up, and poured it out, and counted the money that was found in the house of the Lord.

11 And they gave it out by number and measure into the hands of them that were over the builders of the house of the Lord. And they laid it out to the carpenters and the masons that wrought in the house of the Lord.

12 And made the repairs: and to them that cut stones, and to buy timber, and stones, to be hewed, that the repairs of the house of the Lord might be completely finished, and wheresoever there was need of expenses to uphold the house.

13 But there were not made of the same money for the temple of the Lord, bowls, or fleshhooks, or censers, or trumpets, or any vessel of gold and silver, of the money that was brought into the temple of the Lord.

14 For it was given to them that did the work, that the temple of the Lord might be repaired.

15 And they reckoned not with the men that received the money to distribute it to the workmen: but they bestowed it faithfully.

16 But the money for trespass, and the money for sins, they brought not into the temple of the Lord, because it was for the priests.

17 [1] Then Hazael king of Syria went up and fought against Geth, and took it and set his face to go up to Jerusalem.

18 Wherefore Joas king of Juda took all the sanctified things, which Josaphat, and Joram, and Ochozias, his fathers the kings of Juda had dedicated to holy uses, and which he himself had offered: and all the silver that could be found in the treasures of the temple of the Lord, and in the king's

CHAP. 12. [1] 2 Par. 24, 23.

Ver. 21. *The city of David.* He was buried in the same city with his fathers, but not in the sepulchres of the kings (2 Par. 14).

CHAP. 13. Ver. 6. *A grove.* A place dedicated to the worship of idols.

palace: and sent it to Hazael king of Syria. And he went off from Jerusalem.

19 And the rest of the acts of Joas, and all that he did, are they not written in the book of the words of the days of the kings of Juda?

20 And his servants arose, and conspired among themselves, and slew Joas, in the house of Mello in the descent of Sella.

21 For Josachar the son of Semaath, and Jozabad the son of Somer his servant struck him; and he died. And they buried him with his fathers in the city of David: and Amasias his son reigned in his stead.

CHAPTER 13

The reign of Joachaz and of Joas kings of Israel. The last acts and death of Eliseus the prophet. A dead man is raised to life by the touch of his bones.

IN the three and twentieth year of Joas son of Ochozias king of Juda, Joachaz the son of Jehu reigned over Israel in Samaria, seventeen years.

2 And he did evil before the Lord, and followed the sins of Jeroboam the son of Nabat, who made Israel to sin: and he departed not from them.

3 And the wrath of the Lord was kindled against Israel, and he delivered them into the hand of Hazael the king of Syria, and into the hand of Benadad the son of Hazael, all days.

4 But Joachaz besought the face of the Lord; and the Lord heard him, for he saw the distress of Israel, because the king of Syria had oppressed them.

5 And the Lord gave Israel a saviour: and they were delivered out of the hand of the king of Syria. And the children of Israel dwelt in their pavilions as yesterday and the day before.

6 But yet they departed not from the sins of Jeroboam, who made Israel to sin; but walked in them. And there still remained a grove also in Samaria.

7 And Joachaz had no more left of the people than fifty horsemen, and ten chariots, and ten thousand footmen: for the king of Syria had slain them, and had brought them low as dust by thrashing in the barnfloor.

8 But the rest of the acts of Joachaz, and all that he did, and his valour, are they not written in the book of the words of the days of the kings of Israel?

9 And Joachaz slept with his fathers, and they buried him in Samaria: and Joas his son reigned in his stead.

10 In the seven and thirtieth year of Joas king of Juda, Joas the son of Joachaz reigned over Israel in Samaria sixteen years.

11 And he did that which is evil in the sight of the Lord. He departed not

from all the sins of Jeroboam the son of Nabat, who made Israel to sin; but he walked in them.

12 But the rest of the acts of Joas, and all that he did, and his valour wherewith he fought against Amasias king of Juda, are they not written in the book of the words of the days of the kings of Israel?

13 And Joas slept with his fathers: and Jeroboam sat upon his throne. But Joas was buried in Samaria with the kings of Israel.

14 Now Eliseus was sick of the illness whereof he died. And Joas king of Israel went down to him, and wept before him, and said: O my father, my father, the chariot of Israel and the guider thereof.

15 And Eliseus said to him: Bring a bow and arrows. And when he had brought him a bow, and arrows,

16 He said to the king of Israel: Put thy hand upon the bow. And when he had put his hand, Eliseus put his hands over the king's hands,

17 And said: Open the window to the east. And when he had opened it, Eliseus said: Shoot an arrow. And he shot. And Eliseus said: The arrow of the Lord's deliverance, and the arrow of the deliverance from Syria. And thou shalt strike the Syrians in Aphec, till thou consume them.

18 And he said: Take the arrows. And when he had taken them, he said to him: Strike with an arrow upon the ground. And he struck three times and stood still.

19 And the man of God was angry with him, and said: If thou hadst smitten five or six or seven times, thou hadst smitten Syria even to utter destruction; but now three times shalt thou smite it.

20 And Eliseus died, and they buried him. And the rovers from Moab came into the land the same year.

21 ¹ And some that were burying a man, saw the rovers, and cast the body into the sepulchre of Eliseus. And when it had touched the bones of Eliseus, the man came to life, and stood upon his feet.

22 Now Hazael king of Syria afflicted Israel all the days of Joachaz.

23 And the Lord had mercy on them, and returned to them because of his covenant, which he had made with Abraham and Isaac and Jacob. And he would not destroy them, nor utterly cast them away, unto this present time.

24 And Hazael king of Syria died, and Benadad his son reigned in his stead.

25 Now Joas the son of Joachaz, took the cities out of the hand of Benadad,

the son of Hazael, which he had taken out of the hand of Joachaz his father by war. Three times did Joas beat him; and he restored the cities to Israel.

CHAPTER 14

Amasias reigneth in Juda. He overcometh the Edomites. Is overcome by Joas king of Israel. Jeroboam the second reigneth in Israel.

IN the second year of Joas son of Joachaz, king of Israel, reigned Amasias son of Joas king of Juda.

2 ¹ He was five and twenty years old when he began to reign: and nine and twenty years he reigned in Jerusalem. The name of his mother was Joadan of Jerusalem.

3 And he did that which was right before the Lord, but yet not like David his father. He did according to all things that Joas his father did.

4 But this only, that he took not away the high places: for yet the people sacrificed and burnt incense in the high places.

5 And when he had possession of the kingdom, he put his servants to death that had slain the king his father.

6 But the children of the murderers he did not put to death, according to that which is written in the book of the law of Moses, wherein the Lord commanded, saying: ² The fathers shall not be put to death for the children, neither shall the children be put to death for the fathers: but every man shall die for his own sins.

7 He slew of Edom in the valley of the Saltpits ten thousand men, and took the rock by war, and called the name thereof Jectehel, unto this day.

8 Then Amasias sent messengers to Joas son of Joachaz, son of Jehu king of Israel, saying: Come let us see one another.

9 And Joas king of Israel sent again to Amasias king of Juda, saying: A thistle of Libanus sent to a cedar tree, which is in Libanus, saying: Give thy daughter to my son to wife. And the beasts of the forest, that are in Libanus, passed and trod down the thistle.

10 Thou hast beaten and prevailed over Edom, and thy heart hath lifted thee up: be content with the glory, and sit at home. Why provokest thou evil,

CHAP. 13. ¹ Ecclus. 48, 14. CHAP. 14. ¹ 2 Par. 25, 1. ² Deut. 24, 16; Ezech. 18, 20.

Ver. 19. *If thou hadst smitten five or six or seven times.* By this it appears that God had revealed to the prophet that the king should overcome the Syrians as many times as he should then strike on the ground; but as he had not at the same time revealed to him how often the king would strike, the prophet was concerned to see that he struck but thrice.

CHAP. 14. Ver. 8. *Let us see one another.* This was a challenge to fight.

that thou shouldst fall, and Juda with thee?

11 But Amasias did not rest satisfied. So Joas king of Israel went up; and he and Amasias king of Juda saw one another in Bethsames a town in Juda.

12 And Juda was put to the worst before Israel: and they fled every man to their dwellings.

13 But Joas king of Israel took Amasias, king of Juda, the son of Joas, the son of Ochozias, in Bethsames; and brought him into Jerusalem. And he broke down the wall of Jerusalem, from the gate of Ephraim to the gate of the corner, four hundred cubits.

14 And he took all the gold, and silver, and all the vessels, that were found in the house of the Lord, and in the king's treasures, and hostages: and returned to Samaria.

15 But the rest of the acts of Joas, which he did, and his valour, wherewith he fought against Amasias king of Juda, are they not written in the book of the words of the days of the kings of Israel?

16 And Joas slept with his fathers, and was buried in Samaria, with the kings of Israel. And Jeroboam his son reigned in his stead.

17 And Amasias the son of Joas king of Juda lived, after the death of Joas son of Joachaz king of Israel fifteen years.

18 And the rest of the acts of Amasias, are they not written in the book of the words of the days of the kings of Juda?

19 Now they made a conspiracy against him in Jerusalem: and he fled to Lachis. And they sent after him to Lachis; and killed him there.

20 And they brought him away upon horses: and he was buried in Jerusalem with his fathers in the city of David.

21 ³ And all the people of Juda took Azarias, who was sixteen years old, and made him king instead of his father Amasias.

22 He built Elath, and restored it to Juda, after that the king slept with his fathers.

23 In the fifteenth year of Amasias son of Joas king of Juda, reigned Jeroboam the son of Joas king of Israel in Samaria, one and forty years.

24 And he did that which was evil before the Lord. He departed not from all the sins of Jeroboam the son of Nabat, who made Israel to sin.

³ 2 Par. 26, 1.   ⁴ Num. 13, 21.   ⁵ Jonas, 1, 1. CHAP. 15. ¹ 2 Par. 26, 21.

Ver. 25. *Opher*. In the tribe of Zabulon. CHAP. 15. Ver. 1. *Azarias*. Otherwise called Ozias. Ver. 5. *A leper*. In punishment of his usurping the priestly function (2 Par. 26).

25 He restored the borders of ⁴ Israel from the entrance of Emath, unto the sea of the wilderness, according to the word of the Lord the God of Israel, which he spoke by his servant ⁵ Jonas the son of Amathi, the prophet, who was of Geth, which is in Opher.

26 For the Lord saw the affliction of Israel that it was exceeding bitter, and that they were consumed even to them that were shut up in prison, and the lowest persons, and that there was no one to help Israel.

27 And the Lord did not say that he would blot out the name of Israel from under heaven: but he saved them by the hand of Jeroboam the son of Joas.

28 But the rest of the acts of Jeroboam, and all that he did, and his valour, wherewith he fought, and how he restored Damascus, and Emath to Juda in Israel, are they not written in the book of the words of the days of the kings of Israel?

29 And Jeroboam slept with his fathers the kings of Israel, and Zacharias his son reigned in his stead.

CHAPTER 15

The reign of Azarias, and Joatham in Juda: and of Zacharias, Sellum, Manahem, Phaceia, and Phacee in Israel.

IN the seven and twentieth year of Jeroboam, king of Israel, reigned Azarias son of Amasias, king of Juda.

2 He was sixteen years old when he began to reign, and he reigned two and fifty years in Jerusalem. The name of his mother was Jechelia of Jerusalem.

3 And he did that which was pleasing before the Lord, according to all that his father Amasias had done.

4 But the high places he did not destroy: for the people sacrificed and burnt incense in the high places.

5 ¹ And the Lord struck the king, so that he was a leper unto the day of his death: and he dwelt in a free house apart. But Joatham the king's son governed the palace, and judged the people of the land.

6 And the rest of the acts of Azarias, and all that he did, are they not written in the book of the words of the days of the kings of Juda?

7 And Azarias slept with his fathers: and they buried him with his ancestors in the city of David. And Joatham his son reigned in his stead.

8 In the eight and thirtieth year of Azarias king of Juda, reigned Zacharias son of Jeroboam over Israel in Samaria six months.

9 And he did that which is evil before the Lord, as his fathers had done: he departed not from the sins of Jero-

boam the son of Nabat, who made Israel to sin.

10 And Sellum the son of Jabes conspired against him; and struck him publicly; and killed him; and reigned in his place.

11 Now the rest of the acts of Zacharias, are they not written in the book of the words of the days of the kings of Israel?

12 ²This was the word of the Lord, which he spoke to Jehu, saying: Thy children to the fourth generation shall sit upon the throne of Israel. And so it came to pass.

13 Sellum the son of Jabes began to reign in the nine and thirtieth year of Azarias king of Juda: and reigned one month in Samaria.

14 And Manahem the son of Gadi went up from Thersa. And he came into Samaria; and struck Sellum the son of Jabes in Samaria; and slew him; and reigned in his stead.

15 And the rest of the acts of Sellum, and his conspiracy, which he made, are they not written in the book of the words of the days of the kings of Israel?

16 Then Manahem destroyed Thapsa and all that were in it, and the borders thereof from Thersa, because they would not open to him. And he slew all the women thereof that were with child, and ripped them up.

17 In the nine and thirtieth year of Azarias king of Juda, reigned Manahem son of Gadi over Israel ten years in Samaria.

18 And he did that which was evil before the Lord: he departed not from the sins of Jeroboam the son of Nabat, who made Israel to sin, all his days.

19 And Phul king of the Assyrians came into the land: and Manahem gave Phul a thousand talents of silver, to aid him and to establish him in the kingdom.

20 And Manahem laid a tax upon Israel, on all that were mighty and rich, to give the king of the Assyrians, each man fifty sicles of silver. So the king of the Assyrians turned back, and did not stay in the land.

21 And the rest of the acts of Manahem, and all that he did, are they not written in the book of the words of the days of the kings of Israel?

22 And Manahem slept with his fathers: and Phaceia his son reigned in his stead.

23 In the fiftieth year of Azarias king of Juda reigned Phaceia the son of Manahem over Israel in Samaria two years.

24 And he did that which was evil before the Lord: he departed not from the sins of Jeroboam the son of Nabat, who made Israel to sin.

25 And Phacee the son of Romelia, his captain, conspired against him, and smote him in Samaria, in the tower of the king's house, near Argob, and near Arie: and with him fifty men of the sons of the Galaadites. And he slew him and reigned in his stead.

26 And the rest of the acts of Phaceia, and all that he did, are they not written in the book of the words of the days of the kings of Israel?

27 In the two and fiftieth year of Azarias king of Juda reigned Phacee the son of Romelia over Israel in Samaria twenty years.

28 And he did that which was evil before the Lord: he departed not from the sins of Jeroboam the son of Nabat, who made Israel to sin.

29 In the days of Phacee king of Israel came Theglathphalasar king of Assyria, and took Aion, and Abel Domum Maacha, and Janoe, and Cedes, and Asor, and Galaad, and Galilee, and all the land of Nephtali: and carried them captives into Assyria.

30 Now Osee son of Ela conspired, and formed a plot against Phacee the son of Romelia; and struck him; and slew him; and reigned in his stead, in the twentieth year of Joatham the son of Ozias.

31 But the rest of the acts of Phacee and all that he did, are they not written in the book of the words of the days of the kings of Israel?

32 In the second year of Phacee the son of Romelia king of Israel reigned Joatham son of Ozias king of Juda.

33 He was five and twenty years old when he began to reign, and he reigned sixteen years in Jerusalem. The name of his mother was Jerusa, the daughter of Sadoc.

34 And he did that which was right before the Lord: according to all that his father Ozias had done, so did he.

35 But the high places he took not away: the people still sacrificed and burnt incense in the high places. He built the highest gate of the house of the Lord.

36 But the rest of the acts of Joatham, and all that he did, are they not written in the book of the words of the days of the kings of Juda?

37 In those days, the Lord began to send into ⁴ Juda Rasin king of Syria, and Phacee the son of Romelia.

---

² 4 Kings, 10, 30.   ³ 2 Par. 27, 1.   ⁴ Isai. 7, 1.

Ver. 30. *In the twentieth year of Joatham.* That is, in the twentieth year, from the beginning of Joatham's reign. The sacred writer chooses rather to follow here this date, than to speak of the years of Achaz, who had not yet been mentioned.

38 And Joatham slept with his fathers, and was buried with them in the city of David his father: and Achaz his son reigned in his stead.

CHAPTER 16

The wicked reign of Achaz. The kings of Syria and Israel war against him. He hireth the king of the Assyrians to assist him. He causeth an altar to be made after the pattern of that of Damascus.

IN the seventeenth year of Phacee the son of Romelia, reigned Achaz the son of Joatham king of Juda.

2 ¹ Achaz was twenty years old when he began to reign, and he reigned sixteen years in Jerusalem. He did not that which was pleasing in the sight of the Lord his God, as David his father.

3 But he walked in the way of the kings of Israel. Moreover he consecrated also his son, making him pass through the fire according to the idols of the nations: which the Lord destroyed before the children of Israel.

4 He sacrificed also and burnt incense in the high places, and on the hills, and under every green tree.

5 ² Then Rasin king of Syria, and Phacee son of Romelia king of Israel came up to Jerusalem to fight. And they besieged Achaz; but were not able to overcome him.

6 At that time Rasin king of Syria restored Aila to Syria, and drove the men of Juda out of Aila: and the Edomites came into Aila, and dwelt there unto this day.

7 And Achaz sent messengers to Theglathphalasar king of the Assyrians, saying: I am thy servant, and thy son. Come up, and save me out of the hand of the king of Syria, and out of the hand of the king of Israel, who are risen up together against me.

8 And when he had gathered together the silver and gold that could be found in the house of the Lord, and in the king's treasures, he sent it for a present to the king of the Assyrians.

9 And he agreed to his desire: for the king of the Assyrians went up against Damascus, and laid it waste. And he carried away the inhabitants thereof to Cyrene: but Rasin he slew.

10 And king Achaz went to Damascus to meet Theglathphalasar king of the Assyrians. And when he had seen the altar of Damascus, king Achaz sent to Urias the priest a pattern of it, and its

likeness according to all the work thereof.

11 And Urias the priest built an altar according to all that king Achaz had commanded from Damascus. So did Urias the priest, until king Achaz came from Damascus.

12 And when the king was come from Damascus, he saw the altar and worshipped it: and went up and offered holocausts, and his own sacrifice,

13 And offered libations, and poured the blood of the peace offerings, which he had offered upon the altar.

14 But the altar of brass that was before the Lord, he removed from the face of the temple, and from the place of the altar, and from the place of the temple of the Lord: and he set it at the side of the altar toward the north.

15 And king Achaz commanded Urias the priest, saying: Upon the great altar offer the morning holocaust, and the evening sacrifice, and the king's holocaust, and his sacrifice, and the holocaust of the whole people of the land, and their sacrifices, and their libations. And all the blood of the holocaust, and all the blood of the victim thou shalt pour out upon it: but the altar of brass shall be ready at my pleasure.

16 So Urias the priest did according to all that king Achaz had commanded him.

17 And king Achaz took way the graven bases, and the laver that was upon them: and he took down the sea from the brazen oxen that held it up, and put it upon a pavement of stone.

18 The Musach also for the sabbath, which he had built in the temple: and the king's entry from without he turned into the temple of the Lord, because of the king of the Assyrians.

19 Now the rest of the acts of Achaz, which he did, are they not written in the book of the words of the days of the kings of Juda?

20 And Achaz slept with his fathers, and was buried with them in the city of David. ³ And Ezechias his son reigned in his stead.

CHAPTER 17

The reign of Osee. The Israelites for their sins are carried into captivity. Other inhabitants are sent to Samaria, who make a mixture of religion.

IN the twelfth year of Achaz king of Juda, Osee the son of Ela reigned in Samaria over Israel nine years.

2 And he did evil before the Lord: but not as the kings of Israel that had been before him.

3 ¹ Against him came up Salmanasar

CHAP. 16. ¹ 2 Par. 28, 1. ² Isai. 7, 1. ³ 2 Par. 28, 27. CHAP. 17. ¹ 4 Kings, 18, 9; Tob. 1, 2.

CHAP. 16. Ver. 18. *Musach*. The covert, or pavilion, or tribune, for the king.

CHAP. 17. Ver. 1. *In the twelfth year of Achaz, king of Juda*. He began to reign before: but was not in quiet possession of the kingdom to the twelfth year of Achaz.

king of the Assyrians: and Osee bcame his servant, and paid him tribute.

4 And when the king of the Assyrians found that Osee endeavouring to rebel had sent messengers to Sua the king of Egypt, that he might not pay tribute to the king of the Assyrians, as he had done every year, he besieged him, bound him, and cast him into prison.

5 And he went through all the land: and going up to Samaria, he besieged it three years.

6 ² And in the ninth year of Osee, the king of the Assyrians took Samaria, and carried Israel away to Assyria. And he placed them in Hala and Habor by the river of Gozan, in the cities of the Medes.

7 For so it was that the children of Israel had sinned against the Lord their God, who brought them out of the land of Egypt, from under the hand of Pharao king of Egypt. And they worshipped strange gods.

8 And they walked according to the way of the nations which the Lord had destroyed in the sight of the children of Israel and of the kings of Israel; because they had done in like manner.

9 And the children of Israel offended the Lord their God with things that were not right: and built them high places in all their cities, from the tower of the watchmen to the fenced city.

10 And they made them statues and groves on every high hill, and under every shady tree.

11 And they burnt incense there upon altars after the manner of the nations which the Lord had removed from their face. And they did wicked things, provoking the Lord.

12 And they worshipped abominations, concerning which the Lord had commanded them that they should not do this thing.

13 And the Lord testified to them in Israel and in Juda by the hand of all the prophets and seers, saying: ³ Return from your wicked ways, and keep my precepts, and ceremonies, according to all the law which I commanded your fathers; and as I have sent to you in the hand of my servants the prophets.

14 And they hearkened not, but hardened their necks like to the neck of their fathers, who would not obey the Lord their God.

15 And they rejected his ordinances and the covenant that he made with their fathers, and the testimonies which he testified against them. And they followed vanities, and acted vainly. And they followed the nations that were round about them, concerning which the Lord had commanded them that they should not do as they did.

16 And they forsook all the precepts of the Lord their God. And they made to themselves two molten calves, and groves, and adored all the host of heaven. And they served Baal.

17 And they consecrated their sons and their daughters through fire. And they gave themselves to divinations, and soothsayers. And they delivered themselves up to do evil before the Lord, to provoke him.

18 And the Lord was very angry with Israel, and removed them from his sight: and there remained only the tribe of Juda.

19 But neither did Juda itself keep the commandments of the Lord their God: but they walked in the errors of Israel, which they had wrought.

20 And the Lord cast off all the seed of Israel, and afflicted them, and delivered them into the hand of spoilers, till he cast them away from his face:

21 ⁴ Even from that time when Israel was rent from the house of David, and made Jeroboam son of Nabat their king. For Jeroboam separated Israel from the Lord, and made them commit a great sin.

22 And the children of Israel walked in all the sins of Jeroboam, which he had done. And they departed not from them.

23 ⁵ Till the Lord removed Israel from his face, as he had spoken in the hand of all his servants the prophets. And Israel was carried away out of their land to Assyria, unto this day.

24 And the king of the Assyrians brought people from Babylon, and from Cutha, and from Avah, and from Emath, and from Sepharvaim: and placed them in the cities of Samaria instead of the children of Israel. And they possessed Samaria, and dwelt in the cities thereof.

25 And when they began to dwell there, they feared not the Lord: and the Lord sent lions among them, which killed them.

26 And it was told the king of the Assyrians, and it was said: The nations which thou hast removed, and made to dwell in the cities of Samaria know not the ordinances of the God of the land. And the Lord hath sent lions among them: and behold they kill them, because they know not the manner of the God of the land.

27 And the king of the Assyrians commanded, saying: Carry thither one of the priests whom you brought from thence captive. And let him go, and dwell with them: and let him teach them the ordinances of the God of the land.

---

² 4 Kings, 18, 10. ³ Jer. 25, 5. ⁴ 3 Kings, 12, 19. ⁵ Jer. 25, 9.

28 So one of the priests who had been carried away captive from Samaria, came and dwelt in Bethel; and taught them how they should worship the Lord.

29 And every nation made gods of their own, and put them in the temples of the high places, which the Samaritans had made: every nation in their cities where they dwelt.

30 For the men of Babylon made Sochothbenoth: and the Cuthites made Nergel: and the men of Emath made Asima:

31 And the Hevites made Nebahaz and Tharthac. And they that were of Sepharvaim burnt their children in fire, to Adramelech and Anamelech the gods of Sepharvaim.

32 And nevertheless they worshipped the Lord. And they made to themselves, of the lowest of the people, priests of the high places: and they placed them in the temples of the high places.

33 And when they worshipped the Lord, they served also their own gods according to the custom of the nations out of which they were brought to Samaria.

34 Unto this day they followed the old manner: they fear not the Lord, neither do they keep his ceremonies, and judgments, and law, and the commandment, which the Lord commanded the children of Jacob, whom he surnamed Israel: [6]

35 With whom he made a covenant, and charged them, saying: You shall not fear strange gods, nor shall you adore them, nor worship them, nor sacrifice to them.

36 But the Lord your God, who brought you out of the land of Egypt with great power, and a stretched out arm, him shall you fear, and him shall you adore, and to him shall you sacrifice.

37 And the ceremonies, and judgments, and law, and the commandment, which he wrote for you, you shall observe to do them always: and you shall not fear strange gods.

38 And the covenant that he made with you, you shall not forget: neither shall ye worship strange gods,

39 But fear the Lord your God: and he shall deliver you out of the hand of all your enemies.

40 But they did not hearken: but did according to their old custom.

41 So these nations feared the Lord, but nevertheless served also their idols:

[6] Gen. 32, 28. CHAP. 18. [1] 2 Par. 28, 27; 29, 1. [2] Num. 21, 9. [3] 4 Kings, 17, 6; Tob. 1, 2. [4] 2 Par. 32, 1; Ecclus. 48, 20; Isai. 36, 1.

CHAP. 18. Ver. 4. *And he called its name Nohestan.* That is, *their brass; or a little brass.* So he called it in contempt, because they had made an idol of it.

their children also and grandchildren, as their fathers did, so do they unto this day.

CHAPTER 18

The reign of Ezechias. He abolisheth idolatry and prospereth. Sennacherib cometh up against him. Rabsaces soliciteth the people to revolt. And blasphemeth the Lord.

IN [1] the third year of Osee the son of Ela, king of Israel, reigned Ezechias the son of Achaz, king of Juda.

2 He was five and twenty years old when he began to reign: and he reigned nine and twenty years in Jerusalem. The name of his mother was Abi the daughter of Zacharias.

3 And he did that which was good before the Lord, according to all that David his father had done.

4 He destroyed the high places, and broke the statues in pieces, and cut down the groves, and broke the brazen serpent, [2] which Moses had made. For till that time the children of Israel burnt incense to it: and he called its name Nohestan.

5 He trusted in the Lord the God of Israel: so that after him there was none like him among all the kings of Juda, nor any of them that were before him.

6 And he stuck to the Lord, and departed not from his steps: but kept his commandments, which the Lord commanded Moses.

7 Wherefore the Lord also was with him: and in all things, to which he went forth, he behaved himself wisely. And he rebelled against the king of the Assyrians, and served him not.

8 He smote the Philistines as far as Gaza, and all their borders, from the tower of the watchmen to the fenced city.

9 [3] In the fourth year of king Ezechias, which was the seventh year of Osee the son of Ela, king of Israel, Salmanasar king of the Assyrians came up to Samaria, and besieged it,

10 And took it. For after three years, in the sixth year of Ezechias, that is, in the ninth year of Osee king of Israel, Samaria was taken.

11 And the king of the Assyrians carried away Israel into Assyria, and placed them in Hala and in Habor by the rivers of Gozan in the cities of the Medes:

12 Because they hearkened not to the voice of the Lord their God, but transgressed his covenant. All that Moses the servant of the Lord commanded, they would not hear nor do.

13 [4] In the fourteenth year of king Ezechias, Sennacherib king of the Assyrians came up against the fenced cities of Juda: and took them.

14 Then Ezechias king of Juda sent messengers to the king of the Assyrians to Lachis, saying: I have offended, depart from me; and all that thou shalt put upon me, I will bear. And the king of the Assyrians put a tax upon Ezechias king of Juda, of three hundred talents of silver, and thirty talents of gold.

15 And Ezechias gave all the silver that was found in the house to the Lord, and in the king's treasures.

16 At that time Ezechias broke the doors of the temple of the Lord, and the plates of gold which he had fastened on them, and gave them to the king of the Assyrians.

17 And the king of the Assyrians sent Tharthan and Rabsaris, and Rabsaces from Lachis to king Ezechias with a strong army to Jerusalem. And they went up and came to Jerusalem: and they stood by the conduit of the upper pool, which is in the way of the fuller's field.

18 And they called for the king: and there went out to them Eliacim the son of Helcias, who was over the house, and Sobna the scribe, and Joahe the son of Asaph, the recorder.

19 And Rabsaces said to them: Speak to Ezechias: Thus saith the great king, the king of the Assyrians: What is this confidence, wherein thou trustest?

20 Perhaps thou hast taken counsel, to prepare thyself for battle. On whom dost thou trust, that thou darest to rebel?

21 Dost thou trust in Egypt, a staff of a broken reed, upon which if a man lean, it will break and go into his hand, and pierce it? So is Pharao king of Egypt, to all that trust in him.

22 But if you say to me: We trust in the Lord our God: Is it not he, whose high places and altars Ezechias hath taken away; and hath commanded Juda and Jerusalem: You shall worship before this altar in Jerusalem?

23 Now therefore come over to my master the king of the Assyrians: and I will give you two thousand horses, and see whether you be able to have riders for them.

24 And how can you stand against one lord of the least of my master's servants? Dost thou trust in Egypt for chariots and for horsemen?

25 Is it without the will of the Lord that I am come up to this place to destroy it? The Lord said to me: Go up to this land and destroy it.

26 Then Eliacim the son of Helcias, and Sobna, and Joahe said to Rabsaces: We pray thee speak to us thy servants in Syriac: for we understand that tongue. And speak not to us in the Jews' language, in the hearing of the people that are upon the wall.

27 And Rabsaces answered them, saying: Hath my master sent me to thy master and to thee, to speak these words, and not rather to the men that sit upon the wall, that they may eat their own dung, and drink their urine with you?

28 Then Rabsaces stood, and cried out with a loud voice in the Jews' language, and said: Hear the words of the great king, the king of the Assyrians.

29 Thus saith the king: Let not Ezechias deceive you: for he shall not be able to deliver you out of my hand.

30 Neither let him make you trust in the Lord, saying: The Lord will surely deliver us; and this city shall not be given into the hand of the king of the Assyrians.

31 Do not hearken to Ezechias. For thus saith the king of the Assyrians: Do with me that which is for your advantage, and come out to me. And every man of you shall eat of his own vineyard, and of his own fig tree: and you shall drink water of your own cisterns,

32 Till I come, and take you away to a land, like to your own land, a fruitful land, and plentiful in wine, a land of bread and vineyards, a land of olives and oil and honey; and you shall live, and not die. Hearken not to Ezechias, who deceiveth you, saying: The Lord will deliver us.

33 Have any of the gods of the nations delivered their land from the hand of the king of Assyria?

34 [5] Where is the god of Emath, and of Arphad? Where is the god of Sepharvaim, of Ana, and of Ava? [6] Have they delivered Samaria out of my hand?

35 Who are they among all the gods of the nations, that have delivered their country out of my hand, that the Lord may deliver Jerusalem out of my hand?

36 But the people held their peace, and answered him not a word: for they had received commandment from the king that they should not answer him.

37 And Eliacim the son of Helcias, who was over the house, and Sobna the scribe, and Joahe the son of Asaph, the recorder, came to Ezechias, with their garments rent, and told him the words of Rabsaces.

CHAPTER 19

Ezechias is assured of God's help by Isaias the prophet. The king of the Assyrians still threateneth and blasphemeth. Ezechias prayeth, and God promiseth to protect Jerusalem. An angel destroyeth the army of the Assyrians. Their king returneth to Ninive, and is slain by his two sons.

[5] 4 Kings, 19, 13; Isai. 10, 9; 37, 13. [6] 4 Kings, 17, 24.

AND ¹ when king Ezechias heard these words, he rent his garments, and covered himself with sackcloth, and went into the house of the Lord.

2 And he sent Eliacim, who was over the house, and Sobna the scribe, and the ancients of the priests covered with sackcloths, to Isaias, the prophet, the son of Amos.

3 And they said to him: Thus saith Ezechias: This day is a day of tribulation, and of rebuke, and of blasphemy. The children are come to the birth; and the woman in travail hath not strength.

4 It may be the Lord thy God will hear all the words of Rabsaces whom the king of the Assyrians his master hath sent to reproach the living God and to reprove with words which the Lord thy God hath heard: and do thou offer prayer for the remnants that are found.

5 So the servants of king Ezechias came to Isaias.

6 And Isaias said to them: Thus shall you say to your master: Thus saith the Lord: Be not afraid for the words which thou hast heard with which the servants of the king of the Assyrians have blasphemed me.

7 Behold I will send a spirit upon him, and he shall hear a message, and shall return into his own country: and I will make him fall by the sword in his own country.

8 And Rabsaces returned, and found the king of the Assyrians besieging Lobna: for he had heard that he was departed from Lachis.

9 And when he heard of Theraca king of Ethiopia, Behold, he is come out to fight with thee; and was going against him, he sent messengers to Ezechias, saying:

10 Thus shall you say to Ezechias king of Juda: Let not thy God deceive thee, in whom thou trustest. And do not say: Jerusalem shall not be delivered into the hands of the king of the Assyrians.

11 Behold thou hast heard what the kings of the Assyrians have done to all countries: how they have laid them waste. And canst thou alone be delivered?

12 Have the gods of the nations de-

CHAP. 19. ¹ Isai. 37, 1.
CHAP. 19. Ver. 23. *Carmel.* A pleasant fruitful hill in the forest. These expressions are figurative, signifying under the names of mountains and forests, the kings and provinces whom the Assyrians had triumphed over.
Ver. 25. *I have formed it.* All thy exploits, in which thou takest pride, are no more than what I have decreed; and are not to be ascribed to thy wisdom or strength, but to my will and ordinance: who have given to thee to take and destroy so many fenced cities, and to carry terror wherever thou comest.—*Heaps of ruin.* Literally, *ruin of hills.*

livered any of them, whom my fathers have destroyed, to wit, Gozan, and Haran, and Reseph, and the children of Eden that were in Thelassar?

13 Where is the king of Emath, and the king of Arphad, and the king of the city of Sepharvaim, of Ana and of Ava?

14 And when Ezechias had received the letter of the hand of the messengers, and had read it, he went up to the house of the Lord, and spread it before the Lord.

15 And he prayed in his sight, saying: O Lord God of Israel, who sitteth upon the cherubims, thou alone art the God of all the kings of the earth. Thou madest heaven and earth.

16 Incline thy ear, and hear: open, O Lord, thy eyes, and see: and hear all the words of Sennacherib, who hath sent to upbraid unto us the living God.

17 Of a truth, O Lord, the kings of the Assyrians have destroyed nations, and the lands of them all.

18 And they have cast their gods into the fire. For they were not gods, but the works of men's hands of wood and stone: and they destroyed them.

19 Now therefore, O Lord our God, save us from his hand, that all the kingdoms of the earth may know, that thou art the Lord the only God.

20 And Isaias the son of Amos sent to Ezechias, saying: Thus saith the Lord the God of Israel: I have heard the prayer thou hast made to me concerning Sennacherib king of the Assyrians.

21 This is the word, that the Lord hath spoken of him: The virgin daughter of Sion hath despised thee, and laughed thee to scorn: the daughter of Jerusalem hath wagged her head behind thy back.

22 Whom hast thou reproached, and whom hast thou blasphemed? Against whom hast thou exalted thy voice, and lifted up thy eyes on high? Against the holy one of Israel.

23 By the hand of thy servants thou hast reproached the Lord, and hast said: With the multitude of my chariots I have gone up to the height of the mountains, to the top of Libanus, and have cut down its tall cedars, and its choice fir trees. And I have entered into the furthest parts thereof, and the forest of its Carmel.

24 I have cut down, and I have drunk strange waters: and have dried up with the soles of my feet all the shut up waters.

25 Hast thou not heard what I have done from the beginning? From the days of old I have formed it, and now

I have brought it to effect: that fenced cities of fighting men should be turned to heaps of ruin.

26 And the inhabitants of them, were weak of hand: they trembled and were confounded: they became like the grass of the field, and the green herb on the tops of houses, which withered before it came to maturity.

27 Thy dwelling and thy going out, and thy coming in, and thy way I knew before, and thy rage against me.

28 Thou hast been mad against me, and thy pride hath come up to my ears. Therefore I will put a ring in thy nose, and a bit between thy lips: and I will turn thee back by the way, by which thou camest.

29 And to thee, O Ezechias, this shall be a sign: [2] Eat this year what thou shalt find: and in the second year, such things as spring of themselves: but in the third year sow and reap: plant vineyards, and eat the fruit of them.

30 And whatsoever shall be left of the house of Juda, shall take root downward, and bear fruit upward.

31 For out of Jerusalem shall go forth a remnant, and that which shall be saved out of mount Sion: the zeal of the Lord of hosts shall do this.

32 Wherefore thus saith the Lord concerning the king of the Assyrians: He shall not come into this city, nor shoot an arrow into it, nor come before it with shield, nor cast a trench about it.

33 By the way that he came, he shall return: and into this city he shall not come, saith the Lord.

34 And I will protect this city, and will save it for my own sake, and for David my servant's sake.

35 [3] And it came to pass that night that an angel of the Lord came, and slew in the camp of the Assyrians a hundred and eighty-five thousand. And when he arose early in the morning, he saw all the bodies of the dead.

36 And Sennacherib king of the Assyrians departing went away: And he returned and abode in Ninive.

37 [4] And as he was worshipping in the temple of Nesroch his god, Adramelech and Sarasar his sons slew him with the sword. And they fled into the land of the Armenians: and Asarhaddon his son reigned in his stead.

CHAPTER 20

Ezechias being sick, is told by Isaias that he shall die. Praying to God, he obtaineth longer life, and in confirmation thereof receiveth a sign by the sun's returning back. He sheweth all his treasures to the ambassadors of the king of Babylon. Isaias reproving him for it, foretelleth the Babylonish captivity.

IN [1] those days Ezechias was sick unto death. And Isaias the son of Amos the prophet came and said to him: Thus saith the Lord God: Give charge concerning thy house, for thou shalt die, and not live.

2 And he turned his face to the wall, and prayed to the Lord, saying:

3 I beseech thee, O Lord, remember how I have walked before thee in truth, and with a perfect heart, and have done that which is pleasing before thee. And Ezechias wept with much weeping.

4 And before Isaias was gone out of the middle of the court, the word of the Lord came to him, saying:

5 Go back, and tell Ezechias the captain of my people: Thus saith the Lord the God of David thy father: I have heard thy prayer, and I have seen thy tears: and behold I have healed thee. On the third day thou shalt go up to the temple of the Lord.

6 And I will add to thy days fifteen years: and I will deliver thee and this city out of the hand of the king of the Assyrians: and I will protect this city for my own sake, and for David my servant's sake.

7 And Isaias said: Bring me a lump of figs. And when they had brought it, and laid it upon his boil, he was healed.

8 And Ezechias had said to Isaias: What shall be the sign that the Lord will heal me, and that I shall go up to the temple of the Lord the third day?

9 And Isaias said to him: This shall be the sign from the Lord, that the Lord will do the word which he hath spoken: Wilt thou that the shadow go forward ten lines, or that it go back so many degrees?

10 And Ezechias said: It is an easy matter for the shadow to go forward ten lines; and I do not desire that this be done: but let it return back ten degrees.

11 And Isaias the prophet called upon the Lord; and he brought the shadow ten degrees backwards by the lines, by which it had already gone down in the dial of Achaz.

12 [2] At that time, Berodach Baladan, the son of Baladan, king of the Babylonians, sent letters and presents to Ezechias: for he had heard that Ezechias had been sick.

13 And Ezechias rejoiced at their coming: and he showed them the house of his aromatical spices, and the gold and the silver, and divers precious odours, and ointments, and the house of his vessels, and all that he had in his treasures. There was nothing in his

[2] Isai. 37, 30. [3] Tob. 1, 21; Ecclus. 48, 24; Isai. 37, 36; 1 Mach. 7, 41; 2 Mach. 8, 19. [4] Tob. 1, 24. CHAP. 20. [1] 2 Par. 32, 24; Isai. 38, 1.

house, nor in all his dominions that Ezechias shewed them not.

14 And Isaias the prophet came to king Ezechias, and said to him: What said these men? Or from whence came they to thee? And Ezechias said to him: From a far country they came to me out of Babylon.

15 And he said: What did they see in thy house? Ezechias said: They saw all the things that are in my house; there is nothing among my treasures that I have not shewn them.

16 And Isaias said to Ezechias: Hear the word of the Lord.

17 Behold the days shall come, that all that is in thy house, and that thy fathers have laid up in store unto this day, shall be carried into Babylon. Nothing shall be left, saith the Lord.

18 And of thy sons also that shall issue from thee, whom thou shalt beget, they shall take away: and they shall be eunuchs in the palace of the king of Babylon.

19 Ezechias said to Isaias: The word of the Lord, which thou hast spoken, is good. Let peace and truth be in my days.

20 And the rest of the acts of Ezechias and all his might, and how he made a pool, and a conduit, and brought waters into the city, are they not written in the book of the words of the days of the kings of Juda?

21 And Ezechias slept with his fathers: and Manasses his son reigned in his stead.

CHAPTER 21

The wickedness of Manasses. God's threats by his prophets. His wicked son Amon succeedeth him, and is slain by his servants.

MANASSES [1] was twelve years old when he began to reign, and he reigned five and fifty years in Jerusalem: the name of his mother was Haphsiba.

2 And he did evil in the sight of the Lord, according to the idols of the nations, which the Lord destroyed from before the face of the children of Israel.

3 [2] And he turned, and built up the high places which Ezechias his father had destroyed. And he set up altars to Baal, and made groves, as Achab king of Israel had done. And he adored all the host of heaven, and served them.

4 And he built altars in the house of the Lord, of which the Lord said: [3] In Jerusalem I will put my name.

5 And he built altars for all the host

of heaven in the two courts of the temple of the Lord.

6 And he made his son pass through fire. And he used divination, and observed omens, and appointed pythons, and multiplied soothsayers to do evil before the Lord, and to provoke him.

7 He set also an idol of the grove, which he had made, in the temple of the Lord; [4] concerning which the Lord said to David, and to Solomon his son: In this temple, and in Jerusalem, which I have chosen out of all the tribes of Israel, I will put my name for ever.

8 And I will no more make the feet of Israel to be moved out of the land which I gave to their fathers: only if they will observe to do all that I have commanded them according to the law which my servant Moses commanded them.

9 But they hearkened not: but were seduced by Manasses, to do evil more than the nations which the Lord destroyed before the children of Israel.

10 And the Lord spoke in the hand of his servants, the prophets, saying:

11 [5] Because Manasses king of Juda hath done these most wicked abominations, beyond all that the Amorrhites did before him, and hath made Juda also to sin with his filthy doings.

12 Therefore thus saith the Lord the God of Israel: Behold I will bring on evils upon Jerusalem and Juda; that whosoever shall hear of them, both his ears shall tingle.

13 And I will stretch over Jerusalem the line of Samaria, and the weight of the house of Achab. And I will efface Jerusalem, as tables are wont to be effaced: and I will erase and turn it, and draw the pencil often over the face thereof.

14 And I will leave the remnants of my inheritance, and will deliver them into the hands of their enemies. And they shall become a prey, and a spoil to all their enemies.

15 Because they have done evil before me, and have continued to provoke me, from the day that their fathers came out of Egypt, even unto this day.

16 [6] Moreover Manasses shed also very much innocent blood, till he filled Jerusalem up to the mouth: besides his sins, wherewith he made Juda to sin, to do evil before the Lord.

17 Now the rest of the acts of Manasses, and all that he did, and his sin which he sinned, are they not written in the book of the words of the days of the kings of Juda?

18 And Manasses slept with his fathers, and was buried in the garden of his own house, in the garden of Oza: and Amon his son reigned in his stead.

---

[2] Isai. 39, 1. CHAP. 21. [1] 2 Par. 33, 1. [2] 2 Par. 33, 3. [3] 2 Kings, 7, 10. [4] 2 Kings, 7, 26; 3 Kings, 8, 16; 9, 5. [5] Jer. 15, 4. [6] 4 Kings, 24, 4.

CHAP. 21. Ver. 6. *Pythons.* That is, diviners by spirits.

19 Two and twenty years old was Amon when he began to reign, and he reigned two years in Jerusalem. The name of his mother was Messalemeth the daughter of Harus of Jeteba.

20 And he did evil in the sight of the Lord, as Manasses his father had done.

21 And he walked in all the way in which his father had walked. And he served the abominations which his father had served, and he adored them:

22 And forsook the Lord the God of his fathers: and walked not in the way of the Lord.

23 And his servants plotted against him, and slew the king in his own house.

24 But the people of the land slew all them that had conspired against king Amon: and made Josias his son their king in his stead.

25 But the rest of the acts of Amon which he did, are they not written in the book of the words of the days of the kings of Juda?

26 And they buried him in his sepulchre in the garden of Oza: and his son Josias reigned in his stead.

CHAPTER 22

Josias repaireth the temple. The book of the law is found, upon which they consult the Lord, and are told that great evils shall fall upon them, but not in the time of Josias.

JOSIAS [1] was eight years old when he began to reign: he reigned one and thirty years in Jerusalem. The name of his mother was Idida, the daughter of Hadaia of Besecath.

2 And he did that which was right in the sight of the Lord, and walked in all the ways of David his father: he turned not aside to the right hand, or to the left.

3 And in the eighteenth year of king Josias, the king sent Saphan the son of Assia, the son of Messulam, the scribe of the temple of the Lord, saying to him:

4 Go to Helcias the high priest, that the money may be put together which is brought into the temple of the Lord, which the doorkeepers of the temple have gathered of the people.

5 And let it be given to the workmen by the overseers of the house of the Lord: and let them distribute it to those that work in the temple of the Lord, to repair the temple:

6 That is, to carpenters and masons, and to such as mend breaches: and that timber may be bought, and stones out of the quarries, to repair the temple of the Lord.

7 But let there be no reckoning made

with them of the money which they receive: but let them have it in their power, and in their trust.

8 And Helcias the high priest said to Saphan the scribe: [2] I have found the book of the law in the house of the Lord. And Helcias gave the book to Saphan, and he read it.

9 And Saphan the scribe came to the king, and brought him word again concerning that which he had commanded, and said: Thy servants have gathered together the money that was found in the house of the Lord, and they have given it to be distributed to the workmen, by the overseers of the works of the temple of the Lord

10 And Saphan the scribe told the king, saying: Helcias the priest hath delivered to me a book. And when Saphan had read it before the king,

11 And the king had heard the words of the law of the Lord: he rent his garments.

12 And he commanded Helcias the priest, and Ahicam the son of Saphan, and Achobor the son of Micha, and Saphan the scribe, and Asaia the king's servant, saying:

13 Go and consult the Lord for me, and for the people, and for all Juda, concerning the words of this book which is found. For the great wrath of the Lord is kindled against us, because our fathers have not hearkened to the words of this book, to do all that is written for us.

14 So Helcias the priest, and Ahicam, and Achobor, and Saphan, and Asaia, went to Holda the prophetess the wife of Sellum the son of Thecua, the son of Araas keeper of the wardrobe, who dwelt in Jerusalem in the Second: and they spoke to her.

15 And she said to them: Thus saith the Lord the God of Israel: Tell the man that sent you to me:

16 Thus saith the Lord: Behold, I will bring evils upon this place, and upon the inhabitants thereof, all the words of the law which the king of Juda hath read.

17 Because they have forsaken me, and have sacrificed to strange gods, provoking me by all the works of their hands: therefore my indignation shall be kindled against this place, and shall not be quenched.

18 But to the king of Juda, who sent you to consult the Lord, thus shall you say: Thus saith the Lord the God of Israel: Forasmuch as thou hast heard the words of the book,

---

CHAP. 22. [1] 2 Par. 34, 1.   [2] 2 Par. 44, 14.

CHAP. 22. Ver. 8. *The book of the law.* That is, Deuteronomy.

Ver. 14. *The Second.* A street, or part of the city, so called; in Hebrew, *Massem.*

19 And thy heart hath been moved to fear, and thou hast humbled thyself, before the Lord, hearing the words against this place, and the inhabitants thereof, to wit, that they should become a wonder and a curse, and thou hast rent thy garments, and wept before me. I also have heard thee, saith the Lord.

20 Therefore I will gather thee to thy fathers: and thou shalt be gathered to thy sepulchre in peace, that thy eyes may not see all the evils which I will bring upon this place.

CHAPTER 23

Josias readeth the law before all the people. They promise to observe it. He abolisheth all idolatry: celebrateth the phase: is slain in battle by the king of Egypt. The short reign of Joachaz, in whose place Joakim is made king.

AND [1] they brought the king word again what she had said. And he sent; and all the ancients of Juda and Jerusalem were assembled to him.

2 And the king went up to the temple of the Lord, and all the men of Juda, and all the inhabitants of Jerusalem with him, the priests and the prophets, and all the people, both little and great. And in the hearing of them all he read all the words of the book of the covenant, which was found in the house of the Lord.

3 And the king stood upon the step: and made a covenant with the Lord, to walk after the Lord, and to keep his commandments, and his testimonies, and his ceremonies, with all their heart, and with all their soul, and to perform the words of this covenant, which were written in that book. And the people agreed to the covenant.

4 And the king commanded Helcias the high priest, and the priests of the second order, and the doorkeepers, [2] to cast out of the temple of the Lord all the vessels that had been made for Baal, and for the grove, and for all the host of heaven. And he burnt them without Jerusalem in the valley of Cedron: and he carried the ashes of them to Bethel.

5 And he destroyed the soothsayers, whom the kings of Juda had appointed to sacrifice in the high places in the cities of Juda, and round about Jerusalem: them also that burnt incense to Baal, and to the sun, and to the moon, and to the twelve signs, and to all the host of heaven.

6 And he caused the grove to be carried out from the house of the Lord without Jerusalem to the valley of Cedron. And he burnt it there, and reduced it to dust, and cast the dust upon the graves of the common people.

7 He destroyed also the pavilions of the effeminate, which were in the house of the Lord, for which the women wove as it were little dwellings for the grove.

8 And he gathered together all the priests out of the cities of Juda. And he defiled the high places, where the priests offered sacrifice, from Gabaa to Bersabee. And he broke down the altars of the gates that were in the entering in of the gate of Josue governor of the city, which was on the left hand of the gate of the city.

9 However the priests of the high places came not up to the altar of the Lord in Jerusalem: but only ate of the unleavened bread among their brethren.

10 And he defiled Topheth, which is in the valley of the son of Ennom: that no man should consecrate there his son or his daughter through fire to Moloch.

11 And he took away the horses which the kings of Juda had given to the sun, at the entering in of the temple of the Lord, near the chamber of Nathanmelech the eunuch, who was in Pharurim: and he burnt the chariots of the sun with fire.

12 And the altars that were upon the top of the upper chamber of Achaz, which the kings of Juda had made, and the altars which Manasses had made in the two courts of the temple of the Lord, the king broke down. And he ran from thence, and cast the ashes of them into the torrent Cedron.

13 The high places also that were at Jerusalem on the right side of the Mount of Offence, [3] which Solomon king of Israel had built to Astaroth the idol of the Sidonians, and to Chamos the scandal of Moab, and to Melchom the abomination of the children of Ammon, the king defiled.

14 And he broke in pieces the statues, and cut down the groves: and he filled their places with the bones of dead men.

15 [4] Moreover the altar also that was at Bethel, and the high place, which Jeroboam the son of Nabat, who made Israel to sin, had made: both the altar and the high place he broke down and burnt, and reduced to powder, and burnt the grove.

16 And as Josias turned himself, he saw there the sepulchres that were in the mount: and he sent and took the bones out of the sepulchres, and burnt them upon the altar, and defiled it according to the word of the Lord, which

CHAP. 23. [1] 2 Par. 34, 28. [2] Ecclus. 49, 3. [3] 3 Kings, 11, 7. [4] 3 Kings, 13, 32.

CHAP. 23. Ver. 3. *The king stood upon the step.* That is, his tribune, or tribunal, a more eminent place, from whence he might be seen and heard by the people.

the man of God spoke, who had foretold these things.

17 [5] And he said: What is that monument which I see? And the men of that city answered: It is the sepulchre of the man of God, who came from Juda, and foretold these things which thou hast done upon the altar of Bethel.

18 And he said: Let him alone, let no man move his bones. So his bones were left untouched with the bones of the prophet that came out of Samaria.

19 Moreover all the temples of the high places, which were in the cities of Samaria, which the kings of Israel had made to provoke the Lord, Josias took away. And he did to them according to all the acts that he had done in Bethel.

20 And he slew all the priests of the high places, that were there, upon the altars: and he burnt men's bones upon them: and returned to Jerusalem.

21 [6] And he commanded all the people, saying: Keep the phase to the Lord your God, according as it is written in the book of this covenant.

22 Now there was no such a phase kept from the days of the judges, who judged Israel, nor in all the days of the kings of Israel, and of the kings of Juda,

23 As was this phase that was kept to the Lord in Jerusalem, in the eighteenth year of king Josias.

24 Moreover the diviners by spirits, and soothsayers, and the figures of idols, and the uncleannesses, and the abominations, that had been in the land of Juda and Jerusalem, Josias took away: that he might perform the words of the law, that were written in the book which Helcias the priest had found in the temple of the Lord.

25 There was no king before him like unto him, that returned to the Lord with all his heart, and with all his soul, and with all his strength, according to all the law of Moses: neither after him did there arise any like him.

26 But yet the Lord turned not away from the wrath of his great indignation, wherewith his anger was kindled against Juda: because of the provocations, wherewith Manasses had provoked him.

27 [7] And the Lord said: I will remove Juda also from before my face, as I have removed Israel. And I will cast off this city Jerusalem, which I chose, and the house, of which I said: My name shall be there.

28 Now the rest of the acts of Josias, and all that he did, are they not written in the book of the words of the days of the kings of Juda?

29 [8] In his days Pharao Nechao king of Egypt went up against the king of Assyria to the river Euphrates. And king Josias went to meet him: and was slain at Mageddo, when he had seen him.

30 And his servants carried him dead from Mageddo. And they brought him to Jerusalem, and buried him in his own sepulchre. And the people of the land took Joachaz the son of Josias: and they anointed him, and made him king in his father's stead.

31 [9] Joachaz was three and twenty years old when he began to reign: and he reigned three months in Jerusalem. The name of his mother was Amital, the daughter of Jeremias of Lobna.

32 And he did evil before the Lord, according to all that his fathers had done.

33 And Pharao Nechao bound him at Rebla, which is in the land of Emath, that he should not reign in Jerusalem. And he set a fine upon the land, of a hundred talents of silver, and a talent of gold.

34 And Pharao Nechao made Eliacim the son of Josias king in the room of Josias his father: and turned his name to Joakim. And he took Joachaz away and carried him into Egypt: and he died there.

35 And Joakim gave the silver and the gold to Pharao, after he had taxed the land for every man, to contribute according to the commandment of Pharao. And he exacted both the silver and the gold of the people of the land, of every man according to his ability: to give to Pharao Nechao.

36 [10] Joakim was five and twenty years old when he began to reign: and he reigned eleven years in Jerusalem. The name of his mother was Zebida the daughter of Phadaia of Ruma.

37 And he did evil before the Lord according to all that his fathers had done.

CHAPTER 24

The reign of Joakim, Joachin, and Sedecias.

IN his days, Nabuchodonosor king of Babylon came up, and Joakim became his servant three years. Then again he rebelled against him.

2 And the Lord sent against him the rovers of the Chaldees, and the rovers of Syria, and the rovers of Moab, and the rovers of the children of Ammon. And he sent them against Juda, to destroy it, [1] according to the word of the Lord, which he had spoken by his servants the prophets.

[5] 3 Kings, 13, 1. [6] 2 Par. 35, 1. [7] . Kings, 24, 2.
[8] 2 Par. 35, 20. [9] 2 Par. 36, 2. [10] 2 Par. 36, 5.
Chap. 24. [1] 4 Kings, 23, 27.

Chap. 24. Ver. 2. *The Lord sent against him the rovers. Latrunculos.* Bands or parties of men, who pillaged and plundered wherever they came.

3 And this came by the word of the Lord against Juda, to remove them from before him, for all the sins of Manasses which he did:

4 And for the innocent blood that he shed, filling Jerusalem with innocent blood. And therefore the Lord would not be appeased.

5 But the rest of the acts of Joakim, and all that he did, are they not written in the book of the words of the days of the kings of Juda? And Joakim slept with his fathers.

6 And Joachin his son reigned in his stead.

7 And the king of Egypt came not again any more out of his own country: for the king of Babylon had taken all that had belonged to the king of Egypt, from the river of Egypt, unto the river Euphrates.

8 Joachin was eighteen years old when he began to reign, and he reigned three months in Jerusalem. The name of his mother was Nohesta the daughter of Elnathan of Jerusalem.

9 And he did evil before the Lord, according to all that his father had done.

10 [2] At that time the servants of Nabuchodonosor king of Babylon came up against Jerusalem: and the city was surrounded with their forts.

11 And Nabuchodonosor king of Babylon came to the city with his servants to assault it.

12 And Joachin king of Juda went out to the king of Babylon, he, and his mother, and his servants, and his nobles, and his eunuchs. And the king of Babylon received him in the eighth year of his reign.

13 And he brought out from thence all the treasures of the house of the Lord, and the treasures of the king's house. And he cut in pieces all the vessels of gold which Solomon king of Israel had made in the temple of the Lord, according to the word of the Lord.[3]

14 And he carried away all Jerusalem; and all the princes; and all the valiant men of the army, to the number of ten thousand into captivity; and every artificer and smith. And none were left, but the poor sort of the people of the land.

15 [4] And he carried away Joachin into Babylon, and the king's mother, and the king's wives, and his eunuchs. And the judges of the land he carried into captivity from Jerusalem into Babylon.

16 And all the strong men, seven thousand, and the artificers, and the smiths, a thousand, all that were valiant men and fit for war: and the king of Babylon led them captives into Babylon.

17 [5] And he appointed Matthanias his uncle in his stead: and called his name Sedecias.

18 Sedecias was one and twenty years old when he began to reign: and he reigned eleven years in Jerusalem. The name of his mother was Amital, the daughter of Jeremias of Lobna.

19 And he did evil before the Lord, according to all that Joakim had done.

20 For the Lord was angry against Jerusalem and against Juda, till he cast them out from his face. And Sedecias revolted from the king of Babylon.

CHAPTER 25

Jerusalem is besieged and taken by Nabuchodonosor. Sedecias is taken. The city and temple are destroyed. Godolias, who is left governor, is slain. Joachin is exalted by Evilmerodach.

AND [1] it came to pass in the ninth year of his reign, in the tenth month, the tenth day of the month, that Nabuchodonosor king of Babylon came, he and all his army against Jerusalem. And they surrounded it; and raised works round about it.

2 And the city was shut up and besieged till the eleventh year of king Sedecias.

3 The ninth day of the month. And a famine prevailed in the city; and there was no bread for the people of the land.

4 And a breach was made into the city: and all the men of war fled in the night between the two walls by the king's garden (now the Chaldees besieged the city round about). And Sedecias fled by the way that leadeth to the plains of the wilderness.

5 And the army of the Chaldees pursued after the king, and overtook him in the plains of Jericho. And all the warriors that were with him were scattered, and left him.

6 So they took the king, and brought him to the king of Babylon to Reblatha; and he gave judgment upon him.

7 And he slew the sons of Sedecias before his face; and he put out his eyes, and bound him with chains, and brought him to Babylon.

8 In the fifth month, the eleventh day of the month, that is, the nineteenth year of the king of Babylon, came Nabuzardan commander of the army, a servant of the king of Babylon, into Jerusalem.

---

[2] Dan. 1, 1. [3] Isai. 39, 6. [4] 2 Par. 36, 10; Esther, 2, 6; 11, 4; Ezech. 17, 12; Jer. 24, 1; 39, 2. [5] Jer. 37, 1; 52, 1. CHAP. 25. [1] Jer. 39, 4; 52, 4.

9 [2] And he burnt the house of the Lord, and the king's house, and the houses of Jerusalem: and every house he burnt with fire.

10 And all the army of the Chaldees, which was with the commander of the troops, broke down the walls of Jerusalem round about.

11 And Nabuzardan the commander of the army, carried away the rest of the people that remained in the city, and the fugitives that had gone over to the king of Babylon, and the remnant of the common people.

12 But of the poor of the land he left some dressers of vines and husbandmen.

13 [3] And the pillars of brass that were in the temple of the Lord, and the bases, and the sea of brass which was in the house of the Lord, the Chaldees broke in pieces: and carried all the brass of them to Babylon.

14 They took away also the pots of brass, and the mazers, and the forks, and the cups, and the mortars, and all the vessels of brass with which they ministered.

15 Moreover also the censers, and the bowls, such as were of gold in gold, and such as were of silver in silver, the general of the army took away.

16 That is, two pillars, one sea, and the bases which Solomon had made in the temple of the Lord. The brass of all these vessels was without weight.

17 [4] One pillar was eighteen cubits high; and the chapiter of brass which was upon it was three cubits high. And the network, and the pomegranates that were upon the chapiter of the pillar, were all of brass. And the second pillar had the like adorning.

18 And the general of the army took Seraias the chief priest, and Sophonias the second priest, and three doorkeepers.

19 And out of the city one eunuch, who was captain over the men of war: and five men of them that had stood before the king, whom he found in the city: and Sopher the captain of the army who exercised the young soldiers of the people of the land: and threescore men of the common people, who were found in the city.

20 These Nabuzardan the general of the army took away, and carried them to the king of Babylon to Reblatha.

21 And the king of Babylon smote them, and slew them at Reblatha in the land of Emath. So Juda was carried away out of their land.

22 But over the people that remained in the land of Juda, which Nabuchodonosor king of Babylon had left, he gave the government to Godolias the son of Ahicam the son of Saphan.

23 And when all the captains of the soldiers had heard this, they and the men that were with them, to wit, that the king of Babylon had made Godolias governor, they came to Godolias to Maspha: Ismael the son of Nathanias, and Johanan the son of Caree, and Saraia the son of Thanehumeth the Netophathite, and Jezonias the son of Maachathi: they and their men.

24 And Godolias swore to them and to their men, saying: Be not afraid to serve the Chaldees. Stay in the land, and serve the king of Babylon; and it shall be well with you.

25 But it came to pass in the seventh month, that Ismael the son of Nathanias the son of Elisama, of the seed royal, came, and ten men with him; and smote Godolias so that he died. And also the Jews and the Chaldees that were with him in Maspha.

26 And all the people both little and great, and the captains of the soldiers, rising up went to Egypt, fearing the Chaldees.

27 [5] And it came to pass in the seven and thirtieth year of the captivity of Joachim king of Juda, in the twelfth month the seven and twentieth day of the month: Evilmerodach king of Babylon, in the year that he began to reign, lifted up the head of Joachin king of Juda out of prison.

28 And he spoke kindly to him: and he set his throne above the throne of the kings that were with him in Babylon.

29 And he changed his garments which he had in prison: and he ate bread always before him, all the days of his life.

30 And he appointed him a continual allowance, which was also given him by the king day by day, all the days of his life.

[2] Ps. 73, 7. [3] Jer. 27, 19. [4] 3 Kings, 7, 15; 2 Par. 3, 15; Jer. 52, 21. [5] Jer. 52, 31.

THE BOOK OF
PARALIPOMENON

These Books are called by the Greek interpreters, Paralipomenon, (Παραλει-πόμενον,) *that is, of things left out, or omitted: because they are a kind of a supplement of such things as were passed over in the books of the Kings. The Hebrews call them* Dibre Haijamin, *that is,* The Words of the Days, *or* The Chronicles.—*Not that they are the books which are so often quoted in the* Kings, *under the title of* The Words of the Days of the Kings of Israel, *and* The Words of the Days of the Kings of Juda; *for the books of Paralipomenon were written after the books of Kings: but because in all probability they have been abridged from those* ancient words of the days, *by Esdras or some other sacred writer.*

CHAPTER 1

The genealogy of the patriarchs down to Abraham. The posterity of Abraham and of Esau.

ADAM, [1] Seth, Enos,

2 Cainan, Malaleel, Jared,

3 Henoc, Mathusale, Lamech.

4 Noe, Sem, Cham, and Japheth.

5 The sons of Japheth: Gomer, and Magog, and Madai, and Javan, Thubal, Mosoch, Thiras.

6 And the sons of Gomer: Ascenez, and Riphath, and Thogorma.

7 And the sons of Javan: Elisa and Tharsis, Cethim and Dodanim.

8 The sons of Cham: Chus, and Mesrai, and Phut, and Chanaan.

9 And the sons of Chus: Saba, and Hevila, Sabatha, and Regma, and Saba-thaca. And the sons of Regma: Saba, and Dadan.

10 Now Chus begot [2] Nemrod. He began to be mighty upon earth.

11 But Mesraim begot Ludim, and Anamim, and Laabim, and Nephtuim,

12 Phetrusim also, and Casluim: from whom came the Philistines, and Caphtorim.

13 And Chanaan begot Sidon his firstborn, and the Hethite,

14 And the Jebusite, and the Amor-rhite, and the Gergesite,

15 And the Hevite, and the Aracite, and the Sinite,

16 And the Aradian, and the Sama-rite, and the Hamathite.

17 The sons of Sem: [3] Elam, and Asur, and Arphaxad, and Lud, and Aram, and Hus, and Hul, and Gether, and Mosoch.

18 And Arphaxad begot Sale, and Sale begot Heber.

19 And to Heber were born two sons. The name of the one was Phaleg, because in his days the earth was divided; and the name of his brother was Jectan.

20 And Jectan begot Elmodad, and Saleph, and Asarmoth, and Jare,

21 And Adoram, and Usal, and Decla,

22 And Hebal, and Abimael, and Saba,

23 And Ophir, and Hevila, and Jo-bab. All these are the sons of Jectan.

24 Sem, Arphaxad, Sale,

25 Heber, Phaleg, Ragau,

26 Serug, Nachor, Thare,

27 Abram, [4] this is Abraham.

28 And the sons of Abraham, Isaac and Ismahel.

29 And these are the generations of them. The firstborn of [5] Ismahel, Naba-joth: then Cedar, and Adbeel, and Mabsam.

30 And Masma, and Duma, Massa, Hadad, and Thema,

31 Jetur, Naphis, Cedma. These are the sons of Ismahel.

32 And the sons of Cetura, Abra-ham's concubine, whom she bore: Zam-ran, Jecsan, Madan, Madian, Jesboc, and Sue. And the sons of Jecsan, Saba, and Dadan. And the sons of Dadan: Assurim, and Latussim, and Laomin.

33 And the sons [6] of Madian: Epha, and Epher, and Henoch, and Abida, and Eldaa. All these are the sons of Cetura.

34 [7] And Abraham begot Isaac: and his sons were Esau and Israel.

35 The sons of [8] Esau: Eliphaz, Ra-huel, Jehus, Ihelom, and Core.

36 The sons of Eliphaz: Theman, Omar, Sephi, Gathan, Cenez, and by Thamna, Amalec.

37 The sons of Rahuel: Nahath, Zara, Samma, Meza.

38 The sons of Seir: Lotan, Sobal, Sebeon, Ana, Dison, Eser, Disan.

CHAP. 1. [1] Gen. 2, 7; 4, 25; 5, 6, 9. [2] Gen. 10, 8. [3] Gen. 10, 22; 11, 10. [4] Gen. 11, 26. [5] Gen. 25, 13. [6] Gen. 25, 4. [7] Gen. 25, 19. [8] Gen. 36, 10.

CHAP. 1. Ver. 32. *Concubine.* She was his law-ful wife, but of an inferior degree.

39 The sons of Lotan: Hori, Homam. And the sister of Lotan was Thamna.

40 The sons of Sobal: Alian, and Manahath, and Ebal, Sephi, and Onam. The sons of Sebeon: Aia, and Ana. The son of Ana: Dison.

41 The sons of Dison: Hamram, and Eseban, and Jethran, and Charan.

42 The sons of Eser: Balaan, and Zavan, and Jacan. The sons of Disan: Hus and Aran.

43 Now these are the kings that reigned in the land of Edom, before there was a king over the children of Israel: Bale the son of Beor; and the name of his city was Denaba.

44 And Bale died, and Jobab the son of Zare of Bosra, reigned in his stead.

45 And when Jobab also was dead, Husam of the land of the Themanites reigned in his stead.

46 And Husam also died, and Adad the son of Badad reigned in his stead; and he defeated the Madianites in the land of Moab: and the name of his city was Avith.

47 And when Adad also was dead, Semla of Masreca reigned in his stead.

48 Semla also died, and Saul of Rohoboth, which is near the river, reigned in his stead.

49 And when Saul was dead, Balanan the son of Achobor reigned in his stead.

50 He also died, and Adad reigned in his stead: and the name of his city was Phau. And his wife was called Meetabel the daughter of Matred, the daughter of Mezaab.

51 And after the death of Adad, there began to be dukes in Edom instead of kings: duke Thamna, duke Alva, duke Jetheth,

52 Duke Oolibama, duke Ela, duke Phinon,

53 Duke Cenez, due Theman, duke Mabsar,

54 Duke Magdiel, duke Hiram. These *are* the dukes of Edom.

CHAPTER 2

The twelve tribes of Israel. The genealogy of Juda down to David. Other genealogies of the tribe of Juda.

AND [1] these are the sons of Israel: Ruben, Simeon, Levi, Juda, Issachar, and Zabulon,

2 Dan, Joseph, Benjamin, Nephtali, Gad, and Aser.

3 The sons of [2] Juda: Her, Onan, and Sela. These three were born to him of the Chanaanitess the daughter of Sue. And Her, the firstborn of Juda, was wicked in the sight of the Lord, and he slew him.

4 [3] And Thamar his daughter-in-law bore him Phares and Zara. So all the sons of Juda were five.

5 And the sons of Phares were Hesron, and Hamul.

6 And the sons also of Zare, Zamri, and Ethan, and Eman, and Chalchal, and Dara, five in all.

7 And the sons of Charmi: Achar, who troubled Israel, and sinned by the theft of the anathema.

8 The sons of Ethan: Azarias.

9 And the sons of [5] Hesron that were born to him: Jerameel, and Ram, and Calubi.

10 And Ram begot Aminadab, and Aminadab begot Nahasson, prince of the children of Juda.

11 And Nahasson begot Salma, the father of Booz.

12 And Booz begot Obed, and Obed begot Isai.

13 [6] And Isai begot Eliab his firstborn, the second Abinadab, the third Simmaa,

14 The fourth, Nathanael, the fifth Raddai,

15 The sixth Asom, the seventh David.

16 And their sisters were Sarvia, and Abigail. The sons of Sarvia: Abisai, Joab, and Asael, three.

17 And Abigail bore Amasa, whose father was Jether the Ismahelite.

18 And Caleb the son of Hesron took a wife named Azuba, of whom he had Jerioth: and her sons were Jaser, and Sobab, and Ardon.

19 And when Azuba was dead, Caleb took to wife Ephrata: who bore him Hur.

20 And Hur begot Uri: and Uri begot Bezeleel.

21 And afterwards Hesron went in to the daughter of Machir the father of Galaad, and took her to wife when he was threescore years old: and she bore him Segub.

22 And Segub begot Jair, and he had three and twenty cities in the land of Galaad.

23 And he took Gessur, and Aram the towns of Jair, and Canath, and the villages thereof, threescore cities. All

CHAP. 2. [1] Gen. 29, 32; 30, 5; 35, 22. [2] Gen. 38, 3; 46, 12. [3] 1 Par. 4, 1; Matt. 1, 3. [4] Jos. 7, 1. [5] Ruth, 4, 19. [6] 1 Kings, 16, 6, 9; 17, 12.

CHAP. 2. Ver. 7. *Achar,* alias Achan (Jos. 7). —*The anathema.* The thing devoted or accursed, viz, the spoils of Jericho.

Ver. 10. *Ram.* He is commonly called *Aram.* But it is to be observed here, once for all, that it was a common thing among the Hebrews for the same persons to have different names: and that it is not impossible among so many proper names, as here occur in the first nine chapters of this book, that the transcribers of the ancient Hebrew copies may have made some slips in the orthography.

Ver. 18. *Caleb,* alias Calubi (ver. 9).

these, the sons of Machir father of Galaad.

24 And when Hesron was dead, Caleb went in to Ephrata. Hesron also had to wife Abia, who bore him Ashur the father of Thecua.

25 And the sons of Jerameel the first born of Hesron were Ram his firstborn, and Buna, and Aram, and Asom, and Achia.

26 And Jerameel married another wife, named Atara, who was the mother of Onam.

27 And the sons of Ram the firstborn of Jerameel, were Moos, Jamin, and Achar.

28 And Onam had sons Semei, and Jada. And the sons of Semei; Nadab, and Abisur.

29 And the name of Abisur's wife was Abihail, who bore him Ahobban, and Molid.

30 And the sons of Nadab were Saled, and Apphaim. And Saled died without children.

31 But the son of Apphaim was Jesi: and Jesi begot Sesan. And Sesan begot Oholai.

32 And the sons of Jada the brother of Semei: Jether, and Jonathan. And Jether also died without children.

33 But Jonathan begot Phaleth, and Ziza. These were the sons of Jerameel.

34 And Sesan had no sons, but daughters and a servant an Egyptian named Jeraa.

35 And he gave him his daughter to wife: and she bore him Ethei.

36 And Ethei begot Nathan, and Nathan begot Zabad.

37 And Zabad begot Ophlal, and Ophlal begot Obed.

38 Obed begot Jehu, Jehu begot Azarias.

39 Azarias begot Helles, and Helles begot Elasa.

40 Elasa begot Sisamoi, Sisamoi begot Sellum,

41 Sellum begot Icamia, and Icamia begot Elisama.

42 Now the sons of Caleb the brother of Jerameel were Mesa his firstborn, who was the father of Siph: and the sons of Maresa father of Hebron.

43 And the sons of Hebron: Core, and Thaphua, and Recem, and Samma.

44 And Samma begot Raham, the father of Jercaam, and Recem begot Sammai.

45 The son of Sammai: Maon. And Maon was the father of Bethsur.

46 And Epha the concubine of Caleb bore Haran, and Mosa, and Gezez. And Haran begot Gezcz.

47 And the sons of Jahaddai: Rogom, and Joathan, and Gesan, and Phalet, and Epha, and Saaph.

48 And Maacha the concubine of Caleb bore Saber, and Tharana.

49 And Saaph the father of Madmena begot Sue the father of Machbena, and the father of Gabaa. And the daughter of Caleb was Achsa.

50 These were the sons of Caleb, the son of Hur the firstborn of Ephrata; Sobal the father of Cariathiarim,

51 Salma the father of Bethlehem, Hariph the father of Bethgader.

52 And Sobal the father of Cariathiarim had sons: he that saw half of the places of rest.

53 And of the kindred of Cariathiarim, the Jethrites, and Aphuthites, and Semathites, and Maserites. Of them came the Saraites, and Esthaolites.

54 The sons of Salma, Bethlehem, and Netophathi, the crowns of the house of Joab, and half of the place of rest of Sarai.

55 And the families of the scribes that dwell in Jabes, singing and making melody, and abiding in tents. These are the Cinites, who came of Calor (Chamath) father of the house of Rechab.

CHAPTER 3

The genealogy of the house of David.

NOW [1] these were the sons of David that were born to him in Hebron: the firstborn Amnon of Achinoam the Jezrahelitess: the second Daniel of Abigail the Carmelitess:

2 The third Absalom the son of Maacha the daughter of Tolmai king of Gessur: the fourth Adonias the son of Aggith:

3 The fifth Saphatias of Abital: the sixth Jethrahem of Egla his wife.

4 So six sons were born to him in Hebron, where he reigned seven years and six months. And in Jerusalem he reigned three and thirty years.

5 [2] And these sons were born to him in Jerusalem: Simmaa, and Sobab, and Nathan, and Solomon four of Bethsabee the daughter of Ammiel.

6 Jebaar also, and Elisama,

7 And Eliphaleth, and Noge, and Nepheg, and Japhia,

8 And Elisama, and Eliada, and Elipheleth, nine:

9 All these the sons of David, beside the sons of the concubines. And they had a sister Thamar.

CHAP. 3. 1 2 Kings, 3, 2. 2 2 Kings, 5, 14.

Ver. 52. *He that saw half of the places of rest.* The Latin interpreter seems to have given us here, instead of the proper names, the meaning of those names in the Hebrew. He has done in like manner, ver. 55.

CHAP. 3. Ver. 9. *The concubines.* The inferior wives.

10 And Solomon's son was Roboam: whose son Abia begot Asa. And his son was Josaphat,

11 The father of Joram. And Joram begot Ochozias, of whom was born Joas.

12 And his son Amasias begot Azarias. And Joathan the son of Azarias

13 Begot Achaz, the father of Ezechias, of whom was born Manasses.

14 And Manasses begot Amon the father of Josias.

15 And the sons of Josias were, the firstborn Johanan, the second Joakim, the third Sedecias, the fourth Sellum.

16 [3] Of Joakim was born Jechonias, and Sedecias.

17 The sons of Jechonias were Asir, Salathiel,

18 Melchiram, Phadaia, Senneser and Jecemia, Sama, and Nadabia.

19 Of Phadaia, were born Zorobabel and Semei. Zorobabel begot Mosollam, Hananias, and Salomith their sister:

20 Hasaba also, and Ohol, and Barachias, and Hasadias, Josabhesed, five.

21 And the son of Hananias *was* Phaltias the father of Jeseias, whose son was Raphaia. And his son was Arnan, of whom was born Obdia, whose son was Sechenias.

22 The son of Sechenias, *was* Semeia, whose sons were Hattus, and Jegaal, and Baria, and Naaria, and Saphat, six in number.

23 The sons of Naaria, Elioenai, and Ezechias, and Ezricam, three.

24 The sons of Elioenai, Oduia, and Eliasub, and Pheleia, and Accub, and Johanan, and Dalaia, and Anani, seven.

CHAPTER 4

Other genealogies of Juda and of Simeon, and their victories.

THE [1] sons of Juda: Phares, Hesron, and Charmi, and Hur, and Sobal.

2 And Raia the son of Sobal begot Jahath, of whom were born Ahumai, and Laad. These are the families of Sarathi.

3 And this *is* the posterity of Etam: Jezrahel, and Jesema, and Jedebos: and the name of their sister was Asalelphuni.

4 And Phanuel the father of Gedor, and Ezar the father of Hosa. These are the sons of Hur the firstborn of Ephratha the father of Bethlehem.

5 And Assur the father of Thecua had two wives, Halaa, and Naara:

6 And Naara bore him Ozam, and Hepher, and Themani, and Ahasthari: these are the sons of Naara.

7 And the sons of Halaa: Sereth, Isaar, and Ethnan.

8 And Cos begot Anob, and Soboba, and the kindred of Aharehel the son of Arum.

9 And Jabes was more honourable than any of his brethren, and his mother called his name Jabes, saying: Because I bore him with sorrow.

10 And Jabes called upon the God of Israel, saying: If blessing thou wilt bless me, and wilt enlarge my borders, and thy hand be with me, and thou save me from being oppressed by evil. And God granted him the things he prayed for.

11 And Caleb the brother of Sua begot Mahir, who was the father of Esthon.

12 And Esthon begot Bethrapha, and Phesse, and Tehinna father of the city of Naas: these are the men of Recha.

13 And the sons of Cenez were Othoniel and Saraia. And the sons of Othoniel: Hathath, and Maonathi.

14 Maonathi begot Ophra, and Saraia begot Joab the father of the Valley of artificers: for artificers were there.

15 And the sons of Caleb the son of Jephone, were Hir, and Ela, and Naham. And the sons of Ela: Cenez.

16 The sons also of Jaleleel: Ziph, and Zipha, Thiria, and Asrael.

17 And the sons of Esra: Jether, and Mered, and Epher, and Jalon; and he begot Mariam, and Sammai, and Jesba the father of Esthamo.

18 And his wife Judaia bore Jared the father of Gedor, and Heber the father of Socho, and Icuthiel the father of Zanoe. And these are the sons of Bethia the daughter of Pharao, whom Mered took to wife.

19 And the sons of his wife Odaia the sister of Naham the father of Celia: Garmi, and Esthamo, who was of Machathi.

20 The sons also of Simon: Amnon, and Rinna the son of Hanan, and Thilon. And the sons of Jesi: Zoheth, and Benzoheth.

21 The sons of [2] Sela the son of Juda: Her the father of Lecha, and Laada the father of Maresa, and the families of the house of them that wrought fine linen in the House of oath.

22 And he that made the sun to stand, and the men of Lying, and Secure, and Burning, who were princes in Moab, and who returned into Lahem. Now these are things of old.

[3] Matt. 1, 11. CHAP. 4. [1] Gen. 38, 3; 46, 12; 1 Par. 2, 4; Matt. 1, 3. [2] Gen. 38, 5.

Ver. 22. *Six.* Counting the father in the number.

CHAP. 4. Ver. 9. *Jabes.* That is, *sorrowful.*

Ver. 22. *He that made the sun to stand.* That is, *Joazim,* the meaning of whose name in Hebrew is, *he that made the sun to stand.* In like

23 These are the potters, and they dwelt in Plantations, and Hedges, with the king for his works, and they abode there.

24 The sons of [3] Simeon: Namuel, and Jamin, Jarib, Zara, Saul:

25 Sellum his son, Mapsam his son, Masma his son.

26 The sons of Masma: Hamuel his son, Zachur his son, Semei his son.

27 The sons of Semei were sixteen, and six daughters: but his brethren had not many sons; and the whole kindred could not reach to the sum of the children of Juda.

28 And they dwelt in Bersabee, and Molada, and Hasarsuhal,

29 And in Bala, and in Asom, and in Tholad,

30 And in Bathuel, and in Horma, and in Siceleg,

31 And in Bethmarchaboth, and in Hasarsusim, and in Bethberai, and in Saarim. These were their cities unto the reign of David.

32 Their towns also were Etam, and Aen, Remmon, and Thochen, and Asan, five cities.

33 And all their villages round about these cities as far as Baal. This was their habitation, and the distribution of their dwellings.

34 And Mosabab, and Jemlech, and Josa, the son of Amasias,

35 And Joel, and Jehu the son of Josabia the son of Saraia the son of Asiel,

36 And Elioenai, and Jacoba, and Isuhaia, and Asaia, and Adiel, and Ismiel, and Banaia,

37 Ziza also the son of Sephei the son of Allon the son of Idaia the son of Semri the son of Samaia.

38 These were named princes in their kindreds, and in the houses of their families were multiplied exceedingly.

39 And they went forth to enter into Gador as far as to the east side of the valley, to seek pastures for their flocks.

40 And they found fat pastures, and very good, and a country spacious, and quiet, and fruitful, in which some of the race of Cham had dwelt before.

41 And these whose names are written above, came in the days of Ezechias king of Juda: and they beat down their tents, and slew the inhabitants that were found there, and utterly destroyed them unto this day: and they dwelt in their place, because they found there fat pastures.

42 Some also of the children of Simeon, five hundred men, went into mount Seir, having for their captains Phaltias and Naaria and Raphaia and Oziel the sons of Jesi.

43 And they slew the remnant of the Amalecites, who had been able to escape; and they dwelt there in their stead unto this day.

CHAPTER 5
Genealogies of Ruben and Gad. Their victories over the Agarites. Their captivity.

NOW the sons of Ruben the firstborn of Israel, (for he was his firstborn: but forasmuch as [1] he defiled his father's bed, his first birthright was given to the sons of Joseph the son of Israel, and he was not accounted for the firstborn.

2 But of the race of Juda, who was the strongest among his brethren, came the princes: but the first birthright was accounted to Joseph.)

3 The sons then of [2] Ruben the firstborn of Israel were Enoch, and Phallu, Esron, and Charmi.

4 The sons of Joel: Samaia his son, Gog his son, Semei his son,

5 Micha his son, Reia his son, Baal his son,

6 Beera his son, whom Thelgathphalnasar [3] king of the Assyrians carried away captive, and he was prince in the tribe of Ruben.

7 And his brethren, and all his kindred, when they were numbered by their families, had for princes Jehiel, and Zacharias.

8 And Bala the son of Azaz, the son of Samma, the son of Joel, dwelt in Aroer as far as Nebo, and Beelmeon.

9 And eastward he had his habitation as far as the entrance of the desert, and the river Euphrates. For they possessed a great number of cattle in the land of Galaad.

10 And in the days of Saul they fought against the Agarites, and slew them, and dwelt in their tents in their stead, in all the country, that looketh to the east of Galaad.

11 And the children of Gad dwelt over against them in the land of Basan, as far as Selcha:

12 Johel the chief, and Saphan the second, and Janai, and Saphat in Basan.

[3] Gen. 46, 10. CHAP. 5. [1] Gen. 35, 22; 49, 4. [2] Gen. 46, 9; Exod. 6, 14; Num. 26, 5. [3] 4 Kings, 15, 29.

manner the following names, *Lying* (Chozeba), *Secure* (Joas), and *Burning* (Saraph), are substituted in place of the Hebrew names of the same signification.

Ver. 23. *Plantation and Hedges.* These are the proper names of the places where they dwelt. In Hebrew *Atharim* and *Gadira.*

CHAP. 5. Ver. 2. *Accounted to Joseph.* That is, as to the double portion, which belonged to the firstborn; but the princely dignity was given to Juda, and the priesthood to Levi.

13 And their brethren according to the houses of their kindreds, *were* Michael, and Mosollam, and Sebe, and Jorai, and Jacan, and Zie, and Heber, seven.

14 These were the sons of Abihail, the son of Huri, the son of Jara, the son of Galaad, the son of Michael, the son of Jesisi, the son of Jeddo, the son of Buz.

15 And their brethren the sons of Abdiel, the son of Guni, chief of the house in their families.

16 And they dwelt in Galaad, and in Basan and in the towns thereof, and in all the suburbs of Saron, unto the borders.

17 All these were numbered in the days of Joathan king of Juda, and in the days of Jeroboam king of Israel.

18 The sons of Ruben, and of Gad, and of the half tribe of Manasses, fighting men, bearing shields, and swords, and bending the bow, and trained up to battles, four and forty thousand seven hundred and threescore that went out to war.

19 They fought against the Agarites: but the Itureans, and Naphis, and Nodab,

20 Gave them help. And the Agarites were delivered into their hands, and all that were with them, because they called upon God in the battle: and he heard them, because they had put their faith in him.

21 And they took all that they possessed, of camels fifty thousand, and of sheep two hundred and fifty thousand, and of asses two thousand, and of men a hundred thousand souls.

22 And many fell down slain: for it was the battle of the Lord. And they dwelt in their stead till the captivity.

23 And the children of the half tribe of Manasses possessed the land, from the borders of Basan unto Baal, Hermon, and Sanir, and mount Hermon; for their number was great.

24 And these were the heads of the house of their kindred: Epher, and Jesi, and Eliel, and Esriel, and Jeremia, and Odoia, and Jediel; most valiant and powerful men, and famous chiefs in their families.

25 But they forsook the God of their fathers, and went astray after the gods of the people of the land, whom God destroyed before them.

26 And the God of Israel stirred up the spirit of Phul [4] king of the Assyrians, and the spirit of Thelgathphalnasar king of Assur. And he carried away Ruben, and Gad, and the half tribe of Manasses, and brought them to Lahela, and to Habor, and to Ara, and to the river of Gozan, unto this day.

CHAPTER 6

The genealogies of Levi, and of Aaron. The cities of the Levites.

THE [1] sons of Levi were Gerson, Caath, and Merari.

2 The sons of Caath: Amram, Isaar, Hebron, and Oziel.

3 The children of Amram: Aaron, Moses, and Mary. The sons of Aaron: Nadab and Abiu, Eleazar and Ithamar.

4 Eleazar begot Phinees, and Phinees begot Abisue.

5 And Abisue begot Bocci, and Bocci begot Ozi.

6 Ozi begot Zaraias, and Zaraias begot Maraioth.

7 And Maraioth begot Amarias, and Amarias begot Achitob.

8 Achitob begot Sadoc, and Sadoc begot Achimaas.

9 Achimaas begot Azarias, Azarias begot Johanan.

10 Johanan begot Azarias. This is he that executed the priestly office in the house which Solomon built in Jerusalem.

11 And Azarias begot Amarias and Amarias begot Achitob.

12 And Achitob begot Sadoc, and Sadoc begot Sellum.

13 Sellum begot Helcias, and Helcias begot Azarias,

14 Azarias begot Saraias, and Saraias begot Josedec.

15 Now Josedec went out, when the Lord carried away Juda, and Jerusalem, by the hands of Nabuchodonosor.

16 So the sons of [2] Levi were Gerson, Caath, and Merari.

17 And these are the names of the sons of Gerson: Lobni and Semei.

18 The sons of Caath: Amram, and Isaar, and Hebron, and Oziel.

19 The sons of Merari: Moholi and Musi. And these are the kindreds of Levi according to their families.

20 Of Gerson: Lobni his son, Jahath his son, Zamma his son,

21 Joah his son, Addo his son, Zara his son, Jethrai his son.

22 The sons of Caath: Aminadab his son, Core his son, Asir his son,

23 Elcana his son, Abiasaph his son, Asir his son,

24 Thahath his son, Uriel his son, Ozias his son, Saul his son.

25 The sons of Elcana: Amasai, and Achimoth,

26 And Elcana. The sons of Elcana: Sophai his son, Nahath his son,

27 Eliab his son, Jeroham his son, Elcana his son.

[4] 4 Kings, 15, 19, 29. CHAP. 6. [1] Gen. 46, 11; 1 Par. 23, 6. [2] Exod. 6, 16.

28 The sons of Samuel: the firstborn Vasseni, and Abia.

29 And the sons of Merari: Moholi, Lobni his son, Semei his son, Oza his son,

30 Sammaa his son, Haggia his son, Asaia his son.

31 There are they, whom David set over the singing men of the house of the Lord, after that the ³ ark was placed.

32 And they ministered before the tabernacle of the testimony, with singing, until Solomon built the house of the Lord in Jerusalem; and they stood according to their order in the ministry.

33 And these are they that stood with their sons, of the sons of Caath: Hemam a singer, the son of Joel, the son of Samuel,

34 The son of Elcana, the son of Jeroham, the son of Eliel, the son of Thohu,

35 The son of Suph, the son of Elcana, the son of Mahath, the son of Amasai,

36 The son of Elcana, the son of Johel, the son of Azarias, the son of Sophonias,

37 The son of Thahath, the son of Asir, the son of Abiasaph, the son of Core,

38 The son of Isaar, the son of Caath, the son of Levi, the son of Israel.

39 And his brother Asaph, who stood on his right hand; Asaph the son of Barachias, the son of Samaa,

40 The son of Michael, the son of Basaia, the son of Melchia,

41 The son of Athanai, the son of Zara, the son of Adaia,

42 The son of Ethan, the son of Zamma, the son of Semei,

43 The son of Jeth, the son of Gerson, the son of Levi.

44 And the sons of Merari their brethren, on the left hand; Ethan the son of Cusi, the son of Abdi, the son of Meloch,

45 The son of Hasabia, the son of Amasai, the son of Helcias,

46 The son of Amasai, the son of Boni, the son of Somer,

47 The son of Moholi, the son of Musi, the son of Merari, the son of Levi.

48 Their brethren also the Levites, who were appointed for all the ministry of the tabernacle of the house of the Lord.

49 But Aaron and his sons offered burnt offerings upon the altar of holocausts, and upon the altar of incense, for every work of the holy of holies: and to pray for Israel according to all that

³ 2 Kings, 6, 1, 17. ⁴ Jos. 21, 21.

Moses the servant of God had commanded.

50 And these are the sons of Aaron: Eleazar his son, Phinees his son, Abisue his son,

51 Bocci his son, Ozi his son, Zarahia his son,

52 Meraioth his son, Amarias his son, Achitob his son,

53 Sadoc his son, Achimaas his son.

54 And these are their dwelling places by the towns and confines, to wit, of the sons of Aaron, of the families of the Caathites: for they fell to them by lot.

55 And they gave them Hebron in the land of Juda, and the suburbs thereof round about:

56 But the fields of the city, and the villages to Caleb son of Jephone.

57 And to the sons of Aaron they gave the cities for refuge, Hebron, and Lobna, and the suburbs thereof:

58 And Jether and Esthemo, with their suburbs, and Helon, and Dabir with their suburbs:

59 Asan also, and Bethsames, with their suburbs.

60 And out of the tribe of Benjamin: Gabee and its suburbs, Almath with its suburbs, Anathoth also with its suburbs: all their cities throughout their families were thirteen.

61 And to the sons of Caath that remained of their kindred they gave, out of the half tribe of Manasses ten cities in possession.

62 And to the sons of Gerson by their families, out of the tribe of Issachar, and out of the tribe of Aser, and out of the tribe of Nephtali, and out of the tribe of Manasses in Basan, thirteen cities.

63 And to the sons of Merari by their families, out of the tribe of Ruben, and out of the tribe of Gad, and out of the tribe of Zabulon, they gave by lot twelve cities.

64 And the children of Israel gave to the Levites the cities, and their suburbs.

65 And they gave them by lot, out of the tribe of the sons of Juda, and out of the tribe of the sons of Simeon, and out of the tribe of the sons of Benjamin, these cities which they called by their names.

66 And to them that were of the kindred of the sons of Caath, ⁴ and the cities in their borders were of the tribe of Ephraim.

67 And they gave the cities of refuge Sichem with its suburbs in mount Ephraim, and Gazer with its suburbs;

68 Jecmaan also with its suburbs, and Beth-horon in like manner;

69 Helon also with its suburbs, and Gethremmon in like manner.

70 And out of the half tribe of Manasses, Aner and its suburbs, Baalam and its suburbs: to wit, to them that were left of the family of the sons of Caath.

71 And to the sons of Gersom, out of the kindred of the half tribe of Manasses, Gaulon, in Basan, and its suburbs, and Astharoth with its suburbs.

72 Out of the tribe of Issachar, Cedes and its suburbs, and Dabercth with its suburbs;

73 Ramoth also and its suburbs, and Anem with its suburbs.

74 And out of the tribe of Aser: Masal with its suburbs, and Abdon in like manner;

75 Hucac also and its suburbs, and Rohol with its suburbs.

76 And out of the tribe of Nephtali, Cedes in Galilee and its suburbs, Hamon with its suburbs, and Cariathaim and its suburbs.

77 And to the sons of Merari that remained, out of the tribe of Zabulon, Remmono and its suburbs, and Thabor with its suburbs.

78 Beyond the Jordan also over against Jericho, on the east side of the Jordan, out of the tribe of Ruben, Bosor in the wilderness with its suburbs, and Jassa with its suburbs;

79 Cademoth also and its suburbs, and Mephaath with its suburbs.

80 Moreover also out of the tribe of Gad, Ramoth in Galaad and its suburbs, and Manaim with its suburbs;

81 Hesebon also with its suburbs, and Jazer with its suburbs.

CHAPTER 7

Genealogies of Issachar, Benjamin, Nephtali, Manasses, Ephraim, and Aser.

NOW [1] the sons of Issachar were Thola, and Phua, Jasub and Simeron, four.

2 The sons of Thola: Ozi, and Raphaia, and Jeriel, and Jemai, and Jebsem, and Samuel, chiefs of the houses of their kindreds. Of the posterity of Thola were numbered in the days of David, two and twenty thousand six hundred most valiant men.

3 The sons of Ozi: Izrahia, of whom were born Michael, and Obadia, and Joel, and Jesia, five all great men.

4 And there were with them by their families and peoples, six and thirty thousand most valiant men ready for war: for they had many wives and children.

5 Their brethren also throughout all the house of Issachar, were numbered

fourscore and seven thousand most valiant men for war.

6 The sons of [2] Benjamin were Bela, and Bechor, and Jadihel, three.

7 The sons of Bela: Esbon, and Ozi, and Ozial, and Jerimoth and Urai, five chiefs of their families, and most valiant warriors; and their number was twenty-two thousand and thirty-four.

8 And the sons of Bechor were Zamira, and Joas, and Eliezer, and Elioenai, and Amai, and Jerimoth, and Abia, and Anathoth, and Almath: all these were the sons of Bechor.

9 And they were numbered by the families, heads of their kindreds, most valiant men for war, twenty thousand and two hundred.

10 And the son of Jadihel: Balan. And the sons of Balan; Jehus, and Benjamin, and Aod, and Chanana, and Zethan, and Tharsis, and Ahisahar.

11 All these were sons of Jadihel, heads of their kindreds, most valiant men, seventeen thousand and two hundred fit to go out to war.

12 Sepham also and Hapham the sons of Hir: and Hasim the sons of Aher.

13 [3] And the sons of Nephtali were Jasiel, and Guni, and Jezer, and Sellum, sons of Bala.

14 And the son of Manasses, Ezriel. And his concubine the Syrian bore Machir the father of Galaad.

15 And Machir took wives for his sons Happhim, and Saphan: and he had a sister named Maacha. The name of the second was Salphaad, and Salphaad had daughters.

16 And Maacha the wife of Machir bore a son, and she called his name Phares. And the name of his brother was Sares: and his sons were Ulam and Recen.

17 And the son of Ulam, Baden. These are the sons of Galaad, the son of Machir, the son of Manasses.

18 And his sister named Queen bore Goodlyman, and Abiezer, and Mohola.

19 And the sons of Semida were Ahiu, and Sechem, and Leci, and Aniam.

20 And the sons of Ephraim were Suthala, Bared his son, Thahath his son, Elada his son, Thahath his son, and his son Zabad,

21 And his son Suthala, and his son Ezer and Elad. And the men of Geth born in the land slew them, because they came down to invade their possessions.

22 And Ephraim their father mourned many days, and his brethren came to comfort him.

CHAP. 7. [1] Gen. 46, 13. [2] Gen. 46, 21. [3] Gen. 46, 24.

23 And he went in to his wife: and she conceived and bore a son. And he called his name Beria, because he was born when it went evil with his house:

24 And his daughter was Sara, who built Bethoron, the nether and the upper, and Ozensara.

25 And Rapha was his son, and Reseph, and Thale, of whom was born Thaan,

26 Who begot Laadan. And his son was Ammiud, who begot Elisama,

27 Of whom was born Nun, who had Josue for his son.

28 And their possessions and habitations were Bethel with her daughters, and eastward Noran, and westward Gazer and her daughters, Sichem also with her daughters, as far as Asa with her daughters.

29 And by the borders of the sons of Manasses, Bethsan and her daughters, Thanach and her daughters, Mageddo and her daughters, Dor and her daughters. In these dwelt the children of Joseph, the son of Israel.

30 The children of ⁴ Aser were Jemna, and Jesua, and Jessui, and Baria, and Sara their sister.

31 And the sons of Baria: Haber, and Melchiel; he is the father of Barsaith.

32 And Heber begot Jephlat, and Somer, and Hotham, and Suaa their sister.

33 The sons of Jephlat: Phosech, and Chamaal, and Asoth: these are the sons of Jephlat.

34 And the sons of Somer: Ahi, and Roaga, and Haba, and Aram.

35 And the sons of Helem his brother: Supha, and Jemna, and Selles, and Amal.

36 The sons of Supha: Sue, Hernapher, and Sual, and Beri, and Jamra.

37 Bosor and Hod, and Samma, and Salusa, and Jethran, and Bera.

38 The sons of Jether: Jephone, and Phaspha, and Ara.

39 And the sons of Olla: Aree, and Haniel, and Resia.

40 All these were sons of Aser, heads of their families, choice and most valiant captains of captains. And the number of them that were of the age that was fit for war, was six and twenty thousand.

CHAPTER 8

The posterity of Benjamin is further declared down to Saul. His issue.

NOW ¹ Benjamin begot Bale his firstborn, Asbel the second, Ahara the third,

⁴ Gen. 46, 17. Chap. 8. ¹ Gen. 46, 21; 1 Par. 7, 6.

Chap. 7. Ver. 23. *Beria.* This name signifies *in evil* or *in affliction.*

2 Nohaa the fourth, and Rapha the fifth.

3 And the sons of Bale were Addar, and Gera, and Abiud,

4 And Abisue, and Naaman, and Ahoe,

5 And Gera, and Sephuphan, and Huram.

6 These are the sons of Ahod, heads of families that dwelt in Gabaa, who were removed into Manahath.

7 And Naaman, and Achia, and Gera he removed them, and begot Oza, and Ahiud.

8 And Saharim begot in the land of Moab, after he sent away Husim and Bara his wives.

9 And he begot of Hodes his wife Jobab, and Sebia, and Mosa, and Molchom,

10 And Jehus, and Sechia, and Marma. These were his sons heads of their families.

11 And Mehusim begot Abitob, and Elphaal.

12 And the sons of Elphaal were Heber, and Misaam, and Samad: who built Ono, and Lod, and its daughters.

13 And Baria, and Sama were heads of their kindreds that dwelt in Aialon: these drove away the inhabitants of Geth.

14 And Ahio, and Sesac, and Jerimoth,

15 And Zabadia, and Arod, and Heder,

16 And Michael, and Jespha, and Joha, the sons of Baria.

17 And Zabadia, and Mosollam, and Hezeci, and Heber,

18 And Jesamari, and Jezlia, and Jobab, sons of Elphaal,

19 And Jacim, and Zechri, and Zabdi,

20 And Elioenai, and Selethai, and Elial,

21 And Adaia, and Baraia, and Samareth, the sons of Semei.

22 And Jespham, and Heber, and Eliel,

23 And Abdon, and Zechri, and Hanan,

24 And Hanania, and Elam, and Anathothia.

25 And Jephdaia, and Phanuel, the sons of Sesac.

26 And Samsari, and Sohoria, and Otholia,

27 And Jersia, and Elia, and Zechri, the sons of Jeroham.

28 These were the chief fathers, and heads of their families who dwelt in Jerusalem.

29 And ² at Gabaon dwelt Abigabaon; and the name of his wife was Maacha.

30 And his firstborn son Abdon, and Sur, and Cis, and Baal, and Nadab,

31 And Gedor, and Ahio, and Zacher, and Macelloth.

32 And Macelloth begot Samaa: and they dwelt over against their brethren in Jerusalem with their brethren.

33 And ³ Ner begot Cis, and Cis begot Saul. And Saul begot Jonathan and Melchisua, and Abinadab, and Esbaal.

34 And the son of Jonathan was Meribbaal. And Meribbaal begot Micha.

35 And the sons of Micha were Phithon, and Melech, and Tharaa, and Ahaz.

36 And Ahaz begot Joada. And Joada begot Alamath, and Azmoth, and Zamri. And Zamri begot Mosa.

37 And Mosa begot Banaa, whose son was Rapha, of whom was born Elasa, who begot Asel.

38 And Asel had six sons whose names were Ezricam, Bochru, Ismahel, Saria, Obdia, and Hanan. All these were the sons of Asel.

39 And the sons of Esec, his brother were Ulam the firstborn, and Jehus the second, and Eliphalet the third.

40 And the sons of Ulam were most valiant men, and archers of great strength: and they had many sons and grandsons, even to a hundred and fifty. All these were children of Benjamin.

CHAPTER 9

The Israelites, priests, and Levites, who first dwelt in Jerusalem after the captivity. A repetition of the genealogy of Saul.

AND all Israel was numbered: and the sum of them was written in the book of the kings of Israel, and Juda. And they were carried away to Babylon for their transgression.

2 Now the first that dwelt in their possessions, and in their cities, were the Israelites, and the priests, and the Levites, and the Nathineans.

3 And in Jerusalem dwelt of the children of Juda, and of the children of Benjamin, and of the children of Ephraim, and of Manasses.

4 Othei the son of Ammiud, the son of Amri, the son of Omrai, the son of Bonni, of the sons of Phares the son of Juda.

5 And of Siloni: Asaia the firstborn, and his sons.

6 And of the sons of Zara: Jehuel, and their brethren, six hundred and ninety.

7 And of the sons of Benjamin: Salo the son of Mosollam, the son of Oduia, the son of Asana.

8 And Jobania the son of Jeroham. And Ela the son of Ozi, the son of Mochori. And Mosallam the son of Saphatias, the son of Rahuel, the son of Jebania.

9 And their brethren by their families, nine hundred and fifty-six. All these were heads of their families, by the houses of their fathers.

10 And of the priests: Jedaia, Joiarib, and Jachin:

11 And Azarias the son of Helcias, the son of Mosollam, the son of Sadoc, the son of Maraioth, the son of Achitob, high priest of the house of God.

12 And Adaias the son of Jeroham, the son of Phassur, the son of Melchias. And Maasai the son of Adiel, the son of Jezra, the son of Mosollam, the son of Mosollamith, the son of Emmer.

13 And their brethren heads in their families a thousand seven hundred and threescore, very strong and able men for the work of the ministry in the house of God.

14 And of the Levites: Semeia the son of Hassub, the son of Ezricam, the son of Hasebia of the sons of Merari.

15 And Bacbacar the carpenter, and Galal, and Mathania the son of Micha, the son of Zechri, the son of Asaph.

16 And Obdia the son of Semeia, the son of Galal, the son of Idithun. And Barachia the son of Asa, the son of Elcana, who dwelt in the suburbs of Netophati.

17 And the porters were Sellum, and Accub, and Telmon, and Ahiman: and their brother Sellum was the prince.

18 Until that time, in the king's gate eastward, the sons of Levi waited by their turns.

19 But Sellum the son of Core, the son of Abiasaph, the son of Core, with his brethren and his father's house, the Corites were over the works of the service, keepers of the gates of the tabernacle: and their families in turns were keepers of the entrance of the camp of the Lord.

20 And Phinees the son of Eleazar was their prince before the Lord.

21 And Zacharias the son of Mosollamia was porter of the gate of the tabernacle of the testimony.

22 All these that were chosen to be porters at the gates were two hundred and twelve: and they were registered in their proper towns: whom David and Samuel the seer appointed in their trust.

23 As well them as their sons, to keep

CHAP. 8. Ver. 33. *Esbaal*, alias Isboseth.
Ver. 34. *Meribbaal*. Otherwise Miphiboseth (2 Kings, 4, 4).
CHAP. 9. Ver. 2. *Nathineans*. These were the posterity of the Gabaonites, whose office was to bring wood, water, &c., for the service of the temple.

the gates of the house of the Lord, and the tabernacle by their turns.

24 In four quarters were the porters: that is to say, toward the east, and west, and north, and south.

25 And their brethren dwelt in villages; and came upon their sabbath days from time to time.

26 To these four Levites were committed the whole number of the porters. And they were over the chambers, and treasures, of the house of the Lord.

27 And they abode in their watches round about the temple of the Lord: that when it was time, they might open the gates in the morning.

28 And some of their stock had the charge of the vessels for the ministry: for the vessels were both brought in and carried out by number.

29 Some of them also had the instruments of the sanctuary committed unto them: and the charge of the fine flour, and wine, and oil, and frankincense, and spices.

30 And the sons of the priests made the ointments of the spices.

31 And Mathathias a Levite, the firstborn of Sellum the Corite, was overseer of such things as were fried in the fryingpan.

32 And some of the sons of Caath their brethren, were over the loaves of proposition, to prepare always new for every sabbath.

33 These are the chief of the singing men of the families of the Levites, who dwelt in the chambers, by the temple, that they might serve continually day and night in their ministry.

34 The heads of the Levites, princes in their families, abode in Jerusalem.

35 And [1] in Gabaon dwelt Jehiel the father of Gabaon, and the name of his wife was Maacha.

36 His firstborn son Abdon, and Sur, and Cis, and Baal, and Ner, and Nadab,

37 Gedor also, and Ahio, and Zacharias, and Macelloth.

38 And Macelloth begot Samaan: these dwelt over against their brethren in Jerusalem, with their brethren.

39 [2] Now Ner begot Cis: and Cis begot Saul: and Saul begot Jonathan and Melchisua, and Abinadab, and Esbaal.

40 And the son of Jonathan, was Meribbaal: and Meribbaal begot Micha.

41 And the sons of Micha were Phithon, and Melech, and Tharaa, and Ahaz.

42 And Ahaz begot Jara, and Jara begot Alamath, and Azmoth, and Zamri. And Zamri begot Mosa.

43 And Mosa begot Banaa: whose son Raphaia begot Elasa: of whom was born Asel.

44 And Asel had six sons whose names are, Ezricam, Bochru, Ismahel, Saria, Obdia, Hanan: these are the sons of Asel.

CHAPTER 10

Saul is slain for his sins. He is buried by the men of Jabes.

NOW [1] the Philistines fought against Israel; and the men of Israel fled from before the Philistines; and fell down wounded in mount Gelboe.

2 And the Philistines drew near pursuing after Saul, and his sons. And they killed Jonathan, and Abinadab, and Melchisua the sons of Saul.

3 And the battle grew hard against Saul: and the archers reached him, and wounded him with arrows.

4 And Saul said to his armourbearer: Draw thy sword, and kill me: lest these uncircumcised come, and mock me. But his armourbearer would not, for he was struck with fear. So Saul took his sword, and fell upon it.

5 And when his armourbearer saw it, to wit, that Saul was dead, he also fell upon his sword and died.

6 So Saul died, and his three sons: and all his house fell together.

7 And when the men of Israel, that dwelt in the plains, saw this, they fled. And Saul and his sons being dead, they forsook their cities, and were scattered up and down. And the Philistines came, and dwelt in them.

8 And the next day the Philistines taking away the spoils of them that were slain, found Saul and his sons lying on mount Gelboe.

9 And when they had stripped him, and cut off his head, and taken away his armour, they sent it into their land, to be carried about, and shewn in the temples of the idols and to the people.

10 And his armour they dedicated in the temple of their god, and his head they fastened up in the temple of Dagon.

11 And when the men of Jabes Galaad had heard this, to wit, all that the Philistines had done to Saul,

12 All the valiant men of them arose, and took the bodies of Saul and of his sons, and brought them to Jabes, and buried their bones under the oak that was in Jabes. And they fasted seven days.

13 So Saul died for his iniquities: because he transgressed the [2] commandment of the Lord, which he had commanded, and kept it not, [3] and moreover consulted also a witch,

CHAP. 9. [1] 1 Par. 8, 29. [2] Par. 8, 33. CHAP. 10.
[1] 1 Kings, 31, 1. [2] Exod. 17, 14; 1 Kings, 15, 8.
[3] 1 Kings, 28, 8.

14 And trusted not in the Lord. Therefore he slew him, and transferred his kingdom to David the son of Isai.

CHAPTER 11

David is made king. He taketh the castle of Sion. A catalogue of his valiant men.

THEN [1] all Israel gathered themselves to David in Hebron, saying: We are thy bone, and thy flesh:

2 Yesterday also, and the day before when Saul was king, thou wast he that leddest out and broughtest in Israel. For the Lord thy God said to thee: Thou shalt feed my people Israel, and thou shalt be ruler over them.

3 So all. the ancients of Israel came to the king to Hebron: and David made a covenant with them before the Lord. And they anointed him king over Israel, according to the word of the Lord which he spoke in the hand of Samuel.

4 And David and all Israel went to Jerusalem, [2] which is Jebus, where the Jebusites were the inhabitants of the land.

5 And the inhabitants of Jebus said to David: Thou shalt not come in here. But David took the castle of Sion, which is the city of David.

6 And he said: Whosoever shall first strike the Jebusites, shall be the head and chief captain. And Joab the son of Sarvia went up first, and was made the general.

7 And David dwelt in the castle: and therefore it was called the city of David.

8 And he built the city round about from Mello all round; and Joab built the rest of the city.

9 And David went on growing and increasing: and the Lord of hosts was with him.

10 [3] These are the chief of the valiant men of David, who helped him to be made king over all Israel, according to the word of the Lord, which he spoke to Israel.

11 And this is the number of the heroes of David: Jesbaam the son of Hachamoni the chief among the thirty. He lifted up his spear against three hundred wounded by him at one time.

12 And after him was Eleazar his uncle's son, the Ahohite, who was one of the three mighties.

13 He was with David in Phesdomim, when the Philistines were gathered to that place to battle: and the field of that country was full of barley, and the people fled from before the Philistines.

14 But these men stood in the midst of the field, and defended it. And they slew the Philistines, and the Lord gave a great deliverance to his people.

15 [4] And three of the thirty captains went down to the rock, wherein David was, to the cave of Odollam, when the Philistines encamped in the valley of Raphaim.

16 [5] And David was in a hold, and the garrison of the Philistines in Bethlehem.

17 And David longed, and said: O that some man would give me water of the cistern of Bethlehem, which is in the gate.

18 And these three broke through the midst of the camp of the Philistines, and drew water out of the cistern of Bethlehem, which was in the gate, and brought it to David to drink. And he would not drink of it, but rather offered it to the Lord.

19 Saying: God forbid that I should do this in the sight of my God, and should drink the blood of these men; for with the danger of their lives they have brought me the water. And therefore he would not drink. These things did the three most valiant.

20 And Abisai the brother of Joab, he was chief of three; and he lifted up his spear against three hundred whom he slew; and he was renowned among the three,

21 And illustrious among the second three, and their captain. But yet he attained not to the first three.

22 Banaias the son of Joiada, a most valiant man, of Cabseel, who had done many acts. He slew the two ariels of Moab: and he went down, and killed a lion in the midst of a pit in the time of snow.

23 And he slew an Egyptian, whose stature was of five cubits, and who had a spear like a weaver's beam. And he went down to him with a staff, and plucked away the spear, that he held in his hand, and slew him with his own spear.

24 These things did Banaias the son of Joiada, who was renowned among the three valiant ones,

25 And the first among the thirty. But yet to the three he attained not. And David made him of his council.

26 Moreover the most valiant men of the army, were Asahel brother of Joab, and Elchanan the son of his uncle of Bethlehem,

27 Sammoth an Arorite, Helles a Phalonite,

28 Ira the son of Acces a Thecuite, Abiezer an Anathothite,

CHAP. 11. [1] 2 Kings, 5, 1. [2] 2 Kings, 5, 6. [3] 2 Kings, 23, 8. [4] 2 Kings, 23, 13. [5] 2 Kings, 23, 14.

CHAP. 11. Ver. 22. *Two ariels.* That is, two lions, or lion-like men; for Ariel in Hebrew signifies a lion.

29 Sobbochai a Husathite, Ilai an Ahohite,

30 Maharai a Netophathite, Heled the son of Baana a Netophathite,

31 Ethai the son of Ribai of Gabaath of the sons of Benjamin, Banai a Pharathonite,

32 Hurai of the torrent Gaas, Abiel an Arbathite, Azmoth a Bauramite, Eliaba a Salabonite,

33 The sons of Assem a Gezonite, Jonathan the son of Sage an Ararite,

34 Ahiam the son of Sachar an Ararite,

35 Eliphal the son of Ur,

36 Hepher a Mecherathite, Ahia a Phelonite,

37 Hesro a Carmelite, Naarai the son of Azbai,

38 Joel the brother of Nathan, Mibahar the son of Agarai.

39 Selec an Ammonite, Naharai a Berothite, the armourbearer of Joab the son of Sarvia.

40 Ira a Jethrite, Gareb a Jethrite,

41 Urias a Hethite, Zabad the son of Oholi,

42 Adina the son of Siza a Rubenite the prince of the Rubenites, and thirty with him,

43 Hanan the son of Maacha, and Josaphat a Mathanite,

44 Ozia an Astarothite, Samma, and Jehiel the sons of Hotham an Arorite,

45 Jedihel the son of Zamri, and Joha his brother a Thosaite,

46 Eliel a Mahumite, and Jeribai, and Josaia the sons of Elnaim, and Jethma a Moabite, Eliel, and Obed, and Jasiel of Masobia.

CHAPTER 12

Who followed David when he fled from Saul. And who came to Hebron to make him king.

NOW these are they that came to David to Siceleg, [1] while he yet fled from Saul the son of Cis. And they were most valiant and excellent warriors,

2 Bending the bow, and using either hand in hurling stones with slings, and shooting arrows: of the brethren of Saul of Benjamin.

3 The chief was Ahiezer, and Joas, the sons of Samaa of Gabaath, and Jaziel, and Phallet, the sons of Azmoth, and Beracha, and Jehu an Anathothite.

4 And Samaias of Gabaon, the stoutest amongst the thirty and over the thirty: Jeremias, and Jeheziel, and Johanan, and Jezabad of Gaderoth:

5 And Eluzai, and Jerimuth, and Baalia, and Samaria, and Saphatia the Haruphite:

6 Elcana, and Jesia, and Azareel, and Joezer, and Jesbaam of Carehim:

7 And Joela, and Zabadia, the sons of Jeroham of Gedor.

8 From Gaddi also there went over to David, when he lay hid in the wilderness most valiant men, and excellent warriors, holding shield and spear. Their faces were like the faces of a lion; and they were swift like the roebucks on the mountains.

9 Ezer the chief, Obdias the second, Eliab the third,

10 Masmana the fourth, Jeremias the fifth,

11 Ethi the sixth, Eliel the seventh,

12 Johanan the eighth, Elzebad the ninth,

13 Jerenias the tenth, Machbani the eleventh,

14 These *were* of the sons of Gad, captains of the army. The least of them was captain over a hundred soldiers, and the greatest over a thousand.

15 These are they who passed over the Jordan in the first month, when it is used to flow over its banks: and they put to flight all that dwelt in the valleys both toward the east and toward the west.

16 And there came also of the men of Benjamin and of Juda to the hold, in which David abode,

17 And David went out to meet them, and said: If you are come peaceably to me to help me, let my heart be joined to you. But if you plot against me for my enemies whereas I have no iniquity in my hands, let the God of our fathers see, and judge.

18 But the spirit came upon Amasai the chief among thirty, and he said: We are thine, O David, and for thee, O son of Isai. Peace, Peace be to thee, and peace to thy helpers. For thy God helpeth thee. So David received them, and made them captains of the band.

19 And there were some of Manasses that went over to David, when he came with the Philistines against Saul to fight. But he did not fight with them: [2] because the lords of the Philistines taking counsel sent him back, saying: With the danger of our heads he will return to his master Saul.

20 So when he went back to Siceleg, there fled to him of Manasses, Ednas, and Jozabad, and Jedihel, and Michael, and Ednas, and Jozabad, and Eliu, and Salathi, captains of thousands in Manasses.

21 These helped David against the rovers: for they were all most valiant men, and were made commanders in the army.

22 Moreover day by day there came

some to David to help him till they became a great number, like the army of God.

23 And this is the number of the chiefs of the army who came to David, when he was in Hebron, [3] to transfer to him the kingdom of Saul, according to the word of the Lord.

24 The sons of Juda bearing shield and spear, six thousand eight hundred well appointed to war.

25 Of the sons of Simeon valiant men for war, seven thousand one hundred.

26 Of the sons of Levi, four thousand six hundred.

27 And Joiada prince of the race of Aaron, and with him three thousand seven hundred.

28 Sadoc also a young man of excellent disposition, and the house of his father, twenty-two principal men.

29 And of the sons of Benjamin the brethren of Saul, three thousand: for hitherto a great part of them followed the house of Saul.

30 And of the sons of Ephraim, twenty thousand eight hundred, men of great valour renowned in their kindreds.

31 And of the half tribe of Manasses, eighteen thousand: every one by their names, came to make David king.

32 Also of the sons of Issachar men of understanding, that knew all times to order what Israel should do, two hundred principal men: and all the rest of the tribe followed their counsel.

33 And of Zabulon such as went forth to battle, and stood in array well appointed with armour for war, there came fifty thousand to his aid, with no double heart.

34 And of Nephtali, a thousand leaders: and with them seven and thirty thousand, furnished with shield and spear.

35 Of Dan also, twenty-eight thousand six hundred prepared for battle.

36 And of Aser, forty thousand going forth to fight, and challenging in battle.

37 And on the other side of the Jordan of the sons of Ruben, and of Gad, and of the half of the tribe of Manasses, a hundred and twenty thousand, furnished with arms for war.

38 All these men of war well appointed to fight came with a perfect heart to Hebron, to make David king over all Israel. And all the rest also of Israel were of one heart to make David king.

39 And they were there with David three days eating and drinking: for their brethren had prepared for them.

40 Moreover they that were near them, even as far as Issachar, and Zabulon, and Nephtali, brought loaves on asses, and on camels, and on mules, and on oxen, to eat: meal, figs, raisins, wine, oil, and oxen, and sheep in abundance: for there was joy in Israel.

CHAPTER 13

The ark is brought from Cariathiarim. Oza for touching it is struck dead.

AND David consulted with the captains of thousands, and of hundreds, and with all the commanders.

2 And he said to all the assembly of Israel: If it please you, and if the words which I speak come from the Lord our God, let us send to the rest of our brethren into all the countries of Israel, and to the priests, and the Levites, that dwell in the suburbs of the cities, to gather themselves to us.

3 And let us bring again the ark of our God to us: for we sought it not in the days of Saul.

4 And all the multitude answered that it should be so: for the word pleased all the people.

5 So David assembled all Israel from Sihor of Egypt, even to the entering into Emath, [1] to bring the ark of God from Cariathiarim.

6 And David went up with all the men of Israel to the hill of Cariathiarim which is in Juda, to bring thence the ark of the Lord God sitting upon the cherubims, where his name is called upon.

7 And they carried the ark of God upon a new cart, out of the house of Abinadab. And Oza and his brother drove the cart.

8 And David and all Israel played before God with all their might: with hymns, and with harps, and with psalteries, and timbrels, and cymbals, and trumpets,

9 And when they came to the floor of Chidon, Oza put forth his hand, to hold up the ark: for the ox being wanton had made it lean a little on one side.

10 And the Lord was angry with Oza, and struck him, because he had touched the ark. And he died there before the Lord.

11 And David was troubled because the Lord had divided Oza: and he called that place the Breach of Oza to this day.

12 And he feared God at that time, saying: How can I bring in the ark of God to me?

13 And therefore he brought it not home to himself, that is, into the city

[3] 2 Kings, 5, 12. CHAP. 13. [1] 2 Kings, 6, 2.
CHAP. 13. Ver. 9. *Chidon.* Otherwise Nachon.

of David, but carried it aside into the house of Obededom the Gethite.

14 And the ark of God remained in the house of Obededom three months: and the Lord blessed his house, and all that he had.

CHAPTER 14

David's house, and children. His victories over the Philistines.

AND [1] Hiram king of Tyre sent messengers to David, and cedar trees, and masons, and carpenters, to build him a house.

2 And David perceived that the Lord had confirmed him king over Israel, and that his kingdom was exalted over his people Israel.

3 [2] And David took other wives in Jerusalem: and he begot sons, and daughters.

4 Now these are the names of them that were born to him in Jerusalem: Samua, and Sobad, Nathan, and Solomon.

5 Jebahar, and Elisua, and Eliphalet,

6 And Noga, and Napheg, and Japhia,

7 Elisama, and Baaliada, and Eliphalet.

8 [3] And the Philistines hearing that David was anointed king over all Israel, went all up to seek him: and David heard of it, and went out against them.

9 And the Philistines came and spread themselves in the vale of Raphaim.

10 And David consulted the Lord, saying: Shall I go up against the Philistines, and wilt thou deliver them into my hand? And the Lord said to him: Go up, and I will deliver them into thy hand.

11 And when they were come to Baalpharasim, David defeated them there. And he said: God hath divided my enemies by my hand, as waters are divided. And therefore the name of that place was called Baalpharasim.

12 And they left there their gods; and David commanded that they should be burnt.

13 Another time also the Philistines made an irruption, and spread themselves abroad in the valley.

14 And David consulted God again; and God said to him: Go not up after them; turn away from them, and come upon them over against the pear trees.

15 And when thou shalt hear the sound of one going in the tops of the pear trees, then shalt thou go out to

battle. For God is gone out before thee to strike the army of the Philistines.

16 And David did as God had commanded him, and defeated the army of the Philistines, slaying them from Gabaon to Gazera.

17 And the name of David became famous in all countries; and the Lord made all nations fear him.

CHAPTER 15

The ark is brought into the city of David, with great solemnity. Michol derideth David's devotion.

HE made also houses for himself in the city of David: and built a place for the ark of God, and pitched a tabernacle for it.

2 Then David said: No one ought to carry the ark of God, but the Levites, whom the Lord hath chosen to carry it, and to minister unto himself for ever.

3 And he gathered all Israel together into Jerusalem, that the ark of God might be brought into its place, which he had prepared for it.

4 And the sons of Aaron also, and the Levites.

5 Of the children of Caath, Uriel was the chief: and his brethren a hundred and twenty.

6 Of the sons of Merari, Asaia the chief: and his brethren two hundred and twenty.

7 Of the sons of Gersom, Joel the chief: and his brethren a hundred and thirty.

8 Of the sons of Elisaphan, Semeias the chief: and his brethren two hundred.

9 Of the sons of Hebron, Eliel the chief: and his brethren eighty.

10 Of the sons of Oziel, Aminadab the chief: and his brethren a hundred and twelve.

11 And David called Sadoc, and Abiathar the priests, and the Levites, Uriel, Asaia, Joel, Semeia, Eliel, and Aminadab.

12 And he said to them: You that are the heads of the Levitical families, be sanctified with your brethren; and bring the ark of the Lord the God of Israel to the place, which is prepared for it:

13 [1] Lest as the Lord at first struck us, because you were not present, the same should now also come to pass, by our doing some thing against the law.

14 So the priests and the Levites were sanctified, to carry the ark of the Lord the God of Israel.

15 [2] And the sons of Levi took the ark of God, as Moses had commanded, according to the word of the Lord, upon their shoulders, with the staves.

CHAP. 14. [1] 2 Kings, 5, 11. [2] 2 Kings, 5, 13. [3] 2 Kings, 5, 17. CHAP. 15. [1] 1 Par. 13, 10. [2] Num. 4, 15.

16 And David spoke to the chiefs of the Levites, to appoint some of their brethren to be singers with musical instruments, to wit, on psalteries, and harps, and cymbals, that the joyful noise might resound on high.

17 And they appointed Levites, Heman the son of Joel: and of his brethren Asaph the son of Barachias: and of the sons of Merari, their brethren, Ethan the son of Casaia.

18 And with them their brethren: in the second rank, Zacharias, and Ben, and Jaziel, and Semiramoth, and Jahiel, and Ani, and Eliab, and Banaias, and Maasias, and Mathathias, and Eliphalu, and Macenias, and Obededom, and Jehiel, the porters.

19 Now the singers, Hemar, Asaph, and Ethan, sounded with cymbals of brass.

20 And Zacharias, and Oziel, and Semiramoth, and Jehiel, and Ani, and Eliab, and Maasias, and Banaias, sung mysteries upon psalteries.

21 And Mathathias, and Eliphalu, and Macenias and Obededom, and Jehiel, and Ozaziu, sung a song of victory for the octave upon harps.

22 And Chonenias chief of the Levites, presided over the prophecy, to give out the tunes: for he was very skilful.

23 And Barachias, and Elcana, were doorkeepers of the ark.

24 And Sebenias, and Josaphat, and Nathanael, and Amasai, and Zacharias, and Banaias, and Eliezer the priests, sounded with trumpets, before the ark of God: and Obededom and Jehias were porters of the ark.

25 [3] So David and all the ancients of Israel, and the captains over thousands, went to bring the ark of the covenant of the Lord out of the house of Obededom with joy.

26 And when God had helped the Levites who carried the ark of the covenant of the Lord, they offered in sacrifice seven oxen, and seven rams.

27 And David was clothed with a robe of fine linen, and all the Levites that carried the ark, and the singing men, and Chonenias the ruler of the prophecy among the singers: and David also had on him an ephod of linen.

28 And all Israel brought the ark of the covenant of the Lord with joyful shouting, and sounding with the sound of the cornet, and with trumpets, and cymbals, and psalteries, and harps.

29 And when the ark of the covenant of the Lord was come to the city of David, Michol the daughter of Saul looking out at a window, saw king David dancing and playing; and she despised him in her heart.

CHAPTER 16

The ark is placed in the tabernacle. Sacrifice is offered. David blesseth the people, disposeth the offices of Levites, and maketh a psalm of praise to God.

SO [1] they brought the ark of God, and set it in the midst of the tent, which David had pitched for it. And they offered holocausts and peace offerings before God.

2 And when David had made an end of offering holocausts and peace offerings, he blessed the people in the name of the Lord.

3 And he divided to all and every one, both men and women, a loaf of bread, and a piece of roasted beef, and flour fried with oil.

4 And he appointed Levites to minister before the ark of the Lord, and to remember his works, and to glorify, and praise the Lord God of Israel.

5 Asaph the chief, and next after him Zacharias: moreover Jahiel, and Semiramoth, and Jehiel, and Mathathias, and Eliab, and Banaias, and Obededom: and Jehiel over the instruments of psaltery, and harps: and Asaph sounded with cymbals:

6 But Banaias, and Jaziel the priests, to sound the trumpet continually before the ark of the covenant of the Lord.

7 In that day David made Asaph the chief to give praise to the Lord with his brethren.

8 [2] Praise ye the Lord, and call upon his name: make known his doings among the nations.

9 Sing to him, yea, sing praises to him: and relate all his wondrous works.

10 Praise ye his holy name: let the heart of them rejoice, that seek the Lord.

11 Seek ye the Lord, and his power: seek ye his face evermore.

12 Remember his wonderful works, which he hath done: his signs, and the judgments of his mouth.

13 O ye seed of Israel his servants: ye children of Jacob his chosen.

14 He is the Lord our God: his judgments are in all the earth.

15 Remember for ever his covenant: the word, which he commanded to a thousand generations.

16 The covenant which he made with Abraham: and his oath to Isaac.

17 And he appointed the same to Jacob for a precept: and to Israel for an everlasting covenant:

[3] 2 Kings, 6, 12. Chap. 16. [1] 2 Kings, 6, 17. [2] Ps. 104, 1; Isai. 12, 4.

Chap. 15. Ver. 22. *Tho prophecy, to give out the tunes.* Singing praises to God is here called *prophecy:* the more, because these singers were often inspired men.

18 Saying: To thee will I give the land of Chanaan: the lot of your inheritance.

19 When they were but a small number: very few and sojourners in it.

20 And they passed from nation to nation: and from a kingdom to another people.

21 He suffered no man to do them wrong: and reproved kings for their sake.

22 [3] Touch not my anointed: and do no evil to my prophets.

23 [4] Sing ye to the Lord, all the earth: shew forth from day to day his salvation.

24 Declare his glory among the Gentiles: his wonders among all people.

25 For the Lord is great and exceedingly to be praised: and he is to be feared above all gods.

26 For all the gods of the nations are idols: but the Lord made the heavens.

27 Praise and magnificence are before him: strength and joy in his place.

28 Bring ye to the Lord, O ye families of the nations: bring ye to the Lord glory and empire.

29 Give to the Lord glory to his name; bring up sacrifice, and come ye in his sight: and adore the Lord in holy becomingness.

30 Let all the earth be moved at his presence: for he hath founded the world immoveable.

31 Let the heavens rejoice, and the earth be glad: and let them say among the nations: The Lord hath reigned.

32 Let the sea roar, and the fulness thereof: let the fields rejoice, and all things that are in them.

33 Then shall the trees of the wood give praise before the Lord: because he is come to judge the earth.

34 Give ye glory to the Lord, for he is good: for his mercy endureth for ever.

35 And say ye: Save us, O God our saviour: and gather us together; and deliver us from the nations: that we may give glory to thy holy name, and may rejoice in singing thy praises.

36 Blessed be the Lord the God of Israel from eternity to eternity. And let all the people say, Amen, and a hymn to God.

37 So he left there before the ark of the covenant of the Lord, Asaph and his brethren to minister in the presence of the ark continually day by day, and in their courses.

38 And Obededom, with his brethren sixty-eight: and Obededom the son of Idithun, and Hosa he appointed to be porters.

39 And Sadoc the priest, and his brethren priests, before the tabernacle of the Lord in the high place, which was in Gabaon.

40 That they should offer holocausts to the Lord upon the altar of holocausts continually, morning and evening, according to all that is written in the law of the Lord, which he commanded Israel.

41 And after him Heman, and Idithun, and the rest that were chosen, every one by his name to give praise to the Lord: because his mercy endureth for ever.

42 And Heman and Idithun sounded the trumpet, and played on the cymbals, and all kinds of musical instruments to sing praises to God. And the sons of Idithun he made porters.

43 And all the people returned to their houses: and David to bless also his own house.

CHAPTER 17

David's purpose to build a temple, is rewarded by most ample promises. David's thanksgiving.

NOW [1] when David was dwelling in his house, he said to Nathan the prophet: Behold I dwell in a house of cedar; and the ark of the covenant of the Lord is under skins.

2 And Nathan said to David: Do all that is in thy heart: for God is with thee.

3 Now that night the word of God came to Nathan, saying:

4 Go, and speak to David my servant: Thus saith the Lord: Thou shalt not build me a house to dwell in.

5 For I have not remained in a house from the time that I brought up Israel, to this day: but I have been always changing places in a tabernacle, and in a tent,

6 Abiding with all Israel. Did I ever speak to any one, of all the judges of Israel, whom I charged to feed my people, saying: Why have you not built me a house of cedar?

7 Now therefore thus shalt thou say to my servant David: Thus saith the Lord of hosts: I took thee from the pastures, from following the flock, that thou shouldst be ruler of my people Israel.

8 And I have been with thee whithersoever thou hast gone: and have slain all thy enemies before thee, and have made thee a name like that of one of the great ones that are renowned in the earth.

9 And I have given a place to my people Israel. They shall be planted, and shall dwell therein, and shall be

[3] Ps. 104, 15. [4] Ps. 95, 1. CHAP. 17. [1] 2 Kings, 7, 2.

moved no more: neither shall the children of iniquity waste them, as at the beginning,

10 Since the days that I gave judges to my people Israel, and have humbled all thy enemies. And I declare to thee, that the Lord will build thee a house.

11 And when thou shalt have ended thy days to go to thy fathers, I will raise up thy seed after thee, which shall be of thy sons: and I will establish his kingdom.

12 He shall build me a house: and I will establish his throne for ever.

13 I will be to him a father, and he shall be to me a son: and I will not take my mercy away from him, as I took it from him that was before thee.

14 But I will settle him in my house, and in my kingdom for ever: and his throne shall be most firm for ever.

15 According to all these words, and according to all this vision, so did Nathan speak to David.

16 And king David came and sat before the Lord, and said: Who am I, O Lord God, and what is my house, that thou shouldst give such things to me?

17 But even this hath seemed little in thy sight: and therefore thou hast also spoken concerning the house of thy servant for the time to come; and hast made me remarkable above all men, O Lord God.

18 What can David add more, seeing thou hast thus glorified thy servant, and known him?

19 O Lord, for thy servant's sake, according to thy own heart, thou hast shewn all this magnificence, and wouldst have all the great things to be known.

20 O Lord, there is none like thee: and there is no other God beside thee, of all whom we have heard of with our ears.

21 For what other nation is there upon earth like thy people Israel, whom God went to deliver, and make a people for himself: and by his greatness and terrors cast out nations before their face whom he had delivered out of Egypt?

22 And thou hast made thy people Israel to be thy own people for ever: and thou, O Lord, art become their God.

23 Now therefore, O Lord, let the word which thou hast spoken to thy servant, and concerning his house, be established for ever: and do as thou hast said.

24 And let thy name remain and be magnified for ever. And let it be said: The Lord of hosts is God of Israel, and the house of David his servant remaineth before him.

25 For thou, O Lord my God, hast revealed to the ear of thy servant, that thou wilt build him a house: and therefore thy servant hath found confidence to pray before thee.

26 And now, O Lord, thou art God: and thou hast promised to thy servant such great benefits.

27 And thou hast begun to bless the house of thy servant ,that it may be always before thee: for seeing thou blessest it, O Lord, it shall be blessed for ever.

CHAPTER 18

David's victories. His chief officers.

AND ¹it came to pass after this, that David defeated the Philistines, and humbled them, and took away Geth, and her daughters out of the hands of the Philistines,

2 And he defeated Moab: and the Moabites were made David's servants, and brought him gifts.

3 At that time David defeated also Adarezer king of Soba of the land of Hemath, when he went to extend his dominions as far as the river Euphrates.

4 And David took from him a thousand chariots, and seven thousand horsemen, and twenty thousand footmen: and he houghed all the chariot horses, only a hundred chariots, which he reserved for himself.

5 And the Syrians of Damascus came also to help Adarezer king of Soba: and David slew of them likewise two and twenty thousand men.

6 And he put a garrison in Damascus, that Syria also should serve him, and bring gifts. And the Lord assisted him in all things to which he went.

7 And David took the golden quivers which the servants of Adarezer had: and he brought them to Jerusalem.

8 Likewise out of Thebath and Chun, cities of Adarezer, he brought very much brass, of which Solomon made the brazen sea, and the pillars, and the vessels of brass.

9 Now when Thou king of Hemath heard that David had defeated all the army of Adarezer king of Soba,

10 He sent Adoram his son to king David, to desire peace of him, and to congratulate him that he had defeated and overthrown Adarezer: for Thou was an enemy to Adarezer.

11 And all the vessels of gold, and silver, and brass king David consecrated to the Lord, with the silver and gold which he had taken from all the nations: as well from Edom, and from Moab, and from the sons of Ammon, as from the Philistines, and from Amalec.

CHAP. 18. ¹ 2 Kings, 8, 1.

12 And Abisai the son of Sarvia slew of the Edomites in the vale of the salt-pits, eighteen thousand.

13 And he put a garrison in Edom, that Edom should serve David. And the Lord preserved David in all things to which he went.

14 So David reigned over all Israel, and executed judgment and justice among all his people.

15 And Joab the son of Sarvia was over the army: and Josaphat the son of Ahilud recorder.

16 And Sadoc the son of Achitob, and Achimelech the son of Abiathar, were the priests: and Susa, scribe.

17 And Banaias the son of Joiada was over the bands of the Cerethi, and the Phelethi: and the sons of David were chief about the king.

CHAPTER 19

The Ammonites abuse David's ambassadors. Both they and their confederates are overthrown.

NOW [1] it came to pass that Naas the king of the children of Ammon died, and his son reigned in his stead.

2 And David said: I will shew kindness to Hanon the son of Naas: for his father did a favour to me. And David sent messengers to comfort him upon the death of his father. But when they were come into the land of the children of Ammon, to comfort Hanon,

3 The princes of the children of Ammon said to Hanon: Thou thinkest perhaps that David to do honour to thy father hath sent comforters to thee; and thou dost not take notice, that his servants are come to thee to consider, and search, and spy out thy land.

4 Wherefore Hanon shaved the heads and beards of the servants of David, and cut away their garments from the buttocks to the feet, and sent them away.

5 And when they were gone, they sent word to David, who sent to meet them (for they had suffered a great affront), and ordered them to stay at Jericho till their beards grew and then to return.

6 And when the children of Ammon saw that they had done an injury to David, Hanon and the rest of the people sent a thousand talents of silver, to hire them chariots and horsemen out of Mesopotamia, and out of Syria Maacha, and out of Soba.

7 And they hired two and thirty thousand chariots, and the king of

CHAP. 19. [1] 2 Kings, 10, 1. CHAP. 20. [1] 2 Kings, 10, 7; 11, 1.

CHAP. 19. Ver. 18. *Seven thousand chariots.* That is, of men who fought in chariots.

Maacha, with his people. And they came and camped over against Medaba. And the children of Ammon gathered themselves together out of their cities, and came to battle.

8 And when David heard of it, he sent Joab, and all the army of valiant men.

9 And the children of Ammon came out and put their army in array before the gate of the city: and the kings, that were come to their aid, stood apart in the field.

10 Wherefore Joab understanding that the battle was set against him before and behind, chose out the bravest men of all Israel, and marched against the Syrians.

11 And the rest of the people he delivered into the hand of Abisai his brother: and they went against the children of Ammon.

12 And he said: If the Syrians be too strong for me, then thou shalt help me; but if the children of Ammon be too strong for thee, I will help thee.

13 Be of good courage, and let us behave ourselves manfully for our people, and for the cities of our God: and the Lord will do that which is good in his sight.

14 So Joab and the people that were with him, went against the Syrians to the battle. And he put them to flight.

15 And the children of Ammon seeing that the Syrians were fled, they likewise fled from Abisai his brother, and went into the city. And Joab also returned to Jerusalem.

16 But the Syrians, seeing that they had fallen before Israel, sent messengers, and brought to them the Syrians that were beyond the river. And Sophach, general of the army of Adarezer, was their leader.

17 And it was told David, and he gathered together all Israel, and passed the Jordan, and came upon them, and put his army in array against them; and they fought with him.

18 But the Syrian fled before Israel. And David slew of the Syrians seven thousand chariots, and forty thousand footmen, and Sophach the general of the army.

19 And when the servants of Adarezer saw themselves overcome by Israel, they went over to David, and served him: and Syria would not help the children of Ammon any more.

CHAPTER 20

Rabba is taken. Other victories over the Philistines.

AND [1] it came to pass after the course of a year, at the time that kings go out to battle, Joab gathered together an army and the strength of the troops: and wasted the land of the children of Ammon: and went and besieged Rabba. But David stayed at Jerusalem, when Joab smote Rabba, and destroyed it.

2 And David took the crown of Melchom from his head, and found in it a talent weight of gold, and most precious stones: and he made himself a diadem of it. He took also the spoils of the city which were very great.

3 And the people that were therein he brought out: and made harrows, and sleds, and chariots of iron to go over them, so that they were cut and bruised to pieces. In this manner David dealt with all the cities of the children of Ammon: and he returned with all his people to Jerusalem.

4 ² After this there arose a war at Gazer against the Philistines: in which Sabachai the Husathite slew Saphai of the race of Raphaim, and humbled them.

5 Another battle also was fought against the Philistines, in which Adeodatus the son of Saltus a Bethlehemite slew the brother of Goliath the Gethite, the staff of whose spear was like a weaver's beam.

6 There was another battle also in Geth, in which there was a man of great stature, whose fingers and toes were four and twenty, six on each hand and foot: who also was born of the stock of Rapha.

7 He reviled Israel: but Jonathan the son of Samaa the brother of David slew him. These were the sons of Rapha in Geth, who fell by the hand of David and his servants.

CHAPTER 21

David's sin in numbering the people is punished by a pestilence. It ceaseth upon his offering sacrifice in the thrashingfloor of Ornan.

AND ¹ Satan rose up against Israel: and moved David to number Israel.

2 And David said to Joab, and to the rulers of the people: Go, and number Israel from Bersabee even to Dan: and bring me the number of them that I may know it.

3 And Joab answered: The Lord make his people a hundred times more than they are! But, my lord the king, are they not all thy servants? Why doth my lord seek this thing, which may be imputed as a sin to Israel?

4 But the king's word rather prevailed: and Joab departed, and went through all Israel, and returned to Jerusalem.

5 And he gave David the number of them, whom he had surveyed. And all the number of Israel was found to be eleven hundred thousand men that drew the sword: and of Juda four hundred and seventy thousand fighting men.

6 But Levi and Benjamin he did not number: for Joab unwillingly executed the king's orders.

7 And God was displeased with this thing that was commanded: and he struck Israel.

8 And David said to God: I have sinned exceedingly in doing this. I beseech thee take away the iniquity of thy servant, for I have done foolishly.

9 And the Lord spoke to Gad the seer of David, saying:

10 Go, and speak to David, and tell him: Thus saith the Lord: I give thee the choice of three things. Choose one which thou wilt, and I will do it to thee.

11 And when Gad was come to David, he said to him: Thus saith the Lord: Choose which thou wilt:

12 Either three years' famine: or three months to flee from thy enemies, and not to be able to escape their sword: or three days to have the sword of the Lord, and pestilence in the land, and the angel of the Lord destroying in all the coasts of Israel. Now therefore see what I shall answer him who sent me.

13 And David said to Gad: I am on every side in a great strait; but it is better for me to fall into the hands of the Lord, for his mercies are many, than into the hands of men.

14 So the Lord sent a pestilence upon Israel. And there fell of Israel seventy thousand men.

15 And he sent an angel to Jerusalem, to strike it. And as he was striking it, the Lord beheld; and took pity for the greatness of the evil; and said to the angel that destroyed: It is enough. Now stop thy hand. And the angel of the Lord stood by the thrashingfloor of Ornan the Jebusite.

16 And David lifting up his eyes, saw the angel of the Lord standing between heaven and earth, with a drawn sword in his hand, turned against Jerusalem. And both he and the ancients clothed in haircloth, fell down flat on the ground.

² 2 Kings, 21, 18. Chap. 21. ¹ 2 Kings, 24, 1; 1 Par. 27, 24.

Chap. 21. Ver. 5. *The number.* The difference of the numbers here and 2 Kings 24 is to be accounted for, by supposing the greater number to be that which was really found, and the lesser to be that which Joab gave in.

Ver. 12. *Three years' famine.* Which joined with the three foregoing years of famine mentioned, 2 Kings 21, and the seventh year of the land's resting would make up the seven years proposed by the prophet (2 Kings, 24, 13).

Ver. 15. *Ornan.* Otherwise Areuna.

17 And David said to God: Am not I he that commanded the people to be numbered? It is I that have sinned. It is I that have done the evil. But as for this flock, what hath it deserved? O Lord my God, let thy hand be turned, I beseech thee, upon me, and upon my father's house: and let not thy people be destroyed.

18 And the angel of the Lord commanded Gad to tell David, to go up, and build an altar to the Lord God in the thrashingfloor of Ornan the Jebusite.

19 And David went up, according to the word of Gad, which he spoke to him in the name of the Lord.

20 Now when Ornan looked up, and saw the angel, he and his four sons hid themselves: for at that time he was thrashing wheat in the floor.

21 And as David was coming to Ornan, Ornan saw him, and went out of the thrashingfloor to meet him, and bowed down to him with his face to the ground.

22 And David said to him: Give me this place of thy thrashingfloor, that I may build therein an altar to the Lord: but thou shalt take of me as much money as it is worth, that the plague may cease from the people.

23 And Ornan said to David: Take it, and let my lord the king do all that pleaseth him: and moreover the oxen also I give for a holocaust, and the drays for wood, and the wheat for the sacrifice. I will give it all willingly.

24 And king David said to him: It shall not be so, but I will give thee money as much as it is worth: for I must not take it from thee, and so offer to the Lord holocausts free cost.

25 So David gave to Ornan for the place, six hundred sicles of gold of just weight.

26 [2] And he built there an altar to the Lord: and he offered holocausts, and peace offerings: and he called upon the Lord. And he heard him by sending fire from heaven upon the altar of the holocaust.

27 And the Lord commanded the angel: and he put up his sword again into the sheath.

28 And David, seeing that the Lord had heard him in the thrashingfloor of Ornan the Jebusite, forthwith offered victims there.

29 But the tabernacle of the Lord, [3] which Moses made in the desert, and the altar of holocausts, was at that time in the high place of Gabaon.

[2] 2 Par. 3, 1. [3] Exod. 36, 2. CHAP. 22. [1] 2 Par. 3, 1. [2] 2 Kings, 7, 1. [3] 2 Kings, 7, 13; 3 Kings, 5, 5; 2 Kings, 7, 14; Heb. 1, 5.

Ver. 25. *Six hundred sicles.* This was the price of the whole place, on which the temple was afterwards built; but the price of the oxen was fifty sicles of silver (2 Kings, 24, 24).

30 And David could not go to the altar there to pray to God: for he was seized with an exceeding great fear, seeing the sword of the angel of the Lord.

CHAPTER 22

David having prepared all necessaries, chargeth Solomon to build the temple and the princes to assist him.

THEN David said: [1] This is the house of God, and this is the altar for the holocaust of Israel.

2 And he commanded to gather together all the proselytes of the land of Israel, and out of them he appointed stonecutters to hew stones and polish them, to build the house of God.

3 And David prepared in abundance iron for the nails of the gates, and for the closures and joinings: and of brass an immense weight.

4 And the cedar trees were without number, which the Sidonians, and Tyrians brought to David.

5 And David said: Solomon my son is very young and tender, and the house which I would have to be built to the Lord must be such as to be renowned in all countries; therefore I will prepare him necessaries. And therefore before his death he prepared all the charges.

6 And he called for Solomon his son: and commanded him to build a house to the Lord the God of Israel.

7 And David said to Solomon: My son, it was my desire to have built a house to the name of the Lord my God.[2]

8 But the word of the Lord came to me, saying: Thou hast shed much blood, and fought many battles; so thou canst not build a house to my name, after shedding so much blood before me.

9 The son, that shall be born to thee, shall be a most quiet man: for I will make him rest from all his enemies round about. And therefore he shall be called Peaceable: and I will give peace and quietness to Israel all his days.

10 [3] He shall build a house to my name. And he shall be a son to me: and I will be a father to him. And I will establish the throne of his kingdom over Israel for ever.

11 Now then, my son, the Lord be with thee: and do thou prosper, and build the house to the Lord thy God, as he hath spoken of thee.

12 The Lord also give thee wisdom and understanding, that thou mayest be able to rule Israel, and to keep the law of the Lord thy God.

13 For then thou shalt be able to prosper, if thou keep the commandments and judgments, which the Lord commanded Moses to teach Israel.

Take courage and act manfully: fear not, nor be dismayed.

14 Behold I in my poverty have prepared the charges of the house of the Lord, of gold a hundred thousand talents, and of silver a million of talents. But of brass, and of iron there is no weight, for the abundance surpasseth all account: timber also and stones I have prepared for all the charges.

15 Thou hast also workmen in abundance, hewers of stones, and masons, and carpenters, and of all trades the most skilful in their work,

16 In gold, and in silver, and in brass, and in iron, whereof there is no number. Arise then, and be doing: and the Lord will be with thee.

17 David also charged all the princes of Israel, to help Solomon his son,

18 Saying: You see, that the Lord your God is with you, and hath given you rest round about, and hath delivered all your enemies into your hands; and the land is subdued before the Lord, and before his people.

19 Give therefore your hearts and your souls to seek the Lord your God. And arise, and build a sanctuary to the Lord God, that the ark of the covenant of the Lord, and the vessels consecrated to the Lord, may be brought into the house, which is built to the name of the Lord.

CHAPTER 23

David appointeth Solomon king. The distribution of the Levites and their offices.

AND David, being old and full of days, made Solomon his son king over Israel.

2 And he gathered together all the princes of Israel, and the priests and Levites.

3 And the Levites were numbered from the age of thirty years, and upwards: and there were found of them thirty-eight thousand men.

4 Of these twenty-four thousand were chosen, and distributed unto the ministry of the house of the Lord: and six thousand were the overseers and judges.

5 Moreover four thousand were porters: and as many singers, singing to the Lord with the instruments which he had made to sing with.

6 ¹ And David distributed them into courses by the families of the sons of Levi: to wit, of Gerson, and of Caath, and of Merari.

7 The sons of Gerson were Leedan and Semei.

8 The sons of Leedan: the chief Jahiel, and Zethan, and Joel, three.

9 The sons of Semei: Salomith, and Hosiel, and Aran, three: these were the heads of the families of Leedan.

10 And the sons of Semei were Leheth, and Ziza, and Jaus, and Baria: these were the sons of Semei, four.

11 And Leheth was the first, Ziza the second: but Jaus and Baria had not many children; and therefore they were counted in one family, and in one house.

12 The sons of Caath were Amram, and Isaar, Hebron, and Oziel four.

13 ² The sons of Amram, Aaron, and Moses. ³ And Aaron was separated to minister in the holy of holies, he and his sons for ever, and to burn incense before the Lord, according to his ceremonies, and to bless his name for ever.

14 The sons also of Moses, the man of God, were numbered in the tribe of Levi.

15 The sons ⁴ of Moses *were* Gersom and Eliezer.

16 The sons of Gersom: Subuel the first.

17 And the sons of Eliezer were: Rohobia the first. And Eliezer had no more sons; but the sons of Rohobia were multiplied exceedingly.

18 The sons of Isaar: Salomith the first.

19 The sons of Hebron: Jeriau the first, Amarias the second, Jahaziel the third, Jecmaan the fourth.

20 The sons of Oziel: Micha the first, Jesia the second.

21 The sons of Merari: Moholi, and Musi. The sons of Moholi: Eleazar and Cis.

22 And Eleazar died, and had no sons but daughters: and the sons of Cis their brethren took them.

23 The sons of Musi: Moholi, and Eder, and Jerimoth, three.

24 These are the sons of Levi in their kindreds and families, princes by their courses: and the number of every head that did the works of the ministry of the house of the Lord from twenty years old and upward.

25 For David said: The Lord, the God of Israel, hath given rest to his people, and a habitation in Jerusalem for ever.

26 And it shall not be the office of the Levites to carry any more the tabernacle, and all the vessels for the service thereof.

27 So according to the last precepts of David, the sons of Levi are to be numbered from twenty years old and upward.

28 And they are to be under the hand of the sons of Aaron for the service of

CHAP. 23. ¹¹ Par. 6, 1. ² 1 Par. 6, 3. ³ Heb. 5, 4. ⁴ Exod. 2, 22; 18, 3, 4.

the house of the Lord, in the porches, and in the chambers, and in the place of purification, and in the sanctuary, and in all the works of the ministry of the temple of the Lord.

29 And the priests have the charge of the loaves of proposition, and of the sacrifice of fine flour, and of the unleavened cakes, and of the fryingpan, and of the roasting, and of every weight and measure.

30 And the Levites are to stand in the morning to give thanks, and to sing praises to the Lord: and in like manner in the evening:

31 As well in the oblation of the holocausts of the Lord, as in the sabbaths, and in the new moons, and the rest of the solemnities, according to the number and ceremonies prescribed for every thing, continually before the Lord.

32 And let them keep the observances of the tabernacle of the covenant, and the ceremonies of the sanctuary, and the charge of the sons of Aaron their brethren, that they may minister in the house of the Lord.

CHAPTER 24

The divisions of the priests into four and twenty courses, to serve in the temple. The chiefs of the Levites.

NOW these were the divisions of the sons of Aaron: The sons of Aaron: Nadab, and Abiu, and Eleazar, and Ithamar.

2 ¹ But Nadab and Abiu died before their father, and had no children: so Eleazar and Ithamar did the office of the priesthood.

3 And David distributed them, that is, Sadoc of the sons of Eleazar, and Ahimelech of the sons of Ithamar, according to their courses and ministry.

4 And there were found many more of the sons of Eleazar among the principal men than of the sons of Ithamar. And he divided them so, that there were of the sons of Eleazar sixteen chief men by their families: and of the sons of Ithamar eight by their families and houses.

5 And he divided both the families one with the other by lot: for there were princes of the sanctuary, and princes of God, both of the sons of Eleazar, and of the sons of Ithamar.

6 And Semeias the son of Nathanael the scribe, a Levite, wrote them down before the king and the princes, and Sadoc the priest, and Ahimelech the son of Abiathar, and the princes also of the priestly and Levitical families. One house, which was over the rest, of Elcazar: and another house, which had the rest under it, of Ithamar.

7 Now the first lot came forth to Joiarib, the second to Jedei,

8 The third to Harim, the fourth to Seorim,

9 The fifth to Melchia, the sixth to Maiman,

10 The seventh to Accos, the eighth to Abia,

11 The ninth to Jesua, the tenth to Sechenia,

12 The eleventh to Eliasib, the twelfth to Jacim,

13 The thirteenth to Hoppha, the fourteenth to Isbaab,

14 The fifteenth to Belga, the sixteenth to Emmer,

15 The seventeenth to Hezir, the eighteenth to Aphses,

16 The nineteenth to Pheteia, the twentieth to Hezechiel,

17 The one and twentieth to Jachin, the two and twentieth to Gamul,

18 The three and twentieth to Dalaiau, the four and twentieth to Maaziau.

19 These are their courses according to their ministries, to come into the house of the Lord, and according to their manner, under the hand of Aaron their father: as the Lord, the God of Israel, had commanded.

20 Now of the rest of the sons of Levi, there was of the sons of Amram, Subaal: and of the sons of Subael, Jehedeia.

21 Also of the sons of Rohobia, the chief Jesias.

22 And the son of Isaar, Salemoth, and the son of Salemoth, Jahath.

23 And his son Jeriau the first, Amarias the second, Jahaziel the third, Jecmaan the fourth.

24 The son of Oziel, Micha: the son of Micha, Samir.

25 The brother of Micha, Jesia: and the son of Jesia, Zacharias.

26 The sons of Merari, Moholi and Musi: the son of Oziau, Benno.

27 The son also of Merari, Oziau: and Soam, and Zacchur, and Hebri.

28 And the son of Moholi, Eleazar, who had no sons.

29 And the son of Cis, Jeramael,

30 The sons of Musi, Moholi, Eder, and Jerimoth. These are the sons of Levi according to the houses of their families.

31 And they also cast lots over against their brethren, the sons of Aaron, before David the king, and Sadoc, and Ahimelech, and the princes of the priestly and Levitical families, both the elder and the younger. The lot divided all equally.

CHAP. 24. ¹ Lev. 10, 2; Num. 3, 4.

CHAPTER 25

The number and divisions of the musicians.

MOREOVER David and the chief officers of the army separated for the ministry the sons of Asaph, and of Heman, and of Idithun: to prophesy with harps, and with psalteries, and with cymbals according to their number serving in their appointed office.

2 Of the sons of Asaph: Zacchur, and Joseph, and Nathania, and Asarela, sons of Asaph; under the hand of Asaph prophesying near the king.

3 And of Idithun: the sons of Idithun, Godolias, Sori, Jeseias, and Hasabias, and Mathathias, six; under the hand of their father Idithun, who prophesied with a harp to give thanks and to praise the Lord.

4 Of Heman also: the sons of Heman, Bocciau, Mathaniau, Oziel, Subuel, and Jerimoth, Hananias, Hanani, Eliatha, Geddelthi, and Romemthiezer, and Jesbacassa, Mellothi, Othir, Mahazioth.

5 All these were the sons of Heman the seer of the king in the words of God, to lift up the horn. And God gave to Heman fourteen sons and three daughters.

6 All these under their father's hand were distributed to sing in the temple of the Lord, with cymbals, and psalteries, and harps, for the service of the house of the Lord, near the king: to wit, Asaph, and Idithun, and Heman.

7 And the number of them with their brethren, that taught the song of the Lord, all the teachers, were two hundred and eighty-eight.

8 And they cast lots by their courses, the elder equally with the younger, the learned and the unlearned together.

9 And the first lot came forth to Joseph, who was of Asaph. The second to Godolias: to him and his sons, and his brethren, twelve.

10 The third to Zacchur: to his sons and his brethren, twelve.

11 The fourth to Isari: to his sons and his brethren, twelve.

12 The fifth to Nathania: to his sons and his brethren, twelve.

13 The sixth to Bocciau: to his sons and his brethren, twelve.

14 The seventh to Isreela: to his sons and his brethren, twelve.

15 The eighth to Jesaia: to his sons and his brethren, twelve.

16 The ninth to Mathanaias: to his sons and his brethren, twelve.

17 The tenth to Semeias: to his sons and his brethren, twelve.

18 The eleventh to Azareel: to his sons and his brethren, twelve.

19 The twelfth to Hasabia: to his sons and his brethren, twelve.

20 The thirteenth to Subael: to his sons and his brethren, twelve.

21 The fourteenth to Mathathias: to his sons and his brethren, twelve.

22 The fifteenth to Jerimoth: to his sons and his brethren, twelve.

23 The sixteenth to Hananias: to his sons and his brethren, twelve.

24 The seventeenth to Jesbacassa: to his sons and his brethren, twelve.

25 The eighteenth to Hanani: to his sons and his brethren, twelve.

26 The nineteenth to Mellothi: to his sons and his brethren, twelve.

27 The twentieth to Eliatha: to his sons and his brethren, twelve.

28 The one and twentieth to Othir: to his sons and his brethren, twelve.

29 The two and twentieth to Geddelthi: to his sons and his brethren, twelve.

30 The three and twentieth to Mahazioth: to his sons and his brethren, twelve.

31 The four and twentieth to Romemthiezer: to his sons and his brethren, twelve.

CHAPTER 26

The divisions of the porters. Offices of other Levites.

AND the divisions of the porters: of the Corites Meselemia, the son of Core, of the sons of Asaph.

2 The sons of Meselemia: Zacharias the firstborn, Jadihel the second, Zabadias the third, Jathanael the fourth,

3 Elam the fifth, Johanan the sixth, Elioenai the seventh.

4 And the sons of Obededom: Semeias the firstborn, Jozabad the second, Joaha the third, Sachar the fourth, Nathanael the fifth,

5 Ammiel the sixth, Issachar the seventh, Phollathi the eighth: for the Lord had blessed him.

6 And to Semei his son were born sons, heads of their families: for they were men of great valour.

7 The sons then of Semeias: Othni, and Raphael, and Obed, Elizabad, and his brethren: most valiant men. And Eliu, and Samachias.

8 All these of the sons of Obededom: they, and their sons, and their brethren, most able men for service, sixty-two of Obededom.

9 And the sons of Meselemia, and their brethren, strong men, *were* eighteen.

10 And of Hosa, that is, of the sons of Merari: Semri the chief (for he had

not a firstborn, and therefore his father made him chief),

11 Helcias the second, Tabelias the third, Zacharias the fourth. All these, the sons, and the brethren of Hosa, were thirteen.

12 Among these were the divisions of the porters, so that the chiefs of the wards, as well as their brethren, always ministered in the house of the Lord.

13 And they cast lots equally, both little and great, by their families for every one of the gates.

14 And the lot of the east fell to Selemias. But to his son Zacharias, a very wise and learned man, the north gate fell by lot.

15 And to Obededom and his sons that towards the south: in which part of the house was the council of the ancients.

16 To Sephim, and Hosa towards the west, by the gate which leadeth to the way of the ascent: ward against ward.

17 Now towards the east were six Levites: and towards the north four a day: and towards the south likewise four a day: and where the council was, two and two.

18 In the cells also of the porters toward the west four in the way: and two at every cell.

19 These are the divisions of the porters of the sons of Core and of Merari.

20 Now Achias was over the treasures of the house of God, and the holy vessels.

21 The sons of Ledan, the sons of Gersonni: of Ledan were heads of the families, of Ledan, and Gersonni, Jehieli.

22 The sons of Jehieli: Zathan and Joel, his brethren over the treasures of the house of the Lord,

23 With the Amramites, and Isaarites, and Hebronites, and Ozielites.

24 And Subael the son of Gersom, the son of Moses, was chief over the treasures.

25 His brethren also: Eliezer, whose son Rohobia, and his son Isaias, and his son Joram, and his son Zechri, and his son Selemith.

26 Which Selemith and his brethren were over the treasures of the holy things, which king David, and the heads of families, and the captains over thousands and over hundreds, and the captains of the host had dedicated:

27 Out of the wars, and the spoils won in battles, which they had consecrated to the building and furniture of the temple of the Lord.

28 And all these things that Samuel the seer, and Saul the son of Cis, and Abner the son of Ner, and Joab the son of Sarvia, had sanctified. And whosoever had sanctified those things, they were under the hand of Selemith and his brethren.

29 But Chonenias and his sons were over the Isaarites, for the business abroad over Israel, to teach them and judge them.

30 And of the Hebronites Hasabias, and his brethren most able men, a thousand seven hundred, had the charge over Israel beyond the Jordan westward, in all the works of the Lord, and for the service of the king.

31 And the chief of the Hebronites was Jeria, according to their families and kindreds. In the fortieth year of the reign of David they were numbered; and there were found most valiant men in Jazer Galaad,

32 And his brethren of stronger age: two thousand seven hundred chiefs of families. And king David made them rulers over the Rubenites and the Gadites, and the half tribe of Manasses, for all the services of God, and the kings.

CHAPTER 27

The twelve captains for every month. The twelve princes of the tribes. David's several officers.

NOW the children of Israel according to their number, the heads of families, captains of thousands and of hundreds, and officers, that served the king according to their companies, who came in and went out every month in the year, under every chief were four and twenty thousand.

2 Over the first company the first month Jesboam, the son of Zabdiel was chief: and under him were four and twenty thousand,

3 Of the sons of Phares, the chief of all the captains in the host in the first month.

4 The company of the second month was under Dudia, an Ahohite: and after him was another named Macelloth, who commanded a part of the army of four and twenty thousand.

5 And the captain of the third company for the third month, was Banaias the son of Joiada the priest: and in his division were four and twenty thousand.

6 This is that Banaias the most valiant among the thirty, and above the thirty. And Amizabad his son commanded his company.

7 The fourth, for the fourth month, was Asahel the brother of Joab, and

Zabadias his son after him: and in his company were four and twenty thousand.

8 The fifth captain for the fifth month, was Samaoth, a Jezerite: and his company were four and twenty thousand.

9 The sixth, for the sixth month, was Hira the son of Acces, a Thecuite: and in his company were four and twenty thousand.

10 The seventh, for the seventh month, was Helles, a Phallonite of the sons of Ephraim: and in his company were four and twenty thousand.

11 The eighth, for the eighth month, was Sobochai, a Husathite of the race of Zarahi: and in his company were four and twenty thousand.

12 The ninth, for the ninth month, was Abiezer, an Anathothite of the sons of Jemini: and in his company were four and twenty thousand.

13 The tenth, for the tenth month, was Marai, who was a Netophathite of the race of Zarai: and in his company were four and twenty thousand.

14 The eleventh, for the eleventh month, was Banaias, a Pharathonite of the sons of Ephraim: and in his company were four and twenty thousand.

15 The twelfth, for the twelfth month, was Holdai, a Netophathite, of the race of Gothoniel: and in his company were four and twenty thousand.

16 Now the chiefs over the tribes of Israel were these: Over the Rubenites, Eliezer the son of Zechri was ruler: Over the Simeonites, Saphatias the son of Maacha:

17 Over the Levites, Hasabias the son of Camuel: Over the Aaronites, Sadoc:

18 Over Juda, Eliu the brother of David: Over Isaachar, Amri the son of Michael:

19 Over the Zabulonites, Jesmaias the son of Adias: Over the Nephtalites, Jerimoth the son of Ozriel:

20 Over the sons of Ephraim, Osee the son of Ozaziu: Over the half tribe of Manasses, Joel the son of Phadaia:

21 And over the half tribe of Manasses in Galaad, Jaddo the son of Zacharias: And over Benjamin, Jasiel the son of Abner:

22 And over Dan, Ezrihel the son of Jeroham. These were the princes of the children of Israel.

23 But David would not number them from twenty years old and under: because the Lord had said that he would multiply Israel like the stars of heaven.

24 [1] Joab the son of Sarvia began to number, but he finished not: because upon this there fell wrath upon Israel. And therefore the number of them that were numbered was not registered in the chronicles of king David.

25 And over the king's treasures was Azmoth the son of Adiel. And over those stores which were in the cities, and in the villages, and in the castles, was Jonathan the son of Ozias.

26 And over the tillage, and the husbandmen, who tilled the ground, was Ezri the son of Chelub.

27 And over the dressers of the vineyards, was Semeias, a Romathite. And over the wine cellars, Zabdias, an Aphonite.

28 And over the oliveyards and the fig groves, which were in the plains, was Balanam, a Gederite. And over the oil cellars, Joas.

29 And over the herds that fed in Saron, was Setrai, a Saronite. And over the oxen in the valleys, Saphat the son of Ali.

30 And over the camels, Ubil, an Ishmahelite. And over the asses, Jadias, a Meronathite.

31 And over the sheep Jaziz, an Agarene. All these were the rulers of the substance of king David.

32 And Jonathan David's uncle, a counselor, a wise and learned man: he and Jahiel the son of Hachamoni were with the king's sons.

33 And Achitophel was the king's counsellor: and Chusai the Arachite, the king's friend.

34 And after Achitophel was Joiada the son of Banaias, and Abiathar. And the general of the king's army was Joab.

CHAPTER 28

David's speech, in a solemn assembly. His exhortation to Solomon. He giveth him a pattern of the temple.

AND David assembled all the chief men of Israel, the princes of the tribes, and the captains of the companies, who waited on the king: and the captains over thousands, and over hundreds: and them who had the charge over the substance and possessions of the king: and his sons with the officers of the court, and the men of power: and all the bravest of the army at Jerusalem.

2 And the king rising up and standing said: Hear me, my brethren and my people. I had a thought to have built a house, in which the ark of the Lord and the footstool of our God might rest: and I prepared all things for the building.

3 And God said to me: [1] Thou shalt not build a house to my name; because thou art a man of war, and hast shed blood.

CHAP. 27. [1] 1 Par. 21, 2. CHAP. 28. [1] 2 Kings, 7, 13.

4 But the Lord God of Israel chose me of all the house of my father, to be king over Israel for ever. For of Juda he chose the princes: and of the house of Juda, my father's house: and among the sons of my father, it pleased him to choose me king over all Israel.

5 [2] And among my sons (for the Lord hath given me many sons) he hath chosen Solomon my son, to sit upon the throne of the kingdom of the Lord over Israel.

6 And he said to me: Solomon thy son shall build my house and my courts. For I have chosen him to be my son: and I will be a father to him.

7 And I will establish his kingdom for ever, if he continue to keep my commandments, and my judgments, as at this day.

8 Now then before all the assembly of Israel, in the hearing of our God, keep ye, and seek all the commandments of the Lord our God: that you may possess the good land; and may leave it to your children after you for ever.

9 And thou, my son Solomon, know the God of thy father, and serve him with a perfect heart, and a willing mind. [3] For the Lord searcheth all hearts, and understandeth all the thoughts of minds. If thou seek him, thou shalt find him: but if thou forsake him, he will cast thee off for ever.

10 Now therefore seeing the Lord hath chosen thee to build the house of the sanctuary, take courage, and do it.

11 And David gave to Solomon his son a description of the porch, and of the temple, and of the treasures, and of the upper floor, and of the inner chambers, and of the house for the mercy seat:

12 As also of all the courts, which he had in his thought, and of the chambers round about, for the treasures of the house of the Lord, and for the treasures of the consecrated things:

13 And of the divisions of the priests and of the Levites, for all the works of the house of the Lord, and for all the vessels of the service of the temple of the Lord.

14 Gold by weight for every vessel for the ministry. And silver by weight according to the diversity of the vessels and uses.

15 He gave also gold for the golden candlesticks, and their lamps, according to the dimensions of every candlestick, and the lamps thereof. In like manner also he gave silver by weight for the silver candlesticks, and for their lamps according to the diversity of the dimensions of them.

16 He gave also gold for the tables of proposition, according to the diversity of the tables: in like manner also silver for other tables of silver.

17 For fleshhooks also, and bowls, and censers of fine gold, and for little lions of gold, according to the measure he gave by weight for every lion. In like manner also for lions of silver he set aside a different weight of silver.

18 And for the altar of incense, he gave the purest gold: and to make the likeness of the chariot of the cherubims spreading their wings, and covering the ark of the covenant of the Lord.

19 All these things, said he, came to me written by the hand of the Lord, that I might understand all the works of the pattern.

20 And David said to Solomon his son: Act like a man, and take courage, and do. Fear not, and be not dismayed: for the Lord my God will be with thee, and will not leave thee, nor forsake thee, till thou hast finished all the work for the service of the house of the Lord.

21 Behold the courses of the priests and the Levites, for every ministry of the house of the Lord, stand by thee, and are ready: and both the princes, and the people know how to execute all thy commandments.

CHAPTER 29

David by word and example encourageth the princes to contribute liberally to the building of the temple. His thanksgiving, prayer, and sacrifices. His death.

AND king David said to all the assembly: Solomon, my son, whom alone God hath chosen, is as yet young and tender; and the work is great, for a house is prepared, not for man, but for God.

2 And I with all my ability have prepared the expenses for the house of my God. Gold for vessels of gold, and silver for vessels of silver, brass for things of brass, iron for things of iron, wood for things of wood: and onyx stones, and stones like alabaster, and of divers colours, and all manner of precious stones, and marble of Paros in great abundance.

3 Now over and above the things which I have offered into the house of my God I give, of my own proper goods, gold and silver for the temple of my God, beside what things I have prepared for the holy house.

4 Three thousand talents of gold of the gold of Ophir: and seven thousand talents of refined silver, to overlay the walls of the temple.

5 And gold for wheresoever there is need of gold: and silver for wheresoever there is need of silver, for the works to

[2] Wisd. 9, 7.   [3] Ps. 7, 10.

be made by the hands of the artificers. Now, if any man is willing to offer, let him fill his hand to-day, and offer what he pleaseth to the Lord.

6 Then the heads of the families, and the princes of the tribes of Israel, and the captains of thousands and of hundreds, and the overseers of the king's possessions promised.

7 And they gave for the works of the house of the Lord: of gold, five thousand talents, and ten thousand solids: of silver, ten thousand talents: and of brass, eighteen thousand talents: and of iron, a hundred thousand talents.

8 And all they that had stones gave them to the treasures of the house of the Lord, by the hand of Jahiel the Gersonite.

9 And the people rejoiced, when they promised their offerings willingly: because they offered them to the Lord with all their heart. And David the king rejoiced also with a great joy.

10 And he blessed the Lord before all the multitude; and he said: Blessed art thou, O Lord, the God of Israel, our father from eternity to eternity.

11 Thine, O Lord, is magnificence, and power, and glory, and victory: and to thee is praise. For all that is in heaven, and in earth, is thine. Thine is the kingdom, O Lord, and thou art above all princes

12 Thine are riches, and thine is glory: thou hast dominion over all. In thy hand is power and might: in thy hand greatness, and the empire of all things.

13 Now therefore, our God, we give thanks to thee :and we praise thy glorious name.

14 Who am I, and what is my people, that we should be able to promise thee all these things? All things are thine: and we have given thee what we received of thy hand.

15 For we are sojourners before thee, and strangers, as *were* all our fathers. [1] Our days upon earth are as a shadow: and there is no stay.

16 O Lord our God, all this store that we have prepared to build thee a house for thy holy name is from thy hand: and all things are thine.

17 I know, my God, that thou provest hearts, and lovest simplicity. Wherefore I also in the simplicity of my heart, have joyfully offered all these things: and I have seen with great joy thy people, which are here present, offer thee their offerings.

18 O Lord God of Abraham, and of Isaac, and of Israel, our fathers, keep for ever this will of their heart: and let this mind remain always for the worship of thee.

19 And give to Solomon my son a perfect heart, that he may keep thy commandments, thy testimonies, and do all things: and thy ceremonies, build the house, for which I have provided the charges.

20 And David commanded all the assembly: Bless ye the Lord our God. And all the assembly blessed the Lord the God of their fathers. And they bowed themselves and worshipped God, and then the king.

21 And they sacrificed victims to the Lord: and they offered holocausts the next day, a thousand bullocks, a thousand rams, a thousand lambs, with their libations, and with every thing prescribed most abundantly for all Israel.

22 And they ate, and drank before the Lord that day with great joy. [2] And they anointed the second time Solomon the son of David. And they anointed him to the Lord to be prince, and Sadoc to be high priest.

23 And Solomon sat on the throne of the Lord as king instead of David his father. And he pleased all: and all Israel obeyed him.

24 And all the princes, and men of power, and all the sons of king David gave their hand, and were subject to Solomon the king.

25 And the Lord magnified Solomon over all Israel: and gave him the glory of a reign, such as no king of Israel had before him.

26 So David the son of Isai reigned over all Israel.

27 [3] And the days that he reigned over Israel, were forty years: in Hebron he reigned seven years: and in Jerusalem three and thirty years.

28 And he died in a good age, full of days, and riches, and glory. And Solomon his son reigned in his stead.

29 Now the acts of king David first and last are written in the book of Samuel the seer, and in the book of Nathan the prophet, and in the book of Gad the seer:

30 And of all his reign, and his valour, and of the times that passed under him, either in Israel, or in all the kingdoms of the countries.

CHAP. 29. [1] Wisd. 2, 5.   [2] 3 Kings, 1, 34.   [3] 3 Kings, 2, 11.

THE SECOND BOOK OF

PARALIPOMENON

CHAPTER 1

Solomon offereth sacrifices at Gabaon. His choice of wisdom which God giveth him.

AND [1] Solomon the son of David was strengthened in his kingdom: and the Lord his God was with him, and magnified him to a high degree.

2 And Solomon gave orders to all Israel, to the captains of thousands, and of hundreds, and to the rulers, and to the judges of all Israel, and the heads of the families.

3 And he went with all the multitude to the high place of Gabaon, where was the tabernacle of the covenant of the Lord, which Moses the servant of God made, in the wilderness.

4 [2] For David had brought the ark of God from Cariathiarim to the place, which he had prepared for it, and where he had pitched a tabernacle for it; that is, in Jerusalem.

5 And the altar of brass, [3] which Beseleel the son of Uri the son of Hur had made, was there before the tabernacle of the Lord. And Solomon and all the assembly sought it.

6 And Solomon went up thither to the brazen altar, before the tabernacle of the covenant of the Lord, and offered up on it a thousand victims.

7 And behold that night God appeared to him, saying: Ask what thou wilt that I should give thee.

8 And Solomon said to God: Thou hast shewn great kindness to my father David; and hast made me king in his stead.

9 Now therefore, O Lord God, let thy word be fulfilled, which thou hast promised to David my father: for thou hast made me king over thy great people, which is as innumerable as the dust of the earth.

10 [4] Give me wisdom and knowledge that I may come in and go out before thy people: for who can worthily judge this thy people, which is so great?

11 And God said to Solomon: Because this choice hath pleased thy heart, and thou hast not asked riches, and wealth, and glory, nor the lives of them that hate thee, nor many days of life: but hast asked wisdom and knowledge, to be able to judge my people, over which I have made thee king,

12 Wisdom and knowledge are granted to thee: and I will give thee riches, and wealth, and glory, so that none of the kings before thee, nor after thee, shall be like thee.

13 Then Solomon came from the high place of Gabaon to Jerusalem before the tabernacle of the covenant, and reigned over Israel.

14 [5] And he gathered to himself chariots and horsemen: and he had a thousand four hundred chariots, and twelve thousand horsemen: and he placed them in the cities of the chariots, and with the king in Jerusalem.

15 And the king made silver and gold to be in Jerusalem as stones, and cedar trees as sycamores, which grow in the plains in great multitude.

16 And there were horses brought him from Egypt, and from Coa, by the king's merchants, who went, and bought at a price.

17 A chariot of four horses for six hundred pieces of silver, and a horse for a hundred and fifty. In like manner, market was made in all the kingdoms of the Hethites, and of the kings of Syria.

CHAPTER 2

Solomon's embassage to Hiram, who sends him a skilful workman and timber.

AND Solomon determined to build a house to the name of the Lord, and a palace for himself.

2 And he numbered out seventy thousand men to bear burdens, and eighty thousand to hew stones in the mountains, and three thousand six hundred to oversee them.

3 [1] He sent also to Hiram king of Tyre, saying: As thou didst with David my father, and didst send him cedars, to build him a house, in which he dwelt:

4 So do with me: that I may build a house to the name of the Lord my God, to dedicate it to burn incense before him, and to perfume with aromatical spices, and for the continual setting forth of bread, and for the holocausts, morning and evening, and on the sab-

CHAP. 1. [1] 3 Kings, 3, 1. [2] 2 Kings, 6, 17; 1 Par. 16, 1. [3] Exod. 38, 8. [4] Wisd. 9, 10. [5] 3 Kings, 10, 26. CHAP. 2. [1] 3 Kings, 5, 2.

baths, and on the new moons, and the solemnities of the Lord our God for ever, which are commanded for Israel.

5 For the house which I desire to build, is great: for our God is great above all gods.

6 Who then can be able to build him a worthy house? If heaven, and the heaven of heavens cannot contain him: who am I that I should be able to build him a house? But to this end only, that incense may be burnt before him.

7 Send me therefore a skilful man, that knoweth how to work in gold, and in silver, in brass, and in iron, in purple, in scarlet and in blue, and that hath skill in engraving, with the artificers, which I have with me in Judea and Jerusalem, whom David my father provided.

8 Send me also cedars, and fir trees, and pine trees from Libanus: for I know that thy servants are skilful in cutting timber in Libanus. And my servants shall be with thy servants,

9 To provide me timber in abundance. For the house which I desire to build, is to be exceeding great, and glorious.

10 And I will give thy servants the workmen that are to cut down the trees, for their food, twenty thousand cores of wheat, and as many cores of barley, and twenty thousand measures of wine, and twenty thousand measures of oil.

11 And Hiram king of Tyre sent a letter to Solomon, saying: Because the Lord hath loved his people, therefore he hath made thee king over them.

12 And he added, saying: Blessed be the Lord the God of Israel, who made heaven and earth, who hath given to king David a wise and knowing son, endued with understanding and prudence, to build a house to the Lord, and a palace for himself.

13 I therefore have sent thee my father Hiram, a wise and most skilful man,

14 The son of a woman of the daughters of Dan, whose father was a Tyrian, who knoweth how to work in gold, and in silver, in brass, and in iron, and in marble, and in timber, in purple also, and violet, and silk and scarlet: and who knoweth to grave all sort of graving, and to devise ingeniously all that there may be need of in the work with thy artificers, and with the artificers of my lord David thy father.

15 The wheat therefore, and the barley, and the oil, and the wine, which thou, my lord, hast promised, send to thy servants.

16 And we will cut down as many trees out of Libanus, as thou shalt want, and will convey them in floats by sea to Joppe: and it will be thy part to bring them thence to Jerusalem.

17 And Solomon numbered all the proselytes in the land of Israel, after the numbering which David his father had made: and they were found a hundred and fifty-three thousand and six hundred.

18 And he set seventy thousand of them to carry burdens on their shoulders: and eighty thousand to hew stones in the mountains: and three thousand and six hundred to be overseers of the work of the people.

CHAPTER 3

The plan and ornaments of the temple. The cherubims, the veil, and the pillars.

AND [1] Solomon began to build the house of the Lord in Jerusalem, in mount Moria, which had been shewn to David his father, in the place which David had prepared in the [2] thrashingfloor of Ornan the Jebusite.

2 And he began to build in the second month, in the fourth year of his reign.

3 Now these are the foundations, which Solomon laid, to build the house of God. The length by the first measure sixty cubits, the breadth twenty cubits.

4 And the porch in the front, which was extended in length according to the measure of the breadth of the house, twenty cubits. And the height was a hundred and twenty cubits. And he overlaid it within with pure gold.

5 And the greater house he ceiled with deal boards, and overlaid them with plates of fine gold throughout: and he graved in them palm trees, and like little chains interlaced with one another.

6 He paved also the floor of the temple with most precious marble, of great beauty.

7 And the gold of the plates with which he overlaid the house, and the beams thereof, and the posts, and the walls, and the doors, was of the finest. And he graved cherubims on the walls.

8 He made also the house of the Holy of Holies: the length of it according to the breadth of the temple, twenty cubits, and the breadth of it in like manner twenty cubits. And he overlaid it with plates of gold, amounting to about six hundred talents.

9 He made also nails of gold: and the weight of every nail was fifty sicles. The upper chambers also he overlaid with gold.

10 He made also in the house of the Holy of Holies two cherubims of image work: and he overlaid them with gold.

CHAP. 3. [1] 3 Kings, 6, 1. [2] 2 Kings, 24, 21; 1 Par. 21, 26.

11 The wings of the cherubims were extended twenty cubits, so that one wing was five cubits long, and reached to the wall of the house: and the other was also five cubits long, and reached to the wing of the other cherub.

12 In like manner the wing of the other cherub was five cubits long, and reached to the wall: and his other wing was five cubits long, and touched the wing of the other cherub.

13 So the wings of the two cherubims were spread forth, and were extended twenty cubits. And they stood upright on their feet, and their faces were turned toward the house without.

14 [3] He made also a veil of violet, purple, scarlet, and silk: and wrought in it cherubims.

15 [4] He made also before the doors of the temple two pillars, which were five and thirty cubits high: and their chapiters were five cubits.

16 He made also as it were little chains in the oracle; and he put them on the heads of the pillars. And a hundred pomegranates, which he put between the little chains.

17 These pillars he put at the entrance of the temple, one on the right hand, and the other on the left. That which was on the right hand, he called Jachin: and that on the left hand, Booz.

CHAPTER 4

The altar of brass. The molten sea upon twelve oxen. The ten loaves, the candlesticks and other vessels and ornaments of the temple.

HE made also an altar of brass twenty cubits long, and twenty cubits broad, and ten cubits high.

2 [1] Also a molten sea of ten cubits from brim to brim, round in compass. It was five cubits high, and a line of thirty cubits compassed it round about.

3 And under it there was the likeness of oxen; and certain engravings on the outside of ten cubits compassed the belly of the sea, as it were with two rows.

4 And the oxen were cast. And the sea itself was set upon the twelve oxen: three of which looked toward the north: and other three toward the west: and other three toward the south: and the other three that remained toward the east. And the sea stood upon them; and the hinder parts of the oxen were inward under the sea.

5 Now the thickness of it was a handbreadth; and the brim of it was like the brim of a cup, or of a crisped lily: and it held three thousand measures.

6 He made also ten lavers: and he set five on the right hand, and five on the left, to wash in them all such things as they were to offer for holocausts. But the sea was for the priests to wash in.

7 And he made ten golden candlesticks, according to the form which they were commanded to be made by: and he set them in the temple, five on the right hand, and five on the left.

8 Moreover also ten tables: and he set them in the temple, five on the right side, and five on the left. Also a hundred bowls of gold.

9 He made also the court of the priests, and a great hall, and doors in the hall, which he covered with brass.

10 And he set the sea on the right side over against the east toward the south.

11 And Hiram made caldrons, and fleshhooks, and bowls: and finished all the king's work in the house of God.

12 That is to say: the two pillars, and the pommels, and the chapiters, and the network, to cover the chapiters over the pommels:

13 And four hundred pomegranates, and two wreaths of network, so that two rows of pomegranates were joined to each wreath, to cover the pommels, and the chapiters of the pillars.

14 He made also bases, and lavers, which he set upon the bases:

15 One sea, and twelve oxen under the sea:

16 And the caldrons, and fleshhooks, and bowls. All the vessels did Hiram his father make for Solomon in the house of the Lord of the finest brass.

17 In the country near the Jordan did the king cast them, in a clay ground between Sochot and Saredatha.

18 And the multitude of vessels was innumerable, so that the weight of the brass was not known.

19 And Solomon made all the vessels for the house of God, and the golden altar, and the tables, upon which were the loaves of proposition;

20 The candlesticks also of most pure gold with their lamps to give light before the oracle, according to the manner.

21 And certain flowers, and lamps, and golden tongs. All were made of the finest gold.

22 The vessels also for the perfumes, and the censers, and the bowls, and the mortars, of pure gold. And he graved the doors of the inner temple, that is, for the Holy of Holies. And the doors of the temple without *were* of gold. And thus all the work was finished which Solomon made in the house of the Lord.

[3] Matt. 27, 51. [4] Jer. 52, 20. CHAP. 4. [1] 3 Kings, 7, 23.

CHAPTER 5

The ark is brought with great solemnity into the temple. The temple is filled with the glory of God.

THEN [1] Solomon brought in all the things that David his father had vowed; the silver, and the gold, and all the vessels, he put among the treasures of the house of God.

2 [2] And after this he gathered together the ancients of Israel, and all the princes of the tribes, and the heads of the families, of the children of Israel to Jerusalem, to bring the ark of the covenant of the Lord out of the city of David, which is Sion.

3 And all the men of Israel came to the king in the solemn day of the seventh month.

4 And when all the ancients of Israel were come the Levites took up the ark.

5 And brought it in, together with all the furniture of the tabernacle. And the priests with the Levites carried the vessels of the sanctuary, which were in the tabernacle.

6 And king Solomon and all the assembly of Israel, and all that were gathered together before the ark, sacrificed rams, and oxen without number: so great was the multitude of the victims.

7 And the priests brought in the ark of the covenant of the Lord into its place; that is, to the oracle of the temple, into the Holy of Holies under the wings of the cherubims;

8 So that the cherubims spread their wings over the place, in which the ark was set, and covered the ark itself and its staves.

9 Now the ends of the staves wherewith the ark was carried, because they were something longer, were seen before the oracle: but if a man were a little outward, he could not see them. So the ark has been there unto this day.

10 And there was nothing else in the ark but the two tables which Moses put there at Horeb, when the Lord gave the law to the children of Israel, at their coming out of Egypt.

11 Now when the priests were come out of the sanctuary (for all the priests that could be found there, were sanctified, and as yet at that time the courses and orders of the ministries were not divided among them),

12 Both the Levites and the singing men, that is, both they that were under Asaph, and they that were under Heman, and they that were under Idithun, with their sons, and their brethren, clothed with fine linen, sounded with cymbals, and psalteries, and harps, standing on the east side of the altar:

and with them a hundred and twenty priests, sounding with trumpets.

13 So when they all sounded together, both with trumpets, and voice, and cymbals, and organs, and with divers kind of musical instruments, and lifted up their voice on high the sound was heard afar off. So that when they began to praise the Lord, and to say: Give glory to the Lord for he is good, for his mercy endureth for ever, the house of God was filled with a cloud.

14 Nor could the priests stand and minister by reason of the cloud. For the glory of the Lord had filled the house of God.

CHAPTER 6

Solomon's blessings and prayer.

THEN [1] Solomon said: The Lord promised that he would dwell in a cloud.

2 But I have built a house to his name, that he might dwell there for ever.

3 And the king turned his face, and blessed all the multitude of Israel (for all the multitude stood attentive); and he said:

4 Blessed be the Lord the God of Israel, who hath accomplished in deed that which he spoke to David my father, saying:

5 From the day that I brought my people out of the land of Egypt, I chose no city among all the tribes of Israel, for a house to be built in it to my name. Neither chose I any other man, to be the ruler of my people Israel.

6 But I chose Jerusalem, that my name might be there: and I chose David to set him over my people Israel.

7 And whereas David my father had a mind to build a house to the name of the Lord the God of Israel,

8 The Lord said to him: Forasmuch as it was thy will to build a house to my name, thou hast done well indeed in having such a will.

9 But thou shalt not build the house: but thy son, who shall come out of thy loins, he shall build a house to my name.

10 The Lord therefore hath accomplished his word which he spoke. And I am risen up in the place of David my father, and sit upon the throne of Israel, as the Lord promised: and have built a house to the name of the Lord God of Israel.

11 And I have put in it the ark, wherein is the covenant of the Lord, which he made with the children of Israel.

12 And he stood before the altar of

<hr>

CHAP. 5. ¹ 3 Kings, 7, 51. ² 3 Kings, 8, 1. CHAP. 6. ¹ 3 Kings, 8, 12.

the Lord, in presence of all the multitude of Israel, and stretched forth his hands.

13 For Solomon had made a brazen scaffold, and had set it in the midst of the temple, which was five cubits long, and five cubits broad, and three cubits high: and he stood upon it. Then kneeling down in the presence of all the multitude of Israel, and lifting up his hands towards heaven,

14 [2] He said: O Lord God of Israel, there is no God like thee in heaven nor in earth: who keepest covenant and mercy with thy servants, that walk before thee with all their hearts:

15 Who hast performed to thy servant David my father all that thou hast promised him: and hast accomplished in fact, what thou hast spoken with thy mouth; as also the present time proveth.

16 Now then, O Lord God of Israel, fulfil to thy servant David my father, whatsoever thou hast promised him, saying: There shall not fail thee a man in my sight, to sit upon the throne of Israel; yet so that thy children take heed to their ways, and walk in my law, as thou hast walked before me.

17 And now, Lord God of Israel, let thy word be established which thou hast spoken to thy servant David.

18 Is it credible then that God should dwell with men on the earth? If heaven and the heavens of heavens do not contain thee, how much less this house, which I have built?

19 But to this end only it is made, that thou mayest regard the prayer of thy servant and his supplication, O Lord my God: and mayest hear the prayers which thy servant poureth out before thee.

20 That thou mayest open thy eyes upon this house, day and night, upon the place wherein thou hast promised that thy name should be called upon,

21 And that thou wouldst hear the prayer which thy servant prayeth in it. Hearken then to the prayers of thy servant, and of thy people Israel. Whosoever shall pray in this place, hear thou from thy dwelling place, that is, from heaven, and shew mercy.

22 If any man sin against his neighbour, and come to swear against him, and bind himself with a curse before the altar in this house:

23 Then hear thou from heaven, and do justice to thy servants, so as to requite the wicked by making his wickedness fall upon his own head, and to revenge the just, rewarding him according to his justice.

24 If thy people Israel be overcome by their enemies (for they will sin against thee), and being converted shall do penance, and call upon thy name, and pray to thee in this place:

25 Then hear thou from heaven, and forgive the sin of thy people Israel, and bring them back into the land, which thou gavest to them and their fathers.

26 If the heavens be shut up, and there fall no rain by reason of the sins of the people, and they shall pray to thee in this place, and confess to thy name, and be converted from their sins, when thou dost afflict them:

27 Then hear thou from heaven, O Lord, and forgive the sins of thy servants and of thy people Israel, and teach them the good way, in which they may walk; and give rain to thy land which thou hast given to thy people to possess.

28 [3] If a famine arise in the land, or a pestilence or blasting, or mildew, or locusts, or caterpillars; or if their enemies waste the country, and besiege the cities, whatsoever scourge or infirmity shall be upon them:

29 Then if any of thy people Israel, knowing his own scourge and infirmity, shall pray, and shall spread forth his hands in this house:

30 Hear thou from heaven, from thy high dwelling place, and forgive, and render to every one according to his ways, which thou knowest him to have in his heart (for thou only knowest the hearts of the children of men);

31 That they may fear thee, and walk in thy ways, all the days that they live upon the face of the land, which thou hast given to our fathers.

32 If the stranger also, who is not of thy people Israel, come from a far country, for the sake of thy great name, and thy strong hand, and thy stretched out arms, and adore in this place:

33 Hear thou from heaven, thy firm dwelling place, and do all that which that stranger shall call upon thee for; that all the people of the earth may know thy name, and may fear thee, as thy people Israel, and may know, that thy name is invoked upon this house, which I have built.

34 If thy people go out to war against their enemies, by the way that thou shalt send them, and adore thee towards the way of this city, which thou hast chosen, and the house which I have built to thy name:

35 Then hear thou from heaven their prayers, and their supplications, and revenge them.

36 And if they sin against thee ([4] for there is no man that sinneth not), and

thou be angry with them, and deliver them up to their enemies, and they lead them away captive to a land, either afar off, or near at hand;

37 And if they be converted in their heart in the land to which they were led captive, and do penance, and pray to thee in the land of their captivity, saying: We have sinned, we have done wickedly, we have dealt unjustly;

38 And return to thee with all their heart, and with all their soul, in the land of their captivity, to which they were led away, and adore thee towards the way of their own land which thou gavest their fathers, and of the city, which thou hast chosen, and the house which I have built to thy name:

39 Then hear thou from heaven, that is, from thy firm dwelling place, their prayers, and do judgment, and forgive thy people, although they have sinned.

40 For thou art my God: let thy eyes, I beseech thee, be open, and let thy ears be attentive to the prayer that is made in this place.

41 [5] Now, therefore, arise, O Lord God, into thy resting place, thou and the ark of thy strength: let thy priests, O Lord God, put on salvation, and thy saints rejoice in good things.

42 O Lord God, turn not away the face of thy anointed: remember the mercies of David thy servant.

CHAPTER 7

Fire from heaven consumeth the sacrifices. The solemnity of the dedication of the temple. God signifieth his having heard Solomon's prayer: yet so if he continue to serve him.

AND when Solomon had made an end of his prayer, fire came down from heaven, and consumed the holocausts and the victims. And the majesty of the Lord filled the house.

2 [1] Neither could the priest enter into the temple of the Lord; because the majesty of the Lord had filled the temple of the Lord.

3 Moreover all the children of Israel saw the fire coming down, and the glory of the Lord upon the house. And falling down with their faces to the ground, upon the stone pavement, they adored and praised the Lord: because he is good, because his mercy endureth for ever.

4 And the king and all the people sacrificed victims before the Lord.

5 [2] And king Solomon offered a sacrifice of twenty-two thousand oxen, and one hundred and twenty thousand rams: and the king and all the people dedicated the house of God.

6 And the priests stood in their offices: and the Levites with the instruments of music of the Lord, which king David made to praise the Lord: because his mercy endureth for ever, singing the hymns of David by their ministry. And the priests sounded with trumpets before them; and all Israel stood.

7 Solomon also sanctified the middle of the court before the temple of the Lord. For he offered there the holocausts and the fat of the peace offerings: because the brazen altar which he had made could not hold the holocausts, and the sacrifices, and the fat.

8 And Solomon kept the solemnity at that time seven days, and all Israel with him, a very great congregation, from the entrance of Emath to the torrent of Egypt.

9 And he made on the eighth day a solemn assembly, because he had kept the dedication of the altar seven days, and had celebrated the solemnity, seven days.

10 So, on the three and twentieth day of the seventh month he sent away the people to their dwellings, joyful and glad for the good that the Lord had done to David, and to Solomon, and to all Israel his people.

11 [3] And Solomon finished the house of the Lord, and the king's house, and all that he had designed in his heart to do, in the house of the Lord, and in his own house; and he prospered.

12 And the Lord appeared to him by night, and said: I have heard thy prayer, and I have chosen this place to myself for a house of sacrifice.

13 If I shut up heaven, and there fall no rain, or if I give orders, and command the locust to devour the land, or if I send pestilence among my people:

14 And my people, upon whom my name is called, being converted, shall make supplication to me, and seek out my face, and do penance for their most wicked ways: then will I hear from heaven, and will forgive their sins and will heal their land.

15 My eyes also shall be open, and my ears attentive to the prayer of him that shall pray in this place.

16 For I have chosen, and have sanctified this place, that my name may be there for ever: and my eyes and my heart may remain there perpetually.

17 And as for thee, if thou walk before me, as David thy father walked, and do according to all that I have commanded thee, and keep my justices and my judgments:

18 I will raise up the throne of thy kingdom, as I promised to David thy

[5] Ps. 131, 8. CHAP. 7. [1] 2 Mach. 2, 8. [2] 3 Kings, 8, 63. [3] 3 Kings, 9, 1.

father, saying: There shall not fail thee a man of thy stock to be ruler in Israel.

19 But if you turn away, and forsake my justices, and my commandments, which I have set before you, and shall go and serve strange gods, and adore them,

20 I will pluck you up by the root out of my land which I have given you: and this house which I have sanctified to my name, I will cast away from before my face, and will make it a byword, and an example among all nations.

21 And this house shall be for a proverb to all that pass by. And they shall be astonished and say: Why hath the Lord done thus to this land, and to this house?

22 And they shall answer: Because they forsook the Lord, the God of their fathers, who brought them out of the land of Egypt, and laid hold on strange gods, and adored them, and worshipped them: therefore all these evils are come upon them.

CHAPTER 8

Solomon's buildings and other acts.

AND ¹at the end of twenty years after Solomon had built the house of the Lord and his own house:

2 He built the cities which Hiram had given to Solomon, and caused the children of Israel to dwell there.

3 He went also into Emath Suba, and possessed it.

4 And he built Palmira in the desert: and he built other strong cities in Emath.

5 And he built Beth-horon the upper, and Beth-horon the nether, walled cities with gates and bars and locks.

6 Balaath also, and all the strong cities that were Solomon's, and all the cities of the chariots, and the cities of the horsemen. All that Solomon had a mind, and designed, he built in Jerusalem, and in Libanus, and in all the land of his dominion.

7 All the people that were left of the Hethites, and the Amorrhites, and the Pherezites, and the Hevites, and the Jebusites, that were not of the stock of Israel:

8 Of their children, and of the posterity, whom the children of Israel had not slain, Solomon made to be the tributaries, unto this day.

9 But of the children of Israel he set none to serve in the king's works: for they were men of war, and chief captains, and rulers of his chariots and horsemen.

10 And all the chief captains of king Solomon's army were two hundred and fifty, who taught the people.

11 And he removed the daughter of Pharao from the city of ²David, to the house which he had built for her. For the king said: My wife shall not dwell in the house of David king of Israel, for it is sanctified: because the ark of the Lord came into it.

12 Then Solomon offered holocausts to the Lord upon the altar of the Lord, which he had built before the porch,

13 That every day an offering might be made on it according to the ordinance of Moses: in the sabbaths: and on the new moons: and on the festival days three times a year, that is to say, in the feast of unleavened bread, and in the feast of weeks, and in the feast of tabernacles.

14 And he appointed according to the order of David his father the offices of the priests in their ministries: and the Levites in their order to give praise, and minister before the priests according to the duty of every day: and the porters in their divisions by gate and gate. For so David, the man of God, had commanded.

15 And the priests and Levites departed not from the king's commandments, as to any thing that he had commanded, and as to the keeping of the treasures.

16 Solomon had all charges prepared, from the day that he founded the house of the Lord, until the day wherein he finished it.

17 Then Solomon went to Asiongaber, and to Ailath, on the coast of the Red Sea, which is in the land of Edom.

18 And Hiram sent him ships by the hands of his servants, and skilful mariners. And they went with Solomon's servants to Ophir: and they took thence four hundred and fifty talents of gold, and brought it to king Solomon.

CHAPTER 9

The queen of Saba admireth the wisdom of Solomon. His riches and glory. His death.

AND ¹when the queen of Saba heard of the fame of Solomon, she came to try him with hard questions at Jerusalem, with great riches, and camels, which carried spices, and abundance of gold, and precious stones. And when she was come to Solomon, she proposed to him all that was in her heart.

2 And Solomon explained to her all that she proposed: and there was not any thing that he did not make clear unto her.

3 And when she had seen these things, to wit, the wisdom of Solomon, and the house which he had built.

4 And the meats of his table, and the dwelling places of his servants, and the attendance of his officers, and their apparel, his cupbearers also, and their garments, and the victims which he offered in the house of the Lord: there was no more spirit in her, she was so astonished.

5 And she said to the king: The word is true which I heard in my country of thy virtues and wisdom.

6 I did not believe them that told it, until I came, and my eyes had seen, and I had proved that scarce one half of thy wisdom had been told me. Thou hast exceeded the same with thy virtues.

7 Happy are thy men, and happy are thy servants, who stand always before thee, and hear thy wisdom.

8 Blessed be the Lord thy God, who hath been pleased to set thee on his throne, king of the Lord thy God. Because God loveth Israel, and will preserve them for ever: therefore hath he made thee king over them, to do judgment and justice.

9 And she gave to the king a hundred and twenty talents of gold, and spices in great abundance, and most precious stones. There were no such spices as these which the queen of Saba gave to king Solomon.

10 And the servants also of Hiram, with the servants of Solomon, brought gold from Ophir, and thyine trees, and most precious stones.

11 And the king made of the thyine trees stairs in the house of the Lord, and in the king's house, and harps and psalteries for the singing men: never were there seen such trees in the land of Juda.

12 And king Solomon gave to the queen of Saba all that she desired, and that she asked, and many more things than she brought to him. So she returned, and went to her own country with her servants.

13 And the weight of the gold, that was brought to Solomon every year, was six hundred and sixty-six talents of gold:

14 Besides the sum which the deputies of divers nations, and the merchants, were accustomed to bring, and all the kings of Arabia, and the lords of the lands, who brought gold and silver to Solomon.

15 And king Solomon made two hundred golden spears, of the sum of six hundred pieces of gold, which went to every spear:

16 And three hundred golden shields of three hundred pieces of gold, which went to the covering of every shield. And the king put them in the armoury, which was compassed with a wood.

17 The king also made a great throne of ivory, and overlaid it with pure gold:

18 And six steps to go up to the throne: and a footstool of gold: and two arms one on either side: and two lions standing by the arms:

19 Moreover twelve other little lions standing upon the steps on both sides. There was not such a throne in any kingdom.

20 And all the vessels of the king's table were of gold; and the vessels of the house of the forest of Libanus were of the purest gold. For no account was made of silver in those days.

21 For the king's ships went to Tharsis with the servants of Hiram, once in three years: and they brought thence gold and silver, and ivory, and apes, and peacocks.

22 And Solomon was magnified above all the kings of the earth for riches and glory.

23 And all the kings of the earth desired to see the face of Solomon, that they might hear the wisdom which God had given in his heart.

24 And every year they brought him presents: vessels of silver and of gold, and garments, and armour, and spices, and horses, and mules.

25 And Solomon had forty thousand horses in the stables, and twelve thousand chariots, and horsemen; and he placed them in the cities of the chariots, and where the king was in Jerusalem.

26 And he exercised authority over all the kings from the river Euphrates to the land of the Philistines, and to the borders of Egypt.

27 And he made silver as plentiful in Jerusalem as stones: and cedars as common as the sycamores, which grow in the plains.

28 And horses were brought to him out of Egypt, and out of all countries.

29 Now the rest of the acts of Solomon first and last are written in the words of Nathan the prophet, and in the books of Ahias the Silonite, and in the vision of Addo the seer, against Jeroboam the son of Nabat.

30 And Solomon reigned in Jerusalem over all Israel forty years.

31 And he slept with his fathers. And they buried him in the city of David: and Roboam his son reigned in his stead.

CHAPTER 10

Roboam answereth the people roughly: upon which ten tribes revolt.

AND [1] Roboam went to Sichem: for thither all Israel were assembled to make him king.

2 And when Jeroboam the son of Nabat, who was in Egypt (for he was fled thither from Solomon), heard it, forthwith he returned.

3 And they sent for him; and he came with all Israel. And they spoke to Roboam, saying:

4 Thy father oppressed us with a most grievous yoke; do thou govern us with a lighter hand than thy father, who laid upon us a heavy servitude, and ease some thing of the burden, that we may serve thee.

5 And he said to them: Come to me again after three days. And when the people were gone,

6 He took counsel with the ancients, who had stood before his father Solomon, while he yet lived, saying: What counsel give you to me, that I may answer the people?

7 And they said to him: If thou please this people, and soothe them with kind words, they will be thy servants for ever.

8 But he forsook the counsel of the ancients, and began to treat with the young men, that had been brought up with him, and were in his train.

9 And he said to them: What seemeth good to you? Or what shall I answer this people, who have said to me: Ease the yoke which thy father laid upon us?

10 But they answered as young men and brought up with him in pleasures, and said: Thus shalt thou speak to the people, that said to thee: Thy father made our yoke heavy, do thou ease it. Thus shalt thou answer them: My little finger is thicker than the loins of my father.

11 My father laid upon you a heavy yoke: and I will add more weight to it. My father beat you with scourges: but I will beat you with scorpions.

12 So Jeroboam and all the people came to Roboam the third day, as he commanded them.

13 And the king answered roughly, leaving the counsel of the ancients.

14 And he spoke according to the advice of the young men: My father laid upon you a heavy yoke, which I will make heavier. My father beat you with scourges: but I will beat you with scorpions.

15 And he condescended not to the people's requests: for it was the will of God, that his word might be [2] fulfilled,

which he had spoken by the hand of Ahias the Silonite to Jeroboam the son of Nabat.

16 And all the people upon the king's speaking roughly, said thus unto him: We have no part in David, nor inheritance in the son of Isai. Return to thy dwellings, O Israel: and do thou, O David, feed thy own house. And Israel went away to their dwellings.

17 But Roboam reigned over the children of Israel that dwelt in the cities of Juda.

18 And king Roboam sent Aduram, who was over the tributes. And the children of Israel stoned him; and he died. And king Roboam made haste to get up into his chariot, and fled into Jerusalem.

19 And Israel revolted from the house of David unto this day.

CHAPTER 11
Roboam's reign. His kingdom is strengthened.

AND [1] Roboam came to Jerusalem, and called together all the house of Juda and of Benjamin, a hundred and fourscore thousand chosen men and warriors, to fight against Israel, and to bring back his kingdom to him.

2 And the word of the Lord came to Semeias the man of God, saying:

3 Speak to Roboam the son of Solomon, the king of Juda, and to all Israel, in Juda and Benjamin:

4 Thus saith the Lord: You shall not go up, nor fight against your brethren. Let every man return to his own house, for by my will this thing has been done. And when they heard the word of the Lord, they returned, and did not go against Jeroboam.

5 And Roboam dwelt in Jerusalem, and built walled cities in Juda.

6 And he built Bethlehem, and Etam, and Thecue,

7 And Bethsur, and Socho, and Odollam,

8 And Geth, and Maresa, and Ziph,

9 And Aduram, and Lachis, and Azecha:

19 Saraa also, and Aialon, and Hebron, which are in Juda and Benjamin, well fenced cities.

11 And when he had enclosed them with walls, he put in them governors and storehouses of provisions, that is, of oil and wine.

12 Moreover in every city he made an armoury of shields and spears; and he fortified them with great diligence; and he reigned over Juda, and Benjamin,

13 And the priests and Levites, that

were in all Israel, came to him out of all their seats,

14 Leaving their suburbs, and their possessions, and passing over to Juda, and Jerusalem; because Jeroboam and his sons had cast them off from executing the priestly office to the Lord.

15 And he made to himself priests for the high places, and for the devils, and for the calves which he had made.

16 Moreover out of all the tribes of Israel, whosoever gave their heart to seek the Lord the God of Israel, came into Jerusalem to sacrifice their victims before the Lord, the God of their fathers.

17 And they strengthened the kingdom of Juda, and established Roboam the son of Solomon for three years: for they walked in the ways of David and of Solomon, only three years.

18 And Roboam took to wife Mahalath the daughter of Jerimoth, the son of David: and Abihail the daughter of Eliab, the son of Isai.

19 And they bore him sons, Jehus, and Somorias, and Zoom.

20 And after her, he married Maacha the daughter of Absalom, who bore him Abia, and Ethai, and Ziza, and Salomith.

21 And Roboam loved Maacha, the daughter of Absalom, above all his wives and concubines. For he had married eighteen wives, and threescore concubines. And he begot eight and twenty sons, and threescore daughters.

22 But he put at the head of them Abia the son of Maacha, to be the chief ruler over all his brethren: for he meant to make him king,

23 Because he was wiser and mightier than all his sons, and in all the countries of Juda, and of Benjamin, and in all the walled cities. And he gave them provisions in abundance; and he sought many wives.

CHAPTER 12

Roboam for his sins is delivered up into the hands of the king of Egypt. Sesac carrieth away all the treasures of the temple.

AND when the kingdom of Roboam was strengthened and fortified, he forsook the law of the Lord, and all Israel with him.

2 And in the fifth year [1] of the reign of Roboam, Sesac king of Egypt came up against Jerusalem (because they had sinned against the Lord)

3 With twelve hundred chariots and threescore thousand horsemen. And the people were without number that came with him out of Egypt, to wit, Libyans, and Troglodites, and Ethiopians.

4 And he took the strongest cities in Juda, and came to Jerusalem.

5 And Semeias the prophet came to Roboam, and to the princes of Juda, that were gathered together in Jerusalem, fleeing from Sesac. And he said to them: Thus saith the Lord: You have left me, and I have left you in the hand of Sesac.

6 And the princes of Israel, and the king, being in a consternation, said: The Lord is just.

7 And when the Lord saw that they were humbled, the word of the Lord came to Semeias, saying: Because they are humbled, I will not destroy them, and I will give them a little help, and my wrath shall not fall upon Jerusalem by the hand of Sesac.

8 But yet they shall serve him, that they may know the difference between my service, and the service of a kingdom of the earth.

9 So Sesac king of Egypt departed from Jerusalem, taking away the treasures of the house of the Lord, and of the king's house. And he took all with him, and the golden shields that Solomon had made;

10 Instead of which the king made brazen ones, and delivered them to the captains of the shieldbearers, who guarded the entrance of the palace.

11 And when the king entered into the house of the Lord, the shieldbearers came and took them, and brought them back again to their armoury.

12 But yet because they were humbled, the wrath of the Lord turned away from them, and they were not utterly destroyed: for even in Juda there were found good works.

13 [2] King Roboam therefore was strengthened in Jerusalem, and reigned. He was one and forty years old when he began to reign; and he reigned seventeen years in Jerusalem, the city which the Lord chose out of all the tribes of Israel, to establish his name there. And the name of his mother was Naama, an Ammonitess.

14 But he did evil, and did not prepare his heart to seek the Lord.

15 Now the acts of Roboam first and last are written in the books of Semeias the prophet, and of Addo the seer, and diligently recorded. And there was war between Roboam and Jeroboam all their days.

16 And Roboam slept with his fathers; and was buried in the city of David. And Abia his son reigned in his stead.

CHAP. 12. [1] 3 Kings, 14, 25. [2] 3 Kings, 14, 21.

CHAPTER 13

Abia's reign. His victory over Jeroboam.

IN [1] the eighteenth year of king Jeroboam, Abia reigned over Juda.

2 Three years he reigned in Jerusalem. And his mother's name was Michaia, the daughter of Uriel of Gabaa. And there was war between Abia and Jeroboam.

3 [2] And when Abia had begun battle, and had with him four hundred thousand most valiant and chosen men, Jeroboam put his army in array against him, eight hundred thousand men, who were also chosen and most valiant for war.

4 And Abia stood upon mount Semeron, which was in Ephraim, and said: Hear me, O Jeroboam, and all Israel:

5 Do you not know that the Lord God of Israel gave to David the kingdom over Israel for ever, to him and to his sons by a covenant of salt?

6 And Jeroboam the son of Nabat, the servant of Solomon the son of David, rose up, [3] and rebelled against his lord:

7 And there were gathered to him vain men, and children of Belial. And they prevailed against Roboam the son of Solomon: for Roboam was unexperienced, and of a fearful heart, and could not resist them.

8 And now you say that you are able to withstand the kingdom of the Lord, which he possesseth by the sons of David: and you have a great multitude of people, and golden calves, which Jeroboam hath made you for gods.

9 [4] And you have cast out the priests of the Lord, the sons of Aaron, and the Levites: and you have made your priests, like all the nations of the earth. Whosoever cometh and consecrateth his hand with a bullock of the herd, and with seven rams, is made a priest of those who are no gods.

10 But the Lord is our God, whom we forsake not; and the priests who minister to the Lord are the sons of Aaron; and the Levites are in their order.

11 And they offer holocausts to the Lord, every day, morning and evening, and incense made according to the ordinance of the law. And the loaves are set forth on a most clean table. And there is with us the golden candlestick, and the lamps thereof, to be lighted always in the evening: for we keep the

precepts of the Lord our God, whom you have forsaken.

12 Therefore God is the leader in our army, and his priests who sound with trumpets, and resound against you. O children of Israel, fight not against the Lord the God of your fathers; for it is not good for you.

13 While he spoke these things, Jeroboam caused an ambushment to come about behind him. And while he stood facing the enemies, he encompassed Juda, who perceived it not, with his army.

14 And when Juda looked back, they saw the battle coming upon them both before and behind; and they cried to the Lord. And the priests began to sound with the trumpets:

15 And all the men of Juda shouted. And behold when they shouted, God terrified Jeroboam, and all Israel that stood against Abia and Juda.

16 And the children of Israel fled before Juda: and the Lord delivered them into their hand.

17 And Abia and his people slew them with a great slaughter: and there fell wounded of Israel five hundred thousand valiant men.

18 And the children of Israel were brought down, at that time and the children of Juda were exceedingly strengthened, because they had trusted in the Lord the God of their fathers.

19 And Abia pursued after Jeroboam, and took cities from him: Bethel and her daughters, and Jesana with her daughters, Ephron also and her daughters.

20 And Jeroboam was not able to resist any more, in the days of Abia: and the Lord struck him, and he died.

21 But Abia, being strengthened in his kingdom, took fourteen wives: and begot two and twenty sons, and sixteen daughters.

22 And the rest of the acts of Abia, and of his ways and works, are written diligently in the book of Addo the prophet.

CHAPTER 14

The reign of Asa. His victory over the Ethiopians.

AND [1] Abia slept with his fathers; and they buried him in the city of David: and Asa his son reigned in his stead. In his days the land was quiet ten years.

2 And Asa did that which was good and pleasing in the sight of his God: and he destroyed the altars of foreign worship, and the high places.

3 And broke the statues, and cut down the groves.

CHAP. 13. [1] 3 Kings. 15, 2. [2] 3 Kings. 15, 7. [3] 3 Kings. 11, 26. [4] 3 Kings. 12, 31. CHAP. 14. [1] 3 Kings. 15, 8.

CHAP. 13. Ver. 2. *Michaia.* Otherwise Maacha. Her father had also two names, namely, Absalom, or Abessalom, and Uriel.

Ver. 5. *A covenant of salt.* That is, a firm and perpetual covenant. See Num. 18, 19.

4 And he commanded Juda to seek the Lord the God of their fathers, and to do the law, and all the commandments.

5 And he took away out of all the cities of Juda the altars, and temples; and reigned in peace.

6 He built also strong cities in Juda: for he was quiet, and there had no wars risen in his time, the Lord giving peace.

7 And he said to Juda: Let us build these cities, and compass them with walls, and fortify them with towers, and gates, and bars, while all is quiet from wars, because we have sought the Lord the God of our fathers, and he hath given us peace round about. So they built, and there was no hinderance in building.

8 And Asa had in his army of men that bore shields and spears, of Juda three hundred thousand, and of Benjamin that bore shields and drew bows, two hundred and eighty thousand. All these were most valiant men.

9 And Zara, the Ethiopian, came out against them with his army of ten hundred thousand men, and with three hundred chariots. And he came as far as Maresa.

10 And Asa went out to meet him, and set his army in array for battle in the vale of Sephata, which is near Maresa.

11 And he called upon the Lord God, and said: [2] Lord, there is no difference with thee, whether thou help with few, or with many. Help us, O Lord our God: for with confidence in thee, and in thy name, we are come against this multitude. O Lord thou art our God. Let not man prevail against thee.

12 And the Lord terrified the Ethiopians before Asa and Juda: and the Ethiopians fled.

13 And Asa and the people that were with him pursued them to Gerara. And the Ethiopians fell even to utter destruction: for the Lord slew them, and his army fought against them, and they were destroyed. And they took abundance of spoils.

14 And they took all the cities round about Gerara: for a great fear was come upon all men. And they pillaged the cities, and carried off much booty.

15 And they destroyed the sheepcotes, and took an infinite number of cattle, and of camels: and returned to Jerusalem.

CHAPTER 15

The prophecy of Azarias. Asa's covenant with God. He deposeth his mother.

AND the spirit of God came upon Azarias the son of Oded.

2 And he went out to meet Asa, and said to him: Hear ye me, Asa, and all Juda and Benjamin: The Lord is with you, because you have been with him. If you seek him, you shall find: but if you forsake him, he will forsake you.

3 And many days shall pass in Israel, without the true God, and without a priest a teacher, and without the law.

4 And when in their distress they shall return to the Lord the God of Israel, and shall seek him, they shall find him.

5 At that time there shall be no peace to him that goeth out and cometh in: but terrors on every side among all the inhabitants of the earth.

6 For nation shall fight against nation, and city against city: for the Lord will trouble them with all distress.

7 Do you therefore take courage, and let not your hands be weakened: for there shall be a reward for your work.

8 And when Asa had heard the words, and the prophecy of Azarias the son of Oded, the prophet, he took courage, and took away the idols out of all the land of Juda, and out of Benjamin, and out of the cities of mount Ephraim, which he had taken; and he dedicated the altar of the Lord, which was before the porch of the Lord.

9 And he gathered together all Juda and Benjamin, and the strangers with them, of Ephraim, and Manasses, and Simeon: for many were come over to him out of Israel, seeing that the Lord his God was was with him.

10 And when they were come to Jerusalem in the third month, in the fifteenth year of the reign of Asa,

11 They sacrificed to the Lord in that day of the spoils, and of the prey, that they had brought, seven hundred oxen, and seven thousand rams.

12 And he went in to confirm as usual the covenant, that they should seek the Lord the God of their fathers with all their heart, and with all their soul.

13 And if any one, said he, seek not the Lord the God of Israel, let him die, whether little or great, man or woman.

14 And they swore to the Lord with a loud voice with joyful shouting, and with sound of trumpets, and sound of cornets:

15 All that were in Juda with a curse. For with all their heart they swore, and with all their will they sought him, and they found him; and the Lord gave them rest round about.

16 Moreover Maacha the mother of king Asa he deposed from the royal authority, because she had made in a grove an idol of Priapus. And he en-

2 1 Kings, 14, 6.

tirely destroycd it, and breaking it into pieces burnt it at the torrent Cedron.

17 But high places were left in Israel: nevertheless the heart of Asa was perfect all his days.

18 And the things which has father had vowed, and he himself had vowed, he brought into the house of the Lord: gold and silver, and vessels of divers uses.

19 And there was no war unto the five and thirtieth year of the kingdom of Asa.

CHAPTER 16

Asa is reproved for seeking help from the Syrians. His last acts and death.

AND in the six and thirtieth year of his kingdom, Baasa the king of Israel came up against Juda, and built a wall about Rama, that no one might safely go out or come in of the kingdom of Asa.

2 Then Asa brought out silver and gold out of the treasures of the house of the Lord, and of the king's treasures, and sent to Benadad king of Syria, who dwelt in Damascus, saying:

3 There is a league between me and thee, as there was between my father and thy father. Wherefore I have sent thee silver and gold, that thou mayst break thy league with Baasa king of Israel, and make him depart from me.

4 And when Benadad heard this, he sent the captains of his armies against the cities of Israel. And they took Ahion, and Dan, and Abelmaim, and all the walled cities of Nephtali.

5 And when Baasa heard of it, he left off the building of Rama, and interrupted his work.

6 Then king Asa took all Juda. And they carried away from Rama the stones, and the timber that Baasa had prepard for the building: and he built with them Gabaa, and Maspha.

7 At that time, Hanani the prophet came to Asa king of Juda, and said to him: Because thou hast had confidence in the king of Syria, and not in the Lord thy God, therefore hath the army of the king of Syria escaped out of thy hand.

8 [1] Were not the Ethiopians, and the Libyans much more numerous in chariots, and horsemen, and an exceeding great multitude: yet, because thou trustedst in the Lord, he delivered them into thy hand?

9 For the eyes of the Lord behold all the earth, and give strength to those

CHAP. 16. [1] Par. 14, 9.

CHAP. 16. Ver. 1. *Six and thirtieth year of his kingdom.* That is, of the kingdom of Juda, taking the date of it from the beginning of the reign of Roboam.

who with a perfect heart trust in him. Wherefore, thou hast done foolishly, and for this cause from this time wars shall arise against thee.

10 And Asa was angry with the seer, and commanded him to be put in prison: for he was greatly enraged because of this thing. And he put to death many of the people at that time.

11 But the works of Asa the first and last are written in the book of the kings of Juda and Israel.

12 And Asa fell sick in the nine and thirtieth year of his reign, of a most violent pain in his feet. And yet in his illness he did not seek the Lord, but rather trusted in the skill of physicians.

13 And he slept with his fathers: and he died in the one and fortieth year of his reign.

14 And they buried him in his own sepulchre, which he had made for himself in the city of David. And they laid him on his bed, full of spices and odoriferous ointments, which were made by the art of the perfumers. And they burnt them over him with very great pomp.

CHAPTER 17

Josaphat's reign. His care for the instruction of his people. His numerous forces.

AND Josaphat his son reigned in his stead, and grew strong against Israel.

2 And he placed numbers of soldiers in all the fortified cities of Juda. And he put garrisons in the land of Juda, and in the cities of Ephraim, which Asa his father had taken.

3 And the Lord was with Josaphat: because he walked in the first ways of David his father; and trusted not in Baalim,

4 But in the God of his father; and walked in his commandments, and not according to the sins of Israel.

5 And the Lord established the kingdom in his hand; and all Juda brought presents to Josaphat. And he acquired immense riches, and much glory.

6 And when his heart had taken courage for the ways of the Lord, he took away also the high places and the groves out of Juda.

7 And in the third year of his reign, he sent of his princes, Benhail, and Abdias, and Zacharias, and Nathanael, and Micheas, to teach in the cities of Juda.

8 And with them the Levites, Semeias, and Nathanias, and Zabadias, and Asael, and Semiramoth, and Jonathan, and Adonias, and Tobias, and Thobadonias, Levites. And with them Elisama, and Joram, priests.

9 And they taught the people in

Juda, having with them the book of the law of the Lord: and they went about all the cities of Juda, and instructed the people.

10 And the fear of the Lord came upon all the kingdoms of the lands that were round about Juda: and they durst not make war against Josaphat.

11 The Philistines also brought presents to Josaphat, and tribute in silver. And the Arabians brought him cattle, seven thousand seven hundred rams, and as many he-goats.

12 And Josaphat grew, and became exceeding great: and he built in Juda houses like towers, and walled cities.

13 And he prepared many works in the cities of Juda. And he had warriors, and valiant men in Jerusalem.

14 Of whom this is the number of the houses and families of every one: in Juda captains of the army, Ednas the chief, and with him three hundred thousand most valiant men.

15 After him Johanan the captain, and with him two hundred and eighty thousand.

16 And after him was Amasias the son of Zechri, consecrated to the Lord, and with him were two hundred thousand valiant men.

17 After him was Eliada, valiant in battle, and with him two hundred thousand armed with bow and shield.

18 After him also was Jozabad, and with him a hundred and eighty thousand ready for war.

19 All these were at the hand of the king, beside others, whom he had put in the walled cities, in all Juda.

CHAPTER 18

Josaphat accompanies Achab in his expedition against Ramoth. Achab is slain, as Micheas had foretold.

NOW Josaphat was rich and very glorious, and was joined by affinity to Achab.

2 And he went down to him after some years to Samaria. And Achab at his coming killed sheep and oxen in abundance, for him and the people that came with him: and he persuaded him to go up to Ramoth Galaad.

3 And Achab king of Israel said to Josaphat king of Juda: Come with me to Ramoth Galaad. And he answered him: Thou art as I am, and my people as thy people, and we will be with thee in the war.

4 And Josaphat said to the king of Israel: Inquire, I beseech thee, at present the word of the Lord.

5 So the king of Israel gathered together of the prophets four hundred men. And he said to them: Shall we go to Ramoth Galaad to fight, or shall we forbear? But they said: Go up, and God will deliver it into the king's hand.

6 And Josaphat said: Is there not here a prophet of the Lord, that we may inquire also of him?

7 And the king of Israel said to Josaphat: There is one man, of whom we may ask the will of the Lord: but I hate him; for he never prophesieth good to me, but always evil. And it is Micheas the son of Jemla. And Josaphat said: Speak not thus, O king.

8 And the king of Israel called one of the eunuchs, and said to him: Call quickly Micheas the son of Jemla.

9 Now the king of Israel, and Josaphat king of Juda, both sat on their thrones, clothed in royal robes: and they sat in the open court by the gate of Samaria. And all the prophets prophesied before them.

10 And Sedecias the son of Chanaana made him horns of iron, and said: Thus saith the Lord: With these shalt thou push Syria, till thou destroy it.

11 And all the prophets prophesied in like manner, and said: Go up to Ramoth Galaad; and thou shalt prosper; and the Lord will deliver them into the king's hand.

12 And the messenger that went to call Micheas, said to him: Behold the words of all the prophets with one mouth declare good to the king. I beseech thee therefore let not thy word disagree with them: and speak thou also good success.

13 And Micheas answered him: As the Lord liveth, whatsoever my God shall say to me, that will I speak.

14 So he came to the king; and the king said to him: Micheas, shall we go to Ramoth Galaad to fight, or forbear? And he answered him: Go up, for all shall succeed prosperously, and the enemies shall be delivered into your hands.

15 And the king said: I adjure thee again and again to say nothing but the truth to me, in the name of the Lord.

16 Then he said: I saw all Israel scattered in the mountains, like sheep without a shepherd. And the Lord said: These have no masters. Let every man return to his own house in peace.

17 And the king of Israel said to Josaphat: Did I not tell thee that this man would not prophesy me any good, but evil?

18 Then he said: Hear ye therefore the word of the Lord: I saw the Lord sitting on his throne, and all the army of heaven standing by him on the right hand and on the left.

19 And the Lord said: Who shall deceive Achab king of Israel, that he may go up and fall in Ramoth Galaad? And when one spoke in this manner, and another otherwise:

20 There came forth a spirit, and stood before the Lord, and said: I will deceive him. And the Lord said to him: By what means wilt thou deceive him?

21 And he answered: I will go out, and be a lying spirit in the mouth of all his prophets. And the Lord said: Thou shalt deceive, and shalt prevail. Go out, and do so.

22 Now therefore behold the Lord hath put a spirit of lying in the mouth of all thy prophets: and the Lord hath spoken evil against thee.

23 And Sedecias the son of Chanaana came and struck Micheas on the cheek and said: Which way went the spirit of the Lord from me, to speak to thee?

24 And Micheas said: Thou thyself shalt see in that day, when thou shalt go in from chamber to chamber, to hide thyself.

25 And the king of Israel commanded, saying: Take Micheas, and carry him to Amon the governor of the city, and to Joas the son of Amelech,

26 And say: Thus saith the king: Put this fellow in prison, and give him bread and water in a small quantity till I return in peace.

27 And Micheas said: If thou return in peace, the Lord hath not spoken by me. And he said: Hear, all ye people.

28 So the king of Israel and Josaphat king of Juda went up to Ramoth Galaad.

29 And the king of Israel said to Josaphat: I will change my dress, and so I will go to the battle: but put thou on thy own garments. And the king of Israel, having changed his dress, went to the battle.

30 Now the king of Syria had commanded the captains of his cavalry, saying: Fight ye not with small, or great, but with the king of Israel only.

31 So when the captains of the cavalry saw Josaphat, they said: This is the king of Israel. And they surrounded him to attack him. But he cried to the Lord; and he helped him, and turned them away from him.

32 For when the captains of the cavalry saw that he was not the king of Israel, they left him.

33 And it happened that one of the people shot an arrow at a venture, and struck the king of Israel between the neck and the shoulders; and he said to his chariot man: Turn thy hand, and carry me out of the battle, for I am wounded.

34 And the fight was ended that day. But the king of Israel stood in his chariot against the Syrians until the evening, and died at the sunset.

CHAPTER 19

Josaphat's charge to the judges and to the Levites.

AND Josaphat king of Juda returned to his house in peace to Jerusalem.

2 And Jehu the son of Hanani, the seer, met him and said to him: Thou helpest the ungodly; and thou art joined in friendship with them that hate the Lord: and therefore thou didst deserve indeed the wrath of the Lord.

3 But good works are found in thee, because thou hast taken away the groves out of the land of Juda, and hast prepared thy heart to seek the Lord the God of thy fathers.

4 And Josaphat dwelt at Jerusalem: and he went out again to the people from Bersabee to mount Ephraim, and brought them back to the Lord the God of their fathers.

5 And he set judges of the land in all the fenced cities of Juda, in every place.

6 And charging the judges, he said: Take heed what you do: for you exercise not the judgment of man, but of the Lord. And whatsoever you judge, it shall redound to you.

7 Let the fear of the Lord be with you, and do all things with diligence. For there is no iniquity with the Lord our God, ¹nor respect of persons, nor desire of gifts.

8 In Jerusalem also Josaphat appointed Levites, and priests and chiefs of the families of Israel, to judge the judgment and the cause of the Lord, for the inhabitants thereof.

9 And he charged them, saying: Thus shall you do in the fear of the Lord faithfully, and with a perfect heart.

10 Every cause that shall come to you of your brethren, that dwell in their cities, between kindred and kindred, wheresoever there is question concerning the law, the commandment, the ceremonies, the justifications: shew it them, that they may not sin against the Lord, and that wrath may not come upon you and your brethren. And so doing you shall not sin.

11 And Amarias the priest your high priest shall be chief in the things which regard God; and Zabadias the son of Ismahel, who is ruler in the house of Juda, shall be over those matters which

CHAP. 19. ¹ Deut. 10, 17; Wisd. 6, 8; Ecclus. 35, 15; Acts, 10, 34; Rom. 2, 11; Gal. 2, 6; Eph. 6, 9; Col. 3, 25; 1 Peter, 1, 17.

CHAP. 18. Ver. 19. *Who shall deceive.* See the annotations, 3 Kings, 22.

belong to the king's office. And you have before you the Levites for masters. Take courage and do diligently; and the Lord will be with you in good things.

CHAPTER 20

The Ammonites, Moabites, and Syrians combine against Josaphat. He seeketh God's help by public prayer and fasting. A prophet foretelleth that God will fight for his people. The enemies destroy one another. Josaphat with his men gathereth the spoils. He reigneth in peace; but his navy perisheth, for his society with wicked Ochozias.

AFTER this the children of Moab, and the children of Ammon, and with them of the Ammonites, were gathered together to fight against Josaphat.

2 And there came messengers, and told Josaphat, saying: There cometh a great multitude against thee from beyond the sea, and out of Syria. And behold they are in Asasonthamar, which is Engaddi.

3 And Josaphat being seized with fear betook himself wholly to pray to the Lord: and he proclaimed a fast for all Juda.

4 And Juda gathered themselves together to pray to the Lord: and all came out of their cities to make supplication to him.

5 And Josaphat stood in the midst of the assembly of Juda, and Jerusalem, in the house of the Lord, before the new court,

6 And said: O Lord God of our fathers, thou art God in heaven, and rulest over all the kingdoms and nations. In thy hand is strength and power; and no one can resist thee.

7 Didst not thou our God kill all the inhabitants of this land before thy people Israel, and gavest it to the seed of Abraham thy friend for ever?

8 And they dwelt in it, and built in it a sanctuary to thy name, saying:

9 If evils fall upon us, the sword of judgment, or pestilence, or famine, we will stand in thy presence before this house, in which thy name is called upon: and we will cry to thee in our afflictions. And thou wilt hear, and save us.

10 ¹ Now therefore behold the children of Ammon, and of Moab, and mount Seir (through whose lands thou didst not allow Israel to pass, when they came out of Egypt, but they turned aside from them, and slew them not)

11 Do the contrary, and endeavour to cast us out of the possession which thou hast delivered to us.

12 O our God, wilt thou not then judge them? As for us, we have not

strength enough to be able to resist this multitude, which cometh violently upon us. But as we know not what to do, we can only turn our eyes to thee.

13 And all Juda stood before the Lord with their little ones, and their wives, and their children.

14 And Jahaziel the son of Zacharias, the son of Banaias, the son of Jehiel, the son of Mathanias, a Levite of the sons of Asaph, was *there*, upon whom the spirit of the Lord came in the midst of the multitude.

15 And he said: Attend ye, all Juda, and you that dwell in Jerusalem, and thou king Josaphat: Thus saith the Lord to you: Fear ye not, and be not dismayed at this multitude. For the battle is not yours, but God's.

16 To-morrow you shall go down against them: for they will come up by the ascent named Sis. And you shall find them at the head of the torrent, which is over against the wilderness of Jeruel.

17 It shall not be you that shall fight: but only stand with confidence, and you shall see the help of the Lord over you, O Juda, and Jerusalem: fear ye not, nor be you dismayed: to-morrow you shall go out against them, and the Lord will be with you.

18 Then Josaphat, and Juda, and all the inhabitants of Jerusalem fell flat on the ground before the Lord, and adored him.

19 And the Levites of the sons of Caath, and of the sons of Core, praised the Lord the God of Israel with a loud voice, on high.

20 And they rose early in the morning, and went out through the desert of Thecua. And as they were marching, Josaphat standing in the midst of them, said: Hear me, ye men of Juda, and all the inhabitants of Jerusalem. Believe in the Lord your God, and you shall be secure. Believe his prophets, and all things shall succeed well.

21 And he gave counsel to the people, and appointed the singing men of the Lord, to praise him by their companies, and to go before the army, and with one voice to say: ² Give glory to the Lord, for his mercy endureth for ever.

22 And when they began to sing praises, the Lord turned their ambushments upon themselves: that is to say, of the children of Ammon, and of Moab, and of mount Seir, who were come out to fight against Juda; and they were slain.

23 For the children of Ammon, and of Moab, rose up against the inhabi-

CHAP. 20. ¹ Deut. 2, 1.   ² Ps. 135, 1.

tants of mount Seir, to kill and destroy them. And when they had made an end of them, they turned also against one another, and destroyed one another.

24 And when Juda came to the watch tower, that looketh toward the desert, they saw afar off all the country, for a great space, full of dead bodies; and that no one was left that could escape death.

25 Then Josaphat came, and all the people with him to take away the spoils of the dead. And they found among the dead bodies, stuff of various kinds, and garments, and most precious vessels. And they took them for themselves, insomuch that they could not carry all, nor in three days take away the spoils; the booty was so great.

26 And on the fourth day, they were assembled in the valley of Blessing. For there they blessed the Lord; and therefore they called that place the valley of Blessing until this day.

27 And every man of Juda, and the inhabitants of Jerusalem returned, and Josaphat at their head, into Jerusalem, with great joy, because the Lord had made them rejoice over their enemies.

28 And they came into Jerusalem with psalteries, and harps, and trumpets into the house of the Lord.

29 And the fear of the Lord fell upon all the kingdoms of the lands when they heard that the Lord had fought against the enemies of Israel.

30 And the kingdom of Josaphat was quiet, and God gave him peace round about.

31 ³ And Josaphat reigned over Juda. And he was five and thirty years old when he began to reign: and he reigned five and twenty years in Jerusalem. And the name of his mother was Azuba the daughter of Selahi.

32 And he walked in the way of his father Asa, and departed not from it, doing the things that were pleasing before the Lord.

33 But yet he took not away the high places: and the people had not yet turned their heart to the Lord the God of their fathers.

34 But the rest of the acts of Josaphat, first and last, are written in the words of Jehu the son of Hanani, which he digested into the books of the kings of Israel.

35 After these things Josaphat king of Juda made friendship with Ochozias king of Israel, whose works were very wicked.

36 And he was partner with him in making ships, to go to Tharsis: and they made the ships in Asiongaber.

37 And Eliezer the son of Dodau of Maresa prophesied to Josaphat, saying: Because thou hast made a league with Ochozias, the Lord hath destroyed thy works. And the ships are broken. And they could not go to Tharsis.

CHAPTER 21

Joram's wicked reign. His punishment and death.

AND ¹ Josaphat slept with his fathers; and was buried with them in the city of David. And Joram his son reigned in his stead.

2 And he had brethren, the sons of Josaphat, Azarias, and Jahiel, and Zacharias, and Azaria, and Michael, and Saphatias. All these were the sons of Josaphat king of Juda.

3 And their father gave them great gifts of silver, and of gold, and pensions, with strong cities in Juda: but the kingdom he gave to Joram, because he was the eldest.

4 So Joram rose up over the kingdom of his father: and when he had established himself, he slew all his brethren with the sword, and some of the princes of Israel.

5 Joram was two and thirty years old when he began to reign: and he reigned eight years in Jerusalem.

6 ² And he walked in the ways of the kings of Israel, as the house of Achab had done: for his wife was a daughter of Achab. And he did evil in the sight of the Lord.

7 But the Lord would not destroy the house of David: because of the covenant which he had made with him: and because he had promised to give a lamp to him, and to his sons for ever.

8 In those days Edom revolted ³ from being subject to Juda, and made themselves a king.

9 And Joram went over with his princes, and all his cavalry with him, and rose in the night, and defeated the Edomites who had surrounded him and all the captains of his cavalry.

10 However, Edom revolted from being under the dominion of Juda unto this day. At that time, Lobna also revolted, from being under his hand. For he had forsaken the Lord the God of his fathers.

11 Moreover he built also high places in the cities of Juda: and he made the inhabitants of Jerusalem to commit fornication, and Juda to transgress.

12 And there was a letter brought him from Elias the prophet, in which it was written: Thus saith the Lord, the God of David thy father: Because thou hast not walked in the ways of

³ 3 Kings, 22, 41. Chap. 21. ¹ 3 Kings, 22, 51.
² 4 Kings, 8, 16. ³ Gen. 27, 40.

Josaphat thy father, nor in the ways of Asa king of Juda,

13 But hast walked in the ways of the kings of Israel, and hast made Juda and the inhabitants of Jerusalem to commit fornication, imitating the fornication of the house of Achab: moreover also thou hast killed thy brethren, the house of thy father, better men than thyself:

14 Behold the Lord will strike thee with a great plague, with all thy people, and thy children, and thy wives, and all thy substance.

15 And thou shalt be sick of a very grievous disease of thy bowels, till thy vital parts come out by little and little every day.

16 And the Lord stirred up against Joram the spirit of the Philistines, and of the Arabians, who border on the Ethiopians.

17 And they came up into the land of Juda, and wasted it. And they carried away all the substance that was found in the king's house: his sons also, and his wives; so that there was no son left him but Joachaz, who was the youngest.

18 And besides all this, the Lord struck him with an incurable disease in his bowels.

19 And as day came after day, and time rolled on, two whole years passed. Then after being wasted with a long consumption, so as to void his very bowels, his disease ended with his life. And he died of a most wretched illness; and the people did not make a funeral for him according to the manner of burning, as they had done for his ancestors.

20 He was two and thirty years old when he began his reign; and he reigned eight years in Jerusalem. And he walked not rightly. And they buried him in the city of David: but not in the sepulchres of the kings.

CHAPTER 22

The reign and death of Ochozias. The tyranny of Athalia.

AND ¹ the inhabitants of Jerusalem made Ochozias his youngest son king in his place: for the rovers of the Arabians, who had broke in upon the camp, had killed all that were his elder brothers. So Ochozias the son of Joram king of Juda reigned.

2 Ochozias was forty-two years old when he began to reign: and he reigned one year in Jerusalem. And the name of his mother was Athalia the daughter of Amri.

3 He also walked in the ways of the house of Achab: for his mother pushed him on to do wickedly.

4 So he did evil in the sight of the Lord, as the house of Achab did: for they were his counsellors after the death of his father, to his destruction.

5 And he walked after their counsels. And he went with Joram the son of Achab king of Israel, to fight against Hazael king of Syria, at Ramoth Galaad: and the Syrians wounded Joram.

6 And he returned to be healed in Jezrahel: for he received many wounds in the foresaid battle. And Ochozias the son of Joram king of Juda went down to visit Joram the son of Achab in Jezrahel where he lay sick.

7 For it was the will of God against Ochozias that he should come to Joram: and when he was come should go out also against Jehu the son of Namsi, whom the Lord had anointed to destroy the house of Achab.

8 So when Jehu was rooting out the house of Achab, he found the princes of Juda, and the sons of the brethren of Ochozias, who served him: and he slew them.

9 And he sought for Ochozias himself, and took him lying hid in Samaria. And when he was brought to him, he killed him. And they buried him, because he was the son of Josaphat, who had sought the Lord with all his heart. And there was no more hope that any one should reign of the race of Ochozias.

10 ² For Athalia his mother, seeing that her son was dead, rose up, and killed all the royal family of the house of Joram.

11 But Josabeth the king's daughter took Joas the son of Ochozias, and stole him from among the king's sons that were slain. And she hid him with his nurse in a bedchamber. Now Josabeth that hid him, was daughter of king Joram, wife of Joiada the high priest, and sister of Ochozias. And therefore Athalia did not kill him.

12 And he was with them hid in the house of God six years, during which Athalia reigned over the land.

CHAPTER 23

Joiada the high priest causeth Joas to be made king, Athalia to be slain, and idolatry to be destroyed.

AND ¹ in the seventh year Joiada being encouraged, took the captains of hundreds: to wit, Azarias the son of Jeroham, and Ismahel the son of Johanan, and Azarias the son of

CHAP. 22. ¹ 4 Kings, 8, 25. ² 4 Kings, 11, 1.
CHAP. 23. ¹ 4 Kings, 11, 4.

CHAP. 21. Ver. 17. *Joachaz.* Otherwise Ochozias.

CHAP. 22. Ver. 2. *Forty-two.* Otherwise divers Greek Bibles read *thirty-two,* agreeably to 4 Kings, 8, 17.

Obed, and Maasias the son of Adaias, and Elisaphat the son of Zechri; and made a covenant with them.

2 And they went about Juda, and gathered together the Levites out of all the cities of Juda, and the chiefs of the families of Israel; and they came to Jerusalem.

3 And all the multitude made a covenant with the king in the house of God. And Joiada said to them: Behold the king's son shall reign, as the Lord hath said of the sons of David.

4 And this is the thing that you shall do:

5 A third part of you that come to the sabbath, of the priests, and of the Levites, and of the porters, shall be at the gates: and a third part at the king's house: and a third at the gate that is called the Foundation. But let all the rest of the people be in the courts of the house of the Lord.

6 And let no one come into the house of the Lord, but the priests, and they that minister of the Levites. Let them only come in, because they are sanctified: and let all the rest of the people keep the watches of the Lord.

7 And let the Levites be round about the king, every man with his arms; and if any other come into the temple, let him be slain. And let them be with the king, both coming in and going out.

8 So the Levites, and all Juda did according to all that Joiada the high priest had commanded. And they took every one his men that were under him, and that came in by the course of the sabbath, with those who had fulfilled the sabbath, and were to go out. For Joiada the high priest permitted not the companies to depart, which were accustomed to succeed one another every week.

9 And Joida the priest gave to the captains the spears, and the shields, and targets of king David, which he had dedicated in the house of the Lord.

10 And he set all the people with swords in their hands, from the right side of the temple to the left side of the temple, before the altar, and the temple, round about the king.

11 And they brought out the king's son, and put the crown upon him, and the testimony, and gave him the law to hold in his hand. And they made him king: and Joiada the high priest and his sons anointed him. And they prayed for him, and said: God save the king.

12 Now when Athalia heard the noise of the people running and praising the

CHAP. 24. ¹ 4 Kings, 11, 21; 12, 1.

CHAP. 23. Ver. 5. *To the sabbath.* That is, to perform in your weeks the functions of your office, or the weekly watches.

king, she came in to the people, into the temple of the Lord.

13 And when she saw the king standing upon the step in the entrance, and the princes, and the companies about him, and all the people of the land rejoicing, and sounding with trumpets, and playing on instruments of divers kinds, and the voice of those that praised, she rent her garments, and said: Treason, treason.

14 And Joiada the high priest going out to the captains, and the chiefs of the army, said to them: Take her forth without the precinct of the temple; and when she is without, let her be killed with the sword. For the priest commanded that she should not be killed in the house of the Lord.

15 And they laid hold on her by the neck: and when she was come within the horse gate of the palace, they killed her there.

16 And Joiada made a covenant between himself and all the people, and the king, that they should be the people of the Lord.

17 And all the people went into the house of Baal, and destroyed it: and they broke down his altars and his idols. And they slew Mathan the priest of Baal before the altars.

18 And Joiada appointed overseers in the house of the Lord, under the hands of the priests and the Levites, whom David had distributed in the house of the Lord: to offer holocausts to the Lord, as it is written in the law of Moses, with joy and singing, according to the disposition of David.

19 He appointed also porters in the gates of the house of the Lord, that none who was unclean in any thing should enter in.

20 And he took the captains of hundreds, and the most valiant men, and the chiefs of the people, and all the people of the land: and they brought down the king from the house of the Lord, and brought him through the upper gate into the king's house, and set him on the royal throne.

21 And all the people of the land rejoiced, and the city was quiet: but Athalia was slain with the sword.

CHAPTER 24

Joas reigneth well all the days of Joiada. Afterwards falleth into idolatry and causeth Zacharias to be slain. He is slain himself by his servants.

JOAS ¹ was seven years old when he began to reign: and he reigned forty years in Jerusalem. The name of his mother was Sebia of Bersabee.

2 And he did that which is good be-

fore the Lord all the days of Joiada the priest.

3 And Joiada took for him two wives, by whom he had sons and daughters.

4 After this Joas had a mind to repair the house of the Lord.

5 And he assembled the priests, and the Levites, and said to them: Go out to the cities of Juda, and gather of all Israel money to repair the temple of your God, from year to year; and do this with speed. But the Levites were negligent.

6 And the king called Joiada the chief, and said to him: Why hast thou not taken care to oblige the Levites to bring in out of Juda and Jerusalem the money that was appointed by Moses the servant of the Lord for all the multitude of Israel to bring into the tabernacle of the testimony?

7 For that wicked woman Athalia and her children have destroyed the house of God and adorned the temple of Baal with all the things that had been dedicated in the temple of the Lord.

8 And the king commanded, and they made a chest: and set it by the gate of the house of the Lord on the outside.

9 And they made a proclamation in Juda and Jerusalem, that every man should bring to the Lord ² the money which Moses the servant of God appointed for all Israel in the desert.

10 And all the princes, and all the people rejoiced: and going in they contributed and cast so much into the chest of the Lord, that it was filled.

11 And when it was time to bring the chest before the king by the hands of the Levites (for they saw there was much money), the king's scribe, and he whom the high priest had appointed went in: and they poured out the money that was in the chest: and they carried back the chest to its place. And thus they did from day to day; and there was gathered an immense sum of money.

12 And the king and Joiada gave it to those who were over the works of the house of the Lord. But they hired with it stonecutters and artificers of every kind of work, to repair the house of the Lord: and such as wrought in iron and brass, to uphold what began to be falling.

13 And the workmen were diligent; and the breach of the walls was closed up by their hands; and they set up the house of the Lord in its former state, and made it stand firm.

14 And when they had finished all the works, they brought the rest of the money before the king and Joiada: and with it were made vessels for the temple, for the ministry, and for holocausts and bowls, and other vessels of gold and silver. And holocausts were offered in the house of the Lord continually all the days of Joiada.

15 But Joiada grew old, and was full of days, and died when he was a hundred and thirty years old.

16 And they buried him in the city of David among the kings, because he had done good to Israel, and to his house.

17 And after the death of Joiada the princes of Juda went in, and worshipped the king: and he was soothed by their services and hearkened to them.

18 And they forsook the temple of the Lord the God of their fathers, and served groves and idols: and wrath came upon Juda and Jerusalem for this sin.

19 And he sent prophets to them to bring them back to the Lord, and they would not give ear when they testified against them.

20 The spirit of God then came upon Zacharias the son of Joiada the priest. And he stood in the sight of the people, and said to them: Thus saith the Lord God: Why transgress you the commandment of the Lord which will not be for your good, and have forsaken the Lord, to make him forsake you?

21 And they gathered themselves together against him, and stoned him at the king's commandment in the court of the house of the Lord.

22 And king Joas did not remember the kindness that Joiada his father had done to him; ³ but killed his son. And when he died, he said: The Lord see, and require it.

23 ⁴ And when a year was come about, the army of Syria came up against him. And they came to Juda and Jerusalem, and killed all the princes of the people; and they sent all the spoils to the king of Damascus.

24 And whereas there came a very small number of the Syrians, the Lord delivered into their hands an infinite multitude, because they had forsaken the Lord the God of their fathers. And on Joas they executed shameful judgments.

25 And departing they left him in great diseases. And his servants rose up against him, for revenge of the blood of the son of Joiada the priest. And they slew him in his bed: and he died. And they buried him in the city of David, but not in the sepulchres of the kings.

26 Now the men that conspired

² Exod. 30, 12. ³ Matt. 23, 25. ⁴ 3 Kings, 12, 17.

against him were Zabad the son of Sem-maath an Ammonitess, and Jozabad the son of Semarith a Moabitess.

27 And concerning his sons, and the sum of money which was gathered under him, and the repairing the house of God, they are written more diligently in the book of kings. And Amasias his son reigned in his stead.

CHAPTER 25

Amasias's reign. He beginneth well, but endeth ill. He is overthrown by Joas, and slain by his own people.

AMASIAS [1] was five and twenty years old when he began to reign; and he reigned nine and twenty years in Jerusalem. The name of his mother was Joadan of Jerusalem.

2 And he did what was good in the sight of the Lord: but yet not with a perfect heart.

3 And when he saw himself strengthened in his kingdom, he put to death the servants that had slain the king his father.

4 But he slew not their children, as it is written in the book of the law of Moses, where the Lord commanded, saying: [2] The fathers shall not be slain for the children, nor the children for their fathers; but every man shall die for his own sin.

5 Amasias therefore gathered Juda together, and appointed them by families, and captains of thousands and of hundreds, in all Juda, and Benjamin. And he numbered them from twenty years old and upwards, and found three hundred thousand young men that could go out to battle, and could hold the spear and shield.

6 He hired also of Israel a hundred thousand valiant men, for a hundred talents of silver.

7 But a man of God came to him, and said: O king, let not the army of Israel go out with thee. For the Lord is not with Israel, and all the children of Ephraim.

8 And if thou think that battles consist in the strength of the army, God will make thee to be overcome by the enemies, for it belongeth to God, both to help, and to put to flight.

9 And Amasias said to the man of God: What will then become of the hundred talents which I have given to the soldiers of Israel? And the man of God answered him: The Lord is rich enough to be able to give thee much more than this.

10 Then Amasias separated the army that came to him out of Ephraim, to go home again: but they being much en-raged against Juda, returned to their own country.

11 And Amasias taking courage led forth his people, and went to the vale of saltpits, and slew of the children of Seir ten thousand.

12 And other ten thousand men the sons of Juda took, and brought to the steep of a certain rock, and cast them down headlong from the top. And they all were broken to pieces.

13 But that army which Amasias had sent back, that they should not go with him to battle, spread themselves among the cities of Juda, from Samaria to Bethhoron, and having killed three thousand took away much spoil.

14 But Amasias, after he had slain the Edomites, set up the gods of the children of Seir, which he had brought thence, to be his gods: and adored them, and burnt incense to them.

15 Wherefore the Lord, being angry against Amasias, sent a prophet to him, to say to him: Why hast thou adored gods that have not delivered their own people out of thy hand?

16 And when he spoke these things, he answered him: Art thou the king's counsellor? Be quiet lest I kill thee. And the prophet departing, said: I know that God is minded to kill thee, because thou hast done this evil, and moreover hast not hearkened to my counsel.

17 Then Amasias king of Juda, taking very bad counsel, sent to Joas the son of Joachaz the son of Jehu, king of Israel, saying: Come, Let us see one another.

18 But he sent back the messengers, saying: The thistle that is in Libanus, sent to the cedar in Libanus, saying: Give thy daughter to my son to wife. And behold the beasts that were in the wood of Libanus passed by, and trod down the thistle.

19 Thou hast said: I have overthrown Edom, and therefore thy heart is lifted up with pride. Stay at home: Why dost thou provoke evil against thee, that both thou shouldst fall and Juda with thee?

20 Amasias would not hearken to him, because it was the Lord's will that he should be delivered into the hands of enemies, because of the gods of Edom.

21 So Joas king of Israel went up; and they presented themselves to be seen by one another. And Amasias king of Juda was in Bethsames of Juda.

22 And Juda fell before Israel; and they fled to their dwellings.

23 And Joas king of Israel took Amasias king of Juda, the son of Joas, the son of Joachaz, in Bethsames, and brought him to Jerusalem: and broke down the walls thereof, from the gate

CHAP. 25. [1] 4 Kings, 14, 2. [2] Deut. 24, 16; 4 Kings, 14, 6; Ezech. 18, 20.

of Ephraim to the gate of the corner, four hundred cubits.

24 And he took all the gold and silver, and all the vessels, that he found in the house of God, and with Obededom, and in the treasures of the king's house. Moreover also the sons of the hostages, he brought back to Samaria.

25 And Amasias the son of Joas king of Juda lived, after the death of Joas the son of Joachaz king of Israel, fifteen years.

26 Now the rest of the acts of Amasias, the first and last, are written in the book of the kings of Juda and Israel.

27 And after he revolted from the Lord, they made a conspiracy against him in Jerusalem. And he fled into Lachis; and they sent, and killed him there.

28 And they brought him back upon horses, and buried him with his fathers in the city of David.

CHAPTER 26

Ozias reigneth prosperously, till he invadeth the priests' office, upon which he is struck with a leprosy.

AND ¹ all the people of Juda took his son Ozias, who was sixteen years old, and made him king in the room of Amasias his father.

2 He built Ailath, and restored it to the dominion of Juda, after that the king slept with his fathers.

3 Ozias was sixteen years old when he began to reign; and he reigned two and fifty years in Jerusalem. The name of his mother was Jechelia of Jerusalem.

4 And he did that which was right in the eyes of the Lord, according to all that Amasias his father had done.

5 And he sought the Lord in the days of Zacharias that understood and saw God: and as long as he sought the Lord, he directed him in all things.

6 Moreover he went forth and fought against the Philistines, and broke down the wall of Geth, and the wall of Jabnia, and the wall of Azotus. And he built towns in Azotus, and among the Philistines.

7 And God helped him against the Philistines, and against the Arabians, that dwelt in Gurbaal, and against the Ammonites.

8 And the Ammonites gave gifts to Ozias: and his name was spread abroad even to the entrance of Egypt for his frequent victories.

9 And Ozias built towers in Jerusalem over the gate of the corner, and over the gate of the valley, and the

rest, in the same side of the wall: and fortified them.

10 And he built towers in the wilderness, and dug many cisterns, for he had much cattle both in the plains, and in the waste of the desert. He had also vineyards and dressers of vines in the mountains, and in Carmel: for he was a man that loved husbandry.

11 And the army of his fighting men, that went out to war, was under the hand of Jehiel the scribe, and Maasias the doctor, and under the hand of Henanias, who was one of the king's captains.

12 And the whole number of the chiefs by the families of valiant men were two thousand six hundred.

13 And the whole army under them, three hundred and seven thousand five hundred: who were fit for war, and fought for the king against the enemy.

14 And Ozias prepared for them, that is, for the whole army, shields, and spears, and helmets, and coats of mail, and bows, and slings to cast stones.

15 And he made in Jerusalem engines of diverse kinds, which he placed in the towers, and in the corners of the walls, to shoot arrows, and great stones. And his name went forth far abroad: for the Lord helped him, and had strengthened him.

16 But when he was made strong, his heart was lifted up to his destruction: and he neglected the Lord his God. And going into the temple of the Lord, he had a mind to burn incense upon the altar of incense.

17 And immediately Azarias the priest going in after him, and with him fourscore priests of the Lord, most valiant men,

18 Withstood the king and said: It doth not belong to thee, Ozias, to burn incense to the Lord, but to the priests, that is, to the sons of Aaron, ² who are consecrated for this ministry. Go out of the sanctuary: do not despise: for this thing shall not be accounted to thy glory by the Lord God.

19 And Ozias was angry, and holding in his hand the censer to burn incense, threatened the priests. And presently there rose a leprosy in his forehead before the priests, in the house of the Lord at the altar of incense.

20 And Azarias the high priest, and all the rest of the priests looked upon him, and saw the leprosy in his forehead; and they made haste to thrust him out. Yea himself also being frightened, hasted to go out, because he had quickly felt the stroke of the Lord.

21 ³ And Ozias the king was a leper

CHAP. 26. ¹ 4 Kings, 14, 21. ² Exod. 30, 7. ³ 4 Kings, 15, 5.

unto the day of his death. And he dwelt in a house apart, being full of the leprosy for which he had been cast out of the house of the Lord. And Joatham his son governed the king's house, and judged the people of the land.

22 But the rest of the acts of Ozias, first and last, were written by Isaias the son of Amos, the prophet.

23 And Ozias slept with his fathers: and they buried him in the field of the royal sepulchres, because he was a leper. And Joatham his son reigned in his stead.

CHAPTER 27
Joatham's good reign.

JOATHAM [1] was five and twenty years old when he began to reign, and he reigned sixteen years in Jerusalem. The name of his mother was Jerusa the daughter of Sadoc.

2 And he did that which was right before the Lord, according to all that Ozias his father had done: only that he entered not into the temple of the Lord, and the people still transgressed.

3 He built the high gate of the house of the Lord, and on the wall of Ophel he built much.

4 Moreover he built cities in the mountains of Juda, and castles and towers in the forests.

5 He fought against the king of the children of Ammon, and overcame them: and the children of Ammon gave him at that time a hundred talents of silver, and ten thousand measures of wheat, and as many measures of barley. So much did the children of Ammon give him in the second and third year.

6 And Joatham was strengthened, because he had his way directed before the Lord his God.

7 Now the rest of the acts of Joatham, and all his wars, and his works, are written in the book of the kings of Israel and Juda.

8 He was five and twenty years old when he began to reign; and he reigned sixteen years in Jerusalem.

9 And Joatham slept with his fathers; and they buried him in the city of David. And Achaz his son reigned in his stead.

CHAPTER 28
The wicked and unhappy reign of Achaz.

ACHAZ [1] was twenty years old when he began to reign; and he reigned sixteen years in Jerusalem. He did not that which was right in the sight of the Lord as David his father had done;

2 But walked in the ways of the kings

of Israel. Moreover also he cast statues for Baalim.

3 It was he that burnt incense in the valley of Benennom, and consecrated his sons in the fire, according to the manner of the nations which the Lord slew at the coming of the children of Israel.

4 He sacrificed also, and burnt incense in the high places, and on the hills, and under every green tree.

5 And the Lord his God delivered him into the hands of the king of Syria, who defeated him, and took a great booty out of his kingdom, and carried it to Damascus. He was also delivered into the hands of the king of Israel, who overthrew him with a great slaughter.

6 For Phacee the son of Romelia slew of Juda a hundred and twenty thousand in one day, all valiant men: because they had forsaken the Lord the God of their fathers.

7 At the same time Zechri, a powerful man of Ephraim, slew Maasias the king's son, and Ezricam the governor of his house, and Elcana who was next to the king.

8 And the children of Israel carried away of their brethren two hundred thousand women, boys, and girls, and an immense booty. And they brought it to Samaria.

9 At that time there was a prophet of the Lord there, whose name was Oded. And he went out to meet the army that came to Samaria, and said to them: Behold the Lord the God of your fathers being angry with Juda, hath delivered them into your hands; and you have butchered them cruelly, so that your cruelty hath reached up to heaven.

10 Moreover you have a mind to keep under the children of Juda and Jerusalem for your bondmen and bondwomen, which ought not to be done: for you have sinned in this against the Lord your God.

11 But hear ye my counsel, and release the captives that you have brought of your brethren; because a great indignation of the Lord hangeth over you.

12 Then some of the chief men of the sons of Ephraim: Azarias the son of Johanan, Barachias the son of Mosollamoth, Ezechias the son of Sellum, and Amasa the son of Adali, stood up against them that came from the war.

13 And they said to them: You shall not bring in the captives hither, lest we sin against the Lord. Why will you add to our sins, and heap up upon our former offences? For the sin is great, and the fierce anger of the Lord hangeth over Israel.

14 So the soldiers left the spoils, and

CHAP. 27. [1] 4 Kings, 15, 33. CHAP. 28. [1] 4 Kings, 16, 2.

all that they had taken, before the princes and all the multitude.

15 And the men, whom we mentioned above, rose up and took the captives, and with the spoils clothed all them that were naked. And when they had clothed and shod them, and refreshed them with meat and drink, and anointed them because of their labour, and had taken care of them, they set such of them as could not walk, and were feeble, upon beasts, and brought them to Jericho the city of palm trees to their brethren. And then returned to Samaria.

16 At that time king Achaz sent to the king of the Assyrians asking help.

17 And the Edomites came and slew many of Juda, and took a great booty.

18 The Philistines also spread themselves among the cities of the plains, and to the south of Juda: and they took Bethsames, and Aialon, and Gaderoth, and Socho, and Thamnan, and Gamzo, with their villages; and they dwelt in them.

19 For the Lord had humbled Juda because of Achaz the king of Juda: for he had stripped it of help, and had contemned the Lord.

20 And he brought against him Thelgathphalnasar [2] king of the Assyrians, who also afflicted him, and plundered him without any resistance.

21 And Achaz stripped the house of the Lord, and the house of the kings, and of the princes, and gave gifts to the king of the Assyrians. And yet it availed him nothing.

22 Moreover also in the time of his distress he increased contempt against the Lord. King Achaz, himself by himself,

23 Sacrificed victims to the gods of Damascus that struck him. And he said: The gods of the kings of Syria help them; and I will appease them with victims, and they will help me. Whereas on the contrary they were the ruin of him, and of all Israel.

24 Then Achaz having taken away all the vessels of the house of God, and broken them, shut up the doors of the temple of God, and made himself altars in all the corners of Jerusalem.

25 And in all the cities of Juda he built altars to burn frankincense: and he provoked the Lord the God of his fathers to wrath.

26 But the rest of his acts, and all his works first and last are written in the book of the kings of Juda and Israel.

27 And Achaz slept with his fathers, and they buried him in the city of Jerusalem. For they received him not into the sepulchres of the kings of Israel. And Ezechias his son reigned in his stead.

CHAPTER 29

Ezechias purifieth the temple, and restoreth religion.

NOW [1] Ezechias began to reign, when he was five and twenty years old; and he reigned nine and twenty years in Jerusalem. The name of his mother was Abia, the daughter of Zacharias.

2 And he did that which was pleasing in the sight of the Lord, according to all that David his father had done.

3 In the first year and month of his reign he opened the doors of the house of the Lord, and repaired them.

4 And he brought the priests and the Levites, and assembled them in the east street.

5 And he said to them: Hear me, ye Levites, and be sanctified; purify the house of the Lord the God of your fathers; and take away all filth out of the sanctuary.

6 Our fathers have sinned and done evil in the sight of the Lord God, forsaking him: they have turned away their faces from the tabernacle of the Lord, and turned their backs.

7 They have shut up the doors that were in the porch, and put out the lamps. And have not burnt incense, nor offered holocausts in the sanctuary of the God of Israel.

8 Therefore the wrath of the Lord hath been stirred up against Juda and Jerusalem: and he hath delivered them to trouble, and to destruction, and to be hissed at, as you see with your eyes.

9 Behold, our fathers are fallen by the sword: our sons, and our daughters, and wives are led away captives for this wickedness.

10 Now therefore I have a mind that we make a covenant with the Lord the God of Israel: and he will turn away the wrath of his indignation from us.

11 My sons, be not negligent. The Lord hath chosen you to stand before him, and to minister to him, and to worship him, and to burn incense to him.

12 Then the Levites arose: Mahath the son of Amasai, and Joel the son of Azarias, of the sons of Caath: and of the sons of Merari, Cis the son of Abdi, and Azarias the son of Jalaleel: and of the sons of Gerson, Joah the son of Zemma, and Eden the son of Joah:

13 And of the sons of Elisaphan, Samri, and Jahiel. Also of the sons of Asaph, Zacharias, and Mathanias.

[2] 4 Kings, 16, 10.   CHAP. 29.   [1] 4 Kings, 18, 1.

CHAP. 28.   Ver. 19. *For he had stripped it of help.* That is, Achaz stripped the kingdom of Juda of the divine assistance by his wickedness, and by his introducing idolatry.

14 And of the sons of Heman, Jahiel, and Semei: and of the sons of Idithun, Semeias, and Oziel.

15 And they gathered together their brethren, and sanctified themselves, and went in according to the commandment of the king, and the precept of the Lord, to purify the house of God.

16 And the priests went into the temple of the Lord to sanctify it, and brought out all the uncleanness that they found within to the entrance of the house of the Lord. And the Levites took it away, and carried it out abroad to the torrent Cedron.

17 And they began to cleanse on the first day of the first month; and on the eighth day of the same month they came into the porch of the temple of the Lord. And they purified the temple in eight days; and on the sixteenth day of the same month they finished what they had begun.

18 And they went in to king Ezechias, and said to him: We have sanctified all the house of the Lord, and the altar of holocaust, and the vessels thereof, and the table of proposition with all its vessels,

19 And all the furniture of the temple, which king Achaz in his reign had defiled, after his transgression. And behold they are all set forth before the altar of the Lord.

20 And king Ezechias rising early, assembled all the rulers of the city; and went up into the house of the Lord.

21 And they offered together seven bullocks, and seven rams, and seven lambs, and seven he-goats for sin, for the kingdom, for the sanctuary, for Juda. And he spoke to the priests the sons of Aaron, to offer them upon the altar of the Lord.

22 Therefore they killed the bullocks; and the priests took the blood, and poured it upon the altar. They killed also the rams; and their blood they poured also upon the altar. And they killed the lambs, and poured the blood upon the altar.

23 And they brought the he-goats for sin before the king, and the whole multitude. And they laid their hand upon them:

24 And the priests immolated them, and sprinkled their blood before the altar for an expiation of all Israel: for the king had commanded that the holocaust and the sin offering should be made for all Israel.

25 And he set the Levites in the house of the Lord with cymbals, and psalteries, and harps, according to the regulation of David the king, and of Gad the seer, and of Nathan the prophet:

for it was the commandment of the Lord by the hand of his prophets.

26 And the Levites stood, with the instruments of David, and the priests with trumpets.

27 And Ezechias commanded that they should offer holocausts upon the altar. And when the holocausts were offered, they began to sing praises to the Lord, and to sound with trumpets, and divers instruments which David the king of Israel had prepared.

28 And all the multitude adored: and the singers, and the trumpeters, were in their office till the holocaust was finished.

29 And when the oblation was ended, the king, and all that were with him bowed down and adored.

30 And Ezechias and the princes commanded the Levites to praise the Lord with the words of David, and Asaph the seer. And they praised him with great joy, and bowing the knee adored.

31 And Ezechias added, and said: You have filled your hands to the Lord. Come and offer victims, and praises in the house of the Lord. And all the multitude offered victims, and praises, and holocausts with a devout mind.

32 And the number of the holocausts which the multitude offered, was seventy bullocks, a hundred rams, and two hundred lambs.

33 And they consecrated to the Lord six hundred oxen, and three thousand sheep.

34 But the priests were few, and were not enough to flay the holocausts. Wherefore the Levites their brethren, helped them, till the work was ended, and priests were sanctified. For the Levites are sanctified with an easier rite than the priests.

35 So there were many holocausts, and the fat of peace offerings, and the libations of holocausts: and the service of the house of the Lord was completed.

36 And Ezechias, and all the people rejoiced because the ministry of the Lord was accomplished. For the resolution of doing this thing was taken suddenly.

CHAPTER 30

Ezechias inviteth all Israel to celebrate the pasch. The solemnity is kept fourteen days.

AND Ezechias sent to all Israel and Juda. And he wrote letters to Ephraim and Manasses, that they should come to the house of the Lord in Jerusalem, and keep the phase to the Lord the God of Israel.

2 For the king, taking counsel, and the princes, and all the assembly of

Jerusalem, decreed to keep the phase the second month.

3 For they could not keep it in its time; because there were not priests enough sanctified, and the people was not as yet gathered together to Jerusalem.

4 And the thing pleased the king, and all the people.

5 And they decreed to send messengers to all Israel from Bersabee even to Dan; that they should come, and keep the phase to the Lord the God of Israel in Jerusalem: for many had not kept it as it is prescribed by the law.

6 And the posts went with letters by commandment of the king, and his princes, to all Israel and Juda, proclaiming according to the king's orders: Ye children of Israel, turn again to the Lord, the God of Abraham, and of Isaac, and of Israel. And he will return to the remnant of you that have escaped the hand of the king of the Assyrians.

7 Be not like your fathers, and brethren, who departed from the Lord the God of their fathers: and he hath given them up to destruction, as you see.

8 Harden not your necks, as your fathers did: Yield yourselves to the Lord, and come to his sanctuary, which he hath sanctified for ever. Serve the Lord the God of your fathers; and the wrath of his indignation shall be turned away from you.

9 For if you turn again to the Lord, your brethren, and children shall find mercy before their masters, that have led them away captive. And they shall return into this land: for the Lord your God is merciful, and will not turn away his face from you, if you return to him.

10 So the posts went speedily from city to city, through the land of Ephraim, and of Manasses, even to Zabulon, whilst they laughed at them and mocked them.

11 Nevertheless some men of Aser, and of Manasses, and of Zabulon, yielding to the counsel, came to Jerusalem.

12 But the hand of God was in Juda, to give them one heart to do the word of the Lord, according to the commandment of the king, and of the princes.

13 And much people were assembled to Jerusalem to celebrate the solemnity of the unleavened bread in the second month.

14 And they arose and destroyed the altars that were in Jerusalem, and took away all things in which incense was burnt to idols, and cast them into the torrent Cedron.

15 And they immolated the phase on the fourteenth day of the second month. And the priests and the Levites

being at length sanctified offered holocausts in the house of the Lord.

16 And they stood in their order, according to the disposition and law of Moses the man of God. But the priests received the blood which was to be poured out from the hands of the Levites,

17 Because a great number was not sanctified. And therefore the Levites immolated the phase for them that came not in time to be sanctified to the Lord.

18 For a great part of the people from Ephraim, and Manasses, and Issachar, and Zabulon, that had not been sanctified, ate the phase otherwise than it is written. And Ezechias prayed for them, saying: The Lord who is good will shew mercy,

19 To all them, who with their whole heart seek the Lord the God of their fathers: and will not impute it to them that they are not sanctified.

20 And the Lord heard him, and was merciful to the people.

21 And the children of Israel, that were found at Jerusalem, kept the feast of unleavened bread seven days with great joy, praising the Lord every day: the Levites also, and the priests, with instruments that agreed to their office.

22 And Ezechias spoke to the heart of all the Levites that had good understanding, concerning the Lord. And they ate during the seven days of the solemnity, immolating victims of peace offerings, and praising the Lord the God of their fathers.

23 And it pleased the whole multitude to keep other seven days: which they did with great joy.

24 For Ezechias the king of Juda had given to the multitude a thousand bullocks, and seven thousand sheep. And the princes had given the people a thousand bullocks, and ten thousand sheep. And a great number of priests was sanctified.

25 And all the multitude of Juda with the priests and Levites; and all the assembly, that came out of Israel; and the proselytes of the land of Israel, and that dwelt in Juda, were full of joy.

26 And there was a great solemnity in Jerusalem, such as had not been in that city since the time of Solomon the son of David king of Israel.

27 And the priests and the Levites rose up and blessed the people. and their voice was heard: and their prayer came to the holy dwelling place of heaven.

CHAPTER 31

Idolatry is abolished. Provisions are made for the ministers.

AND when these things had been duly celebrated, all Israel that were found in the cities of Juda went out. And they broke the iols, and cut down the groves, demolished the high places, and destroyed the altars, not only out of all Juda and Benjamin, but out of Ephraim also and Manasses, till they had utterly destroyed them. Then all the children of Israel returned to their possessions and cities.

2 And Ezechias appointed companies of the priests, and the Levites, by their courses, every man in his own office; to wit, both of the priests, and of the Levites: for holocausts, and for peace offerings: to minister, and to praise, and to sing in the gates of the camp of the Lord.

3 And the king's part was, that of his proper substance the holocaust should be offered always morning and evening, and on the sabbaths, and the new moons and the other solemnities, as it is written in the law of Moses.

4 He commanded also the people that dwelt in Jerusalem, to give to the priests, and the Levites their portion, that they might attend to the law of the Lord.

5 Which when it was noised abroad in the ears of the people, the children of Israel offered in abundance the first-fruits of corn, wine, and oil, and honey: and brought the tithe of all things which the ground bringeth forth.

6 Moreover the children of Israel and Juda, that dwelt in the cities of Juda, brought in the tithes of oxen, and sheep, and the tithes of holy things, which they had vowed to the Lord their God: and carrying them all, made many heaps.

7 In the third month they began to lay the foundations of the heaps. and in the seventh month they finished them.

8 And when Ezechias and his princes came in, they saw the heaps; and they blessed the Lord and the people of Israel.

9 And Ezechias asked the priests and the Levites, why the heaps lay so.

10 Azarias the chief priest of the race of Sadoc answered him, saying: Since the firstfruits began to be offered in the house of the Lord, we have eaten, and have been filled, and abundance is left, because the Lord hath blessed his people: and of that which is left is this great store which thou seest.

11 Then Ezechias commanded to prepare storehouses in the house of the Lord. And when they had done so,

12 They brought in faithfully both the firstfruits, and the tithes, and all they had vowed. And the overseer of them was Chonenias the Levite; and Semei his brother was the second.

13 And after him Jehiel, and Azarias, and Nahath, and Asael, and Jerimoth, and Jozabad, and Eliel, and Jesmachias, and Mahath, and Banaias, overseers under the hand of Chonenias, and Semei his brother, by the command-ment of Ezechias the king, and Azarias the high priest of the house of God, to whom all things appertained.

14 But Core the son of Jemna the Levite, the porter of the east gate, was overseer of the things which were freely offered to the Lord, and of the firstfruits and the things dedicated for the Holy of Holies.

15 And under his charge were Eden, and Benjamin, Jesue, and Semeias, and Amarias, and Sechenias, in the cities of the priests, to distribute faithfully por-tions to their brethren, both little and great:

16 Besides the males from three years old and upward: to all that went into the temple of the Lord, and whatsoever there was need of in the ministry, and their offices according to their courses, day by day.

17 To the priests by their families, and to the Levites from the twentieth year and upward, by their classes and companies.

18 And to all the multitude, both to their wives, and to their children both sexes, victuals were given faith-fully out of the things that had been sanctified.

19 Also of the sons of Aaron who were in the fields and in the suburbs of each city, there were men appointed, to distribute portions to all the males, among the priests and the Levites.

20 So Ezechias did all things which we have said in all Juda, and wrought that which was good, and right, and truth, before the Lord his God.

21 In all the service of the ministry of the house of the Lord according to the law and the ceremonies, desiring to seek his God with all his heart. And he did it and prospered.

CHAPTER 32

Sennacherib invadeth Juda. His army is destroyed by an angel. Ezechias recover-eth from his sickness. His other acts.

AFTER [1] these things, and this truth, Sennacherib king of the Assyrians came and entered into Juda, and besieged the fenced cities, desiring to take them.

2 And when Ezechias saw that Sen-nacherib was come, and that the whole

CHAP. 32. [1] 4 Kings, 18, 13; Ecclus. 48, 20; Isai. 36, 1.

force of the war was turning against Jerusalem,

3 He took counsel with the princes, and the most valiant men, to stop up the heads of the springs, that were without the city. And as they were all of this mind,

4 He gathered together a very great multitude; and they stopped up all the springs and the brook, that ran through the midst of the land, saying: Lest the kings of the Assyrians should come, and find abundance of water.

5 He built up also with great diligence all the wall that had been broken down, and built towers upon it, and another wall without. And he repaired Mello in the city of David, and made all sorts of arms and shields.

6 And he appointed captains of the soldiers of the army. And he called them all together in the street of the gate of the city; and spoke to their heart, saying:

7 Behave like men, and take courage: Be not afraid nor dismayed for the king of the Assyrians, nor for all the multitude that is with him. For there are many more with us than with him.

8 For with him is an arm of flesh: with us the Lord our God, who is our helper, and fighteth for us. And the people were encouraged with these words of Ezechias king of Juda.

9 After this, Sennacherib king of the Assyrians sent his servants to Jerusalem (for he with all his army was besieging Lachis), to Ezechias king of Juda, and to all the people that were in the city, saying:

10 Thus saith Sennacherib king of the Assyrians: In whom do you trust, that you sit still besieged in Jerusalem?

11 Doth not Ezechias deceive you, to give you up to die by hunger and thirst, affirming that the Lord your God shall deliver you from the hand of the king of the Assyrians?

12 Is it not this same Ezechias, that hath destroyed his high places, and his altars, and commanded Juda and Jerusalem, saying: You shall worship before one altar, and upon it you shall burn incense?

13 Know you not what I and my fathers have done to all the people of the lands? Have the gods of any nations and lands been able to deliver their country out of my hand?

14 Who is there among all the gods of the nations, which my fathers have destroyed, that could deliver his people out of my hand, that your God should be able to deliver you out of this hand?

15 Therefore let not Ezechias deceive you, nor delude you with a vain persuasion, and do not believe him. For

if no god of all the nations and kingdoms could deliver his people out of my hand, and out of the hand of my fathers, consequently neither shall your God be able to deliver you out of my hand.

16 And many other things did his servants speak against the Lord God, and against Ezechias his servant.

17 He wrote also letters full of blasphemy against the Lord the God of Israel. And he spoke against him: As the gods of other nations could not deliver their people out of my hand, so neither can the God of Ezechias deliver his people out of this hand.

18 Moreover he cried out with a loud voice, in the Jews' tongue, to the people that sat on the walls of Jerusalem, that he might frighten them, and take the city.

19 And he spoke against the God of Jerusalem, as against the gods of the people of the earth, the works of the hands of men.

20 And Ezechias the king, and Isaias the prophet, the son of Amos, prayed against this blasphemy, and cried out to heaven.

21 [2] And the Lord sent an angel, who cut off all the stout men and the warriors, and the captains of the army of the king of the Assyrians. And he returned with disgrace into his own country. And when he was come into the house of his god, his sons that came out of his bowels slew him with the sword.

22 And the Lord saved Ezechias and the inhabitants of Jerusalem, out of the hand of Sennacherib king of the Assyrians, and out of the hand of all, and gave them treasures on every side.

23 Many also brought victims and sacrifices to the Lord to Jerusalem, and presents to Ezechias king of Juda. And he was magnified thenceforth in the sight of all nations.

24 [3] In those days, Ezechias was sick even to death; and he prayed to the Lord. And he heard him, and gave him a sign.

25 But he did not render again according to the benefits which he had received, for his heart was lifted up: and wrath was enkindled against him, and against Juda and Jerusalem.

26 And he humbled himself afterwards, because his heart had been lifted up, both he and the inhabitants of Jerusalem: and therefore the wrath of the Lord came not upon them in the days of Ezechias.

27 And Ezechias was rich, and very glorious; and he gathered himself great

[2] Tob. 1, 21.   [3] 4 Kings, 20, 1; Isai. 38, 1.

treasures of silver and of gold, and of precious stones, of spices, and of arms of all kinds, and of vessels of great price.

28 Storehouses also of corn, of wine, and of oil, and stalls for all beasts, and folds for cattle.

29 And he built himself cities. For he had flocks of sheep, and herds without number: for the Lord had given him very much substance.

30 This same Ezechias was he that stopped the upper source of the waters of Gihon, and turned them away underneath toward the west of the city of David. In all his works he did prosperously what he would.

31 But yet in the embassy of the princes of Babylon, that were sent to him, to inquire of the wonder that had happened upon the earth, God left him that he might be tempted, and all things might be made known that were in his heart.

32 Now the rest of the acts of Ezechias, and of his mercies, are written in the vision of Isaias the son of Amos the prophet and in the book of the kings of Juda and Israel.

33 And Ezechias slept with his fathers, and they buried him above the sepulchres of the sons of David: and all Juda, and all the inhabitants of Jerusalem celebrated his funeral. And Manasses his son reigned in his stead.

CHAPTER 33

Manasses for his manifold wickedness is led captive to Babylon. He repenteth, and is restored to his kingdom, and destroyeth idolatry. His successor Amon is slain by his servants.

MANASSES [1] was twelve years old when he began to reign; and he reigned fifty-five years in Jerusalem.

2 And he did evil before the Lord, according to all the abominations of the nations, which the Lord cast out before the children of Israel:

3 And he turned, and built again the high places which Ezechias his father had destroyed. And he built altars to Baalim, and made groves; and he adored all the host of heaven, and worshipped them.

4 He built also altars in the house of the Lord, whereof the Lord had said: [2] In Jerusalem shall my name be for ever.

5 And he built them for all the host of heaven in the two courts of the house of the Lord.

6 And he made his sons to pass

through the fire in the valley of Benennom. He observed dreams, followed divinations, gave himself up to magic arts, had with him magicians and enchanters: and he wrought many evils before the Lord, to provoke him to anger.

7 [3] He set also a graven and a molten statue in the house of God, of which God had said to David, and to Solomon his son: In this house, and in Jerusalem, which I have chosen out of all the tribes of Israel, will I put my name for ever.

8 And I will not make the foot of Israel to be removed out of the land which I have delivered to their fathers: yet so if they will take heed to do what I have commanded them, and all the law, and the ceremonies, and judgments, by the hand of Moses.

9 So Manasses seduced Juda, and the inhabitants of Jerusalem, to do evil beyond all the nations which the Lord had destroyed before the face of the children of Israel.

10 And the Lord spoke to him, and to his people: and they would not hearken.

11 Therefore he brought upon them the captains of the army of the king of the Assyrians. And they took Manasses, and carried him bound with chains and fetters to Babylon.

12 And after that he was in distress he prayed to the Lord his God: and did penance exceedingly before the God of his fathers.

13 And he entreated him, and besought him earnestly. And he heard his prayer, and brought him again to Jerusalem into his kingdom. And Manasses knew that the Lord was God.

14 After this, he built a wall without the city of David, on the west side of Gihon in the valley, from the entering in of the fish gate round about to Ophel, and raised it up to a great height. And he appointed captains of the army in all the fenced cities of Juda.

15 And he took away the strange gods, and the idol out of the house of the Lord: the altars also which he had made in the mount of the house of the Lord, and in Jerusalem. And he cast them all out of the city.

16 And he repaired the altar of the Lord, and sacrificed upon it victims, and peace offerings, and praise: and he commanded Juda to serve the Lord the God of Israel.

17 Nevertheless the people still sacrificed in the high places to the Lord their God.

18 But the rest of the acts of Manasses, and his prayer to his God, and the words of the seers that spoke to him in the name of the Lord the God

CHAP. 33. [1] 4 Kings, 21, 1. [2] 2 Kings, 7, 10. [3] 3 Kings, 8, 17.

CHAP. 33. Ver. 3. *The host of heaven.* The sun, moon, and stars.

of Israel, are contained in the words of the kings of Israel.

19 His prayer also, and his being heard, and all his sins, and contempt, and places wherein he built high places, and set up groves, and statues before he did penance, are written in the words of Hozai.

20 And Manasses slept with his fathers; and they buried him in his house. And his son Amon reigned in his stead.

21 Amon was two and twenty years old when he began to réign; and he reigned two years in Jerusalem.

22 And he did evil in the sight of the Lord, as Manasses his father had done: and he sacrificed to all the idols which Manasses his father had made, and served them.

23 And he did not humble himself before the Lord, as Manasses his father had humbled himself, but committed far greater sins.

24 And his servants conspired against him, and slew him in his own house.

25 But the rest of the multitude of the people slew them that had killed Amon: and made Josias his son king in his stead.

CHAPTER 34

Josias destroyeth idolatry, repaireth the temple, and reneweth the covenant between God and the people.

JOSIAS [1] was eight years old when he began to reign; and he reigned one and thirty years in Jerusalem.

2 And he did that which was right in the sight of the Lord, and walked in the ways of David his father. He declined not, neither to the right hand, nor to the left.

3 And in the eighth year of his reign, when he was yet a boy, he began to seek the God of his father David: and in the twelfth year after he began to reign, he cleansed Juda and Jerusalem from the high places, and the groves, and the idols, and the graven things.

4 And they broke down before him the altars of Baalim, and demolished the idols that had been set upon them. And he cut down the groves and the graven things, and broke them in pieces: and strewed the fragments upon the graves of them that had sacrificed to them.

5 And he burnt the bones of the priests on the altars of the idols: and he cleansed Juda and Jerusalem.

6 And in the cities of Manasses, and of Ephraim, and of Simeon, even to Nephtali, he demolished all.

7 And when he had destroyed the altars, and the groves, and had broken the idols in pieces, and had demolished all profane temples throughout all the land of Israel, he returned to Jerusalem.

8 Now in the eighteenth year of his reign, when he had cleansed the land, and the temple of the Lord, he sent Saphan the son of Eselias, and Maasias the governor of the city, Joha the son of Joachaz the recorder, to repair the house of the Lord his God.

9 And they came to Helcias the high priest: and received of him the money which had been brought into the house of the Lord, and which the Levites and porters had gathered together from Manasses, and Ephraim, and all the remnant of Israel; and from all Juda, and Benjamin, and the inhabitants of Jerusalem.

10 Which they delivered into the hands of them that were over the workmen in the house of the Lord, to repair the temple, and mend all that was weak.

11 But they gave it to the artificers, and to the masons, to buy, stones out of the quarries, and timber for the couplings of the buildings, and to rafter the houses, which the kings of Juda had destroyed.

12 And they did all faithfully. Now the overseers of the workmen were Jahath and Abdias of the sons of Merari, Zacharias and Mosollam of the sons of Caath, who hastened the work: all Levites skilful to play on instruments.

13 But over them that carried burdens for divers uses were scribes, and masters of the number of the Levites, and porters.

14 Now when they carried out the money that had been brought into the temple of the Lord, Helcias the priest found the book of the law of the Lord, by the hand of Moses.

15 And he said to Saphan the scribe: I have found the book of the law in the house of the Lord. And he delivered it to him.

16 But he carried the book to the king, and told him, saying: Lo, all that thou hast committed to thy servants, is accomplished.

17 They have gathered together the silver that was found in the house of the Lord: and it is given to the overseers of the artificers, and of the workmen, for divers works.

18 Moreover Helcias the priest gave me this book. And he read it before the king.

19 And when he had heard the words of the law, he rent his garments:

20 And he commanded Helcias, and Ahican the son of Saphan, and Abdon the son of Micha, and Saphan the

CHAP. 34. [1] 4 Kings, 22, 1.

scribe, and Asaa the king's servant, saying:

21 Go, and pray to the Lord for me, and for the remnant of Israel, and Juda, concerning all the words of this book, which is found. For the great wrath of the Lord hath fallen upon us, because our fathers have not kept the words of the Lord, to do all things that are written in this book.

22 And Helcias and they that were sent with him by the king, went to Olda the prophetess, the wife of Sellum the son of Thecuath, the son of Hasra keeper of the wardrobe, who dwelt in Jerusalem in the Second part: and they spoke to her the words above mentioned.

23 And she answered them: Thus saith the Lord the God of Israel: Tell the man that sent you to me:

24 Thus saith the Lord: Behold I will bring evils upon this place, and upon the inhabitants thereof, and all the curses that are written in this book which they read before the king of Juda.

25 Because they have forsaken me, and have sacrificed to strange gods, to provoke me to wrath with all the works of their hands, therefore my wrath shall fall upon this place and shall not be quenched.

26 But as to the king of Juda that sent you to beseech the Lord, thus shall you say to him: Thus saith the Lord the God of Israel: Because thou hast heard the words of this book,

27 And thy heart was softened, and thou hast humbled thyself in the sight of God for the things that are spoken against this place, and the inhabitants of Jerusalem, and reverencing my face, hast rent thy garments, and wept before me: I also have heard thee, saith the Lord.

28 For now I will gather thee to thy fathers, and thou shalt be brought to thy tomb in peace: and thy eyes shall not see all the evil that I will bring upon this place, and the inhabitants thereof. [2] They therefore reported to the king all that she had said,

29 And he called together all the ancients of Juda and Jerusalem.

30 And went up to the house of the Lord: and all the men of Juda, and the inhabitants of Jerusalem, the priests and the Levites, and all the people from the least to the greatest. And the king read in their hearing, in the house of the Lord, all the words of the book.

31 And standing up in his tribunal, he made a covenant before the Lord to walk after him, and keep his commandments, and testimonies, and justifica-

tions with all his heart, and with all his soul, and to do the things that were written in that book which he had read.

32 And he adjured all that were found in Jerusalem and Benjamin to do the same. And the inhabitants of Jerusalem did according to the covenant of the Lord the God of their fathers.

33 And Josias took away all the abominations out of all the countries of the children of Israel: and made all that were left in Israel to serve the Lord their God. As long as he lived they departed not from the Lord the God of their fathers.

CHAPTER 35

Josias celebrateth a most solemn pasch. He is slain by the king of Egypt.

AND [1] Josias kept a phase to the Lord in Jerusalem. And it was sacrificed on the fourteenth day of the first month.

2 And he set the priests in their offices, and exhorted them to minister in the house of the Lord.

3 And he spoke to the Levites, by whose instruction all Israel was sanctified to the Lord, saying: Put the ark in the sanctuary of the temple, which Solomon the son of David king of Israel built. For, you shall carry it no more. But minister now to the Lord your God, and to his people Israel.

4 And prepare yourselves by your houses and families, according to your courses, as David king of Israel commanded, and Solomon his son hath written.

5 And serve ye in the sanctuary by the families and companies of Levi.

6 And being sanctified kill the phase, and prepare your brethren, that they may do according to the words which the Lord spoke by the hand of Moses.

7 And Josias gave to all the people that were found there in the solemnity of the phase, of lambs and of kids of the flocks, and of other small cattle, thirty thousand, and of oxen, three thousand. All these were of the king's substance.

8 And his princes willingly offered what they had vowed, both to the people and to the priests and the Levites. Moreover Helcias, and Zacharias, and Jahiel, rulers of the house of the Lord, gave to the priests to keep the phase two thousand six hundred small cattle, and three hundred oxen.

9 And Chonenias, and Semeias, and Nathanael, his brethren, and Hasabias, and Jehiel, and Jozabad, princes of the Levites, gave to the rest of the Levites to celebrate the phase five thousand small cattle, and five hundred oxen.

[2] 4 Kings, 23, 1. CHAP. 35. [1] 4 Kings, 26, 21.

10 And the ministry was prepared, and the priests stood in their office: the Levites also in *their* companies, according to the king's commandment.

11 And the phase was immolated: and the priests sprinkled the blood with their hand, and the Levites flayed the holocausts.

12 And they separated them to give them by the houses and families of every one, and to be offered to the Lord, as it is written in the book of Moses. And with the oxen they did in like manner.

13 And they roasted the phase with fire, according to that which is written in the law: but the victims of peace offerings they boiled in caldrons, and kettles, and pots; and they distributed them speedily among all the people.

14 And afterwards they made ready for themselves, and for the priests: for the priests were busied in offering of holocausts and the fat until night. Wherefore the Levites prepared for themselves, and for the priests the sons of Aaron last.

15 And the singers the sons of Asaph stood in their order, according to the commandment of David, and Asaph, and Heman, and Idithun, the prophets of the king. And the porters kept guard at every gate, so as not to depart one moment from their service. And therefore their brethren the Levites prepared meats for them.

16 So all the service of the Lord was duly accomplished that day, both in keeping the phase, and offering holocausts upon the altar of the Lord, according to the commandment of king Josias.

17 And the children of Israel that were found there kept the phase at that time, and the feast of unleavened bread seven days.

18 There was no phase like to this in Israel, from the days of Samuel the prophet: neither did any of all the kings of Israel keep such a phase as Josias kept, with the priests, and the Levites, and all Juda, and Israel that were found, and the inhabitants of Jerusalem.

19 In the eighteenth year of the reign of Josias was his phase celebrated.

20 ² After that Josias had repaired the temple, Nechao king of Egypt came up to fight in Charcamis by the Euphrates: and Josias went out to meet him.

21 But he sent messengers to him, saying: What have I to do with thee, O king of Juda? I come not against thee this day, but I fight against another house, to which God hath commanded me to go in haste. Forbear to do against God, who is with me, lest he kill thee.

22 Josias would not return, but prepared to fight against him, and hearkened not to the words of Nechao from the mouth of God, ³ but went to fight in the field of Magedo.

23 And there he was wounded by the archers. And he said to his servants: Carry me out of the battle, for I am grievously wounded.

24 And they removed him from the chariot into another, that followed him after the manner of kings: and they carried him away to Jerusalem. And he died, and was buried in the monument of his fathers. And all Juda and Jerusalem mourned for him,

25 Particularly Jeremias: whose lamentations for Josias all the singing men and singing women repeat unto this day. And it became like a law in Israel: Behold it is found written in the Lamentations.

26 Now the rest of the acts of Josias and of his mercies, according to what was commanded by the law of the Lord:

27 And his works first and last, are written in the book of the kings of Juda and Israel.

CHAPTER 36

The reigns of Joachaz, Joakim, Joachin, and Sedecias. The captivity of Babylon released at length by Cyrus.

THEN ¹ the people of the land took Joachaz the son of Josias, and made him king instead of his father in Jerusalem.

2 Joachaz was three and twenty years old when he began to reign; and he reigned three months in Jerusalem.

3 And the king of Egypt came to Jerusalem, and deposed him, and condemned the land in a hundred talents of silver, and a talent of gold.

4 And he made ² Eliakim his brother king in his stead, over Juda and Jerusalem: and he turned his name to Joakim. But he took Joachaz with him, and carried him away into Egypt.

5 Joakim was five and twenty years old when he began to reign; and he reigned eleven years in Jerusalem. And he did evil before the Lord his God.

6 Against him came up Nabuchodonosor king of the Chaldeans, and led him bound in chains into Babylon.

7 And he carried also thither the vessels of the Lord, and put them in his temple.

8 But the rest of the acts of Joakim, and his abominations, which he wrought, and the things that were found in him, are contained in the book

² 4 Kings, 23, 29.   ³ Zach. 12, 11.   Chap. 36.   ¹ 4 Kings, 23, 30.   ² Matt. 1, 11.

of the kings of Juda and Israel. And Joachin his son reigned in his stead.

9 Joachin was eight years old when he began to reign; and he reigned three months and ten days in Jerusalem. And he did evil in the sight of the Lord.

10 And at the return of the year, king Nabuchodonosor sent, and brought him to Babylon, carrying away at the same time the most precious vessels of the house of the Lord. ³And he made Sedecias his uncle king over Juda and Jerusalem.

11 Sedecias was one and twenty years old when he began to reign; and he reigned eleven years in Jerusalem.

12 And he did evil in the eyes of the Lord his God, and did not reverence the face of Jeremias the prophet speaking to him from the mouth of the Lord.

13 He also revolted from king Nabuchodonosor, who had made him swear by God. And he hardened his neck and his heart, from returning to the Lord the God of Israel.

14 Moreover all the chief of the priests, and the people wickedly transgressed according to all the abominations of the Gentiles: and they defiled the house of the Lord, which he had sanctified to himself in Jerusalem.

15 And the Lord the God of their fathers sent to them, by the hand of his messengers, rising early, and daily admonishing them: because he spared his people and his dwelling place.

16 But they mocked the messengers of God, and despised his words, and misused the prophets, until the wrath of the Lord arose against his people, and there was no remedy.

17 For he brought upon them the king of the Chaldeans: and he slew their young men with the sword in the house of his sanctuary. He had no compassion on young man, or maiden, old man, or even him that stooped for age; but he delivered them all into his hands.

18 And all the vessels of the house of the Lord, great and small, and the treasures of the temple and of the king and of the princes he carried away to Babylon.

19 And the enemies set fire to the house of God, and broke down the wall of Jerusalem, burnt all the towers; and whatsoever was precious they destroyed.

20 Whosoever escaped the sword, was led into Babylon: and there served the king and his sons till the reign of the king of Persia.

21 That the word of the Lord by the mouth of Jeremias might be fulfilled, and the land might keep her sabbaths. For all the days of the desolation she kept a sabbath, till the seventy years were expired.

22 'But in the first year of Cyrus king of the Persians, to fulfil the word of the Lord, which he had spoken by the mouth of Jeremias, the Lord stirred up the heart of Cyrus king of the Persians: who commanded it to be proclaimed through all his kingdom, and by writing also, saying:

23 Thus saith Cyrus king of the Persians: All the kingdoms of the earth hath the Lord the God of heaven given to me; and he hath charged me to build him a house in Jerusalem, which is in Judea. Who is there among you of all his people? The Lord his God be with him, and let him go up.

THE FIRST BOOK OF

ESDRAS

This Book taketh its name from the writer: who was a holy priest, and doctor of the law. He is called by the Hebrews, Ezra.

CHAPTER 1

Cyrus king of Persia releaseth God's people from their captivity, with license to return and build the temple in Jerusalem. He restoreth the holy vessels which Nabuchodonosor had taken from thence.

³ 4 Kings, 24, 17; Jer. 37, 1. ⁴ Esd. 1, 1; 6, 3; Jer. 25, 12; 29, 10. CHAP. 1. ¹ 2 Par. 36, 22; Jer. 25, 12; 29, 10.

CHAP. 36. Ver. 9. *Eight years old.* He was associated by his father to the kingdom, when he was but eight years old; but after his father's death, when he reigned alone, he was eighteen years old (4 Kings, 24, 8).

IN the first year ¹ of Cyrus king of the Persians, that the word of the Lord by the mouth of Jeremias might be fulfilled, the Lord stirred up the spirit of Cyrus king of the Persians: and he made a proclamation throughout all his kingdom, and in writing also, saying:

2 Thus saith Cyrus king of the Persians: The Lord the God of heaven hath given to me all the kingdoms of the earth, and he hath charged me to build him a house in Jerusalem, which is in Judea.

3 Who is there among you of all his people? His God be with him. Let him go up to Jerusalem, which is in Judea, and build the house of the Lord the God of Israel. He is the God that is in Jerusalem.

4 And let all the rest in all places, wheresoever they dwell, help him every man from his place, with silver and gold, and goods, and cattle, besides that which they offer freely to the temple of God which is in Jerusalem.

5 Then rose up the chief of the fathers of Juda and Benjamin, and the priests, and Levites, and every one whose spirit God had raised up, to go up to build the temple of the Lord which was in Jerusalem.

6 And all they that were round about helped their hands with vessels of silver and gold, with goods, and with beasts, and with furniture, besides what they had offered on their own accord.

7 And king Cyrus brought forth the vessels of the temple of the Lord, which Nabuchodonosor had taken from Jerusalem, and had put them in the temple of his god.

8 Now Cyrus king of Persia brought them forth by the hand of Mithridates the son of Gazabar, and numbered them to Sassabasar the prince of Juda.

9 And this is the number of them: thirty bowls of gold: a thousand bowls of silver: nine and twenty knives: thirty cups of gold.

10 Silver cups of a second sort, four hundred and ten: other vessels, a thousand.

11 All the vessels of gold and silver, five thousand four hundred. All these Sassabasar brought with them that came up from the captivity of Babylon to Jerusalem.

CHAPTER 2

The number of them that returned to Judea. Their oblations.

NOW [1] these are the children of the province, that went out of the captivity, which Nabuchodonosor king of Babylon had carried away to Babylon, and who returned to Jerusalem and Juda, every man to his city.

2 Who came with Zorobabel: Josue, Nehemia, Saraia, Rahelaia, Mardochai, Belsan, Mesphar, Beguai, Rehum, Baana. The number of the men of the people of Israel:

3 The children of Pharos, two thousand one hundred seventy-two.

4 The children of Sephatia, three hundred seventy-five.

5 The children of Area, seven hundred seventy-five.

6 The children of Phahath Moab, of the children of Josue: Joab two thousand eight hundred twelve.

7 The children of Elam, a thousand two hundred fifty-four.

8 The children of Zethua, nine hundred forty-five.

9 The children of Zachai, seven hundred sixty.

10 The children of Bani, six hundred forty-two.

11 The children of Bebai, six hundred twenty-three.

12 The children of Azgad, a thousand two hundred twenty-two.

13 The children of Adonicam, six hundred sixty-six.

14 The children of Beguai, two thousand fifty-six.

15 The children of Adin, four hundred fifty-four.

16 The children of Ather, who were of Ezechias, ninety-eight.

17 The children of Besai, three hundred and twenty-three.

18 The children of Jora, a hundred and twelve.

19 The children of Hasum, two hundred twenty-three.

20 The children of Gebbar, ninety-five.

21 The children of Bethlehem, a hundred twenty-three.

22 The men of Netupha, fifty-six.

23 The men of Anathoth, a hundred twenty-eight.

24 The children of Azmaveth, forty-two.

25 The children of Cariathiarim, Cephira, and Beroth, seven hundred forty-three.

26 The children of Rama and Gabaa, six hundred twenty-one.

27 The men of Machmas, a hundred twenty-two.

28 The men of Bethel and Hai, two hundred twenty-three.

29 The children of Nebo, fifty-two.

30 The children of Megbis, a hundred fifty-six.

31 The children of the other Elam, a thousand two hundred fifty-four.

32 The children of Harim, three hundred and twenty.

33 The children of Lod, Hadid and Ono, seven hundred twenty-five.

34 The children of Jericho, three hundred forty-five.

35 The children of Senaa, three thousand six hundred thirty.

36 The priests: The children of Jadaia of the house of Josue, nine hundred seventy-three.

CHAP. 2. [1] 2 Esd. 7, 6.
CHAP. 1. Ver. 8. *Sassabasar.* Otherwise *Zorobabel.*

37 The children of Emmer, a thousand fifty-two.

38 The children of Pheshur, a thousand two hundred forty-seven.

39 The children of Harim, a thousand and seventeen.

40 The Levites: The children of Josue and of Cedmihel, the children of Odovia, seventy-four.

41 The singing men: The children of Asaph, a hundred twenty-eight.

42 The children of the porters: The children of Sellum, the children of Ater, the children of Telmon, the children of Accub, the children of Hatita, the children of Sobai. In all a hundred thirty-nine.

43 The Nathinites: The children of Siha, the children of Hasupha, the children of Tabbaoth,

44 The children of Ceros, the children of Sia, the children of Phadon,

45 The children of Lebana, the children of Hegaba, the children of Accub,

46 The children of Hagab, the children of Semlai, the children of Hanan,

47 The children of Gaddel, the children of Gaher, the children of Raaia,

48 The children of Rasin, the children of Necoda, the children of Gazam.

49 The children of Asa, the children of Phasea, the children of Besee,

50 The children of Asena, the children of Munim, the children of Nephusim,

51 The children of Bacbuc, the children of Hacupha, the children of Harhur,

52 The children of Besluth, the children of Mahida, the children of Harsa,

53 The children of Bercos, the children of Sisara, the children of Thema,

54 The children of Nasia, the children of Hatipha,

55 The children of the servants of Solomon: The children of Sotai, the children of Sopheret, the children of Pharuda,

56 The children of Jala, the children of Dercon, the children of Geddel,

57 The children of Saphatia, the children of Hatil, the children of Phochereth, which were of Asebaim, the children of Ami.

58 All the Nathinites, and the chil-

2 2 Esd. 7, 65.

CHAP. 2. Ver. 64. *Forty-two thousand three hundred and sixty.* Those who are reckoned up above of the tribes of Juda, Benjamin, and Levi, fall short of this number. The rest, who must be taken in to make up the whole sum, were of the other tribes.

CHAP. 3. Ver. 2. *Josue.* Or Jesus (Jeshua) the son of Josedec; he was the high priest, at that time.

dren of the servants of Solomon, three hundred ninety-two.

59 And these are they that came up from Thelmela, Thelharsa, Cherub, and Adon, and Emer. And they could not shew the house of their fathers and their seed, whether they were of Israel.

60 The children of Dalaia, the children of Tobia, the children of Necoda, six hundred fifty-two.

61 And of the children of the priests: the children of Hobia, the children of Accos, the children of Berzellai, who took a wife of the daughters of Berzellai, the Galaadite, and was called by their name.

62 These sought the writing of their genealogy, and found it not: and they were cast out of the priesthood.

63 [2] And Athersatha said to them, that they should not eat of the holy of holies, till there arose a priest learned and perfect.

64 All the multitudes as one man, *were* forty-two thousand three hundred and sixty:

65 Besides their men-servants, and women-servants, of whom there were seven thousand three hundred and thirty-seven; and among them singing men, and singing women, two hundred.

66 Their horses, seven hundred thirty-six: their mules, two hundred forty-five:

67 Their camels, four hundred thirty-five: their asses, six thousand seven hundred and twenty.

68 And some of the chief of the fathers, when they came to the temple of the Lord, which is in Jerusalem, offered freely to the house of the Lord to build it in its place.

69 According to their ability, they gave towards the expenses of the work, sixty-one thousand solids of gold, five thousand pounds of silver, and a hundred garments for the priests.

70 So the priests and the Levites, and some of the people, and the singing men, and the porters, and the Nathinites dwelt in their cities, and all Israel in their cities.

CHAPTER 3

An altar is built for sacrifice, the feast of tabernacles is solemnly celebrated, and the foundations of the temple are laid.

AND now the seventh month was come, and the children of Israel were in their cities. And the people gathered themselves together as one man to Jerusalem.

2 And Josue the son of Josedec rose up, and his brethren the priests, and Zorobabel the son of Salathiel, and his brethren: and they built the altar of

the God of Israel that they might offer holocausts upon it, as it is written in the law of Moses the man of God.

3 And they set the altar of God upon its bases, while the people of the lands round about put them in fear: and they offered upon it a holocaust to the Lord morning and evening.

4 And they kept the feast of tabernacles, as it is written: and offered the holocaust every day orderly according to the commandment, the duty of the day in its day.

5 And afterwards the continual holocaust, both on the new moons, and on all the solemnities of the Lord, that were consecrated, and on all in which a freewill offering was made to the Lord.

6 From the first day of the seventh month they began to offer holocausts to the Lord: but the temple of God was not yet founded.

7 And they gave money to hewers of stones and to masons: and meat and drink and oil to the Sidonians and Tyrians, to bring cedar trees from Libanus to the sea of Joppe, according to the orders which Cyrus king of the Persians had given them.

8 And in the second year of their coming to the temple of God in Jerusalem, the second month, Zorobabel the son of Salathiel, and Josue the son of Josedec, and the rest of their brethren, the priests, and the Levites, and all that were come from the captivity to Jerusalem began. And they appointed Levites from twenty years old and upward, to hasten forward the work of the Lord.

9 Then Josue and his sons and his brethren, Cedmihel, and his sons, and the children of Juda, as one man, stood to hasten them that did the work in the temple of God: the sons of Henadad, and their sons, and their brethren the Levites.

10 And when the masons laid the foundations of the temple of the Lord, the priests stood in their ornaments with trumpets: and the Levites the sons of Asaph with cymbals, to praise God by the hands of David king of Israel.

11 And they sung together hymns, and praise to the Lord: because he is good; for his mercy endureth for ever towards Israel. And all the people shouted with a great shout, praising the Lord, because the foundations of the temple of the Lord were laid.

12 But many of the priests and the Levites, and the chief of the fathers and the ancients that had seen the former temple, when they had the foundation of this temple before their eyes, wept with a loud voice. And many shouting for joy lifted up their voice.

13 So that one could not distinguish the voice of the shout of joy, from the noise of the weeping of the people: for one with another the people shouted with a loud shout, and the voice was heard afar off.

CHAPTER 4

The Samaritans by their letter to the king hinder the building.

NOW the enemies of Juda and Benjamin heard that the children of the captivity were building a temple to the Lord the God of Israel.

2 And they came to Zorobabel, and the chief of the fathers, and said to them: Let us build with you, for we seek your God as ye do. Behold we have sacrificed to him, since the days of Asor Haddan king of Assyria, who brought us hither.

3 But Zorobabel, and Josue, and the rest of the chief of the fathers of Israel said to them: You have nothing to do with us to build a house to our God; but we ourselves alone will build to the Lord our God, as Cyrus king of the Persians hath commanded us.

4 Then the people of the land hindered the hands of the people of Juda, and troubled them in building.

5 And they hired counsellors against them, to frustrate their design all the days of Cyrus king of Persia, even until the reign of Darius king of the Persians.

6 And in the reign of Assuerus, in the beginning of his reign, they wrote an accusation against the inhabitants of Juda and Jerusalem.

7 And in the days of Artaxerxes, Beselam, Mithridates, and Thabeel, and the rest that were in the council wrote to Artaxerxes king of the Persians: and the letter of accusation was written in Syriac, and was read in the Syrian tongue.

8 Reum Beelteem, and Samsai the scribe wrote a letter from Jerusalem to king Artaxerxes, in this manner:

9 Reum Beelteem, and Samsai the scribe, and the rest of their counsellors, the Dinites, and the Apharsathacites, the Therphalites, the Apharsites, the Erchuites, the Babylonians, the Susanechites, the Dievites, and the Elamites:

10 And the rest of the nations, whom the great and glorious Asenaphar brought over and made to dwell in the cities of Samaria and in the rest of the countries of this side of the river in peace.

11 (This is the copy of the letter, which they sent to him): To Artax-

CHAP. 4. Ver. 6. *Assuerus.* Otherwise called Cambyses the son and successor of Cyrus. He is also in the following verse named Artaxerxes, a name common to almost all the kings of Persia.

erxes the king, thy servants, the men that are on this side of the river send greeting.

12 Be it known to the king, that the Jews, who came up from thee to us, are come to Jerusalem a rebellious and wicked city, which they are building, setting up the ramparts thereof and repairing the walls.

13 And now be it known to the king, that if this city be built up, and the walls thereof repaired, they will not pay tribute nor toll, nor yearly revenues: and this loss will fall upon the kings.

14 But we remembering the salt that we have eaten in the palace, and because we count it a crime to see the king wronged, have therefore sent and certified the king,

15 That search may be made in the books of the histories of thy fathers. And thou shalt find written in the records; and shalt know that this city is a rebellious city, and hurtful to the kings and provinces, and that wars were raised therein of old time. For which cause also the city was destroyed.

16 We certify the king, that if this city be built, and the walls thereof repaired, thou shalt have no possession on this side of the river.

17 The king sent word to Reum Beelteem and Samsai the scribe, and to the rest that were in their council, inhabitants of Samaria, and to the rest beyond the river, sending greeting and peace:

18 The accusation, which you have sent to us, hath been plainly read before me.

19 And I commanded; and search hath been made. And it is found, that this city of old time hath rebelled against kings, and seditions and wars have been raised therein.

20 For there have been powerful kings in Jerusalem: who have had dominion over all the country that is beyond the river, and have received tribute, and toll, and revenues.

21 Now therefore hear the sentence: Hinder those men, that this city be not built, till further orders be given by me.

22 See that you be not negligent in executing this, lest by little and little the evil grow to the hurt of the kings.

23 Now the copy of the edict of king Artaxerxes was read before Reum Beelteem, and Samsai the scribe, and their counsellors. And they went up in haste to Jerusalem to the Jews, and hindered them with arm and power.

24 Then the work of the house of the Lord in Jerusalem was interrupted, and ceased till the second year of the reign of Darius king of the Persians.

CHAPTER 5

By the exhortation of Aggeus, and Zacharias, the people proceed in building the temple. Which their enemies strive in vain to hinder.

NOW Aggeus the prophet, and Zacharias the son of Addo, prophesied to the Jews that were in Judea and Jerusalem, in the name of the God of Israel.

2 Then rose up Zorobabel the son of Salathiel, and Josue the son of Josedec, and began to build the temple of God in Jerusalem: and with them were the prophets of God helping them.

3 And at the same time came to them Thathanai, who was governor beyond the river, and Stharbuzanai, and their counsellors; and said thus to them: Who hath given you counsel to build this house, and to repair the walls thereof?

4 In answer to which, we gave them the names of the men who were the promoters of that building.

5 But the eye of their God was upon the ancients of the Jews, and they could not hinder them. And it was agreed that the matter should be referred to Darius, and then they should give satisfaction concerning that accusation.

6 The copy of the letter that Thathanai governor of the country beyond the river, and Stharbuzanai, and his counsellors the Arphasachites, who dwelt beyond the river, sent to Darius the king.

7 The letter which they sent him, was written thus: To Darius the king all peace.

8 Be it known to the king, that we went to the province of Judea, to the house of the great God, which they are building with unpolished stones; and timber is. laid in the walls. And this work is carried on diligently, and advanceth in their hands.

9 And we asked those ancients, and said to them thus: Who hath given you authority to build this house, and to repair these walls?

10 We asked also of them their names, that we might give thee notice: and we have written the names of the men that are the chief among them.

11 And they answered us in these words, saying: We are the servants of the God of heaven and earth; and we are building a temple that was built these many years ago, and which a great king of Israel built and set up.

12 But after that our fathers had provoked the God of heaven to wrath, he delivered them into the hands of Nabuchodonosor the king of Babylon the Chaldean: and he destroyed this house, and carried away the people to Babylon.

13 But in the first year of Cyrus the king of Babylon, king Cyrus set forth a decree, that this house of God should be built.

14 And the vessels also of gold and silver of the temple of God, which Nabuchodonosor had taken out of the temple, that was in Jerusalem, and had brought them to the temple of Babylon, king Cyrus brought out of the temple of Babylon. And they were delivered to one Sassabasar, whom also he appointed governor,

15 And said to him: Take these vessels, and go, and put them in the temple that is in Jerusalem, and let the house of God be built in its place.

16 Then came this same Sassabasar, and laid the foundations of the temple of God in Jerusalem, and from that time until now it is in building, and is not yet finished.

17 Now therefore if it seem good to the king, let him search in the king's library, which is in Babylon, whether it hath been decreed by Cyrus the king, that the house of God in Jerusalem should be built: and let the king send his pleasure to us concerning this matter.

CHAPTER 6

King Darius favoureth the building and contributeth to it.

THEN king Darius gave orders; and they searched in the library of the books that were laid up in Babylon,

2 And there was found in Ecbatana, which is a castle in the province of Media, a book in which this record was written.

3 In the first year of Cyrus the king: Cyrus the king decreed, that the house of God should be built, which is in Jerusalem, in the place where they may offer sacrifices; and that they lay the foundations that may support the height of threescore cubits, and the breadth of threescore cubits,

4 Three rows of unpolished stones, and so rows of new timber. And the charges shall be given out of the king's house.

5 And also let the golden and silver vessels of the temple of God which Nabuchodonosor took out of the temple of Jerusalem, and brought to Babylon, be restored, and carried back to the temple of Jerusalem to their place, which also were placed in the temple of God.

6 Now therefore Thathanai, governor of the country beyond the river, Stharbuzanai, and your counsellors the Apharsachites, who are beyond the river, depart far from them,

7 And let that temple of God be built by the governor of the Jews, and by

their ancients, that they may build that house of God in its place.

8 I also have commanded what must be done by those ancients of the Jews, that the house of God may be built: to wit, that of the king's chest, that is, of the tribute that is paid out of the country beyond the river, the charges be diligently given to those men, lest the work be hindered.

9 And if it shall be necessary, let calves also, and lambs, and kids, for holocausts to the God of heaven, wheat, salt, wine, and oil; according to the custom of the priests that are in Jerusalem, be given them day by day, that there be no complaint in any thing.

10 And let them offer oblations to the God of heaven, and pray for the life of the king, and of his children.

11 And I have made a decree: That if any whosoever, shall alter this commandment, a beam be taken from his house, and set up, and he be nailed upon it, and his house be confiscated.

12 And may the God, that hath caused his name to dwell there, destroy all kingdoms, and the people that shall put out their hand to resist, and to destroy the house of God, that is in Jerusalem. I Darius have made the decree, which I will have diligently complied with.

13 So then Thathanai, governor of the country beyond the river, and Stharbuzanai, and his counsellors diligently executed what Darius the king had commanded.

14 And the ancients of the Jews built, and prospered according to the prophecy of Aggeus the prophet, and of Zacharias the son of Addo. And they built and finished, by the commandment of the God of Israel, and by the commandment of Cyrus, and Darius, and Artaxerxes, kings of the Persians.

15 And they were finishing this house of God until the third day of the month of Adar, which was in the sixth year of the reign of king Darius.

16 And the children of Israel, the priests and the Levites, and the rest of the children of the captivity kept the dedication of the house of God with joy.

17 And they offered at the dedication of the house of God, a hundred calves, two hundred rams, four hundred lambs: and for a sin offering for all Israel twelve he-goats, according to the number of the tribes of Israel.

18 And they set the priests in their divisions, and the Levites in their courses over the works of God in Jerusalem, [1] as it is written in the book of Moses.

CHAP. 6. [1] Num. 3, 6; 8, 9.

19 And the children of Israel of the captivity kept the phase, on the fourteenth day of the first month.

20 For all the priests and the Levites were purified as one man: all were clean to kill the phase for all the children of the captivity, and for their brethren the priests, and themselves.

21 And the children of Israel that were returned from captivity, and all that had separated themselves from the filthiness of the nations of the earth to them, to seek the Lord the God of Israel, did eat.

22 And they kept the feast of unleavened bread seven days with joy; for the Lord had made them joyful, and had turned the heart of the king of Assyria to them, that he should help their hands in the work of the house of the Lord the God of Israel.

CHAPTER 7

Esdras goeth up to Jerusalem to teach, and assist the people, with a gracious decree of Artaxerxes.

NOW after these things in the reign of Artaxerxes king of the Persians, Esdras the son of Saraias, the son of Azarias, the son of Helcias,

2 The son of Sellum, the son of Sadoc, the son of Achitob,

3 The son of Amarias, the son of Azarias, the son of Maraioth,

4 The son of Zarahias, the son of Ozi, the son of Bocci,

5 The son of Abisue, the son of Phinees, the son of Eleazar, the son of Aaron the priest from the beginning.

6 This Esdras went up from Babylon, and he was a ready scribe in the law of Moses, which the Lord God had given to Israel. And the king granted him all his request, according to the hand of the Lord his God upon him.

7 And there went up some of the children of Israel, and of the children of the priests, and of the children of the Levites, and of the singing men, and of the porters, and of the Nathinites to Jerusalem, in the seventh year of Artaxerxes the king.

8 And they came to Jerusalem in the fifth month, in the seventh year of the king.

9 For upon the first day of the first month he began to go up from Babylon; and on the first day of the fifth month he came to Jerusalem, according to the good hand of his God upon him.

10 For Esdras had prepared his heart to seek the law of the Lord, and to do and to teach in Israel the commandments and judgment.

11 And this is the copy of the letter of the edict, which king Artaxerxes gave to Esdras the priest, the scribe instructed in the words and commandments of the Lord, and his ceremonies in Israel.

12 Artaxerxes, king of kings, to Esdras the priest, the most learned scribe of the law of the God of heaven, greeting:

13 It is decreed by me, that all they of the people of Israel, and of the priests and of the Levites in my realm, that are minded to go into Jerusalem, should go with thee.

14 For thou art sent from before the king, and his seven counsellors, to visit Judea and Jerusalem according to the law of thy God, which is in thy hand.

15 And to carry the silver and gold, which the king and his counsellors have freely offered to the God of Israel, whose tabernacle is in Jerusalem.

16 And all the silver and gold that thou shalt find in all the province of Babylon, and that the people is willing to offer, and that the priests shall offer of their own accord to the house of their God, which is in Jerusalem,

17 Take freely: and buy diligently with this money, calves, rams, lambs, with the sacrifices and libations of them. And offer them upon the altar of the temple of your God, that is in Jerusalem.

18 And if it seem good to thee, and to thy brethren to do any thing with the rest of the silver and gold, do it according to the will of your God.

19 The vessels also, that are given thee for the sacrifice of the house of thy God, deliver thou in the sight of God in Jerusalem.

20 And whatsoever more there shall be need of for the house of thy God, how much soever thou shalt have occasion to spend, it shall be given out of the treasury, and the king's exchequer, and by me.

21 I Artaxerxes the king have ordered and decreed to all the keepers of the public chest, that are beyond the river, that whatsoever Esdras the priest, the scribe of the law of the God of heaven, shall require of you, you give it without delay:

22 Unto a hundred talents of silver, and unto a hundred cores of wheat, and unto a hundred bates of wine, and unto a hundred bates of oil, and salt without measure.

23 All that belongeth to the rites of the God of heaven, let it be given diligently in the house of the God of heaven: lest his wrath should be enkindled against the realm of the king, and of his sons.

24 We give you also to understand concerning all the priests, and the Le-

vites, and the singers, and the porters, and the Nathinites, and ministers of the house of this God, that you have no authority to impose toll or tribute, or custom upon them.

25 And thou Esdras, according to the wisdom of thy God, which is in thy hand, appoint judges and magistrates, that may judge all the people that is beyond the river, that is: for them who know the law of thy God. Yea and the ignorant teach ye freely.

26 And whosoever will not do the law of thy God, and the law of the king diligently, judgment shall be executed upon him, either unto death, or unto banishment, or to the confiscation of goods, or at least to prison.

27 Blessed be the Lord the God of our fathers, who had put this in the king's heart, to glorify the house of the Lord, which is in Jerusalem,

28 And hath inclined his mercy toward me before the king and his counsellors, and all the mighty princes of the king. And I being strengthened by the hand of the Lord my God, which was upon me, gathered together out of Israel chief men to go up with me.

CHAPTER 8

The companions of Esdras. The fast which he appointed. They bring the holy vessels into the temple.

NOW these are the chiefs of families, and the genealogy of them, who came up with me from Babylon in the reign of Artaxerxes the king.

2 Of the sons of Phinees, Gersom. Of the sons of Ithamar, Daniel. Of the sons of David, Hattus.

3 Of the sons of Sechenias, the son of Pharos, Zacharias: and with him were numbered a hundred and fifty men.

4 Of the sons of Phahath Moab, Eleoenai the son of Zareha: and with him two hundred men.

5 Of the sons of Sechenias, the son of Ezechiel: and with him three hundred men.

6 Of the sons of Adan, Abed the son of Jonathan: and with him fifty men.

7 Of the sons of Alam, Isaias the son of Athalias: and with him seventy men.

8 Of the sons of Saphatia: Zebodia the son of Michael: and with him eighty men.

9 Of the sons of Joab, Obedia the son of Jahiel: and with him two hundred and eighteen men.

10 Of the sons of Selomith, the son of Josphia: and with him a hundred and sixty men.

11 Of the sons of Bebai, Zacharias the son of Bebai: and with him eight and twenty men.

12 Of the sons of Azgad, Joanan the son of Eccetan: and with him a hundred and ten men.

13 Of the sons of Adonicam, who were the last (and these are their names: Eliphelet, and Jehiel, and Samaias): and with them sixty men.

14 Of the sons of Begui, Uthai and Zachur: and with him seventy men.

15 And I gathered them together to the river, which runneth down to Ahava, and we stayed there three days. And I sought among the people and among the priests for the sons of Levi, and found none there.

16 So I sent Eliezer, and Ariel, and Semeias, and Elnathan, and Jarib, and another Elnathan, and Nathan, and Zacharias, and Mosollam, chief men; and Joiarib, and Elnathan, wise men.

17 And I sent them to Eddo, who is chief in the place of Chasphia; and I put in their mouth the words that they should speak to Eddo, and his brethren the Nathinites in the place of Chasphia, that they should bring us ministers of the house of our God.

18 And by the good hand of our God upon us, they brought us a most learned man of the sons of Moholi the son of Levi the son of Israel: and Sarabias and his sons, and his brethren, eighteen.

19 And Hasabias, and with him Isaias of the sons of Merari, and his brethren, and his sons, twenty.

20 And of the Nathinites, whom David, and the princes gave for the service of the Levites: Nathinites, two hundred and twenty. All these were called by their names.

21 And I proclaimed there a fast by the river Ahava, that we might afflict ourselves before the Lord our God, and might ask of him a right way for us, and for our children, and for all our substance.

22 For I was ashamed to ask the king for aid and for horsemen, to defend us from the enemy in the way. Because we had said to the king: The hand of our God is upon all them that seek him in goodness; and his power and strength, and wrath upon all them that forsake him.

23 And we fasted, and besought our God for this: and it fell out prosperously unto us.

24 And I separated twelve of the chief of the priests, Sarabias, and Hasabias: and with them ten of their brethren.

Chap. 8. Ver. 21. *And I proclaimed a fast.* It is not enough to part from Babylon, that is, figuratively from sin, but we must also do works of penance; and therefore Esdras here proclaimed an extraordinary fast to those that were come from captivity. This shews that fasting was commanded and practised from the earliest times.

25 And I weighed unto them the silver and gold, and the vessels consecrated for the house of our God, which the king and his counsellors, and his princess, and all Israel, that were found, had offered.

26 And I weighed to their hands six hundred and fifty talents of silver, and a hundred vessels of silver, and a hundred talents of gold.

27 And twenty cups of gold, of a thousand solids, and two vessels of the best shining brass, beautiful as gold.

28 And I said to them: You are the holy ones of the Lord. And the vessels are holy: and the silver and gold, that is freely offered to the Lord the God of our fathers.

29 Watch ye and keep them, till you deliver them by weight before the chief of the priests, and of the Levites, and the heads of the families of Israel in Jerusalem, into the treasure of the house of the Lord.

30 And the priests and the Levites received the weight of the silver and gold, and the vessels, to carry them to Jerusalem to the house of our God.

31 Then we set forward from the river Ahava on the twelfth day of the first month to go to Jerusalem. And the hand of our God was upon us, and delivered us from the hand of the enemy, and of such as lay in wait by the way.

32 And we came to Jerusalem: and we stayed there three days.

33 And on the fourth day the silver, and the gold, and the vessels were weighed in the house of our God by the hand of Meremoth the son of Urias the priest; and with him was Eleazar the son of Phinees; and with them Jozabad the son of Josue, and Noadaia the son of Benoi, Levites.

34 According to the number and weight of every thing. And all the weight was written at that time.

35 Moreover the children of them that had been carried away that were come out of the captivity, offered holocausts to the God of Israel: twelve calves for all the people of Israel, ninety-six rams, seventy-seven lambs, and twelve he-goats for sin: all for a holocaust to the Lord.

36 And they gave the king's edicts to the lords that were from the king's court, and the governors beyond the river. And they furthered the people and the house of God.

CHAP. 9. Vers. 1, 2. This shows how sinful it is to intermarry with those that the Church forbids us, on account of the danger of perversion and falling off from the true faith.
Ver. 8. *A pin*, or *nail*. Here this signifies a small settlement or holding; which Esdras begs for, to preserve even a part of the people, who, by their great iniquity, had incurred the anger of God.

CHAPTER 9

Esdras mourneth for the transgression of the people. His confession and prayer.

AND after these things were accomplished, the princes came to me, saying: The people of Israel, and the priests and Levites have not separated themselves from the people of the lands, and from their abominations: namely, of the Chanaanites, and the Hethites, and the Pherezites, and the Jebusites, and the Ammonites, and the Moabites, and the Egyptians, and the Amorrhites.

2 For they have taken of their daughters for themselves and for their sons; and they have mingled the holy seed with the people of the lands. And the hand of the princes and magistrates hath been first in this transgression.

3 And when I had heard this word, I rent my mantle and my coat, and plucked off the hairs of my head and my beard: and I sat down mourning.

4 And there were assembled to me all that feared the God of Israel, because of the transgression of those that were come from the captivity. And I sat sorrowful, until the evening sacrifice.

5 And at the evening sacrifice I rose up from my affliction, and having rent my mantle and my garment, I fell upon my knees, and spread out my hands to the Lord my God:

6 And said: My God, I am confounded and ashamed to lift up my face to thee. For our iniquities are multiplied over our heads; and our sins are grown up even unto heaven,

7 From the days of our fathers. And we ourselves also have sinned grievously unto this day: and for our iniquities we, and our kings, and our priests have been delivered into the hands of the kings of the lands, and to the sword, and to captivity, and to spoil, and to confusion of face, as it is at this day.

8 And now, as little, and for a moment, has our prayer been made before the Lord our God, to leave us a remnant, and give us a pin in his holy place: and that our God would enlighten our eyes, and would give us a little life in our bondage.

9 For we are bondmen, and in our bondage our God hath not forsaken us, but hath extended mercy upon us before the king of the Persians, to give us life, and to set up the house of our God, and to rebuild the desolations thereof, and to give us a fence in Juda and Jerusalem.

10 And now, O our God, what shall we say after this? For we have forsaken thy commandments,

11 Which thou hast commanded by

the hand of thy servants the prophets, saying: The land which you go to possess, is an unclean land, according to the uncleanness of the people, and of other lands, with their abominations, who have filled it from mouth to mouth with their filth.

12 ¹ Now therefore give not your daughters to their sons: and take not their daughters for your sons. And seek not their peace, nor their prosperity for ever: that you may be strengthened, and may eat the good things of the land, and may have your children your heirs for ever.

13 And after all that is come upon us, for our most wicked deeds, and our great sin, seeing that thou our God hast saved us from our iniquity, and hast given us a deliverance as at this day,

14 That we should not turn away, nor break thy commandments, nor join in marriage with the people of these abominations. Art thou angry with us unto utter destruction, not to leave us a remnant to be saved?

15 O Lord God of Israel, thou art just: for we remain yet to be saved as at this day. Behold we are before thee in our sin: for there can be no standing before thee in this matter.

CHAPTER 10

Order is given for discharging strange women. The names of the guilty.

NOW when Esdras was thus praying, and beseeching, and weeping, and lying before the temple of God, there was gathered to him of Israel an exceeding great assembly of men and women and children: and the people wept with much lamentation.

2 And Sechenias the son of Jehiel of the sons of Elam answered, and said to Esdras: We have sinned against our God, and have taken strange wives of the people of the land. And now if there be repentance in Israel concerning this,

3 Let us make a covenant with the Lord our God, to put away all the wives, and such as are born of them, according to the will of the Lord, and of them that fear the commandment of the Lord our God. Let it be done according to the law.

4 Arise, it is thy part to give orders: and we will be with thee. Take courage, and do it.

5 So Esdras arose, and made the chiefs of the priests and of the Levites, and all Israel, to swear that they would do according to this word. And they swore.

6 And Esdras rose up from before the house of God, and went to the chamber of Johanan the son of Eliasib, and en-

tered in thither. He ate no bread, and drank no water: for he mourned for the transgression of them that were come out of the captivity.

7 And proclamation was made in Juda and Jerusalem to all the children of the captivity, that they should assemble together into Jerusalem.

8 And that whosoever would not come within three days, according to the counsel of the princes and the ancients, all his substance should be taken away; and he should be cast out of the company of them that were returned from captivity.

9 Then all the men of Juda and Benjamin gathered themselves together to Jerusalem within three days, in the ninth month, the twentieth day of the month. And all the people sat in the street of the house of God, trembling, because of the sin and the rain.

10 And Esdras the priest stood up, and said to them: You have transgressed, and taken strange wives, to add to the sins of Israel.

11 And now make confession to the Lord the God of your fathers; and do his pleasure; and separate yourselves from the people of the land, and from your strange wives.

12 And all the multitude answered and said with a loud voice: According to thy word unto us, so be it done.

13 But as the people are many; and it is time of rain; and we are not able to stand without; and it is not a work of one day or two (for we have exceedingly sinned in this matter) :

14 Let rulers be appointed in all the multitude. And in all our cities, let them that have taken strange wives come at the times appointed, and with them the ancients and the judges of every city, until the wrath of our God be turned away from us for this sin.

15 Then Jonathan the son of Azahel, and Jaasia the son of Thecua were appointed over this: and Mesollam and Sebethai, Levites, helped them.

16 And the children of the captivity did so. And Esdras the priest, and the men heads of the families in the houses of their fathers, and all by their names, went and sat down in the first day of the tenth month to examine the matter.

17 And they made an end with all the men that had taken strange wives by the first day of the first month.

18 And there were found among the sons of the priests that had taken strange wives: Of the sons of Josue the son of Josedec, and his brethren, Maasia, and Eliezer, and Jarib, and Godolia.

19 And they gave their hands to put

CHAP. 9. ¹ Deut. 7, 3.

away their wives, and to offer for their offence a ram of the flock.

20 And of the sons of Emmer, Hanani, and Zebedia.

21 And of the sons of Harim, Maasia, and Elia, and Semeia, and Jehiel, and Ozias.

22 And of the sons of Pheshur, Elioenai, Maasia, Ismael, Nathanael, Jozabed, and Elasa.

23 And of the sons of the Levites, Jozabed, and Semei, and Celaia, the same is Calita, Phataia, Juda, and Eliezer.

24 And of the singing men, Elisiab. And of the porters, Sellum, and Telem, and Uri.

25 And of Israel, of the sons of Pharos, Remeia, and Jezia, and Melchia, and Miamin, and Eliezer, and Melchia, and Banea.

26 And of the sons of Elam, Mathania, Zacharias, and Jehiel, and Abdi, and Jerimoth, and Elia.

27 And of the sons of Zethua, Elioenai, Eliasib, Mathania, Jerimuth, and Zabad, and Aziaza.

28 And of the sons of Babai, Johanan, Hanania, Zabbai, Athalai.

29 And of the sons of Bani, Mosollam, and Melluch, and Adaia, Jasub, and Saal, and Ramoth.

30 And of the sons of Phahath, Moab, Edna, and Chalal, Banaias, and Maasias, Mathanias, Beseleel, Bennui, and Manasse.

31 And of the sons of Herem, Eliezer, Josue, Melchias, Semeias, Simeon,

32 Benjamin, Maloch, Samarias.

33 And of the sons of Hasom, Mathanai, Mathatha, Zabad, Eliphelet, Jermai, Manasse, Semei.

34 Of the sons of Bani, Maaddi, Amram, and Uel,

35 Baneas, and Badaias, Cheliau,

36 Vania, Marimuth, and Eliasib,

37 Mathanias, Mathania, and Jasi,

38 And Bani, and Bennui, Semei,

39 And Salmias, and Nathan, and Adaias,

40 And Mechnedebai, Sisai, Sarai,

41 Ezrel, and Selemiau, Semeria,

42 Sellum, Amaria, Joseph.

43 Of the sons of Nebo, Jehiel, Mathathias, Zabad, Zabina, Jeddu, and Joel, and Banaia.

44 All these had taken strange wives: and there were among them women that had borne children.

THE BOOK OF

NEHEMIAS

WHICH IS CALLED

THE SECOND OF ESDRAS

This book takes its name from the writer, who was cupbearer to Artaxerxes (surnamed Longimanus) king of Persia, and was sent by him with a commission to rebuild the walls of Jerusalem. It is also called the second book of Esdras; because it is a continuation of the history, begun by Esdras, of the state of the people of God after their return from captivity.

CHAPTER 1

Nehemias hearing the miserable state of his countrymen in Judea lamenteth, fasteth, and prayeth to God for their relief.

THE words of Nehemias the son of Helchias. And it came to pass in the month of Casleu, in the twentieth year, as I was in the castle of Susa,

2 That Hanani one of my brethren came, he and some men of Juda; and I asked them concerning the Jews, that remained and were left of the captivity, and concerning Jerusalem.

3 And they said to me: They that have remained, and are left of the captivity there in the province, are in great affliction and reproach. And the wall of Jerusalem is broken down, and the gates thereof are burnt with fire.

4 And when I had heard these words, I sat down, and wept, and mourned for many days: and I fasted, and prayed before the face of the God of heaven,

5 And I said: [1] I beseech thee, O Lord God of heaven, strong, great, and terrible, who keepest covenant and mercy with those that love thee and keep thy commandments:

6 Let thy ears be attentive, and thy eyes open, to hear the prayer of thy servant, which I pray before thee now, night and day, for the children of Israel thy servants. And I confess the sins of the children of Israel, by which they have sinned against thee: I and my father's house have sinned.

7 We have been seduced by vanity, and have not kept thy commandments and ceremonies and judgments, which thou hast commanded thy servant Moses.

8 Remember the word that thou commandedst to Moses thy servant, saying: If you shall transgress, I will scatter you abroad among the nations:

9 But if you return to me, and keep my commandments, and do them, though you should be led away to the uttermost parts of the world, I will gather you from thence, and bring you back to the place which I have chosen for my name to dwell there.

10 And these are thy servants, and thy people: whom thou hast redeemed by thy great strength, and by thy mighty hand.

11 I beseech thee, O Lord, let thy ear be attentive to the prayer of thy servant, and to the prayer of thy servants who desire to fear thy name. And direct thy servant this day: and give him mercy before this man. For I was the king's cupbearer.

CHAPTER 2

Nehemias with commission from king Artaxerxes cometh to Jerusalem. He exhorteth the Jews to rebuild the walls.

AND it came to pass in the month of Nisan, in the twentieth year of Artaxerxes the king, that wine was before him: and I took up the wine, and gave it to the king. And I was as one languishing away before his face.

2 And the king said to me: Why is thy countenance sad, seeing thou dost not appear to be sick? This is not without cause, but some evil, I know not what, is in thy heart. And I was seized with an exceeding great fear.

3 And I said to the king: O king, live for ever: Why should not my countenance be sorrowful, seeing the city of the place of the sepulchres of my fathers is desolate, and the gates thereof are burnt with fire?

4 Then the king said to me: For what dost thou make request? And I prayed to the God of heaven.

5 And I said to the king: If it seem good to the king, and if thy servant hath found favour in thy sight: that thou wouldst send me into Judea to the city of the sepulchre of my father, and I will build it.

6 And the king said to me, and the queen that sat by him: For how long shall thy journey be, and when wilt thou return? And it pleased the king; and he sent me. And I fixed him a time.

7 And I said to the king: If it seem good to the king, let him give me letters to the governors of the country beyond the river, that they convey me over till I come into Judea:

8 And a letter to Asaph the keeper of the king's forest, to give me timber that I may cover the gates of the tower of the house, and the walls of the city, and the house that I shall enter into. And the king gave me according to the good hand of my God with me.

9 And I came to the governors of the country beyond the river, and gave them the king's letters. And the king had sent with me captains of soldiers, and horsemen.

10 And Sanaballat the Horonite, and Tobias the servant, the Ammonite, heard it: and it grieved them exceedingly, that a man was come, who sought the prosperity of the children of Israel.

11 And I came to Jerusalem, and was there three days.

12 And I arose in the night, I and some few men with me, and I told not any man what God had put in my heart to do in Jerusalem; and there was no beast with me, but the beast that I rode upon.

13 And I went out by night by the gate of the valley, and before the dragon fountain, and to the dung gate: and I viewed the wall of Jerusalem which was broken down, and the gates thereof which were consumed with fire.

14 And I passed to the gate of the fountain, and to the king's aqueduct: and there was no place for the beast on which I rode to pass.

15 And I went up in the night by the torrent, and viewed the wall. and going back I came to the gate of the valley, and returned.

16 But the magistrates knew not whither I went, or what I did: neither had I as yet told any thing to the Jews, or to the priests, or to the nobles, or to the magistrates, or to the rest that did the work.

17 Then I said to them: You know the affliction wherein we are, because Jerusalem is desolate and the gates thereof are consumed with fire. Come,

CHAP. 1. [1] Dan. 9, 4.

and let us build up the walls of Jerusalem, and let us be no longer a reproach.

18 And I shewed them how the hand of my God was good with me, and the king's words which he had spoken to me. And I said: Let us rise up, and build. And their hands were strengthened in good.

19 But Sanaballat the Horonite, and Tobias the servant, the Ammonite, and Gossem the Arabian heard of it; and they scoffed at us, and despised us, and said: What is this thing that you do? Are you going to rebel against the king?

20 And I answered them, and said to them: The God of heaven he helpeth us, and we are his servants. Let us rise up and build: but you have no part, nor justice, nor remembrance in Jerusalem.

CHAPTER 3

They begin to build the walls. The names and order of the builders.

THEN Eliasib the high priest arose, and his brethren the priests, and they built the flock gate. They sanctified it, and set up the doors thereof: even unto the tower of a hundred cubits they sanctified it, unto the tower of Hananeel.

2 And next to him the men of Jericho built. And next to them built Zachur the son of Amri.

3 But the fish gate the sons of Asnaa built: they covered it, and set up the doors thereof, and the locks, and the bars. And next to them built Marimuth the son of Urias the son of Accus.

4 And next to him built Mosollam the son of Barachias, the son of Merezebel. And next to them built Sadoc the son of Baana.

5 And next to them the Thecuites built: but their great men did not put their necks to the work of their Lord.

6 And Joiada the son of Phasea, and Mosollam the son of Besodia built the old gate: they covered it and set up the doors thereof, and the locks, and the bars.

7 And next to them built Meltias the Gabaonite, and Jadon the Meronathite, the men of Gabaon and Maspha, for the governor that was in the country beyond the river.

8 And next to him built Eziel the son of Araia the goldsmith. And next to him built Ananias the son of the perfumer: and they left Jerusalem unto the wall of the broad street.

9 And next to him built Raphaia the son of Hur, lord of the street of Jerusalem.

10 And next to him Jedaia the son of Haromaph, over against his own house. And next to him built Hattus the son of Hasebonia.

11 Melchias the son of Herem, and Hasub the son of Phahath Moab, built half the street, and the tower of the furnaces.

12 And next to him built Sellum the son of Alohes, lord of half the street of Jerusalem, he and his daughters.

13 And the gate of the valley Hanun built, and the inhabitants of Zanoe: they built it, and set up the doors thereof, and the locks, and the bars, and a thousand cubits in the wall unto the gate of the dunghill.

14 And the gate of the dunghill Melchias the son of Rechab built, lord of the street of Bethacharam: he built it, and set up the doors thereof, and the locks, and the bars.

15 And the gate of the fountain Sellum the son of Cholhoza built, lord of the street of Maspha: he built it, and covered it, and set up the doors thereof, and the locks, and the bars, and the walls of the pool of Siloe unto the king's guard, and unto the steps that go down from the city of David.

16 After him built Nehemias the son of Azboc, lord of half the street of Bethsur: as far as over against the sepulchre of David, and to the pool that was built with great labour, and to the house of the mighty.

17 After him built the Levites, Rehum the son of Benni. After him built Hasebias, lord of half the street of Ceila in his own street.

18 After him built their brethren, Bavai the son of Enadad, lord of half Ceila.

19 And next to him Aser the son of Josue, lord of Maspha, built another measure, over against the going up of the strong corner.

20 After him, in the mount, Baruch the son of Zachai built another measure, from the corner to the door of the house of Eliasib the high priest.

21 After him Merimuth the son of Urias the son of Haccus, built another measure, from the door of the house of Eliasib to the end of the house of Eliasib.

22 And after him built the priests, the men of the plains of the Jordan.

23 After him built Benjamin and Hasub, over against their own house. And after him built Azarias the son of Maasias the son of Ananias, over against his house.

24 After him built Bennui the son of Hanadad another measure, from the

house of Azarias unto the bending; and unto the corner.

25 Phalel, the son of Ozi, over against the bending and the tower, which lieth out from the king's high house, that is, in the court of the prison. After him Phadaia the son of Pharos.

26 And the Nathinites dwelt in Ophel, as far as over against the water gate toward the east, and the tower that stood out.

27 After him the Thecuites built another measure over against, from the great tower that standeth out unto the wall of the temple.

28 And upward from the horse gate the priests built, every man over against his house.

29 After them built Sadoc the son of Emmer over against his house. And after him built Semaia the son of Sechenias, keeper of the east gate.

30 After him built Hanania the son of Selemia, and Hanun the sixth son of Seleph, another measure. After him built Mosollam the son of Barachias over against his treasury. After him Melcias the goldsmith's son built unto the house of the Nathinites and of the sellers of small wares, over against the judgment gate, and unto the chamber of the corner.

31 And within the chamber of the corner of the flock gate, the goldsmiths and the merchants built.

CHAPTER 4

The building is carried on notwithstanding the opposition of their enemies.

AND it came to pass, that when Sanaballat heard that we were building the wall he was angry. And being moved exceedingly he scoffed at the Jews;

2 And said before his brethren, and the multitude of the Samaritans: What are the silly Jews doing? Will the Gentiles let them alone? Will they sacrifice and make an end in a day? Are they able to raise stones out of the heaps of the rubbish, which are burnt?

3 Tobias also the Ammonite who was by him said: Let them build; if a fox go up, he will leap over their stone wall.

4 Hear thou our God, for we are despised. Turn their reproach upon their own head, and give them to be despised in a land of captivity.

5 Cover not their iniquity, and let not their sin be blotted out from before thy face, because they have mocked thy builders.

6 So we built the wall, and joined it all together unto the half thereof: and the heart of the people was excited to work.

7 And it came to pass, when Sanaballat, and Tobias, and the Arabians, and the Ammonites, and the Azotians heard that the walls of Jerusalem were made up, and the breaches began to be closed, that they were exceedingly angry.

8 And they all assembled themselves together, to come, and to fight against Jerusalem, and to prepare ambushes.

9 And we prayed to our God, and set watchmen upon the wall day and night against them.

10 And Juda said: The strength of the bearer of burdens is decayed, and the rubbish is very much; and we shall not be able to build the wall.

11 And our enemies said: Let them not know, nor understand, till we come in the midst of them, and kill them, and cause the work to cease.

12 And it came to pass, that when the Jews that dwelt by them came and told us ten times, out of all the places from whence they came to us:

13 I set the people in the place behind the wall round about in order, with their swords, and spears, and bows.

14 And I looked and rose up. And I said to the chief men and the magistrates, and to the rest of the common people: Be not afraid of them. Remember the Lord who is great and terrible: and fight for your brethren, your sons, and your daughters, and your wives, and your houses.

15 And it came to pass, when our enemies heard that the thing had been told us, that God defeated their counsel. And we returned all of us to the walls, every man to his work.

16 And it came to pass from that day forward, that half of their young men did the work, and half were ready for to fight, with spears, and shields, and bows, and coats of mail: and the rulers were behind them in all the house of Juda.

17 Of them that built on the wall and that carried burdens, and that laded: with one of his hands he did the work, and with the other he held a sword.

18 For every one of the builders was girded with a sword about his reins. And they built, and sounded with a trumpet by me.

19 And I said to the nobles, and to the magistrates, and to the rest of the common people: The work is great and wide; and we are separated on the wall, one far from another.

20 In what place soever you shall hear the sound of the trumpet, run all thither unto us. Our God will fight for us.

21 And let us do the work: and let one half of us hold our spears from the rising of the morning till the stars appear.

22 At that time also I said to the people: Let every one with his servant stay in the midst of Jerusalem; and let us take our turns in the night, and by day, to work.

23 Now I and my brethren, and my servants, and the watchmen that followed me, did not put off our clothes: only every man stripped himself when he was to be washed.

CHAPTER 5

Nehemias blameth the rich, for their op-pressing the poor. His exhortation, and bounty to his countrymen.

NOW there was a great cry of the people, and of their wives against their brethren the Jews.

2 And there were some that said: Our sons and our daughters are very many. Let us take up corn for the price of them; and let us eat and live.

3 And there were some that said: Let us mortgage our lands, and our vineyards, and our houses; and let us take corn because of the famine.

4 And others said: Let us borrow money for the king's tribute; and let us give up our fields and vineyards.

5 And now our flesh is as the flesh of our brethren; and our children as their children. Behold we bring into bondage our sons and our daughters; and some of our daughters are bondwomen already. Neither have we wherewith to redeem them; and our fields and our vineyards other men possess.

6 And I was exceedingly angry when I heard their cry according to these words.

7 And my heart thought with myself; and I rebuked the nobles and magistrates, and said to them: Do you every one exact usury of your brethren? And I gathered together a great assembly against them.

8 And I said to them: We, as you know, have redeemed according to our ability our brethren the Jews, that were sold to the Gentiles; and will you then sell your brethren, for us to redeem them? And they held their peace, and found not what to answer.

9 And I said to them: The thing you do is not good. Why walk you not in the fear of our God, that we be not exposed to the reproaches of the Gentiles our enemies?

10 Both I and my brethren, and my servants, have lent money and corn to many. Let us all agree not to call for it again: let us forgive the debt that is owing to us.

11 Restore ye to them this day their fields, and their vineyards, and their oliveyards, and their houses. And the hundredth part of the money, and of the corn, the wine, and the oil, which you were wont to exact of them, give it rather for them.

12 And they said: We will restore, and we will require nothing of them; and we will do as thou sayest. And I called the priests and took an oath of them, to do according to what I had said.

13 Moreover I shook my lap, and said: So may God shake every man that shall not accomplish this word, out of his house, and out of his labours. Thus may he be shaken out and become empty. And all the multitude said: Amen. And they praised God. And the people did according to what was said.

14 And from the day, in which the king commanded me to be governor in the land of Juda, from the twentieth year even to the two and thirtieth year of Artaxerxes the king, for twelve years, I and my brethren did not eat the yearly allowance that was due to the governors.

15 But the former governors that had been before me, were chargeable to the people; and took of them in bread, and wine, and in money, every day forty sicles: and their officers also oppressed the people. But I did not so for the fear of God.

16 Moreover I built in the work of the wall; and I bought no land; and all my servants were gathered together to the work.

17 The Jews also and the magistrates to the number of one hundred and fifty men, were at my table, besides them that came to us from among the nations that were round about us.

18 And there was prepared for me day by day one ox, and six choice rams, besides fowls: and once in ten days I gave store of divers wines, and many other things. Yet I did not require my yearly allowance as governor: for the people were very much impoverished.

19 Remember me, O my God, for good according to all that I have done for this people.

CHAPTER 6

The enemies seek to terrify Nehemias. He proceedeth and finisheth the wall.

AND it came to pass, when Sanaballat, and Tobias, and Gossem the Arabian, and the rest of our enemies, heard that I had built the wall, and that there was no breach left in it (though at that time I had not set up the doors in the gates:

2 Sanaballat and Gossem sent to me, saying: Come, and let us make a league together in the villages, in the plain of Ono. But they thought to do me mischief.

3 And I sent messengers to them, saying: I am doing a great work, and I cannot come down, lest it be neglected whilst I come and go down to you.

4 And they sent to me, according to this word, four times: and I answered them after the same manner.

5 And Sanaballat sent his servant to me the fifth time according to the former word; and he had a letter in his hand written in this manner:

6 It is reported amongst the Gentiles, and Gossem hath said it, that thou and the Jews think to rebel; and therefore thou buildest the wall and hast a mind to set thyself king over them. For which end

7 Thou hast also set up prophets, to preach of thee at Jerusalem, saying: There is a king in Judea. The king will hear of these things. Therefore come now, that we may take counsel together.

8 And I sent to them, saying: There is no such thing done as thou sayest: but thou feignest these things out of thy own heart.

9 For all these men thought to frighten us, thinking that our hands would cease from the work, and that we would leave off. Wherefore I strengthened my hands the more.

10 And I went into the house of Samaia the son of Delaia the son of Metabeel, privately. And he said: Let us consult together in the house of God in the midst of the temple. And let us shut the doors of the temple; for they will come to kill thee, and in the night they will come to slay thee.

11 And I said: Should such a man as I flee? And who is there that being as I am, would go into the temple to save his life? I will not go in.

12 And I understood that God had not sent him: but that he had spoken to me as if he had been prophesying; and Tobias, and Sanaballat had hired him.

13 For he had taken money, that I being afraid should do this thing and sin; and they might have some evil to upbraid me withal.

14 Remember me, O Lord, for Tobias and Sanaballat, according to their works of this kind: and Noadias the prophet, and the rest of the prophets that would have put me in fear.

15 But the wall was finished the five and twentieth day of the month of Elul, in two and fifty days.

16 And it came to pass when all our enemies heard of it, that all nations which were round about us were afraid and were cast down within themselves: for they perceived that this work was the work of God.

17 Moreover in those days many letters were sent by the principal men of the Jews to Tobias, and from Tobias there came letters to them.

18 For there were many in Judea sworn to him: because he was the son-in-law of Sechenias the son of Area, and Johanan his son had taken to wife the daughter of Mosollam the son of Barachias.

19 And they praised him also before me, and they related my words to him. And Tobias sent letters to put me in fear.

CHAPTER 7

Nehemias appointeth watchmen in Jerusalem. The list of those who came first from Babylon.

NOW [1] after the wall was built, and I had set up the doors, and numbered the porters and singing men, and Levites:

2 I commanded Hanani my brother, and Hananias ruler of the house of Jerusalem (for he seemed as a sincere man, and one that feared God above the rest).

3 And I said to them: Let not the gates of Jerusalem be opened till the sun be hot. And while they were yet standing by, the gates were shut, and barred: and I set watchmen of the inhabitants of Jerusalem, every one by their courses, and every man over against his house.

4 And the city was very wide and great; and the people few in the midst thereof; and the houses were not built.

5 But God had put in my heart, and I assembled the princes and magistrates and common people, to number them. And I found a book of the number of them who came up at first, and therein it was found written:

6 [2] These are the children of the province, who came up from the captivity of them that had been carried away, whom Nabuchodonosor the king of Babylon had carried away, and who returned into Judea, every one into his own city.

7 Who came with Zorobabel: Josue, Nehemias, Azarias, Raamias, Nahamani, Mardochai, Belsam, Mespharath, Begoia, Nahum, Baana. The number of the men of the people of Israel:

8 The children of Pharos, two thousand one hundred seventy-two.

9 The children of Sephatia, three hundred seventy-two.

CHAP. 7. [1] Ecclus. 49, 15. [2] 1 Esd. 2, 1.

10 The children of Area, six hundred fifty-two.

11 The children of Phahath Moab of the children of Josue and Joab, two thousand eight hundred eighteen.

12 The children of Elam, one thousand two hundred fifty-four.

13 The children of Zethua, eight hundred forty-five.

14 The children of Zachai, seven hundred sixty.

15 The children of Bannui, six hundred forty-eight.

16 The children of Bebai, six hundred twenty-eight.

17 The children of Azgad, two thousand three hundred twenty-two.

18 The children of Adonicam, six hundred sixty-seven.

19 The children of Beguai, two thousand sixty-seven.

20 The children of Adin, six hundred fifty-five.

21 The children of Ater, children of Hezechias, ninety-eight.

22 The children of Hasem, three hundred twenty-eight.

23 The children of Besai, three hundred twenty-four.

24 The children of Hareph, a hundred and twelve.

25 The children of Gabaon, ninety-five.

26 The children of Bethlehem, and Netupha, a hundred eighty-eight.

27 The men of Anathoth, a hundred twenty-eight.

28 The men of Bethazmoth, forty-two.

29 The men of Cariathiarim, Cephira, and Beroth, seven hundred forty-three.

30 The men of Rama and Geba, six hundred twenty-one.

31 The men of Machmas, a hundred twenty-two.

32 The men of Bethel and Hai, a hundred twenty-three.

33 The men of the other Nebo, fifty-two.

34 The men of the other Elam, one thousand two hundred fifty-four.

35 The children of Harem, three hundred and twenty.

36 The children of Jericho, three hundred forty-five.

37 The children of Lod, of Hadid and Ono, seven hundred twenty-one.

38 The children of Senaa, three thousand nine hundred thirty.

39 The priests: The children of Idaia in the house of Josue, nine hundred and seventy-three.

40 The children of Emmer, one thousand fifty-two.

41 The children of Phashur, one thousand two hundred forty-seven.

42 The children of Arem, one thousand and seventeen. The Levites

43 The children of Josue and Cedmihel, the sons

44 Of Oduia, seventy-four. The singing men:

45 The children of Asaph, a hundred forty-eight.

46 The porters: The children of Sellum, the children of Ater, the children of Telmon, the children of Accub, the children of Hatita, the children of Sobai, a hundred thirty-eight.

47 The Nathinites: The children of Soha, the children of Hasupha, the children of Tebbaoth,

48 The children of Ceros, the children of Siaa, the children of Phadon, the children of Lebana, the children of Hagaba, the children of Selmai,

49 The children of Hanan, the children of Geddel, the children of Gaher,

50 The children of Raaia, the children of Rasin, the children of Necoda,

51 The children of Gezem, the children of Asa, the children of Phasea,

52 The children of Besai, the children of Munim, the children of Nephussim,

53 The children of Bacbuc, the children of Hacupha, the children of Harhur,

54 The children of Besloth, the children of Mahida, the children of Harsa,

55 The children of Bercos, the children of Sisara, the children of Thema,

56 The children of Nasia, the children of Hatipha.

57 The children of the servants of Solomon: The children of Sothai, the children of Sophereth, the children of Pharida,

58 The children of Jahala, the children of Darcon, the children of Jeddel,

59 The children of Saphatia, the children of Hatil, the children of Phochereth, who was born of Sabaim the son of Amon.

60 All the Nathinites, and the children of the servants of Solomon, three hundred ninety-two.

61 And these are they that came up from Telmela, Thelharsa, Cherub, Addon, and Emmer; and could not shew the house of their fathers, nor their seed, whether they were of Israel:

62 The children of Dalaia, the children of Tobia, the children of Necoda, six hundred forty-two.

63 And of the priests: The children of Habia, the children of Accos, the

children of Berzellai, who took a wife of the daughters of Berzellai the Galaadite; and he was called by their name.

64 These sought their writing in the record, and found it not: and they were cast out of the priesthood.

65 And Athersatha said to them, that they should not eat of the Holies of Holies, until there stood up a priest learned and skilful.

66 All the multitude as it were one man, forty-two thousand three hundred sixty,

67 Beside their men-servants and women-servants, who were seven thousand three hundred thirty-seven: and among them singing men, and singing women, two hundred forty-five.

68 Their horses, seven hundred thirty-six. Their mules, two hundred forty-five:

69 Their camels, four hundred thirty-five. Their asses, six thousand seven hundred and twenty.

Hitherto is related what was written in the record. From this place forward goeth on the history of Nehemias.

70 And some of the heads of the families gave unto the work. Athersatha gave into the treasure a thousand drams of gold, fifty bowls, and five hundred and thirty garments for priests.

71 And some of the heads of families gave to the treasure of the work, twenty thousand drams of gold, and two thousand two hundred pounds of silver.

72 And that which the rest of the people gave, was twenty thousand drams of gold, and two thousand pounds of silver, and sixty-seven garments for priests.

73 And the priests, and the Levites, and the porters, and the singing men, and the rest of the common people, and the Nathinites, and all Israel dwelt in their cities.

CHAPTER 8

Esdras readeth the law before the people. Nehemias comforteth them. They celebrate the feast of tabernacles.

AND the seventh month came: and the children of Israel were in their cities. And all the people were gathered together as one man to the street which is before the water gate: and they spoke to Esdras the scribe, to bring the book of the law of Moses, which the Lord had commanded to Israel.

2 Then Esdras the priest brought the law before the multitude of men and women, and all those that could understand, in the first day of the seventh month.

3 And he read it plainly in the street that was before the water gate, from the morning until midday, before the men, and the women, and all those that could understand: and the ears of all the people were attentive to the book.

4 And Esdras the scribe stood upon a step of wood, which he had made to speak upon. And there stood by him Mathathias, and Semeia, and Ania, and Uria, and Helcia, and Maasia, on his right hand: and on the left, Phadaia, Misael, and Melchia, and Hasum, and Hasbadana, Zacharia and Mosollam.

5 And Esdras opened the book before all the people: for he was above all the people. And when he had opened it, all the people stood.

6 And Esdras blessed the Lord the great God. And all the people answered: Amen, Amen; lifting up their hands. And they bowed down, and adored God with their faces to the ground.

7 Now Josue, and Bani, and Serebia, Jamin, Accub, Sephtai, Odia, Maasia, Celtia, Azarias, Jozabed, Hanan, Phalaia, the Levites, made silence among the people to hear the law: and the people stood in their place.

8 And they read in the book of the law of God distinctly and plainly to be understood: and they understood when it was read.

9 And Nehemias (he is Athersatha) and Esdras the priest and scribe, and the Levites who interpreted to all the people, said: This is a holy day to the Lord our God: do not mourn, nor weep. For all the people wept, when they heard the words of the law.

10 And he said to them: Go, eat fat meats, and drink sweet wine, and send portions to them that have not prepared for themselves; because it is the holy day of the Lord, and be not sad. For the joy of the Lord is our strength.

11 And the Levites stilled all the people, saying: Hold your peace, for the day is holy, and be not sorrowful.

12 So all the people went to eat and drink, and to send portions, and to make great mirth: because they understood the words that he had taught them.

13 And on the second day the chiefs of the families of all the people, the priests, and the Levites were gathered together to Esdras the scribe, that he should interpret to them the words of the law.

14 And they found written in the law, that the Lord had commanded by the

CHAP. 7. Ver. 70. *Athersatha* That is, Nehemias; as appears from chap. 12. Either that he was so called at the court of the king of Persia, where he was cupbearer: or that, as some think, this name signifies *governor;* and he was at that time governor of Judea.

hand of Moses, that the children of Israel should dwell in tabernacles, on the feast, in the seventh month.

15 And that they should proclaim and publish the word in all their cities, and in Jerusalem, saying: Go forth to the mount, and fetch branches of olive, and branches of beautiful wood, branches of myrtle, and branches of palm, and branches of thick trees, to make tabernacles, as it is written.

16 And the people went forth, and brought. And they made themselves tabernacles every man on the top of his house, and in their courts, and in the courts of the house of God, and in the street of the water gate, and in the street of the gate of Ephraim.

17 And all the assembly of them that were returned from the captivity ¹ made tabernacles, and dwelt in tabernacles. For since the days of Josue the son of Nun the children of Israel had not done so, until that day. And there was exceeding great joy.

18 And he read in the book of the law of God day by day, from the first day till the last. And they kept the solemnity seven days, and in the eighth day a solemn assembly according to the manner.

CHAPTER 9

The people repent with fasting and sackcloth. The Levites confess God's benefits, and the people's ingratitude. They pray for them, and make a covenant with God.

AND in the four and twentieth day of the month the children of Israel came together with fasting and with sackcloth, and earth upon them.

2 And the seed of the children of Israel separated themselves from every stranger: and they stood, and confessed their sins, and the iniquities of their fathers.

3 And they rose up to stand: and they read in the book of the law of the Lord their God, four times in the day. And four times they confessed, and adored the Lord their God.

4 And there stood up upon the step of the Levites, Josue, and Bani, and Cedmihel, Sabania, Bonni, Sarebias, Bani, and Chanani: and they cried with a loud voice to the Lord their God.

5 And the Levites, Josue and Cedmihel, Bonni, Hasebnia, Serebia, Oduia, Sebnia, and Phathahia, said: Arise,

bless the Lord your God from eternity to eternity: and blessed be the high name of thy glory with all blessing and praise.

6 Thou thyself, O Lord alone, thou hast made heaven, and the heaven of heavens, and all the host thereof: the earth and all things that are in it: the seas and all that are therein. And thou givest life to all these things, and the host of heaven adoreth thee.

7 Thou, O Lord God, art he who chosest Abram, ¹ and broughtest him forth out of the fire of the Chaldeans, and gavest him the name of Abraham.

8 And thou didst find his heart faithful before thee. And thou madest a covenant with him, to give him the land of the Chanaanite, of the Hethite, and of the Amorrhite, and of the Pherezite, and of the Jebusite, and of the Gergezite, to give it to his seed. And thou hast fulfilled thy words, because thou art just.

9 And thou sawest the affliction of our fathers in Egypt: and thou didst hear their cry by the Red Sea.

10 And thou shewedst signs and wonders upon Pharao, and upon all his servants, and upon the people of his land: for thou knewest that they dealt proudly against them. And thou madest thyself a name, as it is at this day.

11 And thou didst divide the sea before them, and they passed through the midst of the sea on dry land: but their persecutors thou threwest into the depth, as a stone into mighty waters.

12 And in a pillar of a cloud thou wast their leader by day, and in a pillar of fire by night, that they might see the way by which they went.

13 Thou camest down also to mount Sinai, and didst speak with them from heaven: and thou gavest them right judgments, and the law of truth, ceremonies, and good precepts.

14 Thou madest known to them thy holy sabbath, and didst prescribe to them commandments, and ceremonies, and the law, by the hand of Moses thy servant.

15 And thou gavest them bread from heaven in their hunger, and broughtest forth water for them out of the rock in their thirst. And thou saidst to them that they should go in, and possess the land, upon which thou hadst lifted up thy hand to give it them.

16 But they and our fathers dealt proudly, and hardened their necks, and hearkened not to thy commandments.

17 And they would not hear, and they remembered not thy wonders which thou hadst done for them. And they

CHAP. 8. ¹ Lev. 23, 39. CHAP. 9. ¹ Gen. 11, 31.

CHAP. 9. Ver. 7. *The fire of the Chaldeans.* The city of *Ur* in Chaldea, the name of which signifies *fire.* Or out of the fire of the tribulations and temptations to which he was there exposed.—The ancient Rabbins understood this literally, affirming that Abram was cast into the fire by the idolaters, and brought out by a miracle without any hurt.

Ver. 17. *And gave the head.* That is, they set their *head,* or were bent to return to Egypt.

hardened their necks, and gave the head to return to their bondage, as it were by contention. But thou, a forgiving God, gracious, and merciful, long-suffering, and full of compassion, didst not forsake them.

18 Yea, when they had made also to themselves a molten calf, and had said: This is thy God, that brought thee out of Egypt; and had committed great blasphemies.

19 Yet thou, in thy many mercies, didst not leave them in the desert. The pillar of the cloud departed not from them by day to lead them in the way, and the pillar of fire by night to shew them the way by which they should go.

20 And thou gavest them thy good Spirit to teach them; and thy manna thou didst not withhold from their mouth; and thou gavest them water for their thirst.

21 Forty years didst thou feed them in the desert, and nothing was wanting to them: their garments did not grow old, and their feet were not worn.

22 And thou gavest them kingdoms, and nations, and didst divide lots for them. And they possessed the land of Sehon, and the land of the king of Hesebon, and the land of Og king of Basan.

23 And thou didst multiply their children as the stars of heaven: and broughtest them to the land concerning which thou hadst said to their fathers, that they should go in and possess it.

24 And the children came and possessed the land: and thou didst humble before them the inhabitants of the land, the Chanaanites, and gavest them into their hands, with their kings, and the people of the land, that they might do with them as it pleased them.

25 And they took strong cities and a fat land, and possessed houses full of all goods: cisterns made by others, vineyards, and oliveyards, and fruit trees in abundance. And they ate, and were filled, and became fat, and abounded with delight in thy great goodness.

26 But they provoked thee to wrath, and departed from thee, and threw thy law behind their backs. And they killed thy prophets, who admonished them earnestly to return to thee. And they were guilty of great blasphemies.

27 And thou gavest them into the hands of their enemies, and they afflicted them. And in the time of their tribulation they cried to thee; and thou heardest from heaven. And according to the multitude of thy tender mercies thou gavest them saviours, to save them from the hands of their enemies.

28 But after they had rest, they returned to do evil in thy sight: and thou leftest them in the hand of their enemies, and they had dominion over them. Then they returned, and cried to thee: and thou heardest from heaven, and deliveredst them many times in thy mercies.

29 And thou didst admonish them to return to thy law. But they dealt proudly, and hearkened not to thy commandments, but sinned against thy judgments, which if a man do, he shall live in them. And they withdrew the shoulder, and hardened their neck, and would not hear.

30 And thou didst forbear with them for many years, and didst testify against them by thy spirit, by the hand of thy prophets. And they heard not; and thou didst deliver them into the hand of the people of the lands.

31 Yet in thy very many mercies thou didst not utterly consume them, nor forsake them: because thou art a merciful and gracious God.

32 Now therefore our God, great, strong, and terrible, who keepest covenant and mercy, turn not away from thy face all the labour which hath come upon us: upon our kings, and our princes, and our priests, and our prophets, and our fathers, and all the people, from the days of the king of Assur, until this day.

33 And thou art just in all things that have come upon us: because thou hast done truth, but we have done wickedly.

34 Our kings, our princes, our priests, and our fathers have not kept thy law, and have not minded thy commandments, and thy testimonies which thou hast testified among them.

35 And they have not served thee in their kingdoms, and in thy manifold goodness, which thou gavest them, and in the large and fat land, which thou deliveredst before them: nor did they return from their most wicked devices.

36 Behold we ourselves this day are bondmen: and the land, which thou gavest our fathers, to eat the bread thereof, and the good things thereof; and we ourselves are servants in it.

37 And the fruits thereof grow up for the kings, whom thou hast set over us for our sins; and they have dominion over our bodies, and over our beasts, according to their will; and we are in great tribulation.

38 And because of all this we ourselves make a covenant, and write it: and our princes, our Levites, and our priests sign it.

CHAPTER 10

The names of the subscribers to the covenant, and the contents of it.

AND the subscribers were Nehemias Athersatha the son of Hachelai, and Sedecias,

2 Saraias, Azarias, Jeremias,

3 Pheshur, Amarias, Melchias,

4 Hattus, Sebenia, Melluch,

5 Harem, Merimuth, Obdias,

6 Daniel, Genthon, Baruch,

7 Mosollam, Abia, Miamin,

8 Maazia, Belgia, Semeia: these were priests.

9 And the Levites; Josue the son of Azanias, Bennui of the sons of Henadad, Cedmihel,

10 And their brethren, Sebenia, Oduia, Celita, Phalaia, Hanan,

11 Micha, Rohob, Hasebia,

12 Zachur, Serebia, Sabania,

13 Odaia, Bani, Baninu.

14 The heads of the people: Pharos, Phahath Moab, Elam, Zethu, Bani,

15 Bonni, Azgad, Bebai,

16 Adonia, Begoai, Adin,

17 Ater, Hezecia, Azur,

18 Odaia, Hasum, Besai,

19 Hareph, Anathoth, Neba,

20 Megphias, Mosollam, Hazir,

21 Mesizabel, Sadoc, Jeddua,

22 Pheltia, Hanan, Anaia,

23 Osee, Hanania, Hasub,

24 Alohes, Phalea, Sobec,

25 Rehum, Hasebna, Maasia,

26 Echaia, Hanan, Anan,

27 Melluch, Haran, Baana.

28 And the rest of the people, priests, Levites, porters, and singing men, Nathinites, and all that had separated themselves from the people of the lands to the law of God, their wives, their sons, and their daughters.

29 All that could understand promising for their brethren, with their chief men. And they came to promise and swear that they would walk in the law of God, which he gave in the hand of Moses the servant of God: that they would do and keep all the commandments of the Lord our God, and his judgments and his ceremonies.

30 And that we would not give our daughters to the people of the land, nor take their daughters for our sons.

31 And if the people of the land bring in things to sell, or any things for use, to sell them on the sabbath day, that we would not buy them of them on the sabbath, or on the holy day. And that we would leave the seventh year, and the exaction of every hand.

32 And we made ordinances for ourselves, to give the third part of a sicle every year for the work of the house of our God:

33 For the loaves of proposition, and for the continual sacrifice, and for a continual holocaust on the sabbaths, on the new moons, on the set feasts, and for the holy things, and for the sin offering: that atonement might be made for Israel, and for every use of the house of our God.

34 And we cast lots among the priests, and the Levites, and the people for the offering of wood, that it might be brought into the house of our God by the houses of our fathers at set times, from year to year: to burn upon the altar of the Lord our God, as it is written in the law of Moses.

35 And that we would bring the firstfruits of our land, and the firstfruits of all fruit of every tree, from year to year, in the house of our Lord.

36 And the firstborn of our sons, and of our cattle, as it is written in the law. and the firstlings of our oxen, and of our sheep, to be offered in the house of our God, to the priests who minister in the house of our God.

37 And that we would bring the firstfruits of our meats, and of our libations, and the fruit of every tree, of the vintage also and of oil to the priests, to the storehouse of our God; and the tithes of our ground to the Levites. The Levites also shall receive the tithes of our works out of all the cities.

38 And the priest, the son of Aaron, shall be with the Levites in the tithes of the Levites; and the Levites shall offer the tithe of their tithes in the house of our God, to the storeroom into the treasure house.

39 For the children of Israel and the children of Levi shall carry to the treasury the firstfruits of corn, of wine, and of oil. And the sanctified vessels shall be there, and the priests, and the singing men, and the porters and ministers. And we will not forsake the house of our God.

CHAPTER 11

Who were the inhabitants of Jerusalem, and the other cities.

AND the princes of the people dwelt at Jerusalem: but the rest of the people cast lots, to take one part in ten to dwell in Jerusalem the holy city; and nine parts in the *other* cities.

2 And the people blessed all the men that willingly offered themselves to dwell in Jerusalem.

3 These therefore are the chief men of the province, who dwelt in Jerusalem, and in the cities of Juda. And every one

dwelt in his possession, in their cities: Israel, the priests, the Levites, the Nathinites, and the children of the servants of Solomon.

4 And in Jerusalem there dwelt some of the children of Juda, and some of the children of Benjamin. Of the children of Juda, Athaias the son of Aziam, the son of Zacharias, the son of Amarias, the son of Saphatias, the son of Malaleel. Of the sons of Phares:

5 Maasia the son of Baruch, the son of Cholhoza, the son of Hazia, the son of Adaia, the son of Joiarib, the son of Zacharias, the son of the Silonite.

6 All these the sons of Phares, who dwelt in Jerusalem, were four hundred sixty-eight valiant men.

7 And these are the children of Benjamin: Sellum the son of Mosollam, the son of Joed, the son of Phadaia, the son of Colaia, the son of Masia, the son of Etheel, the son of Isaia.

8 And after him Gebbai, Sellai: nine hundred twenty-eight.

9 And Joel the son of Zechri their ruler: and Judas the son of Senua was second over the city.

10 And of the priests Idaia the son of Joarib, Jachin,

11 Saraia the son of Helcias, the son of Mosollam, the son of Sadoc, the son of Meraioth the son of Achitob, the prince of the house of God.

12 And their brethren that do the works of the temple: eight hundred twenty-two. And Adaia the son of Jeroham, the son of Phelelia, the son of Amsi, the son of Zacharias, the son of Pheshur, the son of Melchias.

13 And his brethren the chiefs of the fathers: two hundred forty-two. And Amassai the son of Azreel, the son of Ahazi, the son of Mosollamoth, the son of Emmer,

14 And their brethren who were very mighty: a hundred twenty-eight. And their ruler Zabdiel son of the mighty.

15 And of the Levites: Semeia the son of Hasub, the son of Azaricam, the son of Hasabia, the son of Boni,

16 And Sabathai and Jozabed, who were over all the outward business of the house of God, of the princes of the Levites.

17 And Mathania the son of Micha, the son of Zebedei, the son of Asaph, was the principal man to praise, and to give glory in prayer, and Becbecia the second, one of his brethren, and Abda the son of Samua, the son of Galal, the son of Idithun.

18 All the Levites in the holy city were two hundred eighty-four.

19 And the porters: Accub, Telmon, and their brethren, who kept the doors: a hundred seventy-two.

20 And the rest of Israel, the priests and the Levites were in all the cities of Juda, every man in his possession.

21 And the Nathinites that dwelt in Ophel, and Siaha, and Gaspha of the Nathinites.

22 And the overseer of the Levites in Jerusalem, was Azzi the son of Bani, the son of Hasabia, the son of Mathania, the son of Micha. Of the sons of Asaph, were the singing men in the ministry of the house of God.

23 For the king's commandment was concerning them, and an order among the singing men day by day.

24 And Phathahia the son of Mesezebel of the children of Zara the son of Juda was at the hand of the king, in all matters concerning the people.

25 And in the houses through all their countries. Of the children of Juda, some dwelt at Cariath-Arbe, and in the villages thereof: and at Dibon, and in the villages thereof: and at Cabseel, and in the villages thereof:

26 And at Jesue, and at Molada, and at Bethphaleth:

27 And at Hasersual, and at Bersabee, and in the villages thereof:

28 And at Siceleg, and at Mochona, and in the villages thereof:

29 And at Remmon, and at Saraa, and at Jerimuth,

30 Zanoa, Odollam, and in their villages: at Lachis and its dependencies: and at Azeca and the villages thereof. And they dwelt from Bersabee unto the valley of Ennom.

31 And the children of Benjamin from Geba, at Mechmas, and at Hai, and at Bethel, and in the villages thereof:

32 At Anathoth, Nob, Anania,

33 Asor, Rama, Gethaim,

34 Hadid, Seboim, and Neballat, Lod,

35 And Ono the valley of craftsmen.

36 And of the Levites were portions of Juda and Benjamin.

CHAPTER 12

The priests, and Levites that came up with Zorobabel. The succession of high priests. The solemnity of the dedication of the wall.

NOW these are the priests and the Levites, that went up with Zorobabel the son of Salathiel, and Josue: Saraia, Jeremias, Esdras,

2 Amaria, Melluch, Hattus,

3 Sebenias, Rheum, Merimuth,

4 Addo, Genthon, Abia,

5 Miamin, Madia, Belga,

6 Semeia, and Joiarib, Idaia, Sellum, Amoc, Helcias,

7 Idaia. These were the chief of the priests, and of their brethren in the days of Josue.

8 And the Levites: Jesua, Bennui, Cedmihel, Sarebia, Juda, Mathanias. They and their brethren were over the hymns.

9 And Becbecia, and Hanni, and their brethren every one in his office.

10 And Josue begot Joacim, and Joacim begot Eliasib, and Eliasib begot Joiada,

11 And Joiada begot Jonathan, and Jonathan begot Jeddoa.

12 And in the days of Joacim the priests and heads of the families were: Of Saraia, Maraia: of Jeremias, Hanania:

13 Of Esdras, Mosollam: and of Amaria, Johanan:

14 Of Milicho, Jonathan: of Sebenia, Joseph:

15 Of Haram, Edna: of Maraioth, Helci:

16 Of Adaia, Zacharia: of Genthon, Mosollam:

17 Of Abia, Zechri: of Miamin and Moadia, Phelti:

18 Of Belga, Sammua of Semaia, Jonathan:

19 Of Joiarib, Mathanai: of Jodaia, Azzi:

20 Of Sellai, Celai: of Amoc, Heber:

21 Of Helcias, Hasebia: of Idaia, Nathanael.

22 The Levites the chiefs of the families in the days of Eliasib, and Joiada, and Johanan, and Jeddoa, were recorded: and the priests in the reign of Darius the Persian.

23 The sons of Levi, heads of the families, were written in the book of Chronicles, even unto the days of Jonathan the son of Eliasib.

24 Now the chief of the Levites were Hasebia, Serebia, and Josue the son of Cedmihel. And their brethren by their courses: to praise and to give thanks according to the commandment of David the man of God, and to wait equally in order.

25 Mathania, and Becbecia, Obedia, and Mosollam, Telmon, Accub, were keepers of the gates and of the entrances before the gates.

26 These were in the days of Joacim the son of Josue, the son of Josedec, and in the days of Nehemias the governor, and of Esdras the priest and scribe.

27 And at the dedication of the wall of Jerusalem they sought the Levites out of all their places, to bring them to Jerusalem, and to keep the dedication, and to rejoice with thanksgiving,

and with singing, and with cymbals and psalteries and harps.

28 And the sons of the singing men were gathered together out of the plain country about Jerusalem, and out of the villages of Nethuphati:

29 And from the house of Galgal, and from the countries of Geba and Azmaveth. For the singing men had built themselves villages round about Jerusalem.

30 And the priests and the Levites were purified: and they purified the people, and the gates, and the wall.

31 And I made the princes of Juda go up upon the wall, and I appointed two great choirs to give praise. And they went on the right hand upon the wall toward the dunghill gate.

32 And after them went Osaias, and half of the princes of Juda:

33 And Azarias, Esdras, and Mosollam, Judas, and Benjamin, and Semeia, and Jeremias.

34 And of the sons of the priests with trumpets, Zacharias the son of Jonathan, the son of Semeia, the son of Mathania, the son of Michaia, the son of Zechur, the son of Asaph:

35 And his brethren Semeia, and Azareel, Malalai, Galalai, Maai, Nathanael, and Judas, and Hanani, with the musical instruments of David the man of God: and Esdras the scribe before them at the fountain gate.

36 And they went up over against them by the stairs of the city of David, at the going up of the wall of the house of David, and to the water gate eastward.

37 And the second choir of them that gave thanks went on the opposite side. And I after them; and the half of the people upon the wall, and upon the tower of the furnaces, even to the broad wall,

38 And above the gate of Ephraim, and above the old gate, and above the fish gate and the tower of Hananeel, and the tower of Emath, and even to the flock gate. And they stood still in the watch gate.

39 And the two choirs of them that gave praise stood still at the house of God: and I and the half of the magistrates with me.

40 And the priests, Eliachim, Maasia, Miamin, Michea, Elioenai, Zacharia, Hanania with trumpets,

41 And Maasia, and Semeia, and Eleazar, and Azzi, and Johanan, and Melchia, and Elam, and Ezer. And the singers sung loud, and Jezraia was their overseer.

42 And they sacrificed on that day great sacrifices, and they rejoiced: for

God had made them joyful with great joy. Their wives also and their children rejoiced; and the joy of Jerusalem was heard afar off.

43 They appointed also in that day men over the storehouses of the treasure, for the libations, and for the firstfruits, and for the tithes: that the rulers of the city might bring them in by them in honour of thanksgiving, for the priests and Levites. For Juda was joyful in the priests and Levites that assisted.

44 And they kept the watch of their God, and the observance of expiation. And the singing men, and the porters, according to the commandment of David, and of Solomon his son.

45 For in the days of David and Asaph from the beginning there were chief singers appointed, to praise with canticles and give thanks to God.

46 And all Israel, in the days of Zorobabel, and in the days of Nehemias, gave portions to the singing men, and to the porters, day by day. And they sanctified the Levites: and the Levites sanctified the sons of Aaron.

CHAPTER 13

Divers abuses are reformed.

AND [1] on that day they read in the book of Moses in the hearing of the people. And therein was found written, that the Ammonites and the Moabites should not come in to the church of God for ever.

2 Because they met not the children of Israel with bread and water: and they hired against them Balaam, to curse them; and our God turned the curse into blessing.

3 And it came to pass, when they had heard the law, that they separated every stranger from Israel.

4 And over this thing was Eliasib the priest, who was set over the treasury of the house of our God, and was near akin to Tobias.

5 And he made him a great storeroom, where before him they laid up gifts, and frankincense, and vessels, and the tithes of the corn, of the wine, and of the oil, the portions of the Levites, and of the singing men, and of the porters, and the firstfruits of the priests.

6 But in all this time I was not in Jerusalem, because in the two and thirtieth year of Artaxerxes king of Babylon, I went to the king, and after certain days I asked the king.

7 And I came to Jerusalem, and I understood the evil that Eliasib had done for Tobias, to make him a storehouse in the courts of the house of God.

8 And it seemed to me exceeding evil. And I cast forth the vessels of the house of Tobias out of the storehouse.

9 And I commanded and they cleansed the storehouses. And I brought thither again the vessels of the house of God, the sacrifice, and the frankincense.

10 And I perceived that the portions of the Levites had not been given them: and that the Levites, and the singing men, and they that ministered were fled away every man to his own country.

11 And I pleaded the matter against the magistrates, and said: Why have we forsaken the house of God? And I gathered them together, and I made them to stand in their places.

12 And all Juda brought the tithe of the corn, and the wine, and the oil into the storehouses.

13 And we set over the storehouses Selemias the priest, and Sadoc the scribe, and of the Levites Phadaia; and next to them Hanan the son of Zachur, the son of Mathania. For they were approved as faithful; and to them were committed the portions of their brethren.

14 Remember me, O my God, for this thing: and wipe not out my kindnesses, which I have done relating to the house of my God and his ceremonies.

15 In those days, I saw in Juda some treading the presses on the sabbath, and carrying sheaves, and lading asses with wine, and grapes, and figs, and all manner of burthens, and bringing them into Jerusalem on the sabbath day. And I charged them that they should sell on a day on which it was lawful to sell.

16 Some Tyrians also dwelt there, who brought fish, and all manner of wares. And they sold them on the sabbaths to the children of Juda in Jerusalem.

17 And I rebuked the chief men of Juda, and said to them: What is this evil thing that you are doing, profaning the sabbath day?

18 Did not our fathers do these things, and our God brought all this evil upon us, and upon this city? And you bring more wrath upon Israel by violating the sabbath.

19 And it came to pass, that when the gates of Jerusalem were at rest on the sabbath day, I spoke. And they shut the gates: and I commanded that they should not open them till after the sabbath. And I set some of my servants

---

CHAP. 13. [1] Deut. 23, 3.

CHAP. 12. Ver. 46. *Sanctified.* That is, they gave them that which by the law was set aside, and sanctified for their use.

CHAP. 13. Ver. 4. *Over this thing.* Or, he was faulty in this thing, or in this kind.

at the gates, that none should bring in burthens on the sabbath day.

20 So the merchants, and they that sold all kinds of wares, stayed without Jerusalem once or twice.

21 And I charged them, and I said to them: Why stay you before the wall? If you do so another time, I will lay hands on you. And from that time they came no more on the sabbath.

22 I spoke also to the Levites that they should be purified, and should come to keep the gates, and to sanctify the sabbath day. For this also remember me, O my God: and spare me according to the multitude of thy tender mercies.

23 In those days also I saw Jews that married wives: women of Azotus, and of Ammon, and of Moab.

24 And their children spoke half in the speech of Azotus, and could not speak the Jews' language; but they spoke according to the language of this and that people.

25 And I chid them, and laid my curse upon them. And I beat some of them, and shaved off their hair, and made them swear by God that they would not give their daughters to their sons, nor take their daughters for their sons, nor for themselves, saying:

26 [2] Did not Solomon king of Israel sin in this kind of thing? And surely among many nations, there was not a king like him. And he was beloved of his God, and God made him king over all Israel: [3] and yet women of other countries brought even him to sin.

27 And shall we also be disobedient and do all this great evil: to transgress against our God, and marry strange women?

28 And one of the sons of Joiada the son of Eliasib the high priest, was son-in-law to Sanaballat the Horonite: and I drove him from me.

29 Remember them, O Lord my God, that defile the priesthood, and the law of priests and Levites.

30 So I separated from them all strangers: and I appointed the courses of the priests and the Levites, every man in his ministry:

31 And for the offering of wood at times appointed, and for the firstfruits. Remember me, O my God, unto good. Amen.

THE BOOK OF

TOBIAS

This Book takes its name from the holy man Tobias, whose wonderful virtues are herein recorded. It contains most excellent documents of great piety, extraordinary patience, and of a perfect resignation to the will of God. His humble prayer was heard, and the angel Raphael was sent to relieve him. He is thankful and praises the Lord, calling on the children of Israel to do the same. Having lived to the age of one hundred and two years, he exhorts his son and grandsons to piety, foretells the destruction of Ninive, and the rebuilding of Jerusalem. He dies happily.

CHAPTER 1

Tobias's early piety. His works of mercy, particularly in burying the dead.

TOBIAS of the tribe and city of Nephtali (which is in the upper parts of Galilee above Naasson, beyond the way that leadeth to the west, having on the right hand the city of Sephet),

2 [1] When he was made captive in the days of Salmanasar king of the Assyrians, even in his captivity, forsook not the way of truth:

3 But every day gave all he could get to his brethren, his fellow captives, that were of his kindred.

4 And when he was younger than any of the tribe of Nephtali, yet did he no childish thing in his work.

5 Moreover when all went to the golden calves [2] which Jeroboam king of Israel had made, he alone fled the company of all:

6 And went to Jerusalem to the temple of the Lord; and there adored the Lord God of Israel, offering faithfully all his firstfruits, and his tithes,

7 So that in the third year he gave all his tithes to the proselytes and strangers.

8 These and such like things did he

observe when but a boy according to the law of God.

9 But when he was a man, he took to wife Anna of his own tribe, and had a son by her, whom he called after his own name.

10 And from his infancy he taught him to fear God, and to abstain from all sin.

11 And when by the captivity he with his wife and his son and all his tribe was come to the city of Ninive,

12 (When all ate of the meats of the Gentiles) he kept his soul and never was defiled with their meats.

13 And because he was mindful of the Lord with all his heart, God gave him favour in the sight of Salmanasar the king.

14 And he gave him leave to go whithersoever he would, with liberty to do whatever he had a mind.

15 He therefore went to all that were in captivity, and gave them wholesome admonitions.

16 And when he was come to Rages a city of the Medes, and had ten talents of silver of that with which he had been honoured by the king:

17 And when amongst a great multitude of his kindred, he saw Gabelus in want, who was one of his tribe, taking a note of his hand he gave him the aforesaid sum of money.

18 But after a long time, Salmanasar the king being dead, when Sennacherib his son, who reigned in his place, had a hatred for the children of Israel:

19 Tobias daily went among all his kindred, and comforted them, and distributed to every one as he was able, out of his goods.

20 He fed the hungry, and gave clothes to the naked, and was careful to bury the dead, and they that were slain.

21 And when [3] king Sennacherib was come back, fleeing from Judea by reason of the slaughter that God had made about him for his blasphemy, and being angry slew many of the children of Israel, Tobias buried their bodies.

22 But when it was told the king, he commanded him to be slain, and took away all his substance.

23 But Tobias fleeing naked away with his son and with his wife, lay concealed: for many loved him.

24 [4] But after forty-five days, the king was killed by his own sons.

25 And Tobias returned to his house: and all his substance was restored to him.

CHAPTER 2

Tobias leaveth his dinner to bury the dead. He loseth his sight by God's permission, for manifestation of his patience.

BUT after this, when there was a festival of the Lord, and a good dinner was prepared in Tobias's house,

2 He said to his son: Go, and bring some of our tribe that fear God, to feast with us.

3 And when he had gone, returning he told him, that one of the children of Israel lay slain in the street. And he forthwith leaped up from his place at the table, and left his dinner, and came fasting to the body.

4 And taking it up he carried it privately to his house, that after the sun was down, he might bury him cautiously.

5 And when he had hid the body, he ate bread with mourning and fear,

6 Remembering the word which the Lord spoke by [1] Amos the prophet: Your festival days shall be turned into lamentation and mourning.

7 So when the sun was down, he went and buried him.

8 Now all his neighbours blamed him, saying: Once already commandment was given for thee to be slain because of this matter; and thou didst scarce escape the sentence of death. And dost thou again bury the dead?

9 [2] But Tobias fearing God more than the king, carried off the bodies of them that were slain, and hid them in his house, and at midnight buried them.

10 Now it happened one day that, being wearied with burying, he came to his house and cast himself down by the wall and slept.

11 And as he was sleeping, hot dung out of a swallow's nest fell upon his eyes, and he was made blind.

12 Now this trial the Lord therefore permitted to happen to him, that an example might be given to posterity of his patience, as also of holy Job.

13 For whereas he had always feared God from his infancy, and kept his commandments, he repined not against God because the evil of blindness had befallen him:

14 But continued immoveable in the fear of God, giving thanks to God all the days of his life.

15 For as the kings insulted over holy Job, so his relations and kinsmen mocked at his life, saying:

16 Where is thy hope, for which thou gavest alms, and buriedst the dead?

17 But Tobias rebuked them, saying: Speak not so.

18 For we are the children of saints,

---

[3] 4 Kings. 19, 35; Ecclus. 48, 24; 2 Mach. 8, 19.   [4] 4 Kings, 19, 37; 2 Par. 32, 21; Isai. 37, 38. CHAP. 2. [1] Amos, 8, 10; 1 Mach. 1, 41. [2] Tob. 1, 21.

CHAP. 2. Ver. 15. *Kings.* So Job's three friends are here called, because they were princes in their respective territories.

and look for that life which God will give to those that never change their faith from him.

19 Now Anna his wife went daily to weaving work; and she brought home what she could get for their living by the labour of her hands.

20 Whereby it came to pass that she received a young kid, and brought it home.

21 And when her husband heard it bleating, he said: ³ Take heed, lest perhaps it be stolen: restore ye it to its owners, for it is not lawful for us either to eat or to touch any thing that cometh by theft.

22 ⁴ At these words his wife being angry answered: It is evident thy hope is come to nothing, and thy alms now appear.

23 And with these and other such like words she upbraided him.

CHAPTER 3

The prayer of Tobias, and of Sara, in their several afflictions are heard by God. The angel Raphael is sent to relieve them.

THEN Tobias sighed, and began to pray with tears,

2 Saying: Thou art just, O Lord, and all thy judgments are just; and all thy ways mercy, and truth, and judgment.

3 And now, O Lord, think of me, and take not revenge of my sins: neither remember my offences, nor those of my parents.

4 ¹ For we have not obeyed thy commandments: therefore are we delivered to spoil, and to captivity and death, and are made a fable, and a reproach to all nations, amongst which thou hast scattered us.

5 And now, O Lord, great are thy judgments, because we have not done according to thy precepts, and have not walked sincerely before thee.

6 And now, O Lord, do with me according to thy will, and command my spirit to be received in peace: for it is better for me to die, than to live.

7 Now it happened on the same day, that Sara daughter of Raguel, in Rages a city of the Medes, received a reproach from one of her father's servant maids,

8 Because she had been given to seven husbands, and a devil named Asmodeus had killed them, at their first going in unto her.

9 So when she reproved the maid for her fault, she answered her, saying: May we never see son, or daughter

³ Deut. 22, 1. ⁴ Job. 2, 9. CHAP. 3. ¹ Deut. 28, 15.

CHAP. 3. Ver. 7. *Rages.* In the Greek it is *Ecbatana,* which was also called Rages. For there were two cities in Media, of the name of Rages. Raguel dwelt in one of them, and Gabelus in the other.

of thee upon the earth, thou murderer of thy husbands.

10 Wilt thou kill me also, as thou hast already killed seven husbands? At these words she went into an upper chamber of her house: and for three days and three nights did neither eat nor drink.

11 But continuing in prayer with tears, she besought God that he would deliver her from this reproach.

12 And it came to pass on the third day, when she was making an end of her prayer, blessing the Lord,

13 She said: Blessed is thy name, O God of our fathers: who when thou hast been angry, wilt shew mercy, and in the time of tribulation forgivest the sins of them that call upon thee.

14 To thee, O Lord, I turn my face: to thee I direct my eyes.

15 I beg, O Lord, that thou loose me from the bond of this reproach, or else take me away from the earth.

16 Thou knowest, O Lord, that I never coveted a husband, and have kept my soul clean from all lust.

17 Never have I joined myself with them that play: neither have I made myself partaker with them that walk in lightness.

18 But a husband I consented to take, with thy fear, not with my lust.

19 And either I was unworthy of them; or they perhaps were not worthy of me: because perhaps thou hast kept me for another man.

20 For thy counsel is not in man's power.

21 But this every one is sure of that worshippeth thee, that his life, if it be under trial, shall be crowned: and if it be under tribulation, it shall be delivered: and if it be under correction, it shall be allowed to come to thy mercy.

22 For thou art not delighted in our being lost: because after a storm thou makest a calm, and after tears and weeping thou pourest in joyfulness.

23 Be thy name, O God of Israel, blessed for ever.

24 At that time the prayers of them both were heard in the sight of the glory of the most high God.

25 And the holy angel of the Lord, Raphael, was sent to heal them both, whose prayers at one time were rehearsed in the sight of the Lord.

CHAPTER 4

Tobias thinking he shall die, giveth his son godly admonitions. He telleth him of money he had lent to a friend.

THEREFORE when Tobias thought that his prayer was heard that he might die, he called to him Tobias his son.

2 And he said to him: Hear, my son, the words of my mouth, and lay them as a foundation in thy heart.

3 When God shall take my soul, thou shalt bury my body: [1] and thou shalt honour thy mother all the days of her life.

4 For thou must be mindful what and how great perils she suffered for thee in her womb.

5 And when she also shall have ended the time of her life, bury her by me.

6 And all the days of thy life have God in thy mind. And take heed thou never consent to sin, nor transgress the commandments of the Lord our God.

7 [2] Give alms out of thy substance, and turn not away thy face from any poor person: for so it shall come to pass that the face of the Lord shall not be turned from thee.

8 [3] According to thy ability be merciful.

9 If thou have much give abundantly: if thou have little, take care even so to bestow willingly a little.

10 For thus thou storest up to thyself a good reward for the day of necessity.

11 [4] For alms deliver from all sin, and from death, and will not suffer the soul to go into darkness.

12 Alms shall be a great confidence before the most high God, to all them that give it.

13 [5] Take heed to keep thyself, my son, from all fornication: and beside thy wife never endure to know a crime.

14 Never suffer pride to reign in thy mind, or in thy words: [6] for from it all perdition took its beginning.

15 [7] If any man hath done any work for thee, immediately pay him his hire: and let not the wages of thy hired servant stay with thee at all.

16 [8] See thou never do to another what thou wouldst hate to have done to thee by another.

17 [9] Eat thy bread with the hungry and the needy: and with thy garments cover the naked.

18 Lay out thy bread and thy wine upon the burial of a just man: and do not eat and drink thereof with the wicked.

19 Seek counsel always of a wise man.

20 Bless God at all times: and desire of him to direct thy ways, and that all thy counsels may abide in him.

21 I tell thee also, my son, that I lent ten talents of silver, while thou wast yet a child, to Gabelus, in Rages a city of the Medes, and I have a note of his hand with me.

22 Now therefore inquire how thou mayst go to him, and receive of him the foresaid sum of money, and restore to him the note of his hand.

23 Fear not, my son: we lead indeed a poor life; [10] but we shall have many good things, if we fear God, and depart from all sin, and do that which is good.

CHAPTER 5

Young Tobias seeking a guide for his journey, the angel Raphael, in shape of a man, undertaketh this office.

THEN Tobias answered his father, and said: I will do all things, father, which thou hast commanded me.

2 But how I shall get this money, I cannot tell. He knoweth not me, and I know not him. What token shall I give him? Nor did I ever know the way which leadeth thither.

3 Then his father answered him, and said: I have a note of his hand with me, which when thou shalt shew him, he will presently pay it.

4 But go now, and seek thee out some faithful man, to go with thee for his hire: that thou mayest receive it, while I yet live.

5 Then Tobias going forth, found a beautiful young man, standing girded, and as it were ready to walk.

6 And not knowing that he was an angel of God, he saluted him, and said: From whence art thou, good young man?

7 But he answered: Of the children of Israel. And Tobias said to him: Knowest thou the way that leadeth to the country of the Medes?

8 And he answered: I know it; and I have often walked through all the ways thereof; and I have abode with Gabelus our brother, who dwelleth at Rages a city of the Medes, which is situate in the mount of Ecbatana.

9 And Tobias said to him: Stay for me. I beseech thee, till I tell these same things to my father.

10 Then Tobias going in told all these things to his father. Upon which his father being in admiration, desired that he would come in unto him.

11 So going in he saluted him, and said: Joy be to thee always.

12 And Tobias said: What manner of joy shall be to me, who sit in darkness, and see not the light of heaven?

CHAP. 4. [1] Exod. 20, 12; Ecclus. 7, 29. [2] Prov. 3, 9; Ecclus. 4, 1; 14, 23; Luke, 14, 13. [3] Ecclus. 35, 12. [4] Ecclus. 29, 15. [5] 1 Thess. 4, 3. [6] Gen. 3, 5. [7] Lev. 19, 13; Deut. 24, 14. [8] Matt. 7, 12; Luke, 6, 31. [9] Luke, 14, 13. [10] Rom. 8, 17.

13 And the young man said to him: Be of good courage; thy cure from God is at hand.

14 And Tobias said to him: Canst thou conduct my son to Gabelus at Rages, a city of the Medes? And when thou shalt return, I will pay thee thy hire.

15 And the angel said to him: I will conduct him thither, and bring him back to thee.

16 And Tobias said to him: I pray thee, tell me, of what family, or what tribe art thou?

17 And Raphael the angel answered: Dost thou seek the family of him thou hirest, or the hired servant himself to go with thy son?

18 But lest I should make thee uneasy, I am Azarias, the son of the great Ananias.

19 And Tobias answered: Thou art of a great family. But I pray thee be not angry that I desired to know thy family.

20 And the angel said to him: I will lead thy son safe, and bring him to thee again safe.

21 And Tobias answering, said: May you have a good journey; and God be with you in your way; and his angel accompany you.

22 Then all things being ready, that were to be carried in their journey, Tobias bade his father and his mother farewell: and they set out both together.

23 ¹ And when they were departed, his mother began to weep, and to say: Thou hast taken the staff of our old age, and sent him away from us.

24 I wish the money for which thou hast sent him, had never been.

25 For our poverty was sufficient for us, that we might account it as riches, that we saw our son.

26 And Tobias said to her: Weep not. Our son will arrive thither safe, and will return safe to us; and thy eyes shall see him.

27 For I believe that the good angel of God doth accompany him, and doth order all things well that are done about him, so that he shall return to us with joy.

28 At these words his mother ceased weeping, and held her peace.

CHAP. 5. ¹ Tob. 10, 4. CHAP. 6. ¹ Num. 27, 8; 36. 8.

CHAP. 5. Ver. 18. *Azarias.* The angel took the form of Azarias: and therefore might call himself by the name of the man whom he personated. *Azarias,* in Hebrew, signifies *the help of God,* and *Ananias the grace of God.*
CHAP. 6. Ver. 8. *Its heart. The liver* (ver. 19). God was pleased to give to these things a virtue against those proud spirits, to make them, who affected to be like the Most High, subject to such mean corporeal creatures as instruments of his power.

CHAPTER 6

By the angel's advice young Tobias taketh hold on a fish that assaulteth him. Reserveth the heart, the gall, and the liver for medicines. They lodge at the house of Raguel, whose daughter Sara, Tobias is to marry. She had before been married to seven husbands, who were all slain by a devil.

AND Tobias went forward; and the dog followed him. And he lodged the first night by the river of Tigris.

2 And he went out to wash his feet: and behold a monstrous fish came up to devour him.

3 And Tobias being afraid of him, cried out with a loud voice, saying: Sir, he cometh upon me.

4 And the angel said to him: Take him by the gill, and draw him to thee. And when he had done so, he drew him out upon the land: and he began to pant before his feet.

5 Then the angel said to him: Take out the entrails of this fish, and lay up his heart, and his gall, and his liver for thee. For these are necessary for useful medicines.

6 And when he had done so, he roasted the flesh thereof, and they took it with them in the way. The rest they salted as much as might serve them, till they came to Rages the city of the Medes.

7 Then Tobias asked the angel, and said to him: I beseech thee, brother Azarias, tell me what remedies are these things good for, which thou hast bid me keep of the fish?

8 And the angel answering, said to him: If thou put a little piece of its heart upon coals, the smoke thereof driveth away all kind of devils, either from man or from woman, so that they come no more to them.

9 And the gall is good for anointing the eyes, in which there is a white speck: and they shall be cured.

10 And Tobias said to him: Where wilt thou that we lodge?

11 And the angel answering, said: Here is one whose name is Raguel, a near kinsman of thy tribe. And he hath a daughter named Sara: but he hath no son nor any other daughter beside her.

12 ¹ All his substance is due to thee: and thou must take her to wife.

13 Ask her therefore of her father: and he will give her thee to wife.

14 Then Tobias answered, and said: I hear that she hath been given to seven husbands, and they all died. Moreover I have heard, that a devil killed them.

15 Now I am afraid, lest the same

thing should happen to me also: and whereas I am the only child of my parents, I should bring down their old age with sorrow to hell.

16 Then the angel Raphael said to him: Hear me, and I will shew thee who they are, over whom the devil can prevail.

17 For they who in such manner receive matrimony, as to shut out God from themselves, and from their mind, and to give themselves to their lust, as the horse and mule, which have not understanding: over them the devil hath power.

18 But thou when thou shalt take her, go into the chamber: and for three days keep thyself continent from her, and give thyself to nothing else but to prayers with her.

19 And on that night lay the liver of the fish on the fire: and the devil shall be driven away.

20 But the second night, thou shalt be admitted into the society of the holy Patriarchs.

21 And the third night, thou shalt obtain a blessing that sound children may be born of you.

22 And when the third night is past, thou shalt take the virgin with the fear of the Lord, moved rather for love of children than for lust: that in the seed of Abraham thou mayest obtain a blessing in children.

CHAPTER 7

They are kindly entertained by Raguel.
Tobias demandeth Sara to wife.

AND they went to Raguel, and Raguel received them with joy.

2 And Raguel looking upon Tobias, said to Anna his wife: How like is this young man to my cousin!

3 And when he had spoken these words, he said: Whence are ye young men our brethren?

4 But they said: We are of the tribe of Nephtali, of the captivity of Ninive.

5 And Raguel said to them: Do you know Tobias my brother? And they said: We know him.

6 And when he was speaking many good things of him, the angel said to Raguel: Tobias concerning whom thou inquirest is this young man's father.

7 And Raguel went to him, and kissed him with tears; and weeping upon his neck, said: A blessing be upon thee, my son, because thou art the son of a good and most virtuous man.

8 And Anna his wife, and Sara their daughter wept.

9 And after they had spoken, Raguel commanded a sheep to be killed, and a

feast to be prepared. And when he desired them to sit down to dinner,

10 Tobias said: I will not eat nor drink here this day, unless thou first grant me my petition, and promise to give me Sara thy daughter.

11 Now whon Raguel heard this, he was afraid, knowing what had happened to those seven husbands, that went in unto her. And he began to fear lest it might happen to him also in like manner. And as he was in suspense, and gave no answer to his petition,

12 The angel said to him: Be not afraid to give her to this man, for to him who feareth God is thy daughter due to be his wife. Therefore another could not have her.

13 Then Raguel said: I doubt not but God hath regarded my prayers and tears in his sight.

14 And I believe he hath therefore made you come to me, that this maid might be married to one of her own kindred, ¹ according to the law of Moses: and now doubt not but I will give her to thee.

15 And taking the right hand of his daughter, he gave it into the right hand of Tobias, saying: The God of Abraham, and the God of Isaac, and the God of Jacob, be with you. And may he join you together, and fulfil his blessing in you.

16 And taking paper they made a writing of the marriage.

17 And afterwards they made merry, blessing God.

18 And Raguel called to him Anna his wife, and bade her prepare another chamber.

19 And she brought Sara her daughter in thither: and she wept.

20 And she said to her: Be of good cheer, my daughter. The Lord of heaven give thee joy for the trouble thou hast undergone.

CHAPTER 8

Tobias burneth part of the fish's liver, and
Raphael bindeth the devil. Tobias and
Sara pray.

AND after they had supped, they brought in the young man to her.

2 And Tobias, remembering the angel's word, took out of his bag part of the liver, and laid it upon burning coals.

3 Then the angel Raphael took the devil, and bound him in the desert of upper Egypt.

4 Then Tobias exhorted the virgin, and said to her: Sara, arise, and let us pray to God to-day, and to-morrow, and

CHAP. 7. ¹ Num. 36, 6.

Ver. 15. *To hell.* That is, to the place where the souls of the good were kept before the coming of Christ.

thc next day: because for these three nights we are joined to God. And when the third night is over, we will be in our own wedlock.

5 For we are the children of saints: and we must not be joined together like heathens that know not God.

6 So they both arose, and prayed earnestly both together that health might be given them,

7 And Tobias said: Lord God of our fathers, may the heavens and the earth, and the sea, and the fountains, and the rivers, and all thy creatures that are in them, bless thee.

8 ¹ Thou madest Adam of the slime of the earth: and gavest him Eve for a helper.

9 And now, Lord, thou knowest, that not for fleshly lust do I take my sister to wife, but only for the love of posterity, in which thy name may be blessed for ever and ever.

10 Sara also said: Have mercy on us, O Lord, have mercy on us: and let us grow old both together in health.

11 And it came to pass about the cock-crowing, Raguel ordered his servants to be called for. And they went with him together to dig a grave.

12 For he said: Lest perhaps it may have happened to him, in like manner as it did to the other seven husbands, that went in unto her.

13 And when they had prepared the pit, Raguel went back to his wife, and said to her:

14 Send one of thy maids, and let her see if he be dead, that I may bury him before it be day.

15 So she sent one of her maidservants, who went into the chamber, and found them safe and sound, sleeping both together.

16 And returning she brought the good news. And Raguel and Anna his wife blessed the Lord,

17 And said: We bless thee, O Lord God of Israel, because it hath not happened as we suspected.

18 For thou hast shewn thy mercy to us: and hast shut out from us the enemy that persecuted us.

19 And thou hast taken pity upon two only children. Make them, O Lord, bless thee more fully: and to offer up to thee a sacrifice of thy praise, and of thcir health; that all nations may know thou alone art God in all the earth.

20 And immediately Raguel commanded his servants to fill up the pit they made, before it was day.

21 And he spoke to his wife to make ready a feast, and prepare all kind of

provisions that are necessary for such as go a journey.

22 He caused also two fat kine, and four wethers to be killed, and a banquet to be prepared for all his neighbours, and all his friends.

23 And Raguel adjured Tobias, to abide with him two weeks.

24 And of all things which Raguel possessed, he gave one half to Tobias: and made a writing, that the half that remained should after their decease come also to Tobias.

CHAPTER 9

The angel Raphael goeth to Gabelus, receiveth the money, and bringeth him to the marriage.

THEN Tobias called the angel to him, whom he took to be a man, and said to him: Brother Azarias, I pray thee hearken to my words.

2 If I should give myself to be thy servant, I should not make a worthy return for thy care.

3 However, I beseech thee, to take with thee beasts and servants, and to go to Gabelus to Rages the city of the Medes: and to restore to him his note of hand, and receive of him the money, and desire him to come to my wedding.

4 For thou knowest that my father numbereth the days: and if I stay one day more, his soul will be afflicted.

5 And indeed thou seest how Raguel hath adjured me, whose adjuring I cannot despise.

6 Then Raphael took four of Raguel's servants, and two camels, and went to Rages the city of the Medes: and finding Gabelus, gave him his note of hand, and received of him all the money.

7 And he told him concerning Tobias, the son of Tobias, all that had been done: and made him come with him to the wedding.

8 And when he was come into Raguel's house he found Tobias sitting at the table. And he leaped up, and they kissed each other. And Gabelus wept, and blessed God,

9 And said: The God of Israel bless thee: because thou art the son of a very good and just man, and that feareth God, and doth almsdeeds.

10 And may a blessing come upon thy wife and upon your parents.

11 And may you scc your children, and your children's children, unto the third and fourth generation. And may your seed be blessed by the God of Israel, who reigneth for ever and ever.

12 And when all had said, Amen, they went to the feast: but the marriage feast they celebrated also with the fear of the Lord.

CHAPTER 10

The parents lament the long absence of their son Tobias. He sets out to return.

BUT as Tobias made longer stay upon occasion of the marriage, Tobias his father was solicitous, saying: Why thinkest thou doth my son tarry, or why is he detained there?

2 Is Gabelus dead, thinkest thou, and no man will pay him the money?

3 And he began to be exceeding sad, both he and Anna his wife with him. And they began both to weep together: because their son did not return to them on the day appointed.

4 [1] But his mother wept and was quite disconsolate, and said: Woe, woe is me! My son, why did we send thee to go to a strange country, the light of our eyes, the staff of our old age, the comfort of our life, the hope of our posterity?

5 We having all things together in thee alone, ought not to have let thee go from us.

6 And Tobias said to her: Hold thy peace, and be not troubled: our son is safe. That man with whom we sent him is very trusty.

7 But she could by no means be comforted: but daily running out looked round about, and went into all the ways by which there seemed any hope he might return, that she might if possible see him coming afar off.

8 But Raguel said to his son-in-law: Stay here, and I will send a messenger to Tobias thy father, that thou art in health.

9 And Tobias said to him: I know that my father and mother now count the days; and their spirit is grievously afflicted within them.

10 And when Raguel had pressed Tobias with many words, and he by no means would hearken to him, he delivered Sara unto him, and half of all his substance in men-servants and women-servants, in cattle, in camels, and in kine, and in much money: and sent him away safe and joyful from him,

11 Saying: The holy angel of the Lord be with you in your journey, and bring you through safe, and that you may find all things well about your parents, and my eyes may see your children before I die.

12 And the parents taking their daughter kissed her, and let her go:

13 Admonishing her to honour her father and mother in law, to love her husband, to take care of the family, to govern the house, and to behave herself irreprehensibly.

CHAPTER 11

Tobias anointeth his father's eyes with the fish's gall. He recovereth his sight.

AND as they were returning they came to Charan, which is in the midway to Ninive, the eleventh day.

2 And the angel said: Brother Tobias, thou knowest how thou didst leave thy father.

3 If it please thee therefore, let us go before: and let the family follow softly after us, together with thy wife, and with the beasts.

4 And as this their going pleased him, Raphael said to Tobias: Take with thee of the gall of the fish, for it will be necessary. So Tobias took some of that gall and departed.

5 But Anna sat beside the way daily, on the top of a hill, from whence she might see afar off.

6 And while she watched his coming from that place, she saw him afar off, and presently perceived it was her son coming. And returning she told her husband, saying: Behold thy son cometh.

7 And Raphael said to Tobias: As soon as thou shalt come into thy house, forthwith adore the Lord thy God; and giving thanks to him, go to thy father and kiss him.

8 And immediately anoint his eyes with this gall of the fish, which thou carriest with thee. For be assured that his eyes shall be presently opened, and thy father shall see the light of heaven, and shall rejoice in the sight of thee.

9 Then the dog, which had been with them in the way, ran before; and coming as if he had brought the news, shewed his joy by his fawning and wagging his tail.

10 And his father that was blind, rising up, began to run, stumbling with his feet: and giving a servant his hand, went to meet his son.

11 And receiving him kissed him, as did also his wife. And they began to weep for joy.

12 And when they had adored God, and given him thanks, they sat down together.

13 Then Tobias taking of the gall of the fish, anointed his father's eyes.

14 And he stayed about half an hour: and a white skin began to come out of his eyes, like the skin of an egg.

15 And Tobias took hold of it, and

CHAP. 10. [1] Tob. 5, 23.

CHAP. 11. Ver. 9. *The dog.* This may seem a very minute circumstance to be recorded in sacred history: but as we learn from our Saviour (Matt. 5, 18), there are *iotas* and *tittles* in the word of God: that is to say, things that appear minute, but which have indeed a deep and mysterious meaning in them.

drew it from his eyes. And immediately he recovered his sight.

16 And they glorified God both he and his wife and all that knew him.

17 And Tobias said: I bless thee, O Lord God of Israel, because thou hast chastised me, and thou hast saved me. And behold I see Tobias my son.

18 And after seven days Sara his son's wife, and all the family arrived safe: and the cattle, and the camels, and an abundance of money of his wife's: and that money also which he had received of Gabelus.

19 And he told his parents all the benefits of God, which he had done to him by the man that conducted him.

20 And Achior and Nabath the kinsmen of Tobias came, rejoicing for Tobias, and congratulating with him for all the good things that God had done for him.

21 And for seven days they feasted and rejoiced all with great joy.

CHAPTER 12

Raphael maketh himself known.

THEN Tobias called to him his son, and said to him: What can we give to this holy man, that is come with thee?

2 Tobias answering, said to his father: Father, what wages shall we give him? Or what can be worthy of his benefits?

3 He conducted me and brought me safe again; he received the money of Gabelus; he caused me to have my wife; and he chased from her the evil spirit. He gave joy to her parents; myself he delivered from being devoured by the fish; thee also he hath made to see the light of heaven; and we are filled with all good things through him. What can we give him sufficient for these things?

4 But I beseech thee, my father, to desire him, that he would vouchsafe to accept of one half of all things that have been brought.

5 So the father and the son calling him, took him aside: and began to desire him that he would vouchsafe to accept of half of all things that they had brought.

6 Then he said to them secretly: Bless ye the God of heaven, give glory to him in the sight of all that live, because he hath shewn his mercy to you.

7 For it is good to hide the secret of a king: but honourable to reveal and confess the works of God.

8 Prayer is good with fasting and alms: more than to lay up treasures of gold:

CHAP. 13. ¹ Deut. 32, 39; 1 Kings, 2, 6; Wisd. 16, 18.

9 For alms delivereth from death: and the same is that which purgeth away sins, and maketh to find mercy and life everlasting.

10 But they that commit sin and iniquity are enemies to their own soul.

11 I discover then the truth unto you: and I will not hide the secret from you.

12 When thou didst pray with tears, and didst bury the dead, and didst leave thy dinner, and hide the dead by day in thy house, and bury them by night, I offered thy prayer to the Lord.

13 And because thou wast acceptable to God, it was necessary that temptation should prove thee.

14 And now the Lord hath sent me to heal thee, and to deliver Sara thy son's wife from the devil.

15 For I am the angel Raphael, one of the seven, who stand before Lord.

16 And when they had heard these things, they were troubled: and being seized with fear they fell upon the ground on their face.

17 And the angel said to them: Peace be to you. Fear not.

18 For when I was with you, I was there by the will of God: bless ye him, and sing praises to him.

19 I seemed indeed to eat and to drink with you: but I use an invisible meat and drink, which cannot be seen by men.

20 It is time therefore that I return to him that sent me: but bless ye God, and publish all his wonderful works.

21 And when he had said these things, he was taken from their sight: and they could see him no more.

22 Then they lying prostrate for three hours upon their face, blessed God: and rising up, they told all his wonderful works.

CHAPTER 13

Tobias the father praiseth God, exhorting all Israel to do the same. Prophesieth the restoration and better state of Jerusalem.

AND Tobias the elder opening his mouth, blessed the Lord, and said: Thou art great, O Lord, for ever, and thy kingdom is unto all ages.

2 ¹For thou scourgest, and thou savest: thou leadest down to hell, and bringest up again: and there is none that can escape thy hand.

3 Give glory to the Lord, ye children of Israel: and praise him in the sight of the Gentiles.

4 Because he hath therefore scattered you among the Gentiles, who know not him, that you may declare his wonderful works: and make them know

that there is no other almighty God besides him.

5 He hath chastised us for our iniquities: and he will save us for his own mercy.

6 See then what he hath done with us, and with fear and trembling give ye glory to him: and extol the eternal King of worlds in your works.

7 As for me, I will praise him in the land of my captivity: because he hath shewn his majesty toward a sinful nation.

8 Be converted, therefore, ye sinners: and do justice before God, believing that he will shew his mercy to you.

9 And I and my soul will rejoice in him.

10 Bless ye the Lord, all his elect: keep days of joy, and give glory to him.

11 Jerusalem, city of God, the Lord hath chastised thee for the works of thy hands.

12 Give glory to the Lord for thy good things, and bless the God eternal: that he may rebuild his tabernacle in thee, and may call back all the captives to thee: and thou mayst rejoice for ever and ever.

13 Thou shalt shine with a glorious light: and all the ends of the earth shall worship thee.

14 [2] Nations from afar shall come to thee: and shall bring gifts: and shall adore the Lord in thee: and shall esteem thy land as holy.

15 For they shall call upon the great name in thee.

16 They shall be cursed that shall despise thee: and they shall be condemned that shall blaspheme thee. And blessed shall they be that shall build thee up.

17 But thou shalt rejoice in thy children: because they shall all be blessed, and shall be gathered together to the Lord.

18 Blessed are all they that love thee, and that rejoice in thy peace.

19 My soul, bless thou the Lord: because the Lord our God hath delivered Jerusalem his city from all her troubles.

20 Happy shall I be if there shall remain of my seed, to see the glory of Jerusalem.

21 [3] The gates of Jerusalem shall be built of sapphire, and of emerald: and all the walls thereof round about of precious stones.

22 All its streets shall be paved with white and clean stones: and Alleluia shall be sung in its streets.

23 Blessed be the Lord, who hath exalted it: and may he reign over it for ever and ever, Amen.

CHAPTER 14

Old Tobias dieth at the age of a hundred and two years, after exhorting his son and grandsons to piety, foreshewing that Ninive shall be destroyed, and Jerusalem, rebuilt. The younger Tobias returneth with his family to Raguel, and dieth happily as he had lived.

AND the words of Tobias were ended. And after Tobias was restored to his sight, he lived two and forty years, and saw the children of his grandchildren.

2 And after he had lived a hundred and two years, he was buried honourably in Ninive.

3 For he was six and fifty years old when he lost the sight of his eyes, and sixty when he recovered it again.

4 And the rest of his life was in joy: and with great increase of the fear of God he departed in peace.

5 And at the hour of his death he called unto him his son Tobias and his children, seven young men, his grandsons, and said to them:

6 The destruction of Ninive is at hand: for the word of the Lord must be fulfilled. [1] And our brethren, that are scattered abroad from the land of Israel, shall return to it.

7 And all the land thereof that is desert shall be filled with people: and the house of God which is burnt in it, shall again be rebuilt. And all that fear God shall return thither.

8 And the Gentiles shall leave their idols, and shall come into Jerusalem, and shall dwell in it.

9 And all the kings of the earth shall rejoice in it, adoring the King of Israel.

10 Hearken therefore, my children, to your father. Serve the Lord in truth, and seek to do the things that please him.

11 And command your children that they do justice and almsdeeds: and that they be mindful of God, and bless him at all times in truth, and with all their power.

12 And now, children, hear me, and do not stay here: but as soon as you shall bury your mother by me in one sepulchre, without delay direct your steps to depart hence.

13 For I see that its iniquity will bring it to destruction.

14 And it came to pass that after the death of his mother, Tobias de-

[2] Isai. 60, 5. [3] Apoc. 21, 19. CHAP. 14. [1] Esd. 3. 8.

CHAP. 13. Ver. 11. *Jerusalem.* What is prophetically delivered here, and in the following chapter, with relation to Jerusalem, is partly to be understood of the rebuilding the city after the captivity: and partly of the spiritual Jerusalem, which is the church of Christ, and the eternal Jerusalem in heaven.

parted out of Ninive with his wife, and children, and children's children, and returned to his father and mother in law.

15 And he found them in health in a good old age: and he took care of them, and he closed their eyes. And all the inheritance of Raguel's house came to him: and he saw his children's children to the fifth generation.

16 And after he had lived ninety-nine years in the fear of the Lord, with joy they buried him.

17 And all his kindred, and all his generation continued in good life, and in holy conversation, so that they were acceptable both to God, and to men, and to all that dwelt in the land.

THE BOOK OF
JUDITH

The sacred writer of this Book is generally believed to be the high priest Eliachim (called also Joachim). The transactions herein related, most probably happened in his days, and in the reign of Manasses, after his repentance and return from captivity. It takes its name from that illustrious woman, by whose virtue and fortitude, and armed with prayer, the children of Israel were preserved from the destruction threatened them by Holofernes and his great army. It finishes with her canticle of thanksgiving to God.

CHAPTER 1

Nabuchodonosor king of the Assyrians overcometh Arphaxad king of the Medes.

NOW Arphaxad king of the Medes had brought many nations under his dominions: and he built a very strong city, which he called Ecbatana,

2 Of stones squared and hewed. He made the walls thereof seventy cubits broad, and thirty cubits high: and the towers thereof he made a hundred cubits high. But on the square of them, each side was extended the space of twenty feet.

3 And he made the gates thereof according to the height of the towers:

4 And he glorified as a mighty one in the force of his army and in the glory of his chariots.

5 Now in the twelfth year of his reign, Nabuchodonosor king of the Assyrians, who reigned in Ninive the great city, fought against Arphaxad and overcame him,

6 In the great plain which he called Ragua, about the Euphrates, and the Tigris, and the Jadason: in the plain of Erioch the king of the Elicians.

CHAP. 1. Ver. 1. *Arphaxad*. He was probably the same as is called *Dejoces* by Herodotus; to whom he attributes the building of Ecbatana, the capital city of Media.

Ver. 5. *Nabuchodonosor*. Not the king of Babylon, who took and destroyed Jerusalem, but another of the same name, who reigned in Ninive: and is called by profane historians *Saosduchin*. He succeeded Asarhaddon in the kingdom of the Assyrians, and was contemporary with Manasses king of Juda.

7 Then was the kingdom of Nabuchodonosor exalted, and his heart was elevated. And he sent to all that dwelt in Cilicia and Damascus, and Libanus,

8 And to the nations that are in Carmelus, and Cedar, and to the inhabitants of Galilee in the great plain of Asdrelon,

9 And to all that were in Samaria, and beyond the river Jordan even to Jerusalem, and all the land of Jesse till you come to the borders of Ethiopia.

10 To all these Nabuchodonosor king of the Assyrians, sent messengers.

11 But they all with one mind refused, and sent them back empty, and rejected them without honour.

12 Then king Nabuchodonosor being angry against all that land, swore by his throne and kingdom that he would revenge himself of all those countries.

CHAPTER 2

Nabuchodonosor sendeth Holofernes to waste the countries of the west.

IN the thirteenth year of the reign of Nabuchodonosor, the two and twentieth day of the first month, the word was given out in the house of Nabuchodonosor king of the Assyrians, that he would revenge himself.

2 And he called all the ancients, and all the governors, and his officers of war, and communicated to them the secret of his counsel.

3 And he said that his thoughts were to bring all the earth under his empire.

4 And when this saying pleased them all, Nabuchodonosor, the king, called Holofernes the general of his armies,

5 And said to him: Go out against all the kingdoms of the west, and against them especially that despised my commandment.

6 Thy eye shall not spare any kingdom: and all the strong cities thou shalt bring under my yoke.

7 Then Holofernes called the captains, and officers of the power of the Assyrians. And he mustered men for the expedition, as the king commanded him: a hundred and twenty thousand fighting men on foot, and twelve thousand archers, horsemen.

8 And he made all his warlike preparations to go before with a multitude of innumerable camels, with all provisions sufficient for the armies in abundance, and herds of oxen, and flocks of sheep, without number.

9 He appointed corn to be prepared out of all Syria in his passage.

10 But gold and silver he took out of the king's house in great abundance.

11 And he went forth he and all the army, with the chariots, and horsemen, and archers, who covered the face of the earth, like locusts.

12 And when he had passed through the borders of the Assyrians, he came to the great mountains of Ange, which are on the left of Cilicia. And he went up to all their castles, and took all the strong places.

13 And he took by assault the renowned city of Melothus, and pillaged all the children of Tharsis, and the children of Ismahel, who were over against the face of the desert, and on the south of the land of Cellon.

14 And he passed over the Euphrates, and came into Mesopotamia: and he forced all the stately cities that were there, from the torrent of Mambre, till one comes to the sea.

15 And he took the borders thereof, from Cilicia to the coasts of Japheth, which are towards the south.

16 And he carried away all the children of Madian, and stripped them of all their riches: and all that resisted him he slew with the edge of the sword.

17 And after these things he went down into the plains of Damascus in the days of the harvest; and he set all the corn on fire; and he caused all the trees and vineyards to be cut down.

18 And the fear of them fell upon all the inhabitants of the land.

CHAPTER 3

Many submit themselves to Holofernes. He destroyeth their cities, and their gods, that Nabuchodonosor only might be called God.

THEN the kings and the princes of all the cities and provinces, of Syria, Mesopotamia, and Syria, Sobol, and Libya, and Cilicia sent their ambassadors, who coming to Holofernes, said:

2 Let thy indignation towards us cease. For it is better for us to live and serve Nabuchodonosor the great king, and be subject to thee, than to die and to perish, or suffer the miseries of slavery.

3 All our cities and our possessions, all mountains and hills, and fields, and herds of oxen, and flocks of sheep, and goats, and horses, and camels, and all our goods, and families are in thy sight.

4 Let all we have be subject to thy law.

5 Both we and our children are thy servants.

6 Come to us a peaceable lord, and use our service as it shall please thee.

7 Then he came down from the mountains with horsemen, in great power, and made himself master of every city, and all the inhabitants of the land.

8 And from all the cities he took auxiliaries, valiant men, and chosen for war.

9 And so great a fear lay upon all those provinces that the inhabitants of all the cities, both princes and nobles, as well as the people, went out to meet him at his coming.

10 And received him with garlands, and lights, and dances, and timbrels, and flutes.

11 And though they did these things, they could not for all that mitigate the fierceness of his heart.

12 For he both destroyed their cities, and cut down their groves.

13 For Nabuchodonosor the king had commanded him to destroy all the gods of the earth; that he only might be called God by those nations which could be brought under him by the power of Holofernes.

14 And when he had passed through all Syria, Sobal, and all Apamea, and all Mesopotamia, he came to the Idumeans into the land of Gabaa.

15 And he took possession of their cities, and stayed there for thirty days, in which days he commanded all the troops of his army to be united.

CHAPTER 4

The children of Israel prepare themselves to resist Holofernes. They cry to the Lord for help.

WHEN the children of Israel, who dwelt in the land of Juda, hearing these things, were exceedingly afraid of him.

2 Dread and horror seized upon their minds, lest he should do the same to Jerusalem and to the temple of the Lord, that he had done to other cities and their temples.

3 And they sent into all Samaria round about, as far as Jericho; and seized upon all the tops of the mountains.

4 And they compassed their towns with walls, and gathered together corn for provision for war.

5 And Eliachim the priest wrote to all that were over against Esdrelon, which faceth the great plain near Dothain, and to all by whom there might be a passage of way, that they should take possession of the ascents of the mountains, by which there might be any way to Jerusalem, and should keep watch where the way was narrow between the mountains.

6 And the children of Israel did as the priest of the Lord Eliachim had appointed them.

7 And all the people cried to the Lord with great earnestness: and they humbled their souls in fastings, and prayers, both they and their wives.

8 And the priests put on haircloths; and they caused the little children to lie prostrate before the temple of the Lord. And the altar of the Lord they covered with haircloth.

9 And they cried to the Lord the God of Israel with one accord, that their children might not be made a prey, and their wives carried off, and their cities destroyed, and their holy things profaned; and that they might not be made a reproach to the Gentiles.

10 Then Eliachim the high priest of the Lord went about all Israel and spoke to them,

11 Saying: Know ye that the Lord will hear your prayers, if you continue with perseverance in fastings and prayers in the sight of the Lord.

12 Remember Moses the servant of the Lord, who overcame Amalec that trusted in his own strength, and in his power, and in his army, and in his shields, and in his chariots, and in his horsemen, not by fighting with the sword, but by holy prayers.

13 [1] So shall all the enemies of Israel

be, if you persevere in this work which you have begun.

14 So they being moved by this exhortation of his, prayed to the Lord, and continued in the sight of the Lord.

15 So that even they who offered the holocausts to the Lord, offered the sacrifices to the Lord, girded with haircloths, and with ashes upon their head.

16 And they all begged of God with all their heart, that he would visit his people Israel.

CHAPTER 5

Achior gives Holofernes an account of the people of Israel.

AND it was told Holofernes the general of the army of the Assyrians, that the children of Israel prepared themselves to resist, and had shut up the ways of the mountains.

2 And he was transported with exceeding great fury and indignation: and he called all the princes of Moab and the leaders of Ammon.

3 And he said to them: Tell me what is this people that besetteth the mountains; or what are their cities, and of what sort, and how great? Also what is their power, or what is their multitude: or who is the king over their warfare?

4 And why they above all that dwell in the east, have despised us, and have not come out to meet us, that they might receive us with peace?

5 Then Achior captain of all the children of Ammon answering, said: If thou vouchsafe, my lord, to hear, I will tell the truth in thy sight concerning this people, that dwelleth in the mountains. And there shall not a false word come out of my mouth.

6 This people is of the offspring of the Chaldeans.

7 [1] They dwelt first in Mesopotamia, because they would not follow the gods of their fathers, who were in the land of the Chaldeans.

8 Wherefore forsaking the ceremonies of their fathers, which consisted in the worship of many gods,

9 They worshipped one God of heaven, [2] who also commanded them to depart from thence, and to dwell in Charan. And when there was a famine over all the land, [3] they went down into Egypt; and there for four hundred years were so multiplied, that the army of them could not be numbered.

10 And when the king of Egypt oppressed them, and made slaves of them to labour in clay and brick, in the building of his cities, they cried to their Lord: and he struck the whole land of Egypt with divers plagues.

CHAP. 4. [1] Exod. 17, 12. CHAP. 5. [1] Gen. 11, 31. [2] Gen. 12, 1. [3] Gen. 46, 6.

11 ⁴ And when the Egyptians had cast them out from them, and the plague had ceased from them; and they had a mind to take them again, and bring them back to their service,

12 ⁵ The God of heaven opened the sea to them in their flight, so that the waters were made to stand firm as a wall on either side: and they walked through the bottom of the sea and passed it dry foot.

13 And when an innumerable army of the Egyptians pursued after them in that place, they were so overwhelmed with the waters, that there was not one left, to tell what had happened to posterity.

14 And after they came out of the Red Sea, they abode in the deserts of mount Sina, in which never man could dwell, or son of man rested.

15 There bitter fountains were made sweet for them to drink: and for forty years they received food from heaven.

16 Wheresoever they went in; without bow and arrow, and without shield and sword, their God fought for them and overcame.

17 And there was no one that triumphed over this people, but when they departed from the worship of the Lord their God.

18 But as often as beside their own God, they worshipped any other, they were given to spoil, and to the sword, and to reproach.

19 And as often as they were penitent for having revolted from the worship of their God, the God of heaven gave them power to resist.

20 So they overthrew the king of the Chanaanites, and of the Jebusites, and of the Pherezites, and of the Hethites, and of the Hevites, and of the Amorrhites, and all the mighty ones in Hesebon: and they possessed their lands, and their cities.

21 And as long as they sinned not in the sight of their God, it was well with them: for their God hateth iniquity.

22 And even some years ago when they had revolted from the way which God had given them to walk therein, they were destroyed in battles by many nations: and very many of them were led away captive into a strange land.

23 But of late returning to the Lord their God, from the different places wherein they were scattered, they are come together and are gone up into all these mountains, and possess Jerusalem again, where their holies are.

24 Now therefore, my lord, search if there be any iniquity of theirs in the sight of their God. Let us go up to them because their God will surely deliver them to thee: and they shall be brought under the yoke of thy power:

25 But if there be no offence of this people in the sight of their God, we cannot resist them, because their God will defend them: and we shall be a reproach to the whole earth.

26 And it came to pass, when Achior had ceased to speak these words, all the great men of Holofernes were angry. And they had a mind to kill him, saying to each other:

27 Who is this, that saith the children of Israel can resist king Nabuchodonosor, and his armies: men unarmed, and without force, and without skill in the art of war?

28 That Achior therefore may know that he deceiveth us, let us go up into the mountains. And when the bravest of them shall be taken, then shall he with them be stabbed with the sword.

29 That every nation may know that Nabuchodonosor is god of the earth, and besides him there is no other.

CHAPTER 6

Holofernes in great rage sendeth Achior to Bethulia, there to be slain with the Israelites.

AND it came to pass when they had left off speaking, that Holofernes being in a violent passion, said to Achior:

2 Because thou hast prophesied unto us, saying: That the nation of Israel is defended by their God. To shew thee that there is no God, but Nabuchodonosor:

3 When we shall slay them all as one man, then thou also shalt die with them by the sword of the Assyrians; and all Israel shall perish with thee.

4 And thou shalt find that Nabuchodonosor is lord of the whole earth. And then the sword of my soldiers shall pass through thy sides; and thou shalt be stabbed and fall among the wounded of Israel; and thou shalt breathe no more till thou be destroyed with them.

5 But if thou think thy prophecy true, let not thy countenance sink. And let the paleness that is in thy face, depart from thee, if thou imaginest these my words cannot be accomplished.

6 And that thou mayst know that thou shalt experience these things together with them, behold from this hour thou shalt be associated to their people, that when they shall receive punishment they deserve from my sword, thou mayst fall under the same vengeance.

7 Then Holofernes commanded his servants to take Achior, and to lead him

⁴ Exod. 12, 33.   ⁵ Exod. 14, 29.

to Bethulia, and to deliver him into the hands of the children of Israel.

8 And the servants of Holofernes taking him, went through the plains: but when they came near the mountains, the slingers came out against them.

9 Then turning out of the way by the side of the mountain, they tied Achior to a tree, hand and foot, and so left him bound with ropes and returned to their master.

10 And the children of Israel coming down from Bethulia, came to him, and loosing him they brought him to Bethulia: and setting him in the midst of the people, asked him what was the matter, that the Assyrians had left him bound.

11 In those days the rulers there, were Ozias the son of Micha of the tribe of Simeon, and Charmi, called also Gothoniel.

12 And Achior related in the midst of the ancients, and in the presence of all the people, all that he had said, being asked by Holofernes: and how the people of Holofernes would have killed him for this word.

13 And how Holofernes himself being angry had commanded him to be delivered for this cause to the Israelites: that when he should overcome the children of Israel, then he might command Achior also himself to be put to death by diverse torments, for having said: The God of heaven is their defender.

14 [1] And when Achior had declared all these things, all the people fell upon their faces, adoring the Lord: and all of them together mourning and weeping poured out their prayers with one accord to the Lord.

15 Saying: O Lord God of heaven and earth, behold their pride, and look on our low condition, and have regard to the face of thy saints; and shew that thou forsakest not them that trust on thee, and that thou humblest them that presume of themselves, and glory in their own strength.

16 So when their weeping was ended, and the people's prayer, in which they continued all the day, was concluded, they comforted Achior,

17 Saying: The God of our fathers, whose power thou hast set forth, will make this return to thee, that thou rather shalt see their destruction.

18 And when the Lord our God shall give this liberty to his servants, let God be with thee also in the midst of us: that as it shall please thee, so thou with all thine mayst converse with us.

Chap. 6. [1] Judith, 5, 26.

Chap. 6. Ver. 21. *The church.* That is, the synagogue or place where they met for prayer.

19 Then Ozias, after the assembly was broken up, received him into his house, and made him a great supper.

20 And all the ancients were invited: and they refreshed themselves together after their fast was over.

21 And afterwards all the people were called together: and they prayed all the night long within the church, desiring help of the God of Israel.

CHAPTER 7

Holofernes besiegeth Bethulia. The distress of the besieged.

BUT Holofernes on the next day gave orders to his army, to go up against Bethulia.

2 Now there were in his troops a hundred and twenty thousand footmen, and two and twenty thousand horsemen, besides the preparations of those men who had been taken, and who had been brought away out of the provinces and cities of all the youth.

3 All these prepared themselves together to fight against the children of Israel. And they came by the hillside to the top, which looketh toward Dothain, from the place which is called Belma, unto Chelmon, which is over against Esdrelon.

4 But the children of Israel, when they saw the multitude of them, prostrated themselves upon the ground, putting ashes upon their heads, praying with one accord, that the God of Israel would shew his mercy upon his people.

5 And taking their arms of war, they posted themselves at the places, which by a narrow pathway lead directly between the mountains: and they guarded them all day and night.

6 Now Holofernes, in going round about, found that the fountain which supplied them with water, ran through an aqueduct without the city on the south side. And he commanded their aqueduct to be cut off.

7 Nevertheless there were springs not far from the walls, out of which they were seen secretly to draw water, to refresh themselves a little rather than to drink their fill.

8 But the children of Ammon and Moab came to Holofernes, saying: The children of Israel trust not in their spears, nor in their arrows; but the mountains are their defence, and the steep hills and precipices guard them.

9 Wherefore that thou mayst overcome them without joining battle, set guards at the springs that they may not draw water out of them: and thou shalt destroy them without sword, or at least being wearied out they will yield up their city, which they suppose, because

it is situate in the mountains, to be impregnable.

10 And these words pleased Holofernes, and his officers: and he placed all round about a hundred men at every spring.

11 And when they had kept this watch for full twenty days, the cisterns, and the reserve of waters failed among all the inhabitants of Bethulia, so that there was not within the city, enough to satisfy them, no not for one day: for water was daily given out to the people by measure.

12 Then all the men and women, young men, and children, gathering themselves together to Ozias, all together with one voice,

13 Said: [1] God be judge between us and thee, for thou hast done evil against us, in that thou wouldst not speak peaceably with the Assyrians, and for this cause God hath sold us into their hands.

14 And therefore there is no one to help us, while we are cast down before their eyes in thirst, and sad destruction.

15 And now assemble ye all that are in the city, that we may of our own accord yield ourselves all up to the people of Holofernes.

16 For it is better, that being captives we should live and bless the Lord, than that we should die, and be a reproach to all flesh, after we have seen our wives and our infants die before our eyes.

17 We call to witness this day heaven and earth, and the God of our fathers, who taketh vengeance upon us according to our sins, conjuring you to deliver now the city into the hand of the army of Holofernes, that our end may be short by the edge of the sword, which is made longer by the drought of thirst.

18 And when they had said these things, there was great weeping and lamentation of all in the assembly. And for many hours with one voice they cried to God, saying:

19 [2] We have sinned with our fathers, we have done unjustly, we have committed iniquity.

20 Have thou mercy on us, because thou art good, or punish our iniquities by chastising us thyself: and deliver not them that trust in thee to a people that knoweth not thee.

21 That they may not say among the Gentiles: Where is their God?

22 And when being wearied with these cries, and tired with these weepings, they held their peace,

23 Ozias rising up all in tears, said: Be of good courage, my brethren, and let us wait these five days for mercy from the Lord.

24 For perhaps he will put a stop to his indignation, and will give glory to his own name.

25 But if after five days be past there come no aid, we will do the things which you have spoken.

CHAPTER 8

The character of Judith. Her discourse to the ancients.

NOW it came to pass, when Judith a widow had heard these words, who was the daughter of Merari, the son of Idox, the son of Joseph, the son of Ozias, the son of Elai, the son of Jamnor, the son of Gedeon, the son of Raphaim, the son of Achitob, the son of Melchias, the son of Enan, the son of Nathanias, the son of Salathiel, the son of Simeon, the son of Ruben.

2 And her husband was Manasses, who died in the time of the barley harvest.

3 For he was standing over them that bound sheaves in the field; and the heat came upon his head. And he died in Bethulia his own city, and was buried there with his fathers.

4 And Judith his relict was a widow now three years and six months.

5 And she made herself a private chamber in the upper part of her house, in which she abode shut up with her maids.

6 And she wore haircloth upon her loins, and fasted all the days of her life, except the sabbaths, and new moons, and the feasts of the house of Israel.

7 And she was exceedingly beautiful: and her husband left her great riches, and very many servants, and large possessions of herds of oxen, and flocks of sheep.

8 And she was greatly renowned among all, because she feared the Lord very much: neither was there any one that spoke an ill word of her.

9 When therefore she had heard that Ozias had promised that he would deliver up the city after the fifth day, she sent to the ancients Chabri and Charmi.

10 And they came to her, and she said to them: What is this word, by which Ozias hath consented to give up the city to the Assyrians, if within five days there come no aid to us?

CHAP. 7. [1] Exod. 5, 21. [2] Ps. 105, 6.

CHAP. 8. Ver. 1. *Simeon the son of Ruben.* In the Greek, it is *the son of Israel.* For Simeon the patriarch, from whom Judith descended, was not the son, but the brother of Ruben. It seems more probable that the Simeon and the Ruben here mentioned are not the patriarchs: but two of the descendants of the patriarch Simeon: and that the genealogy of Judith, recorded in this place, is not carried up so high as the patriarchs. No more than that of Elcana the father of Samuel, 1 Kings, 1, 1, and that of king Saul, 1 Kings, 9, 1.

11 And who are you that tempt the Lord?

12 This is not a word that may draw down mercy, but rather that may stir up wrath, and enkindle indignation.

13 You have set a time for the mercy of the Lord: and you have appointed him a day, according to your pleasure.

14 But forasmuch as the Lord is patient, let us be penitent for this same thing, and with many tears let us beg his pardon.

15 For God will not threaten like man, nor be inflamed to anger like the son of man.

16 And therefore let us humble our souls before him. And continuing in an humble spirit in his service,

17 Let us ask the Lord with tears, that according to his will so he would shew his mercy to us: that as our heart is troubled by their pride, so also we may glorify in our humility.

18 For we have not followed the sins of our fathers, who forsook their God, and worshipped strange gods.

19 For which crime they were given up to their enemies, to the sword, and to pillage, and to confusion: but we know no other God but him.

20 Let us humbly wait for his consolation: and the Lord our God will require our blood of the afflictions of our enemies. And he will humble all the nations that shall rise up against us, and bring them to disgrace.

21 And now, brethren, as you are the ancients among the people of God, and their very soul resteth upon you: comfort their hearts by your speech, that they may be mindful how our fathers were tempted that they might be proved, whether they worshipped their God truly.

22 ¹ They must remember how our father Abraham was tempted, and being proved by many tribulations, was made the friend of God.

23 So Isaac, so Jacob, so Moses, and all that have pleased God, passed through many tribulations, remaining faithful.

24 But they that did not receive the trials with the fear of the Lord, but uttered their impatience and the reproach of their murmuring against the Lord,

25 ² Were destroyed by the destroyer, and perished by serpents.

26 As for us therefore let us not revenge ourselves for these things which we suffer.

27 But esteeming these very punishments to be less than our sins deserve, let us believe that these scourges of the Lord, with which like servants we are chastised, have happened for our amendment, and not for our destruction.

28 And Ozias and the ancients said to her: All things which thou hast spoken are true; and there is nothing to be reprehended in thy words.

29 Now therefore pray for us; for thou art a holy woman, and one fearing God.

30 And Judith said to them: As you know that what I have been able to say is of God:

31 So that which I intend to do, prove ye if it be of God; and pray that God may strengthen my design.

32 You shall stand at the gate this night; and I will go out with my maidservant. And pray ye, that, as you have said, in five days the Lord may look down upon his people Israel.

33 But I desire that you search not into what I am doing: and till I bring you word let nothing else be done but to pray for me to the Lord our God.

34 And Ozias the prince of Juda said to her: Go in peace; and the Lord be with thee to take revenge of our enemies. So returning they departed.

CHAPTER 9
Judith's prayer, to beg of God to fortify her in her undertaking.

AND when they were gone, Judith went into her oratory: and putting on haircloth, laid ashes on her head. And falling down prostrate before the Lord, she cried to the Lord, saying:

2 O Lord God of my father Simeon, ¹ who gavest him a sword to execute vengeance against strangers, who had defiled by their uncleanness, and uncovered the virgin unto confusion:

3 And who gavest their wives to be made a prey, and their daughters into captivity: and all their spoils to be divided to thy servants, who were zealous with thy zeal: assist, I beseech thee, O Lord God, me a widow.

4 For thou hast done the things of old, and hast devised one thing after another: and what thou hast designed hath been done.

5 For all thy ways are prepared; and in thy providence thou hast placed thy judgments.

CHAP. 8. ¹ Gen. 22, 1. ² 1 Cor. 10, 9. CHAP. 9. ¹ Gen. 34, 26. ² Exod. 14, 9.

CHAP. 9. Ver. 2. *Gavest him a sword.* The justice of God is here praised, in punishing by the sword of Simeon the crime of the Sichemites: and not the act of Simeon, which was justly condemned by his father (Gen. 49, 5). Though even with regard to this act, we may distinguish between his zeal against the crime committed by the ravishers of his sister, which zeal may be considered just: and the manner of his punishing that crime, which was irregular and excessive.

6 ² Look upon the camp of the Assyrians now, as thou wast pleased to look upon the camp of the Egyptians, when they pursued armed after thy servants, trusting in their chariots, and in their horsemen, and in a multitude of warriors.

7 But thou lookedst over their camp, and darkness wearied them.

8 The deep held their feet: and the waters overwhelmed them.

9 So may it be with these also, O Lord, who trust in their multitude, and in their chariots, and in their pikes, and in their shields, and in their arrows, and glory in their spears;

10 And know not that thou art our God, who destroyest wars from the beginning. And the Lord is thy name.

11 Lift up thy arm as from the beginning, and crush their power with thy power. Let their power fall in their wrath, who promise themselves to violate thy sanctuary, and defile the dwelling place of thy name, and to beat down with their sword the horn of thy altar.

12 Bring to pass, O Lord, that his pride may be cut off with his own sword.

13 Let him be caught in the net of his own eyes in my regard: and do thou strike him by the graces of the words of my lips.

14 Give me constancy in my mind, that I may despise him: and fortitude that I may overthrow him.

15 ³ For this will be a glorious monument for thy name, when he shall fall by the hand of a woman.

16 For thy power, O Lord, is not in a multitude, nor is thy pleasure in the strength of horses, nor from the beginning have the proud been acceptable to thee: but the prayer of the humble and the meek hath always pleased thee.

17 O God of the heavens, creator of the waters, and Lord of the whole creation: hear me a poor wretch, making supplication to thee, and presuming of thy mercy.

18 Remember, O Lord, thy covenant, and put thou words in my mouth, and strengthen the resolution in my heart: that thy house may continue in thy holiness.

19 And all nations may acknowledge that thou art God: and there is no other besides thee.

CHAPTER 10

Judith goeth out towards the camp, and is taken, and brought to Holofernes.

AND it came to pass, when she had ceased to cry to the Lord, that she rose from the place wherein she lay prostrate before the Lord.

2 And she called her maid: and going down into her house she took off her haircloth, and put away the garments of her widowhood.

3 And she washed her body, and anointed herself with the best ointment, and plaited the hair of her head, and put a bonnet upon her head, and clothed herself with the garments of her gladness, and put sandals on her feet, and took her bracelets, and lilies, and earlets, and rings, and adorned herself with all her ornaments.

4 And the Lord also gave her more beauty: because all this dressing up did not proceed from sensuality, but from virtue. And therefore the Lord increased this her beauty, so that she appeared to all men's eyes incomparably lovely.

5 And she gave to her maid a bottle of wine to carry, and a vessel of oil, and parched corn, and dry figs, and bread and cheese, and went out.

6 And when they came to the gate of the city, they found Ozias, and the ancients of the city waiting.

7 And when they saw her they were astonished, and admired her beauty exceedingly.

8 But they asked her no question. Only they let her pass, saying: The God of our fathers give thee grace. And may he strengthen all the counsel of thy heart with his power, that Jerusalem may glory in thee; and thy name may be in the number of the holy and just.

9 And they that were there said, all with one voice: So be it, so be it.

10 But Judith praying to the Lord, passed through the gates, she and her maid.

11 And it came to pass, when she went down the hill, about break of day, that the watchmen of the Assyrians met her, and stopped her, saying: Whence comest thou? Or whither goest thou?

12 And she answered: I am a daughter of the Hebrews, and I am fled from them, because I knew they would be made a prey to you, because they despised you, and would not of their own accord yield themselves, that they might find mercy in your sight.

13 For this reason I thought with myself, saying: I will go to the presence of the prince Holofernes, that I may tell him their secrets, and shew him by

³ Judges, 4, 21; 5, 26.

CHAP. 10. Ver. 12. *Because I knew.* In this and the following chapter, some things are related to have been said by Judith, which seem hard to reconcile with truth. But all that is related in scripture of the servants of God is not approved by the scripture; and even the saints in their good enterprises may sometimes slip into venial sins.

what way he may take them, without the loss of one man of his army.

14 And when the men had heard her words, they beheld her face. And their eyes were amazed, for they wondered exceedingly at her beauty.

15 And they said to her: Thou hast saved thy life by taking this resolution, to come down to our lord.

16 And be assured of this, that when thou shalt stand before him, he will treat thee well: and thou wilt be most acceptable to his heart. And they brought her to the tent of Holofernes, telling him of her.

17 And when she was come into his presence, forthwith Holofernes was caught by his eyes.

18 And his officers said to him: Who can despise the people of the Hebrews, who have such beautiful women, that we should not think it worth our while for their sakes to fight against them?

19 And Judith seeing Holofernes sitting under a canopy, which was woven of purple and gold, with emeralds and precious stones:

20 After she had looked on his face, bowed down to him, prostrating herself to the ground. And the servants of Holofernes lifted her up, by the command of their master.

CHAPTER 11

Judith's speech to Holofernes.

THEN Holofernes said to her: Be of good comfort, and fear not in thy heart; for I have never hurt a man that was willing to serve Nabuchodonosor the king.

2 And if thy people had not despised me, I would never have lifted up my spear against them.

3 But now tell me, for what cause hast thou left them: and why it hath pleased thee to come to us?

4 And Judith said to him: Receive the words of thy handmaid; for if thou wilt follow the words of thy handmaid, the Lord will do with thee a perfect thing.

5 For as Nabuchodonosor the king of the earth liveth, and his power liveth which is in thee for chastising of all straying souls: not only men serve him through thee, but also the beasts of the field obey him.

6 For the industry of thy mind is spoken of among all nations: and it is told through the whole world, that thou only art excellent, and mighty in all his kingdom; and thy discipline is cried up in all provinces.

7 [1] It is known also what Achior said:

nor are we ignorant of what thou hast commanded to be done to him.

8 For it is certain that our God is so offended with sins, that he hath sent word by his prophets to the people, that he will deliver them up for their sins.

9 And because the children of Israel know they have offended their God, thy dread is upon them.

10 Moreover also a famine hath come upon them: and for drought of water they are already to be counted among the dead.

11 And they have a design even to kill their cattle, and to drink the blood of them.

12 And the consecrated things of the Lord their God, which God forbade them to touch, in corn, wine, and oil, these have they purposed to make use of: and they design to consume the things which they ought not to touch with their hands. Therefore because they do these things, it is certain they will be given up to destruction.

13 And I, thy handmaid, knowing this, am fled from them; and the Lord hath sent me to tell thee these very things.

14 For I, thy handmaid, worship God even now that I am with thee: and thy handmaid will go out. And I will pray to God,

15 And he will tell me when he will repay them for their sins: and I will come and tell thee, so that I may bring thee through the midst of Jerusalem. And thou shalt have all the people of Israel, as sheep that have no shepherd; and there shall not so much as one dog bark against thee.

16 Because these things are told me by the providence of God;

17 And because God is angry with them, I am sent to tell these very things to thee.

18 And all these words pleased Holofernes, and his servants. And they admired her wisdom; and they said one to another:

19 There is not such another woman upon earth in look, in beauty, and in sense of words.

20 And Holofernes said to her: God hath done well who sent thee before the people, that thou mightest give them into our hands.

21 And because thy promise is good, if thy God shall do this for me, he shall also be my God. And thou shalt be great in the house of Nabuchodonosor: and thy name shall be renowned through all the earth.

CHAPTER 12

Judith goeth out in the night to pray. She is invited to a banquet with Holofernes.

WHEN he ordered that she should go in where his treasures were laid up: and bade her tarry there. And he appointed what should be given her from his own table.

2 And Judith answered him and said: Now I cannot eat of these things which thou commandest to be given me, lest sin come upon me: but I will eat of the things which I have brought.

3 And Holofernes said to her: If these things which thou hast brought with thee fail thee, what shall we do for thee?

4 And Judith said: As thy soul liveth, my lord, thy handmaid shall not spend all these things till God do by my hand that which I have purposed. And his servants brought her into the tent which he had commanded.

5 And when she was going in, she desired that she might have liberty to go out at night and before day, to prayer, and to beseech the Lord.

6 And he commanded his chamberlains, that she might go out and in, to adore her God as she pleased, for three days.

7 And she went out in the nights into the valley of Bethulia, and washed herself in a fountain of water.

8 And as she came up, she prayed to the Lord the God of Israel, that he would direct her way to the deliverance of his people.

9 And going in, she remained pure in the tent, until she took her own meat in the evening.

10 And it came to pass on the fourth day, that Holofernes made a supper for his servants, and said to Vagao his eunuch: Go, and persuade that Hebrew woman, to consent of her own accord to dwell with me.

11 For it is looked upon as shameful among the Assyrians, if a woman mock a man, by doing so as to pass free from him.

12 Then Vagao went in to Judith, and said: Let not my good maid be afraid to go in to my lord, that she may be honoured before his face, that she may eat with him and drink wine and be merry.

13 And Judith answered him: Who am I, that I should gainsay my lord?

14 All that shall be good and best before his eyes, I will do. And whatsoever shall please him, that shall be best to me all the days of my life.

15 And she arose and dressed herself out with her garments: and going in she stood before his face.

16 And the heart of Holofernes was smitten, for he was burning with the desire of her.

17 And Holofernes said to her: Drink now, and sit down and be merry; for thou hast found favour before me.

18 And Judith said: I will drink my lord, because my life is magnified this day above all my days.

19 And she took and ate and drank before him what her maid had prepared for her.

20 And Holofernes was made merry on her occasion, and drank exceeding much wine, so much as he had never drunk in his life.

CHAPTER 13

Judith cutteth off the head of Holofernes, and returneth to Bethulia.

AND when it was grown late, his servants made haste to their lodgings: and Vagao shut the chamber doors, and went his way.

2 And they were all overcharged with wine.

3 And Judith was alone in the chamber.

4 But Holofernes lay on his bed, fast asleep, being exceedingly drunk.

5 And Judith spoke to her maid to stand without before the chamber, and to watch.

6 And Judith stood before the bed praying with tears; and the motion of her lips in silence,

7 Saying: Strengthen me, O Lord God of Israel, and in this hour look on the works of my hands, that as thou hast promised, thou mayst raise up Jerusalem thy city. And that I may bring to pass that which I have purposed, having a belief that it might be done by thee.

8 And when she had said this, she went to the pillar that was at his bed's head, and loosed his sword that hung tied upon it.

9 And when she had drawn it out, she took him by the hair of his head, and said: Strengthen me, O Lord God, at this hour.

10 And she struck twice upon his neck, and cut off his head, and took off his canopy from the pillars, and rolled away his headless body.

11 And after a while she went out, and delivered the head of Holofernes to her maid, and bade her put it into her wallet.

12 And they two went out according to their custom, as it were to prayer. And they passed the camp; and having compassed the valley, they came to the gate of the city.

13 And Judith from afar off cried to the watchmen upon the walls: Open the gates, for God is with us, who hath shewn his power in Israel.

14 And it came to pass, when the men had heard her voice, that they called the ancients of the city.

15 And all ran to meet her from the least to the greatest: for they now had no hopes that she would come.

16 And lighting up lights they all gathered round about her. And she went up to a higher place, and commanded silence to be made. And when all had held their peace,

17 Judith said: Praise ye the Lord our God, who hath not forsaken them that hope in him.

18 And by me his handmaid he hath fulfilled his mercy, which he promised to the house of Israel: and he hath killed the enemy of his people by my hand this night.

19 Then she brought forth the head of Holofernes out of the wallet, and shewed it them, saying: Behold the head of Holofernes the general of the army of the Assyrians; and behold his canopy, wherein he lay in his drunkenness, where the Lord our God slew him by the hand of a woman.

20 But as the same Lord liveth, his angel hath been my keeper both going hence, and abiding there, and returning from thence hither. And the Lord hath not suffered me his handmaid to be defiled: but hath brought me back to you without pollution of sin, rejoicing for his victory, for my escape, and for your deliverance.

21 [1] Give all of you glory to him, because he is good: because his mercy endureth for ever.

22 And they all adored the Lord, and said to her: The Lord hath blessed thee by his power, because by thee he hath brought our enemies to nought.

23 And Ozias, the prince of the people of Israel, said to her: Blessed art thou, O daughter, by the Lord the most high God, above all women upon the earth.

24 Blessed be the Lord who made heaven and earth, who hath directed thee to the cutting off the head of the prince of our enemies.

25 Because he hath so magnified thy name this day, that thy praise shall not depart out of the mouth of men who shall be mindful of the power of the Lord, for ever: for that thou hast not spared thy life, by reason of the distress and tribulation of thy people; but hast prevented our ruin in the presence of our God.

26 And all the people said: So be it. So be it.

27 And Achior being called for came: and Judith said to him: The God of Israel, to whom thou gavest testimony,

that he revengeth himself of his enemies, he hath cut off the head of all the unbelievers this night by my hand.

28 And that thou mayst find that it is so, behold the head of Holofernes, who in the contempt of his pride despised the God of Israel, and threatened thee with death, saying: When the people of Israel shall be taken, I will command thy sides to be pierced with a sword.

29 Then Achior seeing the head of Holofernes, being seized with a great fear he fell on his face upon the earth; and his soul swooned away.

30 But after he had recovered his spirits, he fell down at her feet, and reverenced her, and said:

31 Blessed art thou by thy God in every tabernacle of Jacob; for in every nation which shall hear thy name, the God of Israel shall be magnified on occasion of thee.

CHAPTER 14

The Israelites assault the Assyrians, who finding their general slain, are seized with a panic fear.

AND Judith said to all the people: Hear me, my brethren; hang ye up this head upon our walls.

2 And as soon as the sun shall rise, let every man take his arms: and rush ye out, not as going down beneath, but as making an assault.

3 Then the watchmen must needs run to awake their prince for the battle.

4 And when the captains of them shall run to the tent of Holofernes, and shall find him without his head, wallowing in his blood, fear shall fall upon them.

5 And when you shall know that they are fleeing, go after them securely: for the Lord will destroy them under your feet.

6 And Achior seeing the power that the God of Israel had wrought, leaving the religion of the Gentiles, he believed God, and circumcised the flesh of his foreskin, and was joined to the people of Israel, with all the succession of his kindred until this present day.

7 And immediately at break of day, they hung up the head of Holofernes upon the walls. And every man took his arms: and they went out with a great noise and shouting.

8 And the watchmen seeing this, ran to the tent of Holofernes.

9 And they that were in the tent came, and made a noise before the door of the chamber to awake him: endeavouring by art to break his rest, that

CHAP. 13. [1] Ps. 105, 1; 106, 1.

Holofernes might awake, not by their calling him, but by their noise.

10 For no man durst knock, or open and go into the chamber of the general of the Assyrians.

11 But when his captains and tribunes were come, and all the chiefs of the army of the king of the Assyrians, they said to the chamberlains:

12 Go in, and awake him; for the mice, coming out of their holes, have presumed to challenge us to fight.

13 Then Vagao going into his chamber, stood before the curtain, and made a clapping with his hands. For he thought that he was sleeping with Judith.

14 But when with hearkening, he perceived no motion of one lying, he came near to the curtain; and lifting up, and seeing the body of Holofernes, lying upon the ground, without the head, weltering in his blood, he cried out with a loud voice, with weeping, and rent his garments.

15 And he went into the tent of Judith; and not finding her, he ran out to the people,

16 And said: One Hebrew woman hath made confusion in the house of king Nabuchodonosor. For behold Holofernes lieth upon the ground; and his head is not upon him.

17 Now when the chiefs of the army of the Assyrians had heard this, they all rent their garments: and an intolerable fear and dread fell upon them; and their minds were troubled exceedingly.

18 And there was a very great cry in the midst of their camp.

CHAPTER 15

The Assyrians flee. The Hebrews pursue after them, and are enriched by their spoils.

AND when all the army heard that Holofernes was beheaded, courage and counsel fled from them. And being seized with trembling and fear, they thought only to save themselves by flight.

2 So that no one spoke to his neighbour, but hanging down the head, leaving all things behind, they made haste to escape from the Hebrews, who, as they heard, were coming armed upon them: and fled by the ways of the fields and the paths of the hills.

3 So the children of Israel seeing them fleeing, followed after them. And they went down sounding with trumpets and shouting after them.

4 And because the Assyrians were not united together, they went without order in their flight. But the children of Israel pursuing in one body, defeated all that they could find.

5 And Ozias sent messengers through all the cities and countries of Israel.

6 And every country, and every city, sent their chosen young men armed after them. And they pursued them with the edge of the sword until they came to the extremities of their confines.

7 And the rest that were in Bethulia went into the camp of the Assyrians, and took away the spoils, which the Assyrians in their flight had left behind them: and they were laden exceedingly.

8 But they that returned conquerors to Bethulia, brought with them all things that were theirs, so that there was no numbering of their cattle, and beasts, and all their moveables, insomuch that from the least to the greatest all were made rich by their spoils.

9 And Joachim the high priest came from Jerusalem to Bethulia with all his ancients to see Judith.

10 And when she was come out to him, they all blessed her with one voice, saying: Thou art the glory of Jerusalem, thou art the joy of Israel, thou art the honour of our people.

11 For thou hast done manfully, and thy heart has been strengthened, because thou hast loved chastity, and after thy husband hast not known any other. Therefore also the hand of the Lord hath strengthened thee, and therefore thou shalt be blessed for ever.

12 And all the people said: So be it. So be it.

13 And thirty days were scarce sufficient for the people of Israel to gather up the spoils of the Assyrians.

14 But all those things that were proved to be the peculiar goods of Holofernes, they gave to Judith in gold, and silver and garments and precious stones, and all household stuff: and they all were delivered to her by the people.

15 And all the people rejoiced with the women, and virgins, and young men, playing on instruments and harps.

CHAPTER 16

The canticle of Judith. Her virtuous life and death.

THEN Judith sung this canticle to the Lord, saying:

2 Begin ye to the Lord with timbrels, sing ye to the Lord with cymbals, tune unto him a new psalm: extol and call upon his name.

3 The Lord putteth an end to wars: the Lord in his name.

4 He hath set his camp in the midst

of his people, to deliver us from the hand of all our enemies.

5 The Assyrian came out of the mountains from the north in the multitude of his strength: his multitude stopped up the torrents; and their horses covered the valleys.

6 He bragged that he would set my borders on fire, and kill my young men with the sword: to make my infants a prey, and my virgins captives.

7 But the almighty Lord hath struck him, and hath delivered him into the hands of a woman, and hath slain him.

8 For their mighty one did not fall by young men: neither did the sons of Titan strike him, nor tall giants oppose themselves to him. But Judith the daughter of Merari weakened him with the beauty of her face.

9 For she put off her the garments of widowhood, and put on her the garments of joy, to give joy to the children of Israel.

10 She anointed her face with ointment, and bound up her locks with a crown: she took a new robe to deceive him.

11 Her sandals ravished his eyes, her beauty made his soul her captive: with a sword she cut off his head.

12 The Persians quaked at her constancy: and the Medes at her boldness.

13 Then the camp of the Assyrians howled, when my lowly ones appeared, parched with thirst.

14 The sons of the damsels have pierced them through: and they have killed them like children fleeing away. They perished in battle before the face of the Lord my God.

15 Let us sing a hymn to the Lord: let us sing a new hymn to our God.

16 O Adonai, Lord, greatest art thou, and glorious in thy power: and no one can overcome thee.

17 [1] Let all thy creatures serve thee: because thou hast spoken, and they were made: thou didst send forth thy spirit, and they were created. And there is no one that can resist thy voice.

18 The mountains shall be moved from the foundations with the waters: the rocks shall melt as wax before thy face.

19 But they that fear thee, shall be great with thee in all things.

20 Woe be to the nation that riseth up against my people: for the Lord almighty will take revenge on them. In the day of judgment he will visit them:

21 For he will give fire, and worms into their flesh, that they may burn, and may feel for ever.

22 And it came to pass after these things, that all the people, after the victory, came to Jerusalem to adore the Lord: and as soon as they were purified, they all offered holocausts, and vows, and their promises.

23 And Judith offered for an anathema of oblivion all the arms of Holofernes, which the people gave her, and the canopy that she had taken away out of his chamber.

24 And the people were joyful in the sight of the sanctuary: and for three months the joy of this victory was celebrated with Judith.

25 And after those days every man returned to his house. And Judith was made great in Bethulia; and she was most renowned in all the land of Israel.

26 And chastity was joined to her virtue, so that she knew no man all the days of her life, after the death of Manasses her husband.

27 And on festival days she came forth with great glory.

28 And she abode in her husband's house a hundred and five years, and made her handmaid free. And she died, and was buried with her husband in Bethulia.

29 And all the people mourned for seven days.

30 And all the time of her life there was none that troubled Israel, nor many years after her death.

31 But the day of the festivity of this victory is received by the Hebrews in the number of holy days, and is religiously observed by the Jews from that time until this day.

CHAP. 16. [1] Ps. 32, 9.

CHAP. 16. Ver. 23. *An anathema of oblivion:* That is, a gift or offering made to God, by the way of an everlasting monument, to prevent the oblivion of forgetting so great a benefit.

THE BOOK OF

ESTHER

This Book takes its name from Queen Esther, whose history is here recorded. The general opinion of almost all commentators on the Holy Scriptures makes Mardochai the writer of it: which also may be collected below from chap. 9, ver. 20.

CHAPTER 1

King Assuerus maketh a great feast. Queen Vasthi being sent for refuseth to come. For which disobedience she is deposed.

IN the days of Assuerus, who reigned from India to Ethiopia, over a hundred and twenty-seven provinces:

2 When he sat on the throne of his kingdom, the city Susan was the capital of his kingdom.

3 Now in the third year of his reign he made a great feast for all the princes, and for his servants, for the most mighty of the Persians, and the nobles of the Medes, and the governors of the provinces in his sight:

4 That he might shew the riches of the glory of his kingdom, and the greatness, and boasting of his power: for a long time, to wit, for a hundred and fourscore days.

5 And when the days of the feast were expired, he invited all the people that were found in Susan, from the greatest to the least: and commanded a feast to be made seven days in the court of the garden, and of the wood, which was planted by the care and hand of the king.

6 And there were hung up on every side sky-coloured, and green, and violet hangings, fastened with cords of silk, and of purple: which were put into rings of ivory, and were held up with marble pillars. The beds also were of gold and silver, placed in order upon a floor paved with porphyry and white marble: which was embellished with painting of wonderful variety.

7 And they that were invited, drank in golden cups: and the meats were brought in divers vessels, one after another. Wine also in abundance and of the best was presented, as was worthy of a king's magnificence.

8 Neither was there any one to compel them to drink that were not willing: but as the king had appointed, who set over every table one of his nobles, that every man might take what he would.

9 Also Vasthi the queen made a feast for the women in the palace, where king Assuerus was used to dwell.

10 Now on the seventh day, when the king was merry, and after very much drinking was well warmed with wine, he commanded Mauman, and Bazatha, and Harbona, and Bagatha, and Abgatha, and Zethar, and Charcas, the seven eunuchs that served in his presence,

11 To bring in queen Vasthi before the king, with the crown set upon her head: to shew her beauty to all the people and the princes. For she was exceeding beautiful.

12 But she refused, and would not come at the king's commandment, which he had signified to her by the eunuchs. Whereupon the king, being angry, and inflamed with a very great fury,

13 Asked the wise men, who according to the custom of the kings, were always near his person, and all he did was by their counsel, who knew the laws, and judgments of their forefathers:

14 (Now the chief and nearest him were, Charsena, and Sethar, and Admatha, and Tharsis, and Mares, and Marsana, and Mamuchan, seven princes of the Persians, and of the Medes, who saw the face of the king, and were used to sit first after him):

15 What sentence ought to pass upon Vasthi the queen, who had refused to obey the commandment of king Assuerus, which he had sent to her by the eunuchs?

16 And Mamuchan answered, in the hearing of the king and the princes: Queen Vasthi hath not only injured the king, but also all the people and princes that are in all the provinces of king Assuerus.

17 For this deed of the queen will go abroad to all women, so that they will despise their husbands, and will say: King Assuerus commanded that queen Vasthi should come in to him, and she would not.

18 And by this example all the wives of the princes of the Persians and the Medes will slight the commandments of their husbands. Wherefore the king's indignation is just.

19 If it please thee, let an edict go out from thy presence, and let it be written according to the law of the Persians and of the Medes, which must not be altered: That Vasthi come in no more to the king; but another, that is better than her, be made queen in her place.

20 And let this be published through all the provinces of thy empire (which is very wide): and let all wives, as well of the greater as of the lesser, give honour to their husbands.

21 His counsel pleased the king and the princes. And the king did according to the counsel of Mamuchan.

22 And he sent letters to all the provinces of his kingdom, as every nation could hear and read, in divers languages and characters, that the husbands should be rulers and masters in their houses: and that this should be published to every people.

CHAPTER 2

Esther is advanced to be queen. Mardochai detecteth a plot against the king.

AFTER this, when the wrath of king Assuerus was appeased, he remembered Vasthi, and what she had done and what she had suffered.

2 And the king's servants and his officers said: Let young women be sought for the king, virgins and beautiful,

3 And let some persons be sent through all the provinces to look for beautiful maidens and virgins. And let them bring them to the city of Susan, and put them into the house of the women under the hand of Egeus the eunuch, who is the overseer and keeper of the king's women. And let them receive women's ornaments, and other things necessary for their use.

4 And whosoever among them all shall please the king's eyes, let her be queen instead of Vasthi. The word pleased the king: and he commanded it should be done as they had suggested.

5 There was a man in the city of Susan, a Jew, named Mardochai, [1] the son of Jair, the son of Semei, the son of Cis, of the race of Jemini,

6 Who had been carried away from Jerusalem at the time that Nabuchodonosor king of Babylon carried away [2] Jechonias king of Juda.

7 And he had brought up his brother's daughter Edissa, who by

another name was called Esther. Now she had lost both her parents: and was exceeding fair and beautiful. And her father and mother being dead, Mardochai adopted her for his daughter.

8 And when the king's ordinance was noised abroad, and according to his commandment many beautiful virgins were brought to Susan, and were delivered to Egeus the eunuch: Esther also among the rest of the maidens was delivered to him to be kept in the number of the women.

9 And she pleased him, and found favour in his sight. And he commanded the eunuch to hasten the women's ornaments, and to deliver to her her part, and seven of the most beautiful maidens of the king's house: and to adorn and deck out both her and her waiting maids.

10 And she would not tell him her people nor her country. For Mardochai had charged her to say nothing at all of that:

11 And he walked every day before the court of the house, in which the chosen virgins were kept, having a care for Esther's welfare, and desiring to know what would befall her.

12 Now when every virgin's turn came to go in to the king, after all had been done for setting them off to advantage, it was the twelfth month. So that for six months they were anointed with oil of myrrh; and for other six months they used certain perfumes and sweet spices.

13 And when they were going in to the king, whatsoever they asked to adorn themselves they received. And being decked out, as it pleased them, they passed from the chamber of the women to the king's chamber.

14 And she that went in at evening, came out in the morning: and from thence she was conducted to the second house, that was under the hand of Susagaz the eunuch, who had the charge over the king's concubines. Neither could she return any more to the king, unless the king desired it, and had ordered her by name to come.

15 And as the time came orderly about, the day was at hand, when Esther, the daughter of Abihail the brother of Mardochai, whom he had adopted for his daughter, was to go in to the king. But she sought not women's ornaments, but whatsoever Egeus the eunuch the keeper of the virgins had a mind, he gave her to adorn her. For she was exceeding fair: and her incredible beauty made her appear agreeable and amiable in the eyes of all.

16 So she was brought to the cham-

ber of king Assuerus, the tenth month, which is called Tebeth, in the seventh year of his reign.

17 And the king loved her more than all the women: and she had favour and kindness before him above all the women. And he set the royal crown on her head, and made her queen instead of Vasthi.

18 And he commanded a magnificent feast to be prepared for all the princes, and for his servants, for the marriage and wedding of Esther. And he gave rest to all the provinces, and bestowed gifts according to princely magnificence.

19 And when the virgins were sought the second time, and gathered together, Mardochai stayed at the king's gate,

20 Neither had Esther as yet declared her country and people, according to his commandment. For whatsoever he commanded, Esther observed: and she did all things in the same manner as she was wont at that time when he brought her up, a little one.

21 At that time, therefore, when Mardochai abode at the king's gate, Bagathan and Thares, two of the king's eunuchs, who were porters, and presided in the first entry of the palace, were angry. And they designed to rise up against the king, and to kill him.

22 And Mardochai had notice of it, and immediately he told it to queen Esther: and she to the king in Mardochai's name, who had reported the thing unto her.

23 It was inquired into, and found out: and they were both hanged on a gibbet. And it was put in the histories, and recorded in the chronicles before the king.

CHAPTER 3

Aman, advanced by the king is offended at Mardochai, and therefore procureth the king's decree to destroy the whole nation of the Jews.

AFTER these things, king Assuerus advanced Aman, the son of Amadathi, who was of the race of Agag. And he set his throne above all the princes that were with him.

2 And all the king's servants, that were at the doors of the palace, bent their knees, and worshipped Aman: for so the emperor had commanded them. Only Mardochai did not bend his knee, nor worship him.

3 And the king's servants that were chief at the doors of the palace said to him: Why dost thou alone not observe the king's commandment?

4 And when they were saying this often, and he would not hearken to them, they told Aman, desirous to know whether he would continue in his resolution: for he had told them that he was a Jew.

5 Now when Aman had heard this, and had proved by experience that Mardochai did not bend his knee to him, nor worship him, he was exceeding angry.

6 And he counted it nothing to lay his hands upon Mardochai alone. For he had heard that he was of the nation of the Jews: and he chose rather to destroy all the nation of the Jews that were in the kingdom of Assuerus.

7 In the first month (which is called Nisan) in the twelfth year of the reign of Assuerus, the lot was cast into an urn, which in Hebrew is called Phur, before Aman, on what day and what month the nation of the Jews should be destroyed. And there came out the twelfth month, which is called Adar.

8 And Aman said to king Assuerus: There is a people scattered through all the provinces of thy kingdom, and separated one from another, that use new laws and ceremonies, and moreover despise the king's ordinances: and thou knowest very well that it is not expedient for thy kingdom that they should grow insolent by impunity.

9 If it please thee, decree that they may be destroyed: and I will pay ten thousand talents to thy treasurers.

10 And the king took the ring that he used, from his own hand, and gave it to Aman, the son of Amadathi of the race of Agag, the enemy of the Jews,

11 And he said to him: As to the money which thou promisest, keep it for thyself. And as to the people, do with them as seemeth good to thee.

12 And the king's scribes were called in the first month Nisan, on the thirteenth day of the same month. And they wrote, as Aman had commanded, to all the king's lieutenants, and to the judges of the provinces, and of divers nations, as every nation could read, and hear according to their different languages, in the name of king Assuerus. And the letters, sealed with his ring,

13 Were sent by the king's messengers to all provinces, to kill and destroy all the Jews, both young and old, little children, and women, in one day, that is, on the thirteenth of the twelfth month, which is called Adar: and to make a spoil of their goods.

14 And the contents of the letters were to this effect, that all provinces might know and be ready against that day.

15 The couriers that were sent made haste to fulfil the king's commandment. And immediately the edict was hung up

in Susan: the king and Aman feasting together, and all the Jews that were in the city weeping.

CHAPTER 4

Mardochai desireth Esther to petition the king for the Jews. They join in fasting and prayer.

NOW when Mardochai had heard these things, he rent his garments, and put on sackcloth, strewing ashes on his head. And he cried with a loud voice in the street in the midst of the city, shewing the anguish of his mind.

2 And he came lamenting in this manner even to the gate of the palace: for no one clothed with sackcloth might enter the king's court.

3 And in all provinces, towns, and places, to which the king's cruel edict was come, there was great mourning among the Jews, with fasting, wailing, and weeping, many using sackcloth and ashes for their bed.

4 Then Esther's maids and her eunuchs went in, and told her. And when she heard it she was in a consternation. And she sent a garment, to clothe him, and to take away the sackcloth: but he would not receive it.

5 And she called for Athach the eunuch, whom the king had appointed to attend upon her: and she commanded him to go to Mardochai, and learn of him why he did this.

6 And Athach going out went to Mardochai, who was standing in the street of the city, before the palace gate.

7 And Mardochai told him all that had happened: how Aman had promised to pay money into the king's treasures, to have the Jews destroyed.

8 He gave him also a copy of the edict which was hanging up in Susan: that he should shew it to the queen, and admonish her to go in to the king, and to entreat him for her people.

9 And Athach went back and told Esther all that Mardochai had said.

10 She answered him, and bade him say to Mardochai:

11 All the king's servants, and all the provinces that are under his dominion, know, that whosoever, whether man, or woman, cometh into the king's inner court, who is not called for, is immediately to be put to death without any delay: except the king shall hold out the golden sceptre to him, in token of clemency, that so he may live. How then can I go in to the king, who for these thirty days now have not been called unto him?

12 And when Mardochai had heard this,

13 He sent word to Esther again, saying: Think not that thou mayst save thy life only, because thou art in the king's house, more than all the Jews.

14 For if thou wilt now hold thy peace, the Jews shall be delivered by some other occasion: and thou, and thy father's house, shall perish. And who knoweth whether thou art not therefore come to the kingdom, that thou mightest be ready in such a time as this?

15 And again Esther sent to Mardochai in these words:

16 Go, and gather together all the Jews whom thou shalt find in Susan: and pray ye for me. Neither eat nor drink for three days and three nights: and I with my handmaids will fast in like manner. And then I will go in to the king, against the law, not being called: and expose myself to death and to danger.

17 So Mardochai went, and did all that Esther had commanded him.

CHAPTER 5

Esther is graciously received. She inviteth the king and Aman to dinner. Aman prepareth a gibbet for Mardochai.

AND on the third day Esther put on her royal apparel, and stood in the inner court of the king's house, over against the king's hall. Now he sat upon his throne in the hall of the palace, over against the door of the house.

2 And when he saw Esther the queen standing, she pleased his eyes, and he held out toward her the golden sceptre which he held in his hand. And she drew near, and kissed the top of his sceptre.

3 And the king said to her: What wilt thou, Queen Esther? What is thy request? If thou shouldst even ask one half of the kingdom, it shall be given to thee.

4 But she answered: If it please the king, I beseech thee to come to me this day, and Aman with thee, to the banquet which I have prepared.

5 And the king said forthwith: Call ye Aman quickly, that he may obey Esther's will. So the king and Aman came to the banquet which the queen had prepared for them.

6 And the king said to her, after he had drunk wine plentifully: What dost thou desire should be given thee? And for what thing askest thou? Although thou shouldst ask the half of my kingdom, thou shalt have it.

7 And Esther answered: My petition and request is this:

8 If I have found favour in the king's sight; and if it please the king to give me what I ask, and to fulfil my petition; let the king and Aman come to the ban-

quet which I have prepared them; and to-morrow I will open my mind to the king.

9 So Aman went out that day joyful and merry. And when he saw Mardochai sitting before the gate of the palace, and that he not only did not rise up to honour him, but did not so much as move from the place where he sat, he was exceedingly angry.

10 But dissembling his anger, and returning into his house, he called together to him his friends, and Zares his wife.

11 And he declared to them the greatness of his riches, and the multitude of his children, and with how great glory the king had advanced him above all his princes and servants.

12 And after this he said: Queen Esther also hath invited no other to the banquet with the king, but me. And with her I am also to dine to-morrow with the king:

13 And whereas I have all these things, I think I have nothing, so long as I see Mardochai the Jew sitting before the king's gate.

14 Then Zares his wife and the rest of his friends answered him: Order a great beam to be prepared, fifty cubits high. And in the morning, speak to the king, that Mardochai may be hanged upon it. And so thou shalt go full of joy with the king to the banquet. The counsel pleased him: and he commanded a high gibbet to be prepared.

CHAPTER 6

The king hearing of the good service done him by Mardochai, commandeth Aman to honour him next to the king, which he performeth.

THAT night the king passed without sleep: and he commanded the histories and chronicles of former times to be brought him. And when they were reading them before him,

2 They came to that place where it was written, how Mardochai had discovered the treason of Bagathan and Thares the eunuchs, who sought to kill king Assuerus.

3 And when the king heard this, he said: What honour and reward hath Mardochai received for this fidelity? His servants and minister said to him: He hath received no reward at all.

4 And the king said immediately: Who is in the court? For Aman was coming in to the inner court of the king's house, to speak to the king; that he might order Mardochai to be hanged upon the gibbet which was prepared for him.

5 The servants answered: Aman standeth in the court. And the king said: Let him come in.

6 And when he was come in, he said to him: What ought to be done to the man whom the king is desirous to honour? But Aman thinking in his heart, and supposing that the king would honour no other but himself,

7 Answered: The man whom the king desireth to honour,

8 Ought to be clothed with the king's apparel, and to be set upon the horse that the king ridest upon, and to have the royal crown upon his head.

9 And let the first of the king's princes and nobles hold his horse. And going through the street of the city, proclaim before him and say: Thus shall he be honoured, whom the king hath a mind to honour.

10 And the king said to him: Make haste and take the robe and the horse; and do as thou hast spoken to Mardochai the Jew, who sitteth before the gates of the palace. Beware thou pass over any of those things which thou hast spoken.

11 So Aman took the robe and the horse, and arraying Mardochai in the street of the city, and setting him on the horse, went before him, and proclaimed: This honour is he worthy of, whom the king hath a mind to honour.

12 But Mardochai returned to the palace gate: and Aman made haste to go to his house, mourning and having his head covered.

13 And he told Zares his wife, and his friends, all that had befallen him. And the wise men whom he had in counsel, and his wife answered him: If Mardochai be of the seed of the Jews, before whom thou hast begun to fall, thou canst not resist him: but thou shalt fall in his sight.

14 As they were yet speaking, the king's eunuchs came, and compelled him to go quickly to the banquet which the queen had prepared.

CHAPTER 7

Esther's petition for herself and her people. Aman is hanged upon the gibbet he had prepared for Mardochai.

SO the king and Aman went in, to drink with the queen.

2 And the king said to her again the second day, after he was warm with wine: What is thy petition, Esther, that it may be granted thee? And what wilt thou have done: although thou ask the half of my kingdom, thou shalt have it.

CHAP. 6. Ver. 3. *No reward at all.* He received some presents from the king (chap. 12, 5); but these were so inconsiderable in the opinion of the courtiers, that they esteemed them as nothing at all.

3 Then she answered: If I have found favour in thy sight, O king, and if it please thee, give me my life for which I ask, and my people for which I request.

4 For we are given up, I and my people, to be destroyed, to be slain, and to perish. And would God we were sold for bondmen and bondwomen: the evil might be borne with, and I would have mourned in silence. But now we have an enemy, whose cruelty redoundeth upon the king.

5 And king Assuerus answered and said: Who is this, and of what power, that he should do these things?

6 And Esther said: It is this Aman that is our adversary and most wicked enemy. Aman hearing this was forthwith astonished, not being able to bear the countenance of the king and of the queen.

7 But the king being angry rose up, and went from the place of the banquet into the garden set with trees. Aman also rose up to entreat Esther the queen for his life: for he understood that evil was prepared for him by the king.

8 And when the king came back out of the garden set with trees, and entered into the place of the banquet, he found Aman was fallen upon the bed on which Esther lay. And he said: He will force the queen also in my presence, in my own house. The word was not yet gone out of the king's mouth: and immediately they covered his face.

9 And Harbona, one of the eunuchs that stood waiting on the king, said: Behold the gibbet which he hath prepared for Mardochai, who spoke for the king, standeth in Aman's house, being fifty cubits high. And the king said to him: Hang him upon it.

10 So Aman was hanged on the gibbet, which he had prepared for Mardochai: and the king's wrath ceased.

CHAPTER 8

Mardochai is advanced. Aman's letters are reversed.

ON that day king Assuerus gave the house of Aman, the Jews' enemy, to queen Esther: and Mardochai came in before the king. For Esther had confessed to him that he was her uncle.

2 And the king took the ring which he had commanded to be taken again from Aman, and gave it to Mardochai. And Esther set Mardochai over her house.

3 And not content with these things, she fell down at the king's feet and wept: and speaking to him besought him, that he would give orders that the malice of Aman the Agagite, and his most wicked devices which he had invented against the Jews, should be of no effect.

4 But he, as the manner was, held out the golden sceptre with his hand, which was the sign of clemency. And she arose up and stood before him.

5 And said: If it please the king, and if I have found favour in his sight, and my request be not disagreeable to him, I beseech thee, that the former letters of Aman the traitor and enemy of the Jews, by which he commanded that they should be destroyed in all the king's provinces, may be reversed by new letters.

6 For how can I endure the murdering and slaughter of my people?

7 And king Assuerus answered Esther the queen, and Mardochai the Jew: I have given Aman's house to Esther; and I have commanded him to be hanged on a gibbet, because he durst lay hands on the Jews.

8 Write ye therefore to the Jews, as it pleaseth you, in the king's name: and seal the letters with my ring. For this was the custom, that no man durst gainsay the letters which were sent in the king's name, and were sealed with his ring.

9 Then the king's scribes and secretaries were called for (now it was the time of the third month which is called Siban) the three and twentieth day of the month, and letters were written, as Mardochai had a mind, to the Jews, and to the governors, and to the deputies, and to the judges, who were rulers over the hundred and twenty-seven provinces, from India even to Ethiopia: to province and province, to people and people, according to their languages and characters: and to the Jews, according as they could read and hear.

10 And these letters which were sent in the king's name, were sealed with his ring, and sent by posts: who were to run through all the provinces, to prevent the former letters with new messages.

11 And the king gave orders to them, to speak to the Jews in every city, and to command them to gather themselves together, and to stand for their lives, and to kill and destroy all their enemies with their wives and children and all their houses, and to take their spoil.

12 And one day of revenge was appointed through all the provinces, to wit, the thirteenth of the twelfth month Adar.

13 And this was the content of the letter, that it should be notified in all lands and peoples that were subject to the empire of king Assuerus, that the Jews were ready to be revenged of their enemies.

14 So the swift posts went out carrying the messages: and the king's edict was hung up in Susan.

15 And Mardochai going forth out of the palace, and from the king's presence, shone in royal apparel: to wit, of violet and sky colour, wearing a golden crown on his head, and clothed with a cloak of silk and purple. And all the city rejoiced and was glad.

16 But to the Jews a new light seemed to rise: joy, honour, and dancing.

17 And in all peoples, cities, and provinces, whithersoever the king's commandments came, there was wonderful rejoicing, feasts and banquets, and keeping holy day: insomuch that many of other nations and religion joined themselves to their worship and ceremonies. For a great dread of the name of the Jews had fallen upon all.

CHAPTER 9

The Jews kill their enemies that would have killed them. The days of Phurim are appointed to be kept holy.

SO on the thirteenth day of the twelfth month, which as we have said above is called Adar, when all the Jews were designed to be massacred, and their enemies were greedy after their blood, the case being altered, the Jews began to have the upper hand, and to revenge themselves of their adversaries.

2 And they gathered themselves together in every city, and town, and place, to lay their hands on their enemies, and their persecutors. And no one durst withstand them: for the fear of their power had gone through every people.

3 And the judges of the provinces, and the governors, and lieutenants, and every one in dignity, that presided over every place and work, extolled the Jews for fear of Mardochai.

4 For they knew him to be prince of the palace, and to have great power. And the fame of his name increased daily, and was spread abroad through all men's mouths.

5 So the Jews made a great slaughter of their enemies, and killed them, repaying according to what they had prepared to do to them.

6 Insomuch that even in Susan they killed five hundred men, besides the ten sons of Aman the Agagite, the enemy of the Jews. Whose names are these:

7 Pharsandatha, and Delphon, and Esphatha,

8 And Phoratha, and Adalia, and Aridatha,

9 And Phermesta, and Arisai, and Aridai, and Jezatha.

10 And when they had slain them, they would not touch the spoils of their goods.

11 And presently the number of them that were killed in Susan was brought to the king.

12 And he said to the queen: The Jews have killed five hundred men in the city of Susan, besides the ten sons of Aman. How many dost thou think they have slain in all the provinces? What askest thou more, and what wilt thou have me to command to be done?

13 And she answered: If it please the king, let it be granted to the Jews, to do to-morrow in Susan as they have done to-day, and that the ten sons of Aman may be hanged upon gibbets.

14 And the king commanded that it should be so done. And forthwith the edict was hung up in Susan: and the ten sons of Aman were hanged.

15 And on the fourteenth day of the month Adar, the Jews gathered themselves together and they killed in Susan three hundred men. But they took not their substance.

16 Moreover through all the provinces that were subject to the king's dominion, the Jews stood for their lives and slew their enemies and persecutors. Insomuch that the number of them that were killed amounted to seventy-five thousand: and no man took any of their goods.

17 Now the thirteenth day of the month Adar was the first day with them all of the slaughter; and on the fourteenth day they left off. Which they ordained to be kept holy day, so that all times hereafter they should celebrate it with feasting, joy, and banquets.

18 But they that were killing in the city of Susan were employed in the slaughter on the thirteenth and fourteenth day of the same month: and on the fifteenth day they rested. And therefore they appointed that day to be a holy day of feasting and gladness.

19 But those Jews that dwelt in towns not walled and in villages, appointed the fourteenth day of the month Adar for banquets and gladness: so as to rejoice on that day, and send one another portions of their banquets and meats.

20 And Mardochai wrote all these things, and sent them comprised in letters to the Jews that abode in all the king's provinces, both those that lay near and those afar off.

21 That they should receive the four-

CHAP. 9. Ver. 1. *To revenge themselves.* The Jews on this occasion, by authority from the king, were made executioners of the public justice, for punishing by death a crime worthy of death, viz., a malicious conspiracy for extirpating their whole nation.

teenth and fifteenth day of the month Adar for holy days, and always at the return of the year should celebrate them with solemn honour:

22 Because on those days the Jews revenged themselves of their enemies, and their mourning and sorrow were turned into mirth and joy. And that these should be days of feasting and gladness, in which they should send one to another portions of meats, and should give gifts to the poor.

23 And the Jews undertook to observe with solemnity all they had begun to do at that time, which Mardochai by letters had commanded to be done.

24 For Aman, the son of Amadathi of the race of Agag, the enemy and adversary of the Jews, had devised evil against them, to kill them and destroy them: and had cast Phur, that is, the lot.

25 And afterwards Esther went in to the king, beseeching him that his endeavours might be made void by the king's letters: and the evil that he had intended against the Jews might return upon his own head. And so both he and his sons were hanged upon gibbets.

26 And since that time these days are called Phurim, that is, of lots: because Phur, that is, the lot, was cast into the urn. And all things that were done are contained in the volume of this epistle, that is, of this book.

27 And the things that they suffered, and that were afterwards changed, the Jews took upon themselves and their seed, and upon all that had a mind to be joined to their religion, so that it should be lawful for none to pass these days without solemnity which the writing testifieth, and certain times require, as the years continually succeed one another.

28 These are the days which shall never be forgot: and which all provinces in the whole world shall celebrate throughout all generations. Neither is there any city wherein the days of Phurim, that is, of lots, must not be observed by the Jews, and by their posterity, which is bound to these ceremonies.

29 And Esther the queen, the daughter of Abihail, and Mardochai the Jew, wrote also a second epistle, that with all diligence this day should be established a festival for the time to come.

30 And they sent to all the Jews that were in the hundred and twenty-seven provinces of king Assuerus, that they should have peace, and receive truth.

31 And observe the days of lots, and celebrate them with joy in their proper time, as Mardochai and Esther had appointed. And they undertook them to be observed by themselves and by their seed, fasts, and cries, and the days of lots,

32 And all things which are contained in the history of this book, which is called Esther.

CHAPTER 10

Assuerus's greatness. Mardochai's dignity.

AND king Assuerus made all the land and all the islands of the sea, tributary.

2 And his strength and his empire, and the dignity and greatness whereof he exalted Mardochai, are written in the books of the Medes, and of the Persians.

3 And how Mardochai, of the race of the Jews, was next after king Assuerus: and great among the Jews, and acceptable to the people of his brethren, seeking the good of his people, and speaking those things which were for the welfare of his seed.

4 Then Mardochai said: God hath done these things.

5 I remember a dream that I saw, which signified these same things: and nothing thereof hath failed.

6 The little fountain which grew into a river, and was turned into a light, and into the sun, and abounded into many waters, is Esther, whom the king married, and made queen.

7 But the two dragons are I and Aman.

8 The nations that were assembled are they that endeavoured to destroy the name of the Jews.

9 And my nation is Israel, who cried to the Lord: and the Lord saved his people. And he delivered us from all evils, and hath wrought great signs and wonders among the nations.

10 And he commanded that there should be two lots: one of the people of God, and the other of all the nations.

11 And both lots came to the day appointed already from that time before God to all nations.

12 And the Lord remembered his people, and had mercy on his inheritance.

13 And these days shall be observed in the month of Adar, on the fourteenth, and fifteenth day of the same month, with all diligence, and joy of the people gathered into one assembly, throughout all the generations hereafter of the people of Israel.

CHAP. 10. Ver. 4. *Mardochai.* Here St. Jerome advertiseth the reader, that what follows is not in the Hebrew: but is found in the Septuagint Greek edition, which the seventy-two interpreters translated out of the Hebrew, or added by the inspiration of the Holy Ghost.

Ver. 5. *A dream.* This dream was prophetical and extraordinary: otherwise the general rule is not to observe dreams.

CHAPTER 11

The dream of Mardochai, which in the ancient Greek and Latin Bibles was in the beginning of the book, but was detached by St. Jerome, and put in this place.

IN the fourth year of the reign of Ptolemy and Cleopatra, Dositheus, who said he was a priest, and of the Levitical race, and Ptolemy his son brought this epistle of Phurim, which they said Lysimachus the son of Ptolemy had interpreted in Jerusalem.

2 In the second year of the reign of Artaxerxes the Great, in the first day of the month Nisan, Mardochai the son of Jair, the son of Semei, the son of Cis, of the tribe of Benjamin:

3 A Jew who dwelt in the city of Susan, a great man and among the first of the king's court, had a dream.

4 ¹ Now he was of the number of the captives whom Nabuchodonosor king of Babylon had carried away from Jerusalem with Jechonias king of Juda.

5 And this was his dream: Behold there were voices, and tumults, and thunders, and earthquakes, and a disturbance upon the earth.

6 ² And behold two great dragons came forth ready to fight one against another.

7 And at their cry all nations were stirred up to fight against the nation of the just.

8 And that was a day of darkness and danger, of tribulation and distress, and great fear upon the earth.

9 And the nation of the just was troubled fearing their own evils, and was prepared for death.

10 And they cried to God: and as they were crying, a little fountain grew into a very great river, and abounded into many waters.

11 The light and the sun rose up: and the humble were exalted, and they devoured the glorious.

12 And when Mardochai had seen this, and arose out of his bed, he was thinking what God would do: and he kept it fixed in his mind, desirous to know what the dream should signify.

CHAPTER 12

Mardochai detects the conspiracy of the two eunuchs.

AND ¹ he abode at that time in the king's court, with Bagatha and Thara the king's eunuchs, who were porters of the palace.

2 And when he understood their designs, and had diligently searched into their projects, he learned that they went about to lay violent hands on king Artaxerxes: and he told the king thereof.

3 Then the king had them both examined, and after they had confessed, commanded them to be put to death.

4 But the king made a record of what was done: and Mardochai also committed the memory of the thing to writing.

5 And the king commanded him to abide in the court of the palace, and gave him presents for the information.

6 But Aman the son of Amadathi the Bugite was in great honour with the king: and sought to hurt Mardochai and his people, because of the two eunuchs of the king who were put to death.

CHAPTER 13

A copy of a letter sent by Aman to destroy the Jews. Mardochai's prayer for the people.

AND this was the copy of the letter: Artaxerxes, the great king who reigneth from India to Ethiopia, to the princes and governors of the hundred and twenty-seven provinces, that are subject to his empire, greeting:

2 Whereas I reigned over many nations, and had brought all the world under my dominion, I was not willing to abuse the greatness of my power, but to govern my subjects with clemency and lenity, that they might live quietly without any terror, and might enjoy peace, which is desired by all men.

3 But when I asked my counsellors how this might be accomplished, one that excelled the rest in wisdom and fidelity, and was second after the king, Aman by name,

4 Told me that there was a people scattered through the whole world, which used new laws, and acted against the customs of all nations, despised the commandments of kings, and violated by their opposition the concord of all nations.

5 Wherefore having learned this, and seeing one nation in opposition to all mankind using perverse laws, and going against our commandments, and disturbing the peace and concord of the provinces subject to us,

6 We have commanded that all whom Aman shall mark out (who is chief over all the provinces, and second after the king, and whom we honour as a father), shall be utterly destroyed by their enemies, with their wives and children (and that none shall have pity on them), on the fourteenth day of the twelfth month Adar of this present year:

7 That these wicked men going down to hell in one day, may restore to our

---

CHAP. 11. ¹ 4 Kings, 24, 15; Esther, 2, 6. ² Esther, 10, 7. CHAP. 12. ¹ Esther, 2, 21; 6, 2.

empire the peace which they had disturbed.

8 But Mardochai besought the Lord, remembering all his works,

9 And said: O Lord, Lord, Almighty King, for all things are in thy power: and there is none that can resist thy will, if thou determine to save Israel.

10 Thou hast made heaven and earth, and all things that are under the cope of heaven.

11 Thou art Lord of all: and there is none that can resist thy majesty.

12 Thou knowest all things: and thou knowest that it was not out of pride and contempt, or any desire of glory, that I refused to worship the proud Aman

13 (For I would willingly and readily for the salvation of Israel have kissed even the steps of his feet):

14 But I feared lest I should transfer the honour of my God to a man, and lest I should adore any one except my God.

15 And now, O Lord, O King, O God of Abraham, have mercy on thy people, because our enemies resolve to destroy us, and extinguish thy inheritance.

16 Despise not thy portion, which thou hast redeemed for thyself out of Egypt.

17 Hear my supplication, and be merciful to thy lot and inheritance. And turn my mourning into joy, that we may live and praise thy name, O Lord. And shut not the mouths of them that sing to thee.

18 And all Israel with like mind and supplication cried to the Lord, because they saw certain death hanging over their heads.

CHAPTER 14

The prayer of Esther for herself and her people.

QUEEN Esther also, fearing the danger that was at hand, had recourse to the Lord.

2 And when she had laid away her royal apparel, she put on garments suitable for weeping and mourning. Instead of divers precious ointments, she covered her head with ashes and dung: and she humbled her body with fasts. And all the places in which before she was accustomed to rejoice, she filled with her torn hair.

3 And she prayed to the Lord the God of Israel, saying: O my Lord, who alone art our king, help me a desolate woman, and who have no other helper but thee.

4 My danger is in my hands.

CHAP. 14. 1 Deut. 4, 20, 34; 32, 9.

5 [1] I have heard of my father that thou, O Lord, didst take Israel from among all nations, and our fathers from all their predecessors, to possess them as an everlasting inheritance. And thou hast done to them as thou hast promised.

6 We have sinned in thy sight: and therefore thou hast delivered us into the hands of our enemies:

7 For we have worshipped their gods. Thou art just, O Lord.

8 And now they are not content to oppress us with most hard bondage, but attributing the strength of their hands to the power of their idols,

9 They design to change thy promises, and destroy thy inheritance, and shut the mouths of them that praise thee, and extinguish the glory of thy temple and altar:

10 That they may open the mouths of Gentiles, and praise the strength of idols, and magnify for ever a carnal king.

11 Give not, O Lord, thy sceptre to them that are not, lest they laugh at our ruin. But turn their counsel upon themselves: and destroy him that hath begun to rage against us.

12 Remember, O Lord, and shew thyself to us in the time of our tribulation: and give me boldness, O Lord, king of gods, and of all power.

13 Give me a well ordered speech in my mouth, in the presence of the lion: and turn his heart to the hatred of our enemy; that both he himself may perish, and the rest that consent to him.

14 But deliver us by thy hand: and help me, who have no other helper, but thee, O Lord, who hast the knowledge of all things.

15 And thou knowest that I hate the glory of the wicked, and abhor the bed of the uncircumcised, and of every stranger.

16 Thou knowest my necessity; that I abominate the sign of my pride and glory, which is upon my head in the days of my public appearance, and detest it as a menstruous rag, and wear it not in the days of my silence;

17 And that I have not eaten at Aman's table nor hath the king's banquet pleased me; and that I have not drunk the wine of the drink offerings;

18 And that thy handmaid hath never rejoiced, since I was brought hither unto this day, but in thee, O Lord, the God of Abraham.

19 O God, who art mighty above all, hear the voice of them, that have no other hope: and deliver us from the hand of the wicked. And deliver me from my fear.

CHAPTER 15

Esther comes into the king's presence. She is terrified, but God turns his heart.

AND he commanded her (no doubt but he was Mardochai) to go to the king, and petition for her people, and for her country.

2 Remember (said he) the days of thy low estate, how thou wast brought up by my hand, because Aman, the second after the king, hath spoken against us unto death.

3 And do thou call upon the Lord; and speak to the king for us; and deliver us from death.

4 And on the third day she laid away the garments she wore, and put on her glorious apparel.

5 And glittering in royal robes, after she had called upon God the Ruler and Saviour of all, she took two maids with her.

6 And upon one of them she leaned, as if for delicateness and overmuch tenderness she were not able to bear up her own body.

7 And the other maid followed her lady, bearing up her train flowing on the ground.

8 But she with a rosy colour in her face, and with gracious and bright eyes, hid a mind full of anguish and exceeding great fear.

9 So going in she passed through all the doors in order, and stood before the king, where he sat upon his royal throne, clothed with his royal robes, and glittering with gold and precious stones. And he was terrible to behold.

10 And when he had lifted up his countenance, and with burning eyes had shewn the wrath of his heart, the queen sunk down. And her colour turned pale: and she rested her weary head upon her handmaid.

11 And God changed the king's spirit into mildness; and all in haste and in fear, he leaped from his throne, and holding her up in his arms, till she came to herself, caressed her with these words:

12 What is the matter, Esther? I am thy brother. Fear not.

13 Thou shalt not die: for this law is not made for thee, but for all others.

14 Come near then; and touch the sceptre.

15 And as she held her peace, he took the golden sceptre, and laid it upon her neck, and kissed her, and said: Why dost thou not speak to me?

16 She answered: [1] I saw thee, my lord, as an angel of God: and my heart was troubled for fear of thy majesty.

17 For thou, my lord, art very admirable: and thy face is full of graces.

18 And while she was speaking, she fell down again, and was almost in a swoon.

19 But the king was troubled: and all his servants comforted her.

CHAPTER 16

A copy of the king's letter in favour of the Jews.

THE [1] great king Artaxerxes, from India to Ethiopia, to the governors and princes of a hundred and twenty-seven provinces, which obey our command, sendeth greeting.

2 Many [2] have abused unto pride the goodness of princes and the honour that hath been bestowed upon them:

3 And not only endeavour to oppress the king's subjects; but not bearing the glory that is given them, take in hand to practise also against them that gave it.

4 Neither are they content not to return thanks for benefits received, and to violate in themselves the laws of humanity: but they think they can also escape the justice of God who seeth all things.

5 And they break out into so great madness, as to endeavour to undermine by lies such as observe diligently the offices committed to them, and do all things in such manner as to be worthy of all men's praise:

6 While with crafty fraud they deceive the ears of princes that are well meaning, and judge of others by their own nature.

7 Now this is proved both from ancient histories, and by the things which are done daily, how the good designs of kings are depraved by the evil suggestions of certain men.

8 Wherefore we must provide for the peace of all provinces.

9 Neither must you think, if we command different things, that it cometh of the levity of our mind; but that we give sentence according to the quality and necessity of times, as the profit of the commonwealth requireth.

10 Now that you may more plainly understand what we say, [3] Aman the son of Amadathi, a Macedonian both in mind and country, and having nothing of the Persian blood, but with his cruelty staining our goodness, was received being a stranger by us:

11 And found our humanity so great towards him, that he was called our

CHAP. 15. [1] Gen. 33, 10. CHAP. 16. [1] Esther, 11, 2. [2] Esther, 3, 10. [3] Esther, 3, 1.

CHAP. 16: Ver. 1: *From India to Ethiopia.* That is, who reigneth from India to Ethiopia.

father; and was worshipped by all as the next man after the king.

12 But he was so far puffed up with arrogancy as to go about to deprive us of our kingdom and life.

13 For with certain new and unheard of devices he hath sought the destruction of Mardochai, by whose fidelity and good services our life was saved, and of Esther the partner of our kingdom, with all their nation.

14 Thinking that after they were slain, he might work treason against us left alone without friends: and might transfer the kingdom of the Persians to the Macedonians.

15 But we have found that the Jews, who were by that most wicked man appointed to be slain, are in no fault at all: but contrariwise, use just laws,

16 And are the children of the highest and greatest, and the ever living God, by whose benefit the kingdom was given both to our fathers and to us, and is kept unto this day.

17 Wherefore know ye that those letters which he sent in our name, are void and of no effect.

18 For which crime both he himself that devised it, and all his kindred,

hang on gibbets, before the gates of this city Susan: not we, but God repaying him as he deserved.

19 But this edict, which we now send, shall be published in all cities, that the Jews may freely follow their own laws.

20 And you shall aid them that they may kill those who had prepared themselves to kill them, on the thirteenth day of the twelfth month, which is called Adar.

21 For the almighty God hath turned this day of sadness and mourning into joy to them.

22 Wherefore you shall also count this day among other festival days, and celebrate it with all joy. That it may be known also in times to come,

23 That all they who faithfully obey the Persians, receive a worthy reward for their fidelity: but they that are traitors to their kingdom, are destroyed for their wickedness.

24 And let every province and city, that will not be partaker of this solemnity, perish by the sword and by fire, and be destroyed in such manner as to be made unpassable, both to men and beasts, for an example of contempt and disobedience.

THE BOOK OF

JOB

This Book takes its name from the holy man of whom it treats, who, according to the more probable opinion, was of the race of Esau, and the same as Jobab, king of Edom, mentioned Gen. 36, 33. It is uncertain who was the writer of it. Some attribute it to Job himself; others to Moses or some one of the prophets. In the Hebrew it is written in verse, from the beginning of the third chapter to the forty-second chapter.

CHAPTER 1

Job's virtue and riches. Satan by permission from God strippeth him of all his substance. His patience.

THERE was a man in the land of Hus, whose name was Job: and that man was simple and upright, and fearing God, and avoiding evil.

Chap. 1. Ver. 1. *Hus.* The land of Hus was a part of Edom; as appears from Lam. 4, 21.—*Simple.* That is, innocent, sincere, and without guile.

Ver. 4. *And made a feast by houses.* That is, each made a feast in his own house and had *his day,* inviting the others, and their sisters.

Ver. 5. *Blessed.* For greater horror of the very thought of blasphemy, the scripture both here and ver. 11, and in the following chapter, ver. 5 and 9, uses the word *bless* to signify its contrary.

2 And there were born to him seven sons and three daughters.

3 And his possession was seven thousand sheep, and three thousand camels, and five hundred yoke of oxen, and five hundred she-asses, and a family exceeding great: and this man was great among all the people of the East.

4 And his sons went and made a feast by houses, every one in his day. And sending they called their three sisters to eat and drink with them.

5 And when the days of their feasting were gone about, Job sent to them, and sanctified them: and rising up early offered holocausts for every one of them. For he said: Lest perhaps my

sons have sinned, and have blessed God in their hearts. So did Job all days.

6 Now on a certain day, when the sons of God came to stand before the Lord, Satan also was present among them.

7 And the Lord said to him: Whence comest thou? And he answered and said: I have gone round about the earth, and walked through it.

8 And the Lord said to him: Hast thou considered my servant Job, that there is none like him in the earth, a simple and upright man, and fearing God, and avoiding evil?

9 And Satan answering, said: Doth Job fear God in vain?

10 Hast not thou made a fence for him, and his house, and all his substance round about: blessed the works of his hands, and his possession hath increased on the earth?

11 But stretch forth thy hand a little, and touch all that he hath: and see if he blesseth thee not to thy face.

12 Then the Lord said to Satan: Behold, all that he hath is in thy hand; only put not forth thy hand upon his person. And Satan went forth from the presence of the Lord.

13 Now upon a certain day when his sons and daughters were eating and drinking wine in the house of their eldest brother,

14 There came a messenger to Job, and said: The oxen were ploughing, and the asses feeding beside them;

15 And the Sabeans rushed in, and took all away, and slew the servants with the sword. And I alone have escaped to tell thee.

16 And while he was yet speaking, another came, and said: The fire of God fell from heaven and striking the sheep and the servants, hath consumed them. And I alone have escaped to tell thee.

17 And while he also was yet speaking, there came another, and said: The Chaldeans made three troops, and have fallen upon the camels, and taken them. Moreover they have slain the servants with the sword. And I alone have escaped to tell thee.

18 He was yet speaking, and behold another came in, and said: Thy sons and daughters were eating and drinking wine in the house of their elder brother.

19 A violent wind came on a sudden from the side of the desert, and shook the four corners of the house. And it fell upon thy children; and they are dead. And I alone have escaped to tell thee.

20 Then Job rose up, and rent his garments: and having shaven his head

fell down upon the ground and worshipped,

21 And said: [1] Naked came I out of my mother's womb, and naked shall I return thither. The Lord gave, and the Lord hath taken away. As it hath pleased the Lord so is it done. Blessed be the name of the Lord.

22 In all these things Job sinned not by his lips; nor spoke he any foolish thing against God.

CHAPTER 2

Satan, by God's permission, striketh Job with ulcers from head to foot. His patience is still invincible.

AND it came to pass, when on a certain day the sons of God came, and stood before the Lord, and Satan came among them, and stood in his sight,

2 That the Lord said to Satan: Whence comest thou? And he answered and said: I have gone round about the earth, and walked through it.

3 And the Lord said to Satan: Hast thou considered my servant Job, that there is none like him in the earth, a man simple, and upright, and fearing God, and avoiding evil, and still keeping his innocence? But thou hast moved me against him, that I should afflict him without cause.

4 And Satan answered, and said: Skin for skin, and all that a man hath he will give for his life.

5 But put forth thy hand, and touch his bone and his flesh: and then thou shalt see that he will bless thee to thy face.

6 And the Lord said to Satan: Behold he is in thy hand; but yet save his life.

7 So Satan went forth from the presence of the Lord, and struck Job with a very grievous ulcer, from the sole of the foot even to the top of his head.

8 And he took a potsherd and scraped the corrupt matter, sitting on a dunghill.

9 And his wife said to him: Dost thou still continue in thy simplicity? Bless God, and die.

10 And he said to her: Thou hast spoken like one of the foolish women. If we have received good things at the hand of God, why should we not receive

CHAP. 1. [1] Ecclus. 5, 14; 1 Tim. 6, 7.

Ver. 6. *The sons of God. The angels.—Satan.* This passage represents to us in a figure, accommodated to the ways and understandings of men. 1. The restless endeavours of Satan against the servants of God; 2. That he can do nothing without God's permission; 3. That God doth not permit him to tempt them above their strength: but assists them by his divine grace in such manner, that the vain efforts of the enemy only serve to illustrate their virtue and increase their merit.

evil? In all these things Job did not sin with his lips.

11 Now when Job's three friends heard all the evil that had befallen him, they came every one from his own place: Eliphaz the Themanite, and Baldad the Suhite, and Sophar the Naamathite. For they had made an appointment to come together and visit him, and comfort him.

12 And when they had lifted up their eyes afar off, they knew him not. And crying out they wept: and rending their garments they sprinkled dust upon their heads towards heaven.

13 And they sat with him on the ground seven days and seven nights: and no man spoke to him a word. For they saw that his grief was very great.

CHAPTER 3

Job expresseth his sense of the miseries of man's life, by cursing the day of his birth.

AFTER this Job opened his mouth, and cursed his day.

2 And he said:

3 [1] Let the day perish wherein I was born, and the night in which it was said: A man child is conceived.

4 Let that day be turned into darkness. Let not God regard it from above: and let not the light shine upon it.

5 Let darkness, and the shadow of death cover it, let a mist overspread it; and let it be wrapped up in bitterness.

6 Let a darksome whirlwind seize upon that night: let it not be counted in the days of the year, nor numbered in the months.

7 Let that night be solitary, and not worthy of praise.

8 Let them curse it who curse the day, who are ready to raise up a Leviathan.

9 Let the stars be darkened with the mist thereof: let it expect light and not see it, nor the rising of the dawning of the day.

10 Because it shut not up the doors of the womb that bore me, nor took away evils from my eyes.

11 Why did I not die in the womb? Why did I not perish when I came out of the belly?

12 Why received upon the knees? Why suckled at the breasts?

13 For now I should have been asleep and still; and should have rest in my sleep.

14 With kings and consuls of the

CHAP. 3. [1] Jer. 20, 14.

CHAP. 3. Ver. 1. *Cursed his day. Job cursed* the day of his birth, not by way of wishing evil to any thing of God's creation; but only to express in a stronger manner his sense of human miseries in general, and of his own calamities in particular.

earth, who build themselves solitudes:

15 Or with princes, that possess gold, and fill their houses with silver.

16 Or as a hidden untimely birth, I should not be, or as they that being conceived have not seen the light.

17 There the wicked cease from tumult, and there the wearied in strength are at rest.

18 And they sometime bound together without disquiet, have not heard the voice of the oppressor.

19 The small and great are there: and the servant *is* free from his master.

20 Why is light given to him that is in misery, and life to them that are in bitterness of soul?

21 That look for death, and it cometh not, as they that dig for a treasure:

22 And that rejoice exceedingly when they have found the grave.

23 To a man whose way is hidden, and God hath surrounded him with darkness?

24 Before I eat, I sigh: and as overflowing waters, so *is* my roaring.

25 For the fear which I feared hath come upon me: and that which I was afraid of hath befallen me.

26 Have I not dissembled? Have I not kept silence? Have I not been quiet? And indignation is come upon me.

CHAPTER 4

Eliphaz charges Job with impatience, and pretends that God never afflicts the innocent.

THEN Eliphaz the Themanite answered, and said:

2 If we begin to speak to thee, perhaps thou wilt take it ill: but who can withhold the words he hath conceived?

3 Behold thou hast taught many, and thou hast strengthened the weary hands.

4 Thy words have confirmed them that were staggering, and thou hast strengthened the trembling knees.

5 But now the scourge is come upon thee, and thou faintest. It hath touched thee, and thou art troubled.

6 Where is thy fear, thy fortitude, thy patience, and the perfection of thy ways?

7 Remember, I pray thee, who ever perished being innocent? Or when were the just destroyed?

8 On the contrary I have seen those who work iniquity, and sow sorrows, and reap them,

9 Perishing by the blast of God, and consumed by the spirit of his wrath.

10 The roaring of the lion, and the

voice of the lioness, and the teeth of the whelps of lions are broken.

11 The tiger hath perished for want of prey: and the young lions are scattered abroad.

12 Now there was a word spoken to me in private; and my ears by stealth as it were received the veins of its whisper

13 In the horror of a vision by night, when deep sleep is wont to hold men,

14 Fear seized upon me, and trembling: and all my bones were affrighted.

15 And when a spirit passed before me, the hair of my flesh stood up.

16 There stood one whose countenance I knew not, an image before my eyes: and I heard the voice as it were of a gentle wind:

17 ¹ Shall man be justified in comparison of God; or shall a man be more pure than his maker?

18 ² Behold they that serve him are not steadfast: and in his angels he found wickedness:

19 How much more shall they that dwell in houses of clay, who have an earthly foundation, be consumed as with the moth?

20 From morning till evening they shall be cut down: and because no one understandeth, they shall perish for ever.

21 And they that shall be left, shall be taken away from them. They shall die, and not in wisdom.

CHAPTER 5

Eliphaz proceeds in his charge, and exhorts Job to acknowledge his sins.

CALL now if there be any that will answer thee, and turn to some of the saints.

2 Anger indeed killeth the foolish: and envy slayeth the little one.

3 I have seen a fool with a strong root: and I cursed his beauty immediately.

4 His children shall be far from safety, and shall be destroyed in the gate: and there shall be none to deliver them.

5 His harvest the hungry shall eat: and the armed man shall take him by violence; and the thirsty shall drink up his riches.

6 Nothing upon earth is done without a cause: and sorrow doth not spring out of the ground.

7 Man is born to labour, and the bird to fly.

8 Wherefore I will pray to the Lord, and address my speech to God.

9 Who doth great things and unsearchable and wonderful things without number.

10 Who giveth rain upon the face of the earth, and watereth all things with waters.

11 Who setteth up the humble on high, and comforteth with health those that mourn.

12 Who bringeth to nought the designs of the malignant, so that their hands cannot accomplish what they had begun.

13 ¹ Who catcheth the wise in their craftiness, and disappointeth the counsel of the wicked.

14 They shall meet with darkness in the day, and grope at noonday as in the night.

15 But he shall save the needy from the sword of their mouth, and the poor from the hand of the violent.

16 And to the needy there shall be hope: but iniquity shall draw in her mouth.

17 Blessed is the man whom God correcteth: refuse not therefore the chastising of the Lord.

18 For he woundeth, and cureth: he striketh, and his hands shall heal.

19 In six troubles he shall deliver thee: and in the seventh, evil shall not touch thee.

20 In famine he shall deliver thee from death: and in battle, from the hand of the sword.

21 Thou shalt be hidden from the scourge of the tongue: and thou shalt not fear calamity when it cometh.

22 In destruction and famine thou shalt laugh: and thou shalt not be afraid of the beasts of the earth.

23 But thou shalt have a covenant with the stones of the lands: and the beasts of the earth shall be at peace with thee.

24 And thou shalt know that thy tabernacle is in peace: and visiting thy beauty thou shalt not sin.

25 Thou shalt know also that thy seed shall be multiplied: and thy offspring like the grass of the earth.

26 Thou shalt enter into the grave in abundance, as a heap of wheat is brought in its season.

27 Behold, this is even so, as we have searched out. Which thou having heard, consider it thoroughly in thy mind.

CHAPTER 6

Job maintains his innocence, and complains of his friends.

BUT Job answered, and said:

2 O that my sins, whereby I have

CHAP. 4. ¹ Job. 25, 4. ² Job. 15, 15; 2 Peter, 2, 4; Jude, 6. CHAP. 5. ¹ 1 Cor. 3, 19.

CHAP. 4. Ver. 17. *Shall man be justified in comparison of God.* These are the words which Eliphaz had heard from an angel, which, ver. 15, he calls a *spirit.*

deserved wrath, and the calamity that I suffer, were weighed in a balance.

3 As the sand of the sea this would appear heavier: therefore my words are full of sorrow.

4 For the arrows of the Lord are in me, the rage whereof drinketh up my spirit: and the terrors of the Lord war against me.

5 Will the wild ass bray when he hath grass? Or will the ox low when he standeth before a full manger?

6 Or can an unsavoury thing be eaten, that is not seasoned with salt? Or can a man taste that which when tasted bringeth death?

7 The things which before my soul would not touch, now, through anguish are my meats.

8 Who will grant that my request may come: and that God may give me what I look for?

9 And that he that hath begun may destroy me: that he may let loose his hand, and cut me off?

10 And that this may be my comfort, that afflicting me with sorrow, he spare not: nor I contradict the words of the Holy One.

11 For what is my strength, that I can hold out? Or what is my end that I should keep patience?

12 My strength is not the strength of stones: nor is my flesh of brass.

13 Behold there is no help for me in myself; and my familiar friends also are departed from me.

14 He that taketh away mercy from his friend, forsaketh the fear of the Lord.

15 My brethren have passed by me, as the torrent that passeth swiftly in the valleys.

16 They that fear the hoar frost, the snow shall fall upon them.

17 At the time when they shall be scattered they shall perish: and after it groweth hot they shall be melted out of their place.

18 The paths of their steps are entangled: they shall walk in vain, and shall perish.

19 Consider the paths of Thema, the ways of Saba, and wait a little while.

20 They are confounded, because I have hoped: they are come also even unto me, and are covered with shame.

21 Now you are come: and now seeing my affliction you are afraid.

22 Did I say: Bring to me, and give me of your substance?

23 Or: Deliver me from the hand of the enemy, and rescue me out of the hand of the mighty?

24 Teach me, and I will hold my peace: and if I have been ignorant in any thing, instruct me.

25 Why have you detracted the words of truth, whereas there is none of you that can reprove me?

26 You dress up speeches only to rebuke: and you utter words to the wind.

27 You rush in upon the fatherless: and you endeavour to overthrow your friend.

28 However finish what you have begun: give ear, and see whether I lie.

29 Answer, I beseech you, without contention: and speaking that which is just, judge ye.

30 And you shall not find iniquity in my tongue: neither shall folly sound in my mouth.

CHAPTER 7

Job declares the miseries of man's life. He addresses himself to God.

THE life of man upon earth is a warfare, and his days are like the days of a hireling.

2 As a servant longeth for the shade, as the hireling looketh for the end of his work;

3 So I also have had empty months, and have numbered to myself wearisome nights.

4 If I lie down to sleep, I shall say: When shall I arise? And again I shall look for the evening, and shall be filled with sorrows even till darkness.

5 My flesh is clothed with rottenness and the filth of dust: my skin is withered and drawn together.

6 My days have passed more swiftly than the web is cut by the weaver, and are consumed without any hope.

7 Remember that my life is but wind: and my eyes shall not return to see good things.

8 Nor shall the sight of man behold me. Thy eyes are upon me, and I shall be no more.

9 As a cloud is consumed, and passeth away: so he that shall go down to hell shall not come up.

10 Nor shall he return any more into his house: neither shall his place know him any more.

11 Wherefore I will not spare my mouth, I will speak in the affliction of my spirit: I will talk with the bitterness of my soul.

CHAP. 6. Ver. 2. *My sins.* He does not mean to compare his sufferings with his real sins: but with the imaginary crimes which his friends imputed to him: and especially with his *wrath*, or *grief*, expressed in the third chapter, which they so much accused. Though, as he tells them here, it bore no proportion with the greatness of his calamity.

12 Am I a sea, or a whale, that thou hast enclosed me in a prison?

13 If I say: My bed shall comfort me, and I shall be relieved speaking with myself on my couch:

14 Thou wilt frighten me with dreams and terrify me with visions.

15 So that my soul rather chooseth hanging: and my bones death.

16 I have done with hope. I shall now live no longer. Spare me, for my days are nothing.

17 What is a man that thou shouldst magnify him? Or why dost thou set thy heart upon him?

18 Thou visitest him early in the morning; and thou provest him suddenly.

19 How long wilt thou not spare me, nor suffer me to swallow down my spittle?

20 I have sinned. What shall I do to thee, O keeper of men? Why hast thou set me opposite to thee, and I am become burdensome to myself?

21 Why dost thou not remove my sin, and why dost thou not take away my iniquity? Behold now I shall sleep in the dust: and if thou seek me in the morning, I shall not be.

CHAPTER 8

Baldad, under pretence of defending the justice of God, accuses Job, and exhorts him to return to God.

THEN Baldad the Suhite answered, and said:

2 How long wilt thou speak these things: and how long shall the words of thy mouth be like a strong wind?

3 Doth God pervert judgment: or doth the Almighty overthrow that which is just?

4 Although thy children have sinned against him, and he hath left them in the hand of their iniquity:

5 Yet if thou wilt arise early to God, and wilt beseech the Almighty:

6 If thou wilt walk clean and upright: he will presently awake unto thee, and will make the dwelling of thy justice peaceable.

7 Insomuch, that if thy former things were small, thy latter things would be multiplied exceedingly.

8 For inquire of the former generation: and search diligently into the memory of the fathers

9 (For we are but of yesterday, and are ignorant [1] that our days upon earth are but a shadow):

10 And they shall teach thee. They shall speak to thee, and utter words out of their hearts.

11 Can the rush be green without moisture, or a sedge-bush grow without water?

12 When it is yet in flower, and is not plucked up with the hand, it withereth before all herbs.

13 Even so are the ways of all that forget God: and the hope of the hypocrite shall perish.

14 His folly shall not please him: and his trust shall be like the spider's web.

15 He shall lean upon his house, and it shall not stand. He shall prop it up, and it shall not rise.

16 He seemeth to have moisture before the sun cometh: and at his rising his blossom shall shoot forth.

17 His roots shall be thick upon a heap of stones: and among the stones he shall abide.

18 If one swallow him up out of his place, he shall deny him, and shall say: I know thee not.

19 For this is the joy of his way, that others may spring again out of the earth.

20 God will not cast away the simple, nor reach out his hand to the evildoer:

21 Until thy mouth be filled with laughter, and thy lips with rejoicing.

22 They that hate thee shall be clothed with confusion: and the dwelling of the wicked shall not stand.

CHAPTER 9

Job acknowledges God to be just, although he often afflicts the innocent.

AND Job answered, and said:

2 Indeed I know it is so, and that man cannot be justified compared with God.

3 If he will contend with him, he cannot answer him one for a thousand.

4 He is wise in heart, and mighty in strength. Who hath resisted him, and hath had peace?

5 He hath removed mountains, and they whom he overthrew in his wrath, knew it not.

6 He shaketh the earth out of her place, and the pillars thereof tremble.

7 He commandeth the sun and it riseth not: and shutteth up the stars as it were under a seal.

8 He alone spreadeth out the heavens: and walketh upon the waves of the sea.

9 He maketh Arcturus, and Orion, and Hyades, and the inner parts of the south.

10 He doth things great and incom-

CHAP. 8. [1] Job. 14, 2; Ps. 143, 3.

CHAP. 9. Ver. 9. *Arcturus and Orion and Hyades.* These are names of stars or constellations. In Hebrew, Ash, Cesil, and Cimah. See note chap. 38, ver. 31.

prehensible and wonderful: of which is like myself: nor one that may be there is no number.

11 If he come to me, I shall not see him: if he depart I shall not understand.

12 If he examine on a sudden, who shall answer him? Or, who can say: Why dost thou so?

13 God, whose wrath no man can resist, and under whom they stoop that bear up the world.

14 What am I then, that I should answer him, and have words with him?

15 I, who although I should have any just thing, would not answer, but would make supplication to my judge.

16 And if he should hear me when I call, I should not believe that he had heard my voice.

17 For he shall crush me in a whirlwind and multiply my wounds, even without cause.

18 He alloweth not my spirit to rest: and he filleth me with bitterness.

19 If strength be demanded, he is most strong: if equity of judgment, no man dare bear witness for me.

20 If I would justify myself, my own mouth shall condemn me: if I would shew myself innocent, he shall prove me wicked.

21 Although I should be simple, even this my soul shall be ignorant of: and I shall be weary of my life.

22 One thing there is that I have spoken: Both the innocent and the wicked he consumeth.

23 If he scourge, let him kill at once, and not laugh at the pains of the innocent.

24 The earth is given into the hand of the wicked: he covereth the face of the judges thereof. And if it be not he, who is it then?

25 My days have been swifter than a post: they have fled away and have not seen good.

26 They have passed by as ships carrying fruits, as an eagle flying to the prey.

27 If I say: I will not speak so: I change my face, and am tormented with sorrow.

28 I feared all my works, knowing that thou didst not spare the offender.

29 But, if so also, I am wicked, why have I laboured in vain?

30 If I be washed as it were with snow waters, and my hands shall shine ever so clean:

31 Yet thou shalt plunge me in filth; and my garments shall abhor me.

32 For I shall not answer a man that

Ver. 17. *Without cause.* That is, without my knowing the cause: or without any crime of mine.

is like myself: nor one that may be heard with me equally in judgment.

33 There is none that may be able to reprove both, and to put his hand between both.

34 Let him take his rod away from me: and let not his fear terrify me.

35 I will speak, and will not fear him: for I cannot answer while I am in fear.

CHAPTER 10

Job laments his afflictions and begs to be delivered.

MY soul is weary of my life: I will let go my speech against myself. I will speak in the bitterness of my soul.

2 I will say to God: Do not condemn me. Tell me why thou judgest me so.

3 Doth it seem good to thee that thou shouldst calumniate me, and oppress me, the work of thy own hands, and help the counsel of the wicked?

4 Hast thou eyes of flesh? Or, shalt thou see as man seeth?

5 Are thy days as the days of man, and are thy years as the times of men:

6 That thou shouldst inquire after my iniquity and search after my sin?

7 And shouldst know that I have done no wicked thing, whereas there is no man that can deliver out of thy hand.

8 Thy hands have made me and fashioned me wholly round about. And dost thou thus cast me down headlong on a sudden?

9 Remember, I beseech thee, that thou hast made me as the clay, and thou wilt bring into dust again.

10 Hast thou not milked me as milk, and curdled me like cheese?

11 Thou hast clothed me with skin and flesh. Thou hast put me together with bones and sinews.

12 Thou hast granted me life and mercy; and thy visitation hath preserved my spirit.

13 Although thou conceal these things in thy heart, yet I know that thou rememberest all things.

14 If I have sinned and thou hast spared me for an hour: why dost thou not suffer me to be clean from my iniquity?

15 And if I be wicked, woe unto me: and if just, I shall not lift up my head, being filled with affliction and misery.

16 And for pride thou wilt take me as a lioness, and returning thou tormentest me wonderfully.

17 Thou renewest thy witnesses against me, and multipliest thy wrath upon me; and pains war against me.

18 Why didst thou bring me forth

out of the womb? O that I had been consumed that eye might not see me!

19 I should have been as if I had not been, carried from the womb to the grave.

20 Shall not the fewness of my days be ended shortly? Suffer me, therefore, that I may lament my sorrow a little,

21 Before I go, and return no more: to a land that is dark and covered with the mist of death:

22 A land of misery and darkness, where the shadow of death, and no order, but everlasting horrow dwelleth.

CHAPTER 11

Sophar reproves Job, for justifying himself, and invites him to repentance.

THEN Sophar the Naamathite answered, and said:

2 Shall not he that speaketh much, hear also? Or shall a man full of talk be justified?

3 Shall men hold their peace to thee only? And when thou hast mocked others, shall no man confute thee?

4 For thou hast said: My word is pure, and I am clean in thy sight.

5 And I wish that God would speak with thee, and would open his lips to thee,

6 That he might shew thee the secrets of wisdom, and that his law is manifold: and thou mightest understand that he exacteth much less of thee than thy iniquity deserveth.

7 Peradventure thou wilt comprehend the steps of God, and wilt find out the Almighty perfectly?

8 He is higher than heaven, and what wilt thou do? He is deeper than hell, and how wilt thou know?

9 The measure of him is longer than the earth, and broader than the sea.

10 If he shall overturn all things, or shall press them together, who shall contradict him?

11 For he knoweth the vanity of men: and when he seeth iniquty, doth he not consider it?

12 A vain man is lifted up into pride, and thinketh himself born free like a wild ass's colt.

13 But thou hast hardened thy heart, and hast spread thy hands to him.

14 If thou wilt put away from thee the iniquity that is in thy hand, and let not injustice remain in thy tabernacle:

15 Then mayst thou lift up thy face without spot; and thou shalt be steadfast and shalt not fear.

16 Thou shalt also forget misery, and remember it only as waters that are passed away.

17 And brightness, like that of the noonday, shall arise to thee at evening. And when thou shalt think thyself consumed, thou shalt rise as the day star.

18 And thou shalt have confidence, hope being set before thee: and being buried thou shalt sleep secure.

19 [1] Thou shalt rest, and there shall be none to make thee afraid: and many shall entreat thy face.

20 [2] But the eyes of the wicked shall decay: and the way to escape shall fail them, and their hope the abomination of the soul.

CHAPTER 12

Job's reply to Sophar. He extols God's power and wisdom.

THEN Job answered, and said:

2 Are you then men alone; and shall wisdom die with you?

3 [1] I also have a heart as well as you: for who is ignorant of these things, which you know?

4 [2] He that is mocked by his friends as I, shall call upon God: and he will hear him. For the simplicity of the just man is laughed to scorn.

5 The lamp, despised in the thoughts of the rich, is ready for the time appointed.

6 [3] The tabernacles of robbers abound, and they provoke God boldly; whereas it is he that hath given all into their hands.

7 But ask now the beasts, and they shall teach thee: and the birds of the air, and they shall tell thee.

8 Speak to the earth, and it shall answer thee: and the fishes of the sea shall tell.

9 Who is ignorant that the hand of the Lord hath made all these things?

10 In whose hand is the soul of every living thing, and the spirit of all flesh of man.

11 [4] Doth not the ear discern words, and the palate of him that eateth, the taste?

12 In the ancient is wisdom: and in length of days prudence.

13 With him is wisdom and strength: he hath counsel and understanding.

14 [5] If he pull down, there is no man that can build up. If he shut up a man, there is none that can open.

15 If he withhold the waters, all things shall be dried up: and if he send them out, they shall overturn the earth.

16 With him is strength and wisdom: he knoweth both the deceiver and him that is deceived.

CHAP. 11. [1] Lev. 26, 6. [2] Lev. 26, 16. CHAP. 12. [1] Job. 20, 2. [2] Prov. 14, 2. [3] Ps. 43, 11; 48, 7. [4] Job. 34, 3. [5] Isai. 22, 22; Apoc. 3, 7.

17 He bringeth counsellors to a foolish end, and judges to insensibility.

18 He looseth the belt of kings, and girdeth their loins with a cord.

19 He leadeth away priests without glory, and overthroweth nobles.

20 He changeth the speech of the true speakers, and taketh away the doctrine of the aged.

21 He poureth contempt upon princes, and relieveth them that were oppressed.

22 He discovereth deep things out of darkness, and bringeth up to light the shadow of death.

23 He multiplieth nations, and destroyeth them, and restoreth them again after they were overthrown.

24 He changeth the heart of the princes of the people of the earth, and deceiveth them, that they walk in vain where there is no way.

25 They shall grope as in the dark, and not in the light: and he shall make them stagger like men that are drunk.

CHAPTER 13

Job persists in maintaining his innocence. He reproves his friends.

BEHOLD my eye hath seen all these things, and my ear hath heard them: and I have understood them all.

2 According to your knowledge I also know: neither am I inferior to you.

3 But yet I will speak to the Almighty: and I desire to reason with God.

4 Having first shewn that you are forgers of lies and maintainers of perverse opinions.

5 And I wish you would hold your peace, that you might be thought to be wise men.

6 Hear ye therefore my reproof: and attend to the judgment of my lips.

7 Hath God any need of your lie, that you should speak deceitfully for him?

8 Do you accept his person, and do you endeavour to judge for God?

9 Or shall it please him, from whom nothing can be concealed? Or shall he be deceived as a man, with your deceitful dealings?

10 He shall reprove you, because in secret you accept his person.

11 As soon as he shall move himself, he shall trouble you: and his dread shall fall upon you.

12 Your remembrance shall be compared to ashes: and your necks shall be brought to clay.

13 Hold your peace, a little while,

that I may speak whatsoever my mind shall suggest to me.

14 Why do I tear my flesh with my teeth, and carry my soul in my hands?

15 Although he should kill me, I will trust in him. But yet I will reprove my ways in his sight;

16 And he shall be my saviour: for no hypocrite shall come before his presence.

17 Hear ye my speech: and receive with your ears hidden truths.

18 If I shall be judged, I know that I shall be found just.

19 Who is he that will plead against me? Let him come. Why am I consumed holding my peace?

20 Two things only do not to me, and then from thy face I shall not be hid.

21 Withdraw thy hand far from me: and let not thy dread terrify me.

22 Call me, and I will answer thee: or else I will speak, and do thou answer me.

23 How many are my iniquities and sins? Make me know my crimes and offences?

24 Why hidest thou thy face, and thinkest me thy enemy?

25 Against a leaf, that is carried away with the wind, thou shewest thy power: and thou pursuest a dry straw.

26 For thou writest bitter things against me, and wilt consume me for the sins of my youth.

27 Thou hast put my feet in the stocks, and hast observed all my paths, and hast considered the steps of my feet:

28 Who am to be consumed as rottenness, and as a garment that is motheaten.

CHAPTER 14

Job declares the shortness of man's days. He professes his belief of a resurrection.

MAN, born of a woman, living for a short time, is filled with many miseries.

2 [1] Who cometh forth like a flower, and is destroyed, and fleeth as a shadow, and never continueth in the same state.

3 And dost thou think it meet to open thy eyes upon such an one, and to bring him into judgment with thee?

4 [2] Who can make him clean that is conceived of unclean seed? Is it not thou who only art?

5 The days of man are short, and the number of his months is with thee: thou hast appointed his bounds which cannot be passed.

6 Depart a little from him, that he

CHAP. 14. [1] Job. 8, 9; Ps. 143, 4. [2] Ps. 50, 4.

may rest, until his wished for day come, as that of the hireling.

7 A tree hath hope. If it be cut, it groweth green again, and the boughs thereof sprout.

8 If its root be old in the earth, and its stock be dead in the dust:

9 At the scent of water, it shall spring, and bring forth leaves, as when it was first planted.

10 But man when he shall be dead, and stripped, and consumed, I pray you where is he?

11 As if the waters should depart out of the sea, and an emptied river should be dried up:

12 So man when he is fallen asleep shall not rise again; till the heavens be broken, he shall not awake, nor rise up out of his sleep.

13 Who will grant me this, that thou mayst protect me in hell, and hide me till thy wrath pass, and appoint me a time when thou wilt remember me?

14 Shall man that is dead, thinkest thou, live again? All the days in which I am now in warfare, I expect until my change come.

15 Thou shalt call me, and I will answer thee: to the work of thy hands thou shalt reach out thy right hand.

16 [3] Thou indeed hast numbered my steps: but spare my sins.

17 Thou hast sealed up my offences as it were in a bag, but hast cured my iniquity.

18 A mountain falling cometh to nought: and a rock is removed out of its place.

19 Waters wear away the stones: and with inundation the ground by little and little is washed away. So in like manner thou shalt destroy man.

20 Thou hast strengthened him for a little while, that he may pass away for ever: thou shalt change his face and shalt send him away.

21 Whether his children come to honour or dishonour, he shall not understand.

22 But yet his flesh, while he shall live, shall have pain: and his soul shall mourn over him.

CHAPTER 15

Eliphaz returns to the charge against Job, and describes the wretched state of the wicked.

AND Eliphaz the Themanite answered, and said:

2 Will a wise man answer as if he were speaking in the wind, and fill his stomach with burning heat?

3 Thou reprovest him by words, who is not equal to thee: and thou speakest that which is not good for thee.

4 As much as is in thee, thou hast made void fear, and hast taken away prayers from before God.

5 For thy iniquity hath taught thy mouth: and thou imitatest the tongue of blasphemers.

6 Thy own mouth shall condemn thee, and not I: and thy own lips shall answer thee.

7 Art thou the first man that was born, or wast thou made before the hills?

8 Hast thou heard God's counsel, and shall his wisdom be inferior to thee?

9 What knowest thou that we are ignorant of? What dost thou understand that we know not?

10 [1] There are with us also aged and ancient men, much elder than thy fathers.

11 Is it a great matter that God should comfort thee? But thy wicked words hinder this.

12 Why doth thy heart elevate thee, and why dost thou stare with thy eyes, as if they were thinking great things?

13 Why doth thy spirit swell against God, to utter such words out of thy mouth?

14 What is man that he should be without spot, and he that is born of a woman that he should appear just?

15 [2] Behold among his saints none is unchangeable: and the heavens are not pure in his sight.

16 How much more is man abominable and unprofitable, who drinketh iniquity like water?

17 I will shew thee. Hear me, and I will tell thee what I have seen.

18 Wise men confess and hide not their fathers.

19 To whom alone the earth was given: and no stranger hath passed among them.

20 The wicked man is proud all his days; and the number of the years of his tyranny is uncertain.

21 The sound of dread is always in his ears: and when there is peace, he always suspecteth treason.

22 He believeth not that he may return from darkness to light, looking round about for the sword on every side.

23 When he moveth himself to seek bread, he knoweth that the day of darkness is ready at his hand.

[3] Job. 31, 4; 34, 31; Prov. 5, 21. CHAP. 15. [1] Ecclus. 18, 8. [2] Job. 4, 18.

CHAP. 14. Ver. 13. *That thou mayst protect me in hell.* That is, in the state of the dead; and in the place where the souls are kept waiting for their Redeemer.

CHAP. 15. Ver. 4. *Thou hast made void fear.* That is, cast off the fear of offending God.

Ver. 18. *Wise men confess and hide not their fathers.* That is, the knowledge and documents they have received from their fathers they are not ashamed to own.

24 Tribulation shall terrify him, and distress shall surround him, as a king that is prepared for the battle.

25 For he hath stretched out his hand against God, and hath strengthened himself against the Almighty.

26 He hath run against him with his neck raised up, and is armed with a fat neck.

27 Fatness hath covered his face, and the fat hangeth down on his sides.

28 He hath dwelt in desolate cities, and in desert houses that are reduced into heaps.

29 He shall not be enriched; neither shall his substance continue; neither shall he push his root in the earth.

30 He shall not depart out of darkness. The flame shall dry up his branches: and he shall be taken away by the breath of his own mouth.

31 He shall not believe, being vainly deceived by error, that he may be redeemed with any price.

32 Before his days be full he shall perish: and his hands shall wither away.

33 He shall be blasted as a vine when its grapes are in the first flower, and as an olive tree that casteth its flower.

34 For the congregation of the hypocrite is barren: and fire shall devour their tabernacles, who love to take bribes.

35 [3] He hath conceived sorrow, and hath brought forth iniquity: and his womb prepareth deceits.

CHAPTER 16

Job expostulates with his friends and appeals to the judgment of God.

THEN Job answered, and said:
2 I have often heard such things as these: you are all troublesome comforters.

3 Shall windy words have no end? Or is it any trouble to thee to speak?

4 I also could speak like you: and would God your soul were for my soul.

5 I would comfort you also with words, and would wag my head over you.

6 I would strengthen you with my mouth, and would move my lips, as sparing you.

7 But what shall I do? If I speak, my pain will not rest: and if I hold my peace, it will not depart from me.

8 But now my sorrow hath oppressed me: and all my limbs are brought to nothing.

9 My wrinkles bear witness against me: and a false speaker riseth up against my face, contradicting me.

[3] Ps. 7, 15; Isai. 59, 4.

CHAP. 17. Ver. 2. *Not sinned.* That is, I am not guilty of such sins as they charge me with.

10 He hath gathered together his fury against me; and threatening me he hath gnashed with his teeth upon me. My enemy hath beheld me with terrible eyes.

11 They have opened their mouths upon me, and reproaching me they have struck me on the cheek; they are filled with my pains.

12 God hath shut me up with the unjust man: and hath delivered me into the hands of the wicked.

13 I that was formerly so wealthy am all on a sudden broken to pieces. He hath taken me by my neck: he hath broken me, and hath set me up to be his mark.

14 He hath compassed me round about with his lances; he hath wounded my loins; he hath not spared; and hath poured out my bowels on the earth.

15 He hath torn me with wound upon wound: he hath rushed in upon me like a giant.

16 I have sowed sackcloth upon my skin, and have covered my flesh with ashes.

17 My face is swollen with weeping; and my eyelids are dim.

18 These things have I suffered without the iniquity of my hand, when I offered pure prayers to God.

19 O earth, cover not thou my blood: neither let my cry find a hiding place in thee.

20 For behold my witness is in heaven: and he that knoweth my conscience is on high.

21 My friends *are* full of words: my eye poureth out tears to God.

22 And O that a man might so be judged with God, as the son of man is judged with his companion!

23 For behold short years pass away: and I am walking in a path by which I shall not return.

CHAPTER 17

Job's hope in God. He expects rest in death.

MY spirit shall be wasted; my days shall be shortened: and only the grave remaineth for me.

2 I have not sinned: and my eye abideth in bitterness.

3 Deliver me, O Lord, and set me beside thee: and let any man's hand fight against me.

4 Thou hast set their heart far from understanding: therefore they shall not be exalted.

5 He promiseth a prey to his companions: and the eyes of his children shall fail.

6 He hath made me as it were a byword of the people: and I am an example before them.

7 My eye is dim through indignation: and my limbs are brought as it were to nothing.

8 The just shall be astonished at this: and the innocent shall be raised up against the hypocrite.

9 And the just man shall hold on his way: and he that hath clean hands shall be stronger and stronger.

10 Wherefore be you all converted, and come: and I shall not find among you any wise man.

11 My days have passed away, my thoughts are dissipated, tormenting my heart.

12 They have turned night into day: and after darkness I hope for light again.

13 If I wait, hell is my house: and I have made my bed in darkness.

14 I have said to rottenness: Thou art my father: to worms, My mother and my sister.

15 Where is now then my expectation: and who considereth my patience?

16 All that I have shall go down into the deepest pit: thinkest thou that there at least I shall have rest?

CHAPTER 18

Baldad again reproves Job. He describes the miseries of the wicked.

THEN Baldad the Suhite answered, and said:

2 How long will you throw out words? Understand first, and so let us speak.

3 Why are we reputed as beasts, and counted vile before you?

4 Thou that destroyest thy soul in thy fury, shall the earth be forsaken for thee; and shall rocks be removed out of their place?

5 Shall not the light of the wicked be extinguished, and the flame of his fire not shine?

6 The light shall be dark in his tabernacle: and the lamp that is over him shall be put out.

7 The step of his strength shall be straitened: and his own counsel shall cast him down headlong.

8 For he hath thrust his feet into a net, and walketh in its meshes.

9 The sole of his foot shall be held in a snare: and thirst shall burn against him.

10 A gin is hidden for him in the earth: and his trap upon the path.

11 Fears shall terrify him on every side, and shall entangle his feet.

12 Let his strength be wasted with famine: and let hunger invade his ribs.

13 Let it devour the beauty of his skin: let the firstborn death consume his arms.

14 Let his confidence be rooted out of his tabernacle: and let destruction tread upon him like a king.

15 Let the companions of him that is not, dwell in his tabernacle: let brimstone be sprinkled in his tent.

16 Let his roots be dried up beneath: and his harvest destroyed above.

17 [1] Let the memory of him perish from the earth: and let not his name be renowned in the streets.

18 He shall drive him out of light into darkness, and shall remove him out of the world.

19 His seed shall not subsist, nor his offspring among his people, nor any remnants in his country.

20 They that come after him shall be astonished at his day: and horror shall fall upon them that went before.

21 These then are the tabernacles of the wicked: and this the place of him that knoweth not God.

CHAPTER 19

Job complains of the cruelty of his friends. He describes his own sufferings and his belief of a future resurrection.

THEN Job answered, and said:

2 How long do you afflict my soul, and break me in pieces with words?

3 Behold, these ten times you confound me, and are not ashamed to oppress me.

4 For if I have been ignorant, my ignorance shall be with me.

5 But you set yourself up against me, and reprove me with my reproaches.

6 At least now, understand that God hath not afflicted me with an equal judgment, and compassed me with his scourges.

7 Behold I shall cry suffering violence, and no one will hear: I shall cry aloud, and there is none to judge.

8 He hath hedged in my path round about, and I cannot pass: and in my way he hath set darkness.

9 He hath stripped me of my glory, and hath taken the crown from my head.

10 He hath destroyed me on every side, and I am lost. And he hath taken away my hope, as from a tree that is plucked up.

CHAP. 18. [1] Prov. 2, 22.

Ver. 13. *Hell.* Sheol. The region of the dead.
Ver. 16. *Deepest pit.* Literally, *hell.*

CHAP. 19. Ver. 6. *With an equal judgment.* St. Gregory explains these words thus: Job being a just man, and truly considering his own life, thought that his affliction was greater than his sins deserved: and in that respect, that the punishment was not equal, yet it was just, as coming from God, who gives a *crown of justice* to those who suffer for righteousness' sake, and proves the just with tribulations, as gold is tried by fire.

11 His wrath is kindled against me: and he hath counted me as his enemy.

12 His troops have come together, and have made themselves a way by me, and have besieged my tabernacle round about.

13 He hath put my brethren far from me: and my acquaintance like strangers have departed from me.

14 My kinsmen have forsaken me: and they that knew me have forgotten me.

15 They that dwell in my house and my maid-servants have counted me as a stranger: and I have been like an alien in their eyes.

16 I called my servant, and he gave me no answer: I entreated him with my own mouth.

17 My wife hath abhorred my breath, and I entreated the children of my womb.

18 Even fools despised me: and when I was gone from them, they spoke against me.

19 They that were sometime my counsellors have abhorred me: and he whom I loved most is turned against me.

20 The flesh being consumed, my bone hath cleaved to my skin, and nothing but lips are left about my teeth.

21 Have pity on me, have pity on me, at least you my friends, because the hand of the Lord hath touched me.

22 Why do you persecute me as God, and glut yourselves with my flesh?

23 Who will grant me that my words may be written? Who will grant me that they may be marked down in a book?

24 With an iron pen and in a plate of lead, or else be graven with an instrument in flint stone?

25 For I know that my Redeemer liveth, and in the last day I shall rise out of the earth.

26 And I shall be clothed again with my skin: and in my flesh I shall see my God.

27 Whom I myself shall see, and my eyes shall behold; and not another. This my hope is laid up in my bosom.

28 Why then do you say now: Let us persecute him, and let us find occasion of word against him?

29 Flee then from the face of the sword; for the sword is the revenger

Chap. 20. ¹ Ecclus. 5, 9.

Ver. 25, 26, and 27 shew Job's explicit belief in his Redeemer, and also of the resurrection of the flesh, not as one tree riseth in place of another, but that the selfsame flesh shall rise at the last day, by the power of God, changed in quality but not in substance, every one to receive sentence according to his works in this life.

Chap. 20. Ver. 18. *According to the multitude of his devices.* That is, his stratagems to gratify his passions and to oppress and destroy the poor.

of iniquities. And know ye that there is a judgment.

CHAPTER 20

Sophar declares the shortness of the prosperity of the wicked and their sudden downfall.

THEN Sophar the Naamathite answered, and said:

2 Therefore various thoughts succeed one another in me, and my mind is hurried away to different things.

3 The doctrine with which thou reprovest me, I will hear: and the spirit of my understanding shall answer for me.

4 This I know from the beginning, since man was placed upon the earth,

5 That the praise of the wicked is short, and the joy of the hypocrite but for a moment.

6 If his pride mount up even to heaven, and his head touch the clouds:

7 In the end he shall be destroyed like a dunghill; and they that had seen him, shall say: Where is he?

8 As a dream that fleeth away he shall not be found: he shall pass as a vision of the night:

9 The eyes that had seen him shall see him no more: neither shall his place any more behold him.

10 His children shall be oppressed with want: and his hands shall render to him his sorrow.

11 His bones shall be filled with the vices of his youth: and they shall sleep with him in the dust.

12 For when evil shall be sweet in his mouth, he will hide it under his tongue.

13 He will spare it, and not leave it, and will hide it in his throat.

14 His bread in his belly shall be turned into the gall of asps within him.

15 The riches which he hath swallowed, he shall vomit up: and God shall draw them out of his belly.

16 He shall suck the head of asps: and the viper's tongue shall kill him.

17 (Let him not see the streams of the river, the brooks of honey and of butter.)

18 He shall be punished for all that he did, and yet shall not be consumed: according to the multitude of his devices so also shall he suffer.

19 Because he broke in and stripped the poor. He hath violently taken away a house which he did not build:

20 ¹ And yet his belly was not filled. And when he hath the things he coveted, he shall not be able to possess them.

21 There was nothing left of his

meat: and therefore nothing shall continue of his goods.

22 When he shall be filled, he shall be straitened, he shall burn: and every sorrow shall fall upon him.

23 May his belly be filled, that *God* may send forth the wrath of his indignation upon him, and rain down his war upon him.

24 He shall flee from weapons of iron, and shall fall upon a bow of brass.

25 The sword *is* drawn out, and cometh forth from its scabbard, and glittereth in his bitterness. The terrible ones shall go and come upon him.

26 All darkness is hid in his secret places. A fire that is not kindled shall devour him: he shall be afflicted when left in his tabernacle.

27 The heavens shall reveal his iniquity: and the earth shall rise up against him.

28 The offspring of his house shall be exposed: he shall be pulled down in the day of God's wrath.

29 This is the portion of a wicked man from God: and the inheritance of his doings from the Lord.

CHAPTER 21

Job shews that the wicked often prosper in this world, even to the end of their life. But that their judgment is in another world.

THEN Job answered, and said:

2 Hear, I beseech you, my words: and do penance.

3 Suffer me, and I will speak: and after, if you please, laugh at my words.

4 Is my debate against man, that I should not have just reason to be troubled?

5 Hearken to me, and be astonished: and lay your finger on your mouth.

6 As for me, when I remember, I am afraid: and trembling taketh hold on my flesh.

7 [1] Why then do the wicked live, are they advanced, and strengthened with riches?

8 Their seed continueth before them: a multitude of kinsmen, and of children's children in their sight.

9 Their houses are secure and peaceable: and the rod of God is not upon them.

10 Their cattle have conceived, and failed not: their cow has calved, and is not deprived of her fruit.

11 Their little ones go out like a flock: and their children dance and play.

12 They take the timbrel and the harp, and rejoice at the sound of the organ.

13 They spend their days in wealth. And in a moment they go down to hell.

14 Who have said to God: Depart from us. We desire not the knowledge of thy ways.

15 [2] Who is the Almighty, that we should serve him? And what doth it profit us if we pray to him?

16 Yet because their good things are not in their hand, may the counsel of the wicked be far from me.

17 How often shall the lamp of the wicked be put out, and a deluge come upon them: and he shall distribute the sorrows of his wrath?

18 They shall be as chaff before the face of the wind, and as ashes which the whirlwind scattereth.

19 God shall lay up the sorrow of the father for his children: and when he shall repay, then shall he know.

20 His eyes shall see his own destruction: and he shall drink of the wrath of the Almighty.

21 For what is it to him what befalleth his house after him: and if the number of his months be diminished by one half?

22 Shall any one teach God knowledge, who judgeth those that are high?

23 One man dieth strong and hale, rich and happy.

24 His bowels are full of fat, and his bones are moistened with marrow.

25 But another dieth in bitterness of soul without any riches.

26 And yet they shall sleep together in the dust, and worms shall cover them.

27 Surely I know your thoughts, and your unjust judgments against me.

28 For you say: Where is the house of the prince? And where are the dwelling places of the wicked?

29 Ask any one of them that go by the way: and you shall perceive that he knoweth these same things.

30 Because the wicked man is reserved to the day of destruction: and he shall be brought to the day of wrath.

31 Who shall reprove his way to his face? And who shall repay him what he hath done?

32 He shall be brought to the graves, and shall watch in the heap of the dead.

33 He hath been acceptable to the gravel of Cocytus. And he shall draw

CHAP. 21. [1] Jer. 12, 1; Hab. 2, 5. [2] Mal. 3, 14.

CHAP. 21. Ver. 33. *Acceptable to the gravel of Cocytus.* The Hebrew word, which St. Jerome has here rendered by the name *Cocytus* (which the poets represent as a river in hell), signifies a *valley* or a *torrent:* and in this place, is taken for the low region of death and hell: which willingly, as it were, receives the wicked at their death: who are ushered in by innumerable others that have gone before them; and are followed by multitudes above number.

every man after him; and there are innumerable before him.

34 How then do ye comfort me in vain, whereas your answer is shewn to be repugnant to truth?

CHAPTER 22

Eliphaz falsely imputes many crimes to Job. He promises him prosperity if he will repent.

THEN Eliphaz the Themanite answered, and said:

2 Can man be compared with God, even though he were of perfect knowledge?

3 What doth it profit God if thou be just? Or what dost thou give him if thy way be unspotted?

4 Shall he reprove thee for fear, and come with thee into judgment?

5 And not for thy manifold wickedness, and thy infinite iniquities?

6 For thou hast taken away the pledge of thy brethren without cause, and stripped the naked of their clothing.

7 Thou hast not given water to the weary: thou hast withdrawn bread from the hungry.

8 In the strength of thy arm thou didst possess the land, and being the most mighty thou holdest it.

9 Thou hast sent widows away empty: and the arms of the fatherless thou hast broken in pieces.

10 Therefore art thou surrounded with snares: and sudden fear troubleth thee.

11 And didst thou think that thou shouldst not see darkness, and that thou shouldst not be covered with the violence of overflowing waters?

12 Dost not thou think that God is higher than heaven, and is elevated above the height of the stars?

13 And thou sayst: What doth God know? And he judgeth as it were through a mist.

14 The clouds are his covert, and he doth not consider our things: and he walketh about the poles of heaven.

15 Dost thou desire to keep the path of ages, which wicked men have trodden?

16 Who were taken away before their time: and a flood hath overthrown their foundation.

17 Who said to God: Depart from us: and looked upon the Almighty as if he could do nothing:

18 Whereas he had filled their houses with good things. Whose way of thinking be far from me.

19 [1] The just shall see, and shall rejoice: and the innocent shall laugh them to scorn.

20 Is not their exaltation cut down, and hath not fire devoured the remnants of them?

21 Submit thyself then to him, and be at peace: and thereby thou shalt have the best fruits.

22 Receive the law of his mouth, and lay up his words in thy heart.

23 If thou wilt return to the Almighty, thou shalt be built up, and shalt put away iniquity far from thy tabernacle.

24 He shall give for earth flint, and for flint torrents of gold.

25 And the Almighty shall be against thy enemies: and silver shall be heaped together for thee.

26 Then shalt thou abound in delights in the Almighty: and shalt lift up thy face to God.

27 Thou shalt pray to him, and he will hear thee: and thou shalt pay vows.

28 Thou shalt decree a thing, and it shall come to thee: and light shall shine in thy ways.

29 [2] For he that hath been humbled shall be in glory: and he that shall bow down his eyes, he shall be saved.

30 The innocent shall be saved: and he shall be saved by the cleanness of his hands.

CHAPTER 23

Job wishes to be tried at God's tribunal.

THEN Job answered, and said:

2 Now also my words are in bitterness, and the hand of my scourge is more grievous than my mourning.

3 Who will grant me that I might know and find him, and come even to his throne?

4 I would set judgment before him, and would fill my mouth with complaints.

5 That I might know the words that he would answer me, and understand what he would say to me.

6 I would not that he should contend with me with much strength, nor overwhelm me with the weight of his greatness.

7 Let him propose equity against me: and let my judgment come to victory.

8 But if I go to the east, he appeareth not: if to the west, I shall not understand him.

9 If to the left hand, what shall I do? I shall not take hold on him. If I turn myself to the right hand, I shall not see him.

10 But he knoweth my way, and has tried me as gold that passeth through the fire.

CHAP. 22. [1] Ps. 106, 42. [2] Prov. 29, 23.

11 My foot hath followed his steps: I have kept his way, and have not declined from it.

12 I have not departed from the commandments of his lips: and the words of his mouth I have hid in my bosom.

13 For he is alone, and no man can turn away his thought. And whatsoever his soul hath desired, that hath he done.

14 And when he shall have fulfilled his will in me, many other like things are also at hand with him.

15 And therefore I am troubled at his presence: and when I consider him I am made pensive with fear.

16 God hath softened my heart: and the Almighty hath troubled me.

17 For I have not perished because of the darkness that hangs over me: neither hath the mist covered my face.

CHAPTER 24

God's providence often suffers the wicked to go on a long time in their sins. He punisheth them in another life.

TIMES are not hid from the Almighty: but they that know him, know not his days.

2 Some have removed landmarks, have taken away flocks by force, and fed them.

3 They have driven away the ass of the fatherless, and have taken away the widow's ox for a pledge.

4 They have overturned the way of the poor, and have oppressed together the meek of the earth.

5 Others like wild asses in the desert go forth to their work: by watching for a prey they get bread for their children.

6 They reap the field that is not their own: and gather the vintage of his vineyard whom by violence they have oppressed.

7 They send men away naked, taking away their clothes who have no covering in the cold:

8 Who are wet with the showers of the mountains, and having no covering embrace the stones.

9 They have violently robbed the fatherless, and stripped the poor common people.

10 From the naked and them that go without clothing, and from the hungry, they have taken away the ears of corn.

11 They have taken their rest at noon among the stores of them who after having trodden the winepresses suffer thirst.

12 Out of the cities they have made men to groan. And the soul of the wounded hath cried out: and God doth not suffer it to pass unrevenged.

13 They have been rebellious to the light, they have not known his ways: neither have they returned by his paths.

14 The murderer riseth at the very break of day; he killeth the needy, and the poor man: but in the night he will be as a thief.

15 The eye of the adulterer observeth darkness, saying: No eye shall see me. And he will cover his face.

16 He diggeth through houses in the dark, as in the day they had appointed for themselves: and they have not known the light.

17 If the morning suddenly appear, it is to them the shadow of death: and they walk in darkness as if it were in light.

18 He is light upon the face of the water. Cursed be his portion on the earth. Let him not walk by the way of the vineyards.

19 Let him pass from the snow waters to excessive heat: and his sin even to hell.

20 Let mercy forget him: may worms be his sweetness. Let him be remembered no more, but be broken in pieces as an unfruitful tree.

21 For he hath fed the barren that beareth not: and to the widow he hath done no good.

22 He hath pulled down the strong by his might: and when he standeth up, he shall not trust to his life.

23 [1] God hath given him place for penance: and he abuseth it unto pride. But his eyes are upon his ways.

24 They are lifted up for a little while and shall not stand, and shall be brought down as all things, and shall be taken away: and as the tops of the ears of corn they shall be broken.

25 And if it be not so, who can convince me that I have lied, and set my words before God?

CHAPTER 25

Baldad represents the justice of God, before whom no man can be justified.

THEN Baldad the Suhite answered, and said:

2 Power and terror are with him, who maketh peace in his high places.

3 Is there any numbering of his soldiers? And upon whom shall not his light arise?

4 Can man be justified compared with God; or he that is born of a woman appear clean?

5 Behold even the moon doth not shine, and the stars are not pure, in his sight.

6 How much less man that is rottenness, and the son of man who is a worm?

CHAP. 24. [1] Apoc. 2, 21.

CHAPTER 26

Job declares his sentiment of the wisdom and power of God.

THEN Job answered, and said:
2 Whose helper art thou? Is it of him that is weak? And dost thou hold up the arm of him that has no strength?

3 To whom hast thou given counsel? Perhaps to him that hath no wisdom: and thou hast shewn thy very great prudence.

4 Whom hast thou desired to teach? Was it not him that made life?

5 Behold the giants groan under the waters, and they that dwell with them.

6 Hell is naked before him: and there is no covering for destruction.

7 He stretched out the north over the empty space, and hangeth the earth upon nothing.

8 He bindeth up the waters in his clouds, so that they break not out and fall down together.

9 He withholdeth the face of his throne, and spreadeth his cloud over it.

10 He hath set bounds about the waters, till light and darkness come to an end.

11 The pillars of heaven tremble and dread at his beck.

12 By his power the seas are suddenly gathered together; and his wisdom has struck the proud one.

13 His spirit hath adorned the heavens: and his obstetric hand brought forth the winding serpent.

14 Lo, these things are said in part, of his ways: and seeing we have heard scarce a little drop of his word, who shall be able to behold the thunder of his greatness?

CHAPTER 27

Job persists in asserting his own innocence, and that hypocrites will be punished in the end.

JOB also added, taking up his parable, and said:

2 As God liveth, who hath taken away my judgment, and the Almighty, who hath brought my soul to bitterness,

3 As long as breath remaineth in me, and the spirit of God in my nostrils,

4 My lips shall not speak iniquity, neither shall my tongue contrive lying.

CHAP. 27. [1] Ps. 48, 18.

CHAP. 26. Ver. 13. *His obstetric hand brought forth the winding serpent.* That is, the omnipotent power of God: which brought forth all things created in time, but conceived in the Divine mind from all eternity. The *winding serpent*, a constellation of fixed stars winding round the north pole, called *Draco.* This appears from the foregoing part of the same verse, *His spirit hath adorned the heavens*,

5 God forbid that I should judge you to be just: till I die I will not depart from my innocence.

6 My justification, which I have begun to hold, I will not forsake: for my heart doth not reprehend me in all my life.

7 Let my enemy be as the ungodly: and my adversary as the wicked one.

8 For what is the hope of the hypocrite if through covetousness he take by violence, and God deliver not his soul?

9 Will God hear his cry, when distress shall come upon him?

10 Or can he delight himself in the Almighty, and call upon God at all times?

11 I will teach you by the hand of God, what the Almighty hath, and I will not conceal it.

12 Behold you all know it; and why do you speak vain things without cause?

13 This is the portion of a wicked man with God, and the inheritance of the violent, which they shall receive of the Almighty.

14 If his sons be multiplied, they shall be for the sword: and his grandsons shall not be filled with bread.

15 They that shall remain of him, shall be buried in death: and his widows shall not weep.

16 If he shall heap together silver as earth, and prepare raiment as clay,

17 He shall prepare indeed; but the just man shall be clothed with it: and the innocent shall divide the silver.

18 He hath built his house as a moth: and as a keeper he hath made a booth.

19 [1] The rich man when he shall sleep shall take away nothing with him: he shall open his eyes and find nothing.

20 Poverty like water shall take hold on him: a tempest shall oppress him in the night.

21 A burning wind shall take him up, and carry him away: and as a whirlwind shall snatch him from his place.

22 And he shall cast upon him, and shall not spare. Out of his hand he would willingly flee.

23 He shall clasp his hands upon him, and shall hiss at him, beholding his place.

CHAPTER 28

Man's industry searcheth out many things. True wisdom is taught by God alone.

SILVER hath beginnings of its veins: and gold hath a place wherein it is melted.

2 Iron is taken out of the earth: and stone melted with heat is turned into brass.

3 He hath set a time for darkness, and the end of all things he con-

sidereth: the stone also that is in the dark and the shadow of death.

4 The flood divideth from the people that are on their journey, those whom the food of the needy man hath forgotten and who cannot be come at.

5 The land, out of which bread grew in its place, hath been overturned with fire.

6 The stones of it are the place of sapphires: and the clods of it are gold.

7 The bird hath not known the path: neither hath the eye of the vulture beheld it.

8 The children of the merchants have not trodden it: neither hath the lioness passed by it.

9 He hath stretched forth his hand to the flint: he hath overturned mountains from the roots.

10 In the rocks he hath cut out rivers: and his eye hath seen every precious thing.

11 The depths also of rivers he hath searched: and hidden things he hath brought forth to light.

12 But where is wisdom to be found? And where is the place of understanding?

13 Man knoweth not the price thereof: neither is it found in the land of them that live in delights.

14 The depth saith: It is not in me. And the sea saith: It is not with me.

15 ¹ The finest gold shall not purchase it: neither shall silver be weighed in exchange for it.

16 It shall not be compared with the dyed colours of India, or with the most precious stone sardonyx, or the sapphire.

17 Gold or crystal cannot equal it: neither shall any vessels of gold be changed for it.

18 High and eminent things shall not be mentioned in comparison of it: but wisdom is drawn out of secret places.

19 The topaz of Ethiopia shall not be equal to it: neither shall it be compared to the cleanest dyeing.

20 Whence then cometh wisdom? And where is the place of understanding?

21 It is hid from the eyes of all living: and the fowls of the air know it not.

22 Destruction and death have said: With our ears we have heard the fame thereof.

23 God understandeth the way of it: and he knoweth the place thereof.

24 For he beholdeth the ends of the world: and looketh on all things that are under heaven.

25 Who made a weight for the winds, and weighed the waters by measure.

26 When he gave a law for the rain, and a way for the sounding storms.

27 Then he saw it; and declared, and prepared, and searched it.

28 And he said to man: Behold the fear of the Lord, that is wisdom. And to depart from evil is understanding.

CHAPTER 29

Job relates his former happiness, and the respect that all men shewed him.

JOB also added, taking up his parable, and said:

2 Who will grant me that I might be according to the months past, according to the days in which God kept me?

3 When his lamp shined over my head: and I walked by his light in darkness?

4 As I was in the days of my youth, when God was secretly in my tabernacle?

5 When the Almighty was with me: and my servants round about me?

6 When I washed my feet with butter: and the rock poured me out rivers of oil?

7 When I went out to the gate of the city: and in the street they prepared me a chair?

8 The young men saw me, and hid themselves: and the old men rose up and stood.

9 The princes ceased to speak, and laid the finger on their mouth.

10 The rulers held their peace; and their tongue cleaved to their throat.

11 The ear that heard me blessed me: and the eye that saw me gave witness to me.

12 Because I had delivered the poor man that cried out; and the fatherless, that had no helper.

13 The blessing of him that was ready to perish came upon me; and I comforted the heart of the widow.

14 I was clad with justice: and I clothed myself with my judgment, as with a robe and a diadem.

15 I was an eye to the blind, and a foot to the lame.

16 I was the father of the poor: and the cause which I knew not, I searched out most diligently.

17 I broke the jaws of the wicked man: and out of his teeth I took away the prey.

18 And I said: I shall die in my nest, and as a palm tree shall multiply my days.

19 My root is opened beside the waters: and dew shall continue in my harvest.

CHAP. 28. ¹ Wisd. 7, 9.

20 My glory shall always be renewed: and my bow in my hand shall be repaired.

21 They that heard me waited for my sentence, and being attentive held their peace at my counsel.

22 To my words they durst add nothing: and my speech dropped upon them.

23 They waited for me as for rain: and they opened their mouth as for a latter shower.

24 If at any time I laughed on them, they believed not: and the light of my countenance fell not on earth.

25 If I had a mind to go to them, I sat first. And when I sat as a king, with his army standing about him, yet I was a comforter of them that mourned.

CHAPTER 30

Job shews the wonderful change of his temporal estate, from welfare to great calamity.

BUT now the younger in time scorn me, whose fathers I would not have set with the dogs of my flock.

2 The strength of whose hands was to me as nothing: and they were thought unworthy of life itself.

3 Barren with want and hunger, they gnawed in the wilderness: disfigured with calamity and misery.

4 And they ate grass and barks of trees: and the root of junipers was their food.

5 Who snatched up these things out of the valleys: and when they had found any of them, they ran to them with a cry.

6 They dwelt in the desert places of torrents, and in caves of earth, or upon the gravel.

7 They pleased themselves among these kind of things, and counted it delightful to be under the briers.

8 The children of foolish and base men, and not appearing at all upon the earth.

9 Now I am turned into their song, and am become their byword.

10 They abhor me and flee far from me, and are not afraid to spit in my face.

11 For he hath opened his quiver, and hath afflicted me, and hath put a bridle into my mouth.

12 At the right hand of my rising, my calamities forthwith arose. They have overthrown my feet, and have

CHAP. 30. Ver. 1. *But now the younger in time:* that is, younger than I am, and as it were obscure, whom I was conspicuous and in magnificence; they now look down on me.

Ver. 29. *Brother of dragons.* Imitating these creatures in their lamentable noise.

overwhelmed me with their paths as with waves.

13 They have destroyed my ways, they have lain in wait against me, and they have prevailed: and there was none to help.

14 They have rushed in upon me, as when a wall is broken, and a gate opened: and have rolled themselves down to my miseries.

15 I am brought to nothing. As a wind thou hast taken away my desire: and my posterity hath passed away like a cloud.

16 And now my soul fadeth within myself: and the days of affliction possess me.

17 In the night my bone is pierced with sorrows: and they that feed upon me do not sleep.

18 With the multitude of them my garment is consumed: and they have girded me about, as with the collar of my coat.

19 I am compared to dirt: and am likened to embers and ashes.

20 I cry to thee, and thou hearest me not: I stand up, and thou dost not regard me.

21 Thou art changed to be cruel toward me: and in the hardness of thy hand thou art against me.

22 Thou hast lifted me up, and set me as it were upon the wind: and thou hast mightily dashed me.

23 I know that thou wilt deliver me to death, where a house is appointed for every one that liveth.

24 But yet thou stretchest not forth thy hand to their consumption: and if they shall fall down thou wilt save.

25 I wept heretofore for him that was afflicted: and my soul had compassion on the poor.

26 I expected good things, and evils are come upon me: I waited for light, and darkness broke out.

27 My inner parts have boiled without any rest: the days of affliction have prevented me.

28 I went mourning without indignation; I rose up, and cried in the crowd.

29 I was the brother of dragons, and companion of ostriches.

30 My skin is become black upon me: and my bones are dried up with heat.

31 My harp is turned to mourning: and my organ into the voice of those that weep.

CHAPTER 31

Job, to defend himself from the unjust judgments of his friends, gives a sincere account of his own virtues.

I MADE a covenant with my eyes, that I would not so much as think upon a virgin.

2 For what part should God from above have in me, and *what* inheritance the Almighty from on high?

3 Is not destruction to the wicked, and aversion to them that work iniquity?

4 Doth not he consider my ways, and number all my steps?

5 If I have walked in vanity, and my foot hath made haste to deceit:

6 Let him weigh me in a just balance, and let God know my simplicity.

7 If my step hath turned out of the way, and if my heart hath followed my eyes, and if a spot hath cleaved to my hands:

8 Then let me sow and let another eat: and let my offspring be rooted out.

9 If my heart hath been deceived upon a woman, and if I have laid wait at my friend's door:

10 Let my wife be the harlot of another; and let other men lie with her.

11 For this is a heinous crime, and a most grievous iniquity.

12 It is a fire that devoureth even to destruction, and rooteth up all things that spring.

13 If I have despised to abide judgment with my man-servant, or my maid-servant, when they had any controversy against me:

14 For what shall I do when God shall rise to judge? And when he shall examine, what shall I answer him?

15 Did not he that made me in the womb make him also? And did not one and the same form me in the womb?

16 If I have denied to the poor what they desired, and have made the eyes of the widow wait:

17 If I have eaten my morsel alone, and the fatherless hath not eaten thereof:

18 (For from my infancy mercy grew up with me: and it came out with me from my mother's womb):

19 If I have despised him that was perishing for want of clothing, and the poor man that had no covering:

20 If his sides have not blessed me, and if he were not warmed with the fleece of my sheep:

21 If I have lifted up my hand against the fatherless, even when I saw myself superior in the gate:

22 Let my shoulder fall from its joint, and let my arm with its bones be broken.

23 For I have always feared God as waves swelling over me; and his weight I was not able to bear.

24 If I have thought gold my strength, and have said to fine gold: My confidence:

25 If I have rejoiced over my great riches, and because my hand had gotten much:

26 If I beheld the sun when it shined, and the moon going in brightness:

27 And my heart in secret hath rejoiced, and I have kissed my hand with my mouth

28 (Which is a very great iniquity, and a denial against the most high God):

29 If I have been glad at the downfall of him that hated me, and have rejoiced that evil had found him

30 (For I have not given my mouth to sin, by wishing a curse to his soul).

31 If the men of my tabernacle have not said: Who will give us of his flesh that we may be filled?

32 The stranger did not stay without, my door was open to the traveller.

33 If as a man I have hid my sin, and have concealed my iniquity in my bosom:

34 If I have been afraid at a very great multitude, and the contempt of kinsmen hath terrified me: and I have not rather held my peace, and not gone out of the door:

35 Who would grant me a hearer, that the Almighty may hear my desire; and that he himself that judgeth would write a book,

36 That I may carry it on my shoulder, and put it about me as a crown?

37 At every step of mine I would pronounce it, and offer it as to a prince.

38 If my land cry against me, and with it the furrows thereof mourn:

39 If I have eaten the fruits thereof without money, and have afflicted the soul of the tillers thereof:

40 Let thistles grow up to me instead of wheat, and thorns instead of barley.

The words of Job are ended.

CHAPTER 32

Eliu is angry both with Job and his friends. He boasts of himself.

SO these three men ceased to answer Job, because he seemed just to himself.

2 And Eliu the son of Barachel the Buzite, of the kindred of Ram, was angry and was moved to indignation. Now he was angry against Job, because he said he was just before God.

3 And he was angry with his friends, because they had not found a reason-

CHAP. 31. Ver. 26. *If I beheld the sun.* If I behold the sun and moon with admiration, knowing them to be created and governed by the power of God, I call on my adversaries to produce any thing against me, whereby I could be charged with worshipping the sun or moon.

able answer, but only had condemned Job.

4 So Eliu waited while Job was speaking, because they were his elders that were speaking.

5 But when he saw that the three were not able to answer, he was exceedingly angry.

6 Then Eliu the son of Barachel the Buzite answered, and said: I am younger in days, and you are more ancient; therefore hanging down my head, I was afraid to shew you my opinion.

7 For I hoped that greater age would speak, and that a multitude of years would teach wisdom.

8 But, as I see, there is a spirit in men, and the inspiration of the Almighty giveth understanding.

9 They that are aged are not the wise men: neither do the ancients understand judgment.

10 Therefore I will speak: Hearken to me; I also will shew you my wisdom.

11 For I have waited for your words; I have given ear to your wisdom, as long as you were disputing in words.

12 And as long as I thought you said some thing, I considered. But, as I see, there is none of you that can convince Job, and answer his words.

13 Lest you should say: We have found wisdom. God hath cast him down, not man.

14 He hath spoken nothing to me: and I will not answer him according to your words.

15 They were afraid, and answered no more: and they left off speaking.

16 Therefore because I have waited, and they have not spoken: they stood, and answered no more:

17 I also will answer my part, and will shew my knowledge.

18 For I am full of matter to speak of, and the spirit of my bowels straiteneth me.

19 Behold, my belly is as new wine which wanteth vent, which bursteth the new vessels.

20 I will speak and take breath a little: I will open my lips, and will answer.

21 I will not accept the person of man: and I will not level God with man.

22 For I know not how long I shall continue, and whether after a while my Maker may take me away.

CHAP. 32. Ver. 21. *I will not level God with man.* Here Eliu considers that Job hath put himself on a level with God, by the manner he assumed to justify his own life in speaking to God as if he spoke to an equal: Eliu expresses in the following ver. 22 his fear of punishment hereafter for such an attempt.

CHAPTER 33
Eliu blames Job for asserting his own innocence.

HEAR therefore, O Job, my speeches: and hearken to all my words.

2 Behold now I have opened my mouth: let my tongue speak within my jaws.

3 My words are from my upright heart: and my lips shall speak a pure sentence.

4 The spirit of God made me: and the breath of the Almighty gave me life.

5 If thou canst, answer me: and stand up against my face.

6 Behold God hath made me as well as thee, and of the same clay I also was formed.

7 But yet let not my wonder terrify thee, and let not my eloquence be burdensome to thee.

8 Now thou hast said in my hearing, and I have heard the voice of thy words:

9 I am clean, and without sin. I am unspotted, and there is no iniquity in me.

10 Because he hath found complaints against me, therefore he hath counted me for his enemy.

11 He hath put my feet in the stocks, he hath observed all my paths.

12 Now this is the thing in which thou art not justified. I will answer thee, that God is greater than man.

13 Dost thou strive against him, because he hath not answered thee to all words?

14 God speaketh once, and repeateth not the selfsame thing the second time.

15 By a dream in a vision by night, when deep sleep falleth upon men, and they are sleeping in their beds,

16 Then he openeth the ears of men, and teaching instructeth them in what they are to learn.

17 That he may withdraw a man from the things he is doing, and may deliver him from pride.

18 Rescuing his soul from corruption: and his life from passing to the sword.

19 He rebuketh also by sorrow in the bed; and he maketh all his bones to wither.

20 Bread becometh abominable to him in his life, and to his soul the meat which before he desired.

21 His flesh shall be consumed away: and his bones that were covered shall be made bare.

22 His soul hath drawn near to corruption: and his life to the destroyers.

23 If there shall be an angel speak-

ing for him, one among thousands, to declare man's uprightness,

24 He shall have mercy on him, and shall say: Deliver him, that he may not go down to corruption. I have found wherein I may be merciful to him.

25 His flesh is consumed with punishments: let him return to the days of his youth.

26 He shall pray to God, and he will be gracious to him. And he shall set his face with joy: and he will render to man his justice.

27 He shall look upon men, and shall say: I have sinned, and indeed I have offended, and I have not received what I have deserved.

28 He hath delivered his soul from going into destruction, that it may live and see the light.

29 Behold, all these things God worketh three times within every one.

30 That he may withdraw their souls from corruption, and enlighten them with the light of the living.

31 Attend, Job, and hearken to me: and hold thy peace, whilst I speak.

32 But if thou hast any thing to say, answer me. Speak: for I would have thee to appear just.

33 And if thou have not, hear me. Hold thy peace, and I will teach thee wisdom.

CHAPTER 34

Eliu charges Job with blasphemy. He sets forth the power and justice of God.

AND Eliu continued his discourse, and said:

2 Hear ye, wise men, my words, and ye learned, hearken to me:

3 ¹ For the ear trieth words, and the mouth discerneth meats by the taste.

4 Let us choose to us judgment: and let us see among ourselves what is the best.

5 For Job hath said: I am just, and God hath overthrown my judgment.

6 For in judging me there is a lie: my arrow is violent without any sin.

7 What man is there like Job, who drinketh up scorning like water?

8 Who goeth in company with them that work iniquity, and walketh with wicked men?

9 For he hath said: Man shall not please God, although he run with him.

10 Therefore, ye men of understanding, hear me. Far from God be wickedness; and iniquity from the Almighty.

11 For he will render to a man his work: and according to the ways of every one he will reward them.

12 For in very deed God will not con-demn without cause: neither will the Almighty pervert judgment.

13 What other hath he appointed over the earth? Or whom hath he set over the world which he made?

14 If he turn his heart to him, he shall draw his spirit and breath unto himself.

15 All flesh shall perish together: and man shall return into ashes.

16 If then thou hast understanding, hear what is said: and hearken to the voice of my words.

17 Can he be healed that loveth not judgment? And how dost thou so far condemn him that is just?

18 Who saith to the king: *Thou art an* apostate. Who calleth rulers, ungodly:

19 ² Who accepteth not the persons of princes: nor hath regarded the tyrant, when he contended against the poor man. For all are the work of his hands.

20 They shall suddenly die, and the people shall be troubled at midnight: and they shall pass, and take away the violent without hand.

21 For his eyes are upon the ways of men: and he considereth all their steps.

22 There is no darkness, and there is no shadow of death, where they may be hid who work iniquity.

23 For it is no longer in the power of man to enter into judgment with God.

24 He shall break in pieces many and innumerable, and shall make others to stand in their stead.

25 For he knoweth their works. And therefore he shall bring night on them, and they shall be destroyed.

26 He hath struck them, as being wicked, in open sight.

27 Who as it were on purpose have revolted from him, and would not understand all his ways:

28 So that they caused the cry of the needy to come to him. And he heard the voice of the poor.

29 For when he granteth peace, who is there that can condemn? When he hideth his countenance, who is there that can behold him, whether it regard nations, or all men?

30 Who maketh a man that is a hypocrite to reign for the sins of the people?

31 Seeing then I have spoken of God, I will not hinder thee in thy turn.

32 If I have erred, teach thou me: if I have spoken iniquity, I will add no more.

CHAP. 34. ¹ Job, 12, 11. ² Deut. 10, 17; 2 Par. 19, 7; Wisd. 6, 8; Ecclus. 35, 16; Acts, 10, 34; Rom. 2, 11; Gal. 2, 6; Eph. 6, 9; Col. 3, 25; 1 Peter, 1, 17.

33 Doth God require it of thee, because it hath displeased thee? For thou begannest to speak, and not I. But if thou know any thing better, speak.

34 Let men of understanding speak to me: and let a wise man hearken to me.

35 But Job hath spoken foolishly: and his words sound not discipline.

36 My father, let Job be tried even to the end: cease not from the man of iniquity.

37 Because he addeth blasphemy upon his sins, let him be tied fast in the mean time amongst us. And then let him provoke God to judgment with his speeches.

CHAPTER 35

Eliu declares that the good or evil done by man cannot reach God.

MOREOVER Eliu spoke these words: 2 Doth thy thought seem right to thee, that thou shouldst say: I am more just than God?

3 For thou saidst: That which is right doth not please thee: or what will it profit thee if I sin?

4 Therefore I will answer thy words, and thy friends with thee.

5 Look up to heaven and see, and behold the sky, that it is higher than thee.

6 If thou sin, what shalt thou hurt him? And if thy iniquities be multiplied, what shalt thou do against him?

7 And if thou do justly, what shalt thou give him, or what shall he receive of thy hand?

8 Thy wickedness may hurt a man that is like thee: and thy justice may help the son of man.

9 By reason of the multitude of oppressors they shall cry out: and shall wail for the violence of the arm of tyrants.

10 And he hath not said: Where is God, who made me, who hath given songs in the night?

11 Who teacheth us more than the beasts of the earth, and instructeth us more than the fowls of the air.

12 There shall they cry: and he will not hear, because of the pride of evil men.

13 God therefore will not hear in vain: and the Almighty will look into the causes of every one.

14 Yea when thou shalt say: He considereth not: be judged before him, and expect him.

CHAP. 36. Ver. 16. *Out of the narrow mouth.* That is, out of hell, whose entrance is narrow, and its depth bottomless; but figuratively meant here, that is, from his miseries and calamity to be restored to his former state of happiness.

15 For he doth not now bring on his fury: neither doth he revenge wickedness exceedingly.

16 Therefore Job openeth his mouth in vain, and multiplieth words without knowledge.

CHAPTER 36

Eliu proceeds in setting forth the justice and power of God.

ELIU also proceeded, and said: 2 Suffer me a little, and I will shew thee: for I have yet somewhat to speak in God's behalf.

3 I will repeat my knowledge from the beginning: and I will prove my Maker just.

4 For indeed my words are without a lie: and perfect knowledge shall be proved to thee.

5 God doth not cast away the mighty, whereas he himself also is mighty.

6 But he saveth not the wicked: and he giveth judgment to the poor.

7 He will not take away his eyes from the just; and he placeth kings on the throne for ever: and they are exalted.

8 And if they shall be in chains, and be bound with the cords of poverty:

9 He shall shew them their works, and their wicked deeds, because they have been violent.

10 He also shall open their ear, to correct them: and shall speak, that they may return from iniquity.

11 If they shall hear and observe, they shall accomplish for their days in good, and their years in glory.

12 But if they hear not, they shall pass by the sword: and shall be consumed in folly.

13 Dissemblers and crafty men prove the wrath of God: neither shall they cry when they are bound.

14 Their soul shall die in a storm, and their life among the effeminate.

15 He shall deliver the poor out of his distress, and shall open his ear in affliction.

16 Therefore he shall set thee at large out of the narrow mouth, and which hath no foundation under it: and the rest of thy table shall be full of fatness.

17 Thy cause hath been judged as that of the wicked. Cause and judgment thou shalt recover.

18 Therefore let not anger overcome thee to oppress any man: neither let multitude of gifts turn thee aside.

19 Lay down thy greatness without tribulation, and all the mighty of strength.

20 Prolong not the night that people may come up for them.

21 Beware thou turn not aside to

iniquity: for this thou hast begun to follow after misery.

22 Behold, God is high in his strength: and none is like him among the law-givers.

23 Who can search out his ways? Or who can say to him: Thou hast wrought iniquity?

24 Remember that thou knowest not his work, concerning which men have sung.

25 All men see him: every one beholdeth afar off.

26 Behold, God is great, exceeding our knowledge: the number of his years is inestimable.

27 He lifteth up the drops of rain, and poureth out showers like floods:

28 Which flow from the clouds that cover all above.

29 If he will spread out clouds as his tent,

30 And lighten with his light from above, he shall cover also the ends of the sea.

31 For by these he judgeth people, and giveth food to many mortals.

32 In his hands he hideth the light, and commandeth it to come again.

33 He sheweth his friend concerning it, that it is his possession, and that he may come up to it.

CHAPTER 37

Eliu goes on in his discourse, shewing God's wisdom and power, by his wonderful works.

AT this my heart trembleth, and is moved out of its place.

2 Hear ye attentively the terror of his voice, and the sound that cometh out of his mouth.

3 He beholdeth under all the heavens: and his light is upon the ends of the earth.

4 After it a noise shall roar: he shall thunder with the voice of his majesty, and shall not be found out, when his voice shall be heard.

5 God shall thunder wonderfully with his voice, he that doth great and unsearchable things.

6 He commandeth the snow to go down upon the earth, and the winter rain, and the shower of his strength.

7 He sealeth up the hand of all men, that every one may know his works.

8 Then the beast shall go into his covert, and shall abide in his den.

9 Out of the inner parts shall a tempest come, and cold out of the north.

10 When God bloweth there cometh frost: and again the waters are poured out abundantly.

11 Corn desireth clouds, and the clouds spread their light:

12 Which go round about, whithersoever the will of him that governeth them shall lead them, to whatsoever he shall command them upon the face of the whole earth:

13 Whether in one tribe, or in his own land, or in what place soever of his mercy he shall command them to be found.

14 Hearken to these things, Job: Stand, and consider the wondrous works of God.

15 Dost thou know when God commanded the rains, to shew his light of his clouds?

16 Knowest thou the great paths of the clouds, and the perfect knowledges?

17 Art not thy garments hot when the south wind blows upon the earth?

18 Thou perhaps hast made the heavens with him, which are most strong, as if they were of molten brass.

19 Shew us what we may say to him: for we are wrapped up in darkness.

20 Who shall tell him the things I speak? Even if a man shall speak, he shall be swallowed up.

21 But now they see not the light: the air on a sudden shall be thickened into clouds, and the wind shall pass and drive them away.

22 Cold cometh out of the north: and to God praise with fear.

23 We cannot find him worthily. He is great in strength, and in judgment, and in justice: and he is ineffable.

24 Therefore men shall fear him: and all that seem to themselves to be wise shall not dare to behold him.

CHAPTER 38

God interposes and shews from the things he hath made, that man cannot comprehend his power and wisdom.

THEN the Lord answered Job out of a whirlwind, and said:

2 Who is this that wrappeth up sentences in unskilful words?

3 Gird up thy loins like a man. I will ask thee, and answer thou me.

4 Where wast thou when I laid the foundations of the earth? Tell me if thou hast understanding.

Ver. 21. *For this thou hast begun to follow after misery.* Eliu charges Job, that notwithstanding his misery, he does not fear God as he ought: but in his judgment, falls into iniquity.

Chap. 37. Ver. 7. *He sealeth up.* When he sends those *showers of his strength*, that is, those storms of rain, *he seals up*, that is, he shuts up the hands of men from their usual works abroad, and confines them within doors, to consider *his* works: or to forecast *their* works, that is, what they themselves are to do.

Ver. 20. *He shall be swallowed up.* All that man can say when he speaks of God, is so little and inconsiderable in comparison with the subject, that man is lost, and as it were swallowed up, in so immense an ocean.

Chap. 38. Ver. 1. *The Lord.* That is, an angel speaking in the name of the Lord.

5 Who hath laid the measures thereof, if thou knowest? Or who hath stretched the line upon it?

6 Upon what are its bases grounded? Or who laid the corner stone thereof,

7 When the morning stars praised me together, and all the sons of God made a joyful melody?

8 Who shut up the sea with doors, when it broke forth as issuing out of the womb:

9 When I made a cloud the garment thereof, and wrapped it in a mist as in swaddling bands?

10 I set my bounds around it, and made it bars and doors:

11 And I said: Hitherto thou shalt come, and shalt go no further. And here thou shalt break thy swelling waves.

12 Didst thou since thy birth command the morning, and shew the dawning of the day its place?

13 And didst thou hold the extremities of the earth shaking them? And hast thou shaken the ungodly out of it?

14 The seal shall be restored as clay, and shall stand as a garment.

15 From the wicked their light shall be taken away: and the high arm shall be broken.

16 Hast thou entered into the depths of the sea, and walked in the lowest parts of the deep?

17 Have the gates of death been opened to thee, and hast thou seen the darksome doors?

18 Hast thou considered the breadth of the earth? Tell me, if thou knowest all things?

19 Where is the way where light dwelleth; and where is the place of darkness?

20 That thou mayst bring every thing to its own bounds, and understand the paths of the house thereof.

21 Didst thou know then that thou shouldst be born? And didst thou know the number of thy days?

22 Hast thou entered into the storehouses of the snow? Or hast thou beheld the treasures of the hail,

23 Which I have prepared for the time of the enemy, against the day of battle and war?

24 By what way is the light spread, and heat divided upon the earth?

25 Who gave a course to violent showers, or a way for noisy thunder:

26 That it should rain on the earth without man in the wilderness, where no mortal dwelleth:

27 That it should fill the desert and desolate land, and should bring forth green grass?

28 Who is the father of rain? Or who begot the drops of dew?

29 Out of whose womb came the ice? And the frost from heaven who hath gendered it?

30 The waters are hardened like a stone: and the surface of the deep is congealed.

31 Shalt thou be able to join together the shining stars the Pleiades, or canst thou stop the turning about of Arcturus?

32 Canst thou bring forth the day star in its time, and make the evening star to rise upon the children of the earth?

33 Dost thou know the order of heaven? And canst thou set down the reason thereof on the earth?

34 Canst thou lift up thy voice to the clouds, that an abundance of waters may cover thee?

35 Canst thou send lightnings? And will they go, and will they return and say to thee: Here we are?

36 Who hath put wisdom in the heart of man? Or who gave the cock understanding?

37 Who can declare the order of the heavens? Or who can make the harmony of heaven to sleep?

38 When was the dust poured on the earth, and the clods fastened together?

39 Wilt thou take the prey for the lioness, and satisfy the appetite of her whelps,

40 When they couch in the dens and lie in wait in holes?

41 [1] Who provideth food for the raven, when her young ones cry to God, wandering about, because they have no meat?

CHAPTER 39

The wonders of the power and providence of God in many of his creatures.

KNOWEST thou the time when the wild goats bring forth among the rocks? Or hast thou observed the hinds when they fawn?

2 Hast thou numbered the months of their conceiving, or knowest thou the time when they bring forth?

3 They bow themselves to bring forth young; and they cast them, and send forth roarings.

4 Their young are weaned and go to

CHAP. 38. [1] Ps. 146, 9.

Ver. 31. *Pleiades.* Hebrew, *Cimah.* A cluster of seven stars in the constellation *Taurus* or the *Bull. Arcturus,* a bright star in the constellation *Bootes.* The Hebrew name *Cesil,* is variously interpreted; by some, *Orion;* by others, the *Great Bear* is understood.

Ver. 36. *Understanding.* That instinct by which he distinguishes the times of crowing in the night.

feed: they go forth, and return not to them.

5 Who hath sent out the wild ass free, and who hath loosed his bonds?

6 To whom I have given a house in the wilderness, and his dwellings in the barren land.

7 He scorneth the multitude of the city, he heareth not the cry of the driver.

8 He looketh round about the mountains of his pasture, and seeketh for every green thing.

9 Shall the rhinoceros be willing to serve thee, or will he stay at thy crib?

10 Canst thou bind the rhinoceros with thy thong to plough, or will he break the clods of the valleys after thee?

11 Wilt thou have confidence in his great strength, and leave thy labours to him?

12 Wilt thou trust him that he will render thee the seed, and gather it into thy barnfloor?

13 The wing of the ostrich is like the wings of the heron, and of the hawk.

14 When she leaveth her eggs on the earth, thou perhaps wilt warm them in the dust?

15 She forgetteth that the foot may tread upon them, or that the beasts of the field may break them.

16 She is hardened against her young ones, as though they were not hers. She hath laboured in vain, no fear constraining her.

17 For God hath deprived her of wisdom: neither hath he given her understanding.

18 When time shall be, she setteth up her wings on high: she scorneth the horse and his rider.

19 Wilt thou give strength to the horse, or clothe his neck with neighing?

20 Wilt thou lift him up like the locusts? The glory of his nostrils in terror.

21 He breaketh up the earth with his hoof; he pranceth boldly; he goeth forward to meet armed men.

22 He despiseth fear; he turneth not his back to the sword.

23 Above him shall the quiver rattle; the spear and shield shall glitter.

24 Chasing and raging he swalloweth the ground: neither doth he make account when the noise of the trumpet soundeth.

25 When he heareth the trumpet he saith: Ha, ha. He smelleth the battle afar off, the encouraging of the captains, and the shouting of the army.

26 Doth the hawk wax feathered by thy wisdom, spreading her wings to the south?

27 Will the eagle mount up at thy command, and make her nest in high places?

28 She abideth among the rocks, and dwelleth among cragged flints, and stony hills, where there is no access.

29 From thence she looketh for the prey, and her eyes behold afar off.

30 Her young ones shall suck up blood: and wheresoever the carcass shall be, she is immediately there.

31 And the Lord went on, and said to Job:

32 Shall he that contendeth with God be so easily silenced? Surely he that reproveth God, ought to answer him.

33 Then Job answered the Lord, and said:

34 What can I answer, who have spoken inconsiderately? I will lay my hand upon my mouth.

35 One thing I have spoken, which I wish I had not said: and another, to which I will add no more.

CHAPTER 40

Of the power of God in the behemoth and the leviathan.

AND the Lord answering Job out of the whirlwind, said:

2 Gird up thy loins like a man. I will ask thee, and do thou tell me.

3 Wilt thou make void my judgment? And condemn me, that thou mayst be justified?

4 And hast thou an arm like God? And canst thou thunder with a voice like him?

5 Clothe thyself with beauty, and set thyself up on high: and be glorious, and put on goodly garments.

6 Scatter the proud in thy indignation: and behold every arrogant man, and humble him.

7 Look on all that are proud, and confound them: and crush the wicked in their place.

8 Hide them in the dust together: and plunge their faces into the pit.

9 Then I will confess that thy right hand is able to save thee.

10 Behold behemoth whom I made with thee. He eateth grass like an ox.

11 His strength is in his loins, and his force in the navel of his belly.

CHAP. 39. Ver. 34. *Spoken inconsiderately.* If we discuss all Job's words (saith St. Gregory), we shall find nothing impiously spoken; as may be gathered from the words of the Lord himself, chap. 42, ver. 7, 8; but what was reprehensible in him, was the manner of expressing himself at times, speaking too much of his own afflictions, and too little of God's goodness towards him, which here he acknowledges as *inconsiderate.*

CHAP. 40. Ver. 10. *Behemoth.* In Hebrew, *behema,* which signifies in general an *animal;* but many authors explain, that here it is put for the *elephant.*

12 He setteth up his tail like a cedar: the sinews of his testicles are wrapped together.

13 His bones are like pipes of brass, his gristle like plates of iron.

14 He is the beginning of the ways of God, who made him: he will apply his sword.

15 To him the mountains bring forth grass: there all the beasts of the field shall play.

16 He sleepeth under the shadow, in the covert of the reed, and in moist places.

17 The shades cover his shadow: the willows of the brook shall compass him about.

18 Behold, he will drink up a river, and not wonder: and he trusteth that the Jordan may run into his mouth.

19 In his eyes as with a hook he shall take him, and bore through his nostrils with stakes.

20 Canst thou draw out the leviathan with a hook? Or canst thou tie his tongue with a cord?

21 Canst thou put a ring in his nose, or bore through his jaw with a buckle?

22 Will he make many supplications to thee, or speak soft words to thee?

23 Will he make a covenant with thee? And wilt thou take him to be a servant for ever?

24 Shalt thou play with him as with a bird, or tie him up for thy handmaids?

25 Shall friends cut him in pieces? Shall merchants divide him?

26 Wilt thou fill nets with his skin, and the cabins of fishes with his head?

27 Lay thy hand upon him. Remember the battle; and speak no more.

28 Behold his hope shall fail him: and in the sight of all he shall be cast down.

CHAPTER 41

A further description of the leviathan.

I WILL not stir him up, like one that is cruel. For who can resist my countenance?

Ver. 14. *He will apply his sword.* This text is variously explained: some explain the *sword*, the horn given to the animal for his defence: others, the power that God hath given to man to slay him, notwithstanding his great size and strength.
Ver. 20. *Leviathan.* The whale or some sea monster.
CHAP. 41. Ver. 16. *Angels*, Elim, Hebrew: which signifies here, the mighty, the most valiant, shall fear this monstrous fish, and in their fear shall seek to be purified.
Ver. 21. *Under him.* He shall not value the beams of the sun; and gold to him shall be like mire.
Ver. 23. *The deep as growing old.* Growing hoary, as it were with the froth which he leaves behind him.
Ver. 25. *He is king.* He is superior in strength to all that are great and strong amongst living creatures: mystically it is understood of the devil, who is king over all the proud.

2 Who hath given me before that I should repay him? All things that are under heaven are mine.

3 I will not spare him, nor his mighty words, and framed to make supplication.

4 Who can discover the face of his garment? Or who can go into the midst of his mouth?

5 Who can open the doors of his face? His teeth are terrible round about.

6 His body is like molten shields, shut close up with scales pressing upon one another.

7 One is joined to another, and not so much as any air can come between them.

8 They stick one to another and they hold one another fast, and shall not be separated.

9 His sneezing is like the shining of fire: and his eyes like the eyelids of the morning.

10 Out of his mouth go forth lamps, like torches of lighted fire.

11 Out of his nostrils goeth smoke, like that of a pot heated and boiling.

12 His breath kindleth coals: and a flame cometh forth out of his mouth.

13 In his neck strength shall dwell: and want goeth before his face.

14 The members of his flesh cleave one to another. He shall send lightnings against him, and they shall not be carried to another place.

15 His heart shall be as hard as a stone, and as firm as a smith's anvil.

16 When he shall raise him up, the angels shall fear: and being affrighted shall purify themselves.

17 When a sword shall lay at him, it shall not be able to hold, nor a spear, nor a breastplate.

18 For he shall esteem iron as straw, and brass as rotten wood.

19 The archer shall not put him to flight: the stones of the sling are to him like stubble.

20 As stubble will he esteem the hammer: and he will laugh him to scorn who shaketh the spear.

21 The beams of the sun shall be under him: and he shall strew gold under him like mire.

22 He shall make the deep sea to boil like a pot, and shall make it as when ointments boil.

23 A path shall shine after him: he shall esteem the deep as growing old.

24 There is no power upon earth that can be compared with him who was made to fear no one.

25 He beholdeth every high thing. He is king over all the children of pride.

CHAPTER 42

Job submits himself. God pronounces in his favour. Job offers sacrifice for his friends. He is blessed with riches and children, and dies happily.

THEN Job answered the Lord, and said:

2 I know that thou canst do all things, and no thought is hid from thee.

3 Who is this that hideth counsel without knowledge? Therefore I have spoken unwisely, and things that above measure exceeded my knowledge.

4 Hear, and I will speak: I will ask thee, and do thou tell me.

5 With the hearing of the ear, I have heard thee: but now my eye seeth thee.

6 Therefore I reprehend myself, and do penance in dust and ashes.

7 And after the Lord had spoken these words to Job, he said to Eliphaz the Themanite: My wrath is kindled against thee, and against thy two friends, because you have not spoken the thing that is right before me, as my servant Job hath.

8 Take unto you therefore seven oxen, and seven rams, and go to my servant Job, and offer for yourselves a holocaust. And my servant Job shall pray for you. His face I will accept, that folly be not imputed to you: for you have not spoken right things before me, as my servant Job hath.

9 So Eliphaz the Themanite, and Baldad the Suhite, and Sophar the Naamathite went, and did as the Lord had spoken to them. And the Lord accepted the face of Job.

10 The Lord also was turned at the penance of Job, when he prayed for his friends. And the Lord gave Job twice as much as he had before.

11 And all his brethren came to him, and all his sisters, and all that knew him before. And they ate bread with him in his house, and bemoaned him, and comforted him upon all the evil that God had brought upon him. And every man gave him one ewe, and one earring of gold.

12 And the Lord blessed the latter end of Job more than his beginning. And he had fourteen thousand sheep, and six thousand camels, and a thousand yoke of oxen, and a thousand she-asses.

13 And he had seven sons, and three daughters.

14 And he called the name of one Dies, and the name of the second Cassia, and the name of the third Cornustibii.

15 And there were not found in all the earth women so beautiful as the daughters of Job: and their father gave them inheritance among their brethren.

16 And Job lived after these things, a hundred and forty years: and he saw his children, and his children's children, unto the fourth generation. And he died, an old man and full of days.

THE BOOK OF

PSALMS

The Psalms are called by the Hebrews TEHILLIM, *that is, Hymns of Praise. The author, of a great part of them, at least, was king David: but many are of opinion that some of them were made by Asaph and others whose names are prefixed in the titles.*

PSALM 1

Beatus vir

The happiness of the just and the evil state of the wicked.

BLESSED *is* the man who hath not walked in the counsel of the ungodly, nor stood in the way of sinners, nor sat in the chair of pestilence.

2 [1] But his will is in the law of the Lord: and on his law he shall meditate day and night.

3 [2] And he shall be like a tree which is planted near the running waters, which shall bring forth its fruit, in due season.

And his leaf shall not fall off: and all whatsoever he shall do shall prosper.

4 Not so the wicked, not so: but like the dust, which the wind driveth from the face of the earth.

5 Therefore the wicked shall not rise again in judgment: nor sinners in the council of the just.

6 For the Lord knoweth the way of the just: and the way of the wicked shall perish.

PSALM 1. [1] Jos. 1, 8. [2] Jer. 17, 8.

PSALM 2

Quare fremuerunt

The vain efforts of persecutors against Christ and his church.

WHY [1]have Gentiles raged: and the people devised vain things?

2 The kings of the earth stood up, and the princes met together, against the Lord and against his Christ.

3 Let us break their bonds asunder: and let us cast away their yoke from us.

4 He that dwelleth in heaven shall laugh at them: and the Lord shall deride them.

5 Then shall he speak to them in his anger, and trouble them in his rage.

6 But I am appointed king by him over Sion his holy mountain, preaching his commandment.

7 [2]The Lord hath said to me: Thou art my son; this day have I begotten thee.

8 Ask of me, and I will give thee the Gentiles for thy inheritance, and the utmost parts of the earth for thy possession.

9 [3]Thou shalt rule them with a rod of iron and shalt break them in pieces like a potter's vessel.

10 And now, O ye kings, understand: receive instruction, you that judge the earth.

11 Serve ye the Lord with fear: and rejoice unto him with trembling.

12 Embrace discipline: lest at any time the Lord be angry, and you perish from the just way.

13 When his wrath shall be kindled in a short time, blessed are all they that trust in him.

PSALM 3

Domine, quid multiplicati

The prophet's danger and delivery from his son Absalom: mystically, the passion and resurrection of Christ.

1 The psalm of David when he fled from the face of his son Absalom. [2 Kings 15.]

2 **W**HY, O Lord, are they multiplied that afflict me? Many are they who rise up against me.

PSALM 2. [1] Acts. 4, 25. [2] Acts, 13, 33; Heb. 1, 5; 5, 5. [3] Apoc.2, 27; 19, 15. PSALM 4. [1] Eph. 4, 26.

PSALM 4. Ver. 1. *Unto the end.* Or, as St. Jerome renders it (*victori*), *to him that overcometh:* which some understand of *the chief musician,* to whom they suppose the psalms, which bear that title, were given to be sung. We rather understand the psalms thus inscribed to refer to Christ, who is the *end of the law,* and the *great conqueror* of death and hell, and to the New Testament.—*In verses* (*in carminibus*). In the Hebrew, it is *neghinoth,* supposed by some to be a musical instrument, with which this psalm was to be sung.—*For David,* or *to David,* τῷ Δαδίδ; that is, inspired to David himself, or to be sung.

PSALM 5. Ver. 1. *For her that obtaineth the inheritance.* That is, for the church of Christ.

3 Many say to my soul: There is no salvation for him in his God.

4 But thou, O Lord, art my protector, my glory, and the lifter up of my head.

5 I have cried to the Lord with my voice: and he hath heard me from his holy hill.

6 I have slept and have taken my rest: and I have risen up, because the Lord hath protected me.

7 I will not fear thousands of the people, surrounding me. Arise, O Lord; save me, O my God.

8 For thou hast struck all them who are my adversaries without cause: thou hast broken the teeth of sinners.

9 Salvation is of the Lord: and thy blessing is upon thy people.

PSALM 4

Cum invocarem

The prophet teacheth us to flee to God in tribulation, with confidence in him.

1 Unto the end, in verses. A psalm for David.

2 **W**HEN I called upon him, the God of my justice heard me: when I was in distress, thou hast enlarged me. Have mercy on me: and hear my prayer.

3 O ye sons of men, how long will you be dull of heart? Why do you love vanity, and seek after lying?

4 Know ye also that the Lord hath made his holy one wonderful: the Lord will hear me when I shall cry unto him.

5 [1]Be ye angry, and sin not: the things you say in your hearts, be sorry for them upon your beds.

6 Offer up the sacrifice of justice, and trust in the Lord: many say, Who sheweth us good things?

7 The light of thy countenance, O Lord, is signed upon us: thou hast given gladness in my heart.

8 By the fruit of their corn, their wine, and oil, they are multiplied.

9 In peace in the selfsame I will sleep, and I will rest:

10 For thou, O Lord, singularly hast settled me in hope.

PSALM 5

Verba mea auribus

A prayer to God against the iniquities of men.

1 Unto the end, for her that obtaineth the inheritance. A psalm for David.

2 **G**IVE ear, O Lord, to my words: understand my cry.

3 Hearken to the voice of my prayer, O my King and my God.

4 For to thee will I pray: O Lord, in the morning thou shalt hear my voice.

5 In the morning I will stand before thee, and will see: because thou art not a God that willest iniquity.

6 Neither shall the wicked dwell near thee: nor shall the unjust abide before thy eyes.

7 Thou hatest all the workers of iniquity: thou wilt destroy all that speak a lie.

The bloody and the deceitful man the Lord will abhor.

8 But as for me in the multitude of thy mercy,

I will come into thy house; I will worship towards thy holy temple, in thy fear.

9 Conduct me, O Lord, in thy justice: because of my enemies, direct my way in thy sight.

10 For there is no truth in their mouth: their heart is vain.

11 [1] Their throat is an open sepulchre: they dealt deceitfully with their tongues: judge them, O God.

Let them fall from their devices: according to the multitude of their wickedness cast them out: for they have provoked thee, O Lord.

12 But let all them be glad that hope in thee: they shall rejoice for ever, and thou shalt dwell in them.

And all they that love thy name shall glory in thee:

13 For thou wilt bless the just.

O Lord, thou hast crowned us, as with a shield of thy good will.

PSALM 6

Domine, ne in furore

A prayer of a penitent sinner, under the scourge of God. The first penitential psalm.

1 Unto the end, in verses. A psalm for David, for the octave.

2 O LORD, rebuke me not in thy indignation, nor chastise me in thy wrath.

3 Have mercy on me, O Lord, for I am weak: heal me, O Lord, for my bones are troubled.

4 And my soul is troubled exceedingly: but thou, O Lord, how long?

5 Turn to me, O Lord, and deliver my soul: O save me for thy mercy's sake.

6 For there is no one in death, that is mindful of thee: and who shall confess to thee in hell?

7 I have laboured in my groanings, every night I will wash my bed: I will water my couch with my tears.

8 My eye is troubled through indignation: I have grown old amongst all my enemies.

9 [1] Depart from me, all ye workers of iniquity: for the Lord hath heard the voice of my weeping.

10 The Lord hath heard my supplication: the Lord hath received my prayer.

11 Let all my enemies be ashamed and be very much troubled: let them be turned back and be ashamed very speedily.

PSALM 7

Domine, Deus meus

David, trusting in the justice of his cause, prayeth for God's help against his enemies.

1 The psalm of David which he sung to the Lord, for the words of Chusi the son of Jemini. [2 Kings, 16.]

2 O LORD my God, in thee have I put my trust: save me from all them that persecute me, and deliver me.

3 Lest at any time he seize upon my soul like a lion, while there is no one to redeem me, nor to save.

4 O Lord my God, if I have done this thing, if there be iniquity in my hands:

5 If I have rendered to them that repaid me evils, let me deservedly fall empty before my enemies.

6 Let the enemy pursue my soul, and take it, and tread down my life on the earth, and bring down my glory to the dust.

7 Rise up, O Lord, in thy anger: and be thou exalted in the borders of my enemies.

And arise, O Lord my God, in the precept which thou hast commanded: 8 and a congregation of people shall surround thee.

And for their sakes, return thou on high.

9 The Lord judgeth the people.

Judge me, O Lord, according to my justice, and according to my innocence in me.

10 The wickedness of sinners shall be brought to nought, and thou shalt direct the just: [1] the searcher of hearts and reins is God.

11 Just is my help from the Lord: who saveth the upright of heart.

12 God is a just judge, strong and patient: Is he angry every day?

13 Except you will be converted, he will brandish his sword: he hath bent his bow, and made it ready.

14 And in it he hath prepared the

PSALM 5. [1] Ps. 13, 3; 139, 4; Rom. 3, 13. PSALM 6. [1] Matt. 7, 23; 25, 41; Luke, 13, 27. PSALM 7. [1] 1 Par. 28, 9; Jer. 11, 20; 17, 10; 20, 12.

PSALM 6. Ver. 1. *For the octave.* That is, to be sung on an instrument of eight strings. St. Augustine understands it mystically, of the last resurrection, and the world to come which is, it were, the octave, or eighth day, after the seven days of this mortal life; and for this octave sinners must dispose themselves, like David by bewailing their sins whilst they are here upon earth.

instruments of death: he hath made ready his arrows for them that burn.

15 ²Behold he hath been in labour with injustice; he hath conceived sorrow, and brought forth iniquity.

16 He hath opened a pit and dug it: and he is fallen into the hole he made.

17 His sorrow shall be turned on his own head: and his iniquity shall come down upon his crown.

18 I will give glory to the Lord according to his justice: and will sing to the name of the Lord the most high.

PSALM 8
Domine, Dominus noster

God is wonderful in his works. Especially in mankind, singularly exalted by the incarnation of Christ.

1 Unto the end, for the presses. A psalm for David.

2 O LORD our Lord: how admirable is thy name in the whole earth! For thy magnificence is elevated above the heavens.

3 Out of the mouth of infants and of sucklings thou hast perfected praise, because of thy enemies: that thou mayst destroy the enemy and the avenger.

4 For I will behold thy heavens, the works of thy fingers: the moon and the stars which thou hast founded.

5 What is man that thou art mindful of him? Or the son of man that thou visitest him?

6 ¹Thou hast made him a little less than the angels: thou hast crowned him with glory and honour, 7 and hast set him over the works of thy hands.

8 ²Thou hast subjected all things under his feet: all sheep and oxen, moreover the beasts also of the fields.

9 The birds of the air, and the fishes of the sea that pass through the paths of the sea.

10 O Lord our Lord: how admirable is thy name in all the earth!

PSALM 9
Confitebor tibi, Domine

The church praiseth God for his protection against her enemies.

1 Unto the end, for the hidden things of the Son. A psalm for David.

2 I WILL give praise to thee, O Lord, with my whole heart: I will relate all thy wonders.

3 I will be glad and rejoice in thee: I will sing to thy name, O thou most high.

4 When my enemy shall be turned back: they shall be weakened and perish before thy face.

5 For thou hast maintained my judgment and my cause: thou hast sat on the throne, who judgest justice.

6 Thou hast rebuked the Gentiles, and the wicked one hath perished: thou hast blotted out their name for ever and ever.

7 The swords of the enemy have failed unto the end: and their cities thou hast destroyed.

Their memory hath perished with a noise: 8 but the Lord remaineth for ever.

He hath prepared his throne in judgment: 9 and he shall judge the world in equity, he shall judge the people in justice.

10 And the Lord is become a refuge for the poor: a helper in due time in tribulation.

11 And let them trust in thee who know thy name: for thou hast not forsaken them that seek thee, O Lord.

12 Sing ye to the Lord, who dwelleth in Sion: declare his ways among the Gentiles:

13 For requiring their blood he hath remembered them: he hath not forgotten the cry of the poor.

14 Have mercy on me, O Lord: see my humiliation *which I suffer* from my enemies.

15 Thou that liftest me up from the gates of death, that I may declare all thy praises in the gates of the daughter of Sion.

16 I will rejoice in thy salvation: the Gentiles have stuck fast in the destruction which they prepared.

Their foot hath been taken in the very snare which they hid.

17 The Lord shall be known when he executeth judgments: the sinner hath been caught in the works of his own hands.

18 The wicked shall be turned into hell, all the nations that forget God.

19 For the poor man shall not be forgotten to the end: the patience of the poor shall not perish for ever.

20 Arise, O Lord, let not man be strengthened: let the Gentiles be judged in thy sight.

21 Appoint, O Lord, a lawgiver over them: that the Gentiles may know themselves to be *but men.*

---

2 Job, 15, 35; Isai. 59, 4. PSALM 8. ¹ Heb. 2, 7. ² Gen. 1, 28; 1 Cor. 15, 26.

PSALM 7. Ver. 14. *For them that burn.* That is, against the persecutors of his saints.

PSALM 8. Ver. 1. *The presses.* In Hebrew, *Gittith,* supposed to be a musical instrument.

PSALM 9. Ver. 1. *The hidden things of the Son.* The humility and sufferings of Christ, the *Son* of God, and of good Christians, who are his *sons* by adoption, are called *hidden things,* with regard to the children of this world, who know not the value and merit of them.

Ver. 21. Here the late Hebrew doctors divide

Psalm 10 according to the Hebrews.

1 Why, O Lord, hast thou retired afar off? *Why* dost thou slight *us* in our wants, in *the time* of trouble?

2 Whilst the wicked man is proud, the poor is set on fire: they are caught in the counsels which they devise.

3 For the sinner is praised in the desires of his soul: and the unjust man is blessed.

4 The sinner hath provoked the Lord: according to the multitude of his wrath he will not seek *him:*

5 God is not before his eyes: his ways are filthy at all times.

Thy judgments are removed from his sight: he shall rule over all his enemies.

6 For he hath said in his heart: I shall not be moved from generation to generation, *and shall be* without evil.

7 [1] His mouth is full of cursing, and of bitterness, and of deceit: under his tongue *are* labour and sorrow.

8 He sitteth in ambush with the rich in private places, that he may kill the innocent.

9 His eyes are upon the poor man: he lieth in wait in secret like a lion in his den.

He lieth in ambush that he may catch the poor man: to catch the poor, whilst he draweth him to him.

10 In his net he will bring him down: he will crouch and fall, when he shall have power over the poor.

11 For he hath said in his heart: God hath forgotten; he hath turned away his face not to see to the end.

12 Arise, O Lord God, let thy hand be exalted: forget not the poor.

13 Wherefore hath the wicked provoked God? For he hath said in his heart: He will not require *it.*

14 Thou seest *it,* for thou considerest labour and sorrow: that thou mayst deliver them into thy hands.

To thee is the poor *man* left: thou wilt be a helper to the orphan.

15 Break thou the arm of the sinner and of the malignant: his sin shall be sought, and shall not be found.

16 The Lord shall reign to eternity, yea, for ever and ever: ye Gentiles shall perish from his land.

17 The Lord hath heard the desire of the poor: thy ear hath heard the preparation of their heart.

18 To judge for the fatherless and for the humble, that man may no more presume to magnify himself upon earth.

PSALM 10

In Domino confido

The just man's confidence in God in the midst of persecutions.

---

1 Unto the end. A psalm for David.

2 IN the Lord I put my trust: How then do you say to my soul, Get thee away from hence to the mountain like a sparrow?

3 For, lo, the wicked have bent their bow; they have prepared their arrows in the quiver, to shoot in the dark the upright of heart.

4 For they have destroyed the things which thou hast made: but what has the just man done?•

5 [1] The Lord *is* in his holy temple: the Lord's throne is in heaven.

His eyes look on the poor man: his eyelids examine the sons of men.

6 The Lord trieth the just and the wicked: but he that loveth iniquity hateth his own soul.

7 He shall rain snares upon sinners: fire and brimstone and storms of winds *shall be* the portion of their cup.

8 For the Lord is just and hath loved justice: his countenance hath beheld righteousness.

PSALM 11

Salvum me fac

The prophet calls for God's help against the wicked.

1 Unto the end; for the octave. A psalm for David.

2 SAVE me, O Lord, for there is now no saint: truths are decayed from among the children of men.

3 They have spoken vain things every one to his neighbour: *with* deceitful lips *and* with a double heart have they spoken.

4 May the Lord destroy all deceitful lips, and the tongue that speaketh proud things.

5 Who have said: We will magnify our tongue; our lips are our own. Who is Lord over us?

6 By reason of the misery of the needy and the groans of the poor, now will I arise, saith the Lord.

I will set him in safety; I will deal confidently in his regard.

7 [1] The words of the Lord are pure words: *as* silver tried by the fire, purged from the earth, refined seven times.

8 Thou, O Lord, wilt preserve us: and keep us from this generation for ever.

9 The wicked walk round about:

PSALM 9. [1] Ps. 13, 3; Rom. 3, 14. PSALM 10.
[1] Hab. 2, 20. PSALM 11. [1] Prov. 30, 5.

this psalm into two, making ver 22 the beginning of Psalm 10. And again they join Psalms 146 and 147 into one, in order that the whole number of psalms should not exceed 150. And in this manner the psalms are numbered in the Protestant Bible.

according to thy highness, thou hast multiplied the children of men.

PSALM 12

Usquequo, Domine

A prayer in tribulation.

1 Unto the end. A psalm for David.

HOW long, O Lord, wilt thou forget me unto the end? How long dost thou turn away thy face from me?

2 How long shall I take counsels in my soul, sorrow in my heart all the day?

3 How long shall my enemy be exalted over me? 4 Consider, and hear me, O Lord my God.

Enlighten my eyes that I never sleep in death; 5 lest at any time my enemy say: I have prevailed against him.

They that trouble me will rejoice when I am moved: 6 but I have trusted in thy mercy.

My heart shall rejoice in thy salvation: I will sing to the Lord, who giveth me good things: yea I will sing to the name of the Lord the most high.

PSALM 13

Dixit insipiens (1)

The general corruption of man before our redemption by Christ.

1 Unto the end. A psalm for David.

THE fool hath said in his heart: [1] There is no God.

They are corrupt, and are become abominable in their ways: there is none that doth good, no, not one.

2 The Lord hath looked down from heaven upon the children of men, to see if there be any that understand and seek God.

3 They are all gone aside, they are become unprofitable together: there is none that doth good, no, not one.

Their throat is an open sepulchre: with their tongues they acted deceitfully; the poison of asps is under their lips.

Their mouth is full of cursing and bitterness; their feet are swift to shed blood.

Destruction and unhappiness in their ways: and the way of peace they have not known. There is no fear of God before their eyes.

4 Shall not all they know that work iniquity, who devour my people as they eat bread?

5 They have not called upon the Lord: there have they trembled for fear where there was no fear.

PSALM 13. [1] Ps. 52, 1.

PSALM 15. Ver. 1. *The inscription of a title,* That is, of a pillar or monument, στηλογραφία: which is as much as to say, that this psalm is most worthy to be engraved on an everlasting monument.

6 For the Lord is in the just generation: you have confounded the counsel of the poor man, but the Lord is his hope.

7 Who shall give out of Sion the salvation of Israel? When the Lord shall have turned away the captivity of his people, Jacob shall rejoice and Israel shall be glad.

PSALM 14

Domine, quis habitabit

What kind of men shall dwell in the heavenly Sion.

1 A psalm of David.

LORD, who shall dwell in thy tabernacle? Or who shall rest in thy holy hill?

2 He that walketh without blemish, and worketh justice:

3 He that speaketh truth in his heart: who hath not used deceit in his tongue:

Nor hath done evil to his neighbour: nor taken up a reproach against his neighbours.

4 In his sight the malignant is brought to nothing: but he glorifieth them that fear the Lord.

He that sweareth to his neighbour, and deceiveth not; 5 he that hath not put out his money to usury, nor taken bribes against the innocent.

He that doeth these things shall not be moved for ever.

PSALM 15

Conserva me, Domine

Christ's future victory and triumph over the world and death.

1 The inscription of a title to David himself.

PRESERVE me, O Lord, for I have put my trust in thee. 2 I have said to the Lord: Thou art my God, for thou hast no need of my goods.

3 To the saints, who are in his land, he hath made wonderful all my desires in them.

4 Their infirmities were multiplied: afterwards they made haste.

I will not gather together their meetings for blood *offerings:* nor will I be mindful of their names by my lips.

5 The Lord is the portion of my inheritance and of my cup: it is thou that wilt restore my inheritance to me.

6 The lines are fallen unto me in goodly places: for my inheritance is goodly to me.

7 I will bless the Lord who hath given me understanding: moreover my reins also have corrected me even till night.

8 [1] I set the Lord always in my sight: for he is at my right hand, that I be not moved.

9 Therefore my heart hath been glad, and my tongue hath rejoiced: moreover my flesh also shall rest in hope.

10 [2] Because thou wilt not leave my soul in hell; nor wilt thou give thy holy one to see corruption.

11 Thou hast made known to me the ways of life; thou shalt fill me with joy with thy countenance: at thy right hand are delights even to the end.

PSALM 16

Exaudi, Domine, justitiam

A just man's prayer in tribulation against the malice of his enemy.

1 The prayer of David.

HEAR, O Lord, my justice: attend to my supplication.

Give ear unto my prayer, *which proceedeth* not from deceitful lips.

2 Let my judgment come forth from thy countenance: let thy eyes behold the things that are equitable.

3 Thou hast proved my heart, and visited it by night, thou hast tried me by fire: and iniquity hath not been found in me.

4 That my mouth may not speak the works of men: for the sake of the words of thy lips, I have kept hard ways.

5 Perfect thou my goings in thy paths: that my footsteps be not moved.

6 I have cried *to thee,* for thou, O God, hast heard me: O incline thy ear unto me, and hear my words.

7 Shew forth thy wonderful mercies; thou who savest them that trust in thee.

8 From them that resist thy right hand keep me, as the apple of thy eye.

Protect me under the shadow of thy wings, 9 From the face of the wicked who have afflicted me.

My enemies have surrounded my soul: 10 they have shut up their fat: their mouth hath spoken proudly.

11 They have cast me forth and now they have surrounded me: they have set their eyes bowing down to the earth.

12 They have taken me, as a lion prepared for the prey: and as a young lion dwelling in secret places.

13 Arise, O Lord, disappoint him and supplant him; deliver my soul from the wicked one: thy sword 14 from the enemies of thy hand.

O Lord, divide them from the few of the earth in their life: their belly is filled from thy hidden *stores.*

They are full of children: and they have left to their little ones the rest *of their substance.*

15 But as for me, I will appear before thy sight in justice: I shall be satisfied when thy glory shall appear.

PSALM 17

Diligam te, Domine

David's thanks to God for his delivery from all his enemies.

1 Unto the end, for David the servant of the Lord, who spoke to the Lord the words of this canticle, in the day that the Lord delivered him from the hands of all his enemies, and from. the hand of Saul. [2 Kings, 22.]

2 I WILL love thee, O Lord, my strength:

3 The Lord *is my* firmament, my refuge, and my deliverer.

[1] My God *is* my helper: and in him will I put my trust.

My protector and the horn of my salvation and my support.

4 Praising, I will call upon the Lord: and I shall be saved from my enemies.

5 The sorrows of death surrounded me: and the torrents of iniquity troubled me.

6 The sorrows of hell encompassed me: and the snares of death prevented me.

7 In my affliction I called upon the Lord: and I cried to my God.

And he heard my voice from his holy temple: and my cry before him came into his ears.

8 The earth shook and trembled: the foundations of the mountains were troubled and were moved, because he was angry with them.

9 There went up a smoke in his wrath: and a fire flamed from his face: coals were kindled by it.

10 He bowed the heavens, and came down: and darkness *was* under his feet.

11 And he ascended upon the cherubim, and he flew: he flew upon the wings of the winds.

12 And he made darkness his covert, his pavilion round about him: dark waters in the clouds of the air.

13 At the brightness *that was* before

PSALM 15. [1] Acts, 2, 25. [2] Acts, 2, 31; 13, 35.
PSALM 17. [1] Heb. 2, 13.

PSALM 16. Ver. 10. *Their fat.* That is, their bowels of compassion: for they have none for me. Ver. 14. *Divide them from the few.* That is, cut them off from *the earth,* and the *few* trifling things thereof; which they are so proud of. Or *divide them from the few;* that is, from thy elect, who are but *few;* that they may no longer have it in their power to oppress them. It is not meant by way of a curse or imprecation; but, as many other the like passages in the psalms, by way of a prediction, or prophecy of what should come upon them in punishment of their wickedness.—*Thy hidden stores.* Thy secret treasures, out of which thou furnishest those earthly goods, which with a bountiful hand thou hast distributed both to the good and the bad.

him the clouds passed: hail and coals of fire.

14 And the Lord thundered from heaven, and the Highest gave his voice: hail and coals of fire.

15 And he sent forth his arrows, and he scattered them: he multiplied lightnings, and troubled them.

16 Then the fountains of waters appeared: and the foundations of the world were discovered:

At thy rebuke, O Lord, at the blast of the spirit of thy wrath.

17 He sent from on high, and took me: and received me out of many waters.

18 He delivered me from my strongest enemies, and from them that hated me: for they were too strong for me.

19 They prevented me in the day of my affliction: and the Lord became my protector.

20 And he brought me forth into a large place: he saved me, because he was well pleased with me.

21 And the Lord will reward me according to my justice; and will repay me according to the cleanness of my hands:

22 Because I have kept the ways of the Lord; and have not done wickedly against my God.

23 For all his judgments are in my sight: and his justices I have not put away from me.

24 And I shall be spotless with him: and shall keep myself from my iniquity.

25 And the Lord will reward me according to my justice; and according to the cleanness of my hands before his eyes.

26 With the holy, thou wilt be holy: and with the innocent man thou wilt be innocent.

27 And with the elect thou wilt be elect: and with the perverse thou wilt be perverted.

28 For thou wilt save the humble people; but wilt bring down the eyes of the proud.

29 For thou lightest my lamp, O Lord: O my God, enlighten my darkness.

30 For by thee I shall be delivered from temptation; and through my God I shall go over a wall.

31 As for my God, his way is undefiled: the words of the Lord are fire tried. He is the protector of all that trust in him.

32 For who is God but the Lord? Or who is God but our God?

33 God who hath girt me with strength; and made my way blameless.

34 ²Who hath made my feet like the feet of harts: and who setteth me upon high places.

35 ³Who teacheth my hands to war: and thou hast made my arms like a brazen bow.

36 And thou hast given me the protection of thy salvation: and thy right hand hath held me up.

And thy discipline hath corrected me unto the end: and thy discipline, the same shall teach me.

37 Thou hast enlarged my steps under me; and my feet are not weakened.

38 I will pursue after my enemies, and overtake them: and I will not turn again till they are consumed.

39 I will break them, and they shall not be able to stand: they shall fall under my feet.

40 And thou hast girded me with strength unto battle: and hast subdued under me them that rose up against me.

41 And thou hast made my enemies turn their back upon me: and hast destroyed them that hated me.

42 They cried: but there was none to save them. To the Lord: but he heard them not.

43 And I shall beat them as small as the dust before the wind: I shall bring them to nought, like the dirt in the streets.

44 Thou wilt deliver me from the contradictions of the people: thou wilt make me head of the Gentiles.

45 A people which I knew not hath served me: at the hearing of the ear they have obeyed me.

46 The children that are strangers have lied to me: strange children have faded away, and have halted from their paths.

47 The Lord liveth, and blessed be my God: and let the God of my salvation be exalted.

48 O God, who avengest me, and subduest the people under me, my deliverer from my enemies.

49 ⁴And thou wilt lift me up above them that rise up against me: from the unjust man thou wilt deliver me.

50 ⁵Therefore will I give glory to thee, O Lord, among the nations: and I will sing a psalm to thy name.

51 Giving great deliverance to his king, and shewing mercy to David his anointed: and to his seed for ever.

² 2 Kings, 22, 34. ³ 2 Kings, 22, 35. ⁴ 2 Kings, 22, 49. ⁵ 2 Kings, 22, 50; Rom. 15, 9.

PSALM 18

Cœli enarrant

The works of God shew forth his glory. His law is greatly to be esteemed and loved.

1 Unto the end. A psalm for David.

2 THE heavens shew forth the glory of God: and the firmament declareth the work of his hands.

3 Day to day uttereth speech: and night to night sheweth knowledge.

4 There are no speeches nor languages, where their voices are not heard.

5 [1] Their sound hath gone forth into all the earth: and their words unto the ends of the world.

6 He hath set his tabernacle in the sun: [2] and he, as a bridegroom coming out of his bride chamber,

Hath rejoiced as a giant to run the way. 7 His going out is from the end of heaven.

And his circuit even to the end thereof: and there is no one that can hide himself from his heat.

8 The law of the Lord is unspotted, converting souls: the testimony of the Lord is faithful, giving wisdom to little ones.

9 The justices of the Lord are right, rejoicing hearts: the commandment of the Lord is lightsome, enlightening the eyes.

10 The fear of the Lord is holy, enduring for ever and ever: the judgments of the Lord are true, justified in themselves,

11 More to be desired than gold and many precious stones: and sweeter than honey and the honeycomb.

12 For thy servant keepeth them: *and* in keeping them there is a great reward.

13 Who can understand sins? From my secret ones cleanse me, O Lord:

14 and from those of others spare thy servant.

If they shall have no dominion over me, then shall I be without spot: and I shall be cleansed from the greatest sin.

15 And the words of my mouth shall be such as may please: and the meditation of my heart always in thy sight.

O Lord, my helper, and my redeemer.

PSALM 19

Exaudiat te Dominus

A prayer for the king.

1 Unto the end. A psalm for David.

2 MAY the Lord hear thee in the day of tribulation: may the name of the God of Jacob protect thee.

3 May he send thee help from the sanctuary: and defend thee out of Sion.

4 May he be mindful of all thy sacrifices: and may thy whole burnt offering be made fat.

5 May he give thee according to thy own heart; and confirm all thy counsels.

6 We will rejoice in thy salvation; and in the name of our God we shall be exalted.

7 The Lord fulfil all thy petitions: now have I known that the Lord hath saved his anointed.

He will hear him from his holy heaven: the salvation of his right hand *is* in powers.

8 Some *trust* in chariots, and some in horses: but we will call upon the name of the Lord our God.

9 They are bound and have fallen; but we are risen and are set upright.

O Lord, save the king: and hear us in the day that we shall call upon thee.

PSALM 20

Domine, in virtute

Praise to God for Christ's exaltation after his passion.

1 Unto the end. A psalm for David.

2 IN thy strength, O Lord, the king shall joy: and in thy salvation he shall rejoice exceedingly.

3 Thou hast given him his heart's desire: and hast not withholden from him the will of his lips.

4 For thou hast prevented him with blessings of sweetness: thou hast set on his head a crown of precious stones.

5 He asked life of thee: and thou hast given him length of days for ever and ever.

6 His glory is great in thy salvation: glory and great beauty shalt thou lay upon him.

7 For thou shalt give him to be a blessing for ever and ever: thou shalt make him joyful in gladness with thy countenance.

8 For the king hopeth in the Lord: and through the mercy of the most High he shall not be moved.

9 Let thy hand be found by all thy enemies: let thy right hand find out all them that hate thee.

10 Thou shalt make them as an oven of fire, in the time of thy anger. The Lord shall trouble them in his wrath: and fire shall devour them.

11 Their fruit shalt thou destroy

PSALM 18. [1] Rom. 10, 18. [2] Luke, 24, 46.

PSALM 19. Ver. 7. *The salvation of his right hand is in powers.* That is, in strength. His right hand is strong and mighty to save them that trust in him.

from the earth: and their seed from among the children of men.

12 For they have intended evils against thee: they have devised counsels which they have not been able to establish.

13 For thou shalt make them turn their back: in thy remnants thou shalt prepare their face.

14 Be thou exalted, O Lord, in thy own strength: we will sing and praise thy power.

PSALM 21

Deus Deus meus

Christ's passion. The conversion of the Gentiles.

1 Unto the end, for the morning protection. A psalm for David.

2 O GOD, [1] my God, look upon me: Why hast thou forsaken me?

For from my salvation are the words of my sins.

3 O my God, I shall cry by day, and thou wilt not hear: and by night, and it shall not be reputed as folly in me.

4 But thou dwellest in the holy place, the praise of Israel.

5 In thee have our fathers hoped: they have hoped, and thou hast delivered them.

6 They cried to thee, and they were saved: they trusted in thee, and were not confounded.

7 But I am a worm and no man: the reproach of men and the outcast of the people.

8 [2] All they that saw me have laughed me to scorn: they have spoken with the lips and wagged the head.

9 [3] He hoped in the Lord, let him deliver him: let him save him, seeing he delighteth in him.

10 For thou art he that hast drawn me out of the womb: my hope from the breasts of my mother. 11 I was cast upon thee from the womb.

From my mother's womb thou art my God: 12 depart not from me.

For tribulation is very near: for there is none to help *me*.

13 Many calves have surrounded me: fat bulls have besieged me.

PSALM 21. [1] Matt. 27, 46; Mark, 15, 34. [2] Matt. 27, 39; Mark, 15, 29. [3] Matt. 27, 43. [4] Matt. 27, 35; John, 19, 23, 24. [5] Heb. 2, 12.

PSALM 20. Ver. 13. *In thy remnants thou shalt prepare their face.* Or thou shalt set thy remnants against their faces. That is, thou shalt make them see what punishments *remain* for them hereafter from thy justice. Instead of *remnants*, St. Jerome renders it *funes*, that is, *cords* or *strings*, *viz.*, of the *bow* of divine justice, from which God directs his *arrows* against the *faces* of his enemies.

PSALM 21. Ver. 2. *The words of my sins.* That is, the sins of the world, which I have taken upon myself, cry out against me and are the cause of all my sufferings.

14 They have opened their mouths against me, as a lion ravening and roaring.

15 I am poured out like water; and all my bones are scattered.

My heart is become like wax melting in the midst of my bowels.

16 My strength is dried up like a potsherd, and my tongue hath cleaved to my jaws: and thou hast brought me down into the dust of death.

17 For many dogs have encompassed me: the council of the malignant hath besieged me.

They have dug my hands and feet. 18 They have numbered all my bones.

And they have looked and stared upon me. 19 [4] They parted my garments amongst them: and upon my vesture they cast lots.

20 But thou, O Lord, remove not thy help to a distance from me: look towards my defence.

21 Deliver, O God, my soul from the sword: my only one from the hand of the dog.

22 Save me from the lion's mouth: and my lowness from the horns of the unicorns.

23 [5] I will declare thy name to my brethren: in the midst of the church will I praise thee.

24 Ye that fear the Lord, praise him: all ye the seed of Jacob, glorify him.

25 Let all the seed of Israel fear him: because he hath not slighted nor despised the supplication of the poor man.

Neither hath he turned away his face from me: and when I cried to him he heard me.

26 With thee is my praise in a great church: I will pay my vows in the sight of them that fear him.

27 The poor shall eat and shall be filled: and they shall praise the Lord that seek him: their hearts shall live for ever and ever.

28 All the ends of the earth shall remember, and shall be converted to the Lord:

And all the kindreds of the Gentiles shall adore in his sight.

29 For the kingdom is the Lord's; and he shall have dominion over the nations.

30 All the fat ones of the earth have eaten and have adored: all they that go down to the earth shall fall before him.

31 And to him my soul shall live: and my seed shall serve him.

32 There shall be declared to the Lord a generation to come: and the heavens shall shew forth his justice to a people that shall be born, which the Lord hath made.

PSALM 22
Dominus regit me
God's spiritual benefits to faithful souls.

1 A psalm for David.

THE [1] Lord ruleth me: and I shall want nothing. 2 He hath set me in a place of pasture.

He hath brought me up on the water of refreshment: 3 he hath converted my soul.

He hath led me on the paths of justice, for his own name's sake.

4 For though I should walk in the midst of the shadow of death, I will fear no evils, for thou art with me.

Thy rod and thy staff: they have comforted me.

5 Thou hast prepared a table before me, against them that afflict me.

Thou hast anointed my head with oil; and my chalice which inebriated *me*, how goodly is it!

6 And thy mercy will follow me all the days of my life.

And that I may dwell in the house of the Lord unto length of days.

PSALM 23
Domini est terra
Who are they that shall ascend to heaven. Christ's triumphant ascension thither.

1 On the first day of the week. A psalm for David.

THE [1] earth is the Lord's and the fulness thereof: the world and all they that dwell therein.

2 For he hath founded it upon the seas; and hath prepared it upon the rivers.

3 Who shall ascend into the mountain of the Lord: or who shall stand in his holy place?

4 The innocent in hands, and clean of heart, who hath not taken his soul in vain, nor sworn deceitfully to his neighbour.

5 He shall receive a blessing from the Lord, and mercy from God his Saviour.

6 This is the generation of them that seek him, of them that seek the face of the God of Jacob.

7 Lift up your gates, O ye princes, and be ye lifted up, O eternal gates: and the King of Glory shall enter in.

8 Who is this King of Glory? The Lord who is strong and mighty: the Lord mighty in battle.

9 Lift up your gates, O ye princes, and be ye lifted up, O eternal gates: and the King of Glory shall enter in.

10 Who is this King of Glory? The Lord of hosts, he is the King of Glory.

PSALM 24
Ad te, Domine, levavi
A prayer for grace, mercy, and protection against our enemies.

1 Unto the end. A psalm for David.

TO thee, O Lord, have I lifted up my soul. 2 In thee, O my God, I put my trust; let me not be ashamed.

3 Neither let my enemies laugh at me: for none of them that wait on thee shall be confounded.

4 Let all them be confounded that act unjust things without cause.

Shew, O Lord, thy ways to me, and teach me thy paths.

5 Direct me in thy truth, and teach me; for thou art God my Saviour, and on thee have I waited all the day long.

6 Remember, O Lord, thy bowels of compassion: and thy mercies that are from the beginning of the world.

7 The sins of my youth and my ignorances do not remember.

According to thy mercy remember thou me: for thy goodness' sake, O Lord.

8 The Lord is sweet and righteous: therefore he will give a law to sinners in the way.

9 He will guide the mild in judgment: he will teach the meek his ways.

10 All the ways of the Lord are mercy and truth: to them that seek after his covenant and his testimonies.

11 For thy name's sake, O Lord, thou wilt pardon my sin: for it is great.

12 Who is the man that feareth the Lord? He hath appointed him a law in the way he hath chosen.

13 His soul shall dwell in good things: and his seed shall inherit the land.

14 The Lord is a firmament to them that fear him: and his covenant shall be made manifest to them.

15 My eyes are ever towards the Lord: for he shall pluck my feet out of the snare.

16 Look thou upon me, and have mercy on me; for I am alone and poor.

17 The troubles of my heart are multiplied: deliver me from my necessities.

18 See my abjection and my labour; and forgive me all my sins.

19 Consider my enemies for they are multiplied, [1] and have hated me with an unjust hatred.

20 Keep thou my soul, and deliver me: I shall not be ashamed, for I have hoped in thee.

PSALM 22. [1] Isai. 40, 11; Jer. 23, 5; Ezech. 34, 11, 23; 1 Peter, 2, 25; 5, 3. PSALM 23. [1] Ps. 49, 12; 1 Cor. 10, 26. PSALM 24. [1] John, 15, 25.

PSALM 22. Ver. 1. *Ruleth me.* In Hebrew, *Is my shepherd*, to feed, guide, and govern me.

21 The innocent and the upright have adhered to me: because I have waited on thee.

22 Deliver Israel, O God, from all his tribulations.

PSALM 25

Judica me, Domine

David's prayer to God in his distress, to be delivered, that he may come to worship him in his tabernacle.

1 Unto the end. A psalm for David.

JUDGE me, O Lord, for I have walked in my innocence: and I have put my trust in the Lord, and shall not be weakened.

2 Prove me, O Lord, and try me: burn my reins and my heart.

3 For thy mercy is before my eyes: and I am well pleased with thy truth.

4 I have not sat with the council of vanity: neither will I go in with the doers of unjust things.

5 I have hated the assembly of the malignant: and with the wicked I will not sit.

6 I will wash my hands among the innocent: and will compass thy altar, O Lord.

7 That I may hear the voice of thy praise: and tell of all thy wondrous works.

8 I have loved, O Lord, the beauty of thy house: and the place where thy glory dwelleth.

9 Take not away my soul, O God, with the wicked: nor my life with bloody men:

10 In whose hands are iniquities: their right hand is filled with gifts.

11 But as for me, I have walked in my innocence: redeem me, and have mercy on me.

12 My foot hath stood in the direct way: in the churches I will bless thee, O Lord.

PSALM 26

Dominus illuminatio.

David's faith and hope in God.

1 The psalm of David before he was anointed.

THE Lord is my light and my salvation: Whom shall I fear?

The Lord is the protector of my life: Of whom shall I be afraid?

2 Whilst the wicked draw near against me, to eat my flesh.

My enemies that trouble me, have themselves been weakened, and have fallen.

3 If armies in camp should stand together against me, my heart shall not fear.

If a battle should rise up against me, in this will I be confident.

4 One thing I have asked of the Lord, this will I seek after: that I may dwell in the house of the Lord all the days of my life.

That I may see the delight of the Lord: and may visit his temple.

5 For he hath hidden me in his tabernacle: in the day of evils, he hath protected me in the secret place of his tabernacle.

6 He hath exalted me upon a rock: and now he hath lifted up my head above my enemies.

I have gone round, and have offered up in his tabernacle a sacrifice of jubilation: I will sing, and recite a psalm to the Lord.

7 Hear, O Lord, my voice, with which I have cried to thee: have mercy on me and hear me.

8 My heart hath said to thee: My face hath sought thee. Thy face, O Lord, will I still seek.

9 Turn not away thy face from me: decline not in thy wrath from thy servant.

Be thou my helper, forsake me not; do not thou despise me, O God my Saviour.

10 For my father and my mother have left me: but the Lord hath taken me up.

11 Set me, O Lord, a law in thy way, and guide me in the right path, because of my enemies.

12 Deliver me not over to the will of them that trouble me; for unjust witnesses have risen up against me, and iniquity hath lied to itself.

13 I believe to see the good things of the Lord in the land of the living.

14 Expect the Lord: do manfully. And let thy heart take courage: and wait thou for the Lord.

PSALM 27

Ad te, Domine, clamabo

David's prayer that his enemies may not prevail over him.

1 A psalm for David himself.

UNTO thee will I cry, O Lord: O my God, be not thou silent to me; lest if thou be silent to me, I become like them that go down into the pit.

2 Hear, O Lord, the voice of my supplication: when I pray to thee, when I lift up my hands to thy holy temple.

3 Draw me not away together with the wicked: and with the workers of iniquity destroy me not.

Who speak peace with their neighbour: but evils *are* in their hearts.

4 Give them according to their works: and according to the wickedness of their inventions.

According to the works of their hands give thou to them: render to them their reward.

5 Because they have not understood the works of the Lord and the operations of his hands: thou shalt destroy them, and shalt not build them up.

6 Blessed be the Lord: for he hath heard the voice of my supplication.

7 The Lord is my helper and my protector: in him hath my heart confided, and I have been helped.

And my flesh hath flourished again: and with my will I will give praise to him.

8 The Lord is the strength of his people, and the protector of the salvation of his anointed.

9 Save, O Lord, thy people and bless thy inheritance: and rule them and exalt them for ever.

PSALM 28

Afferte Domino

An invitation to glorify God, with a commemoration of his mighty works.

1 A psalm for David, at the finishing of the tabernacle.

BRING to the Lord, O ye children of God: bring to the Lord the offspring of rams.

2 Bring to the Lord glory and honour: bring to the Lord glory to his name: adore ye the Lord in his holy court.

3 The voice of the Lord *is* upon the waters; the God of majesty hath thundered: The Lord *is* upon many waters.

4 The voice of the Lord *is in* power: the voice of the Lord in magnificence.

5 The voice of the Lord breaketh the cedars: yea, the Lord shall break the cedars of Libanus,

6 And shall reduce them to pieces: as a calf of Libanus, and as the beloved son of unicorns.

7 The voice of the Lord divideth the flame of fire. 8 The voice of the Lord shaketh the desert: and the Lord shall shake the desert of Cades.

9 The voice of the Lord prepareth the stags. And he will discover the thick *woods:* and in his temple all shall speak *his* glory.

10 The Lord maketh the flood to dwell: and the Lord shall sit king for ever.

The Lord will give strength to his people: the Lord will bless his people with peace.

PSALM 29

Exaltabo te, Domine

David praiseth God for his deliverance and his merciful dealings with him.

1 A psalm of a canticle, at the dedication of David's house.

2 **I** WILL extol thee, O Lord, for thou hast upheld me: and hast not made my enemies to rejoice over me.

3 O Lord my God, I have cried to thee: and thou hast healed me.

4 Thou hast brought forth, O Lord, my soul from hell: thou hast saved me from them that go down into the pit.

5 Sing to the Lord, O ye his saints: and give praise to the memory of his holiness.

6 For wrath is in his indignation; and life in his *good* will.

In the evening weeping shall have place: and in the morning gladness.

7 And in my abundance I said: I shall never be moved.

8 O Lord, in thy favour, thou gavest strength to my beauty.

Thou turnedst away thy face from me: and I became troubled.

9 To thee, O Lord, will I cry: and I will make supplication to my God.

10 What profit is there in my blood, whilst I go down to corruption?

Shall dust confess to thee or declare thy truth?

11 The Lord hath heard, and hath had mercy on me: the Lord became my helper.

12 Thou hast turned for me my mourning into joy: thou hast cut my sackcloth and hast compassed me with gladness.

13 To the end that my glory may sing to thee, and I may not regret: O Lord my God, I will give praise to thee for ever.

PSALM 30

In te, Domine, speravi

A prayer of a just man under affliction.

1 Unto the end. A psalm for David, in an ecstasy.

2 **I**N thee, O Lord, have I hoped, let me never be confounded: deliver me in thy justice.

3 Bow down thy ear to me: make haste to deliver me.

Be thou unto me a God, a protector, and a house of refuge, to save me.

4 For thou art my strength and my refuge; and for thy name's sake thou wilt lead me and nourish me.

Psalm 28. Ver. 6. *Shall reduce them to pieces.* In Hebrew, *Shall make them to skip like a calf.* The psalmist here describes the effects of thunder (which he calls the voice of the Lord) which sometimes breaks down the tallest and strongest trees, and makes their broken branches, as it were, to *skip.* All this is to be understood mystically of the powerful voice of God's word in his church, which has broken the pride of the great ones of this world, and brought many of them meekly and joyfully to submit their necks to the sweet yoke of Christ.

5 Thou wilt bring me out of this snare which they have hidden for me: for thou art my protector.

6 [1] Into thy hands I commend my spirit: thou hast redeemed me, O Lord, the God of truth.

7 Thou hast hated them that regard vanities to no purpose.

But I have hoped in the Lord: 8 I will be glad and rejoice in thy mercy.

For thou hast regarded my humility: thou hast saved my soul out of distresses.

9 And thou hast not shut me up in the hands of the enemy: thou hast set my feet in a spacious place.

10 Have mercy on me, O Lord, for I am afflicted: my eye is troubled with wrath, my soul, and my belly.

11 For my life is wasted with grief: and my years in sighs.

My strength is weakened through poverty: and my bones are disturbed.

12 I am become a reproach among all my enemies, and very much to my neighbours; and a fear to my acquaintance.

They that saw me without fled from me. 13 I am forgotten as one dead from the heart.

I am become as a vessel that is destroyed. 14 For I have heard the blame of many that dwell round about.

While they assembled together against me, they consulted to take away my life.

15 But I have put my trust in thee, O Lord. I said: Thou art my God; 16 My lots are in thy hands.

Deliver me out of the hands of my enemies, and from them that persecute me.

17 Make thy face to shine upon thy servant: save me in thy mercy.

18 Let me not be confounded, O Lord: for I have called upon thee.

Let the wicked be ashamed, and be brought down to hell. 19 Let deceitful lips be made dumb.

Which speak iniquity against the just, with pride and abuse.

20 O how great is the multitude of thy sweetness, O Lord, which thou hast hidden for them that fear thee!

Which thou hast wrought for them that hope in thee, in the sight of the sons of men!

21 Thou shalt hide them in the secret of thy face from the disturbance of men.

Thou shalt protect them in thy tabernacle from the contradiction of tongues.

22 Blessed be the Lord: for he hath shewn his wonderful mercy to me in a fortified city.

23 But I said in the excess of my mind: I am cast away from before thy eyes.

Therefore thou hast heard the voice of my prayer when I cried to thee.

24 O love the Lord, all ye his saints: for the Lord will require truth and will repay them abundantly that act proudly.

25 Do ye manfully, and let your heart be strengthened, all ye that hope in the Lord.

PSALM 31

Beati quorum

The second penitential psalm.

1 To David himself, understanding.

BLESSED [1] are they whose iniquities are forgiven: and whose sins are covered.

2 Blessed is the man to whom the Lord hath not imputed sin: and in whose spirit there is no guile.

3 Because I was silent my bones grew old; whilst I cried out all the day long.

4 For day and night thy hand was heavy upon me: I am turned in my anguish, whilst the thorn is fastened.

5 I have acknowledged my sin to thee: and my injustice I have not concealed.

[3] I said: I will confess against myself my injustice to the Lord. And thou hast forgiven the wickedness of my sin.

6 For this shall every one that is holy pray to thee in a seasonable time.

And yet in a flood of many waters, they shall not come nigh unto him.

7 Thou art my refuge from the trouble which hath encompassed me: my joy, deliver me from them that surround me.

8 I will give thee understanding and I will instruct thee in this way, in which thou shalt go: I will fix my eyes upon thee.

9 Do not become like the horse and the mule who have no understanding.

With bit and bridle bind fast their jaws, who come not near unto thee.

10 Many are the scourges of the sinner: but mercy shall encompass him that hopeth in the Lord.

11 Be glad in the Lord, and rejoice, ye just: and glory, all ye right of heart.

PSALM 30. [1] Luke, 23, 46. PSALM 31. [1] Rom. 4, 7. [2] Isai. 65, 24.

PSALM 31. Ver. 3. *Because I was silent.* That is, whilst I kept silence, by concealing, or refusing to confess my sins, thy hand was heavy upon me.

Ver. 4. *I am turned.* That is, I turn and roll about in my bed to seek for ease in my pain whilst the thorn of thy justice pierces my flesh, and sticks fast in me. Or, *I am turned:* that is, I am converted to thee, my God, by being brought to a better understanding by thy chastisements. In the Hebrew it is, *my moisture is turned into the droughts of the summer.*

PSALM 32

Exultate, justi

An exhortation to praise God, and to trust in him.

1 A psalm for David.

R EJOICE in the Lord, O ye just: praise becometh the upright.

2 Give praise to the Lord on the harp; sing to him with the psaltery, the instrument of ten strings.

3 Sing to him a new canticle: sing well unto him with a loud noise.

4 For the word of the Lord is right: and all his works are *done* with faithfulness.

5 He loveth mercy and judgment; the earth is full of the mercy of the Lord.

6 By the word of the Lord the heavens were established; and all the power of them by the spirit of his mouth:

7 Gathering together the waters of the sea, as in a vessel; laying up the depths in storehouses.

8 Let all the earth fear the Lord: and let all the inhabitants of the world be in awe of him.

9 [1] For he spoke and they were made: he commanded and they were created.

10 The Lord bringeth to nought the counsels of nations; and he rejecteth the devices of people, and casteth away the counsels of princes.

11 But the counsel of the Lord standeth for ever: the thoughts of his heart to all generations.

12 Blessed is the nation whose God is the Lord: the people whom he hath chosen for his inheritance.

13 The Lord hath looked from heaven: he hath beheld all the sons of men.

14 From his habitation which he hath prepared, he hath looked upon all that dwell on the earth.

15 He who hath made the hearts of every one of them: who understandeth all their works.

16 The king is not saved by a great army: nor shall the giant be saved by his own great strength.

17 Vain is the horse for safety: neither shall he be saved by the abundance of his strength.

18 Behold the eyes of the Lord are on them that fear him: and on them that hope in his mercy.

19 To deliver their souls from death and feed them in famine.

20 Our soul waiteth for the Lord: for he is our helper and protector.

21 For in him our heart shall rejoice: and in his holy name we have trusted.

22 Let thy mercy, O Lord, be upon us, as we have hoped in thee.

PSALM 33

Benedicam Dominum

An exhortation to the praise, and service of God.

1 For David, when he changed his countenance before Achimelech, who dismissed him, and he went his way. [1 Kings 21.]

2 I WILL bless the Lord at all times: his praise shall be always in my mouth.

3 In the Lord shall my soul be praised: let the meek hear and rejoice.

4 O magnify the Lord with me; and let us extol his name together.

5 I sought the Lord, and he heard me; and he delivered me from all my troubles.

6 Come ye to him and be enlightened: and your faces shall not be confounded.

7 This poor man cried and the Lord heard him: and saved him out of all his troubles.

8 The angel of the Lord shall encamp round about them that fear him: and shall deliver them.

9 O taste, and see that the Lord is sweet: blessed is the man that hopeth in him.

10 Fear the Lord, all ye his saints: for there is no want to them that fear him.

11 [1] The rich have wanted, and have suffered hunger: but they that seek the Lord shall not be deprived of any good.

12 Come, children, hearken to me: I will teach you the fear of the Lord.

13 [2] Who is the man that desireth life, who loveth to see good days?

14 Keep thy tongue from evil, and thy lips from speaking guile.

15 Turn away from evil and do good: seek after peace and pursue it.

16 The eyes of the Lord are [3] upon the just: and his ears unto their prayers.

17 But the countenance of the Lord is against them that do evil things: to cut off the remembrance of them from the earth.

18 The just cried, and the Lord heard them: and delivered them out of all their troubles.

19 The Lord is nigh unto them that are of a contrite heart: and he will save the humble of spirit.

20 Many are the afflictions of the just; but out of them all will the Lord deliver them.

21 The Lord keepeth all their bones: not one of them shall be broken.

22 The death of the wicked is very

PSALM 32. [1] Gen. 1, 8; Judith, 16, 17. PSALM 33. [1] Luke 1, 52. [2] 1 Peter, 3, 10. [3] Ecclus. 15, 20; Heb. 4, 13.

evil: and they that hate the just shall be guilty.

23 The Lord will redeem the souls of his servants: and none of them that trust in him shall offend.

PSALM 34

Judica, Domine, nocentes me

David, in the person of Christ, prayeth against his persecutors: prophetically foreshewing the punishments that shall fall upon them.

1 For David himself.

JUDGE thou, O Lord, them that wrong me: overthrow them that fight against me.

2 Take hold of arms and shield: and rise up to help me.

3 Bring out the sword, and shut up the way against them that persecute me. Say to my soul: I am thy salvation.

4 ¹ Let them be confounded and ashamed that seek after my soul.

Let them be turned back and be confounded that devise evil against me.

5 Let them become as dust before the wind: and let the angel of the Lord straiten them.

6 Let their way become dark and slippery: and let the angel of the Lord pursue them.

7 For without cause they have hidden their net for me unto destruction: without cause they have upbraided my soul.

8 Let the snare which he knoweth not come upon him: and let the net which he hath hidden catch him: and into that very snare let them fall.

9 But my soul shall rejoice in the Lord, and shall be delighted in his salvation.

10 All my bones shall say: Lord, who is like to thee?

Who deliverest the poor from the hand of them that are stronger than he: the needy and the poor from them that strip him.

11 Unjust witnesses rising up have asked me things I knew not.

12 They repaid me evil for good: to the depriving me of my soul.

13 But as for me, when they were troublesome to me, I was clothed with haircloth.

I humbled my soul with fasting: and my prayer shall be turned into my bosom.

14 As a neighbour and as an own brother, so did I please: as one mourning and sorrowful, so was I humbled.

15 But they rejoiced against me, and

came together: scourges were gathered together upon me, and I knew not.

16 They were separated and repented not: they tempted me, they scoffed at me with scorn, they gnashed upon me with their teeth.

17 Lord, when wilt thou look upon me? Rescue thou my soul from their malice: my only one from the lions.

18 I will give thanks to thee in a great church: I will praise thee in a strong people.

19 Let not them that are my enemies wrongfully rejoice over me: ² who have hated me without cause and wink with the eyes.

20 For they spoke indeed peaceably to me: and speaking in the anger of the earth they devised guile.

21 And they opened their mouth wide against me; they said: Well done, well done, our eyes have seen it.

22 Thou hast seen, O Lord: be not thou silent. O Lord, depart not from me.

23 Arise, and be attentive to my judgment: to my cause, my God and my Lord.

24 Judge me, O Lord my God, according to thy justice: and let them not rejoice over me.

25 Let them not say in their hearts: It is well, it is well, to our mind. Neither let them say: We have swallowed him up.

26 Let them blush and be ashamed together, who rejoice at my evils.

Let them be clothed with confusion and shame, who speak great things against me.

27 Let them rejoice and be glad, who are well pleased with my justice; and let them say always: The Lord be magnified, who delights in the peace of his servant.

28 And my tongue shall meditate thy justice: thy praise all the day long.

PSALM 35

Dixit injustus

The malice of sinners and the goodness of God.

1 Unto the end, for the servant of God, David himself.

2 THE unjust hath said within himself that he would sin: there is no fear of God before his eyes.

3 ¹ For in his sight he hath done deceitfully, that his iniquity may be found unto hatred.

4 The words of his mouth are iniquity and guile: he would not understand that he might do well.

5 He hath devised iniquity on his bed: he hath set himself on every way

PSALM 34. ¹ Ps. 39, 15. ² John, 15, 25. PSALM 35. ¹ Ps. 13, 3.

PSALM 35. Ver. 3. *Unto hatred.* That is, hateful to God.

that is not good: but evil he hath not hated.

6 O Lord, thy mercy is in heaven: and thy truth *reacheth* even to the clouds.

7 Thy justice is as the mountains of God: thy judgments are a great deep.

Men and beasts thou wilt preserve, O Lord: 8 O how hast thou multiplied thy mercy, O God!

But the children of men shall put their trust under the covert of thy wings.

9 They shall be inebriated with the plenty of thy house; and thou shalt make them drink of the torrent of thy pleasure.

10 For with thee is the fountain of life: and in thy light we shall see light.

11 Extend thy mercy to them that know thee: and thy justice to them that are right in heart.

12 Let not the foot of pride come to me: and let not the hand of the sinner move me.

13 There the workers of iniquity are fallen: they are cast out, and could not stand.

PSALM 36
Noli æmulari
An exhortation to despise this world and the short prosperity of the wicked, and to trust in Providence.

1 A psalm for David himself.

BE not emulous of evildoers; nor envy them that work iniquity.

2 For they shall shortly wither away as grass: and as the green herbs shall quickly fall.

3 Trust in the Lord, and do good, and dwell in the land: and thou shalt be fed with its riches.

4 Delight in the Lord: and he will give thee the requests of thy heart.

5 Commit thy way to the Lord, and trust in him: and he will do it.

6 And he will bring forth thy justice as the light, and thy judgment as the noonday. 7 Be subject to the Lord and pray to him.

Envy not the man who prospereth in his way: the man who doth unjust things.

8 Cease from anger, and leave rage: have no emulation to do evil.

9 For evildoers shall be cut off: but they that wait upon the Lord, they shall inherit the land.

10 For yet a little while, and the wicked shall not be: and thou shalt seek his place, and shalt not find it.

11 [1] But the meek shall inherit the land: and shall delight in abundance of peace.

12 The sinner shall watch the just

man: and shall gnash upon him with his teeth.

13 But the Lord shall laugh at him: for he forseeth that his day shall come.

14 The wicked have drawn out the sword: they have bent their bow.

To cast down the poor and needy, to kill the upright of heart.

15 Let their sword enter into their own hearts: and let their bow be broken.

16 Better is a little to the just than the great riches of the wicked.

17 For the arms of the wicked shall be broken in pieces: but the Lord strengtheneth the just.

18 The Lord knoweth the days of the undefiled: and their inheritance shall be for ever.

19 They shall not be confounded in the evil time: and in the days of famine they shall be filled, 20 because the wicked shall perish.

And the enemies of the Lord, presently after they shall be honoured and exalted, shall come to nothing and vanish like smoke.

21 The sinner shall borrow, and not pay again: but the just sheweth mercy and shall give.

22 For such as bless him shall inherit the land: but such as curse him shall perish.

23 With the Lord shall the steps of a man be directed: and he shall like well his way.

24 When he shall fall he shall not be bruised, for the Lord putteth his hand under him.

25 I have been young, and now am old: and I have not seen the just forsaken, nor his seed seeking bread.

26 He sheweth mercy, and lendeth all the day long; and his seed shall be in blessing.

27 Decline from evil and do good: and dwell for ever and ever.

28 For the Lord loveth judgment and will not forsake his saints: they shall be preserved for ever.

The unjust shall be punished: and the seed of the wicked shall perish.

29 But the just shall inherit the land, and shall dwell therein for evermore.

30 [2] The mouth of the just shall meditate wisdom: and his tongue shall speak judgment.

31 [3] The law of his God is in his heart: and his steps shall not be supplanted.

32 The wicked watcheth the just man, and seeketh to put him to death.

33 But the Lord will not leave him in

PSALM 36. [1] Matt. 5, 4. [2] Prov. 31, 26. [3] Isai. 51, 7.

his hands; nor condemn him when he shall be judged.

34 Expect the Lord and keep his way: and he will exalt thee to inherit the land. When the sinners shall perish thou shalt see.

35 I have seen the wicked highly exalted, and lifted up like the cedars of Libanus.

36 And I passed by, and lo, he was not: and I sought him and his place was not found.

37 Keep innocence, and behold justice: for there are remnants for the peaceable man.

38 But the unjust shall be destroyed together: the remnants of the wicked shall perish.

39 But the salvation of the just is from the Lord: and he is their protector in the time of trouble.

40 And the Lord will help them and deliver them: and he will rescue them from the wicked, and save them, because they have hoped in him.

PSALM 37

Domine, ne in furore

A prayer of a penitent for the remission of his sins. The third penitential psalm.

1 A psalm for David. For a remembrance of the sabbath.

2 REBUKE [1] me not, O Lord, in thy indignation: nor chastise me in thy wrath.

3 For thy arrows are fastened in me: and thy hand hath been strong upon me.

4 There is no health in my flesh, because of thy wrath: there is no peace for my bones, because of my sins.

5 For my iniquities are gone over my head: and as a heavy burden are become heavy upon me.

6 My sores are putrified and corrupted, because of my foolishness.

7 I am become miserable, and am bowed down even to the end: I walked sorrowful all the day long.

8 For my loins are filled with illusions: and there is no health in my flesh.

9 I am afflicted and humbled exceedingly: I roared with the groaning of my heart.

10 Lord, all my desire is before thee: and my groaning is not hidden from thee.

11 My heart is troubled, my strength hath left me: and the light of my eyes itself is not with me.

12 My friends and my neighbours

PSALM 37. [1] Ps. 6, 2.

PSALM 37. Ver. 1. *For a remembrance.* Namely, of our miseries and sins. To be sung on the sabbath day.

have drawn near, and stood against me. And they that were near me stood afar off.

13 And they that sought my soul used violence.

And they that sought evils to me spoke vain things, and studied deceits all the day long.

14 But I, as a deaf man, heard not: and as a dumb man not opening his mouth.

15 And I became as a man that heareth not: and that hath no reproofs in his mouth.

16 For in thee, O Lord, have I hoped: thou wilt hear me, O Lord my God.

17 For I said: Lest at any time my enemies rejoice over me, and whilst my feet are moved, they speak great things against me.

18 For I am ready for scourges: and my sorrow is continually before me.

19 For I will declare my iniquity: and I will think for my sin.

20 But my enemies live, and are stronger than I: and they that hate me wrongfully are multiplied.

21 They that render evil for good, have detracted me, because I followed goodness.

22 Forsake me not, O Lord my God: do not thou depart from me.

23 Attend unto my help, O Lord, the God of my salvation.

PSALM 38

Dixi custodiam

A just man's peace and patience in his sufferings from considering the vanity of the world and the providence of God.

1 Unto the end. For Idithun himself, a canticle of David.

2 I SAID: I will take heed to my ways, that I sin not with my tongue. I have set a guard to my mouth, when the sinner stood against me.

3 I was dumb, and was humbled, and kept silence from good things: and my sorrow was renewed.

4 My heart grew hot within me: and in my meditation a fire shall flame out.

5 I spoke with my tongue: O Lord, make me know my end,

And what is the number of my days: that I may know what is wanting to me.

6 Behold thou hast made my days measurable: and my substance is as nothing before thee.

And indeed all things are vanity: every man living.

7 Surely man passeth as an image: yea, and he is disquieted in vain.

He storeth up: and he knoweth not for whom he shall gather these things.

8 And now what is my hope? Is it

not the Lord? And my substance is with thee.

9 Deliver thou me from all my iniquities: thou hast made me a reproach to the fool.

10 I was dumb, and I opened not my mouth, because thou hast done it. 11 Remove thy scourges from me.

The strength of thy hand hath made me faint in rebukes: 12 thou hast corrected man for iniquity.

And thou hast made his soul to waste away like a spider: surely in vain is any man disquieted.

13 Hear my prayer, O Lord, and my supplication: give ear to my tears.

Be not silent: for I am a stranger with thee, and a sojourner as all my fathers were.

14 O forgive me, that I may be refreshed, before I go hence, and be no more.

PSALM 39

Expectans expectavi

Christ's coming and redeeming of mankind.

1 Unto the end. A psalm for David himself.

2 **W**ITH expectation I have waited for the Lord: and he was attentive to me.

3 And he heard my prayers, and brought me out of the pit of misery and the mire of dregs.

And he set my feet upon a rock, and directed my steps.

4 And he put a new canticle into my mouth, a song to our God.

Many shall see and shall fear: and they shall hope in the Lord.

5 Blessed is the man whose trust is in the name of the Lord; and who hath not had regard to vanities and lying follies.

6 Thou hast multiplied thy wonderful works, O Lord my God: and in thy thoughts there is no one like to thee.

I have declared, and I have spoken: they are multiplied above number.

7 [1] Sacrifice and oblation thou didst not desire: but thou hast pierced ears for me.

Burnt offering and sin offering thou didst not require: 8 then said I, Behold I come.

In the head of the book it is written of me 9 that I should do thy will: O my God, I have desired *it*, and thy law in the midst of my heart.

10 I have declared thy justice in a great church. Lo, I will not restrain my lips. O Lord, thou knowest it.

11 I have not hid thy justice within my heart: I have declared thy truth and thy salvation.

I have not concealed thy mercy and thy truth from a great council.

12 Withhold not thou, O Lord, thy tender mercies from me: thy mercy and thy truth have always upheld me.

13 For evils without number have surrounded me; my iniquities have overtaken me, and I was not able to see.

They are multiplied above the hairs of my head: and my heart hath forsaken me.

14 Be pleased, O Lord, to deliver me: [2] look down, O Lord, to help me.

15 [3] Let them be confounded and ashamed together, that seek after my soul to take it away.

Let them be turned backward and be ashamed, that desire evils to me.

16 Let them immediately bear their confusion, that say to me: 'Tis well, 'tis well.

17 Let all that seek thee rejoice and be glad in thee: and let such as love thy salvation say always: The Lord be magnified.

18 But I am a beggar and poor: the Lord is careful for me.

Thou art my helper and my protector: O my God, be not slack.

PSALM 40

Beatus qui intelligit

The happiness of him that shall believe in Christ, notwithstanding the humility and poverty in which he shall come. The malice of his enemies, especially of the traitor Judas.

1 Unto the end. A psalm for David himself.

2 **B**LESSED is he that understandeth concerning the needy and the poor: the Lord will deliver him in the evil day.

3 The Lord preserve him and give him life, and make him blessed upon the earth: and deliver him not up to the will of his enemies.

4 The Lord help him on his bed of sorrow: thou hast turned all his couch in his sickness.

5 I said: O Lord, be thou merciful to me. Heal my soul, for I have sinned against thee.

6 My enemies have spoken evils against me: When shall he die and his name perish?

7 And if he came in to see *me*, he spoke vain things: his heart gathered together iniquity to itself.

PSALM 39. [1] Heb. 10, 5. [2] Ps. 69, 2. [3] Ps. 34, 4.

PSALM 39. Ver. 13. *My iniquities.* That is, the sins of all mankind, which I have taken upon me.

Ver. 16. *'Tis well.* The Hebrew here is an interjection of insult and derision, like the Vah (Matt. 27, 49).

He went out and spoke to the same purpose.

8 All my enemies whispered together against me: they devised evils to me.

9 They determined against me an unjust word: Shall he that sleepeth rise again no more?

10 [1] For even the man of my peace, in whom I trusted, who ate my bread, hath greatly supplanted me.

11 But thou, O Lord, have mercy on me, and raise me up again: and I will requite them.

12 By this I know that thou hast had a good will for me: because my enemy shall not rejoice over me.

13 But thou hast upheld me by reason of my innocence: and hast established me in thy sight for ever.

14 Blessed be the Lord, the God of Israel, from eternity to eternity. So be it. So be it.

PSALM 41

Quemadmodum desiderat

The fervent desire of the just after God. Hope in afflictions.

1 Unto the end. Understanding for the sons of Core.

2 **A**S the hart panteth after the fountains of water; so my soul panteth after thee, O God.

3 My soul hath thirsted after the strong living God. When shall I come and appear before the face of God?

4 My tears have been my bread day and night, whilst it is said to me daily: Where is thy God?

5 These things I remembered, and poured out my soul in me: for I shall go over into the place of the wonderful tabernacle, even to the house of God: With the voice of joy and praise; the noise of one feasting.

6 Why art thou sad, O my soul? And why dost thou trouble me?

Hope in God, for I will still give praise to him: the salvation of my countenance, 7 and my God.

My soul is troubled within myself: therefore will I remember thee from the land of Jordan and Hermoniim, from the little hill.

8 Deep calleth on deep, at the noise of thy flood-gates.

All thy heights and thy billows have passed over me.

9 In the daytime the Lord hath commanded his mercy: and a canticle to him in the night.

With me *is* prayer to the God of my life. 10 I will say to God: Thou art my support.

Why hast thou forgotten me? And

PSALM 40. [1] Acts, 1, 16.

why go I mourning, whilst my enemy afflicteth me?

11 Whilst my bones are broken, my enemies who trouble me have reproached me;

Whilst they say to me day by day: Where is thy God?

12 Why art thou cast down, O my soul? And why dost thou disquiet me?

Hope thou in God, for I will still give praise to him: the salvation of my countenance, and my God.

PSALM 42

Judica me, Deus

The prophet aspireth after the temple and altar of God.

1 A psalm for David.

JUDGE me, O God, and distinguish my cause from the nation that is not holy: deliver me from the unjust and deceitful man.

2 For thou art God my strength: Why hast thou cast me off? And why do I go sorrowful whilst the enemy afflicteth me?

3 Send forth thy light and thy truth: they have conducted me, and brought me unto thy holy hill, and into thy tabernacles.

4 And I will go in to the altar of God: to God who giveth joy to my youth.

5 To thee, O God, my God, I will give praise upon the harp: Why art thou sad, O my soul? And why dost thou disquiet me?

6 Hope in God, for I will still give praise to him: the salvation of my countenance, and my God.

PSALM 43

Deus auribus nostris

The church commemorates former favours, and present afflictions. She prays for succour.

1 Unto the end. For the sons of Core, to give understanding.

2 **W**E have heard, O God, with our ears: our fathers have declared to us,

The work thou hast wrought in their days, and in the days of old.

3 Thy hand destroyed the Gentiles, and thou plantedst them: thou didst afflict the people and cast them out.

4 For they got not the possession of the land by their own sword: neither did their own arm save them.

But thy right hand and thy arm, and the light of thy countenance: because thou wast pleased with them.

5 Thou art thyself my king and my God, who commandest the saving of Jacob.

6 Through thee we will push down

our enemies with the horn: and through thy name we will despise them that rise up against us.

7 For I will not trust in my bow: neither shall my sword save me.

8 But thou hast saved us from them that afflict us: and hast put them to shame that hate us.

9 In God shall we glory all the day long: and in thy name we will give praise for ever.

10 But now thou hast cast us off, and put us to shame: and thou, O God, wilt not go out with our armies.

11 Thou hast made us turn our back to our enemies: and they that hated us plundered for themselves.

12 Thou hast given us up like sheep to be eaten: thou hast scattered us among the nations.

13 Thou hast sold thy people for no price: and there was no reckoning in the exchange of them.

14 Thou hast made us a reproach to our neighbours: a scoff and derision to them that are round about us.

15 Thou hast made us a byword among the Gentiles: a shaking of the head among the people.

16 All the day long my shame is before me: and the confusion of my face hath covered me,

17 At the voice of him that reproacheth and detracteth me: at the face of the enemy and persecutor.

18 All these things have come upon us: yet we have not forgotten thee: and we have not done wickedly in thy covenant.

19 And our heart hath not turned back: neither hast thou turned aside our steps from thy way.

20 For thou hast humbled us in the place of affliction: and the shadow of death hath covered us.

21 If we have forgotten the name of our God, and if we have spread forth our hands to a strange god:

22 Shall not God search out these things: for he knoweth the secrets of the heart?

[1] Because for thy sake we are killed all the day long: we are counted as sheep for the slaughter.

23 Arise, why sleepest thou, O Lord? Arise, and cast us not off to the end.

24 Why turnest thou thy face away and forgettest our want and our trouble?

25 For our soul is humbled down to the dust: our belly cleaveth to the earth.

26 Arise, O Lord: Help us and redeem us for thy name's sake.

PSALM 44

Eructavit cor meum

The excellence of Christ's kingdom, and the endowments of his church.

1 Unto the end. For them that shall be changed. For the sons of Core. For understanding. A canticle for the Beloved.

2 MY heart hath uttered a good word: I speak my works to the king.

My tongue is the pen of a scrivener that writeth swiftly.

3 Thou art beautiful above the sons of men: grace is poured abroad in thy lips; therefore hath God blessed thee for ever.

4 Gird thy sword upon thy thigh, O thou most mighty.

5 With thy comeliness and thy beauty set out: proceed prosperously, and reign.

Because of truth and meekness and justice: and thy right hand shall conduct thee wonderfully.

6 Thy arrows are sharp: under thee shall people fall, into the hearts of the king's enemies.

7 [1] Thy throne, O God, is for ever and ever: the sceptre of thy kingdom is a sceptre of uprightness.

8 Thou hast loved justice, and hated iniquity: therefore God, thy God, hath anointed thee with the oil of gladness above thy fellows.

9 Myrrh and stacte and cassia perfume thy garments, from the ivory houses: out of which 10 the daughters of kings have delighted thee in thy glory.

The queen stood on thy right hand, in gilded clothing; surrounded with variety.

11 Hearken, O daughter, and see, and incline thy ear: and forget thy people and thy father's house.

12 And the king shall greatly desire thy beauty; for he is the Lord thy God, and him they shall adore.

13 And the daughters of Tyre with gifts, yea, all the rich among the people, shall entreat thy countenance.

14 All the glory of the king's daughter is within in golden borders, 15 clothed round about with varieties.

After her shall virgins be brought to the king: her neighbours shall be brought to thee.

16 They shall be brought with gladness and rejoicing: they shall be brought into the temple of the king.

PSALM 43. [1] Rom. 8, 36. PSALM 44. [1] Heb. 1, 8.

PSALM 44. Ver. 1. *For them that shall be changed.* That is, for souls happily changed, by being converted to God.—*The Beloved.* Our Lord Jesus Christ.

17 Instead of thy fathers, sons are born to thee: thou shalt make them princes over all the earth.

18 They shall remember thy name throughout all generations.

Therefore shall people praise thee for ever: yea, for ever and ever.

PSALM 45

Deus noster refugium

The church in persecution trusteth in the protection of God.

1 Unto the end. For the sons of Core, for the hidden.

2 OUR God is our refuge and strength: a helper in troubles, which have found us exceedingly.

3 Therefore we will not fear when the earth shall be troubled; and the mountains shall be removed into the heart of the sea.

4 Their waters roared and were troubled with his strength.

5 The stream of the river maketh the city of God joyful: the most High hath sanctified his own tabernacle.

6 God is in the midst thereof, it shall not be moved: God will help it in the morning early.

7 Nations were troubled, and kingdoms were bowed down: he uttered his voice, the earth trembled.

8 The Lord of armies is with us: the God of Jacob is our protector.

9 Come and behold ye the works of the Lord, what wonders he hath done upon earth: 10 making wars to cease even to the end of the earth.

He shall destroy the bow, and break the weapons: and the shield he shall burn in the fire.

11 Be still and see that I am God. I will be exalted among the nations, and I will be exalted in the earth.

12 The Lord of armies is with us: the God of Jacob is our protector.

PSALM 46

Omnes gentes, plaudite

The Gentiles are invited to praise God for the establishment of the kingdom of Christ.

1 Unto the end. For the sons of Core.

2 O CLAP your hands, all ye nations: shout unto God with the voice of joy,

3 For the Lord is high, terrible: a great king over all the earth.

4 He hath subdued the people under us: and the nations under our feet.

5 He hath chosen for us his inheritance, the beauty of Jacob which he hath loved.

PSALM 46. ¹ 2 Kings, 6, 15.

6 ¹ God is ascended with jubilee: and the Lord with the sound of trumpet.

7 Sing praises to our God, sing ye: sing praises to our king, sing ye.

8 For God is the king of all the earth: sing ye wisely.

9 God shall reign over the nations: God sitteth on his holy throne.

10 The princes of the people are gathered together, with the God of Abraham: for the strong gods of the earth are exceedingly exalted.

PSALM 47

Magnus Dominus

God is greatly to be praised for the establishment of his church.

1 A psalm of a canticle. For the sons of Core. On the second day of the week.

2 GREAT is the Lord, and exceedingly to be praised in the city of our God, in his holy mountain.

3 With the joy of the whole earth is mount Sion founded, on the sides of the north, the city of the great king.

4 In her houses shall God be known, when he shall protect her.

5 For behold the kings of the earth assembled themselves: they gathered together.

6 So they saw: and they wondered, they were troubled, they were moved.

7 Trembling took hold of them.

There were pains as of a woman in labour. 8 With a vehement wind thou shalt break in pieces the ships of Tharsis.

9 As we have heard, so have we seen, in the city of the Lord of hosts, in the city of our God: God hath founded it for ever.

10 We have received thy mercy, O God, in the midst of thy temple.

11 According to thy name, O God, so also is thy praise unto the ends of the earth: thy right hand is full of justice.

12 Let mount Sion rejoice, and the daughters of Juda be glad; because of thy judgments, O Lord.

13 Surround Sion, and encompass her: tell ye in her towers.

14 Set your hearts on her strength: and distribute her houses, that ye may relate it in another generation.

15 For this is God, our God unto eternity, and for ever and ever. He shall rule us for evermore.

PSALM 48

Audite hæc, omnes gentes

The folly of worldlings, who live on in sin, without thinking of death or hell.

1 Unto the end. A psalm for the sons of Core.

2 ℏEAR these things, all ye nations: give ear, all ye inhabitants of the world.

3 All you that are earthborn, and you sons of men: both rich and poor together.

4 My mouth shall speak wisdom: and the meditation of my heart understanding.

5 [1] I will incline my ear to a parable; I will open my proposition on the psaltery.

6 Why shall I fear in the evil day? The iniquity of my heel shall encompass me.

7 They that trust in their own strength, and glory in the multitude of their riches.

8 No brother *can* redeem, *nor* shall man redeem: he shall not give to God his ransom,

9 Nor the price of the redemption of his soul: and shall labour for ever 10 and shall still live unto the end.

11 He shall not see destruction, when he shall see the wise dying: the senseless and the fool shall perish together.

And they shall leave their riches to strangers: 12 and their sepulchres shall be their houses for ever.

Their dwelling places to all generations: they have called their lands by their names.

13 And man when he was in honour did not understand: he is compared to senseless beasts, and is become like to them.

14 This way of theirs is a stumblingblock to them: and afterwards they shall delight in their mouth.

15 They are laid in hell like sheep: death shall feed upon them.

And the just shall have dominion over them in the morning: and their help shall decay in hell from their glory.

16 But God will redeem my soul from the hand of hell, when he shall receive me.

17 Be not thou afraid when a man shall be made rich, and when the glory of his house shall be increased.

18 For when he shall die he shall take nothing away: nor shall his glory descend with him.

19 For in his lifetime his soul will be blessed: and he will praise thee when thou shalt do well to him.

20 He shall go in to the generations of his fathers: and he shall never see light.

21 Man when he was in honour did not understand: he hath been compared to senseless beasts, and made like to them.

PSALM 49
Deus deorum
The coming of Christ, who prefers virtue and inward purity before the blood of victims.

1 A psalm for Asaph.

THE God of gods, the Lord hath spoken: and he hath called the earth.

From the rising of the sun, to the going down thereof: 2 out of Sion the loveliness of his beauty.

3 God shall come manifestly: our God *shall come*, and shall not keep silence.

A fire shall burn before him: and a mighty tempest *shall be* round about him.

4 He shall call heaven from above, and the earth, to judge his people.

5 Gather ye together his saints to him: who set his covenant before sacrifices.

6 And the heaven shall declare his justice: for God is judge.

7 Hear, O my people, and I will speak: O Israel, and I will testify to thee: I am God, thy God.

8 I will not reprove thee for thy sacrifices: and thy burnt offerings are always in my sight.

PSALM 48. [1] Ps. 77, 2; Matt. 13, 35.

PSALM 48. Ver. 6. *The iniquity of my heel.* That is, the iniquity of my steps or *ways*: or the *iniquity* of my *pride*, with which as with the *heel*, I have spurned and kicked at my neighbours: or the iniquity of my *heel*, that is, the iniquity in which I shall be found in death. The meaning of this verse is: Why should I now indulge those passions and sinful affections, or commit now those sins, which will cause me so much fear and anguish in the evil day; when the sorrows of death shall compass me, and the perils of hell shall find me?

Ver. 7. *They that trust in their own strength.* As much as to say: Let them fear that trust in their strength or riches: for they have great reason to fear, seeing that no brother or other man, how much a friend soever, can by any price or labour rescue them from death.

Ver. 9. *And shall labour for ever.* This seems to be a continuation of the foregoing sentence: as much as to say no man can by any price or ransom prolong his life, that so he may still continue to *labour here*, and *live to the end* of the world. Others understand it of the eternal sorrows, and dying *life* of hell, which is the dreadful consequence of dying in sin.

Ver. 11. *He shall not see destruction.* Or, *Shall not he see destruction?* As much as to say, however thoughtless he may be of his death, he must not expect to escape, since even the wise and the good are not exempt from dying.

Ver. 12. *They have called their lands by their names.* That is, they have left their names on their graves, which alone remain of their lands.

Ver. 14. *They shall delight in their mouth.* Notwithstanding the wretched way in which they walk, they shall applaud themselves with their mouths, and glory in their doings.

Ver. 15. *In the morning.* That is, in the resurrection to a new life; when the just shall judge and condemn the wicked.—*From their glory.* That is, when their short-lived glory in this world shall be past, and be no more.

9 I will not take calves out of thy house: nor he-goats out of thy flocks.

10 For all the beasts of the woods are mine: the cattle on the hills, and the oxen.

11 I know all the fowls of the air: and with me is the beauty of the field.

12 If I should be hungry, I would not tell thee: for the world is mine, and the fulness thereof.

13 Shall I eat the flesh of bullocks? Or shall I drink the blood of goats?

14 Offer to God the sacrifice of praise: and pay thy vows to the most High.

15 And call upon me in the day of trouble: I will deliver thee, and thou shalt glorify me.

16 But to the sinner God hath said: Why dost thou declare my justices, and take my covenant in thy mouth?

17 Seeing thou hast hated discipline: and hast cast my words behind thee.

18 If thou didst see a thief thou didst run with him: and with adulterers thou hast been a partaker.

19 Thy mouth hath abounded with evil: and thy tongue framed deceits.

20 Sitting thou didst speak against thy brother, and didst lay a scandal against thy mother's son.

21 These things hast thou done, and I was silent.

Thou thoughtest unjustly that I should be like to thee: *but* I will reprove thee, and set before thy face.

22 Understand these things, you that forget God: lest he snatch you *away*, and there be none to deliver you.

23 The sacrifice of praise shall glorify me: and there is the way by which I will shew him the salvation of God.

PSALM 50

Miserere

The repentance and confession of David after his sin. The fourth penitential psalm.

1 Unto the end. A psalm of David, 2 when Nathan the prophet came to him, after he had sinned with Bethsabee. [2 Kings, 12.]

3 HAVE mercy on me, O God, according to thy great mercy.

And according to the multitude of thy tender mercies, blot out my iniquity.

4 Wash me yet more from my iniquity, and cleanse me from my sin.

5 For I know my iniquity, and my sin is always before me.

6 To thee only have I sinned, and have done evil before thee: [1] that thou mayst be justified in thy words, and mayst overcome when thou art judged.

PSALM 50. [1] Rom. 3, 4. [2] Lev. 14; Num. 19.

7 For behold I was conceived in iniquities: and in sins did my mother conceive me.

8 For behold thou hast loved truth: the uncertain and hidden things of thy wisdom thou hast made manifest to me.

9 [2] Thou shalt sprinkle me with hyssop, and I shall be cleansed: thou shalt wash me, and I shall be made whiter than snow.

10 To my hearing thou shalt give joy and gladness: and the bones that have been humbled shall rejoice.

11 Turn away thy face from my sins: and blot out all my iniquities.

12 Create a clean heart in me, O God: and renew a right spirit within my bowels.

13 Cast me not away from thy face: and take not thy holy spirit from me.

14 Restore unto me the joy of thy salvation: and strengthen me with a perfect spirit.

15 I will teach the unjust thy ways: and the wicked shall be converted to thee.

16 Deliver me from blood, O God, thou God of my salvation: and my tongue shall extol thy justice.

17 O Lord, thou wilt open my lips: and my mouth shall declare thy praise.

18 For if thou hadst desired sacrifice, I would indeed have given it: with burnt offerings thou wilt not be delighted.

19 A sacrifice to God is an afflicted spirit: a contrite and humbled heart, O God, thou wilt not despise.

20 Deal favourably, O Lord, in thy good will with Sion; that the walls of Jerusalem may be built up.

21 Then shalt thou accept the sacrifice of justice, oblations and whole burnt offerings: then shall they lay calves upon thy altar.

PSALM 51

Quid gloriaris

David condemneth the wickedness of Doeg, and foretelleth his destruction.

1 Unto the end. Understanding for David, 2 when Doeg the Edomite came and told Saul: David went to the house of Achimelech. [1 Kings, 22, 9.]

3 WHY dost thou glory in malice, thou that art mighty in iniquity?

4 All the day long thy tongue hath devised injustices: as a sharp razor, thou hast wrought deceit.

5 Thou hast loved malice more than goodness: and iniquity rather than to speak righteousness.

6 Thou hast loved all the words of ruin, O deceitful tongue.

7 Therefore will God destroy thee for ever. He will pluck thee out, and remove thee from thy dwelling place: and thy root out of the land of the living.

8 The just shall see and fear, and shall laugh at him, and say: 9 Behold the man that made not God his helper:

But trusted in the abundance of his riches, and prevailed in his vanity.

10 But I, as a fruitful olive tree in the house of God, have hoped in the mercy of God for ever, yea for ever and ever.

11 I will praise thee for ever, because thou hast done it: and I will wait on thy name, for it is good in the sight of thy saints.

PSALM 52

Dixit insipiens (2)

The general corruption of man before the coming of Christ.

1 Unto the end. For Maeleth. Understandings to David.

T HE fool said in his heart: [1] There is no God.

2 They are corrupted, and become abominable in iniquities: there is none that doth good.

3 God looked down from heaven on the children of men: to see if there were any that did understand, or did seek God.

4 [2] All have gone aside, they are become unprofitable together: there is none that doth good, no not one.

5 Shall not all the workers of iniquity know, who eat up my people as they eat bread?

6 They have not called upon God: there have they trembled for fear, where there was no fear.

For God hath scattered the bones of them that please men: they have been confounded, because God hath despised them.

7 Who will give out of Sion the salvation of Israel? When God shall bring back the captivity of his people, Jacob shall rejoice, and Israel shall be glad.

PSALM 53

Deus, in nomine tuo

A prayer for help in distress.

1 Unto the end. In verses. Understanding for David. 2 When the men of Ziph had come and said to Saul: Is not David hidden with us? [1 Kings, 23, 19.]

3 S AVE me, O God, by thy name: and judge me in thy strength.

4 O God, hear my prayer: give ear to the word of my mouth.

5 For strangers have risen up against me, and the mighty have sought after

my soul: and they have not set God before their eyes.

6 For behold God is my helper: and the Lord is the protector of my soul.

7 Turn back the evils upon my enemies; and cut them off in thy truth.

8 I will freely sacrifice to thee, and will give praise, O God, to thy name: because it is good:

9 For thou hast delivered me out of all trouble: and my eye hath looked down upon my enemies.

PSALM 54

Exaudi, Deus

A prayer of a just man under persecution from the wicked. It agrees to Christ persecuted by the Jews, and betrayed by Judas.

1 Unto the end. In verses. Understanding for David.

2 H EAR, O God, my prayer and despise not my supplication: 3 be attentive to me and hear me.

I am grieved in my exercise; and am troubled, 4 at the voice of the enemy, and at the tribulation of the sinner.

For they have cast iniquities upon me: and in wrath they were troublesome to me.

5 My heart is troubled within me: and the fear of death is fallen upon me.

6 Fear and trembling are come upon me: and darkness hath covered me.

7 And I said: Who will give me wings like a dove, and I will fly and be at rest?

8 Lo, I have gone far off, flying away; and I abode in the wilderness.

9 I waited for him that hath saved me from pusillanimity of spirit and a storm.

10 Cast down, O Lord, *and* divide their tongues: for I have seen iniquity and contradiction in the city.

11 Day and night shall iniquity surround it upon its walls: and in the midst thereof are labour 12 and injustice.

And usury and deceit have not departed from its streets.

13 For if my enemy had reviled me, I would verily have borne with it.

And if he that hated me had spoken great things against me, I would perhaps have hidden myself from him.

14 But thou a man of one mind, my guide, and my familiar,

PSALM 52. [1] Ps. 13, 1. [2] Rom. 3, 12.

PSALM 52. Ver. 1. *Maeleth*, or Machalath. A musical instrument, or a chorus of musicians, for St. Jerome renders it, *per chorum*.

Ver. 6. *God hath scattered the bones of them that please men.* That is, God has brought to nothing the strength of all those that seek to please men, to the prejudice of their duty to their Maker.

15 Who didst take sweet meats together with me: in the house of God we walked with consent.

16 Let death come upon them: and let them go down alive into hell.

For there is wickedness in their dwellings: in the midst of them.

17 But I have cried to God: and the Lord will save me.

18 Evening and morning, and at noon, I will speak and declare: and he shall hear my voice.

19 He shall redeem my soul in peace from them that draw near to me: for among many they were with me.

20 God shall hear: and the Eternal shall humble them.

For there is no change with them, and they have not feared God: 21 he hath stretched forth his hand to repay.

They have defiled his covenant, 22 they are divided by the wrath of his countenance: and his heart hath drawn near.

His words are smoother than oil, and the same are darts.

23 ¹ Cast thy care upon the Lord, and he shall sustain thee: he shall not suffer the just to waver for ever.

24 But thou, O God, shalt bring them down into the pit of destruction.

Bloody and deceitful men shall not live out half their days. But I will trust in thee, O Lord.

PSALM 55
Miserere mei, Deus
A prayer of David in danger and distress.

1 Unto the end. For a people that is removed at a distance from the sanctuary. For David, for an inscription of a title (*or pillar*) when the Philistines held him in Geth.

2 HAVE mercy on me, O God, for man hath trodden me under

PSALM 54. ¹ Matt. 6, 25; Luke, 12, 22; 1 Peter, 5, 7.

PSALM 54. Ver. 16. *Let death come upon them.* This and such like imprecations which occur in the psalms are delivered prophetically; that is, by way of foretelling the punishments which shall fall upon the wicked from divine justice, and approving the righteous ways of God: but not by way of ill will, or uncharitable curses, which the law of God disallows.
Ver. 19. *Among many.* That is, they that *drew near* to attack me were *many* in company, all combined to fight against me.
Ver. 22. *They are divided.* Dispersed, scattered, and brought to nothing by the wrath of God, who looks with indignation on their wicked and deceitful ways.
PSALM 55. Ver. 4. *The height of the day.* That is, even at noonday, when the sun is the highest, I am still in danger.
Ver. 5. *My words.* The words or promises God has made in my favour.
Ver. 8. *For nothing shalt thou save them.* That is, since they lie in wait to ruin my soul, thou shalt for no consideration favour or assist them, but execute thy justice upon them.
PSALM 56. Ver. 1. *Destroy not.* Suffer me not to be destroyed.

foot. All the day long he hath afflicted me fighting against me.

3 My enemies have trodden on me all the day long; for they are many that make war against me.

4 From the height of the day I shall fear: but I will trust in thee.

5 In God I will praise my words, in God I have put my trust: I will not fear what flesh can do against me.

6 All the day long they detested my words: all their thoughts *were* against me unto evil.

7 They will dwell and hide *themselves:* they will watch my heel.

As they have waited for my soul, 8 for nothing shalt thou save them: in thy anger thou shalt break the people in pieces.

O God, 9 I have declared to thee my life: thou hast set my tears in thy sight,

As also in thy promise. 10 Then shall my enemies be turned back.

In what day soever I shall call upon thee, behold I know thou art my God.

11 In God will I praise the word, in the Lord will I praise *his* speech. In God have I hoped: I will not fear what man can do to me.

12 In me, O God, are vows to thee, which I will pay, praises to thee:

13 Because thou hast delivered my soul from death, my feet from falling: that I may please in the sight of God, in the light of the living.

PSALM 56
Miserere mei, Deus
The prophet prays in his affliction, and praises God for his delivery.

1 Unto the end. Destroy not. For David, for an inscription of a title, when he fled from Saul into the cave. [1 Kings, 24.]

2 HAVE mercy on me, O God, have mercy on me: for my soul trusteth in thee.

And in the shadow of thy wings will I hope, until iniquity pass away.

3 I will cry to God the most High: to God who hath done good to me.

4 He hath sent from heaven and delivered me: he hath made them a reproach that trod upon me.

God hath sent his mercy and his truth: 5 and he hath delivered my soul from the midst of the young lions. I slept troubled.

The sons of men, whose teeth are weapons and arrows, and their tongue a sharp sword.

6 Be thou exalted, O God, above the heavens, and thy glory above all the earth.

7 They prepared a snare for my feet: and thy bowed down my soul.

They dug a pit before my face: and they are fallen into it.

8 My heart is ready, O God, my heart is ready: I will sing, and rehearse a psalm.

9 Arise, O my glory. Arise psaltery and harp: I will arise early.

10 I will give praise to thee, O Lord, among the people: I will sing a psalm to thee among the nations.

11 For thy mercy is magnified even to the heavens: and thy truth unto the clouds.

12 Be thou exalted, O God, above the heavens: and thy glory above all the earth.

PSALM 57
Si vere utique

David reproveth the wicked and foretelleth their punishment.

1 Unto the end. Destroy not. For David, for an inscription of a title.

2 IF in very deed you speak justice: judge right things, ye sons of men.

3 For in your heart you work iniquity: your hands forge injustice in the earth.

4 The wicked are alienated from the womb; they have gone astray from the womb: they have spoken false things.

5 Their madness is according to the likeness of a serpent: like the deaf asp that stoppeth her ears:

6 Which will not hear the voice of the charmers; nor of the wizard that charmeth wisely.

7 God shall break in pieces their teeth in their mouth: the Lord shall break the grinders of the lions.

8 They shall come to nothing, like water running down: he hath bent his bow till they be weakened.

9 Like wax that melteth they shall be taken away: fire hath fallen on them, and they shall not see the sun.

10 Before your thorns could know the brier; he swalloweth them up, as alive, in his wrath.

11 The just shall rejoice when he shall see the revenge: he shall wash his hands in the blood of the sinner.

12 And man shall say: If indeed there be fruit to the just: there is indeed a God that judgeth them on the earth.

PSALM 58
Eripe me

A prayer to be delivered from the wicked, with confidence in God's help and protection. It agrees to Christ and his enemies the Jews.

1 Unto the end. Destroy not. For David for an inscription of a title, when Saul sent and watched his house to kill him. [1 Kings, 19.]

2 DELIVER me from my enemies, O my God; and defend me from them that rise up against me.

3 Deliver me from them that work iniquity: and save me from bloody men.

4 For behold they have caught my soul: the mighty have rushed in upon me.

5 Neither is it my iniquity, nor my sin, O Lord: without iniquity have I run, and directed *my steps.*

6 Rise up thou to meet me, and behold: even thou, O Lord, the God of hosts, the God of Israel.

Attend to visit all the nations: have no mercy on all them that work iniquity.

7 They shall return at evening, and shall suffer hunger like dogs: and shall go round about the city.

8 Behold they shall speak with their mouth, and a sword *is* in their lips: for, Who, *say they,* hath heard *us?*

9 But thou, O Lord, shalt laugh at them: thou shalt bring all the nations to nothing.

10 I will keep my strength to thee: for thou art my protector. 11 My God, his mercy shall prevent me.

12 God shall let me see over my enemies: slay them not, lest at any time my people forget.

Scatter them by thy power: and bring them down, O Lord, my protector:

13 *For* the sin of their mouth, and the word of their lips: and let them be taken in their pride.

And for their cursing and lying they shall be talked of 14 when they are consumed, when they are consumed by *thy* wrath: and they shall be no more.

And they shall know that God will rule Jacob and all the ends of the earth.

15 They shall return at evening and shall suffer hunger like dogs: and shall go round about the city.

16 They shall be scattered abroad to eat: and shall murmur if they be not filled.

17 But I will sing thy strength: and will extol thy mercy in the morning.

For thou art become my support and my refuge, in the day of my trouble.

18 Unto thee, O my helper, will I sing, for thou art God my defence: My God, my mercy.

PSALM 59
Deus, repulisti nos

After many afflictions, the church of Christ shall prevail.

PSALM 57. Ver. 10. *Before your thorns.* That is, before your thorns grow up, so as to become strong briers, they shall be overtaken and consumed by divine justice, swallowing them up, *as it were, alive in his wrath.*

Ver. 11. *Shall wash his hands.* Shall applaud the justice of God, and take occasion from the consideration of the punishment of the wicked to wash and cleanse his hands from sin.

1 Unto the end. For them that shall be changed. For the inscription of a title, to David himself, for doctrine, 2 when he set fire to Mesopotamia of Syria and Sobal; and Joab returned and slew of Edom, in the vale of the saltpits, twelve thousand men. [2 Kings, 8.]

3 O GOD, thou hast cast us off, and hast destroyed us; thou hast been angry, and hast had mercy on us.

4 Thou hast moved the earth, and hast troubled it: heal thou the breaches thereof, for it has been moved.

5 Thou hast shewn thy people hard things: thou hast made us drink the wine of sorrow.

6 Thou hast given a warning to them that fear thee: that they may flee from before the bow,

That thy beloved may be delivered.
7 Save me with thy right hand, and hear me.

8 God hath spoken in his holy *place*: I will rejoice, and I will divide Sichem; and will mete out the vale of tabernacles.

9 Galaad is mine, and Manasses is mine: and Ephraim *is* the strength of my head.

Juda is my king: 10 Moab is the pot of my hope.

Into Edom will I stretch out my shoe: to me the foreigners are made subject.

11 Who will bring me into the strong city? Who will lead me into Edom?

12 Wilt not thou, O God, who hast cast us off? And wilt not thou, O God, go out with our armies?

13 Give us help from trouble: for vain is the salvation of man.

14 Through God we shall do mightily: and he shall bring to nothing them that afflict us.

PSALM 60
Exaudi, Deus
A prayer for the coming of the kingdom of Christ, which shall have no end.

1 Unto the end. In hymns, for David.

2 HEAR, O God, my supplication: be attentive to my prayer.

3 To thee have I cried from the ends

PSALM 61. [1] Matt. 16, 27; Rom. 2, 6; 1 Cor. 3, 8; Gal. 6, 5.

PSALM 59. Ver. 10. *The pot of my hope.* Or *my watering pot.* That is, a vessel for meaner uses, by being reduced to serve me, even in the meanest employments.—*Foreigners.* So the Philistines are called, who had no kindred with the Israelites; whereas the Edomites, Moabites, &c., were originally of the same family.

PSALM 61. Ver. 10. *Are liars in the balances.* They are so vain and light that, if they are put into the scales, they will be found to be of no weight and to be mere lies, deceit, and vanity. Or, *They are liars in their balances,* by weighing things by false weights, and preferring the temporal before the eternal.

of the earth: when my heart was in anguish, thou hast exalted me on a rock.

Thou hast conducted me. 4 For thou hast been my hope: a tower of strength against the face of the enemy.

5 In thy tabernacle I shall dwell for ever: I shall be protected under the covert of thy wings.

6 For thou, my God, hast heard my prayer: thou hast given an inheritance to them that fear thy name.

7 Thou wilt add days to the days of the king: his years even to generation and generation.

8 He abideth for ever in the sight of God. His mercy and truth who shall search?

9 So will I sing a psalm to thy name for ever and ever: that I may pay my vows from day to day.

PSALM 61
Nonne Deo
The prophet encourageth himself and all others to trust in God, and serve him.

1 Unto the end. For Idithun, a psalm of David.

2 SHALL not my soul be subject to God? For from him is my salvation:

3 For he is my God and my saviour. *He is* my protector; I shall be moved no more.

4 How long do you rush in upon a man? You all kill, as if *you were thrusting down* a leaning wall, and a tottering fence.

5 But they have thought to cast away my price. I am in thirst. They blessed with their mouth, but cursed with their heart.

6 But be thou, O my soul, subject to God: for from him is my patience.

7 For he is my God and my saviour: *he is* my helper, I shall not be moved.

8 In God is my salvation and my glory: *he is* the God of my help, and my hope is in God.

9 Trust in him, all ye congregation of people: pour out your hearts before him. God is our helper for ever.

10 But vain are the sons of men, the sons of men are liars in the balances: that by vanity they may together deceive.

11 Trust not in iniquity, and cover not robberies: if riches abound, set not your heart upon them.

12 God hath spoken once. These two things have I heard, that power belongeth to God, 13 and mercy to thee, O Lord: [1] for thou wilt render to every man according to his works.

PSALM 62

Deus Deus meus, ad te

The prophet aspireth after God.

1 A psalm of David when he was in the desert of Edom.

2 O GOD, my God: to thee do I watch at break of day. For thee my soul hath thirsted. For thee my flesh, O how many ways!

3 In a desert land, and where there is no way and no water: so in the sanctuary have I come before thee, to see thy power and thy glory.

4 For thy mercy is better than lives: thee my lips shall praise.

5 Thus will I bless thee *all* my life long: and in thy name I will lift up my hands.

6 Let my soul be filled as with marrow and fatness: and my mouth shall praise thee with joyful lips.

7 If I have remembered thee upon my bed, I will meditate on thee in the morning: 8 because thou hast been my helper.

And I will rejoice under the covert of thy wings. 9 My soul hath stuck close to thee: thy right hand hath received me.

10 But they have sought my soul in vain: they shall go into the lower parts of the earth:

11 They shall be delivered into the hands of the sword: they shall be the portions of foxes.

12 But the king shall rejoice in God; all they shall be praised that swear by him: because the mouth is stopped of them that speak wicked things.

PSALM 63

Exaudi Deus orationem

A prayer in affliction, with confidence in God that he will bring to nought the machinations of persecutors.

1 Unto the end. A psalm for David.

2 HEAR, O God, my prayer, when I make supplication to thee: deliver my soul from the fear of the enemy.

3 Thou hast protected me from the assembly of the malignant: from the multitudes of the workers of iniquity.

4 For they have whetted their

PSALM 63. Ver. 7. *A deep heart.* That is, crafty, subtle, deep projects and designs; which nevertheless shall not succeed; for God *shall be exalted* in bringing them to nought by his wisdom and power.

Ver. 8. *The arrows of children are their wounds.* That is, the wounds, stripes, or blows, they seek to inflict upon the just, are but like the weak efforts of children's arrows, which can do no execution: and *their tongues,* that is, their speeches against them, come to nothing.

PSALM 64. Ver. 1. *Of the captivity.* That is, the people of the captivity of Babylon. This is not in the Hebrew, but is found in the ancient translation of the Septuagint.

tongues like a sword: they have bent their bow, a bitter thing, 5 to shoot in secret the undefiled.

6 They will shoot at him on a sudden, and will not fear: they are resolute in wickedness.

They have talked of hiding snares; they have said: Who shall see them?

7 They have searched after iniquities: they have failed in their search.

Man shall come to a deep heart: 8 and God shall be exalted.

The arrows of children are their wounds: 9 and their tongues against them are made weak.

All that saw them were troubled; 10 and every man was afraid.

And they declared the works of God: and understood his doings.

11 The just shall rejoice in the Lord, and shall hope in him: and all the upright in heart shall be praised.

PSALM 64

Te decet

God is to be praised in his church, to which all nations shall be called.

1 To the end. A psalm of David. The canticle of Jeremias and Ezechiel to the people of the captivity, when they began to go out.

2 A HYMN, O God, becometh thee in Sion: and a vow shall be paid to thee in Jerusalem.

3 O hear my prayer: all flesh shall come to thee.

4 The words of the wicked have prevailed over us: and thou wilt pardon our transgressions.

5 Blessed is he whom thou hast chosen and taken to thee: he shall dwell in thy courts.

We shall be filled with the good things of thy house: holy is thy temple, 6 wonderful in justice.

Hear us, O God our Saviour, *who art* the hope of all the ends of the earth, and in the sea afar off.

7 Thou who preparest the mountains by thy strength, being girded with power: 8 who troublest the depth of the sea, the noise of its waves.

The Gentiles shall be troubled, 9 and they that dwell in the uttermost borders shall be afraid at thy signs: thou shalt make the outgoings of the morning and of the evening to be joyful.

10 Thou hast visited the earth, and hast plentifully watered it: thou hast many ways enriched it.

The river of God is filled with water: thou hast prepared their food; for so is its preparation.

11 Fill up plentifully the streams thereof; multiply its fruits. It shall spring up and rejoice in its showers.

12 Thou shalt bless the crown of the year of thy goodness: and thy fields shall be filled with plenty.

13 The beautiful places of the wilderness shall grow fat: and the hills shall be girded about with joy.

14 The rams of the flock are clothed: and the vales shall abound with corn. They shall shout; yea, they shall sing a hymn.

PSALM 65
Jubilate Deo
An invitation to praise God.

1 Unto the end. A canticle of a psalm of the resurrection.

SHOUT with joy to God, all the earth: 2 sing ye a psalm to his name: give glory to his praise.

3 Say unto God: How terrible are thy works, O Lord! in the multitude of thy strength thy enemies shall lie to thee.

4 Let all the earth adore thee and sing to thee: let it sing a psalm to thy name.

5 Come and see the works of God; *who* is terrible in his counsels over the sons of men.

6 Who turneth the sea into dry land: in the river they shall pass on foot. There shall we rejoice in him.

7 Who by his power ruleth for ever His eyes behold the nations: let not them that provoke *him* be exalted in themselves.

8 O bless our God, ye Gentiles: and make the voice of his praise to be heard.

9 Who hath set my soul to live: and hath not suffered my feet to be moved.

10 For thou, O God, hast proved us: thou hast tried us by fire, as silver is tried.

11 Thou hast brought us into a net: thou hast laid afflictions on our back: 12 thou hast set men over our heads.

We have passed through fire and water: and thou hast brought us out into a refreshment.

13 I will go into thy house with burnt offerings: I will pay thee my vows, 14 which my lips have uttered.

And my mouth hath spoken, when I was in trouble.

15 I will offer up to thee holocausts full of marrow, with burnt offerings of rams: I will offer to thee bullocks with goats.

16 Come and hear, all ye that fear God: and I will tell you what great things he hath done for my soul.

17 I cried to him with my mouth: and I extolled him with my tongue.

18 If I have looked at iniquity in my heart, the Lord will not hear me.

19 Therefore hath God heard me, and hath attended to the voice of my supplication.

20 Blessed be God, who hath not turned away my prayer, nor his mercy from me.

PSALM 66
Deus misereatur
A prayer for the propagation of the church.

1 Unto the end. In hymns, a psalm of a canticle for David.

MAY God have mercy on us, and bless us: may he cause the light of his countenance to shine upon us: and may he have mercy on us.

3 That we may know thy way upon earth: thy salvation in all nations.

4 Let people confess to thee, O God: let all people give praise to thee.

5 Let the nations be glad and rejoice: for thou judgest the people with justice, and directest the nations upon earth.

6 Let the people, O God, confess to thee; let all the people give praise to thee: 7 the earth hath yielded her fruit:

May God, our God bless us. 8 May God bless us: and all the ends of the earth fear him.

PSALM 67
Exurgat Deus
The glorious establishment of the church of the New Testament, prefigured by the benefits bestowed on the people of Israel.

1 Unto the end. A psalm of a canticle for David himself.

LET God arise, and let his enemies be scattered: and let them that hate him flee from before his face.

3 As smoke vanisheth, so let them vanish away: as wax melteth before the fire, so let the wicked perish at the presence of God.

4 And let the just feast and rejoice before God: and be delighted with gladness.

5 Sing ye to God: sing a psalm to his name: make a way for him who ascendeth upon the west. The Lord is his name.

Rejoice ye before him: *but the wicked* shall be troubled at his presence. 6 *who is* the father of orphans, and the judge of widows.

God in his holy place: 7 God who maketh *men* of one manner to dwell in a house.

PSALM 67. Ver. 5. *Who ascendeth upon the west. Super occasum.* St. Gregory understands it of Christ, who after his going down, like the sun, in the west, by his passion and death, ascended more glorious, and carried all before him. St. Jerome renders it, *who ascendeth,* or cometh up, *through the deserts.*
Ver. 7. *Of one manner.* That is, agreeing in faith, unanimous in love, and following the same manner of discipline. It is verified in the

Who bringeth out them that were bound in strength; in like manner them that provoke, that dwell in sepulchres.

8 O God, when thou didst go forth in the sight of thy people, when thou didst pass through the desert:

9 The earth was moved, and the heavens dropped at the presence of the God of Sina, at the presence of the God of Israel.

10 Thou shalt set aside for thy inheritance a free rain, O God; and it was weakened, but thou hast made it perfect.

11 In it shall thy animals dwell; in thy sweetness, O God, thou hast provided for the poor.

12 The Lord shall give the word to them that preach good tidings with great power.

13 The king of powers *is* of the beloved, of the beloved; and the beauty of the house shall divide spoils.

14 If you sleep among the midst of lots, *you shall be as the* wings of a dove covered with silver, and the hinder parts of her back with the paleness of gold.

15 When he that is in heaven appointeth kings over her, they shall be whited with snow in Selmon. 16 The mountain of God is a fat mountain:

A curdled mountain, a fat mountain.

17 Why suspect, ye curdled mountains?

A mountain in which God is well pleased to dwell: for there the Lord shall dwell unto the end.

18 The chariot of God is attended by ten thousands; thousands of them that rejoice. The Lord is among them in Sina, in the holy place.

19 Thou hast ascended on high; thou hast led captivity captive; thou hast received gifts in men.

Yea for those also that do not believe, the dwelling of the Lord God.

20 Blessed be the Lord day by day: the God of our salvation will make our journey prosperous to us.

21 Our God is the God of salvation: and of the Lord, of the Lord, are the issues from death.

22 But God shall break the heads of his enemies: the hairy crown of them that walk on in their sins.

23 The Lord said: I will turn *them* from Basan; I will turn them into the depth of the sea:

24 That thy foot may be dipped in the blood of thy enemies; the tongue of thy dogs be red with the same.

25 They have seen thy goings, O God, the goings of my God: of my king who is in *his* sanctuary.

26 Princes went before joined with singers, in the midst of young damsels playing on timbrels.

27 In the churches bless ye God the Lord, from the fountains of Israel.

28 There *is* Benjamin a youth, in ecstasy of mind.

The princes of Juda *are* their leaders: the princes of Zabulon, the princes of Nephthali.

---

servants of God living together in his *house*, which is the church (1 Tim. 3, 5).—*Them that were bound.* The power and mercy of God appears in his bringing out of their captivity those that were strongly *bound* in their sins: and in restoring to his grace those whose behaviour had been most *provoking*; and who by their evil habits were not only dead, but buried in their *sepulchres*.

Ver. 10. *A free rain.* The manna, which rained plentifully from heaven, in favour of God's *inheritance*, that is, of his people Israel: which *was weakened* indeed under a variety of afflictions, but was *made perfect* by God; that is, was still supported by divine providence, and brought on to the promised land. It agrees particularly to the church of Christ, his true *inheritance*, which is plentifully watered with the *free rain* of heavenly grace; and through many *infirmities*, that is, crosses and tribulations, is *made perfect*, and fitted for eternal glory.

Ver. 11. *In it shall thy animals dwell.* That is, in this church, which is thy fold and thy *inheritance*, shall thy *animals*, thy sheep, *dwell;* where thou hast plentifully provided for them.

Ver. 12. *To them that preach good tidings. Evangelizantibus.* That is, to the preachers of the gospel; who receiving the *word* from the Lord, shall with great power and efficacy preach throughout the world the glad tidings of a Saviour, and of eternal salvation through him.

Ver. 13. *The king of powers.* That is, the mighty King, the Lord of hosts, is *of the beloved, of the beloved;* that is, is on the side of Christ, *his most beloved* son: and his *beautiful house*, viz., the church, in which God dwells forever, shall by her spiritual conquests *divide the spoils* of many nations. The Hebrew (as it now stands pointed) is thus rendered, *The kings of armies have fled, they have fled, and she that dwells*

at home (or *the beauty of the house*) *shall divide the spoils.*

Ver. 14. *If you sleep among the midst of lots. Inter medios cleros.* That is, in such dangers and persecutions, as if your enemies were casting *lots* for your goods and persons: or in the midst of the *lots* (*inter medios terminos*, as St. Jerome renders it), that is, upon the very bounds or borders of the dominions of your enemies: you shall be secure nevertheless under the divine protection and shall be enabled to fly away, like a dove, with glittering wings and feathers shining like the palest and most precious gold; that is, with great increase of virtue, and glowing with the fervour of charity.

Ver. 15. *Kings over her.* That is, pastors and rulers over his church, the apostles and their successors. Then by their ministry shall men be made whiter than the snow which lies on the top of the high mountain Selmon.

Ver. 16. *The mountain of God.* The church, which (Isai. 2, 2) is called *The mountain of the house of the Lord upon the top of mountains.* It is here called a *fat* and *a curdled mountain;* that is to say, most fruitful, and enriched by the spiritual gifts and graces of the Holy Ghost.

Ver. 17. *Why suspect, ye curdled mountains!* Why do you suppose or imagine there may be any other such curdled mountains? You are mistaken: the mountain thus favoured by God is but one; and this same he has chosen for his dwelling for ever.

Ver. 18. *The chariot of God.* God descending to give his law on mount Sina: as also Jesus Christ his Son, ascending into heaven, to send from thence the Holy Ghost, to punish his new law, is attended with ten thousands, that is, with an innumerable multitude of joyful angels.

Ver. 19. *Led captivity captive.* Carrying away with thee to heaven those who before had been

29 Command thy strength, O God: confirm, O God, what thou hast wrought in us.

30 From thy temple in Jerusalem, kings shall offer presents to thee.

31 Rebuke the wild beasts of the reeds, the congregation of bulls with the kine of the people; *who seek* to exclude them who are tried with silver.

Scatter thou the nations that delight in wars. 32 Ambassadors shall come out of Egypt: Ethiopia shall soon stretch out her hands to God.

33 Sing to God, ye kingdoms of the earth: sing ye to the Lord:

Sing ye to God, 34 who mounteth above the heaven of heavens, to the east.

Behold he will give to his voice the voice of power. 35 Give ye glory to God for Israel: his magnificence, and his power *is* in the clouds.

36 God is wonderful in his saints: the God of Israel is he who will give power and strength to his people. Blessed be God.

PSALM 68
Salvum me fac, Deus

Christ in his passion declareth the greatness of his sufferings, and the malice of his persecutors the Jews. He foretelleth their reprobation.

1 Unto the end. For them that shall be changed. For David.

2 SAVE me, O God: for the waters are come in even unto my soul.

3 I stick fast in the mire of the deep: and there is no sure standing.

PSALM 68. [1] John, 2, 17. [2] Rom. 15, 3.

the captives of Satan; and receiving from God the Father gifts to be distributed to men; even to those who were before unbelievers.

Ver. 21. *The issues from death.* The Lord alone is master of the *issues*, by which we may escape *from death.*

Ver. 23. *I will turn them from Basan.* I will cast out my enemies from their rich possessions, signified by *Basan,* a fruitful country; and I will drive them *into the depth of the sea:* and make such a slaughter of them, that the feet of my servants may be dyed in their blood.

Ver. 25. *Thy goings.* Thy ways, thy proceedings, by which thou didst formerly take possession of the promised land in favour of thy people; and shalt afterwards of the whole world, which thou shalt subdue to thy Son.

Ver. 26. *Princes.* The apostles, the first converters of nations; attended by numbers of perfect souls, singing the divine praises, and virgins consecrated to God.

Ver. 27. *From the fountains of Israel.* From whom both Christ and his apostles sprung. By Benjamin, the holy fathers on this place understand St. Paul, who was of that tribe, named here *a youth,* because he was the last called to the apostleship. By the princes of Juda, Zabulon, and Nephthali, we may understand the other apostles, who were of the tribe of Juda; or of the tribes of Zabulon, and Nephthali, where our Lord began to preach (Matt 4, 13).

Ver. 29. *Command thy strength.* Give orders that thy strength may be always with us.

Ver. 31. *Rebuke the wild beasts of the reeds:* or *the wild beasts,* which lie hid in the *reeds.*

I am come into the depth of the sea: and a tempest hath overwhelmed me.

4 I have laboured with crying; my jaws are become hoarse: my eyes have failed, whilst I hope in my God.

5 They are multiplied above the hairs of my head, who hate me without cause.

My enemies are grown strong who have wrongfully persecuted me: then did I pay that which I took not away.

6 O God, thou knowest my foolishness: and my offences are not hidden from thee:

7 Let not them be ashamed for me, who look for thee, O Lord, the Lord of hosts.

Let them not be confounded on my account, who seek thee, O God of Israel.

8 Because for thy sake I have borne reproach: shame hath covered my face.

9 I am become a stranger to my brethren, and an alien to the sons of my mother.

10 [1] For the zeal of thy house hath eaten me up: [2] and the reproaches of them that reproached thee are fallen upon me.

11 And I covered my soul in fasting: and it was made a reproach to me.

12 And I made haircloth my garment: and I became a byword to them.

13 They that sat in the gate spoke against me: and they that drank wine made me their song.

14 But as for me, my prayer *is* to thee, O Lord; *for* the time of *thy* good pleasure, O God.

That is, the devils, who hide themselves in order to surprise their prey. Or, by *wild beasts,* are here understood persecutors, who, for all their attempts against the Church, are but as *weak reeds,* which cannot prevail against them who are supported by the strength of the Almighty. The same are also called *the congregation of bulls* (from their rage against the Church) who assemble together all their *kine,* that is, the people their subjects, to exclude if they can, from Christ and his inheritance, his constant confessors, who are like silver tried by fire.

Ver. 32. *Ambassadors shall come.* It is a prophecy of the conversion of the Gentiles, and by name of the Egyptians and Ethiopians.

Ver. 34. *To the east.* From mount Olivet, which is on the east side of Jerusalem.—*The voice of power.* That is, he will make *his voice to be a powerful voice;* by calling from death to life, such as were dead in mortal sin: as at the last day he will by the power of his voice call all the dead from their graves.

PSALM 68. Ver. 1. *For them that shall be changed.* A psalm for Christian converts, to remember the passion of Christ.

Ver. 2. *The waters.* Of afflictions and sorrows. *My soul is sorrowful even unto death* (Matt. 26, 38).

Ver. 5. *I pay that which I took not away.* Christ in his passion made restitution of what he had not taken away, by suffering the punishment due to our sins, and so repairing the injury we had done to God.

Ver. 6. *My foolishness and my offences.* The transgressions which my enemies impute to me: or the follies and sins of men, which I have taken upon myself.

In the multitude of thy mercy hear me, in the truth of thy salvation.

15 Draw me out of the mire, that I may not stick fast: deliver me from them that hate me, and out of the deep waters.

16 Let not the tempest of water drown me, nor the deep swallow me up: and let not the pit shut her mouth upon me.

17 Hear me, O Lord, for thy mercy is kind; look upon me according to the multitude of thy tender mercies.

18 And turn not away thy face from thy servant: for I am in trouble. Hear me speedily.

19 Attend to my soul, and deliver it: save me because of my enemies.

20 Thou knowest my reproach, and my confusion, and my shame.

21 In thy sight are all they that afflict me: my heart hath expected reproach and misery.

And I looked for one that would grieve together with me, but there was none: and for one that would comfort me, and I found none.

22 ³ And they gave me gall for my food: and in my thirst they gave me vinegar to drink.

23 ⁴ Let their table become as a snare before them, and a recompense, and a stumbling-block.

24 Let their eyes be darkened that they see not: and their back bend thou down always.

25 Pour out thy indignation upon them: and let thy wrathful anger take hold of them.

26 ⁵ Let their habitation be made desolate: and let there be none to dwell in their tabernacles.

27 Because they have persecuted him whom thou hast smitten: and they have added to the grief of my wounds.

28 Add thou iniquity upon their iniquity: and let them not come into thy justice.

29 Let them be blotted out of the book of the living: and with the just let them not be written.

30 But I am poor and sorrowful: thy salvation, O God, hath set me up.

31 I will praise the name of God with a canticle: and I will magnify him with praise.

32 And it shall please God better than a young calf, that bringeth forth horns and hoofs.

33 Let the poor see and rejoice: seek ye God, and your soul shall live.

34 For the Lord hath heard the poor: and hath not despised his prisoners.

35 Let the heavens and the earth praise him: the sea, and every thing that creepeth therein.

36 For God will save Sion: and the cities of Juda shall be built up.

And they shall dwell there, and acquire it by inheritance.

37 And the seed of his servants shall possess it: and they that love his name shall dwell therein.

PSALM 69

Deus in adjutorium

A prayer in persecution.

1 Unto the end. A psalm for David, to bring to remembrance that the Lord saved him.

2 O GOD, come to my assistance; O Lord, make haste to help me.

3 Let them be confounded and ashamed that seek my soul.

4 Let them be turned backward and blush for shame, that desire evils to me.

Let them be presently turned away blushing for shame, that say to me: 'Tis well, 'tis well.

5 Let all that seek thee rejoice and be glad in thee. And let such as love thy salvation say always: The Lord be magnified.

6 But I am needy and poor: O God, help me.

Thou art my helper and my deliverer: O Lord, make no delay.

PSALM 70

In te, Domine

A prayer for perseverance.

1 A psalm for David. Of the sons of Jonadab, and the former captives.

IN thee, O Lord, I have hoped: let me never be put to confusion. 2 Deliver me in thy justice and rescue me.

Incline thy ear unto me, and save me.

3 Be thou unto me a God, a protector, and a place of strength: that thou mayst make me safe.

For thou art my firmament and my refuge.

³ Matt. 27, 48.   ⁴ Rom. 11, 9.   ⁵ Acts, 1, 20.

Ver. 23. *Let their table become as a snare.* What here follows in the style of an imprecation, is a prophecy of the wretched state to which the Jews should be reduced in punishment of their wilful obstinacy.

Ver. 36. *Sion.* The catholic church. *The cities of Juda.* Her places of worship, which shall be established throughout the world. And *there,* namely, in this church of Christ, shall his servants dwell.

PSALM 69. Ver. 4. *'Tis well, 'tis well. Euge, euge.* St. Jerome renders it, *vah, vah!* which is the voice of one insulting and deriding. Some understand it as a detestation of deceitful flatterers.

PSALM 70. Ver. 1. *Of the sons of Jonadab.* The Rechabites, of whom see Jer. 35. By this addition of the seventy-two interpreters, we gather that this psalm was usually sung in the synagogue, in the person of the Rechabites, and of those who were first carried away into captivity.

4 Deliver me, O my God, out of the hand of the sinner, and out of the hand of the transgressor of the law and of the unjust.

5 For thou art my patience, O Lord: my hope, O Lord, from my youth.

6 By thee have I been confirmed from the womb: from my mother's womb thou art my protector.

Of thee shall I continually sing. 7 I am become unto many as a wonder: but thou art a strong helper.

8 Let my mouth be filled with praise, that I may sing thy glory: thy greatness all the day long.

9 Cast me not off in the time of old age: when my strength shall fail, do not thou forsake me.

10 For my enemies have spoken against me: and they that watched my soul have consulted together,

11 Saying: God hath forsaken him. Pursue and take him, for there is none to deliver him.

12 O God, be not thou far from me: O my God, make haste to my help.

13 Let them be confounded and come to nothing that detract my soul: let them be covered with confusion and shame that seek my hurt.

14 But I will always hope, and will add to all thy praise.

15 My mouth shall shew forth thy justice: thy salvation all the day long. Because I have not known learning,

16 I will enter into the powers of the Lord: O Lord, I will be mindful of thy justice alone.

17 Thou hast taught me, O God, from my youth: and till now I will declare thy wonderful works.

18 And unto old age and grey hairs: O God, forsake me not,

Until I shew forth thy arm to all the generation that is to come:

Thy power, 19 and thy justice, O God, even to the highest great things thou hast done: O God, who is like to thee?

20 How great troubles hast thou shewn me, many and grievous: and turning thou hast brought me to life, and hast brought me back again from the depths of the earth.

21 Thou hast multiplied thy magnificence; and turning *to me* thou hast comforted me.

22 For I will also confess to thee thy truth with the instruments of psaltery.

Ver. 15. *Learning.* As much as to say, I build not upon human learning, but only on the power and justice of God.

PSALM 71. Ver. 16. *A firmament on the earth.* This may be understood of the church of Christ, ever firm and visible, and of the flourishing condition of its congregation.

O God, I will sing to thee with the harp, thou holy one of Israel.

23 My lips shall greatly rejoice, when I shall sing to thee: and my soul which thou hast redeemed.

24 Yea and my tongue shall meditate on thy justice all the day: when they shall be confounded and put to shame that seek evils to me.

PSALM 71

Deus, judicium tuum

A prophecy of the coming of Christ, and of his kingdom: prefigured by Solomon and his happy reign.

1 A psalm on Solomon.

2 GIVE to the king thy judgment, O God: and to the king's son thy justice:

To judge thy people with justice, and thy poor with judgment.

3 Let the mountains receive peace for the people: and the hills justice.

4 He shall judge the poor of the people: and he shall save the children of the poor: and he shall humble the oppressor.

5 And he shall continue with the sun, and before the moon, throughout all generations.

6 He shall come down like rain upon the fleece: and as showers falling gently upon the earth.

7 In his days shall justice spring up, and abundance of peace, till the moon be taken away.

8 And he shall rule from sea to sea: and from the river unto the ends of the earth.

9 Before him the Ethiopians shall fall down: and his enemies shall lick the ground.

10 The kings of Tharsis and the islands shall offer presents: the kings of the Arabians and of Saba shall bring gifts.

11 And all kings of the earth shall adore him: all nations shall serve him.

12 For he shall deliver the poor from the mighty: and the needy that had no helper.

13 He shall spare the poor and needy: and he shall save the souls of the poor.

14 He shall redeem their souls from usuries and iniquity: and their names shall be honourable in his sight.

15 And he shall live, and to him shall be given of the gold of Arabia. For him they shall always adore: they shall bless him all the day.

16 And there shall be a firmament on the earth on the tops of mountains: above Libanus shall the fruit thereof

be exalted. And *they* of the city shall flourish like the grass of the earth.

17 Let his name be blessed for evermore: his name continueth before the sun.

And in him shall all the tribes of the earth be blessed: all nations shall magnify him.

18 Blessed be the Lord, the God of Israel who alone doth wonderful things.

19 And blessed be the name of his majesty for ever: and the whole earth shall be filled with his majesty. So be it. So be it.

20 The praises of David, the son of Jesse, are ended.

PSALM 72

Quam bonus Israel Deus

The temptation of the weak, upon seeing the prosperity of the wicked, is overcome by the consideration of the justice of God, who will quickly render to every one according to his works.

1 A psalm for Asaph.

HOW good is God to Israel: to them that are of a right heart!

2 But my feet were almost moved: my steps had wellnigh slipped.

3 Because I had a zeal on occasion of the wicked, seeing the prosperity of sinners.

4 For there is no regard to their death: nor *is there* strength in their stripes.

5 They are not in the labour of men: neither shall they be scourged like *other* men.

6 Therefore pride hath held them fast: they are covered with their iniquity and their wickedness.

7 Their iniquity hath come forth, as it were from fatness: they have passed into the affection of the heart.

8 They have thought and spoken wickedness: they have spoken iniquity on high.

9 They have set their mouth against heaven. and their tongue hath passed through the earth.

10 Therefore will my people return here: and full days shall be found in them.

11 And they said: How doth God know? And is there knowledge in the most High?

12 Behold these are sinners; and *yet* abounding in the world they have obtained riches.

13 And I said: Then have I in vain justified my heart, and washed my hands among the innocent.

14 And I have been scourged all the day; and my chastisement hath been in the mornings.

15 If I said: I will speak thus; behold I should condemn the generation of thy children.

16 I studied that I might know this thing: it is a labour in my sight:

17 Until I go into the sanctuary of God, and understand concerning their last ends.

18 But indeed for deceits thou hast put it to them: when they were lifted up thou hast cast them down.

19 How are they brought to desolation? They have suddenly ceased to be: they have perished by reason of their iniquity.

20 As the dream of them that awake, O Lord; *so* in thy city thou shalt bring their image to nothing.

21 For my heart hath been inflamed, and my reins have been changed: 22 and I am brought to nothing, and I knew not.

23 I am become as a beast before thee: and I *am* always with thee.

24 Thou hast held me by my right hand; and by thy will thou hast conducted me: and with thy glory thou hast received me.

25 For what have I in heaven? And besides thee what do I desire upon earth?

26 *For thee* my flesh and my heart hath fainted away. Thou art the God of my heart, and the God that is my portion for ever.

27 For behold they that go far from thee shall perish: thou hast destroyed all them that are disloyal to thee.

28 But it is good for me to adhere to my God, to put my hope in the Lord God:

That I may declare all thy praises, in the gates of the daughter of Sion.

PSALM 73

Ut quid, Deus

A prayer of the church under grievous persecutions.

1 Understanding for Asaph.

O GOD, why hast thou cast us off unto the end? Why is thy wrath

Ver. 20. *Are ended.* By this it appears that this psalm, though placed here, was in order of time the last of those which David composed.

PSALM 72. Ver. 7. *Fatness.* Abundance and temporal prosperity, which hath encouraged them in their iniquity, and made them give themselves up to their irregular affections.

Ver. 10. *Return here.* The weak among the servants of God will be apt often to return to this thought, and will be shocked when they consider the *full days,* that is, the long and prosperous life of the wicked; and will be tempted to make the reflections against providence which are set down in the following verses.

Ver. 15. *If I said.* That is, if I should indulge such thoughts as these.

Ver. 18. *Thou hast put it to them.* In punishment of their deceits, or for deceiving them, thou hast brought evils upon them in their last end, which, in their prosperity they never apprehended.

enkindled against the sheep of thy pasture?

2 Remember thy congregation, which thou hast possessed from the beginning:

The sceptre of thy inheritance *which* thou hast redeemed: Mount Sion in which thou hast dwelt.

3 Lift up thy hands against their pride unto the end; *see* what things the enemy hath done wickedly in the sanctuary.

4 And they that hate thee have made their boasts, in the midst of thy solemnity.

They have set up their ensigns for signs: 5 and they knew not both in the going out and on the highest top.

As with axes in a wood of trees, 6 they have cut down at once the gates thereof: with axe and hatchet they have brought it down.

7 ¹ They have set fire to thy sanctuary: they have defiled the dwelling place of thy name on the earth.

8 They said in their heart, the *whole* kindred of them together: Let us abolish all the festival days of God from the land.

9 Our signs we have not seen: there is now no prophet: and he will know us no more.

10 How long, O God, shall the enemy reproach? *Is* the adversary to provoke thy name for ever?

11 Why dost thou turn away thy hand? And thy right hand out of the midst of thy bosom for ever?

PSALM 73. ¹ 4 Kings, 25, 9. ² Luke, 1, 68.

PSALM 73. Ver. 4. *Their ensigns.* They have fixed their colours for signs and trophies, both on the gates, and on the highest top of the temple: and *they knew not,* that is, they regarded not the sanctity of the place. This psalm manifestly foretells the time of the Machabees, and the profanation of the temple by Antiochus.

Ver. 13. *The sea firm.* By making the waters of the Red Sea stand like firm walls, whilst Israel passed through: and destroying the Egyptians called here *dragons* from their cruelty, in the same waters, with their king: casting up their bodies on the shore to be stripped by the Ethiopians inhabiting in those days the coast of Arabia.

Ver. 15. *Ethan rivers.* That is, *rivers which run with strong streams.* This was verified in Jordan (Jos. 3,), and in Arnon (Num. 21, 14).

Ver. 20. *The obscure of the earth.* Mean and ignoble wretches *have been filled,* that is, enriched, with *houses of iniquity,* that is, with our estates and possessions, which they have unjustly acquired.

PSALM 74. Ver. 1. *Corrupt not.* It is believed to have been the beginning of some ode or hymn, to the tune of which this psalm was to be sung. St. Augustine and other fathers take it to be an admonition of the spirit of God, not to faint or fail in our hope: but to persevere with constancy in good, because God will not fail in his due time to render to every man according to his works.

Ver. 3. *When I shall take a time.* In proper times: particularly at the last day, when *the earth* shall *melt* away at the presence of the great Judge: the same who originally laid the foundations of it, and as it were established its pillars.

12 ² But God is our king before ages: he hath wrought salvation in the midst of the earth.

13 Thou by thy strength didst make the sea firm: thou didst crush the heads of the dragons in the waters.

14 Thou hast broken the heads of the dragon: thou hast given him to be meat for the people of the Ethiopians.

15 Thou hast broken up the fountains and the torrents: thou hast dried up the Ethan rivers.

16 Thine is the day, and thine is the night: thou hast made the morning light and the sun.

17 Thou hast made all the borders of the earth: the summer and the spring were formed by thee.

18 Remember this, the enemy hath reproached the Lord: and a foolish people hath provoked thy name.

19 Deliver not up to beasts the souls that confess to thee: and forget not to the end the souls of thy poor.

20 Have regard to thy covenant: for they that are the obscure of the earth have been filled with dwellings of iniquity.

21 Let not the humble be turned away with confusion: the poor and needy shall praise thy name.

22 Arise, O God, judge thy own cause: remember thy reproaches with which the foolish man hath reproached thee all the day.

23 Forget not the voices of thy enemies: the pride of them that hate thee ascendeth continually.

PSALM 74

Confitebimur tibi

There is a just judgment to come. Wherefore let the wicked take care.

1 Unto the end. Corrupt not. A psalm of a canticle for Asaph.

2 **W**E will praise thee, O God: we will praise, and we will call upon thy name.

We will relate thy wondrous works.
3 When I shall take a time, I will judge justices.

4 The earth is melted, and all that dwell therein: I have established the pillars thereof.

5 I said to the wicked: Do not act wickedly. And to the sinners: Lift not up the horn.

6 Lift not up your horn on high: speak not iniquity against God.

7 For neither from the east, nor from the west, nor from the desert hills: 8 for God is the judge.

One he putteth down, and another he lifteth up. 9 For in the hand of the

Lord there is a cup of strong wine full of mixture.

And he hath poured it out from this to that: but the dregs thereof are not emptied: all the sinners of the earth shall drink.

10 But I will declare for ever: I will sing to the God of Jacob.

11 And I will break all the horns of sinners: but the horns of the just shall be exalted.

PSALM 75

Notus in Judæa

God is known in his church: and exerts his power in protecting it. It alludes to the slaughter of the Assyrians, in the days of king Ezechias.

1 Unto the end. In praises. A psalm for Asaph: a canticle to the Assyrians.

2 IN Judæa God is known: his name is great in Israel.

3 And his place is in peace: and his abode in Sion:

4 There hath he broken the powers of bows: the shield, the sword, and the battle.

5 Thou enlightenest wonderfully from the everlasting hills. 6 All the foolish of heart were troubled.

They have slept their sleep: and all the men of riches have found nothing in their hands.

7 At thy rebuke, O God of Jacob, they have all slumbered that mounted on horseback.

8 Thou art terrible, and who shall resist thee? From that time thy wrath.

9 Thou hast caused judgment to be heard from heaven: the earth trembled and was still,

10 When God arose in judgment, to save all the meek of the earth.

11 For the thought of man shall give praise to thee: and the remainders of the thought shall keep holiday to thee.

12 Vow ye, and pay to the Lord your God: all you that are round about him bring presents.

To him that is terrible: 13 even to him who taketh away the spirit of princes: to the terrible with the kings of the earth.

PSALM 76

Voce mea

The faithful have recourse to God in trouble of mind, with confidence in his mercy and power.

1 Unto the end. For Idithun. A psalm of Asaph.

2 I CRIED to the Lord with my voice, to God with my voice; and he gave ear to me.

3 In the day of my trouble I sought

God, with my hands *lifted up* to him in the night: and I was not deceived.

My soul refused to be comforted: 4 I remembered God, and was delighted, and was exercised; and my spirit swooned away.

5 My eyes prevented the watches: I was troubled, and I spoke not.

6 I thought upon the days of old: and I had in my mind the eternal years.

7 And I meditated in the night with my own heart: and I was exercised, and I swept my spirit.

8 Will God then cast off for ever? Or will he never be more favourable again?

9 Or will he cut off his mercy for ever, from generation to generation?

10 Or will God forget to shew mercy? Or will he in his anger shut up his mercies?

11 And I said: Now have I begun. This is the change of the right hand of the most High.

12 I remembered the works of the Lord: for I will be mindful of thy wonders from the beginning.

13 And I will meditate on all thy works: and will be employed in thy inventions.

14 Thy way, O God, is in the holy *place*. Who is the great God like our God? 15 Thou art the God that dost wonders.

Thou hast made thy power known among the nations: 16 with thy arm thou hast redeemed thy people, the children of Jacob and of Joseph.

17 The waters saw thee, O God, the waters saw thee: and they were afraid, and the depths were troubled.

18 Great was the noise of the waters: the clouds sent out a sound.

For thy arrows pass: 19 the voice of thy thunder in a wheel.

Thy lightnings enlightened the world: the earth shook and trembled.

20 Thy way is in the sea, and thy paths in many waters: and thy footsteps shall not be known.

21 [1] Thou hast conducted thy people like sheep, by the hand of Moses and Aaron.

PSALM 77

Attendite

God's great benefits to the people of Israel, notwithstanding their ingratitude.

1 Understanding for Asaph.

ATTEND, O my people, to my law: incline your ears to the words of my mouth.

2 I will open my mouth in parables:

PSALM 76. [1] Exod. 14, 29.

PSALM 75. Ver. 8. *From that time.* From the time that thy wrath shall break out.

I will utter propositions from the beginning.

3 How great things have we heard and known, and our fathers have told us.

4 They have not been hidden from their children, in another generation.

Declaring the praises of the Lord, and his powers, and his wonders which he hath done.

5 And he set up a testimony in Jacob: and made a law in Israel.

How great things he commanded our fathers, that they should make the same known to their children: 6 that another generation might know them.

The children that should be born, and should rise up and declare them to their children.

7 That they may put their hope in God and may not forget the works of God: and may seek his commandments.

8 That they may not become like their fathers, a perverse and exasperating generation;

A generation that set not their heart aright: and whose spirit was not faithful to God.

9 The sons of Ephraim who bend and shoot with the bow: they have turned back in the day of battle.

10 They kept not the covenant of God: and in his law they would not walk.

11 And they forgot his benefits, and his wonders that he had shewn them.

12 Wonderful things did he do in the sight of their fathers: in the land of Egypt, in the field of Tanis.

13 [1] He divided the sea and brought them through: and he made the waters to stand as in a vessel.

14 And he conducted them with a cloud by day: and all the night with a light of fire.

15 [2] He struck the rock in the wilderness: and gave them to drink, as out of the great deep.

16 He brought forth water out of the rock: and made streams run down as rivers.

17 And they added yet more sin against him: they provoked the most High to wrath in the place without water.

18 And they tempted God in their hearts, by asking meat for their desires.

19 And they spoke ill of God. They said: Can God furnish a table in the wilderness?

20 Because he struck the rock, and the waters gushed out, and the streams overflowed.

Can he also give bread, or provide a table for his people?

21 [3] Therefore the Lord heard, and was angry: and a fire was kindled against Jacob, and wrath came up against Israel.

22 Because they believed not in God: and trusted not in his salvation.

23 And he had commanded the clouds from above: and had opened the doors of heaven.

24 [4] And had rained down manna upon them to eat: and had given them the bread of heaven.

25 [5] Man ate the bread of angels: he sent them provisions in abundance.

26 [6] He removed the south wind from heaven: and by his power brought in the southwest wind.

27 And he rained upon them flesh as dust: and feathered fowls like as the sand of the sea.

28 And they fell in the midst of their camp, round about their pavilions.

29 So they did eat, and were filled exceedingly: and he gave them their desire. 30 They were not defrauded of that which they craved.

[7] As yet their meat was in their mouth: 31 and the wrath of God came upon them.

And he slew the fat ones amongst them: and brought down the chosen men of Israel.

32 In all these things they sinned still: and they believed not for his wondrous works.

33 And their days were consumed in vanity, and their years in haste.

34 When he slew them, then they sought him: and they returned, and came to him early in the morning.

35 And they remembered that God was their helper: and the most high God their redeemer.

36 And they loved him with their mouth: and with their tongue they lied unto him.

37 But their heart was not right with him: nor were they counted faithful in his covenant.

38 But he is merciful and will forgive their sins: and will not destroy them.

And many a time did he turn away his anger: and did not kindle all his wrath.

39 And he remembered that they are flesh: a wind that goeth and returneth not.

PSALM 77. [1] Exod. 14, 22. [2] Exod. 17, 6; Ps. 104, 41. [3] Num. 11, 1. [4] Exod. 16, 4; Num. 11, 7. [5] John, 6, 31; 1 Cor. 10, 3. [6] Num. 11, 31. [7] Num. 11, 33.

PSALM 77. Ver. 2. *Propositions.* Deep and mysterious sayings. By this it appears that the historical facts of ancient times, commemorated in this psalm, were deep and *mysterious:* as being figures of great truths appertaining to the time of the New Testament.

40 How often did they provoke him in the desert: and move him to wrath in the place without water!

41 And they turned back and tempted God: and grieved the holy one of Israel.

42 They remembered not his hand, in the day that he redeemed them from the hand of him that afflicted them:

43 How he wrought his signs in Egypt, and his wonders in the field of Tanis.

44 ⁸ And he turned their rivers into blood: and their showers that they might not drink.

45 ⁹ He sent amongst them divers sorts of flies, which devoured them: ¹⁰ and frogs which destroyed them.

46 ¹¹ And he gave up their fruits to the blast, and their labours to the locust.

47 ¹² And he destroyed their vineyards with hail, and their mulberry trees with hoarfrost.

48 And he gave up their cattle to the hail, and their stock to the fire.

49 And he sent upon them the wrath of his indignation: indignation and wrath and trouble, which he sent by evil angels.

50 He made a way for a path to his anger. He spared not their souls from death, and their cattle he shut up in death.

51 ¹³ And he killed all the firstborn in the land of Egypt: the firstfruits of all their labour in the tabernacles of Cham.

52 And he took away his own people as sheep: and guided them in the wilderness like a flock.

53 And he brought them out in hope, and they feared not. ¹⁴ And the sea overwhelmed their enemies.

54 And he brought them into the mountain of his sanctuary: the mountain which his right hand had purchased.

¹⁵ And he cast out the Gentiles before them: and by lot divided to them their land by a line of distribution.

55 And he made the tribes of Israel to dwell in their tabernacles.

56 Yet they tempted and provoked the most high God: and they kept not his testimonies.

57 And they turned away, and kept not the covenant: even like their fathers they were turned aside as a crooked bow.

58 They provoked him to anger on their hills: and moved him to jealousy with their graven things.

59 God heard, and despised *them*: and he reduced Israel exceedingly, *as it were* to nothing.

60 ¹⁶ And he put away the tabernacle of Silo, his tabernacle where he dwelt among men.

61 And he delivered their strength into captivity: and their beauty into the hands of the enemy.

62 And he shut up his people under the sword: and he despised his inheritance.

63 Fire consumed their young men: and their maidens were not lamented.

64 Their priests fell by the sword: and their widows did not mourn.

65 And the Lord was awaked as one out of sleep, and like a mighty man that hath been surfeited with wine.

66 And he smote his enemies on the hinder parts: he put them to an everlasting reproach.

67 And he rejected the tabernacle of Joseph: and chose not the tribe of Ephraim.

68 But he chose the tribe of Juda, Mount Sion which he loved.

69 And he built his sanctuary as of unicorns, in the land which he founded for ever.

70 And he chose his servant David, and took him from the flocks of sheep: he brought him from following the ewes great with young,

71 To feed Jacob his servant, and Israel his inheritance.

72 And he fed them in the innocence of his heart: and conducted them by the skilfulness of his hands.

PSALM 78

Deus, venerunt gentes

The church in time of persecution prayeth for relief. This psalm seems to belong to the time of the Machabees.

1 A psalm for Asaph.

O GOD, the heathens are come into thy inheritance: They have defiled thy holy temple: they have made Jerusalem as a place to keep fruit.

2 They have given the dead bodies of thy servants to be meat for the fowls of the air: the flesh of thy saints for the beasts of the earth.

3 They have poured out their blood as water, round about Jerusalem: and there was none to bury them.

4 We are become a reproach to our neighbours: a scorn and derision to them that are round about us.

5 How long, O Lord, wilt thou be

⁸ Exod. 7, 20. ⁹ Exod. 8, 24. ¹⁰ Exod. 8, 6. ¹¹ Exod. 10, 15. ¹² Exod. 9, 25. ¹³ Exod. 12, 29. ¹⁴ Exod. 14, 27. ¹⁵ Jos. 13, 6, 7. ¹⁶ 1 Kings, 4, 4; Jer. 7, 12, 14; 26, 6.

Ver. 69. *As of unicorns.* That is, firm and strong like the horn of the *unicorn.* That is one of the chiefest of the *propositions* of this psalm, foreshewing the firm establishment of the one, true, and everlasting sanctuary of God, in his Church.

angry for ever? Shall thy zeal be kindled like a fire?

6 [1] Pour out thy wrath upon the nations that have not known thee: and upon the kingdoms that have not called upon thy name.

7 Because they have devoured Jacob, and have laid waste his place.

8 [2] Remember not our former iniquities. Let thy mercies speedily prevent us, for we are become exceeding poor.

9 Help us, O God, our saviour: and for the glory of thy name, O Lord, deliver us: and forgive us our sins for thy name's sake.

10 Lest they should say among the Gentiles: Where is their God? And let him be made known among the nations before our eyes,

By the revenging the blood of thy servants, which hath been shed. 11 Let the sighing of the prisoners come in before thee.

According to the greatness of thy arm, take possession of the children of them that have been put to death.

12 And render to our neighbours sevenfold in their bosom: the reproach wherewith they have reproached thee, O Lord.

13 But we thy people, and the sheep of thy pasture, will give thanks to thee for ever.

We will shew forth thy praise, unto generation and generation.

PSALM 79
Qui regis Israel

A prayer for the church in tribulation, commemorating God's former favours.

1 Unto the end. For them that shall be changed. A testimony for Asaph. A psalm.

2 GIVE ear, O thou that rulest Israel: thou that leadest Joseph like a sheep.

Thou that sittest upon the cherubims: shine forth 3 before Ephraim, Benjamin, and Manasses.

Stir up thy might: and come to save us.

4 Convert us, O God, and shew us thy face: and we shall be saved.

5 O Lord God of hosts, how long wilt thou be angry against the prayer of thy servant?

6 How long wilt thou feed us with the bread of tears, and give us for our drink tears in measure?

7 Thou hast made us to be a contradiction to our neighbours: and our enemies have scoffed at us.

8 O God of hosts, convert us, and shew thy face: and we shall be saved.

9 Thou hast brought a vineyard out of Egypt: thou hast cast out the Gentiles and planted it.

10 Thou wast the guide of its journey in its sight: thou plantedst the roots thereof. And it filled the land.

11 The shadow of it covered the hills: and the branches thereof the cedars of God.

12 It stretched forth its branches unto the sea, and its boughs unto the river.

13 Why hast thou broken down the hedge thereof, so that all they who pass by the way do pluck it?

14 The boar out of the wood hath laid it waste: and a singular wild beast hath devoured it.

15 Turn again, O God of hosts. Look down from heaven, and see, and visit this vineyard:

16 And perfect the same which thy right hand hath planted: and upon the son of man whom thou hast confirmed for thyself.

17 Things set on fire and dug down shall perish at the rebuke of thy countenance.

18 Let thy hand be upon the man of thy right hand: and upon the son of man whom thou hast confirmed for thyself.

19 And we depart not from thee. Thou shalt quicken us: and we will call upon thy name.

20 O Lord God of hosts, convert us, and shew thy face: and we shall be saved.

PSALM 80
Exultate Deo

An invitation to a solemn praising of God.

1 Unto the end. For the winepresses, a psalm for Asaph himself.

2 REJOICE to God our helper: sing aloud to the God of Jacob.

3 Take a psalm, and bring hither the timbrel: the pleasant psaltery with the harp.

4 Blow up the trumpet on the new moon, on the noted day of your solemnity.

5 For it is a commandment in Israel, and a judgment to the God of Jacob.

6 [1] He ordained it for a testimony in Joseph, when he came out of the land of Egypt: he heard a tongue which he knew not.

7 He removed his back from the burdens: his hands had served in baskets.

8 Thou calledst upon me in affliction,

and I delivered thee: I heard thee in the secret place of tempest: [2] I proved thee at the waters of contradiction.

9 Hear, O my people, and I will testify to thee. O Israel, if thou wilt hearken to me, 10 there shall be [3] no new god in thee: neither shalt thou adore a strange god.

11 For I am the Lord thy God, who brought thee out of the land of Egypt. Open thy mouth wide, and I will fill it.

12 But my people heard not my voice: and Israel hearkened not to me.

13 [4] So I let them go according to the desires of their heart: they shall walk in their own inventions.

14 [5] If my people had heard me, if Israel had walked in my ways:

15 I should soon have humbled their enemies, and laid my hand on them that troubled them.

16 The enemies of the Lord have lied to him: and their time shall be for ever.

17 And he fed them with the fat of wheat, and filled them with honey out of the rock.

PSALM 81

Deus stetit

An exhortation to judges and men in power.

1 A psalm for Asaph.

GOD hath stood in the congregation of gods: and *being* in the midst of *them* he judgeth gods.

2 How long will you judge unjustly, and accept the persons of the wicked?

3 Judge for the needy and fatherless: do justice to the humble and the poor.

4 [1] Rescue the poor: and deliver the needy out of the hand of the sinner.

5 They have not known nor understood: they walk on in darkness. All the foundations of the earth shall be moved.

6 [2] I have said: You are gods, and all of you the sons of the most High.

7 But you like men shall die: and shall fall like one of the princes.

8 Arise, O God, judge thou the earth: for thou shalt inherit among all the nations.

PSALM 82

Deus, quis similis

A prayer against the enemies of God's church.

1 A canticle of a psalm for Asaph.

2 O GOD, who shall be like to thee? Hold not thy peace, neither be thou still, O God.

3 For lo, thy enemies have made a noise: and they that hate thee have lifted up the head.

4 They have taken a malicious coun-sel against thy people: and have consulted against thy saints.

5 They have said: Come and let us destroy them, so that they be not a nation. And let the name of Israel be remembered no more.

6 For they have contrived with one consent: they have made a covenant together against thee, 7 the tabernacles of the Edomites, and the Ismahelites:

Moab, and the Agarens, 8 Gebal, and Ammon, and Amalec: the Philistines, with the inhabitants of Tyre.

9 Yea, and the Assyrian also is joined with them: they are come to the aid of the sons of Lot.

10 Do to them [1] as thou didst to Madian [2] and to Sisara: as to Jabin at the brook of Cisson.

11 *Who* perished at Endor, and became as dung for the earth.

12 [3] Make their princes like Oreb, [4] and Zeb, and Zebee, and Salmana.

All their princes, 13 who have said: Let us possess the sanctuary of God for an inheritance.

14 O my God, make them like a wheel: and as stubble before the wind.

15 As fire which burneth the wood: and as a flame burning mountains:

16 So shalt thou pursue them with thy tempest: and shalt trouble them in thy wrath.

17 Fill their faces with shame: and they shall seek thy name, O Lord.

18 Let them be ashamed and troubled for ever and ever: and let them be confounded and perish.

19 And let them know that the Lord is thy name. Thou alone art the most High over all the earth.

PSALM 83

Quam dilecta

The soul aspireth after heaven. Rejoiceth in the mean time, in being in the communion of God's church upon earth.

1 Unto the end. For the winepresses, a psalm for the sons of Core.

2 HOW lovely are thy tabernacles, O Lord of hosts: 3 My soul longeth and fainteth for the courts of the Lord.

My heart and my flesh have rejoiced in the living God.

4 For the sparrow hath found herself

[2] Exod. 17, 5. [3] Exod. 20, 3. [4] Acts, 14, 15. [5] Bar. 3, 13. PSALM 81. [1] Prov. 24, 11. [2] John, 10, 34. PSALM 82. [1] Judges, 7, 22. [2] Judges, 4, 15. [3] Judges, 7, 25. [4] Judges, 8, 21.

Ver. 8. *In the secret place of tempest,* Heb. *Of thunder.* When thou soughtest to *hide* thyself from the *tempest:* or, when I came down to mount Sina, *hidden* from thy eyes in a storm *of thunder.*

Ver. 16. *Their time shall be for ever.* Impenitent sinners shall suffer for ever.

a house, and the turtle a nest for herself where she may lay her young ones: Thy altars, O Lord of hosts: My king and my God.

5 Blessed are they that dwell in thy house, O Lord: they shall praise thee for ever and ever.

6 Blessed is the man whose help is from thee. In his heart he hath disposed to ascend by steps, 7 in the vale of tears, in the place which he hath set.

8 For the lawgiver shall give a blessing; they shall go from virtue to virtue: the God of gods shall be seen in Sion.

9 O Lord God of hosts, hear my prayer: give ear, O God of Jacob.

10 Behold, O God our protector: and look on the face of thy Christ.

11 For better is one day in thy courts above thousands.

I have chosen to be an abject in the house of my God, rather than to dwell in the tabernacles of sinners.

12 For God loveth mercy and truth: the Lord will give grace and glory.

13 He will not deprive of good things them that walk in innocence. O Lord of hosts, blessed is the man that trusteth in thee.

PSALM 84
Benedixisti, Domine
The coming of Christ, to bring peace and salvation to man.

1 Unto the end. For the sons of Core, a psalm.

2 LORD, thou hast blessed thy land: thou hast turned away the captivity of Jacob.

3 Thou hast forgiven the iniquity of thy people: thou hast covered all their sins.

4 Thou hast mitigated all thy anger: thou hast turned away from the wrath of thy indignation.

5 Convert us, O God our saviour: and turn off thy anger from us.

6 Wilt thou be angry with us for ever? Or wilt thou extend thy wrath from generation to generation?

7 Thou wilt turn, O God, and bring us to life: and thy people shall rejoice in thee.

8 Shew us, O Lord, thy mercy; and grant us thy salvation.

PSALM 85. ¹ Joel, 2, 13.

PSALM 83. Ver. 6. *In his heart he hath disposed to ascend by steps. Ascensiones in corde suo disposuit.* As *by steps* men *ascended* to the temple of God, situated on a hill; so the good Christian *ascends* towards the eternal temple by certain *steps* of virtue *disposed* or ordered within the heart: and this whilst he lives as yet in the body, in this *vale of tears, the place which* man hath *set:* that is, which he hath brought himself to, being cast out of paradise for his sin.

PSALM 85. Ver. 2. *I am holy.* I am by my office and profession dedicated to thy service.

9 I will hear what the Lord God will speak in me: for he will speak peace unto his people.

And unto his saints: and unto them that are converted to the heart.

10 Surely his salvation is near to them that fear him: that glory may dwell in our land.

11 Mercy and truth have met each other: justice and peace have kissed.

12 Truth is sprung out of the earth: and justice hath looked down from heaven.

13 For the Lord will give goodness: and our earth shall yield her fruit.

14 Justice shall walk before him: and shall set his steps in the way.

PSALM 85
Inclina, Domine
A prayer for God's grace to assist us to the end.

1 A prayer for David himself.

INCLINE thy ear, O Lord, and hear me: for I am needy and poor.

2 Preserve my soul, for I am holy: save thy servant, O my God, that trusteth in thee.

3 Have mercy on me, O Lord, for I have cried to thee all the day. 4 Give joy to the soul of thy servant, for to thee, O Lord, I have lifted up my soul.

5 ¹ For thou, O Lord, art sweet and mild, and plenteous in mercy to all that call upon thee.

6 Give ear, O Lord, to my prayer: and attend to the voice of my petition.

7 I have called upon thee in the day of my trouble: because thou hast heard me.

8 There is none among the gods like unto thee, O Lord: and there is none according to thy works.

9 All the nations thou hast made shall come and adore before thee, O Lord: and they shall glorify thy name.

10 For thou art great and dost wonderful things: thou art God alone.

11 Conduct me, O Lord, in thy way, and I will walk in thy truth: let my heart rejoice that it may fear thy name.

12 I will praise thee, O Lord my God, with my whole heart: and I will glorify thy name for ever:

13 For thy mercy is great towards me: and thou hast delivered my soul out of the lower hell.

14 O God, the wicked are risen up against me, and the assembly of the mighty have sought my soul: and they have not set thee before their eyes.

15 And thou, O Lord, *art* a God of compassion, and merciful: patient, and of much mercy, and true.

16 O look upon me, and have mercy

on me: give thy command to thy servant, and save the son of thy handmaid.

17 Shew me a token for good, that they who hate me may see, and be confounded: because thou, O Lord, hast helped me and hast comforted me.

PSALM 86
Fundamenta ejus
The glory of the church of Christ.

1 For the sons of Core, a psalm of a canticle.

THE foundations thereof *are* in the holy mountains:

2 The Lord loveth the gates of Sion above all the tabernacles of Jacob.

3 Glorious things are said of thee: O city of God.

4 I will be mindful of Rahab and of Babylon knowing me.

Behold the foreigners, and Tyre, and the people of the Ethiopians, these were there.

5 Shall not Sion say: *This* man and *that* man is born in her? And the Highest himself hath founded her.

6 The Lord shall tell in *his* writings of peoples and of princes: of them that have been in her.

7 The dwelling in thee is as it were of all rejoicing.

PSALM 87
Domine, Deus salutis
A prayer of one under grievous affliction. It agrees to Christ in his passion, and alludes to his death and burial.

1 A canticle of a psalm for the sons of Core. Unto the end, for Maheleth, to answer understanding of Eman the Ezrahite.

2 O LORD, the God of my salvation: I have cried in the day and in the night, before thee.

3 Let my prayer come in before thee: incline thy ear to my petition.

4 For my soul is filled with evils: and my life hath drawn nigh to hell.

5 I am counted among them that go down to the pit: I am become as a man without help, 6 free among the dead.

Like the slain sleeping in the sepulchres, whom thou rememberest no more: and they are cast off from thy hand.

7 They have laid me in the lower pit: in the dark places, and in the shadow of death.

8 Thy wrath is strong over me: and all thy waves thou hast brought in upon me.

9 Thou hast put away my acquaintance far from me: they have set me an abomination to themselves.

I was delivered up, and came not forth: 10 my eyes languished through poverty.

All the day I cried to thee, O Lord: I stretched out my hands to thee.

11 Wilt thou shew wonders to the dead? Or shall physicians raise to life, and give praise to thee?

12 Shall any one in the sepulchre declare thy mercy: and thy truth in destruction?

13 Shall thy wonders be known in the dark: and thy justice in the land of forgetfulness?

14 But I, O Lord, have cried to thee: and in the morning my prayer shall prevent thee.

15 Lord, why castest thou off my prayer? Why turnest thou away thy face from me?

16 I am poor, and in labours from my youth: and being exalted have been humbled and troubled.

17 Thy wrath hath come upon me: and thy terrors have troubled me.

18 They have come around about me like water all the day: they have compassed me about together.

19 Friend and neighbour thou hast put far from me: and my acquaintance, because of misery.

PSALM 88
Misericordias Domini
The perpetuity of the church of Christ, in consequence of the promise of God. Which, notwithstanding, God permits her to suffer sometimes most grievous afflictions.

1 Of understanding. For Ethan the Ezrahite.

2 THE mercies of the Lord I will sing for ever.

I will shew forth thy truth with my mouth to generation and generation.

3 For thou hast said: Mercy shall be built up for ever in the heavens. Thy truth shall be prepared in them.

4 I have made a covenant with my elect, [1] I have sworn to David my servant: 5 Thy seed will I settle for ever.

And I will build up thy throne unto generation and generation.

6 The heavens shall confess thy won-

PSALM 88. [1] 2 Kings, 7, 12.

PSALM 86. Ver. 1. *The holy mountains.* The apostles and prophets (Eph. 2, 20).

Ver. 4. *Rahab.* Egypt. To this Sion, which is the church of God, many shall resort from all nations.

Ver. 5. *Shall not Sion say, &c.* The meaning is, that *Sion*, that is, the church, shall not only be able to commemorate *this* or *that* particular person of renown born in her, but also to glory in great multitudes of people and princes of her communion; who have been foretold in the writings of the prophets, and registered in the writings of the apostles.

PSALM 87. Ver. 1. *Maheleth.* A musical instrument, or chorus of musicians, to answer one another.—*Understanding.* Or a psalm of instruction, composed by *Eman the Ezrahite*, or by David, in his name.

ders, O Lord: and thy truth in the church of the saints.

7 For who in the clouds can be compared to the Lord? Or who among the sons of God shall be like to God?

8 God, who is glorified in the assembly of the saints: great and terrible above all them that are about him.

9 O Lord God of hosts, who is like to thee? Thou art mighty, O Lord, and thy truth is round about thee.

10 Thou rulest the power of the sea: and appeasest the motion of the waves thereof.

11 Thou hast humbled the proud one, as one that is slain: with the arm of thy strength thou hast scattered thy enemies.

12 [2] Thine are the heavens, and thine is the earth: the world and the fulness thereof thou hast founded: 13 the north and the sea thou hast created.

Thabor and Hermon shall rejoice in thy name: 14 thy arm is with might.

Let thy hand be strengthened, and thy right hand be exalted: 15 justice and judgment are the preparation of thy throne.

Mercy and truth shall go before thy face. 16 Blessed is the people that knoweth jubilation.

They shall walk, O Lord, in the light of thy countenance, 17 and in thy name they shall rejoice all the day: and in thy justice they shall be exalted.

18 For thou art the glory of their strength: and in thy good pleasure shall our horn be exalted.

19 For our protection is of the Lord, and of our king the holy one of Israel.

20 Then thou spokest in a vision to thy saints, and saidst: I have laid help upon one that is mighty, and have exalted one chosen out of my people.

21 [3] I have found David my servant: with my holy oil I have anointed him.

22 For my hand shall help him: and my arm shall strengthen him.

23 The enemy shall have no advantage over him: nor the son of iniquity have power to hurt him.

24 And I will cut down his enemies before his face; and them that hate him I will put to flight.

25 And my truth and my mercy *shall be* with him: and in my name shall his horn be exalted.

26 And I will set his hand in the sea: and his right hand in the rivers.

[2] Gen. 1, 1. [3] 1 Kings, 16, 1, 12; Acts, 13, 22. [4] 2 Kings, 7, 16. [5] 2 Kings, 7, 11.

PSALM 88. Ver. 40. *Overthrown the covenant.* All this seems to relate to the time of the captivity of Babylon, in which, for the sins of the people and their princes, God seemed to have set aside for a while the covenant he made with David.

27 He shall cry out to me: Thou art my father, my God, and the support of my salvation.

28 And I will make him my firstborn, high above the kings of the earth.

29 I will keep my mercy for him for ever: and my covenant faithful to him.

30 And I will make his seed to endure for evermore: and his throne as the days of heaven.

31 And if his children forsake my law, and walk not in my judgments:

32 If they profane my justices: and keep not my commandments:

33 I will visit their iniquities with a rod: and their sins with stripes.

34 But my mercy I will not take away from him: nor will I suffer my truth to fail.

35 Neither will I profane my covenant: and the words that proceed from my mouth I will not make void.

36 Once have I sworn by my holiness: I will not lie unto David. 27 His seed shall endure for ever.

38 [4] And his throne as the sun before me, and as the moon perfect for ever: and a faithful witness in heaven.

39 But thou hast rejected and despised: thou hast been angry with thy anointed.

40 Thou hast overthrown the covenant of thy servant: thou hast profaned his sanctuary on the earth.

41 Thou hast broken down all his hedges: thou hast made his strength fear.

42 All that pass by the way have robbed him: he is become a reproach to his neighbours.

43 Thou hast set up the right hand of them that oppress him: thou hast made all his enemies to rejoice.

44 Thou hast turned away the help of his sword: and hast not assisted him in battle.

45 Thou hast made his purification to cease: and thou hast cast his throne down to the ground.

46 Thou hast shortened the days of his time: thou hast covered him with confusion.

47 How long, O Lord, turnest thou away unto the end? Shall thy anger burn like fire?

48 Remember what my substance is: for hast thou made all the children of men in vain?

49 Who is the man that shall live, and not see death: that shall deliver his soul from the hand of hell?

50 Lord, where are thy ancient mercies, according to [5] what thou didst swear to David in thy truth?

51 Be mindful, O Lord, of the re-

proach of thy servants (which I have held in my bosom) of many nations:

52 Wherewith thy enemies have reproached, O Lord; wherewith they have reproached the change of thy anointed.

53 Blessed be the Lord for evermore. So be it. So be it.

PSALM 89

Domine, refugium

A prayer for the mercy of God, recounting the shortness and miseries of the days of man.

1 A prayer of Moses, the man of God.

LORD, thou hast been our refuge from generation to generation.

2 Before the mountains were made, or the earth and the world was formed; from eternity and to eternity thou art God.

3 Turn not man away to be brought low. And thou hast said: Be converted, O ye sons of men.

4 For a thousand years in thy sight *are* as yesterday, which is past. And as a watch in the night: 5 things that are counted nothing, shall their years be.

6 In the morning *man* shall grow up like grass; in the morning he shall flourish and pass away: in the evening he shall fall, grow dry, and wither.

7 For in thy wrath we have fainted away: and are troubled in thy indignation.

8 Thou hast set our iniquities before thy eyes: our life in the light of thy countenance.

9 For all our days are spent: and in thy wrath we have fainted away. Our years shall be considered as a spider: 10 ¹ the days of our years in them are threescore and ten years. But if in the strong *they be* fourscore years: and what is more of them is labour and sorrow.

For mildness is come upon us: and we shall be corrected.

11 Who knoweth the power of thy anger, and for thy fear 12 can number thy wrath?

So make thy right hand known: and men learned in heart, in wisdom.

13 Return, O Lord: How long? And be entreated in favour of thy servants.

14 We are filled in the morning with thy mercy: and we have rejoiced, and are delighted all our days.

15 We have rejoiced for the days in which thou hast humbled us: for the years in which we have seen evils.

16 Look upon thy servants and upon their works: and direct their children.

17 And let the brightness of the Lord our God be upon us, and direct thou the works of our hands over us; yea, the work of our hands do thou direct.

PSALM 90

Qui habitat

The just is secure under the protection of God.

1 The praise of a canticle. For David.

HE that dwelleth in the aid of the most High, shall abide under the protection of the God of Heaven.

2 He shall say to the Lord: Thou art my protector and my refuge: my God, in him will I trust.

3 For he hath delivered me from the snare of the hunters: and from the sharp word.

4 He will overshadow thee with his shoulders: and under his wings thou shalt trust.

5 His truth shall compass thee with a shield: thou shalt not be afraid of the terror of the night.

6 Of the arrow that flieth in the day, of the business that walketh about in the dark: of invasion, or of the noonday devil.

7 A thousand shall fall at thy side, and ten thousand at thy right hand: but it shall not come nigh thee.

8 But thou shalt consider with thy eyes: and shalt see the reward of the wicked.

9 Because thou, O Lord, art my hope: thou hast made the most High thy refuge.

10 There shall no evil come to thee: nor shall the scourge come near thy dwelling.

11 ¹ For he hath given his angels charge over thee, to keep thee in all thy ways.

12 In their hands they shall bear thee up, lest thou dash thy foot against a stone.

13 Thou shalt walk upon the asp and the basilisk: and thou shalt trample under foot the lion and the dragon.

14 Because he hoped in me I will deliver him: I will protect him because he hath known my name.

15 He shall cry to me, and I will hear him: I am with him in tribulation, I will deliver him, and I will glorify him.

PSALM 89. ¹ Ecclus. 18, 8. PSALM 90. ¹ Matt. 4, 6; Luke, 4, 10.

PSALM 89. Ver. 3. *Turn not man away.* Suffer him not quite to perish from thee, since thou art pleased to call upon him to be converted to thee.

Ver. 9. *As a spider.* As frail and weak as *a spider's* web; and miserable withal, whilst like *a spider* we spend our bowels in weaving webs to catch flies.

Ver. 10. *Mildness is come upon us.* God's *mildness corrects us;* inasmuch as he deals *kindly* with us, in shortening the days of this miserable life; and so weaning our affections from all its transitory enjoyments, and teaching us *true wisdom.*

16 I will fill him with length of days: and I will shew him my salvation.

PSALM 91

Bonum est confiteri

God is to be praised for his wondrous works.

1 A psalm of a canticle. On the sabbath day.

2 IT is good to give praise to the Lord: and to sing to thy name, O most High.

3 To shew forth thy mercy in the morning, and thy truth in the night:

4 Upon an instrument of ten strings, upon the psaltery: with a canticle upon the harp.

5 For thou hast given me, O Lord, a delight in thy doings: and in the works of thy hands I shall rejoice.

6 O Lord, how great are thy works! Thy thoughts are exceeding deep.

7 The senseless man shall not know: nor will the fool understand these things.

8 When the wicked shall spring up as grass: and all the workers of iniquity shall appear,

That they may perish for ever and ever. 9 But thou, O Lord, art most high for evermore.

10 For behold thy enemies, O Lord, for behold thy enemies shall perish: and all the workers of iniquity shall be scattered.

11 But my horn shall be exalted like that of the unicorn: and my old age in plentiful mercy.

12 My eye also hath looked down upon my enemies: and my ear shall hear *of the downfall* of the malignant that rise up against me.

13 The just shall flourish like the palm tree: he shall grow up like the cedar of Libanus.

14 They that are planted in the house of the Lord shall flourish in the courts of the house of our God.

15 They shall still increase in a fruitful old age: and shall be well treated, 16 that they may shew,

That the Lord our God is righteous, and there is no iniquity in him.

PSALM 92

Dominus regnavit

The glory and stability of the kingdom, that is, of the church of Christ.

Praise *in the way* of a canticle. For David himself. On the day before the sabbath, when the earth was founded.

PSALM 93. Ver. 13. *Rest from the evil days.* That thou mayst mitigate the sorrows, to which he is exposed, during the short and evil days of his mortality.
Ver. 15. *Until justice be turned into judgment.* By being put in execution; which will be agreeable to *all the upright* in heart.

1 THE Lord hath reigned, he is clothed with beauty: the Lord is clothed with strength, and hath girded himself.

For he hath established the world which shall not be moved.

2 Thy throne is prepared from of old: thou art from everlasting.

3 The floods have lifted up, O Lord: the floods have lifted up their voice.

The floods have lifted up their waves, 4 with the noise of many waters.

Wonderful are the surges of the sea: wonderful is the Lord on high.

5 Thy testimonies are become exceedingly credible. Holiness becometh thy house, O Lord, unto length of days.

PSALM 93

Deus ultionum

God shall judge and punish the oppressors of his people.

A psalm for David himself. On the fourth day of the week.

1 THE Lord is the God to whom revenge belongeth: the God of revenge hath acted freely.

2 Lift up thyself, thou that judgest the earth: render a reward to the proud.

3 How long shall sinners, O Lord: how long shall sinners glory?

4 Shall they utter, and speak iniquity: shall all speak who work injustice?

5 Thy people, O Lord, they have brought law: and they have afflicted thy inheritance.

6 They have slain the widow and the stranger: and they have murdered the fatherless.

7 And they have said: The Lord shall not see; neither shall the God of Jacob understand.

8 Understand, ye senseless among the people: and, you fools, be wise at last.

9 He that planted the ear, shall he not hear? Or he that formed the eye, doth he not consider?

10 He that chastiseth nations, shall he not rebuke: he that teacheth man knowledge?

11 The Lord knoweth the thoughts of men, that they are vain.

12 Blessed is the man whom thou shalt instruct, O Lord: and shalt teach him out of thy law.

13 That thou mayst give him rest from the evil days: till a pit be dug for the wicked.

14 For the Lord will not cast off his people: neither will he forsake his own inheritance.

15 Until justice be turned into judg-

ment: and they that are near it are all the upright in heart.

16 Who shall rise up for me against the evildoers? Or who shall stand with me against the workers of iniquity?

17 Unless the Lord had been my helper, my soul had almost dwelt in hell.

18 If I said: My foot is moved: thy mercy, O Lord, assisted me.

19 According to the multitude of my sorrows in my heart, thy comforts have given joy to my soul.

20 Doth the seat of iniquity stick to thee, who framest labour in commandment?

21 They will hunt after the soul of the just, and will condemn innocent blood.

22 But the Lord is my refuge: and my God the help of my hope.

23 And he will render them their iniquity: and in their malice he will destroy them. The Lord our God will destroy them.

PSALM 94
Venite exultemus

An invitation to adore and serve God, and to hear his voice.

Praise of a canticle. For David himself.

1 COME let us praise the Lord with joy: let us joyfully sing to God our saviour.

2 Let us come before his presence with thanksgiving; and make a joyful noise to him with psalms.

3 For the Lord is a great God, and a great King above all gods.

4 For in his hand are all the ends of the earth: and the heights of the mountains are his.

5 For the sea is his, and he made it: and his hands formed the dry land.

6 Come let us adore and fall down: and weep before the Lord that made us.

7 For he is the Lord our God: and we are the people of his pasture and the sheep of his hand.

8 [1] To-day if you shall hear his voice, harden not your hearts:

9 As in the provocation, according to the day of temptation in the wilderness: where your fathers tempted me, they proved me, and saw my works.

10 [2] Forty years long was I offended with that generation, and I said: These always err in heart.

11 And these men have not known my ways: [3] so I swore in my wrath that they shall not enter into my rest.

PSALM 95
Cantate Domino

An exhortation to praise God for the coming of Christ and his kingdom.

1 A canticle for David himself. When the house was built after the captivity.

SING ye to the Lord a new canticle: sing to the Lord, all the earth.

2 Sing ye to the Lord and bless his name: shew forth his salvation from day to day.

3 Declare his glory among the Gentiles: his wonders among all people.

4 For the Lord is great, and exceedingly to be praised: he is to be feared above all gods.

5 For all the gods of the Gentiles are devils: but the Lord made the heavens.

6 Praise and beauty are before him: holiness and majesty in his sanctuary.

7 Bring ye to the Lord, O ye kindreds of the Gentiles, bring ye to the Lord glory and honour: 8 bring to the Lord glory unto his name.

Bring up sacrifices, and come into his courts: 9 adore ye the Lord in his holy court.

Let all the earth be moved at his presence. 10 Say ye among the Gentiles: The Lord hath reigned.

For he hath corrected the world, which shall not be moved: he will judge the people with justice.

11 Let the heavens rejoice, and let the earth be glad, let the sea be moved, and the fulness thereof: 12 the fields and all things that are in them shall be joyful.

Then shall all the trees of the woods rejoice 13 before the face of the Lord, because he cometh: because he cometh to judge the earth.

He shall judge the world with justice, and the people with his truth.

PSALM 96
Dominus regnavit

All are invited to rejoice at the glorious coming and reign of Christ.

1 For the same David. When his land was restored again to him.

THE Lord hath reigned, let the earth rejoice: let many islands be glad.

2 Clouds and darkness *are* round about him: justice and judgment *are* the establishment of his throne.

PSALM 94. [1] Heb. 3, 7; 4, 7. [2] Num. 14, 34. [3] Heb. 4, 3.

Ver. 20. *Doth the seat of iniquity stick to thee.* That is, wilt thou, O God, who art always just, admit of the *seat of iniquity;* that is, of injustice, or unjust, judges, to have any partnership with thee? Thou *who framest,* or makest, *labour in commandment,* that is, thou who obligest us to *labour* with all diligence to keep thy *commandments.*

PSALM 95. Ver. 1. *When the house was built.* Alluding to that time, and then ordered to be sung: but principally relating to the building of the church of Christ, after our redemption from the captivity of Satan.

PSALM 96. Ver. 2. *Clouds and darkness.* The

3 A fire shall go before him, and shall burn his enemies round about.

4 His lightnings have shone forth to the world: the earth saw and trembled.

5 The mountains melted like wax, at the presence of the Lord: at the presence of the Lord of all the earth.

6 The heavens declared his justice: and all people saw his glory.

7 [1] Let them be all confounded that adore graven things, and that glory in their idols.

[2] Adore him, all you his angels: 8 Sion heard, and was glad.

And the daughters of Juda rejoiced, because of thy judgments, O Lord.

9 For thou art the most high Lord over all the earth: thou art exalted exceedingly above all gods.

10 [3] You that love the Lord, hate evil: the Lord preserveth the souls of his saints, he will deliver them out of the hand of the sinner.

11 Light is risen to the just: and joy to the right of heart.

12 Rejoice, ye just, in the Lord: and give praise to the remembrance of his holiness.

PSALM 97
Cantate Domino

All are again invited to praise the Lord, for the victories of Christ.

1 A psalm for David himself.

SING ye to the Lord a new canticle: because he hath done wonderful things.

PSALM 96. [1] Exod. 20, 4; Lev. 26, 1; Deut. 5, 8. [2] Heb. 1, 6. [3] Amos, 5, 15; Rom. 12, 9. PSALM 97. [1] Isai. 52, 10; 63, 8; Luke, 3, 6.
coming of Christ in the clouds with great terror and majesty to judge the world, is here prophesied.
PSALM 98. Ver. 1. *Let the people be angry.* Though many enemies rage, and the whole earth be stirred up to oppose the reign of Christ, he shall still prevail.
Ver. 4. *Loveth judgment.* Requireth discretion. *Directions.* Most right and just laws to *direct men.*
Ver. 5. *Adore his footstool.* The ark of the covenant was called, in the Old Testament, God's *footstool:* over which he was understood to sit, on his propitiatory, or mercy seat, as on a throne, between the wings of the cherubims, in the sanctuary: to which the children of Israel paid a great veneration. But as this psalm evidently relates to Christ, and the New Testament, where the ark has no place, the holy fathers understand this text, of the worship paid by the church to the body and blood of Christ in the sacred mysteries: inasmuch as the humanity of Christ is, as it were, the footstool of the divinity. So St. Ambrose (L. 3. De Spiritu Sancto, c. xii.). And St. Augustine upon this psalm.
Ver. 6. *Moses and Aaron among his priests.* By this it is evident, that Moses also was a priest, and indeed the chief priest, inasmuch as he consecrated Aaron, and offered sacrifice for him (Lev. 8). So that his pre-eminence over Aaron makes nothing for lay church headship.
Ver. 8. *All their inventions.* That is, all the enterprises of their enemies against them, as in the case of Core, Dathan and Abiron.

His right hand hath wrought for him salvation: and his arm *is* holy.

2 [1] The Lord hath made known his salvation: he hath revealed his justice in the sight of the Gentiles.

3 He hath remembered his mercy and his truth toward the house of Israel.

All the ends of the earth have seen the salvation of our God.

4 Sing joyfully to God, all the earth: make melody, rejoice and sing.

5 Sing praise to the Lord on the harp, on the harp, and with the voice of a psalm: 6 with long trumpets, and sound of cornet.

Make a joyful noise before the Lord our king. 7 Let the sea be moved and the fulness thereof: the world and they that dwell therein.

8 The rivers shall clap their hands; the mountains shall rejoice together 9 at the presence of the Lord: because he cometh to judge the earth.

He shall judge the world with justice, and the people with equity.

PSALM 98
Dominus regnavit

The reign of the Lord in Sion, that is, of Christ in his church.

1 A psalm for David himself.

THE Lord hath reigned, let the people be angry: he that sitteth on the cherubims, let the earth be moved.

2 The Lord *is* great in Sion, and high above all people.

3 Let them give praise to thy great name, for it is terrible and holy: 4 and the king's honour loveth judgment.

Thou hast prepared directions: thou hast done judgment and justice in Jacob.

5 Exalt ye the Lord our God: and adore his footstool, for it is holy.

6 Moses and Aaron among his priests: and Samuel among them that call upon his name.

They called upon the Lord, and he heard them: 7 he spoke to them in the pillar of the cloud.

They kept his testimonies and the commandment which he gave them.

8 Thou didst hear them, O Lord our God: thou wast a merciful God to them, and taking vengeance on all their inventions.

9 Exalt ye the Lord our God, and adore at his holy mountain: for the Lord our God is holy.

PSALM 99
Jubilate Deo

All are invited to rejoice in God the Creator of all.

1 A psalm of praise.

2 SING joyfully to God, all the earth: serve ye the Lord with gladness.

Come in before his presence with exceeding great joy.

3 Know ye that the Lord he is God: he made us, and not we ourselves.

We are his people and the sheep of his pasture. 4 Go ye into his gates with praise, into his courts with hymns: and give glory to him.

Praise ye his name, 5 for the Lord is sweet: his mercy endureth for ever, and his truth to generation and generation.

PSALM 100

Misericordiam et judicium

The prophet exhorteth all by his examples to follow mercy and justice.

1 A psalm for David himself.

MERCY and judgment I will sing to thee, O Lord.

I will sing, 2 and I will understand in the unspotted way, when thou shalt come to me.

I walked in the innocence of my heart, in the midst of my house.

3 I did not set before my eyes any unjust thing: I hated the workers of iniquities.

4 The perverse heart did not cleave to me: and the malignant, that turned aside from me, I would not know.

5 The man that in private detracted his neighbour, him did I persecute.

With him that had a proud eye and an unsatiable heart, I would not eat.

6 My eyes were upon the faithful of the earth, to sit with me: the man that walked in the perfect way, he served me.

7 He that worketh pride shall not dwell in the midst of my house: he that speaketh unjust things did not prosper before my eyes.

8 In the morning I put to death all the wicked of the land: that I might cut off all the workers of iniquity from the city of the Lord.

PSALM 101

Domine, exaudi

A prayer for one in affliction. The fifth penitential psalm.

1 The prayer of the poor man, when he was anxious, and poured out his supplication before the Lord.

2 HEAR, O Lord, my prayer: and let my cry come to thee.

3 Turn not away thy face from me: in the day when I am in trouble, incline thy ear to me.

In what day soever I shall call upon thee, hear me speedily.

4 For my days are vanished like smoke: and my bones are grown dry like fuel for the fire.

5 I am smitten as grass, and my heart is withered: because I forgot to eat my bread.

6 Through the voice of my groaning, my bone hath cleaved to my flesh.

7 I am become like to a pelican of the wilderness: I am like a night raven in the house.

8 I have watched, and am become as a sparrow all alone on the housetop.

9 All the day long my enemies reproached me and they that praised me did swear against me.

10 For I did eat ashes like bread, and mingled my drink with weeping.

11 Because of thy anger and indignation: for having lifted me up thou hast thrown me down.

12 My days have declined like a shadow: and I am withered like grass.

13 But thou, O Lord, endurest for ever: and thy memorial to all generations.

14 Thou shalt arise and have mercy on Sion: for it is time to have mercy on it, for the time is come.

15 For the stones thereof have pleased thy servants: and they shall have pity on the earth thereof.

16 And the Gentiles shall fear thy name, O Lord, and all the kings of the earth thy glory.

17 For the Lord hath built up Sion: and he shall be seen in his glory.

18 He hath had regard to the prayer of the humble: and he hath not despised their petition.

19 Let these things be written unto another generation: and the people that shall be created shall praise the Lord:

20 Because he hath looked forth from his high sanctuary: from heaven the Lord hath looked upon the earth.

21 That he might hear the groans of them that are in fetters: that he might release the children of the slain:

22 That they may declare the name of the Lord in Sion; and his praise in Jerusalem.

23 When the people assemble together, and kings, to serve the Lord.

24 He answered him in the way of his strength: Declare unto me the fewness of my days.

25 Call me not away in the midst of

PSALM 100. Ver. 2. *I will understand.* That is, I will apply my mind, I will do my endeavour, to know and to follow the *perfect way* of thy commandments: not trusting to my own strength, but relying on thy *coming to me* by thy grace.

PSALM 101. Ver. 7. *A pelican.* I am become through grief like birds that affect solitude and darkness.

Ver. 24. *He answered him in the way of his*

my days: thy years are unto generation and generation.

26 In the beginning, O Lord, thou foundedst the earth: and the heavens are the works of thy hands.

27 They shall perish but thou remainest: and all of them shall grow old like a garment:

And as a vesture thou shalt change them, and they shall be changed. 28 But thou art always the selfsame: and thy years shall not fail.

29 The children of thy servants shall continue: and their seed shall be directed for ever.

PSALM 102

Benedic, anima

Thanksgiving to God for his mercies.

1 For David himself.

BLESS the Lord, O my soul: and let all that is within me bless his holy name.

2 Bless the Lord, O my soul: and never forget all he hath done for thee.

3 Who forgiveth all thy iniquities: who healeth all thy diseases.

4 Who redeemeth thy life from destruction: who crowneth thee with mercy and compassion.

5 Who satisfieth thy desire with good things: thy youth shall be renewed like the eagle's.

6 The Lord doth mercies, and judgment for all that suffer wrong.

7 He hath made his ways known to Moses: his wills to the children of Israel.

8 ¹ The Lord is compassionate and merciful: longsuffering and plenteous in mercy.

9 He will not always be angry: nor will he threaten for ever.

10 He hath not dealt with us according to our sins: nor rewarded us according to our iniquities.

11 For according to the height of the heaven above the earth, he hath strengthened his mercy towards them that fear him.

12 As far as the east is from the west, so far hath he removed our iniquities from us.

13 As a father hath compassion on his children, so hath the Lord compassion on them that fear him: 14 for he knoweth our frame.

PSALM 102. ¹ Exod. 34, 6; Num. 14, 18. PSALM 103. ¹ Heb. 1, 7.

strength. That is, the people, mentioned in the foregoing verse, or *the penitent,* in whose person this psalm is delivered, *answered the Lord in the way of his strength;* that is, according to the best of his power and strength. Or, when he was in the flower of his age and strength, inquiring after the *fewness of his days:* to know if he should live long enough to see the happy restoration of Sion.

He remembereth that we are dust.

15 Man's days are as grass: as the flower of the field so shall he flourish.

16 For the spirit shall pass in him, and he shall not be: and he shall know his place no more.

17 But the mercy of the Lord is from eternity and unto eternity, upon them that fear him.

And his justice unto children's children, 18 to such as keep his covenant,

And are mindful of his commandments to do them.

19 The Lord hath prepared his throne in heaven: and his kingdom shall rule over all.

20 Bless the Lord, all ye his angels: you that are mighty in strength, and execute his word, hearkening to the voice of his orders.

21 Bless the Lord, all ye his hosts: you ministers of his that do his will.

22 Bless the Lord, all his works: in every place of his dominion, O my soul, bless thou the Lord.

PSALM 103

Benedic, anima

God is to be praised for his mighty works and wonderful providence.

1 For David himself.

BLESS the Lord, O my soul: O Lord my God, thou art exceedingly great.

Thou hast put on praise and beauty: 2 and art clothed with light as with a garment.

Who stretchest out the heaven like a pavilion: 3 who coverest the higher rooms thereof with water.

Who makest the clouds thy chariot: who walkest upon the wings of the winds.

4 ¹ Who makest thy angels spirits: and thy ministers a burning fire.

5 Who hast founded the earth upon its own bases: it shall not be moved for ever and ever.

6 The deep like a garment is its clothing: above the mountains shall the waters stand.

7 At thy rebuke they shall flee: at the voice of thy thunder they shall fear.

8 The mountains ascend, and the plains descend into the place which thou hast founded for them.

9 Thou hast set a bound which they shall not pass over: neither shall they return to cover the earth.

10 Thou sendest forth springs in the vales: between the midst of the hills the waters shall pass.

11 All the beasts of the field shall drink: the wild asses shall expect in their thirst.

12 Over them the birds of the air shall dwell: from the midst of the rocks they shall give forth their voices.

13 Thou waterest the hills from thy upper rooms: the earth shall be filled with the fruit of thy works:

14 Bringing forth grass for cattle, and herb for the service of men.

That thou mayst bring bread out of the earth: 15 and that wine may cheer the heart of man.

That he may make the face cheerful with oil: and that bread may strengthen man's heart.

16 The trees of the field shall be filled, and the cedars of Libanus which he hath planted: 17 there the sparrows shall make their nests.

The highest of them is the house of the heron. 18 The high hills are a refuge for the harts, the rock for the irchins.

19 He hath made the moon for seasons: the sun knoweth his going down.

20 Thou hast appointed darkness, and it is night: in it shall all the beasts of the woods go about:

21 The young lions roaring after their prey, and seeking their meat from God.

22 The sun ariseth, and they are gathered together: and they shall lie down in their dens.

23 Man shall go forth to his work, and to his labour until the evening.

24 How great are thy works, O Lord! Thou hast made all things in wisdom: the earth is filled with thy riches.

25 *So is* this great sea, which stretcheth wide its arms: there are creeping things without number, creatures little and great. 26 There the ships shall go.

This sea dragon which thou hast formed to play therein. 27 All expect of thee that thou give them food in season.

28 What thou givest to them they shall gather up: when thou openest thy hand, they shall all be filled with good.

29 But if thou turnest away thy face, they shall be troubled: thou shalt take away their breath, and they shall fail, and shall return to their dust.

30 Thou shalt send forth thy spirit, and they shall be created: and thou shalt renew the face of the earth.

31 May the glory of the Lord endure for ever: the Lord shall rejoice in his works.

32 He looketh upon the earth, and maketh it tremble: he toucheth the mountains, and they smoke.

33 [2] I will sing to the Lord as long as I live: I will sing praise to my God while I have my being.

34 Let my speech be acceptable to him: but I will take delight in the Lord.

35 Let sinners be consumed out of the earth, and the unjust, so that they be no more. O my soul, bless thou the Lord.

PSALM 104
Confitemini Domino
A thanksgiving to God for his benefits to his people Israel.

Alleluia.

GIVE [1] glory to the Lord, and call upon his name: declare his deeds among the Gentiles.

2 Sing to him, yea sing praises to him: relate all his wondrous works.

3 Glory ye in his holy name: let the heart of them rejoice that seek the Lord.

4 Seek ye the Lord, and be strengthened: seek his face evermore.

5 Remember his marvellous works which he hath done: his wonders, and the judgments of his mouth.

6 O ye seed of Abraham his servant; ye sons of Jacob his chosen.

7 He is the Lord our God: his judgments are in all the earth.

8 He hath remembered his covenant for ever: the word which he commanded to a thousand generations.

9 [2] Which he made to Abraham; and his oath to Isaac:

10 And he appointed the same to Jacob for a law, and to Israel for an everlasting testament:

11 Saying: To thee will I give the land of Chanaan, the lot of your inheritance.

12 When they were but a small number: *yea* very few, and sojourners therein:

13 And they passed from nation to nation, and from *one* kingdom to another people.

14 He suffered no man to hurt them: and he reproved kings for their sakes.

15 [3] Touch ye not my anointed: and do no evil to my prophets.

16 And he called a famine upon the land: and he broke in pieces all the support of bread.

17 He sent a man before them: [4] Joseph, *who* was sold for a slave.

18 [5] They humbled his feet in fetters: the iron pierced his soul, 19 until his word came.

The word of the Lord inflamed him. 20 [6] The king sent, and he released him: the ruler of the people, and he set him at liberty.

21 He made him master of his house, and ruler of all his possession.

22 That he might instruct his princes as himself, and teach his ancients wisdom.

23 [7] And Israel went into Egypt: and Jacob was a sojourner in the land of Cham.

24 [8] And he increased his people exceedingly: and strengthened them over their enemies.

25 He turned their heart to hate his people: and to deal deceitfully with his servants.

26 [9] He sent Moses his servant: Aaron, the man whom he had chosen.

27 [10] He gave them power to shew his signs and his wonders, in the land of Cham.

28 [11] He sent darkness, and made it obscure: and grieved not his words.

29 [12] He turned their waters into blood and destroyed their fish.

30 [13] Their land brought forth frogs, in the inner chambers of their kings.

31 [14] He spoke, and there came divers sorts of flies and sciniphs in all their coasts.

32 He gave them hail for rain, a burning fire in the land.

33 And he destroyed their vineyards and their fig trees: and he broke in pieces the trees of their coasts.

34 [15] He spoke, and the locust came, and the bruchus, of which there was no number.

35 And they devoured all the grass in their land and consumed all the fruit of their ground.

36 [16] And he slew all the firstborn in their land: the firstfruits of all their labour.

37 [17] And he brought them out with

---

[7] Gen. 46, 6. [8] Exod. 1, 7; Acts, 7, 17. [9] Exod. 3, 10; 4, 29. [10] Exod. 7, 10. [11] Exod. 10, 21. [12] Exod. 7, 20. [13] Exod. 8, 6. [14] Exod. 8, 16, 24. [15] Exod. 10, 12. [16] Exod. 12, 29. [17] Exod. 12, 35. [18] Exod. 13, 21; Ps. 77, 14; 1 Cor. 10, 1. [19] Exod. 16, 13. [20] Num. 20, 11. [21] Gen. 17, 7. PSALM 105. [1] Judith, 13, 21. [2] Ecclus. 43, 35. [3] Judith, 7, 19. [4] Exod. 14, 22. [5] Exod. 14, 27.

PSALM 104. Ver. 25. *He turned their heart.* Not that God (who is never the author of sin) moved the Egyptians to hate and persecute his people; but that the Egyptians took occasion of hating and envying them, from the sight of the benefits which God bestowed upon them.

Ver. 28. *Grieved not his words.* That is, he was not wanting to fulfil his words: or he did not grieve Moses and Aaron, the carriers of his words: or he did not *grieve his words,* that is, *his sons,* the children of Israel, who enjoyed light whilst the Egyptians were oppressed with darkness.

Ver. 31. *Sciniphs.* See the annotation, Exod. 8, 16.

Ver. 34. *Bruchus,* an insect of the locust kind.

Ver. 45. *His justifications.* That is, his commandments; which here, and in many other places of the scripture, are called *justifications,* because the keeping of them makes man just. The Protestants render it by the word *statutes,* in favour of their doctrine, which does not allow good works to justify.

---

silver and gold: and there was not among their tribes one that was feeble.

38 Egypt was glad when they departed: for the fear of them lay upon them.

39 [18] He spread a cloud for their protection, and fire to give them light in the night.

40 [19] They asked, and the quail came: and he filled them with the bread of heaven.

41 [20] He opened the rock, and waters flowed: rivers ran down in the dry land.

42 [21] Because he remembered his holy word, which he had spoken to his servant Abraham.

43 And he brought forth his people with joy, and his chosen with gladness.

44 And he gave them the lands of the Gentiles; and they possessed the labours of the people:

45 That they might observe his justifications and seek after his law.

PSALM 105

Confitemini Domino

A confession of the manifold sins and ingratitudes of the Israelites.

Alleluia.

GIVE [1] glory to the Lord, for he is good: for his mercy endureth for ever.

2 [2] Who shall declare the powers of the Lord? Who shall set forth all his praises?

3 Blessed are they that keep judgment and do justice at all times.

4 Remember us, O Lord, in the favour of thy people: visit us with thy salvation.

5 That we may see the good of thy chosen, that we may rejoice in the joy of thy nation: that thou mayst be praised with thy inheritance.

6 [3] We have sinned with our fathers: we have acted unjustly, we have wrought iniquity.

7 Our fathers understood not thy wonders in Egypt. They remembered not the multitude of thy mercies:

And they provoked to wrath going up to the sea, even the Red Sea.

8 And he saved them for his own name's sake: that he might make his power known.

9 [4] And he rebuked the Red Sea, and it was dried up: and he led them through the depths, as in a wilderness.

10 And he saved them from the hand of them that hated them: and he redeemed them from the hand of the enemy.

11 [5] And the water covered them that afflicted them: there was not one of them left.

12 And they believed his words: and they sang his praises.

13 They had quickly done, they forgot his works: and they waited not for his counsel.

14 [6] And they coveted their desire in the desert: and they tempted God in the place without water.

15 [7] And he gave them their request: and sent fulness into their souls.

16 And they provoked Moses in the camp, Aaron the holy one of the Lord.

17 [8] The earth opened and swallowed up Dathan: and covered the congregation of Abiron.

18 And a fire was kindled in their congregation: the flame burned the wicked.

19 [9] They made also a calf in Horeb: and they adored the graven thing.

20 And they changed their glory into the likeness of a calf that eateth grass.

21 They forgot God, who saved them, who had done great things in Egypt, 22 wondrous works in the land of Cham, terrible things in the Red Sea.

23 [10] And he said that he would destroy them, had not Moses his chosen stood before him in the breach:

To turn away his wrath, lest he should destroy them. 24 And they set at nought the desirable land.

They believed not his word. 25 and they murmured in their tents: they hearkened not to the voice of the Lord.

26 [11] And he lifted up his hand over them, to overthrow them in the desert;

27 And to cast down their seed among the nations, and to scatter them in the countries.

28 They also were initiated to Beelphegor: and ate the sacrifices of the dead.

29 And they provoked him with their inventions: and destruction was multiplied among them.

30 [12] Then Phinees stood up, and pacified him: and the slaughter ceased.

31 And it was reputed to him unto justice, to generation and generation for evermore.

32 [13] They provoked him also at the waters of contradiction: and Moses was afflicted for their sakes, 33 because they exasperated his spirit.

And he distinguished with his lips.

34 They did not destroy the nations of which the Lord spoke unto them.

35 And they were mingled among the heathens, and learned their works, 36 and served their idols: and it became a stumbling-block to them.

37 And they sacrificed their sons, and their daughters to devils.

38 And they shed innocent blood: the blood of their sons and of their daughters which they sacrificed to the idols of Chanaan.

And the land was polluted with blood, 39 and was defiled with their works: and they went aside after their own inventions.

40 And the Lord was exceedingly angry with his people: and he abhorred his inheritance.

41 And he delivered them into the hands of the nations: and they that hated them had dominion over them.

42 And their enemies afflicted them: and they were humbled under their hands. 43 Many times did he deliver them:

But they provoked him with their counsel. And they were brought low by their iniquities.

44 And he saw when they were in tribulation: and he heard their prayer.

45 [14] And he was mindful of his covenant: and repented according to the multitude of his mercies.

46 And he gave them unto mercies, in the sight of all those that had made them captives.

47 Save us, O Lord, our God, and gather us from among the nations:

That we may give thanks to thy holy name, and may glory in thy praise.

48 Blessed be the Lord, the God of Israel, from everlasting to everlasting. And let all the people say: So be it. So be it.

PSALM 106

Confitemini Domino

All are invited to give thanks to God for his perpetual providence over men.

Alleluia.

GIVE glory to the Lord, for he is good: for his mercy endureth for ever.

2 Let them say *so* that have been redeemed by the Lord: whom he hath redeemed from the hand of the enemy and gathered out of the countries.

3 From the rising and from the setting of the sun, from the north, and from the sea.

4 They wandered in a wilderness, in a place without water: they found not the way of a city for their habitation.

---

[6] Exod. 17, 2.   [7] Num. 11, 31.   [8] Num. 16, 32.   [9] Exod. 32, 4.   [10] Exod. 32, 10.   [11] Num. 14, 32.   [12] Num. 25, 7.   [13] Num. 20, 10.   [14] Deut. 30, 1.

PSALM 105. Ver. 28. *Initiated.* That is, they dedicated, or consecrated themselves to the idol of the Moabites and Madianites, called Beelphegor, or Baal-Peor (Num 25, 3).—*The dead.* That is, idols *without life.*

Ver. 33. *He distinguished with his lips.* Moses, by occasion of the people's rebellion and incredulity, was guilty of *distinguishing with his lips;* when, instead of speaking to the rock, as God had commanded, he said to the people, with a certain hesitation in his faith, *Hear ye, rebellious and incredulous: Can we from this rock bring out water for you?* (Num. 20, 10).

5 They were hungry and thirsty: their soul fainted in them.

6 And they cried to the Lord in their tribulation: and he delivered them out of their distresses.

7 And he led them into the right way: that they might go to a city of habitation.

8 Let the mercies of the Lord give glory to him: and his wonderful works to the children of men.

9 For he hath satisfied the empty soul: and hath filled the hungry soul with good things.

10 Such as sat in darkness and in the shadow of death: bound in want and in iron.

11 Because they had exasperated the words of God: and provoked the counsel of the most High:

12 And their heart was humbled with labours: they were weakened, and there was none to help them.

13 Then they cried to the Lord in their affliction: and he delivered them out of their distresses.

14 And he brought them out of darkness and the shadow of death: and broke their bonds in sunder.

15 Let the mercies of the Lord give glory to him: and his wonderful works to the children of men.

16 Because he hath broken gates of brass and burst iron bars.

17 He took them out of the way of their iniquity: for they were brought low for their injustices.

18 Their soul abhorred all manner of meat: and they drew nigh even to the gates of death.

19 And they cried to the Lord in their affliction: and he delivered them out of their distresses.

20 He sent his word, and healed them: and delivered them from their destructions.

21 Let the mercies of the Lord give glory to him: and his wonderful works to the children of men.

22 And let them sacrifice the sacrifice of praise: and declare his works with joy.

23 They that go down to the sea in ships, doing business in the great waters:

24 These have seen the works of the Lord, and his wonders in the deep.

25 He said the word, and there arose a storm of wind: and the waves thereof were lifted up.

26 They mount up to the heavens, and they go down to the depths: their soul pined away with evils.

27 They were troubled, and reeled

PSALM 106. [1] Job. 22, 19.

like a drunken man: and all their wisdom was swallowed up.

28 And they cried to the Lord in their affliction: and he brought them out of their distresses.

29 And he turned the storm into a breeze: and its waves were still.

30 And they rejoiced because they were still: and he brought them to the haven which they wished for.

31 Let the mercies of the Lord give glory to him: and his wonderful works to the children of men.

32 And let them exalt him in the church of the people: and praise him in the chair of the ancients.

33 He hath turned rivers into a wilderness: and the sources of waters into dry ground:

34 A fruitful land into barrenness: for the wickedness of them that dwell therein.

35 He hath turned a wilderness into pools of waters: and a dry land into water springs.

36 And hath placed there the hungry: and they made a city for their habitation.

37 And they sowed fields, and planted vineyards: and they yielded fruit of birth.

38 And he blessed them, and they were multiplied exceedingly: and their cattle he suffered not to decrease.

39 Then they were brought to be few: and they were afflicted through the trouble of evils and sorrow.

40 Contempt was poured forth upon *their* princes: and he caused them to wander where there was no passing, and out of the way.

41 And he helped the poor out of poverty: and made *him* families like a *flock of* sheep.

42 [1] The just shall see, and shall rejoice: and all iniquity shall stop her mouth.

43 Who is wise, and will keep these things: and will understand the mercies of the Lord?

PSALM 107

Paratum cor meum

The prophet praiseth God for benefits received.

1 A canticle of a psalm for David himself.

2 **M**Y heart is ready, O God, my heart is ready: I will sing, and will give praise, with my glory.

3 Arise, my glory: arise, psaltery and harp. I will arise in the morning early.

4 I will praise thee, O Lord, among the people: and I will sing unto thee among the nations.

5 For thy mercy is great above the

heavens: and thy truth even unto the clouds.

6 Be thou exalted, O God, above the heavens, and thy glory over all the earth: 7 that thy beloved may be delivered.

Save with thy right hand and hear me. 8 God hath spoken in his holiness.

I will rejoice, and I will divide Sichem: and I will mete out the vale of tabernacles.

9 Galaad is mine: and Manasses is mine: and Ephraim the protector of my head.

Juda is my king: 10 Moab the pot of my hope.

Over Edom I will stretch out my shoe: the aliens are become my friends.

11 Who will bring me into the strong city? Who will lead me into Edom?

12 Wilt not thou, O God, who hast cast us off? And wilt not thou, O God, go forth with our armies?

13 O grant us help from trouble: for vain is the help of man.

14 Through God we shall do mightily: and he will bring our enemies to nothing.

PSALM 108

Deus, laudem meam

David in the person of Christ, prayeth against his persecutors, more especially the traitor Judas: foretelling and approving his just punishment for his obstinacy in sin, and final impenitence.

1 Unto the end. A psalm for David.

2 O GOD, be not thou silent in my praise: for the mouth of the wicked and the mouth of the deceitful man is opened against me.

3 They have spoken against me with deceitful tongues; and they have compassed me about with words of hatred; and have have fought against me without cause.

4 Instead of making me a return of love, they detracted me: but I gave myself to prayer.

5 And they repaid me evil for good: and hatred for my love.

6 Set thou the sinner over him: and may the devil stand at his right hand.

7 When he is judged, may he go out condemned: and may his prayer be turned to sin.

8 May his days be few: and his bishopric let another take.

9 May his children be fatherless: and his wife a widow.

10 Let his children be carried about vagabonds, and beg: and let them be cast out of their dwellings.

11 May the usurer search all his substance: and let strangers plunder his labours.

12 May there be none to help him: nor any to pity his fatherless offspring.

13 May his posterity be cut off: in one generation may his name be blotted out.

14 May the iniquity of his fathers be remembered in the sight of the Lord: and let not the sin of his mother be blotted out.

15 May they be before the Lord continually: and let the memory of them perish from the earth. 16 Because he remembered not to shew mercy:

17 But persecuted the poor man and the beggar, and the broken in heart, to put him to death.

18 And he loved cursing, and it shall come unto him: and he would not have blessing, and it shall be far from him.

And he put on cursing, like a garment: and it went in like water into his entrails, and like oil in his bones.

19 May it be unto him like a garment which covereth him: and like a girdle with which he is girded continually.

20 This is the work of them who detract me before the Lord: and who speak evils against my soul.

21 But thou, O Lord, do with me for thy name's sake: because thy mercy is sweet.

Do thou deliver me, 22 for I am poor and needy: and my heart is troubled within me.

23 I am taken away like the shadow when it declineth: and I am shaken off as locusts.

24 My knees are weakened through fasting: and my flesh is changed for oil.

25 And I am become a reproach to them: they saw me and they shaked their heads.

26 Help me, O Lord my God: save me according to thy mercy.

27 And let them know that this is thy hand: and *that* thou, O Lord, hast done it.

28 They will curse and thou wilt bless: let them that rise up against me be confounded: but thy servant shall rejoice.

29 Let them that detract me be clothed with shame: and let them be covered with their confusion as with a double cloak.

30 I will give great thanks to the

PSALM 108. Ver. 6. *Set thou the sinner over him.* Give to the devil, that arch-sinner, power over him: let him enter into him, and possess him. The imprecations, contained in the thirty verses of this psalm, are opposed to the thirty pieces of silver for which Judas betrayed our Lord; and are to be taken as prophetic denunciations of the evils that should befall the traitor and his accomplices the Jews; and not properly as curses.

Ver. 24. *For oil. Propter oleum.* The meaning is, my flesh is changed, being perfectly emaciated, and dried up, as having lost all its oil or fatness.

Lord with my mouth, and in the midst of many I will praise him:

31 Because he hath stood at the right hand of the poor, to save my soul from persecutors.

PSALM 109

Dixit Dominus

Christ's exaltation and everlasting priesthood.

1 A psalm for David.

THE [1] Lord said to my Lord: Sit thou at my right hand:

2 Until I make thy enemies thy footstool.

2 The Lord will send forth the sceptre of thy power out of Sion: rule thou in the midst of thy enemies.

3 With thee is the principality in the day of thy strength, in the brightness of the saints: from the womb before the day star I begot thee.

4 The Lord hath sworn, and he will not repent: [3] Thou art a priest for ever according to the order of Melchisedech.

5 The Lord at thy right hand hath broken kings in the day of his wrath.

6 He shall judge among nations, he shall fill ruins: he shall crush the heads in the land of many.

7 He shall drink of the torrent in the way: therefore shall he lift up the head.

PSALM 110

Confitebor tibi, Domine

God is to be praised for his graces and benefits to his church.

Alleluia.

I WILL praise thee, O Lord, with my whole heart; in the council of the just, and in the congregation.

2 Great are the works of the Lord: sought out according to all his wills.

3 His work is praise and magnificence: and his justice continueth for ever and ever.

4 He hath made a remembrance of his wonderful works, being a merciful and gracious Lord: 5 he hath given food to them that fear him.

He will be mindful for ever of his covenant: 6 he will shew forth to his people the power of his works.

7 That he may give them the inheritance of the Gentiles: the works of his hands are truth and judgment.

8 All his commandments are faith-

ful: confirmed for ever and ever, made in truth and equity.

9 He hath sent redemption to his people: he hath commanded his covenant for ever.

Holy and terrible is his name: 10 [1] the fear of the Lord is the beginning of wisdom.

A good understanding to all that do it: his praise continueth for ever and ever.

PSALM 111

Beatus vir

The good man is happy.

Alleluia. Of the returning of Aggeus and Zacharias.

BLESSED is the man that feareth the Lord: he shall delight exceedingly in his commandments.

2 His seed shall be mighty upon earth: the generation of the righteous shall be blessed.

3 Glory and wealth *shall* be in his house: and his justice remaineth for ever and ever.

4 To the righteous a light is risen up in darkness: *he is* merciful, and compassionate and just.

5 Acceptable is the man that sheweth mercy and lendeth: he shall order his words with judgment, 6 because he shall not be moved for ever.

7 The just shall be in everlasting remembrance: he shall not fear the evil hearing.

His heart is ready to hope in the Lord, 8 his heart is strengthened: he shall not be moved until he look over his enemies.

9 He hath distributed, he hath given to the poor: his justice remaineth for ever and ever; his horn shall be exalted in glory.

10 The wicked shall see and shall be angry, he shall gnash with his teeth and pine away: the desire of the wicked shall perish.

PSALM 112

Laudate, pueri

God is to be praised for his regard to the poor and humble.

Alleluia.

PRAISE the Lord, ye children: praise ye the name of the Lord.

2 Blessed be the name of the Lord: from henceforth now and for ever.

3 [1] From the rising of the sun unto the going down of the same, the name of the Lord is worthy of praise.

4 The Lord is high above all nations: and his glory above the heavens.

5 Who is as the Lord our God, who dwelleth on high, 6 and looketh down

PSALM 109. [1] Matt. 22, 44. [2] 1 Cor. 25, 25; Heb. 1, 13; 10, 13. [3] John, 12, 34; Heb. 5, 6; 7, 17. PSALM 110. [1] Prov. 1, 7; 9, 10; Ecclus. 1, 16. PSALM 112. [1] Mal. 1, 11.

PSALM 111. *Of the returning.* This is in the Greek and Latin, but not in the Hebrew. It signifies that this psalm was proper to be sung at the time of the return of the people from their captivity; to inculcate to them, how happy they might be, if they would be constant in the service of God.

on the low things in heaven and in earth?

7 Raising up the needy from the earth: and lifting up the poor out of the dunghill.

8 That he may place him with princes: with the princes of his people.

9 Who maketh a barren woman to dwell in a house: the joyful mother of children.

PSALM 113

In exitu Israel

God hath shewn his power in delivering his people. Idols are vain. The Hebrews divide this into two psalms.

Alleluia.

WHEN [1] Israel went out of Egypt, the house of Jacob from a barbarous people:

2 Judea was made his sanctuary, Israel his dominion.

3 The sea saw and fled: Jordan was turned back.

4 The mountains skipped like rams: and the hills like the lambs of the flock.

5 What ailed thee, O thou sea, that thou didst flee? And thou, O Jordan, that thou wast turned back?

6 Ye mountains, that ye skipped like rams, and ye hills, like lambs of the flock?

7 At the presence of the Lord the earth was moved: at the presence of the God of Jacob:

8 Who turned the rock into pools of water, and the stony hill into fountains of waters.

1 Not to us, O Lord, not to us: but to thy name give glory.

2 For thy mercy, and for thy truth's sake: lest the Gentiles should say: Where is their God?

3 But our God is in heaven: he hath done all things whatsoever he would.

4 [2] The idols of the Gentiles are silver and gold, the works of the hands of men.

5 [3] They have mouths and speak not: they have eyes and see not.

6 They have ears and hear not: they have noses and smell not.

7 They have hands and feel not, they have feet and walk not: neither shall they cry out through their throat.

8 Let them that make them become like unto them: and all such as trust in them.

9 The house of Israel hath hoped in the Lord: he is their helper and their protector.

10 The house of Aaron hath hoped in the Lord: he is their helper and their protector.

11 They that fear the Lord have hoped in the Lord: he is their helper and their protector.

12 The Lord hath been mindful of us, and hath blessed us.

He hath blessed the house of Israel: he hath blessed the house of Aaron.

13 He hath blessed all that fear the Lord, both little and great.

14 May the Lord add blessings upon you: upon you, and upon your children.

15 Blessed be you of the Lord: who made heaven and earth.

16 The heaven of heaven is the Lord's: but the earth he has given to the children of men.

17 [4] The dead shall not praise thee, O Lord: nor any of them that go down to hell.

18 But we that live bless the Lord: from this time now and for ever.

PSALM 114

Dilexi

The prayer of a just man in affliction, with a lively confidence in God.

Alleluia.

I HAVE loved, because the Lord will hear the voice of my prayer.

2 Because he hath inclined his ear unto me: and in my days I will call upon him.

3 The sorrows of death have compassed me: and the perils of hell have found me.

I met with trouble and sorrow: 4 and I called upon the name of the Lord.

O Lord, deliver my soul. 5 The Lord is merciful and just, and our God sheweth mercy.

6 The Lord is the keeper of little ones. I was humbled, and he delivered me.

7 Turn, O my soul, into thy rest: for the Lord hath been bountiful to thee.

8 For he hath delivered my soul from death: my eyes from tears, my feet from falling.

9 I will please the Lord in the land of the living.

PSALM 115

Credidi

This in the Hebrew is joined with the foregoing psalm, and continues to express the faith and gratitude of the psalmist.

Alleluia.

10 **I** HAVE [1] believed, therefore have I spoken: but I have been humbled exceedingly.

11 I said in my excess: [2] Every man is a liar.

PSALM 113. [1] Exod. 13, 3. [2] Ps. 134, 15. [3] Wisd. 15, 15. [4] Bar. 2, 17. PSALM 115. [1] 2 Cor. 4, 13. [2] Rom. 3, 4.

12 What shall I render to the Lord for all the things that he hath rendered to me?

13 I will take the chalice of salvation: and I will call upon the name of the Lord.

14 I will pay my vows to the Lord before all his people. 15 Precious in the sight of the Lord is the death of his saints.

16 O Lord, for I am thy servant: I am thy servant, and the son of thy handmaid.

Thou hast broken my bonds. 17 I will sacrifice to thee the sacrifice of praise: and I will call upon the name of the Lord.

18 I will pay my vows to the Lord in the sight of all his people: 19 in the courts of the house of the Lord, in the midst of thee, O Jerusalem.

PSALM 116

Laudate Dominum

All nations are called upon to praise God for his mercy and truth.

Alleluia.

PRAISE [1] the Lord, all ye nations: praise him, all ye people.

2 For his mercy is confirmed upon us: [2] and the truth of the Lord remaineth for ever.

PSALM 117

Confitemini Domino

The psalmist praiseth God for his delivery from evils. Putteth his whole trust in him. Foretelleth the coming of Christ.

Alleluia.

GIVE praise to the Lord, for he is good: for his mercy endureth for ever.

2 Let Israel now say, that he is good: that his mercy endureth for ever.

3 Let the house of Aaron now say: that his mercy endureth for ever.

4 Let them that fear the Lord now say: that his mercy endureth for ever.

5 In my trouble I called upon the Lord: and the Lord heard me, and enlarged me.

6 The Lord is my helper: I will not fear what man can do unto me.

7 [1] The Lord is my helper: and I will look over my enemies.

8 It is good to confide in the Lord, rather than to have confidence in man.

9 It is good to trust in the Lord, rather than to trust in princes.

10 All nations compassed me about: and in the name of the Lord I have been revenged on them.

11 Surrounding me they compassed me about: and in the name of the Lord I have been revenged on them.

12 They surrounded me like bees, and they burned like fire among thorns: and in the name of the Lord I was revenged on them.

13 Being pushed I was overturned that I might fall: but the Lord supported me.

14 [2] The Lord is my strength and my praise: and he is become my salvation.

15 The voice of rejoicing and of salvation is in the tabernacles of the just.

16 The right hand of the Lord hath wrought strength: the right hand of the Lord hath exalted me: the right hand of the Lord hath wrought strength.

17 I shall not die, but live: and shall declare the works of the Lord.

18 The Lord chastising hath chastised me: but he hath not delivered me over to death.

19 Open ye to me the gates of justice: I will go in to them, and give praise to the Lord. 20 This is the gate of the Lord: the just shall enter into it.

21 I will give glory to thee because thou hast heard me: and art become my salvation.

22 [3] The stone which the builders rejected: the same is become the head of the corner.

23 This is the Lord's doing: and it is wonderful in our eyes.

24 This is the day which the Lord hath made: let us be glad and rejoice therein.

25 O Lord, save me: O Lord, give good success. 26 Blessed be he that cometh in the name of the Lord.

We have blessed you out of the house of the Lord. 27 The Lord is God, and he hath shone upon us.

Appoint a solemn day, with shady boughs, even to the horn of the altar.

28 Thou art my God, and I will praise thee: thou art my God, and I will exalt thee.

I will praise thee, because thou hast heard me and art become my salvation.

29 O praise ye the Lord, for he is good: for his mercy endureth for ever.

PSALM 118

Beati immaculati

Of the excellence of virtue consisting in the love and observance of the commandments of God.

Alleluia.

ALEPH.

BLESSED are the undefiled in the way: who walk in the law of the Lord.

PSALM 116. [1] Rom. 15, 11. [2] John, 12, 34. PSALM 117. [1] Heb. 13, 6. [2] Exod. 15, 2. [3] Isai. 28, 16; Matt. 21, 42; Luke, 20, 17; Acts, 4, 11; Rom. 9, 33; 1 Peter, 2, 7.

2 Blessed are they that search his testimonies: that seek him with their whole heart.

3 For they that work iniquity have not walked in his ways.

4 Thou hast commanded thy commandments to be kept most diligently.

5 O that my ways may be directed to keep thy justifications!

6 Then shall I not be confounded, when I shall look into all thy commandments.

7 I will praise thee with uprightness of heart, when I shall have learned the judgments of thy justice.

8 I will keep thy justifications: O do not thou utterly forsake me!

BETH.

9 By what doth a young man correct his way? By observing thy words.

10 With my whole heart have I sought after thee: let me not stray from thy commandments.

11 Thy words have I hidden in my heart, that I may not sin against thee.

12 Blessed art thou, O Lord: teach me thy justifications.

13 With my lips I have pronounced all the judgments of thy mouth.

14 I have been delighted in the way of thy testimonies, as in all riches.

15 I will meditate on thy commandments: and I will consider thy ways.

16 I will think of thy justifications: I will not forget thy words.

GIMEL.

17 Give bountifully to thy servant, enliven me: and I shall keep thy words.

18 Open thou my eyes: and I will consider the wondrous things of thy law.

19 I am a sojourner on the earth: hide not thy commandments from me.

20 My soul hath coveted to long for thy justifications, at all times.

21 Thou hast rebuked the proud: they are cursed who decline from thy commandments.

22 Remove from me reproach and contempt: because I have sought after thy testimonies.

23 For princes sat, and spoke against me: but thy servant was employed in thy justifications.

24 For thy testimonies are my meditation: and thy justifications my counsel.

DALETH.

25 My soul hath cleaved to the pavement: quicken thou me according to thy word.

26 I have declared my ways, and thou hast heard me: teach me thy justifications.

27 Make me to understand the way of thy justifications: and I shall be exercised in thy wondrous works.

28 My soul hath slumbered through heaviness: strengthen thou me in thy words.

29 Remove from me the way of iniquity: and out of thy law have mercy on me.

30 I have chosen the way of truth: thy judgments I have not forgotten.

31 I have stuck to thy testimonies, O Lord: put me not to shame.

32 I have run the way of thy commandments, when thou didst enlarge my heart.

HE.

33 Set before me for a law the way of thy justifications, O Lord: and I will always seek after it.

34 Give me understanding, and I will search thy law: and I will keep it with my whole heart.

35 Lead me into the path of thy commandments: for this same I have desired.

36 Incline my heart into thy testimonies and not to covetousness.

37 Turn away my eyes that they may not behold vanity: quicken me in thy way.

38 Establish thy word to thy servant, in thy fear.

39 Turn away my reproach, which I have apprehended: for thy judgments are delightful.

40 Behold I have longed after thy precepts: quicken me in thy justice.

VAU.

41 Let thy mercy also come upon me, O Lord: thy salvation according to thy word.

42 So shall I answer them that reproach me in any thing: that I have trusted in thy words.

43 And take not thou the word of truth utterly out of my mouth: for in thy words, I have hoped exceedingly.

44 So shall I always keep thy law, for ever and ever.

PSALM 118. *Aleph.* The first eight verses of this psalm in the original begin with *Aleph*, which is the name of the first letter of the Hebrew alphabet. The second eight verses begin with *Beth*, the name of the second letter of the Hebrew alphabet; and so to the end of the whole alphabet, in all twenty-two letters, each letter having eight verses. This order is variously expounded by the holy fathers; which shews the difficulty of understanding the holy scriptures, and consequently with what humility, and submission to the Church they are to be read.

Ver. 2. *His testimonies.* The commandments of God are called his *testimonies*, because they testify his holy will unto us. Note here, that in almost every verse of this psalm (which in number are one hundred and seventy-six) the word and law of God, and the love and observance of it, is perpetually inculcated, under a variety of denominations, all signifying the same thing.

45 And I walked at large: because I have sought after thy commandments.

46 And I spoke of thy testimonies before kings: and I was not ashamed.

47 I meditated also on thy commandments, which I loved:

48 And I lifted up my hands to thy commandments, which I loved. And I was exercised in thy justifications.

ZAIN.

49 Be thou mindful of thy word to thy servant: in which thou hast given me hope.

50 This hath comforted me in my humiliation: because thy word hath enlivened me.

51 The proud did iniquitously altogether: but I declined not from thy law.

52 I remembered, O Lord, thy judgments of old: and I was comforted.

53 A fainting hath taken hold of me, because of the wicked that forsake thy law.

54 Thy justifications were the subject of my song in the place of my pilgrimage.

55 In the night I have remembered thy name, O Lord: and have kept thy law.

56 This happened to me: because I sought after thy justifications.

HETH.

57 O Lord, my portion. I have said, I would keep thy law.

58 I entreated thy face with all my heart: have mercy on me according to thy word.

59 I have thought on my ways: and turned my feet unto thy testimonies.

60 I am ready, and am not troubled: that I may keep thy commandments.

61 The cords of the wicked have encompassed me: but I have not forgotten thy law.

62 I rose at midnight to give praise to thee: for the judgments of thy justification.

63 I am a partaker with all them that fear thee: and that keep thy commandments.

64 The earth, O Lord, is full of thy mercy: teach me thy justifications.

TETH.

65 Thou hast done well with thy servant, O Lord, according to thy word.

66 Teach me goodness and discipline and knowledge: for I have believed thy commandments.

67 Before I was humbled I offended: therefore have I kept thy word.

68 Thou art good: and in thy goodness teach me thy justifications.

69 The iniquity of the proud hath been multiplied over me: but I will seek thy commandments with my whole heart.

70 Their heart is curdled like milk: but I have meditated on thy law.

71 It is good for me that thou hast humbled me: that I may learn thy justifications.

72 The law of thy mouth is good to me, above thousands of gold and silver.

JOD.

73 Thy hands have made me and formed me: give me understanding, and I will learn thy commandments.

74 They that fear thee shall see me and shall be glad: because I have greatly hoped in thy words.

75 I know, O Lord, that thy judgments are equity: and in thy truth thou hast humbled me.

76 O let thy mercy be for my comfort, according to thy word unto thy servant!

77 Let thy tender mercies come unto me, and I shall live: for thy law is my meditation.

78 Let the proud be ashamed, because they have done unjustly towards me: but I will be employed in thy commandments.

79 Let them that fear thee turn to me: and they that know thy testimonies.

80 Let my heart be undefiled in thy justifications, that I may not be confounded.

CAPH.

81 My soul hath fainted after thy salvation: and in thy word I have very much hoped.

82 My eyes have failed for thy word, saying: When wilt thou comfort me?

83 For I am become like a bottle in the frost. I have not forgotten thy justifications.

84 How many are the days of thy servant? When wilt thou execute judgment on them that persecute me?

85 The wicked have told me fables: but not as thy law.

86 All thy statutes are truth. They have persecuted me unjustly: do thou help me.

87 They had almost made an end of me upon earth: but I have not forsaken thy commandments.

88 Quicken thou me according to thy mercy: and I shall keep the testimonies of thy mouth.

LAMED.

89 For ever, O Lord, thy word standeth firm in heaven:

90 Thy truth unto all generations. Thou hast founded the earth, and it continueth.

91 By thy ordinance the day goeth on: for all things serve thee.

92 Unless thy law had been my meditation, I had then perhaps perished in my abjection.

93 Thy justifications I will never forget: for by them thou hast given me life.

94 I am thine. Save thou me: for I have sought thy justifications.

95 The wicked have waited for me to destroy me: *but* I have understood thy testimonies.

96 I have seen an end of all perfection: thy commandment is exceeding broad.

MEM.

97 O how have I loved thy law, O Lord! It is my meditation all the day.

98 Through thy commandment, thou hast made me wiser than my enemies: for it is ever with me.

99 I have understood more than all my teachers: because thy testimonies are my meditation.

100 I have had understanding above ancients: because I have sought thy commandments.

101 I have restrained my feet from every evil way: that I may keep thy words.

102 I have not declined from thy judgments: because thou hast set me a law.

103 How sweet are thy words to my palate! More than honey to my mouth!

104 By thy commandments I have had understanding: therefore have I hated every way of iniquity.

NUN.

105 Thy word is a lamp to my feet, and a light to my paths.

106 I have sworn: and am determined to keep the judgments of thy justice.

107 I have been humbled, O Lord, exceedingly: quicken thou me according to thy word.

108 The free offerings of my mouth make acceptable, O Lord: and teach me thy judgments.

109 My soul is continually in my hands and I have not forgotten thy law.

110 Sinners have laid a snare for me: but I have not erred from thy precepts.

111 I have purchased thy testimonies for an inheritance for ever: because they are the joy of my heart.

112 I have inclined my heart to do thy justifications for ever, for the reward.

SAMECH.

113 I have hated the unjust: and have loved thy law.

114 Thou art my helper and my protector: and in thy word I have greatly hoped.

115 Depart from me, ye malignant: and I will search the commandments of my God.

116 Uphold me according to thy word, and I shall live: and let me not be confounded in my expectation.

117 Help me, and I shall be saved: and I will meditate always on thy justifications.

118 Thou hast despised all them that fall off from thy judgments: for their thought is unjust.

119 I have accounted all the sinners of the earth prevaricators: therefore have I loved thy testimonies.

120 Pierce thou my flesh with thy fear: for I am afraid of thy judgments.

AIN.

121 I have done judgment and justice: give me not up to them that slander me.

122 Uphold thy servant unto good: let not the proud calumniate me.

123 My eyes have fainted after thy salvation: and for the word of thy justice.

124 Deal with thy servant according to thy mercy: and teach me thy justifications.

125 I am thy servant: give me understanding that I may know thy testimonies.

126 It is time, O Lord, to do: they have dissipated thy law.

127 Therefore have I loved thy commandments above gold and the topaz.

128 Therefore was I directed to all thy commandments: I have hated all wicked ways.

PHE.

129 Thy testimonies are wonderful: therefore my soul hath sought them.

130 The declaration of thy words giveth light: and giveth understanding to little ones.

131 I opened my mouth, and panted: because I longed for thy commandments.

132 Look thou upon me and have mercy on me: according to the judgment of them that love thy name.

133 Direct my steps according to thy word: and let no iniquity have dominion over me.

134 Redeem me from the calumnies of men: that I may keep thy commandments.

135 Make thy face to shine upon thy servant: and teach me thy justifications.

136 My eyes have sent forth springs of water: because they have not kept thy law.

SADE.

137 Thou art just, O Lord: and thy judgment is right.

138 Thou hast commanded justice thy testimonies: and thy truth exceedingly.

139 My zeal hath made me pine away: because my enemies forgot thy words.

140 Thy word is exceedingly refined: and thy servant hath loved it.

141 I am very young and despised; *but* I forget not thy justifications.

142 Thy justice is justice for ever: and thy law is the truth.

143 Trouble and anguish have found me: thy commandments are my meditation.

144 Thy testimonies are justice for ever: give me understanding and I shall live.

COPH.

145 I cried with my whole heart: Hear me, O Lord. I will seek thy justifications.

146 I cried unto thee: Save me that I may keep thy commandments.

147 I prevented the dawning of the day, and cried: because in thy words I very much hoped.

148 My eyes to thee have prevented the morning: that I might meditate on thy words.

149 Hear thou my voice, O Lord, according to thy mercy: and quicken me according to thy judgment.

150 They that persecute me have drawn nigh to iniquity: but they are gone far off from thy law.

151 Thou art near, O Lord: and all thy ways are truth.

152 I have known from the beginning concerning thy testimonies: that thou hast founded them for ever.

RES.

153 See my humiliation and deliver me: for I have not forgotten thy law.

154 Judge my judgment and redeem me: quicken thou me for thy word's sake.

155 Salvation is far from sinners; because they have not sought thy justifications.

156 Many, O Lord, are thy mercies: quicken me according to thy judgment.

157 Many are they that persecute me and afflict me; *but* I have not declined from thy testimonies.

158 I beheld the transgressors, and I pined away; because they kept not thy word.

159 Behold, I have loved thy commandments, O Lord: quicken me thou in thy mercy.

160 The beginning of thy words is truth: all the judgments of thy justice are for ever.

SIN.

161 Princes have persecuted me without cause: and my heart hath been in awe of thy words.

162 I will rejoice at thy words, as one that hath found great spoil.

163 I have hated and abhorred iniquity; but I have loved thy law.

164 Seven times a day I have given praise to thee, for the judgments of thy justice.

165 Much peace have they that love thy law: and to them there is no stumbling-block.

166 I looked for thy salvation, O Lord: and I loved thy commandments.

167 My soul hath kept thy testimonies: and hath loved them exceedingly.

168 I have kept thy commandments and thy testimonies: because all my ways are in thy sight.

TAU.

169 Let my supplication, O Lord, come near in thy sight: give me understanding according to thy word.

170 Let my request come in before thee: deliver thou me according to thy word.

171 My lips shall utter a hymn: when thou shalt teach me thy justifications.

172 My tongue shall pronounce thy word: because all thy commandments are justice.

173 Let thy hand be with me to save me: for I have chosen thy precepts.

174 I have longed for thy salvation, O Lord: and thy law is my meditation.

175 My soul shall live and shall praise thee: and thy judgments shall help me.

176 I have gone astray like a sheep that is lost: seek thy servant, because I have not forgotten thy commandments.

PSALM 119

Ad Dominum

A prayer in tribulation.

A gradual canticle.

IN my trouble I cried to the Lord: and he heard me.

2 O Lord, deliver my soul from wicked lips, and a deceitful tongue.

PSALM 119. *A gradual canticle.* The following psalms, in number fifteen, are called *gradual psalms*, or *canticles*, from the *word gradus*, signifying steps, ascensions, or degrees: either be-

3 What shall be given to thee, or what shall be added to thee, to a deceitful tongue?

4 The sharp arrows of the mighty, with coals that lay waste.

5 Woe is me, that my sojourning is prolonged! I have dwelt with the inhabitants of Cedar: 6 my soul hath been long a sojourner.

7 With them that hated peace I was peaceable: when I spoke to them they fought against me without cause.

PSALM 120
Levavi oculos
God is the keeper of his servants.

A gradual canticle.

I HAVE lifted up my eyes to the mountains, from whence help shall come to me.

2 My help is from the Lord, who made heaven and earth.

3 May he not suffer thy foot to be moved: neither let him slumber that keepeth thee.

4 Behold he shall neither slumber nor sleep, that keepeth Israel.

5 The Lord is thy keeper: the Lord is thy protection upon thy right hand.

6 The sun shall not burn thee by day: nor the moon by night.

7 The Lord keepeth thee from all evil: may the Lord keep thy soul.

8 May the Lord keep thy coming in and thy going out: from henceforth now and for ever.

PSALM 121
Lætatus sum in his
The desire and hope of the just for the coming of the kingdom of God, and the peace of his church.

A gradual canticle.

I REJOICED at the things that were said to me: We shall go into the house of the Lord.

2 Our feet were standing in thy courts, O Jerusalem.

3 Jerusalem, which is built as a city, which is compact together.

4 For thither did the tribes go up, the tribes of the Lord: the testimony of Israel, to praise the name of the Lord.

5 Because their seats have sat in judgment, seats upon the house of David.

6 Pray ye for the things that are for the peace of Jerusalem: and abundance for them that love thee.

7 Let peace be in thy strength: and abundance in thy towers.

8 For the sake of my brethren, and of my neighbours, I spoke peace of thee.

9 Because of the house of the Lord our God, I have sought good things for thee.

PSALM 122
Ad te levavi
A prayer in affliction, with confidence in God.

A gradual canticle.

TO thee have I lifted up my eyes: who dwellest in heaven.

2 Behold as the eyes of servants are on the hands of their masters,

As the eyes of the handmaid are on the hands of her mistress: so are our eyes unto the Lord our God, until he have mercy on us.

3 Have mercy on us, O Lord, have mercy on us: for we are greatly filled with contempt.

4 For our soul is greatly filled: *we are* a reproach to the rich, and contempt to the proud.

PSALM 123
Nisi quia Dominus
The church giveth glory to God for her deliverance from the hands of her enemies.

A gradual canticle.

IF it had not been that the Lord was with us, let Israel now say: 2 If it had not been that the Lord was with us,

When men rose up against us: 3 perhaps they had swallowed us up alive.

When their fury was enkindled against us: 4 perhaps the waters had swallowed us up.

5 Our soul hath passed through a torrent: perhaps our soul had passed through a water insupportable.

6 Blessed be the Lord, who hath not given us to be a prey to their teeth.

7 Our soul hath been delivered as a sparrow out of the snare of the fowlers. The snare is broken: and we are delivered.

8 Our help is in the name of the Lord, who made heaven and earth.

PSALM 124
Qui confidunt
The just are always under God's protection.
A gradual canticle.

cause they were appointed to be sung on the *fifteen steps,* by which the people *ascended* to the temple: or, that in the singing of them the voice was to be raised by certain *steps or ascensions:* or that they were to be sung by the people returning from their captivity and *ascending* to Jerusalem, which was seated amongst mountains. The holy fathers, in a mystical sense, understand these steps, or ascensions, of the degrees by which Christians spiritually ascend to virtue and perfection; and to the true temple of God in the heavenly Jerusalem.

THEY that trust in the Lord *shall be* as mount Sion: he shall not be moved for ever that dwelleth 2 in Jerusalem.

Mountains are round about it: so the Lord is round about his people, from henceforth now and for ever.

3 For the Lord will not leave the rod of sinners upon the lot of the just: that the just may not stretch forth their hands to iniquity.

4 Do good, O Lord, to those that are good, and to the upright of heart.

5 But such as turn aside into bonds, the Lord shall lead out with the workers of iniquity. Peace upon Israel.

PSALM 125

In convertendo

The people of God rejoice at their delivery from captivity.

A gradual canticle.

WHEN the Lord brought back the captivity of Sion, we became like men comforted.

2 Then was our mouth filled with gladness: and our tongue with joy.

Then shall they say among the Gentiles: The Lord hath done great things for them.

3 The Lord hath done great things for us: we are become joyful.

4 Turn again our captivity, O Lord, as a stream in the south.

5 They that sow in tears shall reap in joy.

6 Going, they went and wept, casting their seeds.

7 But coming, they shall come with joyfulness, carrying their sheaves.

PSALM 126

Nisi Dominus

Nothing can be done without God's grace and blessing.

A gradual canticle of Solomon.

UNLESS the Lord build the house, they labour in vain that build it. Unless the Lord keep the city, he watcheth in vain that keepeth it.

2 It is vain for you to rise before light: rise ye after you have sitten, you that eat the bread of sorrow.

When he shall give sleep to his beloved, 3 behold the inheritance of the Lord are children: the reward, the fruit of the womb.

4 As arrows in the hand of the mighty, so the children of them that have been shaken.

5 Blessed is the man that hath filled the desire with them: he shall not be

PSALM 126. Ver. 2. *It is vain for you to rise before light.* That is, your early rising, your labour and worldly solicitude, will be *vain*, will avail you nothing, without the light, grace, and blessing of God.

confounded when he shall speak to his enemies in the gate.

PSALM 127

Beati omnes

The fear of God is the way to happiness.

A gradual canticle.

BLESSED are all they that fear the Lord: that walk in his ways.

2 For thou shalt eat the labours of thy hands: blessed art thou, and it shall be well with thee.

3 Thy wife as a fruitful vine, on the sides of thy house.

Thy children as olive plants, round about thy table.

4 Behold, thus shall the man be blessed that feareth the Lord.

5 May the Lord bless thee out of Sion: and mayst thou see the good things of Jerusalem all the days of thy life.

6 And mayst thou see thy children's children, peace upon Israel.

PSALM 128

Sæpe expugnaverunt

The church of God is invincible. Her persecutors come to nothing.

A gradual canticle.

OFTEN have they fought against me from my youth, let Israel now say.

2 Often have they fought against me from my youth: but they could not *prevail* over me.

3 The wicked have wrought upon my back: they have lengthened their iniquity.

4 The Lord *who* is just will cut the necks of sinners. 5 Let them all be confounded and turned back that hate Sion.

6 Let them be as grass upon the tops of houses, which withereth before it be plucked up:

7 Wherewith the mower filleth not his hand, nor he that gathereth sheaves his bosom.

8 And they that passed by have not said: The blessing of the Lord be upon you. We have blessed you in the name of the Lord.

PSALM 129

De profundis

A prayer of a sinner, trusting in the mercies of God. The sixth penitential psalm.

A gradual canticle.

OUT of the depths I have cried to thee, O Lord: 2 Lord, hear my voice.

Let thy ears be attentive to the voice of my supplication.

3 If thou, O Lord, wilt mark iniquities: Lord, who shall stand it?

4 For with thee there is merciful forgiveness: and by reason of thy law, I have waited for thee, O Lord.

My soul hath relied on his word: 5 my soul hath hoped in the Lord.

6 From the morning watch even until night, let Israel hope in the Lord.

7 Because with the Lord there is mercy: and with him plentiful redemption.

And he shall redeem Israel from all his iniquities.

PSALM 130
Domine, non est
The prophet's humility.
A gradual canticle of David.

LORD, my heart is not exalted: nor are my eyes lofty.

Neither have I walked in great matters: nor in wonderful things above me.

2 If I was not humbly minded, but exalted my soul:

As a child that is weaned is towards his mother, so reward in my soul.

3 Let Israel hope in the Lord: from henceforth now and for ever.

PSALM 131
Memento, Domine
A prayer for the fulfilling of the promise made to David.
A gradual canticle.

O LORD, remember David: and all his meekness.

2 How he swore to the Lord, he vowed a vow to the God of Jacob:

3 ¹ If I shall enter into the tabernacle of my house: if I shall go up into the bed wherein I lie:

4 If I shall give sleep to my eyes, or slumber to my eyelids,

5 Or rest to my temples: until I find out a place for the Lord, a tabernacle for the God of Jacob.

6 Behold we have heard of it in Ephrata: we have found it in the fields of the wood.

7 We will go into his tabernacle: we will adore in the place where his feet stood.

8 ² Arise, O Lord, into thy resting place: thou and the ark, which thou hast sanctified.

9 Let thy priests be clothed with justice: and let thy saints rejoice.

10 For thy servant David's sake, turn not away the face of thy anointed.

11 The Lord hath sworn truth to David, and he will not make it void: ³ Of the fruit of thy womb I will set upon thy throne.

12 If thy children will keep my covenant, and these my testimonies which I shall teach them.

Their children also for evermore shall sit upon thy throne.

13 For the Lord hath chosen Sion: he hath chosen it for his dwelling.

14 This is my rest for ever and ever: here will I dwell, for I have chosen it.

15 Blessing I will bless her widow: I will satisfy her poor with bread.

16 I will clothe her priests with salvation: and her saints shall rejoice with exceeding great joy.

17 ⁴ There will I bring forth a horn to David: I have prepared a lamp for my anointed.

18 His enemies I will clothe with confusion: but upon him shall my sanctification flourish.

PSALM 132
Ecce quam bonum
The happiness of brotherly love and concord.
A gradual canticle of David.

BEHOLD how good and how pleasant it is for brethren to dwell together in unity:

2 Like the precious ointment on the head, that ran down upon the beard, the beard of Aaron,

Which ran down to the skirt of his garment: 3 As the dew of Hermon, which descendeth upon mount Sion.

For there the Lord hath commanded blessing, and life for evermore.

PSALM 133
Ecce nunc benedicite
An exhortation to praise God continually.
A gradual canticle.

BEHOLD now bless ye the Lord: all ye servants of the Lord:

Who stand in the house of the Lord, in the courts of the house of our God.

2 In the nights lift up your hands to the holy places: and bless ye the Lord.

3 May the Lord out of Sion bless thee, he that made heaven and earth.

PSALM 134
Laudate nomen
An exhortation to praise God. The vanity of idols.
Alleluia.

PRAISE ye the name of the Lord: O you *his* servants, praise the Lord:

PSALM 131. ¹ 2 Kings, 7, 2. ² 2 Par. 6, 41. ³ 2 Kings, 7, 12; Luke, 1, 55; Acts, 2, 30. ⁴ Mal. 3, 1; Luke, 1, 69.

PSALM 131. Ver. 6. *We have heard of it in Ephrata.* When I was young, and lived in Bethlehem, otherwise called *Ephrata,* I heard of God's tabernacle and ark, and had a devout desire of seeking it; and accordingly I found it at *Cariathiarim,* the city of the woods: where is was till it was removed to Jerusalem (1 Par. xiii.).

2 You that stand in the house of the Lord: in the courts of the house of our God.

3 Praise ye the Lord, for the Lord is good: sing ye to his name, for it is sweet.

4 For the Lord hath chosen Jacob unto himself: Israel for his own possession.

5 For I have known that the Lord is great: and our God is above all gods.

6 Whatsoever the Lord pleased he hath done, in heaven, in earth, in the sea, and in all the deeps.

7 [1] He bringeth up clouds from the end of the earth: he hath made lightnings for the rain.

He bringeth forth winds out of his stores: 8 [2] he slew the firstborn of Egypt from man even unto beast.

9 He sent forth signs and wonders in the midst of thee, O Egypt: upon Pharao, and upon all his servants.

10 [3] He smote many nations, and slew mighty kings:

11 [4] Sehon king of the Amorrhites, and Og king of Basan, and all the kingdoms of Chanaan.

12 And gave their land for an inheritance: for an inheritance to his people Israel.

13 Thy name, O Lord, is for ever: thy memorial, O Lord, unto all generations.

14 For the Lord will judge his people: and will be entreated in favour of his servants.

15 [5] The idols of the Gentiles are silver and gold, the works of men's hands.

16 [6] They have a mouth, but they speak not. They have eyes, but they see not.

17 They have ears, but they hear not. Neither is there any breath in their mouths.

18 Let them that make them be like to them: and every one that trusteth in them.

19 Bless the Lord, O house of Israel: bless the Lord, O house of Aaron.

20 Bless the Lord, O house of Levi: you that fear the Lord, bless the Lord.

21 Blessed be the Lord out of Sion, who dwelleth in Jerusalem.

PSALM 135

Confitemini Domino

God is to be praised for his wonderful works.

Psalm 134. [1] Jer. 10, 13. [2] Exod. 12, 29. [3] Jos. 12, 1, 7. [4] Num. 21, 24, 34. [5] Ps. 113. 4. [6] Wisd. 15, 15. Psalm 135. [1] Gen. 1, 1. [2] Exod. 12, 29. [3] Exod. 13, 17. [4] Exod. 14, 28. [5] Num. 21, 24. [6] Num. 21, 33. [7] Jos. 13, 7.

Psalm 135. Ver. 1, 2, and 3. *Praise the Lord.* By this invitation to praise the Lord, thrice repeated, we profess the Blessed Trinity, One God in three distinct Persons, the Father, and the Son, and the Holy Ghost.

Alleluia.

PRAISE the Lord, for he is good: for his mercy endureth for ever:

2 Praise ye the God of gods: for his mercy endureth for ever.

3 Praise ye the Lord of lords: for his mercy endureth for ever.

4 Who alone doth great wonders: for his mercy endureth for ever.

5 [1] Who made the heavens in understanding: for his mercy endureth for ever.

6 Who established the earth above the waters: for his mercy endureth for ever.

7 Who made the great lights: for his mercy endureth for ever.

8 The sun to rule the day: for his mercy endureth for ever.

9 The moon and the stars to rule the night: for his mercy endureth for ever.

10 [2] Who smote Egypt with their firstborn: for his mercy endureth for ever.

11 [3] Who brought out Israel from among them: for his mercy endureth for ever.

12 With a mighty hand and with a stretched out arm: for his mercy endureth for ever.

13 Who divided the Red Sea into parts: for his mercy endureth for ever.

14 And brought out Israel through the midst thereof: for his mercy endureth for ever.

15 [4] And overthrew Pharao and his host in the Red Sea: for his mercy endureth for ever.

16 Who led his people through the desert: for his mercy endureth for ever.

17 Who smote great kings: for his mercy endureth for ever.

18 [5] And slew strong kings: for his mercy endureth for ever.

19 Sehon king of the Amorrhites: for his mercy endureth for ever.

20 [6] And Og king of Basan: for his mercy endureth for ever.

21 [7] And he gave their land for an inheritance: for his mercy endureth for ever.

22 For an inheritance to his servant Israel: for his mercy endureth for ever.

23 For he was mindful of us in our affliction: for his mercy endureth for ever.

24 And he redeemed us from our enemies: for his mercy endureth for ever.

25 Who giveth food to all flesh: for his mercy endureth for ever.

26 Give glory to the God of heaven: for his mercy endureth for ever.

27 Give glory to the Lord of lords: for his mercy endureth for ever.

PSALM 136

Super flumina

The lamentation of the people of God in their captivity in Babylon.

A psalm of David. For Jeremias.

UPON the rivers of Babylon, there we sat and wept: when we remembered Sion.

2 On the willows in the midst thereof we hung up our instruments. 3 For there they that led us into captivity required of us the words of songs.

And they that carried us away, said: Sing ye to us a hymn of the songs of Sion.

4 How shall we sing the song of the Lord in a strange land?

5 If I forget thee, O Jerusalem, let my right hand be forgotten.

6 Let my tongue cleave to my jaws, if I do not remember thee:

If I make not Jerusalem the beginning of my joy.

7 Remember, O Lord, the children of Edom, in the day of Jerusalem:

Who say: Rase it, rase it, even to the foundation thereof.

8 O daughter of Babylon, miserable: blessed *shall he be* who shall repay thee thy payment which thou hast paid us.

9 Blessed be he that shall take and dash thy little ones against the rock.

PSALM 137

Confitebor tibi

Thanksgiving to God for his benefits.

For David himself.

I WILL praise thee, O Lord, with my whole heart: for thou hast heard the words of my mouth.

I will sing praise to thee in the sight of the angels: 2 I will worship towards thy holy temple, and I will give glory to thy name.

For thy mercy, and for thy truth: for thou hast magnified thy holy name above all.

3 In what day soever I shall call upon thee, hear me. Thou shalt multiply strength in my soul.

4 May all the kings of the earth give glory to thee: for they have heard all the words of thy mouth.

5 And let them sing in the ways of the Lord: for great is the glory of the Lord.

6 For the Lord is high, and looketh on the low: and the high he knoweth afar off.

7 If I shall walk in the midst of tribulation, thou wilt quicken me: and

thou hast stretched forth thy hand against the wrath of my enemies: and thy right hand hath saved me.

8 The Lord will repay for me: thy mercy, O Lord, endureth for ever. O despise not the works of thy hands.

PSALM 138

Domine, probasti

God's special providence over his servants.

Unto the end. A psalm of David.

LORD, thou hast proved me, and known me: 2 thou hast known my sitting down, and my rising up.

3 Thou hast understood my thoughts afar off: my path and my line thou hast searched out.

4 And thou hast foreseen all my ways: for there is no speech in my tongue.

5 Behold, O Lord, thou hast known all things, the last and those of old: thou hast formed me, and hast laid thy hand upon me.

6 Thy knowledge is become wonderful to me: it is high, and I cannot reach to it.

7 Whither shall I go from thy spirit? Or whither shall I flee from thy face?

8 [1] If I ascend into heaven, thou art there: if I descend into hell, thou art present.

9 If I take my wings early in the morning, and dwell in the uttermost parts of the sea:

10 Even there also shall thy hand lead me: and thy right hand shall hold me.

11 And I said: Perhaps darkness shall cover me, and night shall be my light in my pleasures.

12 But darkness shall not be dark to thee, and night shall be light as the day: the darkness thereof, and the light thereof are alike *to thee*.

13 For thou hast possessed my reins: thou hast protected me from my mother's womb.

14 I will praise thee, for thou art fearfully magnified: wonderful are thy works, and my soul knoweth right well.

15 My bone is not hidden from thee, which thou hast made in secret: and my substance in the lower parts of the earth.

PSALM 138. [1] Amos, 9, 2.

PSALM 136. *For Jeremias.* For the time of Jeremias, and the captivity of Babylon.

Ver. 9. *Dash thy little ones.* In the spiritual sense, we dash the little ones of Babylon against the rock, when we mortify our passions, and stifle the first motions of them, by a speedy recourse to the rock which is Christ.

PSALM 138. Ver. 4. *There is no speech in my tongue.* That is, unknown to thee. Or, though there is no speech in my tongue, yet my whole interior and my most secret thoughts are known to thee.

16 Thy eyes did see my imperfect being, and in thy book all shall be written: days shall be formed, and no one in them.

17 But to me thy friends, O God, are made exceedingly honourable: their principality is exceedingly strengthened.

18 I will number them, and they shall be multiplied above the sand. I rose up and am still with thee.

19 If thou wilt kill the wicked, O God: Ye men of blood, depart from me:

20 Because you say in thought: They shall receive thy cities in vain.

21 Have I not hated them, O Lord, that hated thee: and pined away because of thy enemies?

22 I have hated them with a perfect hatred: and they are become enemies to me.

23 Prove me, O God, and know my heart: examine me and know my paths.

24 And see if there be in me the way of iniquity: and lead me in the eternal way.

PSALM 139
Eripe me, Domine
A prayer to be delivered from the wicked.

1 Unto the end. A psalm of David.

2 DELIVER me, O Lord, from the evil man: rescue me from the unjust man.

3 Who have devised iniquities in their hearts: all the day long they designed battles.

4 [1]They have sharpened their tongues like a serpent: the venom of asps is under their lips.

5 Keep me, O Lord, from the hand of the wicked: and from unjust men deliver me,

Who have proposed to supplant my steps. 6 The proud have hidden a net for me:

And they have stretched out cords for a snare. They have laid for me a stumbling-block by the wayside.

PSALM 139. [1] Ps. 5, 11; Rom. 3, 13.

Ver. 20. *Because you say in thought.* Depart from me, you wicked, who plot against the servants of God, and think to cast them out of the cities of their habitation; as if *they have received them in vain,* and to no purpose.

Ver. 22. *I have hated them.* Not with an hatred of malice, but a zeal for the observance of God's commandments; which he saw were despised by the wicked, who are to be considered enemies to God.

PSALM 140. Ver. 5. *Let not the oil of the sinner.* That is, the flattery, or deceitful praise.—*For my prayer shall still be against the things with which they are well pleased.* So far from coveting their praises, who are never well pleased but with things that are evil, I shall continually pray to be preserved from such things as they are delighted with.

Ver. 6. *Their judges have been swallowed up.* Their rulers, or chiefs, quickly vanish and perish, like ships dashed against the rocks, and swallowed up by the waves. Let them then hear my words, for they are powerful and will prevail; or, as it is in the Hebrew, *for they are sweet.*

---

7 I said to the Lord: Thou art my God. Hear, O Lord, the voice of my supplication.

8 O Lord, Lord, the strength of my salvation: thou hast overshadowed my head in the day of battle.

9 Give me not up, O Lord, from my desire to the wicked: they have plotted against me. Do not thou forsake me, lest they should triumph.

10 The head of them compassing me about: the labour of their lips shall overwhelm them.

11 Burning coals shall fall upon them. Thou wilt cast them down into the fire: in miseries they shall not be able to stand.

12 A man full of tongue shall not be established in the earth: evil shall catch the unjust man unto destruction.

13 I know that the Lord will do justice to the needy: and will revenge the poor.

14 But as for the just, they shall give glory to thy name: and the upright shall dwell with thy countenance.

PSALM 140
Domine, clamavi
A prayer against sinful words, and deceitful flatterers.

A psalm of David.

I HAVE cried to thee, O Lord, hear me: hearken to my voice, when I cry to thee.

2 Let my prayer be directed as incense in thy sight: the lifting up of my hands, as evening sacrifice.

3 Set a watch, O Lord, before my mouth: and a door round about my lips.

4 Incline not my heart to evil words: to make excuses in sins.

With men that work iniquity: and I will not communicate with the choicest of them.

5 The just man shall correct me in mercy, and shall reprove me: but let not the oil of the sinner fatten my head.

For my prayer also *shall still be* against the things with which they are well pleased: 6 their judges falling upon the rock have been swallowed up.

They shall hear my words, for they have prevailed. 7 As when the thickness of the earth is broken up upon the ground:

Our bones are scattered by the side of hell. 8 But to thee, O Lord, Lord, are my eyes: in thee have I put my trust. Take not away my soul.

9 Keep me from the snare, which they have laid for me: and from the stumbling-blocks of them that work iniquity.

10 The wicked shall fall in his net. I am alone until I pass.

PSALM 141
Voce mea

A prayer of David in extremity of danger.

1 Of understanding. For David. A prayer when he was in the cave (1 Kings, 24).

2 I CRIED [1] to the Lord with my voice: with my voice I made supplication to the Lord.

3 In his sight I pour out my prayer: and before him I declare my trouble.

4 When my spirit failed me, then thou knewest my paths.

In this way wherein I walked they have hidden a snare for me.

5 I looked on my right hand, and beheld: and there was no one that would know me.

Flight hath failed me: and there is no one that hath regard to my soul:

6 I cried to thee, O Lord. I said: Thou art my hope, my portion in the land of the living.

7 Attend to my supplication: for I am brought very low.

Deliver me from my persecutors: for they are stronger than I.

8 Bring my soul out of prison, that I may praise thy name: the just wait for me, until thou reward me.

PSALM 142
Domine, exaudi

The psalmist in tribulation calleth upon God for his delivery. The seventh penitential psalm.

1 A psalm of David when his son Absalom pursued him (2 Kings, 17).

HEAR, O Lord, my prayer: give ear to my supplication in thy truth: hear me in thy justice.

2 And enter not into judgment with thy servant: for in thy sight no man living shall be justified.

3 For the enemy hath persecuted my soul: he hath brought down my life to the earth.

He hath made me to dwell in darkness as those that have been dead of old: 4 and my spirit is in anguish within me. My heart within me is troubled.

5 I remembered the days of old: I meditated on all thy works: I meditated upon the works of thy hands.

6 I stretched forth my hands to thee: my soul is as earth without water unto thee.

7 Hear me speedily, O Lord: my spirit hath fainted away.

Turn not away thy face from me, lest I be like unto them that go down into the pit.

8 Cause me to hear thy mercy in the morning: for in thee have I hoped.

Make the way known to me, wherein I should walk: for I have lifted up my soul to thee.

9 Deliver me from my enemies, O Lord. To thee have I fled. 10 Teach me to do thy will, for thou art my God.

Thy good spirit shall lead me into the right land. 11 For thy name's sake, O Lord, thou wilt quicken me in thy justice.

Thou wilt bring my soul out of trouble: 12 and in thy mercy thou wilt destroy my enemies.

And thou wilt cut off all them that afflict my soul: for I am thy servant.

PSALM 143
Benedictus Dominus

The prophet praiseth God, and prayeth to be delivered from his enemies. No worldly happiness is to be compared with that of serving God.

A psalm of David against Goliath.

BLESSED *be* the Lord my God, who teacheth my hands to fight, and my fingers to war.

2 My mercy, and my refuge: my support, and my deliverer.

My protector, and I have hoped in him: who subdueth my people under me.

3 Lord, what is man, that thou art made known to him? Or the son of man, that thou makest account of him?

4 Man is like to vanity: [1] his days pass away like a shadow.

5 Lord, bow down thy heavens and descend: touch the mountains, and they shall smoke.

6 Send forth lightning, and thou shalt scatter them: shoot out thy arrows, and thou shalt trouble them.

7 Put forth thy hand from on high: take me out, and deliver me from many waters: from the hand of strange children.

8 Whose mouth hath spoken vanity: and their right hand is the right hand of iniquity.

9 To thee, O God, I will sing a new canticle: on the psaltery *and* an instrument of ten strings I will sing praises to thee.

10 Who givest salvation to kings: who hast redeemed thy servant David from the malicious sword.

11 Deliver me,

And rescue me out of the hand of strange children. Whose mouth hath

---

PSALM 141. [1] Ps. 76, 2. PSALM 143. [1] Job. 8, 9; 14, 2.

Ver. 10. *I am alone. Singularly* protected by the Almighty, *until I pass* all their nets and snares.

spoken vanity: and their right hand is the right hand of iniquity.

12 Whose sons are as new plants in their youth:

Their daughters decked out, adorned round about after the similitude of a temple:

13 Their storehouses full, flowing out of this into that:

Their sheep fruitful in young, abounding in their goings forth: 14 their oxen fat.

There is no breach of wall, nor passage, nor crying out in their streets.

15 They have called the people happy, that hath these things: *but* happy is that people whose God is the Lord.

PSALM 144

Exaltabo te, Deus

A psalm of praise to the infinite majesty of God.

Praise. For David himself.

I WILL extol thee, O God my king: and I will bless thy name for ever. Yea, for ever and ever.

2 Every day will I bless thee: and I will praise thy name for ever. Yea, for ever and ever.

3 Great is the Lord, and greatly to be praised: and of his greatness there is no end.

4 Generation and generation shall praise thy works: and they shall declare thy power.

5 They shall speak of the magnificence of the glory of thy holiness: and shall tell thy wondrous works.

6 And they shall speak of the might of thy terrible acts: and shall declare thy greatness.

7 They shall publish the memory of the abundance of thy sweetness: and shall rejoice in thy justice.

8 The Lord is gracious and merciful: patient and plenteous in mercy.

9 The Lord is sweet to all: and his tender mercies are over all his works.

10 Let all thy works, O Lord, praise thee: and let thy saints bless thee.

11 They shall speak of the glory of thy kingdom: and shall tell of thy power:

12 To make thy might known to the sons of men: and the glory of the magnificence of thy kingdom.

13 Thy kingdom is a kingdom of all ages: and thy dominion endureth throughout all generations.

The Lord is faithful in all his words: and holy in all his works.

14 The Lord lifteth up all that fall: and setteth up all that are cast down

15 The eyes of all hope in thee, O Lord: and thou givest them meat in due season.

16 Thou openest thy hand: and fillest with blessing every living creature.

17 The Lord is just in all his ways: and holy in all his works.

18 The Lord is nigh unto all them that call upon him: to all that call upon him in truth.

19 He will do the will of them that fear him: and he will hear their prayer, and save them.

20 The Lord keepeth all them that love him: but all the wicked he will destroy.

21 My mouth shall speak the praise of the Lord: and let all flesh bless his holy name for ever. Yea, for ever and ever.

PSALM 145

Lauda, anima

We are not to trust in men, but in God alone.

1 Alleluia. Of Aggeus and Zacharias.

2 PRAISE [1] the Lord, O my soul: in my life I will praise the Lord: I will sing to my God as long as I shall be.

Put not your trust in princes: 3 in the children of men, in whom there is no salvation.

4 His spirit shall go forth, and he shall return into his earth: in that day all their thoughts shall perish.

5 Blessed is he who hath the God of Jacob for his helper, whose hope is in the Lord his God 6 [2] Who made heaven and earth, the sea, and all things that are in them.

7 Who keepeth truth for ever: who executeth judgment for them that suffer wrong: who giveth food to the hungry.

The Lord looseth them that are fettered: 8 the Lord enlighteneth the blind.

The Lord lifted up them that are cast down: the Lord loveth the just.

9 The Lord keepeth the strangers. He will support the fatherless and the widow: and the ways of sinners he will destroy.

10 The Lord shall reign for ever: thy God, O Sion, unto generation and generation.

PSALM 146

Laudate Dominum

An exhortation to praise God for his benefits.

Alleluia.

PRAISE ye the Lord, because psalm is good: to our God be joyful and comely praise.

PSALM 145. [1] Ps. 144, 2. [2] Acts, 14, 14; Apoc. 14, 7.

2 The Lord buildeth up Jerusalem: he will gather together the dispersed of Israel.

3 Who healeth the broken of heart: and bindeth up their bruises.

4 Who telleth the number of the stars: and calleth them all by their names.

5 Great is our Lord, and great is his power: and of his wisdom there is no number.

6 The Lord lifteth up the meek: and bringeth the wicked down even to the ground.

7 Sing ye to the Lord with praise: sing to our God upon the harp.

8 Who covereth the heaven with clouds, and prepareth rain for the earth.

Who maketh grass to grow on the mountains, and herbs for the service of men.

9 Who giveth to beasts their food, and to the young ravens that call upon him.

10 He shall not delight in the strength of the horse: nor take pleasure in the legs of a man.

11 The Lord taketh pleasure in them that fear him: and in them that hope in his mercy.

PSALM 147

Lauda, Jerusalem

The church is called upon to praise God for his peculiar graces and favours to his people. In the Hebrew, this psalm is joined to the foregoing.

Alleluia.

12 PRAISE the Lord, O Jerusalem: praise thy God, O Sion.

13 Because he hath strengthened the bolts of thy gates: he hath blessed thy children within thee.

14 Who hath placed peace in thy borders: and filleth thee with the fat of corn.

15 Who sendeth forth his speech to the earth: his word runneth swiftly.

16 Who giveth snow like wool: scattereth mists like ashes.

17 He sendeth his crystal like morsels: Who shall stand before the face of his cold?

18 He shall send out his word, and shall melt them: his wind shall blow, and the waters shall run.

19 Who declareth his word to Jacob: his justices and his judgments to Israel.

20 He hath not done in like manner to every nation: and his judgments he hath not made manifest to them. Alleluia.

PSALM 148

Laudate Dominum de cælis

All creatures are invited to praise their Creator.

Alleluia.

PRAISE ye the Lord from the heavens: praise ye him in the high places.

2 Praise ye him, all his angels: praise ye him, all his hosts.

3 Praise ye him, O sun and moon: praise him, all ye stars and light.

4 [1]Praise him, ye heavens of heavens: and let all the waters that are above the heavens 5 praise the name of the Lord.

For he spoke, and they were made: he commanded, and they were created.

6 He hath established them for ever, and for ages of ages: he hath made a decree, and it shall not pass away.

7 Praise the Lord from the earth: ye dragons, and all ye deeps:

8 Fire, hail, snow, ice, stormy winds which fulfil his word:

9 Mountains and all hills: fruitful trees and all cedars:

10 Beasts and all cattle: serpents and feathered fowls:

11 Kings of the earth and all people: princes and all judges of the earth:

12 Young men and maidens. Let the old with the younger, praise the name of the Lord: 13 for his name alone is exalted.

14 The praise of him is above heaven and earth: and he hath exalted the horn of his people.

A hymn to all his saints: to the children of Israel, a people approaching to him. Alleluia.

PSALM 149

Cantate Domino

The church is particularly bound to praise God.

Alleluia.

SING ye to the Lord a new canticle: let his praise be in the church of the saints.

2 Let Israel rejoice in him that made him: and let the children of Sion be joyful in their king.

3 Let them praise his name in choir: let them sing to him with the timbrel and the psaltery.

4 For the Lord is well pleased with his people: and he will exalt the meek unto salvation.

5 The saints shall rejoice in glory: they shall be joyful in their beds.

6 The high praises of God shall be in

<small>PSALM 148. [1] Dan. 3, 59, 60.</small>

<small>PSALM 147. Ver. 17. *He sendeth his crystal.* That is, his *ice.* Some understand it of *hail,* which is, as it were, *ice,* divided into particles or morsels.</small>

their mouth: and two-edged swords in their hands:

7 To execute vengeance upon the nations, chastisements among the people:

8 To bind their kings with fetters, and their nobles with manacles of iron:

9 To execute upon them the judgment that is written. This glory is to all his saints. Alleluia.

PSALM 150

Laudate Dominum in sanctis

An exhortation to praise God with all sorts of instruments.

Alleluia.

PRAISE ye the Lord in his holy places: praise ye him in the firmament of his power.

2 Praise ye him for his mighty acts: praise ye him according to the multitude of his greatness.

3 Praise him with sound of trumpet: praise him with psaltery and harp.

4 Praise him with timbrel and choir: praise him with strings and organs.

5 Praise him on high sounding cymbals: praise him on cymbals of joy. Let every spirit praise the Lord. Alleluia.

THE BOOK OF
PROVERBS

This book is so called, because it consists of wise and weighty sentences, regulating the morals of men, and directing them to wisdom and virtue. And these sentences are also called PARABLES, *because great truths are often couched in them under certain figures and similitudes.*

CHAPTER 1

The use and end of the proverbs. An exhortation to flee the company of the wicked, and to hearken to the voice of wisdom.

THE parables of Solomon, the son of David, king of Israel.

2 To know wisdom, and instruction:

3 To understand the words of prudence: and to receive the instruction of doctrine, justice, and judgment, and equity:

4 To give subtilty to little ones, to the young man knowledge and understanding.

5 A wise man shall hear and shall be wiser: and he that understandeth shall possess governments.

6 He shall understand a parable, and the interpretation: the words of the wise, and their mysterious sayings.

7 [1] The fear of the Lord is the beginning of wisdom. Fools despise wisdom and instruction.

8 My son, hear the instruction of thy father, and forsake not the law of thy mother:

9 That grace may be added to thy head, and a chain of gold to thy neck.

10 My son, if sinners shall entice thee, consent not to them.

11 If they shall say: Come with us. Let us lie in wait for blood: let us hide snares for the innocent without cause:

12 Let us swallow him up alive like hell, and whole as one that goeth down into the pit.

13 We shall find all precious substance: we shall fill our houses with spoils.

14 Cast in thy lot with us: let us all have one purse.

15 My son, walk not thou with them: restrain thy foot from their paths.

16 [2] For their feet run to evil, and make haste to shed blood.

17 But a net is spread in vain before the eyes of them that have wings.

18 And they themselves lie in wait for their own blood, and practise deceits against their own souls.

19 So the ways of every covetous man destroy the souls of the possessors.

20 Wisdom preacheth abroad: she uttereth her voice in the streets.

21 At the head of multitudes she crieth out, in the entrance of the gates of the city she uttereth her words, saying:

22 O children, how long will you love childishness, and fools covet those things which are hurtful to themselves, and the unwise hate knowledge?

23 Turn ye at my reproof: behold I will utter my spirit to you, and will shew you my words.

24 [3] Because I called, and you refused. I stretched out my hand, and there was none that regarded.

25 You have despised all my counsel, and have neglected my reprehensions.

CHAP. 1. [1] Ps. 110, 10; Ecclus. 1, 16. [2] Isai. 59, 7. [3] Isai. 65, 12; 66, 4; Jer. 7, 13.

26 I also will laugh in your destruction, and will mock when that shall come to you which you feared.

27 When sudden calamity shall fall on you, and destruction, as a tempest, shall be at hand: when tribulation and distress shall come upon you.

28 Then shall they call upon me, and I will not hear: they shall rise in the morning and shall not find me.

29 Because they have hated instruction, and received not the fear of the Lord,

30 Nor consented to my counsel, but despised all my reproof:

31 Therefore they shall eat the fruit of their own way and shall be filled with their own devices.

32 The turning away of little ones shall kill them, and the prosperity of fools shall destroy them.

33 But he that shall hear me shall rest without terror, and shall enjoy abundance, without fear of evils.

CHAPTER 2

The advancement of wisdom. The evils from which it delivers.

MY son, if thou wilt receive my words, and wilt hide my commandments with thee,

2 That thy ear may hearken to wisdom: incline thy heart to know prudence.

3 For if thou shalt call for wisdom and incline thy heart to prudence:

4 If thou shalt seek her as money, and shalt dig for her as for a treasure:

5 Then shalt thou understand the fear of the Lord, and shalt find the knowledge of God.

6 Because the Lord giveth wisdom: and out of his mouth cometh prudence and knowledge.

7 He will keep the salvation of the righteous and protect them that walk in simplicity.

8 Keeping the paths of justice, and guarding the way of saints.

9 Then shalt thou understand justice, and judgment, and equity, and every good path.

10 If wisdom shall enter into thy heart, and knowledge please thy soul:

11 Counsel shall keep thee, and prudence shall preserve thee.

12 That thou mayst be delivered from the evil way, and from the man that speaketh perverse things:

13 Who leave the right way, and walk by dark ways:

14 Who are glad when they have done evil, and rejoice in most wicked things:

15 Whose ways are perverse, and their steps infamous.

16 That thou mayst be delivered from the strange women, and from the stranger, who softeneth her words;

17 And forsaketh the guide of her youth;

18 And hath forgotten the covenant of her God: for her house inclineth unto death, and her paths to hell.

19 None that go in unto her shall return again: neither shall they take hold of the paths of life,

20 That thou mayst walk in a good way: and mayst keep the paths of the just.

21 For they that are upright shall dwell in the earth: and the simple shall continue in it.

22 [1] But the wicked shall be destroyed from the earth: and they that do unjustly shall be taken away from it.

CHAPTER 3

An exhortation to the praise of virtue.

MY son, forget not my law: and let thy heart keep my commandments.

2 For they shall add to thee length of days: and years of life and peace.

3 Let not mercy and truth leave thee. Put them about thy neck, and write them in the tables of thy heart:

4 And thou shalt find grace and good understanding before God and men.

5 Have confidence in the Lord with all thy heart, and lean not upon thy own prudence.

6 In all the ways think on him: and he will direct thy steps.

7 [1] Be not wise in thy own conceit. Fear God, and depart from evil:

8 For it shall be health to thy navel, and moistening to thy bones.

9 [2] Honour the Lord with thy substance, and give him of the first of all thy fruits:

10 And thy barns shall be filled with abundance, and thy presses shall run over with wine.

11 [3] My son, reject not the correction of the Lord, and do not faint when thou art chastised by him.

12 For whom the Lord loveth, he chastiseth: and as a father in the son he pleaseth himself.

13 Blessed is the man that findeth wisdom, and is rich in prudence.

14 The purchasing thereof is better than the merchandise of silver: and her fruit than the chiefest and purest gold.

15 She is more precious than all

CHAP. 2. [1] Job, 18, 17. CHAP. 3. [1] Rom. 12, 16. [2] Tob. 4, 7; Luke, 14, 13. [3] Heb. 12, 5; Apoc. 3, 19.

riches: and all the things that are desired are not to be compared with her.

16 Length of days is in her right hand: and in her left hand riches and glory.

17 Her ways are beautiful ways: and all her paths are peaceable.

18 She is a tree of life to them that lay hold on her: and he that shall retain her is blessed.

19 The Lord by wisdom hath founded the earth, hath established the heavens by prudence.

20 By his wisdom the depths have broken out, and the clouds grow thick with dew.

21 My son, let not these things depart from thy eyes: keep the law and counsel:

22 And there shall be life to thy soul, and grace to thy mouth.

23 Then shalt thou walk confidently in thy way: and thy foot shall not stumble.

24 If thou sleep, thou shalt not fear: thou shalt rest, and thy sleep shall be sweet.

25 Be not afraid of sudden fear, nor of the power of the wicked falling upon thee.

26 For the Lord will be at thy side, and will keep thy foot that thou be not taken.

27 Do not withhold him from doing good, who is able. If thou art able, do good thyself also.

28 Say not to thy friend: Go, and come again, and to-morrow I will give to thee: when thou canst give at present.

29 Practise not evil against thy friend, when he hath confidence in thee.

30 Strive not against a man without cause, when he hath done thee no evil.

31 ⁴ Envy not the unjust man, and do not follow his ways:

32 For every mocker is an abomination to the Lord: and his communication is with the simple.

33 Want is from the Lord in the house of the wicked: but the habitations of the just shall be blessed.

34 He shall scorn the scorners: and to the meek he will give grace.

35 The wise shall possess glory: the promotion of fools is disgrace.

CHAPTER 4

A further exhortation to seek after wisdom.

HEAR, ye children, the instruction of a father: and attend that you may know prudence.

⁴ Ps. 36, 1.

2 I will give you a good gift. Forsake not my law.

3 For I also was my father's son, tender and as an only son in the sight of my mother.

4 And he taught me, and said: Let thy heart receive my words; keep my commandments, and thou shalt live.

5 Get wisdom, get prudence: forget not, neither decline from the words of my mouth.

6 Forsake her not, and she shall keep thee: love her, and she shall preserve thee.

7 The beginning of wisdom, get wisdom: and with all thy possession purchase prudence.

8 Take hold on her, and she shall exalt thee: thou shalt be glorified by her, when thou shalt embrace her.

9 She shall give to thy head increase of graces, and protect thee with a noble crown.

10 Hear, O my son, and receive my words, that years of life may be multiplied to thee.

11 I will shew thee the way of wisdom. I will lead thee by the paths of equity.

12 Which when thou shalt have entered, thy steps shall not be straitened: and when thou runnest thou shalt not meet a stumbling-block.

13 Take hold on instruction: leave it not. Keep it, because it is thy life.

14 Be not delighted in the paths of the wicked: neither let the way of evil men please thee.

15 Flee from it, pass not by it: go aside, and forsake it.

16 For they sleep not except they have done evil: and their sleep is taken away unless they have made some to fall.

17 They eat the bread of wickedness, and drink the wine of iniquity.

18 But the path of the just, as a shining light, goeth forwards and increaseth even to perfect day.

19 The way of the wicked is darksome: they know not where they fall.

20 My son, hearken to my words: and incline thy ear to my sayings.

21 Let them not depart from thy eyes: keep them in the midst of thy heart.

22 For they are life to those that find them, and health to all flesh.

23 With all watchfulness keep thy heart, because life issueth out from it.

24 Remove from thee a froward mouth: and let detracting lips be far from thee.

25 Let thy eyes look straight on: and let thy eyelids go before thy steps.

26 Make straight the path for thy feet: and all thy ways shall be established.

27 Decline not to the right hand, nor to the left. Turn away thy foot from evil. For the Lord knoweth the ways that are on the right hand: but those are perverse which are on the left hand. But he will make thy courses straight: he will bring forward thy ways in peace.

CHAPTER 5
An exhortation to fly unlawful lust and the occasions of it.

MY son, attend to my wisdom: and incline thy ear to my prudence.

2 That thou mayst keep thoughts, and thy lips may preserve instruction. Mind not the deceit of a woman.

3 For the lips of a harlot are like a honeycomb dropping, and her throat is smoother than oil.

4 But her end is bitter as wormwood, and sharp as a two-edged sword.

5 Her feet go down into death: and her steps go in as far as hell.

6 They walk not by the path of life: her steps are wandering, and unaccountable.

7 Now therefore, my son, hear me, and depart not from the words of my mouth.

8 Remove thy way far from her: and come not nigh the doors of her house.

9 Give not thy honour to strangers, and thy years to the cruel.

10 Let strangers be filled with thy strength, and thy labours be in another man's house;

11 And thou mourn at the last, when thou shalt have spent thy flesh and thy body; and say:

12 Why have I hated instruction, and my heart consented not to reproof,

13 And have not heard the voice of them that taught me, and have not inclined my ear to masters?

14 I have almost been in all evil, in the midst of the church and of the congregation.

15 Drink water out of thy own cistern, and the streams of thy own well.

16 Let thy fountains be conveyed abroad, and in the streets divide thy waters.

17 Keep them to thyself alone: neither let strangers be partakers with thee.

18 Let thy vein be blessed, and rejoice with the wife of thy youth:

19 Let her be thy dearest hind, and most agreeable fawn: let her breasts inebriate thee at all times; be thou delighted continually with her love.

20 Why art thou seduced, my son, by a strange woman, and art cherished in the bosom of another?

21 [1] The Lord beholdeth the ways of man and considereth all his steps.

22 His own iniquities catch the wicked: and he is fast bound with the ropes of his own sins.

23 He shall die, because he hath not received instruction: and in the multitude of his folly he shall be deceived.

CHAPTER 6
Documents on several heads.

MY son, if thou be surety for thy friend, thou hast engaged fast thy hand to a stranger.

2 Thou art ensnared with the words of thy mouth, and caught with thy own words.

3 Do therefore, my son, what I say, and deliver thyself: because thou art fallen into the hand of thy neighbour. Run about, make haste, stir up thy friend.

4 Give not sleep to thy eyes: neither let thy eyelids slumber.

5 Deliver thyself as a doe from the hand, and as a bird from the hand of the fowler.

6 Go to the ant, O sluggard, and consider her ways, and learn wisdom:

7 Which, although she hath no guide, nor master, nor captain,

8 Provideth her meat for herself in the summer, and gathereth her food in the harvest.

9 How long wilt thou sleep, O sluggard? When wilt thou rise out of thy sleep?

10 [1] Thou wilt sleep a little, thou wilt slumber a little, thou wilt fold thy hands a little to sleep:

11 And want shall come upon thee, as a traveller, and poverty as a man armed. But if thou be diligent, thy harvest shall come as a fountain, and want shall flee far from thee.

12 A man that is an apostate, an unprofitable man, walketh with a perverse mouth.

13 He winketh with the eyes, presseth with the foot, speaketh with the finger.

14 With a wicked heart he deviseth evil: and at all times he soweth discord.

15 To such a one his destruction shall presently come: and he shall suddenly be destroyed, and shall no longer have any remedy.

16 Six things there are, which the Lord hateth, and the seventh his soul detesteth:

CHAP. 5. [1] Job, 14, 16; 31, 4; 34, 21. CHAP. 6. [1] Prov. 24, 33.

17 Haughty eyes, a lying tongue, hands that shed innocent blood,

18 A heart that deviseth wicked plots, feet that are swift to run into mischief,

19 A deceitful witness that uttereth lies, and him that soweth discord among brethren.

20 My son, keep the commandments of thy father, and forsake not the law of thy mother.

21 Bind them in thy heart continually, and put them about thy neck.

22 When thou walkest, let them go with thee: when thou sleepest, let them keep thee; and when thou awakest, talk with them.

23 Because the commandment is a lamp, and the law a light, and reproofs of instruction are the way of life:

24 That they may keep thee from the evil woman, and from the flattering tongue of the stranger.

25 Let not thy heart covet her beauty: be not caught with her winks.

26 For the price of a harlot is scarce one loaf: but the woman catcheth the precious soul of a man.

27 Can a man hide fire in his bosom, and his garments not burn?

28 Or can he walk upon hot coals, and his feet not be burnt?

29 So he that goeth in to his neighbour's wife shall not be clean when he shall touch her.

30 The fault is not so great when a man hath stolen: for he stealeth to fill his hungry soul.

31 And if he be taken he shall restore sevenfold, and shall give up all the substance of his house.

32 But he that is an adulterer, for the folly of his heart shall destroy his own soul.

33 He gathereth to himself shame and dishonour, and his reproach shall not be blotted out:

34 Because the jealousy and rage of the husband will not spare in the day of revenge.

35 Nor will he yield to any man's prayers: nor will he accept for satisfaction ever so many gifts.

CHAPTER 7

The love of wisdom is the best perservative from being led astray by temptation.

CHAP. 6. Ver. 30. *The fault is not so great when a man hath stolen.* The sin of theft is not so great as to be compared with adultery: especially when a person pressed with hunger (which is the case here spoken of) steals to satisfy nature. Moreover, the damage done by theft may much more easily be repaired than the wrong done by adultery. But this does not hinder but that theft also is a mortal sin, forbidden by one of the ten commandments.

M Y son, keep my words, and lay up my precepts with thee. Son,

2 Keep my commandments, and thou shalt live. And my law, as the apple of thy eye,

3 Bind it upon thy fingers, write it upon the tables of thy heart.

4 Say to wisdom: Thou art my sister. And call prudence thy friend:

5 That she may keep thee from the woman that is not thine, and from the stranger who sweeteneth her words.

6 For I look out of the window of my house through the lattice,

7 And I see little ones. I behold a foolish young man,

8 Who passeth through the street by the corner, and goeth nigh the way of her house,

9 In the dark, when it grows late, in the darkness and obscurity of the night,

10 And behold a woman meeteth him in harlot's attire, prepared to deceive souls; talkative and wandering;

11 Not bearing to be quiet, not able to abide still at home;

12 Now abroad, now in the streets, now lying in wait near the corners.

13 And catching the young man, she kisseth him, and with an impudent face, flattereth, saying:

14 I vowed victims for prosperity; this day I have paid my vows.

15 Therefore I am come out to meet thee, desirous to see thee; and I have found thee.

16 I have woven my bed with cords; I have covered it with painted tapestry, brought from Egypt.

17 I have perfumed my bed with myrrh, aloes, and cinnamon.

18 Come, let us be inebriated with the breasts, and let us enjoy the desired embraces, till the day appear.

19 For my husband is not at home: he is gone a very long journey.

20 He took with him a bag of money: he will return home the day of the full moon.

21 She entangled him with many words, and drew him away with the flattery of her lips.

22 Immediately he followeth her as an ox led to be a victim, and as a lamb playing the wanton, and not knowing that he is drawn like a fool to bonds,

23 Till the arrow pierce his liver: as if a bird should make haste to the snare, and knoweth not that his life is in danger.

24 Now therefore, my son, hear me, and attend to the words of my mouth.

25 Let not thy mind be drawn away in her ways: neither be thou deceived with her paths.

26 For she hath cast down many wounded: and the strongest have been slain by her.

27 Her house is the way to hell, reaching even to the inner chambers of death.

CHAPTER 8

The preaching of wisdom. Her excellence.

DOTH not wisdom cry aloud, and prudence put forth her voice?

2 Standing in the top of the highest places by the way, in the midst of the paths,

3 Beside the gates of the city, in the very doors she speaketh, saying:

4 O ye men, to you I call, and my voice is to the sons of men.

5 O little ones, understand subtilty, and ye unwise, take notice.

6 Hear, for I will speak of great things: and my lips shall be opened to preach right things.

7 My mouth shall meditate truth: and my lips shall hate wickedness.

8 All my words are just. There is nothing wicked nor perverse in them.

9 They are right to them that understand, and just to them that find knowledge.

10 Receive my instruction, and not money: choose knowledge rather than gold.

11 For wisdom is better than all the most precious things: and whatsoever may be desired cannot be compared to it.

12 I, wisdom, dwell in counsel, and am present in learned thoughts.

13 The fear of the Lord hateth evil. I hate arrogance, and pride, and every wicked way, and a mouth with a double tongue.

14 Counsel and equity is mine: prudence is mine: strength is mine.

15 By me kings reign, and lawgivers decree just things,

16 By me princes rule, and the mighty decree justice.

17 I love them that love me: and they that in the morning early watch for me shall find me.

18 With me are riches and glory, glorious riches and justice.

19 For my fruit is better than gold and the precious stone, and my blossoms than choice silver.

20 I walk in the way of justice, in the midst of the paths of judgment:

21 That I may enrich them that love me, and may fill their treasures.

22 The Lord possessed me in the beginning of his ways, before he made any thing from the beginning.

23 I was set up from eternity, and of old before the earth was made.

24 The depths were not as yet, and I was already conceived: neither had the fountains of waters as yet sprung out.

25 The mountains with their huge bulk had not as yet been established: before the hills I was brought forth.

26 He had not yet made the earth, nor the rivers, nor the poles of the world.

27 When he prepared the heavens, I was present: when with a certain law and compass he enclosed the depths:

28 When he established the sky above, and poised the fountains of waters:

29 When he compassed the sea with its bounds, and set a law to the waters that they should not pass their limits: when he balanced the foundations of the earth:

30 I was with him forming all things: and was delighted every day, playing before him at all times;

31 Playing in the world. And my delights *were* to be with the children of men.

32 Now therefore, ye children, hear me: Blessed are they that keep my ways.

33 Hear instruction and be wise, and refuse it not.

34 Blessed is the man that heareth me, and that watcheth daily at my gates, and waiteth at the posts of my doors.

35 He that shall find me shall find life, and shall have salvation from the Lord.

36 But he that shall sin against me shall hurt his own soul. All that hate me love death.

CHAPTER 9

Wisdom invites all to her feast. Folly calls another way.

WISDOM hath built herself a house: she hath hewn her out seven pillars.

2 She hath slain her victims, mingled her wine, and set forth her table.

3 She hath sent her maids to invite to the tower, and to the walls of the city:

4 Whosoever is a little one, let him come to me. And to the unwise she said:

5 Come, eat my bread, and drink the wine which I have mingled for you.

6 Forsake childishness, and live, and walk by the ways of prudence.

7 He that teacheth a scorner doth an

injury to himself: and he that rebuketh a wicked man getteth himself a blot.

8 Rebuke not a scorner lest he hate thee. Rebuke a wise man, and he will love thee.

9 Give an occasion to a wise man, and wisdom shall be added to him. Teach a just man, and he shall make haste to receive it.

10 [1] The fear of the Lord is the beginning of wisdom: and the knowledge of the holy is prudence.

11 For by me shall thy days be multiplied: and years of life shall be added to thee.

12 If thou be wise, thou shalt be so to thyself: and if a scorner, thou alone shalt bear the evil.

13 A foolish woman and clamorous, and full of allurements, and knowing nothing at all,

14 Sat at the door of her house, upon a seat, in a high place of the city,

15 To call them that pass by the way, and go on their journey:

16 He that is a little one, let him turn to me. And to the fool she said:

17 Stolen waters are sweeter, and hidden bread is more pleasant.

18 And he did not know that giants are there: and that her guests are in the depths of hell.

THE PARABLES OF SOLOMON

CHAPTER 10

In the twenty following chapters are contained many wise sayings and axioms, relating to wisdom and folly, virtue and vice.

A WISE son maketh the father glad: but a foolish son is the sorrow of his mother.

2 [1] Treasures of wickedness shall profit nothing: but justice shall deliver from death.

3 The Lord will not afflict the soul of the just with famine: and he will disappoint the deceitful practices of the wicked.

4 The slothful hand hath wrought poverty: but the hand of the industrious getteth riches.

He that trusteth to lies feedeth the winds: and the same runneth after birds that fly away.

5 He that gathered in the harvest is a wise son: but he that snorteth in the summer is the son of confusion.

6 The blessing of the Lord is upon the head of the just: but iniquity covereth the mouth of the wicked.

7 The memory of the just is with

praises: and the name of the wicked shall rot.

8 The wise of heart receiveth precepts: a fool is beaten with lips.

9 He that walketh sincerely, walketh confidently: but he that perverteth his ways shall be manifest.

10 [2] He that winketh with the eye shall cause sorrow: and the foolish in lips shall be beaten.

11 The mouth of the just is a vein of life: and the mouth of the wicked covereth iniquity.

12 Hatred stirreth up strifes: [3] and charity covereth all sins.

13 In the lips of the wise is wisdom found: and a rod on the back of him that wanteth sense.

14 Wise men lay up knowledge: but the mouth of the fool is next to confusion.

15 The substance of a rich man is the city of his strength: the fear of the poor is their poverty.

16 The work of the just is unto life: but the fruit of the wicked, unto sin.

17 The way of life, to him that observeth correction: but he that forsaketh reproofs goeth astray.

18 Lying lips hide hatred: he that uttereth reproach is foolish.

19 In the multitude of words there shall not want sin: but he that refraineth his lips is most wise.

20 The tongue of the just is as choice silver: but the heart of the wicked is nothing worth.

21 The lips of the just teach many: but they that are ignorant shall die in the want of understanding.

22 The blessing of the Lord maketh men rich: neither shall affliction be joined to them.

23 A fool worketh mischief as it were for sport: but wisdom is prudence to a man.

24 That which the wicked feareth shall come upon him: to the just their desire shall be given.

25 As a tempest that passeth, so the wicked shall be no more: but the just is as an everlasting foundation.

26 As vinegar to the teeth, and smoke to the eyes, so is the sluggard to them that sent him.

27 The fear of the Lord shall prolong days: and the years of the wicked shall be shortened.

28 The expectation of the just is joy: but the hope of the wicked shall perish.

29 The strength of the upright is the way of the Lord: and fear to them that work evil.

30 The just shall never be moved: but the wicked shall not dwell on the earth.

CHAP. 9. [1] Ps. 110, 10; Prov. 1, 7; Ecclus. 1, 16. CHAP. 10. [1] Prov. 11, 4. [2] Ecclus. 27, 25. [3] 1 Cor. 13, 4; 1 Peter, 4, 8.

31 The mouth of the just shall bring forth wisdom: the tongue of the perverse shall perish.

32 The lips of the just consider what is acceptable: and the mouth of the wicked uttereth perverse things.

CHAPTER 11

A DECEITFUL [1] balance is an abomination before the Lord: and a just weight is his will.

2 Where pride is, there also shall be reproach: [2] but where humility is, there also is wisdom.

3 The simplicity of the just shall guide them: and the deceitfulness of the wicked shall destroy them.

4 [3] Riches shall not profit in the day of revenge: but justice shall deliver from death.

5 The justice of the upright shall make his way prosperous: and the wicked man shall fall by his own wickedness.

6 The justice of the righteous shall deliver them: and the unjust shall be caught in their own snares.

7 When the wicked man is dead, there shall be no hope any more: and the expectation of the solicitous shall perish.

8 The just is delivered out of distress: and the wicked shall be given up for him.

9 The dissembler with his mouth deceiveth his friend: but the just shall be delivered by knowledge.

10 When it goeth well with the just the city shall rejoice: and when the wicked perish there shall be praise.

11 By the blessing of the just the city shall be exalted: and by the mouth of the wicked it shall be overthrown.

12 He that despiseth his friend is mean of heart: but the wise man will hold his peace.

13 He that walketh deceitfully revealeth secrets: but he that is faithful concealeth the thing committed to him by his friend.

14 Where there is no governor, the people shall fall: but there is safety where there is much counsel.

15 He shall be afflicted with evil, that is surety for a stranger: but he that is aware of the snares shall be secure.

16 A gracious woman shall find glory: and the strong shall have riches.

17 A merciful man doth good to his own soul: but he that is cruel casteth off even his own kindred.

18 The wicked maketh an unsteady work: but to him that soweth justice, there is a faithful reward.

19 Clemency prepareth life: and the pursuing of evil things, death.

20 A perverse heart is abominable to the Lord: and his will is in them that walk sincerely.

21 Hand in hand the evil man shall not be innocent: but the seed of the just shall be saved.

22 A golden ring in a swine's snout, a woman fair and foolish.

23 The desire of the just is all good: the expectation of the wicked is indignation.

24 Some distribute their own goods, and grow richer: others take away what is not their own, and are always in want.

25 The soul which blesseth shall be made fat: and he that inebriateth shall be inebriated also himself.

26 He that hideth up corn shall be cursed among the people: but a blessing upon the head of them that sell.

27 Well doth he rise early who seeketh good things: but he that seeketh after evil things shall be oppressed by them.

28 He that trusteth in his riches shall fall: but the just shall spring up as a green leaf.

29 He that troubleth his own house, shall inherit the winds: and the fool shall serve the wise.

30 The fruit of the just man is a tree of life: and he that gaineth souls, is wise.

31 [4] If the just man receive in the earth, how much more the wicked and the sinner.

CHAPTER 12

HE that loveth correction loveth knowledge: but he that hateth reproof is foolish.

2 He that is good shall draw grace from the Lord: but he that trusteth in his own devices doth wickedly.

3 Men shall not be strengthened by wickedness: and the root of the just shall not be moved.

4 A diligent woman is a crown to her husband: and she that doth things worthy of confusion is a rottenness in his bones.

5 The thoughts of the just are judgments: and the counsels of the wicked are deceitful.

6 The words of the wicked lie in wait for blood: the mouth of the just shall deliver them.

7 Turn the wicked, and they shall not be: but the house of the just shall stand firm.

8 A man shall be known by his learning: but he that is vain and foolish shall be exposed to contempt.

CHAP. 11. [1] Prov. 20, 10. [2] Prov. 15, 33. [3] Prov. 10, 2. [4] 1 Peter, 4, 18.

9 ¹ Better is the poor man that provideth for himself, than he that is glorious and wanteth bread.

10 The just regardeth the lives of his beasts: but the bowels of the wicked are cruel.

11 ² He that tilleth his land shall be satisfied with bread: but he that pursueth idleness is very foolish.

He that is delighted in passing his time over wine leaveth a reproach in his strong holds.

12 The desire of the wicked is the fortification of evil men: but the root of the just shall prosper.

13 For the sins of the lips, ruin draweth nigh to the evil man: but the just shall escape out of distress.

14 By the fruit of his own mouth shall a man be filled with good things: and according to the works of his hands it shall be repaid him.

15 The way of a fool is right in his own eyes: but he that is wise hearkeneth unto counsels.

16 A fool immediately sheweth his anger: but he that dissembleth injuries is wise.

17 He that speaketh that which he knoweth sheweth forth justice: but he that lieth is a deceitful witness.

18 There is that promiseth, and is pricked as it were with a sword of conscience: but the tongue of the wise is health.

19 The lip of truth shall be steadfast for ever: but he that is a hasty witness frameth a lying tongue.

20 Deceit is in the heart of them that think evil things: but joy followeth them that take counsels of peace.

21 Whatsoever shall befall the just men, it shall not make him sad: but the wicked shall be filled with mischief.

22 Lying lips are an abomination to the Lord: but they that deal faithfully please him.

23 A cautious man concealeth knowledge: and the heart of fools publisheth folly.

24 The hand of the valiant shall bear rule: but that which is slothful shall be under tribute.

25 Grief in the heart of a man shall bring him low: but with a good word he shall be made glad.

26 He that neglecteth a loss for the sake of a friend, is just: but the way of the wicked shall deceive them.

27 The deceitful man shall not find gain: but the substance of a just man shall be precious gold.

28 In the path of justice is life: but the by-way leadeth to death.

CHAP. 12. ¹ Ecclus. 10, 30. ² Ecclus. 20, 30.

CHAPTER 13

A WISE son *heareth* the doctrine of *his* father: but he that is a scorner heareth not when he is reproved.

2 Of the fruit of his own mouth shall a man be filled with good things: but the soul of transgressors is wicked.

3 He that keepeth his mouth keepeth his soul: but he that hath no guard on his speech shall meet with evils.

4 The sluggard willeth and willeth not: but the soul of them that work shall be made fat.

5 The just shall hate a lying word: but the wicked confoundeth, and shall be confounded.

6 Justice keepeth the way of the innocent: but wickedness overthroweth the sinner.

7 One is as it were rich, when he hath nothing: and another is as it were poor, when he hath great riches.

8 The ransom of a man's life *are* his riches: but he that is poor beareth not reprehension.

9 The light of the just giveth joy: but the lamp of the wicked shall be put out.

10 Among the proud there are always contentions: but they that do all things with counsel are ruled by wisdom.

11 Substance got in haste shall be diminished: but that which by little and little is gathered with the hand shall increase.

12 Hope that is deferred afflicteth the soul: desire when it cometh is a tree of life.

13 Whosoever speaketh ill of any thing, bindeth himself for the time to come: but he that feareth the commandment shall dwell in peace.

Deceitful souls go astray in sins: the just are merciful, and shew mercy.

14 The law of the wise *is* a fountain of life, that he may decline from the ruin of death.

15 Good instruction shall give grace: in the way of scorners is a deep pit.

16 The prudent man doth all things with counsel: but he that is a fool layeth open his folly.

17 The messenger of the wicked shall fall into mischief: but a faithful ambassador is health.

18 Poverty and shame to him that refuseth instruction: but he that yieldeth to reproof shall be glorified.

19 The desire that is accomplished delighteth the soul: fools hate them that flee from evil things.

20 He that walketh with the wise shall be wise: a friend of fools shall become like to them.

21 Evil pursueth sinners: and to the just good shall be repaid.

22 The good man leaveth heirs, sons, and grandsons: and the substance of the sinner is kept for the just.

23 Much food is in the tillage of fathers: but for others it is gathered without judgment.

24 [1] He that spareth the rod hateth his son: but he that loveth him correcteth him betimes.

25 The just eateth and filleth his soul: but the belly of the wicked is never to be filled.

CHAPTER 14

A WISE woman buildeth her house: but the foolish will pull down with her hands that also which is built.

2 He that walketh in the right way, and feareth God, [1] is despised by him that goeth by an infamous way.

3 In the mouth of a fool is the rod of pride: but the lips of the wise preserve them.

4 Where there are no oxen, the crib is empty: but where there is much corn, there the strength of the ox is manifest.

5 A faithful witness will not lie: but a deceitful witness uttereth a lie.

6 A scorner seeketh wisdom, and findeth it not: the learning of the wise is easy.

7 Go against a foolish man, and he knoweth not the lips of prudence.

8 The wisdom of a discreet man is to understand his way: and the imprudence of fools erreth.

9 A fool will laugh at sin: but among the just grace shall abide.

10 The heart that knoweth the bitterness of his own soul, in his joy the stranger shall not intermeddle.

11 The house of the wicked shall be destroyed: but the tabernacles of the just shall flourish.

12 There is a way which seemeth just to a man: but the ends thereof lead to death.

13 Laughter shall be mingled with sorrow: and mourning taketh hold of the end of joy.

14 A fool shall be filled with his own ways: and the good man shall be above him.

15 The innocent believeth every word: the discreet man considereth his steps.

No good shall come to the deceitful son: but the wise servant shall prosper in his dealings, and his way shall be made straight.

16 A wise man feareth and declineth from evil: the fool leapeth over and is confident.

17 The impatient man shall work folly: and the crafty man is hateful.

18 The childish shall possess folly: and the prudent shall look for knowledge.

19 The evil shall fall down before the good: and the wicked before the gates of the just.

20 The poor man shall be hateful even to his own neighbour: but the friends of the rich are many.

21 He that despiseth his neighbour sinneth: but he that sheweth mercy to the poor shall be blessed.

He that believeth in the Lord loveth mercy.

22 They err that work evil: but mercy and truth prepare good things.

23 In much work there shall be abundance: but where there are many words, there is oftentimes want.

24 The crown of the wise is their riches: the folly of fools, imprudence.

25 A faithful witness delivereth souls: and the double dealer uttereth lies.

26 In the fear of the Lord is confidence of strength: and there shall be hope for his children.

27 The fear of the Lord is a fountain of life, to decline from the ruin of death.

28 In the multitude of people is the dignity of the king: and in the small number of people the dishonour of the prince.

29 He that is patient is governed with much wisdom: but he that is impatient exalteth his folly.

30 Soundness of heart is the life of the flesh: but envy is the rottenness of the bones.

31 [2] He that oppresseth the poor upbraideth his Maker: but he that hath pity on the poor honoureth him.

32 The wicked man shall be driven out in his wickedness: but the just hath hope in his death.

33 In the heart of the prudent resteth wisdom: and it shall instruct all the ignorant.

34 Justice exalteth a nation: but sin maketh nations miserable.

35 A wise servant is acceptable to the king: he that is good for nothing shall feel his anger.

CHAPTER 15

A MILD [1] answer breaketh wrath: but a harsh word stirreth up fury.

2 The tongue of the wise adorneth knowledge: but the mouth of fools bubbleth out folly.

CHAP. 13. [1] Prov. 23, 13. CHAP. 14. [1] Job, 12, 4. [2] Prov. 17, 5. CHAP. 15. [1] Prov. 25, 15.

3 The eyes of the Lord in every place behold the good and the evil.

4 A peaceable tongue is a tree of life: but that which is immoderate shall crush the spirit.

5 A fool laugheth at the instruction of his father: but he that regardeth reproofs shall become prudent.

In abundant justice there is the greatest strength: but the devices of the wicked shall be rooted out.

6 The house of the just is very much strength: and in the fruits of the wicked is trouble.

7 The lips of the wise shall disperse knowledge: the heart of fools shall be unlike.

8 [2] The victims of the wicked are abominable to the Lord: the vows of the just are acceptable.

9 The way of the wicked is an abomination to the Lord: he that followeth justice is beloved by him.

10 Instruction is grievous to him that forsaketh the way of life: he that hateth reproof shall die.

11 Hell and destruction are before the Lord. How much more the hearts of the children of men!

12 A corrupt man loveth not one that reproveth him: nor will he go to the wise.

13 [3] A glad heart maketh a cheerful countenance: but by grief of mind the spirit is cast down.

14 The heart of the wise seeketh instruction: and the mouth of fools feedeth on foolishness.

15 All the days of the poor are evil: a secure mind is like a continual feast.

16 Better is a little with the fear of the Lord, than great treasures without content.

17 It is better to be invited to herbs with love, than to a fatted calf with hatred.

18 A passionate man stirreth up strifes: he that is patient appeaseth those that are stirred up.

19 The way of the slothful is as a hedge of thorns; the way of the just is without offence.

20 A wise son maketh a father joyful: but the foolish man despiseth his mother.

[2] Prov. 21, 27; Ecclus. 34, 21.   [3] Prov. 16, 24; 17, 22.   [4] Prov. 16, 6.   CHAP. 16.   [1] Prov. 16, 9.   [2] Prov. 20, 24; 21, 2.   [3] Prov. 15, 27.

CHAP. 16. Ver. 1. *It is the part of man to prepare the soul.* That is, a man should prepare in his heart and soul what he is to say; but after all, it must be the Lord that must govern his tongue, to speak to the purpose. Not that we can think any thing of good without God's grace; but that after we have (with God's grace) thought and prepared within our souls what we would speak, if God does not govern our tongue, we shall not succeed in what we speak.

21 Folly is joy to the fool: and the wise man maketh straight his steps.

22 Designs are brought to nothing where there is no counsel: but where there are many counsellors, they are established.

23 A man rejoiceth in the sentence of his mouth: and a word in due time is best.

24 The path of life is above for the wise, that he may decline from the lowest hell.

25 The Lord will destroy the house of the proud: and will strengthen the borders of the widow.

26 Evil thoughts are an abomination to the Lord: and pure words most beautiful shall be confirmed by him.

27 He that is greedy of gain troubleth his own house: but he that hateth bribes shall live.

[4] By mercy and faith sins are purged away: and by the fear of the Lord every one declineth from evil.

28 The mind of the just studieth obedience: the mouth of the wicked overfloweth with evils.

29 The Lord is far from the wicked: and he will hear the prayers of the just.

30 The light of the eyes rejoiceth the soul: a good name maketh the bones fat.

31 The ear that heareth the reproofs of life shall abide in the midst of the wise.

32 He that rejecteth instruction despiseth his own soul: but he that yieldeth to reproof possesseth understanding.

33 The fear of the Lord *is* the lesson of wisdom: and humility goeth before glory.

CHAPTER 16

IT [1] is the part of man to prepare the soul: and of the Lord to govern the tongue.

2 [2] All the ways of a man are open to his eyes: the Lord is the weigher of spirits.

3 Lay open thy works to the Lord: and thy thoughts shall be directed.

4 The Lord hath made all things for himself: the wicked also for the evil day.

5 Every proud man is an abomination to the Lord: though hand should be joined to hand, he is not innocent.

The beginning of a good way is to do justice; and this is more acceptable with God than to offer sacrifices.

6 [3] By mercy and truth iniquity is redeemed: and by the fear of the Lord men depart from evil.

7 When the ways of man shall please the Lord, he will convert even his enemies to peace.

8 Better is a little with justice, than great revenues with iniquity.

9 [4] The heart of man disposeth his way: but the Lord must direct his steps.

10 Divination is in the lips of the king: his mouth shall not err in judgment.

11 Weight and balance are judgments of the Lord: and his work all the weights of the bag.

12 They that act wickedly are abominable to the king: for the throne is established by justice.

13 Just lips are the delight of kings: he that speaketh right things shall be loved.

14 The wrath of a king *is as* messengers of death: and the wise man will pacify it.

15 In the cheerfulness of the king's countenance is life: and his clemency is like the latter rain.

16 Get wisdom, because it is better than gold: and purchase prudence, for it is more precious than silver.

17 The path of the just departeth from evils: he that keepeth his soul keepeth his way.

18 Pride goeth before destruction: and the spirit is lifted up before a fall.

19 It is better to be humbled with the meek than to divide spoils with the proud.

20 The learned in word shall find good things: and he that trusteth in the Lord is blessed.

21 The wise in heart shall be called prudent: and he that is sweet in words shall attain to greater things.

22 Knowledge is a fountain of life to him that possesseth it: the instruction of fools *is* foolishness.

23 The heart of the wise shall instruct his mouth: and shall add grace to his lips.

24 [5] Well ordered words are *as* a honeycomb: sweet to the soul, and health to the bones.

25 There is a way that seemeth to a man right: and the ends thereof lead to death.

26 The soul of him that laboureth laboureth for himself, because his mouth hath obliged him to it.

27 The wicked man diggeth evil: and in his lips is a burning fire.

28 A perverse man stirreth up quarrels: and one full of words separateth princes.

29 An unjust man allureth his friend: and leadeth him into a way that is not good.

30 He that with fixed eyes deviseth wicked things, biting his lips, bringeth evil to pass.

31 Old age is a crown of dignity, when it is found in the ways of justice.

32 The patient man is better than the valiant: and he that ruleth his spirit, than he that taketh cities.

33 Lots are cast into the lap: but they are disposed of by the Lord.

CHAPTER 17

BETTER is a dry morsel with joy, than a house full of victims with strife.

2 [1] A wise servant shall rule over foolish sons: and shall divide the inheritance among the brethren.

3 As silver is tried by fire, and gold in the furnace: so the Lord trieth the hearts.

4 The evil man obeyeth an unjust tongue: and the deceitful hearkeneth to lying lips.

5 [2] He that despiseth the poor reproacheth his Maker: and he that rejoiceth at another man's ruin shall not be unpunished.

6 Children's children are the crown of old men: and the glory of children are their fathers.

7 Eloquent words do not become a fool: nor lying lips a prince.

8 The expectation of him that expecteth *is* a most acceptable jewel, whithersoever he turneth himself, he understandeth wisely.

9 He that concealeth a transgression seeketh friendships: he that repeateth it again separateth friends.

10 A reproof availeth more with a wise man, than a hundred stripes with a fool.

11 An evil man always seeketh quarrels: but a cruel angel shall be sent against him.

12 It is better to meet a bear robbed of her whelps than a fool trusting in his own folly.

13 [3] He that rendereth evil for good, evil shall not depart from his house.

14 The beginning of quarrels is *as when one* letteth out water: before he suffereth reproach he forsaketh judgment.

15 [4] He that justifieth the wicked, and he that condemneth the just, both are abominable before God.

16 What doth it avail a fool to have riches, seeing he cannot buy wisdom?

He that maketh his house high seeketh a downfall: and he that refuseth to learn shall fall into evils.

[4] Prov. 16, 1. [5] Prov. 15, 13; 17, 22. CHAP. 17. [1] Ecclus. 10, 28. [2] Prov. 14, 31. [3] Rom. 12, 17; 1 Thess. 5, 15; 1 Peter, 3, 9. [4] Isai. 5, 23.

17 He that is a friend loveth at all times: and a brother is proved in distress.

18 A foolish man will clap hands, when he is surety for his friend.

19 He that studieth discords loveth quarrels: and he that exalteth his door seeketh ruin.

20 He that is of a perverse heart shall not find good: and he that perverteth his tongue shall fall into evil.

21 A fool is born to his own disgrace: and even his father shall not rejoice in a fool.

22 [5] A joyful mind maketh age flourishing: a sorrowful spirit drieth up the bones.

23 The wicked man taketh gifts out of the bosom, that he may pervert the paths of judgment.

24 [6] Wisdom shineth in the face of the wise: the eyes of fools are in the ends of the earth.

25 A foolish son is the anger of the father: and the sorrow of the mother that bore him.

26 It is no good thing to do hurt to the just: nor to strike the prince who judgeth right.

27 [7] He that setteth bounds to his words is knowing and wise: and the man of understanding is of a precious spirit.

28 Even a fool, if he will hold his peace, shall be counted wise: and if he close his lips, a man of understanding.

CHAPTER 18

HE that hath a mind to depart from a friend seeketh occasions: he shall ever be subject to reproach.

2 A fool receiveth not the words of prudence: unless thou say those things which are in his heart.

3 The wicked man, when he is come into the depth of sins, contemneth: but ignominy and reproach follow him.

4 [1] Words from the mouth of a man are as deep water: and the fountain of wisdom as an overflowing stream.

5 It is not good to accept the person of the wicked: to decline from the truth of judgment.

6 The lips of a fool intermeddle with strife: and his mouth provoketh quarrels.

7 The mouth of a fool is his destruction: and his lips are the ruin of his soul.

8 The words of the double tongued are as if they were harmless: and they reach even to the inner parts of the bowels.

Fear casteth down the slothful: and the souls of the effeminate shall be hungry.

9 He that is loose and slack in his work is the brother of him that wasteth his own works.

10 The name of the Lord is a strong tower: the just runneth to it, and shall be exalted.

11 The substance of the rich man is the city of his strength: and as a strong wall compassing him about.

12 [2] Before destruction, the heart of a man is exalted: and before he be glorified, it is humbled.

13 [3] He that answereth before he heareth sheweth himself to be a fool and worthy of confusion.

14 The spirit of a man upholdeth his infirmity. But a spirit that is easily angered, who can bear!

15 A wise heart shall acquire knowledge: and the ear of the wise seeketh instruction.

16 A man's gift enlargeth his way and maketh him room before princes.

17 The just is first accuser of himself: his friend cometh, and shall search him.

18 The lot suppresseth contentions: and determineth even between the mighty.

19 A brother that is helped by his brother is like a strong city: and judgments are like the bars of cities.

20 Of the fruit of a man's mouth shall his belly be satisfied: and the offspring of his lips shall fill him.

21 Death and life are in the power of the tongue: they that love it shall eat the fruits thereof.

22 He that hath found a good wife hath found a good thing and shall receive a pleasure from the Lord. He that driveth away a good wife driveth away a good thing: but he that keepeth an adulteress is foolish and wicked.

23 The poor will speak with supplications: and the rich will speak roughly.

24 A man amiable in society shall be more friendly than a brother.

CHAPTER 19

BETTER is the poor man that walketh in his simplicity than a rich man that is perverse in his lips and unwise.

2 [1] Where there is no knowledge of the soul, there is no good: and he that is hasty with his feet shall stumble.

3 The folly of a man supplanteth his steps: and he fretteth in his mind against God.

4 Riches make many friends: but

from the poor man, even they whom he had, depart.

5 ² A false witness shall not be unpunished: and he that speaketh lies shall not escape.

6 Many honour the person of him that is mighty: and are friends of him that giveth gifts.

7 The brethren of the poor man hate him: moreover also his friends have departed far from him.

He that followeth after words only shall have nothing.

8 But he that possesseth a mind loveth his own soul: and he that keepeth prudence shall find good things.

9 A false witness shall not be unpunished: and he that speaketh lies shall perish.

10 Delicacies are not seemly for a fool: nor for a servant to have rule over princes.

11 The learning of a man is known by patience: and his glory is to pass over wrongs.

12 As the roaring of a lion, so also is the anger of a king: and his cheerfulness as the dew upon the grass.

13 A foolish son is the grief of his father: and a wrangling wife is like a roof continually dropping through.

14 House and riches are given by parents: but a prudent wife is properly from the Lord.

15 Slothfulness casteth into a deep sleep: and an idle soul shall suffer hunger.

16 He that keepeth the commandment keepeth his own soul: but he that neglecteth his own way shall die.

17 He that hath mercy on the poor lendeth to the Lord: and he will repay him.

18 Chastise thy son, despair not: but to the killing of him set not thy soul.

19 He that is impatient shall suffer damage: and when he shall take away he shall add another thing.

20 Hear counsel and receive instruction, that thou mayst be wise in thy latter end.

21 There are many thoughts in the heart of a man: but the will of the Lord shall stand firm.

22 A needy man is merciful: and better is the poor than the lying man.

23 The fear of the Lord is unto life: and he shall abide in fulness without being visited with evil.

24 ³ The slothful hideth his hand under his armpit: and will not so much as bring it to his mouth.

25 ⁴ The wicked man being scourged, the fool shall be wiser: but if thou rebuke a wise. man he will understand discipline.

26 He that afflicteth his father and chaseth away his mother is infamous and unhappy.

27 Cease not, O my son, to hear instruction: and be not ignorant of the words of knowledge.

28 An unjust witness scorneth judgment: and the mouth of the wicked devoureth iniquity.

29 Judgments are prepared for scorners: and striking hammers for the bodies of fools.

CHAPTER 20

𝕎INE is a luxurious thing, and drunkenness riotous: whosoever is delighted therewith shall not be wise.

2 As the roaring of a lion, so also is the dread of a king: he that provoketh him sinneth against his own soul.

3 It is an honour for a man to separate himself from quarrels: but all fools are meddling with reproaches.

4 Because of the cold, the sluggard would not plough: he shall beg therefore in the summer, and it shall not be given him.

5 ¹ Counsel in the heart of a man is like deep water: but a wise man will draw it out.

6 Many men are called merciful. But who shall find a faithful man!

7 The just that walketh in his simplicity, shall leave behind him blessed children.

8 The king, that sitteth on the throne of judgment scattereth away all evil with his look.

9 ² Who can say: My heart is clean. I am pure from sin?

10 ³ Diverse weights and diverse measures, both are abominable before God.

11 By his inclinations a child is known, if his works be clean and right.

12 The hearing ear, and the seeing eye, the Lord hath made them both.

13 Love not sleep, lest poverty oppress thee: open thy eyes, and be filled with bread.

14 It is nought, it is nought, saith every. buyer: and when he is gone away, then he will boast.

15 There is gold, and a multitude of jewels: but the lips of knowledge are a precious vessel.

16 ⁴ Take away the garment of him that is surety for a stranger: and take a pledge from him for strangers.

17 The bread of lying is sweet to a man: but afterwards his mouth shall be filled with gravel.

² Dan. 13, 61. ³ Prov. 26, 15. ⁴ Prov. 21, 11. CHAP. 20. ¹ Prov. 18, 4. ² 3 Kings, 8, 46; 2 Par. 6, 36; Eccles. 7, 21; 1 John, 1, 8. ³ Prov. 11, 1; 20, 23. ⁴ Prov. 27, 13.

18 Designs are strengthened by counsels: and wars are to be managed by governments.

19 Meddle not with him that revealeth secrets, and walketh deceitfully, and openeth wide his lips.

20 [5] He that curseth his father and mother, his lamp shall be put out in the midst of darkness.

21 The inheritance gotten hastily in the beginning, in the end shall be without a blessing.

22 [6] Say not: I will return evil. Wait for the Lord and he will deliver thee.

23 [7] Diverse weights are an abomination before the Lord: a deceitful balance is not good.

24 [8] The steps of man are guided by the Lord. But who is the man that can understand his own way!

25 It is ruin to a man to devour holy ones, and after vows to retract.

26 A wise king scattereth the wicked, and bringeth over them the wheel.

27 The spirit of a man is the lamp of the Lord, which searcheth all the hidden things of the bowels.

28 Mercy and truth preserve the king: and his throne is strengthened by clemency.

29 The joy of young men is their strength: and the dignity of old men, their grey hairs.

30 The blueness of a wound shall wipe away evils: and stripes in the more inward parts of the belly.

CHAPTER 21

AS the divisions of waters, so the heart of the king is in the hand of the Lord: whithersoever he will he shall turn it.

2 [1] Every way of a man seemeth right to himself: but the Lord weigheth the hearts.

3 To do mercy and judgment pleaseth the Lord more than victims.

4 Haughtiness of the eyes is the enlarging of the heart: the lamp of the wicked is sin.

5 The thoughts of the industrious always bring forth abundance: but every sluggard is always in want.

6 He that gathereth treasures by a lying tongue is vain and foolish: and shall stumble upon the snares of death.

7 The robberies of the wicked shall be their downfall, because they would not do judgment.

8 The perverse way of a man is strange: but as for him that is pure, his work is right.

9 [2] It is better to sit in a corner of the housetop than with a brawling woman and in a common house.

10 The soul of the wicked desireth evil: he will not have pity on his neighbour.

11 [3] When a pestilent man is punished, the little one will be wiser: and if he follow the wise, he will receive knowledge.

12 The just considereth seriously the house of the wicked, that he may withdraw the wicked from evil.

13 He that stoppeth his ear against the cry of the poor shall also cry himself and shall not be heard.

14 A secret present quencheth anger: and a gift in the bosom the greatest wrath.

15 It is joy to the just to do judgment: and dread to them that work iniquity.

16 A man that shall wander out of the way of doctrine shall abide in the company of the giants.

17 He that loveth good cheer shall be in want: he that loveth wine and fat things shall not be rich.

18 The wicked is delivered up for the just: and the unjust for the righteous.

19 [4] It is better to dwell in a wilderness than with a quarrelsome and passionate woman.

20 There is a treasure to be desired and oil, in the dwelling of the just: and the foolish man shall spend it.

21 He that followeth justice and mercy shall find life, justice, and glory.

22 The wise man hath scaled the city of the strong: and hath cast down the strength of the confidence thereof.

23 He that keepeth his mouth and his tongue keepeth his soul from distress.

24 The proud and the arrogant is called ignorant, who in anger worketh pride.

25 Desires kill the slothful: for his hands have refused to work at all.

26 He longeth and desireth all the day: but he that is just will give, and will not cease.

27 [5] The sacrifices of the wicked are abominable, because they are offered of wickedness.

28 A lying witness shall perish: an obedient man shall speak of victory.

29 The wicked man impudently hardeneth his face: but he that is righteous correcteth his way.

30 There is no wisdom, there is no prudence, there is no counsel against the Lord.

31 The horse is prepared for the day of battle: but the Lord giveth safety.

[5] Exod. 21, 17; Lev. 20, 9; Matt. 15, 4. [6] Rom. 12, 17; 1 Thess. 5, 15; 1 Peter, 3, 9. [7] Prov. 20, 10. [8] Prov. 16, 2. CHAP. 21. [1] Prov. 16, 2; 20, 24. [2] Prov. 25, 24. [3] Prov. 19, 25. [4] Prov. 21, 9; Ecclus. 25, 23. [5] Prov. 15, 8; Ecclus. 34, 21.

CHAPTER 22

A GOOD[1] name is better than great riches: and good favour is above silver and gold.

2 [2] The rich and poor have met one another: the Lord is the maker of them both.

3 The prudent man saw the evil, and hid himself: the simple passed on, and suffered loss.

4 The fruit of humility is the fear of the Lord: riches and glory and life.

5 Arms and swords are in the way of the perverse: but he that keepeth his own soul departeth far from them.

6 It is a proverb: A young man according to his way. Even when he is old he will not depart from it.

7 The rich ruleth over the poor: and the borrower is servant to him that lendeth.

8 He that soweth iniquity shall reap evils: and with the rod of his anger he shall be consumed.

9 [3] He that is inclined to mercy shall be blessed: for of his bread he hath given to the poor.

He that maketh presents shall purchase victory and honour: but he carrieth away the souls of the receivers.

10 Cast out the scoffer, and contention shall go with him: and quarrels and reproaches shall cease.

11 He that loveth cleanness of heart, for the grace of his lips, shall have the king for his friend.

12 The eyes of the Lord preserve knowledge: and the words of the unjust are overthrown.

13 The slothful man saith: There is a lion without, I shall be slain in the midst of the streets.

14 The mouth of a strange woman is a deep pit: he whom the Lord is angry with shall fall into it.

15 Folly is bound up in the heart of a child: and the rod of correction shall drive it away.

16 He that oppresseth the poor, to increase his own riches, shall himself give to one that is richer, and shall be in need.

17 Incline thy ear and hear the words of the wise: and apply thy heart to my doctrine.

18 It shall be beautiful for thee, if thou keep it in thy bowels: and it shall flow in thy lips.

19 That thy trust may be in the Lord, wherefore I have also shewn it to thee this day.

20 Behold I have described it to thee three manner of ways, in thoughts and knowledge:

21 That I might shew thee the certainty, and the words of truth, to answer out of these to them that sent thee.

22 Do no violence to the poor, because he is poor: and do not oppress the needy in the gate:

23 Because the Lord will judge his cause, and will afflict them that have afflicted his soul.

24 Be not a friend to an angry man: and do not walk with a furious man:

25 Lest perhaps thou learn his ways and take scandal to thy soul.

26 Be not with them that fasten down their hands and that offer themselves sureties for debts:

27 For if thou have not wherewith to restore, what cause is there that he should take the covering from thy bed?

28 Pass not beyond the ancient bounds which thy fathers have set.

29 Hast thou seen a man swift in his work? He shall stand before kings and shall not be before those that are obscure.

CHAPTER 23

WHEN thou shalt sit to eat with a prince, consider diligently what is set before thy face.

2 And put a knife to thy throat, if it be so that thou have thy soul in thy own power.

3 Be not desirous of his meats, in which is the bread of deceit.

4 Labour not to be rich: but set bounds to thy prudence.

5 Lift not up thy eyes to riches which thou canst not have: because they shall make themselves wings like those of an eagle, and shall fly towards heaven.

6 Eat not with an envious man, and desire not his meats:

7 Because like a soothsayer, and diviner, he thinketh that which he knoweth not. Eat and drink, will he say to thee: and his mind is not with thee.

8 The meats which thou hadst eaten, thou shalt vomit up: and shalt loose thy beautiful words.

9 Speak not in the ears of fools: because they will despise the instruction of thy speech.

10 Touch not the bounds of little ones: and enter not into the field of the fatherless.

11 For their near kinsman is strong: and he will judge their cause against thee.

12 Let thy heart apply itself to instruction: and thy ears to words of knowledge.

CHAP. 22. [1] Ecclus. 7, 2. [2] Prov. 29, 13. [3] Ecclus. 31, 28.

13 ¹Withhold not correction from a child: for if thou strike him with the rod, he shall not die.

14 Thou shalt beat him with the rod: and deliver his soul from hell.

15 My son, if thy mind be wise, my heart shall rejoice with thee:

16 And my reins shall rejoice, when thy lips shall speak what is right.

17 ²Let not thy heart envy sinners: but be thou in the fear of the Lord all the day long.

18 Because thou shalt have hope in the latter end: and thy expectation shall not be taken away.

19 Hear thou, my son, and be wise: and guide thy mind in the way.

20 Be not in the feasts of great drinkers, nor in their revellings, who contribute flesh to eat.

21 Because they that give themselves to drinking and that club together shall be consumed: and drowsiness shall be clothed with rags.

22 Hearken to thy father that begot thee: and despise not thy mother when she is old.

23 Buy truth, and do not sell wisdom and instruction and understanding.

24 The father of the just rejoiceth greatly: he that hath begotten a wise son shall have joy in him.

25 Let thy father, and thy mother be joyful: and let her rejoice that bore thee.

26 My son, give me thy heart: and let thy eyes keep my ways.

27 For a harlot is a deep ditch: and a strange woman is a narrow pit.

28 She lieth in wait in the way as a robber: and him whom she shall see unwary, she will kill.

29 Who hath woe? Whose father hath woe? Who hath contentions? Who falls into pits? Who hath wounds without cause? Who hath redness of eyes?

30 Surely they that pass their time in wine, and study to drink off their cups.

31 Look not upon the wine when it is yellow, when the colour thereof shineth in the glass. It goeth in pleasantly:

32 But in the end, it will bite like a snake, and will spread abroad poison like a basilisk.

33 Thy eyes shall behold strange women: and thy heart shall utter perverse things.

34 And thou shalt be as one sleeping in the midst of the sea, and as a pilot fast asleep, when the stern is lost.

35 And thou shalt say: They have beaten me, but I was not sensible of pain: they drew me, and I felt not. When shall I awake, and find wine again?

CHAPTER 24

SEEK ¹not to be like evil men: neither desire to be with them.

2 Because their mind studieth robberies: and their lips speak deceits.

3 By wisdom the house shall be built: and by prudence it shall be strengthened.

4 By instruction the storerooms shall be filled with all precious and most beautiful wealth.

5 A wise man is strong: and a knowing man, stout and valiant.

6 Because war is managed by due ordering: and there shall be safety where there are many counsels.

7 Wisdom is too high for a fool: in the gate he shall not open his mouth.

8 He that deviseth to do evils shall be called a fool.

9 The thought of a fool is sin: and the detracter is the abomination of men.

10 If thou lose hope being weary in the day of distress, thy strength shall be diminished.

11 ²Deliver them that are led to death: and those that are drawn to death forbear not to deliver.

12 If thou say: I have not strength enough. He that seeth into the heart, he understandeth, and nothing deceiveth the keeper of thy soul: and he shall render to a man according to his works.

13 ³Eat honey, my son, because it is good: and the honeycomb, most sweet to thy throat.

14 So also is the doctrine of wisdom to thy soul. Which when thou hast found, thou shalt have hope in the end: and thy hope shall not perish.

15 Lie not in wait, nor seek after wickedness in the house of the just: nor spoil his rest.

16 For a just man shall fall seven times and · shall rise again: but the wicked shall fall down into evil.

17 When thy enemy shall fall, be not glad: and in his ruin let not thy heart rejoice.

18 Lest the Lord see, and it displease him, and he turn away his wrath from him.

19 Contend not with the wicked: nor seek to be like the ungodly.

20 For evil men have no hope of things to come: and the lamp of the wicked shall be put out.

21 My son, fear the Lord and the

CHAP. 23. ¹ Prov. 13, 24; Ecclus. 30, 1; Prov. 29, 15. ² Prov. 24, 1. CHAP. 24. ¹ Prov. 23, 17. ³ Ps. 81, 1. ⁴ Prov. 25, 16, 27.

king: and have nothing to do with detracters.

22 For their destruction shall rise suddenly. And who knoweth the ruin of both!

23 These things also to the wise: It is not good to have respect to persons in judgment.

24 They that say to the wicked man: Thou art just, shall be cursed by the people; and the tribes shall abhor them.

25 They that rebuke him shall be praised: and a blessing shall come upon them.

26 He shall kiss the lips, who answereth right words.

27 Prepare thy work without, and diligently till thy ground: that afterward thou mayst build thy house.

28 Be not witness without cause against thy neighbour: and deceive not any man with thy lips.

29 ⁵ Say not: I will do to him as he hath done to me. I will render to every one according to his work.

30 I passed by the field of the slothful man, and by the vineyard of the foolish man:

31 And behold it was all filled with nettles, and thorns had covered the face thereof, and the stone wall was broken down.

32 Which when I had seen, I laid it up in my heart: and by the example I received instruction.

33 Thou wilt sleep a little, said I, thou wilt slumber a little; thou wilt fold thy hands a little to rest:

34 And poverty shall come to thee as a runner: and beggary as an armed man.

CHAPTER 25

THESE are also parables of Solomon, which the men of Ezechias king of Juda copied out.

2 It is the glory of God to conceal the word, and the glory of kings to search out the speech.

3 The heaven above, and the earth beneath, and the heart of kings is unsearchable.

4 Take away the rust from silver: and there shall come forth a most pure vessel.

5 Take away wickedness from the face of the king: and his throne shall be established with justice.

6 Appear not glorious before the king, and stand not in the place of great men.

7 For it is better that it should be said to thee: Come up hither; than that thou shouldst be humbled before the prince.

8 The things which thy eyes have seen, utter not hastily in a quarrel: lest afterward thou mayst not be able to make amends, when thou hast dishonoured thy friend.

9 Treat thy cause with thy friend, and discover not the secret to a stranger:

10 Lest he insult over thee, when he hath heard it, and cease not to upbraid thee.

Grace and friendship deliver a man: keep these for thyself, lest thou fall under reproach.

11 To speak a word in due time is like apples of gold on beds of silver.

12 As an earring of gold and a bright pearl, so is he that reproveth the wise, and the obedient ear.

13 ¹ As the cold of snow in the time of harvest, so is a faithful messenger to him that sent him: for he refresheth his soul.

14 As clouds, and wind, when no rain followeth, so is the man that boasteth, and doth not fulfil his promises.

15 By patience a prince shall be appeased: ² and a soft tongue shall break hardness.

16 Thou hast found honey. Eat what is sufficient for thee, lest being glutted therewith thou vomit it up.

17 Withdraw thy foot from the house of thy neighbour, lest having his fill he hate thee.

18 A man that beareth false witness against his neighbour is like a dart and a sword and a sharp arrow.

19 To trust to an unfaithful man in the time of trouble is like a rotten tooth, and weary foot,

20 And one that looseth his garment in cold weather.

As vinegar upon nitre, so is he that singeth songs to a very evil heart. As a moth doth by a garment, and a worm by the wood: so the sadness of a man consumeth the heart.

21 ³ If thy enemy be hungry, give him to eat: if he thirst, give him water to drink:

22 For thou shalt heap hot coals upon his head; and the Lord will reward thee.

23 The north wind driveth away rain, as doth a sad countenance a backbiting tongue.

24 ⁴ It is better to sit in a corner of the housetop than with a brawling woman, and in a common house.

25 As cold water to a thirsty soul, so is good tidings from a far country.

26 A just man falling down before

---

⁴ Lev. 19, 15; Deut. 1, 17; 16, 19; Ecclus. 42, 1. ⁵ Prov. 20, 22. CHAP. 25. ¹ Prov. 26, 6. ² Prov. 15, 1. ³ Rom. 12, 20. ⁴ Prov. 21, 9.

the wicked is as a fountain troubled with the foot and a corrupted spring.

27 As it is not good for a man to eat much honey, [5] so he that is a searcher of majesty shall be overwhelmed by glory.

28 As a city that lieth open and is not compassed with walls, so is a man that cannot refrain his own spirit in speaking.

CHAPTER 26

AS snow in summer and rain in harvest, so glory is not seemly for a fool.

2 As a bird flying to other places and a sparrow going here or there, so a curse uttered without cause shall come upon a man.

3 A whip for a horse and a snaffle for an ass: [1] and a rod for the back of fools.

4 Answer not a fool according to his folly, lest thou be made like him.

5 Answer a fool according to his folly, lest he imagine himself to be wise.

6 [2] He that sendeth words by a foolish messenger is lame of feet and drinketh iniquity.

7 As a lame man hath fair legs in vain, so a parable is unseemly in the mouth of fools.

8 As he that casteth a stone into the heap of Mercury, so is he that giveth honour to a fool.

9 As if a thorn should grow in the hand of a drunkard, so is a parable in the mouth of fools.

10 Judgment determineth causes: and he that putteth a fool to silence appeaseth anger.

11 [3] As a dog that returneth to his vomit, so is the fool that repeateth his folly.

12 Hast thou seen a man wise in his own conceit? There shall be more hope of a fool than of him.

13 The slothful man saith: There is a lion in the way and a lioness in the roads.

14 As a door turneth upon its hinges, so doth the slothful upon his bed.

15 [4] The slothful hideth his hand under his armpit: and it grieveth him to turn it to his mouth.

16 The sluggard is wiser in his own conceit than seven men that speak sentences.

17 As he that taketh a dog by the ears, so is he that passeth by in anger and meddleth with another man's quarrel.

18 As he is guilty that shooteth arrows and lances unto death:

19 So is the man that hurteth his friend deceitfully, and when he is taken, saith: I did it in jest.

20 When the wood faileth, the fire shall go out: and when the talebearer is taken away contentions shall cease.

21 As coals are to burning coals, and wood to fire, [5] so an angry man stirreth up strife.

22 The words of a talebearer *are* as it were simple, but they reach to the innermost parts of the belly.

23 Swelling lips joined with a corrupt heart are like an earthen vessel adorned with silver dross.

24 An enemy is known by his lips, when in his heart he entertaineth deceit.

25 When he shall speak low, trust him not: because there are seven mischiefs in his heart.

26 He that covereth hatred deceitfully, his malice shall be laid open in the public assembly.

27 He that diggeth a pit shall fall into it: and he that rolleth a stone, it shall return to him.

28 A deceitful tongue loveth not truth: and a slippery mouth worketh ruin.

CHAPTER 27

BOAST not for to-morrow, for thou knowest not what the day to come may bring forth.

2 Let another praise thee, and not thy own mouth: a stranger, and not thy own lips.

3 [1] A stone is heavy, and sand weighty: but the anger of a fool is heavier than them both.

4 Anger hath no mercy, nor fury when it breaketh forth. And who can bear the violence of one provoked!

5 Open rebuke is better than hidden love.

6 Better are the wounds of a friend than the deceitful kisses of an enemy.

7 [2] A soul that is full shall tread upon the honeycomb: and a soul that is hungry shall take even bitter for sweet.

8 As a bird that wandereth from her nest, so is a man that leaveth his place.

9 Ointment and perfumes rejoice the

[5] Ecclus. 3, 22. CHAP. 26. [1] Prov. 23, 13. [2] Prov. 25, 13. [3] 2 Peter, 2, 22. [4] Prov. 19, 24. [5] Prov. 15, 18. CHAP. 27. [1] Ecclus. 22, 18. [2] Job. 6, 7.

CHAP. 25. Ver. 27. *Majesty.* That is, of God. For to search into that incomprehensible *Majesty*, and to pretend to sound the depth of the wisdom of God, is exposing our weak understanding to be blinded with an excess of light and glory, which it cannot comprehend.

CHAP. 26. Ver. 2. *As a bird.* The meaning is, that a curse uttered without cause shall do no harm to the person that is cursed, but will return upon him that curseth, as whithersoever a bird flies, it returns to its own nest.

Ver. 4. *Answer not a fool according to his folly.* That is, so as to imitate him, but only so as to reprove his folly.

Ver. 8. *The heap of Mercury.* The heap of stones at the foot of this idol.

heart: and the good counsels of a friend are sweet to the soul.

10 Thy own friend and thy father's friend, forsake not: and go not into thy brother's house in the day of thy affliction.

Better is a neighbour that is near, than a brother afar off.

11 Study wisdom, my son, and make my heart joyful, that thou mayst give an answer to him that reproacheth.

12 The prudent man seeing evil hideth himself: little ones passing on have suffered losses.

13 [8] Take away his garment that hath been surety for a stranger: and take from him a pledge for strangers.

14 He that blesseth his neighbour with a loud voice, rising in the night, shall be like to him that curseth.

15 [4] Roofs dropping through in a cold day and a contentious woman are alike.

16 He that retaineth her is as he that would hold the wind, and shall call in the oil of his right hand.

17 Iron sharpeneth iron, so a man sharpeneth the countenance of his friend.

18 He that keepeth the fig tree shall eat the fruit thereof: and he that is the keeper of his master shall be glorified.

19 As the faces of them that look therein shine in the water, so the hearts of men are laid open to the wise.

20 Hell and destruction are never filled: [5] So the eyes of men are never satisfied.

21 [6] As silver is tried in the finingpot and gold in the furnace: so a man is tried by the mouth of him that praiseth.

The heart of the wicked seeketh after evils: but the righteous heart seeketh after knowledge.

22 Though thou shouldst bray a fool in the mortar, as when a pestle striketh upon sodden barley, his folly would not be taken from him.

23 Be diligent to know the countenance of thy cattle: and consider thy own flocks.

24 For thou shalt not always have power: but a crown shall be given to generation and generation.

25 The meadows are open and the green herbs have appeared, and the hay is gathered out of the mountains.

26 [7] Lambs are for thy clothing: and kids for the price of the field.

27 Let the milk of the goats be enough for thy food, and for the necessities of thy house, and for maintenance for thy handmaids.

CHAPTER 28

THE wicked man fleeth, when no man pursueth: but the just, bold as a lion, shall be without dread.

2 For the sins of the land many are the princes thereof: and for the wisdom of a man, and the knowledge of those things that are said, the life of the prince shall be prolonged.

3 A poor man that oppresseth the poor is like a violent shower, which bringeth a famine.

4 They that forsake the law praise the wicked man: they that keep it are incensed against him.

5 Evil men think not on judgment: but they that seek after the Lord take notice of all things.

6 [1] Better is the poor man walking in his simplicity than the rich in crooked ways.

7 He that keepeth the law is a wise son: but he that feedeth gluttons shameth his father.

8 He that heapeth together riches by usury and loan gathereth them for him that will be bountiful to the poor.

9 He that turneth away his ears from hearing the law, his prayer shall be an abomination.

10 He that deceiveth the just in a wicked way shall fall in his own destruction: and the upright shall possess his goods.

11 The rich man seemeth to himself wise: but the poor man that is prudent shall search him out.

12 In the joy of the just there is great glory: when the wicked reign, men are ruined.

13 He that hideth his sins shall not prosper: but he that shall confess and forsake them shall obtain mercy.

14 Blessed is the man that is always fearful: but he that is hardened in mind shall fall into evil.

15 As a roaring lion, and a hungry bear, so is a wicked prince over the poor people.

16 A prince void of prudence shall oppress many by calumny: but he that hateth covetousness shall prolong his days.

17 A man that doth violence to the blood of a person, if he flee even to the pit, no man will stay him.

18 He that walketh uprightly shall be saved: he that is perverse in his ways shall fall at once.

19 [2] He that tilleth his ground shall be filled with bread: but he that followeth idleness shall be filled with poverty.

20 A faithful man shall be much praised: [3] but he that maketh haste to be rich shall not be innocent.

3 Prov. 20, 16.   4 Prov. 19, 13.   5 Ecclus. 14, 9. 6 Prov. 17, 3.   7 1 Tim. 6, 8.   Chap. 28.   1 Prov. 19, 1.   2 Prov. 12, 11; Ecclus. 20, 30.   3 Prov. 13, 11; 20, 21; 28, 22.

21 He that hath respect to a person in judgment doth not well: such a man even for a morsel of bread forsaketh the truth.

22 A man, that maketh haste to be rich, and envieth others is ignorant that poverty shall come upon him.

23 He that rebuketh a man shall afterward find favour with him, more than he that by a flattering tongue deceiveth *him*.

24 He that stealeth any thing from his father, or from his mother, and saith: This is no sin, is the partner of a murderer.

25 He that boasteth, and puffeth up up himself, stirreth up quarrels: but he that trusteth in the Lord shall be healed.

26 He that trusteth in his own heart is a fool: but he that walketh wisely, he shall be saved.

27 He that giveth to the poor shall not want: he that despiseth his entreaty shall suffer indigence.

28 When the wicked rise up, men shall hide themselves: when they perish, the just shall be multiplied.

CHAPTER 29

THE man that with a stiff neck despiseth him that reproveth him shall suddenly be destroyed: and health shall not follow him.

2 When just men increase, the people shall rejoice: when the wicked shall bear rule, the people shall mourn.

3 A man that loveth wisdom rejoiceth his father: but he that maintaineth harlots shall squander away his substance.

4 A just king setteth up the land: a covetous man shall destroy it.

5 A man that speaketh to his friend with flattering and dissembling words spreadeth a net for his feet.

6 A snare shall entangle the wicked man when he sinneth: and the just shall praise and rejoice.

7 The just taketh notice of the cause of the poor: the wicked is void of knowledge.

8 Corrupt men bring a city to ruin: but wise men turn away wrath.

9 If a wise man contend with a fool, whether he be angry or laugh, he shall find no rest.

10 Bloodthirsty men hate the upright: but just men seek his soul.

11 A fool uttereth all his mind: a wise man deferreth, and keepeth it till afterwards.

12 A prince that gladly heareth lying words hath all his servants wicked.

13 [1] The poor man and the creditor have met one another: the Lord is the enlightener of them both.

14 The king that judgeth the poor in truth, his throne shall be established for ever.

15 [2] The rod and reproof give wisdom: but the child that is left to his own will bringeth his mother to shame.

16 When the wicked are multiplied, crimes shall be multiplied: but the just shall see their downfall.

17 Instruct thy son: and he shall refresh thee and shall give delight to thy soul.

18 When prophecy shall fail, the people shall be scattered abroad: but he that keepeth the law is blessed.

19 A slave will not be corrected by words: because he understandeth what thou sayest, and will not answer.

20 Hast thou seen a man hasty to speak? Folly is rather to be looked for than his amendment.

21 He that nourisheth his servant delicately from his childhood, afterwards shall find him stubborn.

22 A passionate man provoketh quarrels: and he that is easily stirred up to wrath shall be more prone to sin.

23 [3] Humiliation followeth the proud: and glory shall uphold the humble of spirit.

24 He that is partaker with a thief hateth his own soul: he heareth one putting him to his oath, and discovereth not.

25 He that feareth man shall quickly fall: he that trusteth in the Lord shall be set on high.

26 Many seek the face of the prince: but the judgment of every one cometh forth from the Lord.

27 The just abhor the wicked man: and the wicked loathe them that are in the right way.

The son that keepeth the word, shall be free from destruction.

CHAPTER 30

The wise man thinketh humbly of himself. His prayer and sentiments upon certain virtues and vices

THE words of Gatherer the son of Vomiter. The vision which the man spoke with whom God is, and who, being strengthened by God abiding with him, said:

CHAP. 29. [1] Prov. 22, 2. [2] Prov. 23, 13; 29, 17. [3] Job. 22, 29.

CHAP. 30. Ver. 1. *Gatherer the son of Vomiter,* or, as it is in the Latin, *Congregans* the son of *Vomens.* The Latin interpreter has given us in this place the signification of the Hebrew names, instead of the names themselves, which are in the Hebrew, *Agur the son of Jakeh.* But whether this *Agur* be the same person as *Solomon,* as many think, or a different person, whose doctrine was adopted by Solomon, and inserted among his parables or proverbs, is uncertain.

2 I am the most foolish of men, and the wisdom of men is not with me.

3 I have not learned wisdom, and have not known the science of saints.

4 Who hath ascended up into heaven, and descended? Who hath held the wind in his hands? Who hath bound up the waters together as in a garment? Who hath raised up all the borders of the earth? What is his name, and what is the name of his son, if thou knowest?

5 ¹Every word of God is fire tried: he is a buckler to them that hope in him.

6 ²Add not any thing to his words, lest thou be reproved, and found a liar.

7 Two things I have asked of thee: deny them not to me before I die.

8 Remove far from me vanity and lying words. Give me neither beggary nor riches. Give me only the necessaries of life.

9 Lest perhaps being filled, I should be tempted to deny, and say: Who is the Lord? Or being compelled by poverty, I should steal, and forswear the name of my God.

10 Accuse not a servant to his master, lest he curse thee, and thou fall.

11 *There is* a generation that curseth their father, and doth not bless their mother.

12 A generation that are pure in their own eyes, and yet are not washed from their filthiness.

13 A generation, whose eyes are lofty and their eyelids lifted up on high.

14 A generation that for teeth hath swords, and grindeth with their jaw teeth: to devour the needy from off the earth, and the poor from among men.

15 The horseleech hath two daughters that say: Bring, bring.

There are three things that never are satisfied. And the fourth never saith: It is enough.

16 Hell, and the mouth of the womb, and the earth which is not satisfied with water. And the fire never saith: It is enough.

17 The eye that mocketh at his father and that despiseth the labour of his mother in bearing him, let the ravens of the brooks pick it out, and the young eagles eat it.

18 Three things are hard to me, and the fourth I am utterly ignorant of.

19 The way of an eagle in the air, the way of a serpent upon a rock, the way of a ship in the midst of the sea, and the way of a man in youth.

20 Such is also the way of an adulterous woman, who eateth, and wipeth her mouth, and saith: I have done no evil.

21 By three things the earth is disturbed, and the fourth it cannot bear:

22 By a slave when he reigneth: by a fool when he is filled with meat:

23 By an odious woman when she is married: and by a bondwoman when she is heir to her mistress.

24 There are four very little things of the earth, and they are wiser than the wise:

25 The ants, a feeble people, which provide themselves food in the harvest:

26 The rabbit, a weak people, which maketh its bed in the rock:

27 The locust which hath no king, yet they all go out by their bands:

28 The stellio which supporteth itself on hands, and dwelleth in king's houses.

29 There are three things which go well, and the fourth that walketh happily:

30 A lion, the strongest of beasts, who hath no fear of any thing he meeteth:

31 A cock girded about the loins: and a ram: and a king, whom none can resist.

32 There is that hath appeared a fool after he was lifted up on high: for if he had understood, he would have laid his hand upon his mouth.

33 And he that strongly squeezeth the paps to bring out milk straineth out butter: and he that violently bloweth his nose bringeth out blood: and he that provoketh wrath bringeth forth strife.

CHAPTER 31

An exhortation to chastity, temperance, and works of mercy. The praise of a wise woman.

THE words of king Lamuel. The vision wherewith his mother instructed him.

2 What, O my beloved: What, O the beloved of my womb: What, O the beloved of my vows?

3 Give not thy substance to women, and thy riches to destroy kings.

4 Give not to kings, O Lamuel, give not wine to kings: because there is no secret where drunkenness reigneth:

5 And lest they drink and forget judgments, and pervert the cause of the children of the poor.

CHAP. 30. ¹ Ps. 11, 7. ² Deut. 4, 2; 12, 32.

Ver. 5. *Is fire tried:* that is, most pure, like gold purified by fire.

Ver. 15. *The horseleech.* Consupiscence, which hath two daughters that are never satisfied, lust and avarice.

Ver. 28. *The stellio.* A kind of house lizard marked with spots like stars, from whence it has its name.

CHAP. 31. Ver. 1. *Lamuel.* This name signifies *God with him,* and is supposed to have been one of the names of Solomon.

6 Give strong drink to them that are sad: and wine to them that are grieved in mind:

7 Let them drink, and forget their want, and remember their sorrow no more.

8 Open thy mouth for the dumb, and for the causes of all the children that pass.

9 Open thy mouth, decree that which is just: and do justice to the needy and poor.

10 Who shall find a valiant woman? Far and from the uttermost coasts is the price of her.

11 The heart of her husband trusteth in her: and he shall have no need of spoils.

12 She will render him good, and not evil, all the days of her life.

13 She hath sought wool and flax, and hath wrought by the counsel of her hands.

14 She is like the merchant's ship: she bringeth her bread from afar.

15 And she hath risen in the night, and given a prey to her household, and victuals to her maidens.

16 She hath considered a field, and bought it: with the fruit of her hands she hath planted a vineyard.

17 She hath girded her loins with strength, and hath strengthened her arm.

18 She hath tasted and seen that her traffic is good: her lamp shall not be put out in the night.

19 She hath put out her hand to strong things: and her fingers have taken hold of the spindle.

20 She hath opened her hand to the needy, and stretched out her hands to the poor.

21 She shall not fear for her house in the cold of snow: for all her domestics are clothed with double garments.

22 She hath made for herself clothing of tapestry: fine linen, and purple is her covering.

23 Her husband is honourable in the gates, when he sitteth among the senators of the land.

24 She made fine linen, and sold it, and delivered a girdle to the Chanaanite.

25 Strength and beauty are her clothing: and she shall laugh in the latter day.

26 She hath opened her mouth to wisdom: and the law of clemency is on her tongue.

27 She hath looked well to the paths of her house, and hath not eaten her bread idle.

28 Her children rose up, and called her blessed: her husband, and he praised her.

29 Many daughters have gathered together riches: thou hast surpassed them all.

30 Favour is deceitful, and beauty is vain: the woman that feareth the Lord, she shall be praised.

31 Give her of the fruit of her hands: and let her works praise her in the gates.

ECCLESIASTES

This Book is called Ecclesiastes, or the Preacher, (in Hebrew, Coheleth,) because in it Solomon, as an excellent preacher, settled forth the vanity of the things of this world, in order to withdraw the hearts and affections of men from such empty toys.

CHAPTER 1

The vanity of all temporal things.

THE words of Ecclesiastes, the son of David, king of Jerusalem.

2 Vanity of vanities, said Ecclesiastes: vanity of vanities, and all is vanity.

3 What hath a man more of all his labour that he taketh under the sun?

4 *One* generation passeth away, and

Ver. 24. *The Chanaanite. Chanaanite,* in Hebrew, signifies *a merchant.*

---

another generation cometh: but the earth standeth for ever.

5 The sun riseth, and goeth down, and returneth to his place: and there rising again,

6 Maketh his round by the south, and turneth again to the north: the spirit goeth forward, surveying all places round about, and returneth to his circuits.

7 All the rivers run into the sea, yet the sea doth not overflow: unto the place from whence the rivers come they return, to flow again.

8 All things are hard: man cannot explain them by word. The eye is not filled with seeing, neither is the ear filled with hearing.

9 What is it that hath been? The same thing that shall be. What is it that hath been done? The same that shall be done.

10 Nothing under the sun is new, neither is any man able to say: Behold this is new. For it hath already gone before in the ages that were before us.

11 There is no remembrance of former things: nor indeed of those things which hereafter are to come, shall there be any remembrance with them that shall be in the latter end.

12 I, Ecclesiastes, was king over Israel in Jerusalem,

13 And I proposed in my mind to seek and search out wisely concerning all things that are done under the sun. This painful occupation hath God given to the children of men, to be exercised therein.

14 I have seen all things that are done under the sun: and behold all is vanity and vexation of spirit.

15 The perverse are hard to be corrected: and the number of fools is infinite.

16 I have spoken in my heart, saying: Behold I am become great, and have gone beyond all in wisdom that were before me in Jerusalem. And my mind hath contemplated many things wisely: and I have learned.

17 And I have given my heart to know prudence, and learning, and errors, and folly: and I have perceived that in these also there was labour and vexation of spirit,

18 Because in much wisdom there is much indignation: and he that addeth knowledge addeth also labour.

CHAPTER 2

The vanity of pleasures, riches, and worldly labours.

I SAID in my heart: I will go and abound with delights, and enjoy good things. And I saw that this also was vanity.

2 Laughter I counted error; and to mirth I said: Why art thou vainly deceived?

3 I thought in my heart to withdraw my flesh from wine, that I might turn my mind to wisdom and might avoid folly: till I might see what was profitable for the children of men, and what they ought to do under the sun, all the days of their life.

4 I made me great works: I built me houses, and planted vineyards.

5 I made gardens and orchards, and set them with trees of all kinds,

6 And I made me ponds of water, to water therewith the wood of the young trees.

7 I got me men-servants and maid-servants, and had a great family: and herds of oxen, and great flocks of sheep, above all that were before me in Jerusalem.

8 [1] I heaped together for myself silver and gold, and the wealth of kings and provinces: I made me singing men and singing women, and the delights of the sons of men, cups and vessels to serve to pour out wine.

9 And I surpassed in riches all that were before me in Jerusalem: my wisdom also remained with me.

10 And whatsoever my eyes desired, I refused them not: and I withheld not my heart from enjoying every pleasure, and delighting itself in the things which I had prepared. And I esteemed this my portion, to make use of my own labour.

11 And when I turned myself to all the works which my hands had wrought and to the labours wherein I had laboured in vain, I saw in all things vanity and vexation of mind, and that nothing was lasting under the sun.

12 I passed further to behold wisdom, and errors and folly: (What is man, said I, that he can follow the King his maker?)

13 And I saw that wisdom excelled folly, as much as light differeth from darkness.

14 [2] The eyes of a wise man are in his head: the fool walketh in darkness. And I learned that they were to die both alike.

15 And I said in my heart: If the death of the fool and mine shall be one, what doth it avail me that I have applied myself more to the study of wisdom? And speaking with my own mind, I perceived that this also was vanity.

16 For there shall be no remembrance of the wise no more than of the fool, for ever: and the times to come shall cover all things together with oblivion. The learned dieth in like manner as the unlearned.

17 And therefore I was weary of my life, when I saw that all things under the sun are evil, and all vanity and vexation of spirit.

18 Again I hated all my application wherewith I had earnestly laboured under the sun, being like to have an heir after me,

19 Whom I know not whether he

will be a wise man or a fool: and he shall have rule over all my labours with which I have laboured and been solicitous. And is there any thing so vain?

20 Wherefore I left off, and my heart renounced labouring any more under the sun.

21 For when a man laboureth in wisdom and knowledge and carefulness, he leaveth what he hath gotten to an idle man: so this also is vanity and a great evil.

22 For what profit shall a man have of all his labour and vexation of spirit, with which he hath been tormented under the sun?

23 All his days are full of sorrows and miseries: even in the night he doth not rest in mind. And is not this vanity?

24 Is it not better to eat and drink, and to shew his soul good things of his labours? And this is from the hand of God.

25 Who shall so feast and abound with delights as I?

26 God hath given to a man that is good in his sight, wisdom and knowledge and joy: but to the sinner he hath given vexation and superfluous care, to heap up and to gather together, and to give it to him that hath pleased God. But this also is vanity and a fruitless solicitude of the mind.

CHAPTER 3

All human things are liable to perpetual changes. We are to rest on God's providence and cast away fruitless cares.

ALL things have their season: and in their times all things pass under heaven.

2 A time to be born, and a time to die. A time to plant, and a time to pluck up that which is planted.

3 A time to kill, and a time to heal. A time to destroy, and a time to build.

4 A time to weep, and a time to laugh. A time to mourn, and a time to dance.

5 A time to scatter stones, and a time to gather. A time to embrace, and a time to be far from embrace.

6 A time to get, and a time to lose. A time to keep, and a time to cast away.

7 A time to rend, and a time to sew. A time to keep silence, and a time to speak.

8 A time to love, and a time of hatred. A time of war, and a time of peace.

9 What hath man more of his labour?

CHAP. 3. Ver. 19. *Man hath nothing more than beast.* That is, as to the life of the body.
Ver. 21. *Who knoweth if the spirit of the children of Adam ascend upward?* That is, no one knows experimentally: since no one in this life can see a spirit. But as to the spirit of the beasts, which is merely *animal*, and becomes extinct by the death of the beast, who can tell the manner it acts so as to give life and motion, and by death to descend downward, that is, to be no more?

10 I have seen the trouble which God hath given the sons of men to be exercised in it.

11 He hath made all things good in their time, and hath delivered the world to their consideration; so that man cannot find out the work which God hath made from the beginning to the end.

12 And I have known that there was no better thing than to rejoice and to do well in this life.

13 For every man that eateth and drinketh, and seeth good of his labour, this is the gift of God.

14 I have learned that all the works which God hath made continue for ever: we cannot add any thing, nor take away from those things which God hath made that he may be feared.

15 That which hath been made, the same continueth: the things that shall be have already been: and God restoreth that which is past.

16 I saw under the sun in the place of judgment, wickedness: and in the place of justice, iniquity.

17 And I said in my heart: God shall judge both the just and the wicked: and then shall be the time of every thing.

18 I said in my heart concerning the sons of men, that God would prove them and shew them to be like beasts.

19 Therefore the death of man and of beasts is one: and the condition of them both is equal. As man dieth, so they also die. All things breathe alike, and man hath nothing more than beast. All things are subject to vanity.

20 And all things go to one place: of earth they were made, and into earth they return together.

21 Who knoweth if the spirit of the children of Adam ascend upward, and if the spirit of the beasts descend downward?

22 And I have found that nothing is better than for a man to rejoice in his work: and that this is his portion. For who shall bring him to know the things that shall be after him?

CHAPTER 4

Other instances of human miseries.

I TURNED myself to other things: and I saw the oppressions that are done under the sun, and the tears of the innocent. And they had no comforter; and they were not able to resist their violence, being destitute of help from any.

2 And I praised the dead rather than the living.

3 And I judged him happier than them both that is not yet born, nor

hath seen the evils that are done under the sun.

4 Again I considered all the labours of men; and I remarked that their industries are exposed to the envy of their neighbour. So in this also there is vanity and fruitless care.

5 The fool foldeth his hands together, and eateth his own flesh, saying:

6 Better is a handful with rest, than both hands full with labour, and vexation of mind.

7 Considering, I found also another vanity under the sun:

8 There is but one, and he hath not a second, no child, no brother, and yet he ceaseth not to labour. Neither are his eyes satisfied with riches, neither doth he reflect, saying: For whom do I labour, and defraud my soul of good things? In this also is vanity and a grievous vexation.

9 It is better therefore that two should be together than one: for they have the advantage of their society.

10 If one fall he shall be supported by the other. Woe to him that is alone: for, when he falleth, he hath none to lift him up.

11 And if two lie together, they shall warm one another: How shall one alone be warmed?

12 And if a man prevail against one two shall withstand him: a threefold cord is not easily broken.

13 Better is a child that is poor and wise than a king that is old and foolish, who knoweth not to forsee for hereafter.

14 Because out of prison and chains sometimes a man cometh forth to a kingdom: and another born king is consumed with poverty.

15 I saw all men living, that walk under the sun with the second young man, who shall rise up in his place.

16 The number of the people, of all that were before him, is infinite: and they that shall come afterwards shall not rejoice in him. But this also is vanity and vexation of spirit.

17 Keep thy foot when thou goest into the house of God, and draw nigh to hear. [1] For much better is obedience than the victims of fools, who know not what evil they do.

CHAPTER 5

Caution in words. Vows are to be paid. Riches are often pernicious but the moderate use of them is the gift of God.

SPEAK not any thing rashly, and let not thy heart be hasty to utter a word before God. For God is in heaven, and thou upon earth: therefore let thy words be few.

2 Dreams follow many cares: and in many words shall be found folly.

3 If thou hast vowed any thing to God, defer not to pay it. For an unfaithful and foolish promise displeaseth him: but whatsoever thou hast vowed, pay it.

4 And it is much better not to vow than after a vow not to perform the things promised.

5 Give not thy mouth to cause thy flesh to sin; and say not before the angel: There is no providence. Lest God be angry at thy words and destroy all the works of thy hands.

6 Where there are many dreams, there are many vanities, and words without number: but do thou fear God.

7 If thou shalt see the oppressions of the poor, and violent judgments, and justice perverted, in the province, wonder not at this matter: for he that is high hath another higher, and there are others still higher than these.

8 Moreover, there is the king that reigneth over all the land subject to him.

9 A covetous man shall not be satisfied with money: and he that loveth riches shall reap no fruit from them. So this also is vanity.

10 Where there are great riches, there are also many to eat them. And what doth it profit the owner, but that he seeth the riches with his eyes?

11 Sleep is sweet to a labouring man, whether he eat little or much: but the fulness of the rich will not suffer him to sleep.

12 [1] There is also another grievous evil which I have seen under the sun: riches kept to the hurt of the owner.

13 For they are lost with very great affliction: he hath begotten a son who shall be in extremity of want.

14 [2] As he came forth naked from his mother's womb, so shall he return: and shall take nothing way with him of his labour.

15 A most deplorable evil: As he came, so shall he return. What then doth it profit him that he hath laboured for the wind?

16 All the days of his life, he eateth in darkness, and in many cares, and in misery and sorrow.

17 This therefore hath seemed good to me, that a man should eat and drink, and enjoy the fruit of his labour, wherewith he hath laboured under the sun, all the days of his life, which God hath given him: and this is his portion.

18 And every man to whom God hath given riches and substance, and hath

given him power to eat thereof, and to enjoy his portion, and to rejoice of his labour: this is the gift of God.

19 For he shall not much remember the days of his life, because God entertained his heart with delight.

CHAPTER 6
The misery of the covetous man.

THERE is also another evil which I have seen under the sun, and that frequent among men:

2 A man to whom God hath given riches and substance and honour, and his soul wanteth nothing of all that he desireth: yet God doth not give him power to eat thereof, but a stranger shall eat it up. This is vanity and a great misery.

3 If a man beget a hundred children, and live many years, and attain to a great age, and his soul make no use of the goods of his substance, and he be without burial: of this man I pronounce, that the untimely born is better than he.

4 For he came in vain, and goeth to darkness, and his name shall be wholly forgotten.

5 He hath not seen the sun, nor known the distance of good and evil.

6 Although he lived two thousand years, and hath not enjoyed good things: do not all make haste to one place?

7 All the labour of man is for his mouth: but his soul shall not be filled.

8 What hath the wise man more than the fool? And what the poor man, but to go thither where there is life?

9 Better it is to see what thou mayst desire than to desire that which thou canst not know. But this also is vanity and presumption of spirit.

10 ¹ He that shall be, his name is already called: and it is known that he is man and cannot contend in judgment with him that is stronger than himself.

11 There are many words that have much vanity in disputing.

CHAPTER 7
Prescriptions against worldly vanities. Mortification, patience, and seeking wisdom.

WHAT needeth a man to seek things that are above him, whereas he knoweth not what is profitable for him in his life, in all the

days of his pilgrimage, and the time that passeth like a shadow? Or who can tell him what shall be after him under the sun?

2 ¹ A good name is better than precious ointments: and the day of death than the day of one's birth.

3 It is better to go to the house of mourning, than to the house of feasting: for in that we are put in mind of the end of all, and the living thinketh what is to come.

4 Anger is better than laughter: because by the sadness of the countenance the mind of the offender is corrected.

5 The heart of the wise is where there is mourning: and the heart of fools where there is mirth.

6 It is better to be rebuked by a wise man than to be deceived by the flattery of fools.

7 For as the crackling of thorns burning under a pot, so is the laughter of a fool. Now this also is vanity.

8 Oppression troubleth the wise and shall destroy the strength of his heart.

9 Better is the end of a speech than the beginning. Better is the patient man than the presumptuous.

10 Be not quickly angry: for anger resteth in the bosom of a fool.

11 Say not: What thinkest thou is the cause that former times were better than they are now? For this manner of question is foolish.

12 Wisdom with riches is more profitable and bringeth more advantage to them that see the sun.

13 For as wisdom is a defence, so money is a defence: but learning and wisdom excel in this, that they give life to him that possesseth them.

14 Consider the works of God, that no man can correct whom he hath despised.

15 In the good day enjoy good things, and beware beforehand of the evil day. For God hath made both the one and the other, that man may not find against him any just complaint.

16 These things also I saw in the days of my vanity: A just man perisheth in his justice, and a wicked man liveth a long time in his wickedness.

17 Be not over just. And be not more wise than is necessary, lest thou become stupid.

18 Be not overmuch wicked. And be not foolish, lest thou die before thy time.

19 It is good that thou shouldst hold up the just, yea and from him withdraw not thy hand: for he that feareth God, neglecteth nothing.

20 Wisdom hath strengthened the wise more than ten princes of the city.

CHAP. 6. ¹ 1 Kings, 13, 14; and 3 Kings, 13, 2.
CHAP. 7. ¹ Prov. 22, 1.

CHAP. 7. Ver. 4. *Anger.* That is, correction, or just wrath and zeal against evil.
Ver. 17. *Over just.* That is, by an excessive rigour in censuring the ways of God in bearing with the wicked.
Ver. 18. *Be not overmuch wicked.* That is, lest by the greatness of your sin you leave no room for mercy.

21 [2]For there is no just man upon earth, that doth good, and sinneth not.

22 But do not apply thy heart to all words that are spoken: lest perhaps thou hear thy servant reviling thee.

23 For thy conscience knoweth that thou also hast often spoken evil of others.

24 I have tried all things in wisdom. I have said: I will be wise. And it departed farther from me,

25 Much more than it was. *It is a* great depth. Who shall find it out?

26 I have surveyed all things with my mind, to know, and consider, and seek out wisdom and reason: and to know the wickedness of the fool and the error of the imprudent:

27 And I have found a woman more bitter than death, who is the hunter's snare: and her heart is a net, and her hands are bands. He that pleaseth God shall escape from her: but he that is a sinner shall be caught by her.

28 Lo, this have I found, said Ecclesiastes, weighing one thing after another, that I might find out the account,

29 Which yet my soul seeketh: and I have not found it. One man among a thousand I have found: a woman among them all I have not found.

30 Only this I have found, that God made man right, and he hath entangled himself with an infinity of questions. Who is as the wise man? And who hath known the resolution of the word?

CHAPTER 8

True wisdom is to observe God's command-
ments. The ways of God are unsearch-
able.

THE [1] wisdom of a man shineth in his countenance: and the most mighty will change his face.

2 I observe the mouth of the king, and the commandments of the oath of God.

3 Be not hasty to depart from his face, and do not continue in an evil work. For he will do all that pleaseth him:

4 And his word is full of power. Neither can any man say to him: Why dost thou so?

5 He that keepeth the commandment shall find no evil. The heart of a wise man understandeth time and answer.

6 There is a time and opportunity for every business: and great affliction for man.

7 Because he is ignorant of things past, and things to come he cannot know by any messenger.

8 It is not in man's power to stop the spirit; neither hath he power in the day of death; neither is he suffered to rest when war is at hand; neither shall wickedness save the wicked.

9 All these things I have considered, and applied my heart to all the works that are done under the sun. Sometimes one man ruleth over another to his own hurt.

10 I saw the wicked buried: who also when they were yet living were in the holy place, and were praised in the city as men of just works. But this also is vanity.

11 For, because sentence is not speedily pronounced against the evil, the children of men commit evils without any fear.

12 But though a sinner do evil a hundred times, and by patience be borne withal, I know from thence that it shall be well with them that fear God, who dread his face.

13 But let it not be well with the wicked, neither let his days be prolonged: but as a shadow let them pass away that fear not the face of the Lord.

14 There is also another vanity, which is done upon the earth. There are just men to whom evils happen, as though they had done the works of the wicked: and there are wicked men who are as secure as though they had the deeds of the just. But this also I judge most vain.

15 Therefore I commended mirth, because there was no good for a man under the sun but to eat and drink and be merry; and that he should take nothing else with him of his labour in the days of his life, which God hath given him under the sun.

16 And I applied my heart to know wisdom, and to understand the distraction that is upon earth: for there are some that day and night take no sleep with their eyes.

17 And I understood that man can find no reason of all those works of God that are done under the sun: and the more he shall labour to seek, so much the less shall he find: yea, though the wise man shall say that he knoweth *it,* he shall not be able to find *it.*

CHAPTER 9

Man knows not certainly that he is in God's
grace. After death no more work or merit.

[2] 3 Kings, 8, 46; 2 Par. 6, 36; Prov. 20, 9; 1 John, 1, 8. CHAP. 8. [1] Eccles. 2, 14.

Ver. 30. *Of the word.* That is, of this obscure and difficult matter.

CHAP. 8. Ver. 15. *No good for a man.* Some commentators think the wise man here speaks in the person of the libertine: representing the objections of these men against Divine Providence, and the inferences they draw from thence, which he takes care afterwards to refute. But it may also be said, that his meaning is to commend the moderate use of the goods of this world, preferably to the cares and solicitudes of worldlings, their attachment to vanity and curiosity, and their presumptuously diving into the unsearchable ways of Divine Providence.

LL these things have I considered in my heart, that I might carefully understand them. There are just men and wise men, and their works are in the hand of God: and yet man knoweth not whether he be worthy of love, or hatred.

2 But all things are kept uncertain for the time to come; because all things equally happen to the just and to the wicked, to the good and to the evil, to the clean and to the unclean, to him that offereth victims, and to him that despiseth sacrifices. As the good is, so also is the sinner: as the perjured, so he also that sweareth truth.

3 This is a very great evil among all things that are done under the sun, that the same things happen to all men: whereby also the hearts of the children of men are filled with evil and with contempt while they live, and afterwards they shall be brought down to hell.

4 There is no man that liveth always, or that hopeth for this: a living dog is better than a dead lion.

5 For the living know that they shall die, but the dead know nothing more. Neither have they a reward any more: for the memory of them is forgotten.

6 Their love also, and their hatred, and their envy, are all perished: neither have they any part in this world and in the work that is done under the sun.

7 Go then, and eat thy bread with joy, and drink thy wine with gladness: because thy works please God.

8 At all times let thy garments be white: and let not oil depart from thy head.

9 Live joyfully with the wife whom thou lovest, all the days of thy unsteady life, which are given to thee under the sun, all the time of thy vanity: for this is thy portion in life, and in thy labour wherewith thou labourest under the sun.

10 Whatsoever thy hand is able to do, do it earnestly: for neither work, nor reason, nor wisdom, nor knowledge, shall be in hell, whither thou art hastening.

11 I turned me to another thing; and I saw that under the sun, the race is not to the swift, nor the battle to the strong, nor bread to the wise, nor riches to the learned, nor favour to the skilful: but time and chance in all.

CHAP. 9. [1] Eccles. 7, 20. CHAP. 10. [1] Prov. 26, 27; Ecclus. 26, 29.

CHAP. 9. Ver. 5. *Know nothing more.* That is, as to the transactions of this world, in which they have now no part, unless it be revealed to them; neither have they any knowledge or power now of doing any thing to secure their eternal state (if they have not taken care of it in their lifetime) : nor can they now procure themselves any good, as the living always may do, by the grace of God.

12 Man knoweth not his own end: but as fishes are taken with the hook, and as birds are caught with the snare, so men are taken in the evil time, when it shall suddenly come upon them.

13 This wisdom also I have seen under the sun: and it seemed to me to be very great.

14 A little city, and few men in it. There came against it a great king, and invested it, and built bulwarks round about it: and the siege was perfect.

15 Now there was found in it a man poor and wise, and he delivered the city by his wisdom: and no man afterward remembered that poor man.

16 And I said that wisdom is better than strength: How then is the wisdom of the poor man slighted, and his words not heard?

17 The words of the wise are heard in silence, more than the cry of a prince among fools.

18 [1] Better is wisdom, than weapons of war: and he that shall offend in one shall lose many good things.

CHAPTER 10

Observations on wisdom and folly, ambition and detraction.

YING flies spoil the sweetness of the ointment. Wisdom and glory is more precious than a small and short-lived folly.

2 The heart of a wise man is in his right hand, and the heart of a fool is in his left hand.

3 Yea, and the fool when he walketh in the way, whereas he himself is a fool, esteemeth all men fools.

4 If the spirit of him that hath power ascend upon thee, leave not thy place: because care will make the greatest sins to cease.

5 There is an evil that I have seen under the sun, as it were by an error, proceeding from the face of the prince:

6 A fool set in high dignity, and the rich sitting beneath.

7 I have seen servants upon horses: and princes walking on the ground as servants.

8 [1] He that diggeth a pit shall fall into it: and he that breaketh a hedge, a serpent shall bite him.

9 He that removeth stones shall be hurt by them: and he that cutteth trees shall be wounded by them.

10 If the iron be blunt, and be not as before, but be made blunt, with much labour it shall be sharpened: and after industry shall follow wisdom.

11 If a serpent bite in silence, he is nothing better that backbiteth secretly.

12 The words of the mouth of a wise

man are grace: but the lips of a fool shall throw him down headlong.

13 The beginning of his words is folly: and the end of his talk is a mischievous error.

14 A fool multiplieth words. A man cannot tell what hath been before him. And what shall be after him, who can tell him?

15 The labour of fools shall afflict them that know not how to go to the city.

16 Woe to thee, O land, when thy king is a child, and when the princes eat in the morning.

17 Blessed is the land, whose king is noble, and whose princes eat in due season, for refreshment, and not for riotousness.

18 By slothfulness a building shall be brought down, and through the weakness of hands the house shall drop through.

19 For laughter they make bread and wine, that the living may feast: and all things obey money.

20 Detract not the king, no, not in thy thought; and speak not evil of the rich man in thy private chamber: because even the birds of the air will carry thy voice, and he that hath wings will tell what thou hast said.

CHAPTER 11

Exhortation to works of mercy, while we have time, to diligence in good, and to the remembrance of death and judgment.

CAST thy bread upon the running waters: for after a long time thou thou shalt find it again.

2 Give a portion to seven, and also to eight: for thou knowest not what evil shall be upon the earth.

3 If the clouds be full, they will pour out rain upon the earth. If the tree fall to the south, or to the north, in what place soever it shall fall, there shall it be.

4 He that observeth the wind shall not sow: and he that considereth the clouds shall never reap.

5 As thou knowest not what is the way of the spirit, nor how the bones are joined together in the womb of her that is with child: so thou knowest not the works of God, who is the maker of all.

6 In the morning sow thy seed, and in the evening let not thy hand cease: for thou knowest not which may rather spring up, this or that: and if both together; it shall be the better.

7 The light is sweet: and it is delightful for the eyes to see the sun.

8 If a man live many years, and have rejoiced in them all, he must remember the darksome time, and the many days: which, when they shall come, the things past shall be accused of vanity.

9 Rejoice therefore, O young man, in thy youth, and let thy heart be in that which is good in the days of thy youth, and walk in the ways of thy heart, and in the sight of thy eyes: and know that for all these God will bring thee into judgment.

10 Remove anger from thy heart, and put away evil from thy flesh. For youth and pleasure are vain.

CHAPTER 12

The Creator is to be remembered in the days of our youth. All worldly things are vain. We should fear God and keep his commandments.

REMEMBER thy Creator in the days of thy youth, before the time of affliction come, and the years draw nigh of which thou shalt say: They please me not.

2 Before the sun and the light, and the moon and the stars be darkened, and the clouds return after the rain:

3 When the keepers of the house shall tremble, and the strong men shall stagger, and the grinders shall be idle in a small number, and they that look through the holes shall be darkened,

4 And they shall shut the doors in the street: when the grinder's voice shall be low, and they shall rise up at the voice of the bird, and all the daughters of music shall grow deaf.

5 And they shall fear high things, and they shall be afraid in the way. The almond tree shall flourish, the locust shall be made fat, and the caper tree shall be destroyed: because man shall go into the house of his eternity, and the mourners shall go round about in the street.

6 Before the silver cord be broken, and the golden fillet shrink back, and the pitcher be crushed at the fountain, and the wheel be broken upon the cistern,

7 And the dust return into its earth, from whence it was, and the spirit return to God, who gave it.

CHAP. 11. Ver. 3. *If the tree fall.* The state of the soul is unchangeable when once she comes to heaven or hell: and a soul that departs this life in the state of grace shall never fall from grace: as on the other side, a soul that dies out of the state of grace shall never come to it. But this does not exclude a place of temporal punishments for such souls as die in the state of grace, yet not so as to be entirely pure: and therefore they *shall be saved*, indeed, *yet so as by fire* (1 Cor. 3, 13, 14, 15).

CHAP. 12. Ver. 2. *Before the sun.* That is, before old age: the effects of which upon all the senses and faculties are described in the following verses, under a variety of figures.

8 Vanity of vanities said Ecclesiastes, and all things *are* vanity.

9 And whereas Ecclesiastes was very wise, he taught the people, and declared the things that he had done: and seeking out, he set forth many parables.

10 He sought profitable words: and wrote words most right, and full of truth.

11 The words of the wise are as goads, and as nails deeply fastened in, which by the counsel of masters are given from one shepherd.

12 More than these, my son, require not. Of making many books there is no end: and much study is an affliction of the flesh.

13 Let us all hear together the conclusion of the discourse. Fear God, and keep his commandments: for this is all man:

14 And all things that are done, God will bring into judgment for every error, whether it be good or evil.

SOLOMON'S
CANTICLE OF CANTICLES

This Book is called the Canticle of Canticles, *that is to say, the most excellent of all canticles: because it is full of high mysteries, relating to the happy union of Christ and his Spouse: which is here begun by love, and is to be eternal in heaven. The Spouse of Christ is the Church: more especially as to the happiest part of it, namely, perfect souls, every one of which is his beloved, but, above all others, his Immaculate and ever blessed Virgin Mother.*

CHAPTER 1

The spouse aspires to an union with Christ. Their mutual love for one another.

LET him kiss me with the kiss of his mouth: for thy breasts are better than wine,

2 Smelling sweet of the best ointments. Thy name *is as* oil poured out: therefore young maidens have loved thee.

3 Draw me: we will run after thee to the odour of thy ointments. The king hath brought me into his storerooms: we will be glad and rejoice in

Ver. 13. *All man.* The whole business and duty of man.
Ver. 14. *Error.* Or, hidden and secret thing.
CHAP. 1. Ver. 1. *Let him kiss me.* The church, the spouse of Christ, prays that he may love and have peace with her, which the spouse prefers to every thing howsoever delicious: and therefore expresses (ver. 2) that *young maidens,* that is the souls of the faithful, *have loved thee.*
Ver. 3. *Draw me.* That is, with thy grace: otherwise I should not be able to come to thee. This metaphor shews that we cannot of ourselves come to Christ our Lord, unless he draws us by his grace, which is laid up in his *storerooms:* that is, in the mysteries of Faith, which God in his goodness and love for mankind hath revealed, first by his servant Moses in the Old Law in figure only, and afterwards in reality by his only begotten Son Jesus Christ.
Ver. 4. *I am black but beautiful.* That is, the church of Christ founded in humility appearing outwardly afflicted, and as it were black and contemptible; but inwardly, that is, in its doctrine and morality, fair and beautiful.
Ver. 7. *If thou know not thyself.* Christ encourages his spouse to follow and watch her flock: and though she know not entirely the power at hand to assist her, he tells her, ver. 8, *my company of horsemen,* that is, his angels, are always watching and protecting her. And in the following verses he reminds her of the virtues and gifts with which he has endowed her.

thee, remembering thy breasts more than wine. The righteous love thee.

4 I am black but beautiful, O ye daughters of Jerusalem, as the tents of Cedar, as the curtains of Solomon.

5 Do not consider me that I am brown, because the sun hath altered my colour: the sons of my mother have fought against me. They have made me the keeper in the vineyards: my vineyard I have not kept.

6 Shew me, O thou whom my soul loveth, where thou feedest, where thou liest in the midday, lest I begin to wander after the flocks of thy companions.

7 If thou know not thyself, O fairest among women, go forth, and follow after the steps of the flocks, and feed thy kids beside the tents of the shepherds.

8 To my company of horsemen, in Pharao's chariots, have I likened thee, O my love.

9 Thy cheeks are beautiful as the turtle-dove's, thy neck as jewels.

10 We will make thee chains of gold, inlaid with silver.

11 While the king was at his repose, my spikenard sent forth the odour thereof.

12 A bundle of myrrh *is* my beloved to me: he shall abide between my breasts.

13 A cluster of cypress my love is to me: in the vineyards of Engaddi.

14 Behold thou art fair, O my love,

behold thou art fair: thy eyes are as those of doves.

15 Behold thou art fair, my beloved, and comely. Our bed is flourishing.

16 The beams of our houses are of cedar, our rafters of cypress trees.

CHAPTER 2

Christ caresses his spouse. He invites her to him.

I AM the flower of the field, and the lily of the valleys.

2 As the lily among thorns, so is my love among the daughters.

3 As the apple tree among the trees of the woods, so is my beloved among the sons. I sat down under his shadow, whom I desired: and his fruit was sweet to my palate.

4 He brought me into the cellar of wine: he set in order charity in me.

5 Stay me up with flowers, compass me about with apples: because I languish with love.

6 His left hand is under my head, and his right hand shall embrace me.

7 I adjure you, O ye daughters of Jerusalem, by the roes and the harts of the fields, that you stir not up, nor make the beloved to awake, till she please.

8 The voice of my beloved. Behold he cometh leaping upon the mountains, skipping over the hills.

9 My beloved is like a roe or a young hart. Behold he standeth behind our wall, looking through the windows, looking through the lattices.

10 Behold, my beloved speaketh to me: Arise, make haste, my love, my dove, my beautiful one, and come.

11 For winter is now past, the rain is over and gone.

12 The flowers have appeared in our land: the time of pruning is come: the voice of the turtle is heard in our land:

13 The fig tree hath put forth her green figs: the vines in flower yield their sweet smell. Arise, my love, my beautiful one, and come.

14 My dove in the clefts of the rock, in the hollow places of the wall, shew me thy face. Let thy voice sound in my ears: for thy voice is sweet and thy face comely.

15 Catch us the little foxes that destroy the vines: for our vineyard hath flourished.

16 My beloved to me, and I to him who feedeth among the lilies,

17 Till the day break, and the shadows retire. Return: be like, my beloved, to a roe, or to a young hart upon the mountains of Bether.

CHAPTER 3

The spouse seeks Christ. The glory of his humanity.

IN my bed by night I sought him whom my soul loveth: I sought him, and found him not.

2 I will rise and will go about the city. In the streets and the broad ways I will seek him whom my soul loveth. I sought him, and I found him not.

3 The watchmen who keep the city found me: Have you seen him whom my soul loveth?

4 When I had a little passed by them, I found him whom my soul loveth. I held him: and I will not let him go, till I bring him into my mother's house, and into the chamber of her that bore me.

5 I adjure you, O daughters of Jerusalem, by the roes and the harts of the fields, that you stir not up nor awake my beloved, till she please.

6 Who is she that goeth up by the desert, as a pillar of smoke of aromatical spices, of myrrh and frankincense, and of all the powders of the perfumer?

7 Behold threescore valiant ones of the most valiant of Israel surrounded the bed of Solomon!

8 All holding swords, and most expert in war: every man's sword upon his thigh, because of fears in the night.

9 King Solomon hath made him a litter of the wood of Libanus.

10 The pillars thereof he made of silver, the seat of gold, the going up of purple: the midst he covered with charity for the daughters of Jerusalem.

11 Go forth, ye daughters of Sion, and see king Solomon in the diadem wherewith his mother crowned him in the day of his espousals, and in the day of the joy of his heart.

CHAP. 2. Ver. 1. *I am the flower of the field.* Christ professes himself the flower of mankind, yea, the Lord of all creatures: and, ver. 2, declares the excellence of his spouse, the true church above all other societies, which are to be considered as thorns.

Ver. 8. *The voice of my beloved.* That is, the preaching of the gospel surmounting difficulties figuratively here expressed by *mountains* and *little hills.*

Ver. 15. *Catch us the little foxes.* Christ commands his pastors to catch false teachers, by holding forth their fallacy and erroneous doctrine, which like foxes would bite and destroy the vines.

CHAP. 3. Ver. 1. *In my bed by night.* The Gentiles as in the dark, and seeking in heathen delusion what they could not find, the true God, until Christ revealed his doctrine to them by his *watchmen* (ver. 3), that is, by the apostles, and teachers, by whom they were converted to the true faith. And holding that faith firmly, the spouse (the Catholic Church) declares, ver. 4, That she *will not let him go, till* she *bring him into* her *mother's house,* that it, till at last, the JEWS also shall find him.

CHAPTER 4

Christ sets forth the graces of his spouse.
He declares his love for her.

HOW beautiful art thou, my love, how beautiful art thou! Thy eyes are doves' eyes, besides what is hid within. Thy hair is as flocks of goats which come up from mount Galaad.

2 Thy teeth as flocks of *sheep*, that are shorn, which come up from the washing, all with twins: and there is none barren among them.

3 Thy lips are as a scarlet lace: and thy speech sweet. Thy cheeks are as a piece of pomegranate, besides that which lieth hid within.

4 Thy neck is as the tower of David, which is built with bulwarks: a thousand bucklers hang upon it, all the armour of valiant men.

5 Thy two breasts like two young roes that are twins, which feed among the lilies.

6 Till the day break and the shadows retire, I will go to the mountain of myrrh and to the hill of frankincense.

7 Thou art all fair, O my love, and there is not a spot in thee.

8 Come from Libanus, my spouse, come from Libanus, come: thou shalt be crowned from the top of Amana, from the top of Sanir and Hermon, from the dens of the lions, from the mountains of the leopards.

9 Thou hast wounded my heart, my sister, *my* spouse: thou hast wounded my heart with one of thy eyes, and with one hair of thy neck.

10 How beautiful are thy breasts, my sister, *my* spouse! thy breasts are more beautiful than wine, and the sweet smell

CHAP. 4. Ver. 1. *How beautiful art thou.* Christ again praises the beauties of his church, which through the whole of this chapter are exemplified by a variety of metaphors, setting forth her purity, her simplicity, and her stability.

Ver. 5. *Thy two breasts.* Mystically to be understood: the love of God and the love of our neighbour, which are so united as *twins which feed among the lilies:* that is, the love of God and our neighbour, feeds on the divine mysteries and the holy sacraments, left by Christ to his spouse to feed and nourish her children.

Ver. 12. *A garden enclosed.* Figuratively the church is enclosed, containing only the faithful. *A fountain sealed up.* That none can drink of its waters, that is, the graces and spiritual benefits of the holy sacraments, but those who are within its walls.

CHAP. 5. Ver. 1. *Let my beloved come into his garden. Garden,* mystically the church of Christ, abounding with *fruit,* that is, the good works of the elect.

Ver. 4. *My beloved put his hand through the key hole.* The spouse of Christ, his church, at times as it were penned up by its persecutors, and in fears, expecting the divine assistance, here signified by *his hand:* and ver. 6, *but he had turned aside and was gone,* that is, Christ permitting a further trial of suffering: and again, ver. 7, *the keepers,* signifying the violent and cruel persecutors of the church taking her *veil,* despoiling the church of its places of worship and ornaments for the divine service.

of thy ointments above all aromatical spices.

11 Thy lips, my spouse, are a dropping honeycomb, honey and milk are under thy tongue; and the smell of thy garments, as the smell of frankincense.

12 My sister, *my* spouse, is a garden enclosed, a garden enclosed, a fountain sealed up.

13 Thy plants are a paradise of pomegranates with the fruits of the orchard. Cypress with spikenard,

14 Spikenard and saffron, sweet cane and cinnamon, with all the trees of Libanus, myrrh and aloes, with all the chief perfumes.

15 The fountain of gardens: the well of living waters, which run with a strong stream from Libanus.

16 Arise, O north wind, and come, O south wind: blow through my garden, and let the aromatical spices thereof flow.

CHAPTER 5

Christ calls his spouse. She languished with love, and describes him by his graces.

LET my beloved come into his garden, and eat the fruit of his apple trees. I am come into my garden, O my sister, *my* spouse. I have gathered my myrrh, with my aromatical spices. I have eaten the honeycomb with my honey. I have drunk my wine with my milk. Eat, O friends, and drink, and be inebriated, my dearly beloved.

2 I sleep, and my heart watcheth. The voice of my beloved knocking. Open to me, my sister, my love, my dove, my undefiled: for my head is full of dew, and my locks of the drops of the nights.

3 I have put off my garment, how shall I put it on? I have washed my feet, how shall I defile them?

4 My beloved put his hand through the *key* hole, and my bowels were moved at his touch.

5 I arose up to open to my beloved: my hands dropped with myrrh, and my fingers were full of the choicest myrrh.

6 I opened the bolt of my door to my beloved: but he had turned aside, and was gone. My soul melted when he spoke. I sought him and found him not: I called, and he did not answer me.

7 The keepers that go about the city found me. They struck me and wounded me. The keepers of the walls took away my veil from me.

8 I adjure you, O daughters of Jerusalem, if you find my beloved, that you tell him that I languish with love.

9 What manner of one is thy beloved of the beloved, O thou most beautiful among women? What manner of one

is thy beloved of the beloved, that thou hast so adjured us?

10 My beloved is white and ruddy, chosen out of thousands.

11 His head *is as* the finest gold: his locks *as* the branches of palm trees, black as a raven.

12 His eyes as doves upon brooks of waters, which are washed with milk, and sit beside the plentiful streams.

13 His cheeks are as beds of aromatical spices set by the perfumers. His lips are as lilies dropping choice myrrh.

14 His hands *are* turned *and as* of gold, full of hyacinths. His belly *as* of ivory, set with sapphires.

15 His legs as pillars of marble, that are set upon bases of gold. His form as of Libanus, excellent as the cedars.

16 His throat most sweet, and he is all lovely. Such is my beloved, and he is my friend, O ye daughters of Jerusalem.

17 Whither is thy beloved gone, O thou most beautiful among women? Whither is thy beloved turned aside, and we will seek him with thee?

CHAPTER 6
The spouse of Christ is but one. She is fair and terrible.

MY beloved is gone down into his garden, to the bed of aromatical spices, to feed in the gardens and to gather lilies.

2 I to my beloved, and my beloved to me, who feedeth among the lilies.

3 Thou art beautiful, O my love, sweet and comely as Jerusalem: terrible as an army set in array.

4 Turn away thy eyes from me, for they have made me flee away. Thy hair as as a flock of goats that appear from Galaad.

5 Thy teeth as a flock of sheep, which come up from the washing, all with twins: and there is none barren among them.

6 Thy cheeks *are* as the bark of a pomegranate, beside what is hidden within thee.

7 There are threescore queens, and fourscore concubines, and young maidens without number.

8 One is my dove: my perfect one is *but* one. She is the only one of her mother, the chosen of her that bore her. The daughters saw her and declared her most blessed: the queens and concubines, and they praised her.

9 Who is she that cometh forth as the morning rising, fair as the moon, bright as the sun, terrible as an army set in array?

10 I went down into the garden of nuts to see the fruits of the valleys, and to look if the vineyards had flourished and the pomegranates budded.

11 I knew not: my soul troubled me for the chariots of Aminadab.

12 Return, return, O Sulamitess: return, return, that we may behold thee.

CHAPTER 7
A further description of the graces of the church the spouse of Christ.

WHAT shalt thou see in the Sulamitess but the companies of camps? How beautiful are thy steps in shoes, O prince's daughter! The joints of thy thighs are like jewels, that are made by the hand of a skilful workman.

2 Thy navel is like a round bowl never wanting cups. Thy belly is like a heap of wheat, set about with lilies.

3 Thy two breasts *are* like two young roes that are twins.

4 Thy neck as a tower of ivory. Thy eyes like the fishpools in Hesebon, which are in the gate of the daughter of the multitude. Thy nose *is* as the tower of Libanus that looketh toward Damascus.

5 Thy head is like Carmel: and the hairs of thy head as the purple of the king bound in the channels.

6 How beautiful art thou, and how comely, my dearest, in delights!

7 Thy stature is like to a palm tree and thy breasts to clusters of grapes.

8 I said: I will go up into the palm tree, and will take hold of the fruit thereof: and thy breasts shall be as the clusters of the vine, and the odour of thy mouth like apples.

9 Thy throat like the best wine, worthy for my beloved to drink, and for his lips and his teeth to ruminate.

10 I to my beloved, and his turning is toward me.

Ver. 10. *My beloved.* In this and the following verses, the church mystically describes Christ to those who know him not, that is, to infidels in order to convert them to the true faith.

CHAP. 6. Ver. 1. *My beloved is gone down into his garden.* Christ, pleased with the good works of his holy and devout servants labouring in his garden, is always present with them: but the words *is gone down,* are to be understood, that after trying his Church by permitting persecution, he comes to her assistance and she rejoices at his coming.

Ver. 8. *One is my dove.* That is, my church is *one,* and she only is *perfect* and *blessed.*

Ver. 9. *Who is she.* Here is a beautiful metaphor describing the church from the beginning. As, *the morning rising,* signifying the church before the written law; *fair as the moon,* shewing her under the written law of Moses: *bright as the sun,* under the light of the gospel: and *terrible as an army,* the power of Christ's church against its enemies.

CHAP. 7. Ver. 1. *How beautiful are thy steps.* By these metaphors are signified the power and mission of the church in propagating the true faith.

Ver. 5. *Thy head is like Carmel.* Christ, the invisible head of his church, is here signified.

11 Come, my beloved, let us go forth into the field, let us abide in the villages.

12 Let us get up early to the vineyards, let us see if the vineyard flourish, if the flowers be ready to bring forth fruits, if the pomegranates flourish: there will I give thee my breasts.

13 The mandrakes give a smell. In our gates are all fruits: the new and the old, my beloved, I have kept for thee.

CHAPTER 8

The love of the church to Christ: his love to her.

WHO shall give thee to me for my brother, sucking the breasts of my mother, that I may find thee without, and kiss thee, and now no man may despise me?

2 I will take hold of thee, and bring thee into my mother's house: there thou shalt teach me, and I will give thee a cup of spiced wine and new wine of my pomegranates.

3 His left hand under my head, and his right hand shall embrace me.

4 I adjure you, O daughters of Jeru-

CHAP. 8. Ver. 3. *His left hand.* Words of the church to Christ—*His left hand,* signifying the Old Testament and his *right hand,* the New.

Ver. 5. *Who is this.* The angels with admiration behold the Gentiles converted to the faith: *coming up from the desert,* that is, coming from heathenism and false worship: *flowing with delights,* that is, abounding with good works which are pleasing to God: *leaning on her beloved,* on the promise of Christ to his church, *that the gates of hell should not prevail against it;* and supported by his grace conferred by the sacraments.—*Under the apple tree I raised thee up,* that is: Christ redeemed the Gentiles at the foot of the cross, where the synagogue of the Jews (the mother church) *was corrupted* by their denying him, and crucifying him.

Ver. 8. *Our sister is little.* Mystically signifies the Jews, who are to *be spoken to:* that is, converted towards the end of the world, and then shall become *a wall,* that is, a part of the building, the church of Christ.

salem, that you stir not up, nor awake my love till she please.

5 Who is this that cometh up from the desert, flowing with delights, leaning upon her beloved? Under the apple tree I raised thee up: there thy mother was corrupted: there she was defloured that bore thee.

6 Put me as a seal upon thy heart, as a seal upon thy arm: for love is strong as death, jealousy as hard as hell. The lamps thereof *are* fire and flames.

7 Many waters cannot quench charity, neither can the floods drown it: if a man should give all the substance of his house for love, he shall despise it as nothing.

8 Our sister is little, and hath no breasts. What shall we do to our sister in the day when she is to be spoken to?

9 If she be a wall, let us build upon it bulwarks of silver: if she be a door, let us join it together with boards of cedar.

10 I am a wall: and my breasts are as a tower, since I am become in his presence as one finding peace.

11 The peaceable had a vineyard, in that which hath people: he let out the same to keepers: every man bringeth for the fruit thereof a thousand pieces of silver.

12 My vineyard is before me. A thousand are for thee, the peaceable, and two hundred for them that keep the fruit thereof.

13 Thou that dwellest in the gardens, the friends hearken: make me hear thy voice.

14 Flee away, O my beloved, and be like to the roe, and to the young hart upon the mountains of aromatical spices.

THE BOOK OF
WISDOM

This Book is so called, because it treats of the excellence of WISDOM, *the means to obtain it, and the happy fruits it produces. It is written in the person of Solomon and contains his sentiments. But it is uncertain who was the writer. It abounds with instructions and exhortations to kings and all magistrates to minister justice in the commonwealth, teaching all kinds of virtues under the general names of justice and wisdom. It contains also many prophecies of Christ's coming, passion, resurrection, and other Christian mysteries. The whole may be divided into three parts. In the first six chapters, the author admonishes all superiors to love and exercise justice and wisdom. In the next three, he teacheth that wisdom proceedeth only from God, and is procured by prayer and a good life. In the other ten chapters, he sheweth the excellent effects and utility of wisdom and justice.*

CHAPTER 1

An exhortation to seek God sincerely, who cannot be deceived, and desireth not our death.

LOVE [1] justice, you that are the judges of the earth. Think of the Lord in goodness, and seek him in simplicity of heart.

2 [2] For he is found by them that tempt him not: and he sheweth himself to them that have faith in him.

3 For perverse thoughts separate from God: and his power, when it is tired, reproveth the unwise.

4 For wisdom will not enter into a malicious soul, nor dwell in a body subject to sins.

5 For the Holy Spirit of discipline will flee from the deceitful, and will withdraw himself from thoughts that are without understanding: and he shall not abide when iniquity cometh in.

6 [3] For the spirit of wisdom is benevolent, and will not acquit the evil speaker from his lips: [4] for God is witness of his reins, and he is a true searcher of his heart, and a hearer of his tongue.

7 [5] For the spirit of the Lord hath filled the whole world: and that which containeth all things hath knowledge of the voice.

8 Therefore he that speaketh unjust things cannot be hid: neither shall the chastising judgment pass him by.

9 For inquisition shall be made into the thoughts of the ungodly: and the hearing of his words shall come to God, to the chastising of his iniquities.

10 For the ear of jealousy heareth all things, and the tumult of murmuring shall not be hid.

11 Keep yourselves therefore from murmuring which profiteth nothing,

and refrain your tongue from detraction: for an obscure speech shall not go for nought, and the mouth that belieth killeth the soul.

12 Seek not death in the error of your life: neither procure ye destruction by the works of your hands.

13 [6] For God made not death: neither hath he pleasure in the destruction of the living.

14 For he created all things that they might be, and he made the nations of the earth for health: and there is no poison of destruction in them, nor kingdom of hell upon the earth.

15 For justice is perpetual and immortal.

16 But the wicked with works and words have called it [7] to them: and esteeming it a friend have fallen away, and have made a covenant with it: because they are worthy to be of the part thereof.

CHAPTER 2

The vain reasonings of the wicked. Their persecuting the just, especially the Son of God.

FOR they have said, reasoning with themselves, *but* not right: [1] The time of our life is short and tedious, and in the end of a man there is no remedy, and no man hath been known to have returned from hell.

2 For we are born of nothing, and after this we shall be as if we had not been: for the breath in our nostrils is smoke, and speech a spark to move our heart.

3 Which being put out, our body shall be ashes, and our spirit shall be

CHAP. 1. [1] 3 Kings, 3, 9; Isai. 56, 1. [2] 2 Par. 15, 2. [3] Gal. 5, 22. [4] Jer. 17, 10. [5] Isai. 6, 3. [6] Ezech. 18, 32; 33, 11. [7] Isai. 28, 15. CHAP. 2. [1] Job. 7, 1; 14, 1.

poured abroad as soft air, and our life shall pass away as the trace of a cloud, and shall be dispersed as a mist which is driven away by the beams of the sun and overpowered with the heat thereof.

4 And our name in time shall be forgotten, and no man shall have any remembrance of our works.

5 ² For our time is as the passing of a shadow, and there is no going back of our end: for it is fast sealed, and no man returneth.

6 ³ Come therefore, and let us enjoy the good things that are present: and let us speedily use the creatures as in youth.

7 Let us fill ourselves with costly wine and ointments: and let not the flower of the time pass by us.

8 Let us crown ourselves with roses, before they be withered: let no meadow escape our riot.

9 Let none of us go without his part in luxury: let us everywhere leave tokens of joy: for this is our portion, and this our lot.

10 Let us oppress the poor just man, and not spare the widow, nor honour the ancient grey hairs of the aged.

11 But let our strength be the law of justice: for that which is feeble is found to be nothing worth.

12 Let us therefore lie in wait for the just, because he is not for our turn, and he is contrary to our doings, and upbraideth us with transgressions of the law, and divulgeth against us the sins of our way of life.

13 ⁴ He boasteth that he hath the knowledge of God, and calleth himself the son of God.

14 ⁵ He is become a censurer of our thoughts.

15 He is grievous unto us, even to behold: for his life is not like other men's and his ways are very different.

16 We are esteemed by him as triflers: and he abstaineth from our ways as from filthiness, and he preferreth the latter end of the just, and glorieth that he hath God for his father.

17 Let us see then if his words be true, and let us prove what shall happen to him: and we shall know what his end shall be.

18 ⁶ For if he be the true son of God, he will defend him and will deliver him from the hands of his enemies.

19 Let us examine him by outrages and tortures, that we may know his meekness and try his patience.

20 ⁷ Let us condemn him to a most shameful death: for there shall be respect had unto him by his words.

21 These things they thought, and were deceived: for their own malice blinded them.

22 And they knew not the secrets of God, nor hoped for the wages of justice, nor esteemed the honour of holy souls.

23 ⁸ For God created man incorruptible, and to the image of his own likeness he made him.

24 ⁹ But, by the envy of the devil, death came into the world:

25 And they follow him that are of his side.

CHAPTER 3

The happiness of the just, and the unhappiness of the wicked.

BUT ¹ the souls of the just are in the hand of God: and the torment of death shall not touch them.

2 ² In the sight of the unwise they seemed to die: and their departure was taken for misery.

3 And their going away from us, for utter destruction: but they are in peace.

4 And though in the sight of men they suffered torments, their hope is full of immortality.

5 Afflicted in few things, in many they shall be well rewarded: because God hath tried them, and found them worthy of himself.

6 As gold in the furnace he hath proved them, and as a victim of a holocaust he hath received them: and in time there shall be respect had to them.

7 ³ The just shall shine, and shall run to and fro like sparks among the reeds.

8 ⁴ They shall judge nations, and rule over people: and their Lord shall reign for ever.

9 They that trust in him shall understand the truth, and they that are faithful in love shall rest in him: for grace and peace is to his elect.

10 But the wicked shall be punished according to their own devices: who have neglected the just, and have revolted from the Lord.

11 For he that rejecteth wisdom, and discipline is unhappy: and their hope is vain, and their labours without fruit, and their works unprofitable.

12 Their wives are foolish, and their children wicked.

13 Their offspring is cursed: for happy is the barren and the undefiled that hath not known bed in sin. She shall have fruit in the visitation of holy souls.

14 ⁵ And the eunuch, that hath not

² 1 Par. 29, 15.   ³ Isai. 22, 13; 56, 12; 1 Cor. 15, 32.   ⁴ Matt. 27, 43.   ⁵ John, 7, 7.   ⁶ Ps. 21, 9.   ⁷ Jer. 11, 19.   ⁸ Gen. 1, 27; 2, 7; 5, 1; Ecclus. 17, 1.   ⁹ Gen. 3, 1.   CHAP. 3.   ¹ Deut. 33, 3.   ² Wisd. 5, 4.   ³ Matt. 13, 43.   ⁴ 1 Cor. 6, 2.

wrought iniquity with his hands, nor thought wicked things against God: for the precious gift of faith shall be given to him, and a most acceptable lot in the temple of God.

15 For the fruit of good labours is glorious, and the root of wisdom never faileth.

16 But the children of adulterers shall not come to perfection, and the seed of the unlawful bed shall be rooted out.

17 And if they live long, they shall be nothing regarded, and their last old age shall be without honour.

18 And if they die quickly, they shall have no hope, nor speech of comfort in the day of trial.

19 For dreadful are the ends of a wicked race.

CHAPTER 4

The difference between the chaste and the adulterous generations, and between the death of the just and the wicked.

O HOW beautiful is the chaste generation with glory, for the memory thereof is immortal: because it is known both with God and with men.

2 When it is present, they imitate it: and they desire it when it hath withdrawn itself. And it triumpheth crowned for ever, winning the reward of undefiled conflicts.

3 But the multiplied brood of the wicked shall not thrive, and bastard slips shall not take deep root, nor any fast foundation.

4 [1] And if they flourish in branches for a time, yet, standing not fast, they shall be shaken with the wind, and through the force of winds they shall be rooted out.

5 For the branches not being perfect, shall be broken: and their fruits shall be unprofitable, and sour to eat, and fit for nothing.

6 For the children that are born of unlawful beds are witnesses of wickedness against their parents in their trial.

7 But the just man, if he be prevented with death, shall be in rest.

8 For venerable old age is not that of long time, nor counted by the number of years: but the understanding of a man is grey hairs.

9 And a spotless life is old age.

10 [2] He pleased God and was beloved: and living among sinners he was translated.

11 He was taken away lest wickedness should alter his understanding, or deceit beguile his soul.

12 For the bewitching of vanity obscureth good things, and the wandering of concupiscence overturneth the innocent mind.

13 Being made perfect in a short space, he fulfilled a long time:

14 For his soul pleased God. Therefore he hastened to bring him out of the midst of iniquities. But the people see this, and understand not, nor lay up such things in their hearts:

15 That the grace of God, and his mercy is with his saints, and that he hath respect to his chosen.

16 But the just that is dead, condemneth the wicked that are living; and youth soon ended, the long life of the unjust.

17 For they shall see the end of the wise man, and shall not understand what God hath designed for him, and why the Lord hath set him in safety.

18 They shall see him and shall despise him: but the Lord shall laugh them to scorn.

19 And they shall fall after this without honour, and be a reproach among the dead for ever. For he shall burst them puffed up and speechless, and shall shake them from the foundations: and they shall be utterly laid waste. They shall be in sorrow and their memory shall perish.

20 They shall come with fear at the thought of their sins: and their iniquities shall stand against them to convict them.

CHAPTER 5

The fruitless repentance of the wicked in another world. The reward of the just.

THEN shall the just stand with great constancy against those that have afflicted them and taken away their labours.

2 These seeing it, shall be troubled with terrible fear, and shall be amazed at the suddenness of their unexpected salvation.

3 Saying within themselves, repenting, and groaning for anguish of spirit: These are they whom we had some time in derision and for a parable of reproach.

4 [1] We fools esteemed their life madness and their end without honour.

5 Behold how they are numbered among the children of God, and their lot is among the saints.

6 Therefore we have erred from the way of truth, and the light of justice hath not shined unto us, and the sun of understanding hath not risen upon us.

7 We wearied ourselves in the way of iniquity and destruction, and have

5 Isai. 56, 3. Chap. 4. 1 Jer. 17, 6; Matt. 7, 27. 2 Heb. 11, 5. Chap. 5. 1 Wisd. 3, 2.

walked through hard ways: but the way of the Lord we have not known.

8 What hath pride profited us? Or what advantage hath the boasting of riches brought us?

9 [2] All those things are passed away like a shadow, and like a post that runneth on,

10 [3] And as a ship that passeth through the waves: whereof when it is gone by, the trace cannot be found, nor the path of its keel in the waters.

11 Or as when a bird flieth through the air, of the passage of which no mark can be found, but only the sound of the wings beating the light air and parting it by the force of her flight; she moved her wings, and hath flown through, and there is no mark found afterwards of her way.

12 Or as when an arrow is shot at a mark, the divided air presently cometh together again, so that the passage thereof is not known.

13 So we also being born, forthwith ceased to be, and have been able to shew no mark of virtue: but are consumed in our wickedness.

14 Such things as these the sinners said in hell.

15 [4] For the hope of the wicked is as dust which is blown away with the wind: and as a thin froth which is dispersed by the storm, and a smoke that is scattered abroad by the wind: and as the remembrance of a guest of one day that passeth by.

16 But the just shall live for evermore: and their reward is with the Lord, and the care of them with the most High.

17 Therefore shall they receive a kingdom of glory and a crown of beauty, at the hand of the Lord: for with his right hand he will cover them, and with his holy arm he will defend them.

18 [5] And his zeal will take armour: and he will arm the creature for the revenge of his enemies.

19 He will put on justice as a breastplate, and will take true judgment instead of a helmet.

20 He will take equity for an invincible shield.

21 And he will sharpen his severe wrath for a spear: and the whole world shall fight with him against the unwise.

22 Then shafts of lightning shall go directly from the clouds. As from a bow well bent, they shall be shot out, and shall fly to the mark.

23 And thick hail shall be cast upon them from the stone casting wrath: the water of the sea shall rage against them, and the rivers shall run together in a terrible manner.

24 A mighty wind shall stand up against them, and as a whirlwind shall divide them: and their iniquity shall bring all the earth to a desert. And wickedness shall overthrow the thrones of the mighty.

CHAPTER 6

An address to princes to seek after wisdom. She is easily found by those that seek her.

WISDOM [1] is better than strength: and a wise man is better than a strong man.

2 Hear therefore, ye kings, and understand: learn, ye that are judges of the ends of the earth.

3 Give ear, you that rule the people, and that please yourselves in multitudes of nations:

4 [2] For power is given you by the Lord, and strength by the most High. Who will examine your works, and search out your thoughts:

5 Because being ministers of his kingdom, you have not judged rightly, nor kept the law of justice, nor walked according to the will of God.

6 Horribly and speedily will he appear to you: for a most severe judgment shall be for them that bear rule.

7 For to him that is little, mercy is granted: but the mighty shall be mightily tormented.

8 [3] For God will not except any man's person, neither will he stand in awe of any man's greatness: for he made the little and the great, and he hath equally care of all.

9 But a greater punishment is ready for the more mighty.

10 To you, therefore, O kings, are these my words: that you may learn wisdom, and not fall from it.

11 For they that have kept just things justly shall be justified: and they that have learned these things shall find what to answer.

12 Covet ye therefore my words, and love them: and you shall have instruction.

13 Wisdom is glorious, and never fadeth away, and is easily seen by them that love her, and is found by them that seek her.

14 She preventeth them that covet her, so that she first sheweth herself unto them.

15 He that awaketh early to seek her shall not labour: for he shall find her sitting at his door.

16 To think therefore upon her is

perfect understanding: and he that watcheth for her shall quickly be secure.

17 For she goeth about seeking such as are worthy of her: and she sheweth herself to them cheerfully in the ways and meeteth them with all providence.

18 For the beginning of her is the most true desire of discipline.

19 And the care of discipline is love: and love is the keeping of her laws: and the keeping of her laws is the firm foundation of incorruption:

20 And incorruption bringeth near to God.

21 Therefore the desire of wisdom bringeth to the everlasting kingdom.

22 If then your delight be in thrones and sceptres, O ye kings of the people, love wisdom, that you may reign for ever.

23 Love the light of wisdom, all ye that bear rule over peoples.

24 Now what wisdom is, and what her origin, I will declare. And I will not hide from you mysteries of God, but will seek her out from the beginning of her birth, and bring the knowledge of her to light, and will not pass over the truth.

25 Neither will I go with consuming envy: for such a man shall not be partaker of wisdom.

26 Now the multitude of the wise is the welfare of the whole world: and a wise king is the upholding of the people.

27 Receive therefore instruction by my words: and it shall be profitable to you.

CHAPTER 7

The excellence of wisdom. How she is to be found.

I MYSELF also am a mortal man, like all *others*, and of the race of him, that was first made of the earth: and in the womb of thy mother I was fashioned to be flesh.

2 In the time of ten months I was compacted in blood, of the seed of man, [1] and the pleasure of sleep concurring.

3 And being born I drew in the common air, and fell upon the earth, that is made alike: and the first voice which I uttered was crying, as all *others* do.

4 I was nursed in swaddling clothes, and with great cares.

5 For none of the kings had any other beginning of birth.

6 [2] For all men have one entrance into life, and the like going out.

7 Wherefore I wished, and understanding was given me: and I called upon God, and the spirit of wisdom came upon me.

8 And I preferred her before king-doms and thrones, and esteemed riches nothing in comparison of her.

9 [3] Neither did I compare unto her any precious stone: for all gold in comparison of her is as a little sand, and silver in respect to her shall be counted as clay.

10 I loved her above health and beauty, and chose to have her instead of light: for her light cannot be put out.

11 [4] Now all good things came to me together with her, and innumerable riches through her hands,

12 And I rejoiced in all these: for this wisdom went before me, and I knew not that she was the mother of them all.

13 Which I have learned without guile, and communicate without envy, and her riches I hide not.

14 For she is an infinite treasure to men: which they that use, become the friends of God, being commended for the gift of discipline.

15 And God hath given to me to speak as I would, and to conceive thoughts worthy of those things that are given me: because he is the guide of wisdom, and the director of the wise.

16 For in his hand are both we, and our words, and all wisdom, and the knowledge and skill of works.

17 For he hath given me the true knowledge of the things that are: to know the disposition of the whole world, and the virtues of the elements;

18 The beginning, and ending, and midst of the times, the alterations of their courses, and the changes of seasons;

19 The revolutions of the year, and the dispositions of the stars;

20 The natures of living creatures, and rage of wild beasts, the force of winds, and reasonings of men, the diversities of plants, and the virtues of roots.

21 And all such things as are hid and not foreseen, I have learned: for wisdom, which is the worker of all things, taught me.

22 For in her is the spirit of understanding: holy, one, manifold, subtile, eloquent, active, undefiled, sure, sweet, loving that which is good, quick, which nothing hindereth, beneficent,

23 Gentle, kind, steadfast, assured, secure, having all power, overseeing all things, and containing all spirits, intelligible, pure, subtile.

24 For wisdom is more active than all active things: and reacheth everywhere by reason of her purity.

25 For she is a vapour of the power

CHAP. 7. [1] Job. 10, 10. [2] Job. 1, 21; 1 Tim. 6, 7. [3] Job. 28, 15; Prov. 8, 11. [4] 3 Kings, 3, 13; Matt. 6, 33.

of God and a certain pure emanation of the glory of the almighty God: and therefore no defiled thing cometh into her.

26 ⁵ For she is the brightness of eternal light, and the unspotted mirror of God's majesty, and the image of his goodness.

27 And being but one, she can do all things: and remaining in herself the same, she reneweth all things and through nations conveyeth herself into holy souls. She maketh the friends of God and prophets.

28 For God loveth none but him that dwelleth with wisdom.

29 For she is more beautiful than the sun, and above all the order of the stars: being compared with the light, she is found before it.

30 For after this cometh night: but no evil can overcome wisdom.

CHAPTER 8

Further praises of wisdom. Her fruits.

SHE reacheth therefore from end to end mightily and ordereth all things sweetly.

2 Her have I loved, and have sought her out from my youth, and have desired to take her for my spouse: and I became a lover of her beauty.

3 She glorifieth her nobility by being conversant with God: yea, and the Lord of all things hath loved her.

4 For it is she that teacheth the knowledge of God and is the chooser of his works.

5 And if riches be desired in life, what is richer than wisdom, which maketh all things?

6 And if sense do work, who is a more artful worker than she of those things that are?

7 And if a man love justice, her labours have great virtues. For she teacheth temperance and prudence and justice and fortitude, which are such things as men can have nothing more profitable in life.

8 And if a man desire much knowledge, she knoweth things past, and judgeth of things to come: she knoweth the subtilties of speeches and the solutions of arguments: she knoweth signs and wonders before they be done, and the events of times and ages.

9 I purposed therefore to take her to me to live with me: knowing that she will communicate to me of her good things and will be a comfort in my cares and grief.

10 For her sake I shall have glory among the multitude, and honour with the ancients, though I be young:

11 And I shall be found of a quick conceit in judgment and shall be admired in the sight of the mighty; and the faces of princes shall wonder at me.

12 They shall wait for me when I hold my peace and they shall look upon me when I speak; and if I talk much they shall lay their hands on their mouths.

13 Moreover, by the means of her I shall have immortality: and shall leave behind me an everlasting memory to them that come after me.

14 I shall set the people in order: and nations shall be subject to me.

15 Terrible kings hearing shall be afraid of me: among the multitude I shall be found good, and valiant in war.

16 When I go into my house, I shall repose myself with her: for her conversation hath no bitterness, nor her company any tediousness, but joy and gladness.

17 Thinking these things with myself and pondering them in my heart: that to be allied to wisdom is immortality,

18 And that there is great delight in her friendship, and inexhaustible riches in the works of her hands and in the exercise of conference with her, wisdom and glory in the communication of her words; I went about seeking, that I might take her to myself.

19 And I was a witty child and had received a good soul.

20 And whereas I was more good, I came to a body undefiled.

21 And as I knew that I could not otherwise be continent, except God gave it, and this also was a point of wisdom, to know whose gift it was: I went to the Lord, and besought him, and said with my whole heart:

CHAPTER 9

Solomon's prayer for wisdom.

GOD ¹ of my fathers, and Lord of mercy, who hast made all things with thy word,

2 And by thy wisdom hast appointed man, that he should have dominion over the creature that was made by thee,

3 That he should order the world according to equity and justice, and execute justice with an upright heart:

4 Give me wisdom that sitteth by thy throne, and cast me not off from among thy children:

5 ² For I am thy servant and the son of thy handmaid, a weak man, and of short time, and falling short of the understanding of judgment and laws.

6 For if one be perfect among the children of men, yet if thy wisdom be

⁵ Heb. 1, 3. Chap. 9. ¹ 1 Kings, 3, 9. ² Ps. 115, 16.

not with him, he shall be nothing regarded.

7 ³ Thou hast chosen me to be king of thy people and a judge of thy sons and daughters.

8 And hast commanded me to build a temple on thy holy mount, and an altar in the city of thy dwelling place, a resemblance of thy holy tabernacle, which thou hast prepared from the beginning.

9 ⁴ And thy wisdom with thee, which knoweth thy works, which then also was present when thou madest the world, and knew what was agreeable to thy eyes, and what was right in thy commandments:

10 Send her out of thy holy heaven, and from the throne of thy majesty, that she may be with me, and may labour with me, that I may know what is acceptable with thee.

11 For she knoweth and understandeth all things, and shall lead me soberly in my works, and shall preserve me by her power.

12 So shall my works be acceptable, and I shall govern thy people justly, and shall be worthy of the throne of my father.

13 ⁵ For who among men is he that can know the counsel of God? Or who can think what the will of God is?

14 For the thoughts of mortal men are fearful, and our counsels uncertain.

15 For the corruptible body is a load upon the soul: and the earthly habitation presseth down the mind that museth upon many things.

16 And hardly do we guess aright at things that are upon earth: and with labour do we find the things that are before us. But the things that are in heaven, who shall search out?

17 And who shall know thy thought, except thou give wisdom, and send thy Holy Spirit from above.

18 And so the ways of them that are upon earth may be corrected, and men may learn the things that please thee?

19 For by wisdom they were healed, whosoever hath pleased thee, O Lord, from the beginning.

CHAPTER 10

What wisdom did for Adam, Noe, Abraham, Lot, Jacob, Joseph, and the people of Israel.

SHE ¹ preserved him, that was first formed by God, the father of the world, when he was created alone,

2 ² And she brought him out of his sin and gave him power to govern all things.

3 ³ But when the unjust went away from her in his anger, he perished by

the fury wherewith he murdered his brother.

4 ⁴ For whose cause, when water destroyed the earth, wisdom healed it again, directing the course of the just by contemptible wood.

5 ⁵ Moreover when the nations had conspired together to consent to wickedness, she knew the just, and preserved him without blame to God, and kept him strong against the compassion for his son.

6 ⁶ She delivered the just man who fled from the wicked that were perishing, when the fire came down upon Pentapolis:

7 Whose land for a testimony of their wickedness is desolate and smoketh to this day; and the trees bear fruits that ripen not; and a standing pillar of salt is a monument of an incredulous soul.

8 For regarding not wisdom, they did not only slip in this that they were ignorant of good things, but they left also unto men a memorial of their folly, so that in the things in which they sinned they could not so much as lie hid.

9 But wisdom hath delivered from sorrow them that attend upon her.

10 ⁷ She conducted the just, when he fled from his brother's wrath, through the right ways, and shewed him the kingdom of God, and gave him the knowledge of the holy things, made him honourable in his labours, and accomplished his labours.

11 In the deceit of them that overreached him, she stood by him and made him honourable.

12 She kept him safe from his enemies, and she defended him from seducers, and gave him a strong conflict, that he might overcome and know that wisdom is mightier than all.

13 ⁸ She forsook not the just when he was sold, but delivered him from sinners. She went down with him into the pit.

14 ⁹ And in bands she left him not, till she brought him the sceptre of the kingdom, and power against those that oppressed him: and shewed them to be

³ 1 Par. 28, 4, 5; 2 Par. 1, 9. ⁴ Prov. 8, 22, 27; John, 1, 1. ⁵ Isai. 40, 13; Rom. 11, 34; 1 Cor. 2, 16. CHAP. 10. ¹ Gen. 1, 27. ² Gen. 2, 7. ³ Gen. 4, 8. ⁴ Gen. 7, 6. ⁵ Gen. 12, 2. ⁶ Gen. 19, 17, 22. ⁷ Gen. 28, 5, 10. ⁸ Gen. 37, 28. ⁹ Gen. 41, 40; Acts, 7, 9.

CHAP. 10. Ver. 3. *The unjust.* Cain.
Ver. 4. *For whose cause.* That is, for the wickedness of the race of Cain.—*The just.* Noe.
Ver. 5. *She knew the just.* She found out and approved Abraham.—*And kept him strong.* Gave him strength to stand firm against the efforts of his natural tenderness, when he was ordered to sacrifice his son.
Ver. 6. *The just man.* Lot.—*Pentapolis.* The land of the five cities, Sodom, Gomorrha, &c.
Ver. 10. *The just.* Jacob.
Ver. 12. *Conflict.* That is, with the angel.
Ver. 13. *The just when he was sold.* Joseph.

liars that had accused him, and gave him everlasting glory.

15 [10] She delivered the just people and blameless seed, from the nations that oppressed them.

16 She entered into the soul of the servant of God and stood against dreadful kings in wonders and signs.

17 And she rendered to the just the wages of their labours and conducted them in a wonderful way: and she was to them for a covert by day and for the light of stars by night:

18 [11] And she brought them through the Red Sea and carried them over through a great water.

19 But their enemies she drowned in the sea, and from the depth of hell she brought them out. [12] Therefore the just took the spoils of the wicked.

20 [13] And they sung to thy holy name, O Lord: and they praised with one accord thy victorious hand.

21 For wisdom opened the mouth of the dumb and made the tongues of infants eloquent.

CHAPTER 11

Other benefits of wisdom to the people of God.

SHE [1] prospered their works in the hands of the holy prophet.

2 They went through wildernesses that were not inhabited: and in desert places they pitched their tents.

3 [2] They stood against their enemies and revenged themselves of their adversaries.

4 [3] They were thirsty, and they called upon thee: and water was given them out of the high rock, and a refreshment of their thirst out of the hard stone.

5 For by what things their enemies were punished, when their drink failed them, while the children of Israel abounded therewith and rejoiced:

6 By the same things they in their need were benefited.

7 For instead of a fountain of an ever

---

[10] Exod. 1, 11. [11] Exod. 14, 22; Ps. 77, 13. [12] Exod. 12, 35. [13] Exod. 15, 1. CHAP. 11. [1] Exod. 16, 1. [2] Exod. 17, 13. [3] Num. 20, 11. [4] Wisd. 12, 24. [5] Lev. 26, 22; Wisd. 16, 1; Jer. 8, 17.

Ver. 16. *The servant of God.* Moses.
CHAP. 11. Ver. 1. *The holy prophet.* Moses.
Ver. 3. *Their enemies.* The Amalecites.
Ver. 5. *By what things.* The meaning is, that God, who wrought a miracle to punish the Egyptians by thirst, when he turned all their waters into blood (at which time the Israelites, who were exempt from those plagues, had plenty of water), wrought another miracle in favour of his own people in their thirst, by giving them water out of the rock.
Ver. 14. *By their punishments.* That is, that the Israelites had been benefited and miraculously favoured in the same kind in which they had been punished.
Ver. 16. *Dumb beasts,* namely, frogs, sciniphs, flies, and locusts.

---

running river, thou gavest human blood to the unjust.

8 And whilst they were diminished for a manifest reproof of their murdering the infants, thou gavest to thine abundant water, unlooked for:

9 Shewing by the thirst that was then how thou didst exalt thine and didst kill their adversaries.

10 For when they were tried, and chastised with mercy they knew how the wicked were judged with wrath and tormented.

11 For thou didst admonish and try them as a father: but the others, as a severe king, thou didst examine and condemn.

12 For whether absent or present, they were tormented alike.

13 For a double affliction came upon them, and a groaning for the remembrance of things past.

14 For, when they heard that by their punishments the others were benefited, they remembered the Lord, wondering at the end of what was come to pass.

15 For whom they scorned before, when he was thrown out at the time of his being wickedly exposed to perish, him they admired in the end, when they saw the event: their thirsting being unlike to that of the just.

16 But for the foolish devices of their iniquity, [4] because some being deceived worshipped dumb serpents and worthless beasts, thou didst send upon them a multitude of dumb beasts for vengeance:

17 That they might know that by what things a man sinneth, by the same also he is tormented.

18 For thy almighty hand, which made the world of matter without form, was not unable to send upon them a multitude of bears, or fierce lions,

19 Or unknown beasts of a new kind, full of rage: either breathing out a fiery vapour, [5] or sending forth a stinking smoke, or shooting horrible sparks out of their eyes:

20 Whereof not only the hurt might be able to destroy them, but also the very sight might kill them through fear.

21 Yea, and without these, they might have been slain with one blast, persecuted by their own deeds, and scattered by the breath of thy power: but thou hast ordered all things in measure, and number, and weight.

22 For great power always belonged to thee alone: and who shall resist the strength of thy arm?

23 For the whole world before thee is as the least grain of the balance, and

as a drop of the morning dew that falleth down upon the earth.

24 But thou hast mercy upon all, because thou canst do all things, and overlookest the sins of men for the sake of repentance.

25 For thou lovest all things that are, and hatest none of the things which thou hast made: for thou didst not appoint or make any thing, hating it.

26 And how could any thing endure, if thou wouldst not, or be preserved, if not called by thee?

27 But thou sparest all: because they are thine, O Lord, who lovest souls.

CHAPTER 12

God's wisdom and mercy in his proceedings with the Chanaanites.

O HOW good and sweet is thy spirit, O Lord, in all things!

2 And therefore thou chastisest them that err, by little and little: and admonishest them, and speakest to them concerning the things wherein they offend: that leaving their wickedness, they may believe in thee, O Lord.

3 [1] For those ancient inhabitants of thy holy land, whom thou didst abhor,

4 Because they did works hateful to thee by their sorceries and wicked sacrifices;

5 And *those* merciless murderers of their own children, and eaters of men's bowels, and devourers of blood from the midst of thy consecration;

6 And *those* parents sacrificing with their own hands helpless souls: it was thy will to destroy by the hands of our parents,

7 That the land which of all is most dear to thee might receive a worthy colony of the children of God.

8 Yet even those thou sparedst as men, and didst send wasps, forerunners of thy host, to destroy them by little and little.

9 Not that thou wast unable to bring the wicked under the just by war, or by cruel beasts, or with one rough word to destroy them at once:

10 [2] But executing thy judgments by degrees thou gavest them place of repentance, not being ignorant that they were a wicked generation, and their malice natural, and that their thought could never be changed.

11 For it was a cursed seed from the beginning: neither didst thou for fear of any one give pardon to their sins.

12 For who shall say to thee: What hast thou done? Or who shall withstand thy judgment? Or who shall come before thee *to be* a revenger of wicked men? Or who shall accuse thee, if the nations perish, which thou hast made?

13 For there is no other God but thou, [3] who hast care of all, that thou shouldst shew that thou dost not give judgment unjustly.

14 Neither shall king nor tyrant in thy sight inquire about them whom thou hast destroyed.

15 For so much then as thou art just, thou orderest all things justly: thinking it not agreeable to thy power to condemn him who deserveth not to be punished.

16 For thy power is the beginning of justice: and because thou art Lord of all, thou makest thyself gracious to all.

17 For thou shewest thy power, when men will not believe thee to be absolute in power; and thou convincest the boldness of them that know thee not.

18 But thou being master of power, judgest with tranquillity; and with great favour disposest of us: for thy power is at hand when thou wilt.

19 But thou hast taught thy people by such works that they must be just and humane, and hast made thy children to be of a good hope: because in judging thou givest place for repentance for sins.

20 For if thou didst punish the enemies of thy servants, and that deserved to die, with so great deliberation, giving them time and place whereby they might be changed from their wickedness:

21 With what circumspection hast thou judged thy own children, to whose parents thou hast sworn and made covenants of good promises?

22 Therefore, whereas thou chastisest us, thou scourgest our enemies very many ways, to the end that when we judge we may think on thy goodness: and when we are judged, we may hope for thy mercy.

23 Wherefore, thou hast also greatly tormented them who in their life have lived foolishly and unjustly, by the same things which they worshipped.

24 [4] For they went astray for a long time in the ways of error, holding those things for gods which are the most worthless among beasts, living after the manner of children without understanding.

25 Therefore thou hast sent a judgment upon them, as senseless children, to mock them.

26 But they that were not amended

CHAP. 12. [1] Deut. 9, 3; 12, 29; 18, 12. [2] Exod. 23, 30; Deut. 7, 22. [3] 1 Peter, 5, 7. [4] Wisd. 11, 16; Rom. 1, 23.

CHAP. 12. Ver. 5. *From the midst of thy consecration.* Literally *sacrament.* That is, the land sacred to thee, in which thy temple was to be established, and man's redemption to be wrought.

by mockeries and reprehensions experienced the worthy judgment of God.

27 For seeing with indignation that they suffered by those very things which they took for gods, when they were destroyed by the same, they acknowledged him the true God, whom in time past they denied that they knew: for which cause the end also of their condemnation came upon them.

CHAPTER 13

Idolaters are inexcusable. Those most of all that worship for gods the works of the hands of men.

BUT ¹ all men are vain, in whom there is not the knowledge of God: and who by these good things that are seen could not understand him that is. Neither by attending to the works have acknowledged who was the workman:

2 ² But have imagined, either the fire, or the wind, or the swift air, or the circle of the stars, or the great water, or the sun and moon, to be the gods that rule the world.

3 With whose beauty, if they being delighted, took them to be gods: let them know how much the Lord of them is more beautiful than they. For the first author of beauty made all those things.

4 Or if they admired their power and their effects, let them understand by them that he that made them, is mightier than they:

5 For by the greatness of the beauty, and of the creature, the creator of them may be seen, so as to be known thereby.

6 But yet as to these they are less to be blamed. For they perhaps err, seeking God, and desirous to find him.

7 ³ For being conversant among his works, they search: and they are persuaded that the things are good which are seen.

8 But then again they are not to be pardoned.

9 For if they were able to know so much as to make a judgment of the world, how did they not more easily find out the Lord thereof?

10 But unhappy are they, and their hope is among the dead, who have called gods the works of the hands of men, gold and silver, the invention of art, and the resemblances of beasts, or an unprofitable stone, the work of an ancient hand.

11 ⁴ Or if an artist, a carpenter, hath cut down a tree proper for his use in the wood, and skilfully taken off all the

bark thereof, and with his art diligently formeth a vessel profitable for the common uses of life,

12 And useth the chips of his work to dress his meat:

13 And taking what was left thereof, which is good for nothing, being a crooked piece of wood and full of knots, carveth it diligently when he hath nothing else to do, and by the skill of his art fashioneth it and maketh it like the image of a man,

14 Or the resemblance of some beast, laying it over with vermilion, and painting it red, and covering every spot that is in it:

15 And maketh a convenient dwelling place for it, and setting it in a wall and fastening it with iron,

16 Providing for it, lest it should fall, knowing that it is unable to help itself: for it is an image, and hath need of help.

17 And then maketh prayer to it, inquiring concerning his substance and his children, or his marriage. And he is not ashamed to speak to that which hath no life.

18 And for health he maketh supplication to the weak, and for life prayeth to that which is dead, and for help calleth upon that which is unprofitable:

19 And for a good journey he petitioneth him that cannot walk: and for getting, and for working, and for the event of all things he asketh him that is unable to do any thing.

CHAPTER 14

The beginning of worshipping idols. The effects thereof.

AGAIN, another, designing to sail, and beginning to make his voyage through the raging waves, calleth upon a piece of wood more frail than the wood that carrieth him.

2 For this the desire of gain devised, and the workman built it by his skill.

3 But thy providence, O Father, governeth it: ¹ for thou hast made a way even in the sea, and a most sure path among the waves,

4 Shewing that thou art able to save out of all things, yea, though a man went to sea without art.

5 But that the works of thy wisdom might not be idle: therefore men also trust their lives even to a little wood, and passing over the sea by ship are saved.

6 ² And from the beginning also when the proud giants perished, the hope of the world fleeing to a vessel which was governed by thy hand, left to the world seed of generation.

CHAP. 13. ¹ Rom. 1, 18. ² Deut. 4, 19; 17, 3. ³ Rom. 1, 21. ⁴ Isai. 44, 12; Jer. 10, 3. CHAP. 14. ¹ Exod. 14, 22. ² Gen. 6, 4; 7, 7. ³ Ps. 113, 4; Bar. 6, 3.

7 For blessed is the wood by which justice cometh.

8 [3] But the idol that is made by hands is cursed, as well it as he that made it: he because he made it; and it because, being frail, it is called a god.

9 But to God the wicked and his wickedness are hateful alike.

10 For that which is made, together with him that made it, shall suffer torments.

11 Therefore, there shall be no respect had even to the idols of the Gentiles: because the creatures of God are turned to an abomination, and a temptation to the souls of men, and a snare to the feet of the unwise.

12 For the beginning of fornication is the devising of idols: and the invention of them is the corruption of life.

13 For neither were they from the beginning: neither shall they be for ever.

14 For by the vanity of men they came into the world: and therefore they shall be found to come shortly to an end.

15 For a father, being afflicted with bitter grief, made to himself the image of his son who was quickly taken away: and him who then had died as a man, he began now to worship as a god, and appointed him rites and sacrifices, among his servants.

16 Then in process of time, wicked custom prevailing, this error was kept as a law; and statues were worshipped by the commandment of tyrants.

17 And those whom men could not honour in presence, because they dwelt far off, they brought their resemblance from afar, and made an express image of the king whom they had a mind to honour: that by this their diligence they might honour as present him that was absent.

18 And to the worshipping of these, the singular diligence also of the artificer helped to set forward the ignorant.

19 For he, being willing to please him that employed him, laboured with all his art, to make the resemblance in the best manner.

20 And the multitude of men, carried away by the beauty of the work, took him now for a god that a little before was but honoured as a man.

21 And this was the occasion of deceiving human life: for men serving either their affection, or their kings, gave the incommunicable name to stones and wood.

22 And it was not enough for them to err about the knowledge of God: but whereas they lived in a great war of ignorance, they call so many and so great evils peace.

23 [4] For either they sacrifice their own children, or use hidden sacrifices, or keep watches full of madness,

24 So that now they neither keep life, nor marriage undefiled: but one killeth another through envy or grieveth him by adultery.

25 And all things are mingled together, blood, murder, theft and dissimulation, corruption and unfaithfulness, tumults and perjury, disquieting of the good,

26 Forgetfulness of God, defiling of souls, changing of nature, disorder in marriage, and the irregularity of adultery and uncleanness.

27 For the worship of abominable idols is the cause, and the beginning and end, of all evil.

28 For either they are mad when they are merry: or they prophesy lies, or they live unjustly, or easily forswear themselves.

29 For whilst they trust in idols, which are without life, though they swear amiss, they look not to be hurt.

30 But for two things they shall be justly punished, because they have thought not well of God, giving heed to idols, and have sworn unjustly, in guile despising justice.

31 For it is not the power of them by whom they swear, but the just vengeance of sinners, always punisheth the transgression of the unjust.

CHAPTER 15

The servants of God praise him who hath delivered them from idolatry, and condemn both the makers and the worshippers of idols.

BUT thou, our God, art gracious and true, patient, and ordering all things in mercy.

2 For if we sin, we are thine, knowing thy greatness: and if we sin not, we know that we are counted with thee.

3 For to know thee is perfect justice: and to know thy justice and thy power is the root of immortality.

4 For the invention of mischievous men hath not deceived us, nor the shadow of a picture, a fruitless labour, a graven figure with divers colours.

5 The sight whereof enticeth the fool to lust after it: and he loveth the lifeless figure of a dead image.

6 The lovers of evil things deserve to have no better things to trust in, both they that make them, and they that love them, and they that worsip them.

7 [1] The potter also, tempering soft

4 Deut. 18, 10; Jer. 7, 6. CHAP. 15. 1 Rom. 9, 21.

earth, with labour fashioneth every vessel for our service, and of the same clay he maketh both vessels that are for clean uses, and likewise such as serve to the contrary: but what is the use of these vessels, the potter is the judge.

8 And of the same clay by a vain labour he maketh a god: he who a little before was made of earth himself, and a little after returneth to the same out of which he was taken, when his life which was lent him shall be called for again.

9 But his care is, not that he shall labour, nor that his life is short, but he striveth with the goldsmiths and silversmiths: and he endeavoureth to do like the workers in brass, and counteth it a glory to make vain things.

10 For his heart is ashes, and his hope vain earth, and his life more base than clay:

11 Forasmuch as he knew not his maker, and him that inspired into him the soul that worketh, and that breathed into him a living spirit.

12 Yea, and they have counted our life a pastime and the business of life to be gain, and that we must be getting every way, even out of evil.

13 For that man knoweth that he offendeth above all others, who of earthly matter maketh brittle vessels, and graven *gods.*

14 But all the enemies of thy people, that hold them in subjection, are foolish, and unhappy, and proud beyond measure.

15 ²For they have esteemed all the idols of the heathens for gods, which neither have the use of eyes to see, nor noses to draw breath, nor ears to hear, nor fingers of hands to handle, and, as for their feet, they are slow to walk.

16 For man made them: and he that borroweth his own breath fashioned them. For no man can make a god like to himself.

17 For, being mortal himself, he formeth a dead thing with his wicked hands. For he is better than they whom he worshippeth, because he indeed hath lived, though he were mortal, but they never.

18 Moreover they worship also the vilest creatures: but things without sense, compared to these, are worse than they.

² Ps. 113, 5; 134, 16. CHAP. 16. ¹ Num. 11, 31.
² Num. 21, 6. ³ Exod. 8, 24; 10, 4; Apoc. 9, 7.
⁴ Deut. 32, 39; 1 Kings, 2, 6; Tob. 13, 2. ⁵ Exod. 9, 23.

CHAP. 16. Ver. 3. *They indeed desiring food.* He means the Egyptians; who were restrained even from that food which was necessary, by the frogs and the flies that were sent amongst them, and spoiled all their meats.—*But these.* The Israelites.

Ver. 6. *Sign of salvation.* The brazen serpent, an emblem of Christ our Saviour.

19 Yea, neither by sight can any man see good of these beasts. But they have fled from the praise of God and from his blessing.

CHAPTER 16

God's different dealings with the Egyptians and with his own people.

FOR these things, and by the like things to these, they were worthily punished, and were destroyed by a multitude of beasts.

2 Instead of which punishment, dealing well with thy people, ¹ thou gavest them their desire of delicious food, of a new taste, preparing for them quails for their meat:

3 To the end that they indeed, desiring food, by means of those things that were shewn and sent among them, might loathe even that which was necessary to satisfy their desire. But these, after suffering want for a short time, tasted a new meat.

4 For it was requisite that inevitable destruction should come upon them that exercised tyranny: but to these it should only be shewn how their enemies were destroyed.

5 ²For, when the fierce rage of beasts came upon these, they were destroyed with the bitings of crooked serpents.

6 But thy wrath endured not for ever, but they were troubled for a short time, for their correction, having a sign of salvation to put them in remembrance of the commandment of thy law.

7 For he that turned to it, was not healed by that which he saw, but by thee, the Saviour of all.

8 And in this thou didst shew to our enemies that thou art he who deliverest from all evil.

9 ³For the bitings of locusts and of flies killed them; and there was found no remedy for their life: because they were worthy to be destroyed by such things.

10 But not even the teeth of venomous serpents overcame thy children: for thy mercy came and healed them.

11 For they were examined for the remembrance of thy words: and were quickly healed, lest falling into deep forgetfulness, they might not be able to use thy help.

12 For it was neither herb, nor mollifying plaster, that healed them, but thy word, O Lord, which healeth all things.

13 ⁴For it is thou, O Lord, that hast power of life and death, and leadest down to the gates of death, and bringest back again.

14 A man indeed killeth through malice, and when the spirit is gone

forth, it shall not return, neither shall he call back the soul that is received:

15 But it is impossible to escape thy hand.

16 [5] For the wicked that denied to know thee were scourged by the strength of thy arm, being persecuted by strange waters, and hail, and rain, and consumed by fire.

17 And which was wonderful, in water, which extinguished all things, the fire had more force: for the world fighteth for the just.

18 For at one time, the fire was mitigated, that the beasts which were sent against the wicked might not be burned; but that they might see and perceive that they were persecuted by the judgment of God.

19 And at another time the fire, above its own power, burned in the midst of water, to destroy the fruits of a wicked land.

20 [6] Instead of which things thou didst feed thy people with the food of angels, and gavest them bread from heaven, prepared without labour; having in it all that is delicious and the sweetness of every taste.

21 For thy sustenance shewed thy sweetness to thy children, and serving every man's will, it was turned to what every man liked.

22 [7] But snow and ice endured the force of fire, and melted not: that they might know that fire burning in the hail and flashing in the rain destroyed the fruits of the enemies.

23 But this same again, that the just might be nourished, did even forget its own strength.

24 For the creature serving thee, the Creator, is made fierce against the unjust for their punishment; and abateth its strength for the benefit of them that trust in thee.

25 Therefore even then it was transformed into all things, and was obedient to thy grace that nourisheth all, according to the will of them that desired it of thee:

26 That thy children, O Lord, [8] whom thou lovedst, might know that it is not the growing of fruits that nourisheth men, but thy word preserveth them that believe in thee.

27 For that which could not be destroyed by fire, being warmed with a little sunbeam, presently melted away:

28 That it might be known to all, that we ought to prevent the sun to bless thee and adore thee at the dawning of the light.

29 For the hope of the unthankful shall melt away as the winter's ice; and shall run as unprofitable water.

CHAPTER 17
The Egyptian darkness.

FOR thy judgments, O Lord, are great, and thy words cannot be expressed: therefore undisciplined souls have erred.

2 [1] For while the wicked thought to be able to have dominion over the holy nation, *they themselves being* fettered with the bonds of darkness and a long night, shut up in their houses, lay *there* exiled from the eternal providence.

3 And while they thought to lie hid in their obscure sins, they were scattered under a dark veil of forgetfulness, being horribly afraid and troubled with exceeding great astonishment.

4 For neither did the den that held them keep them from fear: for noises coming down troubled them, and sad visions appearing to them, affrighted them.

5 And no power of fire could give them light: neither could the bright flames of the stars enlighten that horrible night.

6 But there appeared to them a sudden fire, very dreadful: and being struck with the fear of that face which was not seen, they thought the things which they saw to be worse.

7 [2] And the delusions of their magic art were put down: and their boasting of wisdom was reproachfully rebuked.

8 For they who promised to drive away fears and troubles from a sick soul were sick themselves of a fear worthy to be laughed at.

9 For though no terrible thing disturbed them: yet being scared with the passing by of beasts and hissing of serpents, they died for fear: and denying that they saw the air, which could by no means be avoided.

10 For whereas wickedness is fearful, it beareth witness of its condemnation: for a troubled conscience always forecasteth grievous things.

11 For fear is nothing else but a yielding up of the succours from thought.

12 And while there is less expectation from within, the greater doth it count the ignorance of that cause which bringeth the torment.

13 But they that during that night, in which nothing could be done, and which came upon them from the lowest and deepest hell, slept the same sleep,

14 Were sometimes molested with the

---

[6] Exod. 16, 14; Num. 11, 7; Ps. 77, 25; John, 6, 31. [7] Exod. 9, 24. [8] Deut. 8, 3; Matt. 4, 4. CHAP. 17. [1] Exod. 10, 23. [2] Exod. 7, 22; 8, 7.

Ver. 17. *The fire had more force*, namely, when the fire and hail mingled together laid waste the land of Egypt.

fear of monsters, sometimes fainted away, their soul failing them: for a sudden and unlooked for fear was come upon them.

15 Moreover, if any of them had fallen down, he was kept shut up in prison without irons.

16 For if any one were a husbandman, or a shepherd, or a labourer in the field, and was suddenly overtaken, he endured a necessity from which he could not fly.

17 For they were all bound together with one chain of darkness. Whether it were a whistling wind, or the melodious voice of birds among the spreading branches of trees, or a fall of water running down with violence,

18 Or the mighty noise of stones tumbling down, or the running that could not be seen of beasts playing together, or the roaring voice of wild beasts, or a rebounding echo from the highest mountains: these things made them to swoon for fear.

19 For the whole world was enlightened with a clear light; and none were hindered in their labours.

20 But over them only was spread a heavy night, an image of that darkness which was to come upon them. But they were to themselves more grievous than the darkness.

CHAPTER 18

The slaughter of the firstborn in Egypt. The efficacy of Aaron's intercession, in the sedition on occasion of Core.

BUT [1] thy saints had a very great light, and they heard their voice indeed, but did not see their shape. And because they also did not suffer the same things, they glorified thee.

2 And they that before had been wronged gave thanks, because they were not hurt now: and asked this gift, that there might be a difference.

3 [2] Therefore, they received a burning pillar of fire for a guide of the way which they knew not: and thou gavest them a harmless sun of a good entertainment.

4 The others indeed were worthy to be deprived of light and imprisoned in darkness, who kept thy children shut

CHAP. 18. [1] Exod. 10, 23. [2] Exod. 14, 24; Ps. 77, 14; 104, 39. [3] Exod. 1, 16; 2, 3. [4] Exod. 14, 27. [5] Exod. 12, 30. [6] Num. 16, 46.

CHAP. 18. Ver. 3. *A harmless sun.* A light that should not hurt or molest them; but that should be an agreeable guest to them.
Ver. 5. *One child.* Moses.
Ver. 9. *Of good men.* That is, of the patriarchs. Their children, the Israelites, offered in private the sacrifice of the paschal lamb; and were regulating what they were to do in their journey, when that last and most dreadful plague was coming upon their enemies.
Ver. 12. *The noblest offspring.* That is the firstborn.

up, by whom the pure light of the law was to be given to the world.

5 [3] And whereas they thought to kill the babes of the just, one child being cast forth and saved to reprove them, thou tookest away a multitude of their children [4] and destroyedst them all together in a mighty water.

6 For that night was known before by our fathers, that assuredly knowing what oaths they had trusted to, they might be of better courage.

7 So thy people received the salvation of the just and destruction of the unjust.

8 For as thou didst punish the adversaries, so thou didst also encourage and glorify us.

9 For the just children of good men were offering sacrifice secretly; and they unanimously ordered a law of justice: That the just should receive both good and evil alike, singing now the praises of the fathers.

10 But on the other side there sounded an ill according cry of the enemies: and a lamentable mourning was heard for the children that were bewailed.

11 [5] And the servant suffered the same punishment as the master: and a common man suffered in like manner as the king.

12 So all alike had innumerable dead, with one kind of death. Neither were the living sufficient to bury them; for in one moment the noblest offspring of them was destroyed.

13 For whereas they would not believe any thing before by reason of the enchantments, then first, upon the destruction of the firstborn, they acknowledged the people to be of God.

14 For while all things were in quiet silence and the night was in the midst of her course,

15 Thy almighty word leapt down from heaven from thy royal throne, as a fierce conqueror into the midst of the land of destruction,

16 *With* a sharp sword carrying thy unfeigned commandment. And he stood and filled all things with death: and standing on the earth reached even to heaven.

17 Then suddenly visions of evil dreams troubled them: and fears unlooked for came upon them.

18 And one thrown here, another there, half dead, shewed the cause of his death.

19 For the visions that troubled them foreshewed these things, lest they should perish and not know why they suffered these evils.

20 But the just also were afterwards touched by an assault of death, and there was a disturbance of the multi-

tude in the wilderness: but thy wrath did not long continue.

21 [6] For a blameless man made haste to pray for the people, bringing forth the shield of his ministry, prayer, and by incense making supplication, withstood the wrath, and put an end to the calamity, shewing that he was thy servant.

22 And he overcame the disturbance, not by strength of body, nor with force of arms, but, with a word, he subdued him that punished them, alleging the oaths and covenant made with the fathers.

23 For when they were now fallen down dead by heaps, one upon another, he stood between and stayed the assault, and cut off the way to the living.

24 [7] For in the priestly robe which he wore was the whole world: and in the four rows of the stones the glory of the fathers was graven, and thy majesty was written upon the diadem of his head.

25 And to these the destroyer gave place, and was afraid of them: for the proof only of wrath was enough.

CHAPTER 19

Why God shewed no mercy to the Egyptians. His favour to the Israelites. All creatures obey God's orders for the service of the good, and the punishment of the wicked.

BUT as to the wicked, even to the end, there came upon them wrath without mercy. For he knew before also what they would do.

2 For when they had given them leave to depart, and had sent them away with great care, they repented, and pursued after them.

3 [1] For whilst they were yet mourning and lamenting at the graves of the dead, they took up another foolish device: and pursued them as fugitives whom they had pressed to be gone.

4 For a necessity, of which they were worthy, brought them to this end. And they lost the remembrance of those things which had happened, that their punishment might fill up what was wanting to their torments,

5 And that thy people might wonderfully pass through; but they might find a new death.

6 For every creature according to its kind was fashioned again *as* from the beginning, obeying thy commandments, that thy children might be kept without hurt:

7 [7] For a cloud overshadowed their camp, and where water was before, dry land appeared, and in the Red Sea a way without hinderance, and out of the great deep a springing field:

8 Through which all the nation passed which was protected with thy hand, seeing thy miracles and wonders.

9 For they fed on their food like horses, and they skipped like lambs, praising thee, O Lord, who hadst delivered them.

10 For they were yet mindful of those things which had been done in the time of their sojourning: how the ground brought forth flies instead of cattle, and how the river cast up a multitude of frogs instead of fishes.

11 [2] And at length they saw a new generation of birds, when being led by their appetite they asked for delicate meats:

12 For to satisfy their desire, the quail came up to them from the sea. And punishments came upon the sinners, not without foregoing signs by the force of thunders: for they suffered justly according to their own wickedness.

13 For they exercised a more detestable inhospitality *than any*. Others indeed received not strangers unknown to them: but these brought their guests into bondage that had deserved well of them.

14 And not only so, but in another respect also they were worse: for the others against their will received the strangers.

15 But these grievously afflicted them whom they had received with joy, and who lived under the same laws.

16 But they were struck with blindness, [3] as those others were at the doors of the just man, when they were covered with sudden darkness: and every one sought the passage of his own door.

17 For while the elements are changed in themselves, as in an instrument the sound of the quality is changed, yet all keep their sound: which may clearly be perceived by the very sight.

18 For the things of the land were turned into things of the water: and the things that before swam in the water passed upon the land.

19 The fire had power in water above its own virtue: and the water forgot its quenching nature.

20 On the other side, the flames wasted not the flesh of corruptible animals walking therein: neither did they melt that good food which was apt to melt as ice. For in all things thou didst magnify thy people, O Lord, and didst honour them, and didst not despise them: but didst assist them at all times, and in every place.

[7] Exod. 28, 6. CHAP. 19. [1] Exod. 14, 15. [2] Exod. 16, 13; Num. 11, 31; Wisd. 16, 2. [3] Gen. 19, 11.

CHAP. 19. Ver. 17. *Elements are changed.* The meaning is, that whatever changes God wrought in the elements by miracles in favour of his people, they still kept their harmony by obeying his will.

Ver. 20. *That good food.* The manna.

ECCLESIASTICUS

This Book is so called from a Greek word that signifies THE PREACHER: *because, like an excellent preacher, it gives admirable lessons of all virtues. The author was Jesus the son of Sirach of Jerusalem, who flourished about two hundred years before Christ. As it was written after the times of Esdras, it is not in the Jewish canon; but it is received as canonical and divine by the Catholic Church, instructed by apostolical tradition, and directed by the spirit of God. It was first written in the Hebrew, but afterwards translated into Greek by another Jesus, the grandson of the author, whose prologue to this book is the following:*

THE PROLOGUE.

THE knowledge of many and great things hath been shewn us by the law, and the prophets, and others that have followed them: for which things Israel is to be commended for doctrine and wisdom, because not only they that speak must needs be skilful, but strangers also, both speaking and writing, may *by their means* become most learned. My grandfather Jesus, after he had much given himself to a diligent reading of the law, and the prophets, and other books, that were delivered to us from our fathers, had a mind also to write something himself, pertaining to doctrine and wisdom: that such as are desirous to learn, and are made knowing in these things, may be more and more attentive in mind, and be strengthened to live according to the law. I entreat you therefore to come with benevolence, and to read with attention, and to pardon us for those things wherein we may seem, while we follow the image of wisdom, to come short in the composition of words; for the Hebrew words have not the same force in them when translated into another tongue. And not only these, but the law also itself, and the prophets, and the rest of the books, have no small difference, when they are spoken in their own language. For in the eight and thirtieth year, coming into Egypt, when Ptolemy Evergetes was king, and continuing there a long time, I found there books left, of no small nor contemptible learning. Therefore, I thought it good, and necessary for me to bestow some diligence and labour, to interpret this book; and with much watching and study, in some space of time, I brought the book to an end, and set it forth for the service of them that are willing to apply their mind, and to learn how they ought to conduct themselves who propose to lead their life according to the law of the Lord.

CHAPTER 1

All wisdom is from God, and is given to them that fear and love God.

ALL [1] wisdom is from the Lord God, and hath been always with him, and is before all time.

2 Who hath numbered the sand of the sea, and the drops of rain, and the days of the world? Who hath measured the height of heaven, and the breadth of the earth, and the depth of the abyss?

3 Who hath searched out the wisdom of God that goeth before all things?

4 Wisdom hath been created before all things, and the understanding of prudence from everlasting.

5 The word of God on high is the fountain of wisdom: and her ways are everlasting commandments.

6 To whom hath the root of wisdom been revealed: and who hath known her wise counsels?

7 To whom hath the discipline of wisdom been revealed and made manifest? And who hath understood the multiplicity of her steps?

8 There is one most high Creator, Almighty, and a powerful king, and greatly to be feared, who sitteth upon his throne, and is the God of dominion.

9 He created her in the Holy Ghost, and saw her, and numbered her, and measured her.

10 And he poured her out upon all his works, and upon all flesh, according to his gift: and hath given her to them that love him.

11 The fear of the Lord is honour, and glory, and gladness, and a crown of joy.

12 The fear of the Lord shall delight the heart: and shall give joy, and gladness, and length of days.

13 With him that feareth the Lord, it shall go well in the latter end: and in the day of his death he shall be blessed.

14 The love of God is honourable wisdom.

15 And they to whom she shall shew herself love her by the sight and by the knowledge of her great works.

16 [2] The fear of the Lord is the beginning of wisdom, and was created with the faithful in the womb. It walketh with chosen women, and is known with the just and faithful.

17 The fear of the Lord is the religiousness of knowledge.

18 Religiousness shall keep and justify the heart: it shall give joy and gladness.

19 It shall go well with him that

CHAP. 1. [1] 3 Kings, 3, 9; 4, 29. [2] Ps. 110, 10; Prov. 1, 7; 9, 10.

feareth the Lord: and in the days of his end he shall be blessed.

20 To fear God is the fulness of wisdom: and fulness is from the fruits thereof.

21 She shall fill all her house with her increase, and the storehouses with her treasures.

22 The fear of the Lord is a crown of wisdom, filling up peace and the fruit of salvation.

23 And it hath seen, and numbered her: but both are the gifts of God.

24 Wisdom shall distribute knowledge and understanding of prudence: and exalteth the glory of them that hold her.

25 The root of wisdom is to fear the Lord: and the branches thereof are long-lived.

26 In the treasures of wisdom is understanding, and religiousness of knowledge: but to sinners wisdom is an abomination.

27 The fear of the Lord driveth out sin.

28 For he that is without fear, cannot be justified: for the wrath of his high spirits is his ruin.

29 A patient man shall bear for a time, and afterwards joy shall be restored to him.

30 A good understanding will hide his words for a time: and the lips of many shall declare his wisdom.

31 In the treasures of wisdom is the signification of discipline:

32 But the worship of God is an abomination to a sinner.

33 Son, if thou desire wisdom, keep justice: and God will give her to thee.

34 For the fear of the Lord is wisdom and discipline: and that which is agreeable to him

35 Is faith, and meekness: and he will fill up his treasures.

36 Be not incredulous to the fear of the Lord: and come not to him with a double heart.

37 Be not a hypocrite in the sight of men: and let not thy lips be a stumbling-block to thee.

38 Watch over them, lest thou fall and bring dishonour upon thy soul,

39 And God discover thy secrets, and cast thee down in the midst of the congregation:

40 Because thou camest to the Lord wickedly, and thy heart is full of guile and deceit.

CHAPTER 2

God's servants must look for temptations and must arm themselves with patience and confidence in God.

SON, [1] when thou comest to the service of God, stand in justice and in fear: and prepare thy soul for temptation.

2 Humble thy heart, and endure: incline thy ear, and receive the words of understanding: and make not haste in the time of clouds.

3 Wait on God with patience: join thyself to God and endure, that thy life may be increased in the latter end.

4 Take all that shall be brought upon thee: and in thy sorrow endure, and in thy humiliation keep patience.

5 [2] For gold and silver are tried in the fire, but acceptable men in the furnace of humiliation.

6 Believe God, and he will recover thee and direct thy way: and trust in him. Keep his fear, and grow old therein.

7 Ye that fear the Lord, wait for his mercy: and go not aside from him, lest ye fall.

8 Ye that fear the Lord, believe him: and your reward shall not be made void.

9 Ye that fear the Lord, hope in him: and mercy shall come to you for your delight.

10 Ye that fear the Lord, love him: and your hearts shall be enlightened.

11 My children, behold the generations of men: and know ye that no one hath hoped in the Lord and hath been confounded.

12 [3] For who hath continued in his commandment, and hath been forsaken? Or who hath called upon him, and he despised him?

13 For God is compassionate and merciful, and will forgive sins in the day of tribulation: and he is a protector to all that seek him in truth.

14 Woe to them that are of a double heart, and to wicked lips, and to the hands that do evil, [4] and to the sinner that goeth on the earth two ways.

15 Woe to them that are fainthearted, who believe not God: and therefore they shall not be protected by him.

16 Woe to them that have lost patience, and that have forsaken the right ways, and have gone aside into crooked ways.

17 And what will they do when the Lord shall begin to examine?

18 They that fear the Lord will not be incrudulous to his word: [5] and they that love him will keep his way.

CHAP. 2. [1] Matt. 4, 1; 2 Tim. 3, 12. [2] Wisd. 3, 6. [3] Ps. 30, 1. [4] 3 Kings, 18, 21. [5] John, 14, 23

19 They that fear the Lord will seek after the things that are well pleasing to him: and they that love him shall be filled with his law.

20 They that fear the Lord will prepare their hearts: and in his sight will sanctify their souls.

21 They that fear the Lord keep his commandments: and will have patience even until his visitation.

22 Saying: If we do not penance, we shall fall into the hands of the Lord, and not into the hands of men.

23 For according to his greatness, so also is his mercy with him.

CHAPTER 3

Lessons concerning the honour of parents, and humility, and avoiding curiosity.

THE sons of wisdom *are* the church of the just: and their generation, obedience and love.

2 Children, hear the judgment of your father: and so do that you may be saved.

3 For God hath made the father honourable to the children: and, seeking the judgment of the mothers hath confirmed *it* upon the children.

4 He that loveth God shall obtain pardon for *his* sins by prayer, and shall refrain himself from them, and shall be heard in the prayer of days.

5 And he that honoureth his mother is as one that layeth up a treasure.

6 He that honoureth his father shall have joy in *his own* children: and in the day of his prayer he shall be heard.

7 He that honoureth his father shall enjoy a long life: and he that obeyeth the father shall be comfort to his mother.

8 He that feareth the Lord honoureth his parents and will serve them as his masters that brought him into the world.

9 [1] Honour thy father, in work and word, and all patience:

10 That a blessing may come upon thee from him, and his blessing may remain in the latter end.

11 [2] The father's blessing establisheth the houses of the children: but the mother's curse rooteth up the foundation.

12 Glory not in the dishonour of thy father: for his shame is no glory to thee.

13 For the glory of a man is from the honour of his father: and a father without honour is the disgrace of the son.

14 Son, support the old age of thy father: and grieve him not in his life;

15 And if his understanding fail, have patience with him, and despise him not when thou art in thy strength: for the relieving of the father shall not be forgotten.

16 For good shall be repaid to thee for the sin of thy mother.

17 And in justice thou shalt be built up, and in the day of affliction thou shalt be remembered: and thy sins shall melt away as the ice in the fair warm weather.

18 Of what an evil fame is he that forsaketh his father! And he is cursed of God that angereth his mother.

19 My son, do thy works in meekness: and thou shalt be beloved above the glory of men.

20 [3] The greater thou art, the more humble thyself in all things: and thou shalt find grace before God:

21 For, great is the power of God alone: and he is honoured by the humble.

22 [4] Seek not the things that are too high for thee, and search not into things above thy ability: but the things that God hath commanded thee, think on them always, and in many of his works be not curious.

23 For it is not necessary for thee to see with thy eyes those things that are hid.

24 In unnecessary matters be not over curious: and in many of his works thou shalt not be inquisitive.

25 For many things are shewn to thee above the understanding of men:

26 And the suspicion of them hath deceived many, and hath detained their minds in vanity.

27 A hard heart shall fear evil at the last: and he that loveth danger shall perish in it.

28 A heart that goeth two ways shall not have success: and the perverse of heart shall be scandalized therein.

29 A wicked heart shall be laden with sorrows: and the sinner will add sin to sin.

30 The congregation of the proud shall not be healed: for the plant of wickedness shall take root in them, and it shall not be perceived.

31 The heart of the wise is understood in wisdom: and a good ear will hear wisdom with all desire.

32 A wise heart, and which hath understanding, will abstain from sins: and in the works of justice shall have success.

CHAP. 3. [1] Exod. 20, 12; Deut. 5, 16; Matt. 15, 4; Mark, 7, 10; Eph. 6, 2. [2] Gen. 27, 27; 49, 2. [3] Phil. 2, 3. [4] Prov. 25, 27.

33 [5] Water quencheth a flaming fire: and alms resisteth sins.

34 And God provideth for him that sheweth favour: he remembereth him afterwards, and in the time of his fall he shall find a sure stay.

CHAPTER 4

An exhortation to works of mercy, and to the love of wisdom.

SON [1] defraud not the poor of alms: and turn not away thy eyes from the poor.

2 Despise not the hungry soul: and provoke not the poor in his want.

3 Afflict not the heart of the needy: and defer not to give to him that is in distress.

4 Reject not the petition of the afflicted: and turn not away thy face from the needy.

5 Turn not away thy eyes from the poor for fear of anger: and leave not to them that ask of thee to curse thee behind thy back.

6 For the prayer of him that curseth thee in the bitterness of *his* soul shall be heard: for he that made him will hear him.

7 Make thyself affable to the congregation of the poor, and humble thy soul to the ancient, and bow thy head to a great man.

8 Bow down thy ear cheerfully to the poor, and pay what thou owest, and answer him peaceable words with mildness.

9 Deliver him that suffereth wrong out of the hand of the proud: and be not fainthearted in thy soul.

10 In judging be merciful to the fatherless as a father, and as a husband to their mother.

11 And thou shalt be as the obedient son of the most High: and he will have mercy on thee more than a mother.

12 Wisdom inspireth life into her children, and protecteth them that seek after her, and will go before *them* in the way of justice.

13 And he that loveth her loveth life: and they that watch for her shall embrace her sweetness.

14 They that hold her fast shall inherit life: and whithersoever she entereth, God will give a blessing.

15 They that serve her shall be servants to the holy one: and God loveth them that love her.

16 He that hearkeneth to her shall judge nations: and he that looketh upon her shall remain secure.

17 If he trust to her, he shall inherit her: and his generation shall be in assurance.

18 For she walketh with him in temptation: and at the first she chooseth him.

19 She will bring upon him fear and dread and trial: and she will scourge him with the affliction of her discipline, till she try him by her laws, and trust his soul.

20 Then she will strengthen him, and make a straight way to him, and give him joy.

21 And will disclose her secrets to him: and will heap upon him treasures of knowledge and understanding of justice.

22 But if he go astray, she will forsake him, and deliver him into the hands of his enemy.

23 Son, observe the time, and fly from evil.

24 For thy soul be not ashamed to say the truth.

25 For there is a shame that bringeth sin, and there is a shame that bringeth glory and grace.

26 Accept no person against thy own person, nor against thy soul a lie.

27 Reverence not thy neighbour in his fall:

28 And refrain not to speak in the time of salvation. Hide not thy wisdom in her beauty.

29 For by the tongue wisdom is discerned: and understanding, and knowledge, and learning, by the word of the wise: and steadfastness, in the works of justice.

30 In nowise speak against the truth: but be ashamed of the lie of thy ignorance.

31 Be not ashamed to confess thy sins, [2] but submit not thyself to every man for sin.

32 Resist not against the face of the mighty: and do not strive against the stream of the river.

33 Strive for justice for thy soul, and even unto death fight for justice: and God will overthrow thy enemies for thee.

34 Be not hasty in thy tongue: and slack and remiss in thy works.

35 Be not as a lion in thy house, terrifying them of thy household and oppressing them that are under thee.

36 Let not thy hand be stretched out to receive, and shut when thou shouldst give.

---

[5] Dan. 4, 24. CHAP. 4. [1] Tob. 4, 7. [2] Ecclus. 6, 6.

CHAP. 4. Ver. 18. *In temptation.* The meaning is, that before wisdom will choose any for her favourite, she will try them by leading them through contradictions, afflictions, and temptations; the usual noviceship of the children of God.

CHAPTER 5

We must not presume of our wealth or strength, nor of the mercy of God, to go on in sin. We must be steadfast in virtue and truth.

SET not thy heart upon unjust possessions, and say not: I have enough to live on; for it shall be of no service in the time of vengeance and darkness.

2 Follow not in thy strength the desires of thy heart.

3 And say not: How mighty am I? And who shall bring me under for my deeds? For God will surely take revenge.

4 Say not: I have sinned, and what harm hath befallen me? For the most High is a patient rewarder.

5 Be not without fear about sin forgiven: and add not sin upon sin.

6 And say not: The mercy of the Lord is great; he will have mercy on the multitude of my sins.

7 ¹ For mercy and wrath quickly come from him: and his wrath looketh upon sinners.

8 Delay not to be converted to the Lord: and defer it not from day to day.

9 For his wrath shall come on a sudden: and in the time of vengeance he will destroy thee.

10 ² Be not anxious for goods unjustly gotten: for they shall not profit thee in the day of calamity and revenge.

11 Winnow not with every wind, and go not into every way: for so is every sinner proved by a double tongue.

12 Be steadfast in the way of the Lord, and in the truth of thy judgment, and in knowledge: and let the word of peace and justice keep with thee.

13 Be meek to hear the word, that thou mayst understand: and return a true answer with wisdom.

14 If thou have understanding, answer *thy* neighbour: but if not, let thy hand be upon thy mouth, lest thou be surprised in an unskilful word, and be confounded.

15 Honour and glory is in the word of the wise: but the tongue of the fool is his ruin.

16 Be not called a whisperer: and be not taken in thy tongue, and confounded.

17 For confusion and repentance is upon a thief, and an evil mark of disgrace upon the double tongued: but to the whisperer, hatred and enmity and reproach.

18 Justify alike the small and the great.

_{CHAP. 5. ¹ Prov. 10, 6. ² Prov. 11, 4. CHAP. 6. ¹ Rom. 12, 16; Phil. 2, 3.}

CHAPTER 6

Of true and false friends. Of the fruits of wisdom.

INSTEAD of a friend, become not an enemy to thy neighbour: for an evil man shall inherit reproach and shame. So shall every sinner that is envious and double tongued.

2 ¹ Extol not thyself in the thoughts of thy soul like a bull: lest thy strength be quashed by folly,

3 And it eat up thy leaves, and destroy thy fruit, and thou be left as a dry tree in the wilderness.

4 For a wicked soul shall destroy him that hath it, and maketh him to be a joy to his enemies, and shall lead him into the lot of the wicked.

5 A sweet word multiplieth friends and appeaseth enemies: and a gracious tongue in a good man aboundeth.

6 Be in peace with many: but let one of a thousand be thy counsellor.

7 If thou wouldst get a friend, try him before thou taketh him, and do not credit him easily.

8 For there is a friend for his own occasion: and he will not abide in the day of thy trouble.

9 And there is a friend that turneth to enmity; and there is a friend that will disclose hatred and strife and reproaches.

10 And there is a friend, a companion at the table: and he will not abide in the day of distress.

11 A friend, if he continue steadfast, shall be to thee as thyself: and shall act with confidence among them of thy household.

12 If he humble himself before thee, and hide himself from thy face, thou shalt have unanimous friendship for good.

13 Separate thyself from thy enemies: and take heed of thy friends.

14 A faithful friend is a strong defence: and he that hath found him hath found a treasure.

15 Nothing can be compared to a faithful friend: and no weight of gold and silver is able to countervail the goodness of his fidelity.

16 A faithful friend is the medicine of life and immortality: and they that fear the Lord shall find him.

17 He that feareth God shall likewise have good friendship: because according to him shall his friend be.

18 My son, from thy youth up, receive instruction: and even to thy grey hairs thou shalt find wisdom.

19 Come to her as one that plougheth and soweth: and wait for her good fruits.

20 For in working about her thou shalt labour a little and shalt quickly eat of her fruits.

21 How very unpleasant is wisdom to the unlearned! And the unwise will not continue with her.

22 She shall be to them as a mighty stone of trial: and they will cast her from them before it be long.

23 For the wisdom of doctrine is according to her name: and she is not manifest unto many. But with them to whom she is known, she continueth even to the sight of God.

24 Give ear, my son, and take wise counsel: and cast not away my advice.

25 Put thy feet into her fetters, and thy neck into her chains.

26 Bow down thy shoulder, and bear her: and be not grieved with her bands.

27 Come to her with all thy mind: and keep her ways with all thy power.

28 Search for her, and she shall be made known to thee: and when thou hast gotten her, let her not go.

29 For in the latter end thou shalt find rest in her: and she shall be turned to thy joy.

30 Then shall her fetters be a strong defence for thee, and a firm foundation, and her chain a robe of glory.

31 For in her is the beauty of life: and her bands are a healthful binding.

32 Thou shalt put her on as a robe of glory: and thou shalt set her upon thee as a crown of joy.

33 My son, if thou wilt attend to me, thou shalt learn: and if thou wilt apply thy mind, thou shalt be wise.

34 If thou wilt incline thy ear, thou shalt receive instruction: and if thou love to hear, thou shalt be wise.

35 [2] Stand in the multitude of ancients that are wise, and join thyself from thy heart to their wisdom: that thou mayst hear every discourse of God, and the sayings of praise may not escape thee.

36 And if thou see a man of understanding, go to him early in the morning: and let thy foot wear the steps of his doors.

37 [3] Let thy thoughts be upon the precepts of God, and meditate continually on his commandments: and he will give thee a heart; and the desire of wisdom shall be given to thee.

CHAPTER 7

Religious and moral duties.

D O no evils: and no evils shall lay hold of thee.

2 Depart from the unjust: and evils shall depart from thee.

3 My son, sow not evils in the furrows of injustice: and thou shalt not reap them sevenfold.

4 Seek not of the Lord a preeminence, nor of the king the seat of honour.

5 [1] Justify not thyself before God, for he knoweth the heart: and desire not to appear wise before the king.

6 Seek not to be made a judge unless thou have strength enough to extirpate iniquities: lest thou fear the person of the powerful, and lay a stumbling-block for thy integrity.

7 Offend not against the multitude of a city, neither cast thyself in upon the people,

8 [2] Nor bind sin to sin: for even in one thou shalt not be unpunished.

9 Be not fainthearted in thy mind.

10 Neglect not to pray and to give alms.

11 Say not: God will have respect to the multitude of my gifts, and when I offer to the most high God, he will accept my offerings.

12 Laugh no man to scorn in the bitterness of his soul: [3] for there is one that humbleth and exalteth, God who seeth all.

13 Devise not a lie against thy brother: neither do the like against thy friend.

14 Be not willing to make any manner of lie: for the custom thereof is not good.

15 Be not full of words in a multitude of ancients: and repeat not the word in thy prayer.

16 Hate not laborious works, nor husbandry ordained by the most High.

17 Number not thyself among the multitude of the disorderly.

18 Remember wrath: for it will not tarry long.

19 Humble thy spirit very much: for the vengeance on the flesh of the ungodly is fire and worms.

20 Do not transgress against thy friend deferring money, nor despise thy dear brother for the sake of gold.

21 Depart not from a wise and good wife, whom thou hast gotten in the fear of the Lord: for the grace of her modesty is above gold.

22 [4] Hurt not the servant that worketh faithfully, nor the hired man that giveth thee his life.

23 Let a wise servant be dear to thee as thy own soul: defraud him not of liberty, nor leave him needy.

24 Hast thou cattle? Have an eye to

[2] Ecclus. 8, 9.   [3] Ps. 1, 2.   CHAP. 7.   [1] Job, 9, 2; Ps. 142, 2; Eccles. 7, 17; Luke, 18, 11.   [2] Ecclus. 12, 7.   [3] 1 Kings, 2, 7.   [4] Lev. 19, 13.

CHAP. 7. Ver. 15. *Repeat not.* Make not much babbling by repetition of words: but aim more at fervour of heart.

them: and if they be for thy profit, keep them with thee.

25 Hast thou children? Instruct them, and bow down their neck from their childhood.

26 Hast thou daughters? Have a care of their body, and shew not thy countenance gay towards them.

27 Marry thy daughter *well*, and thou shalt do a great work. And give her to a wise man.

28 If thou hast a wife according to thy soul, cast her not off: and to her that is hateful, trust not thyself. With thy whole heart,

29 ⁵ Honour thy father, and forget not the groanings of thy mother.

30 Remember that thou hadst not been born but through them: and make a return to them as they have done for thee.

31 With all thy soul fear the Lord, and reverence his priests.

32 With all thy strength love him that made thee: and forsake not his ministers.

33 ⁶ Honour God with all thy soul, and give honour to the priests, and purify thyself with thy arms.

34 Give them their portion, ⁷ as it is commanded thee, of the firstfruits and of purifications: and for thy negligences purify thyself with a few.

35 Offer to the Lord the gift of thy shoulders, and the sacrifice of sanctification, and the firstfruits of the holy things.

36 And stretch out thy hand to the poor, that thy expiation and thy blessing may be perfected.

37 A gift hath grace in the sight of all the living: and restrain not grace from the dead.

38 ⁸ Be not wanting in comforting them that weep: and walk with them that mourn.

39 ⁹ Be not slow to visit the sick: for by these things thou shalt be confirmed in love.

40 In all thy works remember thy last end, and thou shalt never sin.

CHAPTER 8

Other lessons of wisdom and virtue.

STRIVE not with a powerful man, lest thou fall into his hands.

2 ¹ Contend not with a rich man, lest he bring an action against thee.

3 ² For gold and silver hath destroyed many, and hath reached even to the heart of kings, and perverted them.

4 Strive not with a man that is full of tongue: and heap not wood upon his fire.

5 Communicate not with an ignorant man, lest he speak ill of thy family.

6 Despise not a man that turneth away from sin, ³ nor reproach him therewith: remember that we are all worthy of reproof.

7 ⁴ Despise not a man in his old age; for we also shall become old.

8 Rejoice not at the death of thy enemy; knowing that we all die, and are not willing that others should rejoice at our death.

9 ⁵ Despise not the discourse of them that are ancient and wise: but acquaint thyself with their proverbs.

10 For of them thou shalt learn wisdom, and instruction of understanding, and to serve great men without blame.

11 Let not the discourse of the ancients escape thee: for they have learned of their fathers:

12 For of them thou shalt learn understanding, and to give an answer in time of need.

13 Kindle not the coals of sinners by rebuking them: lest thou be burnt with the flame of the fire of their sins.

14 Stand not against the face of an injurious person: lest he sit as a spy to entrap thee in thy words.

15 ⁶ Lend not to a man that is mightier than thyself: and, if thou lendest, count it as lost.

16 Be not surety above thy power: and, if thou be surety, think as if thou wert to pay it.

17 Judge not against a judge: for he judgeth according to that which is just.

18 ⁷ Go not on the way, with a bold man, lest he burden thee with his evils. For he goeth according to his own will: and thou shalt perish together with his folly.

19 ⁸ Quarrel not with a passionate man: and go not into the desert with a bold man. For blood is as nothing in his sight: and where there is no help he will overthrow thee.

20 Advise not with fools: for they cannot love but such things as please them.

21 Before a stranger do no matter of counsel: for thou knowest not what he will bring forth.

22 Open not thy heart to every man:

---

⁵ Tob. 4, 3. ⁶ Deut. 12, 18. ⁷ Lev. 2, 3; Num. 18, 15. ⁸ Rom. 12, 15. ⁹ Matt. 25, 36. CHAP. 8. ¹ Matt. 5, 25. ² Ecclus. 31, 6. ³ 2 Cor. 2, 6; Gal. 6, 1. ⁴ Lev. 19, 32. ⁵ Ecclus. 6, 35. ⁶ Ecclus. 29, 4. ⁷ Gen. 4, 8. ⁸ Prov. 22, 24.

Ver. 33. *Thy arms.* That is, with all thy power, or else by gifts (brachiis), are here signified the *right shoulders* of the victims, which by the law fell to the priests.

Ver. 37. *And restrain not grace from the dead.* That is, withhold not from them the benefit of alms, prayers, and sacrifices. Such was the doctrine and practice of the church of God even in the time of the Old Testament. And the same has always been continued from the days of the apostles in the church of the New Testament.

lest he repay thee with an evil turn, and speak reproachfully to thee.

CHAPTER 9

Cautions with regard to women and dangerous conversations.

BE not jealous over the wife of thy bosom: lest she shew in thy regard the malice of a wicked lesson.

2 Give not the power of thy soul to a woman: lest she enter upon thy strength, and thou be confounded.

3 Look not upon a woman that hath a mind for many: lest thou fall into her snares.

4 Use not much the company of her that is a dancer, and hearken not to her: lest thou perish by the force of her charms.

5 [1] Gaze not upon a maiden: lest her beauty be a stumbling-block to thee.

6 [2] Give not thy soul to harlots in any point: lest thou destroy thyself and thy inheritance.

7 Look not round about thee in the ways of the city: nor wander up and down in the streets thereof.

8 [3] Turn away thy face from a woman dressed up: and gaze not about upon another's beauty.

9 For many have perished by the beauty of a woman, and hereby lust is enkindled as a fire.

10 Every woman that is a harlot shall be trodden upon as dung in the way.

11 Many by admiring the beauty of another man's wife have become reprobate: for her conversation burneth as fire.

12 Sit not at all with another man's wife: nor repose upon the bed with her.

13 And strive not with her over wine: lest thy heart decline towards her, and by thy blood thou fall into destruction.

14 Forsake not an old friend: for the new will not be like to him.

15 A new friend is as new wine: it shall grow old, and thou shalt drink it with pleasure.

16 [4] Envy not the glory and riches of a sinner: for thou knowest not what his ruin shall be.

17 Be not pleased with the wrong done by the unjust: knowing that even to hell the wicked shall not please.

18 Keep thee far from the man that hath power to kill: so thou shalt not suspect the fear of death.

19 And if thou come to him, commit no fault: lest he take away thy life.

20 Know it to be a communication with death: for thou art going in the midst of snares and walking upon the arms of them that are grieved.

21 According to thy power beware of thy neighbour: and treat with the wise and prudent.

22 Let just men be thy guests: and let thy glory be in the fear of God.

23 And let the thought of God be in thy mind: and all thy discourse on the commandments of the Highest.

24 Works shall be praised for the hand of the artificers, and the prince of the people for the wisdom of his speech: but the word of the ancients for the sense.

25 A man full of tongue is terrible in his city: and he that is rash in his word shall be hateful.

CHAPTER 10

The virtues and vices of men in power. The great evil of pride.

A WISE judge shall judge his people: and the government of a prudent man shall be steady.

2 [1] As the judge of the people is himself, so also are his ministers: and what manner of man the ruler of a city is, such also are they that dwell therein.

3 [2] An unwise king shall be the ruin of his people: and cities shall be inhabited through the prudence of the rulers.

4 The power of the earth is in the hand of God: and in his time he will raise up a profitable ruler over it.

5 The prosperity of man is in the hand of God: and upon the person of the scribe he shall lay his honour.

6 Remember not any injury done thee by thy neighbour: [3] and do thou nothing by deeds of injury.

7 Pride is hateful before God and men: and all iniquity of nations is execrable.

8 [4] A kingdom is translated from one people to another, because of injustices and wrongs and injuries and divers deceits.

9 But nothing is more wicked than the covetous man. Why is earth and ashes proud?

10 There is not a more wicked thing than to love money: for such a one setteth even his own soul to sale; because while he liveth he hath cast away his bowels.

11 All power is of short life. A long sickness is troublesome to the physician.

12 The physician cutteth off a short sickness: so also a king is to-day, and to-morrow he shall die.

CHAP. 9. [1] Gen. 6, 2. [2] Prov. 5, 2. [3] Gen. 34, 2; 2 Kings, 11, 4; 13, 1; Matt. 5, 28. [4] Judges, 9, 4; 2 Kings, 15, 10. CHAP. 10. [1] Prov. 29, 12. [2] 3 Kings, 12, 13. [3] Lev. 19, 13. [4] Dan. 4, 14.

CHAP. 10. Ver. 1. *Judge his people.* In the Greek it is *instruct* his people.
Ver. 5. *The scribe.* That is, the man that is wise and learned in the law.

13 For when a man shall die, he shall inherit serpents, and beasts, and worms.

14 The beginning of the pride of man is to fall off from God:

15 Because his heart is departed from him that made him. [5] For pride is the beginning of all sin: he that holdeth it shall be filled with maledictions and it shall ruin him in the end.

16 Therefore hath the Lord disgraced the assemblies of the wicked, and hath utterly destroyed them.

17 God hath overturned the thrones of proud princes: and hath set up the meek in their stead.

18 God hath made the roots of proud nations to wither: and hath planted the humble of these nations.

19 The Lord hath overthrown the lands of the Gentiles: and hath destroyed them even to the foundation.

20 He hath made some of them to wither away, and hath destroyed them: and hath made the memory of them to cease from the earth.

21 God hath abolished the memory of the proud: and hath preserved the memory of them that are humble in mind.

22 Pride was not made for men: nor wrath for the race of women.

23 That seed of men shall be honoured, which feareth God: but that seed shall be dishonoured, which transgresseth the commandments of the Lord.

24 In the midst of brethren their chief is honourable: so shall they that fear the Lord be in his eyes.

25 The fear of God is the glory of the rich, *and* of the honourable, and of the poor.

26 Despise not a just man that is poor: and do not magnify a sinful man that is rich.

27 The great man, and the judge, and the mighty is in honour: and there is none greater than he that feareth God.

28 [6] They that are free shall serve a servant that is wise: [7] and a man that is prudent and well instructed will not murmur when he is reproved; and he that is ignorant shall not be honoured.

29 Extol not thyself in doing thy work: and linger not in the time of distress.

30 [8] Better is he that laboureth and aboundeth in all things, than he that boasteth himself and wanteth bread.

31 My son, keep thy soul in meekness: and give it honour according to its desert.

32 Who will justify him that sinneth against his own soul? And who will honour him that dishonoureth his own soul?

33 The poor man is glorified by his discipline and fear: and there is a man that is honoured for his wealth.

34 But he that is glorified in poverty, how much more in wealth? And he that is glorified in wealth, let him fear poverty.

CHAPTER 11

Lessons of humility and moderation in all things.

THE [1] wisdom of the humble shall exalt his head, and shall make him sit in the midst of great men.

2 [2] Praise not a man for his beauty: neither despise a man for his look.

3 The bee is small among flying things: but her fruit hath the chiefest sweetness.

4 [3] Glory not in apparel at any time, and be not exalted in the day of thy honour: for the works of the Highest only are wonderful, and his works are glorious, and secret, and hidden.

5 Many tyrants have sat on the throne: and he whom no man would think on hath worn the crown.

6 [4] Many mighty men have been greatly brought down: and the glorious have been delivered into the hand of others.

7 Before thou inquire, blame no man: and when thou hast inquired, reprove justly.

8 [5] Before thou hear, answer not a word: and interrupt not others in the midst of their discourse.

9 Strive not in a matter which doth not concern thee: and sit not in judgment with sinners.

10 My son, meddle not with many matters: [6] and if thou be rich, thou shalt not be free from sin. For if thou pursue after, thou shalt not overtake: and if thou run before, thou shalt not escape.

11 [7] There is an ungodly man that laboureth, and maketh haste, and is in sorrow, and is so much the more in want.

12 Again, there is an inactive man that wanteth help, is very weak in ability, and full of poverty:

13 [8] Yet the eye of God hath looked upon him for good, and hath lifted him up from his low estate, and hath exalted his head. And many have wondered at him, and have glorified God.

14 [9] Good things and evil, life and

[5] Prov. 18, 12. [6] Prov. 17, 2. [7] 2 Kings, 12, 13. [8] Prov. 12, 9. CHAP. 11. [1] Gen. 41, 40; Dan. 6, 3; John, 7, 18. [2] 1 Kings, 16, 7; 2 Cor. 10, 10; James, 2, 1, 9. [3] Acts, 12, 21, 22. [4] 1 Kings, 15, 28; Esther, 6, 7. [5] Prov. 18, 13. [6] 1 Tim. 6, 9. [7] Eccles. 4, 8. [8] Job, 42, 10. [9] Job, 2, 10.

death, poverty and riches, are from God.

15 Wisdom and discipline, and the knowledge of the law are with God. Love and the ways of good things are with him.

16 Error and darkness are created with sinners: and they that glory in evil things grow old in evil.

17 The gift of God abideth with the just: and his advancement shall have success for ever.

18 There is one that is enriched by living sparingly: and this is the portion of his reward.

19 In that he saith: [10] I have found me rest, and now I will eat of my goods alone.

20 And he knoweth not what time shall pass, and that death approacheth, and that he must leave all to others, and shall die.

21 Be steadfast in thy covenant, and be conversant therein: and grow old in the work of thy commandments.

22 Abide not in the works of sinners: but trust in God, and stay in thy place.

23 For it is easy in the eyes of God on a sudden to make the poor man rich.

24 The blessing of God maketh haste to reward the just: and in a swift hour his blessing beareth fruit.

25 Say not: What need I, and what good shall I have by this?

26 Say not: I am sufficient for myself; and what shall I be made worse by this?

27 [11] In the day of good things be not unmindful of evils: and in the day of evils be not unmindful of good things.

28 For it is easy before God in the day of death to reward every one according to his ways.

29 The affliction of an hour maketh one forget great delights: and in the end of a man is the disclosing of his works.

30 Praise not any man before death, for a man is known by his children.

31 Bring not every man into thy house: for many are the snares of the deceitful.

32 For, as corrupted bowels send forth stinking breath, and as the partridge is brought into the cage, and as the roe into the snare: so also is the heart of the proud, and as a spy that looketh on the fall of his neighbour.

33 For he lieth in wait and turneth good into evil, and on the elect he will lay a blot.

34 Of one spark cometh a great fire, and of one deceitful man much blood: and a sinful man lieth in wait for blood.

35 Take heed to thyself of a mis-chievous man, for he worketh evils: lest he bring upon thee reproach for ever.

36 Receive a stranger in, and he shall overthrow thee with a whirlwind, and shall turn thee out of thy own.

CHAPTER 12

We are to be liberal to the just and not to trust the wicked.

IF thou do good, know to whom thou dost it: and there shall be much thanks for thy good deeds.

2 Do good to the just, and thou shalt find great recompense: and if not of him, assuredly of the Lord.

3 For there is no good for him that is always occupied in evil and that giveth no alms: for the Highest hateth sinners and hath mercy on the penitent.

4 [1] Give to the merciful and uphold not the sinner, God will repay vengeance to the ungodly and to sinners, and keep them against the day of vengeance.

5 Give to the good: and receive not a sinner.

6 Do good to the humble, and give not to the ungodly: hold back thy bread, and give it not to him, lest thereby he overmaster thee.

7 For thou shalt receive twice as much evil for all the good thou shalt have done to him. For the Highest also hateth sinners, and will repay vengeance to the ungodly.

8 A friend shall not be known in prosperity: and an enemy shall not be hidden in adversity.

9 In the prosperity of a man, his enemies are grieved: and a friend is known in his adversity.

10 Never trust thy enemy: for as a brass pot his wickedness rusteth.

11 Though he humble himself and go crouching, yet take good heed and beware of him.

12 Set him not by thee, neither let him sit on thy right hand, lest he turn into thy place and seek to take thy seat: and at the last thou acknowledge my words, and be pricked with my sayings.

13 Who will pity an enchanter struck by a serpent, or any that come near wild beasts? So is it with him that keepeth company with a wicked man, and is involved in his sins.

14 For an hour he will abide with thee: but if thou begin to decline, he will not endure it.

15 [2] An enemy speaketh sweetly with his lips: but in his heart he lieth in wait to throw thee into a pit.

16 An enemy weepeth with his eyes:

[10] Luke, 12, 19.   [11] Ecclus. 18, 25.   CHAP. 12. [1] Gal. 6, 10.   [2] Jer. 41, 6.

but if he find an opportunity he will not be satisfied with blood.

17 And if evils come upon thee, thou shalt find him there first.

18 An enemy hath tears in his eyes, and, while he pretendeth to help thee, will undermine thy feet.

19 He will shake his head, and clap his hands, and whisper much, and change his countenance.

CHAPTER 13

Cautions in the choice of company.

HE [1] that toucheth pitch shall be defiled with it: and he that hath fellowship with the proud shall put on pride.

2 He shall take a burden upon him that hath fellowship with one more honourable than himself. And have no fellowship with one that is richer than thyself.

3 What agreement shall the earthen pot have with the kettle? For if they knock one against the other, it shall be broken.

4 The rich man hath done wrong, and yet he will fume: but the poor is wronged and must hold his peace.

5 If thou give, he will make use of thee: and if thou have nothing, he will forsake thee.

6 If thou have any thing, he will live with thee, and will make thee bare: and he will not be sorry for thee.

7 If he have need of thee he will deceive thee, and smiling upon thee will put thee in hope. He will speak thee fair, and will say: What wantest thou?

8 And he will shame thee by his meats, till he have drawn thee dry twice or thrice, and at last he will laugh at thee: and afterward when he seeth thee, he will forsake thee and shake his head at thee.

9 Humble thyself to God, and wait for his hands.

10 Beware that thou be not deceived into folly and be humbled.

11 Be not lowly in thy wisdom: lest being humbled thou be deceived into folly.

12 If thou be invited by one that is mightier, withdraw thyself: for so he will invite thee the more.

13 Be not troublesome *to him*, lest thou be put back: and keep not far from him, lest thou be forgotten.

14 Affect not to speak with him as an equal: and believe not his many words. For by much talk he will sift thee, and smiling will examine thee concerning thy secrets.

15 His cruel mind will lay up thy words: and he will not spare to do thee hurt and to cast thee into prison.

16 Take heed to thyself, and attend diligently to what thou hearest: for thou walkest in danger of thy ruin.

17 When thou hearest those things, see as it were in sleep: and thou shalt awake.

18 Love God all thy life: and call upon him for thy salvation.

19 Every beast loveth its like: so also every man him that is nearest to himself.

20 All flesh shall consort with the like to itself: and every man shall associate himself to his like.

21 If the wolf shall at any time have fellowship with the lamb, so the sinner with the just.

22 [2] What fellowship hath a holy man with a dog, or what part hath the rich with the poor?

23 The wild ass is the lion's prey in the desert: so also the poor are devoured by the rich.

24 And as humility is an abomination to the proud: so also the rich man abhorreth the poor.

25 When a rich man is shaken, he is kept up by his friends: but when a poor man is fallen down, he is thrust away even by his acquaintance.

26 When a rich man hath been deceived, he hath many helpers: he hath spoken proud things, and they have justified him.

27 The poor man was deceived, and he is rebuked also: he hath spoken wisely, and could have no place.

28 The rich man spoke, and all held their peace: and what he said they extol even to the clouds.

29 The poor man spoke, and they say: Who is this? And if he stumble, they will overthrow him.

30 Riches are good to him that hath no sin in his conscience: and poverty is very wicked in the mouth of the ungodly.

31 The heart of a man changeth his countenance, either for good, or for evil.

32 The token of a good heart and a good countenance thou shalt hardly find, and with labour.

CHAPTER 14

The evil of avarice. Works of mercy are recommended, and the love of wisdom.

BLESSED [1] is the man that hath not slipped by a word out of his mouth and is not pricked with the remorse of sin.

2 Happy is he that hath had no sadness of his mind, and who is not fallen from his hope.

CHAP. 13. [1] Ecclus. 7, 2. [2] 2 Cor. 6, 14. CHAP. 14. [1] Ecclus. 19, 17.

3 Riches are not comely for a covetous man and a niggard. And what should an envious man do with gold?

4 He that gathereth together by wronging his own soul, gathereth for others: and another will squander away his goods in rioting.

5 He that is evil to himself, to whom will he be good? And he shall not take pleasure in his goods.

6 There is none worse than he that envieth himself: and this is the reward of his wickedness:

7 And if he do good, he doth it ignorantly and unwillingly: and at the last he discovereth his wickedness.

8 The eye of the envious is wicked: and he turneth away his face, and despiseth his own soul.

9 The eye of the covetous man *is* insatiable in his portion of iniquity: he will not be satisfied till he consume his own soul, drying it up.

10 An evil eye is towards evil things: and he shall not have his fill of bread, but shall be needy and pensive at his own table.

11 My son, if thou have any thing, do good to thyself, and offer to God worthy offerings.

12 Remember that death is not slow, and that the covenant of hell hath been shewn to thee: for the covenant of this world shall surely die.

13 [2] Do good to thy friend before thou die: and according to thy ability, stretching out thy hand, give to the poor.

14 Defraud not thyself of the good day: and let not the part of a good gift overpass thee.

15 Shalt thou not leave to others to divide by lot thy sorrows and labours?

16 Give and take, and justify thy soul.

17 Before thy death work justice: for in hell there is no finding food.

18 [3] All flesh shall fade as grass, and as the leaf that springeth out on a green tree.

19 Some grow, and some fall off: so is the generation of flesh and blood. One cometh to an end, and another is born.

20 Every work that is corruptible shall fail in the end: and the worker thereof shall go with it.

21 And every excellent work shall be justified: and the worker thereof shall be honoured therein.

22 [4] Blessed is the man that shall continue in wisdom, and that shall meditate in his justice, and in his mind shall think of the all seeing eye of God.

23 He that considereth her ways in his heart and hath understanding in her secrets, who goeth after her as one that traceth, and stayeth in her ways:

24 He who looketh in at her windows, and hearkeneth at her door:

25 He that lodgeth near her house, and fastening a pin in her walls shall set up his tent nigh unto her, where good things shall rest in his lodging for ever.

26 He shall set his children under her shelter: and shall lodge under her branches:

27 He shall be protected under her covering from the heat: and shall rest in her glory.

CHAPTER 15

Wisdom embraceth them that fear God. God is not the author of sin.

HE that feareth God will do good: and he that possesseth justice shall shall lay hold on her.

2 And she will meet him as an honourable mother: and will receive him as a wife married of a virgin.

3 With the bread of life and understanding, she shall feed him: [1] and give him the water of wholesome wisdom to drink. And she shall be made strong in him: and he shall not be moved.

4 And she shall hold him fast, and he shall not be confounded: and she shall exalt him among his neighbours.

5 And in the midst of the church she shall open his mouth, and shall fill him with the spirit of wisdom and understanding, and shall clothe him with a robe of glory.

6 She shall heap upon him a treasure of joy and gladness, and shall cause him to inherit an everlasting name.

7 But foolish men shall not obtain her, and wise men shall meet her. Foolish men shall not see her: for she is far from pride and deceit.

8 Lying men shall not be mindful of her: but men that speak truth shall be found with her, and shall advance, even till they come to the sight of God.

9 Praise is not seemly in the mouth of a sinner:

10 For wisdom came forth from God. For praise shall be with the wisdom of God and shall abound in a faithful mouth: and the sovereign Lord will give praise unto it.

11 Say not: It is through God, that she is not with me. For, do not thou the things that he hateth.

12 Say not: He hath caused me to err. For, he hath no need of wicked men.

---

[2] Ecclus. 4, 1; Tob. 4, 7; Luke, 16, 9. [3] Isai. 40, 6; James, 1, 10; 1 Peter, 1, 24. [4] Ps. 1, 2. CHAP. 15. [1] John, 4, 10.

CHAP. 14. Ver. 12. *The covenant of hell.* The decree by which all are to go down to the regions of death.

13 The Lord hateth all abomination of error: and they that fear him shall not love it.

14 God made man from the beginning, and left him in the hand of his own counsel.

15 He added his commandments and precepts.

16 [2] If thou wilt keep the commandments and perform acceptable fidelity for ever, they shall preserve thee.

17 He hath set water and fire before thee: stretch forth thy hand to which thou wilt.

18 [3] Before man is life and death, good and evil: that which he shall choose shall be given him.

19 For the wisdom of God is great, and he is strong in power, seeing all men without ceasing.

20 [4] The eyes of the Lord are towards them that fear him: and he knoweth all the work of man.

21 He hath commanded no man to do wickedly: and he hath given no man license to sin.

22 For he desireth not a multitude of faithless and unprofitable children.

CHAPTER 16

It is better to have none than many wicked children. Of the justice and mercy of God. His ways are unsearchable.

REJOICE not in ungodly children, if they be multiplied: neither be delighted in them, if the fear of God be not with them.

2 Trust not to their life: and respect not their labours.

3 For better is one that feareth God, than a thousand ungodly children.

4 And it is better to die without children, than to leave ungodly children.

5 By one that is wise a country shall be inhabited: the tribe of the ungodly shall become desolate.

6 Many such things hath my eyes seen: and greater things than these my ear hath heard.

7 [1] In the congregation of sinners a fire shall be kindled: and in an unbelieving nation wrath shall flame out.

8 [2] The ancient giants did not obtain pardon for their sins, who were destroyed trusting to their own strength.

9 And he spared not the place where Lot sojourned: but abhorred them for the pride of their word.

10 He had not pity on them, destroying the whole nation that extolled themselves in their sins.

11 [3] So did he with the six hundred thousand footmen, who were gathered together in the hardness of their heart: and if one had been stiffnecked, it is a wonder if he had escaped unpunished.

12 For mercy and wrath are with him. *He is* mighty to forgive, and to pour out indignation.

13 According as his mercy is, so his correction judgeth a man according to his works.

14 The sinner shall not escape in his rapines: and the patience of him that sheweth mercy shall not be put off.

15 [4] All mercy shall make a place for every man according to the merit of his works, and according to the wisdom of his sojournment.

16 Say not: I shall be hidden from God, and who shall remember me from on high?

17 In such a multitude I shall not be known. For what is my soul in such an immense creation?

18 Behold the heaven, and the heavens of heavens, the deep, and all the earth, and the things that are in them, shall be moved in his sight,

19 The mountains also, and the hills and the foundations of the earth: when God shall look upon them, they shall be shaken with trembling.

20 And in all these things the heart is senseless: and every heart is understood by him.

21 And his ways who shall understand, and the storm which no eye of man shall see?

22 For many of his works are hidden: but the works of his justice who shall declare or who shall endure? For the testament is far from some, and the examination of all is in the end.

23 He that wanteth understanding thinketh vain things: and the foolish and erring man thinketh foolish things.

24 Hearken to me, my son, and learn the discipline of understanding, and attend to my words in thy heart.

25 And I will shew forth good doctrine in equity and will seek to declare wisdom. And attend to my words in thy heart, whilst with equity of spirit I tell thee the virtues that God hath put upon his works from the beginning, and I shew forth in truth his knowledge.

26 The works of God are done in judgment from the beginning: and from the making of them he distinguished their parts and their beginnings in their generations.

27 He beautified their works for ever. They have neither hungered nor la-

---

[2] Matt. 19, 17; John, 3, 31, 32. [3] Jer. 21, 8. [4] Ps. 33, 16; Heb. 4, 13. CHAP. 16. [1] Ecclus. 21, 10. [2] Gen. 6, 4. [3] Num. 14, 23, 24; 26, 51. [4] Rom. 2, 6.

CHAP. 16. Ver. 11. *Six hundred thousand footmen.* The children of Israel whom he sentenced to die in the wilderness. Num. 14.

boured: and they have not ceased from their works.

28 Nor shall any of them straiten his neighbour at any time.

29 Be not thou incredulous to his word.

30 After this God looked upon the earth, and filled it with his goods.

31 The soul of every living thing hath shewn forth before the face thereof, and into it they return again.

CHAPTER 17

The creation and favour of God to man. An exhortation to turn to God.

GOD [1] created man of the earth, and made him after his own image.

2 And he turned him into it again, and clothed him with strength according to himself.

3 He gave him the number of his days and time, and gave him power over all things that are upon the earth.

4 He put the fear of him upon all flesh: and he had dominion over beasts and fowls.

5 [2] He created of him a helpmate like to himself: he gave them counsel, and a tongue, and eyes, and ears, and a heart to devise: and he filled them with the knowledge of understanding.

6 He created in them the science of the spirit: he filled their heart with wisdom, and shewed them both good and evil.

7 He set his eye upon their hearts to shew them the greatness of his works:

8 That they might praise the name which he hath sanctified, and glory in his wondrous acts: that they might declare the glorious things of his works.

9 Moreover, he gave them instructions, and the law of life for an inheritance.

10 He made an everlasting covenant with them, and he shewed them his justice and judgments.

11 And their eye saw the majesty of his glory: and their ears heard his glorious voice. And he said to them: Beware of all iniquity.

12 And he gave to every one of them commandment concerning his neighbour.

13 Their ways are always before him: they are not hidden from his eyes.

14 [3] Over every nation he set a ruler.

15 And Israel was made the manifest portion of God.

16 And all their works are as the sun in the sight of God: and his eyes are continually upon their ways.

17 Their covenants were not hid by their inquity: and all their iniquities are in the sight of God.

18 [4] The alms of a man is as a signet with him: and shall preserve the grace of a man as the apple of the eye.

19 [5] And afterward he shall rise up and shall render them their reward, to every one upon their own head: and shall turn *them* down into the bowels of the earth.

20 But to the penitent he hath given the way of justice: and he hath strengthened them that were fainting in patience, and hath appointed to them the lot of truth.

21 Turn to the Lord: and forsake thy sins.

22 Make thy prayer before the face of the Lord: and offend less.

23 Return to the Lord, and turn away from thy injustice: and greatly hate abomination.

24 And know the justices and judgments of God: and stand firm in the lot set before thee, and in prayer to the most high God.

25 Go to the side of the holy age, [6] with them that live and give praise to God.

26 Tarry not in the error of the ungodly: give glory before death. Praise perisheth from the dead as nothing.

27 Give thanks whilst thou art living. Whilst thou art alive and in health thou shalt give thanks, and shalt praise God, and shalt glory in his mercies.

28 How great is the mercy of the Lord, and his forgiveness to them that turn to him!

29 For all things cannot be in men, because the son of man is not immortal, and they are delighted with the vanity of evil.

30 What is brighter than the sun! Yet it shall be eclipsed. Or what is more wicked than that which flesh and blood hath invented! And this shall be reproved.

31 He beholdeth the power of the height of heaven: and all men are earth and ashes.

CHAPTER 18

God's works are wonderful. We must serve him, and not our lusts.

HE [1] that liveth for ever created all things together. God only shall be justified, and he remaineth an invincible king for ever.

CHAP. 17. [1] Gen. 1, 27; 5, 1. [2] Gen. 2, 18. [3] Rom. 13, 1. [4] Ecclus. 29, 6, 15. [5] Matt. 25, 35. [6] Ps. 6, 6; Isai. 38, 19. CHAP. 18. [1] Gen. 1, 1.

Ver. 31. *Shewn forth.* The glory and power of God upon the earth.
CHAP. 17. Ver. 11. *Their eye saw.* When he gave the law on mount Sinai.
Ver. 22. *Offend less (minue offendicula).* That is, remove sins and the occasions of sins.
Ver. 25. *Go to the side.* Fly from the side of Satan and sin, and join with the holy ones, that follow God and godliness.

2 Who is able to declare his works?

3 For who shall search out his glorious acts?

4 And who shall shew forth the power of his majesty? Or, who shall be able to declare his mercy?

5 Nothing may be taken away, nor added: neither is it possible to find out the glorious works of God.

6 When a man hath done, then shall he begin: and when he leaveth off, he shall be at a loss.

7 What is man, and what is his grace? And what is his good, or what is his evil?

8 [2] The number of the days of men at the most are a hundred years. As a drop of water of the sea are they esteemed: and as a pebble of the sand. So are a few years compared to eternity.

9 Therefore God is patient in them, and poureth forth his mercy upon them.

10 He hath seen the presumption of their heart that it is wicked: and hath known their end that it is evil.

11 Therefore hath he filled up his mercy in their favour: and hath shewn them the way of justice.

12 The compassion of man is toward his neighbour: but the mercy of God is upon all flesh.

13 He hath mercy, and teacheth, and correcteth, as a shepherd doth his flock.

14 He hath mercy on him that receiveth the discipline of mercy, and that maketh haste in his judgments.

15 My son, in thy good deeds, make no complaint: and when thou givest any thing, add not grief by an evil word.

16 Shall not the dew assuage the heat? So also the good word is better than the gift.

17 Lo, is not a word better than a gift? But both *are* with a justified man.

18 A fool will upbraid bitterly: and a gift of one ill taught consumeth the eyes.

19 Before judgment prepare thee justice: and learn before thou speak.

20 Before sickness take a medicine, [3] and before judgment examine thyself: and thou shalt find mercy in the sight of God.

21 Humble thyself before thou art sick: and in the time of sickness shew thy conversation.

22 [4] Let nothing hinder thee from praying always, and be not afraid to be justified even to death: for the reward of God continueth for ever.

23 Before prayer prepare thy soul: and be not as a man that tempteth God.

24 [5] Remember the wrath that shall be at the last day, and the time of repaying when he shall turn away his face.

25 [6] Remember poverty in the time of abundance, and the necessities of poverty in the day of riches.

26 From the morning until the evening the time shall be changed: and all these are swift in the eyes of God.

27 A wise man will fear in every thing, and in the days of sins will beware of sloth.

28 Every man of understanding knoweth wisdom, and will give praise to him that findeth her.

29 They that were of good understanding in words have also done wisely themselves: and have understood truth and justice: and have poured forth proverbs and judgments.

30 [7] Go not after thy lusts: but turn away from thy own will.

31 If thou give to thy soul her desires, she will make thee a joy to thy enemies.

32 Take no pleasure in riotous assemblies, be they ever so small: for their concertation is continual.

33 Make not thyself poor by borrowing to contribute to feasts when thou hast nothing in thy purse: for thou shalt be an enemy to thy own life.

CHAPTER 19

Admonitions against sundry vices.

A WORKMAN that is a drunkard shall not be rich: and he that contemneth small things shall fall by little and little.

2 [1] Wine and women make wise men fall off, and shall rebuke the prudent:

3 And he that joineth himself to harlots will be wicked. Rottenness and worms shall inherit him, and he shall be lifted up for a greater example, and his soul shall be taken away out of the number.

4 [2] He that is hasty to give credit is light of heart and shall be lessened: and he that sinneth against his own soul shall be despised.

5 He that rejoiceth in iniquity shall be censured, and he that hateth chastisement shall have less life: and he that hateth babbling extinguisheth evil.

6 He that sinneth against his own soul shall repent: and he that is delighted with wickedness shall be condemned.

7 Rehearse not again a wicked and harsh word: and thou shalt not fare the worse.

8 Tell not thy mind to friend or foe:

[2] Ps. 89, 10. [3] 1 Cor. 11, 28. [4] Luke, 18, 1; 1 Thess. 5, 17. [5] Ecclus. 7, 18. [6] Ecclus. 11, 27. [7] Rom. 6, 12, 13; 13, 14. Chap. 19. [1] Gen. 19, 33; 2 Kings, 11, 1. [2] Jos. 9, 15; 22, 11.

Chap. 18. Ver. 6. *Then shall he begin.* God is so great and incomprehensible, that when man has done all that he can to find out his greatness and boundless perfections, he is still to begin: for what he has found out, is but a mere nothing in comparison with his infinity.

and if there be a sin with thee, disclose it not.

9 For he will hearken to thee, and will watch thee, and as it were defending *thy* sin he will hate thee, and so will he be with thee always.

10 Hast thou heard a word against thy neighbour? Let it die within thee, trusting that it will not burst thee.

11 At the hearing of a word the fool is in travail, as a woman groaning in the bringing forth a child.

12 As an arrow that sticketh in a man's thigh: so is a word in the heart of a fool.

13 [3] Reprove a friend, lest he may not have understood, and say: I did it not. Or if he did it, that he may do it no more.

14 Reprove thy neighbour, for it may be he hath not said it: and if he hath said it, that he may not say it again.

15 Admonish thy friend: for there is often a fault committed.

16 And believe not every word. There is one, that slippeth with the tongue, but not from his heart.

17 [4] For who is there that hath not offended with his tongue? Admonish thy neighbour before thou threaten him.

18 And give place to the fear of the most High: for the fear of God is all wisdom. And therein is to fear God: and the disposition of the law is in all wisdom.

19 But the learning of wickedness is not wisdom: and the device of sinners is not prudence.

20 There is a subtle wickedness, and the same is detestable: and there is a man that is foolish, wanting in wisdom.

21 Better is a man that hath less wisdom, and wanteth understanding, with the fear *of God*, than he that aboundeth in understanding, and transgresseth the law of the most High.

22 There is an exquisite subtilty: and the same is unjust.

23 And there is one that uttereth an exact word telling the truth. There is one that humbleth himself wickedly, and his interior is full of deceit.

24 And there is one that submitteth himself exceedingly with a great lowliness. And there is one that casteth down his countenance, and maketh as if he did not see that which is unknown.

25 And if he be hindered from sinning for want of power, if he shall find opportunity to do evil, he will do it.

26 A man is known by his look: and a wise man, when thou meetest him, is known by his countenance.

27 The attire of the body, and the laughter of the teeth, and the gait of the man, shew what he is.

28 There is a lying rebuke in the anger of an injurious man: and there is a judgment that is not allowed to be good. And there is one that holdeth his peace: he is wise.

CHAPTER 20

Rules with regard to correction, discretion, and avoiding lies.

HOW much better is it to reprove, than to be angry: and not to hinder him that confesseth in prayer.

2 [1] The lust of an eunuch shall deflour a young maiden:

3 So is he that by violence executeth unjust judgment.

4 How good is it, when thou art reproved, to shew repentance: for so thou shalt escape wilful sin.

5 There is one that holdeth his peace, that is found wise: and there is another that is hateful, that is bold in speech.

6 There is one that holdeth his peace, because he knoweth not what to say: and there is another that holdeth his peace, knowing the proper time.

7 A wise man will hold his peace till he see opportunity: but a babbler and a fool will regard no time.

8 He that useth many words shall hurt his own soul: and he that taketh authority to himself unjustly shall be hated.

9 There is success in evil things to a man without discipline: and there is a finding that turneth to loss.

10 There is a gift that is not profitable: and there is a gift, the recompense of which is double.

11 There is an abasement because of glory: and there is one that shall lift up his head from a low estate.

12 There is that buyeth much for a small price, and restoreth the same sevenfold.

13 A man wise in words shall make himself beloved: but the graces of fools shall be poured out.

14 The gift of the fool shall do thee no good: for his eyes are sevenfold.

15 He will give a few things, and upbraid much: and the opening of his mouth is the kindling of a fire.

16 To-day a man lendeth, and to-morrow he asketh it again: such a man as this is hateful.

17 A fool shall have no friend: and there shall be no thanks for his good deeds.

18 For they that eat his bread are of a false tongue. How often, and how many will laugh him to scorn!

[3] Lev. 19, 17; Matt. 18, 15; Luke, 17, 3. [4] James, 3, 8. Chap. 20. [1] Ecclus. 30, 21.

19 For he doth not distribute with right understanding that which was to be had: in like manner also that which was not to be had.

20 The slipping of a false tongue *is* as one that falleth on the pavement: so the fall of the wicked shall come speedily.

21 A man without grace is as a vain fable: it shall be continually in the mouth of the unwise.

22 A parable coming out of a fool's mouth shall be rejected: for he doth not speak it in due season.

23 There is that is hindered from sinning through want: and in his rest he shall be pricked.

24 There is that will destroy his own soul through shamefacedness: and by occasion of an unwise person he will destroy it: and by respect of person he will destroy himself.

25 There is that for bashfulness promiseth to his friend: and maketh him his enemy for nothing.

26 A lie is a foul blot in a man: and yet it will be continually in the mouth of men without discipline.

27 A thief is better than a man that is always lying: but both of them shall inherit destruction.

28 The manners of lying men are without honour: and their confusion is with them without ceasing.

29 A wise man shall advance himself with his words: and a prudent man shall please the great ones.

30 He that tilleth his land shall make a high heap of corn: and he that worketh justice shall be exalted: and he that pleaseth great men shall escape iniquity.

31 [2] Presents and gifts blind the eyes of judges: and make them dumb in the mouth, so that they cannot correct.

32 [3] Wisdom that is hid, and treasure that is not seen: what profit is there in them both?

33 Better is he that hideth his folly than the man that hideth his wisdom.

CHAPTER 21

Cautions against sin in general, and some sins in particular.

MY son, hast thou sinned? Do so no more: but for thy former sins also pray that they may be forgiven thee.

2 Flee from sins as from the face of a serpent: for if thou comest near them, they will take hold of thee.

3 The teeth thereof are the teeth of a lion, killing the souls of men.

4 All iniquity is like a two-edged sword: there is no remedy for the wound thereof.

5 Injuries and wrongs will waste riches, and the house that is very rich shall be brought to nothing by pride: so the substance of the proud shall be rooted out.

6 The prayer out of the mouth of the poor shall reach the ears *of God:* and judgment shall come for him speedily.

7 He. that hateth to be reproved *walketh in* the trace of a sinner: and he that feareth God will turn to his own heart.

8 He that is mighty by a bold tongue is known afar off: but a wise man knoweth to slip by him.

9 He that buildeth his house at other men's charges is as he that gathereth himself stones to *build* in the winter.

10 [1] The congregation of sinners is like tow heaped together: and the end of them is a flame of fire.

11 The way of sinners is made plain with stones: and in their end is hell, and darkness, and pains.

12 He that keepeth justice shall get the understanding thereof.

13 The perfection of the fear of God is wisdom and understanding.

14 He that is not wise in good will not be taught.

15 But there is a wisdom that aboundeth in evil: and there is no understanding where there is bitterness.

16 The knowledge of a wise man shall abound like a flood: and his counsel continueth like a fountain of life.

17 The heart of a fool is like a broken vessel: and no wisdom at all shall it hold.

18 A man of sense will praise every wise word he shall hear, and will apply it to himself: the luxurious man hath heard it, and it shall displease him; and he will cast it behind his back.

19 The talking of a fool is like a burden in the way: but in the lips of the wise, grace shall be found.

20 The mouth of the prudent is sought after in the church: and they will think upon his words in their hearts.

21 As a house that is destroyed, so is wisdom to a fool: and the knowledge of the unwise is as words without sense.

22 Doctrine to a fool is as fetters on the feet: and like manacles on the right hand.

23 A fool lifteth up his voice in laughter: but a wise man will scarce laugh low to himself.

24 Learning to the prudent is as an ornament of gold: and like a bracelet upon his right arm.

[2] Exod. 23, 8; Deut. 16, 19. [3] Ecclus. 41, 17.
Chap. 21. [1] Ecclus. 16, 7.

25 The foot of a fool is soon in his neighbour's house: but a man of experience will be abashed at the person of the mighty.

26 A fool will peep through the window into the house: but he that is well taught will stand without.

27 It is the folly of a man to hearken at the door: and a wise man will be grieved with the disgrace.

28 The lips of the unwise will be telling foolish things: but the words of the wise shall be weighed in a balance.

29 The heart of fools is in their mouth: and the mouth of wise men is in their heart.

30 While the ungodly curseth the devil, he curseth his own soul.

31 The talebearer shall defile his own soul, and shall be hated by all: and he that shall abide with him shall be hateful. The silent and wise man shall be honoured.

CHAPTER 22

Wise sayings on divers subjects.

THE sluggard is pelted with a dirty stone: and all men will speak of his disgrace.

2 The sluggard is pelted with the dung of oxen: and every one that toucheth him will shake his hands.

3 A son ill taught is the confusion of the father: and a *foolish* daughter shall be to his loss.

4 A wise daughter shall bring an inheritance to her husband: but she that confoundeth becometh a disgrace to her father.

5 She that is bold shameth both her father and husband, and will not be inferior to the ungodly: and shall be disgraced by them both.

6 A tale out of time is like music in mourning: but the stripes and instruction of wisdom are never out of time.

7 He that teacheth a fool is like one that glueth a potsherd together.

8 He that telleth a word to him that heareth not is like one that waketh a man out of a deep sleep.

9 He speaketh with one that is asleep, who uttereth wisdom to a fool: and in the end of the discourse he saith: Who is this?

10 [1] Weep for the dead, for his light hath failed: and weep for the fool, for his understanding faileth.

11 Weep but a little for the dead, for he is at rest.

12 For the wicked life of a wicked fool is worse than death.

13 [2] The mourning for the dead is seven days: but for a fool and an ungodly man all the days of their life.

14 Talk not much with a fool: and go not with him that hath no sense.

15 Keep thyself from him, that thou mayst not have trouble: and thou shalt not be defiled with his sin.

16 Turn away from him, and thou shalt find rest: and shalt not be wearied out with his folly.

17 What is heavier than lead? And what other name hath he but fool?

18 [3] Sand and salt, and a mass of iron is easier to bear than a man without sense, that is both foolish and wicked.

19 A frame of wood bound together in the foundation of a building shall not be loosed: so neither shall the heart that is established by advised counsel.

20 The thought of him that is wise at all times shall not be depraved by fear.

21 As pales set in high places and plasterings made without cost will not stand against the face of the wind:

22 So also a fearful heart in the imagination of a fool shall not resist against the violence of fear.

23 As a fearful heart in the thought of a fool at all times will not fear: so neither shall he that continueth always in the commandments of God.

24 He that pricketh the eye bringeth out tears: and he that pricketh the heart bringeth forth resentment.

25 He that flingeth a stone at birds shall drive them away: so he that upbraideth his friend breaketh friendship.

26 Although thou hast drawn a sword at a friend, despair not: for there may be a returning. To a friend,

27 If thou hast opened a sad mouth, fear not: for there may be a reconciliation. Except upbraiding, and reproach, and pride, and disclosing of secrets, or a treacherous wound: for in all these cases a friend will flee away.

28 Keep fidelity with a friend in his poverty, that in his prosperity also thou mayst rejoice.

29 In the time of his trouble continue faithful to him: that thou mayst also be heir with him in his inheritance.

30 As the vapour of a chimney and the smoke of the fire goeth up before the fire: so also injurious words, and reproaches, and threats, before blood.

31 I will not be ashamed to salute a friend: neither will I hide myself from

---

Chap. 22. [1] Ecclus. 38, 16. [2] Gen. 1, 10. [3] Prov. 27, 3.

Chap. 21. Ver. 30. *While the ungodly.* He condemneth and curseth himself: inasmuch as by sin he takes part with the devil, and is, at it were, his member and subject.

Chap. 22. Ver. 10. *For the fool.* In the language of the Holy Ghost, he is styled a *fool,* that turns away from God to follow vanity and sin. And what is said by the wise man against *fools* is meant of such fools as these.

his face. And if any evil happened to me by him, I will bear it:

32 But every one that shall hear it will beware of him.

33 [4] Who will set a guard before my mouth, and a sure seal upon my lips, that I fall not by them, and that my tongue destroy me not?

CHAPTER 23

A prayer for grace to flee sin. Cautions against profane swearing and other vices.

O LORD, Father, and sovereign ruler of my life, leave me not to their counsel: nor suffer me to fall by them.

2 Who will set scourges over my thoughts, and the discipline of wisdom over my heart, that they spare me not in their ignorances, and that their sins may not appear:

3 Lest my ignorances increase, and my offences be multiplied, and my sins abound, and I fall before my adversaries, and my enemy rejoice over me?

4 O Lord, Father, and God of my life, leave me not to their devices.

5 Give me not haughtiness of my eyes, and turn away from me all coveting.

6 Take from me the greediness of the belly, and let not the lusts of the flesh take hold of me: and give me not over to a shameless and foolish mind.

7 Hear, O ye children, the discipline of the mouth: and he that will keep it shall not perish by his lips, nor be brought to fall into most wicked works.

8 A sinner is caught in his own vanity: and the proud and the evil speakers shall fall thereby.

9 [1] Let not thy mouth be accustomed to swearing: for in it there are many falls.

10 And let not the naming of God be usual in thy mouth, and meddle not with the names of saints: for thou shalt not escape free from them.

11 For as a slave daily put to the question is never without a blue mark: so every one that sweareth and nameth shall not be wholly pure from sin.

12 A man that sweareth much shall be filled with iniquity: and a scourge shall not depart from his house.

13 And if he make it void, his sin shall be upon him: and if he dissemble it, he offendeth double.

14 And if he swear in vain, he shall

[4] Ps. 140, 3. CHAP. 23. [1] Exod. 20, 7; Matt. 5, 33. [2] 2 Kings, 16, 7. [3] Isai. 29, 15. [4] Lev. 20, 10; Deut. 22, 21.

CHAP. 23. Ver. 1. *By them.* The tongue and the lips, mentioned in the last verse of the foregoing chapter.

Ver. 2. *That they spare me not in their ignorances.* That is, that the scourges and discipline of wisdom may restrain the *ignorances,* that is, the slips and offences which are usually committed by the tongue and the lips.

not be justified: for his house shall be filled with his punishment.

15 There is also another speech opposite to death: let it not be found in the inheritance of Jacob.

16 For from the merciful all these things shall be taken away: and they shall not wallow in sins.

17 Let not thy mouth be accustomed to indiscreet speech: for therein is the word of sin.

18 Remember thy father and thy mother: for thou sittest in the midst of great men.

19 Lest God forget thee in their sight, and thou, by thy daily custom, be infatuated and suffer reproach: and wish that thou hadst not been born, and curse the day of thy nativity.

20 [2] The man that is accustomed to opprobrious words will never be corrected all the days of his life.

21 Two sorts of men multiply sins, and the third bringeth wrath and destruction.

22 A hot soul is a burning fire: it will never be quenched, till it devour some thing.

23 And a man that is wicked in the mouth of his flesh will not leave off till he hath kindled a fire.

24 To a man that is a fornicator all bread is sweet: he will not be weary of sinning unto the end.

25 Every man that passeth beyond his own bed, despising his own soul, and saying: [3] Who seeth me?

26 Darkness compasseth me about, and the walls cover me, and no man seeth me. Whom do I fear? The Most High will not remember my sins.

27 And he understandeth not that his eye seeth all things: for such a man's fear driveth from him the fear of God, and the eyes of men fearing him.

28 And he knoweth not that the eyes of the Lord are far brighter than the sun, beholding round about all the ways of men, and the bottom of the deep, and looking into the hearts of men, into the most hidden parts.

29 For all things were known to the Lord God, before they were created: so also after they were perfected he beholdeth all things.

30 This man shall be punished in the streets of the city, and he shall be chased as a colt: and where he suspected not, he shall be taken.

31 And he shall be in disgrace with all men: because he understood not the fear of the Lord.

32 [4] So every woman also that leaveth her husband, and bringeth in an heir by another.

33 For, first, she hath been unfaithful to the law of the most High: and secondly, she hath offended against her husband: thirdly, she hath fornicated in adultery, and hath gotten her children of another man.

34 This woman shall be brought into the assembly: and inquisition shall be made of her children.

35 Her children shall not take root: and her branches shall bring forth no fruit.

36 She shall leave her memory to be cursed: and her infamy shall not be blotted out.

37 And they that remain shall know that there is nothing better than the fear of God: and that there is nothing sweeter than to have regard to the commandments of the Lord.

38 It is great glory to follow the Lord: for length of days shall be received from him.

CHAPTER 24

Wisdom praiseth herself. Her origin, her dwelling, her dignity, and her fruits.

ꟺISDOM shall praise her own self, and shall be honoured in God, and shall glory in the midst of her people,

2 And shall open her mouth in the churches of the most High, and shall glorify herself in the sight of his power.

3 And in the midst of her own people she shall be exalted, and shall be admired in the holy assembly.

4 And in the multitude of the elect she shall have praise. And among the blessed she shall be blessed, saying:

5 I came out of the mouth of the most High, the firstborn before all creatures.

6 I made that in the heavens there should rise light that never faileth, and as a cloud I covered all the earth.

7 I dwelt in the highest places, and my throne is in a pillar of a cloud.

8 I alone have compassed the circuit of heaven, and have penetrated into the bottom of the deep, and have walked in the waves of the sea,

9 And have stood in all the earth. And in every people,

10 And in every nation I have had the chief rule.

11 And by my power I have trodden under my feet the hearts of all the high and low: and in all these I sought rest, and I shall abide in the inheritance of the Lord.

12 Then the creator of all things commanded and said to me: and he that made me rested in my tabernacle.

13 And he said to me: Let thy dwelling be in Jacob, and thy inheritance in Israel, and take root in my elect.

14 ¹From the beginning, and before the world, was I created, and unto the world to come I shall not cease to be: and in the holy dwelling place I have ministered before him.

15 And so was I established in Sion, and in the holy city likewise I rested: and my power *was* in Jerusalem.

16 And I took root in an honourable people, and in the portion of my God his inheritance: and my abode is in the full assembly of saints.

17 I was exalted like a cedar in Libanus, and as a cypress tree on Mount Sion.

18 I was exalted like a palm tree in Cades, and as a rose plant in Jericho.

19 As a fair olive tree in the plains, and as a plane tree by the water in the streets, was I exalted.

20 I gave a sweet smell like cinnamon, and aromatical balm: I yielded a sweet odour like the best myrrh.

21 And I perfumed my dwelling as storax, and galbanum, and onyx, and aloes, and as the frankincense not cut: and my odour is as the purest balm.

22 I have stretched out my branches as the turpentine tree: and my branches are of honour and grace.

23 As the vine I have brought forth a pleasant odour: and my flowers are the fruit of honour and riches.

24 I am the mother of fair love, and of fear, and of knowledge, and of holy hope.

25 In me is all grace of the way and of the truth: in me is all hope of life and of virtue.

26 Come over to me, all ye that desire me: and be filled with my fruits.

27 For my spirit is sweet above honey: and my inheritance above honey and the honeycomb.

28 My memory is unto everlasting generations.

29 ²They that eat me shall yet hunger: and they that drink me shall yet thirst.

30 He that hearkeneth to me shall not be confounded: and they that work by me shall not sin.

31 They that explain me shall have life everlasting.

32 All these things are the book of life, and the covenant of the most High, and the knowledge of truth.

33 Moses commanded a law in the precepts of justices, and an inheritance to the house of Jacob, and the promises to Israel.

34 He appointed to David his servant to raise up of him a most mighty king,

CHAP. 24. ¹ Prov. 8, 22. ² John, 6, 35. ³ Gen. 2, 11.

CHAP. 24. Ver. 34. *A most mighty king,* namely, Christ, who by his gospel, like an overflowing river, has enriched the earth with heavenly wisdom.

and sitting on the throne of glory for ever.

35 [3] Who filleth up wisdom as the Phison, and as the Tigris in the days of the new fruits.

36 Who maketh understanding to abound as the Euphrates: [4] who multiplied it as the Jordan in the time of harvest.

37 Who sendeth knowledge as the light, and riseth up as Gehon in the time of the vintage.

38 Who first hath perfect knowledge of her: and a weaker shall not search her out.

39 For her thoughts are more vast than the sea: and her counsels more deep than the great ocean.

40 I, wisdom, have poured out rivers.

41 I, like a brook out of a river of a mighty water: I, like a channel of a river, and like an aqueduct, came out of paradise.

42 I said: I will water my garden of plants, and I will water abundantly the fruits of my meadow.

43 And behold my brook became a great river, and my river came near to a sea.

44 For I make doctrine to shine forth to all as the morning light: and I will declare it afar off.

45 I will penetrate to all the lower parts of the earth, and will behold all that sleep, and will enlighten all that hope in the Lord.

46 I will yet pour out doctrine as prophecy, and will leave it to them that seek wisdom, and will not cease to instruct their offspring even to the holy age.

47 [5] See ye that I have not laboured for myself only, but for all that seek out the truth.

CHAPTER 25

Documents of wisdom on several subjects.

WITH three things my spirit is pleased, which are approved before God and men:

2 The concord of brethren, and the love of neighbours, and man and wife that agree well together.

3 Three sorts my soul hateth, and I am greatly grieved at their life:

4 A poor man that is proud: a rich man that is a liar; an old man that is a fool and doting.

5 The things that thou hast not gathered in thy youth, how shalt thou find them in thy old age?

[4] Jos. 3, 15. [5] Ecclus. 33, 18. CHAP. 25. [1] Ecclus. 26, 1. [2] Ecclus. 14, 1; 19, 16; James, 3, 2. [3] Prov. 21, 19. [4] Ecclus. 42, 6.

Ver. 38. *Who first hath perfect knowledge of her.* Christ was the first that had perfect knowledge of heavenly wisdom.

6 O how comely is judgment for a grey head, and for ancients to know counsel!

7 O how comely is wisdom for the aged, and understanding and counsel to men of honour!

8 Much experience is the crown of old men: and the fear of God is their glory.

9 Nine things that are not to be imagined by the heart have I magnified, and the tenth I will utter to men with my tongue.

10 A man that hath joy of his children: and he that liveth and seeth the fall of his enemies.

11 [1] Blessed is he that dwelleth with a wise woman, [2] and that hath not slipped with his tongue, and that hath not served such as are unworthy of him.

12 Blessed is he that findeth a true friend, and that declareth justice to an ear that heareth.

13 How great is he that findeth wisdom and knowledge! But there is none above him that feareth the Lord.

14 The fear of God hath set itself above all things.

15 Blessed is the man to whom it is given to have the fear of God. He that holdeth it, to whom shall he be likened?

16 The fear of God is the beginning of his love: and the beginning of faith is to be fast joined unto it.

17 The sadness of the heart is every plague: and the wickedness of a woman is all evil.

18 And a man will choose any plague, but the plague of the heart:

19 And any wickedness, but the wickedness of a woman:

20 And any affliction, but the affliction from them that hate him:

21 And any revenge, but the revenge of enemies.

22 There is no head worse than the head of a serpent:

23 And there is no anger above the anger of a woman. [3] It will be more agreeable to abide with a lion and a dragon, than to dwell with a wicked woman.

24 The wickedness of a woman changeth her face: and she darkeneth her countenance as a bear, and sheweth it like sackcloth. In the midst of her neighbours,

25 Her husband groaned, and hearing he sighed a little.

26 All malice is short to the malice of a woman: let the lot of sinners fall upon her.

27 As the climbing of a sandy way is to the feet of the aged, so is a wife full of tongue to a quiet man.

28 Look not upon a woman's beauty, and desire not a woman for beauty.

29 ‘ A woman's anger, and impudence, and confusion is great.

30 A woman, if she have superiority, is contrary to her husband.

31 A wicked woman abateth the courage, and maketh a heavy countenance and a wounded heart.

32 Feeble hands and disjointed knees, a woman doth not make her husband happy.

33 ⁵ From the woman came the beginning of sin, and by her we all die.

34 Give no issue to thy water, no, not a little: nor to a wicked woman liberty to gad abroad.

35 If she walk not at thy hand, she will confound thee in the sight of thy enemies.

36 Cut her off from thy flesh, lest she always abuse thee.

CHAPTER 26

Of good and bad women.

HAPPY is the husband of a good wife: for the number of his years is double.

2 A virtuous woman rejoiceth her husband: and shall fulfil the years of his life in peace.

3 A good wife is a good portion: she shall be given in the portion of them that fear God, to a man for *his* good deeds.

4 Rich or poor, if his heart is good, his countenance shall be cheerful at all times.

5 Of three things my heart hath been afraid, and at the fourth my face hath trembled:

6 The accusation of a city, and the gathering together of the people,

7 And a false calumny. All *are* more grievous than death.

8 A jealous woman is the grief and mourning of the heart.

9 With a jealous woman is a scourge of the tongue which communicateth with all.

10 As a yoke of oxen that is moved to and fro, so also is a wicked woman: he that hath hold of her is as he that taketh hold of a scorpion.

11 A drunken woman is a great wrath: and her reproach and shame shall not be hid.

12 The fornication of a woman shall be known by the haughtiness of her eyes, and by her eyelids.

13 ¹ On a daughter that turneth not away herself, set a strict watch: lest finding an opportunity she abuse herself.

14 Take heed of the impudence of her eyes: and wonder not if she slight thee.

15 She will open her mouth as a thirsty traveller to the fountain, and will drink of every water near her, and will sit down by every hedge, and open her quiver against every arrow: until she fail.

16 The grace of a diligent woman shall delight her husband, and shall fat his bones.

17 Her discipline is the gift of God.

18 *Such is* a wise and silent woman: *and* there is nothing so much worth as a well instructed soul.

19 A holy and shamefaced woman is grace upon grace.

20 And no price is worthy of a continent soul.

21 As the sun when it riseth to the world in the high places of God, so is the beauty of a good wife for the ornament of her house.

22 As the lamp shining upon the holy candlestick, so is the beauty of the face in a ripe age.

23 As golden pillars upon bases of silver, so are the firm feet upon the soles of a steady woman.

24 As everlasting foundations upon a solid rock, so the commandments of God in the heart of a holy woman.

25 At two things my heart is grieved, and the third bringeth anger upon me:

26 A man of war fainting through poverty: and a man of sense despised:

27 And he that passeth over from justice to sin. God hath prepared such an one for the sword.

28 Two sorts of *callings* have appeared to me hard and dangerous: a merchant is hardly free from negligence, and a huckster shall not be justified from the sins of the lips.

CHAPTER 27

Dangers of sin from several heads. The fear of God is the best preservative. He that diggeth a pit, shall fall into it.

THROUGH poverty many have sinned: and he that seeketh to be enriched turneth away his eye.

2 As a stake sticketh fast in the midst of the joining of stones, so also, in the midst of selling and buying sin shall stick fast.

3 Sin shall be destroyed with the sinner.

---

⁵ Gen. 3, 6. CHAP. 26. ¹ Ecclus. 42, 11.

CHAP. 26. Ver. 28. *From negligence.* That is, from the neglect of the service of God: because the eager pursuit of the mammon of this world, is apt to make men of that calling forget the great duties of loving God above all things, and their neighbours as themselves.—*A huckster*, or, a retailer of wine. Men of that profession are both greatly exposed to danger of sin themselves, and are too often accessory to the sins of others.

4 Unless thou hold thyself diligently in the fear of the Lord, thy house shall quickly be overthrown.

5 As when one sifteth with a sieve, the dust will remain: so will the perplexity of a man in his thoughts.

6 The furnace trieth the potter's vessels: and the trial of affliction just men.

7 As the dressing of a tree sheweth the fruit thereof, so a word out of the thought of the heart of man.

8 Praise not a man before he speaketh: for this is the trial of men.

9 If thou followest justice, thou shalt obtain her, and shalt put her on as a long robe of honour: and thou shalt dwell with her. And she shall protect thee for ever: and in the day of acknowledgment thou shalt find a strong foundation.

10 Birds resort unto their like: so truth will return to them that practise her.

11 The lion always lieth in wait for prey: so do sins for them that work iniquities.

12 A holy man continueth in wisdom as the sun: but a fool is changed as the moon.

13 In the midst of the unwise keep in the word till its time: but be continually among men that think.

14 The discourse of sinners is hateful: and their laughter is at the pleasures of sin.

15 The speech that sweareth much shall make the hair of the head stand upright: and its irreverence shall make one stop his ears.

16 In the quarrels of the proud is the shedding of blood: and their cursing is a grievous hearing.

17 He that discloseth the secret of a friend loseth his credit: and shall never find a friend to his mind.

18 Love thy neighbour: and be joined to him with fidelity.

19 But if thou discover his secrets, follow no more after him.

20 For as a man that destroyeth his friend, so also is he that destroyeth the friendship of his neighbour.

21 And as one that letteth a bird go out of his hand so hast thou let thy neighbour go: and thou shalt not get him again.

22 Follow after him no more, for he is gone afar off: he is fled, as a roe escaped out of the snare; because his soul is wounded.

23 Thou canst no more bind him up. And of a curse there is reconciliation:

24 But to disclose the secrets of a friend leaveth no hope to an unhappy soul.

25 He that winketh with the eye forgeth wicked things: and no man will cast him off.

26 In the sight of thy eyes he will sweeten his mouth, and will admire thy words: but at the last he will writhe his mouth, and on thy words he will lay a stumbling-block.

27 I have hated many things, but not like him: and the Lord will hate him.

28 If one cast a stone on high, it will fall upon his own head: and the deceitful stroke will wound the deceitful.

29 He that diggeth a pit shall fall into it: and he that setteth a stone for his neighbour shall stumble upon it: and he that layeth a snare for another shall perish in it.

30 A mischievous counsel shall be rolled back upon the author: and he shall not know from whence it cometh to him.

31 Mockery and reproach are of the proud: and vengeance as a lion shall lie in wait for him.

32 They shall perish in a snare that are delighted with the fall of the just: and sorrow shall consume them before they die.

33 Anger and fury are both of them abominable: and the sinful man shall be subject to them.

CHAPTER 28
Lessons against revenge and quarrels. The evils of the tongue.

HE [1] that seeketh to revenge himself shall find vengeance from the Lord: and he will surely keep his sins *in remembrance.*

2 Forgive thy neighbour if he hath hurt thee: and then shall thy sins be forgiven to thee when thou prayest.

3 Man to man reserveth anger: And doth he seek remedy of God?

4 He hath no mercy on a man like himself: And doth he entreat for his own sins?

5 He that is but flesh, nourisheth anger: And doth he ask forgiveness of God? Who shall obtain pardon for his sins?

6 Remember thy last things, and let enmity cease:

7 For corruption and death hang over in his commandments.

8 Remember the fear of God: and be not angry with thy neighbour.

CHAP. 28. [1] Deut. 32, 35; Matt. 6, 14; Mark, 11, 25; Rom. 12, 19.

CHAP. 27. Ver. 23. *And of a curse there is reconciliation.* That is, it is easier to obtain a reconciliation after a curse than after disclosing a secret.

CHAP. 28. Ver. 7. *In his commandments.* Supply the sentence out of the Greek thus: Remember corruption and death, and *abide in the commandments.*

9 Remember the covenant of the most High: and overlook the ignorance of thy neighbour.

10 Refrain from strife: and thou shalt diminish *thy* sins.

11 For a passionate man kindleth strife: and a sinful man will trouble his friends and bring in debate in the midst of them that are at peace.

12 For as the wood of the forest is, so the fire burneth: and as a man's strength is, so shall his anger be: and according to his riches, he shall increase his anger.

13 A hasty contention kindleth a fire: and a hasty quarrel sheddeth blood: and a tongue that beareth witness bringeth death.

14 If thou blow the spark, it shall burn as a fire: and if thou spit upon it, it shall be quenched. Both come out of the mouth.

15 The whisperer and the double tongued is accursed: for he hath troubled many that were at peace.

16 The tongue of a third person hath disquieted many and scattered them from nation to nation.

17 It hath destroyed the strong cities of the rich and hath overthrown the houses of great men.

18 It hath cut in pieces the forces of people and undone strong nations.

19 The tongue of a third person hath cast out valiant women and deprived them of their labours.

20 He that hearkeneth to it shall never have rest: neither shall he have a friend in whom he may repose.

21 The stroke of a whip maketh a blue mark: but the stroke of the tongue will break the bones.

22 Many have fallen by the edge of the sword: but not so many as have perished by their own tongue.

23 Blessed is he that is defended from a wicked tongue, that hath not passed into the wrath thereof, and that hath not drawn the yoke thereof, and hath not been bound in its bands.

24 For its yoke is a yoke of iron: and its bands are bands of brass.

25 The death thereof is a most evil death: and hell is preferable to it.

26 Its continuance shall not be for a long time, but it shall possess the ways of the unjust: and the just shall not be burnt with its flame.

27 They that forsake God shall fall into it: and it shall burn in them, and shall not be quenched. And it shall be sent upon them as a lion: and as a leopard it shall tear them.

28 Hedge in thy ears with thorns, hear not a wicked tongue, and make doors and bars to thy mouth.

29 Melt down thy gold and silver, and make a balance for thy words, and a just bridle for thy mouth.

30 And take heed lest thou slip with thy tongue and fall in the sight of thy enemies who lie in wait for thee; and thy fall be incurable unto death.

CHAPTER 29

Of charity in lending money, and justice in repaying. Of alms, and of being surety.

HE that sheweth mercy lendeth to his neighbour: and he that is stronger in hand keepeth the commandments.

2 Lend to thy neighbour in the time of his need: and pay thou thy neighbour again in due time.

3 Keep thy word and deal faithfully with him: and thou shalt always find that which is necessary for thee.

4 Many have looked upon a thing lent as a thing found and have given trouble to them that helped them.

5 Till they receive, they kiss the hands of the lender, and in promises they humble their voice.

6 But when they should repay, they will ask time, and will return tedious and murmuring words, and will complain of the time.

7 And if he be able to pay, he will stand off: he will scarce pay one half, and will count it as if he had found it.

8 But if not, he will defraud him of his money: and he shall get him for an enemy without cause.

9 And he will pay him with reproaches and curses: and instead of honour and good turn will repay him injuries.

10 Many have refused to lend, not out of wickedness: but they were afraid to be defrauded without cause.

11 But yet towards the poor be thou more hearty: and delay not to shew him mercy.

12 Help the poor because of the commandment: and send him not away empty handed because of his poverty.

13 Lose thy money for thy brother and thy friend: and hide it not under a stone to be lost.

14 [1] Place thy treasure in the commandments of the most High: and it shall bring thee more profit than gold.

15 Shut up alms in the heart of the poor: and it shall obtain help for thee against all evil.

16 Better than the shield of the mighty and better than the spear:

17 It shall fight for thee against thy enemy.

CHAP. 29. [1] Tob. 4, 11; Ecclus. 17, 18.

CHAP. 29. Ver. 1. *And he that is stronger in hand.* That is, he that is hearty and bountiful in lending to his neighbour in his necessity.

18 A good man is surety for his neighbour: and he that hath lost shame will leave *him* to himself.

19 Forget not the kindness of thy surety: for he hath given his life for thee.

20 The sinner and the unclean fleeth from his surety.

21 A sinner attributeth to himself the goods of his surety: and he that is of an unthankful mind will leave him that delivered him.

22 A man is surety for his neighbour: and when he hath lost all shame, he shall forsake him.

23 Evil suretyship hath undone many of good estate: and hath tossed them as a wave of the sea.

24 It hath made powerful men to go from place to place round about: and they have wandered in strange countries.

25 A sinner that transgresseth the commandment of the Lord shall fall into an evil suretyship: and he that undertaketh many things shall fall into judgment.

26 Recover thy neighbour according to thy power: and take heed to thyself that thou fall not.

27 The chief thing for man's life is water, and bread, and clothing, and a house to cover shame.

28 ²Better is the poor man's fare under a roof of boards than sumptuous cheer abroad in another man's house.

29 Be contented with little instead of much: and thou shalt not hear the reproach of going abroad.

30 It is a miserable life to go as a guest from house to house: for where a man is a stranger, he shall not deal confidently nor open his mouth.

31 He shall entertain and feed and give drink to the unthankful, and moreover he shall hear bitter words:

32 Go, stranger, and furnish the table, and give others to eat what thou hast in thy hand.

33 Give place to the honourable presence of my friends; for I want my house, my brother being to be lodged with me.

34 These things are grievous to a man of understanding: the upbraiding of houseroom, and the reproaching of the lender.

CHAPTER 30

Of correction of children. Health is better than wealth. Excessive grief is hurtful.

HE ¹that loveth his son frequently chastiseth him: that he may rejoice in his latter end and not grope after the doors of his neighbours.

² Ecclus. 39, 31. Chap. 30. ¹ Prov. 13, 24; 23, 13. ² Deut. 6, 7. ³ Ecclus. 7, 25. ⁴ Dan. 14, 6. ⁵ Ecclus. 20, 2. ⁶ Prov. 12, 15, 13; 17, 22.

2 He that instructeth his son shall be praised in him and shall glory in him in the midst of them of his household.

3 ²He that teacheth his son maketh his enemy jealous: and in the midst of his friends he shall glory in him.

4 His father is dead, and he is as if he were not dead: for he hath left one behind that is like himself.

5 While he lived, he saw and rejoiced in him: and when he died, he was not sorrowful, neither was he confounded before his enemies.

6 For he left behind him a defender of his house against his enemies, and one that will requite kindness to his friends.

7 For the souls of his sons he shall bind up his wounds: and at every cry his bowels shall be troubled.

8 A horse not broken becometh stubborn: and a child left to himself will become headstrong.

9 Give thy son his way, and he shall make thee afraid: play with him, and he shall make thee sorrowful.

10 Laugh not with him: lest thou have sorrow, and at the last thy teeth be set on edge.

11 Give him not liberty in his youth: and wink not at his devices.

12 ³Bow down his neck while he is young, and beat his sides while he is a child: lest he grow stubborn, and regard thee not, and so be a sorrow of heart to thee.

13 Instruct thy son, and labour about him: lest his lewd behaviour be an offence to thee.

14 Better is a poor man who is sound and strong of constitution than a rich man who is weak and afflicted with evils.

15 Health of the soul in holiness of justice is better than all gold and silver: and a sound body than immense revenues.

16 There is no riches above the riches of the health of the body: and there is no pleasure above the joy of the heart.

17 Better is death than a bitter life: and everlasting rest than continual sickness.

18 Good things that are hidden in a mouth that is shut are as messes of meat set about a grave.

19 ⁴What good shall an offering do to an idol? For it can neither eat, nor smell.

20 So is he that is persecuted by the Lord, bearing the reward of his iniquity.

21 ⁵He seeth with his eyes and groaneth, as an eunuch embracing a virgin and sighing.

22 ⁶Give not up thy soul to sadness: and afflict not thy self in thy own counsel.

23 The joyfulness of the heart is the life of a man and a never failing treasure of holiness: and the joy of a man is length of life.

24 Have pity on thy own soul, pleasing God, and contain thyself. Gather up thy heart in his holiness: and drive away sadness far from thee.

25 [7] For sadness hath killed many: and there is no profit in it.

26 Envy and anger shorten a man's days: and pensiveness will bring old age before the time.

27 A cheerful and good heart is always feasting: for his banquets are prepared with diligence.

CHAPTER 31

Of the desire of riches, and of moderation in eating and drinking.

WATCHING for riches consumeth the flesh: and the thought thereof driveth away sleep.

2 The thinking beforehand turneth away the understanding: and a grievous sickness maketh the soul sober.

3 The rich man hath laboured in gathering riches together: and when he resteth he shall be filled with his goods.

4 The poor man hath laboured in his low way of life: and in the end he is still poor.

5 He that loveth gold shall not be justified: and he that followeth after corruption shall be filled with it.

6 [1] Many have been brought to fall for gold: and the beauty thereof hath been their ruin.

7 Gold is a stumbling-block to them that sacrifice to it. Woe to them that eagerly follow after it: and every fool shall perish by it.

8 Blessed is the rich man that is found without blemish: and that hath not gone after gold nor put his trust in money nor in treasures.

9 Who is he, and we will praise him? For he hath done wonderful things in his life.

10 Who hath been tried thereby, and made perfect, he shall have glory everlasting. He that could have transgressed, and hath not transgressed: and could do evil things and hath not done them.

11 Therefore are his goods established in the Lord: and all the church of the saints shall declare his alms.

12 Art thou set at a great table? Be not the first to open thy mouth upon it.

13 Say not: There are many things which are upon it.

14 Remember that a wicked eye is evil.

15 What is created more wicked than an eye? Therefore shall it weep over all the face when it shall see.

16 Stretch not out thy hand first: lest being disgraced with envy thou be put to confusion.

17 Be not hasty in a feast.

18 Judge of the disposition of thy neighbour by thyself.

19 Use as a frugal man the things that are set before thee: lest if thou eatest much, thou be hated.

20 Leave off first, for manners' sake and exceed not: lest thou offend.

21 And if thou sittest among many, reach not thy hand out first of all: and be not the first to ask for drink.

22 How sufficient is a little wine for a man well taught! And in sleeping thou shalt not be uneasy with it: and thou shalt feel no pain.

23 Watching and choler and gripes are with an intemperate man:

24 Sound and wholesome sleep with a moderate man. He shall sleep till morning: and his soul shall be delighted with him.

25 And if thou hast been forced to eat much, arise, go out, and vomit: and it shall refresh thee, and thou shalt not bring sickness upon thy body.

26 Hear me, my son, and despise me not: and in the end thou shalt find my words.

27 In all thy works be quick: and no infirmity shall come to thee.

28 The lips of many shall bless him that is liberal of his bread: and the testimony of his truth is faithful.

29 Against him that is niggardly of his bread, the city will murmur: and the testimony of his niggardliness is true.

30 Challenge not them that love wine: [2] for wine hath destroyed very many.

31 Fire trieth hard iron: so wine drunk to excess shall rebuke the hearts of the proud.

32 Wine taken with sobriety is equal life to men: if thou drink it moderately, thou shalt be sober.

33 What is his life who is diminished with wine?

34 What taketh away life? Death.

35 [3] Wine was created from the beginning to make men joyful, and not to make them drunk.

36 Wine drunken with moderation is the joy of the soul and the heart.

37 Sober drinking is health to soul and body.

38 Wine drunken with excess raiseth quarrels and wrath and many ruins.

[7] 2 Cor. 7, 10. CHAP. 31. [1] Ecclus. 8, 3. [2] Judith 13, 4. [3] Ps. 103, 15; Prov. 31, 4.

39 Wine drunken with excess is bitterness of the soul.

40 The heat of drunkenness is the stumbling-block of the fool, lessening strength and causing wounds.

41 Rebuke not thy neighbour in a banquet of wine: and despise him not in his mirth.

42 Speak not to him words of reproach: and press him not in demanding again.

CHAPTER 32

Lessons for superiors and inferiors. Advantages of fearing God, and doing nothing without counsel.

HAVE they made thee ruler? Be not lifted up: be among them as one of them.

2 Have care of them, and so sit down: and when thou hast acquitted thyself of all thy charge, take thy place.

3 That thou mayest rejoice for them, and receive a crown as an ornament of grace, and get the honour of the contribution.

4 Speak, thou that art elder: for it becometh thee

5 To speak the first word with careful knowledge: and hinder not music.

6 Where there is no hearing, pour not out words: and be not lifted up out of season with thy wisdom.

7 A concert of music in a banquet of wine is as a carbuncle set in gold.

8 As a signet of an emerald in a work of gold: so is the melody of music with pleasant and moderate wine.

9 Hear in silence: and for thy reverence good grace shall come to thee.

10 Young man, scarcely speak in thy own cause.

11 If thou be asked twice, let thy answer be short.

12 In many things be as if thou wert ignorant: and hear in silence and withal seeking.

13 In the company of great men take not upon thee: and when the ancients are present, speak not much.

14 Before a storm goeth lightning: and before shamefacedness goeth favour: and for thy reverence good grace shall come to thee

15 And at the time of rising be not slack: but be first to run home to thy house. And there withdraw thyself, and there take thy pastime.

16 And do what thou hast a mind, but not in sin or proud speech.

17 And for all these things bless the Lord that made thee and that replenisheth thee with all his good things.

CHAP. 33. [1] Ecclus. 21, 17.
CHAP. 32. Ver. 27. *In faith.* That is, follow sincerely thy soul in her faith and conscience.

18 He that feareth the Lord will receive his discipline: and they that will seek him early shall find a blessing.

19 He that seeketh the law shall be filled with it: and he that dealeth deceitfully shall meet with a stumbling-block therein.

20 They that fear the Lord shall find just judgment, and shall kindle justice as a light.

21 A sinful man will flee reproof and will find an excuse according to his will.

22 A man of counsel will not neglect understanding: a strange and proud man will not dread fear:

23 Even after he hath done with fear without counsel, he shall be controlled by the things of his own seeking.

24 My son, do thou nothing without counsel: and thou shalt not repent when thou hast done.

25 Go not in the way of ruin: and thou shalt not stumble against the stones. Trust not thyself to a rugged way: lest thou set a stumbling-block to thy soul.

26 And beware of thy own children: and take heed of them of thy household.

27 In every work of thine regard thy soul in faith: for this is the keeping of the commandments.

28 He that believeth God taketh heed to the commandments: and he that trusteth in him shall fare never the worse.

CHAPTER 33

The fear of God is the best security. Times and men are in the hands of God. Take care of thyself as long as thou livest, and look to thy servants.

NO evils shall happen to him that feareth the Lord: but in temptation God will keep him and deliver him from evils.

2 A wise man hateth not the commandments and justices: and he shall not be dashed in pieces as a ship in a storm.

3 A man of understanding is faithful to the law of God: and the law is faithful to him.

4 He that cleareth up a question shall prepare what to say: and so, having prayed, he shall be heard, and shall keep discipline, and then he shall answer.

5 [1] The heart of a fool is as a wheel of a cart: and his thoughts are like a rolling axletree.

6 A friend that is a mocker is like a stallion horse: he neigheth under every one that sitteth upon him.

7 Why doth one day excel another, and one light another, and one year another year, when all come of the sun?

8 By the knowledge of the Lord they

were distinguished, the sun being made and keeping his commandment.

9 And he ordered the seasons and holidays of them: and in them they celebrated festivals at an hour.

10 Some of them God made high and great days, and some of them he put in the number of ordinary days. And all men are from the ground [2] and out of the earth, from whence Adam was created.

11 With much knowledge the Lord hath divided them and diversified their ways.

12 Some of them hath he blessed and exalted: and some of them hath he sanctified and set near himself: and some of them hath he cursed and brought low and turned them from their station.

13 [3] As the potter's clay is in his hand, to fashion and order it:

14 All his ways are according to his ordering. So man is in the hand of him that made him: and he will render to him according to his judgment.

15 Good is set against evil, and life against death: so also is the sinner against a just man. And so look upon all the works of the most High. Two and two, and one against another.

16 And I awaked last of all, and as one that gathereth after the grape-gatherers.

17 In the blessing of God I also have hoped: and as one that gathereth grapes, have I filled the winepress.

18 [4] See that I have not laboured for myself only: but for all that seek discipline.

19 Hear me, ye great men, and all ye people: and hearken with your ears, ye rulers of the church.

20 Give not to son or wife, brother or friend, power over thee while thou livest; and give not thy estate to another: lest thou repent, and thou entreat for the same.

21 As long as thou livest and hast breath in thee, let no man change thee.

22 For it is better that thy children should ask of thee than that thou look toward the hands of thy children.

23 In all thy works keep the pre-eminence.

24 Let no stain sully thy glory. In the time when thou shalt end the days of thy life and in the time of thy decease, distribute thy inheritance.

25 Fodder and a wand and a burden are for an ass: bread and correction and work for a slave.

26 He worketh under correction and seeketh to rest: let his hands be idle, and he seeketh liberty.

27 The yoke and the thong bend a stiff neck: and continual labours bow a slave.

28 Torture and fetters are for a malicious slave: send him to work, that he be not idle.

29 For idleness hath taught much evil.

30 Set him to work: for so it is fit for him. And if he be not obedient, bring him down with fetters: but be not excessive towards any one, and do no grievous thing without judgment.

31 [5] If thou have a faithful servant, let him be to thee as thy own soul: treat him as a brother: because in the blood of thy soul thou hast gotten him.

32 If thou hurt him unjustly, he will run away.

33 And if he rise up and depart, thou knowest not whom to ask, and in what way to seek him.

CHAPTER 34

The vanity of dreams. The advantage of experience and of the fear of God.

THE hopes of a man that is void of understanding are vain and deceitful: and dreams lift up fools.

2 The man that giveth heed to lying visions is like to him that catcheth at a shadow and followeth after the wind.

3 The vision of dreams is the resemblance of one thing to another: as when a man's likeness is before the face of a man.

4 What can be made clean by the unclean? And what truth can come from that which is false?

5 Deceitful divinations and lying omens and the dreams of evildoers are vanity:

6 And the heart fancieth as that of a woman in travail. Except it be a vision sent forth from the most High, set not thy heart upon them.

7 For dreams have deceived many: and they have failed that put their trust in them.

8 The word of the law shall be fulfilled without a lie: and wisdom shall be made plain in the mouth of the faithful.

9 What doth he know that hath not been tried? A man that hath much experience shall think of many things: and he that hath learned many things shall shew forth understanding.

10 He that hath no experience knoweth little: and he that hath been experienced in many things multiplieth prudence.

[2] Gen. 2, 7.   [3] Rom. 9, 21.   [4] Ecclus. 24, 47. [5] Ecclus. 7, 23.

CHAP. 33. Ver. 21. *Change thee.* That is, so as to have this power over thee.
Ver. 23. *The pre-eminence.* That is, be master in thy own house, and part not with thy authority.

11 He that hath not been tried, what manner of things doth he know? He that hath been surprised shall abound with subtlety.

12 I have seen many things by travelling, and many customs of things.

13 Sometimes I have been in danger of death for these things: and I have been delivered by the grace of God.

14 The spirit of those that fear God is sought after: and by his regard shall be blessed.

15 For their hope is on him that saveth them: and the eyes of God are upon them that love him.

16 He that feareth the Lord shall tremble at nothing and shall not be afraid: for he is his hope.

17 The soul of him that feareth the Lord is blessed.

18 To whom doth he look, and who is his strength?

19 [1] The eyes of the Lord are upon them that fear him. He is their powerful protector and strong stay, a defence from the heart and a cover from the sun at noon,

20 A preservation from stumbling and a help from falling: he raiseth up the soul and enlighteneth the eyes and giveth health and life and blessing.

21 [2] The offering of him that sacrificeth of a thing wrongfully gotten is stained: and the mockeries of the unjust are not acceptable.

22 The Lord is only for them that wait upon him in the way of truth and justice.

23 [3] The most High approveth not the gifts of the wicked: neither hath he respect to the oblations of the unjust; nor will he be pacified for sins by the multitude of their sacrifices.

24 He that offereth sacrifice of the goods of the poor is as one that sacrificeth the son in the presence of his father.

25 The bread of the needy is the life of the poor: he that defraudeth them thereof is a man of blood.

26 He that taketh away the bread gotten by sweat is like him that killeth his neighbour.

27 He that sheddeth blood [4] and he that defraudeth the labourer of his hire are brothers.

28 When one buildeth up and another pulleth down what profit have they but the labour?

29 When one prayeth and another curseth whose voice will God hear?

30 He that washeth himself after touching the dead, if he toucheth him again, what doth his washing avail?

31 [5] So a man that fasteth for his sins, and doth the same again, what doth his humbling himself profit him? Who will hear his prayer?

CHAPTER 35

What sacrifices are pleasing to God.

HE that keepeth the law multiplieth offerings.

2 [1] It is a wholesome sacrifice to take heed to the commandments, and to depart from all iniquity.

3 And to depart from injustices is to offer a propitiatory sacrifice for injustices, and a begging of pardon for sins.

4 He shall return thanks, that offereth fine flour: and he that doth mercy offereth sacrifice.

5 [2] To depart from iniquity is that which pleaseth the Lord: and to depart from injustice is an entreaty for sins.

6 [3] Thou shalt not appear empty in the sight of the Lord.

7 For all these things are to be done because of the commandment of God.

8 The oblation of the just maketh the altar fat: and is an odour of sweetness in the sight of the most High.

9 The sacrifice of the just is acceptable: and the Lord will not forget the memorial thereof.

10 Give glory to God with a good heart: and diminish not the firstfruits of thy hands.

11 [4] In every gift shew a cheerful countenance: and sanctify thy tithes with joy.

12 Give to the most High according to what he hath given to thee: and with a good eye do according to the ability of thy hands.

13 For the Lord maketh recompense and will give thee seven times as much.

14 [5] Do not offer wicked gifts: for such he will not receive.

15 And look not upon an unjust sacrifice, for the Lord is judge: [6] and there is not with him respect of person.

16 The Lord will not accept any person against a poor man: and he will hear the prayer of him that is wronged.

17 He will not despise the prayers of the fatherless: nor the widow, when she poureth out her complaint.

18 Do not the widow's tears run down the cheek, and her cry against him that causeth them to fall?

19 For from the cheek they go up even to heaven: and the Lord that heareth will not be delighted with them.

CHAP. 34. [1] Ps. 33, 16. [2] Prov. 21, 27. [3] Prov. 15, 8. [4] Deut. 24, 14; Ecclus. 7, 21. [5] 2 Peter, 2, 21. CHAP. 35. [1] 1 Kings, 15, 22. [2] Jer. 7, 3; 26, 13. [3] Exod. 23, 15; 34, 20; Deut. 16, 16. [4] 2 Cor. 9, 7; Tob. 4, 9. [5] Lev. 22, 21; Deut. 15, 21. [6] Deut. 10, 17; 2 Par. 19, 7; Job, 34, 19; Wisd. 6, 8; Rom. 2, 11; Gal. 2, 6; Col. 3, 25; Acts, 10, 34; 1 Peter, 1, 17.

20 He that adoreth God with joy shall be accepted: and his prayer shall approach even to the clouds.

21 The prayer of him that humbleth himself shall pierce the clouds: and till it come nigh he will not be comforted: and he will not depart till the most High behold.

22 And the Lord will not be slack: but will judge for the just and will do judgment. And the Almighty will not have patience with them: that he may crush their back.

23 And he will repay vengeance to the Gentiles, till he have taken away the multitude of the proud, and broken the sceptres of the unjust:

24 Till he have rendered to men according to their deeds, and according to the works of Adam, and according to his presumption:

25 Till he have judged the cause of his people. And he shall delight the just with his mercy.

26 The mercy of God is beautiful in the time of affliction, as a cloud of rain in the time of drought.

CHAPTER 36

A prayer for the church of God. Of a good heart, and a good wife.

HAVE mercy upon us, O God of all, and behold us, and shew us the light of thy mercies.

2 And send thy fear upon the nations that have not sought after thee: that they may know that there is no God beside thee, and that they may shew forth thy wonders.

3 Lift up thy hand over the strange nations: that they may see thy power.

4 For as thou hast been sanctified in us in their sight, so thou shalt be magnified among them in our presence:

5 That they may know thee, as we also have known thee; that there is no God beside thee, O Lord.

6 Renew thy signs, and work new miracles.

7 Glorify thy hand and thy right arm.

8 Raise up indignation and pour out wrath.

9 Take away the adversary and crush the enemy.

10 Hasten the time and remember the end, that they may declare thy wonderful works.

11 Let him that escapeth be consumed by the rage of the fire: and let them perish that oppress thy people.

12 Crush the head of the princes of the enemies that say: There is no other beside us.

13 Gather together all the tribes of Jacob, that they may know that there is no God besides thee, and may declare thy great works: and thou shalt inherit them as from the beginning.

14 Have mercy on thy people, upon whom thy name is invoked: and upon Israel, [1] whom thou hast raised up to be thy firstborn.

15 Have mercy on Jerusalem, the city which thou hast sanctified, the city of thy rest.

16 Fill Sion with thy unspeakable words, and thy people with thy glory.

17 Give testimony to them that are thy creatures from the beginning: and raise up the prophecies which the former prophets spoke in thy name.

18 Reward them that patiently wait for thee, that thy prophets may be found faithful: and hear the prayers of thy servants,

19 [2] According to the blessing of Aaron over thy people. And direct us into the way of justice: and let all know that dwell upon the earth, that thou art God, the beholder of all ages.

20 The belly will devour all meat: yet one is better than another.

21 The palate tasteth venison: and the wise heart false speeches.

22 A perverse heart will cause grief: and a man of experience will resist it.

23 A woman will receive every man: yet one daughter is better than another.

24 The beauty of a woman cheereth the countenance of her husband: and a man desireth nothing more.

25 If she have a tongue that can cure, and likewise mitigate and shew mercy: her husband is not like other men.

26 He that possesseth a good wife beginneth a possession: she is a help like to himself and a pillar of rest.

27 Where there is no hedge, the possession shall be spoiled: and where there is no wife, he mourneth that is in want.

28 Who will trust him that hath no rest, and that lodgeth wheresoever the night taketh him: as a robber well appointed, that skippeth from city to city.

CHAPTER 37

Of the choice of friends and counsellors.

EVERY friend will say: I also am his friend. But there is a friend that is only a friend in name. Is not this a grief even to death?

2 But a companion and a friend shall be turned to an enemy.

CHAP. 36. [1] Exod. 4, 22. [2] Num. 6, 24.

CHAP. 36. Ver. 23. *A woman will receive every man.* That is, any man that her parents propose to her to marry, though she does not like him, but marries in obedience to her parents, who make the choice for her.

3 O wicked presumption, whence camest thou, to cover the earth with thy malice and deceitfulness?

4 There is a companion who rejoiceth with his friend in his joys: but in the time of trouble, he will be against him.

5 There is a companion who condoleth with his friend for his belly's sake: and he will take up a shield against the enemy.

6 Forget not thy friend in thy mind: and be not unmindful of him in thy riches.

7 Consult not with him that layeth a snare for thee: and hide thy counsel from them that envy thee.

8 Every counsellor giveth out counsel: but there is one that is a counsellor for himself.

9 Beware of a counsellor, and know before what need he hath: for he will devise to his own mind.

10 Lest he thrust a stake into the ground and say to thee:

11 Thy way is good: and then stand on the other side to see what shall befall thee.

12 Treat not with a man without religion concerning holiness, nor with an unjust man concerning justice, nor with a woman touching her of whom she is jealous, nor with a coward concerning war, nor with a merchant about traffic, nor with a buyer of selling, nor with an envious man of giving thanks,

13 Nor with the ungodly of piety, nor with the dishonest of honesty, nor with the field labourer of every work.

14 Nor with him that worketh by the year of the finishing of the year, nor with an idle servant of much business: give no heed to these in any matter of counsel.

15 But be continually with a holy man, whomsoever thou shalt know to observe the fear of God.

16 Whose soul is according to thy own soul: and who, when thou shalt stumble in the dark, will be sorry for thee.

17 And establish within thyself a heart of good counsel: for there is no other thing of more worth to thee than it.

18 The soul of a holy man discovereth sometimes true things: more than seven watchmen that sit in a high place to watch.

19 But above all these things, pray to the most High, that he may direct thy way in truth.

20 In all thy works let the true word go before thee, and steady counsel before every action.

21 A wicked word shall change the heart, out of which four manner of things arise: Good and evil, life and death. And the tongue is continually the ruler of them. There is a man that is subtle and a teacher of many, and yet is unprofitable to his own soul.

22 A skilful man hath taught many: and is sweet to his own soul.

23 He that speaketh sophistically is hateful: he shall be destitute of every thing.

24 Grace is not given him from the Lord: for he is deprived of all wisdom.

25 There is a wise man that is wise to his own soul: and the fruit of his understanding is commendable.

26 A wise man instructeth his own people: and the fruits of his understanding are faithful.

27 A wise man shall be filled with blessings: and they that see shall praise him.

28 The life of a man is in the number of his days: but the days of Israel are innumerable.

29 A wise man shall inherit honour among his people: and his name shall live for ever.

30 My son, prove thy soul in thy life: and if it be wicked, give it no power.

31 For all things are not expedient for all: and every kind pleaseth not every soul.

32 Be not greedy in any feasting: and pour not out thyself upon any meat:

33 For in many meats, there will be sickness, and greediness will turn to choler.

34 By surfeiting many have perished: but he that is temperate, shall prolong life.

CHAPTER 38

Of physicians and medicines. What is to be done in sickness, and how we are to mourn for the dead. Of the employments of labourers and artificers.

ᴴONOUR the physician for the need thou hast of him: for the most High hath created him.

2 For all healing is from God: and he shall receive gifts of the king.

3 The skill of the physician shall lift up his head: and in the sight of great men he shall be praised.

4 The most High hath created medicines out of the earth: and a wise man will not abhor them.

5 ¹ Was not bitter water made sweet with wood?

6 The virtue of these things is come to the knowledge of men: and the most High hath given knowledge to men,

that he may be honoured in his wonders.

7 By these he shall cure and shall allay their pains: and *of these* the apothecary shall make sweet confections and shall make up ointments of health. And of his works there shall be no end:

8 For the peace of God *is* over all the face of the earth.

9 [2]My son, in thy sickness, neglect not thyself: but pray to the Lord and he shall heal thee.

10 Turn away from sin and order thy hands aright: and cleanse thy heart from all offence.

11 Give a sweet savour and a memorial of fine flour, and make a fat offering: and then give place to the physician.

12 For the Lord created him: and let him not depart from thee, for his works are necessary.

13 For there is a time when thou must fall into their hands.

14 And they shall beseech the Lord that he would prosper what they give for ease and remedy, for their conversation.

15 He that sinneth in the sight of his Maker shall fall into the hands of the physician.

16 My son, shed tears over the dead, and begin to lament as if thou hadst suffered some great harm: and according to judgment cover his body and neglect not his burial.

17 And for *fear of* being ill spoken of, weep bitterly for a day: and then comfort thyself in thy sadness.

18 And make mourning for him, according to his merit, for a day, or two, for fear of detraction.

19 [3]For of sadness cometh death, and it overwhelmeth the strength: and the sorrow of the heart boweth down the neck.

20 In withdrawing aside sorrow remaineth: and the substance of the poor is according to his heart.

21 Give not up thy heart to sadness, but drive it from thee: and remember the latter end.

22 Forget *it* not, for there is no returning: and thou shalt do him no good, and shalt hurt thyself.

23 Remember my judgment: for thine also shall be so. Yesterday for me, and to-day for thee.

24 [4]When the dead is at rest, let his remembrance rest: and comfort him in the departing of his spirit.

25 The wisdom of a scribe cometh by his time of leisure: and he that is less in action shall receive wisdom.

26 With what wisdom shall he be furnished that holdeth the plough and that glorieth in the goad, that driveth the oxen therewith, and is occupied in their labours: and his whole talk is about the offspring of bulls?

27 He shall give his mind to turn up furrows: and his care is to give the kine fodder.

28 So every craftsman and workmaster that laboureth night and day, *he* who maketh graven seals, and by his continual diligence varieth the figure: he shall give his mind to the resemblance of the picture, and by his watching shall finish the work.

29 So doth the smith sitting by the anvil and considering the iron work. The vapour of the fire wasteth his flesh: and he fighteth with the heat of the furnace.

30 The noise of the hammer is always in his ears: and his eye is upon the pattern of the vessel he maketh.

31 He setteth his mind to finish his work: and his watching to polish *them* to perfection.

32 So doth the potter sitting at his work, turning the wheel about with his feet, who is always carefully set to his work, and maketh all his work by number.

33 He fashioneth the clay with his arm, and boweth down his strength before his feet.

34 He shall give his mind to finish the glazing: and his watching to make clean the furnace.

35 All these trust to their hands: and every one is wise in his own art.

36 Without these a city is not built.

37 And they shall not dwell, nor walk about therein: and they shall not go up into the assembly.

38 Upon the judges' seat they shall not sit, and the ordinance of judgment they shall not understand: neither shall they declare discipline and judgment, and they shall not be found where parables are spoken.

39 But they shall strengthen the state of the world: and their prayer shall be in the work of their craft, applying their soul, and searching in the law of the most High.

CHAPTER 39

The exercises of the wise man. The Lord is to be glorified for his works.

THE wise man will seek out the wisdom of all the ancients and will be occupied in the prophets.

2 He will keep the sayings of re-

[2] Isai. 38, 3.   [3] Prov. 15, 13; 17, 22.   [4] 2 Kings, 12, 21.

Снар. 38. Ver. 25. *A scribe.* That is, a doctor of the law, or, a learned man.

nowned men and will enter withal into the subtilties of parables.

3 He will search out the hidden meaning of proverbs and will be conversant in the secrets of parables.

4 He shall serve among great men, and appear before the governor.

5 He shall pass into strange countries: for he shall try good and evil among men.

6 He will give his heart to resort early to the Lord that made him and he will pray in the sight of the most High.

7 He will open his mouth in prayer and will make supplication for his sins.

8 For if it shall please the great Lord, he will fill him with the spirit of understanding.

9 And he will pour forth the words of his wisdom as showers: and in his prayer he will confess to the Lord.

10 And he shall direct his counsel, and his knowledge: and in his secrets shall he meditate.

11 He shall shew forth the discipline he hath learned: and shall glory in the law of the covenant of the Lord.

12 Many shall praise his wisdom: and it shall never be forgotten.

13 The memory of him shall not depart away: and his name shall be in request from generation to generation.

14 Nations shall declare his wisdom: and the church shall shew forth his praise.

15 If he continue, he shall leave a name above a thousand: and if he rest, it shall be to his advantage.

16 I will yet meditate that I may declare: for I am filled as with a *holy* transport.

17 By a voice he saith: Hear me, ye divine offspring, and bud forth as the rose planted by the brooks of waters.

18 Give ye a sweet odour as frankincense.

19 Send forth flowers, as the lily, and yield a smell, and bring forth leaves in grace, and praise with canticles, and bless the Lord in his works.

20 Magnify his name, and give glory to him with the voice of your lips, and with the canticles of your mouths, and with harps. And in praising him, you shall say in this manner:

21 ¹ All the works of the Lord are exceeding good.

22 ² At his word the waters stood as a heap: and at the words of his mouth the receptacles of waters.

23 For at his commandment favour is shewn: and there is no diminishing of his salvation.

24 The works of all flesh are before him: and there is nothing hid from his eyes.

25 He seeth from eternity to eternity: and there is nothing wonderful before him.

26 There is no saying: What is this, or what is that? For all things shall be sought in their time.

27 His blessing hath overflowed like a river:

28 ³ And as a flood hath watered the earth. So shall his wrath inherit the nations that have not sought after him:

29 ⁴ Even as he turned the waters into a dry land, and the earth was made dry, and his ways were made plain for their journey: so to sinners *they are* stumbling-blocks in his wrath.

30 Good things were created for the good from the beginning: so for the wicked, good and evil things.

31 ⁵ The principal things necessary for the life of men, are: Water, fire, and iron, salt, milk, and bread of flour, and honey, and the cluster of the grape, and oil, and clothing.

32 All these things shall be for good to the holy: so to the sinners and the ungodly they shall be turned into evil.

33 There are spirits that are created for vengeance: and in their fury they lay on grievous torments.

34 In the time of destruction they shall pour out their force: and they shall appease the wrath of him that made them.

35 Fire, hail, famine, and death: all these were created for vengeance.

36 The teeth of beasts and scorpions and serpents: and the sword taking vengeance upon the ungodly, unto destruction.

37 In his commandments they shall feast, and they shall be ready upon earth when need is: and when their time is come they shall not transgress his word.

38 Therefore from the beginning I was resolved: and I have meditated and thought on these things, and left them in writing.

39 ⁶ All the works of the Lord are good: and he will furnish every work in due time.

40 It is not to be said: This is worse than that. For all shall be well approved in their time.

41 Now therefore with the whole heart and mouth praise ye him: and bless the name of the Lord.

Chap. 39. ¹ Gen. 1, 31; Mark, 7, 37. ² Gen. 8, 3. ³ Gen. 7, 21. ⁴ Exod. 14, 21. ⁵ Ecclus. 29, 28. ⁶ Gen. 1, 31; Mark, 7, 37.

Chap. 39. Ver. 17. *Ye divine offspring.* He that speaks to the children of Israel, the people of God: whom he exhorts to bud forth and flourish with virtue.

CHAPTER 40

The miseries of the life of man are relieved by the grace of God and his fear.

GREAT labour is created for all men: and a heavy yoke is upon the children of Adam, from the day of their coming out of their mother's womb, until the day of their burial into the mother of all.

2 Their thoughts and fears of the heart, their imagination of things to come, and the day of their end.

3 From him that sitteth on a glorious throne, unto him that is humbled in earth and ashes:

4 From him that weareth purple and beareth the crown, even to him that is covered with rough linen: wrath, envy, trouble, unquietness and the fear of death, continual anger and strife.

5 And in the time of rest upon his bed, the sleep of the night changeth his knowledge.

6 A little and as nothing is his rest. And afterward in sleep, as in the day of keeping watch.

7 He is troubled in the vision of his heart, as if he had escaped in the day of battle. In the time of his safety, he rose up and wondereth that there is no fear.

8 Such things happen to all flesh, from man even to beast: and upon sinners are sevenfold more.

9 [1] Moreover, death and bloodshed, strife and sword, oppressions, famine and affliction and scourges.

10 All these things are created for the wicked: [2] and for their sakes came the flood.

11 [3] All things that are of the earth shall return to the earth again: [4] and all waters shall return to the sea.

12 All bribery and injustice shall be blotted out: and fidelity shall stand for ever.

13 The riches of the unjust shall be dried up like a river: and shall pass away with a noise like a great thunder in rain.

14 While he openeth his hands he shall rejoice: but transgressors shall pine away in the end.

15 The offspring of the ungodly shall not bring forth many branches, and make a noise as unclean roots upon the top of a rock.

16 The weed growing over every water, and at the bank of the river, shall be pulled up before all grass.

17 Grace is like a paradise in blessings: and mercy remaineth for ever.

18 The life of a labourer that is content with what he hath shall be sweet: and in it thou shalt find a treasure.

19 Children and the building of a city shall establish a name: but a blameless wife shall be counted above them both.

20 Wine and music rejoice the heart: but the love of wisdom is above them both.

21 The flute and the psaltery make a sweet melody: but a pleasant tongue is above them both.

22 The eye desireth favour and beauty: but more than these green sown fields.

23 A friend and companion meeting together in season: but above them both is a wife with her husband.

24 Brethren are a help in the time of trouble: but mercy shall deliver more than they.

25 Gold and silver make the feet stand sure: but wise counsel is above them both.

26 Riches and strength lift up the heart: but above these is the fear of the Lord.

27 There is no want in the fear of the Lord: and it needeth not to seek for help.

28 The fear of the Lord is like a paradise of blessing: and they have covered it above all glory.

29 My son, in thy lifetime be not indigent: for it is better to die than to want.

30 The life of him that looketh toward another man's table is not to be counted a life: for he feedeth his soul with another man's meat.

31 But a man, well instructed and taught, will look to himself.

32 Begging will be sweet in the mouth of the unwise: but in his belly there shall burn a fire.

CHAPTER 41

Of the remembrance of death. Of an evil and of a good name. Of what things we ought to be ashamed.

O DEATH, how bitter is the remembrance of thee to a man that hath peace in his possessions!

2 To a man that is at rest, and whose ways are prosperous in all things, and that is yet able to take meat!

3 O death, thy sentence is welcome to the man that is in need, and to him whose strength faileth:

4 Who is in a decrepit age, and that is in care about all things: and to the distrustful that loseth patience.

5 Fear not the sentence of death. Remember what things have been before thee, and what shall come after thee: this sentence is from the Lord upon all flesh.

CHAP. 40. [1] Ecclus. 39, 35, 36. [2] Gen. 7, 10. [3] Ecclus. 41, 13. [4] Eccles. 1, 7.

6 And what shall come upon thee by the good pleasure of the most High, whether ten, or a hundred, or a thousand years.

7 For among the dead there is no accusing of life.

8 The children of sinners become children of abominations: and they that converse near the houses of the ungodly.

9 The inheritance of the children of sinners shall perish: and with their posterity shall be a perpetual reproach.

10 The children will complain of an ungodly father, because for his sake they are in reproach.

11 Woe to you, ungodly men, who have forsaken the law of the most high Lord.

12 And if you be born, you shall be born in malediction: and if you die, in malediction shall be your portion.

13 ¹ All things that are of the earth shall return into the earth: so the ungodly shall from malediction to destruction.

14 The mourning of men is about their body: but the name of the ungodly shall be blotted out.

15 Take care of a good name: for this shall continue with thee, more than a thousand treasures precious and great.

16 A good life hath its number of days: but a good name shall continue for ever.

17 My children, keep discipline in peace. ² For wisdom that is hid, and a treasure that is not seen, what profit is there in them both?

18 Better is the man that hideth his folly than the man that hideth his wisdom.

19 Wherefore have a shame of these things I am now going to speak of.

20 For it is not good to keep all shamefacedness: and all things do not please all men in opinion.

21 Be ashamed of fornication before father and mother: and of a lie before a governor and a man in power:

22 Of an offence before a prince, and a judge: of iniquity before a congregation and a people:

23 Of injustice before a companion and friend: and, in regard to the place where thou dwellest,

24 Of theft, and of the truth of God and the covenant: of leaning with thy elbow over meat: and of deceit in giving and taking:

25 Of silence before them that salute thee: of looking upon a harlot: and of turning away thy face from thy kinsman:

26 (Turn not away thy face from thy neighbour): and of taking away a portion and not restoring.

27 ³ Gaze not upon another man's wife: and be not inquisitive after his handmaid: and approach not her bed.

28 *Be ashamed* of upbraiding speeches before friends: and after thou hast given, upbraid not.

CHAPTER 42

Of what things we ought not to be ashamed. Cautions with regard to women. The works and greatness of God.

REPEAT not the word which thou hast heard and disclose not the thing that is secret: so shalt thou be truly without confusion and shalt find favour before all men. Be not ashamed of any of these things, ¹ and accept no person to sin thereby:

2 Of the law of the most High, and of his covenant, and of judgment to justify the ungodly,

3 Of the affair of companions and travellers, and of the gift of inheritance of friends,

4 Of exactness of balance and weights, of getting much or little:

5 Of the corruption of buying, and of merchants, and of much correction of children, and to make the side of a wicked slave to bleed.

6 Sure keeping is good over a wicked wife.

7 Where there are many hands, shut up and deliver all things in number and weight: and put all in writing that thou givest out or receivest in.

8 Be not ashamed to inform the unwise and foolish and the aged, that are judged by young men: and thou shalt be well instructed in all things and well approved in the sight of all men living.

9 The father waketh for the daughter when no man knoweth, and the care for her taketh away his sleep: when she is young, lest she pass away the flower of her age, and when she is married, lest she should be hateful.

10 In her virginity, lest she should be corrupted and be found with child in her father's house: and having a husband, lest she should misbehave herself, or at the least become barren.

11 Keep a sure watch over a shameless daughter. Lest at any time she make thee become a laughing-stock to

CHAP. 41. Ver. 19. *Have a shame.* That is to say, be ashamed of doing any of these things, which I am now going to mention: for though sometimes shamefacedness is not to be indulged, yet it is often good and necessary, as in the following cases.

thy enemies and a byword in the city and a reproach among the people: and she make thee ashamed before all the multitude.

12 Behold not everybody's beauty: and tarry not among women.

13 For from garments cometh a moth: and from a woman the iniquity of a man.

14 For better is the iniquity of a man, than a woman doing a good turn and a woman bringing shame and reproach.

15 I will now remember the works of the Lord: and I will declare the things I have seen. By the words of the Lord are his works.

16 The sun giving light hath looked upon all things: and full of the glory of the Lord is his work.

17 Hath not the Lord made the saints to declare all his wonderful works, which the Lord Almighty hath firmly settled to be established for his glory.

18 He hath searched out the deep and the heart of men: and considered their crafty devices.

19 For the Lord knoweth all knowledge and hath beheld the signs of the world. He declareth the things that are past and the things that are to come, and revealeth the traces of hidden things.

20 No thought escapeth him: and no word can hide itself from him.

21 He hath beautified the glorious works of his wisdom: and he is from eternity to eternity. And to him nothing may be added.

22 Nor can he be diminished: and he hath no need of any counsellor.

23 O how desirable are all his works: and what we can know is *but* as a spark!

24 All these things live and remain for ever: and for every use all things obey him.

25 All things are double, one against another: and he hath made nothing defective.

26 He hath established the good things of every one. And who shall be filled with beholding his glory?

CHAPTER 43

The works of God are exceedingly glorious and wonderful. No man is able sufficiently to praise him.

THE firmament on high is his beauty, the beauty of heaven with its glorious shew.

2 The sun when he appeareth shewing forth at his rising: an admirable instrument, the work of the most High.

3 At noon he burneth the earth, and who can abide his burning heat? As

one keeping a furnace in the works of heat.

4 The sun, three times as much, burneth the mountains, breathing out fiery vapours: and shining with his beams, he blindeth the eyes.

5 Great is the Lord that made him: and at his words he hath hastened his course.

6 And the moon in all in her season is for a declaration of times and a sign of the world.

7 From the moon is the sign of the festival day, a light that decreaseth in her perfection.

8 The month is called after her name, increasing wonderfully in her perfection.

9 Being an instrument of the armies on high, shining gloriously in the firmament of heaven.

10 The glory of the stars is the beauty of heaven: the Lord enlighteneth the world on high.

11 By the words of the holy one they shall stand in judgment: and shall never fail in their watches.

12 Look upon the rainbow, and bless him that made it: [1] it is very beautiful in its brightness.

13 It encompasseth the heaven about the circle of its glory: the hands of the most High have displayed it.

14 By his commandment he maketh the snow to fall apace: and sendeth forth swiftly the lightnings of his judgment.

15 Through this are the treasures opened: and the clouds fly out like birds.

16 By his greatness he hath fixed the clouds: and the hailstones are broken.

17 At his sight shall the mountains be shaken: and at his will the south wind shall blow.

18 The noise of his thunder shall strike the earth: so *doth* the northern storm and the whirlwind:

19 And as the birds lighting upon the earth, he scattereth snow: and the falling thereof is as the coming down of locusts.

20 The eye admireth at the beauty of the whiteness thereof: and the heart is astonished at the shower thereof.

21 He shall pour frost as salt upon the earth: and when it freezeth, it shall become like the tops of thistles.

22 The cold north wind bloweth, and the water is congealed into crystal; upon every gathering together of

Chap. 43. [1] Gen. 9, 13.

Chap. 42. Ver. 14. *Better is the iniquity.* That is, there is, commonly speaking, less danger to be apprehended to the soul from the churlishness, or injuries we receive from men, than from the flattering favours and familiarity of women.

waters it shall rest and shall clothe the waters as a breastplate.

23 And it shall devour the mountains and burn the wilderness and consume all that is green as with fire.

24 A present remedy of all is the speedy coming of a cloud: and a dew that meeteth it, by the heat that cometh, shall overpower it.

25 At his word the wind is still, and with his thought he appeaseth the deep: and the Lord hath planted islands therein.

26 Let them that sail on the sea tell the dangers thereof: and when we hear with our ears, we shall admire.

27 There are great and wonderful works: a variety of beasts and of all living things, and the monstrous creatures of whales.

28 Through him is established the end of their journey: and by his word all things are regulated.

29 We shall say much, and yet shall want words: but the sum of our words is, He is all.

30 What shall we be able to do to glorify him? For the Almighty himself is above all his works.

31 The Lord is terrible and exceeding great: and his power is admirable.

32 Glorify the Lord as much as ever you can: for he will yet far exceed and his magnificence is wonderful.

33 Blessing the Lord, exalt him as much as you can: for he is above all praise.

34 When you exalt him put forth all your strength and be not weary: for you can never go far enough.

35 [2] Who shall see him, and declare him? And who shall magnify him as he is from the beginning?

36 There are many things hidden from us that are greater than these: for we have seen but a few of his works.

37 But the Lord hath made all things: and to the godly he hath given wisdom.

CHAPTER 44

The praise of the holy fathers, in particular of Enoch, Noe, Abraham, Isaac, and Jacob.

LET us now praise men of renown, and our fathers in their generation.

2 The Lord hath wrought great glory through his magnificence from the beginning.

3 Such as have borne rule in their dominions, men of great power and endued with their wisdom, shewing

forth in the prophets the dignity of prophets,

4 And ruling over the present people, and by the strength of wisdom *instructing* the people in most holy words.

5 Such as by their skill sought out musical tunes and published canticles of the scriptures.

6 Rich men in virtue, studying beautifulness: living at peace in their houses.

7 All these have gained glory in their generations and were praised in their days.

8 They that were born of them have left a name behind them, that their praises might be related:

9 And there are some of whom there is no memorial: who are perished, as if they had never been, and are become as if they had never been born, and their children with them.

10 But these were men of mercy, whose godly deeds have not failed.

11 Good things continue with their seed.

12 Their posterity are a holy inheritance: and their seed hath stood in the covenants.

13 And their children for their sakes remain for ever: their seed and their glory shall not be forsaken.

14 Their bodies are buried in peace: and their name liveth unto generation and generation.

15 Let the people shew forth their wisdom: and the church declare their praise.

16 [1] Henoch pleased God, and was translated into paradise, that he may give repentance to the nations.

17 [2] Noe was found perfect, just: and in the time of wrath he was made a reconciliation.

18 Therefore was there a remnant left to the earth, when the flood came.

19 [3] The covenants of the world were made with him, that all flesh should no more be destroyed with the flood.

20 [4] Abraham *was* the great father of a multitude of nations, and there was not found the like to him in glory, who kept the law of the most High and was in covenant with him.

21 [5] In his flesh he established the covenant: [6] and in temptation he was found faithful.

22 Therefore by an oath he gave him glory in his posterity, that he should increase as the dust of the earth.

23 And that he would exalt his seed as the stars, and they should inherit from sea to sea and from the river to the ends of the earth.

[2] Ps. 105, 2. CHAP. 44. [1] Gen. 5, 24; Heb. 11, 5. [2] Gen. 9, 9. [3] Gen. 6, 14; 7, 1; Heb. 11, 7. [4] Gen. 12, 2; 15, 5; 17, 4. [5] Gen. 17, 10; Gal. 3, 6. [6] Gen. 22, 1.

24 And he did in like manner with Isaac, for the sake of Abraham his father.

25 The Lord gave him the blessing of all nations: and confirmed his covenant upon the head of Jacob.

26 He acknowledged him in his blessings and gave him an inheritance and divided him his portion in twelve tribes.

27 And he preserved for him men of mercy that found grace in the eyes of all flesh.

CHAPTER 45

The praise of Moses, of Aaron, and of Phinees.

MOSES [1] was beloved of God and men: whose memory is in benediction.

2 He made him like the saints in glory and magnified him in the fear of his enemies and with his words he made prodigies to cease.

3 [2] He glorified him in the sight of kings and gave him commandments in the sight of his people and shewed him his glory.

4 [3] He sanctified him in his faith and meekness and chose him out of all flesh.

5 For he heard him and his voice, and brought him into a cloud.

6 And he gave him commandments before his face and a law of life and instruction, that he might teach Jacob his covenant and Israel his judgments.

7 He exalted Aaron his brother, and like to himself of the tribe of Levi.

8 He made an everlasting covenant with him and gave him the priesthood of the nation and made him blessed in glory.

9 And he girded him about with a glorious girdle and clothed him with a robe and crowned him with majestic attire.

10 He put upon him a garment to the feet and breeches and an ephod: and he compassed him with many little bells of gold all round about,

11 [4] That as he went there might be a sound, and a noise made that might be heard in the temple, for a memorial to the children of his people.

12 He gave him a holy robe of gold and blue and purple, a woven work of a wise man, endued with judgment and truth:

13 Of twisted scarlet, the work of an artist, with precious stones cut and set in gold, and graven by the work of a lapidary, for a memorial, according to the number of the tribes of Israel.

14 And a crown of gold upon his mitre, wherein was engraved Holiness,

an ornament of honour, a work of power, and delightful to the eyes for its beauty.

15 Before him there were none so beautiful, even from the beginning.

16 No stranger was ever clothed with them, but only his children alone, and his grandchildren for ever.

17 His sacrifices were consumed with fire every day.

18 [5] Moses filled his hands and anointed him with holy oil.

19 This was made to him for an everlasting testament, and to his seed as the days of heaven, to execute the office of the priesthood, and to have praise, and to glorify his people in his name.

20 He chose him out of all men living to offer sacrifice to God, incense, and a good savour, for a memorial to make reconciliation for his people.

21 And he gave him power in his commandments, in the covenants of his judgments: that he should teach Jacob his testimonies and give light to Israel in his law.

22 [6] And strangers stood up against him: and through envy the men that were with Dathan and Abiron compassed him about in the wilderness, and the congregation of Core in their wrath.

23 The Lord God saw and it pleased him not: and they were consumed in his wrathful indignation.

24 He wrought wonders upon them and consumed them with a flame of fire.

25 And he added glory to Aaron and gave him an inheritance and divided unto him the firstfruits of the increase of the earth.

26 He prepared them bread in the first place unto fulness: for, the sacrifices also of the Lord they shall eat, which he gave to him and to his seed.

27 But he shall not inherit among the people in the land, and he hath no portion among the people: for he himself is his portion and inheritance.

28 [7] Phinees the son of Eleazar is the third in glory, by imitating him in the fear of the Lord.

29 And he stood up in the shameful fall of the people: in the goodness and readiness of his soul he appeased God for Israel.

30 Therefore he made to him a covenant of peace, to be the prince of the sanctuary and of his people, that the dignity of priesthood should be to him and to his seed for ever.

CHAP. 45. [1] Exod. 11, 3. [2] Exod. 6, 7, 8. [3] Num. 12, 3, 7; Heb. 3, 2, 5. [4] Exod. 28, 35. [5] Lev. 8, 12. [6] Num. 16, 1, 3. [7] Num. 25, 7; 1 Mach. 2, 26, 54.

31 And a covenant to David the king, the son of Jesse, of the tribe of Juda, an inheritance to him and to his seed, that he might give wisdom into our heart to judge his people in justice, that their good things might not be abolished. And he made their glory in their nation everlasting.

CHAPTER 46

The praise of Josue, of Caleb, and of Samuel.

VALIANT in war was Jesus, the son of Nave, who was successor of Moses among the prophets, who was great according to his name,

2 Very great for the saving the elect of God, to overthrow the enemies that rose up against them, that he might get the inheritance for Israel.

3 How great glory did he gain when he lifted up his hands and stretched out swords against the cities!

4 Who before him hath so resisted? For the Lord himself brought the enemies.

5 ¹ Was not the sun stopped in his anger, and one day made as two?

6 He called upon the most high Sovereign when the enemies assaulted him on every side: and the great and holy God heard him by hailstones of exceeding great force.

7 He made a violent assault against the nation of his enemies: and in the descent he destroyed the adversaries.

8 That the nations might know his power, that it is not easy to fight against God. And he followed the mighty one.

9 ² And in the days of Moses he did a work of mercy, he and Caleb the son of Jephone, in standing against the enemy and withholding the people from sins and appeasing the wicked murmuring.

10 And they two being appointed, were delivered out of the danger from among the number of six hundred thousand men on foot: to bring them into their inheritance, into the land that floweth with milk and honey.

11 And the Lord gave strength also to Caleb: and his strength continued even to his old age, so that he went up to the high places of the land. And his seed obtained it for an inheritance:

12 That all the children of Israel

might see that it is good to obey the holy God.

13 Then all the judges, every one by name, whose heart was not corrupted, who turned not away from the Lord:

14 That their memory might be blessed, and their bones spring up out of their place,

15 And their name continue for ever, the glory of the holy men remaining unto their children.

16 Samuel, the prophet of the Lord, the beloved of the Lord his God, established a new government and anointed princes over his people.

17 By the law of the Lord he judged the congregation, and the God of Jacob beheld: and by his fidelity he was proved a prophet.

18 And he was known to be faithful in his words, because he saw the God of light:

19 ³ And called upon the name of the Lord Almighty, in fighting against the enemies who beset him on every side, when he offered a lamb without blemish.

20 And the Lord thundered from heaven and with a great noise made his voice to be heard.

21 And he crushed the princes of the Tyrians and all the lords of the Philistines.

22 ⁴ And before the time of the end of his life in the world, he protested before the Lord and his anointed: money, or any thing else, ⁵ even to a shoe, he had not taken of any man, and no man did accuse him.

23 And after this he slept. ⁶ And he made known to the king, and shewed him the end of his life: and he lifted up his voice from the earth in prophecy, to blot out the wickedness of the nation.

CHAPTER 47

The praise of Nathan, of David, and of Solomon. Of his fall and punishment.

THEN ¹ Nathan the prophet arose in the days of David.

2 And as the fat taken away from the flesh, so was David *chosen* from among the children of Israel.

3 ² He played with lions as with lambs: and with bears he did in like manner as with the lambs of the flock, in his youth.

4 ³ Did not he kill the giant, and take away reproach from his people?

5 In lifting up his hand, with the stone in the sling he beat down the boasting of Goliath.

6 For he called upon the Lord the Almighty: and he gave strength in his right hand, to take away the mighty

CHAP. 46. ¹ Jos. 10, 14. ² Num. 14, 6. ³ 1 Kings, 7. ⁴ 1 Kings, 12. ⁵ Gen. 14, 28. ⁶ 1 Kings, 38, 18. CHAP. 47. ¹ 2 Kings, 12, 1. ² 1 Kings, 17, 34. ³ 1 Kings, 17, 49. ⁴ 1 Kings, 18, 7.

CHAP. 46. Ver. 1. *Jesus the son of Nave.* So Josue is named in the Greek Bibles. For *Josue* and *Jesus* signify the same thing, namely, *Saviour.*

Ver. 7. *And in the descent.* Of Beth-horon (Jos. 10).

warrior and to set up the horn of his nation.

7 ⁴So in ten thousand did he glorify him: and praise him in the blessings of the Lord, in offering to him a crown of glory:

8 For he destroyed the enemies on every side and extirpated the Philistines, the adversaries, unto this day: he broke their horn for ever.

9 In all his works he gave thanks to the holy one and to the most High, with words of glory.

10 With his whole heart he praised the Lord and loved God that made him: and he gave him power against his enemies:

11 And he set singers before the altar: and by their voices he made sweet melody.

12 And to the festivals he added beauty and set in order the solemn times even to the end of his life: that they should praise the holy name of the Lord and magnify the holiness of God in the morning.

13 ⁵The Lord took away his sins and exalted his horn for ever: and he gave him a covenant of the kingdom and a throne of glory in Israel.

14 After him arose up a wise son: and for his sake he cast down all the power of the enemies.

15 ⁶Solomon reigned in days of peace: and God brought all his enemies under him, that he might build a house in his name and prepare a sanctuary for ever. O, how wise wast thou in thy youth!

16 ⁷And thou wast filled as a river with wisdom: and thy soul covered the earth:

17 And thou didst multiply riddles in parables. Thy name went abroad to the islands far off: and thou wast beloved in thy peace.

18 The countries wondered at thee for thy canticles and proverbs and parables and interpretations:

19 And at the name of the Lord God, whose surname is, God of Israel.

20 ⁸Thou didst gather gold as copper, and didst multiply silver as lead,

21 And thou didst bow thyself to women: and by thy body thou wast brought under subjection.

22 Thou hast stained thy glory and defiled thy seed, so as to bring wrath upon thy children and to have thy folly kindled:

23 That thou shouldst make the kingdom to be divided, ⁹and out of Ephraim a rebellious kingdom to rule.

24 But God will not leave off his mercy: and he will not destroy, nor abolish his own works. Neither will he

cut up by the roots the offspring of his elect: and he will not utterly take away the seed of him that loveth the Lord.

25 Wherefore he gave a remnant to Jacob, and to David of the same stock.

26 And Solomon had an end with his fathers.

27 And he left behind him of his seed, the folly of the nation:

28 Even Roboam that had little wisdom, who turned away the people through his counsel.

29 ¹⁰And Jeroboam the son of Nabat, who caused Israel to sin, and shewed Ephraim the way of sin: and their sins were multiplied exceedingly.

30 They removed them far away from their land.

31 And they sought out all iniquities: till vengeance came upon them and put an end to all their sins.

CHAPTER 48

The praises of Elias, of Eliseus, of Ezechias, and of Isaias.

AND ¹Elias the prophet stood up, as a fire: and his word burnt like a torch.

2 He brought a famine upon them: and they that provoked him in their envy, were reduced to a small number, for they could not endure the commandments of the Lord.

3 ²By the word of the Lord he shut up the heaven: and he brought down fire from heaven thrice.

4 Thus was Elias magnified in his wondrous works. And who can glory like to thee,

5 ³Who raisedst up a dead man from below, from the lot of death, by the word of the Lord God?

6 Who broughtest down kings to destruction: and brokest easily their power in pieces, and the glorious from their bed.

7 Who heardest judgment in Sina: and in Horeb the judgments of vengeance.

8 Who anointedst kings to penance: and madest prophets successors after thee.

9 ⁴Who wast taken up in a whirlwind of fire, in a chariot of fiery horses.

10 Who art registered in the judgments of times to appease the wrath of the Lord, ⁵to reconcile the heart of the father to the son and to restore the tribes of Jacob.

11 Blessed are they that saw thee and were honoured with thy friendship.

⁵ 2 Kings, 12, 13. ⁶ 3 Kings, 3, 1. ⁷ 3 Kings, 4, 31. ⁸ 3 Kings, 10, 27. ⁹ 3 Kings, 12, 16. ¹⁰ 3 Kings, 12, 28. CHAP. 48. ¹ 3 Kings, 17, 1. ² 3 Kings, 17, 1; 4 Kings, 1, 10, 12. ³ 3 Kings, 17, 22. ⁴ 4 Kings, 2, 11. ⁵ Mal. 4, 6. ⁶ 4 Kings, 2, 11. ⁷ 4 Kings, 13, 21.

12 For we live only in our life, but after death our name shall not be such.

13 ⁶Elias was indeed covered with the whirlwind: and his spirit was filled up in Eliseus. In his days he feared not the prince: and no man was more powerful than he.

14 No word could overcome him: 'and after death his body prophesied.

15 In his life he did great wonders: and in death he wrought miracles.

16 For all this, the people repented not: neither did they depart from their sins till they were cast out of their land and were scattered through all the earth.

17 And there was left but a small people: and a prince in the house of David.

18 Some of these did that which pleased God, but others committed many sins.

19 Ezechias fortified his city and brought in water into the midst thereof: and he digged a rock with iron and made a well for water.

20 ⁸In his days, Sennacherib came up and sent Rabsaces: and lifted up his hand against them. And he stretched out his hand against Sion: and became proud through his power.

21 Then their hearts and hands trembled: and they were in pain as women in travail.

22 And they called upon the Lord, who is merciful: and spreading their hands, they lifted them up to heaven. And the holy Lord God quickly heard their voice.

23 He was not mindful of their sins, neither did he deliver them up to their enemies: but he purified them by the hand of Isaias, the holy prophet.

24 ⁹He overthrew the army of the Assyrians: and the angel of the Lord destroyed them.

25 For Ezechias did that which pleased God and walked valiantly in the way of David his father, which Isaias, the great prophet, and faithful in the sight of God, had commanded him.

26 ¹⁰In his days, the sun went backward: and he lengthened the king's life.

27 With a great spirit he saw the things that are to come to pass at last: and comforted the mourners in Sion.

28 He shewed what should come to pass for ever, and secret things, before they came.

⁶ 4 Kings. 18, 13. ⁷ 4 Kings, 19, 35; Tob. 1, 21; Isai. 37, 36; 1 Mach. 7, 41; 2 Mach. 8, 19. ¹⁰ 4 Kings, 20, 11; Isai. 38, 8. CHAP. 49. ¹ 4 Kings, 22, 1. ² 4 Kings, 25, 9. ³ Ezech. 1, 4. ⁴ 1 Esd. 3, 2; Agg. 1, 14; 2, 3, 5; 22, 24. ⁵ Zach. 3, 1. ⁶ Gen. 41, 40; 42, 3; 45, 5; 50, 20.

CHAPTER 49

The praise of Josias, of Jeremias, Ezechiel, and the twelve prophets. Also of Zorobabel, Jesus the son of Josedech, Nehemias, Enoch, Joseph, Seth, Sem, and Adam.

THE ¹memory of Josias is like the composition of a sweet smell made by the art of a perfumer.

2 His remembrance shall be sweet as honey in every mouth, and as music at a banquet of wine.

3 He was directed by God unto the repentance of the nation: and he took away the abominations of wickedness.

4 And he directed his heart towards the Lord: and in the days of sinners he strengthened godliness.

5 Except David and Ezechias and Josias, all committed sin.

6 For the kings of Juda forsook the law of the most High and despised the fear of God.

7 So they gave their kingdom to others, and their glory to a strange nation.

8 ²They burnt the chosen city of holiness and made the streets thereof desolate: according to the prediction of Jeremias.

9 For they treated him evil who was consecrated a prophet from his mother's womb, to overthrow and pluck up and destroy, and to build again and renew.

10 ³It was Ezechiel that saw the glorious vision, which was shewn him upon the chariot of cherubims.

11 For he made mention of the enemies under the figure of rain, and of doing good to them that shewed right ways.

12 And may the bones of the twelve prophets spring up out of their place, for they strengthened Jacob and redeemed themselves by strong faith!

13 ⁴How shall we magnify Zorobabel, for he was as a signet on the right hand?

14 ⁵In like manner, Jesus the son of Josedec? Who in their days built the house and set up a holy temple to the Lord, prepared for everlasting glory.

15 And let Nehemias be a long time remembered, who raised up for us our walls that were cast down, and set up the gates and the bars: who rebuilt our houses.

16 No man was born upon earth like Henoch: for he also was taken up from the earth.

17 ⁶Nor as Joseph, who was a man born prince of his brethren, the support of his family, the ruler of his brethren, the stay of the people.

18 And his bones were visited: and after death they prophesied.

19 ⁷ Seth and Sem obtained glory among men: and above every soul Adam in the beginning.

CHAPTER 50

The praises of Simon the high priest. The conclusion.

SIMON ¹ the high priest, the son of Onias, who in his life propped up the house and in his days fortified the temple.

2 By him also the height of the temple was founded: the double building and the high walls of the temple.

3 In his days the wells of water flowed out: and they were filled as the sea above measure.

4 He took care of his nation and delivered it from destruction.

5 He prevailed to enlarge the city and obtained glory in his conversation with the people and enlarged the entrance of the house and the court.

6 He shone in his days as the morning star in the midst of a cloud, and as the moon at the full.

7 And as the sun when it shineth, so did he shine in the temple of God.

8 And as the rainbow giving light in the bright clouds, and as the flower of roses in the days of the spring, and as the lilies that are on the brink of the water, and as the sweet smelling frankincense in the time of summer.

9 As a bright fire, and frankincense burning in the fire.

10 As a massy vessel of gold, adorned with every precious stone.

11 As an olive tree budding forth, and a cypress tree rearing itself on high, when he put on the robe of glory and was clothed with the perfection of power.

12 When he went up to the holy altar, he honoured the vesture of holiness.

13 And when he took the portions out of the hands of the priests, he himself stood by the altar. And about him was the ring of his brethren: and as the cedar planted in mount Libanus,

14 And as branches of palm trees, they stood round about him: and all the sons of Aaron in their glory.

15 And the oblation of the Lord was in their hands, before all the congregation of Israel: and, finishing his service on the altar, to honour the offering of the most high King,

16 He stretched forth his hand to make a libation, and offered of the blood of the grape.

17 He poured out at the foot of the altar a divine odour to the most high Prince.

18 Then the sons of Aaron shouted: they sounded with beaten trumpets and made a great noise to be heard for a remembrance before God.

19 Then all the people together made haste, and fell down to the earth upon their faces, to adore the Lord their God and to pray to the Almighty God, the most High.

20 And the singers lifted up their voices: and in the great house the sound of sweet melody was increased.

21 And the people in prayer besought the Lord, the most High, until the worship of the Lord was perfected, and they had finished their office.

22 Then coming down, he lifted up his hands over all the congregation of the children of Israel, to give glory to God with his lips and to glory in his name.

23 And he repeated his prayer, willing to shew the power of God.

24 And now pray ye to the God of all, who hath done great things in all the earth, who hath increased our days from our mother's womb, and hath done with us according to his mercy.

25 May he grant us joyfulness of heart, and that there be peace in our days in Israel for ever:

26 That Israel may believe that the mercy of God is with us, to deliver us in his days.

27 There are two nations which my soul abhorreth, and the third is no nation, which I hate:

28 They that sit on mount Seir, and the Philistines, and the foolish people that dwell in Sichem.

29 Jesus, the son of Sirach, of Jerusalem, hath written in this book doctrine of wisdom and instruction, who renewed wisdom from his heart.

30 Blessed is he that is conversant in these good things: and he that layeth them up in his heart shall be wise always.

31 For if he do them, he shall be strong to do all things: because the light of God guideth his steps.

---

⁷ Gen. 4, 25. CHAP. 50. ¹ Mach. 12, 7; 2 Mach. 3, 4.

CHAP. 49. Ver. 18. *They prophesied.* That is, by their being carried out of Egypt they verified the prophetic prediction of Joseph. Gen. 50.

CHAP. 50. Ver. 11. *Clothed with the perfection of power.* That is, with all the vestments denoting his dignity and authority.

Ver. 27. *Abhorreth.* With a holy indignation, as enemies of God and persecutors of his people. Such were then the Edomites who abode in mount Seir, the Philistines, and the Samaritans who dwelt in Sichem, and had their schismatical temple in that neighbourhood.

CHAPTER 51

A prayer of praise and thanksgiving.

A PRAYER of Jesus, the son of Sirach. I will give glory to thee, O Lord, O King, and I will praise thee, O God my Saviour.

2 I will give glory to thy name: for thou hast been a helper and protector to me.

3 And hast preserved my body from destruction, from the snare of an unjust tongue, and from the lips of them that forge lies: and in the sight of them that stood by thou hast been my helper.

4 And thou hast delivered me, according to the multitude of the mercy of thy name, from them that did roar, prepared to devour:

5 Out of the hands of them that sought my life, and from the gates of afflictions which compassed me about:

6 From the oppression of the flame which surrounded me, and in the midst of the fire I was not burnt:

7 From the depth of the belly of hell: and from an unclean tongue: and from lying words: from an unjust king: and from a slanderous tongue.

8 My soul shall praise the Lord even to death.

9 And my life was drawing near to hell beneath.

10 They compassed me on every side: and there was no one that would help me. I looked for the succour of men: and there was none.

11 I remembered thy mercy, O Lord, and thy works, which are from the beginning of the world.

12 How thou deliverest them that wait for thee, O Lord, and savest them out of the hands of the nations.

13 Thou hast exalted my dwelling place upon the earth: and I have prayed for death to pass away.

14 I called upon the Lord, the father of my Lord, that he would not leave me in the day of my trouble, and in the time of the proud, without help.

15 I will praise thy name continually and will praise it with thanksgiving. And my prayer was heard.

16 And thou hast saved me from destruction: and hast delivered me from the evil time.

17 Therefore I will give thanks, and praise thee, and bless the name of the Lord.

18 When I was yet young, before I wandered about, I sought for wisdom openly in my prayer.

19 I prayed for her before the temple and unto the very end I will seek after her: and she flourished as a grape soon ripe.

20 My heart delighted in her, my foot walked in the right way: from my youth up I sought after her.

21 I bowed down my ear a little, and received her.

22 I found much wisdom in myself: and I profited much therein.

23 To him that giveth me wisdom will I give glory.

24 For I have determined to follow her: I have had a zeal for good and shall not be confounded.

25 My soul hath wrestled for her: and in doing it I have been confirmed.

26 I stretched forth my hands on high: and I bewailed my ignorance of her.

27 I directed my soul to her: and in knowledge I found her.

28 I possessed my heart with her from the beginning: therefore I shall not be forsaken.

29 My entrails were troubled in seeking her: therefore shall I possess a good possession.

30 The Lord hath given me a tongue for my reward: and with it I will praise him.

31 Draw near to me, ye unlearned: and gather yourselves, together into the house of discipline.

32 Why are ye slow? And what do you say of these things? Your souls are exceeding thirsty.

33 I have opened my mouth, and have spoken: buy her for yourselves without silver,

34 And submit your neck to the yoke: and let your soul receive discipline. For she is near at hand to be found.

35 Behold with your eyes how I have laboured a little and have found much rest to myself.

36 Receive ye discipline as a great sum of money: and possess abundance of gold by her.

37 Let your soul rejoice in his mercy: and you shall not be confounded in his praise.

38 Work your work before the time: and he will give you your reward in his time.

THE PROPHECY OF

ISAIAS

This inspired writer is called by the Holy Ghost, the great prophet (Ecclesiasticus 48, 25), from the greatness of his prophetic spirit, by which he hath foretold so long before, and in so clear a manner, the coming of Christ, the mysteries of our redemption, the calling of the Gentiles, and the glorious establishment, and perpetual flourishing of the church of Christ: insomuch that he may seem to have been rather an evangelist than a prophet. His very name is not without mystery; for ISAIAS *in Hebrew signifies* SALVATION OF THE LORD, *or* JESUS IS THE LORD. *He was, according to the tradition of the Hebrews, of the blood royal of the kings of Juda: and after a most holy life, ended his days by a glorious martyrdom; being sawed in two, at the command of his wicked son-in-law, King Manasses, for reproving his evil ways.*

CHAPTER 1

The prophet complains of the sins of Juda and Jerusalem. He exhorts them to a sincere conversion.

THE vision of Isaias, the son of Amos, which he saw concerning Juda and Jerusalem in the days of Ozias, Joathan, Achaz and Ezechias, kings of Juda.

2 Hear, O ye heavens, and give ear, O earth, for the Lord hath spoken. I have brought up children [1] and exalted them: but they have despised me.

3 The ox knoweth his owner and the ass his master's crib: but Israel hath not known me and my people hath not understood.

4 Woe to the sinful nation, a people laden with iniquity, a wicked seed, ungracious children: they have forsaken the Lord, they have blasphemed the Holy One of Israel, they are gone away backwards.

5 For what shall I strike you any more, you that increase transgression? The whole head is sick, and the whole heart is sad.

6 From the sole of the foot unto the top of the head, there is no soundness therein: wounds and bruises and swelling sores. They are not bound up, nor dressed nor fomented with oil.

7 [2] Your land is desolate, your cities are burnt with fire, your country strangers devour before your face: and it shall be desolate as when wasted by enemies.

8 And the daughter of Sion shall be left as a covert in a vineyard, and as a lodge in a garden of cucumbers, and as a city that is laid waste.

9 [3] Except the Lord of hosts had left us seed, [4] we had been as Sodom: and we should have been like to Gomorrha.

10 Hear the word of the Lord, ye rulers of Sodom: give ear to the law of our God, ye people of Gomorrha.

11 [5] To what purpose do you offer me the multitude of your victims, saith the Lord? I am full, I desire not holocausts of rams and fat of fatlings and blood of calves and lambs and buck-goats.

12 When you came to appear before me, who required these things at your hands, that you should walk in my courts?

13 Offer sacrifice no more in vain: incense is an abomination to me. The new moons and the sabbaths and other festivals I will not abide: your assemblies are wicked.

14 My soul hateth your new moons and your solemnities: they are become troublesome to me. I am weary of bearing them.

15 And when you stretch forth your hands, I will turn away my eyes from you: and when you multiply prayer, I will not hear. [6] For your hands are full of blood.

16 [7] Wash yourselves: be clean. Take away the evil of your devices from my eyes. Cease to do perversely.

17 Learn to do well. Seek judgment. Relieve the oppressed. Judge for the fatherless. Defend the widow.

18 And then come and accuse me, saith the Lord. If your sins be as scarlet, they shall be made as white as snow: and if they be red as crimson, they shall be white as wool.

19 If you be willing and will hearken to me, you shall eat the good things of the land.

20 But if you will not and will provoke me to wrath, the sword shall de-

CHAP. 1. [1] Osee. 11, 3. [2] Isai. 5. 6. [3] Rom. 9, 29. [4] Gen. 19, 24. [5] Jer. 6, 20; Amos. 5, 22. [6] Isai. 59, 3. [7] 1 Peter, 3, 11.

vour you: because the mouth of the Lord hath spoken it.

21 How is the faithful city, that was full of judgment, become a harlot? Justice dwelt in it, but now murderers.

22 Thy silver is turned into dross: thy wine is mingled with water.

23 Thy princes are faithless, companions of thieves: they all love bribes, they run after rewards. ⁸ They judge not for the fatherless: and the widow's cause cometh not in to them.

24 Therefore saith the Lord, the God of hosts, the mighty one of Israel: Ah! I will comfort myself over my adversaries, and I will be revenged of my enemies.

25 And I will turn my hand to thee, and I will clean purge away thy dross, and I will take away all thy tin.

26 And I will restore thy judges as they were before and thy counsellors as of old. After this thou shalt be called the city of the just, a faithful city.

27 Sion shall be redeemed in judgment: and they shall bring her back in justice.

28 And he shall destroy the wicked and the sinners together: and they that have forsaken the Lord, shall be consumed:

29 For they shall be confounded for the idols to which they have sacrificed. And you shall be ashamed of the gardens which you have chosen,

30 When you shall be as an oak with the leaves falling off and as a garden without water.

31 And your strength shall be as the ashes of tow, and your work as a spark. And both shall burn together: and there shall be none to quench it.

CHAPTER 2

All nations shall flow to the church of Christ. The Jews shall be rejected for their sins. Idolatry shall be destroyed.

THE word that Isaias the son of Amos saw, concerning Juda and Jerusalem.

2 ¹ And in the last days the mountain of the house of the Lord shall be

---

⁸ Jer. 5, 28. CHAP. 2. ¹ Mich. 4, 1.

CHAP. 2. Ver. 2. *The last days.* The whole time of the new law, from the coming of Christ till the end of the world, is called in the scripture *the last days;* because no other age or time shall come after it, but only eternity.—*On the top of mountains.* This shews the perpetual visibility of the church of Christ: for a mountain upon the top of mountains cannot be hid.

Ver. 18. *Idols shall be utterly destroyed.* Or *utterly pass away.* This was verified by the establishment of Christianity. And by this and other texts of the like nature, the wild system of some modern sectaries is abundantly confuted, who charge the whole Christian church with worshipping idols for many ages.

prepared on the top of mountains, and it shall be exalted above the hills: and all nations shall flow unto it.

3 And many people shall go, and say: Come, and let us go up to the mountain of the Lord and to the house of the God of Jacob: and he will teach us his ways, and we will walk in his paths. For the law shall come forth from Sion: and the word of the Lord from Jerusalem.

4 And he shall judge the Gentiles and rebuke many people: and they shall turn their swords into ploughshares and their spears into sickles. Nation shall not lift up sword against nation: neither shall they be exercised any more to war.

5 O house of Jacob, come ye: and let us walk in the light of the Lord.

6 For thou hast cast off thy people, the house of Jacob: because they are filled as in times past, and have had soothsayers as the Philistines, and have adhered to strange children.

7 Their land is filled with silver and gold: and there is no end of their treasures.

8 And their land is filled with horses: and their chariots are innumerable. Their land also is full of idols: they have adored the work of their own hands, which their own fingers have made.

9 And man hath bowed himself down: and man hath been debased. Therefore forgive them not.

10 Enter thou into the rock and hide thee in the pit: from the face of the fear of the Lord and from the glory of his majesty.

11 The lofty eyes of man are humbled, and the haughtiness of men shall be made to stoop: and the Lord alone shall be exalted in that day.

12 Because the day of the Lord of hosts *shall be* upon every one that is proud and highminded, and upon every one that is arrogant: and he shall be humbled.

13 And upon all the tall and lofty cedars of Libanus, and upon all the oaks of Basan.

14 And upon all the high mountains, and upon all the elevated hills.

15 And upon every high tower, and every fenced wall.

16 And upon all the ships of Tharsis, and upon all that is fair to behold.

17 And the loftiness of men shall be bowed down: and the haughtiness of men shall be humbled. And the Lord alone shall be exalted in that day.

18 And idols shall be utterly destroyed.

19 [2] And they shall go into the holes of rocks and into the caves of the earth, from the face of the fear of the Lord and from the glory of his majesty, when he shall rise up to strike the earth.

20 In that day a man shall cast away his idols of silver and his idols of gold, which he had made for himself to adore, moles and bats.

21 And he shall go into the clefts of rocks and into the holes of stones, from the face of the fear of the Lord and from the glory of his majesty, when he shall rise up to strike the earth.

22 Cease ye therefore from the man, whose breath is in his nostrils, for he is reputed high.

CHAPTER 3

The confusion and other evils that shall come upon the Jews for their sins. The pride of their women shall be punished.

FOR behold, the sovereign, the Lord of hosts, shall take away from Jerusalem and from Juda the valiant and the strong, the whole strength of bread, and the whole strength of water:

2 The strong man and the man of war, the judge and the prophet, and the cunning man, and the ancient:

3 The captain over fifty, and the honourable in countenance, and the counsellor, and the architect, and the skilful in eloquent speech.

4 [1] And I will give children to be their princes: and the effeminate shall rule over them.

5 And the people shall rush one upon another, and every man against his neighbour: the child shall make a tumult against the ancient, and the base against the honourable.

6 For a man shall take hold of his brother, one of the house of his father, *saying:* Thou hast a garment. Be thou our ruler: and let this ruin be under thy hand.

7 In that day he shall answer, saying: I am no healer and in my house there is no bread nor clothing: make me not ruler of the people.

8 For Jerusalem is ruined, and Juda is fallen: because their tongue and their devices are against the Lord, to provoke the eyes of his majesty.

9 The shew of their countenance hath answered them: and they have proclaimed abroad their sin as Sodom, and they have not hid it. Woe to their souls, for evils are rendered to them.

10 Say to the just man that it is well: for he shall eat the fruit of his doings.

11 Woe to the wicked unto evil: for the reward of his hands shall be given him.

12 As for my people, their oppressors have stripped them, and women have ruled over them. O my people, [2] they that call thee blessed, the same deceive thee and destroy the way of thy steps.

13 The Lord standeth up to judge: and he standeth to judge the people.

14 The Lord will enter into judgment with the ancients of his people and its princes. For you have devoured the vineyard: and the spoil of the poor is in your house.

15 Why do you consume my people, and grind the faces of the poor? Saith the Lord, the God of hosts.

16 And the Lord said: Because the daughters of Sion are haughty, and have walked with stretched out necks and wanton glances of their eyes, and made a noise as they walked with their feet, and moved in a set pace:

17 The Lord will make bald the crown of the head of the daughters of Sion: and the Lord will discover their hair.

18 In that day, the Lord will take away the ornaments of shoes, and little moons:

19 And chains, and necklaces, and bracelets, and bonnets:

20 And bodkins, and ornaments of the legs, and tablets, and sweet balls, and earrings:

21 And rings, and jewels hanging on the forehead:

22 And changes of apparel, and short cloaks, and fine linen, and crisping pins:

23 And looking-glasses, and lawns, and headbands, and fine veils.

24 And instead of a sweet smell, there shall be stench: and instead of a girdle, a cord. And instead of curled hair, baldness: and instead of a stomacher, haircloth.

25 Thy fairest men also shall fall by the sword: and thy valiant ones in battle.

26 And her gates shall lament and mourn: and she shall sit desolate on the ground.

CHAPTER 4

After an extremity of evils that shall fall upon the Jews, a remnant shall be comforted by Christ.

AND in that day, seven women shall take hold of one man, saying: We will eat our own bread, and wear our own apparel: only let us be called by thy name. Take away our reproach.

2 In that day, the bud of the Lord

---

[2] Osee, 10, 8; Luke, 23, 30; Apoc. 6, 16. **CHAP. 3.** [1] Ecclus. 10, 16. [2] Ezech. 13, 18.

CHAP. 4. Ver. 2. *The bud of the Lord.* That is, Christ.

shall be in magnificence and glory: and the fruit of the earth *shall* be high and a great joy to them that shall have escaped of Israel.

3 And it shall come to pass, that every one that shall be left in Sion, and that shall remain in Jerusalem, shall be called holy: every one that is written in life in Jerusalem.

4 If the Lord shall wash away the filth of the daughters of Sion, and shall wash away the blood of Jerusalem out of the midst thereof, by the spirit of judgment and by the spirit of burning.

5 And the Lord will create, upon every place of mount Sion and where he is called upon, a cloud by day and a smoke and the brightness of a flaming fire in the night: for over all the glory *shall be* a protection.

6 And there shall be a tabernacle for a shade in the daytime from the heat, and for a security and covert from the whirlwind and from rain.

CHAPTER 5

The reprobation of the Jews is foreshewn under the parable of a vineyard. A woe is pronounced against sinners. The army God shall send against them.

I [1] WILL sing to my beloved the canticle of my cousin concerning his vineyard. My beloved had a vineyard on a hill in a fruitful place.

2 And he fenced it in, and picked the stones out of it, and planted it with the choicest vines, and built a tower in the midst thereof, and set up a winepress therein. And he looked that it should bring forth grapes: and it brought forth wild grapes.

3 And now, O ye inhabitants of Jerusalem, and ye men of Juda, judge between me and my vineyard.

4 What is there that I ought to do more to my vineyard, that I have not done to it? Was it that I looked that it should bring forth grapes, and it hath brought forth wild grapes?

5 And now I will shew you what I will do to my vineyard. I will take away the hedge thereof, and it shall be wasted: I will break down the wall thereof, and it shall be trodden down.

6 And I will make it desolate. It shall not be pruned and it shall not be digged: but briers and thorns shall come up. And I will command the clouds to rain no rain upon it.

7 For the vineyard of the Lord of hosts is the house of Israel: and the man of Juda, his pleasant plant. And

CHAP. 5. [1] Jer. 2, 21; Matt. 21, 33. [2] Amos. 6, 6. [3] Prov. 3, 7; Rom. 12, 16.

CHAP. 5. Ver. 1. *My cousin.* So the prophet calls Christ, as being of his family and kindred, by descending from the house of David.—*On a hill.* Literally, *in the horn, the son of oil.*

I looked that he should do judgment, and behold iniquity: and do justice, and behold a cry.

8 Woe to you that join house to house and lay field to field, even to the end of the place: Shall you alone dwell in the midst of the earth?

9 These things are in my ears, saith the Lord of hosts: Unless many great and fair houses shall become desolate, without an inhabitant.

10 For ten acres of vineyard shall yield one little measure: and thirty bushels of seed shall yield three bushels.

11 Woe to you that rise up early in the morning to follow drunkenness and to drink till the evening, to be inflamed with wine.

12 The harp and the lyre and the timbrel and the pipe and wine *are* in your feasts: and the work of the Lord you regard not, nor do you consider the works of his hands.[2]

13 Therefore is my people led away captive, because they had not knowledge: and their nobles have perished with famine, and their multitude were dried up with thirst.

14 Therefore hath hell enlarged her soul and opened her mouth without any bounds: and their strong ones and their people and their high and glorious ones shall go down into it.

15 And man shall be brought down, and man shall be humbled, and the eyes of the lofty shall be brought low.

16 And the Lord of hosts shall be exalted in judgment: and the holy God shall be sanctified in justice.

17 And the lambs shall feed according to their order: and strangers shall eat the deserts turned into fruitfulness.

18 Woe to you that draw iniquity with cords of vanity, and sin as the rope of a cart.

19 That say: Let him make haste, and let his work come quickly, that we may see it: and let the counsel of the Holy One of Israel come that we may know it.

20 Woe to you that call evil good, and good evil: that put darkness *for* light, and light *for* darkness: that put bitter for sweet, and sweet for bitter.

21 [3] Woe to you that are wise in your own eyes, and prudent in your own conceits.

22 Woe to you that are mighty to drink wine, and stout men at drunkenness:

23 That justify the wicked for gifts, and take away the justice of the just from him.

24 Therefore as the tongue of the fire devoureth the stubble, and the heat of the flame consumeth it: so shall their

root be as ashes, and their bud shall go up as dust. For they have cast away the law of the Lord of hosts, and have blasphemed the word of the Holy One of Israel.

25 Therefore is the wrath of the Lord kindled against his people, and he hath stretched out his hand upon them, and struck them: and the mountains were troubled, and their carcasses became as dung in the midst of the streets. For all this his anger is not turned away, but his hand is stretched out still.

26 And he will lift up a sign to the nations afar off, and will whistle to them from the ends of the earth: and behold they shall come with speed swiftly.

27 There is none that shall faint, nor labour among them. They shall not slumber nor sleep: neither shall the girdle of their loins be loosed, nor the latchet of their shoes be broken.

28 Their arrows are sharp, and all their bows bent. The hoofs of their horses shall be like the flint, and their wheels like the violence of a tempest.

29 Their roaring like that of a lion: they shall roar like young lions. Yea, they shall roar and take hold of the prey, and they shall keep fast hold of it, and there shall be none to deliver it.

30 And they shall make a noise against them, that day, like the roaring of the sea. We shall look towards the land, and behold darkness of tribulation: and the light is darkened with the mist thereof.

CHAPTER 6

A glorious vision, in which the prophet's lips are cleansed. He foretelleth the obstinacy of the Jews.

IN the year that king Ozias died, I saw the Lord sitting upon a throne high and elevated: and his train filled the temple.

2 Upon it stood the seraphims: the one had six wings, and the other had six wings: with two they covered his face, and with two they covered his feet, and with two they flew.

3 And they cried one to another, and said: [1] Holy, Holy, Holy, the Lord God of hosts, all the earth is full of his glory.

4 And the lintels of the doors were moved at the voice of him that cried: and the house was filled with smoke.

5 And I said: Woe *is* me, because I have held my peace; because I am a man of unclean lips, and I dwell in the midst of a people that hath unclean lips, and I have seen with my eyes the King the Lord of hosts.

6 And one of the seraphims flew to me: and in his hand was a live coal,

which he had taken with the tongs off the altar.

7 And he touched my mouth, [2] and said: Behold this hath touched thy lips, and thy iniquities shall be taken away, and thy sin shall be cleansed.

8 And I heard the voice of the Lord, saying: Whom shall I send, and who shall go for us? And I said: Lo, here am I. Send me.

9 And he said: Go, and thou shalt say to this people: [3] Hearing, hear and understand not: and see the vision and know it not.

10 Blind the heart of this people, and make their ears heavy, and shut their eyes: lest they see with their eyes and hear with their ears and understand with their heart and be converted, and I heal them.

11 And I said: How long, O Lord? And he said: Until the cities be wasted without inhabitant, and the houses without man, and the land shall be left desolate.

12 And the Lord shall remove men far away: and she shall be multiplied that was left in the midst of the earth.

13 And there shall be still a tithing therein: and she shall turn, and shall be made a show as a turpentine tree, and as an oak that spreadeth its branches. That which shall stand therein shall be a holy seed.

CHAPTER 7

The prophet assures king Achaz that the two kings his enemies shall not take Jerusalem. A virgin shall conceive and bear a son.

AND it came to pass in the days of Achaz the son of Joathan, the son of Ozias king of Juda, that Rasin king of Syria, and Phacee the son of Romelia king of Israel, came up to Jerusalem, to fight against it: but they could not prevail over it.

2 And they told the house of David, saying: Syria hath rested upon Ephraim; and his heart was moved, and the heart of his people, as the trees of the woods are moved with the wind.

3 And the Lord said to Isaias: Go forth to meet Achaz, thou and Jasub thy son that is left, to the conduit of the upper pool, [2] in the way of the fuller's field.

4 And thou shalt say to him: See thou be quiet: fear not, and let not thy heart be afraid of the two tails of these firebrands, smoking with the wrath of the fury of Rasin king of Syria, and of the son of Romelia.

CHAP. 6. [1] Apoc. 4, 8. [2] Jer. 1, 9. [3] Matt. 13, 14; Mark, 4, 12; Luke, 8, 10; John, 12, 40; Acts, 28, 26; Rom. 11, 8. CHAP. 7. [1] 4 Kings, 16, 5. [2] 4 Kings, 18, 17.

5 Because Syria hath taken counsel against thee, unto the evil of Ephraim and the son of Romelia, saying:

6 Let us go up to Juda, and rouse it up, and draw it away to us, and make the son of Tabeel king in the midst thereof.

7 Thus saith the Lord God: It shall not stand, and this shall not be.

8 But the head of Syria is Damascus, and the head of Damascus is Rasin: and within threescore and five years, Ephraim shall cease to be a people:

9 And the head of Ephraim is Samaria, and the head of Samaria the son of Romelia. If you will not believe, you shall not continue.

10 And the Lord spoke again to Achaz, saying:

11 Ask thee a sign of the Lord thy God, either unto the depth of hell, or unto the height above.

12 And Achaz said: I will not ask, and I will not tempt the Lord.

13 And he said: Hear ye therefore, O house of David: Is it a small thing for you to be grievous to men, that you are grievous to my God also?

14 Therefore the Lord himself shall give you a sign. [3] Behold a virgin shall conceive and bear a son: and his name shall be called Emmanuel.

15 He shall eat butter and honey, that he may know to refuse the evil, and to choose the good.

16 For before the child know to refuse the evil, and to choose the good, the land which thou abhorrest shall be forsaken of the face of her two kings.

17 The Lord shall bring upon thee, and upon thy people, and upon the house of thy father, days that have not come since the time of the separation of Ephraim from Juda, with the king of the Assyrians.

18 And it shall come to pass in that day, that the Lord shall hiss for the fly that is in the uttermost parts of the rivers of Egypt, and for the bee that is in the land of Assyria.

19 And they shall come and shall all of them rest in the torrents of the valleys, and in the holes of the rocks, and upon all places set with shrubs, and in all hollow places.

20 In that day the Lord shall shave with a razor that is hired by them that are beyond the river, by the king of the Assyrians, the head and the hairs of the feet, and the whole beard.

21 And it shall come to pass in that day that a man shall nourish a young cow and two sheep.

22 And for the abundance of milk he shall eat butter: for, butter and honey shall every one eat that shall be left in the midst of the land.

23 And it shall come to pass in that day that every place where there were a thousand vines at a thousand pieces of silver shall become thorns and briers.

24 With arrows and with bows they shall go in thither: for briers and thorns shall be in all the land.

25 And as for all the hills that shall be raked with a rake, the fear of thorns and briers shall not come thither, but they shall be for the ox to feed on, and the lesser cattle to tread upon.

CHAPTER 8

The name of a child that is to be born. Many evils shall come upon the Jews for their sins.

AND the Lord said to me: Take thee a great book, and write in it with a man's pen. Take away the spoils with speed: quickly take the prey.

2 And I took unto me faithful witnesses, Urias the priest, and Zacharias the son of Barachias.

3 And I went to the prophetess: and she conceived, and bore a son. And the Lord said to me: Call his name, Hasten to take away the spoils: Make haste to take away the prey.

4 For before the child know to call his father and his mother, the strength of Damascus and the spoils of Samaria shall be taken away before the king of the Assyrians.

5 And the Lord spoke to me again, saying:

6 Forasmuch as this people hath cast away the waters of Siloe, that go with silence, and hath rather taken Rasin and the son of Romelia:

7 Therefore, behold the Lord will bring upon them the waters of the river, strong and many, the king of the Assyrians and all his glory. And he shall come up over all his channels and shall overflow all his banks,

8 And shall pass through Juda, overflowing, and going over shall reach even to the neck. And the stretching out of his wings shall fill the breadth of thy land, O Emmanuel.

9 Gather yourselves together, O ye people: and be overcome, and give ear, all ye lands afar off. Strengthen yourselves, and be overcome: gird yourselves, and be overcome.

10 Take counsel together, and it shall be defeated: speak a word, and it shall not be done: because God is with us.

11 For thus saith the Lord to me: As he hath taught me, with a strong arm, that I should not walk in the way of this people, saying:

[3] Matt. 1, 23; Luke, 1, 31.

12 Say ye not: A conspiracy. For all that this people speaketh, is a conspiracy. Neither fear ye their fear, nor be afraid.

13 Sanctify the Lord of hosts himself: and let him be your fear; and let him be your dread.

14 And he shall be a sanctification to you: ¹ but for a stone of stumbling and for a rock of offence to the two houses of Israel, for a snare and a ruin to the inhabitants of Jerusalem.

15 And very many of them shall stumble and fall, and shall be broken in pieces, and shall be snared and taken.

16 Bind up the testimony, seal the law among my disciples.

17 And I will wait for the Lord who hath hid his face from the house of Jacob: and I will look for him.

18 Behold I and my children, whom the Lord hath given me for a sign, and for a wonder in Israel from the Lord of hosts, who dwelleth in mount Sion.

19 And when they shall say to you: Seek of pythons and of diviners, who mutter in their enchantments: should not the people seek of their God, for the living of the dead?

20 To the law rather, and to the testimony. And if they speak not according to this word, they shall not have the morning light.

21 And they shall pass by it; they shall fall, and be hungry. And when they shall be hungry, they will be angry, and curse their king and their God, and look upwards.

22 And they shall look to the earth, and behold trouble and darkness, weakness and distress, and a mist following them: and they cannot fly away from their distress.

CHAPTER 9

What joy shall come after afflictions by the birth and kingdom of Christ which shall flourish for ever. Judgments upon Israel for their sins.

AT ¹ the first time, the land of Zabulon and the land of Nephtali was lightly touched: and at the last the way of the sea beyond the Jordan of the Galilee of the Gentiles was heavily loaded.

2 The people that walked in darkness have seen a great light: to them that dwelt in the region of the shadow of death, light is risen.

3 Thou hast multiplied the nation, *and* hast not increased the joy. They shall rejoice before thee, as they that rejoice in the harvest, as conquerors rejoice after taking a prey, when they divide the spoils.

4 For the yoke of their burden, and the rod of their shoulder, and the sceptre of their oppressor, thou hast overcome, ² as in the day of Madian.

5 For every violent taking of spoils, with tumult, and garment mingled with blood, shall be burnt and be fuel for the fire.

6 For a CHILD IS BORN to us, and a son is given to us, and the government is upon his shoulder: and his name shall be called, Wonderful, Counsellor, God the Mighty, the Father of the world to come, the Prince of Peace.

7 His empire shall be multiplied, and there shall be no end of peace. He shall sit upon the throne of David, and upon his kingdom: to establish it and strengthen it with judgment and with justice, from henceforth and for ever. The zeal of the Lord of hosts will perform this.

8 The Lord sent a word into Jacob: and it hath lighted upon Israel.

9 And all the people of Ephraim shall know, and the inhabitants of Samaria, that say in the pride and haughtiness of their heart:

10 The bricks are fallen down, but we will build with square stones: they have cut down the sycamores, but we will change them for cedars.

11 And the Lord shall set up the enemies of Rasin over him, ³ and shall bring on his enemies in a crowd:

12 The Syrians from the east, and the Philistines from the west: and they shall devour Israel with open mouth. For all this his indignation is not turned away: but his hand is stretched out still.

13 And the people are not returned to him who hath struck them, and have not sought after the Lord of hosts.

14 And the Lord shall destroy out of Israel the head and the tail, him that bendeth down, and him that holdeth back, in one day.

15 The aged and honourable, he is the head: and the prophet that teaches lies, he is the tail.

16 And they that call this people blessed shall cause them to err: and they that are called blessed shall be thrown down headlong.

17 Therefore the Lord shall have no joy in their young men: neither shall he have mercy on their fatherless and widows. For every one is a hypocrite and wicked, and every mouth hath

Chap. 8. ¹ Luke, 2, 34; Rom. 9, 32; 1 Peter, 2, 8. Chap. 9. ¹ Matt. 4, 15. ² Judges, 7, 22. ³ 4 Kings, 16, 9.

Chap. 8. Ver. 19. *Seek of pythons.* That is, people pretending to tell future things by a prophesying spirit. *Should not the people seek of their God, for the living of the dead?* Here is signified, that it is to God we should pray to be directed, and not to seek of the *dead*, (that is, of fortunetellers dead in sin,) for the health of the living.

spoken folly. For all this his indignation is not turned away: but his hand is stretched out still.

18 For wickedness is kindled as a fire. It shall devour the brier and the thorn, and shall kindle in the thicket of the forest: and it shall be wrapped up in smoke ascending on high.

19 By the wrath of the Lord of hosts the land is troubled, and the people shall be as fuel for the fire: no man shall spare his brother.

20 And he shall turn to the right hand, and shall be hungry: and shall eat on the left hand, and shall not be filled. Every one shall eat the flesh of his own arm: Manasses Ephraim, and Ephraim Manasses, and they together shall be against Juda.

21 After all these things his indignation is not turned away: but his hand is stretched out still.

CHAPTER 10

Woe to the makers of wicked laws. The Assyrians shall be a rod for punishing Israel. For their pride they shall be destroyed, and a remnant of Israel saved.

WOE to them that make wicked laws: and when they write, write injustice:

2 To oppress the poor in judgment, and do violence to the cause of the humble of my people: that widows might be their prey, and that they might rob the fatherless.

3 What will you do in the day of visitation, and of the calamity which cometh from afar? To whom will ye flee for help? And where will ye leave your glory,

4 That you be not bowed down under the bond, and fall with the slain? In all these things his anger is not turned away: but his hand is stretched out still.

5 Woe to the Assyrian: he is the rod and the staff of my anger, and my indignation is in their hands.

6 I will send him to a deceitful nation: and I will give him a charge against the people of my wrath, to take away the spoils, and to lay hold on the prey, and to tread them down like the mire of the streets.

7 But he shall not take it so, and his heart shall not think so: but his heart shall be set to destroy and to cut off nations not a few.

CHAP. 10. ¹ 4 Kings, 19, 35; Isai. 37, 36. ² Isai. 11, 11; Rom. 9, 27.

CHAP. 10. Ver. 22. *A remnant of them shall be converted.* This was partly verified in the children of Israel who remained after the devastations of the Assyrians, in the time of king Ezechias: and partly in the conversion of a remnant of the Jews to the faithful of Christ.— *The consumption abridged. That is, the number of them cut short and reduced to few,* shall flourish in abundance of justice.

8 For he shall say:

9 Are not my princes as so many kings? Is not Calano as Charcamis, and Emath as Arphad? Is not Samaria as Damascus?

10 As my hand hath found the kingdoms of the idol, so also their idols of Jerusalem, and of Samaria.

11 Shall I not, as I have done to Samaria and her idols, so do to Jerusalem and her idols?

12 And it shall come to pass, that when the Lord shall have performed all his works in Mount Sion and in Jerusalem, I will visit the fruit of the proud heart of the king of ¹ Assyria and the glory of the haughtiness of his eyes.

13 For he hath said: By the strength of my own hand I have done it, and by my own wisdom I have understood. And I have removed the bounds of the people, and have taken the spoils of the princes, and as a mighty man have pulled down them that sat on high.

14 And my hand hath found the strength of the people as a nest: and as eggs are gathered, that are left, so have I gathered all the earth. And there was none that moved the wing, or opened the mouth, or made the least noise.

15 Shall the axe boast itself against him that cutteth with it? Or shall the saw exalt itself against him by whom it is drawn? As if a rod should lift itself up against him that lifeth it, up, and a staff exalt itself, which is but wood.

16 Therefore the sovereign Lord, the Lord of hosts, shall send leanness among his fat ones: and under his glory shall be kindled a burning, as it were the burning of a fire.

17 And the light of Israel shall be as a fire, and the Holy One thereof as a flame: and his thorns and his briers shall be set on fire and shall be devoured in one day.

18 And the glory of his forest and of his beautiful hill, shall be consumed from the soul even to flesh: and he shall run away through fear.

19 And they that remain of the trees of his forest shall be so few that they shall easily be numbered, and a child shall write them down.

20 And it shall come to pass in that day that the remnant of Israel and they that shall escape of the house of Jacob shall lean no more upon him that striketh them: but they shall lean upon the Lord, the Holy One of Israel, in truth.

21 The remnant shall be converted, the remnant, I say, of Jacob, to the mighty God.

22 ² For if thy people, O Israel, shall be as the sand of the sea, a remnant of them shall be converted: the con-

sumption abridged shall overflow with justice.

23 For the Lord God of hosts shall make a consumption, and an abridgment in the midst of all the land.

24 Therefore, thus saith the Lord, the God of hosts: O my people that dwellest in Sion, be not afraid of the Assyrian: he shall strike thee with his rod, and he shall lift up his staff over thee in the way of Egypt.

25 For yet a little and a very little while: and my indignation shall cease, and my wrath shall be upon their wickedness.

26 [3] And the Lord of hosts shall raise up a scourge against him, [4] according to the slaughter of Madian in the rock of Oreb, and his rod over the sea. And he shall lift it up in the way of Egypt.

27 And it shall come to pass in that day, that his burden shall be taken away from off thy shoulder, and his yoke from off thy neck: and the yoke shall putrefy at the presence of the oil.

28 He shall come into Aiath, he shall pass into Magron: at Machmas he shall lay up his carriages.

29 They have passed in haste: Gaba is our lodging, Rama was astonished, Gabaath of Saul fled away.

30 Lift up thy voice, O daughter of Gallim: attend, O Laisa, poor Anathoth.

31 Medemena is removed. Ye inhabitants of Gabim, take courage:

32 It is yet day enough, to remain in Nobe. He shall shake his hand against the mountain of the daughter of Sion, the hill of Jerusalem.

33 Behold the sovereign Lord of hosts shall break the earthen vessel with terror. And the tall of stature shall be cut down: and the lofty shall be humbled.

34 And the thickets of the forest shall be cut down with iron: and Libanus with its high ones shall fall.

CHAPTER 11

Of the spiritual kingdom of Christ, to which all nations shall repair.

AND [1] there shall come forth a rod out of the root of Jesse: and a flower shall rise up out of his root.

2 And the spirit of the Lord shall rest upon him: the spirit of wisdom and of understanding, the spirit of counsel and of fortitude, the spirit of knowledge and of godliness.

3 And he shall be filled with the spirit of the fear of the Lord. He shall not judge according to the sight of the eyes, nor reprove according to the hearing of the ears.

4 But he shall judge the poor with justice, and shall reprove with equity for the meek of the earth. [2] And he shall

strike the earth with the rod of his mouth: and with the breath of his lips he shall slay the wicked.

5 And justice shall be the girdle of his loins: and faith the girdle of his reins.

6 [3] The wolf shall dwell with the lamb: and the leopard shall lie down with the kid. The calf and the lion and the sheep shall abide together: and a little child shall lead them.

7 The calf and the bear shall feed, their young ones shall rest, together: and the lion shall eat straw like the ox.

8 And the sucking child shall play on the hole of the asp: and the weaned child shall thrust his hand into the den of the basilisk.

9 They shall not hurt, nor shall they kill in all my holy mountain: for the earth is filled with the knowledge of the Lord, as the covering waters of the sea.

10 [4] In that day, the root of Jesse, who standeth for an ensign of the people, him the Gentiles shall beseech: and his sepulchre shall be glorious.

11 And it shall come to pass in that day, that the Lord shall set his hand the second time to possess the remnant of his people, which shall be left from the Assyrians, and from Egypt, and from Phetros, and from Ethiopia, and from Elam, and from Sennaar, and from Emath, and from the islands of the sea.

12 And he shall set up a standard unto the nations: and shall assemble the fugitives of Israel and shall gather together the dispersed of Juda, from the four quarters of the earth.

13 And the envy of Ephraim shall be taken away, and the enemies of Juda shall perish: Ephraim shall not envy Juda, and Juda shall not fight against Ephraim.

14 But they shall fly upon the shoulders of the Philistines by the sea: they together shall spoil the children of the east. Edom, and Moab shall be under the rule of their hand: and the children of Ammon shall be obedient.

15 And the Lord shall lay waste the tongue of the sea of Egypt and shall lift up his hand over the river in the strength of his spirit: and he shall strike it in the seven streams, so that men may pass through it in their shoes.

16 And there shall be a highway for the remnant of my people, which shall be left from the Assyrians: as there was for Israel in the day that he came up out of the land of Egypt.

---

[3] Isai. 37, 36. [4] Judges, 7, 25. Chap. 11. [1] Acts, 13, 23; Isai. 53, 2. [2] 2 Thess. 2, 8. [3] Isai. 65, 25. [4] Rom. 15, 12.

Ver. 27. *At the presence of the oil.* That is, by the sweet unction of divine mercy.

Ver. 28. *Into Aiath.* Here the prophet describes the march of the Assyrians under Sennacherib, and the terror they should carry with them; and how they should suddenly be destroyed.

CHAPTER 12

A canticle of thanksgiving for the benefits of Christ.

AND thou shalt say in that day: I will give thanks to thee, O Lord, for thou wast angry with me. Thy wrath is turned away: and thou hast comforted me.

2 Behold, God is my saviour: I will deal confidently, and will not fear, [1] because the Lord is my strength and my praise: and he is become my salvation.

3 You shall draw waters with joy out of the saviour's fountains.

4 And you shall say in that day: Praise ye the Lord, and call upon his name. Make his works known among the people: remember that his name is high.

5 Sing ye to the Lord, for he hath done great things: shew this forth in all the earth.

6 Rejoice, and praise, O thou habitation of Sion: for great is he that is in the midst of thee, the Holy One of Israel.

CHAPTER 13

The desolation of Babylon.

THE burden of Babylon, which Isaias the son of Amos saw.

2 Upon the dark mountain lift ye up a banner. Exalt the voice, lift up the hand, and let the rulers go into the gates.

3 I have commanded my sanctified ones and have called my strong ones in my wrath, them that rejoice in my glory.

4 The noise of a multitude in the mountains, as it were of many people: the noise of the sound of kings, of nations gathered together. The Lord of hosts hath given charge to the troops of war,

5 To them that come from a country afar off, from the end of heaven: the Lord and the instruments of his wrath, to destroy the whole land.

6 Howl ye, for the day of the Lord is near: it shall come as a destruction from the Lord.

7 Therefore shall all hands be faint: and every heart of man shall melt,

8 And shall be broken. Gripings and pains shall take hold of them: they shall be in pain as a woman in labour. Every one shall be amazed at his neighbour: their countenances shall be as faces burnt.

9 Behold, the day of the Lord shall come, a cruel day, and full of indignation and of wrath and fury, to lay the land desolate, and to destroy the sinners thereof out of it.

10 [1] For the stars of heaven and their brightness shall not display their light: the sun shall be darkened in his rising, and the moon shall not shine with her light.

11 And I will visit the evils of the world, and against the wicked for their iniquity: and I will make the pride of infidels to cease, and will bring down the arrogancy of the mighty.

12 A man shall be more precious than gold: yea a man than the finest of gold.

13 For this, I will trouble the heaven: and the earth shall be moved out of her place: for the indignation of the Lord of hosts, and for the day of his fierce wrath.

14 And they shall be as a doe fleeing away, and as a sheep: and there shall be none to gather them together. Every man shall turn to his own people, and every one shall flee to his own land.

15 Every one that shall be found shall be slain: and every one that shall come to their aid shall fall by the sword.

16 [2] Their infants shall be dashed in pieces before their eyes, their houses shall be pillaged, and their wives shall be ravished.

17 Behold I will stir up the Medes against them, who shall not seek silver, nor desire gold.

18 But with their arrows they shall kill the children, and shall have no pity upon the sucklings of the womb: and their eye shall not spare their sons.

19 And that Babylon, glorious among kingdoms, the famous pride of the Chaldeans, [3] shall be even as the Lord destroyed Sodom and Gomorrha.

20 It shall no more be inhabited for ever, and it shall not be founded unto generation and generation: neither shall the Arabian pitch his tents there, nor shall shepherds rest there.

21 But wild beasts shall rest there, and their houses shall be filled with serpents: and ostriches shall dwell there, and the hairy ones shall dance there.

22 And owls shall answer one another there, in the houses thereof, and sirens in the temples of pleasure.

CHAPTER 14

The restoration of Israel after their captivity. The parable or song insulting over the king of Babylon. A prophecy against the Philistines.

HER time is near at hand, and her days shall not be prolonged. For the Lord will have mercy on Jacob, and will yet choose out of Israel, and will

CHAP. 12. [1] Exod. 15, 2; Ps. 117, 14. CHAP. 13. [1] Ezech. 32, 7; Joel, 2, 10; 3, 15; Matt. 24, 29; Mark, 13, 24; Luke, 21, 25. [2] Ps. 136, 9. [3] Gen. 19, 24.

CHAP. 13. Ver. 1. *The burden of Babylon.* That is, *a prophecy against Babylon.*

make them rest upon their own ground. And the stranger shall be joined with them, and shall adhere to the house of Jacob.

2 And the people shall take them and bring them into their place: and the house of Israel shall possess them in the land of the Lord for servants and hand-maids. And they shall make them captives that had taken them: and shall subdue their oppressors.

3 And it shall come to pass in that day, that when God shall give thee rest from thy labour, and from thy vexation, and from the hard bondage wherewith thou didst serve before,

4 Thou shalt take up this parable against the king of Babylon, and shalt say: How is the oppressor come to nothing, the tribute hath ceased?

5 The Lord hath broken the staff of the wicked, the rod of the rulers,

6 That struck the people in wrath with an incurable wound, that brought nations under in fury, that persecuted in a cruel manner.

7 The whole earth is quiet and still: it is glad and hath rejoiced.

8 The fir trees also have rejoiced over thee, and the cedars of Libanus, *saying:* Since thou hast slept, there hath none come up to cut us down.

9 Hell below was in an uproar to meet thee at thy coming: it stirred up the giants for thee. All the princes of the earth are risen up from their thrones, all the princes of nations.

10 All shall answer and say to thee: Thou also art wounded as well as we. Thou art become like unto us.

11 Thy pride is brought down to hell: thy carcass is fallen down. Under thee shall the moth be strewed, and worms shall be thy covering.

12 How art thou fallen from heaven, O Lucifer, who didst rise in the morning? How art thou fallen to the earth, that didst wound the nations?

13 And thou saidst in thy heart: I will ascend into heaven. I will exalt my throne above the stars of God. I will sit in the mountain of the covenant, in the sides of the north.

14 I will ascend above the height of the clouds. I will be like the most High.

15 But yet thou shalt be brought down to hell, into the depth of the pit.

16 They that shall see thee shall turn toward thee and behold thee. Is this the man that troubled the earth, that shook kingdoms,

17 That made the world a wilderness and destroyed the cities thereof, that opened not the prison to his prisoners?

18 All the kings of the nations have all of them slept in glory, every one in his own house.

19 But thou art cast out of thy grave, as an unprofitable branch, defiled, and wrapped up among them that were slain by the sword: and art gone down to the bottom of the pit, as a rotten carcass.

20 Thou shalt not keep company with them, even in burial: for thou hast destroyed thy land, thou hast slain thy people: the seed of the wicked shall not be named for ever.

21 Prepare his children for slaughter, for the iniquity of their fathers: they shall not rise up, nor inherit the land, nor fill the face of the world with cities.

22 And I will rise up against them, saith the Lord of hosts: and I will destroy the name of Babylon, and the remains, and the bud, and the offspring, saith the Lord.

23 And I will make it a possession for the ericius, and pools of waters: and I will sweep it and wear it out with a besom, saith the Lord of hosts.

24 The Lord of hosts hath sworn, saying: Surely as I have thought, so shall it be. And as I have purposed,

25 So shall it fall out: That I will destroy the Assyrian in my land, and upon my mountains tread him under foot. And his yoke shall be taken away from them: and his burden shall be taken off their shoulder.'

26 This is the counsel that I have purposed upon all the earth: and this is the hand that is stretched out upon all nations.

27 For the Lord of hosts hath decreed, and who can disannul it? And his hand is stretched out, and who shall turn it away?

28 In the year that king Achaz died, was this burden:

29 Rejoice not thou, whole Philistia, that the rod of him that struck thee is broken in pieces: for out of the root of the serpent shall come forth a basilisk, and his seed shall swallow the bird.

30 And the firstborn of the poor shall be fed, and the poor shall rest with confidence: and I will make thy root perish with famine, and I will kill thy remnant.

31 Howl, O gate: cry, O city. All Philistia is thrown down: for a smoke shall come from the north, and there is none that shall escape his troop.

32 And what shall be answered to the messengers of the nations? That the

Chap. 14. Ver. 12. *O Lucifer.* O day star. All this, according to the letter, is spoken of the king of Babylon. It may also be applied, in a spiritual sense, to Lucifer the prince of devils, who was created a bright angel, but fell by pride and rebellion against God.

Lord hath founded Sion, and the poor of his people shall hope in him.

CHAPTER 15
A prophecy of the desolation of the Moabites.

THE burden of Moab. Because in the night Ar of Moab is laid waste, it is silent: because the wall of Moab is destroyed in the night, it is silent.

2 The house is gone up, and Dibon to the high places, to mourn over Nabo: and over Medaba Moab hath howled. ¹ On all their heads shall be baldness, and every beard shall be shaven.

3 In their streets they are girded with sackcloth: on the tops of their houses, and in their streets, all shall howl and come down weeping.

4 Hesebon shall cry and Eleale: their voice is heard even to Jasa. For this shall the well-appointed men of Moab howl, his soul shall howl to itself.

5 My heart shall cry to Moab, the bars thereof *shall flee* unto Segor, a heifer of three years old. For by the ascent of Luith they shall go up weeping: and in the way of Oronaim they shall lift up a cry of destruction.

6 For the waters of Nemrim shall be desolate, for the grass is withered away: the spring is faded, all the greenness is perished.

7 According to the greatness of their work is their visitation also: they shall lead them to the torrent of the willows.

8 For the cry is gone round about the border of Moab: the howling thereof unto Gallim, and unto the well of Elim the cry thereof.

9 For the waters of Dibon are filled with blood. For I will bring more upon Dibon: the lion upon them that shall flee of Moab, and upon the remnant of the land.

CHAPTER 16
The prophet prayeth for Christ's coming. The affliction of the Moabites for their pride.

SEND forth, O Lord, the Lamb, the ruler of the earth, from Petra of the desert, to the mount of the daughter of Sion.

2 And it shall come to pass that, as a bird fleeing away, and as young ones flying out of the nest, so shall the daughters of Moab be in the passage of Arnon.

3 Take counsel, gather a council: make thy shadow as the night in the

midday; hide them that flee; and betray not them that wander about.

4 My fugitives shall dwell with thee: O Moab, be thou a covert to them from the face of the destroyer: for the dust is at an end; the wretch is consumed; he hath failed that trod the earth under foot.

5 And a throne shall be prepared in mercy: and one shall sit upon it in truth in the tabernacle of David, judging and seeking judgment, and quickly rendering that which is just.

6 ¹ We have heard of the pride of Moab: he is exceeding proud. His pride and his arrogancy and his indignation is more than his strength.

7 Therefore shall Moab howl to Moab: every one shall howl. To them that rejoice upon the brick walls, tell ye their stripes.

8 For the suburbs of Hesebon are desolate, and the lords of the nations have destroyed the vineyard of Sabama: the branches thereof have reached even to Jazer: they have wandered in the wilderness; the branches thereof are left; they are gone over the sea.

9 Therefore I will lament with the weeping of Jazer the vineyard of Sabama: I will water thee with my tears, O Hesebon and Eleale: for the voice of the treaders hath rushed in upon thy vintage and upon thy harvest.

10 And gladness and joy shall be taken away from Carmel: and there shall be no rejoicing nor shouting in the vineyards. He shall not tread out wine in the press that was wont to tread it out: the voice of the treaders I have taken away.

11 Wherefore my bowels shall sound like a harp for Moab, and my inward parts for the brick wall.

12 And it shall come to pass, when it is seen that Moab is wearied on his high places, that he shall go in to his sanctuaries to pray, and shall not prevail.

13 This is the word that the Lord spoke to Moab from that time:

14 And now the Lord hath spoken, saying: In three years, as the years of a hireling, the glory of Moab shall be taken away for all the multitude of the people; and it shall be left small and feeble, not many.

CHAPTER 17
Judgments upon Damascus and Samaria. The overthrow of the Assyrians.

THE burden of Damascus. Behold Damascus shall cease to be a city, and shall be as a ruinous heap of stones.

2 The cities of Aroer shall be left for flocks: and they shall rest there, and

CHAP. 15. ¹ Jer. 48, 37; Ezech. 7, 18. CHAP. 16. ¹ Jer. 48, 29.

CHAP. 15. Ver. 7. *Torrent of the willows.* That is, as some say, the waters of Babylon: others render it, a valley of the Arabians.

CHAP. 16. Ver. 10. *Carmel.* This name is often taken to signify a fair and fruitful hill or field, such as Mount Carmel is.

there shall be none to make them afraid.

3 And aid shall cease from Ephraim, and the kingdom from Damascus: and the remnant of Syria shall be as the glory of the children of Israel, saith the Lord of hosts.

4 And it shall come to pass in that day, that the glory of Jacob shall be made thin, and the fatness of his flesh shall grow lean.

5 And it shall be as when one gathereth in the harvest that which remaineth, and his arm shall gather the ears of corn: and it shall be as he that seeketh ears in the vale of Raphaim.

6 And the fruit thereof that shall be left upon it shall be as one cluster of grapes, and as the shaking of the olive tree, two or three berries in the top of a bough, or four or five upon the top of the tree, saith the Lord the God of Israel.

7 In that day, man shall bow down himself to his Maker: and his eyes shall look to the Holy One of Israel.

8 And he shall not look to the altars which his hands made: and he shall not have respect to the things that his fingers wrought, such as groves and temples.

9 In that day, his strong cities shall be forsaken, as the ploughs, and the corn that were left before the face of the children of Israel: and thou shalt be desolate.

10 Because thou hast forgotten God thy saviour, and hast not remembered thy strong helper: therefore shalt thou plant good plants and shalt sow strange seed.

11 In the day of thy planting shall be the wild grape, and in the morning thy seed shall flourish: the harvest is taken away in the day of inheritance and shall grieve thee much.

12 Woe to the multitude of many people, like the multitude of the roaring sea: and the tumult of crowds, like the noise of many waters.

13 Nations shall make a noise like the noise of waters overflowing: but he shall rebuke him, and he shall flee far off. And he shall be carried away as the dust of the mountains before the wind, and as a whirlwind before a tempest.

14 In the time of the evening, behold there shall be trouble: the morning shall come, and he shall not be. This is the portion of them that have wasted us, and the lot of them that spoiled us.

CHAPTER 18

A woe to the Ethiopians, who fed Israel with vain hopes. Their future conversion.

WOE to the land, the winged cymbal, which is beyond the rivers of Ethiopia,

2 That sendeth ambassadors by the sea, and in vessels of bulrushes upon the waters. Go, ye swift angels, to a nation rent and torn in pieces: to a terrible people, after which there is no other: to a nation expecting and trodden under foot, whose land the rivers have spoiled.

3 All ye inhabitants of the world, who dwell on the earth, when the sign shall be lifted up on the mountains, you shall see, and you shall hear the sound of the trumpet.

4 For thus saith the Lord to me: I will take my rest, and consider in my place, as the noon light is clear, and as a cloud of dew in the day of harvest.

5 For before the harvest it was all flourishing, and it shall bud without perfect ripeness, and the sprigs thereof shall be cut off with pruning hooks: and what is left shall be cut away and shaken out.

6 And they shall be left together to the birds of the mountains and the beasts of the earth: and the fowls shall be upon them all the summer, and all the beasts of the earth shall winter upon them.

7 At that time shall a present be brought to the Lord of hosts, from a people rent and torn in pieces: from a terrible people, after which there hath been no other: from a nation expecting, expecting, and trodden under foot, whose land the rivers have spoiled, to the place of the name of the Lord of hosts, to Mount Sion.

CHAPTER 19

The punishment of Egypt. Their call to the church.

THE burden of Egypt. Behold the Lord will ascend upon a swift cloud and will enter into Egypt. And the idols of Egypt shall be moved at his presence, and the heart of Egypt shall melt in the midst thereof.

2 And I will set the Egyptians to fight against the Egyptians: and they shall fight brother against brother, and friend against friend, city against city, kingdom against kingdom.

3 And the spirit of Egypt shall be broken in the bowels thereof, and I will cast down their counsel: and they shall consult their idols, and their diviners, and their wizards and soothsayers.

4 And I will deliver Egypt into the hand of cruel masters: and a strong king shall rule over them, saith the Lord the God of hosts.

CHAP. 17. Ver. 9. *That were left*, namely, by the Chanaanites, when the children of Israel came into their land.
Ver. 12. *The multitude.* This, and all that follows to the end of the chapter, relates to the Assyrian army under Sennacherib.
CHAP. 18. Ver. 2. *Angels.* Or messengers.

5 And the water of the sea shall be dried up: and the river shall be wasted and dry.

6 And the rivers shall fail: the streams of the banks shall be diminished and be dried up. The reed and the bulrush shall wither away.

7 The channel of the river shall be laid bare from its fountain, and every thing sown by the water shall be dried up. It shall wither away and shall be no more.

8 The fishers also shall mourn, and all that cast a hook into the river shall lament: and they that spread nets upon the waters shall languish away.

9 They shall be confounded that wrought in flax, combing and weaving fine linen.

10 And its watery places shall be dry: all they *shall mourn* that made pools to take fishes.

11 The princes of Tanis are become fools, the wise counsellors of Pharao have given foolish counsel. How will you say to Pharao: I am the son of the wise, the son of ancient kings?

12 Where are now thy wise men? Let them tell thee, and shew what the Lord of hosts hath purposed upon Egypt.

13 The princes of Tanis are become fools, the princes of Memphis are gone astray: they have deceived Egypt, the stay of the people thereof.

14 The Lord hath mingled in the midst thereof the spirit of giddiness: and they have caused Egypt to err in all its works, as a drunken man staggereth and vomiteth.

15 And there shall be no work for Egypt, to make head or tail, him that bendeth down, or that holdeth back.

16 In that day, Egypt shall be like unto women: and they shall be amazed and afraid, because of the moving of the hand of the Lord of hosts, which he shall move over it.

17 And the land of Juda shall be a terror to Egypt: every one that shall remember it shall tremble, because of the counsel of the Lord of hosts, which he hath determined concerning it.

18 [1] In that day, there shall be five cities in the land of Egypt, speaking the language of Chanaan, and swearing by the Lord of hosts. One shall be called the city of the sun.

19 In that day, there shall be an altar of the Lord in the midst of the land of Egypt, and a monument of the Lord at the borders thereof.

20 It shall be for a sign and for a testimony to the Lord of hosts, in the land of Egypt. For they shall cry to the Lord because of the oppressor: and he

shall send them a Saviour and a defender, to deliver them.

21 And the Lord shall be known by Egypt: and the Egyptians shall know the Lord in that day, and shall worship him with sacrifices and offerings. And they shall make vows to the Lord and perform them.

22 And the Lord shall strike Egypt with a scourge, and shall heal it. And they shall return to the Lord: and he shall be pacified towards them and heal them.

23 In that day, there shall be a way from Egypt to the Assyrians: and the Assyrian shall enter into Egypt, and the Egyptian to the Assyrians. And the Egyptians shall serve the Assyrian.

24 In that day shall Israel be the third to the Egyptian and the Assyrian: a blessing in the midst of the land.

25 Which the Lord of hosts hath blessed, saying: Blessed be my people of Egypt, and the work of my hands to the Assyrian. But Israel is my inheritance.

CHAPTER 20

The ignominious captivity of the Egyptians and the Ethiopians.

IN the year that Thartan entered into Azotus, when Sargon the king of the Assyrians had sent him, and he had fought against Azotus, and had taken it:

2 At that same time, the Lord spoke by the hand of Isaias the son of Amos, saying: [1] Go, and loose the sackcloth from off thy loins, and take off thy shoes from thy feet. And he did so, and went naked and barefoot.

3 And the Lord said: As my servant Isaias hath walked, naked and barefoot, it shall be a sign and a wonder of three years upon Egypt, and upon Ethiopia,

4 So shall the king of the Assyrians lead away the prisoners of Egypt, and the captivity of Ethiopia, young and old. naked and barefoot, with their buttocks uncovered to the shame of Egypt.

5 And they shall be afraid, and ashamed of Ethiopia their hope, and of Egypt their glory.

6 And the inhabitants of this isle shall say in that day: Lo, this was our hope, to whom we fled for help, to deliver us from the face of the king of the Assyrians. And how shall we be able to escape?

CHAPTER 21

The destruction of Babylon by the Medes and Persians. A prophecy against the Edomites and the Arabians.

THE burden of the desert of the sea. As whirlwinds come from the

---

CHAP. 19. [1] Ezech. 30. CHAP. 20. [1] Zach. 13, 4; Matt. 3, 4.

south, it cometh from the desert, from a terrible land.

2 A grievous vision is told me: He that is unfaithful dealeth unfaithfully; and he that is a spoiler, spoileth. Go up, O Elam, besiege, O Mede: I have made all the mourning thereof to cease.

3 Therefore are my loins filled with pain: anguish hath taken hold of me as the anguish of a woman in labour. I fell down at the hearing of it: I was troubled at the seeing of it.

4 My heart failed, darkness amazed me: Babylon, my beloved, is become a wonder to me.

5 Prepare the table: behold in the watchtower them that eat and drink. Arise, ye princes, take up the shield.

6 For thus hath the Lord said to me: Go, and set a watchman: and whatsoever he shall see, let him tell.

7 And he saw a chariot with two horsemen, a rider upon an ass, and a rider upon a camel: and he beheld them diligently with much heed.

8 And a lion cried out: I am upon the watchtower of the Lord, standing continually by day: ¹ and I am upon my ward, standing whole nights.

9 Behold this man cometh, the rider upon the chariot with two horsemen. And he answered and said: ² Babylon is fallen, she is fallen, and all the graven gods thereof are broken unto the ground.

10 O my thrashing, and the children of my floor, that which I have heard of the Lord of hosts, the God of Israel, I have declared unto you.

11 The burden of Duma calleth to me out of Seir: Watchman, what of the night? Watchman, what of the night?

12 The watchman said: The morning cometh, also the night. If you seek, seek: return, come.

13 The burden in Arabia. In the forest at evening you shall sleep, in the paths of Dedanim.

14 Meeting the thirsty bring him water, you that inhabit the land of the south: meet with bread him that fleeth.

15 For they are fled from before the swords, from the sword that hung over them, from the bent bow, from the face of a grievous battle.

16 For thus saith the Lord to me: Within a year, according to the years of a hireling, all the glory of Cedar shall be taken away.

17 And the residue of the number of strong archers of the children of Cedar shall be diminished: for the Lord the God of Israel hath spoken it.

CHAPTER 22

The prophet laments the devastation of Juda. He foretells the deprivation of Sobna, and the substitution of Eliacim, a figure of Christ.

THE burden of the valley of vision. What aileth thee also, that thou too art wholly gone up to the housetops?

2 Full of clamour, a populous city, a joyous city: thy slain are not slain by the sword, nor dead in battle.

3 All the princes are fled together, and are bound hard: all that were found are bound together. They are fled far off.

4 Therefore have I said: Depart from me, I will weep bitterly. Labour not to comfort me, for the devastation of the daughter of my people.

5 For it is a day of slaughter and of treading down, and weeping to the Lord the God of hosts in the valley of vision: searching the wall, and magnificent upon the mountain.

6 And Elam took the quiver, the chariot of the horseman: and the shield was taken down from the wall.

7 And thy choice valleys shall be full of chariots: and the horsemen shall place themselves in the gate.

8 And the covering of Juda shall be discovered: and thou shalt see in that day the armoury of the house of the forest.

9 And you shall see the breaches of the city of David, that they are many. And you have gathered together the waters of the lower pool.

10 And have numbered the houses of Jerusalem, and broken down houses to fortify the wall.

11 ¹ And you made a ditch between the two walls for the water of the old pool: and you have not looked up to the maker thereof, nor regarded him even at a distance, that wrought it long ago.

CHAP. 21. ¹ Hab. 2, 1. ² Jer. 51, 8; Apoc. 14, 8. CHAP. 22. ¹ 4 Kings, 20, 20; 2 Par. 32, 30.

CHAP. 21. Ver. 1. *The desert of the sea.* So Babylon is here called, because from a city as full of people as the sea is with water, it was become a desert.

Ver. 2. *O Elam.* That is, O Persia.

Ver. 7. *A rider upon an ass.* These two riders are the kings of the Persians and Medes.

Ver. 8. *And a lion cried out.* That is, I (Isaias), seeing the approaching ruin of Babylon, have cried out as a lion roaring.

Ver. 11. *Duma.* That is, Idumea, or Edom.

Ver. 16. *Cedar.* Arabia.

CHAP. 22. Ver. 1. *The valley of vision.* Jerusalem. The temple of Jerusalem was built upon mount *Moria,* or the mountain *of vision.* But the city is here called *the valley of vision:* either because it was lower than the temple, or because of the low condition to which it was to be reduced.

12 And the Lord, the God of hosts, in that day shall call to weeping and to mourning: to baldness and to girding with sackcloth.

13 And behold joy and gladness, killing calves and slaying rams, eating flesh and drinking wine: ² Let us eat and drink; for to-morrow we shall die.

14 And the voice of the Lord of hosts was revealed in my ears: Surely this iniquity shall not be forgiven you till you die, saith the Lord God of hosts.

15 Thus saith the Lord God of hosts: Go, get thee in to him that dwelleth in the tabernacle, to Sobna who is over the temple: and thou shalt say to him:

16 What dost thou here, or as if thou wert somebody here? For thou hast hewed thee out a sepulchre here; thou hast hewed out a monument carefully in a high place, a dwelling for thyself in a rock.

17 Behold the Lord will cause thee to be carried away, as a cock is carried away: and he will lift thee up as a garment.

18 He will crown thee with a crown of tribulation: he will toss thee like a ball into a large and spacious country. There shalt thou die: and there shall the chariot of thy glory be, the shame of the house of thy Lord.

19 And I will drive thee out from thy station, and depose thee from thy ministry.

20 And it shall come to pass in that day, that I will call my servant Eliacim, the son of Helcias.

21 And I will clothe him with thy robe, and will strengthen him with thy girdle, and will give thy power into his hand: and he shall be as a father to the inhabitants of Jerusalem, and to the house of Juda.

22 ³ And I will lay the key of the house of David upon his shoulder: and he shall open, and none shall shut: and he shall shut, and none shall open.

23 And I will fasten him as a peg in a sure place: and he shall be for a throne of glory to the house of his father.

24 And they shall hang upon him all the glory of his father's house, divers kinds of vessels, every little vessel: from the vessels of cups even to every instrument of music.

25 In that day, saith the Lord of hosts, shall the peg be removed, that was fastened in the sure place. And it shall be broken and shall fall: and that which hung thereon shall perish, because the Lord hath spoken it.

² Wisd. 2, 6; Isai. 56, 12; 1 Cor. 15, 32. ³ Apoc. 3, 7; Job, 12, 14.

CHAPTER 23

The destruction of Tyre. It shall be repaired again after seventy years.

THE burden of Tyre. Howl, ye ships of the sea, for the house is destroyed, from whence they were wont to come: from the land of Cethim it is revealed to them.

2 Be silent, you that dwell in the island: the merchants of Sidon, passing over the sea, have filled thee.

3 The seed of the Nile in many waters, the harvest of the river is her revenue: and she is become the mart of the nations.

4 Be thou ashamed, O Sidon: for the sea speaketh, even the strength of the sea, saying: I have not been in labour; nor have I brought forth, nor have I nourished up young men, nor brought up virgins.

5 When it shall be heard in Egypt, they will be sorry: when they shall hear of Tyre.

6 Pass over the seas, howl, ye inhabitants of the island.

7 Is not this your city, which gloried from of old in her antiquity? Her feet shall carry her afar to sojourn.

8 Who hath taken this counsel against Tyre, that was formerly crowned, whose merchants were princes, and her traders the nobles of the earth?

9 The Lord of hosts hath designed it, to pull down the pride of all glory and bring to disgrace all the glorious ones of the earth.

10 Pass thy land as a river, O daughter of the sea: thou hast a girdle no more.

11 He stretched out his hand over the sea: he troubled kingdoms. The Lord hath given a charge against Chanaan, to destroy the strong ones thereof.

12 And he said: Thou shalt glory no more, O virgin daughter of Sidon, who art oppressed. Arise and sail over to Cethim: there also thou shalt have no rest.

13 Behold the land of the Chaldeans. There was not such a people: the Assyrian founded it. They have led away the strong ones thereof into captivity, they have destroyed the houses thereof, they have brought it to ruin.

14 Howl, O ye ships of the sea, for your strength is laid waste.

15 And it shall come to pass in that day that thou, O Tyre, shalt be forgotten, seventy years, according to the days of one king: but after seventy years, there shall be unto Tyre as the song of a harlot.

16 Take a harp, go about the city, thou harlot that hast been forgotten: sing well, sing many a song, that thou mayst be remembered.

17 And it shall come to pass after seventy years, that the Lord will visit Tyre and will bring her back again to her traffic: and she shall commit fornication again with all the kingdoms of the world upon the face of the earth.

18 And her merchandise and her hire shall be sanctified to the Lord. They shall not be kept in store nor laid up: for her merchandise shall be for them that shall dwell before the Lord, that they may eat unto fulness and be clothed for a continuance.

CHAPTER 24

The judgments of God upon all the sinners of the world. A remnant shall joyfully praise him.

BEHOLD the Lord shall lay waste the earth, and shall strip it, and shall afflict the face thereof and scatter abroad the inhabitants thereof.

2 [1] And it shall be as with the people, so with the priest: and as with the servant, so with his master: as with the handmaid, so with her mistress: as with the buyer, so with the seller: as with the lender, so with the borrower: as with him that calleth for his money, so with him that oweth.

3 With desolation shall the earth be laid waste, and it shall be utterly spoiled: for the Lord hath spoken this word.

4 The earth mourned and faded away and is weakened: the world faded away: the height of the people of the earth is weakened.

5 And the earth is infected by the inhabitants thereof: because they have transgressed the laws, they have changed the ordinance, they have broken the everlasting covenant.

6 Therefore shall a curse devour the earth: and the inhabitants thereof shall sin. And therefore they that dwell therein shall be mad: and few men shall be left.

7 The vintage hath mourned: the vine hath languished away: all the merry-hearted have sighed.

8 The mirth of timbrels hath ceased: the noise of them that rejoice is ended: the melody of the harp is silent.

9 They shall not drink wine with a song: the drink shall be bitter to them that drink it.

10 The city of vanity is broken down: every house is shut up: no man cometh in.

11 There shall be a crying for wine in the streets: all mirth is forsaken: the joy of the earth is gone away.

12 Desolation is left in the city and calamity shall oppress the gates.

13 For it shall be thus in the midst of the earth, in the midst of the people, as if a few olives that remain should be shaken out of the olive tree: or grapes, when the vintage is ended.

14 These shall lift up their voice and shall give praise: when the Lord shall be glorified, they shall make a joyful noise from the sea.

15 Therefore glorify ye the Lord in instruction: the name of the Lord God of Israel in the islands of the sea.

16 From the ends of the earth we have heard praises, the glory of the just one. And I said: My secret to myself, my secret to myself. Woe is me! The prevaricators have prevaricated: and with the prevarication of transgressors they have prevaricated.

17 Fear and the pit and the snare *are* upon thee, O thou inhabitant of the earth.

18 And it shall come to pass, [2] that he that shall flee from the noise of the fear shall fall into the pit: and he that shall rid himself out of the pit shall be taken in the snare: for the flood-gates from on high are opened, and the foundations of the earth shall be shaken.

19 With breaking shall the earth be broken, with crushing shall the earth be crushed, with trembling shall the earth be moved.

20 With shaking shall the earth be shaken as a drunken man, and shall be removed as the tent of one night. And the iniquity thereof shall be heavy upon it: and it shall fall and not rise again.

21 And it shall come to pass, that in that day the Lord shall visit upon the host of heaven, on high, and upon the kings of the earth, on the earth.

22 And they shall be gathered together as in the gathering of one bundle into the pit. And they shall be shut up there in prison: and after many days they shall be visited.

23 [3] And the moon shall blush, and the sun shall be ashamed, when the Lord of hosts shall reign in mount Sion and in Jerusalem, and shall be glorified in the sight of his ancients.

CHAPTER 25

A canticle of thanksgiving for God's judgments and benefits.

O LORD, thou art my God. I will exalt thee, and give glory to thy

CHAP. 24. [1] Osee, 4, 9. [2] Jer. 48, 44. [3] Joel, 2, 31; Acts, 2, 20.

CHAP. 23. Ver. 18. *Sanctified to the Lord.* This alludes to the conversion of the Gentiles.

CHAP. 24. Ver. 21. *The host of heaven on high.* The stars, which in many places of the Scripture are so called. Some commentators explain that these words here signify the demons of the air.

name: for thou hast done wonderful things, thy designs of old, faithful. Amen.

2 For thou hast reduced the city to a heap, the strong city to ruin, the house of strangers: to be no city and to be no more built up for ever.

3 Therefore shall a strong people praise thee: the city of mighty nations shall fear thee.

4 Because thou hast been a strength to the poor, a strength to the needy in his distress, a refuge from the whirlwind, a shadow from the heat. For the blast of the mighty is like a whirlwind beating against a wall.

5 Thou shalt bring down the tumult of strangers, as heat in thirst: and as with heat under a burning cloud, thou shalt make the branch of the mighty to wither away.

6 And the Lord of hosts shall make unto all people, in this mountain, a feast of fat things: a feast of wine, of fat things full of marrow, of wine purified from the lees.

7 And he shall destroy in this mountain the face of the bond with which all people were tied and the web that he began over all nations.

8 He shall cast death down headlong for ever. [1] And the Lord God shall wipe away tears from every face. And the reproach of his people he shall take away from off the whole earth. For the Lord hath spoken it.

9 And they shall say in that day: Lo, this is our God: we have waited for him, and he will save us. This is the Lord: we have patiently waited for him, we shall rejoice and be joyful in his salvation.

10 For the hand of the Lord shall rest in this mountain: and Moab shall be trodden down under him, as straw is broken in pieces with the wain.

11 And he shall stretch forth his hands under him, as he that swimmeth stretcheth forth his hands to swim: and he shall bring down his glory with the dashing of his hands.

12 And the bulwarks of thy high walls shall fall and be brought low, and shall be pulled down to the ground, even to the dust.

CHAPTER 26

A canticle of thanks for the deliverance of God's people.

IN that day shall this canticle be sung in the land of Juda. Sion, the city of our strength: a saviour, a wall and a bulwark shall be set therein.

Chap. 25. [1] Apoc. 7, 17; 21, 4.

Chap. 25. Ver. 10. *Moab.* That is, the reprobate, whose eternal punishment, from which they can no way escape, is described under these figures.

2 Open ye the gates: and let the just nation, that keepeth the truth, enter in.

3 The old error is passed away, thou wilt keep peace: peace, because we have hoped in thee.

4 You have hoped in the Lord for evermore: in the Lord God, mighty for ever.

5 For he shall bring down them that dwell on high: the high city he shall lay low. He shall bring it down even to the ground: he shall pull it down even to the dust.

6 The foot shall tread it down: the feet of the poor, the steps of the needy.

7 The way of the just is right: the path of the just is right to walk in.

8 And in the way of thy judgments, O Lord, we have patiently waited for thee: thy name, and thy remembrance *are* the desire of the soul.

9 My soul hath desired thee in the night: yea, and with my spirit within me in the morning early I will watch to thee. When thou shalt do thy judgments on the earth, the inhabitants of the world shall learn justice.

10 Let us have pity on the wicked: but he will not learn justice. In the land of the saints he hath done wicked things: and he shall not see the glory of the Lord.

11 Lord, let thy hand be exalted, and let them not see: let the envious people see and be confounded: and let fire devour thy enemies.

12 Lord, thou wilt give us peace: for thou hast wrought all our works for us.

13 O Lord our God, other lords besides thee have had dominion over us: only in thee let us remember thy name.

14 Let not the dead live, let not the giants rise again: therefore hast thou visited and destroyed them, and hast destroyed all their memory.

15 Thou hast been favourable to the nation, O Lord: thou hast been favourable to the nation. Art thou glorified? Thou hast removed all the ends of the earth far off.

16 Lord, they have sought after thee in distress: in the tribulation of murmuring thy instruction was with them.

17 As a woman with child, when she draweth near the time of her delivery, is in pain and crieth out in her pangs: so are we become in thy presence, O Lord.

18 We have conceived and been as it were in labour, and have brought forth wind. We have not wrought salvation on the earth: therefore the inhabitants of the earth have not fallen.

19 Thy dead men shall live, my slain shall rise again. Awake, and give praise, ye that dwell in the dust. For thy dew is the dew of the light: and the land of

the giants thou shalt pull down into ruin.

20 Go, my people, enter into thy chambers, shut thy doors upon thee, hide thyself a little for a moment; until the indignation pass away.

21 [1] For behold the Lord will come out of his place, to visit the iniquity of the inhabitant of the earth against him: and the earth shall disclose her blood and shall cover her slain no more.

CHAPTER 27

The punishment of the oppressors of God's people. The Lord's favour to his church.

IN that day, the Lord with his hard and great strong sword shall visit leviathan the bar serpent, and leviathan the crooked serpent: and shall slay the whale that is in the sea.

2 In that day, there shall be singing to the vineyard of pure wine.

3 I am the Lord that keep it, I will suddenly give it drink: lest any hurt come to it, I keep it night and day.

4 There is no indignation in me. Who shall make me a thorn and a brier in battle? Shall I march against it? Shall I set it on fire together?

5 Or rather shall it take hold of my strength? Shall it make peace with me? Shall it make peace with me?

6 When they shall rush in unto Jacob, Israel shall blossom and bud: and they shall fill the face of the world with seed.

7 Hath he struck him according to the stroke of him that struck him? Or is he slain, as he killed them that were slain by him?

8 In measure against measure, when it shall be cast off, thou shalt judge it. He hath meditated with his severe spirit in the day of heat.

9 Therefore upon this shall the iniquity of the house of Jacob be forgiven: and this is all the fruit, that the sin thereof should be taken away. when he shall have made all the stones of the altar as burnt stones broken in pieces. The groves and temples shall not stand.

10 For the strong city shall be desolate: the beautiful city shall be forsaken and shall be left as a wilderness. There the calf shall feed: and there shall he lie down and shall consume its branches.

11 Its harvest shall be destroyed with drought, women shall come and teach it: for it is not a wise people. Therefore he that made it shall not have mercy on it: and he that formed it shall not spare it.

12 And it shall come to pass that in that day the Lord will strike from the channel of the river even to the torrent of Egypt: and you shall be gathered together one by one, O ye children of Israel.

13 And it shall come to pass that in that day a noise shall be made with a great trumpet: and they that were lost shall come from the land of the Assyrians, and they that were outcasts in the land of Egypt. And they shall adore the Lord in the holy mount in Jerusalem.

CHAPTER 28

The punishment of the Israelites, for their pride, intemperance and contempt of religion. Christ the corner stone.

WOE to the crown of pride, to the drunkards of Ephraim, and to the fading flower, the glory of his joy, who were on the head of the fat valley, staggering with wine.

2 Behold the Lord is mighty and strong, as a storm of hail: a destroying whirlwind, as the violence of many waters overflowing and sent forth upon a spacious land.

3 The crown of pride of the drunkards of Ephraim shall be trodden under feet.

4 And the fading flower, the glory of his joy, who is on the head of the fat valley, shall be as a hasty fruit before the ripeness of autumn: which when he that seeth it shall behold, as soon as he taketh it in his hand, he will eat it up.

5 In that day, the Lord of hosts shall

CHAP. 26. [1] Mich. 1, 3.

CHAP. 26. Ver. 21. *Shall cover her slain no more.* This is said with relation to the martyrs and their happy resurrection.

CHAP. 27. Ver. 1. *Leviathan.* That is, the devil, the great enemy of the people of God. He is called the *bar serpent* from his strength, and the *crooked serpent* from his wiles, and the *whale of the sea* from the tyranny he exercises in the sea of this world. He was spiritually slain by the death of Christ, when his power was destroyed.

Ver. 3. *I will suddenly give it drink.* Or, as the Hebrew may also be rendered, *I will continually water it.*

Ver. 4. *No indignation in me.* That is, against the church: nor shall I become as *a thorn or brier* in its regard, or *march against it,* or *set it on fire:* but it shall always *take fast hold of me* and keep an everlasting *peace with me.*

Ver. 6. *When they shall rush in.* Some understand this of the enemies of the true Israel, that shall invade it in vain. Others of the spiritual invasion made by the apostles of Christ.

Ver. 7. *Hath he struck him?* Hath God punished the carnal persecuting Jews, in proportion to their doings against Christ and his saints?

Ver. 8. *When it shall be cast off.* When the synagogue shall be cast off, thou shalt judge it in measure, and in proportion to its crimes.—*He hath meditated.* God hath designed severe punishments in the day of his wrath.

Ver. 9. *Of the house of Jacob.* Namely, of such of them as shall be converted.

Ver. 10. *The strong city.* Jerusalem.

Ver. 13. *A great trumpet.* The preaching of the gospel for the conversion of the Jews

CHAP. 28. Ver. 1. *Ephraim.* That is, the kingdom of the ten tribes.—*The head of the fat valley.* Samaria, situate on a hill, having under it a most fertile valley.

be a crown of glory and a garland of joy to the residue of his people:

6 And a spirit of judgment to him that sitteth in judgment, and strength to them that return out of the battle to the gate.

7 But these also have been ignorant through wine, and through drunkenness have erred: the priest and the prophet have been ignorant through drunkenness. They are swallowed up with wine, they have gone astray in drunkenness, they have not known him that seeth, they have been ignorant of judgment.

8 For all tables were full of vomit and filth, so that there was no more place.

9 Whom shall he teach knowledge? And whom shall he make to understand the hearing? Them that are weaned from the milk, that are drawn away from the breasts.

10 For command, command again; command, command again; expect, expect again; expect, expect again: a little there, a little there.

11 ¹ For with the speech of lips and with another tongue, he will speak to this people.

12 To whom he said: This is my rest. Refresh the weary, and this is my refreshing. And they would not hear.

13 And the word of the Lord shall be to them: Command, command again; command, command again: expect, expect again; expect, expect again: a little there, a little there: that they may go, and fall backward, and be broken, and snared, and taken.

14 Wherefore, hear the word of the Lord, ye scornful men, who rule over my people that is in Jerusalem.

15 For you have said: We have entered into a league with death, and we have made a covenant with hell. When the overflowing scourge shall pass through, it shall not come upon us: for we have placed our hope in lies, and by falsehood we are protected.

16 ² Therefore thus saith the Lord

CHAP. 28. ¹ 1 Cor. 14, 21. ² Ps. 117, 22; Matt. 21, 42; Acts, 4, 11; Rom. 9, 33; 1 Peter, 2, 6. ³ 2 Kings, 5, 20; 1 Par. 14, 11. ⁴ Jos. 10, 13.

Ver. 7. *These also.* The kingdom of Juda.
Ver. 10. *Command, command again.* This is said in the person of the Jews, resisting the repeated commands of God and still putting him off.
Ver. 16. *A stone in the foundations.* That is, Christ.—*Let him not hasten.* Let him expect his coming with patience.
Ver. 20. *The bed is straitened.* It is too narrow to hold two: God will have the bed of our heart all to himself.
Ver. 21. *As in the mountain.* As the Lord fought against the Philistines in Baal Pharasim, 2 Kings 5, and against the Chanaanites, in the valley of Gabaon, Jos. 10.
Ver. 29. *This also.* Such also is the proceeding of the Lord with his land, and the divers seeds he sows therein.
CHAP. 29. Ver. 1. *Ariel.* This word signifies,

God: Behold, I will lay a stone in the foundations of Sion, a tried stone, a corner stone, a precious stone, founded in the foundation. He that believeth, let him not hasten.

17 And I will set judgment in weight, and justice in measure: and hail shall overturn the hope of falsehood, and waters shall overflow *its* protection.

18 And your league with death shall be abolished, and your covenant with hell shall not stand. When the overflowing scourge shall pass, you shall be trodden down by it.

19 Whensoever it shall pass through, it shall take you away, because in the morning early it shall pass through, in the day and in the night: and vexation alone shall make you understand what you hear.

20 For the bed is straitened so that one must fall out: and a short covering cannot cover both.

21 ³ For the Lord shall stand up as in the mountain of divisions: ⁴ he shall be angry as in the valley which is in Gabaon: that he may do his work, his strange work: that he may perform his work, his work is strange to him.

22 And now do not mock, lest your bonds be tied strait. For I have heard of the Lord the God of hosts a consumption and a cutting short upon all the earth.

23 Give ear, and hear my voice: hearken, and hear my speech.

24 Shall the ploughman, plough all the day to sow, shall he open and harrow his ground?

25 Will he not, when he hath made plain the surface thereof, sow gith, and scatter cummin, and put wheat in order, and barley and millet and vetches in their bounds?

26 For he will instruct him in judgment: his God will teach him.

27 For gith shall not be thrashed with saws, neither shall the cart wheel turn about upon cummin: but gith shall be beaten out with a rod, and cummin with a staff.

28 But bread corn shall be broken small; but the thrasher shall not thrash it for ever: neither shall the cart wheel hurt it, nor break it with its teeth.

29 This also is come forth from the Lord God of hosts, to make his counsel wonderful, and magnify justice.

CHAPTER 29

God's heavy judgments upon Jerusalem for their blind obstinacy. A prophecy of the conversion of the Gentiles.

ᗯOE to Ariel, to Ariel the city which David took! Year is added to year: the solemnities are at an end.

2 And I will make a trench about Ariel, and it shall be in sorrow and mourning, and it shall be to me as Ariel.

3 And I will make a circle round about thee, and will cast up a rampart against thee, and raise up bulwarks to besiege thee,

4 Thou shalt be brought down: thou shalt speak out of the earth. And thy speech shall be heard out of the ground: and thy voice shall be from the earth like that of the python: and out of the ground thy speech shall mutter.

5 And the multitude of them that fan thee shall be like small dust: and as ashes passing away, the multitude of them that have prevailed against thee.

6 And it shall be at an instant suddenly. A visitation shall come from the Lord of hosts in thunder, and with earthquake, and with a great noise of whirlwind and tempest, and with the flame of devouring fire.

7 And the multitude of all nations that have fought against Ariel shall be as the dream of a vision by night, and all that have fought, and besieged and prevailed against it.

8 And as he that is hungry dreameth and eateth, but when he is awake, his soul is empty: and as he that is thirsty dreameth and drinketh, and after he is awake, is yet faint with thirst, and his soul is empty: so shall be the multitude of all the Gentiles that have fought against mount Sion.

9 Be astonished and wonder: waver and stagger: be drunk, and not with wine: stagger, and not with drunkenness.

10 For the Lord hath mingled for you the spirit of a deep sleep: he will shut up your eyes: he will cover your prophets and princes, that see visions.

11 And the vision of all shall be unto you as the words of a book that is sealed, which when they shall deliver to one that is learned, they shall say: Read this. And he shall answer: I cannot, for it is sealed.

12 And the book shall be given to one that knoweth no letters, and it shall be said to him: Read. And he shall answer: I know no letters.

13 [1] And the Lord said: Forasmuch as this people draw near me with their mouth, and with their lips glorify me, but their heart is far from me, and they have feared me with the commandment and doctrines of men:

14 Therefore, behold I will proceed to cause an admiration in this people, by a great and wonderful miracle: [2] for wisdom shall perish from their wise men, and the understanding of their prudent men shall be hid.

15 Woe to you that are deep of heart,

to hide your counsel from the Lord! And their works are in the dark, and they say: [3] Who seeth us, and who knoweth us?

16 This thought of yours is perverse: as if the clay should think against the potter, and the work should say to the maker thereof: Thou madest me not. Or the thing framed should say to him that fashioned it: Thou understandest not.

17 Is it not yet a very little while, and Libanus shall be turned into charmel, and charmel shall be esteemed as a forest?

18 And in that day the deaf shall hear the words of the book: and out of darkness and obscurity the eyes of the blind shall see.

19 And the meek shall increase their joy in the Lord: and the poor men shall rejoice in the Holy One of Israel.

20 For he that did prevail hath failed; the scorner is consumed; and they are all cut off that watched for iniquity:

21 That made men sin by word, and supplanted him that reproved them in the gate, and declined in vain from the just.

22 Therefore, thus saith the Lord to the house of Jacob, he that redeemeth Abraham: Jacob shall not now be confounded, neither shall his countenance now be ashamed:

23 But when he shall see his children, the work of my hands in the midst of him, sanctifying my name. And they shall sanctify the Holy One of Jacob: and shall glorify the God of Israel.

24 And they that erred in spirit shall know understanding: and they that murmured shall learn the law.

CHAPTER 30

The people are blamed for their confidence in Egypt. God's mercies towards his church. The punishment of sinners.

WOE to you, apostate children, saith the Lord, that you would take counsel, and not of me: and would begin a web, and not by my spirit, that you might add sin upon sin.

2 Who walk to go down into Egypt, and have not asked at my mouth: hoping for help in the strength of Pharao and trusting in the shadow of Egypt.

3 And the strength of Pharao shall be to your confusion: and the confidence of the shadow of Egypt to your shame.

CHAP. 29. [1] Matt. 15, 8; Mark, 7, 6. [2] 1 Cor. 1, 19; Abd. 1, 8. [3] Ecclus. 23, 26.

the lion of God, and here is taken for the strong city of Jerusalem.

Ver. 17. *Charmel.* This word signifies *a fruitful field.*

4 For thy princes were in Tanis, and thy messengers came even to Hanes.

5 They were all confounded at a people that could not profit them: they were no help, nor to any profit, but to confusion and to reproach.

6 The burden of the beasts of the south. In a land of trouble and distress, from whence come the lioness and the lion, the viper and the flying basilisk, they carry their riches upon the shoulders of beasts and their treasures upon the bunches of camels, to a people that shall not be able to profit them.

7 [1] For Egypt shall help in vain, and to no purpose. Therefore have I cried concerning this: It is pride only. Sit still.

8 Now therefore go in *and* write for them upon box, and note it diligently in a book: and it shall be in the latter days for a testimony for ever.

9 For it is a people that provoketh to wrath, and lying children, children that will not hear the law of God.

10 Who say to the seers: See not. And to them that behold: Behold not for us those things that are right. Speak unto us pleasant things: see errors for us.

11 Take away from me the way: turn away the path from me. Let the Holy One of Israel cease from before us.

12 Therefore thus saith the Holy One of Israel: Because you have rejected this word and have trusted in oppression and tumult and have leaned upon it:

13 Therefore shall this iniquity be to you as a breach that falleth and is found wanting in a high wall. For the destruction thereof shall come on a sudden, when it is not looked for.

14 And it shall be broken small, as the potter's vessel is broken all to pieces with mighty breaking: and there shall not a sherd be found of the pieces thereof, wherein a little fire may be carried from the hearth, or a little water be drawn out of the pit.

15 For thus saith the Lord God, the Holy One of Israel: If you return and be quiet, you shall be saved. In silence and in hope shall your strength be. And you would not,

16 But have said: No, but we will flee to horses. Therefore shall you flee. And we will mount upon swift ones. Therefore shall they be swifter that shall pursue after you.

17 A thousand men shall flee for fear of one: and for fear of five shall you flee, till you be left, as the mast of a ship on the top of a mountain and as an ensign upon a hill.

18 Therefore the Lord waiteth that he may have mercy on you, and therefore shall he be exalted sparing you: because the Lord is the God of judgment. Blessed are all they that wait for him.

19 For the people of Sion shall dwell in Jerusalem. Weeping thou shalt not weep: he will surely have pity on thee. At the voice of thy cry, as soon as he shall hear, he will answer thee.

20 And the Lord will give you spare bread and short water: and will not cause thy teacher to flee away from thee any more; and thy eyes shall see thy teacher.

21 And thy ears shall hear the word of one admonishing thee behind thy back: This is the way; walk ye in it. And go not aside, neither to the right hand, nor to the left.

22 And thou shalt defile the plates of thy graven things of silver, and the garment of thy molten things of gold: and shalt cast them away as the uncleanness of a menstruous woman. Thou shalt say to it: Get thee hence.

23 And rain shall be given to thy seed, wheresoever thou shalt sow in the land: and the bread of the corn of the land shall be most plentiful and fat. The lamb in that day shall feed at large in thy possession.

24 And thy oxen, and the ass colts that till the ground, shall eat mingled provender as it was winnowed in the floor.

25 And there shall be upon every high mountain, and upon every elevated hill, rivers of running waters in the day of the slaughter of many, when the tower shall fall.

26 And the light of the moon shall be as the light of the sun, and the light of the sun shall be sevenfold, as the light of seven days: in the day when the Lord shall bind up the wound of his people and shall heal the stroke of their wound.

27 Behold the name of the Lord cometh from afar. His wrath burneth and is heavy to bear: his lips are filled with indignation, and his tongue as a devouring fire.

28 His breath as a torrent overflowing even to the midst of the neck: to destroy the nations unto nothing, and the bridle of error that was in the jaws of the people.

29 You shall have a song as in the night of the sanctified solemnity, and joy of heart, as when one goeth with a pipe to come into the mountain of the Lord, to the Mighty One of Israel.

30 And the Lord shall make the glory of his voice to be heard, and shall shew the terror of his arm, in the threatening

of wrath and the flame of devouring fire: he shall crush to pieces with whirlwind and hailstones.

31 For at the voice of the Lord the Assyrian shall fear being struck with the rod.

32 And the passage of the rod shall be strongly grounded, which the Lord shall make to rest upon him with timbrels and harps: and in great battles he shall overthrow them.

33 For Topheth is prepared from yesterday, prepared by the king, deep and wide. The nourishment thereof is fire and much wood: the breath of the Lord as a torrent of brimstone kindling it.

CHAPTER 31

The folly of trusting to Egypt, and forgetting God. He will fight for his people against the Assyrians.

WOE to them that go down to Egypt for help, trusting in horses, and putting their confidence in chariots because they are many, and in horsemen because they are very strong: and have not trusted in the Holy One of Israel, and have not sought after the Lord.

2 But he that is the wise one hath brought evil, and hath not removed his words: and he will rise up against the house of the wicked, and against the aid of them that work iniquity.

3 Egypt is man, and not God: and their horses, flesh, and not spirit. And the Lord shall put down his hand, and the helper shall fall, and he that is helped shall fall, and they shall all be confounded together.

4 For thus saith the Lord to me: Like as the lion roareth, and the lion's whelp upon his prey; and when a multitude of shepherds shall come against him, he will not fear at their voice, nor be afraid of their multitude: so shall the Lord of hosts come down to fight upon Mount Sion and upon the hill thereof.

5 As birds flying, so will the Lord of hosts protect Jerusalem, protecting and delivering, passing over and saving.

6 Return as you had deeply revolted, O children of Israel.

7 For in that day a man shall cast away his idols of silver and his idols of gold, which your hands have made for you to sin.

8 ¹ And the Assyrian shall fall by the sword, not of a man, and the sword, not of a man, shall devour him: and he shall flee, not at the face of the sword. And his young men shall be tributaries.

9 And his strength shall pass away with dread: and his princes fleeing shall be afraid. The Lord hath said it, whose fire is in Sion, and his furnace in Jerusalem.

CHAPTER 32

The blessings of the reign of Christ. The desolation of the Jews and prosperity of the church of Christ.

BEHOLD a king shall reign in justice: and princes shall rule in judgment.

2 And a man shall be as when one is hid from the wind, and hideth himself from a storm: as rivers of waters in drought, and the shadow of a rock that standeth out in a desert land.

3 The eyes of them that see shall not be dim: and the ears of them that hear shall hearken diligently.

4 And the heart of fools shall understand knowledge: and the tongue of stammerers shall speak readily and plain.

5 The fool shall no more be called prince: neither shall the deceitful be called great.

6 For the fool will speak foolish things, and his heart will work iniquity, to practise hypocrisy and speak to the Lord deceitfully, and to make empty the soul of the hungry and take away drink from the thirsty.

7 The vessels of the deceitful are most wicked: for he hath framed devices to destroy the meek with lying words, when the poor man speaketh judgment.

8 But the prince will devise such things as are worthy of a prince: and he shall stand above the rulers.

9 Rise up, ye rich women, and hear my voice, ye confident daughters, give ear to my speech.

10 For after days and a year, you that are confident shall be troubled: for the vintage is at an end, the gathering shall come no more.

11 Be astonished, ye rich women, be troubled, ye confident ones: strip you and be confounded, gird your loins.

12 Mourn for your breasts, for the delightful country, for the fruitful vineyard.

13 Upon the land of my people shall thorns and briers come up. How much more upon all the houses of joy, of the city that rejoiced!

14 For the house is forsaken, the multitude of the city is left, darkness and obscurity are come upon its dens for ever. A joy of wild asses, the pastures of flocks,

15 Until the spirit be poured upon us from on high. And the desert shall

CHAP. 31. ¹ Isai. 37, 36; 4 Kings, 19, 35; 2 Par. 32, 21.

CHAP. 30. Ver. 33. *Topheth.* It is the same as *Gehenna,* and is taken for hell.

be as a charmel: and charmel shall be counted for a forest.

16 And judgment shall dwell in the wilderness: and justice shall sit in charmel.

17 And the work of justice shall be peace: and the service of justice quietness and security for ever.

18 And my people shall sit in the beauty of peace, and in the tabernacles of confidence, and in wealthy rest.

19 But hail shall be in the descent of the forest: and the city shall be made very low.

20 Blessed are ye that sow upon all waters, sending thither the foot of the ox and the ass.

CHAPTER 33

God's revenge against the enemies of his church. The happiness of the heavenly Jerusalem.

WOE to thee that spoilest! Shalt not thou thyself also be spoiled? And thou that despisest, shalt not thyself also be despised? When thou shalt have made an end of spoiling, thou shalt be spoiled: when being wearied thou shalt cease to despise, thou shalt be despised.

2 O Lord, have mercy on us, for we have waited for thee: be thou our arm in the morning, and our salvation in the time of trouble.

3 At the voice of the angel the people fled: and at the lifting up thyself the nations are scattered.

4 And your spoils shall be gathered together as the locusts are gathered: as when the ditches are full of them.

5 The Lord is magnified, for he hath dwelt on high: he hath filled Sion with judgment and justice.

6 And there shall be faith in thy times, riches of salvation, wisdom and knowledge: the fear of the Lord is his treasure.

7 Behold they that see shall cry without: the angels of peace shall weep bitterly.

8 The ways are made desolate, no one passeth by the road, the covenant is made void. He hath rejected the cities, he hath not regarded the men.

9 The land hath mourned and languished: Libanus is confounded and

become foul. And Saron is become as a desert: and Basan and Carmel are shaken.

10 Now will I rise up, saith the Lord. Now will I be exalted: now will I lift up myself.

11 You shall conceive heat, you shall bring forth stubble: your breath as fire shall devour you.

12 And the people shall be as ashes after a fire: as a bundle of thorns they shall be burnt with fire.

13 Hear, you that are far off, what I have done: and you that are near, know my strength.

14 The sinners in Sion are afraid, trembling hath seized upon the hypocrites. Which of you can dwell with devouring fire? Which of you shall dwell with everlasting burnings?

15 [1] He that walketh in justices and speaketh truth, that casteth away avarice by oppression and shaketh his hands from all bribes, that stoppeth his ears lest he hear blood and shutteth his eyes that he may see no evil.

16 He shall dwell on high: the fortifications of rocks shall be his highness. Bread is given him: his waters are sure.

17 His eyes shall see the king in his beauty: they shall see the land far off.

18 Thy heart shall meditate fear. [2] Where is the learned? Where is he that pondereth the words of the law? Where *is* the teacher of little ones?

19 The shameless people thou shalt not see, the people of profound speech: so that thou canst not understand the eloquence of his tongue, in whom there is no wisdom.

20 Look upon Sion, the city of our solemnity: thy eyes shall see Jerusalem, a rich habitation, a tabernacle that cannot be removed. Neither shall the nails thereof be taken away for ever: neither shall any of the chords thereof be broken.

21 Because only there our Lord is magnificent: a place of rivers, very broad and spacious streams. No ship with oars shall pass by it: neither shall the great galley pass through it.

22 For the Lord is our judge, the Lord is our lawgiver, the Lord is our king: he will save us.

23 Thy tacklings are loosed, and they shall be of no strength: thy mast shall be in such condition that thou shalt not be able to spread the flag. Then shall the spoils of much prey be divided: the lame shall take the spoil.

24 Neither shall he that is near say: I am feeble. The people that dwell therein shall have their iniquity taken away from them.

CHAP. 33. [1] Ps. 14, 2. [2] 1 Cor. 1, 20.

CHAP. 33. Ver. 1. *That spoilest.* This is particularly directed to Sennacherib.

Ver. 7. *The angels of peace.* The messengers or deputies sent to negotiate a peace.

Ver. 21. *Of rivers.* He speaks of the rivers of endless joys that flow from the throne of God to water the heavenly Jerusalem, where no enemy's ship can come.

Ver. 23. *Thy tacklings.* He speaks of the enemies of the church, under the allegory of a ship that is disabled.

CHAPTER 34

The general judgment of the wicked.

COME near, ye Gentiles, and hear: and hearken, ye people. Let the earth hear, and all that is therein, the world, and every thing that cometh forth of it.

2 For the indignation of the Lord is upon all nations, and his fury upon all their armies: he hath killed them and delivered them to slaughter.

3 Their slain shall be cast forth, and out of their carcasses shall rise a stink: the mountains shall be melted with their blood.

4 And all the host of the heavens shall pine away, and the heavens shall be folded together as a book: and all their host shall fall down, as the leaf falleth from the vine and from the fig tree.

5 For my sword is inebriated in heaven: behold it shall come down upon Idumea, and upon the people of my slaughter unto judgment.

6 The sword of the Lord is filled with blood. It is made thick with the blood of lambs and buck-goats, with the blood of rams full of marrow: for there is a victim of the Lord in Bosra and a great slaughter in the land of Edom.

7 And the unicorns shall go down with them, and the bulls with the mighty: their land shall be soaked with blood, and their ground with the fat of fat ones.

8 For it is the day of the vengeance of the Lord, the year of recompenses of the judgment of Sion.

9 And the streams thereof shall be turned into pitch, and the ground thereof into brimstone: and the land thereof shall become burning pitch.

10 Night and day, it shall not be quenched: the smoke thereof shall go up for ever. From generation to generation it shall lie waste: none shall pass through it for ever and ever.

11 The bittern and ericius shall possess it, and the ibis and the raven shall dwell in it: and a line shall be stretched out upon it to bring it to nothing, and a plummet unto desolation.

12 The nobles thereof shall not be there. They shall call rather upon the king: and all the princes thereof shall be nothing.

13 And thorns and nettles shall grow up in its houses, and the thistle in the fortresses thereof: and it shall be the habitation of dragons and the pasture of ostriches.

14 And demons and monsters shall meet, and the hairy ones shall cry out one to another. There hath the lamia lain down and found rest for herself.

15 There hath the ericius had its hole and brought up its young ones, and hath dug round about and cherished them in the shadow thereof. Thither are the kites gathered together one to another.

16 Search ye diligently in the book of the Lord, and read: not one of them was wanting, one hath not sought for the other. For that which proceedeth out of my mouth, he hath commanded: and his spirit it hath gathered them.

17 And he hath cast the lot for them, and his hand hath divided it to them by line. They shall possess it for ever: from generation to generation they shall dwell therein.

CHAPTER 35

The joyful flourishing of Christ's kingdom. In his church shall be a holy and secure way.

THE land that was desolate and impassable shall be glad: and the wilderness shall rejoice and shall flourish like the lily.

2 It shall bud forth and blossom, and shall rejoice with joy and praise. The glory of Libanus is given to it: the beauty of Carmel, and Saron. They shall see the glory of the Lord and the beauty of our God.

3 Strengthen ye the feeble hands, and confirm the weak knees.

4 Say to the fainthearted: Take courage, and fear not. Behold your God will bring the revenge of recompense. God himself will come and will save you.

5 Then shall the eyes of the blind be opened: and the ears of the deaf shall be unstopped.

6 Then shall the lame man leap as a hart, and the tongue of the dumb shall be free. For waters are broken out in the desert, and streams in the wilderness.

7 And that which was dry land shall become a pool, and the thirsty land springs of water. In the dens where dragons dwelt before shall rise up the verdure of the reed and the bulrush.

8 And a path and a way shall be there, and it shall be called the holy way: the unclean shall not pass over it. And this shall be unto you a straight way, so that fools shall not err therein.

9 No lion shall be there, nor shall

CHAP. 34. Ver. 4. *And all the host of the heavens.* That is, the sun, moon, and stars.

Ver. 5. *Idumea.* Under the name of *Idumea,* or *Edom,* a people that were enemies of the Jews, are here understood the wicked in general, the enemies of God and his church.

Ver. 7. *The unicorns.* That is, the great and mighty.

Ver. 8. *The year of recompenses.* When the persecutors of Sion, that is, of the church, shall receive their reward.

any mischievous beast go up by it, nor be found there: but they shall walk *there* that shall be delivered.

10 And the redeemed of the Lord shall return, and shall come into Sion with praise: and everlasting joy shall be upon their heads. They shall obtain joy and gladness: and sorrow and mourning shall flee away.

CHAPTER 36

Sennacherib invades Juda. His blasphemies.

AND it came to pass in the fourteenth year [1] of king Ezechias, that Sennacherib, king of the Assyrians, came up against all the fenced cities of Juda and took them.

2 And the king of the Assyrians sent Rabsaces from the Lachis to Jerusalem, to king Ezechias, with a great army: and he stood by the conduit of the upper pool in the way of the fuller's field.

3 And there went out to him Eliacim the son of Helcias, who was over the house, and Sobna the scribe, and Joahe the son of Asaph, the recorder.

4 And Rabsaces said to them: Tell Ezechias: Thus saith the great king, the king of the Assyrians: What is this confidence wherein thou trustest?

5 Or with what counsel or strength dost thou prepare for war? On whom dost thou trust, that thou art revolted from me?

6 Lo, thou trustest upon this broken staff of a reed, upon Egypt: upon which if a man lean, it will go into his hand and pierce it. So is Pharao king of Egypt to all that trust in him.

7 But if thou wilt answer me: We trust in the Lord our God; Is it not he whose high places and altars Ezechias hath taken away, and hath said to Juda and Jerusalem: You shall worship before this altar?

8 And now deliver thyself up to my lord the king of the Assyrians, and I will give thee two thousand horses: and thou wilt not be able on thy part to find riders for them.

9 And how wilt thou stand against the face of the judge of one place, of the least of my master's servants? But if thou trust in Egypt, in chariots and in horsemen:

10 And am I now come up without the Lord against this land to destroy it? The Lord said to me: Go up against this land and destroy it.

11 And Eliacim and Sobna and Joahe said to Rabsaces: Speak to thy servants in the Syrian tongue, for we understand it. Speak not to us in the Jews' language in the hearing of the people that are upon the wall.

12 And Rabsaces said to them: Hath my master sent me to thy master and to thee, to speak all these words; and not rather to the men that sit on the wall: that they may eat their own dung and drink their urine with you?

13 Then Rabsaces stood, and cried out with a loud voice in the Jews' language, and said: Hear the words of the great king, the king of the Assyrians.

14 Thus saith the king: Let not Ezechias deceive you, for he shall not be able to deliver you.

15 And let not Ezechias make you trust in the Lord, saying: The Lord will surely deliver us, *and* this city shall not be given into the hands of the king of the Assyrians.

16 Do not hearken to Ezechias, for thus said the king of the Assyrians: Do with me that which is for your advantage, and come out to me, and eat ye every one of his vine, and every one of his fig tree, and drink ye every one the water of his cistern,

17 Till I come and take you away to a land, like to your own, a land of corn and of wine, a land of bread and vineyards.

18 Neither let Ezechias trouble you, saying: The Lord will deliver us. Have any of the gods of the nations delivered their land out of the hand of the king of the Assyrians?

19 Where is the god of Emath and of Arphad? Where is the god of Sepharvaim? Have they delivered Samaria out of my hand?

20 Who is there among all the gods of these lands that hath delivered his country out of my hand, that the Lord may deliver Jerusalem out of my hand?

21 [2] And they held their peace, and answered him not a word. For the king had commanded, saying: Answer him not.

22 And Eliacim the son of Helcias, that was over the house, and Sobna, the scribe, and Joahe the son of Asaph the recorder, went in to Ezechias, with their garments rent, and told him the words of Rabsaces.

CHAPTER 37

Ezechias, his mourning and prayer. God's promise of protection. The Assyrian army is destroyed. Sennacherib is slain.

AND [1] it came to pass, when king Ezechias had heard it, that he rent his garments and covered himself with sackcloth and went into the house of the Lord.

2 And he sent Eliacim, who was over the house, and Sobna the scribe, and the ancients of the priests, covered with

CHAP. 36. [1] 4 Kings, 18, 13; 2 Par. 32, 1; Ecclus. 48, 20. [2] 4 Kings, 18, 36. CHAP. 37. [1] 4 Kings, 19, 1.

sackcloth, to Isaias the son of Amos the prophet.

3 And they said to him: Thus saith Ezechias: This day is a day of tribulation and of rebuke and of blasphemy: for the children are come to the birth, and there is not strength to bring forth.

4 It may be the Lord thy God will hear the words of Rabsaces, whom the king of the Assyrians his master hath sent to blaspheme the living God and to reproach with words which the Lord thy God hath heard: wherefore lift up thy prayer for the remnant that is left.

5 And the servants of Ezechias came to Isaias.

6 And Isaias said to them: Thus shall you say to your master: Thus saith the Lord: Be not afraid of the words that thou hast heard, with which the servants of the king of the Assyrians have blasphemed me.

7 Behold, I will send a spirit upon him, and he shall hear a message and shall return to his own country: and I will cause him to fall by the sword in his own country.

8 And Rabsaces returned, and found the king of the Assyrians besieging Lobna. ² For he had heard that he was departed from Lachis.

9 And he heard say about Tharaca the king of Ethiopia: He is come forth to fight against thee. And when he heard it, he sent messengers to Ezechias, saying:

10 Thus shall you speak to Ezechias the king of Juda, saying: Let not thy God deceive thee, in whom thou trustest, saying: Jerusalem shall not be given into the hands of the king of the Assyrians.

11 Behold thou hast heard all that the kings of the Assyrians have done to all countries which they have destroyed: and canst thou be delivered?

12 Have the gods of the nations delivered them whom my fathers have destroyed, Gozam and Haram and Reseph and the children of Eden that were in Thalassar?

13 Where is the king of Emath, and the king of Arphad, and the king of the city of Sepharvaim, of Ana, and of Ava? ³

14 And Ezechias took the letter from the hand of the messengers and read it, and went up to the house of the Lord: and Ezechias spread it before the Lord.

15 And Ezechias prayed to the Lord, saying:

16 O Lord of hosts, God of Israel, who sittest upon the cherubims, Thou alone art the God of all the kingdoms of the earth: Thou hast made heaven and earth.

17 Incline, O Lord, thy ear, and hear: open, O Lord, thy eyes, and see. And hear all the words of Sennacherib, which he hath sent to blaspheme the living God.

18 For of a truth, O Lord, the kings of the Assyrians have laid waste lands, and their countries.

19 And they have cast their gods into the fire. For they were not gods, but the works of men's hands, of wood and stone: and they broke them in pieces.

20 And now, O Lord our God, save us out of his hand: and let all the kingdoms of the earth know that thou only art the Lord.

21 And Isaias the son of Amos sent to Ezechias, saying: Thus saith the Lord the God of Israel: For the prayer thou hast made to me concerning Sennacherib the king of the Assyrians:

22 This is the word which the Lord hath spoken of him: The virgin, the daughter of Sion, hath despised thee and laughed thee to scorn: the daughter of Jerusalem hath wagged the head after thee.

23 Whom hast thou reproached, and whom hast thou blasphemed, and against whom hast thou exalted thy voice, and lifted up thy eyes on high? Against the Holy One of Israel.

24 By the hand of thy servants thou hast reproached the Lord, and hast said: With the multitude of my chariots I have gone up to the height of the mountains, to the top of Libanus: and I will cut down its tall cedars and its choice fir trees, and will enter to the top of its height, to the forest of its Carmel.

25 I have digged, and drunk water: and have dried up with the sole of my foot all the rivers shut up in banks.

26 Hast thou not heard what I have done to him of old? From the days of old I have formed it: and now I have brought it to effect: and it hath come to pass that hills fighting together and fenced cities should be destroyed.

27 The inhabitants of them were weak of hand: they trembled and were confounded. They became like the grass of the field and the herb of the pasture, and like the grass of the housetops, which withered before it was ripe.

28 I know thy dwelling, and thy going out, and thy coming in, and thy rage against me.

29 When thou wast mad against me, thy pride came up to my ears: therefore I will put a ring in thy nose and a bit between thy lips: and I will turn thee back by the way by which thou camest.

² 4 Kings, 19, 8. ³ 4 Kings, 18, 34.

CHAP. 37. Ver. 24. *Carmel.* See these figurative expressions explained in the annotations on the nineteenth chapter of the fourth book of Kings.

30 But to thee this shall be a sign: Eat this year the things that spring of themselves, and in the second year eat fruits; but in the third year sow and reap, and plant vineyards, and eat the fruit of them.

31 And that which shall be saved of the house of Juda and which is left shall take root downward and shall bear fruit upward.

32 For out of Jerusalem shall go forth a remnant, and salvation from mount Sion. The zeal of the Lord of hosts shall do this.

33 Wherefore thus saith the Lord concerning the king of the Assyrians: He shall not come into this city, nor shoot an arrow into it, nor come before it with shield, nor cast a trench about it.

34 By the way that he came, he shall return, and into this city he shall not come, saith the Lord.

35 And I will protect this city and will save it, for my own sake and for the sake of David my servant.

36 ⁴ And the angel of the Lord went out, and slew in the camp of the Assyrians a hundred and eighty-five thousand. And they arose in the morning, and behold they were all dead corpses.

37 And Sennacherib the king of the Assyrians went out and departed; and returned and dwelt in Ninive.

38 And it came to pass, as he was worshipping in the temple of Nesroch his god, that Adramelech and Sarasar his sons slew him with the sword. And they fled into the land of Ararat: and Asarhaddon his son reigned in his stead.

CHAPTER 38

Ezechias being advertised that he shall die, obtains by prayer a prolongation of his life, in confirmation of which the sun goes back. The canticle of Ezechias.

IN ¹ those days, Ezechias was sick even to death, and Isaias the son of Amos the prophet came unto him, and said to him: Thus saith the Lord: Take order with thy house, for thou shalt die, and not live.

2 And Ezechias turned his face toward the wall and prayed to the Lord,

3 And said: I beseech thee, O Lord, remember how I have walked before thee in truth, and with a perfect heart, and have done that which is good in thy sight. And Ezechias wept with great weeping.

4 And the word of the Lord came to Isaias, saying:

5 Go and say to Ezechias: Thus saith the Lord the God of David thy father: I have heard thy prayer, and I have seen thy tears: behold I will add to thy days fifteen years.

6 And I will deliver thee and this city out of the hand of the king of the Assyrians: and I will protect it.

7 And this shall be a sign to thee from the Lord, that the Lord will do this word which he hath spoken:

8 ² Behold I will bring again the shadow of the lines, by which it is now gone down in the sun dial of Achaz with the sun, ten lines backward. And the sun returned ten lines by the degrees by which it was gone down.

9 The writing of Ezechias king of Juda, when he had been sick and was recovered of his sickness.

10 I said: In the midst of my days I shall go to the gates of hell. I sought for the residue of my years.

11 I said: I shall not see the Lord God in the land of the living. I shall behold man no more, nor the inhabitant of rest.

12 My generation is at an end; and it is rolled away from me, as a shepherd's tent. My life is cut off, as by a weaver: whilst I was yet but beginning, he cut me off. From morning even to night thou wilt make an end of me.

13 I hoped till morning: as a lion so hath he broken all my bones. From morning even to night thou wilt make an end of me.

14 I will cry like a young swallow, I will meditate like a dove: my eyes are weakened looking upward. Lord, I suffer violence, answer thou for me.

15 What shall I say, or what shall he answer for me, whereas he himself hath done it? I will recount to thee all my years in the bitterness of my soul.

16 O Lord, if man's life be such, and the life of my spirit be in such things as these, thou shalt correct me and make me to live.

17 Behold in peace is my bitterness most bitter. But thou hast delivered my soul that it should not perish: thou hast cast all my sins behind thy back.

18 For hell shall not confess to thee, neither shall death praise thee: nor shall they that go down into the pit look for thy truth.

19 The living, the living, he shall give praise to thee, as I do this day: the father shall make thy truth known to the children.

20 O Lord, save me, and we will sing our psalms all the days of our life in the house of the Lord.

21 Now Isaias had ordered that they should take a lump of figs and lay it as

---

⁴ Isai. 31, 8; 4 Kings, 19, 35; Tob. 1, 21; Ecclus. 48, 24; 1 Mach. 7, 41; 2 Mach. 8, 19. CHAP. 38. ¹ 4 Kings, 20, 1; 2 Par. 32, 24. ² Ecclus. 48, 26.

CHAP. 38. Ver. 10. *Hell,* Sheol or Hades, the region of the dead.

a plaster upon the wound, and that he should be healed.

22 And Ezechias had said: What shall be the sign that I shall go up to the house of the Lord?

CHAPTER 39

Ezechias shews all his treasures to the ambassadors of Babylon. Upon which Isaias foretells the Babylonish captivity.

AT [1] that time Merodach Baladan, the son of Baladan king of Babylon, sent letters and presents to Ezechias: for he had heard that he had been sick and was recovered.

2 And Ezechias rejoiced at their coming: and he shewed them the storehouses of his aromatical spices and of the silver and of the gold and of the sweet odours and of the precious ointment, and all the storehouses of his furniture, and all things that were found in his treasures. There was nothing in his house nor in all his dominion that Ezechias shewed them not.

3 Then Isaias the prophet came to king Ezechias, and said to him: What said these men, and from whence came they to thee? And Ezechias said: From a far country they came to me, from Babylon.

4 And he said: What saw they in thy house? And Ezechias said: All things that are in my house have they seen. There was not any thing which I have not shewn them in my treasures.

5 And Isaias said to Ezechias: Hear the word of the Lord of hosts.

6 Behold the days shall come, that all that is in thy house, and that thy fathers have laid up in store until this day, shall be carried away into Babylon: there shall not any thing be left, saith the Lord.

7 And of thy children, that shall issue from thee, whom thou shalt beget, they shall take away: and they shall be eunuchs in the palace of the king of Babylon.

8 And Ezechias said to Isaias: The word of the Lord, which he hath spoken, is good. And he said: Only let peace and truth be in my days.

CHAPTER 40

The prophet comforts the people with the promise of the coming of Christ to forgive their sins. God's almighty power and majesty.

BE comforted, be comforted, my people, saith your God.

2 Speak ye to the heart of Jerusalem, and call to her: for her evil is come to an end, her iniquity is forgiven. [1] She hath received of the hand of the Lord double for all her sins.

3 [2] The voice of one crying in the desert: Prepare ye the way of the Lord, make straight in the wilderness the paths of our God.

4 Every valley shall be exalted and every mountain and hill shall be made low: and the crooked shall become straight, and the rough ways plain.

5 And the glory of the Lord shall be revealed: and all flesh together shall see, that the mouth of the Lord hath spoken.

6 The voice of one, saying: Cry. And I said: What shall I cry? [3] All flesh is grass, and all the glory thereof as the flower of the field.

7 The grass is withered and the flower is fallen, because the spirit of the Lord hath blown upon it. Indeed the people is grass.

8 The grass is withered and the flower is fallen: but the word of our Lord endureth for ever.

9 Get thee up upon a high mountain, thou that bringest good tidings to Sion. Lift up thy voice with strength, thou that bringest good tidings to Jerusalem. Lift it up: fear not. Say to the cities of Juda: Behold your God.

10 Behold the Lord God shall come with strength: and his arm shall rule. Behold his reward is with him and his work is before him.

11 [4] He shall feed his flock like a shepherd. He shall gather together the lambs with his arm and shall take them up in his bosom, and he himself shall carry them that are with young.

12 Who hath measured the waters in the hollow of his hand and weighed the heavens with his palm? Who hath poised with three fingers the bulk of the earth and weighed the mountains in scales and the hills in a balance?

13 [5] Who hath forwarded the spirit of the Lord? Or who hath been his counsellor, and hath taught him?

14 With whom hath he consulted: and who hath instructed him, and taught him the path of justice, and taught him knowledge, and shewed him the way of understanding?

15 Behold the Gentiles are as a drop of a bucket, and are counted as the smallest grain of a balance: behold the islands are as a little dust.

16 And Libanus shall not be enough to burn, nor the beasts thereof sufficient for a burnt offering.

17 All nations are before him as if they had no being at all, and are counted to him as nothing and vanity.

18 [6] To whom then have you likened

God? Or what image will you make for him?

19 Hath the workman cast a graven *statue?* Or hath the goldsmith formed it with gold, or the silversmith with plates of silver?

20 He hath chosen strong wood, and that will not rot: the skilful workman seeketh how he may set up an idol that may not be moved.

21 Do you not know? Hath it not been heard? Hath it not been told you from the beginning? Have you not understood the foundations of the earth?

22 It is he that sitteth upon the globe of the earth, and the inhabitants thereof are as locusts: [7] he that stretcheth out the heavens as nothing and spreadeth them out as a tent to dwell in.

23 He that bringeth the searchers of secrets to nothing, that hath made the judges of the earth as vanity.

24 And surely their stock was neither planted, nor sown, nor rooted in the earth. Suddenly he hath blown upon them, and they are withered: and a whirlwind shall take them away as stubble.

25 And to whom have ye likened me or made me equal, saith the Holy One?

26 Lift up your eyes on high, and see who hath created these things, who bringeth out their host by number and calleth them all by their names. By the greatness of his might and strength and power, not one of them was missing.

27 Why sayest thou, O Jacob, and speakest, O Israel: My way is hid from the Lord and my judgment is passed over from my God?

28 Knowest thou not, or hast thou not heard? The Lord is the everlasting God, who hath created the ends of the earth. He shall not faint nor labour, neither is there any searching out of his wisdom.

29 It is he that giveth strength to the weary, and increaseth force and might to them that are not.

30 Youths shall faint and labour: and young men shall fall by infirmity.

31 But they that hope in the Lord shall renew their strength. [8] They shall take wings as eagles; they shall run and not be weary; they shall walk and not faint.

CHAPTER 41
The reign of the just one. The vanity of idols.

LET the islands keep silence before me, and the nations take new strength. Let them come near, and

[7] Gen. 1, 6.   [8] Ps. 10, 5.   CHAP. 41.   [1] Isai. 44, 6; 48, 12; Apoc. 1, 8, 17; 22, 13.

then speak: let us come near to judgment together.

2 Who hath raised up the just one from the east, hath called him to follow him? He shall give the nations in his sight, and he shall rule over kings: he shall give *them* as the dust to his sword, as stubble driven by the wind, to his bow.

3 He shall pursue them, he shall pass in peace: no path shall appear after his feet.

4 Who hath wrought and done these things, calling the generations from the beginning? [1] I, the Lord. I am the first and the last.

5 The islands saw it, and feared: the ends of the earth were astonished; they drew near, and came.

6 Every one shall help his neighbour, and shall say to his brother: Be of good courage.

7 The coppersmith striking with the hammer encouraged him that forged at that time, saying: It is ready for soldering. And he strengthened it with nails, that it should not be moved.

8 But thou Israel, art my servant, Jacob whom I have chosen, the seed of Abraham my friend:

9 In whom I have taken thee from the ends of the earth, and from the remote parts thereof have called thee, and said to thee: Thou art my servant. I have chosen thee and have not cast thee away.

10 Fear not, for I am with thee: turn not aside, for I am thy God. I have strengthened thee and have helped thee: and the right hand of my just one hath upheld thee.

11 Behold all that fight against thee shall be confounded and ashamed: they shall be as nothing; and the men shall perish that strive against thee.

12 Thou shalt seek them, and shalt not find the men that resist thee. They shall be as nothing: and as a thing consumed the men that war against thee.

13 For I am the Lord thy God, who take thee by the hand, and say to thee: Fear not. I have helped thee.

14 Fear not, thou worm of Jacob, you that are dead, of Israel. I have helped thee, saith the Lord, and thy Redeemer the Holy One of Israel.

15 I have made thee as a new thrashing wain, with teeth like a saw. Thou shalt thrash the mountains, and break them in pieces: and shalt make the hills as chaff.

16 Thou shalt fan them, and the wind shall carry them away, and the whirlwind shall scatter them. And thou shalt rejoice in the Lord: in the Holy One of Israel thou shalt be joyful.

17 The needy and the poor seek for waters, and there are none: their tongue hath been dry with thirst. I the Lord will hear them: I the God of Israel will not forsake them.

18 I will open rivers in the high hills, and fountains in the midst of the plains: I will turn the desert into pools of waters, and the impassable land into streams of waters.

19 I will plant in the wilderness the cedar and the thorn and the myrtle and the olive tree: I will set in the desert the fir tree, the elm, and the box tree together:

20 That they may see and know, and consider, and understand together that the hand of the Lord hath done this, and the Holy One of Israel hath created it.

21 Bring your cause near, saith the Lord: bring hither, if you have any thing *to allege*, saith the King of Jacob.

22 Let them come and tell us all things that are to come, tell us the former things what they were: and we will set our heart *upon them*, and shall know the latter end of them. And tell us the things that are to come,

23 Shew the things that are to come hereafter: and we shall know that ye are gods. Do ye also good or evil, if you can: and let us speak and see together.

24 Behold, you are of nothing, and your work of that which hath no being: he that hath chosen you is an abomination.

25 I have raised up *one* from the north: and he shall come from the rising of the sun. He shall call upon my name: and he shall make princes to be as dirt, and as the potter treading clay.

26 Who hath declared from the beginning, that we may know? And from time of old, that we may say: Thou art just? There is none that sheweth, nor that foretelleth, nor that heareth your words.

27 The first shall say to Sion: Behold they are here, and to Jerusalem I will give an evangelist.

28 And I saw: and there was no one even among them to consult, or who, when I asked, could answer a word.

29 Behold they are all in the wrong, and their works are vain: their idols are wind and vanity.

CHAPTER 42

The office of Christ. The preaching of the gospel to the Gentiles. The blindness and reprobation of the Jews.

BEHOLD [1] my servant: I will uphold him. My elect: my soul delighteth in him. I have given my spirit upon him: he shall bring forth judgment to the Gentiles.

2 He shall not cry, nor have respect to person: neither shall his voice be heard abroad.

3 The bruised reed he shall not break, and smoking flax he shall not quench: he shall bring forth judgment unto truth.

4 He shall not be sad nor troublesome, till he set judgment in the earth: and the islands shall wait for his law.

5 Thus saith the Lord God that created the heavens and stretched them out: that established the earth and the things that spring out of it: that giveth breath to the people upon it, and spirit to them that tread thereon.

6 I, the Lord, have called thee in justice, and taken thee by the hand, and preserved thee. [2] And I have given thee for a covenant of the people, for a light of the Gentiles:

7 That thou mightest open the eyes of the blind, and bring forth the prisoner out of prison, and them that sit in darkness out of the prison house.

8 [3] I, the Lord: this is my name. I will not give my glory to another, nor my praise to graven things.

9 The things that were first, behold they are come: and new things do I declare. Before they spring forth, I will make you hear them.

10 Sing ye to the Lord a new song: his praise is from the ends of the earth. You that go down to the sea, and all that are therein: ye islands, and ye inhabitants of them.

11 Let the desert and the cities thereof be exalted: Cedar shall dwell in houses. Ye inhabitants of Petra, give praise: they shall cry from the top of the mountains.

12 They shall give glory to the Lord, and shall declare his praise in the islands.

13 The Lord shall go forth as a mighty man: as a man of war shall he stir up zeal. He shall shout and cry: he shall prevail against his enemies.

14 I have always held my peace, I have kept silence, I have been patient. I will speak now as a woman in labour: I will destroy, and swallow up at once.

15 I will lay waste the mountains and hills, and will make all their grass to wither: and I will turn rivers into islands and will dry up the standing pools.

16 And I will lead the blind into the way which they know not: and in the

CHAP. 42. [1] Matt. 12, 18. [2] Isai. 49, 6. [3] Isai. 48, 11.

CHAP. 41. Ver. 19. *The thorn.* In Hebrew, the *shitta,* or *setim,* a tree resembling the white thorn.

CHAP. 42. Ver. 1. *My servant.* Christ, who according to his humanity, is the srevant of God.
Ver. 11. *Petra.* A city that gives name to Arabia Petræa.

paths which they were ignorant of I will make them walk. I will make darkness light before them, and crooked things straight. These things have I done to them, and have not forsaken them.

17 They are turned back. Let them be greatly confounded that trust in a graven thing, that say to a molten thing: You are our god.

18 Hear, ye deaf, and, ye blind, behold that you may see.

19 Who is blind, but my servant? Or deaf, but he to whom I have sent my messengers? Who is blind, but he that is sold? Or who is blind, but the servant of the Lord?

20 Thou that seest many things, wilt thou not observe them? Thou that hast ears open, wilt thou not hear?

21 And the Lord was willing to sanctify him, and to magnify the law and exalt it.

22 But this is a people that is robbed and wasted. They are all the snare of young men, and they are hid in the houses of prisons. They are made a prey, and there is none to deliver them: a spoil, and there is none that saith: Restore.

23 Who is there among you that will give ear to this, that will attend and hearken for times to come?

24 Who hath given Jacob for a spoil, and Israel to robbers? Hath not the Lord himself, against whom we have sinned? And they would not walk in his ways: and they have not hearkened to his law.

25 And he hath poured out upon him the indignation of his fury and a strong battle: and hath burnt him round about, and he knew not: and set him on fire, and he understood not.

CHAPTER 43

God comforts his church, promising to protect her for ever. He expostulates with the Jews for their ingratitude.

AND now thus saith the Lord that created thee, O Jacob, and formed thee, O Israel: Fear not, for I have redeemed thee, and called thee by thy name. Thou art mine.

2 When thou shalt pass through the waters, I will be with thee: and the rivers shall not cover thee. When thou shalt walk in the fire, thou shalt not be burnt: and the flames shall not burn in thee.

3 For I am the Lord thy God, the Holy One of Israel, thy Saviour: I have given Egypt for thy atonement, Ethiopia and Saba for thee.

4 Since thou becamest honourable in my eyes, thou art glorious. I have loved thee: and I will give men for thee, and people for thy life.

5 Fear not, for I am with thee. I will bring thy seed from the east, and gather thee from the west.

6 I will say to the north: Give up. And to the south: Keep not back: bring my sons from afar, and my daughters from the ends of the earth.

7 And every one that calleth upon my name, I have created him for my glory: I have formed him and made him.

8 Bring forth the people that are blind, and have eyes: that are deaf, and have ears.

9 All the nations are assembled together and the tribes are gathered. Who among you can declare this, and shall make us hear the former things? Let them bring forth their witnesses, let them be justified, and hear, and say: It is truth.

10 You are my witnesses, saith the Lord, and my servant whom I have chosen: that you may know and believe me, and understand that I myself am. Before me there was no God formed: and after me there shall be none.

11 [1]I am, I am, the Lord: and there is no saviour besides me.

12 I have declared and have saved. I have made it heard, and there was no strange one among you. You are my witnesses, saith the Lord: and I am God.

13 And from the beginning I am the same: and there is none that can deliver out of my hand. I will work, and who shall turn it away?

14 Thus saith the Lord your redeemer, the Holy One of Israel: For your sake I sent to Babylon; and have brought down all their bars and the Chaldeans glorying in their ships.

15 I *am* the Lord, your Holy One, the Creator of Israel, your King.

16 Thus saith the Lord, who made a way in the sea and a path in the mighty waters,

17 Who brought forth the chariot and the horse, the army and the strong. They lay down to sleep together, and they shall not rise again: they are broken as flax and are extinct.

18 Remember not former things, and look not on things of old.

19 [2]Behold I do new things: and now they shall spring forth. Verily, you shall know them: I will make a way in the wilderness and rivers in the desert.

20 The beast of the field shall glorify me, the dragons and the ostriches: because I have given waters in the wilderness, rivers in the desert, to give drink to my people, to my chosen.

CHAP. 43. [1] Osee, 13, 4. [2] 2 Cor. 5, 17; Apoc. 21, 5.

21 This people have I formed for myself: they shall shew forth my praise.

22 *But* thou hast not called upon me, O Jacob: neither hast thou laboured about me, O Israel.

23 Thou hast not offered me the ram of thy holocaust, nor hast thou glorified me with thy victims. I have not caused thee to serve with oblations, nor wearied thee with incense.

24 Thou hast bought me no sweet cane with money: neither hast thou filled me with the fat of thy victims. But thou hast made me to serve with thy sins: thou hast wearied me with thy iniquities.

25 I am, I am he that blot out thy iniquities for my own sake: and I will not remember thy sins.

26 Put me in remembrance, and let us plead together: tell if thou hast any thing to justify thyself.

27 Thy first father sinned: and thy teachers have transgressed against me.

28 And I have profaned the holy princes: I have given Jacob to slaughter and Israel to reproach.

CHAPTER 44

God's favour to his church. The folly of idolatry. The people shall be delivered from captivity.

AND [1] now hear, O Jacob, my servant, and Israel whom I have chosen.

2 Thus saith the Lord that made and formed thee, thy helper from the womb: Fear not, O my servant Jacob, and thou most righteous whom I have chosen.

3 For I will pour out waters upon the thirsty ground and streams upon the dry land: I will pour out my spirit upon thy seed and my blessing upon thy stock.

4 And they shall spring up among the herbs, as willows beside the running waters.

5 One shall say: I am the Lord's: and another shall call himself by the name of Jacob: and another shall subscribe with his hand, To the Lord, and surname himself by the name of Israel.

6 Thus saith the Lord, the king of Israel and his redeemer, the Lord of hosts: [2] I am the First, and I am the Last: and besides me there is no God.

7 Who is like to me? Let him call and declare: and let him set before me the order, since I appointed the ancient people. And the things to come, and that shall be hereafter, let them shew unto them.

8 Fear ye not, neither be ye troubled. From that time I have made thee to hear, and have declared: You are my witnesses. Is there a God besides me, a maker whom I have not known?

9 The makers of idols are all of them nothing: and their best beloved things shall not profit them. They are their witnesses, that they do not see nor understand, that they may be ashamed.

10 Who hath formed a god, and made a graven thing that is profitable for nothing?

11 Behold, all the partakers thereof shall be confounded: for the makers are men. They shall all assemble together: they shall stand and fear, and shall be confounded together.

12 [3] The smith hath wrought with his file: with coals and with hammers he hath formed it, and hath wrought with the strength of his arm. He shall hunger and faint, he shall drink no water, and shall be weary.

13 The carpenter hath stretched out his rule, he hath formed it with a plane. He hath made it with corners and hath fashioned it round with the compass: and he hath made the image of a man, as it were, a beautiful man, dwelling in a house.

14 He hath cut down cedars, taken the holm and the oak that stood among the trees of the forest. He hath planted the pine tree which the rain hath nourished:

15 And it hath served men for fuel. He took thereof and warmed himself, and he kindled it and baked bread. But of the rest he made a god and adored it: he made a graven thing and bowed down before it.

16 Part of it he burnt with fire, and with part of it he dressed his meat. He boiled pottage, and was filled, and was warmed, and said: Aha, I am warm, I have seen the fire.

17 But the residue thereof he made a god and a graven thing for himself: he boweth down before it and adoreth it and prayeth unto it, saying: Deliver me, for thou art my God.

18 They have not known, nor understood: for their eyes are covered that they may not see and that they may not understand with their heart.

19 They do not consider in their mind, nor know, nor have the thought to say: I have burnt part of it in the fire, and I have baked bread. Upon the coals thereof I have broiled flesh and have eaten. And of the residue thereof shall I make an idol? Shall I fall down before the stock of a tree?

20 Part thereof is ashes. His foolish heart adoreth it, and he will not save his soul, nor say: Perhaps there is a lie in my right hand.

21 Remember these things, O Jacob, and Israel, for thou art my servant. I

CHAP. 44. [1] Jer. 30, 10; 46, 27. [2] Isai. 41, 4; 48, 12; Apoc. 1, 8, 17; 22, 13. [3] Wisd. 13, 11.

have formed thee: thou art my servant. O Israel, forget me not.

22 I have blotted out thy iniquities as a cloud and thy sins as a mist: return to me, for I have redeemed thee.

23 Give praise, O ye heavens, for the Lord hath shewn mercy: shout with joy, ye ends of the earth. Ye mountains, resound with praise, thou, O forest, and every tree therein: for the Lord hath redeemed Jacob, and Israel shall be glorified.

24 Thus saith the Lord, thy redeemer, and thy maker from the womb: I am the Lord, that make all things, that alone stretch out the heavens, that establish the earth. And there is none with me.

25 That make void the tokens of diviners and make the soothsayers mad. That turn the wise backward, and that make their knowledge foolish.

26 That raise up the word of my servant and perform the counsel of my messengers, who say to Jerusalem: Thou shalt be inhabited; and to the cities of Juda: You shall be built, and I will raise up the wastes thereof.

27 Who say to the deep: Be thou desolate, and I will dry up thy rivers.

28 Who say to Cyrus: Thou art my shepherd, and thou shalt perform all my pleasure. Who say to Jerusalem: Thou shalt be built. And to the temple: The foundations shall be laid.

CHAPTER 45

A prophecy of Cyrus, as a figure of Christ, the great deliverer of God's people.

THUS saith the Lord to my anointed Cyrus, whose right hand I have taken hold of, to subdue nations before his face, and to turn the back of kings, and to open the doors before him: and the gates shall not be shut.

2 I will go before thee and will humble the great ones of the earth. I will break in pieces the gates of brass and will burst the bars of iron.

3 And I will give thee hidden treasures and the concealed riches of secret places: that thou mayest know that I am the Lord who call thee by thy name, the God of Israel.

4 For the sake of my servant Jacob and Israel my elect, I have even called thee by thy name. I have made a likeness of thee: and thou hast not known me.

5 I am the Lord, and there is none else: there is no God besides me. I girded thee: and thou hast not known me:

6 That they may know who are from the rising of the sun, and they who are from the west, that there is none besides me. I am the Lord: and there is none else:

7 I form the light and create darkness. I made peace and create evil. I, the Lord, that do all these things.

8 Drop down dew, ye heavens, from above: and let the clouds rain the just. Let the earth be opened and bud forth a saviour: and let justice spring up together. I the Lord have created him.

9 [1] Woe to him that gainsayeth his maker, a sherd of the earthen pots. Shall the clay say to him that fashioneth it: What art thou making, and thy work is without hands?

10 Woe to him that saith to his father: Why begettest thou? And to the woman: Why dost thou bring forth?

11 Thus saith the Lord, the Holy One of Israel, his maker: Ask me of things to come, concerning my children, and concerning the work of my hands give ye charge to me.

12 I made the earth: and I created man upon it. My hand stretched forth the heavens: and I have commanded all their host.

13 I have raised him up to justice and I will direct all his ways. He shall build my city and let go my captives, not for ransom, nor for presents, saith the Lord, the God of hosts.

14 Thus saith the Lord: The labour of Egypt and the merchandise of Ethiopia, and of Sabaim men of stature, shall come over to thee and shall be thine. They shall walk after thee, they shall go bound with manacles. And they shall worship thee and shall make supplication to thee: Only in thee is God; and there is no God besides thee.

15 Verily thou art a hidden God, the God of Israel, the Saviour.

16 They are all confounded and ashamed: the forgers of errors are gone together into confusion.

17 Israel is saved in the Lord with an eternal salvation: you shall not be confounded, and you shall not be ashamed for ever and ever.

18 For thus saith the Lord that created the heavens, God himself that formed the earth and made it, the very maker thereof, who did not create it in vain, who formed it to be inhabited: I *am* the Lord; and there is no other.

19 I have not spoken in secret, in a dark place of the earth. I have not said to the seed of Jacob: Seek me in vain. I am the Lord that speak justice, that declare right things.

20 Assemble yourselves, and come, and draw near together, ye that are

---

CHAP. 45. [1] Jer. 13, 6; Rom. 9, 20.

CHAP. 45. Ver. 7. *Create evil.* The evils of afflictions and punishments, but not the evil of sin.

saved of the Gentiles. They have no knowledge that set up the wood of their graven work and pray to a god that cannot save.

21 Tell ye (and come, and consult together: Who hath declared this from the beginning? *Who* hath foretold this from that time? Have not I, the Lord, and there is no God else besides me? A just God and a saviour, there is none besides me.

22 Be converted to me, and you shall be saved, all ye ends of the earth: for I am God, and there is no other.

23 I have sworn by myself: the word of justice shall go out of my mouth and shall not return.

24 [2] For every knee shall be bowed to me: and every tongue shall swear.

25 Therefore shall he say: In the Lord are my justices and empire; they shall come to him, and all that resist him shall be confounded.

26 In the Lord shall all the seed of Israel be justified and praised.

CHAPTER 46

The idols of Babylon shall be destroyed. Salvation is promised through Christ.

BEL is broken: Nebo is destroyed. Their idols are put upon beasts and cattle, your burdens of heavy weight even unto weariness.

2 They are consumed and are broken together: they could not save him that carried them; and they themselves shall go into captivity.

3 Hearken unto me, O house of Jacob, all the remnant of the house of Israel, who are carried by my bowels, are borne up by my womb.

4 Even to *your* old age I am the same, and to your grey hairs I will carry *you*. I have made *you*, and I will bear: I will carry and will save.

5 To whom have you likened me, and made me equal, and compared me, and made me like?

6 You that contribute gold out of the bag, and weigh out silver in the scales: and hire a goldsmith to make a god: and they fall down and worship.

7 [1] They bear him on their shoulders and carry him and set him in his place: and he shall stand and shall not stir out of his place. Yea, when they shall cry also unto him, he shall not hear: he shall not save them from tribulation.

8 Remember this and be ashamed: return, ye transgressors, to the heart.

9 Remember the former age, for I am God and there is no God beside: neither is there the like to me.

10 Who shew from the beginning the things that shall be at last, and from ancient times the things that as

yet are not done, saying: My counsel shall stand, and all my will shall be done.

11 Who call a bird from the east, and from a far country the man of my own will. And I have spoken and will bring it to pass: I have created, and I will do it. Hear me, O ye hardhearted, who are far from justice.

12 I have brought my justice near: it shall not be afar off, and my salvation shall not tarry. I will give salvation in Sion and my glory in Israel.

CHAPTER 47

God's judgment upon Babylon.

COME down, sit in the dust, O virgin daughter of Babylon: sit on the ground. There is no throne for the daughter of the Chaldeans, for thou shalt no more be called delicate and tender.

2 Take a millstone and grind meal. Uncover thy shame, strip thy shoulder, make bare thy legs, pass over the rivers.

3 [1] Thy nakedness shall be discovered and thy shame shall be seen: I will take vengeance, and no man shall resist me.

4 Our redeemer, the Lord of hosts is his name, the Holy One of Israel.

5 Sit thou silent and get thee into darkness, O daughter of the Chaldeans: for thou shalt no more be called the lady of kingdoms.

6 I was angry with my people, I have polluted my inheritance, and have given them into thy hand. Thou hast shewn no mercy to them: upon the ancient thou hast laid thy yoke exceeding heavy.

7 And thou hast said: I shall be a lady for ever. Thou hast not laid these things to thy heart, neither hast thou remembered thy latter end.

8 And now hear these things, thou that art delicate and dwellest confidently, that sayest in thy heart: [2] I am, and there is none else besides me; I shall not sit as a widow, and I shall not know barrenness.

9 [3] These two things shall come upon thee suddenly in one day: barrenness and widowhood. All things are come upon thee because of the multitude of thy sorceries and for the great hardness of thy enchanters.

10 And thou hast trusted in thy wickedness, and hast said: There is none that seeth me. Thy wisdom and thy knowledge, this hath deceived thee. And thou hast said in thy heart: I am, and besides me there is no other.

11 Evil shall come upon thee: and

[2] Rom. 14, 11; Phil. 2, 10. CHAP. 46. [1] Bar. 6, 25. CHAP. 47. [1] Nah. 3, 5. [2] Apoc. 18, 7. [3] Isai. 51, 19.

thou shalt not know the rising thereof. And calamity shall fall violently upon thee, which thou canst not keep off. Misery shall come upon thee suddenly, which thou shalt not know.

12 Stand now with thy enchanters and with the multitude of thy sorceries, in which thou hast laboured from thy youth; if so be it may profit thee any thing, or if thou mayst become stronger.

13 Thou hast failed in the multitude of thy counsels. Let now the astrologers stand and save thee, they that gazed at the stars and counted the months, that from them they might tell the things that shall come to thee.

14 Behold they are as stubble, fire hath burnt them, they shall not deliver themselves from the power of the flames: there are no coals wherewith they may be warned, nor fire, that they may sit thereat.

15 Such are all the things become to thee, in which thou hast laboured: thy merchants from thy youth, every one hath erred in his own way. There is none that can save thee.

CHAPTER 48

He reproaches the Jews for their obstinacy. He will deliver them out of their captivity, for his own name's sake.

HEAR ye these things, O house of Jacob, you that are called by the name of Israel and are come forth out of the waters of Juda, you who swear by the name of the Lord and make mention of the God of Israel, *but* not in truth, nor in justice.

2 For they are called of the holy city and are established upon the God of Israel: the Lord of hosts is his name.

3 The former things of old I have declared. And they went forth out of my mouth, and I have made them to be heard. I did them suddenly, and they came to pass.

4 For I knew that thou art stubborn, and thy neck is as an iron sinew, and thy forehead as brass.

5 I foretold thee of old, before they came to pass I told thee, lest thou shouldst say: My idols have done these things, and my graven and molten things have commanded them.

6 See now all the things which thou hast heard. But have you declared them? I have shewn thee new things from that time: and things are kept which thou knowest not.

7 They are created now, and not of old: and before the day, when thou

heardest them not, lest thou shouldst say: Behold I knew them.

8 Thou hast neither heard nor known: neither was thy ear opened of old. For I know that transgressing thou wilt transgress: and I have called thee a transgressor from the womb.

9 For my name's sake I will remove my wrath far off: and for my praise I will bridle thee, lest thou shouldst perish.

10 Behold I have refined thee, but not as silver: I have chosen thee in the furnace of poverty.

11 For my own sake, for my own sake: will I do it, that I may not be blasphemed: [1] and I will not give my glory to another.

12 Hearken to me, O Jacob, and thou, Israel, whom I call: [2] I am he, I am the First, and I am the Last.

13 My hand also hath founded the earth, and my right hand hath measured the heavens: I shall call them, and they shall stand together.

14 Assemble yourselves together, all you, and hear. Who among them hath declared these things? The Lord hath loved him: he will do his pleasure in Babylon, and his arm *shall be* on the Chaldeans.

15 I, even I, have spoken and called him. I have brought him, and his way is made prosperous.

16 Come ye near unto me and hear this: I have not spoken in secret from the beginning. From the time before it was done, I was there: and now the Lord God hath sent me, and his spirit.

17 Thus saith the Lord, thy redeemer, the Holy One of Israel: I am the Lord thy God that teach thee profitable things, that govern thee in the way that thou walkest.

18 O that thou hadst hearkened to my commandments: thy peace had been as a river, and thy justice as the waves of the sea.

19 And thy seed had been as the sand, and the offspring of thy bowels like the gravel thereof: his name should not have perished, nor have been destroyed from before my face.

20 [3] Come forth out of Babylon, flee ye from the Chaldeans, declare it with the voice of joy: make this to be heard, and speak it out even to the ends of the earth. Say: The Lord hath redeemed his servant Jacob.

21 They thirsted not in the desert when he led them out. [4] He brought forth water out of the rock for them: and he clove the rock, and the waters gushed out.

22 [5] There is no peace to the wicked, saith the Lord.

CHAP. 48. [1] Isai. 42, 8. [2] Isai. 41, 4; 44, 6; Apoc. 1, 8, 17; 22, 13. [3] Jer. 51, 6; Apoc. 18, 4. [4] Exod. 17, 6; Num. 20, 11. [5] Isai. 57, 21.

CHAPTER 49

Christ shall bring the Gentiles to salvation.
God's love to his church is perpetual.

GIVE ear, ye islands, and hearken, ye people from afar. ¹ The Lord hath called me from the womb: from the bowels of my mother he hath been mindful of my name.

2 ² And he hath made my mouth like a sharp sword. In the shadow of his hand he hath protected me and hath made me as a chosen arrow. In his quiver he hath hidden me.

3 And he said to me: Thou art my servant Israel, for in thee will I glory.

4 And I said: I have laboured in vain, I have spent my strength without cause and in vain. Therefore my judgment is with the Lord, and my work with my God.

5 And now saith the Lord, that formed me from the womb to be his servant, that I may bring back Jacob unto him. And Israel will not be gathered together. And I am glorified in the eyes of the Lord: and my God is made my strength.

6 And he said: It is a small thing that thou shouldst be my servant, to raise up the tribes of Jacob and to convert the dregs of Israel. ³ Behold, I have given thee to be the light of the Gentiles, that thou mayst be my salvation even to the farthest part of the earth.

7 Thus saith the Lord, the redeemer of Israel, his Holy One, to the soul that is despised, to the nation that is abhorred, to the servant of rulers: Kings shall see, and princes shall rise up and adore for the Lord's sake, because he is faithful, and for the Holy One of Israel who hath chosen thee.

8 Thus saith the Lord: ⁴ In an acceptable time I have heard thee, and in the day of salvation I have helped thee. And I have preserved thee and given thee to be a covenant of the people, that thou mightest raise up the earth and possess the inheritances that were destroyed.

9 That thou mightest say to them that are bound: Come forth. And to them that are in darkness: Shew yourselves. They shall feed in the ways: and their pastures shall be in every plain.

10 ⁵ They shall not hunger, nor thirst: neither shall the heat nor the sun strike them. For he that is merciful to them shall be their shepherd, and at the fountains of waters he shall give them drink.

11 And I will make all my mountains a way: and my paths shall be exalted.

12 Behold these shall come from afar: and behold these from the north and from the sea, and these from the south country.

13 Give praise, O ye heavens, and rejoice, O earth; ye mountains, give praise with jubilation: because the Lord hath comforted his people and will have mercy on his poor ones.

14 And Sion said: The Lord hath forsaken me, and the Lord hath forgotten me.

15 Can a woman forget her infant, so as not to have pity on the son of her womb? And if she should forget, yet will not I forget thee.

16 Behold, I have graven thee in my hands: ⁶ thy walls are always before my eyes.

17 Thy builders are come: they that destroy thee and make thee waste shall go out of thee.

18 ⁷ Lift up thy eyes round about, and see. All these are gathered together; they are come to thee. I live, saith the Lord. Thou shalt be clothed with all these as with an ornament: and as a bride thou shalt put them about thee.

19 For thy deserts and thy desolate places and the land of thy destruction shall now be too narrow by reason of the inhabitants: and they that swallowed thee up shall be chased far away.

20 The children of thy barrenness shall still say in thy ears: The place is too strait for me. Make me room to dwell in.

21 And thou shalt say in thy heart: Who hath begotten these? I was barren and brought not forth, led away and captive: and who hath brought up these? I *was* destitute and alone: and these, where were they?

22 Thus saith the Lord God: Behold I will lift up my hand to the Gentiles and will set up my standard to the people. And they shall bring thy sons in their arms and carry thy daughters upon their shoulders.

23 And kings shall be thy nursing fathers, and queens thy nurses. They shall worship thee with their face toward the earth: and they shall lick up the dust of thy feet. ⁸ And thou shalt know that I am the Lord: for they shall not be confounded that wait for him.

24 Shall the prey be taken from the strong? Or can that which was taken by the mighty be delivered?

25 For thus saith the Lord: Yea verily. Even the captivity shall be

CHAP. 49. ¹ Jer. 1, 5; al. 1, 15. ² Isai. 51, 16; Eph. 6, 16; Heb. 4, 12; Apoc. 1, 16. ³ Isai. 42, 6; Acts. 13, 47. ⁴ 2 Cor. 6, 2. ⁵ Apoc. 7, 16. ⁶ Exod. 13, 9. ⁷ Isai. 60, 4. ⁸ Ps. 71, 9; Isai. 40, 14.

taken away from the strong: and that which was taken by the mighty shall be delivered. But I will judge those that have judged thee: and thy children I will save.

26 And I will feed thy enemies with their own flesh: and they shall be made drunk with their own blood, as with new wine. And all flesh shall know that I am the Lord that save thee, and thy Redeemer, the Mighty One of Jacob.

CHAPTER 50

The synagogue shall be divorced for her iniquities. Christ for her sake will endure ignominious afflictions.

THUS saith the Lord: What is this bill of the divorce of your mother, with which I have put her away? Or who is my creditor, to whom I sold you? Behold you are sold for your iniquities: and for your wicked deeds have I put your mother away.

2 Because I came, and there was not a man: I called, and there was none that would hear. [1] Is my hand shortened and become little, that I cannot redeem? Or is there no strength in me to deliver? Behold at my rebuke I will make the sea a desert, I will turn the rivers into dry land: the fishes shall rot for want of water and shall die for thirst.

3 I will clothe the heavens with darkness and will make sackcloth their covering.

4 The Lord hath given me a learned tongue, that I should know how to uphold by word him that is weary. He wakeneth in the morning: in the morning he wakeneth my ear, that I may hear him as a master.

5 The Lord God hath opened my ear, and I do not resist: I have not gone back.

6 [2] I have given my body to the strikers, and my cheeks to them that plucked them: I have not turned away my face from them that rebuked me and spit upon me.

7 The Lord God is my helper: therefore am I not confounded. Therefore have I set my face as a most hard rock: and I know that I shall not be confounded.

8 [3] He is near that justifieth me. Who will contend with me? Let us stand together. Who is my adversary? Let him come near to me.

9 Behold the Lord God *is* my helper: who is he that shall condemn me? Lo, they shall all be destroyed as a garment: the moth shall eat them up.

10 Who is there among you that feareth the Lord, that heareth the voice of his servant, that hath walked in darkness, and hath no light? Let him hope in the name of the Lord and lean upon his God.

11 Behold all you that kindle a fire, encompassed with flames, walk in the light of your fire and in the flames which you have kindled. This is done to you by my hand: you shall sleep in sorrows.

CHAPTER 51

An exhortation to trust in Christ. He shall protect the children of his church.

GIVE ear to me, you that follow that which is just, and you that seek the Lord. Look unto the rock whence you are hewn and to the hole of the pit from which you are dug out.

2 Look unto Abraham your father and to Sara that bore you: for I called him alone, and blessed him, and multiplied him.

3 The Lord therefore will comfort Sion: and will comfort all the ruins thereof. And he will make her desert as a place of pleasure and her wilderness as the garden of the Lord. Joy and gladness shall be found therein, thanksgiving and the voice of praise.

4 Hearken unto me, O my people, and give ear to me, O my tribes: [1] for a law shall go forth from me, and my judgment shall rest to be a light of the nations.

5 My just one is near at hand, my saviour is gone forth, and my arms shall judge the people. The islands shall look for me and shall patiently wait for my arm.

6 Lift up your eyes to heaven, and look down to the earth beneath: for the heavens shall vanish like smoke, and the earth shall be worn away like a garment, and the inhabitants thereof shall perish in like manner. [2] But my salvation shall be for ever: and my justice shall not fail.

7 Hearken to me, you that know what is just, my people who have my law in your heart: fear ye not the reproach of men and be not afraid of their blasphemies.

8 For the worm shall eat them up as a garment and the moth shall consume them as wool: but my salvation shall be for ever, and my justice from generation to generation.

9 Arise, arise, put on strength, O thou arm of the Lord: arise as in the days of old, in the ancient generations. Hast not thou struck the proud one, *and* wounded the dragon?

10 [3] Hast not thou dried up the sea, the water of the mighty deep: who madest the depth of the sea a way, that the delivered might pass over?

CHAP. 50. [1] Isai. 59, 1. [2] Matt. 26, 67. [3] Rom. 8, 33. CHAP. 51. [1] Isai. 2, 3. [2] Ps. 36, 39. [3] Exod. 14, 21.

11 And now they that are redeemed by the Lord shall return and shall come into Sion singing praises: and joy everlasting *shall be* upon their heads. They shall obtain joy and gladness: sorrow and mourning shall flee away.

12 I, I myself, will comfort you. Who art thou, that thou shouldst be afraid of a mortal man and of the son of man who shall wither away like grass?

13 And thou hast forgotten the Lord thy maker, who stretched out the heavens and founded the earth: and thou hast been afraid continually all the day at the presence of his fury who afflicted thee, and had prepared himself to destroy thee. Where is now the fury of the oppressor?

14 He shall quickly come that is going to open *unto you* and he shall not kill unto utter destruction: neither shall his bread fail.

15 But I am the Lord thy God, who trouble the sea, and the waves thereof swell. The Lord of hosts is my name.

16 [4] I have put my words in thy mouth and have protected thee in the shadow of my hand, that thou mightest plant the heavens and found the earth and mightest say to Sion: Thou art my people.

17 Arise, arise, stand up, O Jerusalem, which hast drunk at the hand of the Lord the cup of his wrath; thou hast drunk even to the bottom of the cup of dead sleep, and thou hast drunk even to the dregs.

18 There is none that can uphold her among all the children that she hath brought forth: and there is none that taketh her by the hand among all the children that she hath brought up.

19 [5] There are two things that have happened to thee: Who shall be sorry for thee? Desolation and destruction and the famine and the sword: Who shall comfort thee?

20 Thy children are cast forth, they have slept at the head of all the ways, as the wild ox that is snared: full of the indignation of the Lord, of the rebuke of thy God.

21 Therefore hear this, thou poor little one, and thou that art drunk but not with wine.

22 Thus saith thy Sovereign, the Lord and thy God, who will fight for his people: Behold I have taken out of thy hand the cup of dead sleep, the dregs of the cup of my indignation. Thou shalt not drink it again any more.

23 And I will put it in the hand of them that have oppressed thee and have said to thy soul: Bow down, that we may go over. And thou hast laid thy body as the ground and as a way to them that went over.

CHAPTER 52

Under the figure of the deliverance from the Babylonish captivity, the church is invited to rejoice for her redemption from sin. Christ's kingdom shall be exalted.

ARISE, arise, put on thy strength, O Sion, put on the garments of thy glory, O Jerusalem, the city of the Holy One: for henceforth the uncircumcised and unclean shall no more pass through thee.

2 Shake thyself from the dust, arise, sit up, O Jerusalem: loose the bonds from off thy neck, O captive daughter of Sion.

3 For thus saith the Lord: You were sold gratis, and you shall be redeemed without money.

4 For thus saith the Lord God: [1] My people went down into Egypt at the beginning to sojourn there; and the Assyrian hath oppressed them without any cause at all.

5 And now what have I here, saith the Lord, for my people is taken away gratis? They that rule over them treat them unjustly, saith the Lord, and [2] my name is continually blasphemed all the day long.

6 Therefore my people shall know my name in that day: for I myself that spoke, behold I am here.

7 [3] How beautiful upon the mountains are the feet of him that bringeth good tidings and that preacheth peace, of him that sheweth forth good, that preacheth salvation, that saith to Sion: Thy God shall reign!

8 The voice of thy watchmen. They have lifted up their voice, they shall praise together: for they shall see eye to eye when the Lord shall convert Sion.

9 Rejoice and give praise together, O ye deserts of Jerusalem, for the Lord hath comforted his people: he hath redeemed Jerusalem.

10 The Lord hath prepared his holy arm in the sight of all the Gentiles: [4] and all the ends of the earth shall see the salvation of our God.

11 Depart, depart, go ye out from thence: [5] touch no unclean thing. Go out of the midst of her. Be ye clean, you that carry the vessels of the Lord.

12 For you shall not go out in a tumult: neither shall you make haste by flight. For the Lord will go before you: and the God of Israel will gather you together.

13 Behold my servant shall understand: he shall be exalted and extolled, and shall be exceeding high.

4 Isai. 49, 2. 5 Isai. 47, 9. CHAP. 52. 1 Gen. 46, 6. 2 Ezech. 36, 20; Rom. 2, 24. 3 Nah. 1, 15; Rom. 10, 15. 4 Ps. 97, 3. 5 2 Cor. 6, 17.

14 As many have been astonished at thee, so shall his visage be inglorious among men and his form among the sons of men.

15 He shall sprinkle many nations: kings shall shut their mouth at him. [6] For they to whom it was not told of him have seen: and they that heard not have beheld.

CHAPTER 53

A prophecy of the passion of Christ.

WHO [1] hath believed our report? And to whom is the arm of the Lord revealed?

2 And he shall grow up as a tender plant before him, and as a root out of a thirsty ground. There is no beauty in him, nor comeliness: and we have seen him, and there was no sightliness, that we should be desirous of him:

3 [2] Despised and the most abject of men, a man of sorrows and acquainted with infirmity: and his look *was* as it were hidden and despised. Whereupon we esteemed him not.

4 [3] Surely he hath borne our infirmities and carried our sorrows: and we have thought him as it were a leper, and as one struck by God and afflicted.

5 [4] But he was wounded for our iniquities: he was bruised for our sins. The chastisement of our peace *was* upon him: and by his bruises we are healed.

6 All we like sheep have gone astray, every one hath turned aside into his own way: and the Lord hath laid on him the iniquity of us all.

7 He was offered because it was his own will, and he opened not his mouth. He shall be led as a sheep to the slaughter and shall be dumb as a lamb before his shearer, [5] and he shall not open his mouth.

8 He was taken away from distress and from judgment. Who shall declare his generation? Because he is cut off out of the land of the living: for the wickedness of my people have I struck him.

9 And he shall give the ungodly for his burial and the rich for his death: [6] because he hath done no iniquity, neither was there deceit in his mouth.

10 And the Lord was pleased to bruise him in infirmity. If he shall lay down his life for sin, he shall see a long-lived seed: and the will of the Lord shall be prosperous in his hand.

11 Because his soul hath laboured,

he shall see and be filled. By his knowledge shall this my just servant justify many: and he shall bear their iniquities.

12 Therefore will I distribute to him very many, and he shall divide the spoils of the strong: because he hath delivered his soul unto death [7] and was reputed with the wicked. And he hath borne the sins of many [8] and hath prayed for the transgressors.

CHAPTER 54

The Gentiles, who were barren before, shall multiply in the church of Christ, from which God's mercy shall never depart.

GIVE [1] praise, O thou barren, that bearest not; sing forth praise and make a joyful noise, thou that didst not travail with child: for many are the children of the desolate, more than of her that hath a husband, saith the Lord.

2 Enlarge the place of thy tent and stretch out the skins of thy tabernacles. Spare not: lengthen thy cords and strengthen thy stakes.

3 For thou shalt pass on to the right hand and to the left: and thy seed shall inherit the Gentiles and shall inhabit the desolate cities.

4 Fear not, for thou shalt not be confounded nor blush. For thou shalt not be put to shame, because thou shalt forget the shame of thy youth and shalt remember no more the reproach of thy widowhood.

5 For he that made thee shall rule over thee. [2] The Lord of hosts is his name: and thy Redeemer, the Holy One of Israel, shall be called the God of all the earth.

6 For the Lord hath called thee as a woman forsaken and mourning in spirit: and as a wife cast off from her youth, said thy God.

7 For a small moment have I forsaken thee: but with great mercies will I gather thee.

8 In a moment of indignation have I hid my face a little while from thee: but with everlasting kindness have I had mercy on thee, said the Lord, thy Redeemer.

9 [3] This thing is to me as in the days of Noe, to whom I swore that I would no more bring in the waters of Noe upon the earth: so have I sworn not to be angry with thee and not to rebuke thee.

10 For the mountains shall be moved, and the hills shall tremble: but my mercy shall not depart from thee, and the covenant of my peace shall not be moved, said the Lord that hath mercy on thee.

[6] Rom. 15, 21. CHAP. 53. [1] John, 12, 38; Rom. 10, 16. [2] Mark, 9, 11. [3] Matt. 8, 17. [4] 1 Cor. 15, 3. [5] Matt. 26, 63; Acts, 8, 32. [6] 1 Peter, 2, 22; 1 John, 3, 5. [7] Mark, 15, 28; Luke, 22, 37. [8] Luke, 23, 34. CHAP. 54. [1] Luke, 23, 29; Gal. 4, 27. [2] Luke, 1, 32. [3] Gen. 9, 11.

11 O poor little one, tossed with tempest, without all comfort: behold I will lay thy stones in order and will lay thy foundations with sapphires,

12 And I will make thy bulwarks of jasper, and thy gates of graven stones, and all thy borders of desirable stones.

13 * All thy children *shall be* taught of the Lord: and great shall be the peace of thy children.

14 And thou shalt be founded in justice. Depart far from oppression, for thou shalt not fear: and from terror, for it shall not come near thee.

15 Behold, an inhabitant shall come, who was not with me: he that was a stranger to thee before shall be joined to thee.

16 Behold, I have created the smith that bloweth the coals in the fire and bringeth forth an instrument for his work: and I have created the killer to destroy.

17 No weapon that is formed against thee shall prosper: and every tongue that resisteth thee in judgment, thou shalt condemn. This is the inheritance of the servants of the Lord and their justice with me, saith the Lord.

CHAPTER 55

God promises abundance of spiritual graces to the faithful that shall believe in Christ out of all nations and sincerely serve him.

ALL [1] you that thirst, come to the waters: and you that have no money, make haste, buy and eat. Come ye: buy wine and milk without money and without any price.

2 Why do you spend money for that which is not bread and your labour for that which doth not satisfy you? Hearken diligently to me and eat that which is good: and your soul shall be delighted in fatness.

3 Incline your ear and come to me. Hear and your soul shall live. And I will make an everlasting covenant with you, [2] the faithful mercies of David.

4 Behold I have given him for a witness to the people, for a leader and a master to the Gentiles.

5 Behold thou shalt call a nation which thou knewest not: and the nations that knew not thee shall run to thee, because of the Lord thy God, and for the Holy One of Israel; for he hath glorified thee.

6 Seek ye the Lord while he may be found: call upon him while he is near.

7 Let the wicked forsake his way and the unjust man his thoughts, and let him return to the Lord; and he will have mercy on him: and to our God; for he is bountiful to forgive.

8 For my thoughts are not your thoughts: nor your ways my ways, saith the Lord.

9 For as the heavens are exalted above the earth, so are my ways exalted above your ways, and my thoughts above your thoughts.

10 And as the rain and the snow come down from heaven, and return no more thither, but soak the earth and water it, and make it to spring and give seed to the sower and bread to the eater:

11 So shall my word be, which shall go forth from my mouth. It shall not return to me void, but it shall do whatsoever I please and shall prosper in the things for which I sent it.

12 For you shall go out with joy and be led forth with peace. The mountains and the hills shall sing praise before you: and all the trees of the country shall clap their hands.

13 Instead of the shrub, shall come up the fir tree, and instead of the nettle, shall come up the myrtle tree: and the Lord shall be named for an everlasting sign that shall not be taken away.

CHAPTER 56

God invites all to keep his commandments. The Gentiles that keep them shall be the people of God. The Jewish pastors are reproved.

THUS [1] saith the Lord: Keep ye judgment and do justice, for my salvation is near to come and my justice to be revealed.

2 Blessed is the man that doth this, and the son of man that shall lay hold on this: that keepeth the sabbath from profaning it, that keepeth his hands from doing any evil.

3 And let not the son of the stranger, that adhereth to the Lord, speak, saying: The Lord will divide and separate me from his people. And let not the eunuch say: Behold I am a dry tree.

4 For thus saith the Lord to the eunuchs: They that shall keep my sabbaths and shall choose the things that please me and shall hold fast my covenant,

5 I will give to them, in my house and within my walls, a place and a name better than sons and daughters. I will give them an everlasting name which shall never perish.

6 And the children of the stranger that adhere to the Lord, to worship him and to love his name, to be his servants; every one that keepeth the sabbath from profaning it and that holdeth fast my covenant:

⁴ John, 6, 45. Chap. 55. ¹ John, 7, 37; Ecclus. 51, 33; Apoc. 22, 17; Jer. 15, 16; Ezech. 3, 3; Prov. 9, 5. ² Acts, 13, 34. Chap. 56. ¹ Wisd. 1, 1; Matt. 23, 23.

7 I will bring them into my holy mount and will make them joyful in my house of prayer. Their holocausts and their victims shall please me upon my altar: [2] for my house shall be called the house of prayer, for all nations.

8 The Lord God, [3] who gathereth the scattered of Israel, saith: I will still gather unto him his congregation.

9 All ye beasts of the field, come to devour, all ye beasts of the forest.

10 [4] His watchmen are all blind. They are all ignorant: dumb dogs not able to bark, seeing vain things, sleeping, and loving dreams.

11 And most impudent dogs, they never had enough: the shepherds themselves knew no understanding. All have turned aside into their own way, [5] every one after his own gain, from the first even to the last.

12 Come, let us take wine and be filled with drunkenness: and it shall be as to-day, so also to-morrow, and much more.

CHAPTER 57

The infidelity of the Jews. Their idolatry. Promises to humble penitents.

THE just perisheth and no man layeth it to heart: and men of mercy are taken away, because there is none that understandeth; for the just man is taken away from before the face of evil.

2 Let peace come: let him rest in his bed that hath walked in his uprightness.

3 But draw near hither, you, sons of the sorceress, the seed of the adulterer and of the harlot.

4 Upon whom have you jested? Upon whom have you opened your mouth wide and put out your tongue? Are not you wicked children, a false seed,

5 Who seek your comfort in idols under every green tree, sacrificing children in the torrents, under the high rocks?

6 In the parts of the torrent is thy portion. This is thy lot. And thou hast poured out libations to them, thou hast offered sacrifice. Shall I not be angry at these things?

7 Upon a high and lofty mountain thou hast laid thy bed and hast gone up thither to offer victims.

8 And behind the door and behind the post thou hast set up thy remembrance: for thou hast discovered thyself near me and hast received an adulterer. Thou hast enlarged thy bed

and made a covenant with them: thou hast loved their bed with open hand.

9 And thou hast adorned thyself for the king with ointment and hast multiplied thy perfumes. Thou hast sent thy messengers far off and wast debased even to hell.

10 Thou hast been wearied in the multitude of thy ways: *yet* thou saidst not: I will rest. Thou hast found life of thy hand: therefore thou hast not asked.

11 For whom hast thou been solicitous and afraid, that thou hast lied and hast not been mindful of me, nor thought on me in thy heart? For I am silent and as one that seeth not: and thou hast forgotten me.

12 I will declare thy justice: and thy works shall not profit thee.

13 When thou shalt cry, let thy companies deliver thee: but the wind shall carry them all off, a breeze shall take them away. But he that putteth his trust in me shall inherit the land and shall possess my holy mount.

14 And I will say: [1] Make a way. Give free passage. Turn out of the path. Take away the stumbling-blocks out of the way of my people.

15 For thus saith the High and the Eminent that inhabiteth eternity. And his name is Holy, who dwelleth in the high and holy place and with a contrite and humble spirit, to revive the spirit of the humble and to revive the heart of the contrite.

16 For I will not contend for ever, neither will I be angry unto the end: because the spirit shall go forth from my face, and breathings I will make.

17 For the iniquity of his covetousness I was angry: and I struck him. I hid my face from thee and was angry: and he went away wandering in his own heart.

18 I saw his ways, and I healed him and brought him back and restored comforts to him and to them that mourn for him.

19 I created the fruit of the lips, peace, peace to him that is far off, and to him that is near, said the Lord: and I healed him.

20 But the wicked are like the raging sea which cannot rest: and the waves thereof cast up dirt and mire.

21 [2] There is no peace to the wicked, saith the Lord God.

CHAPTER 58

God rejects the hypocritical fasts of the Jews, recommends works of mercy and sincere godliness.

CRY, cease not, lift up thy voice like a trumpet, and shew my people

[2] Jer. 7, 11; Matt. 21, 13; Mark, 11, 17; Luke, 19, 46. [3] John, 11, 52. [4] Ezech. 3, 17; 32, 2, 6, 7. [5] Jer. 6, 13; 8, 10. CHAP. 57. [1] Isai. 62, 10. [2] Isai. 48, 22.

their wicked doings and the house of Jacob their sins.

2 For they seek me from day to day and desire to know my ways, as a nation that hath done justice and hath not forsaken the judgment of their God. They ask of me the judgments of justice: they are willing to aproach to God.

3 Why have we fasted: and thou hast not regarded? Have we humbled our souls: and thou hast not taken notice? Behold in the day of your fast your own will is found: and you exact of all your debtors.

4 Behold you fast for debates and strife, and strike with the fist wickedly. Do not fast as *you have done* until this day, to make your cry to be heard on high.

5 ¹ Is this such a fast as I have chosen: For a man to afflict his soul for a day? Is this it: To wind his head about like a circle and to spread sackcloth and ashes? Wilt thou call this a fast and a day acceptable to the Lord?

6 Is not this rather the fast that I have chosen? Loose the bands of wickedness, undo the bundles that oppress. Let them that are broken go free: and break asunder every burden.

7 ² Deal thy bread to the hungry and bring the needy and the harbourless into thy house: when thou shalt see one naked, cover him and despise not thy own flesh.

8 Then shall thy light break forth as the morning, and thy health shall speedily arise, and thy justice shall go before thy face, and the glory of the Lord shall gather thee up.

9 Then shalt thou call, and the Lord shall hear; thou shalt cry, and he shall say: Here I am. If thou wilt take away the chain out of the midst of thee and cease to stretch out the finger and to speak that which profiteth not.

10 When thou shalt pour out thy soul to the hungry and shalt satisfy the afflicted soul, then shall thy light rise up in darkness, and thy darkness shall be as the noonday.

11 And the Lord will give thee rest continually and will fill thy soul with brightness and deliver thy bones: and thou shalt be like a watered garden and like a fountain of water whose waters shall not fail.

12 ³ And the places that have been desolate for ages shall be built in thee. Thou shalt raise up the foundations of generation and generation: and thou shalt be called the repairer of the fences, turning the paths into rest.

13 If thou turn away thy foot from the sabbath, from doing thy own will in my holy day and call the sabbath delightful and the holy of the Lord

glorious and glorify him, while thou dost not thy own ways and thy own will is not found, to speak a word:

14 Then shalt thou be delighted in the Lord, and I will lift thee up above the high places of the earth and will feed thee with the inheritance of Jacob thy father. For the mouth of the Lord hath spoken it.

CHAPTER 59

The dreadful evil of sin is displayed, as the great obstacle to all good from God. Yet he will send a Redeemer and make an everlasting covenant with his church.

BEHOLD ¹ the hand of the Lord is not shortened that it cannot save: neither is his ear heavy that it cannot hear.

2 But your iniquities have divided between you and your God: and your sins have hid his face from you that he should not hear.

3 ² For your hands are defiled with blood and your fingers with iniquity: your lips have spoken lies and your tongue uttereth iniquity.

4 There is none that calleth upon justice, neither is there any one that judgeth truly: but they trust in a mere nothing and speak vanities. They have conceived labour and brought forth iniquity.

5 They have broken the eggs of asps ³ and have woven the webs of spiders. He that shall eat of their eggs shall die: and that which is brought out shall be hatched into a basilisk.

6 Their webs shall not be for clothing: neither shall they cover themselves with their works. Their works are unprofitable works: and the work of iniquity is in their hands.

7 ⁴ Their feet run to evil and make haste to shed innocent blood: their thoughts are unprofitable thoughts. Wasting and destruction are in their ways.

8 They have not known the way of peace, and there is no judgment in their steps. Their paths are become crooked to them: every one that treadeth in them knoweth no peace.

9 Therefore is judgment far from us and justice shall not overtake us. We looked for light, and behold darkness: brightness, and we have walked in the dark.

10 We have groped for the wall, and like the blind we have groped as if we had no eyes. We have stumbled at noonday as in darkness: *we are* in dark places as dead *men*.

CHAP. 58. ¹ Zach. 7, 5. ² Ezech. 18, 7, 16; Matt. 25, 35. ³ Isai. 61, 4. CHAP. 59. ¹ Num. 11, 23; Isai. 50, 2. ² Isai. 1, 15. ³ Job, 8, 4. ⁴ Prov. 1, 16; Rom. 3, 15.

11 We shall roar all of us like bears and shall lament as mournful doves. We have looked for judgment; and there is none: for salvation; and it is far from us.

12 For our iniquities are multiplied before thee and our sins have testified against us: for our wicked doings are with us and we have known our iniquities.

13 In sinning and lying against the Lord. And we have turned away so that we went not after our God, but spoke calumny and transgression: we have conceived and uttered from the heart words of falsehood.

14 And judgment is turned away backward and justice hath stood far off: because truth hath fallen down in the street and equity could not come in.

15 And truth hath been forgotten: and he that departed from evil, lay open to be a prey. And the Lord saw, and it appeared evil in his eyes, because there is no judgment.

16 And he saw that there is not a man: and he stood astonished, because there is none to oppose himself. And his own arms brought salvation to him and his own justice supported him.

17 ⁵ He put on justice as a breastplate, and a helmet of salvation upon his head: he put on the garments of vengeance and was clad with zeal as with a cloak.

18 As unto revenge, as it were to repay wrath to his adversaries and a reward to his enemies: he will repay the like to the islands.

19 And they from the west shall fear the name of the Lord: and they from the rising of the sun, his glory: when he shall come as a violent stream which the spirit of the Lord driveth on:

20 ⁶ And there shall come a redeemer to Sion and to them that return from iniquity in Jacob, saith the Lord.

21 This is my covenant with them, saith the Lord: My spirit that is in thee and my words that I have put in thy mouth shall not depart out of thy mouth, nor out of the mouth of thy seed, nor out of the mouth of thy seed's seed, saith the Lord, from henceforth and for ever.

CHAPTER 60

The light of true faith shall shine forth in the church of Christ and shall be spread through all nations and continue for all ages.

⁵ Eph. 6, 17; 1 Thess. 5, 8. ⁶ Rom. 11, 26. CHAP. 60. ¹ Isai. 49, 18. ² Apoc. 21, 25.

CHAP. 59. Ver. 21. *This is my covenant.* Note here a clear promise of perpetual orthodoxy to the church of Christ.

ARISE, be enlightened, O Jerusalem: for thy light is come, and the glory of the Lord is risen upon thee.

2 For, behold, darkness shall cover the earth and a mist the people: but the Lord shall arise upon thee and his glory shall be seen upon thee.

3 And the Gentiles shall walk in thy light, and kings in the brightness of thy rising.

4 ¹ Lift up thy eyes round about and see: all these are gathered together, they are come to thee. Thy sons shall come from afar and thy daughters shall rise up at thy side.

5 Then shalt thou see and abound, and thy heart shall wonder and be enlarged: when the multitude of the sea shall be converted to thee, the strength of the Gentiles shall come to thee.

6 The multitude of camels shall cover thee, the dromedaries of Madian and Epha. All they from Saba shall come, bringing gold and frankincense and shewing forth praise to the Lord.

7 All the flocks of Cedar shall be gathered together unto thee: the rams of Nabaioth shall minister to thee. They shall be offered upon my acceptable altar: and I will glorify the house of my majesty.

8 Who are these that fly as clouds, and as doves to their windows?

9 For, the islands wait for me, and the ships of the sea in the beginning: that I may bring thy sons from afar, their silver and their gold with them, to the name of the Lord thy God and to the Holy One of Israel, because he hath glorified thee.

10 And the children of strangers shall build up thy walls, and their kings shall minister to thee: for in my wrath have I struck thee and in my reconciliation have I had mercy upon thee.

11 ² And thy gates shall be open continually: they shall not be shut day nor night, that the strength of the Gentiles may be brought to thee, and their kings may be brought.

12 For the nation and the kingdom that will not serve thee shall perish: and the Gentiles shall be wasted with desolation.

13 The glory of Libanus shall come to thee, the fir tree and the box tree and the pine tree together, to beautify the place of my sanctuary: and I will glorify the place of my feet.

14 And the children of them that afflict thee shall come bowing down to thee: and all that slandered thee shall worship the steps of thy feet and shall call thee the City of the Lord, the Sion of the Holy One of Israel.

15 Because thou wast forsaken and

hated, and there was none that passed through thee, I will make thee to be an everlasting glory, a joy unto generation and generation.

16 And thou shalt suck the milk of the Gentiles: and thou shalt be nursed with the breasts of kings. And thou shalt know that I am the Lord thy Saviour and thy Redeemer, the Mighty One of Jacob.

17 For brass I will bring gold, and for iron I will bring silver, and for wood brass, and for stones iron: and I will make thy visitation peace, and thy overseers justice.

18 Iniquity shall no more be heard in thy land, wasting nor destruction in thy borders: and salvation shall possess thy walls, and praise thy gates.

19 [3] Thou shalt no more have the sun for thy light by day, neither shall the brightness of the moon enlighten thee: but the Lord shall be unto thee for an everlasting light, and thy God for thy glory.

20 Thy sun shall go down no more and thy moon shall not decrease. For the Lord shall be unto thee for an everlasting light: and the days of thy mourning shall be ended.

21 And thy people *shall be* all just: they shall inherit the land for ever, the branch of my planting, the work of my hand, to glorify *me*.

22 The least shall become a thousand, and a little one a most strong nation: I, the Lord, will suddenly do this thing in its time.

CHAPTER 61

The office of Christ. The mission of the Apostles. The happiness of their converts.

THE [1] spirit of the Lord is upon me, because the Lord hath anointed me. He hath sent me to preach to the meek, to heal the contrite of heart, and to preach a release to the captives and deliverance to them that are shut up:

2 To proclaim the acceptable year of the Lord and the day of vengeance of our God: [2] to comfort all that mourn:

3 To appoint to the mourners of Sion: and to give them a crown for ashes, the oil of joy for mourning, a garment of praise for the spirit of grief. And they shall be called in it the mighty ones of justice, the planting of the Lord to glorify *him*.

4 [3] And they shall build the places that have been waste from of old, and shall raise up ancient ruins, and shall repair the desolate cities that were destroyed for generation and generation.

5 And strangers shall stand and shall feed your flocks: and the sons of strangers shall be your husbandmen and the dressers of your vines.

6 But you shall be called the priests of the Lord; to you it shall be said: Ye ministers of our God. You shall eat the riches of the Gentiles and you shall pride yourselves in their glory.

7 For your double confusion and shame, they shall praise their part: therefore shall they receive double in their land. Everlasting joy shall be unto them.

8 For I am the Lord that love judgment and hate robbery in a holocaust: and I will make their work in truth; and I will make a perpetual covenant with them.

9 And they shall know their seed among the Gentiles and their offspring in the midst of peoples. All that shall see them shall know them, that these are the seed which the Lord hath blessed.

10 I will greatly rejoice in the Lord, and my soul shall be joyful in my God. For he hath clothed me with the garments of salvation and with the robe of justice he hath covered me: as a bridegroom decked with a crown and as a bride adorned with her jewels.

11 For as the earth bringeth forth her bud and as the garden causeth her seed to shoot forth: so shall the Lord God make justice to spring forth and praise before all the nations.

CHAPTER 62

The prophet will not cease from preaching Christ, to whom all nations shall be converted and whose church shall continue for ever.

FOR Sion's sake I will not hold my peace, and for the sake of Jerusalem I will not rest till her just one come forth as brightness and her saviour be lighted as a lamp.

2 And the Gentiles shall see thy just one, and all kings thy glorious one: and thou shalt be called by a new name which the mouth of the Lord shall name.

3 And thou shalt be a crown of glory in the hand of the Lord and a royal diadem in the hand of thy God.

4 Thou shalt no more be called Forsaken, and thy land shall no more be called Desolate: but thou shalt be called My pleasure in her, and thy land Inhabited. Because the Lord hath been well pleased with thee: and thy land shall be inhabited.

5 For the young man shall dwell with the virgin: and thy children shall dwell in thee. And the bridegroom shall

---

[3] Apoc. 21, 23; 22, 5. CHAP. 61. [1] Luke, 4, 18. [2] Matt. 5, 5. [3] Isai. 58, 12.

CHAP. 60. Ver. 19. *Thou shalt no more.* In this latter part of the chapter, the prophet passes from the illustrious promises made to the church militant on earth, to the glory of the church triumphant in heaven.

rejoice over the bride: and thy God shall rejoice over thee.

6 Upon thy walls, O Jerusalem, I have appointed watchmen, all the day and all the night: they shall never hold their peace. You that are mindful of the Lord, hold not your peace,

7 And give him no silence till he establish, and till he make Jerusalem a praise in the earth.

8 The Lord hath sworn by his right hand and by the arm of his strength: Surely I will no more give thy corn to be meat for thy enemies: and the sons of the strangers shall not drink thy wine, for which thou hast laboured.

9 For they that gather it shall eat it and shall praise the Lord: and they that bring it together shall drink it in my holy courts.

10 Go through, go through the gates, [1] prepare the way for the people, make the road plain, pick out the stones, and lift up the standard to the people.

11 [2] Behold the Lord hath made it to be heard in the ends of the earth. Tell the daughter of Sion: Behold thy Saviour cometh. Behold his reward is with him and his work before him.

12 And they shall call them: The Holy People, The Redeemed of the Lord. But thou shalt be called: A city, sought after and not forsaken.

CHAPTER 63

Christ's victory over his enemies. His mercies to his people. Their complaint.

𝕎HO is this that cometh from Edom, with dyed garments from Bosra, this beautiful one in his robe, walking in the greatness of his strength? I, that speak justice and am a defender to save.

2 [1] Why then is thy apparel red and thy garments like theirs that tread in the winepress?

3 I have trodden the winepress alone: and of the Gentiles there is not a man with me. I have trampled on them in my indignation and have trod-

<hr>

CHAP. 62. [1] Isai. 57, 14. [2] Zach. 9, 9; Matt. 21, 5. CHAP. 63. [1] Apoc. 19, 13. [2] Isai. 34, 8. [3] Exod. 14, 29. [4] Deut. 26, 15; Bar. 2, 16.

CHAP. 63. Ver. 1. *Edom.* Edom and Bosra (a strong city of Edom) are here taken in a mystical sense for the enemies of Christ and his church.

Ver. 15. *They have held back.* This is spoken by the prophet in the person of the Jews at the time when, for their sins, they were given up to their enemies.

Ver. 16. *Abraham hath not known us.* That is, Abraham will not now acknowledge us for his children, by reason of our degeneracy; but thou, O Lord, art our true Father and our Redeemer, and no other can be called our parent in comparison with thee.

Ver. 17. *Made us to err.—Hardened our heart.* The meaning is, that God in punishment of their great and manifold crimes, and their long abuse

den them down in my wrath. And their blood is sprinkled upon my garments: and I have stained all my apparel.

4 [2] For the day of vengeance is in my heart: the year of my redemption is come.

5 I looked about, and there was none to help: I sought, and there was none to give aid. And my own arm hath saved for me: and my indignation itself hath helped me.

6 And I have trodden down the people in my wrath and have made them drunk in my indignation: and have brought down their strength to the earth.

7 I will remember the tender mercies of the Lord, the praise of the Lord for all the things that the Lord hath bestowed upon us: and for the multitude of his good things to the house of Israel, which he hath given them according to his kindness and according to the multitude of his mercies.

8 And he said: Surely they are my people, children that will not deny. So he became their saviour.

9 In all their affliction he was not troubled: and the angel of his presence saved them. In his love, and in his mercy he redeemed them: and he carried them and lifted them up all the days of old.

10 But they provoked to wrath and afflicted the spirit of his Holy One: and he was turned to be their enemy, and he fought against them.

11 And he remembered the days of old, of Moses and of his people: [3] Where is he that brought them up out of the sea, with the shepherds of his flock? Where is he that put in the midst of them the spirit of his Holy One?

12 He that brought out Moses by the right hand, by the arm of his majesty: that divided the waters before them, to make himself an everlasting name.

13 He that led them out through the deep, as a horse in the wilderness that stumbleth not:

14 As a beast that goeth down in the field. The spirit of the Lord was their leader: so didst thou lead thy people to make thyself a glorious name.

15 [4] Look down from heaven and behold from thy holy habitation and the place of thy glory. Where is thy zeal and thy strength, the multitude of thy bowels and of thy mercies? They have held back themselves from me.

16 For thou art our father: and Abraham hath not known us, and Israel hath been ignorant of us. Thou, O Lord, art our father, our redeemer: from everlasting is thy name.

17 Why hast thou made us to err, O

Lord, from thy ways? Why hast thou hardened our heart, that we should not fear thee? Return for the sake of thy servants, the tribes of thy inheritance.

18 They have possessed thy holy people as nothing: our enemies have trodden down thy sanctuary.

19 We are become as in the beginning, when thou didst not rule over us and when we were not called by thy name.

CHAPTER 64

The prophet prays for the release of his people and for the remission of their sins.

O THAT thou wouldst rend the heavens and wouldst come down. The mountains would melt away at thy presence.

2 They would melt as at the burning of fire, the waters would burn with fire: that thy name might be made known to thy enemies, that the nations might tremble at thy presence.

3 When thou shalt do wonderful things, we shall not bear them. Thou didst come down, and at thy presence the mountains melted away.

4 From the beginning of the world they have not heard, nor perceived with the ears: [1] the eye hath not seen, O God, besides thee, what things thou hast prepared for them that wait for thee.

5 Thou hast met him that rejoiceth and doth justice: in thy ways they shall remember thee. Behold thou art angry, and we have sinned: in them we have been always and we shall be saved.

6 And we are all become as one unclean: and all our justices as the rag of a menstruous woman. And we have all fallen as a leaf: and our iniquities, like the wind, have taken us away.

7 There is none that calleth upon thy name: that riseth up and taketh hold of thee. Thou hast hid thy face from us and hast crushed us in the hand of our iniquity.

8 And now, O Lord, thou art our father, and we are clay: and thou art our maker, and we all are the works of thy hands.

9 [2] Be not very angry, O Lord, and remember no longer our iniquity: behold, see we are all thy people.

10 The city of thy sanctuary is become a desert; Sion is made a desert: Jerusalem is desolate.

11 The house of our holiness and of our glory, where our fathers praised thee, is burnt with fire: and all our lovely things are turned into ruins.

12 Wilt thou refrain thyself, O Lord, upon these things? Wilt thou hold thy peace and afflict us vehemently?

CHAPTER 65

The Gentiles shall seek and find Christ, but the Jews will persecute him and be rejected. Only a remnant shall be reserved. The church shall multiply and abound with graces.

THEY [1] have sought me that before asked not *for me:* they have found *me* that sought me not. I said: Behold me, Behold me, to a nation that did not call upon my name.

2 I have spread forth my hands all day to an unbelieving people, who walk in a way that is not good, after their own thoughts.

3 A people that continually provoke me to anger before my face: that immolate in gardens and sacrifice upon bricks.

4 That dwell in sepulchres and sleep in the temple of idols: that eat swine's flesh, and profane broth is in their vessels.

5 That say: Depart from me. Come not near me, because thou art unclean. These shall be smoke in my anger, a fire burning all the day.

6 Behold it is written before me. I will not be silent: but I will render and repay into their bosom

7 Your iniquities and the iniquities of your fathers together, saith the Lord, who have sacrificed upon the mountains and have reproached me upon the hills; and I will measure back their first work in their bosom.

8 Thus saith the Lord: As if a grain be found in a cluster, and it be said: Destroy it not, because it is a blessing. So will I do for the sake of my servants, that I may not destroy the whole.

9 And I will bring forth a seed out of Jacob, and out of Juda a possessor of my mountains: and my elect shall inherit it, and my servants shall dwell there.

10 And the plains shall be turned to folds of flocks, and the valley of Achor into a place for the herds to lie down in, for my people that have sought me.

11 And you that have forsaken the Lord, that have forgotten my holy mount, that set a table for fortune and offer libations upon it,

12 I will number you in the sword, and you shall all fall by slaughter: [2] because I called and you did not answer, I spoke and you did not hear.

CHAP. 64. [1] 1 Cor. 2, 9. [2] Ps. 78, 8. CHAP. 65. [1] Rom. 10, 20. [2] Prov. 1, 24; Isai. 66, 4; Jer. 7, 13. of his mercy and grace, had withdrawn his graces from them, and so given them up to error and hardness of heart.

CHAP. 64. Ver. 6. *Our justices.* That is, the works by which we pretended to make ourselves just. This is spoken particularly of the sacrifices, sacraments, and ceremonies of the Jews, after the death of Christ, and the promulgation of the new law.

And you did evil in my eyes: and you have chosen the things that displease me.

13 Therefore thus saith the Lord God: Behold my servants shall eat, and you shall be hungry: behold my servants shall drink, and you shall be thirsty.

14 Behold my servants shall rejoice, and you shall be confounded: behold my servants shall praise for joyfulness of heart, and you shall cry for sorrow of heart and shall howl for grief of spirit.

15 And you shall leave your name for an execration to my elect. And the Lord God shall slay thee and call his servants by another name,

16 In which he that is blessed upon the earth shall be blessed in God, Amen; and he that sweareth in the earth shall swear by God, Amen: because the former distresses are forgotten and because they are hid from my eyes.

17 ³ For behold I create new heavens and a new earth: and the former things shall not be in remembrance, and they shall not come upon the heart.

18 But you shall be glad and rejoice for ever in these things which I create: for behold I create Jerusalem, a rejoicing, and the people thereof, joy.

19 And I will rejoice in Jerusalem and joy in my people: and the voice of weeping shall no more be heard in her, nor the voice of crying.

20 There shall be no more be an infant of days there, nor an old man that shall not fill up his days: for the child shall die a hundred years old, and the sinner being a hundred years old shall be accursed.

21 And they shall build houses and inhabit them: and they shall plant vineyards and eat the fruits of them.

22 They shall not build and another inhabit; they shall not plant and another eat. For as the days of a tree, so shall be the days of my people: and the works of their hands shall be of long continuance.

23 My elect shall not labour in vain,

³ Isai. 66, 22; Apoc. 21, 1. ⁴ Ps. 31, 5. ⁵ Isai. 11, 6. CHAP. 66. ¹ Acts, 7, 49; 17, 24. ² Prov. 1, 24; Isai. 65, 12; Jer. 7, 13.

CHAP. 66. Ver. 1. *What is this house.* This is a prophecy that the temple should be cast off.
Ver. 3. *He that sacrificeth an ox.* This is a prophecy that the sacrifices which were offered in the old law should be abolished in the new; and that the offering of them should be a crime.— *Remembereth incense,* that is, to offer it in the way of a sacrifice.
Ver. 4. *I will choose their mockeries.* I will turn their mockeries upon themselves, and will cause them to be mocked by their enemies.
Ver. 7. *Before she was in labour.* This relates to the conversion of the Gentiles, who were born, as it were, all on a sudden to the church of God.

nor bring forth in trouble; for they are the seed of the blessed of the Lord, and their posterity with them.

24 ⁴ And it shall come to pass that before they call, I will hear; as they are yet speaking, I will hear.

25 ⁵ The wolf and the lamb shall feed together; the lion and the ox shall eat straw; and dust shall be the serpent's food. They shall not hurt nor kill in all my holy mountain, saith the Lord.

CHAPTER 66
More of the reprobation of the Jews, and of the call of the Gentiles.

THUS ¹ saith the Lord: Heaven is my throne, and the earth my footstool. What is this house that you will build to me? And what is this place of my rest?

2 My hand made all these things, and all these things were made, saith the Lord. But to whom shall I have respect, but to him that is poor and little and of a contrite spirit, and that trembleth at my words?

3 He that sacrificeth an ox is as if he slew a man: he that killeth a sheep in sacrifice, as if he should brain a dog: he that offereth an oblation, as if he should offer swine's blood; he that remembereth incense, as if he should bless an idol. All these things have they chosen in their ways: and their soul is delighted in their abominations.

4 Wherefore, I also will choose their mockeries and will bring upon them the things they feared: ² because I called and there was none that would answer, I have spoken and they heard not; and they have done evil in my eyes and have chosen the things that displease me.

5 Hear the word of the Lord, you that tremble at his word: Your brethren that hate you and cast you out for my name's sake have said: Let the Lord be glorified, and we shall see in your joy. But they shall be confounded.

6 A voice of the people from the city, a voice from the temple, the voice of the Lord that rendereth recompense to his enemies.

7 Before she was in labour, she brought forth: before her time came to be delivered she brought forth a man child.

8 Who hath ever heard such a thing? And who hath seen the like to this? Shall the earth bring forth in one day? Or shall a nation be brought forth at once, because Sion hath been in labour and hath brought forth her children?

9 Shall not I that make others to bring forth children, myself bring forth, saith the Lord? Shall I, that give generation to others be barren, saith the Lord thy God?

10 Rejoice with Jerusalem and be glad with her, all you that love her: rejoice for joy with her, all you that mourn for her.

11 That you may suck and be filled with the breasts of her consolations: that you may milk out and flow with delights, from the abundance of her glory.

12 For thus saith the Lord: Behold I will bring upon her as it were a river of peace, and as an overflowing torrent the glory of the Gentiles, which you shall suck; you shall be carried at the breasts, and upon the knees they shall caress you.

13 As one whom the mother caresseth, so will I comfort you: and you shall be comforted in Jerusalem.

14 You shall see and your heart shall rejoice, [3] and your bones shall flourish like an herb, and the hand of the Lord shall be known to his servants, and he shall be angry with his enemies.

15 For behold the Lord will come with fire, and his chariots are like a whirlwind: to render his wrath in indignation and his rebuke with flames of fire.

16 For the Lord shall judge by fire and by his sword unto all flesh: and the slain of the Lord shall be many.

17 They that were sanctified and thought themselves clean in the gardens behind the gate within, they that did eat swine's flesh and the abomination and the mouse: they shall be consumed together, saith the Lord.

18 But I *know* their works and their thoughts: I come that I may gather them together with all nations and tongues: and they shall come and shall see my glory.

19 And I will set a sign among them, and I will send of them that shall be saved, to the Gentiles into the sea, into Africa and Lydia, them that draw the bow: into Italy and Greece, to the islands afar off, to them that have not heard of me and have not seen my glory. And they shall declare my glory to the Gentiles:

20 And they shall bring all your brethren out of all nations for a gift to the Lord, upon horses and in chariots and in litters and on mules and in coaches, to my holy mountain Jerusalem, saith the Lord, as if the children of Israel should bring an offering in a clean vessel into the house of the Lord.

21 And I will take of them to be priests and Levites, saith the Lord.

22 'For as the new heavens and the new earth, which I will make to stand before me, saith the Lord: so shall your seed stand, and your name.

23 And there shall be month after month and sabbath after sabbath: *and* all flesh shall come to adore before my face, saith the Lord.

24 And they shall go out and see the carcasses of the men that have transgressed against me. [5] Their worm shall not die and their fire shall not be quenched: and they shall be a loathsome sight to all flesh.

THE PROPHECY OF
JEREMIAS

Jeremias, a priest, a native of Anathoth, a priestly city in the tribe of Benjamin, was sanctified from his mother's womb, to be a prophet of God. This office he began to execute when he was yet a child in age. He was in his whole life, according to the signification of his name, Great before the Lord. *He was a special figure of Jesus Christ, in the persecutions he underwent for discharging his duty, in his charity for his persecutors, and in the violent death he suffered at their hands: it being an ancient tradition of the Hebrews, that he was stoned to death by the remnant of the Jews who had retired into Egypt.*

CHAPTER 1

The time, and the calling, of Jeremias. His prophetical visions. God encourages him.

THE words of Jeremias the son of Helcias, of the priests that were in Anathoth, in the land of Benjamin.

2 The word of the Lord which came to him in the days of Josias the son of Amon king of Juda, in the thirteenth year of his reign.

3 And which came *to him* in the days of Joakim the son of Josias king of Juda, unto the end of the eleventh year of Sedecias the son of Josias king of

[3] Ezech. 37. [4] Apoc. 21, 1. [5] Mark, 9, 45.

Juda, even unto the carrying away of Jerusalem captive, in the fifth month.

4 And the word of the Lord came to me, saying:

5 Before I formed thee in the bowels of thy mother, I knew thee: and before thou camest forth out of the womb, I sanctified thee and made thee a prophet unto the nations.

6 And I said: Ah, ah, ah, Lord God, behold, I cannot speak, for I am a child.

7 And the Lord said to me: Say not: I am a child: for thou shalt go to all that I shall send thee, and whatsoever I shall command thee, thou shalt speak.

8 Be not afraid at their presence: for I am with thee to deliver thee, saith the Lord.

9 And the Lord put forth his hand and touched my mouth. [1] And the Lord said to me: Behold I have given my words in thy mouth.

10 Lo, I have set thee this day over the nations, and over kingdoms, to root up [2] and to pull down, and to waste and to destroy, and to build and to plant.

11 And the word of the Lord came to me, saying: What seest thou, Jeremias? And I said: I see a rod watching.

12 And the Lord said to me: Thou hast seen well, for I will watch over my word to perform it.

13 And the word of the Lord came to me a second time, saying: What seest thou? And I said: [3] I see a boiling caldron, and the face thereof from the face of the north.

14 And the Lord said to me: [4] From the north shall an evil break forth upon all the inhabitants of the land.

15 For behold I will call together all the families of the kingdoms of the north, saith the Lord: and they shall come, and shall set every one his throne in the entrance of the gates of Jerusalem and upon all the walls thereof round about and upon all the cities of Juda.

16 And I will pronounce my judgments against them, touching all their wickedness, who have forsaken me and have sacrificed to strange gods and have adored the work of their own hands.

17 Thou therefore gird up thy loins and arise, and speak to them all that I command thee. Be not afraid at their presence: for I will make thee not to fear their countenance.

18 [5] For behold I have made thee this day a fortified city and a pillar of iron

and a wall of brass, over all the land, to the kings of Juda, to the princes thereof and to the priests and to the people of the land.

19 And they shall fight against thee and shall not prevail: for I am with thee, saith the Lord, to deliver thee.

CHAPTER 2

God expostulates with the Jews for their ingratitude and infidelity.

AND the word of the Lord came to me, saying:

2 Go, and cry in the ears of Jerusalem, saying: Thus saith the Lord: I have remembered thee, pitying thy youth and the love of thy espousals, when thou followedst me in the desert, in a land that is not sown.

3 Israel is holy to the Lord, the firstfruits of his increase: all they that devour him offend: evils shall come upon them, saith the Lord.

4 Hear ye the word of the Lord, O house of Jacob, and all ye families of the house of Israel.

5 Thus saith the Lord: [1] What iniquity have your fathers found in me, that they are gone far from me and have walked after vanity and are become vain?

6 And they have not said: Where is the Lord that made us come up out of the land of Egypt, that led us through the desert, through a land uninhabited and unpassable, through a land of drought, and the image of death, through a land wherein no man walked, nor any man dwelt?

7 And I brought you into the land of Carmel, to eat the fruit thereof and the best things thereof: and when ye entered in, you defiled my land and made my inheritance an abomination.

8 The priests did not say: Where is the Lord? And they that held the law knew me not, and the pastors transgressed against me, and the prophets prophesied in Baal and followed idols.

9 Therefore will I yet contend in judgment with you, saith the Lord, and I will plead with your children.

10 Pass over to the isles of Cethim and see, and send into Cedar and consider diligently: and see if there hath been done any thing like this.

11 If a nation hath changed their gods, and indeed they are not gods: but my people have changed their glory into an idol.

12 Be astonished, O ye heavens, at this: and, ye gates thereof, be very desolate, saith the Lord.

13 For my people have done two evils. They have forsaken me, the fountain

CHAP. 1. [1] Isai. 6, 7. [2] Jer. 18, 7. [3] Ezech. 11, 7. [4] Jer. 4, 6. [5] Jer. 6, 27. CHAP. 2. [1] Mich. 6, 3.

CHAP. 2. Ver. 7. *Carmel.* That is, a fruitful, plentiful land.

of living water, and have digged to themselves cisterns, broken cisterns, that can hold no water.

14 Is Israel a bondman, or a home-born slave? Why then is he become a prey?

15 The lions have roared upon him and have made a noise: they have made his land a wilderness. His cities are burnt down: and there is none to dwell in them.

16 The children also of Memphis and of Taphnes have defloured thee, even to the crown of the head.

17 Hath not this been done to thee, because thou hast forsaken the Lord thy God, at that time when he led thee by the way?

18 And now what hast thou to do in the way of Egypt, to drink the troubled water? And what hast thou to do with the way of the Assyrians, to drink the water of the river?

19 Thy own wickedness shall reprove thee, and thy apostasy shall rebuke thee. Know thou, and see that it is an evil and a bitter thing for thee, to have left the Lord thy God, and that my fear is not with thee, saith the Lord, the God of hosts.

20 Of old time thou hast broken my yoke, thou hast burst my bands, and thou saidst: I will not serve. [2] For on every high hill and under every green tree, thou didst prostitute thyself.

21 [3] Yet I planted thee a chosen vineyard, all true seed: how then art thou turned unto me into that which is good for nothing. O strange vineyard?

22 Though thou wash thyself with nitre and multiply to thyself the herb borith, thou art stained in thy iniquity before me, saith the Lord God.

23 How canst thou say: I am not polluted, I have not walked after Baalim? See thy ways in the valleys, know what thou hast done: *as* a swift runner pursuing his course.

24 A wild ass accustomed to the wilderness in the desire of his heart snuffed up the wind of his love: none shall turn her away. All that seek her shall not fail: in her monthly filth they shall find her.

25 Keep thy foot from being bare and thy throat from thirst. But thou saidst: I have lost all hope, I will not do it: for I have loved strangers and I will walk after them.

26 As the thief is confounded when he is taken, so is the house of Israel confounded, they and their kings, their princes, and their priests and their prophets.

27 Saying to a stock: Thou art my father. And to a stone: Thou hast be-gotten me. [4] They have turned their back to me, and not their face: and in the time of their affliction they will say: Arise, and deliver us.

28 Where are the gods, whom thou hast made thee? Let them arise and deliver thee in the time of thy affliction: [5] for according to the number of thy cities were thy gods, O Juda.

29 Why will you contend with me in judgment? You have all forsaken me, saith the Lord.

30 In vain have I struck your children: they have not received correction. Your sword hath devoured your prophets: your generation is like a ravaging lion.

31 See ye the word of the Lord: Am I become a wilderness to Israel, or a lateward springing land? Why then have my people said: We are revolted, we will come to thee no more?

32 Will a virgin forget her ornament, or a bride her stomacher? But my people hath forgotten me days without number.

33 Why dost thou endeavour to shew thy way good to seek *my* love, thou who hast also taught thy malices to be thy ways,

34 And in thy skirts is found the blood of the souls of the poor and innocent? Not in ditches have I found them, but in all places which I mentioned before.

35 And thou hast said: I am without sin and am innocent: and therefore let thy anger be turned away from me. Behold, I will contend with thee in judgment, because thou hast said: I have not sinned.

36 How exceeding base art thou become, going the same ways over again! And thou shalt be ashamed of Egypt, as thou wast ashamed of Assyria.

37 For from thence thou shalt go, and thy hand shall be upon thy head: for the Lord hath destroyed thy trust, and thou shalt have nothing prosperous therein.

CHAPTER 3

God invites the rebel Jews to return to him, with a promise to receive them. He foretells the conversion of the Gentiles.

IT is commonly said: If a man put away his wife, and she go from him and marry another man, shall he return to her any more? Shall not that woman be polluted and defiled? But thou hast prostituted thyself to many lovers. Nevertheless return to me, saith the Lord, and I will receive thee.

[2] Jer. 3, 6.   [3] Isai. 5, 1; Matt. 21, 33.   [4] Jer. 32, 33.   [5] Jer. 11, 13.

Ver. 22. *Borith.* An herb used to clean clothes, and take out spots and dirt.

2 Lift up thy eyes on high, and see where thou hast not prostituted thyself. Thou didst sit in the ways, waiting for them as a robber in the wilderness: and thou hast polluted the land with thy fornications and with thy wickedness.

3 Therefore, the showers were withholden, and there was no lateward rain: thou hadst a harlot's forehead, thou wouldst not blush.

4 Therefore, at the least from this time call to me: Thou art my father, the guide of my virginity:

5 Wilt thou be angry for ever, or wilt thou continue unto the end? Behold, thou hast spoken and hast done evil things and hast been able.

6 And the Lord said to me in the days of king Josias: [1] Hast thou seen what rebellious Israel hath done? She hath gone of herself upon every high mountain and under every green tree and hath played the harlot there.

7 And when she had done all these things, I said: Return to me. And she did not return. And her treacherous sister Juda saw,

8 That because the rebellious Israel had played the harlot, I had put her away and given her a bill of divorce: yet her treacherous sister Juda was not afraid, but went and played the harlot also herself.

9 And by the facility of her fornication she defiled the land and played the harlot with stones and with stocks.

10 And after all this, her treacherous sister Juda hath not returned to me with her whole heart, but with falsehood, saith the Lord.

11 And the Lord said to me: The rebellious Israel hath justified her soul, in comparison of the treacherous Juda.

12 Go, and proclaim these words towards the north. And thou shalt say: Return, O rebellious Israel, saith the Lord, and I will not turn away my face from you: for I am holy, saith the Lord, and I will not be angry for ever.

13 But yet acknowledge thy iniquity, that thou hast transgressed against the Lord thy God: and thou hast scattered thy ways to strangers under every green tree, and hast not heard my voice, saith the Lord.

14 Return, O ye revolting children, saith the Lord: for I am your husband: and I will take you, one of a city, and two of a kindred, and will bring you into Sion.

15 And I will give you pastors according to my own heart: and they shall feed you with knowledge and doctrine.

16 And when you shall be multiplied and increase in the land in those days, saith the Lord, they shall say no more: The ark of the covenant of the Lord. Neither shall it come upon the heart, neither shall they remember it, neither shall it be visited, neither shall that be done any more.

17 At that time Jerusalem shall be called the Throne of the Lord: and all the nations shall be gathered together to it, in the name of the Lord, to Jerusalem, and they shall not walk after the perversity of their most wicked heart.

18 In those days the house of Juda shall go to the house of Israel: and they shall come together out of the land of the north, to the land which I gave to your fathers.

19 But I said: How shall I put thee among the children and give thee a lovely land, the goodly inheritance of the armies of the Gentiles? And I said: Thou shalt call me father and shalt not cease to walk after me.

20 But as a woman that despiseth her lover, so hath the house of Israel despised me, saith the Lord.

21 A voice was heard in the highways, weeping and howling of the children of Israel: because they have made their way wicked, they have forgotten the Lord their God.

22 Return, you rebellious children, and I will heal your rebellions. Behold we come to thee: for thou art the Lord our God.

23 In very deed the hills were liars, and the multitude of the mountains: truly in the Lord our God *is* the salvation of Israel.

24 Confusion hath devoured the labour of our fathers from our youth, their flocks and their herds, their sons and their daughters.

25 We hall sleep in our confusion, and our shame shall cover us, because we have sinned against the Lord our God, we and our fathers from our youth even to this day: and we have not hearkened to the voice of the Lord our God.

CHAPTER 4

An admonition to sincere repentance and circumcision of the heart, with threats of grievous punishment to those that persist in sin.

IF thou wilt return, O Israel, saith the Lord, return to me: if thou wilt take away thy stumbling-blocks out of my sight, thou shalt not be moved.

2 And thou shalt swear: As the Lord liveth, in truth and in judgment and

CHAP. 3. [1] Jer. 2, 20.

CHAP. 3. Ver. 14. *Husband.* That is, Lord.

in justice: and the Gentiles shall bless him and shall praise him.

3 For thus saith the Lord to the men of Juda and Jerusalem: [1] Break up anew your fallow ground, and sow not upon thorns.

4 Be circumcised to the Lord, and take away the foreskins of your hearts, ye men of Juda and ye inhabitants of Jerusalem: lest my indignation come forth like fire and burn, and there be none that can quench it: because of the wickedness of your thoughts.

5 Declare ye in Juda, and make it heard in Jerusalem: speak, and sound with the trumpet in the land. Cry aloud, and say: Assemble yourselves, and let us go into strong cities.

6 Set up the standing in Sion. Strengthen yourselves, stay not: [2] for I bring evil from the north, and great destruction.

7 The lion is come up out of his den, and the robber of nations hath roused himself: he is come forth out of his place to make thy land desolate. Thy cities shall be laid waste, remaining without an inhabitant.

8 For this, gird yourselves with haircloth, lament and howl: for the fierce anger of the Lord is not turned away from us.

9 And it shall come to pass in that day, saith the Lord, that the heart of the king shall perish, and the heart of the princes: and the priests shall be astonished, and the prophets shall be amazed.

10 And I said: Alas, alas, alas, O Lord God, hast thou then deceived this people and Jerusalem, saying: You shall have peace? And behold the sword reacheth even to the soul.

11 At that time, it shall be said to this people and to Jerusalem: A burning wind *is* in the ways that are in the desert of the way of the daughter of my people, not to fan nor to cleanse.

12 A full wind from these *places* shall come to me: and now I will speak my judgments with them.

13 Behold he shall come up as a cloud, and his chariots as a tempest: his horses *are* swifter than eagles. Woe unto us, for we are laid waste!

14 Wash thy heart from wickedness, O Jerusalem, that thou mayst be saved. How long shall hurtful thoughts abide in thee?

15 For a voice of one declaring from Dan, and giving notice of the idol from mount Ephraim.

16 Say ye to the nations: Behold it is heard in Jerusalem that guards are coming from a far country and give out their voice against the cities of Juda.

17 They are set round about her, as keepers of fields: because she hath provoked me to wrath, saith the Lord.

18 [3] Thy ways and thy devices have brought these things upon thee: this is thy wickedness, because it is bitter, because it hath touched thy heart.

19 My bowels, my bowels, are in pain, the senses of my heart are troubled within me. I will not hold my peace, for my soul hath heard the sound of the trumpet, the cry of battle.

20 Destruction upon destruction is called for, and all the earth is laid waste: my tents are destroyed on a sudden and my pavilions in a moment.

21 How long shall I see men fleeing away? How long shall I hear the sound of the trumpet?

22 For my foolish people have not known me: they are foolish and senseless children. They are wise to do evil, but to do good they have no knowledge.

23 I beheld the earth, and lo it was void and nothing: and the heavens, and there was no light in them.

24 I looked upon the mountains, and behold they trembled: and all the hills were troubled.

25 I beheld, and lo there was no man: and all the birds of the air were gone.

26 I looked, and behold Carmel was a wilderness: and all its cities were destroyed at the presence of the Lord and at the presence of the wrath of his indignation.

27 For thus saith the Lord: All the land shall be desolate, but yet I will not utterly destroy.

28 The earth shall mourn, and the heavens shall lament from above: because I have spoken, I have purposed and I have not repented, neither am I turned away from it.

29 At the voice of the horsemen and the archers, all the city is fled away: they have entered into thickets and have climbed up the rocks. All the cities are forsaken, and there dwelleth not a man in them.

30 But when thou art spoiled, what wilt thou do? Though thou clothest thyself with scarlet, though thou deckest thee with ornaments of gold and paintest thy eyes with stibic stone, thou shalt dress thyself out in vain: thy lovers have despised thee, they will seek thy life.

31 For I have heard the voice as of a woman in travail, anguishes as of a woman in labour of a child. The voice of the daughter of Sion, dying away, spreading her hands: Woe is me, for my soul hath fainted because of them that are slain.

CHAP. 4. [1] Osee, 10, 12. [2] Jer. 1, 14. [3] Wisd. 3, 5.

CHAPTER 5

The judgments of God shall fall upon the Jews for their manifold sins.

GO about through the streets of Jerusalem, and see and consider, and seek in the broad places thereof, if you can find a man that executeth judgment and seeketh faith: and I will be merciful unto it.

2 And though they say: The Lord liveth; this also they will swear falsely.

3 O Lord, thy eyes are upon truth: thou hast struck them, and they have not grieved: thou hast bruised them, and they have refused to receive correction. They have made their faces harder than the rock and they have refused to return.

4 But I said: Perhaps these are poor and foolish, that know not the way of the Lord, the judgment of their God.

5 I will go therefore to the great men and will speak to them: for they have known the way of the Lord, the judgment of their God. And behold these have altogether broken the yoke more *and* have burst the bonds.

6 Wherefore a lion out of the wood hath slain them, a wolf in the evening hath spoiled them, a leopard watcheth for their cities: every one that shall go out thence shall be taken, because their transgressions are multiplied, their rebellions are strengthened.

7 How can I be merciful to thee? Thy children have forsaken me and swear by them that are not gods: I fed them to the full, and they committed adultery and rioted in the harlot's house.

8 They are become as amorous horses and stallions: [1] every one neighed after his neighbour's wife.

9 Shall I not visit for these things, saith the Lord? And shall not my soul take revenge on such a nation?

10 Scale the walls thereof and throw them down, but do not utterly destroy: take away the branches thereof, because they are not the Lord's.

11 For the house of Israel and the house of Juda have greatly transgressed against me, saith the Lord.

12 They have denied the Lord and said: It is not he and the evil shall not come upon us. We shall not see the sword and famine.

13 The prophets have spoken in the wind, and there was no word *of God* in them: these things therefore shall befall them.

14 Thus saith the Lord the God of hosts: Because you have spoken this word, behold I will make my words in thy mouth as fire and this people as wood; and it shall devour them.

15 Behold I will bring upon you a nation from afar, O house of Israel, saith the Lord: a strong nation, an ancient nation, a nation whose language thou shalt not know, nor understand what they say.

16 Their quiver is an open sepulchre: they are all valiant.

17 And they shall eat up thy corn and thy bread: they shall devour thy sons and thy daughters: they shall eat up thy flocks and thy herds: they shall eat thy vineyards and thy figs: and with the sword they shall destroy thy strong cities, wherein thou trustest.

18 Nevertheless, in those days, saith the Lord, I will not bring you to utter destruction.

19 [2] And if you shall say: Why hath the Lord our God done all these things to us? Thou shalt say to them: As you have forsaken me and served a strange god in your own land, so shall you serve strangers in a land that is not your own.

20 Declare ye this to the house of Jacob and publish it in Juda, saying:

21 Hear, O foolish people, and without understanding: who have eyes and see not, and ears and hear not.

22 Will not you then fear me? saith the Lord. And will you not repent at my presence? I have set the sand a bound for the sea, an everlasting ordinance which it shall not pass over. And the waves thereof shall toss themselves and shall not prevail: they shall swell, and shall not pass over it.

23 But the heart of this people is become hard of belief and provoking: they are revolted and gone away.

24 And they have not said in their heart: Let us fear the Lord our God, who giveth us the early and the latter rain in due season: who preserveth for us the fulness of the yearly harvest.

25 Your iniquities have turned these things away, and your sins have withholden good things from you.

26 For among my people are found wicked men that lie in wait as fowlers, setting snares and traps to catch men.

27 As a net is full of birds, so their houses are full of deceit: therefore are they become great and enriched.

28 They are grown gross and fat: and have most wickedly transgressed my words. [2] They have not judged the cause of the widow, they have not managed the cause of the fatherless, and they have not judged the judgment of the poor.

29 Shall I not visit for these things, saith the Lord? Or shall not my soul take revenge on such a nation?

CHAP. 5. [1]Ezech. 22, 11. [2] Jer. 16, 10. [3] Isai. 1, 23; Zach. 7, 10.

30 Astonishing and wonderful things have been done in the land.

31 The prophets prophesied falsehood, and the priests clapped their hands: and my people loved such things. What then shall be done in the end thereof?

CHAPTER 6

The evils that threaten Jerusalem. She is invited to return and walk in the good way, and not to rely on sacrifice without obedience.

STRENGTHEN yourselves, ye sons of Benjamin, in the midst of Jerusalem, and sound the trumpet in Thecua, and set up the standard over Bethacarem: for evil is seen out of the north, and a great destruction.

2 I have likened the daughter of Sion to a beautiful and delicate woman.

3 The shepherds shall come to her with their flocks: they have pitched *their* tents against her round about: every one shall feed them that are under his hand.

4 Prepare ye war against her: arise, and let us go up at midday. Woe unto us, for the day is declined, for the shadows of the evening are grown longer.

5 Arise, and let us go up in the night and destroy her houses.

6 For thus saith the Lord of hosts: Hew down her trees, cast up a trench about Jerusalem. This is the city to be visited: all oppression is in the midst of her.

7 As a cistern maketh its water cold, so hath she made her wickedness cold. Violence and spoil shall be heard in her: infirmity and stripes are continually before me.

8 Be thou instructed, O Jerusalem, lest my soul depart from thee, lest I make thee desolate, a land uninhabited.

9 Thus saith the Lord of hosts: They shall gather the remains of Israel, as in a vine, even to one cluster: turn back thy hand, as a grapegatherer into the basket.

10 To whom shall I speak? And to whom shall I testify, that he may hear? Behold, their ears are uncircumcised and they cannot hear. Behold the word of the Lord is become unto them a reproach: and they will not receive it.

11 Therefore am I full of the fury of the Lord, I am weary with holding in. Pour it out upon the child abroad and upon the council of the young men together: for man and woman shall be taken, the ancient and he that is full of days.

12 And their houses shall be turned over to others, with their lands and their wives together: for I will stretch forth my hand upon the inhabitants of the land, saith the Lord.

13 [1]For from the least of them even to the greatest, all are given to covetousness: and from the prophet even to the priest, all are guilty of deceit.

14 And they healed the breach of the daughter of my people disgracefully, saying: Peace, peace. And there was no peace.

15 They were confounded, because they committed abomination: yea rather, they were not confounded with confusion and they knew not how to blush. Wherefore they shall fall among them that fall: in the time of their visitation they shall fall down, saith the Lord.

16 Thus saith the Lord: Stand ye on the ways, and see, and ask for the old paths, which is the good way, and walk ye in it: [2]and you shall find refreshment for your souls. And they said: We will not walk.

17 And I appointed watchmen over you, saying: Hearken ye to the sound of the trumpet. And they said: We will not hearken.

18 Therefore hear, ye nations, and know, O congregation, what great things I will do to them.

19 Hear, O earth: Behold I will bring evils upon this people, the fruits of their own thoughts: because they have not heard my words and they have cast away my law.

20 [3]To what purpose do you bring me frankincense from Saba, and the sweet smelling cane from a far country? Your holocausts are not acceptable, nor are your sacrifices pleasing to me.

21 Therefore thus saith the Lord: Behold I will bring destruction upon this people, by which fathers and sons together shall fall, neighbour and kinsman shall perish.

22 Thus saith the Lord: Behold a people cometh from the land of the north, and a great nation shall rise up from the ends of the earth.

23 They shall lay hold on arrow and shield: they are cruel and will have no mercy. Their voice shall roar like the sea: and they shall mount upon horses, prepared as men for war, against thee, O daughter of Sion.

24 We have heard the fame thereof, our hands grow feeble: anguish hath taken hold of us, as a woman in labour.

25 Go not out into the fields, nor walk in the highway: for the sword of the enemy *and* fear is on every side.

26 Gird thee with sackcloth, O daughter of my people, and sprinkle thee with ashes: make thee mourning as for

CHAP. 6. [1] Isai. 56, 11; Jer. 8, 10. [2] Matt. 11, 29. [3] Isai. 1, 11.

an only son, a bitter lamentation, because the destroyer shall suddenly come upon us.

27 I have set thee for a strong trier among my people: and thou shalt know, and prove their way.

28 All these princes go out of the way: they walk deceitfully, *they are* brass and iron, they are all corrupted.

29 The bellows have failed, the lead is consumed in the fire, the founder hath melted in vain: for their wicked deeds are not consumed.

30 Call them reprobate silver, for the Lord hath rejected them.

CHAPTER 7

The temple of God shall not protect a sinful people, without a sincere conversion. The Lord will not receive the prayers of the prophet for them, because they are obstinate in their sins.

THE word that came to Jeremias from the Lord, saying:

2 Stand in the gate of the house of the Lord, and proclaim there this word, and say: Hear ye the word of the Lord, all ye men of Juda that enter in at these gates to adore the Lord.

3 Thus saith the Lord of hosts, the God of Israel: [1] Make your ways and your doings good: and I will dwell with you in this place.

4 Trust not in lying words, saying: The temple of the Lord, the temple of the Lord, it is the temple of the Lord.

5 For if you will order well your ways and your doings: if you will execute judgment between a man and his neighbour;

6 If you oppress not the stranger, the fatherless, and the widow, and shed not innocent blood in this place, and walk not after strange gods to your own hurt:

7 I will dwell with you in this place: in the land, which I gave to your fathers from the beginning and for evermore.

8 Behold you put your trust in lying words which shall not profit you:

9 To steal, to murder, to commit adultery, to swear falsely, to offer to Baalim, and to go after strange gods, which you know not.

10 And you have come and stood before me in this house, in which my name is called upon, and have said: We are

delivered, because we have done all these abominations.

11 [2] Is this house then, in which my name hath been called upon, in your eyes become a den of robbers? I, I am he: I have seen *it,* saith the Lord.

12 Go ye to my place in Silo, where my name dwelt from the beginning: and see what I did to it for the wickedness of my people Israel.

13 And now, because you have done all these works, saith the Lord: and I have spoken to you, rising up early and speaking, and you have not heard: [3] and I have called you, and you have not answered:

14 [4] I will do to this house, in which my name is called upon, and in which you trust, and to the place which I have given you and your fathers, as I did to Silo.

15 And I will cast you away from before my face, as I have cast away all your brethren, the whole seed of Ephraim.

16 [5] Therefore, do not thou pray for this people, nor take to thee praise and supplication for them: and do not withstand me: for I will not hear thee.

17 Seest thou not what they do in the cities of Juda and in the streets of Jerusalem?

18 The children gather wood, and the fathers kindle the fire, and the women knead the dough, to make cakes to the queen of heaven, and to offer libations to strange gods, and to provoke me to anger.

19 Do they provoke me to anger, saith the Lord? Is it not themselves, to the confusion of their own countenance?

20 Therefore thus saith the Lord God: Behold my wrath and my indignation is enkindled against this place, upon men and upon beasts, and upon the trees of the field, and upon the fruits of the land: and it shall burn and shall not be quenched.

21 Thus saith the Lord of hosts, the God of Israel: Add your burnt offerings to your sacrifices and eat ye the flesh.

22 For I spoke not to your fathers, and I commanded them not, in the day that I brought them out of the land of Egypt, concerning the matter of burnt offerings and sacrifices.

23 But this thing I commanded them, saying: Hearken to my voice, and I will be your God and you shall be my people. And walk ye in all the way that I have commanded you, that it may be well with you.

24 But they hearkened not, nor inclined their ear: but walked in their own will and in the perversity of their

CHAP. 7. [1] Jer. 26, 13. [2] Matt. 21, 13; Mark. 11, 17; Luke, 19, 46. [3] Prov. 1, 24; Isai. 65, 12. [4] 1 Kings, 4, 2, 10. [5] Jer. 11, 14; 14, 11.

CHAP. 7. Ver. 18. *The queen of heaven.* That is, the moon, which they worshipped under that name.

Ver. 22. *I commanded them not.* Not such sacrifices as the Jews at this time offered, without obedience; which was the thing principally commanded: so that in comparison with it, the offering of the holocausts and sacrifices was of small account.

wicked heart, and went backward and not forward,

25 From the day that their fathers came out of the land of Egypt even to this day. And I have sent to you all my servants the prophets from day to day, rising up early and sending.

26 And they have not hearkened to me nor inclined their ear: but have hardened their neck [6] and have done worse than their fathers.

27 And thou shalt speak to them all these words, but they will not hearken to thee: and thou shalt call them, but they will not answer thee.

28 And thou shalt say to them: This is a nation which hath not hearkened to the voice of the Lord their God nor received instruction. Faith is lost and is taken away out of their mouth.

29 Cut off thy hair, and cast it away: and take up a lamentation on high: for the Lord hath rejected and forsaken the generation of his wrath,

30 Because the children of Juda have done evil in my eyes, saith the Lord. They have set their abominations in the house in which my name is called upon, to pollute it.

31 And they have built the high places of Topheth, which is in the valley of the son of Ennom, to burn their sons and their daughters in the fire: which I commanded not nor thought on in my heart.

32 Therefore, behold the days shall come, saith the Lord, and it shall no more be called Topheth, nor the valley of the son of Ennom: but the valley of slaughter. And they shall bury in Topheth, because there is no place.

33 And the carcass of this people shall be meat for the fowls of the air and for the beasts of the earth, and there shall be none to drive them away.

34 [7] And I will cause to cease out of the cities of Juda and out of the streets of Jerusalem, the voice of joy and the voice of gladness, the voice of the bridegroom and the voice of the bride: for the land shall be desolate.

CHAPTER 8

Other evils that shall fall upon the Jews for their impenitence.

AT that time, saith the Lord, they shall cast out the bones of the kings of Juda, and the bones of the princes thereof, and the bones of the priests, and the bones of the prophets, and the bones of the inhabitants of Jerusalem, out of their graves.

2 And they shall spread them abroad to the sun and the moon and all the host of heaven, whom they have loved and whom they have served and after whom they have walked and whom they have sought and adored. They shall not be gathered, and they shall not be buried: they shall be as dung upon the face of the earth.

3 And death, shall be chosen rather than life by all that shall remain of this wicked kindred, in all places which are left, to which I have cast them out, saith the Lord of hosts.

4 And thou shalt say to them: Thus saith the Lord: Shall not he that falleth rise again? And he that is turned away, shall he not turn again?

5 Why then is this people in Jerusalem turned away with a stubborn revolting? They have laid hold on lying and have refused to return.

6 I attended and hearkened; no man speaketh what is good. There is none that doth penance for his sin, saying: What have I done? They are all turned to their own course, as a horse rushing to the battle.

7 The kite in the air hath known her time: the turtle and the swallow and the stork have observed the time of their coming: but my people have not known the judgment of the Lord.

8 How do you say: We are wise, and the law of the Lord is with us? Indeed the lying pen of the scribes hath wrought falsehood.

9 The wise men are confounded, they are dismayed and taken: for they have cast away the word of the Lord, and there is no wisdom in them.

10 [1] Therefore will I give their women to strangers, their fields to others for an inheritance: because from the least even to the greatest all follow covetousness: from the prophet even to the priest all deal deceitfully.

11 And they healed the breach of the daughter of my people disgracefully, saying, Peace, Peace, when there was no peace.

12 They are confounded, because they have committed abomination: yea rather they are not confounded with confusion and they have not known how to blush. Therefore shall they fall among them that fall: in the time of their visitation they shall fall, saith the Lord.

13 Gathering I will gather them together, saith the Lord. There is no grape on the vines, and there are no figs on the fig tree, the leaf is fallen: and I have given them the things that are passed away.

14 Why do we sit still? Assemble yourselves, and let us enter into the fenced city, and let us be silent there.

For the Lord our God hath put us to silence and hath given us [2] water of gall to drink: for we have sinned against the Lord.

15 [3] We looked for peace, and no good came: *for* a time of healing, and behold fear.

16 The snorting of his horses was heard from Dan, all the land was moved at the sound of the neighing of his warriors: and they came and devoured the land and all that was in it, the city and its inhabitants.

17 For behold I will send among you serpents, basilisks, against which there is no charm: and they shall bite you, saith the Lord.

18 My sorrow is above sorrow: my heart mourneth within me.

19 Behold the voice of the daughter of my people from a far country: Is not the Lord in Sion, or is not her king in her? Why then have they provoked me to wrath with their idols and strange vanities?

20 The harvest is past, the summer is ended, and we are not saved.

21 For the affliction of the daughter of my people, I am afflicted and made sorrowful: astonishment hath taken hold on me.

22 Is there no balm in Galaad? Or is there no physician there? Why then is not the wound of the daughter of my people closed?

CHAPTER 9

The prophet laments the miseries of his people, and their sins, which are the cause of them. He exhorts them to repentance.

WHO will give water to my head and a fountain of tears to my eyes, and I will weep day and night for the slain of the daughter of my people?

2 Who will give me in the wilderness a lodging place of wayfaring men, and I will leave my people and depart from them, because they are all adulterers, an assembly of transgressors?

3 And they have bent their tongue, as a bow, for lies and not for truth: they have strengthened themselves upon the earth: for they have proceeded from evil to evil, and me they have not known, saith the Lord.

4 Let every man take heed of his neighbour, and let him not trust in any brother of his: for every brother will utterly supplant, and every friend will walk deceitfully.

5 And a man shall mock his brother, and they will not speak the truth: for they have taught their tongue to speak

lies, they have laboured to commit iniquity.

6 Thy habitation is in the midst of deceit: through deceit they have refused to know me, saith the Lord.

7 Therefore thus saith the Lord of hosts: Behold I will melt and try them. For what else shall I do before the daughter of my people?

8 [1] Their tongue is a piercing arrow: it hath spoken deceit. With his mouth one speaketh peace with his friend, and secretly he lieth in wait for him.

9 Shall I not visit *them* for these things, saith the Lord? Or shall not my soul be revenged on such a nation?

10 For the mountains I will take up weeping and lamentation, and for the beautiful places of the desert, mourning: because they are burnt up, for that there is not a man that passeth through them. And they have not heard the voice of the owner: from the fowl of the air to the beasts, they are gone away and departed.

11 And I will make Jerusalem to be heaps of sand and dens of dragons: and I will make the cities of Juda desolate for want of an inhabitant.

12 Who is the wise man, that may understand this, and to whom the word of the mouth of the Lord may come that he may declare this, why the land hath perished and is burnt up like a wilderness which none passeth through?

13 And the Lord said: Because they have forsaken my law which I gave them, and have not heard my voice, and have not walked in it.

14 But they have gone after the perverseness of their own heart, and after Baalim, which their fathers taught them.

15 Therefore thus saith the Lord of hosts the God of Israel: [3] Behold I will feed this people with wormwood and give them water of gall to drink.

16 And I will scatter them among the nations which they and their fathers have not known: and I will send the sword after them till they be consumed.

17 Thus saith the Lord of hosts, the God of Israel: Consider ye, and call for the mourning women, and let them come: and send to them that are wise women, and let them make haste:

18 Let them hasten and take up a lamentation for us: let our eyes shed tears and our eyelids run down with waters.

19 For a voice of wailing is heard out of Sion: How are we wasted and greatly confounded? Because we have left the land, because our dwellings are cast down.

[2] Jer. 9, 15. [3] Jer. 14, 19. CHAP. 9. [1] Ps. 27, 3.
[2] Jer. 23, 15.

20 Hear therefore, ye women, the word of the Lord, and let your ears receive the word of his mouth: and teach your daughters wailing, and every one her neighbour mourning.

21 For death is come up through our windows: it is entered into our houses, to destroy the children from without, the young men from the streets.

22 Speak: Thus saith the Lord: Even the carcass of man shall fall as dung upon the face of the country, and as grass behind the back of the mower, and there is none to gather it.

23 Thus saith the Lord: [3] Let not the wise man glory in his wisdom, and let not the strong man glory in his strength, and let not the rich man glory in his riches:

24 But let him that glorieth glory in this, that he understandeth and knoweth me, for I am the Lord that exercise mercy and judgment and justice in the earth: for these things please me, saith the Lord.

25 Behold, the days come, saith the Lord, and I will visit upon every one that hath the foreskin circumcised.

26 Upon Egypt, and upon Juda, and upon Edom, and upon the children of Ammon, and upon Moab, and upon all that have their hair polled round, that dwell in the desert: for all the nations are uncircumcised in the flesh, but all the house of Israel are uncircumcised in the heart.

CHAPTER 10

Neither stars nor idols are to be feared, but the great Creator of all things. The chastisement of Jerusalem for her sins.

HEAR ye the word which the Lord hath spoken concerning you, O house of Israel.

2 Thus saith the Lord: Learn not according to the ways of the Gentiles: and be not afraid of the signs of heaven which the heathens fear.

3 For the laws of the people are vain: [1] for the work of the hand of the workman hath cut a tree out of the forest with an axe.

4 He hath decked it with silver and gold: he hath put it together with nails and hammers, that it may not fall asunder.

5 They are framed after the likeness of a palm tree and shall not speak: they must be carried to be removed, because they cannot go. Therefore fear them not, for they can neither do evil nor good.

6 [2] There is none like to thee, O Lord: Thou art great, and great is thy name in might.

7 [3] Who shall not fear thee, O king of nations, for thine is the glory? Among all the wise men of the nations and in all their kingdoms there is none like unto thee.

8 They shall be all proved together to be senseless and foolish: the doctrine of their vanity is wood.

9 Silver spread into plates is brought from Tharsis, and gold from Ophaz: the work of the artificer and of the hand of the coppersmith: violet and purple is their clothing: all these things are the work of artificers.

10 But the Lord is the true God: he is the living God and the everlasting king. At his wrath the earth shall tremble, and the nations shall not be able to abide his threatening.

11 Thus then shall you say to them: The gods that have not made heaven and earth, let them perish from the earth and from among those places that are under heaven.

12 [4] He that maketh the earth by his power, that prepareth the world by his wisdom and stretcheth out the heavens by his knowledge:

13 At his voice he giveth a multitude of waters in the heaven and lifteth up the clouds from the ends of the earth. [5] He maketh lightnings for rain and bringeth forth the wind out of his treasures.

14 Every man is become a fool for knowledge, every artist is confounded in his graven *idol:* for what he hath cast is false, and there is no spirit in them.

15 They are vain things and a ridiculous work: in the time of their visitation they shall perish.

16 The portion of Jacob is not like these: for it is he who formed all things and Israel is the rod of his inheritance. The Lord of hosts is his name.

17 Gather up thy shame out of the land, thou that dwellest in a siege.

18 For thus saith the Lord: Behold I will cast away far off the inhabitants of the land at this time: and I will afflict them, so that they may be found.

19 Woe is me for my destruction: my wound is very grievous. But I said: Truly this is my own evil, and I will bear it.

20 My tabernacle is laid waste, all my cords are broken: my children are gone out from me and they are not: there is none to stretch forth my tent any more, and to set up my curtains.

21 Because the pastors have done foolishly and have not sought the Lord: therefore have they not understood and all their flock is scattered.

[3] 1 Cor. 1, 31; 2 Cor. 10, 17. CHAP. 10. [1] Wisd. 13, 11; 14, 8. [2] Mich 7, 18. [3] Apoc. 15, 4. [4] Gen. 1, 1; Jer. 51, 15. [5] Ps. 134, 7; Jer. 51, 16.

22 Behold the sound of a noise cometh, a great commotion out of the land of the north: to make the cities of Juda a desert and a dwelling for dragons.

23 I know, O Lord, that the way of a man is not his: neither is it in a man to walk and to direct his steps.

24 Correct me, O Lord, but yet with judgment: and not in thy fury, lest thou bring me to nothing.

25 Pour out thy indignation upon the nations that have not known thee, and upon the provinces that have not called upon thy name: because they have eaten up Jacob and devoured him and consumed him, and have destroyed his glory.

CHAPTER 11

The prophet proclaims the covenant of God and denounces evils to the obstinate transgressors of it. The conspiracy of the Jews against him, a figure of their conspiracy against Christ.

THE word that came from the Lord to Jeremias, saying:

2 Hear ye the words of this covenant, and speak to the men of Juda and to the inhabitants of Jerusalem.

3 And thou shalt say to them: Thus saith the Lord, the God of Israel: Cursed is the man that shall not hearken to the words of this covenant.

4 Which I commanded your fathers in the day that I brought them out of the land of Egypt, from the iron furnace, saying: Hear ye my voice, and do all things that I command you: and you shall be my people, and I will be your God:

5 That I may accomplish the oath which I swore to your fathers, to give them a land flowing with milk and honey, as it is this day. And I answered and said: Amen, O Lord.

6 And the Lord said to me: Proclaim aloud all these words in the cities of Juda and in the streets of Jerusalem, saying: Hear ye the words of the covenant and do them:

7 For protesting I conjured your fathers in the day that I brought them out of the land of Egypt even to this day: rising early, I conjured them, and said: Hearken ye to my voice.

CHAP. 11. [1] Jer. 2, 28. [2] Jer. 7, 16; 14, 11. [3] Jer. 17, 10; 20, 12.

CHAP. 10. Ver. 23. *The way of a man is not his.* The meaning is, that notwithstanding man's free will, yet he can do no good without God's help, nor evil without his permission. So that, in the present case, all the evils which Nabuchodonosor was about to bring upon Jerusalem could not have come but by the will of God.

CHAP. 11. Ver. 20. *Sabaoth.* That is, of hosts or armies, a name frequently given to God in the scriptures.—*Thy revenge.* This was rather a prediction of what was to happen, with an approbation of the divine justice, than an imprecation.

8 And they obeyed not, nor inclined their ear: but walked every one in the perverseness of his own wicked heart. And I brought upon them all the words of this covenant which I commanded them to do: but they did them not.

9 And the Lord said to me: A conspiracy is found among the men of Juda, and among the inhabitants of Jerusalem.

10 They are returned to the former iniquities of their fathers who refused to hear my words: so these likewise have gone after strange gods, to serve them. The house of Israel and the house of Juda have made void my covenant which I made with their fathers.

11 Wherefore thus saith the Lord: Behold I will bring in evils upon them, which they shall not be able to escape: and they shall cry to me, and I will not hearken to them.

12 And the cities of Juda and the inhabitants of Jerusalem shall go and cry to the gods to whom they offer sacrifice: and they shall not save them in the time of their affliction.

13 [1] For according to the number of thy cities were thy gods, O Juda: and according to the number of the streets of Jerusalem thou hast set up altars of confusion, altars to offer sacrifice to Baalim.

14 [2] Therefore, do not thou pray for this people, and do not take up praise and prayer for them: for I will not hear them in the time of their cry to me, in the time of their affliction.

15 What is the meaning that my beloved hath wrought much wickedness in my house? Shall the holy flesh take away from thee thy crimes in which thou hast boasted?

16 The Lord called thy name, a plentiful olive tree, fair, fruitful, and beautiful: at the noise of a word, a great fire was kindled in it and the branches thereof are burnt.

17 And the Lord of hosts that planted thee hath pronounced evil against thee: for the evils of the house of Israel and of the house of Juda which they have done to themselves, to provoke me, offering sacrifice to Baalim.

18 But thou, O Lord, hast shewn me, and I have known: then thou shewedst me their doings.

19 And I was as a meek lamb that is carried to be a victim: and I knew not that they had devised counsels against me, saying: Let us put wood on his bread and cut him off from the land of the living, and let his name be remembered no more.

20 [3] But thou, O Lord of Sabaoth, who judgest justly and triest the reins and the hearts, let me see thy revenge

on them: for to thee have I revealed my cause.

21 Therefore thus saith the Lord to the men of Anathoth, who seek thy life and say: Thou shalt not prophesy in the name of the Lord and thou shalt not die in our hands.

22 Therefore thus saith the Lord of hosts: Behold I will visit upon them: their young men shall die by the sword, their sons and their daughters shall die by famine.

23 And there shall be no remains of them: for I will bring in evil upon the men of Anathoth, the year of their visitation.

CHAPTER 12

The prosperity of the wicked shall be but for a short time. The desolation of the Jews for their sins. Their return from their captivity.

THOU indeed, O Lord, art just, if I plead with thee, [1] but yet I will speak what is just to thee; [2] Why doth the way of the wicked prosper? Why is it well with all them that transgress and do wickedly?

2 Thou hast planted them, and they have taken root: they prosper and bring forth fruit: thou art near in their mouth and far from their reins.

3 And thou, O Lord, hast known me, thou hast seen me and proved my heart with thee: gather them together as sheep for a sacrifice, and prepare them for the day of slaughter.

4 How long shall the land mourn and the herb of every field wither for the wickedness of them that dwell therein? The beasts and the birds are consumed: because they have said: He shall not see our last end.

5 If thou hast been wearied with running with footmen, how canst thou contend with horses? And if thou hast been secure in a land of peace, what wilt thou do in the swelling of the Jordan?

6 For even thy brethren and the house of thy father, even they have fought against thee and have cried after thee with full voice. Believe them not when they speak good things to thee.

7 I have forsaken my house, I have left my inheritance, I have given my dear soul into the hand of her enemies.

8 My inheritance is become to me as a lion in the wood: it hath cried out against me. Therefore have I hated it.

9 Is my inheritance to me as a speckled bird? Is it as a bird dyed throughout? Come ye, assemble yourselves, all ye beasts of the earth, make haste to devour.

10 Many pastors have destroyed my vineyard: they have trodden my portion under foot, they have changed my delightful portion into a desolate wilderness.

11 They have laid it waste, and it hath mourned for me. With desolation is all the land made desolate, because there is none that considereth in the heart.

12 The spoilers are come upon all the ways of the wilderness, for the sword of the Lord shall devour from one end of the land to the other end thereof: there is no peace for all flesh.

13 They have sown wheat and reaped thorns: they have received an inheritance, and it shall not profit them: you shall be ashamed of your fruits, because of the fierce wrath of the Lord.

14 Thus saith the Lord against all my wicked neighbours that touch the inheritance that I have shared out to my people Israel: Behold I will pluck them out of their land, and I will pluck the house of Juda out of the midst of them.

15 And when I shall have plucked them out, I will return and have mercy on them: and I will bring them back, every man to his inheritance and every man into his land.

16 And it shall come to pass, if they will be taught and will learn the ways of my people, to swear by my name: The Lord liveth, as they have taught my people to swear by Baal: that they shall be built up in the midst of my people.

17 But if they will not hear, I will utterly pluck out and destroy that nation, saith the Lord.

CHAPTER 13

Under the figure of a linen girdle is foretold the destruction of the Jews. Their obstinacy in sin brings all miseries upon them.

THUS saith the Lord to me: Go, and get thee a linen girdle, and thou shalt put it about thy loins and shalt not put it into water.

2 And I got a girdle according to the word of the Lord and put it about my loins.

3 And the word of the Lord came to me the second time, saying:

4 Take the girdle which thou hast got, which is about thy loins, and arise. Go to the Euphrates and hide it there in a hole of the rock.

5 And I went and hid it by the Euphrates, as the Lord had commanded me.

6 And it came to pass after many

CHAP. 12. [1] Ps. 51, 6. [2] Job, 21, 7; Heb. 1, 13.

days that the Lord said to me: Arise, go to the Euphrates, and take from thence the girdle which I commanded thee to hide there.

7 And I went to the Euphrates, and digged, and took the girdle out of the place where I had hid it: and behold the girdle was rotten, so that it was fit for no use.

8 And the word of the Lord came to me, saying:

9 Thus saith the Lord: After this manner will I make the pride of Juda and the great pride of Jerusalem to rot.

10 This wicked people, that will not hear my words and that walk in the perverseness of their heart and have gone after strange gods to serve them and to adore them: and they shall be as this girdle which is fit for no use.

11 For as the girdle sticketh close to the loins of a man, so have I brought close to me all the house of Israel and all the house of Juda, saith the Lord: that they might be my people, and for a name, and for a praise, and for a glory. But they would not hear.

12 Thou shalt speak therefore to them this word: Thus saith the Lord, the God of Israel: Every bottle shall be filled with wine. And they shall say to thee: Do we not know that every bottle shall be filled with wine?

13 And thou shalt say to them: Thus saith the Lord: Behold I will fill all the inhabitants of this land, and the kings of the race of David that sit upon his throne, and the priests, and the prophets, and all the inhabitants of Jerusalem, with drunkenness.

14 And I will scatter them every man from his brother, and fathers and sons in like manner, saith the Lord. I will not spare and I will not pardon: nor will I have mercy, but to destroy them.

15 Hear ye, and give ear: Be not proud, for the Lord hath spoken.

16 Give ye glory to the Lord your God, before it be dark and before your feet stumble upon the dark mountains. You shall look for light, and he will turn it into the shadow of death and into darkness.

17 But if you will not hear this, my soul shall weep in secret for *your* pride: [1] weeping it shall weep, and my eyes shall run down with tears, because the flock of the Lord is carried away captive.

18 Say to the king and to the queen: Humble yourselves, sit down: for the crown of your glory is come down from your head.

19 The cities of the south are shut up, and there is none to open them: all

Juda is carried away captive with an entire captivity.

20 Lift up your eyes and see, you that come from the north. Where is the flock that is given thee, thy beautiful cattle?

21 What wilt thou say when he shall visit thee? For thou hast taught them against thee and instructed *them* against thy own head. Shall not sorrows lay hold on thee, as a woman in labour?

22 And if thou shalt say in thy heart: Why are these things come upon me? [2] For the greatness of thy iniquity, thy nakedness is discovered, the soles of thy feet are defiled.

23 If the Ethiopian can change his skin or the leopard his spots: you also may do well when you have learned evil.

24 And I will scatter them as stubble, which is carried away by the wind in the desert.

25 This *is* thy lot and the portion of thy measure from me, saith the Lord, because thou hast forgotten me and hast trusted in falsehood.

26 Wherefore, I have also bared thy thighs against thy face: and thy shame hath appeared.

27 I have seen thy adulteries and thy neighing, the wickedness of thy fornication and thy abominations upon the hills in the field. Woe to thee, Jerusalem! Wilt thou not be made clean after me? How long yet?

CHAPTER 14

A grievous famine. The prophet's prayer on that occasion. Evils denounced to false prophets. The prophet mourns for his people.

THE word of the Lord that came to Jeremias, concerning the words of the drought.

2 Judea hath mourned, and the gates thereof are fallen and are become obscure on the ground, and the cry of Jerusalem is gone up.

3 The great ones sent their inferiors to the water: they came to draw, they found no water, they carried back their vessels empty: they were confounded and afflicted and covered their heads.

4 For the destruction of the land, because there came no rain upon the earth, the husbandmen were confounded: they covered their heads.

5 Yea, the hind also brought forth in the field and left it, because there was no grass.

6 And the wild asses stood upon the rocks, they snuffed up the wind like dragons: their eyes failed, because there was no grass.

7 If our iniquities have testified

against us, O Lord, do thou it for thy name's sake, for our rebellions are many: we have sinned against thee.

8 O expectation of Israel, the Saviour thereof in time of trouble: Why wilt thou be as a stranger in the land and as a wayfaring man turning in to lodge?

9 Why wilt thou be as a wandering man, as a mighty man that cannot save? But thou, O Lord, art among us, and thy name is called upon by us: forsake us not.

10 Thus saith the Lord to this people that have loved to move their feet and have not rested and have not pleased the Lord: He will now remember their iniquities and visit their sins.

11 And the Lord said to me: [1] Pray not for this people for *their* good.

12 When they fast, I will not hear their prayers: and if they offer holocausts and victims, I will not receive them: for I will consume them by the sword and by famine and by the pestilence.

13 And I said: Ah, ah, ah, O Lord God, the prophets say to them: [2] You shall not see the sword, and there shall be no famine among you, but he will give you true peace in this place.

14 And the Lord said to me: [3] The prophets prophesy falsely in my name. I sent them not, neither have I commanded them, nor have I spoken to them: they prophesy unto you a lying vision and divination and deceit and the seduction of their own heart.

15 Therefore, thus saith the Lord, concerning the prophets that prophesy in my name, whom I did not send, that say: Sword and famine shall not be in this land. By sword and famine shall those prophets be consumed.

16 And the people to whom they prophesy shall be cast out in the streets of Jerusalem because of the famine and the sword, and there shall be none to bury them, they and their wives, their sons and their daughters. And I will pour out their own wickedness upon them.

17 And thou shalt speak this word to them: [4] Let my eyes shed down tears night and day and let them not cease, because the virgin daughter of my people is afflicted with a great affliction, with an exceeding grievous evil.

18 If I go forth into the fields, behold the slain with the sword: and if I enter into the city, behold them that are consumed with famine. The prophet also and the priest are gone into a land which they knew not.

19 Hast thou utterly cast away Juda, or hath thy soul abhorred Sion? Why then hast thou struck us, so that there is no healing for us? [5] We have looked

for peace, and there is no good: and for the time of healing, and behold trouble.

20 We acknowledge, O Lord, our wickedness, the iniquities of our fathers, because we have sinned against thee.

21 Give us not to be a reproach, for thy name's sake, and do not disgrace in us the throne of thy glory. Remember: break not thy covenant with us.

22 Are there any among the graven things of the Gentiles that can send rain? Or can the heavens give showers? Art not thou the Lord our God, whom we have looked for? For thou hast made all these things.

CHAPTER 15

God is determined to punish the Jews for their sins. The prophet's complaint and God's promise to him.

AND the Lord said to me: If Moses and Samuel shall stand before me, my soul is not towards this people. Cast them out from my sight and let them go forth.

2 And if they shall say unto thee: Whither shall we go forth? Thou shalt say to them: Thus saith the Lord: [1] Such as are for death, to death: and such as *are* for the sword, to the sword: and such as *are* for famine, to famine: and such as *are* for captivity, to captivity.

3 And I will visit them with four kinds, saith the Lord: The sword to kill, and the dogs to tear, and the fowls of the air and the beasts of the earth, to devour and to destroy.

4 And I will give them up to the rage of all the kingdoms of the earth: [2] because of Manasses the son of Ezechias the king of Juda, for all that he did in Jerusalem.

5 For who shall have pity on thee, O Jerusalem? Or who shall bemoan thee? Or who shall go to pray for thy peace?

6 Thou hast forsaken me, saith the Lord, thou art gone backward: and I will stretch out my hand against thee, and I will destroy thee. I am weary of entreating thee.

7 And I will scatter them with a fan in the gates of the land: I have killed and destroyed my people, and yet they are not returned from their ways.

8 Their widows are multiplied unto me above the sand of the sea: I have brought upon them against the mother of the young man a spoiler at noonday: I have cast a terror on a sudden upon the cities.

9 [3] She that hath borne seven is become weak, her soul hath fainted away,

CHAP. 14. [1] Jer. 7, 16; 11, 14. [2] Jer. 5, 12; 23, 17. [3] Jer. 29, 9. [4] Lam. 1, 16; 2, 18. [5] Jer. 8, 15. CHAP. 15. [1] Zach. 11, 9. [2] 4 Kings, 21, 2-11. [3] 1 Kings, 2, 5.

'her sun is gone down while it was yet day: she is confounded and ashamed. And the residue of them I will give up to the sword in the sight of their enemies, saith the Lord.

10 Woe is me, my mother! Why hast thou borne me, a man of strife, a man of contention to all the earth? I have not lent on usury, neither hath any man lent to me on usury: *yet* all curse me.

11 The Lord saith to *me:* Assuredly it shall be well with thy remnant, assuredly I shall help thee in the time of affliction and in the time of tribulation, against the enemy.

12 Shall iron be allied with the iron from the north and the brass?

13 Thy riches and thy treasures I will give unto spoil for nothing, because of all thy sins, even in all thy borders.

14 And I will bring thy enemies out of a land which thou knowest not, for a fire is kindled in my rage: it shall burn upon you.

15 O Lord, thou knowest, remember me, and visit me, and defend me from them that persecute me: do not defend me in thy patience, know that for thy sake I have suffered reproach.

16 Thy words were found, and I did eat them: and thy word was to me a joy and gladness of my heart, for thy name is called upon me, O Lord God of hosts.

17 [5] I sat not in the assembly of jesters, nor did I make a boast of the presence of thy hand: I sat alone, because thou hast filled me with threats.

18 [6] Why is my sorrow become perpetual, and my wound desperate so as to refuse to be healed? It is become to me as the falsehood of deceitful waters that cannot be trusted.

19 Therefore thus saith the Lord: If thou wilt be converted, I will convert thee, and thou shalt stand before my face: and if thou wilt separate the precious from the vile, thou shalt be as my mouth. They shall be turned to thee, and thou shalt not be turned to them.

20 And I will make thee to this people as a strong wall of brass: and they shall fight against thee and shall not

---

prevail. For I am with thee to save thee and to deliver thee, saith the Lord.

21 And I will deliver thee out of the hand of the wicked, and I will redeem thee out of the hand of the mighty.

CHAPTER 16

The prophet is forbid to marry. The Jews shall be utterly ruined for their idolatry, but shall at length be released from their captivity, and the Gentiles shall be converted.

AND the word of the Lord came to me, saying:

2 Thou shalt not take thee a wife: neither shalt thou have sons and daughters in this place.

3 For thus saith the Lord, concerning the sons and daughters that are born in this place, and concerning their mothers that bore them, and concerning their fathers of whom they were born in this land:

4 They shall die by the death of grievous illnesses: they shall not be lamented and they shall not be buried: they shall be as dung upon the face of the earth: and they shall be consumed with the sword and with famine: and their carcasses shall be meat for the fowls of the air and for the beasts of the earth.

5 For thus saith the Lord: Enter not into the house of feasting, neither go thou to mourn, nor to comfort them: because I have taken away my peace from this people, saith the Lord, *my* mercy and commiserations.

6 Both the great and the little shall die in this land. They shall not be buried nor lamented: and men shall not cut themselves nor make themselves bald for them.

7 And they shall not break bread among them to him that mourneth, to comfort him for the dead: neither shall they give them to drink of the cup, to comfort them for their father and mother.

8 And do not thou go into the house of feasting, to sit with them and to eat and drink:

9 For thus saith the Lord of hosts, the God of Israel: Behold I will take away out of this place in your sight, and in your days, the voice of mirth and the voice of gladness, the voice of the bridegroom and the voice of the bride.

10 And when thou shalt tell this people all these words and they shall say to thee: [1] Wherefore hath the Lord pronounced against us all this great evil? What is our iniquity, and what is our sin, that we have sinned against the Lord our God?

11 Thou shalt say to them: Because

---

[4] Amos, 8, 9. [5] Ps. 1, 1; 25, 4. [6] Jer. 30, 15.
CHAP. 16. [1] Jer. 5, 19.

CHAP. 15. Ver. 12. *Shall iron be allied.* Shall the *iron,* that is, the strength of Judea, stand against the stronger iron of the north, that is, of Babylon: or enter into an alliance upon equal footing with it? No certainly: but it must be broken by it.

Ver. 15. *Do not defend me in thy patience.* That is, let not thy patience and longsuffering, which thou usest towards sinners, keep thee from making haste to my assistance.

your fathers forsook me, saith the Lord, and went after strange gods and served them and adored them: and they forsook me and kept not my law.

12 [2] And you also have done worse than your fathers: for behold every one of you walketh after the perverseness of his evil heart, so as not to hearken to me.

13 So I will cast you forth out of this land, into a land which you know not, nor your fathers: and there you shall serve strange gods, day and night, which shall not give you any rest.

14 Therefore, behold the days come, saith the Lord, when it shall be said no more: The Lord liveth, that brought forth the children of Israel out of the land of Egypt:

15 But, The Lord liveth, that brought the children of Israel out of the land of the north and out of all the lands to which I cast them out. And I will bring them again into their land, which I gave to their fathers.

16 Behold, I will send many fishers, saith the Lord, and they shall fish them: and after this, I will send them many hunters, and they shall hunt them from every mountain and from every hill and out of the holes of the rocks.

17 For my eyes *are* upon all their ways: they are not hid from my face, and their iniquity hath not been hid from my eyes.

18 And I will repay first their double iniquities and their sins: because they have defiled my land with the carcasses of their idols, and they have filled my inheritance with their abominations.

19 O Lord, my might and my strength and my refuge in the day of tribulation: to thee the Gentiles shall come from the ends of the earth and shall say: Surely our fathers have possessed lies, a vanity which hath not profited them.

20 Shall a man make gods unto himself, and they are no gods?

21 Therefore behold I will this once cause them to know, I will shew them my hand and my power: and they shall know that my name *is* the Lord.

CHAPTER 17

For their obstinacy in sin the Jews shall be led captive. He is cursed that trusteth in flesh. God alone searcheth the heart, giving to every one as he deserves. The prophet prayeth to be delivered from his enemies and preacheth up the observance of the sabbath.

THE sin of Juda is written with a pen of iron, with the point of a diamond: *it is* graven upon the table

of their heart, upon the horns of their altars.

2 When their children shall remember their altars and their groves and their green trees upon the high mountains,

3 Sacrificing in the field: I will give thy strength and all thy treasures to the spoil, *and* thy high places for sin in all thy borders.

4 And thou shalt be left stripped of thy inheritance which I gave thee; and I will make thee serve thy enemies in a land which thou knowest not. Because thou hast kindled a fire in my wrath, it shall burn for ever.

5 Thus saith the Lord: [1] Cursed be the man that trusteth in man and maketh flesh his arm, and whose heart departeth from the Lord!

6 [2] For he shall be like tamaric in the desert, and he shall not see when good shall come: but he shall dwell in dryness in the desert, in a salt land, and not inhabited.

7 Blessed be the man that trusteth in the Lord, and the Lord shall be his confidence.

8 [3] And he shall be as a tree that is planted by the waters, that spreadeth out its roots towards moisture: and it shall not fear when the heat cometh. And the leaf thereof shall be green, and in the time of drought it shall not be solicitous: neither shall it cease at any time to bring forth fruit.

9 The heart is perverse above all things and unsearchable. Who can know it?

10 I *am* the Lord, [4] who search the heart and prove the reins: who give to every one according to his way and according to the fruit of his devices.

11 *As* the partridge hath hatched *eggs* which she did not lay: *so is* he that hath gathered riches, and not by right. In the midst of his days he shall leave them: and in his latter end he shall be a fool.

12 A high and glorious throne from the beginning *is* the place of our sanctification.

13 O Lord, the hope of Israel: All that forsake thee shall be confounded: they that depart from thee shall be written in the earth: because they have forsaken the Lord, the vein of living waters.

14 Heal me, O Lord, and I shall be healed: save me, and I shall be saved: for thou art my praise.

[2] Jer. 7, 26. Chap. 17. [1] Isai. 30, 2; 31, 1; Jer. 48, 7. [2] Jer. 48, 6. [3] Ps. 1, 3. [4] 1 Kings, 16, 7; Ps. 7, 10; Apoc. 2, 28.

Chap. 17. Ver. 6. *Tamaric.* A barren shrub that grows in the driest parts of the wilderness.

15 Behold they say to me: Where is the word of the Lord? Let it come.

16 And I am not troubled, following thee for my pastor: and I have not desired the day of man, thou knowest. That which went out of my lips hath been right in thy sight.

17 Be not thou a terror unto me: thou art my hope in the day of affliction.

18 Let them be confounded that persecute me, and let not me be confounded: let them be afraid, and let not me be afraid: bring upon them the day of affliction and with a double destruction destroy them.

19 Thus saith the Lord to me: Go, and stand in the gate of the children of the people, by which the kings of Juda come in and go out, and in all the gates of Jerusalem.

20 And thou shalt say to them: Hear the word of the Lord, ye kings of Juda, and all Juda, and all the inhabitants of Jerusalem, that enter in by these gates.

21 Thus saith the Lord: Take heed to your souls and carry no burdens on the sabbath day: and bring them not in by the gates of Jerusalem.

22 And do not bring burdens out of your houses on the sabbath day: neither do ye any work. Sanctify the sabbath day, as I commanded your fathers.

23 But they did not hear nor incline their ear: but hardened their neck, that they might not hear me and might not receive instruction.

24 And it shall come to pass, if you will hearken to me, saith the Lord, to bring in no burdens by the gates of this city on the sabbath day, and if you will sanctify the sabbath day, to do no work therein:

25 Then shall there enter in by the gates of this city kings and princes, sitting upon the throne of David and riding in chariots and on horses, they and their princes, the men of Juda and the inhabitants of Jerusalem: and this city shall be inhabited for ever.

26 And they shall come from the cities of Juda and from the places round about Jerusalem and from the land of Benjamin and from the plains and from the mountains and from the south, bringing holocausts and victims and sacrifices and frankincense: and they shall bring in an offering into the house of the Lord.

CHAP. 18. [1] Isai. 45; 9; Rom. 9, 20. [2] Jer. 1, 10. [3, 4] Kings, 17, 13; Jer. 25, 5; 35, 15; Jonas, 3, 9.
Ver. 18. *Let them be confounded.* Such expressions as these in the writings of the prophets are not to be understood as imprecations proceeding from malice or desire of revenge: but as prophetic predictions of evils that were about to fall upon impenitent sinners and approbations of the ways of divine justice.

27 But if you will not hearken to me, to sanctify the sabbath day, and not to carry burdens, and not to bring them in by the gates of Jerusalem on the sabbath day: I will kindle a fire in the gates thereof. And it shall devour the houses of Jerusalem: and it shall not be quenched.

CHAPTER 18

As clay in the hand of the potter, so is Israel in God's hand. He pardoneth penitents and punisheth the obstinate. They conspire against Jeremias, for which he denounceth to them the miseries that hang over them.

THE word that came to Jeremias from the Lord, saying:

2 Arise, and go down into the potter's house: and there thou shalt hear my words.

3 And I went down into the potter's house: and behold he was doing a work on the wheel.

4 And the vessel was broken which he was making of clay with his hands: and turning he made another vessel, as it seemed good in his eyes to make it.

5 Then the word of the Lord came to me, saying:

6 [1] Cannot I do with you as this potter, O house of Israel, saith the Lord? Behold as clay *is* in the hand of the potter, so are you in my hand, O house of Israel.

7 I will suddenly speak against a nation and against a kingdom [2] to root out and to pull down and to destroy it.

8 If that nation against which I have spoken shall repent of their evil, I also will repent of the evil that I have thought to do to them.

9 And I will suddenly speak of a nation and of a kingdom, to build up and plant it.

10 If it shall do evil in my sight, that it obey not my voice, I will repeat of the good that I have spoken to do unto it.

11 Now therefore tell the men of Juda and the inhabitants of Jerusalem, saying: Thus saith the Lord: Behold I frame evil against you and devise a device against you. [3] Let every man of you return from his evil way: and make ye your ways and your doings good.

12 And they said: We have no hopes, for we will go after our own thoughts and we will do every one according to the perverseness of his evil heart.

13 Therefore thus saith the Lord: Ask among the nations: Who hath heard such horrible things as the virgin of Israel hath done to excess?

14 Shall the snow of Libanus fail from the rock of the field? Or can the cold waters that gush out and run down be taken away?

15 Because my people have forgotten me, sacrificing in vain, and stumbling in their ways, in ancient paths, to walk by them in a way not trodden:

16 ⁴ That their land might be given up to desolation and to a perpetual hissing. Every one that shall pass by it shall be astonished and wag his head.

17 As a burning wind will I scatter them before the enemy. I will shew them the back and not the face, in the day of their destruction.

18 And they said: Come, and let us invent devices against Jeremias, for the law shall not perish from the priest, nor counsel from the wise, nor the word from the prophet. Come, and let us strike him with the tongue, and let us give no heed to all his words.

19 Give heed to me, O Lord, and hear the voice of my adversaries.

20 Shall evil be rendered for good, because they have digged a pit for my soul? Remember that I have stood in thy sight, to speak good for them, and to turn away thy indignation from them.

21 Therefore, deliver up their children to famine and bring them into the hands of the sword. Let their wives be bereaved of children and widows: and let their husbands be slain by death. Let their young men be stabbed with the sword in battle.

22 Let a cry be heard out of their houses: for thou shalt bring the robber upon them suddenly, because they have digged a pit to take me and have hid snares for my feet.

23 But thou, O Lord, knowest all their counsel against me unto death. Forgive not their iniquity, and let not their sin be blotted out from thy sight. Let them be overthrown before thy eyes: in the time of thy wrath do thou destroy them.

CHAPTER 19

Under the type of breaking a potter's vessel, the prophet foresheweth the desolation of the Jews for their sins.

THUS saith the Lord: Go, and take a potter's earthen bottle, *and take* of the ancients of the people, and of the ancients of the priests.

2 And go forth into the valley of the son of Ennom, which is by the entry of the earthen gate: and there thou shalt proclaim the words that I shall tell thee.

3 And thou shalt say: Hear the word of the Lord, O ye kings of Juda and ye inhabitants of Jerusalem. Thus saith the Lord of hosts, the God of Israel: Behold, I will bring an affliction upon this place: so that whosoever shall hear it, his ears shall tingle.

4 Because they have forsaken me and have profaned this place and have sacrificed therein to strange gods, whom neither they nor their fathers knew, nor the kings of Juda. And they have filled this place with the blood of innocents.

5 And they have built the high places of Baalim, to burn their children with fire for a holocaust to Baalim: which I did not command, nor speak of, neither did it once come into my mind.

6 Therefore, behold the days come, saith the Lord, that this place shall no more be called Topheth, nor the valley of the son of Ennom, but the valley of slaughter.

7 And I will defeat the counsel of Juda and of Jerusalem in this place: and I will destroy them with the sword in the sight of their enemies and by the hands of them that seek their lives: and I will give their carcasses to be meat for the fowls of the air and for the beasts of the earth.

8 ¹ And I will make this city an astonishment and a hissing: every one that shall pass by it shall be astonished and shall hiss because of all the plagues thereof.

9 And I will feed them with the flesh of their sons and with the flesh of their daughters: and they shall eat every one the flesh of his friend in the siege, and in the distress wherewith their enemies, and they that seek their lives shall straiten them.

10 And thou shalt break the bottle in the sight of the men that shall go with thee.

11 And thou shalt say to them: Thus saith the Lord of hosts: Even so will I break this people and this city, as the potter's vessel is broken which cannot be made whole again: and they shall be buried in Topheth, because there is no other place to bury in.

12 Thus will I do to this place, saith the Lord, and to the inhabitants thereof: and I will make this city as Topheth.

13 And the houses of Jerusalem and the houses of the kings of Juda shall be unclean as the place of Topheth: all the houses upon whose roofs they have sacrificed to all the host of heaven and have poured out drink offerings to strange gods.

14 Then Jeremias came from Topheth, whither the Lord had sent him to prophesy: and he stood in the court of the house of the Lord and said to all the people:

---

⁴ Jer. 19, 8; 49, 18; 50, 13. Cʜᴀᴘ. 19. ¹ Jer. 18, 10; 49, 13; 50, 13.

Cʜᴀᴘ. 18. Ver 20. *Remember.* This is spoken in the person of Christ, persecuted by the Jews, and prophetically denouncing the evils that should fall upon them in punishment of their crimes.

15 Thus saith the Lord of hosts, the God of Israel: Behold I will bring in upon this city and upon all the cities thereof all the evils that I have spoken against it: because they have hardened their necks, that they might not hear my words.

CHAPTER 20

The prophet is persecuted. He denounces captivity to his persecutors and bemoans himself.

NOW Phassur the son of Emmer, the priest, who was appointed chief in the house of the Lord, heard Jeremias prophesying these words.

2 And Phassur struck Jeremias the prophet and put him in the stocks that were in the upper gate of Benjamin, in the house of the Lord.

3 And when it was light the next day, Phassur brought Jeremias out of the stocks. And Jeremias said to him: The Lord hath not called thy name Phassur, but Fear on every side.

4 For thus saith the Lord: Behold I will deliver thee up to fear, thee and all thy friends. And they shall fall by the sword of their enemies, and thy eyes shall see *it*. And I will give all Juda into the hand of the king of Babylon: and he shall carry them away to Babylon and shall strike them with the sword.

5 And I will give all the substance of this city, and all its labour, and every precious thing thereof, and all the treasures of the kings of Juda will I give into the hands of their enemies: and they shall pillage them and take them away and carry them to Babylon.

6 But thou, Phassur, and all that dwell in thy house shall go into captivity. And thou shalt go to Babylon, and there thou shalt die, and there thou shalt be buried, thou and all thy friends, to whom thou hast prophesied a lie.

7 Thou hast deceived me, O Lord, and I am deceived: thou hast been stronger than I, and thou hast pre-

CHAP. 20. [1] Jer. 23, 40. [2] Jer. 11, 20; 17, 10. [3] Job, 3, 3.

CHAP. 20. Ver. 3. *Phassur*. This name signifies *increase* and *principality*: and therefore is here changed to *Magor-Missabib*, or *Fear on every side*, to denote the evils that should come upon him in punishment of his opposing the word of God.
Ver. 7. *Thou hast deceived me*. The meaning of the prophet, is not to charge God with any untruth; but what he calls *deceiving* was only the concealing from him, when he accepted of the prophetical commission, the greatness of the evils which the execution of that commission was to bring upon him.
Ver. 12. *Let me see*. This prayer proceeded not from hatred or ill will, but from zeal of justice.
Ver. 14. *Cursed be the day*. In these, and the following words of the prophet, there is a certain figure of speech to express with more energy the greatness of the evils to which his birth had exposed him.

vailed. I am become a laughing-stock all the day: all scoff at me.

8 For I am speaking now this long time, crying out *against* iniquity and I often proclaim devastation: and the word of the Lord is made a reproach to me and a derision, all the day.

9 Then I said: I will not make mention of him nor speak any more in his name. And there came in my heart as a burning fire, shut up in my bones: and I was wearied, not being able to bear it.

10 For I heard the reproaches of many, and terror on every side: Persecute him, and, Let us persecute him: from all the men that were my familiars and continued at my side: if by any means he may be deceived and we may prevail against him and be revenged on him.

11 But the Lord is with me as a strong warrior: therefore they that persecute me shall fall and shall be weak. They shall be greatly confounded, [1] because they have not understood the everlasting reproach which never shall be effaced.

12 And thou, O Lord of hosts, [2] prover of the just, who seest the reins and the heart: let me see, I beseech thee, thy vengeance on them, for to thee I have laid open my cause.

13 Sing ye to the Lord, praise the Lord: because he hath delivered the soul of the poor out of the hand of the wicked.

14 [3] Cursed be the day wherein I was born: let not the day in which my mother bore me be blessed.

15 Cursed be the man that brought the tidings to my father, saying: A man child is born to thee: and made him greatly rejoice.

16 Let that man be as the cities which the Lord hath overthrown, and hath not repented: let him hear a cry in the morning and howling at noontide:

17 Who slew me not from the womb, that my mother might have been my grave, and her womb an everlasting conception.

18 Why came I out of the womb to see labour and sorrow, and that my days should be spent in confusion?

CHAPTER 21

The prophet's answer to the messengers of Sedecias, when Jerusalem was besieged.

THE word that came to Jeremias from the Lord, when king Sedecias sent unto him Phassur, the son of Melchias, and Sophonias, the son of Maasias the priest, saying:

2 Inquire of the Lord for us: for

Nabuchodonosor king of Babylon maketh war against us: if so be the Lord will deal with us according to all his wonderful works, that he may depart from us.

3 And Jeremias said to them: Thus shall you say to Sedecias:

4 Thus saith the Lord, the God of Israel: Behold, I will turn back the weapons of war that are in your hands, and with which you fight against the king of Babylon and the Chaldeans that besiege you round about the walls: and I will gather them together in the midst of this city.

5 And I myself will fight against you with an outstretched hand, and with a strong arm, and in fury, and in indignation, and in great wrath.

6 And I will strike the inhabitants of this city: men and beasts shall die of a great pestilence.

7 And after this, saith the Lord, I will give Sedecias the king of Juda, and his servants, and his people, and such as are left in this city from the pestilence and the sword and the famine, into the hand of Nabuchodonosor the king of Babylon, and into the hand of their enemies, and into the hand of them that seek their life: and he shall strike them with the edge of the sword, and he shall not be moved to pity nor spare them nor shew mercy to them.

8 And to this people thou shalt say: Thus saith the Lord: Behold I set before you the way of life and the way of death.

9 [1] He that shall abide in this city shall die by the sword and by the famine and by the pestilence: but he that shall go out and flee over to the Chaldeans, that besiege you shall live, and his life shall be to him as a spoil.

10 For I have set my face against this city for evil, and not for good, saith the Lord. It shall be given into the hand of the king of Babylon: and he shall burn it with fire.

11 And to the house of the king of Juda: Hear ye the word of the Lord,

12 O house of David, thus saith the Lord: [2] Judge ye judgment in the morning, and deliver him that is oppressed by violence out of the hand of the oppressor: lest my indignation go forth like a fire and be kindled, and there be none to quench it, because of the evil of your ways.

13 Behold I *come* to thee that dwellest in *a* valley upon a rock above a plain, saith the Lord. And you say: Who shall strike us and who shall enter into our houses?

14 But I will visit upon you according to the fruit of your doings, saith the Lord: and I will kindle a fire in the

forest thereof: and it shall devour all things round about it.

CHAPTER 22

An exhortation both to king and people to return to God. The sentence of God upon Joachaz, Joakim, and Jechonias.

THUS saith the Lord: Go down to the house of the king of Juda, and there thou shalt speak this word.

2 And thou shalt say: Hear the word of the Lord, O king of Juda, that sittest upon the throne of David: thou and thy servants and thy people, who enter in by these gates.

3 Thus saith the Lord: [1] Execute judgment and justice: and deliver him that is oppressed out of the hand of the oppressor: and afflict not the stranger, the fatherless and the widow, nor oppress them unjustly: and shed not innocent blood in this place.

4 For if you will do this thing indeed, then shall there enter in by the gates of this house kings of the race of David, sitting upon his throne and riding in chariots and on horses, they and their servants and their people.

5 But if you will not hearken to these words, I swear by myself, saith the Lord, that this house shall become a desolation.

6 For thus saith the Lord to the house of the king of Juda: Thou art to me Galaad, the head of Libanus: *yet* surely I will make thee a wilderness *and* cities not habitable.

7 And I will prepare against thee the destroyer and his weapons: and they shall cut down thy chosen cedars and shall cast them headlong into the fire.

8 And many nations shall pass by this city, and they shall say every man to his neighbour: [2] Why hath the Lord done so to this great city?

9 And they shall answer: Because they have forsaken the covenant of the Lord their God and have adored strange gods and served them.

10 Weep not for him that is dead

CHAP. 21. [1] Jer. 38, 2. [2] Jer. 22, 3. CHAP. 22. [1] Jer. 21, 12. [2] Deut. 29, 24; 3 Kings, 9, 8.

CHAP. 21. Ver. 13. *To thee that dwellest.* He speaks to Jerusalem, confiding in the strength of her situation upon rocks, surrounded with a deep valley.

CHAP. 22. Ver. 1. *Go down.* The contents of this chapter are of a more ancient date than those of the foregoing chapter: for the order of time is not always observed in the writings of the prophets.

Ver. 6. *Galaad the head of Libanus.* By Galaad, a rich and fruitful country, is here signified the royal palace of the kings of the house of David: by Libanus, a high mountain abounding in cedar trees, the populous city of Jerusalem.

Ver. 7. *Prepare.* Literally, *sanctify.*

Ver. 10. *Weep not for him that is dead.* He means the good king Josias, who by death was taken away, so as not to see the miseries of his country.—*Him that goeth away,* namely, *Sellum,* or Joachaz, who was carried captive into Egypt.

nor bemoan him with your tears: lament him that goeth away, for he shall return no more nor see his native country.

11 For thus saith the Lord to Sellum the son of Josias, the king of Juda, who reigned instead of his father, who went forth out of this place: He shall return hither no more.

12 But in the place to which I have removed him, there shall he die: and he shall not see this land any more.

13 Woe to him that buildeth up his house by injustice, and his chambers not in judgment: that will oppress his friend without cause and will not pay him his wages.

14 Who saith: I will build me a wide house and large chambers: who openeth to himself windows and maketh roofs of cedar and painteth them with vermilion.

15 Shalt thou reign, because thou comparest thyself to the cedar? Did not thy father eat and drink, and do judgment and justice, and it was then well with him?

16 He judged the cause of the poor and needy for his own good. Was it not therefore because he knew me, saith the Lord?

17 But thy eyes and thy heart are set upon covetousness and upon shedding innocent blood and upon oppression and running after evil works.

18 Therefore, thus saith the Lord concerning Joakim the son of Josias king of Juda: They shall not mourn for him, Alas, my brother, and, Alas, sister: they shall not lament for him, Alas, my lord, or, Alas, the noble one.

19 He shall be buried with the burial of an ass, rotten and cast forth [3] without the gates of Jerusalem.

20 Go up to Libanus and cry: and lift up thy voice in Basan and cry to them that pass by, for all thy lovers are destroyed.

21 I spoke to thee in thy prosperity: and thou saidst: I will not hear. This hath been thy way from thy youth, because thou hast not heard my voice.

22 The wind shall feed all thy pastors, and thy lovers shall go into captivity: and then shalt thou be confounded and ashamed of all thy wickedness.

23 Thou that sittest in Libanus and makest thy nest in the cedars, how hast thou mourned when sorrows came upon thee, as the pains of a woman in labour?

[3] Jer. 36, 30. CHAP. 23. [1] Ezech. 13, 3; 34, 2.
[2] Jer. 3, 15. [3] Isai. 4, 2; 40, 11; 45, 8; Jer. 33, 11;
Ezech. 34, 10, 11; Dan. 9, 24; John, 1, 45. [4] Deut. 33, 28.

Ver. 30. *Write this man barren.* That is, childless: not that he had no children, but that his children should never sit on the throne of Juda.

24 As I live, saith the Lord, if Jachonias the son of Joakim, the king of Juda, were a ring on my right hand, I would pluck him thence.

25 And I will give thee into the hand of them that seek thy life, and into the hand of them whose face thou fearest, and into the hand of Nabuchodonosor king of Babylon, and into the hand of the Chaldeans.

26 And I will send thee, and thy mother that bore thee, into a strange country, in which you were not born: and there you shall die.

27 And they shall not return into the land, whereunto they lift up their mind to return thither.

28 Is this man Jechonias an earthen and a broken vessel? Is he a vessel wherein is no pleasure? Why are they cast out, he and his seed, and are cast into a land which they know not?

29 O earth, earth, earth, hear the word of the Lord.

30 Thus saith the Lord: Write this man barren, a man that shall not prosper in his days: for there shall not be a man of his seed that shall sit upon the throne of David and have power any more in Juda.

CHAPTER 23

God reproves evil governors and promises to send good pastors and Christ himself the prince of the pastors. He inveighs against false prophets preaching without being sent.

WOE [1] to the pastors that destroy and tear the sheep of my pasture, saith the Lord.

2 Therefore, thus saith the Lord the God of Israel to the pastors that feed my people: You have scattered my flock and driven them away, and have not visited them: behold, I will visit upon you for the evil of your doings, saith the Lord.

3 And I will gather together the remnant of my flock out of all the lands into which I have cast them out. And I will make them return to their own fields: and they shall increase and be multiplied.

4 [2] And I will set up pastors over them, and they shall feed them: they shall fear no more and they shall not be dismayed. And none shall be wanting of their number, saith the Lord.

5 [3] Behold the days come, saith the Lord, and I will raise up to David a just branch. And a king shall reign, and shall be wise, and shall execute judgment and justice in the earth.

6 In those [4] days shall Juda be saved and Israel shall dwell confidently: and this is the name that they shall call him; The Lord, Our Just One.

7 Therefore, behold the days come, saith the Lord, and they shall say no more: The Lord liveth, who brought up the children of Israel out of the land of Egypt:

8 But, [5] The Lord liveth, who hath brought out and brought hither the seed of the house of Israel, from the land of the north and out of all the lands to which I had cast them forth: and they shall dwell in their own land.

9 To the prophets: My heart is broken within me, all my bones tremble: I am become as a drunken man, and as a man full of wine, at the presence of the Lord and at the presence of his holy words.

10 Because the land is full of adulterers, because the land hath mourned by reason of cursing. The fields of the desert are dried up, and their course is become evil, and their strength unlike.

11 For the prophet and the priest are defiled: and in my house I have found their wickedness, saith the Lord.

12 Therefore, their way shall be as a slippery way in the dark: for they shall be driven on and fall therein: for I will bring evils upon them, the year of their visitation, saith the Lord.

13 And I have seen folly in the prophets of Samaria: They prophesied in Baal and deceived my people Israel.

14 And I have seen the likeness of adulterers and the way of lying in the prophets of Jerusalem: and they strengthened the hands of the wicked, that no man should return from his evil doings. They are all become unto me as Sodom, and the inhabitants thereof as Gomorrha.

15 Therefore thus saith the Lord of hosts to the prophets: [6] Behold I will feed them with wormwood and will give them gall to drink: for from the prophets of Jerusalem corruption is gone forth into all the land.

16 Thus saith the Lord of hosts: [7] Hearken not to the words of the prophets that prophesy to you and deceive you. They speak a vision of their own heart and not out of the mouth of the Lord.

17 They say to them that blaspheme me: The Lord hath said, [8] You shall have peace. And to every one that walketh in the perverseness of his own heart they have said: No evil shall come upon you.

18 For who hath stood in the counsel of the Lord and hath seen and heard his word? Who hath considered his word and heard it?

19 [9] Behold the whirlwind of the Lord's indignation shall come forth: and a tempest shall break out and come upon the head of the wicked.

20 The wrath of the Lord shall not return till he execute it and till he accomplish the thought of his heart: in the latter days you shall understand his counsel.

21 [10] I did not send prophets, yet they ran: I have not spoken to them, yet they prophesied.

22 If they had stood in my counsel and had made my words known to my people, I should have turned them from their evil way and from their wicked doings.

23 Am I, think ye, a God at hand, saith the Lord, and not a God afar off?

24 Shall a man be hid in secret places and I not see him, saith the Lord? Do not I fill heaven and earth, saith the Lord?

25 I have heard what the prophets said that prophesy lies in my name and say: I have dreamed, I have dreamed.

26 How long shall this be in the heart of the prophets that prophesy lies and that prophesy the delusions of their own heart?

27 Who seek to make my people forget my name through their dreams, which they tell every man to his neighbour: as their fathers forgot my name for Baal.

28 The prophet that hath a dream, let him tell a dream: and he that hath my word, let him speak my word with truth. What hath the chaff to do with the wheat, saith the Lord?

29 Are not my words as a fire, saith the Lord, and as a hammer that breaketh the rock in pieces?

30 Therefore, behold I *am against* the prophets, saith the Lord: who steal my words every one from his neighbour.

31 Behold I *am against* the prophets, saith the Lord: who use their tongues and say: The Lord saith it.

32 Behold I *am against* the prophets that have lying dreams, saith the Lord, and tell them and cause my people to err by their lying and by their wonders: when I sent them not nor commanded them, who have not profited this people at all, saith the Lord.

33 If therefore this people or the prophet or the priest shall ask thee, saying: What is the burden of the Lord? Thou shalt say to them: You are the burden: for I will cast you away, saith the Lord.

34 And as for the prophet and the priest and the people that shall say:

[5] Jer. 16, 14. [6] Jer. 9, 15. [7] Jer. 27, 9; 29, 8. [8] Jer. 5, 12; 14, 13. [9] Jer. 30, 14. [10] Jer. 27, 15; 29. 9.

CHAP. 23. Ver. 34. *Burden of the Lord.* This expression is here rejected and disallowed, at least for those times: because it was then used in mockery and contempt by the false prophets and unbelieving people, who ridiculed the repeated threats of Jeremias under the name of his *burdens.*

The burden of the Lord: I will visit upon that man and upon his house.

35 Thus shall you say, every one to his neighbour and to his brother: What hath the Lord answered and what hath the Lord spoken?

36 And the burden of the Lord shall be mentioned no more, for every man's word shall be his burden: for you have perverted the words of the living God, of the Lord of hosts our God.

37 Thus shalt thou say to the prophet: What hath the Lord answered thee and what hath the Lord spoken?

38 But if you shall say, The burden of the Lord: therefore thus saith the Lord: Because you have said this word, The burden of the Lord: and I have sent to you, saying: Say not, The burden of the Lord:

39 Therefore, behold I will take you away, carrying you, and will forsake you and the city which I gave to you and to your fathers, out of my presence.

40 [11] And I will bring an everlasting reproach upon you and a perpetual shame which shall never be forgotten.

CHAPTER 24

Under the type of good and bad figs, he foretells the restoration of the Jews that had been carried away captive with Jechonias and the desolation of those that were left behind.

THE Lord showed me: and behold two baskets full of figs, set before the temple of the Lord: after that Nabuchodonosor king of Babylon had carried away Jechonias the son of Joakim the king of Juda, and his chief men, and the craftsmen and engravers of Jerusalem, and had brought them to Babylon.

2 One basket had very good figs, like the figs of the first season: and the other basket had very bad figs, which could not be eaten, because they were bad.

3 And the Lord said to me: What seest thou, Jeremias? And I said: Figs, the good figs, very good: and the bad figs, very bad, which cannot be eaten because they are bad.

4 And the word of the Lord came to me, saying:

5 Thus saith the Lord, the God of Israel: Like these good figs, so will I regard the captives of Juda, whom I have sent forth out of this place into the land of the Chaldeans, for their good.

---

[11] Jer. 20, 11. Chap. 24. [1] Jer. 7, 23; 28, 6.
[2] Jer. 29, 17. Chap. 25. [1] 4 Kings, 17, 13; Jer. 18, 11; 35, 15.

Ver. 39. *Out of my presence.* That is, the Lord declares that out of his presence he will cast them and bring them to captivity for their transgressions.

---

6 And I will set my eyes upon them to be pacified, and I will bring them again into this land. And I will build them up and not pull them down: and I will plant them and not pluck *them* up.

7 And I will give them a heart to know me, that I am the Lord. [1] And they shall be my people, and I will be their God: because they shall return to me with their whole heart.

8 [2] And as the very bad figs, that cannot be eaten because they are bad: thus saith the Lord: So will I give Sedecias the king of Juda and his princes, and the residue of Jerusalem that have remained in this city and that dwell in the land of Egypt.

9 And I will deliver them up to vexation and affliction, to all the kingdoms of the earth: to be a reproach and a byword and a proverb, and to be a curse in all places to which I have cast them out.

10 And I will send among them the sword and the famine and the pestilence: till they be consumed out of the land which I gave to them and their fathers.

CHAPTER 25

The prophet foretells the seventy years' captivity and after that the destruction of Babylon and other nations.

THE word that came to Jeremias concerning all the people of Juda, in the fourth year of Joakim the son of Josias king of Juda (the same is the first year of Nabuchodonosor king of Babylon),

2 Which Jeremias, the prophet spoke to all the people of Juda and to all the inhabitants of Jerusalem, saying:

3 From the thirteenth year of Josias the son of Ammon king of Juda until this day, this is the three and twentieth year, the word of the Lord hath come to me, and I have spoken to you, rising before day and speaking, and you have not hearkened.

4 And the Lord hath sent to you all his servants the prophets, rising early and sending, and you have not hearkened nor inclined your ears to hear.

5 When he said: [1] Return ye, every one from his evil way and from your wicked devices: and you shall dwell in the land which the Lord hath given to you and your fathers for ever and ever.

6 And go not after strange gods to serve them and adore them, nor provoke me to wrath by the works of your hands: and I will not afflict you.

7 And you have not heard me, saith the Lord, that you might provoke me

to anger with the works of your hands, to your own hurt.

8 Therefore, thus saith the Lord of hosts: Because you have not heard my words:

9 Behold I will send, and take all the kindreds of the north, saith the Lord, and Nabuchodonosor the king of Babylon my servant: and I will bring them against this land and against the inhabitants thereof and against all the nations that are round about it: and I will destroy them and make them an astonishment and a hissing and perpetual desolations.

10 And I will take away from them the voice of mirth and the voice of gladness, the voice of the bridegroom and the voice the bride, the sound of the mill and the light of the lamp.

11 ² And all this land shall be a desolation and an astonishment: and all these nations shall serve the king of Babylon seventy years.

12 And when the seventy years shall be expired, I will punish the king of Babylon and that nation, saith the Lord, for their iniquity, and the land of the Chaldeans: and I will make it perpetual desolations.

13 And I will bring upon that land all my words that I have spoken against it, all that is written in this book, all that Jeremias hath prophesied against all nations:

14 For they have served them, whereas they were many nations and great kings: and I will repay them according to their deeds and according to the works of their hands.

15 For thus saith the Lord of hosts, the God of Israel: Take the cup of wine of this fury at my hand. And thou shalt make all the nations to drink thereof, unto which I shall send thee.

16 And they shall drink and be troubled and be mad, because of the sword which I shall send among them.

17 And I took the cup at the hand of the Lord, and I presented it to all the nations to drink of it, to which the Lord sent me:

18 To wit, Jerusalem and the cities of Juda and the kings thereof and the princes thereof: to make them a desolation and an astonishment and a hissing and a curse, as it is at this day.

19 Pharao, the king of Egypt, and his servants and his princes and all his people.

20 And all in general: all the kings of the land of Ausitis, and all the kings of the land of the Philistines and Ascalon and Gaza and Accaron and the remnant of Azotus.

21 And Edom and Moab and the children of Ammon.

22 And all the kings of Tyre and all the kings of Sidon: and the kings of the land of the islands that are beyond the sea.

23 And Dedan and Thema and Buz and all that have their hair cut round.

24 And all the kings of Arabia and all the kings of the west that dwell in the desert.

25 And all the kings of Zambri and all the kings of Elam and all the kings of the Medes.

26 And all the kings of the north far and near, every one against his brother: and all the kingdoms of the earth, which are upon the face thereof. And the king of Sesac shall drink after them.

27 And thou shalt say to them: Thus saith the Lord of hosts, the God of Israel: Drink ye, and be drunken and vomit: and fall and rise no more, because of the sword which I shall send among you.

28 And if they refuse to take the cup at thy hand to drink, thou shalt say to them: Thus saith the Lord of hosts: Drinking you shall drink:

29 ³ For behold I begin to bring evil on the city wherein my name is called upon. And shall you be as innocent and escape free? You shall not escape free: for I will call for the sword upon all the inhabitants of the earth, saith the Lord of hosts.

30 And thou shalt prophesy unto them all these words, and thou shalt say to them: ⁴ The Lord shall roar from on high and shall utter his voice from his holy habitation: roaring he shall roar upon the *place* of his beauty. The shout as it were of them that tread grapes shall be given out against all the inhabitants of the earth.

31 The noise is come even to the ends of the earth, for the Lord entereth into judgment with the nations: he entereth into judgment with all flesh. The wicked I have delivered up to the sword, saith the Lord.

32 Thus saith the Lord of hosts: Behold evil shall go forth from nation to nation: and a great whirlwind shall go forth from the ends of the earth.

33 And the slain of the Lord shall be at that day from one end of the earth even to the other end thereof. They shall not be lamented and they shall not be gathered up, nor buried: they

² 2 Par. 36, 22; 1 Esd. 1, 1; Jer. 26, 6; 29, 10; Dan. 9, 2. ³ 1 Peter, 4, 17. ⁴ Joel, 3, 16; Amos, 1, 2.

CHAP. 25. Ver. 9. *My servant.* So this wicked king is here called: because God made him his instrument in punishing the sins of his people.

Ver. 12. *Punish.* Literally, *visit upon.*

Ver. 26. *Sesac.* That is, Babel or Babylon; which after bringing all these people under her yoke, should quickly fall and be destroyed herself.

shall lie as dung upon the face of the earth.

34 Howl, ye shepherds, and cry, and sprinkle yourselves with ashes, ye leaders of the flock: for the days of your slaughter and your dispersion are accomplished and you shall fall like precious vessels.

35 And the shepherds shall have no way to flee, nor the leaders of the flock to save themselves.

36 A voice of the cry of the shepherds and a howling of the principal of the flock: because the Lord hath wasted their pastures.

37 And the fields of peace have been silent: because of the fierce anger of the Lord.

38 He hath forsaken his covert as the lion, for the land is laid waste: because of the wrath of the dove and because of the fierce anger of the Lord.

CHAPTER 26

The prophet is apprehended and accused by the priests, but discharged by the princes.

IN the beginning of the reign of Joakim the son of Josias king of Juda, came this word from the Lord, saying:

2 Thus saith the Lord: Stand in the court of the house of the Lord and speak to all the cities of Juda, out of which they come to adore in the house of the Lord, all the words which I have commanded thee to speak unto them: leave not out one word.

3 If so be they will hearken and be converted every one from his evil way; that I may repent me of the evil that I think to do unto them for the wickedness of their doings.

4 And thou shalt say to them: Thus saith the Lord: If you will not hearken to me to walk in my law which I have given you:

5 To give ear to the words of my servants the prophets whom I sent to you, rising up early and sending, and you have not hearkened:

6 ¹ I will make this house like Silo: ² and I will make this city a curse to all the nations of the earth.

7 And the priests and the prophets and all the people heard Jeremias speaking these words in the house of the Lord.

8 And when Jeremias had made an

CHAP. 26. ¹ 1 Kings, 4, 2, 10. ² Jer. 7, 12. ³ Jer. 25, 11. ⁴ Jer. 7, 3. ⁵ Mich. 3, 12.

Ver. 38. *The dove.* This is commonly understood of Nabuchodonosor, whose military standard, it is said, was a dove. But the Hebrew word *Jonah,* which is here rendered *a dove,* may also signify a waster or oppressor, which name better agrees to that unmerciful prince; or by comparison, as a dove's flight is the swiftest, so would their destruction come upon them.

end of speaking all that the Lord had commanded him to speak to all the people, the priests and the prophets and all the people laid hold on him, saying: Let him be put to death.

9 Why hath he prophesied in the name of the Lord, saying: This house shall be like Silo, and this city shall be made desolate without an inhabitant? And all the people were gathered together against Jeremias in the house of the Lord.

10 And the princes of Juda heard these words: and they went up from the king's house into the house of the Lord and sat in the entry of the new gate of the house of the Lord.

11 And the priests and the prophets spoke to the princes and to all the people, saying: The judgment of death is for this man, because he hath prophesied against this city, as you have heard with your ears.

12 Then Jeremias spoke to all the princes and to all the people, saying: The Lord sent me to prophesy concerning this house and concerning this city all the words that you have heard.

13 ⁴ Now therefore, amend your ways and your doings, and hearken to the voice of the Lord your God: and the Lord will repent him of the evil that he hath spoken against you.

14 But as for me, behold I am in your hands: do with me what is good and right in your eyes.

15 But know ye and understand, that if you put me to death, you will shed innocent blood against your own selves and against this city and the inhabitants thereof. For in truth the Lord sent me to you, to speak all these words in your hearing.

16 Then the princes and all the people said to the priests and to the prophets: There is no judgment of death for this man: for he hath spoken to us in the name of the Lord our God.

17 And some of the ancients of the land rose up: and they spoke to all the assembly of the people, saying:

18 Micheas of Morasthi was a prophet in the days of Ezechias king of Juda, and he spoke to all the people of Juda, saying: Thus saith the Lord of hosts: ⁵ Sion shall be ploughed like a field, and Jerusalem shall be a heap of stones, and the mountain of the house, the high places of woods.

19 Did Ezechias king of Juda and all Juda condemn him to death? Did they not fear the Lord and beseech the face of the Lord? And the Lord repented the evil that he had spoken against them. Therefore we are doing a great evil against our souls.

20 There was also a man that prophesied in the name of the Lord, Urias the son of Semei of Cariathiarim: and he prophesied against this city and against this land, according to all the words of Jeremias.

21 And Joakim and all his men in power and his princes heard these words: and the king sought to put him to death. And Urias heard it and was afraid, and fled and went into Egypt.

22 And king Joakim sent men into Egypt, Elnathan the son of Achobor, and men with him into Egypt.

23 And they brought Urias out of Egypt: and brought him to king Joakim: and he slew him with the sword: and he cast his dead body into the graves of the common people.

24 So the hand of Ahicam the son of Saphan was with Jeremias, that he should not be delivered into the hands of the people, to put him to death.

CHAPTER 27

The prophet sends chains to divers kings, signifying that they must bend their necks under the yoke of the king of Babylon. The vessels of the temple shall not be brought back till all the rest are carried away.

IN the beginning of the reign of Joakim the son of Josias king of Juda, this work came to Jeremias from the Lord, saying:

2 Thus saith the Lord to me: Make thee bands and chains. And thou shalt put them on thy neck.

3 And thou shalt send them to the king of Edom and to the king of Moab and to the king of the children of Ammon and to the king of Tyre and to the king of Sidon, by the hand of the messengers that are come to Jerusalem to Sedecias the king of Juda.

4 And thou shalt command them to speak to their masters: Thus saith the Lord of hosts, the God of Israel: Thus shall you say to your masters:

5 I made the earth and the men and the beasts that are upon the face of the earth, by my great power and by my stretched out arm: and I have given it to whom it seemed good in my eyes.

6 And now I have given all these lands into the hand of Nabuchodonosor king of Babylon, my servant: moreover also the beasts of the field I have given him to serve him.

7 And all nations shall serve him and his son and his son's son, till the time come for his land and himself: and many nations and great kings shall serve him.

8 But the nation and kingdom that will not serve Nabuchodonosor king of Babylon, and whosoever will not bend his neck under the yoke of the king of Babylon: I will visit upon that nation with the sword and with famine and with pestilence, saith the Lord: till I consume them by his hand.

9 [1] Therefore, hearken not to your prophets and diviners and dreamers and soothsayers and sorcerers, that say to you: You shall not serve the king of Babylon.

10 For they prophesy lies to you: to remove you far from your country and cast you out, and to make you perish.

11 But the nation that shall bend down their neck under the yoke of the king of Babylon and shall serve him: I will let them remain in their own land, saith the Lord. And they shall till it and dwell in it.

12 And I spoke to Sedecias the king of Juda, according to all these words, saying: Bend down your necks under the yoke of the king of Babylon and serve him and his people, and you shall live.

13 Why will you die, thou and thy people, by the sword and by famine and by the pestilence, as the Lord hath spoken against the nation that will not serve the king of Babylon?

14 Hearken not to the words of the prophets that say to you: You shall not serve the king of Babylon. For they tell you a lie.

15 [2] For I have not sent them, saith the Lord, and they prophesy in my name falsely: to drive you out, and that you may perish, both you and the prophets that prophesy to you.

16 I spoke also to the priests and to this people, saying: Thus saith the Lord: Hearken not to the words of your prophets, that prophesy to you, saying: Behold the vessels of the Lord shall now in a short time be brought again from Babylon. For they prophesy a lie unto you.

17 Therefore hearken not to them, but serve the king of Babylon, that you may live. Why should this city be given up to desolation?

18 But if they be prophets and the word of the Lord be in them: let them interpose themselves before the Lord of hosts, that the vessels which were left in the house of the Lord and in the house of the king of Juda and in Jerusalem may not go to Babylon.

19 For thus saith the Lord of hosts

CHAP. 27. [1] Jer. 23, 16; 29, 8. [2] Jer. 14, 14; 23, 21; 29. 9.

CHAP. 27. Ver. 1. *Joakim.* This revelation was made to the prophet in the beginning of the reign of Joakim: but the bands were not sent to the princes here named before the reign of Sedecias, ver. 3.

Ver. 7. *His son.* Evilmerodach, and his son's son, Nabonydus, or Nabonadius, the *Baltassar* of Daniel, chap. 5, and the last of the Chaldean kings.

3 to the pillars and to the sea and to the bases and to the rest of the vessels that remain in this city,

20 Which Nabuchodonosor the king of Babylon did not take, when he carried away Jechonias the son of Joakim the king of Juda, from Jerusalem to Babylon, and all the great men of Juda and Jerusalem.

21 For thus saith the Lord of hosts, the God of Israel, to the vessels that are left in the house of the Lord and in the house of the king of Juda and Jerusalem:

22 They shall be carried to Babylon, and there they shall be until the day of their visitation, saith the Lord: and I will cause them to be brought and to be restored in this place.

CHAPTER 28

The false prophecy of Hananias. He dies that same year, as Jeremias foretold.

AND it came to pass in that year, in the beginning of the reign of Sedecias king of Juda, in the fourth year, in the fifth month, that Hananias the son of Azur, a prophet of Gabaon, spoke to me, in the house of the Lord, before the priests and all the people, saying:

2 Thus saith the Lord of hosts, the God of Israel: I have broken the yoke of the king of Babylon.

3 As yet two years of days, and I will cause all the vessels of the house of the Lord to be brought back into this place, which Nabuchodonosor king of Babylon took away from this place and carried them to Babylon.

4 And I will bring back to this place Jechonias the son of Joakim king of Juda and all the captives of Juda that are gone to Babylon, saith the Lord: for I will break the yoke of the king of Babylon.

5 And Jeremias the prophet said to Hananias the prophet, in the presence of the priests and in the presence of all the people that stood in the house of the Lord:

6 And Jeremias the prophet said: Amen, the Lord do so: the Lord perform thy words, which thou hast prophesied: that the vessels may be brought again into the house of the Lord, and all the captives may return out of Babylon to this place.

7 Nevertheless, hear this word that I speak in thy ears and in the ears of all the people:

8 The prophets that have been before me and before thee from the beginning and have prophesied concerning many countries and concerning great

3 4 Kings, 25, 13.

kingdoms, of war and of affliction and of famine.

9 The prophet that prophesied peace: when his word shall come to pass, the prophet shall be known, whom the Lord hath sent in truth.

10 And Hananias the prophet took the chain from the neck of Jeremias the prophet and broke it.

11 And Hananias spoke in the presence of all the people, saying: Thus saith the Lord: Even so will I break the yoke of Nabuchodonosor the king of Babylon after two full years from off the neck of all the nations.

12 And Jeremias the prophet went his way. And the word of the Lord came to Jeremias, after that Hananias the prophet had broken the chain from off the neck of Jeremias the prophet, saying:

13 Go, and tell Hananias: Thus saith the Lord: Thou hast broken chains of wood, and thou shalt make for them chains of iron.

14 For thus saith the Lord of hosts, the God of Israel: I have put a yoke of iron upon the neck of all these nations, to serve Nabuchodonosor king of Babylon, and they shall serve him. Moreover also I have given him the beasts of the earth.

15 And Jeremias the prophet said to Hananias the prophet: Hear now, Hananias: the Lord hath not sent thee, and thou hast made this people to trust in a lie.

16 Therefore, thus saith the Lord: Behold I will send thee away from off the face of the earth: this year shalt thou die. For thou hast spoken against the Lord.

17 And Hananias the prophet died in that year, in the seventh month.

CHAPTER 29

Jeremias writeth to the captives in Babylon, exhorting them to be easy there and not to hearken to false prophets. That they shall be delivered after seventy years. But those that remain in Jerusalem shall perish by the sword, famine, and pestilence. And that Achab, Sedecias, and Semeias, false prophets, shall die miserably.

NOW these are the words of the letter which Jeremias the prophet sent from Jerusalem to the residue of the ancients that were carried into captivity and to the priests and to the prophets and to all the people whom Nabuchodonosor had carried away from Jerusalem to Babylon:

2 After that Jechonias the king and the queen and the eunuchs and the princes of Juda and of Jerusalem and the craftsmen and the engravers were departed out of Jerusalem:

3 By the hand of Elasa the son of Saphan and Gamarias the son of Helcias, whom Sedecias king of Juda sent to Babylon to Nabuchodonosor king of Babylon, saying:

4 Thus saith the Lord of hosts, the God of Israel, to all that are carried away captives, whom I have caused to be carried away from Jerusalem to Babylon:

5 Build ye houses and dwell in them: and plant orchards and eat the fruit of them.

6 Take ye wives and beget sons and daughters: and take wives for your sons and give your daughters to husbands, and let them bear sons and daughters: and be ye multiplied there, and be not few in number.

7 And seek the peace of the city to which I have caused you to be carried away captives and pray to the Lord for it: for in the peace thereof shall be your peace.

8 For thus saith the Lord of hosts, the God of Israel: [1] Let not your prophets that are in the midst of you and your diviners deceive you, and give no heed to your dreams which you dream:

9 For they prophesy falsely to you in my name: and I have not sent them, saith the Lord.

10 [2] For thus saith the Lord: When the seventy years shall begin to be accomplished in Babylon, I will visit you: and I will perform my good word in your favour, to bring you again to this place.

11 For I know the thoughts that I think towards you, saith the Lord, thoughts of peace and not of affliction, to give you an end and patience.

12 And you shall call upon me, and you shall go: and you shall pray to me, and I will hear you.

13 You shall seek me: and shall find me, when you shall seek me with all your heart.

14 And I will be found by you, saith the Lord: and I will bring back your captivity, and I will gather you out of all nations and from all the places to which I have driven you out, saith the Lord: and I will bring you back from the place to which I caused you to be carried away captive.

15 Because you have said: The Lord hath raised us up prophets in Babylon.

16 For thus saith the Lord to the king that sitteth upon the throne of David and to all the people that dwell in this city, to your brethren that are not gone forth with you into captivity.

17 Thus saith the Lord of hosts: [3] Behold, I will send upon them the sword and the famine and the pestilence: and

I will make them like bad figs that cannot be eaten, because they are very bad.

18 And I will persecute them with the sword and with famine and with the pestilence: and I will give them up unto affliction to all the kingdoms of the earth: to be a curse and an astonishment and a hissing and a reproach to all the nations to which I have driven them out:

19 Because they have not hearkened to my words, saith the Lord: which I sent to them by my servants the prophets, rising by night and sending: and you have not heard, saith the Lord.

20 Hear ye therefore the word of the Lord, all ye of the captivity, whom I have sent out from Jerusalem to Babylon.

21 Thus saith the Lord of hosts, the God of Israel, to Achab the son of Colias and to Sedecias the son of Maasias, who prophesy unto you in my name falsely: Behold I will deliver them up into the hands of Nabuchodonosor the king of Babylon. And he shall kill them before your eyes.

22 And of them shall be taken up a curse by all the captivity of Juda that are in Babylon, saying: The Lord make thee like Sedecias and like Achab whom the king of Babylon fried in the fire:

23 Because they have acted folly in Israel and have committed adultery with the wives of their friends and have spoken lying words in my name, which I commanded them not. I am the judge and the witness, saith the Lord.

24 And to Semeias the Nehelamite thou shalt say:

25 Thus saith the Lord of hosts, the God of Israel: Because thou hast sent letters in thy name to all the people that are in Jerusalem and to Sophonias the son of Maasias the priest and to all the priests, saying:

26 The Lord hath made thee priest instead of Joiada the priest, that thou shouldst be ruler in the house of the Lord over every man that raveth and prophesieth, to put him in the stocks and into prison.

27 And now why hast thou not rebuked Jeremias the Anathothite who prophesieth to you?

28 For he hath also sent to us in Babylon, saying: It is a long time: build ye houses and dwell in them, and plant gardens and eat the fruits of them.

29 So Sophonias the priest read this letter in the hearing of Jeremias the prophet.

30 And the word of the Lord came to Jeremias, saying:

CHAP. 29. [1] Jer. 14, 14; 23, 16; 27, 15. [2] Jer. 25, 12; 2 Par. 36, 21; 1 Esd. 1, 1; Dan. 9, 2. [3] Jer. 24, 9, 10.

31 Send to all them of the captivity, saying: Thus saith the Lord to Semeias the Nehelamite: Behold Semeias hath prophesied to you and I sent him not, and hath caused you to trust in a lie:

32 Therefore thus saith the Lord: Because I will visit upon Semeias the Nehelamite and upon his seed. He shall not have a man to sit in the midst of this people and he shall not see the good that I will do to my people, saith the Lord: because he hath spoken treason against the Lord.

CHAPTER 30

God will deliver his people from their captivity. Christ shall be their king, and his church shall be glorious for ever.

THIS is the word that came to Jeremias from the Lord, saying:

2 Thus saith the Lord, the God of Israel, saying: Write thee all the words that I have spoken to thee in a book.

3 For behold the days come, saith the Lord, and I will bring again the captivity of my people Israel and Juda, saith the Lord: and I will cause them to return to the land which I gave to their fathers, and they shall possess it.

4 And these are the words that the Lord hath spoken to Israel and to Juda:

5 For thus saith the Lord: We have heard a voice of terror: there is fear and no peace.

6 Ask ye, and see if a man bear children? Why then have I seen every man with his hands on his loins, like a woman in labour, and all faces are turned yellow?

7 ¹Alas, for that day *is* great: neither is there the like to it. And it is the time of tribulation to Jacob: but he shall be saved out of it.

8 And it shall come to pass in that day, saith the Lord of hosts, that I will break his yoke from off thy neck and will burst his hands: and strangers shall no more rule over him.

9 But they shall serve the Lord their God and David their king, whom I will raise up to them.

10 ²Therefore, fear thou not, my servant Jacob, saith the Lord, neither be dismayed, O Israel: for behold, I will save thee from a country afar off, and thy seed from the land of their captivity. And Jacob shall return and be at rest and abound with all good things: and there shall be none whom he may fear.

11 For I am with thee, saith the Lord, to save thee: for I will utterly consume all the nations among which I have scattered thee. But I will not utterly consume thee: but I will chastise thee in judgment, that thou mayst not seem to thyself innocent.

12 For thus saith the Lord: Thy bruise is incurable, thy wound is very grievous.

13 There is none to judge the judgment to bind it up: thou hast no healing medicines.

14 All thy lovers have forgotten thee and will not seek after thee: ³ for I have wounded thee with the wound of an enemy, with a cruel chastisement: by reason of the multitude of thy iniquities, thy sins are hardened.

15 Why criest thou for thy affliction? Thy sorrow is incurable: for the multitude of thy iniquity and for thy hardened sins, I have done these things to thee.

16 Therefore all they that devour thee shall be devoured: and all thy enemies shall be carried into captivity: and they that waste thee shall be wasted: and all that prey upon thee will I give for a prey.

17 For I will close up thy scar and will heal thee of thy wounds, saith the Lord. Because they have called thee, O Sion, an outcast: This is she that hath none to seek after her.

18 Thus saith the Lord: Behold I will bring back the captivity of the pavilions of Jacob and will have pity on his houses, and the city shall be built in her high place, and the temple shall be founded according to the order thereof.

19 And out of them shall come forth praise and the voice of them that play: and I will multiply them, and they shall not be made few: and I will glorify them, and they shall not be lessened.

20 And their children shall be as from the beginning and their assembly shall be permanent before me: and I will visit against all that afflict them.

21 And their leader shall be of themselves: and their prince shall come forth from the midst of them. And I will bring him near, and he shall come to me: for who is this that setteth his heart to approach to me, saith the Lord?

22 And you shall be my people: and I will be your God.

23 Behold the whirlwind of the Lord, *his fury going forth, a violent storm.* It shall rest upon the head of the wicked.

24 The Lord will not turn away the wrath of his indignation till he have executed and performed the thought of his heart. In the latter days you shall understand these things.

CHAP. 30. ¹ Joel, 2, 11; Amos, 5, 18; Soph. 1, 15. ² Isai. 43, 1; 44, 2; Luke, 1, 70. ³ Jer. 23, 19.

CHAP. 30. Ver. 9. *David.* That is, Christ of the house of David.

CHAPTER 31

The restoration of Israel. Rachel shall cease from mourning. The new covenant. The church shall never fail.

AT that time, saith the Lord, I will be the God of all the families of Israel: and they shall be my people.

2 Thus saith the Lord: The people that were left and escaped from the sword found grace in the desert: Israel shall go to his rest.

3 The Lord hath appeared from afar to me. Yea, I have loved thee with an everlasting love: therefore have I drawn thee, taking pity *on thee.*

4 And I will build thee again, and thou shalt be built, O virgin of Israel. Thou shalt again be adorned with thy timbrels and shalt go forth in the dances of them that make merry.

5 Thou shalt yet plant vineyards in the mountains of Samaria: the planters shall plant, and they shall not gather the vintage before the time.

6 For there shall be a day, in which the watchmen on mount Ephraim, shall cry: [1] Arise, and let us go up to Sion to the Lord our God.

7 For thus saith the Lord: Rejoice ye in the joy of Jacob and neigh before the head of the Gentiles. Shout ye and sing, and say: Save, O Lord, thy people, the remnant of Israel.

8 Behold I will bring them from the north country and will gather them from the ends of the earth: and among them shall be the blind and the lame, the woman with child and she that is bringing forth, together, a great company of them returning hither.

9 They shall come with weeping: and I will bring them back in mercy. And I will bring them through the torrents of waters in a right way: and they shall not stumble in it. For I am a father to Israel, and Ephraim is my firstborn.

10 Hear the word of the Lord, O ye nations, and declare *it* in the islands that are afar off, and say: He that scattered Israel will gather him: and he will keep him as the shepherd *doth* his flock.

11 For the Lord hath redeemed Jacob and delivered him out of the hand of one that was mightier than he.

12 And they shall come and shall give praise in mount Sion: and they shall flow together to the good things of the Lord, for the corn and wine and oil and the increase of cattle and herds. And their soul shall be as a watered garden: and they shall be hungry no more.

13 Then shall the virgin rejoice in the dance, the young men and old men together: and I will turn their mourn-ing into joy and will comfort them and make them joyful after their sorrow.

14 And I will fill the soul of the priests with fatness: and my people shall be filled with my good things, saith the Lord.

15 Thus saith the Lord: [2] A voice was heard on high of lamentation, of mourning and weeping, of Rachel weeping for her children and refusing to be comforted for them, because they are not.

16 Thus saith the Lord: Let thy voice cease from weeping and thy eyes from tears, for there is a reward for thy work, saith the Lord: and they shall return out of the land of the enemy.

17 And there is hope for thy last end, saith the Lord: and the children shall return to their own borders.

18 Hearing, I heard Ephraim when he went into captivity. Thou hast chastised me: and I was instructed, as a young bullock unaccustomed to the yoke. Convert me, and I shall be converted: for thou art the Lord my God.

19 For after thou didst convert me, I did penance: and after thou didst show unto me, I struck my thigh. I am confounded and ashamed, because I have borne the reproach of my youth.

20 Surely Ephraim is an honourable son to me, surely he is a tender child: for since I spoke of him, I will still remember him. Therefore are my bowels troubled for him: pitying, I will pity him, saith the Lord.

21 Set thee up a watchtower: make to thee bitterness: direct thy heart into the right way wherein thou hast walked. Return, O virgin of Israel, return to these thy cities.

22 How long wilt thou be dissolute in deliciousness, O wandering daughter? For the Lord hath created a new thing upon the earth: A WOMAN SHALL COMPASS A MAN.

23 Thus saith the Lord of hosts, the God of Israel: As yet shall they say this word in the land of Juda and in the cities thereof, when I shall bring back their captivity: The Lord bless thee, the beauty of justice, the holy mountain.

24 And Juda and all his cities shall dwell therein together: the husbandmen and they that drive the flocks.

25 For I have inebriated the weary soul: and I have filled every hungry soul.

26 Upon this I was as it were awaked out of a sleep, and I saw, and my sleep was sweet to me.

27 Behold the days come, saith the Lord: and I will sow the house of Israel and the house of Juda with the seed of men and with the seed of beasts.

CHAP. 31. [1] Isai. 2, 3; Mich. 4, 2. [2] Matt. 2, 18.

28 And as I have watched over them, to pluck up and to throw down and to scatter and destroy and afflict: so will I watch over them, to build up and to plant them, saith the Lord.

29 In those days they shall say no more. [3] The fathers have eaten a sour grape, and the teeth of the children are set on edge.

30 But every one shall die for his own iniquity: every man that shall eat the sour grape, his teeth shall be set on edge.

31 [4] Behold the days shall come, saith the Lord, and I will make a new covenant with the house of Israel and with the house of Juda:

32 Not according to the covenant which I made with their fathers, in the day that I took them by the hand to bring them out of the land of Egypt: the covenant which they made void, and I had dominion over them, saith the Lord.

33 But this shall be the covenant that I will make with the house of Israel after those days, saith the Lord: [5] I will give my law in their bowels and I will write it in their heart: and I will be their God, and they shall be my people.

34 And they shall teach no more every man his neighbour, and every man his brother, saying: Know the Lord. For all shall know me from the least of them even to the greatest, saith the Lord: [6] for I will forgive their iniquity and I will remember their sin no more.

35 Thus saith the Lord, who giveth the sun for the light of the day, the order of the moon and of the stars for the light of the night: who stirreth up the sea, and the waves thereof roar. The Lord of hosts is his name.

36 If these ordinances shall fail before me, saith the Lord: then also the seed of Israel shall fail, so as not to be a nation before me for ever.

37 Thus saith the Lord: If the heavens above can be measured and the foundations of the earth searched out beneath, I also will cast away all the seed of Israel for all that they have done, saith the Lord.

38 Behold the days come, saith the Lord, that the city shall be built to the Lord from the tower of Hanameel even to the gate of the corner.

39 And the measuring line shall go out farther in his sight upon the hill Gareb: and it shall compass Goatha,

40 And the whole valley of dead bodies and of ashes, and all the country of death, even to the torrent Cedron and to the corner of the horse gate to-

wards the east, the Holy of the Lord. It shall not be plucked up and it shall not be destroyed any more for ever.

CHAPTER 32

Jeremias by God's commandment purchases a field of his kinsman and prophesies the return of the people out of captivity and the everlasting covenant God will make with his church.

THE word that came to Jeremias from the Lord in the tenth year of Sedecias king of Juda: the same is the eighteenth year of Nabuchodonosor.

2 At that time, the army of the king of Babylon besieged Jerusalem: and Jeremias the prophet was shut up in the court of the prison which was in the house of the king of Juda.

3 For Sedecias king of Juda had shut him up, saying: Why dost thou prophesy, saying: Thus saith the Lord: Behold I will give this city into the hand of the king of Babylon, and he shall take it?

4 And Sedecias king of Juda shall not escape out of the hand of the Chaldeans: but he shall be delivered into the hands of the king of Babylon. And he shall speak to him mouth to mouth, and his eyes shall see his eyes.

5 And he shall lead Sedecias to Babylon: and he shall be there till I visit him, saith the Lord. But if you will fight against the Chaldeans, you shall have no success.

6 And Jeremias said: The word of the Lord came to me, saying:

7 Behold, Hanameel, the son of Sellum thy cousin, shall come to thee, saying: Buy thee my field which is in Anathoth, for it is thy right to buy it, being next akin.

8 And Hanameel, my uncle's son, came to me, according to the word of the Lord, to the entry of the prison, and said to me: Buy my field which is in Anathoth in the land of Benjamin, for the right of inheritance is thine, and thou art next of kin to possess it. And I understood that this was the word of the Lord.

9 And I bought the field of Hanameel, my uncle's son, that is in Anathoth: and I weighed him the money, seven staters and ten pieces of silver.

10 And I wrote it in a book and sealed it and took witnesses: and I weighed him the money in the balances.

11 And I took the deed of the purchase that was sealed and the stipulations and the ratifications with the seals that were on the outside.

12 And I gave the deed of the purchase to Baruch the son of Neri the son of Maasias, in the sight of Hanameel my uncle's son, in the presence of the

[3] Ezech. 18, 2. [4] Heb. 8, 8. [5] Heb. 10, 16. [6] Acts, 10, 43.

witnesses that subscribed the book of the purchase, and before all the Jews that sat in the court of the prison.

13 And I charged Baruch before them, saying:

14 Thus saith the Lord of hosts, the God of Israel: Take these writings, this deed of the purchase that is sealed up, and this deed that is open: and put them in an earthen vessel, that they may continue many days.

15 For thus saith the Lord of hosts, the God of Israel: Houses and fields and vineyards shall be possessed again in this land.

16 And after I had delivered the deed of purchase to Baruch the son of Neri, I prayed to the Lord, saying:

17 Alas, alas, alas, O Lord God, behold thou hast made heaven and earth by thy great power and thy stretched out arm: no word shall be hard to thee.

18 [1] Thou shewest mercy unto thousands and returnest the iniquity of the fathers into the bosom of their children after them. O most mighty, great, and powerful: the Lord of hosts is thy name.

19 Great in counsel and incomprehensible in thought: whose eyes are open upon all the ways of the children of Adam to render unto every one according to his ways and according to the fruit of his devices.

20 Who hast set signs and wonders in the land of Egypt even until this day, and in Israel, and amongst men, and hast made thee a name as at this day.

21 And hast brought forth thy people Israel out of the land of Egypt with signs and with wonders and with a strong hand and a stretched out arm and with great terror.

22 And hast given them this land which thou didst swear to their fathers to give them, a land flowing with milk and honey.

23 And they came in and possessed it: but they obeyed not thy voice and they walked not in thy law. And they did not any of those things that thou didst command them to do: and all these evils are come upon them.

24 Behold works are built up against the city to take it: and the city is given into the hands of the Chaldeans who fight against it, by the sword and the famine and the pestilence. And what thou hast spoken is all come to pass, as thou thyself seest.

25 And sayest thou to me, O Lord God: Buy a field for money and take witnesses, whereas the city is given into the hands of the Chaldeans?

26 And the word of the Lord came to Jeremias, saying:

27 Behold I am the Lord the God of all flesh: Shall any thing be hard for me?

28 Therefore thus saith the Lord: Behold I will deliver this city into the hands of the Chaldeans and into the hands of the king of Babylon, and they shall take it.

29 And the Chaldeans that fight against this city shall come and set it on fire and burn it, with the houses upon whose roofs they offered sacrifice to Baal and poured out drink offerings to strange gods, to provoke me to wrath.

30 For the children of Israel and the children of Juda have continually done evil in my eyes from their youth: the children of Israel who even till now provoke me with the work of their hands, saith the Lord.

31 For this city hath been to me a provocation and indignation from the day that they built it until this day in which it shall be taken out of my sight.

32 Because of all the evil of the children of Israel and of the children of Juda which they have done, provoking me to wrath, they and their kings, their princes and their priests and their prophets, the men of Juda and the inhabitants of Jerusalem.

33 And they have turned their backs to me, and not their faces, when I taught them early in the morning and instructed them: and they would not hearken to receive instruction.

34 [2] And they have set their idols in the house in which my name is called upon, to defile it.

35 And they have built the high places of Baal which are in the valley of the son of Ennom, to consecrate their sons and their daughters to Moloch: which I commanded them not, neither entered it into my heart that they should do this abomination and cause Juda to sin.

36 And now, therefore, thus saith the Lord, the God of Israel, to this city, whereof you say that it shall be delivered into the hands of the king of Babylon by the sword and by famine and by pestilence:

37 Behold I will gather them together out of all the lands to which I have cast them out in my anger and in my wrath and in my great indignation: and I will bring them again into this place and will cause them to dwell securely.

38 And they shall be my people, and I will be their God.

39 And I will give them one heart and one way, that they may fear me all days: and that it may be well with them and with their children after them.

CHAP. 32. [1] Exod. 34, 7. [2] 4 Kings, 21, 4.

40 And I will make an everlasting covenant with them and will not cease to do them good: and I will give my fear in their heart, that they may not revolt from me.

41 And I will rejoice over them when I shall do them good: and I will plant them in this land in truth, with my whole heart and with all my soul.

42 For thus saith the Lord: As I have brought upon this people all this great evil, so will I bring upon them all the good that I now speak to them.

43 And fields shall be purchased in this land, whereof you say that it is desolate, because there remaineth neither man nor beast, and it is given into the hands of the Chaldeans.

44 Fields shall be bought for money, and deeds shall be written and sealed, and witnesses shall be taken, in the land of Benjamin and round about Jerusalem, in the cities of Juda and in the cities on the mountains and in the cities on the plains and in the cities that are towards the south: for I will bring back their captivity, saith the Lord.

CHAPTER 33

God promises reduction from captivity and other blessings, especially the coming of Christ, whose reign in his church shall be glorious and perpetual.

AND the word of the Lord came to Jeremias the second time, while he was yet shut up in the court of the prison, saying:

2 Thus saith the Lord, who will do and will form it and prepare it. The Lord is his name.

3 Cry to me and I will hear thee: and I will shew thee great things and sure things which thou knowest not.

4 For thus saith the Lord, the God of Israel, to the house of this city and to the houses of the king of Juda which are destroyed and to the bulwarks and to the sword.

5 Of them that come to fight with the Chaldeans and to fill them with the dead bodies of the men whom I have slain in my wrath and in my indignation, hiding my face from this city because of all their wickedness.

6 Behold I will close their wounds and give them health, and I will cure them: and I will reveal to them the prayer of peace and truth.

CHAP. 33. Ver. 6. *The prayer of peace.* That is, the peace and welfare which they pray for.

Ver. 17. *There shall not be cut off from David.* This was verified in Christ, who is of the house of David and whose kingdom in his church shall have no end.

Ver. 18. *Neither shall there be cut off from the priests.* This promise relates to the Christian priesthood, which shall also continue for ever:

7 And I will bring back the captivity of Juda and the captivity of Jerusalem: and I will build them as from the beginning.

8 And I will cleanse them from all their iniquity whereby they have sinned against me: and I will forgive all their iniquities whereby they have sinned against me and despised me.

9 And it shall be to me a name and a joy and a praise and a gladness before all the nations of the earth that shall hear of all the good things which I will do to them: and they shall fear and be troubled for all the good things and for all the peace that I will make for them.

10 Thus saith the Lord: There shall be heard again in this place (which you say is desolate because there is neither man nor beast in the cities of Juda and without Jerusalem, which are desolate without man and without inhabitant and without beast)

11 The voice of joy and the voice of gladness, the voice of the bridegroom and the voice of the bride, the voice of them that shall say: Give ye glory to the Lord of hosts, for the Lord is good, for his mercy endureth for ever. And of them that shall bring their vows into the house of the Lord: for I will bring back the captivity of the land as at the first, saith the Lord.

12 Thus saith the Lord of hosts: There shall be again in this place that is desolate without man and without beast, and in all the cities thereof, an habitation of shepherds causing their flocks to lie down.

13 And in the cities on the mountains and in the cities of the plains and in the cities that are towards the south: and in the land of Benjamin and round about Jerusalem and in the cities of Juda shall the flocks pass again under the hand of him that numbered them, saith the Lord.

14 Behold the days come, saith the Lord, that I will perform the good word that I have spoken to the house of Israel and to the house of Juda.

15 In those days and at that time I will make the bud of justice to spring forth unto David: and he shall do judgment and justice in the earth.

16 In those days shall Juda be saved and Jerusalem shall dwell securely. And this is the name that they shall call him. The Lord our just one.

17 For thus saith the Lord: There shall not be cut off from David a man to sit upon the throne of the house of Israel.

18 Neither shall there be cut off from the priests and Levites a man before my face to offer holocausts and

to burn sacrifices and to kill victims continually.

19 And the word of the Lord came to Jeremias, saying:

20 Thus saith the Lord: If my covenant with the day can be made void, and my covenant with the night, that there should not be day and night in their season:

21 Also my covenant with David my servant may be made void, that he should not have a son to reign upon his throne, and *with the* Levites and priests, my ministers.

22 As the stars of heaven cannot be numbered, nor the sand of the sea be measured: so will I multiply the seed of David my servant and the Levites my ministers.

23 And the word of the Lord came to Jeremias, saying:

24 Hast thou not seen what this people hath spoken, saying: The two families which the Lord had chosen are cast off: and they have despised my people, so that it is no more a nation before them?

25 Thus saith the Lord: If I have not set my covenant between day and night, and laws to heaven and earth:

26 Surely I will also cast off the seed of Jacob and of David my servant, so as not to take any of his seed to be rulers of the seed of Abraham, Isaac and Jacob. For I will bring back their captivity and will have mercy on them.

CHAPTER 34

The prophet foretells that Sedecias shall fall into the hands of Nabuchodonosor. God's sentence upon the princes and people that had broken his covenant.

THE word that came to Jeremias from the Lord, (when Nabuchodonosor king of Babylon and all his army and all the kingdoms of the earth that were under the power of his hand and all the people fought against Jerusalem and against all the cities thereof,) saying:

2 Thus saith the Lord, the God of Israel: Go, and speak to Sedecias king of Juda, and say to him: Thus saith the Lord: Behold I will deliver this city into the hands of the king of Babylon, and he shall burn it with fire.

3 And thou shalt not escape out of his hand, but thou shalt surely be taken: and thou shalt be delivered into his hand. And thy eyes shall see the eyes of the king of Babylon, and his mouth shall speak with thy mouth and thou shalt go to Babylon.

4 Yet hear the word of the Lord, O Sedecias king of Juda: Thus saith the

Lord to thee: Thou shalt not die by the sword.

5 But thou shalt die in peace: and according to the burnings of thy fathers, the former kings that were before thee, so shall they burn thee. And they shall mourn for thee, saying: Alas, Lord! For I have spoken the word, saith the Lord.

6 And Jeremias the prophet spoke all these words to Sedecias the king of Juda in Jerusalem.

7 And the army of the king of Babylon fought against Jerusalem and against all the cities of Juda that were left, against Lachis and against Azecha: for these remained of the cities of Juda, fenced cities.

8 The word that came to Jeremias from the Lord, after that king Sedecias had made a covenant with all the people in Jerusalem making a proclamation:

9 That every man should let his man-servant, and every man his maid-servant, being a Hebrew man or a Hebrew woman, go free: and that they should not lord it over them, to wit, over the Jews their brethren.

10 And all the princes and all the people who entered into the covenant heard that every man should let his man-servant, and every man his maid-servant, go free and should no more have dominion over them. And they obeyed and let them go free.

11 But afterwards they turned, and brought back again their servants and their handmaids, whom they had let go free, and brought them into subjection as men-servants and maid-servants.

12 And the word of the Lord came to Jeremias from the Lord, saying:

13 Thus saith the Lord the God of Israel: I made a covenant with your fathers in the day that I brought them out of the land of Egypt, out of the house of bondage, saying:

14 [1] At the end of seven years, let ye go every man his brother, being a Hebrew, who hath been sold to thee, so he shall serve thee six years: and thou shalt let him go free from thee. And your fathers did not hearken to me, nor did they incline their ear.

15 And you turned to day and did that which was right in my eyes, in proclaiming liberty every one to his brother: and you made a covenant in

CHAP. 34. [1] Exod. 21, 2; Deut. 15, 12.

the functions of which (more especially the great sacrifice of the altar) are here expressed by the name of holocausts and other offerings of the law, which were so many figures of the Christian sacrifice.

Ver. 24. *Two families.* The families of the kings and priests.

CHAP. 34. Ver. 5. *Die in peace.* That is, by natural death.

my sight, in the house upon which my name is invocated.

16 And you are fallen back and have defiled my name: and you have brought back again every man his man-servant, and every man his maid-servant, whom you had let go free and set at liberty: and you have brought them into subjection to be your servants and handmaids.

17 Therefore thus saith the Lord: You have not hearkened to me in proclaiming liberty every man to his brother and every man to his friend: behold I proclaim a liberty for you, saith the Lord, to the sword, to the pestilence and to the famine: and I will cause you to be removed to all the kingdoms of the earth.

18 And I will give the men that have transgressed my covenant and have not performed the words of the covenant which they agreed to in my presence, when they cut the calf in two ² and passed between the parts thereof:

19 The princes of Juda and the princes of Jerusalem, the eunuchs and the priests and all the people of the land that passed between the parts of the calf.

20 And I will give them into the hands of their enemies and into the hands of them that seek their life: and their dead bodies shall be for meat to the fowls of the air and to the beasts of the earth.

21 And Sedecias the king of Juda and his princes, I will give into the hands of their enemies and into the hands of them that seek their lives and into the hands of the armies of the king of Babylon which are gone from you.

22 Behold I will command, saith the Lord, and I will bring them again to this city: and they shall fight against it and take it and burn it with fire. And I will make the cities of Juda a desolation, without an inhabitant.

CHAPTER 35

The obedience of the Rechabites condemns the disobedience of the Jews. The reward of the Rechabites.

THE word that came to Jeremias from the Lord, in the days of Joakim the son of Josias king of Juda, saying:

2 Go to the house of the Rechabites, and speak to them, and bring them into the house of the Lord, into one of the chambers of the treasures: and thou shalt give them wine to drink.

3 And I took Jezonias the son of

<hr>

² Gen. 15, 10. Chap. 35. ¹⁴ Kings, 10, 15. ² Jer. 18, 11; 25, 5.

Chap. 35. Ver. 2. *Rechabites*. These were of the race of Jethro, father-in-law to Moses.

Jeremias the son of Habsanias and his brethren and all his sons and the whole house of the Rechabites.

4 And I brought them into the house of the Lord, to the treasure house of the sons of Hanan the son of Jegedelias, the man of God, which was by the treasure house of the princes, above the treasure of Maasias the son of Sellum, who was keeper of the entry.

5 And I set before the sons of the house of the Rechabites pots full of wine and cups: and I said to them: Drink ye wine.

6 And they answered: We will not drink wine, because Jonadab, the son of Rechab, ¹ our father, commanded us, saying: You shall drink no wine, neither you nor your children, for ever.

7 Neither shall ye build houses, nor sow seed, nor plant vineyards, nor have any: but you shall dwell in tents all your days, that you may live many days upon the face of the earth, in which you are strangers:

8 Therefore we have obeyed the voice of Jonadab the son of Rechab, our father, in all things that he commanded us: so as to drink no wine all our days, neither we, nor our wives, nor our sons, nor our daughters:

9 Nor to build houses to dwell in, nor to have vineyard or field or seed:

10 But we have dwelt in tents and have been obedient according to all that Jonadab our father commanded us.

11 But when Nabuchodonosor king of Babylon came up to our land, we said: Come, let us go into Jerusalem, from the face of the army of the Chaldeans and from the face of the army of Syria: and we have remained in Jerusalem.

12 And the word of the Lord came to Jeremias, saying:

13 Thus saith the Lord of hosts, the God of Israel: Go, and say to the men of Juda and to the inhabitants of Jerusalem: Will you not receive instruction, to obey my words, saith the Lord?

14 The words of Jonadab the son of Rechab, by which he commanded his sons not to drink wine, have prevailed: and they have drunk none to this day, because they have obeyed the commandment of their father: but I have spoken to you, rising early and speaking, and you have not obeyed me.

15 And I have sent to you all my servants the prophets, rising early, and sending and saying: ² Return ye every man from his wicked way and make your ways good, and follow not strange gods nor worship them: and you shall dwell in the land which I gave you and your fathers. And you have not inclined your ear, nor hearkened to me.

16 So the sons of Jonadab the son of Rechab have constantly kept the commandment of their father which he commanded them: but this people hath not obeyed me.

17 Therefore thus saith the Lord of hosts, the God of Israel: Behold I will bring upon Juda and upon all the inhabitants of Jerusalem all the evil that I have pronounced against them: because I have spoken to them and they have not heard, I have called to them, and they have not answered me.

18 And Jeremias said to the house of the Rechabites: Thus saith the Lord of hosts, the God of Israel: Because you have obeyed the commandment of Jonadab your father and have kept all his precepts and have done all that he commanded you:

19 Therefore thus saith the Lord of hosts, the God of Israel: There shall not be wanting a man of the race of Jonadab the son of Rechab, standing before me for ever.

CHAPTER 36

Jeremias sends Baruch to read his prophecies in the temple. The book is brought to king Joakim who burns it. The prophet denounces his judgment and causes Baruch to write a new copy.

AND it came to pass in the fourth year of Joakim the son of Josias king of Juda that this word came to Jeremias by the Lord, saying:

2 Take thee a roll of a book: and thou shalt write in it all the words that I have spoken to thee against Israel and Juda and against all the nations, from the day that I spoke to thee, from the days of Josias, even to this day.

3 If so be, when the house of Juda shall hear all the evils that I purpose to do unto them, that they may return every man from his wicked way: and I will forgive their iniquity and their sin.

4 So Jeremias called Baruch the son of Nerias: and Baruch wrote from the mouth of Jeremias all the words of the Lord which he spoke to him, upon the roll of a book.

5 And Jeremias commanded Baruch, saying: I am shut up and cannot go into the house of the Lord.

6 Go thou in therefore, and read out of the volume which thou hast written from my mouth the words of the Lord, in the hearing of all the people in the house of the Lord, on the fasting day: and also thou shalt read them in the hearing of all Juda that come out of their cities:

7 If so be they may present their supplications before the Lord and may return every one from his wicked way. For great is the wrath and indignation which the Lord hath pronounced against this people.

8 And Baruch the son of Nerias did according to all that Jeremias the prophet had commanded him, reading out of the volume the words of the Lord in the house of the Lord.

9 And it came to pass in the fifth year of Joakim the son of Josias king of Juda, in the ninth month, that they proclaimed a fast before the Lord to all the people in Jerusalem and to all the people that were come together out of the cities of Juda to Jerusalem.

10 And Baruch read out of the volume the words of Jeremias, in the house of the Lord, in the treasury of Gamarias the son of Saphan the scribe, in the upper court, in the entry of the new gate of the house of the Lord, in the hearing of all the people.

11 And when Micheas the son of Gamarias the son of Saphan had heard out of the book all the words of the Lord,

12 He went down into the king's house to the secretary's chamber: and behold all the princes sat there, Elisama the scribe, and Dalaias the son of Semeias, and Elnathan the son of Achobor, and Gamarias the son of Saphan, and Sedecias the son of Hananias, and all the princes.

13 And Micheas told them all the words that he had heard when Baruch read out of the volume in the hearing of the people.

14 Therefore all the princes sent Judi the son of Nathanias, the son of Selemias, the son of Chusi, to Baruch, saying: Take in thy hand the volume in which thou hast read in the hearing of the people and come. So Baruch the son of Nerias took the volume in his hand and came to them.

15 And they said to him: Sit down and read these things in our hearing. And Baruch read in their hearing.

16 And when they had heard all the words, they looked upon one another with astonishment and they said to Baruch: We must tell the king all these words.

17 And they asked him, saying: Tell us how didst thou write all these words from his mouth.

18 And Baruch said to them: With his mouth he pronounced all these words as if he were reading to me. And I wrote in a volume with ink.

19 And the princes said to Baruch: Go, and hide thou and Jeremias, and let no man know where you are.

CHAP. 36. Ver. 5. *Shut up*. Not that the prophet was now in prison; for the contrary appears from ver. 19, but that he kept himself shut up, by reason of the persecutions he had lately met with. See chap. 26.

20 And they went into the king into the court: but they laid up the volume in the chamber of Elisama the scribe. And they told all the words in the hearing of the king.

21 And the king sent Judi that he should take the volume: who, bringing it out of the chamber of Elisama the scribe, read it in the hearing of the king and of all the princes that stood about the king.

22 Now the king sat in the winter house, in the ninth month: and there was a hearth before him, full of burning coals.

23 And when Judi had read three or four pages, he cut it with the penknife: and he cast it into the fire that was upon the hearth, till all the volume was consumed with the fire that was on the hearth.

24 And the king and all his servants that heard all these words were not afraid, nor did they rend their garments.

25 But yet Elnathan and Dalaias and Gamarias spoke to the king, not to burn the book: and he heard them not.

26 And the king commanded Jeremiel the son of Amelech and Saraias the son of Ezriel and Selemias the son of Abdeel, to take up Baruch the scribe and Jeremias, the prophet: but the Lord hid them.

27 And the word of the Lord came to Jeremias the prophet, after that the king had burnt the volume and the words that Baruch had written from the mouth of Jeremias, saying:

28 Take thee again another volume and write in it all the former words that were in the first volume which Joakim the king of Juda hath burnt.

29 And thou shalt say to Joakim the king of Juda: Thus saith the Lord: Thou hast burnt that volume, saying: Why hast thou written therein and said: The king of Babylon shall come speedily and shall lay waste this land and shall cause to cease from thence man and beast?

30 Therefore thus saith the Lord against Joakim the king of Juda: He shall have none to sit upon the throne of David: and his dead body shall be cast out to the heat by day and to the frost by night.

31 And I will punish him and his seed and his servants, for their iniquities: and I will bring upon them and upon the inhabitants of Jerusalem and upon

CHAP. 37. ¹ 4 Kings, 24, 17; Jer. 52, 1. ² 1 Par. 36, 15.

Ver. 30. *He shall have none.* Because his son Joachin or Jechonias, within three months after the death of his father, was carried away to Babylon, so that his reign is not worthy of notice.

the men of Juda all the evil that I have pronounced against them, but they have not heard.

32 And Jeremias took another volume and gave it to Baruch the son of Nerias the scribe: who wrote in it from the mouth of Jeremias all the words of the book which Joakim the king of Juda had burnt with fire. And there were added besides many more words than had been before.

CHAPTER 37

Jeremias prophesies that the Chaldeans, who had departed from Jerusalem, would return and burn the city. He is cast into prison. His conference with Sedecias.

NOW king Sedecias the ¹ son of Josias reigned instead of Jechonias the son of Joakim: whom Nabuchodonosor king of Babylon made king in the land of Juda.

2 ² But neither he nor his servants nor the people of the land did obey the words of the Lord that he spoke in the hand of Jeremias the prophet.

3 And king Sedecias sent Juchal the son of Selemias and Sophonias the son of Maasias the priest to Jeremias the prophet, saying: Pray to the Lord our God for us.

4 Now Jeremias walked freely in the midst of the people: for they had not as yet cast him into prison. And the army of Pharao was come out of Egypt: and the Chaldeans that besieged Jerusalem, hearing these tidings, departed from Jerusalem.

5 And the word of the Lord came to Jeremias the prophet, saying:

6 Thus saith the Lord, the God of Israel: Thus shall you say to the king of Juda who sent you to inquire of me: Behold the army of Pharao, which is come forth to help you, shall return into their own land, into Egypt.

7 And the Chaldeans shall come again and fight against this city and take it and burn it with fire.

8 Thus saith the Lord: Deceive not your souls, saying: The Chaldeans shall surely depart and go away from us: for they shall not go away.

9 But if you should even beat all the army of the Chaldeans that fight against you, and there should be left of them some wounded men: they shall rise up, every man from his tent, and burn this city with fire.

10 Now when the army of the Chaldeans was gone away from Jerusalem, because of Pharao's army,

11 Jeremias went forth out of Jerusalem to go into the land of Benjamin: and to divide a possession there in the presence of the citizens.

12 And when he was come to the gate of Benjamin, the captain of the gate, who was there in his turn, was one named Jerias, the son of Selemias, the son of Hananias: and he took hold of Jeremias the prophet, saying: Thou art fleeing to the Chaldeans.

13 And Jeremias answered: It is not so. I am not fleeing to the Chaldeans. But he hearkened not to him: so Jerias took Jeremias and brought him to the princes.

14 Wherefore, the princes were angry with Jeremias, and they beat him and cast him into the prison that was in the house of Jonathan the scribe: for he was chief over the prison.

15 So Jeremias went into the house of the prison and into the dungeon: and Jeremias remained there many days.

16 Then Sedecias the king, sending, took him, and asked him secretly in his house, and said: Is there, thinkest thou, any word from the Lord? And Jeremias said: There is. And he said: Thou shalt be delivered into the hands of the king of Babylon.

17 And Jeremias said to king Sedecias: In what way have I offended against thee or thy servants or thy people, that thou hast cast me into prison?

18 Where are your prophets that prophesied to you, and said: The king of Babylon shall not come against you and against this land?

19 Now therefore hear, I beseech thee, my lord the king. Let my petition be accepted in thy sight: and send me not back into the house of Jonathan the scribe, lest I die there.

20 Then king Sedecias commanded that Jeremias should be committed into the entry of the prison, and that they should give him daily a piece of bread, beside broth, till all the bread in the city were spent. And Jeremias remained in the entry of the prison.

CHAPTER 38

The prophet at the instance of the great men is cast into a filthy dungeon. He is drawn out by Abdemelech and has another conference with the king.

NOW Saphatias the son of Mathan and Gedelias the son of Phassur and Juchal the son of Selemias and Phassur the son of Melchias heard the words that Jeremias spoke to all the people, saying:

2 Thus saith the Lord: [1] Whosoever shall remain in this city shall die by the sword and by famine and by pestilence: but he that shall go forth to the Chaldeans shall live, and his life shall be safe, and he shall live.

3 Thus saith the Lord: This city shall surely be delivered into the hand of the army of the king of Babylon, and he shall take it.

4 And the princes said to the king: We beseech thee that this man may be put to death: for on purpose he weakeneth the hands of the men of war that remain in this city and the hands of the people, speaking to them according to these words. For this man seeketh not peace to this people, but evil.

5 And king Sedecias said: Behold he is in your hands: for it is not lawful for the king to deny you any thing.

6 Then they took Jeremias and cast him into the dungeon of Melchias the son of Amelech, which was in the entry of the prison: and they let down Jeremias by ropes into the dungeon, wherein there was no water but mire. And Jeremias sunk into the mire.

7 Now Abdemelech the Ethiopian, an eunuch that was in the king's house, heard that they had put Jeremias in the dungeon: but the king was sitting in the gate of Benjamin.

8 And Abdemelech went out of the king's house and spoke to the king, saying:

9 My lord the king, these men have done evil in all that they have done against Jeremias the prophet, casting him into the dungeon to die there with hunger, for there is no more bread in the city.

10 Then the king commanded Abdemelech the Ethiopian, saying: Take from hence thirty men with thee and draw up Jeremias the prophet out of the dungeon, before he die.

11 So Abdemelech, taking the men with him, went into the king's house that was under the storehouse: and he took from thence old rags and old rotten things, and he let them down by cords to Jeremias into the dungeon.

12 And Abdemelech the Ethiopian said to Jeremias: Put these old rags and these rent and rotten things under thy arms and upon the cords. And Jeremias did so.

13 And they drew up Jeremias with the cords and brought him forth out of the dungeon. And Jeremias remained in the entry of the prison.

14 And king Sedecias sent and took Jeremias the prophet to him to the third gate that was in the house of the Lord. And the king said to Jeremias: I will ask thee a thing. Hide nothing from me.

15 Then Jeremias said to Sedecias: If I shall declare it to thee, wilt thou not put me to death? And if I give thee counsel, thou wilt not hearken to me.

16 Then king Sedecias swore to Jere-

mias, in private, saying: As the Lord liveth, that made us this soul, I will not put thee to death, nor will I deliver thee into the hands of these men that seek thy life.

17 And Jeremias said to Sedecias: Thus saith the Lord of hosts, the God of Israel: If thou wilt take a resolution and go out to the princes of the king of Babylon, thy soul shall live and this city shall not be burnt with fire: and thou shalt be safe and thy house.

18 But if thou wilt not go out to the princes of the king of Babylon, this city shall be delivered into the hands of the Chaldeans. And they shall burn it with fire: and thou shalt not escape out of their hands.

19 And king Sedecias said to Jeremias: I am afraid because of the Jews that are fled over to the Chaldeans: lest I should be delivered into their hands and they should abuse me.

20 But Jeremias answered: They shall not deliver thee. Hearken I beseech thee, to the word of the Lord which I speak to thee, and it shall be well with thee: and thy soul shall live.

21 But if thou wilt not go forth, this is the word which the Lord hath shewn me.

22 Behold all the women that are left in the house of the king of Juda shall be brought out to the princes of the king of Babylon. And they shall say: Thy men of peace have deceived thee and have prevailed against thee. They have plunged thy feet in the mire and in a slippery place: and they have departed from thee.

23 And all thy wives and thy children shall be brought out to the Chaldeans. And thou shalt not escape their hands, but thou shalt be taken by the hand of the king of Babylon: and he shall burn this city with fire.

24 Then Sedecias said to Jeremias: Let no man know these words, and thou shalt not die.

25 But if the princes shall hear that I have spoken with thee, and shall come to thee and say to thee: Tell us what thou hast said to the king. Hide it not from us, and we will not kill thee. And also what the king said to thee.

26 Thou shalt say to them: I presented my supplication before the king that he would not command me to be carried back into the house of Jonathan, to die there.

27 So all the princes came to Jeremias and asked him: and he spoke to them according to all the words that

CHAP. 38. Ver. 22. *Thy men of peace. Viri pacifici tui.* That is, thy false friends promising thee peace and happiness and by their evil counsels involving thee in misery.

the king had commanded him. And they left him: for nothing had been heard.

28 But Jeremias remained in the entry of the prison until the day that Jerusalem was taken. And it came to pass that Jerusalem was taken.

CHAPTER 39

After two years' siege Jerusalem is taken. Sedecias is carried before Nabuchodonosor, who kills his sons in his sight and then puts out his eyes. Jerusalem is set at liberty.

IN the ninth year [1] of Sedecias king of Juda, in the tenth month, came Nabuchodonosor king of Babylon and all his army to Jerusalem, and they besieged it.

2 And in the eleventh year of Sedecias, in the fourth month, the fifth day of the month, the city was opened.

3 And all the princes of the king of Babylon came in and sat in the middle gate: Neregel, Sereser, Semegarnabu, Sarsachim, Rabsares, Neregel, Serezer, Rebmag, and all the rest of the princes of the king of Babylon.

4 And when Sedecias the king of Juda and all the men of war saw them, they fled: and they went forth in the night out of the city, by the way of the king's garden and by the gate that was between the two walls: and they went out to the way of the desert.

5 But the army of the Chaldeans pursued after them: and they took Sedecias in the plain of the desert of Jericho. And when they had taken him, they brought him to Nabuchodonosor king of Babylon, to Reblatha, which is in the land of Emath: and he gave judgment upon him.

6 And the king of Babylon slew the sons of Sedecias, in Reblatha, before his eyes: and the king of Babylon slew all the nobles of Juda.

7 He also put out the eyes of Sedecias: and bound him with fetters, to be carried to Babylon.

8 And the Chaldeans burnt the king's house and the houses of the people, with fire, and they threw down the wall of Jerusalem.

9 And Nabuzardan the general of the army, carried away captive to Babylon the remnant of the people that remained in the city, and the fugitives that had gone over to him, and the rest of the people that remained.

10 But Nabuzardan the general left some of the poor people, that had nothing at all, in the land of Juda: and he gave them vineyards and cisterns at that time.

11 Now Nabuchodonosor king of

Babylon had given charge to Nabuzardan the general concerning Jeremias, saying:

12 Take him and set thy eyes upon him and do him no harm: but as he hath a mind, so do with him.

13 Therefore Nabuzardan the general sent: and Nabusezban and Rabsares and Neregel and Sereser and Rebmag and all the nobles of the king of Babylon.

14 Sent and took Jeremias out of the court of the prison and committed him to Godolias the son of Ahicam the son of Saphan, that he might go home and dwell among the people.

15 But the word of the Lord came to Jeremias, when he was yet shut up in the court of the prison, saying: Go, and tell Abdemelech the Ethiopian, saying:

16 Thus saith the Lord of hosts, the God of Israel: Behold I will bring my words upon this city unto evil and not unto good: and they shall be *accomplished* in thy sight in that day.

17 And I will deliver thee in that day, saith the Lord: and thou shalt not be given into the hands of the men whom thou fearest.

18 But delivering, I will deliver thee, and thou shalt not fall by the sword: but thy life shall be saved for thee, because thou hast put thy trust in me, saith the Lord.

CHAPTER 40

Jeremias remains with Godolias the governor, who receives all the Jews that resort to him.

THE word that came to Jeremias from the Lord, after that Nabuzardan the general had let him go from Rama, when he had taken him, being bound with chains, among all them that were carried away from Jerusalem and Juda and were carried to Babylon.

2 And the general of the army, taking Jeremias, said to him: The Lord thy God hath pronounced this evil upon this place.

3 And he hath brought it. And the Lord hath done as he hath said: because you have sinned against the Lord and have not hearkened to his voice, and this word is come upon you.

4 Now then behold I have loosed thee this day from the chains which were upon thy hands. If it please thee to come with me to Babylon, come, and I will set my eyes upon thee: but if it do not please thee to come with me to Babylon, stay here. Behold all the land is before thee, as thou shalt choose: and whither it shall please thee to go, thither go.

5 And come not with me: but dwell with Godolias the son of Ahicam the son of Saphan, whom the king of Babylon hath made governor over the cities of Juda. Dwell therefore with him in the midst of the people: or whithersoever it shall please thee to go, go. And the general of the army gave him victuals and presents and let him go.

6 And Jeremias went to Godolias the son of Ahicam to Masphath: and dwelt with him in the midst of the people that were left in the land.

7 And when all the captains of the army that were scattered through the countries, they and their companions, had heard that the king of Babylon had made Godolias the son of Ahicam governor of the country and that he had committed unto him men and women and children and of the poor of the land them that had not been carried away captive to Babylon:

8 They came to Godolias to Masphath: and Ismahel the son of Nathanias, and Johanan and Jonathan, the sons of Caree, and Sareas the son of Thanehumeth, and the children of Ophi that were of Netophathi, and Jezonias the son of Maachati, they and their men.

9 [1] And Godolias the son of Ahicam the son of Saphan swore to them and to their companions, saying: Fear not to serve the Chaldeans. Dwell in the land and serve the king of Babylon, and it shall be well with you.

10 Behold I dwell in Masphath, that I may answer the commandment of the Chaldeans that are sent to us: but as for you, gather ye the vintage and the harvest and the oil, and lay it up in your vessels, and abide in your cities which you hold.

11 Moreover all the Jews that were in Moab and among the children of Ammon and in Edom and in all the countries, when they heard that the king of Babylon had left a remnant in Judea, and that he had made Godolias the son of Ahicam the son of Saphan ruler over them:

12 All the Jews, I say, returned out of all the places to which they had fled. And they came into the land of Juda to Godolias to Masphath: and they gathered wine and a very great harvest.

13 Then Johanan the son of Caree and all the captains of the army that had been scattered about in the countries came to Godolias to Masphath.

14 And they said to him: Know that Baalis, the king of the children of Ammon, hath sent Ismahel the son of Nathanias to kill thee. And Godolias the son of Ahicam believed them not.

15 But Johanan the son of Caree

spoke to Godolias privately in Masphath, saying: I will go and I will kill Ismahel the son of Nathanias, *and* no man shall know it, lest he kill thee, and all the Jews be scattered that are gathered unto thee, and the remnant of Juda perish.

16 And Godolias the son of Ahicam said to Johanan the son of Caree: Do not this thing: for what thou sayst of Ismahel is false.

CHAPTER 41
Godolias is slain. The Jews that were with him are apprehensive of the Chaldeans.

AND it came to pass in the seventh month, that Ismahel the son of Nathanias, the son of Elisama of the royal blood, and the nobles of the king, and ten men with him, came to Godolias the son of Ahicam into Masphath: and they ate bread there together in Masphath.

2 And Ismahel the son of Nathanias arose, and the ten men that were with him, and they struck Godolias the son of Ahicam, the son of Saphan, with the sword, and slew him whom the king of Babylon had made governor over the land.

3 Ismahel slew also all the Jews that were with Godolias in Masphath and the Chaldeans that were found there and the soldiers.

4 And on the second day after he had killed Godolias, no man yet knowing it,

5 There came some from Sichem and from Silo and from Samaria, fourscore men, with their beards shaven and their clothes rent and mourning: and they had offerings and incense in their hand, to offer in the house of the Lord.

6 And Ismahel the son of Nathanias went forth from Masphath to meet them, weeping all along as he went. And when he had met them, he said to them: Come to Godolias the son of Ahicam.

7 And when they were come to the midst of the city, Ismahel the son of Nathanias slew them *and cast them into* the midst of the pit, he and the men that were with him.

8 But ten men were found among them that said to Ismahel: Kill us not: for we have stores in the field, of wheat and barley and oil and honey. And he forbore and slew them not with their brethren.

9 And the pit into which Ismahel cast all the dead bodies of the men whom he slew because of Godolias, is the same that king Asa made for fear of Baasa the king of Israel: the same did Ismahel the son of Nathanias fill with them that were slain.

10 Then Ismahel carried away captive all the remnant of the people that were in Masphath: the king's daughters and all the people that remained in Masphath, whom Nabuzardan the general of the army had committed to Godolias the son of Ahicam. And Ismahel the son of Nathanias took them: and he departed, to go over to the children of Ammon.

11 But Johanan the son of Caree and all the captains of the fighting men that were with him heard of the evil that Ismahel the son of Nathanias had done.

12 And taking all the men, they went out to fight against Ismahel the son of Nathanias: and they found him by the great waters that are in Gabaon.

13 And when all the people that were with Ismahel had seen Johanan the son of Caree and all the captains of the fighting men that were with him, they rejoiced.

14 And all the people whom Ismahel had taken went back to Masphath: and they returned and went to Johanan the son of Caree.

15 But Ismahel the son of Nathanias fled with eight men from the face of Johanan and went to the children of Ammon.

16 Then Johanan the son of Caree and all the captains of the soldiers that were with him took all the remnant of the people whom they had recovered from Ismahel the son of Nathanias, from Masphath, after that he had slain Godolias the son of Ahicam: valiant men for war and the women and the children and the eunuchs, whom he had brought back from Gabaon.

17 And they departed and sat as sojourners in Chamaam, which is near Bethlehem: in order to go forward and enter into Egypt,

18 From the face of the Chaldeans: for they were afraid of them, because Ismahel the son of Nathanias had slain Godolias the son of Ahicam, whom the king of Babylon had made governor in the land of Juda.

CHAPTER 42
Jeremias assures the remnant of the people that, if they will stay in Juda, they shall be safe, but if they go down into Egypt, they shall perish.

THEN all the captains of the warriors and Johanan the son of Caree and Jezonias the son of Osaias and the rest of the people, from least to the greatest, came near.

2 And they said to Jeremias the prophet: Let our supplication fall before thee. And pray thou for us to the Lord thy God for all this remnant: for we are left but a few of many, as thy eyes do behold us.

3 And let the Lord thy God shew us the way by which we may walk and the thing that we must do.

4 And Jeremias the prophet said to them: I have heard *you*. Behold I will pray to the Lord your God according to your words: and whatsoever thing he shall answer me, I will declare it to you. And I will hide nothing from you.

5 And they said to Jeremias: The Lord be witness between us of truth and faithfulness, if we do not according to every thing for which the Lord thy God shall send thee to us.

6 Whether it be good or evil, we will obey the voice of the Lord our God, to whom we send thee: that it may be well with us when we shall hearken to the voice of the Lord our God.

7 Now after ten days, the word of the Lord came to Jeremias.

8 And he called Johanan the son of Caree and all the captains of the fighting men that were with him and all the people from the least to the greatest.

9 And he said to them: Thus saith the Lord, the God of Israel, to whom you sent me to present your supplications before him:

10 If you will be quiet and remain in this land, I will build you up and not pull you down: I will plant you and not pluck you up. For now I am appeased for the evil that I have done to you.

11 Fear not because of the king of Babylon, of whom you are greatly afraid. Fear not, saith the Lord: for I am with you, to save you and to deliver you from his hand.

12 And I will shew mercies to you and will take pity on you and will cause you to dwell in your own land.

13 But if you say: We will not dwell in this land, neither will we hearken to the voice of the Lord our God,

14 Saying: No, but we will go into the land of Egypt, where we shall see no war nor hear the sound of the trumpet nor suffer hunger: and there we will dwell.

15 For this now hear the word of the Lord, ye remnant of Juda: Thus saith the Lord of hosts, the God of Israel: If you set your faces to go into Egypt and enter in to dwell there:

16 The sword which you fear shall overtake you there in the land of Egypt: and the famine whereof you are afraid shall cleave to you in Egypt: and there you shall die.

17 And all the men that set their faces to go into Egypt to dwell there shall die by the sword and by famine and by pestilence: none of them shall remain nor escape from the face of the evil that I will bring upon them.

18 For thus saith the Lord of hosts, the God of Israel: As my anger and my indignation hath been kindled against the inhabitants of Jerusalem: so shall my indignation be kindled against you, when you shall enter into Egypt. And you shall be an execration and an astonishment and a curse and a reproach: and you shall see this place no more.

19 This is the word of the Lord concerning you, O ye remnant of Juda: Go ye not into Egypt. Know certainly that I have adjured you this day.

20 For you have deceived your own souls: for you sent me to the Lord our God, saying: Pray for us to the Lord our God, and according to all that the Lord our God shall say to thee, so declare unto us, and we will do it.

21 And now I have declared it to you this day: and you have not obeyed the voice of the Lord your God with regard to all the things for which he hath sent me to you.

22 Now therefore know certainly that you shall die by the sword and by famine and by pestilence, in the place to which you desire to go to dwell there.

CHAPTER 43

The Jews, contrary to the orders of God by the prophet, go into Egypt, carrying Jeremias with them. He foretells the devastation of that land by the king of Babylon.

AND it came to pass, that when Jeremias had made an end of speaking to the people all the words of the Lord their God, for which the Lord their God had sent him to them, all these words:

2 Azarias the son of Osaias and Johanan the son of Caree and all the proud men made answer, saying to Jeremias: Thou tellest a lie. The Lord our God hath not sent thee, saying: Go not into Egypt to dwell there.

3 But Baruch the son of Nerias setteth thee on against us, to deliver us into the hands of the Chaldeans, to kill us and to cause us to be carried away captives to Babylon.

4 So Johanan the son of Caree and all the captains of the soldiers and all the people obeyed not the voice of the Lord, to remain in the land of Juda.

5 But Johanan the son of Caree and all the captains of the soldiers took all the remnant of Juda that were returned out of all nations, to which they had before been scattered, to dwell in the land of Juda:

CHAP. 42. Ver. 6. *Good or evil.* That is, agreeable or disagreeable.

Ver. 10. *I am appeased for the evil that I have done to you.* That is, I am appeased, as I have sufficiently punished you, and now I am reconciled with you.

6 Men and women and children and the king's daughters and every soul which Nabuzardan the general had left with Godolias the son of Ahicam the son of Saphan, and Jeremias the prophet, and Baruch the son of Nerias.

7 And they went into the land of Egypt: for they obeyed not the voice of the Lord. And they came as far as Taphnis.

8 And the word of the Lord came to Jeremias in Taphnis, saying:

9 Take great stones in thy hand: and thou shalt hide them in the vault that is under the brick wall at the gate of Pharao's house in Taphnis, in the sight of the men of Juda.

10 And thou shalt say to them: Thus saith the Lord of hosts, the God of Israel: Behold I will send and take Nabuchodonosor the king of Babylon my servant and I will set his throne over these stones which I have hid. And he shall set his throne over them.

11 And he shall come and strike the land of Egypt: such as are for death, to death: and such as are for captivity, to captivity: and such as are for the sword, to the sword.

12 And he shall kindle a fire in the temples of the gods of Egypt: and he shall burn them: and he shall carry them away captives. And he shall array himself with the land of Egypt, as a shepherd putteth on his garment: and he shall go forth from thence in peace.

13 And he shall break the statues of the house of the sun that are in the land of Egypt; and the temples of the gods of Egypt he shall burn with fire.

CHAPTER 44

The prophet's admonition to the Jews in Egypt against idolatry is not regarded. He denounces to them their destruction.

THE word that came to Jeremias, concerning all the Jews that dwelt in the land of Egypt, dwelling in Magdal and in Taphnis and in Memphis and in the land of Phatures, saying:

2 Thus saith the Lord of hosts, the God of Israel: You have seen all this evil that I have brought upon Jerusalem and upon all the cities of Juda. And behold they are desolate this day. and there is not an inhabitant in them:

3 Because of the wickedness which they have committed, to provoke me to wrath, and to go and offer sacrifice and worship other gods which neither they nor you nor your fathers knew.

4 And I sent to you all my servants the prophets, rising early and sending. and saying: Do not commit this abominable thing which I hate.

5 But they heard not nor inclined their ear to turn from their evil ways and not to sacrifice to strange gods.

6 Wherefore my indignation and my fury was poured forth and was kindled in the cities of Juda and in the streets of Jerusalem: and they are turned to desolation and waste, as at this day.

7 And now thus saith the Lord of hosts, the God of Israel: Why do you commit this great evil against your own souls, that there should die of you man and woman, child and suckling, out of the midst of Juda, and no remnant should be left you:

8 In that you provoke me to wrath with the works of your hands, by sacrificing to other gods in the land of Egypt, into which you are come to dwell there: and that you should perish and be a curse and a reproach to all the nations of the earth?

9 Have you forgotten the evils of your fathers and the evils of the kings of Juda and the evils of their wives and your evils and the evils of your wives, that they have done in the land of Juda and in the streets of Jerusalem?

10 They are not cleansed even to this day: neither have they feared nor walked in the law of the Lord nor in my commandments which I set before you and your fathers.

11 Therefore thus saith the Lord of hosts, the God of Israel: ¹ Behold I will set my face upon you for evil: and I will destroy all Juda.

12 And I will take the remnant of Juda that have set their faces to go into the land of Egypt and to dwell there: and they shall be all consumed in the land of Egypt. They shall fall by the sword and by the famine: and they shall be consumed from the least even to the greatest. By the sword and by the famine shall they die: and they shall be for an execration and for a wonder and for a curse and for a reproach.

13 And I will visit them that dwell in the land of Egypt, as I have visited Jerusalem, by the sword and by famine and by pestilence.

14 And there shall be none that shall escape and remain of the remnant of the Jews that are gone to sojourn in the land of Egypt, and that shall return into the land of Juda, to which they have a desire to return to dwell there. There shall none return but they that shall flee.

15 Then all the men that knew that their wives sacrificed to other gods, and all the women of whom there stood by a great multitude, and all the people of them that dwelt in the land of Egypt

in Phatures, answered Jeremias, saying:

16 As for the word which thou hast spoken to us in the name of the Lord, we will not hearken to thee:

17 But we will certainly do every word that shall proceed out of our own mouth, to sacrifice to the queen of heaven and to pour out drink offerings to her, as we and our fathers have done, our kings and our princes in the cities of Juda and in the streets of Jerusalem: and we were filled with bread, and it was well with us, and we saw no evil.

18 But since we left off to offer sacrifice to the queen of heaven and to pour out drink offerings to her, we have wanted all things and have been consumed by the sword and by famine.

19 And if we offer sacrifice to the queen of heaven and pour out drink offerings to her: did we make cakes to worship her, to pour out drink offerings to her, without our husbands?

20 And Jeremias spoke to all the people, to the men and to the women and to all the people which had given him that answer, saying:

21 Was it not the sacrifice that you offered in the cities of Juda and in the streets of Jerusalem, you and your fathers, your kings and your princes, and the people of the land, which the Lord hath remembered: and hath it not entered into his heart?

22 So that the Lord could no longer bear, because of the evil of your doings and because of the abominations which you have committed. Therefore your land is become a desolation and an astonishment and a curse, without an inhabitant, as at this day.

23 Because you have sacrificed to idols and have sinned against the Lord, and have not obeyed the voice of the Lord, and have not walked in his law and in his commandments and in his testimonies: therefore are these evils come upon you, as at this day.

24 And Jeremias said to all the people and to all the women: Hear ye the word of the Lord, all Juda, you that dwell in the land of Egypt.

25 Thus saith the Lord of hosts, the God of Israel, saying: You and your wives have spoken with your mouth and fulfilled with your hands, saying: Let us perform our vows which we have made, to offer sacrifice to the queen of heaven and to pour out drink offerings to her. You have fulfilled your vows and have performed them indeed.

26 Therefore hear ye the word of the Lord, all Juda, you that dwell in the land of Egypt: Behold I have sworn by my great name, saith the Lord, that my name shall no more be named in the mouth of any man of Juda, in the land of Egypt, saying: The Lord God liveth.

27 Behold I will watch over them for evil and not for good: and all the men of Juda that are in the land of Egypt shall be consumed by the sword and by famine till there be an end of them.

28 And a few men that shall flee from the sword shall return out of the land of Egypt into the land of Juda: and all the remnant of Juda that are gone into the land of Egypt to dwell there shall know whose word shall stand, mine or theirs.

29 And this shall be a sign to you, saith the Lord, that I will punish you in this place: that you may know that my words shall be accomplished indeed against you for evil.

30 Thus saith the Lord: Behold I will deliver Pharao Ephree king of Egypt into the hand of his enemies and into the hand of them that seek his life: as I delivered Sedecias king of Juda into the hand of Nabuchodonosor the king of Babylon his enemy and that sought his life.

CHAPTER 45

The prophet comforts Baruch in his affliction.

THE word that Jeremias the prophet spoke to Baruch the son of Nerias, when he had written these words in a book, out of the mouth of Jeremias, in the fourth year of Joakim the son of Josias king of Juda, saying:

2 Thus saith the Lord the God of Israel to thee, Baruch:

3 Thou hast said: Woe is me, wretch that I am, for the Lord hath added sorrow to my sorrow! I am wearied with my groans and I find no rest.

4 Thus saith the Lord: Thus shalt thou say to him: Behold, them whom I have built, I do destroy: and them whom I have planted, I do pluck up, and all this land.

5 And dost thou seek great things for thyself? Seek not: for behold I will bring evil upon all flesh, saith the Lord. But I will give thee thy life and save thee in all places whithersoever thou shalt go.

CHAPTER 46

A prophecy against Egypt. The Jews shall return from captivity.

THE word of the Lord that came to Jeremias the prophet, against the Gentiles,

2 Against Egypt, against the army of Pharao Nechao king of Egypt which was by the river Euphrates in Charcamis, whom Nabuchodonosor the

CHAP. 44. Ver. 17. *The queen of heaven.* The moon, which they worshipped under this name.

king of Babylon defeated, in the fourth year of Joakim the son of Josias king of Juda.

3 Prepare ye the shield and buckler and go forth to battle.

4 Harness the horses and get up, ye horsemen. Stand forth with helmets, furbish the spears, put on coats of mail.

5 What then? I have seen them dismayed and turning their backs, their valiant ones slain. They fled apace and they looked not back: terror was round about, saith the Lord.

6 Let not the swift flee away nor the strong think to escape: they are overthrown and fallen down, towards the north, by the river Euphrates.

7 Who is this that cometh up as a flood: and his streams swell like those of rivers?

8 Egypt riseth up like a flood, and the waves thereof shall be moved as rivers. And he shall say: I will go up and will cover the earth. I will destroy the city and its inhabitants.

9 Get ye up on horses and glory in chariots: and let the valiant men come forth, the Ethiopians and the Libyans that hold the shield and the Lydians that take and shoot arrows.

10 For this is the day of the Lord, the God of hosts, a day of vengeance, that he may revenge himself of his enemies. The sword shall devour and shall be filled and shall be drunk with their blood: for there is a sacrifice of the Lord God of hosts in the north country, by the river Euphrates.

11 Go up into Galaad and take balm, O virgin daughter of Egypt: in vain dost thou multiply medicines. There shall be no cure for thee.

12 The nations have heard of thy disgrace and thy howling hath filled the land: for the strong hath stumbled against the strong, and both are fallen together.

13 The word that the Lord spoke to Jeremias the prophet, how Nabuchodonosor king of Babylon should come and strike the land of Egypt:

14 Declare ye to Egypt and publish it in Magdal, ¹ and let it be known in Memphis and in Taphnis. Say ye: Stand up and prepare thyself: for the sword shall devour all round about thee.

15 Why are thy valiant men come to nothing? They stood not: because the Lord hath overthrown them.

16 He hath multiplied them that fall, and one hath fallen upon another. And they shall say: Arise, and let us return to our own people and to the land of our nativity, from the sword of the dove.

17 Call ye the name of Pharao king of Egypt: A tumult time hath brought.

18 As I live (saith the King, whose name is the Lord of hosts), as Thabor is among the mountains and as Carmel by the sea, so shall he come.

19 Furnish thyself to go into captivity, thou daughter inhabitant of Egypt: for Memphis shall be made desolate and shall be forsaken and uninhabited.

20 Egypt is like a fair and beautiful heifer: there shall come from the north one that shall goad her.

21 Her hirelings also that lived in the midst of her, like fatted calves, are turned back and are fled away together. And they could not stand: for the day of their slaughter is come upon them, the time of their visitation.

22 Her voice shall sound like brass: for they shall hasten with an army, and with axes they shall come against her, as hewers of wood.

23 They shall cut down her forest, saith the Lord, which cannot be counted: they are multiplied above locusts and are without number.

24 The daughter of Egypt is confounded and delivered into the hand of the people of the north.

25 The Lord of hosts, the God of Israel, hath said: Behold I will visit upon the tumult of Alexandria and upon Pharao and upon Egypt and upon her gods, and upon her kings, and upon Pharao, and upon them that trust in him.

26 And I will deliver them into the hand of them that seek their lives and into the hand of Nabuchodonosor king of Babylon and into the hand of his servants: and afterwards it shall be inhabited, ² as in the days of old, saith the Lord.

27 ³ And thou, my servant Jacob, fear not, and be not thou dismayed, O Israel: for behold I will save thee from afar off, and thy seed out of the land of thy captivity. And Jacob shall return and be at rest and prosper: and there shall be none to terrify him.

28 And thou, my servant Jacob, fear not, saith the Lord: because I am with thee. For I will consume all the nations to which I have cast thee out: but thee I will not consume. But I will correct thee in judgment: neither will I spare thee, as if thou wert innocent.

CHAPTER 47

A prophecy of the desolation of the Philistines, of Tyre, Sidon, Gaza and Ascalon.

CHAP. 46. ¹ Jer. 44, 1. ² Ezech. 20, 13. ³ Isai. 43, 1; 44, 2.

CHAP. 46. Ver. 16. The dove. See the annotation on chap. 25, ver. 38.

Ver. 25. Visit upon. That is, punish.—Alexandria. In the Hebrew, No, which was the ancient name of the city, to which Alexander gave afterwards the name of Alexandria.

THE word of the Lord that came to Jeremias the prophet against the people of Palestine, before Pharao took Gaza.

2 Thus saith the Lord: Behold there come up waters out of the north, and they shall be as an overflowing torrent. And they shall cover the land and all that is therein, the city and the inhabitants thereof. Then the men shall cry, and all the inhabitants of the land shall howl.

3 At the noise of the marching of arms and of his soldiers, at the rushing of his chariots and the multitude of his wheels. The fathers have not looked back to the children, for feebleness of hands,

4 Because of the coming of the day in which all the Philistines shall be laid waste, and Tyre and Sidon shall be destroyed, with all the rest of their helpers. For the Lord hath wasted the Philistines, [1] the remnant of the isle of Cappadocia.

5 Baldness is come upon Gaza: Ascalon hath held her peace with the remnant of their valley. How long shalt thou cut thyself?

6 O thou sword of the Lord, how long wilt thou not be quiet? Go into thy scabbard: rest and be still.

7 How shall it be quiet when the Lord hath given it a charge against Ascalon and against the countries thereof by the sea side, and there hath made an appointment for it?

CHAPTER 48

A prophecy of the desolation of Moab for their pride. But their captivity shall at last be released.

AGAINST [1] Moab, thus saith the Lord of hosts, the God of Israel: Woe to Nabo, for it is laid waste and confounded: Cariathaim is taken: the strong city is confounded and hath trembled.

2 There is no more rejoicing in Moab over Hesebon: they have devised evil. Come and let us cut it off from being a nation. Therefore shalt thou in silence hold thy peace, and the sword shall follow thee.

3 A voice of crying from Oronaim: waste, and great destruction.

4 Moab is destroyed: proclaim a cry for her little ones.

5 For by the ascent of Luith shall the mourner go up with weeping: for in the descent of Oronaim the enemies have heard a howling of destruction.

6 Flee, save your lives: and be [2] as heath in the wilderness.

7 For because thou hast trusted in thy bulwarks and in thy treasures, thou also shalt be taken: and Chamos shall go into captivity, his priests and his princes together.

8 And the spoiler shall come upon every city, and no city shall escape. And the valleys shall perish and the plains shall be destroyed: for the Lord hath spoken.

9 Give a flower to Moab, for in its flower it shall go out: and the cities thereof shall be desolate and uninhabited.

10 Cursed be he that doth the work of the Lord deceitfully: and cursed be he that withholdeth his sword from blood.

11 Moab hath been fruitful from his youth and hath rested upon his lees: and hath not been poured out from vessel to vessel, nor hath gone into captivity. Therefore his taste hath remained in him and his scent is not changed.

12 Therefore, behold the days come, saith the Lord, and I will send him men that shall order and overturn his bottles: and they shall cast him down and shall empty his vessels and break their bottles one against another.

13 And Moab shall be ashamed of Chamos, [3] as the house of Israel was ashamed of Bethel, in which they trusted.

14 How do you say: [4] We are valiant, and stout men in battle?

15 Moab is laid waste, and they have cast down her cities, and her choice young men are gone down to the slaughter: saith the king, whose name is the Lord of hosts.

16 The destruction of Moab is near to come: the calamity thereof shall come on exceeding swiftly.

17 Comfort him, all you that are round about him. And all you that know his name, say: How is the strong staff broken, the beautiful rod?

18 Come down from thy glory and sit in thirst, O dwelling of the daughter of Dibon: because the spoiler of Moab is come up to thee, he hath destroyed thy bulwarks.

19 Stand in the way and look out, O habitation of Aroer: inquire of him that fleeth and say to him that hath escaped: What is done?

CHAP. 47. [1] Deut. 2, 23; Amos, 9, 7. CHAP. 48. [1] Jer. 27,; Ezech. 25. [2] Jer. 17, 6. [3] 3 Kings, 12, 29. [4] Isai. 16, 6.

CHAP. 48. Ver. 7. *Chamos.* The idol of the Moabites.
Ver. 10. *Deceitfully.* In the Greek, *negligently.* The *work of God* here spoken of is the punishment of the Moabites.
Ver. 11. *Moab hath been fruitful.* That is, rich and flourishing. *And hath rested upon his lees.* That is, remained in its bad morals: as wine not decanted has its lees mixed and remains muddy.
Ver. 13. *Of Bethel.* That is, of their golden calf which they worshipped in Bethel.

20 Moab is confounded, because he is overthrown. Howl ye and cry: tell ye it in Arnon that Moab is wasted.

21 And judgment is come upon the plain country: upon Helon and upon Jasa and upon Mephaath.

22 And upon Dibon and upon Nabo and upon the house of Deblathaim,

23 And upon Cariathaim and upon Bethgamul and upon Bethmaon,

24 And upon Carioth and upon Bosra and upon all the cities of the land of Moab, far or near.

25 The horn of Moab is cut off and his arm is broken, saith the Lord.

26 Make him drunk, because he lifted up himself against the Lord: and Moab shall dash his hand in his own vomit, and he also shall be in derision.

27 For Israel hath been a derision unto thee: as though thou hadst found him amongst thieves: for thy words therefore, which thou hast spoken against him, thou shalt be led away captive.

28 Leave the cities and dwell in the rock, you that dwell in Moab: and be ye like the dove that maketh her nest in the mouth of the hole in the highest place.

29 ⁵ We have heard the pride of Moab, he is exceeding proud: his haughtiness and his arrogancy and his pride and the loftiness of his heart.

30 I know, saith the Lord, his boasting and that the strength thereof is not according to it: neither hath it endeavoured to do according as it was able.

31 Therefore will I lament for Moab and I will cry out to all Moab, for the men of the brick wall that mourn.

32 O vineyard of Sabama, I will weep for thee with the mourning of Jazer: thy branches are gone over the sea. They are come even to the sea of Jazer: the robber hath rushed in upon thy harvest and thy vintage.

33 ⁶ Joy and gladness is taken away from Carmel and from the land of Moab, and I have taken away the wine out of the presses: the treader of the grapes shall not sing the accustomed cheerful tune.

34 From the cry of Hesebon even to Eleale and to Jasa, they have uttered their voice: from Segor to Oronaim, as a heifer of three years old. The waters also of Nemrim shall be very bad.

35 And I will take away from Moab, saith the Lord, him that offereth in the high places and that sacrificeth to his gods.

36 Therefore my heart shall sound for Moab like pipes: and my heart shall sound like pipes for the men of the brick wall. Because he hath done more than he could, therefore they have perished.

37 ⁷ For every head *shall be* bald and every beard shall be shaven: all hands shall be tied together and upon every back there shall be haircloth.

38 Upon all the housetops of Moab and in the streets thereof general mourning: because I have broken Moab as an useless vessel, saith the Lord.

39 How is it overthrown and they have howled! How hath Moab bowed down the neck and is confounded! And Moab shall be a derision and an example to all round about him.

40 Thus saith the Lord: Behold he shall fly as an eagle and shall stretch forth his wings to Moab.

41 Carioth is taken and the strong holds are won: and the heart of the valiant men of Moab in that day shall be as the heart of a woman in labour.

42 And Moab shall cease to be a people: because he hath gloried against the Lord.

43 Fear and the pit and the snare *come* upon thee, O inhabitant of Moab, saith the Lord.

44 ⁸ He that shall flee from the fear shall fall into the pit: and he that shall get up out of the pit shall be taken in the snare: for I will bring upon Moab the year of their visitation, saith the Lord.

45 They that fled from the snare stood in the shadow of Hesebon: but there came a fire out of Hesebon and a flame out of the midst of Seon, and it shall devour part of Moab and the crown of the head of the children of tumult.

46 Woe to thee, Moab, thou hast perished, O people of Chamos: for thy sons, and thy daughters are taken captives.

47 And I will bring back the captivity of Moab in the last days, saith the Lord. Hitherto the judgments of Moab.

CHAPTER 49

The like desolation of Ammon, of Idumea, of the Syrians, of the Agarenes and of the Elamites.

AGAINST ¹ the children of Ammon. Thus saith the Lord: Hath Israel no sons? Or hath he no heir? Why then hath Melchom inherited Gad, and his people dwelt in his cities?

---

⁵ Isai. 16, 6. ⁶ Isai. 16, 10. ⁷ Isai. 15, 2; Ezech. 7, 18. ⁸ Isai. 24, 18. CHAP. 49. ¹ Jer. 27; Ezech. 25.

Ver. 25. *The horn of Moab is cut off.* That is the strength of Moab is cut off. A metaphor drawn from animals whose strength is in their horns.

Ver. 43. *Fear.* That is, the sword of the enemy. *The pit.* That is, unforeseen calamities. *The snare.* That is, the ambushes laid by the enemy. CHAP. 49. Ver. 1. *Melchom.* The idol of the Ammonites.

2 Therefore, behold the days come, saith the Lord, and I will cause the noise of war to be heard in Rabbath of the children of Ammon, and it shall be destroyed into a heap and her daughters shall be burnt with fire: and Israel shall possess them that have possessed him, saith the Lord.

3 Howl, O Hesebon, for Hai is wasted. Cry, ye daughters of Rabbath, gird yourselves with haircloth, mourn and go about by the hedges: for Melchom shall be carried into captivity, his priests and his princes together.

4 Why gloriest thou in the valleys? Thy valley hath flowed away, O delicate daughter, that hast trusted in thy treasures and hast said: Who shall come to me?

5 Behold, I will bring a fear upon thee, saith the Lord God of hosts, from all that are round about thee. And you shall be scattered every one out of one another's sight: neither shall there be any to gather together them that flee.

6 And afterwards I will cause the captives of the children of Ammon to return, saith the Lord.

7 Against Edom. Thus saith the Lord of hosts: Is wisdom no more in Theman? Counsel is perished from her children: their wisdom is become unprofitable.

8 Flee and turn your backs, go down into the deep hole, ye inhabitants of Dedan: for I have brought the destruction of Esau upon him, the time of his visitation.

9 If grapegatherers had come to thee, would they not have left a bunch? If thieves in the night, they would have taken what was enough for them.

10 But I have made Esau bare, I have revealed his secrets: and he cannot be hid. His seed is laid waste, and his brethren and his neighbours: and he shall not be.

11 Leave thy fatherless children: I will make them live. And thy widows shall hope in me.

12 For thus saith the Lord: Behold they whose judgment was not to drink of the cup shall certainly drink: and shalt thou come off as innocent? Thou shalt not come off as innocent, but drinking thou shalt drink.

13 For I have sworn by myself, saith the Lord, that Bosra shall become a desolation and a reproach and a desert and a curse: and all her cities shall be everlasting wastes.

14 [2] I have heard a rumour from the Lord, and an ambassador is sent to the nations: Gather yourselves together and come against her, and let us rise up to battle.

15 For behold, I have made thee a little one among the nations, despicable among men.

16 Thy arrogancy hath deceived thee, and the pride of thy heart, O thou that dwellest in the clefts of the rocks and endeavourest to lay hold on the height of the hill: [3] but though thou shouldst make thy nest as high as an eagle, I will bring thee down from thence, saith the Lord.

17 And Edom shall be desolate: every one that shall pass by it shall be astonished and shall hiss at all its plagues.

18 [4] As Sodom was overthrown and Gomorrha and the neighbours thereof, saith the Lord: there shall not a man dwell there and there shall no son of man inhabit it.

19 Behold one shall come up as a lion from the swelling of the Jordan, against the strong and beautiful: for I will make him run suddenly upon her. And who shall be the chosen one whom I may appoint over her? For who is like to me and who shall abide me? [5] And who is that shepherd that can withstand my countenance?

20 Therefore hear ye the counsel of the Lord which he hath taken concerning Edom and his thoughts which he hath thought concerning the inhabitants of Theman. Surely the little ones of the flock shall cast them down: of a truth they shall destroy them with their habitation.

21 The earth is moved at the noise of their fall: the cry of their voice is heard in the Red Sea.

22 Behold, he shall come up as an eagle and fly: and he shall spread his wings over Bosra: and in that day the heart of the valiant ones of Edom shall be as the heart of a woman in labour.

23 Against Damascus. Emath is confounded and Arphad: for they have heard very bad tidings: they are troubled as in the sea: through care they could not rest.

24 Damascus is undone: she is put to flight; trembling hath seized on her. Anguish and sorrows have taken her as a woman in labour.

25 How have they forsaken the city of renown, the city of joy!

26 Therefore her young men shall fall in her streets: and all the men of war shall be silent in that day, saith the Lord of hosts.

27 And I will kindle a fire in the wall of Damascus: and it shall devour the strong holds of Benadad.

28 Against Cedar and against the kingdoms of Asor which Nabuchodo-

_____
[2] Abd. 1, 1. [3] Abd. 1, 4. [4] Gen. 19, 24. [5] Job, 12, 1.

Ver. 28. *Cedar* and *Asor* were parts of Arabia, which with Moab, Ammon, Edom, &c., were all brought under the yoke of Nabuchodonosor.

nosor king of Babylon destroyed. Thus saith the Lord: Arise and go ye up to Cedar and waste the children of the east.

29 They shall take their tents and their flocks: and shall carry off for themselves their curtains and all their vessels and their camels: and they shall call fear upon them round about.

30 Flee ye, get away speedily, sit in deep holes, you that inhabit Asor, saith the Lord: for Nabuchodonosor king of Babylon hath taken counsel against you and hath conceived designs against you.

31 Arise and go up to a nation that is at ease and that dwelleth securely, saith the Lord: they have neither gates nor bars: they dwell alone.

32 And their camels shall be for a spoil and the multitude of their cattle for a booty: and I will scatter into every wind them that have their hair cut round: and I will bring destruction upon them from all their confines, saith the Lord.

33 And Asor shall be a habitation for dragons, desolate for ever: no man shall abide there, nor son of man inhabit it.

34 The word of the Lord that came to Jeremias the prophet against Elam, in the beginning of the reign of Sedecias king of Juda, saying:

35 Thus saith the Lord of hosts: Behold I will break the bow of Elam and their chief strength.

36 And I will bring upon Elam the four winds from the four quarters of heaven: and I will scatter them into all these winds: and there shall be no nation to which the fugitives of Elam shall not come.

37 And I will cause Elam to be afraid before their enemies and in the sight of them that seek their life: and I will bring evil upon them, my fierce wrath, saith the Lord: and I will send the sword after them till I consume them.

38 And I will set my throne in Elam and destroy kings and princes from thence, saith the Lord.

39 But in the latter days I will cause the captives of Elam to return, saith the Lord.

CHAPTER 50

Babylon, which hath afflicted the Israelites, after their restoration shall be utterly destroyed.

THE word that the Lord hath spoken against Babylon and against the land of the Chaldeans, in the hand of Jeremias the prophet.

Ver. 34. *Elam.* A part of Persia.

CHAP. 50. Ver. 2. *Bel.* Bel and Merodach were worshipped for gods by the men of Babylon.

Ver. 3. *A nation.* The Medes.

2 Declare ye among the nations and publish it, lift up a standard: proclaim and conceal it not. Say: Babylon is taken, Bel is confounded, Merodach is overthrown, their graven things are confounded, their idols are overthrown.

3 For a nation is come up against her out of the north, which shall make her land desolate. And there shall be none to dwell therein from man even to beast: yea they are removed and gone away.

4 In those days and at that time, saith the Lord, the children of Israel shall come, they and the children of Juda together: going and weeping, they shall make haste and shall seek the Lord their God.

5 They shall ask the way to Sion: their faces *are* hitherward. They shall come and shall be joined to the Lord by an everlasting covenant which shall never be forgotten.

6 My people have been a lost flock: their shepherds have caused them to go astray and have made them wander in the mountains. They have gone from mountain to hill: they have forgotten their resting place.

7 All that found them have devoured them: and their enemies said: We have not sinned *in so doing,* because, they have sinned against the Lord, the beauty of justice, and against the Lord, the hope of their fathers.

8 Remove out of the midst of Babylon and go forth out of the land of the Chaldeans: and be ye as kids at the head of the flock.

9 For behold, I raise up and will bring against Babylon an assembly of great nations from the land of the north: and they shall be prepared against her, and from thence she shall be taken. Their arrows, like those of a mighty man, a destroyer, shall not return in vain.

10 And Chaldea shall be made a prey: all that waste her shall be filled, saith the Lord.

11 Because you rejoice and speak great things, pillaging my inheritance: because you are spread abroad as calves upon the grass and have bellowed as bulls.

12 Your mother is confounded exceedingly and she that bore you is made even with the dust: behold, she shall be the last among the nations, a wilderness unpassable and dry.

13 Because of the wrath of the Lord, it shall not be inhabited but shall be wholly desolate: every one that shall pass by Babylon shall be astonished and shall hiss at all her plagues.

14 Prepare yourselves against Babylon round about, all you that bend the

bow. Fight against her, spare not arrows: because she hath sinned against the Lord.

15 Shout against her, she hath every where given her hand, her foundations are fallen, her walls are thrown down: for it is the vengeance of the Lord. Take vengeance upon her. As she hath done, so do to her.

16 Destroy the sower out of Babylon and him that holdeth the sickle in the time of harvest. For fear of the sword of the dove every man shall return to his people and every one shall flee to his own land.

17 Israel is a scattered flock, the lions have driven him away: first the king of Assyria devoured him, and last this Nabuchodonosor king of Babylon hath broken his bones.

18 Therefore thus saith the Lord of hosts, the God of Israel: Behold I will visit the king of Babylon and his land, as I have visited the king of Assyria.

19 And I will bring Israel again to his habitation: and he shall feed on Carmel and Bason, and his soul shall be satisfied in mount Ephraim and Galaad.

20 In those days and at that time, saith the Lord, the iniquity of Israel shall be sought for, and there shall be none: and the sin of Juda, and there shall none be found: for I will be merciful to them whom I shall leave.

21 Go up against the land of the rulers and punish the inhabitants thereof, waste and destroy all behind them, saith the Lord: and do according to all that I have commanded thee.

22 A noise of war in the land and a great destruction.

23 How is the hammer of the whole earth broken, and destroyed! How is Babylon turned into a desert among the nations!

24 I have caused thee to fall into a snare and thou art taken, O Babylon: and thou wast not aware of it. Thou art found and caught, because thou hast provoked the Lord.

25 The Lord hath opened his armoury and hath brought forth the weapons of his wrath: for the Lord, the God of hosts, hath a work to be done in the land of the Chaldeans.

26 Come ye against her from the uttermost borders: open, that they may go forth that shall tread her down: take the stones out of the way and make heaps and destroy her: and let nothing of her be left.

27 Destroy all her valiant men, let them go down to the slaughter. Woe to them, for their day is come, the time of their visitation.

28 The voice of them that flee and of them that have escaped out of the land of Babylon: to declare in Sion the revenge of the Lord our God, the revenge of his temple.

29 Declare to many against Babylon, to all that bend the bow: stand together against her round about and let none escape: pay her according to her work: [1] according to all that she hath done, do ye to her: for she hath lifted up herself against the Lord, against the Holy One of Israel.

30 Therefore shall her young men fall in her streets: and all her men of war shall hold their peace in that day, saith the Lord.

31 Behold I *come against* thee, O proud one, saith the Lord, the God of hosts: for thy day is come, the time of thy visitation.

32 And the proud one shall fall, he shall fall down, and there shall be none to lift him up: and I will kindle a fire in his cities and it shall devour all round about him.

33 Thus saith the Lord of hosts: The children of Israel and the children of Juda are oppressed together: all that have taken them captives hold them fast. They will not let them go.

34 Their redeemer is strong: the Lord of hosts is his name. He will defend their cause in judgment, to terrify the land and to disquiet the inhabitants of Babylon.

35 A sword is upon the Chaldeans, saith the Lord, and upon the inhabitants of Babylon and upon her princes and upon her wise men.

36 A sword upon her diviners, and they shall be foolish: a sword upon her valiant ones, and they shall be dismayed.

37 A sword upon their horses and upon their chariots and upon all the people that are in the midst of her, and they shall become as women. A sword upon her treasures, and they shall be made a spoil.

38 A drought upon her waters, and they shall be dried up: because it is a land of idols, and they glory in monstrous things.

39 Therefore shall dragons dwell there with the fig fauns: and ostriches shall dwell therein. And it shall be no more inhabited for ever: neither shall it be built up from generation to generation.

CHAP. 50. [1] Jer. 51, 49.

Ver. 16. *The dove.* Or the *destroyer,* for the Hebrew word signifies either the one or the other.

Ver. 39. *Fig fauns.* Monsters of the desert, or demons in monstrous shapes: such as the ancients called *fauns* and *satyrs.* As they imagined them to live upon wild figs, they called them *fauni ficarii,* or *fig fauns.*

40 [2] As the Lord overthrew Sodom and Gomorrha and their neighbour cities, saith the Lord: no man shall dwell there, neither shall the son of man inhabit it.

41 Behold a people cometh from the north and a great nation, and many kings shall rise from the ends of the earth.

42 They shall take the bow and the shield: they are cruel and unmerciful. Their voice shall roar like the sea and they shall ride upon horses, like a man prepared for battle: against thee, O daughter of Babylon.

43 The king of Babylon hath heard the report of them and his hands are grown feeble: anguish hath taken hold of him, pangs as a woman in labour.

44 [3] Behold he shall come up like a lion from the swelling of the Jordan to the strong and beautiful: for I will make him run suddenly upon her. And who shall be the chosen one whom I may appoint over her? For who is like to me and who shall bear up against me? [4] And who is that shepherd that can withstand my countenance?

45 Therefore, hear ye the counsel of the Lord which he hath taken against Babylon and his thoughts which he hath thought against the land of the Chaldeans. Surely the little ones of the flocks shall pull them down: of a truth their habitation shall be destroyed with them.

46 At the noise of the taking of Babylon the earth is moved and the cry is heard amongst the nations.

CHAPTER 51

The miseries that shall fall upon Babylon from the Medes. The destruction of her idols.

THUS saith the Lord: Behold I will raise up as it were a pestilential wind against Babylon and against the inhabitants thereof who have lifted up their heart against me.

2 And I will send to Babylon fanners, and they shall fan her and shall destroy her land: for they are come upon her on every side in the day of her affliction.

3 Let not him that bendeth bend his bow, and let not him go up that is armed with a coat of mail: spare not her young men, destroy all her army.

4 And the slain shall fall in the land of the Chaldeans and the wounded in the regions thereof.

5 For Israel and Juda have not been forsaken by their God, the Lord of hosts: but their land hath been filled with sin against the Holy One of Israel.

6 Flee ye from the midst of Babylon and let every one save his own life, be not silent upon her iniquity: for it is the time of revenge from the Lord. He will render unto her what she hath deserved.

7 Babylon hath been a golden cup in the hand of the Lord, that made all the earth drunk: the nations have drunk of her wine, and therefore they have staggered.

8 [1] Babylon is suddenly fallen and destroyed: howl for her, take balm for her pain, if so she may be healed.

9 We would have cured Babylon, but she is not healed: let us forsake her and let us go every man to his own land: because her judgment hath reached even to the heavens and is lifted up to the clouds.

10 The Lord hath brought forth our justices: Come, and let us declare in Sion the work of the Lord our God.

11 Sharpen the arrows, fill the quivers, the Lord hath raised up the spirit of the kings of the Medes: and his mind is against Babylon to destroy it, because it is the vengeance of the Lord, the vengeance of his temple.

12 Upon the walls of Babylon set up the standard, strengthen the watch: set up the watchmen, prepare the ambushes: for the Lord hath both purposed and done all that he spoke against the inhabitants of Babylon.

13 O thou that dwellest upon many waters, rich in treasures, thy end is come for thy entire destruction.

14 [2] The Lord of hosts hath sworn by himself, saying: I will fill thee with men as with locusts, and they shall lift up a joyful shout against thee.

15 [3] He that made the earth by his power, that hath prepared the world by his wisdom and stretched out the heavens by his understanding.

16 When he uttereth his voice the waters are multiplied in heaven: he lifteth up the clouds from the ends of the earth, he hath turned lightning into rain and hath brought forth the wind out of his treasures.

17 Every man is become foolish by *his* knowledge: every founder is confounded by his idol, for what he hath cast is a lie, and there is no breath in them.

18 They are vain works and worthy to be laughed at: in the time of their visitation they shall perish.

19 The portion of Jacob is not like them: for he that made all things he it is, and Israel is the sceptre of his inheritance: the Lord of hosts is his name.

20 Thou dashest together for me the weapons of war, and with thee I will dash nations together and with thee I will destroy kingdoms:

21 And with thee I will break in pieces the horse and his rider, and with thee I will break in pieces the chariot and him that getteth up into it:

22 And with thee I will break in pieces man and woman, and with thee I will break in pieces the old man and the child, and with thee I will break in pieces the young man and the virgin:

23 And with thee I will break in pieces the shepherd and his flock, and with thee I will break in pieces the husbandman and his yoke of oxen, and with thee I will break in pieces captains and rulers.

24 And I will render to Babylon and to all the inhabitants of Chaldea all their evil, that they have done in Sion, before your eyes, saith the Lord.

25 Behold I *come against* thee, thou destroying mountain, saith the Lord, which corruptest the whole earth: and I will stretch out my hand upon thee and will roll thee down from the rocks and will make thee a burnt mountain.

26 And they shall not take of thee a stone for the corner, nor a stone for foundations, but thou shalt be destroyed for ever, saith the Lord.

27 Set ye up a standard in the land: sound with the trumpet among the nations: prepare the nations against her: call together against her the kings of Ararat, Menni and Ascenez: number Taphsar against her, bring the horse as the stinging locust.

28 Prepare the nations against her, the kings of Media, their captains and all their rulers and all the land of their dominion.

29 And the land shall be in a commotion and shall be troubled: for the design of the Lord against Babylon shall awake, to make the land of Babylon desert and uninhabitable.

30 The valiant men of Babylon have forborne to fight, they have dwelt in holds: their strength hath failed and they are become as women: her dwelling places are burnt, her bars are broken.

31 One running post shall meet another and messenger shall meet messenger: to tell the king of Babylon that his city is taken from one end to the other:

32 And that the fords are taken and the marshes are burnt with fire and the men of war are affrighted.

33 For thus saith the Lord of hosts. the God of Israel: The daughter of Babylon is like a thrashingfloor. This is the time of her thrashing: yet a little while, and the time of her harvest shall come.

34 Nabuchodonosor king of Babylon hath eaten me up: he hath devoured me: he hath made me as an empty vessel: he hath swallowed me up like a dragon: he hath filled his belly with my delicate meats and he hath cast me out.

35 The wrong done to me and my flesh *be* upon Babylon, saith the habitation of Sion: and my blood upon the inhabitants of Chaldea, saith Jerusalem.

36 Therefore thus saith the Lord: Behold I will judge thy cause and will take vengeance for thee, and I will make her sea desolate [4] and will dry up her spring.

37 And Babylon shall be reduced to heaps, a dwelling place for dragons, an astonishment and a hissing, because there is no inhabitant.

38 They shall roar together like lions: they shall shake their manes like young lions.

39 In their heat I will set them drink: and I will make them drunk, [5] that they may slumber, and sleep an everlasting sleep, and awake no more, saith the Lord.

40 I will bring them down like lambs to the slaughter and like rams with kids.

41 How is Sesach taken and the renowned one of all the earth surprised? How is Babylon become an astonishment among the nations?

42 The sea is come up over Babylon: she is covered with the multitude of the waves thereof.

43 Her cities are become an astonishment, a land uninhabited and desolate, a land wherein none can dwell, nor son of man pass through it.

44 And I will visit against Bel in Babylon and I will bring forth out of his mouth that which he had swallowed down: and the nations shall no more flow together to him, for the wall also of Babylon shall fall.

45 Go out of the midst of her, my people: that every man may save his life from the fierce wrath of the Lord.

46 And lest your hearts faint, and ye fear for the rumour that shall be heard in the land: and a rumour shall come in one year, and after this year *another* rumour: and iniquity in the land, and ruler upon ruler.

47 Therefore, behold the days come, and I will visit the idols of Babylon: and her whole land shall be confounded and all her slain shall fall in the midst of her.

---

[4] Jer. 50, 38. [5] Jer. 51, 57.

48 And the heavens and the earth and all things that are in them shall give praise for Babylon: for spoilers shall come to her from the north, saith the Lord.

49 And as Babylon caused that there should fall slain in Israel: so of Babylon there shall fall slain in all the earth.

50 You that have escaped the sword, come away, stand not still: remember the Lord afar off and let Jerusalem come into your mind.

51 We are confounded, because we have heard reproach: shame hath covered our faces, because strangers are come upon the sanctuaries of the house of the Lord.

52 Therefore, behold the days come, saith the Lord, and I will visit her graven things: and in all her land the wounded shall groan:

53 If Babylon should mount up to heaven and establish her strength on high: from me there should come spoilers upon her, saith the Lord.

54 The noise of a cry from Babylon and great destruction from the land of the Chaldeans:

55 Because the Lord hath laid Babylon waste and destroyed out of her the great voice. And their wave shall roar like many waters: their voice hath made a noise.

56 Because the spoiler is come upon her, that is, upon Babylon, and her valiant men are taken, and their bow is weakened: because the Lord, who is a strong revenger, will surely repay.

57 And I will make her princes drunk, and her wise men and her captains and her rulers and her valiant men: and they shall sleep an everlasting sleep and shall awake no more, saith the king whose name is Lord of hosts.

58 Thus saith the Lord of hosts: That broad wall of Babylon shall be utterly broken down, and her high gates shall be burnt with fire, and the labours of the people shall come to nothing, and of the nations shall go to the fire and shall perish.

59 The word that Jeremias the prophet commanded Saraias the son of Nerias, the son of Maasias, when he went with king Sedecias to Babylon, in the fourth year of his reign. Now Saraias was chief over the prophecy.

60 And Jeremias wrote in one book all the evil that was to come upon Babylon: all these words that are written against Babylon.

61 And Jeremias said to Saraias: When thou shalt come into Babylon and shalt see and shalt read all these words.

CHAP. 52. ¹ 4 Kings, 24, 18; 2 Par. 36, 11. ² 4 Kings, 25, 1; Jer. 39, 1.

62 Thou shalt say: O Lord, thou hast spoken against this place to destroy it, so that there should be neither man nor beast to dwell therein and that it should be desolate for ever.

63 And when thou shalt have made an end of reading this book, thou shalt tie a stone to it and shalt throw it into the midst of the Euphrates.

64 And thou shalt say: Thus shall Babylon sink, and she shall not rise up from the affliction that I will bring upon her, and she shall be utterly destroyed. Thus far are the words of Jeremias.

CHAPTER 52

A recapitulation of the reign of Sedecias and the destruction of Jerusalem. The number of the captives.

SEDECIAS ¹ was one and twenty years old when he began to reign: and he reigned eleven years in Jerusalem: and the name of his mother was Amital, the daughter of Jeremias of Lobna.

2 And he did that which was evil in the eyes of the Lord, according to all that Joakim had done.

3 For the wrath of the Lord was against Jerusalem and against Juda, till he cast them out from his presence: and Sedecias revolted from the king of Babylon.

4 ² And it came to pass in the ninth year of his reign, in the tenth month, the tenth day of the month, that Nabuchodonosor the king of Babylon came, he and all his army, against Jerusalem: and they besieged it and built forts against it round about.

5 And the city was besieged until the eleventh year of king Sedecias.

6 And in the fourth month, the ninth day of the month, a famine overpowered the city: and there was no food for the people of the land.

7 And the city was broken up, and the men of war fled and went out of the city in the night by the way of the gate that is between the two walls and leadeth to the king's garden (the Chaldeans besieging the city round about): and they went by the way that leadeth to the wilderness.

8 But the army of the Chaldeans pursued after the king. And they overtook Sedecias in the desert which is near Jericho: and all his companions were scattered from him.

9 And when they had taken the king, they carried him to the king of Babylon to Reblatha, which is in the land of Emath: and he gave judgment upon him.

10 And the king of Babylon slew the sons of Sedecias before his eyes: and

he slew all the princes of Juda in Reblatha.

11 And he put out the eyes of Sedecias and bound him with fetters. And the king of Babylon brought him into Babylon: and he put him in prison till the day of his death.

12 And in the fifth month, the tenth day of the month, the same is the nineteenth year of Nabuchodonosor king of Babylon, came Nabuzardan the general of the army, who stood before the king of Babylon in Jerusalem.

13 And he burnt the house of the Lord and the king's house and all the houses of Jerusalem: and every great house he burnt with fire.

14 And all the army of the Chaldeans that were with the general broke down all the wall of Jerusalem round about.

15 But Nabuzardan the general carried away captives some of the poor people and of the rest of the common sort who remained in the city and of the fugitives that were fled over to the king of Babylon and the rest of the multitude.

16 But of the poor of the land, Nabuzardan the general left some for vinedressers and for husbandmen.

17 The Chaldeans also broke in pieces the brazen pillars that were in the house of the Lord and the bases and the sea of brass that was in the house of the Lord: and they carried all the brass of them to Babylon.

18 And they took the caldrons and the fleshhooks and the psalteries and the bowls and the little mortars and all the brazen vessels that had been used in the ministry: and

19 The general took away the pitchers and the censers and the pots and the basins and the candlesticks and the mortars and the cups: as many as were of gold, in gold: and as many as were of silver, in silver:

20 And the two pillars and one sea and twelve oxen of brass that were under the bases, which king Solomon had made in the house of the Lord. There was no weight of the brass of all these vessels.

21 And concerning the pillars, one pillar was eighteen cubits high, and a cord of twelve cubits compassed it about: but the thickness thereof was four fingers, and it was hollow within.

22 And chapiters of brass were upon both: and the height of one chapiter was five cubits: and network and pome-

granates were upon the chapiters round about, all of brass. The same of the second pillar and the pomegranates.

23 And there were ninety-six pomegranates hanging down: and the pomegranates, being a hundred in all, were compassed with network.

24 And the general took Saraias the chief priest and Sophonias the second priest and the three keepers of the entry.

25 He also took out of the city one eunuch that was chief over the men of war: and seven men of them that were near the king's person, that were found in the city: and a scribe, an officer of the army, who exercised the young soldiers: and threescore men of the people of the land that were found in the midst of the city.

26 And Nabuzardan the general took them and brought them to the king of Babylon, to Reblatha.

27 And the king of Babylon struck them and put them to death in Reblatha, in the land of Emath: and Juda was carried away captive out of his land.

28 This is the people whom Nabuchodonosor carried away captive: In the seventh year, three thousand and twenty-three Jews.

29 In the eighteenth year of Nabuchodonosor, eight hundred and thirty-two souls from Jerusalem.

30 In the three and twentieth year of Nabuchodonosor, Nabuzardan the general carried away of the Jews seven hundred *and* forty-five souls. So all the souls were four thousand six hundred.

31 And it came to pass in the seven and thirtieth [3] year of the captivity of Joachin king of Juda, in the twelfth month, the five and twentieth day of the month, that Evilmerodach king of Babylon, in the first year of his reign, lifted up the head of Joachin king of Juda and brought him forth out of prison.

32 And he spoke kindly to him and he set his throne above the thrones of the kings that were with him in Babylon.

33 And he changed his prison garments: and he ate bread before him always all the days of his life.

34 And for his diet a continual provision was allowed him by the king of Babylon, every day a portion, until the day of his death, all the days of his life.

3 4 Kings, 25, 27.

THE LAMENTATIONS OF

JEREMIAS

In these JEREMIAS laments in a most pathetical manner the miseries of his people, and the destruction of Jerusalem and the temple, in Hebrew verses, beginning with different letters according to the order of the Hebrew alphabet.

And it came to pass, after Israel was carried into captivity and Jerusalem was desolate, that Jeremias the prophet sat weeping, and mourned with this lamentation over Jerusalem. And with a sorrowful mind, sighing and moaning, he said:

CHAPTER 1

Aleph. HOW doth the city sit solitary that was full of people! *How* is the mistress of the Gentiles become as a widow: the princes of provinces made tributary!

2 *Beth.* ¹Weeping she hath wept in the night, and her tears are on her cheeks. There is none to comfort her among all them that were dear to her: all her friends have despised her and are become her enemies.

3 *Ghimel.* Juda hath removed her dwelling place, because of her affliction and the greatness of her bondage: she hath dwelt among the nations and she hath found no rest: all her persecutors have taken her in the midst of straits.

4 *Daleth.* The ways of Sion mourn, because there are none that come to the solemn feast: all her gates are broken down: her priests sigh: her virgins are in affliction and she is oppressed with bitterness.

5 *He.* Her adversaries are become her lords, her enemies are enriched: because the Lord hath spoken against her for the multitude of her iniquities. Her children are led into captivity, before the face of the oppressor.

6 *Vau.* And from the daughter of Sion all her beauty is departed: her princes are become like rams that find no pastures: and they are gone away without strength before the face of the pursuer.

7 *Zain.* Jerusalem hath remembered the days of her affliction and prevarication of all her desirable things which she had from the days of old, when her people fell in the enemy's hand and there was no helper. The enemies have seen her and have mocked at her sabbaths.

CHAP. 1. ¹ Jer. 42, 17. ² Jer. 14, 17.

And it came to pass. This preface was not written by Jeremias, but was added by the seventy interpreters, to give the reader to understand upon what occasion the Lamentations were published.

8 *Heth.* Jerusalem hath grievously sinned, therefore is she become unstable. All that honoured her have despised her, because they have seen her shame: but she sighed and turned backword.

9 *Teth.* Her filthiness is on her feet and hath not remembered her end: she is wonderfully cast down, not having a comforter. Behold, O Lord, my affliction, because the enemy is lifted up.

10 *Jod.* The enemy hath put out his hand to all her desirable things: for she hath seen the Gentiles enter into her sanctuary, of whom thou gavest commandment that they should not enter into thy church.

11 *Caph.* All her people sigh, they seek bread: they have given all their precious things for food to relieve the soul. See, O Lord, and consider, for I am become vile.

12 *Lamed.* O all ye that pass by the way, attend, and see if there be any sorrow like to my sorrow: for he hath made a vintage of me, as the Lord spoke in the day of his fierce anger.

13 *Mem.* From above he hath sent fire into my bones and hath chastised me: he hath spread a net for my feet, he hath turned me back: he hath made me desolate, wasted with scrrow all the day long.

14 *Nun.* The yoke of my iniquities hath watched: they are folded together in his hand and put upon my neck. My strength is weakened: the Lord hath delivered me into a hand out of which I am not able to rise.

15 *Samech.* The Lord hath taken away all my mighty men out of the midst of me: he hath called against me the time, to destroy my chosen men: the Lord hath trodden the winepress for the virgin daughter of Juda.

16 *Ain.* ²Therefore do I weep and my eyes run down with water, because the comforter, the relief of my soul, is far from me: my children are desolate because the enemy hath prevailed.

17 *Phe.* Sion hath spread forth her hands, there is none to comfort her: the Lord hath commanded against Jacob, his enemies are round about him: Jerusalem is as a menstruous woman among them.

18 *Sade.* The Lord is just, for I have provoked his mouth to wrath: hear, I pray you, all ye people, and see my sorrow: my virgins and my young men are gone into captivity.

19 *Coph.* I called for my friends, but they deceived me: my priests and my ancients pined away in the city, while they sought their food to relieve their souls.

20 *Res.* Behold, O Lord, for I am in distress, my bowels are troubled: my heart is turned within me, for I am full of bitterness: abroad the sword destroyeth and at home there is death alike.

21 *Sin.* They have heard that I sigh, and there is none to comfort me: all my enemies have heard of my evil, they have rejoiced that thou hast done it. Thou hast brought a day of consolation, and they shall be like unto me.

22 *Thau.* Let all their evil be present before thee: and make vintage of them, as thou hast made vintage of me for all my iniquities: for my sighs are many and my heart is sorrowful.

CHAPTER 2

Aleph. **N**OW hath the Lord covered with obscurity the daughter of Sion in his wrath! *How hath* he cast down from heaven to the earth the glorious one of Israel and hath not remembered his footstool in the day of his anger!

2 *Beth.* The Lord hath cast down headlong and hath not spared all that was beautiful in Jacob: he hath destroyed in his wrath the strong holds of the virgin of Juda and brought them down to the ground: he hath made the kingdom unclean, and the princes thereof.

3 *Ghimel.* He hath broken in his fierce anger all the horn of Israel: he hath drawn back his right hand from before the enemy: and he hath kindled in Jacob as it were a flaming fire devouring round about.

4 *Daleth.* He hath bent his bow as an enemy, he hath fixed his right hand as an adversary: and he hath killed all that was fair to behold in the tabernacle of the daughter of Sion: he hath poured out his indignation like fire.

5 *He.* The Lord is become as an enemy: he hath cast down Israel headlong, he hath overthrown all the walls thereof: he hath destroyed his strong holds and hath multiplied in the daughter of Juda the afflicted, both men and women.

6 *Vau.* And he hath destroyed his tent as a garden, he hath thrown down his tabernacle. The Lord hath caused feasts and sabbaths to be forgotten in Sion and hath delivered up king and priest to reproach and to the indignation of his wrath.

7 *Zain.* The Lord hath cast off his altar, he hath cursed his sanctuary: he hath delivered the walls of the towers thereof into the hand of the enemy. They have made a noise in the house of the Lord, as in the day of a solemn feast.

8 *Heth.* The Lord hath purposed to destroy the wall of the daughter of Sion: he hath stretched out his line and hath not withdrawn his hand from destroying. And the bulwark hath mourned, and the wall hath been destroyed together.

9 *Teth.* Her gates are sunk into the ground: he hath destroyed and broken her bars: her king and her princes *are* among the Gentiles: the law is no more, and her prophets have found no vision from the Lord.

10 *Jod.* The ancients of the daughter of Sion sit upon the ground, they have held their peace: they have sprinkled their heads with dust, they are girded with haircloth: the virgins of Jerusalem hang down their heads to the ground.

11 *Caph.* My eyes hath failed with weeping, my bowels are troubled: my liver is poured out upon the earth, for the destruction of the daughter of my people, when the children and the sucklings fainted away in the streets of the city.

12 *Lamed.* They said to their mothers: Where is corn and wine? when they fainted away as the wounded in the streets of the city: when they breathed out their souls in the bosoms of their mothers.

13 *Mem.* To what shall I compare thee, or to what shall I liken thee, O daughter of Jerusalem? To what shall I equal thee, that I may comfort thee, O virgin daughter of Sion? For great as the sea is thy destruction: Who shall heal thee?

14 *Nun.* Thy prophets have seen false and foolish things for thee: and they have not laid open thy iniquity, to excite thee to penance: but they have seen for thee false revelations and banishments.

CHAP. 2. Ver. 7. *He hath cursed his sanctuary.* That is, he permitted his sanctuary to be destroyed, as if it had not been consecrated, but execrable.

15 *Samech*. All they that passed by the way have clapped their hands at thee: they have hissed and wagged their heads at the daughter of Jerusalem, saying: Is this the city of perfect beauty, the joy of all the earth?

16 *Phe*. All thy enemies have opened their mouth against thee: they have hissed and gnashed with the teeth, and have said: We will swallow her up. Lo, this is the day which we looked for: we have found it, we have seen it.

17 [1] *Ain*. The Lord hath done that which he purposed, he hath fulfilled his word which he commanded in the days of old: he hath destroyed and hath not spared, and he hath caused the enemy to rejoice over thee and hath set up the horn of thy adversaries.

18 *Sade*. Their heart cried to the Lord upon the walls of the daughter of Sion: [2] Let tears run down like a torrent day and night: give thyself no rest, and let not the apple of thy eye cease.

19 *Coph*. Arise, give praise in the night, in the beginning of the watches: pour out thy heart like water before the face of the Lord: lift up thy hands to him for the life of thy little children that have fainted for hunger at the top of all the streets.

20 *Res*. Behold, O Lord, and consider whom thou hast thus dealt with. Shall women then eat their own fruit, their children of a span long? Shall the priest and the prophet be slain in the sanctuary of the Lord?

21 *Sin*. The child and the old man lie without on the ground: my virgins and my young men are fallen by the sword. Thou hast slain them in the day of thy wrath: thou hast killed and shewn them no pity.

22 *Thau*. Thou hast called as to a festival those that should terrify me round about, and there was none in the day of the wrath of the Lord that escaped and was left: those that I brought up and nourished, my enemy hath consumed them.

CHAPTER 3

Aleph.   I AM the man that see my poverty by the rod of his indignation.

2 *Aleph*. He hath led me and brought me into darkness, and not into light.

3 *Aleph*. Only against me he hath turned and turned again his hand all the day.

4 *Beth*. My skin and my flesh he hath made old: he hath broken my bones.

5 *Beth*. He hath built round about

me: and he hath compassed me with gall and labour.

6 *Beth*. He hath set me in dark places, as those that are dead for ever.

7 *Ghimel*. He hath built against me round about, that I may not get out: he hath made my fetters heavy.

8 *Ghimel*. Yea, and when I cry and entreat, he hath shut out my prayer.

9 *Ghimel*. He hath shut up my ways with square stones: he hath turned my paths upside down.

10 *Daleth*. He is become to me as a bear lying in wait: as a lion in secret places.

11 *Daleth*. He hath turned aside my paths and hath broken me in pieces: he hath made me desolate.

12 *Daleth*. He hath bent his bow and set me as a mark for his arrows.

13 *He*. He hath shot into my reins the daughters of his quiver.

14 *He*. I am made a derision to all my people, their song all the day long.

15 *He*. He hath filled me with bitterness, he hath inebriated me with wormwood.

16 *Vau*. And he hath broken my teeth one by one: he hath fed me with ashes.

17 *Vau*. And my soul is removed far off from peace: I have forgotten good things.

18 *Vau*. And I said: My end and my hope is perished from the Lord.

19 *Zain*. Remember my poverty and transgression, the wormwood and the gall.

20 *Zain*. I will be mindful and remember: and my soul shall languish within me.

21 *Zain*. These things I shall think over in my heart: therefore will I hope.

22 *Heth*. The mercies of the Lord that we are not consumed: because his commiserations have not failed.

23 *Heth*. *They are* new *every* morning: great is thy faithfulness.

24 *Heth*. The Lord is my portion, said my soul: therefore will I wait for him.

25 *Teth*. The Lord is good to them that hope in him, to the soul that seeketh him. •

26 *Teth*. It is good to wait with silence for the salvation of God.

27 *Teth*. It is good for a man, when he hath borne the yoke from his youth.

28 *Jod*. He shall sit solitary and hold his peace: because he hath taken it up upon himself.

29 *Jod*. He shall put his mouth in the dust, if so be there may be hope.

30 *Jod*. He shall give his cheek to him that striketh him: he shall be filled with reproaches.

CHAP. 2. [1] Lev. 26, 14; Deut. 28, 15. [2] Jer. 14, 17; Lament. 1, 16.

31 *Caph.* For the Lord will not cast off for ever.

32 *Caph.* For if he hath cast off, he will also have mercy, according to the multitude of his mercies.

33 *Caph.* For he hath not willingly afflicted nor cast off the children of men.

34 *Lamed.* To crush under his feet all the prisoners of the land,

35 *Lamed.* To turn aside the judgment of a man before the face of the most High,

36 *Lamed.* To destroy a man wrongfully in his judgment, the Lord hath not approved.

37 [1] *Mem.* Who is he that hath commanded a thing to be done, when the Lord commandeth it not?

38 *Mem.* Shall not both evil and good proceed out of the mouth of the Highest?

39 *Mem.* Why hath a living man murmured, man *suffering* for his sins?

40 *Nun.* Let us search our ways, and seek and return to the Lord.

41 *Nun.* Let us lift up our hearts with our hands to the Lord in the heavens.

42 *Nun.* We have done wickedly and provoked *thee* to wrath: therefore thou art inexorable.

43 *Samech.* Thou hast covered in thy wrath and hast struck us: thou hast killed and hast not spared.

44 *Samech.* Thou hast set a cloud before thee, that *our* prayer may not pass through.

45 *Samech.* Thou hast made me an outcast and refuse in the midst of the people.

46 *Phe.* All *our* enemies have opened their mouths against us.

47 *Phe.* Prophecy is become to us a fear and a snare and destruction.

48 *Phe.* My eye hath run down with streams of water for the destruction of the daughter of my people.

49 *Ain.* My eye is afflicted and hath not been quiet, because there was no rest:

50 *Ain.* Till the Lord regarded and looked down from the heavens.

51 *Ain.* My eye hath wasted my soul, because of all the daughters of my city.

52 *Sade.* My enemies have chased me and caught me like a bird, without cause.

53 *Sade.* My life is fallen into the pit, and they have laid a stone over me.

54 *Sade.* Waters have flowed over my head. I said: I am cut off.

55 *Coph.* I have called upon thy name, O Lord, from the lowest pit.

56 *Coph.* Thou hast heard my voice:

turn not away thy ear from my sighs and cries.

57 *Coph.* Thou drewest near in the day when I called upon thee. Thou saidst: Fear not.

58 *Res.* Thou hast judged, O Lord, the cause of my soul, *thou the* Redeemer of my life.

59 *Res.* Thou hast seen, O Lord, their iniquity against me: judge thou my judgment.

60 *Res.* Thou hast seen all their fury *and* all their thoughts against me.

61 *Sin.* Thou hast heard their reproach, O Lord, all their imaginations against me:

62 *Sin.* The lips of them that rise up against me and their devices against me all the day.

63 *Sin.* Behold their sitting down and their rising up: I am their song.

64 *Thau.* Thou shalt render them a recompense, O Lord, according to the works of their hands.

65 *Thau.* Thou shalt give them a buckler of heart, thy labour.

66 *Thau.* Thou shalt persecute them in anger and shalt destroy them from under the heavens, O Lord.

CHAPTER 4

Aleph. HOW is the gold become dim, the finest colour is changed, the stones of the sanctuary are scattered in the top of every street!

2 *Beth.* The noble sons of Sion and they that were clothed with the best gold: how are they esteemed as earthen vessels, the work of the potter's hands?

3 *Ghimel.* Even the sea monsters have drawn out the breast, they have given suck to their young: the daughter of my people is cruel, like the ostrich in the desert.

4 *Daleth.* The tongue of the sucking child hath stuck to the roof of his mouth for thirst: the little ones have asked for bread, and there was none to break it unto them.

5 *He.* They that were fed delicately have died in the streets; they that were brought up in scarlet have embraced the dung.

6 *Vau.* And the iniquity of the daughter of my people is made greater than the sin of Sodom, [1] which was overthrown in a moment, and hands took nothing in her.

7 *Zain.* Her Nazarites were whiter than snow, purer than milk, more ruddy than the old ivory, fairer than the sapphire.

8 *Heth.* Their face is *now* made

CHAP. 3. [1] Amos, 3, 6. CHAP. 4. [1] Gen. 19, 24.
Ver. 65. *A buckler of heart.* That is, affliction.
—*Labour.* That is, punishment.

blacker than coals and they are not known in the streets: their skin hath stuck to their bones. It is withered and is become like wood.

9 *Teth.* It was better with them that were slain by the sword than with them that died with hunger: for these pined away being consumed for want of the fruits of the earth.

10 *Jod.* The hands of the pitiful women have sodden their own children: they were their meat in the destruction of the daughter of my people.

11 *Caph.* The Lord hath accomplished his wrath, he hath poured out his fierce anger and he hath kindled a fire in Sion: and it hath devoured the foundations thereof.

12 *Lamed.* The kings of the earth and all the inhabitants of the world would not have believed that the adversary and the enemy should enter in by the gates of Jerusalem.

13 *Mem.* For the sins of her prophets and the iniquities of her priests that have shed the blood of the just in the midst of her.

14 *Nun.* They have wandered as blind men in the streets, they were defiled with blood: and when they could not *help walking* in it they held up their skirts.

15 *Samech.* Depart, you that are defiled, they cried out to them: Depart, get ye hence, touch not: for they quarrelled, and being removed, they said among the Gentiles: He will no more dwell among them.

16 *Phe.* The face of the Lord hath divided them, he will no more regard them: they respected not the persons of the priests, neither had they pity on the ancient.

17 *Ain.* While we were yet standing, our eyes failed, expecting help for us in vain, when we looked attentively towards a nation that was not able to save.

18 *Sade.* Our steps have slipped in the way of our streets, our end draweth near: our days are fulfilled, for our end is come.

19 *Coph.* Our persecutors were swifter than the eagles of the air: they pursued us upon the mountains, they lay in wait for us in the wilderness.

20 *Res.* The breath of our mouth, Christ the Lord, is taken in our sins. To whom we said: Under thy shadow we shall live among the Gentiles.

21 *Sin.* Rejoice and be glad, O daughter of Edom, that dwellest in the land

of Hus: to thee also shall the cup come, thou shalt be made drunk and naked.

22 *Thau.* Thy iniquity is accomplished, O daughter of Sion, he will no more carry thee away into captivity: he hath visited thy iniquity, O daughter of Edom, he hath discovered thy sins.

THE PRAYER OF JEREMIAS
THE PROPHET
CHAPTER 5

REMEMBER, O Lord, what is come upon us: consider and behold our reproach.

2 Our inheritance is turned to aliens: our houses to strangers.

3 We are become orphans without a father: our mothers are as widows.

4 We have drunk our water for money: we have bought our wood.

5 We were dragged by the necks: we were weary and no rest was given us.

6 We have given our hand to Egypt and to the Assyrians, that we might be satisfied with bread.

7 Our fathers have sinned and are not: and we have borne their iniquities.

8 Servants have ruled over us: there was none to redeem us out of their hand.

9 We fetched our bread at the peril of our lives, because of the sword in the desert.

10 Our skin was burnt as an oven, by reason of the violence of the famine.

11 They oppressed the women in Sion and the virgins in the cities of Juda.

12 The princes were hanged up by their hand: they did not respect the persons of the ancient.

13 They abused the young men indecently: and the children fell under the wood.

14 The ancients have ceased from the gates: the young men from the choir of the singers.

15 The joy of our heart is ceased: our dancing is turned into mourning.

16 The crown is fallen from our head. Woe to us, because we have sinned!

17 Therefore is our heart sorrowful: therefore are our eyes become dim.

18 For mount Sion, because it is destroyed: foxes have walked upon it.

19 But thou, O Lord, shalt remain for ever: thy throne from generation to generation.

20 Why wilt thou forget us for ever? *Why* wilt thou forsake us for a long time?

21 Convert us, O Lord, to thee, and we shall be converted: renew our days, as from the beginning.

22 But thou hast utterly rejected us: thou art exceedingly angry against us.

THE PROPHECY OF

BARUCH

BARUCH *was a man of noble extraction and learned in the law, secretary and disciple to the prophet* JEREMIAS, *and a sharer in his labours and persecutions. For this reason the ancient fathers have considered this book as a part of the prophecy of* JEREMIAS *and have usually quoted it under his name.*

CHAPTER 1

The Jews of Babylon send the book of Baruch with money to Jerusalem, requesting their brethren there to offer sacrifice, and to pray for the king and for them, acknowledging their manifold sins.

AND these are the words of the book which Baruch the son of Nerias, the son of Maasias, the son of Sedecias, the son of Sedei, the son of Helcias, wrote in Babylonia.

2 In the fifth year, in the seventh day of the month, at the time that the Chaldeans took Jerusalem and burnt it with fire.

3 And Baruch read the words of this book in the hearing of Jechonias the son of Joakim king of Juda, and in the hearing of all the people that came to *hear* the book,

4 And in the hearing of the nobles, the sons of the kings, and in the hearing of the ancients, and in the hearing of the people, from the least even to the greatest of them that dwelt in Babylonia, by the river Sedi.

5 And when they heard it they wept and fasted and prayed before the Lord.

6 And they made a collection of money according to every man's power.

7 And they sent *it* to Jerusalem, to Joakim the priest, the son of Helcias, the son of Salom, and to the priests and to all the people that were found with him in Jerusalem:

8 At the time when he received the vessels of the temple of the Lord, which had been taken away out of the temple, to return them into the land of Juda, the tenth day of the month Sivan: the silver vessels which Sedecias the son of Josias king of Juda had made:

9 After that Nabuchodonosor the king of Babylon had carried away Jechonias and the princes and all the powerful men and the people of the land from Jerusalem and brought them bound to Babylon.

10 And they said: Behold we have sent you money. Buy with it holocausts and frankincense and make meat offer-

ings and offerings for sin at the altar of the Lord our God:

11 And pray ye for the life of Nabuchodonosor the king of Babylon and for the life of Balthasar his son, that their days may be upon earth as the days of heaven:

12 And that the Lord may give us strength and enlighten our eyes, that we may live under the shadow of Nabuchodonosor the king of Babylon and under the shadow of Balthasar his son, and may serve them many days, and may find favour in their sight.

13 And pray ye for us to the Lord our God: for we have sinned against the Lord our God, and his wrath is not turned away from us even to this day.

14 And read ye this book which we have sent to you to be read in the temple of the Lord on feasts and proper days.

15 [1] And you shall say: To the Lord our God *belongeth* justice, but to us confusion of our face: as it is come to pass at this day to all Juda and to the inhabitants of Jerusalem,

16 To our kings and to our princes and to our priests and to our prophets and to our fathers.

17 [2] We have sinned before the Lord our God and have not believed him nor put our trust in him:

18 And we were not obedient to him and we have not hearkened to the voice of the Lord our God, to walk in his commandments which he hath given us.

19 From the day that he brought our fathers out of the land of Egypt, even to this day, we were disobedient to the Lord our God: and going astray we turned away from hearing his voice.

20 [3] And many evils have cleaved to us, and the curses which the Lord foretold by Moses his servant: who brought our fathers out of the land of Egypt, to give us a land flowing with milk and honey, as at this day.

21 And we have not hearkened to the voice of the Lord our God according to

CHAP. 1. [1] Bar. 2, 6. [2] Dan. 9, 5. [3] Deut. 28, 15.

all the words of the prophets whom he sent to us.

22 And we have gone away every man after the inclinations of his own wicked heart, to serve strange gods and to do evil in the sight of the Lord our God.

CHAPTER 2

A further confession of the sins of the people and of the justice of God.

WHEREFORE the Lord our God hath made good his word that he spoke to us and to our judges that have judged Israel and to our kings and to our princes, and to all Israel and Juda:

2 That the Lord would bring upon us great evils, *such* as never happened under heaven, as they have come to pass in Jerusalem, [1] according to the things that are written in the law of Moses:

3 That a man should eat the flesh of his own son and the flesh of his own daughter.

4 And he hath delivered them up to be under the hand of all the kings that are round about us, to be a reproach and desolation among all the people among whom the Lord hath scattered us.

5 And we are brought under and *are* not uppermost: because we have sinned against the Lord our God by not obeying his voice.

6 [2] To the Lord our God *belongeth* justice: but to us and to our fathers confusion of face, as at this day.

7 For the Lord hath pronounced against us all these evils that are come upon us:

8 And we have not entreated the face of the Lord our God, that we might return every one of us from our most wicked ways.

9 And the Lord hath watched over us for evil and hath brought it upon us: for the Lord is just in all his works which he hath commanded us.

10 And we have not hearkened to his voice to walk in the commandments of the Lord which he hath set before us.

11 [3] And now, O Lord God of Israel, who hast brought thy people out of the land of Egypt with a strong hand and with signs and with wonders and with thy great power and with a mighty arm, and hast made thee a name as at this day:

12 We have sinned, we have done wickedly, we have acted unjustly, O Lord our God, against all thy justices.

CHAP. 2. [1] Deut. 28, 53. [2] Bar. 1, 15. [3] Dan. 9, 15. [4] Deut. 26, 15; Isai. 63, 15. [5] Isai. 37, 17; 64, 9. [6] Ps. 113, 17.

CHAP. 2. Ver. 17. *Justice.* They that are in hell shall not give justice to God; that is, they shall not acknowledge and glorify his justice as penitent sinners do upon earth.

13 Let thy wrath be turned away from us: for we are left a few among the nations where thou hast scattered us.

14 Hear, O Lord, our prayers and our petitions and deliver us for thy own sake: and grant that we may find favour in the sight of them that have led us away:

15 That all the earth may know that thou art the Lord our God and that thy name is called upon Israel and upon his posterity.

16 [4] Look down upon us, O Lord, from thy holy house, and incline thy ear and hear us.

17 [5] Open thy eyes and behold. [6] For the dead that are in hell, whose spirit is taken away from their bowels, shall not give glory and justice to the Lord:

18 But the soul that is sorrowful for the greatness of evil *she hath done* and goeth bowed down and feeble, and the eyes that fail, and the hungry soul giveth glory and justice to thee the Lord.

19 For it is not for the justices of our fathers that we pour out our prayers and beg mercy in thy sight, O Lord our God:

20 But because thou hast sent out thy wrath and thy indignation upon us, as thou hast spoken by the hand of thy servants the prophets, saying:

21 Thus saith the Lord: Bow down your shoulder and your neck and serve the king of Babylon: and you shall remain in the land which I have given to your fathers.

22 But if you will not hearken to the voice of the Lord your God, to serve the king of Babylon: I will cause you to depart out of the cities of Juda and from without Jerusalem.

23 And I will take away from you the voice of mirth and the voice of joy and the voice of the bridegroom and the voice of the bride; and all the land shall be without any footstep of inhabitants.

24 And they hearkened not to thy voice, to serve the king of Babylon: and thou hast made good thy words, which thou spokest by the hands of thy servants the prophets that the bones of our kings and the bones of our fathers should be removed out of their place:

25 And behold they are cast out to the heat of the sun and to the frost of the night: and they have died in grievous pains, by famine and by the sword and in banishment.

26 And thou hast made the temple in which thy name was called upon as it is at this day, for the iniquity of the house of Israel and the house of Juda.

27 And thou hast dealt with us, O

Lord our God, according to all thy goodness and according to all that great mercy of thine:

28 As thou spokest by the hand of thy servant Moses, in the day when thou didst command him to write thy law before the children of Israel,

29 Saying: [7] If you will not hear my voice, this great multitude shall be turned into a very small number among the nations where I will scatter them:

30 For I know that the people will not hear me, for they are a people of a stiff neck. But they shall turn to their heart in the land of their captivity:

31 And they shall know that I am the Lord their God: and I will give them a heart, and they shall understand: and ears, and they shall hear.

32 And they shall praise me in the land of their captivity and shall be mindful of my name.

33 And they shall turn away themselves from their stiff neck and from their wicked deeds: for they shall remember the way of their fathers that sinned against me.

34 And I will bring them back again into the land which I promised with an oath to their fathers, Abraham, Isaac, and Jacob: and they shall be masters thereof. And I will multiply them, and they shall not be diminished.

35 And I will make with them another covenant that *shall be* everlasting, to be their God, and they shall be my people. And I will no more remove my people, the children of Israel, out of the land that I have given them.

CHAPTER 3

They pray for mercy, acknowledging that they are justly punished for forsaking true wisdom. A prophecy of Christ.

AND now, O Lord Almighty, the God of Israel, the soul in anguish and the troubled spirit crieth to thee:

2 Hear, O Lord, and have mercy, for thou art a merciful God: and have pity on us, for we have sinned before thee.

3 For thou remainest for ever: and shall we perish everlastingly?

4 O Lord Almighty, the God of Israel, hear now the prayer of the dead of Israel and of their children that have sinned before thee and have not hearkened to the voice of the Lord their God, wherefore evils have cleaved fast to us.

5 Remember not the iniquities of our fathers, but think upon thy hand and upon thy name at this time:

6 For thou art the Lord our God, and we will praise thee, O Lord:

7 Because for this end thou hast put thy fear in our hearts, to the intent that we should call upon thy name and

praise thee in our captivity: for we are converted from the iniquity of our fathers, who sinned before thee.

8 And behold we are at this day in our captivity, whereby thou hast scattered us to be a reproach and a curse and an offence, according to all the iniquities of our fathers who departed from thee, O Lord our God.

9 Hear, O Israel, the commandments of life: give ear, that thou mayst learn wisdom.

10 How happeneth it, O Israel, that thou art in thy enemies' land?

11 Thou art grown old in a strange country: thou art defiled with the dead: thou art counted with them that go down into hell!

12 Thou hast forsaken the fountain of wisdom.

13 For if thou hadst walked in the way of God, thou hadst surely dwelt in peace for ever.

14 Learn where is wisdom, where is strength, where is understanding: that thou mayst know also where is length of days and life, where is the light of the eyes and peace.

15 Who hath found out her place? And who hath gone in to her treasures?

16 Where are the princes of the nations, and they that rule over the beasts that are upon the earth?

17 That take their diversion with the birds of the air?

18 That hoard up silver and gold, wherein men trust, and there is no end of their getting? Who work in silver and are solicitous, and their works are unsearchable?

19 They are cut off and are gone down to hell, and others are risen up in their place.

20 Young men have seen the light and dwelt upon the earth: but the way of knowledge they have not known,

21 Nor have they understood the paths thereof, neither have their children received it: it is far from their face.

22 It hath not been heard of in the land of Chanaan: neither hath it been seen in Theman.

23 The children of Agar also that search after the wisdom that is of the earth, the merchants of Merrha and of Theman, and the tellers of fables and searchers of prudence and understanding: but the way of wisdom they have not known, neither have they remembered her paths.

24 O Israel, how great is the house of

[7] Lev. 26, 14; Deut. 28, 15.

CHAP. 3. Ver. 22. *Theman.* The capital city of Edom.

Ver. 23. *Agar.* The mother of the *Ismaelites.*

God, and how vast is the place of his possession!

25 It is great and hath no end: *it is* high and immense.

26 There were the giants, those renowed men that were from the beginning, of great stature, expert in war.

27 The Lord chose not them: neither did they find the way of knowledge. Therefore did they perish.

28 And because they had not wisdom, they perished through their folly.

29 Who hath gone up into heaven and taken her and brought her down from the clouds?

30 Who hath passed over the sea and found her and brought her preferably to chosen gold?

31 There is none that is able to know her ways, nor that can search out her paths:

32 But he that knoweth all things knoweth her and hath found her out with his understanding: he that prepared the earth for evermore and filled it with cattle and fourfooted beasts:

33 He that sendeth forth light, and it goeth: and hath called it, and it obeyeth him with trembling.

34 And the stars have given light in their watches and rejoiced.

35 They were called, and they said: Here we are. And with cheerfulness they have shined forth to him that made them.

36 This is our God, and there shall no other be accounted of in comparison of him.

37 He found out all the way of knowledge and gave it to Jacob his servant and to Israel his beloved.

38 Afterwards, he was seen upon earth and conversed with men.

CHAPTER 4

The prophet exhorts to the keeping of the law of wisdom and encourages the people to be patient and to hope for their deliverance.

THIS is the book of the commandments of God, and the law that is for ever. All they that keep it shall come to life: but they that have forsaken it, to death.

2 Return, O Jacob, and take hold of it: walk in the way by its brightness, in the presence of the light thereof.

3 Give not thy honour to another, nor thy dignity to a strange nation.

4 We are happy, O Israel: because the things that are pleasing to God are made known to us.

Ver. 38. *Was seen upon earth.* By the mystery of the Incarnation, by means of which the son of God came visibly amongst us and conversed with men. The prophets often speak of things to come as if they were past, to express the certainty of the event of the things foretold.

5 Be of good comfort, O people of God, the memorial of Israel.

6 You have been sold to the Gentiles, not for your destruction: but because you provoked God to wrath, you are delivered to your adversaries.

7 For you have provoked him who made you, the eternal God, offering sacrifice to devils and not to God.

8 For you have forgotten God who brought you up, and you have grieved Jerusalem that nursed you.

9 For she saw the wrath of God coming upon you, and she said: Give ear, all you that dwell near Sion, for God hath brought upon me great mourning:

10 For I have seen the captivity of my people, of my sons and my daughters, which the Eternal hath brought upon them.

11 For I nourished them with joy: but I sent them away with weeping and mourning.

12 Let no man rejoice over me, a widow and desolate: I am forsaken of many for the sins of my children, because they departed from the law of God.

13 And they have not known his justices nor walked by the ways of God's commandments: neither have they entered by the paths of his truth and justice.

14 Let them that dwell about Sion come and remember the captivity of my sons and daughters, which the Eternal hath brought upon them.

15 For he hath brought a nation upon them from afar, a wicked nation and of a strange tongue:

16 Who have neither reverenced the ancient nor pitied children, and have carried away the beloved of the widow, and have left *me* all alone without children.

17 But as for me, what help can I give you?

18 But he that hath brought the evils upon you, he will deliver you out of the hands of your enemies.

19 Go your way, my children, go your way: for I am left alone.

20 I have put off the robe of peace and have put upon me the sackcloth of supplication, and I will cry to the most High in my days.

21 Be of good comfort, my children. Cry to the Lord: and he will deliver you out of the hand of the princes your enemies.

22 For my hope is in the Eternal that he will save you: and joy is come upon me from the Holy One, because of the mercy which shall come to you from our everlasting Saviour.

23 For I sent you forth with mourning and weeping: but the Lord will bring you back to me with joy and gladness for ever.

24 For as the neighbours of Sion have now seen your captivity from God: so shall they also shortly see your salvation from God, which shall come upon you with great honour and everlasting glory.

25 My children, suffer patiently the wrath that is come upon you. For thy enemy hath persecuted thee: but thou shalt quickly see his destruction and thou shalt get up upon his neck.

26 My delicate ones have walked rough ways, for they were taken away as a flock made a prey by the enemies.

27 Be of good comfort, my children and cry to the Lord: for you shall be remembered by him that hath led you away.

28 For, as it was your mind to go astray from God: so when you return again, you shall seek him ten times as much.

29 For he that hath brought evils upon you shall bring you everlasting joy again with your salvation.

30 Be of good heart, O Jerusalem: for he exhorteth thee that named thee.

31 The wicked that have afflicted thee shall perish: and they that have rejoiced at thy ruin shall be punished.

32 The cities which thy children have served shall be punished: and she that received thy sons.

33 For as she rejoiced at thy ruin and was glad of thy fall: so shall she be grieved for her own desolation.

34 And the joy of her multitude shall be cut off: and her gladness shall be turned to mourning.

35 For fire shall come upon her from the Eternal, long to endure: and she shall be inhabited by devils for a great time.

36 [1] Look about thee, O Jerusalem, towards the east, and behold the joy that cometh to thee from God.

37 For behold thy children come whom thou sentest away scattered: they come gathered together from the east even to the west, at the word of the Holy One, rejoicing for the honour of God.

CHAPTER 5

Jerusalem is invited to rejoice and behold the return of her children out of their captivity.

PUT off, O Jerusalem, the garment of thy mourning and affliction: and put on the beauty and honour of that everlasting glory which thou hast from God.

2 God will clothe thee with the double garment of justice and will set a crown on thy head of everlasting honour.

3 For God will shew his brightness in thee to every one under heaven.

4 For thy name shall be named to thee by God for ever: the peace of justice and honour of piety.

5 Arise, O Jerusalem, and stand on high, and look about towards the east, [1] and behold thy children gathered together from the rising to the setting sun, by the word of the Holy One, rejoicing in the remembrance of God.

6 For they went out from thee on foot, led by the enemies: but the Lord will bring them to thee, exalted with honour as children of the kingdom.

7 For God hath appointed to bring down every high mountain and the everlasting rocks and to fill up the valleys, to make them even with the ground: that Israel may walk diligently to the honour of God.

8 Moreover the woods and every sweet-smelling tree have overshadowed Israel by the commandment of God.

9 For God will bring Israel with joy in the light of his majesty, with mercy and justice that cometh from him.

CHAPTER 6

The epistle of Jeremias to the captives, as a preservative against idolatry.

A COPY [1] of the epistle that Jeremias sent to them that were to be led away captives into Babylon by the king of Babylon, to declare to them according to what was commanded him by God.

1 FOR the sins that you have committed before God, you shall be carried away captives into Babylon by Nabuchodonosor the king of Babylon.

2 And when you are come into Babylon, you shall be there many years and for a long time, even to seven generations: and after that I will bring you away from thence with peace.

3 [2] But now, you shall see in Babylon gods of gold and of silver and of stone and of wood, borne upon shoulders, causing fear to the Gentiles.

4 Beware therefore that you imitate not the doings of others and be afraid and the fear of them seize upon you.

5 But when you see the multitude behind and before, adoring them, say you in your hearts: Thou oughtest to be adored, O Lord.

CHAP. 4. [1] Bar. 5, 5. CHAP. 5. [1] Bar. 4, 36.
CHAP. 6. [1] Jer. 25, 9. [2] Isai. 44, 10.

CHAP. 4. Ver. 32. *She that received.* That is, Babylon.
CHAP. 6. Ver. 2. *Seven generations.* That is, seventy years.

6 For my angel is with you, and I myself will demand an account of your souls.

7 For their tongue that is polished by the craftsmen and themselves, laid over with gold and silver, are false things, and they cannot speak.

8 And as if it were for a maiden that loveth to go gay: so do they take gold and make them up.

9 Their gods have golden crowns upon their heads: whereof the priests secretly convey away from them gold and silver and bestow it on themselves.

10 Yea, and they give thereof to prostitutes, and they dress out harlots: and again, when they receive it of the harlots, they adorn their gods.

11 And these gods cannot defend themselves from the rust and the moth.

12 But when they have covered them with a purple garment, they wipe their face because of the dust of the house which is very much among them.

13 This holdeth a sceptre as a man, as a judge of the country, but cannot put to death one that offendeth him.

14 And this hath in his hand a sword or an axe, but cannot save himself from war or from robbers: whereby be it known to you that they are not gods.

15 Therefore, fear them not. For as a vessel that a man uses when it is broken becometh useless, even so are their gods.

16 When they are placed in the house, their eyes are full of dust by the feet of them that go in.

17 And as the gates are made sure on every side upon one that hath offended the king, or like a dead man carried to the grave, so do the priests secure the doors with bars and locks, lest they be stripped by thieves.

18 They light candles to them, and in great number, of which they cannot see one: but they are like beams in the house.

19 And they say that the creeping things which are of the earth gnaw their hearts, while they eat them and their garments, and they feel it not.

20 Their faces are black with the smoke that is made in the house.

21 Owls and swallows and other birds fly upon their bodies and upon their heads, and cats in like manner.

22 Whereby you may know that they are no gods. Therefore fear them not.

23 The gold also which they have is for shew, but, except a man wipe off the rust, they will not shine: for neither when they were molten did they feel it.

24 Men buy them at a high price, whereas there is no breath in them.

25 [3] And having not the use of feet,

[3] Isai. 46, 7.

they are carried upon shoulders, declaring to men how vile they are. Be they confounded also that worship them.

26 Therefore if they fall to the ground they rise not up again of themselves, nor if a man set them upright will they stand by themselves: but their gifts shall be set before them, as to the dead.

27 The things that are sacrificed to them, their priests sell and abuse: in like manner also their wives take part of them, but give nothing of it either to the sick or to the poor.

28 The childbearing and menstruous women touch their sacrifices. Knowing therefore by these things that they are not gods, fear them not.

29 For how can they be called gods? Because women set offerings before the gods of silver and of gold and of wood:

30 And priests sit in their temples, having their garments rent and their heads and beards shaven and nothing upon their heads.

31 And they roar and cry before their gods, as men do at the feast when one is dead.

32 The priests take away their garments and clothe their wives and their children.

33 And whether it be evil that one doth unto them or good, they are not able to recompense it: neither can they set up a king nor put him down.

34 In like manner they can neither give riches nor requite evil. If a man make a vow to them and perform it not, they cannot require it.

35 They cannot deliver a man from death: nor save the weak from the mighty.

36 They cannot restore the blind man to his sight: nor deliver a man from distress.

37 They shall not pity the widow: nor do good to the fatherless.

38 Their gods of wood and of stone and of gold and of silver are like the stones that are hewn out of the mountains: and they that worship them shall be confounded.

39 How then is it to be supposed, or to be said, that they are gods?

40 Even the Chaldeans themselves dishonour them: who when they hear of one dumb that cannot speak, they present him to Bel, entreating him that he may speak,

41 As though they could be sensible that have no motion themselves. And they, when they shall perceive this, will leave them: for their gods themselves have no sense.

42 The women also with cords about

them sit in the ways burning olive stones.

43 And when any one of them, drawn away by some passenger, lieth with him, she upbraideth her neighbour that she was not thought as worthy as herself, nor her cord broken.

44 But all things that are done about them are false: How is it then to be thought, or to be said, that they are gods?

45 And they are made by workmen and by goldsmiths. They shall be nothing else but what the priests will have them to be.

46 For the artificers themselves that make them are of no long continuance. Can those things then that are made by them be gods?

47 But they have left false things and reproach to them that come after.

48 For when war cometh upon them or evils, the priests consult with themselves where they may hide themselves with them.

49 How then can they be thought to be gods that can neither deliver themselves from war nor save themselves from evils?

50 For seeing they are but of wood and laid over with gold and with silver, it shall be known hereafter that they are false things by all nations and kings: and it shall be manifest that they are no gods, but the work of men's hands, and that there is no work of God in them.

51 Whence therefore is it known that they are not gods, but the work of men's hands, and no work of God is in them?

52 They cannot set up a king over the land nor give rain to men.

53 They determine no causes nor deliver countries from oppression; because they can do nothing and are as daws between heaven and earth.

54 For when fire shall fall upon the house of *these* gods of wood and of silver and of gold their priests indeed will flee away and be saved: but they themselves shall be burnt in the midst like beams.

55 And they cannot withstand a king and war. How then can it be supposed or admitted that they are gods?

56 Neither are these gods of wood and of stone and laid over with gold and with silver able to deliver themselves from thieves or robbers. They that are stronger than them

57 Shall take from them the gold and silver and the raiment wherewith they are clothed and shall go their way: neither shall they help themselves.

58 Therefore it is better to be a king that sheweth his power: or else a profitable vessel in the house, with which the owner thereof will be well satisfied: or a door in the house to keep things safe that are therein, than such false gods.

59 The sun and the moon and the stars, being bright and sent forth for profitable uses, are obedient.

60 In like manner the lightning, when it breaketh forth, is easy to be seen: and after the same manner the wind bloweth in every country.

61 And the clouds when God commandeth them to go over the whole world do that which is commanded them.

62 The fire also being sent from above to consume mountains and woods doth as it is commanded. But these neither in shew nor in power are like to any one of them.

63 Wherefore it is neither to be thought nor to be said that they are gods: since they are neither able to judge causes nor to do any good to men.

64 Knowing therefore that they are not gods, fear them not.

65 For neither can they curse kings nor bless them.

66 Neither do they shew signs in the heaven to the nations, nor shine as the sun, nor give light as the moon.

67 Beasts are better than they, which can fly under a covert and help themselves.

68 Therefore there is no manner of appearance that they are gods: so fear them not.

69 For as a scarecrow in a garden of cucumbers keepeth nothing, so are their gods of wood and of silver and laid over with gold.

70 They are no better than a white thorn in a garden, upon which every bird sitteth. In like manner also their gods of wood and laid over with gold and with silver are like to a dead body cast forth in the dark.

71 By the purple also and the scarlet which are motheaten upon them, you shall know that they are not gods. And they themselves at last are consumed and shall be a reproach in the country.

72 Better therefore is the just man that hath no idols: for he shall be far from reproach.

Ver. 56. *They that are stronger than them.* That is, robbers and thieves are stronger than these idols, being things without life or motion.

THE PROPHECY OF

EZECHIEL

EZECHIEL, *whose name signifies the* STRENGTH OF GOD, *was of the priestly race and of the number of the captives that were carried away to Babylon with king Joachin. He was contemporary with Jeremias, prophesied to the same effect in Babylon as Jeremias did in Jerusalem, and is said to have ended his days in like manner, by martyrdom.*

CHAPTER 1

The time of Ezechiel's prophecy. He sees a glorious vision.

NOW it came to pass in the thirtieth year, in the fourth *month*, on the fifth *day* of the month, when I was in the midst of the captives [1] by the river Chobar, the heavens were opened, and I saw the visions of God.

2 On the fifth day of the month, the same was the fifth year of the captivity of king Joachin,

3 The word of the Lord came to Ezechiel the priest, the son of Buzi, in the land of the Chaldeans, by the river Chobar: and the hand of the Lord was there upon him.

4 And I saw, and behold a whirlwind came out of the north, and a great cloud, and a fire infolding *it!* And brightness was about it, and out of the midst thereof, that is, out of the midst of the fire, as it were the resemblance of amber.

5 And in the midst thereof the likeness of four living creatures: and this was their appearance. There was the likeness of a man in them.

6 Every one had four faces, and every one four wings.

7 Their feet were straight feet, and the sole of their foot was like the sole of a calf's foot: and they sparkled like the appearance of glowing brass.

8 And *they* had the hands of a man under their wings on *their* four sides:

and they had faces and wings on the four sides,

9 And the wings of one were joined to the wings of another. They turned not when they went: but every one went straight forward.

10 And as for the likeness of their faces: there was the face of a man, and the face of a lion on the right side of all the four, and the face of an ox on the left side of all the four, and the face of an eagle over all the four.

11 And their faces and their wings were stretched upward: two wings of every one were joined, and two covered their bodies.

12 And every one of them went straight forward. Whither the impulse of the spirit was to go, thither they went: and they turned not when they went.

13 And as for the likeness of the living creatures: their appearance was like that of burning coals of fire, and like the appearance of lamps. This was the vision running to and fro in the midst of the living creatures, a bright fire and lightning going forth from the fire.

14 And the living creatures ran and returned like flashes of lightning.

15 Now as I beheld the living creatures, there appeared upon the earth by the living creatures one wheel with four faces.

16 And the appearance of the wheels and the work of them was like the appearance of the sea: and the four had all one likeness. And their appearance and their work *was* as it were a wheel in the midst of a wheel.

17 When they went, they went by their four parts: and they turned not when they went.

18 The wheels had also a size and a height and a dreadful appearance: [2] and the whole body was full of eyes round about all the four.

19 And when the living creatures went the wheels also went together by them: and when the living creatures

CHAP. 1. [1] Ezech. 3, 23; 10, 20; 43, 3. [2] Ezech. 10, 12.

CHAP. 1. Ver. 1. *The thirtieth year.* Either of the age of Ezechiel; or, as others will have it, from the solemn covenant made in the eighteenth year of the reign of Josias. 4 Kings, 23.

Ver. 5. *Living creatures.* Cherubims (as appears from Ecclesiasticus, 49, 10) represented to the prophet under these mysterious shapes, as supporting the throne of God, and as it were drawing his chariot. All this chapter appeared so obscure and full of mysteries to the ancient Hebrews that, as we learn from St. Jerome (Ep. ad Paulin.), they suffered none to read it before they were thirty years old.

Ver. 17. *When they went, they went by their four parts.* That is, indifferently to any of their sides, either forward or backward: to the right or to the left.

were lifted up from the earth the wheels also were lifted up with them.

20 Whithersoever the spirit went, thither as the spirit went the wheels also were lifted up withal and followed it: for the spirit of life was in the wheels.

21 When those went these went, and when those stood these stood, and when those were lifted up from the earth the wheels also were lifted up together and followed them: for the spirit of life was in the wheels.

22 And over the heads of the living creatures was the likeness of the firmament, as the appearance of crystal, terrible to behold, and stretched out over their heads above.

23 And under the firmament were their wings straight, the one toward the other. Every one with two wings covered his body, and the other was covered in like manner.

24 And I heard the noise of their wings, like the noise of many waters, as it were the voice of the most high God. When they walked, it was like the voice of a multitude, like the noise of an army: and when they stood, their wings were let down.

25 For when a voice came from above the firmament that was over their heads, they stood and let down their wings.

26 And above the firmament that was over their heads was the likeness of a throne, as the appearance of the sapphire stone: and upon the likeness of the throne was a likeness as of the appearance of a man above upon it.

27 And I saw as it were the resemblance of amber, as the appearance of fire within it round about: from his loins and upward, and from his loins downward, I saw as it were the resemblance of fire shining round about.

28 As the appearance of the rainbow when it is in a cloud on a rainy day: this was the appearance of the brightness round about.

CHAPTER 2

The prophet receives his commission.

THIS was the vision of the likeness of the glory of the Lord. And I saw, and I fell upon my face, and I heard the voice of one that spoke. And he said to me: Son of man, stand upon thy feet, and I will speak to thee.

2 And the spirit entered into me after that he spoke to me: and he set me upon my feet, and I heard him speaking to me,

3 And saying: Son of man, I send thee to the children of Israel, to a rebellious people that hath revolted from me. They and their fathers have transgressed my covenant even unto this day.

4 And they to whom I send thee are children of a hard face and of an obstinate heart: and thou shalt say to them: Thus saith the Lord God:

5 If so be they at least will hear, and if so be they will forbear, for they are a provoking house: and they shall know that there hath been a prophet in the midst of them.

6 And thou, O son of man, fear not, neither be thou afraid of their words: for thou art among unbelievers and destroyers, and thou dwellest with scorpions. Fear not their words, neither be thou dismayed at their looks: for they are a provoking house.

7 And thou shalt speak my words to them, if perhaps they will hear and forbear: for they provoke me to anger.

8 But thou, O son of man, hear all that I say to thee: and do not thou provoke me, as that house provoketh me. Open thy mouth, and eat what I give thee.

9 And I looked, and behold a hand was sent to me, wherein was a book rolled up. And he spread it before me.
[1] And it was written within and without: and there were written in it lamentations and canticles and woe.

CHAPTER 3

The prophet eats the book and receives further instructions. The office of a watchman.

AND he said to me: Son of man, eat all that thou shalt find: eat this book and go speak to the children of Israel.

2 And I opened my mouth, and he caused me to eat that book:

3 And he said to me: Son of man, thy belly shall eat, and thy bowels shall be filled with this book which I give thee.
[1] And I did eat it: and it was sweet as honey in my mouth.

4 And he said to me: Son of man, go to the house of Israel, and thou shalt speak my words to them.

5 For thou art not sent to a people of a profound speech and of an unknown tongue, *but* to the house of Israel:

6 Nor to many nations of a strange speech and of an unknown tongue, whose words thou canst not understand: and if thou wert sent to them, they would hearken to thee.

CHAP. 2. [1] Apoc. 5, 1. CHAP. 3. [1] Apoc. 10, 9, 10.

CHAP. 3. Ver. 1. *Eat this book and go speak to the children of Israel.* By this eating of the book was signified the diligent attention and affection with which we are to receive and embrace the word of God; and to let it, as it were, sink into our interior by devout meditation.

7 But the house of Israel will not hearken to thee, because they will not hearken to me: for all the house of Israel are of a hard forehead and an obstinate heart.

8 Behold I have made thy face stronger than their faces: and thy forehead harder than their foreheads.

9 I have made thy face like an adamant and like flint. Fear them not, neither be thou dismayed at their presence: for they are a provoking house.

10 And he said to me: Son of man, receive in thy heart and hear with thy ears all the words that I speak to thee:

11 And go get thee in to them of the captivity, to the children of thy people: and thou shalt speak to them and shalt say to them: Thus saith the Lord: If so be they will hear and will forbear.

12 And the spirit took me up, and I heard behind me the voice of a great commotion, *saying:* Blessed *be* the glory of the Lord from his place.

13 And the noise of the wings of the living creatures striking one against another, and the noise of the wheels following the living creatures, and the noise of a great commotion.

14 The spirit also lifted me and took me up: and I went away in bitterness in the indignation of my spirit: for the hand of the Lord was with me, strengthening me.

15 And I came to them of the captivity, to the heap of new corn, to them that dwelt by the river Chobar, and I sat where they sat: and I remained there seven days, mourning in the midst of them.

16 And at the end of seven days the word of the Lord came to me, saying:

17 [2] Son of man, I have made thee a watchman to the house of Israel: and thou shalt hear the word out of my mouth and shalt tell it them from me.

18 If, when I say to the wicked, Thou shalt surely die: thou declare it not to him nor speak *to him* that he may be converted from his wicked way and live, the same wicked man shall die in his iniquity but I will require his blood at thy hand.

19 But if thou give warning to the wicked, and he be not converted from his wickedness and from his evil way: he indeed shall die in his iniquity but thou hast delvered thy soul.

20 Moreover, if the just man shall turn away from his justice and shall commit iniquity: I will lay a stumblingblock before him. He shall die, because thou hast not given him warning. He shall die in his sin and his justices which he hath done, shall not be remembered. But I will require his blood at thy hand.

21 But if thou warn the just man, that the just may not sin, and he doth not sin: living he shall live because thou hast warned him, and thou hast delivered thy soul.

22 And the hand of the Lord was upon me, and he said to me: Rise *and* go forth into the plain, and there I will speak to thee.

23 And I rose up and went forth into the plain: and behold the glory of the Lord stood there, like the glory which [3] I saw by the river Chobar. And I fell upon my face.

24 And the spirit entered into me and set me upon my feet: and he spoke to me and said to me: Go in and shut thyself up in the midst of thy house.

25 And thou, O son of man, behold they shall put bands upon thee, and they shall bind thee with them: and thou shalt not go forth from the midst of them.

26 And I will make thy tongue stick fast to the roof of thy mouth, and thou shalt be dumb, *and* not as a man that reproveth: because they are a provoking house.

27 But when I shall speak to thee, I will open thy mouth, and thou shalt say to them: Thus saith the Lord God: He that heareth, let him hear: and he that forbeareth, let him forbear. For they are a provoking house.

CHAPTER 4

A prophetic description of the siege of Jerusalem and of the famine that shall reign there.

AND thou, O son of man, take thee a tile and lay it before thee: and draw upon it the plan of the city of Jerusalem.

2 And lay siege against it and build forts and cast up a mount and set a camp against it and place battering rams round about *it.*

3 And take unto thee an iron pan and set it for a wall of iron between thee and the city and set thy face resolutely against it: and it shall be besieged, and thou shalt lay siege against it. It is a sign to the house of Israel.

4 And thou shalt sleep upon thy left side and shalt lay the iniquities of the house of Israel upon it, according to the number of the days that thou shalt sleep upon it, and thou shalt take upon thee their iniquity.

5 And I have laid upon thee the years of their iniquity, according to the number of the days, three hundred and

[2] Ezech. 33, 7. [3] Ezech. 1, 3.

Ver. 15. *The heap of new corn.* It was the name of a place; in Hebrew, *tel abib.*

ninety days: and thou shalt bear the iniquity of the house of Israel.

6 And when thou hast accomplished this, thou shalt sleep again upon thy right side, [1] and thou shalt take upon thee the iniquity of the house of Juda forty days: a day for a year, yea, a day for a year, I have appointed to thee.[2]

7 And thou shalt turn thy face to the siege of Jerusalem, and thy arm shall be stretched out: and thou shalt prophesy against it.

8 Behold I have encompassed thee with bands: and thou shalt not turn thyself from one side to the other till thou hast ended the days of thy siege.

9 And take to thee wheat and barley and beans and lentils and millet and fitches, and put them in one vessel, and make thee bread thereof according to the number of the days that thou shalt lie upon thy side: three hundred and ninety days shalt thou eat thereof.

10 And thy meat that thou shalt eat shall be in weight twenty staters a day: from time to time thou shalt eat it.

11 And thou shalt drink water by measure, the sixth part of a hin: from time to time thou shalt drink it.

12 And thou shalt eat it as barley bread baked under the ashes: and thou shalt cover it in their sight with the dung that cometh out of a man.

13 And the Lord said: So shall the children of Israel [3] eat their bread all filthy among the nations whither I will cast them out.

14 And I said: Ah, ah, ah, O Lord God, behold my soul hath not been defiled, and from my infancy even till now, I have not eaten any thing that died of itself or was torn by beasts, and no unclean flesh hath entered into my mouth.

15 And he said to me: Behold I have given thee neat's dung for man's dung and thou shalt make thy bread therewith.

16 And he said to me: Son of man: [4] Behold, I will break in pieces the staff of bread in Jerusalem. And they shall eat bread by weight and with care: and they shall drink water by measure and in distress.

17 So that when bread and water fail, every man may fall against his brother, and they may pine away in their iniquities.

CHAPTER 5

The judgments of God upon the Jews are foreshewn under the type of the prophet's hair.

AND thou, son of man, take thee a sharp knife that shaveth the hair: and cause it to pass over thy head

and over thy beard: and take thee a balance to weigh in. And divide the *hair*.

2 A third part thou shalt burn with fire in the midst of the city, according to the fulfilling of the days of the siege: and thou shalt take a third part and cut it in pieces with the knife all round about: and the other third part thou shalt scatter in the wind, and I will draw out the sword after them.

3 And thou shalt take thereof a small number and shalt bind them in the skirt of thy cloak.

4 And thou shalt take of them again and shalt cast them in the midst of the fire and shalt burn them with fire: and out of it shall come forth a fire into all the house of Israel.

5 Thus saith the Lord God: This is Jerusalem. I have set her in the midst of the nations and the countries round about her.

6 And she hath despised my judgments, so as to be more wicked than the Gentiles; and my commandments, more than the countries that are round about her: for they have cast off my judgments and have not walked in my commandments.

7 Therefore thus saith the Lord God: Because you have surpassed the Gentiles that are round about you and have not walked in my commandments and have not kept my judgments and have not done according to the judgments of the nations that are round about you:

8 Therefore thus saith the Lord God: Behold I *come* against thee and I myself will execute judgments in the midst of thee in the sight of the Gentiles.

9 And I will do in thee that which I have not done and the like to which I will do no more: because of all thy abominations.

10 Therefore the fathers shall eat the sons in the midst of thee, and the sons shall eat their fathers: and I will execute judgments in thee, and I will scatter thy whole remnant into every wind.

11 Therefore *as* I live, saith the Lord God: Because thou hast violated my sanctuary with all thy offences and with all thy abominations: I will also break thee in pieces, and my eye shall not spare, and I will not have any pity.

12 A third part of thee shall die with the pestilence and shall be consumed with famine in the midst of thee: and a third part of thee shall fall by the sword round about thee: and a third part of thee will I scatter into every

CHAP. 4. [1] Num. 13, 34. [2] Jer. 52, 30. [3] Osee, 9, 4. [4] Ezech. 5, 16; 14, 13.

CHAP. 4. Ver. 11. *Hin.* That is, a measure of liquids containing about ten pints.

wind, and I will draw out a sword after them.

13 [1] And I will accomplish my fury and will cause my indignation to rest upon them, and I will be comforted: and they shall know that I the Lord have spoken it in my zeal, when I shall have accomplished my indignation in them.

14 And I will make thee desolate and a reproach among the nations that are round about thee, in the sight of every one that passeth by.

15 And thou shalt be a reproach and a scoff, an example and an astonishment amongst the nations that are round about thee, when I shall have executed judgments in thee in anger and in indignation and in wrathful rebukes.

16 I the Lord have spoken it. When I shall send upon them the grievous arrows of famine which shall bring death and which I will send to destroy you, I will gather together famine against you: [2] and I will break among you the staff of bread.

17 And I will send in upon you famine and evil beasts unto utter destruction: and pestilence, and blood shall pass through thee: and I will bring in the sword upon thee. I the Lord have spoken it.

CHAPTER 6

*The punishment of Israel for their idolatry.
A remnant shall be blessed.*

AND the word of the Lord came to me, saying:

2 Son of man, set thy face towards the mountains of Israel and prophesy against them.

3 And say: [1] Ye mountains of Israel, hear the word of the Lord God: Thus saith the Lord God to the mountains and to the hills and to the rocks and the valleys: Behold, I will bring upon you the sword and I will destroy your high places.

4 And I will throw down your altars, and your idols shall be broken in pieces: and I will cast down your slain before your idols.

5 And I will lay the dead carcasses of the children of Israel before your idols: and I will scatter your bones round about your altars,

6 In all your dwelling places. The cities shall be laid waste and the high places shall be thrown down and destroyed, and your altars shall be abolished and shall be broken in pieces: and your idols shall be no more, and your temples shall be destroyed, and your works shall be defaced.

CHAP. 5. [1] Zach. 1, 8. [2] Ezech. 4, 16; 14, 13.
CHAP. 6. [1] Ezech. 36, 1.

7 And the slain shall fall in the midst of you: and you shall know that I am the Lord.

8 And I will leave in you some that shall escape the sword among the nations when I shall have scattered you through the countries.

9 And they that are saved of you shall remember me amongst the nations to which they are carried captives: because I have broken their heart that was faithless and revolted from me and their eyes that went a fornicating after their idols: and they shall be displeased with themselves because of the evils which they have committed in all their abominations.

10 And they shall know that I the Lord have not spoken in vain that I would do this evil to them.

11 Thus saith the Lord God: Strike with thy hand and stamp with thy foot and say: Alas, for all the abominations of the evils of the house of Israel: for they shall fall by the sword, by the famine, and by the pestilence.

12 He that is far off shall die of the pestilence: and he that is near shall fall by the sword: and he that remaineth and is besieged shall die by the famine: and I will accomplish my indignation upon them.

13 And you shall know that I am the Lord, when your slain shall be amongst your idols, round about your altars, in every high hill and on all the tops of mountains and under every woody tree and under every thick oak, the place where they burnt sweet smelling frankincense to all their idols.

14 And I will stretch forth my hand upon them: and I will make the land desolate and abandoned, from the desert of Deblatha, in all their dwelling places: and they shall know that I am the Lord.

CHAPTER 7

The final desolation of Israel from which few shall escape.

AND the word of the Lord came to me, saying:

2 And thou son of man, thus saith the Lord God to the land of Israel: The end is come, the end is come upon the four quarters of the land.

3 Now is an end come upon thee. And I will send my wrath upon thee and I will judge thee according to thy ways: and I will set all thy abominations against thee.

4 And my eye shall not spare thee, and I will shew thee no pity: but I will lay thy ways upon thee, and thy abominations shall be in the midst of thee: and you shall know that I am the Lord.

5 Thus saith the Lord God: One affliction, behold an affliction is come.

6 The end is come, the end is come, it hath awaked against thee: behold it is come.

7 Destruction is come upon thee that dwellest in the land: the time is come, the day of slaughter is near, and not of the joy of mountains.

8 Now very shortly I will pour out my wrath upon thee and I will accomplish my anger in thee: and I will judge thee according to thy ways and I will lay upon thee all thy crimes.

9 And my eye shall not spare, neither will I shew mercy: but I will lay thy ways upon thee, and thy abominations shall be in the midst of thee. And you shall know that I am the Lord that strike.

10 Behold the day, behold it is come: destruction is gone forth, the rod hath blossomed, pride hath budded.

11 Iniquity is risen up into a rod of impiety: nothing of them *shall remain*, nor of their people, nor of the noise of them: and there shall be no rest among them.

12 The time is come, the day is at hand: let not the buyer rejoice, nor the seller mourn: for wrath is upon all the people thereof.

13 For the seller shall not return to that which he hath sold, although their life be yet among the living. For the vision which regardeth all the multitude thereof shall not go back; neither shall man be strengthened in the iniquity of his life.

14 Blow the trumpet, let all be made ready. Yet there is none to go to the battle: for my wrath shall be upon all the people thereof.

15 The sword without, and the pestilence and the famine within: he that is in the field shall die by the sword: and they that are in the city shall be devoured by the pestilence and the famine.

16 And such of them as shall flee shall escape: and they shall be in the mountains like doves of the valleys, all of them trembling, every one for his iniquity.

17 All hands shall be made feeble and all knees shall run with water.

18 [1] And they shall gird themselves with haircloth, and fear shall cover them, and shame shall be upon every face and baldness upon all their heads.

19 Their silver shall be cast forth and their gold shall become a dunghill. [2] Their silver and their gold shall not be able to deliver them in the day of the wrath of the Lord. They shall not satisfy their soul and their bellies shall not be filled: because it hath been the stumbling-block of their iniquity.

20 And they have turned the ornament of their jewels into pride and have made of it the images of their abominations and idols: therefore I have made it an uncleanness to them.

21 And I will give it into the hands of strangers for spoil and to the wicked of the earth for a prey: and they shall defile it.

22 And I will turn away my face from them, and they shall violate my secret *place:* and robbers shall enter into it and defile it.

23 Make a shutting up: for the land is full of the judgment of blood and the city is full of iniquity.

24 And I will bring the worst of the nations and they shall possess their houses: and I will make the pride of the mighty to cease and they shall possess their sanctuary.

25 When distress cometh upon them, they will seek for peace, and there shall be none.

26 Trouble shall come upon trouble, and rumour upon rumour, and they shall seek a vision of the prophet: and the law shall perish from the priest and counsel from the ancients.

27 The king shall mourn and the prince shall be clothed with sorrow and the hands of the people of the land shall be troubled. I will do to them according to their way and will judge them according to their judgments: and they shall know that *I am* the Lord.

CHAPTER 8

The prophet sees in a vision the abominations committed in Jerusalem, which determine the Lord to spare them no longer.

AND it came to pass in the sixth year, in the sixth month, in the fifth day of the month, *as* I sat in my house and the ancients of Juda sat before me, that the hand of the Lord God fell there upon me.

2 And I saw, and behold a likeness as the appearance of fire: from the appearance of his loins and downward, fire: and from his loins and upward, as the appearance of brightness, as the appearance of amber.

3 [1] And the likeness of a hand was put forth and took me by a lock of my head: and the spirit lifted me up between the earth and the heaven and brought me in the vision of God into Jerusalem,

CHAP. 7. [1] Isai. 15, 2; Jer. 48, 37. [2] Prov. 11, 4; Soph. 1, 18; Ecclus. 5, 10, 13. CHAP. 8. [1] Dan. 14 35.

CHAP. 7. Ver. 22. *Secret place.* That is, the inward sanctuary, the Holy of Holies.
Ver. 23. *Make a shutting up.* In Hebrew, a chain, namely, for imprisonment and captivity.

near the inner gate that looked toward the north, where was set the idol of jealousy, to provoke to jealousy.

4 And behold the glory of the God of Israel *was* there, according to the vision which I had seen in the plain.

5 And he said to me: Son of man, lift up thy eyes towards the way of the north. And I lifted up my eyes towards the way of the north: and behold on the north side of the gate of the altar the idol of jealousy in the very entry.

6 And he said to me: Son of man, dost thou see, thinkest thou, what these are doing, the great abominations that the house of Israel committeth here, that I should depart far off from my sanctuary? And turn thee yet again and thou shalt see greater abominations.

7 And he brought me in to the door of the court: and I saw, and behold a hole in the wall.

8 And he said to me: Son of man, dig in the wall. And when I had digged in the wall, behold a door.

9 And he said to me: Go in and see the wicked abominations which they commit here.

10 And I went in and saw, and behold every form of creeping things and of living creatures, the abomination: and all the idols of the house of Israel were painted on the wall all round about.

11 And seventy men of the ancients of the house of Israel and Jezonias the son of Saaphan stood in the midst of them that stood before the pictures. And every one had a censer in his hand: and a cloud of smoke went up from the incense.

12 And he said to me: Surely thou seest, O son of man, what the ancients of the house of Israel do in the dark, every one in private in his chamber: for they say: The Lord seeth us not, the Lord hath forsaken the earth.

13 And he said to me: If thou turn thee again, thou shalt see greater abominations which these commit.

14 And he brought me in by the door of the gate of the Lord's house which looked to the north: and behold women sat there mourning for Adonis.

CHAP. 9. [1] Exod. 12, 7; Apoc. 7, 3.

CHAP. 8. Ver. 14. *Adonis.* The favourite of Venus, slain by a wild boar, as feigned by the heathen poets, and which being here represented by an idol, is lamented by the female worshippers of that goddess. In the Hebrew the name is Tammuz.

CHAP. 9. Ver. 4. *Mark Thau.* *Thau,* or *Tau,* is the last letter in the Hebrew alphabet, and signifies *a sign,* or *a mark;* which is the reason why some translators render this place *Set a mark,* or *Mark a mark,* without specifying what this mark was. But St. Jerome, and other interpreters, conclude it was the form of the letter *Thau,* which in the ancient Hebrew character, was the form of a cross.

15 And he said to me: Surely thou hast seen, O son of man: but turn thee again *and* thou shalt see greater abominations than these.

16 And he brought me into the inner court of the house of the Lord: and behold at the door of the temple of the Lord, between the porch and the altar, were about five and twenty men having their backs towards the temple of the Lord and their faces to the east: and they adored towards the rising of the sun.

17 And he said to me: Surely thou hast seen, O son of man. Is this a light thing to the house of Juda, that they should commit these abominations which they have committed here: because they have filled the land with iniquity *and* have turned to provoke me to anger? And behold they put a branch to their nose.

18 Therefore I also will deal with them in my wrath: my eye shall not spare them, neither will I shew mercy: and when they shall cry to my ears with a loud voice, I will not hear them.

CHAPTER 9

All are ordered to be destroyed that are not marked in their foreheads. God will not be entreated for them.

AND he cried in my ears with a loud voice, saying: The visitations of the city are at hand, and every one hath a destroying weapon in his hand.

2 And behold six men came from the way of the upper gate which looketh to the north: and each one had his weapon of destruction in his hand. And there was one man in the midst of them clothed with linen, with a writer's inkhorn at his reins. And they went in and stood by the brazen altar.

3 And the glory of the Lord of Israel went up from the cherub upon which he was, to the threshold of the house: and he called to the man that was clothed with linen and had a writer's inkhorn at his loins.

4 And the Lord said to him: Go through the midst of the city, through the midst of Jerusalem, [1] and mark Thau upon the foreheads of the men that sigh and mourn for all the abominations that are committed in the midst thereof.

5 And to the others he said in my hearing: Go ye after him through the city and strike: let not your eyes spare nor be ye moved with pity.

6 Utterly destroy old and young, maidens, children and women: but upon whomsoever you shall see Thau, kill him not. And begin ye at my sanctuary. So they began at the ancient men who were before the house.

7 And he said to them: Defile the house and fill the courts with the slain. Go ye forth. And they went forth and slew them that were in the city.

8 And the slaughter being ended, I was left: and I fell upon my face, and crying I said: Alas, alas, alas, O Lord God, wilt thou then destroy all the remnant of Israel by pouring out thy fury upon Jerusalem?

9 And he said to me: The iniquity of the house of Israel and of Juda is exceeding great, and the land is filled with blood, and the city is filled with perverseness. For they have said: The Lord hath forsaken the earth, and, The Lord seeth not.

10 Therefore neither shall my eye spare nor will I have pity: I will requite their way upon their head.

11 And behold the man that was clothed with linen, that had the inkhorn at his back, returned the word, saying: I have done as thou hast commanded me.

CHAPTER 10

Fire is taken from the midst of the wheels under the cherubims and scattered over the city. A description of the cherubims.

AND I saw, and behold in the firmament that was over the heads of the cherubims, there appeared over them as it were the sapphire stone, as the appearance of the likeness of a throne.

2 And he spoke to the man that was clothed with linen, and said: Go in between the wheels that are under the cherubims and fill thy hand with the coals of fire that are between the cherubims and pour them out upon the city. And he went in, in my sight.

3 And the cherubims stood on the right side of the house when the man went in, and a cloud filled the inner court.

4 And the glory of the Lord was lifted up from above the cherub to the threshold of the house: and the house was filled with the cloud, and the court was filled with the brightness of the glory of the Lord.

5 And the sound of the wings of the cherubims was heard even to the outward court as the voice of God Almighty speaking.

6 And when he had commanded the man that was clothed with linen, saying: Take fire from the midst of the wheels that are between the cherubims: he went in and stood beside the wheel.

7 And one cherub stretched out his arm from the midst of the cherubims to the fire that was between the cherubims: and he took and put it into the hands of him that was clothed with linen. Who took it and went forth.

8 And there appeared in the cherubims the likeness of a man's hand under their wings.

9 And I saw, and behold *there were* four wheels by the cherubims: one wheel by one cherub, and another wheel by another cherub: and the appearance of the wheels was to the sight like the chrysolite stone.

10 And as to their appearance, all four were alike: as if a wheel were in the midst of a wheel.

11 And when they went, they went by four ways: and they turned not when they went: but to the place whither they first turned the rest also followed and did not turn back.

12 And their whole body and their necks and their hands and their wings and the circles were full of eyes, round about the four wheels.

13 And these wheels he called Voluble, in my hearing.

14 And every one had four faces: one face *was* the face of a cheruib: and the second face, the face of a man: and in the third was the face of a lion: and in the fourth the face of an eagle.

15 And the cherubims were lifted up: this is the living creature that I had seen by the river Chobar.

16 And when the cherubims went, the wheels also went by them: and when the cherubims lifted up their wings to mount up from the earth, the wheels stayed not behind but were by them.

17 When they stood, these stood: and when they were lifted up, these were lifted up: for the spirit of life was in them.

18 And the glory of the Lord went forth from the threshold of the temple and stood over the cherubims.

19 And the cherubims lifting up their wings were raised from the earth before me: and as they went out, the wheels also followed. And it stood in the entry of the east gate of the house of the Lord: and the glory of the God of Israel was over them.

20 [1] This is the living creature which I saw under the God of Israel by the river Chobar: and I understood that they were cherubims.

21 Each one had four faces and each one had four wings: and the likeness of a man's hand was under their wings.

CHAP. 10.   [1] Ezech. 1, 1, 3.
CHAP. 10.   Ver. 11. *By four ways.* That is, by any of the four ways, forward, backward, to the right or to the left.
Ver. 13. *Voluble.* That is, *rolling wheels,* galgal.

22 And as to the likeness of their faces, they were the same faces which I had seen by the river Chobar, and their looks, and the impulse of every one to go straight forward.

CHAPTER 11

A prophecy against the presumptuous assurance of the great ones. A remnant shall be saved and receive a new spirit and a new heart.

AND the spirit lifted me up and brought me into the east gate of the house of the Lord, which looketh towards the rising of the sun: and behold in the entry of the gate five and twenty men. And I saw in the midst of them Jezonias the son of Azur and Pheltias the son of Banaias, princes of the people.

2 And he said to me: Son of man, these are the men that study iniquity and frame a wicked counsel in this city,

3 Saying: Were not houses lately built? This *city* is the caldron, and we the flesh.

4 Therefore prophesy against them, prophesy, thou son of man.

5 And the spirit of the Lord fell upon me, and said to me: Speak: Thus saith the Lord: Thus have you spoken, O house of Israel, for I know the thoughts of your heart.

6 You have killed a great many in this city and you have filled the streets thereof with the slain.

7 Therefore thus saith the Lord God: Your slain, whom you have laid in the midst thereof, they are the flesh, and this is the caldron: and I will bring you forth out of the midst thereof.

8 You have feared the sword and I will bring the sword upon you, saith the Lord God.

CHAP. 11. ¹ Jer. 31, 33; Ezech. 36, 26.

CHAP: 11. Ver. 3. *Were not houses lately built?* These men despised the predictions and threats of the prophets who declared to them from God that the city should be destroyed and the inhabitants carried into captivity; and they made use of this kind of argument against the prophets, that the city, so far from being like to be destroyed, had lately been augmented by the building of new houses; from whence they further inferred, by way of a proverb, using the similitude of a caldron, out of which the flesh is not taken till it is thoroughly boiled and fit to be eaten, that they should not be carried away out of their city, but there end their days in peace. Ver. 10. *In the borders of Israel.* They pretended that they should die in peace in Jerusalem. God tells them it should not be so; but that they should be judged and condemned and fall by the sword in the borders of Israel: namely, in Reblatha in the land of Emath, where all their chief men were put to death by order of Nabuchodonosor. 4 Kings 25, and Jer. 52, 10, 27. Ver. 15. *Thy brethren.* He speaks of them that had been carried away captives before, who were despised by them that remained in Jerusalem: but as the prophet here declares to them from God, should be in a more happy condition than they and after some time return from their captivity.

9 And I will cast you out of the midst thereof and I will deliver you into the hand of the enemies and I will execute judgments upon you.

10 You shall fall by the sword: I will judge you in the borders of Israel and you shall know that I am the Lord.

11 This shall not be as a caldron to you, and you shall not be as flesh in the midst thereof: I will judge you in the borders of Israel.

12 And you shall know that I am the Lord: because you have not walked in my commandments and have not done my judgments, but you have done according to the judgments of the nations that are round about you.

13 And it came to pass when I prophesied, that Pheltias the son of Banaias died: and I fell down upon my face and cried with a loud voice and said: Alas, alas, alas, O Lord God: Wilt thou make an end of all the remnant of Israel?

14 And the word of the Lord came to me, saying:

15 Son of man, thy brethren, thy brethren, thy kinsmen and all the house of Israel, all they to whom the inhabitants of Jerusalem have said: Get ye far from the Lord, the land is given in possession to us.

16 Therefore thus saith the Lord God: Because I have removed them far off among the Gentiles and because I have scattered them among the countries, I will be to them a little sanctuary in the countries whither they are come.

17 Therefore speak *to them:* Thus saith the Lord God: I will gather you from among the peoples and assemble you out of the countries wherein you are scattered and I will give you the land of Israel.

18 And they shall go in thither and shall take away all the scandals and all the abominations thereof from thence.

19 ¹ And I will give them one heart and will put a new spirit in their bowels: and I will take away the stony heart out of their flesh and will give them a heart of flesh:

20 That they may walk in my commandments and keep my judgments and do them: and that they may be my people and I may be their God.

21 But *as for them* whose heart walketh after their scandals and abominations, I will lay their way upon their head, saith the Lord God.

22 And the cherubims lifted up their wings and the wheels with them: and the glory of the God of Israel was over them.

23 And the glory of the Lord went

up from the midst of the city and stood over the mount that is on the east side of the city.

24 And the spirit lifted me up and brought me into Chaldea, to them of the captivity, in vision, by the spirit of God: and the vision which I had seen was taken up from me.

25 And I spoke to them of the captivity all the words of the Lord which he had shewn me.

CHAPTER 12

The prophet foresheweth by signs, the captivity of Sedecias and the desolation of the people, all which shall quickly come to pass.

AND the word of the Lord came to me, saying:

2 Son of man, thou dwellest in the midst of a provoking house: who have eyes to see and see not, and ears to hear and hear not: for they are a provoking house.

3 Thou, therefore, O son of man, prepare thee all necessaries for removing, and remove by day in their sight. And thou shalt remove out of thy place to another place in their sight, if so be they will regard it: for they are a provoking house.

4 And thou shalt bring forth thy furniture, as the furniture of one that is removing by day in their sight: and thou shalt go forth in the evening in their presence, as one goeth forth that removeth his dwelling.

5 Dig thee a way through the wall before their eyes: and thou shalt go forth through it.

6 In their sight thou shalt be carried out upon men's shoulders: thou shalt be carried out in the dark. Thou shalt cover thy face and shalt not see the ground: for I have set thee for a sign of things to come to the house of Israel.

7 I did therefore as he had commanded me: I brought forth my goods by day, as the goods of one that removeth, and in the evening I digged through the wall with my hand. And I went forth in the dark and was carried on men's shoulders in their sight.

8 And the word of the Lord came to me in the morning, saying:

9 Son of man, hath not the house of Israel, the provoking house, said to thee: What art thou doing?

10 Say to them: Thus saith the Lord God: This burden concerneth my prince that is in Jerusalem and all the house of Israel that are among them.

11 Say: I am a sign of things to come to you. As I have done, so shall it be done to them. They shall be removed from their dwellings and go into captivity.

12 And the prince that is in the midst of them shall be carried on shoulders: he shall go forth in the dark. They shall dig through the wall to bring him out: his face shall be covered, that he may not see the ground with his eyes.

13 [1] And I will spread my net over him, and he shall be taken in my net: and I will bring him into Babylon, into the land of the Chaldeans. And he shall not see it: and there he shall die.

14 And all that are about him, his guards and his troops, I will scatter into every wind: and I will draw out the sword after them.

15 And they shall know that I am the Lord when I shall have dispersed them among the nations and scattered them in the countries.

16 And I will leave a few men of them from the sword and from the famine and from the pestilence: that they may declare all their wicked deeds among the nations whither they shall go. And they shall know that I am the Lord.

17 And the word of the Lord came to me, saying:

18 Son of man, eat thy bread in trouble and drink thy water in hurry and sorrow.

19 And say to the people of the land: Thus saith the Lord God to them that dwell in Jerusalem in the land of Israel: They shall eat their bread in care and drink their water in desolation: that the land may become desolate from the multitude that is therein, for the iniquity of all that dwell therein.

20 And the cities that are now inhabited shall be laid waste and the land shall be desolate: and you shall know that I am the Lord.

21 And the word of the Lord came to me, saying:

22 Son of man, what is this proverb that you have in the land of Israel, saying: The days shall be prolonged and every vision shall fail?

23 Say to them therefore: Thus saith the Lord God: I will make this proverb to cease, neither shall it be any more a common saying in Israel. And tell them that the days are at hand and the effect of every vision.

24 For there shall be no more any vain visions nor doubtful divination in the midst of the children of Israel.

25 For I the Lord will speak: and what word soever I shall speak, it shall come to pass and shall not be prolonged any more: but in your days, ye

---

CHAP. 12. [1] Ezech. 17, 20.

CHAP. 12. Ver. 13. *He shall not see it.* Because his eyes shall be put out by Nabuchodonosor.

provoking house, I will speak the word and will do it, saith the Lord God.

26 And the word of the Lord came to me, saying:

27 Son of man, behold the house of Israel, they that say: The vision that this man seeth is for many days to come: and this man prophesieth of times afar off.

28 Therefore say to them: Thus saith the Lord God: Not one word of mine shall be prolonged any more. The word that I shall speak shall be accomplished, saith the Lord God.

CHAPTER 13

God declares against false prophets and prophetesses that deceive the people with lies.

AND the word of the Lord came to me, saying:

2 Son of man, prophesy thou against the prophets of Israel that prophesy. And thou shalt say to them that prophesy out of their own heart: Hear ye the word of the Lord.

3 Thus saith the Lord God: [1] Woe to the foolish prophets that follow their own spirit and see nothing.

4 Thy prophets, O Israel, were like foxes in the deserts.

5 You have not gone up to face the enemy, nor have you set up a wall for the house of Israel, to stand in battle in the day of the Lord.

6 They see vain things and they foretell lies, saying: The Lord saith: whereas the Lord hath not sent them. And they have persisted to confirm what they have said.

7 Have you not seen a vain vision and spoken a lying divination? And you say: The Lord saith: whereas I have not spoken.

8 Therefore thus saith the Lord God: Because you have spoken vain things and have seen lies, therefore behold I come against you, saith the Lord God.

9 And my hand shall be upon the prophets that see vain things and that divine lies. They shall not be in the council of my people, nor shall they be written in the writing of the house of Israel: neither shall they enter into the land of Israel. And you shall know that I am the Lord God.

10 Because they have deceived my people, saying: Peace: and there is no

CHAP. 13. [1] Jer. 23, 1; Ezech. 14, 9; 34, 2.

CHAP. 13. Ver. 10. *Peace and there is no peace.* By making people easy in their sins and promising them impunity.—*They gave life to their souls.* That is, they flattered them with promises of life, peace and security.

Ver. 19. *Violated me.* That is, dishonoured and discredited me.—*To kill souls.* That is, to sentence souls to death, which are not to die, and to promise life to them who are not to live.

peace. And the people built up a wall: and they daubed it with dirt without straw.

11 Say to them that daub without tempering, that it shall fall: for there shall be an overflowing shower, and I will cause great hailstones to fall violently from above and a stormy wind to throw it down.

12 Behold, when the wall is fallen, shall it not be said to you: Where is the daubing wherewith you have daubed it?

13 Therefore thus saith the Lord God: Lo, I will cause a stormy wind to break forth in my indignation: and there shall be an overflowing shower in my anger, and great hailstones in my wrath to consume.

14 And I will break down the wall that you have daubed with untempered mortar: and I will make it even with the ground, and the foundation thereof shall be laid bare. And it shall fall and shall be consumed in the midst thereof: and you shall know that I am the Lord.

15 And I will accomplish my wrath upon the wall and upon them that daub it without tempering the mortar, and I will say to you: The wall is no more, and they that daub it are no more.

16 Even the prophets of Israel that prophesy to Jerusalem and that see visions of peace for her: and there is no peace, saith the Lord God.

17 And thou, son of man, set thy face against the daughters of thy people that prophesy out of their own heart: and do thou prophesy against them,

18 And say: Thus saith the Lord God: Woe to them that sew cushions under every elbow and make pillows for the heads of *persons of* every age to catch souls: and when they caught the souls of my people, they gave life to their souls.

19 And they violated me among my people for a handful of barley and a piece of bread, to kill souls which should not die and to save souls alive which should not live, telling lies to my people that believe lies.

20 Therefore thus saith the Lord God: Behold I *declare against* your cushions wherewith you catch flying souls: and I will tear them off from your arms: and I will let go the souls that you catch, the souls that should fly.

21 And I will tear your pillows and will deliver my people out of your hands: neither shall they be any more in your hands to be a prey. And you shall know that I am the Lord.

22 Because with lies you have made the heart of the just to mourn, whom I have not made sorrowful: and have

strengthened the hands of the wicked, that he should not return from his evil way and live.

23 Therefore you shall not see vain things nor divine divinations any more: and I will deliver my people out of your hand. And you shall know that I am the Lord.

CHAPTER 14

God suffers the wicked to be deceived in punishment of their wickedness. The evils that shall come upon them for their sins, from which they shall not be delivered by the prayers of Noe, Daniel and Job. But a remnant shall be preserved.

AND some of the ancients of Israel came to me and sat before me.

2 And the word of the Lord came to me, saying:

3 Son of man, these men have placed their uncleannesses in their hearts, and have set up before their face the stumbling-block of their iniquity: and shall I answer when they inquire of me?

4 Therefore speak to them, and say to them: Thus saith the Lord God: Man, man of the house of Israel, that shall place his uncleannesses in his heart and set up the stumbling-block of his iniquity before his face and shall come to the prophet inquiring of me by him, I the Lord will answer him according to the multitude of his uncleannesses:

5 That the house of Israel may be caught in their own heart, with which they have departed from me through all their idols.

6 Therefore say to the house of Israel: Thus saith the Lord God: Be converted and depart from your idols and turn away your faces from all your abominations.

7 For every man of the house of Israel and every stranger among the proselytes in Israel, if he separate himself from me and place his idols in his heart and set the stumbling-block of his iniquity before his face and come to the prophet to inquire of me by him: I the Lord will answer him by myself.

8 And I will set my face against that man and will make him an example and a proverb and will cut him off from the midst of my people. And you shall know that I am the Lord.

9 [1] And when the prophet shall err and speak a word: I the Lord have deceived that prophet. And I will stretch forth my hand upon him and will cut him off from the midst of my people Israel.

10 And they shall bear their iniquity. According to the iniquity of him that

inquireth, so shall the iniquity of the prophet be.

11 That the house of Israel may go no more astray from me, nor be polluted with all their transgressions: but may be my poeple and I may be their God, saith the Lord of hosts.

12 And the word of the Lord came to me, saying:

13 Son of man, when a land shall sin against me, so as to transgress grievously, I will stretch forth my hand upon it [2] and will break the staff of the bread thereof: and I will send famine upon it and will destroy man and beast out of it.

14 And if these three men, Noe, Daniel and Job, shall be in it: they shall deliver their own souls by their justice, saith the Lord of hosts.

15 And if I shall bring mischievous beasts also upon the land to waste it, and it be desolate so that there is none that can pass because of the beasts:

16 If these three men shall be in it, as I live, saith the Lord, they shall deliver neither sons nor daughters: but they only shall be delivered and the land shall be made desolate.

17 Or, if I bring the sword upon that land and say to the sword: Pass through the land: and I destroy man and beast out of it:

18 And these three men be in the midst thereof: as I live, saith the Lord God, they shall deliver neither sons nor daughters, but they themselves alone shall be delivered.

19 Or, if I also send the pestilence upon that land and pour out my indignation upon it in blood to cut off from it man and beast:

20 And Noe and Daniel and Job be in the midst thereof: as I live, saith the Lord God, they shall deliver neither son nor daughter, but they shall only deliver their own souls by their justice.

21 For thus saith the Lord: Although I shall send in upon Jerusalem my four grievous judgments, the sword and the famine and the mischievous beasts and the pestilence, to destroy out of it man and beast,

---

CHAP. 14. [1] Ezech. 13, 3. [2] Ezech. 4, 16; 5, 16.

CHAP. 14. Ver. 3. *Uncleannesses.* That is, their filthy idols, upon which they have set their hearts and which are a stumbling-block to their souls.
Ver. 4. *Man, man.* That is, every *man*, an Hebrew expression.
Ver. 9. *The prophet shall err.* He speaks of false prophets, answering out of their own heads and according to their own corrupt inclinations. —*I have deceived that prophet.* God Almighty *deceives* false prophets: partly by withdrawing his light from them and abandoning them to their own corrupt inclinations which push them on to prophesy such things as are agreeable to those who consult them: and partly by disappointing them and causing all things to happen contrary to what they have said.

22 Yet there shall be left in it some that shall be saved, who shall bring away their sons and daughters. Behold they shall come among you, and you shall see their way and their doings: and you shall be comforted concerning the evil that I have brought upon Jerusalem, in all things that I have brought upon it.

23 And they shall comfort you, when you shall see their ways and their doings: and you shall know that I have not done without cause all that I have done in it, saith the Lord God.

CHAPTER 15

As a vine cut down is fit for nothing but the fire, so it shall be with Jerusalem, for her sins.

AND the word of the Lord came to me, saying:

2 Son of man, what shall be made of the wood of the vine, out of all the trees of the woods that are among the trees of the forests?

3 Shall wood be taken of it to do any work, or shall a pin be made of it for any vessel to hang thereon?

4 Behold it is cast into the fire for fuel: the fire hath consumed both ends thereof, and the midst thereof is reduced to ashes. Shall it be useful for any work?

5 Even when it was whole, it was not fit for work: How much less, when the fire hath devoured and consumed it shall any work be made of it?

6 Therefore thus saith the Lord God: As the vine tree among the trees of the forests which I have given to the fire to be consumed, so will I deliver up the inhabitants of Jerusalem.

7 And I will set my face against them. They shall go out from fire: and fire shall consume them. And you shall know that I am the Lord, when I shall have set my face against them,

8 And I shall have made their land a wilderness and desolate, because they have been transgressors, saith the Lord God.

CHAPTER 16

Under the figure of an unfaithful wife, God upbraids Jerusalem with her ingratitude and manifold disloyalties, but promiseth mercy by a new covenant.

AND the word of the Lord came to me, saying:

2 Son of man, make known to Jerusalem her abominations.

3 And thou shalt say: Thus saith the Lord God to Jerusalem: Thy root and thy nativity is of the land of Chanaan. Thy father was an Amorrhite and thy mother a Cethite.

4 And when thou wast born, in the day of thy nativity thy navel was not cut, neither wast thou washed with water for thy health, nor salted with salt, nor swaddled with clouts.

5 No eye had pity on thee to do any of these things for thee, out of compassion to thee: but thou wast cast out upon the face of the earth in the abjection of thy soul, in the day that thou wast born.

6 And passing by thee, I saw that thou wast trodden under foot in thy own blood. And I said to thee when thou wast in thy blood: Live. I have said to thee: Live in thy blood.

7 I caused thee to multiply as the bud of the field: and thou didst increase and grow great and advancedst and camest to woman's ornament. Thy breasts were fashioned and thy hair grew: and thou wast naked and full of confusion.

8 And I passed by thee and saw thee: and behold thy time was the time of lovers: and I spread my garment over thee and covered thy ignominy. And I swore to thee and I entered into a covenant with thee, saith the Lord God. And thou becamest mine.

9 And I washed thee with water and cleansed away thy blood from thee: and I anointed thee with oil.

10 And I clothed thee with embroidery and shod thee with violet coloured shoes: and I girded thee about with fine linen and clothed thee with fine garments.

11 I decked thee also with ornaments and put bracelets on thy hands and a chain about thy neck.

12 And I put a jewel upon thy forehead and earrings in thy ears and a beautiful crown upon thy head.

13 And thou wast adorned with gold and silver, and wast clothed with fine linen and embroidered work and many colours: thou didst eat fine flour and honey and oil: and wast made exceeding beautiful and wast advanced to be a queen.

14 And thy renown went forth among the nations for thy beauty: for thou wast perfect through my beauty which I had put upon thee, saith the Lord God.

15 But trusting in thy beauty, thou playedst the harlot because of thy renown and thou hast prostituted thyself to every passenger, to be his.

16 And taking of thy garments thou hast made thee high places sewed to-

CHAP. 16. Ver. 2. *Make known to Jerusalem.* That is, by letters, for the prophet was then in Babylon.

Ver. 11. *I decked thee also with ornaments.* That is, with spiritual benefits, giving you a law with sacrifices, sacraments and other holy rites.

gether on each side: and hast played the harlot upon them, as hath not been done before nor shall be hereafter.

17 And thou tookest thy beautiful vessels, of my gold and my silver which I gave thee, and thou madest thee images of men and hast committed fornication with them.

18 And thou tookest thy garments of divers colours and coveredst them: and settest my oil and my sweet incense before them.

19 And my bread which I gave thee, the fine flour and oil and honey, wherewith I fed thee, thou hast set before them for a sweet odour: and it was done, saith the Lord God.

20 And thou hast taken thy sons and thy daughters, whom thou hast borne to me, and hast sacrificed the same to them to be devoured. Is thy fornication small?

21 Thou hast sacrificed and given my children to them, consecrating them *by fire.*

22 And after all thy abominations and fornications, thou hast not remembered the days of thy youth, when thou wast naked and full of confusion, trodden under foot in thy own blood.

23 And it came to pass after all thy wickedness (Woe, Woe to thee, saith the Lord God)

24 That thou didst also build thee a common stew and madest thee a brothel house in every street.

25 At every head of the way thou hast set up a sign of thy prostitution, and hast made thy beauty to be abominable, and hast prostituted thyself to every one that passed by, and hast multiplied thy fornications.

26 And thou hast committed fornication with the Egyptians thy neighbours, *men* of large bodies, and hast multiplied thy fornications to provoke me.

27 Behold, I will stretch out my hand upon thee and will take away thy justification: and I will deliver thee up to the will of the daughters of the Philistines that hate thee, that are ashamed of thy wicked way.

28 Thou hast also committed fornication with the Assyrians, because thou wast not yet satisfied: and after thou hadst played the harlot with them, even so thou wast not contented.

29 Thou hast also multiplied thy fornications in the land of Chanaan with the Chaldeans: and neither so wast thou satisfied.

30 Wherein shall I cleanse thy heart, saith the Lord God, seeing thou dost all these the works of a shameless prostitute?

31 Because thou hast built thy brothel house at the head of every way and thou hast made thy high place in every street: and wast not as a harlot that by disdain enhanceth her price,

32 But as an adulteress that bringeth in strangers over her husband.

33 Gifts are given to all harlots: but thou hast given hire to all thy lovers, and thou hast given them gifts to come to thee from every side, to commit fornication with thee.

34 And it hath happened in thee contrary to the custom of women in thy fornications, and after thee there shall be no *such* fornication: for in that thou gavest rewards and didst not take rewards, the contrary hath been done in thee.

35 Therefore, O harlot, hear the word of the Lord.

36 Thus saith the Lord God: Because thy money hath been poured out and thy shame discovered through thy fornications with thy lovers and with the idols of thy abominations, by the blood of thy children whom thou gavest them:

37 Behold, I will gather together all thy lovers with whom that hast taken pleasure and all whom thou hast loved with all whom thou hast hated: and I will gather them together against thee on every side and will discover thy shame in their sight: and they shall see all thy nakedness.

38 [1] And I will judge thee as adulteresses and they that shed blood are judged: and I will give thee blood in fury and jealousy.

39 And I will deliver thee into their hands: and they shall destroy thy brothel house and throw down thy stews. And they shall strip thee of thy garments and shall take away the vessels of thy beauty and leave thee naked and full of disgrace.

40 And they shall bring upon thee a multitude: and they shall stone thee with stones and shall slay thee with their swords.

41 [2] And they shall burn thy houses with fire and shall execute judgments upon thee in the sight of many women: and thou shalt cease from fornication and shalt give no hire any more.

42 And my indignation shall rest in thee and my jealousy shall depart from thee: and I will cease and be angry no more.

43 Because thou hast not remem-

CHAP. 16.   [1] Ezech. 23, 10.   [2] 4 Kings, 25, 9.

Ver. 21. *Thou hast sacrificed.* As there is nothing more base and abominable than the crimes mentioned throughout this chapter, so the infidelities of the Israelites in forsaking God and sacrificing even their children to idols are strongly figured by these allegories.

bered the days of thy youth, but hast provoked me in all these things: wherefore I also have turned thy ways upon thy head, saith the Lord God, and I have not done according to thy wicked deeds in all thy abominations.

44 Behold every one that useth a common proverb shall use this against thee, saying: As the mother *was*, so also *is* her daughter.

45 Thou art thy mother's daughter, that cast off her husband and her children: and thou art the sister of thy sisters, who cast off their husbands and their children. Your mother was a Cethite, and your father an Amorrhite.

46 And thy elder sister *is* Samaria, she and her daughters that dwell at thy left hand: and thy younger sister that dwelleth at thy right hand *is* Sodom and her daughters.

47 But neither hast thou walked in their ways, nor hast thou done a little less *than they* according to their wickednesses: thou hast done almost more wicked things than they in all thy ways.

48 *As* I live, saith the Lord God, thy sister Sodom herself and her daughters have not done as thou hast done and thy daughters.

49 [3] Behold this was the iniquity of Sodom thy sister, pride, fulness of bread and abundance, and the idleness of her and of her daughters: and they did not put forth their hand to the needy and to the poor.

50 And they were lifted up and committed abominations before me: and I took them away, as thou hast seen.

51 And Samaria committed not half thy sins: but thou hast surpassed them with thy crimes and hast justified thy sisters by all thy abominations which thou hast done.

52 Therefore, do thou also bear thy confusion, thou that hast surpassed thy sisters with thy sins, doing more wickedly than they: for they are justified above thee. Therefore be thou also

[3] Gen. 19, 24.

Ver. 49. *This was the iniquity of Sodom.* That is, these were the steps by which the Sodomites came to fall into those abominations for which they were destroyed. For pride, gluttony and idleness are the highroad to all kinds of lust: especially when they are accompanied with a neglect of the works of mercy.

Ver. 53. *I will bring back.* This relates to the conversion of the Gentiles out of all nations, and of many of the Jews, to the church of Christ.

Ver. 55. *Ancient state.* That is, to their former state of liberty and their ancient possessions. In the spiritual sense, to the true liberty and the happy inheritance of the children of God, through faith in Christ.

CHAP. 17. Ver. 3. *A large eagle.* Nabuchodonosor king of Babylon.—*Came to Libanus.* That is, to Jerusalem.—*Took away the marrow of the cedar.* King Jechonias.

Ver. 4. *Chanaan.* This name, which signifies traffic, is not taken here for Palestine, but for Chaldea: and the city of merchants here mentioned is Babylon.

confounded and bear thy shame, thou that hast justified thy sisters.

53 And I will bring back and restore them by bringing back Sodom, with her daughters, and by bringing back Samaria and her daughters: and I will bring those that return of thee in the midst of them.

54 That thou mayest bear thy shame and mayest be confounded in all that thou hast done, comforting them.

55 And thy sister Sodom and her daughters shall return to their ancient state: and Samaria and her daughters shall return to their ancient state: and thou and thy daughters shall return to your ancient state.

56 And Sodom thy sister was not heard of in thy mouth, in the day of thy pride,

57 Before thy malice was laid open: as *it is* at this time, making thee a reproach of the daughters of Syria and of all the daughters of Palestine round about thee, that encompass thee on all sides.

58 Thou hast borne thy wickedness and thy disgrace, saith the Lord God.

59 For thus saith the Lord God: I will deal with thee as thou hast despised the oath, in breaking the covenant:

60 And I will remember my covenant with thee in the days of thy youth: and I will establish with thee an everlasting covenant.

61 And thou shalt remember thy ways and be ashamed when thou shalt receive thy sisters, thy elder and thy younger: and I will give them to thee for daughters, but not by thy covenant.

62 And I will establish my covenant with thee: and thou shalt know that I am the Lord,

63 That thou mayest remember and be confounded and mayest no more open thy mouth because of thy confusion, when I shall be pacified toward thee for all that thou hast done, saith the Lord God.

CHAPTER 17

The parable of the two eagles and the vine. A promise of the cedar of Christ and his church.

AND the word of the Lord came to me, saying:

2 Son of man, put forth a riddle and speak a parable to the house of Israel,

3 And say: Thus saith the Lord God: A large eagle with great wings, long-limbed, full of feathers and of variety, came to Libanus and took away the marrow of the cedar.

4 He cropped off the top of the twigs thereof and carried it away into

the land of Chanaan: and he set it in a city of merchants.

5 And he took of the seed of the land and put it in the ground for seed, that it might take a firm root over many waters: he planted it on the surface of the earth.

6 And it sprung up and grew into a spreading vine of low stature: and the branches thereof looked towards him and the roots thereof were under him. So it became a vine and grew into branches and shot forth sprigs.

7 And there was another large eagle, with great wings and many feathers: and behold this vine, bending as it were her roots towards him, stretched forth her branches to him, that he might water it by the furrows of her plantation.

8 It was planted in a good ground upon many waters, that it might bring forth branches and bear fruit, that it might become a large vine.

9 Say thou: Thus saith the Lord God: Shall it prosper then? Shall he not pull up the roots thereof and strip off its fruit and dry up all the branches it hath shot forth and make it wither: and this without a strong arm or many people to pluck it up by the root?

10 Behold, it is planted. Shall it prosper then? Shall it not be dried up when the burning wind shall touch it, and shall it not wither in the furrows where it grew?

11 And the word of the Lord came to me, saying:

12 Say to the provoking house: Know you not what these things mean? Tell them: Behold the king of Babylon cometh to Jerusalem: and he shall take away the king and the princes thereof and carry them with him to Babylon.

13 And he shall take one of the king's seed and make a covenant with him and take an oath of him. Yea, and he shall take away the mighty men of the land.

14 That it may be a low kingdom and not lift itself up, but keep his covenant and observe it.

15 But he hath revolted from him and sent ambassadors to Egypt, that it might give him horses and much people. And shall he that hath done thus prosper or be saved? And shall he escape that hath broken the covenant?

16 As I live, saith the Lord God: In the place where the king dwelleth that made him king, whose oath he hath made void and whose covenant he broke, even in the midst of Babylon, shall he die.

17 And not with a great army nor with much people shall Pharao fight against him: when he shall cast up mounts and build forts, to cut off many souls.

18 For he had despised the oath, breaking his covenant, and behold he hath given his hand: and, having done all these things, he shall not escape.

19 Therefore, thus saith the Lord God: As I live, I will lay upon his head the oath he hath despised and the covenant he hath broken.

20 [1] And I will spread my net over him and he shall be taken in my net: and I will bring him into Babylon and will judge him there for the transgression by which he hath despised me.

21 And all his fugitives with all his bands shall fall by the sword: and the residue shall be scattered into every wind. And you shall know that I the Lord have spoken.

22 Thus saith the Lord God: I myself will take of the marrow of the high cedar and will set it: I will crop off a tender twig from the top of the branches thereof and I will plant it on a mountain high and eminent.

23 On the high mountains of Israel will I plant it: and it shall shoot forth into branches and shall bear fruit, and it shall become a great cedar. And all birds shall dwell under it, and every fowl shall make its nest under the shadow of the branches thereof.

24 And all the trees of the country shall know that I the Lord have brought down the high tree and exalted the low tree: and have dried up the green tree and have caused the dry tree to flourish. I the Lord have spoken and have done it.

CHAPTER 18

One man shall not bear the sins of another, but every one his own. If a wicked man truly repent, he shall be saved: and if a just man leave his justice, he shall perish.

AND the word of the Lord came to me, saying: What is the meaning

2 That you use among you this parable as a proverb in the land of Israel, saying: [3] The fathers have eaten sour grapes and the teeth of the children are set on edge?

3 As I live, saith the Lord God, this

CHAP. 17. [1] Ezech. 12, 13; 32, 3. CHAP. 18. [1] Jer. 31, 29.

Ver. 5. *Of the seed of the land.* Sedecias, whom he made king.

Ver. 6. *Towards him.* Nabuchodonosor, to whom Sedecias swore allegiance.

Ver. 7. *Another large eagle.* The king of Egypt.

Ver. 12. *Shall take away,* or *hath taken away.* For all this was now done.

Ver. 22. *Of the marrow of the high cedar.* Of the royal stock of David.—*A tender twig.* Jesus Christ, whom God hath planted in mount Sion, that is, the high mountain of his church, to which all nations flow.

parable shall be no more to you a proverb in Israel.

4 Behold all souls are mine: as the soul of the father, so also the soul of the son is mine: the soul that sinneth, the same shall die.

5 And if a man be just and do judgment and justice:

6 And hath not eaten upon the mountains nor lifted up his eyes to the idols of the house of Israel: and hath not defiled his neighbour's wife, nor come near to a menstruous woman:

7 And hath not wronged any man but hath restored the pledge to the debtor: hath taken nothing away by violence: [2] hath given his bread to the hungry and hath covered the naked with a garment:

8 Hath not lent upon usury, nor taken any increase: hath withdrawn his hand from iniquity and hath executed true judgment between man and man:

9 Hath walked in my commandments and kept my judgments, to do truth: he is just, he shall surely live, saith the Lord God.

10 And if he beget a son that is a robber, a shedder of blod, and that hath done some one of these things:

11 Though he doth not all these things, but that eateth upon the mountains and that defileth his neighbour's wife:

12 That grieveth the needy and the poor: that taketh away by violence: that restoreth not the pledge: and that lifteth up his eyes to idols: that committeth abomination:

13 That giveth upon usury and that taketh an increase: Shall such a one live? He shall not live. Seeing he hath done all these detestable things, he shall surely die: his blood shall be upon him.

14 But if he beget a son who, seeing all his father's sins, which he hath done, is afraid and shall not do the like to them:

15 That hath not eaten upon the mountains nor lifted up his eyes to the idols of the house of Israel and hath not defiled his neighbour's wife:

16 And hath not grieved any man, nor withholden the pledge, nor taken away with violence: but hath given his bread to the hungry and covered the naked with a garment:

17 That hath turned away his hand from injuring the poor, hath not taken usury and increase: but hath executed my judgments and hath walked in my commandments: this man shall not die for the iniquity of his father, but living he shall live.

18 As for his father, because he oppressed and offered violence to his brother and wrought evil in the midst of his people, behold he is dead in his own iniquity.

19 And you say: Why hath not the son borne the iniquity of his father? Verily, because the son hath wrought judgment and justice, hath kept all my commandments and done them, living, he shall live.

20 [3] The soul that sinneth the same shall die: the son shall not bear the iniquity of the father, and the father shall not bear the iniquity of the son. The justice of the just shall be upon him, and the wickedness of the wicked shall be upon him.

21 But if the wicked do penance for all his sins which he hath committed and keep all my commandments and do judgment and justice, living he shall live, and shall not die.

22 I will not remember all his iniquities that he hath done: in his justice which he hath wrought, he shall live.

23 [4] Is it my will that a sinner should die, saith the Lord God, and not that he should be converted from his ways and live?

24 But, if the just man turn himself away from his justice and do iniquity according to all the abominations which the wicked man useth to work, shall he live? All his justices which he hath done shall not be remembered: in the prevarication by which he hath prevaricated and in his sin which he hath committed, in them he shall die.

25 And you have said: [5] The way of the Lord is not right. Hear ye, therefore, O house of Israel: Is it my way that is not right, and are not rather your ways perverse?

26 For when the just turneth himself away from his justice and committeth iniquity, he shall die therein: in the injustice that he hath wrought he shall die.

27 And when the wicked turneth himself away from his wickedness, which he hath wrought, and doeth judgment and justice, he shall save his soul alive.

28 Because he considereth and turneth away himself from all his iniquities which he hath wrought, he shall surely live and not die.

29 And the children of Israel say: The way of the Lord is not right. Are

[2] Isai. 58, 7; Matt. 25, 35. [3] Deut. 24, 16; 4 Kings, 14, 6; 2 Par. 25, 4. [4] Ezech. 18, 32; 33, 11; 2 Peter, 3, 9. [5] Ezech. 33, 20.

CHAP. 18. Ver. 6. *Not eaten upon the mountains.* That is, of the sacrifices there offered to idols.

Ver. 9. *To do truth.* That is, to act according to truth; for the Hebrews called everything that was just, truth.

not my ways right, O house of Israel, and are not rather your ways perverse?

30 Therefore will I judge every man according to his ways, O house of Israel, saith the Lord God. [6] Be converted and do penance for all your iniquities: and iniquity shall not be your ruin.

31 Cast away from you all your transgressions, by which you have transgressed, and make to yourselves a new heart and a new spirit: and why will you die, O house of Israel?

32 [7] For I desire not the death of him that dieth, saith the Lord God, return ye and live.

CHAPTER 19

The parable of the young lions and of the vine that is wasted.

MOREOVER, take thou up a lamentation for the princes of Israel,

2 And say: Why did thy mother the lioness lie down among the lions *and* bring up her whelps in the midst of young lions?

3 And she brought out one of her whelps, and he became a lion: and he learned to catch the prey and to devour men.

4 And the nations heard of him and took him, but not without receiving wounds: and they brought him in chains into the land of Egypt.

5 But she, seeing herself weakened and that her hope was lost, took one of her young lions *and* set him up for a lion.

6 And he went up and down among the lions and became a lion: and he learned to catch the prey and to devour men.

7 He learned to make widows and to lay waste their cities: and the land became desolate and the fulness thereof, by the noise of his roaring.

8 And the nations came together against him on every side out of the provinces, and they spread their net over him. In their wounds he was taken:

9 And they put him into a cage. They brought him in chains to the king of Babylon: and they cast him into prison, that his voice should no more be heard upon the mountains of Israel.

10 Thy mother *is* like a vine in thy blood planted by the water: her fruit and her branches have grown out of many waters.

11 And she hath strong rods to make sceptres for them that bear rule: and her stature was exalted among the branches: and she saw her height in the multitude of her branches.

12 But she was plucked up in wrath and cast on the ground: [1] and the burn-ing wind dried up her fruit. Her strong rods are withered and dried up: the fire hath devoured her.

13 And now she is transplanted into the desert, in a land not passable and dry.

14 And a fire is gone out from a rod of her branches, which hath devoured her fruit: so that she now hath no strong rod to be a sceptre of rulers. This is a lamentation, and it shall be for a lamentation.

CHAPTER 20

God refuses to answer the ancients of Israel inquiring by the prophet. But by him setteth his benefits before their eyes and their heinous sins, threatening yet greater punishments, but still mixed with mercy.

AND it came to pass in the seventh year, in the fifth *month*, the tenth day of the month, there came men of the ancients of Israel to inquire of the Lord: and they sat before me

2 And the word of the Lord came to me, saying:

3 Son of man, speak to the ancients of Israel, and say to them: Thus saith the Lord God: Are you come to inquire of me? As I live, I will not answer you, saith the Lord God.

4 If thou judgest them, if thou judgest, O son of man, declare to them the abominations of their fathers.

5 And say to them: Thus saith the Lord God: In the day when I chose Israel and lifted up my hand for the race of the house of Jacob, and appeared to them in the land of Egypt and lifted up my hand for them saying: I *am* the Lord your God:

6 In that day, I lifted up my hand for them, to bring them out of the land of Egypt, into a land which I had provided for them, flowing with milk and honey, which excelleth amongst all lands.

7 And I said to them: Let every man cast away the scandals of his eyes, and defile not yourselves with the idols of Egypt. I *am* the Lord your God.

8 But they provoked me and would not hearken to me: they did not every man cast away the abominations of his eyes, neither did they forsake the idols of Egypt. And I said I would pour out

[6] Matt. 3, 2; Luke, 3, 3.   [7] Ezech. 18, 23; 33, 11; 2 Peter, 3, 9. CHAP. 19. [1] Osee, 13, 15.

CHAP. 19. Ver. 2. *Thy mother the lioness.* Jerusalem.
Ver. 3. *One of her whelps.* Joachaz, otherwise Sellum.
Ver. 5. *One of her young lions.* Joakim.
CHAP. 20. Ver. 4. *If thou judgest them.* Or, if thou wilt enter into the cause and plead against them.
Ver. 7. *Scandals. Offensiones.* That is, the abominations or idols, to the worship of which they were allured by their eyes.

my indignation upon them and accomplish my wrath against them in the midst of the land of Egypt.

9 But I did *otherwise* for my name's sake, that it might not be violated before the nations, in the midst of whom they were, and among whom I made myself known to them, to bring them out of the land of Egypt.

10 Therefore I brought them out from the land of Egypt and brought them into the desert.

11 ¹ And I gave them my statutes, and I shewed them my judgments, which, if a man do, he shall live in them.

12 ² Moreover, I gave them also my sabbaths, to be a sign between me and them: and that they might know that I am the Lord that sanctify them.

13 But the house of Israel provoked me in the desert: they walked not in my statutes and they cast away my judgments, which if a man do, he shall live in them, and they grievously violated my sabbaths. I said therefore that I would pour out my indignation upon them in the desert and would consume them.

14 But I spared them for the sake of my name, lest it should be profaned before the nations from which I brought them out in their sight.

15 So I lifted up my hand over them in the desert, not to bring them into the land which I had given them flowing with milk and honey, the best of all lands.

16 Because they cast off my judgments and walked not in my statutes and violated my sabbaths: for their heart went after idols.

17 Yet my eye spared them, so that I destroyed them not: neither did I consume them in the desert.

18 And I said to their children in the wilderness: Walk not in the statutes of your fathers and observe not their judgments, nor be ye defiled with their idols.

19 I *am* the Lord your God: Walk ye in my statutes, and observe my judgments and do them.

20 And sanctify my sabbaths: that they may be a sign between me and you, and that you may know that I am the Lord your God.

21 But their children provoked me,

Chap. 20. ¹ Lev. 18, 5; Rom. 10, 5. ² Exod. 20, 8; 31, 13; Deut. 5, 12.

Ver. 25. *Statutes that were not good.* The laws and ordinances of their enemies, or those imposed upon them by that cruel tyrant the devil, to whose power they were delivered up for their sins.

Ver. 26. *I polluted them.* That is, I gave them up to such blindness, in punishment of their offences, as to pollute themselves with the blood of all their firstborn, whom they offered up to their idols in compliance with their wicked devices.

they walked not in my commandments nor observed my judgments to do them, which if a man do, he shall live in them: and they violated my sabbaths. And I threatened to pour out my indignation upon them and to accomplish my wrath in them in the desert.

22 But I turned away my hand and wrought for my name's sake, that it might not be violated before the nations out of which I brought them forth in their sight.

23 Again I lifted up my hand upon them in the wilderness, to disperse them among the nations and scatter them through the countries:

24 Because they had not done my judgments and had cast off my statutes and had violated my sabbaths, and their eyes had been after the idols of their fathers.

25 Therefore I also gave them statutes that were not good, and judgments, in which they shall not live.

26 And I polluted them in their own gifts, when they offered all that opened the womb, for their offences. And they shall know that I am the Lord.

27 Wherefore speak to the house of Israel, O son of man, and say to them: Thus saith the Lord God: Moreover in this also your fathers blasphemed me, when they had despised and contemned me;

28 And I had brought them into the land for which I lifted up my hand to give it them. They saw every high hill and every shady tree, and there they sacrificed their victims: and there they presented the provocation of their offerings: and there they set their sweet odours and poured forth their libations.

29 And I said to them: What meaneth the high place to which you go? And the name thereof was called Highplace even to this day.

30 Wherefore say to the house of Israel: Thus saith the Lord God: Verily, you are defiled in the way of your fathers and you commit fornication with their abominations.

31 And you defile yourselves with all your idols unto this day, in the offering of your gifts, when you make your children pass through the fire. And shall I answer you, O house of Israel? *As* I live, saith the Lord God, I will not answer you.

32 Neither shall the thought of your mind come to pass, by which you say: We will be as the Gentiles and as the families of the earth, to worship stocks and stones.

33 *As* I live, saith the Lord God, I will reign over you with a strong hand and with a stretched out arm and with fury poured out.

34 And I will bring you out from the people, and I will gather you out of the countries in which you are scattered. I will reign over you with a strong hand and with a stretched out arm and with fury poured out.

35 And I will bring you into the wilderness of people: and there will I plead with you face to face.

36 As I pleaded against your fathers in the desert of the land of Egypt; even so will I judge you, saith the Lord God.

37 And I will make you subject to my sceptre and will bring you into the bands of the covenant.

38 And I will pick out from among you the transgressors and the wicked and will bring them out of the land where they sojourn: and they shall not enter into the land of Israel. And you shall know that I am the Lord.

39 And as for you, O house of Israel: thus saith the Lord God: Walk ye every one after your idols and serve them. But if in this also you hear me not, but defile my holy name any more with your gifts and with your idols:

40 In my holy mountain, in the high mountain of Israel, saith the Lord God, there shall all the house of Israel serve me; all of them, I say, in the land in which they shall please me. And there will I require your firstfruits and the chief of your tithes with all your sanctifications.

41 I will accept of you for an odour of sweetness, when I shall have brought you out from the people and shall have gathered you out of the lands into which you are scattered: and I will be sanctified in you in the sight of the nations.

42 And you shall know that I am the Lord, when I shall have brought you into the land of Israel, into the land for which I lifted up my hand to give it to your fathers.

43 And there you shall remember your ways and all your wicked doings with which you have been defiled: and you shall be displeased with yourselves in your own sight for all your wicked deeds which you committed.

44 And you shall know that I am the Lord, when I shall have done well by you for my own name's sake and not according to your evil ways nor according to your wicked deeds, O house of Israel, saith the Lord God.

45 And the word of the Lord came to me, saying:

46 Son of man, set thy face against the way of the south, and drop towards the south, and prophesy against the forest of the south field.

47 And say to the south forest: Hear the word of the Lord: Thus saith the Lord God: Behold I will kindle a fire in thee and will burn in thee every green tree and every dry tree. The flame of the fire shall not be quenched: and every face shall be burned in it, from the south even to the north.

48 And all flesh shall see that I the Lord have kindled it: and it shall not be quenched.

49 And I said: Ah, ah, ah, O Lord God, they say of me: Doth not this man speak by parables?

CHAPTER 21

The destruction of Jerusalem by the sword is further described. The ruin also of the Ammonites is foreshewn. And finally Babylon, the destroyer of others, shall be destroyed.

AND the word of the Lord came to me, saying:

2 Son of man, set thy face toward Jerusalem, and let thy speech flow towards the holy places, and prophesy against the land of Israel:

3 And say to the land of Israel: Thus saith the Lord God: Behold I come against thee, and I will draw forth my sword out of its sheath and will cut off in thee the just and the wicked.

4 And forasmuch as I have cut off in thee the just and the wicked, therefore shall my sword go forth out of its sheath against all flesh, from the south even to the north.

5 That all flesh may know that I the Lord have drawn my sword out of its sheath not to be turned back.

6 And thou, son of man, mourn with the breaking of thy loins, and with bitterness sigh before them.

7 And when they shall say to thee: Why mournest thou? Thou shalt say: For that which I hear: because it cometh, and every heart shall melt, and all hands shall be made feeble, and every spirit shall faint, and water shall run down every knee. Behold it cometh, and it shall be done, saith the Lord God.

Ver. 35. *The wilderness of people.* That is, a desert in which there are no people.

Ver. 39. *Walk ye every one.* It is not an allowance, much less a commandment, to serve idols; but a figure of speech, by which God would have them to understand that, if they would walk after their idols, they must not pretend to serve him at the same time: for that he would by no means suffer such a mixture of worship.

Ver. 40. *In my holy mountain.* The foregoing verse, to make the sense complete, must be understood so as to condemn and reject that mixture of worship which the Jews then followed. In this verse God promises to the true Israelites, especially to those of the Christian church, that they shall serve him in another manner, in his holy mountain, the spiritual Sion, and shall be accepted of by him.

Ver. 46. *Of the south.* Jerusalem lay towards the south of Babylon (where the prophet then was), and is here called *the forest of the south field* and is threatened with utter desolation.

8 And the word of the Lord came to me, saying:

9 Son of man, prophesy and say: Thus saith the Lord God: Say: The sword, the sword, is sharpened and furbished.

10 It is sharpened to kill victims: it is furbished that it may glitter. Thou removest the sceptre of my son: thou hast cut down every tree.

11 And I have given it to be furbished, that it may be handled: this sword is sharpened and it is furbished, that it may be in the hand of the slayer.

12 Cry and howl, O son of man, for this *sword* is upon my people: it is upon all the princes of Israel that are fled. They are delivered up to the sword with my people: strike therefore upon thy thigh,

13 Because it is tried: and that when it shall overthrow the sceptre, and it shall not be, saith the Lord God.

14 Thou therefore, O son of man, prophesy and strike thy hands together: and let the sword be doubled, and let the sword of the slain be tripled. This is the sword of a great slaughter that maketh them stand amazed.

15 And languish in heart, and that multiplieth ruins. In all their gates I have set the dread of the sharp sword, the sword that is furbished to glitter, that is made ready for slaughter.

16 Be thou sharpened: go to the right hand or to the left, which way soever thou hast a mind to set thy face.

17 And I will clap my hands together and will satisfy my indignation: I, the Lord, have spoken.

18 And the word of the Lord came to me, saying:

19 And thou son of man, set thee two ways for the sword of the king of Babylon to come: both shall come forth out

of the land. And with his hand he shall draw lots: he shall consult at the head of the way of the city.

20 Thou shalt make a way that the sword may come to Rabbath of the children of Ammon and to Juda, unto Jerusalem the strong city.

21 For the king of Babylon stood in the highway, at the head of two ways, seeking divination, shuffling arrows: he inquired of the idols and consulted entrails.

22 On his right hand was the divination for Jerusalem, to set battering rams, to open the mouth in slaughter, to lift up the voice in howling, to set engines against the gates, to cast up a mount to build forts.

23 And he shall be in their eyes as one consulting the oracle in vain and imitating the leisure of sabbaths: but he will call to remembrance the iniquity that they may be taken.

24 Therefore thus saith the Lord God: Because you have remembered your iniquity and have discovered your prevarications, and your sins have appeared in all your devices: because, I say, you have remembered, you shall be taken with the hand.

25 But thou profane wicked prince of Israel, whose day is come, that hath been appointed in the time of iniquity:

26 Thus saith the Lord God: Remove the diadem, take off the crown. Is it not this that hath exalted the low one, and brought down him that was high?

27 I will shew it to be iniquity, iniquity, iniquity: but this was not done till he came to whom judgment belongeth, and I will give it him.

28 ¹ And thou son of man, prophesy and say: Thus saith the Lord God concerning the children of Ammon and concerning their reproach. And thou shalt say: O sword, O sword, come out of the scabbard to kill, be furbished to destroy and to glitter,

29 Whilst they see vain things in thy regard and divine lies: to bring thee upon the necks of the wicked that are wounded, whose appointed day is come in the time of iniquity.

30 Return into thy sheath. I will judge thee in the place wherein thou wast created, in the land of thy nativity.

31 And I will pour out upon thee my indignation: in the fire of my rage will I blow upon thee and will give thee into the hands of men that are brutish and contrive thy destruction.

32 Thou shalt be fuel for the fire, thy blood shall be in the midst of the land: thou shalt be forgotten. For I, the Lord, have spoken *it*.

CHAP. 21. ¹ Gen. 49, 10.

CHAP. 21. Ver. 10. *Thou removest the sceptre of my son.* He speaks (according to St. Jerome) to the *sword* of Nabuchodonosor, which was about to remove the sceptre of Israel, whom God here calls his *son*.

Ver. 25. *Thou profane.* He speaks to king Sedecias, who had broken his oath, and was otherwise a wicked prince.

Ver. 26. *Is it not this that hath exalted the low one?* The royal crown of Juda had exalted Sedecias from a private state and condition to the sovereign power, as the loss of it had brought down Jechonias.

Ver. 27. *I will shew it to be iniquity.* I will overturn it, that is, the crown of Juda, for the manifold iniquities of the kings: but it shall not be utterly removed till Christ come whose right it is, and who shall reign in the spiritual house of Jacob, that is, in his church, for evermore.

Ver. 28. *Concerning their reproach.* By which they had reproached and insulted over the Jews, at the time of the destruction of Jerusalem.

Ver. 30. *Return into thy sheath.* The sword of Babylon, after raging against many nations, was shortly to be judged and destroyed at home by the Medes and Persians.

CHAPTER 22

The general corruption of the inhabitants of Jerusalem, for which God will consume them as dross in his furnace.

AND the word of the Lord came to me, saying:

2 And thou son of man, dost thou not judge, dost thou not judge the city of blood?

3 And thou shalt shew her all her abominations and shalt say: Thus saith the Lord God: *This is* the city that sheddeth blood in the midst of her, that her time may come: and that hath made idols against herself, to defile herself.

4 Thou art become guilty in thy blood which thou hast shed and thou art defiled in thy idols which thou hast made: and thou hast made thy days to draw near and hast brought on the time of thy years. Therefore have I made thee a reproach to the Gentiles and a mockery to all countries.

5 Those that are near and those that are far from thee shall triumph over thee: thou filthy one, infamous, great in destruction.

6 Behold, the princes of Israel: every one hath employed his arm in thee to shed blood.

7 They have abused father and mother in thee: they have oppressed the stranger in the midst of thee: they have grieved the fatherless and widow in thee.

8 Thou hast despised my sanctuaries and profaned my sabbaths.

9 Slanderers have been in thee to shed blood and they have eaten upon the mountains in thee: they have committed wickedness in the midst of thee.

10 They have discovered the nakedness of their father in thee, they have humbled the uncleanness of the menstruous woman in thee.

11 [1] And every one hath committed abomination with his neighbour's wife, and the father-in-law wickedly defiled his daughter-in-law: the brother hath oppressed his sister, the daughter of his father, in thee.

12 They have taken gifts in thee to shed blood: thou hast taken usury and increase and hast covetously oppressed thy neighbours: and thou hast forgotten me, saith the Lord God.

13 Behold, I have clapped my hands at thy covetousness which thou hast exercised: and at the blood that hath been shed in the midst of thee.

14 Shall thy heart endure or shall thy hands prevail, in the days which I will bring upon thee: I, the Lord, have spoken and will do it.

15 And I will disperse thee in the nations and will scatter thee among the countries, and I will put an end to thy uncleanness in thee.

16 And I will possess thee in the sight of the Gentiles, and thou shalt know that I am the Lord.

17 And the word of the Lord came to me, saying:

18 Son of man, the house of Israel is become dross to me. All these are brass and tin and iron and lead in the midst of the furnace: they are become the dross of silver.

19 Therefore, thus saith the Lord God: Because you are all turned into dross, therefore, behold I will gather you together in the midst of Jerusalem.

20 As they gather silver and brass and tin and iron and lead in the midst of the furnace: that I may kindle a fire in it to melt it: so will I gather you together in my fury and in my wrath and will take my rest, and I will melt you down.

21 And I will gather you together and will burn you in the fire of my wrath: and you shall be melted in the midst thereof.

22 As silver is melted in the midst of the furnace, so shall you be in the midst thereof: and you shall know that I am the Lord, when I have poured out my indignation upon you.

23 And the word of the Lord came to me, saying:

24 Son of man, say to her: Thou art a land that is unclean and not rained upon in the day of wrath.

25 There is a conspiracy of prophets in the midst thereof: like a lion that roareth and catcheth the prey, they have devoured souls, they have taken riches and hire, they have made many widows in the midst thereof.

26 Her priests have despised my law and have defiled my sanctuaries: they have put no difference between holy and profane, nor have distinguished between the polluted and the clean, and they have turned away their eyes from my sabbaths: and I was profaned in the midst of them.

27 [2] Her princes in the midst of her are like wolves ravening the prey to shed blood and to destroy souls and to run after gains through covetousness.

28 And her prophets have daubed them without tempering *the mortar,* seeing vain things and divining lies unto them, saying: Thus saith the Lord God: when the Lord hath not spoken.

29 The people of the land have used oppression and committed robbery: they afflicted the needy and poor and

CHAP. 22. [1] Jer. 5, 8. [2] Mich. 3, 11; Soph. 3, 3.

they oppressed the stranger by calumny without judgment.

30 And I sought among them for a man that might set up a hedge and stand in the gap before me in favour of the land, that I might not destroy it: and I found none.

31 And I poured out my indignation upon them: in the fire of my wrath I consumed them. I have rendered their way upon their own head, saith the Lord God.

CHAPTER 23

Under the names of the two harlots, Oolla and Ooliba, are described the manifold disloyalties of Samaria and Jerusalem, with the punishment of them both.

AND the word of the Lord came to me, saying:

2 Son of man, there were two women, daughters of one mother.

3 And they committed fornication in Egypt: in their youth they committed fornication. There were their breasts pressed down, and the teats of their virginity were bruised.

4 And their names were Oolla the elder and Ooliba her younger sister: and I took them, and they bore sons and daughters. Now for their names: Samaria is Oolla and Jerusalem is Ooliba.

5 And Oolla committed fornication against me and doted on her lovers, on the Assyrians that came to her,

6 Who were clothed with blue, princes and rulers, beautiful youths, all horsemen, mounted upon horses.

7 And she committed her fornications with those chosen men, all sons of the Assyrians: and she defiled herself with the uncleanness of all them on whom she doted.

8 Moreover also, she did not forsake her fornications which she had committed in Egypt: for they also lay with her in her youth and they bruised the breasts of her virginity and poured out their fornication upon her.

9 Therefore have I delivered her into the hands of her lovers, into the hands of the sons of the Assyrians, upon whose lust she doted.

10 ¹They discovered her disgrace,

Chap. 23. ¹ Ezech. 16, 38.

Chap. 23. Ver. 3. *Committed fornication.* That is, idolatry.

Ver. 4. *Oolla and Ooliba.* God calls the kingdom of Israel, *Oolla,* which signifies *their own habitation,* because they separated themselves from his temple: and the kingdom of Juda, *Ooliba,* which signifies *his habitation in her,* because of his temple among them in Jerusalem.

Ver. 5. *On the Assyrians.* That is, the idols of the Assyrians: for all that is said ·in this chapter of the fornications of Israel and Juda is to be understood, in a spiritual sense, of their disloyalty to the Lord, by worshipping strange gods.

took away her sons and daughters, and slew her with the sword: and they became infamous women and they executed judgments in her.

11 And when her sister Ooliba saw this, she was mad with lust more than she: and she carried her fornication beyond the fornication of her sister,

12 Impudently prostituting herself to the children of the Assyrians, the princes and rulers that came to her, clothed with divers colours, to the horsemen that rode upon horses, and to young men, all of great beauty.

13 And I saw that she was defiled and that they both took one way.

14 And she increased her fornications: and when she had seen men painted on the wall, the images of the Chaldeans set forth in colours,

15 And girded with girdles about their reins, and with dyed turbans on their heads, the resemblance of all the captains, the likeness of the sons of Babylon and of the land of the Chaldeans wherein they were born,

16 She doted upon them with the lust of her eyes and she sent messengers to them into Chaldea.

17 And when the sons of Babylon were come to her to the bed of love, they defiled her with their fornications, and she was polluted by them and her soul was glutted with them.

18 And she discovered her fornications and discovered her disgrace: and my soul was alienated from her, as my soul was alienated from her sister.

19 For she multiplied her fornications, remembering the days of her youth, in which she played the harlot in the land of Egypt.

20 And she was mad with lust after lying with them whose flesh is as the flesh of asses: and whose issue is as the issue of horses.

21 And thou hast renewed the wickedness of thy youth, when thy breasts were pressed in Egypt and the paps of thy virginity broken.

22 Therefore, Ooliba, thus saith the Lord God: Behold I will raise up against thee all thy lovers with whom thy soul hath been glutted, and I will gather them together against thee round about.

23 The children of Babylon and all the Chaldeans, the nobles, and the kings and princes, all the sons of the Assyrians, beautiful young men, all the captains and rulers, the princes of princes and the renowned horsemen.

24 And they shall come upon thee well appointed with chariot and wheel, a multitude of people: they shall be armed against thee on every side with

breastplate and buckler and helmet: and I will set judgment before them, and they shall judge thee by their judgments.

25 And I will set my jealousy against thee, which they shall execute upon thee with fury. They shall cut off thy nose and thy ears: and what remains shall fall by the sword. They shall take thy sons and thy daughters, and thy residue shall be devoured by fire.

26 And they shall strip thee of thy garments and take away the instruments of thy glory.

27 And I will put an end to thy wickedness in thee and thy fornication *brought* out of the land of Egypt: neither shalt thou lift up thy eyes to them nor remember Egypt any more.

28 For thus saith the Lord God: Behold, I will deliver thee into the hands of them whom thou hatest, into their hands with whom thy soul hath been glutted.

29 And they shall deal with thee in hatred, and they shall take away all thy labours and shall let thee go naked and full of disgrace; and the disgrace of thy fornication shall be discovered, thy wickedness and thy fornications.

30 They have done these things to thee, because thou hast played the harlot with the nations among which thou wast defiled with their idols.

31 Thou hast walked in the way of thy sister, and I will give her cup into thy hand.

32 Thus saith the Lord God: Thou shalt drink thy sister's cup, deep and wide: thou shalt be had in derision and scorn, which containeth very much.

33 Thou shalt be filled with drunkenness and sorrow: with the cup of grief and sadness, with the cup of thy sister Samaria.

34 And thou shalt drink it and shalt drink it up even to the dregs, and thou shalt devour the fragments thereof: thou shalt rend thy breasts. Because I have spoken *it*, saith the Lord God.

35 Therefore thus saith the Lord God: Because thou hast forgotten me and hast cast me off behind thy back, bear thou also thy wickedness and thy fornications.

36 And the Lord spoke to me, saying: Son of man, dost thou judge Oolla and Ooliba, and dost thou declare to them their wicked deeds?

37 Because they have committed adultery, and blood is in their hands, and they have committed fornication with their idols: moreover also their children, whom they bore to me, they have offered to them to be devoured.

38 Yea, and they have done this to me. They polluted my sanctuary on the same day and profaned my sabbaths.

39 And when they sacrificed their children to their idols and went into my sanctuary the same day to profane it: they did these things even in the midst of my house.

40 They sent for men coming from afar, to whom they had sent a messenger: and behold they came. For whom thou didst wash thyself and didst paint thy eyes and wast adorned with women's ornaments.

41 Thou sattest on a very fine bed, and a table was decked before thee: whereupon thou didst set my incense and my ointment.

42 And there was in her the voice of a multitude rejoicing: and to some that were brought of the multitude of men and that came from the desert, they put bracelets on their hands and beautiful crowns on their heads.

43 And I said to her that was worn out in her adulteries: Now will this woman still continue in her fornication.

44 And they went in to her, as to a harlot: so went they in unto Oolla and Ooliba, wicked women.

45 They therefore are just men: these shall judge them as adulteresses are judged, and as shedders of blood are judged: because they are adulteresses, and blood is in their hands.

46 For thus saith the Lord God: Bring a multitude upon them and deliver them over to tumult and rapine:

47 And let the people stone them with stones, and let them be stabbed with their swords. They shall kill their sons and daughters, and their houses they shall burn with fire.

48 And I will take away wickedness out of the land: and all women shall learn not to do according to the wickedness of them.

49 And they shall render your wickedness upon you, and you shall bear the sins of your idols: and you shall know that I am the Lord God.

CHAPTER 24

Under the parable of a boiling pot is shewn the utter destruction of Jerusalem, for which the Jews at Babylon shall not dare to mourn.

AND the word of the Lord came to me in the ninth year, in the tenth month, the tenth day of the month, saying:

2 Son of man, write thee the name of this day, on which the king of Babylon hath set himself against Jerusalem to-day.

3 And thou shalt speak by a figure,

CHAP. 23. Ver. 45. *Just men.* That is, ministers of the Divine justice.

a parable, to the provoking house and say to them: Thus saith the Lord God: Set on a pot, set it on, I say, and put water into it.

4 Heap together into it the pieces thereof, every good piece, the thigh and the shoulder, choice pieces and full of bones.

5 Take the fattest of the flock and lay together piles of bones under it: the seething thereof is boiling hot and the bones thereof are thoroughly sodden in the midst of it.

6 Therefore thus saith the Lord God: Woe to the bloody city, to the pot whose rust is in it, and its rust is not gone out of it. Cast it out piece by piece: there hath no lot fallen upon it.

7 For her blood is in the midst of her, she hath shed it upon the smooth rock: she hath not shed it upon the ground, that it might be covered with dust.

8 And that I might bring my indignation upon her and take my vengeance. I have shed her blood upon the smooth rock, that it should not be covered.

9 Therefore thus saith the Lord God: [1] Woe to the bloody city, of which I will make a great bonfire.

10 Heap together the bones which I will burn with fire: the flesh shall be consumed and the whole composition shall be sodden and the bones shall be consumed.

11 Then set it empty upon burning coals, that it may be hot and the brass thereof may be melted: and let the filth of it be melted in the midst thereof and let the rust of it be consumed.

12 Great pains have been taken, and the great rust thereof is not gone out, not even by fire.

13 Thy uncleanness is execrable: because I desired to cleanse thee, and thou art not cleansed from thy filthiness. Neither shalt thou be cleansed, before I cause my indignation to rest in thee.

14 I, the Lord, have spoken. It shall come to pass, and I will do it: I will not pass by, nor spare, nor be pacified. I will judge thee according to thy ways and according to thy doings, saith the Lord.

15 And the word of the Lord came to me, saying:

16 Son of man, behold I take from thee the desire of thy eyes with a stroke: and thou shalt not lament nor weep: neither shall thy tears dun down.

17 Sigh in silence, make no mourning for the dead: let the tire of thy head be upon thee and thy shoes on thy feet, and cover not thy face nor eat the meat of mourners.

18 So I spoke to the people in the morning, and my wife died in the evening: and I did in the morning as he had commanded me.

19 And the people said to me: Why dost thou not tell us what these things mean that thou doest?

20 And I said to them: The word of the Lord came to me, saying:

21 Speak to the house of Israel: Thus saith the Lord God: Behold I will profane my sanctuary, the glory of your realm and the thing that your eyes desire and for which your soul feareth: your sons, and your daughters, whom you have left, shall fall by the sword.

22 And you shall do as I have done: you shall not cover your faces nor shall you eat the meat of mourners.

23 You shall have crowns on your heads and shoes on your feet: you shall not lament nor weep, but you shall pine away for your iniquities, and every one shall sigh with his brother.

24 And Ezechiel shall be unto you for a sign of things to come: according to all that he hath done, so shall you do, when this shall come to pass. And you shall know that I am the Lord God.

25 And thou, O son of man, behold in the day wherein I will take away from them their strength and the joy of their glory and the desire of their eyes upon which their souls rest, their sons and their daughters.

26 In that day when he that escapeth shall come to thee to tell thee:

27 In that day, I say, shall thy mouth be opened to him that hath escaped, and thou shalt speak and shalt be silent no more: and thou shalt be unto them for a sign of things to come. And you shall know that I am the Lord.

CHAPTER 25

A prophecy against the Ammonites, Moabites, Edomites, and Philistines, for their malice against the Israelites.

AND the word of the Lord came to me, saying:

2 Son of man, set thy face against the children of Ammon, and thou shalt prophesy of them.

3 [1] And thou shalt say to the children of Ammon: Hear ye the word of the Lord God: Thus saith the Lord God: Because thou hast said: Ha, ha, upon my sanctuary, because it was profaned: and upon the land of Israel, because it was laid waste: and upon the house of Juda, because they are led into captivity:

4 Therefore will I deliver thee to the men of the east for an inheritance, and they shall place their sheepcotes in thee and shall set up their tents in thee.

Chap. 24. [1] Nah. 3, 1; Hab. 2, 12. Chap. 25. [1] Jer. 27, 3; 49, 1.

They shall eat thy fruits: and they shall drink thy milk.

5 And I will make Rabbath a stable for camels, and the children of Ammon a couching place for flocks: and you shall know that I am the Lord.

6 For thus saith the Lord God: Because thou hast clapped thy hands and stamped with thy foot, and hast rejoiced with all thy heart against the land of Israel:

7 Therefore, behold I will stretch forth my hand upon thee and will deliver thee to be the spoil of nations and will cut thee off from among the people and destroy thee out of the lands and break thee in pieces: and thou shalt know that I am the Lord.

8 Thus saith the Lord God: Because Moab and Seir have said: Behold the house of Juda is like all other nations:

9 Therefore, behold I will open the shoulder of Moab from the cities, from his cities, I say, and his borders, the noble cities of the land of Bethiesimoth and Beelmeon and Cariathaim,

10 To the people of the east with the children of Ammon: and I will give it them for an inheritance, that there may be no more any remembrance of the children of Ammon among the nations.

11 And I will execute judgments in Moab: and they shall know that I am the Lord.

12 ² Thus saith the Lord God: Because Edom hath taken vengeance to revenge herself of the children of Juda, and hath greatly offended, and hath sought revenge of them:

13 Therefore thus saith the Lord God: I will stretch forth my hand upon Edom and will take away out of it man and beast and will make it desolate from the south: and they that are in Dedan shall fall by the sword.

14 And I will lay my vengeance upon Edom by the hand of my people Israel: and they shall do in Edom according to my wrath and my fury: and they shall know my vengeance, saith the Lord God.

15 Thus saith the Lord God: Because the Philistines have taken vengeance and have revenged themselves with all their mind, destroying and satisfying old enmities:

16 Therefore thus saith the Lord God: Behold I will stretch forth my hand upon the Philistines and will kill the killers and will destroy the remnant of the sea coast.

17 And I wil execute great vengeance upon them, rebuking them in fury: and they shall know that I am the Lord, when I shall lay my vengeance upon them.

CHAPTER 26

A prophecy of the destruction of the famous city of Tyre by Nabuchodonosor.

AND it came to pass in the eleventh year, the first day of the month, that the word of the Lord came to me, saying:

2 Son of man, because Tyre hath said of Jerusalem: Aha, the gates of the people are broken, she is turned to me: I shall be filled, *now* she is laid waste.

3 Therefore thus saith the Lord God: Behold I come against thee, O Tyre, and I will cause many nations to come up to thee, as the waves of the sea rise up.

4 And they shall break down the walls of Tyre and destroy the towers thereof: and I will scrape her dust from her and make her like a smooth rock.

5 She shall be a drying place for nets in the midst of the sea, because I have spoken *it,* saith the Lord God: and she shall be a spoil to the nations.

6 Her daughters also that are in the field shall be slain by the sword: and they shall know that I am the Lord.

7 For thus saith the Lord God: Behold I will bring against Tyre Nabuchodonosor king of Babylon, the king of kings, from the north, with horses and chariots and horsemen and companies and much people.

8 Thy daughters that are in the field he shall kill with the sword: and he shall compass thee with forts and shall cast up a mount round about: and he shall lift up the buckler against thee.

9 And he shall set engines of war and battering rams against thy walls and shall destroy thy towers with his arms.

10 By reason of the multitude of his horses, their dust shall cover thee: thy walls shall shake at the noise of the horsemen and wheels and chariots: when they shall go in at thy gates, as by the entrance of a city that is destroyed.

11 With the hoofs of his horses he shall tread down all thy streets: thy people he shall kill with the sword, and thy famous statues shall fall to the ground.

12 They shall waste thy riches, they shall make a spoil of thy merchandise, and they shall destroy thy walls and pull down thy fine houses: and they shall lay thy stones and thy timber and thy dust in the midst of the waters.

13 ¹ And I will make the multitude of thy songs to cease, and the sound of thy harps shall be heard no more.

² Jer. 49, 7. CHAP. 26. ¹ Jer. 7, 34.

CHAP. 25. Ver. 5. *Rabbath.* The capital city of the Ammonites, which was afterwards called *Philadelphia.*

14 And I will make thee like a naked rock: thou shalt be a drying place for nets, neither shalt thou be built any more. For I have spoken it, saith the Lord God.

15 Thus saith the Lord God to Tyre: Shall not the islands shake at the sound of thy fall and the groans of thy slain when they shall be killed in the midst of thee?

16 Then all the princes of the sea shall come down from their thrones, and take off their robes and cast away their broidered garments and be clothed with astonishment: they shall sit on the ground and with amazement shall wonder at thy sudden fall.

17 And taking up a lamentation over thee, they shall say to thee: How art thou fallen, that dwellest in the sea, renowned city that wast strong in the sea, with thy inhabitants whom all did dread?

18 Now shall the ships be astonished in the day of thy terror: and the islands in the sea shall be troubled because no one cometh out of thee.

19 For thus saith the Lord God: When I shall make thee a desolate city like the cities that are not inhabited: and shall bring the deep upon thee, and many waters shall cover thee:

20 And when I shall bring thee down with those that descend into the pit, to the everlasting people, and shall set thee in the lowest parts of the earth, as places desolate of old, with them that are brought down into the pit, that thou be not inhabited: and when I shall give glory in the land of the living,

21 I will bring thee to nothing, and thou shalt not be: and if thou be sought for, thou shalt not be found any more for ever, saith the Lord God.

CHAPTER 27

A description of the glory and riches of Tyre, and of her irrecoverable fall.

AND the word of the Lord came to me, saying:

2 Thou therefore, O son of man, take up a lamentation for Tyre:

3 And say to Tyre that dwelleth at the entry of the sea, being the mart of the people for many islands: Thus saith the Lord God: O Tyre, thou hast said: I am of perfect beauty.

4 And situate in the heart of the sea. Thy neighbours that built thee have perfected thy beauty:

5 With fir trees of Sanir they have built thee, with all sea planks: they

CHAP. 27. Ver. 5. *Sea planks.* That is, timber brought by sea to build the city.
Ver. 11. *The Pygmeans.* That is, strong and valiant men. In Hebrew, *Gammadim.*
Ver. 16. *Chodchod.* It is the Hebrew name for some precious stone, but of what kind in particular interpreters are not agreed.

have taken cedars from Libanus to make thee masts.

6 They have cut thy oars out of the oaks of Basan: and they have made thee benches of Indian ivory and cabins with things brought from the islands of Italy.

7 Fine broidered linen from Egypt was woven for thy sail, to be spread on thy mast: blue and purple from the islands of Elisa were made thy covering.

8 The inhabitants of Sidon and the Arabians were thy rowers: thy wise men, O Tyre, were thy pilots.

9 The ancients of Gebal and the wise men thereof furnished mariners for the service of thy various furniture: all the ships of the sea and their mariners were thy factors.

10 The Persians and Lydians and the Libyans were thy soldiers in thy army: they hung up the buckler and the helmet in thee for thy ornament.

11 The men of Arad were with thy army upon thy walls round about: the Pygmeans also that were in thy towers hung up their quivers on thy walls round about: they perfected thy beauty.

12 The Carthaginians, thy merchants, supplied thy fairs with a multitude of all kinds of riches with silver, iron, tin and lead.

13 Greece, Thubal and Mosoch, they were thy merchants: they brought to thy people slaves and vessels of brass.

14 From the house of Thogorma they brought horses and horsemen and mules to thy market.

15 The men of Dedan were thy merchants, many islands *were* the traffic of thy hand: they exchanged for thy price teeth of ivory and ebony.

16 The Syrian was thy merchant: by reason of the multitude of thy works, they set forth precious stones and purple and broidered works and fine linen and silk and chodchod in thy market.

17 Juda and the land of Israel, they were thy merchants with the best corn: they set forth balm and honey and oil and rosin in thy fairs.

18 The men of Damascus were thy merchants in the multitude of thy works, in the multitude of divers riches, in rich wine, in wool of the best colour.

19 Dan and Greece and Mosel have set forth in thy marts wrought iron: stacte and calamus were in thy market.

20 The men of Dedan were thy merchants in tapestry for seats.

21 Arabia and all the princes of Cedar, they were the merchants of thy hand: thy merchants came to thee with lambs and rams and kids.

22 The sellers of Saba and Reema, they were thy merchants: with all the best spices and precious stones and

gold, which they set forth in thy market.

23 Haran and Chene and Eden *were* thy merchants; Saba, Assur and Chelmad sold to thee.

24 They were thy merchants in divers manners, with bales of blue *cloth* and of embroidered work and of precious riches, which were wrapped up and bound with cords: they had cedars also in thy merchandise.

25 The ships of the sea were thy chief in thy merchandise: and thou wast replenished and glorified exceedingly in the heart of the sea.

26 Thy rowers have brought thee into great waters: the south wind hath broken thee in the heart of the sea.

27 Thy riches and thy treasures and thy manifold furniture, thy mariners and thy pilots who kept thy goods and were chief over thy people. Thy men of war also that were in thee, with all thy multitude that is in the midst of thee shall fall in the heart of the sea in the day of thy ruin.

28 Thy fleets shall be troubled at the sound of the cry of thy pilots.

29 And all that handled the oar shall come down from their ships: the mariners and all the pilots of the sea shall stand upon the land.

30 And they shall mourn over thee with a loud voice and shall cry bitterly: and they shall cast up dust upon their heads and shall be sprinkled with ashes.

31 And they shall shave themselves bald for thee and shall be girded with haircloth: and they shall weep for thee with bitterness of soul, with most bitter weeping.

32 And they shall take up a mournful song for thee and shall lament thee: What *city* is like Tyre, which is become silent in the midst of the sea:

33 Which by thy merchandise that went from thee by sea didst fill many people: which by the multitude of thy riches, and of thy people didst enrich the kings of the earth?

34 Now thou art destroyed by the sea, thy riches are in the bottom of the waters, and all the multitude that was in the midst of thee is fallen.

35 All the inhabitants of the islands are astonished at thee: and all their kings being struck with the storm have changed their countenance.

36 The merchants of people have hissed at thee. Thou art brought to nothing, and thou shalt never be any more.

CHAPTER 28

The king of Tyre, who affected to be like to God, shall fall under the like sentence with Lucifer. The judgment of Sidon. The restoration of Israel.

AND the word of the Lord came to me, saying:

2 Son of man, say to the prince of Tyre: Thus saith the Lord God: Because thy heart is lifted up and thou hast said: I am God, and I sit in the chair of God in the heart of the sea: whereas thou art a man and not God: and hast set thy heart as if it were the heart of God.

3 Behold, thou art wiser than Daniel: no secret is hid from thee.

4 In thy wisdom and thy understanding thou hast made thyself strong: and hast gotten gold and silver into thy treasures.

5 By the greatness of thy wisdom and by thy traffic thou hast increased thy strength: and thy heart is lifted up with thy strength.

6 Therefore, thus saith the Lord God: Because thy heart is lifted up as the heart of God:

7 Therefore behold, I will bring upon thee strangers, the strongest of the nations: and they shall draw their swords against the beauty of thy wisdom and they shall defile thy beauty.

8 They shall kill thee and bring thee down: and thou shalt die the death of them that are slain in the heart of the sea.

9 Wilt thou yet say before them that slay thee: I am God; whereas thou art a man and not God, in the hand of them that slay thee?

10 Thou shalt die the death of the uncircumcised by the hand of strangers: for I have spoken it, saith the Lord God.

11 And the word of the Lord came to me, saying: Son of man, take up a lamentation upon the king of Tyre:

12 And say to him: Thus saith the Lord God: Thou wast the seal of resemblance, full of wisdom and perfect in beauty.

13 Thou wast in the pleasures of the paradise of God: every precious stone *was* thy covering: the sardius, the topaz and the jasper, the chrysolite and the onyx and the beryl, the sapphire and the carbuncle and the emerald: gold the work of thy beauty: and thy pipes were prepared in the day that thou wast created.

Chap. 28. Ver. 3. *Thou art wiser than Daniel.* In thy own conceit. The wisdom of Daniel was so much celebrated in his days that it became a proverb amongst the Chaldeans when any one would express an extraordinary wisdom to say he was *as wise as Daniel.*

Ver. 12. *Thou wast the seal of resemblance.* The king of Tyre, by his dignity and his natural perfections, bore in himself a certain resemblance of God, by reason of which he might be called *the seal of resemblance.* But what is here said to him is commonly understood of Lucifer, the king over all the children of pride.

14 Thou, a cherub stretched out and protecting, and I set thee in the holy mountain of God: thou hast walked in the midst of the stones of fire.

15 Thou wast perfect in thy ways from the day of thy creation, until iniquity was found in thee.

16 By the multitude of thy merchandise, thy inner parts were filled with iniquity and thou hast sinned: and I cast thee out from the mountain of God and destroyed thee, O covering cherub, out of the midst of the stones of fire.

17 And thy heart was lifted up with thy beauty: thou hast lost thy wisdom in thy beauty: I have cast thee to the ground: I have set thee before the face of kings, that they might behold thee.

18 Thou hast defiled thy sanctuaries by the multitude of thy iniquities and by the iniquity of thy traffic. Therefore I will bring forth a fire from the midst of thee, to devour thee: and I will make thee as ashes upon the earth in the sight of all that see thee.

19 All that shall see thee among the nations shall be astonished at thee: thou art brought to nothing and thou shalt never be any more.

20 And the word of the Lord came to me, saying:

21 Son of man, set thy face against Sidon: and thou shalt prophesy of it,

22 And shalt say: Thus saith the Lord God: Behold I come against thee, Sidon, and I will be glorified in the midst of thee. And they shall know that I am the Lord when I shall execute judgments in her and shall be sanctified in her.

23 And I will send into her pestilence and blood in her streets: and they shall fall being slain by the sword on all sides in the midst thereof. And they shall know that I am the lord.

24 And the house of Israel shall have no more a stumbling-block of bitterness nor a thorn causing pain on every side round about them, of them that are against them. And they shall know that I am the Lord God.

25 Thus saith the Lord God: When I shall have gathered together the house of Israel out of the people among whom they are scattered, I will be sanctified in them before the Gentiles: and they shall dwell in their own land, which I gave to my servant Jacob.

26 And they shall dwell therein secure, and they shall build houses and shall plant vineyards and shall dwell

CHAP. 29. ¹ Isai. 36, 6.

Ver. 14. *A cherub stretched out.* That is, thy wings extended. This alludes to the figure of the cherubims in the sanctuary, which with *stretched out* wings *covered* the ark.—*The stones of fire.* That is, bright and precious stones which sparkle like fire.

with confidence, when I shall have executed judgments upon all that are their enemies round about. And they shall know that I am the Lord their God.

CHAPTER 29

The king of Egypt shall be overthrown and his kingdom wasted. It shall be given to Nabuchodonosor for his service against Tyre.

IN the tenth year, the tenth month, the eleventh day of the month, the word of the Lord came to me, saying:

2 Son of man, set thy face against Pharao king of Egypt: and thou shalt prophesy of him and of all Egypt.

3 Speak and say: Thus saith the Lord God: Behold, I *come* against thee, Pharao king of Egypt, thou great dragon that liest in the midst of thy rivers and sayest: The river is mine and I made myself.

4 But I will put a bridle in thy jaws, and I will cause the fish of thy rivers to stick to thy scales. And I will draw thee out of the midst of thy rivers, and all thy fish shall stick to thy scales.

5 And I will cast thee forth into the desert, and all the fish of thy river. Thou shalt fall upon the face of the earth, thou shalt not be taken up nor gathered together: I have given thee for meat to the beasts of the earth and to the fowls of the air.

6 And all the inhabitants of Egypt shall know that I am the Lord: ¹ because thou hast been a staff of a reed to the house of Israel.

7 When they took hold of thee with the hand thou didst break and rend all their shoulder: and when they leaned upon thee thou brokest and weakenedst all their loins.

8 Therefore, thus saith the Lord God: Behold, I will bring the sword upon thee and cut off man and beast out of thee.

9 And the land of Egypt shall become a desert and a wilderness. And they shall know that I am the Lord. Because thou hast said: The river is mine, and I made it.

10 Therefore, behold I *come* against thee and thy rivers: and I will make the land of Egypt utterly desolate *and* wasted by the sword, from the tower of Syene even to the borders of Ethiopia.

11 The foot of man shall not pass through it, neither shall the foot of beasts go through it: nor shall it be inhabited during forty years.

12 And I will make the land of Egypt desolate in the midst of the lands that are desolate, and the cities thereof in the midst of the cities that are destroyed: and they shall be desolate for

forty years. And I will scatter the Egyptians among the nations and will disperse them through the countries.

13 For thus saith the Lord God: At the end of forty years I will gather the Egyptians from the people among whom they had been scattered.

14 And I will bring back the captivity of Egypt and will place them in the land of Phatures, in the land of their nativity: and they shall be there a low kingdom.

15 It shall be the lowest among other kingdoms and it shall no more be exalted over the nations: and I will diminish them that they shall rule no more over the nations.

16 And they shall be no more a confidence to the house of Israel, teaching iniquity that they may flee and follow them. And they shall know that I am the Lord God.

17 And it came to pass in the seven and twentieth year, in the first *month*, in the first of the month, that word of the Lord came to me, saying:

18 Son of man, Nabuchodonosor king of Babylon hath made his army to undergo hard service against Tyre: every head was made bald and every shoulder was peeled: and there hath been no reward given him nor his army, for Tyre, for the service that he rendered me against it.

19 Therefore thus saith the Lord God: Behold, I will set Nabuchodonosor the king of Babylon in the land of Egypt. ²And he shall take her multitude and take the booty thereof for a prey and rifle the spoils thereof: and it shall be wages for his army.

20 And for the service that he hath done me against it, I have given him the land of Egypt, because he hath laboured for me, saith the Lord God.

21 In that day, a horn shall bud forth to the house of Israel, and I will give thee an open mouth in the midst of them. And they shall know that I am the Lord.

CHAPTER 30

The desolation of Egypt and her helpers. All her cities shall be wasted.

AND ¹the word of the Lord came to me, saying:

2 Son of man, prophesy and say: Thus saith the Lord God: Howl ye, Woe, woe to the day!

3 For the day is near, yea the day of the Lord is near, a cloudy day: it shall be the time of the nations.

4 And the sword shall come upon Egypt: and there shall be dread in Ethiopia, when the wounded shall fall in Egypt, and the multitude thereof

shall be taken away, and the foundations thereof shall be destroyed.

5 Ethiopia and Libya and Lydia and all the rest of the crowd and Chub and the children of the land of the covenant shall fall with them by the sword.

6 Thus saith the Lord God: They also that uphold Egypt shall fall and the pride of her empire shall be brought down: from the tower of Syene shall they fall in it by the sword, saith the Lord, the God of hosts.

7 And they shall be desolate in the midst of the lands that are desolate, and the cities thereof shall be in the midst of the cities that are wasted.

8 And they shall know that I am the Lord: when I shall have set a fire in Egypt, and all the helpers thereof shall be destroyed.

9 In that day shall messengers go forth from my face in ships to destroy the confidence of Ethiopia: and there shall be dread among them in the day of Egypt, because it shall certainly come.

10 Thus saith the Lord God: I will make the multitude of Egypt to cease by the hand of Nabuchodonosor the king of Babylon.

11 He and his people with him, the strongest of nations, shall be brought to destroy the land: and they shall draw their swords upon Egypt and shall fill the land with the slain.

12 And I will make the channels of the rivers dry and will deliver the land into the hand of the wicked: and will lay waste the land and all that is therein by the hands of strangers. I the Lord have spoken it.

13 ²Thus saith the Lord God: I will also destroy the idols and I will make an end of the idols of Memphis: and there shall be no more a prince of the land of Egypt: and I will cause a terror in the land of Egypt.

14 And I will destroy the land of Phatures and will make a fire in Taphnis and will execute judgments in Alexandria.

15 And I will pour out my indignation upon Pelusium, the strength of Egypt, and will cut off the multitude of Alexandria.

16 And I will make a fire in Egypt: Pelusium shall be in pain like a woman in labour, and Alexandria shall be laid waste, and in Memphis there shall be daily distresses.

17 The young men of Heliopolis and

---

² Jer. 46, 2.　CHAP. 30.　¹ Jer. 43, 44, 46.　² Zach. 13, 2.

CHAP. 30. Ver. 14. *Alexandria.* In the Hebrew, *No:* which was the ancient name of that city, afterwards rebuilt by Alexander the Great and from his name called Alexandria.

of Bubastus shall fall by the sword: and they themselves shall go into captivity.

18 And in Taphnis the day shall be darkened, when I shall break there the sceptres of Egypt, and the pride of her power shall cease in her. A cloud shall cover her and her daughters shall be led into captivity.

19 And I will execute judgments in Egypt. And they shall know that I *am* the Lord.

20 And it came to pass in the eleventh year, in the first month, in the seventh day of the month, that the word of the Lord came to me, saying:

21 Son of man, I have broken the arm of Pharao king of Egypt: and behold it is not bound up to be healed, to be tied up with clothes and swathed with linen, that it might recover strength and hold the sword.

22 Therefore, thus saith the Lord God: Behold, I *come* against Pharao king of Egypt, and I will break into pieces his strong arm which is already broken: and I will cause the sword to fall out of his hand.

23 And I will disperse Egypt among the nations and scatter them through the countries.

24 And I will strengthen the arms of the king of Babylon and will put my sword in his hand. And I will break the arms of Pharao, and they shall groan bitterly being slain before his face.

25 And I will strengthen the arms of the king of Babylon, and the arms of Pharao shall fall. And they shall know that I am the Lord, when I shall have given my sword into the hand of the king of Babylon, and he shall have stretched it forth upon the land of Egypt.

26 And I will disperse Egypt among the nations and will scatter them through the countries. And they shall know that I am the Lord.

CHAPTER 31

The Assyrian empire fell for their pride. The Egyptian shall fall in like manner.

AND it came to pass in the eleventh year, the third month, the first day of the month, that the word of the Lord came to me, saying:

2 Son of man, speak to Pharao king of Egypt and to his people: To whom art thou like in thy greatness?

3 Behold, the Assyrian was like a cedar in Libanus, with fair branches and full of leaves, of a high stature, and

CHAP. 31. Ver. 11. *I have delivered.* Here the time past is put for the future, *I shall deliver.*— *The mighty one.* Nabuchodonosor, who conquered both the Assyrians and Egyptians.

his top was elevated among the thick boughs.

4 The waters nourished him, the deep set him up on high, the streams thereof ran round about his roots, and it sent forth its rivulets to all the trees of the country.

5 Therefore was his height exalted above all the trees of the country: and his branches were multiplied and his boughs were elevated, because of many waters.

6 And when he had spread forth his shadow, all the fowls of the air made their nests in his boughs, and all the beasts of the forest brought forth their young under his branches, and the assembly of many nations dwelt under his shadow.

7 And he was most beautiful for his greatness and for the spreading of his branches: for his root was near great waters.

8 The cedars in the paradise of God were not higher than he: the fir trees did not equal his top: neither were the plane trees to be compared with him for branches. No tree in the paradise of God was like him in his beauty.

9 For I made him beautiful and thick set with many branches: and all the trees of pleasure that were in the paradise of God, envied him.

10 Therefore thus saith the Lord God: Because he was exalted in height and shot up his top, green and thick, and his heart was lifted up in his height:

11 I have delivered him into the hands of the mighty one of the nations. He shall deal with him: I have cast him out according to his wickedness.

12 And strangers and the most cruel of the nations shall cut him down and cast him away upon the mountains, and his boughs shall fall in every valley, and his branches shall be broken on every rock of the country: and all the people of the earth shall depart from his shadow and leave him.

13 All the fowls of the air dwelt upon his ruins and all the beasts of the field were among his branches.

14 For which cause none of the trees by the waters shall exalt themselves for their height, nor shoot up their tops among the thick branches and leaves, neither shall any of them that are watered stand up in their height: for they are all delivered unto death to the lowest parts of the earth, in the midst of the children of men, with them that go down into the pit.

15 Thus saith the Lord God: In the day when he went down to hell, I brought in mourning, I covered him with the deep: and I withheld its rivers

and restrained the many waters. Libanus grieved for him, and all the trees of the field trembled.

16 I shook the nations with the sound of his fall, when I brought him down to hell with them that descend into the pit: and all the trees of pleasure, the choice and best in Libanus, all that were moistened with waters, were comforted in the lowest parts of the earth.

17 For they also shall go down with him to hell, to them that are slain by the sword: and the arm of every one shall sit down under his shadow in the midst of the nations.

18 To whom art thou like, O thou that art famous and lofty among the trees of pleasure? Behold, thou art brought down with the trees of pleasure to the lowest parts of the earth: thou shalt sleep in the midst of the uncircumcised, with them that are slain by the sword. This is Pharao and all his multitude, saith the Lord God.

CHAPTER 32

The prophet's lamentation for the king of Egypt.

AND it came to pass in the twelfth year, in the twelfth month, in the first day of the month, that the word of the Lord came to me, saying:

2 Son of man, take up a lamentation for Pharao the king of Egypt, and say to him: Thou art like the lion of the nations and the dragon that is in the sea: and thou didst push with the horn in thy rivers and didst trouble the waters with thy feet and didst trample upon their streams.

3 Therefore, thus saith the Lord God: [1] I will spread out my net over thee with the multitude of many people and I will draw thee up in my net,

4 And I will throw thee out on the land. I will cast thee away into the open field: and I will cause all the fowls of the air to dwell upon thee: and I will fill the beasts of all the earth with thee.

5 And I will lay thy flesh upon the mountains and will fill thy hills with thy corruption.

6 And I will water the earth with thy stinking blood upon the mountains: and the valleys shall be filled with thee.

7 [2] And I will cover the heavens when thou shalt be put out, and I will make the stars thereof dark. I will cover the sun with a cloud and the moon shall not give her light.

8 I will make all the lights of heaven to mourn over thee: and I will cause darkness upon thy land, saith the Lord God, when thy wounded shall fall in the midst of the land, saith the Lord God.

9 And I shall provoke to anger the heart of many people when I shall have brought in thy destruction among the nations, upon the lands which thou knowest not.

10 And I will make many people to be amazed at thee, and their kings shall be horribly afraid for thee, when my sword shall begin to fly upon their faces: and they shall be astonished on a sudden, every one for his own life, in the day of their ruin.

11 For thus saith the Lord God: The sword of the king of Babylon shall come upon thee,

12 By the swords of the mighty I will overthrow thy multitude: all these nations are invincible. And they shall waste the pride of Egypt, and the multitude thereof shall be destroyed.

13 I will destroy also all the beasts thereof that were beside the great waters: and the foot of man shall trouble them no more, neither shall the hoof of beasts trouble them.

14 Then will I make their waters clear and cause their rivers to run like oil, saith the Lord God:

15 When I shall have made the land of Egypt desolate and the land shall be destitute of her fulness: when I shall have struck all the inhabitants thereof. And they shall know that I am the Lord.

16 This is the lamentation, and they shall lament therewith: the daughters of the nations shall lament therewith: for Egypt and for the multitude thereof they shall lament therewith, saith the Lord God.

17 And it came to pass in the twelfth year, in the fifteenth day of the month, that the word of the Lord came to me, saying:

18 Son of man, sing a mournful song for the multitude of Egypt, and cast her down, *both* her and the daughters of the mighty nations, to the lowest part of the earth, with them that go down into the pit.

19 Whom dost thou excel in beauty? Go down and sleep with the uncircumcised.

20 They shall fall in the midst of them that are slain with the sword: the sword is given, they have drawn her down and all her people.

21 The most mighty among the strong ones shall speak to him from the midst of hell, they that went down with his helpers and slept uncircumcised, slain by the sword.

22 Assur is there and all his multitude: their graves are round about him, all of them slain and that fell by the sword.

CHAP. 32. [1] Ezech. 12, 13; 17, 20. [2] Isai. 13, 10; Joel, 2, 10; 3, 15; Matt. 24, 29.

23 Whose graves are set in the lowest parts of the pit. And his multitude lay round about his grave: all of them slain and fallen by the sword, they that heretofore spread terror in the land of the living.

24 There is Elam and all his multitude round about his grave, all of them slain and fallen by the sword: that went down uncircumcised to the lowest parts of the earth, that caused their terror in the land of the living, and that have borne their shame with them that go down into the pit.

25 In the midst of the slain they have set him a bed among all his people: their graves are round about him. All these are uncircumcised and slain by the sword: for they spread their terror in the land of the living and have borne their shame with them that descend into the pit: they are laid in the midst of the slain.

26 There is Mosoch and Thubal and all their multitude: their graves are round about him: all of them uncircumcised and slain and fallen by the sword, though they spread their terror in the land of the living.

27 And they shall not sleep with the brave and with them that fell uncircumcised, that went down to hell with their weapons and laid their swords under their heads, and their iniquities were in their bones, because they were the terror of the mighty in the land of the living.

28 So thou also shalt be broken in the midst of the uncircumcised and shalt sleep with them that are slain by the sword.

29 There is Edom and her kings and all her princes: who with their army are joined with them that are slain by the sword and have slept with the uncircumcised and with them that go down into the pit.

30 There are all the princes of the north and all the hunters: who were brought down with the slain, fearing, and confounded in their strength: who slept uncircumcised with them that are slain by the sword and have borne their shame with them that go down into the pit.

31 Pharao saw them and he was comforted concerning all his multitude which was slain by the sword: Pharao and all his army, saith the Lord God:

32 Because I have spread my terror in the land of the living, and he hath slept in the midst of the uncircumcised with them that are slain by the sword: Pharao and all his multitude, saith the Lord God.

CHAP. 33. ¹ Ezech. 3, 17. ² Ezech. 18, 32.

CHAPTER 33

The duty of the watchman appointed by God. The justice of God's ways. His judgments upon the Jews.

AND the word of the Lord came to me, saying:

2 Son of man, speak to the children of thy people, and say to them: When I bring the sword upon a land, if the people of the land take a man, one of their meanest, and make him a watchman over them:

3 And he see the sword coming upon the land and sound the trumpet and tell the people:

4 Then he that heareth the sound of the trumpet, whosoever he be, and doth not look to himself, if the sword come and cut him off: his blood shall be upon his own head.

5 He heard the sound of the trumpet and did not look to himself: his blood shall be upon him. But if he look to himself, he shall save his life.

6 And if the watchman see the sword coming and sound not the trumpet, and the people look not to themselves and the sword come and cut off a soul from among them: he indeed is taken away in his iniquity, but I will require his blood at the hand of the watchman.

7 ¹ So thou, O son of man, I have made thee a watchman to the house of Israel: therefore thou shalt hear the word from my mouth and shalt tell it them from me.

8 When I say to the wicked: O wicked man, thou shalt surely die: if thou dost not speak to warn the wicked man from his way, that wicked man shall die in his iniquity, but I will require his blood at thy hand.

9 But if thou tell the wicked man, that he may be converted from his ways, and he be not converted from his way: he shall die in his iniquity, but thou hast delivered thy soul.

10 Thou therefore, O son of man, say to the house of Israel: Thus you have spoken, saying: Our iniquities and our sins are upon us and we pine away in them. How then can we live?

11 ² Say to them: As I live, saith the Lord God, I desire not the death of the wicked, but that the wicked turn from his way and live. Turn ye, turn ye from your evil ways: and why will you die, O house of Israel?

12 Thou therefore, O son of man, say to the children of thy people: The justice of the just shall not deliver him in what day soever he shall sin: and the wickedness of the wicked shall not hurt him in what day soever he shall turn from his wickedness: and the just shall

not be able to live in his justice in what day soever he shall sin.

13 Yea, if I shall say to the just that he shall surely live, and he, trusting in his justice, commit iniquity: all his justices shall be forgotten and in his iniquity, which he hath committed, in the same shall he die.

14 And if I shall say to the wicked: Thou shalt surely die: and he do penance for his sin and do judgment and justice,

15 And if that wicked man restore the pledge and render what he had robbed and walk in the commandments of life and do no unjust thing: he shall surely live and shall not die.

16 None of his sins, which he hath committed, shall be imputed to him. He hath done judgment and justice: he shall surely live.

17 And the children of thy people have said: The way of the Lord is not equitable: whereas their own way is unjust.

18 For when the just shall depart from his justice and commit iniquities, he shall die in them.

19 And when the wickedness shall depart from his wickedness and shall do judgments and justice, he shall live in them.

20 ³ And you say: The way of the Lord is not right. I will judge every one of you according to his ways, O house of Israel.

21 And it came to pass in the twelfth year of our captivity, in the tenth month, in the fifth day of the month, that there came to me one that was fled from Jerusalem, saying: The city is laid waste.

22 And the hand of the Lord had been upon me in the evening, before he that was fled came: and he opened my mouth till he came to me in the morning and, my mouth being opened, I was silent no more.

23 And the word of the Lord came to me, saying:

24 Son of man, they that dwell in these ruinous places in the land of Israel, speak, saying: Abraham was one and he inherited the land, but we are many, the land is given us in possession.

25 Therefore say to them: Thus saith the Lord God: You that eat with the blood and lift up your eyes to your uncleannesses and that shed blood: shall you possess the land by inheritance?

26 You stood on your swords, you have committed abominations, and every one hath defiled his neighbour's wife: and shall you possess the land by inheritance?

27 Say thou thus to them: Thus saith the Lord God: As I live they that dwell in the ruinous places shall fall by the sword, and he that is in the field shall be given to the beasts to be devoured: and they that are in holds and caves shall die of the pestilence.

28 And I will make the land a wilderness and a desert, and the proud strength thereof shall fail, and the mountains of Israel shall be desolate, because there is none to pass by them.

29 And they shall know that I am the Lord, when I shall have made their land waste and desolate, for all their abominations which they have committed.

30 And thou, son of man: the children of thy people that talk of thee by the walls and in the doors of the houses and speak one to another, each man to his neighbour, saying: Come and let us hear what is the word that cometh forth from the Lord.

31 And they come to thee, as if a people were coming in: and my people sit before thee and hear thy words and do them not: for they turn them into a song of their mouth, and their heart goeth after their covetousness.

32 And thou art to them as a musical song which is sung with a sweet and agreeable voice: and they hear thy words and do them not.

33 And when that which was foretold shall come to pass (for behold it is coming), then shall they know that a prophet hath been among them.

CHAPTER 34

Evil pastors are reproved. Christ the true pastor shall come, and gather together his flock from all parts of the earth and preserve it for ever.

AND the word of the Lord came to me, saying:

2 Son of man, prophesy concerning the shepherds of Israel: prophesy, and say to the shepherds: Thus saith the Lord God: ¹ Woe to the shepherds of Israel that fed themselves! Should not the flocks be fed by the shepherds?

3 You ate the milk and you clothed yourselves with the wool and you killed that which was fat: but my flock you did not feed.

4 The weak you have not strengthened and that which was sick you have not healed: that which was broken you have not bound up and that which was driven away you have not brought again: neither have you sought that

³ Ezech. 18, 25. CHAP. 34. ¹ Jer. 23, 1; Ezech. 13, 3.

CHAP. 34. Ver. 2. *Shepherds.* That is, princes, magistrates, chief priests, and scribes.

which was lost: but you ruled over them with rigour and with a high hand.

5 And my sheep were scattered because there was no shepherd: and they became the prey of all the beasts of the field and were scattered.

6 My sheep have wandered in every mountain and in every high hill: and my flocks were scattered upon the face of the earth. And there was none that sought them: there was none, I say, that sought them.

7 Therefore, ye shepherds, hear the word of the Lord:

8 *As* I live, saith the Lord God, forasmuch as my flocks have been made a spoil and my sheep are become a prey to all the beasts of the field, because there was no shepherd: for my shepherds did not seek after my flock, but the shepherds fed themselves and fed not my flocks:

9 Therefore, ye shepherds, hear the word of the Lord:

10 Thus saith the Lord God: Behold I myself *come* upon the shepherds. I will require my flock at their hand and I will cause them to cease from feeding the flock any more: neither shall the shepherds feed themselves any more. And I will deliver my flock from their mouth and it shall no more be meat for them.

11 For thus saith the Lord God: Behold I myself will seek my sheep and will visit them.

12 As the shepherd visiteth his flock in the day when he shall be in the midst of his sheep that were scattered, so will I visit my sheep and will deliver them out of all the places where they have been scattered in the cloudy and dark day.

13 And I will bring them out from the peoples and will gather them out of the countries and will bring them to their own land: and I will feed them in the mountains of Israel, by the rivers and in all the habitations of the land.

14 I will feed them in the most fruitful pastures, and their pastures shall be in the high mountains of Israel. There shall they rest on the green grass and be fed in fat pastures upon the mountains of Israel.

15 I will feed my sheep and I will cause them to lie down, saith the Lord God.

16 I will seek that which was lost: and that which was driven away, I will bring again. And I will bind up that

---

2 Isai. 40, 11; Osee, 3, 5; John, 1, 45; 10, 11, 14.
Ver. 23. *David.* Christ, who is of the house of David.
Ver. 29. *A bud of renown. Germen nominatum.* He speaks of Christ our Lord, the illustrious bud of the house of David, renowned over all the earth. See Jer. 33, 15.

---

which was broken and I will strengthen that which was weak, and that which was fat and strong I will preserve: and I will feed them in judgment.

17 And as for you, O my flocks, thus saith the Lord God: Behold I judge between cattle, and cattle of rams and of he-goats.

18 Was it not enough for you to feed upon good pastures? But you must also tread down with your feet the residue of your pastures: and when you drank the clearest water you troubled the rest with your feet.

19 And my sheep were fed with that which you had trodden with your feet: and they drank what your feet had troubled.

20 Therefore thus saith the Lord God to you: Behold, I myself will judge between the fat cattle and the lean.

21 Because you thrusted with sides and shoulders, and struck all the weak cattle with your horns till they were scattered abroad:

22 I will save my flock and it shall be no more a spoil, and I will judge between cattle and cattle.

23 ² AND I WILL SET UP ONE SHEPHERD OVER THEM: and he shall feed them, even my servant David. He shall feed them, and he shall be their shepherd.

24 And I the Lord will be their God: and my servant David the prince in the midst of them. I the Lord have spoken *it.*

25 And I will make a covenant of peace with them and will cause the evil beasts to cease out of the land: and they that dwell in the wilderness shall sleep secure in the forests.

26 And I will make them a blessing round about my hill and I will send down the rain in its season: there shall be showers of blessing.

27 And the tree of the field shall yield its fruit and the earth shall yield her increase and they shall be in their land without fear: and they shall know that I am the Lord, when I shall have broken the bonds of their yoke and shall have delivered them out of the hand of those that rule over them.

28 And they shall be no more for a spoil to the nations, neither shall the beasts of the earth devour them: but they shall dwell securely without any terror.

29 And I will raise up for them a bud of renown: and they shall be no more consumed with famine in the land, neither shall they bear any more the reproach of the Gentiles.

30 And they shall know that I the Lord their God am with them and *that*

they *are* my people, the house of Israel: saith the Lord God.

31 ³ And you, my flocks, the flocks of my pasture are men: and I am the Lord your God, saith the Lord God.

CHAPTER 35

The judgment of Mount Seir for their hatred of Israel.

AND the word of the Lord came to me, saying:

2 Son of man, set thy face against mount Seir and prophesy concerning it and say to it:

3 Thus saith the Lord God: Behold I come against thee, mount Seir, and I will stretch forth my hand upon thee and I will make thee desolate and waste.

4 I will destroy thy cities and thou shalt be desolate. And thou shalt know that I am the Lord.

5 Because thou hast been an everlasting enemy and hast shut up the children of Israel in the hands of the sword in the time of their affliction, in the time of their last iniquity.

6 Therefore as I live, saith the Lord God, I will deliver thee up to blood, and blood shall pursue thee: and whereas thou hast hated blood, blood shall pursue thee.

7 And I will make mount Seir waste and desolate: and I will take away from it him that goeth and him that returneth.

8 And I will fill his mountains with his men that are slain: in thy hills and in thy valleys and in thy torrents they shall fall that are slain with the sword.

9 I will make thee everlasting desolations and thy cities shall not be inhabited. And thou shalt know that I am the Lord God.

10 Because thou hast said: The two nations and the two lands shall be mine, and I will possess them by inheritance: whereas the Lord was there.

11 Therefore, as I live, saith the Lord God, I will do according to thy wrath and according to thy envy which thou hast exercised in hatred to them: and I will be made known by them when I shall have judged thee.

12 And thou shalt know that I the Lord have heard all thy reproaches that thou hast spoken against the mountains of Israel, saying: They are desolate, they are given to us to consume.

13 And you rose up against me with your mouth and have derogated from me by your words: I have heard them.

14 Thus saith the Lord God: When the whole earth shall rejoice I will make thee a wilderness.

15 As thou hast rejoiced over the inheritance of the house of Israel, because it was laid waste, so will I do to thee. Thou shalt be laid waste, O mount Seir, and all Idumea. And they shall know that I am the Lord.

CHAPTER 36

The restoration of Israel, not for their merits, but by God's special grace. Christ's baptism.

AND thou, son of man, prophesy to the mountains of Israel, and say: ¹ Ye mountains of Israel, hear the word of the Lord.

2 Thus saith the Lord God: Because the enemy hath said of you: Aha, the everlasting heights are given to us for an inheritance.

3 Therefore prophesy and say: Thus saith the Lord God: Because you have been desolate and trodden under foot on every side and made an inheritance to the rest of the nations and are become the subject of the talk and the reproach of the people:

4 Therefore, ye mountains of Israel, hear the word of the Lord God: Thus saith the Lord God to the mountains and to the hills, to the brooks and to the valleys and to desolate places and ruinous walls and to the cities that are forsaken, that are spoiled and derided by the rest of the nations round about.

5 Therefore thus saith the Lord God: In the fire of my zeal I have spoken of the rest of the nations and of all Edom, who have taken my land to themselves for an inheritance, with joy and with all the heart and with the mind, and have cast it out to lay it waste.

6 Prophesy therefore concerning the land of Israel and say to the mountains and to the hills, to the ridges and to the valleys: Thus saith the Lord God: Behold I have spoken in my zeal and in my indignation, because you have borne the shame of the Gentiles.

7 Therefore thus saith the Lord God: I have lifted up my hand, that the Gentiles who are round about you shall themselves bear their shame.

8 But as for you, O mountains of Israel, shoot ye forth your branches and yield your fruit to my people of Israel: for they are at hand to come.

9 For lo I am for you and I will turn to you, and you shall be ploughed and sown.

10 And I will multiply men upon you and all the house of Israel: and the cities shall be inhabited and the ruinous places shall be repaired.

³ John, 10, 11. Chap. 36. ¹ Ezech. 6, 3.

11 And I will make you abound with men and with beasts: and they shall be multiplied and increased. And I will settle you as from the beginning and will give you greater gifts than you had from the beginning. And you shall know that I am the Lord.

12 And I will bring men upon you, my people Israel: and they shall possess thee for their inheritance. And thou shalt be their inheritance and shalt no more henceforth be without them.

13 Thus saith the Lord God: Because they say of you: Thou art a devourer of men and one that suffocatest thy nation:

14 Therefore thou shalt devour men no more nor destroy thy nation any more, saith the Lord God:

15 Neither will I cause men to hear in thee the shame of the nations any more, nor shalt thou bear the reproach of the people nor lose thy nation any more, saith the Lord God.

16 And the word of the Lord came to me, saying:

17 Son of man, when the house of Israel dwelt in their own land, they defiled it with their ways and with their doings: their way was before me like the uncleanness of a menstruous woman.

18 And I poured out my indignation upon them for the blood which they had shed upon the land: and with their idols they defiled it.

19 And I scattered them among the nations: and they are dispersed through the countries. I have judged them according to their ways and their devices.

20 And when they entered among the nations whither they went, [2] they profaned my holy name, when it was said of them: This is the people of the Lord and they are come forth out of his land.

21 And I have regarded my own holy name which the house of Israel hath profaned among the nations to which they went in.

22 Therefore thou shalt say to the house of Israel: Thus saith the Lord God: It is not for your sake that I will do this, O house of Israel, but for my holy name's sake, which you have profaned among the nations whither you went.

23 And I will sanctify my great name which was profaned among the Gentiles, which you have profaned in the midst of them: that the Gentiles may know that I am the Lord, saith the Lord of hosts, when I shall be sanctified in you before their eyes.

24 For I will take you from among the Gentiles and will gather you together out of all the countries and will bring you into your own land.

25 And I will pour upon you clean water and you shall be cleansed from all your filthiness: and I will cleanse you from all your idols.

26 [3] And I will give you a new heart and put a new spirit within you: and I will take away the stony heart out of your flesh and will give you a heart of flesh.

27 And I will put my spirit in the midst of you: and I will cause you to walk in my commandments and to keep my judgments and do them.

28 And you shall dwell in the land which I gave to your fathers: and you shall be my people and I will be your God.

29 And I will save you from all your uncleannesses: and I will call for corn and will multiply it, and will lay no famine upon you.

30 And I will multiply the fruit of the tree and the increase of the field, that you bear no more the reproach of famine among the nations.

31 And you shall remember your wicked ways and your doings that were not good: and your iniquities and your wicked deeds shall displease you.

32 It is not for your sakes that I will do this, saith the Lord God, be it known to you: be confounded and ashamed at your own ways, O house of Israel.

33 Thus saith the Lord God: In the day that I shall cleanse you from all your iniquities and shall cause the cities to be inhabited and shall repair the ruinous places,

34 And the desolate land shall be tilled, which before was waste in the sight of all that passed by,

35 They shall say: This land *that was* untilled is become as a garden of pleasure: and the cities that were abandoned and desolate and destroyed are peopled and fenced.

36 And the nations that shall be left round about you shall know that I the Lord have built up what was destroyed and planted what was desolate: that I the Lord have spoken and done it.

37 Thus saith the Lord God: Moreover in this shall the house of Israel find me, that I will do *it* for them. I will multiply them as a flock of men.

38 As a holy flock, as the flock of Jerusalem in her solemn feasts: so shall the waste cities be full of flocks of men.

---

[2] Isai. 52, 5; Rom. 2, 24. [3] Ezech. 11, 19.

CHAP. 36. Ver. 15. *Nor lose thy nation any more.* This whole promise principally relates to the Church of Christ and God's perpetual protection of her: for as to the carnal Jews, they have been removed out of their land these sixteen hundred years.

And they shall know that I am the Lord.

CHAPTER 37

A vision of the resurrection of dry bones, foreshewing the deliverance of the people from their captivity. Juda and Israel shall be all one kingdom under Christ. God's everlasting covenant with the church.

THE hand of the Lord was upon me and brought me forth in the spirit of the Lord and set me down in the midst of a plain that was full of bones.

2 And he led me about through them on every side. Now they were very many upon the face of the plain and they were exceeding dry.

3 And he said to me: Son of man, dost thou think these bones shall live? And I answered: O Lord God, thou knowest.

4 And he said to me: Prophesy concerning these bones and say to them: Ye dry bones, hear the word of the Lord.

5 Thus saith the Lord God to these bones: Behold, I will send spirit into you and you shall live.

6 And I will lay sinews upon you and will cause flesh to grow over you and will cover you with skin: and I will give you spirit and you shall live. And you shall know that I am the Lord.

7 And I prophesied as he had commanded me: and as I prophesied there was a noise, and behold a commotion. And the bones came together, each one to its joint.

8 And I saw, and behold the sinews and the flesh came up upon them, and the skin was stretched out over them: but there was no spirit in them.

9 And he said to me: Prophesy to the spirit, prophesy, O son of man, and say to the spirit: Thus saith the Lord God: Come, spirit, from the four winds and blow upon these slain and let them live again.

10 And I prophesied as he had commanded me: and the spirit came into them, and they lived: and they stood up upon their feet, an exceeding great army.

11 And he said to me: Son of man: All these bones are the house of Israel. They say: Our bones are dried up and our hope is lost and we are cut off.

12 Therefore prophesy and say to them: Thus saith the Lord God: Behold I will open your graves and will bring you out of your sepulchres, O my people, and will bring you into the land of Israel.

13 And you shall know that I am the Lord: when I shall have opened your sepulchres and shall have brought you out of your graves, O my people.

14 And shall have put my spirit in you. And you shall live and I shall make you rest upon your own land. And you shall know that I the Lord have spoken and done it, saith the Lord God:

15 And the word of the Lord came to me, saying:

16 And thou, son of man, take thee a stick and write upon it: Of Juda and of the children of Israel his associates. And take another stick and write upon it: For Joseph, the stick of Ephraim, and for all the house of Israel and of his associates.

17 And join them one to the other into one stick: and they shall become one in thy hand.

18 And when the children of thy people shall speak to me, saying: Wilt thou not tell us what thou meanest by this?

19 Say to them: Thus saith the Lord God: Behold, I will take the stick of Joseph which is in the hand of Ephraim, and the tribes of Israel that are associated with him, and I will put them together with the stick of Juda and will make them one stick: and they shall be one in his hand.

20 And the sticks whereon thou hast written shall be in thy hand, before their eyes.

21 And thou shalt say to them: Thus saith the Lord God: Behold, I will take the children of Israel from the midst of the nations whither they are gone, and I will gather them on every side and will bring them to their own land.

22 [1] And I will make them one nation in the land on the mountains of Israel, and one king shall be king over them all. And they shall no more be two nations: neither shall they be divided any more into two kingdoms.

23 Nor shall they be defiled any more with their idols nor with their abominations nor with all their iniquities: and I will save them out of all the places in which they have sinned, and I will cleanse them. And they shall be my people, and I will be their God.

24 [2] And my servant David shall be king over them: and they shall have one shepherd. They shall walk in my judgments and shall keep my commandments and shall do them.

25 And they shall dwell in the land which I gave to my servant Jacob, wherein your fathers dwelt: and they shall dwell in it, they and their children and their children's children, forever. And David my servant shall be their prince for ever.

CHAP. 37. [1] John, 10, 16. [2] Isai. 40, 11; Jer. 23, 5; Ezech. 34, 23; Dan. 9, 24; John, 1, 45.

CHAP. 37. Ver. 5. *Spirit.* That is, soul, life, and breath.

26 [3] And I will make a covenant of peace with them: it shall be an everlasting covenant with them. And I will establish them and will multiply them and will set my sanctuary in the midst of them for ever.

27 And my tabernacle shall be with them: and I will be their God, and they shall be my people.

28 And the nations shall know that I am the Lord, the sanctifier of Israel, when my sanctuary shall be in the midst of them for ever.

CHAPTER 38

Gog shall persecute the church in the latter days. He shall be overthrown.

AND the word of the Lord came to me, saying:

2 [1] Son of man, set thy face against Gog, the land of Magog, the chief prince of Mosoch and Thubal: and prophesy of him.

3 And say to him: Thus saith the Lord God: Behold, I *come* against thee, O Gog, the chief prince of Mosoch and Thubal.

4 And I will turn thee about and I will put a bit in thy jaws and I will bring thee forth, and all thy army, horses and horsemen, all clothed with coats of mail, a great multitude, armed with spears and shields and swords.

5 The Persians, Ethiopians and Libyans with them, all with shields and helmets.

6 Gomer and all his bands, the house of Thogorma, the northern parts and all his strength, and many peoples with thee.

7 Prepare and make thyself ready, and all thy multitude that is assembled about thee, and be thou commander over them.

8 After many days thou shalt be visited: at the end of years thou shalt come to the land that is returned from the sword and is gathered out of many nations, to the mountains of Israel which have been continually waste: but it hath been brought forth out of the nations and they shall all of them dwell securely in it.

9 And thou shalt go up and come like a storm and like a cloud to cover the land, thou and all thy bands, and many people with thee.

[3] Ps. 109, 4; 116, 2; John, 12, 34. CHAP. 38. [1] Ezech. 39, 1; Apoc. 20, 7. [2] Matt. 24, 29; Luke, 21, 25.

CHAP. 38. Ver. 2. *Gog.* This name, which signifies *hidden* or *covered*, is taken in this place, either for the persecutors of the church of God in general, or some arch-persecutor in particular: such as Antichrist shall be in the latter days. See Apoc. 20, 8. And what is said of the punishment of Gog is verified by the unhappy ends of these persecutors. *Magog.* Scythia or Tartary, from whence the Turks and other enemies of the Church of Christ originally sprung.

10 Thus saith the Lord God: In that day projects shall enter into thy heart and thou shalt conceive a mischievous design.

11 And thou shalt say: I will go up to the land which is without a wall, I will come to them that are at rest and dwell securely: all these dwell without a wall, they have no bars nor gates:

12 To take spoils and lay hold on the prey, to lay thy hand upon them that had been wasted and afterwards restored, and upon the people that is gathered together out of the nations, which hath begun to possess and to dwell in the midst of the earth.

13 Saba and Dedan and the merchants of Tharsis and all the lions thereof shall say to thee: Art thou come to take spoils? Behold, thou hast gathered thy multitude to take a prey, to take silver and gold and to carry away goods and substance and to take rich spoils.

14 Therefore, thou son of man, prophesy and say to Gog: Thus saith the Lord God: Shalt thou not know in that day when my people of Israel shall dwell securely?

15 And thou shalt come out of thy place from the northern parts, thou and many people with thee, all of them riding upon horses, a great company and a mighty army.

16 And thou shalt come upon my people of Israel like a cloud, to cover the earth. Thou shalt be in the latter days and I will bring thee upon my land: that the nations may know me when I shall be sanctified in thee, O Gog, before their eyes.

17 Thus saith the Lord God: Thou then art he of whom I have spoken in the days of old by my servants the prophets of Israel, who prophesied in the days of those times that I would bring thee upon them.

18 And it shall come to pass in that day, in the day of the coming of Gog upon the land of Israel, saith the Lord God, that my indignation shall come up in my wrath.

19 And I have spoken in my zeal and in the fire of my anger, that in that day there shall be a great commotion upon the land of Israel:

20 [2] So that the fishes of the sea and the birds of the air and the beasts of the field and every creeping thing that creepeth upon the ground and all men that are upon the face of the earth shall be moved at my presence: and the mountains shall be thrown down, and the hedges shall fall, and every wall shall fall to the ground.

21 And I will call in the sword against him in all my mountains,

saith the Lord God: every man's sword shall be pointed against his brother.

22 And I will judge him with pestilence and with blood and with violent rain and vast hailstones: I will rain fire and brimstone upon him and upon his army and upon the many nations that are with him.

23 And I will be magnified and I will be sanctified and I will be known in the eyes of many nations. And they shall know that I am the Lord.

CHAPTER 39

God's judgments upon Gog. God's people were punished for their sins but shall be favoured with everlasting kindness.

AND thou, son of man, prophesy against Gog and say: Thus saith the Lord God: Behold, I *come* against thee, O Gog, the chief prince of Mosoch and Thubal.

2 And I will turn thee round and I will lead thee out and will make thee go up from the northern parts and will bring thee upon the mountains of Israel.

3 And I will break thy bow in thy left hand and I will cause thy arrows to fall out of thy right hand.

4 Thou shalt fall upon the mountains of Israel, thou and all thy bands and thy nations that are with thee: I have given thee to the wild beasts, to the birds and to every fowl and to the beasts of the earth, to be devoured.

5 Thou shalt fall upon the face of the field: for I have spoken *it*, saith the Lord God.

6 And I will send a fire on Magog and on them that dwell confidently in the islands. And they shall know that I am the Lord.

7 And I will make my holy name known in the midst of my people Israel: and my holy name shall be profaned no more. And the Gentiles shall know that I am the Lord, the Holy One of Israel.

8 Behold it cometh and it is done, saith the Lord God: this is the day whereof I have spoken.

9 And the inhabitants shall go forth of the cities of Israel and shall set on fire and burn the weapons, the shields and the spears, the bows and the arrows and the handstaves and the pikes: and they shall burn them with fire seven years.

10 And they shall not bring wood out of the countries nor cut down out of the forests: for they shall burn the weapons with fire and shall make a prey of them to whom they had been a prey, and they shall rob those that robbed them, saith the Lord God.

11 And it shall come to pass in that day that I will give Gog, a noted place for a sepulchre in Israel, the valley of the passengers on the east of the sea, which shall cause astonishment in them that pass by. And there shall they bury Gog and all his multitude: and it shall be called the valley of the multitude of Gog.

12 And the house of Israel shall bury them for seven months to cleanse the land.

13 And all the people of the land shall bury him and it shall be unto them a noted day wherein I was glorified, saith the Lord God.

14 And they shall appoint men to go continually about the land to bury and to seek out them that were remaining upon the face of the earth, that they may cleanse it. And after seven months they shall begin to seek.

15 And they shall go about passing through the land. And when they shall see the bone of a man, they shall set up a sign by it, till the buriers bury it in the valley of the multitude of Gog.

16 And the name of the city *shall be* Amona: and they shall cleanse the land.

17 And thou, O son of man, saith the Lord God, say to every fowl and to all the birds and to all the beasts of the field: Assemble yourselves, make haste, come together from every side to my victim which I slay for you, a great victim upon the mountains of Israel: to eat flesh, and drink blood.

18 You shall eat the flesh of the mighty and you shall drink the blood of the princes of the earth, of rams and of lambs and of he-goats and bullocks and of all that are well fed and fat.

19 And you shall eat the fat till you be full and shall drink blood till you be drunk of the victim which I shall slay for you.

20 And you shall be filled at my table with horses and mighty horsemen and all the men of war, saith the Lord God.

21 And I will set my glory among the nations: and all nations shall see my judgment that I have executed and my hand that I have laid upon them.

22 And the house of Israel shall know that I am the Lord their God from that day and forward.

23 And the nations shall know that the house of Israel were made captives for their iniquity, because they forsook me and I hid my face from them and I delivered them into the hands of their enemies and they fell all by the sword.

24 I have dealt with them according to their uncleanness and wickedness and hid my face from them.

25 Therefore, thus saith the Lord

God: Now will I bring back the captivity of Jacob and will have mercy on all the house of Israel: and I will be jealous for my holy name.

26 And they shall bear their confusion and all the transgressions wherewith they have transgressed against me, when they shall dwell in their land securely, fearing no man:

27 And I shall have brought them back from among the nations and shall have gathered them together out of the lands of their enemies and shall be sanctified in them in the sight of many nations.

28 [1] And they shall know that I am the Lord their God: because I caused them to be carried away among the nations and I have gathered them together unto their own land and have not left any of them there.

29 And I will hide my face no more from them, for I have poured out my spirit upon all the house of Israel, saith the Lord God.

CHAPTER 40

The prophet sees in a vision the rebuilding of the temple. The dimensions of several parts thereof.

IN the five and twentieth year of our captivity, in the beginning of the year, the tenth day of the month, the fourteenth year after the city was destroyed: in the selfsame day the hand of the Lord was upon me and he brought me thither.

2 In the visions of God he brought me into the land of Israel and set me upon a very high mountain: upon which there was as the building of a city, bending towards the south.

3 And he brought me in thither, and behold a man whose appearance was like the appearance of brass, with a line of flax in his hand and a measuring reed in his hand: and he stood in the gate.

4 And this man said to me: Son of man, see with thy eyes and hear with thy ears and set thy heart upon all that I shall shew thee: for thou art brought hither that they may be shewn to thee. Declare all that thou seest to the house of Israel.

5 And behold, *there was* a wall on the outside of the house round about and in the man's hand a measuring reed of six cubits and a handbreadth: and he measured the breadth of the building one reed and the height of one reed.

CHAP. 39.   [1] Ezech. 36, 23.

CHAP. 40.   Ver. 17. *There were chambers. Gazophylacia,* so called, because the priests and Levites kept in them the stores and vessels that belonged to the temple.

6 And he came to the gate that looked toward the east and he went up the steps thereof and he measured the breadth of the threshold of the gate one reed: that is, one threshold was one reed broad.

7 And *every* little chamber *was* one reed long and one reed broad: and between the little chambers *were* five cubits.

8 And the threshold of the gate by the porch of the gate within was one reed.

9 And he measured the porch of the gate eight cubits and the front thereof two cubits: and the porch of the gate was inward.

10 And the little chambers of the gate that looked eastward *were* three on this side and three on that side: all three were of one measure and the fronts of one measure on both parts.

11 And he measured the breadth of the threshold of the gate ten cubits: and the length of the gate thirteen cubits:

12 And the border before the little chambers one cubit: and one cubit was the border on both sides. And the little chambers were six cubits on this side and that side.

13 And he measured the gate from the roof of one little chamber to the roof of another, in breadth five and twenty cubits: door against door.

14 He made also fronts of sixty cubits: and to the front the court of the gate on every side round about.

15 And before the face of the gate, which reached even to the face of the porch of the inner gate, fifty cubits.

16 And slanting windows in the little chambers and in their fronts, which were within the gate on every side round about: and in like manner there were also in the porches windows round about within and before the fronts the representation of palm trees.

17 And he brought me into the outward court, and behold *there were* chambers and a pavement of stone in the court round about: thirty chambers encompassed the pavement.

18 And the pavement in the front of the gates according to the length of the gates was lower.

19 And he measured the breadth from the face of the lower gate to the front of the inner court without, a hundred cubits to the east and to the north.

20 He measured also both the length and the breadth of the gate of the outward court which looked northward.

21 And the little chambers thereof, three on this side and three on that side: and the front thereof and the

porch thereof according to the measure of the former gate, fifty cubits long and five and twenty cubits broad.

22 And the windows thereof and the porch and the gravings, according to the measure of the gate that looked to the east: and they went up to it by seven steps, and a porch was before it.

23 And the gate of the inner court was over against the gate of the north and that of the east: and he measured from gate to gate a hundred cubits.

24 And he brought me out to the way of the south, and behold the gate that looked to the south: and he measured the front thereof and the porch thereof according to the former measures.

25 And the windows thereof and the porches round about, as the other windows: the length was fifty cubits and the breadth five and twenty cubits.

26 And there were seven steps to go up to it, and a porch before the doors thereof. And there were graven palm trees, one on this side and another on that side, in the front thereof.

27 And there was a gate of the inner court towards the south: and he measured from gate to gate towards the south a hundred cubits.

28 And he brought me into the inner court at the south gate: and he measured the gate according to the former measures,

29 The little chamber thereof and the front thereof and the porch thereof, with the same measures. And the windows thereof and the porch thereof round about: it was fifty cubits in length and five and twenty cubits in breadth.

30 And the porch round about was five and twenty cubits long and five cubits broad.

31 And the porch thereof to the outward court and the palm trees thereof in the front: and there were eight steps to go up to it.

32 And he brought me into the inner court by the way of the east: and he measured the gate according to the former measures.

33 The little chamber thereof and the front thereof and the porch thereof as before. And the windows thereof and the porch thereof round about: it was fifty cubits long and five and twenty cubits broad.

34 And the porch thereof, that is, of the outward court, and the graven palm trees in the front thereof on this side and on that side: and the going up thereof was by eight steps.

35 And he brought me into the gate that looked to the north: and he meas-

ured according to the former measures.

36 The little chamber thereof and the front thereof and the porch thereof and the windows thereof round about: it was fifty cubits long and five and twenty cubits broad.

37 And the porch thereof looked to the outward court: and the graving of palm trees in the front thereof was on this side and on that side: and the going up to it was by eight steps.

38 And at every chamber was a door in the forefronts of the gates: there they washed the holocaust.

39 And in the porch of the gate were two tables on this side and two tables on that side: that the holocaust and the sin offering and the trespass offering might be slain thereon.

40 And on the outward side which goeth up to the entry of the gate that looketh toward the north were two tables: and at the other side before the porch of the gate were two tables.

41 Four tables were on this side and four tables on that side: at the sides of the gate were eight tables, upon which they slew the victims.

42 And the four tables for the holocausts were made of square stones: one cubit and a half long and one cubit and a half broad and one cubit high: to lay the vessels upon, in which the holocaust and the victim is slain.

43 And the borders of them were of one handbreadth, turned inwards round about: and upon the tables was the flesh of the offering.

44 And without the inner gate were the chambers of the singing men, in the inner court which was on the side of the gate that looketh to the north: and their prospect was towards the south, one at the side of the east gate, which looketh toward the north.

45 And he said to me: This chamber which looketh toward the south shall be for the priests that watch in the wards of the temple.

46 But the chamber that looketh towards the north shall be for the priests that watch over the ministry of the altar. These are the sons of Sadoc who among the sons of Levi come near to the Lord to minister to him.

47 And he measured the court, a hundred cubits long and a hundred cubits broad, foursquare, and the altar that was before the face of the temple.

48 And he brought me into the porch of the temple: and he measured the porch, five cubits on this side and five cubits on that side: and the breadth of the gate, three cubits on this side and three cubits on that side.

49 And the length of the porch was

twenty cubits and the breadth eleven cubits, and there were eight steps to go up to it. And there were pillars in the fronts: one on this side and another on that side.

CHAPTER 41

A description of the temple and of all the parts of it.

AND he brought me into the temple and he measured the fronts, six cubits broad on this side and six cubits on that side, the breadth of the tabernacle.

2 And the breadth of the gate was ten cubits: and the sides of the gate five cubits on this side and five cubits on that side. And he measured the length thereof forty cubits and the breadth twenty cubits.

3 Then going inward he measured the front of the gate two cubits: and the gate six cubits and the breadth of the gate seven cubits.

4 And he measured the length thereof twenty cubits and the breadth twenty cubits, before the face of the temple: and he said to me: This is the Holy of Holies.

5 And he measured the wall of the house six cubits and the breadth of *every* side *chamber* four cubits, round about the house on every side.

6 And the side chambers one by another were twice thirty-three: and they bore outwards, that they might enter in through the wall of the house in the sides round about, to hold in and not to touch the wall of the temple.

7 And there was a broad passage round about, going up by winding stairs, and it led into the upper loft of the temple all round. Therefore was the temple broader in the higher parts: and so from the lower parts they went to the higher by the midst.

8 And I saw in the house the height round about the foundations of the side chambers which were the measure of a reed, the space of six cubits:

9 And the thickness of the wall for

the side chamber without which was five cubits: and the inner house was within the side chambers of the house.

10 And between the chambers was the breadth of twenty cubits round about the house on every side.

11 And the door of the side chambers was turned towards the place of prayer: one door was toward the north and another door was toward the south: and the breadth of the place for prayer *was* five cubits round about.

12 And the building that was separate and turned to the way that looked toward the sea was seventy cubits broad: and the wall of the building, five cubits thick round about and ninety cubits long.

13 And he measured the length of the house, a hundred cubits: and the separate building and the walls thereof, a hundred cubits in length.

14 And the breadth before the face of the house and of the separate place toward the east, a hundred cubits.

15 And he measured the length of the building over against it, which was separated at the back of *it, and* the galleries on both sides, a hundred cubits: and the inner temple and the porches of the court:

16 The thresholds and the oblique windows and the galleries round about on three sides, over against the threshold of every one, and floored with wood all round about. And the ground *was* up to the windows, and the windows were shut over the doors.

17 And even to the inner house and without, all the wall round about, within and without, by measure.

18 And there were cherubims and palm trees wrought, so that a palm tree was between a cherub and a cherub: and *every* cherub had two faces.

19 And the face of a man was toward the palm trees on one side and the face of a lion was toward the palm tree on the other side: set forth through all the house round about.

20 From the ground even to the upper parts of the gate were cherubims and palm trees, wrought in the wall of the temple.

21 The threshold was foursquare and the face of the sanctuary, sight to sight.

22 The altar of wood was three cubits high: and the length thereof was two cubits: and the corners thereof and the length thereof and the walls thereof were of wood. And he said to me: This is the table before the Lord.

23 And there were two doors in the temple and in the sanctuary.

24 And in the two doors on both sides were two little doors which were folded

CHAP. 41. Ver. 1. *The temple.* This plan of a temple, which was here shewn to the prophet in a vision, partly had relation to the material temple, which was to be rebuilt, and partly, in a mystical sense, to the spiritual temple of God, the Church of Christ.

Ver. 6. *One by another,* or *one over another:* literally, *side to side,* or *side upon side.*

Ver. 9. *And the inner house was within the side chambers of the house.* Because these side chambers were in the very walls of the temple all round. Or, it may also be rendered (more agreeably to the Hebrew) so as to signify that the thickness of the wall for the side chamber within was the same as that of the wall without, that is, equally five cubits.

Ver. 21. *The threshold was foursquare.* That is, the gate of the temple *was foursquare:* and so placed as to answer the gate of the sanctuary within.

within each other: for there were two
wickets on both sides of the doors.

25 And there were cherubims also
wrought in the doors of the temple and
the figures of palm trees, like as were
made on the walls: for which cause also
the planks were thicker in the front of
the porch without.

26 Upon which were the oblique windows and the representation of palm
trees, on this side and on that side, in
the sides of the porch, according to the
sides of the house and the breadth of
the walls.

CHAPTER 42
*A description of the courts, chambers and
other places belonging to the temple.*

AND he brought me forth into the
outward court by the way that
leadeth to the north: and he brought
me into the chamber that was over
against the separate building and over
against the house toward the north.

2 In the face of the north door was
the length of a hundred cubits and the
breadth of fifty cubits:

3 Over against the twenty cubits of
the inner court and over against the
pavement of the outward court that
was paved with stone, where there was
a gallery joined to a triple gallery.

4 And before the chambers *was* a
walk ten cubits broad, looking to the
inner parts of a way of one cubit. And
their doors were toward the north,

5 Where were the store chambers
lower above: because they bore up the
galleries which appeared above out of
them from the lower parts and from the
midst of the building.

6 For they were of three stories and
had not pillars as the pillars of the
courts: therefore did they appear above
out of the lower places and out of the
middle places, fifty cubits from the
ground.

7 And the outward wall that went
about by the chambers, which were
towards the outward court on the forepart of the chambers, was fifty cubits
long.

8 For the length of the chambers of
the outward court was fifty cubits: and
the length before the face of the temple,
a hundred cubits.

9 And there was under these chambers an entrance from the east, for
them that went into them out of the
outward court,

10 In the breadth of the outward
wall of the court that was toward the
east, over against the separate building: and there were chambers before
the building.

11 And the way before them *was* like
the chambers which were toward the
north: they were as long as they, and
as broad as they: and all the going in
to them and their fashions and their
doors were alike,

12 According to the doors of the
chambers that were towards the south.
There was a door in the head of the
way, which way was before the porch,
separated towards the east as one entereth in.

13 And he said to me: The chambers
of the north and the chambers of the
south, which are before the separate
building: they are holy chambers, in
which the priests shall eat that approach to the Lord into the Holy of
Holies: there they shall lay the most
holy things and the offering for sin and
for trespass: for it is a holy place.

14 And when the priests shall have
entered in, they shall not go out of the
holy places into the outward court: but
there they shall lay their vestments
wherein they minister, for they are
holy. And they shall put on other garments, and so they shall go forth to the
people.

15 Now when he had made an end
of measuring the inner house, he
brought me out by the way of the gate
that looked toward the east: and he
measured it on every side round about.

16 And he measured toward the east
with the measuring reed, five hundred
reeds with the measuring reed round
about.

17 And he measured toward the
north, five hundred reeds with the
measuring reed round about.

18 And towards the south, he measured five hundred reeds with the measuring reed round about.

19 And toward the west, he measured five hundred reeds with the measuring reed.

20 By the four winds he measured
the wall thereof on every side round
about, five hundred cubits long and
five hundred cubits broad, making a
separation between the sanctuary and
the place of the people.

CHAPTER 43
*The glory of God returns to the new temple.
The Israelites shall no more profane
God's name by idolatry. The prophet is
commanded to shew them the dimensions
and form of the temple and of the altar,
with the sacrifices to be offered thereon.*

AND he brought me to the gate
that looked towards the east.

2 And behold the glory of the God
of Israel came in by the way of the
east: and his voice was like the voice
of many waters and the earth shone
with his majesty.

3 ¹ And I saw the vision according to the appearance which I had seen when he came to destroy the city: and the appearance was according to the vision ² which I had seen by the river Chobar. And I fell upon my face.

4 And the majesty of the Lord went into the temple by the way of the gate that looked to the east.

5 And the spirit lifted me up and brought me into the inner court: and behold the house was filled with the glory of the Lord.

6 And I heard one speaking to me out of the house: and the man that stood by me

7 Said to me: Son of man, the place of my throne and the place of the soles of my feet, where I dwell in the midst of the children of Israel for ever. And the house of Israel shall no more profane my holy name, they and their kings, by their fornications and by the carcasses of their kings and by the high places.

8 They who have set their threshold by my threshold and their posts by my posts: and there was *but* a wall between me and them. And they profaned my holy name by the abominations which they committed: for which reason I consumed them in my wrath.

9 Now therefore, let them put away their fornications and the carcasses of their kings far from me: and I will dwell in the midst of them for ever.

10 But thou, son of man, shew to the house of Israel the temple, and let them be ashamed of their iniquities and let them measure the building

11 And be ashamed of all that they have done. Shew them the form of the house and of the fashion thereof, the goings out and the comings in, and the whole plan thereof and all its ordinances and all its order and all its laws. And thou shalt write it in their sight, that they may keep the whole form thereof and its ordinances and do them.

12 This is the law of the house upon the top of the mountain: All its border round about is most holy: this then is the law of the house.

13 And these are the measures of the altar by the truest cubit, which is a cubit and a handbreadth: the bottom thereof was a cubit and the breadth a cubit: and the border thereof unto its edge and round about, one hand-

breadth: and this was the trench of the altar.

14 And from the bottom of the ground to the lowest brim, two cubits and the breadth of one cubit: and from the lesser brim to the greater brim, four cubits and the breadth of one cubit.

15 And the Ariel itself was four cubits: and from the Ariel upward were four horns.

16 And the Ariel was twelve cubits long and twelve cubits broad, four-square, with equal sides.

17 And the brim was fourteen cubits long and fourteen cubits broad in the four corners thereof: and the crown round about it was half a cubit and the bottom of it, one cubit round about: and its steps turned toward the east.

18 And he said to me: Son of man, thus saith the Lord God: These are the ceremonies of the altar, in what day soever it shall be made: that holocausts may be offered upon it and blood poured out.

19 And thou shalt give to the priests and the Levites that are of the race of Sadoc who approach to me, saith the Lord God, to offer to me a calf of the herd for sin.

20 And thou shalt take of his blood and shalt put it upon the four horns thereof and upon the four corners of the brim and upon the crown round about: and thou shalt cleanse, and expiate it.

21 And thou shalt take the calf that is offered for sin: and thou shalt burn him in a separate place of the house without the sanctuary.

22 And in the second day thou shalt offer a he-goat without blemish for sin: and they shall expiate the altar, as they expiated it with the calf.

23 And when thou shalt have made an end of the expiation thereof, thou shalt offer a calf of the herd without blemish and a ram of the flock without blemish.

24 And thou shalt offer them in the sight of the Lord: and the priests shall put salt upon them and shall offer them a holocaust to the Lord.

25 Seven days shalt thou offer a he-goat for sin daily: they shall offer also a calf of the herd and a ram of the flock without blemish.

26 Seven days shall they expiate the altar and shall cleanse it: and they shall consecrate it.

27 And the days being expired, on the eighth day and thenceforward, the priests shall offer your holocausts upon the altar and the peace offerings: and I will be pacified towards you, saith the Lord God.

CHAP. 43. ¹ Ezech. 9, 1. ² Ezech. 1, 1.

CHAP. 43. Ver. 15. *The Ariel.* That is, the altar itself, or rather the highest part of it, upon which the burnt offerings were laid. In the Hebrew it is *Harel,* that is, *the mountain of God:* but in the following verse *Haariel,* that is, *the lion of God;* a figure, from its consuming and as it were devouring the sacrifices, as a lion devours its prey.

Ver. 26. *Consecrate it.* Literally, *fill its hand,* that is, dedicate and apply it to holy service.

CHAPTER 44

The east gate of the sanctuary shall be always shut. The uncircumcised shall not enter into the sanctuary, nor the Levites that have served idols, but the sons of Sadoc shall do the priestly functions, who stood firm in the worst of times.

AND he brought me back to the way of the gate of the outward sanctuary, which looked towards the east: and it was shut.

2 And the Lord said to me: This gate shall be shut. It shall not be opened and no man shall pass through it: because the Lord the God of Israel hath entered in by it. And it shall be shut

3 For the prince. The prince himself shall sit in it, to eat bread before the Lord: he shall enter in by the way of the porch of the gate and shall go out by the same way.

4 And he brought me by the way of the north gate, in the sight of the house: and I saw, and behold the glory of the Lord filled the house of the Lord. And I fell on my face.

5 And the Lord said to me: Son of man, attend with thy heart and behold with thy eyes and hear with thy ears all that I say to thee concerning all the ceremonies of the house of the Lord and concerning all the laws thereof: and mark well the ways of the temple with all the goings out of the sanctuary.

6 And thou shalt say to the house of Israel that provoketh me: Thus saith the Lord God: Let all your wicked doings suffice you, O house of Israel:

7 In that you have brought in strangers, uncircumcised in heart and uncircumcised in flesh, to be in my sanctuary and to defile my house: and you offer my bread, the fat and the blood: and you have broken my covenant by all your wicked doings.

8 And you have not kept the ordinances of my sanctuary: but you have set keepers of my charge in my sanctuary for yourselves.

9 Thus saith the Lord God: No stranger, uncircumcised in heart and uncircumcised in flesh, shall enter into my sanctuary, no stranger that is in the midst of the children of Israel.

10 Moreover the Levites that went away far from me when the children of Israel went astray and have wandered from me after their idols and have borne their iniquity:

11 They shall be officers in my sanctuary and doorkeepers of the gates of the house and ministers to the house: they shall slay the holocausts and the victims of the people: and they shall stand in their sight, to minister to them.

12 Because they ministered to them before their idols and were a stumbling-block of iniquity to the house of Israel: therefore have I lifted up my hand against them, saith the Lord God, and they shall bear their iniquity.

13 And they shall not come near to me to do the office of priest to me, neither shall they come near to any of my holy things that are by the Holy of Holies: but they shall bear their shame and their wickednesses which they have committed.

14 And I will make them doorkeepers of the house, for all the service thereof and for all that shall be done therein.

15 But the priests and Levites, the sons of Sadoc, who kept the ceremonies of my sanctuary when the children of Israel went astray from me, they shall come near to me to minister to me: and they shall stand before me, to offer me the fat and the blood, saith the Lord God.

16 They shall enter into my sanctuary and they shall come near to my table, to minister unto me and to keep my ceremonies.

17 And when they shall enter in at the gates of the inner court, they shall be clothed with linen garments: neither shall any woollen come upon them when they minister in the gates of the inner court and within.

18 They shall have linen mitres on their heads and linen breeches on their loins: and they shall not be girded with *any thing that causeth* sweat.

19 And when they shall go forth to the outward court to the people, they shall put off their garments wherein they ministered and lay them up in the store chamber of the sanctuary. And they shall clothe themselves with other garments: and they shall not sanctify the people with their vestments.

20 Neither shall they shave their heads nor wear long hair: but they shall only poll their heads.

21 And no priest shall drink wine when he is to go into the inner court.

22 [1] Neither shall they take to wife a widow, nor one that is divorced: but they shall take virgins of the seed of the house of Israel. But they may take a widow also, that is the widow of a priest.

23 And they shall teach my people the difference between holy and profane and shew them how to discern between clean and unclean.

CHAP. 44. [1] Lev. 21, 14.

CHAP. 44. Ver. 19. *Shall not sanctify the people with their vestments.* By exposing them to the danger of touching the sacred vestments, which none were to touch but they that were sanctified.

24 And when there shall be a controversy, they shall stand in my judgments and shall judge: they shall keep my laws and my ordinances in all my solemnities and sanctify my sabbaths.

25 And they shall come near no dead person, lest they be defiled, only their father and mother and son and daughter and brother and sister that hath not had another husband: for whom they may become unclean.

26 And after one is cleansed, they shall reckon unto him seven days.

27 And in the day that he goeth into the sanctuary, to the inner court, to minister unto me in the sanctuary, he shall offer for his sin, saith the Lord God.

28 [2] And they shall have no inheritance: I am their inheritance. Neither shall you give them any possession in Israel: for I am their possession.

29 They shall eat the victim both for sin and for trespass: and every vowed thing in Israel shall be theirs.

30 [3] And the firstfruits of all the firstborn and all the libations of all things that are offered shall be the priest's: and you shall give the firstfruits of your meats to the priest, that he may return a blessing upon thy house.

31 [4] The priests shall not eat of any thing that is dead of itself or caught by a beast, whether it be fowl or cattle.

CHAPTER 45

Portions of land for the sanctuary, for the city and for the prince. Ordinances for the prince.

AND when you shall begin to divide the land by lot, separate ye firstfruits of the Lord, a portion of the land *to be* holy, in length twenty-five thousand and in breadth ten thousand: it shall be holy in all the borders thereof round about.

2 And there shall be for the sanctuary on every side five hundred by five hundred, foursquare round about: and fifty cubits for the suburbs thereof round about.

3 And with this measure thou shalt measure the length of five and twenty thousand and the breadth of ten thousend. And in it shall be the temple and the Holy of Holies.

4 The holy portion of the land shall be for the priests, the ministers of the sanctuary, who come near to the ministry of the Lord: and it shall be a place

[2] Num. 18, 20; Deut. 18, 1. [3] Ex. 22, 29. [4] Lev. 22, 8. CHAP. 45. [1] Ex. 30, 13; Lev. 27, 25; Num. 3, 47.

CHAP. 45. Ver. 1. *Twenty-five thousand.* Reeds or cubits.
Ver. 11. *The ephi and the bate.* These measures were of equal capacity, but the *bate* served for liquids and the *ephi* for dry things.

for their houses and for the holy place of the sanctuary.

5 And five and twenty thousand of length and ten thousand of breadth shall be for the Levites that minister in the house: they shall possess twenty store chambers.

6 And you shall appoint the possession of the city, five thousand broad and five and twenty thousand long, according to the separation of the sanctuary, for the whole house of Israel.

7 For the prince also, on the one side and on the other side, according to the separation of the sanctuary and according to the possession of the city, over against the separation of the sanctuary and over against the possession of the city: from the side of the sea even to the sea and from the side of the east even to the east. And the length according to every part from the west border to the east border.

8 He shall have a portion of the land in Israel: and the princes shall no more rob my people but they shall give the land to the house of Israel according to their tribes.

9 Thus saith the Lord God: Let it suffice you, O princes of Israel. Cease from iniquity and robberies, and execute judgment and justice: separate your confines from my people, saith the Lord God.

10 You shall have just balances and a just ephi and a just bate.

11 The ephi and the bate shall be equal and of one measure: that the bate may contain the tenth part of a core and the ephi the tenth part of a core: their weight shall be equal according to the measure of a core.

12 [1] And the sicle hath twenty obols. Now twenty sicles and five and twenty sicles and fifteen sicles make a mna.

13 And these are the firstfruits which you shall take: the sixth part of an ephi of a core of wheat and the sixth part of an ephi of a core of barley.

14 The measure of oil also: a bate of oil is the tenth part of a core: and ten bates make a core: for ten bates fill a core.

15 And one ram out of a flock of two hundred, of those that Israel feedeth for sacrifice and for holocausts and for peace offerings, to make atonement for them, saith the Lord God.

16 All the people of the land shall be bound to these firstfruits for the prince in Israel.

17 And the prince shall give the holocaust and the sacrifice and the libations on the feasts and on the new moons and on the sabbaths and on all the solemnities of the house of Israel:

he shall offer the sacrifice for sin and the holocaust and the peace offerings to make expiation for the house of Israel.

18 Thus saith the Lord God: In the first month, the first of the month, thou shalt take a calf of the herd without blemish, and thou shalt expiate the sanctuary.

19 And the priest shall take of the blood of the sin offering: and he shall put it on the posts of the house and on the four corners of the brim of the altar and on the posts of the gate of the inner court.

20 And so shalt thou do in the seventh day of the month, for every one that hath been ignorant and hath been deceived by error: and thou shalt make expiation for the house.

21 In the first month, the fourteenth day of the month, you shall observe the solemnity of the pasch: seven days unleavened bread shall be eaten.

22 And the prince on that day shall offer, for himself and for all the people of the land, a calf for sin.

23 And in the solemnity of the seven days he shall offer for a holocaust to the Lord seven calves and seven rams without blemish daily for seven days: and for sin a he-goat daily.

24 And he shall offer the sacrifice of an ephi for every calf and an ephi for every ram and a hin of oil for every ephi.

25 In the seventh month, in the fifteenth day of the month, in the solemn feast, he shall do the like for the seven days: as well in regard to the sin offering, as to the holocaust and the sacrifice and the oil.

CHAPTER 46

Other ordinances for the prince and for the sacrifices.

THUS saith the Lord God: The gate of the inner court that looketh toward the east shall be shut the six days on which work is done; but on the sabbath day it shall be opened, yea, and on the day of the new moon it shall be opened.

2 And the prince shall enter by the way of the porch of the gate from without and he shall stand at the threshold of the gate: and the priests shall offer his holocaust and his peace offerings: and he shall adore upon the threshold of the gate and shall go out: but the gate shall not be shut till the evening.

3 And the people of the land shall adore at the door of that gate before the Lord on the sabbaths and on the new moons.

4 And the holocaust that the prince shall offer to the Lord on the sabbath day shall be six lambs without blemish and a ram without blemish:

5 And the sacrifice of an ephi for a ram, but for the lambs what sacrifice his hand shall allow: and a hin of oil for every ephi.

6 And on the day of the new moon a calf of the herd without blemish: and the six lambs and the rams shall be without blemish.

7 And he shall offer in sacrifice an ephi for a calf, an ephi also for a ram: but for the lambs, as his hand shall find: and a hin of oil for every ephi.

8 And when the prince is to go in, let him go in by the way of the porch of the gate: and let him go out the same way.

9 But when the people of the land shall go in before the Lord in the solemn feasts, he that goeth in by the north gate to adore shall go out by the way of the south gate: and he that goeth in by the way of the south gate shall go out by the way of the north gate: he shall not return by the way of the gate whereby he came in but shall go out at that over against it.

10 And the prince in the midst of them shall go in when they go in and go out when they go out.

11 And in the fairs and in the solemnities there shall be the sacrifice of an ephi to a calf and an ephi to a ram: and to the lambs, the sacrifice shall be as his hand shall find: and a hin of oil to every ephi.

12 But when the prince shall offer a voluntary holocaust or voluntary peace offerings to the Lord, the gate that looketh towards the east shall be opened to him: and he shall offer his holocaust and his peace offerings as it is wont to be done on the sabbath day: and he shall go out and the gate shall be shut after he is gone forth.

13 And he shall offer every day, for a holocaust to the Lord, a lamb of the same year without blemish: he shall offer it always in the morning.

14 And he shall offer the sacrifice for it morning by morning, the sixth part of an ephi, and the third part of a hin of oil to be mingled with the fine flour: a sacrifice to the Lord by ordinance continual and everlasting.

15 He shall offer the lamb and the sacrifice and the oil, morning by morning: an everlasting holocaust.

16 Thus saith the Lord God: If the prince give a gift to any of his sons, the inheritance of it shall go to his children: they shall possess it by inheritance.

17 But if he give a legacy out of his

inheritance to one of his servants, it shall be his until the year of release and it shall return to the prince: but his inheritance shall go to his sons.

18 And the prince shall not take of the people's inheritance by violence nor of their possession: but out of his own possession he shall give an inheritance to his sons: that my people be not dispersed every man from his possession.

19 And he brought me in by the entry that was at the side of the gate, into the chambers of the sanctuary that were for the priests, which looked toward the north. And there was a place bending to the west.

20 And he said to me: This is the place where the priests shall boil the sin offering and the trespass offering: where they shall dress the sacrifice, that they may not bring it out into the outward court and the people be sanctified.

21 And he brought me into the outward court and he led me about by the four corners of the court: and behold there was a little court in the corner of the court: to every corner of the court there was a little court.

22 In the four corners of the court were little courts disposed, forty cubits long and thirty broad: all the four were of one measure.

23 And there was a wall round about compassing the four little courts: and there were kitchens built under the rows round about.

24 And he said to me: This is the house of the kitchens wherein the ministers of the house of the Lord shall boil the victims of the people.

CHAPTER 47

The vision of the holy waters issuing out from under the temple. The borders of the land to be divided among the twelve tribes.

AND he brought me again to the gate of the house, and behold waters issued out from under the threshold of the house toward the east, for the forefront of the house looked toward the east: but the waters came down to the right side of the temple to the south part of the altar.

2 And he led me out by the way of the north gate and he caused me to turn to the way without the outward gate, to the way that looked toward the east: and behold there ran out waters on the right side.

3 And when the man that had the line in his hand went out towards the east, he measured a thousand cubits: and he brought me through the water up to the ankles.

4 And again he measured a thousand: and he brought me through the water up to the knees.

5 And he measured a thousand and he brought me through the water up to the loins. And he measured a thousand and it was a torrent which I could not pass over: for the waters were risen so as to make a deep torrent which could not be passed over.

6 And he said to me: Surely thou hast seen, O son of man. And he brought me out and he caused me to turn to the bank of the torrent.

7 And when I had turned myself, behold on the bank of the torrent were very many trees on both sides.

8 And he said to me: These waters that issue forth toward the hillocks of sand to the east and go down to the plains of the desert shall go into the sea and shall go out, and the waters shall be healed.

9 And every living creature that creepeth whithersoever the torrent shall come shall live: and there shall be fishes in abundance after these waters shall come thither: and they shall be healed, and all things shall live to which the torrent shall come.

10 And the fishers shall stand over these *waters*. From Engaddi even to Engallim there shall be drying of nets: there shall be many sorts of the fishes thereof, as the fishes of the great sea, a very great multitude.

11 But on the shore thereof and in the fenny places they shall not be healed, because they shall be turned into saltpits.

12 And by the torrent on the banks thereof on both sides shall grow all trees that bear fruit: their leaf shall not fall off and their fruit shall not fail. Every month shall they bring forth firstfruits, because the waters thereof shall issue out of the sanctuary: and the fruits thereof shall be for food, and the leaves thereof for medicine.

13 Thus saith the Lord God: This is the border by which you shall possess the land according to the twelve tribes of Israel: for Joseph hath a double portion.

14 And you shall possess it, every man in like manner as his brother: concerning which I lifted up my hand to give it to your fathers. And this land shall fall unto you for a possession.

CHAP. 47. Ver. 1. *Waters.* These waters are not to be understood literally (for there were none such that flowed from the temple): but mystically, of the baptism of Christ and of his doctrine and his grace. The trees that grow on the banks are Christian virtues: the fishes are Christians that spiritually live in and by these holy waters: the fishermen are the apostles and apostolic preachers: the fenny places, where there is no health, are such as by being out of the church are separated from these waters of life.

15 And this is the border of the land: toward the north side, from the great sea by the way of Hethalon, as men go to Sedada,

16 Emath, Berotha, Sabarim, which is between the border of Damascus and the border of Emath, the house of Tichon, which is by the border of Auran.

17 And the border from the sea even to the court of Enan shall be the border of Damascus, and from the north to the north: the border of Emath, *this is* the north side.

18 And the east side *is* from the midst of Auran and from the midst of Damascus and from the midst of Galaad and from the midst of the land of Israel, Jordan making the bound to the east sea: and *thus* you shall measure the east side.

19 And the south side southward is from Thamar even to the waters of contradiction of Cades and the torrent even to the great sea: and this is the south side southward.

20 And the side toward the sea *is* the great sea from the borders straight on till thou come to Emath: this is the side of the sea.

21 And you shall divide this land unto you by the tribes of Israel:

22 And you shall divide it by lot for an inheritance to you and to the strangers that shall come over to you that shall beget children among you: and they shall be unto you as men of the same country born among the children of Israel: they shall divide the possession with you in the midst of the tribes of Israel.

23 And in what tribe soever the stranger shall be, there shall you give him possession, saith the Lord God.

CHAPTER 48

The portions of the twelve tribes, of the sanctuary, of the city and of the prince. The dimensions and gates of the city.

AND these are the names of the tribes from the borders of the north, by the way of Hethalon, as they go to Emath, the court of Enan, the border of Damascus northward, by the way of Emath. And from the east side thereof to the sea shall be one portion for Dan.

2 And by the border of Dan, from the east side even to the side of the sea, one portion for Aser:

3 And by the border of Aser, from the east side even to the side of the sea, one portion for Nephthali.

4 And by the border of Nephthali, from the east side even to the side of the sea, one portion for Manasses.

5 And by the border of Manasses, from the east side even to the side of the sea, one portion for Ephraim.

6 And by the border of Ephraim, from the east side even to the side of the sea, one portion for Ruben.

7 And by the border of Ruben, from the east side even to the side of the sea, one portion for Juda.

8 And by the border of Juda, from the east side even to the side of the sea, shall be the firstfruits which you shall set apart, five and twenty thousand in breadth, and in length as every one of the portions from the east side to the side of the sea. And the sanctuary shall be in the midst thereof.

9 The firstfruits which you shall set apart for the Lord *shall be* the length of five and twenty thousand and the breadth of ten thousand.

10 And these shall be the firstfruits of the sanctuary for the priests: toward the north, five and twenty thousand in length, and toward the sea, ten thousand in breadth, and toward the east also, ten thousand in breadth, and toward the south, five and twenty thousand in length. And the sanctuary of the Lord shall be in the midst thereof.

11 The sanctuary shall be for the priests of the sons of Sadoc, who kept my ceremonies and went not astray, when the children of Israel went astray, as the Levites also went astray.

12 And for them shall be the firstfruits of the firstfruits of the land, holy of holies, by the border of the Levites.

13 And the Levites in like manner *shall have* by the borders of the priests five and twenty thousand in length and ten thousand in breadth. All the length *shall be* five and twenty thousand and the breadth ten thousand.

14 And they shall not sell thereof nor exchange: neither shall the firstfruits of the land be alienated, because they are sanctified to the Lord.

15 But the five thousand that remain in the breadth over against the five and twenty thousand shall be a profane place for the city, for dwelling and for suburbs: and the city shall be in the midst thereof.

16 And these are to the measures thereof: on the north side, four thousand and five hundred: and on the south side, four thousand and five hundred: and on the east side, four thousand and five hundred: and on the west side, four thousand and five hundred.

17 And the suburbs of the city shall be to the north, two hundred and fifty, and to the south, two hundred and fifty, and to the east, two hundred and fifty, and to the sea, two hundred and fifty.

18 And the residue in length by the firstfruits of the sanctuary, ten thousand toward the east and ten thousand toward the west, shall be as the firstfruits of the sanctuary; and the fruits thereof shall be for bread to them that serve the city.

19 And they that serve the city shall serve it out of all the tribes of Israel.

20 All the firstfruits, of five and twenty thousand by five and twenty thousand, foursquare, shall be set apart for the firstfruits of the sanctuary and for the possession of the city.

21 And the residue shall be for the prince, on every side of the firstfruits of the sanctuary and of the possession of the city, over against the five and twenty thousand of the firstfruits, unto the east border: toward the sea also, over against the five and twenty thousand unto the border of the sea, shall likewise be the portion of the prince: and the firstfruits of the sanctuary and the sanctuary of the temple shall be in the midst thereof.

22 And from the possession of the Levites and from the possession of the city which are in the midst of the prince's portions, what shall be to the border of Juda and to the border of Benjamin shall also belong to the prince.

23 And for the rest of the tribes: from the east side to the west side, one portion for Benjamin.

24 And over against the border of Benjamin, from the east side to the west side, one portion for Simeon.

Chap. 48. Ver. 35. *The Lord is there.* This name is here given to the city, that is, to the church of Christ, because the Lord is always with her till the end of the world. Matt. 28, 20.

25 And by the border of Simeon, from the east side to the west side, one portion for Issachar.

26 And by the border of Issachar, from the east side to the west side, one portion for Zabulon.

27 And by the border of Zabulon, from the east side to the side of the sea, one portion for Gad.

28 And by the border of Gad, the south side southward: and the border shall be from Thamar, even to the waters of contradiction of Cades, the inheritance over against the great sea.

29 This is the land which you shall divide by lot to the tribes of Israel and these are the portions of them: saith the Lord God.

30 And these are the goings out of the city: on the north side thou shalt measure four thousand and five hundred.

31 And the gates of the city according to the names of the tribes of Israel, three gates on the north side, the gate of Ruben one, the gate of Juda one, the gate of Levi one.

32 And at the east side, four thousand and five hundred: and three gates, the gate of Joseph one, the gate of Benjamin one, the gate of Dan one.

33 And at the south side, thou shalt measure four thousand and five hundred: and three gates, the gate of Simeon one, the gate of Issachar one, the gate of Zabulon one.

34 And at the west side, four thousand and five hundred: and their three gates, the gate of Gad one, the gate of Aser one, the gate of Nephthali one.

35 Its circumference was eighteen thousand. And he name of the city from that day: THE LORD IS THERE.

THE PROPHECY OF

DANIEL

DANIEL, *whose name signifies* THE JUDGMENT OF GOD, *was of the royal blood of the kings of Juda and one of those that were first of all carried away into captivity. He was so renowned for wisdom and knowledge, that it became a proverb among the Babylonians, As wise as Daniel* (Ezech. 28, 3). *And his holiness was so great from his very childhood, that at the time when he was as yet but a young man, he is joined by the Spirit of God with Noe and Job, as three persons-most eminent for virtue and sanctity* (Ezech. 14). *He is not commonly numbered by the Hebrews among the prophets, because he lived at court and in high station in the world: but if we consider his many clear predictions of things to come, we shall find that no one better deserves the name and title of a prophet, which also has been given him by the Son of God himself* (Matt. 24, Mark 13, Luke 21).

CHAPTER 1

Daniel and his companions are taken into the palace of the king of Babylon. They abstain from his meat and wine, and succeed better with pulse and water. Their excellence and wisdom.

IN the third year of the reign of Joakim king of Juda, Nabuchodonosor king of Babylon came to Jerusalem and besieged it.

2 And the Lord delivered into his hands Joakim the king of Juda and part of the vessels of the house ¹ of God: and he carried them away into the land of Sennaar, to the house of his god: and the vessels he brought into the treasure house of his god.

3 And the king spoke to Asphenez the master of the eunuchs, that he should bring in *some* of the children of Israel and of the king's seed and of the princes,

4 Children in whom there was no blemish, well favoured and skilful in all wisdom, acute in knowledge and instructed in science, and such as might stand in the king's palace, that he might teach them the learning, and the tongue of the Chaldeans.

5 And the king appointed them a daily provision, of his own meat and of the wine of which he drank himself, that being nourished three years, afterwards they might stand before the king.

6 Now there were among them, of the children of Juda, Daniel, Ananias, Misael and Azarias.

7 And the master of the eunuchs gave them names: to Daniel, Baltassar: to Ananias, Sidrach: to Misael, Misach: and to Azarias, Abdenago.

8 But Daniel purposed in his heart that he would not be defiled with the king's table nor with the wine which he drank: and he requested the master of the eunuchs that he might not be defiled.

9 And God gave to Daniel grace and mercy in the sight of the prince of the eunuchs.

10 And the prince of the eunuchs said to Daniel: I fear my lord the king who hath appointed you meat and drink: who if he should see your faces leaner than those of the other youths your equals, you shall endanger my head to the king.

11 And Daniel said to Malasar, whom the prince of the eunuchs had ap-pointed over Daniel, Ananias, Misael and Azarias:

12 Try, I beseech thee, thy servants for ten days, and let pulse be given us to eat and water to drink:

13 And look upon our faces and the faces of the children that eat of the king's meat: and as thou shalt see, deal with thy servants.

14 And when he had heard these words, he tried them for ten days.

15 And after ten days their faces appeared fairer and fatter than all the children that ate of the king's meat.

16 So Malasar took their portions and the wine that they should drink: and he gave them pulse.

17 And to these children God gave knowledge and understanding in every book and wisdom: but to Daniel the understanding *also* of all visions and dreams.

18 And when the days were ended, after which the king had ordered they should be brought in: the prince of the eunuchs brought them in before Nabuchodonosor.

19 And when the king had spoken to them, there were not found among them all such as Daniel, Ananias, Misael and Azarias: and they stood in the king's presence.

20 And in all matters of wisdom and understanding that the king inquired of them, he found them ten times better than all the diviners and wise men that were in all his kingdom.

21 ² And Daniel continued even to the first year of king Cyrus.

CHAPTER 2

Daniel, by divine revelation, declares the dream of Nabuchodonosor and the interpretation of it. He is highly honoured by the king.

IN the second year of the reign of Nabuchodonosor, Nabuchodonosor had a dream and his spirit was terrified: and his dream went out of his mind.

2 Then the king commanded to call together the diviners and the wise men

CHAP. 1. ¹ Jer. 25, 1. ² Dan. 6, 28.

CHAP. 1. Ver. 2. *His god. Bel* or *Belus*, the principal idol of the Chaldeans.
Ver. 8. *Be defiled.* Either by eating meat forbidden by the law, or which had before been offered to idols.
Ver. 12. *Pulse.* That is, pease, beans, and such like.
CHAP. 2. Ver. 1. *The second year.* From the death of his father Nabopolassar: for he had reigned before as partner with his father in the empire.

and the magicians and the Chaldeans: to declare to the king his dreams: so they came and stood before the king.

3 And the king said to them: I saw a dream: and being troubled in mind I know not what I saw.

4 And the Chaldeans answered the king in Syriac: O king, live for ever. Tell to thy servants thy dream and we will declare the interpretation thereof.

5 And the king answering said to the Chaldeans: The thing is gone out of my mind. Unless you tell me the dream and the meaning thereof, you shall be put to death and your houses shall be confiscated.

6 But if you tell the dream and the meaning of it, you shall receive of me rewards and gifts and great honour: therefore tell me the dream and the interpretation thereof.

7 They answered again and said: Let the king tell his servants the dream, and we will declare the interpretation of it.

8 The king answered, and said: I know for certain that you seek to gain time, since you know that the thing is gone from me.

9 If therefore you tell me not the dream, there is one sentence concerning you, that you have also framed a lying interpretation and full of deceit, to speak before me till the time pass away. Tell me therefore the dream, that I may know that you also give a true interpretation thereof.

10 Then the Chaldeans answered before the king, and said: There is no man upon earth that can accomplish thy word, O king: neither doth any king, though great and mighty, ask such a thing of any diviner or wise man or Chaldean.

11 For the thing that thou askest, O king, is difficult: nor can any one be found that can shew it before the king, except the gods, whose conversation is not with men.

12 Upon hearing this, the king, in fury and in great wrath, commanded that all the wise men of Babylon should be put to death.

13 And the decree being gone forth the wise men were slain: and Daniel and his companions were sought for to be put to death.

14 Then Daniel inquired concerning the law and the sentence, of Arioch the general of the king's army who was gone forth to kill the wise men of Babylon.

15 And he asked him that had re-

ceived the orders of the king why so cruel a sentence was gone forth from the face of the king. And when Arioch had told the matter to Daniel,

16 Daniel went in and desired of the king that he would give him time to resolve the question and declare it to the king.

17 And he went into his house and told the matter to Ananias and Misael and Azarias, his companions:

18 To the end that they should ask mercy at the face of the God of heaven concerning this secret, and that Daniel and his companions might not perish with the rest of the wise men of Babylon.

19 Then was the mystery revealed to Daniel by a vision in the night: and Daniel blessed the God of heaven,

20 And speaking he said: Blessed be the name of the Lord from eternity and for evermore: for wisdom and fortitude are his.

21 And he changeth times and ages: taketh away kingdoms and establisheth them, giveth wisdom to the wise and knowledge to them that have understanding.

22 He revealeth deep and hidden things and knoweth what is in darkness: and light is with him.[1]

23 To thee, O God of our fathers, I give thanks and I praise thee, because thou hast given me wisdom and strength: and now thou hast shewn me what we desired of thee, for thou hast made known to us the king's discourse.

24 After this Daniel went in to Arioch, to whom the king had given orders to destroy the wise men of Babylon, and he spoke thus to him: Destroy not the wise men of Babylon: bring me in before the king and I will tell the solution to the king.

25 Then Arioch in haste brought in Daniel to the king and said to him: I have found a man of the children of the captivity of Juda, that will resolve the question to the king.

26 The king answered and said to Daniel whose name was Baltassar: Thinkest thou indeed that thou canst tell me the dream that I saw and the interpretation thereof?

27 And Daniel made answer before the king and said: The secret that the king desireth to know, none of the wise men or the philosophers or the diviners or the soothsayers can declare to the king.

28 But there is a God in heaven that revealeth mysteries, who hath shewn to thee, O king Nabuchodonosor, what is to come to pass in the latter times. Thy dream and the visions of thy head upon thy bed are these:

CHAP. 2. [1] Cor. 4, 5; 1 John, 1, 6; John, 1, 9; 8. 12.

Ver. 2. *The Chaldeans.* That is, the astrologers that pretended to divine by stars.

29 Thou, O king, didst begin to think in thy bed what should come to pass hereafter: and he that revealeth mysteries shewed thee what shall come to pass.

30 To me also this secret is revealed, not by any wisdom that I have more than all men alive: but that the interpretation might be made manifest to the king, and thou mightest know the thoughts of thy mind.

31 Thou, O king, sawest, and behold *there was* as it were a great statue. This statue, which was great and high, tall of stature, stood before thee, and the look thereof was terrible.

32 The head of this statue was of fine gold, but the breast and the arms of silver, and the belly and the thighs of brass:

33 And the legs of iron, the feet part of iron and part of clay.

34 Thus thou sawest, till a stone was cut out of a mountain without hands: and it struck the statue upon the feet thereof that were of iron and of clay and broke them in pieces.

35 Then was the iron, the clay, the brass, the silver and the gold broken to pieces together, and became like the chaff of a summer's thrashingfloor. And they were carried away by the wind: and there was no place found for them. But the stone that struck the statue became a great mountain and filled the whole earth.

36 This is the dream: we will also tell the interpretation thereof before thee, O king.

37 Thou art a king of kings: and the God of heaven hath given thee a kingdom and strength and power and glory:

38 And all places wherein the children of men and the beasts of the field do dwell. He hath also given the birds of the air into thy hand and hath put all things under thy power: thou therefore art the head of gold.

39 And after thee shall rise up another kingdom, inferior to thee, of silver: and another third kingdom of brass, which shall rule over all the world.

40 And the fourth kingdom shall be as iron. As iron breaketh into pieces and subdueth all things, so shall that break and destroy all these.

41 And whereas thou sawest the feet, and the toes, part of the potter's clay and part of iron: the kingdom shall be divided, but yet it shall take its origin from the iron, according as thou sawest the iron mixed with the miry clay.

42 And as the toes of the feet were part of iron and part of clay, the king-dom shall be partly strong and partly broken.

43 And whereas thou sawest the iron mixed with miry clay, they shall be mingled indeed together with the seed of man, but they shall not stick fast one to another, as iron cannot be mixed with clay.

44 But in the days of those kingdoms the God of heaven will set up a kingdom that shall never be destroyed: and his kingdom shall not be delivered up to another people. And it shall break in pieces and shall consume all these kingdoms: and itself shall stand for ever.

45 According as thou sawest that the stone was cut out of the mountain without hands and broke in pieces the clay and the iron and the brass and the silver and the gold, the great God hath shewn the king what shall come to pass hereafter. And the dream is true, and the interpretation thereof is faithful.

46 Then king Nabuchodonosor fell on his face and worshipped Daniel and commanded that they should offer in sacrifice to him victims and incense.

47 And the king spoke to Daniel and said: Verily your God is the God of gods and Lord of kings and a revealer of hidden things: seeing thou couldst discover this secret.

48 Then the king advanced Daniel to a high station and gave him many and great gifts: and he made him governor over all the provinces of Babylon, and chief of the magistrates over all the wise men of Babylon.

49 And Daniel requested of the king, and he appointed Sidrach, Misach and Abdenago over the works of the province of Babylon: but Daniel himself was in the king's palace.

CHAPTER 3

Nabuchodonosor sets up a golden statue which he commands all to adore. The three children for refusing to do it are cast into the fiery furnace, but are not hurt by the flames. Their prayer and canticle of praise.

KING Nabuchodonosor made a statue of gold, of sixty cubits high and six cubits broad: and he set it up in the plain of Dura of the province of Babylon.

2 Then Nabuchodonosor the king sent to call together the nobles, the

Ver. 39. *Another kingdom.* That of the Medes and Persians. *Third kingdom.* That of Alexander the Great.

Ver. 40. *The fourth kingdom.* Some understand this of the successors of Alexander, the kings of Syria and Egypt, others of the Roman empire and its civil wars.

Ver. 44. *A kingdom.* The kingdom of Christ in the Catholic Church, which cannot be destroyed.

magistrates and the judges, the captains, the rulers and governors, and all the chief men of the provinces, to come to the dedication of the statue which king Nabuchodonosor had set up.

3 Then the nobles, the magistrates and the judges, the captains and rulers, and the great men that were placed in authority, and all the princes of the provinces, were gathered together to come to the dedication of the statue which king Nabuchodonosor had set up. And they stood before the statue which king Nabuchodonosor had set up.

4 Then a herald cried with a strong voice: To you it is commanded, O nations, tribes, and languages:

5 That in the hour that you shall hear the sound of the trumpet and of the flute and of the harp, of the sackbut and of the psaltery and of the symphony and of all kind of music; ye fall down and adore the golden statue which king Nabuchodonosor hath set up.

6 But if any man shall not fall down and adore, he shall the same hour be cast into a furnace of burning fire.

7 Upon this therefore, at the time when all the people heard the sound of the trumpet, the flute and the harp, of the sackbut and the psaltery, of the symphony and of all kind of music: all the nations, tribes and languages fell down and adored the golden statue which king Nabuchodonosor had set up.

8 And presently at that very time some Chaldeans came and accused the Jews,

9 And said to king Nabuchodonosor: O king, live for ever.

10 Thou, O king, hast made a decree that every man that shall hear the sound of the trumpet, the flute and the harp, of the sackbut and the psaltery, of the symphony and of all kind of music shall prostrate himself and adore the golden statue:

11 And that if any man shall not fall down and adore, he should be cast into a furnace of burning fire.

12 Now there are certain Jews whom thou hast set over the works of the province of Babylon, Sidrach, Misach and Abdenago: these men, O king, have slighted thy decree. They worship not thy gods, nor do they adore the golden statue thou hast set up.

CHAP. 3. Ver. 24. *And they walked.* Here St. Jerome takes notice, that from this verse, to ver. 91, was not in the Hebrew in his time. But as it was in all the Greek Bibles, (which were originally translated from the Hebrew,) it is more than probable that it had been formerly in the Hebrew, or rather in the Chaldaic, in which the book of Daniel was written. But this is certain: that it is, and has been of old, received by the church and read as canonical scripture in her liturgy and divine offices.

13 Then Nabuchodonosor, in fury and in wrath, commanded that Sidrach, Misach and Abdenago should be brought: who immediately were brought before the king.

14 And Nabuchodonosor the king spoke to them and said: Is it true, O Sidrach, Misach and Abdenago, that you do not worship my gods, nor adore the golden statue that I have set up?

15 Now therefore if you be ready, at what hour soever you shall hear the sound of the trumpet, flute, harp, sackbut and psaltery and symphony and of all kind of music, prostrate yourselves and adore the statue which I have made: but if you do not adore, you shall be cast the same hour into the furnace of burning fire. And who is the God that shall deliver you out of my hand?

16 Sidrach, Misach and Abdenago answered and said to king Nabuchodonosor: We have no occasion to answer thee concerning this matter.

17 For behold our God, whom we worship, is able to save us from the furnace of burning fire and to deliver us out of thy hands, O king.

18 But if he will not, be it known to thee, O king, that we will not worship thy gods nor adore the golden statue which thou hast set up.

19 Then was Nabuchodonosor filled with fury: and the countenance of his face was changed against Sidrach, Misach and Abdenago: and he commanded that the furnace should be heated seven times more than it had been accustomed to be heated.

20 And he commanded the strongest men that were in his army to bind the feet of Sidrach, Misach and Abdenago and to cast them into the furnace of burning fire.

21 And immediately these men were bound and were cast into the furnace of burning fire, with their coats and their caps and their shoes and their garments.

22 For the king's commandment was urgent and the furnace was heated exceedingly. And the flame of the fire slew those men that had cast in Sidrach, Misach and Abdenago.

23 But these three men, that is, Sidrach, Misach and Abdenago, fell down bound in the midst of the furnace of burning fire.

24 And they walked in the midst of the flame, praising God and blessing the Lord.

25 Then Azarias standing up prayed in this manner: and, opening his mouth in the midst of the fire, he said:

26 Blessed art thou, O Lord, the God

of our fathers, and thy name is worthy of praise and glorious for ever:

27 For thou art just in all that thou hast done to us, and all thy works are true, and thy ways right, and all thy judgments true.

28 For thou hast executed true judgments in all the things that thou hast brought upon us and upon Jerusalem the holy city of our fathers: for according to truth and judgment, thou hast brought all these things upon us for our sins.

29 For we have sinned and committed iniquity, departing from thee: and we have trespassed in all things.

30 And we have not hearkened to thy commandments, nor have we observed nor done as thou hadst commanded us, that it might go well with us.

31 Wherefore all that thou hast brought upon us and every thing that thou hast done to us, thou hast done in true judgment:

32 And thou hast delivered us into the hands of our enemies *that are* unjust and most wicked and prevaricators, and to a king unjust and most wicked beyond all that are upon the earth.

33 And now we cannot open our mouths: we are become a shame and reproach to thy servants and to them that worship thee.

34 Deliver us not up for ever, we beseech thee, for thy name's sake, and abolish not thy covenant.

35 And take not away thy mercy from us, for the sake of Abraham thy beloved and Isaac thy servant and Israel thy holy one:

36 To whom thou hast spoken, promising that thou wouldst multiply their seed as the stars of heaven and as the sand that is on the sea shore.

37 For we, O Lord, are diminished more than any nation and are brought low in all the earth this day for our sins.

38 Neither is there at this time prince or leader or prophet or holocaust or sacrifice or oblation or incense or place of firstfruits before thee,

39 That we may find thy mercy: nevertheless in a contrite heart and humble spirit let us be accepted.

40 As in holocausts of rams and bullocks and as in thousands of fat lambs: so let our sacrifice be made in thy sight this day that it may please thee: for there is no confusion to them that trust in thee.

41 And now we follow thee with all our heart and we fear thee and seek thy face.

42 Put us not to confusion, but deal with us according to thy meekness and according to the multitude of thy mercies.

43 And deliver us according to thy wonderful works, and give glory to thy name, O Lord.

44 And let all them be confounded that shew evils to thy servants: let them be confounded in all thy might, and let their strength be broken.

45 And let them know that thou art the Lord, the only God, and glorious over all the world.

46 Now the king's servants that had cast them in ceased not to heat the furnace with brimstone and tow and pitch and dry sticks,

47 And the flame mounted up above the furnace nine and forty cubits:

48 And it broke forth and burnt such of the Chaldeans as it found near the furnace:

49 But the angel of the Lord went down with Azarias and his companions into the furnace. And he drove the flame of the fire out of the furnace:

50 And made the midst of the furnace like the blowing of a wind bringing dew. And the fire touched them not at all, nor troubled them, nor did them any harm.

51 Then these three as with one mouth praised and glorified and blessed God in the furnace, saying:

52 Blessed art thou, O Lord the God of our fathers: and worthy to be praised and glorified and exalted above all for ever: and blessed is the holy name of thy glory and worthy to be praised and exalted above all in all ages.

53 Blessed art thou in the holy temple of thy glory: and exceedingly to be praised and exceeding glorious for ever.

54 Blessed art thou on the throne of thy kingdom, and exceedingly to be praised and exalted above all for ever.

55 Blessed art thou, that beholdest the depths and sittest upon the cherubims: and worthy to be praised and exalted above all for ever.

56 Blessed art thou in the firmament of heaven: and worthy of praise and glorious for ever.

57 All ye works of the Lord, bless the Lord: praise and exalt him above all for ever.

58 O ye angels of the Lord, bless the Lord: praise and exalt him above all for ever.

59 [1] O ye heavens, bless the Lord: praise and exalt him above all for ever.

60 O all ye waters that are above the heavens, bless the Lord: praise and exalt him above all for ever.

Chap. 3. [1] Ps. 148, 4.

61 O all ye powers of the Lord, bless the Lord: praise and exalt him above all for ever.

62 O ye sun and moon, bless the Lord: praise and exalt him above all for ever.

63 O ye stars of heaven, bless the Lord: praise and exalt him above all for ever.

64 O every shower and dew, bless ye the Lord: praise and exalt him above all for ever.

65 O all ye spirits of God, bless the Lord: praise and exalt him above all for ever.

66 O ye fire and heat, bless the Lord: praise and exalt him above all for ever.

67 O ye cold and heat, bless the Lord: praise and exalt him above all for ever.

68 O ye dews and hoar frosts, bless the Lord: praise and exalt him above all for ever.

69 O ye frost and cold, bless the Lord: praise and exalt him above all for ever:

70 O ye ice and snow, bless the Lord: praise and exalt him above all for ever.

71 O ye nights and days, bless the Lord: praise and exalt him above all for ever.

72 O ye light and darkness, bless the Lord: praise and exalt him above all for ever.

73 O ye lightnings and clouds, bless the Lord: praise and exalt him above all for ever.

74 O let the earth bless the Lord: let it praise and exalt him above all for ever.

75 O ye mountains and hills, bless the Lord: praise and exalt him above all for ever.

76 O all ye things that spring up in the earth, bless the Lord: praise and exalt him above all for ever.

77 O ye fountains, bless the Lord: praise and exalt him above all for ever.

78 O ye seas and rivers, bless the Lord: praise and exalt him above all for ever.

79 O ye whales and all that move in the waters, bless the Lord: praise and exalt him above all for ever.

80 O all ye fowls of the air, bless the Lord: praise and exalt him above all for ever.

81 O all ye beasts and cattle, bless the Lord: praise and exalt him above all for ever.

82 O ye sons of men, bless the Lord: praise and exalt him above all for ever.

83 O let Israel bless the Lord: let them praise and exalt him above all for ever.

84 O ye priests of the Lord, bless the Lord: praise and exalt him above all for ever.

85 O ye servants of the Lord, bless the Lord: praise and exalt him above all for ever.

86 O ye spirits and souls of the just, bless the Lord: praise and exalt him above all for ever.

87 O ye holy and humble of heart, bless the Lord: praise and exalt him above all for ever.

88 O Ananias, Azarias and Misael, bless ye the Lord: praise and exalt him above all for ever. For he hath delivered us from hell and saved us out of the hand of death and delivered us out of the midst of the burning flame and saved us out of the midst of the fire.

89 O give thanks to the Lord, because he is good: because his mercy endureth for ever and ever.

90 O all ye religious, bless the Lord, the God of gods: praise him and give him thanks, because his mercy endureth for ever and ever.

91 Then Nabuchodonosor the king was astonished and rose up in haste and said to his nobles: Did we not cast three men bound into the midst of the fire? They answered the king and said: True, O king.

92 He answered and said: Behold I see four men loose and walking in the midst of the fire. And there is no hurt in them: and the form of the fourth is like the Son of God.

93 Then Nabuchodonosor came to the door of the burning fiery furnace and said: Sidrach, Misach and Abdenago, ye servants of the most high God, go ye forth, and come. And immediately Sidrach, Misach and Abdenago went out from the midst of the fire.

94 And the nobles and the magistrates and the judges and the great men of the king being gathered together, considered these men, that the fire had no power on their bodies and that not a hair of their head had been singed, nor their garments altered, nor the smell of the fire had passed on them.

95 Then Nabuchodonosor breaking forth, said: Blessed be the God of them, to wit, of Sidrach, Misach and Abdenago, who hath sent his angel and delivered his servants that believed in him: and they changed the king's word and delivered up their bodies that they might not serve nor adore any god, except their own God.

96 By me therefore this decree is made, that every people, tribe and tongue, which shall speak blasphemy against the God of Sidrach, Misach and

Abdenago, shall be destroyed, and their houses laid waste: for there is no other God that can save in this manner.

97 Then the king promoted Sidrach, Misach and Abdenago, in the province of Babylon.

98 Nabuchodonosor the king, to all peoples, nations and tongues, that dwell in all the earth. Peace be multiplied unto you.

99 The most high God hath wrought signs and wonders toward me. It hath seemed good to me therefore to publish

100 His signs, because they are great, and his wonders, because they are mighty: and his kingdom is an everlasting kingdom, [2] and his power to all generations.

CHAPTER 4

Nabuchodonosor's dream, by which the judgments of God are denounced against him for his pride, is interpreted by Daniel and verified by the event.

I NABUCHODONOSOR was at rest in my house and flourishing in my palace:

2 I saw a dream that affrighted me: and my thoughts in my bed and the visions of my head troubled me.

3 Then I set forth a decree that all the wise men of Babylon should be brought in before me and that they should shew me the interpretation of the dream.

4 Then came in the diviners, the wise men, the Chaldeans and the soothsayers, and I told the dream before them. But they did not shew me the interpretation thereof,

5 Till *their* colleague Daniel came in before me, whose name is Baltassar, according to the name of my god, who hath in him the spirit of the holy gods: and I told the dream before him.

6 Baltassar, prince of the diviners, because I know that thou hast in thee the spirit of the holy gods and that no secret is impossible to thee: tell me the visions of my dreams that I have seen and the interpretation of them.

7 This was the vision of my head in my bed. I saw, and behold a tree in the midst of the earth: and the height thereof was exceeding great.

8 The tree was great and strong: and the height thereof reached unto heaven: the sight thereof was even to the ends of all the earth.

9 Its leaves were most beautiful and its fruit exceeding much, and in it was food for all: under it dwelt cattle and beasts, and in the branches thereof the fowls of the air had their abode. And all flesh did eat of it.

10 I saw in the vision of my head

upon my bed: and behold a watcher and a holy one came down from heaven.

11 He cried aloud, and said thus: Cut down the tree and chop off the branches thereof: shake off its leaves and scatter its fruits: let the beasts fly away that are under it and the birds from its branches.

12 Nevertheless, leave the stump of its roots in the earth, and let it be tied with a band of iron and of brass, among the grass that is without, and let it be wet with the dew of heaven, and let its portion be with the wild beasts in the grass of the earth.

13 Let his heart be changed from man's and let a beast's heart be given him: and let seven times pass over him.

14 This is the decree by the sentence of the watchers and the word and demand of the holy ones, till the living know that the most High ruleth in the kingdom of men. And he will give it to whomsoever it shall please him: and he will appoint the basest [1] man over it.

15 I, king Nabuchodonosor, saw this dream: thou, therefore, O Baltassar, tell me quickly the interpretation: for all the wise men of my kingdom are not able to declare the meaning of it to me. But thou art able, because the spirit of the holy gods is in thee.

16 Then Daniel, whose name was Baltassar, began silently to think within himself for about one hour: and his thoughts troubled him. But the king answering, said: Baltassar, let not the dream and the interpretation thereof trouble thee. Baltassar answered, and said: My lord, the dream be to them that hate thee, and the interpretation thereof to thy enemies.

17 The tree which thou sawest which was high and strong, whose height reached to the skies and the sight thereof into all the earth:

18 And the branches thereof were most beautiful and its fruit exceeding much, and in it was food for all, under which the beasts of the field dwelt, and

[2] Dan. 4, 31; 7, 14. CHAP 4. [1] Kings, 2, 8; 16, 11, etc.

Ver. 98. *Nabuchodonosor.* These last three verses are a kind of preface to the following chapter, which is written in the style of an epistle from the king.

CHAP. 4. Ver. 5. *Baltassar, according to the name of my god.* He says this, because the name of *Baltassar*, or *Belteshazzar*, is derived from the name of *Bel*, the chief god of the Babylonians.

Ver. 10. *A watcher.* A vigilant angel, perhaps the guardian of Israel.

Ver. 13. *Let his heart be changed.* It does not appear by scripture that Nabuchodonosor was changed from human shape, much less that he was changed into an ox; but only that he lost his reason and became mad, and in this condition remained abroad in the company of beasts, eating grass like an ox, till his hair grew in such manner as to resemble the feathers of eagles, and his nails to be like birds' claws.

the birds of the air had their abode in its branches.

19 It is thou, O king, who art grown great and become mighty: for thy greatness hath grown and hath reached to heaven, and thy power unto the ends of the earth.

20 And whereas the king saw a watcher and a holy one come down from heaven, and say: Cut down the tree and destroy it, but leave the stump of the roots thereof in the earth, and let it be bound with iron and brass among the grass without, and let it be sprinkled with the dew of heaven, and let his feeding be with the wild beasts, till seven times pass over him.

21 This is the interpretation of the sentence of the most High which is come upon my lord the king.

22 They shall cast thee out from among men and thy dwelling shall be with cattle and with wild beasts: [2] and thou shalt eat grass as an ox and shalt be wet with the dew of heaven: and seven times shall pass over thee, till thou know that the most High ruleth over the kingdom of men and giveth it to whomsoever he will.

23 But whereas he commanded that the stump of the roots thereof, that is, of the tree, should be left: thy kingdom shall remain to thee after thou shalt have known that power is from heaven.

24 Wherefore, O king, let my counsel be acceptable to thee, [3] and redeem thou thy sins with alms and thy iniquities with works of mercy to the poor: perhaps he will forgive thy offences.

25 All these things came upon king Nabuchodonosor.

26 At the end of twelve months he was walking in the palace of Babylon.

27 And the king answered and said: Is not this the great Babylon which I have built to be the seat of the kingdom, by the strength of my power and in the glory of my excellence?

28 And while the word was yet in the king's mouth, a voice came down from heaven: To thee, O king Nabuchodonosor, it is said: Thy kingdom shall pass from thee,

29 And they shall cast thee out from among men: and thy dwelling shall be with cattle and wild beasts. Thou shalt eat grass like an ox, and seven times

[2] Dan. 5, 21. [3] Ecclus. 3, 33. [4] Dan. 3, 100. [5] Jer. 23, 13; Ps. 115, 3.

Ver. 34. I Nabuchodonosor. From this place some commentators infer that this king became a true convert and, dying not long after, was probably saved.

CHAP. 5. Ver. 1. Baltasar. He is believed to be the same as Nabonydus, the last of the Chaldean kings, grandson to Nabuchodonosor. He is called his son, ver. 2, 11, etc., according to the style of the scriptures, because he was a descendant from him.

shall pass over thee, till thou know that the most High ruleth in the kingdom of men and giveth it to whomsoever he will.

30 The same hour the word was fulfilled upon Nabuchodonosor, and he was driven away from among men and did eat grass like an ox, and his body was wet with the dew of heaven: till his hairs grew like the feathers of eagles and his nails like birds' claws.

31 Now at the end of the days, I Nabuchodonosor lifted up my eyes to heaven, and my sense was restored to me. And I blessed the most High and I praised and glorified him that liveth for ever: [4] for his power is an everlasting power, and his kingdom is to all generations.

32 And all the inhabitants of the earth are reputed as nothing before him: for he doth according to his will, [5] as well with the powers of heaven, as among the inhabitants of the earth. And there is none that can resist his hand and say to him: Why hast thou done it?

33 At the same time my sense returned to me: and I came to the honour and glory of my kingdom. And my shape returned to me: and my nobles, and my magistrates sought for me. And I was restored to my kingdom: and greater majesty was added to me.

34 Therefore I Nabuchodonosor do now praise and magnify and glorify the King of heaven: because all his works are true, and his ways judgments, and them that walk in pride he is able to abase.

CHAPTER 5

Baltasar's profane banquet. His sentence is denounced by a handwriting on the wall, which Daniel reads and interprets.

BALTASAR the king made a great feast for a thousand of his nobles: and every one drank according to his age.

2 And being now drunk he commanded that they should bring the vessels of gold and silver which Nabuchodonosor his father had brought away out of the temple that was in Jerusalem, that the king and his nobles and his wives and his concubines might drink in them.

3 Then were the golden and silver vessels brought which he had brought away out of the temple that was in Jerusalem: and the king and his nobles, his wives and his concubines, drank in them.

4 They drank wine and praised their gods of gold and of silver, of brass, of iron and of wood and of stone.

5 In the same hour there appeared

fingers, as it were of the hand of a man, writing over against the candlestick upon the surface of the wall of the king's palace: and the king beheld the joints of the hand that wrote.

6 Then was the king's countenance changed, and his thoughts troubled him: and the joints of his loins were loosed, and his knees struck one against the other.

7 And the king cried out aloud to bring in the wise men, the Chaldeans and the soothsayers. And the king spoke and said to the wise men of Babylon: Whosoever shall read this writing and shall make known to me the interpretation thereof shall be clothed with purple and shall have a golden chain on his neck and shall be the third man in my kingdom.

8 Then came in all the king's wise men: but they could neither read the writing nor declare the interpretation to the king.

9 Wherewith king Baltasar was much troubled and his countenance was changed: and his nobles also were troubled.

10 Then the queen, on occasion of what happened to the king and his nobles, came into the banquet house: and she spoke and said: O king, live for ever: let not thy thoughts trouble thee, neither let thy countenance be changed.

11 There is a man in thy kingdom that hath the spirit of the holy gods in him, and in the days of thy father knowledge and wisdom were found in him. For king Nabuchodonosor thy father appointed him prince of the wise men, enchanters, Chaldeans and soothsayers, thy father, I say, O king:

12 Because a greater spirit and knowledge and understanding and interpretation of dreams and shewing of secrets and resolving of difficult things were found in him, that is, in Daniel, whom the king named Baltassar. Now therefore let Daniel be called for, and he will tell the interpretation.

13 Then Daniel was brought in before the king. And the king spoke and said to him: Art thou Daniel of the children of the captivity of Juda, whom my father the king brought out of Judea?

14 I have heard of thee that thou hast the spirit of the gods: and that excellent knowledge and understanding and wisdom are found in thee.

15 And now the wise men the magicians have come in before me to read this writing and shew me the interpretation thereof: and they could not declare to me the meaning of this writing.

16 But I have heard of thee, that

thou canst interpret obscure things and resolve difficult things: now if thou art able to read the writing and to shew me the interpretation thereof, thou shalt be clothed with purple and shalt have a chain of gold about thy neck and shalt be the third prince in my kingdom.

17 To which Daniel made answer and said before the king: Thy rewards be to thyself, and the gifts of thy house give to another: but the writing I will read to thee, O king, and shew thee the interpretation thereof.

18 O king, the most high God gave to Nabuchodonosor thy father a kingdom and greatness and glory and honour.

19 And for the greatness that he gave to him, all people, tribes and languages trembled and were afraid of him: whom he would, he slew: and whom he would, he destroyed: and whom he would, he set up: and whom he would, he brought down.

20 But when his heart was lifted up and his spirit hardened unto pride, he was put down from the throne of his kingdom and his glory was taken away.

21 [1] And he was driven out from the sons of men, and his heart was made like the beasts, and his dwelling was with the wild asses, and he did eat grass like an ox, and his body was wet with the dew of heaven: till he knew that the most High ruled in the kingdom of men and that he will set over it whomsoever it shall please him.

22 Thou also his son, Baltasar, hast not humbled thy heart, whereas thou knewest all these things:

23 But hast lifted thyself up against the Lord of heaven: and the vessels of his house have been brought before thee: and thou and thy nobles and thy wives and thy concubines have drunk wine in them: and thou hast praised the gods of silver and of gold and of brass, of iron and of wood and of stone, that neither see nor hear nor feel: but the God who hath thy breath in his hand and all thy ways, thou hast not glorified.

24 Wherefore he hath sent the part of the hand which hath written this that is set down.

25 And this is the writing that is written: MANE, THECEL, PHARES.

26 And this is the interpretation of the word. MANE: God hath numbered thy kingdom and hath finished it.

27 THECEL: Thou art weighed in the balance and art found wanting.

28 PHARES: Thy kingdom is divided and is given to the Medes and Persians.

CHAP. 5. [1] Dan. 4, 22.

Ver. 10. *The queen.* Not the wife, but the mother of the king.

29 Then by the king's command Daniel was clothed with purple, and a chain of gold was put about his neck: and it was proclaimed of him that he had power as the third man in the kingdom.

30 The same night, Baltasar the Chaldean king was slain.

31 And Darius the Mede succeeded to the kingdom, being threescore and two years old.

CHAPTER 6

Daniel is promoted by Darius. His enemies procure a law forbidding prayer. For the transgression of this law, Daniel is cast into the lion's den, but miraculously delivered.

IT seemed good to Darius and he appointed over the kingdom a hundred and twenty governors to be over his whole kingdom.

2 And three princes over them, of whom Daniel was one: that the governors might give an account to them and the king might have no trouble.

3 And Daniel excelled all the princes and governors: because a greater spirit of God was in him.

4 And the king thought to set him over all the kingdom: whereupon the princes and the governors sought to find occasion against Daniel with regard to the king. And they could find no cause nor suspicion, because he was faithful: and no fault nor suspicion was found in him.

5 Then these men said: We shall not find any occasion against this Daniel, unless perhaps concerning the law of his God.

6 Then the princes and the governors craftily suggested to the king, and spoke thus unto him: King Darius, live for ever.

7 All the princes of the kingdom, the magistrates and governors, the senators and judges, have consulted together, that an imperial decree and an edict be published: That whosoever shall ask any petition of any god or man, for thirty days, but of thee, O king, shall be cast into the den of lions.

8 Now, therefore, O king, confirm the sentence, [1] and sign the decree: that what is decreed by the Medes and Persians may not be altered, nor any man be allowed to transgress it.

9 So king Darius set forth the decree and established it.

10 Now when Daniel knew this, that is to say, that the law was made, he went into his house: and opening the

CHAP. 6. [1] Esther, 1, 19. [2] 1 Mach. 2, 60.

Ver. 31. *Darius.* He is called *Cyaxares* by the historians and was the son of Astyages and uncle to Cyrus.

windows in his upper chamber towards Jerusalem, he knelt down three times a day and adored and gave thanks before his God, as he had been accustomed to do before.

11 Wherefore those men carefully watching him, found Daniel praying and making supplication to his God.

12 And they came and spoke to the king concerning the edict: O king, hast thou not decreed, that every man that should make a request to any of the gods or men, for thirty days, but to thyself, O king, should be cast into the den of the lions? And the king answered them, saying: The word is true according to the decree of the Medes and Persians, which it is not lawful to violate.

13 Then they answered and said before the king: Daniel, who is of the children of the captivity of Juda, hath not regarded thy law nor the decree that thou hast made: but three times a day he maketh his prayer.

14 Now when the king had heard these words, he was very much grieved: and in behalf of Daniel he set his heart to deliver him and even till sunset he laboured to save him.

15 But those men perceiving the king's design, said to him: Know thou, O king, that the law of the Medes and Persians is, that no decree which the king hath made may be altered.

16 Then the king commanded, and they brought Daniel and cast him into the den of the lions. And the king said to Daniel: Thy God, whom thou always servest, he will deliver thee.

17 And a stone was brought and laid upon the mouth of the den: which the king sealed with his own ring and with the ring of his nobles, that nothing should be done against Daniel.

18 And the king went away to his house and laid himself down without taking supper. And meat was not set before him: and even sleep departed from him.

19 Then the king, rising very early in the morning, went in haste to the lions' den.

20 And coming near to the den, he cried with a lamentable voice to Daniel, and said to him: Daniel, servant of the living God, hath thy God, whom thou servest always, been able, thinkest thou, to deliver thee from the lions?

21 And Daniel answering the king, said: O king, live for ever.

22 [2] My God hath sent his angel and hath shut up the mouths of the lions, and they have not hurt me: forasmuch as before him justice hath been found in me. Yea and before thee, O king, I have done no offence.

23 Then was the king exceeding glad for him, and he commanded that Daniel should be taken out of the den. And Daniel was taken out of the den: and no hurt was found in him, because he believed in his God.

24 And by the king's commandment, those men were brought that had accused Daniel: and they were cast into the lions' den, they and their children and their wives: and they did not reach the bottom of the den, before the lions caught them and broke all their bones in pieces.

25 Then king Darius wrote to all people, tribes and languages, dwelling in the whole earth: PEACE be multiplied unto you.

26 It is decreed by me, that in all my empire and my kingdom all men dread and fear the God of Daniel. For he is the living and eternal God for ever: and his kingdom shall not be destroyed, and his power shall be for ever.

27 He is the deliverer and saviour, doing signs and wonders in heaven and in earth: who hath delivered Daniel out of the lions' den.

28 ³ Now Daniel continued unto the reign of Darius and the reign of Cyrus the Persian.

CHAPTER 7

Daniel's vision of the four beasts, signifying four kingdoms, of God sitting on his throne, and of the opposite kingdoms of Christ and Antichrist.

IN the first year of Baltasar king of Babylon, Daniel saw a dream: and the vision of his head *was* upon his bed. And writing the dream, he comprehended it in few words: and relating the sum of it in short, he said:

2 I saw in my vision by night, and behold the four winds of the heaven strove upon the great sea.

3 And four great beasts, different one from another, came up out of the sea.

4 The first was like a lioness and had the wings of an eagle: I beheld till her wings were plucked off, and she was lifted up from the earth and stood upon her feet as a man, and the heart of a man was given to her.

5 And behold another beast like a bear stood up on one side: and there were three rows in the mouth thereof and in the teeth thereof, and thus they said to it: Arise, devour much flesh.

6 After this I beheld, and lo, another like a leopard, and it had upon it four wings as of a fowl: and the beast had four heads and power was given to it.

7 After this I beheld in the vision of the night, and lo, a fourth beast, terrible and wonderful and exceeding strong. It had great iron teeth, eating and breaking in pieces and treading down the rest with its feet: and it was unlike to the other beasts which I had seen before it and had ten horns.

8 I considered the horns, and behold another little horn sprung out of the midst of them: and three of the first horns were plucked up at the presence thereof. And behold eyes like the eyes of a man were in this horn, and a mouth speaking great things.

9 I beheld till thrones were placed and the Ancient of days sat. His garment was white as snow and the hair of his head like clean wool: his throne like flames of fire: the wheels of it like a burning fire.

10 A swift stream of fire issued forth from before him: ¹ thousands of thousands ministered to him, and ten thousand times a hundred thousand stood before him. The judgment sat and the books were opened.

11 I beheld because of the voice of the great words which that horn spoke: and I saw that the beast was slain and the body thereof was destroyed and given to the fire to be burnt:

12 And that the power of the other beasts was taken away: and that times of life were appointed them for a time and a time.

13 I beheld therefore in the vision of the night, and lo, one like the son of man came with the clouds of heaven. And he came even to the Ancient of days: and they presented him before him.

14 And he gave him power and glory and a kingdom: and all peoples, tribes and tongues shall serve him. ² His power is an everlasting power that shall not be taken away: and his kingdom that shall not be destroyed.

15 My spirit trembled: I, Daniel, was affrighted at these things, and the visions of my head troubled me.

16 I went near to one of them that stood by and asked the truth of him concerning all these things, and he told me the interpretation of the words and instructed me:

17 These four great beasts are four

³ Dan. 1, 21. CHAP. 7. ¹ Apoc. 5, 11. ² Dan. 3, 100; 4, 31; Mich. 4, 7; Luke, 1, 32.

CHAP. 7. Ver. 3. *Four great beasts.* The Chaldean, Persian, Grecian and Roman empires. But some rather choose to understand the fourth beast of the successors of Alexander the Great, more especially of them that reigned in Asia and Syria.

Ver. 7. *Ten horns.* That is, ten kingdoms, (as Apoc. 17, 12,) among which the empire of the fourth beast shall be parcelled. Or ten kings or the number of the successors of Alexander, as figures of such as shall be about the time of Antichrist.

Ver. 8. *Another little horn.* This is commonly understood of Antichrist. It may also be applied to that great persecutor Antiochus Epiphanes, as a figure of Antichrist.

kingdoms which shall arise out of the earth.

18 But the saints of the most high God shall take the kingdom: and they shall possess the kingdom for ever and ever.

19 After this, I would diligently learn concerning the fourth beast, which was very different from all and exceeding terrible. His teeth and claws were of iron: he devoured and broke in pieces, and the rest he stamped upon with his feet:

20 And concerning the ten horns that he had on his head: and concerning the other that came up, before which three horns fell: and of that horn that had eyes and a mouth speaking great things and was greater than the rest.

21 I beheld, and lo, that horn made war against the saints and prevailed over them,

22 Till the Ancient of days came and gave judgment to the saints of the most High, and the time came, and the saints obtained the kingdom.

23 And thus he said: The fourth beast shall be the fourth kingdom upon earth, which shall be greater than all the kingdoms and shall devour the whole earth and shall tread it down and break it in pieces.

24 And the ten horns of the same kingdom shall be ten kings: and another shall rise up after them, and he shall be mightier than the former, and he shall bring down three kings.

25 And he shall speak words against the High One and shall crush the saints of the most High. And he shall think himself able to change times and laws: and they shall be delivered into his hand until a time and times and half a time.

26 And judgment shall sit, that his power may be taken away and be broken in pieces and perish even to the end.

27 And that the kingdom and power

and the greatness of the kingdom, under the whole heaven, may be given to the people of the saints of the most High. Whose kingdom is an everlasting kingdom, and all kings shall serve him and shall obey him.

28 Hitherto is the end of the word. I Daniel was much troubled with my thoughts and my countenance was changed in me: but I kept the word in my heart.

CHAPTER 8

Daniel's vision of the ram and he-goat interpreted by the angel Gabriel.

IN the third year of the reign of king Baltasar, a vision appeared to me. I, Daniel, after what I had seen in the beginning,

2 Saw in my vision when I was in the castle of Susa, which is in the province of Elam: and I saw in the vision that I was over the gate of Ulai.

3 And I lifted up my eyes and saw: and behold a ram stood before the water, having *two* high horns, and one higher than the other and growing up. Afterward

4 I saw the ram pushing with his horns against the west and against the north and against the south: and no beasts could withstand him nor be delivered out of his hand: and he did according to his own will and became great.

5 And I understood: and behold a he-goat came from the west on the face of the whole earth, and he touched not the ground: and the he-goat had a notable horn between his eyes.

6 And he went up to the ram that had the horns, which I had seen standing before the gate: and he ran towards him in the force of his strength.

7 And when he was come near the ram, he was enraged against him and struck the ram and broke his two horns. And the ram could not withstand him: and when he had cast him down on the ground, he stamped upon him, and none could deliver the ram out of his hand.

8 And the he-goat became exceeding great. And when he was grown the great horn was broken: and there came up four horns under it towards the four winds of heaven.

9 And out of one of them came forth a little horn: and it became great against the south and against the east and against the strength.

10 And it was magnified even unto the strength of heaven: and it threw down of the strength and of the stars and trod upon them.

11 And it was magnified even to the prince of the strength: and it took

---

Ver. 25. *A time and times and half a time.* That is, three years and a half; which is supposed to be the length of the duration of the persecution of Antichrist.

CHAP. 8. Ver. 8. *A ram.* The empire of the Medes and Persians.

Ver. 5. *A he-goat.* The empire of the Greeks, or Macedonians.—*He touched not the ground.* He conquered all before him with so much rapidity that he seemed rather to fly than to walk upon the earth.—*A notable horn.* Alexander the Great.

Ver. 8. *Four horns.* Seleucus, Antigonus, Philip, and Ptolemeus, the successors of Alexander, who divided his empire among them.

Ver. 9. *A little horn.* Antiochus Epiphanes, a descendant of *Seleucus.* He grew against the south and the east, by his victories over the kings of Egypt and Armenia: and *against the strength,* that is, against Jerusalem and the people of God.

Ver. 10. *Unto the strength of heaven:* or, *against the strength of heaven.* So are here called the army of the Jews, the people of God.

away from him the continual sacrifice and cast down the place of his sanctuary.

12 And strength was given him against the continual sacrifice, because of sins: and truth shall be cast down on the ground, and he shall do and shall prosper.

13 And I heard one of the saints speaking, and one saint said to another, I know not to whom that was speaking: How long shall be the vision, concerning the continual sacrifice and the sin of the desolation that is made: and the sanctuary and the strength be trodden under foot?

14 And he said to him: Unto evening and morning, two thousand three hundred days: and the sanctuary shall be cleansed.

15 And it came to pass when I Daniel saw the vision and sought the meaning, that behold there stood before me as it were the appearance of a man.

16 And I heard the voice of a man between Ulai: and he called and said: Gabriel, make this man to understand the vision.

17 And he came and stood near where I stood: and when he was come, I fell on my face trembling. And he said to me: Understand, O son of man, for in the time of the end the vision shall be fulfilled.

18 And when he spoke to me, I fell flat on the ground: and he touched me and set me upright,

19 And he said to me: I will shew thee what things are to come to pass in the end of the malediction, for the time hath its end.

20 The ram, which thou sawest with horns, is the king of the Medes and Persians.

21 And the he-goat is the king of the Greeks, and the great horn that was between his eyes, the same is the first king.

22 But whereas when that was broken, there arose up four for it: four kings shall rise up of his nation, but not with his strength.

23 And after their reign, when iniquities shall be grown up, there shall arise a king of a shameless face and understanding dark sentences.

24 And his power shall be strengthened, but not by his own force: and he shall lay all things waste and shall prosper and do more than can be believed. And he shall destroy the mighty and the people of the saints,

25 According to his will: and craft shall be successful in his hand. And his heart shall be puffed up, and in the abundance of all things he shall kill many: and he shall rise up against the

prince of princes and shall be broken without hand.

26 And the vision of the evening and the morning, which was told, is true. Thou therefore seal up the vision, because it shall come to pass after many days.

27 And I Daniel languished and was sick for some days: and when I was risen up, I did the king's business. And I was astonished at the vision, and there was none that could interpret it.

CHAPTER 9

Daniel's confession and prayer. Gabriel informs him concerning the seventy weeks to the coming of Christ.

IN the first year of Darius the son of Assuerus of the seed of the Medes, who reigned over the kingdom of the Chaldeans:

2 The first year of his reign, I Daniel understood by books the [1] number of the years, concerning which the word of the Lord came to Jeremias the prophet, that seventy years should be accomplished of the desolation of Jerusalem.

3 And I set my face to the Lord my God, to pray and make supplication with fasting and sackcloth and ashes.

4 And I prayed to the Lord my God, and I made my confession and said: [2] I beseech thee, O Lord God, great and terrible, who keepest the covenant and mercy to them that love thee and keep thy commandments.

5 [3] We have sinned, we have committed iniquity, we have done wickedly and have revolted: and we have gone aside from thy commandments and thy judgments.

6 We have not hearkened to thy servants the prophets, that have spoken in thy name to our kings, to our princes, to our fathers, and to all the people of the land.

7 To thee, O Lord, justice: but to us, confusion of face, as at this day to the men of Juda and to the inhabitants of Jerusalem and to all Israel, to them that are near, and to them that are far off in all the countries whither thou hast driven them for their iniquities by which they have sinned against thee.

8 O Lord, to us *belongeth* confusion of face, to our princes and to our fathers, that have sinned.

9 But to thee, the Lord our God, mercy and forgiveness, for we have departed from thee.

CHAP. 9. [1] Jer. 25, 11; 29, 10. [2] 2 Esd. 1, 5. [3] Bar. 1, 17.

Ver. 14. *Unto evening and morning, two thousand three hundred days.* That is, six years and almost four months: which was the whole time from the beginning of the persecution of Antiochus till his death.

10 And we have not hearkened to the voice of the Lord our God, to walk in his law, which he set before us by his servants the prophets.

11 And all Israel have transgressed thy law and have turned away from hearing thy voice. And the malediction and the curse [4] which is written in the book of Moses the servant of God is fallen upon us, because we have sinned against him.

12 And he hath confirmed his words which he spoke against us and against our princes that judged us, that he would bring in upon us a great evil, such as never was under all the heaven, according to that which hath been done in Jerusalem.

13 As it is written in the law of Moses, all this evil is come upon us: and we entreated not thy face, O Lord our God, that we might turn from our iniquities and think on thy truth.

14 And the Lord hath watched upon the evil and hath brought it upon us. The Lord our God is just in all his works which he hath done: for we have not hearkened to his voice.

15 [5] And now, O Lord our God, who hast brought forth thy people out of the land of Egypt with a strong hand and hast made thee a name as at this day: we have sinned, we have committed iniquity,

16 O Lord, against all thy justice. Let thy wrath and thy indignation be turned away, I beseech thee, from thy city Jerusalem and from thy holy mountain. For by reason of our sins and the iniquities of our fathers, Jerusalem and thy people are a reproach to all that are round about us.

[4] Deut. 17, 14.   [5] Bar. 2, 11; Exod. 14, 22.   [6] Jer. 25, 29; Ps. 48, 2, 9; 101, 3.   [7] Dan. 8, 16.   [8] Matt. 24, 15; John, 1, 45.

CHAP. 9. Ver. 21. *The man Gabriel.* The angel Gabriel in the shape of a man.

Ver. 23. *Man of desires,* that is, ardently praying for the Jews then in captivity.

Ver. 24. *Seventy weeks,* namely, of years, (or seventy times seven, that is, 490 years,) *are shortened;* that is, fixed and determined, so that the time shall be no longer.

Ver. 25. *From the going forth of the word.* That is, from the twentieth year of king Artaxerxes, when by his commandment Nehemias rebuilt the walls of Jerusalem, (2 Esd. 2). From which time, according to the best chronology, there were just sixty-nine weeks of years, that is, 483 years to the baptism of Christ, when he first began to preach and execute the office of Messias.—*In straitness of times (angustia temporum):* which may allude both to the difficulties and opposition they met with in building: and to the shortness of the time in which they finished the wall—fifty-two days.

Ver. 26. *A people with their leader.* The Romans under Titus.

Ver. 27. *In the half of the week,* or, *in the middle of the week.* Because Christ preached three years and a half: and then by his sacrifice upon the cross abolished all the sacrifices of the law.—*The abomination of desolation.* Some understand this of the profanation of the temple by the crimes of the Jews, and by the bloody faction of the zealots. Others of the bringing in

17 Now therefore, O our God, hear the supplication of thy servant and his prayers: and shew thy face upon thy sanctuary which is desolate, for thy own sake.

18 Incline, O my God, thy ear and hear: open thy eyes and see our desolation and the city upon which thy name is called: [6] for it is not for our justifications that we present our prayers before thy face, but for the multitude of thy tender mercies.

19 O Lord, hear: O Lord, be appeased. Hearken and do. Delay not for thy own sake, O my God: because thy name is invocated upon thy city and upon thy people.

20 Now while I was yet speaking and praying and confessing my sins and the sins of my people of Israel and presenting my supplications in the sight of my God, for the holy mountain of my God:

21 As I was yet speaking in prayer, behold the man Gabriel, whom I had seen in the vision at the beginning, [7] flying swiftly, touched me at the time of the evening sacrifice.

22 And he instructed me and spoke to me and said: O Daniel, I am now come forth to teach thee, that thou mightest understand.

23 From the beginning of thy prayers the word came forth: and I am come to shew it to thee, because thou art a man of desires. Therefore, do thou mark the word and understand the vision.

24 [8] Seventy weeks are shortened upon thy people and upon thy holy city, that transgression may be finished and sin may have an end and iniquity may be abolished and everlasting justice may be brought and vision and prophecy may be fulfilled and the Saint of Saints may be anointed.

25 Know thou therefore and take notice: *that* from the going forth of the word to build up Jerusalem again, unto Christ the prince, there shall be seven weeks and sixty-two weeks: and the street shall be built again, and the walls in straitness of times.

26 And after sixty-two weeks Christ shall be slain: and the people that shall deny him shall not be his. And a people, with their leader that shall come, shall destroy the city and the sanctuary: and the end thereof shall be waste, and after the end of the war the appointed desolation.

27 And he shall confirm the covenant with many, in one week: and in the half of the week the victim and the sacrifice shall fail: and there shall be in the temple the abomination of desolation. And the desolation shall continue even to the consummation and to the end.

CHAPTER 10

Daniel having humbled himself by fasting and penance seeth a vision, with which he is much terrified, but he is comforted by an angel.

IN the third year of Cyrus king of the Persians, a word was revealed to Daniel surnamed Baltassar, and a true word and great strength. And he understood the word: for there is need of understanding in a vision.

2 In those days I Daniel mourned the days of three weeks.

3 I ate no desirable bread, and neither flesh nor wine entered into my mouth: neither was I anointed with ointment till the days of three weeks were accomplished.

4 And in the four and twentieth day of the first month, I was by the great river which is the Tigris.

5 And I lifted up my eyes and I saw: and behold a man clothed in linen, and his loins were girded with the finest gold.

6 And his body was like the chrysolite, and his face as the appearance of lightning, and his eyes as a burning lamp: and his arms and all downward even to the feet, like in appearance to glittering brass: and the voice of his word like the voice of a multitude.

7 And I Daniel alone saw the vision: for the men that were with me saw it not: but an exceeding great terror fell upon them, and they fled away and hid themselves.

8 And I being left alone saw this great vision: and there remained no strength in me, and the appearance of my countenance was changed in me, and I fainted away and retained no strength.

9 And I heard the voice of his words: and when I heard, I lay in a consternation upon my face, and my face was close to the ground.

10 And behold a hand touched me and lifted me up upon my knees and upon the joints of my hands

11 And he said to me: Daniel, thou man of desires, understand the words that I speak to thee and stand upright: for I am sent now to thee. And when he had said this word to me I stood trembling.

12 And he said to me: Fear not, Daniel. For from the first day that thou didst set thy heart to understand, to afflict thyself in the sight of thy God, thy words have been heard: and I am come for thy words.

13 But the prince of the kingdom of the Persions resisted me one and twenty days: and behold Michael, one of the chief princes, came to help me, and I

remained there by the king of the Persians.

14 But I am come to teach thee what things shall befall thy people in the latter days: for as yet the vision is for days.

15 And when he was speaking such words to me, I cast down my countenance to the ground and held my peace.

16 And behold, as it were the likeness of a son of man touched my lips: then I opened my mouth and spoke and said to him that stood before me: O my Lord, at the sight of thee my joints are loosed and no strength hath remained in me.

17 And how can the servant of my lord speak with my lord? For no strength remaineth in me: moreover my breath is stopped.

18 Therefore he that looked like a man touched me again and strengthened me.

19 And he said: Fear not, O man of desires, peace be to thee. Take courage and be strong. And when he spoke to me, I grew strong. And I said: Speak, O my lord, for thou hast strenghtened me.

20 And he said: Dost thou know wherefore I am come to thee? And now I will return, to fight against the prince of the Persians. When I went forth, there appeared the prince of the Greeks coming.

21 But I will tell thee what is set down in the scripture of truth: and none is my helper in all these things but [1] Michael your prince.

CHAPTER 11

The angel declares to Daniel many things to come with regard to the Persian and Grecian kings, more especially with regard to Antiochus as a figure of Antichrist.

AND from the first year of Darius the Mede, I stood up that he might be strengthened and confirmed.

2 And now I will shew thee the truth. Behold there shall stand yet three kings in Persia, and the fourth shall be enriched exceedingly above them all: and when he shall be grown mighty by his

CHAP. 10. [1] Apoc. 12, 7.
thither the ensigns and standard of the pagan Romans. Others, in fine, distinguish three different times of desolation: that under Antiochus; that when the temple was destroyed by the Romans; and the last near the end of the world under Antichrist. To all which, as they suppose, this prophecy may have a relation.
CHAP. 10. Ver. 13. *The prince.* That is, the angel guardian of Persia, who according to his office, seeking the spiritual good of the Persians, was desirous that many of the Jews should remain among them.
Ver. 21. *Michael your prince.* The guardian general of the church of God.
CHAP. 11. Ver. 2. *Three kings.* Cambyses, Smerdes Magus and Darius, the son of Hystaspes.—*The fourth.* Xerxes.

riches, he shall stir up all against the kingdom of Greece.

3 But there shall rise up a strong king and shall rule with great power: and he shall do what he pleaseth.

4 And when he shall come to his height, his kingdom shall be broken: and it shall be divided towards the four winds of the heaven, but not to his posterity nor according to his power with which he ruled. For his kingdom shall be rent in pieces, even for strangers, beside these.

5 And the king of the south shall be strengthened, and one of his princes shall prevail over him, and he shall rule with great power: for his dominion shall be great.

6 And after the end of years they shall be in league together: and the daughter of the king of the south shall come to the king of the north to make friendship: but she shall not obtain the strength of the arm, neither shall her seed stand. And she shall be given up, and her young men that brought her, and they that strengthened her in *these* times.

7 And a plant of the bud of her roots shall stand up: and he shall come with an army and shall enter into the province of the king of the north. And he shall abuse them and shall prevail.

8 And he shall also carry away captive into Egypt their gods and their

CHAP. 11. [1] Isai. 19, 1.
Ver. 3. *A strong king.* Alexander.
Ver. 5. *The king of the south.* Ptolemeus the son of Lagus, king of Egypt, which lies south of Jerusalem.—*One of his princes,* that is, one of Alexander's princes, *shall prevail over him:* that is, shall be stronger than the king of Egypt. He speaks of Seleucus Nicator, king of Asia and Syria, whose successors are here called the kings of the north, because their dominions lay to the north in respect to Jerusalem.
Ver. 6. *The daughter of the king of the south.* Berenice, daughter of Ptolemeus Philadelphus, given in marriage to Antiochus Theos, grandson of Seleucus.
Ver. 7. *A plant.* Ptolemeus Evergetes, the son of Philadelphus.
Ver. 8. *The king of the north.* Seleucus Callinicus.
Ver. 10. *His sons.* Seleucus Ceraunius and Antiochus the Great, the sons of Callinicus.—*He shall come.* Antiochus the Great.
Ver. 11. *The king of the south.* Ptolemeus Philopator, son of Evergetes.
Ver. 16. *He shall come upon him.* Antiochus shall come upon the king of the south.—*The glorious land.* Judea.
Ver. 17. *All his kingdom.* All the kingdom of Ptolemeus Epiphanes, son of Philopator. — *A daughter of women.* That is, a most beautiful woman, his daughter Cleopatra.—*To overthrow it.* The kingdom of Epiphanes: but his policy shall not succeed; for Cleopatra shall take more to heart the interest of her husband than that of her father.
Ver. 18. *The prince of his reproach.* Scipio the Roman general, called the prince of his reproach, because he overthrew Antiochus and obliged him to submit to very dishonourable terms, before he would *cease* from the war.
Ver. 20. *One most vile.* Seleucus Philopator, who sent Heliodorus to plunder the temple and was shortly after slain by the same Heliodorus.

graven things and their precious vessels of gold and silver: he shall prevail against the king of the north.

9 And the king of the south shall enter into the kingdom and shall return to his own land.

10 And his sons shall be provoked, and they shall assemble a multitude of great forces: and he shall come with haste like a flood. And he shall return and be stirred up: and he shall join battle with his forces.

11 And the king of the south being provoked shall go forth and shall fight against the king of the north and shall prepare an exceeding great multitude: and a multitude shall be given into his hand.

12 And he shall take a multitude, and his heart shall be lifted up, and he shall cast down many thousands. But he shall not prevail.

13 For the king of the north shall return and shall prepare a multitude much greater than before: and in the end of times and years he shall come in haste with a great army and much riches.

14 [1] And in those times many shall rise up against the king of the south: and the children of prevaricators of thy people shall lift up themselves to fulfil the vision. And they shall fall.

15 And the king of the north shall come and shall cast up a mount and shall take the best fenced cities: and the arms of the south shall not withstand. And his chosen ones shall rise up to resist; and they shall not have strength.

16 And he shall come upon him and do according to his pleasure: and there shall be none to stand against his face. And he shall stand in the glorious land: and it shall be consumed by his hand.

17 And he shall set his face to come to possess all his kingdom and he shall make upright *conditions* with him: and he shall give him a daughter of women to overthrow it: and she shall not stand, neither shall she be for him.

18 And he shall turn his face to the islands and shall take many: and he shall cause the prince of his reproach to cease: and his reproach shall be turned upon him.

19 And he shall turn his face to the empire of his own land: and he shall stumble and fall and shall not be found.

20 And there shall stand up in his place, one most vile and unworthy of kingly honour: and in a few days he shall be destroyed, not in rage nor in battle.

21 And there shall stand up in his place one despised, and the kingly

honour shall not be given him: and he shall come privately and shall obtain the kingdom by fraud.

22 And the arms of the fighter shall be overcome before his face, and shall be broken: yea also the prince of the covenant.

23 And after friendships, he will deal deceitfully with him: and he shall go up and shall overcome with a small people.

24 And he shall enter into rich and plentiful cities: and he shall do that which his fathers never did, nor his fathers' fathers: he shall scatter their spoils and their prey and their riches, and shall forecast devices against the best fenced places: and this until a time.

25 And his strength and his heart shall be stirred up against the king of the south with a great army: and the king of the south shall be stirred up to battle with many and very strong succours: and they shall not stand, for they shall form designs against him.

26 And they that eat bread with him shall destroy him, and his army shall be overthrown: and many shall fall down slain.

27 And the heart of the two kings shall be to do evil, and they shall speak lies at one table, and they shall not prosper: because as yet the end is unto another time.

28 And he shall return into his land with much riches: and his heart *shall* be against the holy covenant, and he shall succeed and shall return into his own land.

29 At the time appointed he shall return and he shall come to the south: but the latter time shall not be like the former.

30 And the galleys and the Romans shall come upon him: and he shall be struck and shall return and shall have indignation against the covenant of the sanctuary. And he shall succeed: and he shall return and shall devise against them that have forsaken the covenant of the sanctuary.

31 And arms shall stand on his part and they shall defile the sanctuary of strength and shall take away the continual sacrifice: and they shall place *there* the abomination unto desolation.

32 And such as deal wickedly against the covenant shall deceitfully dissemble: but the people that know their God shall prevail and succeed.

33 And they that are learned among the people shall teach many: and they shall fall by the sword and by fire and by captivity and by spoil for *many* days.

34 And when they shall have fallen

they shall be relieved with a small help: and many shall be joined to them deceitfully.

35 And some of the learned shall fall, that they may be tried and may be chosen and made white even to the appointed time: because yet there shall be another time.

36 And the king shall do according to his will, and he shall be lifted up and shall magnify himself against every god: and he shall speak great things against the God of gods and shall prosper till the wrath be accomplished. For the determination is made.

37 And he shall make no account of the God of his fathers: and he shall follow the lust of women and he shall not regard any gods: for he shall rise up against all things.

38 But he shall worship the god Maozim in his place: and a god whom his fathers knew not he shall worship with gold and silver and precious stones and things of great price.

39 And he shall do this to fortify Maozim with a strange god whom he hath acknowledged: and he shall increase glory and shall give them power over many and shall divide the land gratis.

40 And at the time prefixed the king of the south shall fight against him and the king of the north shall come against him like a tempest, with chariots and with horsemen and with a great navy: and he shall enter into the countries and shall destroy and pass through.

41 And he shall enter into the glorious land, and many shall fall: and these only shall be saved out of his hand, Edom and Moab and the principality of the children of Ammon.

42 And he shall lay his hand upon the lands: and the land of Egypt shall not escape.

43 And he shall have power over the treasures of gold and of silver and all

Ver. 21. *One despised.* Antiochus Epiphanes, who at first was *despised* and not received for king. What is here said of this prince is accommodated by St. Jerome and others to Antichrist; of whom this Antiochus was a figure.

Ver. 22. *Of the fighter.* That is, of them that shall oppose him and shall fight against him. *The prince of the covenant,* or *of the league.* The chief of them that conspired against him: or the king of Egypt his most powerful adversary.

Ver. 25. *The king.* Ptolemeus Philometor.

Ver. 30. *The galleys and the Romans.* Popilius and the other Roman ambassadors, who came in galleys and obliged him to depart from Egypt.

Ver. 31. *They shall place* there *the abomination.* The idol of Jupiter Olympius which Antiochus ordered to be set up in the sanctuary of the temple, which is here called the *sanctuary of strength,* from the Almighty that was worshipped there.

Ver. 38. *The God Maozim.* That is, the god of *forces* or *strong holds.*

Ver. 39. *And he shall increase glory.* He shall bestow honours, riches and lands, upon them that shall worship his god.

the precious things of Egypt: and he shall pass through Libya and Ethiopia.

44 And tidings out of the east and out of the north shall trouble him: and he shall come with a great multitude to destroy and slay many.

45 And he shall fix his tabernacle Apadno between the seas, upon a glorious and holy mountain: and he shall come even to the top thereof, and none shall help him.

CHAPTER 12

Michael shall stand up for the people of God. With other things relating to Antichrist and the end of the world.

BUT [1] at that time shall Michael rise up, the great prince, who standeth for the children of thy people: and a time shall come such as never was from the time that nations began even until that time. And at that time shall thy people be saved, every one that shall be found written in the book.

2 And many of those that sleep in the dust of the earth shall awake: [2] some unto life everlasting, and others unto reproach, to see *it* always.

3 But they that are learned [3] shall shine as the brightness of the firmament: and they that instruct many to justice, as stars for all eternity.

4 But thou, O Daniel, shut up the words and seal the book, even to the time appointed. Many shall pass over, and knowledge shall be manifold.

5 And I Daniel looked, and behold as it were two others stood: one on this side upon the bank of the river, and another on that side, on the other bank of the river.

6 And I said to the man that was clothed in linen, that stood upon the waters of the river: How long shall it be to the end of these wonders?

7 And I heard the man that was clothed in linen, that stood upon the waters of the river: [4] when he had lifted up his right hand and his left hand to heaven and had sworn by him that liveth for ever, that *it should be* unto a time and times and half a time. And when the scattering of the band of the

CHAP. 12. [1] Apoc. 12, 7. [2] Matt. 25, 46; John, 5, 29. [3] Wisd. 3, 7. [4] Apoc. 10, 5.

Ver. 45. *Apadno.* Some take it for the proper name of a place: others, from the Hebrew, translate it *his palace.*

CHAP. 12. Ver. 3. *Learned.* Namely, in the law of God and true wisdom, which consists in knowing and loving God.

CHAP. 13. This history of Susanna, in all the ancient Greek and Latin Bibles, was placed in the beginning of the book of Daniel till St. Jerome, in his translation, detached it from thence, because he did not find it in the Hebrew: which is also the case of the history of Bel and the Dragon. But both the one and the other are received by the Catholic Church and were from the very beginning a part of the Christian Bible.

holy people shall be accomplished, all these things shall be finished.

8 And I heard and understood not. And I said: O my lord, what shall be after these things?

9 And he said: Go, Daniel, because the words are shut up and sealed until the appointed time.

10 Many shall be chosen and made white and shall be tried as fire: and the wicked shall deal wickedly. And none of the wicked shall understand: but the learned shall understand.

11 And from the time when the continual sacrifice shall be taken away and the abomination unto desolation shall be set up, there shall be a thousand two hundred ninety days.

12 Blessed is he that waiteth and cometh unto a thousand three hundred thirty-five days.

13 But go thou thy ways until the time appointed: and thou shalt rest and stand in thy lot unto the end of the days.

CHAPTER 13

The history of Susanna and the two elders.

NOW there was a man that dwelt in Babylon, and his name was Joakim:

2 And he took a wife whose name was Susanna, the daughter of Helcias, a very beautiful woman and one that feared God.

3 For her parents being just, had instructed their daughter according to the law of Moses.

4 Now Joakim was very rich and had an orchard near his house: and the Jews resorted to him, because he was the most honourable of them all.

5 And there were two of the ancients of the people appointed judges that year, of whom the Lord said: Iniquity came out from Babylon from the ancient judges that seemed to govern the people.

6 These men frequented the house of Joakim: and all that had any matters of judgment came to them.

7 And when the people departed away at noon, Susanna went in and walked in her husband's orchard.

8 And the old men saw her going in every day and walking: and they were inflamed with lust towards her.

9 And they perverted their own mind and turned away their eyes that they might not look unto heaven nor remember just judgments.

10 So they were both wounded with the love of her. Yet they did not make known their grief one to the other:

11 For they were ashamed to declare

to one another their lust, being desirous to have to do with her.

12 And they watched carefully every day to see her. And one said to the other:

13 Let us now go home, for it is dinner time. So going out they departed one from another.

14 And turning back again, they came both to the same place, and, asking one another the cause, they acknowledged their lust; and then they agreed upon a time when they might find her alone.

15 And it fell out, as they watched a fit day, she went in on a time, as yesterday and the day before, with two maids only and was desirous to wash herself in the orchard: for it was hot weather.

16 And there was nobody there, but the two old men that had hid themselves and were beholding her.

17 So she said to the maids: Bring me oil and washing balls and shut the doors of the orchard, that I may wash me.

18 And they did as she bade them: and they shut the doors of the orchard and went out by a back door to fetch what she had commanded them: and they knew not that the elders were hid within.

19 Now when the maids were gone forth, the two elders arose and ran to her and said:

20 Behold the doors of the orchard are shut and nobody seeth us and we are in love with thee: wherefore consent to us and lie with us.

21 But if thou wilt not, we will bear witness against thee that a young man was with thee and therefore thou didst send away thy maids from thee.

22 Susanna sighed and said: I am straitened on every side: for if I do this thing, it is death to me: and if I do it not, I shall not escape your hands.

23 But it is better for me to fall into your hands without doing it than to sin in the sight of the Lord.

24 With that Susanna cried out with a loud voice: and the elders also cried out against her.

25 And one *of them* ran to the door of the orchard and opened it.

26 So when the servants of the house heard the cry in the orchard, they rushed in by the back door to see what was the matter.

27 But after the old men had spoken the servants were greatly ashamed: for never had there been any such word said of Susanna. And on the next day,

28 When the people were come to Joakim her husband, the two elders also came full of wicked device against Susanna, to put her to death.

29 And they said before the people: Send to Susanna daughter of Helcias, the wife of Joakim. And presently they sent.

30 And she came with her parents and children and all her kindred.

31 Now Susanna was exceeding delicate and beautiful to behold.

32 But those wicked men commanded that her face should be uncovered (for she was covered) that so at least they might be satisfied with her beauty.

33 Therefore her friends and all her acquaintance wept.

34 But the two elders rising up in the midst of the people laid their hands upon her head.

35 And she weeping looked up to heaven: for her heart had confidence in the Lord.

36 And the elders said: As we walked in the orchard alone, this woman came in with two maids and shut the doors of the orchard and sent away the maids from her.

37 Then a young man that was there hid came to her and lay with her.

38 But we that were in a corner of the orchard, seeing this wickedness, ran up to them: and we saw them lie together.

39 And him indeed we could not take because he was stronger than us: and opening the doors he leaped out:

40 But having taken this woman, we asked who the young man was: but she would not tell us. Of this thing we are witnesses.

41 The multitude believed them as being the elders and the judges of the people: and they condemned her to death.

42 Then Susanna cried out with a loud voice and said: O eternal God, who knowest hidden things, who knowest all things before they come to pass,

43 Thou knowest that they have borne false witness against me: and behold I must die, whereas I have done none of these things which these men have maliciously forged against me.

44 And the Lord heard her voice.

45 And when she was led to be put to death, the Lord raised up the holy spirit of a young boy, whose name was Daniel.

46 And he cried out with a loud voice: I am clear from the blood of this woman.

47 Then all the people, turning themselves towards him, said: What meaneth this word that thou hast spoken?

48 But he standing in the midst of them, said: Are ye so foolish, ye children of Israel, that without examination or knowledge of the truth, you have condemned a daughter of Israel?

49 Return to judgment: for they have borne false witness against her.

50 So all the people turned again in haste, and the old men said to him: Come and sit thou down among us and shew it us, seeing God hath given thee the honour of old age.

51 And Daniel said to the people: Separate these two far from one another: and I will examine them.

52 So when they were put asunder one from the other, he called one of them and said to him: O thou that art grown old in evil days, now are thy sins come *out* which thou hast committed before.

53 In judging unjust judgments, oppressing the innocent and letting the guilty to go free, whereas the Lord saith: ¹ The innocent and the just thou shalt not kill.

54 Now then, if thou sawest her, tell me under what tree thou sawest them conversing together. He said: Under a mastic tree.

55 And Daniel said: Well hast thou lied against thine own head: for behold the angel of God, having received the sentence of him, shall cut thee in two.

56 And having put him aside, he commanded that the other should come. And he said to him: O thou seed of Chanaan and not of Juda, beauty hath deceived thee and lust hath perverted thy heart:

57 Thus did you do to the daughters of Israel: and they for fear conversed with you. But a daughter of Juda would not abide your wickedness.

58 Now therefore tell me, under what tree didst thou take them conversing together. And he answered: Under a holm tree.

59 And Daniel said to him: Well hast thou also lied against thy own head: for the angel of the Lord waiteth with a sword to cut thee in two and to destroy you.

60 With that all the assembly cried out with a loud voice. And they blessed God who saveth them that trust in him.

61 And they rose up against the two elders (for Daniel had convicted them of false witness by their own mouth) and they did to them as they had

maliciously dealt against their neighbour,

62 ² To fulfil the law of Moses. And they put them to death, and innocent blood was saved in that day.

63 But Helcias and his wife praised God for their daughter Susanna, with Joakim her husband and all her kindred, because there was no dishonesty found in her.

64 And Daniel became great in the sight of the people, from that day and thenceforward.

65 And king Astyages was gathered to his fathers: and Cyrus the Persian received his kingdom.

CHAPTER 14

The history of Bel and of the great serpent worshipped by the Babylonians.

AND Daniel was the king's guest and was honoured above all his friends.

2 Now the Babylonians had an idol called Bel: and there were spent upon him every day twelve great measures of fine flour and forty sheep and sixty vessels of wine.

3 The king also worshipped him and went every day to adore him: but Daniel adored his God. And the king said to him: Why dost thou not adore Bel?

4 And he answered and said to him: Because I do not worship idols made with hands, but the living God that created heaven and earth and hath power over all flesh.

5 And the king said to him: Doth not Bel seem to thee to be a living god? Seest thou not how much he eateth and drinketh every day?

6 Then Daniel smiled and said: O king, be not deceived, for this is but clay within, and brass without: neither hath he eaten at any time.

7 And the king being angry called for his priests, and said to them: If you tell me not who it is that eateth up these expenses, you shall die.

8 But if you can shew that Bel eateth these things, Daniel shall die, because he hath blasphemed against Bel. And Daniel said to the king: Be it done according to thy word.

9 Now the priests of Bel were seventy, besides their wives and little ones and children. And the king went with Daniel into the temple of Bel.

10 And the priests of Bel said: Behold we go out: and do thou, O king, set on the meats and make ready the wine and shut the door fast and seal it with thy own ring:

11 And when thou comest in the morning, if thou findest not that Bel

CHAP. 13. ¹ Exod. 23, 7. ² Deut. 19, 18, 19.

CHAP. 14. Ver. 1. *The king's guest.* It seems most probable that the king here spoken of was Evilmerodach, the son and successor of Nabuchodonosor and a great favourer of the Jews.

hath eaten up all, we will suffer death, or else Daniel that hath lied against us.

12 And they little regarded it: because they had made under the table a secret entrance, and they always came in by it and consumed those things.

13 So it came to pass after they were gone out, the king set the meats before Bel. And Daniel commanded his servants, and they brought ashes. And he sifted them all over the temple before the king. And going forth they shut the door, and having sealed it with the king's ring, they departed.

14 But the priests went in by night, according to their custom, with their wives and their children: and they ate and drank up all.

15 And the king arose early in the morning, and Daniel with him.

16 And the king said: Are the seals whole, Daniel? And he answered: They are whole, O king.

17 And as soon as he had opened the door, the king looked upon the table, and cried out with a loud voice: Great art thou, O Bel, and there is not any deceit with thee.

18 And Daniel laughed: and he held the king that he should not go in. And he said: Behold the pavement, mark whose footsteps these are.

19 And the king said: I see the footsteps of men and women and children. And the king was angry.

20 Then he took the priests and their wives and their children; and they shewed him the private doors by which they came in and consumed the things that were on the table.

21 The king therefore put them to death and delivered Bel into the power of Daniel, who destroyed him and his temple.

22 And there was a great dragon in that place, and the Babylonians worshipped him.

23 And the king said to Daniel: Behold thou canst not say now that this is not a living god: adore him therefore.

24 And Daniel said: I adore the Lord my God for he is the living God. But that is no living god.

25 But give me leave, O king, and I will kill this dragon without sword or club. And the king said: I give thee leave.

26 Then Daniel took pitch and fat and hair, and boiled them together: and he made lumps and put them into the dragon's mouth. And the dragon burst asunder. And he said: Behold him whom you worshipped.

27 And when the Babylonians had heard this they took great indignation:

and being gathered together against the king, they said: The king is become a Jew. He hath destroyed Bel, he hath killed the dragon, and he hath put the priests to death.

28 And they came to the king and said: Deliever us Daniel, or else we will destroy thee and thy house.

29 And the king saw that they pressed upon him violently: and being constrained by necessity he delivered Daniel to them.

30 And they cast him into the den of lions: and he was there six days.

31 And in the den there were seven lions, and they had given to them two carcasses every day and two sheep: but then they were not given unto them that they might devour Daniel.

32 Now there was in Judea a prophet called Habacuc, and he had boiled pottage and had broken bread in a bowl and was going into the field, to carry it to the reapers.

33 And the angel of the Lord said to Habacuc: Carry the dinner which thou hast into Babylon to Daniel who is in the lions' den.

34 And Habacuc said: Lord, I never saw Babylon, nor do I know the den.

35 [1] And the angel of the Lord took him by the top of his head and carried him by the hair of his head and set him in Babylon over the den in the force of his spirit.

36 And Habacuc cried, saying: O Daniel, thou servant of God, take the dinner that God hath sent thee.

37 And Daniel said: Thou hast remembered me, O God, and thou hast not forsaken them that love thee.

38 And Daniel arose and ate. And the angel of the Lord presently set Habacuc again in his own place.

39 And upon the seventh day, the king came to bewail Daniel: and he came to the den and looked in. And behold Daniel was sitting in the midst of the lions.

40 And the king cried out with a loud voice, saying: Great art thou, O Lord, the God of Daniel. And he drew him out of the lions' den.

41 But those that had been the cause of his destruction, he cast into the den: and they were devoured in a moment before him.

CHAP. 14. [1] Ezech. 8, 3.

Ver. 30. *The den of lions.* Daniel was twice cast into the den of lions: once under Darius the Mede, because he had transgressed the king's edict, by praying three times a day; and another time under Evilmerodach by a sedition of the people. This time he remained six days in the lions' den; the other time only one night.

Ver. 32. *Habacuc.* The same, as some think, whose prophecy is found among the lesser prophets: but others believe him to be different.

42 Then the king said: Let all the inhabitants of the whole earth fear the God of Daniel: for he is the Saviour, working signs and wonders in the earth: who hath delivered Daniel out of the lions' den.

THE PROPHECY OF

OSEE

Osee, *or* Hosea, *whose name signifies* A saviour, *was the first in the order of time among those who are commonly called Lesser Prophets, because their prophecies are short. He prophesied in the kingdom of Israel, that is, of the ten tribes, about the same time that Isaias prophesied in the kingdom of Juda.*

CHAPTER 1

By marrying a harlot, and by the names of his children, the prophet sets forth the crimes of Israel and their punishment. He foretells their redemption by Christ.

THE word of the Lord, that came to Osee the son of Beeri, in the days of Ozias, Joathan, Achaz *and* Ezechias, kings of Juda, and in the days of Jeroboam the son of Joas, king of Israel.

2 The beginning of the Lord's speaking by Osee. And the Lord said to Osee: Go, take thee a wife of fornications. And have of her children of fornications: for the land by fornication shall depart from the Lord.

3 So he went and took Gomer the daughter of Debelaim: and she conceived and bore him a son.

4 And the Lord said to him: Call his name Jezrahel: for yet a little while, and I will visit the blood of Jezrahel upon the house of Jehu, and I will cause to cease the kingdom of the house of Israel.

5 And in that day I will break in pieces the bow of Israel in the valley of Jezrahel.

6 And she conceived again and bore a daughter, and he said to him: Call her name, Without mercy: for I will not add any more to have mercy on the house of Israel, but I will utterly forget them.

7 And I will have mercy on the house of Juda and I will save them by the Lord their God: and I will not save them by bow, nor by sword, nor by battle, nor by horses, nor by horsemen.

8 And she weaned her that was *called,* Without mercy. And she conceived and bore a son.

9 And he said: Call his name, Not my people: for you are not my people, and I will not be yours.

10 And the number of the children of Israel shall be as the sand of the sea that is without measure and shall not be numbered. [1] And it shall be in the place where it shall be said to them: You are not my people: it shall be said to them: *Ye are* the sons of the living God.

11 And the children of Juda and the children of Israel shall be gathered together: and they shall appoint themselves one head and shall come up out of the land: for great is the day of Jezrahel.

CHAPTER 2

Israel is justly punished for leaving God. The abundance of grace in the church of Christ.

SAY ye to your brethren, *You are* my people: and to your sister, *Thou hast obtained mercy.*

2 Judge your mother, judge *her:* because she is not my wife, and I am not her husband. Let her put away her fornications from her face and adulteries from between her breasts.

3 Lest I strip her naked and set her as in the day that she was born: and I will make her as a wilderness and will set her as a land that none can pass through and will kill her with drought.

Chap. 1. [1] Rom. 9, 26.

Chap. 1. Ver. 2. *A wife of fornications.* That is, a wife that hath been given to fornication. This was to represent the Lord's proceedings with his people Israel, who, by spiritual fornication were continually offending him.—*Children of fornications.* So called from the character of their mother, if not also from their own wicked dispositions.

Ver. 6. *Without mercy.* Lo-Ruhamah.
Ver. 9. *Not my people.* Lo-ammi.
Ver. 10. *The number,* namely, of the true Israelites, the children of the church of Christ.
Ver. 11. *One head,* Christ.—*Great is the day of Jezrahel.* That is, of the seed of God; for *Jezrahel* signifies the seed of God.
Chap. 2. Ver. 1. *Say to your brethren,* or, *Call your brethren, My people: and your sister, Her that hath obtained mercy.* This is connected with the latter end of the foregoing chapter and relates to the converts of Israel.
Ver. 2. *Your mother.* The synagogue.

4 And I will not have mercy on her children: for they are the children of fornications.

5 For their mother hath committed fornication, she that conceived them is covered with shame. For she said: I will go after my lovers that give me my bread and my water, my wool and my flax, my oil and my drink.

6 Wherefore behold I will hedge up thy way with thorns and I will stop it up with a wall: and she shall not find her paths.

7 And she shall follow after her lovers and shall not overtake them: and she shall seek them and shall not find. And she shall say: I will go and return to my first husband, because it was better with me then, than now.

8 And she did not know that I gave her corn and wine and oil, and multiplied her silver and gold, which they have used in the service of Baal.

9 Therefore will I return and take away my corn in its season and my wine in its season, and I will set at liberty my wool and my flax which covered her disgrace.

10 And now I will lay open her folly in the eyes of her lovers: and no man shall deliver her out of my hand.

11 And I will cause all her mirth to cease: her solemnities, her new moons, her sabbaths and all her festival times.

12 And I will destroy her vines and her fig trees, of which she said: These are my rewards which my lovers have given me. And I will make her as a forest, and the beasts of the field shall devour her.

13 And I will visit upon her the days of Baalim, to whom she burnt incense and decked herself out with her earrings and with her jewels and went after her lovers and forgot me, saith the Lord.

14 Therefore, behold I will allure her and will lead her into the wilderness: and I will speak to her heart.

15 And I will give her vinedressers out of the same place, and the valley of Achor for an opening of hope: and she shall sing there according to the days of her youth and according to the days of her coming up out of the land of Egypt.

16 And it shall be in that day, saith the Lord, that she shall call me, My husband: and she shall call me no more, Baali.

17 And I will take away the names of Baalim out of her mouth: and she shall no more remember their name.

18 And in that day I will make a covenant with them, with the beasts of the field and with the fowls of the air

and with the creeping things of the earth: and I will destroy the bow and the sword and war out of the land: and I will make them sleep secure.

19 And I will espouse thee to me for ever: and I will espouse thee to me in justice and judgment and in mercy and in commiserations.

20 And I will espouse thee to me in faith: and thou shalt know that I am the Lord.

21 And it shall come to pass in that day: I will hear, saith the Lord, I will hear the heavens. And they shall hear the earth.

22 And the earth shall hear the corn and the wine and the oil. And these shall hear Jezrahel.

23 And I will sow her unto me in the earth: and I will have mercy on her that was without mercy.

24 [1] And I will say to that which was not my people: Thou art my people. And they shall say: Thou art my God.

CHAPTER 3

The prophet is commanded again to love an adulteress, to signify God's love to the synagogue. The wretched state of the Jews for a long time till at last they shall be converted.

AND the Lord said to me: Go yet again and love a woman beloved of her friend and an adulteress: as the Lord loveth the children of Israel, and they look to strange gods and love the husks of the grapes.

2 And I bought her to me for fifteen pieces of silver and for a core of barley and for half a core of barley.

3 And I said to her: Thou shalt wait for me many days. Thou shalt not play the harlot and thou shalt be no man's: and I also will wait for thee.

4 For the children of Israel shall sit

Chap. 2. [1] Rom. 9, 26; 1 Peter, 2, 10.

Ver. 14. *I will allure her.* After all her disloyalties, I will still allure her by my grace, and send her *vinedressers,* namely, the apostles; originally her own children, who shall *open* to her the gates of hope; as heretofore at her coming into the land of promise, she had all good success after she had satisfied the divine justice by the execution of Achan in the *valley of Achor* (Jos. 7.).

Ver. 16. *My husband.* In Hebrew, Ishi. *Baali,* my lord. The meaning of this verse is that, whereas *Ishi* and *Baali* were used indifferently in those days by wives speaking to their husbands, the synagogue, whom God was pleased to consider as his spouse, should call him only *Ishi,* and abstain from the name of *Baali,* because of its affinity with the name of the idol Baal.

Ver. 17. *Baalim.* It is the plural number of Baal: for there were divers idols of Baal.

Ver. 19. *I will espouse thee.* This relates to the happy espousals of Christ with his church, which shall never be dissolved.

Ver. 21. *Hear the heavens.* All shall conspire in favour of the church, which in the following verse is called *Jezrahel,* that is, *the seed of God.*

Ver. 24. *That which was not my people.* This relates to the conversion of the Gentiles.

many days without king and without prince and without sacrifice and without altar and without ephod and without theraphim.

5 [1] And after this the children of Israel shall return and shall seek the Lord their God and David their king: and they shall fear the Lord and his goodness in the last days.

CHAPTER 4

God's judgment against the sins of Israel. Juda is warned not to follow their example.

HEAR the word of the Lord, ye children of Israel: for the Lord shall enter into judgment with the inhabitants of the land. For there is no truth, and there is no mercy, and there is no knowledge of God in the land.

2 Cursing and lying and killing and theft and adultery have overflowed: and blood hath touched blood.

3 Therefore shall the land mourn and every one that dwelleth in it shall languish, with the beasts of the field and with the fowls of the air: yea, the fishes of the sea also shall be gathered together.

4 But yet let not any man judge, and let not a man be rebuked: for thy people are as they that contradict the priest.

5 And thou shalt fall to-day, and the prophet also shall fall with thee: in the night I have made thy mother to be silent.

6 My people have been silent, because they had no knowledge. Because thou hast rejected knowledge, I will reject thee, that thou shalt not do the office of priesthood to me: and because thou hast forgotten the law of thy God, I also will forget thy children.

7 According to the multitude of them so have they sinned against me: I will change their glory into shame.

8 They shall eat the sins of my people and shall lift up their souls to their iniquity.

9 [1] And there shall be like people like priest: and I will visit their ways upon them and I will repay them their devices.

10 And they shall eat and shall not

be filled: they have committed fornication and have not ceased: because they have forsaken the Lord in not observing *his law*.

11 Fornication and wine and drunkenness take away the understandig.

12 My people have consulted their stocks and their staff hath declared unto them: for the spirit of fornication hath deceived them and they have committed fornication against their God.

13 They offered sacrifice upon the tops of the mountains and burnt incense up the hills: under the oak and the poplar and the turpentine tree, because the shadow thereof was good: therefore shall you daughters commit fornication and your spouses shall be adulteresses.

14 I will not visit upon your daughters when they shall commit fornication and upon your spouses when they shall commit adultery: because themselves conversed with harlots and offered sacrifice with the effeminate: and the people that doth not understand shall be beaten.

15 If thou play the harlot, O Israel, at least let not Juda offend: and go ye not into Galgal and come not up into Bethaven and do not swear: The Lord liveth.

16 For Israel hath gone astray like a wanton heifer: now will the Lord feed them, as a lamb in a spacious place.

17 Ephraim is a partaker with idols: let him alone.

18 Their banquet is separated, they have gone astray by fornication: they that should have protected them have loved to bring shame upon them.

19 The wind hath bound them up in its wings: and they shall be confounded because of their sacrifices.

CHAPTER 5

God's threats against the priests, the people and princes of Israel for their idolatry.

HEAR ye this, O priests, and hearken, O ye house of Israel, and ear, O house of the king: for there is a judgment against you, because you have been a snare to them whom you should have watched over and a net spread upon Thabor.

2 And you have turned aside victims into the depth: and I *am* the teacher of them all.

3 I know Ephraim, and Israel is not hid from me: for now Ephraim hath committed fornication, Israel is defiled.

4 They will not set their thoughts to return to their God: for the spirit of fornication is in the midst of them, and they have not known the Lord.

CHAP. 3. [1] Ezech. 34, 23. CHAP. 4. [1] Isai. 24, 2.

CHAP. 3. Ver. 4. *Theraphim*, Images or representations.

Ver. 5. *David their king*. That is, Christ, who is of the house of David.

CHAP. 4. Ver. 4. *Let not any man judge*. As if he would say: It is in vain to strive with them or reprove them, they are so obstinate in evil.

Ver. 15. *Galgal* and *Bethaven*. Places where idols were worshipped. *Bethel*, which signifies *the house of God*, is called by the prophet, *Bethaven*, that is, the *house of vanity*, from Jeroboam's golden calf that was worshipped there.

CHAP. 5. Ver. 1. *O priests*. What is said to *priests* in this prophecy is chiefly understood of the priests of the kingdom of Israel, who were not true priests of the race of Aaron, but served the calves at Bethel and Dan.

5 And the pride of Israel shall answer in his face: and Israel and Ephraim shall fall in their iniquity. Juda also shall fall with them.

6 With their flocks and with their herds, they shall go to seek the Lord and shall not find him: he is withdrawn from them.

7 They have transgressed against the Lord, for they have begotten children *that are* strangers: now shall a month devour them with their portions.

8 Blow ye the cornet in Gabaa, the trumpet in Rama: howl ye in Bethaven, behind thy back, O Benjamin.

9 Ephraim shall be in desolation in the day of rebuke: among the tribes of Israel I have shewn that which shall surely be.

10 The princes of Juda are become as they that take up the bound: I will pour out my wrath upon them like water.

11 Ephraim is under oppression *and* broken in judgment: because he began to go after filthiness.

12 And I *will be* like a moth to Ephraim: and like rottenness to the house of Juda.

13 And Ephraim saw his sickness, and Juda his band. And Ephraim went to the Assyrian and sent to the avenging king: and he shall not be able to heal you: neither shall he be able to take off the band from you.

14 For I will be like a lioness to Ephraim and like a lion's whelp to the house of Juda. I, I, will catch and go: I will take away, and there is none that can rescue.

15 I will go and return to my place, until you are consumed and seek my face.

CHAPTER 6

Affliction shall be a means to bring many to Christ. A complaint of the untowardness of the Jews. God loves mercy more than sacrifice.

IN their affliction they will rise early to me: Come, and let us return to the Lord:

2 For he hath taken us, and he will heal us: he will strike, and he will cure us.

3 [1] He will revive us after two days: on the third day he will raise us up and we shall live in his sight. We shall know and we shall follow on, that we may know the Lord. His going forth is prepared as the morning light and he will come to us as the early and the latter rain to the earth.

4 What shall I do to thee, O Ephraim? What shall I do to thee, O Juda? Your mercy *is* as a morning cloud and as the dew that goeth away in the morning.

5 For this reason have I hewed *them* by the prophets, I have slain them by the words of my mouth: and the judgments shall go forth as the light.

6 [2] For I desired mercy and not sacrifice: and the knowledge of God more than holocausts.

7 But they, like Adam, have transgressed the covenant: there have they dealt treacherously against me.

8 Galaad *is* a city of workers of idols, supplanted with blood.

9 And like the jaws of highway robbers, they conspire with the priests who murder in the way those that pass out of Sichem: for they have wrought wickedness.

10 I have seen a horrible thing in the house of Israel: the fornications of Ephraim there. Israel is defiled.

11 And thou also, O Juda, set thee a harvest, when I shall bring back the captivity of my people.

CHAPTER 7

The manifold sins of Israel and of their kings hinder the Lord from healing them.

WHEN I would have healed Israel, the iniquity of Ephraim was discovered, and the wickedness of Samaria, for they have committed falsehood: and the thief is come in to steal, the robber is without.

2 And lest they may say in their hearts that I remember all their wickedness, their own devices now have beset them about: they have been done before my face.

3 They have made the king glad with their wickedness: and the princes with their lies.

4 They are all adulterers, like an oven heated by the baker: the city rested a little from the mingling of the leaven, till the whole was leavened.

5 The day of our king, the princes began to be mad with wine: he stretched out his hand with scorners.

CHAP. 6. [1] 1 Cor. 15, 4. [2] 1 Kings, 15, 22; Eccles. 4, 17; Matt. 9, 13.

Ver. 7. *Children that are strangers.* That is, aliens from God: and therefore they are threatened with speedy destruction.

Ver. 10. *As they that take up the bound.* That is, they that remove the boundary, encroaching on the property of their neighbours: figuratively, their going beyond the boundary of the laws of God.

CHAP. 6. Ver. 8. *Supplanted with blood.* That is, undermined and brought to ruin, for shedding of blood: and, as it is signified in the following verse, for *conspiring with the priests* (of Bethel) like robbers, to *murder in the way* such as *passed out of Sichem* to go towards the temple of Jerusalem. Or else *supplanted with blood*, signifies flowing in such manner with blood, as to suffer none to walk there without imbruing the *soles* of their feet in blood.

CHAP. 7. Ver. 3. *Made the king glad.* To please Jeroboam and their other kings, they have given themselves up to the wicked worship of idols, which are mere falsehood and lies.

6 Because they have applied their heart like an oven, when he laid snares for them. He slept all the night baking them: in the morning he himself was heated as a flaming fire.

7 They were all heated like an oven and have devoured their judges: all their kings have fallen: there is none amongst them that calleth unto me.

8 Ephraim himself is mixed among the nations: Ephraim is become as bread baked under the ashes, that is not turned.

9 Strangers have devoured his strength and he knew it not: yea, grey hairs also are spread about upon him and he is ignorant of it.

10 And the pride of Israel shall be humbled before his face: and they have not returned to the Lord their God, nor have they sought him in all these.

11 And Ephraim is become as a dove that is decoyed not having a heart: they called upon Egypt, they went to the Assyrians.

12 And when they shall go, I will spread my net upon them: I will bring them down as the fowl of the air: I will strike them as their congregation hath heard.

13 Woe to them, for they have departed from me: they shall be wasted because they have transgressed against me. And I redeemed them: and they have spoken lies against me.

14 And they have not cried to me with their heart, but they howled in their beds: they have thought upon wheat and wine, they are departed from me.

15 And I have chastised them and strengthened their arms: and they have imagined evil against me.

16 They returned, that they might be without yoke: they became like a deceitful bow: their princes shall fall by the sword, for the rage of their tongue. This is their derision in the land of Egypt.

CHAPTER 8

The Israelites are threatened with destruction for their impiety and idolatry.

LET there be a trumpet in thy throat, like an eagle upon the house of the Lord: because they have transgressed my covenant and have violated my law.

2 They shall call upon me: O my God, we, Israel, know thee.

3 Israel hath cast off the thing that is good: the enemy shall pursue him.

4 They have reigned, but not by me: they have been princes, and I knew not: of their silver and their gold they have made idols to themselves, that they might perish.

5 Thy calf, O Samaria, is cast off: my wrath is kindled against them. How long will they be incapable of being cleansed?

6 For itself also is *the invention* of Israel: a workman made it. And it is no god: for the calf of Samaria shall be turned to spiders' webs.

7 For they shall sow wind and reap a whirlwind. There is no standing stalk in it, the bud shall yield no meal; and if it should yield, strangers shall eat it.

8 Israel is swallowed up: now is he become among the nations like an unclean vessel.

9 For they are gone up to Assyria, a wild ass alone by himself: Ephraim hath given gifts to his lovers.

10 But even though they shall have hired the nations, now will I gather them together: and they shall rest a while from the burden of the king and the princes.

11 Because Ephraim hath made many altars to sin: altars are become to him unto sin.

12 I shall write to him my manifold laws, which have been accounted as foreign.

13 They shall offer victims, they shall sacrifice flesh and shall eat it, and the Lord will not receive them: now will he remember their iniquity and will visit their sins: they shall return to Egypt.

14 And Israel hath forgotten his Maker and hath built temples: and Juda hath built many fenced cities. And I will send a fire upon his cities: and it shall devour the houses thereof.

CHAPTER 9

The distress and captivity of Israel for their sins and idolatry.

REJOICE not, O Israel: rejoice not as the nations *do:* for thou hast committed fornication against thy God, thou hast loved a reward upon every corn-floor.

2 The floor and the winepress shall not feed them: and the wine shall deceive them.

3 They shall not dwell in the Lord's land: Ephraim is returned to Egypt and hath eaten unclean things among the Assyrians.

4 They shall not offer wine to the Lord, neither shall they please him: their sacrifices shall be like the bread of mourners: all that shall eat it shall be defiled. For their bread is life for their soul: it shall not enter into the house of the Lord.

5 What will you do in the solemn day, in the day of the feast of the Lord?

6 For behold they are gone because of destruction: Egypt shall gather them together, Memphis shall bury them: nettles shall inherit their beloved silver, the bur shall be in their tabernacles.

7 The days of visitation are come, the days of repaying are come: know ye, O Israel, that the prophet was foolish, the spiritual man was mad for the multitude of thy iniquity and the multitude of thy madness.

8 The watchman of Ephraim *was* with my God: the prophet is become a snare of ruin upon all his ways: madness is in the house of his God.

9 ¹They have sinned deeply, as in the days of Gabaa: he will remember their iniquity and will visit their sin.

10 I found Israel like grapes in the desert, I saw their fathers like the first-fruits of the fig tree in the top thereof: but they went in to Beelphegor and alienated themselves to *that* confusion and became abominable, as those things *were*, which they loved.

11 As for Ephraim, their glory hath flown away like a bird, from the birth and from the womb and from the conception.

12 And though they should bring up their children, I will make them without children among men: yea, and woe to them, when I shall depart from them.

13 Ephraim, as I saw, was a Tyre founded in beauty: and Ephraim shall bring out his children to the murderer.

14 Give them, O Lord. What wilt thou give them? Give them a womb without children and dry breasts.

15 ²All their wickedness is in Galgal, for there I hated them: for the wickedness of their devices I will cast them forth out of my house. I will love them no more: all their princes are revolters.

16 Ephraim is struck, their root is dried up, they shall yield no fruit. And if they should have issue, I will slay the best beloved fruit of their womb.

17 My God will cast them away, because they hearkened not to him: and they shall be wanderers among the nations.

CHAPTER 10

After many benefits, great affliction shall fall upon the ten tribes for their ingratitude to God.

ISRAEL, a vine full of branches, the fruit is agreeable to it: according to the multitude of his fruit he hath multiplied altars: according to the plenty of his land he hath abounded with idols.

2 Their heart is divided: now they shall perish: he shall break down their idols, he shall destroy their altars.

3 For now they shall say: We have no king, because we fear not the Lord. And what shall a king do to us?

4 You speak words of an unprofitable vision and you shall make a covenant: and judgment shall spring up as bitterness in the furrows of the field.

5 The inhabitants of Samaria have worshipped the kine of Bethaven: for the people thereof have mourned over it, and the wardens of its temple *that* rejoiced over it in its glory, because it is departed from it.

6 For itself also is carried into Assyria, a present to the avenging king. Shame shall fall upon Ephraim: and Israel shall be confounded in his own will.

7 Samaria hath made her king to pass as froth upon the face of the water.

8 And the high places of the idol, the sin of Israel, shall be destroyed: the bur and the thistle shall grow up over their altars: and they shall say to the mountains: ¹Cover us; and to the hills: Fall upon us.

9 ²From the days of Gabaa, Israel hath sinned: there they stood: the battle in Gabaa against the children of iniquity shall not overtake them.

10 According to my desire I will chastise them: and the nations shall be gathered together against them, when they shall be chastised for their two iniquities.

11 Ephraim is a heifer taught to love to tread out corn, but I passed over upon the beauty of her neck. I will ride upon Ephraim: Juda shall plough, Jacob shall break the furrows for himself.

12 ³Sow for yourselves in justice and reap in the mouth of mercy, break up your fallow ground: but the time to seek the Lord is, when he shall come that shall teach you justice.

13 You have ploughed wickedness, you have reaped iniquity, you have eaten the fruit of lying: because thou hast trusted in thy ways, in the multitude of thy strong ones.

14 A tumult shall arise among thy people and all thy fortresses shall be

---

CHAP. 9. ¹ Judges, 19, 25. ² 1 Kings, 8, 5. CHAP. 10. ¹ Isai. 2, 19; Luke, 23, 30; Apoc. 6, 16. ² Judges, 20, 1. ³ Jer. 4, 3.

CHAP. 10. Ver. 5. *The kine of Bethaven.* The golden calves of Jeroboam.
Ver. 6. *Itself also is carried.* One of the golden calves was given by king Manahem, to Phul, king of the Assyrians, to engage him to stand by him.
Ver. 10. *Their two iniquities.* Their two calves.
Ver. 14. *As Salmana,* king of the Midianites, *was destroyed by the house,* that is, by the followers *of him that judged Baal;* that is, of Gideon, who threw down the altar of Baal and was therefore called Jerubaal. See Judges 6 and 8.

destroyed as [4] Salmana was destroyed by the house of him that judged Baal in the day of battle: the mother being dashed in pieces upon her children.

15 So hath Bethel done to you, because of the evil of your iniquities.

CHAPTER 11

God proceeds in threatening Israel for their ingratitude. Yet he will not utterly destroy them.

AS the morning passeth, so hath the king of Israel passed away. Because Israel was a child and [1] I loved him: and I called my son out of Egypt

2 As they called them, they went away from before their face: they offered victims to Baalim and sacrificed to idols.

3 And I was like a foster father to Ephraim, I carried them in my arms: and they knew not that I healed them.

4 I will draw them with the cords of Adam, with the bands of love: and I will be to them as one that taketh off the yoke on their jaws: and I put his meat to him that he might eat.

5 He shall not return into the land of Egypt, but the Assyrian shall be his king: because they would not be converted.

6 The sword hath begun in his cities: and it shall consume his chosen men and shall devour their heads.

7 And my people shall long for my return: but a yoke shall be put upon them together, which shall not be taken off.

8 How shall I deal with thee, O Ephraim? Shall I protect thee, O Israel? [2] How shall I make thee as Adama? Shall I set thee as Seboim? My heart is turned within me: my repentance is stirred up.

9 I will not execute the fierceness of my wrath: I will not return to destroy Ephraim: because I am God and not man: the holy one in the midst of thee: and I will not enter into the city.

10 They shall walk after the Lord. He shall roar as a lion: because he shall

[4] Judges, 8, 12. CHAP. 11. [1] Matt. 2, 15. [2] Gen. 19, 24. CHAP. 12. [1] Gen. 25, 25; 32, 24. [2] Gen. 28, 5. [3] Exod. 14, 21, 22.

CHAP. 11. Ver. 1. *I called my son*, Israel. But as the calling of Israel out of Egypt was a figure of the calling of Christ from thence; therefore this text is also applicable to Christ, as we learn from Matt. 2, 15.

Ver. 2. *They called.* Moses and Aaron called; but they went away after other gods and would not hear.

Ver. 8. *Adama.* Adama and Seboim were two cities in the neighbourhood of Sodom and underwent the like destruction.

CHAP. 12. Ver. 11. *If Galaad be an idol.* That is, if Galaad with all its idols and sacrifices be like a mere idol itself, being brought to nothing by Theglathphalasar: how vain is it to expect that the idols worshipped in Galgal shall be of any service to the tribes that remain.

roar and the children of the sea shall fear.

11 And they shall fly away like a bird out of Egypt and like a dove out of the land of the Assyrians: and I will place them in their own houses, saith the Lord.

12 Ephraim hath compassed me about with denials and the house of Israel with deceit: but Juda went down as a witness with God and is faithful with the saints.

CHAPTER 12

Israel is reproved for sin. God's favours to them.

EPHRAIM feedeth on the wind and followeth the *burning* heat: all the day long he multiplied lies and desolation: and he hath made a covenant with the Assyrians and carried oil into Egypt.

2 Therefore there is a judgment of the Lord with Juda and a visitation for Jacob: he will render to him according to his ways and according to his devices.

3 [1] In the womb he supplanted his brother: and by his strength he had success with an angel.

4 And he prevailed over the angel and was strengthened: he wept and made supplication to him: he found him in Bethel, and there he spoke with us.

5 Even the Lord, the God of hosts, the Lord *is* his memorial.

6 Therefore turn thou to thy God: keep mercy and judgment, and hope in thy God always.

7 *He is like* Chanaan, there is a deceitful balance in his hand: he hath loved oppression.

8 And Ephraim said: But yet I am become rich, I have found me an idol: all my labours shall not find me the iniquity that I have committed.

9 And I *that am* the Lord thy God from the land of Egypt will yet cause thee to dwell in tabernacles, as in the days of the feast.

10 And I have spoken by the prophets and I have multiplied visions and I have used similitudes by the ministry of the prophets.

11 If Galaad be an idol, then in vain were they in Galgal offering sacrifices with bullocks: for their altars also are as heaps in the furrows of the field.

12 [2] Jacob fled into the country of Syria, and Israel served for a wife and was a keeper for a wife.

13 [3] But the Lord by a prophet brought Israel out of Egypt: and he was preserved by a prophet.

14 Ephraim hath provoked me to

wrath with his bitterness, and his blood shall come upon him: and his Lord will render his reproach unto him.

CHAPTER 13

The judgments of God upon Israel for their sins. Christ shall one day redeem them.

ᙡHEN Ephraim spoke, a horror seized Israel: and he sinned in Baal and died.

2 And now they have sinned more and more: and they have made to themselves a molten thing of their silver as the likeness of idols: the whole is the work of craftsmen: to these they say: Sacrifice men, ye that adore calves.

3 Therefore they shall be as a morning cloud and as the early dew that passeth away, as the dust that is driven with a whirlwind out of the floor and as the smoke out of the chimney.

4 ¹ But I *am* the Lord thy God from the land of Egypt: and thou shalt know no God but me, and there is no saviour beside me.

5 I knew thee in the desert, in the land of the wilderness.

6 According to their pastures they were filled and were made full: and they lifted up their heart and have forgotten me.

7 And I will be to them as a lioness, as a leopard in the way of the Assyrians.

8 I will meet them as a bear that is robbed of her whelps and I will rend the inner parts of their liver: and I will devour them there as a lion. The beast of the field shall tear them.

9 Destruction is thy own, O Israel: thy help is only in me.

10 Where is thy king? Now especially let him save thee in all thy cities. And thy judges, of whom thou saidst: ² Give me kings and princes.

11 I will give thee a king in my wrath and will take *him* away in my indignation.

12 The iniquity of Ephraim is bound up: his sin is hidden.

13 The sorrows of a woman in labour shall come upon him, he is an unwise son: for now he shall not stand in the breach of the children.

14 I will deliver them out of the hand of death. I will redeem them from death. ³ O death, I will be thy death; O hell, I will be thy bite. Comfort is hidden from my eyes:

15 Because he shall make a separation between brothers. ⁴ The Lord will bring a burning wind that shall rise from the desert, and it shall dry up his springs and shall make his fountain desolate: and he shall carry off the treasure of every desirable vessel.

CHAPTER 14

Samaria shall be destroyed. An exhortation to repentance. God's favour through Christ to the penitent.

ᒪET Samaria perish, because she hath stirred up her God to bitterness. Let them perish by the sword, let their little ones be dashed: and let the women with child be ripped up.

2 Return, O Israel, to the Lord thy God: for thou hast fallen down by thy iniquity.

3 Take with you words and return to the Lord and say to him: Take away all iniquity and receive the good: and we will render the calves of our lips.

4 Assyria shall not save us, we will not ride upon horses, neither will we say any more: The works of our hands are our gods. For thou wilt have mercy on the fatherless that is in thee.

5 I will heal their breaches, I will love them freely: for my wrath is turned away from them.

6 I will be as the dew: Israel shall spring as the lily and his root shall shoot forth as that of Libanus.

7 His branches shall spread and his glory shall be as the olive tree: and his smell as that of Libanus.

8 They shall be converted that sit under his shadow: they shall live upon wheat and they shall blossom as a vine: his memorial shall be as the wine of Libanus.

9 Ephraim *shall say,* What have I to do any more with idols? I will hear him and I will make him flourish like a green fir tree: from me is thy fruit found.

10 Who is wise, and he shall understand these things? Prudent, and he shall know these things? For the ways of the Lord are right and the just shall walk in them: but the transgressors shall fall in them.

CHAP. 13. ¹ Isai. 43, 11. ² 1 Kings, 8, 5. ³ 1 Cor. 15, 54: Heb. 2, 14. ⁴ Ezech. 19, 12.

CHAP. 14. Ver. 1. *Perish, because she hath stirred up her God to bitterness.* It is not a curse or imprecation, but a prophecy of what should come to pass.

THE PROPHECY OF

JOEL

JOEL, *whose name, according to St. Jerome, signifies* THE LORD GOD, *or, as others say,* THE COMING DOWN OF GOD, *prophesied about the same time in the kingdom of Judea as Osee did in the kingdom of Israel. He foretells under figures the great evils that were coming upon the people for their sins: earnestly exhorts them to repentance: and comforts them with the promise of a teacher of justice, that is, of Christ Jesus our Lord, and of the coming down of his holy Spirit.*

CHAPTER 1

The prophet describes the judgments that shall fall upon the people and invites them to fasting and prayer.

THE word of the Lord that came to Joel, the son of Phatuel.

2 Hear this, ye old men, and give ear, all ye inhabitants of the land: Did this ever happen in your days or in the days of your fathers?

3 Tell ye of this to your children: and let your children tell their children, and their children to another generation.

4 That which the palmerworm hath left, the locust hath eaten: and that which the locust hath left, the bruchus hath eaten: and that which the bruchus hath left, the mildew hath destroyed.

5 Awake, ye that are drunk, and weep and mourn all ye that take delight in drinking sweet wine: for it is cut off from your mouth.

6 For a nation is come up upon my land, strong and without number: his teeth are like the teeth of a lion and his cheek teeth as of a lion's whelp.

7 He hath laid my vineyard waste and hath pilled off the bark of my fig tree: he hath stripped it bare and cast it away: the branches thereof are made white.

8 Lament like a virgin girded with sackcloth for the husband of her youth.

9 Sacrifice and libation is cut off from the house of the Lord: the priests, the Lord's ministers, have mourned.

10 The country is destroyed, the ground hath mourned: for the corn is wasted, the wine is confounded, the oil hath languished.

11 The husbandmen are ashamed, the vinedressers have howled for the wheat and for the barley, because the harvest of the field is perished.

12 The vineyard is confounded and the fig tree hath languished: the pomegranate tree and the palm tree and the apple tree and all the trees of the field are withered: because joy is withdrawn from the children of men.

13 Gird yourselves and lament, O ye priests: howl, ye ministers of the altars. Go in, lie in sackcloth, ye ministers of my God: because sacrifice and libation is cut off from the house of your God.

14 [1] Sanctify ye a fast, call an assembly, gather together the ancents, all the inhabitants of the land into the house of your God: and cry ye to the Lord:

15 Ah, ah, ah, for the day: because the day of the Lord is at hand, and it shall come like destruction from the mighty.

16 Is not your food cut off before your eyes: joy and gladness from the house of our God?

17 The beasts have rotted in their dung, the barns are destroyed, the storehouses are broken down: because the corn is confounded.

18 Why did the beast groan, why did the herds of cattle low? Because there is no pasture for them: yea, and the flocks of sheep are perished.

19 To thee, O Lord, will I cry: because fire hath devoured the beautiful places of the wilderness and the flame hath burnt all the trees of the country.

20 Yea and the beasts of the field have looked up to thee, as a garden bed that thirsteth after rain: for the springs of waters are dried up and fire hath devoured the beautiful places of the wilderness.

CHAP. 1. [1] Joel, 2, 15.

CHAP. 1. Ver. 4. *That which the palmerworm hath left.* Some understand this literally of the desolation of the land by these insects: others understand it of the different invasions of the Chaldeans or other enemies.

CHAPTER 2

The prophet foretells the terrible day of the Lord, exhorts sinners to a sincere conversion, and comforts God's people with promises of future blessings under Christ.

BLOW ye the trumpet in Sion, sound an alarm in my holy mountain, let all the inhabitants of the land tremble: because the day of the Lord cometh, because it is nigh at hand.

2 A day of darkness and of gloominess, a day of clouds and whirlwinds: a numerous and strong people as the morning spread upon the mountains: the like to it hath not been from the beginning, nor shall be after it even to the years of generation and generation.

3 Before the face thereof a devouring fire, and behind it a burning flame: the land is like a garden of pleasure before it, and behind it a desolate wilderness: neither is there any one that can escape it.

4 The appearance of them is as the appearance of horses: and they shall run like horsemen.

5 They shall leap like the noise of chariots upon the tops of mountains. like the noise of a flame of fire devouring the stubble, as a strong people prepared to battle.

6 At their presence, the people shall be in grievous pains: all faces shall be made like a kettle.

7 They shall run like valiant men: like men of war they shall scale the wall: the men shall march every one on his way, and they shall not turn aside from their ranks.

8 No one shall press upon his brother: they shall walk every one in his path: yea, and they shall fall through the windows and shall take no harm.

9 They shall enter into the city, they shall run upon the wall, they shall climb up the houses, they shall come in at the windows as a thief.

10 At their presence, the earth hath trembled, the heavens are moved: [1] the sun and moon are darkened and the stars have withdrawn their shining.

11 And the Lord hath uttered his voice before the face of his army: for his armies are exceeding great, for they are strong and execute his word: [2] for the day of the Lord is great and very terrible: and who can stand it?

12 Now therefore saith the Lord: Be converted to me with all your heart, in fasting and in weeping and in mourning.

13 And rend your hearts and not your garments, and turn to the Lord your God: [3] for he is gracious and mer-ciful, patient and rich in mercy, and ready to repent of the evil.

14 [4] Who knoweth but he will return and forgive and leave a blessing behind him, sacrifice and libation to the Lord your God?

15 Blow the trumpet in Sion: [5] sanctify a fast, call a solemn assembly,

16 Gather together the people, sanctify the church, assemble the ancients, gather together the little ones and them that suck at the breasts: let the bridegroom go forth from his bed and the bride out of her bride chamber.

17 Between the porch and the altar the priests the Lord's ministers shall weep and shall say: Spare, O Lord, spare thy people: and give not thy inheritance to reproach, that the heathen should rule over them. Why should they say among the nations: Where is their God?

18 The Lord hath been zealous for his land and hath spared his people.

19 And the Lord answered and said to his people: Behold I will send you corn and wine and oil, and you shall be filled with them: and I will no more make you a reproach among the nations.

20 And I will remove far off from you the northern *enemy:* and I will drive him into a land unpassable and desert, with his face towards the east sea and his hinder part towards the utmost sea: and his stench shall ascend and his rottenness shall go up, because he hath done proudly.

21 Fear not, O land, be glad and rejoice: for the Lord hath done great things.

22 Fear not, ye beasts of the fields: for the beautiful places of the wilderness are sprung, for the tree hath brought forth its fruit: the fig tree and the vine have yielded their strength.

23 And you, O children of Sion, rejoice and be joyful in the Lord your God: because he hath given you a teacher of justice, and he will make the early and the latter rain to come down to you as in the beginning.

24 And the floors shall be filled with wheat, and the presses shall overflow with wine and oil.

25 And I will restore to you the years

CHAP. 2. [1] Isai. 13, 10; Ezech. 32, 7; Joel, 3, 15; Matt. 24, 29; Mark, 13, 24; Luke, 21, 25. [2] Jer. 30, 7; Amos, 5, 18; Soph. 1, 15. [3] Ps. 85, 5; John, 4, 2. [4] John, 3, 9. [5] Joel, 1, 14.

CHAP. 2. Ver. 1. *The day of the Lord.* That is, the time when he will execute justice upon sinners.
Ver. 2. *A numerous and strong people.* The Assyrians or Chaldeans. Others understand all this of an army of locusts laying waste the land.
Ver. 20. *The northern enemy.* Some understand this of Holofernes and his army: others, of the locusts.

which the locust and the bruchus and the mildew, and the palmerworm have eaten: my great host which I sent upon you.

26 And you shall eat in plenty and shall be filled: and you shall praise the name of the Lord your god who hath done wonders with you: and my people shall not be confounded for ever.

27 And you shall know that I am in the midst of Israel: and I *am* the Lord your God, and there is none besides: and my people shall not be confounded for ever.

28 And it shall come to pass after this, [6] that I will pour out my spirit upon all flesh: and your sons and your daughters shall prophesy: your old men shall dream dreams, and your young men shall see visions.

29 Moreover upon my servants and handmaids in those days I will pour forth my spirit.

30 And I will shew wonders in heaven: and in earth, blood and fire and vapour of smoke.

31 [7] The sun shall be turned into darkness and the moon into blood: before the great and dreadful day of the Lord doth come.

32 And it shall come to pass, [8] that every one that shall call upon the name of the Lord shall be saved: for in mount Sion, and in Jerusalem shall be salvation, as the Lord hath said, and in the residue whom the Lord shall call.

CHAPTER 3

The Lord shall judge all nations in the valley of Josaphat. The evils that shall fall upon the enemies of God's people. His blessing upon the church of the saints.

FOR behold in those days and in that time when I shall bring back the captivity of Juda and Jerusalem:

2 I will gather together all nations and will bring them down into the valley of Josaphat: and I will plead with them there for my people and for my inheritance Israel, whom they have scattered among the nations and have parted my land.

3 And they have cast lots upon my people: and the boy they have put in the stews, and the girl they have sold for wine, that they might drink.

4 But what have you to do with me,

O Tyre and Sidon and all the coast of the Philistines? Will you revenge yourselves on me, I will very soon return you a recompense upon your own head.

5 For you have taken away my silver and my gold: and my desirable and most beautiful things you have carried into your temples.

6 And the children of Juda and the children of Jerusalem you have sold to the children of the Greeks, that you might remove them far off from their own country.

7 Behold, I will raise them up out of the place wherein you have sold them: and I will return your recompense upon your own heads.

8 And I will sell your sons and your daughters by the hands of the children of Juda: and they shall sell them to the Sabeans, a nation far off, for the Lord hath spoken it.

9 Proclaim ye this among the nations: prepare war, rouse up the strong: let them come, let all the men of war come up.

10 Cut your ploughshares into swords and your spades into spears. Let the weak say: I am strong.

11 Break forth and come, all ye nations, from round about, and gather yourselves together: there will the Lord cause all thy strong ones to fall down.

12 Let them arise and let the nations come up into the valley of Josaphat: for there I will sit to judge all nations round about.

13 [1] Put ye in the sickles, for the harvest is ripe: come and go down, for the press is full, the vats run over: for their wickedness is multiplied.

14 Nations, nations in the valley of destruction: for the day of the Lord is near in the valley of destruction.

15 [2] The sun and the moon are darkened: and the stars have withdrawn their shining.

16 [3] And the Lord shall roar out of Sion and utter his voice from Jerusalem: and the heavens and the earth shall be moved: and the Lord shall be the hope of his people and the strength of the children of Israel.

17 And you shall know that I am the Lord your God, dwelling in Sion my holy mountain: and Jerusalem shall be holy and strangers shall pass through it no more.

18 And it shall come to pass in that day, that the mountains shall drop down sweetness and the hills shall flow with milk: and waters shall flow through all the rivers of Juda: and a fountain shall come forth of the house of the Lord, and shall water the torrent of thorns.

---

[6] Isai. 44, 3; Acts, 2, 17. [7] Joel, 2, 10; Matt. 24, 29; Luke, 21, 25; Acts, 2, 20. [8] Rom. 10, 13. CHAP. 3. [1] Apoc. 14, 15. [2] Joel, 2, 10, 31. [3] Jer. 25, 30; Amos 1, 2; Amos 9, 13.

CHAP. 3. Ver. 18. *A fountain shall come forth of the house of the Lord.* The fountain of grace in the church militant and of glory in the church triumphant: which shall water *the torrent* or valley *of thorns,* that is, the souls that before, like barren ground brought forth nothing but *thorns;* or that were afflicted with the *thorns* of crosses and tribulations.

19 Egypt shall be a desolation and Edom a wilderness destroyed: because they have done unjustly against the children of Juda and have shed innocent blood in their land.

20 And Judea shall be inhabited for ever, and Jerusalem to generation and generation

21 And I will cleanse their blood which I had not cleansed: and the Lord will dwell in Sion.

THE PROPHECY OF

AMOS

AMOS *prophesied in Israel about the same time as Osee, and was called from following the cattle to denounce God's judgments to the people of Israel and the neighbouring nations, for their repeated crimes in which they continued without repentance.*

CHAPTER 1

The prophet threatens Damascus, Gaza, Tyre, Edom and Ammon with the judgments of God, for their obstinacy in sin.

THE words of Amos, who was among the herdsmen of Thecua: which he saw concerning Israel in the days of Ozias king of Juda and in the days of Jeroboam the son of Joas king of Israel, [1] two years before the earthquake.

2 And he said: [2] The Lord will roar from Sion and utter his voice from Jerusalem: and the beautiful places of the shepherds have mourned, and the top of Carmel is withered.

3 Thus saith the Lord: For three crimes of Damascus, and for four, I will not convert it: because they have thrashed Galaad with iron wains.

4 And I will send a fire into the house of Azael: and it shall devour the houses of Benadad.

5 And I will break the bar of Damascus: and I will cut off the inhabitants from the plain of the idol, and him that holdeth the sceptre from the house of pleasure: and the people of Syria shall be carried away to Cyrene, saith the Lord.

6 Thus saith the Lord: For three crimes of Gaza, and for four, I will not convert it: because they have carried away a perfect captivity to shut them up in Edom.

7 And I will send a fire on the wall of Gaza: and it shall devour the houses thereof.

8 And I will cut off the inhabitant from Azotus and him that holdeth the sceptre from Ascalon, and I will turn my hand against Accaron, and the rest of the Philistines shall perish, saith the Lord God.

9 Thus saith the Lord: For three crimes of Tyre, and for four, I will not convert it: because they have shut up an entire captivity in Edom and have not remembered the covenant of brethren.

10 And I will send a fire upon the wall of Tyre: and it shall devour the houses thereof.

11 Thus saith the Lord: For three crimes of Edom, and for four, I will not convert it: because he hath pursued his brother with the sword and hath cast off all pity and hath carried on his fury and hath kept his wrath to the end.

12 I will send a fire into Theman: and it shall devour the houses of Bosra.

13 Thus saith the Lord: For three crimes of the children of Ammon, and for four, I will not convert him: because he hath ripped up the women with child of Galaad to enlarge his border.

14 And I will kindle a fire in the wall of Rabba: and it shall devour the houses thereof, with shouting in the day of battle and with a whirlwind in the day of trouble.

15 And Melchom shall go into cap-

CHAP. 1. [1] Zach. 14, 5. [2] Jer. 25, 30; Joel, 3, 16.
Ver. 20. *Judea—and Jerusalem.* That is, the spiritual Jerusalem, the Church of Christ.
CHAP. 1. Ver. 1. *The earthquake.* Many understand this of a great *earthquake*, which they say was felt at the time that king Ozias attempted to offer incense in the temple. But the best chronologists prove that the earthquake here spoken of must have been before that time: because Jeroboam the second, under whom Amos prophesied, was dead long before that attempt of Ozias.
Ver. 3. *For three crimes—and for four.* That is, for their many unrepented of crimes. *I will not convert it.* That is, I will not spare them, nor turn away the punishments I design to inflict upon them.
Ver. 15. *Melchom.* The god or idol of the Ammonites, otherwise called Moloch and Melech: which in Hebrew signifies a *king,* and Melchom *their king.*

tivity, both he and his princes together, saith the Lord.

CHAPTER 2

The judgments with which God threatens Moab, Juda and Israel for their sins and their ingratitude.

THUS saith the Lord. For three crimes of Moab, and for four, I will not convert him: because he hath burnt the bones of the king of Edom even to ashes.

2 And I will send a fire into Moab: and it shall devour the houses of Carioth. And Moab shall die with a noise, with the sound of the trumpet.

3 And I will cut off the judge from the midst thereof and will slay all his princes with him, saith the Lord.

4 Thus saith the Lord: For three crimes of Juda, and for four, I will not convert him: because he hath cast away the law of the Lord and hath not kept his commandments: for their idols have caused them to err, after which their fathers have walked.

5 And I will send a fire into Juda: and it shall devour the houses of Jerusalem.

6 Thus saith the Lord: For three crimes of Israel, and for four, I will not convert him: because he hath sold the just man for silver and the poor man for a pair of shoes.

7 They bruise the heads of the poor upon the dust of the earth and turn aside the way of the humble: and the son and his father have gone to the *same* young woman, to profane my holy name.

8 And they sat down upon garments laid to pledge by every altar and drank the wine of the condemned in the house of their God.

9 [1] Yet I cast out the Amorrhite before their face: whose height was like the height of cedars and who was strong as an oak: and I destroyed his fruit from above and his roots beneath.

10 [2] It is I that brought you up out of the land of Egypt, and that led you forty years through the wilderness, that you might possess the land of the Amorrhite.

11 And I raised up of your sons for prophets and of your young men for

CHAP. 2. [1] Num. 21, 24; Deut. 2, 24. [2] Exod. 14, 22; Deut. 8, 14.

CHAP. 2. Ver. 13. *I will screak.* Unable to bear any longer the enormous load of your sins. The Spirit of God, as St. Jerome takes notice, accommodates himself to the education of the prophet and inspires him with comparisons taken from country affairs.

CHAP. 3. Ver. 2. *Visit upon.* That is, punish.

Ver. 6. *Evil in a city.* He speaks of the *evil* of punishments of war, famine, pestilence, desolation, and so forth, but not of the *evil* of sin, of which God is not the author.

Nazarites. Is it not so, O ye children of Israel, saith the Lord?

12 And you will present wine to the Nazarites: and command the prophets, saying: Prophesy not.

13 Behold, I will screak under you as a wain screaketh that is laden with hay.

14 And flight shall perish from the swift and the valiant shall not possess his strength: neither shall the strong save his life.

15 And he that holdeth the bows shall not stand and the swift of foot shall not escape: neither shall the rider of the horse save his life.

16 And the stout of heart among the valiant shall flee away naked in that day, saith the Lord.

CHAPTER 3

The evils that shall fall upon Israel for their sins.

HEAR the word that the Lord hath spoken concerning you, O ye children of Israel: concerning the whole family that I brought up out of the land of Egypt, saying:

2 You only have I known of all the families of the earth: therefore will I visit upon you all your iniquities.

3 Shall two walk together except they be agreed?

4 Will a lion roar in the forest, if he have no prey? Will the lion's whelp cry out of his den, if he have taken nothing?

5 Will the bird fall into the snare upon the earth, if there be no fowler? Shall the snare be taken up from the earth, before it hath taken somewhat?

6 Shall the trumpet sound in a city and the people not be afraid? Shall there be evil in a city, which the Lord hath not done?

7 For the Lord God doth nothing without revealing his secret to his servants the prophets.

8 The lion shall roar: Who will not fear? The Lord God hath spoken: Who shall not prophesy?

9 Publish it in the houses of Azotus and in the houses of the land of Egypt, and say: Assemble yourselves upon the mountains of Samaria, and behold the many follies in the midst thereof, and them that suffer oppression in the inner rooms thereof.

10 And they have not known to do the right thing, saith the Lord, storing up iniquity and robberies in their houses.

11 Therefore thus saith the Lord God: The land shall be in tribulation and shall be compassed about: and thy

strength shall be taken away from thee, and thy houses shall be spoiled.

12 Thus saith the Lord: As if a shepherd should get out of the lion's mouth two legs or the tip of the ear: so shall the children of Israel be taken out that dwell in Samaria, in a piece of a bed and in the couch of Damascus.

13 Hear ye and testify in the house of Jacob, saith the Lord the God of hosts:

14 That in the day when I shall begin to visit the transgressions of Israel, I will visit upon him and upon the altars of Bethel: and the horns of the altars shall be cut off and shall fall to the ground.

15 And I will strike the winter house with the summer house: and the houses of ivory shall perish, and many houses shall be destroyed, saith the Lord.

CHAPTER 4

The Israelites are reproved for their oppressing the poor, for their idolatry and their incorrigibleness.

HEAR this word, ye fat kine that are in the mountains of Samaria, you that oppress the needy and crush the poor, that say to your masters: Bring, and we will drink.

2 The Lord God hath sworn by his holiness that lo the days shall come upon you, when they shall lift you up on pikes and what shall remain of you in boiling pots.

3 And you shall go out at the breaches one over against the other: and you shall be cast forth into Armon, saith the Lord.

4 Come ye to Bethel and do wickedly, to Galgal and multiply transgressions: and bring in the morning your victims, your tithes in three days.

5 And offer a sacrifice of praise with leaven: and call free offerings, and proclaim it: for so you would do, O children of Israel, saith the Lord God.

6 Whereupon I also have given you dulness of teeth in all your cities and want of bread in all your places: yet you have not returned to me, saith the Lord.

7 I also have withholden the rain from you, when there were yet three months to the harvest: and I caused it to rain upon one city and caused it not to rain upon another city. One piece was rained upon: and the piece whereupon I rained not withered.

8 And two and three cities went to one city to drink water and were not filled: yet you returned not to me, saith the Lord.

9 ¹ I struck you with a burning wind and with mildew: the palmerworm

hath eaten up your many gardens and your vineyards, your olive groves and fig groves: yet you returned not to me, saith the Lord.

10 I sent death upon you in the way of Egypt: I slew your young men with the sword, even to the captivity of your horses: and I made the stench of your camp to come up into your nostrils: yet you returned not to me, saith the Lord.

11 I destroyed *some* of you, ² as God destroyed Sodom and Gomorrha, and you were as a firebrand plucked out of the burning: yet you returned not to me, saith the Lord.

12 Therefore I will do these things to thee, O Israel: and after I shall have done these things to thee, be prepared to meet thy God, O Israel.

13 For behold he that formeth the mountains and createth the wind and declareth his word to man, he that maketh the morning mist and walketh upon the high places of the earth: the Lord, the God of hosts, is his name.

CHAPTER 5

A lamentation for Israel. An exhortation to return to God.

HEAR ye this word which I take up concerning you for a lamentation. The house of Israel is fallen: and it shall rise no more.

2 The virgin of Israel is cast down upon her land: there is none to raise her up.

3 For thus saith the Lord God: The city out of which came forth a thousand, there shall be left in it a hundred: and out of which there came a hundred, there shall be left in it ten, in the house of Israel.

4 For thus saith the Lord to the house of Israel: Seek ye me, and you shall live.

5 But seek not Bethel and go not into Galgal, neither shall you pass over to Bersabee: for Galgal shall go into captivity and Bethel shall be unprofitable.

6 Seek ye the Lord and live, lest the house of Joseph be burnt with fire: and it shall devour, and there shall be none to quench Bethel.

7 You that turn judgment into wormwood and forsake justice in the land.

8 *Seek* him that maketh **Arcturus**

CHAP. 4. ¹ Agg. 2, 18. ² Gen. 19, 24.
CHAP. 4. Ver. 1. *Fat kine.* He means the great ones that lived in plenty and wealth.
Ver. 3. *Armon.* A foreign country: some understand it of Armenia.
CHAP. 5. Ver. 5. *Bethel—Galgal—Bersabee.* The places where they worshipped their idols.
Ver. 8. *Arcturus and Orion.* Arcturus is a bright star in the north: Orion a beautiful constellation in the south.

and Orion, and that turneth darkness into morning, and that changeth day into night: [1] that calleth the waters of the sea and poureth them out upon the face of the earth: The Lord is his name.

9 He that with a smile bringeth destruction upon the strong and waste upon the mighty.

10 They have hated him that rebuketh in the gate: and have abhorred him that speaketh perfectly.

11 Therefore because you robbed the poor and took the choice prey from him: [2] you shall build houses with square stone and shall not dwell in them: you shall plant most delightful vineyards and shall not drink the wine of them.

12 Because I know your manifold crimes and your grievous sins: enemies of the just, taking bribes, and oppressing the poor in the gate.

13 Therefore the prudent shall keep silence at that time: for it is an evil time.

14 Seek ye good and not evil, that you may live: and the Lord the God of hosts, will be with you, as you have said.

15 [3] Hate evil and love good and establish judgment in the gate: it may be the Lord, the God of hosts, may have mercy on the remnant of Joseph.

16 Therefore thus saith the Lord, the God of hosts, the sovereign Lord: In every street *there shall be* wailing. And in all places that are without they shall say: Alas, alas! And they shall call the husbandman to mourning and such as are skilful in lamentation to lament.

17 And in all vineyards there shall be wailing: because I will pass through in the midst of thee, saith the Lord.

18 [4] Woe to them that desire the day of the Lord! To what end is it for you? The day of the Lord *is* darkness and not light.

19 As if a man should flee from the face of a lion, and a bear should meet him: or enter into the house and lean with his hand upon the wall, and a serpent should bite him.

20 Shall not the day of the Lord be darkness and not light: and obscurity, and no brightness in it?

21 [5] I hate and have rejected your

CHAP. 5. [1] Amos, 9, 6. [2] Soph. 1, 13. [3] Ps. 96, 10; Rom. 12, 9. [4] Jer. 30, 7; Joel, 2, 11; Soph. 1, 15. [5] Isai. 1, 11; Jer. 6, 20; Mal. 1, 12. [6] Acts, 7, 42. CHAP. 6. [1] Luke, 6, 24. [2] Jer. 51, 14.

Ver. 9. *With a smile.* That is, with all ease, and without making any effort.
Ver. 25. *Did you offer.* Except the sacrifices that were offered at the first, in the dedication of the tabernacle, the Israelites offered no sacrifices in the desert.
Ver. 26. *A tabernacle.* All this alludes to the idolatry which they committed when they were drawn away by the daughters of Moab to the worship of their gods (Num. 25).

festivities: and I will not receive the odour of your assemblies.

22 And if you offer me holocausts and your gifts, I will not receive them: neither will I regard the vows of your fat beasts.

23 Take away from me the tumult of thy songs: and I will not hear the canticles of thy harp.

24 But judgment shall be revealed as water, and justice as a mighty torrent.

25 [6] Did you offer victims and sacrifices to me in the desert for forty years, O house of Israel?

26 But you carried a tabernacle for your Moloch, and the image of your idols, the star of your god, which you made to yourselves.

27 And I will cause you to go into captivity beyond Damascus, saith the Lord: the God of hosts is his name.

CHAPTER 6

The desolation of Israel for their pride and luxury.

WOE [1] to you that are wealthy in Sion, and to you that have confidence in the mountain of Samaria: ye great men, heads of the people, that go in with state into the house of Israel.

2 Pass ye over to Chalane and see, and go from thence into Emath the great: and go down into Geth of the Philistines and to all the best kingdoms of these: if their border be larger than your border.

3 You that are separated unto the evil day and that approach to the throne of iniquity;

4 You that sleep upon beds of ivory and are wanton on your couches: that eat the lambs out of the flock and the calves out of the midst of the herd;

5 You that sing to the sound of the psaltery: they have thought themselves to have instruments of music like David;

6 That drink wine in bowls and anoint themselves with the best ointments: and they are not concerned for the affliction of Joseph.

7 Wherefore now they shall go captive at the head of them that go into captivity: and the faction of the luxurious ones shall be taken away.

8 [2] The Lord God hath sworn by his own soul, saith the Lord, the God of hosts: I detest the pride of Jacob and I hate his houses and I will deliver up the city with the inhabitants thereof.

9 And if there remain ten men in one house, they also shall die.

10 And a man's kinsman shall take him up and shall burn him, that he may carry the bones out of the house. And he shall say to him that is in the inner

rooms of the house: Is there yet any with thee?

11 And he shall answer: There is an end. And he shall say to him: Hold thy peace and mention not the name of the Lord.

12 For behold the Lord hath commanded: and he will strike the greater house with breaches and the lesser house with clefts.

13 Can horses run upon the rocks or can any one plough with buffles? for you have turned judgment into bitterness and the fruit of justice into wormwood.

14 You that rejoice in a thing of nought: you that say: Have we not taken unto us horns by our own strength?

15 But behold, I will raise up a nation against you, O house of Israel, saith the Lord, the God of hosts; and they shall destroy you from the entrance of Emath even to the torrent of the desert.

CHAPTER 7

The prophet sees, in three visions evils coming upon Israel. He is accused of treason by the false priest of Bethel.

THESE things the Lord God shewed to me: and behold the locust was formed in the beginning of the shooting up of the latter rain, and lo, *it was* the latter rain after the king's mowing.

2 And it came to pass that when they had made an end of eating the grass of the land, I said: O Lord God, be merciful, I beseech thee: Who shall raise up Jacob, for he is very little?

3 The Lord had pity upon this. It shall not be, said the Lord.

4 These things the Lord God shewed to me: and behold the Lord called for judgment unto fire, and it devoured the great deep and ate up a part at the same time.

5 And I said: O Lord God, cease, I beseech thee: Who shall raise up Jacob, for he is a little one?

6 The Lord had pity upon this. Yea this also shall not be, said the Lord God.

7 These things the Lord shewed to me: and behold the Lord *was* standing upon a plastered wall, and in his hand a mason's trowel.

8 And the Lord said to me: What seest thou, Amos? And I said: A mason's trowel. And the Lord said: Behold, I will lay down the trowel in the midst of my people Israel. I will plaster them over no more.

9 And the high places of the idol shall be thrown down, and the sanctuaries of Israel shall be laid waste: and I will rise up against the house of Jeroboam with the sword.

10 And Amasias, the priest of Bethel, sent to Jeroboam king of Israel, saying: Amos hath rebelled against thee in the midst of the house of Israel: the land is not able to bear all his words.

11 For thus saith Amos: Jeroboam shall die by the sword and Israel shall be carried away captive out of their own land.

12 And Amasias said to Amos: Thou seer, go, flee away into the land of Juda: and eat bread there and prophesy there.

13 But prophesy not again any more in Bethel: because it is the king's sanctuary and it is the house of the kingdom.

14 And Amos answered and said to Amasias. I am not a prophet, nor am I the son of a prophet: but I am a herdsman plucking wild figs.

15 And the Lord took me when I followed the flock, and the Lord said to me: Go, prophesy to my people Israel.

16 And now hear thou the word of the Lord. Thou sayest: Thou shalt not prophesy against Israel, and thou shalt not drop *thy word* upon the house of the idol.

17 Therefore thus saith the Lord: Thy wife shall play the harlot in the city, and thy sons and thy daughters shall fall by the sword, and thy land shall be measured by a line: and thou shalt die in a polluted land, and Israel shall go into captivity out of their land.

CHAPTER 8

Under the figure of a hook, which bringeth down the fruit, the approaching desolation of Israel is foreshadowed for their avarice and injustices.

THESE things the Lord shewed to me: and behold a hook to draw down the fruit.

2 And he said: What seest thou, Amos? And I said: A hook to draw down fruit. And the Lord said to me: The end is come upon my people Israel: I will not again pass them any more.

3 And the hinges of the temple shall

CHAP. 7. Ver. 1. *The locust.* These judgments by locusts and fire, which, by the prophet's intercession, were moderated, signify the former invasions of the Assyrians under Phul and Theglathphalasar, before the utter desolation of Israel by Salmanasar.
Ver. 11. *Jeroboam shall die by the sword.* The prophet did not say this; but that the Lord would *rise up against the house of Jeroboam with the sword:* which was verified, when Zacharias, the son and successor of Jeroboam, was slain by the sword (4 Kings, 15, 10).
Ver. 14. *I am not a prophet.* That is, I am not a prophet by education: nor is prophesying my calling or profession: but I am a herdsman, whom God was pleased to send hither to prophesy to Israel.
Ver. 16. *The house of the idol.* That is, of the calf worshipped in Bethel.

screak in that day, saith the Lord God.
Many shall die: silence shall be cast in
every place.

4 Hear this, you that crush the poor
and make the needy of the land to fail,

5 Saying: When will the month be
over, and we shall sell our wares: and
the sabbath, and we shall open the
corn: that we may lessen the measure
and increase the sicle and may convey
in deceitful balances,

6 That we may possess the needy for
money and the poor for a pair of shoes
and may sell the refuse of the corn?

7 The Lord hath sworn against the
pride of Jacob: Surely I will never
forget all their works.

8 Shall not the land tremble for this
and every one mourn that dwelleth
therein, and rise up altogether as a
river, and be cast out, and run down
as the river of Egypt?

9 And it shall come to pass in that
day, saith the Lord God, that the sun
shall go down at midday, and I will
make the earth dark in the day of light.

10 ¹And I will turn your feasts into
mourning and all your songs into lamentation: and I will bring up sackcloth upon every back of yours and baldness upon every head: and I will make
it as the mourning of an only son, and
the latter end thereof as a bitter day.

11 Behold the days come, saith the
Lord, and I will send forth a famine
into the land: not a famine of bread,
nor a thirst of water, but of hearing the
word of the Lord.

12 And they shall move from sea to
sea and from the north to the east:
they shall go about seeking the word
of the Lord and shall not find it.

13 In that day the fair virgins and
the young men shall faint for thirst.

14 They that swear by the sin of
Samaria, and say: Thy God, O Dan,
liveth, and the way of Bersabee liveth.
And they shall fall and shall rise no
more.

CHAPTER 9

The certainty of the desolation of Israel.
The restoring of the tabernacle of David
and the conversion of the Gentiles to the
church, which shall flourish for ever.

I SAW the Lord standing upon the
altar, and he said: Strike the hinges

CHAP. 8. ¹ Tob. 2, 6; 1 Mach. 1, 41. CHAP. 9.
¹ Ps. 138, 8. ² Jer. 44, 11. ³ Amos, 5, 8. ⁴ Deut.
2, 23; Jer. 47, 4. ⁵ Acts, 15, 16. ⁶ Joel, 3, 18.

CHAP. 9. Ver. 6. *His ascension.* That is, his
throne.—*His bundle.* That is, his church bound
up together by the bands of one faith and communion.
Ver. 7. *As the children of the Ethiopians.* That
is, as black as they, by your iniquities.
Ver. 13. *Shall overtake.* By this is meant the
great abundance of spiritual blessings, which, as
it were, by a constant succession, shall enrich the
Church of Christ.

and let the lintels be shook: for there
is covetousness in the head of them all,
and I will slay the last of them with the
sword. There shall be no flight for
them: they shall flee, and he that shall
flee of them shall not be delivered.

2 ¹Though they go down even to hell,
thence shall my hand bring them out:
and though they climb up to heaven,
thence will I bring them down.

3 And though they be hid in the top
of Carmel, I will search and take them
away from thence: and though they
hide themselves from my eyes in the
depth of the sea, there will I command
the serpent: and he shall bite them.

4 And if they go into captivity before
their enemies, there will I command the
sword, and it shall kill them.² And I
will set my eyes upon them for evil
and not for good.

5 And the Lord, the God of hosts,
is he who toucheth the earth, and it
shall melt and all that dwell therein
shall mourn: and it shall rise up as
a river and shall run down as the river
of Egypt.

6 He that buildeth his ascension in
heaven and hath founded his bundle
upon the earth, ³who calleth the waters
of the sea and poureth them out upon
the face of the earth: the Lord is his
name.

7 Are not you as the children of
the Ethiopians unto me, O children
of Israel, saith the Lord? Did not I
bring up Israel, out of the land of
Egypt, ⁴and the Philistines out of Cappadocia, and the Syrians out of Cyrene?

8 Behold the eyes of the Lord God
are upon the sinful kingdom, and I will
destroy it from the face of the earth:
but yet I will not utterly destroy the
house of Jacob, saith the Lord.

9 For behold I will command and I
will sift the house of Israel among all
nations, as corn is sifted in a sieve: and
there shall not a little stone fall to the
ground.

10 All the sinners of my people shall
fall by the sword: they who say: The
evils shall not approach and shall not
come upon us.

11 In that day ⁵I will raise up the
tabernacle of David, that is fallen: and
I will close up the breaches of the walls
thereof and repair what was fallen: and
I will rebuild it as in the days of old.

12 That they may possess the remnant of Edom and all nations, because
my name is invoked upon them: saith
the Lord that doth these things.

13 Behold the days come, saith the
Lord, when the ploughman shall overtake the reaper and the treader of
grapes him that soweth seed: and ⁶the

mountains shall drop sweetness, and every hill shall be tilled.

14 And I will bring back the captivity of my people Israel: and they shall build the abandoned cities and inhabit *them:* and they shall plant vineyards and drink the wine of them: and shall make gardens and eat the fruits of them. And I will plant them upon their own land: and I will no more pluck them out of their land which I have given them, saith the Lord thy God.

THE PROPHECY OF
ABDIAS

ABDIAS, *whose name is interpreted* THE SERVANT OF THE LORD, *is believed to have prophesied about the same time as Osee, Joel, and Amos: though some of the Hebrews, who believe him to be the same with Achab's steward, make him much more ancient. His prophecy is the shortest of any in number of words, but yields to none, says St. Jerome, in the sublimity of mysteries. It contains but one chapter.*

CHAPTER 1

The destruction of Edom for their pride and the wrongs they did to Jacob. The salvation and victory of Israel.

THE vision of Abdias. Thus saith the Lord God of Edom: [1] We have heard a rumour from the Lord, and he hath sent an ambassador to the nations: Arise, and let us rise up to battle against him.

2 Behold I have made thee small among the nations: thou art exceeding contemptible.

3 The pride of thy heart hath lifted thee up, who dwellest in the clefts of the rocks and settest up thy throne on high: who sayest in thy heart: Who shall bring me down to the ground?

4 Though thou be exalted as an eagle and though thou set thy nest among the stars: thence will I bring thee down, saith the Lord.

5 If thieves had gone in to thee, if robbers by night, how wouldst thou have have held thy peace? Would they not have stolen till they had enough? If the grape-gatherers had come in to thee, would they not have left thee at least a cluster?

6 How have they searched Esau! How have they sought out his hidden things!

7 They have sent thee out even to the border: all the men of thy confederacy have deceived thee: the men of thy peace have prevailed against thee: they that eat with thee shall lay snares under thee: there is no wisdom in him.

8 [2] Shall not I in that day, saith the Lord, destroy the wise out of Edom and understanding out of the mount of Esau?

9 And thy valiant men of the south shall be afraid that man may be cut off from the mount of Esau.

10 [3] For the slaughter and for the iniquity against thy brother Jacob, confusion shall cover thee and thou shalt perish for ever.

11 In the day when thou stoodest against him, when strangers carried away his army captive and foreigners entered into his gates and cast lots upon Jerusalem: thou also wast as one of them.

12 But thou shalt not look on in the day of thy brother, in the day of his leaving his country: and thou shalt not rejoice over the children of Juda in the day of their destruction: and thou shalt not magnify thy mouth in the day of distress.

13 Neither shalt thou enter into the gate of my people in the day of their ruin: neither shalt thou also look on in his evils in the day of his calamity: and thou shalt not be sent out against his army in the day of his desolation.

14 Neither shalt thou stand in the crossways to kill them that flee: and thou shalt not shut up them that remain of him in the day of tribulation.

15 For the day of the Lord is at hand upon all nations: as thou hast done, so shall it be done to thee: he will turn thy reward upon thy own head.

16 For as you have drunk upon my

CHAP. 1. [1] Jer. 49, 14. [2] Isai. 29, 14; 1 Cor. 1, 19. [3] Gen. 27, 42.

CHAP. 1. Ver. 12. *Thou shalt not look, or, thou shouldst not.* It is a reprehension for what they had done, and at the same time a declaration that these things should not pass unpunished.— *Thou shalt not magnify thy mouth.* That is, thou shalt not speak arrogantly against the children of Juda as insulting them in their distress.

holy mountain, so all nations shall drink continually: and they shall drink and sup up, and they shall be as though they were not.

17 And in mount Sion shall be salvation, and it shall be holy: and the house of Jacob shall possess those that possessed them.

18 And the house of Jacob shall be a fire and the house of Joseph a flame and the house of Esau stubble: and they shall be kindled in them and shall devour them: and there shall be no remains of the house of Esau, for the Lord hath spoken it.

19 And they that are toward the south shall inherit the mount of Esau, and they that are in the plains, the Philistines: and they shall possess the country of Ephraim and the country of Samaria: and Benjamin shall possess Galaad.

20 And the captivity of this host of the children of Israel, all the places of the Chanaanites even to Sarepta: and the captivity of Jerusalem that is in Bosphorus shall possess the cities of the south.

21 And saviours shall come up into mount Sion to judge the mount of Esau: and the kingdom shall be for the Lord.

THE PROPHECY OF
JONAS

JONAS *prophesied in the reign of Jeroboam the second: as we learn from* 4 *Kings,* 14, 25. *To whom also he foretold his success in restoring all the borders of Israel. He was of Geth Opher in the tribe of Zabulon, and consequently of Galilee: which confutes that assertion of the Pharisees,* (John 7, 52), *that no prophet ever rose out of Galilee. He prophesied and prefigured in his own person the death and resurrection of* CHRIST: *and was the only one among the prophets that was sent to preach to the Gentiles.*

CHAPTER 1

Jonas, being sent to preach in Ninive, fleeth away by sea. A tempest riseth, of which he being found, by lot, to be the cause, is cast into the sea which thereupon is calmed.

NOW the word of the Lord came to Jonas the son of Amathi, saying:

2 Arise, and go to Ninive the great city and preach in it: for the wickedness thereof is come up before me.

3 And Jonas rose up to flee into Tharsis from the face of the Lord: and he went down to Joppe and found a ship going to Tharsis. And he paid the fare thereof and went down into it, to go with them to Tharsis from the face of the Lord.

4 But the Lord sent a great wind into the sea: and a great tempest was raised in the sea, and the ship was in danger to be broken.

5 And the mariners were afraid and the men cried to their god: and they cast forth the wares that were in the ship into the sea, to lighten it of them: and Jonas went down into the inner part of the ship and fell into a deep sleep.

6 And the shipmaster came to him and said to him: Why art thou fast asleep? Rise up, call upon thy God, if so be that God will think of us, that we may not perish.

7 And they said every one to his fellow: Come, and let us cast lots, that we may know why this evil is upon us. And they cast lots: and the lot fell upon Jonas.

8 And they said to him: Tell us for what cause this evil is upon us. What is thy business? Of what country art thou and whither goest thou? Or of what people art thou?

9 And he said to them: I am a Hebrew, and I fear the Lord the God of heaven, who made both the sea and the dry land.

10 And the men were greatly afraid, and they said to him: Why hast thou done this? (For the men knew that he fled from the face of the Lord: because he had told them.)

11 And they said to him: What shall we do to thee, that the sea may be

CHAP. 1. Ver. 2. *Ninive.* The capital city of the Assyrian empire.

Ver. 3. *Tharsis.* Which some take to be Tharsus of Cilicia, others to be Tartessus of Spain, others to be Carthage.

Ver. 5. *A deep sleep.* This is a lively image of the insensibility of sinners, fleeing from God and threatened on every side with his judgments, and yet sleeping as if they were secure.

calm to us? For the sea flowed and swelled.

12 And he said to them: Take me up and cast me into the sea, and the sea shall be calm to you: for I know that for my sake this great tempest is upon you.

13 And the men rowed hard to return to land: but they were not able, because the sea tossed and swelled upon them.

14 And they cried to the Lord and said: We beseech thee, O Lord, let us not perish for this man's life, and lay not upon us innocent blood: for thou, O Lord, hast done as it pleased thee.

15 And they took Jonas and cast him into the sea: and the sea ceased from raging.

16 And the men feared the Lord exceedingly and sacrificed victims to the Lord and made vows.

CHAPTER 2

Jonas is swallowed up by a great fish. He prayeth with confidence in God, and the fish casteth him out on the dry land.

NOW the Lord prepared a great fish to swallow up Jonas: [1] and Jonas was in the belly of the fish three days and three nights.

2 And Jonas prayed to the Lord his God out of the belly of the fish.

3 And he said: [2] I cried out of my affliction to the Lord: and he heard me. I cried out of the belly of hell: and thou hast heard my voice.

4 And thou hast cast me forth into the deep in the heart of the sea, and a flood hath compassed me: all thy billows and thy waves have passed over me.

5 And I said: I am cast away out of the sight of thy eyes: but yet I shall see thy holy temple again.

6 [3] The waters compassed me about even to the soul: the deep hath closed me round about: the sea hath covered my head.

7 I went down to the lowest parts of the mountains: the bars of the earth have shut me up for ever: and thou wilt bring up my life from corruption, O Lord my God.

8 When my soul was in distress within me, I remembered the Lord: that my prayer may come to thee, unto thy holy temple.

9 They that are vain and observe vanities forsake their own mercy.

10 But I with the voice of praise will sacrifice to thee: I will pay whatsoever I have vowed for *my* salvation to the Lord.

11 And the Lord spoke to the fish: and it vomited out Jonas upon the dry land.

CHAPTER 3

Jonas is sent again to preach in Ninive. Upon their fasting and repentance, God recalleth the sentence by which they were to be destroyed.

AND the word of the Lord came to Jonas the second time, saying:

2 Arise, and go to Ninive the great city: and preach in it the preaching that I bid thee.

3 And Jonas arose and went to Ninive, according to the word of the Lord: now Ninive was a great city of three days' journey.

4 And Jonas began to enter into the city one day's journey: and he cried, and said: Yet forty days, and Ninive shall be destroyed.

5 [1] And the men of Ninive believed in God: and they proclaimed a fast and put on sackcloth from the greatest to the least.

6 And the word came to the king of Ninive: and he rose up out of his throne and cast away his robe from him and was clothed with sackcloth and sat in ashes.

7 And he caused it to be proclaimed and published in Ninive from the mouth of the king and of his princes, saying: Let neither men nor beasts, oxen nor sheep, taste any thing: let them not feed nor drink water.

8 And let men and beasts be covered with sackcloth and cry to the Lord with all their strength: and let them turn every one from his evil way and from the iniquity that is in their hands.

9 [2] Who can tell if God will turn and forgive and will turn away from his fierce anger: and we shall not perish?

10 And God saw their works, that they were turned from their evil way: and God had mercy with regard to the evil which he had said that he would do to them, and he did it not.

CHAPTER 4

Jonas, repining to see that his prophecy is not fulfilled, is reproved by the type of the ivy.

AND Jonas was exceedingly troubled, and was angry.

CHAP. 2. [1] Matt. 12, 40; 16, 4; Luke, 11, 30; 1 Cor. 15, 4. [2] Ps. 119, 1. [3] Ps. 68, 1. CHAP. 3. [1] Matt. 12, 41; Luke, 11, 32. [2] Jer. 11, 8; Joel, 2, 14.

CHAP. 2. Ver. 11. *Spoke to the fish.* God's speaking to the fish was nothing else but his will, which all things obey.

CHAP. 3. Ver. 3. *Of three days' journey.* By the computation of some ancient historians, Ninive was about fifty miles round: so that to go through all the chief streets and public places was three days' journey.

CHAP. 4. Ver. 1. *Was exceedingly troubled.* His concern was lest he should pass for a false prophet; or rather, lest God's word, by this occasion, might come to be slighted and disbelieved.

2 And he prayed to the Lord and said: I beseech thee, O Lord, is not this what I said, when I was yet in my own country? Therefore I went before to flee into Tharsis: ¹ for I know that thou art a gracious and merciful God, patient and of much compassion and easy to forgive evil.

3 And now, O Lord, I beseech thee take my life from me: for it is better for me to die than to live.

4 And the Lord said: Dost thou think thou hast reason to be angry?

5 Then Jonas went out of the city and sat toward the east side of the city. And he made himself a booth there: and he sat under it in the shadow, till he might see what would befall the city.

6 And the Lord God prepared an ivy, and it came up over the head of Jonas, to be a shadow over his head and to cover him (for he was fatigued): and Jonas was exceeding glad of the ivy.

7 But God prepared a worm, when the morning arose on the following day: and it struck the ivy and it withered.

8 And when the sun was risen, the Lord commanded a hot and burning wind. And the sun beat upon the head of Jonas, and he broiled with the heat: and he desired for his soul that he might die and said: It is better for me to die than to live.

9 And the Lord said to Jonas: Dost thou think thou hast reason to be angry, for the ivy? And he said: I am angry with reason even unto death.

10 And the Lord said: Thou art grieved for the ivy, for which thou hast not laboured nor made it to grow, which in one night came up and in one night perished.

11 And shall not I spare Ninive, that great city, in which there are more than a hundred and twenty thousand persons that know not how to distinguish between their right hand and their left, and many beasts?

THE PROPHECY OF
MICHEAS

MICHEAS, of Morasti, a little town in the tribe of Juda, was contemporary with the prophet Isaias, whom he resembles both in his spirit and his style. He is different from the prophet Micheas mentioned in the third book of Kings, chap. 22. For that Micheas lived in the days of king Achab, one hundred and fifty years before the time of Ezechias, under whom this Micheas prophesied.

CHAPTER 1

Samaria for her sins shall be destroyed by the Assyrians. They shall also invade Juda and Jerusalem.

THE word of the Lord that came to Micheas the Morasthite, in the days of Joathan, Achaz and Ezechias, kings of Juda: which he saw concerning Samaria and Jerusalem.

2 ¹ Hear, all ye people: and let the earth give ear, and all that is therein. And let the Lord God be a witness to you, the Lord from his holy temple.

3 ² For behold the Lord will come forth out of his place: and he will come down and will tread upon the high places of the earth.

4 And the mountains shall be melted under him: and the valleys shall be cleft, as wax before the fire and as waters that run down a steep place.

5 For the wickedness of Jacob is all this, and for the sins of the house of Israel. What is the wickedness of Jacob? Is it not Samaria? And what are the high places of Juda? Are they not Jerusalem?

6 And I will make Samaria as a heap of stones in the field when a vineyard is planted: and I will bring down the stones thereof into the valley and will lay her foundations bare.

7 And all her graven things shall be cut in pieces and all her wages shall be burnt with fire and I will bring to destruction all her idols. For they were gathered together of the hire of a harlot, and unto the hire of a harlot they shall return.

Chap. 4. ¹ Ps. 85, 5; Joel, 2, 13. Chap. 1. ¹ Deut. 32, 1; Isai. 1, 2. ² Isai. 26, 21.

Ver. 6. *The Lord God prepared an ivy.* Hederam. In the Hebrew it is Kikajon, which some render a *gourd*: others a *palmerist* or *palma Christi.*

Chap. 1. Ver. 7. *Her wages.* That is, her donaries or presents offered to her idols: or the hire of all her traffic and labour.—*Of the hire of a harlot.* They were gathered together by one idolatrous city, Samaria; and they shall be carried away to another idolatrous city, Ninive.

8 Therefore will I lament and howl: I will go stripped and naked: I will make a wailing like the dragons and a mourning like the ostriches.

9 Because her wound is desperate, because it is come even to Juda: it hath touched the gate of my people even to Jerusalem.

10 Declare ye it not in Geth, weep ye not with tears: in the house of dust sprinkle yourselves with dust.

11 And pass away, O thou that dwellest in the beautiful place, covered with thy shame: she went not forth that dwelleth in the confines: the house adjoining shall receive mourning from you, which stood by herself.

12 For she is become weak unto good that dwelleth in bitterness: for evil is come down from the Lord into the gate of Jerusalem.

13 A tumult of chariots hath astonished the inhabitants of Lachis: it is the beginning of sin to the daughter of Sion, for in thee were found the crimes of Israel.

14 Therefore shall she send messengers to the inheritance of Geth: the houses of lying to deceive the kings of Israel.

15 Yet will I bring an heir to thee that dwellest in Maresa: even to Odollam shall the glory of Israel come.

16 Make thee bald and be polled for thy delicate children: enlarge thy baldness as the eagle: for they are carried into captivity from thee.

CHAPTER 2

The Israelites by their crying injustices provoke God to punish them. He shall at last restore Jacob.

WOE to you that devise that which is unprofitable and work evil in your beds: in the morning light they execute it, because their hand is against God.

2 And they have coveted fields and taken them by violence, and houses they have forcibly taken away: and oppressed a man and his house, a man and his inheritance.

3 Therefore thus saith the Lord: Behold, I devise an evil against this family, from which you shall not withdraw your necks: and you shall not walk haughtily, for this is a very evil time.

4 In that day a parable shall be taken up upon you, and a song shall be sung with melody by them that say: We are laid waste and spoiled: the portion of my people is changed. How shall he depart from me, whereas he is returning that will divide our land?

5 Therefore thou shalt have none that shall cast the cord of a lot in the assembly of the Lord.

6 Speak ye not, saying: It shall not drop upon these; confusion shall not take them.

7 The house of Jacob saith: Is the spirit of the Lord straitened, or are these his thoughts? Are not my words good to him that walketh uprightly?

8 But my people, on the contrary, are risen up as an enemy: you have taken away the cloak off from the coat, and them that passed harmless you have turned to war.

9 You have cast out the women of my people from their houses in which they took delight: you have taken my praise for ever from their children.

Ver. 9. *It that touched the gate.* That is, the destruction of Samaria shall be followed by the invasion of my people of Juda, and the Assyrians shall come and lay all waste even to the confines of Jerusalem.

Ver. 10. *Declare ye it not in Geth.* That is, amongst the Philistines, lest they rejoice at your calamity.—*Weep ye not.* Keep in your tears, that you may not give your enemies an occasion of insulting over you; but in your own houses, or in your *house of dust,* your *earthly habitation, sprinkle yourselves with dust* and put on the habit of penitents. Some take the house of *dust* (in Hebrew, *Aphrah*) to be the proper name of a city.

Ver. 11. *Thou that dwellest in the beautiful place,* that is, in *Samaria.* In the Hebrew the *beautiful place* is expressed by the word *Sapir,* which some take for the proper name of a city.—*She went not forth,* that is, they that dwelt in the confines came not forth, but kept themselves within, for fear.—*The house adjoining.* Namely, Judea, and Jerusalem, neighbours to Samaria and partners in her sins, shall share also in her *mourning* and calamity; though they have pretended to *stand by themselves,* trusting in their strength.

Ver. 12. *She is become weak.* Jerusalem is become weak unto any good; because she dwells in the bitterness of sin.

Ver. 13. *It is the beginning.* That is, Lachis was the first city of Juda that learned from Samaria the worship of idols and communicated it to Jerusalem.

Ver. 14. *Therefore shall she send.* Lachis shall send to Geth for help: but in vain: for Geth, instead of helping, shall be found to be a *house of lying* and *deceit* to Israel.

Ver. 15. *An heir. Maresa* (which was the name of a city of Juda) signifies *inheritance:* but here God by his prophet tells the Jews that he will bring them *an heir* to take possession of their *inheritance* and that the *glory of Israel* shall be obliged to give place and to retire even to *Odollam,* a city in the extremity of their dominions. And therefore he exhorts them to penance in the following verse.

CHAP. 2. Ver. 4. *How shall he depart.* How do you pretend to say that the Assyrian is departing, when indeed he is coming to divide our lands amongst his subjects?

Ver. 5. *Thou shalt have none.* Thou shalt have no longer any lot or inheritance in the land of the people of the Lord.

Ver. 6. *It shall not drop.* That is, the prophecy shall not come upon these. Such were the sentiments of the people that were unwilling to believe the threats of the prophets.

Ver. 8. *You have taken away.* You have even stripped people of their necessary garments, and have treated such as were innocently passing on the way as if they were at war with you.

Ver. 9. *You have cast out.* Either by depriving them of their houses or by your crimes, given occasion to their being carried away captives, and to their children, by that means, never learning to praise the Lord.

10 Arise ye and depart, for there is no rest here for you. For that uncleanness of *the land*, it shall be corrupted with a grievous corruption.

11 Would God I were not a man that hath the spirit, and that I rather spoke a lie! I will let drop to thee of wine and of drunkenness: and it shall be this people upon whom it shall drop.

12 I will assemble and gather together all of thee, O Jacob: I will bring together the remnant of Israel. I will put them together as a flock in the fold, *as the* sheep in the midst of the sheepcotes: they shall make a tumult by reason of the multitude of men.

13 For he shall go up that shall open the way before them. They shall divide and pass through the gate and shall come in by it: and their king shall pass before them, and the Lord at the head of them.

CHAPTER 3

For the sins of the rich oppressing the poor, of false prophets flattering for lucre and of judges perverting justice, Jerusalem and the temple shall be destroyed.

AND I said: Hear, O ye princes of Jacob and ye chiefs of the house of Israel: Is it not your part to know judgment?

2 You that hate good and love evil, that violently pluck off their skins from them and their flesh from their bones.

3 Who have eaten the flesh of my people and have flayed their skin from off them: and have broken and chopped their bones as for the kettle and as flesh in the midst of the pot.

4 Then shall they cry to the Lord and he will not hear them: and he will hide his face from them at that time, as they have behaved wickedly in their devices.

5 Thus saith the Lord concerning the prophets that make my people err, that bite with their teeth and preach peace: and if a man give not something into their mouth, they prepare war against him.

6 Therefore night shall be to you instead of vision and darkness to you instead of divination and the sun

Chap. 3. ¹ Ezech. 22, 27; Soph. 3, 3. ² Jer. 26, 18.
Chap. 4. ¹ Isai. 2, 2.

Ver. 11. *Would God.* The prophet could have wished, out of his love to his people, that he might be deceived in denouncing to them these evils that were to fall upon them: but by conforming himself to the will of God, he declares to them that he is sent to prophesy, literally to *let drop* upon them, the wine of God's indignation with which they should be made drunk, that is, stupefied and cast down.

Ver. 12. *In the midst of the sheepcotes.* That is, in the sheepfold.

Chap. 4. Ver. 3. *Neither shall they learn.* The law of Christ is a law of peace; and all his true subjects, as much as lies in them, love and keep peace with all the world.

shall go down upon the prophets: and the day shall be darkened over them.

7 And they shall be confounded that see visions and the diviners shall be confounded: and they shall all cover their faces, because there is no answer of God.

8 But yet I am filled with the strength of the spirit of the Lord, with judgment and power: to declare unto Jacob his wickedness and to Israel his sin.

9 Hear this, ye princes of the house of Jacob and ye judges of the house of Israel: you that abhor judgment and pervert all that is right.

10 You that build up Sion with blood and Jerusalem with iniquity.

11 ¹ Her princes have judged for bribes and her priests have taught for hire and her prophets divined for money: and they leaned upon the Lord, saying: Is not the Lord in the midst of us? No evil shall come upon us.

12 Therefore, because of you, ² Sion shall be ploughed as a field and Jerusalem shall be as a heap of stones and the mountain of the temple as the high places of the forests.

CHAPTER 4

The glory of the church of Christ by the conversion of the Gentiles. The Jews shall be carried captives to Babylon and be delivered again.

AND ¹ it shall come to pass in the last days that the mountain of the house of the Lord shall be prepared in the top of mountains and high above the hills: and people shall flow to it.

2 And many nations shall come in haste and say: Come, let us go up to the mountain of the Lord and to the house of the God of Jacob: and he will teach us of his ways and we will walk in his paths. For the law shall go forth out of Sion, and the word of the Lord out of Jerusalem.

3 And he shall judge among many people and rebuke strong nations afar off: and they shall beat their swords into ploughshares and their spears into spades. Nation shall not take sword against nation: neither shall they learn war any more.

4 And every man shall sit under his vine and under his fig tree, and there shall be none to make them afraid: for the mouth of the Lord of hosts hath spoken.

5 For all people will walk every one in the name of his god: but we will walk in the name of the Lord our God for ever and ever.

6 In that day, saith the Lord, I will gather up her that halteth: and her

that I had cast out, I will gather up: and her whom I had afflicted.

7 [2] And I will make her that halted, a remnant, and her that hath been afflicted, a mighty nation. [3] And the Lord will reign over them in mount Sion, from this time now and for ever.

8 And thou, O cloudy tower of the flock of the daughter of Sion, unto thee shall it come: yea, the first power shall come, the kingdom to the daughter of Jerusalem.

9 Now, why art thou drawn together with grief? Hast thou no king in thee, or is thy counsellor perished, because sorrow hath taken thee as a woman in labour?

10 Be in pain and labour, O daughter of Sion, as a woman that bringeth forth: for now shalt thou go out of the city and shalt dwell in the country and shalt come even to Babylon. There thou shalt be delivered: there the Lord will redeem thee out of the hand of thy enemies.

11 And now many nations are gathered together against thee, and they say: Let her be stoned and let our eye look upon Sion.

12 But they have not known the thoughts of the Lord and have not understood his counsel: because he hath gathered them together as the hay of the floor.

13 Arise and tread, O daughter of Sion: for I will make thy horn iron and thy hoofs I will make brass: and thou shalt beat in pieces many peoples and shalt immolate the spoils of them to the Lord, and their strength to the Lord of the whole earth.

CHAPTER 5

The birth of Christ in Bethlehem. His reign and spiritual conquests.

NOW shalt thou be laid waste, O daughter of the robber. They have laid siege against us: with a rod shall they strike the cheek of the judge of Israel.

2 [1] AND THOU, BETHLEHEM Ephrata, art a little one among the thousands of Juda: out of thee shall he come forth unto me that is to be the ruler in Israel: and his going forth *is* from the beginning, from the days of eternity.

3 Therefore will he give them up even till the time wherein she that travaileth shall bring forth: and the remnant of his brethren shall be converted to the children of Israel.

4 And he shall stand and feed in the strength of the Lord, in the height of the name of the Lord his God: and they shall be converted, for now shall he be magnified even to the ends of the earth.

5 And this man shall be *our* peace when the Assyrian shall come into our land and when he shall set his foot in our houses: and we shall raise against him seven shepherds and eight principal men.

6 And they shall feed the land of Assyria with the sword and the land of Nemrod with the spears thereof: and he shall deliver us from the Assyrian when he shall come into our land and when he shall tread in our borders.

7 And the remnant of Jacob shall be in the midst of many peoples as a dew from the Lord and as drops upon the grass, which waiteth not for man nor tarrieth for the children of men.

8 And the remnant of Jacob shall be among the Gentiles in the midst of many peoples as a lion among the beasts of the forests and as a young lion among the flocks of sheep: who when he shall go through and tread down and take, there is none to deliver.

9 Thy hand shall be lifted up over thy enemies: and all thy enemies shall be cut off.

10 And it shall come to pass in that day, saith the Lord, that I will take away thy horses out of the midst of thee and will destroy thy chariots.

11 And I will destroy the cities of thy land and will throw down all thy strong holds: and I will take away sorceries out of thy hand, and there shall be no divinations in thee.

12 And I will destroy thy graven things and thy statues out of the midst

[2] Soph. 3, 19. [3] Dan. 7, 14; Luke, 1, 32. CHAP. 5. [1] Matt. 2, 6; John, 7, 42.

CHAP. 5. Ver. 1. *Daughter of the robber.* Some understand this of Babylon which robbed and pillaged the temple of God: others understand it of Jerusalem, by reason of the many rapines and oppressions committed there.

Ver. 2. *His going forth.* That is, he who *as man* shall be born in thee, *as God* was born of his Father from all eternity.

Ver. 5. *The Assyrian.* That is, the persecutors of the church, who are here called Assyrians by the prophet, because the Assyrians were at that time the chief enemies and persecutors of the people of God.—*Seven shepherds.* The pastors of God's church and the defenders of the faith. The number *seven* in scriptures is taken to signify many: and when *eight* is joined with it, we are to understand that the number will be very great.

Ver. 6. *They shall feed.* They shall make spiritual conquests in the lands of their persecutors, with the *sword of the spirit, which is the word of God* (Eph. 6, 17).

Ver. 7. *The remnant of Jacob.* The apostles and the first preachers of the Jewish nation; whose doctrine, like dew, shall make the plants of the converted Gentiles grow up, without waiting for any man to cultivate them by human learning.

Ver. 8. *As a lion.* This denotes the fortitude of these first preachers and their success in their spiritual enterprises.

Ver. 10. *I will take away thy horses.* Some understand this and all that follows to the end of the chapter as addressed to the enemies of the church. But it may as well be understood of the converts to the church who should no longer put their trust in any of these things.

of thee: and thou shalt no more adore the works of thy hands.

13 And I will pluck up thy groves out of the midst of thee and will crush thy cities.

14 And I will execute vengeance in wrath and in indignation among all the nations that have not given ear.

CHAPTER 6

God expostulates with the Jews for their ingratitude and sins, for which they shall be punished.

HEAR ye what the Lord saith: Arise, contend thou in judgment against the mountains, and let the hills hear thy voice.

2 Let the mountains hear the judgment of the Lord, and the strong foundations of the earth: for the Lord will enter into judgment with his people and he will plead against Israel.

3 ¹O my people, what have I done to thee or in what have I molested thee? Answer thou me.

4 For I brought thee up out of the land of Egypt and delivered thee out of the house of slaves: and I sent before thy face Moses and Aaron and Mary.

5 ²O my people, remember, I pray thee, what Balach the king of Moab purposed: and what Balaam the son of Beor answered him, from Setim to Galgal, that thou mightest know the justices of the Lord.

6 What shall I offer to the Lord that is worthy? Wherewith shall I kneel before the high God? Shall I offer holocausts unto him and calves of a year old?

7 May the Lord be appeased with thousands of rams or with many thousands of fat he-goats? Shall I give my firstborn for my wickedness, the fruit of my body for the sin of my soul?

8 I will shew thee, O man, what is good and what the Lord requireth of thee: ³Verily, to do judgment, and to love mercy, and to walk solicitous with thy God.

9 The voice of the Lord crieth to the city and salvation shall be to them that

CHAP. 6. ¹ Jer. 2, 5. ² Num. 22, 23. ³ Zach. 7, 9; Matt. 23, 23; Deut. 6, 2; 26, 16. ⁴ Deut. 28, 38; Agg. 1, 6. CHAP. 7. ¹ Matt. 10, 35. ² Matt. 10, 36.

CHAP. 6. Ver. 1. *The mountains.* That is, the great ones, the princes of the people.
Ver. 5. *From Setim to Galgal.* He puts them in mind of the favour he did them in not suffering them to be quite destroyed by the evil purpose of Balach and the wicked counsel of Balaam: and then gives them a hint of the wonders he wrought in order to bring them into the Land of Promise, by stopping the course of the Jordan, in their march from Setim to Galgal.
Ver. 6. *What shall I offer.* This is spoken in the person of the people, desiring to be informed what they are to do to please God.
Ver. 10. *Full of wrath.* That is, highly provoking in the sight of God.
Ver. 16. *The statutes of Amri.* The wicked ways of Amri and Achab, idolatrous kings.

fear thy name. Hear, O ye tribes, and who shall approve it?

10 As yet there is a fire in the house of the wicked, the treasures of iniquity and a scant measure full of wrath.

11 Shall I justify wicked balances and the deceitful weights of the bag?

12 By which her rich men were filled with iniquity, and the inhabitants thereof have spoken lies: and their tongue was deceitful in their mouth.

13 And I therefore began to strike thee with desolation for thy sins.

14 Thou shalt eat, but shalt not be filled: and thy humiliation *shall be* in the midst of thee. And thou shalt take hold, but shalt not save: and those whom thou shalt save, I will give up to the sword.

15 ⁴Thou shalt sow, but shalt not reap: thou shalt tread the olives, but shalt not be anointed with the oil: and the new wine, but shalt not drink the wine.

16 For thou hast kept the statutes of Amri and all the works of the house of Achab: and thou hast walked according to their wills, that I should make thee a desolation and the inhabitants thereof a hissing: and you shall bear the reproach of my people.

CHAPTER 7

The prophet laments that, notwithstanding all his preaching, the generality are still corrupt in their manners, wherefore their desolation is at hand. Yet they shall be restored again and prosper and all mankind shall be redeemed by Christ.

WOE is me, for I am become as one that gleaneth in autumn the grapes of the vintage. There is no cluster to eat: my soul desired the firstripe figs.

2 The holy man is perished out of the earth and there is none upright among men: they all lie in wait for blood. Every one hunteth his brother to death.

3 The evil of their hands they call good: the prince requireth and the judge is for giving: and the great man hath uttered the desire of his soul, and they have troubled it.

4 He that is best among them is as a brier: and he that is righteous, as the thorn of the hedge. The day of thy inspection, thy visitation, cometh: now shall be their destruction.

5 Believe not a friend and trust not in a prince; keep the doors of thy mouth from her that sleepeth in thy bosom.

6 ¹For the son dishonoureth the father and the daughter riseth up against her mother, the daughter-in-law against her mother-in-law: ²and a man's enemies are they of his own houschold.

7 But I will look towards the Lord, I will wait for God my Saviour: my God will hear me.

8 Rejoice not, thou, my enemy, over me, because I am fallen. I shall arise. When I sit in darkness the Lord is my light.

9 I will bear the wrath of the Lord, because I have sinned against him, until he judge my cause and execute judgment for me. He will bring me forth into the light: I shall behold his justice.

10 And my enemy shall behold and she shall be covered with shame, who saith to me: Where is the Lord thy God? My eyes shall look down upon her: now shall she be trodden under foot as the mire of the streets.

11 The day *shall come* that thy walls may be built up: in that day shall the law be far removed.

12 In that day they shall come even from Assyria to thee and to the fortified cities: and from the fortified cities even to the river, and from sea to sea, and from mountain to mountain.

13 And the land shall be made desolate, because of the inhabitants thereof and for the fruit of their devices.

14 Feed thy people with thy rod, the flock of thy inheritance, them that dwell alone in the forest in the midst of Carmel: they shall feed in Basan and Galaad, according to the days of old.

15 According to the days of thy coming out of the land of Egypt, I will shew him wonders.

16 The nations shall see and shall be confounded at all their strength: they shall put the hand upon the mouth, their ears shall be deaf.

17 They shall lick the dust like serpents, as the creeping things of the earth: they shall be disturbed in their houses: they shall dread the Lord our God and shall fear thee.

18 [3] Who is a God like to thee, who takest away iniquity and passest by the sin of the remnant of thy inheritance? He will send his fury in no more, because he delighteth in mercy.

19 He will turn again and have mercy on us: he will put away our iniquities and he will cast all our sins into the bottom of the sea.

20 Thou wilt perform the truth to Jacob, the mercy to Abraham: which thou hast sworn to our fathers from the days of old.

THE PROPHECY OF
NAHUM

NAHUM, *whose name signifies a comforter, was a native of Elcese or Elcesai, supposed to be a little town in Galilee. He prophesied after the ten tribes were carried into captivity and foretold the utter destruction of Ninive by the Babylonians and Medes, which happened in the reign of Josias.*

CHAPTER 1

The majesty of God, his goodness to his people and severity to his enemies.

THE burden of Ninive. The book of the vision of Nahum the Elcesite.

2 The Lord is a jealous God and a revenger: the Lord is a revenger and hath wrath: the Lord taketh vengeance on his adversaries and he is angry with his enemies.

3 The Lord is patient and great in power and will not cleanse and acquit *the guilty*. The Lord's ways *are* in a tempest and a whirlwind: and clouds *are* the dust of his feet.

4 He rebuketh the sea and drieth it up and bringeth all the rivers to be a desert. Basan languisheth and Carmel: and the flower of Libanus fadeth away.

5 The mountains trembled at him,

and the hills are made desolate: and the earth hath quaked at his presence, and the world and all that dwell therein.

6 Who can stand before the face of his indignation? And who shall resist in the fierceness of his anger? His indignation is poured out like fire: and the rocks are melted by him.

7 The Lord is good and giveth strength in the day of trouble and knoweth them that hope in him.[1]

8 But with a flood that passeth by he will make an utter end of the place thereof: and darkness shall pursue his enemies.

[3] Jer. 10, 6; Acts, 10, 43. CHAP. 1. [1] 2 Tim. 11, 9.

CHAP. 7. Ver. 10. *She shall be covered.* Babylon, *my enemy,* shall be covered.

Ver. 11. *The law.* Namely, of thy enemies, who have tyrannized over thee.

Ver. 13. *The land.* That is, Babylon.

CHAP. 1. Ver. 8. *Of the place thereof.* Ninive.

9 What do ye devise against the Lord? He will make an utter end: there shall not rise a double affliction.

10 For as thorns embrace one another, so while they are feasting and drinking together they shall be consumed as stubble that is fully dry.

11 Out of thee shall come forth one that imagineth evil against the Lord, contriving treachery in his mind.

12 Thus saith the Lord: Though they were perfect and many of them so, yet thus shall they be cut off, and he shall pass. I have afflicted thee and I will afflict thee no more.

13 And now I will break in pieces his rod with which he struck thy back and I will burst thy bonds asunder.

14 And the Lord will give a commandment concerning thee that no more of thy name shall be sown. I will destroy the graven and molten thing out of the house of thy God: I will make *it* thy grave, for thou art disgraced.

15 [2] Behold upon the mountains the feet of him that bringeth good tidings and that preacheth peace. O Juda, keep thy festivals and pay thy vows, for Belial shall no more pass through thee again: he is utterly cut off.

CHAPTER 2

God sends his armies against Ninive to destroy it.

HE is come up that shall destroy before thy face, that shall keep the siege: watch the way, fortify thy loins, strengthen thy power exceedingly.

2 For the Lord hath rendered the pride of Jacob as the pride of Israel: because the spoilers have laid them waste and have marred their vine branches.

---

[2] Isai. 3, 7; Rom. 10, 15. CHAP. 2. [1] Mich. 7, 11. CHAP. 3. [1] Ezech. 24, 9; Hab. 2, 12.

Ver. 11. *Shall come forth one.* Some understand this of Sennacherib. But as his attempt against the people seems to have been prior to the prophecy of Nahum, we may better understand it of Holofernes.

Ver. 12. *Though they were perfect.* That is, however strong or numerous their forces may be, they shall be cut off; and their prince or leader shall pass away and disappear.

Ver. 14. *Will give a commandment.* That is, a decree, *concerning thee,* O king of Ninive.

Ver. 15. *Belial.* The wicked one, namely, the Assyrian.

CHAP. 2. Ver. 2. *Hath rendered the pride of Jacob.* He hath punished Jacob for his pride: and therefore Ninive must not expect to escape. Or else, *rendering the pride of Jacob* means rewarding, that is, punishing Ninive for the pride they exercised against Jacob.

Ver. 3. *Of his mighty men.* He speaks of the Chaldeans and Medes sent to destroy Ninive. *Stupefied (consopiti).* That is, they drive on furiously like men intoxicated with wine.

Ver. 5. *Stumble in their march.* By running hastily on.

---

3 The shield of his mighty men is like fire, the men of the army are clad in scarlet, the reins of the chariot are flaming in the day of his preparation, and the drivers are stupefied.

4 They are in confusion in the ways, the chariots jostle one against another in the streets: their looks are like torches, like lightning running to and fro.

5 He will muster up his valiant men, they shall stumble in their march: they shall quickly get upon the walls thereof and a covering shall be prepared.

6 The gates of the rivers are opened, and the temple is thrown down to the ground.

7 And the soldier is led away captive: and her bondowmen were led away mourning as doves, murmuring in their hearts.

8 And as for Ninive, her waters are like a great pool: but the men flee away. *They cry:* Stand, stand. But there is none that will return back.

9 Take ye the spoil of the silver, take the spoil of the gold: for there is no end of the riches of all the precious furniture.

10 She is destroyed and rent and torn: the heart melteth and the knees fail and all the lions lose strength: and the faces of them all *are* as the blackness of a kettle.

11 Where is now the dwelling of the lions and the feeding place of the young lions, to which the lion went, to enter in thither, the young lion, and there was none to make them afraid?

12 The lion caught enough for his whelps and killed for his lionesses: and he filled his holes with prey and his den with rapine.

13 Behold I *come* against thee, saith the Lord of hosts, and I will burn thy chariots even to smoke: and the sword shall devour thy young lions. And I will cut off thy prey out of the land: and the voice of thy messengers shall be heard no more.[1]

CHAPTER 3

The miserable destruction of Ninive.

WOE [1] to thee, O city of blood, all full of lies and violence: rapine shall not depart from thee.

2 The noise of the whip and the noise of the rattling of the wheels and of the neighing horse and of the running chariot and of the horsemen coming up,

3 And of the shining sword and of the glittering spear and of a multitude slain and of a grievous destruction: and there is no end of carcasses, and they shall fall down on their *dead* bodies.

4 Because of the multitude of the

fornications of the harlot that was beautiful and agreeable and that made use of witchcraft, that sold nations through her fornications and families through her witchcrafts.

5 Behold I *come* against thee, saith the Lord of hosts: ² and I will discover thy shame to thy face and will shew thy nakedness to the nations and thy shame to kingdoms.

6 And I will cast abominations upon thee and will disgrace thee and will make an example of thee.

7 And it shall come to pass that every one that shall see thee shall flee from thee and shall say: Ninive is laid waste. Who shall bemoan thee? Whence shall I seek a comforter for thee?

8 Art thou better than the populous Alexandria that dwelleth among the rivers? Waters are round about it: the sea is its riches, the waters are its walls.

9 Ethiopia and Egypt *were* the strength thereof, and there is no end: Africa and the Libyans were thy helpers.

10 Yet she also was removed and carried into captivity: her young children were dashed in pieces at the top of every street and they cast lots upon her nobles and all her great men were bound in fetters.

11 Therefore thou also shalt be made drunk and shalt be despised: and thou shalt seek help from the enemy.

12 All thy strong holds shall be like fig trees with their green figs: if they be shaken, they shall fall into the mouth of the eater.

13 Behold thy people in the midst of thee *are* women: the gates of thy land shall be set wide open to thy enemies: the fire shall devour thy bars.

14 Draw thee water for the siege, build up thy bulwarks: go into the clay and tread, work it and make brick.

15 There shall the fire devour thee: thou shalt perish by the sword, it shall devour thee like the bruchus: assemble together like the bruchus, make thyself many like the locust.

16 Thou hast multiplied thy merchandises above the stars of heaven: the bruchus hath spread himself and flown away.

17 Thy guards are like the locusts: and thy little ones like the locusts of locusts which swarm on the hedges in the day of cold: the sun arose and they flew away, and their place was not known where they were.

18 Thy shepherds have slumbered, O king of Assyria, thy princes shall be buried: thy people are hid in the mountains, and there is none to gather them together.

19 Thy destruction is not hidden thy wound is grievous: all that have heard the fame of thee have clapped their hands over thee: for upon whom hath not thy wickedness passed continually?

THE PROPHECY OF
HABACUC

HABACUC *was a native of Bezocher and prophesied in Juda, some time before the invasion of the Chaldeans, which he foretold. He lived to see this prophecy fulfilled and for many years after, according to the general opinion which supposes him to be the same that was brought by the Angel to Daniel in Babylon*

CHAPTER 1

The prophet complains of the wickedness of the people. God reveals to him the vengeance he is going to take of them by the Chaldeans.

THE burden that Habacuc the prophet saw.

2 How long, O Lord, shall I cry, and thou wilt not hear? Shall I cry out to thee suffering violence, and thou wilt not save?

3 Why hast thou shewn me iniquity and grievance, to see rapine and injus-

tice before me? And there is a judgment, but opposition is more powerful.

4 Therefore the law is torn in pieces and judgment cometh not to the end. Because the wicked prevaileth against

² Isai. 47, 3.

CHAP. 3. Ver. 8. *Populous Alexandria. No-Ammon.* A populous city of Egypt destroyed by the Chaldeans and afterwards rebuilt by Alexander and called Alexandria. Others suppose *No-Ammon* to be the same as *Diospolis.*
Ver. 17. *The locusts of locusts.* The young locusts.
CHAP. 1. Ver. 1. *Burden.* Such prophecies more especially are called *burdens* as threaten grievous evils and punishments.

the just, therefore wrong judgment goeth forth.

5 ¹ Behold ye among the nations and see: wonder and be astonished; for a work is done in your days which no man will believe when it shall be told.

6 For behold, I will raise up the Chaldeans, a bitter and swift nation, marching upon the breadth of the earth, to possess the dwelling places that are not their own.

7 They are dreadful and terrible: from themselves shall their judgment and their burden proceed.

8 Their horses are lighter than leopards and swifter than evening wolves; and their horsemen shall be spread abroad. For their horsemen shall come from afar: they shall fly as an eagle that maketh haste to eat.

9 They shall all come to the prey: their face is like a burning wind and they shall gather together captives as the sand.

10 And *their prince* shall triumph over kings and princes shall be his laughing-stock: and he shall laugh at every strong hold and shall cast up a mount and shall take it.

11 Then shall his spirit be changed and he shall pass and fall: this is his strength of his god.

12 Wast thou not from the beginning, O Lord my God, my holy one, and we shall not die? Lord, thou hast appointed him for judgment and made him strong for correction.

13 Thy eyes are too pure to behold evil, and thou canst not look on iniquity. Why lookest thou upon them that do unjust things and holdest thy peace when the wicked devoureth the man that is more just than himself?

14 And thou wilt make men as the fishes of the sea and as the creeping things that have no ruler.

CHAP. 1. ¹ Acts, 13, 41. CHAP. 2. ¹ John, 3, 36; Rom. 1, 17; Gal. 3, 11; Heb. 10, 38.

Ver. 11. *Then shall his spirit.* The spirit of the king of Babylon. It alludes to the judgment of God upon Nabuchodonosor, recorded Dan. 4, and to the speedy fall of the Chaldean empire.

CHAP. 2. Ver. 1. *Will stand.* Waiting to see what the Lord will answer to my complaint that the Chaldeans, who are worse than the Jews and who attribute all their success to their own strength, or to their idols, should nevertheless prevail over the people of the Lord. The Lord's answer is that the prophet must wait with patience and faith: that all should be set right in due time and the enemies of God and his people punished according to their deserts.

Ver. 5. *As wine deceiveth.* By affording only a short passing pleasure, followed by the evils and disgrace that are the usual consequences of drunkenness: so shall it be with the proud enemies of the people of God, whose success affordeth them only a momentary pleasure, followed by innumerable and everlasting evils.

Ver. 6. *Thick clay.* Ill-gotten goods, that, like mire, both burden and defile the soul.

15 He lifted up all them with his hook, he drew them in his drag and gathered them into his net: for this he will be glad and rejoice.

16 Therefore will he offer victims to his drag and he will sacrifice to his net: because through them his portion is made fat and his meat dainty.

17 For this cause therefore he spreadeth his net and will not spare continually to slay the nations.

CHAPTER 2

The prophet is admonished to wait with faith. The enemies of God's people shall assuredly be punished.

I WILL stand upon my watch and fix my foot upon the tower: and I will watch, to see what will be said to me and what I may answer to him that reproveth me.

2 And the Lord answered me and said: Write the vision and make it plain upon tables: that he that readeth it may run over it.

3 For as yet the vision is far off and it shall appear at the end and shall not lie: if it make any delay, wait for it, for it shall surely come and it shall not be slack.

4 Behold, he that is unbelieving, his soul shall not be right in himself: ¹ but the just shall live in his faith.

5 And as wine deceiveth him that drinketh *it,* so shall the proud man be: and he shall not be honoured. Who hath enlarged his desire like hell and is never satisfied: but will gather together unto him all nations and heap together unto him all people.

6 Shall not all these take up a parable against him and a dark speech concerning him? And it shall be said: Woe to him that heapeth together that which is not his own. How long also doth he load himself with thick clay?

7 Shall they not rise up suddenly that shall bite thee and they be stirred up that shall tear thee, and thou shalt be a spoil to them?

8 Because thou hast spoiled many nations, all that shall be left of the people shall spoil thee: because of men's blood and for the iniquity of the land, of the city and of all that dwell therein.

9 Woe to him that gathereth together an evil covetousness to his house that his nest may be on high, and thinketh he may be delivered out of the hand of evil.

10 Thou hast devised confusion to thy house: thou has cut off many people, and thy soul hath sinned.

11 For the stone shall cry out of the

wall: and the timber that is between the joints of the building, shall answer.

12 [2] Woe to him that buildeth a town with blood and prepareth a city by iniquity!

13 Are not these things from the Lord of hosts? For the people shall labour in a great fire and the nations in vain: and they shall faint.

14 For the earth shall be filled, that men may know the glory of the Lord, as waters covering the sea.

15 Woe to him that giveth drink to his friend and presenteth his gall and maketh him drunk, that he may behold his nakedness!

16 Thou art filled with shame instead of glory: drink thou also and fall fast asleep. The cup of the right hand of the Lord shall compass thee, and shameful vomiting *shall be* on thy glory.

17 For the iniquity of Libanus shall cover thee and the ravaging of beasts shall terrify them, because of the blood of men and of the iniquity of the land and of the city and of all that dwell therein.

18 What doth the graven thing avail, because the maker thereof hath graven it, a molten and a false image, because the forger thereof hath trusted in a thing of his own forging, to make dumb idols?

19 Woe to him that saith to wood: Awake. To the dumb stone. Arise. Can it teach? Behold, it is laid over with gold and silver and there is no spirit in the bowels thereof.

20 [3] But the Lord is in his holy temple: let all the earth keep silence before him.

CHAPTER 3

1 A PRAYER OF HABACUC THE PROPHET FOR IGNORANCES.

2 O LORD, I have heard thy hearing and was afraid.

O Lord, thy work, in the midst of the years bring it to life.

In the midst of the years thou shalt make it known: when thou art angry, thou wilt remember mercy.

3 God will come from the south: and the holy one from mount Pharan:

His glory covered the heavens: and the earth is full of his praise.

4 His brightness shall be as the light: horns *are* in his hands:

There is his strength hid. 5 Death shall go before his face:

And the devil shall go forth before his feet.

6 He stood and measured the earth. He beheld and melted the nations:

and the ancient mountains were crushed to pieces.

The hills of the world were bowed down by the journeys of his eternity.

7 I saw the tents of Ethiopia for *their* iniquity: the curtains of the land of Madian shall be troubled.

8 Wast thou angry, O Lord, with the rivers? Or was thy wrath upon the rivers? Or thy indignation in the sea?

Who will ride upon thy horses? And thy chariots are salvation.

9 Thou wilt surely take up thy bow: *according* to the oaths which thou hast spoken to the tribes.

[2] Ezech. 24, 9; Nah. 3, 1. [3] Ps. 10, 5.

Ver. 13. *Are not these things.* That is, shall not these punishments that are here recorded come from the Lord upon him that is guilty of such crimes.—*The people shall labour.* Namely, the enemies of God's people.

Ver. 17. *The iniquity of Libanus.* That is, the iniquity committed by the Chaldeans against the temple of God, signified here by the name of Libanus.

CHAP. 3. Ver. 1. *For ignorances.* That is, for the sins of his people. In the Hebrew, it is *Sigionoth;* which some take to signify a musical instrument or tune, with which this sublime prayer and canticle was to be sung.

Ver. 2. *Thy hearing.* That is, thy oracles, the great and wonderful things thou hast revealed to me which struck me with a reverential fear and awe.—*Thy work.* The great work of the redemption of man, which thou wilt *bring to life* and light *in the midst of the years,* when our calamities and miseries shall be at their height.

Ver. 3. *God will come from the south.* God himself will come to give us his law and to conduct us into the true land of promise; as heretofore he came from the South (in the Hebrew *Theman*) and from mount *Pharan* to give his law to his people in the desert. See Deut. 33, 2.

Ver. 4. *Horns.* That is, strength and power, which, by a Hebrew phrase, are called *horns.* Or *beams of light,* which come forth from his hands. Or it may allude to the cross, in the *horns* of which the *hands of Christ* were fastened, where his *strength was hidden,* by which he overcame the world and drove out *death and the devil.*

Ver. 5. *Death shall go before his face.* Both death and the devil shall be the executioners of his justice against his enemies: as they were heretofore against the Egyptians and Chananites.

Ver. 6. *He beheld.* One look of his eye is enough to melt all the nations and to reduce them to nothing. For all heaven and earth disappear when they come before his light (Apoc. 20, 11).—*The ancient mountains.* By the *mountains* and *hills* are signified the great ones of the world that persecute the church, whose power was quickly crushed by the Almighty.

Ver. 7. *Ethiopia,* the land of the *Blacks,* and *Madian* are here taken for the enemies of God and his people, who shall perish for their iniquity.

Ver. 8. *With the rivers.* He alludes to the wonders wrought heretofore by the Lord in favour of his people Israel, when the waters of *the rivers* of Arnon and Jordan and of the *Red Sea* retired before their face: when he came as it were with *his horses* and *chariots to save* them, when he took up *his bow* for their defence, in consequence of *the oath* he had made to their *tribes.* when the mountains trembled and the *deep* stood with its waves raised up in a heap, as with *hand lifted up* to heaven: when the *sun and the moon stood still* at his command to comply with his anger, not against the rivers and sea, but against the enemies of his people. How much more will he do in favour of his Son and against the enemies of his Church!

Thou wilt divide the rivers of the earth.

10 The mountains saw thee and were grieved: the great body of waters passed away.

The deep put forth its voice: the deep lifted up its hands.

11 The sun and the moon stood still in their habitation, in the light of thy arrows: they shall go in the brightness of thy glittering spear.

12 In thy anger thou wilt tread the earth under foot: in thy wrath thou wilt astonish the nations.

13 Thou wentest forth for the salvation of thy people for salvation with thy Christ.

Thou struckest the head of the house of the wicked: thou hast laid bare his foundation even to the neck.

14 Thou hast cursed his sceptres, the head of his warriors, them that came out as a whirlwind to scatter me.

Their joy was like that of him that devoureth the poor man in secret.

15 Thou madest a way in the sea for thy horses, in the mud of many waters.

16 I have heard and my bowels were troubled: my lips trembled at the voice.

Let rottenness enter into my bones and swarm under me.

That I may rest in the day of tribulation: that I may go up to our people that are girded.

17 For the fig tree shall not blossom and there shall be no spring in the vines. The labour of the olive tree shall fail and the fields shall yield no food. The flock shall be cut off from the fold and there shall be no herd in the stalls.

18 But I will rejoice in the Lord: and I will joy in God my Jesus.

19 The Lord God is my strength and he will make my feet like the feet of harts: and he the conqueror will lead me upon my high places singing psalms.

THE PROPHECY OF

SOPHONIAS

SOPHONIAS, whose name, saith St. Jerome, signifies The Watchman of the Lord or The hidden of the Lord, prophesied in the beginning of the reign of Josias. He was a native of Sarabatha and of the tribe of Simeon, according to the more general opinion. He prophesied the punishments of the Jews for their idolatry and other crimes; also the punishments that were to come on divers nations; the coming of Christ, the conversion of the Gentiles, the blindness of the Jews and their conversion towards the end of the world.

Ver. 13. The head of the house of the wicked.—Such was Pharao heretofore: such shall Antichrist be hereafter.

Ver. 15. Thou madest a way in the sea. To deliver thy people from the Egyptian bondage: and thou shalt work the like wonders in the spiritual way, to rescue the children of the church from their enemies.

Ver. 16. I have heard. Namely, the evils that are now coming upon the Israelites for their sins, and that shall come hereafter upon all impenitent sinners; and the foresight that I have of these miseries makes me willing to die, that I may be at rest before this general tribulation comes, in which all good things shall be withdrawn from the wicked.—That I may go up to our people. That I may join the happy company in the bosom of Abraham, that are girded, that is, prepared for their journey, by which they shall attend their Lord, when he shall ascend into heaven. To which high and happy place, ... Saviour, the great conqueror of death and hell, shall one day bring me rejoicing and singing psalms of praise (ver. 18 and 19).

CHAP. 1. Ver. 2. Gathering, I will gather. That is, I will assuredly take away and wholly consume, either by captivity or death, both men and beasts out of this land.

Ver. 4. The wardens. Of the temples of the idols, Ædituos, in Hebrew, the Chemarims, that is, such as kindle the fires or burn incense.

CHAPTER 1

For divers enormous sins, the kingdom of Juda is threatened with severe judgment.

THE word of the Lord that came to Sophonias the son of Chusi, the son of Godolias, the son of Amarias, the son of Ezechias, in the days of Josias the son of Amon, king of Juda.

2 Gathering, I will gather together all things from off the face of the land, saith the Lord:

3 I will gather man and beast: I will gather the birds of the air and the fishes of the sea. And the ungodly shall meet with ruin: and I will destroy men from off the face of the land, saith the Lord.

4 And I will stretch out my hand upon Juda and upon all the inhabitants of Jerusalem: and I will destroy out of this place the remnant of Baal and the names of the wardens of the temples with the priests.

5 And them that worship the host of heaven upon the tops of houses and them that adore and swear by the Lord and swear by Melchom:

6 And them that turn away from following after the Lord and that have not sought the Lord nor searched after him.

7 Be silent before the face of the Lord God: for the day of the Lord is near, for the Lord hath prepared a victim, he hath sanctified his guests.

8 And it shall come to pass in the day of the victim of the Lord that I will visit upon the princes and upon the king's sons and upon all such as are clothed with strange apparel.

9 And I will visit in that day upon every one that entereth arrogantly over the threshold: them that fill the house of the Lord their God with iniquity and deceit.

10 And there shall be in that day, saith the Lord, the noise of a cry from the fish gate and a howling from the Second and a great destruction from the hills.

11 Howl, ye inhabitants of the Morter. All the people of Chanaan is hush: all are cut off that were wrapped up in silver.

12 And it shall come to pass at that time that I will search Jerusalem with lamps and will visit upon the men that are settled on their lees, that say in their hearts: The Lord will not do good, nor will he do evil.

13 And their strength shall become a booty and their houses as a desert. ¹ And they shall build houses and shall not dwell in them: and they shall plant vineyards and shall not drink the wine of them.

14 The great day of the Lord is near: it is near and exceeding swift. The voice of the day of the Lord is bitter: the mighty man shall there meet with tribulation.

15 ² That day *is* a day of wrath, a day of tribulation and distress, a day of calamity and misery, a day of darkness and obscurity, a day of clouds and whirlwinds,

16 A day of the trumpet and alarm against the fenced cities and against the high bulwarks.

17 And I will distress men and they shall walk like blind men, because they have sinned against the Lord: and their blood shall be poured out as earth and their bodies as dung.

18 ³ Neither shall their silver and their gold be able to deliver them in the day of the wrath of the Lord. ⁴ All the land shall be devoured by the fire of his jealousy: for he shall make even

a speedy destruction of all them that dwell in the land.

CHAPTER 2

An exhortation to repentance. The judgment of the Philistines, of the Moabites and the Ammonites, of the Ethiopians and the Assyrians.

ASSEMBLE yourselves together, be gathered together, O nation not worthy to be loved:

2 Before the decree bring forth the day as dust passing away, before the fierce anger of the Lord come upon you, before the day of the Lord's indignation come upon you.

3 Seek the Lord, all ye meek of the earth, you that have wrought his judgment: seek the just, seek the meek: if by any means you may be hid in the day of the Lord's indignation.

4 For Gaza shall be destroyed and Ascalon shall be a desert: they shall cast out Azotus at noonday and Accaron shall be rooted up.

5 Woe to you that inhabit the sea coast, O nation of reprobates! The word of the Lord upon you, O Chanaan, the land of the Philistines: and I will destroy thee, so that there shall not be an inhabitant.

6 And the sea coast shall be the resting place of shepherds and folds for cattle.

7 And it shall be the portion of him that shall remain of the house of Juda: there they shall feed. In the houses of Ascalon they shall rest in the evening, because the Lord their God will visit them and bring back their captivity.

8 I have heard the reproach of Moab and the blasphemies of the children of Ammon, with which they reproached my people and have magnified themselves upon their borders.

9 Therefore as I live, saith the Lord of hosts, the God of Israel, Moab shall be as Sodom and the children of Ammon as Gomorrha, the dryness of thorns and heaps of salt and a desert even for ever. The remnant of my people shall make a spoil of them and the residue of my nation shall possess them.

10 This shall befall them for their pride: because they have blasphemed

CHAP. 1. ¹ Amos, 5, 11. ² Jer. 30, 7; Joel, 2, 11; Amos, 5, 18. ³ Ezech. 7, 19. ⁴ Soph. 3, 8.

Ver. 5. *Melchom.* The idol of the Ammonites.
Ver. 10. *The Second.* A part of the city so called.
Ver. 11. *The Morter. Maktesh.* A valley in or near Jerusalem.—*The people of Chanaan.* So he calls the Jews, from their following the wicked ways of the Chanaanites.
Ver. 12. *Settled on their lees.* That is, the wealthy and such as live at their ease, resting upon their riches, like wine upon the lees.

and have been magnified against the people of the Lord of hosts.

11 The Lord shall be terrible upon them and shall consume all the gods of the earth: and they shall adore him, every man from his own place, all the islands of the Gentiles.

12 You, Ethiopians, also shall be slain with my sword.

13 And he will stretch out his hand upon the north and will destroy Assyria: and he will make the beautiful city a wilderness and as a place not passable and as a desert.

14 [1] And flocks shall lie down in the midst thereof, all the beasts of the nations: and the bittern and the urchin shall lodge in the threshold thereof. The voice of the singing *bird* in the window, the raven on the upper post: for I will consume her strength.

15 This is the glorious city that dwelt in security, that said in her heart: I am, and there is none beside me. How is she become a desert, a place for beasts to lie down in! Every one that passeth by her, shall hiss and wag his hand.

CHAPTER 3

A woe to Jerusalem for her sins. A prophecy of the conversion of the Gentiles, and of the poor of Israel. God shall be with them. The Jews shall be converted at last.

WOE to the provoking and redeemed city, the dove.

2 She hath not hearkened to the voice, neither hath she received discipline: she hath not trusted in the Lord, she drew not near to her God.

3 [1] Her princes *are* in the midst of her as roaring lions, her judges *are* evening wolves: they left nothing for the morning.

4 Her prophets *are* senseless men without faith, her priests have polluted the sanctuary: they have acted unjustly against the law.

5 The just Lord *is* in the midst thereof, he will not do iniquity: in the morning, in the morning, he will bring his judgment to light and it shall not be hid: but the wicked man hath not known shame.

6 I have destroyed the nations, and their towers are beaten down: I have made their ways desert so that there is none that passeth by. Their cities are desolate. There is not a man remaining nor any inhabitant.

7 I said: Surely thou wilt fear me, thou wilt receive correction: and her

dwelling shall not perish for all things wherein I have visited her. But they rose early and corrupted all their thoughts.

8 Wherefore expect me, saith the Lord, in the day of my resurrection that is to come; for my judgment *is* to assemble the Gentiles and to gather the kingdoms and to pour upon them my indignation, all my fierce anger: [2] For with the fire of my jealousy shall all the earth be devoured.

9 Because then I will restore to the people a chosen lip, that all may call upon the name of the Lord and may serve him with one shoulder.

10 From beyond the rivers of Ethiopia shall my suppliants, the children of my dispersed people, bring me an offering.

11 In that day thou shalt not be ashamed for all thy doings wherein thou hast transgressed against me: for then I will take away out of the midst of thee thy proud boasters and thou shalt no more be lifted up because of my holy mountain.

12 And I will leave in the midst of thee a poor and needy people: and they shall hope in the name of the Lord.

13 The remnant of Israel shall not do iniquity nor speak lies, nor shall a deceitful tongue be found in their mouth: for they shall feed and shall lie down, and there shall be none to make them afraid.

14 Give praise, O daughter of Sion: shout, O Israel: be glad, and rejoice with all thy heart, O daughter of Jerusalem.

15 The Lord hath taken away thy judgments, he hath turned away thy enemies. The king of Israel the Lord *is* in the midst of thee: thou shalt fear evil no more.

16 In that day it shall be said to Jerusalem: Fear not. To Sion: Let not thy hands be weakened.

17 The Lord thy God in the midst of thee *is* mighty: he will save, he will rejoice over thee with gladness, he will be silent in his love, he will be joyful over thee in praise.

18 The triflers that were departed from the law, I will gather together, because they were of thee: that thou mayest no more suffer reproach for them.

19 Behold I will cut off all that have afflicted thee at that time: and I will save her that halteth and will gather her that was cast out: and I will get them praise and a name in all the land where they had been put to confusion.

20 At that time, when I will bring

CHAP. 2. [1] Isai. 34, 11. CHAP. 3. [1] Ezech. 22, 27; Mich. 3, 11. [2] Soph. 1, 18.

CHAP. 2. Ver. 13. *The beautiful city.* Ninive, which was destroyed soon after this, namely, in the sixteenth year of the reign of Josias.

you and at the time that I will gather you: for I will give you a name and praise among all the people of the earth, when I shall have brought back your captivity before your eyes, saith the Lord.

THE PROPHECY OF
AGGEUS

AGGEUS *was one of those that returned from the captivity of Babylon in the first year of the reign of king Cyrus. He was sent by the Lord in the second year of the reign of king Darius, the son of Hystaspes, to exhort Zorobabel the prince of Juda and Jesus the high priest to the building of the temple, which they had begun but left off again through the opposition of the Samaritans. In consequence of this exhortation they proceeded in the building and finished the temple. And the prophet was commissioned by the Lord to assure them that this second temple should be more glorious than the former, because the Messiah should honour it with his presence: signifying withal how much the church of the New Testament should excel that of the Old Testament.*

CHAPTER 1

The people are reproved for neglecting to build the temple. They are encouraged to set about the work.

IN ¹ the second year of Darius the king, in the six month, in the first day of the month, the word of the Lord came by the hand of Aggeus the prophet, to Zorobabel, the son of Salathiel, governor of Juda, and to Jesus the son of Josedec, the high priest, saying:

2 Thus saith the Lord of hosts, saying: This people saith: The time is not yet come for building the house of the Lord.

3 And the word of the Lord came by the hand of Aggeus the prophet, saying:

4 Is it time for you to dwell in ceiled houses, and this house lie desolate?

5 And now thus saith the Lord of hosts: Set your hearts to consider your ways.

6 ² You have sowed much and brought in little: you have eaten but have not had enough: you have drunk but have not been filled with drink: you have clothed yourselves but have not been warmed: and he that hath earned wages put them into a bag with holes.

7 Thus saith the Lord of hosts: Set your hearts upon your ways.

8 Go up to the mountains, bring timber and build the house: and it shall be acceptable to me and I shall be glorified saith the Lord.

9 You have looked for more and behold it became less, and you brought it home and I blowed it away. Why, saith the Lord of hosts? Because my house is desolate and you make haste every man to his own house.

10 Therefore the heavens over you were stayed from giving dew and the earth was hindered from yielding her fruits.

11 And I called for a drought upon the land and upon the mountains and upon the corn and upon the wine and upon the oil and upon all that the ground bringeth forth and upon men and upon beasts and upon all the labour of the hands.

12 Then Zorobabel the son of Salathiel and Jesus the son of Josedec, the high priest, and all the remnant of the people hearkened to the voice of the Lord their God and to the words of Aggeus the prophet, as the Lord their God sent him to them: and the people feared before the Lord.

13 And Aggeus, the messenger of the Lord, *as* one of the messengers of the Lord, spoke, saying to the people: I am with you, saith the Lord.

14 And the Lord stirred up the spirit of Zorobabel the son of Salathiel governor of Juda and the spirit of Jesus the son of Josedec, the high priest, and the spirit of all the rest of the people: and they went in and did the work in the house of the Lord of hosts their God.

CHAPTER 2

Christ by his coming shall make the latter temple more glorious than the former. The blessing of God shall reward their labour in building. God's promise to Zorobabel.

CHAP. 1. ¹ 1 Esd. 5, 1. ² Deut. 28, 38; Mich. 6, 15.

IN the four and twentieth day of the month, in the sixth month, in the second year of Darius the king, *they* began.

2 *And* in the seventh month, the word of the Lord came by the hand of Aggeus the prophet, saying:

3 Speak to Zorobabel the son of Salathiel the governor of Juda and to Jesus the son of Josedec, the high priest, and to the rest of the people, saying:

4 Who is left among you, that saw this house in its first glory? And how do you see it now? Is it not *in comparison to that* as nothing in your eyes?

5 Yet now take courage, O Zorobabel, saith the Lord, and take courage, O Jesus the son of Josedec, the high priest, and take courage all ye people of the land, saith the Lord of hosts: and perform (for I am with you, saith the Lord of hosts)

6 The word that I covenanted with you when you came out of the land of Egypt. And my spirit shall be in the midst of you: fear not.

7 For thus saith the Lord of hosts: ¹ Yet one little while, and I will move the heaven and the earth and the sea and the dry land.

8 And I will move all nations: AND THE DESIRED OF ALL NATIONS SHALL COME: and I will fill this house with glory, saith the Lord of hosts.

9 The silver is mine and the gold is mine, saith the Lord of hosts.

10 Great shall be the glory of this last house more than of the first, saith the Lord of hosts: and in this place I will give peace, saith the Lord of hosts.

11 In the four and twentieth day of the ninth month, in the second year of Darius the king, the word of the Lord came to Aggeus the prophet, saying:

12 Thus saith the Lord of hosts: Ask the priests the law, saying:

CHAP. 2. ¹ Heb. 12, 26. ² Amos, 4, 9. ³ Ecclus. 49, 13.

CHAP. 2. Ver. 14. *By occasion of a soul.* That is, by having touched the dead; in which case, according to the prescription of the law (Num. 19, 13, 22), a person not only became unclean himself but made every thing that he touched unclean. The prophet applies all this to the people, whose souls remained unclean by neglecting the temple of God, and therefore were not sanctified by the flesh they offered in sacrifice: but rather defiled their sacrifices by approaching to them in the state of uncleanness.

Ver. 24. *O Zorobabel.* This promise principally relates to Christ, who was of the seed of Zorobabel.

13 If a man carry sanctified flesh in the skirt of his garment and touch with his skirt bread or pottage or wine or oil or any meat: shall it be sanctified? And the priests answered and said: No.

14 And Aggeus said: If one that is unclean by occasion of a soul touch any of all these things, shall it be defiled? And the priests answered and said: It shall be defiled.

15 And Aggeus answered and said: So *is* this people and so *is* this nation before my face, saith the Lord, and so *is* all the work of their hands: and all that they have offered there shall be defiled.

16 And now consider in your hearts, from this day and upward, before there was a stone laid upon a stone in the temple of the Lord.

17 When you went to a heap of twenty bushels and they became ten: and when you went into the press to press out fifty vessels and they became twenty.

18 ² I struck you with a blasting wind and all the works of your hand with the mildew and with hail: yet there was none among you that returned to me, saith the Lord.

19 Set your hearts from this day and henceforward, from the four and twentieth day of the ninth month, from the day that the foundations of the temple of the Lord were laid: *and* lay it up in your hearts.

20 Is the seed as yet sprung up? Or hath the vine and the fig tree and the pomegranate and the olive tree as yet flourished? From this day, I will bless *you.*

21 And the word of the Lord came a second time to Aggeus in the four and twentieth day of the month, saying:

22 Speak to Zorobabel, the governor of Juda, saying: I will move both heaven and earth.

23 And I will overthrow the throne of kingdoms and will destroy the strength of the kingdom of the Gentiles: and I will overthrow the chariot and him that rideth therein. And the horses and their riders shall come down, every one by the sword of his brother.

24 In that day, saith the Lord of hosts, I will take thee, ³ O Zorobabel the son of Salathiel, my servant, saith the Lord, and will make thee as a signet: for I have chosen thee, saith the Lord of hosts.

THE PROPHECY OF
ZACHARIAS

ZACHARIAS *began to prophesy in the same year as Aggeus, and upon the same occasion. His prophecy is full of mysterious figures and promises of blessings, partly relating to the synagogue, and partly to the church of Christ.*

CHAPTER 1

The prophet exhorts the people to return to God and declares his visions, by which he puts them in hopes of better times.

IN the eighth month, in the second year of king Darius, the word of the Lord came to Zacharias the son of Barachias, the son of Addo, the prophet, saying:

2 The Lord hath been exceeding angry with your fathers.

3 And thou shalt say to them: Thus saith the Lord of hosts: ¹ Turn ye to me, saith the Lord of hosts, and I will turn to you, saith the Lord of hosts.

4 Be not as your fathers, to whom the former prophets have cried, saying: Thus saith the Lord of hosts: Turn ye from your evil ways and from your wicked thoughts: but they did not give ear, neither did they hearken to me, saith the Lord.

5 Your fathers, where are they? And the prophets, shall they live always?

6 But yet my words and my ordinances, which I gave in charge to my servants the prophets, did they not take hold of your fathers? And they returned and said: As the Lord of hosts thought to do to us according to our ways and according to our devices, so he hath done to us.

7 In the four and twentieth day of the eleventh month which is called Sabbath, in the second year of Darius, the word of the Lord came to Zacharias the son of Barachias, the son of Addo, the prophet, saying:

8 I saw by night, and behold a man riding upon a red horse: and he stood among the myrtle trees that were in the bottom: and behind him were horses, red, speckled, and white.

9 And I said: What are these, my lord? And the angel that spoke in me said to me: I will shew thee what these are.

10 And the man that stood among the myrtle trees answered and said: These are they whom the Lord hath sent to walk through the earth.

11 And they answered the angel of the Lord that stood among the myrtle trees, and said: We have walked through the earth, and behold all the earth is inhabited and is at rest.

12 And the angel of the Lord answered and said: O Lord of hosts, how long wilt thou not have mercy on Jerusalem and on the cities of Juda, with which thou hast been angry? This is now the seventieth year.

13 And the Lord answered the angel that spoke in me good words, comforable words.

14 And the angel that spoke in me said to me: Cry thou, saying: Thus saith the Lord of hosts: ² I am zealous for Jerusalem and Sion with a great zeal.

15 And I am angry with a great anger with the wealthy nations: for I was angry a little, but they helped forward the evil.

16 Therefore thus saith the Lord: I will return to Jerusalem in mercies. My house shall be built in it, saith the Lord of hosts: and the building line shall be stretched forth upon Jerusalem.

17 Cry yet, saying: Thus saith the Lord of hosts: My cities shall yet flow with good things: and the Lord will yet comfort Sion and will yet choose Jerusalem.

18 And I lifted up my eyes, and saw: and behold four horns.

CHAP. I. ¹Isai. 21, 12; 31, 6; 45, 22; Jer. 3, 12; Ezech. 18, 30; 20, 7; 33, 11; Osee, 14, 2; Joel, 2, 12; Mal. 3, 7. ²Zach. 8, 2.

CHAP. 1. Ver. 8. *A man.* An angel in the shape of a man. It was probably St. Michael, the guardian angel of the church of God.

Ver. 10. *These are they.* The guardian angels of provinces and nations.

Ver. 12. *The seventieth year.* Namely, from the beginning of the siege of Jerusalem, in the ninth year of king Sedecias, to the second year of king Darius. These seventy years of the desolation of Jerusalem and the cities of Juda are different from the seventy years of captivity foretold by Jeremias; which began in the fourth year of Joakim and ended in the first year of king Cyrus.

Ver. 18, 20. *Four horns—four smiths.* The four horns represent the empires or kingdoms that persecute and oppress the people of God: the *four smiths* or *carpenters* (for *faber* may signify either) represent those whom God makes his instruments in bringing to nothing the power of persecutors.

19 And I said to the angel that spoke to me: What are these? And he said to me: These are the horns that have scattered Juda and Israel and Jerusalem.

20 And the Lord shewed me four smiths.

21 And I said: What come these to do? And he spoke, saying: These are the horns which have scattered Juda every man apart, and none of them lifted up his head. And these are come to fray them, to cast down the horns of the nations that have lifted up the horn upon the land of Juda to scatter it.

CHAPTER 2

Under the name of Jerusalem, he proph-esieth the progress of the church of Christ, by the conversion of some Jews and many Gentiles.

AND I lifted up my eyes and saw: and behold a man with a measuring line in his hand.

2 And I said: Whither goest thou? And he said to me: To measure Jerusalem and to see how great is the breadth thereof and how great the length thereof.

3 And behold the angel that spoke in me went forth: and another angel went out to meet him.

4 And he said to him: Run, speak to this young man, saying: Jerusalem shall be inhabited without walls, by reason of the multitude of men and of the beasts in the midst thereof.

5 And I will be to it, saith the Lord, a wall of fire round about: and I will be in glory in the midst thereof.

6 O, O flee ye out of the land of the north, saith the Lord: for I have scattered you into the four winds of heaven, saith the Lord.

7 O Sion, flee, thou that dwellest with the daughter of Babylon.

8 For thus saith the Lord of hosts: After the glory, he hath sent me to the nations that have robbed you: for he

that toucheth you toucheth the apple of my eye.

9 For behold I lift up my hand upon them, and they shall be a prey to those that served them: and you shall know that the Lord of hosts sent me.

10 Sing praise and rejoice, O daughter of Sion: for behold I come and I will dwell in the midst of thee: saith the Lord.

11 And many nations shall be joined to the Lord in that day: and they shall be my people: and I will dwell in the midst of thee. And thou shalt know that the Lord of hosts hath sent me to thee.

12 And the Lord shall possess Juda his portion in the sanctified land: and he shall yet choose Jerusalem.

13 Let all flesh be silent at the presence of the Lord: for he is risen up out of his holy habitation.

CHAPTER 3

In a vision Satan appeareth accusing the high priest. He is cleansed from his sins. Christ is promised and great fruit from his passion.

AND the Lord shewed me Jesus the high priest standing before the angel of the Lord: and Satan stood on his right hand to be his adversary.

2 And the Lord said to Satan: The Lord rebuke thee, O Satan, and the Lord that chose Jerusalem rebuke thee. Is not this a brand plucked out of the fire?

3 And Jesus was clothed with filthy garments: and he stood before the face of the angel.

4 Who answered and said to them that stood before him, saying: Take away the filthy garments from him. And he said to him: Behold I have taken away thy iniquity and have clothed thee with change of garments.

5 And he said: Put a clean mitre upon his head. And they put a clean mitre upon his head and clothed him with garments: and the angel of the Lord stood.

6 And the angel of the Lord protested to Jesus, saying:

7 Thus saith the Lord of hosts: If thou wilt walk in my ways and keep my charge, thou also shalt judge my house and shalt keep my courts. And I will give thee some of them that are now present here to walk *with thee.*

8 Hear, O Jesus, thou high priest, thou and thy friends that dwell before thee, for they are portending men: for behold, [1] I WILL BRING MY SERVANT THE ORIENT.

9 For behold the stone that I have laid before Jesus: upon one stone there

CHAP. 3. [1] Luke, 1, 78.

CHAP. 2. Ver. 4. *Jerusalem shall be inhabited without walls.* This must be understood of the spiritual Jerusalem, the church of Christ.

CHAP. 3. Ver. 1. *Jesus,* or Josue, the son of Josedec, the high priest of that time.

Ver. 3. *With filthy garments.* Negligences and sins.

Ver. 7. *I will give thee.* Angels to attend and assist thee.

Ver. 8. *Portending men.* That is, men, who by words and actions are so foreshew things that are to come.—*My servant the Orient.* Christ, who according to his humanity is the servant of God, is called *the Orient* from his rising like the sun in the east to enlighten the world.

Ver. 9. *The stone.* Another emblem of Christ, the rock, foundation, and corner stone of his church.—*Seven eyes.* The manifold providence of Christ over his church, or the seven gifts of the Spirit of God.—*One day.* The day of the

are seven eyes. Behold I will grave the graving thereof, saith the Lord of hosts: and I will take away the iniquity of that land in one day.

10 In that day, saith the Lord of hosts, every man shall call his friend under the vine and under the fig tree.

CHAPTER 4

The vision of the golden candlestick and seven lamps and of the two olive trees. Zorobabel shall finish the building of the temple.

AND the angel that spoke in me came again: and he waked me, as a man that is wakened out of his sleep.

2 And he said to me: What seest thou? And I said: I have looked, and behold a candlestick all of gold, and its lamp upon the top of it: and the seven lights thereof upon it: and seven funnels for the lights that were upon the top thereof.

3 And two olive trees over it: one upon the right side of the lamp and the other upon the left side thereof.

4 And I answered and said to the angel that spoke in me, saying: What are these things, my lord?

5 And the angel that spoke in me answered and said to me: Knowest thou not what these things are? And I said: No, my lord.

6 And he answered and spoke to me, saying: This is the word of the Lord to Zorobabel, saying: Not with an army nor by might, but by my spirit, saith the Lord of hosts.

7 Who art thou, O great mountain, before Zorobabel? Thou shalt become a plain: and he shall bring out the chief stone and shall give equal grace to the grace thereof.

8 And the word of the Lord came to me, saying:

9 The hands of Zorobabel have laid the foundations of this house, and his hands shall finish it: and you shall know that the Lord of hosts hath sent me to you.

10 For who hath despised little days? And they shall rejoice and shall see the tin plummet in the hand of Zorobabel. These are the seven eyes of the Lord that run to and fro through the whole earth.

11 And I answered and said to him: What are these two olive trees upon the right side of the candlestick and upon the left side thereof?

12 And I answered again and said to him: What are the two olive branches that are by the two golden beaks, in which are the funnels of gold?

13 And he spoke to me, saying: Knowest thou not what these are? And I said: No, my lord.

14 And he said: These are two sons of oil who stand before the Lord of the whole earth.

CHAPTER 5

The vision of the flying volume and of the woman in the vessel.

AND I turned and lifted up my eyes: and I saw, and behold a volume flying.

2 And he said to me: What seest thou? And I said: I see a volume flying. The length thereof is twenty cubits, and the breadth thereof ten cubits.

3 And he said to me: This is the curse that goeth forth over the face of the earth. For every thief shall be judged as is there written: and every one that sweareth in like manner shall be judged by it.

4 I will bring it forth, saith the Lord of hosts: and it shall come to the house of the thief and to the house of him that sweareth falsely by my name: and it shall remain in the midst of his house and shall consume it with the timber thereof and the stones thereof.

5 And the angel went forth that spoke in me. And he said to me: Lift up thy eyes and see what this is that goeth forth.

6 And I said: What is it? And he said: This is a vessel going forth. And he said: This is their eye in all the earth.

passion of Christ, the source of all our good: when this precious stone shall be graved, that is, cut and pierced, with whips, thorns, nails, and spear.

CHAP. 4. Ver. 2. *A candlestick.* The temple of God that was then in building and in a more sublime sense the Church of Christ.

Ver. 6. *To Zorobabel.* This vision was in favour of Zorobabel, to assure him of success in the building of the temple which he had begun, signified by the candlestick; the lamp of which, without any other industry, was supplied with oil, dropping from the two olive trees and distributed by the seven funnels or pipes, to maintain the seven lights.

Ver. 7. *Great mountain.* So he calls the opposition made by the enemies of God's people; which nevertheless, without any army or might on their side, was quashed by divine providence.— *Shall give equal grace.* Shall add grace to grace, or beauty to beauty.

Ver. 10. *Little days.* That is, these small and feeble beginnings of the temple of God.— *The tin plummet.* Literally, *the stone of tin.* He means the builder's plummet which Zorobabel shall hold in his hand for the finishing the building.— *The seven eyes.* The providence of God, that oversees and orders all things.

Ver. 14. *Two sons of oil.* That is, the two anointed ones of the Lord, Jesus the high priest and Zorobabel the prince.

CHAP. 5. Ver. 1. *A volume.* That is, a parchment, according to the form of the ancient books, which, from being rolled up, were called *volumes.*

Ver. 6. *This is their eye.* This is what they fix their *eye* upon: or this is a resemblance and figure of them, that is, of sinners.

7 And behold a talent of lead was carried: and behold a woman sitting in the midst of the vessel.

8 And he said: This is wickedness. And he cast her into the midst of the vessel and cast the weight of lead upon the mouth thereof.

9 And I lifted up my eyes and looked: and behold there came out two women, and wind was in their wings, and they had wings like the wings of a kite: and they lifted up the vessel between the earth and the heaven.

10 And I said to the angel that spoke in me: Whither do these carry the vessel?

11 And he said to me: That a house may be built for it in the land of Sennaar and that it may be established and set there upon its own basis.

CHAPTER 6

The vision of the four chariots. Crowns are ordered for Jesus the high priest, as a type of Christ.

AND I turned and lifted up my eyes and saw: and behold four chariots came out from the midst of two mountains: and the mountains *were* mountains of brass.

2 In the first chariot were red horses: and in the second chariot black horses.

3 And in the third chariot white horses: and in the fourth chariot grisled horses, and strong ones.

4 And I answered and said to the angel that spoke in me: What are these, my lord?

5 And the angel answered and said to me: These are the four winds of the heaven which go forth to stand before the Lord of all the earth.

CHAP. 6. ¹ Luke, 1, 78.
Ver. 11. *The land of Sennaar.* Where *Babel* or *Babylon* was built (Gen. 11), where note, that *Babylon* in holy writ is often taken for the city of the devil: that is, for the whole congregation of the wicked: as *Jerusalem* is taken for the city and people of God.
CHAP. 6. Ver. 1. *Four chariots.* The four great empires of the Chaldeans, Persians, Grecians, and Romans. Or perhaps by the fourth chariot are represented the kings of Egypt and of Asia, the descendants of Ptolomeus and Seleucus.
Ver. 6. *The land of the north.* So *Babylon* is called, because it lay to the north in respect of Jerusalem. The black horses, that is, the Medes and Persians, and after them Alexander and his Greeks, signified by the white horses, went thither because they, conquering Babylon, executed upon it the judgments of God, which is signified (ver. 8) by the expression of *quieting his spirit.—The land of the south.* Egypt, which lay to the south of Jerusalem and was occupied first by Ptolomeus and then by the Romans.
Ver. 13. *Between them both.* That is, he shall unite in himself the two offices or dignities of king and priest.
CHAP. 7. Ver. 3. *The fifth month.* They fasted on the tenth day of the fifth month; because on that day the temple was burnt. Therefore they inquire whether they are to continue that fast, after the temple is rebuilt. See this query answered in the 10th verse of the following chapter.

6 That in which were the black horses went forth into the land of the north: and the white went forth after them: and the grisled went forth to the land of the south.

7 And they that were most strong went out and sought to go and to run to and fro through all the earth. And he said: Go, walk throughout the earth. And they walked throughout the earth.

8 And he called me and spoke to me, saying: Behold they that go forth into the land of the north have quieted my spirit in the land of the north.

9 And the word of the Lord came to me, saying:

10 Take of them of the captivity, of Holdai and of Tobias and of Idaias. Thou shalt come in that day and shalt go into the house of Josias, the son of Sophonias, who came out of Babylon.

11 And thou shalt take gold and silver and shalt make crowns: and thou shalt set them on the head of Jesus the son of Josedec, the high priest.

12 And thou shalt speak to him, saying: Thus saith the Lord of hosts, saying: ¹ Behold a man, the Orient is his name. And under him shall he spring up and shall build a temple to the Lord.

13 Yea, he shall build a temple to the Lord: and he shall bear the glory and shall sit and rule upon his throne: and he shall be a priest upon his throne: and the counsel of peace shall be between them both.

14 And the crowns shall be to Helem and Tobias and Idaias and to Hem, the son of Sophonias, a memorial in the temple of the Lord.

15 And they that are far off shall come and shall build in the temple of the Lord: and you shall know that the Lord of hosts sent me to you. But this shall come to pass, if hearing you will hear the voice of the Lord your God.

CHAPTER 7

The people inquire concerning fasting. They are admonished to fast from sin.

AND it came to pass in the fourth year of king Darius, that the word of the Lord came to Zacharias, in the fourth day of the ninth month, which is Casleu.

2 When Sarasar and Rogommelech and the men that were with him sent to the house of God, to entreat the face of the Lord:

3 To speak to the priests of the house of the Lord of hosts and to the prophets, saying: Must I weep in the fifth month or must I sanctify myself as I have now done for many years?

4 And the word of the Lord of hosts came to me, saying:

5 Speak to all the people of the land and to the priests, saying: ¹ When you fasted and mourned in the fifth and the seventh month for these seventy years, did you keep a fast unto me?

6 And when you did eat and drink, did you not eat for yourselves and drink for yourselves?

7 Are not these the words which the Lord spoke by the hand of the former prophets, when Jerusalem as yet was inhabited and was wealthy, both itself and the cities round about it, and there were inhabitants towards the south and in the plain?

8 And the word of the Lord came to Zacharias, saying:

9 Thus saith the Lord of hosts, saying: ² Judge ye true judgment and shew ye mercy and compassion every man to his brother.

10 ³ And oppress not the widow and the fatherless and the stranger and the poor: and let not a man devise evil in his heart against his brother.

11 But they would not hearken: and they turned away the shoulder to depart: and they stopped their ears, not to hear.

12 And they made their heart as the adamant stone, lest they should hear the law and the words which the Lord of hosts sent in his spirit by the hand of the former prophets: so a great indignation came from the Lord of hosts.

13 And it came to pass as he spoke: and they heard not. So shall they cry: and I will not hear, saith the Lord of hosts.

14 And I dispersed them throughout all kingdoms which they know not: and the land was left desolate behind them, so that no man passed through or returned. And they changed the delightful land into a wilderness.

CHAPTER 8

Joyful promises to Jerusalem, fully verified in the church of Christ.

AND the word of the Lord of hosts came to me, saying:

2 Thus saith the Lord of hosts: I have been jealous for Sion with a great jealousy, and with a great indignation have I been jealous for her.

3 Thus saith the Lord of hosts: I am returned to Sion: and I will dwell in the midst of Jerusalem. And Jerusalem shall be called: The City of Truth and the Mountain of the Lord of Hosts, The Sanctified Mountain.

4 Thus saith the Lord of hosts: There shall yet old men and old women dwell in the streets of Jerusalem, and

every man with his staff in his hand through multitude of days.

5 And the streets of the city shall be full of boys and girls, playing in the streets thereof.

6 Thus saith the Lord of hosts: If it seem hard in the eyes of the remnant of this people in those days, shall it be hard in my eyes, saith the Lord of hosts?

7 Thus saith the Lord of hosts: Behold I will save my people from the land of the east and from the land of the going down of the sun.

8 And I will bring them: and they shall dwell in the midst of Jerusalem: and they shall be my people. And I will be their God in truth and in justice.

9 Thus saith the Lord of hosts: Let your hands be strengthened, you that hear in these days these words by the mouth of the prophets, in the day that the house of the Lord of hosts was founded, that the temple might be built.

10 For before those days there was no hire for men, neither was there hire for beasts, neither was there peace to him that came in nor to him that went out, because of the tribulation: and I let all men go every one against his neighbour.

11 But now I will not deal with the remnant of this people according to the former days, saith the Lord of hosts.

12 But there shall be the seed of peace: the vine shall yield her fruit and the earth shall give her increase and the heavens shall give their dew. And I will cause the remnant of this people to possess all these things.

13 And it shall come to pass that as you were a curse among the Gentiles, O house of Juda and house of Israel, so will I save you: and you shall be a blessing. Fear not: let your hands be strengthened.

14 For thus saith the Lord of hosts: As I purposed to afflict you, when your fathers had provoked me to wrath, saith the Lord,

15 And I had no mercy: so turning again I have thought in these days to do good to the house of Juda and Jerusalem. Fear not.

16 These then are the things which you shall do: ¹ Speak ye truth every one to his neighbour: judge ye truth and judgment of peace in your gates.

17 And let none of you imagine evil in your hearts against his friend: and love not a false oath. For all these are the things that I hate, saith the Lord.

18 And the word of the Lord of hosts came to me, saying:

CHAP. 7. ¹ Isai. 58, 5. ² Mich. 6, 8; Matt. 23, 23. ³ Exod. 22, 22; Isai. 1, 23; Jer. 5, 28. CHAP. 8. ¹ Eph. 4, 25.

19 Thus saith the Lord of hosts: The fast of the fourth month and the fast of the fifth and the fast of the seventh and the fast of the tenth shall be to the house of Juda joy and gladness and great solemnities: only love ye truth and peace.

20 Thus saith the Lord of hosts: Until people come and dwell in many cities,

21 And the inhabitants go one to another, saying: Let us go and entreat the face of the Lord and let us seek the Lord of hosts: I also will go.

22 And many peoples and strong nations shall come to seek the Lord of hosts in Jerusalem and to entreat the face of the Lord.

23 Thus saith the Lord of hosts: In those days, wherein ten men of all languages of the Gentiles shall take hold and shall hold fast the skirt of one that is a Jew, saying: We will go with you, for we have heard that God is with you.

CHAPTER 9

God will defend his church and bring over even her enemies to the faith. The meek coming of Christ, to bring peace, to deliver the captives by his blood, and to give us all good things.

THE burden of the word of the Lord in the land of Hadrach and of Damascus, the rest thereof: for the eye of man and of all the tribes of Israel is the Lord's.

2 Emath also in the borders thereof and Tyre and Sidon: for they have taken to themselves to be exceeding wise.

3 And Tyre hath built herself a strong hold and heaped together silver

---

CHAP. 9. [1] Isai. 62, 11; Matt. 21, 5.

CHAP. 8. Ver. 19. *The fast of the fourth month.* They fasted on the ninth day of the *fourth* month, because on that day Nabuchodonosor took Jerusalem (Jer. 52, 6). On the tenth day of the *fifth* month, because on that day the temple was burnt (Jer. 52, 12). On the third day of the *seventh* month, for the murder of Godolias (Jer. 41, 2). And on the tenth day of the *tenth* month, because on that day the Chaldeans began to besiege Jerusalem (4 Kings, 25, 1). All these fasts, if they will be obedient for the future, shall be changed, as is here promised, into joyful solemnities.

Ver. 23. *Ten men.* Many of the Gentiles became proselytes to the Jewish religion before Christ: but many more were converted to Christ by the apostles and other preachers of the Jewish nation.

CHAP. 9. Ver. 1. *Hadrach.* Syria.

Ver. 7. *His blood.* It is spoken of the Philistines and particularly of Azotus (where the temple of Dagon was) and *contains a prophecy of the* conversion of that people from their bloody sacrifices and abominations to the worship of the true God.

Ver. 8. *That serve me in war.* The Machabees.

Ver. 13. *Thy sons, O Sion.* The apostles, who, in the spiritual way, conquered the Greeks, and subdued them to Christ.

Ver. 16. *Holy stones.* The apostles, who shall be as pillars and monuments in the church.

---

as earth, and gold as the mire of the streets.

4 Behold the Lord shall possess her and shall strike her strength in the sea: and she shall be devoured with fire.

5 Ascalon shall see and shall fear: and Gaza, and shall be very sorrowful: and Accaron, because her hope is confounded. And the king shall perish from Gaza: and Ascalon shall not be inhabited.

6 And the divider shall sit in Azotus: and I will destroy the pride of the Philistines.

7 And I will take away his blood out of his mouth and his abominations from between his teeth: and even he shall be left to our God. And he shall be as a governor in Juda, and Accaron as a Jebusite.

8 And I will encompass my house with them that serve me in war, going and returning: and the oppressor shall no more pass through them. For now I have seen with my eyes.

9 [1] Rejoice greatly, O daughter of Sion, shout for joy, O daughter of Jerusalem: BEHOLD THY KING will come to thee, the just and saviour. He is poor and riding upon an ass and upon a colt, the foal of an ass.

10 And I will destroy the chariot out of Ephraim and the horse out of Jerusalem: and the bow for war shall be broken. And he shall speak peace to the Gentiles: and his power shall be from sea to sea, and from the rivers even to the end of the earth.

11 Thou also, by the blood of thy testament, hast sent forth thy prisoners out of the pit wherein is no water.

12 Return to the strong hold, ye prisoners of hope: I will render thee double, as I declare to-day.

13 Because I have bent Juda for me as a bow, I have filled Ephraim: and I will raise up thy sons, O Sion, above thy sons, O Greece: and I will make thee as the sword of the mighty.

14 And the Lord God shall be seen over them and his dart shall go forth as lightning: and the Lord God will sound the trumpet and go in the whirlwind of the south.

15 The Lord of hosts will protect them: and they shall devour and subdue with the stones of the sling. And drinking they shall be inebriated as it were with wine: and they shall be filled as bowls and as the horns of the altar.

16 And the Lord their God will save them in that day, as the flock of his people: for holy stones shall be lifted up over his land.

17 For what is the good thing of him and what is his beautiful thing, but the corn of the elect and wine springing forth virgins?

CHAPTER 10

God is to be sought to, and not idols. The victories of his church, which shall arise originally from the Jewish nation.

ASK ye of the Lord rain in the latter season: and the Lord will make snows and will give them showers of rain, to every one grass in the field.

2 For the idols have spoken what was unprofitable and the diviners have seen a lie and the dreamers have spoken vanity: they comforted in vain. Therefore they were led away as a flock: they shall be afflicted, because they have no shepherd.

3 My wrath is kindled against the shepherds and I will visit upon the buck-goats: for the Lord of hosts hath visited his flock, the house of Juda, and hath made them as the horse of his glory in the battle.

4 Out of him shall come forth the corner, out of him the pin, out of him the bow of battle, out of him every exacter together.

5 And they shall be as mighty men, treading under foot the mire of the ways in battle. And they shall fight, because the Lord is with them: and the riders of horses shall be confounded.

6 And I will strengthen the house of Juda and save the house of Joseph: and I will bring them back again, because I will have mercy on them. And they shall be as they were when I had cast them off: for I am the Lord their God and will hear them.

7 And they shall be as the valiant men of Ephraim: and their heart shall rejoice as through wine: and their children shall see and shall rejoice: and their heart shall be joyful in the Lord.

8 I will whistle for them and I will gather them together, because I have redeemed them: and I will multiply them as they were multiplied before.

9 And I will sow them among peoples: and from afar they shall remember me: and they shall live with their children and shall return.

10 And I will bring them back out of the land of Egypt and will gather them from among the Assyrians and will bring them to the land of Galaad and Libanus: and place shall not be found for them.

11 And he shall pass over the strait of the sea and shall strike the waves in the sea: and all the depths of the river shall be confounded ¹and the

pride of Assyria shall be humbled and the sceptre of Egypt shall depart.

12 I will strengthen them in the Lord: and they shall walk in his name, saith the Lord.

CHAPTER 11

The destruction of Jerusalem and the temple. God's dealings with the Jews, and their reprobation.

OPEN thy gates, O Libanus, and let fire devour thy cedars.

2 Howl, thou fir tree, for the cedar is fallen, for the mighty are laid waste: howl, ye oaks of Basan, because the fenced forest is cut down.

3 The voice of the howling of the shepherds, because their glory is laid waste: the voice of the roaring of the lions, because the pride of the Jordan is spoiled.

4 Thus saith the Lord my God: Feed the flock of the slaughter,

5 Which they that possessed slew and repented not, and they sold them, saying: Blessed be the Lord, we are become rich. And their shepherds spared them not.

6 And I will no more spare the inhabitants of the land, saith the Lord: behold I will deliver the men, every one into his neighbour's hand and into the hand of his king. And they shall destroy the land: and I will not deliver it out of their hand.

7 And I will feed the flock of slaughter for this, O ye poor of the flock. And I took unto me two rods. One I called Beauty, and the other I called a Cord: and I fed the flock.

8 And I cut off three shepherds in one month, and my soul was straitened

CHAP. 10. ¹ Apoc. 16, 12; Isai. 11, 15.

Ver. 17. *The corn.* His most excellent gift is the blessed Eucharist, called here *The corn,* that is, the bread *of the elect;* and the *wine springing forth virgins,* that is, *making virgins* to bud or spring forth, as it were, like flowers among thorns; because it has a wonderful efficacy to give and preserve purity.

CHAP. 11. Ver. 1. *O Libanus.* So Jerusalem, and more particularly the temple, is called by the prophets, from its height and from its being built of the cedars of Libanus.—*Thy cedars.* Thy princes and chief men.

Ver. 6. *Every one into his neighbour's hand.* This alludes to the last siege of Jerusalem in which the different factions of the Jews destroyed one another and they that remained fell into the hands of their king, that is, of the Roman emperor, of whom they had said (John 19, 25) *We have no king but Cæsar.*

Ver. 7. *Two rods.* Or shepherd's staves, meaning the different ways of God's dealing with his people; the one, by sweet means, called the rod of *Beauty;* the other, by bands and punishments, called the *Cord.* And where both these rods are made of no use or effect by the obstinacy of sinners, the rods are broken, and such sinners are given up to a reprobate sense, as the Jews were.

Ver. 8. *Three shepherds in one month.* That is, in a very short time. By these *three shepherds* probably are meant the latter princes and high priests of the Jews, whose reign was short.

in their regard: for their soul also varied in my regard.

9 And I said: I will not feed you. That which dieth, let it die: and that which is cut off, let it be cut off: and let the rest devour every one the flesh of his neighbour.

10 And I took my rod that was called Beauty: and I cut it asunder to make void my covenant which I had made with all people.

11 And it was made void in that day: and so the poor of the flock that keep for me understood that it is the word of the Lord.

12 And I said to them: If it be good in your eyes, bring hither my wages: and if not, be quiet. ¹ And they weighed for my wages thirty pieces of silver.

13 And the Lord said to me: Cast it to the statuary, a handsome price, that I was prized at by them. And I took the thirty pieces of silver and I cast them into the house of the Lord, to the statuary.

14 And I cut off my second rod that was called a Cord, that I might break the brotherhood between Juda and Israel.

15 And the Lord said to me: Take to thee yet the instruments of a foolish shepherd.

16 For behold I will raise up a shepherd in the land, who shall not visit what is forsaken nor seek what is scattered nor heal what is broken nor nourish that which standeth: and he shall eat the flesh of the fat ones and break their hoofs.

17 O shepherd and idol, that forsaketh the flock: the sword upon his arm and upon his right eye. His arm shall quite wither away: and his right eye shall be utterly darkened.

CHAPTER 12

God shall protect his church against her persecutors. The mourning of Jerusalem.

THE burden of the word of the Lord upon Israel. Thus saith the Lord, who stretched forth the heavens and layeth the foundations of the earth and formeth the spirit of man in him.

CHAP. 11. ¹ Matt. 27, 9. CHAP. 12. ¹ John, 19, 37. ² 2 Par. 35, 22.

Ver. 13. *The statuary.* The Hebrew word signifies also *a potter.*

Ver. 15. *A foolish shepherd.* This was to represent the foolish (that is, the wicked) princes and priests that should rule the people, before their utter desolation.

CHAP. 12. Ver. 2. *A lintel of surfeiting.* That is, a door into which they shall seek to enter, to glut themselves with blood: but they shall stumble and fall like men stupefied with wine. It seems to allude to the times of Antiochus and to the victories of the Machabees.

Ver. 11. *Adadremmon.* A place near Mageddon, where the good king Josias was slain and much lamented by his people.

2 Behold I will make Jerusalem a lintel of surfeiting to all the people round about: and Juda also shall be in the siege against Jerusalem.

3 And it shall come to pass in that day that I will make Jerusalem a burdensome stone to all people. All that shall lift it up shall be rent and torn: and all the kingdoms of the earth shall be gathered together against her.

4 In that day, saith the Lord, I will strike every horse with astonishment and his rider with madness: and I will open my eyes upon the house of Juda and will strike every horse of the nations with blindness.

5 And the governors of Juda shall say in their heart: Let the inhabitants of Jerusalem be strengthened for me in the Lord of hosts, their God.

6 In that day I will make the governors of Juda like a furnace of fire amongst wood and as a firebrand amongst hay: and they shall devour all the people round about, to the right hand and to the left. And Jerusalem shall be inhabited again in her own place in Jerusalem.

7 And the Lord shall save the tabernacles of Juda, as in the beginning: that the house of David and the glory of the inhabitants of Jerusalem may not boast and magnify themselves against Juda.

8 In that day shall the Lord protect the inhabitants of Jerusalem: and he that hath offended among them in that day shall be as David: and the house of David, as that of God, as an angel of the Lord in their sight.

9 And it shall come to pass in that day that I will seek to destroy all the nations that come against Jerusalem.

10 And I will pour out upon the house of David and upon the inhabitants of Jerusalem the spirit of grace and of prayers: ¹ and they shall look upon me, whom they have pierced. And they shall mourn for him as one mourneth for an only son: and they shall grieve over him, as the manner is to grieve for the death of the firstborn.

11 In that day there shall be a great lamentation in Jerusalem, ² like the lamentation of Adadremmon in the plain of Mageddon.

12 And the land shall mourn, families and families apart: the families of the house of David apart and their women apart.

13 The families of the house of Nathan apart and their women apart: the families of the house of Levi apart and their women apart: the families of Semei apart and their women apart.

14 All the rest of the families, fami-

lies and families apart and their women apart.

CHAPTER 13

The fountain of Christ. Idols and false prophets shall be extirpated. Christ shall suffer. His people shall be tried by fire.

IN that day there shall be a fountain open to the house of David and to the inhabitants of Jerusalem: for the washing of the sinner and of the unclean woman.

2 ¹ And it shall come to pass in that day, saith the Lord of hosts, that I will destroy the names of idols out of the earth, and they shall be remembered no more: and I will take away the false prophets and the unclean spirit out of the earth.

3 And it shall come to pass that when any man shall prophesy any more, his father and his mother that brought him into the world shall say to him: Thou shalt not live, because thou hast spoken a lie in the name of the Lord. And his father and his mother his parents, shall thrust him through when he shall prophesy.

4 And it shall come to pass in that day that the prophets shall be confounded, every one by his own vision, when he shall prophesy: neither shall they be clad with a garment of sackcloth, to deceive.

5 But he shall say: I am no prophet. I am a husbandman: for Adam is my example from my youth.

6 And they shall say to him: What are these wounds in the midst of thy hands? And he shall say: With these I was wounded in the house of them that loved me.

7 Awake, O sword, against my shepherd and against the man that cleaveth to me, saith the Lord of hosts. ² Strike the shepherd, and the sheep shall be scattered. And I will turn my hand to the little ones.

8 And they shall be in all the earth, saith the Lord: two parts in it shall be scattered and shall perish, but the third part shall be left therein.

9 And I will bring the third part through the fire and will refine them as silver is refined: and I will try them as gold is tried. They shall call on my name, and I will hear them. I will say: Thou art my people. And they shall say: The Lord is my God.

CHAPTER 14

After the persecutions of the church shall follow great prosperity. Persecutors shall be punished, as shall all that will not serve God in his church.

BEHOLD the days of the Lord shall come: and thy spoils shall be divided in the midst of thee.

2 And I will gather all nations to Jerusalem to battle: and the city shall be taken, and the houses shall be rifled, and the women shall be defiled: and half of the city shall go forth into captivity. And the rest of the people shall not be taken away out of the city.

3 Then the Lord shall go forth and shall fight against those nations, as when he fought in the day of battle.

4 And his feet shall stand in that day upon the mount of Olives, which is over against Jerusalem toward the east: and the mount of Olives shall be divided in the midst thereof to the east and to the west with a very great opening: and half of the mountains shall be separated to the north, and half thereof to the south.

5 And you shall flee to the valley of those mountains, for the valley of the mountains shall be joined even to the next: and you shall flee ¹ as you fled from the face of the earthquake in the days of Ozias king of Juda: and the Lord my God shall come, and all the saints with him.

6 And it shall come to pass in that day, that there shall be no light, but cold and frost.

7 And there shall be one day, which is known to the Lord, not day nor night: and in the time of the evening there shall be light.

8 And it shall come to pass in that day that living waters shall go out from Jerusalem: half of them to the east sea and half of them to the last sea: they shall be in summer and in winter.

9 And the Lord shall be king over all the earth. In that day there shall be one Lord, and his name shall be one.

10 And all the land shall return even to the desert, from the hill to Remmon to the south of Jerusalem: and she shall be exalted and shall dwell in her

CHAP. 13. ¹ Ezech. 30, 13. ² Matt. 26, 31; Mark, 14, 27. CHAP. 14. ¹ Amos. 1, 1.

CHAP. 14. Ver. 2. *I will gather.* This seems to be a prophecy of what was done by Antiochus.

Ver. 6. *No light.* In that dismal time of persecution of Antiochus, when it was *neither day nor night* (ver. 7): because they neither had the comfortable light of the day nor the repose of the night.

Ver. 7. *In the time of the evening there shall be light.* An unexpected light shall arise by the means of the Machabees, when things shall seem to be at the worst.

Ver. 8. *Living waters.* The gospel of Christ.

Ver. 10. *All the land shall return.* This, in some measure, was verified by the means of the Machabees: but is rather to be taken in a spiritual sense, as relating to the propagation of the church and kingdom of Christ, the true Jerusalem, which alone shall never fall under the anathema of destruction or God's curse.

own place, from the gate of Benjamin even to the place of the former gate, and even to the gate of the corners: and from the tower of Hananeel even to the king's winepresses.

11 And people shall dwell in it, and there shall be no more an anathema: but Jerusalem shall sit secure.

12 And this shall be the plague wherewith the Lord shall strike all nations that have fought against Jerusalem: the flesh of every one shall consume away while they stand upon their feet, and their eyes shall consume away in their holes, and their tongue shall consume away in their mouth.

13 In that day there shall be a great

Ver. 12. *The flesh of every one shall consume.* Such judgments as these have often fallen upon the persecutors of God's church, as appears by many instances in history.
Ver. 14. *Even Juda.* The carnal Jews and other false brothers shall join in persecuting the church.
Ver. 15. *Shall be like this destruction.* That is, the beasts shall be destroyed as well as the men: the common soldiers as well as their leaders.
Ver. 16. *They that shall be left.* That is, many of them that persecuted the church shall be converted to its faith and communion.—*To keep the feast of tabernacles.* This feast was kept by the Jews in memory of their sojourning forty years in the desert, in their way to the land of promise. And in the spiritual sense is duly kept by all such Christians as in their earthly pilgrimage are continually advancing towards their true home, the heavenly Jerusalem, by the help of the sacraments and sacrifice of the church. And they that neglect this must not look for the kind showers of divine grace to give fruitfulness to their souls.
Ver. 20. *That which is upon the bridle.* The golden ornaments of the bridles shall be turned into offerings in the house of God. And there shall be an abundance of caldrons and phials for the sacrifices of the temple; by which is meant, under a figure, the great resort there shall be to the temple, that is, to the church of Christ, and her sacrifice.
Ver. 21. *The merchant shall be no more.* Or, as some render it, *The Chanaanite shall be no more,* that is, the profane and unbelievers shall have no title to be in the house of the Lord. Or there shall be no occasion for buyers or sellers of oxen, or sheep or doves, in the house of God, such as Jesus Christ cast out of the temple.

tumult from the Lord among them: and a man shall take the hand of his neighbour, and his hand shall be clasped upon his neighbour's hand.

14 And even Juda shall fight against Jerusalem: and the riches of all nations round about shall be gathered together, gold and silver and garments in great abundance.

15 And the destruction of the horse and of the mule and of the camel and of the ass and of all the beasts that shall be in those tents shall be like this destruction.

16 And all they that shall be left of all nations that came against Jerusalem shall go up from year to year to adore the King, the Lord of hosts, and to keep the feast of tabernacles.

17 And it shall come to pass that he shall not go up of the families of the land to Jerusalem to adore the King, the Lord of hosts, there shall be no rain upon them.

18 And if the family of Egypt go not up nor come: neither shall it be upon them. But there shall be destruction wherewith the Lord will strike all nations that will not go up to keep the feast of tabernacles.

19 This shall be the sin of Egypt, and this the sin of all nations that will not go up to keep the feast of tabernacles.

20 In that day that which is upon the bridle of the horse shall be holy to the Lord: and the caldrons in the house of the Lord shall be as the phials before the altar.

21 And every caldron in Jerusalem and Juda shall be sanctified to the Lord of hosts: and all that sacrifice shall come, and take of them and shall seethe in them: and the merchant shall be no more in the house of the Lord of hosts in that day.

THE PROPHECY OF

MALACHIAS

MALACHIAS, *whose name signifies The Angel of the Lord, was contemporary with Nehemias, and by some is believed to have been the same person as Esdras. He was the last of the prophets, in the order of time, and flourished about four hundred years before Christ. He foretells the coming of Christ, the reprobation of the Jews and their sacrifices, and the calling of the Gentiles who shall offer up to God in every place an acceptable sacrifice.*

CHAPTER 1

God reproaches the Jews with their ingratitude and the priests for not offering pure sacrifices. He will accept of the sacrifice that shall be offered in every place among the Gentiles.

THE burden of the word of the Lord to Israel by the hand of Malachias.

2 I have loved you, saith the Lord. And you have said: Wherein hast thou loved us? Was not Esau brother to Jacob, saith the Lord, and [1] I have loved Jacob,

3 But have hated Esau? And I have made his mountains a wilderness and given his inheritance to the dragons of the desert.

4 But if Edom shall say: We are destroyed, but we will return and build up what hath been destroyed: thus saith the Lord of hosts: They shall build up, and I will throw down. And they shall be called the borders of wickedness and the people with whom the Lord is angry for ever.

5 And your eyes shall see, and you shall say: The Lord be magnified upon the border of Israel.

6 The son honoureth the father and the servant his master. If then I be a father, where is my honour? And if I be a master, where is my fear, saith the Lord of hosts?

7 To you, O priests, that despise my name and have said: Wherein have we despised thy name? You offer polluted bread upon my altar and you say: Wherein have we polluted thee? In that you say: The table of the Lord is contemptible.

8 If you offer the blind for sacrifice is it not evil? And if you offer the lame and the sick, is it not evil? Offer it to thy prince, if he will be pleased with it or if he will regard thy face, saith the Lord of hosts.

9 And now beseech ye the face of God, that he may have mercy on you (for by your hand hath this been done) : if by any means he will receive your faces, saith the Lord of hosts.

10 Who is there among you that will shut the doors and will kindle the fire on my altar gratis? I have no pleasure in you, saith the Lord of hosts: and I will not receive a gift of your hand.

11 [2] For from the rising of the sun even to the going down, my name is great among the Gentiles: and in every place there is sacrifice and there is offered to my name a clean oblation. For my name is great among the Gentiles, saith the Lord of hosts.

12 And you have profaned it in that you say: The table of the Lord is defiled; and that which is laid thereupon is contemptible, with the fire that devoureth it.

13 And you have said: Behold of *our* labour: and you puffed it away, saith the Lord of hosts. And you brought in of rapine the lame and the sick, and brought in an offering. Shall I accept it at your hands, saith the Lord?

14 Cursed is the deceitful man that hath in his flock a male and making a vow offereth in sacrifice that which is feeble to the Lord: for I am a great King, saith the Lord of hosts, and my name is dreadful among the Gentiles.

CHAP. 1. [1] Rom. 9, 13. [2] Ps. 112, 3.

CHAP. 1. Ver. 2. *I have loved Jacob.* I have preferred his posterity, to make them my chosen people and to lead them with my blessings, without any merit on their part and though they have been always ungrateful; whilst I have rejected Esau and executed severe judgments upon his posterity. Not that God punished Esau or his posterity beyond their desert: but that by his free election and grace he loved Jacob and favoured his posterity above their deserts. (See the annotations upon Rom. 9.)

Ver. 11. *A clean oblation.* The precious body and blood of Christ in the Eucharistic sacrifice.

Ver. 13. *Behold of our labour.* You pretended *labour* and weariness, when you brought your offering and so made it of no value, by offering it with an evil mind. Moreover, what you offered was both defective in itself and gotten by rapine and extortion.

CHAPTER 2

The priests are sharply reproved for ne-
glecting their covenant. The evil of
marrying with idolaters and too easily
putting away their wives.

AND now, O ye priests, this commandment is to you.

2 ¹ If you will not hear and if you will not lay it to heart, to give glory to my name, saith the Lord of hosts, I will send poverty upon you and will curse your blessings: yea I will curse them, because you have not laid it to heart.

3 Behold, I will cast the shoulder to you and I will scatter upon your face the dung of your solemnities: and it shall take you away with it.

4 And you shall know that I sent you this commandment, that my covenant might be with Levi, saith the Lord of hosts.

5 My covenant was with him of life and peace, and I gave him fear: and he feared me, and he was afraid before my name.

6 The law of truth was in his mouth and iniquity was not found in his lips: he walked with me in peace and in equity and turned many away from iniquity.

7 For the lips of the priest shall keep knowledge, and they shall seek the law at his mouth: because he is the angel of the Lord of hosts.

8 But you have departed out of the way and have caused many to stumble at the law: you have made void the covenant of Levi, saith the Lord of hosts.

9 Therefore have I also made you contemptible and base before all people, as you have not kept my ways and have accepted persons in the law.

10 ² Have we not all one father? Hath not one God created us? Why then doth every one of us despise his brother, violating the covenant of our fathers?

11 Juda hath transgressed, and abomination hath been committed in Israel and in Jerusalem: for Juda hath

profaned the holiness of the Lord which he loved and hath married the daughter of a strange God.

12 The Lord will cut off the man that hath done this, both the master, and the scholar, out of the tabernacles of Jacob, and him that offereth an offering to the Lord of hosts.

13 And this again have you done: you have covered the altar of the Lord with tears, with weeping and bellowing, so that I have no more a regard to sacrifice, neither do I accept any atonement at your hands.

14 And you have said: For what cause? Because the Lord hath been witness between thee and the wife of thy youth whom thou hast despised: yet she was thy partner and the wife of thy covenant.

15 Did not one make *her,* and she is the residue of his spirit? And what doth one seek, but the seed of God? Keep then your spirit and despise not the wife of thy youth.

16 When thou shalt hate her, put her away, saith the Lord the God of Israel: but iniquity shall cover his garment, saith the Lord of hosts. Keep your spirit and despise not.

17 You have wearied the Lord with your words, and you said: Wherein have we wearied him? In that you say: Every one that doth evil is good in the sight of the Lord and such please him: or surely where is the God of judgment?

CHAPTER 3

Christ shall come to his temple and purify
the priesthood. They that continue in
their evil ways shall be punished, but
true penitents shall receive a blessing.

BEHOLD ¹ I send my angel, and he shall prepare the way before my face. And presently the Lord whom you seek, and the angel of the testament whom you desire shall come to his temple. Behold he cometh, saith the Lord of hosts.

2 And who shall be able to think of the day of his coming? And who shall stand to see him? For he is like a refining fire and like the fuller's herb.

3 And he shall sit refining and cleansing the silver, and he shall purify the sons of Levi and shall refine them as gold and as silver: and they shall offer sacrifices to the Lord in justice.

4 And the sacrifice of Juda and of Jerusalem shall please the Lord, as in the days of old and in the ancient years.

5 And I will come to you in judgment and will be a speedy witness against sorcerers and adulterers and false

CHAP. 2. ¹ Lev. 26, 14; Deut. 28, 15. ² Matt. 23, 9; Eph. 4, 6. CHAP. 3. ¹ Matt. 11, 10; Mark, 1, 2; Luke, 1, 17; 7, 27.

CHAP. 2. Ver. 3. *I will cast the shoulder to you.* I will cast away the *shoulder* which in the law was appointed to be your portion and fling it at you in my anger: and will reject both you and your festivals like dung.

Ver. 7. *The angel.* The minister and messenger.

Ver. 13. *With tears.* By occasion of your wives whom you have put away and who came to weep and lament before the altar.

Ver. 16. *Iniquity shall cover his garment.* Namely, of every man that putteth away his wife without just cause; notwithstanding that God permitted it in the law, to prevent the evil of murder.

CHAP. 3. Ver. 1. *My angel.* John the Baptist, the messenger or God and forerunner of Christ.

swearers and them that oppress the hireling in his wages, the widows and the fatherless: and oppress the stranger and have not feared me, saith the Lord of hosts.

6 For I am the Lord and I change not: and you the sons of Jacob are not consumed.

7 For from the days of your fathers you have departed from my ordinances and have not kept *them:* ²Return to me, and I will return to you, saith the Lord of hosts. And you have said: Wherein shall we return?

8 Shall a man afflict God? For you afflict me. And you have said: Wherein do we afflict thee? In tithes and in first-fruits.

9 And you are cursed with want, and you afflict me, even the whole nation of you.

10 Bring all the tithes into the store-house that there may be meat in my house: and try me in this, saith the Lord, if I open not unto you the flood-gates of heaven and pour you out a blessing even to abundance.

11 And I will rebuke for your sakes the devourer, and he shall not spoil the fruit of your land: neither shall the vine in the field be barren, saith the Lord of hosts.

12 And all nations shall call you blessed: for you shall be a delightful land, saith the Lord of hosts.

13 ³Your words have been unsufferable to me, saith the Lord.

14 And you have said: What have we spoken against thee? You have said: He laboureth in vain that serveth God, and what profit is it that we have kept his ordinances and that we have walked sorrowful before the Lord of hosts?

15 Wherefore now we call the proud people happy, for they that work wickedness are built up: and they have tempted God and are preserved.

16 Then they that feared the Lord spoke every one with his neighbour: and the Lord gave ear and heard it. And a book of remembrance was writ-

ten before him for them that fear the Lord and think on his name.

17 And they shall be my special possession, saith the Lord of hosts, in the day that I do *judgment:* and I will spare them, as a man spareth his son that serveth him.

18 And you shall return and shall see the difference between the just and the wicked: and between him that serveth God and him that serveth him not.

CHAPTER 4

The judgment of the wicked and reward of the just. An exhortation to observe the law. Elias shall come for the conversion of the Jews.

FOR behold the day shall come kindled as a furnace: and all the proud and all that do wickedly shall be stubble. And the day that cometh shall set them on fire, saith the Lord of hosts: it shall not leave them root, nor branch.

2 ¹But unto you that fear my name the Sun of justice shall arise, and health in his wings: and you shall go forth and shall leap like calves of the herd.

3 And you shall tread down the wicked when they shall be ashes under the sole of your feet in the day that I do *this,* saith the Lord of hosts.

4 ²Remember the law of Moses my servant which I commanded him in Horeb for all Israel, the precepts and judgments.

5 ³Behold I will send you Elias the prophet, before the coming of the great and dreadful day of the Lord.

6 And he shall turn the heart of the fathers to the children and the heart of the children to their fathers: lest I come, and strike the earth with anathema.

² Zach. 1, 3. ³ John, 21, 14. CHAP. 4. ¹ Luke, 1, 78. ² Exod. 20; Deut. 4, 5, 6. ³ Matt. 17, 10; Mark, 9, 10; Luke, 1, 17.

CHAP. 4. Ver. 6. *He shall turn the heart.* By bringing over the Jews to the faith of Christ, he shall reconcile them to their fathers, the patriarchs and prophets; whose hearts for many ages have been turned away from them, because of their refusing to believe in Christ.—*With anathema.* In the Hebrew, *Cherem,* that is, with utter destruction.

THE FIRST BOOK OF

MACHABEES

These books are so called because they contain the history of the people of God under the command of Judas Machabeus and his brethren: and he, as some will have it, was surnamed Machabeus, from carrying in his ensigns or standards those words of Exodus 15, 11, Who is like to thee among the strong, O Lord: in which the initial letters in the Hebrew are M. C. B. E. I. It is not known who was the author of these books. But as to their authority, though they are not received by the Jews, saith St. Augustine (lib. 18, De Civ. Dei, c. 36), they are received by the Church, who, in settling her canon of the scriptures, chose rather to be directed by the tradition she had received from the Apostles of Christ than by that of the scribes and Pharisees. And as the Church has declared these two Books canonical, even in two general councils, those of Florence and Trent, there can be no doubt of their authenticity.

CHAPTER 1

The reign of Alexander and his successors. Antiochus rifles and profanes the temple of God, and persecutes unto death all that will not forsake the law of God and the religion of their fathers.

NOW it came to pass after that Alexander the *son of* Philip the Macedonian, who first reigned in Greece, coming out of the land of Cethim, had overthrown Darius king of the Persians and Medes:

2 He fought many battles and took the strong holds of all and slew the kings of the earth.

3 And he went through even to the ends of the earth and took the spoils of many nations. And the earth was quiet before him.

4 And he gathered a power and a very strong army: and his heart was exalted and lifted up.

5 And he subdued countries of nations, and princes: and they became tributaries to him.

6 And after these things, he fell down upon his bed and knew that he should die.

7 And he called his servants the nobles that were brought up with him from his youth: and he divided his kingdom among them while he was yet alive.

CHAP. 1. Ver. 7. *Divided his kingdom.* This is otherwise related by Quintus Curtius; though he acknowledges that divers were of that opinion and that it had been delivered by some authors. But here we find from the sacred text that he was in error.

Ver. 11. *Antiochus the Illustrious. Epiphanes,* the younger son of Antiochus the Great, who usurped the kingdom, to the prejudice of his nephew Demetrius, son of his elder brother Seleucus Philopator.—*Of the kingdom of the Greeks.* Counting, not from the beginning of the reign of Alexander, but from the first year of Seleucus Nicator.

Ver. 16. That is, uncircumcised.

8 And Alexander reigned twelve years: and he died.

9 And his servants made themselves kings every one in his place.

10 And they all put crowns upon themselves after his death, and their sons after them many years: and evils were multiplied in the earth.

11 And there came out of them a wicked root, Antiochus the Illustrious, the son of king Antiochus who had been a hostage at Rome: and he reigned in the hundred and thirty-seventh year of the kingdom of the Greeks.

12 In those days there went out of Israel wicked men and they persuaded many, saying: Let us go and make a covenant with the heathens that are round about us. for since we departed from them many evils have befallen us.

13 And the word seemed good in their eyes.

14 And some of the people determined to do this and went to the king: and he gave them license to do after the ordinances of the heathens.

15 And they built a place of exercise in Jerusalem, according to the laws of the nations:

16 And they made themselves prepuces and departed from the holy covenant and joined themselves to the heathens and were sold to do evil.

17 And the kingdom was established before Antiochus: and he had a mind to reign over the land of Egypt, that he might reign over two kingdoms.

18 And he entered into Egypt with a great multitude, with chariots and elephants and horsemen and a great number of ships:

19 And he made war against Ptolemee king of Egypt: but Ptolemee

was afraid at his presence and fled, and many were wounded unto death.

20 And he took the strong cities in the land of Egypt: and he took the spoils of the land of Egypt.

21 And after Antiochus had ravaged Egypt in the hundred and forty-third year, he returned and went up against Israel.

22 And he went up to Jerusalem with a great multitude.

23 And he proudly entered into the sanctuary and took away the golden altar and the candlestick of light and all the vessels thereof and the table of proposition and the pouring vessels and the vials and the little mortars of gold and the veil and the crowns and the golden ornament that was before the temple: and he broke them all in pieces.

24 And he took the silver and gold, and the precious vessels: and he took the hidden treasures which he found. And when he had taken all away he departed into his own country.

25 And he made a great slaughter of men and spoke very proudly.

26 And there was great mourning in Israel and in every place where they were.

27 And the princes and the ancients mourned, and the virgins and the young men were made feeble, and the beauty of the women was changed.

28 Every bridegroom took up lamentation: and the bride that sat in the marriage bed, mourned.

29 And the land was moved for the inhabitants thereof: and all the house of Jacob was covered with confusion.

30 And after two full years the king sent the chief collector of *his* tributes to the cities of Juda: and he came to Jerusalem with a great multitude.

31 And he spoke to them peaceable words in deceit: and they believed him.

32 And he fell upon the city suddenly and struck it with a great slaughter and destroyed much people in Israel.

33 And he took the spoils of the city and burnt it with fire: and threw down the houses thereof and the walls thereof round about.

34 And they took the women captive, and the children and the cattle they possessed.

35 And they built the city of David with a great and strong wall and with strong towers and made it a fortress for them.

36 And they placed there a sinful nation, wicked men: and they fortified themselves therein. And they stored up armour and victuals and gathered together the spoils of Jerusalem.

37 And laid them up there. And they became a great snare.

38 And this was a place to lie in wait against the sanctuary and an evil devil in Israel.

39 And they shed innocent blood round about the sanctuary and defiled the holy place.

40 And the inhabitants of Jerusalem fled away by reason of them, and the city was made the habitation of strangers: and she became a stranger to her own seed and her children forsook her.

41 Her sanctuary was desolate like a wilderness, [1] her festival days were turned into mourning, her sabbaths into reproach, her honours were brought to nothing.

42 Her dishonour was increased according to her glory and her excellency was turned into mourning.

43 And king Antiochus wrote to all his kingdom that all the people should be one and every one should leave his own law.

44 And all nations consented according to the word of king Antiochus.

45 And many of Israel consented to his service: and they sacrificed to idols and profaned the sabbath.

46 And the king sent letters by the hands of messengers to Jerusalem and to all the cities of Juda: that they should follow the law of the nations of the earth,

47 And should forbid holocausts and sacrifices and atonements to be made in the temple of God,

48 And should prohibit the sabbath and the festival days, to be celebrated.

49 And he commanded the holy places to be profaned and the holy people of Israel.

50 And he commanded altars to be built, and temples and idols and swine's flesh to be immolated, and unclean beasts:

51 And that they should leave their children uncircumcised and let their souls be defiled with all uncleannesses and abominations to the end that they should forget the law and should change all the justifications of God:

52 And that whosoever would not do according to the word of king Antiochus should be put to death.

53 According to all these words he wrote to his whole kingdom: and he ap-

---

CHAP. 1. [1] Tob. 2, 6; Amos, 8, 10.

Ver. 30. *The chief collector.* Appollonius.

Ver. 35. *The city of David.* That is, the Castle of Sion.

Ver. 38. *An evil devil.* That is, an adversary watching constantly to do harm, as the evil spirit is always watching and seeking whom he may devour.

pointed rulers over the people that should force them to do these things.

54 And they commanded the cities of Juda to sacrifice.

55 Then many of the people were gathered to them that had forsaken the law of the Lord: and they committed evils in the land.

56 And they drove away the people of Israel into lurking holes and into the secret places of fugitives.

57 On the fifteenth day of the month Casleu, in the hundred and forty-fifth year, king Antiochus set up the abominable idol of desolation upon the altar of God: and they built altars throughout all the cities of Juda round about.

58 And they burnt incense and sacrificed at the doors of the houses and in the streets.

59 And they cut in pieces and burnt with fire the books of the law of God.

60 And every one with whom the books of the testament of the Lord were found and whosoever observed the law of the Lord, they put to death, according to the edict of the king.

61 Thus by their power did they deal with the people of Israel that were found in the cities, month after month.

62 And on the five and twentieth day of the month they sacrificed upon the altar of the idol that was over against the altar *of God.*

63 ²Now the women that circumcised their children were slain according to the commandment of king Antiochus.

64 And they hanged the children about their necks in all their houses: and those that had circumcised them, they put to death.

65 And many of the people of Israel determined with themselves that they would not eat unclean things: and they chose rather to die than to be defiled with unclean meats.

66 And they would not break the holy law of God: and they were put to death.

67 And there was very great wrath upon the people.

CHAPTER 2

The zeal and success of Mathathias. His exhortation to his sons at his death.

IN those days arose Mathathias the son of John, the son of Simeon, a priest of the sons of Joarib, from Jerusalem: and he abode in the mountain of Modin.

2 And he had five sons: John who was surnamed Gaddis:

² 2 Mach. 6, 10.

Ver. 57. *The abominable idol.* The statue of Jupiter Olympus.

3 And Simon who was surnamed Thasi:

4 And Judas who was called Machabeus:

5 And Eleazar who was surnamed Abaron: and Jonathan who was surnamed Apphus.

6 These saw the evils that were done in the people of Juda and in Jerusalem.

7 And Mathathias said: Woe is me! Wherefore was I born to see the ruin of my people and the ruin of the holy city, and to dwell there, when it is given into the hands of the enemies?

8 The holy places are come into the hands of strangers: her temple is become as a man without honour.

9 The vessels of her glory are carried away captive: her old men are murdered in the streets and her young men are fallen by the sword of the enemies.

10 What nation hath not inherited her kingdom and gotten of her spoils?

11 All her ornaments are taken away. She that was free is made a slave.

12 And behold our sanctuary and our beauty and our glory is laid waste: and the Gentiles have defiled them.

13 To what end then should we live any longer?

14 And Mathathias and his sons rent their garments: and they covered themselves with haircloth and made great lamentation.

15 And they that were sent from king Antiochus came thither, to compel them that were fled into the city of Modin to sacrifice and to burn incense and to depart from the law of God.

16 And many of the people of Israel consented and came to them: but Mathathias and his sons stood firm.

17 And they that were sent from Antiochus, answering, said to Mathathias: Thou art a ruler and an honourable and great man in this city and adorned with sons and brethren.

18 Therefore, come thou first and obey the king's commandment, as all nations have done, and the men of Juda and they that remain in Jerusalem: and thou and thy sons shall be in the number of the king's friends and enriched with gold and silver and many presents.

19 Then Mathathias answered and said with a loud voice: Although all nations obey king Antiochus, so as to depart every man from the service of the law of his fathers and consent to his commandments:

20 I and my sons and my brethren will obey the law of our fathers.

21 God be merciful unto us: it is not

profitable for us to forsake the law and the justices of God.

22 We will not hearken to the words of king Antiochus: neither will we sacrifice and transgress the commandments of our law, to go another way.

23 Now as he left off speaking these words, there came a certain Jew in the sight of all to sacrifice to the idols upon the altar in the city of Modin, according to the king's commandment.

24 And Mathathias saw and was grieved. And his reins trembled, and his wrath was kindled according to the judgment of the law: and running upon him he slew him upon the altar.

25 Moreover the man whom king Antiochus had sent, who compelled them to sacrifice, he slew at the same time: and pulled down the altar,

26 And showed zeal for the law, [1] as Phinees did by Zamri the son of Salomi.

27 And Mathathias cried out in the city with a loud voice, saying: Every one that hath zeal for the law and maintaineth the testament, let him follow me.

28 So he and his sons fled into the mountains and left all that they had in the city.

29 Then many that sought after judgment and justice went down into the desert.

30 And they abode there, they and their children and their wives and their cattle: because afflictions increased upon them.

31 And it was told to the king's men and to the army that was in Jerusalem in the city of David, that certain men who had broken the king's commandment were gone away into the secret places in the wilderness and that many were gone after them.

32 And forthwith they went out towards them and made war against them on the sabbath day.

33 And they said to them: Do you still resist? Come forth and do according to the edict of king Antiochus: and you shall live.

34 And they said: We will not come forth, neither will we obey the king's edict, to profane the sabbath day.

35 And they made haste to give them battle.

36 But they answered them not: neither did they cast a stone at them nor stopped up the secret places,

37 Saying: Let us all die in our innocency: and heaven and earth shall be witnesses for us, that you put us to death wrongfully.

38 So they gave them battle on the sabbath: and they were slain with their wives and their children and their cattle, to the number of a thousand persons.

39 And Mathathias and his friends heard of it: and they mourned for them exceedingly.

40 And every man said to his neighbour: If we shall do as our brethren have done and not fight against the heathens for our lives and our justifications, they will now quickly root us out of the earth.

41 And they determined in that day, saying: Whosoever shall come up against us to fight on the sabbath day, we will fight against him. And we will not all die, as our brethren that were slain in the secret places.

42 Then was assembled to them the congregation of the Assideans, the stoutest of Israel, every one that had a good will for the law.

43 And all they that fled from the evils joined themselves to them and were a support to them.

44 And they gathered an army and slew the sinners in their wrath and the wicked men in their indignation: and the rest fled to the nations for safety.

45 And Mathathias and his friends went round about: and they threw down the altars.

46 And they circumcised all the children whom they found in the confines of Israel that were uncircumcised: and they did valiantly.

47 And they pursued after the children of pride: and the work prospered in their hands.

48 And they recovered the law out of the hands of the nations and out of the hands of the kings: and they yielded not the horn to the sinner.

49 Now the days drew near that Mathathias should die, and he said to his sons: Now hath pride and chastisement gotten strength, and the time of destruction and the wrath of indignation:

50 Now therefore, O my sons, be ye zealous for the law and give your lives for the covenant of your fathers.

51 And call to remembrance the works of the fathers which they have done in their generations: and you shall receive great glory and an everlasting name.

52 [2] Was not Abraham found faithful in temptation, and it was reputed to him unto justice?

CHAP. 2. [1] Num. 25, 13.   [2] Gen. 22, 2.

CHAP. 2. Ver. 42. *The Assideans.* A set of men that led a religious life and were zealous for the law and worship of God.
Ver. 48. *They yielded not the horn.* That is, they suffered not the power of Antiochus, that man of sin, to abolish the law and religion of God.

53 [3] Joseph in the time of his distress kept the commandment and he was made lord of Egypt.

54 [4] Phinees our father, by being fervent in the zeal of God, received the covenant of an everlasting priesthood.

55 [5] Jesus, whilst he fulfilled the word, was made ruler in Israel.

56 [6] Caleb, for bearing witness before the congregation, received an inheritance.

57 [7] David by his mercy obtained the throne of an everlasting kingdom.

58 [8] Elias, while he was full of zeal for the law, was taken up into heaven.

59 [9] Ananias and Azarias and Misael by believing were delivered out of the flame.

60 [10] Daniel in his innocency was delivered out of the mouth of the lions.

61 And thus consider through all generations that none that trust in him fail in strength.

62 And fear not the words of a sinful man, for his glory is dung and worms:

63 To-day he is lifted up, and tomorrow he shall not be found, because he is returned into his earth and his thought is come to nothing.

64 You therefore, my sons, take courage and behave manfully in the law: for by it you shall be glorious.

65 And behold, I know that your brother Simon is a man of counsel: give ear to him always, and he shall be a father to you.

66 And Judas Machabeus who is valiant and strong from his youth up, let him be the leader of your army: and he shall manage the war of the people.

67 And you shall take to you all that observe the law: and revenge ye the wrong of your people.

68 Render to the Gentiles their reward: and take heed to the precepts of the law.

69 And he blessed them and was joined to his fathers.

70 And he died in the hundred and forty-sixth year: and he was buried by his sons in the sepulchres of his fathers in Modin. And all Israel mourned for him with great mourning.

CHAPTER 3

Judas Machabeus succeeds his father and overthrows Apollonius and Seron. A great army is sent against him out of Syria. He prepares his people for battle by fasting and prayer.

[3] Gen. 41, 40. [4] Num. 25, 13; Ecclus. 45, 28. [5] Jos. 1, 2. [6] Num. 14, 6; Jos. 14, 14. [7] 2 Kings, 2, 4. [8] 4 Kings, 2, 11. [9] Dan. 3, 50. [10] Dan. 6, 22.

Ver. 55. *Jesus.* That is, Josue.

THEN his son Judas, called Machabeus, rose up in his stead.

2 And all his brethren helped him, and all they that had joined themselves to his father: and they fought with cheerfulness the battle of Israel.

3 And he got his people great honour and put on a breastplate as a giant and girt his warlike armour about him in battles and protected the camp with his sword.

4 In his acts he was like a lion and like a lion's whelp roaring for his prey.

5 And he pursued the wicked and sought them out, and them that troubled his people he burnt with fire.

6 And his enemies were driven away for fear of him, and all the workers of iniquity were troubled: and salvation prospered in his hand.

7 And he grieved many kings and made Jacob glad with his works: and his memory is blessed for ever.

8 And he went through the cities of Juda and destroyed the wicked out of them and turned away wrath from Israel.

9 And he was renowned even to the utmost part of the earth: and he gathered them that were perishing.

10 And Apollonius gathered together the Gentiles and a numerous and great army from Samaria, to make war against Israel.

11 And Judas understood it and went forth to meet him. And he overthrew him and killed him: and many fell down slain, and the rest fled away.

12 And he took their spoils: and Judas took the sword of Apollonius and fought with it all his lifetime.

13 And Seron captain of the army of Syria heard that Judas had assembled a company of the faithful and a congregation with him,

14 And he said: I will get me a name and will be glorified in the kingdom and will overthrow Judas and those that are with him that have despised the edict of the king.

15 And he made himself ready: and the host of the wicked went up with him, strong succours, to be revenged of the children of Israel.

16 And they approached even as far as Bethoron. And Judas went forth to meet him with a small company.

17 But when they saw the army coming to meet them they said to Judas: How shall we, being few, be able to fight against so great a multitude and so strong, and we are ready to faint with fasting to-day?

18 And Judas said: It is an easy matter for many to be shut up in the hands of a few: and there is no differ-

ence in the sight of the God of heaven to deliver with a great multitude or with a small company.

19 For the success of war is not in the multitude of the army: but strength cometh from heaven.

20 They come against us with an insolent multitude, and with pride, to destroy us and our wives and our children and to take our spoils.

21 But we will fight for our lives and our laws:

22 And the Lord himself will overthrow them before our face. But as for you, fear them not.

23 And as soon as he had made an end of speaking, he rushed suddenly upon them: and Seron and his host were overthrown before him.

24 And he pursued him by the descent of Bethoron even to the plain: and there fell of them eight hundred men. And the rest fled into the land of the Philistines.

25 And the fear of Judas and of his brethren and the dread *of them* fell upon all the nations round about them.

26 And his fame came to the king: and all nations told of the battles of Judas.

27 Now when king Antiochus heard these words, he was angry in his mind: and he sent and gathered the forces of all his kingdom, an exceeding strong army.

28 And he opened his treasury and gave out pay to the army for a year: and he commanded them that they should be ready for all things.

29 And he perceived that the money of his treasures failed and that the tributes of the country were small because of the dissension and the evil that he had brought upon the land, that he might take away the laws of old times.

30 And he feared that he should not have as formerly enough for charges and gifts, which he had given before with a liberal hand: for he had abounded more than the kings that had been before him.

31 And he was greatly perplexed in mind and purposed to go into Persia and to take tributes of the countries and to gather much money.

32 And he left Lysias, a nobleman of the blood royal, to oversee the affairs of the kingdom, from the river Euphrates even to the river of Egypt:

33 And to bring up his son Antiochus, till he came again.

34 And he delivered to him half the army and the elephants: and he gave him charge concerning all that he would have done and concerning the inhabitants of Judea, and Jerusalem:

35 And that he should send an army against them, to destroy and root out the strength of Israel and the remnant of Jerusalem and to take away the memory of them from that place:

36 And that he should settle strangers to dwell in all their coasts and divide their land by lot.

37 So the king took the half of the army that remained and went forth from Antioch the chief city of his kingdom, in the hundred and forty-seventh year: and he passed over the river Euphrates and went through the higher countries.

38 Then Lysias chose Ptolemee, the son of Dorymenus, and Nicanor and Gorgias, mighty men of the king's friends.

39 And he sent with them forty thousand men and seven thousand horsemen; to go into the land of Juda and to destroy it according to the king's orders.

40 So they went forth with all their power and came and pitched near Emmaus in the plain country.

41 And the merchants of the countries heard the fame of them and they took silver and gold in abundance and servants: and they came into the camp, to buy the children of Israel for slaves. And there were joined to them the forces of Syria and of the land of the strangers.

42 And Judas and his brethren saw that evils were multiplied and that the armies approached to their borders: and they knew the orders the king had given to destroy the people and utterly abolish them.

43 And they said every man to his neighbour: Let us raise up the low condition of our people and let us fight for our people and our sanctuary.

44 And the assembly was gathered that they might be ready for battle: and that they might pray and ask mercy and compassion.

45 Now Jerusalem was not inhabited but was like a desert: there was none of her children that went in or out. And the sanctuary was trodden down: and the children of strangers were in the castle. There was the habitation of the Gentiles: and joy was taken away from Jacob, and the pipe and harp ceased there.

46 And they assembled together and came to Maspha over against Jerusalem: for in Maspha was a place of prayer heretofore in Israel.

47 And they fasted that day and put on haircloth and put ashes upon their heads: and they rent their garments.

48 And they laid open the books of

the law in which the Gentiles searched for the likeness of their idols.

49 And they brought the priestly ornaments and the firstfruits and tithes and stirred up the Nazarites that had fulfilled their days.

50 And they cried with a loud voice toward heaven, saying: What shall we do with these, and whither shall we carry them?

51 For thy holies are trodden down and are profaned: and thy priests are in mourning and are brought low.

52 And behold the nations are come together against us to destroy us: thou knowest what they intend against us.

53 How shall we be able to stand before their face unless thou, O God, help us?

54 Then they sounded with trumpets and cried out with a loud voice.

55 And after this Judas appointed captains over the people, over thousands, and over hundreds, and over fifties, and over tens.

56 [1] And he said to them that were building houses or had betrothed wives or were planting vineyards or were fearful, that they should return every man to his house, according to the law.

57 So they removed the camp and pitched on the south side of Emmaus

58 And Judas said: Gird yourselves and be valiant men and be ready against the morning, that you may fight with these nations that are assembled against us to destroy us and our sanctuary.

59 For it is better for us to die in battle than to see the evils of our nation and of the holies:

60 Nevertheless as it shall be the will of God in heaven so be it done.

CHAPTER 4

Judas routs the king's army. Gorgias flies before him. Lysias comes against him with a great army, but is defeated. Judas cleanses the temple, sets up a new altar, and fortifies the sanctuary.

THEN Gorgias took five thousand men and a thousand of the best horsemen: and they removed out of the camp by night,

2 That they might come upon the camp of the Jews and strike them suddenly. And the men that were of the castle were their guides.

3 And Judas heard of it and rose up, he and the valiant men, to attack the king's forces that were in Emmaus.

CHAP. 3. [1] Deut. 20, 5, 6; Judges, 7, 3. CHAP. 4. [1] Exod. 14. 9.

CHAP. 4. Ver. 4. *The army was dispersed.* That is, in different divisions, not all together encamped.
Ver. 6. *Who neither had armour nor swords.* Such as they wished for.

4 For as yet the army was dispersed from the camp.

5 And Gorgias came by night into the camp of Judas and found no man. And he sought them in the mountains, for he said: These men flee from us.

6 And when it was day, Judas shewed himself in the plain with three thousand men only, who neither had armour nor swords.

7 And they saw the camp of the Gentiles that it was strong, and the men in breastplates and the horsemen round about them. And these were trained up to war.

8 And Judas said to the men that were with him: Fear ye not their multitude, neither be ye afraid of their assault.

9 [1] Remember in what manner our fathers were saved in the Red Sea, when Pharao pursued them with a great army.

10 And now let us cry to heaven: and the Lord will have mercy on us and will remember the covenant of our fathers and will destroy this army before our face this day.

11 And all nations shall know that there is one that redeemeth and delivereth Israel.

12 And the strangers lifted up their eyes and saw them coming against them.

13 And they went out of the camp to battle: and they that were with Judas sounded the trumpet.

14 And they joined battle: and the Gentiles were routed and fled into the plain.

15 But all the hindmost of them fell by the sword. And they pursued them as far as Gezeron, and even to the plains of Idumea and of Azotus and of Jamnia. And there fell of them to the number of three thousand men.

16 And Judas returned again with his army that followed him,

17 And he said to the people: Be not greedy of the spoils. For there is war before us,

18 And Gorgias and his army are near us in the mountain. But stand ye now against our enemies and overthrow them: and you shall take the spoils afterwards with safety.

19 And as Judas was speaking these words, behold part of them appeared looking forth from the mountain.

20 And Gorgias saw that his men were put to flight and that they had set fire to the camp: for the smoke that was seen declared what was done.

21 And when they had seen this, they were seized with great fear, seeing at

the same time Judas and his army in the plain ready to fight.

22 So they all fled away into the land of the strangers.

23 And Judas returned to take the spoils of the camp: and they got much gold and silver and blue silk and purple of the sea and great riches.

24 And returning home they sung a hymn and blessed God in heaven, because he is good, because his mercy endureth for ever.

25 So Israel had a great deliverance that day.

26 And such of the strangers as escaped went and told Lysias all that had happened.

27 And when he heard these things, he was amazed and discouraged: because things had not succeeded in Israel according to his mind and as the king had commanded.

28 So the year following, Lysias gathered together threescore thousand chosen men and five thousand horsemen, that he might subdue them.

29 And they came into Judea and pitched their tents in Bethoron: and Judas met them with ten thousand men.

30 And they saw that the army was strong. And he prayed and said: Blessed art thou, O Saviour of Israel, ² who didst break the violence of the mighty by the hand of thy servant David ³ and didst deliver up the camp of the strangers into the hands of Jonathan the son of Saul and of his armourbearer.

31 Shut up this army in the hands of thy people Israel: and let them be confounded in their host and their horsemen.

32 Strike them with fear and cause the boldness of their strength to languish: and let them quake at their own destruction.

33 Cast them down with the sword of them that love thee: and let all that know thy name praise thee with hymns.

34 And they joined battle: and there fell of the army of Lysias five thousand men.

35 And when Lysias saw that his men were put to flight and how bold the Jews were, and that they were ready either to live or die manfully, he went to Antioch and chose soldiers, that they might come again into Judea with greater numbers.

36 Then Judas, and his brethren said: Behold our enemies are discomfited: let us go up now to cleanse the holy places and to repair them.

37 And all the army assembled together: and they went up into mount Sion.

38 And they saw the sanctuary desolate, and the altar profaned, and the gates burnt, and shrubs growing up in the courts as in a forest or on the mountains, and the chambers joining to the temple thrown down.

39 And they rent their garments and made great lamentation and put ashes on their heads.

40 And they fell down to the ground on their faces, and they sounded with the trumpets of alarm, and they cried towards heaven.

41 Then Judas appointed men to fight against them that were in the castle, till they had cleansed the holy places.

42 And he chose priests without blemish, whose will was set upon the law of God.

43 And they cleansed the holy places and took away the stones that had been defiled into an unclean place.

44 And he considered about the altar of holocausts that had been profaned, what he should do with it.

45 And a good counsel came into their minds, to pull it down: lest it should be a reproach to them, because the Gentiles had defiled it. So they threw it down.

46 And they laid up the stones in the mountain of the temple in a convenient place, till there should come a prophet and give answer concerning them.

47 And they took whole stones according to the law and built a new altar according to the former.

48 And they built up the holy places and the things that were within the temple: and they sanctified the temple and the courts.

49 And they made new holy vessels and brought in the candlestick and the altar of incense and the table into the temple.

50 And they put incense upon the altar and lighted up the lamps that were upon the candlestick: and they gave light in the temple.

51 And they set the loaves upon the table and hung up the veils and finished all the works that they had begun to make.

52 And they arose before the morning on the five and twentieth day of the ninth month (which is the month of Casleu) in the hundred and forty-eighth year.

53 And they offered sacrifice according to the law upon the new altar of holocausts which they had made.

<hr/>

² 1 Kings, 17, 50.   ³ 1 Kings, 14, 13.

54 According to the time and according to the day wherein the heathens had defiled it, in the same was it dedicated anew with canticles and harps and lutes and cymbals.

55 And all the people fell upon their faces and adored and blessed up to heaven him that had prospered them.

56 And they kept the dedication of the altar eight days: and they offered holocausts with joy and sacrifices of salvation and of praise.

57 And they adorned the front of the temple with crowns of gold and escutcheons: and they renewed the gates and the chambers and hanged doors upon them.

58 And there was exceeding great joy among the people: and the reproach of the Gentiles was turned away.

59 ⁴ And Judas and his brethren and all the church of Israel decreed, that the day of the dedication of the altar should be kept in its season from year to year, for eight days, from the five and twentieth day of the month of Casleu, with joy and gladness.

60 They built up also at that time Mount Sion, with high walls and strong towers round about, lest the Gentiles should at any time come and tread it down as they did before.

61 And he placed a garrison there to keep it: and he fortified it to secure Bethsura, that the people might have a defence against Idumea.

CHAPTER 5

Judas and his brethren attack the enemies of their country and deliver them that were distressed. Josephus and Azarias, attempting, contrary to order, to fight against their enemies, are defeated.

NOW it came to pass, when the nations round about heard that the altar and the sanctuary were built up as before, that they were exceeding angry.

2 And they thought to destroy the generation of Jacob that were among them: and they began to kill some of the people and to persecute them.

3 Then Judas fought against the children of Esau in Idumea and them that were in Acrabathane, because they beset the Israelites round about. And he made a great slaughter of them.

4 And he remembered the malice of the children of Bean, who were a snare and a stumbling-block to the people by lying in wait for them in the way.

5 And they were shut up by him in towers: and he set upon them, and devoted them to utter destruction and

⁴ John, 10, 22.

burnt their towers with fire and all that were in them.

6 Then he passed over to the children of Ammon, where he found a mighty power and much people: and Timotheus was their captain.

7 And he fought many battles with them: and they were discomfited in their sight. And he smote them:

8 And he took the city of Gazer and her towns and returned into Judea.

9 And the Gentiles that were in Galaad assembled themselves together against the Israelites that were in their quarters to destroy them: and they fled into the fortress of Datheman.

10 And they sent letters to Judas and his brethren, saying: The heathens that are round about are gathered together against us, to destroy us.

11 And they are preparing to come and take the fortress into which we are fled. And Timotheus is the captain of their host.

12 Now therefore come, and deliver us out of their hands: for many of us are slain.

13 And all our brethren that were in the places of Tubin are killed: and they have carried away their wives and their children, captives, and taken their spoils: and they have slain there almost a thousand men.

14 And while they were yet reading these letters, behold there came other messengers out of Galilee with their garments rent, who related according to these words:

15 Saying that they of Ptolemais and of Tyre and of Sidon were assembled against them. And all Galilee is filled with strangers, in order to consume us.

16 Now when Judas and the people heard these words, a great assembly met together to consider what they should do for their brethren that were in trouble and were assaulted by them.

17 And Judas said to Simon his brother: Choose thee men and go and deliver thy brethren in Galilee: and I and my brother Jonathan will go into the country of Galaad.

18 And he left Joseph, the son of Zacharias, and Azarias, captains of the people, with the remnant of the army in Judea to keep it.

19 And he commanded them, saying: Take ye the charge of this people: but make no war against the heathens till we return.

20 Now three thousand men were allotted to Simon to go into Galilee: and eight thousand to Judas to go into the land of Galaad.

21 And Simon went into Galilee and

fought many battles with the heathens. And the heathens were discomfited before his face: and he pursued them even to the gate of Ptolemais.

22 And there fell of the heathens almost three thousand men: and he took the spoils of them,

23 And he took with him those that were in Galilee and in Arbatis with their wives and children and all that they had: and he brought them into Judea with great joy.

24 And Judas Machabeus and Jonathan his brother passed over the Jordan and went three days' journey through the desert.

25 And the Nabutheans met them them and received them in a peaceable manner and told them all that happened to their brethren in the land of Galaad:

26 And that many of them were shut up in Barasa and in Bosor and in Alima and in Casphor and in Mageth and in Carnaim, all these strong and great cities.

27 Yea, and that they were kept shut up in the rest of the cities of Galaad: and that they had appointed to bring their army on the morrow near to these cities and to take them and to destroy them all in one day.

28 Then Judas and his army suddenly turned their march into the desert to Bosor and took the city: and he slew every male by the edge of the sword and took all their spoils and burnt it with fire.

29 And they removed from thence by night and went till they came to the fortress.

30 And it came to pass that early in the morning, when they lifted up their eyes, behold there were people without number, carrying ladders and engines to take the fortress and assault them.

31 And Judas saw that the fight was begun: and the cry of the battle went up to heaven like a trumpet, and a great cry out of the city.

32 And he said to his host: Fight ye to-day for your brethren.

33 And he came with three companies behind them: and they sounded their trumpets and cried out in prayer.

34 And the host of Timotheus understood that it was Machabeus: and they fled away before his face. And they made a great slaughter of them: and there fell of them in that day almost eight thousand men.

35 And Judas turned aside to Maspha and assaulted and took it: and he slew every male thereof and took the spoils thereof and burnt it with fire.

36 From thence he marched and took Casbon and Mageth and Bosor and the rest of the cities of Galaad.

37 But after this Timotheus gathered another army and camped over against Raphon beyond the torrent.

38 And Judas sent men to view the army: and they brought him word, saying: All the nations, that are round about us, are assembled unto him an army exceeding great.

39 And they have hired the Arabians to help them: and they have pitched their tents beyond the torrent, ready to come to fight against thee. And Judas went to meet them.

40 And Timotheus said to the captains of his army: When Judas and his army come near the torrent of water, if he pass over unto us first, we shall not be able to withstand him: for he will certainly prevail over us.

41 But if he be afraid to pass over and camp on the other side of the river, we will pass over to them and shall prevail against him.

42 Now when Judas came near the torrent of water, he set the scribes of the people by the torrent and commanded them, saying: Suffer no man to stay behind: but let all come to the battle.

43 And he passed over to them first, and all the people after him: and all the heathens were discomfited before them. And they threw away their weapons and fled to the temple that was in Carnaim.

44 And he took that city: and the temple he burnt with fire, with all things that were therein. And Carnaim was subdued and could not stand against the face of Judas.

45 And Judas gathered together all the Israelites that were in the land of Galaad, from the least even to the greatest, and their wives and children, and an army exceeding great, to come into the land of Juda.

46 And they came as far as Ephron. Now this was a great city situate in the way, strongly fortified: and there was no means to turn from it on the right hand or on the left, but the way was through the midst of it.

47 And they that were in the city shut themselves in and stopped up the gates with stones: and Judas sent to them with peaceable words,

48 Saying: Let us pass through your land, to go into our country: and no man shall hurt you. We will only pass through on foot. But they would not open to them.

49 Then Judas commanded proclamation to be made in the camp, that

they should make an assault, every man in the place where he was.

50 And the men of the army drew near: and he assaulted that city all the day and all the night: and the city was delivered into his hands.

51 And they slew every male with the edge of the sword: and he razed the city and took the spoils thereof and passed through all the city over them that were slain.

52 Then they passed over the Jordan to the great plain that is over against Bethsan.

53 And Judas gathered together the hindmost: and he exhorted the people all the way through, till they came into the land of Juda.

54 And they went up to Mount Sion with joy and gladness and offered holocausts, because not one of them was slain till they had returned in peace.

55 Now in the days that Judas and Jonathan were in the land of Galaad, and Simon his brother in Galilee before Ptolemais,

56 Joseph, the son of Zacharias, and Azarias, captain of the soldiers, heard of the good success and the battles that were fought.

57 And he said: Let us also get us a name, and let us go fight against the Gentiles that are round about us.

58 And he gave charge to them that were in his army: and they went towards Jamnia.

59 And Gorgias and his men went out of the city, to give them battle.

60 And Joseph and Azarias were put to flight and were pursued unto the borders of Judea. And there fell, on that day, of the people of Israel about two thousand men: and there was a great overthrow of the people:

61 Because they did not hearken to Judas and his brethren, thinking that they should do manfully.

62 But they were not of the seed of those men by whom salvation was brought to Israel.

63 And the men of Juda were magnified exceedingly, in the sight of all Israel and of all the nations where their name was heard.

64 And people assembled to them with joyful acclamations.

65 Then Judas and his brethren went forth and attacked the children of Esau, in the land toward the south. And he took Chebron and her towns: and he burnt the walls thereof and the towers all round it.

66 And he removed his camp to go into the land of the aliens: and he went through Samaria.

67 In that day some priests fell in battle, while desiring to do manfully, they went out unadvisedly to fight.

68 And Judas turned to Azotus into the land of the strangers: and he threw down their altars: and be burnt the statues of their gods with fire. And he took the spoils of the cities and returned into the land of Juda.

CHAPTER 6

The fruitless repentance and death of Antiochus. His son comes against Judas with a formidable army. He besieges Sion, but at last makes peace with the Jews.

NOW king Antiochus was going through the higher countries, and he heard that the city of Elymais in Persia was greatly renowned and abounding in silver and gold.

2 And that there was in it a temple exceeding rich and coverings of gold and breastplates and shields which king Alexander, son of Philip the Macedonian that reigned first in Greece, had left there.

3 Lo, he came and sought to take the city and to pillage it: but he was not able, because the design was known to them that were in the city.

4 And they rose up against him in battle: and he fled away from thence and departed with great sadness and returned towards Babylonia.

5 And whilst he was in Persia, there came one that told him, how the armies that were in the land of Juda were put to flight:

6 And that Lysias went with a very great power and was put to flight before the face of the Jews: and that they were grown strong by the armour and power and store of spoils which they had gotten out of the camps which they had destroyed:

7 And that they had thrown down the abomination which he had set up upon the altar in Jerusalem: and that they had compassed about the sanctuary with high walls as before, and Bethsura also his city.

8 And it came to pass when the king heard these words, that he was struck with fear and exceedingly moved. And he laid himself down upon his bed and fell sick for grief, because it had not fallen out to him as he imagined.

9 And he remained there many days: for great grief came more and more upon him, and he made account that he should die.

10 And he called for all his friends and said to them: Sleep is gone from my eyes, and I am fallen away, and my heart is cast down for anxiety.

11 And I said in my heart: Into how much tribulation am I come, and into what floods of sorrow, wherein now I am: I that was pleasant and beloved in my power!

12 But now I remember the evils that I have done in Jerusalem, from whence also I took away all the spoils of gold and of silver that were in it, and I sent to destroy the inhabitants of Juda without cause.

13 I know therefore that for this cause these evils have found me: and behold I perish with great grief in a strange land.

14 Then he called Philip, one of his friends: and he made him regent over all his kingdom.

15 And he gave him the crown and his robe and his ring, that he should go to Antiochus his son and should bring him up for the kingdom.

16 So king Antiochus died there in the year one hundred and forty-nine.

17 And Lysias understood that the king was dead: and he set up Antiochus his son to reign, whom he brought up young: and he called his name Eupator.

18 Now they that were in the castle had shut up the Israelites round about the holy place: and they were continually seeking their hurt and to strengthen the Gentiles.

19 And Judas purposed to destroy them: and he called together all the people, to besiege them.

20 And they came together and besieged them in the year one hundred and fifty: and they made battering slings and engines.

21 And some of the besieged got out: and some wicked men of Israel joined themselves unto them.

22 And they went to the king and said: How long dost thou delay to execute the judgment and to revenge our brethren?

23 We determined to serve thy father and to do according to his orders and obey his edicts:

24 And for this they of our nation are alienated from us and have slain as many of us as they could find and have spoiled our inheritances.

25 Neither have they put forth their hand against us only, but also against all our borders.

26 And behold they have approached this day to the castle of Jerusalem to take it: and they have fortified the strong hold of Bethsura.

27 And unless thou speedily prevent them, they will do greater things than these, and thou shalt not be able to subdue them.

28 Now when the king heard this, he was angry: and he called together all his friends and the captains of his army and them that were over the horsemen.

29 There came also to him from other realms and from the islands of the sea hired troops.

30 And the number of his army was an hundred thousand footmen and twenty thousand horsemen and thirty-two elephants, trained to battle.

31 And they went through Idumea and approached to Bethsura and fought many days: and they made engines. But they sallied forth and burnt them with fire and fought manfully.

32 And Judas departed from the castle and removed the camp to Bethzacharam, over against the king's camp.

33 And the king rose before it was light and made his troops march on fiercely towards the way of Bethzacharam. And the armies made themselves ready for the battle: and they sounded the trumpets.

34 And they shewed the elephants the blood of grapes and mulberries, to provoke them to fight.

35 And they distributed the beasts by the legions: and there stood by every elephant a thousand men in coats of mail and with helmets of brass on their heads: and five hundred horsemen set in order were chosen for every beast.

36 These before the time, wheresoever the beast was, they were there: and whithersoever it went, they went: and they departed not from it.

37 And upon the beast there were strong wooden towers which covered every one of them, and engines upon them: and upon every one thirty-two valiant men, who fought from above, and an Indian to rule the beast.

38 And the rest of the horsemen he placed on this side and on that side at the two wings, with trumpets to stir up the army and to hasten them forward that stood thick together in the legions thereof.

39 Now when the sun shone upon the shields of gold and of brass, the mountains glittered therewith: and they shone like lamps of fire.

40 And part of the king's army was distinguished by the high mountains, and the other part by the low places: and they marched on warily and orderly.

41 And all the inhabitants of the

CHAP. 6. Ver. 31. *But they sallied forth.* That is, the citizens of Bethsura sallied forth, and burnt *them,* that is, burnt the *engines* of the besiegers.
Ver. 36. *These before the time.* That is, these were ready for every occasion.

land were moved at the noise of their multitude and the marching of the company and the rattling of the armour: for the army was exceeding great and strong.

42 And Judas and his army drew near for battle: and there fell of the king's army six hundred men.

43 And Eleazar the son of Saura saw one of the beasts harnessed with the king's harness: and it was higher than the other beasts. And it seemed to him that the king was on it.

44 And he exposed himself to deliver his people and to get himself an everlasting name.

45 And he ran up to it boldly in the midst of the legion, killing on the right hand and on the left: and they fell by him on this side and that side.

46 And he went between the feet of the elephant and put himself under it and slew it: and it fell to the ground upon him, and he died there.

47 Then they, seeing the strength of the king and the fierceness of his army, turned away from them.

48 But the king's army went up against them to Jerusalem: and the king's army pitched their tents against Judea and Mount Sion.

49 And he made peace with them that were in Bethsura. And they came forth out of the city, because they had no victuals, being shut up there: for it was the year of rest to the land.

50 And the king took Bethsura: and he placed there a garrison to keep it.

51 And he turned his army against the sanctuary for many days: and he set up there battering slings and engines and instruments to cast fire and engines to cast stones and javelins and pieces to shoot arrows, and slings.

52 And they also made engines against their engines: and they fought for many days.

53 But there were no victuals in the city, because it was the seventh year: and such as had stayed in Judea of them that came from among the nations had eaten the residue of all that which had been stored up.

54 And there remained in the holy places but a few, for the famine had prevailed over them: and they were dispersed every man to his own place.

55 ¹ Now Lysias heard that Philip, whom king Antiochus while he lived had appointed to bring up his son Antiochus, and to reign, to be king,

56 Was returned from Persia and Media, with the army that went with him and that he sought to take upon him the affairs of the kingdom.

CHAP. 6. ¹ 1 Mach. 6, 15.

57 Wherefore he made haste to go and say to the king and to the captains of the army: We decay daily and our provision of victuals is small and the place that we lay siege to is strong: and it lieth upon us to take order for the affairs of the kingdom.

58 Now therefore let us come to an agreement with these men and make peace with them and with all their nation.

59 And let us covenant with them, that they may live according to their own laws as before. For because of our despising their laws, they have been provoked and have done all these things.

60 And the proposal was acceptable in the sight of the king and of the princes: and he sent to them to make peace: and they accepted of it.

61 And the king and the princes swore to them: and they came out of the strong hold.

62 Then the king entered into Mount Sion and saw the strength of the place: and he quickly broke the oath that he had taken and gave commandment to throw down the wall round about.

63 And he departed in haste and returned to Antioch, where he found Philip master of the city: and he fought against him and took the city.

CHAPTER 7

Demetrius is made king and sends Bacchides and Alcimus the priest into Judea, and after them Nicanor, who is slain by Judas with all his army.

IN the hundred and fifty-first year, Demetrius the son of Seleucus departed from the city of Rome and came up with a few men into a city of the sea coast and reigned there.

2 And it came to pass, as he entered into the house of the kingdom of his fathers, that the army seized upon Antiochus and Lysias, to bring them unto him.

3 And when he knew it, he said: Let me not see their face.

4 So the army slew them. And Demetrius sat upon the throne of his kingdom.

5 And there came to him the wicked and ungodly men of Israel: and Alcimus was at the head of them, who desired to be made high priest.

6 And they accused the people to the king, saying: Judas and his brethren have destroyed all thy friends, and he hath driven us out of our land.

7 Now therefore send some man whom thou trustest, and let him go and see all the havock he hath made amongst us and in the king's lands: and

let him punish all his friends and their helpers.

8 Then the king chose Bacchides, one of his friends that ruled beyond the great river in the kingdom, and was faithful to the king: and he sent him,

9 To see the havock that Judas had made. And the wicked Alcimus he made high priest and commanded him to take revenge upon the children of Israel.

10 And they arose and came with a great army into the land of Juda: and they sent messengers and spoke to Judas and his brethren with peaceable words deceitfully.

11 But they gave no heed to their words: for they saw that they were come with a great army.

12 Then there assembled to Alcimus and Bacchides a company of the scribes, to require things that are just:

13 And first the Assideans that were among the children of Israel. And they sought peace of them.

14 For they said: One that is a priest of the seed of Aaron is come. He will not deceive us.

15 And he spoke to them peaceably: and he swore to them, saying: We will do you no harm nor your friends.

16 And they believed him. And he took threescore of them and slew them in one day, according to the word that is written:

17 [1] The flesh of thy saints and the blood of them they have shed round about Jerusalem, and there was none to bury them.

18 Then fear and trembling fell upon all the people: for they said: There is no truth nor justice among them: for they have broken the covenant and the oath which they made.

19 And Bacchides removed the camp from Jerusalem and pitched in Bethzecha: and he sent and took many of them that were fled away from him. And some of the people he killed, and threw them into a great pit.

20 Then he committed the country to Alcimus and left with him troops to help him. So Bacchides went away to the king.

21 But Alcimus did what he could to maintain his chief priesthood.

22 And they that disturbed the people resorted to him: and they got the land of Juda into their power and did much hurt in Israel.

23 And Judas saw all the evils that Alcimus and they that were with him did to the children of Israel, much more than the Gentiles.

24 And he went out into all the coasts of Judea round about and took vengeance upon the men that had revolted: and they ceased to go forth any more into the country.

25 And Alcimus saw that Judas and they that were with him prevailed: and he knew that he could not stand against them: and he went back to the king and accused them of many crimes.

26 [2] And the king sent Nicanor one of his principal lords, who was a great enemy to Israel: and he commanded him to destroy the people.

27 And Nicanor came to Jerusalem with a great army: and he sent to Judas and his brethren deceitfully with friendly words,

28 Saying: Let there be no fighting between me and you. I will come with a few men to see your faces with peace.

29 And he came to Judas and they saluted one another peaceably: and the enemies were prepared to take away Judas by force.

30 And the thing was known to Judas that he was come to him with deceit: and he was much afraid of him and would not see his face any more.

31 And Nicanor knew that his counsel was discovered: and he went out to fight against Judas near Capharsalama.

32 And there fell of Nicanor's army almost five thousand men: and they fled into the city of David.

33 And after this Nicanor went up into mount Sion: and some of the priests and the people came out to salute him peaceably and to shew him the holocausts that were offered for the king.

34 But he mocked and despised them and abused them: and he spoke proudly,

35 And swore in anger, saying: Unless Judas and his army be delivered into my hands, as soon as ever I return in peace, I will burn this house. And he went out in a great rage.

36 And the priests went in and stood before the face of the altar and the temple. And weeping, they said:

37 Thou, O Lord, hast chosen this house for thy name to be called upon therein, that it might be a house of prayer and supplication for thy people.

38 Be avenged of this man and his army: and let them fall by the sword. Remember their blasphemies and suffer them not to continue any longer.

39 Then Nicanor went out from Jerusalem and encamped near to Bethoron: and an army of Syria joined him.

40 But Judas pitched in Adarsa with

CHAP. 7. [1] Ps. 78, 1, 2, 3. [2] 2 Mach. 15, 1.

three thousand men. And Judas prayed, and said:

41 ³ O Lord, when they that were sent by king Sennacherib blasphemed thee, an angel went out and slew of them a hundred and eighty-five thousand.

42 Even so destroy this army in our sight to-day and let the rest know that he hath spoken ill against thy sanctuary: and judge thou him according to his wickedness.

43 And the armies joined battle on the thirteenth day of the month Adar. And the army of Nicanor was defeated: and he himself was first slain in the battle.

44 And when his army saw that Nicanor was slain, they threw away their weapons and fled.

45 And they pursued after them one day's journey from Adazer, even till ye come to Gazara: and they sounded the trumpets after them with signals.

46 And they went forth out of all the towns of Judea round about: and they pushed them with the horns: and they turned again to them. And they were all slain with the sword: and there was not left of them so much as one.

47 And they took the spoils of them for a booty: and they cut off Nicanor's head and his right hand which he had proudly stretched out: and they brought it and hung it up over against Jerusalem.

48 And the people rejoiced exceedingly: and they spent that day with great joy.

49 And he ordained that this day should be kept every year, being the thirteenth of the month of Adar.

50 And the land of Juda was quiet for a short time.

CHAPTER 8

Judas hears of the great character of the Romans. He makes a league with them.

NOW Judas heard of the fame of the Romans, that they are powerful and strong and willingly agree to all things that are requested of them: and that whosoever have come to them, they have made amity with them, and that they are mighty in power.

2 And they heard of their battles and their noble acts, which they had done in Galatia: how they had conquered them and brought them under tribute.

3 And how great things they had done in the land of Spain, and that they had brought under their power the mines of silver and of gold that are there, and had gotten possession of all the place by their counsel and patience:

4 And had conquered places that were very far off from them and kings that came against them from the ends of the earth and had overthrown them with great slaughter: and the rest pay them tribute every year.

5 And that they had defeated in battle Philip and Perses the king of the Ceteans and the rest that had borne arms against them, and had conquered them:

6 And how Antiochus the great king of Asia, who went to fight against them, having a hundred and twenty elephants with horsemen and chariots and a very great army, was routed by them.

7 And how they took him alive and appointed to him, that both he and they that should reign after him should pay a great tribute and that he should give hostages and that which was agreed upon,

8 And the country of the Indians and of the Medes and of the Lydians, some of their best provinces: and those which they had taken from them they gave to king Eumenes.

9 And that they who were in Greece had a mind to go and to destroy them: and they had knowledge thereof.

10 And they sent a general against them and fought with them, and many of them were slain, and they carried away their wives and their children captives and spoiled them and took possession of their land and threw down their walls and brought them to be their servants unto this day.

11 And the other kingdoms and islands that at any time had resisted them, they had destroyed and brought under their power.

12 But with their friends and such as relied upon them, they kept amity, and had conquered kingdoms that were near and that were far off: for all that heard their name were afraid of them.

13 That whom they had a mind to help to a kingdom, those reigned: and whom they would, they deposed from the kingdom: and they were greatly exalted.

14 And none of all these wore a crown or was clothed in purple, to be magnified thereby.

15 And that they had made themselves a senate house and consulted daily three hundred and twenty men that sat in council always for the people, that they might do the things that were right,

---

³ 4 Kings, 19, 35; Tob. 1, 21; Ecclus. 48, 24; Isal. 31, 36, 2 Mach. 8, 19.

Ver. 46. *Horns.* That is, strength.
CHAP. 8. Ver. 2. *They heard.* What is here set down of the history and character of the ancient Romans is not an assertion or affirmation of the sacred writer, but only a relation of what Judas had heard of them.
Ver. 5. *Ceteans.* That is, the Macedonians.
Ver. 8. *Eumenes.* King of Pergamus.

16 And that they committed their government to one man every year, to rule over all their country: and they all obey one: and there is no envy, nor jealousy amongst them.

17 So Judas chose Eupolemus the son of John, the son of Jacob, and Jason the son of Eleazar: and he sent them to Rome to make a league of amnity and confederacy with them.

18 And that they might take off from them the yoke of the Grecians, for they saw that they oppressed the kingdom of Israel with servitude.

19 And they went to Rome, a very long journey. And they entered into the senate house and said:

20 Judas Machabeus and his brethren and the people of the Jews have sent us to you, to make alliance and peace with you, and that we may be registered your confederates and friends.

21 And the proposal was pleasing in their sight.

22 And this is the copy of the writing that they wrote back again, graven in tables of brass, and sent to Jerusalem, that it might be with them there for a memorial of the peace and alliance.

23 GOOD SUCCESS BE TO THE ROMANS, and to the people of the Jews, by sea and by land for ever and far be the sword and enemy from them.

24 But if there come first any war upon the Romans or any of their confederates, in all their dominions:

25 The nation of the Jews shall help them according as the time shall direct, with all their heart.

26 Neither shall they give them, whilst they are fighting, or furnish them with wheat or arms or money or ships, as it hath seemed good to the Romans: and they shall obey their orders, without taking any thing of them.

27 In like manner also if war shall come first upon the nation of the Jews, the Romans shall help them with all their heart, according as the time shall permit them.

28 And there shall not be given to them that come to their aid either wheat or arms or money or ships, as it hath seemed good to the Romans: and they shall observe their orders without deceit.

29 According to these articles did the Romans covenant with the people of the Jews.

30 And if after this one party or the other shall have a mind to add to these *articles* or take away any thing, they may do it at their pleasure: and whatsoever they shall add or take away shall be ratified.

31 Moreover, concerning the evils that Demetrius the king hath done against them, we have written to him, saying: Why hast thou made thy yoke heavy upon our friends and allies, the Jews?

32 If therefore they come again to us complaining of thee, we will do them justice and will make war against thee by sea and land.

CHAPTER 9

Bacchides is sent again into Judea. Judas fights against him with eight hundred men and is slain. Jonathan succeeds him and revenges the murder of his brother John. He fights against Bacchides. Alcimus dies miserably. Bacchides besieges Bethbessen. He is forced to raise the siege and leave the country.

IN the mean time, when Demetrius heard that Nicanor and his army were fallen in battle, he sent again Bacchides and Alcimus into Judea: and the right wing of his army with them.

2 And they took the road that leadeth to Galgal and they camped in Masaloth, which is in Arabella: and they made themselves masters of it and slew many people.

3 In the first month of the hundred and fifty-second year they brought the army to Jerusalem.

4 And they arose and went to Berea with twenty thousand men and two thousand horsemen.

5 Now Judas had pitched his tents in Laisa, and three thousand chosen men with him.

6 And they saw the multitude of the army that they were many: and they were seized with great fear. And many withdrew themselves out of the camp: and there remained of them no more than eight hundred men.

7 And Judas saw that his army slipped away and the battle pressed upon him. And his heart was cast down, because he had not time to gather them together: and he was discouraged.

8 Then he said to them that remained: Let us arise and go against our enemies, if we may be able to fight against them.

9 But they dissuaded him, saying: We shall not be able, but let us save our lives now and return to our brethren. And then we will fight against them: for we are but few.

10 Then Judas said: God forbid we

Ver. 16. *To one man.* There were two consuls: but one only ruled at one time, each in his day.— *No envy.* So Judas had heard: and it was so far true with regard to the ancient Romans that as yet no envy or jealousy had divided them into such open factions and civil wars as they afterwards experienced from the time of Marius and Sylla.

should do this thing and flee away from them: but if our time be come, let us die manfully for our brethren, and let us not stain our glory.

11 And the army removed out of the camp: and they stood over against them. And the horsemen were divided into two troops, and the slingers and the archers went before the army, and they that were in the front *were* all men of valour.

12 And Bacchides was in the right wing: and the legion drew near on two sides. And they sounded the trumpets.

13 And they also that were on Judas' side, even they, also cried out: and the earth shook at the noise of the armies. And the battle was fought from morning even unto the evening.

14 And Judas perceived that the stronger part of the army of Bacchides was on the right side: and all the stout of heart came together with him.

15 And the right wing was discomfited by them: and he pursued them even to the mount Azotus.

16 And they that were in the left wing saw that the right wing was discomfited: and they followed after Judas and them that were with him, at their back:

17 And the battle was hard fought: and there fell many wounded of the one side and of the other.

18 And Judas was slain and the rest fled away.

19 And Jonathan and Simon took Judas their brother and buried him in the sepulchre of their fathers in the city of Modin.

20 And all the people of Israel bewailed him with great lamentation: and they mourned for him many days.

21 And said: How is the mighty man fallen that saved the people of Israel!

22 But the rest of the words of the wars of Judas and of the noble acts that he did and of his greatness are not written: for they were very many.

23 And it came to pass after the death of Judas that the wicked began to put forth their heads in all the confines of Israel: and all the workers of iniquity rose up.

24 In those days there was a very great famine: and they and all their country yielded to Bacchides.

25 And Bacchides chose the wicked men and made them lords of the country.

26 And they sought out and made diligent search after the friends of Judas and brought them to Bacchides: and he took vengeance of them and abused them.

27 And there was a great tribulation in Israel, such as was not since the day, that there was no prophet seen in Israel.

28 And all the friends of Judas came together and said to Jonathan:

29 Since thy brother Judas died, there is not a man like him to go forth against our enemies, Bacchides and them that are the enemies of our nation.

30 Now therefore we have chosen thee this day to be our prince and captain in his stead, to fight our battle.

31 So Jonathan took upon him the government at that time and rose up in the place of Judas his brother.

32 And Bacchides had knowledge of it and sought to kill him.

33 And Jonathan and Simon his brother knew it, and all that were with them: and they fled into the desert of Thecua and they pitched by the water of the lake Asphar,

34 And Bacchides understood it: and he came himself with all his army over the Jordan on the sabbath day.

35 And Jonathan sent his brother, a captain of the people, to desire the Nabutheans his friends, that they would lend them their equipage which was copious.

36 And the children of Jambri came forth out of Madaba and took John and all that he had and went away with them.

37 After this it was told Jonathan and Simon his brother that the children of Jambri made a great marriage and were bringing the bride out of Madaba, the daughter of one of the great princes of Chanaan, with great pomp.

38 And they remembered the blood of John their brother: and they went up and hid themselves under the covert of the mountain.

39 And they lifted up their eyes and saw: and behold a tumult and great preparation: and the bridegroom came forth and his friends and his brethren to meet them with timbrels and musical instruments and many weapons.

40 And they rose up against them from the place where they lay in ambush and slew them: and there fell many wounded. And the rest fled into the mountains: and they took all their spoils.

41 And the marriage was turned into mourning: and the noise of their musical instruments into lamentation.

42 And they took revenge for the blood of their brother: and they returned to the bank of the Jordan.

43 And Bacchides heard it: and he

came on the sabbath day even to the bank of the Jordan with a great power.

44 And Jonathan said to his company: Let us arise and fight against our enemies: for it is not now as yesterday and the day before.

45 For behold the battle is before us, and the water of the Jordan on this side and on that side, and banks and marshes and woods: and there is no place for us to turn aside.

46 [1] Now therefore cry ye to heaven, that ye may be delivered from the hand of your enemies. And they joined battle.

47 And Jonathan stretched forth his hand to strike Bacchides: but he turned away from him backwards.

48 And Jonathan and they that were with him leaped into the Jordan and swam over the Jordan to them.

49 And there fell of Bacchides' side that day a thousand men. And they returned to Jerusalem,

50 And they built strong cities in Judea, the fortress that was in Jericho, and in Ammaus and in Bethoron and in Bethel and Thamnata and Phara and Thopo, with high walls and gates and bars.

51 And he placed garrisons in them, that they might wage war against Israel.

52 And he fortified the city of Bethsura and Gazara and the castle and set garrisons in them and provisions of victuals.

53 And he took the sons of the chief men of the country for hostages and put them in the castle in Jerusalem in custody.

54 Now in the year one hundred and fifty-three, the second month, Alcimus commanded the walls of the inner *court* of the sanctuary to be thrown down and the works of the prophets to be destroyed: and he began to destroy.

55 At that time Alcimus was struck: and his works were hindered and his mouth was stopped and he was taken with a palsy, so that he could no more speak a word nor give order concerning his house.

56 And Alcimus died at that time in great torment.

57 And Bacchides saw that Alcimus was dead: and he returned to the king. And the land was quiet for two years.

58 And all the wicked held a council, saying: Behold Jonathan and they that are with him dwell at ease and without fear. Now therefore let us bring Bacchides hither: and he shall take them all in one night.

59 So they went and gave him counsel.

60 And he arose to come with a great army: and he sent secretly letters to his adherents that were in Judea, to seize upon Jonathan and them that were with him: but they could not, for their design was known to them.

61 And he apprehended of the men of the country, that were the principal authors of the mischief, fifty men and slew them.

62 And Jonathan and Simon and they that were with him retired into Bethbessen, which is in the desert: and he repaired the breaches thereof: and they fortified it.

63 And when Bacchides knew it, he gathered together all his multitude: and sent word to them that were of Judea.

64 And he came and camped above Bethbessen and fought against it many days and made engines.

65 But Jonathan left his brother Simon in the city and went forth into the country and came with a number of men.

66 And he struck Odares and his brethren and the children of Phaseron in their tents: and he began to slay and to increase in forces.

67 But Simon and they that were with him sallied out of the city and burnt the engines.

68 And they fought against Bacchides: and he was discomfited by them. And they afflicted him exceedingly: for his counsel and his enterprise was in vain.

69 And he was angry with the wicked men that had given him counsel to come into their country. And he slew many of them: and he purposed to return with the rest into their country.

70 And Jonathan had knowledge of it: and he sent ambassadors to him to make peace with him and to restore to him the prisoners.

71 And he accepted it willingly and did according to his words and swore that he would do him no harm all the days of his life.

72 And he restored to him the prisoners which he before had taken out of the land of Juda. And he returned and went away into his own country: and he came no more into their borders.

73 So the sword ceased from Israel: and Jonathan dwelt in Machmas. And Jonathan began there to judge the people: and he destroyed the wicked out of Israel.

CHAP. 9. [1] 2 Par. 20, 3.

CHAPTER 10

Alexander Bales sets himself up for king. Both he and Demetrius seek to make Jonathan their friend. Alexander kills Demetrius in battle and honours Jonathan. His victory over Apollonius.

NOW in the hundred and sixtieth year, Alexander the son of Antiochus surnamed the Illustrious came up and took Ptolemais: and they received him and he reigned there.

2 And king Demetrius heard of it and gathered together an exceeding great army and went forth against him to fight.

3 And Demetrius sent a letter to Jonathan with peaceable words, to magnify him.

4 For he said: Let us first make a peace with him before he make one with Alexander against us.

5 For he will remember all the evils that we have done against him and against his brother and against his nation.

6 And he gave him authority to gather together an army and to make arms and that he should be his confederate: and the hostages that were in the castle, he commanded to be delivered to him.

7 And Jonathan came to Jerusalem and read the letters in the hearing of all the people and of them that were in the castle.

8 And they were struck with great fear, because they heard that the king had given him authority to gather together an army.

9 And the hostages were delivered to Jonathan: and he restored them to their parents.

10 And Jonathan dwelt in Jerusalem and began to build and to repair the city.

11 And he ordered workmen to build the walls and mount Sion round about with square stones for fortification: and so they did.

12 And the strangers that were in the strong holds which Bacchides had built fled away.

13 And every man left his place and departed into his own country.

14 Only in Bethsura there remained some of them that had forsaken the law and the commandments of God: for this was a place of refuge for them.

15 And king Alexander heard of the promises that Demetrius had made Jonathan: and they told him of the battles and the worthy acts that he and his brethren had done and the labours that they had endured.

16 And he said: Shall we find such another man? Now therefore we will make him our friend and our confederate.

17 So he wrote a letter and sent it to him according to these words, saying:

18 King Alexander to his brother Jonathan, greeting.

19 We have heard of thee that thou art a man of great power and fit to be our friend:

20 Now therefore we make thee this day high priest of thy nation and that thou be called the king's friend (and he sent him a purple robe, and a crown of gold) and that thou be of one mind with us in our affairs and keep friendship with us.

21 Then Jonathan put on the holy vestment in the seventh month, in the year one hundred and threescore, at the feast day of the tabernacles: and he gathered together an army and made a great number of arms.

22 And Demetrius heard these words and was exceeding sorry and said:

23 What is this that we have done that Alexander hath prevented us to gain the friendship of the Jews to strengthen himself?

24 I also will write to them words of request and offer dignities and gifts, that they may be with me to aid me.

25 And he wrote to them in these words: King Demetrius to the nation of the Jews, greeting.

26 Whereas you have kept covenant with us and have continued in our friendship and have not joined with our enemies, we have heard of it and are glad.

27 Wherefore now continue still to keep fidelity towards us and we will reward you with good things for what you have done in our behalf.

28 And we will remit to you many charges and will give you gifts.

29 And now I free you and all the Jews from tributes: and I release you from the customs of salt and remit the crowns and the thirds of the seed.

30 And the half of the fruit of trees, which is my share, I leave to you from this day forward, so that it shall not be taken of the land of Juda and of the three cities that are added thereto out of Samaria and Galilee, from this day forth and for ever:

31 And let Jerusalem be holy and free, with the borders thereof: and let the tenths and tributes be for itself.

32 I yield up also the power of the castle that is in Jerusalem: and I give it to the high priest, to place therein such men as he shall choose to keep it.

33 And every soul of the Jews that hath been carried captive from the land

of Juda in all my kingdom, I set at liberty freely, that all be discharged from tributes even of their cattle.

34 And I will that all the feasts and the sabbaths and the new moons and the days appointed and three days before the solemn day and three days after the solemn day be all *days* of immunity and freedom for all the Jews that are in my kingdom:

35 And no man shall have power to do any thing against them or to molest any of them, in any cause.

36 And let there be enrolled in the king's army to the number of thirty thousand of the Jews. And allowance shall be made them as is due to all the king's forces: and certain of them shall be appointed to be in the fortresses of the great king.

37 And some of them shall be set over the affairs of the kingdom that are of trust: and let the governors be taken from among themselves and let them walk in their own laws, as the king hath commanded in the land of Juda.

38 And the three cities that are added to Judea out of the country of Samaria, let them be accounted with Judea, that they may be under one and obey no other authority but that of the high priest.

39 Ptolemais and the confines thereof, I give as a free gift to the holy places that are in Jerusalem, for the necessary charges of the holy things.

40 And I give every year fifteen thousand sicles of silver out of the king's accounts, of what belongs to me.

41 And all that is above, which they that were over the affairs the years before had not paid, from this time they shall give it to the works of the house.

42 Moreover the five thousand sicles of silver which they received from the account of the holy places every year shall also belong to the priests that execute the ministry.

43 And whosoever shall flee into the temple that is in Jerusalem and in all the borders thereof, being indebted to the king for any matter, let them be set at liberty: and all that they have in my kingdom, let them have it free.

44 For the building also or repairing the works of the holy places, the charges shall be given out of the king's revenues.

45 For the building also of the walls of Jerusalem and the fortifying thereof round about, the charges shall be given out of the king's account, as also for the building of the walls in Judea.

46 Now when Jonathan, and the people heard these words [1] they gave

no credit to them nor received them: because they remembered the great evil that he had done in Israel, for he had afflicted them exceedingly.

47 And their inclinations were towards Alexander, because he had been the chief promoter of peace in their regard: and him they always helped.

48 And king Alexander gathered together a great army and moved his camp near to Demetrius.

49 And the two kings joined battle and the army of Demetrius fled away: and Alexander pursued after him and pressed them close.

50 And the battle was hard fought till the sun went down: and Demetrius was slain that day.

51 And Alexander sent ambassadors to Ptolemee king of Egypt with words to this effect, saying:

52 Forasmuch as I am returned into my kingdom and am set in the throne of my ancestors and have gotten the dominion and have overthrown Demetrius and possessed our country,

53 And have joined battle with him: and both he and his army have been destroyed by us: and we are placed in the throne of his kingdom:

54 Now therefore let us make friendship one with another. And give me now thy daughter to wife and I will be thy son-in-law and I will give both thee and her gifts worthy of thee.

55 And king Ptolemee answered, saying: Happy is the day wherein thou didst return to the land of thy fathers and sattest in the throne of their kingdom.

56 And now I will do to thee as thou hast written: but meet me at Ptolemais, that we may see one another and I may give her to thee as thou hast said.

57 So Ptolemee went out of Egypt, with Cleopatra his daughter: and he came to Ptolemais in the hundred and sixty-second year.

58 And king Alexander met him and he gave him his daughter Cleopatra: and he celebrated her marriage at Ptolemais, with great glory after the manner of kings.

59 And king Alexander wrote to Jonathan that he should come and meet him.

60 And he went honourably to Ptolemais and he met there the two kings and he gave them much silver, and gold, and presents: and he found favour in their sight.

61 And some pestilent men of Israel,

CHAP. 10. [1] 1 Mach. 7, 11.

CHAP. 10. Ver. 51. *Ptolemee.* Surnamed Philometer.

men of a wicked life, assembled themselves against him to accuse him: and the king gave no heed to them.

62 And he commanded that Jonathan's garments should be taken off and that he should be clothed with purple: and they did so. And the king made him sit by himself.

63 And he said to his princes: Go out with him into the midst of the city and make proclamation that no man complain against him of any matter and that no man trouble him for any manner of cause.

64 So when his accusers saw his glory proclaimed and him clothed with purple they all fled away.

65 And the king magnified him and enrolled him amongst his chief friends and made him governor and partaker of his dominion.

66 And Jonathan returned into Jerusalem with peace and joy.

67 In the year one hundred and sixty-five, Demetrius the son of Demetrius came from Crete into the land of his fathers.

68 And king Alexander heard of it and was much troubled and returned to Antioch.

69 And king Demetrius made Apollonius his general, who was governor of Celesyria: and he gathered together a great army and came to Jamnia: and he sent to Jonathan the high priest,

70 Saying: Thou alone standest against us and I am laughed at and reproached, because thou shewest thy power against us in the mountains.

71 Now therefore, if thou trustest in thy forces, come down to us into the plain, and there let us try one another: for with me is the strength of war.

72 Ask and learn who I am and the rest that help me, who also say that your foot cannot stand before our face, for thy fathers have twice been put to flight in their own land.

73 And now how wilt thou be able to abide the horsemen and so great an army in the plain, where there is no stone nor rock nor place to flee to?

74 Now when Jonathan heard the words of Apollonius he was moved in his mind. And he chose ten thousand men and went out of Jerusalem: and Simon his brother met him to help him.

75 And they pitched their tents near Joppe: but they shut him out of the city, because a garrison of Apollonius was in Joppe. And he laid siege to it.

76 And they that were in the city, being affrighted, opened the gates to him: so Jonathan took Joppe.

77 And Apollonius heard of it and he took three thousand horsemen and a great army.

78 And he went to Azotus as one that was making a journey: and immediately he went forth into the plain, because he had a great number of horsemen and he trusted in them. And Jonathan followed after him to Azotus: and they joined battle.

79 And Apollonius left privately in the camp a thousand horsemen behind them.

80 And Jonathan knew that there was an ambush behind him: and they surrounded his army and cast darts at the people from morning till evening.

81 But the people stood still, as Jonathan had commanded them: and so their horses were fatigued.

82 Then Simon drew forth his army and attacked the legion: for the horsemen were wearied. And they were discomfited by him and fled.

83 And they that were scattered about the plain fled into Azotus and went into Bethdagon their idol's temple, there to save themselves.

84 But Jonathan set fire to Azotus and the cities that were round about it and took the spoils of them and the temple of Dagon: and all them that were fled into it, he burnt with fire.

85 So they that were slain by the sword, with them that were burnt, were almost eight thousand men.

86 And Jonathan removed his army from thence and camped against Ascalon: and they went out of the city to meet him with great honour.

87 And Jonathan returned into Jerusalem with his people, having many spoils.

88 And it came to pass when Alexander the king heard these words that he honoured Jonathan yet more.

89 And he sent him a buckle of gold, as the custom is, to be given to such as are of the royal blood. And he gave him Accaron and all the borders thereof in possession.

CHAPTER 11

Ptolemee invades the kingdom of Alexander. The latter is slain and the former dies soon after. Demetrius honours Jonathan and is rescued by the Jews from his own subjects in Antioch. Antiochus the younger favours Jonathan. His exploits in divers places.

AND the king of Egypt gathered together an army, like the sand that lieth upon the sea shore, and many ships: and he sought to get the kingdom of Alexander by deceit and join it to his own kingdom.

2 And he went out into Syria with peaceable words: and they opened to

him the cities, and met him. For king Alexander had ordered them to go forth to meet him, because he was his father-in-law.

3 Now when Ptolemee entered into the cities he put garrisons of soldiers in every city.

4 And when he came near to Azotus, they shewed him the temple of Dagon that was burnt with fire and Azotus and the suburbs thereof that were destroyed and the bodies that were cast abroad and the graves of them that were slain in the battle which they had made near the way.

5 And they told the king that Jonathan had done these things, to make him odious: but the king held his peace.

6 And Jonathan came to meet the king at Joppe with glory: and they saluted one another and they lodged there.

7 And Jonathan went with the king as far as the river called Eleutherus: and he returned into Jerusalem.

8 And king Ptolemee got the dominion of the cities by the sea side, even to Seleucia: and he devised evil designs against Alexander.

9 And he sent ambassadors to Demetrius, saying: Come, let us make a league between us and I will give thee my daughter whom Alexander hath: and thou shalt reign in the kingdom of thy father.

10 For I repent that I have given him my daughter: for he hath sought to kill me.

11 And he slandered him, because he coveted his kingdom.

12 And he took away his daughter and gave her to Demetrius and alienated himself from Alexander: and his enmities were made manifest.

13 And Ptolemee entered into Antioch and set two crowns upon his head, that of Egypt and that of Asia.

14 Now king Alexander was in Cilicia at that time: because they that were in those places had rebelled.

15 And when Alexander heard of it he came to give him battle: and king Ptolemee brought forth his army and met him with a strong power and put him to flight.

16 And Alexander fled into Arabia, there to be protected: and king Ptolemee was exalted.

17 And Zabdiel the Arabian took off Alexander's head and sent it to Ptolemee.

18 And king Ptolemee died the third day after: and they that were in the strong holds were destroyed by them that were within the camp.

19 And Demetrius reigned in the hundred and sixty-seventh year.

20 In those days Jonathan gathered together them that were in Judea, to take the castle that was in Jerusalem: and they made many engines of war against it.

21 Then some wicked men that hated their own nation went away to king Demetrius and told him that Jonathan was besieging the castle.

22 And when he heard it he was angry: and forthwith he came to Ptolemais and wrote to Jonathan that he should not besiege the castle but should come to him in haste and speak to him.

23 But when Jonathan heard this he bade them besiege it still: and he chose some of the ancients of Israel and of the priests and put himself in danger.

24 And he took gold and silver and raiment and many other presents and went to the king to Ptolemais: and he found favour in his sight.

25 And certain wicked men of his nation made complaints against him.

26 And the king treated him as his predecessors had done before: and he exalted him in the sight of all his friends.

27 And he confirmed him in the high priesthood and all the honours he had before: and he made him the chief of his friends.

28 And Jonathan requested of the king that he would make Judea free from tribute, and the three governments and Samaria and the confines thereof: and he promised him three hundred talents.

29 And the king consented: and he wrote letters to Jonathan of all these things to this effect.

30 King Demetrius to his brother Jonathan and to the nation of the Jews, greeting.

31 We sent you here a copy of the letter which we have written to Lasthenes our parent, concerning you, that you might know it.

32 King Demetrius to Lasthenes his parent, greeting.

33 We have determined to do good to the nation of the Jews who are our friends and keep the things that are just with us, for their good will which they bear towards us.

34 We have ratified therefore unto them all the borders of Judea and the three cities, *Apherema*, Lydda and Ramatha, which are added to Judea, out of Samaria, and all their confines, to be set apart to all them that sacrifice in Jerusalem, instead of the payments

CHAP. 11. Ver. 34. *Apherema* is found only in the Greek version.

which the king received of them every year, and for the fruits of the land and of the trees.

35 And as for other things that belonged to us of the tithes and of the tributes, from this time we discharge them of them: the saltpans also and the crowns that were presented to us.

36 We give all to them: and nothing hereof shall be revoked from this time forth and for ever.

37 Now therefore see that thou make a copy of these things: and let it be given to Jonathan and set upon the holy mountain, in a conspicuous place.

38 And king Demetrius, seeing that the land was quiet before him and nothing resisted him, sent away all his forces, every man to his own place, except the foreign army which he had drawn together from the islands of the nations. So all the troops of his fathers hated him.

39 Now there was one Tryphon who had been of Alexander's party before: who, seeing that all the army murmured against Demetrius, went to Emalchuel the Arabian who brought up Antiochus the son of Alexander.

40 And he pressed him much to deliver him to him that he might be king in his father's place: and he told him all that Demetrius had done and how his soldiers hated him. And he remained there many days.

41 And Jonathan sent to king Demetrius desiring that he would cast out them that were in the castle in Jerusalem and those that were in the strong holds: because they fought against Israel.

42 And Demetrius sent to Jonathan, saying: I will not only do this for thee and for thy people, but I will greatly honour thee and thy nation, when opportunity shall serve.

43 Now therefore thou shalt do well if thou send me men to help me: for all my army is gone from me.

44 And Jonathan sent him three thousand valiant men to Antioch. And they came to the king: and the king was very glad of their coming.

45 And they that were of the city assembled themselves together, to the number of a hundred and twenty thousand men, and would have killed the king.

46 And the king fled into the palace: and they of the city kept the passages of the city and began to fight.

47 And the king called the Jews to his assistance. And they came to him all at once: and they all dispersed themselves through the city.

48 And they slew in that day a hun-

dred thousand men and they set fire to the city and got many spoils that day and delivered the king.

49 And they that were of the city saw that the Jews had got the city as they would: and they were discouraged in their mind and cried to the king, making supplication and saying:

50 Grant us peace: and let the Jews cease from assaulting us and the city.

51 And they threw down their arms and made peace: and the Jews were glorified in the sight of the king and in the sight of all that were in his realm and were renowned throughout the kingdom and returned to Jerusalem with many spoils.

52 So king Demetrius sat in the throne of his kingdom: and the land was quiet before him.

53 And he falsified all whatsoever he had said and alienated himself from Jonathan and did not reward him according to the benefits he had received from him but gave him great trouble.

54 And after this, Tryphon returned, and with him Antiochus the young boy who was made king, and put on the diadem.

55 And there assembled unto him all the hands which Demetrius had sent away: and they fought against Demetrius, who turned his back and fled.

56 And Tryphon took the elephants and made himself master of Antioch.

57 And young Antiochus wrote to Jonathan, saying: I confirm thee in the high priesthood and I appoint thee ruler over the four cities and to be one of the king's friends.

58 And he sent him vessels of gold for his service: and he gave him leave to drink in gold and to be clothed in purple and to wear a golden buckle.

59 And he made his brother Simon governor from the borders of Tyre even to the confines of Egypt.

60 Then Jonathan went forth and passed through the cities beyond the river: and all the forces of Syria gathered themselves to him to help him. And he came to Ascalon: and they met him honourably out of the city.

61 And he went from thence to Gaza: and they that were in Gaza shut him out. And he besieged it and burnt all the suburbs round about and took the spoils.

62 And the men of Gaza made supplication to Jonathan: and he gave them the right hand. And he took their sons for hostages and sent them to Jerusalem: and he went through the country as far as Damascus.

63 And Jonathan heard that the gen-

erals of Demetrius were come treacherously to Cades, which is in Galilee, with a great army, purposing to remove him from the affairs of the kingdom.

64 And he went against them: but left his brother Simon in the country.

65 And Simon encamped against Bethsura and assaulted it many days and shut them up.

66 And they desired him to make peace: and he granted it them. And he cast them out from thence and took the city and placed a garrison in it.

67 And Jonathan and his army encamped by the water of Genesar: and before it was light they were ready in the plain of Asor.

68 And behold the army of the strangers met him in the plain and they laid an ambush for him in the mountains: but he went out against them.

69 And they that lay in ambush rose out of their places and joined battle.

70 And all that were on Jonathan's side fled, and none was left of them but Mathathias the son of Absalom and Judas the son of Calphi, chief captain of the army.

71 And Jonathan rent his garments and cast earth upon his head and prayed.

72 And Jonathan turned again to them to battle: and he put them to flight: and they fought.

73 And they of his part that fled saw *this* and they turned again to him: and they all with him pursued *the enemies* even to Cades to their own camp: and they came even thither.

74 And there fell of the aliens in that day three thousand men: and Jonathan returned to Jerusalem.

CHAPTER 12

Jonathan renews his league with the Romans and Lacedemonians. The forces of Demetrius flee way from him. He is deceived and made prisoner by Tryphon.

AND Jonathan saw that the time served him: and he chose certain men and sent them to Rome, to confirm and to renew the amity with them.

2 And he sent letters to the Spartans and to other places according to the same form.

3 And they went to Rome and entered into the senate house and said: Jonathan the high priest and the nation of the Jews have sent us to renew the amity and alliance as it was before.

4 And they gave them letters to their governors in every place, to conduct them into the land of Juda with peace.

5 And this is a copy of the letters which Jonathan wrote to the Spartans:

6 Jonathan the high priest and the ancients of the nation and the priests and the rest of the people of the Jews to the Spartans, their brethren, greeting.

7 There were letters sent long ago to Onias the high priest from Arius who reigned then among you, to signify that you are our brethren, as the copy here underwritten doth specify.

8 And Onias received the ambassador with honour and received the letters wherein there was mention made of the alliance and amity.

9 We, though we needed none of these things, having for our comfort the holy books that are in our hands,

10 Chose rather to send to you to renew the brotherhood and friendship, lest we should become strangers to you altogether: for there is a long time passed since you sent to us.

11 We therefore at all times without ceasing, both in our festivals and other days wherein it is convenient, remember you in the sacrifices that we offer and in our observances, as it is meet and becoming to remember brethren.

12 And we rejoice at your glory.

13 But we have had many troubles and wars on every side: and the kings that are round about us, have fought against us.

14 But we would not be troublesome to you, nor to the rest of our allies and friends in these wars.

15 For we have had help from heaven and we have been delivered: and our enemies are humbled.

16 We have chosen therefore Numenius the son of Antiochus and Antipater the son of Jason and have sent them to the Romans to renew with them the former amity and alliance.

17 And we have commanded them to go also to you and to salute you and to deliver you our letters concerning the renewing of our brotherhood.

18 And now you shall do well to give us an answer hereto.

19 And this is the copy of the letter which he had sent to Onias:

20 Arius king of the Spartans to Onias the high priest, greeting.

21 It is found in writing concerning the Spartans and the Jews, that they are brethren and that they are of the stock of Abraham.

22 And now since this is come to our knowledge, you do well to write to us of your prosperity.

23 And we also have written back to you: That our cattle, and our possessions are yours: and yours, ours. We therefore have commanded that these things should be told you.

24 Now Jonathan heard that the generals of Demetrius were come again with a greater army than before to fight against him.

25 So he went out from Jerusalem and met them in the land of Amath: for he gave them no time to enter into his country.

26 And he sent spies into their camp: and they came back and brought him word that they designed to come upon them in the night.

27 And when the sun was set, Jonathan commanded his men to watch and to be in arms all night long ready to fight: and he set sentinels round about the camp.

28 And the enemies heard that Jonathan and his men were ready for battle: and they were struck with fear and dread in their heart: and they kindled fires in their camp.

29 But Jonathan and they that were with him knew it not till the morning: for they saw the lights burning.

30 And Jonathan pursued after them but overtook them not: for they had passed the river Eleutherus.

31 And Jonathan turned upon the Arabians that are called Zabadeans: and he defeated them and took the spoils of them.

32 And he went forward and came to Damascus and passed through all that country.

33 Simon also went forth and came as far as Ascalon and the neighbouring fortresses: and he turned aside to Joppe and took possession of it,

34 (For he heard that they designed to deliver the hold to them that took part with Demetrius). And he put a garrison there to keep it.

35 And Jonathan came back and called together the ancients of the people: and he took a resolution with them to build fortresses in Judea

36 And to build up walls in Jerusalem and raise a mount between the castle and the city, to separate it from the city, that so it might have no communication, and that they might neither buy nor sell.

37 And they came together to build up the city: for the wall that was upon the brook towards the east was broken down: and he repaired that which is called Caphetetha.

38 And Simon built Adiada in Sephela and fortified it and set up gates and bars.

39 Now when Tryphon had conceived a design to make himself king of Asia and to take the crown and to stretch out his hand against king Antiochus:

40 Fearing lest Jonathan would not suffer him but would fight against him: he sought to seize upon him and to kill him. So he rose up and came to Bethsan.

41 And Jonathan went out to meet him with forty thousand men chosen for battle and came to Bethsan.

42 Now when Tryphon saw that Jonathan came with a great army, he durst not stretch forth his hand against him,

43 But received him with honour and commended him to all his friends and gave him presents: and he commanded his troops to obey him as himself.

44 And he said to Jonathan: Why hast thou troubled all the people, whereas we have no war?

45 Now therefore send them back to their own houses and choose thee a few men that may be with thee and come with me to Ptolemais: and I will deliver it to thee, and the rest of the strong holds and the army and all that have any charge: and I will return and go away. For this is the cause of my coming.

46 And Jonathan believed him and did as he said and sent away his army: and they departed into the land of Juda.

47 But he kept with him three thousand men: of whom he sent two thousand into Galilee, and one thousand went with him.

48 Now as soon as Jonathan entered into Ptolemais, they of Ptolemais shut the gates of the city and took him: and all them that came in with him they slew with the sword.

49 Then Tryphon sent an army and horsemen into Galilee and into the great plain to destroy all Jonathan's company.

50 But they, when they understood that Jonathan and all that were with him were taken and slain, encouraged one another and went out ready for battle.

51 Then they that had come after them, seeing that they stood for their lives, returned back.

52 Whereupon, they all came peaceably into the land of Juda. And they bewailed Jonathan and them that had been with him, exceedingly: and Israel mourned with great lamentation.

53 Then all the heathens that were round about them sought to destroy them. For they said:

54 They have no prince nor any to help them: now therefore let us make war upon them and take away the memory of them from amongst men.

CHAPTER 13

Simon is made captain general in the room of his brother. Jonathan is slain by Tryphon. Simon is favoured by Demetrius. He taketh Gaza and the castle of Jerusalem.

NOW Simon heard that Tryphon was gathering a very great army, to invade the land of Juda and to destroy it.

2 And seeing that the people was in dread and in fear, he went up to Jerusalem and assembled the people:

3 And exhorted them, saying: You know what great battles I and my brethren and the house of my father have fought for the laws and the sanctuary and the distresses that we have seen:

4 By reason whereof, all my brethren have lost their lives for Israel's sake and I am left alone.

5 And now far be it from me to spare my life in any time of trouble: for I am not better than my brethren.

6 I will avenge then my nation and the sanctuary and our children and wives: for all the heathens are gathered together to destroy us out of mere malice.

7 And the spirit of the people was enkindled as soon as they heard these words.

8 And they answered with a loud voice, saying: Thou art our leader in the place of Judas and Jonathan thy brother.

9 Fight thou our battles: and we will do whatsoever thou shalt say to us.

10 So gathering together all the men of war, he made haste to finish all the walls of Jerusalem: and he fortified it round about.

11 And he sent Jonathan the son of Absalom, and with him a new army, into Joppe: and he cast out them that were in it and himself remained there.

12 And Tryphon removed from Ptolemais with a great army, to invade the land of Juda: and Jonathan was with him in custody.

13 But Simon pitched in Addus, over against the plain.

14 And when Tryphon understood that Simon was risen up in the place of his brother Jonathan and that he meant to join battle with him he sent messengers to him,

15 Saying: We have detained thy brother Jonathan for the money that he owed in the king's account by reason of the affairs which he had the management of.

16 But now send a hundred talents of silver, and his two sons for hostages, that when he is set at liberty he may not revolt from us: and we will release him.

17 Now Simon knew that he spoke deceitfully to him. Nevertheless he ordered the money and the children to be sent: lest he should bring upon himself a great hatred of the people of Israel, who might have said:

18 Because he sent not the money and the children, therefore is he lost.

19 So he sent the children and the hundred talents: and he lied and did not let Jonathan go.

20 And after this, Tryphon entered within the country, to destroy it: and they went about by the way that leadeth to Ador. And Simon and his army marched to every place whithersoever they went.

21 And they that were in the castle sent messengers to Tryphon that he should make haste to come through the desert and send them victuals.

22 And Tryphon made ready all his horsemen to come that night. But there fell a very great snow: and he came not into the country of Galaad.

23 And when he approached to Bascama, he slew Jonathan and his sons there.

24 And Tryphon returned and went into his own country.

25 And Simon sent and took the bones of Jonathan his brother and buried them in Modin, in the city of his fathers.

26 And all Israel bewailed him with great lamentation: and they mourned for him many days.

27 And Simon built over the sepulchre of his father and of his brethren a building lofty to the sight, of polished stone behind and before.

28 And he set up seven pyramids one against another for his father and his mother and his four brethren.

29 And round about these he set great pillars: and upon the pillars arms for a perpetual memory: and by the arms ships carved, which might be seen by all that sailed on the sea.

30 This is the sepulchre that he made in Modin even unto this day.

31 But Tryphon when he was upon a journey with the young king Antiochus treacherously slew him.

32 And he reigned in his place and put on the crown of Asia and brought great evils upon the land.

33 And Simon built up the strong holds of Judea, fortifying them with

CHAP. 13. Ver. 20. *Simon and his army marched to every place whithersoever they went.* That is, whithersoever Tryphon and his horsemen went in order to oppose them.

high towers and great walls and gates and bars: and he stored up victuals in the fortresses.

34 And Simon chose men and sent to king Demetrius, to the end that he should grant an immunity to the land: for all that Tryphon did was to spoil.

35 And king Demetrius, in answer to this request, wrote a letter in this manner:

36 King Demetrius to Simon, the high priest and friend of kings, and to the ancients and to the nation of the Jews, greeting.

37 The golden crown and the palm which you sent, we have received: and we are ready to make a firm peace with you and to write to the king's chief officers to release you the things that we have released.

38 For all that we have decreed in your favour shall stand in force. The strong holds that you have built shall be your own.

39 And as for any oversight or fault committed unto this day, we forgive it and the crown which you owed: and if any other thing were taxed in Jerusalem, now let it not be taxed.

40 And if any of you be fit to be enrolled among ours, let them be enrolled: and let there be peace between us.

41 In the year one hundred and seventy the yoke of the Gentiles was taken off from Israel.

42 And the people of Israel began to write in the instruments and public records: The first year under Simon the high priest, the great captain and prince of the Jews.

43 In those days Simon besieged Gaza and camped round about it: and he made engines, and set them to the city: and he struck one tower, and took it.

44 And they that were within the engine leaped into the city: and there was a great uproar in the city.

45 And they that were in the city went up with their wives and children upon the wall, with their garments rent: and they cried with a loud voice, beseeching Simon to grant them peace.

46 And they said: Deal not with us according to our evil deeds, but according to thy mercy.

47 And Simon being moved did not destroy them: but yet he cast them out of the city and cleansed the houses wherein there had been idols. And then he entered into it with hymns, blessing the Lord.

48 And having cast out of it all uncleanness, he placed in it men that should observe the law: and he fortified it and made it his habitation.

49 But they that were in the castle of Jerusalem were hindered from going out and coming into the country and from buying and selling: and they were straitened with hunger: and many of them perished through famine.

50 And they cried to Simon for peace: and he granted it to them. And he cast them out from thence and cleansed the castle from uncleannesses.

51 And they entered into it the three and twentieth day of the second month, in the year one hundred and seventy-one, with thanksgiving and branches of palm trees and harps and cymbals and psalteries and hymns and canticles: because the great enemy was destroyed out of Israel.

52 And he ordained that these days should be kept every year with gladness.

53 And he fortified the mountain of the temple that was near the castle: and he dwelt there, himself and they that were with him.

54 And Simon saw that John, his son was a valiant man for war: and he made him captain of all the forces: and he dwelt in Gazara.

CHAPTER 14

Demetrius is taken by the king of Persia. Judea flourishes under the government of Simon.

IN the year one hundred and seventy-two, king Demetrius assembled his army and went into Media to get him succours to fight against Tryphon.

2 And Arsaces, the king of Persia and Media, heard that Demetrius was entered within his borders: and he sent one of his princes to take him alive and bring him to him.

3 And he went and defeated the army of Demetrius: and took him and brought him to Arsaces. And he put him into custody.

4 And all the land of Juda was at rest all the days of Simon. And he sought the good of his nation: and his power and his glory pleased them well all *his* days.

5 And with all his glory he took Joppe for a haven and made an entrance to the isles of the sea.

6 And he enlarged the bounds of his nation and made himself master of the country.

7 And he gathered together a great number of captives and had the dominion of Gazara and of Bethsura and of the castle and took away all uncleanness out of it: and there was none that resisted him.

8 And every man tilled his land with

peace: and the land of Juda yielded her increase, and the trees of the fields their fruit.

9 The ancient men sat all in the streets and treated together of the good things of the land: and the young men put on them glory and the robes of war.

10 And he provided victuals for the cities: and he appointed that they should be furnished with amunition, so that the fame of his glory was renowned even to the end of the earth.

11 He made peace in the land: and Israel rejoiced with great joy.

12 And every man sat under his vine and under his fig tree: and there was none to make them afraid.

13 There was none left in the land to fight against them: kings were discomfited in those days.

14 And he strengthened all those of his people that were brought low: and he sought the law and took away every unjust and wicked man.

15 He glorified the sanctuary and multiplied the vessels of the holy places.

16 And it was heard at Rome and as far as Sparta that Jonathan was dead: and they were very sorry.

17 But when they heard that Simon his brother was made high priest in his place and was possessed of all the country and the cities therein:

18 They wrote to him in tables of brass, to renew the friendship and alliance which they had made with Judas and with Jonathan his brethren.

19 And they were read before the assembly in Jerusalem. And this is the copy of the letters that the Spartans sent.

20 The princes and the cities of the Spartans to Simon the high priest and to the ancients and the priests and the rest of the people of the Jews their brethren, greeting.

21 The ambassadors that were sent to our people have told us of your glory and honour and joy: and we rejoiced at their coming.

22 And we registered what was said by them in the councils of the people in this manner: Numenius the son of Antiochus and Antipater the son of Jason, ambassadors of the Jews, came to us to renew the former friendship with us.

23 And it pleased the people to receive the men honourably and to put a copy of their words in the public records, to be a memorial to the people of the Spartans. And we have written a copy of them to Simon the high priest.

24 And after this Simon sent Numenius to Rome, with a great shield of gold of the weight of a thousand pounds, to confirm the league with them. And when the people of Rome had heard

25 These words, they said: What thanks shall we give to Simon and his sons?

26 For he hath restored his brethren and hath driven away in fight the enemies of Israel from them: and they decreed him liberty and registered it in tables of brass and set it upon pillars in mount Sion.

27 And this is a copy of the writing: The eighteenth day of the month Elul, in the year one hundred and seventy-two, being the third year under Simon the high priest at Asaramel,

28 In a great assembly of the priests and of the people and the princes of the nation and the ancients of the country, these things were notified: For as much as there have often been wars in our country,

29 And Simon, the son of Mathathias of the children of Jarib, and his brethren have put themselves in danger and resisted the enemies of their nation, for the maintenance of their holy places and the law, and have raised their nation to great glory.

30 And Jonathan gathered together his nation and was made their high priest: and he was laid to his people.

31 And their enemies desired to tread down and destroy their country and to stretch forth their hands against their holy places.

32 Then Simon resisted and fought for his nation and laid out much of his money and armed the valiant men of his nation and gave them wages.

33 And he fortified the cities of Judea and Bethsura that lieth in the borders of Judea, where the armour of the enemies was before: and he placed there a garrison of Jews.

34 And he fortified Joppe which lieth by the sea and Gazara, which bordereth upon Azotus, wherein the enemies dwelt before: and he placed Jews here and furnished them with all things convenient for their reparation.

35 And the people seeing the acts of Simon and to what glory he meant to bring his nation, made him their prince and high priest, because he had done all these things, and for the justice and faith which he kept to his nation, and for that he sought by all means to advance his people.

36 And in his days things prospered in his hands, so that the heathens were taken away out of their country, and they also that were in the city of David in Jerusalem in the castle, out of which they issued forth and profaned all

places round about the sanctuary and did much evil to its purity.

37 And he placed therein Jews for the defence of the country and of the city: and he raised up the walls of Jerusalem.

38 And king Demetrius confirmed him in the high priesthood.

39 According to these things he made him his friend and glorified him with great glory.

40 For he had heard that the Romans had called the Jews their friends and confederates and brethren and that they had received Simon's ambassadors with honour:

41 And that the Jews and their priests had consented that he should be their prince and high priest for ever, till there should arise a faithful prophet:

42 And that he should be chief over them and that he should have the charge of the sanctuary and that he should appoint rulers over their works and over the country and over the armour and over the strong holds.

43 And that he should have care of the holy places: and that he should be obeyed by all: and that all the writings in the country should be made in his name: and that he should be clothed with purple and gold:

44 And that it should not be lawful for any of the people or of the priests to disannul any of these things or to gainsay his words or to call together an assembly in the country without him: or to be clothed with purple or to wear a buckle of gold:

45 And whosoever shall do otherwise or shall make void any of these things shall be punished.

46 And it pleased all the people to establish Simon and to do according to these words.

47 And Simon accepted thereof and was well pleased to execute the office of the high priesthood and to be captain and prince of the nation of the Jews and of the priests and to be chief over all.

48 And they commanded that this writing should be put in tables of brass and that they should be set up within the compass of the sanctuary, in a conspicuous place:

49 And that a copy thereof should be put in the treasury, that Simon and his sons may have it.

CHAPTER 15

Antiochus son of Demetrius honours Simon. The Romans write to divers nations in favour of the Jews. Antiochus quarrels with Simon and sends troops to annoy him.

AND king Antiochus the son of Demetrius sent letters from the isles of the sea to Simon the priest and prince of the nation of the Jews and to all the people.

2 And the contents were these: King Antiochus to Simon the high priest and to the nation of the Jews, greeting.

3 Forasmuch as certain pestilent men have usurped the kingdom of our fathers: and my purpose is to challenge the kingdom and to restore it to its former estate: and I have chosen a great army and have built ships of war.

4 And I design to go through the country that I may take revenge of them that have destroyed our country and that have made many cities desolate in my realm.

5 Now therefore I confirm unto thee all the oblations which all the kings before me remitted to thee and what other gifts soever they remitted to thee.

6 And I give thee leave to coin thy own money in thy country.

7 And let Jerusalem be holy and free: and all the armour that hath been made and the fortresses which thou has built and which thou keepest in thy hands, let them remain to thee.

8 And all that is due to the king and what should be the king's hereafter, from this present and for ever, is forgiven thee.

9 And when we shall have recovered our kingdom, we will glorify thee and thy nation and temple with great glory, so that your glory shall be made manifest in all the earth.

10 In the year one hundred and seventy-four Antiochus entered into the land of his fathers: and all the forces assembled to him, so that few were left with Tryphon.

11 And king Antiochus pursued after him: and he fled along by the sea coast and came to Dora.

12 For he perceived that evils were gathered together upon him: and his troops had forsaken him.

13 And Antiochus camped above Dora with a hundred and twenty thousand men of war and eight thousand horsemen.

14 And he invested the city: and the ships drew near by sea. And they annoyed the city by land and by sea and suffered none to come in or to go out.

15 And Numenius, and they that had been with him, came from the city of Rome, having letters written to the kings and countries, the contents whereof were these:

16 Lucius, the consul of the Romans, to king Ptolemee, greeting.

17 The ambassadors of the Jews, our friends, came to us, to renew the former friendship and alliance, being sent from Simon the high priest and the people of the Jews.

18 And they brought also a shield of gold of a thousand pounds.

19 It hath seemed good therefore to us to write to the kings and countries, that they should do them no harm nor fight against them, their cities or countries: and that they should give no aid to them that fight against them.

20 And it hath seemed good to us to receive the shield of them.

21 If therefore any pestilent men are fled out of their country to you, deliver them to Simon the high priest, that he may punish them according to their law.

22 These same things were written to king Demetrius and to Attalus and to Ariarathes and to Arsaces,

23 And to all the countries; and to Lampsacus and to the Spartans and to Delus and Myndus and Sicyon and Caria and Samus and Pamphylia and Lycia and Alicarnassus and Cos and Side and Aradus and Rhodes and Phaselis and Gortyna and Gnidus and Cyprus and Cyrene.

24 And they wrote a copy thereof to Simon the high priest and to the people of the Jews.

25 But king Antiochus moved his camp to Dora the second time, assaulting it continually and making engines: and he shut up Tryphon, that he could not go out.

26 And Simon sent to him two thousand chosen men to aid him, silver also and gold and abundance of furniture.

27 And he would not receive them but broke all the covenant that he had made with him before and alienated himself from him.

28 And he sent to him Athenobius, one of his friends, to treat with him, saying: You hold Joppe and Gazara, and the castle that is in Jerusalem, which are cities of my kingdom.

29 Their borders you have wasted: and you have made great havock in the land and have got the dominion of many places in my kingdom.

30 Now therefore deliver up the cities that you have taken and the tributes of the places whereof you have gotten the dominion without the borders of Judea.

31 But if not, give me for them five hundred talents of silver, and for the havock that you have made and the tributes of the cities, other five hundred talents: or else we will come and fight against you.

32 So Athenobius the king's friend came to Jerusalem and saw the glory of Simon and his magnificence in gold and silver and his great equipage: and he was astonished and told him the king's words.

33 And Simon answered him, and said to him: We have neither taken other men's land, neither do we hold that which is other men's: but the inheritance of our fathers, which was for some time unjustly possessed by our enemies.

34 But we having opportunity claim the inheritance of our fathers.

35 And as to thy complaints concerning Joppe and Gazara, they did great harm to the people and to our country: yet for these we will give a hundred talents. And Athenobius answered him not a word:

36 But returning in a rage to the king, made report to him of these words, and of the glory of Simon, and of all that he had seen. And the king was exceeding angry.

37 And Tryphon fled away by ship to Orthosias.

38 And the king appointed Cendebeus captain of the sea coast and gave him an army of footmen and horsemen.

39 And he commanded him to march with his army towards Judea: and he commanded him to build up Gedor and to fortify the gates of the city and to war against the people. But the king himself pusued after Tryphon.

40 And Cendebeus came to Jamnia and began to provoke the people and to ravage Judea and to take the people prisoners and to kill and to build Gedor.

41 And he placed there horsemen, and an army: that they might issue forth and make incursions upon the ways of Judea as the king had commanded him.

CHAPTER 16

The sons of Simon defeat the troops of Antiochus. Simon with two of his sons are treacherously murdered by Ptolemee his son-in-law.

THEN John came up from Gazara and told Simon his father what Cendebeus had done against their people.

CHAP. 15. Ver. 16. *Ptolemee.* Surnamed Physcon, brother and successor to Philometor.
Ver. 22. *Attalus.* Attalus was king of Pergamus; Ariarathes was king of Cappadocia; and Arsaces was king of the Parthians.
CHAP. 16. Ver. 1. *John.* He was afterwards surnamed Hircanus and succeeded his father in both his dignities of high priest and prince. He conquered the Edomites and obliged them to a conformity with the Jews in religion and destroyed the schismatical temple of the Samaritans.

2 And Simon called his two eldest sons, Judas and John, and said to them: I and my brethren and my father's house have fought against the enemies of Israel from your youth even to this day: and things have prospered so well in our hands that we have delivered Israel oftentimes.

3 And now I am old: but be you instead of me and my brethren. And go out and fight for our nation: and the help from heaven be with you.

4 Then he chose out of the country twenty thousand fighting men and horsemen: and they went forth against Cendebeus: and they rested in Modin.

5 And they arose in the morning and went into the plain. And behold a very great army of footmen and horsemen came against them: and there was a running river between them.

6 And he and his people pitched their camp over against them. And he saw that the people were afraid to go over the river: so he went over first. Then the men seeing him passed over after him.

7 And he divided the people and set the horsemen in the midst of the footmen: but the horsemen of the enemies were very numerous.

8 And they sounded the holy trumpets: and Cendebeus and his army were put to flight: and there fell many of them wounded: and the rest fled into the strong hold.

9 At that time Judas, John's brother, was wounded: but John pursued after them, till he came to Cedron, which he had built:

10 And they fled even to the towers that were in the fields of Azotus: and he burnt them with fire. And there fell of them two thousand men: and he returned into Judea in peace.

11 Now Ptolemee the son of Abobus was appointed captain in the plain of Jericho: and he had abundance of silver and gold,

12 For he was son-in-law of the high priest.

13 And his heart was lifted up and he designed to make himself master of the country: and he purposed treachery against Simon, and his sons, to destroy them.

14 Now Simon, as he was going through the cities that were in the country of Judea and taking care for the good ordering of them, went down to Jericho, he and Mathathias and Judas his sons, in the year one hundred and seventy-seven, the eleventh month: the same is the month Sabath.

15 And the son of Abobus received them deceitfully into a little fortress that is called Doch, which he had built: and he made them a great feast and hid men there.

16 And when Simon and his sons had drunk plentifully, Ptolemee and his men rose up and took their weapons and entered into the banqueting place and slew him and his two sons and some of his servants.

17 And he committed a great treachery in Israel and rendered evil for good.

18 And Ptolemee wrote these things, and sent to the king that he should send him an army to aid him, and he would deliver him the country and their cities and tributes.

19 And he sent others to Gazara to kill John: and to the tribunes he sent letters to come to him, and that he would give them silver and gold and gifts.

20 And he sent others to take Jerusalem and the mountain of the temple.

21 Now one running before told John in Gazara that his father and his brethren were slain and that he hath sent men to kill thee also.

22 But when he heard it he was exceedingly afraid: and he apprehended the men that came to kill him and he put them to death: for he knew that they sought to make him away.

23 And as concerning the rest of the acts of John and his wars and the worthy deeds which he bravely achieved and the building of the walls which he made and the things that he did:

24 Behold these are written in the book of the days of his priesthood, from the time that he was made high priest after his father.

Ver. 6. *He.* John.
Ver. 9. *Cedron.* Otherwise called Gedor, the city that Cendebeus was fortifying.

THE SECOND BOOK OF

MACHABEES

This second book of MACHABEES *is not a continuation of the history contained in the first, nor does it come down so low as the first does: but it relates many of the same facts more at large and adds other remarkable particulars, omitted in the first book, relating to the state of the Jews, as well before as under the persecution of Antiochus. The author, who is not the same with that of the first book, has given (as we learn from chap. 2, 20, etc.) a short abstract of what Jason of Cyrene had written in the five volumes, concerning Judas and his brethren. He wrote in Greek and begins with two letters, sent by the Jews of Jerusalem to their brethren in Egypt.*

CHAPTER 1

Letters of the Jews of Jerusalem to them that were in Egypt. They give thanks for their delivery from Antiochus and exhort their brethren to keep the feast of the dedication of the altar and of the miraculous fire.

TO the brethren, the Jews that are throughout Egypt, the brethren, the Jews that are in Jerusalem and in the land of Judea send health and good peace.

2 May God be gracious to you and remember his covenant that he made with Abraham and Isaac and Jacob, his faithful servants.

3 And give you all a heart to worship him and to do his will with a great heart and a willing mind.

4 May he open your heart in his law and in his commandments and send you peace.

5 May he hear your prayers and be reconciled unto you and never forsake you in the evil time.

6 And now here we are praying for you.

7 When Demetrius reigned, in the year one hundred and sixty-nine, we Jews wrote to you in the trouble and violence, that came upon us in those years, after Jason withdrew himself from the holy land and from the kingdom.

8 They burnt the gate and shed innocent blood. Then we prayed to the Lord and were heard: and we offered sacrifices and fine flour and lighted the lamps and set forth the loaves.

9 And now celebrate ye the days of Scenopegia in the month of Casleu.

10 In the year one hundred and eighty-eight, the people that is at Jerusalem and in Judea, and the senate, and Judas, to Aristobolus, the preceptor of king Ptolemee, who is of the stock of the anointed priests, and to the Jews that are in Egypt, health and welfare.

11 Having been delivered by God out of great dangers, we give him great thanks, forasmuch as we have been in war with such a king.

12 For he made numbers of men swarm out of Persia, that have fought against us and the holy city.

13 For when the leader himself was in Persia, and with him a very great army, he fell in the temple of Nanea, being deceived by the counsel of the priests of Nanea.

14 For Antiochus with his friends came to the place, as though he would marry her, and that he might receive great sums of money under the title of a dowry.

15 And when the priests of Nanea had set it forth, and he with a small company had entered into the compass of the temple, they shut the temple

16 When Antiochus was come in: and, opening a secret entrance of the temple, they cast stones and slew the leader and them that were with him and hewed them in pieces: and cutting off their heads they threw them forth.

CHAP. 1. Ver. 9. *Scenopegia.* The *Encenia* or feast of the dedication of the altar, called here *Scenopegia* or feast of tabernacles, from being celebrated with the like solemnity.

Ver. 11. *Such a king.* Antiochus Sidetes, who began to make war upon the Jews, whilst Simon was yet alive (1 Mach. 15, 39). And afterwards besieged Jerusalem under John Hircanus. So that the Judas here mentioned (ver. 10) is not Judas Machabeus, who was dead long before the year 188 of the kingdom of the Greeks, for he died in the year 146 of that epoch (see above, 1 Mach., chap. 2, ver. 70, also the note on chap. 1, ver. 2), but either Judas the eldest son of John Hircanus or Judas the Essene, renowned for the gift of prophecy, who flourished about that time.

Ver. 13. *Nanea.* A Persian goddess, which some have taken for Diana, others for Venus.

17 Blessed be God in all things, who hath delivered up the wicked.

18 Therefore, whereas we purpose to keep the purification of the temple on the five and twentieth day of the month of Casleu, we thought it necessary to signify it to you: that you also may keep the day of Scenopegia and the day of the fire that was given when Nehemias offered sacrifice, after the temple and the altar was built.

19 For when our fathers were led into Persia, the priests that then were worshippers of God took privately the fire from the altar and hid it in a valley where there was a deep pit without water: and there they kept it safe, so that the place was unknown to all men.

20 But when many years had passed and it pleased God that Nehemias should be sent by the king of Persia, he sent some of the posterity of those priests that had hid it, to seek for the fire: and as they told us, they found no fire, but thick water.

21 Then he bade them draw it up and bring it to him: and the priest Nehemias commanded the sacrifices that were laid on to be sprinkled with the same water, both the wood, and the things that were laid upon it.

22 And when this was done and the time came that the sun shone out, which before was in a cloud, there was a great fire kindled, so that all wondered.

23 And all the priests made prayer while the sacrifice was consuming, Jonathan beginning and the rest answering.

24 And the prayer of Nehemias was after this manner: O Lord God, Creator of all things, dreadful and strong, just and merciful, who alone art the good king,

25 Who alone art gracious, who alone art just and almighty and eternal, who deliverest Israel from all evil, who didst choose the fathers and didst sanctify them:

26 Receive the sacrifice for all thy people Israel, and preserve thy own portion, and sanctify it.

27 Gather together our scattered people: deliver them that are slaves to the Gentiles and look upon them that are despised and abhorred: that the Gentiles may know that thou art our God.

28 Punish them that oppress us and that treat us injuriously with pride.

29 Establish thy people in thy holy place, [1] as Moses hath spoken.

30 And the priests sung hymns till the sacrifice was consumed.

31 And when the sacrifice was consumed, Nehemias commanded the water that was left to be poured out upon the great stones.

32 Which being done, there was kindled a flame from them: but it was consumed by the light that shined from the altar.

33 And when this matter became public, it was told to the king of Persia that, in the place where the priests that were led away had hid the fire, there appeared water, with which Nehemias and they that were with him had purified the sacrifices.

34 And the king, considering and diligently examining the matter, made a temple for it, that he might prove what had happened.

35 And when he had proved it, he gave the priests many goods and divers presents: and he took and distributed them to them with his own hand.

36 And Nehemias called this place Nephthar, which is interpreted purification. But many call it Nephi.

CHAPTER 2

A continuation of the second letter. Of Jeremias' hiding the ark at the time of the captivity. The author's preface.

NOW it is found in the descriptions of Jeremias the prophet that he commanded them that went into captivity to take the fire, as it hath been signified, and how he gave charge to them that were carried away into captivity.

2 And how he gave them the law that they should not forget the commandments of the Lord and that they should not err in their minds, seeing the idols of gold and silver and the ornaments of them.

3 And with other such like speeches he exhorted them that they would not remove the law from their heart.

4 It was also contained in the same writing, how the prophet, being warned by God, commanded that the tabernacle and the ark should accompany him, till he came forth to the mountain [1] where Moses went up and saw the inheritance of God.

5 And when Jeremias came thither he found a hollow cave: and he carried in thither the tabernacle and the ark

CHAP. 1. [1] Deut. 30, 3, 5; 2 Mach. 2, 18. CHAP. 2. [1] Deut. 34, 1.

Ver. 19. *Persia.* Babylonia, called here Persia, from being afterwards part of the Persian empire.

Ver. 34. *A temple.* That is, an enclosure, or a wall round about the place where the fire was hid, to separate it from profane uses, to the end that it might be respected as a holy place.

CHAP. 2. Ver. 1. *The descriptions.* That is, the records or memoirs of Jeremias, a work that is now lost.

and the altar of incense and so stopped the door.

6 Then some of them that followed him came up to mark the place: but they could not find it.

7 And when Jeremias perceived it, he blamed them, saying: The place shall be unknown till God gather together the congregation of the people and receive them to mercy.

8 And then the Lord will shew these things: and the majesty of the Lord shall appear and there shall be a cloud, as it was also shewed to Moses, [2] and he shewed it when Solomon prayed that the place might be sanctified to the great God.

9 For he treated wisdom in a magnificent manner: and, like a wise man, he offered the sacrifice of the dedication and of the finishing of the temple.

10 [3] And as Moses prayed to the Lord and fire came down from heaven and consumed the holocaust: [4] so Solomon also prayed and fire came down from heaven and consumed the holocaust.

11 And Moses said: [5] Because the sin offering was not eaten, it was consumed.

12 So Solomon also celebrated the dedication eight days.

13 And these same things were set down in the memoirs and commentaries of Nehemias: and how he made a library and gathered together out of the countries the books both of the prophets and of David and the epistles of the kings and concerning the holy gifts.

14 And in like manner Judas also gathered together all such things as were lost by the war we had: and they are in our possession.

15 Wherefore if you want these things, send some that may fetch them to you.

16 As we are then about to celebrate the purification, we have written unto you: and you shall do well, if you keep the same days.

17 And we hope that God who hath delivered his people and hath rendered to all the inheritance and the kingdom and the priesthood and the sanctuary,

18 [6] As he promised in the law, will shortly have mercy upon us and will gather us together from every land under heaven into the holy place.

19 For he hath delivered us out of great perils and hath cleansed the place.

20 Now as concerning Judas Machabeus and his brethren and the purification of the great temple and the dedication of the altar:

21 As also the wars against Antiochus the Illustrious and his son Eupator:

22 And the manifestations that came from heaven to them that behaved themselves manfully on the behalf of the Jews, so that, being but a few, they made themselves masters of the whole country and put to flight the barbarous multitude:

23 And recovered again the most renowned temple in all the world and delivered the city and restored the laws that were abolished, the Lord with all clemency shewing mercy to them.

24 And all such things have been comprised in five books by Jason of Cyrene, we have attempted to abridge in one book.

25 For considering the multitude of books and the difficulty that they find that desire to undertake the narrations of histories, because of the multitude of the matter,

26 We have taken care for those indeed that are willing to read that it might be a pleasure of mind: and for the studious that they may more easily commit to memory: and that all that read might receive profit.

27 And as to ourselves indeed, in undertaking this work of abridging, we have taken in hand no easy task, yea rather a business full of watching and sweat.

28 But, as they that prepare a feast and seek to satisfy the will of others, for the sake of many, we willingly undergo the labour.

29 Leaving to the authors the exact handling of every particular: and as for ourselves, according to the plan proposed, studying to be brief.

30 For as the master builder of a new house must have care of the whole building, but he that taketh care to paint it must seek out fit things for the adorning of it: so must it be judged for us.

31 For to collect all that is to be known, to put the discourse in order and curiously to discuss every particular point, is the duty of the author of a history:

32 But to pursue brevity of speech and to avoid nice declarations of things is to be granted to him that maketh an abridgment.

33 Here then we will begin the narration: let this be enough by way of a preface. For it is a foolish thing to

[2] 3 Kings, 8, 11; 2 Par. 6, 14. [3] Lev. 9, 24. [4] 2 Par. 7, 1. [5] Lev. 10, 16, 17. [6] Deut. 30, 3, 5; 2 Mach. 1, 29.

Ver. 16. *The purification.* That is, the feast of the purifying or cleansing of the temple.

Ver. 27. *No easy task.* The Spirit of God, that assists the sacred penmen, does not exempt them from labour in seeking out the matter which they are to treat of and the order and manner in which they are to deliver it. So St. Luke wrote his gospel *having diligently attained to all things* (Luke 1, ver. 3).

make a long prologue and to be short in the story itself.

CHAPTER 3

Heliodorus is sent by king Seleucus to take away the treasures deposited in the temple. He is struck by God and healed by the prayers of the high priest.

THEREFORE when the holy city was inhabited with all peace and the laws as yet were very well kept, because of the godliness of Onias the high priest and the hatred his soul had of evil,

2 It came to pass that even the kings themselves and the princes esteemed the place worthy of the highest honour and glorified the temple with very great gifts:

3 So that Seleucus king of Asia allowed out of his revenues all the charges belonging to the ministry of the sacrifices.

4 But one Simon of the tribe of Benjamin, who was appointed overseer of the temple, strove in opposition to the high priest to bring about some unjust thing in the city.

5 And when he could not overcome Onias he went to Apollonius the son of Tharseas, who at that time was governor of Celesyria and Phenicia:

6 And told him that the treasury in Jerusalem was full of immense sums of money, and the common store was infinite, which did not belong to the account of the sacrifices: and that it was possible to bring all into the king's hands.

7 Now when Apollonius had given the king notice concerning the money that he was told of, he called for Heliodorus, who had the charge over his affairs, and sent him with commission to bring him the foresaid money.

8 So Heliodorus forthwith began his journey, under a colour of visiting the cities of Celesyria and Phenicia, but indeed to fulfil the king's purpose.

9 And when he was come to Jerusalem and had been courteously received in the city by the high priest, he told him what information had been given concerning the money and declared the cause for which he was come and asked if these things were so indeed.

10 Then the high priest told him that these were sums deposited and provisions for the subsistence of the widows and the fatherless.

11 And that some part of that which wicked Simon had given intelligence of belonged to Hircanus *son* of Tobias, a man of great dignity: and that the

whole was four hundred talents of silver and two hundred of gold:

12 But that to deceive them who had trusted to the place and temple which is honoured throughout the whole world, for the reverence and holiness of it, was a thing which could not by any means be done.

13 But he, by reason of the orders he had received from the king, said that by all means the money must be carried to the king.

14 So on the day he had appointed, Heliodorus entered in to order this matter. But there was no small terror throughout the whole city.

15 And the priests prostrated themselves before the altar in their priests' vestments and called upon him from heaven who made the law concerning things given to be kept, that he would preserve them safe for them that had deposited them.

16 Now whosoever saw the countenance of the high priest, was wounded in heart: for his face and the changing of his colour declared the inward sorrow of his mind.

17 For the man was so compassed with sadness and horror of the body that it was manifest to them that beheld him what sorrow he had in his heart.

18 Others also came flocking together out of their houses, praying and making public supplication, because the place was like to come into contempt.

19 And the women, girded with haircloth about their breasts, came together in the streets. And the virgins also that were shut up came forth, some to Onias, and some to the walls, and others looked out of the windows.

20 And all, holding up their hands towards heaven, made supplication.

21 For the expectation of the mixed multitude and of the high priest who was in an agony, would have moved any one to pity.

22 And these indeed called upon Almighty God to preserve the things that had been committed to them, safe and sure for those that had committed them.

23 But Heliodorus executed that which he had resolved on, himself being present in the same place with his guard about the treasury.

24 But the spirit of the Almighty God gave a great evidence of his presence, so that all that had presumed to obey him, falling down by the power of God, were struck with fainting and dread.

25 For there appeared to them a

CHAP. 3. Ver. 3. *Seleucus, son of Antiochus the Great and elder brother of Antiochus Epiphanes.*

horse with a terrible rider upon him, adorned with a very rich covering. And he ran fiercely and struck Heliodorus with his fore feet: and he that sat upon him seemed to have armour of gold.

26 Moreover there appeared two other young men, beautiful and strong, bright and glorious, and in comely apparel: who stood by him on either side and scourged him without ceasing with many stripes.

27 And Heliodorus suddenly fell to the ground: and they took him up covered with great darkness: and having put him into a litter they carried him out.

28 So he that came with many servants and all his guard into the aforesaid treasury was carried out, no one being able to help him, the manifest power of God being known.

29 And he indeed by the power of God lay speechless and without all hope of recovery.

30 But they praised the Lord because he had glorified his place. And the temple, that a little before was full of fear and trouble, when the Almighty Lord appeared, was filled with joy and gladness.

31 Then some of the friends of Heliodorus forthwith begged of Onias that he would call upon the Most High to grant him his life, who was ready to give up the ghost.

32 So the high priest, considering that the king might perhaps suspect that some mischief had been done to Heliodorus by the Jews, offered a sacrifice of health for the recovery of the man.

33 And when the high priest was praying, the same young men in the same clothing stood by Heliodorus and said to him: Give thanks to Onias the priest, because for his sake the Lord hath granted thee life.

34 And thou, having been scourged by God, declare unto all men the great works and the power of God. And having spoken thus, they appeared no more.

35 So Heliodorus, after he had offered a sacrifice to God and made great vows to him that had granted him life and given thanks to Onias, taking his troops with him, returned to the king.

36 And he testified to all men the works of the great God, which he had seen with his own eyes.

37 And when the king asked Heliodorus who might be a fit man to be sent yet once more to Jerusalem, he said:

38 If thou hast any enemy or traitor to thy kingdom, send him thither, and thou shalt receive him again scourged, if so be he escape: for there is undoubtedly in that place a certain power of God.

39 For he that hath his dwelling in the heavens is the visitor and protector of that place: and he striketh and destroyeth them that come to do evil to it.

40 And the things concerning Heliodorus and the keeping of the treasury fell out in this manner.

CHAPTER 4

Onias has recourse to the king. The ambition and wickedness of Jason and Menelaus. Onias is treacherously murdered.

BUT Simon, of whom we spoke before, who was the betrayer of the money and of his country, spoke ill of Onias, as though he had incited Heliodorus to do these things and had been the promoter of evils.

2 And he presumed to call him a traitor to the kingdom, who provided for the city and defended his nation and was zealous for the law of God.

3 But when the enmities proceeded so far that murders were also committed by some of Simon's friends:

4 Onias, considering the danger of this contention and that Apollonius, who was the governor of Celesyria and Phenicia, was outrageous, which increased the malice of Simon, went to the king,

5 Not to be an accuser of his countrymen, but with a view to the common good of all the people.

6 For he saw that, except the king took care, it was impossible that matters should be settled in peace or that Simon would cease from his folly.

7 But after the death of Seleucus, when Antiochus, who was called the Illustrious, had taken possession of the kingdom, Jason the brother of Onias ambitiously sought the high priesthood:

8 And went to the king, promising him three hundred and sixty talents of silver and, out of other revenues, fourscore talents.

9 Besides this, he promised also a hundred and fifty more, if he might have license to set him up a place for exercise and a place for youth, and to entitle them that were at Jerusalem, Antiochians.

10 Which when the king had granted and he had gotten the rule into his hands, forthwith he began to bring over his countrymen to the fashion of the heathens.

11 And abolishing those things

which had been decreed of special favour by the kings in behalf of the Jews, by the means of John the father of that Eupolemus, who went ambassador to Rome to make amity and alliance, he disannulled the lawful ordinances of the citizens and brought in fashions that were perverse.

12 For he had the boldness to set up, [1] under the very castle, a place of exercise and to put all the choicest youths in brothel houses.

13 Now this was not the beginning but an increase and progress of heathenish and foreign manners, through the abominable and unheard of wickedness of Jason, that impious wretch and no priest.

14 Insomuch that the priests were not now occupied about the offices of the altar, but, despising the temple and neglecting the sacrifices, hastened to be partakers of the games and of the unlawful allowance thereof and of the exercise of the discus.

15 And setting nought by the honours of their fathers, they esteemed the Grecian glories for the best:

16 For the sake of which they incurred a dangerous contention and followed earnestly their ordinances, and in all things they coveted to be like them who were their enemies and murderers.

17 For acting wickedly against the laws of God doth not pass unpunished: but this the time following will declare.

18 Now when the game that was used every fifth year was kept at Tyre, the king being present,

19 The wicked Jason sent from Jerusalem sinful men to carry three hundred didrachmas of silver for the sacrifice of Hercules. But the bearers thereof desired it might not be bestowed on the sacrifices, because it was not necessary, but might be deputed for other charges.

20 So the money was appointed by him that sent it to the sacrifice of Hercules: but because of them that carried it, was employed for the making of galleys.

21 Now when Apollonius, the son of Mnestheus, was sent into Egypt to treat with the nobles of King Philometor and Antiochus understood that he was wholly excluded from the affairs of the kingdom, consulting his own interest, he departed thence and came to Joppe, and from thence to Jerusalem.

22 Where he was received in a magnificent manner by Jason and the city, and came in with torch lights and with praises. And from thence he returned with his army into Phenicia.

23 Three years afterwards, Jason sent Menelaus, brother of the aforesaid Simon, to carry money to the king and to bring answers from him concerning certain necessary affairs.

24 But he being recommended to the king, when he had magnified the appearance of his power, got the high priesthood for himself, by offering more than Jason by three hundred talents of silver.

25 So having received the king's mandate, he returned, bringing nothing worthy of the high priesthood: but having the mind of a cruel tyrant and the rage of a savage beast.

26 Then Jason, who had undermined his own brother, being himself undermined, was driven out a fugitive into the country of the Ammonites.

27 So Menelaus got the principality: but as for the money he had promised to the king, he took no care, when Sostratus the governor of the castle called for it.

28 For to him appertained the gathering of the taxes: wherefore they were both called before the king.

29 And Menelaus was removed from the priesthood, Lysimachus his brother succeeding: and Sostratus was made governor of the Cyrians.

30 When these things were in doing, it fell out that they of Tharsus and Mallos raised a sedition, because they were given for a gift to Antiochis, the king's concubine.

31 The king therefore went in all haste to appease them, leaving Andronicus, one of his nobles, for his deputy.

32 Then Menelaus, supposing that he had found a convenient time, having stolen certain vessels of gold out of the temple, gave them to Andronicus: and others he had sold at Tyre and in the neighbouring cities.

33 Which when Onias understood, most certainly, he reproved him, keeping himself in a safe place at Antioch beside Daphne.

34 Whereupon Menelaus, coming to Andronicus, desired him to kill Onias. And he went to Onias and gave him his right hand with an oath: and (though he were suspected by him) persuaded him to come forth out of the sanctuary and immediately slew him, without any regard to justice.

35 For which cause, not only the Jews, but also the other nations, conceived indignation and were much grieved for the unjust murder of so great a man.

36 And when the king was come back

from the places of Cilicia, the Jews that were at Antioch, and also the Greeks, went to him: complaining of the unjust murder of Onias.

37 Antiochus therefore was grieved in his mind for Onias and, being moved to pity, shed tears, remembering the sobriety and modesty of the deceased.

38 And being inflamed to anger, he commanded Andronicus to be stripped of his purple and to be led about through all the city: and that in the same place wherein he had committed the impiety against Onias, the sacrilegious wretch should be put to death, the Lord repaying him his deserved punishment.

39 Now when many sacrileges had been committed by Lysimachus in the temple by the counsel of Menelaus, and the rumour of it was spread abroad, the multitude gathered themselves together against Lysimachus, a great quantity of gold being already carried away.

40 Wherefore the multitude making an insurrection, and their minds being filled with anger, Lysimachus armed about three thousand men and began to use violence, one Tyrannus being captain, a man far gone both in age and in madness.

41 But when they perceived the attempt of Lysimachus, some caught up stones, some strong clubs: and some threw ashes upon Lysimachus.

42 And many of them were wounded and some struck down to the ground, but all were put to flight: and as for the sacrilegious fellow himself, they slew him beside the treasury.

43 Now concerning these matters, an accusation was laid against Menelaus.

44 And when the king was come to Tyre, three men were sent from the ancients to plead the cause before him.

45 But Menelaus, being convicted, promised Ptolemee to give him much money to persuade the king to favour him.

46 So Ptolemee went to the king in a certain court where he was, as it were to cool himself, and brought him to be of another mind.

47 So Menelaus who was guilty of all the evil was acquitted by him of the accusations: and those poor men, who, if they had pleaded their cause even before Scythians, should have been judged innocent, were condemned to death.

48 Thus they that prosecuted the cause for the city and for the people and the sacred vessels did soon suffer unjust punishment.

49 Wherefore even the Tyrians being moved with indignation were liberal towards their burial.

50 And so through the covetousness of them that were in power, Menelaus continued in authority, increasing in malice to the betraying of the citizens.

CHAPTER 5

Wonderful signs are seen in the air. Jason's wickedness and end. Antiochus takes Jerusalem and plunders the temple.

AT the same time, Antiochus prepared for a second journey into Egypt.

2 And it came to pass that through the whole city of Jerusalem for the space of forty days there were seen horsemen running in the air, in gilded raiment and armed with spears, like bands of soldiers.

3 And horses set in order by ranks, running one against another, with the shakings of shields, and a multitude of men in helmets, with drawn swords, and casting of darts, and glittering of golden armour and of harnesses of all sorts.

4 Wherefore all men prayed that these prodigies might turn to good.

5 Now when there was gone forth a false rumour, as though Antiochus had been dead, Jason, taking with him no fewer than a thousand men, suddenly assaulted the city: and though the citizens ran together to the wall, the city at length was taken and Menelaus fled into the castle.

6 But Jason slew his countrymen without mercy, not considering that prosperity against one's own kindred is a very great evil, thinking they had been enemies and not citizens, whom he conquered.

7 Yet he did not get the principality, but received confusion at the end, for the reward of his treachery and fled again into the country of the Ammonites.

8 At the last having been shut up by Aretas the king of the Arabians, in order for his destruction, flying from city to city, hated by all men as a forsaker of the laws and execrable as an enemy of his country and countrymen, he was thrust out into Egypt.

9 And he that had driven many out of their country perished in a strange land, going to Lacedemon, as if for kindred sake he should have refuge there:

10 But he that had cast out many unburied, was himself cast forth both unlamented and unburied, neither having foreign burial, nor being partaker of the sepulchre of his fathers.

CHAP. 4. Ver. 45. *Ptolemee.* The son of Dorymenus, a favourite of the king.

11 Now when these things were done, the king suspected that the Jews would forsake the alliance: whereupon departing out of Egypt with a furious mind, he took the city by force of arms.

12 And commanded the soldiers to kill and not to spare any that came in their way and to go up into the houses to slay.

13 Thus there was a slaughter of young and old, a destruction of women and children, and killing of virgins and infants.

14 And there were slain in the space of three whole days fourscore thousand: forty thousand were made prisoners, and as many sold.

15 But this was not enough. He presumed also to enter into the temple, the most holy in all the world, Menelaus, that traitor to the laws and to his country, being his guide.

16 And taking in his wicked hands the holy vessels which were given by other kings and cities for the ornament and the glory of the place, he unworthily handled and profaned them.

17 Thus Antiochus, going astray in mind, did not consider that God was angry for a while because of the sins of the inhabitants of the city: and therefore this contempt had happened to the place.

18 Otherwise had they not been involved in many sins, ¹as Heliodorus, who was sent by king Seleucus to rob the treasury, so this man also, as soon as he had come, had been forthwith scourged and put back from his presumption.

19 But God did not choose the people for the place's sake, but the place for the people's sake.

20 And therefore the place also itself was made partaker of the evils of the people, but afterward shall communicate in the good things thereof. And as it was forsaken in the wrath of Almighty God, shall be exalted again with great glory, when the great Lord shall be reconciled.

21 So when Antiochus had taken away out of the temple a thousand and eight hundred talents, he went back in all haste to Antioch, thinking through pride that he might now make the land navigable and the sea passable on foot: such was the haughtiness of his mind.

22 He left also governors to afflict the people: at Jerusalem, Philip, a Phrygian by birth, but in manners more barbarous than he that set him there:

23 And in Gazarim, Andronicus and Menelaus, who bore a more heavy hand upon the citizens than the rest.

24 And whereas he was set against the Jews, he sent that hateful prince Apollonius with an army of two and twenty thousand men, commanding him to kill all that were of perfect age and to sell the women and the younger sort.

25 Who when he was come to Jerusalem, pretending peace, rested till the holy day of the sabbath: and then, the Jews keeping holiday, he commanded his men to take arms.

26 And he slew all that were come forth to see: and, running through the city with armed men, he destroyed a very great multitude.

27 But Judas Machabeus, who was the tenth, had withdrawn himself into a desert place, and there lived amongst wild beasts in the mountains with his company: and they continued feeding on herbs, that they might not be partakers of the pollution.

CHAPTER 6

Antiochus commands the law to be abolished, sets up an idol in the temple and persecutes the faithful. The martyrdom of Eleazar.

BUT not long after, the king sent a certain old man of Antioch to compel the Jews to depart from the laws of their fathers and of God:

2 And to defile the temple that was in Jerusalem and to call it the temple of Jupiter Olympius: and that in Gazarim of Jupiter Hospitalis, according as they were that inhabited the place.

3 And very bad was this invasion of evils and grievous to all.

4 For the temple was full of the riot and revellings of the Gentiles and of men lying with lewd women. And women thrust themselves of their accord into the holy places and brought in things that were not lawful.

5 The altar also was filled with unlawful things, which were forbidden by the laws.

6 And neither were the sabbaths kept, nor the solemn days of the fathers observed: neither did any man plainly profess himself to be a Jew.

7 But they were led by bitter constraint on the king's birthday to the sacrifices: and when the feast of Bacchus was kept, they were compelled to go about crowned with ivy in honour of Bacchus.

CHAP. 5. ¹ 2 Mach. 3, 25, 27.

CHAP. 5. Ver. 27. *Was the tenth.* That is, he had nine others in his company.

CHAP. 6. Ver. 2. *That in Gazarim.* Namely, the temple of the Samaritans. And as they were originally strangers, the name of *Hospitalis* (which signifies *of* or *belonging to strangers*) was applicable to the idol not up in their temple.

8 And there went out a decree into the neighbouring cities of the Gentiles, by the suggestion of the Ptolemeans, that they also should act in like manner against the Jews, to oblige them to sacrifice:

9 And whosoever would not conform themselves to the ways of the Gentiles should be put to death. Then was misery to be seen.

10 [1] For two women were accused to have circumcised their children: whom, when they had openly led about through the city with the infants hanging at their breasts, they threw down headlong from the walls.

11 And others that had met together in caves that were near and were keeping the sabbath day privately, being discovered by Philip, were burnt with fire, because they made a conscience to help themselves with their hands, by reason of the religious observance of the day.

12 Now I beseech those that shall read this book, that they be not shocked at these calamities, but that they consider the things that happened, not as being for the destruction but for the correction of our nation.

13 For it is a token of great goodness when sinners are not suffered to go on in their ways for a long time, but are presently punished.

14 For, not as with other nations (whom the Lord patiently expecteth, that when the day of judgment shall come he may punish them in the fulness of their sins)

15 Doth he also deal with us, so as to suffer our sins to come to their height and then take vengeance on us.

16 And therefore he never withdraweth his mercy from us: but though he chastise his people with adversity, he forsaketh them not.

17 But let this suffice in a few words for a warning to the readers. And now we must come to the narration.

18 Eleazar, one of the chief of the scribes, a man advanced in years and of a comely countenance, was pressed to open his mouth to eat swine's flesh.

19 But he, choosing rather a most glorious death than a hateful life, went forward voluntarily to the torment.

20 And considering in what manner he was come to it, patiently bearing, he determined not to do any unlawful things for the love of life.

21 But they that stood by, being moved with wicked pity, for the old friendship they had with the man, taking him aside, desired that flesh might be brought which it was lawful for him to eat, that he might make as if he had eaten, as the king had commanded of the flesh of the sacrifice:

22 That by so doing he might be delivered from death. And for the sake of their old friendship with the man they did him this courtesy.

23 But he began to consider the dignity of his age and his ancient years and the inbred honour of his grey head and his good life and conversation from a child: and he answered without delay, according to the ordinances of the holy lay made by God, saying that he would rather be sent into the other world.

24 For it doth not become our age, said he, to dissemble: whereby many young persons might think that Eleazar, at the age of fourscore and ten years, was gone over to the life of the heathens:

25 And so, they, through my dissimulation and for a little time of a corruptible life, should be deceived, and hereby I should bring a stain and a curse upon my old age.

26 For though, for the present time, I should be delivered from the punishments of men, yet should I not escape the hand of the Almighty, neither alive nor dead.

27 Wherefore by departing manfully out of this life, I shall shew myself worthy of my old age:

28 And I shall leave an example of fortitude to young men, if with a ready mind and constancy I suffer an honourable death, for the most venerable and most holy laws. And having spoken thus, he was forthwith carried to execution.

29 And they that led him and had been a little before more mild were changed to wrath for the words he had spoken, which they thought were uttered out of arrogancy.

30 But when he was now ready to die with the stripes, he groaned and said: O Lord, who hast the holy knowledge, thou knowest manifestly that, whereas I might be delivered from death, I suffer grievous pains in body: but in soul am well content to suffer these because I fear thee.

31 Thus did this man die, leaving not only to young men, but also to the whole nation, the memory of his death for an example of virtue and fortitude.

CHAPTER 7

The glorious martyrdom of the seven brethren and their mother.

Chap. 6. [1] 1 Mach. 1, 63.
Ver. 11. *Philip.* The governor of Jerusalem.
Ver. 21. *Wicked pity.* Their pity was *wicked*, inasmuch as it suggested that wicked proposal of saving his life by dissimulation.

IT came to pass also that seven brethren, together with their mother, were apprehended and compelled by the king to eat swine's flesh against the law, for which end they were tormented with whips and scourges.

2 But one of them, who was the eldest, said thus: What wouldst thou ask, or learn of us? We are ready to die rather than to transgress the laws of God, received from our fathers.

3 Then the king, being angry, commanded fryingpans and brazen caldrons to be made hot: which forthwith being heated,

4 He commanded to cut out the tongue of him that had spoken first, and the skin of his head being drawn off, to chop off also the extremities of his hands and feet, the rest of his brethren and his mother looking on.

5 And when he was now maimed in all parts, he commanded him, being yet alive, to be brought to the fire and to be fried in the fryingpan: and while he was suffering therein long torments, the rest, together with the mother, exhorted one another to die manfully,

6 Saying: The Lord God will look upon the truth and will take pleasure in us, [1] as Moses declared in the profession of the canticle: And in his servants he will take pleasure.

7 So, when the first was dead after this manner, they brought the next to make him a mocking stock: and, when they had pulled off the skin of his head with the hair, they asked him if he would eat before he was punished throughout the whole body in every limb.

8 But he answered in his own language and said: I will not do it. Wherefore, he also in the next place received the torments of the first.

9 And when he was at the last gasp, he said thus: Thou indeed, O most wicked man, destroyest us out of this present life: but the King of the world will raise us up, who die for his laws, in the resurrection of eternal life.

10 After him the third was made a mocking stock, and when he was required, he quickly put forth his tongue and courageously stretched out his hands:

11 And said with confidence: These I have from heaven, but for the laws of God I now despise them: because I hope to receive them again from him.

12 So that the king and they that were with him wondered at the young man's courage, because he esteemed the torments as nothing.

CHAP. 7. [1] Deut. 32, 36.

13 And after he was thus dead, they tormented the fourth in the like manner.

14 And when he was now ready to die he spoke thus: It is better, being put to death, by men, to look for hope from God, to be raised up again by him: for, as to thee thou shalt have no resurrection unto life.

15 And when they had brought the fifth, they tormented him. But he looking upon the king,

16 Said: Whereas thou hast power among men, though thou art corruptible, thou dost what thou wilt: but think not that our nation is forsaken by God.

17 But stay patiently a while and thou shalt see his great power, in what manner he will torment thee and thy seed.

18 After him they brought the sixth: and he, being ready to die, spoke thus: Be not deceived without cause: for we suffer these things for ourselves, having sinned against our God, and things worthy of admiration are done to us.

19 But do not think that thou shalt escape unpunished, for that thou hast attempted to fight against God.

20 Now the mother was to be admired above measure and worthy to be remembered by good men, who beheld her seven sons slain in the space of one day and bore it with a good courage, for the hope that she had in God.

21 And she bravely exhorted every one of them in her own language, being filled with wisdom. And joining a man's heart to a woman's thought,

22 She said to them: I know not how you were formed in my womb: for I neither gave you breath, nor soul, nor life: neither did I frame the limbs of every one of you.

23 But the Creator of the world that formed the nativity of man and that found out the origin of all, he will restore to you again in his mercy, both breath and life, as now you despise yourselves for the sake of his laws.

24 Now Antiochus, thinking himself despised and withal despising the voice of the upbraider, when the youngest was yet alive, did not only exhort him by words, but also assured him with an oath, that he would make him a rich and a happy man, and, if he would turn from the laws of his fathers, would take him for a friend and furnish him with things necessary.

25 But when the young man was not moved with these things, the king called the mother and counselled her to deal with the young man to save his life.

26 And when he had exhorted her

with many words, she promised that she would counsel her son.

27 So bending herself towards him, mocking the cruel tyrant, she said in her own language: My son, have pity upon me that bore thee nine months in my womb and gave thee suck three years and nourished thee and brought thee up unto this age.

28 I beseech *thee,* my son, look upon heaven and earth and all that is in them: and consider that God made them out of nothing, and mankind also:

29 So thou shalt not fear this tormentor, but being made a worthy partner with thy brethren, receive death, that in that mercy I may receive thee again with thy brethren.

30 While she was yet speaking these words, the young man said: For whom do you stay? I will not obey the commandment of the king, but the commandment of the law which was given us by Moses.

31 But thou that hast been the author of all mischief against the Hebrews shalt not escape the hand of God.

32 For we suffer thus for our sins.

33 And though the Lord our God is angry with us a little while for our chastisement and correction, yet he will be reconciled again to his servants.

34 But thou, O wicked and of all men most flagitious, be not lifted up without cause with vain hopes, whilst thou art raging against his servants.

35 For thou hast not yet escaped the judgment of the Almighty God who beholdeth all things.

36 For my brethren, having now undergone a short pain, are under the covenant of eternal life: but thou by the judgment of God shalt receive just punishment for thy pride.

37 But I, like my brethren, offer up my life and my body for the laws of our fathers: calling upon God to be speedily merciful to our nation, and that thou by torments and stripes mayst confess that he alone is God.

38 But in me and in my brethren the wrath of the Almighty, which hath justly been brought upon all our nation, shall cease.

39 Then the king, being incensed with anger, raged against him more cruelly than all the rest, taking it grievously that he was mocked.

40 So this man also died undefiled, wholly trusting in the Lord.

41 And last of all, after the sons, the mother also was consumed.

42 But now there is enough said

of the sacrifices and of the excessive cruelties.

CHAPTER 8

Judas Machabeus gathering an army gains divers victories.

BUT Judas Machabeus and they that were with him went privately into the towns: and calling together their kinsmen and friends and taking unto them such as continued in the Jews' religion, they assembled six thousand men.

2 And they called upon the Lord that he would look upon his people that was trodden down by all and would have pity on the temple that was defiled by the wicked:

3 That he would have pity also upon the city that was destroyed, that was ready to be made even with the ground, and would hear the voice of the blood that cried to him:

4 That he would remember also the most unjust deaths of innocent children and the blasphemies offered to his name and would shew his indignation on this occasion.

5 Now when Machabeus had gathered a multitude, he could not be withstood by the heathens: for the wrath of the Lord was turned into mercy.

6 So coming unawares upon the towns and cities, he set them on fire and, taking possession of the most commodious places, he made no small slaughter of the enemies.

7 And especially in the nights he went upon these expeditions: and the fame of his valour was spread abroad everywhere.

8 Then Philip, seeing that the man gained ground by little and little, and that things for the most part succeeded prosperously with him, wrote to Ptolemee the governor of Celesyria and Phenicia, to send aid to the king's affairs.

9 And he with all speed sent Nicanor the son of Patroclus, one of his special friends, giving him no fewer than twenty thousand armed men of different nations, to root out the whole race of the Jews, joining also with him Gorgias, a good soldier and of great experience in matters of war.

10 And Nicanor purposed to raise for the king the tribute of two thousand talents that was to be given to the

CHAP. 8. Ver. 8. *Philip seeing.* The governor of Jerusalem found himself unable to contend with Judas, especially after the victories he had obtained over Apollonius and Seron (1 Mach. 3).

Ver. 9. *Twenty thousand.* The whole number of the forces sent at that time into Judea was 40,000 footmen, and 7,000 horsemen (1 Mach. 3, 30). But only 20,000 are here taken notice of, because there were no more with Nicanor at the time of the battle.

Romans by making so much money of the captive Jews.

11 Wherefore he sent immediately to the cities upon the sea coast, to invite men together to buy up the Jewish slaves, promising that they should have ninety slaves for one talent, not reflecting on the vengeance, which was to follow him from the Almighty.

12 Now when Judas found that Nicanor was coming, he imparted to the Jews that were with him that the enemy was at hand.

13 And some of them, being afraid and distrusting the justice of God, fled away.

14 Others sold all that they had left and withal besought the Lord that he would deliver them from the wicked Nicanor, who had sold them before he came near them:

15 And if not for their sakes, yet for the covenant that he had made with their fathers and for the sake of his holy and glorious name that was invoked upon them.

16 But Machabeus, calling together seven thousand that were with him, exhorted them not to be reconciled to the enemies nor to fear the multitude of the enemies who came wrongfully against them, but to fight manfully:

17 Setting before their eyes the injury they had unjustly done the holy place and also the injury they had done to the city, which had been shamefully abused, besides their destroying the ordinances of the fathers.

18 For, said he, they trust in their weapons and in their boldness: but we trust in the Almighty Lord who at a beck can utterly destroy both them that come against us and the whole world.

19 Moreover he put them in mind also of the helps their fathers had received from God: [1] and how under Sennacherib a hundred and eighty-five thousand had been destroyed.

20 And of the battle that they had fought against the Galatians in Babylonia: how they, being in all but six thousand, when it came to the point and the Macedonians their companions were at a stand, slew a hundred and twenty thousand, because of the help

CHAP. 8. [1] 4 Kings, 19, 35; Tob. 1, 21; Ecclus. 48, 24; Isai. 37, 36; 1 Mach. 7, 41.

Ver. 16. *Seven thousand.* In the Greek it is six thousand. But then three thousand of them had no arms (1 Mach. 4, 6).

Ver. 20. *Galatians.* That is, the *Gauls*, who having ravaged Italy and Greece, poured themselves in upon Asia in immense multitudes, where also they founded the kingdom of Galatia or Gallo-Græcia.

Ver. 24. *Above nine thousand.* Including the three thousand slain in the pursuit.

they had from heaven, and for this they received many favours.

21 With these words they were greatly encouraged and disposed even to die for the laws and their country.

22 So he appointed his brethren captains over each division of his army, Simon and Joseph and Jonathan, giving to each one fifteen hundred men.

23 And after the holy book had been read to them by Esdras and he had given them for a watchword, The help of God: himself leading the first band, he joined battle with Nicanor.

24 And the Almighty being their helper, they slew above nine thousand men: and having wounded and disabled the greater part of Nicanor's army, they obliged them to fly.

25 And they took the money of them that came to buy them: and they pursued them on every side.

26 But they came back for want of time: for it was the day before the sabbath and therefore they did not continue the pursuit.

27 But when they had gathered together their arms and their spoils, they kept the sabbath: blessing the Lord who had delivered them that day, distilling the beginning of mercy upon them.

28 Then after the sabbath they divided the spoils to the feeble and the orphans and the widows: and the rest they took for themselves and their servants.

29 When this was done and they had all made a common supplication, they besought the merciful Lord to be reconciled to his servants unto the end.

30 Moreover, they slew above twenty thousand of them that were with Timotheus and Bacchides who fought against them: and they made themselves masters of the high strong holds: and they divided amongst them many spoils, giving equal portions to the feeble, the fatherless and the widows, yea and the aged also.

31 And when they had carefully gathered together their arms, they laid them all up in convenient places: and the residue of their spoils they carried to Jerusalem.

32 They slew also Philarches who was with Timotheus, a wicked man, who had many ways afflicted the Jews.

33 And when they kept the feast of the victory at Jerusalem, they burnt Callisthenes, that had set fire to the holy gates, who had taken refuge in a certain house, rendering to him a worthy reward for his impieties.

34 But as for that most wicked man

Nicanor, who had brought a thousand merchants to the sale of the Jews,

35 Being through the help of the Lord brought down by them of whom he had made no account, laying aside his garment of glory, fleeing through the midland country, he came alone to Antioch, being rendered very unhappy by the destruction of his army.

36 And he that had promised to levy the tribute for the Romans by the means of the captives of Jerusalem now professed that the Jews had God for their protector and therefore they could not be hurt, because they followed the laws appointed by him.

CHAPTER 9

The wretched end and fruitless repentance of king Antiochus.

AT that time Antiochus returned with dishonour out of Persia.

2 For he had entered into the city called Persepolis and attempted to rob the temple and to oppress the city: but the multitude, running together to arms, put them to flight: and so it fell out that Antiochus being put to flight returned with disgrace.

3 Now when he was come about Ecbatana, he received the news of what had happened to Nicanor and Timotheus.

4 And swelling with anger he thought to revenge upon the Jews the injury done by them that had put him to flight. And therefore he commanded his chariot to be driven without stopping in his journey, the judgment of heaven urging him forward, because he had spoken so proudly, that he would come to Jerusalem and make it a common buryingplace of the Jews.

5 ¹ But the Lord, the God of Israel, that seeth all things, struck him with an incurable and an invisible plague. For as soon as he had ended these words, a dreadful pain in his bowels came upon him and bitter torments of the inner parts.

6 And indeed very justly, seeing he had tormented the bowels of others with many and new torments, albeit he by no means ceased from his malice.

7 Moreover, being filled with pride, breathing out fire in his rage against the Jews and commanding the matter to be hastened, it happened as he was going with violence that he fell from the chariot, so that his limbs were much pained by a grievous bruising of the body.

8 Thus he that seemed to himself to command even the waves of the sea, being proud above the condition of man, and to weigh the heights of the mountains in a balance, now being cast down to the ground. was carried in a litter, bearing witness to the manifest power of God in himself:

9 So that worms swarmed out of the body of this man, and whilst he lived in sorrow and pain, his flesh fell off and the filthiness of his smell was noisome to the army.

10 And the man that thought a little before he could reach to the stars of heaven, no man could endure to carry, for the intolerable stench.

11 And by this means, being brought from his great pride, he began to come to the knowledge of himself, being admonished by the scourge of God, his pains increasing every moment.

12 And when he himself could not now abide his own stench, he spoke thus: It is just to be subject to God and that a mortal man should not equal himself to God.

13 Then this wicked man prayed to the Lord, of whom he was not like to obtain mercy.

14 And the city to which he was going in haste to lay it even with the ground and to make it a common buryingplace, he now desireth to make free.

15 And the Jews whom he said he would not account worthy to be so much as buried, but would give them up to be devoured by the birds and wild beasts, and would utterly destroy them with their children, he now promiseth to make equal with the Athenians.

16 The holy temple also which before he had spoiled, he promiseth to adorn with goodly gifts and to multiply the holy vessels and to allow out of his revenues the charges pertaining to the sacrifices.

17 Yea also, that he would become a Jew himself and would go through every place of the earth and declare the power of God.

18 But his pains not ceasing (for the just judgment of God was come upon him), despairing *of life,* he wrote to the Jews in the manner of a supplication a letter in these words:

19 To his very good subjects, the Jews, Antiochus, king and ruler, wisheth much health and welfare and happiness.

20 If you and your children are well

CHAP. 9. ¹ 2 Par. 16, 9.

Ver. 35. *Laying aside his garment of glory.* That is, his splendid apparel, which he wore through ostentation. He now throws it off, lest he should be known on his flight.

CHAP. 9. Ver. 2. *Persepolis.* Otherwise called Elymais.

Ver. 13. *Of whom he was not like to obtain mercy.* Because his repentance was not for offence committed against God, but barely on account of his present sufferings.

and if all matters go with you to your mind, we give very great thanks.

21 As for me, being infirm, but yet kindly remembering you, returning out of the places of Persia, and being taken with a grievous disease, I thought it necessary to take care for the common good:

22 Not distrusting my life, but having great hope to escape the sickness.

23 But considering that my father also, at what time he led an army into the higher countries, appointed who should reign after him:

24 To the end that if anything contrary to expectation should fall out, or any bad tidings should be brought, they that were in the countries, knowing to whom the whole government was left, might not be troubled.

25 Moreover, considering that neighbouring princes and borderers wait for opportunities and expect what shall be the event, I have appointed my son Antiochus king, whom I often recommended to many of you when I went into the higher provinces: and I have written to him what I have joined here below.

26 I pray you therefore and request of you, that, remembering favours both public and private, you will every man of you continue to be faithful to me and to my son.

27 For I trust that he will behave with moderation and humanity, and following my intentions, will be gracious unto you.

28 Thus the murderer and blasphemer, being grievously struck, as himself had treated others, died a miserable death in a strange country among the mountains.

29 But Philip that was brought up with him carried away his body: and out of fear of the son of Antiochus, went into Egypt to Ptolemee Philometor.

CHAPTER 10

The purification of the temple and city. Other exploits of Judas. His victory over Timotheus.

BUT Machabeus and they that were with him, by the protection of the Lord, recovered the temple and the city again.

2 But he threw down the altars which the heathens had set up in the streets, as also the temples of the idols.

3 And having purified the temple,

CHAP. 10. Ver. 15. *The Jews.* He speaks of them that had fallen from their religion and were enemies of their country, who joining with the Idumeans or Edomites, kept possession of the strong holds and from thence annoyed their countrymen.

they made another altar: and taking fire out of the fiery stones, they offered sacrifices after two years and set forth incense and lamps and the loaves of proposition.

4 And when they had done these things, they besought the Lord, lying prostrate on the ground, that they might no more fall into such evils: but if they should at any time sin, that they might be chastised by him more gently, and not be delivered up to barbarians and blasphemous men.

5 Now upon the same day that the temple had been polluted by the strangers, on the very same day, it was cleansed again, to wit, on the five and twentieth day of the month of Casleu.

6 And they kept eight days with joy, after the manner of the feast of the tabernacles, remembering that not long before they had kept the feast of the tabernacles when they were in the mountains and in dens, like wild beasts.

7 Therefore they *now* carried boughs and green branches and palms for Him that had given them good success in cleansing his place.

8 And they ordained by a common statute and decree that all the nation of the Jews should keep those days every year.

9 And this was the end of Antiochus that was called the Illustrious.

10 But now we will relate the acts of Eupator, the son of that wicked Antiochus, abridging the account of the evils that happened in the wars.

11 For when he was come to the crown, he appointed over the affairs of his realm one Lysias, general of the army of Phenicia and Syria.

12 For Ptolemee that was called Macer, was determined to be strictly just to the Jews, and especially by reason of the wrong that had been done them, and to deal peaceably with them.

13 But being accused for this to Eupator by his friends and being oftentimes called traitor because he had left Cyprus which Philometor had committed to him, and, coming over to Antiochus the Illustrious, had revolted also from him, he put an end to his life by poison.

14 But Gorgias who was governor of the holds, taking with him the strangers, often fought against the Jews.

15 And the Jews that occupied the most commodious hold received those that were driven out of Jerusalem and attempted to make war.

16 Then they that were with Machabeus, beseeching the Lord by prayers to be their helper, made a strong attack upon the strong holds of the Idumeans:

17 And assaulting them with great force, won the holds, killed them that came in the way and slew altogether no fewer than twenty thousand.

18 And whereas some were fled into very strong towers, having all manner of provision to sustain a siege,

19 Machabeus left Simon and Joseph and Zacheus and them that were with them in sufficient number to besiege them and departed to those expeditions which urged more.

20 Now they that were with Simon, being led with covetousness, were persuaded for the sake of money by some that were in the towers: and taking seventy thousand didrachmas, let some of them escape.

21 But when it was told Machabeus what was done, he assembled the rulers of the people and accused those men that they had sold their brethren for money, having let their adversaries escape.

22 So he put these traitors to death and forthwith took the two towers.

23 And having good success in arms and in all things he took in hand, he slew more than twenty thousand in the two holds.

24 But Timotheus who before had been overcome by the Jews, having called together a multitude of foreign troops and assembled horsemen out of Asia, came as though he would take Judea by force of arms.

25 But Machabeus and they that were with him, when he drew near prayed to the Lord, sprinkling earth upon their heads and girding their loins with hair-cloth

26 And lying prostrate at the foot of the altar besought him to be merciful to them and to be an enemy to their enemies and an adversary to their adversaries, as the law saith.

27 And so after prayer taking their arms, they went forth further from the city: and when they were come very near the enemies they rested.

28 But as soon as the sun was risen both sides joined battle: the one part having with their valour the Lord for a surety of victory and success: but the other side making their rage their leader in battle.

29 But when they were in the heat of the engagement, there appeared to the enemies from heaven five men upon horses, comely, with golden bridles, conducting the Jews:

30 Two of whom took Machabeus between them and covered him on every side with their arms and kept him safe: but cast darts and fireballs against the enemy, so that they fell down, being both confounded with blindness and filled with trouble.

31 And there were slain twenty thousand five hundred, and six hundred horsemen.

32 But Timotheus fled into Gazara a strong hold, where Chereas was governor.

33 Then Machabeus and they that were with him, cheerfully laid siege to the fortress four days.

34 But they that were within, trusting to the strength of the place, blasphemed exceedingly and cast forth abominable words.

35 But when the fifth day appeared, twenty young men of them that were with Machabeus, inflamed in their minds because of the blasphemy, approached manfully to the wall and, pushing forward with fierce courage, got up upon it.

36 Moreover, others also getting up after them went to set fire to the towers and the gates and to burn the blasphemers alive.

37 And having for two days together pillaged and sacked the fortress, they killed Timotheus, who was found hid in a certain place: they slew also his brother Chereas and Apollophanes.

38 And when this was done, they blessed the Lord with hymns and thanksgiving, who had done great things in Israel and given them the victory.

CHAPTER 11

Lysias is overthrown by Judas. He sues for peace.

A SHORT time after this, Lysias, the king's lieutenant and cousin, and who had chief charge over all the affairs, being greatly displeased with what had happened,

2 Gathered together fourscore thousand men and all the horsemen, and came against the Jews, thinking to take the city and make it a habitation of the Gentiles:

3 And to make a gain of the temple, as of the other temples of the Gentiles, and to set the high priesthood to sale every year:

4 Never considering the power of God, but puffed up in mind and trusting in the multitude of his foot soldiers and the thousands of his horsemen and his fourscore elephants.

5 So he came into Judea and, approaching to Bethsura, which was in a narrow place, the space of five furlongs

---

CHAP. 10. ¹ 1 Mach. 5, 6.

Ver. 37. *Timotheus.* This man, who was killed at the taking of Gazara, is different from that Timotheus who is mentioned in the fifth chapter of the first book of Machabees and of whom there is mention in the following chapter.

from Jerusalem, he laid siege to that fortress.

6 But when Machabeus and they that were with him understood that the strong holds were besieged, they and all the people besought the Lord with lamentations and tears that he would send a good angel to save Israel.

7 Then Machabeus himself, first taking his arms, exhorted the rest to expose themselves together with him to the danger and to succour their brethren.

8 And when they were going forth together with a willing mind, there appeared at Jerusalem a horseman going before them in white clothing, with golden armour, shaking a spear.

9 Then they all together blessed the merciful Lord and took great courage, being ready to break through not only men but also the fiercest beasts and walls of iron.

10 So they went on courageously, having a helper from heaven and the Lord who shewed mercy to them.

11 And rushing violently upon the enemy, like lions, they slew of them eleven thousand footmen and one thousand six hundred horsemen.

12 And put all the rest to flight. And many of them being wounded, escaped naked: yea and Lysias himself fled away shamefully and escaped.

13 And as he was a man of understanding, considering with himself the loss he had suffered and perceiving that the Hebrews could not be overcome, because they relied upon the help of the Almighty God, he sent to them

14 And promised that he would agree to all things that are just and that he would persuade the king to be their friend.

15 Then Machabeus consented to the request of Lysias, providing for the common good in all things: and whatsoever Machabeus wrote to Lysias concerning the Jews, the king allowed of.

16 For there were letters written to the Jews from Lysias, to this effect: Lysias to the people of the Jews, greeting:

17 John and Abesalom who were sent from you, delivering your writings, requested that I would accomplish those things which were signified by them.

18 Therefore, whatsoever things would be reported to the king I have

represented to him: and he hath granted as much as the matter permitted.

19 If therefore you will keep yourselves loyal in affairs, hereafter also I will endeavour to be a means of your good.

20 But as concerning other particulars, I have given orders by word, both to these and to them that are sent by me, to commune with you.

21 Fare ye well. In the year one hundred and forty-eight, the four and twentieth day of the month of Dioscorus.

22 But the king's letter contained these words: King Antiochus to Lysias his brother, greeting.

23 Our father being translated amongst the gods, we are desirous that they that are in our realm should live quietly and apply themselves diligently to their own concerns.

24 And we have heard that the Jews would not consent to my father to turn to the rites of the Greeks, but that they would keep to their own manner of living: and therefore that they request us to allow them to live after their own laws.

25 Wherefore, being desirous that this nation also should be at rest, we have ordained and decreed that the temple should be restored to them and that they may live according to the custom of their ancestors.

26 Thou shalt do well therefore to send to them and grant them peace, that, our pleasure being known, they may be of good comfort and look to their own affairs.

27 But the king's letter to the Jews was in this manner: King Antiochus to the senate of the Jews and to the rest of the Jews, greeting.

28 If you are well, you are as we desire: we ourselves also are well.

29 Menelaus came to us, saying that you desired to come down to your countrymen that are with us.

30 We grant therefore a safe conduct to all that come and go, until the thirtieth day of the month of Xanthicus.

31 That the Jews may use their own kind of meats and their own laws as before and that none of them any manner of ways be molested for things which have been done by ignorance.

32 And we have sent also Menelaus to speak to you.

33 Fare ye well. In the year one hundred and forty-eight, the fifteenth day of the month of Xanthicus.

34 The Romans also sent them a letter, to this effect. Quintus Memmius and Titus Manilius, ambassadors of the

CHAP. 11. Ver. 21. *In the year* 148. According to the computation followed by the Greeks, which was different from that of the Hebrews, followed by the writer of the First Book of Machabees. However, by this date, as well as by other circumstances, it appears that the expedition of Lysias, mentioned in this chapter, is different from that which is recorded by him (1 Mach. 6).

Romans, to the people of the Jews, greeting.

35 Whatsoever Lysias the king's cousin hath granted you, we also have granted.

36 But touching such things as he thought should be referred to the king, after you have diligently conferred among yourselves, send some one forthwith, that we may decree as it is convenient for you: for we are going to Antioch.

37 And therefore make haste to write back, that we may know of what mind you are.

38 Fare ye well. In the year one hundred and forty-eight, the fifteenth day of the month of Xanthicus.

CHAPTER 12

The Jews are still molested by their neighbours. Judas gains divers victories over them. He orders sacrifice and prayers for the dead.

WHEN these covenants were made, Lysias went to the king and the Jews gave themselves to husbandry.

2 But they that were behind, namely, Timotheus and Apollonius the son of Genneus, also Hieronymus and Demophon, and besides them Nicanor, the governor of Cyprus, would not suffer them to live in peace and to be quiet.

3 The men of Joppe also were guilty of this kind of wickedness: they desired the Jews who dwelt among them to go with their wives and children into the boats which they had prepared, as though they had no enmity to them.

4 Which when they had consented to, according to the common decree of the city, suspecting nothing because of the peace: when they were gone forth into the deep, they drowned no fewer than two hundred of them.

5 But as soon as Judas heard of this cruelty done to his countrymen, he commanded the men that were with him: and after having called upon God the just judge,

6 He came against those murderers of his brethren and set the haven on fire in the night, burnt the boats and slew with the sword them that escaped from the fire.

7 And when he had done these things in this manner, he departed as if he would return again and root out all the Joppites.

8 But when he understood that the men of Jamnia also designed to do in like manner to the Jews that dwelt among them,

9 He came upon the Jamnites also by night and set the haven on fire with the ships, so that the light of the fire was seen at Jerusalem, two hundred and forty furlongs off.

10 And when they were now gone from thence nine furlongs and were marching towards Timotheus, five thousand footmen and five hundred horsemen of the Arabians set upon them.

11 And after a hard fight in which by the help of God they got the victory, the rest of the Arabians, being overcome, besought Judas for peace, promising to give him pastures and to assist him in other things.

12 And Judas thinking that they might be profitable indeed in many things, promised them peace: and after having joined hands, they departed to their tents.

13 He also laid siege to a certain strong city, encompassed with bridges and walls, and inhabited by multitudes of different nations, the name of which is Casphin.

14 But they that were within it, trusting in the strength of the walls and the provision of the victuals, behaved in a more negligent manner and provoked Judas with railing and blaspheming and uttering such words as were not to be spoken.

15 But Machabeus, calling upon the great Lord of the world who without any rams or engines of war threw down the walls of Jericho [1] in the time of Josue, fiercely assaulted the walls.

16 And having taken the city by the will of the Lord, he made an unspeakable slaughter, so that a pool adjoining of two furlongs broad seemed to run with the blood of the slain.

17 From thence they departed seven hundred and fifty furlongs and came to Characa, to the Jews that are called Tubianites.

18 But as for Timotheus, they found him not in those places, for before he had dispatched any thing he went back, having left a very strong garrison in a certain hold.

19 But Dositheus, and Sosipater, who were captains with Machabeus, slew them that were left by Timotheus in the hold, to the number of ten thousand men.

20 And Machabeus, having set in order about him six thousand men and divided them by bands, went forth against Timotheus, who had with him a hundred and twenty thousand footmen and two thousand five hundred horsemen.

21 Now when Timotheus had knowledge of the coming of Judas, he sent

CHAP. 12. [1] Jos. 6, 20.

CHAP. 12. Ver. 15. *Rams.* That is, engines for battering walls, etc., which were used in sieges in those times.

the women and children and the other baggage before him into a fortress called Carnion: for it was impregnable and hard to come at, by reason of the straitness of the places.

22 But when the first band of Judas came in sight, the enemies were struck with fear, by the presence of God who seeth all things: and they were put to flight one from another, so that they were often thrown down by their own companions and wounded with the strokes of their own swords.

23 But Judas was vehemently earnest in punishing the profane, of whom he slew thirty thousand men.

24 And Timotheus himself fell into the hands of the band of Dositheus and Sosipater: and with many prayers he besought them to let him go with his life, because he had the parents and brethren of many of the Jews, who, by his death might happen to be deceived.

25 And when he had given his faith that he would restore them according to the agreement, they let him go without hurt, for the saving of their brethren.

26 Then Judas went away to Carnion, where he slew five and twenty thousand persons.

27 And after he had put to flight and destroyed these, he removed his army to Ephron, a strong city, wherein there dwelt a multitude of divers nations: and stout young men standing upon the walls made a vigorous resistance. And in this place there were many engines of war and a provision of darts.

28 But when they had invocated the Almighty, who with his power breaketh the strength of the enemies, they took the city and slew five and twenty thousand of them that were within.

29 From thence they departed to Scythopolis, which lieth six hundred furlongs from Jerusalem.

30 But the Jews that were among the Scythopolitans testifying that they were used kindly by them and that even in the times of their adversity they had treated them with humanity:

31 They gave them thanks, exhorting them to be still friendly to their nation: and so they came to Jerusalem, the feast of the weeks being at hand.

32 And after Pentecost they marched against Gorgias, the governor of Idumea.

33 And he came out with three thousand footmen and four hundred horsemen.

34 And when they had joined battle, it happened that a few of the Jews were slain.

35 But Dositheus, a horseman, one of Bacenor's *band*, a valiant man, took hold of Gorgias: and when he would have taken him alive, a certain horseman of the Thracians came upon him and cut off his shoulder: and so Gorgias escaped to Maresa.

36 But when they that were with Esdrin had fought long, and were weary, Judas called upon the Lord to be their helper, and leader of the battle.

37 Then beginning in his own language and singing hymns with a loud voice, he put Gorgias' soldiers to flight.

38 So Judas, having gathered together his army, came into the city of Odollam: and when the seventh day came, they purified themselves according to the custom and kept the sabbath in the same place.

39 And the day following, Judas came with his company to take away the bodies of them that were slain and to bury them with their kinsmen in the sepulchres of their fathers.

40 And they found under the coats of the slain some of the donaries of the idols of Jamnia, which the law forbiddeth to the Jews: so that all plainly saw, that for this cause they were slain.

41 Then they all blessed the just judgment of the Lord, who had discovered the things that were hidden.

42 And so betaking themselves to prayers they besought him that the sin which had been committed might be forgotten. But the most valiant Judas exhorted the people to keep themselves from sin, forasmuch as they saw before their eyes what had happened because of the sins of those that were slain.

43 And making a gathering, he sent twelve thousand drachms of silver to Jerusalem for sacrifice to be offered for the sins of the dead, thinking well and religiously concerning the resurrection.

44 (For if he had not hoped that they that were slain should rise again, it would have seemed superfluous and vain to pray for the dead.)

45 And because he considered that they who had fallen asleep with godliness had great grace laid up for them.

46 It is therefore a holy and whole-

Ver. 29. *Scythopolis.* Formerly called *Bethsan.*
Ver. 40. *Of the donaries.* That is, of the votive offerings, which had been hung up in the temples of the idols, which they had taken away when they burnt the port of Jamnia (ver. 9) contrary to the prohibition of the law (Deut. 7, 25).
Ver. 45. *With godliness.* Judas hoped that these men who died fighting for the cause of God and religion, might find mercy: either because they might be excused from mortal sin by ignorance, or might have repented of their sin, at least at their death.
Ver. 46. *It is therefore a holy and wholesome thought to pray for the dead.* Here is an evident

some thought to pray for the dead, that they may be loosed from sins.

CHAPTER 13

Antiochus and Lysias again invade Judea. Menelaus is put to death. The king's great army is worsted twice. The peace is renewed.

IN the year one hundred and forty-nine, Judas understood that Antiochus Eupator was coming with a multitude against Judea,

2 And with him Lysias the regent, who had charge over the affairs *of the realm,* having with him a hundred and ten thousand footmen, five thousand horsemen, twenty-two elephants *and* three hundred chariots armed with hooks.

3 Menelaus also joined himself with them: and with great deceitfulness besought Antiochus, not for the welfare of his country but in hopes that he should be appointed chief ruler.

4 But the King of kings stirred up the mind of Antiochus against the sinner, and upon Lysias suggesting that he was the cause of all the evils, he commanded (as the custom is with them) that he should be apprehended and put to death in the same place.

5 Now there was in that place a tower fifty cubits high, having a heap of ashes on every side. This had a prospect steep down.

6 From thence he commanded the sacrilegious wretch to be thrown down into the ashes, all men thrusting him forward unto death.

7 And by such a law it happened that Menelaus the transgressor of the law was put to death: not having so much as burial in the earth.

8 And indeed very justly: for insomuch as he had committed many sins against the altar of God, the fire and ashes of which were holy, he was condemned to die in ashes.

9 But the king, with his mind full of rage, came on to shew himself worse to the Jews than his father was.

10 Which, when Judas understood, he commanded the people to call upon the Lord day and night, that, as he had always done, so now also he would help them:

11 Because they were afraid to be deprived of the law and of their country and of the holy temple: and that he would not suffer the people that had of late taken breath for a little while to be again in subjection to blasphemous nations.

12 So when they had all done this together and had craved mercy of the Lord with weeping and fasting, lying prostrate on the ground for three days

continually, Judas exhorted them to make themselves ready.

13 But he with the ancients determined, before the king should bring his army into Judea and make himself master of the city, to go out and to commit the event of the thing to the judgment of the Lord.

14 So committing all to God, the creator of the world, and having exhorted his people to fight manfully and to stand up even to death for the laws, the temple, the city, their country and citizens: he placed his army about Modin.

15 And having given his company for a watchword, The Victory of God, with most valiant chosen young men, he set upon the king's quarter by night and slew four thousand men in the camp and the greatest of the elephants, with them that had been upon him,

16 And having filled the camp of the enemies with exceeding great fear and tumult, they went off with good success.

17 Now this was done at the break of day, by the protection and help of the Lord.

18 But the king, having taken a taste of the hardiness of the Jews, attempted to take the strong places by policy.

19 And he marched with his army to Bethsura, which was a strong hold of the Jews: but he was repulsed, he failed, he lost his men.

20 Now Judas sent necessaries to them that were within.

21 But Rhodocus, one of the Jews' army, disclosed the secrets to the enemies, so he was sought out and taken up and put in prison.

22 Again the king treated with them that were in Bethsura: gave his right hand, took theirs and went away.

23 He fought with Judas and was overcome. And when he understood that Philip, who had been left over the affairs, had rebelled at Antioch, he was in a consternation of mind and, entreating the Jews and yielding to them, he swore to all things that seemed reasonable, and, being reconciled, offered sacrifices, honoured the temple and left gifts.

and undeniable proof of the practice of praying for the dead under the old law, which was then strictly observed by the Jews and consequently could not be introduced at that time by Judas, their chief and high priest, if it had not been always their custom.

CHAP. 13. Ver. 2. *A hundred and ten thousand.* The difference between the numbers here set down, and those recorded (1 Mach. 4), is easily accounted for, if we consider that such armies as these are liable to be at one time more numerous than at another; either by sending away large detachments, or being diminished by sickness, or increased by receiving fresh supplies of troops, according to different exigencies or occurrences.

24 He embraced Machabeus and made made him governor and prince from Ptolemais unto the Gerrenians.

25 But when he was come to Ptolemais, the men of that city were much displeased with the conditions of the peace, being angry for fear they should break the covenant.

26 Then Lysias went up to the judgment seat and set forth the reason and appeased the people and returned to Antioch. And thus matters went with regard to the king's coming and his return.

CHAPTER 14

Demetrius challenges the kingdom. Alcimus applies to him to be made high priest. Nicanor is sent into Judea. His dealings with Judas. His threats. The history of Razias.

BUT after the space of three years, Judas and they that were with him understood that Demetrius the son of Seleucus was come up with a great power and a navy, by the haven of Tripolis, to places proper for his purpose

2 And had made himself master of the countries, against Antiochus and his general Lysias.

3 Now one Alcimus, who had been chief priest, but had wilfully defiled himself in the time of mingling *with the heathens*, seeing that there was no safety for him, nor access to the altar,

4 Came to king Demetrius in the year one hundred and fifty, presenting unto him a crown of gold and a palm, and, besides these, some boughs which seemed to belong to the temple. And that day indeed he held his peace.

5 But having gotten a convenient time to further his madness, being called to counsel by Demetrius and asked what the Jews relied upon and what were their counsels,

6 He answered thereunto: They among the Jews that are called Assideans, of whom Judas Machabeus is captain, nourish wars and raise seditions and will not suffer the realm to be in peace.

7 For I also, being deprived of my ancestors' glory (I mean of the high priesthood), am now come hither:

8 Principally indeed out of fidelity to

CHAP. 14. Ver. 3. *Now Alcimus, who had been chief priest.* This Alcimus was of the stock of Aaron, but for his apostasy here mentioned was incapable of the high priesthood. King Antiochus Eupator appointed him in place of the high priest (see above, 1 Mach., chap. 7, ver 9), as Menelaus had been before him set up by Antiochus (above, chap. 4). Yet neither of them were truly high priests; for the true high priesthood was amongst the Machabees, who were also of the stock of Aaron and had strictly held their religion and were ordained according to the rites commanded in the law of Moses.—*Mingling with the heathens.* That is, in their idolatrous worship.

the king's interests, but in the next place also to provide for the good of my countrymen. For all our nation suffereth much from the evil proceedings of those men.

9 Wherefore, O king, seeing thou knowest all these things, take care, I beseech thee, both of the country and of our nation, according to thy humanity which is known to all men,

10 For as long as Judas liveth, it is not possible that the state should be quiet.

11 Now when this man had spoken to this effect, the rest also of the *king's* friends, who were enemies of Judas, incensed Demetrius against him.

12 And forthwith he sent Nicanor, the commander over the elephants, governor into Judea:

13 Giving him in charge to take Judas himself and disperse all them that were with him and to make Alcimus the high priest of the great temple.

14 Then the Gentiles who had fled out of Judea from Judas came to Nicanor by flocks, thinking the miseries and calmities of the Jews to be the welfare of their affairs.

15 Now when the Jews heard of Nicanor's coming and that the nations were assembled against them, they cast earth upon their heads and made supplication to him who chose his people to keep them for ever and who protected his portion by evident signs.

16 Then at the commandment of their captain, they forthwith removed from the place where they were and went to the town of Dessau to meet them.

17 Now Simon, the brother of Judas, had joined battle with Nicanor, but was frightened with the sudden coming of the adversaries.

18 Nevertheless, Nicanor hearing of the valour of Judas' companions and the greatness of courage with which they fought for their country, was afraid to try the matter by the sword.

19 Wherefore he sent Posidonius and Theodotius and Matthias before, to present and receive the right hands.

20 And when there had been a consultation thereupon and the captain had acquainted the multitude with it, they were all of one mind to consent to covenants.

21 So they appointed a day upon which they might commune together by themselves: and seats were brought out and set for each one.

22 But Judas ordered men to be ready in convenient places, lest some mischief might be suddenly practised by the enemies: so they made an agreeable conference.

23 And Nicanor abode in Jerusalem and did no wrong, but sent away the flocks of the multitudes that had been gathered together.

24 And Judas was always dear to him from the heart: and he was well affected to the man.

25 And he desired him to marry a wife and to have children. So he married. He lived quietly and they lived in common.

26 But Alcimus, seeing the love they had one to another and the covenants, came to Demetrius and told him that Nicanor assented to the foreign interest, for that he meant to make Judas, who was a traitor to the kingdom, his successor.

27 Then the king, being in a rage and provoked with this man's wicked accusations, wrote to Nicanor, signifying that he was greatly displeased with the covenant of friendship and that he commanded him nevertheless to send Machabeus prisoner in all haste to Antioch.

28 When this was known, Nicanor was in a consternation and took it grievously that he should make void the articles that were agreed upon, having received no injury from the man.

29 But because he could not oppose the king, he watched an opportunity to comply with the orders.

30 But when Machabeus perceived that Nicanor was more stern to him and that when they met together as usual he behaved himself in a rough manner: and was sensible that this rough behaviour came not of good, he gathered together a few of his men and hid himself from Nicanor.

31 But he, finding himself notably prevented by the man, came to the great and holy temple and commanded the priests that were offering the accustomed sacrifices to deliver him the man.

32 And when they swore unto him that they knew not where the man was whom he sought, he stretched out his hand to the temple

33 And swore, saying: Unless you deliver Judas prisoner to me, I will lay this temple of God even with the ground and will beat down the altar and I will dedicate this temple to Bacchus.

34 And when he had spoken thus he departed. But the priests, stretching forth their hands to heaven, called upon him that was ever the defender of their nation, saying in this manner:

35 Thou, O Lord of all things, who wantest nothing, wast pleased that the temple of thy habitation should be amongst us.

36 Therefore now, O Lord, the Holy of all Holies, keep this house for ever undefiled, which was lately cleansed.

37 Now Razias, one of the ancients of Jerusalem, was accused to Nicanor, a man that was a lover of the city and of good report, who for his affection was called the father of the Jews.

38 This man, for a long time, had held fast his purpose of keeping himself pure in the Jews' religion and was ready to expose his body and life that he might persevere therein.

39 So Nicanor, being willing to declare the hatred that he bore the Jews, sent five hundred soldiers to take him.

40 For he thought by insnaring him to hurt the Jews very much.

41 Now as the multitude sought to rush into his house and to break open the door and to set fire to it, when he was ready to be taken, he struck himself with his sword:

42 Choosing to die nobly rather than to fall into the hands of the wicked and to suffer abuses unbecoming his noble birth.

43 But whereas through haste he missed of giving himself a sure wound, and the crowd was breaking into the doors, he ran boldly to the wall and manfully threw himself down to the crowd:

44 But they quickly making room for his fall, he came upon the midst of the neck.

45 And as he had yet breath in him, being inflamed in mind, he arose: and while his blood ran down with a great stream and he was grievously wounded, he ran through the crowd:

46 And standing upon a steep rock, when he was now almost without blood, grasping his bowels with both hands, he cast them upon the throng, calling upon the Lord of life and spirit to restore these to him again. And so he departed this life.

CHAPTER 15

Judas encouraged by a vision gains a glorious victory over Nicanor. The conclusion.

BUT [1] when Nicanor understood that Judas was in the places of Samaria, he purposed to set upon him with all violence on the sabbath day.

2 And when the Jews that were constrained to follow him, said: Do not act

CHAP. 15. [1] 1 Mach. 7, 26.

Ver. 41. *He struck himself.* St. Augustine, discussing this fact of Razias, says that the holy scripture relates it, but doth not praise it as to be admired or imitated, and that either it was not well done by him or at least not proper in this time of grace.

Ver. 44. *He came upon the midst of the neck. Venit per mediam cervicem.* In the Greek it is κενεῶνα, which signifies a void place, where there is no building.

so fiercely and barbarously, but give honour to the day that is sanctified and reverence him that beholdeth all things:

3 That unhappy man asked if there were a mighty One in heaven that had commanded the sabbath day to be kept.

4 And when they answered: There is the living Lord himself in heaven, the mighty One, that commanded the seventh day to be kept,

5 Then he said: And I am mighty upon the earth and I command to take arms and to do the king's business. Nevertheless he prevailed not to accomplish his design.

6 So Nicanor, being puffed up with exceeding great pride, thought to set up a public monument of his victory over Judas.

7 But Machabeus ever trusted with all hope that God would help them.

8 And he exhorted his people not to fear the coming of the nations, but to remember the help they had before received from heaven, and now to hope for victory from the Almighty.

9 And speaking to them out of the law and the prophets, and withal putting them in mind of the battles they had fought before, he made them more cheerful.

10 Then after he had encouraged them, he shewed withal the falsehood of the Gentiles and their breach of oaths.

11 So he armed every one of them, not with defence of shield and spear, but with very good speeches and exhortations, and told them a dream worthy to be believed, whereby he rejoiced them all.

12 Now the vision was in this manner: Onias who had been high priest, a good and virtuous man, modest in his looks, gentle in his manners and graceful in his speech, and who from a child was exercised in virtues, holding up his hands, prayed for all the people of the Jews.

13 After this, there appeared also another man, admirable for age and glory and environed with great beauty and majesty.

14 Then Onias answering, said: This is a lover of his brethren and of the people of Israel: this is he that prayeth much for the people and for all the holy city, Jeremias, the prophet of God.

15 Whereupon Jeremias stretched forth his right hand and gave to Judas a sword of gold, saying:

16 Take this holy sword, a gift from God, wherewith thou shalt overthrow the adversaries of my people Israel.

^a2 Mach. 8, 19.

17 Thus being exhorted with the words of Judas, which were very good and proper to stir up the courage and strengthen the hearts of the young men, they resolved to fight and to set upon them manfully: that valour might decide the matter, because the holy city and the temple were in danger.

18 For their concern was less for their wives and children and for their brethren and kinsfolk: but their greatest and principal fear was for the holiness of the temple.

19 And they also that were in the city had no little concern for them that were to be engaged in battle.

20 And now when all expected what judgment would be given, and the enemies were at hand and the army was set in array, the beasts and the horsemen ranged in convenient places,

21 Machabeus, considering the coming of the multitude and the divers preparations of armour and the fierceness of the beasts, stretching out his hands to heaven, called upon the Lord that worketh wonders, who giveth victory to them that are worthy, not according to the power of their arms, but according as it seemeth good to him.

22 And in his prayer he said after this manner: ^aThou, O Lord, who didst send thy angel in the time of Ezechias king of Juda and didst kill a hundred and eighty-five thousand of the army of Sennacherib:

23 Send now also, O Lord of heaven, thy good angel before us, for the fear and dread of the greatness of thy arm:

24 That they may be afraid, who come with blasphemy against thy holy people. And thus he concluded his prayer.

25 But Nicanor and they that were with him came forward, with trumpets and songs.

26 But Judas and they that were with him encountered them, calling upon God by prayers.

27 So, fighting with their hands, but praying to the Lord with their hearts, they slew no less than five and thirty thousand, being greatly cheered with the presence of God.

28 And when the battle was over and they were returning with joy, they understood that Nicanor was slain in his armour.

29 Then making a shout and a great noise, they blessed the Almighty Lord in their own language.

30 And Judas, who was altogether ready, in body and mind, to die for his countrymen, commanded that Nicanor's head and his hand with the shoul-

der should be cut off and carried to Jerusalem.

31 And when he was come thither, having called together his countrymen and the priests to the altar, he sent also for them that were in the castle,

32 And shewing them the head of Nicanor and the wicked hand which he had stretched out, with proud boasts, against the holy house of the Almighty God,

33 He commanded also that the tongue of the wicked Nicanor should be cut out and given by pieces to birds, and the hand of the furious man to be hanged up over against the temple.

34 Then all blessed the Lord of heaven, saying: Blessed be he that hath kept his own place undefiled.

35 And he hung up Nicanor's head in the top of the castle, that it might be an evident and manifest sign of the help of God.

36 And they all ordained by a common decree, by no means to let this day pass without solemnity:

37 But to celebrate the thirteenth day of the month of Adar, called, in the Syrian language, the day before Mardochias' day.

38 So these things being done with relation to Nicanor and from that time the city being possessed by the Hebrews, I also will here make an end of my narration.

39 Which if I have done well and as it becometh the history, it is what I desired: but if not so perfectly, it must be pardoned me.

40 For as it is hurtful to drink always wine or always water, but pleasant to use sometimes the one and sometimes the other: so if the speech be always nicely framed, it will not be grateful to the readers. But here it shall be ended.

CHAP. 15. Ver. 39. *If not so perfectly.* This is not said with regard to the truth of the narration, but with regard to the style and manner of writing, which in the sacred penmen is not always the most accurate. (See St. Paul, 2 Cor. 11, 6.)

THE END OF THE OLD TESTAMENT

AN HISTORICAL AND CHRONOLOGICAL TABLE
OF THE OLD TESTAMENT [1]

B. C.	BIBLICAL EVENTS	EVENTS IN CONTEMPORARY HISTORY
?	Creation of the world and of man. The fall of man. The Deluge. The separation of the nations.	
c. 3500		First Egyptian Dynasty.
c. 2900-2750		Fourth Egyptian Dynasty. Pyramids built.
c. 2000	The call of Abraham, the Father of the Jewish People.	Hammurabi unifies Babylonia and writes his famous Laws.
c. 1800	The Israelites settle in Egypt.	The Hyksos, or Shepherd Kings, rule in Egypt. c. 1800-1580.
c. 1415(?)	The Exodus. The Israelites leave Egypt under Moses, wander in the desert for forty years, and finally settle, under Josue, in the Promised Land.	The eighteenth Dynasty rules in Egypt from 1580 to 1328. Egypt at the height of its power. 1380-1360, Tell el Amarna Period.
c. 1460-1420	The Five Books of Moses (Pentateuch) composed. The Book of Josue written after the death of Josue. Many scholars date Exodus c. 1240.	
c. 1400-1100	Judges (military leaders) rule over Israel.	
c. 1100-1011	Samuel and Saul. Composition of the Book of Judges.	
c. 1013-973	Reign of King David. Composition of the Psalms of David and the Book of Ruth. Some of the Psalms belong to a much later date. Ruth may have been written as late as the 5th century B.C.	
c. 973-933	Solomon. Composition of (parts of) Proverbs, and Canticle of Canticles.	Hiram rules over the flourishing maritime kingdom of Tyre in Phoenicia.
o. 933	The Kingdom of David is divided. The Kingdom of Israel in the North with Samaria as capital, including ten tribes. The Kingdom of Juda in the South with Jerusalem as capital, comprising the tribes of Juda and Benjamin.	Sisac (Shishak) invades Juda and Israel in 931. Shishak's Inscription on a temple in Karnak, only allusion found to any of the kings of Israel or Juda upon the Egyptian monuments. In 847 Mesha, King of Moab, inscribes an account of victory over Omri of Israel on the Moabite Stone in a language not differing much from Biblical Hebrew.
c. 780-722	Amos and Osee prophesy in the Kingdom of Israel. Jonas prophesies to the Ninivites. The First and Second Books of Kings are composed.	
c. 800-585	Isaias (759-694), Micheas, Nahum, Habacuc, Sophonias, and Jeremias (628-585) prophesy in the Kingdom of Juda. Jeremias writes the Lamentations, his secretary Baruch, a short prophecy. Job may have been written at this period.	Sennacherib, king of the Assyrians, besieges Jerusalem in the reign of Ezechias (701).
722	The Kingdom of Israel is destroyed by the Assyrians. Sargon II takes Samaria. The people are led away to Babylon and Ninive. The Book of Tobias narrates an episode of the captivity.	
612		Ninive destroyed by the Medes and Chaldeans.

[1] From Introduction to the Bible by Rev. John Laux, M.A.

B. C.	BIBLICAL EVENTS	EVENTS IN CONTEMPORARY HISTORY
587	End of the Kingdom of Juda. Jerusalem captured by Nabuchodonosor (Nebuchadnezzar) of Babylon. All but the poorest of the people deported to Babylon.	Nabuchodonosor II, king of Babylon (606-562).
597-538	*Ezechiel* and *Daniel* prophesy during the captivity of the Jews in Babylon. *Third* and *Fourth Books of Kings* written after 561.	Nabonid and Baltasar (Belshazzar), kings of Babylon (555-538). Babylon taken by Cyrus the Persian (538).
538	First Edict of Cyrus permitting the Jews to return to Jerusalem. *Aggeus* and *Zacharias* prophesy to the returning Jews under Zorobabel (c. 520). Juda a province of the Persian Empire.	Cyrus the Great (538-530).
c. 500	*Abdias* foretells the overthrow of Edom.	
445	Nehemias returns to Jerusalem. Rebuilding of the city walls.	
c. 470-460	*Malachias* prophesies in Jerusalem.	
c. 430-300	*Joel* prophesies. Composition of the *Books of Esdras* and *Nehemias*, of the two *Books of Paralipomenon*, of *Judith* and *Esther.* According to some, *Job* belongs to this period.	
336-323		Alexander the Great, son of Philip of Macedon, becomes king of Macedonia and begins the conquest of the East.
331		The Persian Empire is overthrown by Alexander the Great.
332-198	*Palestine,* a province of the empire of Alexander and (from 320) of Egypt.	Alexander dies at Babylon (323). His empire is divided among his generals. The Hebrew books of the Old Testament translated into Greek at Alexandria (*Septuagint*).
198	Antiochus the Great, king of Syria, defeats Ptolemy Ephiphanes of Egypt and obtains possession of Palestine.	
c. 180	*Ecclesiasticus* written by Sirach. *Ecclesiastes* probably belongs to this period.	
175-164		Antiochus Epiphanes, king of Syria.
168	Antiochus Epiphanes attempts to suppress the religion of the Jews. Public worship is suspended in the Temple for three years.	
167	Rise of the Machabees.	
166-135	The Machabees Mathathias, Judas, Jonathan and Simon rule over the Jews.	
135-105	John Hyrcanus, son of Simon, elected High Priest.	
c. 130	*Ecclesiasticus* translated into Greek.	
c. 120	Composition of the *Second Book of Machabees* (Greek).	
c. 100	Composition of the *Book of Wisdom* (Greek). Composition of the *First Book of Machabees.*	
63	Jerusalem is captured by Pompey. Palestine becomes a part of the Roman province of Syria. The scepter has passed forever from Juda. The Messias is expected.	

AN HISTORICAL AND CHRONOLOGICAL TABLE
OF THE NEW TESTAMENT

A. D.

1 CHRIST is born at Bethlehem, Luke 2. He is circumcised, Luke 2.

The wise men come and adore him, Matt. 2.

He is presented in the temple, Luke 2. Joseph and the Blessed Virgin mother fly with the Child Jesus into Egypt, Matt. 2.

The massacre of the infants by Herod, Matt. 2. Joseph with the Blessed Virgin and her Son, return from Egypt, but for fear of Archelaus, go and live at Nazareth in Galilee, Matt. 2.

12 Jesus is found in the Temple disputing with the doctors when he was twelve years of age, Luke 2.

30 St. John Baptist begins preaching penance, and to baptize. The chiefs of the Jews send messengers to ask if he was not the Messias, John 1.

Jesus himself is baptized by John. A voice from heaven declares him the beloved Son of God; the Holy Ghost comes down like a dove, Matt. 3; Mark 1; Luke 3.

Christ is no sooner baptized, but he retires into a wilderness, where he fasts for forty days. The devil there tempts him. The angels come and minister to him, Matt. 4; Mark. 1; Luke 4.

Christ's first miracle at Cana in Galilee, by turning water into wine, John 2.

31 St. John Baptist is cast into prison, and beheaded by Herod, Matt. 14; Mark 6; Luke 9.

Christ makes choice of twelve of his disciples, whom he calls Apostles. Peter is the first of them, Matt. 10; Mark 3; Luke 6.

Christ's Sermon, or his instructions on the mountain, Matt. 5, 6, and 7. He preaches in Judea and Galilee, casts out devils, cures all manner of diseases and sometimes on the Sabbath days, confutes and puts to confusion his adversaries, who blame him for it, Matt. 12; Luke 14, etc.

31 He raises to life the daughter of Jairus, Matt. 9; Mark 5; Luke 8.

Also the son of the widow of Naim, Luke 7.

He calms the sea by his word, Matt. 8; Mark 4; Luke 8.

He heals the man thirty-eight years ill of a palsy, John 5.

He sends his twelve Apostles to preach, with power of doing miracles, Matt. 10; Mark 6; Luke 9.

He teacheth them to pray, Matt. 6; Luke 11.

He makes choice of seventy-two disciples, Luke 10.

32 He promises to make Peter the head of his Church, to build his Church upon him, to give him the keys of the kingdom of heaven, Matt. 16.

He declares himself the Messias in plain ⲧⲉⲣⲙⲥ ⲧⲟ ⲧⲏⲉ Ⲥⲁⲙⲁⲣⲓⲧⲁⲛ ⲱⲟⲙⲁⲛ, John 4.

He excuseth his disciples for plucking the ears of corn on the second-first Sabbath, Matt. 12.

A. D.

He feeds at one time five thousand men with five loaves, Matt. 14. At another time four thousand with seven loaves, Matt. 15.

He promises to give them his body to be truly meat, etc. Many even of his disciples leave him, looking upon that doctrine as hard and harsh, John 6.

33 His transfiguration, Matt. 17.

The Sunday, or first day of the week, in which he died on the cross, he came riding upon an ass into Jerusalem, Matt. 21.

In the beginning of that week he went daily into the Temple, and in the evenings retired to Bethania, to pray in the garden of Gethsemani, Luke 21, 38, etc.

On Wednesday Judas made a bargain with the chief priests, to deliver him up to them for a sum of money, Matt. 26, 15.

On Thursday he sent his disciples in the afternoon to bring the paschal lamb, offered in the temple, which after sunset he ate with his twelve Apostles, Matt. 26.

He washed their feet, John 13.

After supper he instituted the Blessed Sacrament and Sacrifice of his Body and Blood, Matt. 26.

He gave his Apostles those excellent instructions set down by St. John, 14-17.

Christ's prayer in the garden three times repeated.

He is there seized, being betrayed by Judas.

He is led away to Annas, and then to Caiphas.

He is condemned as guilty of blasphemy to death, for owning himself the Son of God. He is spit upon, buffeted, etc.

On Friday morning they deliver him up to the Roman governor, Pontius Pilate, who sees and declares him innocent, yet fearing not to be thought a friend to Cæsar, condemns him to the death of the Cross.

He dies on the Cross, and is buried. For the history of his Passion, see Matt. 26, 27, 28; Mark 14, 15, 16; Luke 22, 23, 24; John 18, 19, 20.

The miracles at his death, ibid.

He riseth from the dead the third day, ibid.

His different apparitions that very day; and others afterwards, ibid.

He gives his Apostles power to forgive sins, John 20, 23.

He gives to St. Peter the charge over his whole Church, John 21.

He promiseth to be with his Church to the end of the world, Matt. 28.

After forty days he ascends in their sight into heaven, Acts 1.

St. Matthias is chosen an Apostle in the place of Judas the traitor, Acts 1.

The day of Pentecost the Holy Ghost descended upon them, and upon all present with them, in a visible manner, Acts 2.

A. D.

The wonderful change wrought in the Apostles by the coming of the Holy Ghost. Their undaunted courage, Acts 2, etc.

They preach the resurrection of Christ, the necessity of believing in him, of repenting and doing penance.

St. Peter, the chief of the Apostles, converts on one day three thousand, on another five thousand, Acts 2, 41, and 4, 4.

He, with St. John, cures the lame beggar that sat at the gate of the temple, Acts 3, 6.

The new Christians have all things in common. Everyone's necessities are supplied out of the common stock, Acts 4, 32.

Ananias and Saphira, for reserving some part of the money of a field sold, and for lying to the Holy Ghost, fall dead at St. Peter's feet, Acts 5.

The election of the seven deacons, Acts 6.

Saul, by virtue of a commission from the chief priests, persecutes the Christians, Acts 9.

St. Stephen is stoned to death, Acts 7, 58.

The ministers of the gospel, being dispersed, preach in Judea and Samaria, etc.

St. Philip, in Samaria, baptizeth Simon the Magician. He offers money to St. Peter to have the power of giving the Holy Ghost, Acts 8.

34 St. Paul is miraculously converted going to persecute the Christians at Damascus, Acts 9. He presently preacheth Jesus.

St. Peter cures Eneas at Lydda, and raiseth to life Tabitha at Joppa, Acts. 9.

The very shadow of his body cures all diseases, Acts 5, 15.

39 He receives Cornelius the Centurion and other Gentiles with him into the Church, Acts 10.

He is thought to have gone about this time to Antioch in Syria, and to have founded the episcopal See.

41 He preaches in Pontus, Galatia, etc.

St. Barnabas and St. Paul preach at Antioch, where the believers were first called Christians, Acts 11, 26.

42 Herod Agrippa puts to death St. James, the brother of St. John, and imprisons St. Peter, who is miraculously delivered, Acts 12.

St. Matthew, and afterwards St. Mark, wrote their Gospels.

43 St. Paul and Barnabas sent to preach in Pamphylia, Pisidia, Lycaonia. Afterwards in Pontus, Thracia, etc., Acts 13, 14.

48 St. Peter about this time wrote his first Epistle.

49 A dispute between St. Paul and some zealous converts that had been Jews, about the obligation of making even the Gentiles observe the Jewish laws, Acts 15.

St. Paul and Barnabas are sent to Jerusalem, to have this question decided by the Apostles, etc.

A council of the Apostles and Bishops decides the question. St. Peter speaking first, and St. James joining with him. The letter of the council to their brethren the converted Gentiles, Acts 15.

A. D.

51 St. Paul and St. Barnabas separate, Acts 15.

52 St. Paul with Silas goes to Asia. St. Timothy and also St. Luke become his companions. He goes to Philippi in Macedonia, to Thessalonica, to Berea, to Athens. Finds there an altar dedicated to the unknown God, Acts 16, 17.

He writes his first Epistle to the Thessalonians, and the second soon after.

He stays eighteen months at Corinth, Acts 18, 11.

55 He goes to Ephesus. After a short visit to the brethren at Jerusalem, he goes to Antioch; and from thence again into Galatia and Phrygia, and stays three years at Ephesus, and thereabouts, Acts 19.

56 He writes to the Galatians.

57 He writes his first, and soon after his second Epistle to the Corinthians.

He prepares to go to Jerusalem with alms he had gathered, Acts 20 and 21.

He writes to the Romans.

58 He comes to Jerusalem, Acts 21.

The Jews seize St. Paul in the Temple; being beaten and in danger of being murdered by them, he is rescued by Lysias, the tribune, and his soldiers, Acts 21.

Lysias sends him to Felix, the governor of Judea, then at Cæsarea, where he was two years a prisoner.

His discourse before King Agrippa, Felix, etc., Acts 25.

60 Having appealed to the tribunal of Cæsar, he is sent to Rome with other prisoners, Acts 27.

61 A description of his voyage and shipwreck on the coast of Malta. Everyone in the ship is saved, being two hundred and seventy-six persons, Acts 27, 44.

St. James about this time wrote his catholic Epistle.

St. Paul's arrival at Rome. He is kept under custody for two years, with a soldier to guard him, Acts 28.

62 He converts Onesimus, and sends him with his letter to Philemon. He writes to the Philippians and Colossians.

St. James, Bishop of Jerusalem, there martyred.

St. Paul, being set at liberty, writes to the Hebrews.

66 Goes again into Asia. Makes St. Timothy Bishop in Asia, and goes into Macedonia, from whence he writes his first Epistle to Timothy.

68 St. Peter about this time wrote his second Epistle.

About this time St. Peter and St. Paul came to Rome. See Tillemont, etc.

Not long after they were both put in prison, and suffered martyrdom.

St. John about this time came to live in Asia, and governed all those churches for many years.

St. John was put into a caldron of boiling oil at Rome, under Domitian, and banished to the island of Patmos, where he had those wonderful visions of his Apocalypse.

96 He returns to Ephesus, under the Emperor Nerva.

He writes his Gospel.

He dies at Ephesus, under Trajan, about the year 100.

A TABLE OF REFERENCES

A

ABSOLUTION: The power promised and given to the pastors of the Church, Matt. 16, 19; 18, 18; John 20, 22, 23.

ALMSGIVING: Deut. 15, 11; 26, 12; Tob. 4, 7, 11; 12, 8, 9; 14, 11; Ps. 40, 1-4; Prov. 21, 13; 28, 27; Eccles. 11, 1, 2; Ecclus. 3, 33, 34; 4, 1-8; 7, 10, 36; 12, 3; 14, 13-16; 17, 18, 19; 18, 25; 29, 15; Isa. 58, 7-11; Ezech. 18, 16, 17; Dan. 4, 24; Matt. 6, 1-4; 10, 42; 25, 34-46; Luke 3, 11; 11, 41; 12, 33; 14, 13, 14; Acts 10, 4; 20, 35; 2 Cor. 8, 14, 15; 9, 7; Jas. 2, 15, 16; 1 John 3, 17, 18.

ANGELS: Ps. 102, 20, 21; 103, 4; 148, 2; Dan. 7, 10; Heb. 1, 13, 14; 12, 22; Apoc. 5, 11, 12—Our Guardians, Exod. 23, 20, 21; Ps. 90, 11, 12; Zach. 1, 12; Matt. 18, 10; Heb. 1, 14; 12, 22—Fall of the Angels, Job 4, 18; Isa. 14, 12; Luke 10, 18; Jude 6; Apoc. 12, 4; 20, 9.

ANGER: Ps. 4, 5; 36, 8; Prov. 15, 18; 26, 21; 27, 3, 4; 29, 22; Eccles. 7, 4, 10; 11, 10; Ecclus. 8, 19; 25, 23; 27, 33; 28, 3-12; Matt. 5, 22; Eph. 4, 26, 31; Jas. 1, 19, 20.

ANTICHRIST: 2 Thess. 2, 3-11; 1 John 2, 18; 4, 3; 2 John 7.

APOSTACY: Prov. 6, 12-15; Ecclus. 10, 14.

APOSTOLICAL TRADITIONS: 1 Cor. 11, 2; 2 Thess. 2, 14; 3, 6; 2 Tim. 1, 13; 2, 2; 3, 14. *See also* Deut. 32, 7; Ps. 19, 5-7.

AVARICE: Ps. 38, 7; 118, 36; Prov. 15, 27; 28, 16; 29, 4; Eccles. 5, 9, 14; Ecclus. 10, 9, 10; 14, 3; Isa. 5, 8; 57, 17; Hab. 2, 9; Luke 12, 15-21; 1 Cor. 5, 11; 6, 9, 10; Eph. 5, 3, 5; Col. 3, 5; 1 Tim. 6, 9; Heb. 13, 5.

B

BAPTISM: Matt. 28, 19; Mark 16, 15, 16; John 3, 3, 5; Acts 2, 38; Rom. 6, 3-18; 1 Cor. 10, 1, 2; 12, 13; Gal. 3, 27; Eph. 4, 5; Col. 2, 12; Tit. 3, 5; 1 Pet. 1, 3; 3, 21.

BEATITUDES: Matt. 5, 3-11; Luke 6, 20-23.

BIBLE: Prov. 30, 5, 6; Matt. 22, 29; Rom. 15, 4; 2 Tim. 3, 15-17; Heb. 4, 12; 2 Pet. 1, 20, 21—Holy Scripture hard to be understood and not of private interpretation, Acts 8, 31-35; 2 Pet. 1, 20, 21; 3, 16.

BLASPHEMY: Lev. 24, 14, 16; Job 13, 6; Matt. 12, 31; 15, 19; Mark 3, 29; Eph. 4, 31; Col. 3, 8; 1 Tim. 6, 4; 2 Tim. 3, 2; 2 Pet. 2, 12; Jude 10.

BOOK OF LIFE: Exod. 33, 33; Ps. 68, 29; 138, 16; Luke 10, 20.

BURIAL OF THE DEAD: Tob. 1, 20; 4, 3, 5; 12, 12; Ecclus. 38, 16.

C

CELIBACY: Exod. 19, 22; Lev. 21, 6; 1 Kings 21, 4; Isa. 52, 11; Matt. 19, 11, 12; 1 Cor. 7; 2 Tim. 2, 3.

CHARITY. See LOVE OF GOD—LOVE OF OUR NEIGHBOUR.

CHASTITY: Judith 15, 11; Wisd. 4, 1, 2; 8, 21; 1 Tim. 4, 12; 5, 22.

CHRIST: He is the only begotten, the true, and natural Son of God, Matt. 16, 16; John 1, 14; 3, 16, 18; Rom. 8, 32; 1 John 4, 9—The same God with His Father, and equal to Him, John 5, 18, 19, 23; 10, 30; 14, 1, 9, etc.; 16, 14, 15; 17, 10; Phil. 2, 5, 6—True God, John 1, 1; 20, 28, 29; Acts 20, 25; Rom. 9, 5; Tit. 2, 13; 1 John 3, 16; 5, 20; also Isa. 9, 6; 35, 4, 5; Matt. 1, 23; Luke 1, 16, 17; Heb 1, 8—He is the Creator of all things,

John 1, 3, 10, 11; Col. 1, 5, 16, 17; Heb. 1, 2, 10-12; 3, 4—The Lord of glory, 1 Cor. 2, 8—The King of kings and Lord of lords, Apoc. 17, 14; 19, 16—The first and the last, Alpha and Omega, the beginning and the end, the Almighty, Apoc. 1, 7, 8, 17, 18; 2, 8; 22, 12, 13—He died for all, John 3, 16, 17; Rom. 5, 18; 2 Cor. 5, 14, 15; 1 Tim. 2, 3, 4, 5, 6; 4, 10; Heb. 2, 9; 1 John 2, 1, 2—Even for the reprobate, Rom. 14, 15; 1 Cor. 8, 11; 2 Pet. 2, 1.

CHURCH GUIDES and their authority: Deut. 17, 8, 9, etc.; Matt. 18, 17, 18; 28, 18-20; Luke 10, 16; John 14, 16, 17, 26; 16, 13; 20, 21, etc.; Eph. 4, 11, 12, etc.; Heb. 13, 7, 17; 1 John 4, 6.

CHURCH OF CHRIST: Matt. 16, 18; Acts. 5, 11; 16, 5; Rom. 16, 16, 23; 1 Cor. 6, 4; 11, 16; 12, 28; 14, 5; 2 Cor. 8, 18, 23, 24; 11, 8; 12, 13; Eph. 5, 23; Phil. 4, 15; Col. 1, 18; 1 Tim. 3, 5, 15; Jas. 5, 14; Apoc. 1, 11; 22, 16—Types and figures of the Church, Gen. 6, 14; Ps. 79, 9; Cant. 2, 15; 4, 12; Isa. 5, 1; Jer. 2, 21; 12, 10; 13, 24; Matt. 20, 1; Mark 12, 1; Luke 5, 3; 20, 9; Apoc. 14, 15; 21, 2—The Church cannot err, Isa. 29, 22; Matt. 16, 8 ; 28, 20; Luke 22, 32; John 14, 16; 16, 13; 17, 18, 20; 1 Tim. 3, 15; 1 John 2, 27—Christ the Head of the Church, 1 Cor. 12, 12, 27; Eph. 1, 22; 4, 15; 5, 23; Col. 1, 18; 2, 10—Christ's Vicar, Head of the Church on earth, Matt. 18, 17; Luke 22, 32; John 10, 16; 21, 15, 17; 1 Cor. 12, 12; Eph. 3, 6.

CIRCUMCISION: Law of, Gen. 17, 10-14; Lev. 12, 3—Ceased under the New Testament, Rom. 2, 26-29; 3, 30; Col. 2, 11—Of the heart, Deut. 10, 16; Jer. 4, 4; Rom. 2, 29; Col. 2, 11.

COMMUNION. See EUCHARIST.

CONFESSION OF SINS: Num. 5, 6, 7; Matt. 3, 6; Acts 19, 18; Jas. 5, 16—The obligation of confession is gathered from the judiciary power of binding and loosing, forgiving and retaining sins, given to the pastors of Christ's Church, Matt. 18, 18; John 20, 22, 23.

CONFIDENCE IN GOD: Ps. 26, 1; 45, 2, 3; 117, 6, 8; 124, 1; Prov. 3, 5; Wisd. 3, 9; Ecclus. 11, 22; Jer. 17, 5-8; Dan. 3, 40; Luke 12, 32; John 14, 1; 16, 33.

CONFIRMATION: Isa. 44, 3; Joel 2, 28, 29; Luke 24, 49; John 14, 16-20; 16, 7, 13; Acts 1, 4-8; 8, 17; 19, 6; 1 Cor. 2, 11-15; 6, 19; 12, 4-13; Gal. 5, 22-25; Eph. 1, 13; 4, 30; 5, 18; Tit. 3, 5; 1 John 2, 20.

CONTINENCY: Possible, Matt. 19, 11, 12—The vow binding, Deut. 23, 21—The breach of that vow damnable, 1 Tim. 5, 12—The practice commended, 1 Cor. 7, 7, 8, 27, 37, 38, 40—For reasons which particularly have place in the clergy, 1 Cor. 7, 32, 33, 35.

COUNCILS OF THE CHURCH: Gathered in Christ's name, are assisted by Christ, Matt. 18, 20—And by the Holy Ghost, Acts 15, 28—Their decrees are diligently to be observed by the faithful, Acts 15, 41; 16, 4. See CHURCH GUIDES.

CREATION: Gen. 1; 2 Esd. 9, 6; Job 26, 7; Ps. 99, 3; 101, 26, 28; 103, 24; 118, 91; Prov. 3, 19, 20; Eccles. 3, 13; Wisd. 11, 21, 26; Ecclus. 3, 11; 18, 1-5; Isa. 44, 24; Jer. 10, 12, 13; John 1, 3; 5, 17; Acts 4, 24; Rom. 11, 36.

CRUELTY: Prov. 11, 17; 12, 10—To animals, Exod. 23, 19; Deut. 14, 21; 25, 4; Prov. 12, 10; 1 Cor. 9, 9; 1 Tim. 5, 18.

A TABLE OF REFERENCES

D

DEATH: Gen. 3, 17-19; Num. 23, 10; 2 Kings 14, 14; 3 Kings 2, 2; Job 30, 23; 34, 15; Ps. 88, 49; Eccles. 2, 16; 3, 19, 20; 8, 8; 9, 10, 12; 12, 1, 7; Wisd. 1, 13; 2, 23, 24; 3, 1; 4, 7; 7, 6; Ecclus. 7, 40; 10, 12; 14, 18-21; 38, 23; 41, 1-7, 13; John 9, 4; Rom. 5, 12; 1 Cor. 15, 21, 22, 26—Mourning for the Dead, Ecclus. 22, 11; 38, 16, 24; John 11, 45—Praying for the Dead, 2 Mach. 12, 43-46.

DEFRAUDING: Lev. 19, 11; Ecclus. 34, 27; Mark 10, 19; 1 Thess. 4, 6—Labourers of their wages, Jas. 5, 4.

DETRACTION: Prov. 4, 24; 24, 9, 21; 25, 23; 26, 2; Eccles. 10, 11; Wisd. 1, 6, 11; Jas. 4, 11.

DEVIL: Gen. 3; 1 Par. 21, 1; Job 1, 6, 9, 11, 12; 2, 7; Ps. 77, 49; Wisd. 2, 24; Ecclus. 39, 33, 34; Zach. 3, 2; Luke 22, 31; John 13, 2; 2 Cor. 11, 14; 1 Thess. 2, 18; 2 Tim. 2, 26; 1 Pet. 5, 8; Apoc. 2, 10; 12; 20, 7.

DILIGENCE (*See also* SLOTH): Gen. 2, 15; 3, 17-19; Job 5, 7; 34, 11; Ps. 127, 2; Prov. 6, 6, 8; 10, 5; 12, 11; 13, 4; 14, 23; 16, 3; 21, 5; 23, 4; 24, 27; 28, 19; Eccles. 1, 3; 2, 18-22; 3, 22; 4, 7, 8; 5, 11-17; 8, 10; Ecclus. 2, 20-22; 4, 34; 5, 11; 7, 16; 10, 29, 30; 11, 10, 11, 21-28; 16, 15; 51, 38; Isa. 65, 23; Jer. 27, 10; 48, 10; 1 Thess. 4, 10, 11; 2 Thess. 3, 8-12; 2 Tim. 2, 3.

DISCORD: Prov. 6, 16, 19; 17, 19; 30, 33.

DIVORCE: Allowed in the Old Law, Deut. 24, 1-4—Forbidden in the New, Matt. 5, 31, 32; 19, 3-9; Mark 10, 2-12; Luke 16, 18; 1 Cor. 7, 10, 11, 13.

DRUNKENNESS: Prov. 20, 21; 21, 17; 23, 29-35; 26, 11; 31, 4-7; Ecclus. 19, 1, 2; 26, 11; 31, 22, 30-42; Isa. 5, 11, 12, 22; 28, 7; Osee 4, 11; 1 Cor. 5, 11; 6, 10; Eph. 5, 18—Temperance in drinking, Deut. 11, 14; Ps. 103, 15; Prov. 31, 6, 7; Ecclus. 31, 22, 32, 35, 37; 1 Tim. 5, 23.

E

EDIFICATION: Rom. 14, 19; 15, 2; 1 Cor. 14, 12, 26; Eph. 4, 29.

ENVY: Job 5, 2; Prov. 14, 30; 23, 6; 28, 22; Wisd. 2, 24; Ecclus. 14, 3-10.

EUCHARIST: Its Types, Gen. 14, 18; Exod. 16, 13-35; 25, 30; Num. 11, 4, 20; 2 Esd. 9, 15, 20, 21; Ps. 22, 5; 77, 23, 24, 25; 106, 9; 110, 4, 5; Wisd. 16, 20, 21; Zach. 9, 17; Mal. 1, 10, 11; Matt. 15, 32; 22, 2-14; Luke 14, 15-24; John 6, 5-14—Promised by Christ, John 6, 26-67—Its institution, Matt. 26, 26, 28; Mark 14, 22, 24; Luke 22, 19, 20; 1 Cor. 11, 23, 25—Its effects, Luke 14, 15; 24, 30, 31; John 6, 33, 50, 52, 55, 57, 58, 59; 1 Cor. 10, 16, 17; 11, 26—Proofs of Real Presence, Matt. 26, 26, 28; Mark 14, 22, 24; Luke 22, 19, 20; John 6, 51-59; 1 Cor. 10, 16; 11, 24-29—Bad Communions, 1 Cor. 11, 27-32—Communion in one kind sufficient, Luke 24, 30, 31; John 6, 51, 57, 58; Acts 2, 42, 46; 20, 7; Rom. 5, 9; 1 Cor. 10, 17.

EXTREME UNCTION: Jas. 5, 14, 15.

F

FAITH: Gen. 15, 6; Ecclus. 2, 6, 8, 15; 32, 27, 28; 40, 12; Jer. 5, 3; Hab. 2, 4; Matt. 17, 19; 21, 21; Mark 9, 22, 23; 10, 52; 11, 22, 23; 16, 16, 17, 18; Luke 1, 45; 7, 50; 8, 48; 17, 5, 6, 19; 18, 42; John 3, 16, 18, 36; 5, 44; 6, 29, 40; 7, 38; 20, 29; Rom. 1, 17; 4, 3; 10, 10, 11, 17; 14, 23; 1 Cor. 16, 13; 2 Cor. 4, 13; Gal. 2, 16, 20; 3, 6-26; 5, 6; Eph. 4, 5; Heb. 10, 38, 30; 11; 1 Pet. 1, 8, 9; 1 John 5, 4, 5, 10 —Necessary to salvation, Mark 16, 16; Acts 2, 47; 4, 12; Heb. 11, 6—Faith alone does not justify, Jas. 2, 14-24—Nor assure grace and salvation, Rom. 11, 20, 21; 1 Cor. 9, 27; Phil. 2, 12; Apoc. 3, 11.

FALSE CHRISTS (*See also* ANTICHRIST): Matt. 24, 4, 5, 11, 23-28; Mark 13, 5, 6, 21, 22; Luke 17, 23, 24; 21, 8, 9.

FALSE WITNESS: Exod. 20, 16; 23, 1; Deut. 5, 20; Prov. 12, 17, 19; 14, 5, 25; 19, 5, 9, 28; 21, 28; 24, 28; 25, 18; Matt. 19, 18; Mark 10, 19; Luke 18, 20; Rom. 13, 9.

FASTING: 1 Esd. 8, 23; 2 Esd. 1, 4; Dan. 9, 3; Jonas 3, 5; Matt. 9, 15; Mark 2, 20; 9, 28; Luke 5, 35; Acts 13, 3; 14, 22; 2 Cor. 6, 5; 11, 27—Christ's fast, Matt. 4, 2; Luke 4, 2.

FEAR OF GOD: Lev. 19, 14, 22; 25, 17; Deut. 10, 12, 20; Jos. 24, 14; Tob. 4, 23; Judith 16, 19; Job 28, 28; 31, 23; Ps. 24, 1; 30, 20; 33, 10, 12; 110, 5, 10; 111, 1, 2, 3; 144, 19; Prov. 1, 7; 8, 13; 9, 10; 10, 27; 14, 26, 27; 15, 27, 33; 16, 6; 19, 23; 22, 4; 23, 17; 24, 21; 28, 14; 31, 30; Eccles. 8, 12, 13; Ecclus. 1, 11-36; 2, 6-22; 7, 31; 10, 23-27; 15, 1; 16, 3; 21, 7, 13; 23, 37; 25, 13-16; 28, 8; 32, 18; 33, 1; 34, 15-20; 40, 28; Isa. 33, 6; Luke 12, 5; Rom. 11, 20; 1 Pet. 2, 17; 1 John 4, 18.

FEAR OF MAN: Tob. 1, 5, 6; Ps. 24, 20; Prov. 29, 15; Ecclus. 20, 24; Isa. 2, 12; Matt. 10, 33; Mark 8, 38; Luke 9, 26; 12, 4, 8, 9; Rom. 1, 16; 2 Tim. 1, 2; 2, 12.

FLATTERY: Prov. 29, 5; Eccles. 7, 6.

FORNICATION: Deut. 23, 17; Tob. 4, 13; Ecclus. 9, 6, 10; 19, 3; 23, 24; 26, 12; Osee 4, 11; 1 Cor. 6, 13-20; 10, 8; Eph. 5, 3, 5; Col. 3, 5; Heb. 13, 4; Apoc. 21, 8, 27; 22, 15.

FREE WILL OF MAN: Gen. 4, 7; Deut. 30, 15, 19; Jos. 24, 15; Ecclus. 15, 14-18; 1 Cor. 10, 29; 2 Cor. 3, 17; Gal. 5, 13.

FRIENDSHIP: Lev. 19, 18; Job 6, 14; Prov. 3, 28, 29; 6, 1, 2; 11, 12; 17, 17; 19, 4; 25, 9, 10; 27, 9, 10, 17; Ecclus. 6, 1-17; 9, 14, 15; 12, 8, 9; 14, 13; 19, 13, 15; 20, 17; 22, 25-31; 25, 12; 37, 1-6.

G

GLUTTONY: Gen. 25, 29, 34; Prov. 21, 17; 23, 20, 21; Ecclus. 37, 32, 33, 34; Heb. 12, 16, 17.

GOD: A pure spirit and self-existent, Exod. 3, 14, 16; 6, 2; John 4, 24—He is one, Deut. 6, 4; 32, 39; Wisd. 12, 13; Isa. 43, 10; 44, 6; 45, 6; Eph. 4, 5, 6—He is infinite, Job 36, 26; Ps 144, 3; Wisd. 11, 23—Eternal, Job. 36, 26; Ps. 89, 2; 101, 25; Isa. 57, 15; Dan. 7, 14—Unchangeable, Num. 23, 19; Ps. 101, 26; Mal. 3, 6; Jas. 1, 17—Omniscient, 2 Par. 16, 9; Esth. 14, 14; Job 21, 22; 28, 24; 34, 21; Ps. 138, 6; Prov. 16, 2; Ecclus. 39, 24; 42, 18, 20; Dan. 13, 42; 1 Cor. 2, 10; Heb. 4, 13; 1 John 3, 20—Almighty, Gen. 17, 1; Job 9, 13; 11, 10; 23, 13; Prov. 21, 30, 31; Wisd. 11, 22, 23; 16, 13, 15; Isa. 44, 24—His justice, Deut. 32, 4; 1 Kings 26, 23; Job 34, 10, 12, 19; Ps. 10, 8; 118, 75, 137, 142; Eccles. 7, 15; 12, 14; Ecclus. 35, 16; Acts 10, 34, 35; Rom. 11, 22, 33—His mercy, Exod. 20, 6; 34, 6; Num. 14, 18; Ps. 24, 10; 32, 5; 102, 8, 11, 17; 117, 1; 135; 144, 9; Ecclus. 18, 12, 13; Isa. 13, 18; Lam. 3, 31; Hab. 3, 2; Luke 1, 50; Jas. 2, 13—Loves all men, Wisd. 11, 24, 25, 27; 12, 1, 2; Jer. 31, 3; Osee 11, 4; John 3, 16; 16, 27; Rom. 5, 8, 9; 8, 32; 1 Tim. 2, 4— Wills all to be saved, Wisd. 1, 13; Ezech. 18, 32; Matt. 23, 37; John 6, 39, 40; 1 Tim. 2, 4.

GOOD WORKS: Gen. 4, 7; 22, 16, 18; Tob. 12, 9; Ps. 17, 21-24; 18, 8-11; Matt. 5, 11, 12; 10, 42; 16, 27; 1 Cor. 3, 8; 2 Tim. 4, 8; Jas. 2, 14-26.

GRACE: John 1, 17; Rom. 5, 15-20; 6, 14; 9, 16; 2 Cor. 6, 1; 12, 9; Eph. 2, 8; 4, 7; 1 Tim. 4, 14; 2 Tim. 2, 1; Tit. 2, 11, 12; 3, 4-7; Heb. 4, 16; 12, 15, 28; 13, 9, 25; Jas. 4, 6; 1 Pet. 1, 13; 2 Pet. 3, 18.

H

HEAVEN: Ps. 35, 9; 67, 4; Isa. 33, 20; 40, 10; 49, 10; 60, 19, 20, 21; 64, 4; 65, 17; Matt. 22, 30; 25, 46; 1 Cor. 2, 9; Apoc. 7, 15, 16; 21; 22, 1-5.

A TABLE OF REFERENCES

HELL: Wisd. 5, 2-14; 6, 6, 7; Ecclus. 7, 19; Isa. 33, 14; 66, 24; Dan. 12, 2; Matt. 8, 12; 13, 41, 42, 49, 50; 22, 13; 25, 30, 41, 46; Mark 9, 43-47; Luke 13, 27, 28; 16, 22-31; 2 Thess. 1, 8, 9; Apoc. 18, 7, 8; 20, 9-15; 21, 8—Eternity of hell, Isa. 33, 14; Matt. 3, 12; 25, 46; Mark 9, 44, 45; 2 Thess. 1, 9; Apoc. 20, 10.

HERESY: 1 Cor. 11, 18, 19; 1 Tim. 4, 1-5; 2 Tim. 3, 1-9; Tit. 3, 10, 11; 2 Pet. 3, 3, 4; 2 John 7, 11; Jude 17, 18, 19; Apoc. 2, 6, 15.

HOLY GHOST: 2 Kings 23, 2; Matt. 28, 19; Acts 20, 28; 1 Cor. 3, 16; 6, 19, 20; 2 Pet. 1, 21; 1 John 5, 7—Proceeds from the Father and Son, John 15, 26; 16, 14, 15; Rom. 8, 9 —Gifts of the Holy Ghost, Isa. 11, 2, 3— Fruits of the Holy Ghost, Gal. 5, 22, 23.

HOLY ORDERS: Instituted by Christ, Luke 22, 19; John 20, 22, 23—Conferred by imposition of hands, Acts 6, 6; 13, 3; 14, 22—Give grace, 1 Tim. 4, 14; 2 Tim. 1, 6.

HOPE: Job 13, 15; Ps. 5, 12; 7, 2; 16, 7; 30; 31, 10; 33, 9; 36, 3; 37, 16; 61, 9; 70, 5, 14; 72, 28; 90, 9; 129, 5; 130, 3; 141, 6; 144, 15; 145, 5; 146, 11; Prov. 10, 28; 13, 12; 16, 20; 28, 25; 29, 25; Wisd. 3, 4; Ecclus. 2, 6, 9; Isa. 30, 15; 40, 31; Lam. 3, 25; Osee, 12, 6; Rom. 5, 2, 5; 8, 24, 25; Tit. 2, 13; 3, 7; Heb. 7, 19; 1 Pet. 1, 3; 2 Pet. 3, 13; 1 John 3, 3.

HOSPITALITY: Rom. 12, 13; Heb. 13, 2; 1 Pet. 4, 9.

HUMILITY: Judith 9, 13; Ps. 33, 19; 137, 6; Prov. 11, 2; 15, 33; 29, 23; Ecclus. 3, 20-25; Matt. 5, 3; 11, 29; 18, 4; 20, 26, 27; 23, 11, 12; Mark 10, 43, 44; Luke 9, 44; 45, 11; 22, 26; 1 Cor. 10, 12; Phil. 2, 3; Col. 3, 12; Jas. 1, 9, 10; 4, 6, 10; 1 Pet. 5, 5, 6.

HYPOCRISY: Job. 8, 13; 15, 34, 35; 20, 4-7; Ecclus. 1, 37; Matt. 6, 2; 23, 13-33; Luke 11, 30-52; 12, 1.

I

IDLENESS. See DILIGENCE, SLOTH.

IDOLATRY: Exod. 20, 3, 4, 5; Deut. 4, 15-39; 5, 7, 8, 9; Ps. 95, 5; 113, 4-8; 134, 15-18; Wisd. 12, 23-25; 13; 14; 15; Isa. 44, 9-20; Jer. 10, 1-15; Bar. 6; Dan. 14; Acts 17, 29; 1 Cor. 10, 7, 14, 20, 21; 1 John 5, 21.

IMAGES: Commanded by God, Exod. 25, 18, etc.; Num. 21, 8, 9—And placed on each side of the mercy-seat, in the sanctuary, Exod. 37, 7—And in the Temple of Solomon, 2 Par. 3, 10, 11; 3 Kings 6, 23, 32, 35— And this by Divine ordinance, 1 Par. 28, 18, 19—Relative honour to the images of Christ and the Saints authorized, Heb. 11, 21. See also 2 Kings 6, 12-16; 2 Par. 5, 2, etc.; Ps. 98, 5; Phil. 2, 10.

INDULGENCES: The power of granting them, Matt. 16, 18, 19—The use of this power, 2 Cor. 2, 6-8, 10.

J

JEALOUSY: Cant. 8, 6; Ecclus. 9, 1, 16; 26, 8, 9.

JOY: Ps. 29, 6; Prov. 14, 13; 17, 1, 22; Ecclus. 30, 16, 23; Rom. 12, 15; Phil. 3, 1; 4, 4; 1 Thess. 5, 16.

JUDGING OF OTHERS: Matt. 7, 1-5; Mark 4, 24; Luke 6, 37-41; Rom. 2, 1-3; 14, 4; 1 Cor. 4, 3-5; 10, 29; Jas. 2, 1-4; 4, 11-13.

JUDGMENT (THE LAST): Eccles. 3, 17; 8, 11; 12, 14; Isa. 2, 4-19; 3, 13, 14; 13, 6, 9, 10; 24, 23; 34, 4; Jer. 30, 7; Ezech. 7, 2, 3; 32, 7, 10; Dan. 12, 2, 3; Osee 10, 8; Joel, 1, 15; 2; 9, 1, 10; Amos 6, 10, 00; Soph. 1, 15; Zach. 2; 4, 1; Matt. 10, 26; 12, 36, 37; 13, 30-50; 24, 7-42; 25, 31-46; Mark 4, 22; 13, 19-32; 14, 62; Luke 8, 17; 12, 2, 39, 40; 17, 24; 21, 25-36; John 5, 22, 24, 28, 29; 12, 48; Acts 1, 6-21; 10, 12, 17, 31; Rom. 2, 12, 16; 14, 10, 12; 2 Cor. 5, 10; 1 Thess. 4, 15; 5, 1, 2, 3; 2 Tim. 4, 1; Heb. 10, 30, 31, 37; Jas. 5, 9; 1 Pet. 4, 5, 7, 17; 2 Pet. 3, 10; Apoc. 1, 7, 8; 6, 14-17;

9, 6; 11, 18; 14, 7, 15-19; 16, 15; 20, 11-15; 22, 12.

JUSTIFICATION: Rom. 3, 28; Gal. 2, 16, 17.

K

KINDNESS: Prov. 3, 27; Ecclus. 12, 1-7; 14, 5; 29, 19; Matt. 7, 12; Luke 6, 35; Acts 20, 35; Heb. 13, 16; 3 John 11.

L

LOQUACITY. See SPEECH.

LOVE OF GOD: Deut. 6, 5; 11, 1; Ps. 30, 24; 96, 10; Prov. 8, 17; 10, 12; Cant. 8, 6, 7; Wisd. 6, 19; 7, 28; Ecclus. 1, 14; 2, 10, 18, 19; 3, 4; 7, 32; 13, 18; 34, 15; Matt. 10, 37; 22, 37, 38; Mark 12, 30, 31; Luke 10, 27; John 14, 21; 15, 9, 10; Rom. 5, 5; 8, 28-39; 1 Cor. 8, 2, 3; 13, 1-13; 14, 1; 16, 14; Eph. 1, 4; 1 Tim. 1, 5; 6, 11; 1 John 3, 17; 4, 9-21; 5, 1, 2, 3; 2 John 6.

LOVE OF OUR NEIGHBOUR: Exod. 23, 4, 5; Prov. 10, 12; 25, 21; Matt. 5, 43-46; 7, 12; 19, 19; 22, 39; Mark 12, 31, 33; Luke 6, 27, 31-35; John 13, 34, 35; 15, 12; Rom. 12, 10, 20; 13, 8, 9, 10; 1 Cor. 13, 1-14; Gal. 5, 14; 6, 2; Eph. 4, 2; 5, 2; Col. 3, 14; 1 Thess. 4, 9; 1 Tim. 1, 5; 4, 12; Heb. 13, 1; Jas. 2, 8; 1 Pet. 1, 22; 2, 17; 4, 8; 1 John 3, 10-23; 4, 7; 5, 2.

LUKEWARMNESS: Deut. 8, 11; Eccles. 7, 19; 1 Tim. 4, 14; Apoc. 3, 15, 16.

LUXURY: Prov. 20, 1; Eccles. 10, 17; Ecclus. 11, 29; 21, 18; 42, 11; Isa. 3, 16-24; Amos 6, 1-7; Zach. 1, 15; Luke 6, 24; 16, 19-25; Gal. 5, 19, 21; Eph. 5, 18; Jas. 5, 1-5; 1 Pet. 4, 3, 4; 2 Pet. 2, 2, 12, 13.

LYING: Exod. 23, 1, 7; Lev. 19, 11; Job 27, 3, 4; 36, 13; Ps. 5, 7; Prov. 6, 16, 17; 10, 4, 18; 12, 22; 13, 5; 19, 5, 9; 20, 17; 21, 6; 30, 7, 8; Wisd. 1, 11; Ecclus. 4, 26, 30; 7, 13, 14; 20, 26, 27, 28; 34, 4; John 8, 44; Acts 5, 1-10; Col. 3, 9; Jas. 3, 14; 1 John 2, 21; Apoc. 21, 8.

M

MAGIC, MAGICIANS. See SOOTHSAYERS.

MAN: Created to the likeness of God, Gen. 1, 26, 27; 2, 7; Job 10, 9; Wisd. 1, 13, 16; 2, 23 —His fall, Gen. 3; Wisd. 2, 24, 25—Must die, Gen. 3; 2 Kings 14, 14; Job 14, 5, 19; 30, 23; 34, 15; Ps. 88, 49; 89, 6; 102, 16; Eccles. 8, 8; 9, 4; Wisd. 1, 13, 16; 2, 24, 25; 7, 6; Ecclus. 17, 29; 41, 13; Heb. 9, 27—His soul immortal, Job 19, 25, 26, 27; Wisd. 3, 1, 4; Matt. 22, 32; John 8, 51—His proneness to evil, Gen. 6, 5; 8, 21; Rom. 7, 18, 19, 23, 25.

MARRIAGE (MATRIMONY) (See also DIVORCE): Gen. 2, 24; Tob. 10, 12, 13; Ecclus. 7, 27; Matt. 19, 5, 6; Mark 10, 7, 8; 1 Cor. 7; Heb. 13, 4—Matrimony, a Sacrament, Eph. 5, 31, 32.

MASS: The sacrifice prefigured, Gen. 14, 18— Foretold, Mal. 1, 10, 11—Instituted and celebrated by Christ Himself, Luke 22, 19, 20—Attested, 1 Cor. 10, 16, 18-21; Heb. 13, 10. See EUCHARIST, etc.

MEDICINE: Ecclus. 18, 20; 38, 1-15; Matt. 9, 12; Luke 5, 31.

MEEKNESS: Judith 9, 16; Ps. 24, 9; 36, 11; 146, 6; 149, 4; Prov. 3, 34; 15, 1, 4; 16, 19, 24; 25, 15; Ecclus. 3, 19; 4, 8; 5, 13; 6, 5; 10, 17, 31; Isa. 29, 19; 61, 1; Soph. 2, 3; Matt. 5, 4; 11, 29, 30; Eph. 4, 2; 1 Tim. 6, 11; Tit. 3, 1, 2; Jas. 1, 21; 3, 13; 4, 6; 1 Pet. 5, 5.

MERCY (MERCIFUL): Job 31, 18; Prov. 3, 3, 4; 11, 17; 16, 27; 16, 6; 19, 17; 20, 28; 21, 3, 21; 22, 9; Ecclus. 3, 1; Osee 12, 6; Matt. 5, 7; 9, 13; 18, 33, 35; Luke 6, 36; Eph. 4, 32; Col. 3, 12; Jas. 2, 13.

MODESTY (MODERATION): Prov. 2, 4; Gal. 5, 22, 23; Phil. 4, 5; Col. 3, 12; 2 Tim. 2, 25; Tit. 3, 1, 2; Jas. 3, 17; 1 Pet. 3, 8, 16.

MURDERERS: Gen. 9, 5, 6; Exod. 20, 13; 21, 12-23; Lev. 24, 17; Num. 35, 31; Deut. 5, 17;

A TABLE OF REFERENCES

12, 13, 32, 34; 15, 4, 5; 4 Kings 19, 34; 20, 6; Ecclus. 44, 24; Isa. 37, 25—We may pray to them. Tob. 12, 12; Rom. 15, 30; Eph. 6, 19; Col. 4, 3; 1 Thess. 5, 25; 2 Thess. 3, 1; Heb. 13, 18.

SCANDAL-GIVING: Matt. 5, 29, 30; 13, 41, 42; 18, 6-9; Mark 9, 41-46; Luke 17, 1, 2; Rom. 14 13, 21; 1 Cor. 8, 12, 13; 1 John 2, 10.

SELF-DENIAL: 1 Kings 14, 27, 43, 44; 1 Par. 11, 19; Matt. 10, 38; 16, 24; Mark 8, 34; Luke 9, 23; John 12, 25.

SILENCE. *See* SPEECH.

SIN, SINNERS: 1 Kings 2, 25; 3 Kings 8, 16; 2 Par. 6, 36; Tob. 4, 6, 23; 12, 10; Ps. 10, 6; 13, 3, 5; 18, 13, 14; 31, 1, 2, 10; 49, 16, 22; 1, 7; 52, 4; Ecclus. 12, 7; 15, 21, 22; 16, 16-18; 19, 1; 21, 1-11; 26, 25-27; 41, 8, 9; Isa. 59, 2; Jer. 31, 29, 30; Ezech. 18, 2, 4, 20; 1 Mach. 2, 62, 63; Mark 2, 17; Luke 5, 31, 32; Rom. 3, 23; 6, 12, 14; 1 Tim. 1, 15; Jas. 1, 15; 3, 2; 1 John 1, 8-10; 2, 1, 2; 3, 8, 9; 5, 16-18—Original sin, Gen. 2, 17; 3, 6; 8, 21; Job 14, 4; 15, 14; Ps. 50, 7; Ecclus, 17, 30; Rom. 3, 5-23; 5, 12; 7, 8-17; 1 Cor. 15, 21; Gal. 3, 22; 5, 17; Eph. 2, 3-5—Sin against the Holy Ghost, Matt. 12, 31; Mark 3, 29; Luke 11, 15; 12, 10; Heb. 6, 6; 10, 26; 1 John 5, 16—Sins crying for vengeance, Gen. 4, 10; 18, 20; Exod. 22, 23, 27; Ecclus. 35, 18, 19; Jas. 5, 4—Sinner's prayer for pardon, 2 Kings 19, 19, 20; 25, 10, 17; 1 Esd. 9, 6-15; 2 Esd. 1, 5-11; 9, 7-37; Judith 9, 16, 17; Job 3, 3; 13, 23; Ps. 6; 31; 37; 50; 101; 129; 142; Isa. 44, 22; 59, 12, 13; 64, 8, 9; Jer. 17, 24; Matt. 8, 2; Luke 15, 17-19; 18, 13.

SINCERITY: Prov. 8, 13; 13, 8; Ecclus. 5, 17; 28, 15; Jas. 1, 8.

SLOTH (*See also* DILIGENCE): Prov. 6, 6-11; 10, 4, 5, 26; 12, 11, 24; 13, 4; 15, 19; 18, 8, 9; 19, 15, 24; 20, 4; 21, 5, 25; 22, 13; 24, 30-34; 26, 13-16; 28, 19; Eccles. 10, 18; Ecclus. 22, 1, 2; 33, 29; 37, 14; Ezech. 16, 49; Matt. 3, 10; 7, 19; 25, 30; Luke 3, 9; 6, 46; 2 Thess. 3, 8-12; 1 Tim. 5, 13.

SOBRIETY (*See also* DRUNKENNESS): Ecclus. 31, 19, 24, 37; 37, 34; 1 Thess. 5, 6, 8; 1 Tim. 3, 11; 2 Tim. 4, 5; Tit. 2, 6, 12; 1 Pet. 5, 8.

SOOTHSAYERS: Exod. 22, 18; Lev. 19, 31; 20, 6; Deut. 18, 10, 11, 12; Ecclus. 34, 5—Magicians of Egypt, Exod. 8, 7;—The witch of Endor, 1 Kings 28, 7-24;— Elymas the magician, Acts 13, 8-11—Simon Magus, Acts 8, 24.

SPEECH: Soberness of, Ps. 33, 13, 14; 140, 3; Prov. 13, 3; 18, 21; 21, 23; 25, 11; Ecclus. 5, 15; 18, 19; 22, 33; 28, 29; Matt. 12, 34; Luke 6, 45; Jas. 3, 2; 1 Pet. 3, 10—Evils of the tongue, Prov. 17, 4; 25, 28; Ecclus. 1, 37, 40; 4, 34; 9, 25; 19, 16 Jas. 1, 26; 3, 2-12— Loquacity, Prov. 10, 19; 16, 28; 17, 27, 28; 29, 20; Ecclus. 9, 25; 19, 5; 23, 17; 27, 13— Silence, its uses, Prov. 26, 10; Eccles. 9, 17; Isa. 30, 15; Lam. 3, 26; 1 Tim. 2, 11, 12.

SPIRITISM. *See* SOOTHSAYERS.

STEALING: Exod. 20, 15; 22, 1-4; Lev. 19, 11; Deut. 5, 29; Tob. 2, 21; Prov. 28, 24; 29, 24; Ecclus. 5, 17; Matt. 15, 19; 19, 18; Mark 7, 21, 22; 1 Cor. 6, 10; Eph. 4, 28.

T

THE BLESSED VIRGIN MARY: Her dignity, Luke 1, 28, 42, 43; All generations of true Christians shall call her blessed, Luke 1, 48. See for her veneration and invocation what is said above of Angels and Saints.

TEMPERANCE. *See* DRUNKENNESS.

TEMPTATION: Deut. 13, 3; 1 Par. 29, 17; Tob. 2, 12; 3, 21; 12, 13; Judith 8, 21, 22, 24; Job 1, 12; 2, 6; 23, 10; Ps. 25, 2; 65, 10; 138, 23; Prov. 17, 3; Wisd. 3, 5, 6; 14, 11; Ecclus. 2, 1-5; 4, 18-22; 27, 6; 33, 1; 34, 9, 11; Matt. 6, 13; 1 Cor. 10, 13; Jas. 1, 2, 12, 13, 14; 1 Pet. 1, 6; 4, 12; 2 Pet. 2, 9; 1 John 3, 7—Christ's temptation, Matt. 4, 1-11; Luke 4, 1-13.

TEMPTING GOD: Deut. 6, 16; Judith 8, 11; Wisd. 1, 2; Matt. 4, 7; Luke 4, 12; 1 Cor. 10, 9.

TRADITION: Of God, Deut. 32, 7; Prov. 22, 28; Matt. 10, 20; 20, 19; Mark 15, 16; Luke 10, 16; John 16, 12, 13; Acts 15, 41; 1 Cor. 11, 2, 14, 23, 24; Col. 4, 3, 4; 2 Thess. 2, 5, 6, 14; 1 Tim. 6, 20; 2 Tim. 1, 13, 14; 2, 2, 5, 6—Of men, Matt. 15, 2; Mark 7, 5, 9; Gal. 1, 14; 1 Pet. 1, 18.

TRANSUBSTANTIATION. *See* EUCHARIST.

TRINITY (THE BLESSED): Gen. 1, 26; 18, 1, 3; Ps. 32, 6; Isa. 6, 3; Matt. 3, 16; 28, 19; 2 Cor. 13, 13; 1 Pet. 1, 2; 1 John 5, 6; Jude 20.

V

VOWS: Lev. 27, 2; Num. 30, 3-16; Deut. 23, 21-23; Ps. 49, 14; 115, 14, 18; Prov. 20, 25; Eccles, 5, 3, 4.

W

WATCHFULNESS: Deut. 4, 9, 15; Ps. 62, 2; Prov. 8, 17, 34; Cant. 5, 2; Isa. 26, 9; Matt. 24, 42; 25, 13; 26, 41; Mark 13, 33-37; 14, 38; Luke 12, 35-40; 21, 36; 1 Cor. 16, 13; Col. 4, 2; 1 Thess. 5, 6; 2 Tim. 4, 5; 1 Pet. 4, 7; 5, 8; Apoc. 3, 2, 3; 16, 15.

WOMEN (DUTIES OF): 1 Cor. 11, 3, 15; 14, 34, 35; 1 Tim. 2, 9-15; 1 Pet. 3, 1-5—The valiant woman, Prov. 31, 10-31.

WORKS OF MERCY: Lev. 25, 26, 37; Ecclus. 7, 39; Isa. 58, 7, 10, 11; Ezech. 18, 5, 7, 9; Matt. 5, 2; 10, 8; 25, 34-40; Acts 20, 35; Rom. 15, 1; 1 Thess. 5, 14; Heb. 10, 24.

WORLDLINESS: John 12, 31; 14, 17, 30; 15, 18, 19; 16, 8, 20, 33; 17, 9-18, 25; Rom. 12, 2; 1 Cor. 7, 31; Col. 2, 20-22; Jas. 4, 4, 5; 1 John 2, 15, 16, 17; 3, 13; 4, 4, 5, 6; 5, 4, 5, 19.

Z

ZEAL: 3 Kings 19, 10, 14; Ps. 68, 10; 118, 139; Wisd. 1, 10; Ezech. 23, 25.

A TABLE OF THE EPISTLES AND GOSPELS

For all Sundays and Holydays throughout the Year, and also for Many Feasts in the Roman Calendar

It must be observed that the Verses at which the Epistle or Gospel begin and end are set down after the Chapter.

SUNDAYS, ETC.	EPISTLE	GOSPEL
Advent, 1	Rom. 13, 11-14	Luke 21, 25-33
Advent, 2	Rom. 15, 4-13	Matt. 11, 2-10
Advent, 3	Phil. 4, 4-7	John 1, 19-28
Advent, 4	1 Cor. 4, 1-5	Luke 3, 1-6
Christmas, Mass, 1	Tit. 2, 11-15	Luke 2, 1-14
Christmas, Mass, 2	Tit. 3, 4-7	Luke 2, 15-20
Christmas, Mass, 3	Heb. 1, 1-12	John 1, 1-14
St. Stephen	Acts 6, 8-10, and 7, 54-59	Matt. 23, 34-39
St. John	Ecclus. 15, 1-6	John 21, 19-24
Holy Innocents	Apoc. 14, 1-5	Matt. 2, 13-18
St. Thomas of Canterbury	Heb. 5, 1-6	John 10, 11-16
Within Octave of Christmas	Gal. 4, 1-7	Luke 2, 33, 40
St. Sylvester	2 Tim. 4, 1-8	Luke 12, 35-40
New Year	Tit. 2, 11-15	Luke 2, 21
Holy Name of Jesus	Acts 4, 8-12	Luke 2, 21
The Epiphany	Isa. 60, 1-6	Matt. 2, 1-12
Within Octave of Epiphany Holy Family	Rom. 12, 1-5	Luke 2, 42-52
After Epiphany, 2	Rom. 12, 6-16	John 2, 1-11
After Epiphany, 3	Rom. 12, 16-21	Matt. 8, 1-13
After Epiphany, 4	Rom. 13, 8-10	Matt. 8, 23-27
After Epiphany, 5	Col. 3, 12-17	Matt. 13, 24-30
After Epiphany, 6	1 Thess. 1, 2-10	Matt. 13, 31-35
Septuagesima	1 Cor. 9, 24; 10, 5	Matt. 20, 1-16
Sexagesima	2 Cor. 11, 19; 12, 9	Luke 8, 4-15
Quinquagesima	1 Cor. 13, 1-13	Luke 18, 31-43
Ash-Wednesday	Joel 2, 12-19	Matt. 6, 16-21
Lent, 1	2 Cor. 6, 1-10	Matt. 4, 1-11
Lent, 2	1 Thess. 4, 1-7	Matt. 17, 1-9
Lent, 3	Eph. 5, 1-9	Luke 11, 14-28
Lent, 4	Gal. 4, 22-31	John 6, 1-15
Passion Sunday	Heb. 9, 11-15	John 8, 46-59
Palm Sunday	Phil. 2, 5-11	Matt. 21, 1-9, chaps. 26, 27
Maundy-Thursday	1 Cor. 11, 20-32	John 13, 1-15
Good-Friday	Exod. 12, 1-11	John 18 and 19
Holy Saturday	Col. 3, 1-4	Matt. 28, 1-7
Easter Sunday	1 Cor. 5, 7-8	Mark 16, 1-7
Easter Monday	Acts 10, 37-43	Luke 24, 13-35
Easter Tuesday	Acts 13, 26-33	Luke 24, 36-47
Low Sunday	1 John 5, 4-10	John 20, 19-31
After Easter, 2	1 Pet. 2, 21-25	John 10, 11-16
After Easter, 3	1 Pet. 2, 11-19	John 16, 16-22
After Easter, 4	Jas. 1, 17-21	John 16, 5-14
After Easter, 5	Jas. 1, 22, 27	John 16, 23-30
Ascension Day	Acts 1, 1-11	Mark 16, 14-20
Within Octave of Ascension	1 Pet. 4, 7-11	John 15, 26; 16, 4
Whit-Sunday	Acts 2, 1-11	John 14, 23-31
Whit-Monday	Acts 10, 42-48	John 3, 16-21
Whit-Tuesday	Acts 8, 14-17	John 10, 1-10
Trinity Sunday	Rom. 11, 33-36	Matt. 28, 18-20
First Sunday after Pentecost	1 John 4, 8-21	Luke 6, 36-42
Corpus Christi	1 Cor. 11, 23-29	John 6, 56-59
Within Octave of Corpus Christi	1 John 3, 13-18	Luke 14, 16-24
After Pentecost, 3	1 Pet. 5, 6-11	Luke 15, 1-10
After Pentecost, 4	Rom. 8, 18-23	Luke 5, 1-11
After Pentecost, 5	1 Pet. 3, 8-15	Matt. 5, 20-24
After Pentecost, 6	Rom. 6, 3-11	Mark 8, 1-9
After Pentecost, 7	Rom. 6, 19-23	Matt. 7, 15-21

A TABLE OF THE EPISTLES AND GOSPELS

SUNDAYS, ETC.	EPISTLE	GOSPEL
After Pentecost, 8	Rom. 8, 12-17	Luke 16, 1-9
After Pentecost, 9	1 Cor. 10, 6-13	Luke 19, 41-47
After Pentecost, 10	1 Cor. 12, 2-11	Luke 18, 9-14
After Pentecost, 11	1 Cor. 15, 1-10	Mark 7, 31-37
After Pentecost, 12	2 Cor. 3, 4-9	Luke 10, 23-37
After Pentecost, 13	Gal. 3, 16-22	Luke 17, 11-19
After Pentecost, 14	Gal. 5, 16-24	Matt. 6, 24-33
After Pentecost, 15	Gal. 5, 25; 6, 10	Luke 7, 11-16
After Pentecost, 16	Eph. 3, 13-21	Luke 14, 1-11
After Pentecost, 17	Eph. 4, 1-6	Matt. 22, 35-46
After Pentecost, 18	1 Cor. 1, 4-8	Matt. 9, 1-8
After Pentecost, 19	Eph. 4, 23-28	Matt. 22, 1-14
After Pentecost, 20	Eph. 5, 15-21	John 4, 46-53
After Pentecost, 21	Eph. 6, 10-17	Matt. 18, 23-35
After Pentecost, 22	Phil. 1, 6-11	Matt. 22, 15-21
After Pentecost, 23	Phil. 3, 17; 4, 3	Matt. 9, 18-26
After Pentecost, 24	Col. 1, 9-14	Matt. 24, 15-35

FEAST	EPISTLE	GOSPEL
St. Andrew, Nov. 30	Rom. 10, 10-18	Matt. 4, 18-22
Immaculate Conception, Dec. 8	Prov. 8, 22-35	Luke 1, 26-28
St. Thomas, Dec. 21	Eph. 2, 19-22	John 20, 24-29
Conversion of St. Paul, Jan. 25	Acts 9, 1-22	Matt. 19, 27-29
Candlemas Day, Feb. 2	Mal. 3, 1-4	Luke 2, 22-32
St. Matthias, Feb. 24	Acts 1, 15-26	Matt. 11, 25-30
St. Patrick, Mar. 17	Ecclus. 44, 16-27; 45, 3-20	Matt. 25, 14-23
St. Joseph, Mar. 19	Ecclus. 45, 1-6	Matt. 1, 18-21
Annunciation, Mar. 25	Isaias 8, 10-15	Luke 1, 26-38
St. George, Apr. 23	2 Tim. 2, 8-10; 3, 10-12	John 15, 1-7
St. Mark, Apr. 25	Ezech. 1, 10-14	Luke 10, 1-9
SS. Philip and James, May 1	Wis. 5, 1-5	John 14, 1-13
St. Barnabas, June 11	Acts 16, 21-26; 13, 2-3	Matt. 10, 16-22
St. John Baptist, June 24	Isaias 49, 1-3, 5-7	Luke 1, 57-68
SS. Peter and Paul, June 29	Acts 12, 1-11	Matt. 16, 13-19
Visitation of the Blessed Virgin Mary, July 2	Cant. 2, 8-14	Luke 1, 39-47
St. Mary Magdalen, July 22	Cant. 3, 2-5; 8, 6-7	Luke 7, 36-50
St. James, July 25	1 Cor. 4, 9-15	Matt. 20, 20-23
St. Anne, July 26	Prov. 31, 10-31	Matt. 13, 44-52
Transfiguration of Our Lord, Aug. 6	2 Peter 1, 16-19	Matt. 17, 1-9
St. Lawrence, Aug. 10	2 Cor. 9, 6-10	John 12, 24-26
Assumption of the Blessed Virgin Mary, Aug. 15	Ecclus. 24, 11-20	Luke 10, 38-42
St. Bartholomew, Aug. 24	1 Cor. 12, 27-31	Luke 6, 12-19
Nativity of the Blessed Virgin Mary, Sept. 8	Prov. 8, 22-35	Matt. 1- 1-16
St. Matthew, Sept. 21	Ezech. 1, 10-15	Matt. 9, 9-13
St. Michael, Sept 29	Apoc. 1, 1-15	Matt. 18, 1-10
Holy Guardian Angels, Oct. 2	Ex. 23, 20-23	Matt. 18, 1-10
St. Luke, Oct. 18	2 Cor. 8, 16-24	Luke 10, 1-9
SS. Simon and Jude, Oct. 28	Eph. 4, 7-13	John 15, 17-25
Our Lord Jesus Christ, King, Last Sunday in Oct.	Col. 1, 12-20	John 18, 33-37
All Saints, Nov. 1	Apoc. 7, 2-12	Matt. 5, 1-12
All Souls, Nov. 2	1 Cor. 15, 51-57	John 5, 25-29
Presentation of the Blessed Virgin Mary, Nov. 21	Ecclus. 24, 14-16	Luke 11, 27-28

INDEX TO PRACTICAL BIBLE ATLAS.

Maps and Plans.

1.—The Ancient World, showing the distribution of the posterity of Noah.
2.—Western Asia, illustrating the Patriarchal Age.
3.—Egypt and the Peninsula of Sinai, illustrating the Exodus.
4.—Canaan, showing Territory of the Twelve Tribes.
5.—Palestine, illustrating the Old Testament from the time of Judges.
6.—The Kingdom of Judah and Israel.
7. The Kingdoms of David and Solomon.
8.—Assyria, Babylonia and Adjacent Countries, illustrating the Captivity of Judah-Israel.
9.—Upper and Lower Galilee.
10.—Highlands of Judea, showing Environs of Jerusalem.
11.—Jerusalem, Modern and Ancient.
12.—Plan of the Temple and Temple Area, as rebuilt by Herod.
13.—Palestine in the time of Christ.
14.—The Journeys of St. Paul.

List of Names.

NOTE.—*Figures preceding the dash denote the map; the other figures and letters denote the squares on the maps where the places are to be found; thus Abarim 4-C 4 appears on Map No. 4 in the square C 4.*

The Maps in PRACTICAL BIBLE ATLAS have been specially prepared and engraved from the latest surveys.

ABANA, River	5-D 1	Ahlab	9-C 1	Aram naharaim	8-C 1
Abarim	4-C 4	Ai	10-B 1	Ararat (Armenia)	8-B 1
Abdon	4-B 1	Ajalon	4-B; 10-A 4	Ararat, Mount	2-C 2
Abel, *also*		Ajalon, Valley of	10-A 1	Arbela	9-C 2
Abel-beth-maachah		Akrabbim, Ascent of	5-B 6	Archi	10-A 1
Abel-main	5-C 2	Alema	9-E 2	Argob	5-D 2
Abel-meholah	4-B 3	Alemeth	10-B 2	Arimathea	13-B 3
Abel-shittim	5-C 5	Alexandria	14-D 3	Armageddon	13-B 2
Abez	9-B 3	Almon	4-B 4; 10-B 2	Armenia (Ararat)	8-B 1
Abilene	14-F 3	Amalekites	2-A 3	Arnon, River	4-C 5
Accad	8-C 2	Ammon	5-D 5	Aroer	4-C 5
Accho	4-B 2	Ammonites	2-B 3	Arpad	7-D 1
Aceldama	11-C 6	Amorites	2-A 3	Arumah	5-B 4
Achaia	14-C 2	Amphipolis	14-C 1	Arvad	7-C 2
Achmetha	8-D 1	Anaharath	4-B 2; 9-C 3	Ashdod	4-A 4
Achor, Valley of	5-B 5	Ananiah	10-B 2	Asher, Tribe of	4-B 1
Achshaph	4-B 2; 9-B 2	Anathoth	4-B 4; 10-B 2	Ashkelon, Askelon	4-A 4
Achzib	4-B 1; 9-B 1; 10-A 2	Anem	4-B 2; 9-B 3	Ashtaroth	4-C 2
Achzib (Judah)	10-A 2	Antioch (Syria)	14-F 2	Asochis, Plain of	9-C 2
Acra	11-C 4	Antioch (Pisidia)	14-E 2	Asshur	1-D 3; 8-C 1
Adam	4-C 3	Antipatris	13-A 3; 14-F 3	Assos	14-D 2
Adamah	4-B 2; 9-C 2	Aphek	9-D 2; 4-C 2; 4-B 3	Ataroth	4-C 4
Adami-nekeb	9-C 3	Apollonia	14-C 1	Ataroth-adar	10-A 1
Adasa	10-B 1	Appii, Forum	14-A 1	Athens	14-C 2
Adora, Adoraim	4-B 4; 10-A 3	Arab	5-B 6	Attalia	14-E 2
Adramyttium	14-D 2	Arabah	3-C 1	Azmaveth	10-B 1
Adria	14-B 2	Arabia	3-C 2	Azotus	13-A 4
Adullam	4-A 4; 10-A 3	Arad	4-B 5	Azotus, Mount	10-B 1
Acnon	13-B 3	Aram (Syria)	1-C 3; 8-A 1		

1

2

4

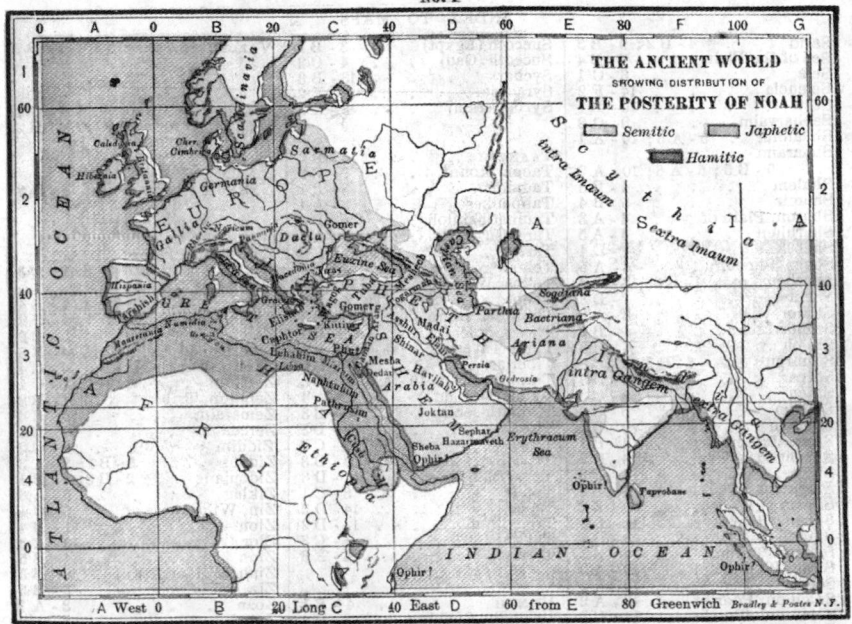

No. 1

THE ANCIENT WORLD
SHOWING DISTRIBUTION OF
THE POSTERITY OF NOAH
Semitic
Japhetic
Hamitic
ATLANTIC OCEAN
EUROPE
Scandinavia
Sarmatia
Germania
Gallia
Hispania
Dacia
Gomer
Euxine Sea
Scythia intra Imaum
Scythia extra Imaum
Sogdiana
Bactriana
Parthia
Ariana
Persia
Gedrosia
India intra Gangem
India extra Gangem
Madai
Ashur
Elam
Shinar
Havilah
Arabia
Mesha
Dedan
Joktan
Sephar
Hazarmaveth
Sheba
Ophir
Erythraeum Sea
AFRICA
Ethiopia
Naphtuhim
Pathrusim
Lubim
Phut
Caphtor
Elishah
Mauretania
Numidia
Ophir?
Taprobane
INDIAN OCEAN
West
Long
East
from
Greenwich
Bradley & Poates N.Y.

No. 2

EUXINE (BLACK) SEA
CASPIAN SEA
Halys
Havilah
MESHECH
TUBAL
ARMENIA
MT. ARARAT
ARARAT
TOGARMAH
Cyrus
Araxes
Euphrates
LYDIA
MAGOG
CILICIA
GOMER
MEDIA
MADAI
ASSYRIA
ASSHUR
Tigris
Nineveh
Rehoboth?
Resen
Calah
Haran
HITTITES
PADAN ARAM
MESOPOTAMIA
ARAM NAHARAIM
Reboboth?
Orontes
SYRIA
ARAM
THE GREAT SEA (Mediterranean)
CYPRUS
KITTIM
Zidon
Tyre
Syrian Desert
BUZ
KEDAR
Jordan
AMMONITES
MOABITES
AMORITES
AMALEKITES
HORITES
UZ
GOSHEN
On
Wilderness of Shur
Wilderness of Paran
Red Sea
EGYPT
Babylon
Babel
Accad
BABYLONIA
SHINAR
Calneh
Erech
CHALDAEA
Ur
Susan
ELAM
SUSIANA
Persian Gulf
WESTERN ASIA
ILLUSTRATING THE
PATRIARCHAL AGE
SCALE OF MILES
0
100
200
300
Longitude
East
from
Greenwich

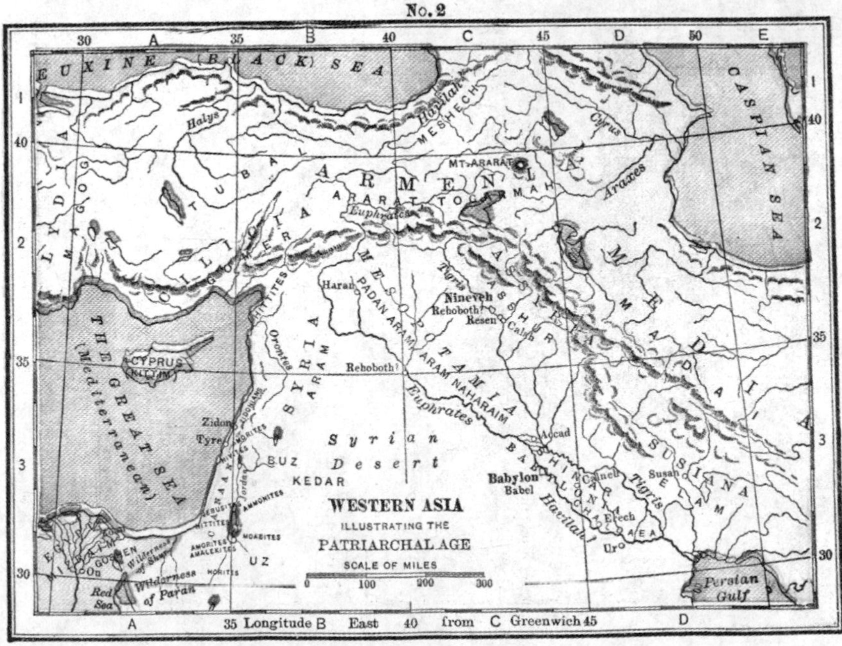

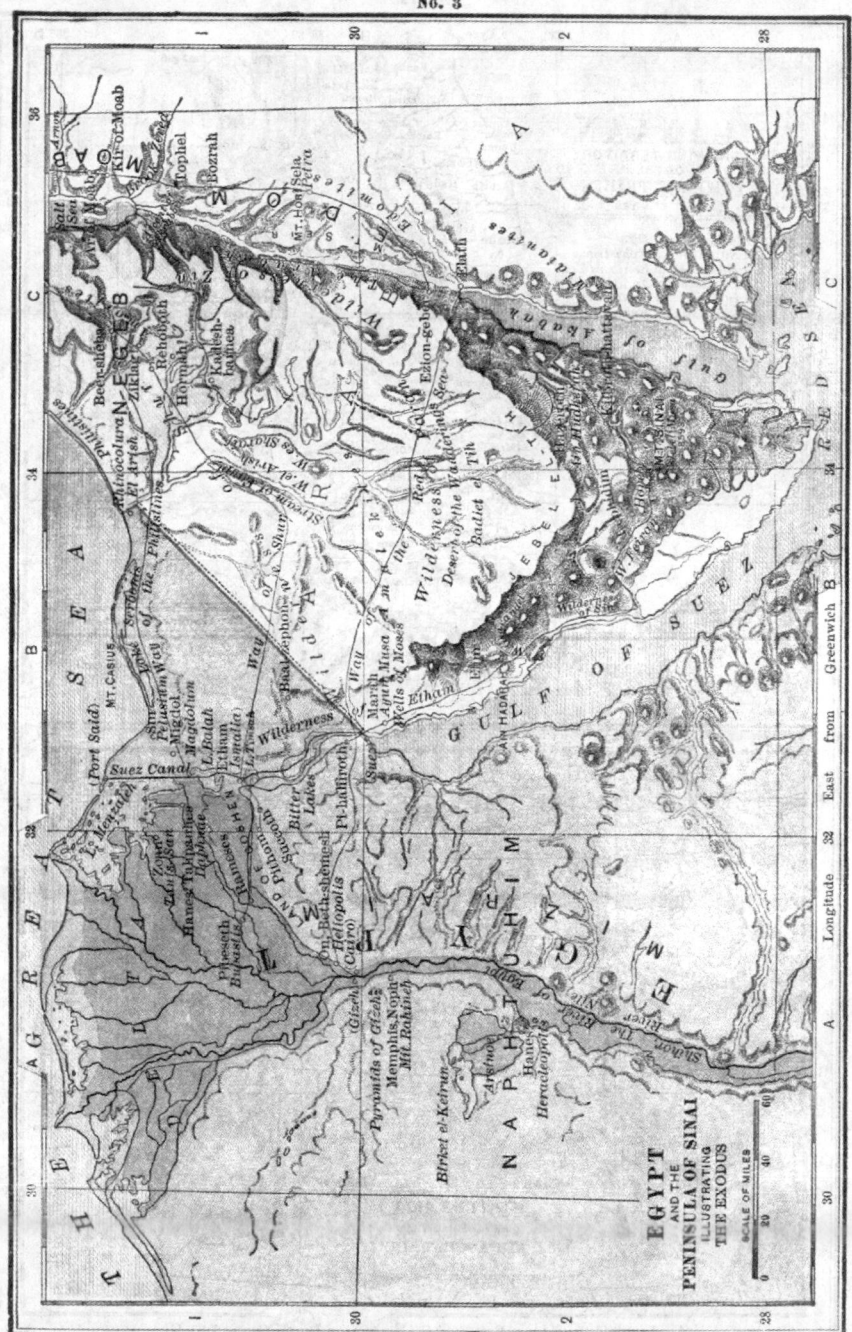

EGYPT
AND THE
PENINSULA OF SINAI
ILLUSTRATING
THE EXODUS

SCALE OF MILES

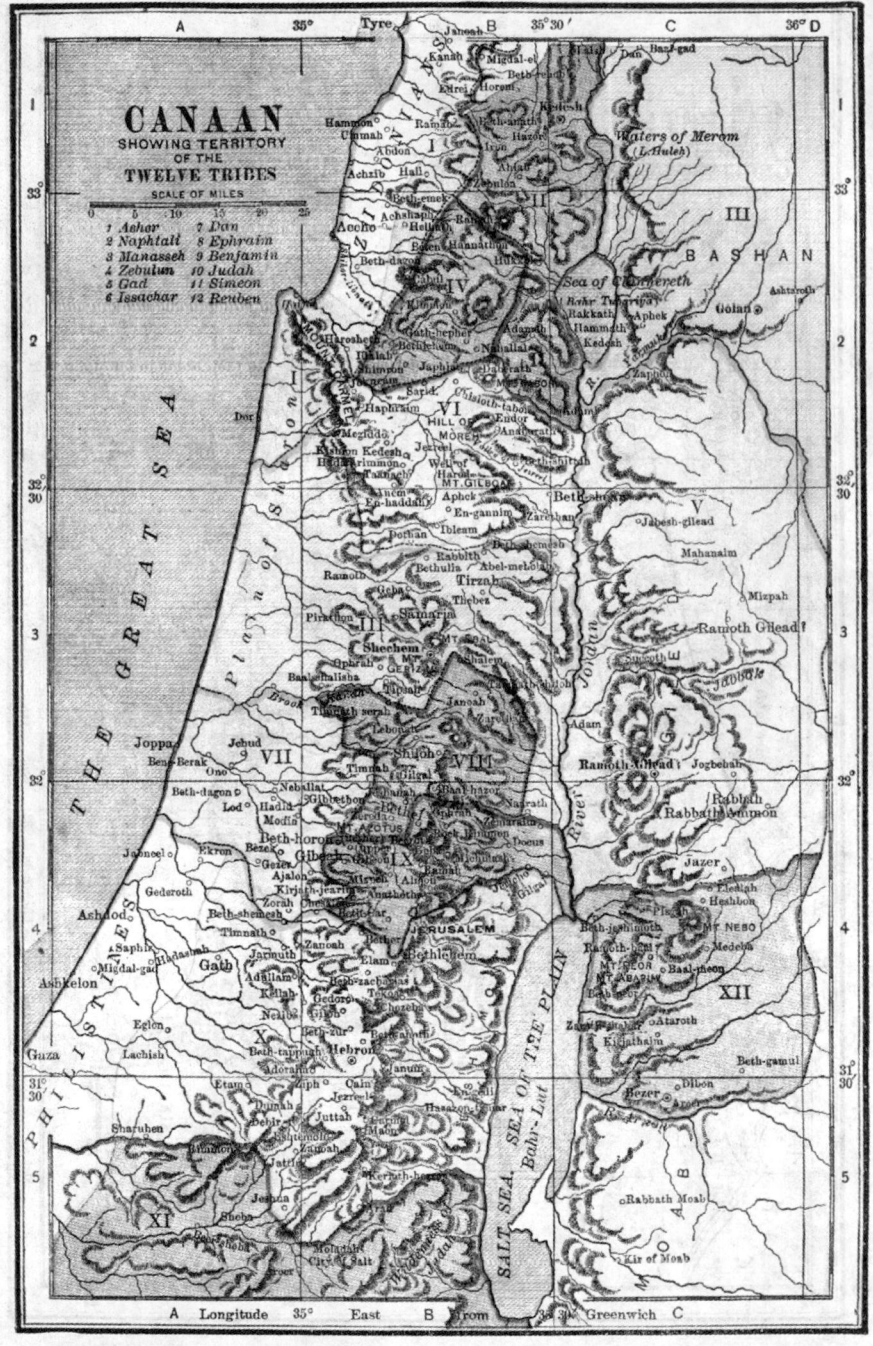

CANAAN

SHOWING TERRITORY
OF THE
TWELVE TRIBES

SCALE OF MILES

0   5   10   15   20   25

1 Asher	7 Dan
2 Naphtali	8 Ephraim
3 Manasseh	9 Benjamin
4 Zebulun	10 Judah
5 Gad	11 Simeon
6 Issachar	12 Reuben

THE GREAT SEA

BASHAN

Waters of Merom
(L. Huleh)

Sea of Chinnereth

PHILISTINES

River Jordan

SALT SEA

SEA OF THE PLAIN

A   Longitude   35°   East   from   35° 30′   Greenwich   C

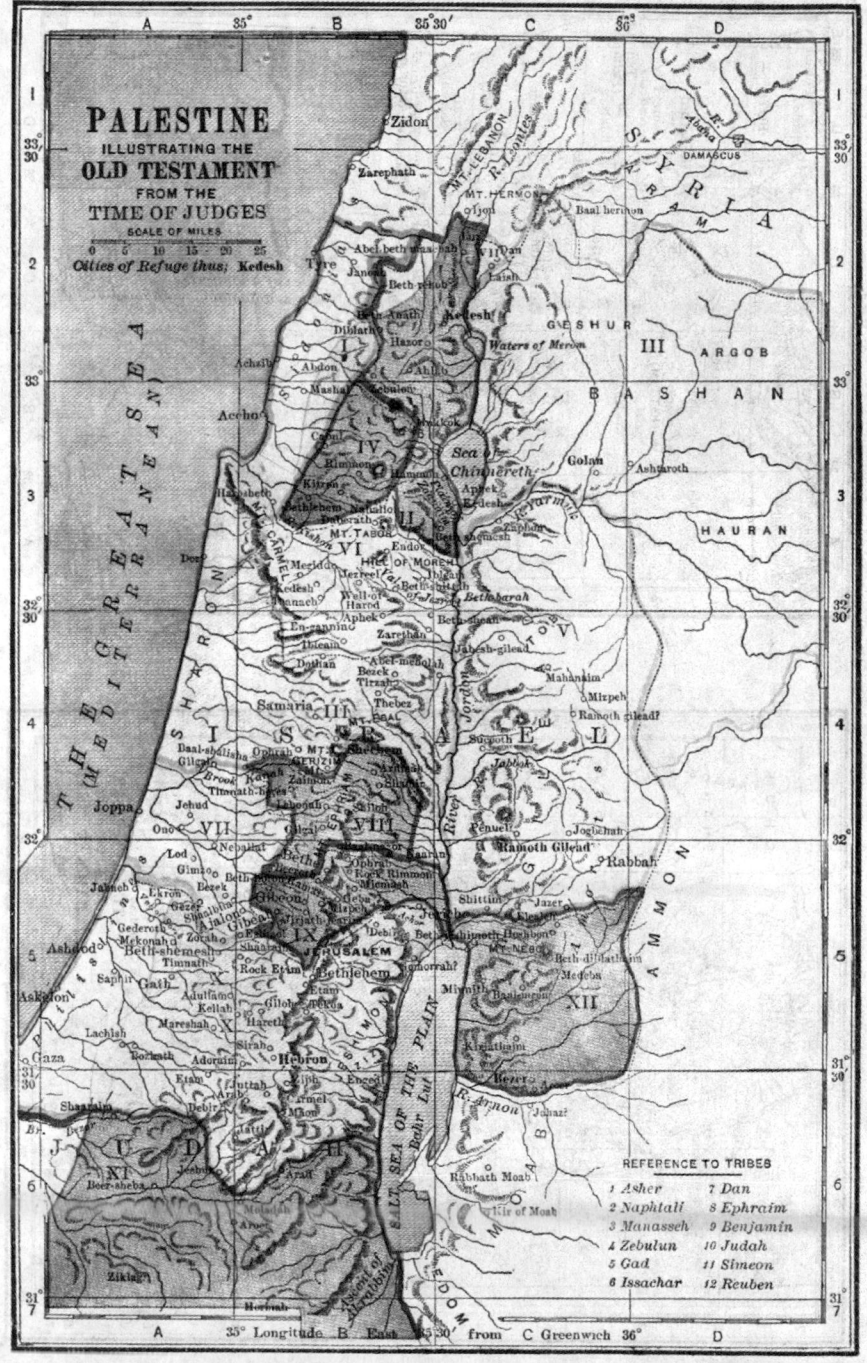

PALESTINE

ILLUSTRATING THE

OLD TESTAMENT

FROM THE

TIME OF JUDGES

SCALE OF MILES

0 5 10 15 20 25

Cities of Refuge thus; **Kedesh**

REFERENCE TO TRIBES

1 *Asher*	7 *Dan*
2 *Naphtali*	8 *Ephraim*
3 *Manasseh*	9 *Benjamin*
4 *Zebulun*	10 *Judah*
5 *Gad*	11 *Simeon*
6 *Issachar*	12 *Reuben*

A   35° Longitude   B   East   35° 30'   from   C   Greenwich   36°   D

No. 7

KINGDOMS
OF
DAVID AND SOLOMON

SCALE OF MILES
0   50   100

THE MEDITERRANEAN SEA

CYPRUS (KITTIM)

Orontes

ZOBA

HAMATH

Berea
Pethor
Arpad
Hamath
Emesa (Kadesh)
Riblah
Tadmor (Palmyra)
Damascus
Argob
Golan
Bashan
Geshur
Tyre
Zidon
Zarephath
Accho
Mt. Carmel
Dor
Bozrah
Salcah
Ramoth-gilead
Jabbok
Gilead
Gath
Shechem
Samaria
Joppa
JERUSALEM
Gaza
Beer-sheba
JUDAH
Ammon
Rabbath Ammon
MOAB
Kir of Moab
Arnon
Ezion-geber
Wilderness of Paran
Wilderness of Zin
Sin
River of Egypt
Horeb
Mt. Sinai
Memphis
EGYPT
Suez Canal
GULF OF SUEZ
Zoan

No. 6

THE KINGDOMS
OF
JUDAH AND ISRAEL

SCALE OF MILES
0 5 10 15 20 25

GESHUR
ARGOB
BASHAN
HAURAN
AMMON
NEGEB

THE GREAT SEA

SEA OF THE PLAIN
OR
SALT SEA

Tyre
Kedesh
Waters of Merom
Chinnereth
Sea of Galilee
Jordan
Golan
Ashtaroth
Kanah
Abel
Dan
Hazor
Ramoth-gilead
Jabesh-gilead
Mahanaim
Succoth
Jabbok
Ramoth-Gilead
Rabbath
Heshbon
Medeba
Dibon
Ar of Moab
Kir of Moab
Mt. Carmel
Dor
Megiddo
Jezreel
Samaria
Shechem
Mt. Gerizim
Mt. Ebal
Shiloh
Bethel
JERUSALEM
Bethlehem
Hebron
Joppa
Gaza
Beer-sheba
SHARON

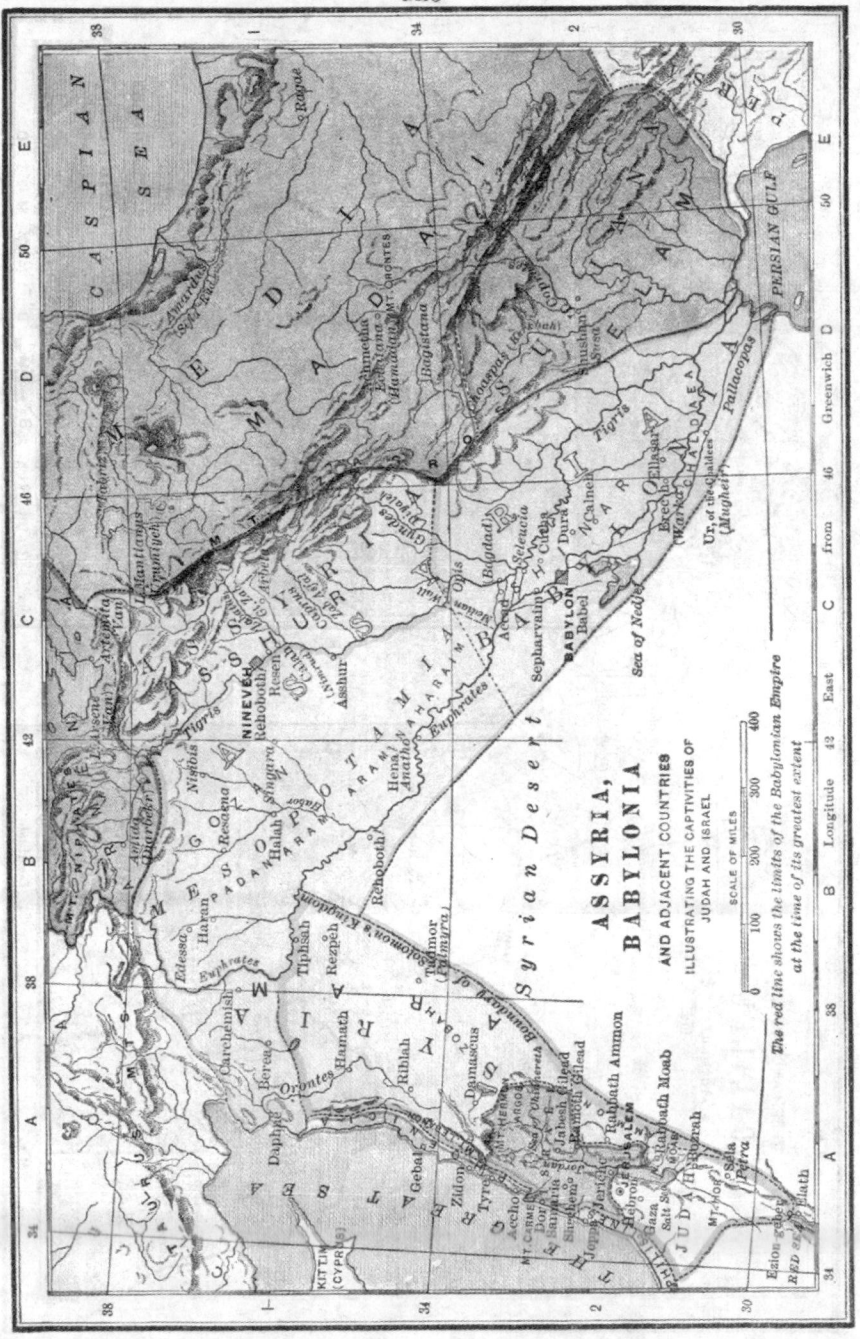

ASSYRIA,
BABYLONIA
AND ADJACENT COUNTRIES
ILLUSTRATING THE CAPTIVITIES OF
JUDAH AND ISRAEL

SCALE OF MILES

The red line shows the limits of the Babylonian Empire
at the time of its greatest extent

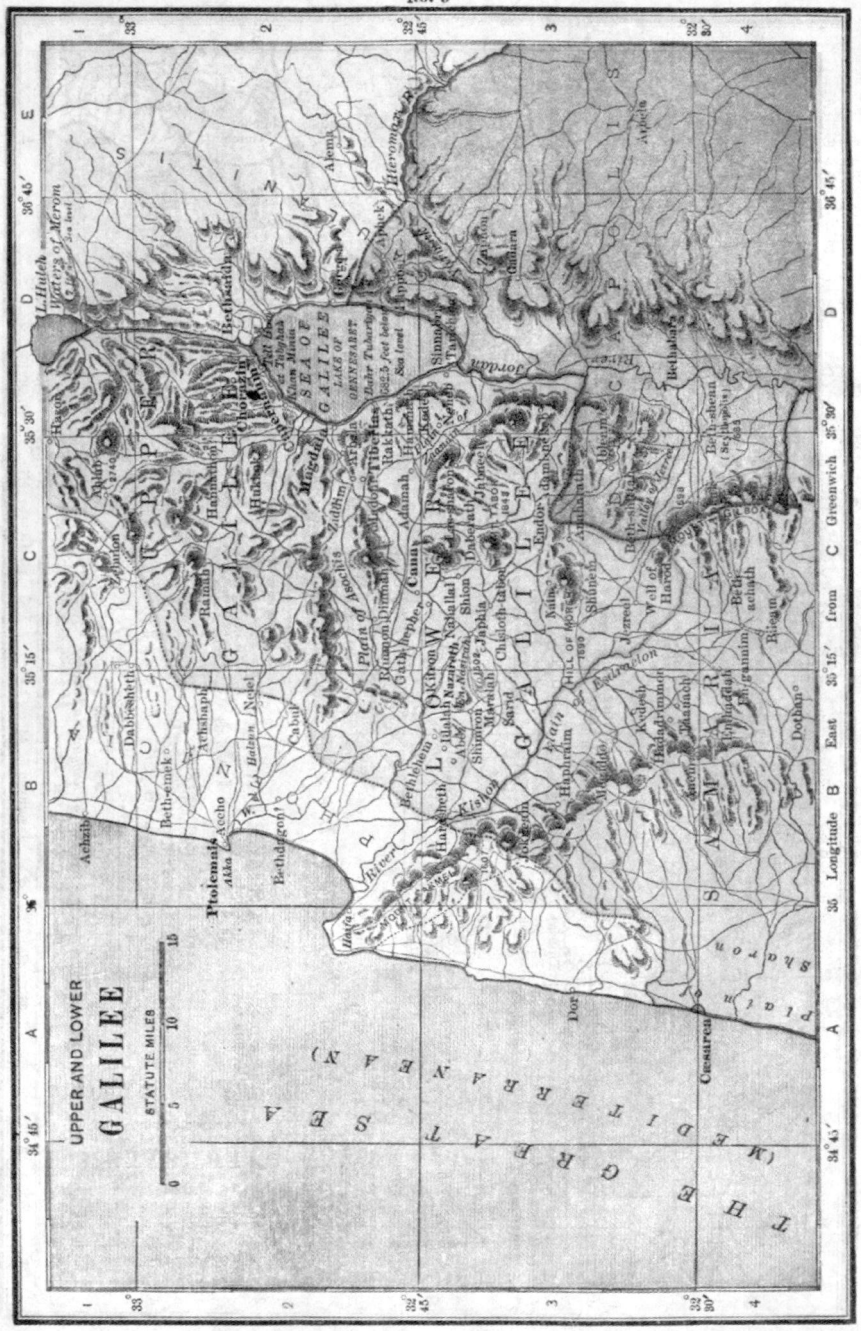

UPPER AND LOWER
GALILEE

STATUTE MILES

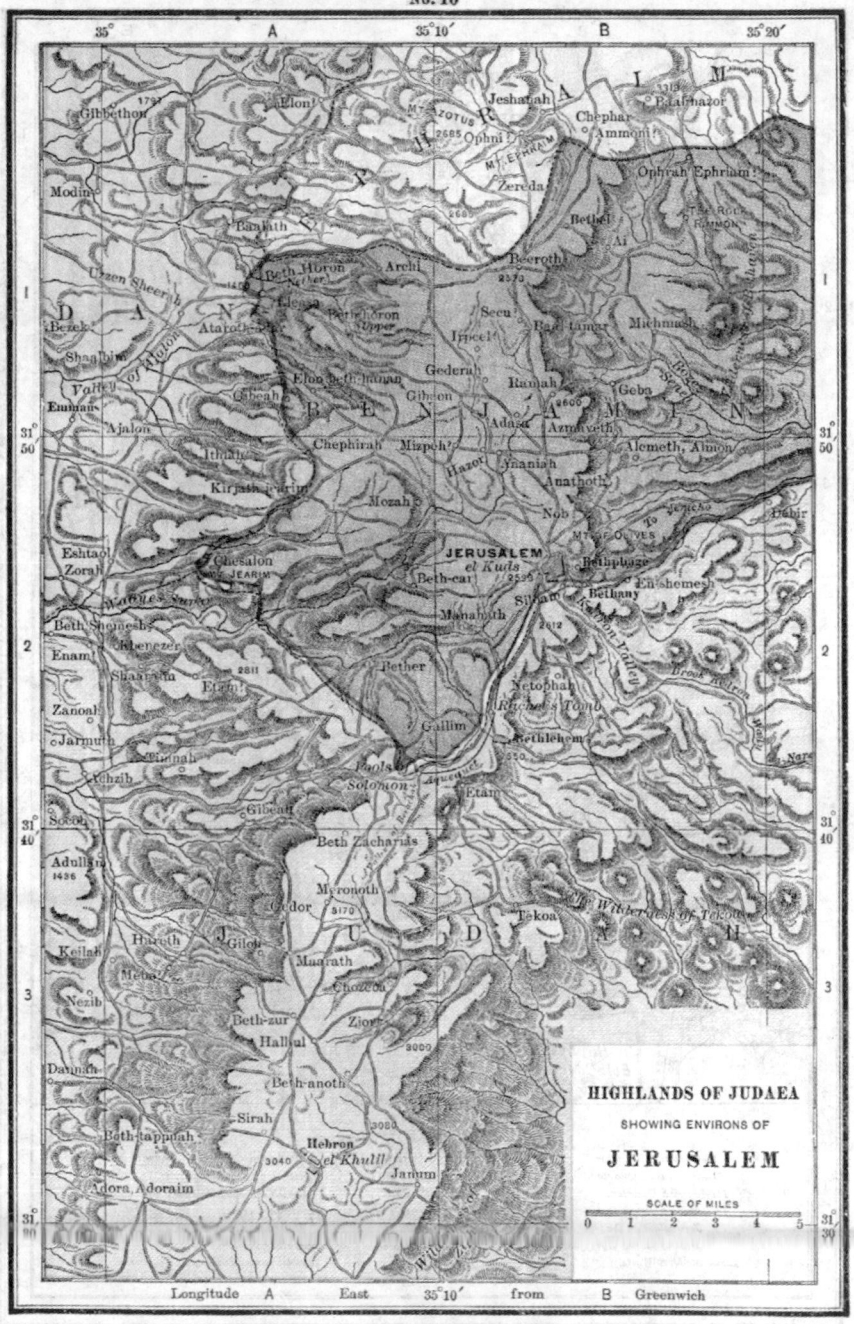

HIGHLANDS OF JUDAEA

SHOWING ENVIRONS OF

JERUSALEM

SCALE OF MILES

0   1   2   3   4   5

Longitude   A   East   35°10′   from   B   Greenwich

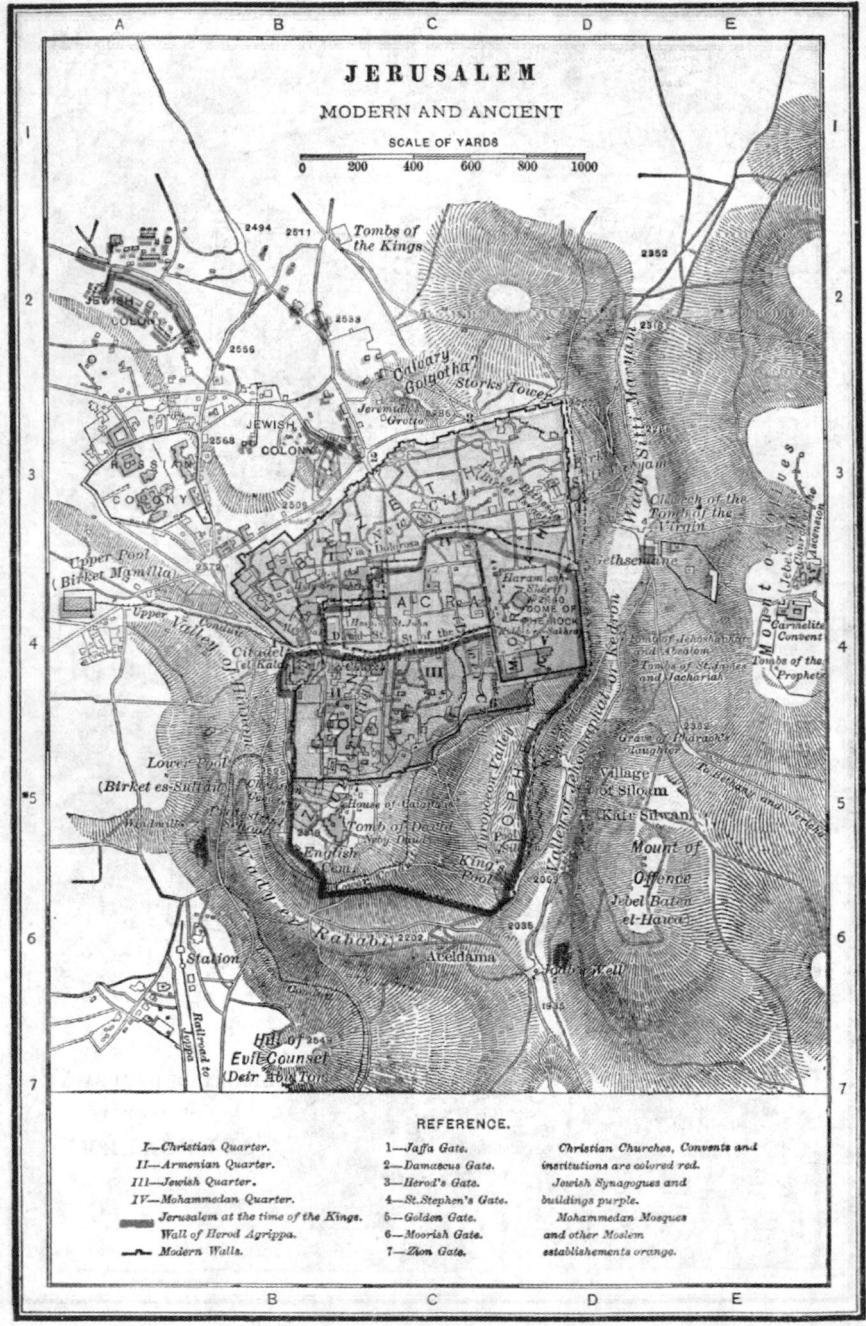

JERUSALEM

MODERN AND ANCIENT

SCALE OF YARDS

0   200   400   600   800   1000

REFERENCE.

I—Christian Quarter.
II—Armenian Quarter.
III—Jewish Quarter.
IV—Mohammedan Quarter.
⬛ Jerusalem at the time of the Kings.
Wall of Herod Agrippa.
— Modern Walls.

1—Jaffa Gate.
2—Damascus Gate.
3—Herod's Gate.
4—St. Stephen's Gate.
5—Golden Gate.
6—Moorish Gate.
7—Zion Gate.

Christian Churches, Convents and
institutions are colored red.
Jewish Synagogues and
buildings purple.
Mohammedan Mosques
and other Moslem
establishements orange.

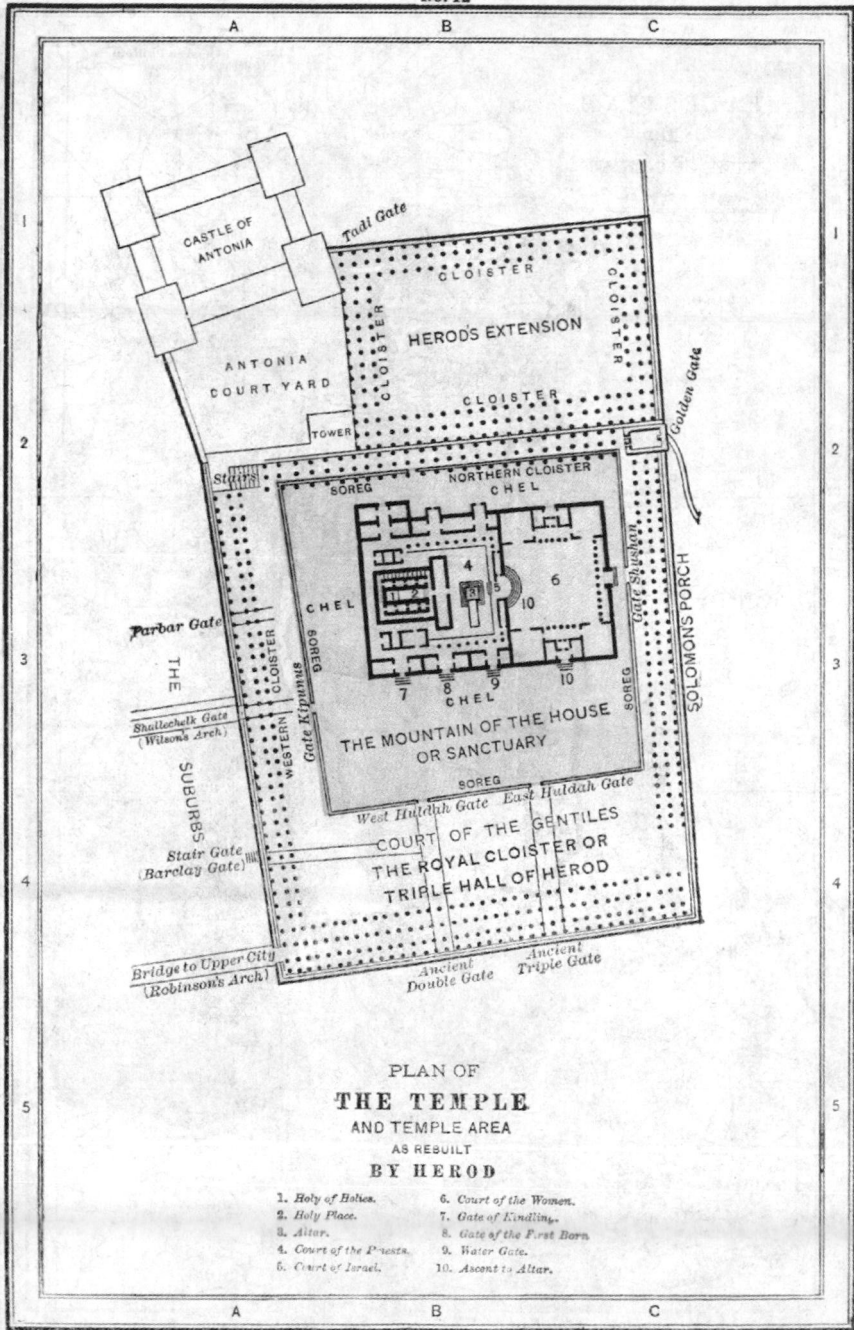

PLAN OF

THE TEMPLE

AND TEMPLE AREA

AS REBUILT

BY HEROD

1. Holy of Holies.
2. Holy Place.
3. Altar.
4. Court of the Priests.
5. Court of Israel.

6. Court of the Women.
7. Gate of Kindling.
8. Gate of the First Born.
9. Water Gate.
10. Ascent to Altar.

No. 13

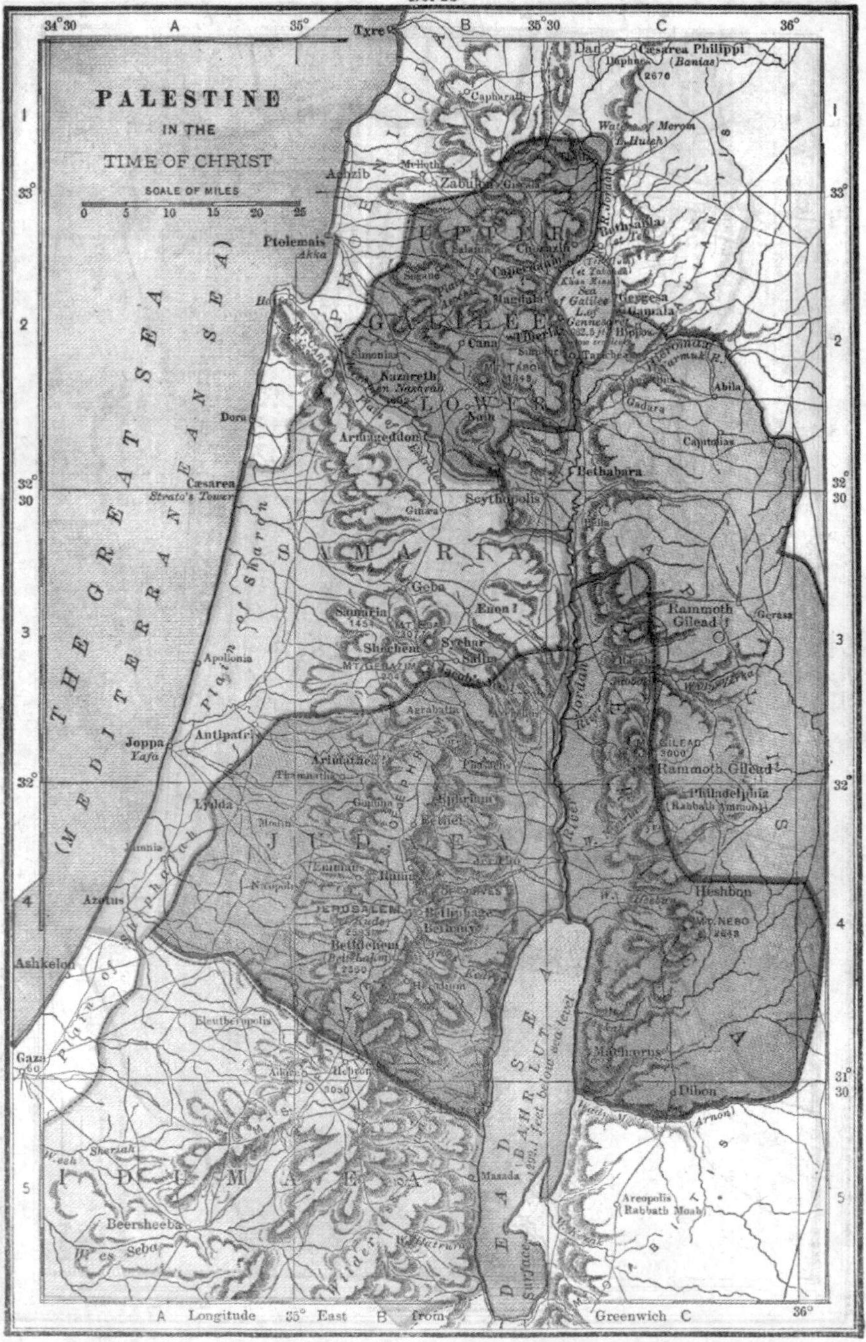

PALESTINE
IN THE
TIME OF CHRIST
SCALE OF MILES
0 5 10 15 20 25
THE GREAT SEA
(MEDITERRANEAN SEA)
Tyre
Dan
Cæsarea Philippi
(Banias)
2676
Waters of Merom
Achzib
Zabulon
Ptolemais
Akka
UPPER
GALILEE
LOWER
Capernaum
Magdala
Tiberias
Cana
Nazareth
Nain
Armageddon
Bethsaida
Gergesa
Gamala
Sea of Galilee
Hippos
Gadara
Abila
Capitolias
Dora
Cæsarea
Strato's Tower
Bethabara
Scythopolis
SAMARIA
Plain of Sharon
Geba
Samaria
Enon
Sychar
Shechem
Salim
MT. GERIZIM
Apollonia
Joppa
Yafa
Antipatris
Arimathea
Lydda
Jamnia
JUDEA
Emmaus
Jerusalem
Bethphage
Bethany
Bethlehem
2550
Herodium
Azotus
Ashkelon
Eleutheropolis
Gaza
Hebron
3030
IDUMAEA
Beersheeba
Masada
Rammoth Gilead
Gerasa
GILEAD
3000
Philadelphia
(Rabbath Ammon)
Heshbon
MT. NEBO
2643
Machaerus
Dibon
Areopolis
Rabbath Moab
Arnon
DEAD SEA
BAHR LUT
Surface 1292.1 feet below sea level
Jordan River
34°30
35°
35°30
36°
32°
32° 30
33°
31° 30
A
B
C
1
2
3
4
5
A Longitude 35° East B from Greenwich C

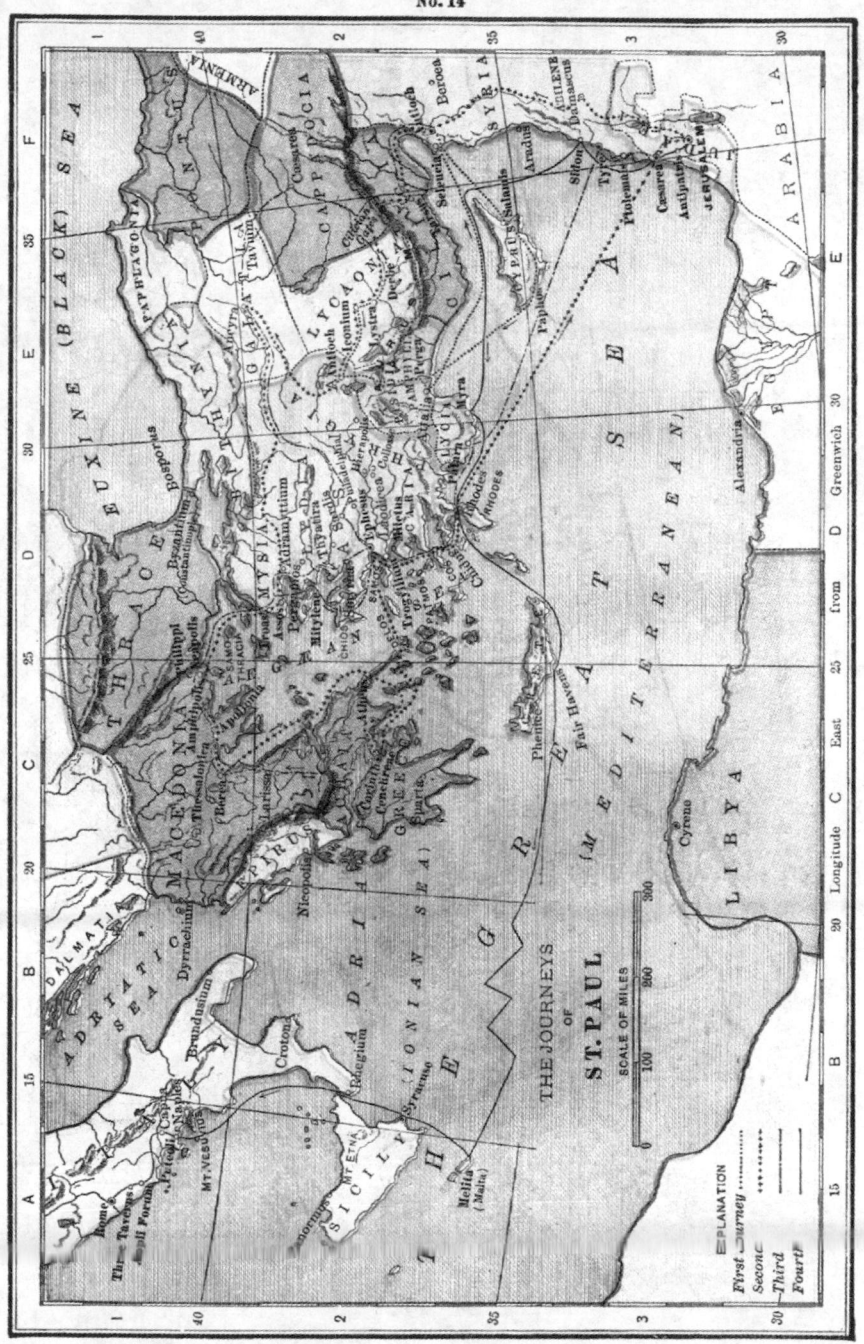

THE JOURNEYS
OF
ST. PAUL.

SCALE OF MILES

EXPLANATION
First Journey ....
Second ++++++++++
Third
Fourth

GOD EXPELS ADAM AND EVE FROM PARADISE

"AND HE CAST OUT ADAM, AND PLACED BEFORE THE PARADISE OF PLEASURE CHERUBIMS, AND A FLAMING SWORD, TURNING EVERY WAY, TO KEEP THE WAY OF THE TREE OF LIFE." — *Gen. 3, 24.*

NOAH AND HIS FAMILY ENTER THE ARK

"AND NOAH WENT IN, AND HIS SONS, HIS WIFE AND THE WIVES OF HIS SONS WITH HIM INTO THE ARK, BECAUSE OF THE WATERS OF THE FLOOD." — *Gen. 7, 7.*

ABRAHAM IS BLESSED BY MELCHISEDECH

"BUT MELCHISEDECH THE KING OF SALEM, BRINGING FORTH BREAD
AND WINE, FOR HE WAS THE PRIEST OF THE MOST HIGH GOD, BLESSED
HIM." — *Gen. 14, 18.19.*

JOSEPH IS SOLD BY HIS BROTHERS

"AND WHEN THE MADIANITE MERCHANTS PASSED BY, THEY DREW HIM
OUT OF THE PIT, AND SOLD HIM TO THE ISMAELITES FOR TWENTY PIECES
OF SILVER: AND THEY LED HIM INTO EGYPT." — *Gen. 37, 28.*

GOD APPEARS TO MOSES IN THE BURNING BUSH

"AND THE LORD APPEARED TO HIM IN A FLAME OF FIRE OUT OF THE
MIDST OF A BUSH: AND HE SAW THAT THE BUSH WAS ON FIRE AND
WAS NOT BURNT." — *Exod. 3, 2.*

THE GLORY OF MOSES

"AND WHEN MOSES CAME DOWN FROM THE MOUNT SINAI, HE HELD THE
TWO TABLES OF THE TESTIMONY: AND HE KNEW NOT THAT HIS FACE
WAS HORNED FROM THE CONVERSATION OF THE LORD." — *Exod. 34, 29.*

THE CONSECRATION OF AARON

"AND HE POURED IT UPON AARON'S HEAD: AND HE
ANOINTED AND CONSECRATED HIM." — *Lev. 8, 12.*

THE PUNISHMENT OF BLASPHEMY

"AND HE THAT BLASPHEMETH THE NAME OF THE LORD, DYING LET HIM DIE. ALL THE MULTITUDE SHALL STONE HIM WHETHER HE BE A NATIVE OR A STRANGER." — *Lev. 24, 16.*

JOSUA HALTS THE SUN

"AND THE SUN AND THE MOON STOOD STILL, TILL THE PEOPLE
REVENGED THEMSELVES OF THEIR ENEMIES." — *Jos. 10, 13.*

THE CONSECRATION OF SAMUEL
"AND THEY IMMOLATED A CALF AND OFFERED THE CHILD TO HELI."
— *1. Kings 1, 25.*

DAVID DANCES BEFORE THE ARK

"AND DAVID DANCED WITH ALL HIS MIGHT BEFORE THE LORD.
AND DAVID WAS GIRDED WITH A LINEN EPHOD."—*2 Kings 6, 14.*

ELIAS ASCENDS TO HEAVEN IN A FIERY CHARIOT

"Behold a fiery chariot, and fiery horses parted them both
asunder: and Elias went up by a whirlwind into heaven."
—4 Kings 2, 11.

AN ANGEL DESTROYS THE ARMY OF SENNACHERIB

"AND THE LORD SENT AN ANGEL WHO CUT OFF ALL THE STOUT MEN AND THE WARRIORS AND THE CAPTAINS OF THE ARMY OF THE KING OF THE ASSYRIANS." — *2 Para. 32, 21.*

TOBIAS BURIES THE DEAD

"SO WHEN THE SUN WAS DOWN, HE WENT AND BURIED HIM."
— *Tob. 2, 7.*

JUDITH BEHEADS HOLOFERNES

"AND WHEN SHE HAD DRAWN IT OUT, SHE TOOK HIM BY THE HAIR OF
THE HEAD AND SAID: STRENGTHEN ME, O LORD GOD, AT THIS HOUR."
— *Jud. 13, 9.*

DAVID SINGS JOYOUSLY UPON THE HARP

"SING YE TO THE LORD WITH PRAISE: SING TO OUR GOD UPON THE HARP."
— Ps. 146, 7.

GOD CLEANSES THE LIPS OF ISAIAS

"AND HE TOUCHED MY MOUTH, AND SAID: BEHOLD THIS HAS TOUCHED THY LIPS, AND THY INIQUITIES SHALL BE TAKEN AWAY, AND THY SINS SHALL BE CLEANSED." — *Is. 6, 7*.

THE KING BURNS THE PROPHECIES OF JEREMIAS

"AND WHEN JUDI HAD READ THREE OR FOUR PAGES, HE CUT IT WITH THE PENKNIFE AND HE CAST IT INTO THE FIRE." — *Jer. 36, 23.*

MARTYRDOM OF A MOTHER AND HER SEVEN SONS

"BUT, I, LIKE MY BRETHREN, OFFER UP MY LIFE AND MY
BODY FOR THE LAWS OF OUR FATHERS." — *2 Mach. 7, 37.*

ADORATION OF THE MAGI

"AND FALLING DOWN THEY ADORED HIM. AND OPENING THEIR TREAS-
URES, THEY OFFERED HIM GIFTS: GOLD, FRANKINCENSE AND MYRRH."
— *Matt. 2, 11.*

CHRIST IS FOUND AMONGST THE DOCTORS

"THEY FOUND HIM IN THE TEMPLE, SITTING IN THE MIDST OF THE
DOCTORS, HEARING THEM AND ASKING THEM QUESTIONS."—*Luke 2, 46.*

MARRIAGE FEAST IN CANA

"JESUS SAITH TO THEM: FILL THE WATER POTS WITH WATER.
AND THEY FILLED THEM UP TO THE BRIM." — *John 2, 7.*

THE SERMON ON THE MOUNT

"AND SEEING THE MULTITUDES, HE WENT UP INTO A MOUNTAIN. AND
WHEN HE WAS SET DOWN, HIS DISCIPLES CAME UNTO HIM."—*Matt. 5, 1.*

THE CENTURION

"AND JESUS HEARING THIS, MARVELLED AND SAID TO THEM THAT FOLLOWED HIM: AMEN, I SAY TO YOU, I HAVE NOT FOUND SO GREAT FAITH IN ISRAEL." — *Matt. 8, 10.*

JESUS CALMS THE WATERS

"Then rising up he commanded the winds and the
sea; and there came a great calm." — *Matt. 8, 26.*

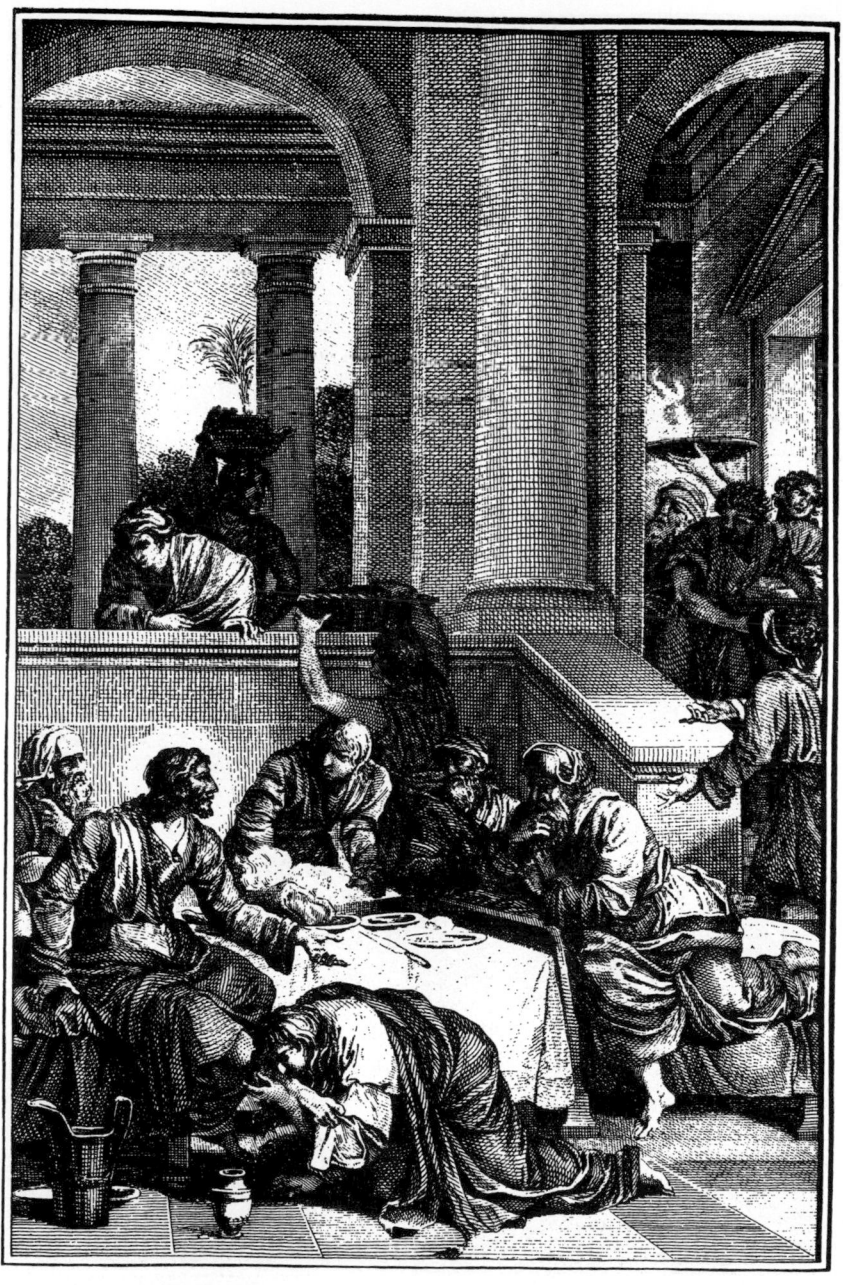

THE SINFUL WOMAN WASHES THE FEET OF JESUS

"SHE BEGAN TO WASH HIS FEET WITH TEARS AND WIPED THEM WITH
THE HAIRS OF HER HEAD AND KISSED HIS FEET AND ANOINTED THEM
WITH OINTMENT." — *Luke 7, 38.*

THE MIRACLE OF THE FIVE LOAVES

"AND JESUS TOOK THE LOAVES: AND WHEN HE HAD GIVEN THANKS, HE DISTRIBUTED TO THEM THAT WERE SET DOWN. IN LIKE MANNER ALSO OF THE FISHES, AS MUCH AS THEY WOULD." — *John 6, 11.*

THE TRANSFIGURATION

"AND BEHOLD THERE APPEARED TO THEM MOSES
AND ELIAS TALKING WITH HIM."—*Matt. 17, 3.*

THE LAST SUPPER

"AND HAVING TAKEN THE CHALICE, GIVING
THANKS, HE GAVE IT TO THEM." — *Mark 14, 23.*

THE CRUCIFIXION OF OUR LORD

"It is consummated." — *John 19, 30.*

Births & Baptisms

First Communions
& Confirmations

THE DESCENT OF THE HOLY GHOST

"AND THEY WERE ALL FILLED WITH THE HOLY GHOST." — *Acts 2, 4.*

THE RESURRECTION OF CHRIST

"FOR AN ANGEL OF THE LORD DESCENDED FROM HEAVEN AND COMING ROLLED BACK THE STONE AND SAT UPON IT."—*Matt. 28, 2.*

Marriages &
Holy Orders

Deaths

The
New Testament
Of Our Lord and Saviour
Jesus Christ

Translated from The Latin Vulgate, diligently
compared with the original Greek, and first
published by the English College at Rheims,
A.D. 1582.

With Annotations, References and an
Historical and Chronological Index.

THE NEW TESTAMENT

THE HOLY GOSPEL OF JESUS CHRIST

ACCORDING TO

ST. MATTHEW

ST. MATTHEW, *one of the twelve Apostles, who from being a publican, that is, a taxgatherer, was called by our Saviour to the Apostleship: in that profession his name was* LEVI (Luke 5, 27, Mark 2, 14). *He was the first of the Evangelists that wrote the Gospel, and that in Hebrew or Syro-Chaldaic which the Jews in Palestine spoke at that time. The original is not now extant; but, as it was translated in the time of the Apostles into Greek, that version was of equal authority. He wrote about six years after our Lord's Ascension.*

CHAPTER 1

The genealogy of Christ. He is conceived and born of a virgin.

THE book of the generation of Jesus Christ, the son of [1] David, the son of Abraham:

2 [2] Abraham begot Isaac. [3] And Isaac begot Jacob. [4] And Jacob begot Judas and his brethren.

3 [5] And Judas begot Phares and Zara of Thamar. [6] And Phares begot Esron. And Esron begot Aram.

4 And Aram begot Aminadab. [7] And Aminadab begot Naasson. And Naasson begot Salmon

5 And Salmon begot Booz of Rahab. [8] And Booz begot Obed of Ruth. And Obed begot Jesse.

6 [9] And Jesse begot David the king. [10] And David the king begot Solomon of her that had been *the wife* of Urias.

7 [11] And Solomon begot Roboam. [12] And Roboam begot Abia. [13] And Abia begot Asa.

8 And Asa begot Josaphat. And Josaphat begot Joram. And Joram begot Ozias.

9 [14] And Ozias begot Joatham. [15] And Joatham begot Achaz. [16] And Achaz begot Ezechias.

10 [17] And Ezechias begot Manasses. [18] And Manasses begot Amon. [19] And Amon begot Josias.

11 [20] And Josias begot Jechonias and his brethren in the transmigration of Babylon.

12 And after the transmigration of Babylon, Jechonias begot Salathiel. And Salathiel begot Zorobabel.

13 And Zorobabel begot Abiud. And Abiud begot Eliacim. And Eliacim begot Azor.

14 And Azor begot Sadoc. And Sadoc begot Achim. And Achim begot Eliud.

15 And Eliud begot Eleazar. And Eleazar begot Mathan. And Mathan begot Jacob.

16 And Jacob begot Joseph, the husband of Mary, of whom was born Jesus, who is called Christ.

17 So all the generations, from Abraham to David are fourteen generations. And from David to the transmigration of Babylon are fourteen generations: and from the transmigration of Babylon to Christ are fourteen generations.

18 Now the generation of Christ was in this wise. [21] When his mother Mary was espoused to Joseph, before they came together, she was found with child, of the Holy Ghost.

19 Whereupon Joseph her husband, being a just man and not willing publicly to expose her, was minded to put her away privately.

20 But while he thought on these things, behold the angel of the Lord appeared to him in his sleep, saying: Joseph, son of David, fear not to take unto thee Mary thy wife, for that which is conceived in her, is of the Holy Ghost.

21 And she shall bring forth a son: [22] and thou shalt call his name JESUS. For he shall save his people from their sins.

22 Now all this was done that it might be fulfilled which the Lord spoke by the prophet, saying:

23 [23] *Behold a virgin shall be with*

CHAP. 1. [1] Luke, 3, 31. [2] Gen. 21, 3. [3] Gen. 25, 25. [4] Gen. 29, 35. [5] Gen. 38, 29; 1 Par. 2, 4. [6] Ruth, 4, 18; 1 Par. 2, 5. [7] Num. 7, 12. [8] Ruth, 4, 21. [9] 2 Kings, 16, 1. [10] 2 Kings, 12, 24. [11] 3 Kings, 11, 43. [12] 3 Kings, 14, 31. [13] 3 Kings, 15, 8. [14] 2 Par. 26, 23. [15] 2 Par. 27, 9. [16] 2 Par. 28, 27. [17] 2 Par. 32, 33. [18] 2 Par. 33, 25. [19] 2 Par. 33, 25. [20] 2 Par. 36, 2. [21] Luke, 1, 27.

CHAP. 1. Ver. 16. *The husband of Mary.* The Evangelist gives us rather the pedigree of St. Joseph than that of the blessed Virgin, to conform to the custom of the Hebrews, who in their genealogies took no notice of women; but as they were near akin, the pedigree of the one sheweth that of the other.

child and bring forth a son: and they shall call his name EMMANUEL, which being interpreted is, God with us.

24 And Joseph rising up from sleep did as the angel of the Lord had commanded him and took unto him his wife.

25 And he knew her not till she brought forth her firstborn son: and he called his name JESUS.

CHAPTER 2

The offerings of the wise men. The flight into Egypt. The massacre of the Innocents.

WHEN ¹ Jesus therefore was born in Bethlehem of Juda, in the days of king Herod, behold, there came wise men from the east to Jerusalem,

2 Saying, Where is he that is born king of the Jews? For we have seen his star in the east, and are come to adore him.

3 And king Herod hearing this was troubled, and all Jerusalem with him.

4 And assembling together all the chief priests and the scribes of the people, he inquired of them where Christ should be born.

5 But they said to him: In Bethlehem of Juda. For so it is written by the prophet:

6 ² *And thou Bethlehem the land of Juda art not the least among the princes of Juda: for out of thee shall come forth the captain that shall rule my people Israel.*

7 Then Herod, privately calling the wise men, learned diligently of them the time of the star which appeared to them.

8 And sending them into Bethlehem, said: Go and diligently inquire after the child, and when you have found him, bring me word again, that I also may come and adore him.

9 Who having heard the king went their way; and behold the star which they had seen in the east went before them until it came and stood over where the child was.

10 And seeing the star they rejoiced with exceeding great joy.

11 And entering into the house, they found the child with Mary his mother. And falling down they adored him. ³ And opening their treasures, they offered him gifts: gold, frankincense, and myrrh.

12 And having received an answer in sleep that they should not return to Herod, they went back another way into their country.

13 And after they were departed, behold an angel of the Lord appeared in sleep to Joseph, saying: Arise, and take the child and his mother and fly into

Egypt: and be there until I shall tell thee. For it will come to pass that Herod will seek the child to destroy him.

14 Who arose and took the child and his mother by night and retired into Egypt. And he was there until the death of Herod:

15 That it might be fulfilled which the Lord spoke by the prophet, saying: ⁴ *Out of Egypt have I called my son.*

16 Then Herod, perceiving that he was deluded by the wise men, was exceeding angry; and sending killed all the men children that were in Bethlehem and in all the borders thereof, from two years old and under, according to the time which he had diligently inquired of the wise men.

17 Then was fulfilled that which was spoken by Jeremias the prophet, saying:

18 ⁵ *A voice in Rama was heard, lamentation and great mourning; Rachel bewailing her children and would not be comforted, because they are not.*

19 But when Herod was dead, behold an angel of the Lord appeared in sleep to Joseph in Egypt,

20 Saying: Arise, and take the child and his mother and go into the land of Israel. For they are dead that sought the life of the child.

21 Who arose and took the child and his mother and came into the land of Israel.

22 But hearing that Archelaus reigned in Judea in the room of Herod his father, he was afraid to go thither: and being warned in sleep retired into the quarters of Galilee.

23 And coming he dwelt in a city called Nazareth: that it might be ful-

²² Luke, 1, 31; Acts, 4, 12. ²³ Isai. 7, 14. CHAP. 2. ¹ Luke, 2, 7. ² Mich. 5, 2; John, 7, 42. ³ Ps. 71, 10. ⁴ Osee, 11, 1. ⁵ Jer. 31, 15.

Ver. 25. *Till she brought forth her firstborn son.* From these words Helvidius and other heretics most impiously inferred that the blessed Virgin Mary had other children besides Christ: but St. Jerome shews, by divers examples, that this expression of the Evangelist was a manner of speaking usual among the Hebrews, to denote by the word *until*, only what is done, without any regard to the future. Thus it is said (Gen. 8, 6, 7) that *Noe sent forth a raven, which went forth and did not return* till *the waters were dried up on the earth.* That is, did not return any more. Also (Isai. 46, 4) God says: *I am* till *you grow old.* Who dare infer that God should then *cease to be?* Also in the first book of Machabees (5, 54), *And they went up to mount Sion with joy and gladness and offered holocausts, because not one of them was slain till they had returned in peace.* That is, not one was slain before or after they had returned.—God saith to his divine Son: *Sit on my right hand* till *I make thy enemies thy footstool.* Shall he sit no longer after his enemies are subdued? Yea and for all eternity. St Jerome also proves by Scripture examples that an *only begotten* son was also called firstborn, or *first begotten:* because according to the law, the *firstborn* males were to be consecrated to God: *Sanctify unto me,* saith the Lord, *every firstborn that openeth the womb among the children of Israel* (Exod. 13, 2).

filled which was said by the prophets: That he shall be called a Nazarene.

CHAPTER 3
The preaching of John. Christ is baptized.

AND in those days cometh John the Baptist preaching in the desert of Judea.

2 And saying: [1] Do penance: for the kingdom of heaven is at hand.

3 For this is he that was spoken of by Isaias the prophet, saying: [2] *A voice of one crying in the desert: Prepare ye the way of the Lord, make straight his paths.*

4 And the same John had his garment of camels' hair and a leathern girdle about his loins: and his meat was locusts and wild honey.

5 [3] Then went out to him Jerusalem and all Judea and all the country about Jordan:

6 And were baptized by him in the Jordan, confessing their sins.

7 And seeing many of the Pharisees and Sadducees [4] coming to his baptism, he said to them: Ye brood of vipers, who hath shewed you to flee from the wrath to come?

8 Bring forth therefore fruit worthy of penance.

9 And think not to say within yourselves: [5] We have Abraham for our father. For I tell you that God is able of these stones to raise up children to Abraham.

10 For now the axe is laid to the root of the trees. Every tree therefore that doth not yield good fruit shall be cut down and cast into the fire.

11 [6] I indeed baptize you in water unto penance: but he that shall come after me is mightier than I, whose shoes I am not worthy to bear. He shall baptize you in the Holy Ghost and fire.

12 Whose fan is in his hand: and he will thoroughly cleanse his floor and gather his wheat into the barn. But the

chaff he will burn with unquenchable fire.

13 [7] Then cometh Jesus from Galilee to the Jordan, unto John, to be baptized by him.

14 But John stayed him, saying: I ought to be baptized by thee, and comest thou to me?

15 And Jesus answering, said to him: Suffer it to be so now. For so it becometh us to fulfil all justice. Then he suffered him.

16 And Jesus being baptized, forthwith came out of the water: and lo, the heavens were opened to him: and he saw the [8] Spirit of God descending as a dove and coming upon him.

17 [9] And behold a voice from heaven, saying: This is my beloved Son, in whom I am well pleased.

CHAPTER 4
Christ's fast of forty days. He is tempted. He begins to preach, to call disciples to him and to work miracles.

THEN [1] Jesus was led by the spirit into the desert to be tempted by the devil.

2 And when he had fasted forty days and forty nights, afterwards he was hungry.

3 And the tempter coming said to him: If thou be the Son of God, command that these stones be made bread.

4 Who answered and said: It is written, [2] *Not in bread alone doth man live, but in every word that proceedeth from the mouth of God.*

5 Then the devil took him up into the holy city and set him upon the pinnacle of the temple,

6 And said to him: If thou be the Son of God, cast thyself down, for it is written: [3] *That he hath given his angels charge over thee, and in their hands shall they bear thee up, lest perhaps thou dash thy foot against a stone.*

7 Jesus said to him: It is written again: [4] *Thou shalt not tempt the Lord thy God.*

8 Again the devil took him up into a very high mountain and shewed him all the kingdoms of the world and the glory of them,

9 And said to him: All these will I give thee, if falling down thou wilt adore me.

10 Then Jesus saith to him: Begone, Satan! For it is written: [5] *The Lord thy God shalt thou adore, and him only shalt thou serve.*

11 Then the devil left him. And behold angels came and ministered to him.

12 And when Jesus had heard that John was delivered up, [6] he retired into Galilee.

13 And leaving the city Nazareth, he came and dwelt in Capharnaum, on

CHAP. 3. [1] Mark, 1, 4; Luke, 3, 3. [2] Isai. 40, 3; Mark, 1, 3; Luke, 3, 4. [3] Mark, 1, 5. [4] Luke, 3, 7. [5] John, 8, 39. [6] Mark, 1, 8; Luke, 3, 16; John, 1, 26; Acts, 1, 5. [7] Mark, 1, 9. [8] Luke, 3, 22 [9] Mark, 1, 26; Luke, 9, 35; 2 Peter, 1, 17. CHAP. 4. [1] Luke, 4, 1. [2] Deut. 8, 3; Luke, 4, 4. [3] Ps. 90, 11. [4] Deut. 6, 16. [5] Deut. 6, 13. [6] Mark, 1, 14; Luke, 4, 14; John, 4, 43.

CHAP. 3. Ver. 2. *Do penance. Pœnitentiam agite,* μετανοεῖτε. which word, according to the use of the scriptures and the holy fathers, does not only signify repentance and amendment of life, but also punishing past sins by fasting and such like penitential exercises.

Ver. 7. *Pharisees and Sadducees.* These were two sects among the Jews: of which the former were for the most part notorious hypocrites; the latter, a kind of freethinkers in matters of religion.

CHAP. 4. Ver. 8. *Shewed him.* That is, pointed out to him where each kingdom lay; and set forth in words what was most glorious and admirable in each of them. Or also, set before his eyes, as it were in a large map, a lively representation of all those kingdoms.

the sea coast, in the borders of Zabulon and of Nephthalim;

14 That it might be fulfilled which was said by Isaias the prophet:

15 [7] Land of Zabulon and land of Nephthalim, the way of the sea beyond the Jordan, Galilee of the Gentiles:

16 The people that sat in darkness hath seen great light: and to them that sat in the region of the shadow of death, light is sprung up.

17 [8] From that time Jesus began to preach and to say: Do penance, for the kingdom of heaven is at hand.

18 And Jesus walking by the sea of Galilee, [9] saw two brethren, Simon who is called Peter and Andrew his brother, casting a net into the sea (for they were fishers).

19 And he saith to them: Come ye after me, and I will make you to be fishers of men.

20 And they immediately leaving their nets, followed him.

21 And going on from thence, he saw two brethren, James the son of Zebedee and John his brother, in a ship with Zebedee their father, mending their nets: and he called them

22 And they forthwith left their nets and father and followed him.

23 And Jesus went about all Galilee, teaching in their synagogues and preaching the gospel of the kingdom and healing all manner of sickness and every infirmity among the people.

24 And his fame went throughout all Syria: and they presented to him all sick people that were taken with divers diseases and torments and such as were possessed by devils and lunatics and those that had the palsy: and he cured them.

25 [10] And much people followed him from Galilee and from Decapolis and from Jerusalem and from Judea and from beyond the Jordan.

CHAPTER 5

Christ's sermon upon the mount. The eight beatitudes.

AND seeing the multitudes, he went up into a mountain. And when he was set down, his disciples came unto him.

2 And opening his mouth, he taught them, saying:

3 [1] Blessed are the poor in spirit: for theirs is the kingdom of heaven.

4 [2] Blessed are the meek: for they shall possess the land.

5 [3] Blessed are they that mourn: for they shall be comforted.

6 Blessed are they that hunger and thirst after justice: for they shall have their fill.

7 Blessed are the merciful: for they shall obtain mercy.

8 [4] Blessed are the clean of heart: for they shall see God.

9 Blessed are the peacemakers: for they shall be called the children of God.

10 [5] Blessed are they that suffer persecution for justice' sake: for theirs is the kingdom of heaven.

11 Blessed are ye when they shall revile you and persecute you and speak all that is evil against you, untruly, for my sake:

12 Be glad and rejoice, for your reward is very great in heaven. For so they persecuted the prophets that were before you.

13 You are the salt of the earth. [6] But if the salt lose its savour, wherewith shall it be salted? It is good for nothing any more but to be cast out and to be trodden on by men.

14 You are the light of the world. A city seated on a mountain cannot be hid.

15 [7] Neither do men light a candle and put it under a bushel, but upon a candlestick, that it may shine to all that are in the house.

16 So let your light shine before men [8] that they may see your good works and glorify your Father who is in heaven.

17 Do not think that I am come to destroy the law or the prophets. I am not come to destroy, but to fulfil.

18 [9] For amen I say unto you, till heaven and earth pass, one jot or one tittle shall not pass of the law, till all be fulfilled.

19 [10] He therefore that shall break one of these least commandments and shall so teach men shall be called the least in the kingdom of heaven. But he that shall do and teach, he shall be called great in the kingdom of heaven.

20 For I tell you, that unless your justice abound [11] more than that of the scribes and Pharisees, you shall not enter into the kingdom of heaven.

21 You have heard that it was said

[7] Isai, 9, 1.   [8] Mark, 1, 15.   [9] Mark, 1, 16; Luke, 5, 2.   [10] Mark, 3, 7; Luke, 6, 17.   CHAP. 5. [1] Luke, 6, 20.   [2] Ps. 36, 11.   [3] Isai. 61, 2.   [4] Ps. 23, 4. [5] 1 Peter, 2, 20; 3, 14; 4, 14.   [6] Mark, 9, 49; Luke, 14, 34.   [7] Mark, 4, 21; Luke, 8, 16; 11, 33.   [8] 1 Peter, 2, 12.   [9] Luke, 16, 17.   [10] James, 2, 10.   [11] Luke, 11, 39.   [12] Exod. 20, 13; Deut. 5, 17.

CHAP. 5. Ver. 3. The poor in spirit. That is, the humble and they whose spirit is not set upon riches.
Ver. 17. To fulfil. By accomplishing all the figures and prophecies; and perfecting all that was imperfect.
Ver. 18. Amen. That is, assuredly of a truth. This Hebrew word, Amen, is here retained by the example and authority of all the four Evangelists. It is used by our Lord as a strong asseveration and affirmation of the truth.
Ver. 20. The scribes and Pharisees. The scribes were the doctors of the law of Moses: the Pharisees were a precise set of men, making profession of a more exact observance of the law and upon that account greatly esteemed among the people.

to them of old: [12] Thou shalt not kill. And whosoever shall kill shall be in danger of the judgment.

22 But I say to you that whosoever is angry with his brother shall be in danger of the judgment. And whosoever shall say to his brother, Raca, shall be in danger of the council. And whosoever shall say, Thou fool, shall be in danger of hell fire.

23 If therefore thou offer thy gift at the altar, and there thou remember that thy brother hath any thing against thee;

24 Leave there thy offering before the altar and go first to be reconciled to thy brother: and then coming thou shalt offer thy gift.

25 [13] Be at agreement with thy adversary betimes, whilst thou art in the way with him: lest perhaps the adversary deliver thee to the judge, and the judge deliver thee to the officer, and thou be cast into prison.

26 Amen I say to thee, thou shalt not go out from thence till thou repay the last farthing.

27 You have heard that it was said to them of old: [14] Thou shalt not commit adultery.

28 But I say to you that whosoever shall look on a woman to lust after her

[13] Luke, 12, 58. [14] Exod. 20, 14. [15] Mark, 9, 46; Matt. 18, 9. [16] Deut. 24, 1; Matt. 19, 7. [17] Mark, 10, 11; Luke, 16, 18; 1 Cor. 7, 10. [18] Exod. 20, 7; Lev. 19, 12; Deut. 5, 11; James, 5, 12. [19] James, 5, 12. [20] Exod. 21, 24; Lev. 24, 20; Deut. 19, 21. [21] Luke, 6, 29. [22] 1 Cor. 6, 7. [23] Deut. 15, 8. [24] Lev. 19, 18. [25] Luke, 6, 27. [26] Rom. 12, 20. [27] Luke, 23, 34; Acts, 7, 59.

Ver. 21. *Shall be in danger of the judgment.* That is, shall deserve to be punished by that lesser tribunal among the Jews, called the *Judgment,* which took cognizance of such crimes.

Ver. 22. *Raca.* A word expressing great indignation or contempt.—*Shall be in danger of the council.* That is, shall deserve to be punished by the highest court of judicature, called the *Council,* or *Sanhedrim,* consisting of seventy-two persons, where the highest causes were tried and judged, which was at Jerusalem.—*Thou fool.* This was then looked upon as a heinous injury, when uttered with contempt, spite or malice: and therefore is here so severely condemned.— *Shall be in danger of hell fire.* Literally, according to the Greek, shall deserve to be cast into the *Gehenna of fire.* Which words our Saviour made use of to express the fire and punishments of hell.

Ver. 29. *Scandalize thee.* That is, if it be a stumbling-block, or occasion of sin to thee. By which we are taught to fly the immediate occasions of sin, though they be as dear to us or as necessary as a hand or an eye.

Ver. 34. *Not to swear at all.* It is not forbid to swear in truth, justice and judgment; to the honour of God, or our own or neighbour's just defence: but only to swear rashly, or profanely, in common discourse and without necessity.

Ver. 39. *Not to resist evil.* What is here commanded is a Christian patience under injuries and affronts and to be willing even to suffer still more rather than to indulge the desire of revenge: but what is further added does not strictly oblige according to the letter, for neither did Christ nor St. Paul turn the other cheek (St. John 18, and Acts 23.

Ver. 46. *The publicans.* These were the gatherers of the public taxes: a set of men, odious and infamous among the Jews, for their extortions and injustice.

hath already committed adultery with her in his heart.

29 [15] And if thy right eye scandalize thee, pluck it out and cast it from thee. For it is expedient for thee that one of thy members should perish, rather than that thy whole body be cast into hell.

30 And if thy right hand scandalize thee, cut it off and cast it from thee. For it is expedient for thee that one of thy members should perish, rather than that thy whole body go into hell.

31 And it hath been said, [16] Whosoever shall put away his wife, let him give her a bill of divorce.

32 But I say to you [17] that whosoever shall put away his wife, excepting for the cause of fornication, maketh her to commit adultery: and he that shall marry her that is put away committeth adultery.

33 Again you have heard that it was said to them of old, [18] Thou shalt not forswear thyself: but thou shalt perform thy oaths to the Lord.

34 But I say to you not to swear at all: neither by heaven, for it is the throne of God:

35 Nor by the earth, for it is his footstool: nor by Jerusalem, for it is the city of the great king.

36 Neither shalt thou swear by thy head, because thou canst not make one hair white or black.

37 [19] But let your speech be: Yea, Yea: No, No. And that which is over and above these is of evil.

38 You have heard that it hath been said: [20] An eye for an eye, and a tooth for a tooth.

39 But I say to you not to resist evil: [21] but if one strike thee on thy right cheek, turn to him also the other:

40 [22] And if a man will contend with thee in judgment and take away thy coat, let go thy cloak also unto him.

41 And whosoever will force thee one mile, go with him other two.

42 [23] Give to him that asketh of thee: and from him that would borrow of thee turn not away.

43 You have heard that it hath been said: [24] Thou shalt love thy neighbour and hate thy enemy.

44 But I say to you: [25] Love your enemies: [26] do good to them that hate you: [27] and pray for them that persecute and calumniate you:

45 That you may be the children of your Father who is in heaven, who maketh his sun to rise upon the good and bad and raineth upon the just and the unjust.

46 For if you love them that love you, what reward shall you have? Do not even the publicans this?

47 And if you salute your brethren only, what do you more? Do not also the heathens this?

48 Be you therefore perfect, as also your heavenly Father is perfect.

CHAPTER 6

A continuation of the sermon on the mount.

TAKE heed that you do not your justice before men, to be seen by them: otherwise you shall not have reward of your Father who is in heaven.

2 Therefore when thou dost an almsdeed, sound not a trumpet before thee, as the hypocrites do in the synagogues and in the streets, that they may be honoured by men: Amen I say to you, they have received their reward.

3 And when thou dost alms, let not thy left hand know what thy right hand doth.

4 That thy alms may be in secret: and thy Father who seeth in secret will repay thee.

5 And when ye pray, ye shall not be as the hypocrites that love to stand and pray in the synagogues and corners of the streets, that they may be seen by men: Amen I say to you, they have received their reward.

6 But thou when thou shalt pray, enter into thy chamber and, having shut the door, pray to thy Father in secret: and thy Father who seeth in secret will repay thee.

7 And when you are praying, speak not much, as the heathens. For they think that in their much speaking they may be heard.

8 Be not you therefore like to them: for your Father knoweth what is needful for you, before you ask him.

9 Thus therefore shall you pray: [1] Our Father who art in heaven. Hallowed be thy name.

10 Thy kingdom come. Thy will be done on earth as it is in heaven.

11 Give us this day our supersubstantial bread.

12 And forgive us our debts, as we forgive our debtors.

13 And lead us not into temptation. But deliver us from evil. Amen.

14 [2] For if you will forgive men their offences, your heavenly Father will forgive you also your offences.

15 But if you will not forgive men, neither will your Father forgive you your offences.

16 And when you fast, be not as the hypocrites, sad. For they disfigure their faces, that they may appear unto men to fast. Amen I say to you, they have received their reward.

17 But thou, when thou fastest anoint thy head, and wash thy face:

18 That thou appear not to men to fast, but to thy Father who is in secret. And thy Father who seeth in secret will repay thee.

19 Lay not up to yourselves treasures on earth: where the rust and moth consume and where thieves break through and steal.

20 [3] But lay up to yourselves treasures in heaven: where neither the rust nor moth doth consume, and where thieves do not break through nor steal.

21 For where thy treasure is, there is thy heart also.

22 [4] The light of thy body is thy eye. If thy eye be single, thy whole body shall be lightsome.

23 But if thy eye be evil, thy whole body shall be darksome. If then the light that is in thee be darkness: the darkness itself how great shall it be!

24 [5] No man can serve two masters. For either he will hate the one and love the other: or he will sustain the one and despise the other. You cannot serve God and mammon.

25 [6] Therefore I say to you, be not solicitous for your life, what you shall eat, nor for your body, what you shall put on. Is not the life more than the meat and the body more than the raiment?

26 Behold the birds of the air, for they neither sow, nor do they reap nor gather into barns: and your heavenly Father feedeth them. Are not you of much more value than they?

27 And which of you by taking thought can add to his stature one cubit?

28 And for raiment why are you solicitous? Consider the lilies of the field, how they grow: they labour not, neither do they spin.

29 But I say to you that not even Solomon in all his glory was arrayed as one of these.

30 And if the grass of the field, which is to-day and to-morrow is cast into the oven, God doth so clothe: how much more you, O ye of little faith?

31 Be not solicitous therefore, say-

CHAP. 6. [1] Luke, 11, 2. [2] Ecclus. 28, 3, 4, 5; Matt. 18, 35; Mark, 11, 25. [3] Luke, 12, 33; 1 Tim. 6, 19. [4] Luke, 11, 34. [5] Luke, 16, 13. [6] Ps. 54, 23; Luke, 12, 22; Phil. 4, 6; 1 Tim. 6, 7; 1 Peter, 5, 7.

CHAP. 6. Ver. 1. *Your justice,* that is, *works of justice;* fasting, prayer, and almsdeeds; which ought to be performed not out of ostentation or a view to please men, but solely to please God. Ver. 11. *Supersubstantial bread.* In St. Luke the same word is rendered *daily bread.* It is understood of the Bread of Life, which we receive in the Blessed Sacrament. Ver. 13. *Lead us not into temptation.* That is, suffer us not to be overcome by temptation. Ver. 24. *Mammon.* That is, riches, worldly interest.

ing, What shall we eat: or, What shall we drink: or, Wherewith shall we be clothed?

32 For after all these things do the heathens seek. For your Father knoweth that you have need of all these things.

33 Seek ye therefore first the kingdom of God and his justice: and all these things shall be added unto you.

34 Be not therefore solicitous for tomorrow: for the morrow will be solicitous for itself. Sufficient for the day is the evil thereof.

CHAPTER 7

The third part of the sermon on the mount.

JUDGE [1] not, that you may not be judged.

2 For with what judgment you judge, you shall be judged: [2] and with what measure you mete, it shall be measured to you again.

3 And why seest thou the mote that is in thy brother's eye; and seest not the beam that is in thy own eye?

4 Or how sayest thou to thy brother: Let me cast the mote out of thy eye; and behold a beam is in thy own eye?

5 Thou hypocrite, cast out first the beam out of thy own eye: and then shalt thou see to cast out the mote out of thy brother's eye.

6 Give not that which is holy to dogs. Neither cast ye your pearls before swine: lest perhaps they trample them under their feet: and turning upon you, they tear you.

7 [3] Ask, and it shall be given you: seek, and you shall find: knock, and it shall be opened to you.

8 For every one that asketh, receiveth: and he that seeketh, findeth: and to him that knocketh, it shall be opened.

9 [4] Or what man is there among you, of whom if his son shall ask bread, will he reach him a stone?

10 Or if he shall ask him a fish, will he reach him a serpent?

11 If you then being evil, know how to give good gifts to your children: how much more will your Father who is in heaven give good things to them that ask him?

12 [5] All things therefore whatsoever you would that men should do to you, do you also to them. For this is the law and the prophets.

13 [6] Enter ye in at the narrow gate:

for wide is the gate and broad is the way that leadeth to destruction: and many there are who go in thereat.

14 How narrow is the gate and strait is the way that leadeth to life: and few there are that find it!

15 Beware of false prophets, who come to you in the clothing of sheep, but inwardly they are ravening wolves.

16 By their fruits you shall know them. Do men gather grapes of thorns, or figs of thistles?

17 Even so every good tree bringeth forth good fruit: and the evil tree bringeth forth evil fruit.

18 A good tree cannot bring forth evil fruit: neither can an evil tree bring forth good fruit.

19 [7] Every tree that bringeth not forth good fruit shall be cut down and shall be cast into the fire.

20 Wherefore by their fruits you shall know them.

21 [8] Not every one that saith to me, Lord, Lord, shall enter into the kingdom of heaven: but he that doth the will of my Father who is in heaven, he shall enter into the kingdom of heaven.

22 Many will say to me in that day: Lord, Lord, have not we prophesied in thy name [9] and cast out devils in thy name and done many miracles in thy name?

23 And then will I profess unto them: I never knew you. [10] Depart from me, you that work iniquity.

24 [11] Every one therefore that heareth these my words and doth them shall be likened to a wise man that built his house upon a rock.

25 And the rain fell and the floods came and the winds blew: and they beat upon that house. And it fell not, for it was founded on a rock.

26 And every one that heareth these my words and doth them not shall be like a foolish man that built his house upon the sand.

27 And the rain fell and the floods came and the winds blew: and they beat upon that house. And it fell: and great was the fall thereof.

28 And it came to pass when Jesus had fully ended these words, the people were in admiration at his doctrine.

29 [12] For he was teaching them as one having power: and not as the scribes and Pharisees.

CHAPTER 8

Christ cleanses the leper, heals the centurion's servant, Peter's mother-in-law, and many others. He stills the storm at sea, drives the devils out of two men possessed and suffers them to go into the swine.

CHAP. 7. [1] Luke, 6, 37; Rom. 2, 1. [2] Mark, 4, 24. [3] Matt. 21, 22; Mark, 11, 24; Luke, 11, 9; John, 14, 13; James, 1, 6. [4] Luke, 11, 11. [5] Tob. 4, 16; Luke, 6, 31. [6] Luke, 13, 24. [7] Matt. 3, 10. [8] Matt. 25, 11; Luke, 6, 46. [9] Acts, 19, 13. [10] Ps. 6, 9; Matt. 25, 41; Luke, 13, 27. [11] Luke, 6, 48; Rom. 2, 13; James, 1, 22. [12] Mark, 1, 22; Luke, 4, 32.

AND when he was come down from the mountain, great multitudes followed him.

2 [1] And behold a leper came and adored him, saying: Lord, if thou wilt, thou canst make me clean.

3 And Jesus stretching forth his hand, touched him, saying: I will. Be thou made clean. And forthwith his leprosy was cleansed.

4 And Jesus saith to him: See thou tell no man: but go, [2] shew thyself to the priest and offer the gift which Moses commanded for a testimony unto them.

5 [3] And when he had entered into Capharnaum, there came to him a centurion, beseeching him,

6 And saying: Lord, my servant lieth at home sick of the palsy and is grievously tormented.

7 And Jesus saith to him: I will come and heal him.

8 And the centurion making answer, said: [4] Lord, I am not worthy that thou shouldst enter under my roof: but only say the word and my servant shall be healed.

9 For I also am a man subject to authority, having under me soldiers; and I say to this, Go, and he goeth, and to another, Come, and he cometh, and to my servant, Do this, and he doeth it.

10 And Jesus hearing this, marvelled and said to them that followed him: Amen I say to you, I have not found so great faith in Israel.

11 And I say to you that many shall come from the [5] east and the west, and shall sit down with Abraham and Isaac and Jacob in the kingdom of heaven;

12 But the children of the kingdom shall be cast out into the exterior darkness. There, shall be weeping and gnashing of teeth.

13 And Jesus said to the centurion: Go, and as thou hast believed so be it done to thee. And the servant was healed at the same hour.

14 And when Jesus was come into Peter's house, he saw his wife's mother lying and sick of a fever.

15 And he touched her hand, and the fever left her: and she arose and ministered to them.

16 [6] And when evening was come, they brought to him many that were possessed with devils: and he cast out the spirits with his word: and all that were sick he healed:

17 That it might be fulfilled, which was spoken by the prophet [7] Isaias, saying: He took our infirmities and bore our diseases.

18 And Jesus seeing great multitudes about him, gave orders to pass over the water.

19 And a certain scribe came and said to him: Master, I will follow thee whithersoever thou shalt go.

20 And Jesus saith to him: [8] The foxes have holes and the birds of the air nests: but the son of man hath not where to lay his head.

21 And another of his disciples said to him: Lord, suffer me first to go and bury my father.

22 But Jesus said to him: Follow me, and let the dead bury their dead.

23 [9] And when he entered into the boat, his disciples followed him.

24 And behold a great tempest arose in the sea, so that the boat was covered with waves but he was asleep.

25 And they came to him and awaked him, saying: Lord, save us, we perish.

26 And Jesus saith to them: Why are you fearful, O ye of little faith? Then rising up he commanded the winds and the sea: and there came a great calm.

27 But the men wondered, saying: What manner of man is this, for the winds and the sea obey him?

28 [10] And when he was come on the other side of the water, into the country of the Gerasenes, there met him two that were possessed with devils, coming out of the sepulchres, exceeding fierce, so that none could pass by that way.

29 And behold they cried out, saying: What have we to do with thee, Jesus Son of God? Art thou come hither to torment us before the time?

30 [11] And there was, not far from them, an herd of many swine feeding.

31 And the devils besought him, saying: If thou cast us out hence, send us into the herd of swine.

32 And he said to them: Go. But they going out went into the swine: and behold the whole herd ran violently down a steep place into the sea: and they perished in the waters.

33 And they that kept them fled: and coming into the city, told every thing and concerning them that had been possessed by the devils.

34 And behold the whole city went out to meet Jesus: [12] and when they saw him, they besought him that he would depart from their coasts.

CHAP. 8. [1] Mark, 1, 40; Luke, 5, 12. [2] Lev. 14, 2. [3] Luke, 7, 1. [4] Luke, 7, 6. [5] Mal. 1, 11. [6] Mark, 1, 32. [7] Isai. 53, 4; 1 Peter, 2, 24. [8] Luke, 9, 58. [9] Mark, 4, 36; Luke, 8, 22. [10] Mark, 5, 1; Luke, 8, 26. [11] Mark, 5, 11; Luke, 8, 32. [12] Mark, 5, 17; Luke, 8, 37.

CHAPTER 9

Christ heals one sick of the palsy, calls Matthew, cures the issue of blood, raises to life the daughter of Jairus, gives sight to two blind men and heals a dumb man possessed by the devil.

AND entering into a boat, he passed over the water and came into his own city.

2 ¹ And behold they brought to him one sick of the palsy lying in a bed. And Jesus, seeing their faith, said to the man sick of the palsy: Be of good heart, son. Thy sins are forgiven thee.

3 And behold some of the scribes said within themselves: He blasphemeth.

4 And Jesus seeing their thoughts, said: Why do you think evil in your hearts?

5 Whether is easier, to say, Thy sins are forgiven thee: or to say, Arise, and walk?

6 But that you may know that the Son of man hath power on earth to forgive sins, (then said he to the man sick of the palsy): Arise, take up thy bed and go into thy house.

7 And he arose and went into his house.

8 And the multitude seeing it, feared, and glorified God that gave such power to men.

9 ² And when Jesus passed on from thence, he saw a man sitting in the custom house, named Matthew; and he saith to him: Follow me. And he arose up and followed him.

10 And it came to pass as he was sitting at meat in the house, behold many publicans and sinners came and sat down with Jesus and his disciples.

11 And the Pharisees seeing it, said to his disciples: Why doth your master eat with publicans and sinners?

12 But Jesus hearing it, said: They that are in health need not a physician, but they that are ill.

13 Go then and learn what this meaneth, ³ *I will have mercy and not sacrifice.* For I am not come to call the just, ⁴ but sinners.

14 Then came to him the disciples of John, saying: ⁵ Why do we and the Pharisees fast often, but thy disciples do not fast?

15 And Jesus said to them: Can the children of the bridegroom mourn, as long as the bridegroom is with them? But the days will come when the bride-groom shall be taken away from them: and then they shall fast.

16 And nobody putteth a piece of raw cloth unto an old garment. For it taketh away the fulness thereof from the garment: and there is made a greater rent.

17 Neither do they put new wine into old bottles. Otherwise the bottles break and the wine runneth out and the bottles perish. But new wine they put into new bottles: and both are preserved.

18 ⁶ As he was speaking these things unto them, behold a certain ruler came and adored him, saying: Lord, my daughter is even now dead; but come, lay thy hand upon her and she shall live.

19 And Jesus rising up followed him, with his disciples.

20 ⁷ And behold a woman who was troubled with an issue of blood twelve years came behind him and touched the hem of his garment.

21 For she said within herself: If I shall touch only his garment, I shall be healed.

22 But Jesus turning and seeing her, said: Be of good heart, daughter. Thy faith hath made thee whole. And the woman was made whole from that hour.

23 And when Jesus was come into the house of the ruler and saw the minstrels and the multitude making a rout,

24 He said: Give place: for the girl is not dead, but sleepeth. And they laughed him to scorn.

25 And when the multitude was put forth, he went in and took her by the hand. And the maid arose.

26 And the fame hereof went abroad into all that country.

27 And as Jesus passed from thence, there followed him two blind men crying out and saying, Have mercy on us, O Son of David.

28 And when he was come to the house, the blind men came to him. And Jesus saith to them: Do you believe, that I can do this unto you? They say to him: Yea, Lord.

29 Then he touched their eyes, saying: According to your faith, be it done unto you.

30 And their eyes were opened. And Jesus strictly charged them, saying: See that no man know this.

31 But they going out, spread his fame abroad in all that country.

32 And when they were gone out, ⁸ behold they brought him a dumb man, possessed with a devil.

33 And after the devil was cast out the dumb man spoke. And the multi-

CHAP. 9. ¹ Mark, 2, 3; Luke, 5, 18. ² Mark, 2, 14; Luke, 5, 27. ³ Osee, 6, 6; Matt. 12, 7. ⁴ 1 Tim. 1, 15. ⁵ Mark, 2, 18; Luke, 5, 33. ⁶ Mark, 5, 23; Luke, 8, 41. ⁷ Mark, 5, 25; Luke, 8, 43. ⁸ Matt. 12, 22; Luke, 11, 14.

CHAP. 9. Ver. 15. *Can the children of the bridegroom.* That, by a Hebraism, signifies the *friends* or *companions* of the bridegroom.

tudes wondered, saying: Never was the like seen in Israel.

34 But the Pharisees said: By the prince of devils he casteth out devils.

35 [9] And Jesus went about all the cities, and towns, teaching in their synagogues, and preaching the gospel of the kingdom and healing every disease and every infirmity.

36 And seeing the multitudes, he had compassion on them: because they were distressed and lying like sheep that have no shepherd.

37 Then he saith to his disciples: [10] The harvest indeed is great, but the labourers are few.

38 Pray ye therefore the Lord of the harvest, that he send forth labourers into his harvest.

CHAPTER 10

Christ sends out his twelve apostles, with the power of miracles. The lessons he gives them.

AND [1] having called his twelve disciples together, he gave them power over unclean spirits, to cast them out and to heal all manner of diseases and all manner of infirmities.

2 And the names of the twelve apostles are these: The first, Simon who is called Peter, and Andrew his brother.

3 James the son of Zebedee and John his brother, Philip and Bartholomew, Thomas and Matthew the publican, and James *the son* of Alpheus, and Thaddeus,

4 Simon the Cananean, and Judas Iscariot, who also betrayed him.

5 These twelve Jesus sent, commanding them, saying: Go ye not into the way of the Gentiles and into the city of the Samaritans enter ye not.

6 But go ye rather [2] to the lost sheep of the house of Israel.

7 And going, preach, saying: The kingdom of heaven is at hand.

8 Heal the sick, raise the dead, cleanse the lepers, cast out devils. Freely have you received: freely give.

9 [3] Do not possess gold, nor silver, nor money in your purses,

10 Nor scrip for your journey, nor two coats, nor shoes, nor a staff. For the workman is worthy of his meat.

11 And into whatsoever city or town you shall enter, inquire who in it is worthy: and there abide till you go thence.

12 And when you come into the house, salute it, saying: Peace be to this house.

13 And if that house be worthy, your peace shall come upon it. But if it be not worthy, your peace shall return to you.

14 And whosoever shall not receive you, nor hear your words: going forth out of that house or city shake off the dust from your feet.

15 Amen I say to you, it shall be more tolerable for the land of Sodom and Gomorrha in the day of judgment than for that city.

16 [4] Behold I send you as sheep in the midst of wolves. Be ye therefore wise as serpents and simple as doves.

17 But beware of men. For they will deliver you up in councils and they will scourge you in their synagogues.

18 And you shall be brought before governors and before kings for my sake, for a testimony to them and to the Gentiles.

19 But when they shall deliver you up, [5] take no thought how or what to speak: for it shall be given you in that hour what to speak.

20 For it is not you that speak, but the Spirit of your Father that speaketh in you.

21 The brother also shall deliver up the brother to death, and the father the son: and the children shall rise up against their parents and shall put them to death.

22 And you shall be hated by all men for my name's sake. But he that shall persevere unto the end, he shall be saved.

23 And when they shall persecute you in this city flee into another. Amen I say to you, you shall not finish all the cities of Israel till the son of man come.

24 [6] The disciple is not above the master, nor the servant above his lord.

25 It is enough for the disciple that he be as his master, and the servant as his lord. If they have called the goodman of the house Beelzebub, how much more them of his household?

26 Therefore fear them not. [7] For nothing is covered that shall not be revealed: nor hid that shall not be known.

27 That which I tell you in the dark, speak ye in the light: and that which you hear in the ear, preach ye upon the house tops.

28 And fear ye not them that kill the body and are not able to kill the soul: but rather fear him that can destroy both soul and body in hell.

29 [8] Are not two sparrows sold for a farthing? And not one of them shall fall on the ground without your Father.

30 But the very hairs of your head are all numbered.

[9] Mark, 6, 6. [10] Luke, 10, 2. CHAP. 10. [1] Mark, 3, 13; Luke, 6, 13; 9, 1. [2] Acts, 13, 46. [3] Mark, 6, 8; Luke, 9; 10, 4. [4] Luke, 10, 3. [5] Luke, 12, 11. [6] Luke, 6, 40; John, 13, 16; 15, 20. [7] Mark, 4, 22; Luke, 8, 17; 12, 2. [8] 2 Kings, 14, 11.

CHAP. 10. Ver. 16. *Simple.* That is, harmless, plain, sincere, and without guile.

31 Fear not therefore: better are you than many sparrows.

32 ⁹ Every one therefore that shall confess me before men, I will also confess him before my Father who is in heaven.

33 But he that shall deny me before men, I will also deny him before my Father who is in heaven.

34 ¹⁰ Do not think that I came to send peace upon earth: I came not to send peace, but the sword.

35 For I came to set a man at variance against his father, and the daughter against her mother, and the daughter-in-law against her mother-in-law.

36 ¹¹ And a man's enemies shall be they of his own household.

37 ¹² He that loveth father or mother more than me is not worthy of me: and he that loveth son or daughter more than me is not worthy of me.

38 ¹³ And he that taketh not up his cross and followeth me is not worthy of me.

39 He that findeth his life shall lose it: ¹⁴ and he that shall lose his life for me shall find it.

40 ¹⁵ He that receiveth you receiveth me: and he that receiveth me receiveth him that sent me.

41 He that receiveth a prophet in the name of a prophet shall receive the reward of a prophet: and he that receiveth a just man in the name of a just man shall receive the reward of a just man.

42 ¹⁶ And whosoever shall give to drink to one of these little ones a cup of cold water only in the name of a disciple, amen I say to you, he shall not lose his reward.

CHAPTER 11

John sends his disciples to Christ who upbraids the Jews with their incredulity and calls to him such as are sensible of their burdens.

AND it came to pass, when Jesus had made an end of commanding

⁹ Mark, 8, 38; Luke, 9, 26; 12, 8; 2 Tim. 2, 12. ¹⁰ Luke, 12, 51. ¹¹ Mich. 7, 6. ¹² Luke, 14, 26. ¹³ Matt. 16, 24; Mark, 8, 34; Luke, 14, 27. ¹⁴ Luke, 9, 24; 17, 33; John, 12, 25. ¹⁵ Luke, 10, 16; John, 13, 20. ¹⁶ Mark, 9, 40. Chap. 11. ¹ Luke, 7, 18. ² Isai. 25, 5. ³ Isai. 61, 1. ⁴ Luke, 7, 24. ⁵ Mal. 3, 1; Mark, 1, 2; Luke, 7, 27. ⁶ Mal. 4, 5.

Ver. 35. *I came to set a man at variance.* Not that this was the end or design of the coming of our Saviour; but that his coming and his doctrine would have this effect, by reason of the obstinate resistance that many would make and of their persecuting all such as should adhere to him.

Chap. 11. Ver. 6. *Scandalized in me.* That is, who shall not take occasion of scandal or offence from my humility and the disgraceful death of the cross which I shall endure.

Ver. 12. *Suffereth violence.* It is not to be obtained but by main force, by using violence upon ourselves, by mortification and penance and resisting our perverse inclinations.

Ver. 14. *He is Elias.* Not in person, but in spirit (Luke, 1, 17).

his twelve disciples, he passed from thence, to teach and preach in their cities.

2 ¹ Now when John had heard in prison the works of Christ, sending two of his disciples, he said to him:

3 Art thou he that are to come, or look we for another?

4 And Jesus making answer said to them: Go and relate to John what you have heard and seen.

5 ² The blind see, the lame walk, the lepers are cleansed, the deaf hear, the dead rise again, ³ the poor have the gospel preached to them.

6 And blessed is he that shall not be scandalized in me.

7 ⁴ And when they went their way, Jesus began to say to the multitudes concerning John: What went you out into the desert to see? A reed shaken with the wind?

8 But what went you out to see? A man clothed in soft garments? Behold they that are clothed in soft garments are in the houses of kings.

9 But what went you out to see? A prophet? Yea, I tell you, and more than a prophet.

10 For this is he of whom it is written: ⁵ *Behold I send my angel before thy face, who shall prepare thy way before thee.*

11 Amen I say to you, there hath not risen among them that are born of women a greater than John the Baptist: yet he that is the lesser in the kingdom of heaven is greater than he.

12 And from the days of John the Baptist until now, the kingdom of heaven suffereth violence and the violent bear it away.

13 For all the prophets and the law prophesied until John:

14 And if you will receive it, ⁶ he is Elias that is to come.

15 He that hath ears to hear, let him hear.

16 But whereunto shall I esteem this generation to be like? It is like to children sitting in the market place.

17 Who crying to their companions say: We have piped to you, and you have not danced: we have lamented, and you have not mourned.

18 For John came neither eating nor drinking. And they say: He hath a devil.

19 The Son of man came eating and drinking. And they say: Behold a man that is a glutton and a wine drinker, a friend of publicans and sinners. And wisdom is justified by her children.

20 Then began he to upbraid the cities wherein were done the most of

his miracles, for that they had not done penance.

21 [7] Woe to thee, Corozain! Woe to thee, Bethsaida! For if in Tyre and Sidon had been wrought the miracles that have been wrought in you, they had long ago done penance in sackcloth and ashes.

22 But I say unto you, it shall be more tolerable for Tyre and Sidon in the day of judgment than for you.

23 And thou Capharnaum, shalt thou be exalted up to heaven? Thou shalt go down even unto hell. For if in Sodom had been wrought the miracles that have been wrought in thee, perhaps it had remained unto this day.

24 But I say unto you that it shall be more tolerable for the hand of Sodom in the day of Judgment than for thee.

25 At that time, Jesus answered and said: I confess to thee, O Father, Lord of heaven and earth, because thou hast hid these things from the wise and prudent and hast revealed them to little ones.

26 Yea, Father: for so hath it seemed good in thy sight.

27 All things are delivered to me by my Father. [8] And no one knoweth the Son, but the Father: neither doth any one know the Father, but the Son and he to whom it shall please the Son to reveal him.

28 Come to me, all you that labour and are burdened: and I will refresh you.

29 Take up my yoke upon you and learn of me, because I am meek, and humble of heart: [9] and you shall find rest to your souls.

30 [10] For my yoke is sweet and my burden light.

CHAPTER 12

Christ reproves the blindness of the Pharisees and confutes their attributing his miracles to Satan.

AT [1] that time, Jesus went through the corn on the sabbath: and his disciples being hungry began to pluck the ears, and to eat.

2 And the Pharisees seeing them, said to him: Behold thy disciples do that which is not lawful to do on the sabbath days.

3 But he said to them: Have you not read [2] what David did when he was hungry, and they that were with him:

4 How he entered into the house of God and did eat the loaves of proposition which it was not lawful for him to eat, nor for them that were with him, [3] but for the priests only?

5 Or have ye not read in the law [4] that on the sabbath days the priests in the temple break the sabbath and are without blame?

6 But I tell you that there is here a greater than the temple.

7 And if you knew what this meaneth: [5] *I will have mercy, and not sacrifice:* you would never have condemned the innocent.

8 For the Son of man is Lord even of the sabbath.

9 And when he had passed from thence, he came into their synagogues.

10 [6] And behold there was a man who had a withered hand. And they asked him, saying: Is it lawful to heal on the sabbath days? that they might accuse him.

11 But he said to them: [7] What man shall there be among you that hath one sheep: and if the same fall into a pit on the sabbath day, will he not take hold on it and lift it up?

12 How much better is a man than a sheep? Therefore it is lawful to do a good deed on the sabbath days.

13 Then he saith to the man: Stretch forth thy hand. And he stretched it forth, and it was restored to health, even as the other.

14 And the Pharisees going out made a consultation against him, how they might destroy him.

15 But Jesus knowing it retired from thence. And many followed him: and he healed them all.

16 And he charged them that they should not make him known.

17 That it might be fulfilled which was spoken by Isaias the prophet, saying:

18 [8] *Behold my servant whom I have chosen, my beloved in whom my soul hath been well pleased. I will put my spirit upon him: and he shall shew judgment to the Gentiles.*

19 *He shall not contend nor cry out: neither shall any man hear his voice in the streets.*

20 *The bruised reed he shall not break: and smoking flax he shall not extinguish: till he send forth judgment unto victory.*

21 *And in his name the Gentiles shall hope.*

22 Then was offered to him one possessed with a devil, blind and dumb: and he healed him, so that he spoke and saw.

23 And all the multitudes were

[7] Luke, 10, 13. [8] John, 6, 46; 7, 28; 8, 19; 10, 15. [9] Jer. 6, 16. [10] 1 John, 5, 3. CHAP. 12. [1] Mark, 2, 23; Luke, 6, 1. [2] 1 Kings, 21, 6. [3] Lev. 24, 9. [4] Num. 28, 9. [5] 1 Kings, 15, 22; Ecclus. 4, 17; Osee, 6, 6; Matt. 9, 13. [6] Mark, 3, 1; Luke, 6, 6. [7] Deut. 22, 4. [8] Isai. 13, 1.

CHAP. 12. Ver. 4. *The loaves of proposition.* So were called the twelve loaves which were placed before the sanctuary in the temple of God.

amazed and said: Is not this the son of David?

24 [9] But the Pharisees hearing it, said: This man casteth not out devils but by Beelzebub the prince of the devils.

25 And Jesus knowing their thoughts, said to them: [10] Every kingdom divided against itself shall be made desolate: and every city or house divided against itself shall not stand.

26 And if Satan cast out Satan, he is divided against himself: how then shall his kingdom stand?

27 And if I by Beelzebub cast out devils, by whom do your children cast them out? Therefore they shall be your judges.

28 But if I by the Spirit of God cast out devils, then is the kingdom of God come upon you.

29 Or how can any one enter into the house of the strong and rifle his goods, unless he first bind the strong? And then he will rifle his house.

30 He that is not with me is against me: and he that gathereth not with me scattereth.

31 [11] Therefore I say to you: Every sin and blasphemy shall be forgiven men, but the blasphemy of the Spirit shall not be forgiven.

32 And whosoever shall speak a word against the Son of man, it shall be forgiven him: but he that shall speak against the Holy Ghost, it shall not be forgiven him, neither in this world, nor in the world to come.

[9] Matt. 9, 34; Mark, 3, 22; Luke, 11, 15. [10] Luke, 11, 17. [11] Mark, 3, 28, 29; Luke, 12, 10. [12] Luke, 6, 45. [13] Matt. 16, 4; Luke, 11, 29; 1 Cor. 1, 22. [14] Jonas, 2, 1. [15] Jonas, 3, 5. [16] 3 Kings, 10, 1; 2 Par. 9, 1. [17] Luke, 11, 24. [18] 2 Peter, 2, 20. [19] Mark, 3, 31; Luke, 8, 19.

Ver. 31. *The blasphemy of the Spirit.* The sin here spoken of is that blasphemy by which the Pharisees attributed the miracles of Christ, wrought by the Spirit of God, to *Beelzebub* the prince of devils. Now this kind of sin is usually accompanied with so much obstinacy and such wilful opposing the Spirit of God and the known truth, that men who are guilty of it are seldom or never converted: and therefore are never forgiven, because they will not repent. Otherwise, there is no sin which God cannot or will not forgive to such as sincerely repent and have recourse to the keys of the church.

Ver. 32. *Nor in the world to come.* From these words St. Augustine (*De Civ. Dei*, lib. 21, c. 13) and St. Gregory (*Dialog.*, 4, c. 39) gather that some sins may be remitted in the world to come; and, consequently, that there is a purgatory or a middle place.

Ver. 36. *Every idle word.* This shews there must be a place of temporal punishment hereafter where these slighter faults shall be punished.

Ver. 38. *A sign.* That is, a miracle from heaven (Luke, 11, 16).

Ver. 40. *Three days.* Not complete days and nights; but part of three days and three nights, taken according to the way that the Hebrews counted their days and nights, that is, from evening to evening.

Ver. 48. *Who is my mother?* That was not spoken by way of slighting his mother, but to shew that we are never to suffer ourselves to be

33 Either make the tree good and its fruit good: or make the tree evil and its fruit evil. For by the fruit the tree is known.

34 O generation of vipers, how can you speak good things, whereas you are evil? [12] For out of the abundance of the heart the mouth speaketh.

35 A good man out of a good treasure bringeth forth good things: and an evil man out of an evil treasure bringeth forth evil things.

36 But I say unto you that every idle word that men shall speak, they shall render an account for it in the day of judgment.

37 For by thy words thou shalt be justified: and by thy words thou shalt be condemned.

38 Then some of the scribes and Pharisees answered him, saying: Master, we would see a sign from thee.

39 Who answering said to them: [13] An evil and adulterous generation seeketh a sign: and a sign shall not be given it, [14] but the sign of Jonas the prophet.

40 For as Jonas was in the whale's belly three days and three nights: so shall the Son of man be in the heart of the earth three days and three nights.

41 [15] The men of Ninive shall rise in judgment with this generation and shall condemn it: because they did penance at the preaching of Jonas. And behold a greater than Jonas here.

42 The queen of the south shall rise in judgment with this generation and shall condemn it: [16] because she came from the ends of the earth to hear the wisdom of Solomon. And behold a greater than Solomon here.

43 [17] And when an unclean spirit is gone out of a man, he walketh through dry places seeking rest and findeth none.

44 Then he saith: I will return into my house from whence I came out. And coming he findeth it empty, swept and garnished.

45 Then he goeth and taketh with him seven other spirits more wicked than himself: and they enter in and dwell there: [18] and the last state of that man is made worse than the first. So shall it be also to this wicked generation.

46 [19] As he was yet speaking to the multitudes, behold his mother and his brethren stood without, seeking to speak to him.

47 And one said to him: Behold thy mother and thy brethren stand without, seeking thee.

48 But he answering him that told him, said: Who is my mother and who are my brethren?

49 And stretching forth his hand towards his disciples, he said: Behold my mother and my brethren.

50 For whosoever shall do the will of my Father that is in heaven, he is my brother, and sister, and mother.

CHAPTER 13

The parables of the sower, of the cockle, of the mustard seed, and others.

THE same day, Jesus going out of the house, sat by the seaside.

2 ¹ And great multitudes were gathered together unto him, so that he went up into a boat and sat: and all the multitude stood on the shore.

3 And he spoke to them many things in parables, saying: Behold the sower went forth to sow.

4 And whilst he soweth, some fell by the way side: and the birds of the air came and ate them up.

5 And other some fell upon stony ground, where they had not much earth: and they sprung up immediately, because they had no deepness of earth.

6 And when the sun was up they were scorched: and because they had not root, they withered away.

7 And others fell among thorns: and the thorns grew up and choked them.

8 And others fell upon good ground: and they brought forth fruit, some an hundredfold, some sixtyfold, and some thirtyfold.

9 He that hath ears to hear, let him hear.

10 And his disciples came and said to him: Why speakest thou to them in parables?

11 Who answered and said to them: Because to you it is given to know the mysteries of the kingdom of heaven: but to them it is not given.

12 ² For he that hath, to him shall be given, and he shall abound: but he that hath not, from him shall be taken away that also which he hath.

13 Therefore do I speak to them in parables: because seeing they see not, and hearing they hear not, neither do they understand.

14 And the prophecy of Isaias is fulfilled in them, so saith: ³ *By hearing you shall hear and shall not understand: and seeing you shall see and shall not perceive.*

15 *For the heart of this people is grown gross, and with their ears they have been dull of hearing, and their eyes they have shut: lest at any time they should see with their eyes and hear with their ears and understand with their heart and be converted; and I should heal them.*

16 But blessed are your eyes because they see, and your ears because they hear.

17 ⁴ For, amen, I say to you, many prophets and just men have desired to see the things that you see and have not seen them, and to hear the things that you hear and have not heard them.

18 Hear you therefore the parable of the sower.

19 When any one heareth the word of the kingdom and understandeth it not, there cometh the wicked one and catcheth away that which was sown in his heart: this is he that received the seed by the way side.

20 And he that received the seed upon stony ground is he that heareth the word and immediately receiveth it with joy.

21 Yet hath he not root in himself, but is only for a time: and when there ariseth tribulation and persecution because of the word, he is presently scandalized.

22 And he that received the seed among thorns is he that heareth the word, and the care of this world and the deceitfulness of riches choketh up the word: and he becometh fruitless.

23 But he that received the seed upon good ground is he that heareth the word and understandeth and beareth fruit and yieldeth the one an hundredfold, and another sixty, and another thirty.

24 ⁵ Another parable he proposed to them, saying: The kingdom of heaven is likened to a man that sowed good seed in his field.

25 But while men were asleep, his enemy came and oversowed cockle among the wheat and went his way.

26 And when the blade was sprung up and had brought forth fruit, then appeared also the cockle.

27 And the servants of the goodman of the house coming said to him: Sir, didst thou not sow good seed in thy field? Whence then hath it cockle?

28 And he said to them: An enemy hath done this. And the servants said to him: Wilt thou that we go and gather it up?

29 And he said: No, lest perhaps gathering up the cockle, you root up the wheat also together with it.

30 Suffer both to grow until the har-

CHAP. 13. ¹ Mark, 4, 1; Luke, 8, 4. ² Matt. 25, 29. ³ Isai. 6, 9; Mark, 4, 12; Luke, 8, 10; John, 12, 40; Acts, 28, 26; Rom. 11, 8. ⁴ Luke, 10, 24. ⁵ Mark, 4, 26.

taken from the service of God by any inordinate affection to our earthly parents: and that that which our Lord chiefly regarded in his mother was her doing the will of his Father in heaven. It may also further allude to the reprobation of the Jews, his carnal kindred, and the election of the Gentiles.

vest, and in the time of the harvest I will say to the reapers: Gather up first the cockle and bind it into bundles to burn, but the wheat gather ye into my barn.

31 ⁶ Another parable he proposed unto them, saying: The kingdom of heaven is like to a grain of mustard seed which a man took and sowed in his field.

32 Which is the least indeed of all seeds: but when it is grown up, it is greater than all herbs and becometh a tree, so that the birds of the air come and dwell in the branches thereof.

33 Another parable he spoke to them: ⁷ The kingdom of heaven is like to leaven which a woman took and hid in three measures of meal, until the whole was leavened.

34 All these things Jesus spoke in parables to the multitudes: and without parables he did not speak to them.

35 That it might be fulfilled which was spoken by the prophet, saying: ⁸ *I will open my mouth in parables, I will utter things hidden from the foundation of the world.*

36 ⁹ Then having sent away the multitudes, he came into the house; and his disciples came to him, saying: Expound to us the parable of the cockle of the field.

37 Who made answer and said to them: He that soweth the good seed is the Son of man.

38 And the field is the world. And the good seed are the children of the kingdom. And the cockle are the children of the wicked one.

39 And the enemy that sowed them is the devil. ¹⁰ But the harvest is the end of the world. And the reapers are the angels.

40 Even as cockle therefore is gathered up and burnt with fire: so shall it be at the end of the world.

41 The Son of man shall send his angels: and they shall gather out of his kingdom all scandals and them that work iniquity.

42 And shall cast them into the furnace of fire. There, shall be weeping and gnashing of teeth.

43 ¹¹ Then shall the just shine as the sun in the kingdom of their Father. He that hath ears to hear, let him hear.

44 The kingdom of heaven is like unto a treasure hidden in a field. Which a man having found, hid it: and for joy thereof goeth and selleth all that he hath and buyeth that field.

45 Again the kingdom of heaven is like to a merchant seeking good pearls.

46 Who, when he had found one pearl of great price, went his way and sold all that he had and bought it.

47 Again the kingdom of heaven is like to a net cast into the sea and gathering together of all kind of fishes.

48 Which, when it was filled, they drew out: and sitting by the shore, they chose out the good into vessels, but the bad they cast forth.

49 So shall it be at the end of the world. The angels shall go out and shall separate the wicked from among the just.

50 And shall cast them into the furnace of fire. There, shall be weeping and gnashing of teeth.

51 Have ye understood all these things? They say to him: Yes.

52 He said unto them: Therefore every scribe instructed in the kingdom of heaven is like to a man that is a householder, who bringeth forth out of his treasure new things and old.

53 And it came to pass when Jesus had finished these parables, he passed from thence.

54 ¹² And coming into his own country, he taught them in their synagogues, so that they wondered and said: How came this man by this wisdom and miracles?

55 ¹³ Is not this the carpenter's son? Is not his mother called Mary, and his brethren James and Joseph and Simon and Jude?

56 And his sisters, are they not all with us? Whence therefore hath he all these things?

57 And they were scandalized in his regard. But Jesus said to them: A prophet is not without honour, save in his own country and in his own house.

58 And he wrought not many miracles there, because of their unbelief.

⁶ Mark, 4, 31; Luke, 13, 19. ⁷ Luke, 13, 21. ⁸ Ps. 77, 2. ⁹ Mark, 4, 34. ¹⁰ Apoc. 14, 15. ¹¹ Wisd. 3, 7; Dan. 12, 3. ¹² Mark, 6, 1; Luke, 4, 16. ¹³ John, 6, 42. CHAP. 14. ¹ Mark, 6, 14; Luke, 9, 7.

CHAP. 13. Ver. 55. *His brethren.* These were the children of Mary the wife of Cleophas, sister to our Blessed Lady (Matt. 27, 56; John, 19, 25), and therefore, according to the usual style of the Scripture, they were called *brethren*, that is, *near relations* to our Saviour.

CHAP. 14. Ver. 1. *Tetrarch.* This word, derived from the Greek, signifies one that rules over the fourth part of a kingdom: as Herod then ruled over Galilee which was but the fourth part of the kingdom of his father.

CHAPTER 14

Herod puts John to death. Christ feeds five thousand in the desert. He walks upon the sea and heals all the diseased with the touch of his garment.

AT ¹ that time, Herod the Tetrarch heard the fame of Jesus.

2 And he said to his servants: This is John the Baptist. He is risen from the dead: and therefore mighty works shew forth themselves in him.

3 [2] For Herod had apprehended John and bound him and put him into prison, because of Herodias, his brother's wife.

4 For John said to him: It is not lawful for thee to have her.

5 And having a mind to put him to death, he feared the people: [3] because they esteemed him as a prophet.

6 But on Herod's birthday, the daughter of Herodias danced before them and pleased Herod.

7 Whereupon he promised with an oath to give her whatsoever she would ask of him.

8 But she, being instructed before by her mother, said: Give me here in a dish the head of John the Baptist.

9 And the king was struck sad: yet because of his oath and for them that sat with him at table, he commanded it to be given.

10 And he sent and beheaded John in the prison.

11 And his head was brought in a dish: and it was given to the damsel: and she brought it to her mother.

12 And his disciples came and took the body and buried it and came and told Jesus.

13 [4] Which when Jesus had heard, he retired from thence by a boat into a desert place apart: and the multitudes having heard of it, followed him on foot out of the cities.

14 And he coming forth saw a great multitude and had compassion on them and healed their sick.

15 And when it was evening, his disciples came to him, saying: This is a desert place and the hour is now past: send away the multitudes, that going into the towns they may buy themselves victuals.

16 But Jesus said to them: They have no need to go. Give you them to eat.

17 They answered him: [5] We have not here but five loaves and two fishes.

18 He said to them: Bring them hither to me.

19 And when he had commanded the multitudes to sit down upon the grass. he took the five loaves and the two fishes: and looking up to heaven, he blessed and brake and gave the loaves to his disciples, and the disciples to the multitudes.

20 And they did all eat and were filled. And they took up what remained, twelve full baskets of fragments.

21 And the number of them that did eat was five thousand men, besides women and children.

22 [6] And forthwith Jesus obliged his disciples to go up into the boat and to go before him over the water, till he dismissed the people.

23 And having dismissed the multitudes, [7] he went into a mountain alone to pray. And when it was evening, he was there alone.

24 But the boat in the midst of the sea was tossed with the waves: for the wind was contrary.

25 And in the fourth watch of the night, he came to them, walking upon the sea.

26 And they, seeing him walking upon the sea, were troubled, saying: It is an apparition. And they cried out for fear.

27 And immediately Jesus spoke to them, saying: Be of good heart. It is I. Fear ye not.

28 And Peter making answer, said: Lord, if it be thou, bid me come to thee upon the waters.

29 And he said: Come. And Peter going down out of the boat walked upon the water to come to Jesus.

30 But seeing the wind strong, he was afraid: and when he began to sink, he cried out, saying: Lord, save me.

31 And immediately Jesus stretching forth his hand took hold of him and said to him: O thou of little faith, why didst thou doubt?

32 And when they were come up into the boat, the wind ceased.

33 And they that were in the boat came and adored him, saying: Indeed thou art the Son of God.

34 [8] And having passed the water, they came into the country of Genesar.

35 And when the men of that place had knowledge of him, they sent into all that country and brought to him all that were diseased.

36 And they besought him that they might touch but the hem of his garment. And as many as touched were made whole.

CHAPTER 15

Christ reproves the scribes. He cures the daughter of the woman of Canaan and many others and feeds four thousand with seven loaves.

THEN [1] came to him from Jerusalem scribes and Pharisees, saying:

2 [2] Why do thy disciples transgress the tradition of the ancients? For they wash not their hands when they eat bread.

3 But he answering, said to them: Why do you also transgress the commandment of God for your tradition? For God said:

[2] Mark, 6, 17; Luke, 3, 19. [3] Matt. 21, 26. [4] Mark, 6, 31; Luke, 9, 10; John, 6, 3. [5] John, 6, 9. [6] Mark, 6, 45. [7] John, 6, 15; Mark, 6, 46. [8] Mark, 6, 53. CHAP. 15. [1] Mark, 7, 1. [2] Mark, 7, 5.

4 [3] *Honour thy father and mother:* [4] And: *He that shall curse father or mother, let him die the death.*

5 But you say: Whosoever shall say to father or mother, The gift whatsoever proceedeth from me, shall profit thee.

6 And he shall not honour his father or his mother: and you have made void the commandment of God for your tradition.

7 Hypocrites, well hath Isaias prophesied of you, saying:

8 [5] *This people honoureth me with their lips: but their heart is far from me.*

9 *And in vain do they worship me, teaching doctrines and commandments of men.*

10 And having called together the multitudes unto him, he said to them: Hear ye and understand.

11 Not that which goeth into the mouth defileth a man: but what cometh out of the mouth, this defileth a man.

12 Then came his disciples, and said to him: Dost thou know that the Phari-

[3] Exod. 20, 12; Deut. 5, 16; Eph. 6, 2. [4] Exod. 21, 17; Lev. 20, 9; Prov. 20, 20. [5] Isai. 29, 13; Mark, 7, 6. [6] John, 15, 2. [7] Luke, 6, 39. [8] Mark, 7, 17. [9] Mark, 7, 24. [10] Matt. 10, 6; John, 10, 3. [11] Isai. 35, 5.

CHAP. 15. Ver. 5. *The gift.* That is, the offering that I shall make to God shall be instead of that which should be expended for thy profit. This tradition of the Pharisees was calculated to enrich themselves by exempting children from giving any further assistance to their parents, if they once offered to the temple and the priests that which should have been the support of their parents. But this was a violation of the law of God and of nature, which our Saviour here condemns.

Ver. 9. *Commandments of men.* The doctrines and commandments here reprehended are such as are either contrary to the law of God (as that of neglecting parents, under pretence of giving to God), or at least are frivolous, unprofitable, and no ways conducing to true piety, as that of often washing hands, without regard to the purity of the heart. But as to rules and ordinances of the holy church, touching fasts, festivals, &c., these are no ways repugnant to, but highly agreeable to God's holy word and all Christian piety. Neither are they to be counted among the *doctrines and commandments of men* because they proceed not from mere human authority; but from that which Christ has established in his church, whose pastors he has commanded us to hear and obey, even as himself (Luke, 10, 16; Matt. 18, 17).

Ver. 11. *Not that which goeth into the mouth.* No uncleanness in meat, nor any dirt contracted by eating it with unwashed hands, can defile the soul: but sin alone, or a disobedience of the heart to the ordinance and will of God. And thus when Adam took the forbidden fruit, it was not the apple which entered into the mouth but the disobedience to the law of God which defiled him. The same is to be said if a Jew, in the time of the old law, had eaten swine's flesh; or a Christian convert, in the days of the apostles, contrary to their ordinance, had eaten blood; or if any of the faithful at present should transgress the ordinance of God's church, by breaking the fasts: for in all these cases the soul would be defiled; not indeed by that which goeth into the mouth, but by the disobedience of the heart in wilfully transgressing the ordinance of God or of those who have their authority from him.

sees, when they heard this word, were scandalized?

13 But he answering, said: [6] Every plant which my heavenly Father hath not planted shall be rooted up.

14 Let them alone: [7] they are blind and leaders of the blind. And if the blind lead the blind, both fall into the pit.

15 [8] And Peter answering, said to him: Expound to us this parable.

16 But he said: Are you also yet without understanding?

17 Do you not understand that whatsoever entereth into the mouth goeth into the belly and is cast out into the privy?

18 But the things which proceed out of the mouth come forth from the heart: and those things defile a man.

19 For from the heart come forth evil thoughts, murders, adulteries, fornications, thefts, false testimonies, blasphemies.

20 These are the things that defile a man. But to eat with unwashed hands doth not defile a man.

21 [9] And Jesus went from thence and retired into the coasts of Tyre and Sidon.

22 And behold a woman of Canaan who came out of those coasts, crying out, said to him: Have mercy on me, O Lord, thou son of David: my daughter is grievously troubled by a devil.

23 Who answered her not a word. And his disciples came and besought him, saying: Send her away, for she crieth after us.

24 And he answering, said: I was not sent [10] but to the sheep that are lost of the house of Israel.

25 But she came and adored him, saying: Lord, help me.

26 Who answering said: It is not good to take the bread of the children and to cast it to the dogs.

27 But she said: Yea, Lord; for the whelps also eat of the crumbs that fall from the table of their masters.

28 Then Jesus answering, said to her: O woman, great is thy faith. Be it done to thee as thou wilt. And her daughter was cured from that hour.

29 And when Jesus had passed away from thence, he came nigh the sea of Galilee. And going up into a mountain, he sat there.

30 [11] And there came to him great multitudes, having with them the dumb, the blind, the lame, the maimed and many others. And they cast them down at his feet. And he healed them:

31 So that the multitudes marvelled, seeing the dumb speak, the lame walk,

the blind see. And they glorified the God of Israel.

32 [12] And Jesus called together his disciples, and said: I have compassion on the multitudes, because they continue with me now three days and have not what to eat. And I will not send them away fasting, lest they faint in the way.

33 And the disciples say unto him: Whence then should we have so many loaves in the desert as to fill so great a multitude?

34 And Jesus said to them: How many loaves have you? But they said: Seven, and a few little fishes.

35 And he commanded the multitude to sit down upon the ground.

36 And taking the seven loaves and the fishes and giving thanks, he brake and gave to his disciples: and the disciples gave to the people.

37 And they did all eat, and had their fill. And they took up seven baskets full, of what remained of the fragments.

38 And they that did eat were four thousand men, beside children and women.

39 And having dismissed the multitude, he went up into a boat and came into the coasts of Magedan.

CHAPTER 16

Christ refuses to show the Pharisees a sign from heaven. Peter's confession is rewarded. He is rebuked for opposing Christ's passion. All his followers must deny themselves.

AND [1] there came to him the Pharisees and Sadducees tempting: and they asked him to shew them a sign from heaven.

2 But he answered and said to them: [2] When it is evening, you say, It will be fair weather, for the sky is red.

3 And in the morning: To-day *there will be* a storm, for the sky is red and lowering. You know then how to discern the face of the sky: and can you not know the signs of the times?

4 [3] A wicked and adulterous generation seeketh after a sign: and a sign shall not be given it, [4] but the sign of Jonas the prophet. And he left them and went away.

5 And when his disciples were come over the water, they had forgotten to take bread.

6 Who said to them: [5] Take heed and beware of the leaven of the Pharisees and Sadducees.

7 But they thought within themselves, saying: Because we have taken no bread.

8 And Jesus knowing it, said: Why do you think within yourselves, O ye

of little faith, for that you have no bread?

9 Do you not yet understand, neither do you remember [6] the five loaves among five thousand men, and how many baskets you took up?

10 [7] Nor the seven loaves among four thousand men, and how many baskets you took up?

11 Why do you not understand that it was not concerning bread I said to you: Beware of the leaven of the Pharisees and Sadducees?

12 Then they understood that he said not that they should beware of the leaven of bread, but of the doctrine of the Pharisees and Sadducees.

13 [8] And Jesus came into the quarters of Cesarea Philippi: and he asked his disciples, saying: Whom do men say that the Son of man is?

14 But they said: [9] Some John the Baptist, and other some Elias, and others Jeremias or one of the prophets.

15 Jesus saith to them: But whom do you say that I am?

16 Simon Peter answered and said: [10] Thou art Christ, the Son of the Living God.

17 And Jesus answering, said to him: Blessed art thou, Simon Bar-Jona: because flesh and blood hath not revealed it to thee, but my Father who is in heaven.

18 [11] And I say to thee: That thou art Peter, and upon this rock I will build my church. And the gates of hell shall not prevail against it.

[12] Mark, 8, 1. CHAP. 16. [1] Mark, 8, 11. [2] Luke, 12, 54. [3] Matt. 12, 39. [4] Jonas, 2, 1. [5] Mark, 8, 15; Luke, 12, 1. [6] Matt. 14, 17; John, 6, 9. [7] Matt. 15, 34. [8] Mark, 8, 27. [9] Mark, 8, 28; Luke, 9, 19. [10] John, 6, 70. [11] John, 12, 42.

CHAP. 16. Ver. 18. *Thou art Peter.* As St. Peter, by divine revelation, here made a solemn profession of his faith of the divinity of Christ; so in recompense of this faith and profession, our Lord here declares to him the dignity to which he is pleased to raise him: namely, that he to whom he had already given the name of *Peter,* signifying a *rock* (John, 1, 42), should be a *rock* indeed, of invincible strength, for the support of the building of the Church; in which building he should be, next to Christ himself, the chief foundation stone, in quality of chief pastor, ruler, and governor; and should have accordingly all fulness of ecclesiastical power, signified by the keys of the kingdom of heaven.— *Upon this rock.* The words of Christ to Peter, spoken in the vulgar language of the Jews which our Lord made use of, were the same as if he had said in English, *Thou art a Rock, and upon this rock I will build my Church.* So that, by the plain course of the words, Peter is here declared to be the rock, upon which the Church was to be built: Christ himself being both the principal foundation and founder of the same. Where also note, that Christ, by building his house, that is, his Church, upon a rock, has thereby secured it against all storms and floods, like the wise builder (Matt. 7, 24, 15).—*The gates of hell.* That is, the powers of darkness and whatever Satan can do, either by himself, or his agents. For as the Church is here likened to a house or fortress, built on a rock; so the adverse powers are likened to a contrary house or fortress, the gates of

19 [12] And I will give to thee the keys of the kingdom of heaven. [13] And whatsoever thou shalt bind upon earth, it shall be bound also in heaven: and whatsoever thou shalt loose on earth, it shall be loosed also in heaven.

20 Then he commanded his disciples that they should tell no one that he was Jesus the Christ.

21 From that time Jesus began to shew to his disciples that he must go to Jerusalem and suffer many things from the ancients and scribes and chief priests: and be put to death and the third day rise again.

22 And Peter taking him, began to rebuke him, saying: Lord, be it far from thee, this shall not be unto thee.

23 Who turning, said to Peter: [14] Go behind me, Satan: thou art a scandal unto me, because thou savourest not the things that are of God, but the things that are of men.

24 Then Jesus said to his disciples: [15] If any man will come after me, let him deny himself and take up his cross and follow me.

25 [16] For he that will save his life shall lose it: and he that shall lose his life for my sake shall find it.

26 For what doth it profit a man, if he gain the whole world and suffer the loss of his own soul? Or what exchange shall a man give for his soul?

27 For the Son of man shall come in the glory of his Father with his angels: [17] and then will he render to every man according to his works.

28 Amen I say to you, [18] there are some of them that stand here that shall not taste death till they see the Son of man coming in his kingdom.

[12] Isai. 22, 22. [13] John, 20, 23. [14] Mark, 8, 33. [15] Matt. 10, 38; Luke, 9, 23; 14, 27. [16] Luke, 17, 33; John, 12, 25. [17] Acts, 17, 31; Rom. 2, 6. [18] Mark, 8, 39; Luke, 9, 28. CHAP. 17. [1] Mark, 9, 1; Luke, 9, 28. [2] Matt. 3, 17; 2 Peter, 1, 17. [3] Mark, 9, 10. [4] Mal. 4, 5. [5] Matt. 9, 14. [6] Matt. 14, 10. [7] Mark, 9, 16; Luke, 9, 38.

which, that is, its whole strength and all the efforts it can make, will never be able to prevail over the City or Church of Christ. By this promise we are fully assured, that neither idolatry, heresy, nor any pernicious error whatsoever shall at any time prevail over the Church of Christ.

Ver. 19. Loose on earth. The loosing the bands of temporal punishments due to sins is called an indulgence; the power of which is here granted.

Ver. 22. And Peter taking him. That is, taking him aside, out of a tender love, respect and zeal for his Lord and Master's honour, began to expostulate with him, as it were to rebuke him, saying, Lord, far be it from thee to suffer death; but the Lord said to Peter (ver. 23), Go behind me, Satan. These words may signify, Begone from me; but the holy Fathers expound them otherwise, that is: Come after me, or follow me. And by these words the Lord would have Peter to follow him in his suffering and not to oppose the divine will by contradiction; for the word Satan means in Hebrew an adversary, or one that opposes.

CHAPTER 17

The transfiguration of Christ. He cures the lunatic child, foretells his passion and pays the didrachma.

AND [1] after six days, Jesus taketh unto him Peter and James, and John his brother, and bringeth them up into a high mountain apart.

2 And he was transfigured before them. And his face did shine as the sun: and his garments became white as snow.

3 And behold there appeared to them Moses and Elias talking with him.

4 And Peter answering, said to Jesus: Lord, it is good for us to be here: if thou wilt, let us make here three tabernacles, one for thee, and one for Moses, and one for Elias.

5 And as he was yet speaking, behold a bright cloud overshadowed them. [2] And lo, a voice out of the cloud, saying: This is my beloved Son in whom I am well pleased. Hear ye him.

6 And the disciples hearing, fell upon their face and were very much afraid.

7 And Jesus came and touched them and said to them: Arise, and fear not.

8 And they lifting up their eyes saw no one but only Jesus.

9 And as they came down from the mountain, Jesus charged them, saying: Tell the vision to no man till the Son of man be risen from the dead.

10 And his disciples asked him, saying: [3] Why then do the scribes say that Elias must come first?

11 But [4] he answering, said to them: Elias indeed shall come and restore all things.

12 But I say to you [5] that Elias is already come: and they knew him not, [6] but have done unto him whatsoever they had a mind. So also the Son of man shall suffer from them.

13 Then the disciples understood, that he had spoken to them of John the Baptist.

14 [7] And when he was come to the multitude, there came to him a man falling down on his knees before him, saying: Lord, have pity on my son, for he is a lunatic and suffereth much: for he falleth often into the fire and often into the water.

15 And I brought him to thy disciples and they could not cure him.

16 Then Jesus answered and said: O unbelieving and perverse generation, how long shall I be with you? How long shall I suffer you? Bring him hither to me.

17 And Jesus rebuked him. And the devil went out of him: and the child was cured from that hour.

18 Then came the disciples to Jesus secretly and said: Why could not we cast him out?

19 Jesus said to them: Because of your unbelief. ⁸ For, amen I say to you, if you have faith as a grain of mustard seed, you shall say to this mountain, Remove from hence hither, and it shall remove; and nothing shall be impossible to you.

20 But this kind is not cast out but by prayer and fasting.

21 And when they abode together in Galilee, Jesus said to them: ⁹ The Son of man shall be betrayed into the hands of men.

22 And they shall kill him: and the third day he shall rise again. And they were troubled exceedingly.

23 And when they were come to Capharnaum, they that received the didrachmas came to Peter and said to him: Doth not your master pay the didrachmas?

24 He said: Yes. And when he was come into the house, Jesus prevented him, saying: What is thy opinion, Simon? The kings of the earth, of whom do they receive tribute or custom? Of their own children, or of strangers?

25 And he said: Of strangers. Jesus said to him: Then the children are free.

26 But that we may not scandalize them, go to the sea and cast in a hook: and that fish which shall first come up, take: and when thou hast opened its mouth, thou shalt find a stater: take that and give it to them for me and thee.

CHAPTER 18

Christ teaches humility, to beware of scandal and to flee the occasions of sin, to denounce to the church incorrigible sinners and to look upon such as refuse to hear the church as heathens. He promises to his disciples the power of binding and loosing and that he will be in the midst of their assemblies. No forgiveness for them that will not forgive.

AT ¹ that hour, the disciples came to Jesus, saying: Who thinkest thou is the greater in the kingdom of heaven?

2 ² And Jesus calling unto him a little child, set him in the midst of them,

3 And said: Amen I say to you, ³ unless you be converted and become as little children, you shall not enter into the kingdom of heaven.

4 Whosoever therefore shall humble himself as this little child, he is the greater in the kingdom of heaven.

5 And he that shall receive one such little child in my name receiveth me.

6 ⁴ But he that shall scandalize one of these little ones that believe in me, it were better for him that a millstone should be hanged about his neck and that he should be drowned in the depth of the sea.

7 Woe to the world because of scandals. For it must needs be that scandals come: but nevertheless woe to that man by whom the scandal cometh.

8 ⁵ And if thy hand or thy foot scandalize thee, cut it off and cast it from thee. It is better for thee to go into life maimed or lame than, having two hands or two feet, to be cast into everlasting fire.

9 And if thy eye scandalize thee, pluck it out and cast it from thee. It is better for thee having one eye to enter into life than, having two eyes, to be cast into hell fire.

10 See that you despise not one of these little ones: for I say to you ⁶ that their angels in heaven always see the face of my Father who is in heaven.

11 ⁷ For the Son of man is come to save that which was lost.

12 ⁸ What think you? If a man have an hundred sheep, and one of them should go astray: doth he not leave the ninety-nine in the mountains and go to seek that which is gone astray?

13 And if it so be that he find it: Amen I say to you, he rejoiceth more for that than for the ninety-nine that went not astray?

14 Even so it is not the will of your Father who is in heaven, that one of these little ones should perish.

15 ⁹ But if thy brother shall offend against thee, go and rebuke him between thee and him alone. If he shall hear thee, thou shalt gain thy brother.

16 And if he will not hear thee: take with thee one or two more, ¹⁰ that in the mouth of two or three witnesses every word may stand.

17 ¹¹ And if he will not hear them: tell the church. And if he will not hear

CHAP. 17. Ver. 19. *As a grain of mustard seed.* That is, a perfect faith; which in its properties and its fruits, resembles the grain of mustard seed, in the parable (Matt. 15, 31).

Ver. 23. *The didrachmas.* A *didrachma* was half a sicle, or half a *stater;* that is, about 15*d.* English. It was a tax laid upon every head for the service of the temple.

CHAP. 18. Ver. 6. *Shall scandalize.* That is, shall put a stumbling-block in their way and cause them to fall into sin.

Ver. 7. *It must needs be.* That is, considering the wickedness and corruption of the world.

Ver. 8. *Scandalize thee.* That is, cause thee to offend.

the church: let him be to thee as the heathen and publican.

18 [12] Amen I say to you, whatsoever you shall bind upon earth shall be bound also in heaven: and whatsoever you shall loose upon earth shall be loosed also in heaven.

19 Again I say to you that if two of you shall consent upon earth concerning any thing whatsoever they shall ask, it shall be done to them by my Father who is in heaven.

20 For where there are two or three gathered together in my name, there am I in the midst of them.

21 Then came Peter unto him and said: [13] Lord, how often shall my brother offend against me, and I forgive him? Till seven times?

22 Jesus saith to him: I say not to thee, till seven times, but till seventy times seven times.

23 Therefore is the kingdom of heaven likened to a king who would take an account of his servants.

24 And when he had begun to take the account, one was brought to him that owed him ten thousand talents.

25 And as he had not wherewith to pay it, his lord commanded that he should be sold, and his wife and children and all that he had, and payment to be made.

26 But that servant falling down besought him, saying: Have patience with me and I will pay thee all.

27 And the lord of that servant, being moved with pity, let him go and forgave him the debt.

28 But when that servant was gone out, he found one of his fellow servants that owed him an hundred pence: and laying hold of him, he throttled him, saying: Pay what thou owest.

29 And his fellow servant, falling down, besought him, saying: Have patience with me and I will pay thee all.

30 And he would not: but went and cast him into prison till he paid the debt.

31 Now his fellow servants, seeing what was done, were very much grieved: and they came and told their lord all that was done.

32 Then his lord called him and said to him: Thou wicked servant, I forgave thee all the debt, because thou besoughtest me:

33 Shouldst not thou then have had compassion also on thy fellow servant, even as I had compassion on thee?

34 And his lord being angry, delivered him to the torturers until he paid all the debt.

35 So also shall my heavenly Father do to you, if you forgive not every one his brother from your hearts.

CHAPTER 19

Christ declares matrimony to be indissoluble. He recommends the making one's self an eunuch for the kingdom of heaven and parting with all things for him. He shews the danger of riches and the reward of leaving all to join him.

AND it came to pass when Jesus had ended these words, he departed from Galilee [1] and came into the coasts of Judea, beyond Jordan.

2 And great multitudes followed him: and he healed them there.

3 [2] And there came to him the Pharisees tempting him and saying: Is it lawful for a man to put away his wife for every cause?

4 Who answering, said to them: Have ye not read that he [3] who made man from the beginning made them male and female? And he said:

5 [4] *For this cause shall a man leave father and mother and shall cleave to his wife: and they two shall be in one flesh.*

6 Therefore now they are not two, but one flesh. What therefore God hath joined together, let no man put asunder.

7 They say to him: [5] Why then did Moses command to give a bill of divorce and to put away?

8 He saith to them: Because Moses by reason of the hardness of your heart permitted you to put away your wives. But from the beginning it was not so.

9 [6] And I say to you that whosoever shall put away his wife, except it be for fornication, and shall marry another, committeth adultery: and he that shall marry her that is put away committeth adultery.

10 His disciples say unto him: If the case of a man with his wife be so, it is not expedient to marry.

11 Who said to them: All men take not this word, but they to whom it is given.

---

[12] John, 20, 23. [13] Luke, 17, 4. CHAP. 19. [1] Mark, 10, 1. [2] Mark, 10, 2. [3] Gen. 1, 27. [4] Gen. 2, 24; 1 Cor. 6, 16; Eph. 5, 31. [5] Deut. 24, 1. [6] Matt. 5, 32; Mark, 10, 11; Luke, 16, 18; 1 Cor. 7, 10.

Ver. 20. *There am I in the midst of them.* This is understood of such assemblies only as are gathered in the name and authority of Christ and in unity of the Church of Christ (St. Cyprian, *De Unitate Ecclesiæ*).

Ver. 24. *Talents.* A talent was seven hundred and fifty ounces of silver, which at the rate of five shillings to the ounce is a hundred and eighty-seven pounds, ten shillings sterling.

Ver. 28. *Pence.* The Roman penny was the eighth part of an ounce, that is, about sevenpence halfpenny English.

CHAP. 19. Ver. 9. *Except it be in the case of fornication, that is, of adultery, the wife may be put away: but even then the husband cannot marry another as long as the wife is living.*

Ver. 11. *All men take not this word.* That is, all receive not the gift of living singly and given.

12 For there are eunuchs who were born so from their mother's womb: and there are eunuchs who were made so by men: and there are eunuchs who have made themselves eunuchs for the kingdom of heaven. He that can take, let him take it.

13 [7] Then were little children presented to him, that he should impose hands upon them and pray. And the disciples rebuked them.

14 But Jesus said to them: [8] Suffer the little children and forbid them not to come to me: for the kingdom of heaven is for such.

15 And when he had imposed hands upon them, he departed from thence.

16 And behold one came and said to him: Good master, what good shall I do that I may have life everlasting?

17 Who said to him: Why askest thou me concerning good? One is good, God. But if thou wilt enter into life, keep the commandments.

18 He said to him: Which? And Jesus said: [9] *Thou shalt do no murder. Thou shalt not commit adultery. Thou shalt not steal, Thou shalt not bear false witness.*

19 *Honour thy father and thy mother.* And: *Thou shalt love thy neighbour as thyself.*

20 The young man saith to him: All these have I kept from my youth. What is yet wanting to me?

21 Jesus saith to him: If thou wilt be perfect, go sell what thou hast and give to the poor and thou shalt have treasure in heaven. And come follow me.

22 And when the young man had heard this word, he went away sad: for he had great possessions.

23 Then Jesus said to his disciples: Amen, I say to you that a rich man shall hardly enter into the kingdom of heaven.

24 And again I say to you: It is easier for a camel to pass through the eye of a needle than for a rich man to enter into the kingdom of heaven.

25 And when they had heard this, the disciples wondered very much, saying: Who then can be saved?

26 And Jesus beholding, said to them: With men this is impossible: but with God all things are possible.

27 Then Peter answering, said to him: Behold we have left all things and have followed thee: what therefore shall we have?

28 And Jesus said to them: Amen, I say to you that you, who have followed me, in the regeneration when the Son of man shall sit on the seat of his ma-

jesty, you also shall sit on twelve seats judging the twelve tribes of Israel.

29 And every one that hath left house or brethren or sisters or father or mother or wife or children or lands, for my name's sake, shall receive an hundredfold and shall possess life everlasting.

30 [10] And many that are first shall be last: and the last shall be first.

CHAPTER 20

The parable of the labourers in the vineyard. The ambition of the two sons of Zebedee. Christ gives sight to two blind men.

THE kingdom of heaven is like to an householder who went out early in the morning to hire labourers into his vineyard.

2 And having agreed with the labourers for a penny a day, he sent them into his vineyard.

3 And going out about the third hour, he saw others standing in the market place idle.

4 And he said to them: Go you also into my vineyard and I will give you what shall be just.

5 And they went their way. And again he went out about the sixth and the ninth hour and did in like manner.

6 But about the eleventh hour he went out and found others standing. And he saith to them: Why stand you here all the day idle?

7 They say to him: Because no man hath hired us. He saith to them: Go you also into my vineyard.

8 And when evening was come, the lord of the vineyard saith to his steward: Call the labourers and pay them their hire, beginning from the last even to the first.

9 When therefore they were come that came about the eleventh hour, they received every man a penny.

10 But when the first also came, they thought that they should receive more: and they also received every man a penny.

11 And receiving it they murmured against the master of the house,

12 Saying: These last have worked but one hour: and thou hast made

[7] Mark, 10, 13; Luke, 18, 15. [8] Matt. 18, 3. [9] Exod. 20, 13. [10] Matt. 20, 16; Mark, 10, 31; Luke, 13, 30.

chastely, unless they pray for the grace of God to enable them to live so. And for some it may be necessary to that end to fast as well as pray: and to those it is given from above.

Ver. 12. *There are eunuchs, who have made themselves eunuchs, for the kingdom of heaven.* This text is not to be taken in the literal sense; but means, that there are such, who have taken a firm and commendable resolution of leading a single and chaste life, in order to serve God in a more perfect state than those who marry: as St. Paul clearly shews (1 Cor. 7, 37, 38).

them equal to us that have borne the burden of the day and the heats.

13 But he answering said to one of them: Friend, I do thee no wrong. Didst thou not agree with me for a penny?

14 Take what is thine and go thy way. I will also give to this last even as to thee.

15 Or, is it not lawful for me to do what I will? Is thy eye evil, because I am good?

16 ¹ So shall the last be first and the first last. For many are called but few chosen.

17 And Jesus going up to Jerusalem, took the twelve disciples apart and said to them:

18 Behold we go up to Jerusalem, and the Son of man shall be betrayed to the chief priests and the scribes: and they shall condemn him to death.

19 And shall deliver him to the Gentiles to be mocked and scourged and crucified: and the third day he shall rise again.

20 ² Then came to him the mother of the sons of Zebedee with her sons, adoring and asking something of him.

21 Who said to her: What wilt thou? She saith to him: Say that these my two sons may sit, the one on thy right hand, and the other on thy left, in thy kingdom.

22 And Jesus answering, said: You know not what you ask. Can you drink the chalice that I shall drink? They say to him: We can.

23 He saith to them: My chalice indeed you shall drink; but to sit on my right or left hand is not mine to give to you, but to them for whom it is prepared by my Father.

24 ³ And the ten, hearing it, were moved with indignation against the two brethren.

25 ⁴ But Jesus called them to him and said: You know that the princes of the Gentiles lord it over them and they that are the greater exercise power upon them.

26 It shall not be so among you: but whosoever will be the greater among you, let him be your minister.

27 And he that will be first among you shall be your servant.

28 ⁵ Even as the Son of man is not come to be ministered unto, but to

minister and to give his life a redemption for many.

29 ⁶ And when they went out from Jericho, a great multitude followed him.

30 And behold two blind men sitting by the way side heard that Jesus passed by. And they cried out, saying: O Lord, thou son of David, have mercy on us.

31 And the multitude rebuked them that they should hold their peace. But they cried out the more, saying: O Lord, thou son of David, have mercy on us.

32 And Jesus stood and called them and said: What will ye that I do to you?

33 They say to him: Lord, that our eyes be opened.

34 And Jesus having compassion on them, touched their eyes. And immediately they saw and followed him.

CHAPTER 21

Christ rides into Jerusalem upon an ass. He casts the buyers and sellers out of the temple, curses the fig tree and puts to silence the priests and scribes.

AND ¹ when they drew nigh to Jerusalem and were come to Bethphage, unto mount Olivet, then Jesus sent two disciples,

2 Saying to them: Go ye into the village that is over against you: and immediately you shall find an ass tied and a colt with her. Loose *them* and bring *them* to me.

3 And if any man shall say anything to you, say ye that the Lord hath need of them. And forthwith he will let them go.

4 Now all this was done that it might be fulfilled which was spoken by the prophet, saying:

5 ² *Tell ye the daughter of Sion: Behold thy king cometh to thee, meek, and sitting upon an ass and a colt, the foal of her that is used to the yoke.*

6 And the disciples going, did as Jesus commanded them.

7 And they brought the ass and the colt and laid their garments upon them and made him sit thereon.

8 And a very great multitude spread their garments in the way: and others cut boughs from the trees and strewed them in the way.

9 And the multitudes that went before and that followed cried, saying: *Hosanna to the son of David:* ³ *Blessed is he that cometh in the name of the Lord: Hosanna in the highest.*

10 And when he was come into Jerusalem, the whole city was moved, saying: Who is this?

11 And the people said: This is Jesus, the prophet from Nazareth of Galilee.

CHAP. 20. ¹ Matt. 19, 30; Mark, 10, 31; Luke, 13, 30. ² Mark, 10, 35. ³ Mark, 10, 41. ⁴ Luke, 22, 25. ⁵ Phil. 2, 7. ⁶ Mark, 10, 46; Luke, 18, 35. CHAP. 21. ¹ Mark, 11, 1; Luke, 19, 29. ² Isai. 62, 11; Zach. 9, 9; John, 12, 15. ³ Ps. 117, 26; Mark, 11, 10; Luke, 19, 38.

CHAP. 20. Ver. 15. *What I will.* That is, with my own, and in matters that depend on my own bounty.

12 'And Jesus went into the temple of God and cast out all them that sold and bought in the temple and overthrew the tables of the money changers and the chairs of them that sold doves.

13 And he saith to them: It is written, [5] *My house shall be called the house of prayer; but you have made it a den of thieves.*

14 And there came to him the blind and the lame in the temple: and he healed them.

15 And the chief priests and scribes, seeing the wonderful things that he did and the children crying in the temple and saying: *Hosanna to the son of David,* were moved with indignation,

16 And said to him: Hearest thou what these say? And Jesus said to them: Yea, have you never read: [6] *Out of the mouth of infants and of sucklings thou hast perfected praise?*

17 And leaving them, he went out of the city into Bethania and remained there.

18 And in the morning, returning into the city, he was hungry.

19 [7] And seeing a certain fig tree by the way side, he came to it and found nothing on it but leaves only. And he saith to it: May no fruit grow on thee henceforward for ever. And immediately the fig tree withered away.

20 [8] And the disciples seeing it wondered, saying: How is it presently withered away?

21 And Jesus answering, said to them: Amen, I say to you, if you shall have faith and stagger not, not only this of the fig tree shall you do, but also if you shall say to this mountain, Take up and cast thyself into the sea, it shall be done.

22 [9] And all things whatsoever you shall ask in prayer believing, you shall receive.

23 And when he was come into the temple, there came to him, as he was teaching, the chief priests and ancients of the people, saying: [10] By what authority dost thou these things? And who hath given thee this authority?

24 Jesus answering, said to them: I also will ask you one word, which if you shall tell me, I will also tell you by what authority I do these things.

25 The baptism of John, whence was it? From heaven or from men? But they thought within themselves, saying:

26 If we shall say, from heaven, he will say to us: Why then did you not believe him? But if we shall say, from men, we are afraid of the multitude: [11] for all held John as a prophet.

27 And answering Jesus, they said: We know not. He also said to them: Neither do I tell you by what authority I do these things.

28 But what think you? A certain man had two sons: and coming to the first, he said: Son, go work to-day in my vineyard.

29 And he answering, said: I will not. But afterwards, being moved with repentance, he went.

30 And coming to the other, he said in like manner. And he answering said: I go, Sir. And he went not.

31 Which of the two did the father's will? They say to him: The first. Jesus saith to them: Amen I say to you that the publicans and the harlots shall go into the kingdom of God before you.

32 For John came to you in the way of justice: and you did not believe him. But the publicans and the harlots believed him: but you, seeing it, did not even afterwards repent, that you might believe him.

33 Hear ye another parable. [12] There was a man, an householder, who planted a vineyard and made a hedge round about it and dug in it a press and built a tower and let it out to husbandmen and went into a strange country.

34 And when the time of the fruits drew nigh, he sent his servants to the husbandmen that they might receive the fruits thereof.

35 And the husbandmen laying hands on his servants, beat one and killed another and stoned another.

36 Again he sent other servants, more than the former; and they did to them in like manner.

37 And last of all he sent to them his son, saying: They will reverence my son.

38 But the husbandmen seeing the son, said among themselves: [13] This is the heir: come, let us kill him, and we shall have his inheritance.

39 And taking him, they cast him forth out of the vineyard and killed him.

40 When therefore the lord of the vineyard shall come, what will he do to those husbandmen?

41 They say to him: He will bring those evil men to an evil end and will let out his vineyard to other husbandmen that shall render him the fruit in due season.

42 Jesus saith to them: Have you never read in the Scriptures: [14] *The*

[4] Mark. 11, 15; Luke, 19, 45; John, 2, 14. [5] Isai. 56, 7; Jer. 7, 11; Luke, 19, 46. [6] Ps. 8, 3. [7] Mark, 11, 13. [8] Mark, 11, 20. [9] Matt. 7, 7; Mark, 11, 24; John, 14, 13; 16, 23. [10] Mark, 11, 28; Luke, 20, 2. [11] Matt. 14, 5. [12] Isai. 5, 1; Jer. 2, 21; Mark, 11, 32; Luke, 20, 9. [13] Matt. 26, 3; 27, 1; John, 11, 53. [14] Ps. 117, 22; Acts, 4, 11; Rom. 9, 33; 1 Peter, 2, 7.

stone which the builders rejected, the same is become the head of the corner? By the Lord this has been done; and it is wonderful in our eyes.

43 Therefore I say to you that the kingdom of God shall be taken from you and shall be given to a nation yielding the fruits thereof.

44 And whosoever shall fall on this stone shall be broken: but on whomsoever it shall fall, it shall grind him to powder.

45 And when the chief priests and Pharisees had heard his parables, they knew that he spoke of them.

46 And seeking to lay hands on him, they feared the multitudes, because they held him as a prophet.

CHAPTER 22

The parable of the marriage feast. Christ orders tribute to be paid to Cæsar. He confutes the Sadducees, shews which is the first commandment in the law and puzzles the Pharisees.

AND Jesus answering, spoke again in parables to them, saying:

2 ¹ The kingdom of heaven is likened to a king who made a marriage for his son.

3 And he sent his servants to call them that were invited to the marriage: and they would not come.

4 Again he sent other servants, saying: Tell them that were invited, Behold, I have prepared my dinner; my beeves and fatlings are killed, and all things are ready. Come ye to the marriage.

5 But they neglected and went their ways, one to his farm and another to his merchandise.

6 And the rest laid hands on his servants and, having treated them contumeliously, put them to death.

7 But when the king had heard of it, he was angry: and sending his armies, he destroyed those murderers and burnt their city.

8 Then he saith to his servants: The marriage indeed is ready; but they that were invited were not worthy.

9 Go ye therefore into the highways; and as many as you shall find, call to the marriage.

10 And his servants going forth into the ways, gathered together all that

CHAP. 22. ¹ Luke, 14, 36; Apoc. 19, 9. ² Matt. 8, 12; 13, 42; 25, 30. ³ Mark, 12, 13; Luke, 20, 20. ⁴ Rom. 13, 7. ⁵ Acts, 23, 6. ⁶ Deut. 25, 5; Mark, 12, 19; Luke, 20, 28.

CHAP. 22. Ver. 16. *The Herodians.* That is, some that belonged to Herod and that joined with him in standing up for the necessity of paying tribute to Cæsar, that is, to the Roman Emperor. Some are of opinion that there was a sect among the Jews called Herodians, from their maintaining that Herod was the Messias.

they found, both bad and good: and the marriage was filled with guests.

11 And the king went in to see the guests: and he saw there a man who had not on a wedding garment.

12 And he saith to him: Friend, how camest thou in hither not having on a wedding garment? But he was silent.

13 Then the king said to the waiters: ² Bind his hands and feet, and cast him into the exterior darkness. There, shall be weeping and gnashing of teeth.

14 For many are called, but few *are* chosen.

15 ³ Then the Pharisees going, consulted among themselves how to insnare him in *his* speech.

16 And they sent to him their disciples with the Herodians, saying: Master, we know that thou art a true speaker and teachest the way of God in truth. Neither carest thou for any man: for thou dost not regard the person of men.

17 Tell us therefore what dost thou think? Is it lawful to give tribute to Cæsar, or not?

18 But Jesus knowing their wickedness, said: Why do you tempt me, ye hypocrites?

19 Shew me the coin of the tribute. And they offered him a penny.

20 And Jesus saith to them: Whose image and inscription is this?

21 They say to him: Cæsar's. Then he saith to them: ⁴ Render therefore to Cæsar the things that are Cæsar's; and to God, the things that are God's.

22 And hearing *this,* they wondered and, leaving him, went their ways.

23 That day there came to him the Sadducees, who say ⁵ there is no resurrection; and asked him,

24 Saying: Master, Moses said ⁶ *If a man die having no son, his brother shall marry his wife and raise up issue to his brother.*

25 Now there were with us seven brethren: and the first having married a wife, died; and not having issue, left his wife to his brother.

26 In like manner the second and the third and so on, to the seventh.

27 And last of all the woman died also.

28 At the resurrection therefore, whose wife of the seven shall she be? For they all had her.

29 And Jesus answering, said to them: You err, not knowing the Scriptures nor the power of God.

30 For in the resurrection they shall neither marry nor be married, but shall be as the angels of God in heaven.

31 And concerning the resurrection of the dead, have you not read that

which was spoken by God, saying to you:

32 [7] *I am the God of Abraham and the God of Isaac and the God of Jacob?* He is not the God of the dead but of the living.

33 And the multitudes hearing it were in admiration at his doctrine.

34 But the Pharisees, hearing that he had silenced the Sadducees, came together.

35 [8] And one of them, a doctor of the law, asked him, tempting him:

36 Master, which is the great commandment in the law?

37 Jesus said to him: [9] *Thou shalt love the Lord thy God with thy whole heart and with thy whole soul and with thy whole mind.*

38 This is the greatest and the first commandment.

39 And the second is like to this: [10] *Thou shalt love thy neighbour as thyself.*

40 On these two commandments dependeth the whole law and the prophets.

41 And the Pharisees being gathered together, Jesus asked them,

42 [11] Saying: What think you of Christ? Whose son is he? They say to him: David's.

43 He saith to them: [12] How then doth David in spirit call him Lord, saying:

44 [13] *The Lord said to my Lord: Sit on my right hand, until I make thy enemies thy footstool?*

45 If David then call him Lord, how is he his son?

46 And no man was able to answer him a word: neither durst any man from that day forth ask him any more questions.

CHAPTER 23

Christ admonishes the people to follow the good doctrine, not the bad example of the scribes and Pharisees. He wrns his disciples not to imitate their ambition and denounces divers woes against them for their hypocrisy and blindness.

THEN Jesus spoke to the multitudes and to his disciples,

2 Saying: [1] The scribes and the Pharisees have sitten on the chair of Moses.

3 All things therefore whatsoever they shall say to you, observe and do: but according to their works do ye not. For they say, and do not.

4 [2] For they bind heavy and insupportable burdens and lay them on men's shoulders; but with a finger of their own they will not move them.

5 And all their works they do for to be seen of men. [3] For they make their phylacteries broad and enlarge their fringes.

6 [4] And they love the first places at feasts and the first chairs in the synagogues,

7 And salutations in the market place, and to be called by men, Rabbi.

8 [5] But be not you called Rabbi. For one is your master: and all you are brethren.

9 [6] And call none your father upon earth: for one is your father, who is in heaven.

10 Neither be ye called masters: for one is your master, Christ.

11 He that is the greatest among you shall be your servant.

12 [7] And whosoever shall exalt himself shall be humbled: and he that shall humble himself shall be exalted.

13 But woe to you, scribes and Pharisees, hypocrites, because you shut the kingdom of heaven against men: for you yourselves do not enter in and those that are going in, you suffer not to enter.

14 Woe to you scribes and Pharisees, hypocrites, [8] because you devour the houses of widows, praying long prayers. For this you shall receive the greater judgment.

15 Woe to you, scribes and Pharisees, hypocrites, because you go round about the sea and the land to make one proselyte. And when he is made, you make him the child of hell twofold more than yourselves.

16 Woe to you, blind guides, that say, Whosoever shall swear by the temple, it is nothing; but he that shall swear by the gold of the temple is a debtor.

17 Ye foolish and blind: for whether is greater, the gold or the temple that sanctifieth the gold?

18 And whosoever shall swear by the altar, it is nothing; but whosoever shall swear by the gift that is upon it is a debtor.

19 Ye blind: for whether is greater,

[7] Exod. 3, 6. [8] Mark, 12, 28; Luke, 10, 25. [9] Deut. 6, 5. [10] Lev. 19, 18; Mark, 12, 31. [11] Mark, 12, 35; Luke, 20, 41. [12] Luke, 20, 42. [13] Ps. 109, 1. CHAP. 23. [1] 2 Esd. 8, 4. [2] Luke, 11, 46; Acts, 15, 10. [3] Num. 15, 38; Deut. 6, 8; 22, 12. [4] Mark, 12, 39; Luke, 11, 43; 20, 46. [5] James, 3, 1. [6] Mal. 1, 6. [7] Luke, 14, 11; 18, 14. [8] Mark, 12, 40; Luke, 20, 47.

CHAP. 23. Ver. 5. *Phylacteries.* That is, parchments, on which they wrote the ten commandments and carried them on their foreheads before their eyes: which the Pharisees affected to wear broader than other men; so to seem more zealous for the law.

Ver. 9, 10. *Call none your father—Neither be ye called masters.* The meaning is that our Father in heaven is incomparably more to be regarded than any father upon earth: and no master to be followed who would lead us away from Christ. But this does not hinder but that we are by the law of God to have a due respect both for our parents and spiritual fathers (1 Cor. 4, 15) and for our masters and teachers.

the gift or the altar that sanctifieth the gift?

20 He therefore that sweareth by the altar sweareth by it and by all things that are upon it.

21 And whosoever shall swear by the temple sweareth by it and by him that dwelleth in it.

22 And he that sweareth by heaven sweareth by the throne of God and by him that sitteth thereon.

23 [9] Woe to you, scribes and Pharisees, hypocrites; because you tithe mint and anise and cummin and have left the weightier things of the law: [10] judgment and mercy and faith. These things you ought to have done and not to leave those undone.

24 Blind guides, who strain out a gnat and swallow a camel.

25 Woe to you, scribes and Pharisees, hypocrites; because you make clean the outside of the cup and of the dish, but within you are full of rapine and uncleanness.

26 Thou blind Pharisee, first make clean the inside of the cup and of the dish, that the outside may become clean.

27 Woe to you, scribes and Pharisees, hypocrites; because you are like to whited sepulchres, which outwardly appear to men beautiful but within are full of dead men's bones and of all filthiness.

28 So you also outwardly indeed appear to men just: but inwardly you are full of hypocrisy and iniquity.

29 Woe to you, scribes and Pharisees, hypocrites, that build the sepulchres of the prophets and adorn the monuments of the just,

30 And say: If we had been in the days of our fathers, we would not have been partakers with them in the blood of the prophets.

31 Wherefore you are witnesses against yourselves, that you are the sons of them that killed the prophets.

32 Fill ye up then the measure of your fathers.

33 [11] You serpents, generation of

vipers, how will you flee from the judgment of hell?

34 Therefore behold I send to you prophets and wise men and scribes: and some of them you will put to death and crucify: and some you will scourge in your synagogues and persecute from city to city.

35 That upon you may come all the just blood that hath been shed upon the earth, [12] from the blood of Abel the just, even unto the blood of [13] Zacharias the son of Barachias, whom you killed between the temple and the altar.

36 Amen I say to you, all these things shall come upon this generation.

37 [14] Jerusalem, Jerusalem, thou that killest the prophets and stonest them that are sent unto thee, how often would I have gathered together thy children, as the hen doth gather her chickens under her wings, and thou wouldst not?

38 Behold, your house shall be left to you, desolate.

39 For I say to you, you shall not see me henceforth till you say: Blessed is he that cometh in the name of the Lord.

CHAPTER 24

Christ foretells the destruction of the temple, with the signs that shall come before it and before the last judgment. We must always watch.

AND [1] Jesus being come out of the temple, went away. And his disciples came to shew him the buildings of the temple.

2 And he answering, said to them: Do you see all these things? Amen I say to you, [2] there shall not be left here a stone upon a stone that shall not be destroyed.

3 And when he was sitting on mount Olivet, the disciples came to him privately, saying: Tell us when shall these things be? And what shall be the sign of thy coming and of the consummation of the world?

4 And Jesus answering, said to them: [3] Take heed that no man seduce you.

5 For many will come in my name saying, I am Christ. And they will seduce many.

6 And you shall hear of wars and rumours of wars. See that ye be not troubled. For these things must come to pass: but the end is not yet.

7 For nation shall rise against nation, and kingdom against kingdom: and there shall be pestilences and famines and earthquakes in places.

8 Now all these are the beginnings of sorrows.

9 [4] Then shall they deliver you up

[9] Luke, 11, 42. [10] Mich. 6, 8; Zach. 7, 9. [11] Matt. 3, 7. [12] Gen. 4, 8; Heb. 11, 4. [13] 2 Par. 24, 22. [14] Luke, 13, 34. CHAP. 24. [1] Mark, 13, 1. [2] Luke, 19, 44. [3] Eph. 5, 6; Col. 2, 18. [4] Matt. 10, 17; Luke, 21, 12; John, 15, 20; 16, 2.

Ver. 29. *Build the sepulchres.* This is not blamed, as if it were in itself evil to build or adorn the monuments of the prophets: but the hypocrisy of the Pharisees is here taxed; who, whilst they pretended to honour the memory of the prophets, were persecuting even unto death the Lord of the prophets.

Ver. 35. *That upon you may come.* Not that they should suffer more than their own sins justly deserved: but that the justice of God should now fall upon them with such a final vengeance, once for all, as might comprise all the different kinds of judgments and punishments that had at any time before been inflicted for the shedding of just blood.

to be afflicted and shall put you to death: and you shall be hated by all nations for my name's sake.

10 And then shall many be scandalized and shall betray one another and shall hate one another.

11 And many falst prophets shall rise and shall seduce many.

12 And because iniquity hath abounded, the charity of many shall grow cold.

13 But he that shall persevere to the end, he shall be saved.

14 And this gospel of the kingdom shall be preached in the whole world, for a testimony to all nations: and then shall the consummation come.

15 [5] When therefore you shall see *the abomination of desolation*, which was spoken of by [6] Daniel the prophet, standing in the holy place: he that readeth let him understand.

16 Then they that are in Judea, let them flee to the mountains:

17 And he that is on the housetop, let him not come down to take any thing out of his house:

18 And he that is in the field, let him not go back to take his coat.

19 And woe to them that are with child and that give suck in those days.

20 But pray that your flight be not in the winter or on the [7] sabbath.

21 For there shall be then great tribulation, such as hath not been from the beginning of the world until now, neither shall be.

22 And unless those days had been shortened, no flesh should be saved: but for the sake of the elect those days shall be shortened.

23 [8] Then if any man shall say to you, Lo here is Christ, or there: do not believe him.

24 For there shall arise false Christs and false prophets and shall shew great signs and wonders, insomuch as to deceive (if possible) even the elect.

25 Behold I have told it to you, beforehand.

26 If therefore they shall say to you, Behold he is in the desert: go ye not out. Behold *he* is in the closets: believe it not.

27 For as lightning cometh out of the east and appeareth even into the west: so shall also the coming of the Son of man be.

28 [9] Wheresoever the body shall be, there shall the eagles also be gathered together.

29 [10] And immediately after the tribulation of those days, the sun shall be darkened and the moon shall not give her light and the stars shall fall from heaven and the powers of heaven shall be moved.

30 And then shall appear the sign of the Son of man in heaven. And then shall all tribes of the earth mourn: [11] and they shall see the Son of man coming in the clouds of heaven with much power and majesty.

31 [12] And he shall send his angels with a trumpet and a great voice: and they shall gather together his elect from the four winds, from the farthest parts of the heavens to the utmost bounds of them.

32 And from the fig tree learn a parable: When the branch thereof is now tender and the leaves come forth, you know that summer is nigh.

33 So you also, when you shall see all these things, know ye that it is nigh, *even* at the doors.

34 Amen I say to you that this generation shall not pass till all these things be done.

35 [13] Heaven and earth shall pass: but my words shall not pass.

36 But of that day and hour no one knoweth: no, not the angels of heaven, but the Father alone.

37 [14] And as in the days of Noe, so shall also the coming of the Son of man be.

38 For, as in the days before the flood they were eating and drinking, marrying and giving in marriage, even till that day in which Noe entered into the ark:

39 And they knew not till the flood came and took them all away: so also shall the coming of the Son of man be.

40 Then two shall be in the field. One shall be taken and one shall be left.

41 Two women shall be grinding at the mill. One shall be taken and one shall be left.

42 Watch ye therefore, because you know not what hour your Lord will come.

43 But this know ye, [15] that, if the goodman of the house knew at what hour the thief would come, he would certainly watch and would not suffer his house to be broken open.

[5] Mark, 13, 14; Luke, 21, 20. [6] Dan. 9, 27. [7] Acts, 1, 12. [8] Mark, 13, 21; Luke, 17, 23. [9] Luke, 17, 37. [10] Isai. 13, 10; Ezech. 32, 7; Joel, 2, 10; 3, 15; Mark, 13, 24; Luke, 21, 25. [11] Apoc. 1, 7. [12] 1 Cor. 15, 52; 1 Thess. 4, 15. [13] Mark, 13, 31. [14] Gen. 7, 7; Luke, 17, 26. [15] Mark, 13, 33; Luke, 12, 39.

CHAP. 24. Ver. 28. *Wheresoever.* The coming of Christ shall be sudden and manifest to all the world, like lightning: and wheresoever he shall come, thither shall all mankind be gathered to him, as eagles are gathered about a dead body.

Ver. 29. *The stars.* Or flaming meteors resembling stars.

Ver. 30. *The sign.* The Cross of Christ.

Ver. 35. *Shall pass.* Because they shall be changed at the end of the world into a new heaven and new earth.

44 Wherefore be you also ready, because at what hour you know not the Son of man will come.

45 Who, thinkest thou, is a faithful and wise servant, whom his lord hath appointed over his family, to give them meat in season?

46 [16] Blessed is that servant, whom when his lord shall come he shall find so doing.

47 Amen I say to you: he shall place him over all his goods.

48 But if that evil servant shall say in his heart: My lord is long a coming:

49 And shall begin to strike his fellow servants and shall eat and drink with drunkards:

50 The lord of that servant shall come in a day that he hopeth not and at an hour that he knoweth not:

51 And shall separate him and appoint his portion with the hypocrites. [17] There, shall be weeping and gnashing of teeth.

CHAPTER 25

The parable of the ten virgins and of the talents. The description of the last judgment.

THEN shall the kingdom of heaven be like to ten virgins, who taking their lamps went out to meet the bridegroom and the bride.

2 And five of them were foolish and five wise.

3 But the five foolish, having taken their lamps, did not take oil with them.

4 But the wise took oil in their vessels with the lamps.

5 And the bridegroom tarrying, they all slumbered and slept.

6 And at midnight there was a cry made: Behold the bridegroom cometh. Go ye forth to meet him.

7 Then all those virgins arose and trimmed their lamps.

8 And the foolish said to the wise: Give us of your oil, for our lamps are gone out.

9 The wise answered, saying: Lest perhaps there be not enough for us and for you, go ye rather to them that sell and buy for yourselves.

10 Now whilst they went to buy the bridegroom came: and they that were ready went in with him to the marriage. And the door was shut.

11 But at last came also the other virgins, saying: Lord, Lord, open to us.

12 But he answering said: Amen I say to you, I know you not.

13 [1] Watch ye therefore, because you know not the day nor the hour.

11 [2] For even as a man going into a far country called his servants and delivered to them his goods;

15 And to one he gave five talents, and to another two, and to another one, to every one according to his proper ability: and immediately he took his journey.

16 And he that had received the five talents went his way and traded with the same and gained other five.

17 And in like manner he that had received the two gained other two.

18 But he that had received the one, going his way, digged into the earth and hid his lord's money.

19 But after a long time the lord of those servants came and reckoned with them.

20 And he that had received the five talents coming brought other five talents, saying: Lord, thou didst deliver to me five talents. Behold I have gained other five over and above.

21 His lord said to him: Well done, good and faithful servant, because thou hast been faithful over a few things, I will place thee over many things. Enter thou into the joy of thy lord.

22 And he also that had received the two talents came and said: Lord, thou deliveredst two talents to me. Behold I have gained other two.

23 His lord said to him: Well done, good and faithful servant: because thou hast been faithful over a few things, I will place thee over many things. Enter thou into the joy of thy lord.

24 But he that had received the one talent came and said: Lord, I know that thou art a hard man; thou reapest where thou hast not sown and gatherest where thou hast not strewed.

25 And being afraid, I went and hid thy talent in the earth. Behold here thou hast that which is thine.

26 And his lord answering, said to him: Wicked and slothful servant, thou knewest that I reap where I sow not and gather where I have not strewed.

27 Thou oughtest therefore to have committed my money to the bankers: and at my coming I should have received my own with usury.

28 Take ye away therefore the talent from him and give it him that hath ten talents.

29 [3] For to every one that hath shall be given, and he shall abound: but from him that hath not, that also which he seemeth to have shall be taken away.

30 And the unprofitable servant, cast ye out into the exterior darkness. There, shall be weeping and gnashing of teeth.

16 Apoc. 16, 15. 17 Matt. 13, 42; 25, 30. CHAP. 25. 1 Mark, 13, 33. 2 Luke, 19, 12. 3 Matt. 13, 12; Mark, 4, 25; Luke, 8, 18; 19, 26.

31 And when the Son of man shall come in his majesty, and all the angels with him, then shall he sit upon the seat of his majesty.

32 And all nations shall be gathered together before him: and he shall separate them one from another, as the shepherd separateth the sheep from the goats:

33 And he shall set the sheep on his right hand, but the goats on his left.

34 Then shall the king say to them that shall be on his right hand: Come, ye blessed of my Father, possess you the kingdom prepared for you from the foundation of the world.

35 [4] For I was hungry, and you gave me to eat: I was thirsty, and you gave me to drink: I was a stranger, and you took me in:

36 Naked, and you covered me; [5] sick, and you visited me: I was in prison, and you came to me.

37 Then shall the just answer him, saying: Lord, when did we see thee hungry and fed thee: thirsty and gave thee drink?

38 And when did we see thee a stranger and took thee in? Or naked and covered thee?

39 Or when did we see thee sick or in prison and came to thee?

40 And the king answering shall say to them: Amen I say to you, as long as you did it to one of these my least brethren, you did it to me.

41 Then he shall say to them also that shall be on his left hand: [6] Depart from me, you cursed, into everlasting fire, which was prepared for the devil and his angels.

42 For I was hungry and you gave me not to eat: I was thirsty and you gave me not to drink.

43 I was a stranger and you took me not in: naked and you covered me not: sick and in prison and you did not visit me.

44 Then they also shall answer him, saying: Lord, when did we see thee hungry or thirsty or a stranger or naked or sick or in prison and did not minister to thee?

45 Then he shall answer them, saying: Amen I say to you, as long as you did it not to one of these least, neither did you do it to me.

46 [7] And these shall go into everlasting punishment: but the just, into life everlasting.

CHAPTER 26

The Jews conspire against Christ. He is anointed by Mary. The treason of Judas. The last supper. The prayer in the garden. The apprehension of our Lord. His treatment in the house of Caiphas.

AND it came to pass, when Jesus had ended all these words, he said to his disciples:

2 [1] You know that after two days shall be the pasch: and the Son of man shall be delivered up to be crucified.

3 Then were gathered together the chief priests and ancients of the people, into the court of the high priest, who was called Caiphas:

4 And they consulted together that by subtilty they might apprehend Jesus and put him to death.

5 But they said: Not on the festival day, lest perhaps there should be a tumult among the people.

6 And when Jesus was in Bethania, in the house of Simon the leper,

7 There came to him a woman having an alabaster box of precious ointment [2] and poured it on his head as he was at table.

8 And the disciples seeing it had indignation, saying: To what purpose is this waste?

9 For this might have been sold for much and given to the poor.

10 And Jesus knowing *it*, said to them: Why do you trouble this woman? For she hath wrought a good work upon me.

11 For the poor you have always with you: but me you have not always.

12 For she in pouring this ointment upon my body hath done it for my burial.

13 Amen I say to you, wheresoever this gospel shall be preached in the whole world, that also which she hath done shall be told for a memory of her.

14 [3] Then went one of the twelve, who was called Judas Iscariot, to the chief priests,

15 And said to them: What will you give me, and I will deliver him unto you? But they appointed him thirty pieces of silver.

16 And from thenceforth he sought opportunity to betray him.

17 [4] And on the first day of the Azymes, the disciples came to Jesus, saying: Where wilt thou that we prepare for thee to eat the pasch?

18 But Jesus said: Go ye into the city to a certain man and say to him: The master saith, My time is near at hand.

[4] Isai. 58, 7; Ezech. 18, 7, 16. [5] Ecclus 7, 39. [6] Ps. 6, 9; Matt. 7, 23; Luke, 13, 27. [7] Dan. 12, 2; John, 5, 29. CHAP. 26. [1] Mark, 14, 1; Luke, 22, 1. [2] Mark, 14, 8; John, 11, 2; 12, 3. [3] Mark, 14, 10; Luke, 22, 3. [4] Mark, 14, 12; Luke, 22, 7.

CHAP. 26. Ver. 11. *Me you have not always.* Not in a visible manner, as when conversant here on earth; and as we have the poor, whom we may daily assist and relieve.
Ver. 17. *Azymes.* Feast of the unleavened bread. *Pasch.* The paschal lamb.

With thee I make the pasch with my disciples.

19 And the disciples did as Jesus appointed to them: and they prepared the pasch.

20 [5] But when it was evening, he sat down with his twelve disciples.

21 And whilst they were eating, he said: Amen I say to you [6] that one of you is about to betray me.

22 And they being very much troubled began every one to say: Is it I, Lord?

23 But he answering said: He that dippeth his hand with me in the dish, he shall betray me.

24 The Son of man indeed goeth, [7] as it is written of him. But woe to that man by whom the Son of man shall be betrayed. It were better for him, if that man had not been born.

25 And Judas that betrayed him answering, said: Is it I, Rabbi? He saith to him: Thou hast said it.

26 [8] And whilst they were at supper, Jesus took bread and blessed and broke and gave to his disciples and said: Take ye and eat. This is my body.

27 And taking the chalice, he gave thanks and gave to them, saying: Drink ye all of this.

28 For this is my blood of the new testament, which shall be shed for many unto remission of sins.

29 And I say to you, I will not drink from henceforth of this fruit of the

[5] Mark, 14, 17; Luke, 22, 14. [6] John, 13, 21. [7] Ps. 40, 10. [8] 1 Cor. 11, 24. [9] Mark, 14, 27; John, 16, 32. [10] Zach. 13, 7. [11] Mark, 14, 28; 16, 7. [12] Mark, 14, 30; John, 13, 38. [13] Mark, 14, 31; Luke, 22, 33. [14] Mark, 14, 43; Luke, 22, 47; John, 18, 3.

Ver. 26. *This is my body.* He does not say, *This is the figure of my body*—but *This is my body.* (2 Council of Nice, *Act.* 6). Neither does he say *In this,* or *With this is my body;* but absolutely, *This is my body:* which plainly implies transubstantiation.

Ver. 27. *Drink ye all of this.* This was spoken to the twelve apostles; who were the *all* then present; and *they all drank of it,* says St. Mark (14, 23). But it no ways follows from these words spoken to the apostles, that all the faithful are here commanded to drink of the chalice: any more than that all the faithful are commanded to consecrate, offer and administer this sacrament; because Christ upon this same occasion and at the same time bid the apostles do so, in these words (Luke, 22, 19), *Do this for a commemoration of me.*

Ver. 28. *Blood of the new testament.* As the old testament was dedicated with the blood of victims, by Moses, in these words: *This is the blood of the testament* (Heb. 9, 20), so here is the dedication and institution of the new testament, in the blood of Christ, here mystically shed by these words: *This is the blood of the new testament.*

Ver. 29. *Fruit of the vine.* These words, by the account of St. Luke (20, 18), were not spoken of the sacramental cup, but of the wine that was drunk with the paschal lamb. Though the sacramental cup might also be called the *fruit of the vine,* because it was consecrated from wine and retains the likeness and all the accidents or qualities of wine.

Ver. 31. *Scandalized in me.* Forasmuch as my being apprehended shall make you all run away and forsake me.

vine until that day when I shall drink it with you new in the kingdom of my Father.

30 And a hymn being said, they went out unto mount Olivet.

31 Then Jesus saith to them: [9] All you shall be scandalized in me this night. For it is writen: [10] *I will strike the shepherd: and the sheep of the flock shall be dispersed.*

32 [11] But after I shall be risen again, I will go before you into Galilee.

33 And Peter answering, said to him: Although all shall be scandalized in thee, I will never be scandalized.

34 Jesus said to him: [12] Amen I say to thee that in this night before the cock crow thou wilt deny me thrice.

35 Peter saith to him: [13] Yea, though I should die with thee, I will not deny thee. And in like manner said all the disciples.

36 Then Jesus came with them into a country place which is called Gethsemani. And he said to his disciples: Sit you here, till I go yonder and pray.

37 And taking with him Peter and the two sons of Zebedee, he began to grow sorrowful and to be sad.

38 Then he saith to them: My soul is sorrowful even unto death. Stay you here and watch with me.

39 And going a little further, he fell upon his face, praying and saying: My Father, if it be possible, let this chalice pass from me. Nevertheless, not as I will but as thou *wilt.*

40 And he cometh to his disciples and findeth them asleep. And he saith to Peter: What? Could you not watch one hour with me?

41 Watch ye: and pray that ye enter not into temptation. The spirit indeed is willing, but the flesh is weak.

42 Again the second time, he went and prayed, saying: My Father, if this chalice may not pass away, but I must drink it, thy will be done.

43 And he cometh again and findeth them sleeping: for their eyes were heavy.

44 And leaving them, he went again: and he prayed the third time, saying the selfsame word.

45 Then he cometh to his disciples and said to them: Sleep ye now and take your rest. Behold the hour is at hand: and the Son of man shall be betrayed into the hands of sinners.

46 Rise: let us go. Behold he is at hand that will betray me.

47 [14] As he yet spoke, behold Judas, one of the twelve, came, and with him a great multitude with swords and clubs, sent from the chief priests and the ancients of the people.

48 And he that betrayed him gave them a sign, saying: Whomsoever I shall kiss, that is he. Hold him fast.

49 And forthwith coming to Jesus, he said: Hail, Rabbi. And he kissed him.

50 And Jesus said to him: Friend, whereto art thou come? Then they came up and laid hands on Jesus and held him.

51 And behold one of them that were with Jesus, stretching forth his hand, drew out his sword: and striking the servant of the high priest, cut off his ear.

52 Then Jesus saith to him: Put up again thy sword into its place: [15] for all that take the sword shall perish with the sword.

53 Thinkest thou that I cannot ask my Father, and he will give me presently more than twelve legions of angels?

54 [16] How then shall the scriptures be fulfilled, that so it must be done?

55 In that same hour, Jesus said to the multitudes: You are come out, as it were to a robber, with swords and clubs to apprehend me. I sat daily with you, teaching in the temple: and you laid not hands on me.

56 Now all this was done that the [17] scriptures of the prophets might be fulfilled. Then the disciples, all [18] leaving him, fled.

57 But they holding Jesus [19] led him to Caiphas the high priest, where the scribes and the ancients were assembled.

58 And Peter followed him afar off, even to the court of the high priest. And going in, he sat with the servants, that he might see the end.

59 And the chief priests and the whole council sought false witness against Jesus, that they might put him to death.

60 And they found not, whereas many false witnesses had come in. And last of all there came two false witnesses:

61 And they said: [20] This man said, I am able to destroy the temple of God and after three days to rebuild it.

62 And the high priest rising up, said to him: Answerest thou nothing to the things which these witness against thee?

63 But Jesus held his peace. And the high priest said to him: I adjure thee by the living God, that thou tell us if thou be the Christ the Son of God.

64 Jesus saith to him: Thou hast said it. Nevertheless I say to you, [21] hereafter you shall see the Son of man sitting on the right hand of the

power of God and coming in the clouds of heaven.

65 Then the high priest rent his garments, saying: He hath blasphemed: What further need have we of witnesses? Behold, now you have heard the blasphemy.

66 What think you? But they answering, said: He is guilty of death.

67 [22] Then did they spit in his face and buffeted him. And others struck his face with the palms of their hands,

68 Saying: Prophesy unto us, O Christ. Who is he that struck thee?

69 [23] But Peter sat without in the court. And there came to him a servant maid, saying: Thou also wast with Jesus the Galilean.

70 But he denied before them all, saying: I know not what thou sayest.

71 And as he went out of the gate, another maid saw him; and she saith to them that were there: This man also was with Jesus of Nazareth.

72 And again he denied with an oath: I know not the man.

73 And after a little while, they came that stood by and said to Peter: Surely thou also art one of them. For even thy speech doth discover thee.

74 Then he began to curse and to swear that he knew not the man. And immediately the cock crew.

75 And Peter remembered the word of Jesus which he had said: Before the cock crow, thou wilt deny me thrice. And going forth, he wept bitterly.

CHAPTER 27

The continuation of the history of the passion of Christ. His death and burial.

AND when morning was come, all the chief priests and ancients of the people took counsel against Jesus, that they might put him to death.

2 [1] And they brought him bound and delivered him to Pontius Pilate the governor.

3 Then Judas, who betrayed him, seeing that he was condemned, repenting himself, brought back the thirty pieces of silver to the chief priests and ancients,

4 Saying: I have sinned in betraying innocent blood. But they said: What is that to us? Look thou to it.

5 And casting down the pieces of silver in the temple, he departed [2] and went and hanged himself with an halter.

[15] Gen. 9, 6; Apoc. 13, 10. [16] Isai. 53, 10. [17] Lam. 4, 20. [18] Mark, 14, 50. [19] Luke, 22, 54; John, 18, 24. [20] John, 2, 19. [21] Matt. 16, 27; Rom. 14, 10; 1 Thess. 4, 16. [22] Isai. 50, 6; Mark, 14, 65. [23] Luke, 22, 55; John, 18, 17. CHAP. 27. [1] Mark, 15, 1; Luke, 23, 1; John, 18, 28. [2] Acts, 1, 18.

6 But the chief priests having taken the pieces of silver, said: It is not lawful to put them into the corbona, because it is the price of blood.

7 And after they had consulted together, they bought with them the potter's field, to be a burying place for strangers.

8 [3] For this cause that field was called Haceldama, that is, The field of blood, even to this day.

9 Then was fulfilled that which was spoken by Jeremias the prophet, saying: [4] And they took the thirty pieces of silver, the price of him that was prized, whom they prized of the children of Israel.

10 And they gave them unto the potter's field, as the Lord appointed to me.

11 And Jesus stood before the governor, [5] and the governor asked him, saying: Art thou the king of the Jews? Jesus saith to him: Thou sayest it.

12 And when he was accused by the chief priests and ancients, he answered nothing.

13 Then Pilate saith to him: Dost not thou hear how great testimonies they allege against thee?

14 And he answered him to never a word, so that the governor wondered exceedingly.

15 Now upon the solemn day the governor was accustomed to release to the people one prisoner, whom they would.

16 And he had then a notorious prisoner that was called Barabbas.

17 They therefore being gathered together, Pilate said: Whom will you that I release to you: Barabbas, or Jesus that is called Christ?

18 For he knew that for envy they had delivered him.

19 And as he was sitting in the place of judgment, his wife sent to him, saying: Have thou nothing to do with that just man; for I have suffered many things this day in a dream because of him.

20 [6] But the chief priests and ancients persuaded the people that they should ask Barabbas and make Jesus away.

21 And the governor answering, said to them: Whether will you of the two to be released unto you? But they said: Barabbas.

22 Pilate saith to them: What shall I do then with Jesus that is called Christ? They say all: Let him be crucified.

23 The governor said to them: Why, what evil hath he done? But they cried out the more, saying: Let him be crucified.

24 And Pilate seeing that he prevailed nothing, but that rather a tumult was made, taking water washed his hands before the people, saying: I am innocent of the blood of this just man. Look you to it.

25 And the whole people answering, said: His blood be upon us and upon our children.

26 Then he released to them Barabbas: and having scourged Jesus, delivered him unto them to be crucified.

27 Then the soldiers of the governor, taking Jesus into the hall, [7] gathered together unto him the whole band.

28 And stripping him, they put a scarlet cloak about him.

29 [8] And platting a crown of thorns, they put it upon his head, and a reed in his right hand. And bowing the knee before him, they mocked him, saying: Hail, King of the Jews.

30 And spitting upon him, they took the reed and struck his head.

31 And after they had mocked him, they took off the cloak from him and put on him his own garments and led him away to crucify him.

32 [9] And going out, they found a man of Cyrene, named Simon: him they forced to take up his cross.

33 [10] And they came to the place that is called Golgotha, which is the place of Calvary.

34 And they gave him wine to drink mingled with gall. And when he had tasted, he would not drink.

35 [11] And after they had crucified him, they divided his garments, casting lots; that it might be fulfilled which was spoken by the prophet, saying: [12] They divided my garments among them; and upon my vesture they cast lots.

36 And they sat and watched him.

37 And they put over his head his cause written: THIS IS JESUS THE KING OF THE JEWS.

38 Then were crucified with him two thieves: one on the right hand and one on the left.

39 And they that passed by blasphemed him, wagging their heads,

40 And saying: [13] Vah, thou that destroyest the temple of God and in three days dost rebuild it: save thy own self. If thou be the Son of God, come down from the cross.

[3] Acts, 1, 19. [4] Zach. 11, 12. [5] Mark, 15, 5; Luke, 23, 3; John, 18, 33. [6] Mark, 15, 11; Luke, 23, 18; John, 18, 40; Acts, 3, 14. [7] Mark, 15, 16; Ps. 21, 17. [8] John, 19, 2. [9] Mark, 15, 21; Luke, 23, 26. [10] Mark, 15, 22; Luke, 23, 33; John, 19, 17. [11] Mark, 15, 24; Luke, 23, 34; John, 19, 23. [12] Ps. 21, 19. [13] John, 2, 19.

CHAP. 27. Ver. 6. Corbona. A place in the temple where the people put in their gifts or offerings.

41 In like manner also the chief priests, with the scribes and ancients, mocking said:

42 He saved others: himself he cannot save. [14] If he be the king of Israel, let him now come down from the cross: and we will believe him.

43 [15] He trusted in God: let him now deliver *him* if he will have him. For he said: I am the Son of God.

44 And the selfsame thing the thieves also that were crucified with him reproached him with.

45 Now from the sixth hour, there was darkness over the whole earth, until the ninth hour.

46 And about the ninth hour, Jesus cried with a loud voice, saying: [16] Eli, Eli, lamma sabacthani? That is, My God, My God, why hast thou forsaken me?

47 And some that stood there and heard said: This man calleth Elias.

48 And immediately one of them running took a sponge and filled it with vinegar and put it on a reed and gave him to drink.

49 And the others said: Let be. Let us see whether Elias will come to deliver him.

50 And Jesus again crying with a loud voice, yielded up the ghost.

51 [17] And behold the veil of the temple was rent in two from the top even to the bottom: and the earth quaked and the rocks were rent.

52 And the graves were opened: and many bodies of the saints that had slept arose,

53 And coming out of the tombs after his resurrection, came into the holy city and appeared to many.

54 Now the centurion and they that were with him watching Jesus, having seen the earthquake and the things that were done, were sore afraid, saying: Indeed this was the Son of God.

55 And there were there many women afar off, who had followed Jesus from Galilee, ministering unto him:

56 Among whom was Mary Magdalen and Mary the mother of James and Joseph and the mother of the sons of Zebedee.

57 [18] And when it was evening, there came a certain rich man of Arimathea, named Joseph, who also himself was a disciple of Jesus.

58 He went to Pilate and asked the body of Jesus. Then Pilate commanded that the body should be delivered.

59 And Joseph taking the body wrapped it up in a clean linen cloth:

60 And laid it in his own new monument, which he had hewed out in a rock. And he rolled a great stone to the door of the monument and went his way.

61 And there was there Mary Magdalen and the other Mary, sitting over against the sepulchre.

62 And the next day, which followed the day of preparation, the chief priests and the Pharisees came together to Pilate,

63 Saying: Sir, we have remembered, that that seducer said, while he was yet alive: After three days I will rise again.

64 Command therefore the sepulchre to be guarded until the third day: lest perhaps his disciples come and steal him away and say to the people: He is risen from the dead. And the last error shall be worse than the first.

65 Pilate saith to them: You have a guard. Go, guard it as you know.

66 And they departing, made the sepulchre sure, sealing the stone and setting guards.

CHAPTER 28

The resurrection of Christ. His commission to his disciples.

AND [1] in the end of the sabbath, when it began to dawn towards the first day of the week, came Mary Magdalen and the other Mary, to see the sepulchre.

2 And behold there was a great earthquake. For an angel of the Lord descended from heaven and coming rolled back the stone and sat upon it.

3 And his countenance was as lightning and his raiment as snow.

4 And for fear of him, the guards were struck with terror and became as dead men.

5 And the angel answering, said to the women: Fear not you; for I know that you seek Jesus who was crucified.

6 He is not here. For he is risen, as he said. Come, and see the place where the Lord was laid.

7 And going quickly, tell ye his disciples that he is risen. And behold he will go before you into Galilee. There you shall see him. Lo, I have foretold it to you.

8 And they went out quickly from the sepulchre with fear and great joy, running to tell his disciples.

9 And behold, Jesus met them, saying: All hail. But they came up and took hold of his feet and adored him.

[14] Wisd. 2, 18. [15] Ps. 21, 9. [16] Ps. 21, 2. [17] 2 Par. 3, 14. [18] Mark, 15, 42; Luke, 23, 50; John, 19, 38. CHAP. 28. [1] Mark, 16, 1; John, 20, 11.

Ver. 02. *The day of preparation.* The eve of the sabbath; so called, because on that day they *prepared* all things necessary, not being allowed so much as to dress their meat on the sabbath day.

10 Then Jesus said to them: Fear not. Go, tell my brethren that they go into Galilee. There they shall see me.

11 Who when they were departed, behold, some of the guards came into the city and told the chief priests all things that had been done.

12 And they being assembled together with the ancients, taking counsel, gave a great sum of money to the soldiers,

13 Saying: Say you, His disciples came by night and stole him away when when we were asleep.

14 And if the governor shall hear of this, we will persuade him and secure you.

15 So they taking the money did as they were taught: and this word was spread abroad among the Jews even unto this day.

16 And the eleven disciples went into Galilee, unto the mountain where Jesus had appointed them.

17 And seeing him they adored: but some doubted.

18 And Jesus coming, spoke to them, saying: All power is given to me in heaven and in earth.

19 ²Going therefore, teach ye all nations: baptizing them in the name of the Father and of the Son of of the Holy Ghost.

20 Teaching them to observe all things whatsoever I have commanded you. And behold I am with you all days, even to the consummation of the world.

THE HOLY GOSPEL OF JESUS CHRIST

ACCORDING TO

ST. MARK

ST. MARK, *the disciple and interpreter of St. Peter (saith St. Jerome), according to what he heard from Peter himself, wrote at Rome a brief Gospel at the request of the Brethren, about ten years after our Lord's Ascension; which when Peter had heard, he approved of it and with his authority published it to the church to be read. Baronius and others say that the original was written in Latin: but the more general opinion is that the Evangelist wrote it in Greek.*

CHAPTER 1

The preaching of John the Baptist. Christ is baptized by him. He calls his disciples and works many miracles.

THE beginning of the gospel of Jesus Christ, the Son of God.

2 As it is written in Isaias the prophet: ¹*Behold I send my angel before thy face, who shall prepare the way before thee.*

2 Mark, 16, 15. CHAP. 1. ¹ Mal. 3, 1. ² Isai. 40, 3; Matt. 3, 3; Luke, 3, 4; John, 1, 23. ³ Matt. 3, 5. ⁴ Matt. 3, 4. ⁵ Lev. 11, 22. ⁶ Matt. 3, 11; Luke, 3, 16; John, 1, 27. ⁷ Acts, 1, 5; 2, 4; 11, 16; 19, 4.

CHAP. 28. Ver. 18, etc. *All power.* See here the warrant and commission of the apostles and their successors, the bishops and pastors of Christ's church. He received from his Father *all power in heaven and in earth:* and in virtue of *this power, he sends them,* even *as his Father sent him* (John 20, 21), to *teach* and *disciple,* μαθητεύειν, not one, but *all nations;* and instruct them in *all truths.* And that he may assist them effectually in the execution of this commission, he promises to be with them, not for three or four hundred years only, but *all days, even to the consummation of the world.* How then could the Catholic Church ever go astray, having always with her pastors, as is here promised, Christ himself who *is the way, the truth, and the life* (John 14)?

3 ²*A voice of one crying in the desert: Prepare ye the way of the Lord, make straight his paths.*

4 John was in the desert, baptizing and preaching the baptism of penance, unto remission of sins.

5 ³And there went out to him all the country of Judea and all they of Jerusalem and were baptized by him in the river of Jordan, confessing their sins.

6 ⁴And John was clothed with camel's hair, an a leathern girdle about his loins: ⁵and he ate locusts and wild honey.

7 And he preached, saying: ⁶There cometh after me one mightier than I, the latchet of whose shoes I am not worthy to stoop down and loose.

8 ⁷I have baptized you with water: but he shall baptize you with the Holy Ghost.

9 And it came to pass, in those days, Jesus came from Nazareth of Galilee and was baptized by John in Jordan.

10 And forthwith coming up out of

the water, he saw the heavens opened [8] and the Spirit as a dove descending and remaining on him.

11 And there came a voice from heaven: Thou art my beloved Son; in thee I am well pleased.

12 [9] And immediately the Spirit drove him out into the desert.

13 And he was in the desert forty days and forty nights, and was tempted by Satan. And he was with beasts: and the angels ministered to him.

14 [10] And after that John was delivered up, Jesus came into Galilee, preaching the gospel of the kingdom of God,

15 And saying: The time is accomplished and the kingdom of God is at hand. Repent and believe the gospel.

16 [11] And passing by the sea of Galilee, he saw Simon and Andrew his brother, casting nets into the sea (for they were fishermen).

17 And Jesus said to them: Come after me; and I will make you to become fishers of men.

18 And immediately leaving their nets, they followed him.

19 And going on from thence a little farther, he saw James the son of Zebedee and John his brother, who also were mending their nets in the ship: 20 And forthwith he called them. And leaving their father Zebedee in the ship with his hired men, they followed him.

21 [12] And they entered into Capharnaum: and forthwith upon the sabbath days going into the synagogue, he taught them.

22 [13] And they were astonished at his doctrine. For he was teaching them as one having power, and not as the scribes.

23 [14] And there was in their synagogue a man with an unclean spirit; and he cried out,

24 Saying: What have we to do with thee, Jesus of Nazareth? Art thou come to destroy us? I know who thou art, the Holy One of God.

25 And Jesus threatened him, saying: Speak no more, and go out of the man.

26 And the unclean spirit, tearing him and crying out with a loud voice, went out of him.

27 And they were all amazed insomuch that they questioned among themselves, saying: What thing is this? What is this new doctrine? For with power he commandeth even the unclean spirits: and they obey him.

28 And the fame of him was spread forthwith into all the country of Galilee.

29 [15] And immediately going out of the synagogue they came into the house of Simon and Andrew, with James and John.

30 And Simon's wife's mother lay in a fit of a fever: and forthwith they tell him of her.

31 And coming to her, he lifted her up, taking her by the hand; and immediately the fever left her, and she ministered unto them.

32 And when it was evening, after sunset, they brought to him all that were ill and that were possessed with devils.

33 And all the city was gathered together at the door.

34 And he healed many that were troubled with divers diseases. [16] And he cast out many devils: and he suffered them not to speak, because they knew him.

35 And rising very early, going out, he went into a desert place: and there he prayed.

36 And Simon and they that were with him followed after him.

37 And when they had found him, they said to him: All seek for thee.

38 And he saith to them: Let us go into the neighbouring towns and cities, that I may preach there also; for to this purpose am I come.

39 And he was preaching in their synagogues and in all Galilee and casting out devils.

40 [17] And there came a leper to him, beseeching him and kneeling down, said to him: If thou wilt thou canst make me clean.

41 And Jesus, having compassion on him, stretched forth his hand and touching him saith to him: I will. Be thou made clean.

42 And when he had spoken, immediately the leprosy departed from him: and he was made clean.

43 And he strictly charged him and forthwith sent him away.

44 And he saith to him: See thou tell no one; but go, shew thyself to the high priest and offer for thy cleansing [18] the things that Moses commanded, for a testimony to them.

45 But he being gone out, began to publish and to blaze abroad the word: so that he could not openly go into the city, but was without in desert places. And they flocked to him from all sides.

----

[8] Luke, 3, 22; John, 1, 32. [9] Matt. 4, 1; Luke, 4, 1. [10] Matt. 4, 12; Luke, 4, 14; John, 4, 43. [11] Matt. 4,13; Luke, 5, 2. [12] Matt. 4, 13; Luke, 4, 31. [13] Matt. 7, 28; Luke, 4, 32. [14] Luke, 4, 33. [15] Matt. 8, 14; Luke, 4, 38. [16] Luke, 4, 41. [17] Matt. 8, 2; Luke, 5, 12. [18] Lev. 14, 2.

CHAPTER 2

Christ heals the sick of the palsy. He calls Matthew and excuses his disciples.

AND ¹again he entered into Capharnaum after some days.

2 And it was heard that he was in the house. And many came together, so that there was no room: no, not even at the door. And he spoke to them the word.

3 ²And they came to him, bringing one sick of the palsy, who was carried by four.

4 And when they could not offer him unto him for the multitude, they uncovered the roof where he was: and opening it, they let down the bed wherein the man sick of the palsy lay.

5 And when Jesus had seen their faith, he saith to the sick of the palsy: Son, thy sins are forgiven thee.

6 And there were some of the scribes sitting there and thinking in their hearts:

7 Why doth this man speak thus? He blasphemeth. ³Who can forgive sins, but God only?

8 Which Jesus presently knowing in his spirit that they so thought within themselves, saith to them: Why think you these things in your hearts?

9 Which is easier, to say to the sick of the palsy: Thy sins are forgiven thee; or to say: Arise, take up thy bed and walk?

10 But that you may know that the Son of man hath power on earth to forgive sins (he saith to the sick of the palsy):

11 I say to thee: Arise. Take up thy bed and go into thy house.

12 And immediately he arose and, taking up his bed, went his way in the sight of all; so that all wondered and glorified God, saying: We never saw the like.

13 And he went forth again to the sea side: and all the multitude came to him. And he taught them.

14 ⁴And when he was passing by, he saw Levi, *the son* of Alpheus, sitting at the receipt of custom; and he saith to him: Follow me. And rising up, he followed him.

15 And it came to pass as he sat at meat in his house, many publicans and sinners sat down together with Jesus and his disciples. For they were many, who also followed him.

16 And the scribes and the Pharisees, seeing that he ate with publicans and sinners, said to his disciples: Why doth your master eat and drink with publicans and sinners?

17 ⁵Jesus hearing this, saith to them: They that are well have no need of a physician, but they that are sick. For I came not to call the just, but sinners.

18 And the disciples of John and the Pharisees used to fast. And they come and say to him: Why do the disciples of John and of the Pharisees fast; but thy disciples do not fast?

19 And Jesus saith to them: Can the children of the marriage fast, as long as the bridegroom is with them? As long as they have the bridegrom with them, they cannot fast.

20 ⁶But the days will come when the bridegroom shall be taken away from them: and then they shall fast in those days.

21 No man seweth a piece of raw cloth to an old garment: otherwise the new piecing taketh away from the old, and there is made a greater rent.

22 And no man putteth new wine into old bottles: otherwise the wine will burst the bottles, and both the wine will be spilled and the bottles will be lost. But new wine must be put into new bottles.

23 ⁷And it came to pass again, as the Lord walked through the corn fields on the sabbath, that his disciples began to go forward and to pluck the ears of corn.

24 And the Pharisees said to him: Behold, why do they on the sabbath day that which is not lawful?

25 And he said to them: ⁸Have you never read what David did when he had need and was hungry, himself and they that were with him?

26 How he went into the house of God, under Abiathar the high priest, and did eat the loaves of proposition, ⁹which was not lawful to eat but for the priests, and gave to them who were with him?

27 And he said to them: The sabbath was made for man, and not for the sabbath.

28 Therefore the Son of man is Lord of the sabbath also.

CHAPTER 3

Christ heals the withered hand. He chooses the twelve. He confutes the blasphemy of the Pharisees.

AND ¹he entered again into the synagogue: and there was a man there who had a withered hand.

2 And they watched him whether he would heal on the sabbath days, that they might accuse him.

3 And he said to the man who had

CHAP. 2. ¹ Matt. 9, 1. ² Luke, 5, 18. ³ Job, 14, 4; Isai. 43, 25. ⁴ Matt. 9, 9; Luke, 5, 27. ⁵ 1 Tim. 1, 15. ⁶ Matt. 9, 15; Luke, 5, 35. ⁷ Matt. 12, 1; Luke, 6, 1. ⁸ 1 Kings, 21, 6. ⁹ Lev. 24, 9. CHAP. 3. ¹ Matt. 12, 10; Luke, 6, 6.

the withered hand: Stand up in the midst.

4 And he saith to them: Is it lawful to do good on the sabbath days, or to do evil? To save life, or to destroy? But they held their peace.

5 And looking round about on them with anger, being grieved for the blindness of their hearts, he saith to the man: Stretch forth thy hand. And he stretched it forth. And his hand was restored unto him.

6 ² And the Pharisees going out, immediately made a consultation with the Herodians against him, how they might destroy him.

7 But Jesus retired with his disciples to the sea; and a great multitude followed him from Galilee and Judea,

8 And from Jerusalem, and from Idumea, and from beyond the Jordan. And they about Tyre and Sidon, a great multitude, hearing the things which he did, came to him.

9 And he spoke to his disciples that a small ship should wait on him, because of the multitude, lest they should throng him.

10 For he healed many, so that they pressed upon him for to touch him, as many as had evils.

11 And the unclean spirits, when they saw him, fell down before him: and they cried, saying:

12 Thou art the Son of God. And he strictly charged them that they should not make him known.

13 ³ And going up into a mountain, he called unto him whom he would himself. And they came to him.

14 And he made that twelve should be with him and that he might send them to preach.

15 And he gave them power to heal sicknesses and to cast out devils.

16 And to Simon he gave the name Peter.

17 And James the son of Zebedee, and John the brother of James; and he named them Boanerges, which is, The sons of thunder.

18 And Andrew and Philip, and Bartholomew and Matthew, and Thomas and James of Alpheus, and Thaddeus and Simon the Cananean.

19 And Judas Iscariot, who also betrayed him.

20 And they come to a house: and the multitude cometh together again, so that they could not so much as eat bread.

21 And when his friends had heard of it, they went out to lay hold on him. For they said: He is become mad.

22 And the scribes who were come down from Jerusalem, said: ⁴ He hath Beelzebub, and by the prince of devils he casteth out devils.

23 And after he had called them together, he said to them in parables: How can Satan cast out Satan?

24 And if a kingdom be divided against itself, that kingdom cannot stand.

25 And if a house be divided against itself, that house cannot stand.

26 And if Satan be risen up against himself, he is divided and cannot stand, but hath an end.

27 No man can enter into the house of a strong man and rob him of his goods, unless he first bind the strong man: and then shall he plunder his house.

28 ⁵ Amen I say to you that all sins shall be forgiven unto the sons of men, and the blasphemies wherewith they shall blaspheme:

29 But he that shall blaspheme against the Holy Ghost shall never have forgiveness, but shall be guilty of an everlasting sin.

30 Because they said: He hath an unclean spirit.

31 And his mother and his brethren came and, standing without, sent unto him, calling him.

32 And the multitude sat about him. And they say to him: Behold thy mother and thy brethren without seek for thee.

33 And answering them, he said: Who is my mother and my brethren?

34 And looking round about on them who sat about him, he saith: Behold my mother and my brethren.

35 For whosoever shall do the will of God, he is my brother and my sister and mother.

CHAPTER 4

The parable of the sower. Christ stills the tempest at sea.

AND ¹ again he began to teach by the sea side. And a great multitude was gathered together unto him, so that he went up into a ship and sat in the sea: and all the multitude was upon the land by the sea side.

2 And he taught them many things in parables and said unto them in his doctrine:

3 Hear ye: Behold, the sower went out to sow.

4 And whilst he sowed, some fell by the way side: and the birds of the air came and ate it up.

5 And other some fell upon stony ground, where it had not much earth:

² Matt. 12, 14. ³ Matt. 10, 1; Luke, 6, 13; 9, 1. ⁴ Matt. 9, 34. ⁵ Matt. 12, 31; Luke, 12, 10; 1 John, 5, 16. CHAP. 4. ¹ Matt. 13, 2; Luke, 8, 4.

and it shot up immediately, because it had no depth of earth.

6 And when the sun was risen, it was scorched: and because it had no root, it withered away.

7 And some fell among thorns: and the thorns grew up and choked it. And it yielded no fruit.

8 And some fell upon good ground and brought forth fruit that grew up and increased and yielded, one thirty, another sixty, and another a hundred.

9 And he said: He that hath ears to hear, let him hear.

10 And when he was alone, the twelve that were with him asked him the parable.

11 And he said to them: To you it is given to know the mystery of the kingdom of God: but to them that are without, all things are done in parables:

12 [2] That seeing they may see and not perceive; and hearing they may hear and not understand: lest at any time they should be converted and their sins should be forgiven them.

13 And he saith to them: Are you ignorant of this parable? And how shall you know all parables?

14 He that soweth, soweth the word.

15 And these are they by the way side, where the word is sown, and as soon as they have heard, immediately Satan cometh and taketh away the word that was sown in their hearts.

16 And these likewise are they that are sown on the stony ground: they who, when they have heard the word, immediately receive it with joy.

17 And they have no root in themselves, but are only for a time: and then when tribulation and persecution ariseth for the word they are presently scandalized.

18 And others there are who are sown among thorns: these are they that hear the word,

19 And the cares of the world [3] and the deceitfulness of riches and the lusts after other things entering in choke the word: and it is made fruitless.

20 And these are they who are sown upon the good ground: they who hear the word and receive it and yield fruit the one thirty, another sixty, and another a hundred.

21 [4] And he said to them: Doth a

candle come in to be put under a bushel or under a bed, and not to be set on a candlestick?

22 [5] For there is nothing hid which shall not be made manifest: neither was it made secret but that it may come abroad.

23 If any man have ears to hear, let him hear.

24 And he said to them: Take heed what you hear. [6] In what measure you shall mete it shall be measured to you again: and more shall be given to you.

25 [7] For he that hath, to him shall be given: and he that hath not, that also which he hath shall be taken away from him.

26 And he said: So is the kingdom of God, as if a man should cast seed into the earth,

27 And should sleep and rise, night and day, and the seed should spring and grow up whilst he knoweth not.

28 For the earth of itself bringeth forth fruit, first the blade, then the ear, afterwards the full corn in the ear.

29 And when the fruit is brought forth, immediately he putteth in the sickle, because the harvest is come.

30 And he said: To what shall we liken the kingdom of God? Or to what parable shall we compare it?

31 [8] It is as a grain of mustard seed: which when it is sown in the earth is less than all the seeds that are in the earth:

32 And when it is sown, it groweth up and becometh greater than all herbs and shooteth out great branches, so that the birds of the air may dwell under the shadow thereof.

33 And with many such parables, he spoke to them the word, according as they were able to hear.

34 And without parable he did not speak unto them: but apart, he explained all things to his disciples.

35 And he saith to them that day, when evening was come: Let us pass over to the other side.

36 [9] And sending away the multitude, they take him even as he was in the ship: and there were other ships with him.

37 And there arose a great storm of wind: and the waves beat into the ship, so that the ship was filled.

38 And he was in the hinder part of the ship, sleeping upon a pillow. And they awake him and say to him: Master, doth it not concern thee that we perish?

39 And rising up, he rebuked the wind and said to the sea: Peace. Be still. And the wind ceased: and there was made a great calm.

---

[2] Isai. 6, 9; Matt. 13, 14; John, 12, 40; Acts, 28, 26; Rom. 11, 8. [3] 1 Tim. 6, 17. [4] Matt. 5, 15; Luke, 8, 16; 11, 33. [5] Matt. 10, 26; Luke, 8, 17. [6] Matt. 7, 2; Luke, 6, 38. [7] Matt. 13, 12; 25, 29; Luke, 8, 18; 19, 26. [8] Matt. 13, 31; Luke, 13, 19. [9] Matt. 8, 23; Luke, 8, 22.

CHAP. 4. Ver. 12. *That seeing they may see.* In punishment of their wilfully *shutting their eyes* (Matt. 13, 15), God justly withdrew those lights and graces which otherwise he would have given them for their effectual conversion.

40 And he said to them: Why are you fearful? Have you not faith yet? And they feared exceedingly. And they said one to another: Who is this (thinkest thou) that both wind and sea obey him?

CHAPTER 5

Christ casts out a legion of devils. He heals the issue of blood and raises the daughter of Jairus to life.

AND ¹ they came over the strait of the sea into the country of the Gerasens.

2 And as he went out of the ship, immediately there met him out of the monuments a man with an unclean spirit,

3 Who had his dwelling in the tombs: and no man now could bind him, not even with chains.

4 For having been often bound with fetters and chains, he had burst the chains and broken the fetters in pieces: and no one could tame him.

5 And he was always day and night in the monuments and in the mountains, crying and cutting himself with stones.

6 And seeing Jesus afar off, he ran and adored him.

7 And crying with a loud voice, he said: What have I to do with thee, Jesus the Son of the Most High God? I adjure thee by God that thou torment me not.

8 For he said unto him: Go out of the man, thou unclean spirit.

9 And he asked him: What is thy name? And he saith to him: My name is Legion, for we are many.

10 And he besought him much that he would not drive him away out of the country.

11 And there was there near the mountain a great herd of swine, feeding.

12 And the spirits besought him, saying: Send us into the swine, that we may enter into them.

13 And Jesus immediately gave them leave. And the unclean spirits going out, entered into the swine. And the herd with great violence was carried headlong into the sea, being about two thousand, and were stifled in the sea.

14 And they that fed them fled and told it in the city and in the fields. And they went out to see what was done.

15 And they came to Jesus. And they see him that was troubled with the devil, sitting, clothed, and well in his wits: and they were afraid.

16 And they that had seen it told them, in what manner he had been dealt with who had the devil: and concerning the swine.

17 And they began to pray him that he would depart from their coasts.

18 And when he went up into the ship, he that had been troubled with the devil began to beseech him that he might be with him.

19 And he admitted him not, but saith to him: Go into thy house to thy friends; and tell them how great things the Lord hath done for thee and hath had mercy on thee.

20 And he went his way and began to publish in Decapolis how great things Jesus had done for him: and all men wondered.

21 And when Jesus had passed again in the ship over the strait, a great multitude assembled together unto him: and he was nigh unto the sea.

22 ² And there cometh one of the rulers of the synagogue named Jairus: and seeing him, falleth down at his feet.

23 And he besought him much, saying: My daughter is at the point of death. Come, lay thy hand upon her, that she may be safe and may live.

24 And he went with him. And a great multitude followed him: and they thronged him.

25 And a woman who was under an issue of blood, twelve years,

26 And had suffered many things from many physicians and had spent all that she had; and was nothing the better, but rather worse,

27 When she had heard of Jesus, came in the crowd behind him and touched his garment.

28 For she said: If I shall touch but his garment, I shall be whole.

29 And forthwith the fountain of her blood was dried up: and she felt in her body that she was healed of the evil.

30 And immediately Jesus knowing in himself the virtue that had proceeded from him, turning to the multitude, said: Who hath touched my garments?

31 And his disciples said to him: Thou seest the multitude thronging thee; and sayest thou who hath touched me?

32 And he looked about to see her who had done this.

33 But the woman fearing and trembling, knowing what was done in her, came and fell down before him and told him all the truth.

34 And he said to her: ³ Daughter, thy faith hath made thee whole. Go in peace: and be thou whole of thy disease.

35 While he was yet speaking, some come from the ruler of the synagogue's

CHAP. 5. ¹ Matt. 8, 28; Luke, 8, 26. ² Matt. 9, 18; Luke, 8, 41. ³ Luke, 7, 50; 8, 48.

house, saying: Thy daughter is dead. Why dost thou trouble the master any further?

36 But Jesus having heard the word that was spoken, saith to the ruler of the synagogue: Fear not, only believe.

37 And he admitted not any man to follow him, but Peter and James and John the brother of James.

38 And they come to the house of the ruler of the synagogue. And he seeth a tumult; and people weeping and wailing much.

39 And going in, he saith to them: Why make you this ado and weep? The damsel is not dead, but sleepeth.

40 And they laughed him to scorn. But he having put them all out, taketh the father and the mother of the damsel and them that were with him, and entereth in where the damsel was lying.

41 And taking the damsel by the hand, he saith to her: Talitha cumi, which is, being interpreted: Damsel (I say to thee) arise.

42 And immediately the damsel rose up and walked: and she was twelve years old. And they were astonished with a great astonishment.

43 And he charged them strictly that no man should know it: and commanded that something should be given her to eat.

CHAPTER 6

Christ teaches at Nazareth. He sends forth the twelve apostles. He feeds five thousand with five loaves and walks upon the sea.

AND [1] going out from thence, he went into his own country; and his disciples followed him.

2 And when the sabbath was come, he began to teach in the synagogue. And many hearing him were in admiration at his doctrine, saying: How came this man by all these things? And what wisdom is this that is given to him, and such mighty works as are wrought by his hands?

3 [2] Is not this the carpenter, the son of Mary, the brother of James and Joseph and Jude and Simon? Are not also his sisters here with us? And they were scandalized in regard of him.

4 And Jesus said to them: 'A prophet is not without honour, but in his own country and in his own house and among his own kindred.

5 And he could not do any miracles there, only that he cured a few that were sick, laying his hands upon them.

6 And he wondered because of their unbelief: and he went through the villages round about teaching.

7 [4] And he called the twelve and began to send them two and two and gave them power over unclean spirits.

8 And he commanded them that they should take nothing for the way, but a staff only: no scrip, no bread, nor money in their purse,

9 [5] But to be shod with sandals, and that they should not put on two coats.

10 And he said to them: Wheresoever you shall enter into an house, there abide till you depart from that place.

11 And whosoever shall not receive you nor hear you: [6] going forth from thence, shake off the dust from your feet for a testimony to them.

12 And going forth they preached that *men* should do penance:

13 And they cast out many devils [7] and anointed with oil many that were sick and healed them.

14 [8] And king Herod heard (for his name was made manifest), and he said: John the Baptist is risen again from the dead; and therefore mighty works shew forth themselves in him.

15 And others said: It is Elias. But others said: It is a prophet, as one of the prophets.

16 Which Herod hearing, said: John whom I beheaded, he is risen again from the dead.

17 [9] For Herod himself had sent and apprehended John and bound him in prison for the sake of Herodias the wife of Philip his brother, because he had married her.

18 For John said to Herod: [10] It is not lawful for thee to have thy brother's wife.

19 Now Herodias laid snares for him and was desirous to put him to death: and could not.

20 For Herod feared John, knowing him to be a just and holy man, and kept him: and when he heard him, did many things. And he heard him willingly.

21 And when a convenient day was come, Herod made a supper for his birthday, for the princes and tribunes and chief men of Galilee.

22 And when the daughter of the same Herodias had come in and had danced and pleased Herod and them that were at table with him, the king

CHAP. 6. ¹ Matt. 13, 54; Luke, 4, 16. ² John, 6, 42. ³ Matt. 13, 57; Luke, 4, 23; John, 4, 44. ⁴ Matt. 10, 1; Mark, 3, 15; Luke, 9, 1. ⁵ Acts, 12, 8. ⁶ Matt. 10, 14; Luke, 9, 5; Acts, 13, 51; 18, 6. ⁷ James, 5, 14. ⁸ Matt. 14, 2 Luke, 9, 7. ⁹ Luke, 3, 19. ¹⁰ Lev. 18, 16.

CHAP. 6. Ver. 5. *He could not.* Not for want of power, but because he would not work miracles in favour of obstinate and incredulous people, who were unworthy of such favours.
Ver. 20. *And kept him.* That is, from the designs of Herodias. Herod, for fear of the people, would not put him to death, though she sought it: and through her daughter she effected her wish.

said to the damsel: Ask of me what thou wilt, and I will give it thee.

23 And he swore to her: Whatsoever thou shalt ask I will give thee, though it be the half of my kingdom.

24 Who when she was gone out, said to her mother: What shall I ask? But she said: The head of John the Baptist.

25 And when she was come in immediately with haste to the king, she asked, saying: I will that forthwith thou give me in a dish the head of John the Baptist.

26 And the king was struck sad. Yet because of his oath and because of them that were with him at table, he would not displease her.

27 But sending an executioner, he commanded that his head should be brought in a dish.

28 And he beheaded him in the prison and brought his head in a dish and gave it to the damsel: and the damsel gave it to her mother.

29 [11] Which his disciples hearing, came and took his body and laid it in a tomb.

30 [12] And the apostles coming together unto Jesus, related to him all things that they had done and taught.

31 And he said to them: [13] Come apart into a desert place and rest a little. For there were many coming and going: and they had not so much as time to eat.

32 And going up into a ship, they went into a desert place apart.

33 And they saw them going away: and many knew. And they ran flocking thither on foot from all the cities and were there before them.

34 [14] And Jesus going out saw a great multitude: and he had compassion on them, because they were as sheep not having a shepherd. And he began to teach them many things.

35 And when the day was now far spent, his disciples came to him, saying: This is a desert place and the hour is not past:

36 [15] Send them away, that going into the next villages and towns, they may buy themselves meat to eat.

37 And he answering said to them: Give you them to eat. And they said to him: Let us go and buy bread for two hundred pence, and we will give them to eat.

38 And he saith to them: How many loaves have you? Go and see. And when they knew, they say: Five, and two fishes.

39 [16] And he commanded them that they should make them all sit down by companies upon the green grass.

40 And they sat down in ranks, by hundreds and by fifties.

41 And when he had taken the five loaves and the two fishes: looking up to heaven, he blessed and broke the loaves, and gave to his disciples to set before them. And the two fishes he divided among them all.

42 And they all did eat and had their fill.

43 And they took up the leavings, twelve full baskets of fragments and of the fishes.

44 And they that did eat were five thousand men.

45 And immediately he obliged his disciples to go up into the ship, that they might go before him over the water to Bethsaida, whilst he dismissed the people.

46 And when he had dismissed them, he went up to the mountain to pray.

47 And when it was late, the ship was in the midst of the sea, and himself alone on the land.

48 [17] And seeing them labouring in rowing (for the wind was against them) and about the fourth watch of the night, he cometh to them, walking upon the sea: and he would have passed by them.

49 But they, seeing him walking upon the sea, thought it was an apparition: and they cried out.

50 For they all saw him and were troubled. And immediately he spoke with them and said to them: Have a good heart. It is I. Fear ye not.

51 And he went up to them into the ship, and the wind ceased. And they were far more astonished within themselves.

52 For they understood not concerning the loaves: for their heart was blinded.

53 [18] And when they had passed over, they came into the land of Genesareth and set to the shore.

54 And when they were gone out of the ship, immediately they knew him:

55 And running through that whole country, they began to carry about in beds those that were sick, where they heard he was.

56 And whithersoever he entered, into towns or into villages or cities, they laid the sick in the streets and besought him that they might touch but the hem of his garment. And as many as touched him were made whole.

CHAPTER 7

Christ rebukes the Pharisees. He heals the daughter of the woman of Chanaan and the man that was deaf and dumb.

[11] Matt. 14, 12. [12] Luke, 9, 10. [13] Matt. 14, 13; Luke, 9, 10; John, 6, 1. [14] Matt. 9, 36; 14, 14. [15] Luke, 9, 12. [16] John, 6, 10. [17] Matt. 14, 25. [18] Matt. 14, 34.

AND there assembled together unto him the Pharisees and some of the scribes, coming from Jerusalem.

2 [1] And when they had seen some of his disciples eat bread with common, that is, with unwashed hands, they found fault.

3 For the Pharisees and all the Jews eat not without often washing their hands, holding the tradition of the ancients.

4 And when they come from the market, unless they be washed, they eat not: and many other things there are that have been delivered to them to observe, the washings of cups and of pots and of brazen vessels and of beds.

5 And the Pharisees and scribes asked him: Why do not thy disciples walk according to the tradition of the ancients, but they eat bread with common hands?

6 But he answering, said to them: Well did Isaias prophesy of you hypocrites, as it is written: [2] *This people honoureth me with their lips, but their heart is far from me.*

7 *And in vain do they worship me, teaching doctrines and precepts of men.*

8 For leaving the commandment of God, you hold the tradition of men, the washing of pots and of cups: and many other things you do like to these.

9 And he said to them: Well do you make void the commandment of God, that you may keep your own tradition.

10 For Moses said: [3] *Honour thy father and thy mother. And* [4] *He that shall curse father or mother, dying let him die.*

11 But you say: If a man shall say to his father or mother, Corban (which is a gift) whatsoever is from me shall profit thee.

12 And further you suffer him not to do any thing for his father or mother,

13 Making void the word of God by your own tradition, which you have given forth. And many other such like things you do.

14 [5] And calling again the multitude unto him, he said to them: Hear ye me all and understand.

15 There is nothing from without a man that entering into him can defile him. But the things which come from a man, those are they that defile a man.

16 If any man have ears to hear, let him hear.

17 And when he was come into the house from the multitude, his disciples asked him the parable.

18 And he saith to them: So are you also without knowledge? Understand you not that every thing from without entering into a man cannot defile him:

19 Because it entereth not into his heart but goeth into his belly and goeth out into the privy, purging all meats?

20 But he said that the things which come out from a man, they defile a man

21 [6] For from within, out of the heart of men, proceed evil thoughts, adulteries, fornications, murders,

22 Thefts, covetousness, wickedness, deceit, lasciviousness, an evil eye, blasphemy, pride, foolishness.

23 All these evil things come from within and defile a man.

24 [7] And rising from thence he went into the coasts of Tyre and Sidon: and entering into a house, he would that no man should know it. And he could not be hid.

25 For a woman as soon as she heard of him, whose daughter had an unclean spirit, came in and fell down at his feet.

26 For the woman was a Gentile, a Syrophenician born. And she besought him that he would cast forth the devil out of her daughter.

27 Who said to her: Suffer first the children to be filled: for it is not good to take the bread of the children and cast it to the dogs.

28 But she answered and said to him: Yea, Lord; for the whelps also eat under the table of the crumbs of the children.

29 And he said to her: For this saying, go thy way. The devil is gone out of thy daughter.

30 And when she was come into her house, she found the girl lying upon the bed and that the devil was gone out.

31 And again going out of the coasts of Tyre, he came by Sidon to the sea of Galilee, through the midst of the coasts of Decapolis.

32 [8] And they bring to him one deaf and dumb: and they besought him that he would lay his hand upon him.

33 And taking him from the multitude apart, he put his fingers into his ears: and spitting, he touched his tongue.

34 And looking up to heaven, he groaned and said to him: Ephpheta, which is, Be thou opened.

35 And immediately his ears were opened and the string of his tongue was loosed and he spoke right.

36 And he charged them that they should tell no man. But the more he

CHAP. 7. [1] Matt. 15, 2. [2] Isai. 29, 13. [3] Exod. 20, 12; Deut. 5, 16; Eph. 6, 2. [4] Exod. 21, 17; Lev. 20, 9; Prov. 20, 20. [5] Matt. 15, 10. [6] Gen. 6, 5. [7] Matt. 15, 21. [8] Matt. 9, 32; Luke, 11, 14.

CHAP. 7. Ver. 7. *Doctrines and precepts of men.* See the annotations on St. Matthew (15, 9, 11).

charged them, so much the more a great deal did they publish it.

37 And so much the more did they wonder, saying: He hath done all things well. He hath made both the deaf to hear and the dumb to speak.

CHAPTER 8

Christ feeds four thousand. He gives sight to a blind man. He foretells his passion.

IN [1] those days again, when there was a great multitude and they had nothing to eat; calling his disciples together, he saith to them:

2 I have compassion on the multitude, for behold they have now been with me three days and have nothing to eat.

3 And if I shall send them away fasting to their home, they will faint in the way: for some of them came from afar off.

4 And his disciples answered him: From whence can any one fill them here with bread in the wilderness?

5 And he asked them: How many loaves have ye? Who said: Seven.

6 And he commanded the people to sit down on the ground. And taking the seven loaves, giving thanks, he broke and gave to his disciples for to set before them. And they set them before the people.

7 And they had a few little fishes: and he blessed them and commanded them to be set before them.

8 And they did eat and were filled: and they took up that which was left of the fragments, seven baskets.

9 And they that had eaten were about four thousand. And he sent them away.

10 And immediately going up into a ship with his disciples, he came into the parts of Dalmanutha.

11 [2] And the Pharisees came forth and began to question with him, asking him a sign from heaven, tempting him.

12 And sighing deeply in spirit, he saith: Why doth this generation seek a sign? Amen, I say to you, a sign shall not be given to this generation.

13 And leaving them, he went up again into the ship and passed to the other side of the water.

14 And they forgot to take bread: and they had but one loaf with them in the ship.

15 And he charged them, saying: Take heed and beware of the leaven of the Pharisees and of the leaven of Herod.

16 And they reasoned among themselves, saying: Because we have no bread.

17 Which Jesus knowing, saith to them: Why do you reason, because you have no bread? Do you not yet know nor understand? Have you still your heart blinded?

18 Having eyes, see you not? And having ears, hear you not? [3] Neither do you remember?

19 When I broke the five loaves among five thousand, how many baskets full of fragments took you up? They say to him: Twelve.

20 When also the seven loaves among four thousand, how many baskets of fragments took you up? And they say to him: Seven.

21 And he said to them: How do you not yet understand?

22 And they came to Bethsaida: and they bring to him a blind man. And they besought him that he would touch him.

23 And taking the blind man by the hand, he led him out of the town: and spitting upon his eyes, laying his hands on him, he asked him if he saw any thing.

24 And looking up, he said: I see men, as it were trees, walking.

25 After that again he laid his hands upon his eyes: and he began to see and was restored, so that he saw all things clearly.

26 And he sent him into his house, saying: Go into thy house, and if thou enter into the town, tell nobody.

27 [4] And Jesus went out, and his disciples into the towns of Cæsarea Philippi. And in the way, he asked his disciples, saying to them: [5] Whom do men say that I am?

28 Who answered him, saying: John the Baptist; but some Elias, and others as one of the prophets.

29 Then he saith to them: But whom do you say that I am? Peter answering said to him: Thou art the Christ.

30 And he strictly charged them that they should not tell any man of him.

31 And he began to teach them that the Son of man must suffer many things and be rejected by the ancients and by the high priests and the scribes: and be killed and after three days rise again.

32 And he spoke the word openly. [6] And Peter taking him began to rebuke him.

33 Who turning about and seeing his disciples, threatened Peter, saying: Go behind me, Satan, because thou savourest not the things that are of God but that are of men.

CHAP. 8. [1] Matt. 15, 32. [2] Matt. 16, 1; Luke, 11, 54. [3] Mark, 6, 41; John, 6, 11. [4] Matt. 16, 13. [5] Luke, 9, 18. [6] Matt. 16, 23.

34 And calling the multitude together with his disciples, he said to them: ⁷ If any man will follow me, let him deny himself and take up his cross and follow me.

35 ⁸ For whosoever will save his life shall lose it: and whosoever shall lose his life for my sake and the gospel shall save it.

36 For what shall it profit a man, if he gain the whole world and suffer the loss of his soul?

37 Or what shall a man give in exchange for his soul?

38 ⁹ For he that shall be ashamed of me and of my words, in this adulterous and sinful generation: the Son of man also will be ashamed of him, when he shall come in the glory of his Father with the holy angels.

39 And he said to them: ¹⁰ Amen I say to you that there are some of them that stand here who shall not taste death till they see the kingdom of God coming in power.

CHAPTER 9

Christ is transfigured. He casts out the dumb spirit. He teaches humility and to avoid scandal.

AND ¹ after six days, Jesus taketh with him Peter and James and John, and leadeth them up into an high mountain apart by themselves, and was transfigured before them.

2 And his garments became shining and exceeding white as snow, so as no fuller upon earth can make white.

3 And there appeared to them Elias with Moses: and they were talking with Jesus.

4 And Peter answering, said to Jesus: Rabbi, it is good for us to be here. And let us make three tabernacles, one for thee, and one for Moses, and one for Elias.

5 For he knew not what he said: for they were struck with fear.

6 And there was a cloud overshadowing them. And a voice came out of the cloud, saying: This is my most beloved Son. Hear ye him.

7 And immediately looking about, they saw no man any more, but Jesus only with them.

8 ² And as they came down from the mountain, he charged them not to tell any man what things they had seen, till the Son of man shall be risen again from the dead.

9 And they kept the word to themselves; questioning together what that should mean, when he shall be risen from the dead.

10 And they asked him, saying: ³ Why then do the Pharisees and scribes say that Elias must come first?

11 Who answering, said to them: Elias, when he shall come first, shall restore all things; and as ⁴ it is written of the Son of man that he must suffer many things and be despised.

12 But I say to you that Elias also is come (and they have done to him whatsoever they would), as it is written of him.

13 And coming to his disciples he saw a great multitude about them and the scribes disputing with them.

14 And presently all the people, seeing Jesus, were astonished and struck with fear; and running to him, they saluted him.

15 And he asked them: What do you question about among you?

16 ⁵ And one of the multitude, answering, said: Master, I have brought my son to thee, having a dumb spirit.

17 Who, wheresoever he taketh him, dasheth him: and he foameth and gnasheth with the teeth and pineth away. And I spoke to thy disciples to cast him out: and they could not.

18 Who answering them, said: O incredulous generation, how long shall I be with you? How long shall I suffer you? Bring him unto me.

19 And they brought him. And when he had seen him, immediately the spirit troubled him: and being thrown down upon the ground, he rolled about foaming.

20 And he asked his father: How long time is it since this hath happened unto him? But he said: From his infancy.

21 And oftentimes hath he cast him into the fire and into the waters to destroy him. But if thou canst do any thing, help us, having compassion on us.

22 And Jesus saith to him: If thou canst believe, all things are possible to him that believeth.

23 And immediately the father of the boy crying out, with tears said: I do believe, Lord. Help my unbelief.

24 And when Jesus saw the multitude running together, he threatened the unclean spirit, saying to him: Deaf and dumb spirit, I command thee, go out of him and enter not any more into him.

25 And crying out and greatly tearing him, he went out of him. And he became as dead, so that many said: He is dead.

⁷ Matt. 10, 38; 16, 24. ⁸ Luke, 9, 23; 14, 27. ⁹ Matt. 10, 33; Luke, 9, 26; 12, 9. ¹⁰ Matt. 16, 28; Luke, 9, 27. CHAP. 9. ¹ Matt. 17, 1; Luke, 9, 28. ² Matt. 17, 9. ³ Mal. 4, 5. ⁴ Isai. 53, 3, 4. ⁵ Luke, 9, 38.

26 But Jesus taking him by the hand, lifted him up. And he arose.

27 And when he was come into the house, his disciples secretly asked him: Why could not we cast him out?

28 And he said to them: This kind can go out by nothing, but by prayer and fasting.

29 And departing from thence, they passed through Galilee: and he would not that any man should know it.

30 [6] And he taught his disciples and said to them: The Son of man shall be betrayed into the hands of men, and they shall kill him; and after that he is killed, he shall rise again the third day.

31 But they understood not the word: and they were afraid to ask him.

32 And they came to Capharnaum. And when they were in the house, he asked them: What did you treat of in the way?

33 But they held their peace, for in the way they had disputed among themselves, [7] which of them should be the greatest.

34 And sitting down, he called the twelve and saith to them: If any man desire to be first, he shall be the last of all and the minister of all.

35 And taking a child, he set him in the midst of them. Whom when he had embraced, he saith to them:

36 Whosoever shall receive one such child as this in my name receiveth me. And whosoever shall receive me receiveth not me but him that sent me.

37 [8] John answered him, saying: Master, we saw one casting out devils in thy name, who followeth not us: and we forbade him.

38 But Jesus said: Do not forbid him. [9] For there is no man that doth a miracle in my name and can soon speak ill of me.

39 For he that is not against you is for you.

40 [10] For whosoever shall give you to drink a cup of water in my name, because you belong to Christ: amen I say to you, he shall not lose his reward.

41 [11] And whosoever shall scandalize one of these little ones that believe in me: it were better for him that a millstone were hanged about his neck and he were cast into the sea.

42 [12] And if thy hand scandalize thee, cut it off: it is better for thee to enter into life, maimed, than having two hands to go into hell, into unquenchable fire:

43 Where their worm dieth not, and the fire is not extinguished.

44 And if thy foot scandalize thee, cut it off: it is better for thee to enter lame into life everlasting than having two feet to be cast into the hell of unquenchable fire:

45 [13] Where their worm dieth not, and the fire is not extinguished.

46 And if thy eye scandalize thee, pluck it out: it is better for thee with one eye to enter into the kingdom of God than having two eyes to be cast into the hell of fire:

47 Where their worm dieth not, and the fire is not extinguished.

48 [14] For every one shall be salted with fire: and every victim shall be salted with salt.

49 [15] Salt is good. But if the salt become unsavoury, wherewith will you season it? Have salt in you: and have peace among you.

CHAPTER 10

Marriage is not to be dissolved. The danger of riches. The ambition of the sons of Zebedee. A blind man is restored to his sight.

AND [1] rising up from thence, he cometh into the coast of Judea beyond the Jordan: and the multitude flocked to him again. And as he was accustomed, he taught them again.

2 And the Pharisees coming to him asked him, tempting him: Is it lawful for a man to put away his wife?

3 But he answering, saith to them: What did Moses command you?

4 Who said: [2] Moses permitted to write a bill of divorce and to put her away.

5 To whom Jesus answering, said: Because of the hardness of your heart, he wrote you that precept.

6 But from the beginning of the creation, [3] God made them male and female.

7 For this cause, [4] a man shall leave his father and mother and shall cleave to his wife.

8 [5] And they two shall be in one flesh. Therefore now they are not two, but one flesh.

9 What therefore God hath joined together, let no man put asunder.

10 And in the house again his disciples asked him concerning the same thing.

11 And he saith to them: Whosoever shall put away his wife and marry another committeth adultery against her.

12 And if the wife shall put away

[6] Matt. 17, 21; Luke, 9, 22, 24. [7] Matt. 18, 1; Luke, 9, 46. [8] Luke, 9, 49. [9] 1 Cor. 12, 3. [10] Matt. 10, 42. [11] Matt. 18, 6; Luke, 17, 2. [12] Matt. 5, 30; 18, 8. [13] Isai. 66, 24. [14] Lev. 2, 13. [15] Matt. 5, 13; Luke, 14, 34. CHAP. 10. [1] Matt. 19, 1. [2] Deut. 24, 1. [3] Gen. 1, 27. [4] Gen. 2, 24; Matt. 19, 5; 1 Cor. 7, 10; Eph. 5, 31. [5] 1 Cor. 6, 16.

her husband and be married to another, she committeth adultery.

13 And they brought to him young children, that he might touch them. And the disciples rebuked them that brought them.

14 Whom when Jesus saw, he was much displeased and saith to them: Suffer the little children to come unto me and forbid them not; for of such is the kingdom of God.

15 Amen I say to you, whosoever shall not receive the kingdom of God as a little child shall not enter into it.

16 And embracing them and laying his hands upon them, he blessed them.

17 And when he was gone forth into the way, a certain man, running up and kneeling before him, asked him: [6] Good Master, what shall I do that I may receive life everlasting?

18 And Jesus said to him: Why callest thou me good? None is good but one, *that is* God.

19 [7] Thou knowest the commandments: *Do not commit adultery, do not kill, do not steal, bear not false witness, do no fraud, honour thy father and mother*.

20 But he answering, said to him: Master, all these things I have observed from my youth.

21 And Jesus, looking on him, loved him and said to him: One thing is wanting unto thee. Go, sell whatsoever thou hast and give to the poor: and thou shalt have treasure in heaven. And come, follow me.

22 Who being struck sad at that saying, went away sorrowful: for he had great possessions.

23 And Jesus looking round about saith to his disciples: How hardly shall they that have riches enter into the kingdom of God!

24 And the disciples were astonished at his words. But Jesus again answering, saith to them: Children, how hard is it for them that trust in riches to enter into the kingdom of God?

25 It is easier for a camel to pass through the eye of a needle than for a rich man to enter into the kingdom of God.

26 Who wondered the more, saying among themselves: Who then can be saved?

27 And Jesus looking on them, saith: With men it is impossible; but not with God. For all things are possible with God.

[6] Matt. 19, 16; Luke, 18, 18. [7] Exod. 20, 13. [8] Matt. 19, 27; Luke, 18, 28. [9] Matt. 19, 30. [10] Luke, 18, 31. [11] Matt. 20, 20. [12] Luke, 22, 25.

CHAP. 10. Ver. 18. *None is good.* Of himself entirely and essentially, but God alone: men may be good also, but only by participation of God's goodness.

28 [8] And Peter began to say unto him: Behold, we have left all things and have followed thee.

29 Jesus answering said: Amen I say to you, there is no man who hath left house or brethren or sisters or father or mother or children or lands, for my sake and for the gospel,

30 Who shall not receive an hundred times as much, now in this time; houses and brethren and sisters and mothers and children and lands, with persecutions: and in the world to come life everlasting.

31 [9] But many that are first shall be last: and the last, first.

32 And they were in the way going up to Jerusalem: and Jesus went before them. And they were astonished and following were afraid. [10] And taking again the twelve, he began to tell them the things that should befall him.

33 *Saying:* Behold we go up to Jerusalem, and the Son of man shall be betrayed to the chief priests and to the scribes and ancients. And they shall condemn him to death and shall deliver him to the Gentiles.

34 And they shall mock him and spit on him and scourge him and kill him: and the third day he shall rise again.

35 [11] And James and John, the sons of Zebedee, come to him, saying: Master, we desire that whatsoever we shall ask, thou wouldst do it for is.

36 But he said to them: What would you that I should do for you?

37 And they said: Grant to us that we may sit, one on thy right hand and the other on thy left hand, in thy glory.

38 And Jesus said to them: You know not what you ask. Can you drink of the chalice that I drink of or be baptized with the baptism wherewith I am baptized?

39 But they said to him: We can. And Jesus saith to them: You shall indeed drink of the chalice that I drink of; and with the baptism wherewith I am baptized you shall be baptized.

40 But to sit on my right hand or on my left is not mine to give to you, but to them for whom it is prepared.

41 And the ten, hearing it, began to be much displeased at James and John.

42 But Jesus calling them, saith to them: [12] You know that they who seem to rule over the Gentiles lord it over them: and their princes have power over them.

43 But it is not so among you: but whosoever will be greater shall be your minister.

44 And whosoever will be first among you shall be the servant of all.

45 For the Son of man also is not come to be ministered unto: but to minister and to give his life a redemption for many.

46 [13] And they came to Jericho. And as he went out of Jericho with his disciples and a very great multitude, Bartimeus the blind man, the son of Timeus, sat by the way side begging.

47 Who when he had heard that it was Jesus of Nazareth, began to cry out and to say: Jesus, Son of David, have mercy on me.

48 And many rebuked him, that he might hold his peace; but he cried a great deal the more: Son of David, have mercy on me.

49 And Jesus, standing still, commanded him to be called. And they call the blind man, saying to him: Be of better comfort. Arise, he calleth thee.

50 Who casting off his garment leaped up and came to him.

51 And Jesus answering, said to him: What wilt thou that I should do to thee? And the blind man said to him: Rabboni. That I may see.

52 And Jesus saith to him: Go thy way. Thy faith hath made thee whole. And immediately he saw and followed him in the way.

CHAPTER 11

Christ enters into Jerusalem upon an ass. He curses the barren fig tree and drives the buyers and sellers out of the temple.

AND [1] when they were drawing near to Jerusalem and to Bethania, at the mount of Olives, he sendeth two of his disciples,

2 And saith to them: Go into the village that is over against you, and immediately at your coming in thither, you shall find a colt tied, upon which no man yet hath sat. Loose him and bring him.

3 And if any man shall say to you: What are you doing? Say ye that the Lord hath need of him. And immediately he will let him come hither.

4 And going their way, they found the colt tied before the gate without, in the meeting of two ways. And they loose him.

5 And some of them that stood there said to them: What do you loosing the colt?

6 Who said to them as Jesus had commanded them. And they let him go with them.

7 [2] And they brought the colt to Jesus. And they lay their garments on him: and he sat upon him

8 And many spread their garments in the way: and others cut down boughs from the trees and strewed them in the way.

9 And they that went before and they that followed cried, saying: [3] *Hosanna: Blessed is he that cometh in the name of the Lord.*

10 *Blessed be the kingdom of our father David that cometh: Hosanna in the highest.*

11 [4] And he entered into Jerusalem, into the temple: and having viewed all things round about, when now the eventide was come, he went out to Bethania with the twelve.

12 And the next day when they came out from Bethania, he was hungry.

13 [5] And when he had seen afar off a fig tree having leaves, he came, if perhaps he might find any thing on it. And when he was come to it, he found nothing but leaves. For it was not the time for figs.

14 And answering he said to it: May no man hereafter eat fruit of thee any more for ever! And his disciples heard it.

15 And they came to Jerusalem. And when he was entered into the temple, he began to cast out them that sold and bought in the temple: and overthrew the tables of the moneychangers and the chairs of them that sold doves.

16 And he suffered not that any man should carry a vessel through the temple.

17 And he taught, saying to them: Is it not written: [6] *My house shall be called the house of prayer to all nations, but you have made it a den of thieves?*

18 Which when the chief priests and the scribes had heard, they sought how they might destroy him. For they feared him, because the whole multitude was in admiration at his doctrine.

19 And when evening was come, he went forth out of the city.

20 And when they passed by in the morning they saw the fig tree dried up from the roots.

21 And Peter remembering, said to him: Rabbi, behold the fig tree which thou didst curse is withered away.

22 And Jesus answering, saith to them: [7] Have the faith of God.

23 Amen I say to you that whosoever shall say to this mountain, Be thou removed and be cast into the sea, and shall not stagger in his heart, but believe that whatsoever he saith shall be done; it shall be done unto him.

24 [8] Therefore I say unto you, all

[13] Matt. 20, 29; Luke, 18, 35. CHAP. 11. [1] Matt. 21, 1; Luke, 19, 29. [2] John, 12, 14. [3] Ps. 117, 26; Matt. 21, 9; Luke, 19, 38. [4] Matt. 21, 10. [5] Matt. 21, 19. [6] Isai. 56, 7; Jer. 7, 11. [7] Matt. 21, 21. [8] Matt. 7, 7; 21, 22.

things, whatsoever you ask when ye pray, believe that you shall receive: and they shall come unto you.

25 ⁹ And when you shall stand to pray, forgive, if you have aught against any man: that your Father also, who is in heaven, may forgive you your sins.

26 But if you will not forgive, neither will your Father that is in heaven forgive you your sins.

27 ¹⁰ And they come again to Jerusalem. And when he was walking in the temple, there come to him the chief priests and the scribes and the ancients.

28 And they say to him: By what authority dost thou these things? And who hath given thee this authority that thou shouldst do these things?

29 And Jesus answering, said to them: I will also ask you one word. And answer you me: and I will tell you by what authority I do these things.

30 The baptism of John, was it from heaven or from men? Answer me.

31 But they thought with themselves, saying: If we say, From heaven; he will say, Why then did you not believe him?

32 If we say, From men, we fear the people. For all men counted John that he was a prophet indeed.

33 And they answering, say to Jesus: We know not. And Jesus answering, saith to them: Neither do I tell you by what authority I do these things.

CHAPTER 12

The parable of the vineyard and husbandmen. Cæsar's right to tribute. The Sadducees are confuted. The first commandment. The widow's mite.

AND ¹ he began to speak to them in parables: A *certain* man planted a vineyard and made a hedge about it and dug a place for the winefat and built a tower and let it to husbandmen: and went into a far country.

2 And at the season he sent to the husbandmen a servant to receive of the husbandmen of the fruit of the vineyard.

3 Who, having laid hands on him, beat and sent him away empty.

4 And again he sent to them another servant: and him they wounded in the head and used him reproachfully.

5 And again he sent another, and him they killed: and many others, of whom some they beat, and others they killed.

6 Therefore, having yet one son, most dear to him, he also sent him unto them last of all, saying: They will reverence my son.

7 But the husbandmen said one to another: This is the heir. Come let us kill him and the inheritance shall be ours.

8 And laying hold on him, they killed him and cast him out of the vineyard.

9 What therefore will the lord of the vineyard do? He will come and destroy *those* husbandmen and will give the vineyard to others.

10 And have you not read this scripture, ² *The stone which the builders rejected, the same is made the head of the corner:*

11 *By the Lord has this been done, and it is wonderful in our eyes.*

12 And they sought to lay hands on him: but they feared the people. For they knew that he spoke this parable to them. And leaving him, they went their way.

13 ³ And they sent to him some of the Pharisees and of the Herodians: that they should catch him in *his* words.

14 Who coming, say to him: Master, we know that thou art a true speaker and carest not for any *man;* for thou regardest not the person of men, but teachest the way of God in truth. Is it lawful to give tribute to Cæsar? Or shall we not give *it?*

15 Who knowing their wiliness, saith to them: Why tempt you me? Bring me a penny that I may see *it.*

16 And they brought it him. And he saith to them: Whose is this image and inscription? They say to him, Cæsar's.

17 And Jesus answering, said to them: ⁴ Render therefore to Cæsar the things that are Cæsar's and to God the things that are God's. And they marvelled at him.

18 ⁵ And there came to him the Sadducees, who say there is no resurrection. And they asked him, saying:

19 Master, Moses wrote unto us ⁶ that if any man's brother die and leave his wife behind him and leave no children, his brother should take his wife and raise up seed to his brother.

20 Now there were seven brethren: and the first took a wife and died leaving no issue.

21 And the second took her and died: and neither did he leave any issue. And the third in like manner.

22 And the seven *all* took her in like manner and did not leave issue. Last of all the woman also died.

23 In the resurrection therefore, when they shall rise again, whose wife

⁹ Matt. 6, 14; 18, 35; Luke, 11, 9. ¹⁰ Luke, 20, 1. CHAP. 12. ¹ Isai. 5, 1; Jer. 2, 21; Matt. 21, 33; Luke, 20, 9. ² Ps. 117, 22; Isai. 28, 16; Matt. 21, 42; Acts, 4, 11; Rom. 9, 43; 1 Peter, 2, 7. ³ Matt. 22, 15; Luke, 20, 20. ⁴ Rom. 13, 7. ⁵ Matt. 22, 23; Luke, 20, 27. ⁶ Deut. 25, 5.

shall she be of them? For the seven had her to wife.

24 And Jesus answering, saith to them: Do ye not therefore err, because you know not the scriptures nor the power of God?

25 For when they shall rise again from the dead, they shall neither marry, nor be married, but are as the angels in heaven.

26 And as concerning the dead that they rise again have you not read in the book of Moses, how in the bush God spoke to him, saying: [7] *I am the God of Abraham and the God of Isaac and the God of Jacob?*

27 He is not the God of the dead, but of the living. You therefore do greatly err.

28 [8] And there came one of the scribes that had heard them reasoning together, and seeing that he had answered them well, asked him which was the first commandment of all.

29 And Jesus answered him: The first commandment of all is, [9] *Hear, O Israel: the Lord thy God is one God.*

30 *And thou shalt love the Lord thy God with thy whole heart and with thy whole soul and with thy whole mind and with thy whole strength.* This is the first commandment.

31 [10] And the second is like to it: *Thou shalt love thy neighbour as thyself.* There is no other commandment greater than these.

32 And the scribe said to him: Well, Master, thou hast said in truth that there is one God and there is no other besides him.

33 And that he should be loved with the whole heart and with the whole understanding and with the whole soul and with the whole strength. And to love one's neighbour as one's self is a greater thing than all holocausts and sacrifices.

34 And Jesus seeing that he had answered wisely, said to him: Thou art not far from the kingdom of God. And no man after that durst ask him any question.

35 And Jesus answering, said, teaching in the temple: How do the scribes say that Christ is the son of David?

36 For David himself saith by the Holy Ghost: [11] *The Lord said to my Lord: Sit on my right hand, until I make thy enemies thy footstool.*

37 David therefore himself calleth him Lord. And whence is he then his son? And a great multitude heard him gladly.

38 And he said to them in his doctrine: [21] Beware of the scribes, who love to walk in long robes and to be saluted in the marketplace,

39 And to sit in the first chairs in the synagogues and to have the highest places at suppers:

40 Who devour the houses of widows under the pretence of long prayer. These shall receive greater judgment.

41 [13] And Jesus sitting over against the treasury, behold how the people cast money into the treasury. And many that were rich cast in much.

42 And there came a certain poor widow: and she cast in two mites, which make a farthing.

43 And calling his disciples together, he saith to them: Amen I say to you, this poor widow hath cast in more than all they who have cast into the treasury.

44 For all they did cast in of their abundance; but she of her want cast in all she had, *even* her whole living.

CHAPTER 13

Christ foretells the destruction of the temple and the signs that shall forerun the day of judgment.

AND [1] as he was going out of the temple, one of his disciples said to him: Master, behold what manner of stones and what buildings *are here.*

2 And Jesus answering, said to him: Seest thou all these great buildings? [3] There shall not be left a stone upon a stone, that shall not be thrown down.

3 And as he sat on the mount of Olivet over against the temple, Peter and James and John and Andrew asked him apart:

4 Tell us, when shall these things be and what shall be the sign when all these things shall begin to be fulfilled?

5 And Jesus answering, began to say to them: [3] Take heed lest any man deceive you.

6 For many shall come in my name saying, I am he: and they shall deceive many.

7 And when you shall hear of wars and rumours of wars, fear ye not. For such things must needs be: but the end is not yet.

8 For nation shall rise against nation and kingdom against kingdom: and there shall be earthquakes in *divers* places and famines. These things *are* the beginning of sorrows.

9 But look to yourselves. For they shall deliver you up to councils: and in the synagogues you shall be beaten: and you shall stand before governors

[7] Exod. 3, 6; Matt. 22, 32. [8] Matt. 22, 35. [9] Deut. 6, 4. [10] Lev. 19, 18; Matt. 22, 39; Rom. 13, 9; Gal. 5, 14; James, 2, 8. [11] Ps. 109, 1; Matt. 22, 44; Luke, 20, 42. [12] Matt. 23, 6; Luke, 11, 43; 20, 46. [13] Luke, 21, 1. CHAP. 13. [1] Matt. 24, 1. [2] Luke, 19, 44; 21, 6. [3] Eph. 5, 6; 2 Thess. 2, 3.

and kings for my sake, for a testimony unto them.

10 And unto all nations the gospel must first be preached.

11 [4] And when they shall lead you and deliver you up, be not thoughtful beforehand what you shall speak: but whatsoever shall be given you in that hour, that speak ye. For it is not you that speak, but the Holy Ghost.

12 And the brother shall betray his brother unto death, and the father his son; and children shall rise up against their parents and shall work their death.

13 And you shall be hated by all men for my name's sake. But he that shall endure unto the end, he shall be saved.

14 [5] And when you shall see the abomination of desolation, standing where it ought not (he that readeth let him understand): then let them that are in Judea flee unto the mountains.

15 And let him that is on the housetop not go down into the house nor enter therein to take any thing out of the house.

16 And let him that shall be in the field not turn back to take up his garment.

17 And woe to them that are with child and that give suck in those days.

18 But pray ye that *these things* happen not in winter.

19 For in those days shall be such tribulations as were not from the beginning of the creation which God created until now: neither shall be.

20 And unless the Lord had shortened the days, no flesh should be saved: but, for the sake of the elect which he hath chosen, he hath shortened the days.

21 [6] And then if any man shall say to you: Lo, here is Christ. Lo, he is here: do not believe.

22 For there will rise up false Christs and false prophets: and they shall shew signs and wonders, to seduce (if it were possible) even the elect.

23 Take you heed therefore: behold, I have foretold you all things.

24 [7] But in those days, after that tribulation, the sun shall be darkened and the moon shall not give her light.

25 And the stars of heaven shall be falling down and the powers that are in heaven shall be moved.

26 And then shall they see the Son of man coming in the clouds, with great power and glory.

27 [8] And then shall he send his angels and shall gather together his elect from the four winds, from the uttermost part of the earth to the uttermost part of heaven.

28 Now of the fig tree learn ye a parable. When the branch thereof is now tender and the leaves are come forth, you know that summer is very near.

29 So you also when you shall see these things come to pass, know ye that it is very nigh, even at the doors.

30 Amen, I say to you that this generation shall not pass until all these things be done.

31 Heaven and earth shall pass away: but my word shall not pass away.

32 But of that day or hour no man knoweth, neither the angels in heaven, nor the Son, but the Father.

33 [9] Take ye heed, watch and pray. For ye know not when the time is.

34 Even as a man who, going into a far country, left his house and gave authority to his servants over every work and commanded the porter to watch.

35 Watch ye therefore (for you know not when the lord of the house cometh, at even, or at midnight, or at the cockcrowing, or in the morning):

36 Lest coming on a sudden, he find you sleeping.

37 And what I say to you, I say to all: Watch.

CHAPTER 14

The first part of the history of the passion of Christ.

NOW [1] the feast of the pasch and of the Azymes was after two days: and the chief priests and the scribes sought how they might by some wile lay hold on him and kill him.

2 But they said: Not on the festival day, lest there should be a tumult among the people.

3 [2] And when he was in Bethania, in the house of Simon the leper, and was at meat, there came a woman having an alabaster box of ointment of precious spikenard. And breaking the alabaster box, she poured it out upon his head.

4 Now there were some that had indignation within themselves and said: Why was this waste of the ointment made?

5 For this ointment might have been sold for more than three hundred pence

4 Matt. 10, 19; Luke, 12, 11; 21, 14. 5 Dan. 9, 27; Matt. 24, 15; Luke, 21, 20. 6 Matt. 24, 23; Luke, 17, 23; 21, 8. 7 Isai. 13, 10; Ezech. 32, 7; Joel, 2, 10. 8 Matt. 24, 31. 9 Matt. 24, 42. CHAP. 14. 1 Matt. 26, 2; Luke, 22, 1. 2 Matt. 26, 6; John, 12, 1.

CHAP. 13. Ver. 32. *Nor the Son.* Not that the Son of God is absolutely ignorant of the day of judgment, but that he knoweth it not, as our teacher; that is, he knoweth it not so as to teach it to us, as not being expedient.

CHAP. 14. Ver. 1. *Azymes.* That is, the feast of the unleavened bread.

and given to the poor. And they murmured against her.

6 But Jesus said: Let her alone. Why do you molest her? She hath wrought a good work upon me.

7 For the poor you have always with you: and whensoever you will, you may do them good: but me you have not always.

8 She hath done what she could: she is come beforehand to anoint my body for the burial.

9 Amen, I say to you, wheresoever this gospel shall be preached in the whole world, that also which she hath done shall be told for a memorial of her.

10 ³ And Judas Iscariot, one of the twelve, went to the chief priests, to betray him to them.

11 Who hearing it were glad: and they promised him they would give him money. And he sought how he might conveniently betray him.

12 ⁴ Now on the first day of the unleavened bread, when they sacrificed the pasch, the disciples say to him: Whither wilt thou that we go and prepare for thee to eat the pasch?

13 And he sendeth two of his disciples and saith to them: Go ye into the city; and there shall meet you a man carrying a pitcher of water. Follow him.

14 And whithersoever he shall go in, say to the master of the house, The master saith, Where is my refectory, where I may eat the pasch with my disciples?

15 And he will shew you a large dining room furnished. And there prepare ye for us.

16 And his disciples went their way and came into the city. And they found as he had told them: and they prepared the pasch.

17 ⁵ And when evening was come, he cometh with the twelve.

18 And when they were at table and eating, Jesus saith: Amen I say to you, ⁶ one of you that eateth with me shall betray me.

19 But they began to be sorrowful and to say to him, one by one: Is it I?

20 Who saith to them: One of the twelve, who dippeth with me his hand in the dish.

21 And the Son of man indeed goeth, as it is written of him: but woe to that man by whom the Son of man shall be betrayed. It were better for him, if that man had not been born.

22 ⁸ And whilst they were eating, Jesus took bread; and blessing, broke and gave to them and said: Take ye. This is my body.

23 And having taken the chalice, giving thanks, he gave it to them. And they all drank of it.

24 And he said to them: This is my blood of the new testament, which shall be shed for many.

25 Amen I say to you that I will drink no more of the fruit of the vine until that day when I shall drink it new in the kingdom of God.

26 And when they had sung an hymn, they went forth to the mount of Olives.

27 And Jesus saith to them: ⁹ You will all be scandalized in my regard this night. For it is written: ¹⁰ *I will strike the shepherd, and the sheep shall be dispersed.*

28 But after I shall be risen again, I will go before you into Galilee.

29 But Peter saith to him: Although all shall be scandalized in thee, yet not I.

30 And Jesus saith to him: Amen I say to thee, to-day, even in this night, before the cock crow twice, thou shalt deny me thrice.

31 But he spoke the more vehemently: Although I should die together with thee, I will not deny thee. And in like manner also said they all.

32 ¹¹ And they came to a farm called Gethsemani. And he saith to his disciples: Sit you here, while I pray.

33 And he taketh Peter and James and John with him: and he began to fear and to be heavy.

34 And he saith to them: My soul is sorrowful even unto death. Stay you here and watch.

35 And when he was gone forward a little, he fell flat on the ground: and he prayed that, if it might be, the hour might pass from him.

36 And he saith: Abba, Father, all things are possible to thee: remove this chalice from me; but not what I will, but what thou wilt.

37 And he cometh and findeth them sleeping. And he saith to Peter: Simon, sleepest thou? Couldst thou not watch one hour?

38 Watch ye: and pray that you enter not into temptation. The spirit indeed is willing, but the flesh is weak.

39 And going away again, he prayed, saying the same words.

40 And when he returned, he found them again asleep (for their eyes were

³ Matt. 26, 14. ⁴ Matt. 26, 17; Luke, 22, 7. ⁵ Matt. 26, 20; Luke, 22, 14. ⁶ John, 13, 21. ⁷ Ps. 40, 10; Acts, 1, 16. ⁸ Matt. 26, 26; 1 Cor. 11, 24. ⁹ John, 16, 32. ¹⁰ Zach. 13, 7. ¹¹ Matt. 26, 36; Luke, 22, 40.
Ver. 30. *Crow twice.* The cocks crow at two different times of the night: about midnight for the first time, and then about the time commonly called the *cock crowing.* This was the *cock crowing* our Saviour spoke of: and therefore the other Evangelists take no notice of the first crowing.

heavy): and they knew not what to answer him.

41 And he cometh the third time and saith to them: Sleep ye now and take *your* rest. It is enough. The hour is come: behold the Son of man shall be betrayed into the hands of sinners.

42 Rise up: let us go. Behold, he that will betray me is at hand.

43 And while he was yet speaking, cometh Judas Iscariot, one of the twelve: [12] and with him a great multitude with swords and staves, from the chief priests and the scribes and the ancients.

44 And he that betrayed him had given them a sign, saying: Whomsoever I shall kiss, that is he. Lay hold on him: and lead him away carefully.

45 And when he was come, immediately going up to him he saith: Hail, Rabbi! And he kissed him.

46 But they laid hands on him and held him.

47 And one of them that stood by drawing a sword, struck a servant of the chief priest and cut off his ear.

48 And Jesus answering, said to them: Are you come out as to a robber, with swords and staves to apprehend me?

49 I was daily with you in the temple teaching: and you did not lay hands on me. But that the scriptures may be fulfilled.

50 [13] Then his disciples, leaving him, all fled away.

51 And a certain young man followed him, having a linen cloth cast about his naked *body*. And they laid hold on him.

52 But he, casting off the linen cloth, fled from them naked.

53 [14] And they brought Jesus to the high priest. And all the priests and the scribes and the ancients assembled together.

54 And Peter followed him afar off, even into the court of the high priest. And he sat with the servants at the fire and warmed himself.

55 [15] And the chief priests and all the council sought for evidence against Jesus, that they might put him to death: and found none.

56 For many bore false witness against him: and their evidences were not agreeing.

57 And some rising up, bore false witness against him, saying:

58 We heard him say, [16] I will destroy this temple made with hands, and within three days I will build another not made with hands.

59 And their witness did not agree.

60 And the high priest rising up in the midst, asked Jesus, saying: Answerest thou nothing to the things that are laid to thy charge by these men?

61 But he held his peace and answered nothing. Again the high priest asked him and said to him: Art thou the Christ, the Son of the Blessed God?

62 And Jesus said to him: I am. [17] And you shall see the Son of man sitting on the right hand of the power of God and coming with the clouds of heaven.

63 Then the high priest rending his garments, saith: What need we any further witnesses?

64 You have heard the blasphemy. What think you? Who all condemned him to be guilty of death.

65 And some began to spit on him and to cover his face and to buffet him and to say unto him: Prophesy. And the servants struck him with the palms of their hands.

66 [18] Now when Peter was in the court below, there cometh one of the maidservants of the high priest.

67 And when she had seen Peter warming himself, looking on him, she saith: Thou also wast with Jesus of Nazareth.

68 But he denied, saying: I neither know nor understand what thou sayest. And he went forth before the court: and the cock crew.

69 [19] And again a maidservant seeing him, began to say to the standers by: This is one of them.

70 But he denied again. [20] And after a while they that stood by said again to Peter: Surely thou art one of them; for thou art also a Galilean.

71 But he began to curse and to swear, *saying:* I know not this man of whom you speak.

72 And immediately the cock crew again. [21] And Peter remembered the word that Jesus had said unto him: Before the cock crow twice, thou shalt thrice deny me. And he began to weep.

CHAPTER 15

The continuation of the history of the passion.

AND [1] straightway in the morning, the chief priests holding a consultation with the ancients and the scribes and the whole council, binding Jesus, led him away and delivered him to Pilate.

[12] Matt. 26, 47; Luke, 22, 47; John, 18, 3. [13] Matt. 26, 56. [14] Matt. 26, 57; Luke, 22, 54; John, 18, 13. [15] Matt. 26, 59. [16] John, 2, 19. [17] Matt. 24, 30; 26, 64. [18] Matt. 26, 69; Luke, 22, 56; John, 18, 17. [19] Matt. 26, 71. [20] Luke, 22, 59; John, 18, 25. [21] Matt. 26, 75; John, 13, 38. Chap. 15. [1] Matt. 27, 1; Luke, 22, 66; John, 18, 28.

2 And Pilate asked him: Art thou the king of the Jews? But he answering, saith to him: Thou sayest *it*.

3 [2] And the chief priests accused him in many things.

4 And Pilate again asked him, saying: Answerest thou nothing? Behold in how many things they accuse thee.

5 But Jesus still answered nothing: so that Pilate wondered.

6 Now on the festival day he was wont to release unto them one of the prisoners, whomsoever they demanded.

7 And there was one called Barabbas, who was put in prison with some seditious men, who in the sedition had committed murder.

8 And when the multitude was come up, they began to desire *that he would do* as he had ever done unto them.

9 And Pilate answered them and said: Will you that I release to you the king of the Jews?

10 For he knew that the chief priests had delivered him up out of envy.

11 But the chief priests moved the people, that he should rather release Barabbas to them.

12 [3] And Pilate again answering, saith to them: What will you then that I do to the king of the Jews?

13 [4] But they again cried out: Crucify him.

14 And Pilate saith to them: Why, what evil hath he done? But they cried out the more: Crucify him.

15 And so Pilate being willing to satisfy the people, released to them Barabbas: and delivered up Jesus, when he had scourged him, to be crucified.

16 [5] And the soldiers led him away into the court of the palace: and they called together the whole band.

17 And they clothe him with purple: and, platting a crown of thorns, they put it upon him.

18 And they began to salute him: Hail, king of the Jews.

19 And they struck his head with a reed: and they did spit on him. And bowing their knees, they adored him.

20 And after they had mocked him, they took off the purple from him and put his own garments on him: and they led him out to crucify him.

21 [6] And they forced one Simon a Cyrenian, who passed by coming out of the country, the father of Alexander and of Rufus, to take up his cross.

22 And they bring him into the place called Golgotha, which being interpreted is, The place of Calvary.

23 And they gave him to drink wine mingled with myrrh. But he took it not.

24 [7] And crucifying him, they divided his garments, casting lots upon them, what every man should take.

25 And it was the third hour: and they crucified him.

26 And the inscription of his cause was written over: THE KING OF THE JEWS.

27 And with him they crucify two thieves: the one on his right hand, and the other on his left.

28 [8] And the scripture was fulfilled, which saith: *And with the wicked he was reputed.*

29 And they that passed by blasphemed him, wagging their heads and saying: [9] Vah, thou that destroyest the temple of God and in three days buildest it up again:

30 Save thyself, coming down from the cross.

31 In like manner also the chief priests, mocking, said with the scribes one to another: He saved others; himself he cannot save.

32 Let Christ the king of Israel come down now from the cross, that we may see and believe. And they that were crucified with him reviled him.

33 And when the sixth hour was come, there was darkness over the whole earth until the ninth hour.

34 And at the ninth hour, Jesus cried out with a loud voice, saying: [10] Eloi, Eloi, lamma sabacthani? Which is, being interpreted: My God, My God, Why hast thou forsaken me?

35 And some of the standers by hearing, said: Behold he calleth Elias.

36 And one running and filling a sponge with vinegar and putting it upon a reed, gave him to drink, saying: Stay, let us see if Elias come to take him down.

37 And Jesus, having cried out with a loud voice, gave up the ghost.

38 And the veil of the temple was rent in two, from the top to the bottom.

39 And the centurion who stood over against him, seeing that crying out in this manner he had given up the ghost, said: Indeed this man was the son of God.

40 [11] And there were also women

[2] Matt. 27, 12; Luke, 23, 2; John, 18, 33. [3] Matt. 27, 22; Luke, 23, 14. [4] John, 18, 40. [5] Matt. 27, 27; John, 19, 2. [6] Matt. 27, 32; Luke, 23, 26. [7] Matt. 27, 35; Luke, 23, 34; John, 19, 23. [8] Isai. 53, 12. [9] John, 2, 19. [10] Ps. 21, 2; Matt. 27, 46. [11] Matt. 27, 55.

CHAP. 15. Ver, 25. *The third hour.* The ancient account divided the day into four parts, which were named from the hour from which they began: the first, third, sixth, and ninth hour. Our Lord was crucified a little before noon; before the *third hour* had quite expired, but when the *sixth hour* was near at hand.

looking on afar off: among whom was Mary Magdalen and Mary the mother of James the Less and of Joseph and Salome.

41 Who also when he was in Galilee followed him [12] and ministered to him, and many other women that came up with him to Jerusalem.

42 [13] And when evening was now come (because it was the Parasceve, that is, the day before the sabbath),

43 Joseph of Arimathea, a noble counsellor, who was also himself looking for the kingdom of God, came and went in boldly to Pilate and begged the body of Jesus.

44 But Pilate wondered that he should be already dead. And sending for the centurion, he asked him if he were already dead.

45 And when he had understood it by the centurion, he gave the body to Joseph.

46 And Joseph, buying fine linen and taking him down, wrapped him up in the fine linen and laid him in a sepulchre which was hewed out of a rock. And he rolled a stone to the door of the sepulchre.

47 And Mary Magdalen and Mary the mother of Joseph, beheld where he was laid.

CHAPTER 16

Christ's resurrection and ascension.

AND [1] when the sabbath was past, Mary Magdalen and Mary *the mother* of James and Salome bought sweet spices, that coming, they might anoint Jesus.

2 And very early in the morning, the first day of the week, they come to the sepulchre, the sun being now risen.

3 And they said one to another: Who shall roll us back the stone from the door of the sepulchre?

4 And looking, they saw the stone rolled back. For it was very great.

5 [2] And entering into the sepulchre, they saw a young man sitting on the right side, clothed with a white robe: and they were astonished.

6 Who saith to them: Be not affrighted. You seek Jesus of Nazareth, who was crucified. He is risen: he is not here. Behold the place where they laid him.

7 But go, tell his disciples and Peter that he goeth before you into Galilee. There you shall see him, [3] as he told you.

8 But they going out, fled from the sepulchre: for a trembling and fear had seized them. And they said nothing to any man: for they were afraid.

9 But he rising [4] early the first first day of the week, appeared first to Mary Magdalen, out of whom he had cast seven devils.

10 She went and told them that had been with him, who were mourning and weeping.

11 And they hearing that he was alive and had been seen by her, did not believe.

12 [5] And after that he appeared in another shape to two of them walking, as they were going into the country.

13 And they going told it to the rest: neither did they believe them.

14 At length he appeared to the eleven as they were at table: and he upbraided them with their incredulity and hardness of heart, because they did not believe them who had seen him after he was risen again.

15 And he said to them: Go ye into the whole world and preach the gospel to every creature.

16 He that believeth and is baptized shall be saved: but he that believeth not shall be condemned.

17 And these signs shall follow them that believe: [6] In my name they shall cast out devils. [7] They shall speak with new tongues.

18 [8] They shall take up serpents: and if they shall drink any deadly thing, it shall not hurt them. [9] They shall lay their hands upon the sick: and they shall recover.

19 And the Lord Jesus, after he had spoken to them, [10] was taken up into heaven and sitteth on the right hand of God.

20 But they going forth preached every where: the Lord working withal, and confirming the word with signs that followed.

[12] Luke, 8, 2. [13] Matt. 27, 57; Luke, 23, 50; John, 19, 38. CHAP. 16. [1] Matt. 28, 1; Luke, 24, 1; John, 20, 1. [2] Matt. 28, 5; Luke, 24, 4; John, 20, 12. [3] Mark, 14, 28. [4] John, 20, 16. [5] Luke, 24, 13. [6] Acts, 16, 18. [7] Acts, 2, 4; 10, 46. [8] Acts, 28, 5. [9] Acts, 28, 8. [10] Luke, 24, 51.

CHAP. 16. Ver. 2. *The sun being now risen.* They set out before it was light, to go to the sepulchre: but the sun was risen when they arrived there. Or, figuratively, the *sun* here spoken of is the *sun of justice*, Christ Jesus our Lord, who was risen before their coming.

THE HOLY GOSPEL OF JESUS CHRIST

ACCORDING TO

ST. LUKE

Sᴛ. Lᴜᴋᴇ *was a native of Antioch, the capital of Syria. He was by profession a physician; and some ancient writers say, that he was very skilful in painting. He was converted by St. Paul and became his disciple and companion in his travels, and fellow-labourer in the ministry of the Gospel. He wrote in Greek, about twenty-four years after our Lord's Ascension.*

CHAPTER 1

The conception of John the Baptist, and of Christ. The visitation and canticle of the Blessed Virgin. The birth of the Baptist and the canticle of Zachary.

FORASMUCH as many have taken in hand to set forth in order a narration of the things that have been accomplished among us,

2 According as they have delivered them unto us, who from the beginning were eyewitnesses and ministers of the word:

3 It seemed good to me also, having diligently attained to all things from the beginning, to write to thee in order, most excellent Theophilus,

4 That thou mayest know the verity of those words in which thou hast been instructed.

5 There was in the days of Herod, the king of Judea, a certain priest named Zachary, [1] of the course of Abia: and his wife was of the daughters of Aaron, and her name Elizabeth.

6 And they were both just before God, walking in all the commandments and justifications of the Lord without blame.

7 And they had no son, for that Elizabeth was barren: and they both were well advanced in years.

8 And it came to pass, when he executed the priestly function in the order of his course before God,

9 According to the custom of the priestly office, it was his lot to offer incense, going into the temple of the Lord.

10 [2] And all the multitude of the people was praying without, at the hour of incense.

11 And there appeared to him an angel of the Lord, standing on the right side of the altar of incense.

12 And Zachary seeing him, was troubled: and fear fell upon him.

13 But the angel said to him: Fear not, Zachary, for thy prayer is heard: and thy wife Elizabeth shall bear thee a son. And thou shalt call his name John.

14 And thou shalt have joy and gladness: and many shall rejoice in his nativity.

15 For he shall be great before the Lord and shall drink no wine nor strong drink: and he shall be filled with the Holy Ghost, even from his mother's womb.

16 And he shall convert many of the children of Israel to the Lord their God.

17 And he shall go before him in the spirit and power of Elias: [3] that he may turn the hearts of the fathers unto the children and the incredulous to the wisdom of the just, to prepare unto the Lord a perfect people.

18 And Zachary said to the angel: Whereby shall I know this? For I am an old man, and my wife is advanced in years.

19 And the angel answering, said to him: I am Gabriel, who stand before God and am sent to speak to thee and to bring thee these good tidings.

20 And behold, thou shalt be dumb and shalt not be able to speak until the day wherein these things shall come to pass: because thou hast not believed my words, which shall be fulfilled in their time.

21 And the people were waiting for Zachary: and they wondered that he tarried so long in the temple.

22 And when he came out, he could not speak to them: and they understood that he had seen a vision in the

Cʜᴀᴘ. 1. [1] 1 Par. 24, 10. [2] Exod. 30, 7; Lev. 16, 17. [3] Mal. 4, 6; Matt. 11, 14.

Cʜᴀᴘ. 1. Ver. 5. *Of the course of Abia.* That is, of the *rank* of Abia, which word in the Greek is commonly put for the employment of *one day;* but here for the functions of a *whole week.* For, by the appointment of David (1 Par. 24), the descendants from Aaron were divided into twenty-four families, of which the eighth was Abia, from whom descended this Zachary, who at this time was in the *week* of his priestly functions.

temple. And he made signs to them and remained dumb.

23 And it came to pass, after the days of his office were accomplished, he departed to his own house.

24 And after those days, Elizabeth his wife conceived and hid herself five months, saying:

25 Thus hath the Lord dealt with me in the days wherein he hath had regard to take away my reproach among men.

26 And in the sixth month, the angel Gabriel was sent from God into a city of Galilee, called Nazareth,

27 To a virgin espoused to a man whose name was Joseph, of the house of David: and the virgin's name was Mary.

28 And the angel being come in, said unto her: Hail, full of grace, the Lord is with thee: blessed art thou among women.

29 Who having heard, was troubled at his saying and thought with herself what manner of salutation this should be.

30 And the angel said to her: Fear not, Mary, for thou hast found grace with God.

31 ⁴Behold thou shalt conceive in thy womb and shalt bring forth a son: ⁵and thou shalt call his name Jesus.

32 He shall be great and shall be called the Son of the Most High. And the Lord God shall give unto him the throne of David his father: ⁶and he shall reign in the house of Jacob for ever.

33 And of his kingdom there shall be no end.

34 And Mary said to the angel: How shall this be done, because I know not man?

35 And the angel answering, said to her: The Holy Ghost shall come upon thee and the power of the Most High shall overshadow thee. And therefore also the Holy which shall be born of thee shall be called the Son of God.

36 And behold thy cousin Elizabeth, she also hath conceived a son in her old age: and this is the sixth month with her that is called barren.

37 Because no word shall be impossible with God.

38 And Mary said: Behold the handmaid of the Lord: be it done to me

according to thy word. And the angel departed from her.

39 And Mary rising up in those days, went into the hill country with haste into a city of Juda.

40 And she entered into the house of Zachary and saluted Elizabeth.

41 And it came to pass that when Elizabeth heard the salutation of Mary, the infant leaped in her womb. And Elizabeth was filled with the Holy Ghost.

42 And she cried out with a loud voice and said: Blessed art thou among women and blessed is the fruit of thy womb.

43 And whence is this to me that the mother of my Lord should come to me?

44 For behold as soon as the voice of thy salutation sounded in my ears, the infant in my womb leaped for joy.

45 And blessed art thou that hast believed, because those things shall be accomplished that were spoken to thee by the Lord.

46 And Mary said: My soul doth magnify the Lord.

47 And my spirit hath rejoiced in God my Saviour.

48 Because he hath regarded the humility of his handmaid: for behold from henceforth all generations shall call me blessed.

49 Because he that is mighty hath done great things to me: and holy is his name.

50 And his mercy is from generation unto generations, to them that fear him.

51 He hath shewed might ⁷in his arm: he hath scattered the proud in the conceit of their heart.

52 He hath put down the mighty from their seat and hath exalted the humble.

53 ⁸He hath filled the hungry with good things: and the rich he hath sent empty away.

54 He hath received Israel his servant, being mindful of his mercy.

55 As he spoke to our fathers: ⁹to Abraham and to his seed for ever.

56 And Mary abode with her about three months. And she returned to her own house.

57 Now Elizabeth's full time of being delivered was come: and she brought forth a son.

58 And her neighbours and kinsfolks heard that the Lord had shewed his great mercy towards her: and they congratulated with her.

59 And it came to pass that on the eighth day they came to circumcise the child: and they called him by his father's name Zachary.

⁴ Isai. 7, 14. ⁵ Luke, 2, 21. ⁶ Dan. 7, 14, 27; Mich. 4, 7. ⁷ Isai. 51, 9; Ps. 32, 10. ⁸ 1 Kings, 2, 5; Ps. 33, 11. ⁹ Gen. 17, 9; 22, 16; Ps. 131, 11; Isai. 41, 8.

Ver. 48. *Shall call me blessed.* These words are a prediction of that honour which the church in all ages should pay to the Blessed Virgin. Let Protestants examine whether they are any way concerned in this prophecy.

60 And his mother answering, said: Not so. But he shall be called John.

61 And they said to her: There is none of thy kindred that is called by this name.

62 And they made signs to his father, how he would have him called.

63 And demanding a writing table, he wrote, [10] saying: John is his name. And they all wondered.

64 And immediately his mouth was opened and his tongue loosed: and he spoke, blessing God.

65 And fear came upon all their neighbours: and all these things were noised abroad over all the hill country of Judea.

66 And all they that had heard them laid them up in their heart, saying: What an one, think ye, shall this child be? For the hand of the Lord was with him.

67 And Zachary his father was filled with the Holy Ghost. And he prophesied, saying:

68 [11] Blessed be the Lord God of Israel: because he hath visited and wrought the redemption of his people.

69 [12] And hath raised up an horn of salvation to us, in the house of David his servant.

70 [13] As he spoke by the mouth of his holy prophets, who are from the beginning.

71 Salvation from our enemies and from the hand of all that hate us.

72 To perform mercy to our fathers and to remember his holy testament.

73 [14] The oath, which he swore to Abraham our father, that he would grant to us.

74 That being delivered from the hand of our enemies, we may serve him without fear:

75 In holiness and justice before him, all our days.

76 And thou, child, shalt be called the prophet of the Highest: for thou shalt go before the face of the Lord to prepare his ways:

77 [15] To give knowledge of salvation to his people, unto the remission of their sins.

78 Through the bowels of the mercy of our God, in which [16] the Orient from on high hath visited us:

79 To enlighten them that sit in darkness and in the shadow of death: to direct our feet into the way of peace.

80 And the child grew and was strengthened in spirit: and was in the deserts until the day of his manifestation to Israel.

CHAPTER 2

The birth of Christ. His presentation in the temple. Simeon's prophecy. Christ, at twelve years of age, is found amongst the doctors.

AND it came to pass that in those days there went out a decree from Cæsar Augustus that the whole world should be enrolled.

2 This enrolling was first made by Cyrinus, the governor of Syria.

3 And all went to be enrolled, every one into his own city.

4 And Joseph also went up from Galilee, out of the city of Nazareth, into Judea, to the city of [1] David, which is called [2] Bethlehem: because he was of the house and family of David,

5 To be enrolled with Mary his espoused wife, who was with child.

6 And it came to pass that when they were there, her days were accomplished that she should be delivered.

7 And she brought forth her firstborn son and wrapped him up in swaddling clothes and laid him in a manger: because there was no room for them in the inn.

8 And there were in the same country shepherds watching and keeping the night watches over their flock.

9 And behold an angel of the Lord stood by them and the brightness of God shone round about them: and they feared with a great fear.

10 And the angel said to them: Fear not; for, behold, I bring you good tidings of great joy that shall be to all the people:

11 For, this day is born to you a Saviour, who is Christ the Lord, in the city of David.

12 And this shall be a sign unto you. You shall find the infant wrapped in swaddling clothes and laid in a manger.

13 And suddenly there was with the angel a multitude of the heavenly army, praising God and saying:

14 Glory to God in the highest: and on earth peace to men of good will.

15 And it came to pass, after the angels departed from them into heav-

---

[10] Luke, 1, 13. [11] Ps. 73, 12. [12] Ps. 131, 17. [13] Jer. 23, 6; 30, 10. [14] Gen. 22, 16; Jer. 31, 33; Heb. 6, 13, 17. [15] Mal. 4, 5; Luke, 1, 17. [16] Zach, 3, 9; 6, 12; Mal. 4, 2. CHAP. 2. [1] 1 Kings, 20, 6. [2] Mich. 5, 2; Matt. 2, 16.

Ver. 69. *Horn of salvation.* That is, *A powerful salvation,* as Dr. Witham translates it. For in the Scripture, by *horn* is generally understood strength and power.

Ver. 78. *The Orient.* It is one of the titles of the Messias, the true light of the world and the sun of justice.

CHAP. 2. Ver. 7. *Her firstborn.* The meaning is, not that she had afterwards any other child; but it is a way of speech among the Hebrews, to call also the *firstborn,* who are the only children (see annotation, Matt. 1, 25).

en, the shepherds said one to another: Let us go over to Bethlehem and let us see this word that is come to pass, which the Lord hath shewed to us.

16 And they came with haste: and they found Mary and Joseph, and the infant lying in the manger.

17 And seeing, they understood of the word that had been spoken to them concerning this child.

18 And all that heard wondered: and at those things that were told them by the shepherds.

19 But Mary kept all these words, pondering *them* in her heart.

20 And the shepherds returned, glorifying and praising God for all the things they had heard and seen, as it was told unto them.

21 ³ And after eight days were accomplished, that the child should be circumcised, his name was called ⁴ JESUS, which was called by the angel before he was conceived in the womb.

22 And after the days of her purification, ⁵ according to the law of Moses, were accomplished, they carried him to Jerusalem, to present him to the Lord:

23 As it is written in the law of the Lord: ⁶ *Every male opening the womb shall be called holy to the Lord:*

24 And to offer a sacrifice, according as it is written ⁷ in the law of the Lord, a pair of turtledoves or two young pigeons:

25 And behold there was a man in Jerusalem named Simeon: and this man was just and devout, waiting for the consolation of Israel. And the Holy Ghost was in him.

26 And he had received an answer from the Holy Ghost, that he should not see death before he had seen the Christ of the Lord.

27 And he came by the Spirit into the temple. And when his parents brought in the child Jesus, to do for him according to the custom of the law,

28 He also took him into his arms and blessed God and said:

29 Now thou dost dismiss thy servant, O Lord, according to thy word in peace:

30 Because my eyes have seen thy salvation,

31 Which thou hast prepared before the face of all peoples:

³ Gen. 17, 12; Lev. 12, 3. ⁴ Matt. 1, 21; Luke. 1, 31. ⁵ Lev. 12, 6. ⁶ Exod. 13, 2; Num. 8, 16. ⁷ Lev. 12, 8. ⁸ Isai. 8, 14; Rom. 9, 33; 1 Peter, 2, 7. ⁹ Exod. 23 ,15; 34, 18; Deut. 16, 1.

Ver. 34. *For the fall.* Christ came for the salvation of all men; but here Simeon prophesies what would come to pass, that *many* through their own wilful blindness and obstinacy would not believe in Christ, nor receive his doctrine, which therefore would be *ruin* to them: but to others a *resurrection*, by their believing in him and obeying his commandments.

32 A light to the revelation of the Gentiles and the glory of thy people Israel.

33 And his father and mother were wondering at those things which were spoken concerning him.

34 And Simeon blessed them and said to Mary his mother: ⁸ Behold this *child* is set for the fall and for the resurrection of many in Israel and for a sign which shall be contradicted.

35 And thy own soul a sword shall pierce, that, out of many hearts thoughts may be revealed.

36 And there was one Anna, a prophetess, the daughter of Phanuel, of the tribe of Aser. She was far advanced in years and had lived with her husband seven years from her virginity.

37 And she was a widow until fourscore and four years: who departed not from the temple, by fastings and prayers serving night and day.

38 Now she, at the same hour, coming in, confessed to the Lord: and spoke of him to all that looked for the redemption of Israel.

39 And after they had performed all things according to the law of the Lord, they returned into Galilee, to their city Nazareth.

40 And the child grew and waxed strong, full of wisdom: and the grace of God was in him.

41 And his parents went every year to Jerusalem, ⁹ at the solemn day of the pasch.

42 And when he was twelve years old, they going up into Jerusalem, according to the custom of the feast,

43 And having fulfilled the days, when they returned, the child Jesus remained in Jerusalem. And his parents knew it not.

44 And thinking that he was in the company, they came a day's journey, and sought him among their kinsfolks and acquaintance.

45 And not finding him, they returned into Jerusalem, seeking him.

46 And it came to pass that, after three days, they found him in the temple, sitting in the midst of the doctors, hearing them and asking them questions.

47 And all that heard him were astonished at his wisdom and his answers.

48 And seeing *him*, they wondered. And his mother said to him: Son, why hast thou done so to us? Behold thy father and I have sought thee sorrowing.

49 And he said to them: How is it that you sought me? Did you not know

that I must be about my father's business?

50 And they understood not the word that he spoke unto them.

51 And he went down with them and came to Nazareth and was subject to them. And his mother kept all these words in her heart.

52 And Jesus advanced in wisdom and age and grace with God and men.

CHAPTER 3

John's mission and preaching. Christ is baptized by him.

NOW in the fifteenth year of the reign of Tiberius Cæsar, Pontius Pilate being governor of Judea, and Herod being tetrarch of Galilee, and Philip his brother tetrarch of Iturea and the country of Trachonitis, and Lysanias tetrarch of Abilina:

2 ¹ Under the high priests Annas and Caiphas: the word of the Lord was made unto John, the son of Zachary, in the desert.

3 ² And he came into all the country about the Jordan, preaching the baptism of penance for the remission of sins.

4 As it was written in the book of the sayings of Isaias the prophet: ³ *A voice of one crying in the wilderness: Prepare ye the way of the Lord, make straight his paths.*

5 *Every valley shall be filled and every mountain and hill shall be brought low: and the crooked shall be made straight, and the rough ways plain.*

6 *And all flesh shall see the salvation of God.*

7 He said therefore to the multitudes that went forth to be baptized by him: ⁴ *Ye offspring of vipers, who hath shewed you to flee from the wrath to come?*

8 Bring forth therefore fruits worthy of penance; and do not begin to say, We have Abraham for our father. For I say unto you that God is able of these stones to raise up children to Abraham.

9 For now the axe is laid to the root of the trees. Every tree therefore that bringeth not forth good fruit shall be cut down and cast into the fire.

10 And the people asked him, saying: What then shall we do?

11 And he answering, said to them: ⁵ He that hath two coats, let him give to him that hath none; and he that hath meat, let him do in like manner.

12 And the publicans also came to be baptized and said to him: Master, what shall we do?

13 But he said to them: Do nothing more than that which is appointed you.

14 And the soldiers also asked him, saying: And what shall we do? And he said to them: Do violence to no man, neither calumniate any man; and be content with your pay.

15 And as the people were of opinion, and all were thinking in their hearts of John, that perhaps he might be the Christ:

16 John answered, saying unto all: ⁶ I indeed baptize you with water; but there shall come one mightier than I, the latchet of whose shoes I am not worthy to loose. ⁷ He shall baptize you with the Holy Ghost and with fire:

17 Whose fan is in his hand: and he will purge his floor and will gather the wheat into his barn: but the chaff he will burn with unquenchable fire.

18 And many other things exhorting, did he preach to the people.

19 ⁸ But Herod the tetrarch, when he was reproved by him for Herodias, his brother's wife, and for all the evils which Herod had done:

20 He added this also above all and shut up John in prison.

21 ⁹ Now it came to pass, when all the people were baptized, that Jesus also being baptized and praying, heaven was opened.

22 And the Holy Ghost descended in a bodily shape, as a dove, upon him. And a voice came from heaven: ¹⁰ Thou art my beloved Son. In thee I am well pleased.

23 And Jesus himself was beginning about the age of thirty years: being (as it was supposed) the son of Joseph, who was of Heli, who was of Mathat,

24 Who was of Levi, who was of Melchi, who was of Janne, who was of Joseph,

25 Who was of Mathathias, who was of Amos, who was of Nahum, who was of Hesli, who was of Nagge,

26 Who was of Mahath, who was of Mathathias, who was of Semei, who was of Joseph, who was of Juda,

27 Who was of Joanna, who was of Reza, who was of Zorobabel, who was of Salathiel, who was of Neri,

28 Who was of Melchi, who was of

CHAP. 3. ¹ Acts, 4, 6. ² Matt. 3, 1; Mark, 1, 4. ³ Isai. 40, 3; John, 1, 23. ⁴ Matt. 3, 7; 23, 33. ⁵ James, 2, 15; 1 John, 3, 17. ⁶ Matt. 3, 11; Mark, 1, 8; John, 1, 26. ⁷ Matt. 3, 11; Acts, 1, 5; 11, 16; 19, 4. ⁸ Matt. 14, 4; Mark, 6, 17. ⁹ Matt. 3, 16; Mark, 1, 10; John, 1, 32. ¹⁰ Matt. 3, 17; 5; Luke, 9, 35; 2 Peter, 1, 17.

CHAP. 3. Ver. 23. *Who was of Heli.* St. Joseph, who by nature was the son of Jacob (Matt. 1, 16), in the account of the law, was son of Heli. For Heli and Jacob were brothers by the same mother; and Heli, who was the elder, dying without issue, Jacob, as the law directed, married his widow. In consequence of such marriage, his son Joseph was reputed in the law the son of Heli.

Addi, who was of Cosan, who was of Helmadan, who was of Her,

29 Who was of Jesus, who was of Eliezer, who was of Jorim, who was of Mathat, who was of Levi,

30 Who was of Simeon, who was of Judas, who was of Joseph, who was of Jona, who was of Eliakim,

31 Who was of Melea, who was of Menna, who was of Mathatha, who was of Nathan, who was of David,

32 Who was of Jesse, who was of Obed, who was of Booz, who was of Salmon, who was of Naasson,

33 Who was of Aminadab, who was of Aram, who was of Esron, who was of Phares, who was of Judas,

34 Who was of Jacob, who was of Isaac, who was of Abraham, who was of Thare, who was of Nachor,

35 Who was of Sarug, who was of Ragau, who was of Phaleg, who was of Heber, who was of Sale,

36 Who was of Cainan, who was of Arphaxad, who was of Sem, who was of Noe, who was of Lamech,

37 Who was of Mathusale, who was of Henoch, who was of Jared, who was of Malaleel, who was of Cainan,

38 Who was of Henos, who was of Seth, who was of Adam, who was of God.

CHAPTER 4

Christ's fasting and temptation. He is persecuted in Nazareth. His miracles in Capharnaum.

AND [1] Jesus being full of the Holy Ghost, returned from the Jordan and was led by the spirit into the desert,

2 For the space of forty days, and was tempted by the devil. And he ate nothing in those days. And when they were ended, he was hungry.

3 And the devil said to him: If thou be the Son of God, say to this stone that it be made bread.

4 And Jesus answered him: It is written [2] that *Man liveth not by bread alone, but by every word of God.*

5 And the devil led him into a high mountain and shewed him all the kingdoms of the world in a moment of time.

6 And he said to him: To thee will I give all this power and the glory of them. For to me they are delivered: and to whom I will, I give them.

7 If thou therefore wilt adore before me, all shall be thine.

8 And Jesus answering said to him. [3] It is written: *Thou shalt adore the Lord thy God, and him only shalt thou serve.*

9 And he brought him to Jerusalem and set him on a pinnacle of the temple and said to him: If thou be the Son of God, cast thyself from hence.

10 [4] For it is written that *He hath given his angels charge over thee, that they keep thee.*

11 And that *In their hands they shall bear thee up, lest perhaps thou dash thy foot against a stone.*

12 And Jesus answering, said to him: It is said: [5] *Thou shalt not tempt the Lord thy God.*

13 And all the temptation being ended, the devil departed from him for a time.

14 [6] And Jesus returned in the power of the spirit, into Galilee: and the fame of him went out through the whole country.

15 And he taught in their synagogues and was magnified by all.

16 [7] And he came to Nazareth, where he was brought up: and he went into the synagogue, according to his custom, on the sabbath day: and he rose up to read.

17 And the book of Isaias the prophet was delivered unto him. And as he unfolded the book, he found the place where it was written:

18 [8] *The spirit of the Lord is upon me. Wherefore he hath anointed me to preach the gospel to the poor: he hath sent me to heal the contrite of heart,*

19 *To preach deliverance to the captives and sight to the blind, to set at liberty them that are bruised, to preach the acceptable year of the Lord and the day of reward.*

20 And when he had folded the book, he restored it to the minister and sat down. And the eyes of all in the synagogue were fixed on him.

21 And he began to say to them: This day is fulfilled this scripture in your ears.

22 And all gave testimony to him. And they wondered at the words of grace that proceeded from his mouth. And they said: Is not this the son of Joseph?

23 And he said to them: Doubtless you will say to me this similitude: Physician, heal thyself. As great things as we have heard done in Capharnaum, do also here in thy own country.

24 And he said: Amen I say to you that no prophet is accepted in his own country.

25 In truth I say to you, [9] there were many widows in the days of Elias in Israel, when heaven was shut up three years and six months, when there was a great famine throughout all the earth.

CHAP. 4. [1] Matt. 4, 1; Mark, 1, 12. [2] Deut. 8, 3; Matt. 4, 4. [3] Deut. 6, 13; 10, 20. [4] Ps. 90, 11. [5] Deut. 6, 16. [6] Matt. 4, 12; Mark, 1, 14. [7] Matt. 13, 54; Mark, 6, 1; John, 4, 45. [8] Isai. 61, 1. [9] 3 Kings, 17, 2.

26 And to none of them was Elias sent, but to Sarepta of Sidon, to a widow woman.

27 [10] And there were many lepers in Israel in the time of Eliseus the prophet: and none of them was cleansed but Naaman the Syrian.

28 And all they in the synagogue, hearing these things, were filled with anger.

29 And they rose up and thrust him out of the city: and they brought him to the brow of the hill whereon their city was built, that they might cast him down headlong.

30 But he passing through the midst of them, went his way.

31 [11] And he went down into Capharnaum, a city of Galilee: and there he taught them on the sabbath days.

32 [12] And they were astonished at his doctrine: for his speech was with power.

33 [13] And in the synagogue there was a man who had an unclean devil: and he cried out with a loud voice,

34 Saying: Let us alone. What have we to do with thee, Jesus of Nazareth? Art thou come to destroy us? I know thee who thou art, the holy one of God.

35 And Jesus rebuked him, saying: Hold thy peace and go out of him. And when the devil had thrown him into the midst, he went out of him and hurt him not at all.

36 And there came fear upon all; and they talked among themselves, saying: What word is this, for with authority and power he commandeth the unclean spirits, and they go out?

37 And the fame of him was published into every place of the country.

38 And Jesus rising up out of the synagogue, went into Simon's house. [14] And Simon's wife's mother was taken with a great fever: and they besought him for her.

39 And standing over her, he commanded the fever: and it left her. And immediately rising, she ministered to them.

40 And when the sun was down, all they that had any sick with divers diseases brought them to him. But he, laying his hands on every one of them, healed them.

41 [15] And devils went out from many, crying out and saying: Thou art the son of God. And rebuking them he suffered them not to speak; for they knew that he was Christ.

42 And when it was day, going out he went into a desert place: and the multitudes sought him, and came unto him. And they stayed him that he should not depart from them.

43 To whom he said: To other cities also I must preach the kingdom of God: for therefore am I sent.

44 And he was preaching in the synagogues of Galilee.

CHAPTER 5

The miraculous draught of fishes. The cure of the leper and of the paralytic. The call of Matthew.

AND it came to pass, that when the multitudes pressed upon him to hear the word of God, he stood by the lake of Genesareth,

2 [1] And saw two ships standing by the lake: but the fishermen were gone out of them and were washing their nets.

3 And going into one of the ships that was Simon's, he desired him to draw back a little from the land. And sitting, he taught the multitudes out of the ship.

4 Now when he had ceased to speak, he said to Simon: Launch out into the deep and let down your nets for a draught.

5 And Simon answering said to him: Master, we have laboured all the night and have taken nothing: but at thy word I will let down the net.

6 And when they had done this, they enclosed a very great multitude of fishes: and their net broke.

7 And they beckoned to their partners that were in the other ship, that they should come and help them. And they came and filled both the ships, so that they were almost sinking.

8 Which when Simon Peter saw, he fell down at Jesus' knees, saying: Depart from me, for I am a sinful man, O Lord.

9 For he was wholly astonished, and all that were with him, at the draught of the fishes which they had taken.

10 And so were also James and John, the sons of Zebedee, who were Simon's partners. And Jesus saith to Simon: Fear not: from henceforth thou shalt catch men.

11 And having brought their ships to land, leaving all things, they followed him.

12 [2] And it came to pass, when he was in a certain city, behold a man full of leprosy who, seeing Jesus and falling on his face, besought him saying: Lord, if thou wilt, thou canst make me clean.

13 And stretching forth *his* hand, he touched him, saying: I will. Be thou cleansed. And immediately the leprosy departed from him.

14 And he charged him that he should tell no man, but: Go, shew thyself to the priest [3] and offer for thy cleansing according as Moses commanded, for a testimony to them.

15 But the fame of him went abroad the more: and great multitudes came together to hear and to be healed by him of their infirmities.

16 And he retired into the desert and prayed.

17 And it came to pass on a certain day, as he sat teaching, that there were also Pharisees and doctors of the law sitting by, that were come out of every town of Galilee and Judea and Jerusalem: and the power of the Lord was to heal them.

18 [4] And behold, men brought in a bed a man who had the palsy: and they sought means to bring him in and to lay him before him.

19 And when they could not find by what way they might bring him in, because of the multitude, they went up upon the roof and let him down through the tiles with his bed into the midst before Jesus.

20 Whose faith when he saw, he said: Man, thy sins are forgiven thee.

21 And the scribes and Pharisees began to think, saying: Who is this who speaketh blasphemies? Who can forgive sins, but God alone?

22 And when Jesus knew their thoughts, answering, he said to them: What is it you think in your hearts?

23 Which is easier to say: Thy sins are forgiven thee; or to say: Arise and walk?

24 But that you may know that the Son of man hath power on earth to forgive sins (he saith to the sick of the palsy), I say to thee: Arise, take up thy bed and go into thy house.

25 And immediately rising up before them, he took up the bed on which he lay: and he went away to his own house, glorifying God.

26 And all were astonished: and they glorified God. And they were filled with fear, saying: We have seen wonderful things to-day.

27 [5] And after these things, he went forth and saw a publican named Levi, sitting at the receipt of custom: and he said to him: Follow me.

28 And leaving all things, he rose up and followed him.

29 And Levi made him a great feast in his own house: and there was a great company of publicans and of others that were at table with them.

30 [6] But the Pharisees and scribes murmured, saying to his disciples: Why do you eat and drink with publicans and sinners?

31 And Jesus answering, said to them: They that are whole need not the physician: but they that are sick.

32 I came not to call the just, but sinners to penance.

33 And they said to him: [7] Why do the disciples of John fast often and make prayers, and the disciples of the Pharisees in like manner; but thine eat and drink?

34 To whom he said: Can you make the children of the bridegroom fast whilst the bridegroom is with them?

35 But the days will come when the bridegroom shall be taken away from them: then shall they fast in those days.

36 And he spoke also a similitude to them: That no man putteth a piece from a new garment upon an old garment; otherwise he both rendeth the new, and the piece taken from the new agreeth not with the old.

37 And no man putteth new wine into old bottles: otherwise the new wine will break the bottles; and it will be spilled and the bottles will be lost.

38 But new wine must be put into new bottles: and both are preserved.

39 And no man drinking old hath presently a mind to new: for he saith: The old is better.

CHAPTER 6

Christ excuses his disciples. He cures upon the sabbath day, chooses the twelve and makes a sermon to them.

AND [1] it came to pass on the second first sabbath that, as he went through the corn fields, his disciples plucked the ears and did eat, rubbing them in their hands.

2 And some of the Pharisees said to them: Why do you that which is not lawful on the sabbath days?

3 And Jesus answering them, said: Have you not read so much as this, what David did, when himself was hungry and they that were with him:

4 [2] How he went into the house of God and took and ate the bread of proposition and gave to them that were with him, which is not lawful to eat [3] but only for the priests?

5 And he said to them: The Son of man is Lord also of the sabbath.

6 And it came to pass also, on another sabbath, that he entered into the

[3] Lev. 14, 4. [4] Matt. 9, 2; Mark, 2, 3. [5] Matt. 9, 9; Mark, 2, 14. [6] Mark, 2, 16. [7] Mark, 2, 18. CHAP. 6. [1] Matt. 12, 1; Mark, 2, 23. [2] 1 Kings, 21, 6. [3] Exod. 29, 32; Lev. 24, 9.

CHAP. 6. Ver. 1. *The second first sabbath.* Some understand this of the sabbath of Pentecost, which was the second in course among the great feasts: others, of a sabbath day that immediately followed any solemn feast.

synagogue and taught. ⁴ And there was a man whose right hand was withered.

7 And the scribes and Pharisees watched if he would heal on the sabbath: that they might find an accusation against him.

8 But he knew their thoughts and said to the man who had the withered hand: Arise and stand forth in the midst. And rising he stood forth.

9 Then Jesus said to them: I ask you, if it be lawful on the sabbath days to do good or to do evil? To save life or to destroy?

10 And looking round about on them all, he said to the man: Stretch forth thy hand. And he stretched it forth. And his hand was restored.

11 And they were filled with madness: and they talked one with another what they might do to Jesus.

12 And it came to pass in those days, that he went out into a mountain to pray: and he passed the whole night in the prayer of God.

13 ⁵ And when day was come, he called unto him his disciples: and he chose twelve of them (whom also he named apostles):

14 Simon, whom he surnamed Peter, and Andrew his brother, James and John, Philip and Bartholomew,

15 Matthew and Thomas, James the son of Alpheus, and Simon who is called Zelotes,

16 And Jude the brother of James, and Judas Iscariot, who was the traitor.

17 And coming down with them, he stood in a plain place: and the company of his disciples and a very great multitude of people from all Judea and Jerusalem and the sea coast, both of Tyre and Sidon,

18 Who were come to hear him and to be healed of their diseases. And they that were troubled with unclean spirits were cured.

19 And all the multitude sought to touch him: for virtue went out from him and healed all.

20 ⁶ And he, lifting up his eyes on his disciples, said: Blessed are ye poor: for yours is the kingdom of God.

21 ⁷ Blessed are ye that hunger now: for you shall be filled. Blessed are ye that weep now: for you shall laugh.

22 ⁸ Blessed shall you be when men shall hate you, and when they shall separate you and shall reproach you and cast out your name as evil, for the Son of man's sake.

23 Be glad in that day and rejoice: for behold, your reward is great in heaven. For according to these things did their fathers to the prophets.

24 ⁹ But woe to you that are rich: for you have your consolation.

25 ¹⁰ Woe to you that are filled: for you shall hunger. Woe to you that now laugh: for you shall mourn and weep.

26 Woe to you when men shall bless you: for according to these things did their fathers to the false prophets.

27 But I say to you that hear: ¹¹ Love your enemies. Do good to them that hate you.

28 Bless them that curse you and pray for them that calumniate you.

29 And to him that striketh thee on the one cheek, offer also the other. And him that taketh away from thee thy cloak, forbid not to take thy coat also.

30 Give to every one that asketh thee: and of him that taketh away thy goods, ask them not again.

31 And as you would that men should do to you, do you also to them in like manner.

32 And if you love them that love you, what thanks are to you? For sinners also love those that love them.

33 And if you do good to them who do good to you, what thanks are to you? For sinners also do this.

34 ¹² And if you lend to them of whom you hope to receive, what thanks are to you? For sinners also lend to sinners, for to receive as much.

35 But love ye your enemies: do good, and lend, hoping for nothing thereby: and your reward shall be great, and you shall be the sons of the Highest. For he is kind to the unthankful and to the evil.

36 Be ye therefore merciful, as your Father also is merciful.

37 ¹³ Judge not: and you shall not be judged. Condemn not: and you shall not be condemned. Forgive: and you shall be forgiven.

38 Give: and it shall be given to you: good measure and pressed down and shaken together and running over shall they give into your bosom. ¹⁴ For with the same measure that you shall mete withal, it shall be measured to you again.

39 And he spoke also to them a similitude: Can the blind lead the blind? Do they not both fall into the ditch?

40 ¹⁵ The disciple is not above his master: but every one shall be perfect, if he be as his master.

41 ¹⁶ And why seest thou the mote in thy brother's eye: but the beam that is in thy own eye considerest not?

---

⁴ Matt. 12, 10; Mark, 3, 1. ⁵ Matt. 10, 1; Mark, 3, 13. ⁶ Matt. 5, 2. ⁷ Matt. 5, 6. ⁸ Matt. 5, 11. ⁹ Ecclus. 31, 8; Amos, 6, 1. ¹⁰ Isai. 65, 13. ¹¹ Matt. 5, 44. ¹² Deut. 15, 8; Matt. 5, 42. ¹³ Matt. 7, 1. ¹⁴ Matt. 7, 2; Mark, 4, 24. ¹⁵ Matt. 10, 24; John, 13, 16. ¹⁶ Matt. 7, 3.

42 Or how canst thou say to thy brother: Brother, let me pull the mote out of thy eye, when thou thyself seest not the beam in thy own eye? Hypocrite, cast first the beam out of thy own eye: and then shalt thou see clearly to take out the mote from thy brother's eye.

43 [17] For there is no good tree that bringeth forth evil fruit: nor an evil tree that bringeth forth good fruit.

44 For every tree is known by its fruit. For men do not gather figs from thorns: nor from a bramble bush do they gather the grape.

45 A good man out of the good treasure of his heart bringeth forth that which is good: and an evil man out of the evil treasure bringeth forth that which is evil. For out of the abundance of the heart the mouth speaketh.

46 And why call you me, [18] Lord, Lord; and do not the things which I say?

47 Every one that cometh to me and heareth my words and doth them, I will shew you to whom he is like.

48 He is like to a man building a house, who digged deep and laid the foundation upon a rock. And when a flood came, the stream beat vehemently upon that house; and it could not shake it: for it was founded on a rock.

49 But he that heareth and doth not is like to a man building his house upon the earth without a foundation: against which the stream beat vehemently. And immediately it fell: and the ruin of that house was great.

CHAPTER 7

Christ heals the centurion's servant. He raises the widow's son to life, answers the messengers sent by John and absolves the penitent sinner.

AND [1] when he had finished all his words in the hearing of the people, he entered into Capharnaum.

2 And the servant of a certain centurion who was dear to him, being sick, was ready to die.

3 And when he had heard of Jesus, he sent unto him the ancients of the Jews, desiring him to come and heal his servant.

4 And when they came to Jesus, they besought him earnestly, saying to him: He is worthy that thou shouldest do this for him.

5 For he loveth our nation: and he hath built us a synagogue.

6 And Jesus went with them. And when he was now not far from the house, the centurion sent his friends to him, saying: [2] Lord, trouble not thyself; for I am not worthy that thou shouldest enter under my roof.

7 For which cause neither did I think myself worthy to come to thee: but say the word, and my servant shall be healed.

8 For I also am a man subject to authority, having under me soldiers: and I say to one, Go, and he goeth; and to another, Come, and he cometh; and to my servant, Do this, and he doth it.

9 Which Jesus hearing, marvelled: and turning about to the multitude that followed him, he said: Amen I say to you, I have not found so great faith, not even in Israel.

10 And they who were sent, being returned to the house, found the servant whole who had been sick.

11 And it came to pass afterwards that he went into a city that is called Naim: and there went with him his disciples and a great multitude.

12 And when he came nigh to the gate of the city, behold a dead man was carried out, the only son of his mother: and she was a widow. And a great multitude of the city was with her.

13 Whom when the Lord had seen, being moved with mercy towards her, he said to her: Weep not.

14 And he came near and touched the bier. And they that carried it stood still. And he said: Young man, I say to thee, arise.

15 And he that was dead sat up and begun to speak. And he gave him to his mother.

16 And there came a fear upon them all: and they glorified God, saying: [3] A great prophet is risen up among us: and, God hath visited his people.

17 And this rumour of him went forth throughout all Judea and throughout all the country round about.

18 And John's disciples told him of all these things.

19 [4] And John called to him two of his disciples and sent them to Jesus, saying: Art thou he that art to come? Or look we for another?

20 And when the men were come unto him, they said: John the Baptist hath sent us to thee, saying: Art thou he that art to come? Or look we for another?

21 (And in that same hour, he cured many of their diseases and hurts and evil spirits: and to many that were blind he gave sight.)

22 And answering, he said to them: Go and relate to John what you have

[17] Matt. 7, 18; 12, 33. [18] Matt. 7, 21; Rom. 2, 13; James, 1, 22. CHAP. 7. [1] Matt. 8, 5. [2] Matt. 8, 8. [3] Luke, 24, 19; John, 4, 19. [4] Matt. 11, 2.

heard and seen: [5] the blind see, the lame walk, the lepers are made clean, the deaf hear, the dead rise again, to the poor the gospel is preached.

23 And blessed is he whosoever shall not be scandalized in me.

24 And when the messengers of John were departed, he began to speak to the multitudes concerning John. What went ye out into the desert to see? A reed shaken with the wind?

25 But what went you out to see? A man clothed in soft garments? Behold they that are in costly apparel and live delicately are in the houses of kings.

26 But what went you out to see? A prophet? Yea, I say to you, and more than a prophet.

27 [6] This is he of whom it is written: Behold I send my angel before thy face, who shall prepare thy way before thee.

28 For I say to you. Amongst those that are born of women, there is not a greater prophet than John the Baptist. But he that is the lesser in the kingdom of God is greater than he.

29 And all the people hearing, and the publicans, justified God, being baptized with John's baptism.

30 But the Pharisees and the lawyers despised the counsel of God against themselves, being not baptized by him.

31 And the Lord said: [7] Whereunto then shall I liken the men of this generation? And to what are they like?

32 They are like to children sitting in the marketplace and speaking one to another and saying: We have piped to you, and you have not danced: we have mourned, and you have not wept.

33 [8] For John the Baptist came neither eating bread nor drinking wine. And you say: He hath a devil.

34 The Son of man is come eating and drinking. And you say: Behold a man that is a glutton and a drinker of wine, a friend of publicans and sinners.

35 And wisdom is justified by all her children.

36 And one of the Pharisees desired him to eat with him. And he went into the house of the Pharisee and sat down to meat.

37 [9] And behold a woman that was in the city, a sinner, when she knew that he sat at meat in the Pharisee's house, brought an alabaster box of ointment.

38 And standing behind at his feet, she began to wash his feet with tears and wiped them with the hairs of her head and kissed his feet and anointed them with the ointment.

39 And the Pharisee, who had invited him, seeing it, spoke within himself, saying: This man, if he were a prophet, would know surely who and what man-

ner of woman this is that toucheth him, that she is a sinner.

40 And Jesus answering, said to him: Simon, I have somewhat to say to thee. But he said: Master, say it.

41 A certain creditor had two debtors: the one owed five hundred pence and the other fifty.

42 And whereas they had not wherewith to pay, he forgave them both. Which therefore of the two loveth him most?

43 Simon answering, said: I suppose that he to whom he forgave most. And he said to him: Thou hast judged rightly.

44 And turning to the woman, he said unto Simon: Dost thou see this woman? I entered into thy house: thou gavest me no water for my feet. But she with tears hath washed my feet; and with her hairs hath wiped them.

45 Thou gavest me no kiss. But she, since she came in, hath not ceased to kiss my feet.

46 My head with oil thou didst not anoint. But she with ointment hath anointed my feet.

47 Wherefore, I say to thee: Many sins are forgiven her, because she hath loved much. But to whom less is forgiven, he loveth less.

48 And he said to her: [10] Thy sins are forgiven thee.

49 And they that sat at meat with him began to say within themselves: Who is this that forgiveth sins also?

50 And he said to the woman: Thy faith had made thee safe. Go in peace.

CHAPTER 8

The parable of the seed. Christ stills the storm at sea, casts out the legion, heals the issue of blood and raises the daughter of Jairus to life.

AND it came to pass afterwards that he travelled through the cities and towns, preaching and evangelizing the kingdom of God: and the twelve with him:

2 And certain women who had been healed of evil spirits and infirmities:

[5] Isai. 35, 5. [6] Mal. 3, 1; Matt. 11, 10; Mark, 1, 2. [7] Matt. 11, 16. [8] Matt. 3, 4; Mark, 1, 6. [9] Matt. 26, 7; Mark, 14, 3; John, 11, 12; 12, 3. [10] Matt. 9, 2.

CHAP. 7. Ver. 29. *Justified God.* That is, praised the justice of God, feared and worshipped God, as just and merciful.

Ver. 36. *One of the Pharisees.* That is, Simon.

Ver. 47. *Many sins are forgiven her, because she hath loved much.* In the scripture an effect sometimes seems attributed to one only cause, when there are divers other concurring dispositions; for the sins of this woman, in this verse, are said to be forgiven, because *she loved much;* but (ver. 50) Christ tells her: *Thy faith hath made thee safe.* Hence in a true conversion are joined faith, hope, love, sorrow for sin and other pious dispositions.

1 Mary who is called Magdalen, out of whom seven devils were gone forth,

3 And Joanna the wife of Chusa, Herod's steward, and Susanna and many others who ministered unto him of their substance.

4 And when a very great multitude was gathered together and hastened out of the cities, unto him, he spoke by a similitude.

5 2 The sower went out to sow his seed. And as he sowed, some fell by the way side. And it was trodden down: and the fowls of the air devoured it.

6 And other some it was fell upon a rock. And as soon as it was sprung up, it withered away, because it had no moisture.

7 And other some fell among thorns. And the thorns growing up with it, choked it.

8 And other some fell upon good ground and, being sprung up, yielded fruit a hundredfold. Saying these things, he cried out: 3 He that hath ears to hear, let him hear.

9 And his disciples asked him what this parable might be.

10 To whom he said: To you it is given to know the mystery of the kingdom of God; but to the rest in parables, that seeing they may not see and hearing may not understand.

11 Now the parable is this: The seed is the word of God.

12 And they by the way side are they that hear: then the devil cometh and taketh the word out of their heart, lest believing they should be saved.

13 Now they upon the rock *are they* who when they hear receive the word with joy: and these have no roots; for they believe for a while and in time of temptation they fall away.

14 And that which fell among thorns are they who have heard and, going their way, are choked with the cares and riches and pleasures of this life and yield no fruit.

15 But that on the good ground are they who in a good and perfect heart, hearing the word, keep it and bring forth fruit in patience.

16 4 Now no man lighting a candle covereth it with a vessel or putteth it under a bed: but setteth it upon a candlestick, that they who come in may see the light.

17 5 For there is not any thing secret that shall not be made manifest, nor hidden that shall not be known and come abroad.

18 Take heed therefore how you hear. 6 For whosoever hath, to him shall be given: and whosoever hath not, that also which he thinketh he hath shall be taken away from him.

19 7 And his mother and brethren came unto him: and they could not come at him for the crowd.

20 And it was told him: Thy mother and thy brethren stand without, desiring to see thee.

21 Who answering, said to them: My mother and my brethren are they who hear the word of God and do it.

22 8 And it came to pass on a certain day that he went into a little ship with his disciples. And he said to them: Let us go over to the other side of the lake. And they launched forth.

23 And when they were sailing, he slept. And there came down a storm of wind upon the lake: and they were filled and were in danger.

24 And they came and awaked him, saying: Master, we perish. But he arising, rebuked the wind and the rage of the water. And it ceased: and there was a calm.

25 And he said to them: Where is your faith? Who being afraid, wondered, saying one to another: Who is this (think you), that he commandeth both the winds and the sea: and they obey him?

26 And they sailed to the country of the Gerasens, which is over against Galilee.

27 And when he was come forth to the land, there met him a certain man who had a devil now a very long time. And he wore no clothes: neither did he abide in a house, but in the sepulchres.

28 And when he saw Jesus, he fell down before him. And crying out with a loud voice, he said: What have I to do with thee, Jesus, Son of the most high God? I beseech thee, do not torment me.

29 For he commanded the unclean spirit to go out of the man. For many times it seized him: and he was bound with chains and kept in fetters: and breaking the bonds, he was driven by the devil into the deserts.

30 And Jesus asked him, saying: What is thy name? But he said: Legion. Because many devils were entered into him.

31 And they besought him that he would not command them to go into the abyss.

32 And there was there a herd of many swine feeding on the mountain: and they besought him that he would

Chap. 8. 1 Mark, 16, 9. 2 Matt. 13, 3; Mark, 4, 3. 3 Isai. 6, 9; Matt. 13, 14; Mark, 4, 12; John, 12, 40; Acts, 28, 26; Rom. 11, 8. 4 Matt. 5, 15; Mark, 4, 21. 5 Matt. 10, 26; 4, 22. 6 Matt. 13, 12; 25, 29. 7 Matt. 12, 46; Mark, 3, 32. 8 Matt. 8, 23; Mark, 4, 36.

Chap. 8. Ver. 10. *Seeing they may not see.* (See the annotation, Mark, 4, 12.)

suffer them to enter into them. And he suffered them.

33 The devils therefore went out of the man and entered into the swine. And the herd ran violently down a steep place into the lake and were stifled.

34 Which when they that fed them saw done, they fled away and told it in the city and in the villages.

35 And they went out to see what was done. And they came to Jesus and found the man out of whom the devils were departed sitting at his feet, clothed and in his right mind. And they were afraid.

36 And they also that had seen told them how he had been healed from the legion.

37 And all the multitude of the country of the Gerasens besought him to depart from them: for they were taken with great fear. And he, going up into the ship, returned back again.

38 Now the man out of whom the devils were departed besought him that he might be with him. But Jesus sent him away, saying:

39 Return to thy house and tell how great things God hath done to thee. And he went through the whole city, publishing how great things Jesus had done to him.

40 And it came to pass that when Jesus was returned, the multitude received him: for they were all waiting for him.

41 [9] And behold there came a man whose name was Jairus: and he was a ruler of the synagogue. And he fell down at the feet of Jesus, beseeching him that he would come into his house:

42 For he had an only daughter, almost twelve years old, and she was dying. And it happened as he went that he was thronged by the multitudes.

43 And there was a certain woman having an issue of blood twelve years, who had bestowed all her substance on physicians and could not be healed by any.

44 She came behind him and touched the hem of his garment: and immediately the issue of her blood stopped.

45 And Jesus said: Who is it that touched me? And all denying, Peter and they that were with him said: Master, the multitudes throng and press thee; and dost thou say, Who touched me?

46 And Jesus said: Somebody hath touched me; for I know that virtue is gone out from me.

47 And the woman seeing that she was not hid, came trembling and fell down before his feet and declared before all the people for what cause she had touched him, and how she was immediately healed.

48 But he said to her: Daughter, thy faith hath made thee whole. Go thy way in peace.

49 As he was yet speaking, there cometh one to the ruler of the synagogue, saying to him: Thy daughter is dead: troubled him not.

50 And Jesus hearing this word, answered the father of the maid: Fear not. Believe only: and she shall be safe.

51 And when he was come to the house, he suffered not any man to go in with him, but Peter and James and John, and the father and mother of the maiden.

52 And all wept and mourned for her. But he said: Weep not. The maid is not dead, but sleepeth.

53 And they laughed him to scorn, knowing that she was dead.

54 But he taking her by the hand, cried out, saying: Maid, arise.

55 And her spirit returned: and she arose immediately. And he bid them give her to eat.

56 And her parents were astonished, whom he charged to tell no man what was done.

CHAPTER 9

Christ sends forth his apostles, feeds five thousand with five loaves, is transfigured and casts out a devil.

THEN [1] calling together the twelve apostles, he gave them power and authority over all devils and to cure diseases.

2 And he sent them to preach the kingdom of God and to heal the sick.

3 [2] And he said to them: Take nothing for your journey, neither staff, nor scrip, nor bread, nor money; neither have two coats.

4 And whatsoever house you shall enter into, abide there and depart not from thence.

5 And whosoever will not receive you, [3] when ye go out of that city, shake off even the dust of your feet, for a testimony against them.

6 And going out, they went about through the towns, preaching the gospel and healing every where.

7 [4] Now Herod, the tetrarch, heard of all things that were done by him. And he was in a doubt, because it was said

8 By some that John was risen from the dead: but by other some, that Elias had appeared: and by others, that one of the old prophets was risen again.

9 And Herod said: John I have beheaded. But who is this of whom I hear such things? And he sought to see him.

10 And the apostles, when they were returned, told him all they had done. And taking them, he went aside into a desert place, apart, which belongeth to Bethsaida.

11 Which when the people knew, they followed him: and he received them and spoke to them of the kingdom of God and healed them who had need of healing.

12 Now the day began to decline. And the twelve came and said to him: ⁵ Send away the multitude, that, going into the towns and villages round about, they may lodge and get victuals; for we are here in a desert place.

13 But he said to them: Give you them to eat. And they said: ⁶ We have no more than five loaves and two fishes; unless perhaps we should go and buy food for all this multitude.

14. Now there were about five thousand men. And he said to his disciples: Make them sit down by fifties in a company.

15 And they did so and made them all sit down.

6 And taking the five loaves and the two fishes, he looked up to heaven and blessed them: and he broke and distributed to his disciples, to set before the multitude.

17 And they did all eat and were filled. And there were taken up of fragments that remained to them, twelve baskets.

18 ⁷ And it came to pass, as he was alone praying, his disciples also were with him: and he asked them, saying: Whom do the people say that I am?

19 But they answered and said: John the Baptist; but some say Elias; and others say that one of the former prophets is risen again.

20 And he said to them: But whom do you say that I am? Simon Peter answering, said: The Christ of God.

21 But he strictly charging them, commanded they should tell this to no man.

22 Saying: ⁸ The Son of man must suffer many things and be rejected by the ancients and chief priests and scribes and be killed and the third day rise again.

23 ⁹ And he said to all: If any man will come after me, let him deny himself and take up his cross daily and follow me.

⁵ Matt. 14, 15; Mark, 6, 36. ⁶ John, 6, 9. ⁷ Matt. 16, 13; Mark, 8, 27. ⁸ Matt. 17, 21; Mark, 8, 31; 9, 30. ⁹ Matt. 10, 38; 16, 24; Mark, 8, 34; Luke, 14, 37. ¹⁰ Luke, 17, 33; John, 12, 25. ¹¹ Matt. 10, 33; Mark, 8, 38; 2 Tim. 2, 12. ¹² Matt. 16, 28; Mark, 8, 39. ¹³ Matt. 17, 1; Mark, 9, 1. ¹⁴ 2 Peter, 1, 17. ¹⁵ Matt. 17, 14; Mark, 9, 16.

24 ¹⁰ For whosoever will save his life shall lose it: for he that shall lose his life for my sake shall save it.

25 For what is a man advantaged, if he gain the whole world and lose himself and cast away himself?

26 ¹¹ For he that shall be ashamed of me and of my words, of him the Son of man shall be ashamed, when he shall come in his majesty and that of his Father and of the holy angels.

27 ¹² But I tell you of a truth: There are some standing here that shall not taste death till they see the kingdom of God.

28 ¹³ And it came to pass, about eight days after these words, that he took Peter and James and John and went up into a mountain to pray.

29 And whilst he prayed, the shape of his countenance was altered and his raiment became white and glittering.

30 And behold two men were talking with him. And they were Moses and Elias,

31 Appearing in majesty. And they spoke of his decease that he should accomplish in Jerusalem.

32 But Peter and they that were with him were heavy with sleep. And waking, they saw his glory and the two men that stood with him.

33 And it came to pass that, as they were departing from him, Peter saith to Jesus: Master, it is good for us to be here; and let us make three tabernacles, one for thee, and one for Moses, and one for Elias: not knowing what he said.

34 And as he spoke these things, there came a cloud and overshadowed them. And they were afraid when they entered into the cloud.

35 And a voice came out of the cloud, saying: ¹⁴ This is my beloved son. Hear him.

36 And whilst the voice was uttered, Jesus was found alone. And they held their peace and told no man in those days any of these things which they had seen.

37 And it came to pass the day following, when they came down from the mountain, there met him a great multitude.

38 ¹⁵ And behold a man among the crowd cried out, saying: Master, I beseech thee, look upon my son, because he is my only one.

39 And lo, a spirit seizeth him, and he suddenly crieth out, and he throweth him down and teareth him. so that he foameth; and bruising him, he hardly departeth from him.

40 And I desired thy disciples to cast him out: and they could not.

41 And Jesus, answering, said: O faithless and perverse generation, how long shall I be with you and suffer you? Bring hither thy son.

42 And as he was coming to him, the devil threw him down and tore him.

43 And Jesus rebuked the unclean spirit and cured the boy and restored him to his father.

44 And all were astonished at the mighty power of God. But while all wondered at all the things he did, he said to his disciples: Lay you up in your hearts these words, for it shall come to pass that the Son of man shall be delivered into the hands of men.

45 But they understood not this word: and it was hid from them, so that they perceived it not. And they were afraid to ask him concerning this word.

46 [16] And there entered a thought into them, which of them should be greater.

47 But Jesus seeing the thoughts of their hearts, took a child and set him by him,

48 And said to them: Whosoever shall receive this child in my name receiveth me; and whosoever shall receive me receiveth him that sent me. For he that is the lesser among you all, he is the greater.

49 And John, answering, said: Master, we saw a certain man casting out devils in thy name: and we forbade him, because he followeth not with us.

50 And Jesus said to him: Forbid *him* not: for he that is not against you is for you.

51 And it came to pass, when the days of his assumption were accomplishing, that he steadfastly set his face to go to Jerusalem.

52 And he sent messengers before his face: and going, they entered into a city of the Samaritans, to prepare for him.

53 And they received him not, because his face was of one going to Jerusalem.

54 And when his disciples, James and John, had seen this, they said: Lord, wilt thou that we command fire to come down from heaven and consume them?

55 And turning, he rebuked them, saying: You know not of what spirit you are.

56 [17] The Son of man came not to destroy souls, but to save. And they went into another town.

57 And it came to pass, as they walked in the way, that a certain man said to him: I will follow thee whithersoever thou goest.

58 [18] Jesus said to him: The foxes have holes, and the birds of the air nests: but the Son of man hath not where to lay his head.

59 But he said to another: Follow me. And he said: Lord, suffer me first to go and to bury my father.

60 And Jesus said to him: Let the dead bury their dead: but go thou and preach the kingdom of God.

61 And another said: I will follow thee, Lord; but let me first take my leave of them that are at my house.

62 Jesus said to him: No man putting his hand to the plough and looking back is fit for the kingdom of God.

CHAPTER 10

Christ sends forth and instructs his seventy-two disciples. The good Samaritan.

AND after these things, the Lord appointed also other seventy-two. And he sent them two and two before his face into every city and place whither he himself was to come.

2 And he said to them: [1] The harvest indeed is great, but the labourers are few. Pray ye therefore the Lord of the harvest that he send labourers into his harvest.

3 Go: [2] Behold I send you as lambs among wolves.

4 [3] Carry neither purse, nor scrip, nor shoes: [4] and salute no man by the way.

5 Into whatsoever house you enter, first say: Peace be to this house.

6 And if the son of peace be there, your peace shall rest upon him: but if not, it shall return to you.

7 And in the same house, remain, eating and drinking such things as they have: [5] for the labourer is worthy of his hire. Remove not from house to house.

8 And into what city soever you enter, and they receive you, eat such things as are set before you.

9 And heal the sick that are therein and say to them: The kingdom of God is come nigh unto you.

10 But into whatsoever city you enter, and they receive you not, going forth into the streets thereof, say:

11 [6] Even the very dust of your city that cleaveth to us, we wipe off against you. Yet know this, that the kingdom of God is at hand.

12 I say to you, it shall be more tolerable at that day for Sodom than for that city.

13 [7] Woe to thee, Corozain! Woe to thee, Bethsaida! For if in Tyre and

Sidon had been wrought the mighty works that have been wrought in you, they would have done penance long ago, sitting in sackcloth and ashes.

14 But it shall be more tolerable for Tyre and Sidon at the judgment than for you.

15 And thou, Capharnaum, which art exalted unto heaven, thou shalt be thrust down to hell.

16 [8] He that heareth you heareth me: and he that despiseth you despiseth me: and he that despiseth me despiseth him that sent me.

17 And the seventy-two returned with joy, saying: Lord, the devils also are subject to us in thy name.

18 And he said to them: I saw Satan like lightning falling from heaven.

19 Behold, I have given you power to tread upon serpents and scorpions and upon all the power of the enemy: and nothing shall hurt you.

20 But yet rejoice not in this, that spirits are subject unto you: but rejoice in this, that your names are written in heaven.

21 [9] In that same hour, he rejoiced in the Holy Ghost and said: I confess to thee, O Father, Lord of heaven and earth, because thou hast hidden these things from the wise and prudent and hast revealed them to little ones. Yea, Father, for so it hath seemed good in thy sight.

22 All things are delivered to me by my Father. And no one knoweth who the Son is, but the Father: and who the Father is, but the Son and to whom the Son will reveal *him*.

23 And turning to his disciples, [10] he said: Blessed are the eyes that see the things which you see.

24 For I say to you that many prophets and kings have desired to see the things that you see and have not seen them; and to hear the things that you hear and have not heard them.

25 [11] And behold a certain lawyer stood up, tempting him and saying, Master, what must I do to possess eternal life?

26 But he said to him: What is written in the law? How readest thou?

27 He answering, said: [12] *Thou shalt love the Lord thy God with thy whole heart and with thy whole soul and with all thy strength and with all thy mind: and thy neighbour as thyself.*

28 And he said to him: Thou hast

answered right. This do: and thou shalt live.

29 But he willing to justify himself, said to Jesus: And who is my neighbour?

30 And Jesus answering, said: A certain man went down from Jerusalem to Jericho and fell among robbers, who also stripped him and having wounded him went away, leaving him half dead.

31 And it chanced, that a certain priest went down the same way: and seeing him, passed by.

32 In like manner also a Levite, when he was near the place and saw him, passed by.

33 But a certain Samaritan, being on his journey, came near him: and seeing him, was moved with compassion:

34 And going up to him, bound up his wounds, pouring in oil and wine: and setting him upon his own beast, brought him to an inn and took care of him.

35 And the next day he took out two pence and gave to the host and said: Take care of him; and whatsoever thou shalt spend over and above, I, at my return, will repay thee.

36 Which of these three, in thy opinion, was neighbour to him that fell among the robbers?

37 But he said: He that shewed mercy to him. And Jesus said to him: Go, and do thou in like manner.

38 Now it came to pass, as they went, that he entered into a certain town: and a certain woman named Martha received him into her house.

39 And she had a sister called Mary, who, sitting also at the Lord's feet, heard his word.

40 But Martha was busy about much serving. Who stood and said: Lord, hast thou no care that my sister hath left me alone to serve? Speak to her therefore, that she help me.

41 And the Lord answering, said to her: Martha, Martha, thou art careful and art troubled about many things:

42 But one thing is necessary. Mary hath chosen the best part, which shall not be taken away from her.

CHAPTER 11

Christ teaches his disciples to pray. He casts out a dumb devil, confutes the Pharisees, and pronounces woes against them for their hypocrisy.

AND it came to pass that as he was in a certain place praying, when he ceased, one of his disciples said to him: Lord, teach us to pray, as John also taught his disciples.

---

[8] Matt. 10, 40; John. 13, 20. [9] Matt. 11, 25.
[10] Matt. 13, 16. [11] Matt. 22, 35; Mark, 12, 23.
[12] Deut. 6, 5.

CHAP. 10. Ver. 21. *He rejoiced in the Holy Ghost.* That is, according to his humanity he rejoiced in the Holy Ghost and gave thanks to his eternal Father.

2 And he said to them: When you pray, say: [1] Father, hallowed be thy name. Thy kingdom come.

3 Give us this day our daily bread.

4 And forgive us our sins, for we also forgive every one that is indebted to us. And lead us not into temptation.

5 And he said to them: Which of you shall have a friend and shall go to him at midnight and shall say to him: Friend, lend me three loaves,

6 Because a friend of mine is come off his journey to me and I have not what to set before him.

7 And he from within should answer and say: Trouble me not; the door is now shut, and my children are with me in bed. I cannot rise and give thee.

8 Yet if he shall continue knocking, I say to you, although he will not rise and give him because he is his friend; yet, because of his importunity, he will rise and give him as many as he needeth.

9 [2] And I say to you: Ask, and it shall be given you: seek, and you shall find: knock, and it shall be opened to you.

10 For every one that asketh receiveth; and he that seeketh findeth; and to him that knocketh it shall be opened.

11 [3] And which of you, if he ask his father bread, will he give him a stone? Or a fish, will he for a fish give him a serpent?

12 Or if he shall ask an egg, will he reach him a scorpion?

13 If you then, being evil, know how to give good gifts to your children, how much more will your Father from heaven give the good Spirit to them that ask him?

14 [4] And he was casting out a devil, and the same was dumb. And when he had cast out the devil, the dumb spoke: and the multitudes were in admiration at it.

15 But some of them said: He casteth out devils [5] by Beelzebub, the prince of devils.

16 And others tempting, asked of him a sign from heaven.

17 But he seeing their thoughts, said to them: Every kingdom divided against itself shall be brought to desolation, and house upon house shall fall.

18 And if Satan also be divided against himself, how shall his kingdom stand? Because you say that through Beelzebub I cast out devils.

19 Now if I cast out devils by Beelzebub, by whom do your children cast them out? Therefore, they shall be your judges.

20 But if I by the finger of God cast out devils, doubtless the kingdom of God is come upon you.

21 When a strong man armed keepeth his court, those things are in peace which he possesseth.

22 But if a stronger than he come upon him and overcome him, he will take away all his armour wherein he trusted and will distribute his spoils.

23 He that is not with me is against me; and he that gathereth not with me scattereth.

24 When the unclean spirit is gone out of a man, he walketh through places without water, seeking rest; and not finding, he saith: I will return into my house whence I came out.

25 And when he is come, he findeth it swept and garnished.

26 Then he goeth and taketh with him seven other spirits more wicked than himself: and entering in they dwell there. And the last state of that man becomes worse than the first.

27 And it came to pass, as he spoke these things, a certain woman from the crowd, lifting up her voice, said to him: Blessed is the womb that bore thee and the paps that gave thee suck.

28 But he said: Yea rather, blessed are they who hear the word of God and keep it.

29 And the multitudes running together, he began to say: [6] This generation is a wicked generation. It asketh a sign: and a sign shall not be given it, but the sign of Jonas the prophet.

30 [7] For as Jonas was a sign to the Ninivites; so shall the Son of man also be to this generation.

31 [8] The queen of the south shall rise in the judgment with the men of this generation and shall condemn them: because she came from the ends of the earth to hear the wisdom of Solomon. And behold more than Solomon here.

32 The men of Ninive shall rise in the judgment with this generation and shall condemn it; [9] because they did penance at the preaching of Jonas. And behold more than Jonas here.

33 [10] No man lighteth a candle and putteth it in a hidden place, nor under a bushel: but upon a candlestick, that they that come in may see the light.

34 [11] The light of thy body is thy eye. If thy eye be single, thy whole body will be lightsome: but if it be evil, thy body also will be darksome.

35 Take heed therefore that the light which is in thee be not darkness.

36 If then thy whole body be lightsome, having no part of darkness: the

CHAP. 11. [1] Matt. 6, 9. [2] Matt. 7, 7; 21, 22; Mark, 11, 24; John, 14, 13; James, 1, 5. [3] Matt. 7, 9. [4] Matt. 9, 32; 12, 22. [5] Matt. 9, 34; Mark, 3, 22. [6] Matt. 12, 39. [7] Jonas, 2, 1. [8] 3 Kings, 10, 1; 2 Par. 9, 1. [9] Jonas, 3, 5. [10] Matt. 5, 15; Mark, 4, 21. [11] Matt. 6, 22.

whole shall be lightsome and, as a bright lamp, shall enlighten thee.

37 And as he was speaking, a certain Pharisee prayed him that he would dine with him. And he going in, sat down to eat.

38 And the Pharisee began to say, thinking within himself, why he was not washed before dinner.

39 And the Lord said to him: [12] Now you, Pharisees, make clean the outside of the cup and of the platter: but your inside is full of rapine and iniquity.

40 Ye fools, did not he that made that which is without make also that which is within?

41 But yet that which remaineth give alms: and behold, all things are clean unto you.

42 But woe to you, Pharisees, because you tithe mint and rue and every herb and pass over judgment and the charity of God. Now these things you ought to have done, and not to leave the other undone.

43 [13] Woe to you, Pharisees, because you love the uppermost seats in the synagogues and salutations in the market-place.

44 Woe to you, because you are as sepulchres that appear not: and men that walk over are not aware.

45 And one of the lawyers answering, saith to him: Master, in saying these things, thou reproachest us also.

46 But he said: [14] Woe to you lawyers also, because you load men with burdens which they cannot bear and you yourselves touch not the packs with one of your fingers.

47 Woe to you who build the monuments of the prophets: and your fathers killed them.

48 Truly you bear witness that you consent to the doings of your fathers. For they indeed killed them: and you build their sepulchres.

49 For this cause also the wisdom of God said: I will send to them prophets and apostles; and some of them they will kill and persecute.

50 That the blood of all the prophets which was shed from the foundation of the world may be required of this generation,

51 [15] From the blood of Abel unto the blood of [16] Zacharias, who was slain between the altar and the temple. Yea I say to you: It shall be required of this generation.

52 Woe to you lawyers, for you have taken away the key of knowledge. You yourselves have not entered in: and those that were entering in, you have hindered.

53 And as he was saying these things to them, the Pharisees and the lawyers began violently to urge him and to oppress his mouth about many things,

54 Lying in wait for him and seeking to catch something from his mouth, that they might accuse him.

CHAPTER 12

Christ warns us against hypocrisy, the fear of the world and covetousness. He admonishes all to watch.

AND when great multitudes stood about him, so that they trod one upon another, he began to say to his disciples: [1] Beware ye of the leaven of the Pharisees, which is hypocrisy.

2 [2] For there is nothing covered that shall not be revealed: nor hidden that shall not be known.

3 For whatsoever things you have spoken in darkness shall be published in the light: and that which you have spoken in the ear in the chambers shall be preached on the housetops.

4 And I say to you, my friends: Be not afraid of them who kill the body and after that have no more that they can do.

5 But I will shew you whom you shall fear: Fear ye him who, after he hath killed, hath power to cast into hell. Yea, I say to you: Fear him.

6 Are not five sparrows sold for two farthings, and not one of them is forgotten before God?

7 Yea, the very hairs of your head are all numbered. Fear not therefore: you are of more value than many sparrows.

8 And I say to you: [3] Whosoever shall confess me before men, him shall the Son of man also confess before the angels of God.

9 But he that shall deny me before men shall be denied before the angels of God.

10 [4] And whosoever speaketh a word against the Son of man, it shall be forgiven him: but to him that shall blaspheme against the Holy Ghost, it shall not be forgiven.

11 And when they shall bring you

---

[12] Matt. 23, 25. [13] Matt. 23, 6; Mark, 12, 39; Luke, 20, 46. [14] Matt. 23, 4. [15] Gen. 4, 8. [16] 2 Par. 24, 22. Chap. 12. [1] Matt. 16, 6; Mark, 8, 15. [2] Matt. 10, 26; Mark, 4, 22. [3] Matt. 10, 32; Mark, 8, 38; 2 Tim. 2, 12. [4] Matt. 12, 32; Mark, 3, 29.

Chap. 11. Ver. 46. *Woe to you lawyers.* He speaks of the doctors of the law of Moses, commonly called the *scribes.*

Ver. 47. *Woe to you who build.* Not that the building of the monuments of the prophets was in itself blameworthy, but only the intention of these unhappy men, who made use of this outward shew of religion and piety as a means to carry on their wicked designs against the Prince of Prophets.

Ver. 53. *Oppress.* That is, *stop.*

into the synagogues and to magistrates and powers, be not solicitous how or what you shall answer, or what you shall say.

12 For the Holy Ghost shall teach you in the same hour what you must say.

13 And one of the multitude said to him: Master, speak to my brother that he divide the inheritance with me.

14 But he said to him: Man, who hath appointed me judge or divider over you?

15 And he said to them: Take heed and beware of all covetousness: for a man's life doth not consist in the abundance of things which he possesseth.

16 And he spoke a similitude to them, saying: [5] The land of a certain rich man brought forth plenty of fruits.

17 And he thought within himself, saying: What shall I do, because I have no room where to bestow my fruits?

18 And he said: This will I do: I will pull down my barns and will build greater; and into them will I gather all things that are grown to me and my goods.

19 And I will say to my soul: Soul, thou hast much goods laid up for many years. Take thy rest: eat, drink, make good cheer.

20 But God said to him: Thou fool, this night do they require thy soul of thee. And whose shall those things be which thou hast provided?

21 So is he that layeth up treasure for himself and is not rich towards God.

22 And he said to his disciples: Therefore I say to you: [6] Be not solicitous for your life, what you shall eat: nor for your body, what you shall put on.

23 The life is more than the meat: and the body is more than the raiment.

24 Consider the ravens, for they sow not, neither do they reap, neither have they storehouse nor barn, and God feedeth them. How much are you more valuable than they?

25 And which of you by taking thought can add to his stature one cubit?

26 If then ye be not able to do so much as the least thing, why are you solicitous for the rest?

27 Consider the lilies, how they grow: they labour not, neither do they spin. But I say to you, not even Solomon in all his glory was clothed like one of these.

28 Now, if God clothe in this manner the grass that is to-day in the field and to-morrow is cast into the oven: how much more you, O ye of little faith?

29 And seek not what you shall eat or what you shall drink: and be not lifted up on high.

30 For all these things do the nations of the world seek. But your Father knoweth that you have need of these things.

31 But seek ye first the kingdom of God and his justice: and all these things shall be added unto you.

32 Fear not, little flock, for it hath pleased your Father to give you a kingdom.

33 [7] Sell what you possess and give alms. Make to yourselves bags which grow not old, [8] a treasure in heaven which faileth not: where no thief approacheth, nor moth corrupteth.

34 For where your treasure is, there will your heart be also.

35 Let your loins be girt and lamps burning in your hands.

36 And you yourselves like to men who wait for their lord, when he shall return from the wedding; that when he cometh and knocketh, they may open to him immediately.

37 Blessed are those servants whom the Lord, when he cometh, shall find watching. Amen I say to you that he will gird himself and make them sit down to meat and passing will minister unto them.

38 And if he shall come in the second watch or come in the third watch and find them so, blessed are those servants.

39 [9] But this know ye, that if the householder did know at what hour the thief would come, he would surely watch and would not suffer his house to be broken open.

40 Be you then also ready: [10] for at what hour you think not the Son of man will come.

41 And Peter said to him: Lord, dost thou speak this parable to us, or likewise to all?

42 And the Lord said: Who (thinkest thou) is the faithful and wise steward, whom his lord setteth over his family, to give them their measure of wheat in due season?

43 Blessed is that servant whom, when his lord shall come, he shall find so doing.

44 Verily I say to you, he will set him over all that he possesseth.

45 But if that servant shall say in his heart: My lord is long a coming; and shall begin to strike the men-servants and maid-servants, and to eat and to drink and be drunk:

46 The lord of that servant will come

[5] Ecclus. 11, 19. [6] Ps. 54, 23; Matt. 6, 25; 1 Peter, 5, 7. [7] Matt. 19, 21. [8] Matt. 6, 20. [9] Matt. 24, 43. [10] Apoc. 16, 15.

in the day that he hopeth not, and at the hour that he knoweth not: and shall separate him and shall appoint him his portion with unbelievers.

47 And that servant, who knew the will of his lord and prepared *not himself* and did not according to his will, shall be beaten with many stripes.

48 But he that knew not and did things worthy of stripes shall be beaten with few stripes. And unto whomsoever much is given, of him much shall be required: and to whom they have committed much, of him they will demand the more.

49 I am come to cast fire on the earth. And what will I, but that it be kindled?

50 And I have a baptism wherewith I am to be baptized. And how am I straitened until it be accomplished?

51 ¹¹ Think ye, that I am come to give peace on earth? I tell you, no; but separation.

52 For there shall be from henceforth five in one house divided: three against two, and two against three.

53 The father *shall be divided* against the son and the son against his father: the mother against the daughter and the daughter against her mother: the mother-in-law against the daughter-in-law and the daughter-in-law against her mother-in-law.

54 ¹² And he said also to the multitudes: When you see a cloud rising from the west, presently you say: A shower is coming. And so it happeneth.

55 And when *ye see* the south wind blow, you say: There will be heat. And it cometh to pass.

56 You hypocrites, you know how to discern the face of the heaven and of the earth: but how is it that you do not discern this time?

57 And why, even of yourselves, do you not judge that which is just?

58 ¹³ And when thou goest with thy adversary to the prince, whilst thou art in the way, endeavour to be delivered from him: lest perhaps he draw thee to the judge, and the judge deliver thee to the exacter, and the exacter cast thee into prison.

59 I say to thee, thou shalt not go out thence until thou pay the very last mite.

CHAPTER 13

The necessity of penance. The barren fig tree. The cure of the infirm woman. The journey to Jerusalem.

AND there were present, at that very time, some that told him of

¹¹ Matt. 10, 34. ¹² Matt. 16, 2. ¹³ Matt. 5, 25. CHAP. 13. ¹ Matt. 13, 31; Mark, 4, 31.

the Galileans, whose blood Pilate had mingled with their sacrifices.

2 And he answering, said to them: Think you that these Galileans were sinners above all the men of Galilee, because they suffered such things?

3 No, I say to you: but unless you shall do penance, you shall all likewise perish.

4 Or those eighteen upon whom the tower fell in Siloe and slew them: think you that they also were debtors above all the men that dwelt in Jerusalem?

5 No, I say to you: but except you do penance, you shall all likewise perish.

6 He spoke also this parable: A certain man had a fig tree planted in his vineyard: and he came seeking fruit on it and found none.

7 And he said to the dresser of the vineyard: Behold, for these three years I come seeking fruit on this fig tree and I find none. Cut it down therefore. Why cumbereth it the ground?

8 But he answering, said to him: Lord, let it alone this year also, until I dig about it and dung it.

9 And if happily it bear fruit: but if not, then after that thou shalt cut it down.

10 And he was teaching in their synagogue on their sabbath.

11 And behold there was a woman who had a spirit of infirmity eighteen years. And she was bowed together: neither could she look upwards at all.

12 Whom when Jesus saw, he called her unto him and said to her: Woman, thou art delivered from thy infirmity.

13 And he laid his hands upon her: and immediately she was made straight and glorified God.

14 And the ruler of the synagogue (being angry that Jesus had healed on the sabbath) answering, said to the multitude: Six days there are wherein you ought to work. In them therefore come and be healed: and not on the sabbath day.

15 And the Lord answering him, said: Ye hypocrites, doth not every one of you, on the sabbath day, loose his ox or his ass from the manger and lead them to water.

16 And ought not this daughter of Abraham, whom Satan hath bound, lo, these eighteen years, be loosed from this bond on the sabbath day?

17 And when he said these things, all his adversaries were ashamed: and all the people rejoiced for all the things that were gloriously done by him.

18 He said therefore: To what is the kingdom of God like, and whereunto shall I resemble it?

19 ¹ It is like to a grain of mustard seed, which a man took and cast into

his garden: and it grew and became a great tree, and the birds of the air lodged in the branches thereof.

20 And again he said: Whereunto shall I esteem the kingdom of God to be like?

21 ² It is like to leaven, which a woman took and hid in three measures of meal, till the whole was leavened.

22 And he went through the cities and towns teaching and making his journey to Jerusalem.

23 And a certain man said to him: Lord, are they few that are saved? But he said to them:

24 ³ Strive to enter by the narrow gate: for many, I say to you, shall seek to enter and shall not be able.

25 ⁴ But when the master of the house shall be gone in and shall shut the door, you shall begin to stand without and knock at the door, saying: Lord, open to us. And he answering, shall say to you: I know you not, whence you are.

26 Then you shall begin to say: We have eaten and drunk in thy presence: and thou hast taught in our streets.

27 And he shall say to you: ⁵ I know you not, whence you are. ⁶ Depart from me, all ye workers of iniquity.

28 There, shall be weeping and gnashing of teeth, when you shall see Abraham and Isaac and Jacob and all the prophets, in the kingdom of God: and you yourselves thrust out.

29 And there shall come from the east and the west and the north and the south: and shall sit down in the kingdom of God.

30 ⁷ And behold, they are last that shall be first: and they are first that shall be last.

31 The same day, there came some of the Pharisees, saying to him: Depart, and get thee hence, for Herod hath a mind to kill thee.

32 And he said to them: Go and tell that fox: Behold, I cast out devils and do cures, to-day and to-morrow, and the third day I am consummated.

33 Nevertheless, I must walk to-day and to-morrow and the day following, because it cannot be that a prophet perish, out of Jerusalem.

34 ⁸ Jerusalem, Jerusalem, that killest the prophets and stonest them that are sent to thee, how often would I have gathered thy children as the bird doth her brood under her wings, and thou wouldest not?

35 Behold your house shall be left to you desolate. And I say to you that you shall not see me till the time come when you shall say: Blessed is he that cometh in the name of the Lord.

CHAPTER 14

Christ heals the dropsical man. The parable of the supper. The necessity of renouncing all to follow Christ.

AND it came to pass, when Jesus went into the house of one of the chief of the Pharisees, on the sabbath day, to eat bread, that they watched him.

2 And behold, there was a certain man before him that had the dropsy.

3 And Jesus answering, spoke to the lawyers and Pharisees, saying: Is it lawful to heal on the sabbath day?

4 But they held their peace. But he taking him, healed him and sent him away.

5 And answering them, he said: Which of you shall have an ass or an ox fall into a pit and will not immediately draw him out, on the sabbath day?

6 And they could not answer him to these things.

7 And he spoke a parable also to them that were invited, marking how they chose the first seats at the table, saying to them:

8 When thou art invited to a wedding, sit not down in the first place, lest perhaps one more honourable than thou be invited by him:

9 And he that invited thee and him, come and say to thee: Give this man place. And then thou begin with shame to take the lowest place.

10 But when thou art invited, go, sit down in the lowest place; that when he who invited thee cometh, he may say to thee: ¹ Friend, go up higher. Then shalt thou have glory before them that sit at table with thee.

11 ² Because every one that exalteth himself shall be humbled: and he that humbleth himself shall be exalted.

12 And he said to him also that had invited him: ³ When thou makest a dinner or a supper, call not thy friends nor thy brethren nor thy kinsmen nor thy neighbours who are rich; lest perhaps they also invite thee again, and a recompense be made to thee.

13 But when thou makest a feast, call the poor, the maimed, the lame and the blind.

14 And thou shalt be blessed, because they have not wherewith to make thee recompense: for recompense shall

² Matt. 13, 33. ³ Matt. 7, 13. ⁴ Matt. 25, 10. ⁵ Matt. 7, 23. ⁶ Ps. 6, 9; Matt. 25, 41. ⁷ Matt. 19, 30; 20, 16; Mark, 10, 31. ⁸ Matt. 23, 37. CHAP. 14. ¹ Prov. 25, 7. ² Matt. 23, 12; Luke, 18, 14. ³ Tob. 4, 7; Prov. 3, 9.

CHAP. 13. Ver. 24. *Shall seek.* Shall desire to be saved; but, for want of taking sufficient pains and of being thoroughly in earnest, shall not attain to it.

be made thee at the resurrection of the just.

15 When one of them that sat at table with him had heard these things, he said to him: Blessed is he that shall eat bread in the kingdom of God.

16 But he said to him: 'A certain man made a great supper and invited many.

17 And he sent his servant at the hour of supper to say to them that were invited, that they should come: for now all things are ready.

18 And they began all at once to make excuse. The first said to him: I have bought a farm and I must needs go out and see it. I pray thee, hold me excused.

19 And another said: I have bought five yoke of oxen and I go to try them. I pray thee, hold me excused.

20 And another said: I have married a wife; and therefore I cannot come.

21 And the servant returning, told these things to his lord. Then the master of the house, being angry, said to his servant: Go out quickly into the streets and lanes of the city; and bring in hither the poor and the feeble and the blind and the lame.

22 And the servant said: Lord, it is done as thou hast commanded; and yet there is room.

23 And the Lord said to the servant: Go out into the highways and hedges, and compel them to come in, that my house may be filled.

24 But I say unto you that none of those men that were invited shall taste of my supper.

25 And there went great multitudes with him. And turning, he said to them:

26 ⁵ If any man come to me, and hate not his father and mother and wife and children and brethren and sisters, yea and his own life also, he cannot be my disciple.

27 ⁶ And whosoever doth not carry his cross and come after me cannot be my disciple.

28 For which of you, having a mind to build a tower, doth not first sit down and reckon the charges that are neces-

⁴ Matt. 22, 2; Apoc. 19, 9. ⁵ Matt. 10, 37. ⁶ Matt. 10, 38; 16, 24; Mark, 8, 34. ⁷ Matt. 5, 13; Mark, 9, 49. CHAP. 15. ¹ Matt. 18, 12.

CHAP. 14. Ver. 26. Hate not. The law of Christ does not allow us to hate even our enemies, much less our parents; but the meaning of the text is, that we must be in such disposition of soul as to be willing to renounce and part with every thing, how near or dear soever it may be to us, that would keep us from following Christ.

CHAP. 15. Ver. 10. Before the angels. By this it is plain that the spirits in heaven have a concern for us below and a joy at our repentance and consequently a knowledge of it.

sary, whether he have wherewithal to finish it:

29 Lest, after he hath laid the foundation and is not able to finish it, all that see it begin to mock him,

30 Saying: This man began to build and was not able to finish.

31 Or, what king, about to go to make war against another king, doth not first sit down and think whether he be able, with ten thousand, to meet him that, with twenty thousand, cometh against him?

32 Or else, while the other is yet afar off, sending an embassy, he desireth conditions of peace.

33 So likewise every one of you that doth not renounce all that he possesseth cannot be my disciple.

34 ⁷ Salt is good. But if the salt shall lose its savour, wherewith shall it be seasoned?

35 It is neither profitable for the land nor for the dunghill: but shall be cast out. He that hath ears to hear, let him hear.

CHAPTER 15

The parables of the lost sheep and of the prodigal son.

NOW the publicans and sinners drew near unto him to hear him.

3 And the Pharisees and the scribes murmured, saying: This man receiveth sinners and eateth with them.

3 And he spoke to them this parable, saying:

4 ¹ What man of you that hath an hundred sheep, and if he shall lose one of them, doth he not leave the ninety-nine in the desert and go after that which was lost, until he find it?

5 And when he hath found it, lay it upon his shoulders, rejoicing?

6 And coming home, call together his friends and neighbours, saying to them: Rejoice with me, because I have found my sheep that was lost?

7 I say to you that even so there shall be joy in heaven upon one sinner that doth penance, more than upon ninety-nine just who need not penance.

8 Or what woman having ten groats, if she lose one groat, doth not light a candle and sweep the house and seek diligently until she find it?

9 And when she hath found it, call together her friends and neighbours, saying: Rejoice with me, because I have found the groat which I had lost.

10 So I say to you, there shall be joy before the angels of God upon one sinner doing penance.

11 And he said: A certain man had two sons.

12 And the younger of them said to his father: Father, give me the portion of substance that falleth to me. And he divided unto them his substance.

13 And not many days after, the younger son, gathering all together, went abroad into a far country: and there wasted his substance, living riotously.

14 And after he had spent all, there came a mighty famine in that country: and he began to be in want.

15 And he went and cleaved to one of the citizens of that country. And he sent him into his farm to feed swine.

16 And he would fain have filled his belly with the husks the swine did eat: and no man gave unto him.

17 And returning to himself, he said: How many hired servants in my father's house abound with bread, and I here perish with hunger!

18 I will arise and will go to my father and say to him: Father, I have sinned against heaven and before thee.

19 I am not worthy to be called thy son: make me as one of thy hired servants.

20 And rising up, he came to his father. And when he was yet a great way off, his father saw him and was moved with compassion and running to him fell upon his neck and kissed him.

21 And the son said to him: Father, I have sinned against heaven and before thee I am not now worthy to be called thy son.

22 And the father said to his servants: Bring forth quickly the first robe and put it on him: and put a ring on his hand and shoes on his feet.

23 And bring hither the fatted calf, and kill it: and let us eat and make merry:

24 Because this my son was dead and is come to life again, was lost and is found. And they began to be merry.

25 Now his elder son was in the field: and when he came and drew nigh to the house, he heard music and dancing.

26 And he called one of the servants and asked what these things meant.

27 And he said to him: Thy brother is come and thy father killed the fatted calf, because he hath received him safe.

28 And he was angry and would not go in. His father therefore coming out began to entreat him.

29 And he answering, said to his father: Behold, for so many years do I serve thee and I have never transgressed thy commandment: and yet thou hast never given me a kid to make merry with my friends.

30 But as soon as this thy son is come, who hath devoured his substance with harlots, thou hast killed for him the fatted calf.

31 But he said to him: Son, thou art always with me; and all I have is thine.

32 But it was fit that we should make merry and be glad: for this thy brother was dead and is come to life again; he was lost, and is found.

CHAPTER 16

The parable of the unjust steward and of the rich man and Lazarus.

AND he said also to his disciples: There was a certain rich man who had a steward: and the same was accused unto him, that he had wasted his goods.

2 And he called him and said to him: How is it that I hear this of thee? Give an account of thy stewardship: for now thou canst be steward no longer.

3 And the steward said within himself: What shall I do, because my lord taketh away from me the stewardship? To dig I am not able; to beg I am ashamed.

4 I know what I will do, that when I shall be removed from the stewardship, they may receive me into their houses.

5 Therefore, calling together every one of his lord's debtors, he said to the first: How much dost thou owe my lord?

6 But he said: An hundred barrels of oil. And he said to him: Take thy bill and sit down quickly and write fifty.

7 Then he said to another: And how much dost thou owe? Who said: An hundred quarters of wheat. He said to him: Take thy bill and write eighty.

8 And the lord commended the unjust steward, forasmuch as he had done wisely: for the children of this world are wiser in their generation than the children of light.

9 And I say to you: Make unto you friends of the mammon of iniquity: that when you shall fail, they may receive you into everlasting dwellings.

10 He that is faithful in that which is least is faithful also in that which is greater: and he that is unjust in that which is little is unjust also in that which is greater.

11 If then you have not been faithful

CHAP. 16. Ver. 9. *Mammon of iniquity.* Mammon signifies *riches.* They are here called the *mammon of iniquity,* because oftentimes ill-gotten, ill-bestowed, or an occasion of evil; and at the best but worldly and false; and not the true riches of a Christian.—*They may receive.* By this we see that the poor servants of God, whom we have relieved by our alms, may hereafter, by their intercession, bring our souls to heaven.

in the unjust mammon, who will trust you with that which is the true?

12 And if you have not been faithful in that which is another's, who will give you that which is your own?

13 [1] No servant can serve two masters: for either he will hate the one and love the other: or he will hold to the one and despise the other. You cannot serve God and mammon.

14 Now the Pharisees, who were covetous, heard all these things: and they derided him.

15 And he said to them: You are they who justify yourselves before men, but God knoweth your hearts. For that which is high to men is an abomination before God.

16 [2] The law and the prophets were until John. From that time the kingdom of God is preached: and every one useth violence towards it.

17 [3] And it is easier for heaven and earth to pass than one tittle of the law to fall.

18 [4] Every one that putteth away his wife and marrieth another committeth adultery: and he that marrieth her that is put away from her husband committeth adultery.

19 There was a certain rich man who was clothed in purple and fine linen and feasted sumptuously every day.

20 And there was a certain beggar, named Lazarus, who lay at his gate, full of sores,

21 Desiring to be filled with the crumbs that fell from the rich man's table. And no one did give him: moreover the dogs came and licked his sores.

22 And it came to pass that the beggar died and was carried by the angels into Abraham's bosom. And the rich man also died: and he was buried in hell.

23 And lifting up his eyes when he was in torments, he saw Abraham afar off and Lazarus in his bosom:

24 And he cried and said: Father Abraham, have mercy on me and send Lazarus, that he may dip the tip of his finger in water to cool my tongue: for I am tormented in this flame.

25 And Abraham said to him: Son,

remember that thou didst receive good things in thy lifetime, and likewise Lazarus evil things: but now he is comforted and thou art tormented.

26 And besides all this, between us and you, there is fixed a great chaos: so that they who would pass from hence to you cannot, nor from thence come hither.

27 And he said: Then, father, I beseech thee that thou wouldst send him to my father's house, for I have five brethren,

28 That he may testify unto them, lest they also come into this place of torments.

29 And Abraham said to him: They have Moses and the prophets. Let them hear them.

30 But he said: No, father Abraham: but if one went to them from the dead, they will do penance.

31 And he said to him: If they hear not Moses and the prophets, neither will they believe, if one rise again from the dead.

CHAPTER 17

Lessons of avoiding scandal and of the efficacy of faith. The ten lepers. The manner of the coming of Christ.

AND [1] he said to his disciples: It is impossible that scandals should not come. But woe to him through whom they come!

2 It were better for him that a millstone were hanged about his neck and he cast into the sea, than that he should scandalize one of these little ones.

3 Take heed to yourselves. [2] If thy brother sin against thee, reprove him: and if he do penance, forgive him.

4 And if he sin against thee seven times a day, and seven times a day be converted unto thee, saying: I repent: forgive him.

5 And the apostles said to the Lord: Increase our faith.

6 [3] And the Lord said: If you had faith like to a grain of mustard seed, you might say to this mulberry tree: Be thou rooted up and be thou transplanted into the sea. And it would obey you.

7 But which of you, having a servant ploughing or feeding cattle, will say to him, when he is come from the field: Immediately go. Sit down to meat.

8 And will not *rather* say to him: Make ready my supper and gird thyself and serve me, whilst I eat and drink; and afterwards thou shalt eat and drink?

9 Doth he thank that servant for doing the things which he commanded him?

10 I think not. So you also, when you

CHAP. 16. [1] Matt. 6, 24. [2] Matt. 11, 12. [3] Matt. 5, 18. [4] Matt. 5, 32; Mark, 10, 11; 1 Cor. 7, 10, 11. CHAP. 17. [1] Matt. 18, 7; Mark, 9, 41. [2] Lev. 19, 17; Ecclus. 19, 13; Matt. 18, 15. [3] Matt. 17, 19.

Ver. 22. *Abraham's bosom.* The place of rest, where the souls of the saints resided till Christ had opened heaven by his death.

CHAP. 17. Ver. 10. *Unprofitable servants.* Because our service is of *no profit* to our master; and he justly claims it as our bounden duty. But though we are *unprofitable to him,* our serving him is not *unprofitable to us;* for he is pleased to give by his grace a value to our good works, which, in consequence of his promise, entitles them to an eternal reward.

shall have done all these things that are commanded you, say: We are unprofitable servants; we have done that which we ought to do.

11 And it came to pass, as he was going to Jerusalem, he passed through the midst of Samaria and Galilee.

12 And as he entered into a certain town, there met him ten men that were lepers, who stood afar off

13 And lifted up their voice, saying: Jesus, Master, have mercy on us.

14 Whom when he saw, he said: ⁴ Go, shew yourselves to the priests. And it came to pass, as they went, they were made clean.

15 And one of them, when he saw that he was made clean, went back with a loud voice glorifying God.

16 And he fell on his face before his feet, giving thanks. And this was a Samaritan.

17 And Jesus answering, said: Were not ten made clean? And where are the nine?

18 There is no one found to return and give glory to God, but this stranger.

19 And he said to him: Arise, go thy way; for thy faith hath made thee whole.

20 And being asked by the Pharisees when the kingdom of God should come, he answered them and said: The kingdom of God cometh not with observation.

21 Neither shall they say: Behold here, or behold there. For lo, the kingdom of God is within you.

22 And he said to his disciples: The days will come when you shall desire to see one day of the Son of man. And you shall not see it.

23 ⁵ And they will say to you: See here, and see there. Go ye not after, nor follow them.

24 For as the lightning that lighteneth from under heaven shineth unto the parts that are under heaven, so shall the Son of man be in his day.

25 But first he must suffer many things and he rejected by this generation.

26 ⁶ And as it came to pass in the days of Noe, so shall it be also in the days of the Son of man.

27 They did eat and drink, they married wives and were given in marriage, until the day that Noe entered into the ark and the flood came and destroyed them all.

28 ⁷ Likewise as it came to pass in the days of Lot. They did eat and drink they bought and sold, they planted and built.

29 And in the day that Lot went out of Sodom, it rained fire and brimstone from heaven and destroyed them all.

30 Even thus shall it be in the day when the Son of man shall be revealed.

31 In that hour, he that shall be on the housetop, and his goods in the house, let him not go down to take them away: and he that shall be in the field, in like manner, let him not return back.

32 Remember Lot's wife.

33 ⁸ Whosoever shall seek to save his life shall lose it: and whosoever shall lose it shall preserve it.

34 I say to you: ⁹ In that night there shall be two men in one bed. The one shall be taken and the other shall be left.

35 Two women shall be grinding together. The one shall be taken and the other shall be left. Two men shall be in the field. The one shall be taken and the other shall be left.

36 They answering, say to him: Where, Lord?

37 Who said to them: Wheresoever the body shall be, thither will the eagles also be gathered together.

CHAPTER 18

We must pray always. The Pharisee and the publican. The danger of riches. The blind man is restored to sight.

AND ¹ he spoke also a parable to them, that we ought always to pray and not to faint,

2 Saying: There was a judge in a certain city, who feared not God nor regarded man.

3 And there was a certain widow in that city; and she came to him, saying: Avenge me of my adversary.

4 And he would not for a long time. But afterwards he said within himself: Although I fear not God nor regard man,

5 Yet because this widow is troublesome to me, I will avenge her, lest continually coming she weary me.

6 And the Lord said: Hear what the unjust judge saith.

7 And will not God revenge his elect who cry to him day and night? And will he have patience in their regard?

8 I say to you that he will quickly revenge them. But yet the Son of man, when he cometh, shall he find, think you, faith on earth?

9 And to some who trusted in them-

⁴ Lev. 14, 2. ⁵ Matt. 24, 23; Mark, 13, 21. ⁶ Gen. 7, 7; Matt. 24, 37. ⁷ Gen. 19, 25. ⁸ Matt. 10, 39; Mark, 8, 35. ⁹ Matt. 24, 40; Luke, 9, 24; John, 12, 25. Снар. 18. ¹ Ecclus. 18, 22; 1 Thess. 5, 17.

Снар. 18. Ver. 3. *Avenge.* That is, do me justice. It is a Hebraism.

selves as just and despised others, he spoke also this parable:

10 Two men went up into the temple to pray: the one a Pharisee and the other a publican.

11 The Pharisee standing, prayed thus with himself: O God, I give thee thanks that I am not as the rest of men, extortioners, unjust, adulterers, as also is this publican.

12 I fast twice in a week: I give tithes of all that I possess.

13 And the publican, standing afar off, would not so much as lift up his eyes towards heaven; but struck his breast, saying: O God, be merciful to me a sinner.

14 I say to you, this man went down into his house justified rather than the other: ² because every one that exalteth himself shall be humbled: and he that humbleth himself shall be exalted.

15 ³ And they brought unto him also infants, that he might touch them. Which when the disciples saw, they rebuked them.

16 But Jesus, calling them together said: Suffer children to come to me and forbid them not: for of such is the kingdom of God.

17 Amen, I say to you: Whosoever shall not receive the kingdom of God as a child shall not enter into it.

18 ⁴ And a certain ruler asked him saying: Good master, what shall I do to possess everlasting life?

19 And Jesus said to him: Why dost thou call me good? None is good but God alone.

20 Thou knowest the commandments: ⁵ Thou shalt not kill: Thou shalt not commit adultery: Thou shalt not steal: Thou shalt not bear false false witness: Honour thy father and mother.

21 Who said: All these things have I kept from my youth.

22 Which when Jesus had heard, he said to him: Yet one thing is wanting to thee. Sell all whatever thou hast and give to the poor: and thou shalt have treasure in heaven. And come, follow me.

23 He having heard these things, became sorrowful: for he was very rich.

24 And Jesus seeing him become sorrowful, said: How hardly shall they that have riches enter into the kingdom of God!

25 For it is easier for a camel to pass through the eye of a needle than for a rich man to enter into the kingdom of God.

26 And they that heard it said: Who then can be saved?

27 He said to them: The things that are impossible with men are possible with God.

28 Then Peter said: Behold, we have left all things and have followed thee.

29 Who said to them: Amen, I say to you, there is no man that hath left home or parents or brethren or wife or children, for the kingdom of God's sake,

30 Who shall not receive much more in this present time, and in the world to come life everlasting.

31 ⁶ Then Jesus took unto him the twelve and said to them: Behold, we go up to Jerusalem; and all things shall be accomplished which were written by the prophets concerning the Son of man.

32 For he shall be delivered to the Gentiles and shall be mocked and scourged and spit upon.

33 And after they have scourged him, they will put him to death. And the third day he shall rise again.

34 And they understood none of these things, and this word was hid from them: and they understood not the things that were said.

35 ⁷ Now it came to pass, when he drew nigh to Jericho, that a certain blind man sat by the way side, begging.

36 And when he heard the multitude passing by, he asked what this meant.

37 And they told him that Jesus of Nazareth was passing by.

38 And he cried out, saying: Jesus, Son of David, have mercy on me.

39 And they that went before rebuked him, that he should hold his peace: but he cried out much more: Son of David, have mercy on me.

40 And Jesus standing, commanded him to be brought unto him. And when he was come near, he asked him,

41 Saying: What wilt thou that I do to thee? But he said: Lord, that I may see.

42 And Jesus said to him: Receive thy sight: thy faith hath made thee whole.

43 And immediately he saw and followed him, glorifying God. And all the people, when they saw it, gave praise to God.

CHAPTER 19

Zacheus entertains Christ. The parable of the pounds. Christ rides upon an ass and weeps over Jerusalem.

AND entering in, he walked through Jericho.

2 And behold, there was a man

² Matt. 23, 12; Luke, 14, 11. ³ Matt. 19, 13; Mark, 10, 13. ⁴ Matt. 19, 16. ⁵ Exod. 20, 13. ⁶ Matt. 20, 17; Mark, 10, 32. ⁷ Matt. 20, 29; Mark, 10, 46.

named Zacheus, who was the chief of the publicans: and he was rich.

3 And he sought to see Jesus who he was: and he could not for the crowd, because he was low of stature.

4 And running before, he climbed up into a sycamore tree, that he might see him: for he was to pass that way.

5 And when Jesus was come to the place, looking up, he saw him and said to him: Zacheus, make haste and come down: for this day I must abide in thy house.

6 And he made haste and came down and received him with joy.

7 And when all saw it, they murmured, saying, that he was gone to be a guest with a man that was a sinner.

8 But Zacheus standing, said to the Lord: Behold, Lord, the half of my goods I give to the poor; and if I have wronged any man of any thing, I restore him fourfold.

9 Jesus said to him: This day is salvation come to this house, because he also is a son of Abraham.

10 ¹ For the Son of man is come to seek and to save that which was lost.

11 As they were hearing these things, he added and spoke a parable, because he was nigh to Jerusalem and because they thought that the kingdom of God should immediately be manifested.

12 He said therefore: ² A certain nobleman went into a far country, to receive for himself a kingdom and to return.

13 And calling his ten servants, he gave them ten pounds and said to them: Trade till I come.

14 But his citizens hated him: and they sent an embassage after him, saying: We will not have this man to reign over us.

15 And it came to pass that he returned, having received the kingdom: and he commanded his servants to be called, to whom he had given the money, that he might know how much every man had gained by trading.

16 And the first came saying: Lord, thy pound hath gained ten pounds.

17 And he said to him: Well done, thou good servant, because thou hast been faithful in a little, thou shalt have power over ten cities.

18 And the second came, saying: Lord, thy pound hath gained five pounds.

19 And he said to him: Be thou also over five cities.

20 And another came, saying: Lord, behold here is thy pound, which I have kept laid up in a napkin.

21 For I feared thee, because thou art an austere man: thou takest up what thou didst not lay down: and thou reapest that which thou didst not sow.

22 He saith to him: Out of thy own mouth I judge thee, thou wicked servant. Thou knewest that I was an austere man, taking up what I laid not down and reaping that which I did not sow.

23 And why then didst thou not give my money into the bank, that at my coming I might have exacted it with usury?

24 And he said to them that stood by: Take the pound away from him and give it to him that hath ten pounds.

25 And they said to him: Lord, he hath ten pounds.

26 ³ But I say to you that to every one that hath shall be given, and he shall abound: and from him that hath not, even that which he hath shall be taken from him.

27 But as for those my enemies, who would not have me reign over them, bring them hither and kill them before me.

28 And having said these things, he went before, going up to Jerusalem.

29 ⁴ And it came to pass, when he was come nigh to Bethphage and Bethania, unto the mount called Olivet, he sent two of his disciples,

30 Saying: Go into the town which is over against you, at your entering into which you shall find the colt of an ass tied, on which no man ever hath sitteth: loose him and bring him hither.

31 And if any man shall ask you: Why do you loose him? You shall say thus unto him: Because the Lord hath need of his service.

32 And they that were sent went their way and found the colt standing, as he said unto them.

33 And as they were loosing the colt, the owners thereof said to them: Why loose you the colt?

34 But they said: Because the Lord hath need of him.

35 ⁵ And they brought him to Jesus And casting their garments on the colt, they set Jesus thereon.

36 And as he went, they spread their clothes underneath in the way.

37 And when he was now coming near the descent of mount Olivet, the whole multitude of his disciples began with joy to praise God with a loud

CHAP. 19. ¹ Matt. 18, 11. ² Matt. 25, 14. ³ Matt. 13, 12; 25, 29; Mark, 4, 25; Luke, 8, 18. ⁴ Matt. 21, 1; Mark, 11, 1. ⁵ John, 12, 14.

CHAP. 19. Ver. 13. *He gave them ten pounds.* In the original, what is here translated a pound is μνᾶ, or in Latin *mina*, in value of our coin, three pounds two shillings and sixpence.

voice, for all the mighty works they had seen,

38 Saying: Blessed be the king who cometh in the name of the Lord! Peace in heaven and glory on high!

39 And some of the Pharisees, from amongst the multitude, said to him: Master, rebuke thy disciples.

40 To whom he said: I say to you that if these shall hold their peace, the stones will cry out.

41 And when he drew near, seeing the city, he wept over it, saying:

42 If thou also hadst known, and that in this thy day, the things that are to thy peace: but now they are hidden from thy eyes.

43 For the days shall come upon thee: and thy enemies shall cast a trench about thee and compass thee round and straiten thee on every side,

44 And beat thee flat to the ground, and thy children who are in thee. [6] And they shall not leave in thee a stone upon a stone: because thou hast not known the time of thy visitation.

45 [7] And entering into the temple, he began to cast out them that sold therein and them that bought.

46 Saying to them: It is written: [8] My house is the house of prayer. But you have made it a den of thieves.

47 And he was teaching daily in the temple. And the chief priests and the scribes and the rulers of the people sought to destroy him.

48 And they found not what to do to him: for all the people were very attentive to hear him.

CHAPTER 20

The parable of the husbandmen. Of paying tribute to Cæsar and of the resurrection of the dead.

AND [1] it came to pass that on one of the days, as he was teaching the people in the temple and preaching the gospel, the chief priests and the scribes, with the ancients, met together,

2 And spoke to him, saying: Tell us by what authority dost thou these things? Or, who is he that hath given thee this authority?

3 And Jesus answering, said to them: I will also ask you one thing. Answer me:

4 The baptism of John, was it from heaven, or of men?

5 But they thought within themselves, saying: If we shall say, From

heaven: he will say: Why then did you not believe in him?

6 But if we say, Of men: the whole people will stone us. For they are persuaded that John was a prophet.

7 And they answered that they knew not whence it was.

8 And Jesus said to them: Neither do I tell you by what authority I do these things.

9 And he began to speak to the people this parable: [2] A certain man planted a vineyard and let it out to husbandmen: and he was abroad for a long time.

10 And at the season he sent a servant to the husbandmen, that they should give him of the fruit of the vineyard. Who, beating him, sent him away empty.

11 And again he sent another servant. But they beat him also and, treating him reproachfully, sent him away empty.

12 And again he sent the third: and they wounded him also and cast him out.

13 Then the lord of the vineyard said: What shall I do? I will send my beloved son. It may be, when they see him, they will reverence him.

14 Whom, when the husbandmen saw, they thought within themselves, saying: This is the heir. Let us kill him, that the inheritance may be ours.

15 So casting him out of the vineyard, they killed him. What therefore will the lord of the vineyard do to them?

16 He will come and will destroy these husbandmen and will give the vineyard to others. Which they hearing, said to him: God forbid.

17 But he looking on them, said: What is this then that is written, [3] *The stone, which the builders rejected, the same is become the head of the corner?*

18 Whosoever shall fall upon that stone shall be bruised: and upon whomsoever it shall fall, it will grind him to powder.

19 And the chief priests and the scribes sought to lay hands on him the same hour: but they feared the people, for they knew that he spoke this parable to them.

20 [4] And being upon the watch, they sent spies, who should feign themselves just, that they might take hold of him in his words, that they might deliver him up to the authority and power of the governor.

21 And they asked him, saying: Master, we know that thou speakest and teachest rightly: and thou dost not re-

[6] Matt. 24, 2; Mark, 13, 2; Luke, 21, 6. [7] Matt. 21, 12; Mark, 11, 15. [8] Isai. 56, 7; Jer. 7, 11. CHAP. 20. [1] Matt. 21, 23; Mark, 14, 27. [2] Isai. 5, 1; Jer. 2, 21; Matt. 21, 3; Mark, 12, 1. [3] Ps. 117, 22; Isai. 28, 16; Matt. 21, 42; Acts, 4, 11; Rom. 9, 33; 1 Peter, 2, 7. [4] Matt. 2, 15; Mark, 12, 13.

spect any person, but teachest the way of God in truth.

22 Is it lawful for us to give tribute to Cæsar, or no?

23 But he, considering their guile, said to them: Why tempt you me?

24 Shew me a penny. Whose image and inscription hath it? They answering, said to him: Cæsar's.

25 And he said to them: [5] Render therefore to Cæsar the things that are Cæsar's: and to God the things that are God's.

26 And they could not reprehend his word before the people: and wondering at his answer, they held their peace.

27 [6] And there came to him some of the Sadducees, who deny that there is any resurrection: and they asked him,

28 Saying: Master, Moses wrote unto us: [7] If any man's brother die, having a wife, and he leave no children, that his brother should take her to wife and raise up seed unto his brother.

29 There were therefore seven brethren: and the first took a wife and died without children.

30 And the next took her to wife: and he also died childless.

31 And the third took her. And in like manner, all the seven: and they left no children and died.

32 Last of all the woman died also.

33 In the resurrection therefore, whose wife of them shall she be? For all the seven had her to wife.

34 And Jesus said to them: The children of this world marry and are given in marriage:

35 But they that shall be accounted worthy of that world and of the resurrection from the dead shall neither be married nor take wives.

36 Neither can they die any more for they are equal to the angels and are the children of God, being the children of the resurrection.

37 Now that the dead rise again, Moses also shewed at the bush, [8] when he called the Lord: The God of Abraham and the God of Isaac and the God of Jacob.

38 For he is not the God of the dead, but of the living: for all live to him.

39 And some of the scribes answering, said to him: Master, thou hast said well.

40 And after that they durst not ask him any more questions.

41 But he said to them: How say they that Christ is the son of David?

42 And David himself saith in the book of Psalms: [9] The Lord said to my Lord, sit thou on my right hand,

43 Till I make thy enemies thy footstool.

44 David then calleth him Lord. And how is he his son?

45 And in the hearing of all the people, he said to his disciples:

46 [10] Beware of the scribes, who desire to walk in long robes and love salutations in the market place and the first chairs in the synagogues and the chief rooms at feasts:

47 Who devour the houses of widows, feigning long prayer. These shall receive greater damnation.

CHAPTER 21

The widow's mites. The signs that should forerun the destruction of Jerusalem and the end of the world.

AND [1] looking on, he saw the rich men cast their gifts into the treasury.

2 And he saw also a certain poor widow casting in two brass mites.

3 And he said: Verily, I say to you that this poor widow hath cast in more than they all.

4 For all these have of their abundance cast into the offerings of God: but she of her want hath cast in all the living that she had.

5 And some saying of the temple that it was adorned with goodly stones and gifts, he said:

6 These things which you see, [2] the days will come in which there shall not be left a stone upon a stone that shall not be thrown down.

7 And they asked him, saying: Master, when shall these things be? And what shall be the sign when they shall begin to come to pass?

8 Who said: Take heed you be not seduced; for many will come in my name, saying: I am he and the time is at hand. Go ye not therefore after them.

9 And when you shall hear of wars and seditions, be not terrified. These things must first come to pass: but the end is not yet presently.

10 Then he said to them: Nation shall rise against nation, and kingdom against kingdom.

11 And there shall be great earthquakes in divers places and pestilences and famines and terrors from heaven: and there shall be great signs.

12 But before all these things, they will lay their hands on you and persecute you, delivering you up to the synagogues and into prisons, dragging you

[5] Rom. 13, 7. [6] Matt. 22, 23; Mark, 12, 18. [7] Deut. 25, 5. [8] Exod. 3, 6. [9] Ps. 109, 1; Matt. 22, 44; Mark, 12, 36. [10] Matt. 23, 6; Mark, 12, 38; Luke, 11, 43. CHAP. 21. [1] Mark, 12, 41. [2] Matt. 24, 2; Mark, 13, 2; Luke, 19, 44.

before kings and governors, for my name's sake.

13 And it shall happen unto you for a testimony.

14 Lay it up therefore in your hearts, not to meditate before how you shall answer:

15 For I will give you a mouth and wisdom, which all your adversaries shall not be able to resist and gainsay.

16 And you shall be betrayed by your parents and brethren and kinsmen and friends: and some of you they will put to death.

17 And you shall be hated by all men for my name's sake.

18 But a hair of your head shall not perish.

19 In your patience you shall possess your souls.

20 [3] And when you shall see Jerusalem compassed about with an army, then know that the desolation thereof is at hand.

21 Then let those who are in Judea flee to the mountains: and those who are in the midst thereof depart out: and those who are in the countries not enter into it.

22 For these are the days of vengeance, that all things may be fulfilled, that are written.

23 But woe to them that are with child and give suck in those days: for there shall be great distress in the land and wrath upon this people.

24 And they shall fall by the edge of the sword and shall be led away captives into all nations: and Jerusalem shall be trodden down by the Gentiles till the times of the nations be fulfilled.

25 [4] And there shall be signs in the sun and in the moon and in the stars; and upon the earth distress of nations, by reason of the confusion of the roaring of the sea and of the waves:

26 Men withering away for fear and expectation of what shall come upon the whole world. For the powers of heaven shall be moved.

27 And then they shall see the Son of man coming in a cloud, with great power and majesty.

28 But when these things begin to come to pass, look up and lift up your heads, [5] because your redemption is at hand.

29 And he spoke to them a similitude. See the fig tree and all the trees:

30 When they now shoot forth their fruit, you know that summer is nigh;

31 So you also, when you shall see

these things come to pass, know that the kingdom of God is at hand.

32 Amen, I say to you, this generation shall not pass away till all things be fulfilled.

33 Heaven and earth shall pass away: but my words shall not pass away.

34 And take heed to yourselves, lest perhaps your hearts be overcharged with surfeiting and drunkenness and the cares of this life: and that day come upon you suddenly.

35 For as a snare shall it come upon all that sit upon the face of the whole earth.

36 Watch ye, therefore, praying at all times, that you may be accounted worthy to escape all these things that are to come and to stand before the Son of man.

37 And in the daytime, he was teaching in the temple: but at night going out, he abode in the mount that is called Olivet.

38 And all the people came early in the morning to him in the temple, to hear him.

CHAPTER 22

The treason of Judas. The last supper. The first part of the history of the passion.

NOW [1] the feast of unleavened bread, which is called the pasch, was at hand.

2 And the chief priests and the scribes sought how they might put Jesus to death: but they feared the people.

3 [2] And Satan entered into Judas, who was surnamed Iscariot, one of the twelve.

4 And he went and discoursed with the chief priests and the magistrates, how he might betray him to them.

5 And they were glad and covenanted to give him money.

6 And he promised. And he sought opportunity to betray him in the absence of the multitude.

7 And the day of the unleavened bread came, on which it was necessary that the pasch should be killed.

8 And he sent Peter and John, saying: Go, and prepare for us the pasch, that we may eat.

9 But they said: Where wilt thou that we prepare?

10 And he said to them: Behold, as you go into the city, there shall meet you a man carrying a pitcher of water: follow him into the house where he entereth in.

11 And you shall say to the goodman of the house: The master saith to thee:

[3] Dan. 9, 27; Matt. 24, 15; Mark, 13, 14. [4] Isai. 13, 19; Ezech. 32, 7; Joel, 2, 10; 3, 7; Matt. 24, 29; Mark, 13, 24. [5] Rom. 8, 23. CHAP. 22. [1] Matt. 26, 2; Mark, 14, 1. [2] Matt. 23, 14; Mark, 14, 10.

Where is the guestchamber, where I may eat the pasch with my disciples?

12 And he will shew you a large dining room, furnished. And there prepare.

13 And they going, found as he had said to them and made ready the pasch.

14 ³ And when the hour was come, he sat down: and the twelve apostles with him.

15 And he said to them: With desire I have desired to eat this pasch with you, before I suffer.

16 For I say to you that from this time I will not eat it, till it be fulfilled in the kingdom of God.

17 And having taken the chalice, he gave thanks and said: Take and divide it among you.

18 For I say to you that I will not drink of the fruit of the vine, till the kingdom of God come.

19 ⁴ And taking bread, he gave thanks and brake and gave to them, saying: This is my body, which is given for you. Do this for a commemoration of me.

20 In like manner, the chalice also, after he had supped, saying: This is the chalice, the new testament in my blood, which shall be shed for you.

21 ⁵ But yet behold: the hand of him that betrayeth me is with me on the table.

22 And the Son of man indeed goeth, ⁶ according to that which is determined: but yet, woe to that man by whom he shall be betrayed.

23 And they began to inquire among themselves, which of them it was that should do this thing.

24 And there was also a strife amongst them, which of them should seem to be the greater.

25 And he said to them: ⁷ The kings of the Gentiles lord it over them; and they that have power over them are called beneficent.

26 But you not so: but he that is the greater among you, let him become as the younger: and he that is the leader, as he that serveth.

27 For which is greater, he that sitteth at table or he that serveth? Is not he that sitteth at table? But I am in the midst of you, as he that serveth.

28 And you are they who have continued with me in my temptations:

29 And I dispose to you, as my Father hath disposed to me, a kingdom;

30 That you may eat and drink at my table, in my kingdom: and may sit upon thrones, judging the twelve tribes of Israel.

31 And the Lord said: Simon, Simon, behold Satan hath desired to have you, that he may sift you as wheat.

32 But I have prayed for thee, that thy faith fail not: and thou, being once converted, confirm thy brethren.

33 Who said to him: Lord, I am ready to go with thee, both into prison and to death.

34 ⁸ And he said: I say to thee, Peter, the cock shall not crow this day, till thou thrice deniest that thou knowest me. And he said to them:

35 ⁹ When I sent you without purse and scrip and shoes, did you want anything?

36 But they said: Nothing. Then said he unto them: But now he that hath a purse, let him take it, and likewise a scrip; and he that hath not, let him sell his coat and buy a sword.

37 For I say to you that this that is written must yet be fulfilled in me. ¹⁰ And with the wicked was he reckoned. For the things concerning me have an end.

38 But they said: Lord, behold, here are two swords. And he said to them: It is enough.

39 ¹¹ And going out, he went, according to his custom, to the mount of Olives. And his disciples also followed him.

40 And when he was come to the place, he said to them: Pray, lest ye enter into temptation.

41 ¹² And he was withdrawn away from them a stone's cast. And kneeling down, he prayed,

42 Saying: Father, if thou wilt, remove this chalice from me: but yet not my will, but thine be done.

43 And there appeared to him an angel from heaven, strengthening him. And being in an agony, he prayed the longer.

44 And his sweat became as drops of blood, trickling down upon the ground.

45 And when he rose up from prayer and was come to the disciples, he found them sleeping for sorrow.

46 And he said to them: Why sleep

³ Matt. 26, 20; Mark, 14, 17. ⁴ 1 Cor. 11, 24. ⁵ Matt. 26, 21; Mark, 14, 20; John, 13, 18. ⁶ Ps. 40, 9. ⁷ Matt. 20, 25; Mark, 10, 42. ⁸ Matt. 26, 34; Mark, 14, 30. ⁹ Matt. 10, 9. ¹⁰ Isai. 53, 12. ¹¹ Matt. 26, 36; Mark, 14, 32; John, 18, 1. ¹² Matt. 26, 39; Mark, 14, 35.

CHAP. 22. Ver. 19. *Do this for a commemoration of me.* This Sacrifice and Sacrament is to be continued in the church, to the end of the world, to shew forth the death of Christ, until he cometh. But this commemoration, or remembrance, is by no means inconsistent with the real presence of his body and blood, under these sacramental veils which represent his death; on the contrary, it is the manner that he himself hath commanded of commemorating and celebrating his death, by offering in sacrifice and receiving in the Sacrament, that body and blood by which we were redeemed.

you? Arise: pray: lest you enter into temptation.

47 [13] As he was yet speaking, behold a multitude; and he that was called Judas, one of the twelve, went before them and drew near to Jesus, for to kiss him.

48 And Jesus said to him: Judas, dost thou betray the Son of man with a kiss?

49 And they that were about him, seeing what would follow, said to him: Lord, shall we strike with the sword?

50 And one of them struck the servant of the high priest and cut off his right ear.

51 But Jesus answering, said: Suffer ye thus far. And when he had touched his ear, he healed him.

52 And Jesus said to the chief priests and magistrates of the temple and the ancients, that were come unto him: Are ye come out, as it were against a thief, with swords and clubs?

53 When I was daily with you in the temple, you did not stretch forth your hands against me: but this is your hour and the power of darkness.

54 [14] And apprehending him, they led him to the high priest's house. But Peter followed afar off.

55 [15] And when they had kindled a fire in the midst of the hall and were sitting about it, Peter was in the midst of them.

56 Whom when a certain servant maid had seen sitting at the light and had earnestly beheld him, she said: This man also was with him.

57 But he denied him, saying: Woman, I know him not.

58 And after a little while, another seeing him, said: Thou also art one of them. But Peter said: O man, I am not.

59 [16] And after the space, as it were of one hour, another certain man affirmed, saying: Of a truth, this man was also with him: for he is also a Galilean.

60 And Peter said: Man, I know not what thou sayest. And immediately, as he was yet speaking, the cock crew.

61 And the Lord turning looked on Peter. And Peter remembered the word of the Lord, as he had said: [17] Before the cock crow, thou shalt deny me thrice.

62 And Peter going out, wept bitterly.

63 And the men that held him mocked him and struck him.

64 And they blindfolded him and smote his face. And they asked him, saying: Prophesy: Who is it that struck thee?

65 And blaspheming, many other things they said against him.

66 [18] And as soon as it was day, the ancients of the people and the chief priests and scribes came together. And they brought him into their council, saying: If thou be the Christ, tell us.

67 And he saith to them: If I shall tell you, you will not believe me.

68 And if I shall also ask you, you will not answer me, nor let me go.

69 But hereafter the Son of man shall be sitting on the right hand of the power of God.

70 Then said they all: Art thou then the Son of God? Who said: You say that I am.

71 And they said: What need we any further testimony? For we ourselves have heard it from his own mouth.

CHAPTER 23

The continuation of the history of the passion.

AND the whole multitude of them, rising up, led him to Pilate.

2 And they began to accuse him, saying: We have found this man perverting our nation [1] and forbidding to give tribute to Cæsar and saying that he is Christ the king.

3 [2] And Pilate asked him, saying: Art thou the king of the Jews? But he answering, said: Thou sayest it.

4 And Pilate said to the chief priests and to the multitudes: I find no cause in this man.

5 But they were more earnest, saying: He stirreth up the people, teaching throughout all Judea, beginning from Galilee to this place.

6 But Pilate hearing Galilee, asked if the man were of Galilee?

7 And when he understood that he was of Herod's jurisdiction, he sent him away to Herod, who was also himself at Jerusalem in those days.

8 And Herod seeing Jesus, was very glad: for he was desirous of a long time to see him, because he had heard many

Ver. 58. *Another.* Observe here, in order to reconcile the four Evangelists, that divers persons concurred in charging Peter with being Christ's disciple; till at length they brought him to deny him thrice. 1. The porteress that let him in, and afterwards, seeing him at the fire, first put the question to him and then positively affirmed that he was with Christ. 2. Another maid accused him to the standers by and gave occasion to the man here mentioned to renew the charge against him, which caused the second denial. 3. Others of the company took notice of his being a Galilean and were seconded by the kinsman of Malchus who affirmed he had seen him in the garden. And this drew on the third denial.

things of him; and he hoped to see some sign wrought by him.

9 And he questioned him in many words. But he answered him nothing.

10 And the chief priests and the scribes stood by, earnestly accusing him.

11 And Herod with his army set him at nought and mocked him, putting on him a white garment: and sent him back to Pilate.

12 And Herod and Pilate were made friends, that same day: for before they were enemies one to another.

13 And Pilate, calling together the chief priests and the magistrates and the people,

14 Said to them: You have presented unto me this man as one that perverteth the people. And behold I, having examined him before you, [3] find no cause in this man, in those things wherein you accuse him.

15 No, nor Herod neither. For, I sent you to him: and behold, nothing worthy of death is done to him.

16 I will chastise him therefore and release him.

17 Now of necessity he was to release unto them one upon the feast day.

18 But the whole multitude together cried out, saying: Away with his man, and release unto us Barabbas:

19 Who, for a certain sedition made in the city and for a murder, was cast into prison.

20 And Pilate again spoke to them, desiring to release Jesus.

21 But they cried again, saying: Crucify him, Crucify him.

22 And he said to them the third time: [4] Why, what evil hath this man done? I find no cause of death in him. I will chastise him therefore and let him go.

23 But they were instant with loud voices, requiring that he might be crucified. And their voices prevailed.

24 And Pilate gave sentence that it should be as they required.

25 And he released unto them him who for murder and sedition had been cast into prison, whom they had desired. But Jesus he delivered up to their will.

26 And as they led him away, they laid hold of one Simon of Cyrene, coming from the country; and they laid the cross on him to carry after Jesus.

27 [5] And there followed him a great multitude of people and of women, who bewailed and lamented him.

28 But Jesus turning to them, said: Daughters of Jerusalem, weep not over me; but weep for yourselves and for your children.

29 For behold, the days shall come, wherein they will say: Blessed are the barren and the wombs that have not borne and the paps that have not given suck.

30 Then shall they begin to say to the mountains: [6] Fall upon us. And to the hills: Cover us.

31 For if in the green wood they do these things, what shall be done in the dry?

32 And there were also two other malefactors led with him to be put to death.

33 [7] And when they were come to the place which is called Calvary, they crucified him there: and the robbers, one on the right hand, and the other on the left.

34 And Jesus said: Father, forgive them, for they know not what they do. But they, dividing his garments, cast lots.

35 And the people stood beholding. And the rulers with them derided him, saying: He saved others; let him save himself, if he be Christ, the elect of God.

36 And the soldiers also mocked him, coming to him and offering him vinegar,

37 And saying: If thou be the king of the Jews, save thyself.

38 And there was also a superscription written over him in letters of Greek and Latin and Hebrew THIS IS THE KING OF THE JEWS.

39 And one of those robbers who were hanged blasphemed him, saying: If thou be. Christ, save thyself and us.

40 But the other answering, rebuked him, saying: Neither dost thou fear God, seeing thou art under the same condemnation?

41 And we indeed justly: for we receive the due reward of our deeds. But this man hath done no evil.

42 And he said to Jesus: Lord, remember me when thou shalt come into thy kingdom.

43 And Jesus said to him: Amen I say to thee: This day thou shalt be with me in paradise.

[3] John, 18, 38; 19, 4. [4] Matt. 27, 23; Mark, 15, 14. [5] Matt. 27, 32; Mark, 15, 21. [6] Isai. 2, 19; Osee, 10, 8; Apoc. 6, 16. [7] Matt. 27, 33; Mark, 15, 22; John, 19, 17.

CHAP. 23. Ver. 43. *In paradise.* That is, in the happy state of rest, joy and peace everlasting. Christ was pleased, by a special privilege, to reward the faith and confession of the penitent thief with a full discharge of all his sins, both as to the guilt and punishment, and to introduce him immediately after death into the happy society of the saints, whose *limbo,* that is, the place of their confinement, was now made a *paradise* by our Lord's going thither.

44 And it was almost the sixth hour: and there was darkness over all the earth until the ninth hour.

45 And the sun was darkened, and the veil of the temple was rent in the midst.

46 And Jesus crying with a loud voice, said: [8] Father, into thy hands I commend my spirit. And saying this, he gave up the ghost.

47 Now, the centurion, seeing what was done, glorified God, saying: Indeed this was a just man.

48 And all the multitude of them that were come together to that sight and saw the things that were done returned, striking their breasts.

49 And all his acquaintance and the women that had followed him from Galilee stood afar off, beholding these things.

50 [9] And behold there was a man named Joseph who was a counsellor, a good and a just man,

51 (The same had not consented to their counsel and doings) of Arimathea, a city of Judea; who also himself looked for the kingdom of God.

52 This man went to Pilate and begged the body of Jesus.

53 And taking him down, he wrapped him in fine linen and laid him in a sepulchre that was hewed in stone, wherein never yet any man had been laid.

54 And it was the day of the Parasceve: and the sabbath drew on.

55 And the women that were come with him from Galilee, following after, saw the sepulchre and how his body was laid.

56 And returning, they prepared spices and ointments: and on the sabbath day they rested, according to the commandment.

CHAPTER 24

Christ's resurrection and manifestation of himself to his disciples.

AND [1] on the first *day* of the week, very early in the morning, they came to the sepulchre, bringing the spices which they had prepared.

2 And they found the stone rolled back from the sepulchre.

3 And going in, they found not the body of the Lord Jesus.

4 And it came to pass, as they were astonished in their mind at this, behold,

8 Ps. 30, 6. 9 Matt. 27, 57; Mark, 15, 43; John, 19, 38. CHAP. 24. 1 Matt. 28, 1; Mark, 16, 2; John, 20, 1. 2 Matt. 16, 21; 17, 21; Mark, 8, 31; 9, 30; Luke, 9, 22. 3 Mark, 16, 12.

Ver. 54. *Parasceve.* That is, the eve, or day of preparation, for the sabbath.

two men stood by them, in shining apparel.

5 And as they were afraid and bowed down their countenance towards the ground, they said unto them: Why seek you the living with the dead?

6 He is not here, but is risen. Remember how he spoke unto you, when he was yet in Galilee,

7 Saying: [2] The Son of man must be delivered into the hands of sinful men and be crucified and the third day rise again.

8 And they remembered his words.

9 And going back from the sepulchre, they told all these things to the eleven and to all the rest.

10 And it was Mary Magdalen and Joanna and Mary of James and the other women that were with them, who told these things to the apostles.

11 And these words seemed to them as idle tales: and they did not believe them.

12 But Peter rising up, ran to the sepulchre and, stooping down, he saw the linen cloths laid by themselves: and went away wondering in himself at that which was come to pass.

13 [3] And behold, two of them went, the same day, to a town which was sixty furlongs from Jerusalem, named Emmaus.

14 And they talked together of all these things which had happened.

15 And it came to pass that while they talked and reasoned with themselves, Jesus himself also, drawing near, went with them.

16 But their eyes were held, that they should not know him.

17 And he said to them: What are these discourses that you hold one with another as you walk and are sad?

18 And the one of them, whose name was Cleophas, answering, said to him: Art thou only a stranger in Jerusalem, and hast not known the things that have been done there in these days?

19 To whom he said: What things? And they said: Concerning Jesus of Nazareth, who was a prophet, mighty in work and word before God and all the people.

20 And how our chief priests and princes delivered him to be condemned to death and crucified him.

21 But we hoped that it was he that should have redeemed Israel. And now besides all this, to-day is the third day since these things were done.

22 Yea and certain women also of our company affrighted us who, before it was light, were at the sepulchre,

23 And not finding his body, came,

saying that they had also seen a vision of angels, who say that he is alive.

24 And some of our people went to the sepulchre and found it so as the women had said: but him they found not.

25 Then he said to them: O foolish and slow of heart to believe in all things which the prophets have spoken.

26 Ought not Christ to have suffered these things and so to enter into his glory?

27 And beginning at Moses and all the prophets, he expounded to them in all the scriptures the things that were concerning him.

28 And they drew nigh to the town whither they were going: and he made as though he would go farther.

29 But they constrained him, saying: Stay with us, because it is towards evening and the day is now far spent. And he went in with them.

30 And it came to pass, whilst he was at table with them, he took bread and blessed and brake and gave to them.

31 And their eyes were opened: and they knew him. And he vanished out of their sight.

32 And they said one to the other: Was not our heart burning within us, whilst he spoke in the way and opened to us the scriptures?

33 And rising up, the same hour, they went back to Jerusalem: and they found the eleven gathered together, and those that were with them,

34 Saying: The Lord is risen indeed and hath appeared to Simon.

35 And they told what things were done in the way: and how they knew him in the breaking of bread.

36 [4] Now, whilst they were speaking these things, Jesus stood in the midst of them and saith to them: Peace be to you. It is I: fear not.

37 But they being troubled and frightened, supposed that they saw a spirit.

38 And he said to them: Why are you troubled, and why do thoughts arise in your hearts?

39 See my hands and feet, that it is I myself. Handle, and see: for a spirit hath not flesh and bones, as you see me to have.

40 And when he had said this, he shewed them his hands and feet.

41 But while they yet believed not and wondered for joy, he said: Have you here any thing to eat?

42 And they offered him a piece of a broiled fish and a honeycomb.

43 And when he had eaten before them, taking the remains, he gave to them.

44 And he said to them: These are the words which I spoke to you while I was yet with you, that all things must needs be fulfilled which are written in the law of Moses and in the prophets and in the psalms, concerning me.

45 Then he opened their understanding, that they might understand the scriptures.

46 And he said to them: [5] Thus it is written, and thus it behoved Christ to suffer and to rise again from the dead, the third day:

47 And that penance and remission of sins should be preached in his name, unto all nations, beginning at Jerusalem.

48 [6] And you are witnesses of these things.

49 [7] And I send the promise of my Father upon you: but stay you in the city till you be endued with power from on high.

50 And he led them out as far as Bethania: and lifting up his hands, he blessed them.

51 [8] And it came to pass, whilst he blessed them, he departed from them and was carried up to heaven.

52 And they adoring went back into Jerusalem with great joy.

53 And they were always in the temple, praising and blessing God. Amen.

[4] Mark, 16, 14; John, 20, 19. [5] Ps. 18, 6. [6] Acts, 1, 8. [7] John, 14, 26. [8] Mark, 16, 19; Acts, 1, 9.

CHAP. 24. Ver. 49. *The promise of my Father.* That is, the Holy Ghost, whom Christ had promised that his Father and he would send (John 14, 26, and 17, 7).

THE HOLY GOSPEL OF JESUS CHRIST

ACCORDING TO

ST. JOHN

St. John *the Apostle and Evangelist was the son of Zebedee and Salome, and brother to James the Greater. He was called the Beloved disciple of Christ and stood by at his Crucifixion. He wrote the Gospel after the other Evangelists, about sixty-three years after our Lord's Ascension. Many things that they had omitted were supplied by him. The original was written in Greek; and by the Greeks he is titled: The Divine. St. Jerome relates that, when he was earnestly requested by the brethren to write the Gospel, he answered he would do it, if by ordering a common fast, they would all put up their prayers together to the Almighty God; which being ended, replenished with the clearest and fullest revelation coming from Heaven, he burst forth into that preface:* IN THE BEGINNING WAS THE WORD.

CHAPTER 1

The divinity and incarnation of Christ. John bears witness of him. He begins to call his disciples.

IN the beginning was the Word: and the Word was with God: and the Word was God.

2 The same was in the beginning with God.

3 All things were made by him: and without him was made nothing that was made.

4 In him was life: and the life was the light of men.

5 And the light shineth in darkness: and the darkness did not comprehend it.

6 ¹ There was a man sent from God, whose name was John.

7 This man came for a witness, to give testimony of the light, that all men might believe through him.

8 He was not the light, but was to give testimony of the light.

9 ² That was the true light, which enlighteneth every man that cometh into this world.

10 He was in the world: ³ and the world was made by him: and the world knew him not.

11 He came unto his own: and his own received him not.

12 But as many as received him, he gave them power to be made the sons of God, to them that believe in his name.

13 Who are born, not of blood, nor of the will of the flesh, nor of the will of man, but of God.

14 ⁴ And the Word was made flesh and dwelt among us (and we saw his glory, the glory as it were of the only begotten of the Father), full of grace and truth.

15 John beareth witness of him and crieth out, saying: This was he of whom I spoke: He that shall come after me is preferred before me: because he was before me.

16 ⁵ And of his fulness we all have received: and grace for grace.

17 For the law was given by Moses: grace and truth came by Jesus Christ.

18 ⁶ No man hath seen God at any time: the only begotten Son who is in the bosom of the Father, he hath declared him.

19 And this is the testimony of John, when the Jews sent from Jerusalem priests and Levites to him, to ask him: Who art thou?

20 And he confessed and did not deny: and he confessed: I am not the Christ.

21 And they asked him: What then? Art thou Elias? And he said: I am not. Art thou the prophet? And he answered: No.

22 They said therefore unto him: Who art thou, that we may give an answer to them that sent us? What sayest thou of thyself?

23 He said: ⁷ *I am the voice of one crying in the wilderness, make straight the way of the Lord,* as said the phophet Isaias.

24 And they that were sent were of the Pharisees.

25 And they asked him and said to him: Why then dost thou baptize, if thou be not Christ, nor Elias, nor the prophet?

CHAP. 1. ¹ Matt. 3, 1; Mark, 1, 2. ² John, 3, 19. ³ Heb. 11, 3. ⁴ Matt. 1, 16; Luke, 2, 7. ⁵ 1 Tim. 6, 17. ⁶ 1 Tim. 6, 16; 1 John, 4, 12. ⁷ Isai. 40, 3; Matt. 3, 3; Mark, 1, 3; Luke, 3, 4.

26 John answered them, saying: [8] I baptize with water: but there hath stood one in the midst of you, whom you know not.

27 [9] The same is he that shall come after me, who is preferred before me: the latchet of whose shoe I am not worthy to loose.

28 These things were done in Bethania, beyond the Jordan, where John was baptizing.

29 The next day, John saw Jesus coming to him; and he saith: Behold the Lamb of God. Behold him who taketh away the sin of the world.

30 This is he of whom I said: After me there comoth a man, who is preferred before me: because he was before me.

31 And I knew him not: but that he may be made manifest in Israel, therefore am I come baptizing with water.

32 And John gave testimony, saying: [10] I saw the Spirit coming down, as a dove from heaven; and he remained upon him.

33 And I knew him not; but he who sent me to baptize with water said to me: He upon whom thou shalt see the Spirit descending and remaining upon him, he it is that baptizeth with the Holy Ghost.

34 And I saw: and I gave testimony that this is the Son of God.

35 The next day again John stood and two of his disciples.

36 And beholding Jesus walking, he saith: Behold the Lamb of God.

37 And the two disciples heard him speak: and they followed Jesus.

38 And Jesus turning and seeing them following him, saith to them: What seek you? Who said to him: Rabbi (which is to say, being interpreted, Master), where dwellest thou?

39 He saith to them: Come and see. They came and saw where he abode: and they stayed with him that day. Now it was about the tenth hour.

40 And Andrew, the brother of Simon Peter, was one of the two who had heard of John and followed him.

41 He findeth first his brother Simon and saith to him: We have found the Messias, which is, being interpreted the Christ.

42 And he brought him to Jesus. And Jesus looking upon him, said: Thou art Simon the son of Jona. Thou shalt be called Cephas, which is interpreted Peter.

43 On the following day, he would go forth into Galilee: and he findeth Philip. And Jesus saith to him: Follow me.

44 Now Philip was of Bethsaida, the city of Andrew and Peter.

45 Philip findeth Nathanael and saith to him: We have found him of whom [11] Moses, in the law [12] and the prophets did write, Jesus the son of Joseph of Nazareth.

46 And Nathanael said to him: Can any thing of good come from Nazareth? Philip saith to him: Come and see.

47 Jesus saw Nathanael coming to him and he saith of him: Behold an Israelite indeed, in whom there is no guile.

48 Nathanael saith to him: Whence knowest thou me? Jesus answered and said to him: Before that Philip called thee, when thou wast under the fig tree, I saw thee.

49 Nathanael answered him and said: Rabbi: Thou art the Son of God. Thou art the King of Israel.

50 Jesus answered and said to him: Because I said unto thee, I saw thee under the fig tree, thou believest: greater things than these shalt thou see.

51 And he saith to him: Amen, amen, I say to you, you shall see the heaven opened and the angels of God ascending and descending upon the Son of man.

CHAPTER 2

Christ changes water into wine. He casts the sellers out of the temple.

AND the third day, there was a marriage in Cana of Galilee: and the mother of Jesus was there.

2 And Jesus also was invited, and his disciples, to the marriage.

3 And the wine failing, the mother of Jesus saith to him: They have no wine.

4 And Jesus saith to her: Woman, what is that to me and to thee? My hour is not yet come.

5 His mother saith to the waiters: Whatsoever he shall say to you, do ye.

6 Now there were set there six waterpots of stone, according to the manner of the purifying of the Jews, containing two or three measures apiece.

[8] Matt. 3, 11. [9] Mark, 1, 7; Luke, 3, 16; Acts, 1, 5; 11, 16; 19, 4. [10] Matt. 3, 16; Mark, 1, 10; Luke, 3, 22. [11] Gen. 49, 10; Deut. 18, 18. [12] Isai. 40, 10; 45, 8; Jer. 23, 5; Ezech. 34, 23; 37, 24; Dan. 9, 24, 25.

CHAP. 2. Ver. 4. *What is that to me.* These words of our Saviour, spoken to his mother, have been understood by some commentators as harsh, they not considering the next following verse: *Whatsoever he shall say to you, do ye,* which plainly shews that his mother knew of the miracle that he was to perform, and that it was at her request he wrought it. Besides the manner of speaking the words as to the tone and the countenance shown at the same time could only be known to those who were present, or from what had followed. For words indicating anger in one tone of voice would be understood quite the reverse in another.

7 Jesus saith to them: Fill the waterpots with water. And they filled them up to the brim.

8 And Jesus saith to them: Draw out now and carry to the chief steward of the feast. And they carried it.

9 And when the chief steward had tasted the water made wine and knew not whence it was, but the waiters knew who had drawn the water: the chief steward calleth the bridegroom,

10 And saith to him: Every man at first setteth forth good wine, and when men have well drunk, then that which is worse. But thou hast kept the good wine until now.

11 This beginning of miracles did Jesus in Cana of Galilee and manifested his glory. And his disciples believed in him.

12 After this, he went down to Capharnaum, he and his mother and his brethren and his disciples: and they remained there not many days.

13 And the pasch of the Jews was at hand: and Jesus went up to Jerusalem.

14 And he found in the temple them that sold oxen and sheep and doves, and the changers of money sitting.

15 And when he had made, as it were, a scourge of little cords, he drove them all out of the temple, the sheep also and the oxen: and the money of the changers he poured out, and the tables he overthrew.

16 And to them that sold doves he said: Take these things hence, and make not the house of my Father a house of traffic.

17 And his disciples remembered, that it was written: ¹ The zeal of thy house hath eaten me up.

18 The Jews, therefore, answered, and said to him: What sign dost thou shew unto us, seeing thou dost these things?

19 Jesus answered and said to them: ² Destroy this temple; and in three days I will raise it up.

20 The Jews then said: Six and forty years was this temple in building; and will thou raise it up in three days?

21 But he spoke of the temple of his body.

22 When therefore he was risen again from the dead, his disciples remembered that he had said this: ³ and they believed the scripture and the word that Jesus had said.

23 Now when he was at Jerusalem,

CHAP. 2. ¹ Ps. 68, 10. ² Mal. 26, 61; 27, 40; Mark, 15, 48; 15, 29. ³ Ps. 3, 6; 56, 9. CHAP. 3. ¹ Ps. 134, 7. ² Num. 21, 9.

CHAP. 3. Ver. 5. *Unless a man be born again.* By these words our Saviour hath declared the necessity of baptism; and by the word *water* it is evident that the application of it is necessary with the words (Matt. 28, 19).

at the pasch, upon the festival day, many believed in his name, seeing his signs which he did.

24 But Jesus did not trust himself unto them: for that he knew all men,

25 And because he needed not that any should give testimony of man: for he knew what was in man.

CHAPTER 3

Christ's discourse with Nicodemus. John's testimony.

AND there was a man of the Pharisees, named Nicodemus, a ruler of the Jews.

2 This man came to Jesus by night and said to him: Rabbi, we know that thou art come a teacher from God; for no man can do these signs which thou dost, unless God be with him.

3 Jesus answered and said to him: Amen, amen, I say to thee, unless a man be born again, he cannot see the kingdom of God.

4 Nicodemus saith to him: How can a man be born when he is old? Can he enter a second time into his mother's womb and be born again?

5 Jesus answered: Amen, amen, I say to thee, unless a man be born again of water and the Holy Ghost, he cannot enter into the kingdom of God.

6 That which is born of the flesh is flesh: and that which is born of the Spirit is spirit.

7 Wonder not that I said to thee: You must be born again.

8 The Spirit breatheth where he will and thou hearest his voice: ¹ but thou knowest not whence he cometh and whither he goeth. So is every one that is born of the Spirit.

9 Nicodemus answered and said to him: How can these things be done?

10 Jesus answered and said to him: Art thou a master in Israel, and knowest not these things?

11 Amen, amen, I say to thee that we speak what we know and we testify what we have seen: and you receive not our testimony.

12 If I have spoken to you earthly things, and you believe not: how will you believe, if I shall speak to you heavenly things?

13 And no man hath ascended into heaven, but he that descended from heaven, the Son of man who is in heaven.

14 ² And as Moses lifted up the serpent in the desert, so must the Son of man be lifted up:

15 That whosoever believeth in him may not perish, but may have life everlasting.

16 [3] For God so loved the world, as to give his only begotten Son: that whosoever believeth in him may not perish, but may have life everlasting.

17 For God sent not his Son into the world, to judge the world: but that the world may be saved by him.

18 He that believeth in him is not judged. But he that doth not believe is already judged: because he believeth not in the name of the only begotten Son of God.

19 And this is the judgment: [4] Because the light is come into the world and men loved darkness rather than the light. For their works were evil.

20 For every one that doth evil hateth the light and cometh not to the light, that his works may not be reproved.

21 But he that doth truth cometh to the light, that his works may be made manifest: because they are done in God.

22 After these things, Jesus and his disciples came into the land of Judea: and there he abode with them [5] and baptized.

23 And John also was baptizing in Ennon near Salim: because there was much water there. And they came and were baptized.

24 For John was not yet cast into prison.

25 And there arose a question between some of John's disciples and the Jews, concerning purification.

26 And they came to John and said to him: Rabbi, he that was with thee beyond the Jordan, [6] to whom thou gavest testimony: behold, he baptizeth and all men come to him.

27 John answered and said: A man cannot receive any thing, unless it be given him from heaven.

28 You yourselves do bear me witness [7] that I said that I am not Christ, but that I am sent before him.

29 He that hath the bride is the bridegroom: but the friend of the bridegroom, who standeth and heareth him, rejoiceth with joy because of the bridegroom's voice. This my joy therefore is fulfilled.

30 He must increase: but I must decrease.

31 He that cometh from above is above all. He that is of the earth, of the earth he is, and of the earth he speaketh. He that cometh from heaven is above all.

32 And what he hath seen and heard, that he testifieth: and no man receiveth his testimony.

33 He that hath received his testi-

mony hath set to his seal that [8] God is true.

34 For he whom God hath sent speaketh the words of God: for God doth not give the Spirit by measure.

35 The Father loveth the Son: and he hath given all things into his hand.

36 [9] He that believeth in the Son hath life everlasting: but he that believeth not the Son shall not see life: but the wrath of God abideth on him.

CHAPTER 4

Christ talks with the Samaritan woman. He heals the ruler's son.

WHEN Jesus therefore understood that the Pharises had heard that Jesus maketh more disciples [1] and baptizeth *more* than John

2 (Though Jesus *himself* did not baptize, but his disciples),

3 He left Judea and went again into Galilee.

4 And he was of necessity to pass through Samaria.

5 He cometh therefore to a city of Samaria, which is called Sichar, near the land [2] which Jacob gave to his son Joseph.

6 Now Jacob's well was there. Jesus therefore, being wearied with his journey, sat thus on the well. It was about the sixth hour.

7 There cometh a woman of Samaria, to draw water. Jesus saith to her: Give me to drink.

8 For his disciples were gone into the city to buy meats.

9 Then that Samaritan woman saith to him: How dost thou, being a Jew; ask of me to drink, who am a Samaritan woman? For the Jews do not communicate with the Samaritans.

10 Jesus answered and said to her: If thou didst know the gift of God and who he is that saith to thee: Give me to drink; thou perhaps wouldst have asked of him, and he would have given thee living water.

11 The woman saith to him: Sir, thou hast nothing wherein to draw, and the well is deep. From whence then hast thou living water?

12 Art thou greater than our father

---

[3] 1 John, 4, 9. [4] John, 1, 9. [5] John, 4, 1. [6] John, 1, 19. [7] John, 1, 20. [8] Rom. 3, 4. [9] 1 John, 5, 10. CHAP. 4. [1] John, 3, 22. [2] Gen. 33, 19; 48, 22; Jos. 24, 32.

Ver. 18. *Is not judged.* He that believeth, that is, by a faith working through charity, is not *judged*, that is, is not *condemned*; but the obstinate *unbeliever* is *judged*, that is, *condemned already*, by retrenching himself from the society of Christ and his church.

Ver. 19. *The judgment.* That is, the cause of his condemnation.

Ver. 21. *He that doth truth,* that is, he that acteth according to truth, which here signifies the Law of God. *Thy law is truth* (Ps. 118, 142).

Jacob, who gave us the well and drank thereof, himself and his children and his cattle?

13 Jesus answered and said to her: Whosoever drinketh of this water shall thirst again: but he that shall drink of the water that I will give him shall not thirst for ever.

14 But the water that I will give him shall become in him a fountain of water, springing up into life everlasting.

15 The woman said to him: Sir, give me this water, that I may not thirst, nor come hither to draw.

16 Jesus saith to her: Go, call thy husband, and come hither.

17 The woman answered and said: I have no husband. Jesus said to her: Thou hast said well: I have no husband.

18 For thou hast had five husbands: and he whom thou now hast is not thy husband. This thou hast said truly.

19 The woman saith to him: Sir, I perceive that thou art a prophet.

20 Our fathers adored on this mountain: and you say ³ that at Jerusalem is the place where men must adore.

21 Jesus saith to her: Woman, believe me that the hour cometh, when you shall neither on this mountain, nor in Jerusalem, adore the Father.

22 ⁴ You adore that which you know not: we adore that which we know. For salvation is of the Jews.

23 But the hour cometh and now is, when the true adorers shall adore the Father in spirit and in truth. For the Father also seeketh such to adore him.

24 ⁵ God is a spirit: and they that adore him must adore him in spirit and in truth.

25 The woman saith to him: I know that the Messias cometh (who is called Christ): therefore, when he is come, he will tell us all things.

26 Jesus saith to her: I am he, who am speaking with thee.

27 And immediately his disciples came. And they wondered that he talked with the woman. Yet no man said: What seekest thou? Or: Why talkest thou with her?

28 The woman therefore left her waterpot and went her way into the city and saith to the men there:

29 Come, and see a man who has told me all things whatsoever I have done. Is not he the Christ?

³ Deut. 12, 5. ⁴ 4 Kings, 17, 41. ⁵ 1 Cor. 3, 17. ⁶ Matt. 9, 37; Luke, 10, 2. ⁷ Matt. 13, 57; Mark, 6, 4; Luke, 4, 24. ⁸ Mark, 4, 12; Mark, 1, 14; Luke, 4, 14. ⁹ John, 2, 9.

CHAP. 4. Ver. 20. *This mountain.* Garizim, where the Samaritans had their schismatical temple.

30 They went therefore out of the city and came unto him.

31 In the mean time, the disciples prayed him, saying: Rabbi, eat.

32 But he said to them: I have meat to eat which you know not.

33 The disciples therefore said one to another: Hath any man brought him to eat?

34 Jesus saith to them: My meat is to do the will of him that sent me, that I may perfect his work.

35 Do not you say: There are yet four months, and then the harvest cometh? Behold, I say to you, lift up your eyes, and see the countries. ⁶ For they are white already to harvest.

36 And he that reapeth receiveth wages and gathereth fruit unto life everlasting: that both he that soweth and he that reapeth may rejoice together.

37 For in this is the saying true: That it is one man that soweth, and it is another that reapeth.

38 I have sent you to reap that in which you did not labour. Others have laboured: and you have entered into their labours.

39 Now of that city many of the Samaritans believed in him, for the word of the woman giving testimony: He told me all things whatsoever I have done.

40 So when the Samaritans were come to him, they desired that he would tarry there. And he abode there two days.

41 And many more believed in him, because of his own word.

42 And they said to the woman: We now believe, not for thy saying: for we ourselves have heard him and know that this is indeed the Saviour of the world.

43 Now after two days, he departed thence and went into Galilee.

44 For ⁷ Jesus himself gave testimony that a prophet hath no honour in his own country.

45 ⁸ And when he was come into Galilee, the Galileans received him, having seen all the things he had done at Jerusalem on the festival day: for they also went to the festival day.

46 He came again therefore into Cana of Galilee, ⁹ where he made the water wine. And there was a certain ruler, whose son was sick at Capharnaum.

47 He having heard that Jesus was come from Judea into Galilee, went to him and prayed him to come down and heal his son: for he was at the point of death.

48 Jesus therefore said to him: Un-

less you see signs and wonders, you believe not.

49 The ruler saith to him: Lord, come down before that my son die.

50 Jesus saith to him: Go thy way. Thy son liveth. The man believed the word which Jesus said to him and went his way.

51 And as he was going down, his servants met him: and they brought word, saying, that his son lived.

52 He asked therefore of them the hour wherein he grew better. And they said to him: Yesterday, at the seventh hour, the fever left him.

53 The father therefore knew that it was at the same hour that Jesus said to him: Thy son liveth. And himself believed, and his whole house.

54 This is again the second miracle that Jesus did, when he was come out of Judea into Galilee.

CHAPTER 5

Christ heals on the sabbath the man languishing thirty-eight years. His discourse upon this occasion.

AFTER these things was a festival day of the Jews: and Jesus went up to Jerusalem.

2 Now there is at Jerusalem a pond, *called* Probatica, which in Hebrew is named Bethsaida, having five porches.

3 In these lay a great multitude of sick, of blind, of lame, of withered: waiting for the moving of the water.

4 And an angel of the Lord descended at certain times into the pond and the water was moved. And he that went down first into the pond after the motion of the water was made whole of whatsoever infirmity he lay under.

5 And there was a certain man there that had been eight and thirty years under his infirmity.

6 Him when Jesus had seen lying, and knew that he had been now a long time, he saith to him: Wilt thou be made whole?

7 The infirm man answered him: Sir, I have no man, when the water is troubled, to put me into the pond. For whilst I am coming, another goeth down before me.

8 Jesus saith to him: Arise, take up thy bed and walk.

9 And immediately the man was made whole: and he took up his bed and walked. And it was the sabbath that day.

10 The Jews therefore said to him that was healed: [1] It is the sabbath. It is not lawful for thee to take up thy bed.

11 He answered them: He that made me whole, he said to me: Take up thy bed and walk.

12 They asked him therefore: Who is that man who said to thee: Take up thy bed and walk?

13 But he who was healed knew not who it was; for Jesus went aside from the multitude standing in the place.

14 Afterwards, Jesus findeth him in the temple and saith to him: Behold thou art made whole: sin no more, lest some worse thing happen to thee.

15 The man went his way and told the Jews that it was Jesus who had made him whole.

16 Therefore did the Jews persecute Jesus, because he did these things on the sabbath.

17 But Jesus answered them: My Father worketh until now; and I work.

18 Hereupon therefore the Jews sought the more to kill him, because he did not only break the sabbath but also said God was his Father, making himself equal to God.

19 Then Jesus answered and said to them: Amen, amen, I say unto you, the Son cannot do any thing of himself, but what he seeth the Father doing: for what things soever he doth, these the Son also doth in like manner.

20 For the Father loveth the Son and sheweth him all things which himself doth: and greater works than these will he shew him, that you may wonder.

21 For as the Father raiseth up the dead and giveth life: so the Son also giveth life to whom he will.

22 For neither does the Father judge any man: but hath given all judgment to the Son.

23 That all men may honour the Son, as they honour the Father. He who honoureth not the Son honoureth not the Father who hath sent him.

24 Amen, amen, I say unto you that he who heareth my word and believeth him that sent me hath life everlasting and cometh not into judgment, but is passed from death to life.

25 Amen, amen, I say unto you, that the hour cometh, and now is, when the dead shall hear the voice of the Son of God: and they that hear shall live.

26 For as the Father hath life in

CHAP. 5. [1] Exod. 20, 11; Jer. 92, 24.

CHAP. 5. Ver. 2. *Probatica.* That is, the sheeppond: either so called, because the sheep were washed therein, that were to be offered up in sacrifice in the temple, or because it was near the sheep gate. That this was a pond where miracles were wrought is evident from the sacred text; and also that the water had no natural virtue to heal, as one only of those put in after the motion of the water was restored to health. For if the water had the healing quality, the others would have the like benefit, being put into it about the same time.

himself, so he hath given to the Son also to have life in himself.

27 And he hath given him power to do judgment, because he is the Son of man.

28 Wonder not at this: for the hour cometh, wherein all that are in the graves shall hear the voice of the Son of God.

29 [2] And they that have done good things shall come forth unto the resurrection of life: but they that have done evil, unto the resurrection of judgment.

30 I cannot of myself do any thing. As I hear, so I judge. And my judgment is just: because I seek not my own will, but the will of him that sent me.

31 If I bear witness of myself, my witness is not true.

32 [3] There is another that beareth witness of me: and I know that the witness which he witnesseth of me is true.

33 You sent to John: and he gave testimony to the truth.

34 But I receive not testimony from man: but I say these things, that you may be saved.

35 He was a burning and a shining light: and you were willing for a time to rejoice in his light.

36 But I have a greater testimony than that of John: for the works which the Father hath given me to perfect the works themselves which I do, give testimony of me, that the Father hath sent me.

37 And the Father himself who hath sent me [4] hath given testimony of me: neither have you heard his voice at any time, [5] nor seen his shape.

38 And you have not his word abiding in you: for whom he hath sent, him you believe not.

39 Search the scriptures: for you think in them to have life everlasting. And the same are they that give testimony of me.

40 And you will not come to me that you may have life.

41 I receive not glory from men.

42 But I know you, that you have not the love of God in you.

43 I am come in the name of my

Father, and you receive me not: if another shall come in his own name, him you will receive.

44 How can you believe, who receive glory one from another: [6] and the glory which is from God alone, you do not seek?

45 Think not that I will accuse you to the Father. There is one that accuseth you, Moses, in whom you trust.

46 For if you did believe Moses, you would perhaps believe me also: [7] for he wrote of me.

47 But if you do not believe his writings, how will you believe my words?

CHAPTER 6

Christ feeds five thousand with five loaves. He walks upon the sea and discourses of the bread of life.

AFTER [1] these things Jesus went over the sea of Galilee, which is that of Tiberias.

2 And a great multitude followed him, because they saw the miracles which he did on them that were diseased.

3 Jesus therefore went up into a mountain: and there he sat with his disciples.

4 Now the pasch, the festival day of the Jews, was near at hand.

5 When Jesus therefore had lifted up his eyes and seen that a very great multitude cometh to him, he said to Philip: Whence shall we buy bread, that these may eat?

6 And this he said to try him: for he himself knew what he would do.

7 Philip answered him: Two hundred pennyworth of bread is not sufficient for them, that every one may take a little.

8 One of his disciples, Andrew, the brother of Simon Peter, saith to him:

9 There is a boy here that hath five barley loaves and two fishes. But what are these among so many?

10 Then Jesus said: Make the men sit down. Now, there was much grass in the place. The men therefore sat down, in number about five thousand.

11 And Jesus took the loaves: and when he had given thanks, he distributed to them that were set down. In like manner also of the fishes, as much as they would.

12 And when they were filled, he said to his disciples: Gather up the fragments that remain, lest they be lost.

13 They gathered up therefore and filled twelve baskets with the fragments of the five barley loaves which remained over and above to them that had eaten.

14 Now those men, when they had

[2] Matt. 25, 46. [3] Matt. 3, 17; John, 1, 15. [4] Matt. 3, 17; 17, 5. [5] Deut. 4, 12. [6] 1 Cor. 4, 3. [7] Gen. 3, 15; 22, 18; 49, 10; Deut. 18, 15. CHAP. 6. [1] Matt. 14, 13; Mark, 6, 32; Luke, 9, 10.

Ver. 29. *Unto the resurrection of judgment.* That is, condemnation.

Ver. 39. Or, *You search the scriptures,* Scrutamini, ἐσευνᾶτε It is not a command for all to read the scriptures; but a reproach to the Pharisees, that reading the scriptures as they did, and thinking to find everlasting life in them, they would not receive him to whom all those scriptures gave testimony and through whom alone they could have that true life.

seen what a miracle Jesus had done said: This is of a truth the prophet that is to come into the world.

15 Jesus therefore, when he knew that they would come to take him by force and make him king, [2] fled again into the mountains, himself alone.

16 And when evening was come, his disciples went down to the sea.

17 And when they had gone up into a ship, they went over the sea to Capharnaum. And it was now dark: and Jesus was not come unto them.

18 And the sea arose, by reason of a great wind that blew.

19 When they had rowed therefore about five and twenty or thirty furlongs, they see Jesus walking upon the sea and drawing nigh to the ship. And they were afraid.

20 But he saith to them: It is I. Be not afraid.

21 They were willing therefore to take him into the ship. And presently the ship was at the land to which they were going.

22 The next day, the multitude that stood on the other side of the sea saw that there was no other ship there but one: and that Jesus had not entered into the ship with his disciples, but that his disciples were gone away alone.

23 But other ships came in from Tiberias, nigh unto the place where they had eaten the bread, the Lord giving thanks.

24 When therefore the multitude saw that Jesus was not there, nor his disciples, they took shipping and came to Capharnaum, seeking for Jesus.

25 And when they had found him on the other side of the sea, they said to him: Rabbi, when camest thou hither?

26 Jesus answered them and said: Amen, amen, I say to you, you seek me. not because you have seen miracles, but because you did eat of the loaves and were filled.

27 Labour not for the meat which perisheth, but for that which endureth unto life everlasting, which the Son of man will give you. [3] For him hath God, the Father, sealed.

28 They said therefore unto him: What shall we do, that we may work the works of God?

29 Jesus answered and said to them: [4] This is the work of God, that you believe in him whom he hath sent.

30 They said therefore to him: What sign therefore dost thou shew that we may see and may believe thee? What dost thou work?

31 Our fathers did eat manna in the desert, as it is written: [5] *He gave them bread from heaven to eat.*

32 Then Jesus said to them: Amen, amen, I say to you; Moses gave you not bread from heaven, but my Father giveth you the true bread from heaven.

33 For the bread of God is that which cometh down from heaven and giveth life to the world.

34 They said therefore unto him: Lord, give us always this bread.

35 And Jesus said to them: I am the bread of life. [6] He that cometh to me shall not hunger: and he that believeth in me shall never thirst.

36 But I said unto you that you also have seen me, and you believe not.

37 All that the Father giveth to me shall come to me: and him that cometh to me, I will not cast out.

38 Because I came down from heaven, not to do my own will but the will of him that sent me.

39 Now this is the will of the Father who sent me: that of all that he hath given me, I should lose nothing; but should raise it up again in the last day.

40 And this is the will of my Father that sent me: that every one who seeth the Son and believeth in him may have life everlasting. And I will raise him up in the last day.

41 The Jews therefore murmured at him, because he had said: I am the living bread which came down from heaven.

42 And they said: [7] Is not this Jesus, the son of Joseph, whose father and mother we know? How then saith he: I came down from heaven?

43 Jesus therefore answered and said to them: Murmur not among yourselves.

44 No man can come to me, except the Father, who hath sent me, draw him. And I will raise him up in the last day.

45 It is written in the prophets: [8] *And they shall all be taught of God.* Every one that hath heard of the Father and hath learned cometh to me.

46 [9] Not that any man hath seen the Father: but he who is of God, he hath seen the Father.

47 Amen, amen, I say unto you: He that believeth in me hath everlasting life.

48 I am the bread of life.

49 [10] Your fathers did eat manna in the desert: and are dead.

50 This is the bread which cometh

[2] Matt. 14, 23; Mark, 6, 46. [3] Matt. 3, 17; 17, 5; John, 1, 32. [4] 1 John, 3, 23. [5] Exod. 16, 14; Num. 11, 7; Ps. 77, 24; Wisd. 16, 20. [6] Ecclus. 24, 29. [7] Matt. 13, 55; Mark, 6, 3. [8] Isai. 54, 13. [9] Matt. 11, 27. [10] Exod. 16, 13.

CHAP. 6. Ver. 44. *Draw him.* Not by compulsion, nor by laying the free will under any necessity, but by the strong and sweet motions of his heavenly grace.

down from heaven: that if any man eat of it, he may not die.

51 I am the living bread which came down from heaven.

52 If any man eat of this bread, he shall live for ever: and the bread that I will give is my flesh, for the life of the world.

53 The Jews therefore strove among themselves, saying: How can this man give us his flesh to eat?

54 Then Jesus said to them: Amen, amen, I say unto you: except you eat the flesh of the Son of man and drink his blood, you shall not have life in you.

55 He that eateth my flesh and drinketh my blood hath everlasting life: and I will raise him up in the last day.

56 [11] For my flesh is meat indeed: and my blood is drink indeed.

57 He that eateth my flesh and drinketh my blood abideth in me: and I in him.

58 As the living Father hath sent me and I live by the Father: so he that eateth me, the same also shall live by me.

59 This is the bread that came down from heaven. Not as your fathers did eat manna and are dead. He that eateth this bread shall live for ever.

60 These things he said, teaching in the synagogue, in Capharnaum.

[11] 1 Cor. 11, 27. [12] John, 3, 13. [13] Matt. 16, 16; Mark, 8, 29; Luke, 9, 20. CHAP. 7. [1] Lev. 23, 34.

Ver. 54. *Except you eat.* To receive the body and blood of Christ, is a divine precept, insinuated in this text, which the faithful fulfil, though they receive but in one kind; because in one kind they receive both body and blood, which cannot be separated from each other. Hence, life eternal is here promised to the worthy receiving, though but in one kind. Ver. 52. *If any man eat of this bread, he shall live for ever; and the bread that I will give, is my flesh for the life of the world.* Ver. 58. *He that eateth me, the same also shall live by me.* Ver. 59. *He that eateth this bread shall live for ever.*

Ver. 63. *If then you shall see.* Christ in mentioning his ascension, by this instance of his power and divinity, would confirm the truth of what he had before asserted; and at the same time correct their gross apprehension of eating his flesh and drinking his blood, in a vulgar and carnal manner, by letting them know he should take his whole body living with him to heaven; and consequently not suffer it to be, as they supposed, divided, mangled and consumed upon earth.

Ver. 64. *The flesh profiteth nothing.* Dead flesh, separated from the spirit in the gross manner they supposed they were to eat his flesh, would profit nothing. Neither doth man's flesh, that is to say, man's natural and carnal apprehension (which refuses to be subject to the spirit and words of Christ), profit any thing. But it would be the height of blasphemy, to say the living flesh of Christ (which we receive in the Blessed Sacrament, with his spirit, that is, with his soul and divinity) profiteth nothing. For if Christ's flesh had profited us nothing, he would never have taken flesh for us, nor died in the flesh for us.—*Are spirit and life.* By proposing to you a heavenly sacrament, in which you shall receive, in a wonderful manner, spirit, grace and life, in its very fountain.

61 Many therefore of his disciples, hearing it, said: This saying is hard; and who can hear it?

62 But Jesus, knowing in himself that his disciples murmured at this, said to them: Doth this scandalize you?

63 If then you shall see [12] the Son of man ascend up where he was before?

64 It is the spirit that quickeneth: the flesh profiteth nothing. The words that I have spoken to you are spirit and life.

65 But there are some of you that believe not. For Jesus knew from the beginning who they were that did not believe and who he was that would betray him.

66 And he said: Therefore did I say to you that no man can come to me, unless it be given him by my Father.

67 After this, many of his disciples went back and walked no more with him.

68 Then Jesus said to the twelve: Will you also go away?

69 And Simon Peter answered him: Lord, to whom shall we go? Thou hast the words of eternal life.

70 [13] And we have believed and have known that thou art the Christ, the Son of God.

71 Jesus answered them: Have not I chosen you twelve? And one of you is a devil.

72 Now he meant Judas Iscariot, the son of Simon: for this same was about to betray him, whereas he was one of the twelve.

CHAPTER 7

Christ goes up to the feast of the tabernacles. He teaches in the temple.

AFTER these things, Jesus walked in Galilee: for he would not walk in Judea, because the Jews sought to kill him.

2 Now the Jews' feast of [1] tabernacles was at hand.

3 And his brethren said to him: Pass from hence and go into Judea, that thy disciples also may see thy works which thou dost.

4 For there is no man that doth any thing in secret, and he himself seeketh to be known openly. If thou do these things, manifest thyself to the world.

5 For neither did his brethren believe in him.

6 Then Jesus said to them: My time is not yet come; but your time is always ready.

7 The world cannot hate you: but me it hateth, because I give testimony of it, that the works thereof are evil.

8 Go you up to this festival day: but

I go not up to this festival day, because my time is not accomplished.

9 When he had said these things, he himself stayed in Galilee.

10 But after his brethren were gone up, then he also went up to the feast not openly, but, as it were, in secret.

11 The Jews therefore sought him on the festival day and said: Where is he?

12 And there was much murmuring among the multitude concerning him. For some said: He is a good man. And others said: No, but he seduceth the people.

13 Yet no man spoke openly of him, for fear of the Jews.

14 Now, about the midst of the feast, Jesus went up into the temple and taught.

15 And the Jews wondered, saying: How doth this man know letters, having never learned?

16 Jesus answered them and said: My doctrine is not mine, but his that sent me.

17 If any man will do the will of him, he shall know of the doctrine, whether it be of God, or whether I speak of myself.

18 He that speaketh of himself seeketh his own glory: but he that seeketh the glory of him that sent him, he is true and there is no injustice in him.

19 ² Did not Moses give you the law, and yet none of you keepeth the law?

20 ³ Why seek you to kill me? The multitude answered and said: Thou hast a devil. Who seeketh to kill thee?

21 Jesus answered and said to them: One work I have done: and you all wonder.

22 Therefore, ⁴ Moses gave you circumcision (not because it is of Moses, ⁵ but of the fathers): and on the sabbath day you circumcise a man.

23 If a man receive circumcision on the sabbath day, that the law of Moses may not be broken: are you angry at me, because I have healed the whole man on the sabbath day?

24 ⁶ Judge not according to the appearance: but judge just judgment.

25 Some therefore of Jerusalem said: Is not this he whom they seek to kill?

26 And behold, he speaketh openly: and they say nothing to him. Have the rulers known for a truth that this is the Christ?

27 But we know this man, whence he is: but when the Christ cometh, no man knoweth, whence he is.

28 Jesus therefore cried out in the temple, teaching and saying: You both know me, and you know whence I am. And I am not come of myself: but he

that sent me is true, whom you know not.

29 I know him, because I am from him: and he hath sent me.

30 They sought therefore to apprehend him: and no man laid hands on him, because his hour was not yet come.

31 But of the people many believed in him and said: When the Christ cometh, shall he do more miracles than this man doth? ·

32 The Pharisees heard the people murmuring these things concerning him: and the rulers and Pharisees sent ministers to apprehend him.

33 Jesus therefore said to them: Yet a little while I am with you: and then I go to him that sent me.

34 ⁷ You shall seek me and shall not find me: and where I am, thither you cannot come.

35 The Jews therefore said among themselves: Whither will he go, that we shall not find him? Will he go unto the dispersed among the Gentiles and teach the Gentiles?

36 What is this saying that he hath said: You shall seek me and shall not find me? And: Where I am, you cannot come?

37 And on the last, ⁸ and great day of the festivity, Jesus stood and cried, saying: If any man thirst, let him come to me and drink.

38 ⁹ He that believeth in me, as the scripture saith: Out of his belly shall flow rivers of living water.

39 Now this he said of the Spirit which they should receive who believed in him: for as yet the Spirit was not given, because Jesus was not yet glorified.

40 Of that multitude therefore, when they had heard these words of his, some said: This is the prophet indeed.

41 Others said: This is the Christ. But some said: Doth the Christ come out of Galilee?

42 ¹⁰ Doth not the scripture say: That Christ cometh of the seed of David and from Bethlehem the town where David was?

43 So there arose a dissension among the people because of him.

44 And some of them would have apprehended him: but no man laid hands upon him.

45 The ministers therefore came to the chief priests and the Pharisees. And they said to them: Why have you not brought him?

46 The ministers answered: Never did man speak like this man.

² Exod. 24, 3. ³ John, 5, 18. ⁴ Lev. 12, 3. ⁵ Gen. 17, 10. ⁶ Deut. 1, 16. ⁷ John, 13, 33. ⁸ Lev. 23, 27. ⁹ Deut. 18, 15; Joel, 2, 28; Acts, 2, 17. ¹⁰ Mich. 5, 2; Matt. 2, 6.

47 The Pharisees therefore answered them: Are you also seduced?

48 Hath any one of the rulers believed in him, or of the Pharisees?

49 But this multitude, that knoweth not the law, are accursed.

50 Nicodemus said to them ([11] he that came to him by night, who was one of them):

51 Doth our law judge any man, unless it first hear him [12] and know what he doth?

52 They answered and said to him: Art thou also a Galilean? Search the scriptures, and see that out of Galilee a prophet riseth not.

53 And every man returned to his own house.

CHAPTER 8

The woman taken in adultery. Christ justifies his doctrine.

ND Jesus went unto mount Olivet. 2. And early in the morning he came again into the temple: and all the people came to him. And sitting down he taught them.

3 And the scribes and Pharisees bring unto him a woman taken in adultery: and they set her in the midst,

4 And said to him: Master, this woman was even now taken in adultery.

5 [1] Now Moses in the law commanded us to stone such a one. But what sayest thou?

6 And this they said tempting him, that they might accuse him. But Jesus bowing himself down, wrote with his finger on the ground.

7 When therefore they continued asking him, he lifted up himself and said to them: [2] He that is without sin among you, let him first cast a stone at her.

8 And again stooping down, he wrote on the ground.

9 But they hearing *this*, went out one by one, beginning at the eldest. And Jesus alone remained, and the woman standing in the midst.

10 Then Jesus lifting up himself, said to her: Woman, where are they that accused thee? Hath no man condemned thee?

11 Who said: No man, Lord. And Jesus said: Neither will I condemn thee. Go, and now sin no more.

12 Again therefore, Jesus spoke to them, saying: [3] I am the light of the world. He that followeth me walketh not in darkness, but shall have the light of life.

13 The Pharisees therefore said to him: Thou givest testimony of thyself. Thy testimony is not true.

14 Jesus answered and said to them: Although I give testimony of myself, my testimony is true: for I know whence I came and whither I go.

15 You judge according to the flesh: I judge not any man.

16 And if I do judge, my judgment is true: because I am not alone, but I and the Father that sent me.

17 And in your law it is written [4] that the testimony of two men is true.

18 I am one that give testimony of myself: and the Father that sent me giveth testimony of me.

19 They said therefore to him: Where is thy Father? Jesus answered: Neither me do you know, nor my Father. If you did know me, perhaps you would know my Father also.

20 These words Jesus spoke in the treasury, teaching in the temple: and no man laid hands on him, because his hour was not yet come.

21 Again therefore Jesus said to them: I go: and you shall seek me. And you shall die in your sin. Whither I go, you cannot come.

22 The Jews therefore said: Will he kill himself, because he said: Whither I go, you cannot come?

23 And he said to them: You are from beneath: I am from above. You are of this world: I am not of this world.

24 Therefore I said to you that you shall die in your sins. For if you believe not that I am he, you shall die in your sin.

25 They said therefore to him: Who art thou? Jesus said to them: The beginning, who also speak unto you.

26 Many things I have to speak and to judge of you. But he that sent me, is [5] true: and the things I have heard of him, these same I speak in the world.

27 And they understood not that he called God his Father.

28 Jesus therefore said to them: When you shall have lifted up the Son of man, then shall you know that I am he and that I do nothing of myself. But as the Father hath taught me, these things I speak.

29 And he that sent me is with me: and he hath not left me alone. For I do always the things that please him.

30 When he spoke these things, many believed in him.

31 Then Jesus said to those Jews who believed him: If you continue in my word, you shall be my disciples indeed.

32 And you shall know the truth: and the truth shall make you free.

---

[11] John, 3, 2. [12] Deut. 17, 8; 19, 15. CHAP. 8.
[1] Lev. 20, 10. [2] Deut. 17, 7. [3] 1 John, 1, 5. [4] Deut. 17, 6; 19, 15; Matt. 18, 16; 2 Cor. 13, 1; Heb. 10, 28. [5] Rom. 3, 4.

33 They answered him: We are the seed of Abraham: and we have never been slaves to any man. How sayest thou: You shall be free?

34 Jesus answered them: Amen, amen, I say unto you [6] that whosoever committeth sin is the servant of sin.

35 Now the servant abideth not in the house for ever: but the son abideth for ever.

36 If therefore the son shall make you free, you shall be free indeed.

37 I know that you are the children of Abraham: but you seek to kill me, because my word hath no place in you.

38 I speak that which I have seen with my Father: and you do the things that you have seen with your father.

39 They answered and said to him: Abraham is our father. Jesus saith to them: If you be the children of Abraham, do the works of Abraham.

40 But now you seek to kill me, a man who have spoken the truth to you, which I have heard of God. This Abraham did not.

41 You do the works of your father. They said therefore to him: We are not born of fornication: we have one Father, *even* God.

42 Jesus therefore said to them: If God were your Father, you would indeed love me. For from God I proceeded and came. For I came not of myself: but he sent me.

43 Why do you not know my speech? Because you cannot hear my word.

44 [7] You are of *your* father the devil. and the desires of your father you will do. He was a murderer from the beginning: and he stood not in the truth, because truth is not in him. When he speaketh a lie, he speaketh of his own: for he is a liar, and the father thereof.

45 But if I say the truth, you believe me not.

46 Which of you shall convince me of sin? If I say the truth to you, why do you not believe me?

47 [8] He that is of God heareth the words of God. Therefore you hear them not, because you are not of God.

48 The Jews therefore answered and said to him: Do not we say well that thou art a Samaritan and hast a devil?

49 Jesus answered: I have not a devil: but I honour my Father. And you have dishonoured me.

50 But I seek not my own glory: there is one that seeketh and judgeth.

51 Amen, amen, I say to you: If any man keep my word, he shall not see death for ever.

52 The Jews therefore said: Now we know that thou hast a devil. Abraham

is dead, and the prophets; and thou sayest: If any man keep my word, he shall not taste death for ever.

53 Art thou greater than our father Abraham who is dead? And the prophets are dead. Whom dost thou make thyself?

54 Jesus answered: If I glorify myself, my glory is nothing. It is my Father that glorifieth me, of whom you say that he is your God.

55 And you have not known him: but I know him. And if I shall say that I know him not, I shall be like to you, a liar. But I do know him and do keep his word.

56 Abraham your father rejoiced that he might see my day: he saw it and was glad.

57 The Jews therefore said to him: Thou art not yet fifty years old. And hast thou seen Abraham?

58 Jesus said to them: Amen, amen, I say to you, before Abraham was made, I AM.

59 They took up stones therefore to cast at him. But Jesus hid himself and went out of the temple.

CHAPTER 9

He gives sight to the man born blind.

AND Jesus passing by, saw a man who was blind from his birth.

2 And his disciples asked him: Rabbi, who hath sinned, this man or his parents, that he should be born blind?

3 Jesus answered: Neither hath this man sinned, nor his parents; but that the works of God should be made manifest in him.

4 I must work the works of him that sent me, whilst it is day: the night cometh, when no man can work.

5 As long as I am in the world, I am the light of the world.

6 When he had said these things, he spat on the ground and made clay of the spittle and spread the clay upon his eyes,

7 And said to him: Go, wash in the pool of Siloe, which is interpreted, Sent. He went therefore and washed: and he came seeing.

8 The neighbours, therefore, and they who had seen him before that he was a beggar, said: Is not this he that sat and begged? Some said: This is he.

9 But others *said:* No, but he is like him. But he said: I am he.

10 They said therefore to him: How were thy eyes opened?

11 He answered: That man that is called Jesus made clay and anointed my

[6] Rom. 6, 15, 16; 2 Peter, 2, 19. [7] 1 John, 3, 8. [8] 1 John, 4, 6.

eyes and said to me: Go to the pool of Siloe and wash. And I went: I washed: and I see.

12 And they said to him: Where is he? He saith: I know not.

13 They bring him that had been blind to the Pharisees.

14 Now it was the sabbath, when Jesus made the clay and opened his eyes.

15 Again therefore the Pharisees asked him how he had received his sight. But he said to them: He put clay upon my eyes: and I washed: and I see.

16 Some therefore of the Pharisees said: This man is not of God, who keepeth not the sabbath. But others said: How can a man that is a sinner do such miracles? And there was a division among them.

17 They say therefore to the blind man again: What sayest thou of him that hath opened thy eyes? And he said: He is a prophet.

18 The Jews then did not believe concerning him, that he had been blind and had received his sight, until they called the parents of him that had received his sight,

19 And asked them, saying: Is this your son, who you say was born blind? How then doth he now see?

20 His parents answered them and said: We know that this is our son and that he was born blind:

21 But how he now seeth, we know not; or who hath opened his eyes, we know not. Ask himself: he is of age. Let him speak for himself.

22 These things his parents said, because they feared the Jews: for the Jews had already agreed among themselves that if any man should confess him to be Christ, he should be put out of the synagogue.

23 Therefore did his parents say: He is of age. Ask himself.

24 They therefore called the man again that had been blind and said to him: Give glory to God. We know that this man is a sinner.

25 He said therefore to them: If he be a sinner, I know not. One thing I know, that whereas I was blind, now I see.

26 They said then to him: What did he to thee? How did he open thy eyes?

27 He answered them: I have told you already, and you have heard. Why would you hear it again? Will you also become his disciples?

28 They reviled him therefore and said: Be thou his disciple; but we are the disciples of Moses.

29 We know that God spoke to Moses: but as to this man, we know not from whence he is.

30 The man answered and said to them: Why, herein is a wonderful thing, that you know not from whence he is, and he hath opened my eyes.

31 Now we know that God doth not hear sinners: but if a man be a server of God and doth his will, him he heareth.

32 From the beginning of the world it hath not been heard, that any man hath opened the eyes of one born blind.

33 Unless this man were of God, he could not do anything.

34 They answered and said to him: Thou wast wholly born in sins; and dost thou teach us? And they cast him out.

35 Jesus heard that they had cast him out. And when he had found him, he said to him: Dost thou believe in the Son of God?

36 He answered, and said: Who is he, Lord, that I may believe in him?

37 And Jesus said to him: Thou hast both seen him; and it is he that talketh with thee.

38 And he said: I believe, Lord. And falling down, he adored him.

39 And Jesus said: For judgment I am come into this world; that they who see not may see; and they who see may become blind.

40 And some of the Pharisees, who were with him, heard: and they said unto him: Are we also blind?

41 Jesus said to them: If you were blind, you should not have sin: but now you say: We see. Your sin remaineth.

CHAPTER 10

Christ is the door and the good shepherd. He and his Father are one.

AMEN, amen, I say to you: He that entereth not by the door into the sheepfold but climbeth up another way, the same is a thief and a robber.

2 But he that entereth in by the door is the shepherd of the sheep.

3 To him the porter openeth: and the sheep hear his voice. And he calleth his own sheep by name and leadeth them out.

4 And when he hath let out his own sheep, he goeth before them: and the

CHAP. 9. Ver. 39. *I am come.* Not that Christ came for that end, that any one should be made blind: but that the Jews, by the abuse of his coming, and by their not receiving him, brought upon themselves this judgment of blindness.

Ver. 41. *If you were blind.* If you were invincibly ignorant and had neither read the scriptures, nor seen my miracles, you would not be guilty of the sin of infidelity: but now, as you boast of your knowledge of the scriptures, you are inexcusable.

sheep follow him, because they know his voice.

5 But a stranger they follow not, but fly from him, because they know not the voice of strangers.

6 This proverb Jesus spoke to them. But they understood not what he spoke to them.

7 Jesus therefore said to them again: Amen, amen, I say to you, I am the door of the sheep.

8 All *others*, as many as have come, are thieves and robbers: and the sheep heard them not.

9 In am the door. By me, if any man enter in, he shall be saved: and he shall go in and go out, and shall find pastures.

10 The thief cometh not, but for to steal and to kill and to destroy. I am come that they may have life and may have it more abundantly.

11 I am the good shepherd. [1] The good shepherd giveth his life for his sheep.

12 But the hireling and he that is not the shepherd, whose own the sheep are not, seeth the wolf coming and leaveth the sheep and flieth: and the wolf catcheth and scattereth the sheep.

13 And the hireling flieth, because he is a hireling: and he hath no care for the sheep.

14 I am the good shepherd: and I know mine, and mine know me.

15 [2] As the Father knoweth me, and I know the Father: and I lay down my life for my sheep.

16 And other sheep I have that are not of this fold: them also I must bring. And they shall hear my voice: and there shall be one fold and one shepherd.

17 Therefore doth the Father love me: [3] because I lay down my life, that I may take it again.

18 No man taketh it away from me: but I lay it down of myself. And I have power to lay it down: and I have power to take it up again. This commandment have I received of my Father.

19 A dissension rose again among the Jews for these words.

20 And many of them said: He hath a devil and is mad. Why hear you him?

21 Others said: These are not the words of one that hath a devil. Can a devil open the eyes of the blind?

22 [4] And it was the feast of the dedication at Jerusalem: and it was winter.

23 And Jesus walked in the temple, in Solomon's porch.

24 The Jews therefore came round about him and said to him: How long dost thou hold our souls in suspense? If thou be the Christ, tell us plainly.

25 Jesus answered them: I speak to you, and you believe not: the works that I do in the name of my Father, they give testimony of me.

26 But you do not believe, because you are not of my sheep.

27 My sheep hear my voice. And I know them: and they follow me.

28 And I give them life everlasting: and they shall not perish for ever. And no man shall pluck them out of my hand.

29 That which my Father hath given me is greater than all: and no one can snatch *them* out of the hand of the Father.

30 I and the Father are ONE.

31 The Jews then took up stones to stone him.

32 Jesus answered them: Many good works I have shewed you from my Father. For which of those works do you stone me?

33 The Jews answered him: For a good work we stone thee not, but for blasphemy; and because that thou, being a man, makest thyself God.

34 Jesus answered them: Is it not written in your law: [5] *I said, you are gods?*

35 If he called them gods to whom the word of God was spoken; and the scripture cannot be broken:

36 Do you say of him whom the Father hath sanctified and sent into the world: Thou blasphemest; because I said: I am the Son of God?

37 If I do not the works of my Father, believe me not.

38 But if I do, though you will not believe me, believe the works: that you may know and believe that the Father is in me and I in the Father.

39 They sought therefore to take him: and he escaped out of their hands.

40 And he went again beyond the Jordan, into that place where John was baptizing first. And there he abode.

41 And many resorted to him: and they said: John indeed did no sign.

42 But all things whatsoever John said of this man were true. And many believed in him.

CHAPTER 11

Christ raises Lazarus to life. The rulers resolve to put him to death.

NOW there was a certain man sick, named Lazarus, of Bethania, of the town of Mary and of Martha her sister.

CHAP. 10. [1] Isai. 40, 11; Ezech. 34, 23; 37, 24. [2] Matt. 11, 27; Luke, 10, 22. [3] Isai. 53, 7. [4] 1 Mach. 4, 56, 59. [5] Ps. 81, 6.

CHAP. 10. VER. 30. *I and the Father are one.* That is, one Divine Nature, but two distinct Persons.

2 (And Mary was she [1] that anointed the Lord with ointment and wiped his feet with her hair: whose brother Lazarus was sick.)

3 His sisters therefore sent to him, saying: Lord, behold, he whom thou lovest is sick.

4 And Jesus hearing it, said to them: This sickness is not unto death, but for the glory of God: that the Son of God may be glorified by it.

5 Now Jesus loved Martha and her sister Mary and Lazarus.

6 When he had heard therefore that he was sick, he still remained in the same place two days.

7 Then after that, he said to his disciples: Let us go into Judea again.

8 The disciples say to him: Rabbi, the Jews but now sought to stone thee. And goest thou thither again?

9 Jesus answered: Are there not twelve hours of the day? If a man walk in the day, he stumbleth not, because he seeth the light of this world:

10 But if he walk in the night, he stumbleth, because the light is not in him.

11 These things he said; and after that he said to them: Lazarus our friend sleepeth; but I go that I may awake him out of sleep.

12 His disciples therefore said: Lord, if he sleep, he shall do well.

13 But Jesus spoke of his death; and they thought that he spoke of the repose of sleep.

14 Then therefore Jesus said to them plainly: Lazarus is dead.

15 And I am glad, for your sakes, that I was not there, that you may believe. But, let us go to him.

16 Thomas therefore, who is called Didymus, said to his fellow disciples Let us also go, that we may die with him.

17 Jesus therefore came: and found that he had been four days already in the grave.

18 (Now Bethania was near Jerusalem, about fifteen furlongs off.)

19 And many of the Jews were come to Martha and Mary, to comfort them concerning their brother.

20 Martha therefore, as soon as she heard that Jesus was come, went to meet him: but Mary sat at home.

21 Martha therefore said to Jesus: Lord, if thou hadst been here, my brother had not died.

22 But now also I know that whatsoever thou wilt ask of God, God will give it thee.

CHAP. 11. [1] Matt. 26, 7; Luke 7, 37; John, 12. 3. [2] Luke, 14, 14; John, 5, 29. [3] John, 6, 40. [4] John, 9, 6.

23 Jesus saith to her: Thy brother shall rise again.

24 Martha saith to him: I know that he shall rise again, [2] in the resurrection at the last day.

25 Jesus said to her: I am the resurrection and the life: [3] he that believeth in me, although he be dead, shall live:

26 And every one that liveth and believeth in me shall not die for ever. Believest thou this?

27 She saith to him: Yea, Lord, I have believed that thou art Christ, the Son of the living God, who art come into this world.

28 And when she had said these things, she went and called her sister Mary secretly, saying: The master is come and calleth for thee.

29 She, as soon as she heard this, riseth quickly and cometh to him.

30 For Jesus was not yet come into the town: but he was still in that place where Martha had met him.

31 The Jews therefore, who were with her in the house and comforted her, when they saw Mary, that she rose up speedily and went out, followed her, saying: She goeth to the grave to weep there.

32 When Mary therefore was come where Jesus was, seeing him, she fell down at his feet and saith to him: Lord, if thou hadst been here, my brother had not died.

33 Jesus, therefore, when he saw her weeping, and the Jews that were come with her weeping, groaned in the spirit and troubled himself,

34 And said: Where have you laid him? They say to him: Lord, come and see.

35 And Jesus wept.

36 The Jews therefore said: Behold how he loved him.

37 But some of them said: [4] Could not he that opened the eyes of the man born blind have caused that this man should not die?

38 Jesus therefore again groaning in himself, cometh to the sepulchre. Now it was a cave; and a stone was laid over it.

39 Jesus saith: Take away the stone. Martha, the sister of him that was dead, saith to him: Lord, by this time he stinketh, for he is now of four days.

40 Jesus saith to her: Did not I say to thee that if thou believe, thou shalt see the glory of God?

41 They took therefore the stone away. And Jesus lifting up his eyes, said: Father, I give thee thanks that thou hast heard me.

42 And I knew that thou hearest me

always; but because of the people who stand about have I said it, that they may believe that thou hast sent me.

43 When he had said these things, he cried with a loud voice: Lazarus, come forth.

44 And presently he that had been dead came forth, bound feet and hands with winding bands. And his face was bound about with a napkin. Jesus said to them: Loose him and let him go.

45 Many therefore of the Jews, who were come to Mary and Martha and had seen the things that Jesus did, believed in him.

46 But some of them went to the Pharisees and told them the things that Jesus had done.

47 The chief priests, therefore, and the Pharisees gathered a council and said: What do we, for this man doth many miracles?

48 If we let him alone so, all will believe in him; and the Romans will come, and take away our place and nation.

49 [5] But one of them, named Caiphas, being the high priest that year, said to them: You know nothing.

50 Neither do you consider that it is expedient for you that one man should die for the people and that the whole nation perish not.

51 And this he spoke not of himself: but being the high priest of that year, he prophesied that Jesus should die for the nation.

52 And not only for the nation, but to gather together in one the children of God that were dispersed.

53 From that day therefore they devised to put him to death.

54 Wherefore Jesus walked no more openly among the Jews: but he went into a country near the desert, unto a city that is called Ephrem. And there he abode with his disciples.

55 And the pasch of the Jews was at hand: and many from the country went up to Jerusalem, before the pasch, to purify themselves.

56 They sought therefore for Jesus: and they discoursed one with another, standing in the temple: What think you that he is not come to the festival day? And the chief priests and Pharisees had given a commandment that, if any man knew where he was, he should tell, that they might apprehend him.

CHAPTER 12

The anointing of Christ's feet. His riding into Jerusalem upon an ass. A voice from heaven.

JESUS [1] therefore, six days before the pasch, came to Bethania, where Lazarus had been dead, whom Jesus raised to life.

2 And they made him a supper there: and Martha served. But Lazarus was one of them that were at table with him.

3 Mary therefore took a pound of ointment of right spikenard, of great price, and anointed the feet of Jesus and wiped his feet with her hair. And the house was filled with the odour of the ointment.

4 Then one of his disciples, Judas Iscariot, he that was about to betray him, said:

5 Why was not this ointment sold for three hundred pence and given to the poor?

6 Now he said this, not because he cared for the poor; but because he was a thief and, having the purse, carried the things that were put therein.

7 Jesus therefore said: Let her alone, that she may keep it against the day of my burial.

8 For the poor you have always with you: but me you have not always.

9 A great multitude therefore of the Jews knew that he was there; and they came, not for Jesus' sake only, but that they might see Lazarus, whom he had raised from the dead.

10 But the chief priests thought to kill Lazarus also:

11 Because many of the Jews, by reason of him, went away and believed in Jesus.

12 And on the next day, a great multitude that was come to the festival day, when they had heard that Jesus was coming to Jerusalem,

13 Took branches of palm trees and went forth to meet him and cried: Hosanna. Blessed is he that cometh in the name of the Lord, the king of Israel.

14 [2] And Jesus found a young ass and sat upon it, as it is written:

15 *Fear not, daughter of Sion: behold, thy king cometh, sitting on an ass's colt.*

16 These things his disciples did not know at the first: but when Jesus was glorified, then they remembered that these things were written of him and that they had done these things to him.

17 The multitude therefore gave testimony, which was with him, when he called Lazarus out of the grave and raised him from the dead.

18 For which reason also the people

[5] John, 18, 14. CHAP. 12. [1] Matt. 26, 6; Mark, 14, 3. [2] Zach. 9, 9; Mark, 11, 7; Luke, 19, 35.

CHAP. 12. Ver. 8. *For the poor.* (See the annotation on Matt. 26, 11.)

came to meet him, because they heard that he had done this miracle.

19 The Pharisees therefore said among themselves: Do you see that we prevail nothing? Behold, the whole world is gone after him.

20 Now there were certain Gentiles among them, who came up to adore on the festival day.

21 These therefore came to Philip, who was of Behsaida of Galilee, and desired him, saying: Sir, we would see Jesus.

22 Philip cometh and telleth Andrew. Again Andrew and Philip told Jesus.

23 But Jesus answered them, saying: The hour is come that the Son of man should be glorified.

24 Amen, amen, I say to you, unless the grain of wheat falling into the ground die,

25 Itself remaineth alone. But if it die it bringeth forth much fruit. ³ He that loveth his life shall lose it and he that hateth his life in this world keepeth it unto life eternal.

26 If any man minister to me, let him follow me: and where I am, there also shall my minister be. If any man minister to me, him will my Father honour.

27 Now is my soul troubled. And what shall I say? Father, save me from this hour. But for this cause I came unto this hour.

28 Father, glorify thy name. A voice therefore came from heaven: I have both glorified and will glorify it again.

29 The multitude therefore that stood and heard said that it thundered. Others said: An angel spoke to him.

30 Jesus answered and said: This voice came not because of me, but for your sakes.

31 Now is the judgment of the world: now shall the prince of this world be cast out.

32 And I, if I be lifted up from the earth, will draw all things to myself.

33 (Now this he said, signifying what death he should die.)

34 The multitude answered him: We have heard ⁴ out of the law that Christ abideth for ever. And how sayest thou: The Son of man must be lifted up? Who is this Son of man?

35 Jesus therefore said to them: Yet a little while, the light is among you. Walk whilst you have the light, and the darkness overtake you not. And he that walketh in darkness knoweth not whither be goeth.

36 Whilst you have the light, believe in the light, that you may be the children of light. These things Jesus spoke: and he went away and hid himself from them.

37 And whereas he had done so many miracles before them, they believed not in him:

38 That the saying of Isaias the prophet might be fulfilled, which he said: ⁵ Lord, who hath believed our hearing? And to whom hath the arm of the Lord been revealed?

39 Therefore they could not believe, because Isaias said again:

40 ⁶ He hath blinded their eyes and hardened their heart, that they should not see with their eyes, nor understand with their heart and be converted: and I should heal them.

41 These things said Isaias, when he saw his glory and spoke of him.

42 However, many of the chief men also believed in him; but because of the Pharisees they did not confess him, that they might not be cast out of the synagogue.

43 For they loved the glory of men more than the glory of God.

44 But Jesus cried and said: He that believeth in me doth not believe in me, but in him that sent me.

45 And he that seeth me, seeth him that sent me.

46 I am come, a light into the world, that whosoever believeth in me may not remain in darkness.

47 And if any man hear my words and keep them not, I do not judge him: for I came not to judge the world, but to save the world.

48 He that despiseth me and receiveth not my words hath one that judgeth him. The word that I have spoken, the same shall judge him in the last day.

49 For I have not spoken of myself: but the Father who sent me, he gave me commandment what I should say and what I should speak.

50 And I know that his commandment is life everlasting. The things therefore that I speak, even as the Father said unto me, so do I speak.

CHAPTER 13

Christ washes his disciples' feet. The treason of Judas. The new commandment of love.

---

³ Matt. 10, 39; 16, 25; Mark, 8, 35; Luke, 9, 24; 17, 33. ⁴ Ps. 109, 4; 116, 2; Isai. 40, 8; Ezech. 37, 25. ⁵ Isai. 53, 1; Rom. 10, 16. ⁶ Isai. 6, 9; Matt. 13, 14; Mark, 4, 12; Luke, 8, 10; Acts, 28, 26; Rom. 11, 8.

Ver. 39. *They could not believe.* Because they would not, saith St. Augustine (Tract, 33, in Joan.). (See the annotation, Mark, 4, 12).

BEFORE [1] the festival day of the pasch, Jesus knowing that his hour was come, that he should pass out of this world to the Father: having loved his own who were in the world, he loved them unto the end.

2 And when supper was done (the devil having now put into the heart of Judas Iscariot, the son of Simon, to betray him),

3 Knowing that the Father had given him all things into his hands and that he came from God and goeth to God,

4 He riseth from supper and layeth aside his garments and, having taken a towel, girded himself.

5 After that, he putteth water into a basin and began to wash the feet of the disciples and to wipe them with the towel wherewith he was girded.

6 He cometh therefore to Simon Peter. And Peter saith to him: Lord, dost thou wash my feet?

7 Jesus answered and said to him: What I do, thou knowest not now; but that shalt know hereafter.

8 Peter saith to him: Thou shalt never wash my feet, Jesus answered him: If I wash thee not, thou shalt have no part with me.

9 Simon Peter saith to him: Lord, not only my feet, but also my hands and my head.

10 Jesus saith to him: He that is washed needeth not but to wash his feet, but is clean wholly. And you are clean, but not all.

11 For he knew who he was that would betray him; therefore he said: You are not all clean.

12 Then after he had washed their feet and taken his garments, being set down again, he said to them: Know you what I have done to you?

13 You call me Master and Lord. And you say well: for so I am.

14 If then I being *your* Lord and Master, have washed your feet; you also ought to wash one another's feet.

15 For I have given you an example, that as I have done to you, so you do also.

16 [2] Amen, amen, I say to you: The servant is not greater than his lord: neither is the apostle greater than he that sent him.

17 If you know these things, you shall be blessed if you do them.

18 I speak not of you all: I know whom I have chosen. But that the scripture may be fulfilled: [3] *He that eateth bread with me shall lift up his heel against me.*

19 At present I tell you, before it come to pass: that when it shall come to pass, you may believe that I am he.

20 ' Amen, amen, I say to you, he that receiveth whomsoever I send receiveth me: and he that receiveth me receiveth him that sent me.

21 When Jesus had said these things, he was troubled in spirit; and he testified, and said: [5] Amen, amen, I say to you, one of you shall betray me.

22 The disciples therefore looked one upon another, doubting of whom he spoke.

23 Now there was leaning on Jesus' bosom one of his disciples, whom Jesus loved.

24 Simon Peter therefore beckoned to him and said to him: Who is it of whom he speaketh?

25 He therefore, leaning on the breast of Jesus, saith to him: Lord, who is it?

26 Jesus answered: He it is to whom I shall reach bread dipped. And when he had dipped the bread, he gave it to Judas Iscariot, *the son* of Simon.

27 And after the morsel, Satan entered into him. And Jesus said to him: That which thou dost, do quickly.

28 Now no man at the table knew to what purpose he said this unto him.

29 For some thought, because Judas had the purse, that Jesus had said to him: Buy those things which we have need of for the festival day: or that he should give something to the poor.

30 He therefore, having received the morsel, went out immediately. And it was night.

31 When he therefore was gone out, Jesus said: Now is the Son of man glorified; and God is glorified in him.

32 If God be glorified in him, God also will glorify him in himself: and immediately will he glorify him.

33 Little children, yet a little while I am with you. [6] You shall seek me. And as I said to the Jews: Whither I go you cannot come; so I say to you now.

CHAP. 13. [1] Matt. 26, 2; Mark, 14, 1; Luke, 22, 1. [2] Matt. 10, 24; Luke, 6, 40; John, 15, 20. [3] Ps. 40, 10. [4] Matt. 10, 40; Luke, 10, 16. [5] Matt. 26, 21; Mark, 14, 18; Luke, 22, 21. [6] John, 7, 34.

CHAP. 13. Ver. 1. *Before the festival day of the pasch.* This was the fourth and last pasch of the ministry of Christ, and according to the common computation, was in the thirty-third year of our Lord: and in the year of the world 4036. Some chronologers are of opinion that our Saviour suffered in the thirty-seventh year of his age: but these different opinions on this subject are of no consequence.

Ver. 27. *That which thou dost, do quickly.* It is not a license, much less a command, to go about his treason: but a signification to him that Christ would not hinder or resist what he was about, do it as soon as he pleased: but was both ready and desirous to suffer for our redemption.

34 [7] A new commandment I give unto you: That you love one another, as I have loved you, that you also love one another.

35 By this shall all men know that you are my disciples, if you have love one for another.

36 Simon Peter saith to him: Lord, whither goest thou? Jesus answered: Whither I go, thou canst not follow me now: but thou shalt follow hereafter.

37 Peter saith to him: Why cannot I follow thee now? [8] I will lay down my life for thee.

38 Jesus answered him: Wilt thou lay down thy life for me? Amen, amen, I say to thee, the cock shall not crow, till thou deny me thrice.

CHAPTER 14

Christ's discourse after his last supper.

LET not your heart be troubled. You believe in God: believe also in me.

2 In my Father's house there are many mansions. If not, I would have told you: because I go to prepare a place for you.

3 And if I shall go and prepare a place for you, I will come again and will take you to myself: that where I am, you also may be.

4 And whither I go you know: and the way you know.

5 Thomas saith to him: Lord, we know not whither thou goest. And how can we know the way?

6 Jesus saith to him: I am the way, and the truth, and the life. No man cometh to the Father, but by me.

7 If you had known me, you would without doubt have known my Father also: and from henceforth you shall know him. And you have seen him.

8 Philip saith to him: Lord, shew us the Father; and it is enough for us.

9 Jesus saith to him: Have I been so long a time with you and have you not known me? Philip, he that seeth me seeth the Father also. How sayest thou: Shew us the Father?

10 Do you not believe that I am in the Father and the Father in me? The

[7] Lev. 19, 18; Matt. 22, 39; John, 15, 12. [8] Matt. 26, 35; Mark, 14, 29; Luke, 22,33. CHAP. 14. [1] Matt. 7, 7; 21, 22; Mark, 11, 24; John, 16, 23.

CHAP. 14. Ver. 16. *Paraclete.* That is, a comforter: or also an advocate; inasmuch as by inspiring prayer, he prays, as it were, in us and pleads for us.—*For ever.* Hence it is evident that this Spirit of truth was not only promised to the persons of the apostles, but also to their successors through all generations.
Ver. 26. *Teach you all things.* Here the Holy Ghost is promised to the apostls and their successors, particularly, in order to teach them all truth and to preserve them from error.

words that I speak to you, I speak not of myself. But the Father who abideth in me, he doth the works.

11 Believe you not that I am in the Father and the Father in me?

12 Otherwise believe for the very works' sake. Amen, amen, I say to you, he that believeth in me, the works that I do, he also shall do: and greater than these shall he do.

13 Because I go to the Father: [1] and whatsoever you shall ask the Father in my name, that will I do: that the Father may be glorified in the Son.

14 If you shall ask me any thing in my name, that I will do.

15 If you love me, keep my commandments.

16 And I will ask the Father: and he shall give you another Paraclete, that he may abide with you for ever:

17 The spirit of truth, whom the world cannot receive, because it seeth him not, nor knoweth him. But you shall know him; because he shall abide with you and shall be in you.

18 I will not leave you orphans: I will come to you.

19 Yet a little while and the world seeth me no more. But you see me: because I live, and you shall live.

20 In that day you shall know that I am in my Father: and you in me, and I in you.

21 He that hath my commandments and keepeth them; he it is that loveth me. And he that loveth me shall be loved of my Father: and I will love him and will manifest myself to him.

22 Judas saith to him, not the Iscariot: Lord, how is it that thou wilt manifest thyself to us, and not to the world?

23 Jesus answered and said to him: If any one love me, he will keep my word. And my Father will love him: and we will come to him and will make our abode with him.

24 He that loveth me not keepeth not my words. And the word which you have heard is not mine; but the Father's who sent me.

25 These things have I spoken to you, abiding with you.

26 But the Paraclete, the Holy Ghost, whom the Father will send in my name, he will teach you all things and bring all things to your mind, whatsoever I shall have said to you.

27 Peace I leave with you: my peace I give unto you: not as the world giveth, do I give unto you. Let not your heart be troubled: nor let it be afraid.

28 You have heard that I said to you: I go away, and I come unto you. If you loved me, you would indeed be glad,

because I go to the Father: for the Father is greater than I.

29 And now I have told you before it come to pass: that when it shall come to pass, you may believe.

30 I will not now speak many things with you. For the prince of this world cometh: and in me he hath not any thing.

31 But that the world may know that I love the Father: [2] and as the Father hath given me commandments, so do I. Arise, let us go hence.

CHAPTER 15

A continuation of Christ's discourse to his disciples.

I AM the true vine: and my Father is the husbandman.

2 Every branch in me that beareth not fruit, he will take away: and every one that beareth fruit, he will purge it, that it may bring forth more fruit.

3 [1] Now you are clean, by reason of the word which I have spoken to you.

4 Abide in me: and I in you. As the branch cannot bear fruit of itself, unless it abide in the vine, so neither can you, unless you abide in me.

5 I am the vine: you the branches. He that abideth in me, and I in him, the same beareth much fruit: for without me you can do nothing.

6 If any one abide not in me, he shall be cast forth as a branch and shall wither: and they shall gather him up and cast him into the fire: and he burneth.

7 If you abide in me and my words abide in you, you shall ask whatever you will: and it shall be done unto you.

8 In this is my Father glorified: that you bring forth very much fruit and become my disciples.

9 As the Father hath loved me, I also have loved you. Abide in my love.

10 If you keep my commandments, you shall abide in my love: as I also have kept my Father's commandments and do abide in his love.

11 These things I have spoken to you, that my joy may be in you, and your joy may be filled.

12 [2] This is my commandment, that you love one another, as I have loved you.

13 Greater love than this no man hath, that a man lay down his life for his friends.

14 You are my friends, if you do the things that I command you.

15 I will not now call you servants: for the servant knoweth not what his lord doth. But I have called you friends: because all things, whatsoever

I have heard of my Father, I have made known to you.

16 You have not chosen me: but I have chosen you; and have appointed you, [3] that you should go and should bring forth fruit; and your fruit should remain: that whatsoever you shall ask of the Father in my name, he may give it you.

17 [4] These things I command you, that you love one another.

18 If the world hate you, know ye that it hath hated me before you.

19 If you had been of the world, the world would love its own: but because you are not of the world, but I have chosen you out of the world, therefore the world hateth you.

20 Remember my word that I said to you: [5] The servant is not greater than his master. If they have persecuted me, [6] they will also persecute you. If they have kept my word, they will keep yours also.

21 But all these things they will do to you for my name's sake: because they know not him that sent me.

22 If I had not come and spoken to them, they would not have sin: but now they have no excuse for their sin.

23 He that hateth me hateth my Father also.

24 If I had not done among them the works that no other man hath done, they would not have sin: but now they have both seen and hated both me and my Father.

25 But that the word may be fulfilled which is written in their law: [7] *they hated me without cause.*

26 [8] But when the Paraclete cometh, whom I will send you from the Father, the Spirit of truth, who proceedeth from the Father, he shall give testimony of me.

27 And you shall give testimony, be-

[2] Acts, 2, 23. CHAP. 15. [1] John, 13, 10. [2] John, 13, 34; Eph. 5, 2; 1 Thess. 4, 9. [3] Matt. 28, 19. [4] 1 John, 3, 11; 4, 7. [5] Matt. 10, 24; John, 13, 16. [6] Matt. 24, 9. [7] Ps. 24, 19. [8] Luke, 24, 49.

Ver. 28. *For the Father is greater than I.* It is evident, that Christ our Lord speaks here of himself as he is made man: for as God he is equal to the Father (Phil. 2). Any difficulty of understanding the meaning of these words will vanish, when the relative circumstances of the text here are considered: for Christ, being at this time shortly to suffer death, signified to his apostles his human nature by these very words: for as God he could not die. And therefore as he was both God and man, it must follow that according to his humanity he was to die, which the apostles were soon to see and believe, as he expresses (ver. 29). *And now I have told you before it come to pass: that when it shall come to pass, you may believe.*

CHAP. 15. Ver. 26. *Whom I will send.* This proves, against the modern Greeks, that the Holy Ghost proceedeth from the Son, as well as from the Father: otherwise he could not be sent by the Son.

cause you are with me from the beginning.

CHAPTER 16

The conclusion of Christ's last discourse to his disciples.

THESE things have I spoken to you, that you may not be scandalized.

2 They will put you out of the synagogues: yea, the hour cometh, that whosoever killeth you will think that he doth a service to God.

3 And these things will they do to you; because they have not known the Father nor me.

4 But these things I have told you, that when the hour shall come, you may remember that I told you of them.

5 But I told you not these things from the beginning, because I was with you. And now I go to him that sent me, and none of you asketh me: Whither goest thou?

6 But because I have spoken these things to you, sorrow hath filled your heart.

7 But I tell you the truth: it is expedient to you that I go. For if I go not, the Paraclete will not come to you: but if I go, I will send him to you.

8 And when he is come, he will convince the world of sin and of justice and of judgment.

9 Of sin: because they believed not in me.

10 And of justice: because I go to the Father: and you shall see me no longer.

11 And of judgment: because the prince of this world is already judged.

12 I have yet many things to say to you: but you cannot bear them now.

13 But when he, the Spirit of truth, is come, he will teach you all truth. For he shall not speak of himself: but what things soever he shall hear, he shall speak. And the things that are to come, he shall shew you.

14 He shall glorify me: because he shall receive of mine and shall shew *it* to you.

15 All things whatsoever the Father hath are mine. Therefore I said that he shall receive of mine and shew *it* to you.

16 A little while, and now you shall

not see me: and again a little while, and you shall see me: because I go to the Father.

17 Then some of his disciples said one to another: What is this that he saith to us: A little while, and you shall not see me; and again a little while, and you shall see me, and, Because I go to the Father?

18 They said therefore: What is this that he saith, A little while? We know not what he speaketh.

19 And Jesus knew that they had a mind to ask him. And he said to them: Of this do you inquire among yourselves, because I said: A little while, and you shall not see me; and again a little while, and you shall see me?

20 Amen, amen, I say to you, that you shall lament and weep, but the world shall rejoice: and you shall be made sorrowful, but your sorrow shall be turned into joy.

21 A woman, when she is in labour, hath sorrow, because her hour is come; but when she hath brought forth the child, she remembereth no more the anguish, for joy that a man is born into the world.

22 So also you now indeed have sorrow: but I will see you again and your heart shall rejoice. And your joy no man shall take from you.

23 And in that day you shall not ask me any thing. [1] Amen, amen, I say to you: if you ask the Father any thing in my name, he will give it you.

24 Hitherto, you have not asked any thing in my name. Ask, and you shall receive; that your joy may be full.

25 These things I have spoken to you in proverbs. The hour cometh when I will no more speak to'you in proverbs, but will shew you plainly of the Father.

26 In that day, you shall ask in my name: and I say not to you that I will ask the Father for you.

27 For the Father himself loveth you, because you have loved me and have believed that I came out from God.

28 I came forth from the Father and am come into the world: again I leave the world and I go to the Father.

29 His disciples say to him: Behold, now thou speakest plainly and speakest no proverb.

30 Now we know that thou knowest all things and thou needest not that any man should ask thee. By this we believe that thou camest forth from God.

31 Jesus answered them: Do you now believe?

32 [2] Behold, the hour cometh, and it is now come, that you shall be scat-

CHAP. 16. [1] Matt. 7, 7; 21, 22; Mark, 11, 24; Luke, 11, 9; John, 14, 13; James, 1, 5. [2] Matt. 26, 31; Mark, 14, 27.

CHAP. 16. Ver. 8. *He will convince the world of sin.* The Holy Ghost, by his coming, brought over many thousands, first, to a sense of their sin in not believing in Christ. Secondly, to a conviction of the justice of Christ, now sitting at the right hand of his Father. And thirdly, to a right apprehension of the judgment prepared for them that choose to follow Satan, who is already judged and condemned.

Ver. 13. *Will teach you all truth.* (See the annotation on chap. 14, ver. 26).

tered every man to his own and shall leave me alone. And yet I am not alone, because the Father is with me.

33 These things I have spoken to you, that in me you may have peace In the world you shall have distress But have confidence. I have overcome the world.

CHAPTER 17

Christ's prayer for his disciples.

THESE things Jesus spoke: and lifting up his eyes to heaven, he said: Father, the hour is come. Glorify thy Son, that thy Son may glorify thee.

2 ¹ As thou hast given him power over all flesh, that he may give eternal life to all whom thou hast given him.

3 Now this is eternal life: That they may know thee, the only true God, and Jesus Christ, whom thou hast sent.

4 I have glorified thee on the earth: I have finished the work which thou gavest me to do.

5 And now glorify thou me, O Father, with thyself, with the glory which I had, before the world was, with thee.

6 I have manifested thy name to the men whom thou hast given me out of the world. Thine they were: and to me thou gavest them. And they have kept thy word.

7 Now they have known that all things which thou hast given me are from thee:

8 Because the words which thou gavest me, I have given to them. And they have received them and have known in very deed that I came out from thee: and they have believed that thou didst send me.

9 I pray for them. I pray not for the world, but for them whom thou hast given me: because they are thine.

10 And all my things are thine, and thine are mine: and I am glorified in them.

11 And now I am not in the world, and these are in the world, and I come to thee. Holy Father, keep them in thy name whom thou hast given me: that they may be one, as we also are.

12 While I was with them, I kept them in thy name. ² Those whom thou gavest me have I kept: and none of them is lost, but the son of perdition ³ that the scripture may be fulfilled.

13 And now I come to thee: and these things I speak in the world, that they may have my joy filled in themselves.

14 I have given them thy word, and the world hath hated them: because they are not of the world, as I also am not of the world.

15 I pray not that thou shouldst take

them out of the world, but that thou shouldst keep them from evil.

16 They are not of the world, as I also am not of the world.

17 Sanctify them in truth. Thy word is truth.

18 As thou hast sent me into the world, I also have sent them into the world.

19 And for them do I sanctify myself, that they also may be sanctified in truth.

20 And not for them only do I pray, but for them also who through their word shall believe in me.

21 That they all may be one, as thou, Father, in me, and I in thee; that they also may be one in us: that the world may believe that thou hast sent me.

22 And the glory which thou hast given me, I have given to them: that they may be one, as we also are one.

23 I in them, and thou in me: that they may be made perfect in one: and the world may know that thou hast sent me and hast loved them, as thou hast also loved me.

24 Father, I will that where I am, they also whom thou hast given me may be with me: that they may see my glory which thou hast given me, because thou hast loved me before the creation of the world.

25 Just Father, the world hath not known thee: but I have known thee. And these have known that thou hast sent me.

26 And I have made known thy name to them and will make it known: that the love wherewith thou hast loved me may be in them, and I in them.

CHAPTER 18

The history of the passion of Christ.

WHEN ¹ Jesus had said these things, he went forth with his disciples over the brook Cedron, where there was a garden, into which he entered with his disciples.

2 And Judas also, who betrayed him, knew the place: because Jesus had often resorted thither together with his disciples.

3 ² Judas therefore having received a band of soldiers and servants from the chief priests and the Pharisees, cometh thither with lanterns and torches and weapons.

4 Jesus therefore, knowing all things that should come upon him, went forth and said to them: Whom seek ye?

5 They answered him: Jesus of Naz-

CHAP. 17. ¹ Matt. 28, 18. ² John, 18, 9. ³ Ps. 108, 8.
CHAP. 18. ¹ 2 Kings, 15, 23; Matt. 26, 36; Mark, 14, 32; Luke, 22, 39. ² Matt. 26, 47; Mark, 14, 43; Luke, 22, 47.

areth. Jesus saith to them: I am he. And Judas also, who betrayed him, stood with them.

6 As soon therefore as he had said to them: I am he; they went backward and fell to the ground.

7 Again therefore he asked them: Whom seek ye? And they said: Jesus of Nazareth.

8 Jesus answered: I have told you that I am he. If therefore you seek me, let these go their way,

9 That the word might be fulfilled which he said: [3] Of them whom thou hast given me, I have not lost any one.

10 Then Simon Peter, having a sword, drew it and struck the servant of the high priest and cut off his right ear. And the name of the servant was Malchus.

11 Jesus therefore said to Peter: Put up thy sword into the scabbard. The chalice which my father hath given me, shall I not drink it?

12 Then the band and the tribune and the servants of the Jews took Jesus and bound him.

13 And they led him away to [4] Annas first, for he was father-in-law to Caiphas, who was the high priest of that year.

14 Now Caiphas was he [5] who had given the counsel to the Jews: That it was expedient that one man should die for the people.

15 And Simon Peter followed Jesus: and so did another disciple. And that disciple was known to the high priest and went in with Jesus into the court of the high priest.

16 But Peter stood at the door without. [6] The other disciple therefore, who was known to the high priest, went out and spoke to the portress and brought in Peter.

17 The maid therefore that was portress saith to Peter: Art not thou also one of this man's disciples? He saith I am not.

18 Now the servants and ministers stood at a fire of coals, because it was cold, and warmed themselves. And with them was Peter also, standing and warming himself.

19 The high priest therefore asked Jesus of his disciples and of his doctrine.

20 Jesus answered him: I have spoken openly to the world. I have always taught in the synagogue and in the temple, whither all the Jews resort: and in secret I have spoken nothing.

21 Why askest thou me? Ask them who have heard what I have spoken unto them. Behold they know what things I have said.

22 And when he had said these things, one of the servants standing by gave Jesus a blow, saying: Answerest thou the high priest so?

23 Jesus answered him: If I have spoken evil, give testimony of the evil; but if well, why strikest thou me?

24 [7] And Annas sent him bound to Caiphas the high priest.

25 And Simon Peter was standing and warming himself. [8] They said therefore to him: Art thou also one of his disciples? He denied it and said: I am not.

26 One of the servants of the high priest (a kinsman to him whose ear Peter cut off) saith to him: Did not I see thee in the garden with him?

27 Again therefore Peter denied: and immediately the cock crew.

28 [9] Then they led Jesus from Caiphas to the governor's hall. And it was morning: and they went not into the hall, [10] that they might not be defiled, but that they might eat the pasch.

29 Pilate therefore went out to them, and said: What accusation bring you against this man?

30 They answered and said to him: If he were not a malefactor, we would not have delivered him up to thee.

31 Pilate therefore said to them: Take him you, and judge him according to your law. The Jews therefore said to him: It is not lawful for us to put any man to death.

32 [11] That the word of Jesus might be fulfilled, which he said, signifying what death he should die.

33 [12] Pilate therefore went into the hall again and called Jesus and said to him: Art thou the king of the Jews?

34 Jesus answered: Sayest thou this thing of thyself, or have others told it thee of me?

35 Pilate answered: Am I a Jew? Thy own nation and the chief priests have delivered thee up to me. What hast thou done?

36 Jesus answered: My kingdom is not of this world. If my kingdom were of this world, my servants would certainly strive that I should not be delivered to the Jews: but now my kingdom is not from hence.

37 Pilate therefore said to him: Art thou a king then? Jesus answered: Thou sayest that I am a king. For this was I born, and for this came I into the world; that I should give testimony to the truth. Every one that is of the truth heareth my voice.

[3] John, 17, 12. [4] Luke, 3, 2. [5] John, 11, 49. [6] Matt. 26, 58; Mark, 14, 54; Luke, 22, 55. [7] Matt. 26, 57; Mark, 14, 53; Luke, 22, 54. [8] Matt. 26, 69; Mark, 14, 67; Luke, 22, 56. [9] Matt. 27, 2; Mark, 15, 1; Luke 23, 1. [10] Acts, 10, 28; 11, 3. [11] Matt. 20, 19. [12] Matt. 27, 11; Mark, 15, 2; Luke, 23, 3. [13] Matt. 27, 15; Mark, 15, 6; Luke, 22, 17.

38 Pilate saith to him: What is truth? And when he said this, he went out again to the Jews and saith to them: I find no cause in him.

39 [13] But you have a custom that I should release one unto you at the pasch. Will you, therefore, that I release unto you the king of the Jews?

40 Then cried they all again, saying: Not this man, but Barabbas. Now Barabbas was a robber.

CHAPTER 19

The continuation of the history of the passion of Christ.

THEN [1] therefore Pilate took Jesus and scourged him.

2 And the soldiers platting a crown of thorns, put it upon his head: and they put on him a purple garment.

3 And they came to him and said: Hail, king of the Jews. And they gave him blows.

4 Pilate therefore went forth again and saith to them: Behold, I bring him forth unto you, that you may know that I find no cause in him.

5 (Jesus therefore came forth, bearing the crown of thorns and the purple garment.) And he saith to them: Behold the Man.

6 When the chief priests, therefore, and the servants had seen him, they cried out, saying: Crucify him, Crucify him. Pilate saith to them: Take him you, and crucify him: for I find no cause in him.

7 The Jews answered him: We have a law; and according to the law he ought to die, because he made himself the Son of God.

8 When Pilate therefore had heard this saying, he feared the more.

9 And he entered into the hall again; and he said to Jesus: Whence art thou? But Jesus gave him no answer.

10 Pilate therefore saith to him: Speakest thou not to me? Knowest thou not that I have power to crucify thee, and I have power to release thee?

11 Jesus answered: Thou shouldst not have any power against me, unless it were given thee from above. Therefore, he that hath delivered me to thee hath the greater sin.

12 And from henceforth Pilate sought to release him. But the Jews cried out, saying: If thou release this man, thou art not Cæsar's friend. For whosoever maketh himself a king speaketh against Cæsar.

13 Now when Pilate had heard these words, he brought Jesus forth and sat down in the judgment seat, in the place that is called Lithostrotos, and in Hebrew Gabbatha.

14 And it was the parasceve of the pasch, about the sixth hour: and he saith to the Jews: Behold your king.

15 But they cried out: Away with him: Away with him: Crucify him. Pilate sath to them: Shall I crucify your king? The chief priests answered: We have no king but Cæsar.

16 Then therefore he delivered him to them to be crucified. And they took Jesus and led him forth.

17 [2] And bearing his own cross, he went forth to the place which is called Calvary, but in Hebrew Golgotha.

18 Where they crucified him, and with him two others, one on each side, and Jesus in the midst.

19 And Pilate wrote a title also: and he put it upon the cross. And the writing was: JESUS OF NAZARETH, THE KING OF THE JEWS.

20 This title therefore many of the Jews did read: because the place where Jesus was crucified was nigh to the city. And it was written in Hebrew, in Greek, and in Latin.

21 Then the chief priests of the Jews said to Pilate: Write not: The King of the Jews. But that he said: I am the King of the Jews.

22 Pilate answered: What I have written, I have written.

23 The soldiers therefore, when they had crucified him, [3] took his garments, (and they made four parts, to every soldier a part) and also his coat. Now the coat was without seam, woven from the top throughout.

24 They said then one to another: Let us not cut, but let us cast lots for it, whose it shall be; that the scripture might be fulfilled, saying: [4] *They have parted my garments among them, and upon my vesture they have cast lot.* And the soldiers indeed did these things.

25 Now there stood by the cross of Jesus, his mother and his mother's sister, Mary of Cleophas, and Mary Magdalen.

26 When Jesus therefore had seen his mother and the disciple standing whom he loved, he saith to his mother: Woman, behold thy son.

27 After that, he saith to the disciple: Behold thy mother. And from that hour, the disciple took her to his own.

[13] Matt. 27, 15; Mark, 15, 6; Luke, 27, 17. CHAP. 19. [1] Matt. 27, 26; Mark, 15, 15. [2] Matt. 27, 33; Mark, 15, 22; Luke, 23, 33. [3] Matt. 27, 35; Mark, 15, 24; Luke, 23, 34. [4] Ps. 21, 19.

CHAP. 19. Ver. 14. *The parasceve of the pasch.* That is, the day before the paschal sabbath. The eve of every sabbath was called the parasceve, or day of preparation. But this was the eve of a high sabbath, namely, that which fell in the paschal week.

28 Afterwards, Jesus knowing that all things were now accomplished, [5] that the scripture might be fulfilled, said: I thirst.

29 Now there was a vessel set there, full of vinegar. And they, putting a sponge full of vinegar about hyssop, put it to his mouth.

30 Jesus therefore, when he had taken the vinegar, said: It is consummated. And bowing his head, he gave up the ghost.

31 Then the Jews (because it was the parasceve), that the bodies might not remain upon the cross on the sabbath day (for that was a great sabbath day), besought Pilate that their legs might be broken: and that they might be taken away.

32 The soldiers therefore came: and they broke the legs of the first, and of the other that was crucified with him.

33 But after they were come to Jesus, when they saw that he was already dead, they did not break his legs.

34 But one of the soldiers with a spear opened his side: and immediately there came out blood and water.

35 And he that saw it hath given testimony: and his testimony is true. And he knoweth that he saith true: that you also may believe.

36 For these things were done that the scripture might be fulfilled: [6] You shall not break a bone of him.

37 And again another scripture saith: [7] They shall look on him whom they pierced.

38 [8] And after these things, Joseph of Arimathea (because he was a disciple of Jesus, but secretly for fear of the Jews), besought Pilate that he might take away the body of Jesus. And Pilate gave leave. He came therefore and took away the body of Jesus.

39 And Nicodemus also came ([9] he who at the first came to Jesus by night), bringing a mixture of myrrh and aloes, about an hundred pound weight.

40 They took therefore the body of Jesus and bound it in linen cloths, with the spices, as the manner of the Jews is to bury.

41 Now there was in the place where he was crucified a garden: and in the garden a new sepulchre, wherein no man yet had been laid.

42 There, therefore, because of the parasceve of the Jews, they laid Jesus: because the sepulchre was nigh at hand.

[5] Ps. 68, 22. [6] Exod. 12, 46; Num. 9, 12. [7] Zach. 12, 10. [8] Matt. 27, 57; Mark, 15, 43; Luke, 23, 50. [9] John, 3, 2. CHAP. 20. [1] Matt. 28, 1; Mark, 16, 1; Luke, 24, 3. [2] Matt. 28, 1; Mark, 16, 2; Luke, 24, 1.

CHAPTER 20

Christ's resurrection and manifestation to his disciples.

AND [1] on the first day of the week, Mary Magdalen cometh early, when it was yet dark, unto the sepulchre: and she saw the stone taken away from the sepulchre.

2 She ran therefore and cometh to Simon Peter and to the other disciple whom Jesus loved and saith to them: They have taken away the Lord out of the sepulchre: and we know not where they have laid him.

3 Peter therefore went out, and that other disciple: and they came to the sepulchre.

4 And they both ran together: and that other disciple did outrun Peter and came first to the sepulchre.

5 And when he stooped down, he saw the linen cloths lying: but yet he went not in.

6 Then cometh Simon Peter, following him, and went into the sepulchre: and saw the linen cloths lying,

7 And the napkin that had been about his head, not lying with the linen cloths, but apart, wrapped up into one place.

8 Then that other disciple also went in, who came first to the sepulchre: and he saw and believed.

9 For as yet they know not the scripture, that he must rise again from the dead.

10 The disciples therefore departed again to their home.

11 [2] But Mary stood at the sepulchre without, weeping. Now as she was weeping, she stooped down and looked into the sepulchre,

12 And she saw two angels in white, sitting, one at the head, and one at the feet, where the body of Jesus had been laid.

13 They say to her: Woman, why weepest thou? She saith to them: Because they have taken away my Lord; and I know not where they have laid him.

14 When she had thus said, she turned herself back and saw Jesus standing: and she knew not that it was Jesus.

15 Jesus saith to her: Woman, why weepest thou? Whom seekest thou? She, thinking that it was the gardener, saith to him: Sir, if thou hast taken him hence, tell me where thou hast laid him: and I will take him away.

16 Jesus saith to her: Mary. She turning, saith to him: Rabboni (which is to say, Master).

17 Jesus saith to her: Do not touch me: for I am not yet ascended to my Father. But go to my brethren and say to them: I ascend to my Father and to your Father, to my God and to your God.

18 Mary Magdalen cometh and telleth the disciples: I have seen the Lord; and these things he said to me.

19 [3] Now when it was late that same day, the first of the week, and the doors were shut, where the disciples wcrc gathered together, for fear of the Jews, Jesus came and stood in the midst and said to them: Peace be to you.

20 And when he had said this, he shewed them his hands and his side. The disciples therefore were glad, when they saw the Lord.

21 He said therefore to them again: Peace be to you. As the Father hath sent me, I also send you.

22 When he had said this, he breathed on them; and he said to them: Receive ye the Holy Ghost.

23 [4] Whose sins you shall forgive, they are forgiven them: and whose sins you shall retain, they are retained.

24 Now Thomas, one of the twelve, who is called Didymus, was not with them when Jesus came.

25 The other disciples therefore said to him: We have seen the Lord. But he said to them: Except I shall see in his hands the print of the nails and put my finger into the place of the nails and put my hand into his side, I will not believe.

26 And after eight days, again his disciples were within, and Thomas with them. Jesus cometh, the doors being shut, and stood in the midst and said: Peace be to you.

27 Then he said to Thomas: Put in thy finger hither and see my hands. And bring hither thy hand and put it into my side. And be not faithless, but believing.

28 Thomas answered and said to him: My Lord and my God.

29 Jesus saith to him: Because thou hast seen me, Thomas, thou hast believed: blessed are they that have not seen and have believed.

30 [5] Many other signs also did Jesus in the sight of his disciples, which are not written in this book.

31 But these are written, that you may believe that Jesus is the Christ, the Son of God: and that believing, you may have life in his name.

CHAPTER 21

Christ manifests himself to his disciples by the sea side and gives Peter the charge of his sheep.

AFTER this, Jesus shewed himself again to the disciples at the sea of Tiberias. And he shewed *himself* after this manner.

2 There were together: Simon Peter and Thomas, who is called Didymus, and Nathanael, who was of Cana of Galilee, and the sons of Zebedee and two others of his disciples.

3 Simon Peter saith to them: I go a fishing. They say to him: We also come with thee. And they went forth and entered into the ship: and that night they caught nothing.

4 But when the morning was come, Jesus stood on the shore: yet the disciples knew not that it was Jesus.

5 Jesus therefore said to them: Children, have you any meat? They answered him: No.

6 He saith to them: Cast the net on the right side of the ship; and you shall find. They cast therefore: and now they were not able to draw it, for the multitude of fishes.

7 That disciple therefore whom Jesus loved said to Peter: It is the Lord. Simon Peter, when he heard that it was the Lord, girt his coat about him (for he was naked) and cast himself into the sea.

8 But the other disciples came in the ship (for they were not far from the land, but as it were two hundred cubits) dragging the net with fishes.

9 As soon then as they came to land, they saw hot coals lying, and a fish laid thereon, and bread.

10 Jesus saith to them: Bring hither of the fishes which you have now caught.

11 Simon Peter went up and drew the net to land, full of great fishes, one hundred and fifty-three. And although there were so many, the net was not broken.

12 Jesus saith to them: Come and dine. And none of them who were at meat, durst ask him: Who art thou? Knowing that it was the Lord.

13 And Jesus cometh and taketh bread and giveth them: and fish in like manner.

14 This is now the third time that Jesus was manifested to his disciples, after he was risen from the dead.

[3] Mark, 16, 14; Luke, 24, 36; 1 Cor. 15, 5. [4] Matt. 18, 18. [5] John, 21, 25.

CHAP. 20. Ver. 19. *The doors were shut.* The same power which could bring Christ's whole body, entire in all its dimensions, through the doors can without the least question make the same body really present in the Sacrament; though both the one and the other be above our comprehension.

Ver. 23. *Whose sins.* See here the commission, stamped by the broad seal of heaven, by virtue of which the pastors of Christ's Church absolve repenting sinners upon their confession.

15 When therefore they had dined, Jesus saith to Simon Peter: Simon, *son* of John, lovest thou me more than these? He saith to him: Yea, Lord, thou knowest that I love thee. He saith to him: Feed my lambs.

16 He saith to him again: Simon, *son* of John, lovest thou me? He saith to him: Yea, Lord, thou knowest that I love thee. He saith to him: Feed my lambs.

17 He said to him the third time: Simon, son of John, lovest thou me? Peter was grieved because he had said to him the third time: Lovest thou me? And he said to him: Lord, thou knowest all things: thou knowest that I love thee. He said to him: Feed my sheep.

18 Amen, amen, I say to thee, [1] When thou wast younger, thou didst gird thyself and didst walk where thou wouldst. But when thou shalt be old, thou shalt stretch forth thy hands, and another shall gird thee and lead thee wither thou wouldst not.

19 And this he said, signifying by what death he should glorify God. And when he had said this, he saith to him: Follow me.

20 Peter turning about, saw that disciple whom Jesus loved following, [2] who also leaned on his breast at supper and said: Lord, who is he that shall betray thee?

21 Him therefore when Peter had seen, he saith to Jesus: Lord, and what *shall* this man *do?*

22 Jesus saith to him: So I will have him to remain till I come, what is it to thee? Follow thou me.

23 This saying therefore went abroad among the brethren, that that disciple should not die. And Jesus did not say to him: He should not die; but: So I will have him to remain till I come, what is it to thee?

24 This is that disciple who giveth testimony of these things and hath written these things: and we know that his testimony is true.

25 [3] But there are also many other things which Jesus did, which, if they were written every one, the world itself, I think, would not be able to contain the books that should be written.

THE ACTS OF
THE APOSTLES

This Book, which, from the first ages, hath been called, The Acts of the Apostles, is not to be considered as a history of what was done by all the Apostles, who were dispersed into different nations; but only a short view of the first establishment of the Christian Church. A part of the preaching and actions of St. Peter are related in the first twelve chapters; and a particular account of St. Paul's apostolical labours in the subsequent chapters. It was written by St. Luke the Evangelist, and the original in Greek. Its history commences from the Ascension of Christ our Lord and ends in the year sixty-three, being a brief account of the Church for the space of about thirty years.

CHAPTER ·1
The ascension of Christ. Matthias is chosen in place of Judas.

Chap. 21. [1] 2 Peter, 1, 14. [2] John, 13, 23. [3] John, 20, 30.

Chap. 21. Ver. 17. *Feed my sheep.* Our Lord had promised the spiritual supremacy to St. Peter (Matt. 16, 9); and here he fulfils that promise, by charging him with the superintendency of all his sheep, without exception; and consequently of his whole flock, that is, of his whole Church.

THE former treatise I made, O Theophilus, of all things which Jesus began to do and to teach,

2 Until the day on which, giving commandments by the Holy Ghost to the apostles whom he had chosen, he was taken up.

3 To whom also he shewed himself alive after his passion, by many proofs, for forty days appearing to them and speaking of the kingdom of God.

4 And eating together with them. [1] he commanded them that they should not depart from Jerusalem, but should wait for the promise of the Father, [2] which you have heard (saith he) by my mouth.

5 For John indeed baptized with water: but you shall be baptized with the Holy Ghost, not many days hence.

6 They therefore who were come together asked him, saying: Lord, wilt thou at this time restore again the kingdom to Israel?

7 But he said to them: It is not for you to know the times or moments, which the Father hath put in his own power:

8 [3] But you shall receive the power of the Holy Ghost coming upon you, [4] and you shall be witnesses unto me in Jerusalem, and in all Judea and Samaria, and even to the uttermost part of the earth.

9 And when he had said these things while they looked on, he was raised up: and a cloud received him out of their sight.

10 And while they were beholding him going up to heaven, behold two men stood by them in white garments.

11 Who also said: Ye men of Galilee, why stand you looking up to heaven? This Jesus who is taken up from you into heaven shall so come as you have seen him going into heaven.

12 Then they returned to Jerusalem from the mount that is called Olivet, which is nigh Jerusalem, within a sabbath day's journey.

13 And when they were come in, they went up into an upper room, where abode Peter and John, James and Andrew, Philip and Thomas, Bartholomew and Matthew, James of Alpheus and Simon Zelotes and Jude the brother of James.

14 All these were persevering with one mind in prayer, with the women and Mary the mother of Jesus, and with his brethren.

15 In those days, Peter, rising up in the midst of the brethren, said (now the number of persons together was about an hundred and twenty):

16 Men, brethren, the scripture must needs be fulfilled, [5] which the Holy Ghost spoke before by the mouth of David concerning Judas, who was the leader of them that apprehended Jesus:

17 Who was numbered with us and had obtained part of this ministry.

18 [6] And he indeed hath possessed a field of the reward of iniquity: and being hanged, burst asunder in the midst and all his bowels gushed out.

19 And it became known to all the inhabitants of Jerusalem: so that the same field was called in their tongue, Haceldama, that is to say, The field of blood.

20 For it is written in the book of Psalms: [7] Let their habitation become desolate, and let there be none to dwell therein. [8] And his bishopric let another take.

21 Wherefore of these men who have companied with us, all the time that the Lord Jesus came in and went out among us,

22 Beginning from the baptism of John, until the day wherein he was taken up from us, one of these must be made a witness with us of his resurrection.

23 And they appointed two: Joseph, called Barsabas, who was surnamed Justus, and Matthias.

24 And praying, they said: Thou, Lord, who knowest the hearts of all men, shew whether of these two thou hast chosen,

25 To take the place of this ministry and apostleship, from which Judas hath by transgression fallen, that he might go to his own place.

26 And they gave them lots: and the lot fell upon Matthias. And he was numbered with the eleven apostles.

CHAPTER 2

The disciples receive the Holy Ghost. Peter's sermon to the people. The piety of the first converts.

AND when the days of the Pentecost were accomplished, they were all together in one place.

2 And suddenly there came a sound from heaven, as of a mighty wind coming: and it filled the whole house where they were sitting.

3 And there appeared to them parted tongues, as it were of fire: and it sat upon every one of them.

4 [1] And they were all filled with the Holy Ghost: and they began to speak with divers tongues, according as the Holy Ghost gave them to speak.

5 Now there were dwelling at Jerusalem, Jews, devout men, out of every nation under heaven.

6 And when this was noised abroad, the multitude came together and were confounded in mind, because that every man heard them speak in his own tongue.

7 And they were all amazed and wondered, saying: Behold, are not all these that speak, Galileans?

CHAP. 1. [1] Luke, 24, 49; John, 14, 26. [2] Matt. 3, 11; Mark, 1, 8; Luke, 3, 16; John, 1, 26. [3] Acts, 2, 2. [4] Luke, 24, 48. [5] Ps. 40, 10; John, 13, 18. [6] Matt. 27, 7. [7] Ps. 68, 26. [8] Ps. 108, 8. CHAP. 2. [1] Matt. 3, 11; Mark, 1, 8; Luke, 3, 16; John, 7, 39; Acts, 1, 8; 11, 16; 19, 6.

8 And how have we heard, every man our own tongue wherein we were born?

9 Parthians and Medes and Elamites and inhabitants of Mesopotamia, Judea and Cappadocia, Pontus and Asia,

10 Phrygia and Pamphylia, Egypt and the parts of Libya about Cyrene, and strangers of Rome,

11 Jews also and proselytes, Cretes and Arabians: we have heard them speak in our own tongues the wonderful works of God.

12 And they were all astonished and wondered, saying one to another: What meaneth this?

13 But others mocking, said: These men are full of new wine.

14 But Peter, standing up with the eleven, lifted up his voice and spoke to them: Ye men of Judea and all you that dwell in Jerusalem, be this known to you and with your ears receive my words.

15 For these are not drunk, as you suppose, seeing it is but the third hour of the day.

16 But this is that which was spoken of by the prophet Joel:

17 ² *And it shall come to pass, in the last days (saith the Lord), I will pour out of my Spirit upon all flesh: and your sons and your daughters shall prophesy: and your young men shall see visions: and your old men shall dream dreams.*

18 *And upon my servants, indeed, and upon my handmaids will I pour out in those days of my spirit: and they shall prophesy.*

19 *And I will shew wonders in the heaven above and signs on the earth beneath: blood and fire and vapour of smoke.*

20 *The sun shall be turned into darkness and the moon into blood, before the great and manifest day of the Lord come.*

21 ³ *And it shall come to pass that whosoever shall call upon the name of the Lord shall be saved.*

22 Ye men of Israel, hear these words: Jesus of Nazareth, a man ap-

² Isai. 44, 3; Joel, 2, 28. ³ Joel, 2, 32; Rom. 10, 13. ⁴ Ps. 15, 8. ⁵ 3 Kings, 2, 10. ⁶ Ps. 131, 11. ⁷ Ps. 15, 10; Acts, 13, 35. ⁸ Ps. 109, 1.

CHAP. 2. Ver. 23. *By the determinate counsel.* God delivered up his Son; and his Son delivered up himself, for the love of us and for the sake of our salvation; and so Christ's being delivered up was holy and was God's own determination. But they who betrayed and crucified him did wickedly, following therein their own malice and the instigation of the devil; not the will and determination of God, who was by no means the author of their wickedness; though he permitted it: because he could, and did draw out of it so great a good as is the salvation of man.

Ver. 24. *Having loosed the sorrows.* Having overcome the grievous pains of death and all the power of hell.

proved of God among you by miracles and wonders and signs, which God did by him, in the midst of you, as you also know:

23 This same being delivered up, by the determinate counsel and foreknowledge of God, you by the hands of wicked men have crucified and slain.

24 Whom God hath raised up, having loosed the sorrows of hell, as it was impossible that he should be holden by it.

25 For David saith concerning him: ⁴ *I foresaw the Lord before my face: because he is at my right hand, that I may not be moved.*

26 *For this my heart hath been glad, and my tongue hath rejoiced: moreover my flesh also shall rest in hope.*

27 *Because thou wilt not leave my soul in hell: nor suffer thy Holy One to see corruption.*

28 *Thou hast made known to me the ways of life: thou shalt make me full of joy with thy countenance.*

29 Ye men, brethren, let me freely speak to you of the patriarch David: ⁵ that he died and was buried; and his sepulchre is with us to this present day.

30 Whereas therefore he was a prophet and knew ⁶ that God hath sworn to him was an oath, that of the fruit of his loins one should sit upon his throne.

31 Forseeing this, he spoke of the resurrection of Christ. ⁷ For neither was he left in hell: neither did his flesh see corruption.

32 This Jesus hath God raised again, whereof all we are witnesses.

33 Being exalted therefore by the right hand of God and having received of the Father the promise of the Holy Ghost, he hath poured forth this which you see and hear.

34 For David ascended not into heaven; but he himself said: ⁸ The Lord saith to my Lord: Sit thou on my right hand,

35 Until I make thy enemies thy footstool.

36 Therefore let all the house of Israel know most certainly that God hath made both Lord and Christ, this same Jesus, whom you have crucified.

37 Now when they had heard these things, they had compunction in their heart and said to Peter and to the rest of the apostles: What shall we do, men *and* brethren?

38 But Peter *said* to them: Do penance: and be baptized every one of you in the name of Jesus Christ, for the remission of your sins. And you shall receive the gift of the Holy Ghost.

39 For the promise is to you and to your children and to all that are far

off, whomsoever the Lord our God shall call.

40 And with very many other words did he testify and exhort them, saying: Save yourselves from this perverse generation.

41 They therefore that received his word were baptized: and there were added in that day about three thousand souls.

42 And they were persevering in the doctrine of the apostles and in the communication of the breaking of bread and in prayers.

43 And fear came upon every soul. Many wonders also and signs were done by the apostles in Jerusalem: and there was great fear in all.

44 And all they that believed were together and had all things common.

45 Their possessions and goods they sold and divided them to all, according as every one had need.

46 And continuing daily with one accord in the temple and breaking bread from house to house, they took their meat with gladness and simplicity of heart:

47 Praising God and having favour with all the people. And the Lord increased daily together such as should be saved.

CHAPTER 3

The miracle upon the lame man, followed by the conversion of many.

NOW Peter and John went up into the temple at the ninth hour of prayer.

2 And a certain man who was lame from his mother's womb was carried: whom they laid every day at the gate of the temple, which is called Beautiful, that he might ask alms of them that went into the temple.

3 He, when he had seen Peter and John, about to go into the temple, asked to receive an alms.

4 But Peter with John, fastening his eyes upon him, said: Look upon us.

5 But he looked earnestly upon them, hoping that he should receive something of them.

6 But Peter said: Silver and gold I have none; but what I have, I give thee. In the name of Jesus Christ of Nazareth, arise and walk.

7 And taking him by the right hand, he lifted him up: and forthwith his feet and soles received strength.

8 And he leaping up, stood and walked and went in with them into the temple, walking and leaping and praising God.

9 And all the people saw him walking and praising God.

10 And they knew him, that it was he who sat begging alms at the Beautiful gate of the temple: and they were filled with wonder and amazement at that which had happened to him.

11 And as he held Peter and John, all the people ran to them, to the porch which is called Solomon's, greatly wondering.

12 But Peter seeing, made answer to the people: Ye men of Israel, why wonder you at this? Or why look you upon us, as if by our strength or power we had made this man to walk?

13 The God of Abraham and the God of Isaac and the God of Jacob, the God of our fathers, hath glorified his Son Jesus, whom you indeed delivered up and denied before the face of Pilate, when he judged he should be released.

14 [1] But you denied the Holy One and the Just: and desired a murderer to be granted unto you.

15 But the author of life you killed, whom God hath raised from the dead: of which we are witnesses.

16 And in the faith of his name, this man, whom you have seen and known, hath his name strengthened. And the faith which is by him hath given this perfect soundness in the sight of you all.

17 And now, brethren, I know that you did it through ignorance: as *did* also your rulers.

18 But those things which God before had shewed by the mouth of all the prophets, that his Christ should suffer, he hath so fulfilled.

19 Be penitent, therefore, and be converted, that your sins may be blotted out.

20 That when the times of refreshment shall come from the presence of the Lord, and he shall send him who hath been preached unto you, Jesus Christ

21 Whom heaven indeed must receive, until the times of the restitution of all things, which God hath spoken by the mouth of his holy prophets, from the beginning of the world.

22 For Moses said: [2] *A prophet shall the Lord your God raise up unto you of your brethren, like unto me: him you shall hear according to all things whatsoever he shall speak to you.*

23 *And it shall be, that every soul which will not hear that prophet shall be destroyed from among the people.*

24 And all the prophets, from Samuel and afterwards, who have spoken, have told of these days.

CHAP. 3. [1] Matt. 27, 20; Mark, 15, 11; Luke, 23, 18; John, 18, 40. [2] Deut. 18, 15.

25 You are the children of the prophets and of the testament which God made to our fathers, saying to Abraham: ³ *And in thy seed shall all the kindreds of the earth be blessed.*

26 To you first, God, raising up his Son, hath sent him to bless you: that every one may convert himself from his wickedness.

CHAPTER 4

Peter and John are apprehended. Their constancy. The church is increased.

AND as they were speaking to the people the priests and the officer of the temple and the Sadducees came upon them,

2 Being grieved that they taught the people and preached in Jesus the resurrection from the dead:

3 And they laid hands upon them and put them in hold till the next day: for it was now evening.

4 But many of them who had heard the word believed: and the number of the men was made five thousand.

5 And it came to pass on the morrow, that their princes and ancients and scribes were gathered together in Jerusalem.

6 And Annas the high priest and Caiphas and John and Alexander: and as many as were of the kindred of the high priest.

7 And setting them in the midst, they asked: By what power or by what name, have you done this?

8 Then Peter, filled with the Holy Ghost, said to them: Ye princes of the people and ancients, hear.

9 If we this day are examined concerning the good deed done to the infirm man, by what means he hath been made whole:

10 Be it known to you all and to all the people of Israel, that by the name of our Lord Jesus Christ of Nazareth, whom you crucified, whom God hath raised from the dead, even by him, this man standeth here before you, whole.

11 ¹ This is *the stone which was rejected by you the builders, which is become the head of the corner.*

12 Neither is there salvation in any other. For there is no other name under heaven given to men, whereby we must be saved.

13 Now seeing the constancy of Peter and of John, understanding that they were illiterate and ignorant men, they wondered: and they knew them that they had been with Jesus.

14 Seeing the man also who had been

healed, standing with them, they could say nothing against it.

15 But they commanded them to go aside out of the council: and they conferred among themselves,

16 Saying: What shall we do to these men? For indeed a miracle hath been done by them, known to all the inhabitants of Jerusalem. It is manifest: and we cannot deny it.

17 But that it may be no farther spread among the people, let us threaten them that they speak no more in this name to any man.

18 And calling them, they charged them not to speak at all, nor teach in the name of Jesus.

19 But Peter and John answering, said to them: If it be just, in the sight of God, to hear you rather than God, judge ye.

20 For we cannot but speak the things which we have seen and heard.

21 But they, threatening, sent them away, not finding how they might punish them, because of the people: for all men glorified what had been done, in that which had come to pass.

22 For the man was above forty years old, in whom that miraculous cure had been wrought.

23 And being let go, they came to their own company and related all that the chief priests and ancients had said to them.

24 Who having heard it, with one accord lifted up their voice to God and said: Lord, thou art he that didst make heaven and earth, the sea and all things that are in them.

25 Who, by the Holy Ghost, by the mouth of our father David, thy servant, hast said: ² *Why did the Gentiles rage: and the people meditate vain things?*

26 *The kings of the earth stood up: and the princes assembled together against the Lord and his Christ.*

27 For of a truth there assembled together in this city against thy holy child Jesus, whom thou hast anointed, Herod, and Pontius Pilate, with the Gentiles and the people of Israel,

28 To do what thy hand and thy counsel decreed to be done.

29 And now, Lord, behold their threatenings: and grant unto thy servants that with all confidence they may speak thy word,

30 By stretching forth thy hand to cures and signs and wonders, to be done by the name of thy holy Son, Jesus.

31 And when they had prayed, the place was moved wherein they were assembled: and they were all filled with the Holy Ghost: and they spoke the word of God with confidence.

³ Gen. 12, 3. Chap. 4. ¹ Ps. 117, 22; Isai. 28, 16; Matt. 21, 42; Mark, 12, 10; Luke, 20, 17; Rom. 9, 32; 1 Peter, 2, 7. ² Ps. 2, 1.

32 And the multitude of believers had but one heart and one soul. Neither did any one say that aught of the things which he possessed was his own: but all things were common unto them.

33 And with great power did the apostles give testimony of the resurrection of Jesus Christ our Lord: and great grace was in them all.

34 For neither was there any one needy among them. For as many as were owners of lands or houses sold them and brought the price of the things they sold,

35 And laid it down before the feet of the apostles. And distribution was made to every one, according as he had need.

36 And Joseph, who, by the apostles, was surnamed Barnabas (which is, by interpretation, The son of consolation), a Levite, a Cyprian born,

37 Having land, sold it and brought the price and laid it at the feet of the apostles.

CHAPTER 5

The judgment of God upon Ananias and Saphira. The apostles are cast into prison.

BUT a certain man named Ananias, with Saphira his wife, sold a piece of land,

2 And by fraud kept back part of the price of the land, his wife being privy thereunto: and bringing a certain part of it, laid it at the feet of the apostles.

3 But Peter said: Ananias, why hath Satan tempted thy heart, that thou shouldst lie to the Holy Ghost and by fraud keep part of the price of the land?

4 Whilst it remained, did it not remain to thee? And after it was sold, was it not in thy power? Why hast thou conceived this thing in thy heart? Thou hast not lied to men, but to God.

5 And Ananias, hearing these words, fell down and gave up the ghost. And there came great fear upon all that heard it.

6 And the young men rising up removed him: and carrying him out buried him.

7 And it was about the space of three hours after, when his wife, not knowing what had happened, came in.

8 And Peter said to her: Tell me, woman, whether you sold the land for so much? And she said: Yea, for so much.

9 And Peter *said* unto her: Why have you agreed together to tempt the spirit of the Lord? Behold the feet of them who have buried thy husband are at the door: and they shall carry thee out.

10 Immediately, she fell down before his feet and gave up the ghost. And the young men coming in found her dead: and carried her out and buried her by her husband.

11 And there came great fear upon the whole church and upon all that heard these things.

12 And by the hands of the apostles were many signs and wonders wrought among the people. And they were all with one accord in Solomon's porch.

13 But of the rest no man durst join himself unto them: but the people magnified them.

14 And the multitude of men and women who believed in the Lord was more increased:

15 Insomuch that they brought forth the sick into the streets and laid them on beds and couches, that, when Peter came, his shadow at the least might overshadow any of them and they might be delivered from their infirmities.

16 And there came also together to Jerusalem a multitude out of the neighbouring cities, bringing sick persons and such as were troubled with unclean spirits: who were all healed.

17 Then the high priest rising up, and all they that were with him (which is the heresy of the Sadducees) were filled with envy.

18 And they laid hands on the apostles and put them in the common prison.

19 But an angel of the Lord by night, opening the doors of the prison and leading them out, said:

20 Go, and standing speak in the temple to the people all the words of this life.

21 Who having heard *this*, early in the morning, entered into the temple and taught. And the high priest coming, and they that were with him, called together the council and all the ancients of the children of Israel: and they sent to the prison to have them brought.

22 But when the ministers came and opening the prison found them not there, they returned and told,

23 Saying: The prison indeed we found shut with all diligence, and the keepers standing before the door: but opening it, we found no man within.

24 Now when the officer of the temple and the chief priests heard these words, they were in doubt concerning them, what would come to pass.

25 But one came and told them: Behold, the men whom you put in prison are in the temple, standing and teaching the people.

26 Then went the officer with the ministers and brought them without violence: for they feared the people, lest they should be stoned.

27 And when they had brought them, they set them before the council. And the high priest asked them,

28 Saying: Commanding, we commanded you that you should not teach in this name. And behold, you have filled Jerusalem with your doctrine: and you have a mind to bring the blood of this man upon us.

29 But Peter and the apostles answering, said: We ought to obey God rather than men.

30 The God of our fathers hath raised up Jesus, whom you put to death, hanging him upon a tree.

31 Him hath God exalted with his right hand, to be Prince and Saviour, to give repentance to Israel and remission of sin.

32 And we are witnesses of these things: and the Holy Ghost, whom God hath given to all that obey him.

33 When they had heard these things, they were cut to the heart: and they thought to put them to death.

34 But one in the council rising up, a Pharisee, named Gamaliel, a doctor of the law, respected by all the people, commanded the men to be put forth a little while.

35 And he said to them: Ye men of Israel, take heed to yourselves what you intend to do, as touching these men.

36 For before these days rose up Theodas, affirming himself to be somebody, to whom a number of men, about four hundred, joined themselves. Who was slain: and all that believed him were scattered and brought to nothing.

37 After this man, rose up Judas of Galilee, in the days of the enrolling, and drew away the people after him. He also perished: and all, even as many as consented to him, were dispersed.

38 And now, therefore, I say to you: Refrain from these men and let them alone. For if this council or this work be of men, it will come to nought:

39 But if it be of God, you cannot overthrow it, lest perhaps you be found even to fight against God. And they consented to him.

40 And calling in the apostles, after they had scourged them, they charged them that they should not speak at all in the name of Jesus. And they dismissed them.

41 And they indeed went from the presence of the council, rejoicing that

CHAP. 6. Ver. 1. *Greeks.* So they called the Jews that were born and brought up in Greece.

they were accounted worthy to suffer reproach for the name of Jesus.

42 And every day they ceased not, in the temple and from house to house, to teach and preach Christ Jesus.

CHAPTER 6

The ordination of the seven deacons. The zeal of Stephen.

AND in those days, the number of the disciples increasing, there arose a murmuring of the Greeks against the Hebrews, for that their widows were neglected in the daily ministration.

2 Then the twelve, calling together the multitude of the disciples, said: It is not reason that we should leave the word of God and serve tables.

3 Wherefore, brethren, look ye out among you seven men of good reputation, full of the Holy Ghost and wisdom, whom we may appoint over this business.

4 But we will give ourselves continually to prayer and to the ministry of the word.

5 And the saying was liked by all the multitude. And they chose Stephen, a man full of faith and of the Holy Ghost, and Philip and Prochorus and Nicanor, and Timon and Parmenas and Nicolas, a proselyte of Antioch.

6 These they set before the apostle: and they praying, imposed hands upon them.

7 And the word of the Lord increased: and the number of the disciples was multiplied in Jerusalem exceedingly. A great multitude also of the priests obeyed the faith.

8 And Stephen, full of grace and fortitude, did great wonders and signs among the people.

9 Now there arose some, of that which is called the synagogue of the Libertines and of the Cyrenians and of the Alexandrians and of them that were of Cilicia and Asia, disputing with Stephen.

10 And they were not able to resist the wisdom and the spirit that spoke.

11 Then they suborned men to say they had heard him speak words of blasphemy against Moses and against God.

12 And they stirred up the people and the ancients and the scribes. And running together, they took him and brought him to the council.

13 And they set up false witnesses, who said: This man ceaseth not to speak words against the holy place and the law.

14 For we have heard him say that

this Jesus of Nazareth shall destroy this place and shall change the traditions which Moses delivered unto us.

15 And all that sat in the council, looking on him, saw his face as if it had been the face of an angel.

CHAPTER 7

Stephen's speech before the council. His martyrdom.

THEN the high priest said: Are these things so?

2 Who said: Ye men, brethren and fathers, hear. The God of glory appeared to our father Abraham, when he was in Mesopotamia, before he dwelt in Charan.

3 And said to him: ¹ *Go forth out of thy country and from thy kindred: and come into the land which I shall shew thee.*

4 Then he went out of the land of the Chaldeans and dwelt in Charan. And from thence, after his father was dead, he removed him into this land, wherein you now dwell.

5 And he gave him no inheritance in it: no, not the pace of a foot. But he promised to give it him in possession, and to his seed after him, when *as yet* he had no child.

6 And God said to him: ² *That his seed should sojourn in a strange country, and that they should bring them under bondage and treat them evil four hundred years.*

7 *And the nation which they shall serve will I judge* (said the Lord): *and after these things they shall go out and shall serve me in this place.*

8 ³ And he gave him the covenant of circumcision. ⁴ And so he begot Isaac and circumcised him the eighth day: and ⁵ Isaac begot Jacob: ⁶ and Jacob, the twelve patriarchs.

9 And the patriarchs, through envy, ⁷ sold Joseph into Egypt. And God was with him,

10 And delivered him out of all his tribulations: ⁸ *and he gave him favour* and wisdom in the sight of Pharao, the king of Egypt. And he appointed him governor over Egypt and over all his house.

11 Now there came a famine upon all Egypt and Chanaan, and great tribulation: and our fathers found no food.

12 ⁹ But when Jacob had heard that there was corn in Egypt, he sent our fathers first.

13 ¹⁰ And at the second time, Joseph was known by his brethren: and his kindred was made known to Pharao.

14 And Joseph sending, called thither Jacob, his father, and all his kindred, seventy-five souls.

15 ¹¹ So Jacob went down into Egypt. And ¹² he died, and our fathers.

16 And they were translated into Sichem and were laid in the sepulchre ¹³ that Abraham bought for a sum of money of the sons of Hemor, the son of Sichem.

17 And when the time of the promise drew near, which God had promised to Abraham, ¹⁴ the people increased and were multiplied in Egypt.

18 Till another king arose in Egypt, who knew not Joseph.

19 This same, dealing craftily with our race, afflicted our fathers, that they should expose their children, to the end they might not be kept alive.

20 ¹⁵ At the same time was Moses born: and he was acceptable to God. Who was nourished three months in his father's house.

21 And when he was exposed, Pharao's daughter took him up and nourished him for her own son.

22 And Moses was instructed in all the wisdom of the Egyptians: and he was mighty in his words and in his deeds.

23 And when he was full forty years old, it came into his heart to visit his brethren, the children of Israel.

24 ¹⁶ And when he had seen one of them suffer wrong, he defended him: and striking the Egyptian, he avenged him who suffered the injury.

25 And he thought that his brethren understood that God by his hand would save them. But they understood it not.

26 ¹⁷ And the day following, he shewed himself to them when they were at strife and would have reconciled them in peace, saying: Men, ye are brethren. Why hurt you one another?

27 But he that did the injury to his neighbour thrust him away, saying: Who hath appointed thee prince and judge over us?

28 What! Wilt thou kill me, as thou didst yesterday kill the Egyptian?

29 And Moses fled upon this word: and was a stranger in the land of Madian, where he begot him two sons.

30 And when forty years were expired, ¹⁸ there appeared to him, in the desert of mount Sina, an angel in a flame of fire in a bush.

CHAP. 7. ¹ Gen. 12, 2. ² Gen. 15, 13. ³ Gen. 17, 10. ⁴ Gen. 21, 2. ⁵ Gen. 25, 25. ⁶ Gen. 29, 32; 35, 22. ⁷ Gen. 37, 28. ⁸ Gen. 41, 37. ⁹ Gen. 42, 2. ¹⁰ Gen. 45, 3. ¹¹ Gen. 46, 5. ¹² Gen. 49, 32. ¹³ Gen. 23, 16; 1, 13; Jos. 24, 32. ¹⁴ Exod. 1, 7. ¹⁵ Exod. 2, 2; Heb. 11, 23. ¹⁶ Exod. 2, 12. ¹⁷ Exod. 2, 13. ¹⁸ Exod. 3, 2.

31 And Moses seeing it wondered at the sight. And as he drew near to view it, the voice of the Lord came unto him, saying:

32 *I am the God of thy fathers: the God of Abraham, the God of Isaac and the God of Jacob.* And Moses being terrified durst not behold.

33 And the Lord said to him: *Loose the shoes from thy feet: for the place wherein thou standest is holy ground.*

34 *Seeing, I have seen the affliction of my people which is in Egypt: and I have heard their groaning and am come down to deliver them. And now come: and I will send thee into Egypt.*

35 This Moses, whom they refused, saying: *Who hath appointed thee prince and judge?* Him God sent to be prince and redeemer, by the hand of the angel who appeared to him in the bush.

36 [19] He brought them out, doing wonders and signs in the land of Egypt and in the Red Sea and in the desert forty years.

37 This is that Moses who said to the children of Israel: [20] *A prophet shall God raise up to you of your own brethren, as myself. Him shall you hear.*

38 [21] This is he that was in the church in the wilderness, with the angel who spoke to him on Mount Sina and with our fathers. Who received the words of life to give unto us.

39 Whom our fathers would not obey: but thrust him away and in their hearts turned back into Egypt,

40 Saying to Aaron: [22] *Make us gods to go before us. For as for this Moses, who brought us out of the land of Egypt, we know not what is become of him.*

41 And they made a calf in those days and offered sacrifices to the idol and rejoiced in the works of their own hands.

42 And God turned and gave them up to serve the host of heaven, as it is written in the books of the prophets: [23] *Did you offer victims and sacrifices to me for forty years, in the desert, O house of Israel?*

43 *And you took unto you the taber-nacle of Moloch and the star of your god Rempham, figures which you made to adore them. And I will carry you away beyond Babylon.*

44 The tabernacle of the testimony was with our fathers in the desert, God ordained for them, [24] speaking to Moses, *that he should make it according to the form which he had seen.*

45 [25] Which also our fathers receiving, brought in with Jesus, into the possession of the Gentiles: whom God drove out before the face of our fathers, unto the days of David,

46 [26] Who found grace before God [27] and desired to find a tabernacle for the God of Jacob.

47 [28] But Solomon built him a house,

48 [29] Yet the most High dwelleth not in houses made by hands, as the prophet saith:

49 [30] *Heaven is my throne and the earth my footstool. What house will you build me (saith the Lord)? Or what is the place of my resting?*

50 *Hath not my hand made all these things?*

51 You stiffnecked and uncircumcised in heart and ears, you always resist the Holy Ghost. As your fathers did, so do you also.

52 Which of the prophets have not your fathers persecuted? And they have slain them who foretold of the coming of the Just One: of whom you have been now the betrayers and murderers.

53 Who have received the law by the disposition of angels and have not kept it.

54 Now hearing these things, they were cut to the heart: and they gnashed with their teeth at him.

55 But he, being full of the Holy Ghost, looking up steadfastly to heaven, saw the glory of God and Jesus standing on the right hand of God. And he said: Behold, I see the heavens opened and the Son of man standing on the right hand of God.

56 And they, crying out with a loud voice, stopped their ears and with one accord ran violently upon him.

57 And casting him forth without the city, they stoned him. And the witnesses laid down their garments at the feet of a young man, whose name was Saul.

58 And they stoned Stephen, invoking and saying: Lord Jesus, receive my spirit.

59 And falling on his knees, he cried with a loud voice, saying: Lord, lay not this sin to their charge. And when he

---

[19] Exod. 7, 8; 9, 10; 11, 4. [20] Deut. 18, 15. [21] Exod. 19, 3. [22] Exod. 32, 1. [23] Amos, 5, 25. [24] Exod. 25, 40. [25] Jos. 3, 14; Heb. 8, 9. [26] 1 Kings, 16, 13. [27] Ps. 131, 5. [28] 3 Kings, 6, 1; 1 Par. 17, 12. [29] Acts, 17, 24. [30] Isai. 66, 1.

CHAP. 7. Ver. 45. *Jesus.* That is, Josue, so called in Greek.

Ver. 48. *Dwelleth not in houses.* That is, so as to stand in need of earthly dwellings, or to be contained or circumscribed by them. Though, otherwise, by his immense divinity, he is in our houses and every where else. And Christ in his humanity dwelt in houses and is now on our altars.

had said this, he fell asleep in the Lord. And Saul was consenting to his death.

CHAPTER 8

Philip converts the Samaritans and baptizes the eunuch.

AND at that time, there was raised a great persecution against the church which was at Jerusalem. And they were all dispersed through the countries of Judea and Samaria, except the apostles.

2 And devout men took order for Stephen's funeral and made great mourning over him.

3 But Saul made havock of the church, entering in from house to house: and dragging away men and women, committed them to prison.

4 They therefore that were dispersed went about preaching the word of God.

5 And Philip, going down to the city of Samaria, preached Christ unto them.

6 And the people with one accord were attentive to those things which were said by Philip, hearing, and seeing the miracles which he did.

7 For many of them who had unclean spirits, crying with a loud voice, went out.

8 And many, taken with the palsy, and that were lame, were healed.

9 There was therefore great joy in that city. Now *there* was a certain man named Simon, who before had been a magician in that city, seducing the people of Samaria, giving out that he was some great one:

10 To whom they all gave ear, from the least to the greatest, saying: This man is the power of God, which is called great.

11 And they were attentive to him, because, for a long time, he had bewitched them with his magical practices.

12 But when they had believed Philip preaching of the kingdom of God, in the name of Jesus Christ, they were baptized, *both* men and women.

13 Then Simon himself believed also and, being baptized, he adhered to Philip. And being astonished, wondered to see the signs and exceeding great miracles which were done.

14 Now, when the apostles, who were in Jerusalem, had heard that Samaria had received the word of God, they sent unto them Peter and John.

15 Who, when they were come, prayed for them that they might receive the Holy Ghost.

16 For he was not as yet come upon any of them: but they were only baptized in the name of the Lord Jesus.

17 Then they laid their hands upon them: and they received the Holy Ghost.

18 And when Simon saw that, by the imposition of the hands of the apostles, the Holy Ghost was given, he offered them money,

19 Saying: Give me also this power, that on whomsoever I shall lay *my* hands, he may receive the Holy Ghost. But Peter said to him:

20 Keep thy money to thyself, to perish with thee: because thou hast thought that the gift of God may be purchased with money.

21 Thou hast no part nor lot in this matter. For thy heart is not right in the sight of God.

22 Do penance therefore for this thy wickedness: and pray to God, that perhaps this thought of thy heart may be forgiven thee.

23 For I see thou art in the gall of bitterness and in the bonds of iniquity.

24 Then Simon answering, said: Pray you for me to the Lord that none of these thngs which you have spoken may come upon me.

25 And they indeed, having testified and preached the word of the Lord, returned to Jerusalem: and preached the gospel to many countries of the Samaritans.

26 Now an angel of the Lord spoke to Philip, saying: Arise, go towards the south, to the way that goeth down from Jerusalem into Gaza: this is desert.

27 And rising up, he went. And behold, a man of Ethiopia, an eunuch, of great authority under Candace the queen of the Ethiopians, who had charge over all her treasures, had come to Jerusalem to adore.

28 And he was returning, sitting in his chariot and reading Isaias the prophet.

29 And the Spirit said to Philip: Go near and join thyself to this chariot.

30 And Philip running thither, heard him reading the prophet Isaias. And he said: Thinkest thou that thou understandest what thou readest?

31 Who said: And how can I, unless some man shew me? And he desired Philip that he would come up and sit with him.

Chap. 8. Ver. 17. *They laid their hands upon them.* The apostles administered the Sacrament of Confirmation, by imposition of hands and prayer: and the faithful thereby received the Holy Ghost. Not but they had received the grace of the Holy Ghost at their Baptism, yet not that plenitude of grace and those spiritual gifts which they afterwards received from bishops in the Sacrament of Confirmation, which strengthened them to profess their faith publicly.

32 And the place of the scripture which he was reading was this: [1] *He was led as a sheep to the slaughter: and like a lamb without voice before his shearer, so openeth he not his mouth.*

33 *In humility his judgment was taken away. His generation who shall declare, for his life shall be taken from the earth?*

34 And the eunuch answering Philip, said: I beseech thee, of whom doth the prophet speak this? Of himself, or of some other man?

35 Then Philip, opening his mouth and beginning at this scripture, preached unto him Jesus.

36 And as they went on their way they came to a certain water. And the eunuch said: See, here is water: What doth hinder me from being baptized?

37 And Philip said: If thou believest with all thy heart, thou mayest. And he answering, said: I believe that Jesus Christ is the Son of God.

38 And he commanded the chariot to stand still. And they went down into the water, both Philip and the eunuch. And he baptized him.

39 And when they were come up out of the water, the Spirit of the Lord took away Philip: and the eunuch saw him no more. And he went on his way rejoicing.

40 But Philip was found in Azotus: and passing through, he preached the gospel to all the cities, till he came to Cæsarea.

CHAPTER 9

Paul's conversion and zeal. Peter heals Eneas and raises up Tabitha to life.

AND [1] Saul, as yet breathing out threatenings and slaughter against the disciples of the Lord, went to the high priest

2 And asked of him letters to Damascus, to the synagogues: that if he found any men and women of this way, he might bring them bound to Jerusalem.

3 [2] And as he went on his journey, it came to pass that he drew nigh to Damascus. And suddenly a light from heaven shined round about him.

4 And falling on the ground, he heard a voice saying to him: Saul, Saul, why persecutest thou me?

5 Who said: Who art thou, Lord?

And he: I am Jesus whom thou persecutest. It is hard for thee to kick against the goad.

6 And he, trembling and astonished, said: Lord, what wilt thou have me to do?

7 And the Lord said to him: Arise and go into the city; and there it shall be told thee what thou must do. Now the men who went in company with him stood amazed, hearing indeed a voice but seeing no man.

8 And Saul arose from the ground: and when his eyes were opened, he saw nothing. But they, leading him by the hands, brought him to Damascus.

9 And he was there three days without sight: and he did neither eat nor drink.

10 Now there was a certain disciple at Damascus, named Ananias. [3] And the Lord said to him in a vision: Ananias. And he said: Behold I am here, Lord.

11 And the Lord *said* to him: Arise and go into the street that is called Strait and seek in the house of Judas, one named Saul of Tarsus. For behold he prayeth.

12 (And he saw a man named Ananias coming in and putting his hands upon him, that he might receive his sight.)

13 But Ananias answered: Lord, I have heard by many of this man, how much evil he hath done to thy saints in Jerusalem.

14 And here he hath authority from the chief priests to bind all that invoke thy name.

15 And the Lord said to him: Go thy way: for this man is to me a vessel of election, to carry my name before the Gentiles and kings and the children of Israel.

16 For I will shew him how great things he must suffer for my name's sake.

17 And Ananias went his way and entered into the house. And laying his hands upon him, he said: Brother Saul, the Lord Jesus hath sent me, he that appeared to thee in the way as thou camest, that thou mayest receive thy sight and be filled with the Holy Ghost.

18 And immediately there fell from his eyes as it were scales: and he received his sight. And rising up, he was baptized.

19 And when he had taken meat, he was strengthened. And he was with the disciples that were at Damascus, for some days.

20 And immediately he preached Jesus in the synagogues, that he is the Son of God.

CHAP. 8. [1] Isai. 53, 7. CHAP. 9. [1] Gal. 1, 13. [2] Acts, 22, 6; 22, 10; 26, 12; 1 Cor. 15, 8; 2 Cor. 12, 2. [3] Acts, 22, 12.

Ver. 37. *If thou believest with all thy heart.* The scripture many times mentions only one disposition, as here *belief*, when others equally necessary are not expressed. These are a sorrow for sins, a firm hope, and the love of God. Moreover, believing with the whole heart signifies a belief of every thing necessary for salvation.

21 And all that heard him were astonished and said: Is not this he who persecuted in Jerusalem those that called upon this name and came hither for that intent, that he might carry them bound to the chief priests?

22 But Saul increased much more in strength and confounded the Jews who dwelt at Damascus, affirming that this is the Christ.

23 And when many days were passed, the Jews consulted together to kill him.

24 But their laying in wait was made known to Saul. ⁴ And they watched the gates also day and night, that they might kill him.

25 But the disciples, taking him in the night, conveyed him away by the wall, letting him down in a basket.

26 And when he was come into Jerusalem, he essayed to join himself to the disciples: and they all were afraid of him, not believing that he was a disciple.

27 But Barnabas took him and brought him to the apostles and told them how he had seen the Lord, and that he had spoken to him: and how in Damascus he had dealt confidently in the name of Jesus.

28 And he was with them, coming in and going out in Jerusalem and dealing confidently in the name of the Lord.

29 He spoke also to the Gentiles and disputed with the Greeks. But they sought to kill him.

30 Which when the brethren had known, they brought him down to Cæsarea and sent him away to Tarsus.

31 Now, the church had peace throughout all Judea and Galilee and Samaria: and was edified, walking in the fear of the Lord: and was filled with the consolation of the Holy Ghost.

32 And it came to pass that Peter, as he passed through, visiting all, came to the saints who dwelt at Lydda.

33 And he found there a certain man named Eneas, who had kept his bed for eight years, who was ill of the palsy.

34 And Peter said to him: Eneas, the Lord Jesus Christ healeth thee. Arise and make thy bed. And immediately he arose.

35 And all that dwelt at Lydda and Saron saw him: who were converted to the Lord.

36 And in Joppe there was a certain disciple named Tabitha, which by interpretation is called Dorcas. This woman was full of good works and almsdeeds which she did.

37 And it came to pass in those days that she was sick and died. Whom when they had washed, they laid her in an upper chamber.

38 And forasmuch as Lydda was nigh to Joppe, the disciples, hearing that Peter was there, sent unto him two men, desiring him that he would not be slack to come unto them.

39 And Peter rising up went with them. And when he was come, they brought him into the upper chamber. And all the widows stood about him, weeping and shewing him the coats and garments which Dorcas made them.

40 And they all being put forth, Peter, kneeling down, prayed. And turning to the body, he said: Tabitha, arise. And she opened her eyes and, seeing Peter, sat up.

41 And giving her his hand, he lifted her up. And when he had called the saints and the widows, he presented her alive.

42 And it was made known throughout all Joppe. And many believed in the Lord.

43 And it came to pass that he abode many days in Joppe, with one Simon a tanner.

CHAPTER 10

Cornelius is received into the church. Peter's vision.

AND there was a certain man in Cæsarea, named Cornelius, a centurion of that which is called the Italian band:

2 A religious man, and fearing God with all his house, giving much alms to the people and always praying to God.

3 This man saw in a vision manifestly, about the ninth hour of the day, an angel of God coming in unto him and saying to him: Cornelius.

4 And he, beholding him, being seized with fear, said: What is it, Lord? And he said to him: Thy prayers and thy alms are ascended for a memorial in the sight of God.

5 And now send men to Joppe: and call hither one Simon, who is surnamed Peter.

6 He lodgeth with one Simon a tanner, whose house is by the sea side. He will tell thee what thou must do.

7 And when the angel who spoke to him was departed, he called two of his household servants and a soldier who feared the Lord, of them that were under him.

8 To whom when he had related all, he sent them to Joppe.

9 And on the next day, whilst they were going on their journey and draw-

⁴ 2 Cor. 11, 32.

ing nigh to the city, Peter went up to the higher parts of the house to pray, about the sixth hour.

10 And being hungry, he was desirous to taste *somewhat*. And as they were preparing, there came upon him an ecstasy of mind.

11 And he saw the heaven opened and a certain vessel descending, as it were a great linen sheet let down by the four corners from heaven to the earth:

12 Wherein were all manner of four-footed beasts and creeping things of the earth and fowls of the air.

13 And there came a voice to him: Arise, Peter. Kill and eat.

14 But Peter said: Far be it from me. For I never did eat any thing that is common and unclean.

15 And the voice spoke to him again the second time: That which God hath cleansed, do not thou call common.

16 And this was done thrice. And presently the vessel was taken up into heaven.

17 Now, whilst Peter was doubting within himself what the vision that he had seen should mean, behold the men who were sent from Cornelius, inquiring for Simon's house, stood at the gate.

18 And when they had called, they asked if Simon, who is surnamed Peter, were lodged there.

19 And as Peter was thinking of the vision, the Spirit said to him: Behold three men seek thee.

20 Arise, therefore: get thee down and go with them, doubting nothing: for I have sent them.

21 Then Peter, going down to the men, said: Behold, I am he whom you seek. What is the cause for which you are come?

22 Who said: Cornelius, a centurion, a just man and one that feareth God, and having good testimony from all the nation of the Jews, received an answer of an holy angel, to send for thee into his house and to hear words of thee.

23 Then bringing them in, he lodged

CHAP. 10. [1] Deut. 10, 17; 2 Par. 19, 7; Job, 34, 19; Wisd. 6, 8; Ecclus. 35, 15; Rom. 2, 11; Gal. 2, 6; Eph. 6, 9; Col. 3, 25; 1 Peter, 1, 17. [2] Luke, 4, 14.

CHAP. 10. Ver. 35. *In every nation*. That is to say, not only Jews, but Gentiles also, of what nation soever, are acceptable to God, if they fear him and work justice. But then true faith is always to be presupposed, *without which* (saith St. Paul, Heb. 11, 6) *it is impossible to please God*. Beware then of the error of those who would infer from this passage that men of all religions may be pleasing to God. For since none but the true religion can be from God, all other religions must be from the father of lies, and therefore highly displeasing to the God of truth.

them. And the day following, he arose and went with them: and some of the brethren from Joppe accompanied him.

24 And the morrow after, he entered into Cæsarea. And Cornelius waited for them, having called together his kinsmen and special friends.

25 And it came to pass that when Peter was come in, Cornelius came to meet him and falling at his feet adored.

26 But Peter lifted him up, saying: Arise: I myself also am a man.

27 And talking with him, he went in and found many that were come together.

28 And he said to them: You know how abominable it is for a man that is a Jew to keep company or to come unto one of another nation: but God hath shewed to me, to call no man common or unclean.

29 For which cause, making no doubt, I came when I was sent for. I ask, therefore, for what cause you have sent for me?

30 And Cornelius said: Four days ago, unto this hour, I was praying in my house, at the ninth hour and behold a man stood before me in white apparel and said:

31 Cornelius, thy prayer is heard and thy alms are had in remembrance in the sight of God.

32 Send therefore to Joppe: and call hither Simon, who is surnamed Peter. He lodgeth in the house of Simon a tanner, by the sea side.

33 Immediately therefore I sent to thee: and thou hast done well in coming. Now, therefore, all we are present in thy sight to hear all things whatsoever are commanded thee by the Lord.

34 And Peter opening his mouth, said: In very deed I perceive [1] that God is not a respecter of persons.

35 But in every nation, he that feareth him and worketh justice is acceptable to him.

36 God sent the word to the children of Israel, preaching peace by Jesus Christ (He is Lord of all).

37 You know the word which hath been published through all Judea: [2] for it began from Galilee, after the baptism which John preached.

38 Jesus of Nazareth: how God anointed him with the Holy Ghost and with power, who went about doing good and healing all that were oppressed by the devil, for God was with him.

39 And we are witnesses of all things that he did in the land of the Jews and in Jerusalem: whom they killed, hanging him upon a tree.

40 Him God raised up the third day: and gave him to be made manifest,

41 Not to all the people, but to witnesses preordained by God, even to us, who did eat and drink with him, after he arose again from the dead.

42 And he commanded us to preach to the people and to testify that it is he who was appointed by God to be judge of the living and of the dead.

43 [3] To him all the prophets give testimony, that by his name all receive remission of sins, who believe in him.

44 While Peter was yet speaking these words, the Holy Ghost fell on all them that heard the word.

45 And the faithful of the circumcision, who came with Peter, were astonished for that the grace of the Holy Ghost was poured out upon the Gentiles also.

46 For they heard them speaking with tongues and magnifying God.

47 Then Peter answered: Can any man forbid water, that these should not be baptized, who have received the Holy Ghost, as well as we?

48 And he commanded them to be baptized in the name of the Lord Jesus Christ. Then they desired him to tarry with them some days.

CHAPTER 11

Peter defends his having received the Gentiles into the church. Many are converted at Antioch.

AND the apostles and brethren, who were in Judea, heard that the Gentiles also had received the word of God.

2 And when Peter was come up to Jerusalem, they that were of the circumcision contended with him,

3 Saying: Why didst thou go in to men uncircumcised and didst eat with them?

4 But Peter began and declared to them the *matter in* order, saying:

5 I was in the city of Joppe praying: and I saw in an ecstasy of mind a vision, a certain vessel descending, as it were a great sheet let down from heaven by four corners. And it came even unto me.

6 Into which looking, I considered and saw fourfooted creatures of the earth and beasts and creeping things and fowls of the air.

7 And I heard also a voice saying to me: Arise, Peter. Kill and eat.

8 And I said: Not so, Lord: for nothing common or unclean hath ever entered into my mouth.

9 And the voice answered again from heaven: What God hath made clean, do not thou call common.

10 And this was done three times. And all were taken up again into heaven.

11 And behold, immediately there were three men come to the house wherein I was, sent to me from Cæsarea.

12 And the Spirit said to me that I should go with them, nothing doubting. And these six brethren went with me also: and we entered into the man's house.

13 And he told us how he had seen an angel in his house, standing and saying to him: Send to Joppe and call hither Simon, who is surnamed Peter,

14 Who shall speak to thee words whereby thou shalt be saved, and all thy house.

15 And when I had begun to speak, the Holy Ghost fell upon them, as upon us also in the beginning.

16 And I remembered the word of the Lord, how that he said: [1] *John indeed baptized with water, but you shall be baptized with the Holy Ghost.*

17 If then God gave them the same grace, as to us also who believed in the Lord Jesus Christ: who was I, that could withstand God?

18 Having heard these things, they held their peace and glorified God, saying: God then hath also to the Gentiles given repentance unto life.

19 Now they who had been dispersed by the persecution that arose on occasion of Stephen went about as far as Phenice and Cyprus and Antioch, speaking the word to none, but to the Jews only.

20 But some of them were men of Cyprus and Cyrene, who, when they were entered into Antioch, spoke also to the Greeks, preaching the Lord Jesus.

21 And the hand of the Lord was with them: and a great number believing, were converted to the Lord.

22 And the tidings came to the ears of the church that was at Jerusalem, touching these things: and they sent Barnabas as far as Antioch.

23 Who, when he was come and had seen the grace of God, rejoiced. And he exhorted them all with purpose of heart to continue in the Lord.

24 For he was a good man and full of the Holy Ghost and of faith. And a great multitude was added to the Lord.

25 And Barnabas went to Tarsus to

[3] Jer. 31, 34; Mich. 7, 18. CHAP. 11. [1] Matt. 3, 11; Mark, 1, 8; Luke, 3, 16; John, 1, 26; Acts, 1, 5; 19, 4.

seek Saul: whom, when he had found, he brought to Antioch.

26 And they conversed there in the church a whole year: and they taught a great multitude, so that at Antioch the disciples were first named Christians.

27 And in these days there came prophets from Jerusalem to Antioch.

28 And one of them named Agabus, rising up, signified by the Spirit that there should be a great famine over the whole world, which came to pass under Claudius.

29 And the disciples, every man according to his ability, purposed to send relief to the brethren who dwelt in Judea.

30 Which also they did, sending it to the ancients, by the hands of Barnabas and Saul.

CHAPTER 12

Herod's persecution. Peter's deliverance by an angel. Herod's punishment.

AND at the same time, Herod the king stretched forth his hands, to afflict some of the church.

2 And he killed James, the brother of John, with the sword.

3 And seeing that it pleased the Jews, he proceeded to take up Peter also. Now it was in the days of the Azymes.

4 And when he had apprehended him, he cast him into prison, delivering him to four files of soldiers, to be kept, intending, after the pasch, to bring him forth to the people.

5 Peter therefore was kept in prison. But prayer was made without ceasing by the church unto God for him.

6 And when Herod would have brought him forth, the same night, Peter was sleeping between two soldiers, bound with two chains: and the keepers before the door kept the prison.

7 And behold an angel of the Lord stood by him and a light shined in the room. And he, striking Peter on the side, raised him up, saying: Arise quickly. And the chains fell off from his hands.

8 And the angel said to him: Gird thyself and put on thy sandals. And he did so. And he said to him: Cast thy garment about thee and follow me.

9 And going out, he followed him. And he knew not that it was true which was done by the angel: but thought he saw a vision.

10 And passing through the first and the second ward, they came to the iron gate that leadeth to the city, which of itself opened to them. And going out, they passed on through one street. And immediately the angel departed from him.

11 And Peter coming to himself, said: Now I know in very deed that the Lord hath sent his angel and hath delivered me out of the hand of Herod and from all the expectation of the people of the Jews.

12 And considering, he came to the house of Mary the mother of John, who was surnamed Mark, where many were gathered together and praying.

13 And when he knocked at the door of the gate, a damsel came to hearken, whose name was Rhode.

14 And as soon as she knew Peter's voice, she opened not the gate for joy: but running in she told that Peter stood before the gate.

15 But they said to her: Thou art mad. But she affirmed that it was so. Then said they: It is his angel.

16 But Peter continued knocking. And when they had opened, they saw him and were astonished.

17 But he, beckoning to them with him hand to hold their peace, told how the Lord had brought him out of prison. And he said: Tell these things to James and to the brethren. And going out, he went into another place.

18 Now when day was come, there was no small stir among the soldiers, what was become of Peter.

19 And when Herod had sought for him and found him not, having examined the keepers, he commanded they should be put to death. And going down from Judea to Cæsarea, he abode there.

20 And he was angry with the Tyrians and the Sidonians. But they with one accord came to him: and, having gained Blastus who was the king's chamberlain, they desired peace, because their countries were nourished by him.

21 And upon a day appointed, Herod being arrayed in kingly apparel, sat in the judgment seat and made an oration to them.

22 And the people made acclamation, saying: It is the voice of a god, and not of a man.

23 And forthwith an angel of the Lord struck him, because he had not given the honour to God: and, being eaten up by worms, he gave up the ghost.

24 But the word of the Lord increased and multiplied.

25 And Barnabas and Saul returned

CHAP. 12. Ver. 3. *Azymes.* The festival of the unleavened bread, or the pasch, which answers to our Easter.

from Jerusalem, [1] having fulfilled their ministry, taking with them John who was surnamed Mark.

CHAPTER 13

Saul and Barnabas are sent forth by the Holy Ghost. They preach in Cyprus and in Antioch of Pisidia.

NOW, there were in the church which was at Antioch prophets and doctors, among whom was Barnabas and Simon who was called Niger, and Lucius of Cyrene and Manahen who was the foster brother of Herod the tetrarch, and Saul.

2 And as they were ministering to the Lord and fasting, the Holy Ghost said to them: Separate me Saul and Barnabas, for the work whereunto I have taken them.

3 Then they, fasting and praying and imposing their hands upon them, sent them away.

4 So they, being sent by the Holy Ghost, went to Seleucia: and from thence they sailed to Cyprus.

5 And when they were come to Salamina, they preached the word of God in the synagogues of the Jews. And they had John also in the ministry.

6 And when they had gone through the whole island, as far as Paphos, they found a certain man, a magician, a false prophet, a Jew, whose name was Bar-jesu:

7 Who was with the proconsul Sergius Paulus, a prudent man. He, sending for Barnabas and Saul, desired to hear the word of God.

8 But Elymas the magician (for so his name is interpreted) withstood them, seeking to turn away the proconsul from the faith.

9 Then Saul, otherwise Paul, filled with the Holy Ghost, looking upon him,

10 Said: O full of all guile and of all deceit, child of the devil, enemy of all justice, thou ceasest not to pervert the right ways of the Lord.

11 And now behold, the hand of the Lord is upon thee: and thou shalt be blind, not seeing the sun for a time. And immediately there fell a mist and darkness upon him: and going about, he sought some one to lead him by the hand.

12 Then the proconsul, when he had seen what was done, believed, admiring at the doctrine of the Lord.

13 Now when Paul and they that were with him had sailed from Paphos, they came to Perge in Pamphylia. And John departing from them, returned to Jerusalem.

14 But they, passing through Perge, came to Antioch in Pisidia: and, entering into the Synagogue on the sabbath day, they sat down.

15 And after the reading of the law and the prophets, the rulers of the synagogue sent to them, saying: Ye men, brethren, if you have any word of exhortation to make to the people, speak.

16 Then Paul rising up and with his hand bespeaking silence, said: Ye men of Israel and you that fear God, give ear.

17 The God of the people of Israel chose our fathers and exalted the people when they were sojourners [1] in the land of Egypt: [2] And with an high arm brought them out from thence:

18 [3] And for the space of forty years endured their manners in the desert:

19 And, destroying seven nations in the land of Chaanan, [4] divided their land among them by lot.

20 As it were, after four hundred and fifty years. [5] And after these things, he gave *unto them* judges, until Samuel the prophet.

21 And after that [6] they desired a king: and God gave them Saul the son of Cis, a man of the tribe of Benjamin, forty years.

22 [7] And when he had removed him, he raised them up David to be king: to whom giving testimony, he said: [8] *I have found David, the son of Jesse, a man according to my own heart, who shall do all my wills.*

23 Of this man's seed, God, [9] according to his promise, hath raised up to Israel a Saviour Jesus:

24 [10] John first preaching, before his coming, the baptism of penance to all the people of Israel.

25 And when John was fulfilling his course, he said: [11] I am not he whom you think me to be. But behold, there cometh one after me, whose shoes of his feet I am not worthy to loose.

26 Men, brethren, children of the stock of Abraham, and whosoever among you fear God: to you the word of this salvation is sent.

27 For they that inhabited Jerusalem and the rulers thereof, not knowing him, nor the voices of the prophets which are read every sabbath, judging him, have fulfilled them.

28 And finding no cause of death in

CHAP. 12. [1] Acts, 11, 30. CHAP. 13. [1] Exod. 1, 1. [2] Exod. 13, 21, 22. [3] Exod. 16, 3. [4] Jos. 14, 2. [5] Judges, 3, 9. [6] 1 Kings, 8, 5; 9, 16; 10, 1. [7] 1 Kings, 13, 14; 16, 13. [8] Ps. 88, 21. [9] Isai. 11, 1. [10] Matt. 3, 1; Mark, 1, 4; Luke, 3, 3. [11] Matt. 3, 11; Mark, 1, 7; John, 1, 27.

him, [12] they desired of Pilate that they might kill him.

29 And when they had fulfilled all things that were written of him, taking him down from the tree, they laid him in a sepulchre.

30 [13] But God raised him up from the dead the third day.

31 Who was seen for many days by them who came up with him from Galilee to Jerusalem, who to this present are his witnesses to the people.

32 And we declare unto you that the promise which was made to our fathers,

33 This same God hath fulfilled to our children, raising up Jesus, as in the second psalm also is written: [14] *Thou art my Son: this day have I begotten thee.*

34 And to shew that he raised him up from the dead, not to return now any more to corruption, he said thus: [15] *I will give you the holy things of David, faithful.*

35 And therefore, in another place also, he saith: [16] *Thou shalt not suffer thy holy one to see corruption.*

36 For David, when he had served in his generation, according to the will of God, [17] slept: and was laid unto his fathers and saw corruption.

37 But he whom God hath raised from the dead saw no corruption.

38 Be it known therefore to you, men, brethren, that through him forgiveness of sins is preached to you: and from all the things from which you could not be justified by the law of Moses.

39 In him every one that believeth is justified.

40 Beware, therefore, lest that come upon you which is spoken in the prophets:

41 [18] *Behold, ye despisers, and wonder and perish: for I work a work in your days, a work which you will not believe, if any man shall tell it you.*

42 And as they went out, they desired them that on the next sabbath they would speak unto them these words.

43 And when the synagogue was broken up, many of the Jews and of the strangers who served God followed Paul and Barnabas: who, speaking to them, persuaded them to continue in the grace of God.

[12] Matt. 27, 20, 23; Mark, 15, 13; Luke, 23, 21, 23; John, 19, 15. [13] Matt. 28; Mark, 16; Luke, 24; John, 20. [14] Ps. 2, 7. [15] Isai. 55, 3. [16] Ps. 15, 10. [17] 3 Kings, 2, 10. [18] Hab. 1, 5. [19] Isai. 49, 6. [20] Matt. 10, 14; Mark, 6, 11; Luke, 9, 5.

CHAP. 13. Ver. 34. *I will give you the holy things.* These are the words of the prophet (Isai. 55, 3). According to the Septuagint, the sense is: *I will faithfully fulfil the promises I made to David.*

44 But the next sabbath day, the whole city almost came together, to hear the word of God.

45 And the Jews, seeing the multitudes, were filled with envy and contradicted those things which were said by Paul, blaspheming.

46 Then Paul and Barnabas said boldly: To you it behoved us first to speak the word of God: but because you reject it and judge yourselves unworthy of eternal life, behold we turn to the Gentiles.

47 For so the Lord hath commanded us: [19] *I have set thee to be the light of the Gentiles; that thou mayest be for salvation unto the utmost part of the earth.*

48 And the Gentiles hearing it were glad and glorified the word of the Lord: and as many as were ordained to life everlasting believed.

49 And the word of the Lord was published throughout the whole country.

50 But the Jews stirred up religious and honourable women and the chief men of the city: and raised persecution against Paul and Barnabas: and cast them out of their coasts.

51 [20] But they, shaking off the dust of their feet against them, came to Iconium.

52 And the disciples were filled with joy and with the Holy Ghost.

CHAPTER 14

Paul and Barnabas preach in Iconium and Lystra. Paul heals a cripple. They are taken for gods. Paul is stoned. They preach in Derbe and Perge.

AND it came to pass in Iconium that they entered together into the synagogue of the Jews and so spoke that a very great multitude both of the Jews and of the Greeks did believe.

2 But the unbelieving Jews stirred up and incensed the minds of the Gentiles against the brethren.

3 A long time therefore they abode there, dealing confidently in the Lord, who gave testimony to the word of his grace, granting signs and wonders to be done by their hands.

4 And the multitude of the city was divided. And some of them indeed held with the Jews, but some with the apostles.

5 And when there was an assault made by the Gentiles and the Jews with their rulers, to use them contumeliously and to stone them:

6 They, understanding it, fled to Lystra and Derbe, cities of Lycaonia, and to the whole country round about: and were there preaching the gospel.

7 And there sat a certain man at Lystra, impotent in his feet, a cripple from his mother's womb, who never had walked.

8 This same heard Paul speaking. Who looking upon him and seeing that he had faith to be healed,

9 Said with a loud voice. Stand upright on thy feet. And he leaped up and walked.

10 And when the multitudes had seen what Paul had done, they lifted up their voice in the Lycaonian tongue, saying: The gods are come down to us in the likeness of men.

11 And they called Barnabas, Jupiter: but Paul, Mercury: because he was chief speaker.

12 The priest also of Jupiter that was before the city, bringing oxen and garlands before the gate, would have offered sacrifice with the people.

13 Which, when the apostles Barnabas and Paul had heard, rending their clothes, they leaped out among the people, crying,

14 And saying: Ye men, why do ye these things? We also are mortals, men like unto you, preaching to you to be converted from these vain things to the living God, [1] who made the heaven and the earth and the sea and all things that are in them:

15 Who in times past suffered all nations to walk in their own ways.

16 Nevertheless he left not himself without testimony, doing good from heaven, giving rains and fruitful seasons, filling our hearts with food and gladness.

17 And speaking these things, they scarce restrained the people from sacrificing to them.

18 Now there came thither certain Jews from Antioch and Iconium; and, persuading the multitude and stoning Paul, drew him out of the city, thinking him to be dead.

19 But as the disciples stood round about him, he rose up and entered into the city: and the next day he departed with Barnabas to Derbe.

20 And when they had preached the gospel to that city and had taught many, they returned again to Lystra and to Iconium and to Antioch:

21 Confirming the souls of the disciples and exhorting them to continue in the faith: and that through many tribulations we must enter into the kingdom of God.

22 And when they had ordained to them priests in every church and had prayed with fasting, they commended

them to the Lord, in whom they believed.

23 And passing through Pisidia, they came into Pamphylia.

24 And having spoken the word of the Lord in Perge, they went down into Attalia.

25 [2] And thence they sailed to Antioch, from whence they had been delivered to the grace of God, unto the work which they accomplished.

26 And when they were come and assembled the church, they related what great things God had done with them and how he had opened the door of faith to the Gentiles.

27 And they abode no small time with the disciples.

CHAPTER 15

A dissension about circumcision. The decision and letter of the council of Jerusalem.

AND [1] some, coming down from Judea, taught the brethren: That, except you be circumcised after the manner of Moses, you cannot be saved.

2 And when Paul and Barnabas had no small contest with them, they determined that Paul and Barnabas and certain others of the other side should go up to the apostles and priests to Jerusalem, about this question.

3 They therefore, being brought on their way by the church, passed through Phenice and Samaria, relating the conversion of the Gentiles. And they caused great joy to all the brethren.

4 And when they were come to Jerusalem, they were received by the church and by the apostles and ancients, declaring how great things God had done with them.

5 But there arose of the sect of the Pharisees some that believed, saying: They must be circumcised and be commanded to observe the law of Moses.

6 And the apostles and ancients assembled to consider of this matter.

7 And when there had been much disputing, Peter, rising up, said to them: [2] Men, brethren, you know that in former days God made choice among us, that by my mouth the Gentiles should hear the word of the gospel and believe.

8 And God, who knoweth the hearts, gave testimony, [3] giving unto them the Holy Ghost, as well as to us:

9 And put no difference between us

CHAP. 14. [1] Gen. 1, 1; Ps. 145, 6; Apoc. 14, 7. [2] Acts, 13, 1. CHAP. 15. [1] Gal. 5, 2. [2] Acts, 10, 20. [3] Acts, 10, 45.

and them, purifying their hearts by faith.

10 Now therefore, why tempt you God to put a yoke upon the necks of the disciples which neither our fathers nor we have been able to bear?

11 But by the grace of the Lord Jesus Christ, we believe to be saved, in like manner as they also.

12 And all the multitude held their peace: and they heard Barnabas and Paul telling what great signs and wonders God had wrought among the Gentiles by them.

13 And after they had held their peace, James answered, saying: Men, brethren, hear me.

14 Simon hath related how God first visited to take of the Gentiles a people to his name.

15 And to this agree the words of the prophets, as it is written:

16 'After these things I will return and will rebuild the tabernacle of David, which is fallen down: and the ruins thereof I will rebuild. And I will set it up:

17 That the residue of men may seek after the Lord, and all nations upon whom my name is invoked, saith the Lord, who doth these things.

18 To the Lord was his own work known from the beginning of the world.

19 For which cause, judge that they who from among the Gentiles are converted to God are not to be disquieted:

20 But that we write unto them, that they refrain themselves from the pollutions of idols and from fornication and from things strangled and from blood.

21 For Moses of old time hath in every city them that preach him in the synagogues, ⁵where he is read every sabbath.

22 Then it pleased the apostles and ancients, with the whole church, to choose men of their own company and to send to Antioch with Paul and Barnabas, namely, Judas, who was surnamed Barsabas, and Silas, chief men among the brethren.

23 Writing by their hands: The apostles and ancients, brethren, to the brethren of the Gentiles that are at Antioch and in Syria and Cilicia, greeting.

24 Forasmuch as we have heard that

⁴ Amos, 9, 11. ⁵ Acts, 13, 27.

CHAP. 15. Ver. 29. *From blood and from things strangled.* The use of these things, though of their own nature indifferent, was here prohibited, to bring the Jews more easily to admit of the society of the Gentiles: and to exercise the latter in obedience. But this prohibition was but temporary and has long since ceased to oblige; more especially in the Western churches.

some going out from us have troubled you with words, subverting your souls, to whom we gave no commandment:

25 It hath seemed good to us, being assembled together, to choose out men and to send them unto you, with our well beloved Barnabas and Paul:

26 Men that have given their lives for the name of our Lord Jesus Christ.

27 We have sent therefore Judas and Silas, who themselves also will, by word of mouth, tell you the same things.

28 For it hath seemed good to the Holy Ghost and to us to lay no further burden upon you than these necessary things:

29 That you abstain from things sacrificed to idols and from blood and from things strangled and from fornication: from which things keeping yourselves, you shall do well. Fare ye well.

30 They therefore, being dismissed, went down to Antioch and, gathering together the multitude, delivered the epistle.

31 Which when they had read, they rejoiced for the consolation.

32 But Judas and Silas, being prophets also themselves, with many words comforted the brethren and confirmed them.

33 And after they had spent some time there, they were let go with peace by the brethren unto them that had sent them.

34 But it seemed good unto Silas to remain there: and Judas alone departed to Jerusalem.

35 And Paul and Barnabas continued at Antioch, teaching and preaching, with many others, the word of the Lord.

36 And after some days, Paul said to Barnabas: Let us return and visit our brethren in all the cities wherein we have preached the word of the Lord, to see how they do.

37 And Barnabas would have taken with them John also, that was surnamed Mark.

38 But Paul desired that he (as having departed from them out of Pamphylia ⁶ and not gone with them to the work) might not be received.

39 And there arose a dissension so that they departed one from another. And Barnabas indeed, taking Mark, sailed to Cyprus.

40 But Paul, choosing Silas, departed, being delivered by the brethren to the grace of God.

41 And he went through Syria and Cilicia, confirming the churches, commanding them to keep the precepts of the apostles and the ancients.

CHAPTER 16

Paul visits the churches. He is called to preach in Macedonia. He is scourged at Philippi.

AND he came to Derbe and Lystra. And behold, there was a certain disciple there named Timothy, the son of a Jewish woman that believed: but his father was a Gentile.

2 To this man the brethren that were in Lystra and Iconium gave a good testimony.

3 Him Paul would have to go along with him: and taking him, he circumcised him, because of the Jews who were in those places. For they all knew that his father was a Gentile.

4 And as they passed through the cities, they delivered unto them the decrees for to keep, that were decreed by the apostles and ancients who were at Jerusalem.

5 And the churches were confirmed in faith and increased in number daily.

6 And when they had passed through Phrygia and the country of Galatia, they were forbidden by the Holy Ghost to preach the word in Asia.

7 And when they were come into Mysia, they attempted to go into Bithynia: and the Spirit of Jesus suffered them not.

8 And when they had passed through Mysia, they went down to Troas.

9 And a vision was shewed to Paul in the night, which was a man of Macedonia standing and beseeching him and saying: Pass over into Macedonia and help us.

10 And as soon as he had seen the vision, immediately we sought to go into Macedonia: being assured that God had called us to preach the gospel to them.

11 And sailing from Troas, we came with a straight course to Samothracia, and the day following to Neapolis.

12 And from thence to Philippi, which is the chief city of part of Macedonia, a colony. And we were in this city some days conferring together.

13 And upon the Sabbath day, we went forth without the gate by a river side, where it seemed that there was prayer: and sitting down, we spoke to the women that were assembled.

14 And a certain woman named Lydia, a seller of purple, of the city of Thyatira, one that worshipped God, did hear: whose heart the Lord opened to attend to those things which were said by Paul.

15 And when she was baptized, and her household, she besought us, saying:

If you have judged me to be faithful to the Lord, come into my house and abide there. And she constrained us.

16 And it came to pass, as we went to prayer, a certain girl having a pythonical spirit met us, who brought to her masters much gain by divining.

17 This same following Paul and us, cried out, saying: These men are the servants of the Most High God, who preach unto you the way of salvation.

18 And this she did many days. But Paul being grieved, turned and said to the spirit: I command thee, in the name of Jesus Christ, to go from her. And he went out the same hour.

19 But her masters, seeing that the hope of their gain was gone, apprehending Paul and Silas, brought them into the market place to the rulers.

20 And presenting them to the magistrates, they said: These men disturb our city, being Jews:

21 And preach a fashion which it is not lawful for us to receive nor observe, being Romans.

22 And the people ran together against them: and [1] the magistrates, rending off their clothes, commanded them to be beaten with rods.

23 And when they had laid many stripes upon them, they cast them into prison, charging the gaoler to keep them diligently.

24 Who having received such a charge, thrust them into the inner prison and made their feet fast in the stocks.

25 And at midnight, Paul and Silas, praying, praised God. And they that were in prison heard them.

26 And suddenly there was a great earthquake, so that the foundations of the prison were shaken. And immediately all the doors were opened and the bands of all were loosed.

27 And the keeper of the prison, awakening out of his sleep and seeing the doors of the prison open, drawing his sword, would have killed himself, supposing that the prisoners had been fled.

28 But Paul cried with a loud voice, saying: Do thyself no harm, for we all are here.

29 Then calling for a light, he went in: and trembling, fell down at the feet of Paul and Silas.

30 And bringing them out, he said: Masters, what must I do, that I may be saved?

31 But they said: Believe in the Lord

CHAP. 16. [1] 2 Cor. 11, 25; Phil. 1, 13; 1 Thess. 2, 2.

CHAP. 16. Ver. 16. *A pythonical spirit.* That is, a spirit pretending to divine and tell fortunes.

Jesus: and thou shalt be saved, and thy house.

32 And they preached the word of the Lord to him and to all that were in his house.

33 And he, taking them the same hour of the night, washed their stripes: and himself was baptized, and all his house immediately.

34 And when he had brought them into his own house, he laid the table for them: and rejoiced with all his house, believing God.

35 And when the day was come, the magistrates sent the serjeants, saying: Let those men go.

36 And the keeper of the prison told these words to Paul: The magistrates have sent to let you go. Now therefore depart. And go in peace.

37 But Paul said to them: They have beaten us publicly, uncondemned, men that are Romans, and have cast us into prison. And now do they thrust us out privately? Not so: but let them come

38 And let us out themselves. And the serjeants told these words to the magistrates. And they were afraid, hearing that they were Romans.

39 And coming, they besought them: and bringing them out, they desired them to depart out of the city.

40 And they went out of the prison and entered into the house of Lydia: and having seen the brethren, they comforted them and departed.

CHAPTER 17

Paul preaches to the Thessalonians and Bereans. His discourse to the Athenians.

AND when they had passed through Amphipolis and Apollonia, they came to Thessalonica, where there was a synagogue of the Jews.

2 And Paul, according to his custom, went in unto them. And for three sabbath days he reasoned with them out of the scriptures:

3 Declaring and insinuating that the Christ was to suffer and to rise again from the dead; and that this is Jesus Christ, whom I preach to you.

4 And some of them believed and were associated to Paul and Silas: and of those that served God and of the Gentiles a great multitude: and of noble women not a few.

CHAP. 17. Ver. 6. *City, Urbem.* In the Greek, οἰκουμένην, the world.

Ver. 11. *More noble.* The Jews of Berea are justly commended for their eagerly embracing the truth and searching the scriptures, to find out the texts alleged by the apostle: which was a far more generous proceeding than that of their countrymen at Thessalonica, who persecuted the preachers of the gospel, without examining the grounds they alleged for what they taught.

5 But the Jews, moved with envy and taking unto them some wicked men of the vulgar sort and making a tumult, set the city in an uproar: and besetting Jason's house, sought to bring them out unto the people.

6 And not finding them, they drew Jason and certain brethren to the rulers of the city, crying: They that set the city in an uproar are come hither also:

7 Whom Jason hath received. And these all do contrary to the decrees of Cæsar, saying that there is another king, Jesus.

8 And they stirred up the people: and the rulers of the city, hearing these things,

9 And having taken satisfaction of Jason and of the rest, they let them go.

10 But the brethren immediately sent away Paul and Silas by night unto Berea. Who, when they were come thither, went into the synagogue of the Jews.

11 Now these were more noble than those in Thessalonica, who received the word with all eagerness, daily searching the scriptures, whether these things were so.

12 And many indeed of them believed: and of honourable women that were Gentiles and of men, not a few.

13 And when the Jews of Thessalonica had knowledge that the word of God was also preached by Paul at Berea, they came thither also, stirring up and troubling the multitude.

14 And then immediately the brethren sent away Paul, to go unto the sea: but Silas and Timothy remained there.

15 And they that conducted Paul brought him as far as Athens: and receiving a commandment from him to Silas and Timothy, that they should come to him with all speed, they departed.

16 Now whilst Paul waited for them at Athens, his spirit was stirred within him, seeing the city wholly given to idolatry.

17 He disputed, therefore, in the synagogue with the Jews and with them that served God: and in the market place, every day, with them that were there.

18 And certain philosophers of the Epicureans and of the Stoics disputed with him. And some said: What is it that this word sower would say? But others: He seemeth to be a setter forth of new gods. Because he preached to them Jesus and the resurrection.

19 And taking him, they brought him to the Areopagus, saying: May we

know what this new doctrine is, which thou speakest of?

20 For thou bringest in certain new things to our ears. We would know therefore what these things mean.

21 (Now all the Athenians and strangers that were there employed themselves in nothing else, but either in telling or in hearing some new thing.)

22 But Paul, standing in the midst of the Areopagus, said: Ye men of Athens, I perceive that in all things you are too superstitious.

23 For passing by and seeing your idols, I found an altar also, on which was written: *To the Unknown God.* What therefore you worship without knowing it, that I preach to you:

24 [1] God, who made the world and all things therein, he being Lord of heaven and earth, dwelleth [2] not in temples made with hands.

25 Neither is he served with men's hands, as though he needed any thing: seeing it is he who giveth to all life and breath and all things:

26 And hath made of one, all mankind, to dwell upon the whole face of the earth, determining appointed times and the limits of their habitation.

27 That they should seek God, if haply they may feel after him or find him, although he be not far from every one of us.

28 For in him we live and move and are; as some also of your own poets said: *For we are also his offspring.*

29 Being therefore the offspring of God, we must not suppose the divinity to be like unto gold or silver or stone, the graving of art and device of man.

30 And God indeed having winked at the times of this ignorance, now declareth unto men that all should every where do penance.

31 Because he hath appointed a day wherein he will judge the world in equity, by the man whom he hath appointed: giving faith to all, by raising him up from the dead.

32 And when they had heard of the resurrection of the dead, some indeed mocked. But others said: We will hear thee again concerning this matter.

33 So Paul went out from among them.

34 But certain men, adhering to him, did believe: among whom was also Dionysius the Areopagite and a woman named Damaris and others with them.

CHAPTER 18

Paul founds the church of Corinth and preaches at Ephesus and in other places. Apollo goes to Corinth.

AFTER these things, departing from Athens, he came to Corinth.

2 And finding a certain Jew, named Aquila, born in Pontus, lately come from Italy, with Priscilla his wife (because that Claudius had commanded all Jews to depart from Rome), he came to them.

3 And because he was of the same trade, he remained with them and wrought. (Now they were tentmakers by trade.)

4 And he reasoned in the synagogue every sabbath, bringing in the name of the Lord Jesus. And he persuaded the Jews and the Greeks.

5 And when Silas and Timothy were come from Macedonia, Paul was earnest in preaching, testifying to the Jews that Jesus is the Christ.

6 But they gainsaying and blaspheming, he shook his garments and said to them: Your blood be upon your own heads: I am clean. From henceforth I will go unto the Gentiles.

7 And departing thence, he entered into the house of a certain man, named Titus Justus, one that worshipped God, whose house was adjoining to the synagogue.

8 And Crispus, the ruler of the synagogue, believed in the Lord, with all his house. And many of the Corinthians hearing, believed and were baptized.

9 And the Lord said to Paul in the night, by a vision: Do not fear, but speak. And hold not thy peace,

10 Because I am with thee and no man shall set upon thee, to hurt thee. For I have much people in this city.

11 And he stayed there a year and six months, teaching among them the word of God.

12 But when Gallio was proconsul of Achaia, the Jews with one accord rose up against Paul and brought him to the judgment seat,

13 Saying: This man persuadeth men to worship God contrary to the law.

14 And when Paul was beginning to open his mouth, Gallio said to the Jews: If it were some matter of injustice or an heinous deed, O Jews, I should with reason bear with you.

15 But if they be questions of word and names and of your law, look you to it. I will not be judge of such things.

16 And he drove them from the judgment seat.

CHAP. 17. [1] Gen. 1. 1. [2] Acts. 7. 48.

Ver. 24. *Dwelleth not in temples.* God is not contained in temples, so as to need them for his dwelling, or any other uses, as the heathens imagined. Yet by his omnipresence, he is both there and every where.

17 And all laying hold on Sosthenes, the ruler of the synagogue, beat him before the judgment seat. And Gallio cared for none of those things.

18 But Paul, when he had stayed yet many days, taking his leave of the brethren, sailed thence into Syria (and with him Priscilla and Aquila), [1] having shorn his head in Cenchræ. For he had a vow.

19 And he came to Ephesus and left them there. But he himself, entering into the synagogue, disputed with the Jews.

20 And when they desired him that he would tarry a longer time, he consented not:

21 But taking his leave and saying: I will return to you again, God willing, he departed from Ephesus.

22 And going down to Cæsarea, he went up to Jerusalem and saluted the church: and so came down to Antioch.

23 And after he had spent some time there, he departed and went through the country of Galatia and Phrygia, in order, confirming all the disciples.

24 Now a certain Jew, named Apollo, born at Alexandria, an eloquent man, came to Ephesus, one mighty in the scriptures.

25 This man was instructed in the way of the Lord: and being fervent in spirit, spoke and taught diligently the things that are of Jesus, knowing only the baptism of John.

26 This man therefore began to speak boldly in the synagogue. Whom when Priscilla and Aquila had heard, they took him to them and expounded to him the way of the Lord more diligently.

27 And whereas he was desirous to go to Achaia, the brethren exhorting wrote to the disciples to receive him. Who, when he was come, helped them much who had believed.

28 For with much vigour he convinced the Jews openly, shewing by the scriptures that Jesus is the Christ.

CHAPTER 19

Paul establishes the church at Ephesus. The tumult of the silversmiths.

AND it came to pass, while Apollo was at Corinth, that Paul, having passed through the upper coasts, came to Ephesus and found certain disciples.

2 And he said to them: Have you received the Holy Ghost since ye believed? But they said to him: We have

not so much as heard whether there be a Holy Ghost.

3 And he said: In what then were you baptized? Who said: In John's baptism.

4 Then Paul said: [1] John baptized the people with the baptism of penance, saying: That they should believe in him who was to come after him, that is to say, in Jesus.

5 Having heard these things, they were baptized in the name of the Lord Jesus.

6 And when Paul had imposed his hands on them, the Holy Ghost came upon them: and they spoke with tongues and prophesied.

7 And all the men were about twelve.

8 And entering into the synagogue, he spoke boldly for the space of three months, disputing and exhorting concerning the kingdom of God.

9 But when some were hardened and believed not, speaking evil of the way of the Lord before the multitude, departing from them, he separated the disciples, disputing daily in the school of one Tyrannus.

10 And this continued for the space of two years, so that all who dwelt in Asia heard the word of the Lord, both Jews and Gentiles.

11 And God wrought by the hand of Paul more than common miracles.

12 So that even there were brought from his body to the sick, handkerchiefs and aprons: and the diseases departed from them: and the wicked spirits went out of them.

13 Now some also of the Jewish exorcists, who went about, attempted to invoke over them that had evil spirits the name of the Lord Jesus, saying: I conjure you by Jesus, whom Paul preacheth.

14 And there were certain men, seven sons of Sceva, a Jew, a chief priest, that did this.

15 But the wicked spirit, answering, said to them: Jesus I know: and Paul I know. But who are you?

16 And the man in whom the wicked spirit was, leaping upon them and mastering them both, prevailed against them, so that they fled out of that house naked and wounded.

17 And this became known to all the Jews and the Gentiles that dwelt at Ephesus. And fear fell on them all: and the name of the Lord Jesus was magnified.

18 And many of them that believed came, confessing and declaring their deeds.

19 And many of them who had followed curious arts brought together

CHAP. 18. [1] Num. 6, 18; Acts, 21, 24. CHAP. 19.
[1] Matt. 3, 11; Mark, 1, 8; Luke, 3, 16; John, 3, 26; Acts, 1, 5; 11, 16.

their books and burnt them before all. And, counting the price of them, they found the money to be fifty thousand pieces of silver.

20 So mightily grew the word of God and was confirmed.

21 And when these things were ended, Paul purposed in the spirit, when he had passed through Macedonia and Achaia, to go to Jerusalem, saying: After I have been there, I must see Rome also.

22 And sending into Macedonia two of them that ministered to him, Timothy and Erastus, he himself remained for a time in Asia.

23 Now at that time there arose no small disturbance about the way of the Lord.

24 For a certain man named Demetrius, a silversmith, who made silver temples for Diana, brought no small gain to the craftsmen.

25 Whom he calling together with the workmen of like occupation, said: Sirs, you know that our gain is by this trade.

26 And you see and hear that this Paul, by persuasion hath drawn away a great multitude, not only of Ephesus, but almost of all Asia, saying: They are not gods which are made by hands.

27 So that not only this our craft is in danger to be set at nought, but also the temple of great Diana shall be reputed for nothing! Yea, and her majesty shall begin to be destroyed, whom all Asia and the world worshippeth.

28 Having heard these things, they were full of anger and cried out, saying: Great is Diana of the Ephesians!

29 And the whole city was filled with confusion. And having caught Gaius and Aristarchus, men of Macedonia, Paul's companions, they rushed with one accord into the theatre.

30 And when Paul would have entered in unto the people, the disciples suffered him not.

31 And some also of the rulers of Asia, who were his friends, sent unto him, desiring that he would not venture himself into the theatre.

32 Now some cried one thing, some another. For the assembly was confused: and the greater part knew not for what cause they were come together.

33 And they drew forth Alexander out of the multitude, the Jews thrusting him forward. And Alexander, beckoning with his hand for silence, would have given the people satisfaction.

34 But as soon as they perceived him to be a Jew, all with one voice, for the space of about two hours, cried out: Great is Diana of the Ephesians!

35 And when the town clerk had appeased the multitudes, he said: Ye men of Ephesus, what man is there that knoweth not that the city of the Ephesians is a worshipper of the great Diana and of Jupiter's offspring?

36 For as much therefore as these things cannot be contradicted, you ought to be quiet and to do nothing rashly.

37 For you have brought hither these men, who are neither guilty of sacrilege nor of blasphemy against your goddess.

38 But if Demetrius and the craftsmen that are with him have a matter against any man, the courts of justice are open: and there are proconsuls. Let them accuse one another.

39 And if you inquire after any other matter, it may be decided in a lawful assembly.

40 For we are even in danger to be called in question for this day's uproar, there being no man guilty (of whom we may give account) of this concourse. And when he had said these things, he dismissed the assembly.

CHAPTER 20

Paul passes through Macedonia and Greece. He raises a dead man to life at Troas. His discourse to the clergy of Ephesus.

AND after the tumult was ceased, Paul calling to him the disciples and exhorting them, took his leave and set forward to go into Macedonia.

2 And when he had gone over those parts and had exhorted them with many words, he came into Greece:

3 Where, when he had spent three months, the Jews laid wait for him, as he was about to sail into Syria. So he took a resolution to return through Macedonia.

4 And there accompanied him Sopater, the son of Pyrrhus, of Berea: and of the Thessalonians, Aristarchus and Secundus: and Gaius of Derbe and Timothy: and of Asia, Tychicus and Trophimus.

5 These, going before, stayed for us at Troas.

6 But we sailed from Philippi after the days of the Azymes and came to them to Troas in five days, where we abode seven days.

7 And on the first day of the week, when we were assembled to break bread, Paul discoursed with them, being to

depart on the morrow. And he continued his speech until midnight.

8 And there were a great number of lamps in the upper chamber where we were assembled.

9 And a certain young man named Eutychus, sitting on the window, being oppressed with a deep sleep (as Paul was long preaching), by occasion of his sleep fell from the third loft down and was taken up dead.

10 To whom, when Paul had gone down, he laid himself upon him and, embracing him, said: Be not troubled, for his soul is in him.

11 Then going up and breaking bread and tasting and having talked a long time to them, until daylight, so he departed.

12 And they brought the youth alive and were not a little comforted.

13 But we going aboard the ship, sailed to Assos, being there to take in Paul. For so he had appointed, himself purposing to travel by land.

14 And when he had met with us at Assos, we took him in and came to Mitylene.

15 And sailing thence, the day following we came over against Chios: and the next day we arrived at Samos: and the day following we came to Miletus.

16 For Paul had determined to sail by Ephesus, lest he should be stayed any time in Asia. For he hasted, if it were possible for him, to keep the day of Pentecost at Jerusalem.

17 And sending from Miletus to Ephesus, he called the ancients of the church.

18 And when they were come to him and were together, he said to them: You know from the first day that I came into Asia, in what manner I have been with you, for all the time.

19 Serving the Lord with all humility and with tears and temptations which befell me by the conspiracies of the Jews:

20 How I have kept back nothing that was profitable to you, but have preached it to you, and taught you publicly, and from house to house,

21 Testifying both to Jews and Gentiles penance towards God and faith in our Lord Jesus Christ.

22 And now, behold, being bound in the spirit, I go to Jerusalem: not knowing the things which shall befall me there:

23 Save that the Holy Ghost in every city witnesseth to me, saying: That bands and afflictions wait for me at Jerusalem.

CHAP. 20. [1] Cor. 4, 12; 2 Thess. 3, 8.

24 But I fear none of these things, neither do I count my life more precious than myself, so that I may consummate my course and the ministry of the word which I received from the Lord Jesus, to testify the gospel of the grace of God.

25 And now behold, I know that all you, among whom I have gone preaching the kingdom of God, shall see my face no more.

26 Wherefore I take you to witness this day that I am clear from the blood of all men.

27 For I have not spread to declare unto you all, the counsel of God.

28 Take heed to yourselves and to the whole flock, wherein the Holy Ghost hath placed you bishops, to rule the Church of God which he hath purchased with his own blood.

29 I know that after my departure ravening wolves will enter in among you, not sparing the flock.

30 And of your own selves shall arise men speaking perverse things, to draw away disciples after them.

31 Therefore watch, keeping in memory that for three years I ceased not with tears to admonish every one of you, night and day.

32 And now I commend you to God and to the word of his grace, who is able to build up and to give an inheritance among all the sanctified.

33 I have not coveted any man's silver, gold or apparel, as

34 You yourselves know. [1] For such things as were needful for me and them that are with me, these hands have furnished.

35 I have shewed you all things, how that so labouring you ought to support the weak and to remember the word of the Lord Jesus, how he said: It is a more blessed thing to give, rather than to receive.

36 And when he had said these things, kneeling down, he prayed with them all.

37 And there was much weeping among them all. And falling on the neck of Paul, they kissed him,

38 Being grieved most of all for the word which he had said, that they should see his face no more. And they brought him on his way to the ship.

CHAPTER 21

Paul goes up to Jerusalem. He is apprehended by the Jews in the temple.

AND when it came to pass that, being parted from them, we set sail, we came with a straight course to

Coos, and the day following to Rhodes: and from thence to Patara.

2 And when we had found a ship sailing over to Phenice, we went aboard and set forth.

3 And when we had discovered Cyrus, leaving it on the left hand, we sailed into Syria and came to Tyre: for there the ship was to unlade her burden.

4 And finding disciples, we tarried there seven days: who said to Paul, through the Spirit, that he should not go up to Jerusalem.

5 And the days being expired, departing we went forward, they all bringing us on our way, with their wives and children, till we were out of the city. And we kneeled down on the shore: and we prayed.

6 And when we had bid one another farewell, we took ship. And they returned home.

7 But we, having finished the voyage by sea, from Tyre came down to Ptolemais: and saluting the brethren, we abode one day with them.

8 And the next day departing, we came to Cæsarea. And entering into the house of Philip the evangelist, [1] who was one of the seven, we abode with him.

9 And he had four daughters, virgins, who did prophesy.

10 And as we tarried there for some days, there came from Judea a certain prophet, named Agabus.

11 Who, when he was come to us, took Paul's girdle: and binding his own feet and hands, he said: Thus saith the Holy Ghost: The man whose girdle this is, the Jews shall bind in this manner in Jerusalem and shall deliver him into the hands of the Gentiles.

12 Which when we had heard, both we and they that were of that place desired him that he would not go up to Jerusalem.

13 Then Paul answered and said: What do you mean, weeping and afflicting my heart? For I am ready not only to be bound, but to die also in Jerusalem, for the name of the Lord Jesus.

14 And when we could not persuade him, we ceased, saying: The will of the Lord be done.

15 And after those days, being prepared, we went up to Jerusalem.

16 And there went also with us some of the disciples from Cæsarea, bringing with them one Mnason a Cyprian, an old disciple, with whom we should lodge.

17 And when we were come to Jerusalem, the brethren received us gladly.

18 And the day following, Paul went in with us unto James: and all the ancients were assembled.

19 Whom when he had saluted, he related particularly what things God had wrought among the Gentiles by his ministry.

20 But they hearing it, glorified God and said to him: Thou seest, brother, how many thousands there are among the Jews that have believed: and they are all zealous for the law.

21 Now they have heard of thee that thou teachest those Jews, who are among the Gentiles to depart from Moses: saying that they ought not to circumcise their children, nor walk according to the custom.

22 What is it therefore? The multitude must needs come together: for they will hear that thou art come.

23 Do therefore this that we say to thee. We have four men, who have a vow on them.

24 Take these and sanctify thyself with them: and bestow on them, [2] that they may shave their heads. And all will know that the things which they have heard of these are false: but that thou thyself also walkest keeping the law.

25 But as touching the Gentiles that believe, [3] we have written, decreeing that they should only refrain themselves from that which has been offered to idols and from blood and from things strangled and from fornication.

26 Then Paul took the men and, the next day being purified with them, entered into the temple, giving notice of the accomplishment of the days of purification, until an oblation should be offered for every one of them.

27 But when the seven days were drawing to an end, those Jews that were of Asia, when they saw him in the temple, stirred up all the people and laid hands upon him, crying out:

28 Men of Israel, help: This is the man that teacheth all men every where against the people and the law and this place; and moreover hath brought in Gentiles into the temple and hath violated this holy place.

29 (For they had seen Trophimus the Ephesian in the city with him, whom they supposed that Paul had brought into the temple.)

30 And the whole city was in an up-

CHAP. 21. [1] Acts, 6, 5; 8 5. [2] Num. 6, 18; Acts, 18, 18. [3] Acts, 15, 20, 29.

CHAP. 21. Ver. 8. *The evangelist.* That is, the preacher of the gospel, the same that before converted the Samaritans and baptized the eunuch (chap. 8), being one of the first seven deacons.

Ver. 24. *Keeping the law.* The law, though now no longer obligatory, was for a time observed by the Christian Jews: to bury, as it were, the synagogue with honour.

roar: and the people ran together. And taking Paul, they drew him out of the temple: and immediately the doors were shut.

31 And as they went about to kill him, it was told the tribune of the band that all Jerusalem was in confusion.

32 Who, forthwith taking with him soldiers and centurions, ran down to them. And when they saw the tribune and the soldiers, they left off beating Paul.

33 Then the tribune, coming near took him and commanded him to be bound with two chains: and demanded who he was and what he had done.

34 And some cried one thing, some another, among the multitude. And when he could not know the certainty for the tumult, he commanded him to be carried into the castle.

35 And when he was come to the stairs, it fell out that he was carried by the soldiers, because of the violence of the people.

36 For the multitude of the people followed after, crying: Away with him!

37 And as Paul was about to be brought into the castle, he saith to the tribune: May I speak something to thee? Who said: Canst thou speak Greek?

38 Art not thou that Egyptian who before these days didst raise a tumult and didst lead forth into the desert four thousand men that were murderers?

39 But Paul said to him: I am a Jew of Tarsus in Cilicia, a citizen of no mean city. And I beseech thee, suffer me to speak to the people.

40 And when he had given him leave, Paul standing on the stairs, beckoned with his hand to the people. And a great silence being made, he spoke unto them in the Hebrew tongue, saying:

CHAPTER 22

Paul declares to the people the history of his conversion. He escapes scourging by claiming the privilege of a Roman citizen.

MEN, brethren and fathers, hear ye the account which I now give unto you.

2 (And when they heard that he spoke to them in the Hebrew tongue, they kept the more silence.)

3 And he saith: I am a Jew, born at Tarsus in Cilicia, but brought up in this city, at the feet of Gamaliel,

CHAP. 22. ¹ Acts, 8, 3. ² Acts, 9, 2. ³ Acts, 8, 3.

CHAP. 22. Ver. 9. *Heard not the voice.* That is, they distinguished not the words: though they heard the voice (Acts. 9, 7).
Ver. 14. *Just One.* Our Saviour, who appeared to St. Paul (Acts, 9, 17).

taught according to the truth of the law of the fathers, zealous for the law, as also all you are this day:

4 ¹ Who persecuted this way unto death, binding and delivering into prisons both men and women,

5 As the high priest doth bear me witness and all the ancients. ² From whom also receiving letters to the brethren, I went to Damascus, that I might bring them bound from thence to Jerusalem to be punished.

6 And it came to pass, as I was going and drawing nigh to Damascus, at mid-day, that suddenly from heaven there shone round about me a great light:

7 And falling on the ground, I heard a voice saying to me: Saul, Saul, why persecutest thou me?

8 And I answered: Who art thou, Lord? And he said to me: I am Jesus of Nazareth, whom thou persecutest.

9 And they that were with me saw indeed the light: but they heard not the voice of him that spoke to me.

10 And I said: What shall I do, Lord? And the Lord said to me: Arise and go to Damascus; and there it shall be told thee of all things that thou must do.

11 And whereas I did not see for the brightness of that light, being led by the hand by my companions, I came to Damascus.

12 And one Ananias, a man according to the law, having testimony of all the Jews who dwelt there,

13 Coming to me and standing by me, said to me: Brother Saul, look up. And I, the same hour, looked upon him.

14 But he said: The God of our fathers hath preordained thee that thou shouldst know his will and see the Just One and shouldst hear the voice from his mouth.

15 For thou shalt be his witness to all men of those things which thou hast seen and heard.

16 And now why tarriest thou? Rise up and be baptized and wash away thy sins, invoking his name.

17 And it came to pass, when I was come again to Jerusalem and was praying in the temple, that I was in a trance,

18 And saw him saying unto me: Make haste and get thee quickly out of Jerusalem: because they will not receive thy testimony concerning me.

19 And I said: Lord, they know ³ that I cast into prison and beat in every synagogue them that believed in thee.

20 And when the blood of Stephen

thy witness was shed, [4] I stood by and consented: and kept the garments of them that killed him.

21 And he said to me: Go, for unto the Gentiles afar off will I send thee.

22 And they heard him until this word and then lifted up their voice, saying: Away with such an one from the earth. For it is not fit that he should live.

23 And as they cried out and threw off their garments and cast dust into the air,

24 The tribune commanded him to be brought into the castle, and that he should be scourged and tortured: to know for what cause they did so cry out against him.

25 And when they had bound him with thongs, Paul saith to the centurion that stood by him: Is it lawful for you to scourge a man that is a Roman and uncondemned?

26 Which the centurion hearing, went to the tribune and told him, saying: What art thou about to do? For this man is a Roman citizen.

27 And the tribune coming, said to him: Tell me. Art thou a Roman? But he said: Yea.

28 And the tribune answered: I obtained the being free of this city with a great sum. And Paul said: But I was born so.

29 Immediately therefore they departed from him that were about to torture him. The tribune also was afraid after he understood that he was a Roman citizen and because he had bound him.

30 But on the next day, meaning to know more diligently for what cause he was accused by the Jews, he loosed him and commanded the priests to come together and all the council: and, bringing forth Paul, he set him before them.

CHAPTER 23

Paul stands before the council. The Jews conspire his death. He is sent away to Cæsarea.

AND Paul, looking upon the council, said: Men, brethren, I have conversed with all good conscience before God until this present day.

2 And the high priest, Ananias, commanded them that stood by him to strike him on the mouth.

3 Then Paul said to him: God shall strike thee, thou whited wall. For, sittest thou to judge me according to the law and, contrary to the law, commandest me to be struck?

4 And they that stood by said: Dost thou revile the high priest of God?

5 And Paul said: I knew not, brethren, that he is the high priest. For it is written: [1] *Thou shalt not speak evil of the prince of thy people.*

6 And Paul, knowing that the one part were Sadducees and the other Pharisees, cried out in the council: Men, brethren, [2] I am a Pharisee, the son of Pharisees: concerning the hope and resurrection of the dead I am called in question.

7 And when he had so said, there arose a dissension between the Pharisees and the Sadducees. And the multitude was divided.

8 [3] For the Sadducees say that there is no resurrection, neither angel, nor spirit: but the Pharisees confess both.

9 And there arose a great cry. And some of the Pharisees rising up, strove, saying: We find no evil in this man. What if a spirit hath spoken to him, or an angel?

10 And when there arose a great dissension, the tribune, fearing lest Paul should be pulled in pieces by them, commanded the soldiers to go down and to take him by force from among them and to bring him into the castle.

11 And the night following, the Lord standing by him, said: Be constant; for as thou hast testified of me in Jerusalem, so must thou bear witness also at Rome.

12 And when day was come, some of the Jews gathered together and bound themselves under a curse, saying that they would neither eat nor drink till they killed Paul.

13 And they were more than forty men that had made this conspiracy.

14 Who came to the chief priests and the ancients and said: We have bound ourselves under a great curse that we will eat nothing till we have slain Paul.

15 Now therefore do you with the council signify to the tribune, that he bring him forth to you, as if you meant to know something more certain touching him. And we, before he come near, are ready to kill him.

16 Which when Paul's sister's son had heard, of their lying in wait, he came and entered into the castle and told Paul.

17 And Paul, calling to him one of the centurions, said: Bring this young man to the tribune; for he hath some thing to tell him.

18 And he, taking him, brought him to the tribune and said: Paul, the prisoner, desired me to bring this

---

[4] Acts, 7, 57. Chap. 23. [1] Exod. 22, 28. [2] Phil. 3, 5. [3] Matt. 22, 23.

Ver. 24. *The tribune.* That is, Lysias.

young man unto thee, who hath something to say to thee.

19 And the tribune, taking him by the hand, went aside with him privately and asked him: What is it that thou hast to tell me?

20 And he said: The Jews have agreed to desire thee that thou wouldst bring forth Paul to-morrow into the council, as if they meant to inquire some thing more certain touching him.

21 But do not thou give credit to them: for there lie in wait for him more than forty men of them, who have bound themselves by oath neither to eat nor to drink, till they have killed him. And they are now ready, looking for a promise from thee.

22 The tribune therefore dismissed the young man, charging him that he should tell no man that he had made known these things unto him.

23 Then having called two centurions, he said to them: Make ready two hundred soldiers to go as far as Cæsarea: and seventy horsemen and two hundred spearmen, for the third hour of the night.

24 And provide beasts, that they may set Paul on and bring him safe to Felix the governor.

25 (For he feared lest perhaps the Jews might take him away by force and kill him: and he should afterwards be slandered, as if he was to take money.) And he wrote a letter after this manner:

26 Claudius Lysias to the most excellent governor, Felix, greeting:

27 This man, being taken by the Jews and ready to be killed by them, I rescued, coming in with an army, understanding that he is a Roman.

28 And meaning to know the cause which they objected unto him, I brought him forth into their council.

29 Whom I found to be accused concerning questions of their law; but having nothing laid to his charge worthy of death or of bands.

30 And when I was told of ambushes that they had prepared for him, I sent him to thee, signifying also to his accusers to plead before thee. Farewell.

31 Then the soldiers, according as it was commanded them, taking Paul, brought him by night to Antipatris.

32 And the next day, leaving the horsemen to go with him, they returned to the castle.

33 Who, when they were come to Cæsarea and had delivered the letter to the governor, did also present Paul before him.

34 And when he had read it and had asked of what province he was and understood that he was of Cilicia:

35 I will hear thee, said he, when thy accusers come. And he commanded him to be kept in Herod's judgment hall.

CHAPTER 24

Paul defends his innocence before Felix the governor. He preaches the faith to him.

AND after five days, the high priest, Ananias, came down with some of the ancients and one Tertullus, an orator, who went to the governor aganst Paul.

2 And Paul being called for, Tertullus began to accuse him, saying: Whereas, through thee we live in much peace and many things are rectified by thy providence,

3 We accept it always and in all places, most excellent Felix, with all thanksgiving.

4 But that I be no further tedious to thee, I desire thee of thy clemency to hear us in a few words.

5 We have found this to be a pestilent man and raising seditions among all the Jews throughout the world: and author of the sedition of the sect of the Nazarenes.

6 Who also hath gone about to profane the temple: whom, we having apprehended, would also have judged according to our law.

7 But Lysias the tribune, coming upon us with great violence, took him away out of our hands;

8 Commanding his accusers to come to thee. Of whom thou mayest thyself, by examination, have knowledge of all these things whereof we accuse him.

9 And the Jews also added and said that these things were so.

10 Then Paul answered (the governor making a sign to him to speak): Knowing that for many years thou hast been judge over this nation, I will with good courage answer for myself.

11 For thou mayest understand that there are yet but twelve days since I went up to adore in Jerusalem:

12 And neither in the temple did they find me disputing with any man or causing any concourse of the people: neither in the synagogues, nor in the city.

13 Neither can they prove unto thee the things whereof they now accuse me.

14 But this I confess to thee that according to the way which they call a heresy, so do I serve the Father and my God, believing all things which are written in the law and the prophets:

15 Having hope in God, which these also themselves look for, that there shall be a resurrection of the just and unjust.

16 And herein do I endeavour to have always a conscience without offence, towards God and towards men.

17 Now after many years, I came to bring alms to my nation and offerings and vows.

18 ¹ In which I was found purified in the temple: neither with multitude nor with tumult.

19 But certain Jews of Asia, who ought to be present before thee and to accuse, if they had anything against me:

20 Or let these men themselves say if they found in me any iniquity, when standing before the council,

21 Except it be for this one voice only that I cried, standing among them: ² Concerning the resurrection of the dead am I judged this day by you.

22 And Felix put them off, having most certain knowledge of this way, saying: When Lysias the tribune shall come down, I will hear you.

23 And he commanded a centurion to keep him: and that he should be easy and that he should not prohibit any of his friends to minister unto him.

24 And after some days, Felix, coming with Drusilla his wife, who was a Jew, sent for Paul and heard of him the faith that is in Christ Jesus.

25 And as he treated of justice and chastity and of the judgment to come, Felix, being terrified, answered: For this time, go thy way: but when I have a convenient time, I will send for thee.

26 Hoping also withal that money should be given him by Paul: for which cause also oftentimes sending for him, he spoke with him.

27 But when two years were ended, Felix had for successor Portius Festus. And Felix being willing to shew the Jews a pleasure, left Paul bound.

CHAPTER 25

Paul appeals to Cæsar. King Agrippa desires to hear him.

NOW when Festus was come into the province, after three days, he went up to Jerusalem from Cæsarea.

2 And the chief priests and principal men of the Jews went unto him against Paul: and they besought him,

3 Requesting favour against him, that he would command him to be brought to Jerusalem, laying wait to kill him in the way.

4 But Festus answered: That Paul was kept in Cæsarea; and that he him-

self would very shortly depart thither.

5 Let them, therefore, saith he, among you that are able, go down with me and accuse him, if there be any crime in the man.

6 And having tarried among them no more than eight or ten days, he went down to Cæsarea. And the next day, he sat in the judgment seat and commanded Paul to be brought.

7 Who being brought, the Jews stood about him, who were come down from Jerusalem, objecting many and grievous causes, which they could not prove:

8 Paul making answer for himself: Neither against the law of the Jews, nor against the temple, nor against Cæsar, have I offended in any thing.

9 But Festus, willing to shew the Jews a pleasure, answering Paul, said: Wilt thou go up to Jerusalem and there be judged of these things before me?

10 Then Paul said: I stand at Cæsar's judgment seat, where I ought to be judged. To the Jews I have done no injury, as thou very well knowest.

11 For if I have injured them or have committed any thing worthy of death, I refuse not to die. But if there be none of these things whereof they accuse me, no man may deliver me to them. I appeal to Cæsar.

12 Then Festus, having conferred with the council, answered: Hast thou appealed to Cæsar? To Cæsar shalt thou go.

13 And after some days, king Agrippa and Bernice came down to Cæsarea to salute Festus.

14 And as they tarried there many days, Festus told the king of Paul, saying: A certain man was left prisoner by Felix.

15 About whom, when I was at Jerusalem, the chief priests and the ancients of the Jews came unto me, desiring condemnation against him.

16 To whom I answered: It is not the custom of the Romans to condemn any man, before that he who is accused have his accusers present and have liberty to make his answer, to clear himself of the things laid to his charge.

17 When therefore they were come hither, without any delay, on the day following, sitting in the judgment seat, I commanded the man to be brought.

18 Against whom, when the accusers stood up, they brought no accusation of things which I thought ill of:

19 But had certain questions of their own superstition against him, and of

one Jesus deceased, whom Paul affirmed to be alive.

20 I therefore being in a doubt of this manner of question, asked him whether he would go to Jerusalem and there be judged of these things.

21 But Paul, appealing to be reserved unto the hearing of Augustus, I commanded him to be kept, till I might send him to Cæsar.

22 And Agrippa said to Festus: I would also hear the man, myself. To-morrow, said he, thou shalt hear him.

23 And on the next day, when Agrippa and Bernice were come with great pomp and had entered into the hall of audience with the tribunes and principal men of the city, at Festus' commandment, Paul was b r o u g h t forth.

24 And Festus saith: King Agrippa and all ye men who are here present with us, you see this man, about whom all the multitude of the Jews dealt with me at Jerusalem, requesting and crying out that he ought not to live any longer.

25 Yet have I found nothing that he hath committed worthy of death. But forasmuch as he himself hath appealed to Augustus, I have determined to send him.

26 Of whom I have nothing certain to write to my lord. For which cause, I have brought him forth before you, and especially before thee, O king Agrippa, that, examination being made, I may have what to write.

27 For it seemeth to me unreasonable to send a prisoner and not to signify the things laid to his charge.

CHAPTER 26

Paul gives an account to Agrippa of his life, conversion and calling.

THEN Agrippa said to Paul: Thou art permitted to speak for thyself. Then Paul, stretching forth his hand, began to make his answer.

2 I think myself happy, O king Agrippa, that I am to answer for myself this day before thee, touching all the things whereof I am accused by the Jews.

3 Especially as thou knowest all, both customs and questions, that are among the Jews. Wherefore I beseech thee to hear me patiently.

4 And my life indeed from my youth, which was from the beginning among my own nation in Jerusalem, all the Jews do know:

5 Having known me from the be-

ginning (if they will give testimony) that according to the most sure sect of our religion I lived, a Pharisee.

6 And now for the hope of the promise that was made by God to the fathers, do I stand subject to judgment:

7 Unto which, our twelve tribes, serving night and day, hope to come. For which hope, O king, I am accused by the Jews.

8 Why should it be thought a thing incredible that God should raise the dead?

9 And I indeed did formerly think that I ought to do many things contrary to the name of Jesus of Nazareth.

10 [1] Which also I did at Jerusalem: and many of the saints did I shut up in prison, having received authority of the chief priests. And when they were put to death, I brought the sentence.

11 And oftentimes punishing them, in every synagogue, I compelled them to blaspheme: and being yet more mad against them, I persecuted them even unto foreign cities.

12 [2] Whereupon, when I was going to Damascus with authority and permission of the chief priest,

13 At midday, O king, I saw in the way a light from heaven, above the brightness of the sun, shining round about me and them that were in company with me.

14 And when we were all fallen down on the ground, I heard a voice speaking to me in the Hebrew tongue: Saul, Saul, why persecutest thou me? It is hard for thee to kick against the goad.

15 And I said: Who art thou, Lord? And the Lord answered: I am Jesus whom thou persecutest.

16 But rise up and stand upon thy feet: for to this end have I appeared to thee, that I may make thee a minister and a witness of those things which thou hast seen and of those things wherein I will appear to thee,

17 Delivering thee from the people and from the nations unto which now I send thee:

18 To open their eyes, that they may be converted from darkness to light and from the power of Satan to God, that they may receive forgiveness of sins and a lot among the saints, by the faith that is in me.

19 Whereupon, O king Agrippa, I was not incredulous to the heavenly vision.

20 [3] But to them first that are at Damascus and at Jerusalem, and unto all the country of Judea, and to the Gentiles did I preach, that they should do penance and turn to God, doing works worthy of penance.

CHAP. 26. [1] Acts, 8, 3. [2] Acts, 9, 2. [3] Acts, 9, 20.

21 For this cause, the Jews, when I was in the temple, [4] having apprehended me, went about to kill me.

22 But being aided by the help of God, I stand unto this day, witnessing both to small and great, saying no other thing than those which the prophets and Moses did say should come to pass:

23 That Christ should suffer and that he should be the first that should rise from the dead and should shew light to the people and to the Gentiles.

24 As he spoke these things and made his answer, Festus said with a loud voice: Paul, thou art beside thyself: much learning doth make thee mad.

25 And Paul said: I am not mad, most excellent Festus, but I speak words of truth and soberness.

26 For the king knoweth of these things, to whom also I speak with confidence. For I am persuaded that none of these things are hidden from him. For neither was any of these things done in a corner.

27 Believest thou the prophets, O king Agrippa? I know that thou believest.

28 And Agrippa said to Paul: In a little thou persuadest me to become a Christian.

29 And Paul said: I would to God that both in a little and in much, not only thou, but also all that hear me, this day, should become such as I also am, except these bands.

30 And the king rose up, and the governor and Bernice and they that sat with them.

31 And when they were gone aside, they spoke among themselves, saying: This man hath done nothing worthy of death or of bands.

32 And Agrippa said to Festus: This man might have been set at liberty, if he had not appealed to Cæsar.

CHAPTER 27

Paul is shipped for Rome. His voyage and shipwreck.

AND when it was determined that he should sail into Italy and that Paul, with the other prisoners, should be delivered to a centurion, named Julius, of the band Augusta,

2 [1] Going on board a ship of Adrumetum, we launched, meaning to sail by the coasts of Asia, Aristarchus, the Macedonian of Thessalonica, continuing with us.

3 And the day following, we came to Sidon. And Julius, treating Paul courteously, permitted him to go to his friends and to take care of himself.

4 And when we had launched from thence, we sailed under Cyprus, because the winds were contrary.

5 And sailing over the sea of Cilicia and Pamphylia, we came to Lystra, which is in Lycia.

6 And there, the centurion, finding a ship of Alexandria sailing into Italy, removed us into it.

7 And when for many days we had sailed slowly and were scarce come over against Gnidus, the wind not suffering us, we sailed near Crete by Salmone.

8 And with much ado sailing by it, we came into a certain place, which is called Good-havens, nigh to which was the city of Thalassa.

9 And when much time was spent and when sailing now was dangerous, because the fast was now past, Paul comforted them,

10 Saying to them: Ye men, I see that the voyage beginneth to be with injury and much damage, not only of the lading and ship, but also of our lives.

11 But the centurion believed the pilot and the master of the ship, more than those things which were said by Paul.

12 And whereas it was not a commodious haven to winter in, the greatest part gave counsel to sail thence, if by any means they might reach Phenice, to winter there, which is a haven of Crete, looking towards the southwest and northwest.

13 And the south wind gently blowing, thinking that they had obtained their purpose, when they had loosed from Asson, they sailed close by Crete.

14 But not long after, there arose against it a tempestuous wind, called Euroaquilo.

15 And when the ship was caught and could not bear up against the wind, giving up the ship to the winds, we were driven.

16 And running under a certain island that is called Cauda, we had much work to come by the boat.

17 Which being taken up, they used helps, undergirding the ship: and fearing lest they should fall into the quicksands, they let down the sail yard and so were driven.

18 And we, being mightily tossed with the tempest, the next day they lightened the ship.

19 And the third day they cast out with their own hands the tacking of the ship.

20 And when neither sun nor stars

4 Acts, 21, 31. CHAP. 27. 1 2 Cor. 11, 25.

appeared for many days and no small storms lay on us, all hope of our being saved was now taken away.

21 And after they had fasted a long time, Paul standing forth in the midst of them, said: You should indeed, O ye men, have hearkened unto me and not have loosed from Crete and have gained this harm and loss.

22 And now I exhort you to be of good cheer. For there shall be no loss of any man's life among you, but only of the ship.

23 For an angel of God, whose I am and whom I serve, stood by me this night,

24 Saying: Fear not, Paul, thou must be brought before Cæsar; and behold, God hath given thee all them that sail with thee.

25 Wherefore, sirs, be of good cheer: for I believe God, that it shall so be, as it hath been told me.

26 And we must come unto a certain island.

27 But after the fourteenth night was come, as we were sailing in Adria, about midnight, the shipmen deemed that they discovered some country.

28 Who also sounding, found twenty fathoms: and going on a little further they found fifteen fathoms.

29 Then fearing lest we should fall upon rough places, they cast four anchors out of the stern: and wished for the day.

30 But as the shipmen sought to fly out of the ship, having let down the boat into the sea, under colour, as though they would have cast anchors out of the forepart of the ship,

31 Paul said to the centurion and to the soldiers: Except these stay in the ship, you cannot be saved.

32 Then the soldiers cut off the ropes of the boat and let her fall off.

33 And when it began to be light Paul besought them all to take meat saying: This day is the fourteenth day that you have waited and continued fasting, taking nothing.

34 Wherefore, I pray you to take some meat for your health's sake; for there shall not an hair of the head of any of you perish.

35 And when he had said these things, taking bread, he gave thanks to God in the sight of them all. And when he had broken it, he began to eat.

36 Then were they all of better cheer: and they also took some meat.

37 And we were in all in the ship two hundred threescore and sixteen souls.

38 And when they had eaten enough,

they lightened the ship, casting the wheat into the sea.

39 And when it was day, they knew not the land. But they discovered a certain creek that had a shore, into which they minded, if they could, to thrust in the ship.

40 And when they had taken up the anchors, they committed themselves to the sea, loosing withal the rudder bands. And hoisting up the mainsail to the wind, they made towards shore.

41 And when we were fallen into a place where two seas met, they run the ship aground. And the forepart indeed, sticking fast, remained unmoveable: but the hinder part was broken with the violence of the sea.

42 And the soldiers' counsel was that they should kill the prisoners, lest any of them, swimming out should escape.

43 But the centurion, willing to save Paul, forbade it to be done. And he commanded that they who could swim should cast themselves first into the sea and save themselves and get to land.

44 And the rest, some they carried on boards and some on those things that belonged to the ship. And so it came to pass that every soul got safe to land.

CHAPTER 28

Paul, after three months' stay in Melita, continues his voyage and arrives at Rome. His conference there with the Jews.

AND when we had escaped, then we knew that the island was called Melita. But the barbarians shewed us no small courtesy.

2 For kindling a fire, they refreshed us all, because of the present rain and of the cold.

3 And when Paul had gathered together a bundle of sticks and had laid them on the fire, a viper, coming out of the heat, fastened on his hand.

4 And when the barbarians saw the beast hanging on his hand, they said one to another: Undoubtedly this man is a murderer, who, though he hath escaped the sea, yet vengeance doth not suffer him to live.

5 And he indeed, shaking off the beast into the fire, suffered no harm.

6 But they supposed that he would begin to swell up and that he would suddenly fall down and die. But expecting long and seeing that there came no harm to him, changing their minds, they said that he was a god.

7 Now in these places were possessions of the chief man of the island,

named Publius: who, receiving us, for three days, entertained us courteously.

8 And it happened that the father of Publius lay sick of a fever and of a bloody flux. To whom Paul entered in. And when he had prayed and laid his hands on him, he healed him.

9 Which being done, all that had diseases in the island came and were healed.

10 Who also honoured us with many honours: and when we were to set sail, they laded us with such things as were necessary.

11 And after three months, we sailed in a ship of Alexandria, that had wintered in the island, whose sign was the Castors.

12 And when we were come to Syracusa, we tarried there three days.

13 From thence, compassing by the shore, we came to Rhegium: and after one day, the south wind blowing, we came the second day to Puteoli:

14 Where, finding brethren, we were desired to tarry with them seven days. And so we went to Rome.

15 And from thence, when the brethren had heard of us, they came to meet us as far as Appii Forum and the Three Taverns. Whom when Paul saw, he gave thanks to God and took courage.

16 And when we were come to Rome, Paul was suffered to dwell by himself, with a soldier that kept him.

17 And after the third day, he called together the chief of the Jews. And when they were assembled, he said to them: Men, brethren, I, having done nothing against the people or the custom of our fathers, was delivered prisoner from Jerusalem into the hands of the Romans.

18 Who, when they had examined me, would have released me, for that there was no cause of death in me.

19 But the Jews contradicting it, I was constrained to appeal unto Cæsar: not that I had anything to accuse my nation of.

20 For this cause therefore I desired to see you and to speak to you. Because

that for the hope of Israel, I am bound with this chain.

21 But they said to him: We neither received letters concerning thee from Judea: neither did any of the brethren that came hither relate or speak any evil of thee.

22 But we desire to hear of thee what thou thinkest: for as concerning this sect, we know that it is every where contradicted.

23 And when they had appointed him a day, there came very many to him unto his lodgings. To whom he expounded, testifying the kingdom of God and persuading them concerning Jesus, out of the law of Moses and the prophets, from morning until evening.

24 And some believed the things that were said: but some believed not.

25 And when they agreed not among themselves, they departed, Paul speaking this one word: Well did the Holy Ghost speak to our fathers by Isaias the prophet,

26 Saying: [1] Go to this people and say to them: With the ear you shall hear and shall not understand: and seeing you shall see and shall not perceive.

27 For the heart of this people is grown gross, and with their ears have they heard heavily, and their eyes they have shut, lest perhaps they should see with their eyes and hear with their ears and understand with their heart and should be converted: and I should heal them.

28 Be it known therefore to you that this salvation of God is sent to the Gentiles: and they will hear it.

29 And when he had said these things, the Jews went out from him, having much reasoning among themselves.

30 And he remained two whole years in his own hired lodging: and he received all that came in to him,

31 Preaching the kingdom of God and teaching the things which concern the Lord Jesus Christ, with all confidence, without prohibition.

CHAP. 28. [1] Isai. 6, 9; Matt. 13, 14; Mark, 4, 12; Luke, 8, 10; John, 12, 40; Rom. 11, 8.

THE EPISTLE OF ST. PAUL THE APOSTLE TO THE

ROMANS

St. Paul wrote this Epistle at Corinth, when he was preparing to go to Jerusalem with the charitable contributions collected in Achaia and Macedonia for the relief of the Christians in Judea; which was about twenty-four years after our Lord's Ascension. It was written in Greek; but at the same time translated into Latin, for the benefit of those who did not understand that language. And though it is not the first of his Epistles in the order of time, yet it is first placed on account of the sublimity of the matter contained in it, of the preeminence of the place to which it was sent, and in veneration of the Church.

CHAPTER 1

He commends the faith of the Romans, whom he longs to see. The philosophy of the heathens, being void of faith and humility, betrayed them into shameful sins.

PAUL, a servant of Jesus Christ, called *to be* an apostle, separated unto the gospel of God.

2 Which he had promised before, by his prophets, in the holy scriptures,

3 Concerning his Son, who was made to him of the seed of David, according to the flesh,

4 Who was predestinated the Son of God in power, according to the spirit of sanctification, by the resurrection of our Lord Jesus Christ from the dead:

5 By whom we have received grace and apostleship for obedience to the faith, in all nations, for his name:

6 Among whom are you also the called of Jesus Christ:

7 To all that are at Rome, the beloved of God, called *to be* saints. Grace to you and peace, from God our Father and from the Lord Jesus Christ.

8 First, I give thanks to my God, through Jesus Christ, for you all: because your faith is spoken of in the whole world.

9 For God is my witness, whom I serve in my spirit in the gospel of his Son, that without ceasing I make a commemoration of you:

10 Always in my prayers making request, if by any means now at length I may have a prosperous journey, by the will of God, to come unto you.

CHAP. 1. [1] Hab. 2, 4; Gal. 3, 11; Heb. 10, 38. [2] Eph. 4, 17.

CHAP. 1. Ver. 4. *Predestinated.* Christ as man, was predestinated to be the Son of God: and declared to be so (as the apostle here signifies) first, by *power*, that is, by his working stupendous miracles; secondly, by the *spirit of sanctification*, that is, by his infinite sanctity; thirdly, by his *resurrection*, or raising himself from the dead.

11 For I long to see you that I may impart unto you some spiritual grace, to strengthen you:

12 That is to say, that I may be comforted together in you by that which is common to us both, your faith and mine.

13 And I would not have you ignorant, brethren, that I have often purposed to come unto you (and have been hindered hitherto) that I might have some fruit among you also, even as among other Gentiles.

14 To the Greeks and to the barbarians, to the wise and to the unwise, I am a debtor.

15 So (as much as in me) I am ready to preach the gospel to you also that are at Rome.

16 For I am not ashamed of the gospel. For it is the power of God unto salvation to every one that believeth: to the Jew first and to the Greek.

17 For the justice of God is revealed therein, from faith unto faith, as it is written: [1] *The just man liveth by faith.*

18 For the wrath of God is revealed from heaven against all ungodliness and injustice of those men that detain the truth of God in injustice:

19 Because that which is known of God is manifest in them. For God hath manifested it unto them.

20 For the invisible things of him from the creation of the world are clearly seen, being understood by the things that are made. His eternal power also and divinity: so that they are inexcusable.

21 [2] Because that, when they knew God, they have not glorified him as God or given thanks: but became vain in their thoughts. And their foolish heart was darkened.

22 For, professing themselves to be wise, they became fools.

23 ³ And they changed the glory of the incorruptible God into the likeness of the image of a corruptible man and of birds, and of fourfooted beasts and of creeping things.

24 Wherefore, God gave them up to the desires of their heart, ⁴ unto uncleanness: to dishonour their own bodies among themselves.

25 Who changed the truth of God into a lie and worshipped and served the creature rather than the Creator, who is blessed for ever. Amen.

26 For this cause, God delivered them up to shameful affections. For their women have changed the natural use into that use which is against nature.

27 And, in like manner, the men also, leaving the natural use of the women, have burned in their lusts, one towards another: men with men, working that which is filthy and receiving in themselves the recompense which was due to their error.

28 And as they liked not to have God in their knowledge, God delivered them up to a reprobate sense, to do those things which are not convenient.

29 Being filled with all iniquity, malice, fornication, avarice, wickedness: full of envy, murder, contention, deceit, malignity: whisperers,

30 Detractors, hateful to God, contumelious, proud, haughty, inventors of evil things, disobedient to parents,

31 Foolish, dissolute: without affection, without fidelity, without mercy.

32 Who, having known the justice of God, did not understand that they who do such things, are worthy of death: and not only they that do them, but they also that consent to them that do them.

CHAPTER 2

The Jews are censured, who make their boast of the law and keep it not. He declares who are the true Jews.

WHEREFORE, thou art inexcusable, O man, whosoever thou art that judgest. ¹ For wherein thou judgest another, thou condemnest thyself. For thou dost the same things which thou judgest.

2 For we know that the judgment of God is, according to truth, against them that do such things.

3 And thinkest thou this, O man, that judgest them who do such things and dost the same, that thou shalt escape the judgment of God?

4 Or despisest thou the riches of his goodness and patience and longsuffering? ² Knowest thou not that the benignity of God leadeth thee to penance?

5 But according to thy hardness and impenitent heart, thou treasurest up to thyself wrath, against the day of wrath and revelation of the just judgment of God:

6 ³ Who will render to every man according to his works.

7 To them indeed who, according to patence in good work, seek glory and honour and incorruption, eternal life:

8 But to them that are contentious and who obey not the truth but give credit to iniquity, wrath and indignation.

9 Tribulation and anguish upon every soul of man that worketh evil: of the Jew first, and also of the Greek.

10 But glory and honour and peace to every one that worketh good: to the Jew first, and also to the Greek.

11 ⁴ For there is no respect of persons with God.

12 For whosoever have sinned without the law shall perish without the law: and whosoever have sinned in the law shall be judged by the law.

13 ⁵ For not the hearers of the law are just before God: but the doers of the law shall be justified.

14 For when the Gentiles, who have not the law, do by nature those things that are of the law; these, having not the law, are a law to themselves.

15 Who shew the work of the law written in their hearts, their conscience bearing witness to them: and their thoughts between themselves accusing or also defending one another,

16 In the day when God shall judge the secrets of men by Jesus Christ, according to my gospel.

17 ⁶ But if thou art called a Jew and restest in the law and makest thy boast of God,

18 And knowest his will ⁷ and approvest the more profitable things, being instructed by the law:

19 Art confident that thou thyself art a guide of the blind, a light of them that are in darkness,

20 An instructor of the foolish, a teacher of infants, having the form of knowledge and of truth in the law.

21 Thou therefore, that teachest another, teachest not thyself: thou, that preachest that men should not steal, stealest.

³ Ps. 105, 20; Jer. 11, 10. ⁴ Gal. 5, 19; Eph. 4, 19; 5, 3; Col. 3, 5; 1 Thess. 2, 3; 4, 7. CHAP. 2. ¹ Mark, 7, 2. ² Wisd. 9, 24; 2 Peter, 3, 9. ³ Matt. 16, 27. ⁴ Deut. 10, 17; 2 Par. 19, 7; Job, 34, 19; Wisd. 6, 8; Eccius. 35, 15; Acts, 10, 34; Eph. 6, 9; Col. 3, 25; 1 Peter, 1, 17. ⁵ Matt. 7, 21; James, 1. 22. ⁶ Apoc. 11, 9. ⁷ Phil. 1, 10.

Ver. 26. *God delivered them up.* Not by being author of their sins, but by withdrawing his grace and so permitting them, in punishment of their pride, to fall into those shameful sins.

22 Thou, that sayest men should not commit adultery, committest adultery: thou, that abhorrest idols, committest sacrilege:

23 Thou, that makest thy boast of the law, by transgression of the law dishonourest God.

24 [8] (For the name of God through you is blasphemed among the Gentiles as it is written.)

25 Circumcision profiteth indeed, if thou keep the law: but if thou be a transgressor of the law, thy circumcision is made uncircumcision.

26 If then, the uncircumcised keep the justices of the law, shall not this uncircumcision be counted for circumcision?

27 [9] And shall not that which by nature is uncircumcision, if it fulfil the law, judge thee, who by the letter and circumcision art a transgressor of the law?

28 [10] For it is not he is a Jew, who is so outwardly: nor is that circumcision which is outwardly in the flesh.

29 But he is a Jew that is one inwardly and the circumcision is that of the heart, in the spirit not in the letter: whose praise is not of men, but of God.

CHAPTER 3

The advantages of the Jews. All men are sinners and none can be justified by the works of the law, but only by the grace of Christ.

WHAT advantage then hath the Jew: or what is the profit of circumcision?

2 Much every way. First indeed, [1] because the words of God were committed to them.

3 For what if some of them have not believed? [2] Shall their unbelief make the faith of God without effect? God forbid!

4 [3] But God is true and every man a liar, as it is written: [4] That thou mayest be justified in thy words and mayest overcome when thou art judged.

5 But if our injustice commend the justice of God, what shall we say? Is God unjust, who executeth wrath?

6 (I speak according to man.) God

[8] Isai. 52, 5; Ezech. 36, 20. [9] Matt. 12, 42. [10] Isai. 48. CHAP. 3. [1] Rom. 9, 4. [2] 2 Tim. 2, 13. [3] John, 3, 33; Ps. 115, 11. [4] Ps. 50, 6. [5] Gal. 3, 22; Rom. 1, 17; 11, 9. [6] Ps. 13, 3. [7] Ps. 5, 11; James, 3, 8. [8] Ps. 139, 4. [9] Ps. 9, 7. [10] Isai. 59, 7; Prov. 1, 16. [11] Ps. 35, 2. [12] Gal. 2, 16.

CHAP. 3. Ver. 4. *God* only *is essentially true.* All men in their own capacity are liable to lies and errors; nevertheless God, who is the *truth,* will make good his promise of keeping his Church in all *truth* (John, 16, 13).

Ver. 10. *There is not any man just.* That is, by virtue either of the law of nature, or of the law of Moses; but only by faith and grace.

forbid! Otherwise how shall God judge this world?

7 For if the truth of God hath more abounded through my lie, unto his glory, why am I also yet judged as a sinner?

8 And not rather (as we are slandered and as some affirm that we say) let us do evil that there may come good? Whose damnation is just.

9 What then? Do we excel them? No, not so. [5] For we have charged both Jews and Greeks, that they are all under sin.

10 As it is written: [6] There is not any man just.

11 There is none that understandeth: there is none that seeketh after God.

12 All have turned out of the way: they are become unprofitable together: there is none that doth good, there is not so much as one.

13 [7] Their throat is an open sepulchre: with their tongues they have dealt deceitfully. [8] The venom of asps is under their lips.

14 [9] Whose mouth is full of cursing and bitterness:

15 [10] Their feet swift to shed blood:

16 Destruction and misery in their ways:

17 And the way of peace they have not known.

18 [11] There is no fear of God before their eyes.

19 [12] Now we know that what things soever the law speaketh, it speaketh to them that are in the law: that every mouth may be stopped and all the world may be made subject to God.

20 Because by the works of the law no flesh shall be justified before him. For by the law is the knowledge of sin.

21 But now, without the law, the justice of God is made manifest, being witnessed by the law and the prophets.

22 Even the justice of God, by faith of Jesus Christ, unto all, and upon all them that believe in him: for there is no distinction.

23 For all have sinned and do need the glory of God.

24 Being justified freely by his grace, through the redemption that is in Christ Jesus,

25 Whom God hath proposed to be a propitiation, through faith in his blood, to the shewing of his justice, for the remission of former sins,

26 Through the forbearance of God, for the shewing of his justice in this time: that he himself may be just and the justifier of him who is of the faith of Jesus Christ.

27 Where is then thy boasting? It is excluded. By what law? Of works? No, but by the law of faith.

28 For we account a man to be justified by faith, without the works of the law.

29 Is he the God of the Jews only? Is he not also of the Gentiles? Yes, of the Gentiles also.

30 For it is one God that justifieth circumcison by faith and uncircumcision through faith.

31 Do we then, destroy the law through faith? God forbid! But we establish the law.

CHAPTER 4

Abraham was not justified by works done, as of himself, but by grace and by faith. And that before he was circumcised. Gentiles, by faith, are his children.

WHAT shall we say then that Abraham hath found, who is our father according to the flesh?

2 For if Abraham were justified by works, he hath whereof to glory, but not before God.

3 For what saith the scripture? [1] *Abraham believed God: and it was reputed to him unto justice.*

4 Now to him that worketh, the reward is not reckoned according to grace but according to debt.

5 But to him that worketh not, yet believeth in him that justifieth the ungodly, his faith is reputed to justice, according to the purpose of the grace of God.

6 As David also termeth the blessedness of a man to whom God reputeth justice without works:

7 *Blessed are they whose [2] iniquities are forgiven: and whose sins are covered.*

8 *Blessed is the man to whom the Lord hath not imputed sin.*

9 This blessedness then, doth it remain in the circumcision only or in the uncircumcision also? For we say that unto Abraham faith was reputed to justice.

10 How then was it reputed? When he was in circumcision or in uncircumcision? Not in circumcision, but in uncircumcision.

11 [3] And he received the sign of circumcision, a seal of the justice of the faith which he had, being uncircumcised: that he might be the father of all them that believe, being uncircumcised: that unto them also it may be reputed to justice:

12 And he might be the father of circumcision; not to them only that are of the circumcision, but to them also

that follow the steps of the faith that is in the uncircumcision of our father Abraham.

13 [4] For not through the law was the promise to Abraham or to his seed, that he should be heir of the world: but through the justice of faith.

14 For if they who are of the law be heirs, faith is made void: the promise is made of no effect.

15 For the law worketh wrath. For where there is no law, neither is there transgression.

16 Therefore is it of faith, that according to grace the promise might be

CHAP. 4. [1] Gen. 15, 6; Gal. 3, 6; James, 2, 23. [2] Ps. 31, 1. [3] Gen. 17, 10, 11. [4] Gal. 3, 18; Heb. 11, 9.

Ver. 28. *By faith.* The faith to which the apostle here attributes man's justification is not a presumptuous assurance of our being justified; but a firm and lively *belief* of all that God has revealed or promised (Heb. 11), *a faith working through charity* in Jesus Christ (Gal. 5, 6); in short, *a faith* which takes in hope, love, repentance and the use of the sacraments. And *the works* which he here excludes are only the *works of the law:* that is, such as are done by the law of nature, or that of Moses, antecedent to the faith of Christ: but by no means, such as follow faith, and proceed from it.

CHAP. 4. Ver. 2. *By works.* Done by his own strength, without the grace of God and faith in him.—*Not before God.* Whatever glory or applause such works might procure from men, they would be of no value in the sight of God.

Ver. 3. *Reputed.* By God, who *reputeth* nothing otherwise than it is. However, we may gather from this word that when we are justified, our justification proceedeth from God's free grace and bounty; and not from any efficacy which any act of ours could have of its own nature, abstracting from God's grace.

Ver. 4. *To him that worketh.* As of his own fund, or by his own strength. Such a man, says the apostle, challenges his reward as a *debt* due to his own performances; whereas he who *worketh not,* that is, who presumeth not upon any works done by his own strength but seeketh justice through faith and grace, is freely justified by God's grace.

Ver. 7. *Blessed are they whose iniquities are forgiven, and whose sins are covered.* That is, blessed are those who, by doing penance, have obtained pardon and remission of their sins; and also are *covered,* that is, newly clothed with the habit of grace and vested with the stole of charity.

Ver. 8. *Blessed is the man to whom the Lord hath not imputed sin.* That is, blessed is the man who hath retained his baptismal innocence, so that no grievous sin can be imputed to him. And, likewise, blessed is the man who, after falling into sin, hath done penance and leads a virtuous life, by frequenting the sacraments necessary for obtaining the grace to prevent a relapse, so that sin is no more imputed to him.

Ver. 9. *In the circumcision.* That is, is it only for the Jews that are circumcised? No, says the apostle, but also for the uncircumcised Gentiles: who, by faith and grace, may come to justice; as Abraham did before he was circumcised.

Ver. 14. *Be heirs.* That is, if *they alone,* who follow the ceremonies of the *law, be heirs* of the blessings promised to Abraham; then that *faith* which was so much praised in him will be found to be of little value. And the very promise will be made void, by which he was promised to be the father, not of the Jews only, but of all nations of believers.

Ver. 15. *The law worketh wrath.* The law, abstracting from faith and grace, worketh wrath occasionally, by being an occasion of many transgressions which provoke God's wrath.

firm to all the seed: not to that only which is of the law, but to that also which is of the faith of Abraham, who is the father of us all,

17 (As it is written: [5] *I have made thee a father of many nations*), before God, whom he believed: who quickeneth the dead and calleth those things that are not, as those that are.

18 Who against hope believed in hope; that he might be made the father of many nations, according to that which was said to him: [6] *So shall thy seed be.*

19 And he was not weak in faith. Neither did he consider his own body, now dead (whereas he was almost an hundred years old), nor the dead womb of Sara.

20 In the promise also of God he staggered not by distrust: but was strengthened in faith, giving glory to God:

21 Most fully knowing that whatsoever he has promised, he is able also to perform.

22 And therefore it was reputed to him unto justice.

23 Now it is not written only for him that it was reputed to him unto justice,

24 But also for us, to whom it shall be reputed, if we believe in him [7] that raised up Jesus Christ, our Lord, from the dead,

25 [8] Who was delivered up for our sins and rose again for our justification.

CHAPTER 5

The grounds we have for hope in Christ. Sin and death came by Adam, grace and life by Christ.

BEING justified therefore by faith, let us have peace with God, through our Lord Jesus Christ:

2 [1] By whom also we have access through faith into this grace wherein we stand: and glory in the hope of the glory of the sons of God.

3 And not only so: but we glory also in tribulation, [2] knowing that tribulation worketh patience;

4 And patience trial; and trial hope;

5 [3] And hope confoundeth not: because the charity of God is poured forth in our hearts, by the Holy Ghost who is given to us.

6 For why did Christ, when as yet we were weak, according to the time, [4] die for the ungodly?

7 For scarce for a just man will one die: yet perhaps for a good man some one would dare to die.

8 But God commendeth his charity towards us: because when as yet we were sinners according to the time.

9 Christ died for us. Much more therefore, being now justified by his blood, shall we be saved from wrath through him.

10 For if, when we were enemies, we were reconciled to God by the death of his Son: much more, being reconciled, shall we be saved by his life.

11 And not only so: but also we glory in God, through our Lord Jesus Christ, by whom we have now received reconciliation.

12 Wherefore as by one man sin entered into this world and by sin death; and so death passed upon all men, in whom all have sinned.

13 For until the law sin was in the world: but sin was not imputed, when the law was not.

14 But death reigned from Adam unto Moses, even over them also who have not sinned, after the similitude of the transgression of Adam, who is a figure of him who was to come.

15 But not as the offence, so also the gift. For if by the offence of one, many died: much more the grace of God and the gift, by the grace of one man, Jesus Christ, hath abounded unto many.

16 And not as it was by one sin, so also is the gift. For judgment indeed was by one unto condemnation: but grace is of many offences unto justification.

17 For if by one man's offence death reigned through one: much more they who receive abundance of grace and of the gift and of justice shall reign in life through one, Jesus Christ.

18 Therefore, as by the offence of one, unto all men to condemnation: so also by the justice of one, unto all men to justification of life.

19 [5] For as by the disobedience of one man, many were made sinners: so also by the obedience of one, many shall be made just.

20 Now the law entered in that sin might abound. And where sin abounded, grace did more abound.

21 That as sin hath reigned to death: so also grace might reign by justice unto life everlasting, through Jesus Christ our Lord.

---

[5] Gen. 17, 4. [6] Gen. 15, 5. [7] 1 Peter, 1, 21. [8] Isai. 53, 6; 1 Peter, 1, 8. CHAP. 5. [1] Eph. 2, 18. [2] James, 1, 3. [3] Ps. 22, 6. [4] Heb. 9, 14; 1 Peter, 3, 18. [5] Phil. 2, 8, 9.

CHAP. 5. Ver. 12. *By one man.* Adam, from whom we all contracted original sin.

Ver. 13. *Not imputed.* That is, men knew not, or made no account of sin; neither was it *imputed* to men in the manner it was afterwards, when they transgressed the known written law of God.

Ver. 20. *That sin might abound.* Not as if the law were given on purpose for sin to abound: but that it so happened through man's perversity, taking occasion of sinning more from the prohibition of sin.

CHAPTER 6

The Christian must die to sin and live to God.

WHAT shall we say, then? Shall we continue in sin, that grace may abound?

2 God forbid! For we that are dead to sin, [1] how shall we live any longer therein?

3 Know you not that all we who are baptized in Christ Jesus are baptized in his death?

4 [2] For we are buried together with him by baptism into death: that, as Christ is risen from the dead by the glory of the Father, [3] so we also may walk in newness of life.

5 For if we have been planted together in the likeness of his death, we shall be also in the likeness of his resurrection.

6 Knowing this, that our old man is crucified with him, that the body of sin may be destroyed, to the end that we may serve sin no longer.

7 For he that is dead is justified from sin.

8 Now, if we be dead with Christ, we believe that we shall live also together with Christ.

9 Knowing that Christ, rising again from the dead, dieth now no more. Death shall no more have dominion over him.

10 For in that he died to sin, he died once: but in that he liveth, he liveth unto God.

11 So do you also reckon that you are dead to sin, but alive unto God, in Christ Jesus our Lord.

12 Let not sin therefore reign in your mortal body, so as to obey the lusts thereof.

13 [4] Neither yield ye your members as instruments of iniquity unto sin: but present yourselves to God, as those that are alive from the dead; and your members as instruments of justice unto God.

14 For sin shall not have dominion over you: for you are not under the law, but under grace.

15 What then? Shall we sin, because we are not under the law, but under grace? God forbid!

16 [5] Know you not that to whom you yield yourselves servants to obey, his servants you are whom you obey, whether it be of sin unto death or of obedience unto justice?

17 But thanks be to God, that you were the servants of sin but have obeyed from the heart unto that form of doctrine into which you have been delivered.

18 Being then freed from sin, we have been made servants of justice.

19 I speak an human thing, because of the infirmity of your flesh. For as you have yielded your members to serve uncleanness and iniquity, unto iniquity: so now yield your members to serve justice, unto sanctification.

20 For when you were the servants of sin, you were free men to justice.

21 What fruit therefore had you then in those things of which you are now ashamed? For the end of them is death.

22 But now being made free from sin and become servants to God, you have your fruit unto sanctification, and the end life everlasting.

23 For the wages of sin is death. But the grace of God, life everlasting in Christ Jesus our Lord.

CHAPTER 7

We are released by Christ from the law, and from the guilt of sin, though the inclination to it still tempts us.

KNOW you not, brethren (for I speak to them that know the law) that the law hath dominion over a man, as long as it liveth?

2 [1] For the woman that hath an husband, whilst her husband liveth is bound to the law. But if her husband be dead, she is loosed from the law of her husband.

3 Therefore, whilst her husband liveth, she shall be called an adulteress, if she be with another man: but if her husband be dead, she is delivered from the law of her husband; so that she is not an adulteress, if she be with another man.

4 Therefore, my brethren, you also are become dead to the law, by the body of Christ: that you may belong to another, who is risen again from the dead that we may bring forth fruit to God.

5 For when we were in the flesh, the passions of sins, which were by the law, did work in our members, to bring forth fruit unto death.

6 But now we are loosed from the

CHAP. 6. [1] 2 Peter, 2, 22. [2] Gal. 3, 27; Col. 2, 12. [3] Eph. 4, 13; Heb. 12, 1; 1 Peter, 2, 1; 4, 2. [4] Col. 3, 5. [5] John, 8, 34; 2 Peter, 2, 19. CHAP. 7. [1] 1 Cor. 7, 39.

CHAP. 6. Ver. 6. *Old man—body of sin.* Our corrupt state, subject to sin and concupiscence, coming to us from Adam, is called our *old man,* as our state, reformed in and by Christ, is called the *new man.* And the vices and sins, which then ruled in us are named *the body of sin.*

CHAP. 7. Ver. 1. *As long as it liveth.* Or, as long as he liveth.

law of death wherein we were detained; so that we should serve in newness of spirit, and not in the oldness of the letter.

7 What shall we say, then? Is the law sin? God forbid! But I do not know sin, but by the law. For I had not known concupiscence, if the law did not say: [2] *Thou shalt not covet.*

8 But sin, taking occasion by the commandment, wrought in me all manner of concupiscence. For without the law sin was dead.

9 And I lived some time without the law. But when the commandment came, sin revived,

10 And I died. And the commandment that was ordained to life, the same was found to be unto death to me.

11 For sin, taking occasion by the commandment, seduced me: and by it killed *me*.

12 [3] Wherefore the law indeed is holy: and the commandment holy and just and good.

13 Was that then which is good made death unto me? God forbid! But sin, that it may appear sin, by that which is good, wrought death in me; that sin, by the commandment, might become sinful above measure.

14 For we know that the law is spiritual. But I am carnal, sold under sin.

15 For that which I work, I understand not. For I do not that good which I will: but the evil which I hate, that I do.

16 If then I do that which I will not, I consent to the law, that it is good.

17 Now then it is no more I that do it: but sin that dwelleth in me.

18 For I know that there dwelleth not in me, that is to say, in my flesh,

2 Exod. 20, 17; Deut. 5, 21. 3 1 Tim. 1, 8. 4 1 Peter, 3, 3, 4. Chap. 8. 1 Acts, 15, 10; 13, 38; Heb. 9, 15.

Ver. 8. *Sin taking occasion.* Sin, or concupiscence, which is called *sin*, because it is from sin and leads to sin, which was asleep before, was wakened by the prohibition: the law not being the cause thereof, nor properly *giving occasion* to it; but *occasion being taken* by our corrupt nature to resist the commandment laid upon us.

Ver. 13. *That it may appear sin*, or *that sin may appear* to be the monster it is, which is even capable to take occasion from that which is good, to work death.

Ver. 15. *I do not that good which I will.* The apostle here describes the disorderly motions of passion and concupiscence; which oftentimes in us get the start of reason: and by means of which even good men suffer in the inferior appetite what their will abhors and are much hindered in the accomplishment of the desires of their spirit and mind. But these evil motions (though they are called the *law of sin*, because they come from original sin and violently tempt and incline to sin), as long as the will does not consent to them, are not sins, because they are not voluntary.

that which is good. For to will is present with me: but to accomplish that which is good, I find not.

19 For the good which I will, I do not: but the evil which I will not, that I do.

20 Now if I do that which I will not, it is no more I that do it: but sin that dwelleth in me.

21 I find then a law, that when I have a will to do good, evil is present with me.

22 For I am delighted with the law of God, [4] according to the inward man:

23 But I see another law in my members, fighting against the law of my mind and captivating me in the law of sin that is in my members.

24 Unhappy man that I am, who shall deliver me from the body of this death?

25 The grace of God, by Jesus Christ our Lord. Therefore, I myself, with the mind serve the law of God: but with the flesh, the law of sin.

CHAPTER 8

There is no condemnation to them that, being justified by Christ, walk not according to the flesh, but according to the spirit. Their strong hope and love of God.

THERE is now therefore no condemnation to them that are in Christ Jesus, who walk not according to the flesh.

2 For the law of the spirit of life, in Christ Jesus, hath delivered me from the law of sin and of death.

3 [1] For what the law could not do, in that it was weak through the flesh, God, sending his own Son in the likeness of sinful flesh and of sin, hath condemned sin in the flesh.

4 That the justification of the law might be fulfilled in us who walk not according to the flesh, but according to the spirit.

5 For they that are according to the flesh mind the things that are of the flesh: but they that are according to the spirit mind the things that are of the spirit.

6 For the wisdom of the flesh is death: but the wisdom of the spirit is life and peace.

7 Because the wisdom of the flesh is an enemy to God. For it is not subject to the law of God: neither can it be.

8 And they who are in the flesh cannot please God.

9 But you are not in the flesh, but in the spirit, if so be that the Spirit of God dwell in you. Now if any man have not the Spirit of Christ, he is none of his.

10 And if Christ be in you, the body indeed is dead, because of sin: but the spirit liveth, because of justification.

11 [2] And if the Spirit of him that raised up Jesus from the dead dwell in you; he that raised up Jesus Christ from the dead shall quicken also your mortal bodies, because of his Spirit that dwelleth in you.

12 Therefore, brethren, we are debtors, not to the flesh to live according to the flesh.

13 For if you live according to the flesh, you shall die: but if by the Spirit you mortify the deeds of the flesh, you shall live.

14 For whosoever are led by the Spirit of God, they are the sons of God.

15 [3] For you have not received the spirit of bondage again in fear: but you have received the spirit of [4] adoption of sons, whereby we cry: Abba (Father).

16 For the Spirit himself giveth testimony to our spirit that we are the sons of God.

17 And if sons, heirs also; heirs indeed of God and joint heirs with Christ: yet so, if we suffer with him, that we may be also glorified with him.

18 For I reckon that the sufferings of this time are not worthy to be compared with the glory to come that shall be revealed in us.

19 For the expectation of the creature waiteth for the revelation of the sons of God.

20 For the creature was made subject to vanity: not willingly, but by reason of him that made it subject, in hope.

21 Because the creature also itself shall be delivered from the servitude of corruption, into the liberty of the glory of the children of God.

22 For we know that every creature groaneth and travaileth in pain, even till now.

23 And not only it, but ourselves also, who have the firstfruits of the Spirit: even we ourselves groan within ourselves, waiting for the adoption of the sons of God, the redemption of our body.

24 For we are saved by hope. But hope that is seen is not hope. For what a man seeth, why doth he hope for?

25 But if we hope for that which we see not, we wait for it with patience.

26 Likewise, the Spirit also helpeth our infirmity. For, we know not what we should pray for as we ought: but the Spirit himself asketh for us with unspeakable groanings.

27 And he that searcheth the hearts knoweth what the Spirit desireth: because he asketh for the saints according to God.

28 And we know that to them that love God all things work together unto good: to such as, according to his purpose, are called to be saints.

29 For whom he foreknew, he also predestinated to be made conformable to the image of his Son: that he might be the firstborn amongst many brethren.

30 And whom he predestinated, them he also called. And whom he called, them he also justified. And whom he justified, them he also glorified.

31 What shall we then say to these things? If God be for us, who is against us?

32 [5] He that spared not even his own Son, but delivered him up for us all, how hath he not also, with him, given us all things?

33 Who shall accuse against the elect of God? God is he that justifieth:

34 Who is he that shall condemn? Christ Jesus that died: yea that is risen also again, who is at the right hand of God, who also maketh intercession for us.

35 Who then shall separate us from the love of Christ? Shall tribulation? Or distress? Or famine? Or nakedness Or danger? Or persecution? Or the sword?

2 Acts, 3, 15; 4, 18; 5, 30; Rom. 4, 24; 1 Cor. 6, 14.   3 2 Tim. 1, 7.   4 Gal. 4, 5.   5 Gen. 22, 12.

CHAP. 8. — Ver. 16. *The Spirit himself.* By the inward motions of divine love and the peace of conscience, which the children of God experience, they have a kind of testimony of God's favour; by which they are much strengthened in their hope of their justification and salvation: but yet not so as to pretend to an absolute assurance, which is not usually granted in this mortal life: during which we are taught to *work out our salvation with fear and trembling* (Phil. 2, 12). And *that he that thinketh himself to stand must take heed lest he fall* (1 Cor. 10, 12). (See also Rom. 11, 20, 21, 22).

Ver. 19. *The expectation of the creature.* He speaks of the corporeal creation, made for the use and service of man and, by occasion of his sin, made subject to vanity, that is, to a perpetual instability, tending to corruption and other defects: so that by a figure of speech it is here said to groan and be in labour and to long for its deliverance, which is then to come, when sin shall reign no more and God shall raise the bodies and unite them to their souls, never more to separate and to be in everlasting happiness in heaven.

Ver. 26. *Asketh for us.* The Spirit is said to ask and desire for the saints and to pray in us; inasmuch as he inspireth prayer and teacheth us to pray.

Ver. 29. *He also predestinated.* That is, God hath preordained that all his elect should be conformable to the image of his Son. We must not here offer to pry into the secrets of God's eternal election: only firmly believe that all our *good*, in time and eternity, flows *originally* from God's free goodness; and all our *evil* from man's free will.

36 (As it is written: *For thy sake we are put to death all the day long. We are accounted as sheep for the slaughter.)*

37 But in all these things we overcome, because of him that hath loved us.

38 For I am sure that neither death, nor life, nor angels, nor principalities, nor powers, nor things present, nor things to come, nor might,

39 Nor height, nor depth, nor any other creature, shall be able to separate us from the love of God which is in Christ Jesus our Lord.

CHAPTER 9

The apostle's concern for the Jews. God's election is free and not confined to their nation.

I SPEAK the truth in Christ: I lie not, my conscience bearing me witness in the Holy Ghost:

2 That I have great sadness and continual sorrow in my heart.

⁰ Ps. 43, 22. CHAP. 9. ¹ Acts, 9, 2; 1 Cor. 15, 9. ² Gen. 21, 12. ³ Gal. 4, 28. ⁴ Gen. 18, 10. ⁵ Gen. 25, 24. ⁶ Gen. 25, 23. ⁷ Mal. 1, 2. ⁸ Exod. 33, 19. ⁹ Exod. 9, 16. ¹⁰ Wisd. 15, 7; Isai. 45, 9; Jer. 18, 6.

Ver. 38. *I am sure.* That is, *I am persuaded:* as it is in the Greek, πεπεισμαι.

CHAP. 9. Ver. 3. *Anathema;* a curse. The apostle's concern and love for his countrymen, the Jews, was so great that he was willing to suffer even an *anathema* or curse, for their sake; or any evil that could come upon him, without his offending God.

Ver. 6. *All are not Israelites.* Not all who are the carnal seed of Israel are true Israelites in God's account: who, as by his free grace he heretofore preferred Isaac before Ismael and Jacob before Esau, so he could and did, by the like free grace, election and mercy, raise up spiritual children by faith to Abraham and Israel, from among the Gentiles and prefer them before the carnal Jews.

Ver. 11. *Not yet born.* By this example of these twins and the preference of the younger to the elder, the drift of the apostle is to show that God, in his election, mercy and grace, is not tied to any particular nation, as the Jews imagined; nor to any prerogative of birth or any foregoing merits. For as, antecedently to his grace, he sees no merits in any, but finds all involved in sin, in the common mass of condemnation and all children of wrath: there is no one whom he might not justly leave in that mass. So that whomsoever he delivers from it, he delivers in his mercy; and whomsoever he leaves in it, he leaves in his justice. As when, of two equally criminal, the king is pleased out of pure mercy to pardon one, whilst he suffers justice to take place in the execution of the other.

Ver. 16. *Not of him that willeth.* That is, by any power or strength of his own, abstracting from the grace of God.

Ver. 17. *To this purpose.* Not that God made him on purpose that he should sin and so be damned: but, foreseeing his obstinacy in sin and the abuse of his own free will, he *raised* him up to be a mighty king, to make a more remarkable example of him: and that his power might be better known and his justice in punishing him published throughout the earth.

Ver. 18. *He hardeneth.* Not by being the cause or author of his sin, but by withholding his grace and so leaving him in his sin, in punishment of his past demerits.

Ver. 21. *The potter.* This similitude is used only to shew that we are not to dispute with our

3 ¹For I wished myself to be an anathema from Christ, for my brethren: who are my kinsmen according to the flesh:

4 Who are Israelites: to whom belongeth the adoption *as* of children and the glory and the testament and the giving of the law and the service *of God* and the promises:

5 Whose are the fathers and of whom is Christ, according to the flesh, who is over all things, God blessed for ever. Amen.

6 Not as though the word of God hath miscarried. For all are not Israelites that are of Israel.

7 Neither are all they that are the seed of Abraham, children: *but in Isaac shall thy seed be called.*

8 That is to say, not they that are the children of the flesh are the children of God: but they ³that are the children of the promise are accounted for the seed.

9 For this is the word of promise: *According to this time will I come. And Sara shall have a son.*

10 And not only she. ⁵But when Rebecca also had conceived at once of Isaac our father.

11 For when the *children* were not yet born, nor had done any good or evil (that the purpose of God according to election might stand):

12 Not of works, but of him that calleth, it was said to her: ⁶*The elder shall serve the younger.*

13 As it is written: ⁷*Jacob I have loved: but Esau I have hated.*

14 What shall we say then? Is there injustice with God? God forbid!

15 For he saith to Moses: ⁸*I will have mercy on whom I will have mercy. And I will shew mercy to whom I will shew mercy.*

16 So then it is not of him that willeth, nor of him that runneth, but of God that sheweth mercy.

17 For the scripture saith to Pharao: ⁹*To this purpose have I raised thee, that I may shew my power in thee and that my name may be declared throughout all the earth.*

18 Therefore he hath mercy on whom he will. And whom he will, he hardeneth.

19 Thou wilt say therefore to me: Why doth he then find fault? For who resisteth his will?

20 O man, who art thou that repliest against God? Shall the thing formed say to him that formed it: Why hast thou made me thus?

21 ¹⁰Or hath not the potter power over the clay, of the same lump, to make

one vessel unto honour and another unto dishonour?

22 What if God, willing to shew his wrath and to make his power known, endured with much patience vessels of wrath, fitted for destruction,

23 That he might shew the riches of his glory on the vessels of mercy which he hath prepared unto glory?

24 Even us, whom also he hath called, not only of the Jews but also of the Gentiles.

25 As in Osee he saith: [11] *I will call that which was not my people, my people; and her that was not beloved, beloved; and her that had not obtained mercy, one that hath obtained mercy.*

26 [12] *And it shall be, in the place where it was said unto them: You are not my people; there they shall be called the sons of the living God.*

27 And Isaias cried out concerning Israel: [13] *If the number of the children of Israel be as the sand of the sea, a remnant shall be saved.*

28 *For he hath finish his word and cut it short in justice: because a short word shall the Lord make upon the earth.*

29 And as Isaias foretold: [14] *Unless the Lord of Sabbath had left us a seed, we had been made as Sodom and we had been like unto Gomorrha.*

30 What then shall we say? That the Gentiles who followed not after justice have attained to justice, even the justice that is of faith.

31 But Israel, by following after the law of justice, is not come unto the law of justice.

32 Why so? Because *they sought it* not by faith, but as it were of works. For they stumbled at the stumbling-stone.

33 As it is written: [15] *Behold I lay in Sion a stumbling-stone and a rock of scandal. And whosoever believeth in him shall not be confounded.*

CHAPTER 10

The end of the law is faith in Christ, which the Jews refusing to submit to, cannot be justified.

BRETHREN, the will of my heart, indeed, and my prayer to God is for them unto salvation.

2 For I bear them witness that they have a zeal of God, but not according to knowledge.

3 For they, not knowing the justice of God and seeking to establish their own, have not submitted themselves to the justice of God.

4 For the end of the law is Christ: unto justice to everyone that believeth.

5 For Moses wrote that the justice which is of the law: [1] *The man that shall do it shall live by it.*

6 But the justice which is of faith, speaketh thus: [2] *Say not in thy heart: Who shall ascend into heaven?* That is to bring Christ down;

7 *Or who shall descend into the deep?* That is, to bring up Christ again from the dead.

8 But what saith the scripture? [3] *The word is nigh thee, even in thy mouth and in thy heart.* This is the word of faith, which we preach.

9 For if thou confess with thy mouth the Lord Jesus and believe in thy heart that God hath raised him up from the dead, thou shalt be saved.

10 For, with the heart, we believe unto justice: but, with the mouth, confession is made unto salvation.

11 For the scripture saith: [4] *Whosoever believeth in him shall not be confounded.*

12 For there is no distinction of the Jew and the Greek: for the same is Lord over all, rich unto all that call upon him.

13 [5] *For whosoever shall call upon the name of the Lord shall be saved.*

14 How then shall they call on him in whom they have not believed? Or how shall they believe him of whom they have not heard? And how shall they hear without a preacher?

15 And how shall they preach unless they be sent, as it is written: [6] *How beautiful are the feet of them that*

[11] Osee, 2, 24; 1 Peter, 2, 10. [12] Osee, 1, 10. [13] Isai. 10, 22. [14] Isai. 1, 9. [15] Isai. 8, 14; 28, 16; 1 Peter, 2, 6. CHAP. 10. [1] Lev. 18, 5; Ezech. 20, 11. [2] Deut. 30, 12. [3] Deut. 30, 14. [4] Isai. 28, 16. [5] Joel, 2, 32; Acts, 2, 21. [6] Isai. 52, 7; Nah. 1, 15.

Maker, nor to reason with him why he does not give as much grace to one as to another; for since the whole lump of our clay is vitiated by sin, it is owing to his goodness and mercy that he makes out of it so many vessels of honour; and it is no more than just that others, in punishment of their unrepented of sins, should be given up to be vessels of dishonour.

Ver. 27. *A remnant.* That is, a small number only of the *children of Israel* shall be converted and saved. How perversely is this text quoted for the salvation of men of all religions, when it speaks only of the converts of the children of Israel!

CHAP. 10. Ver. 3. *The justice of God.* That is, the justice which God giveth us through Christ; as, on the other hand, the Jews' *own justice* is that which they pretended to by their own strength or by the observance of the law, without faith in Christ.

Ver. 9. *Thou shalt be saved.* To confess the Lord Jesus, and to call upon the name of the Lord (ver. 13) is not barely the professing a belief in the person of Christ; but moreover, implies a belief of his whole doctrine and an obedience to his law; without which, the calling him Lord will save no man (Matt. 7, 21).

Ver. 15. *Unless they be sent.* Here is an evident proof against all new teachers, who have all usurped to themselves the ministry without any lawful mission, derived by succession from

preach the gospel of peace, of them that bring glad tidings of good things?

16 But all do not obey the gospel. For Isaias saith: [7] *Lord, who hath believed our report?*

17 Faith then cometh by hearing; and hearing by the word of Christ.

18 But I say: Have they not heard? [8] Yes, verily: *Their sound hath gone forth into all the earth: and their words unto the ends of the whole world.*

19 But I say: Hath not Israel known? First, Moses saith: [9] *I will provoke you to jealousy by that which is not a nation: by a foolish nation I will anger you.*

[10] 20 But Isaias is bold, and saith: *I was found by them that did not seek me. I appeared openly to them that asked not after me.*

21 But to Israel he saith: [11] *All the day long have I spread my hands to a people that believeth not and contradicteth me.*

CHAPTER 11

God hath not cast off all Israel. The Gentiles must not be proud but stand in faith and fear.

I SAY then: Hath God cast away his people? God forbid! For I also am an Israelite of the seed of Abraham, of the tribe of Benjamin.

2 God hath not cast away his people which he foreknew. Know you not what the scripture saith of Elias, how he calleth on God against Israel?

[7] Isai. 53, 1; John, 12, 38. [8] Ps. 18, 5. [9] Deut. 32, 21. [10] Isai. 65, 1. [11] Isai. 65, 2. CHAP. 11. [1] 3 Kings, 19, 10. [2] 3 Kings, 19, 18. [3] Isai. 6, 9, 10; 29, 10; Matt. 13, 14; John, 12, 40; Acts, 28, 26. [4] Ps. 68, 23. [5] Acts, 9, 15; Gal. 2, 7.

the apostles, to whom Christ said (John 20, 21): *As my Father hath sent me, I also send you.*

CHAP. 11. Ver. 4. *Seven thousand.* This is very ill alleged by some against the perpetual visibility of the Church of Christ: the more, because, however the number of the faithful might be abridged by the persecution of Jezabel in the kingdom of the ten tribes, the church was at the same time in a most flourishing condition (under Asa and Josaphat) in the kingdom of Judah.

Ver. 6. *It is not now by works.* If salvation were to come by *works*, done by nature, without faith and grace, salvation would not be a grace or favour, but a debt; but such *dead* works are indeed of no value in the sight of God towards salvation. It is not the same with regard to *works done with*, and *by*, God's grace; for to such works as these, he has promised eternal salvation.

Ver. 8. *God hath given them.* Not by his working or acting in them; but by his permission and by withdrawing his grace in punishment of their obstinacy.

Ver. 11. *That they should fall.* The nation of the Jews is not absolutely and without remedy cast off for ever; but in part only (many thousands of them having been at first converted) and for a time; which fall of theirs, God has been pleased to turn to the good of the Gentiles.

Ver. 20. *Thou standest by faith. Be not highminded, but fear.* We see here that he who standeth by faith may fall from it; and therefore must live in fear, and not in the vain presumption and security of modern sectaries.

3 [1] *Lord, they have slain thy prophets, they have dug down thy altars. And I am left alone: and they seek my life.*

4 But what saith the divine answer to him? [2] *I have left me seven thousand men that have not bowed their knees to Baal.*

5 Even so then, at this present time also, there is a remnant saved according to the election of grace.

6 And if by grace, it is not now by works: otherwise grace is no more grace.

7 What then? That which Israel sought, he hath not obtained: but the election hath obtained it. And the rest have been blinded.

8 As it is written: [3] *God hath given them the spirit of insensibility; eyes that they should not see and ears that they should not hear, until this present day.*

9 And David saith: [4] *Let their table be made a snare and a trap and a stumbling-block and a recompense unto them.*

10 *Let their eyes be darkened, that they may not see: and bow down their back always.*

11 I say then: Have they so stumbled, that they should fall? God forbid! But by their offence salvation is come to the Gentiles, that they may be emulous of them.

12 Now if the offence of them be the riches of the world and the diminution of them the riches of the Gentiles: how much more the fulness of them?

13 For I say to you, Gentiles: [5] As long indeed as I am the apostle of the Gentiles, I will honour my ministry,

14 If, by any means, I may provoke to emulation them who are my flesh and may save some of them.

15 For if the loss of them be the reconciliation of the world, what shall the receiving of them be, but life from the dead?

16 For if the firstfruit be holy, so is the lump also: and if the root be holy, so are the branches.

17 And if some of the branches be broken and thou, being a wild olive, art ingrafted in them and art made partaker of the root and of the fatness of the olive tree:

18 Boast not against the branches. But if thou boast, thou bearest not the root: but the root thee.

19 Thou wilt say then: The branches were broken off that I might be grafted in

20 Well: because of unbelief they were broken off. But thou standest by faith. Be not highminded, but fear.

21 For if God hath not spared the natural branches, *fear* lest perhaps also he spare not thee.

22 See then the goodness and the severity of God: towards them indeed that are fallen, the severity; but towards thee, the goodness of God, if thou abide in goodness. Otherwise thou also shalt be cut off.

23 And they also, if they abide not still in unbelief, shall be grafted in: for God is able to graft them in again.

24 For if thou were cut out of the wild olive tree, which is natural to thee; and, contrary to nature, wert grafted into the good olive tree: how much more shall they that are the natural branches be grafted into their own olive tree?

25 For I would not have you ignorant, brethren, of this mystery ⁶(lest you should be wise in your own conceits) that blindness in part has happened in Israel, until the fulness of the Gentiles should come in.

26 And so all Israel should be saved, as it is written: ⁷ *There shall come out of Sion, he that shall deliver and shall turn away ungodliness from Jacob.*

27 *And this is to them my covenant:* when I shall take away their sins.

28 As concerning the gospel, indeed, they are enemies for your sake: but are touching the election, they are most dear for the sake of the fathers.

29 For the gifts and the calling of God are without repentance.

30 For as you also in times past did not believe God, but now have obtained mercy, through their unbelief:

31 So these also now have not believed, for your mercy, that they also may obtain mercy.

32 For God hath concluded all in unbelief, that he may have mercy on all.

33 O the depth of the riches of the wisdom and of the knowledge of God! How incomprehensible are his judgments, and how unsearchable his ways!

34 ⁸For who hath known the mind of the Lord? Or who hath been his counsellor?

35 Or who hath first given to him, and recompense shall be made him?

36 For of him, and by him, and in him, are all things: to him be glory for ever. Amen.

CHAPTER 12

Lessons of Christian virtues.

I BESEECH you therefore, brethren, by the mercy of God, ¹that you present your bodies a living sacrifice holy, pleasing unto God, your reasonable service.

2 And be not conformed to this world: but be reformed in the newness of your mind, ² that you may prove what is the good and the acceptable and the perfect will of God.

3 For I say, by the grace that is given me, to all that are among you, not to be more wise than it behoveth to be wise, but to be wise unto sobriety ³ and according as God hath divided to every one the measure of faith.

4 For as in one body we have many members, but all the members have not the same office:

5 So we, being many, are one body in Christ; and every one members one of another:

6 And having different gifts, according to the grace that is given us, either prophecy, *to be used* according to the rule of faith;

7 Or ministry, in ministering; or he that teacheth, in doctrine;

8 He that exhorteth, in exhorting; he that giveth, with simplicity; he that ruleth, with carefulness; he that sheweth mercy, with cheerfulness.

9 Let love be without dissimulation. ⁴ Hating that which is evil, cleaving to that which is good,

10 ⁵ Loving one another with the charity of brotherhood: with honour preventing one another.

11 In carefulness not slothful. In spirit fervent. Serving the Lord.

12 Rejoicing in hope. Patient in tribulation. Instant in prayer.

13 Communicating to the necessities of the saints. ⁶ Pursuing hospitality.

14 Bless them that persecute you: bless, and curse not.

15 Rejoice with them that rejoice: weep with them that weep.

16 Being of one mind one towards another. Not minding high things, but consenting to the humble. Be not wise in your own conceits.

⁶ Prov. 3, 7; Isai. 5, 21. ⁷ Isai. 59, 20. ⁸ Wisd. 9, 13; Isai. 40, 13; 1 Cor. 2, 16. CHAP. 12. ¹ Phil. 4, 18. ² Eph. 5, 17; 1 Thess. 4, 3. ³ 1 Cor. 12, 11; Eph. 4, 7. ⁴ Amos. 5, 16. ⁵ Eph. 4, 3; 1 Peter, 2, 17. ⁶ Heb. 13, 2; 1 Peter, 4, 9.

Ver. 22. *Otherwise thou also shalt be cut off.* The Gentiles are here admonished not to be proud nor to glory against the Jews: but to take occasion rather from their fall to fear and to be humble, lest they be cast off. Not that the whole Church of Christ can ever fall from him, having been secured by so many divine promises in holy writ; but that each one in particular may fall. And therefore all in general are to be admonished to beware of that which may happen to any one in particular.

Ver. 29. *For the gifts and the calling of God are without* his repenting himself of them. For the promises of God are unchangeable, nor can he repent of conferring his *gifts.*

Ver. 32. *Concluded all in unbelief.* He hath found all nations, both Jews and Gentiles, in unbelief and sin; not by his causing, but by the abuse of their own free will; so that their calling and election is purely owing to his mercy.

17 To no man rendering evil for evil. [7] Providing good things, not only in the sight of God but also in the sight of all men.

18 [8] If it be possible, as much as is in you, have peace with all men.

19 [9] Revenge not yourselves, my dearly beloved; but give place unto wrath, for it is written: [10] *Revenge is mine, I will repay,* saith the Lord.

20 [11] But *if thy enemy be hungry, give him to eat; if he thirst, give him to drink. For, doing this, thou shalt heap coals of fire upon his head.*

21 Be not overcome by evil: but overcome evil by good.

CHAPTER 13

Lessons of obedience to superiors and mutual charity.

LET [1] every soul be subject to higher powers. For there is no power but from God: and those that are ordained of God.

2 Therefore, he that resisteth the power resisteth the ordinance of God. And they that resist purchase to themselves damnation.

3 For princes are not a terror to the good work, but to the evil. Wilt thou then not be afraid of the power? Do that which is good: and thou shalt have praise from the same.

4 For he is God's minister to thee, for good. But if thou do that which is evil, fear: for he beareth not the sword in vain. For he is God's minister: an avenger to execute wrath upon him that doth evil.

5 Wherefore be subject of necessity: not only for wrath, but also for conscience' sake.

6 For therefore also you pay tribute. For they are the ministers of God, serving unto this purpose.

[7] 2 Cor. 8, 21. [8] Heb. 12, 14. [9] Ecclus. 2, 3; 28, 1. [10] Matt. 5, 39; Deut. 32, 35; Heb. 10, 30. [11] Prov. 25, 21. CHAP. 13. [1] Wisd. 6, 4; 1 Peter, 2, 18. [2] Matt. 22, 21. [3] Exod. 20, 14; Deut. 5, 18. [4] Lev. 19, 18;; Matt. 22, 39; Mark, 12, 31; Gal. 5, 14; James, 2, 8. [5] Luke, 21, 34. [6] Gal. 5, 16; 1 Peter, 2, 11. CHAP. 14. [1] James, 4, 13.

CHAP. 14. Ver. 2. *Eat all things.* That is, without observing the distinction of clean and unclean meats, prescribed by the law of Moses: which was now no longer obligatory. Some weak Christians, converted from among the Jews, as we here gather from the apostle, made a scruple of eating such meats as were deemed unclean by the law (such as swine's flesh), which the stronger sort of Christians did eat without scruple. Now, the apostle, to reconcile them together, exhorts the former not to judge or condemn the latter, using their Christian liberty; and the latter to take care not to despise or scandalize their weaker brethren, either by bringing them to eat what in their conscience they think they should not, or by giving them such offence as to endanger the driving them thereby from the Christian religion.

Ver. 5. *Between day and day.* Still observing the sabbaths and festivals of the law.

7 [2] Render therefore to all men their dues. Tribute, to whom tribute is due: custom, to whom custom: fear, to whom fear: honour, to whom honour.

8 Owe no man any thing, but to love one another. For he that loveth his neighbour hath fulfilled the law.

9 [3] For: *Thou shalt not commit adultery: Thou shalt not kill: Thou shalt not steal: Thou shalt not bear false witness: Thou shalt not covet.* And if there be any other commandment, it is comprised in this word: [4] *Thou shalt love thy neighbour as thyself.*

10 The love of our neighbour worketh no evil. Love therefore is the fulfilling of the law.

11 And that, knowing the season, that it is now the hour for us to rise from sleep. For now our salvation is nearer than when we believed.

12 The night is passed and the day is at hand. Let us therefore cast off the works of darkness and put on the armour of light.

13 Let us walk honestly, as in the day: [5] not in rioting and drunkenness, not in chambering and impurities, not in contention and envy.

14 [6] But put ye on the Lord Jesus Christ: and make not provision for the flesh in its concupiscences.

CHAPTER 14

The strong must bear with the weak. Cautions against judging and giving scandal.

NOW him that is weak in faith, take unto you: not in disputes about thoughts.

2 For one believeth that he may eat all things: but he that is weak, let him eat herbs.

3 Let not him that eateth despise him that eateth not: and he that eateth not, let him not judge him that eateth. For God hath taken him to him.

4 [1] Who art thou that judgest another man's servant? To his own lord he standeth or falleth. And he shall stand: for God is able to make him stand.

5 For one judgeth between day and day: and another judgeth every day. Let every man abound in his own sense.

6 He that regardeth the day regardeth it unto the Lord. And he that eateth eateth to the Lord: for he giveth thanks to God. And he that eateth not, to the Lord he eateth not and giveth thanks to God.

7 For none of us liveth to himself: and no man dieth to himself.

8 For whether we live, we live unto the Lord: or whether we die, we die unto the Lord. Therefore, whether we

live or whether we die, we are the Lord's.

9 For to this end Christ died and rose again: that he might be Lord both of the dead and of the living.

10 But thou, why judgest thou thy brother? Or thou, why dost thou despise thy brother? [2] For we shall all stand before the judgment seat of Christ.

11 For it is written: [3] *As I live,* saith the Lord, *every knee shall bow to me and every tongue shall confess to God.*

12 Therefore every one of us shall render account to God for himself.

13 Let us not therefore judge one another any more. But judge this rather, that you put not a stumbling-block or a scandal in your brother's way.

14 I know, and am confident in the Lord Jesus, that nothing is unclean of itself: but to him that esteemeth any thing to be unclean, to him it is unclean.

15 For if, because of thy meat, thy brother be grieved, thou walkest not now according to charity. [4] Destroy not him with thy meat, for whom Christ died.

16 Let not then our good be evil spoken of.

17 For the kingdom of God is not meat and drink: but justice and peace and joy in the Holy Ghost.

18 For he that in this serveth Christ pleaseth God and is approved of men.

19 Therefore, let us follow after the things that are of peace and keep the things that are of edification, one towards another.

20 Destroy not the work of God for meat. [5] All things indeed are clean: but it is evil for that man who eateth with offence.

21 [6] It is good not to eat flesh and not to drink wine: nor any thing whereby thy brother is offended or scandalized or made weak.

22 Hast thou faith? Have it to thyself before God. Blessed is he that condemneth not himself in that which he alloweth.

23 But he that discerneth, if he eat, is condemned; because not of faith. For all that is not of faith is sin.

CHAPTER 15

He exhorts them to be all of one mind and promises to come and see them.

NOW, we that are stronger ought to bear the infirmities of the weak and not to please ourselves.

2 Let every one of you please his neighbour unto good, to edification.

3 For Christ did not please himself: but, as it is written: [1] *The reproaches of them that reproached thee fell upon me.*

4 For what things soever were written were written for our learning: that, through patience and the comfort of the scriptures, we might have hope.

5 Now the God of patience and of comfort [2] grant you to be of one mind, one towards another, according to Jesus Christ:

6 That with one mind and with one mouth you may glorify God and the Father of our Lord Jesus Christ.

7 Wherefore, receive one another, as Christ also hath received you, unto the honour of God.

8 For I say that Christ Jesus was minister of the circumcision for the truth of God, to confirm the promises made unto the fathers:

9 But that the Gentiles are to glorify God for his mercy, as it is written: [3] *Therefore will I confess to thee, O Lord, among the Gentiles and will sing to thy name.*

10 And again he saith: *Rejoice, ye Gentiles, with his people.*

11 And again: [4] *Praise the Lord, all ye Gentiles: and magnify him, all ye people.*

12 And again, Isaias saith: [5] *There shall be a root of Jesse; and he that shall rise up to rule the Gentiles, in him the Gentiles shall hope.*

13 Now the God of hope fill you with all joy and peace in believing: that you may abound in hope and in the power of the Holy Ghost.

14 And I myself also, my brethren, am assured of you that you also are full of love, replenished with all knowledge, so that you are able to admonish one another.

15 But I have written to you, brethren, more boldly in some sort, as it were putting you in mind, because of the grace which is given me from God,

16 That I should be the minister of Christ Jesus among the Gentiles: sanctifying the gospel of God, that the oblation of the Gentiles may be made acceptable and sanctified in the Holy Ghost.

17 I have therefore glory in Christ Jesus towards God.

[2] 2 Cor. 5, 10. [3] Isai. 45, 24; Phil. 2, 10. [4] 1 Cor. 8, 11. [5] Titus, 1, 15. [6] 1 Cor. 8, 13. CHAP. 15. [1] Ps. 68, 10. [2] 1 Cor. 1, 10. [3] 2 Kings, 22, 50; Ps. 17, 50. [4] Ps. 116, 1. [5] Isai. 11, 10.

Ver. 23. *Discerneth.* That is, distinguisheth between meats and eateth against his conscience what he deems unclean.—*Of faith.* By *faith* is here understood judgment and *conscience,* to act against which is always a sin.

CHAP. 15. Ver. 8. *Minister of the circumcision.* That is, executed his office and *ministry* towards the Jews, the people of the *circumcision.*

18 For I dare not to speak of any of those things which Christ worketh not by me, for the obedience of the Gentiles, by word and deed,

19 By the virtue of signs and wonders, in the power of the Holy Ghost, so that from Jerusalem round about, as far as unto Illyricum, I have replenished the gospel of Christ.

20 And I have so preached this gospel, not where Christ was named, lest I should build upon another man's foundation.

21 But as it is written: ⁶ *They to whom he was not spoken of shall see: and they that have not heard shall understand.*

22 For which cause also, I was hindered very much from coming to you and have been kept away till now.

23 But now, having no more place in these countries and having a great desire these many years past to come unto you,

24 When I shall begin to take my journey into Spain, I hope that, as I pass, I shall see you and be brought on my way thither by you: if first, in part, I shall have enjoyed you.

25 But now I shall go to Jerusalem, to minister unto the saints.

26 For it hath pleased them of Macedonia and Achaia to make a contribution for the poor of the saints that are in Jerusalem.

27 For it hath pleased them: and they are their debtors. ⁷ For, if the Gentiles have been made partakers of their spiritual things, they ought also in carnal things to minister to them.

28 When therefore I shall have accomplished this and consigned to them this fruit, I will come by you into Spain.

29 And I know that when I come to you I shall come in the abundance of the blessing of the gospel of Christ.

30 I beseech you therefore, brethren, through our Lord Jesus Christ and by the charity of the Holy Ghost, that you help me in your prayers for me to God,

31 That I may be delivered from the unbelievers that are in Judea and that the oblation of my service may be acceptable in Jerusalem to the saints.

32 That I may come to you with joy, by the will of God, and may be refreshed with you.

33 Now the God of peace be with you all. Amen.

⁶ Isai. 52, 15. ⁷ 1 Cor. 9, 11. Chap. 16. ¹ Acts, 18, 2, 26.

CHAPTER 16

He concludes with salutations, bidding them beware of all that should oppose the doctrine they had learned.

AND I commend to you Phebe, our sister, who is in the ministry of the church, that is in Cenchræ:

2 That you receive her in the Lord as becometh saints and that you assist her in whatsoever business she shall have need of you. For she also hath assisted many, and myself also.

3 ¹ Salute Prisca and Aquila, my helpers in Christ Jesus

4 (Who have for my life laid down their own necks: to whom not I only give thanks, but also all the churches of the Gentiles),

5 And the church which is in their house. Salute Epenetus, my beloved: who is the firstfruits of Asia in Christ.

6 Salute Mary, who hath laboured much among you.

7 Salute Andronicus and Junias, my kinsmen and fellow prisoners: who are of note among the apostles, who also were in Christ before me.

8 Salute Ampliatus, most beloved to me in the Lord.

9 Salute Urbanus, our helper in Christ Jesus and Stachys, my beloved.

10 Salute Apellas, approved in Christ.

11 Salute them that are of Aristobulus' household. Salute Herodian, my kinsman. Salute them that are of Narcissus' household, who are in the Lord.

12 Salute Tryphæna and Tryphosa, who labour in the Lord. Salute Persis, the dearly beloved, who hath much laboured in the Lord.

13 Salute Rufus, elect in the Lord: and his mother and mine.

14 Salute Asyncritus, Phlegon, Hermas, Patrobas, Hermes: and the brethren that are with them.

15 Salute Philologus and Julia, Nereus and his sister, and Olympias: and all the saints that are with them.

16 Salute one another with an holy kiss. All the churches of Christ salute you.

17 Now I beseech you, brethren, to mark them who make dissensions and offences contrary to the doctrine which you have learned and avoid them.

18 For they that are such serve not Christ our Lord but their own belly: and by pleasing speeches and good words seduce the hearts of the innocent.

19 For your obedience is published in every place. I rejoice therefore in you. But I would have you to be wise in good and simple in evil.

20 And the God of peace crush Satan under your feet speedily. The grace of our Lord Jesus Christ be with you.

21 ²Timothy, my fellow labourer, saluteth you: and Lucius and Jason and Sosipater, my kinsmen.

22 I, Tertius, who wrote this epistle, salute you in the Lord.

23 Caius, my host, and the whole church saluteth you. Erastus, the treasurer of the city, saluteth you: and Quartus, a brother.

24 The grace of our Lord Jesus Christ be with you all. Amen.

25 Now to him that is able to establish you, according to my gospel and the preaching of Jesus Christ, according to the revelation of the mystery which was kept secret from eternity.

26 (Which now is made manifest by the scriptures of the prophets, according to the precept of the eternal God, for the obedience of faith) known among all nations:

27 To God, the only wise, through Jesus Christ, to whom be honour and glory for ever and ever. Amen.

THE FIRST EPISTLE OF ST. PAUL TO THE

CORINTHIANS

St. Paul, having planted the faithful in Corinth, where he had preached a year and a half and converted a great man, went to Ephesus. After being there three years, he wrote this first Epistle to the Corinthians and sent it by the same persons, Stephanus, Fortunatus and Achaicus, who had brought their letter to him. It was written about twenty-four years after our Lord's Ascension and contains several matters appertaining to faith and morals and also to ecclesiastical discipline.

CHAPTER 1

He reproveth their dissensions about their teachers. The world was to be saved by preaching of the cross, and not by human wisdom or eloquence.

PAUL, called to be an apostle of Jesus Christ by the will of God, and Sosthenes a brother,

2 To the church of God that is at Corinth, to them that are sanctified in Christ Jesus, called to be saints, with all that invoke the name of our Lord Jesus Christ in every place of theirs and ours.

3 Grace to you and peace, from God our father and from the Lord Jesus Christ.

4 I give thanks to my God always for you, for the grace of God that is given you in Christ Jesus:

5 That in all things you are made rich in him, in all utterance and in all knowledge;

6 As the testimony of Christ was confirmed in you,

7 So that nothing is wanting to you in any grace, waiting for the manifestation of our Lord Jesus Christ.

8 Who also will confirm you unto the end without crime, in the days of the coming of our Lord Jesus Christ.

9 ¹God is faithful: by whom you are called unto the fellowship of his Son, Jesus Christ our Lord.

10 Now I beseech you, brethren, by the name of our Lord Jesus Christ, that you all speak the same thing and that there be no schisms among you: but that you be perfect in the same mind and in the same judgment.

11 For it hath been signified unto me, my brethren, of you, by them that are of the house of Chloe, that there are contentions among you.

12 Now this I say, that every one of you saith: I indeed am of Paul; and I am ²of Apollo; and I of Cephas; and I of Christ.

---

² Acts, 16, 1. Chap. 1. ¹ 1 Thess. 5, 24. ² Acts, 18, 24.

13 Is Christ divided? Was Paul then crucified for you? Or were you baptized in the name of Paul?

14 I give God thanks, that I baptized none of you [3] but Crisput and Caius:

15 Lest any should say that you were baptized in my name.

16 And I baptized also the household of Stephanas. Besides, I know not whether I baptized any other.

17 For Christ sent me not to baptize, but to preach the gospel: [4] not in wisdom of speech, lest the cross of Christ should be made void.

18 For the word of the cross, to them indeed that perish, is foolishness: but to them that are saved, that is, to us, [5] it is the power of God.

19 For it is written: [6] *I will destroy the wisdom of the wise: and the prudence of the prudent I will reject.*

20 [7] *Where is the wise? Where is the scribe? Where is the disputer of this world?* Hath not God made foolish the wisdom of this world?

21 For, seeing that in the wisdom of God, the world, by wisdom, knew not God, it pleased God, by the foolishness of *our* preaching, to save them that believe.

22 For both the Jews require signs: and the Greeks seek after wisdom.

23 But we preach Christ crucified: unto the Jews indeed a stumbling-block, and unto the Gentiles foolishness:

24 But unto them that are called, both Jews and Greeks, Christ, the power of God and the wisdom of God.

25 For the foolishness of God is wiser than men: and the weakness of God is stronger than men.

26 For see your vocation, brethren, that *there are* not many wise according to the flesh, not many mighty, not many noble.

27 But the foolish things of the world hath God chosen, that he may confound the wise: and the weak things of the world hath God chosen, that he may confound the strong.

28 And the base things of the world and the things that are contemptible, hath God chosen: and things that are not, that he might bring to nought things that are:

29 That no flesh should glory in his sight.

30 But of him are you in Christ Jesus, who of God is made unto us wisdom [8] and justice and sanctification and redemption:

31 That, as it is written: [9] *He that glorieth may glory in the Lord.*

CHAPTER 2

His preaching was not in loftiness of words, but in spirit and power. And the wisdom he taught was not to be understood by the worldly wise or sensual man, but only by the spiritual man.

AND I, brethren, when I came to you, [1] came not in loftiness of speech or of wisdom, declaring unto you the testimony of Christ.

2 For I judged not myself to know anything among you, but Jesus Christ: and him crucified.

3 [2] And I was with you in weakness and in fear and in much trembling.

4 [3] And my speech and my preaching *was* not in the persuasive words of human wisdom, but in shewing of the Spirit and power:

5 That your faith might not stand on the wisdom of men, but on the power of God.

6 Howbeit we speak wisdom among the perfect: yet not the wisdom of this world, neither of the princes of this world that come to nought.

7 But we speak the wisdom of God in a mystery, *a wisdom* which is hidden, which God ordained before the world, unto our glory:

8 Which none of the princes of this world knew. For if they had known it, they would never have crucified the Lord of glory.

9 But, as it is written: [4] *That eye hath not seen, nor ear heard: neither hath it entered into the heart of man, what things God hath prepared for them that love him.*

10 But to us God hath revealed *them,* by his Spirit. For the Spirit searcheth all things, yea, the deep things of God.

11 For what man knoweth the things of a man, but the spirit of a man that is in him? So the things also that are of God, no man knoweth, but the Spirit of God.

12 Now, we have received not the spirit of this world, but the Spirit that is of God: that we may know the things that are given us from God.

13 [5] Which things also we speak: not in the learned words of human wisdom, but in the doctrine of the Spirit, comparing spiritual things with spiritual.

[3] Acts, 18, 8.   [4] 2 Peter, 1, 16; 1 Cor. 2, 1, 4, 13.   [5] Rom. 1, 16.   [6] Isai. 29, 14.   [7] Isai. 33, 18.   [8] Jer. 23, 5.   [9] Jer. 9, 23, 24; 2 Cor. 10, 17.   CHAP. 2.   [1] 1 Cor. 1, 17.   [2] Acts, 18, 3.   [3] 2 Peter, 1, 16.   [4] Isai. 64, 4.   [5] 1 Cor. 1, 17; 2, 1, 4; 2 Peter, 1, 16.

CHAP. 1. Ver. 25. *The foolishness.* That is to say, what appears *foolish* to the world in the ways of God is indeed most wise; and what appears *weak* is indeed above all the strength and comprehension of man.

14 But the sensual man perceiveth not these things that are of the Spirit of God. For it is foolishness to him: and he cannot understand, because it is spiritually examined.

15 But the spiritual man judgeth all things: and he himself is judged of no man.

16 [6] For who hath known the mind of the Lord, that he may instruct him? But we have the mind of Christ.

CHAPTER 3

They must not contend about their teachers, who are but God's ministers and accountable to him. Their works shall be tried by fire.

AND I, brethren, could not speak to you as unto spiritual, but as unto carnal. As unto little ones in Christ.

2 I gave you milk to drink, not meat: for you were not able as yet. But neither indeed are you now able: for you are yet carnal.

3 For, whereas there is among you envying and contention, are you not carnal and walk you not according to man?

4 For while one saith: I indeed am of Paul; and another: I am of Apollo: are you not men? What then is Apollo and what is Paul?

5 The ministers of him whom you have believed: and to every one as the Lord hath given.

6 I have planted, Apollo watered: but God gave the increase.

7 Therefore, neither he that planteth is any thing, nor he that watereth: but God that giveth the increase.

8 Now he that planteth and he that watereth, are one. [1] And every man shall receive his own reward, according to his own labour.

9 For we are God's coadjutors. You are God's husbandry: you are God's building.

10 According to the grace of God that is given to me, as a wise architect, I have laid the foundation: and another buildeth thereon. But let every man take heed how he buildeth thereupon.

11 For other foundation no man can lay, but that which is laid: which is Christ Jesus.

12 Now, if any man build upon this foundation, gold, silver, precious stones, wood, hay, stubble:

13 Every man's work shall be manifest. For the day of the Lord shall declare *it*, because it shall be revealed in fire. And the fire shall try every man's work, of what sort it is.

14 If any man's work abide, which he hath built thereupon, he shall receive a reward.

15 If any man's work burn, he shall suffer loss: but he himself shall be saved, yet so as by fire.

16 Know you not that you are the temple of God and that the Spirit of God dwelleth in you?

17 But if any man violate the temple of God, him shall God destroy. [2] For the temple of God is holy, which you are.

18 Let no man deceive himself. If any man among you seem to be wise in this world, let him become a fool, that he may be wise.

19 For the wisdom of this world is foolishness with God. For it is written: [3] *I will catch the wise in their own craftiness.*

20 And again: [4] *The Lord knoweth the thoughts of the wise, that they are vain.*

21 Let no man therefore glory in men.

22 For all things are yours, whether it be Paul or Apollo or Cephas, or the world, or life, or death, or things present, or things to come. For all are yours.

23 And you are Christ's. And Christ is God's.

[6] Wisd. 9, 13; Isai. 40, 13; Rom. 11, 34. CHAP. 3. [1] Ps. 61, 13; Matt. 16, 27; Rom. 2, 6; Gal. 6, 5. [2] 1 Cor. 6, 19; 2 Cor. 6, 16. [3] Job, 5, 13. [4] Ps. 93, 11.

CHAP. 2. Ver. 14, 15. *The sensual man—the spiritual man.* The *sensual man* is either he who is taken up with sensual pleasures, with carnal and worldly affections: or he who measureth divine mysteries by natural reason, sense and human wisdom only. Now such a man has little or no notion of the things of God. Whereas the *spiritual man* is he who, in the' mysteries of religion, takes not human sense for his guide: but submits his judgment to the decisions of the Church, which he is commanded to hear and obey. For Christ hath promised to remain to the end of the world with his Church and to direct her in all things by the Spirit of truth.

CHAP. 3. Ver. 12. *Upon this foundation.* The foundation is *Christ* and his doctrine: or the true faith in him, working through charity. The building upon this foundation, *gold, silver, and precious stones,* signifies the more perfect preaching and practice of the gospel; the *wood, hay, and stubble,* such preaching as that of the Corinthian teachers (who affected the pomp of words and human eloquence) and such practice as is mixed with much imperfection and many lesser sins. Now the *day* of *the Lord* and his *fiery* trial (in the particular judgment immediately after death) shall make *manifest* of what sort *every man's work* has been: of which, during this life, it is hard to make a judgment. For them, the *fire* of God's judgment *shall try every man's work.* And they, whose *works,* like *wood, hay and stubble,* cannot abide the fire, shall *suffer loss,* these works being found to be of no value; yet they themselves, having built upon the right *foundation* (by living and dying in the true faith and in the state of grace, though with some imperfection), *shall be saved, yet so as by fire;* being liable to this punishment, by reason of the *wood, hay and stubble,* which was mixed with their building.

CHAPTER 4

God's ministers are not to be judged. He reprehends their boasting of their preachers and describes the treatment the apostles every where met with.

LET [1] a man so account of us as of the ministers of Christ and the dispensers of the mysteries of God.

2 Here now it is required among the dispensers that a man be found faithful.

3 But to me it is a very small thing to be judged by you or by man's day. But neither do I judge my own self.

4 For I am not conscious to myself of anything. Yet am I not hereby justified: but he that judgeth me is the Lord.

5 Therefore, judge not before the time: until the Lord come, who both will bring to light the hidden things of darkness and will make manifest the counsels of the hearts. And then shall every man have praise from God.

6 But these things, brethren, I have in a figure transferred to myself and to Apollo, for your sakes: that in us you may learn that one be not puffed up against the other for another, above that which is written.

7 For who distinguished thee? Or what hast thou that thou hast not received, and if thou hast received, why dost thou glory, as if thou hadst not received it?

8 You are now full: you are now become rich: you reign without us; and I would to God you did reign, that we also might reign with you.

9 For I think that God hath set forth us apostles, the last, as it were men appointed to death. We are made a spectacle to the world and to angels and to men.

10 We are fools for Christ's sake, but you are wise in Christ: we are weak, but you are strong: you are honourable, but we without honour.

11 Even unto this hour we both hunger and thirst and are naked and are buffeted and have no fixed abode.

12 [2] And we labour, working with our own hands. We are reviled: and we bless. We are persecuted: and we suffer it.

13 We are blasphemed: and we entreat. We are made as the refuse of this world, the offscouring of all, even until now.

14 I write not these things to confound you: but I admonish you as my dearest children.

15 For if you have ten thousand instructors in Christ, yet not many

fathers. For in Christ Jesus, by the gospel, I have begotten you.

16 Wherefore, I beseech you, be ye followers of me, as I also am of Christ.

17 For this cause have I sent to you Timothy, who is my dearest son and faithful in the Lord. Who will put you in mind of my ways, which are in Christ Jesus: as I teach every where in every church.

18 As if I would not come to you, so some are puffed up.

19 But I will come to you shortly, if the Lord will: and will know, not the speech of them that are puffed up, but the power.

20 For the kingdom of God is not in speech, but in power.

21 What will you? Shall I come to you with a rod? Or in charity and in the spirit of meekness?

CHAPTER 5

He excommunicates the incestuous adulterer and admonishes them to purge out the old leaven.

IT [1] is absolutely heard that there is fornication among you and such fornication as the like is not among the heathens: that one should have his father's wife.

2 And you are puffed up and have not rather mourned: that he might be taken away from among you that hath done this thing.

3 [2] I indeed, absent in body but present in spirit, have already judged, as though I were present, him that hath so done,

4 In the name of our Lord Jesus Christ, you being gathered together and my spirit, with the power of our Lord Jesus:

5 To deliver such a one to Satan for the destruction of the flesh, that the spirit may be saved in the day of our Lord Jesus Christ.

6 Your glorying is not good. [3] Know you not that a little leaven corrupteth the whole lump?

7 Purge out the old leaven, that you may be a new paste, as you are unleavened. For Christ our pasch is sacrificed.

8 Therefore, let us feast, not with the old leaven, nor with the leaven of malice and wickedness: but with the unleavened bread of sincerity and truth.

9 I wrote to you in an epistle not to keep company with fornicators.

10 I mean not with the fornicators of this world or with the covetous or the extortioners or the servers of idols:

otherwise you must needs go out of this world.

11 But now I have written to you, not to keep company, if any man that is named a brother be a fornicator or covetous or a server of idols or a railer or a drunkard or an extortioner: with such a one, not so much as to eat.

12 For what have I to do to judge them that are without? Do not you judge them that are within?

13 For them that are without, God will judge. Put away the evil one from among yourselves.

CHAPTER 6

He blames them for going to law before unbelievers. Of sins that exclude from the kingdom of heaven. The evil of fornication.

D ARE any of you, having a matter against another, go to be judged before the unjust: and not before the saints?

2 Know you not that the saints shall judge this world? And if the world shall be judged by you, are you unworthy to judge the smallest matters?

3 Know you not that we shall judge angels? How much more things of this world?

4 If therefore you have judgments of things pertaining to this world, set them to judge who are the most despised in the church.

5 I speak to your shame. Is it so that there is not among you any one wise man that is able to judge between his brethren?

6 But brother goeth to law with brother: and that before unbelievers.

7 [1] Already indeed there is plainly a fault among you, that you have lawsuits one with another. Why do you not rather take wrong? Why do you not rather suffer yourselves to be defrauded?

8 But you do wrong and defraud: and that to *your* brethren.

9 Know you not that the unjust shall not possess the kingdom of God? Do not err: Neither fornicators nor idolaters nor adulterers:

10 Nor the effeminate nor liers with mankind nor thieves nor covetous nor drunkards nor railers nor extortioners shall possess the kingdom of God.

11 And such some of you were. But you are washed: but you are sanctified: but you are justified: in the name of our Lord Jesus Christ and the Spirit of our God.

12 All things are lawful to me: but all things are not expedient. All things are lawful to me: but I will not be brought under the power of any.

13 Meat for the belly and the belly for the meats: but God shall destroy both it and them. But the body is not for fornication, but for the Lord: and the Lord for the body.

14 Now God hath both raised up the Lord and will raise us up also by his power.

15 Know you not that your bodies are the members of Christ? Shall I then take the members of Christ and make them the members of an harlot? God forbid!

16 Or know you not that he who is joined to a harlot is made one body? [2] For they shall be, saith he, *two in one flesh.*

17 But he who is joined to the Lord is one spirit.

18 Fly fornication. Every sin that a man doth is without the body: but he that committeth fornication sinneth against his own body.

19 Or know you not [3] that your members are the temple of the Holy Ghost, who is in you, whom you have from God: and you are not your own?

20 [4] For you are bought with a great price. Glorify and bear God in your body.

CHAPTER 7

Lessons relating to marriage and celibacy. Virginity is preferable to a married state.

N OW concerning the things whereof you wrote to me: It is good for a man not to touch a woman.

2 But for fear of fornication, let every man have his own wife: and let every woman have her own husband.

3 [1] Let the husband render the debt to his wife: and the wife also in like manner to the husband.

4 The wife hath not power of her own body: but the husband. And in like manner the husband also hath not power of his own body: but the wife.

CHAP. 6. [1] Matt. 5, 39; Luke, 6, 29; Rom. 12, 17; 1 Thess. 4, 6. [2] Gen. 2, 24; Matt. 19, 5; Mark, 10, 8; Eph. 5, 31. [3] 1 Cor. 3, 17; 2 Cor. 6, 16. [4] 1 Cor. 7, 23; 1 Peter, 1, 18. CHAP. 7. [1] 1 Peter, 3, 7.

CHAP. 6. Ver. 7. *A fault.* Lawsuits can hardly ever be without a fault, on the one side or the other; and oftentimes on both sides.

Ver. 12. *All things are lawful.* That is, all *indifferent things* are indeed lawful, inasmuch as they are not prohibited: but oftentimes they are not expedient; as in the case of lawsuits. And much less would it be expedient to be enslaved by an irregular affection to any thing, how indifferent soever.

CHAP. 7. Ver. 2. *Have his own wife.* That is, keep to his wife, which he hath. His meaning is not to exhort the unmarried to marry: on the contrary, he would have them rather continue as they are (ver. 8). But he speaks here to them that are already married; who must not depart from one another but live together as they ought to do in the marriage state.

5 Defraud not one another, except, perhaps, by consent, for a time, that you may give yourselves to prayer: and return together again, lest Satan tempt you for your incontinency.

6 But I speak this by indulgence, not by commandment.

7 For I would that all men were even as myself. But every one hath his proper gift from God: one after this manner, and another after that.

8 But I say to the unmarried and to the widows: It is good for them if they so continue, even as I.

9 But if they do not contain themselves, let them marry. For it is better to marry than to be burnt.

10 But to them that are married, not I, but the Lord, commandeth ² that the wife depart not from her husband.

11 And if she depart, that she remain unmarried or be reconciled to her husband. And let not the husband put away his wife.

12 For to the rest I speak, not the Lord. If any brother hath a wife that believeth not and she consent to dwell with him: let him not put her away.

13 And if any woman hath a husband that believeth not and he consent to dwell with her: let her not put away her husband.

14 For the unbelieving husband is sanctified by the believing wife: and the unbelieving wife is sanctified by the believing husband. Otherwise your children should be unclean: but now they are holy.

15 But if the unbeliever depart, let him depart. For a brother or sister is not under servitude in such cases. But God hath called us in peace.

16 For how knowest thou, O wife, whether thou shalt save thy husband? Or how knowest thou, O man, whether thou shalt save thy wife?

17 But as the Lord hath distributed to every one, as God hath called every one: so let him walk. And so in all churches I teach.

² Matt. 5, 32; 19, 9; Mark, 10, 9; Luke, 16, 18. ³ Eph. 4, 1. ⁴ 1 Cor. 6, 20; 1 Peter, 1, 18.

Ver. 6. *By indulgence.* That is, by a condescension to your weakness.

Ver. 9. *If they do not contain.* This is spoken of such as are free and not of such as, by vow, have given their first faith to God; to whom, if they will use proper means to obtain it, God will never refuse the gift of continency. Some translators have corrupted this text, by rendering it: *If they cannot contain.*

Ver. 12. *I speak, not the Lord.* That is, not by any express commandment or ordinance.

Ver. 14. *Is sanctified.* The meaning is not, that the faith of the husband or the wife is of itself sufficient to put the unbelieving party or their children in the state of grace and salvation; but that it is very often an occasion of their sanctification, by bringing them to the true faith.

18 Is any man called, being circumcised? Let him not procure uncircumcision. Is any man called in uncircumcision? Let him not be circumcised.

19 Circumcision is nothing and uncircumcision is nothing: but the observance of the commandments of God.

20 ³ Let every man abide in the same calling in which he was called.

21 Wast thou called, being a bondman? Care not for it: but if thou mayest be made free, use it rather.

22 For he that is called in the Lord, being a bondman, is the freeman of the Lord. Likewise he that is called, being free, is the bondman of Christ.

23 ⁴ You are bought with a price: be not made the bondslaves of men.

24 Brethren, let every man, wherein he was called, therein abide with God.

25 Now, concerning virgins, I have no commandment of the Lord: but I give counsel, as having obtained mercy of the Lord, to be faithful.

26 I think therefore that this is good for the present necessity: that it is good for a man so to be.

27 Art thou bound to a wife? Seek not to be loosed. Art thou loosed from a wife? Seek not a wife.

28 But if thou take a wife, thou hast not sinned. And if a virgin marry, she hath not sinned: nevertheless, such shall have tribulation of the flesh. But I spare you.

29 This therefore I say, brethren: The time is short. It remaineth, that they also who have wives be as if they had none:

30 And they that weep, as though they wept not: and they that rejoice, as if they rejoiced not: and they that buy, as though they possessed not:

31 And they that use this world, as if they used it not. For the fashion of this world passeth away.

32 But I would have you to be without solicitude. He that is without a wife is solicitous for the things that belong to the Lord: how he may please God.

33 But he that is with a wife is solicitous for the things of the world: how he may please his wife. And he is divided.

34 And the unmarried woman and the virgin thinketh on the things of the Lord: that she may be holy both in body and in spirit. But she that is married thinketh on the things of the world: how she may please her husband.

35 And this I speak for your profit, not to cast a snare upon you, but for

that which is decent and which may give you power to attend upon the Lord, without impediment.

36 But if any man think that he seemeth dishonoured with regard to his virgin, for that she is above the age, and it must so be: let him do what he will. He sinneth not, if she marry.

37 For he that hath determined, being steadfast in his heart, having no necessity, but having power of his own will; and hath judged this in his heart, to keep his virgin, doth well.

38 Therefore, both he that giveth his virgin in marriage doth well: and he that giveth her not doth better.

39 ⁵ A woman is bound by the law as long as her husband liveth: but if her husband die, she is at liberty. Let her marry to whom she will: only in the Lord.

40 But more blessed shall she be, if she so remain, according to my counsel. And I think that I also have the spirit of God.

CHAPTER 8

Though an idol be nothing, yet things offered up to idols are not to be eaten, for fear of scandal.

NOW concerning those things that are sacrificed to idols: we know that we all have knowledge. Knowledge puffeth up: but charity edifieth.

2 And if any man think that he knoweth any thing, he hath not yet known as he ought to know.

3 But if any man love God, the same is known by him.

4 But as for the meats that are sacrificed to idols, we know that an idol is nothing in the world and that there is no God but one.

5 For although there be that are called gods, either in heaven or on earth (for there be gods many and lords many):

6 Yet to us there is but one God, the Father, of whom are all things, and we unto him: and one Lord Jesus Christ, by whom are all things, and we by him.

7 But there is not knowledge in every one. For some until this present, with conscience of the idol, eat as a thing sacrificed to an idol: and their conscience, being weak, is defiled.

8 But meat doth not commend us to God. For neither, if we eat, shall we have the more: nor, if we eat not, shall we have the less.

9 But take heed lest perhaps this your liberty become a stumbling-block to the weak.

10 For if a man see him that hath knowledge sit at meat in the idol's temple, shall not his conscience, being weak, be emboldened to eat those things which are sacrificed to idols?

11 ¹ And through thy knowledge shall the weak brother perish, for whom Christ hath died?

12 Now when you sin thus against the brethren and wound their weak conscience, you sin against Christ.

13 ² Wherefore, if meat scandalize my brother, I will never eat flesh, lest I should scandalize my brother.

CHAPTER 9

The apostle did not make use of his power of being maintained at the charges of those to whom he preached, that he might give no hindrance to the gospel. Of running in the race and striving for the mastery.

AM not I free? Am not I an apostle? Have not I seen Christ Jesus our Lord? Are not you my work in the Lord?

2 And if unto others I be not an apostle, but yet to you I am. For you are the seal of my apostleship in the Lord.

3 My defence with them that do examine me is this.

4 Have not we power to eat and to drink?

5 Have we not power to carry about a woman, a sister, as well as the rest of the apostles and the brethren of the Lord and Cephas?

6 Or I only and Barnabas, have not we power to do this?

7 Who serveth as a soldier, at any time, at his own charges? Who planteth a vineyard and eateth not of the fruit thereof? Who feedeth the flock and eateth not of the milk of the flock?

8 Speak I these things according to man? Or doth not the law also say these things?

⁵ Rom. 7, 2. CHAP. 8. ¹ Rom. 14, 15. ² Rom. 14, 21.

Ver. 36. *Let him do what he will; he sinneth not.* The meaning is not, as libertines would have it, that persons may do what they will and not sin, provided they afterwards marry; but that the father, with regard to the giving his virgin in marriage, may do as he pleaseth; and that it will be no sin to him if she marry.

CHAP. 8. Ver. 1. *Knowledge puffeth up.* Knowledge, without charity and humility, serveth only to puff persons up.

Ver. 5. *Gods many.* Reputed for such among the heathens.

Ver. 13. *If meat scandalize.* That is, if my eating cause my brother to sin.

CHAP. 9. Ver. 5. *A woman, a sister.* Some erroneous translators have corrupted this text by rendering it, *a sister, a wife:* whereas it is certain, St. Paul had no wife (chap. 7, ver. 7, 8) and that he only speaks of such devout women as, according to the custom of the Jewish nation, waited upon the preachers of the gospel and supplied them with necessaries.

9 For it is written in the law of Moses: [1] *Thou shalt not muzzle the mouth of the ox that treadeth out the corn.* Doth God take care for oxen?

10 Or doth he say this indeed for our sakes? For *these things* are written for our sakes: that he that plougheth, should plough in hope and he that thrasheth, in hope to receive fruit.

11 [2] If we have sown unto you spiritual things, is it a great matter if we reap your carnal things?

12 If others be partakers of this power over you, why not we rather? Nevertheless, we have not used this power: but we bear all things, lest we should give any hindrance to the gospel of Christ.

13 [3] Know you not that they who work in the holy place eat the things that are of the holy place; and they that serve the altar partake with the altar?

14 So also the Lord ordained that they who preach the gospel should live by the gospel.

15 But I have used none of these things. Neither have I written these things, that they should be so done unto me: for it is good for me to die rather than that any man should make my glory void.

16 For if I preach the gospel, it is no glory to me: for a necessity lieth upon me. For woe is unto me if I preach not the gospel.

17 For if I do this thing willingly, I have a reward: but if against my will, a dispensation is committed to me.

18 What is my reward then? That preaching the gospel, I may deliver the gospel without charge, that I abuse not my power in the gospel.

19 For whereas I was free as to all, I made myself the servant of all, that I might gain the more.

20 And I became to the Jews a Jew, that I might gain the Jews:

21 To them that are under the law, as if I were under the law (whereas myself was not under the law), that I might gain them that were under the law. To them that were without the law, as if I were without the law (whereas I was not without the law of God, but was in the law of Christ), that I might gain them that were without the law.

22 To the weak I became weak, that I might gain the weak. I became all things to all men, that I might save all.

23 And I do all things for the gospel's sake, that I may be made partaker thereof.

24 Know you not that they that run in the race, all run indeed, but one receiveth the prize. So run that you may obtain.

25 And every one that striveth for the mastery refraineth himself from all things. And they indeed that they may receive a corruptible crown: but we an incorruptible one.

26 I therefore so run, not as at an uncertainty: I so fight, not as one beating the air.

27 But I chastise my body and bring it into subjection: lest perhaps, when I have preached to others, I myself should become a castaway.

CHAPTER 10

By the example of the Israelites, he shews that we are not to build too much upon favours received but to avoid their sins and fly from the service of idols and from things offered to idols.

FOR I would not have you ignorant, brethren, that our fathers were all [1] under the cloud: and all passed through [2] the sea.

2 And all in Moses were baptized, in the cloud and in the sea:

3 [3] And did all eat the same spiritual food:

4 [4] And all drank the same spiritual drink: (And they drank of the spiritual rock that followed them: and the rock was Christ.)

5 But with most of them God was not well pleased: [5] for they were overthrown in the desert.

6 Now these things were done in a figure of us, that we should not covet evil things, [6] as they also coveted.

7 Neither become ye idolaters, as some of them, as it is written: [7] *The people sat down to eat and drink and rose up to play.*

8 Neither let us commit fornication, [8] as some of them that committed fornication: and there fell in one day three and twenty thousand.

9 Neither let us tempt Christ, as some of them tempted and perished by the serpent.

CHAP. 9. [1] Deut. 25, 4; 1 Tim. 5, 18. [2] Rom. 15, 27. [3] Deut. 18, 1. CHAP. 10. [1] Exod. 13, 21; Num. 9, 21. [2] Exod. 14, 22. [3] Exod. 16, 15. [4] Exod. 17, 6; Num. 20, 11. [5] Num. 26, 64, 65. [6] Ps. 105, 14. [7] Exod. 32, 6. [8] Num. 21, 5, 6.

Ver. 16. *It is no glory.* That is, I have nothing to glory of.

Ver. 27. *I chastise.* Here St. Paul shews the necessity of self-denial and mortification, to subdue the flesh and its inordinate desires.

CHAP. 10. Ver. 2. *In Moses.* Under the conduct of Moses, they received baptism in figure, by passing under the cloud and through the sea; and they partook of the body and blood of Christ in figure, by eating of the *manna* (called here a *spiritual food* because it was a figure of the true bread which comes down from heaven), and drinking the water miraculously brought out of the rock, called here a *spiritual rock*, because it was also a figure of Christ.

10 ⁹ Neither do you murmur, as some of them murmured and were destroyed by the destroyer.

11 Now all these things happened to them in figure: and they are written for our correction, upon whom the ends of the world are come.

12 Wherefore, he that thinketh himself to stand, let him take heed lest he fall.

13 Let no temptation take hold on you, but such as is human. And God is faithful, who will not suffer you to be tempted above that which you are able: but will make also with temptation issue, that you may be able to bear it.

14 Wherefore, my dearly beloved, fly from the service of idols.

15 I speak as to wise men: judge ye yourselves what I say.

16 The chalice of benediction which we bless, is it not the communion of the blood of Christ? And the bread which we break, is it not the partaking of the body of the Lord?

17 For we, being many, are one bread, one body: all that partake of one bread.

18 Behold Israel according to the flesh. Are not they that eat of the sacrifices partakers of the altar?

19 What then? Do I say that what is offered in sacrifice to idols is any thing? Or that the idol is any thing?

20 But the things which the heathens sacrifice, they sacrifice to devils and not to God. And I would not that you should be made partakers with devils.

21 You cannot drink the chalice of the Lord and the chalice of devils: you cannot be partakers of the table of the Lord and of the table of devils.

22 Do we provoke the Lord to jealousy? Are we stronger than he? ¹⁰ All things are lawful for me: but all things are not expedient.

23 All things are lawful for me: but all things do not edify.

24 Let no man seek his own, but that which is another's.

25 Whatsoever is sold in the shambles, eat: asking no question for conscience' sake.

26 ¹¹ The earth is the Lord's and the fulness thereof.

27 If any of them that believe not, invite you, and you be willing to go: eat of any thing that is set before you, asking no question for conscience' sake.

28 But if any man say: This has been sacrificed to idols; do not eat of it, for his sake that told it and for conscience' sake.

29 Conscience, I say, not thy own, but the other's. For why is my liberty judged by another man's conscience?

30 If I partake with thanksgiving, why am I evil spoken of for that for which I give thanks?

31 ¹² Therefore, whether you eat or drink, or whatsoever else you do, do all to the glory of God.

32 Be without offence to the Jews and to the Gentiles and to the church of God:

33 As I also in all things please all men, not seeking that which is profitable to myself but to many: that they may be saved.

CHAPTER 11

Women must have a covering over their heads. He blameth the abuses of their love feasts and upon that occasion treats of the Blessed Sacrament.

BE ye followers of me, as I also am of Christ.

2 Now I praise you, brethren, that in all things you are mindful of me and keep my ordinances as I have delivered them to you.

3 But I would have you know ¹ that the head of every man is Christ: and the head of the woman is the man: and the head of Christ is God.

4 Every man praying or prophesying with his head covered disgraceth his head.

5 But every woman praying or prophesying with her head not covered disgraceth her head: for it is all one as if she were shaven.

6 For if a woman be not covered, let her be shorn. But if it be a shame to a woman to be shorn or made bald, let her cover her head.

7 The man indeed ought not to cover his head: because he is the ² image and glory of God. But the woman is the glory of the man.

8 For the man is not of the woman: but the woman of the man.

⁹ Num. 11, 1; 14, 1. ¹⁰ 1 Cor. 6, 12. ¹¹ Ps. 23, 1; Ecclus. 17, 31. ¹² Col. 3, 17. CHAP. 11. ¹ Eph. 5, 23. ² Gen. 1, 26.

Ver. 11. *The ends of the world.* That is, the last ages.

Ver. 13. Or, *no temptation hath taken hold of you,* or come upon you as yet, but what is human, or incident to man.—*Issue,* or a way to escape.

Ver. 16. *Which we bless.* Here the apostle puts them in mind of their partaking of the Body and Blood of Christ in the Sacred Mysteries and becoming thereby one mystical body with Christ. From whence he infers (ver. 21), that they who are made partakers with Christ, by the Eucharistic Sacrifice and Sacrament must not be made partakers with devils by eating of the meats sacrificed to them.

Ver. 17. *One bread.* Or, as it may be rendered, agreeably both to the Latin and Greek: *because the bread is one, all we, being many, are one body, who partake of that one bread.* For it is by our communicating with Christ and with one another in the Blessed Sacrament that we are formed into one mystical body and made, as it were, one bread, compounded of many grains of corn, closely united together.

9 [3] For the man was not created for the woman: but the woman for the man.

10 Therefore ought the woman to have a power over her head, because of the angels.

11 But yet neither is the man without the woman, nor the woman without the man, in the Lord.

12 For as the woman is of the man, so also is the man by the woman: but all things of God.

13 You yourselves judge. Doth it become a woman to pray unto God uncovered?

14 Doth not even nature itself teach you that a man indeed, if he nourish his hair, it is a shame unto him?

15 But if a woman nourish her hair, it is a glory to her; for her hair is given to her for a covering.

16 But if any man seem to be contentious, we have no such custom, nor the Church of God.

17 Now this I ordain: not praising you, that you come together, not for the better, but for the worse.

18 For first of all I hear that when you come together in the church, there are schisms among you. And in part I believe it.

19 For there must be also heresies: that they also, who are approved may be made manifest among you.

20 When you come therefore together into one place, it is not now to eat the Lord's supper.

21 For every one taketh before his own supper to eat. And one indeed is hungry and another is drunk.

[3] Gen. 2, 23. [4] Matt. 26, 26; Mark, 14, 22; Luke, 22, 17. [5] John, 6, 59. [6] 2 Cor. 13, 5. CHAP. 12. [1] Mark, 9, 38.

CHAP. 11. Ver. 10. *A power.* That is, a veil or covering, as a sign that she is under the *power* of her husband: and this, the apostle adds, *because of the angels,* who are present in the assemblies of the faithful.

Ver. 19. *There must be also heresies.* By reason of the pride and perversity of man's heart; not by God's will or appointment; who, nevertheless draws good out of this evil, manifesting, by that occasion, who are the good and firm Christians and making their faith more remarkable.

Ver. 20. *The Lord's supper.* So the apostle here calls the *charity feasts* observed by the primitive Christians. He reprehends the abuses of the Corinthians on these occasions; which were the more criminal, because these feasts were accompanied with the celebrating the Eucharistic Sacrifice and Sacrament.

Ver. 27. *Or drink.* Here erroneous translators corrupted the text, by putting *and drink* (contrary to the original, ἢ πίνη) instead of *or drink.*
—*Guilty of the body.* This demonstrates the real presence of the body and blood of Christ, even to the unworthy communicant; who otherwise could not be *guilty of the body and blood of Christ,* or justly condemned for *not discerning the Lord's body.*

Ver. 28. *Drink of the chalice.* This is not said by way of command, but by way of allowance, namely, where and when it is agreeable to the practice and discipline of the church.

22 What, have you not houses to eat and to drink in? Or despise ye the church of God and put them to shame that have not? What shall I say to you? Do I praise you? In this I praise you not.

23 For I have received of the Lord that which also I delivered unto you, that the Lord Jesus, the same night in which he was betrayed, took bread,

24 And giving thanks, broke and said: [4] Take ye and eat: This is my body, which shall be delivered for you. This do for the commemoration of me.

25 In like manner also the chalice, after he had supped, saying: This chalice is the new testament in my blood. This do ye, as often as you shall drink, for the commemoration of me.

26 For as often as you shall eat this bread and drink the chalice, you shall shew the death of the Lord, until he come.

27 [5] Therefore, whosoever shall eat this bread, or drink the chalice of the Lord unworthily, shall be guilty of the body and of the blood of the Lord.

28 [6] But let a man prove himself: and so let him eat of that bread and drink of the chalice.

29 For he that eateth and drinketh unworthily eateth and drinketh judgment to himself, not discerning the body of the Lord.

30 Therefore are there many infirm and weak among you: and many sleep.

31 But if we would judge ourselves, we should not be judged.

32 But whilst we are judged, we are chastised by the Lord, that we be not condemned with this world.

33 Wherefore, my brethren, when you come together to eat, wait for one another.

34 If any man be hungry, let him eat at home; that you come not together unto judgment. And the rest I will set in order, when I come.

CHAPTER 12

Of the diversity of spiritual gifts. The members of the mystical body, like those of the natural body, must mutually cherish one another.

NOW concerning spiritual things, my brethren, I would not have you ignorant.

2 You know that when you were heathens, you went to dumb idols, according as you were led.

3 Wherefore, I give you to understand [1] that no man, speaking by the Spirit of God, saith Anathema to Jesus. And no man can say The Lord Jesus, but by the Holy Ghost.

4 Now there are diversities of graces, but the same Spirit.

5 And there are diversities of ministries, but the same Lord.

6 And there are diversities of operations, but the same God, who worketh all in all.

7 And the manifestation of the Spirit is given to every man unto profit.

8 To one indeed, by the Spirit, is given the word of wisdom: and to another, the word of knowledge, according to the same Spirit:

9 To another, faith in the same spirit: to another, the grace of healing in one Spirit:

10 To another, the working of miracles: to another, prophecy: to another, the discerning of spirits: to another, *diverse* kinds of tongues: to another, interpretation of speeches.

11 ² But all these things, one and the same Spirit worketh, dividing to every one according as he will.

12 For as the body is one and hath many members; and all the members of the body, whereas they are many, yet are one body: so also *is* Christ.

13 For in one Spirit were we all baptized into one body, whether Jews or Gentiles, whether bond or free: and in one Spirit we have all been made to drink.

14 For the body also is not one member, but many.

15 If the foot should say: Because I am not the hand, I am not of the body: Is it therefore not of the body?

16 And if the ear should say: Because I am not the eye, I am not of the body: Is it therefore not of the body?

17 If the whole body were the eye, where would be the hearing? If the whole were hearing, where would be the smelling?

18 But now God hath set the members, every one of them, in the body as it hath pleased him.

19 And if they all were one member, where would be the body?

20 But now *there are* many members indeed, yet one body.

21 And the eye cannot say to the hand: I need not thy help. Nor again the head to the feet: I have no need of you.

22 Yea, much more those that seem to be the more feeble members of the body are more necessary.

23 And such as we think to be the less honourable members of the body, about these we put more abundant honour: and those that are our un-comely parts have more abundant comeliness.

24 But our comely parts have no need: but God hath tempered the body together, giving to that which wanted the more abundant honour.

25 That there might be no schism in the body; but that the members might be mutually careful one for another.

26 And if one member suffer any thing, all the members suffer with it: or if one member glory, all the members rejoice with it.

27 Now you are the body of Christ and members of member.

28 ³ And God indeed hath set some in the church: first apostles, secondly prophets, thirdly doctors: after that miracles: then the graces of healings, helps, governments, kinds of tongues, interpretations of speeches.

29 Are all apostles? Are all prophets? Are all doctors?

30 Are all *workers of* miracles? Have all the grace of healing? Do all speak with tongues? Do all interpret?

31 But be zealous for the better gifts. And I shew unto you yet a more excellent way.

CHAPTER 13

Charity is to be preferred before all other gifts.

IF I speak with the tongues of men and of angels, and have not charity, I am become as sounding brass, or a tinkling cymbal.

2 And if I should have prophecy and should know all mysteries and all knowledge, and if I should have all faith, so that I could remove mountains, and have not charity, I am nothing.

3 And if I should distribute all my goods to feed the poor, and if I should deliver my body to be burned, and have not charity, it profiteth me nothing.

4 Charity is patient, is kind: charity envieth not, dealeth not perversely, is not puffed up,

5 Is not ambitious, seeketh not her own, is not provoked to anger, thinketh no evil:

6 Rejoiceth not in iniquity, but rejoiceth with the truth:

7 Beareth all things, believeth all things, hopeth all things, endureth all things.

8 Charity never falleth away: whether prophecies shall be made void or tongues shall cease or knowledge shall be destroyed.

² Rom. 12, 3, 6; Eph. 4, 7. ³ Eph. 4, 11.

9 For we know in part: and we prophesy in part.

10 But when that which is perfect is come, that which is in part shall be done away.

11 When I was a child, I spoke as a child, I understood as a child, I thought as a child. But, when I became a man, I put away the things of a child.

12 We see now through a glass in a dark manner: but then face to face. Now I know in part: but then I shall know even as I am known.

13 And now there remain faith, hope and charity, these three: but the greatest of these is charity.

CHAPTER 14

The gift of prophesying is to be preferred before that of speaking strange tongues.

FOLLOW after charity. Be zealous for spiritual gifts: but rather that you may prophesy.

2 For he that speaketh in a tongue speaketh not unto men, but unto God: for no man heareth. Yet by the Spirit he speaketh mysteries.

3 But he that prophesieth speaketh to men unto edification and exhortation and comfort.

4 He that speaketh in a tongue edifieth himself: but he that prophesieth, edifieth the church.

5 And I would have you all to speak with tongues, but rather to prophesy. For greater is he that prophesieth than he that speaketh with tongues: unless perhaps he interpret, that the church may receive edification.

6 But now, brethren, if I come to you speaking with tongues, what shall I profit you, unless I speak to you either in revelation or in knowledge or in prophecy or in doctrine?

7 Even things without life that give sound, whether pipe or harp, except they give a distinction of sounds, how

CHAP. 14. [1] Isai. 28, 11.

CHAP. 14. Ver. 1. *Prophesy.* That is, declare or expound the mysteries of faith.
Ver. 2. *Not unto men.* So as to be *heard,* that is, so as to be understood by them.
Ver. 12. *Of spirits.* Of spiritual gifts.
Ver. 16. *Amen.* The unlearned, not knowing that you are then blessing, will not be qualified to join with you by saying Amen to your blessing. The use or abuse of strange tongues, of which the apostle here speaks, does not regard the public liturgy of the church (in which strange tongues were never used), but certain conferences of the faithful (ver. 26), in which, meeting together, they discovered to one another their various miraculous gifts of the Spirit, common in those primitive times; amongst which the apostle prefers that of prophesying before that of speaking strange tongues, because it was more to the public edification. Where also note, that the Latin, used in our liturgy, is so far from being a strange or unknown tongue, that it is perhaps the best known tongue in the world.

shall it be known what is piped or harped?

8 For if the trumpet give an uncertain sound, who shall prepare himself to the battle?

9 So likewise you, except you utter by the tongue plain speech, how shall it be known what is said? For you shall be speaking into the air.

10 There are, for example, so many kinds of tongues in this world: and none is without voice.

11 If then I know not the power of the voice, I shall be to him to whom I speak a barbarian: and he that speaketh, a barbarian to me.

12 So you also, forasmuch as you are zealous of spirits, seek to abound unto the edifying of the church.

13 And therefore he that speaketh by a tongue, let him pray that he may interpret.

14 For if I pray in a tongue, my spirit prayeth: but my understanding is without fruit.

15 What is it then? I will pray with the spirit, I will pray also with the understanding. I will sing with the spirit, I will sing also with the understanding.

16 Else, if thou shalt bless with the spirit, how shall he that holdeth the place of the unlearned say, Amen, to thy blessing? Because he knoweth not what thou sayest.

17 For thou indeed givest thanks well: but the other is not edified.

18 I thank my God I speak with all your tongues.

19 But in the church I had rather speak five words with my understanding, that I may instruct others also: than ten thousand words in a tongue.

20 Brethren, do not become children in sense. But in malice be children: and in sense be perfect.

21 In the law it is written: [1] *In other tongues and other lips I will speak to this people: and neither so will they hear me, saith the Lord.*

22 Wherefore tongues are for a sign, not to believers but to unbelievers: but prophecies, not to unbelievers but to believers.

23 If therefore the whole church come together into one place, and all speak with tongues, and there come in unlearned persons or infidels, will they not say that you are mad?

24 But if all prophesy, and there come in one that believeth not or an unlearned person, he is convinced of all: he is judged of all.

25 The secrets of his heart are made manifest. And so, falling down on his

face, he will adore God, affirming that God is among you indeed.

26 How is it then, brethren? When you come together, every one of you hath a psalm, hath a doctrine, hath a revelation, hath a tongue, hath an interpretation: let all things be done to edification.

27 If any speak with a tongue, let it be by two, or at the most by three, and in course: and let one interpret.

28 But if there be no interpreter, let him hold his peace in the church and speak to himself and to God.

29 And let the prophets speak, two or three: and let the rest judge.

30 But if any thing be revealed to another sitting, let the first hold his peace.

31 For you may all prophesy, one by one, that all may learn and all may be exhorted.

32 And the spirits of the prophets are subject to the prophets.

33 For God is not the God of dissension, but of peace: as also I teach in all the churches of the saints.

34 Let women keep silence in the churches: for it is not permitted them to speak but to be subject, [2] as also the law saith.

35 But if they would learn anything, let them ask their husbands at home. For it is a shame for a woman to speak in the church.

36 Or did the word of God come out from you? Or came it only unto you?

37 If any seem to be a prophet or spiritual, let him know the things that I write to you, that they are the commandments of the Lord.

38 But if any man know not, he shall not be known.

39 Wherefore, brethren, be zealous to prophesy: and forbid not to speak with tongues.

40 But let all things be done decently and according to order.

CHAPTER 15

Christ's resurrection and ours. The manner of our resurrection.

NOW [1] I make known unto you, brethren, the gospel which I preached to you, which also you have received and wherein you stand.

2 By which also you are saved, if you hold fast after what manner I preached unto you, unless you have believed in vain.

3 For I delivered unto you first of all, which I also received: how that Christ died for our sins, [2] according to the scriptures:

4 [3] And that he was buried: and that

he rose again the third day, according to the scriptures:

5 And that he was seen by Cephas, [4] and after that by the eleven.

6 Then was he seen by more than five hundred brethren at once: of whom many remain until this present, and some are fallen asleep.

7 After that, he was seen by James: then by all the apostles.

8 And last of all, he was seen also by me, as by one born out of due time.

9 [5] For I am the least of the apostles, who am not worthy to be called an apostle, because I persecuted the church of God.

10 But by the grace of God, I am what I am. And his grace in me hath not been void: but I have laboured more abundantly than all they. Yet not I, but the grace of God with me:

11 For whether I or they, so we preach: and so you have believed.

12 Now if Christ be preached, that he arose again from the dead, how do some among you say that there is no resurrection of the dead?

13 But if there be no resurrection of the dead, then Christ is not risen again.

14 And if Christ be not risen again, then is our preaching vain: and your faith is also vain.

15 Yea, and we are found false witnesses of God: because we have given testimony against God, that he hath raised up Christ, whom he hath not raised up, if the dead rise not again.

16 For if the dead rise not again, neither is Christ risen again.

17 And if Christ be not risen again, your faith is vain: for you are yet in your sins.

18 Then they also that are fallen asleep in Christ are perished.

19 If in this life only we have hope in Christ, we are of all men most miserable.

20 But now Christ is risen from the dead, the firstfruits of them that sleep:

21 [6] For by a man *came* death: and by a man the resurrection of the dead.

22 And as in Adam all die, so also in Christ all shall be made alive.

23 [7] But every one in his own order: the firstfruits, Christ: then they that are of Christ, who have believed in his coming.

24 Afterwards the end: when he shall have delivered up the kingdom to God and the Father: when he shall have brought to nought all principality and power and virtue.

[2] Gen. 3, 10. CHAP. 15. [1] Gal. 1, 11. [2] Isai. 53, 5. [3] Jonas, 2, 1. [4] John, 20, 19. [5] Acts, 9, 3; Eph. 3, 3. [6] Col. 1, 18; Apoc. 1, 5. [7] 1 Thess. 4, 15.

25 For he must reign, [8] *until he hath put all his enemies under his feet.*

26 And the enemy, death, shall be destroyed last: [9] *For he hath put all things under his feet.* And whereas he saith:

27 *All things are put under him;* undoubtedly, he is excepted, who put all things under him.

28 And when all things shall be subdued unto him, then the Son also himself shall be subject unto him that put all things under him, that God may be all in all.

29 Otherwise, what shall they do that are baptized for the dead, if the dead rise not again at all? Why are they then baptized for them?

30 Why also are we in danger every hour?

31 I die daily, I protest by your glory, brethren, which I have in Christ Jesus our Lord.

32 If (according to man) I fought with beasts at Ephesus, what doth it profit me, if the dead rise not again? [10] *Let us eat and drink, for to-morrow we shall die.*

33 Be not seduced: *Evil communications corrupt good manners.*

34 Awake, ye just, and sin not. For some have not the knowledge of God. I speak it to your shame.

35 But some man will say: How do the dead rise again? Or with what manner of body shall they come?

36 Senseless man, that which thou sowest is not quickened, except it die first.

37 And that which thou sowest, thou sowest not the body that shall be: but bare grain, as of wheat, or of some of the rest.

38 But God giveth it a body as he will: and to every seed its proper body.

39 All flesh is not the same flesh: but one is the flesh of men, another of beasts, another of birds, another of fishes.

40 And there are bodies celestial and bodies terrestrial: but, one is the glory of the celestial, and another of the terrestrial.

41 One is the glory of the sun, another the glory of the moon, and another the glory of the stars. For star differeth from star in glory.

42 So also is the resurrection of the dead. It is sown in corruption: it shall rise in incorruption.

43 It is sown in dishonour: it shall rise in glory. It is sown in weakness: it shall rise in power.

44 It is sown a natural body: it shall rise a spiritual body. If there be a natural body, there is also a spiritual body, as it is written:

45 [11] *The first man Adam was made into a living soul:* the last Adam into a quickening spirit.

46 Yet that was not first which is spiritual, but that which is natural: afterwards that which is spiritual.

47 The first man *was,* of the earth, earthly: the second man, from heaven, heavenly.

48 Such as *is* the earthly, such also *are* the earthly: and such as *is* the heavenly, such also *are* they that are heavenly.

49 Therefore, as we have borne the image of the earthly, let us bear also the image of the heavenly.

50 Now this I say, brethren, that flesh and blood cannot possess the kingdom of God: neither shall corruption possess incorruption.

51 Behold, I tell you a mystery. We shall all indeed rise again: but we shall not all be changed.

52 In a moment, in the twinkling of an eye, at the last trumpet: for the trumpet shall sound and the dead shall rise again incorruptible. And we shall be changed.

53 For this corruptible must put on incorruption: and this mortal must put on immortality.

54 And when this mortal hath put on immortality, then shall come to pass the saying that is written: [12] *Death is swallowed up in victory.*

55 O death, where *is* thy victory? O death, where *is* thy sting?

56 Now the sting of death is sin: and the power of sin *is* the law.

57 [13] But thanks be to God, who hath given us the victory through our Lord Jesus Christ.

58 Therefore, my beloved brethren, be ye steadfast and unmoveable: always abounding in the work of the Lord, knowing that your labour is not in vain in the Lord.

---

[8] Ps. 109, 1; Heb. 1, 13; 10, 13.   [9] Ps. 8, 8; Heb. 2, 8.   [10] Wisd. 2, 6; Isai. 22, 13; 56, 12.   [11] Gen. 2, 7.   [12] Osee, 13, 14; Heb. 2, 14.   [13] 1 John, 5, 5.

CHAP. 15. Ver. 28. *The Son also himself shall be subject unto him.* That is, the Son will be subject to the Father, according to his human nature, even after the general resurrection: and also the whole mystical body of Christ will be entirely subject to God, obeying him in every thing.

Ver. 29. *That are baptized for the dead.* Some think the apostle here alludes to a ceremony then in use; but others, more probably, to the prayers and penitential labours, performed by the primitive Christians for the souls of the faithful departed; or to the baptism of afflictions and sufferings undergone for sinners spiritually dead.

Ver. 32. *Let us eat and drink.* That is, if we did not believe that we were to rise again from the dead, we might live like the impious and wicked, who have no belief in the resurrection.

CHAPTER 16

Of collection of alms. Admonitions and salutations.

NOW concerning the collections that are made for the saints: as I have given order to the churches of Galatia, so do ye also.

2 On the first day of the week, let every one of you put apart with himself, laying up what it shall well please him: that when I come, the collections be not then to be made.

3 And when I shall be with you, whomsoever you shall approve by letters, them will I send to carry your grace to Jerusalem.

4 And if it be meet that I also go, they shall go with me.

5 Now I will come to you, when I shall have passed through Macedonia. For I shall pass through Macedonia.

6 And with you perhaps I shall abide, or even spend the winter: that you may bring me on my way whithersoever I shall go.

7 For I will not see you now by the way: for I trust that I shall abide with you some time, if the Lord permit.

8 But I will tarry at Ephesus, until Pentecost.

9 For a great door and evident is opened unto me: and many adversaries.

10 Now if Timothy come, see that he be with you without fear: for he worketh the work of the Lord, as I also do.

11 Let no man therefore despise him: but conduct ye him on his way in peace, that he may come to me. For I look for him with the brethren.

12 And touching *our* brother Apollo, I give you to understand that I much entreated him to come unto you with the brethren: and indeed it was not his will at all to come at this time. But he will come when he shall have leisure.

13 Watch ye: stand fast in the faith: do manfully and be strengthened.

14 Let all your things be done in charity.

15 And I beseech you, brethren, you know the house of Stephanas, and of Fortunatus, and of Achaicus, that they are the firstfruits of Achaia, and have dedicated themselves to the ministry of the saints:

16 That you also be subject to such and to every one that worketh with us and laboureth.

17 And I rejoice in the presence of Stephanas and Fortunatus and Achaicus: because that which was wanting on your part, they have supplied.

18 For they have refreshed both my spirit and yours. Know them, therefore, that are such.

19 The churches of Asia salute you. Aquila and Priscilla salute you much in the Lord, with the church that is in their house, with whom I also lodge.

20 All the brethren salute you. Salute one another with a holy kiss.

21 The salutation of *me* Paul, with my own hand.

22 If any man love not our Lord Jesus Christ, let him be anathema, maran-atha.

23 The grace of our Lord Jesus Christ be with you.

24 My charity be with you all in Christ Jesus. Amen.

CHAP. 16. Ver. 22. *Let him be anathema, maran-atha. Anathema* signifies here a thing accursed. *Maran-atha,* according to St. Jerome and St. Chrysostom, signifies, *The Lord is come* already, and therefore is to be taken as an admonition to those who doubted of the resurrection, and to put them in mind that Christ, the judge of the living and the dead, is come already. Others explain *Maran-atha: May our Lord come,* that is, to judge and punish those with exemplary judgments and punishments that do not love the Lord Jesus Christ.

THE SECOND EPISTLE OF ST. PAUL TO THE
CORINTHIANS

In this Epistle St. Paul comforts those who are now reformed by his admonitions to them in the former and absolves the incestuous man on doing penance, whom he had before excommunicated for his crime. Hence he treats of true penance and of the dignity of the ministers of the New Testament. He cautions the faithful against false teachers and the society of infidels. He gives an account of his sufferings and also of the favours and graces which God hath bestowed on him. This second Epistle was written in the same year with the first and sent by Titus from some place in Macedonia.

CHAPTER 1

He speaks of his troubles in Asia. His not coming to them was not out of levity. The constancy and sincerity of his doctrine.

PAUL, an apostle of Jesus Christ by the will of God, and Timothy *our* brother: to the church of God that is at Corinth, with all the saints that are in all Achaia:

2 Grace unto you and peace from God our Father and from the Lord Jesus Christ.

3 ¹ Blessed be the God and Father of our Lord Jesus Christ, the Father of mercies and the God of all comfort:

4 Who comforteth us in all our tribulation, that we also may be able to comfort them who are in all distress, by the exhortation wherewith we also are exhorted by God.

5 For as the sufferings of Christ abound in us: so also by Christ doth our comfort abound.

6 Now whether we be in tribulation, *it is* for your exhortation and salvation: or whether we be comforted, *it is* for your consolation: or whether we be exhorted, *it is* for your exhortation and salvation, which worketh the enduring of the same sufferings which we also suffer.

7 That our hope for you may be steadfast: knowing that as you are partakers of the sufferings, so shall you be also of the consolation.

8 For we would not have you ignorant, brethren, of our tribulation which came to us in Asia: that we were pressed out of measure above *our*

CHAP. 1. ¹ Eph. 1, 3; 1 Peter, 1, 3.

CHAP. 1. Ver. 19. It is, *was in him*. There was no inconstancy in the doctrine of the apostles, sometimes, like modern sectaries, saying, *It is*, and at other times saying, *It is not*. But their doctrine was ever the same, one uniform *yea*, in Jesus Christ, one *Amen*, that is, one *truth* in him.

strength, so that we were weary even of life.

9 But we had in ourselves the answer of death: that we should not trust in ourselves, but in God who raiseth the dead.

10 Who hath delivered and doth deliver us out of so great dangers: in whom we trust that he will *yet* also deliver us,

11 Your helping withal in prayer for us. That for this gift obtained for us, by the means of many persons, thanks may be given by many in our behalf.

12 For our glory is this: the testimony of our conscience, that in simplicity of heart and sincerity of God, and not in carnal wisdom, but in the grace of God, we have conversed in this world: and more abundantly towards you.

13 For we write no other things to you than what you have read and known. And I hope that you shall know unto the end.

14 As also you have known us in part, that we are your glory: as you also are ours, in the day of our Lord Jesus Christ.

15 And in this confidence I had a mind to come to you before, that you might have a second grace:

16 And to pass by you into Macedonia: and again from Macedonia to come to you, and by you to be brought on my way towards Judea.

17 Whereas then I was thus minded, did I use lightness? Or, the things that I purpose, do I purpose according to the flesh, that there should be with me, *It is*, and *It is not?*

18 But God is faithful: for our preaching which was to you, was not, *It is*, and *It is not.*

19 For the Son of God, Jesus Christ, who was preached among you by us,

by me and Sylvanus and Timothy, was not: *It is* and *It is not*. But, *It is*, was in him.

20 For all the promises of God are in him, *It is*. Therefore also by him. Amen to God, unto our glory.

21 Now he that confirmeth us with you in Christ and that hath anointed us, is God:

22 Who also hath sealed us and given the pledge of the Spirit in our hearts.

23 But I call to God to witness upon my soul that, to spare you, I came not any more to Corinth: not because we exercise dominion over your faith: but we are helpers of your joy. For in faith you stand.

CHAPTER 2

He grants a pardon to the incestuous man upon his doing penance.

BUT I determined this with myself, not to come to you again in sorrow.

2 For if I make you sorrowful, who is he then that can make me glad, but the same who is made sorrowful by me?

3 And I wrote this same to you: that I may not, when I come, have sorrow upon sorrow from them of whom I ought to rejoice: having confidence in you all, that my joy is the joy of you all.

4 For out of much affliction and anguish of heart, I wrote to you with many tears: not that you should be made sorrowful: but that you might know the charity I have more abundantly towards you.

5 And if any one have caused grief, he hath not grieved me: but in part, that I may not burden you all.

6 To him who is such a one, this rebuke is sufficient, which is given by many.

7 So that on the contrary, you should rather forgive him and comfort him, lest perhaps such a one be swallowed up with overmuch sorrow.

8 Wherefore, I beseech you that you would confirm your charity towards him.

9 For to this end also did I write, that I may know the experiment of you, whether you be obedient in all things.

10 And to whom you have pardoned any thing, I also. For, what I have pardoned, if I have pardoned any thing, for your sakes have I done it in the person of Christ:

11 That we be not overreached by Satan. For we are not ignorant of his devices.

12 And when I was come to Troas for the gospel of Christ and a door was opened unto me in the Lord,

13 I had no rest in my spirit, because I found not Titus my brother: but bidding them farewell, I went into Macedonia.

14 Now thanks be to God, who always maketh us to triumph in Christ Jesus and manifesteth the odour of his knowledge by us in every place.

15 For we are the good odour of Christ unto God, in them that are saved and in them that perish.

16 To the one indeed the odour of death unto death: but to the others the odour of life unto life. And for these things who is so sufficient?

17 For we are not as many, adulterating the word of God: but with sincerity: but as from God, before God, in Christ we speak.

CHAPTER 3

He needs no commendatory letters. The glory of the ministry of the New Testament.

DO we begin again to commend ourselves? Or do we need (as some do) epistles of commendation to you, or from you?

2 You are our epistle, written in our hearts, which is known and read by all men:

3 Being manifested, that you are the epistle of Christ, ministered by us, and written: not with ink but with the Spirit of the living God: not in tables of stone but in the fleshly tables of the heart.

4 And such confidence we have, through Christ, towards God.

5 Not that we are sufficient to think any thing of ourselves, as of ourselves: but our sufficiency is from God.

6 Who also hath made us fit ministers of the new testament, not in the letter but in the spirit. For the letter killeth: but the spirit quickeneth.

7 Now if the ministration of death, engraven with letters upon stones, was glorious (so that the children of Israel could not steadfastly behold the face of Moses, for the glory of his countenance), which is made void:

8 How shall not the ministration of the spirit be rather in glory?

9 For if the ministration of condemnation be glory, much more the ministration of justice aboundeth in glory.

CHAP. 2. Ver. 10. *I also.* The apostle here granted an indulgence or pardon, *in the person* and by the authority of Christ, to the incestuous Corinthian, whom before he had put under penance; which pardon consisted in a releasing of part of the temporal punishment due to his sin.
Ver. 16. *The odour of death.* The preaching of the apostle, which, by its fragrant odour, brought many to life, was to others, through their own fault, the occasion of death; by their wilfully opposing and resisting that divine call.
CHAP. 3. Ver. 6. *The letter.* Not rightly understood, and taken without the spirit.

10 For even that which was glorious in this part was not glorified by reason of the glory that excelleth.

11 For if that which is done away was glorious, much more that which remaineth is in glory.

12 Having therefore such hope, we use much confidence.

13 ¹ And not as Moses put a veil upon his face, that the children of Israel might not steadfastly look on the face of that which is made void.

14 But their senses were made dull. For, until this present day, the selfsame veil, in the reading of the old testament, remaineth not taken away (because in Christ it is made void).

15 But even until this day, when Moses is read, the veil is upon their heart.

16 But when they shall be converted to the Lord, the veil shall be taken away.

17 ² Now the Lord is a Spirit. And where the Spirit of the Lord is, there is liberty.

18 But we all, beholding the glory of the Lord with open face, are transformed into the same image from glory to glory, as by the Spirit of the Lord.

CHAPTER 4

The sincerity of his preaching. His comfort in his afflictions.

THEREFORE, seeing we have this ministration, according as we have obtained mercy, we faint not.

2 But we renounce the hidden things of dishonesty, not walking in craftiness nor adulterating the word of God: but by manifestation of the truth commending ourselves to every man's conscience, in the sight of God.

3 And if our gospel be also hid, it is hid to them that are lost,

4 In whom the god of this world hath blinded the minds of unbelievers, that the light of the gospel of the glory of Christ, who is the image of God, should not shine unto them.

5 For we preach not ourselves, but Jesus Christ our Lord: and ourselves your servants through Jesus.

6 For God, who commanded the light to shine out of darkness, hath shined in our hearts, to give the light of the knowledge of the glory of God, in the face of Christ Jesus.

7 But we have this t r e a s u r e in earthen vessels, that the excellency may be of the power of God and not of us.

8 In all things we suffer tribulation: but are not distressed. We are straitened: but are not destitute.

9 We suffer persecution: but are not forsaken. We are cast down: but we perish not.

10 Always bearing about in our body the mortification of Jesus, that the life also of Jesus may be made manifest in our bodies.

11 For we who live are always delivered unto death for Jesus' sake: that the life also of Jesus may be made manifest in our mortal flesh.

12 So then death worketh in us: but life in you.

13 But having the same spirit of faith, as it is written: ¹ *I believed, for which cause I have spoken;* we also believe. For which cause we speak also:

14 Knowing that he who raised up Jesus will raise us up also with Jesus and place us with you.

15 For all things *are* for your sakes: that the grace, abounding through many, may abound in thanksgiving unto the glory of God.

16 For which cause we faint not: but though our outward man is corrupted, yet the inward man is renewed day by day.

17 For that which is at present momentary and light of our tribulation worketh for us above measure exceedingly an eternal weight of glory.

18 While we look not at the things which are seen, but at the things which are not seen. For the things which are seen are temporal: but the things which are not seen, are eternal.

CHAPTER 5

He is willing to leave his earthly mansion to be with the Lord. His charity for the Corinthians.

FOR we know, if our earthly house of this habitation be dissolved, that we have a building of God, a house not made with hands, eternal in heaven.

2 For in this also we groan, desiring to be clothed upon with our habitation that is from heaven.

3 ¹ Yet so that we be found clothed, not naked.

4 For we also, who are in this tabernacle, do groan, being burthened; because we would not be unclothed, but clothed upon, that that which is mortal may be swallowed up by life.

5 Now he that maketh us for this very thing is God, who hath given us the pledge of the Spirit.

6 Therefore having always confidence, knowing that while we are in the body we are absent from the Lord.

CHAP. 3. ¹ Exod. 34, 33. ² John, 4, 24. CHAP. 4. ¹ Ps. 115, 1. CHAP. 5. ¹ Apoc. 16, 15.

7 (For we walk by faith and not by sight.)

8 But we are confident and have a good will to be absent rather from the body and to be present with the Lord.

9 And therefore we labour, whether absent or present, to please him.

10 ² We must all be manifested before the judgment seat of Christ, that every one may receive the proper things of the body, according as he hath done, whether it be good or evil.

11 Knowing therefore the fear of the Lord, we use persuasion to men: but to God we are manifest. And I trust also that in your consciences we are manifest.

12 We commend not ourselves again to you, but give you occasion to glory in our behalf: that you may have *somewhat to answer* them who glory in face, and not in heart.

13 For whether we be transported in mind, *it is* to God: or whether we be sober, *it is* for you.

14 For the charity of Christ presseth us: judging this, that if one died for all, then all were dead.

15 And Christ died for all: that they also who live may not now live to themselves, but unto him who died for them and rose again.

16 Wherefore henceforth, we know no man according to the flesh. And if we have known Christ according to the flesh: but now we know him so no longer.

17 If then any be in Christ a new creature, the old things are passed away. ³ Behold all things are made new.

18 But all things *are* of God, who hath reconciled us to himself by Christ and hath given to us the ministry of reconciliation.

19 For God indeed was in Christ, reconciling the world to himself, not imputing to them their sins. And he hath placed in us the word of reconciliation.

20 For Christ therefore we are ambassadors, God as it were exhorting by us. For Christ, we beseech you, be reconciled to God.

21 Him, who knew no sin, he hath made sin for us: that we might be made the justice of God in him.

CHAPTER 6

He exhorts them to a correspondence with God's grace and not to associate with unbelievers.

AND we helping do exhort you that you receive not the grace of God in vain.

2 For he saith: ¹ *In an accepted time have I heard thee and in the day of salvation have I helped thee.* Behold, now is the acceptable time: behold, now is the day of salvation.

3 ² Giving no offence to any man, that our ministry be not blamed.

4 But in all things let us exhibit ourselves ³ as the ministers of God, in much patience, in tribulation, in necessities, in distresses,

5 In stripes, in prisons, in seditions, in labours, in watchings, in fastings,

6 In chastity, in knowledge, in longsuffering, in sweetness, in the Holy Ghost, in charity unfeigned,

7 In the word of truth, in the power of God: by the armour of justice on the right hand and on the left:

8 By honour and dishonour: by evil report and good report: as deceivers and yet true: as unknown and yet known:

9 As dying and behold we live: as chastised and not killed:

10 As sorrowful, yet always rejoicing: as needy, yet enriching many: as having nothing and possessing all things.

11 Our mouth is open to you, O ye Corinthians: our heart is enlarged.

12 You are not straitened in us: but in your own bowels you are straitened.

13 But having the same recompense (I speak as to my children): be you also enlarged.

14 Bear not the yoke with unbelievers. For what participation hath justice with injustice? Or what fellowship hath light with darkness?

15 And what concord hath Christ with Belial? Or what part hath the faithful with the unbeliever?

16 And what agreement hath the temple of God with idols? ⁴ For you are the temple of the living God; as God saith: ⁵ *I will dwell in them and walk among them. And I will be their God: and they shall be my people.*

² Rom. 14, 10. ³ Isai. 43, 19; Apoc. 21, 5. CHAP. 6. ¹ Isai. 49, 8. ² 1 Cor. 10, 32. ³ 1 Cor. 4, 1. ⁴ 1 Cor. 3, 16, 17; 6, 19. ⁵ Lev. 26, 12.

CHAP. 5. Ver. 10. *The proper things of the body.* In the particular judgment, immediately after death, the soul is rewarded or punished according to what it has done in the body.

Ver. 16. *We know no man according to the flesh.* That is, we consider not any man with regard to his nation, family, kindred, or other natural qualities or advantages; but only with relation to Christ and according to the order of divine charity, in God and for God. The apostle adds that, even with respect to Christ himself, he now no longer considers him according to the flesh, by taking a satisfaction in his being his countryman; his affection being now purified from all such earthly considerations.

Ver. 21. *Sin for us.* That is, to be a *sin offering,* a victim for *sin.*

17 ⁶ Wherefore: *Go out from among them and be ye separate,* saith the Lord, *and touch not the unclean thing:* 18 *And I will receive you.* ⁷ *And I will be a Father to you: and you shall be my sons and daughters,* saith the Lord Almighty.

CHAPTER 7

The apostle's affection for the Corinthians. His comfort and joy on their account.

HAVING therefore these promises, dearly beloved, let us cleanse ourselves from all defilement of the flesh and of the spirit, perfecting sanctification in the fear of God.

2 Receive us. We have injured no man: we have corrupted no man: we have overreached no man.

3 I speak not this to your condemnation. For we have said before that you are in our hearts: to die together and to live together.

4 Great is my confidence for you: great is my glorying for you. I am filled with comfort: I exceedingly abound with joy in all our tribulation.

5 For also, when we were come into Macedonia, our flesh had no rest: but we suffered all tribulation. Combats without: fears within.

6 But God, who comforteth the humble, comforted us by the coming of Titus.

7 And not by his coming only, but also by the consolation wherewith he was comforted in you, relating to us your desire, your mourning, your zeal for me: so that I rejoiced the more.

8 For although I made you sorrowful by my epistle, I do not repent. And if I did repent, seeing that the same epistle (although but for a time) did make you sorrowful,

9 Now I am glad: not because you were made sorrowful, but because you were made sorrowful unto penance. For you were made sorrowful according to God, that you might suffer damage by us in nothing.

10 ¹ For the sorrow that is according to God worketh penance, steadfast unto salvation: but the sorrow of the world worketh death.

11 For behold this selfsame thing, that you were made sorrowful according to God, how great carefulness it worketh in you: yea defence, yea indignation, yea fear, yea desire, yea zeal, yea revenge. In all things you have

⁶ Isai. 52, 11. ⁷ Jer. 31, 9. CHAP. 7. ¹ 1 Peter, 2, 19.

CHAP. 7. Ver. 15. *His bowels.* That is, his affection.

CHAP. 8. Ver. 2. *Simplicity.* That is, sincere bounty and charity.

shewed yourselves to be undefiled in the matter.

12 Wherefore, although I wrote to you, it was not for his sake that did the wrong, nor for him that suffered it: but to manifest our carefulness that we have for you

13 Before God. Therefore we were comforted. But in our consolation we did the more abundantly rejoice for the joy of Titus, because his spirit was refreshed by you all.

14 And if I have boasted any thing to him of you, I have not been put to shame: but as we have spoken all things to you in truth, so also our boasting that was made to Titus is found a truth.

15 And his bowels are more abundantly towards you: remembering the obedience of you all, how with fear and trembling you received him.

16 I rejoice that in all things I have confidence in you.

CHAPTER 8

He exhorts them to contribute bountifully to relieve the poor of Jerusalem.

NOW we make known unto you, brethren, the grace of God that hath been given in the churches of Macedonia.

2 That in much experience of tribulation, they have had abundance of joy and their very deep poverty hath abounded unto the riches of their simplicity.

3 For according to their power (I bear them witness) and beyond their power, they were willing:

4 With much entreaty begging of us the grace and communication of the ministry that is done toward the saints.

5 And not as we hoped: but they gave their own selves, first to the Lord, then to us by the will of God;

6 Insomuch, that we desired Titus, that, as he had begun, so also he would finish among you this same grace.

7 That as in all things you abound in faith and word and knowledge and all carefulness, moreover also in your charity towards us: so in this grace also you may abound.

8 I speak not as commanding: but by the carefulness of others, approving also the good disposition of your charity.

9 For you know the grace of our Lord Jesus Christ, that being rich he became poor for your sakes: that through his poverty you might be rich.

10 And herein I give my advice: for this is profitable for you who have be-

gun not only to do but also to be willing, a year ago.

11 Now therefore perform ye it also in deed: that as your mind is forward to be willing, so it may be also to perform, out of that which you have.

12 For if the will be forward, it is accepted according to that which *a man* hath: not according to that which he hath not.

13 For *I mean* not that others should be eased and you burthened, but by an equality.

14 In this present time let your abundance supply their want, that their abundance also may supply your want: that there may be an equality,

15 As it is written: [1] *He that had much had nothing over; and he that had little had no want.*

16 And thanks be to God, who hath given the same carefulness for you in the heart of Titus.

17 For indeed he accepted the exhortation: but, being more careful, of his own will he went unto you.

18 We have sent also with him the brother whose praise is in the gospel through all the churches.

19 And not that only: but he was also ordained by the churches companion of our travels, for this grace, which is administered by us, to the glory of the Lord and our determined will:

20 Avoiding this, lest any man should blame us in this abundance which is administered by us.

21 [2] For we forecast what may be good, not only before God but also before men.

22 And we have sent with them our brother also, whom we have often proved diligent in many things, but now much more diligent: with much confidence in you,

23 Either for Titus, who is my companion and fellow labourer towards you, or our brethren, the apostles of the churches, the glory of Christ.

24 Wherefore shew ye to them, in the sight of the churches, the evidence of your charity and of our boasting on your behalf.

CHAPTER 9

A further exhortation to almsgiving. The fruits of it.

FOR concerning the ministry that is done towards the saints, it is superfluous for me to write unto you.

2 For I know your forward mind: for which I boast of you to the Macedonians, that Achaia also is ready from the year past. And your emulation hath provoked very many.

3 Now I have sent the brethren, that the thing which we boast of concerning you be not made void in this behalf, that (as I have said) you may be ready:

4 Lest, when the Macedonians shall come with me and find you unprepared, we (not to say ye) should be ashamed in this matter.

5 Therefore I thought it necessary to desire the brethren that they would go to you before and prepare this blessing before promised, to be ready, so as a blessing, not as covetousness.

6 Now this I say: He who soweth sparingly shall also reap sparingly: and he who soweth in blessings shall also reap blessings.

7 Every one as he hath determined in his heart, not with sadness or of necessity: [1] *for God loveth a cheerful giver.*

8 And God is able to make all grace abound in you: that ye always, having all sufficiently in all things, may abound to every good work,

9 As it is written: [2] *He hath dispersed abroad, he hath given to the poor: his justice remaineth for ever.*

10 And he that ministereth seed to the sower will both give you bread to eat and will multiply your seed and increase the growth of the fruits of your justice:

11 That being enriched in all things, you may abound unto all simplicity, which worketh through us thanksgiving to God.

12 Because the administration of this office doth not only supply the want of the saints, but aboundeth also by many thanksgivings in the Lord.

13 By the proof of this ministry, glorifying God for the obedience of your confession unto the gospel of Christ and for the simplicity of *your* communicating unto them and unto all.

14 And in their praying for you, being desirous of you, because of the excellent grace of God in you.

15 Thanks be to God for his unspeakable gift.

CHAPTER 10

To stop the calumny and boasting of false apostles, he sets forth the power of his apostleship.

NOW I Paul, myself beseech you, by the mildness and modesty of

Christ: who in presence indeed am lowly among you, but being absent am bold toward you.

2 But I beseech you, that I may not be bold when I am present with that confidence wherewith I am thought to be bold, against some who reckon us as if we walked according to the flesh.

3 For though we walk in the flesh, we do not war according to the flesh.

4 For the weapons of our warfare are not carnal but mighty to God, unto the pulling down of fortifications, destroying counsels,

5 And every height that exalteth itself against the knowledge of God: and bringing into captivity every understanding unto the obedience of Christ:

6 And having in readiness to revenge all disobedience, when your obedience shall be fulfilled.

7 See the things that are according to outward appearance. If any man trust to himself, that he is Christ's let him think this again with himself, that as he is Christ's, so are we also.

8 For if also I should boast somewhat more of our power, which the Lord hath given us unto edification and not for your destruction, I should not be ashamed.

9 But that I may not be thought as it were to terrify you by epistles,

10 (For his epistles indeed, say they, are weighty and strong; but his bodily presence is weak and his speech contemptible):

11 Let such a one think this, that such as we are in word by epistles when absent, such also *we will* be indeed when present.

12 For we dare not match or compare ourselves with some that commend themselves: but we measure ourselves by ourselves and compare ourselves with ourselves.

13 [1] But we will not glory beyond our measure: but according to the measure of the rule which God hath measured to us, a measure to reach even unto you.

14 For we stretch not ourselves beyond our measure, as if we reached not unto you. For we are come as far as to you in the Gospel of Christ.

15 Not glorying beyond measure in other men's labours: but having hope of your increasing faith, to be magnified in you according to our rule abundantly,

CHAP. 10. [1] Eph. 4, 7. [2] Jer. 9, 23; 1 Cor. 1, 31.
CHAP. 11. [1] Gen. 3, 4.

CHAP. 11. Ver. 1. *My folly*. So he calls his reciting his own praises, which, commonly speaking, is looked upon as a piece of folly and vanity; though the apostle was constrained to do it, for the good of the souls committed to his charge.

16 Yea, unto those places that are beyond you to preach the gospel: not to glory in another man's rule, in those things that are made ready to our hand.

17 [2] But he that glorieth, let him glory in the Lord.

18 For not he who commendeth himself is approved: but he, whom God commendeth.

CHAPTER 11

He is forced to commend himself and his labours, lest the Corinthians should be imposed upon by the false apostles.

WOULD to God you could bear with some little of my folly! But do bear with me.

2 For I am jealous of you with the jealousy of God. For I have espoused you to one husband, that I may present you as a chaste virgin to Christ.

3 But I fear lest, [1] as the serpent seduced Eve by his subtilty, so your minds should be corrupted and fall from the simplicity that is in Christ.

4 For if he that cometh preacheth another Christ, whom we have not preached; or if you receive another Spirit, whom you have not received; or another gospel, which you have not received: you might well bear *with him*.

5 For I suppose that I have done nothing less than the great apostles.

6 For although I be rude in speech, yet not in knowledge: but in all things we have been made manifest to you.

7 Or did I commit a fault, humbling myself that you might be exalted, because I preached unto you the gospel of God freely?

8 I have taken from other churches, receiving wages of them for your ministry.

9 And, when I was present with you and wanted, I was chargeable to no man: for that which was wanting to me, the brethren supplied who came from Macedonia. And in all things I have kept myself from being burthensome to you: and so I will keep myself.

10 The truth of Christ is in me, that this glorying shall not be broken off in me in the regions of Achaia.

11 Wherefore? Because I love you not? God knoweth it.

12 But what I do, that I will do: that I may cut off the occasion from them that desire occasion: that wherein they glory, they may be found even as we.

13 For such false apostles are deceitful workmen, transforming themselves into the apostles of Christ.

14 And no wonder: for Satan him-

self transformeth himself into an angel of light.

15 Therefore it is no great thing if his ministers be transformed as the ministers of justice, whose end shall be according to their works.

16 I say again (Let no man think me to be foolish: otherwise take me as one foolish, that I also may glory a little):

17 That which I speak, I speak not according to God: but as it were in foolishness, in this matter of glorying.

18 Seeing that many glory according to the flesh, I will glory also.

19 For you gladly suffer the foolish: whereas yourselves are wise.

20 For you suffer if a man bring you into bondage, if a man devour *you*, if a man take *from you*, if a man be lifted up, if a man strike you on the face.

21 I speak according to dishonour, as if we had been weak in this part, Wherein if any man dare (I speak foolishly), I dare also.

22 They are Hebrews: so am I. They are Israelites: so am I. They are the seed of Abraham: so am I.

23 They are the ministers of Christ (I speak as one less wise): I am more; in many more labours, in prisons more frequently, in stripes above measure, in deaths often.

24 Of the Jews [2] five times did I receive forty *stripes* save one.

25 [3] Thrice was I beaten with rods: [4] once I was stoned: [5] thrice I suffered shipwreck: a night and a day I was in the depth of the sea.

26 In journeying often, in perils of waters, in perils of robbers, in perils from the Gentiles, in perils in the city, in perils in the wilderness, in perils in the sea, in perils from false brethren:

27 In labour and painfulness, in much watchings, in hunger and thirst, in fastings often, in cold and nakedness:

28 Besides those things which are without: my daily instance, the solicitude for all the churches.

29 Who is weak, and I am not weak? Who is scandalized, and I am not on fire?

30 If I must needs glory, I will glory of the things that concern my infirmity.

31 The God and Father of our Lord Jesus Christ, who is blessed for ever, knoweth that I lie not.

32 [6] At Damascus, the governor of the nation under Aretas the king, guarded the city of the Damascenes, to apprehend me.

33 And through a window in a basket was I let down by the wall: and so escaped his hands.

CHAPTER 12

His raptures and revelations. His being buffeted by Satan. His fear for the Corinthians.

IF I must glory (it is not expedient indeed): but I will come to visions and revelations of the Lord.

2 [1] I know a man in Christ: above fourteen years ago (whether in the body, I know not, or out of the body, I know not: God knoweth), such a one caught up to the third heaven.

3 And I know such a man (whether in the body, or out of the body, I know not: God knoweth):

4 That he was caught up into paradise and heard secret words which it is not granted to man to utter.

5 For such an one I will glory: but for myself I will glory nothing but in my infirmities.

6 For though I should have a mind to glory, I shall not be foolish: for I will say the truth. But I forbear, lest any man should think of me above that which he seeth in me, or any thing he heareth from me.

7 And lest the greatness of the revelations should exalt me, there was given me a sting of my flesh, an angel of Satan, to buffet me.

8 For which thing, thrice I besought the Lord that it might depart from me.

9 And he said to me: My grace is sufficient for thee: for power is made perfect in infirmity. Gladly therefore will I glory in my infirmities, that the power of Christ may dwell in me.

10 For which cause I please myself in my infirmities, in reproaches, in necessities, in persecutions, in distresses, for Christ. For when I am weak, then am I powerful.

11 I am become foolish. You have compelled me: for I ought to have been commended by you. For I have no way come short of them that are above measure apostles, although I be nothing.

12 Yet the signs of my apostleship have been wrought on you, in all patience, in signs and wonders and mighty deeds.

[2] Deut. 25. 3. [3] Acts. 16, 22. [4] Acts, 14, 18. [5] Acts, 27, 41. [6] Acts 9, 24. CHAP. 12. [1] Acts, 9, 3.

Ver. 28. *My daily instance.* The labours that come in and press upon me every day.

CHAP. 12. Ver. 9. *Power is made perfect.* The strength and power of God more perfectly shines forth in our weakness and infirmity; as the more weak we are of ourselves, the more illustrious is his grace in supporting us and giving us the victory under all trials and conflicts.

13 For what is there that you have had less than the other churches but that I myself was not burthensome to you? Pardon me this injury.

14 Behold now the third time I am ready to come to you and I will not be burthensome unto you. For I seek not the things that are yours, but you. For neither ought the children to lay up for the parents, but the parents for the children.

15 But I most gladly will spend and be spent myself for your souls: although loving you more, I be loved less.

16 But be it so: I did not burthen you: but being crafty, I caught you by guile.

17 Did I overreach you by any of them whom I sent to you?

18 I desired Titus: and I sent with him a brother. Did Titus overreach you? Did we not walk with the same spirit? Did we not in the same steps?

19 Of old, think you that we excuse ourselves to you? We speak before God in Christ: but all things, my dearly beloved, for your edification.

20 For I fear lest perhaps, when I come, I shall not find you such as I would, and that I shall be found by you such as you would not. Lest perhaps contentions, envyings, animosities, dissensions, detractions, whisperings, swellings, seditions, be among you.

21 Lest again, when I come, God humble me among you: and I mourn many of them that sinned before and have not done penance for the uncleanness and fornication and lasciviousness that they have committed.

CHAPTER 13

He threatens the impenitent, to provoke them to penance.

Chap. 13. ¹ Deut. 19, 15; Matt. 18, 16; John, 8, 17; Heb. 10, 28.

Chap. 13. Ver. 7. *Reprobates.* That is, without proof, by having no occasion of shewing our power in punishing you.

BEHOLD, this is the third time I am coming to you: ¹ In the mouth of two or three witnesses shall every word stand.

2 I have told before and foretell, as present and now absent, to them that sinned before and to all the rest, that if I come again, I will not spare.

3 Do you seek a proof of Christ that speaketh in me, who towards you is not weak, but is mighty in you?

4 For although he was crucified through weakness, yet he liveth by the power of God. For we also are weak in him: but we shall live with him by the power of God towards you.

5 Try your own selves if you be in the faith: prove ye yourselves. Know you not your own selves, that Christ Jesus is in you, unless perhaps you be reprobates?

6 But I trust that you shall know that we are not reprobates.

7 Now we pray God that you may do no evil, not that we may appear approved, but that you may do that which is good and that we may be as reprobates.

8 For we can do nothing against the truth: but for the truth.

9 For we rejoice that we are weak and you are strong. This also we pray for, your perfection.

10 Therefore I write these things, being absent, that, being present, I may not deal more severely, according to the power which the Lord hath given me unto edification and not unto destruction.

11 For the rest, brethren, rejoice, be perfect, take exhortation, be of one mind, have peace. And the God of peace and of love shall be with you.

12 Salute one another with a holy kiss. All the saints salute you.

13 The grace of our Lord Jesus Christ and the charity of God and the communication of the Holy Ghost be with you all. Amen.

THE EPISTLE OF ST. PAUL TO THE
GALATIANS

The Galatians, soon after St. Paul had preached the Gospel to them, were seduced by some false teachers, who had been Jews and who were for obliging all Christians, even those who had been Gentiles, to observe circumcision and the other ceremonies of the Mosaical law. In this Epistle, he refutes the pernicious doctrine of those teachers and also their calumny against his mission and apostleship. The subject matter of this Epistle is much the same as that to the Romans. It was written at Ephesus, about twenty-three years after our Lord's Ascension.

CHAPTER 1

He blames the Galatians for suffering themselves to be imposed upon by new teachers. The apostle's calling.

PAUL, an apostle, not of men, neither by man, but by Jesus Christ and God the Father, who raised him from the dead:

2 And all the brethren who are with me: to the churches of Galatia.

3 Grace be to you, and peace from God the Father and from our Lord Jesus Christ,

4 Who gave himself for our sins, that he might deliver us from this present wicked world, according to the will of God and our Father:

5 To whom is glory for ever and ever Amen.

6 I wonder that you are so soon removed from him that called you into the grace of Christ, unto another gospel.

7 Which is not another: only there are some that trouble you and would pervert the gospel of Christ.

8 But though we, or an angel from heaven, preach a gospel to you besides that which we have preached to you, let him be anathema.

9 As we said before, so now I say again: If any one preach to you a gospel, besides that which you have received, let him be anathema.

10 For do I now persuade men, or God? Or do I seek to please men? If I yet pleased men, I should not be the servant of Christ.

11 ¹For I give you to understand, brethren, that the gospel which was preached by me is not according to man.

12 ²For neither did I receive it of man: nor did I learn it but by the revelation of Jesus Christ.

13 For you have heard of my conversation in time past in the Jews' religion: how that, beyond measure, I persecuted the church of God and wasted it.

14 And I made progress in the Jews' religion above many of my equals in my own nation, being more abundantly zealous for the traditions of my fathers.

15 But when it pleased him who separated me from my mother's womb and called me by his grace,

16 To reveal his Son in me, that I might preach him among the Gentiles: immediately I condescended not to flesh and blood.

17 Neither went I to Jerusalem, to the apostles who were before me: but I went into Arabia, and again I returned to Damascus.

18 Then, after three years, I went to Jerusalem to see Peter: and I tarried with him fifteen days.

19 But other of the apostles I saw none, saving James the brother of the Lord.

20 Now the things which I write to you, behold, before God, I lie not.

21 Afterwards, I came into the regions of Syria and Cilicia.

22 And I was unknown by face to the churches of Judea, which were in Christ:

23 But they had heard only: He, who persecuted us in times past doth now preach the faith which once he impugned.

24 And they glorified God in me.

CHAPTER 2

The apostle's preaching was approved of by the other apostles. The Gentiles were not to be constrained to the observance of the law.

THEN, after fourteen years, I went up again to Jerusalem with Barnabas, taking Titus also with me.

CHAP. 1. ¹ 1 Cor. 15, 1. ² Eph. 3, 3.

2 And I went up according to revelation and communicated to them the gospel which I preach among the Gentiles: but apart to them who seemed to be some thing: lest perhaps I should run or had run in vain.

3 But neither Titus, who was with me, being a Gentile, was compelled to be circumcised.

4 But because of false brethren unawares brought in, who came in privately to spy our liberty which we have in Christ Jesus, that they might bring us into servitude.

5 To whom we yielded not by subjection: no, not for an hour: that the truth of the gospel might continue with you.

6 But of them who seemed to be some thing, (what they were some time, it is nothing to me, [1] God accepteth not the person of man): for to me they that seemed to be some thing added nothing.

7 But contrariwise, when they had seen that to me was committed the gospel of the uncircumcision, as to Peter was that of the circumcision.

8 (For he who wrought in Peter to the apostleship of the circumcision wrought in me also among the Gentiles.)

9 And when they had known the grace that was given to me, James and Cephas and John, who seemed to be pillars, gave to me and Barnabas the right hands of fellowship: that we should go unto the Gentiles, and they unto the circumcision:

10 Only that we should be mindful of the poor: which same thing also I was careful to do.

11 But when Cephas was come to Antioch, I withstood him to the face, because he was to be blamed.

12 For before that some came from James, he did eat with the Gentiles: but when they were come, he withdrew and separated himself, fearing them who were of the circumcision.

13 And to his dissimination the rest of the Jews consented: so that Barnabas also was led by them into that dissimulation.

14 But when I saw that they walked not uprightly unto the truth of the gospel, I said to Cephas before them all: If thou, being a Jew, livest after the manner of the Gentiles and not as the Jews do, how dost thou compel the Gentiles to live as do the Jews?

15 We by nature are Jews: and not of the Gentiles, sinners.

16 But knowing that man is not justified by the works of the law, but by the faith of Jesus Christ, we also believe in Christ Jesus, that we may be justified by the faith of Christ and not by the works of the law: [2] because by the works of the law no flesh shall be justified.

17 But if, while we seek to be justified in Christ, we ourselves also are found sinners, is Christ then the minister of sin? God forbid!

18 For if I build up again the things which I have destroyed, I make myself a prevaricator.

19 For I, through the law, am dead to the law, that I may live to God: with Christ I am nailed to the cross.

20 And I live, now not I: but Christ liveth in me. And that I live now in the flesh: I live in the faith of the Son of God, who loved me and delivered himself for me.

21 I cast not away the grace of God. For if justice be by the law, then Christ died in vain.

CHAPTER 3

The Spirit, and the blessing promised to Abraham cometh not by the law, but by faith.

O SENSELESS Galatians, who hath bewitched you that you should not obey the truth: before whose eyes Jesus Christ hath been set forth, crucified among you?

2 This only would I learn of you: Did you receive the Spirit by the works of the law or by the hearing of faith?

3 Are you so foolish that, whereas you began in the Spirit, you would now be made perfect by the flesh?

4 Have you suffered so great things in vain? If it be yet in vain.

5 He therefore who giveth to you the Spirit and worketh miracles among you: doth he do it by the works of the law or by the hearing of the faith?

CHAP. 2. [1] Deut. 10, 17; Job, 34, 19; Wisd. 6, 8; Ecclus. 35, 15; Acts, 10, 34; Rom. 2, 11; Eph. 6, 9; Col. 3, 25; 1 Peter, 1, 17. [2] Rom. 3, 20.

CHAP. 2. Ver. 7. *The gospel of the uncircumcision.* The preaching of the gospel to the uncircumcised, that is, to the Gentiles. St. Paul was called in an extraordinary manner to be the apostle of the Gentiles; St. Peter, besides his general commission over the whole flock (John, 21, 15), had a peculiar charge of the people of the circumcision, that is, of the Jews.

Ver. 11. *I withstood.* The fault that is here noted in the conduct of St. Peter was only a certain imprudence, in withdrawing himself from the table of the Gentiles, for fear of giving offence to the Jewish converts: but this, in such circumstances, when his so doing might be of ill consequence to the Gentiles, who might be induced thereby to think themselves obliged to conform to the Jewish way of living, to the prejudice of their Christian liberty. Neither was St. Paul's reprehending him any argument against his supremacy; for in such cases an inferior may, and sometimes ought, with respect, to admonish his superior.

6 As it is written: ¹ *Abraham be-lieved God: and it was reputed to him unto justice.*

7 Know ye, therefore, that they who are of faith, the same are the children of Abraham.

8 And the scripture, forseeing that God justifieth the Gentiles by faith, told unto Abraham before: ² *In thee shall all nations be blessed.*

9 Therefore, they that are of faith shall be blessed with faithful Abraham.

10 For as many as are of the works of the law are under a curse. For it is written: ³ *Cursed is every one that abideth not in all things which are written in the book of the law to do them.*

11 But that in the law no man is justified with God, it is manifest: ⁴ because *the just man liveth by faith.*

12 But the law is not of faith: but ⁵ *He that doth those things shall live in them.*

13 Christ hath redeemed us from the curse of the law, being made a curse for us (for it is written: ⁶ *Cursed is every one that hangeth on a tree*).

14 That the blessing of Abraham might come on the Gentiles through Christ Jesus: that we may receive the promise of the Spirit by faith.

15 Brethren (I speak after the manner of man), ⁷ yet a man's testament, if it be confirmed, no man despiseth nor addeth to it.

16 To Abraham were the promises made and to his seed. He saith not: *And to his seeds,* as of many. But as of one: *And to thy seed,* which is Christ.

17 Now this I say: that the testament which was confirmed by God, the law which was made after four hundred and thirty years doth not disannul, to make the promise of no effect.

18 For if the inheritance be of the law, it is no more of promise. But God gave it to Abraham by promse.

19 Why then was the law? It was set because of transgressions, until the seed should come to whom he made the promise, being ordained by angels in the hand of a mediator.

20 Now a mediator is not of one: but God is one.

21 Was the law then against the promises of God? God forbid! For if there had been a law given which could give life, verily justice should have been by the law.

22 ⁸ But the scripture hath concluded all under sin, that the promise, by the faith of Jesus Christ, might be given to them that believe.

23 But before the faith came, we were kept under the law shut up, unto that faith which was to be revealed.

24 Wherefore the law was our pedagogue in Christ: that we might be justified by faith.

25 But after the faith is come, we are no longer under a pedagogue.

26 For you are all the children of God, by faith in Christ Jesus.

27 ⁹ For as many of you as have been baptized in Christ have put on Christ.

28 There is neither Jew nor Greek: there is neither bond nor free: there is neither male nor female. For you are all one in Christ Jesus.

29 And if you be Christ's, then are you the seed of Abraham, heirs according to the promise.

CHAPTER 4

Christ has freed us from the servitude of the law. We are the freeborn sons of Abraham.

NOW I say: As long as the heir is a child, he differeth nothing from a servant, though he be lord of all,

2 But is under tutors and governors until the time appointed by the father.

3 So we also, when we were children, were serving under the elements of the world.

4 But when the fulness of the time was come, God sent his Son, made of a woman, made under the law:

5 That he might redeem them who were under the law: that we might receive the adoption of sons.

6 And because you are sons, God hath sent the Spirit of his Son into your hearts, crying: Abba, Father.

7 Therefore, now he is not a servant, but a son. And if a son, an heir also through God.

8 But then indeed, not knowing God, you served them who, by nature, are not gods.

9 But now, after that you have known God, or rather are known by

CHAP. 3. ¹ Gen. 25, 6; Rom. 4, 3; James, 2, 23. ² Gen. 12, 3; Ecclus. 44, 20. ³ Deut. 27, 26. ⁴ Hab. 2, 4; Rom. 1, 17. ⁵ Lev. 18, 5. ⁶ Deut. 21, 23. ⁷ Heb. 9, 17. ⁸ Rom. 3, 9. ⁹ Rom. 6, 3.

CHAP. 3. Ver. 19. *Because of transgressions.* To restrain them from sin, by fear and threats.— *Ordained by angels.* The law was delivered by angels, speaking in the name and person of God to Moses, who was the *mediator* on this occasion between God and the people.

Ver. 22. *Hath concluded all under sin.* That is, hath declared all to be under sin, from which they could not be delivered but by faith in Jesus Christ, the promised seed.

Ver. 24. *Pedagogue.* That is, schoolmaster, conductor, or instructor.

Ver. 28. *Neither Jew nor Greek.* That is, no distinction of Jew and Greek.

CHAP. 4. Ver. 3. *Under the elements.* That is, under the first rudiments of religion, in which the carnal Jews were trained up: or under those corporeal creatures, used in their manifold rites, sacrifices, and sacraments.

God: how turn you again to the weak and needy elements which you desire to serve again?

10 You observe days and months and times, and years.

11 I am afraid of you, lest perhaps I have laboured in vain among you.

12 Be ye as I, because I also am as you brethren, I beseech you. You have not injured me at all.

13 And you know how, through infirmity of the flesh, I preached the gospel to you heretofore: and your temptation in my flesh

14 You despised not, nor rejected: but received me as an angel of God, even as Christ Jesus.

15 Where is then your blessedness? For I bear you witness that, if it could be done, you would have plucked out your own eyes and would have given them to me.

16 Am I then become your enemy, because I tell you the truth?

17 They are zealous in your regard not well: but they would exclude you, that you might be zealous for them.

18 But be zealous for that which is good in a good thing always: and not only when I am present with you.

19 My little children, of whom I am in labour again, until Christ be formed in you.

20 And I would willingly be present with you now and change my voice: because I am ashamed for you.

21 Tell me, you that desire to be under the law, have you not read the law?

22 For it is written that Abraham had two sons: ¹ the one by a bond-woman ² and the other by a free woman.

23 But he who *was* of the bond-woman was born according to the flesh: but he of the free woman *was* by promise.

24 Which things are said by an allegory. For these are the two testaments. The one from Mount Sina, engendering unto bondage, which is Agar.

25 For Sina is a mountain in Arabia, which hath affinity to that Jerusalem which now is: and is in bondage with her children.

26 But that Jerusalem which is above is free: which is our mother.

27 For it is written: ³ *Rejoice, thou barren, that bearest not: break forth*

CHAP. 4. ¹ Gen. 16, 15. ² Gen. 21, 2. ³ Isai. 54, 1. ⁴ Rom. 9, 8. CHAP. 5. ¹ Acts, 15, 1. ² 1 Cor. 5, 6. ³ Lev. 19, 18; Matt. 22, 39; Rom. 13, 8.

Ver. 10. *You observe days.* He speaks not of the observation of the Lord's day, or other Christian festivals: but either of the superstitious observation of days *lucky* and *unlucky*; or else of the Jewish festivals, to the observance of which certain Jewish teachers sought to induce the Galatians.

and cry, thou that travailest not: for many are the children of the desolate, more than of her that hath a husband.

28 ⁴ Now we, brethren, as Isaac was, are the children of promise.

29 But as then he that was born according to the flesh persecuted him that was after the spirit: so also it is now.

30 But what saith the scripture? *Cast out the bondwoman and her son: for the son of the bondwoman shall not be heir with the sons of the free woman.*

31 So then, brethren, we are not the children of the bondwoman but of the free: by the freedom wherewith Christ has made us free.

CHAPTER 5

He exhorts them to stand to their Christian liberty. Of the fruits of the flesh and of the spirit.

STAND fast and be not held again under the yoke of bondage.

2 ¹ Behold, I Paul tell you, that if you be circumcised, Christ shall profit you nothing.

3 And I testify again to every man circumcising himself that he is a debtor to the whole law.

4 You are made void of Christ, you who are justified in the law: you are fallen from grace.

5 For we in spirit, by faith, wait for the hope of justice.

6 For in Christ Jesus neither circumcision availeth any thing nor uncircumcision: but faith that worketh by charity.

7 You did run well. Who hath hindered you, that you should not obey the truth?

8 This persuasion is not from him that calleth you.

9 ² A little leaven corrupteth the whole lump.

10 I have confidence in you in the Lord that you will not be of another mind: but he that troubleth you shall bear the judgment, whosoever he be.

11 And I, brethren, if I yet preach circumcision, why do I yet suffer persecution? Then is the scandal of the cross made void.

12 I would they were even cut off, who trouble you.

13 For you, brethren, have been called unto liberty. Only make not liberty an occasion to the flesh: but by charity of the spirit serve one another.

14 For all the law is fulfilled in one word: ³ *Thou shalt love thy neighbour as thyself.*

15 But if you bite and devour one

another: take heed you be not consumed one of another.

16 I say to them: [4] Walk in the spirit: and you shall not fulfill the lusts of the flesh.

17 For the flesh lusteth against the spirit: and the spirit against the flesh. For these are contrary one to another: so that you do not the things that you would.

18 But if you are led by the spirit, you are not under the law.

19 Now the works of the flesh are manifest: which are fornication, uncleanness, immodesty, luxury,

20 Idolatry, witchcrafts, enmities, contentions, emulations, wraths, quarrels, dissensions, sects,

21 Envies, murders, drunkenness, revellings, and such like. Of the which I foretell you, as I have foretold to you, that they who do such things shall not obtain the kingdom of God.

22 But the fruit of the Spirit is, charity, joy, peace, patience, benignity, goodness, longanimity,

23 Mildness, faith, modesty, continency, chastity. Against such there is no law.

24 And they that are Christ's have crucified their flesh, with the vices and concupiscences.

25 If we live in the Spirit, let us also walk in the Spirit.

26 Let us not be made desirous of vain glory, provoking one another, envying one another.

CHAPTER 6

He exhorts to charity, humility and all virtue. He glories in nothing but in the cross of Christ.

BRETHREN, and if a man be overtaken in any fault, you, who are spiritual, instruct such a one in the spirit of meekness, considering thyself, lest thou also be tempted.

2 Bear ye one another's burdens: and so you shall fulfil the law of Christ.

3 For if any man think himself to be some thing, whereas he is nothing, he deceiveth himself.

4 But let every one prove his own work: and so he shall have glory in himself only and not in another.

5 [1] For every one shall bear his own burden.

6 And let him that is instructed in the word communicate to him that instructeth him, in all good things.

7 Be not deceived: God is not mocked.

8 For what things a man shall sow, those also shall he reap. For he that soweth in his flesh of the flesh also shall reap corruption. But he that soweth in the spirit of the spirit shall reap life everlasting.

9 [2] And in doing good, let us not fail. For in due time we shall reap, not failing.

10 Therefore, whilst we have time, let us work good to all men, but especially to those who are of the household of the faith.

11 See what a letter I have written to you with my own hand.

12 For as many as desire to please in the flesh, they constrain you to be circumcised, only that they may not suffer the persecution of the cross of Christ.

13 For neither they themselves who are circumcised keep the law: but they will have you to be circumcised, that they may glory in your flesh.

14 But God forbid that I should glory, save in the cross of our Lord Jesus Christ: by whom the world is crucified to me, and I to the world.

15 For in Christ Jesus neither circumcision availeth any thing, nor uncircumcision: but a new creature.

16 And whosoever shall follow this rule, peace on them and mercy: and upon the Israel of God.

17 From henceforth let no man be troublesome to me: for I bear the marks of the Lord Jesus in my body.

18 The grace of our Lord Jesus Christ be with your spirit, brethren. Amen.

[4] 1 Peter, 2, 11. Chap. 6. [1] 1 Cor. 3, 8. [2] 2 Thess. 3, 13.

THE EPISTLE OF ST. PAUL TO THE

EPHESIANS

Ephesus was the capital of Lesser Asia, and celebrated for the temple of Diana, to which the most part of the people of the East went frequently to worship. But St. Paul having preached the Gospel there, for two years the first time and afterwards for about a year, converted many. He wrote this Epistle to them when he was a prisoner in Rome; and sent it by Tychicus. He admonishes them to hold firmly the faith which they had received and warns them, and also those of the neighbouring cities, against the sophistry of philosophers and doctrine of false teachers who were come among them. The matters of faith contained in this Epistle are exceedingly sublime, and consequently very difficult to be understood. It was written about twenty-nine years after our Lord's Ascension.

CHAPTER 1

The great blessings we have received through Christ. He is the head of all the church.

PAUL, an apostle of Jesus Christ, by the will of God, to all the saints who are at Ephesus and to the faithful in Christ Jesus.

2 Grace be to you and peace, from God the Father and from the Lord Jesus Christ.

3 ¹ Blessed be the God and Father of our Lord Jesus Christ, who hath blessed us with spiritual blessings in heavenly *places*, in Christ:

4 As he chose us in him before the foundation of the world, that we should be holy and unspotted in his sight in charity.

5 Who hath predestinated us unto the adoption of children through Jesus Christ unto himself: according to the purpose of his will:

6 Unto the praise of the glory of his grace, in which he hath graced us in his beloved son.

7 In whom we have redemption through his blood, the remission of sins, according to the riches of his grace,

8 Which hath superabounded in us, in all wisdom and prudence,

9 That he might make known unto us the mystery of his will, according to his good pleasure, which he hath purposed in him,

10 In the dispensation of the fulness of times, to re-establsh all things in Christ, that are in heaven and on earth, in him.

11 In whom we also are called by lot, being predestinated according to the purpose of him who worketh all things according to the counsel of his will.

12 That we may be unto the praise of his glory: we who before hoped in Christ:

13 In whom you also, after you had heard the word of truth (the gospel of your salvation), in whom also believing, you were signed with the holy Spirit of promise.

14 Who is the pledge of our inheritance, unto the redemption of acquisition, unto the praise of his glory.

15 Wherefore, I also, hearing of your faith that is in the Lord Jesus and of your love towards all the saints,

16 Cease not to give thanks for you, making commemoration of you in my prayers,

17 That the God of our Lord Jesus Christ, the Father of glory, may give unto you the spirit of wisdom and of revelation, in the knowledge of him:

18 The eyes of your heart enlightened that you may know what the hope is of his calling and what are the riches of the glory of his inheritance in the saints.

19 And what is the exceeding greatness of his power towards us, who believe ² according to the operation of the might of his power,

20 Which he wrought in Christ, raising him up from the dead and setting him on his right hand in the heavenly *places.*

21 Above all principality and power and virtue and dominion and every

CHAP. 1. ¹ 2 Cor. 1, 3; 1 Peter, 1, 3. ² Eph. 3, 7.
CHAP. 1. Ver. 3. *In heavenly places*, or, *in heavenly things. In cœlestibus.*
Ver. 14. *Acquisition*, that is, a purchased possession.

name that is named, not only in this world, but also in that which is to come.

22 [3] And he hath subjected all things under his feet and hath made him head over all the church,

23 Which is his body and the fulness of him who is filled all in all.

CHAPTER 2

All our good comes through Christ. He is our peace.

AND [1] you, when you were dead in your offences and sins,

2 Wherein in time past you walked according to the course of this world, according to the prince of the power of this air, of the spirit that now worketh on the children of unbelief:

3 In which also we all conversed in time past, in the desires of our flesh, fulfilling the will of the flesh and of *our* thoughts, and were by nature children of wrath, even as the rest:

4 But God (who is rich in mercy) for his exceeding charity wherewith he loved us

5 Even when we were dead in sins, hath quickened us together in Christ (by whose grace you are saved)

6 And hath raised us up together and hath made us sit together in the heavinly *places,* through Christ Jesus.

7 That he might shew in the ages to come the abundant riches of his grace, in his bounty towards us in Christ Jesus.

8 For by grace you are saved through faith: and that not of yourselves, for it is the gift of God.

9 Not of works, that no man may glory.

10 For we are his workmanship, created in Christ Jesus in good works, which God hath prepared that we should walk in them.

11 For which cause be mindful that you, being heretofore Gentiles in the flesh, who are called uncircumcision by that which is called circumcision in the flesh, made by hands:

12 That you were at that time without Christ, being aliens from the conversation of Israel and strangers to the testament, having no hope of the promise and without God in this world.

13 But now in Christ Jesus, you, who some time were afar off, are made nigh by the blood of Christ.

14 For he is our peace, who hath made both one, and breaking down the middle wall of partition, the enmities in his flesh:

15 Making void the law of commandments *contained* in decrees: that he might make the two in himself into one new man, making peace

16 And might reconcile both to God in one body by the cross, killing the enmities in himself.

17 And coming, he preached peace to you that were afar off: and peace to them that were nigh.

18 [2] For by him we have access both in one Spirit to the Father.

19 Now therefore you are no more strangers and foreigners: but you are fellow citizens with the saints and the domestics of God,

20 Built upon the foundation of the apostles and prophets, Jesus Christ himself being the chief corner stone:

21 In whom all the building, being framed together, groweth up into an holy temple in the Lord.

22 In whom you also are built together into an habitation of God in the Spirit.

CHAPTER 3

The mystery hidden from former ages was discovered to the apostle, to be imparted to the Gentiles. He prays that they may be strengthened in God.

FOR this cause, I Paul, the prisoner of Jesus Christ, for you Gentiles:

2 If yet you have heard of the dispensation of the grace of God which is given me towards you:

3 How that, according to revelation, the mystery has been made known to me, as I have written above in a few words;

4 As you reading, may understand my knowledge in the mystery of Christ,

5 Which in other generations was not known to the sons of men, as it is now revealed to his holy apostles and prophets in the Spirit:

6 That the Gentiles should be fellow heirs and of the same body: and co-partners of his promise in Christ Jesus, by the gospel

7 Of which I am made a minister, according to the gift of the grace of God, which is given to me [1] according to the operation of his power.

8 [2] To me, the least of all the saints, is given this grace, to preach among the Gentiles the unsearchable riches of Christ:

9 And to enlighten all men, that they may see what is the dispensation of the mystery which hath been hidden from eternity in God who created all things:

10 That the manifold wisdom of God

---

[3] Ps. 8, 8. CHAP. 2. [1] Col. 2, 13. [2] Rom. 5, 2. CHAP. 3. [1] Eph. 1, 19. [2] 1 Cor. 15, 9.

CHAP. 2. Ver. 9. *Not of works,* as of our own growth, or from ourselves; but as from the grace of God.

may be made known to the principalities and powers in heavenly *places* through the church,

11 According to the eternal purpose which he made in Christ Jesus our Lord:

12 In whom we have boldness and access with confidence by the faith of him.

13 Wherefore I pray you not to faint at my tribulations for you, which is your glory.

14 For this cause I bow my knees to the Father of our Lord Jesus Christ,

15 Of whom all paternity in heaven and earth is named:

16 That he would grant you, according to the riches of his glory, to be strengthened by his Spirit with might unto the inward man:

17 That Christ may dwell by faith in your hearts: that, being rooted and founded in charity,

18 You may be able to comprehend, with all the saints, what is the breadth and length and height and depth,

19 To know also the charity of Christ, which surpasseth all knowledge: that you may be filled unto all the fulness of God.

20 Now to him who is able to do all things more abundantly than we desire or understand, according to the power that worketh in us:

21 To him be glory in the church and in Christ Jesus, unto all generations, world without end. Amen.

CHAPTER 4

He exhorts them to unity, to put on the new man, and to fly sin.

I THEREFORE, a prisoner in the Lord, beseech you [1] that you walk worthy of the vocation in which you are called:

2 With all humility and mildness, with patience, supporting one another in charity.

3 [2] Careful to keep the unity of the Spirit in the bond of peace.

4 One body and one Spirit: as you are called in one hope of your calling.

5 One Lord, one faith, one baptism.

6 [3] One God and Father of all, who

CHAP. 4. [1] 1 Cor. 7, 17; Phil. 1, 27. [2] Rom. 12, 10. [3] Mal. 2, 10. [4] Rom. 12, 3; 1 Cor. 12, 11; 2 Cor. 10, 13. [5] Ps. 67, 19. [6] 1 Cor. 12, 28. [7] Rom. 1, 21. [8] Col. 3, 8. [9] Rom. 6, 4. [10] Col. 3, 12.

CHAP. 3. Ver. 15. *All paternity.* Or, *the whole family,* πατριά. God is the Father both of angels and men: whosoever besides is named father is so named with subordination to him.

CHAP. 4. Ver. 11, 13. *Gave some apostles— Until we all meet.* Here it is plainly expressed that Christ has left in his Church a *perpetual* succession of orthodox pastors and teachers, to preserve the faithful in unity and truth.

---

is above all, and through all, and in us all.

7 [4] But to every one of us is given grace, according to the measure of the giving of Christ.

8 Wherefore he saith: [5] *Ascending on high, he led captivity captive: he gave gifts to men.*

9 Now that he ascended, what is it, but because he also descended first into the lower parts of the earth?

10 He that descended is the same also that ascended above all the heavens: that he might fill all things.

11 And he gave some [6] apostles, and some prophets, and other some evangelists, and other some pastors and doctors:

12 For the perfecting of the saints, for the work of the ministry, for the edifying of the body of Christ:

13 Until we all meet into the unity of faith and of the knowledge of the Son of God, unto a perfect man, unto the measure of the age of the fulness of Christ:

14 That henceforth we be no more children, tossed to and fro and carried about with every wind of doctrine, by the wickedness of men, by cunning craftiness by which they lie in wait to deceive.

15 But doing the truth in charity, we may in all things grow up in him who is the head, *even* Christ:

16 From whom the whole body, being compacted and fitly joined together, by what every joint supplieth, according to the operation in the measure of every part, maketh increase of the body, unto the edifying of itself in charity.

17 [7] This then I say and testify in the Lord: That henceforward you walk not as also the Gentiles walk in the vanity of their mind:

18 Having their understanding darkened: being alienated from the life of God through the ignorance that is in them, because of the blindness of their hearts.

19 Who despairing have given themselves up to lasciviousness, unto the working of all uncleanness, unto covetousness.

20 But you have not so learned Christ:

21 If so be that you have heard him and have been taught in him, as the truth is in Jesus:

22 [8] To put off, according to former conversation, the old man, who is corrupted according to the desire of error.

23 [9] And be renewed in the spirit of your mind:

24 [10] And put on the new man, who

according to God is created in justice and holiness of truth.

25 [11] Wherefore, putting away lying, speak ye the truth, every man with his neighbour. For we are members one of another.

26 [12] Be angry: and sin not. Let not the sun go down upon your anger.

27 [13] Give not place to the devil.

28 He that stole, let him now steal no more: but rather let him labour, working with his hands the thing which is good, that he may have something to give to him that suffereth need.

29 Let no evil speech proceed from your mouth: but that which is good, to the edification of faith: that it may administer grace to the hearers.

30 And grieve not the holy Spirit of God: whereby you are sealed unto the day of redemption.

31 Let all bitterness and anger and indignation and clamour and blaspemy be put away from you, with all malice.

32 [14] And be ye kind one to another: merciful, forgiving one another, even as God hath forgiven you in Christ.

CHAPTER 5

Exhortations to a virtuous life. The mutual duties of man and wife, by the example of Christ and of the Church.

BE ye therefore followers of God, as most dear children:

2 [1] And walk in love, as Christ also hath loved us and hath delivered himself for us, an oblation and a sacrifice to God for an odour of sweetness.

3 [2] But fornication and all uncleanness or covetousness, let it not so much as be named among you, as becometh saints:

4 Or obscenity or foolish talking or scurrility, which is to no purpose: but rather giving of thanks.

5 For know you this and understand: That no fornicator or unclean or covetous person (which is a serving of idols) hath inheritance in the kingdom of Christ and of God.

6 [3] Let no man deceive you with vain words. For because of these things cometh the anger of God upon the children of unbelief.

7 Be ye not therefore partakers with them.

8 For you were heretofore darkness, but now light in the Lord. Walk then as children of the light.

9 For the fruit of the light is in all goodness and justice and truth:

10 Proving what is well pleasing to God.

11 And have no fellowship with the unfruitful works of darkness: but rather reprove them.

12 For the things that are done by them in secret, it is a shame even to speak of.

13 But all things that are reproved are made manifest by the light: for all that is made manifest is light.

14 Wherefore he saith: *Rise, thou that sleepest, and arise from the dead: and Christ shall enlighten thee.*

15 See therefore, brethren, how you walk circumspectly: [4] not as unwise, but as wise: redeeming the time,

16 But as wise: redeeming the time, because the days are evil.

17 [5] Wherefore, becoming not unwise: but understanding what is the will of God.

18 And be not drunk with wine, wherein is luxury: but be ye filled with the holy Spirit,

19 Speaking to yourselves in psalms and hymns and spiritual canticles, singing and making melody in your hearts to the Lord:

20 Giving thanks always for all things, in the name of our Lord Jesus Christ, to God and the Father:

21 Being subject one to another, in the fear of Christ.

22 [6] Let women be subject to their husbands, as to the Lord:

23 [7] Because the husband is the head of the wife, as Christ is the head of the church. He *is* the saviour of his body.

24 Therefore as the church is subject to Christ: so also let the wives be to their husbands in all things.

25 [8] Husbands, love your wives, as Christ also loved the church and delivered himself up for it:

26 That he might sanctify it, cleansing it by the laver of water in the word of life:

27 That he might present it to himself, a glorious church, not having spot or wrinkle or any such thing: but that it should be holy and without blemish.

28 So also ought men to love their wives as their own bodies. He that loveth his wife loveth himself.

29 For no man ever hated his own flesh, but nourisheth and cherisheth it, as also Christ doth the church:

30 Because we are members of his body, of his flesh and of his bones.

[11] 1 Peter, 2, 1; Zach. 8, 16. [12] Ps. 4, 5. [13] James, 4, 7. [14] Col. 3, 13. CHAP. 5. [1] John, 13, 34; 15, 12; 1 John, 4, 21. [2] Col. 3, 5. [3] Matt. 24, 4; Mark, 13, 5; Luke, 21, 8; 2 Thess. 2, 3. [4] Col. 4, 5. [5] Rom. 12, 2; 1 Thess. 4, 3. [6] Gen. 3, 16; Col. 3, 18; 1 Peter, 3, 1. [7] 1 Cor. 11, 3. [8] Col 3, 19.

CHAP. 5. Ver. 24. *As the church is subject to Christ.* The church then, according to St. Paul, is ever obedient to Christ and can never fail from him, but will remain faithful to him, unspotted and unchanged, to the end of the world.

31 ⁹ *For this cause shall a man leave his father and mother: and shall cleave to his wife.*¹⁰ *And they shall be two in one flesh.*

32 This is a great sacrament: but I speak in Christ and in the church.

33 Nevertheless, let every one of you in particular love for his wife as himself: and let the wife fear her husband.

CHAPTER 6

Duties of children and servants. The Christian's armour.

CHILDREN, obey your parents in the Lord: for this is just.

2 ¹ *Honour thy father and thy mother,* which is the first commandment with a promise:

3 *That it may be well with thee, and thou mayest be long lived upon earth.*

4 And you, fathers, provoke not your children to anger: but bring them up in the discipline and correction of the Lord.

5 ² Servants, be obedient to them that are your lords according to the flesh, with fear and trembling, in the simplicity of your heart, as to Christ.

6 Not serving to the eye, as it were pleasing men: but, as the servants of Christ, doing the will of God from the heart.

7 With a good will serving, as to the Lord, and not to men.

8 Knowing that whatsoever good thing any man shall do, the same shall he receive from the Lord, whether he be bond or free.

9 And you, masters, do the same things to them, forbearing threatenings: knowing that the Lord both of them and you is in heaven. ³ And there is no respect of persons with him.

⁹ Gen. 2, 24; Matt. 19, 5; Mark, 10, 7. ¹⁰ 1 Cor. 6, 16. ¹ Exod. 20, 12; Deut. 5, 16; Ecclus. 3, 9; Matt. 15, 4; Mark, 7, 10; Col. 3, 20. ² Col. 3, 22; Titus, 2, 9; 1 Peter, 2, 18. ³ Deut. 10, 17; 2 Par. 19, 7; Job, 34, 19; Wisd. 6, 8; Ecclus. 35, 15; Acts, 10, 34; Rom. 2, 11; Col. 3, 25; 1 Peter, 1, 17. ⁴ Isai. 59, 17; 1 Thess. 5, 8. ⁵ Col. 4, 2, 3; 2 Thess. 3, 1.

CHAP. 6. Ver. 12. *High places* or *heavenly places.* That is to say, in the air, the lowest of the celestial regions; in which God permits these wicked spirits or false angels to wander. Ver. 24. *In incorruption.* That is, with a pure and perfect love.

10 Finally, brethren, be strengthened in the Lord and in the might of his power.

11 Put you on the armour of God, that you may be able to stand against the deceits of the devil.

12 For our wrestling is not against flesh and blood: but against principalities and powers, against the rulers of the world of this darkness, against the spirits of wickedness in the high places.

13 Therefore, take unto you the armour of God, that you may be able to resist in the evil day and to stand in all things perfect.

14 Stand therefore, having your loins girt about with truth and having on the breastplate of justice:

15 And your feet shod with the preparation of the gospel of peace.

16 In all things taking the shield of faith, wherewith you may be able to extinguish all the fiery darts of the most wicked one.

17 ⁴ And take unto you the helmet of salvation and the sword of the Spirit (which is the word of God).

18 By all prayer and supplication praying at all times in the spirit: ⁵ and in the same watching with all instance and supplication for all the saints:

19 And for me, that speech may be given me, that I may open my mouth with confidence, to make known the mystery of the gospel,

20 For which I am an ambassador in a chain: so that therein I may be bold to speak according as I ought.

21 But that you also may know the things the concern me *and* what I am doing, Tychicus, my dearest brother and faithful minister in the Lord, will make known to you all things:

22 Whom I have sent to you for this same purpose: that you may know the things concerning us, and that he may comfort your hearts.

23 Peace be to the brethren and charity with faith, from God the Father and the Lord Jesus Christ.

24 Grace *be* with all them that love our Lord Jesus Christ in incorruption. Amen.

THE EPISTLE OF ST. PAUL TO THE

PHILIPPIANS

The Philippians were the first among the Macedonians converted to the faith. They had a great veneration for St. Paul and supplied his wants when he was a prisoner in Rome, sending to him by Epaphroditus, by whom he sent this Epistle; in which he recommends charity, unity and humility and warns them against false teachers, whom he calls dogs and enemies of the cross of Christ. He also returns thanks for their benefactions. It was written about twenty-nine years after our Lord's Ascension.

CHAPTER 1

The apostle's affection for the Philippians.

PAUL and Timothy, the servants of Jesus Christ: to all the saints in Christ Jesus who are at Philippi, with the bishops and deacons.

2 Grace be unto you and peace, from God our Father and from the Lord Jesus Christ.

3 I give thanks to my God in every remembrance of you:

4 Always in all my prayers making supplication for you all with joy:

5 For your communication in the gospel of Christ, from the first day until now.

6 Being confident of this very thing: that he who hath begun a good work in you will perfect it unto the day of Christ Jesus.

7 As it is meet for me to think this for you all, for that I have you in my heart; and that, in my bands and in the defence and confirmation of the gospel, you all are partakers of my joy.

8 For God is my witness how I long after you all in the bowels of Jesus Christ.

9 And this I pray: That your charity may more and more abound in knowledge and in all understanding:

10 That you may approve the better things: that you may be sincere and without offence unto the day of Christ:

11 Filled with the fruit of justice, through Jesus Christ, unto the glory and praise of God.

12 Now, brethren, I desire you should know that the things which have happened to me have fallen out rather to the furtherance of the gospel:

13 So that my bands are made manifest in Christ, in all the court and in all other places.

14 And many of the brethren in the Lord, *growing* confident by my bands, are much more bold to speak the word of God without fear.

15 Some indeed, even out of envy and contention: but some also for good will preach Christ.

16 Some out of charity, knowing that I am set for the defence of the gospel.

17 And some out of contention preach Christ not sincerely: supposing that they raise affliction to my bands.

18 But what then? So that by all means, whether by occasion or by truth, Christ be preached: in this also I rejoice, yea, and will rejoice.

19 For I know that this shall fall out to me unto salvation, through your prayer and the supply of the Spirit of Jesus Christ,

20 According to my expectation and hope. That in nothing I shall be confounded: but with all confidence, as always, so now also, shall Christ be magnified in my body, whether *it be* by life or by death.

21 For to me, to live in Christ: and to die is gain.

22 And if to live in the flesh: this is to me the fruit of labour. And what I shall choose I know not.

23 But I am straitened between two: having a desire to be dissolved and to be with Christ, a thing by far the better.

24 But to abide still in the flesh is needful for you.

25 And having this confidence, I know that I shall abide and continue with you all, for your furtherance and joy of faith:

CHAP. 1. Ver. 22. *This is to me.* His meaning is that, although his dying immediately for Christ would be his gain, by putting him presently in possession of heaven, yet he is doubtful by staying longer in the flesh he should be more beneficial to the souls of his neighbours.

26 That your rejoicing may abound in Christ Jesus for me, by my coming to you again.

27 [1] Only let your conversation be worthy of the gospel of Christ: that, whether I come and see you, or, being absent, may hear of you, that you stand fast in one spirit, with one mind labouring together for the faith of the gospel.

28 And in nothing be ye terrified by the adversaries: which to them is a cause of perdition, but to you of salvation. And this from God.

29 For unto you it is given for Christ, not only to believe in him, but also to suffer for him:

30 Having the same conflict as that which you have seen in me and now have heard of me.

CHAPTER 2

He recommends them to unity and humility, and to work out their salvation with fear and trembling.

IF there be therefore any consolation in Christ, if any comfort of charity, if any society of the spirit, if any bowels of commiseration:

2 Fulfil ye my joy, that you be of one mind, having the same charity, being of one accord, agreeing in sentiment.

3 Let nothing be done through contention: neither by vain glory. But in humility, let each esteem others better than themselves:

4 Each one not considering the things that are his own, but those that are other men's.

5 For let this mind be in you, which was also in Christ Jesus:

6 Who being in the form of God, thought it not robbery to be equal with God:

7 But emptied himself, taking the form of a servant, being made in the likeness of men, and in habit found as a man.

8 [1] He humbled himself, becoming obedient unto death, even to the death of the cross.

9 For which cause, God also hath exalted him and hath given him a name which is above all names:

10 [2] That in the name of Jesus every knee should bow, of those that are in heaven, on earth, and under the earth:

11 And that every tongue should confess that the Lord Jesus Christ is in the glory of God the Father.

CHAP. 1. [1] Eph. 4, 1; Col. 1, 10; 1 Thess. 2, 12.
CHAP. 2. [1] Heb. 2, 9. [2] Isai. 45, 24; Rom. 14, 11.
[3] 1 Peter, 5, 6. [4] Acts, 16, 1. [5] 1 Cor. 13, 5.

CHAP. 2. Ver. 7. *Emptied himself (exinanivit)*, made himself as of no account.
Ver. 12. *With fear.* This is against the false faith and presumptuous security of modern sectaries.

12 Wherefore, my dearly beloved, (as you have always obeyed, not as in my presence only but much more now in my absence) with fear and trembling work out your salvation.

13 For it is God who worketh in you, both to will and to accomplish, according to *his* good will.

14 [3] And do ye all things without murmurings and hesitations:

15 That you may be blameless and sincere children of God, without reproof, in the midst of a crooked and perverse generation: among whom you shine as lights in the world.

16 Holding forth the word of life to my glory in the day of Christ: because I have not run in vain, nor laboured in vain.

17 Yea, and if I be made a victim upon the sacrifice and service of your faith, I rejoice and congratulate with you all.

18 And for the selfsame thing, do you also rejoice and congratulate with me.

19 And I hope in the Lord Jesus [4] to send Timothy unto you shortly, that I also may be of good comfort, when I know the things concerning you.

20 For I have no man so of the same mind, who with sincere affection is solicitous for you.

21 [5] For all seek the things that are their own: not the things that are Jesus Christ's.

22 Now know ye the proof of him: that as a son with the father, so hath he served with me in the gospel.

23 Him therefore I hope to send unto you immediately: so soon as I shall see how it will go with me.

24 And I trust in the Lord that I myself also shall come to you shortly.

25 But I have thought it necessary to send to you Epaphroditus, my brother and fellow labourer and fellow soldier, but your apostle: and he that hath ministered to my wants.

26 For indeed he longed after you all: and was sad, for that you had heard that he was sick.

27 For indeed he was sick, nigh unto death: but God had mercy on him. And not only on him, but on me also, lest I should have sorrow upon sorrow.

28 Therefore, I sent him the more speedily: that seeing him again, you may rejoice, and I may be without sorrow.

29 Receive him therefore with all joy in the Lord: and treat with honour such as he is.

30 Because for the work of Christ he came to the point of death: delivering

his life, that he might fulfil that which on your part was wanting towards my service.

CHAPTER 3

He warneth them against false teachers. He counts all other things loss, that he may gain Christ.

AS to the rest, my brethren, rejoice in the Lord. To write the same things to you, to me indeed *is* not wearisome, but to you *is* necessary.

2 Beware of dogs: beware of evil workers: beware of the concision.

3 For we are the circumcision, who in spirit serve God and glory in Christ Jesus, not having confidence in the flesh.

4 Though I might also have confidence in the flesh. If any other thinketh he may have confidence in the flesh, I more:

5 Being circumcised the eighth day, of the stock of Israel, of the tribe of Benjamin, an Hebrew of the Hebrews. [1] According to the law, a Pharisee:

6 According to zeal, persecuting the church of God: According to the justice that is in the law, conversing without blame.

7 But the things that were gain to me, the same I have counted loss for Christ.

8 Furthermore, I count all things to be but loss for the excellent knowledge of Jesus Christ, my Lord: for whom I have suffered the loss of all things and count them but as dung, that I may gain Christ.

9 And may be found in him, not having my justice, which is of the law, but that which is of the faith of Christ Jesus, which is of God: justice in faith.

10 That I may know him and the power of his resurrection and the fellowship of his sufferings: being made conformable to his death,

11 If by any means I may attain to the resurrection which is from the dead.

12 Not as though I had already attained, or were already perfect: but I follow after, if I may by any means apprehend, wherein I am also apprehended by Christ Jesus.

13 Brethren, I do not count myself to have apprehended. But one thing I do: Forgetting the things that are behind and stretching forth myself to those that are before,

14 I press towards the mark, to the prize of the supernal vocation of God in Christ Jesus.

15 Let us therefore, as many as are perfect, be thus minded: and if in any thing you be otherwise minded, this also God will reveal to you.

16 Nevertheless, whereunto we are come, that we be of the same mind, let us also continue in the same rule.

17 Be ye followers of me, brethren: and observe them who walk so as you have our model.

18 [2] For many walk, of whom I have told you often (and now tell you weeping) that they are enemies of the cross of Christ:

19 Whose end is destruction: whose God is their belly: and *whose* glory is in their shame: who mind earthly things.

20 But our conversation is in heaven: from whence also we look for the Saviour, our Lord Jesus Christ,

21 Who will reform the body of our lowness, made like to the body of his glory, according to the operation whereby also he is able to subdue all things unto himself.

CHAPTER 4

He exhorts them to perseverance in all good and acknowledges their charitable contributions to him.

THEREFORE, my dearly beloved brethren and most desired, my joy and my crown: so stand fast in the Lord, my dearly beloved.

2 I beg of Evodia and I beseech Syntyche to be of one mind in the Lord.

3 And I entreat thee also, my sincere companion, help those women who have laboured with me in the gospel, with Clement and the rest of my fellow labourers, whose names are in the book of life.

4 Rejoice in the Lord always: again, I say, rejoice.

5 Let your modesty be known to all men. The Lord is nigh.

6 Be nothing solicitous: but in every thing, by prayer and supplication, with thanksgiving, let your petitions be made known to God.

7 And the peace of God, which surpasseth all understanding, keep your hearts and minds in Christ Jesus.

8 For the rest, brethren, whatsoever things are true, whatsoever modest, whatsoever just, whatsoever holy, what-

CHAP. 3. [1] Acts, 23, 6. [2] Rom. 16, 17.

CHAP. 3. Ver. 2. *Dogs. That is,* false teachers. CHAP. 4. Ver. 8. *For the rest, brethren, whatsoever things are true.* Here the apostle enumerates general precepts of morality which they ought to practise. *Whatsoever things are true:* in words, in promises, in lawful oaths, and the like, he commands rectitude of mind and sincerity of heart. *Whatsoever modest:* by these words he prescribes gravity in manners, modesty in dress and decency in conversation. *Whatsoever just:* that is, in dealing with others, in buying or selling, in trade or business, to be fair and honest. *Whatsoever holy:* by these words may be understood, that those who are in a religious state professed, or in holy orders, should lead a life of *sanctity* and *chastity*, according to the vows they make: but these words

soever lovely, whatsoever of good fame, if there be any virtue, if any praise of discipline: think on these things.

9 The things which you have both learned and received and heard and seen in me, these do ye: and the God of peace shall be with you.

10 Now I rejoice in the Lord exceedingly that now at length your thought for me hath flourished again, as you did also think; but you were busied.

11 I speak not as it were for want. For I have learned, in whatsoever state I am, to be content therewith.

12 I know both how to be brought low, and I know how to abound (every where and in all things I am instructed) : both to be full and to be hungry: both to abound and to suffer need.

13 I can do all things in him who strengtheneth me.

14 Nevertheless, you have done well in communicating to my tribulation.

15 And you also know, O Philippians, that in the beginning of the gospel, when I departed from Macedonia, no

church communicated with me as concerning giving and receiving, but you only.

16 For unto Thessalonica also you sent once and again for my use.

17 Not that I seek the gift: but I seek the fruit that may abound to your account.

18 But I have all and abound: I am filled, having received from Epaphroditus the things you sent, an odour of sweetness, ¹an acceptable sacrifice, pleasing to God.

19 And may my God supply all your want, according to his riches in glory in Christ Jesus.

20 Now to God and our Father be glory, world without end. Amen.

21 Salute ye every saint in Christ Jesus.

22 The brethren who are with me salute you. All the saints salute you: especially they that are of Cæsar's household.

23 The grace of our Lord Jesus Christ be with your spirit. Amen.

THE EPISTLE OF ST. PAUL TO THE
COLOSSIANS

Colossa was a city of Phrygia, near Laodicea. It does not appear that St. Paul had preached there himself, but that the Colossians were converted by Epaphras, a disciple of the Apostles. However, as St. Paul was the great Apostle of the Gentiles, he wrote this Epistle to the Colossians when he was in prison, and about the same time that he wrote to the Ephesians and Philippians. The exhortations and doctrine it contains are similar to that which is set forth in his Epistle to the Ephesians.

CHAPTER 1

He gives thanks for the grace bestowed upon the Colossians and prays for them. Christ is the head of the church and the peacemaker through his blood. Paul is his minister.

CHAP. 4. ¹ Rom. 12, 1.

being also applied to those in the world indicate the virtuous life they are bound by the divine commandments to follow. *Whatsoever lovely:* that is, to practise those good offices in society that procure us the esteem and good will of our neighbours. *Whatsoever of good fame:* that is, that by our conduct and behaviour we should edify our neighbours and give them good example by our actions. *If there be any virtue, if any praise of discipline:* that those in error, by seeing the morality and good discipline of the true religion, may be converted. And finally, the apostle commands, not only the Philippians, but all Christians, *to think on these things:* that is, to make it their study and concern that the peace of God might be with them.

PAUL, an apostle of Jesus Christ, by the will of God, and Timothy, a brother:

2 To the saints and faithful brethren in Christ Jesus who are at Colossa.

3 Grace be to you and peace, from God our Father and from the Lord Jesus Christ. We give thanks to God and the Father of our Lord Jesus Christ, praying always for you.

4 Hearing your faith in Christ Jesus and the love which you have towards all the saints.

5 For the hope that is laid up for you in heaven, which you have heard in the word of the truth of the gospel,

6 Which is come unto you, as also it is in the whole world and bringeth forth fruit and groweth, even as it does in

you, since the day you heard and knew the grace of God in truth.

7 As you learned of Epaphras, our most beloved fellow servant, who is for you a faithful minister of Christ Jesus:

8 Who also hath manifested to us your love in the spirit.

9 Therefore we also, from the day that we heard it, cease not to pray for you and to beg that you may be filled with the knowledge of his will, in all wisdom and spiritual understanding:

10 That you may walk worthy of God, in all things pleasing; being fruitful in every good work and increasing in the knowledge of God:

11 Strengthened with all might, according to the power of his glory, in all patience and longsuffering with joy,

12 Giving thanks to God the Father, who hath made us worthy to be partakers of the lot of the saints in light:

13 Who hath delivered us from the power of darkness and hath translated us into the kingdom of the Son of his love:

14 In whom we have redemption through his blood, the remission of sins;

15 Who is the image of the invisible God, the firstborn of every creature.

16 [1] For in him were all things created in heaven and on earth, visible and invisible, whether thrones, or dominations, or principalities, or powers. All things were created by him and in him.

17 And he is before all: and by him all things consist.

18 And he is the head of the body, the church: [2] who is the beginning, the firstborn from the dead, that in all things he may hold the primacy:

19 Because in him, it hath well pleased *the Father* that all fulness should dwell:

20 And through him to reconcile all things unto himself, making peace through the blood of his cross, both as to the things that are on earth and the things that are in heaven.

21 And you, whereas you were some time alienated and enemies in mind in evil works:

22 Yet now he hath reconciled in the body of his flesh through death, to present you holy and unspotted and blameless before him:

23 If so ye continue in the faith, grounded and settled, and immoveable from the hope of the gospel which you have heard, which is preached in all the creation that is under heaven: whereof I Paul am made a minister.

24 Who now rejoice in my sufferings for you and fill up those things that are wanting of the sufferings of Christ, in

my flesh, for his body, which is the church:

25 Whereof I am made a minister according to the dispensation of God, which is given me towards you, that I may fulfil the word of God:

26 The mystery which hath been hidden from ages and generations, but now is manifested to his saints,

27 To whom God would make known the riches of the glory of this mystery among the Gentiles, which is Christ, in you the hope of glory.

28 Whom we preach, admonishing every man and teaching every man in all wisdom, that we may present every man perfect in Christ Jesus.

29 Wherein also I labour, striving according to his working which he worketh in me in power.

CHAPTER 2

He warns them against the impostures of the philosophers and the Jewish teachers, that would withdraw them from Christ.

FOR I would have you know what manner of care I have for you and for them that are at Laodicea and whosoever have not seen my face in the flesh:

2 That their hearts may be comforted, being instructed in charity and unto all riches of fulness of understanding, unto the knowledge of the mystery of God the Father and of Christ Jesus:

3 In whom are hid all the treasures of wisdom and knowledge.

4 Now this I say, that no man may deceive you by loftiness of words.

5 [1] For though I be absent in body, yet in spirit I am with you, rejoicing, and beholding your order and the steadfastness of your faith which is in Christ.

6 As therefore you have received Jesus Christ the Lord, walk ye in him:

7 Rooted and built up in him and confirmed in the faith, as also you have learned: abounding in him in thanksgiving.

8 Beware lest any man cheat you by philosophy and vain deceit; according to the tradition of men, according to the elements of the world and not according to Christ.

9 For in him dwelleth all the fulness of the Godhead corporeally.

CHAP. 1. [1] John 1, 3. [2] 1 Cor. 15, 20; Apoc. 1, 5. CHAP. 2. [1] 1 Cor. 5, 3.

CHAP. 1. Ver. 15. *The firstborn.* That is, first begotten; as the Evangelist declares, *the only begotten* of his Father. Hence, St. Chrysostom explains *firstborn,* not first created, as he was not created at all, but born of his Father before all ages; that is, coeval with the Father and with the Holy Ghost.

Ver. 24. *Wanting.* There is no *want* in the sufferings of Christ in himself as *head:* but many sufferings are still *wanting,* or are still to come, in his body the church and his members the faithful.

10 And you are filled in him, who is the head of all principality and power.

11 In whom also you are circumcised with circumcision not made by hand in despoiling of the body of the flesh: but in the circumcision of Christ.

12 Buried with him in baptism: in whom also you are risen again by the faith of the operation of God who hath raised him up from the dead.

13 ² And you, when you were dead in your sins and the uncircumcision of your flesh, he hath quickened together with him, forgiving you all offences:

14 Blotting out the handwriting of the decree that was against us, which was contrary to us. And he hath taken the same out of the way, fastening it to the cross.

15 And despoiling the principalities and powers, he hath exposed them confidently in open shew, triumphing over them in himself.

16 Let no man therefore judge you in meat or in drink or in respect of a festival day or of the new moon or of the sabbaths,

17 Which.are a shadow of things to come: but the body *is* of Christ.

18 ³ Let no man seduce you, willing in humility and religion of angels, walking in the things which he hath not seen, in vain puffed up by the sense of his flesh:

19 And not holding the head, from which the whole body, by joints and

---

² Eph. 2, 1. ³ Matt. 24, 4. Chap. 3. ¹ Eph. 5, 3.
² Rom. 6, 4; Eph. 4, 22; Heb. 12, 1; 1 Peter, 2, 1;
4, 2. ³ Gen. 1, 26.

Chap. 2. Ver. 16. *In meat.* He means with regard to the Jewish observations of the distinction of clean and unclean meats; and of their *festivals, new moons and sabbaths,* as being no longer obligatory.
Ver. 18. *Willing.* That is, by a self willed, self invented, superstitious worship, falsely pretending *humility,* but really proceeding from pride. Such was the worship, that many of the philosophers (against whom St. Paul speaks, ver 8) paid to angels or demons, by sacrificing to them, as carriers of intelligence betwixt God and men; pretending *humility* in so doing, as if God was too great to be addressed by men, and setting aside the mediatorship of Jesus Christ, who is the head both of angels and men. Such also was the worship paid by the ancient heretics, disciples of Simon and Menander, to the angels, whom they believed to be makers and lords of this lower world. This is certain, that they whom the apostle here condemns, did not *hold the head* (ver. 19), that is, Jesus Christ, and his mediatorship; and therefore what he writes here no way touches the Catholic doctrine and practice of desiring our good angels to pray to God for us, through Jesus Christ. St. Jerome understands by the *religion* or service *of angels,* the Jewish religion given by angels and shews all that is here said, to be directed against the Jewish teachers, who sought to subject the new Christians to the observance of the Mosaic law.
Ver. 21. *Touch not.* The meaning is, that Christians should not subject themselves, either to the ordinances of the old law, forbidding touching or tasting things unclean: or to the superstitious invention of heretics, imposing such restraints, under pretence of wisdom, humility or mortification.

---

bands, being supplied with nourishment and compacted, groweth into the increase of God.

20 If then you be dead with Christ from the elements of this world, why do you yet decree as though living in the world?

21 Touch not: taste not: handle not.

22 Which all are unto destruction by the very use, according to the precepts and doctrines of men.

23 Which things have indeed a shew of wisdom in superstition and humility, and not sparing the body: not in any honour to the filling of the flesh.

CHAPTER 3

He exhorts them to put off the old man and to put on the new. The duties of wives and husbands, children and servants.

THEREFORE, if you be risen with Christ, seek the things that are above, where Christ is sitting at the right hand of God.

2 Mind the things that are above, not the things that are upon the earth.

3 For you are dead: and your life is hid with Christ in God.

4 When Christ shall appear, who is your life, then you also shall appear with him in glory.

5 Mortify therefore your members which are upon the earth: ¹ fornication, uncleanness, lust, evil concupiscence and covetousness, which is the service of idols.

6 For which things the wrath of God cometh upon the children of unbelief,

7 In which you also walked some time, when you lived in them.

8 ² But now put you also all away: anger, indignation, malice, blasphemy, filthy speech out of your mouth.

9 Lie not one to another: stripping yourselves of the old man with his deeds,

10 And putting on the new, him who is renewed unto knowledge, ³ according to the image of him that created him.

11 Where there is neither Gentile nor Jew, circumcision nor uncircumcision, Barbarian nor Scythian, bond nor free. But Christ is all and in all.

12 Put ye on therefore, as the elect of God, holy and beloved, the bowels of mercy, benignity, humility, modesty, patience:

13 Bearing with one another and forgiving one another, if any have a complaint against another. Even as the Lord hath forgiven you, so do you also.

14 But above all these things have charity, which is the bond of perfection.

15 And let the peace of Christ rejoice

in your hearts, wherein also you are called in one body. And be ye thankful.

16 Let the word of Christ dwell in you abundantly: in all wisdom, teaching and admonishing one another [4] in psalms, hymns and spiritual canticles, singing in grace in your hearts to God.

17 [5] All whatsoever you do in word or in work, do all in the name of the Lord Jesus Christ, giving thanks to God and the Father by him.

18 [6] Wives, be subject to your husbands, as it behoveth in the Lord.

19 Husbands, love your wives and be not bitter towards them.

20 [7] Children, obey your parents in all things: for this is well pleasing to the Lord.

21 [8] Fathers, provoke not your children to indignation, lest they be discouraged.

22 [9] Servants, obey in all things your masters according to the flesh: not serving to the eye, as pleasing men; but in simplicity of heart, fearing God.

23 Whatsoever you do, do it from the heart: as to the Lord, and not to men:

24 Knowing that you shall receive of the Lord the reward of inheritance. Serve ye the Lord Christ.

25 [10] For he that doth wrong shall receive _for_ that which he hath done wrongfully. And there is no respect of persons with God.

CHAPTER 4

He recommends constant prayer and wisdom. Various salutations.

MASTERS, do to your servants that which is just and equal: knowing that you also have a master in heaven.

2 [1] Be instant in prayer: watching in it with thanksgiving.

3 [2] Praying withal for us also, that God may open unto us a door of speech to speak the mystery of Christ (for which also I am bound):

4 That I may make it manifest as I ought to speak.

5 [3] Walk with wisdom towards them that are without, redeeming the time.

6 Let your speech be always in grace seasoned with salt: that you may know how you ought to answer every man.

7 All the things that concern me, Tychicus, our dearest brother and faithful minister and fellow servant in the Lord, will make known to you.

8 Whom I have sent to you for this same purpose, that he may know the

things that concern you and comfort your hearts:

9 With Onesimus, a most beloved and faithful brother, who is one of you. All things that are done here, they shall make known to you.

10 Aristarchus, my fellow prisoner, saluteth you: and Mark, the cousin german of Barnabas, touching whom you have received commandments. If he come unto you, receive him.

11 And Jesus that is called Justus: who are of the circumcision. These only are my helpers in the kingdom of God: who have been a comfort to me.

12 Epaphras saluteth you, who is one of you, a servant of Christ Jesus, who is always solicitous for you in prayers, that you may stand perfect and full in all the will of God.

13 For I bear him testimony that he hath much labour for you and for them that are at Laodicea and them at Hierapolis.

14 [4] Luke, the most dear physician, saluteth you: and Demas.

15 Salute the brethren who are at Laodicea: and Nymphas and the church that is in his house.

16 And when this epistle shall have been read also in the church of the Laodiceans: and that you read that which is of the Laodiceans.

17 And say to Archippus: Take heed to the ministry which thou hast received in the Lord, that thou fulfil it.

18 The salutation of Paul with my own hand. Be mindful of my bands. Grace be with you. Amen.

[4] Eph. 5, 19. [5] 1 Cor. 10, 31. [6] Eph. 5, 22; 1 Peter, 3, 1. [7] Eph. 6, 1. [8] Eph. 6, 4. [9] Titus, 2, 9; 1 Peter, 2, 18. [10] Rom. 2, 6. CHAP. 4. [1] Luke, 18, 1; 1 Thess. 5, 17. [2] Eph. 6, 19; 2 Thess. 3, 1; Col. 4, 3. [3] Eph. 5, 15. [4] 2 Tim. 4, 11.

CHAP. 4. Ver. 16. _And that you read that which is of the Laodiceans._ What this epistle was is uncertain, and annotators have given different opinions concerning it. Some expound these words of an epistle which St. Paul wrote to the Laodiceans, and is since lost; for that now extant is no more than a collection of sentences out of the other epistles of St. Paul. Therefore it cannot be considered even as a part of that epistle. Others explain that the text means a letter sent to St. Paul by the Laodiceans, which he sends to the Colossians to be read by them. However, this opinion does not seem well founded. Hence it is more probable that St. Paul wrote an epistle from Rome to the Laodiceans, about the same time that he wrote to the Colossians, as he had them both equally at heart, and that he ordered that epistle to be read by the Colossians for their instructions and that, being neighbouring cities, they might communicate to each other what they had received from him: as one epistle might contain some matters not related in the other and would be equally useful for their concern; and more particularly as they were equally disturbed by intruders and false teachers, against which the apostle was anxious to warn them lest they should be infected by their pernicious doctrine.

THE FIRST EPISTLE OF ST. PAUL TO THE

THESSALONIANS

Thessalonica was the capital of Macedonia, in which St. Paul, having preached the Gospel, converted some Jews and a great number of the Gentiles: but the unbelieving Jews, envying his success, raised such a commotion against him that he, and his companion, Sylvanus, were obliged to quit the city. Afterwards he went to Athens, where he heard that the converts in Thessalonica were under a severe persecution ever since his departure; and, lest they should lose their fortitude, he sent Timothy to strengthen and comfort them in their sufferings. In the mean time St. Paul came to Corinth, where he wrote the first Epistle, and also the second to the Thessalonians, both in the same year, being the nineteenth after our Lord's Ascension. These are the first of his Epistles in the order of time.

CHAPTER 1

He gives thanks for the graces bestowed on the Thessalonians.

PAUL and Sylvanus and Timothy to the church of the Thessalonians: in God the Father and in the Lord Jesus Christ.

2 Grace be to you and peace. We give thanks to God always for you all: making a remembrance of you in our prayers without ceasing,

3 Being mindful of the work of your faith and labour and charity: and of the enduring of the hope of our Lord Jesus Christ before God and our Father.

4 Knowing, brethren, beloved of God, your election:

5 For our gospel hath not been unto you in word only, but in power also; and in the Holy Ghost and in much fulness, as you know what manner of men we have been among you for your sakes.

6 And you became followers of us and of the Lord: receiving the word in much tribulation, with joy of the Holy Ghost:

7 So that you were made a pattern to all that believe in Macedonia and in Achaia.

8 For from you was spread abroad the word of the Lord not only in Macedonia and in Achaia but also in every place: your faith which is towards God is gone forth, so that we need not to speak any thing.

9 For they themselves relate of us what manner of entering in we had unto you: and how you turned to God from idols to serve the living and true God

10 And to wait for his Son from

heaven (whom he raised up from the dead), Jesus, who hath delivered us from the wrath to come.

CHAPTER 2

The sincerity of the apostle's preaching the gospel to them and of their receiving it.

FOR yourselves know, brethren our entrance in unto you, that it was not in vain:

2 But having suffered many things before and been shamefully treated, (as you know) at Philippi, [1] we had confidence in our God, to speak unto you the gospel of God in much carefulness.

3 For our exhortation was not of error, nor of uncleanness, nor in deceit.

4 But as we were approved by God that the gospel should be committed to us: even so we speak, not as pleasing men but God, who proveth our hearts.

5 For neither have we used at any time the speech of flattery, as you know: nor taken an occasion of covetousness (God is witness):

6 Nor sought we glory of men, neither of you nor of others.

7 Whereas we might have been burdensome to you, as the apostles of Christ: but we became little ones in the midst of you, as if a nurse should cherish her children:

8 So desirous of you, we would gladly impart unto you not only the gospel of God but also our own souls: because you were become most dear unto us.

9 For you remember, brethren, our labour and toil: [2] working night and day, lest we should be chargeable to any of you, we preached among you the gospel of God.

10 You are witnesses, and God also,

CHAP. 2. [1] Acts, 16, 19. [2] Acts, 20, 24; 1 Cor. 4, 12; 2 Thess. 3, 8.

how holily and justly and without blame we have been to you that have believed:

11 As you know in what manner, entreating and comforting you (as a father doth his children),

12 We testified to every one of you that you would walk worthy of God, who hath called you unto his kingdom and glory.

13 Therefore, we also give thanks to God without ceasing: because, that when you had received of us the word of the hearing of God, you received it not as the word of men, but (as it is indeed) the word of God, who worketh in you that have believed.

14 For you, brethren, are become followers of the churches of God which are in Judea, in Christ Jesus: for you also have suffered the same things from your own countrymen, even as they have from the Jews:

15 Who both killed the Lord Jesus and the prophets, and have persecuted us, and please not God, and are adversaries to all men;

16 Prohibiting us to speak to the Gentiles, that they may be saved, to fill up their sins always: for the wrath of God is come upon them to the end.

17 But we, brethren, being taken away from you for a short time, in sight, not in heart, have hastened the more abundantly to see your face with great desire.

18 For we would have come unto you: I Paul indeed, once and again: but Satan hath hindered us.

19 For what is our hope or joy or crown of glory? Are not you, in the presence of our Lord Jesus Christ at his coming?

20 For you are our glory and joy.

CHAPTER 3

The apostle's concern and love for the Thessalonians.

FOR which cause, forbearing no longer, we thought it good to remain at Athens alone.

2 ¹ And we sent Timothy, our brother and the minister of God in the gospel of Christ, to confirm you and exhort you concerning your faith:

3 That no man should be moved in these tribulations: for yourselves know that we are appointed thereunto.

4 For even when we were with you, we foretold you that we should suffer tribulations: as also it is come to pass, and you know.

5 For this cause also, I, forbearing no longer, sent to know your faith: lest perhaps he that tempteth should have

tempted you; and our labour should be made vain.

6 But now when Timothy came to us from you and related to us your faith and charity, and that you have a good remembrance of us always, desiring to see us as we also to see you:

7 Therefore we were comforted, brethren, in you, in all our necessity and tribulation, by your faith.

8 Because now we live, if you stand in the Lord.

9 For what thanks can we return to God for you, in all the joy wherewith we rejoice for you before our God,

10 Night and day more abundantly praying that we may see your face and may accomplish those things that are wanting to your faith?

11 Now God himself and our Father and our Lord Jesus Christ, direct our way unto you.

12 And may the Lord multiply you and make you abound in charity towards one another and towards all men: as we do also towards you,

13 To confirm your hearts without blame, in holiness, before God and our Father, at the coming of our Lord Jesus Christ, with all his saints. Amen.

CHAPTER 4

He exhorts them to purity and mutual charity. He treats of the resurrection of the dead.

FOR the rest therefore, brethren, we pray and beseech you in the Lord Jesus that, as you have received from us, how you ought to walk and to please God, so also you would walk, that you may abound the more.

2 For you know what precepts I have given to you by the Lord Jesus.

3 ¹ For this is the will of God, your sanctification: That you should abstain from fornication:

4 That every one of you should know how to possess his vessel in sanctification and honour:

5 Not in the passion of lust, like the Gentiles that know not God:

6 And that no man overreach nor circumvent his brother in business: because the Lord is the avenger of all these things, as we have told you before and have testified.

7 For God hath not called us unto uncleanness, but unto sanctification.

8 Therefore, he that despiseth these

CHAP. 3. ¹ Acts, 16, 1. CHAP. 4. ¹ Rom, 12, 2; Eph. 5, 17.

CHAP. 2. Ver. 16. *To fill up their sins.* That is, to fill up the measure of their sins, after which God's justice would punish them. *For the wrath of God is come upon them to the end.* That is, to continue on them to the end.

things, despiseth not man but God, who also hath given his holy Spirit in us.

9 But as touching the charity of brotherhood, we have no need to write to you: [2] for yourselves have learned of God to love one another.

10 For indeed you do it towards all the brethren in all Macedonia. But we entreat you, brethren, that you abound more:

11 And that you use your endeavour to be quiet: and that you do your own business and work with your own hands, as we commanded you: and that you walk honestly towards them that are without: and that you want nothing of any man's.

12 And we will not have you ignorant, brethren, concerning them that are asleep, that you be not sorrowful, even as others who have no hope.

13 For if we believe that Jesus died and rose again: even so them who have slept through Jesus, will God bring with him.

14 For this we say unto you in the word of the Lord, [3] that we who are alive, who remain unto the coming of the Lord, shall not prevent them who have slept.

15 For the Lord himself shall come down from heaven with commandment and with the voice of an archangel and with the trumpet of God: and the dead who are in Christ shall rise first.

16 Then we who are alive, who are left, shall be taken up together with them in the clouds to meet Christ, into the air: and so shall we be always with the Lord.

17 Wherefore, comfort ye one another with these words.

CHAPTER 5

The day of the Lord shall come when least expected. Exhortations to several duties.

BUT of the times and moments, brethren, you need not, that we should write to you:

2 [1] For yourselves know perfectly that the day of the Lord shall so come as a thief in the night.

3 For when they shall say: Peace and security; then shall sudden destruction come upon them, as the pains upon her that is with child. And they shall not escape.

4 But you, brethren, are not in dark-

ness, that that day should overtake you as a thief.

5 For all you are the children of light and children of the day: we are not of the night nor of darkness.

6 Therefore, let us not sleep, as others do: but let us watch, and be sober.

7 For they that sleep, sleep in the night; and they that are drunk, are drunk in the night.

8 But let us, who are of the day, be sober, [2] having on the breast plate of faith and charity and, for a helmet, the hope of salvation.

9 For God hath not appointed us unto wrath: but unto the purchasing of salvation by our Lord Jesus Christ,

10 Who died for us: that, whether we watch or sleep, we may live together with him.

11 For which cause comfort one another and edify one another, as you also do.

12 And we beseech you, brethren, to know them who labour among you and are over you in the Lord and admonish you:

13 That you esteem them more abundantly in charity, for their work's sake. Have peace with them.

14 And we beseech you, brethren, rebuke the unquiet: comfort the feeble minded: support the weak: be patient towards all men.

15 [3] See that none render evil for evil to any man: but ever follow that which is good towards each other and towards all men.

16 Always rejoice.

17 [4] Pray without ceasing.

18 In all things give thanks: for this is the will of God in Christ Jesus concerning you all.

19 Extinguish not the spirit.

20 Despise not prophecies.

21 But prove all things: hold fast that which is good.

22 From all appearance of evil refrain yourselves.

23 And may the God of peace himself sanctify you in all things: that your whole spirit and soul and body may be preserved blameless in the coming of our Lord Jesus Christ.

24 [5] He is faithful who hath called you, who also will do *it*.

25 Brethren, pray for us.

26 Salute all the brethren with a holy kiss.

27 I charge you by the Lord that this epistle be read to all the holy brethren.

28 The grace of our Lord Jesus Christ be with you. Amen.

[2] John, 13, 34; 15, 12, 17; 1 John, 2, 10; 4, 12. [3] 1 Cor. 10, 23. CHAP. 4. [1] 2 Peter, 3, 10; Apoc. 3, 3, 16, 15. [2] Isai. 59, 17; Eph. 6, 14, 17. [3] Prov. 17, 13; 20, 22; Rom. 12, 17; 1 Peter, 3, 9. [4] Ecclus. 18, 22; Luke, 18, 1; Col. 4, 2. [5] 1 Cor. 1, 9.

CHAP. 5. Ver. 14. *The unquiet.* That is, such as are irregular and disorderly.

THE SECOND EPISTLE OF ST. PAUL TO THE
THESSALONIANS

In this Epistle St. Paul admonishes the Thessalonians to be constant in the faith of Christ and not to be terrified by the insinuations of false teachers telling them that the day of judgment was near at hand, as there must come many signs and wonders before it. He bids them to hold firm the traditions received from him, whether by word, or by epistle, and shews them how they may be certain of his letters by the manner he writes.

CHAPTER 1

He gives thanks to God for their faith and constancy and prays for their advancement in all good.

PAUL and Sylvanus and Timothy, to the church of the Thessalonians. In God our Father and the Lord Jesus Christ,

2 Grace unto you: and peace from God our Father and from the Lord Jesus Christ.

3 We are bound to give thanks always to God for you, brethren, as it is fitting, because your faith groweth exceedingly and the charity of every one of you towards each other aboundeth.

4 So that we ourselves also glory in you in the church of God, for your patience and faith, and in all your persecutions and tribulations: which you endure

5 For an example of the just judgment of God, that you may be counted worthy of the kingdom of God, for which also you suffer.

6 Seeing it is a just thing with God to repay tribulation to them that trouble you:

7 And to you who are troubled, rest with us, when the Lord Jesus shall be revealed from heaven with the angels of his power:

8 In a flame of fire, giving vengeance to them who know not God and who obey not the gospel of our Lord Jesus Christ.

9 Who shall suffer eternal punishment in destruction, from the face of the Lord and from the glory of his power:

10 When he shall come to be glorified in his saints and to be made wonderful in all them who have believed; because our testimony was believed upon you in that day.

11 Wherefore also we pray always for you: That our God would make you worthy of his vocation and fulfil all the good pleasure of his goodness and the work of faith in power:

12 That the name of our Lord Jesus may be glorified in you, and you in him, according to the grace of our God and of the Lord Jesus Christ.

CHAPTER 2

The day of the Lord is not to come till the man of sin be revealed. The apostle's traditions are to be observed.

AND we beseech you, brethren, by the coming of our Lord Jesus Christ and of our gathering together unto him:

2 That you be not easily moved from your sense nor be terrified, neither by spirit nor by word nor by epistle, as sent from us, as if the day of the Lord were at hand.

3 ¹ Let no man deceive you by any means: for unless there come a revolt first, and the man of sin be revealed, the son of perdition

4 Who opposeth and is lifted up above all that is called God or that is worshipped, so that he sitteth in the temple of God, shewing himself as if he were God.

5 Remember you not that, when I was yet with you, I told you these things?

CHAP. 2. ¹ Eph. 5, 6.

CHAP. 2. Ver. 3. *A revolt.* This *revolt,* or *falling off,* is generally understood, by the ancient fathers, of a *revolt* from the Roman empire, which was first to be destroyed, before the coming of Antichrist. It may, perhaps, be understood also of a *revolt* of many nations from the Catholic Church; which has, in part, happened already, by the means of Mahomet, Luther, and others, and it may be supposed, will be more general in the days of Antichrist.—*The man of sin.* Here must be meant some particular man, as is evident from the frequent repetition of the Greek article ο *the* man of sin, *the* son of perdition, *the* adversary or opposer ὁ ἀντικείμενος. It agrees to the wicked and great Antichrist, who will come before the end of the world.

Ver. 4. *In the temple.* Either that of Jerusalem which some think he will rebuild; or in some Christian church, which he will pervert to his own worship: as Mahomet has done by the churches of the East.

6 And now you know what withholdeth, that he may be revealed in his time.

7 For the mystery of iniquity already worketh: only that he who now holdeth do hold, until he be taken out of the way.

8 And then that wicked one shall be revealed: [2] whom the Lord Jesus shall kill with the spirit of his mouth and shall destroy with the brightness of his coming: him

9 Whose coming is according to the working of Satan, in all power and signs and lying wonders:

10 And in all seduction of iniquity to them that perish: because they receive not the love of the truth, that they might be saved. Therefore God shall send them the operation of error, to believe lying:

11 That all may be judged who have not believed the truth but have consented to iniquity.

12 But we ought to give thanks to God always for you, brethren, beloved of God, for that God hath chosen you firstfruits unto salvation, in sanctification of the spirit and faith of the truth:

13 Whereunto also he hath called you by our gospel, unto the purchasing of the glory of our Lord Jesus Christ.

14 Therefore, brethren, stand fast: and hold the traditions which you have learned, whether by word or by our epistle.

15 Now our Lord Jesus Christ himself, and God and our Father, who hath loved us and hath given us everlasting consolation and good hope in grace,

16 Exhort your hearts and confirm you in every good work and word.

CHAPTER 3
He begs their prayers and warns them against idleness.

FOR [1] the rest, brethren, pray for us, that the word of God may run

[2] Isai. 11, 4. CHAP. 3. [1] Eph. 6, 19; Col. 4, 3. [2] Acts, 20, 34; 1 Cor. 4, 12; 1 Thess. 2, 9. [3] Gal. 6, 9.

Ver. 10. *God shall send.* That is, God shall suffer them to be deceived by lying wonders and false miracles, in punishment of their not entertaining the love of truth.

Ver. 14. *Traditions.* See here that the unwritten *traditions* of the apostles are no less to be received than their epistles.

CHAP. 3. Ver. 1. *May run.* That is, may spread itself and have free course.

and may be glorified, even as among you:

2 And that we may be delivered from importunate and evil men: for all men have not faith.

3 But God is faithful, who will strengthen and keep you from evil.

4 And we have confidence concerning you in the Lord that the things which we command, you both do and will do.

5 And the Lord direct your hearts, in the charity of God and the patience of Christ.

6 And we charge you, brethren, in the name of our Lord Jesus Christ, that you withdraw yourselves from every brother walking disorderly and not according to the tradition which they have received of us.

7 For yourselves know how you ought to imitate us. For we were not disorderly among you.

8 [2] Neither did we eat any man's bread for nothing: but in labour and in toil we worked night and day, lest we should be chargeable to any of you.

9 Not as if we had not power: but that we might give ourselves a pattern unto you, to imitate us.

10 For also, when we were with you, this we declared to you: that, if any man will not work, neither let him eat.

11 For we have heard there are some among you who walk disorderly: working not at all, but curiously meddling.

12 Now we charge them that are such and beseech them by the Lord Jesus Christ that, working with silence, they would eat their own bread.

13 [3] But you, brethren, be not weary in well doing.

14 And if any man obey not our word by this epistle, note that man and do not keep company with him, that he may be ashamed.

15 Yet do not esteem him as an enemy but admonish him as a brother.

16 Now the Lord of peace himself give you everlasting peace in every place. The Lord be with you all.

17 The salutation of Paul with my own hand: which is the sign in every epistle. So I write.

18 The grace of our Lord Jesus Christ be with you all. Amen.

THE FIRST EPISTLE OF ST. PAUL TO

TIMOTHY

St. Paul writes this Epistle to his beloved Timothy, being then bishop of Ephesus, to instruct him in the duties of a bishop, both in respect to himself and to his charge; and that he ought to be well informed of the good morals of those on whom he was to impose hands: Impose not hands lightly upon any man. He tells him also how he should behave towards his clergy. This Epistle was written about thirty-three years after our Lord's Ascension; but where it was written is uncertain. The more general opinion is, that it was in Macedonia.

CHAPTER 1

He puts Timothy in mind of his charge and blesses God for the mercy he himself had received.

PAUL, an apostle of Jesus Christ, according to the commandment of God our Saviour and of Christ Jesus our hope:

2 ¹ To Timothy, his beloved son in faith. Grace, mercy and peace, from God the Father and from Christ Jesus our Lord.

3 As I desired thee to remain at Ephesus when I went into Macedonia, that thou mightest charge some not to teach otherwise:

4 ² Not to give heed to fables and endless genealogies, which furnish questions rather than the edification of God which is in faith.

5 Now the end of the commandment is charity from a pure heart, and a good conscience, and an unfeigned faith.

6 From which things some, going astray, are turned aside unto vain babbling:

7 Desiring to be teachers of the law: understanding neither the things they say, nor whereof they affirm.

8 ³ But we know that the law is good, if a man use it lawfully.

9 Knowing this: That the law is not made for the just man but for the unjust and disobedient, for the ungodly and for sinners, for the wicked and defiled, for murderers of fathers and murderers of mothers, for manslayers,

10 For fornicators, for them who defile themselves with mankind, for menstealers, for liars, for perjured persons, and whatever other thing is contrary to sound doctrine:

11 Which is according to the gospel of the glory of the blessed God which hath been committed to my trust.

12 I give him thanks who hath strengthened me, *even* to Christ Jesus our Lord, for that he hath counted me faithful, putting me in the ministry:

13 Who before was a blasphemer and a persecutor and contumelious. But I obtained the mercy of God, because I did it ignorantly in unbelief.

14 Now the grace of our Lord hath abounded exceedingly with faith and love, which is in Christ Jesus.

15 A faithful saying and worthy of all acceptation: ⁴ That Christ Jesus came into the world to save sinners, of whom I am the chief.

16 But for this cause have I obtained mercy: that in me first Christ Jesus might shew forth all patience, for the information of them that shall believe in him unto life everlasting.

17 Now to the king of ages, immortal, invisible, the only God, be honour and glory for ever and ever. Amen.

18 This precept, I commend to thee, O son Timothy: according to the prophecies going before on thee, that thou war in them a good warfare,

19 Having faith and a good conscience, which some rejecting have made shipwreck concerning the faith.

20 Of whom is Hymeneus and Alexander, whom I have delivered up to Satan, that they may learn not to blaspheme.

CHAPTER 2

Prayers are to be said for all men, because God wills the salvation of all. Women are not to teach.

I DESIRE therefore, first of all, that supplications, prayers, intercessions and thanksgivings be made for all men:

CHAP. 1. ¹ Acts, 16, 1. ² 1 Tim. 4, 7; 2 Tim. 2, 23; Titus, 3, 9. ³ Rom. 7, 12. ⁴ Matt. 9, 13; Mark, 2, 17.

CHAP. 1. Ver. 9. *The law.* He means, that the just man doth good and avoideth evil, not as *compelled* by the law and merely for fear of the punishment appointed for transgressors; but voluntarily and out of the love of God and virtue, and would do so, though there were no law.

2 For kings and for all that are in high station: that we may lead a quiet and a peaceable life in all piety and chastity.

3 For this is good and acceptable in the sight of God our Saviour,

4 Who will have all men to be saved and to come to the knowledge of the truth.

5 For there is one God: and one mediator of God and men, the man Christ Jesus

6 Who gave himself a redemption for all, a testimony in due times.

7 Whereunto I am appointed a preacher and an apostle (I say the truth, I lie not), a doctor of the Gentiles in faith and truth.

8 I will therefore that men pray in every place, lifting up pure hands, without anger and contention.

9 ¹ In like manner, women also in decent apparel: adorning themselves with modesty and sobriety, not with plaited hair, or gold, or pearls, or costly attire:

10 But, as it becometh women professing godliness, with good works.

11 Let the woman learn in silence with all subjection.

12 ² But I suffer not a woman to teach, nor to use authority over the man: but to be in silence.

13 ³ For Adam was first formed: then Eve.

14 ⁴ And Adam was not seduced: but the woman, being seduced, was in the transgression.

15 Yet she shall be saved through child-bearing: if she continue in faith and love and sanctification with sobriety.

CHAP. 2. ¹ 1 Peter, 3, 3. ² 1 Cor. 14, 34. ³ Gen. 1, 26. ⁴ Gen. 3, 6. CHAP. 3. ¹ Titus, 1, 7. CHAP. 4. ¹ 2 Tim. 3, 1; 2 Peter, 3, 3; Jude, 18.

CHAP. 2. Ver. 5. *One mediator.* Christ is the one and *only mediator of redemption,* who gave himself, as the apostle writes in the following verse, *a redemption* for all. He is also the *only mediator* who stands in need of no other to recommend his petitions to the Father. But this is not against our seeking the prayers and intercessions, as well of the faithful upon earth, as of the saints and angels in heaven, for obtaining mercy, grace and salvation, through Jesus Christ. As St. Paul himself often desired the help of the prayers of the faithful, without any injury to the mediatorship of Jesus Christ.

CHAP. 3. Ver. 2. *Of one wife.* The meaning is, not that every bishop should have a wife (for St. Paul himself had none), but that no one should be admitted to the holy orders of bishop, priest, or deacon, who had been married more than once.

Ver. 6. *A neophyte.* That is, one lately baptized, a young convert.

Ver. 15. *The pillar and ground of the truth.* Therefore the *church of the living God* can never uphold error, nor bring in corruptions, superstition, or idolatry.

CHAPTER 3

What sort of men are to be admitted into the clergy. The church is the pillar of truth.

A FAITHFUL saying: If a man desire the office of a bishop, he desireth a good work.

2 ¹ It behoveth therefore a bishop to be blameless, the husband of one wife, sober, prudent, of good behaviour, chaste, given to hospitality, a teacher,

3 Not given to wine, no striker but modest, not quarrelsome, not covetous: but

4 One that ruleth well his own house, having his children in subjection with all chastity.

5 But if a man know not how to rule his own house, how shall he take care of the church of God?

6 Not a neophyte: lest, being puffed up with pride, he fall into the judgment of the devil.

7 Moreover, he must have a good testimony of them who are without: lest he fall into reproach and the snare of the devil.

8 Deacons in like manner: chaste, not double tongued, not given to much wine, not greedy of filthy lucre:

9 Holding the mystery of faith in a pure conscience.

10 And let these also first be proved: and so let them minister, having no crime.

11 The women in like manner: chaste, not slanderers, but sober, faithful in all things.

12 Let deacons be the husbands of one wife: who rule well their children and their own houses.

13 For they that have ministered well shall purchase to themselves a good degree and much confidence in the faith which is in Christ Jesus.

14 These things I write to thee, hoping that I shall come to thee shortly.

15 But if I tarry long: That thou mayest know how thou oughtest to behave thyself in the house of God, which is the church of the living God, the pillar and ground of the truth.

16 And evidently great is the mystery of godliness, which was manifested in the flesh, was justified in the spirit, appeared unto angels, hath been preached unto the Gentiles, is believed in the world, is taken up in glory.

CHAPTER 4

He warns him against heretics, and exhorts him to the exercise of piety.

NOW the Spirit manifestly saith ¹ that in the last times some shall depart from the faith, giving heed to spirits of error and doctrines of devils,

2 Speaking lies in hypocrisy and having their conscience seared,

3 Forbidding to marry, to abstain from meats, which God hath created to be received with thanksgiving by the faithful and by them that have known the truth.

4 For every creature of God is good, and nothing to be rejected that is received with thanksgiving:

5 For it is sanctified by the word of God and prayer.

6 These things proposing to the brethren, thou shalt be a good minister of Christ Jesus, nourished up in the words of faith and of the good doctrine which thou hast attained unto.

7 ²But avoid foolish and old wives' fables: and exercise thyself unto godliness.

8 For bodily exercise is profitable to little: but godliness is profitable to all things, having promise of the life that now is and of that which is to come.

9 A faithful saying and worthy of all acceptation.

10 For therefore we labour and are reviled, because we hope in the living God, who is the Saviour of all men, especially of the faithful.

11 These things command and teach.

12 Let no man despise thy youth: but be thou an example of the faithful, in word, in conversation, in charity, in faith, in chastity.

13 Till I come, attend unto reading, to exhortation and to doctrine.

14 Neglect not the grace that is in thee: which was given thee by prophecy, with imposition of the hands of the priesthood.

15 Meditate upon these things: be wholly in these things: that thy profiting may be manifest to all.

16 Take heed to thyself and to doctrine: be earnest in them. For in doing this thou shalt both save thyself and them that hear thee.

CHAPTER 5

He gives him lessons concerning widows, and how he is to behave to his clergy.

AN ancient man rebuke not, but entreat him as a father: young men, as brethren:

2 Old women, as mothers: young women, as sisters, in all chastity.

3 Honour widows that are widows indeed.

4 But if any widow have children or grandchildren, let her learn first to govern her own house and to make a return of duty to her parents: for this is acceptable before God.

5 But she that is a widow indeed, and desolate, let her trust in God and continue in supplications and prayers night and day.

6 For she that liveth in pleasures is dead while she is living.

7 And this give in charge, that they may be blameless.

8 But if any man have not care of his own and especially of those of his house, he hath denied the faith and is worse than an infidel.

9 Let a widow be chosen of no less than threescore years of age, who hath been the wife of one husband.

10 Having testimony for her good works, if she have brought up children, if she have received to harbour, if she have washed the saints' feet, if she have ministered to them that suffer tribulation, if she have diligently followed every good work.

11 But the younger widows avoid. For, when they have grown wanton in Christ, they will marry:

12 Having damnation, because they have made void their first faith.

13 And withal being idle they learn to go about from house to house: and are not only idle, but tattlers also and busy bodies, speaking things which they ought not.

14 I will, therefore, that the younger should marry, bear children, be mistresses of families, give no occasion to the adversary to speak evil.

15 For some are already turned aside after Satan.

16 If any of the faithful have widows, let him minister to them, and let not the church be charged: that there may be sufficient for them that are widows indeed.

17 Let the priests that rule well be esteemed worthy of double honour: especially they who labour in the word and doctrine.

18 For the scripture saith: ¹*Thou shalt not muzzle the ox that treadeth out the corn:* and: ²*The labourer is worthy of his reward.*

² 1 Tim. 1, 4; 2 Tim. 2, 23; Titus, 3, 9. CHAP. 5. ¹ Deut. 25, 4; 1 Cor. 9, 9. ² Matt. 10, 10; Luke, 10, 7.

CHAP. 4. Ver. 3. *Forbidding to marry, to abstain from meats.* He speaks of the Gnostics the Marcionites, the Encratites, the Manicheans, and other ancient heretics, who absolutely condemned marriage and the use of all kind of meat; because they pretended that all *flesh* was from an evil principle. Whereas the Church of God, so far from condemning marriage, holds it a holy sacrament and forbids it to none but such as by vow have chosen the better part: and prohibits not the use of any meats whatsoever in proper times and seasons, though she does not judge all kind of diet proper for days of fasting and penance.

CHAP. 5. Ver. 12. *Their first faith.* Their vow, by which they had engaged themselves to Christ,

19 Against a priest receive not an accusation, but under two or three witnesses.

20 Them that sin reprove before all: that the rest also may have fear.

21 I charge thee, before God and Christ Jesus and the elect angels, that thou observe these things without prejudice, doing nothing by declining to either side.

22 Impose not hands lightly upon any man: neither be partaker of other men's sins. Keep thyself chaste.

23 Do not still drink water, but use a little wine for thy stomach's sake and thy frequent infirmities.

24 Some men's sins are manifest, going before to judgment: and some men, they follow after.

25 In like manner also good deeds are manifest: and they that are otherwise cannot be hid.

CHAPTER 6
Duties of servants. The danger of covetousness. Lessons for the rich.

WHOSOEVER are servants under the yoke, let them count their masters worthy of all honour: lest the name of the Lord and *his* doctrine be blasphemed.

2 But they that have believing masters, let them not despise them, because they are brethren: but serve them the rather, because they are faithful and beloved, who are partakers of the benefit. These things teach and exhort.

3 If any man teach otherwise and consent not to the sound words of our Lord Jesus Christ and to that doctrine which is according to godliness,

4 He is proud, knowing nothing, but sick about questions and strifes of words: from which arise envies, contentions, blasphemies, evil suspicions,

5 Conflicts of men corrupted in mind and who are destitute of the truth, supposing gain to be godliness.

6 But godliness with contentment is great gain.

7 [1] For we brought nothing into this

CHAP. 6. [1] Job, 1, 21; Ecclus. 5, 14. [2] Prov. 27, 26. [3] Matt. 27, 11; John, 18, 33, 37. [4] Apoc. 17, 14; 19, 16. [5] John, 1, 18; 1 John, 4, 12. [6] Luke, 12, 21.

world: and certainly we can carry nothing out.

8 [2] But having food and wherewith to be covered, with these we are content.

9 For they that will become rich fall into temptation and into the snare of the devil and into many unprofitable and hurtful desires, which drown men into destruction and perdition.

10 For the desire of money is the root of all evils: which some coveting have erred from the faith and have entangled themselves in many sorrows.

11 But thou, O man of God, fly these things: and pursue justice, godliness, faith, charity, patience, mildness.

12 Fight the good fight of faith. Lay hold on eternal life, whereunto thou art called, and hast confessed a good confession before many witnesses.

13 I charge thee before God who quickeneth all things, and before Christ Jesus who gave testimony [3] under Pontius Pilate, a good confession:

14 That thou keep the commandment without spot, blameless, unto the coming of our Lord Jesus Christ,

15 Which in his times he shall shew, [4] who is the Blessed and only Mighty, the King of kings and Lord of lords:

16 Who only hath immortality and inhabiteth light inaccessible: [5] whom no man hath seen, nor can see: to whom be honour and empire everlasing. Amen.

17 Charge the rich of this world not to be highminded [6] nor to trust in the uncertainty of riches, but in the living God (who giveth us abundantly all things to enjoy):

18 To do good: to be rich in good works: to give easily: to communicate to others:

19 To lay up in store for themselves a good foundation against the time to come, that they may lay hold on the true life.

20 O Timothy, keep that which is committed to thy trust, avoiding the profane novelties of words and oppositions of knowledge falsely so called.

21 Which some promising, have erred concerning the faith. Grace be with thee. Amen.

THE SECOND EPISTLE OF ST. PAUL TO

TIMOTHY

In this Epistle, the Apostle again instructs and admonishes Timothy in what belonged to his office, as in the former; and also warns him to shun the conversation of those who had erred from the truth, describing at the same time their character. He tells him of his approaching death and desires him to come speedily to him. It appears from this circumstance that he wrote this second Epistle in the time of his last imprisonment at Rome and not long before his martyrdom.

CHAPTER 1

He admonishes him to stir up the grace he received by his ordination and not to be discouraged at his sufferings, but to hold firm the sound doctrine of the gospel.

PAUL, an apostle of Jesus Christ, by the will of God, according to the promise of life which is in Christ Jesus:

2 To Timothy, my dearly beloved son. Grace, mercy *and* peace, from God the Father and from Christ Jesus our Lord.

3 I give thanks to God, whom I serve from my forefathers, with a pure conscience, that without ceasing I have a remembrance of thee in my prayers, night and day.

4 Desiring to see thee, being mindful of thy tears, that I may be filled with joy:

5 Calling to mind that faith which is in thee unfeigned, which also dwelt first in thy grandmother Lois and in thy mother Eunice, and I am certain that in thee also.

6 For which cause I admonish thee that thou stir up the grace of God which is in thee by the imposition of my hands.

7 ¹For God hath not given us the spirit of fear: but of power and of love and of sobriety.

8 Be not thou therefore ashamed of the testimony of our Lord, nor of me his prisoner: but labour with the gospel, according to the power of God.

9 Who hath delivered us and called us by his holy calling, ² not according to our own works, but according to his own purpose and grace, which was given us in Christ Jesus before the times of the world:

10 But is now made manifest by the illumination of our Saviour Jesus Christ, who hath destroyed death and hath brought to light life and incorruption by the gospel.

11 Wherefore ³I am appointed a preacher and an apostle and teacher of the Gentiles.

12 For which cause, I also suffer these things: but I am not ashamed. For I know whom I have believed and I am certain that he is able to keep that which I have committed unto him, against that day.

13 Hold the form of sound words which thou hast heard of me: in faith and in the love which is in Christ Jesus.

14 Keep the good thing committed to thy trust by the Holy Ghost who dwelleth in us.

15 Thou knowest this, that all they who are in Asia are turned away from me: of whom are Phigellus and Hermogenes.

16 The Lord give mercy to the ⁴ house of Onesiphorus: because he hath often refreshed me and hath not been ashamed of my chain:

17 But when he was come to Rome, he carefully sought me and found me.

18 The Lord grant unto him to find mercy of the Lord in that day. And in how many things he ministered unto me at Ephesus, thou very well knowest.

CHAPTER 2

He exhorts him to diligence in his office and patience in suffering. The danger of the delusions of heretics.

THOU therefore, my son, be strong in the grace which is in Christ Jesus:

2 And the things which thou hast heard of me by many witnesses, the same commend to faithful men who shall be fit to teach others also.

3 Labour as a good soldier of Christ Jesus.

CHAP. 1. ¹ Rom. 8, 15. ² Titus, 3, 5. ³ 1 Tim. 2, 7. ⁴ 2 Tim. 4, 19.

CHAP. 1. Ver. 9. *Before the times.* That is, the beginning.

Ver. 10. *By the illumination.* That is, by the bright coming and appearing of our Saviour.

4 No man, being a soldier to God, entangleth himself with secular businesses: that he may please him to whom he hath engaged himself.

5 For he also that striveth for the mastery is not crowned, except he strive lawfully.

6 The husbandman that laboureth must first partake of the fruits.

7 Understand what I say: for the Lord will give thee in all things understanding.

8 Be mindful that the Lord Jesus Christ is risen again from the dead, of the seed of David, according to my gospel:

9 Wherein I labour even unto bands, as an evildoer. But the word of God is not bound.

10 Therefore I endure all things for the sake of the elect, that they also may obtain the salvation which is in Christ Jesus, with heavenly glory.

11 A faithful saying: for if we be dead with him, we shall live also with him.

12 If we suffer, we shall also reign with him. ¹ If we deny him, he will also deny us.

13 ² If we believe not, he continueth faithful: he cannot deny himself.

14 Of these things put them in mind, charging them before the Lord. Contend not in words: for it is to no profit, but to the subverting of the hearers.

15 Carefully study to present thyself approved unto God, a workman that needeth not to be ashamed, rightly handling the word of truth.

16 But shun profane and vain babblings: for they grow much towards ungodliness.

17 And their speech spreadeth like a canker: of whom are Hymeneus and Piletus:

18 Who have erred from the truth, saying that the resurrection is past already, and have subverted the faith of some.

19 But the sure foundation of God standeth firm, having this seal: The Lord knoweth who are his; and let every one depart from iniquity who nameth the name of the Lord.

20 But in a great house there are not only vessels of gold and of silver, but also of wood and of earth: and some indeed unto honour, but some unto dishonour.

21 If any man therefore shall cleanse himself from these, he shall be a vessel

CHAP. 2. ¹ Matt. 10, 33; Mark, 8, 38. ² Rom. 3, 3. ³ 1 Tim. 1, 4, 7; Titus, 3, 9. CHAP. 3. ¹ 1 Tim. 4, 1; 2 Peter, 3, 3; Jude, 18. ² Exod. 7, 11. ³ Acts, 14.

CHAP. 3. Ver. 8. Jannes and Mambres. The magicians of king Pharao.

unto honour, sanctified and profitable to the Lord, prepared unto every good work.

22 But flee thou youthful desires: and pursue justice, faith, charity and peace with them that call on the Lord out of a pure heart.

23 ³ And avoid foolish and unlearned questions, knowing that they beget strifes.

24 But the servant of the Lord must not wrangle: but be mild towards all men, apt to teach, patient,

25 With modesty admonishing them that resist the truth: if peradventure God may give them repentance to know the truth;

26 And they may recover themselves from the snares of the devil by whom they are held captive at his will.

CHAPTER 3

The character of heretics of latter days. He exhorts Timothy to constancy. Of the great profit of the knowledge of the scriptures.

KNOW also this, that ¹ in the last days shall come dangerous times.

2 Men shall be lovers of themselves, covetous, haughty, proud, blasphemers, disobedient to parents, ungrateful, wicked,

3 Without affection, without peace, slanderers, incontinent, unmerciful, without kindness,

4 Traitors, stubborn, puffed up, and lovers of pleasures more than of God:

5 Having an appearance indeed of godliness but denying the power thereof. Now these avoid.

6 For of these sort are they who creep into houses and lead captive silly women laden with sins, who are led away with divers desires:

7 Ever learning and never attaining to the knowledge of the truth.

8 Now as ² Jannes and Mambres resisted Moses, so these also resist the truth, men corrupted in mind, reprobate concerning the faith.

9 But they shall proceed no farther: for their folly shall be manifest to all men, as theirs also was.

10 But thou hast fully known my doctrine, manner of life, purpose, faith, longsuffering, love, patience,

11 Persecutions, afflictions: ³ such as came upon me at Antioch, at Iconium and at Lystra: what persecutions I endured. And out of them all the Lord delivered me.

12 And all that will live godly in Christ Jesus shall suffer persecution.

13 But evil men and seducers shall grow worse and worse: erring, and driving into error.

14 But continue thou in those things which thou hast learned and which have been committed to thee. Knowing of whom thou hast learned *them:*

15 And because from thy infancy thou hast known the holy scriptures, which can instruct thee to salvation, by the faith which is in Christ Jesus.

16 ⁴ All scripture, inspired of God, is profitable to teach, to reprove, to correct, to instruct in justice:

17 That the man of God may be perfect, furnished to every good work.

CHAPTER 4

His charge to Timothy. He tells him of his approaching death and desires him to come to him.

I CHARGE thee, before God and Jesus Christ, who shall judge the living and the dead, by his coming and his kingdom:

2 Preach the word: be instant in season, out of season: reprove, entreat, rebuke in all patience and doctrine.

3 For there shall be a time when they will not endure sound doctrine but, according to their own desires, they will heap to themselves teachers, having itching ears:

4 And will indeed turn away their hearing from the truth, but will be turned unto fables.

5 But be thou vigilant: labour in all things: do the work of an evangelist: fulfil thy ministry. Be sober.

For I am even now ready to be sacrificed: and the time of my dissolutions is at hand.

7 I have fought a good fight: I have finished my course: I have kept the faith.

8 As to the rest, there is laid up for me a crown of justice which the Lord the just judge will render to me in that day: and not only to me, but to them also that love his coming. Make haste to come to me quickly.

9 For Demas hath left me, loving this world, and is gone to Thessalonica:

10 Crescens into Galatia, Titus into Dalmatia.

11 ¹ Only Luke is with me. Take Mark and bring him with thee: for he is profitable to me for the ministry.

12 But Tychicus, I have sent to Ephesus.

13 The cloak that I left at Troas, with Carpus, when thou comest, bring with thee: and the books, especially the parchments.

14 Alexander the coppersmith hath done me much evil: the Lord will reward him according to his works:

15 Whom do thou also avoid: for he hath greatly withstood our words.

16 At my first answer, no man stood with me: but all forsook me. May it not be laid to their charge!

17 But the Lord stood by me and strengthened me, that by me the preaching may be accomplished and that all the Gentiles may hear. And I was delivered out of the mouth of the lion.

18 The Lord hath delivered me from every evil work and will preserve me unto his heavenly kingdom. To whom be glory for ever and ever. Amen.

19 Salute Prisca and Aquila ² and the household of Onesiphorus.

20 Erastus remained at Corinth. And Trophimus, I left sick at Miletus.

21 Make haste to come before winter. Eubulus and Pudens and Linus and Claudia and all the brethren, salute thee.

22 The Lord Jesus Christ be with thy spirit. Grace be with you. Amen.

⁴ 2 Peter, 1, 20. CHAP. 4. ¹ Col. 4, 14. ² 2 Tim. 1, 16.

Ver. 16. *All scripture.* Every part of divine scripture is certainly *profitable* for all these ends. But, if we would have the *whole* rule of Christian faith and practice, we must not be content with those Scriptures which Timothy *knew from his infancy,* that is, with the Old Testament alone: nor yet with the New Testament, without taking along with it the traditions of the apostles and the interpretation of the Church, to which the apostles delivered both the book and the true meaning of it.

CHAP. 4. Ver. 5. *An evangelist.* A diligent preacher of the gospel.

THE EPISTLE OF ST. PAUL TO

TITUS

St. Paul, having preached the faith in the island of Crete, he ordained his beloved disciple and companion, Titus, bishop, and left him there to finish the work which he had begun. Afterwards the Apostle, on a journey to Nicopolis, a city of Macedonia, wrote this Epistle to Titus, in which he directs him to ordain bishops and priests for the different cities, shewing him the principal qualities necessary for a bishop. He also gives him particular advice for his own conduct to his flock, exhorting him to hold to strictness of discipline, but seasoned with lenity. It was written about thirty-three years after our Lord's Ascension.

CHAPTER 1

What kind of men he is to ordain priests. Some men are to be sharply rebuked.

PAUL, a servant of God and an apostle of Jesus Christ, according to the faith of the elect of God and the acknowledging of the truth, which is according to godliness:

2 Unto the hope of life everlasting, which God, who lieth not, hath promised before the times of the world:

3 But hath in due times manifested his word in preaching, which is committed to me according to the commandment of God our Saviour:

4 To Titus, my beloved son according to the common faith, grace and peace, from God the Father and from Christ Jesus our Saviour.

5 For this cause I left thee in Crete: that thou shouldest set in order the things that are wanting and shouldest ordain priests in every city, as I also appointed thee:

6 [1] If any be without crime, the husband of one wife, having faithful children, not accused of riot or unruly.

7 For a bishop must be without crime, as the steward of God: not proud, not subject to anger, nor given to wine, no striker, not greedy of filthy lucre:

8 But given to hospitality, gentle, sober, just, holy, continent:

9 Embracing that faithful word which is according to doctrine, that he may be able to exhort in sound doctrine and to convince the gainsayers.

10 For there are also many disobedient, vain talkers and seducers: especially they who are of the circumcision.

11 Who must be reproved, who subvert whole houses, teaching things which they ought not, for filthy lucre's sake.

CHAP. 1. [1] 1 Tim. 3, 2. [2] Rom. 14, 20.
CHAP. 1. Ver. 6. *Of one wife.* (See the note upon 1 Tim. 3, 2.)

12 One of them a prophet of their own, said: *The Cretians are always liars, evil beasts, slothful bellies.*

13 This testimony is true. Wherefore, rebuke them sharply, that they may be sound in the faith:

14 Not giving heed to Jewish fables and commandments of men who turn themselves away from the truth.

15 [2] All things are clean to the clean: but to them that are defiled and to unbelievers, nothing is clean: but both their mind and their conscience are defiled.

16 They profess that they know God: but in ther works they deny *him;* being abominable and incredulous and to every good work reprobate.

CHAPTER 2

How he is to instruct both old and young. The duty of servants. The Christian's rule of life.

BUT speak thou the things that become sound doctrine:

2 That the aged men be sober, chaste, prudent, sound in faith, in love, in patience.

3 The aged women, in like manner, in holy attire, not false accusers, not given to much wine, teaching well:

4 That they may teach the young women to be wise, to love their husbands, to love their children.

5 To be discreet, chaste, sober, having a care of the house, gentle, obedient to their husbands: that the word of God be not blasphemed.

6 Young men, in like manner, exhort that they be sober.

7 In all things shew thyself an example of good works, in doctrine, in integrity, in gravity,

8 The sound word that can not be blamed: that he who is on the contrary part may be afraid, having no evil to say of us.

9 ¹ *Exhort* servants to be obedient to their masters: in all things pleasing, not gainsaying:

10 Not defrauding, but in all things shewing good fidelity, that they may adorn the doctrine of God our Saviour in all things.

11 ² For the grace of God our Saviour hath appeared to all men:

12 Instructing us, that, denying ungodliness and worldly desires, we should live soberly and justly and godly in this world,

13 Looking for the blessed hope and coming of the glory of the great God and our Saviour Jesus Christ.

14 Who gave himself for us, that he might redeem us from all iniquity and might cleanse to himself a people acceptable, a pursuer of good works.

15 These things speak and exhort and rebuke with all authority. Let no man despise thee.

CHAPTER 3

Other instructions and directions for life and doctrine.

ADMONISH them to be subject to princes and powers, to obey at a word, to be ready to every good work.

2 To speak evil of no man, not to be litigious but gentle: shewing all mildness towards all men.

3 For we ourselves also were some time unwise, incredulous, erring, slaves to divers desires and pleasures, living in malice and envy, hateful and hating one another.

4 But when the goodness and kindness of God our Saviour appeared:

5 ¹ Not by the works of justice which we have done, but according to his mercy, he saved us, by the laver of regeneration and renovation of the Holy Ghost.

6 Whom he hath poured forth upon us abundantly, through Jesus Christ our Saviour:

7 That, being justified by his grace, we may be heirs according to hope of life everlasting.

8 It is a faithful saying. And these things I will have thee affirm constantly, that they who believe in God may be careful to excel in good works. These things are good and profitable unto men.

9 ² But avoid foolish questions and genealogies and contentions and strivings about the law. For they are unprofitable and vain.

10 A man that is a heretic, after the first and second admonition, avoid:

11 Knowing that he that is such an one is subverted and sinneth, being condemned by his own judgment.

12 When I shall send to thee Artemas or Tychicus, make haste to come unto me to Nicopolis. For there I have determined to winter.

13 Send forward Zenas the lawyer and Apollo, with care that nothing be wanting to them.

14 And let our men also learn to excel in good works for necessary uses: that they be not unfruitful.

15 All that are with me salute thee. Salute them that love us in the faith. The grace of God be with you all. Amen.

CHAP. 2. ¹ Eph. 6, 5; Col. 7, 22; 1 Peter, 2, 18. ² Titus, 3, 4. CHAP. 3. ¹ 2 Tim. 1, 9. ² 1 Tim. 1, 4; 4, 7; 2 Tim. 2, 23.

CHAP. 3. Ver. 11. *By his own judgment.* Other offenders are judged and cast out of the church by the sentence of the pastors of the same church. Heretics, more unhappy, run out of the church of their own accord, and by doing so give judgment and sentence against their own souls.

THE EPISTLE OF ST. PAUL TO

PHILEMON

Philemon, a noble citizen of Colossa, had a servant named Onesimus, who robbed him and fled to Rome, where he met St. Paul, who was then a prisoner there the first time. The Apostle took compassion on him and received him with tenderness and converted him to the faith; for he was a Gentile before. St. Paul sends him back to his master with this Epistle in his favour: and though he beseeches Philemon to pardon him, yet the Apostle writes with becoming dignity and authority. It contains divers profitable instructions and points out the charity and humanity that masters should have for their servants.

He commends the faith and charity of Philemon and sends back to him his fugitive servant, whom he had converted in prison.

PAUL, a prisoner of Christ Jesus, and Timothy, a brother: to Philemon, our beloved and fellow labourer,

2 And to Appia, our dearest sister, and to Archippus, our fellow soldier, and to the church which is in thy house.

3 Grace to you and peace, from God our Father and from the Lord Jesus Christ.

4 I give thanks to my God, always making a remembrance of thee in my prayers,

5 Hearing of thy charity and faith, which thou hast in the Lord Jesus and towards all the saints:

6 That the communication of thy faith may be made evident in the acknowledgment of every good work that is in you in Christ Jesus.

7 For I have had great joy and consolation in thy charity, because the bowels of the saints have been refreshed by thee, brother.

8 Wherefore, though I have much confidence in Christ Jesus to command thee that which is to the purpose:

9 For charity sake I rather beseech, whereas thou art such a one, as Paul, an old man and now a prisoner also of Jesus Christ.

10 I beseech thee for my son, whom I have begotten in my bands, Onesimus,

11 Who hath been heretofore unprofitable to thee but now is profitable both to me and thee:

12 Whom I have sent back to thee.

And do thou receive him as my own bowels.

13 Whom I would have retained with me, that in thy stead he might have ministered to me in the bands of the gospel.

14 But without thy counsel I would do nothing: that thy good deed might not be as it were of necessity, but voluntary.

15 For perhaps he therefore departed for a season from thee that thou mightest receive him again for ever:

16 Not now as a servant, but instead of a servant, a most dear brother, especially to me. But how much more to thee, both in the flesh and in the Lord?

17 If therefore thou count me a partner, receive him as myself.

18 And if he hath wronged thee in any thing or is in thy debt, put that to my account.

19 I Paul have written it with my own hand: I will repay it: not to say to thee that thou owest me thy own self also.

20 Yea, brother. May I enjoy thee in the Lord! Refresh my bowels in the Lord.

21 Trusting in thy obedience, I have written to thee: knowing that thou wilt also do more than I say.

22 But withal prepare me also a lodging. For I hope that through your prayers I shall be given unto you.

23 There salute thee Epaphras, my fellow prisoner in Christ Jesus:

24 Mark, Aristarchus, Demas and Luke, my fellow labourers.

25 The grace of our Lord Jesus Christ be with your spirit. Amen.

THE EPISTLE OF ST. PAUL TO THE

HEBREWS

St. Paul wrote this Epistle to the Christians in Palestine, the most part of whom being Jews before their conversion, they were called Hebrews. He exhorts them to be thoroughly converted and confirmed in the faith of Christ, clearly shewing them the pre-eminence of Christ's priesthood above the Levitical, and also the excellence of the new law above the old. He commends faith by the example of the ancient fathers: and exhorts them to patience and perseverance and to remain in fraternal charity. It appears from chap. 13 that this Epistle was written in Italy, and probably at Rome, about twenty-nine years after our Lord's Ascension.

CHAPTER 1

God spoke of old by the prophets, but now by his Son, who is incomparably greater than the angels.

GOD, who, at sundry times and in divers manners, spoke in times past to the fathers by the prophets, last of all,

2 In these days, hath spoken to us by his Son, whom he hath appointed heir of all things, by whom also he made the world.

3 ¹ Who being the brightness of his glory and the figure of his substance and upholding all things by the word of his power, making purgation of sins, sitteth on the right hand of the majesty on high:

4 Being made so much better than the angels as he hath inherited a more excellent name than they.

5 For to which of the angels hath he said at any time: ² *Thou art my Son, to-day have I begotten thee?* And again: ³ *I will be to him a Father, and he shall be to me a Son?*

6 And again, when he bringeth in the first begotten into the world, he saith: ⁴ *And let all the angels of God adore him.*

7 And to the angels indeed he saith: ⁵ *He that maketh his angels spirits and his ministers a flame of fire.*

8 But to the Son: ⁶ *Thy throne, O God, is for ever and ever: a sceptre of justice is the sceptre of thy kingdom.*

9 *Thou hast loved justice and hated iniquity: therefore God, thy God, hath anointed thee with the oil of gladness above thy fellows.*

10 And: ⁷ *Thou in the beginning, O Lord, didst found the earth: and the works of thy hands are the heavens.*

11 *They shall perish: but thou shalt continue. And they shall all grow old as a garment.*

12 *And as a vesture shalt thou change them: and they shalt be changed. But thou art the selfsame: and thy years shall not fail.*

13 But to which of the angels said he at any time: ⁸ *Sit on my right hand, until I make thy enemies thy footstool?*

14 Are they not all ministering spirits, sent to minister for them who shall receive the inheritance of salvation?

CHAPTER 2

The transgression of the precepts of the Son of God is far more condemnable than of those of the Old Testament given by angels.

THEREFORE ought we more diligently to observe the things which we have heard, lest perhaps we should let them slip.

2 For if the word spoken by angels became steadfast and every transgression and disobedience received a just recompense of reward:

3 How shall we escape if we neglect so great salvation? Which, having begun to be declared by the Lord, was confirmed unto us by them that heard him.

4 ¹ God also bearing witness by signs and wonders and divers miracles and distributions of the Holy Ghost, according to his own will.

5 For God hath not subjected unto angels the world to come, whereof we speak.

6 But one in a certain place hath testified, saying: ² *What is man, that thou art mindful of him? Or the son of man, that thou visitest him?*

CHAP. 1. ¹ Wisd. 7, 26. ² Ps. 2, 7. ³ 2 Kings, 7, 14. ⁴ Ps. 96, 7. ⁵ Ps. 103, 4. ⁶ Ps. 44, 7. ⁷ Ps. 110, 26. ⁸ Ps. 109, 1; 1 Cor. 15, 25. CHAP. 2. ¹ Mark, 16, 20. ² Ps. 8, 5.

CHAP. 1. Ver. 3. *The figure* (χαραϰτὲϱ). That is, the express image, and most perfect resemblance.—*Making purgation.* That is, having purged away our sins by his passion.

7 *Thou hast made him a little lower than the angels: thou hast crowned him with glory and honour and hast set him over the works of thy hands.*

8 [3] *Thou hast subjected all things under his feet.* For in that he hath subjected all things to him he left nothing not subject to him. But now we see not as yet all things subject to him.

9 [4] But we see Jesus, who was made a little lower than the angels, for the suffering of death, crowned with glory and honour: that, through the grace of God he might taste death for all.

10 For it became him for whom *are* all things and by whom *are* all things, who had brought many children into glory, to perfect the author of their salvation, by *his* passion.

11 For both he that sanctifieth and they who are sanctified *are* all of one. For which cause he is not ashamed to call them brethren, saying:

12 [5] *I will declare thy name to my brethren: in the midst of the church will I praise thee.*

13 And again: [6] *I will put my trust in him.* And again: [7] *Behold I and my children, whom God hath given me.*

14 Therefore because the children are partakers of flesh and blood, he also himself in like manner hath been partaker of the same: that, [8] through death, he might destroy him who had the empire of death, that is to say, the devil:

15 And might deliver them who through the fear of death were all their lifetime subject to servitude.

16 For nowhere doth he take hold of the angels: but of the seed of Abraham he taketh hold.

17 Wherefore, it behoved him in all things to be made like unto his brethren, that he might become a merciful and faithful high priest before God that he might be a propitiation for the sins of the people.

18 For in that wherein he himself hath suffered and been tempted he is able to succour them also that are tempted.

CHAPTER 3

Christ is more excellent than Moses. Wherefore we must adhere to him by faith and obedience.

THEREFORE, holy brethren, partakers of the heavenly vocation,

consider the apostle and high priest of our confession, Jesus:

2 Who is faithful to him that made him, as was also [1] Moses in all his house.

3 For this man was counted worthy of greater glory that Moses, by so much as he that hath built the house hath greater honour than the house.

4 For every house is built by some man: but he that created all things is God.

5 And Moses indeed was faithful in all his house as a servant, for a testimony of those things which were to be said:

6 But Christ, as the Son in his own house: which house are we, if we hold fast the confidence and glory of hope unto the end.

7 Wherefore, as the Holy Ghost saith: [2] *To-day if you shall hear his voice,*

8 *Harden not your hearts, as in the provocation, in the day of temptation in the desert,*

9 *Where your fathers tempted me, proved and saw my works,*

10 *Forty years: for which cause I was offended with this generation. And I said: They always err in heart. And they have not known my ways.*

11 *As I have sworn in my wrath: If they shall enter into my rest.*

12 Take heed, brethren, lest perhaps there be in any of you an evil heart of unbelief, to depart from the living God.

13 But exhort one another every day, whilst it is called *To-day,* that none of you be hardened through the deceitfulness of sin.

14 For we are made partakers of Christ: yet so, if we hold the beginning of his substance firm unto the end.

15 While it is said: *To-day, if you shall hear his voice, harden not your hearts, as in that provocation.*

16 For some who heard did provoke: but not all that came out of Egypt by Moses.

17 And with whom was he offended forty years? Was it not with them that sinned, [3] whose carcasses were overthrown in the desert?

18 And to whom did he swear, that they should not enter into his rest: but to them that were incredulous?

19 And we see that they could not enter in, because of unbelief.

CHAPTER 4

The Christian's rest. We are to enter into it through Jesus Christ.

LET us fear therefore lest, the promise being left of entering into his rest, any of you should be thought to be wanting.

[3] Matt. 28, 18; 1 Cor. 15, 26. [4] Phil. 2, 8. [5] Ps. 21, 23. [6] Ps. 17, 3. [7] Isai. 8, 18. [8] Osee, 13, 14; 1 Cor. 15, 54. CHAP. 3. [1] Num. 12, 7. [2] Ps. 94, 8; Heb. 4, 7. [3] Num. 14, 37.

CHAP. 2. Ver. 10. *Perfect by his passion.* By suffering, Christ was to enter into his glory (Luke 24, 26), which the apostle here calls being made perfect.
Ver. 16. *Nowhere.* That is, he never took upon him the nature of angels, but that of the seed of Abraham.

2 For unto us also it hath been declared in like manner as unto them. But the word of hearing did not profit them, not being mixed with faith of those things they heard.

3 For we, who have believed, shall enter into rest; as he said: [1] *As I have sworn in my wrath: If they shall enter into my rest.* And this indeed when the works from the foundation of the world were finished.

4 For in a certain place he spoke of the seventh day thus: [2] *And God rested the seventh day from all his works.*

5 And in this *place* again: *If they shall enter into my rest.*

6 Seeing then it remaineth that some are to enter into it, and they to whom it was first preached did not enter because of unbelief:

7 Again he limiteth a certain day, saying in David; *To-day,* after so long a time as it is above said: [3] *To-day if you shall hear his voice, harden not your hearts.*

8 For if Jesus had given them rest he would never have afterwards spoken of another day.

9 There remaineth therefore a day of rest for the people of God.

10 For he that is entered into his rest, the same also hath rested from his works, as God did from his.

11 Let us hasten therefore to enter into that rest: lest any man fall into the same example of unbelief

12 For the word of God is living and effectual and more piercing than any two edged sword and reaching unto the division of the soul and the spirit, of the joints also and the marrow: and is a discerner of the thoughts and intents of the heart.

13 [4] Neither is there any creature invisible in his sight: but all things are naked and open to his eyes, to whom our speech is.

14 Having therefore a great high priest that hath passed into the heavens, Jesus the Son of God: let us hold fast our confession.

15 For we have not a high priest who cannot have compassion on our infirmities: but one tempted in all things like as we are, without sin.

16 Let us go therefore with confidence to the throne of grace: that we may obtain mercy and find grace in seasonable aid.

CHAPTER 5

The office of a high priest. Christ is our high priest.

FOR every high priest taken from among men is ordained for men in the things that appertain to God, that

he may offer up gifts and sacrifices for sins:

2 Who can have compassion on them that are ignorant and that err: because he himself also is compassed with infirmity.

3 And therefore he ought, as for the people, so also for himself, to offer for sins.

4 [1] Neither doth any man take the honour to himself, but he that is called by God, as Aaron was.

5 So Christ also did not glorify himself, that he might be made a high priest: but he that said unto him: [2] *Thou art my Son: this day have I begotten thee.*

6 As he saith also in another place: [3] *Thou art a priest for ever, according to the order of Melchisedech.*

7 Who in the days of his flesh, with a strong cry and tears, offering up prayers and supplications to him that was able to save him from death, was heard for his reverence.

8 And whereas indeed he was the Son of God, he learned obedience by the things which he suffered.

9 And being consummated, he became, to all that obey him, the cause of eternal salvation:

10 Called by God a high priest, according to the order of Melchisedech.

11 Of whom we have much to say and hard to be intelligibly uttered: because you are become weak to hear.

12 For whereas for the time you ought to be masters, you have need to be taught again what are the first elements of the words of God: and you are become such as have need of milk and not of strong meat.

13 For every one that is a partaker of milk is unskilful in the word of justice: for he is a little child.

14 But strong meat is for the perfect: for them who by custom have their senses exercised to the discerning of good and evil.

CHAPTER 6

He warns them of the danger of falling by apostasy and exhorts them to patience and perseverance.

WHEREFORE, leaving the word of the beginning of Christ, let us go on to things more perfect: not laying again the foundation of penance from dead works and of faith towards God.

2 Of the doctrine of baptism and im-

CHAP. 4. [1] Ps. 94, 11. [2] Gen. 2, 2. [3] Heb. 3, 7. [4] Ps. 33, 16; Ecclus. 15, 20. CHAP. 5. [1] Exod. 28, 1; 2 Par. 26, 18. [2] Ps. 2, 7. [3] Ps. 109, 4.

CHAP. 4. Ver. 8. *Jesus.* Josue, who in Greek is called Jesus.
CHAP. 6. Ver. 1. *The word of the beginning.* The first rudiments of the Christian doctrine.

position of hands, and of the resurrection of the dead, and of eternal judgment.

3 And this will we do, if God permit.

4 [1] For it is impossible for those who were once illuminated, have tasted also the heavenly gift and were made partakers of the Holy Ghost,

5 Have moreover tasted the good word of God and the powers of the world to come,

6 And are fallen away: to be renewed again to penance, crucifying again to themselves the Son of God and making him a mockery.

7 For the earth, that drinketh in the rain which cometh often upon it and bringeth forth herbs meet for them by whom it is tilled, receiveth blessing from God.

8 But that which bringeth forth thorns and briers is reprobate and very near unto a curse: whose end is to be burnt.

9 But, my dearly beloved, we trust better things of you, and nearer to salvation: though we speak thus.

10 For God is not unjust, that he should forget your work and the love which you have shewn in his name, you who have ministered and do minister to the saints.

11 And we desire that every one of you shew forth the same carefulness to the accomplishing of hope unto the end:

12 That you become not slothful, but followers of them who through faith and patience shall inherit the promises.

13 For God making promises to Abraham, because he had no one greater by whom he might swear, swore by himself,

14 Saying: [2] Unless blessing I shall bless thee and multiplying I shall multiply thee.

15 And so patiently enduring he obtained the promise.

16 For men swear by one greater than themselves: and an oath for confirmation is the end of all their controversy.

17 Wherein God, meaning more abundantly to shew to the heirs of the promise the immutability of his counsel, interposed an oath:

CHAP. 6. [1] Matt. 12, 45; Heb. 10, 26; 2 Peter, 2, 20. [2] Gen. 22, 16. CHAP. 7. [1] Gen. 14, 18. [2] Deut. 18, 3; Jos. 14, 4.

Ver. 4. *It is impossible.* The meaning is, that it is *impossible* for such as have fallen after baptism to be again baptized; and very hard for such as have apostatized from the faith, after having received many graces, to return again to the happy state from which they fell.

CHAP. 7. Ver. 3. *Without father.* Not that he had no father, but that neither his father, nor his pedigree, nor his birth, nor his death, are set down in scripture.

18 That by two immutable things in which it is impossible for God to lie, we may have the strongest comfort, we who have fled for refuge to hold fast the hope set before us.

19 Which we have as an anchor of the soul, sure and firm, and which entereth in even within the veil:

20 Where the forerunner Jesus is entered for us, made a high priest for ever according to the order of Melchisedech.

CHAPTER 7

The priesthood of Christ according to the order of Melchisedech excels the Levitical priesthood and puts an end both to that and to the law.

FOR this Melchisedech *was* king of Salem, priest of the most high God, who met Abraham returning from the slaughter of the kings and blessed him:

2 To whom also Abraham divided the tithes of all: who first indeed by interpretation is king of justice: and then also king of Salem, that is, king of peace:

3 Without father, without mother, without genealogy, having neither beginning of days nor end of life, but likened unto the Son of God, continueth a priest for ever.

4 Now consider how great this man is, to whom also Abraham the patriarch gave tithes out of the principal things.

5 And indeed they that are of the sons of Levi, who receive the priesthood, [2] have commandment to take tithes of the people according to the law, that is to say, of their brethren: though they themselves also came out of the loins of Abraham.

6 But he, whose pedigree is not numbered among them, received tithes of Abraham and blessed him that had the promises.

7 And without all contradiction, that which is less is blessed by the better.

8 And here indeed, men that die receive tithes: but there, he hath witness that he liveth.

9 And (as it may be said) even Levi who received tithes paid tithes in Abraham:

10 For he was yet in the loins of his father when Melchisedech met him.

11 If then perfection was by the Levitical priesthood (for under it the people received the law), what further need was there that another priest should rise according to the order of Melchisedech: and not be called according to the order of Aaron?

12 For the priesthood being translated, it is necessary that a translation also be made of the law.

13 For he of whom these things are spoken is of another tribe, of which no one attended on the altar.

14 For it is evident that our Lord sprung out of Juda: in which tribe Moses spoke nothing concerning priests.

15 And it is yet far more evident: if according to the similitude of Melchisedech there ariseth another priest,

16 Who is made, not according to the law of a carnal commandment, but according to the power of an indissoluble life.

17 For he testifieth: ³ *Thou art a priest for ever according to the order of Melchisedech.*

18 There is indeed a setting aside of the former commandment, because of the weakness and unprofitableness thereof:

19 For the law brought nothing to perfection: but a bringing in of a better hope, by which we draw nigh to God.

20 And inasmuch as it is not without an oath (for the others indeed were made priests without an oath:

21 But this with an oath, by him that said unto him: ⁴ *The Lord hath sworn and he will not repent: Thou art a priest for ever*).

22 By so much is Jesus made a surety of a better testament.

23 And the others indeed were made many priests, because by reason of death they were not suffered to continue:

24 But this, for that he continueth for ever, hath an everlasting priesthood:

25 Whereby he is able also to save for ever them that come to God by him; always living to make intercession for us.

26 For it was fitting that we should have such a high priest, holy, innocent, undefiled, separated from sinners, and made higher than the heavens:

27 Who needeth not daily (as the *other* priests) ⁵ to offer sacrifices, first for his own sins, and then for the people's: for this he did once, in offering himself.

28 For the law maketh men priests, who have infirmity: but the word of the oath (which was since the law) the Son who is perfected for evermore.

CHAPTER 8

More of the excellence of the priesthood of Christ and of the New Testament.

NOW of the things which we have spoken, this is the sum: We have such an high priest who is set on the right hand of the throne of majesty in the heavens,

2 A minister of the holies and of the

true tabernacle, which the Lord hath pitched, and not man.

3 For every high priest is appointed to offer gifts and sacrifices: wherefore it is necessary that he also should have some thing to offer.

4 If then he were on earth, he would not be a priest: seeing that there would be *others* to offer gifts according to the law.

5 Who serve unto the example and shadow of heavenly things. As it was answered to Moses, when he was to finish the tabernacle: ¹ See (saith he) that thou make all things according to the pattern which was shewn thee on the mount.

6 But now he hath obtained a better ministry, by how much also he is a mediator of a better testament which is established on better promises.

7 For if that former had been faultless, there should not indeed a place have been sought for a second.

8 For, finding fault with them, he saith: ² *Behold, the days shall come, saith the Lord: and I will perfect, unto the house of Israel and unto the house of Juda, a new testament:*

9 *Not according to the testament which I made to their fathers, on the day when I took them by the hand to lead them out of the land of Egypt: because they continued not in my testament: and I regarded them not, saith the Lord.*

10 *For this is the testament which I will make to the house of Israel after those days, saith the Lord: I will give my laws into their mind: and in their heart will I write them. And I will be their God: and they shall be my people.*

11 *And they shall not teach every*

³ Ps. 109, 4. ⁴ Ps. 109, 4. ⁵ Lev. 16, 6. CHAP. 8. ¹ Exod. 25, 40; Acts, 7, 44. ² Jer. 31, 31.

Ver. 23. *Many priests.* The apostle notes this difference between the high priests of the law and our high priest, Jesus Christ; that they, being removed by death, made way for their successors: whereas our Lord Jesus is a priest for ever and hath no successors; but liveth and concurreth for ever with his ministers, the priests of the new testament, in all their functions. Also, that no one priest of the law, nor all of them together, could offer that absolute sacrifice of everlasting redemption which our one high priest, Jesus Christ, has offered once, and for ever.

Ver. 25. *Make intercession.* Christ, as man, continually maketh intercession for us, by representing his passion to his Father.

CHAP. 8. Ver. 2. *The holies.* That is, the sanctuary.

Ver. 4. *If then he were on earth.* That is, if he were not of a higher condition than the Levitical order of earthly priests and had not another kind of sacrifice to offer, he should be excluded by them from the priesthood and its functions, which by the law were appropriated to their tribe.

Ver. 5. *Who serve.* The priesthood of the law and its functions were a kind of an example and shadow of what is done by Christ in his Church militant and triumphant, of which the tabernacle was a pattern.

man his neighbour and every man his brother, saying: Know the Lord. For all shall know me, from the least to the greatest of them.

12 Because I will be merciful to their iniquities: and their sins I will remember no more.

13 Now in saying a new, he hath made the former old. And that which decayeth and groweth old is near its end.

CHAPTER 9

The sacrifices of the law were far inferior to that of Christ.

THE former indeed had also justifications of *divine* service and a worldly sanctuary.

2 ¹For there was a tabernacle made the first, wherein were the candlesticks and the table and the setting forth of loaves, which is called the Holy.

3 And after the second veil, the tabernacle which is called the Holy of Holies:

4 Having a golden ² censer and the ark of the testament covered about on every part with gold, in which was a golden pot that had manna and the rod of Aaron that had blossomed and the ³ tables of the testament.

5 And over it were the cherubims of glory overshadowing the propitiatory: of which it is not needful to speak now particularly.

6 Now these things being thus ordered, into the first tabernacle, the priest indeed always entered, accomplishing the offices of sacrifices.

7 But into the second, the high priest alone, ⁴ once a year: not without blood, which he offereth for his own and the people's ignorance:

8 The Holy Ghost signifying this: That the way into the Holies was not yet made manifest, whilst the former tabernacle was yet standing.

9 Which is a parable of the time present: according to which gifts and sacrifices are offered, which cannot, as to the conscience, make him perfect that serveth, only in meats and in drinks,

CHAP. 9. ¹Exod. 26, 1; 36, 8. ²Lev. 16; Num. 16. ³3 Kings, 8, 9; 2 Par. 5, 10. ⁴Exod. 30, 10; Lev. 16, 2. ⁵Lev. 16, 15. ⁶1 Peter, 1, 19; 1 John, 1, 7; Apoc. 1, 5. ⁷Gal. 3, 15. ⁸Exod. 24, 8.

Ver. 11. *They shall not teach.* So great shall be the light and grace of the New Testament, that it shall not be necessary to inculcate to the faithful the belief and knowledge of the true God, for they shall all know him.

Ver. 13. *A new.* Supply *covenant.*

CHAP. 9. Ver. 10. *Of correction.* That is, when Christ should correct and settle all things.

Ver. 12. *Eternal redemption.* By that one sacrifice of his blood, once offered on the cross, Christ our Lord paid and exhibited, once for all, the general price and ransom of all mankind: which no other priest could do.

Ver. 25. *Offer himself often.* Christ shall never more offer himself in sacrifice in that violent, painful and bloody manner, nor can there be any occasion for it: since by that one sacrifice

10 And divers washings and justices of the flesh laid on them until the time of correction.

11 But Christ, being come an high priest of the good things to come, by a greater and more perfect tabernacle, not made with hand, that is, not of this creation:

12 Neither by the blood of goats or of calves, but by his own blood, entered once into the Holies, having obtained eternal redemption.

13 ⁵For if the blood of goats and of oxen and the ashes of an heifer, being sprinkled, sanctify such as are defiled, to the cleansing of the flesh:

14 ⁶How much more shall the blood of Christ, who by the Holy Ghost offered himself unspotted unto God, cleanse our conscience from dead works, to serve the living God?

15 And therefore he is the mediator of the new testament: ⁷that by means of his death for the redemption of those transgressions which were under the former testament, they that are called may receive the promise of eternal inheritance.

16 For where there is a testament the death of the testator must of necessity come in.

17 For a testament is of force after men are dead: otherwise it is as yet of no strength, whilst the testator liveth.

18 Whereupon neither was the first indeed dedicated without blood.

19 For when every commandment of the law had been read by Moses to all the people, he took the blood of calves and goats, with water and scarlet wool and hyssop: and, sprinkled both the book itself and all the people.

20 Saying: ⁸ *This is the blood of the testament which God hath enjoined unto you.*

21 The tabernacle also and all the vessels of the ministry, in like manner, he sprinkled with blood.

22 And almost all things, according to the law, are cleansed with blood: and without shedding of blood there is no remission.

23 It is necessary therefore that the patterns of heavenly things should be cleansed with these: but the heavenly things themselves with better sacrifices than these.

24 For Jesus is not entered into the Holies made with hands, the patterns of the true: but into Heaven itself, that he may appear now in the presence of God for us.

25 Nor yet that he should offer himself often, as the high priest entereth into the Holies every year with the blood of others:

26 For then he ought to have suffered often from the beginning of the world. But now once, at the end of ages, he hath appeared for the destruction of sin by the sacrifice of himself.

27 And as it is appointed unto men once to die, and after this the judgment:

28 [9] So also Christ was offered once to exhaust the sins of many. The second time he shall appear without sin to them that expect him unto salvation.

CHAPTER 10

Because of the insufficiency of the sacrifices of the law, Christ our high priest shed his own blood for us, offering up once for all the sacrifice of our redemption. He exhorts them to perseverance.

FOR the law, having a shadow of the good things to come, not the very image of the things, by the selfsame sacrifices which they offer continually every year, can never make the comers thereunto perfect.

2 For then they would have ceased to be offered: because the worshippers once cleansed should have no conscience of sin any longer.

3 But in them there is made a commemoration of sins every year:

4 For it is impossible that with the blood of oxen and goats sin should be taken away.

5 Wherefore, when he cometh into the world he saith: [1] *Sacrifice and oblation thou wouldst not: but a body thou hast fitted to me.*

6 *Holocausts for sin did not please thee.*

7 *Then said I: Behold I come.* [2] *In the head of the book it is written of me that I should do thy will, O God.*

8 In saying before: *Sacrifices and oblations and holocausts for sin thou wouldest not: neither are they pleasing to thee,* which are offered according to the law.

9 *Then said I: Behold, I come to do thy will, O God:* He taketh away the first, that he may establish that which followeth.

10 In the which will, we are sanctified by the oblation of the body of Jesus Christ once.

11 And every priest indeed standeth daily ministering and often offering the same sacrifices which can never take away sins.

12 But this man, offering one sacrifice for sins, for ever sitteth on the right hand of God,

13 From henceforth expecting [3] until his enemies be made his footstool.

14 For by one oblation he hath perfected for ever them that are sanctified.

15 And the Holy Ghost also doth testify *this* to us. For after that he said:

16 [4] *And this is the testament which I will make unto them after those days,* saith the Lord. *I will give my laws in their hearts and on their minds will I write them:*

17 *And their sins and iniquities I will remember no more.*

18 Now, where there *is* a remission of these, there is no more an oblation for sin.

19 Having therefore, brethren, a confidence in the entering into the holies by the blood of Christ:

20 A new and living way which he hath dedicated for us through the veil, that is to say, his flesh:

21 And a high priest over the house of God:

22 Let us draw near with a true heart, in fulness of faith, having our hearts sprinkled from an evil conscience and our bodies washed with clean water.

23 Let us hold fast the confession of our hope without wavering (for he is faithful that hath promised):

24 And let us consider one another, to provoke unto charity and to good works:

25 Not forsaking our assembly, as some are accustomed: but comforting *one another,* and so much the more as you see the day approaching.

26 [5] For if we sin wilfully after having the knowledge of the truth, there is now left no sacrifice for sins:

27 But a certain dreadful expectation of judgment, and the rage of a fire which shall consume the adversaries.

28 A man making void the law of

[9] Rom. 5, 9; 1 Peter, 3, 18. CHAP. 10. [1] Ps. 39, 7. [2] Ps. 39, 8. [3] Ps. 109, 2; 1 Cor. 15, 25. [4] Jer. 31, 33; Heb. 8, 8. [5] Heb. 6, 4. [6] Deut. 17, 6; Matt. 18, 16; John, 8, 17; 2 Cor. 13, 1.

upon the cross, he has furnished the full ransom, redemption, and remedy for all the sins of the world. But this hinders not that he may offer himself daily in the sacred mysteries in an unbloody manner, for the daily application of that one sacrifice of redemption to our souls.

Ver. 28. *To exhaust.* That is, to empty or draw out to the very bottom, by a plentiful and perfect redemption.

CHAP. 10. Ver. 2. *They would have ceased.* If they had been of themselves perfect to all the intents of redemption and remission, as Christ's death is, there would have been no occasion of so often repeating them: as there is no occasion for Christ's dying any more for our sins.

Ver. 18. *There is no more an oblation for sin.* Where there is a full remission of sins, as in baptism, there is no more occasion for a *sin offering* to be made for such sins already remitted; and as for sins committed afterwards, they can only be remitted in virtue of the one oblation of Christ's death.

Ver. 26. *If we sin wilfully.* He speaks of the sin of wilful apostasy from the known truth, after which, as we cannot be baptized again, we cannot expect to have that abundant remission of sins which Christ purchased by his death, applied to our souls in that ample manner as it is in baptism: but we have rather all manner of reason to look for a dreadful judgment; the more, because apostates from the known truth seldom or never have the grace to return to it.

Moses dieth without any mercy under two [6] or three witnesses:

29 How much more, do you think he deserveth worse punishments, who hath trodden under foot the Son of God and hath esteemed the blood of the testament unclean, by which he was sanctified, and hath offered an affront to the Spirit of grace?

30 For we know him that hath said: [7] *Vengeance belongeth to me, and I will repay. And again: The Lord shall judge his people.*

31 It is a fearful thing to fall into the hands of the living God.

32 But call to mind the former days, wherein, being illuminated you endured a great fight of afflictions.

33 And on the one hand indeed, by reproaches and tribulations, were made a gazingstock: and on the other, became companions of them that were used in such sort.

34 For you both had compassion on them that were in bands and took with joy the being stripped of your own goods, knowing that you have a better and a lasting substance.

35 Do not therefore lose your confidence which hath a great reward.

36 For patience is necessary for you: that, doing the will of God, you may receive the promise.

37 For yet a little and a very little while, and he that is to come will come and will not delay.

38 [8] But my just man liveth by faith: but if he withdraw himself, he shall not please my soul.

39 But we are not the children of withdrawing unto perdition, but of faith to the saving of the soul.

CHAPTER 11

What faith is. Its wonderful fruits and efficacy demonstrated in the fathers.

NOW, faith is the substance of things to be hoped for, the evidence of things that appear not.

2 For by this the ancients obtained a testimony.

3 [1] By faith we understand that the world was framed by the word of God: that from invisible things visible things might be made.

4 [2] By faith Abel offered to God a sacrifice exceeding that of Cain, [3] by

which he obtained a testimony that he was just, God giving testimony to his gifts. And by it he being dead yet speaketh.

5 [4] By faith Henoch was translated that he should not see death: and he was not found because God had translated him. For before his translation he had testimony that he pleased God.

6 But without faith it is impossible to please God. For he that cometh to God must believe that he is: and is a rewarder to them that seek him.

7 [5] By faith Noe, having received an answer concerning those things which as yet were not seen, moved with fear, framed the ark for the saving of his house: by the which he condemned the world and was instituted heir of the justice which is by faith.

8 [6] By faith he that is called Abraham obeyed to go out into a place which he was to receive for an inheritance. And he went out, not knowing whither he went.

9 By faith he abode in the land of promise, as in a strange country, dwelling in cottages, with Isaac and Jacob, the co-heirs of the same promise:

10 For he looked for a city that hath foundations: whose builder and maker is God.

11 [7] By faith also Sara herself, being barren, received strength to conceive seed, even past the time of age: because she believed that he was faithful who had promised,

12 For which cause there sprung even from one (and him as good as dead) as the stars of heaven in multitude and as the sand which is by the sea shore innumerable.

13 All these died according to faith, not having received the promises but beholding them afar off and saluting them and confessing that they are pilgrims and strangers on the earth.

14 For they that say these things do signify that they seek a country.

15 And truly, if they had been mindful of that from whence they came out, they had doubtless time to return.

16 But now they desire a better, that is to say, a heavenly country. Therefore, God is not ashamed to be called their God: for he hath prepared for them a city.

17 [8] By faith Abraham, when he was tried, offered Isaac: and he that had received the promises offered up his only begotten son,

18 (To whom it was said: [9] *In Isaac shall thy seed be called:*)

19 Accounting that God is able to raise up even from the dead. Whereupon also he received him for a parable.

---

[7] Deut. 32, 35; Rom. 12, 19. [8] Hab. 2, 4; Rom. 1, 17; Gal. 3, 11. CHAP. 11. [1] Gen. 1, 4. [2] Gen. 4, 4. [3] Matt. 23, 35. [4] Gen. 5, 24; Ecclus. 44, 16. [5] Gen. 6, 14; Ecclus. 44, 17. [6] Gen. 12, 1. [7] Gen. 17, 19. [8] Gen. 22, 1; Ecclus. 44, 21. [9] Gen. 21, 12; Rom. 9, 7.

CHAP. 11. Ver. 8. *He that is called Abraham.* Or,. Abraham being called.
Ver. 19. *For a parable.* That is, as a *figure* of Christ, slain and coming to life again.

20 [10] By faith also of things to come, Isaac blessed Jacob and Esau.

21 [11] By faith Jacob, dying, blessed each of the sons of Joseph [12] and adored the top of his rod.

22 [13] By faith Joseph, when he was dying, made mention of the going out of the children of Israel and gave commandment concerning his bones.

23 [14] By faith Moses, when he was born, was hid three months by his parents: because they saw he was a comely babe. [15] And they feared not the king's edict.

24 [16] By faith Moses, when he was grown up, denied himself to be the son of Pharao's daughter:

25 Rather choosing to be afflicted with the people of God than to have the pleasure of sin for a time:

26 Esteeming the reproach of Christ greater riches than the treasure of the Egyptians. For he looked unto the reward.

27 By faith he left Egypt, not fearing the fierceness of the king. For he endured, as seeing him that is invisible.

28 [17] By faith he celebrated the pasch and the shedding of the blood: that he who destroyed the firstborn might not touch them.

29 [18] By faith they passed through the Red Sea, as by dry land: which the Egyptians attempting, were swallowed up.

30 [19] By faith the walls of Jericho fell down, by the going round them seven days.

31 [20] By faith Rahab the harlot perished not with the unbelievers, receiving the spies with peace.

32 And what shall I yet say? For the time would fail me to tell of Gedeon, Barac, Samson, Jephthe, David, Samuel, and the prophets:

33 Who by faith conquered kingdoms, wrought justice, obtained promises, stopped the mouths of lions,

34 Quenched the violence of fire, escaped the edge of the sword, recovered strength from weakness, became valiant in battle, put to flight the armies of foreigners.

35 Women received their dead raised to life again. But others were racked, not accepting deliverance, that they might find a better resurrection.

36 And others had trial of mockeries and stripes: moreover also of bands and prisons.

37 They were stoned, they were cut asunder, they were tempted, they were put to death by the sword, they wandered about in sheepskins, in goatskins, being in want, distressed, afflicted:

38 Of whom the world was not worthy: wandering in deserts, in mountains and in dens and in caves of the earth.

39 And all these, being approved by the testimony of faith, received not the promise:

40 God providing some better thing for us, that they should not be perfected without us.

CHAPTER 12

Exhortation to constancy under their crosses. The danger of abusing the graces of the New Testament.

AND therefore we also having so great a cloud of witnesses over our head, [1] laying aside every weight and sin which surrounds us, let us run by patience to the fight proposed to us:

2 Looking on Jesus, the author and finisher of faith, who, having joy set before him, endured the cross, despising the shame, and now sitteth on the right hand of the throne of God.

3 For think diligently upon him that endured such opposition from sinners against himself: that you be not wearied, fainting in your minds.

4 For you have not yet resisted unto blood, striving against sin.

5 And you have forgotten the consolation which speaketh to you, as unto children, saying: [2] *My son, neglect not the discipline of the Lord: neither be thou wearied whilst thou art rebuked by him.*

6 *For whom the Lord loveth, he chastiseth: and he scourgeth every son whom he receiveth.*

7 Persevere under discipline. God dealeth with you as with his sons. For what son is there, whom the father doth not correct?

8 But if you be without chastisement, whereof all are made partakers, then are you bastards and not sons.

9 Moreover, we have had fathers of our flesh for instructors, and we reverenced them. Shall we not much more obey the Father of spirits and live?

[10] Gen. 27, 27, 39. [11] Gen. 48, 15. [12] Gen. 47, 31. [13] Gen. 50, 23. [14] Exod. 2, 2. [15] Exod. 1, 17. [16] Exod. 2, 11. [17] Exod. 12, 21. [18] Exod. 14, 22. [19] Jos. 6, 20. [20] Jos. 2, 3; James, 2, 25. CHAP. 12. [1] Rom. 6, 4; Eph. 4, 22; Col. 3, 8; 1 Peter, 2, 1; 4, 2. [2] Prov. 3, 11; Apoc. 3, 19.

Ver. 21. *Adored the top of his rod.* The apostle here follows the ancient Greek Bible of the seventy interpreters (which translates in this manner, Gen. 47, 31), and alleges this fact of Jacob, in paying a relative honour and veneration to the top of the rod or sceptre of Joseph, as to a figure of Christ's sceptre and kingdom, as an instance and argument of his faith. But some translators, who are no friends to this relative honour, have corrupted the text, by translating it: *he worshipped, leaning upon the top of his staff*, as if this circumstance of James leaning upon his staff were any argument of Jacob's faith or worthy the being thus particularly taken notice of by the Holy Ghost.

10 And they indeed for a few days, according to their own pleasure, instructed us: but he, for our profit, that we might receive his sanctification.

11 Now all chastisement for the present indeed seemeth not to bring with it joy but sorrow: but afterwards it will yield to them that are exercised by it the most peaceable fruit of justice.

12 Wherefore, lift up the hands which hang down and the feeble knees:

13 And make straight steps with your feet: that no one, halting, may go out of the way; but rather be healed.

14 [3] Follow peace with all men and holiness: without which no man shall see God.

15 Looking diligently, lest any man be wanting to the grace of God: lest any root of bitterness springing up do hinder and by it many be defiled:

16 Lest there be any fornicator or profane person, [4] as Esau who for one mess sold his first birthright.

17 For know ye that [5] afterwards, when he desired to inherit the benediction, he was rejected. For he found no place of repentance, although with tears he had sought it.

18 [6] For you are not come to a mountain that might be touched and a burning fire and a whirlwind and darkness and storm

19 And the sound of a trumpet and the voice of words, which they that heard excused themselves, that the word might not be spoken to them.

20 For they did not endure that which was said: [7] And if so much as a beast shall touch the mount, it shall be stoned.

21 And so terrible was that which was seen, Moses said: I am frighted and tremble.

22 But you are come to Mount Sion and to the city of the living God, the heavenly Jerusalem, and to the company of many thousands of angels,

23 And to the church of the firstborn who are written in the heavens, and to God the judge of all, and to the spirits of the just made perfect,

24 And to Jesus the mediator of the new testament, and to the sprinkling of blood which speaketh better than that of Abel.

25 See that you refuse him not that speaketh. For if they escaped not who refused him that spoke upon earth, much more shall not we that turn away from him that speaketh to us from heaven.

26 Whose voice then moved the earth. But now he promiseth, saying: [8] Yet once more: and I will move, not only the earth, but heaven also.

27 And in that he saith: Yet once more, he signifieth the translation of the moveable things as made, that those things may remain which are immoveable.

28 Therefore, receiving an immoveable kingdom, we have grace: whereby let us serve, pleasing God, with fear and reverence.

29 [9] For our God is a consuming fire.

CHAPTER 13

Divers admonitions and exhortations.

LET the charity of the brotherhood abide in you.

2 [1] And hospitality do not forget; for by this some, [2] being not aware of it, have entertained angels.

3 Remember them that are in bands, as if you were bound with them: and them that labour, as being yourselves also in the body.

4 Marriage honourable in all, and the bed undefiled. For fornicators and adulterers God will judge.

5 Let your manners be without covetousness, contented with such things as you have. For he hath said: [3] I will not leave thee: neither will I forsake thee.

6 So that we may confidently say: [4] The Lord is my helper: I will not fear what man shall do to me.

7 Remember your prelates who have spoken the word of God to you: whose faith follow, considering the end of their conversation,

8 Jesus Christ, yesterday, and to-day: and the same for ever.

9 Be not led away with various and strange doctrines. For it is best that the heart be established with grace, not with meats: which have not profited those that walk in them.

10 We have an altar whereof they have no power to eat who serve the tabernacle.

11 [5] For the bodies of those beasts whose blood is brought into the holies

[3] Rom. 12, 18. [4] Gen. 25, 33. [5] Gen. 27, 38.
[6] Exod. 19, 12; 20, 21. [7] Exod. 19, 13. [8] Agg. 2, 7.
[9] Deut. 4, 24. CHAP. 13. [1] Rom. 12, 13; 1 Peter.
4, 9. [2] Gen. 18, 3; 19, 2. [3] Jos. 1, 5. [4] Ps. 117, 6.
[5] Lev. 16, 27.

CHAP. 12. Ver. 17. *He found.* That is, he found no way to bring his father to repent or change his mind, with relation to his having given the blessing to his younger brother Jacob.

CHAP. 13. Ver. 4. Or, *Let marriage be honourable in all.* That is, in *all things* belonging to the marriage state. This is a warning to married people, not to abuse the sanctity of their state, by any liberties or irregularities contrary thereunto. Now it does not follow from this text that all persons are obliged to marry, even if the word *omnibus* were rendered, *in all persons,* instead of *in all things:* for if it was a precept, St. Paul himself would have transgressed it, as he never married. Moreover, those who have already made a vow to God to lead a single life, should they attempt to marry, they would incur their own damnation (1 Tim. 5, 12).

by the high priest for sin are burned without the camp.

12 Wherefore Jesus also, that he might sanctify the people by his own blood, suffered without the gate.

13 Let us go forth therefore to him without the camp, bearing his reproach.

14 [6] For, we have not here a lasting city: but we seek one that is to come.

15 By him therefore let us offer the sacrifice of praise always to God, that is to say, the fruit of lips confessing to his name.

16 And do not forget to do good and to impart: for by such sacrifices God's favour is obtained.

17 Obey your prelates and be subject to them. For they watch as being to render an account of your souls: that they may do this with joy and not with grief. For this is not expedient for you.

18 Pray for us. For we trust we have a good conscience, being willing to behave ourselves well in all things.

19 And I beseech you the more to do this, that I may be restored to you the sooner.

20 And may the God of peace, who brought again from the dead the great pastor of the sheep, our Lord Jesus Christ, in the blood of the everlasting testament,

21 Fit you in all goodness, that you may do his will: doing in you that which is well pleasing in his sight, through Jesus Christ, to whom is glory for ever and ever. Amen.

22 And I beseech you, brethren, that you suffer *this* word of consolation. For I have written to you in a few words.

23 Know ye that our brother Timothy is set at liberty: with whom (if he come shortly) I will see you.

24 Salute all your prelates and all the saints. The brethren from Italy salute you.

25 Grace be with you all. Amen.

THE CATHOLIC EPISTLE OF
ST. JAMES THE APOSTLE

This Epistle is called Catholic or Universal, as formerly were also the two Epistles of St. Peter, the first of St. John and that of St. Jude, because they were not written to any peculiar people or particular person, but to the faithful in general. It was written by the apostle St. James, called the Less, who was also called the brother of our Lord, being his kinsman (for cousins german with the Hebrews were called brothers). He was the first Bishop of Jerusalem. In this Epistle are set forth many precepts appertaining to faith and morals; and particularly, that faith without good works will not save a man and that true wisdom is given only from above. In the fifth chapter he publishes the sacrament of anointing the sick. It was written a short time before his martyrdom, about twenty-eight years after our Lord's Ascension.

CHAPTER 1

The benefit of tribulations. Prayer with faith. God is the author of all good, but not of evil. We must be slow to anger and not hearers only, but doers of the word. Of bridling the tongue and of pure religion.

JAMES, the servant of God and of our Lord Jesus Christ, to the twelve tribes which are scattered abroad, greeting.

2 My brethren, count it all joy, when you shall fall into divers temptations:

3 [1] Knowing that the trying of your faith worketh patience

4 And patience hath a perfect work: that you may be perfect and entire, failing in nothing.

5 But if any of you want wisdom, let him ask of God who giveth to all men abundantly and upbraideth not. And it shall be given him.

6 [2] But let him ask in faith, nothing wavering. For he that wavereth is like a wave of the sea, which is moved and carried about by the wind.

7 Therefore let not that man think that he shall receive any thing of the Lord.

8 A double minded man is inconstant in all his ways.

[6] Mich. 2, 10. CHAP. 1. [1] Rom. 5, 3. [2] Matt. 7, 7; 21, 22; Mark, 11, 24; Luke, 11, 9; John, 14, 13, 16.

Ver. 13. *Let us go forth therefore to him without the camp, bearing his reproach.* That is, bearing his cross. It is an exhortation to them to be willing to suffer with Christ, reproaches, persecutions and even death, if they desire to partake of the benefit of his suffering for man's redemption.

CHAP. 1. Ver. 2. *Into divers temptations.* The word *temptation,* in this epistle, is sometimes taken for trials by afflictions or persecutions, as in this place: at other times, it is to be understood, tempting, enticing, or drawing others into sin.

9 But let the brother of low condition glory in his exaltation:

10 And the rich, in his being low; [3] because as the flower of the grass shall he pass away.

11 For the sun rose with a burning heat and parched the grass: and the flower thereof fell off, and the beauty of the shape thereof perished. So also shall the rich man fade away in his ways.

12 [4] Blessed is the man that endureth temptation: for, when he hath been proved, he shall receive the crown of life which God hath promised to them that love him.

13 Let no man, when he is tempted, say that he is tempted by God. For God is not a tempter of evils: and he tempteth no man.

14 But every man is tempted by his own concupiscence, being drawn away and allured.

15 Then, when concupiscence hath conceived, it bringeth forth sin. But sin, when it is completed, begetteth death.

16 Do not err, therefore, my dearest brethren.

17 Every best gift and every perfect gift is from above, coming down from the Father of lights, with whom there is no change nor shadow of alteration.

18 For of his own will hath he begotten us by the word of truth, that we might be some beginning of his creature.

19 You know, my dearest brethren. [5] And let every man be swift to hear, but slow to speak and slow to anger.

20 For the anger of man worketh not the justice of God.

21 Wherefore, casting away all uncleanness and abundance of naughtiness, with meekness receive the ingrafted word, which is able to save your souls.

22 [6] But be ye doers of the word and not hearers only, deceiving your own selves.

23 For if a man be a hearer of the word and not a doer, he shall be compared to a man beholding his own countenance in a glass.

24 For he beheld himself and went his way and presently forgot what manner of man he was.

25 But he that hath looked into the perfect law of liberty and hath continued therein, not becoming a forgetful hearer but a doer of the work: this man shall be blessed in his deed.

26 And if any man think himself to be religious, not bridling his tongue but deceiving his own heart, this man's religion is vain.

27 Religion clean and undefiled before God and the Father is this: to visit the fatherless and widows in their tribulation and to keep one's self unspotted from this world.

CHAPTER 2

Against respect of persons. The danger of transgressing one point of the law. Faith is dead without works.

MY [1] brethren, have not the faith of our Lord Jesus Christ of glory, with respect of persons.

2 For if there shall come into your assembly a man having a golden ring, in fine apparel; and there shall come in also a poor man in mean attire:

3 And you have respect to him that is clothed with the fine apparel and shall say to him: Sit thou here well; but say to the poor man: Stand thou there, or: Sit under my footstool:

4 Do you not judge within yourselves, and are become judges of unjust thoughts?

5 Hearken, my dearest brethren: Hath not God chosen the poor in this world, rich in faith and heirs of the kingdom which God hath promised to them that love him?

6 But you have dishonoured the poor man. Do not the rich oppress you by might? And do not they draw you before the judgment seats?

7 Do not they blaspheme the good name that is invoked upon you?

8 If then you fulfil the royal law, according to the scriptures: [2] *Thou shalt love thy neighbour as thyself;* you do well.

9 [3] But if you have respect to persons, you commit sin, being reproved by the law as transgressors.

10 [4] And whosoever shall keep the whole law, but offend in one *point,* is become guilty of all.

3 Ecclus. 14, 18; Isai. 40, 6; 1 Peter, 1, 24. 4 Job, 5, 17. 5 Prov. 17, 27. 6 Matt. 7, 21, 24; Rom. 2, 13. CHAP. 2. 1 Lev. 19, 15; Deut. 1, 17; 16, 19; Prov. 24, 23; Ecclus. 42, 1. 2 Lev. 19, 18; Matt. 22, 39; Mark, 12, 31; Rom. 13, 9; Gal. 5, 14. 3 Lev. 19, 15; James, 2, 1. 4 Deut. 1, 18; Matt. 5, 19.

Ver. 18. *Some beginning.* That is, a kind of first fruits of his creatures.

CHAP. 2. Ver. 1. *With respect of persons.* The meaning is that in matters relating to faith, the administering of the sacraments and other spiritual functions in God's Church, there should be no *respect of persons;* but that the souls of the poor should be as much regarded as those of the rich (see Deut. 1, 17).

Ver. 10. *Guilty of all.* That is, he becomes a transgressor of the law in such a manner that the observing of all other points will not avail him to salvation; for he despises the lawgiver and breaks through the great and general commandment of charity, even by one mortal sin. For all the precepts of the law are to be considered as one total and entire law, and as it were a chain of precepts, where, by breaking one link of this chain, the whole chain is broken, or the integrity of the law consisting of a collection of precepts. A sinner, therefore, by a grievous offence against any one precept, incurs eternal punishment; yet the punishment in hell shall be become guilty of all.

11 For he that said: *Thou shalt not commit adultery*, said also: *Thou shalt not kill*. Now if thou do not commit adultery, but shalt kill, thou art become a transgressor of the law.

12 So speak ye and so do, as being to be judged by the law of liberty.

13 For judgment without mercy to him that hath not done mercy. And mercy exalteth itself above judgment.

14 What shall it profit, my brethren, if a man say he hath faith, but hath not works? Shall faith be able to save him?

15 [5] And if a brother or sister be naked and want daily food:

16 And one of you say to them: Go in peace, be ye warmed and filled; yet give them not those things that are necessary for the body, what shall it profit?

17 So faith also, if it have not works, is dead in itself.

18 But some man will say: Thou hast faith, and I have works. Shew me thy faith without works; and I will shew thee, by works, my faith.

19 Thou believest that there is one God. Thou dost well: the devils also believe and tremble.

20 But wilt thou know, O vain man, that faith without works is dead?

21 [6] Was not Abraham our father justified by works, offering up Isaac his son upon the altar?

22 Seest thou that faith did cooperate with his works and by works faith was made perfect?

23 And the scripture was fulfilled. saying: [7] *Abraham believed God, and it was reputed to him to justice, and he was called the friend of God.*

24 Do you see that by works a man is justified, and not by faith only?

25 [8] And in like manner also Rahab the harlot, was not she justified by works, receiving the messengers and sending them out another way?

26 For even as the body without the spirit is dead: so also faith without works is dead.

CHAPTER 3

Of the evils of the tongue. Of the difference between the earthly and heavenly wisdom.

BE [1] ye not many masters, my brethren, knowing that you receive the greater judgment.

2 For in many things we all offend. If any man offend not in word, the same is a perfect man. He is able also with a bridle to lead about the whole body.

3 For if we put bits into the mouths of horses, that they may obey us: and we turn about their whole body.

4 Behold also ships, whereas they are great and are driven by strong winds, yet are they turned about with a small helm, whithersoever the force of the governor willeth.

5 Even so the tongue is indeed a little member and boasteth great things. Behold how small a fire kindleth a great wood.

6 And the tongue is a fire, a world of iniquity. The tongue is placed among our members, which defileth the whole body and inflameth the wheel of our nativity, being set on fire by hell.

7 For every nature of beasts and of birds and of serpents and of the rest is tamed and hath been tamed, by the nature of man.

8 But the tongue no man can tame, an unquiet evil, full of deadly poison.

9 By it we bless God and the Father: and by it we curse men who are made after the likeness of God.

10 Out of the same mouth proceedeth blessing and cursing. My brethren, these things ought not so to be.

11 Doth a fountain send forth, out of the same hole, sweet and bitter water?

12 Can the fig tree, my brethren, bear grapes? Or the vine, figs? So neither can the salt water yield sweet.

13 Who is a wise man and endued with knowledge, among you? Let him shew, by a good conversation, his work in the meekness of wisdom.

14 But if you have bitter zeal, and there be contentions in your hearts: glory not and be not liars against the truth.

15 For this is not wisdom, descending from above: but earthly, sensual, devilish.

16 For where envying and contention is: there is inconstancy and every evil work.

17 But the wisdom that is from above, first indeed is chaste, then peaceable, modest, easy to be persuaded, consenting to the good, full of mercy and good fruits, without judging, without dissimulation.

18 And the fruit of justice is sown in peace, to them that make peace.

CHAPTER 4

The evils that flow from yielding to concupiscence and being friends to this world. Admonitions against pride, detraction and the like.

FROM whence are wars and contentions among you? Are they

[5] 1 John, 3, 17. [6] Gen. 22, 9. [7] Gen. 15, 6; Rom. 4, 3; Gal. 3, 6. [8] Jos. 2, 4; Heb. 11, 31. CHAP. 3. [1] Matt. 23, 8.

greater for those who have been greater sinners, as a greater reward shall be for those in heaven who have lived with greater sanctity and perfection.

not hence, from your concupiscences, which war in your members?

2 You covet, and have not: you kill and envy, and cannot obtain. You contend and war, and you have not: because you ask not.

3 You ask and receive not: because you ask amiss, that you may consume it on your concupiscences.

4 Adulterers, know you not that the friendship of this world is the enemy of God. Whosoever therefore will be a friend of this world becometh an enemy of God.

5 Or do you think that the scripture saith in vain: *To envy doth the spirit covet which dwelleth in you?*

6 But he giveth greater grace. Wherefore he saith: [1] *God resisteth the proud and giveth grace to the humble.*

7 Be subject therefore to God. But resist the devil: and he will fly from you.

8 Draw nigh to God: and he will draw nigh to you. Cleanse your hands, ye sinners, and purify your hearts, ye double minded.

9 Be afflicted and mourn and weep: let your laughter be turned into mourning and your joy into sorrow.

10 Be humbled in the sight of the Lord: and he will exalt you.

11 Detract not one another, my brethren. He that detracteth his brother, or he that judgeth his brother, detracteth the law and judgeth the law. But if thou judge the law, thou art not a doer of the law, but a judge.

12 There is one lawgiver and judge, that is able to destroy and to deliver.

13 [2] But who art thou that judgest thy neighbour? Behold, now you that say: To-day or to-morrow we will go into such a city, and there we will spend a year and will traffic and make our gain.

14 Whereas you know not what shall be on the morrow.

15 For what is your life? It is a vapour which appeareth for a little while and afterwards shall vanish away. For that you should say: If the Lord will, and, If we shall live, we will do this or that.

16 But now you rejoice in your arrogancies. All such rejoicing is wicked.

17 To him therefore who knoweth to do good and doth it not, to him it is sin.

CHAP. 4. [1] Prov. 3, 34; 1 Peter, 5, 5. [2] Rom. 14, 4. CHAP. 5. [1] Matt. 5, 34.

CHAP. 5. Ver. 14. *Let him bring in.* See here a plain warrant of scripture for the Sacrament of Extreme Unction, that any controversy against its institution would be against the express words of the sacred text in the plainest terms.
Ver. 16. *Confess your sins one to another.* That is, to the priests of the church, whom (ver. 14) he had ordered to be called for and

CHAPTER 5

A woe to the rich that oppress the poor. Exhortations to patience and to avoid swearing. Of the anointing the sick, confession of sins and fervour in prayer.

GO to now, ye rich men: weep and howl in your miseries, which shall come upon you.

2 Your riches are corrupted: and your garments are motheaten.

3 Your gold and silver is cankered: and the rust of them shall be for a testimony against you and shall eat your flesh like fire. You have stored up to yourselves wrath against the last days.

4 Behold the hire of the labourers who have reaped down your fields, which by fraud has been kept back by you, crieth: and the cry of them hath entered into the ears of the Lord of Sabaoth.

5 You have feasted upon earth: and in riotousness you have nourished your hearts, in the day of slaughter.

6 You have condemned and put to death the Just One: and he resisted you not.

7 Be patient therefore, brethren, until the coming of the Lord. Behold, the husbandman waiteth for the precious fruit of the earth: patiently bearing till he receive the early and latter *rain.*

8 Be you therefore also patient and strengthen your hearts: for the coming of the Lord is at hand.

9 Grudge not, brethren, one against another, that you may not be judged. Behold the judge standeth before the door.

10 Take, my brethren, for example of suffering evil, of labour and patience, the prophets who spoke in the name of the Lord.

11 Behold, we account them blessed who have endured. You have heard of the patience of Job and you have seen the end of the Lord, that the Lord is merciful and compassionate.

12 But above all things, my brethren, [1] swear not, neither by heaven, nor by the earth, nor by any other oath. But let your speech be: Yea, Yea: No, No: that you fall not under judgment.

13 Is any of you sad? Let him pray: Is he cheerful in mind? Let him sing.

14 Is any man sick among you? Let him bring in the priests of the church, and let them pray over him, anointing him with oil in the name of the Lord.

15 And the prayer of faith shall save the sick man. And the Lord shall raise him up: and if he be in sins, they shall be forgiven him.

16 Confess therefore your sins one to another: and pray one for another,

that you may be saved. For the continual prayer of a just man availeth much.

17 ² Elias was a man passible like unto us: and with prayer he prayed that it might not rain upon the earth. And it rained not for three years and six months.

18 And he prayed again. And the heaven gave rain: and the earth brought forth her fruit.

19 My brethren, if any of you err from the truth and one convert him:

20 He must know that he who causeth a sinner to be converted from the error of his way shall save his soul from death and shall cover a multitude of sins.

THE FIRST EPISTLE OF
ST. PETER THE APOSTLE

The first Epistle of St. Peter, though brief, contains much doctrine concerning Faith, Hope, and Charity, with divers instructions to all persons of what state or condition soever. The Apostle commands submission to rulers and superiors and exhorts all to the practice of a virtuous life in imitation of Christ. This Epistle is written with such apostolical dignity as to manifest the supreme authority with which its writer, the Prince of the Apostles, had been vested by his Lord and Master, Jesus Christ. He wrote it at Rome, which figuratively he calls Babylon, about fifteen years after our Lord's Ascension.

CHAPTER 1

He gives thanks to God for the benefit of our being called to the true faith and to eternal life, into which we are to enter by many tribulations. He exhorts to holiness of life, considering the holiness of God and our redemption by the blood of Christ.

PETER, an apostle of Jesus Christ, to the strangers dispersed through Pontus, Galatia, Cappadocia, Asia and Bithynia, elect,

2 According to the foreknowledge of God the Father, unto the sanctification of the Spirit, unto obedience and sprinkling of the blood of Jesus Christ. Grace unto you and peace be multiplied.

3 ¹ Blessed be the God and Father of our Lord Jesus Christ, who according to his great mercy hath regenerated us unto a lively hope, by the resurrection of Jesus Christ from the dead:

4 Unto an inheritance, incorruptible, and undefiled and that cannot fade, reserved in heaven for you,

5 Who, by the power of God, are kept by faith unto salvation, ready to be revealed in the last time.

6 Wherein you shall greatly rejoice, if now you must be for a little time made sorrowful in divers temptations:

7 That the trial of your faith (much more precious than gold which is tried by the fire) may be found unto praise and glory and honour at the appearing of Jesus Christ.

8 Whom having not seen, you love: in whom also now, though you see him not, you believe and, believing, shall rejoice with joy unspeakable and glorified;

9 Receiving the end of your faith, even the salvation of your souls.

10 Of which salvation the prophets have inquired and diligently searched, who prophesied of the grace to come in you.

11 Searching what or what manner of time the Spirit of Christ in them did signify, when it foretold those sufferings that are in Christ and the glories that should follow.

12 To whom it was revealed that, not to themselves but to you, they ministered those things which are now declared to you by them that have preached the gospel to you: the Holy Ghost being sent down from heaven, on whom the angels desire to look.

13 Wherefore, having the loins of your mind girt up, being sober, trust perfectly in the grace which is offered you in the revelation of Jesus Christ.

14 As children of obedience, not fashioned according to the former desires of your ignorance,

15 But according to him that hath called you, who is holy, be you also in all manner of conversation holy:

16 Because it is written: ² *You shall be holy, for I am holy.*

² 3 Kings, 17, 1; Luke, 4, 25. CHAP. 1. ¹ 2 Cor. 1, 3; Eph. 1, 3.

brought in to the sick; moreover, to confess to persons who had no power to forgive sins would be useless. Hence the precept here means that we must confess to men whom God hath appointed and who, by their ordination and jurisdiction, have received the power of remitting sins in his name.

17 And if you invoke as Father him who, [3] without respect of persons, judgeth according to every one's work: converse in fear during the time of your sojourning here.

18 Knowing that you were not redeemed with corruptible things, as gold or silver, from your vain conversation of the tradition of your fathers:

19 [4] But with the precious blood of Christ, as of a lamb unspotted and undefiled,

20 Foreknown indeed before the foundation of the world, but manifested in the last times for you:

21 Who through him are faithful in God who raised him up from the dead and hath given him glory, that your faith and hope might be in God.

22 Purifying your souls in the obedience of charity, with a brotherly love, from a sincere heart love one another earnestly:

23 Being born again, not of corruptible seed, but incorruptible, by the word of God who liveth and remaineth for ever.

24 [5] For all flesh is as grass and all the glory thereof as the flower of grass. The grass is withered and the flower thereof is fallen away.

25 But the word of the Lord endureth for ever. And this is the word which by the gospel hath been preached unto you.

CHAPTER 2

We are to lay aside all guile and go to Christ the living stone, and, as being now his people, walk worthily of him, with submission to superiors and patience under sufferings.

WHEREFORE, [1] laying away all malice and all guile and dissimulations and envies and all detractions,

2 As newborn babes, desire the rational milk without guile, that thereby you may grow unto salvation:

3 If so be you have tasted that the Lord is sweet.

4 Unto whom coming, as to a living stone, rejected indeed by men but chosen and made honourable by God:

5 Be you also as living stones built up, a spiritual house, a holy priesthood, to offer up spiritual sacrifices, acceptable to God by Jesus Christ.

6 Wherefore it is said in the scripture: [2] Behold, I lay in Sion a chief corner stone, elect, precious. And he that

shall believe in him shall not be confounded.

7 To you therefore that believe, he is honour: but to them that believe not, [3] the stone which the builders rejected, the same is made the head of the corner:

8 And a stone of stumbling and a rock of scandal, to them who stumble at the word, neither do believe, whereunto also they are set.

9 But you are a chosen generation, a kingly priesthood, a holy nation, a purchased people: that you may declare his virtues, who hath called you out of darkness into his marvellous light:

10 [4] Who in time past were not a people: but are now the people of God. Who had not obtained mercy: but now have obtained mercy.

11 [5] Dearly beloved, I beseech you, as strangers and pilgrims, to refrain yourselves from carnal desires which war against the soul,

12 Having your conversation good among the Gentiles: that whereas they speak against you as evildoers, they may, by the good works which they shall behold in you, glorify God in the day of visitation.

13 [6] Be ye subject therefore to every human creature for God's sake: whether it be to the king as excelling,

14 Or to governors as sent by him for the punishment of evildoers and for the praise of the good.

15 For so is the will of God, that by doing well you may put to silence the ignorance of foolish men:

16 As free and not as making liberty a cloak for malice, but as the servants of God.

17 Honour all men. [7] Love the brotherhood. Fear God. Honour the king.

18 [8] Servants, be subject to your masters with all fear, not only to the good and gentle but also to the froward.

19 For this is thankworthy: if, for conscience towards God, a man endure sorrows, suffering wrongfully.

20 For what glory is it, if, committing sin and being buffeted *for it*, you endure? But if doing well you suffer patiently: this is thankworthy before God.

21 For unto this are you called: because Christ also suffered for us, leaving you an example that you should follow his steps.

22 [9] *Who did no sin, neither was guile found in his mouth.*

23 Who, when he was reviled, did not revile: when he suffered, he threatened not, but delivered himself to him that judged him unjustly.

24 [10] Who his own self bore our sins

[2] Lev. 11, 44; 19, 2; 20, 7. [3] Deut. 10, 17; Rom. 2, 11; Gal. 2, 6. [4] 1 Cor. 6, 20; 7, 23; Heb. 9, 14; 1 John, 1, 7; Apoc. 1, 5. [5] Ecclus. 14, 18; Isai. 40, 6; James, 1, 10. CHAP. 2. [1] Rom. 6, 4; Eph. 4, 22; Col. 3, 8; Heb. 12, 1. [2] Isai. 28, 16; Rom. 9, 33. [3] Ps. 117, 22; Isai. 8, 14; Matt. 21, 42; Acts, 4, 11. [4] Osee, 2, 24; Rom. 9, 25. [5] Rom. 13, 14; Gal. 5, 16. [6] Rom. 13, 1. [7] Rom. 12, 10. [8] Eph. 6, 5; Col. 3, 22; Titus, 2, 9. [9] Isai. 53, 9.

in his body upon the tree: that we, being dead to sins, should live to justice: by whose stripes you were healed.

25 For you were as sheep going astray: but you are now converted to the shepherd and bishop of your souls.

CHAPTER 3

How wives are to behave to their husbands. What ornaments they are to seek. Exhortations to divers virtues.

IN ¹ like manner also, let wives be subject to their husbands: that, if any believe not the word, they may be won without the word, by the conversation of the wives,

2 Considering your chaste conversation with fear.

3 ² Whose adorning, let it not be the outward plaiting of the hair, or the wearing of gold, or the putting on of apparel:

4 But the hidden man of the heart, in the incorruptibility of a quiet and a meek spirit which is rich in the sight of God.

5 For after this manner heretofore, the holy women also who trusted in God adorned themselves, being in subjection to their own husbands:

6 ³ As Sara obeyed Abraham, calling him lord: whose daughters you are, doing well and not fearing any disturbance.

7 ⁴ Ye husbands, likewise dwelling with them according to knowledge, giving honour to the female as to the weaker vessel and as to the co-heirs of the grace of life: that your prayers be not hindered.

8 And in fine, be ye all of one mind, having compassion one of another, being lovers of the brotherhood, merciful, modest, humble:

9 ⁵ Not rendering evil for evil, nor railing for railing, but contrariwise, blessing: for unto this are you called, that you may inherit a blessing.

10 ⁶ *For he that will love life and see good days, let him refrain his tongue from evil, and his lips that they speak no guile.*

11 ⁷ *Let him decline from evil and do good: let him seek after peace and pursue it:*

12 *Because the eyes of the Lord are upon the just, and his ears unto their prayers: but the countenance of the Lord upon them that do evil things.*

13 And who is he that can hurt you, if you be zealous of good?

14 ⁸ But if also you suffer any thing for justice' sake, blessed are ye. And be not afraid of their fear: and be not troubled.

15 But sanctify the Lord Christ in your hearts, being ready always to satisfy every one that asketh you a reason of that hope which is in you.

16 ⁹ But with modesty and fear, having a good conscience: that whereas they speak evil of you, they may be ashamed who falsely accuse your good conversation in Christ.

17 For it is better doing well (if such be the will of God) to suffer than doing ill.

18 ¹⁰ Because Christ also died once for our sins, the just for the unjust: that he might offer us to God, being put to death indeed in the flesh, but enlivened in the spirit,

19 In which also coming he preached to those spirits that were in prison:

20 Which had been some time incredulous, ¹¹ when they waited for the patience of God in the days of Noe, when the ark was a building: wherein a few, that is, eight souls, were saved by water.

21 Whereunto baptism, being of the like form, now saveth you also: not the putting away of the filth of the flesh, but the examination of a good conscience towards God by the resurrection of Jesus Christ.

22 Who is on the right hand of God, swallowing down death that we might be made heirs of life everlasting: being gone into heaven, the angels and powers and virtues being made subject to him.

CHAPTER 4

Exhortations to cease from sin, to mutual charity, to do all for the glory of God, to be willing to suffer for Christ.

CHRIST therefore having suffered in the flesh, be you also armed with the same thought: for he that hath suffered in the flesh hath ceased from sins:

2 ¹ That now he may live the rest of his time in the flesh, not after the de-

¹⁰ Isai. 53, 5; 1 John, 3, 5. CHAP. 3. ¹ Eph. 5, 22; Col. 3, 18. ² 1 Tim. 2, 9. ³ Gen. 18, 12. ⁴ 1 Cor. 7, 3. ⁵ Prov. 17, 13; Rom. 12, 17; 1 Thess. 5, 15. ⁶ Ps. 33, 13. ⁷ Isai. 1, 16. ⁸ Matt. 5, 10. ⁹ 1 Peter, 2, 12. ¹⁰ Rom. 5, 6; Heb. 9, 28. ¹¹ Gen. 7, 7; Matt. 24, 37; Luke, 17, 26.

CHAP. 3. Ver. 19. *Spirits that were in prison.* See here a proof of a third place, or middle state of souls: for these spirits in prison, to whom Christ went to preach after his death, were not in heaven; nor yet in the hell of the damned: because heaven is no prison: and Christ did not go to preach to the damned.

Ver. 21. *Whereunto baptism. Baptism* is said to be *of the like form* with the *water* by which Noe was saved, because the one was a figure of the other.—*Not the putting away.* As much as to say that baptism has not its efficacy in order to salvation from its washing away any bodily filth or dirt; but from its purging the conscience from sin, when accompanied with suitable dispositions in the party, to answer the interrogations made at that time, with relation to faith, the renouncing of Satan with all his works and the obedience to God's commandments.

sires of men but according to the will of God.

3 For the time past is sufficient to have fulfilled the will of the Gentiles, for them who have walked in riotousness, lusts, excess of wine, revellings, banquetings and unlawful worshipping of idols.

4 Wherein they think it strange that you run not with them into the same confusion of riotousness: speaking evil *of you.*

5 Who shall render account to him who is ready to judge the living and the dead.

6 For, for this cause was the gospel preached also to the dead: That they might be judged indeed according to men, in the flesh: but may live according to God, in the Spirit.

7 But the end of all is at hand. Be prudent therefore and watch in prayers.

8 But before all things have a constant mutual charity among yourselves: [2] for charity covereth a multitude of sins.

9 [3] Using hospitality one towards another, [4] without murmuring,

10 [5] As every man hath received grace, ministering the same one to another: [6] as good stewards of the manifold grace of God.

11 If any man speak, *let him speak,* as the words of God. If any minister, *let him do it,* as of the power which God administereth: that in all things God may be honoured through Jesus Christ: to whom is glory and empire for ever and ever. Amen.

12 Dearly beloved, think not strange the burning heat which is to try you: as if some new thing happened to you.

13 But if you partake of the sufferings of Christ, rejoice that, when his glory shall be revealed, you may also be glad with exceeding joy.

14 If you be reproached for the name of Christ, you shall be blessed: for that which is of the honour, glory and power of God, and that which is his Spirit, resteth upon you.

15 But let none of you suffer as a murderer or a thief or a railer or a coveter of other men's things.

16 But, if as a Christian, let him not be ashamed: but let him glorify God in that name.

CHAP. 4. [1] Eph. 4, 23. [2] Prov. 10, 12. [3] Rom. 12, 13; Heb. 13, 2. [4] Phil. 2, 14. [5] Rom. 12, 6. [6] 1 Cor. 4, 2. [7] Prov. 11, 31. CHAP. 5. [1] Rom. 12, 10. [2] James, 4, 6. [3] James, 4, 10. [4] Ps. 54, 23; Matt. 6, 25; Luke, 12, 22.

CHAP. 4. Ver. 18. *Scarcely.* That is, not without much labour and difficulty; and because of the dangers which constantly surround, the temptations of the world, of the devil, and of our own corrupt nature.

CHAP. 5. Ver. 1. *The ancients.* That is, the senior priests.

Ver. 13. *Babylon.* Figuratively, Rome.

17 For the time is that judgment should begin at the house of God. And if first at us, what shall be the end of them that believe not the gospel of God?

18 [7] And if the just man shall scarcely be saved, where shall the ungodly and the sinner appear?

19 Wherefore let them also that suffer according to the will of God commend their souls in good deeds to the faithful Creator.

CHAPTER 5

He exhorts both priests and laity to their respective duties and recommends to all humility and watchfulness.

THE ancients therefore that are among you, I beseech who am myself also an ancient and a witness of the sufferings of Christ, as also a partaker of that glory which is to be revealed in time to come:

2 Feed the flock of God which is among you, taking care *of it,* not by constraint but willingly, according to God: not for filthy lucre's sake but voluntarily:

3 Neither as lording it over the clergy but being made a pattern of the flock from the heart.

4 And when the prince of pastors shall appear, you shall receive a never fading crown of glory.

5 In like manner, ye young men, be subject to the ancients. [1] And do you all insinuate humility one to another: for, [2] *God resisteth the proud, but to the humble he giveth grace.*

6 [3] Be you humbled therefore under the mighty hand of God, that he may exalt you in the time of visitation:

7 [4] Casting all your care upon him, for he hath care of you.

8 Be sober and watch: because your adversary the devil, as a roaring lion, goeth about seeking whom he may devour.

9 Whom resist ye, strong in faith: knowing that the same affliction befalls your brethren who are in the world.

10 But the God of all grace, who hath called us unto his eternal glory in Christ Jesus, after you have suffered a little, will himself perfect you and confirm you and establish you.

11 To him be glory and empire, for ever and ever. Amen.

12 By Sylvanus, a faithful brother unto you, as I think, I have written briefly: beseechng and testifying that this is the true grace of God, wherein you stand.

13 The church that is in Babylon, elected together with you, saluteth you. And so doth my son, Mark.

14 Salute one another with a holy kiss. Grace be to all you who are in Christ Jesus. Amen.

THE SECOND EPISTLE OF
ST. PETER THE APOSTLE

In this Epistle St. Peter says (chap. 3): *Behold this second Epistle I write to you: and before* (chap. 1, 14): *Being assured that the laying away of this my tabernacle is at hand. This shews, that it was written a very short time before his martyrdom, which was about thirty-five years after our Lord's Ascension. In this Epistle he admonishes the faithful to be mindful of the great gifts they received from God and to join all other virtues with their faith. He warns them against false teachers, by describing their practices and foretelling their punishments. He describes the dissolution of this world by fire and the day of judgment.*

CHAPTER 1

He exhorts them to join all other virtues with their faith, in order to secure their salvation.

SIMON PETER, servant and apostle of Jesus Christ: to them that have obtained equal faith with us in the justice of our God and Saviour Jesus Christ.

2 Grace to you and peace be accomplished in the knowledge of God and of Christ Jesus our Lord.

3 As all things of his divine power which appertain to life and godliness are given us through the knowledge of him who hath called us by his own proper glory and virtue.

4 By whom he hath given us most great and precious promises: that by these you may be made partakers of the divine nature: flying the corruption of that concupiscence which is in the world.

5 And you, employing all care, minister in your faith, virtue: and in virtue, knowledge:

6 And in knowledge, abstinence: and in abstinence, patience: and in patience, godliness:

7 And in godliness, love of brotherhood: and in love of brotherhood, charity.

8 For if these things be with you and abound, they will make you to be neither empty nor unfruitful in the knowledge of our Lord Jesus Christ.

9 For he that hath not these things with him is blind and groping, having forgotten that he was purged from his old sins.

10 Wherefore, brethren, labour the more, that by good works you may make sure your calling and election. For doing these things, you shall not sin at any time.

11 For so an entrance shall be ministered to you abundantly into the ever-lasting kingdom of our Lord and Saviour Jesus Christ.

12 For which cause, I will begin to put you always in remembrance of these things: though indeed you know them and are confirmed in the present truth.

13 But I think it meet, as long as I am in this tabernacle, to stir you up by putting you in remembrance.

14 Being assured that the laying away of *this* my tabernacle is at hand, according as our Lord Jesus Christ also [1] hath signified to me.

15 And I will endeavour that you frequently have after my decease whereby you may keep a memory of these things.

16 [2] For we have not by following artificial fables made known to you the power and presence of our Lord Jesus Christ: but we were eyewitnesses of his greatness.

17 For he received from God the Father honour and glory, this voice coming down to him from the excellent glory: [3] *This is my beloved Son, in whom I am well pleased. Hear ye him.*

18 And this voice we heard brought from heaven, when we were with him in the holy mount.

19 And we have the more firm prophetical word: whereunto you do well to attend, as to a light that shineth in a dark place, until the day dawn and the day star arise in your hearts.

20 [4] Understanding this first: That

CHAP. 1. [1] John, 21, 19. [2] 1 Cor. 1, 17. [3] Matt. 17, 6. [4] 2 Tim. 3, 16.

CHAP. 1. Ver. 20. *No prophecy of scripture is made by private interpretation.* This shows plainly that the scriptures are not to be expounded by any one's private judgment or private spirit, because every part of the holy scriptures was written by men inspired by the Holy Ghost and declared as such by the Church. Therefore they are not to be interpreted but by the Spirit of God, which he hath left and promised to remain with his Church, to guide her in all truth to the end of the world. Some may tell us that many of our divines interpret the scriptures. They may do so; but they do it always with a submission to the judgment of the Church, and not otherwise.

no prophecy of scripture is made by private interpretation.

21 For prophecy came not by the will of man at any time: but the holy men of God spoke, inspired by the Holy Ghost.

CHAPTER 2

He warns them against false teachers and foretells their punishment.

BUT there were also false prophets among the people, even as there shall be among you lying teachers who shall bring in sects of perdition and deny the Lord who bought them: bringing upon themselves swift destruction.

2 And many shall follow their riotousness, through whom the way of truth shall be evil spoken of.

3 And through covetousness shall they with feigned words make merchandise of you. Whose judgment now of a long time lingereth not: and their perdition slumbereth not.

4 ¹ For if God spared not the angels that sinned, but delivered them, drawn down by infernal ropes to the lower hell, unto torments, to be reserved unto judgment:

5 And spared not the original world, ² but preserved Noe, the eighth person, the preacher of justice, bringing in the flood upon the world of the ungodly.

6 ³ And reducing the cities of the Sodomites and of the Gomorrhites into ashes, condemned them to be overthrown, making them an example to those that should after act wickedly,

7 And delivered just Lot, oppressed by the injustice and lewd conversation of the wicked:

8 For in sight and hearing he was just, dwelling among them who from day to day vexed the just soul with unjust works.

9 The Lord knoweth how to deliver the godly from temptation, but to reserve the unjust unto the day of judgment to be tormented:

10 And especially them who walk after the flesh in the lust of uncleanness and despise government: audacious, self willed, they fear not to bring in sects, blaspheming.

11 Whereas angels, who are greater

in strength and power, bring not against themselves a railing judgment.

12 But these men, as irrational beasts, naturally tending to the snare and to destruction, blaspheming those things which they know not, shall perish in their corruption:

13 Receiving the reward of *their* injustice, counting for a pleasure the delights of a day: stains and spots, sporting themselves to excess, rioting in their feasts with you:

14 Having eyes full of adultery and of sin that ceaseth not: alluring unstable souls: having their heart exercised with covetousness: children of malediction.

15 Leaving the right way, they have gone astray, ⁴ having followed the way of Balaam of Bosor who loved the wages of iniquity,

16 But had a check of his madness, the dumb beast used to the yoke, which, ⁵ speaking with man's voice, forbade the folly of the prophet.

17 ⁶ These are fountains without water and clouds tossed with whirlwinds, to whom the mist of darkness is reserved.

18 For, speaking proud words of vanity, they allure by the desires of fleshly riotousness those who for a little while escape, such as converse in error:

19 Promising them liberty, whereas they themselves are the slaves of corruption. ⁷ For by whom a man is overcome, of the same also he is the slave.

20 For if, flying from the pollutions of the world, through the knowledge of our Lord and Saviour Jesus Christ, ⁸ they *be* again entangled in them and overcome: ⁹ their latter state is become unto them worse than the former.

21 For it had been better for them not to have known the way of justice than, after they have known it, to turn back from that holy commandment which was delivered to them.

22 For, that of the true proverb has happened to them: ¹⁰ The dog is returned to his vomit; and: The sow that was washed to her wallowing in the mire.

CHAPTER 3

Against scoffers denying the second coming of Christ. He declares the sudden dissolution of this world and exhorts to holiness of life.

BEHOLD this second epistle I write to you, my dearly beloved, in which I stir up by way of admonition your sincere mind:

2 That you may be mindful of those words which I told you before from the holy prophets and of your apostles, of the precepts of the Lord and Saviour.

CHAP. 2. ¹ Job. 4, 18; Jude, 6. ² Gen. 7, 1. ³ Gen. 19, 25. ⁴ Jude, 11. ⁵ Num. 22, 28. ⁶ Jude, 12. ⁷ John, 8, 34; Rom. 6, 16, 20. ⁸ Heb. 6, 4. ⁹ Matt. 12, 45. ¹⁰ Prov. 26, 11.

CHAP. 2. Ver. 1. *Sects of perdition.* That is, heresies destructive of salvation.

Ver. 11. *Bring not a railing judgment.* That is, they use no railing nor cursing sentence; not even in their conflicts with the evil angels. (See St. Jude, ver. 9).

Ver. 13. *The delights of a day.* That is, the short delights of this world, in which they place all their happiness.

3 Knowing this first: [1] That in the last days there shall come deceitful scoffers, walking after their own lusts,

4 Saying: [2] Where is his promise or his coming? For since the time that the fathers slept, all things continue as they were from the beginning of the creation.

5 For this they are wilfully ignorant of: That the heavens were before, and the earth out of water and through water, consisting by the word of God:

6 Whereby the world that then was, being overflowed with water, perished.

7 But the heavens and the earth which are now, by the same word are kept in store, reserved unto fire against the day of judgment and perdition of the ungodly men.

8 But of this one thing be not ignorant, my beloved, that one day with the Lord is as a thousand years, and a thousand years as one day.

9 The Lord delayeth not his promise, as some imagine, but dealeth patiently for your sake, not willing that any should perish, but that all should return to penance,

10 [3] But the day of the Lord shall come as a thief, in which the heavens shall pass away with great violence and the elements shall be melted with heat and the earth and the works which are in it shall be burnt up.

11 Seeing then that all these things are to be dissolved, what manner of people ought you to be in holy conversation and godliness?

12 Looking for and hasting unto the coming of the day of the Lord, by which the heavens being on fire shall be dissolved and the elements shall melt with the burning heat?

13 [4] But we look for new heavens and a new earth according to his promises, in which justice dwelleth.

14 Wherefore, dearly beloved, waiting for these things, be diligent that you may be found before him unspotted and blameless in peace.

15 [5] And account the longsuffering of our Lord, salvation: as also our most dear brother Paul, according to the wisdom given him, hath written to you:

16 As also in all *his* epistles, speaking in them of these things; in which are certain things hard to be understood, which the unlearned and unstable wrest, as they do also the other scriptures, to their own destruction.

17 You therefore, brethren, knowing these things before, take heed, lest being led aside by the error of the unwise, you fall from your own steadfastness.

18 But grow in grace and in the knowledge of our Lord and Saviour Jesus Christ. To him be glory both now and unto the day of eternity. Amen.

THE FIRST EPISTLE OF
ST. JOHN THE APOSTLE

The same vein of divine love and charity towards our neighbour, which runs throughout the Gospel written by the beloved disciple and Evangelist, St. John, is found also in his Epistles. He confirms the two principal mysteries of our faith: The mystery of the Trinity, and the mystery of the incarnation of Jesus Christ the Son of God. The sublimity and excellence of the evangelical doctrine he declares: And this commandment we have from God, that he, who loveth God, love also his brother (chap. 4, 21). And again: For this is the charity of God, that we keep his commandments, and: His commandments are not heavy (chap. 5, 3). He shews how to distinguish the children of God from those of the devil: marks out those who should be called Antichrists: describes the turpitude and gravity of sin. Finally, he shews how the sinner may hope for pardon. It was written, according to Baronius' account, sixty-six years after our Lord's Ascension.

CHAPTER 1

He declares what he has seen and heard of Christ who is the life eternal, to the end that we may have fellowship with God and all good through him. Yet so if we confess our sins.

THAT which was from the beginning, which we have heard, which we have seen with our eyes, which we

CHAP. 3. [1] 1 Tim. 4, 1; 2 Tim. 3, 1; Jude, 18. [2] Ezech. 12, 27. [3] 1 Thess. 5, 2; Apoc. 3, 3; 16, 15. [4] Isai. 65, 17; 66, 22; Apoc. 21, 1. [5] Rom. 1, 5.

have looked upon and our hands have handled, of the word of life.

2 For the life was manifested: and we have seen and do bear witness and declare unto you the life eternal, which was with the Father and hath appeared to us.

3 That which we have seen and have heard, we declare unto you: that you also may have fellowship with us and our fellowship may be with the Father and with his Son Jesus Christ.

4 And these things we write to you, that you may rejoice and your joy may be full.

5 And this is the declaration which we have heard from him and declare unto you: ¹ That God is light and in him there is no darkness.

6 If we say that we have fellowship with him and walk in darkness, we lie and do not the truth.

7 But if we walk in the light, as he also is in the light, we have fellowship one with another: ² and the blood of Jesus Christ his Son cleanseth us from all sin.

8 ³ If we say that we have no sin, we deceive ourselves and the truth is not in us.

9 If we confess our sins, he is faithful and just, to forgive us our sins and to cleanse us from all iniquity.

10 If we say that we have not sinned, we make him a liar: and his word is not in us.

CHAPTER 2

Christ is our advocate. We must keep his commandments and love one another. We must not love the world nor give ear to new teachers, but abide by the spirit of God in the church.

MY little children, these things I write to you, that you may not sin. But if any man sin, we have an advocate with the Father, Jesus Christ the just.

2 And he is the propitiation for our sins: and not for ours only, but also for those of the whole world.

3 And by this we know that we have

CHAP. 1. ¹ John, 8, 12. ² Heb. 9, 14; 1 Peter, 1, 19; Apoc. 1, 5. ³ 3 Kings, 8, 46; 2 Par. 6, 36; Prov. 20, 9; Ecclus. 7, 21. CHAP. 2. ¹ John, 13, 34; 15, 12. ² 1 John, 3, 14.

CHAP. 2. Ver. 3. *We have known him, if we keep his commandments.* He speaks of that *practical knowledge* by love and affection which can only be proved by our keeping his commandments; and without which we cannot be said to *know* God, as we should do.
Ver. 8. *A new commandment.* Namely, the commandment of love, which was first given in the old law, but was *renewed* and extended by Christ (see John, 13, 34).
Ver. 18. *It is the last hour.* That is, it is the last age of the world.—*Many Antichrists.* That is, many heretics, enemies of Christ and his church and forerunners of the great Antichrist.
Ver. 19. *They were not of us.* That is, they were not solid, steadfast, genuine Christians; otherwise they would have remained in the church.

known him, if we keep his commandments.

4 He who saith that he knoweth him and keepeth not his commandments is a liar: and the truth is not in him.

5 But he that keepeth his word, in him in very deed the charity of God is perfected. And by this we know that we are in him.

6 He that saith he abideth in him ought himself also to walk even as he walked.

7 Dearly beloved, I write not a new commandment to you, but an old commandment which you had from the beginning. The old commandment is the word which you have heard.

8 ¹ Again a new commandment I write unto you: which thing is true both in him and in you, because the darkness is passed and the true light now shineth.

9 He that saith he is in the light and hateth his brother is in darkness even until now.

10 ² He that loveth his brother abideth in the light: and there is no scandal in him.

11 But he that hateth his brother is in darkness and walketh in darkness and knoweth not whither he goeth: because the darkness hath blinded his eyes.

12 I write unto you, little children, because your sins are forgiven you for his name's sake.

13 I write unto you, fathers, because you have known him who is from the beginning. I write unto you, young men, because you have overcome the wicked one.

14 I write unto you, babes, because you have known the Father. I write unto you, young men, because you are strong, and the word of God abideth in you, and you have overcome the wicked one.

15 Love not the world, nor the things which are in the world. If any man love the world, the charity of the Father is not in him.

16 For all that is in the world is the concupiscence of the flesh and the concupiscence of the eyes and the pride of life, which is not of the Father but is of the world.

17 And the world passeth away and the concupiscence thereof: but he that doth the will of God abideth for ever.

18 Little children, it is the last hour: and as you have heard that Antichrist cometh, even now there are become many Antichrists: whereby we know that it is the last hour.

19 They went out from us but they were not of us. For if they had been of

us, they would no doubt have remained with us: but that they may be manifest, that they are not all of us.

20 But you have the unction from the Holy One and know all things.

21 I have not written to you as to them that know not the truth, but as to them that know it: and that no lie is of the truth.

22 Who is a liar, but he who denieth that Jesus is the Christ? This is Antichrist, who denieth the Father and the Son.

23 Whosoever denieth the Son, the same hath not the Father. He that confesseth the Son hath the Father also.

24 As for you, let that which you have heard from the beginning abide in you. If that abide in you, which you have heard from the beginning, you also shall abide in the Son and in the Father.

25 And this is the promise which he hath promised us, life everlasting.

26 These things have I written to you concerning them that seduce you.

27 And as for you, let the unction, which you have received from him abide in you. And you have no need that any man teach you: but as his unction teacheth you of all things and is truth and is no lie. And as it hath taught you, abide in him.

28 And now, little children, abide in him, that when he shall appear we may have confidence and not be confounded by him at his coming.

29 If you know that he is just, know ye, that every one also who doth justice is born of him.

CHAPTER 3

Of the love of God to us. How we may distinguish the children of God and those of the devil. Of loving one another and of purity of conscience.

BEHOLD what manner of charity the Father hath bestowed upon us, that we should be called and should be the sons of God. Therefore the world knoweth not us, because it knew not him.

2 Dearly beloved, we are now the sons of God: and it hath not yet appeared what we shall be. We know that when he shall appear we shall be like to him: because we shall see him as he is.

3 And every one that hath this hope in him sanctifieth himself, as he also is holy.

4 Whosoever committeth sin committeth also iniquity. And sin is iniquity.

5 And you know that he appeared to take away our sins: [1] and in him there is no sin.

6 Whosoever abideth in him sinneth

not: and whosoever sinneth hath not seen him nor known him.

7 Little children, let no man deceive you. He that doth justice is just, even as he is just.

8 [2] He that committeth sin is of the devil: for the devil sinneth from the beginning. For this purpose the Son of God appeared, that he might destroy the works of the devil.

9 Whosoever is born of God committeth not sin: for his seed abideth in him. And he cannot sin, because he is born of God.

10 In this the children of God are manifest, and the children of the devil. Whosoever is not just is not of God, nor he that loveth not his brother.

11 For this is the declaration which you have heard from the beginning, [3] that you should love one another.

12 Not as [4] Cain, who was of the wicked one and killed his brother. And wherefore did he kill him? Because his own works were wicked: and his brother's just.

13 Wonder not, brethren, if the world hate you.

14 We know that we have passed from death to life, because we love the brethren. [5] He that loveth not abideth in death.

15 Whosoever hateth his brother is a murderer. And you know that no murderer hath eternal life abiding in himself.

16 [6] In this we have known the charity of God, because he hath laid down his life for us: and we ought to lay down our lives for the brethren.

17 [7] He that hath the substance of this world and shall see his brother in

CHAP. 3. [1] Isai. 53, 9; 1 Peter, 2, 22. [2] John, 8, 44. [3] John, 13, 34; 15, 12. [4] Gen. 4, 8. [5] Lev. 19, 17; 1 John, 2, 10. [6] John, 5, 13. [7] Luke, 3, 11; James, 2, 15.

Ver. 20. *The unction from the Holy One.* That is, grace and wisdom from the Holy Ghost.— *Know all things.* The true children of God's church, remaining in unity, under the guidance of their lawful pastors, partake of the grace of the Holy Ghost, promised to the church and her pastors; and have in the church all necessary knowledge and instruction, so as to have no need to seek it elsewhere, since it can be only found in that society of which they are members.

Ver. 27. *You have no need.* You want not to be taught by any of these men, who, under pretence of imparting more knowledge to you, seek to seduce you (ver. 26), since you are sufficiently taught already and have all knowledge and grace in the church, with the unction of the Holy Ghost; which these new teachers have no share in.

CHAP. 3. Ver. 4. *Iniquity* (ἀνομία). Transgression of the law.

Ver. 6. *Sinneth not.* Not mortally (see chap. 1, 8).

Ver. 9. *Committeth not sin.* That is, as long as he keepeth in himself this seed of grace and this divine generation, by which he is born of God. But then he may fall from this happy state, by the abuse of his free will (see Rom. 11, 20-22; 1 Cor. 9, 27; 10, 12; Phil. 2, 12; Apoc. 3, 11).

need and shall shut up his bowels from him: how doth the charity of God abide in him?

18 My little children, let us not love in word nor in tongue, but in deed and in truth.

19 In this we know that we are of the truth and in his sight shall persuade our hearts.

20 For if our heart reprehend us, God is greater than our heart and knoweth all things.

21 Dearly beloved, if our heart do not reprehend us, we have confidence towards God.

22 [8] And whatsoever we shall ask, we shall receive of him: because we keep his commandments and do those things which are pleasing in his sight.

23 [9] And this is his commandment: That we should believe in the name of his Son Jesus Christ and love one another, as he hath given commandment unto us.

24 [10] And he that keepeth his commandments abideth in him, and he in him. And in this we know that he abideth in us by the Spirit which he hath given us.

CHAPTER 4

What spirits are of God, and what are not. We must love one another, because God has loved us.

DEARLY beloved, believe not every spirit: but try the spirits if they be of God: because many false prophets are gone out into the world.

2 By this is the spirit of God known. Every spirit which confesseth that Jesus Christ is come in the flesh is of God:

[8] Matt. 21, 22. [9] John, 6, 29; 17, 3. [10] John, 13, 34; 15, 12. CHAP. 4. [1] John, 8, 47. [2] John, 3, 16. [3] John, 1, 18; 1 Tim. 6, 16. [4] John, 13, 34; 15, 12; Eph. 5, 2.

CHAP. 4. Ver. 1. *Try the spirits.* By examining whether their teaching be agreeable to the rule of the Catholic faith and the doctrine of the church. For as he says (ver. 6), *He that knoweth God heareth us* (the pastors of the church). *By this we know the spirit of truth and the spirit of error.*

Ver. 2. *Every spirit which confesseth.* Not that the confession of this point of faith alone is, at all times, and in all cases, sufficient: but that with relation to that time, and for that part of the Christian doctrine which was then particularly to be confessed, taught and maintained against the heretics of those days, this was the most proper token by which the true teachers might be distinguished from the false.

Ver. 3. *That dissolveth Jesus.* Either by denying his humanity, or his divinity.—*He is now already in the world.* Not in his person, but in his spirit, and in his precursors.

Ver. 18. *Fear is not in charity.* Perfect charity, or love, banisheth *human fear,* that is, the fear of men; as also all *perplexing fear,* which makes men mistrust or despair of God's mercy; and that kind of *servile fear,* which makes them fear the punishment of sin more than the offence offered to God. But it no way excludes the wholesome *fear of God's judgments,* so often recommended in holy writ; nor that *fear and trembling,* with which we are told to work out our salvation (Phil. 2, 12).

3 And every spirit that dissolveth Jesus is not of God. And this is Antichrist, of whom you have heard that he cometh: and he is now already in the world.

4 You are of God, little children, and have overcome him. Because greater is he that is in you, than he that is in the world.

5 [1] They are of the world. Therefore of the world they speak: and the world heareth them.

6 We are of God. He that knoweth God heareth us. He that is not of God heareth us not. By this we know the spirit of truth and the spirit of error.

7 Dearly beloved, let us love one another: for charity is of God. And every one that loveth is born of God and knoweth God.

8 He that loveth not knoweth not God: for God is charity.

9 [2] By this hath the charity of God appeared towards us, because God hath sent his only begotten Son into the world, that we may live by him.

10 In this is charity: not as though we had loved God, but because he hath first loved us, and sent his Son to be a propitiation for our sins.

11 My dearest, if God hath so loved us, we also ought to love one another.

12 [3] No man hath seen God at any time. If we love one another, God abideth in us: and his charity is perfected in us.

13 In this we know that we abide in him, and he in us: because he hath given us of his spirit.

14 And we have seen and do testify that the Father hath sent his Son to be the Saviour of the world.

15 Whosoever shall confess that Jesus is the Son of God, God abideth in him, and he in God.

16 And we have known and have believed the charity which God hath to us. God is charity: and he that abideth in charity abideth in God, and God in him.

17 In this is the charity of God perfected with us, that we may have confidence in the day of judgment: because as he is, we also are in this world.

18 Fear is not in charity: but perfect charity casteth out fear, because fear hath pain. And he that feareth is not perfected in charity.

19 Let us therefore love God: because God first hath loved us.

20 If any man say: I love God, and hateth his brother; he is a liar. For he that loveth not his brother whom he seeth, how can he love God whom he seeth not?

21 [4] And this commandment we have

from God, that he who loveth God love also his brother.

CHAPTER 5

Of them that are born of God, and of true charity. Faith overcomes the world. Three that bear witness to Christ. Of faith in his name and of sin that is and is not to death.

WHOSOEVER believeth that Jesus is the Christ is born of God. And every one that loveth him who begot loveth him also who is born of him.

2 In this we know that we love the children of God: when we love God and keep his commandments.

3 For this is the charity of God: That we keep his commandments. And his commandments are not heavy.

4 For whatsoever is born of God overcometh the world. And this is the victory which overcometh the world: Our faith.

5 ¹ Who is he that overcometh the world, but he that believeth that Jesus is the Son of God?

6 This is he that came by water and blood, Jesus Christ: not by water only but by water and blood. And it is the Spirit which testifieth that Christ is the truth.

7 And there are Three who give testimony in heaven, the Father, the Word, and the Holy Ghost. And these three are one

8 And there are three that give tes-

timony on earth: the spirit and the water and the blood. And these three are one.

9 If we receive the testimony of men, the testimony of God is greater. For this is the testimony of God, which is greater, because he hath testified of his Son.

10 He that believeth in the Son of God hath the testimony of God in himself. ² He that believeth not the Son maketh him a liar: because he believeth not in the testimony which God hath testified of his Son.

11 And this is the testimony that God hath given to us eternal life. And this life is in his Son.

12 He that hath the Son hath life. He that hath not the Son hath not life.

13 These things I write to you that you may know that you have eternal life: you who believe in the name of the Son of God.

14 And this is the confidence which we have towards him: That, whatsoever we shall ask according to his will, he heareth us.

15 And we know that he heareth us whatsoever we ask: we know that we have the petitions which we request of him.

16 He that knoweth his brother to sin a sin *which is* not to death, let him ask: and life shall be given to him who sinneth not to death. There is a sin unto death. For that I say not that any man ask.

CHAP. 5. ¹ 1 John, 4, 15. ² John, 3, 36.

CHAP. 5. Ver. 1. *Is born of God.* That is, is justified and become a child of God by baptism: which is also to be understood; provided the belief of this fundamental article of the Christian faith be accompanied with all the other conditions, which, by the word of God and his appointment, are also required to justification; such as a general belief of all that God has revealed and promised: hope, love, repentance, and a sincere disposition to keep God's holy law and commandments.

Ver. 4. *Our faith.* Not a bare, speculative, or dead faith: but a *faith that worketh by charity* (Gal. 5, 6).

Ver. 6. *Came by water and blood.* Not only to wash away our sins by the *water* of baptism, but by his own *blood.*

Ver. 8. *The spirit and the water and the blood.* As the Father, the Word, and the Holy Ghost, all bear witness to Christ's divinity; so the *spirit,* which he yielded up, crying out with a loud voice upon the cross; and the *water* and *blood* that issued from his side, bear witness to his humanity and *are one;* that is, all agree in one testimony.

Ver. 10. *He that believeth not the Son.* By refusing to believe the testimonies given by the three Divine Persons, that Jesus was the Messias and the true Son of God, by whom eternal *life* is obtained and promised to all that comply with his doctrine. In him we have also this lively *confidence,* that we shall obtain whatever we ask, according to his will, when we ask what is for our good, with perseverance and in the manner we ought. And this we *know* and have experience of, by having obtained the *petitions* that we have made.

Ver. 16. *A sin which is not to death.* It is hard to determine what St. John here calls a sin, *which is not to death,* and a sin which is *unto death.* The difference cannot be the same as betwixt sins

that are called *venial* and *mortal.* For he says, that if a man pray for his brother who commits a sin that *is not to death, life shall be given him:* therefore such a one had before lost the life of grace and been guilty of what is commonly called a mortal sin. And when he speaks of a sin that is *unto death,* and adds these words, *for that I say not that any man ask,* it cannot be supposed that St. John would say this of every mortal sin, but only of some heinous sins, which are very seldom remitted, because such sinners very seldom repent. By *a sin* therefore *which is unto death,* interpreters commonly understand a wilful apostasy from the faith, and from the known truth, when a sinner, hardened by his own ingratitude, becomes deaf to all admonitions, will do nothing for himself, but runs on to a final impenitence. Nor yet does St. John say, that such a sin is never remitted, or cannot be remitted, but only has these words, *for that I say not that any man ask* the remission: that is, though we must pray for all sinners whatsoever, yet men cannot pray for such sinners with such a *confidence* of obtaining always their *petitions,* as St. John said before (ver. 14).

Whatever exposition we follow on this verse, our faith teacheth us from the holy scriptures, that *God desires not the death* of any sinner, but that he be *converted and live* (Ezech. 33, 11). Though men's *sins be as red as scarlet, they shall become as white as snow* (Isai. 3, 18). It is *the will of God that every one come to the knowledge of the truth, and be saved.* There is no sin so great but which God is willing to forgive, and has left a power in his church to remit the most enormous sins; so that no sinner need despair of pardon, nor will any sinner perish, but by his own fault.—*A sin unto death.* Some understand this of *final impenitence,* or of dying in mortal sin; which is the only sin that never can

17 All iniquity is sin. And there is a sin unto death.

18 We know that whosoever is born of God sinneth not: but the generation of God preserveth him and the wicked one toucheth him not.

19 We know that we are of God and the whole world is seated in wickedness.

20 And we know that the Son of God is come. [3] And he hath given us understanding that we may know the true God and may be in his true Son. This is the true God and life eternal.

21 Little children, keep yourselves from idols. Amen.

THE SECOND EPISTLE OF
ST. JOHN THE APOSTLE

The Apostle commends Electa and her family for their steadfastness in the true faith and exhorts them to persevere, lest they lose the reward of their labours. He exhorts them to love one another, but with heretics to have no society, even not to salute them. Although this Epistle is written to a particular person, yet its instructions may serve as a lesson to others, especially to those who, from their connections, situation, or condition in life, are in danger of perversion.

He recommends walking in truth, loving one another and to beware of false teachers.

THE Ancient to the lady Elect and her children, whom I love in the truth: and not I only, but also all they that have known the truth,

2 For the sake of the truth which dwelleth in us and shall be with us for ever.

3 Grace be with you, mercy and peace from God the Father and from Christ Jesus the Son of the Father: in truth and charity.

4 I was exceeding glad that I found of thy children walking in truth, as we have received a commandment from the Father.

5 And now I beseech thee, lady, not as writing a new commandment to thee, but that which we have had from the beginning, [1] that we love one another.

6 And this is charity: That we walk according to his commandments. For this is the commandment that, as you have heard from the beginning, you should walk in the same:

7 For many seducers are gone out into the world who confess not that Jesus Christ is come in the flesh. This is a seducer and an antichrist.

8 Look to yourselves, that you lose not the things which you have wrought: but that you may receive a full reward.

9 Whosoever revolteth and continueth not in the doctrine of Christ hath not God. He that continueth in the doctrine, the same hath both the Father and the Son.

10 If any man come to you and bring not this doctrine, receive him not into the house nor say to him: God speed you.

11 For he that saith unto him: God speed you, communicateth with his wicked works.

12 Having more things to write unto you, I would not by paper and ink: for I hope that I shall be with you and speak face to face, that your joy may be full.

13 The children of thy sister Elect salute thee.

[3] Luke, 24, 45. [1] John, 13, 34; 15, 12.

be remitted. But, it is probable, he may also comprise under this name, the sin of apostasy from the faith, and some other such heinous sins as are seldom and hardly remitted: and therefore he gives little encouragement, to such as pray for these sinners, to expect what they ask.

Ver. 19. *And the whole world is seated in wickedness.* That is, a great part of the world. It may also signify, *is under the wicked one,* meaning the devil, who is elsewhere called the prince of this world, that is, of all the wicked (John, 12, 31).

Ver. 20. *And may be in his true Son. He is,* or: *This is the true God and life eternal.* Which words are a clear proof of Christ's divinity, and as such made use of by the ancient fathers.

Ver. 21. *Keep yourselves from idols.* An admonition to the newly converted Christians, lest conversing with heathens and idolaters, they might fall back into the sin of idolatry, which may be the sin unto death here mentioned by St. John.

Ver. 1. *The Ancient,* that is, the ancient bishop St. John, being the only one of the twelve apostles then living. *To the lady Elect.* Some conjecture that *Electa* might be the name of a family, or of a particular church; but the general opinion is, that it is the proper name of a lady, so eminent for her piety and great charity as to merit this Epistle from St. John.

Ver. 10. *Nor say to him, God speed you.* This admonition is in general to forewarn the faithful of the dangers which may arise from a familiarity with those who have prevaricated and gone from the true faith, and with such as teach false doctrine. But this is not forbidding a charity for all men, by which we ought to wish and pray for the eternal salvation of every one, even of our enemies.

THE THIRD EPISTLE OF
ST. JOHN THE APOSTLE

St. John praises Gaius for his walking in truth and for his charity, complains of the bad conduct of Diotrephes and gives a good testimony to Demetrius.

THE Ancient, to the dearly beloved Gaius, whom I love in truth.

2 Dearly beloved, concerning all things I make *it* my prayer that thou mayest proceed prosperously and fare well, as thy soul doth prosperously.

3 I was exceedingly glad when the brethren came and gave testimony to the truth in thee, even as thou walkest in the truth.

4 I have no greater grace than this, to hear that my children walk in truth.

5 Dearly beloved, thou dost faithfully whatever thou dost for the brethren: and that for strangers.

6 Who have given testimony to thy charity in the sight of the church. Whom thou shalt do well to bring forward on their way in a manner worthy of God:

7 Because, for his name they went out, taking nothing of the Gentiles.

8 We therefore ought to receive such: that we may be fellow helpers of the truth.

9 I had written perhaps to the church: but Diotrephes, who loveth to have the pre-eminence among them, doth not receive us.

10 For this cause, if I come, I will advertise his works which he doth, with malicious words prating against us. And as if these things were not enough for him, neither doth he himself receive the brethren: and them that do receive them he forbiddeth and casteth out of the church.

11 Dearly beloved, follow not that which is evil: but that which is good. He that doth good is of God: he that doth evil hath not seen God.

12 To Demetrius, testimony is given by all, and by the truth itself: yea and we *also* give testimony. And thou knowest that our testimony is true.

13 I had many things to write unto thee: but I would not by ink and pen write to thee.

14 But I hope speedily to see thee: and we will speak mouth to mouth. Peace be to thee. Our friends salute thee. Salute the friends by name.

Ver. 4. *No greater grace.* That is, nothing that gives me greater joy and satisfaction.

Ver. 7. *Taking nothing of the Gentiles.* These ministers of the gospel are commended by St. John, who took nothing from the Gentiles, lest they should seem to preach in order to get money by it.

Ver. 9. *Diotrephes.* This man seemeth to be in power, but not a friend to the faithful; therefore this part of the letter might be an admonition to him from the apostle.

THE CATHOLIC EPISTLE OF
ST. JUDE THE APOSTLE

St. Jude, who wrote this Epistle, was one of the twelve Apostles and brother to St. James the Less. The time it was written is uncertain: only it may be inferred from ver. 17 that few or none of the Apostles were then living, except St. John. He inveighs against the heresies and wicked practices of the Simonians, Nicolaites and Gnostics, describing them and their leaders by strong epithets and similes. He exhorts the faithful to contend earnestly for the faith first delivered to them and to beware of heretics.

He exhorts them to stand to the faith first delivered to them and to beware of heretics.

JUDE, the servant of Jesus Christ and brother of James: to them that are beloved in God the Father and preserved in Jesus Christ and called.

2 Mercy unto you and peace: and charity be fulfilled.

3 Dearly beloved, taking all care to write unto you concerning your common salvation, I was under a necessity to write unto you: to beseech you to contend earnestly for the faith once delivered to the saints.

4 For certain men are secretly entered in (who were written of long ago unto this judgment), ungodly men, turning the grace of our Lord God into riotousness and denying the only sovereign Ruler and our Lord Jesus Christ.

5 I. will therefore admonish you, *though* ye once knew all things, that Jesus, having saved the people out of the land of Egypt, [1] did afterwards destroy them that believed not.

6 And the angels who kept not their principality but forsook their own habitation, [2] he hath reserved under darkness in everlasting chains, unto the judgment of the great day.

7 As Sodom and Gomorrha and the neighbouring cities, in like manner, having given themselves to fornication and going after other flesh, were made an example, suffering the punishment of eternal fire.

8 In like manner, these men also defile the flesh and despise dominion and blaspheme majesty.

9 [3] When Michael the archangel, disputing with the devil, contended about the body of Moses, he durst not bring against him the judgment of railing speech, but said: The Lord command thee.

10 But these men blaspheme whatever things they know not: and what things soever they naturally know, like dumb beasts, in these they are corrupted.

11 Woe unto them! For they have gone in the way of [4] Cain: and after the [5] error of Balaam they have for reward poured out themselves [6] and have perished in the contradiction of Core.

12 These are spots in their banquets, feasting together without fear, feeding themselves: [7] clouds without water, which are carried about by winds: trees of the autumn, unfruitful, twice dead, plucked up by the roots:

13 Raging waves of the sea, foaming out their own confusion: wandering stars, to whom the storm of darkness is reserved for ever.

14 Now of these Enoch also, the seventh from Adam, prophesied, saying: [8] Behold, the Lord cometh with thousands of his saints:

15 To execute judgment upon all and to reprove all the ungodly for all the works of their ungodliness, whereby they have done ungodly: and for all the hard things which ungodly sinners have spoken against God.

16 These are murmurers, full of complaints, walking according to their own

---

[1] Num. 14, 37. [2] 2 Peter, 2, 4; Gen. 19, 24. [3] Zach. 3, 2. [4] Gen. 4, 8. [5] Num. 22, 23. [6] Num. 16, 32. [7] 2 Peter, 2, 17. [8] Apoc. 1, 7.

Ver. 6. *Principality.* That is, the state in which they were first created, their original dignity.

Ver. 8. *Blaspheme majesty.* Speak evil of them that are in dignity; and even utter blasphemies against the divine majesty.

Ver. 9. *Contended.* This contention, which is no where else mentioned in holy writ, was originally known by revelation and transmitted by tradition. It is thought the occasion of it was, that the devil would have had the body buried in such a place and manner as to be worshipped by the Jews with divine honours.—*Command thee.* Or, *Rebuke thee.*

Ver. 11. *Gone in the way.* Heretics follow the way of Cain, by murdering the souls of their brethren; the way of Balaam, by putting a scandal before the people of God, for their own private ends; and the way of Core or Korah, by their opposition to the church governors of divine appointment.

Ver. 14. *Prophesied.* This prophecy was known by tradition.

desires: [9]and their mouth speaketh proud things, admiring persons for gain's sake.

17 But you, my dearly beloved, be mindful of the words [10]which have been spoken before by the apostles of our Lord Jesus Christ:

18 Who told you that in the last time there should come mockers, walking according to their own desires in ungodlinesses.

19 These are they who separate themselves, sensual men, having not the Spirit.

20 But you, my beloved, building yourselves upon your most holy faith, praying in the Holy Ghost,

21 Keep yourselves in the love of God, waiting for the mercy of our Lord Jesus Christ, unto life everlasting.

22 And some indeed reprove, being judged:

23 But others save, pulling *them* out of the fire. And on others have mercy, in fear, hating also the spotted garment which is carnal.

24 Now to him who is able to preserve you without sin and to present you spotless before the presence of his glory with exceeding joy, in the coming of our Lord Jesus Christ:

25 To the only God our Saviour through Jesus Christ our Lord, be glory and magnificence, empire and power, before all ages, and now, and for all ages of ages. Amen.

THE APOCALYPSE
OF ST. JOHN THE APOSTLE

In the first, second, and third chapters of this Book are contained instructions and admonitions which St. John was commanded to write to the seven bishops of the churches in Asia. And in the following chapters, to the end, are contained prophecies of things that are to come to pass in the Church of Christ, particularly towards the end of the world, in the time of Antichrist. It was written in Greek, in the island of Patmos, where St. John was in banishment by order of the cruel emperor Domitian, about sixty-four years after our Lord's Ascension.

CHAPTER 1

St. John is ordered to write to the seven churches in Asia. The manner of Christ's appearing to him.

THE Revelation of Jesus Christ, which God gave unto him, to make known to his servants the things which must shortly come to pass: and signified, sending by his angel to his servant John.

2 Who hath given testimony to the word of God and the testimony of Jesus Christ, what things soever he hath seen.

3 Blessed is he that readeth and heareth the words of this prophecy:

[9] Ps. 16, 10. [10] 1 Tim. 4, 1; 2 Tim. 3, 1; 2 Peter, 3, 3.

Ver. 17. *But you, my dearly beloved, be mindful.* He now exhorts the faithful to remain steadfast in the belief and practice of what they had heard from the apostles, who had also foretold that in aftertimes (*in the last time*) there should be false teachers, *scoffing* and ridiculing all revealed truths, abandoning themselves to their passions and *lusts;* who *separate themselves* from the Catholic communion by heresies and schisms. *Sensual men,* carried away and enslaved by the pleasures of the senses.

Ver. 20, 21. *Building yourselves upon your most holy faith.* Raising by your actions, a spiritual building, founded upon *faith,* upon the *love of God,* and upon hope, whilst you are *waiting* for the *mercies* of God and the reward of *eternal life,* joined with the great duty of *prayer.*

Ver. 22, 23. *And some indeed reprove being judged.* He gives them another instruction to practise charity in endeavouring to convert their neighbour, where they will meet with three sorts of persons: 1. With persons obstinate in their errors and sins. These may be said to be already *judged* and condemned: they are to be sharply reprehended, *reproved* and, if possible, convinced of their error. 2. As to others, you must endeavour to *save them,* by *pulling* them, as it were, *out of the fire,* from the ruin they stand in great danger of. 3. You must *have mercy on others in fear,* when you see them, through ignorance or frailty, in danger of being drawn into the snares of these heretics. With these you must deal more gently and mildly, with a charitable compassion, *hating* always and teaching others to hate *the carnal garment which is spotted,* their sensual and corrupt manners, that defile both the soul and body.

Ver. 24, 25. *Now to him.* St. Jude concludes his epistle with this doxology of praising God and praying to *the only God our Saviour,* which may either signify God the Father, or God as equally agreeing to all the three persons, who are equally the cause of Christ's Incarnation and man's salvation, *through Jesus Christ our Lord,* who, being God from eternity, took upon him our human nature, that he might become our Redeemer.

CHAP. 1. Ver. 1. *The things which must shortly come.* And again it is said (ver. 3): *The time is at hand.* This cannot be meant of all the things prophesied in the Apocalypse, where mention is

and keepeth those things which are written in it. For the time is at hand.

4 John to the seven churches which are in Asia. Grace be unto you and peace, from him [1] that is and that was and that is to come: and from the seven spirits which are before his throne:

5 And from Jesus Christ, who is the faithful witness, [2] the first begotten of the dead and the prince of the kings of the earth, who hath loved us and washed us from our sins [3] in his own blood

6 And hath made us a kingdom and priests to God and his Father. To him be glory and empire for ever and ever. Amen.

7 [4] Behold, he cometh with the clouds, and every eye shall see him: and they also that pierced him. And all the tribes of the earth shall bewail themselves because of him. Even so. Amen.

8 [5] I am Alpha and Omega, the beginning and the end, saith the Lord God, who is and who was and who is to come, the Almighty.

9 I, John, your brother and your partner in tribulation and in the kingdom and patience in Christ Jesus, was in the island which is called Patmos, for the word of God and for the testimony of Jesus.

10 I was in the spirit on the Lord's day and heard behind me a great voice, as of a trumpet,

11 Saying: What thou seest, write in a book and send to the seven churches which are in Asia: to Ephesus and to Smyrna and to Pergamus and to Thyatira and to Sardis and to Philadelphia and to Laodicea.

12 And I turned to see the voice that spoke with me. And being turned, I saw seven golden candlesticks:

13 And in the midst of the seven golden candlesticks, one like to the Son of man, clothed with a garment down to the feet, and girt about the paps with a golden girdle.

14 And his head and his hairs were white, as white wool and as snow. And his eyes were as a flame of fire:

15 And his feet like unto fine brass, as in a burning furnace. And his voice as the sound of many waters.

16 And he had in his right hand seven stars. And from his mouth came out a sharp two-edged sword. And his face was as the sun shineth in his power.

17 And when I had seen him, I fell at his feet as dead. And he laid his right hand upon me, saying: Fear not. [6] I am the First and the Last,

18 And alive, and was dead. And behold I am living for ever and ever and have the keys of death and of hell.

19 Write therefore the things which thou hast seen: and which are: and which must be done hereafter.

20 The mystery of the seven stars, which thou sawest in my right hand and the seven golden candlesticks. The seven stars are the angels of the seven churches. And the seven candlesticks are the seven churches.

CHAPTER 2

Directions what to write to the angels or bishops of Ephesus, Smyrna, Pergamus and Thyatira.

UNTO the angel of the church of Ephesus write: These things saith he who holdeth the seven stars in his right hand, who walketh in the midst of the seven golden candlesticks:

2 I know thy works and thy labour and thy patience and how thou canst not bear them that are evil. And thou hast tried them who say they are apostles and are not: and hast found them liars:

3 And thou hast patience and hast endured for my name and hast not fainted.

4 But I have somewhat against thee, because thou hast left thy first charity.

5 Be mindful therefore from whence thou art fallen: and do penance and do the first works. Or else I come to thee and will move thy candlestick out of its place, except thou do penance.

6 But this thou hast, that thou hatest the deeds of the Nicolaites, which I also hate.

7 He that hath an ear let him hear what the Spirit saith to the churches: To him that overcometh I will give to eat of the tree of life which is in the paradise of my God.

8 And to the angel of the church of Smyrna write: These things saith the First and the Last, who was dead and is alive:

9 I know thy tribulation and thy

CHAP. 1. [1] Exod. 3, 14. [2] 1 Cor. 15, 20; Col. 1, 18. [3] Heb. 9, 14; 1 Peter, 1, 19; 1 John, 1, 7. [4] Isai. 3, 13; Matt. 24, 30; Jude, 14. [5] Isai. 41, 4; 44, 6; 48, 12; Apoc. 21, 6; 22, 13. [6] Isai. 41, 4; 44, 6; 48, 12; Apoc. 21, 6; 22, 13.
made also of the day of judgment and of the glory of heaven at the end of the world. That some things were to come to pass shortly is evident by what is said to the Seven Churches (chaps. 2, 3). Or that the persecutions foretold should begin shortly. Or that these words signified that all time is short and that from the coming of Christ we are now in the last age or *last hour* (see 1 John, 2, 18).
Ver. 8. *I am Alpha and Omega.* These are the names of the first and last letters of the Greek alphabet and signify the same as what follows: *The beginning* and *the end:* the first cause and last end of all beings: *who is and who was and who is to come, the Almighty.* These words signify the true God only and are here applied to our Lord and Saviour Jesus Christ, who is to come again to judge the living and the dead.

poverty: but thou art rich. And thou art blasphemed by them that say they are Jews and are not, but are the synagogue of Satan.

10 Fear none of those things which thou shalt suffer. Behold, the devil will cast some of you into prison, that you may be tried: and you shall have tribulation ten days. Be thou faithful unto death: and I will give thee the crown of life.

11 He that hath an ear, let him hear what the Spirit saith to the churches: He that shall overcome shall not be hurt by the second death.

12 And to the angel of the church of Pergamus write: These things saith he that hath the sharp two-edged sword:

13 I know where thou dwellest, where the seat of Satan is. And thou holdest fast my name and hast not denied my faith. Even in those days *when* Antipas *was* my faithful witness, who was slain among you, where Satan dwelleth.

14 But I have against thee a few things: because thou hast there them that hold the doctrine [1] of Balaam who taught Balac to cast a stumbling-block before the children of Israel, to eat and to commit fornication.

15 So hast thou also them that hold the doctrine of the Nicolaites.

16 In like manner do penance. If not, I will come to thee quickly and will fight against them with the sword of my mouth.

17 He that hath an ear, let him hear what the Spirit saith to the churches: To him that overcometh I will give the hidden manna and will give him a white counter: and in the counter, a new name written, which no man knoweth but he that receiveth it.

18 And to the angel of the church of Thyatira write: These things saith the Son of God, who hath his eyes like to a flame of fire and his feet like to fine brass.

19 I know thy works and thy faith and thy charity and thy ministry and thy patience and thy last works, which are more than the former.

20 But I have against thee a few things: because thou sufferest the woman Jezabel, who calleth herself a prophetess, to teach and to seduce my servants, to commit fornication and to eat of things sacrificed to idols.

21 And I gave her a time that she might do penance: and she will not repent of her fornication.

22 Behold, I will cast her into a bed: and they that commit adultery with her shall be in very great tribulation, except they do penance from their deeds.

23 And I will kill her children with death: and all the churches shall know [2] that I am he that searcheth the reins and hearts. And I will give to every one of you according to your works. But to you I say

24 And to the rest who are at Thyatira: Whosoever have not this doctrine and who have not known the depths of Satan, as they say: I will not put upon you any other burthen.

25 Yet that which you have, hold fast till I come.

26 And he that shall overcome and keep my works unto the end, I will give him power over the nations.

27 And he shall rule them with a rod of iron: and as the vessel of a potter they shall be broken:

28 As I also have received of my Father. And I will give him the morning star.

29 He that hath an ear, let him hear what the Spirit saith to the churches.

CHAPTER 3

Directions what to write to Sardis, Philadelphia and Laodicea.

AND to the angel of the church of Sardis write: These things saith he that hath the seven spirits of God and the seven stars: I know thy works, that thou hast the name of being alive. And thou art dead.

2 Be watchful and strengthen the things that remain, which are ready to die. For I find not thy works full before my God.

3 Have in mind therefore in what manner thou hast received and heard: and observe and do penance: If then thou shalt not watch, [1] I will come to thee as a thief: and thou shalt not know at what hour I will come to thee.

4 But thou hast a few names in Sardis which have not defiled their garments: and they shall walk with me in white, because they are worthy.

5 He that shall overcome shall thus be clothed in white garments: and I will not blot out his name out of the book of life. And I will confess his name before my Father and before his angels.

6 He that hath an ear, let him hear what the Spirit saith to the churches.

7 And to the angel of the church of Philadelphia write: These things saith

CHAP. 2. [1] Num. 24, 3; 25, 2. [2] 1 Kings, 16, 7; Ps. 7, 10; Jer. 11, 20; 17, 10; 20, 12. CHAP. 3. [1] 1 Thess. 5, 2; 2 Peter, 3, 10; Apoc. 16, 15.

CHAP. 2. Ver. 26. *Power over the nations.* This shews that the saints, who are with Christ our Lord in heaven, receive power from him to preside over nations and provinces, as patrons; and shall come with him at the end of the world to execute his will against those who have not kept his commandments.

the Holy One and the true one, [2] he that hath the key of David, he that openeth and no man shutteth, shutteth and no man openeth:

8 I know thy works. Behold, I have given before thee a door opened, which no man can shut: because thou hast a little strength and hast kept my word and hast not denied my name.

9 Behold, I will bring of the synagogue of Satan, who say they are Jews and are not, but do lie. Behold, I will make them to come and adore before thy feet. And they shall know that I have loved thee.

10 Because thou hast kept the word of my patience, I will also keep thee from the hour of temptation, which shall come upon the whole world to try them that dwell upon the earth.

11 Behold, I come quickly: hold fast that which thou hast, that no man take thy crown.

12 He that shall overcome, I will make him a pillar in the temple of my God: and he shall go out no more. And I will write upon him the name of my God and the name of the city of my God, the new Jerusalem, which cometh down out of heaven from my God, and my new name.

13 He that hath an ear, let him hear what the Spirit saith to the churches.

14 And to the angel of the church of Laodicea write: [3] These things saith the Amen, the faithful and true witness, who is the beginning of the creation of God:

15 I know thy works, that thou art neither cold nor hot. I would thou wert cold or hot.

16 But because thou art lukewarm and neither cold nor hot, I will begin to vomit thee out of my mouth.

17 Because thou sayest: I am rich and made wealthy and have need of nothing: and knowest not that thou art wretched and miserable and poor and blind and naked.

18 I counsel thee to buy of me gold, fire tried, that thou mayest be made rich and mayest be clothed in white garments: and that the shame of thy nakedness may not appear. And anoint thy eyes with eyesalve, that thou mayest see.

19 [4] Such as I love, I rebuke and chastise. Be zealous therefore and do penance.

20 Behold, I stand at the gate and knock. If any man shall hear my voice

and open to me the door, I will come in to him and will sup with him: and he with me.

21 To him that shall overcome, I will give to sit with me in my throne: as I also have overcome and am set down with my Father in his throne.

22 He that hath an ear, let him hear what the Spirit saith to the churches.

CHAPTER 4

The vision of the throne of God, the twenty-four ancients and the four living creatures.

AFTER these things, I looked: and behold, a door *was* opened in heaven. And the first voice which I heard, as it were, of a trumpet speaking with me, said: Come up hither and I will shew thee the things which must be done hereafter.

2 And immediately I was in the spirit. And behold, there was a throne set in heaven, and upon the throne one sitting.

3 And he that sat was to the sight like the jasper and the sardine stone. And there was a rainbow round about the throne, in sight like unto an emerald.

4 And round about the throne were four and twenty seats: and upon the seats, four and twenty ancients sitting, clothed in white garments. And on their heads *were* crowns of gold.

5 And from the throne proceeded lightnings and voices and thunders. And there were seven lamps burning before the throne, which are the seven Spirits of God.

6 And in the sight of the throne was, as it were, a sea of glass like to crystal: and in the midst of the throne, and round about the throne, were four living creatures, full of eyes before and behind.

7 And the first living creature was like a lion: and the second living creature like a calf: and the third living creature, having the face, as it were, of a man: and the fourth living creature was like an eagle flying.

8 And the four living creatures had each of them six wings: and round about and within they are full of eyes. And they rested not day and night, saying: [1] Holy, Holy, Holy, Lord God Almighty, who was and who is and who is to come.

9 And when those living creatures gave glory and honour and benediction to him that sitteth on the throne, who liveth for ever and ever:

10 The four and twenty ancients fell down before him that sitteth on the throne and adored him that liveth for

[2] Isai. 22, 22; Job, 12, 14. [3] John, 14, 6. [4] Prov. 3, 11; Heb. 12, 6. CHAP. 4. [1] Isai. 6, 8.

CHAP. 3. Ver. 14. *The Amen.* That is, the true one, the Truth itself; the Word and Son of God. —*The beginning* (ἡ ἀρχή). That is, the principle, the source, and the efficient cause of the whole creation.

ever and ever and cast their crowns before the throne, saying:

11 Thou art worthy, O Lord our God, to receive glory and honour and power. Because thou hast created all things: and for thy will they were and have been created.

CHAPTER 5

The book sealed with seven seals is opened by the Lamb, who thereupon receives adoration and praise from all.

AND I saw, in the right hand of him that sat on the throne, a book, written within and without, sealed with seven seals.

2 And I saw a strong angel, proclaiming with a loud voice: Who is worthy to open the book and to loose the seals thereof?

3 And no man was able, neither in heaven nor on earth nor under the earth, to open the book, nor to look on it.

4 And I wept much, because no man was found worthy to open the book, nor to see it.

5 And one of the ancients said to me: Weep not: behold the lion of the tribe of Juda, the root of David, hath prevailed to open the book and to loose the seven seals thereof.

6 And I saw: and behold in the midst of the throne and of the four living creatures, and in the midst of the ancients, a Lamb standing, as it were slain, having seven horns and seven eyes: which are the seven Spirits of God, sent forth into all the earth.

7 And he came and took the book out of the right hand of him that sat on the throne.

8 And when he had opened the book, the four living creatures and the four and twenty ancients fell down before the Lamb, having every one of them harps and golden vials full of odours, which are the prayers of saints.

9 And they sung a new canticle, saying: Thou art worthy, O Lord, to take the book and to open the seals thereof: because thou wast slain and hast redeemed us to God, in thy blood, out of every tribe and tongue and people and nation:

10 And hast made us to our God a kingdom and priests. And we shall reign on the earth.

11 And I beheld, and I heard the voice of many angels round about the throne and the living creatures and the ancients (and the number of them was [1] thousands of thousands),

12 Saying with a loud voice: The Lamb that was slain is worthy to receive power and divinity and wisdom and strength and honour and glory and benediction.

13 And every creature which is in heaven and on the earth and under the earth, and such as are in the sea, and all that are in them, I heard all saying: To him that sitteth on the throne and to the Lamb, benediction and honour and glory and power, for ever and ever.

14 And the four living creatures said: Amen. And the four and twenty ancients fell down on their faces and adored him that liveth for ever and ever.

CHAPTER 6

What followed upon opening six of the seals.

AND I saw that the Lamb had opened one of the seven seals: and I heard one of the four living creatures, as it were the voice of thunder, saying: Come and see.

2 And I saw: and behold a white horse. And he that sat on him had a bow: and there was a crown given him. And he went forth conquering that he might conquer.

3 And when he had opened the second seal, I heard the second living creature saying: Come and see.

4 And there went out another horse *that was* red. And to him that sat thereon, it was given that he should take peace from the earth: and that they should kill one another. And a great sword was given to him.

5 And when he had opened the third seal, I heard the third living creature saying: Come and see. And behold a black horse. And he that sat on him had a pair of scales in his hand.

6 And I heard, as it were a voice in the midst of the four living creatures, saying: Two pounds of wheat for a penny, and thrice two pounds of barley for a penny: and see thou hurt not the wine and the oil.

7 And when he had opened the fourth seal, I heard the voice of the fourth living creature saying: Come and see.

8 And behold a pale horse: and he that sat upon him, his name was Death. And hell followed him. And power was given to him over the four parts of the earth, to kill with sword, with famine and with death and with the beasts of the earth.

CHAP. 5. [1] Dan. 7, 10.

CHAP. 5. Ver. 8. *The prayers of saints.* Here we see that the saints in heaven offer up to Christ the prayers of the faithful upon earth.

CHAP. 6. Ver. 2. *White horse.* He that sitteth on the white horse is Christ, going forth to subdue the world by his gospel. The other horses that follow represent the judgments and punishment that were to fall on the enemies of Christ and his Church. The red horse signifies war: the black horse, famine; and the pale horse (which has Death for its rider), plagues or pestilence.

9 And when he had opened the fifth seal, I saw under the altar the souls of them that were slain for the word of God and for the testimony which they held.

10 And they cried with a loud voice, saying: How long, O Lord (Holy and True), dost thou not judge and revenge our blood on them that dwell on the earth?

11 And white robes were given, to every one of them one. And it was said to them that they should rest for a little time till their fellow servants and their brethren, who are to be slain even as they, should be filled up.

12 And I saw, when he had opened the sixth seal: and behold there was a great earthquake. And the sun became black as sackcloth of hair: and the whole moon became as blood.

13 And the stars from heaven fell upon the earth, as the fig tree casteth its green figs when it is shaken by a great wind.

14 And the heaven departed as a book folded up. And every mountain, and the islands, were moved out of their places.

15 And the kings of the earth and the princes and tribunes and the rich and the strong and every bondman and every freeman hid themselves in the dens and in the rocks of mountains:

16 And they say to the mountains and the rocks: [1] Fall upon us and hide us from the face of him that sitteth upon the throne and from the wrath of the Lamb.

17 For the great day of their wrath is come. And who shall be able to stand?

CHAPTER 7

The number of them that were marked with the seal of the living God and clothed in white robes.

AFTER these things, I saw four angels standing on the four corners of the earth, holding the four winds of the earth, that they should not blow upon the earth nor upon the sea nor on any tree.

2 And I saw another angel ascending from the rising of the sun, having the sign of the living God. And he cried with a loud voice to the four angels to whom it was given to hurt the earth and the sea,

3 Saying: Hurt not the earth nor the sea nor the trees, till we sign the servants of our God in their foreheads.

4 And I heard the number of them that were signed. An hundred forty-four thousand were signed, of every tribe of the children of Israel.

5 Of the tribe of Juda, twelve thousand signed: Of the tribe of Ruben, twelve thousand signed: Of the tribe of Gad, twelve thousand signed:

6 Of the tribe of Aser, twelve thousand signed: Of the tribe of Nephthali, twelve thousand signed: Of the tribe of Manasses, twelve thousand signed:

7 Of the tribe of Simeon, twelve thousand signed: Of the tribe of Levi, twelve thousand signed: Of the tribe of Issachar, twelve thousand signed:

8 Of the tribe of Zabulon, twelve thousand signed: Of the tribe of Joseph, twelve thousand signed: Of the tribe of Benjamin, twelve thousand signed.

9 After this, I saw a great multitude, which no man could number, of all nations and tribes and peoples and tongues, standing before the throne and in sight of the Lamb, clothed with white robes, and palms in their hands.

10 And they cried with a loud voice, saying: Salvation to our God, who sitteth upon the throne and to the Lamb.

11 And all the angels stood round about the throne and the ancients and the four living creatures. And they fell down before the throne upon their faces and adored God,

12 Saying: Amen. Benediction and glory and wisdom and thanksgiving, honour and power and strength, to our God, for ever and ever. Amen.

13 And one of the ancients answered and said to me: These that are clothed in white robes, who are they? And whence came they?

14 And I said to him: My Lord, thou knowest. And he said to me: These are they who are come out of great tribulation and have washed their robes and have made them white in the blood of the Lamb.

15 Therefore, they are before the throne of God: and they serve him day and night in his temple. And he that sitteth on the throne shall dwell over them.

16 [1] They shall no more hunger nor thirst: neither shall the sun fall on them, nor any heat.

17 For the Lamb, which is in the midst of the throne, shall rule them and shall lead them to the fountains of the waters of life: [2] and God shall wipe all tears from their eyes.

CHAP. 6. [1] Isai. 2, 19; Osee, 10, 8; Luke, 23, 30.
CHAP. 7. [1] Isai. 49, 10. [2] Isai. 25, 8; Apoc. 21, 4.

Ver. 9. *Under the altar.* Christ, as man, is this altar, under which the souls of the martyrs live in heaven, as their bodies are here deposited under our altars.

Ver. 10. *Revenge our blood.* They ask not this out of hatred to their enemies, but out of zeal for the glory of God and a desire that the Lord would accelerate the general judgment and the complete beatitude of all his elect.

CHAPTER 8

The seventh seal is opened. The angels with the seven trumpets.

AND when he had opened the seventh seal, there was silence in heaven, as it were for half an hour.

2 And I saw seven angels standing in the presence of God: and there were given to them seven trumpets.

3 And another angel came and stood before the altar, having a golden censer: and there was given to him much incense, that he should offer of the prayers of all saints, upon the golden altar which is before the throne of God.

4 And the smoke of the incense of the prayers of the saints ascended up before God from the hand of the angel.

5 And the angel took the censer and filled it with the fire of the altar and cast it on the earth: and there were thunders and voices and lightnings and a great earthquake.

6 And the seven angels who had the seven trumpets prepared themselves to sound the trumpet.

7 And the first angel sounded the trumpet: and there followed hail and fire, mingled with blood: and it was cast on the earth. And the third part of the earth was burnt up: and the third part of the trees was burnt up: and all green grass was burnt up.

8 And the second angel sounded the trumpet: and, as it were, a great mountain, burning with fire, was cast into the sea. And the third part of the sea became blood.

9 And the third part of those creatures died which had life in the sea: and the third part of the ships was destroyed.

10 And the third angel sounded the trumpet: and a great star fell from heaven, burning as it were a torch. And it fell on the third part of the rivers and upon the fountains of waters:

11 And the name of the star is called Wormwood. And the third part of the waters became wormwood. And many men died of the waters, because they were made bitter.

12 And the fourth angel sounded the trumpet: and the third part of the sun was smitten, and the third part of the moon, and the third part of the stars, so that the third part of them was darkened. And the day did not shine for a third part of it: and the night in like manner.

13 And I beheld: and heard the voice of one eagle flying through the midst of heaven, saying with a loud voice: Woe, Woe, Woe to the inhabitants of the earth, by reason of the rest of the voices of the three angels, who are yet to sound the trumpet!

CHAPTER 9

Locusts come forth from the bottomless pit. The vision of the army of horsemen.

AND the fifth angel sounded the trumpet: and I saw a star fall from heaven upon the earth. And there was given to him the key of the bottomless pit.

2 And he opened the bottomless pit: and the smoke of the pit arose, as the smoke of a great furnace. And the sun and the air were darkened with the smoke of the pit.

3 And from the smoke of the pit there came out locusts upon the earth. And power was given to them, as the scorpions of the earth have power.

4 And it was commanded them that they should not hurt the grass of the earth nor any green thing nor any tree: but only the men who have not the sign of God on their foreheads.

5 And it was given unto them that they should not kill them: but that they should torment them, five months. And their torment *was* as the torment of a scorpion when he striketh a man.

6 [1] And in these days, men shall seek death and shall not find it. And they shall desire to die: and death shall fly from them.

7 [2] And the shapes of the locusts *were* like unto horses prepared unto battle. And on their heads *were*, as it were,

CHAP. 9. [1] Isai. 2, 19; Osee, 10, 8; Luke, 23, 30. [2] Wisd. 16, 9.

CHAP. 9. Ver. 1. *A star fall.* This may mean the fall and apostasy of great and learned men from the true faith. Or a whole nation falling into error and separating from the church, not having the sign of God in their foreheads.—*And there was given to him the key of the bottomless pit.* That is, to the *angel*, not to the *fallen star.* To this angel was given the power, which is here signified by a *key*, of opening hell.

Ver. 3. *There came out locusts.* These may be devils in Antichrist's time, having the appearance of locusts, but large and monstrous, as here described. Or they may be real locusts, but of an extraordinary size and monstrous shape, such as were never before seen on the earth, sent to torment those *who have not the sign* (or seal) *of God on their foreheads.* Some commentators by these *locusts* understand heretics, and especially those heretics that sprung from Jews, and with them denied the divinity of Jesus Christ; as Theodotus, Praxeas, Noetus, Paul of Samosata, Sabellius, Arius. These were great enemies of the Christian religion; they tormented and infected the souls of men, stinging them *like scorpions,* with the poison of their heresies. Others have explained these *locusts* and other animals, mentioned in different places throughout this sacred and mystical book, in a most absurd, fanciful, and ridiculous manner. They make *Abaddon* the Pope, and the *locusts* to be friars mendicant, and so forth. Here it is thought proper, not to enter any controversy upon that subject, as the inventors of these fancies have been already answered and fully refuted by many controvertists: besides, those who might be imposed on by such chimerical writers are in these days much better informed.

crowns like gold: and their faces *were* as the faces of men.

8 And they had hair as the hair of women: and their teeth were as lions.

9 And they had breastplates as breastplates of iron: and the noise of their wings was as the noise of chariots and many horses running to battle.

10 And they had tails like to scorpions: and there were stings in their tails. And their power was to hurt men, five months. And they had over them

11 A king, the angel of the bottomless pit (whose name in Hebrew is Abaddon and in Greek Apollyon, in Latin Exterminans).

12 One woe is past: and behold there come yet two woes more hereafter.

13 And the sixth angel sounded the trumpet: and I heard a voice from the four horns of the golden altar which is before the eyes of God,

14 Saying to the sixth angel who had the trumpet: Loose the four angels who are bound in the great river Euphrates.

15 And the four angels were loosed, who were prepared for an hour, and a day, and a month, and a year: for to kill the third part of men.

16 And the number of the army of horsemen was twenty thousand times ten thousand. And I heard the number of them.

17 And thus I saw the horses in the vision. And they that sat on them had breastplates of fire and of hyacinth and of brimstone. And the heads of the horses were as the heads of lions: and from their mouths proceeded fire and smoke and brimstone.

18 And by these three plagues was slain the third part of men, by the fire and by the smoke and by the brimstone which issued out of their mouths.

19 For the power of the horses is in their mouths and in their tails. For, their tails are like to serpents and have heads: and with them they hurt.

20 And the rest of the men, who were not slain by these plagues, did not do penance from the works of their hands, that they should not adore devils and idols of gold and silver and brass and stone and wood, which neither can see nor hear nor walk:

21 Neither did they penance from their murders nor from their sorceries nor from their fornication nor from their thefts.

CHAP. 10. [1] Dan. 12, 7. [2] Ezech. 3, 1.

Ver. 11. *Exterminans.* That is, the Destroyer.
CHAP. 10. Ver. 7. *Declared.* Literally *evangelized,* to signify the *good tidings,* agreeable to the Gospel, of the final victory of Christ, and of that eternal life which should be the reward of the temporal sufferings of the martyrs and faithful servants of God.

CHAPTER 10

The cry of a mighty angel. He gives John a book to eat.

AND I saw another mighty angel come down from heaven, clothed with a cloud. And a rainbow *was* on his head: and his face was as the sun, and his feet as pillars of fire.

2 And he had in his hand a little book, open. And he set his right foot upon the sea, and his left foot upon the earth.

3 And he cried with a loud voice as when a lion roareth. And when he had cried, seven thunders uttered their voices.

4 And when the seven thunders had uttered their voices, I was about to write. And I heard a voice from heaven saying to me: Seal up the things which the seven thunders have spoken. And write them not.

5 [1] And the angel whom I saw standing upon the sea and upon the earth lifted up his hand to heaven.

6 And he swore by him that liveth for ever and ever, who created heaven and the things which are therein, and the earth and the things which are in it, and the sea and the things which are therein: That time shall be no longer.

7 But in the days of the voice of the seventh angel, when he shall begin to sound the trumpet, the mystery of God shall be finished, as he hath declared by his servants the prophets.

8 And I heard a voice from heaven, again speaking to me and saying: Go and take the book that is open, from the hand of the angel who standeth upon the sea and upon the earth.

9 And I went to the angel, saying unto him that he should give me the book. And he said to me: [2] Take the book and eat it up. And it shall make thy belly bitter: but in thy mouth it shall be sweet as honey.

10 And I took the book from the hand of the angel and ate it up: and it was in my mouth, sweet as honey. And when I had eaten it, my belly was bitter.

11 And he said to me: Thou must prophesy again to many nations and peoples and tongues and kings.

CHAPTER 11

He is ordered to measure the temple. The two witnesses.

AND there was given me a reed, like unto a rod. And it was said to me: Arise, and measure the temple of God and the altar and them that adore therein.

2 But the court which is without the temple, cast out and measure it not:

because it is given unto the Gentiles. And the holy city they shall tread under foot, two and forty months:

3 And I will give unto my two witnesses: and they shall prophesy, a thousand two hundred sixty days, clothed in sackcloth.

4 These are the two olive trees and the two candlesticks that stand before the Lord of the earth.

5 And if any man will hurt them, fire shall come out of their mouths and shall devour their enemies. And if any man will hurt them, in this manner must he be slain.

6 These have power to shut heaven, that it rain not in the days of their prophecy: and they have power over waters, to turn them into blood and to strike the earth with all plagues, as often as they will.

7 And when they shall have finished their testimony, the beast that ascendeth out of the abyss shall make war against them and shall overcome them and kill them.

8 And their bodies shall lie in the streets of the great city which is called spiritually, Sodom and Egypt: where their Lord also was crucified.

9 And they of the tribes and peoples and tongues and nations shall see their bodies for three days and a half: and they shall not suffer their bodies to be laid in sepulchres.

10 And they that dwell upon the earth shall rejoice over them and make merry: and shall send gifts one to another, because these two prophets tormented them that dwelt upon the earth.

11 And after three days and a half, the spirit of life from God entered into them. And they stood upon their feet: and great fear fell upon them that saw them.

12 And they heard a great voice from heaven, saying to them: Come up hither. And they went up to heaven in a cloud: and their enemies saw them.

13 And at that hour there was made a great earthquake: and the tenth part of the city fell. And there were slain in the earthquake, names of men, seven thousand: and the rest were cast into a fear and gave glory to the God of heaven.

14 The second woe is past: and behold the third woe will come quickly.

15 And the seventh angel sounded the trumpet: and there were great voices in heaven, saying: The kingdom of this world is become our Lord's and his Christ's. And he shall reign for ever and ever. Amen.

16 And the four and twenty ancients who sit on their seats in the sight of God, fell on their faces and adored God, saying:

17 We give thee thanks, O Lord God Almighty, who art and who wast and who art to come: because thou hast taken to thee thy great power, and thou hast reigned.

18 And the nations were angry: and thy wrath is come. And the time of the dead, that they should be judged and that thou shouldest render reward to thy servants the prophets and the saints, and to them that fear thy name, little and great: and shouldest destroy them who have corrupted the earth.

19 And the temple of God was opened in heaven: and the ark of his testament was seen in his temple. And there were lightnings and voices and an earthquake and great hail.

CHAPTER 12

The vision of the woman clothed with the sun and of the great dragon her persecutor.

AND a great sign appeared in heaven: A woman clothed with the sun, and the moon under her feet, and on her head a crown of twelve stars.

2 And being with child, she cried travailing in birth: and was in pain to be delivered.

3 And there was seen another sign in heaven. And behold a great red dragon, having seven heads and ten horns and on his heads seven diadems.

4 And his tail drew the third part of the stars of heaven and cast them to the earth. And the dragon stood before the woman who was ready to be delivered: that, when she should be delivered, he might devour her son.

5 And she brought forth a man child, who was to rule all nations with an iron rod. And her son was taken up to God and to his throne.

6 And the woman fled into the wilderness, where she had a place prepared by God, that there they should feed her, a thousand two hundred sixty days.

7 And there was a great battle in heaven: Michael and his angels fought with the dragon, and the dragon fought, and his angels.

8 And they prevailed not: neither was their place found any more in heaven.

CHAP. 11. Ver. 3. *My two witnesses.* It is commonly understood of Henoch and Elias.

CHAP. 12. Ver. 1. *A woman.* The Church of God. It may also, by allusion, be applied to our Blessed Lady. The Church is clothed with the sun, that is, with Christ: she hath the moon, that is, the changeable things of the world, under her feet: and the twelve stars, with which she is crowned, are the twelve apostles. She is in labour and pain, whilst she brings forth her children, and Christ in them, in the midst of afflictions and persecutions.

9 And that great dragon was cast out, that old serpent, who is called the devil and Satan, who seduceth the whole world. And he was cast unto the earth: and his angels were thrown down with him.

10 And I heard a loud voice in heaven, saying: Now is come salvation and strength and the kingdom of our God and the power of his Christ: because the accuser of our brethren is cast forth, who accused them before our God day and night.

11 And they overcame him by the blood of the Lamb and by the word of the testimony: and they loved not their lives unto death.

12 Therefore, rejoice, O heavens, and you that dwell therein. Woe to the earth and to the sea, because the devil is come down unto you, having great wrath, knowing that he hath but a short time.

13 And when the dragon saw that he was cast unto the earth, he persecuted the woman who brought forth the man child.

14 And there were given to the woman two wings of a great eagle, that she might fly into the desert, unto her place, where she is nourished for a time and times and half a time, from the face of the serpent.

15 And the serpent cast out of his mouth, after the woman, water, as it were a river: that he might cause her to be carried away by the river.

16 And the earth helped the woman: and the earth opened her mouth and swallowed up the river which the dragon cast out of his mouth.

17 And the dragon was angry against the woman: and went to make war with the rest of her seed, who keep the com-

mandments of God and have the testimony of Jesus Christ.

18 And he stood upon the sand of the sea.

CHAPTER 13

Of the beast with seven heads and of a second beast.

AND I saw a beast coming up out of the sea, having seven heads and ten horns: and upon his horns, ten diadems: and upon his heads, names of blasphemy.

2 And the beast which I saw was like a leopard: and his feet were as the feet of a bear, and his mouth as the mouth of a lion. And the dragon gave him his own strength and great power.

3 And I saw one of his heads as it were slain to death: and his death's wound was healed. And all the earth was in admiration after the beast.

4 And they adored the dragon which gave power to the beast. And they adored the beast, saying: Who is like to the beast? And who shall be able to fight with him?

5 And there was given to him a mouth speaking great things and blasphemies: and power was given to him to do, two and forty months.

6 And he opened his mouth unto blasphemies against God, to blaspheme his name and his tabernacle and them that dwell in heaven.

7 And it was given unto him to make war with the saints and to overcome them. And power was given to him over every tribe and people and tongue and nation.

8 And all that dwell upon the earth adored him, whose names are not written in the book of life of the Lamb which was slain from the beginning of the world.

9 If any man have an ear, let him hear.

10 He that shall lead into captivity shall go into captivity: [1] he that shall kill by the sword must be killed by the sword. Here is the patience and the faith of the saints.

11 And I saw another beast coming up out of the earth: and he had two horns, like a lamb: and he spoke as a dragon.

12 And he executed all the power of the former beast in his sight. And he caused the earth and them that dwell therein to adore the first beast, whose wound to death was healed.

13 And he did great signs, so that he made also fire to come down from heaven unto the earth, in the sight of men.

14 And he seduced them that dwell

Ver. 15. *River.* Or, flood.

CHAP. 13. Ver. 1. *A beast.* This first beast, with seven heads and ten horns, is probably the whole company of infidels, enemies and persecutors of the people of God, from the beginning to the end of the world. The seven heads are seven kings, that is, seven principal kingdoms or empires, which have exercised, or shall exercise, tyrannical power over the people of God. Of these, five were then fallen: the Egyptian, Assyrian, Chaldean, Persian, and Grecian monarchies: one was present, the empire of Rome: and the seventh and chiefest was to come, the great Antichrist and his empire. The ten horns may be understood of ten lesser persecutors.

Ver. 3. *One of his heads.* Some understand this of the mortal wound which the idolatry of the Roman empire (signified by the sixth head) received from Constantine; which was, as it were, healed again by Julian the Apostate.

Ver. 6. *His tabernacle.* That is, his Church and his Saints.

Ver. 8. *Slain from the beginning.* In the foreknowledge of God; and inasmuch as all mercy and grace, from the beginning, was given in view of his death and passion.

Ver. 11. *Another beast.* This second beast with two horns may be understood of the heathenish priests and magicians, the principal promoters both of idolatry and persecution.

on the earth, for the signs which were given him to do in the sight of the beast: saying to them that dwell on the earth that they should make the image of the beast which had the wound by the sword and lived.

15 And it was given him to give life to the image of the beast: and that the image of the beast should speak: and should cause that whosoever will not adore the image of the beast should be slain.

16 And he shall make all, both little and great, rich and poor, freemen and bondmen, to have a character in their right hand or on their foreheads:

17 And that no man might buy or sell, but he that hath the character, or the name of the beast, or the number of his name.

18 Here is wisdom. He that hath understanding, let him count the number of the beast. For it is the number of a man: and the number of him is six hundred sixty-six.

CHAPTER 14

Of the Lamb and of the virgins that follow him. Of the judgments that shall fall upon the wicked.

AND I beheld: and lo a Lamb stood upon mount Sion, and with him an hundred forty-four thousand, having his name and the name of his Father written on their foreheads.

2 And I heard a voice from heaven, as the noise of many waters and as the voice of great thunder. And the voice which I heard was as the voice of harpers, harping on their harps.

3 And they sung as it were a new canticle, before the throne and before the four living creatures and the ancients: and no man could say the canticle, but those hundred forty-four thousand who were purchased from the earth.

4 These are they who were not defiled with women: for they are virgins. These follow the Lamb whithersoever he goeth. These were purchased from among men, the firstfruits to God and to the Lamb.

5 And in their mouth there was found no lie: for they are without spot before the throne of God.

6 And I saw another angel flying through the midst of heaven, having the eternal gospel, to preach unto them that sit upon the earth and over every nation and tribe and tongue and people:

7 Saying with a loud voice: Fear the Lord and give him honour, because the hour of his judgment is come. And adore ye him [1] that made heaven and earth, the sea and the fountains of waters.

8 And another angel followed, saying: [2] That great Babylon is fallen, is fallen; which made all nations to drink of the wine of the wrath of her fornication.

9 And the third angel followed them, saying with a loud voice: If any man shall adore the beast and his image and receive his character in his forehead or in his hand,

10 He also shall drink of the wine of the wrath of God, which is mingled with pure wine in the cup of his wrath: and shall be tormented with fire and brimstone in the sight of the holy angels and in the sight of the Lamb.

11 And the smoke of their torments shall ascend up for ever and ever: neither have they rest day nor night, who have adored the beast and his image and whoever receiveth the character of his name.

12 Here is the patience of the saints, who keep the commandments of God and the faith of Jesus.

13 And I heard a voice from heaven, saying to me: Write: Blessed are the dead who die in the Lord. From henceforth now, saith the Spirit, that they may rest from their labours. For their works follow them.

14 And I saw: and behold a white cloud and upon the cloud one sitting like to the Son of man, having on his head a crown of gold and in his hand a sharp sickle.

15 And another angel came out from the temple, crying with a loud voice to him that sat upon the cloud: [3] Thrust in thy sickle and reap, because the hour is come to reap. For the harvest of the earth is ripe.

16 And he that sat on the cloud thrust his sickle into the earth: and the earth was reaped.

17 And another angel came out of the temple which is in heaven, he also having a sharp sickle.

18 And another angel came out from the altar, who had power over fire. And he cried with a loud voice to him that had the sharp sickle, saying: Thrust in thy sharp sickle and gather the clus-

CHAP. 14. [1] Ps. 145, 6; Acts, 14, 14. [2] Isai. 21, 9; Jer. 51, 8. [3] Joel, 3, 13; Matt. 13, 39.

Ver. 18. *Six hundred sixty-six.* The numeral letters of his name shall make up this number.

CHAP. 14. Ver. 8. *Babylon.* By Babylon may be very probably signified all the wicked world in general, which God will punish and destroy after the short time of this mortal life: or it may signify every great city wherein enormous sins and abominations are daily committed; and that when the measure of its iniquities is full, the punishments due to its crimes are poured on it. It may also be some city of the description in the text, that will exist and be destroyed, as here described, towards the end of the world.

Ver. 13. *Die in the Lord.* It is understood of martyrs who die for the Lord.

ters of the vineyard of the earth, because the grapes thereof are ripe.

19 And the angel thrust in his sharp sickle into the earth and gathered the vineyard of the earth and cast it into the great press of the wrath of God:

20 And the press was trodden without the city, and blood came out of the press, up to the horses' bridles, for a thousand and six hundred furlongs.

CHAPTER 15

They that have overcome the beast glorify God. Of the seven angels with the seven vials.

AND I saw another sign in heaven, great and wonderful: seven angels having the seven last plagues. For in them is filled up the wrath of God.

2 And I saw as it were a sea of glass mingled with fire: and them that had overcome the beast and his image and the number of his name, standing on the sea of glass, having the harps of God:

3 And singing the canticle of Moses, the servant of God, and the canticle of the Lamb, saying: Great and wonderful are thy works, O Lord God Almighty. Just and true are thy ways, O King of ages.

4 [1] Who shall not fear thee, O Lord, and magnify thy name? For thou only art holy. For all nations shall come and shall adore in thy sight, because thy judgments are manifest.

5 And after these things, I looked: and behold, the temple of the tabernacle of the testimony in heaven was opened.

6 And the seven angels came out of the temple, having the seven plagues, clothed with clean and white linen and girt about the breasts with golden girdles.

7 And one of the four living creatures gave to the seven angels seven golden vials, full of the wrath of God, who liveth for ever and ever.

8 And the temple was filled with smoke from the majesty of God and from his power. And no man was able to enter into the temple, till the seven plagues of the seven angels were fulfilled.

CHAPTER 16

The seven vials are poured out. The plagues that ensue.

AND I heard a great voice out of the temple, saying to the seven angels: Go and pour out the seven vials of the wrath of God upon the earth.

2 And the first went and poured out his vial upon the earth. And there fell a sore and grievous wound upon men who had the character of the beast: and upon them that adored the image thereof.

3 And the second angel poured out his vial upon the sea. And there came blood as it were of a dead man: and every living soul died in the sea.

4 And the third poured out his vial upon the rivers and the fountains of waters. And there was made blood.

5 And I heard the angel of the waters saying: Thou art just, O Lord, who art and who wast, the Holy One, because thou hast judged these things.

6 For they have shed the blood of saints and prophets: and thou hast given them blood to drink. For they are worthy.

7 And I heard another, from the altar, saying: Yea, O Lord God Almighty, true and just are thy judgments.

8 And the fourth angel poured out his vial upon the sun. And it was given unto him to afflict men with heat and fire.

9 And men were scorched with great heat: and they blasphemed the name of God, who hath power over these plagues. Neither did they penance to give him glory.

10 And the fifth angel poured out his vial upon the seat of the beast. And his kingdom became dark: and they gnawed their tongues for pain.

11 And they blasphemed the God of heaven, because of their pains and wounds: and did not penance for their works.

12 And the sixth angel poured out his vial upon that great river Euphrates and dried up the water thereof, that a way might be prepared for the kings from the rising of the sun.

13 And I saw from the mouth of the dragon and from the mouth of the beast and from the mouth of the false prophet, three unclean spirits like frogs.

14 For they are the spirits of devils, working signs: and they go forth unto the kings of the whole earth, to gather them to battle against the great day of the Almighty God.

15 [1] Behold, I come as a thief. Blessed is he that watcheth and keepeth his garments, lest he walk naked, and they see his shame.

16 And he shall gather them together into a place which in Hebrew is called Armagedon.

17 And the seventh angel poured out his vial upon the air. And there came a great voice out of the temple from the throne, saying: It is done.

CHAP. 15. [1] Jer. 10, 7. CHAP. 16. [1] Matt. 24, 43; Luke, 12, 39; Apoc. 3, 3.

CHAP. 16. Ver. 16. *Armagedon.* That is, the hill of robbers.

18 And there were lightnings and voices and thunders: and there was a great earthquake, such an one as never had been since men were upon the earth, such an earthquake, so great.

19 And the great city was divided into three parts: and the cities of the Gentiles fell. And great Babylon came in remembrance before God, to give her the cup of the wine of the indignation of his wrath.

20 And every island fled away: and the mountains were not found.

21 And great hail, like a talent, came down from heaven upon men: and men blasphemed God, for the plague of the hail: because it was exceeding great.

CHAPTER 17

The description of the great harlot and of the beast upon which she sits.

AND there came one of the seven angels who had the seven vials and spoke with me, saying: Come, I will shew thee the condemnation of the great harlot, who sitteth upon many waters:

2 With whom the kings of the earth have committed fornication. And they who inhabit the earth have been made drunk with the wine of her whoredom.

3 And he took me away in spirit into the desert. And I saw a woman sitting upon a scarlet coloured beast, full of names of blasphemy, having seven heads and ten horns.

4 And the woman was clothed round about with purple and scarlet, and gilt with gold and precious stones and pearls, having a golden cup in her hand, full of the abomination and filthiness of her fornication.

5 And on her forehead a name was written: A mystery: Babylon the great, the mother of the fornications and the abominations of the earth.

6 And I saw the woman drunk with the blood of the saints and with the blood of the martyrs of Jesus. And I wondered, when I had seen her, with great admiration.

7 And the angel said to me: Why dost thou wonder? I will tell thee the mystery of the woman and of the beast which carrieth her, which hath the seven heads and ten horns.

8 The beast which thou sawest, was, and is not, and shall come up out of the bottomless pit and go into destruction. And the inhabitants on the earth (whose names are not written in the book of life from the foundation of the world) shall wonder, seeing the beast that was and is not.

9 And here is the understanding that hath wisdom. The seven heads are seven mountains, upon which the woman sitteth: and they are seven kings.

10 Five are fallen, one is, and the other is not yet come: and when he is come, he must remain a short time.

11 And the beast which was and is not: the same also is the eighth, and is of the seven, and goeth into destruction.

12 And the ten horns which thou sawest are ten kings, who have not yet received a kingdom: but shall receive power as kings, one hour after the beast.

13 These have one design: and their strength and power they shall deliver to the beast.

14 These shall fight with the Lamb, And the Lamb shall overcome them, because he is Lord of lords and King of kings: and they that are with him are called and elect and faithful.

15 And he said to me: The waters which thou sawest, where the harlot sitteth, are peoples and nations and tongues.

16 And the ten horns which thou sawest in the beast: These shall hate the harlot and shall make her desolate and naked and shall eat her flesh and shall burn her with fire.

17 For God hath given into their hearts to do that which pleaseth him: that they give their kingdom to the beast, till the words of God be fulfilled.

18 And the woman which thou sawest is the great city which hath kingdom over the kings of the earth.

CHAPTER 18

The fall of Babylon. Kings and merchants lament over her.

AND after these thngs, I saw another angel come down from

CHAP. 17. ¹ 1 Tim. 6, 15; Apoc. 19, 16.

CHAP. 17. Ver. 5. *A mystery.* That is, a secret; because what follows of the name and title of the great harlot is to be taken in a mystical sense.—*Babylon.* Either the city of the devil in general; or, if this place be to be understood of any particular city, *pagan Rome,* which then and for three hundred years persecuted the church and was the principal seat both of empire and idolatry.

Ver. 8. *The beast which thou sawest.* This beast which supports Babylon may signify the power of the devil: *which was and is not,* being much limited by the coming of Christ, but shall again exert itself under Antichrist. The seven heads of this beast are seven mountains or empires, instruments of his tyranny; of which five were then fallen (see chap. 13, 1, and below, ver. 10). The beast itself is said to be *the eighth, and is of the seven;* because they all act under the devil and by his instigation, so that his power is in them all, yet so as to make up, as it were, an eighth empire, distinct from them all.

Ver. 12. *Ten kings.* Ten lesser kingdoms, enemies also of the Church of Christ; which, nevertheless, shall be made instruments of the justice of God for the punishment of Babylon. Some understand this of the Goths, Vandals, Huns, and other barbarous nations that destroyed the empire of Rome.

heaven, having great power: and the earth was enlightened with his glory.

2 And he cried out with a strong voice, saying: [1] Babylon the great is fallen, is fallen: and is become the habitation of devils and the hold of every unclean spirit and the hold of every unclean and hateful bird:

3 Because all nations have drunk of the wine of the wrath of her fornication; and the kings of the earth have committed fornication with her; and the merchants of the earth have been made rich by the power of her delicacies.

4 And I heard another voice from heaven, saying: Go out from her, my people; that you be not partakers of her sins and that you receive not of her plagues.

5 For her sins have reached unto heaven: and the Lord hath remembered her iniquities.

6 Render to her as she also hath rendered to you: and double unto her double, according to her works. In the cup wherein she hath mingled, mingle ye double unto her.

7 As much as she hath glorified herself and lived in delicacies, so much torment and sorrow give ye to her. Because she saith in her heart: [2] I sit a queen and am no widow: and sorrow I shall not see.

8 Therefore, shall her plagues come in one day, death and mourning and famine. And she shall be burnt with the fire: because God is strong, who shall judge her.

9 And the kings of the earth, who have committed fornication and lived in delicacies with her, shall weep and bewail themselves over her, when they shall see the smoke of her burning:

10 Standing afar off for fear of her torments, saying: Alas! alas! that great city, Babylon, that mighty city: for in one hour is thy judgment come.

11 And the merchants of the earth shall weep and mourn over her: for no man shall buy their merchandise any more.

12 Merchandise of gold and silver and precious stones: and of pearls and fine linen and purple and silk and scarlet: and all thyine wood: and all manner of vessels of ivory: and all manner of vessels of precious stone and of brass and of iron and of marble:

13 And cinnamon and odours and ointment and frankincense and wine and oil and fine flour and wheat and beasts and sheep and horses and chariots: and slaves and souls of men.

14 And the fruits of the desire of thy soul are departed from thee: and all fat and goodly things are perished from thee. And they shall find them no more at all.

15 The merchants of these things, who were made rich, shall stand afar off from her, for fear of her torments, weeping and mourning,

16 And saying: Alas! alas! that great city, which was clothed with fine linen and purple and scarlet and was gilt with gold and precious stones and pearls.

17 For in one hour are so great riches come to nought. And every shipmaster and all that sail into the lake and mariners, and as many as work in the sea, stood afar off,

18 And cried, seeing the place of her burning, saying: What city is like to this great city?

19 And they cast dust upon their heads and cried, weeping and mourning, saying: Alas! alas! that great city, wherein all were made rich, that had ships at sea, by reason of her prices. For, in one hour she is made desolate.

20 Rejoice over her, thou heaven and ye holy apostles and prophets. For God hath judged your judgment on her.

21 And a mighty angel took up a stone, as it were a great millstone, and cast it into the sea, saying: With such violence as this, shall Babylon, that great city, be thrown down and shall be found no more at all.

22 And the voice of harpers and of musicians and of them that play on the pipe and on the trumpet shall no more be heard at all in thee: and no craftsman of any art whatsoever shall be found any more at all in thee: and the sound of the mill shall be heard no more at all in thee:

23 And the light of the lamp shall shine no more at all in thee: and the voice of the bridegroom and the bride shall be heard no more at all in thee. For thy merchants were the great men of the earth: for all nations have been deceived by thy enchantments.

24 And in her was found the blood of prophets and of saints and of all that were slain upon the earth.

CHAPTER 19

The saints glorify God for his judgments on the great harlot. Christ's victory over the beast and the kings of the earth.

AFTER these things, I heard as it were the voice of much people in heaven, saying: Alleluia. Salvation and glory and power is to our God.

2 For true and just are his judgments, who hath judged the great har-

---

CHAP. 18. [1] Isai. 21, 9; Jer. 51, 8; Apoc. 14, 8.
[2] Isai. 47, 8.

lot which corrupted the earth with her fornication and hath revenged the blood of his servants, at her hands.

3 And again they said: Alleluia. And her smoke ascendeth for ever and ever.

4 And the four and twenty ancients and the four living creatures fell down and adored God that sitteth upon the throne, saying: Amen. Alleluia.

5 And a voice came out from the throne, saying: Give praise to our God, all ye his servants: and you that fear him, little and great.

6 And I heard as it were the voice of a great multitude, and as the voice of many waters, and as the voice of great thunders, saying: Alleluia: for the Lord our God, the Almighty, hath reigned.

7 Let us be glad and rejoice and give glory to him. For the marriage of the Lamb is come: and his wife hath prepared herself.

8 And it is granted to her that she should clothe herself with fine linen, glittering and white. For the fine linen are the justifications of saints.

9 And he said to me: Write: ¹ Blessed are they that are called to the marriage supper of the Lamb. And he saith to me: These words of God are true.

10 And I fell down before his feet, to adore him. And he saith to me: See thou do it not. I am thy fellow servant and of thy brethren who have the testimony of Jesus. Adore God. For the testimony of Jesus is the spirit of prophecy.

11 And I saw heaven opened: and behold a white horse. And he that sat upon him was called faithful and true: and with justice doth he judge and fight.

12 And his eyes were as a flame of fire: and on his head were many diadems. And he had a name written, which no man knoweth but himself.

13 ² And he was clothed with a garment sprinkled with blood. And his name is called: THE WORD OF GOD.

14 And the armies that are in heaven followed him on white horses, clothed in fine linen, white and clean.

15 And out of his mouth proceedeth a sharp two-edged sword, that with it he may strike the nations. ³ And he shall rule them with a rod of iron: and he treadeth the winepress of the fierceness of the wrath of God the Almighty.

16 And he hath on his garment and on his thigh written: ⁴ KING OF KINGS AND LORD OF LORDS.

17 And I saw an angel standing in the sun: and he cried with a loud voice, saying to all the birds that did fly through the midst of heaven: Come,

gather yourselves together to the great supper of God:

18 That you may eat the flesh of kings and the flesh of tribunes and the flesh of mighty men and the flesh of horses and of them that sit on them: and the flesh of all freemen and bondmen and of little and of great.

19 And I saw the beast and the kings of the earth and their armies, gathered together to make war with him that sat upon the horse and with his army.

20 And the beast was taken, and with him the false prophet who wrought signs before him, wherewith he seduced them who received the character of the beast and who adored his image. These two were cast alive into the pool of fire, burning with brimstone.

21 And the rest were slain by the sword of him that sitteth upon the horse, which proceedeth out of his mouth: and all the birds were filled with their flesh.

CHAPTER 20

Satan is bound for a thousand years. The souls of the martyrs reign with Christ in the first resurrection. The last attempts of Satan against the church. The last judgment.

AND I saw an angel coming down from heaven, having the key of the bottomless pit and a great chain in his hand.

2 And he laid hold on the dragon, the old serpent, which is the devil and Satan, and bound him for a thousand years.

3 And he cast him into the bottomless pit and shut him up and set a seal upon him, that he should no more seduce the nations till the thousand years be finished. And after that, he must be loosed a little time.

CHAP. 19. ¹ Matt. 22, 2; Luke, 14, 16. ² Isai. 63, 1. ³ Ps. 2, 9. ⁴ 1 Tim. 6, 15; Apoc. 17, 14.

CHAP. 19. Ver. 10. *I fell down before.* St. Augustine is of opinion that this angel appeared in so glorious a manner that St. John took him to be God; and therefore would have given him *divine honour,* had not the angel stopped him by telling him he was but his fellow servant. St. Gregory rather thinks that the veneration offered by St. John was not divine honour, or indeed any other than what might lawfully be given; but was nevertheless refused by the angel, in consideration of the dignity to which our human nature had been raised by the Incarnation of the Son of God and the dignity of St. John, an apostle, prophet and martyr.

CHAP. 20. Ver. 2. *Bound him.* The power of Satan has been very much limited by the Passion of Christ. For a *thousand years;* that is, for the whole time of the New Testament: but especially from the time of the destruction of *Babylon* or pagan Rome, till the new efforts of *Gog* and *Magog* against the church, towards the end of the world. During which time, the souls of the martyrs and saints live and reign with Christ in heaven, in the *first resurrection,* which is that of the soul to the life of glory; as the *second resurrection* will be that of the body, at the day of the general judgment.

4 And I saw seats. And they sat upon them: and judgment was given unto them. And the souls of them that were beheaded for the testimony of Jesus and for the word of God and who had not adored the beast nor his image nor received his character on their foreheads or in their hands. And they lived and reigned with Christ a thousand years.

5 The rest of the dead lived not, till the thousand years were finished. This is the first resurrection.

6 Blessed and holy is he that hath part in the first resurrection. In these the second death hath no power. But they shall be priests of God and of Christ: and shall reign with him a thousand years.

7 And when the thousand years shall be finished, Satan shall be loosed out of his prison and shall go forth and seduce the nations which are over the four quarters of the earth, [1] Gog and Magog: and shall gather them together to battle, the number of whom is as the sand of the sea.

8 And they came upon the breadth of the earth and encompassed the camp of the saints and the beloved city.

9 And there came down fire from God out of heaven and devoured them: and the devil, who seduced them, was cast into the pool of fire and brimstone, where both the beast

10 And the false prophet shall be tormented day and night for ever and ever.

11 And I saw a great white throne and one sitting upon it, from whose face the earth and heaven fled away: and there was no place found for them.

12 And I saw the dead, great and small, standing in the presence of the throne. And the books were opened: and another book was opened, which was the book of life. And the dead were judged by those things which were written in the books, according to their works.

13 And the sea gave up the dead that were in it: and death and hell gave up their dead that were in them. And they were judged, every one according to their works.

14 And hell and death were cast into the pool of fire. This is the second death.

15 And whosoever was not found written in the book of life was cast into the pool of fire.

CHAP. 20. [1] Ezech. 38, 14. CHAP. 21, [1] Isai. 65, 17; 66, 22; 2 Peter, 3, 13. [2] Isai. 25, 8; Apoc. 7, 17. [3] Isai. 43, 19; 2 Cor. 5, 17.

CHAP. 21. Ver. 1. *The first heaven and the first earth was gone*, being changed, not as to their substance, but in their qualities.

CHAPTER 21

The new Jerusalem described.

AND [1] I saw a new heaven and a new earth. For the first heaven and the first earth was gone: and the sea is now no more.

2 And I, John, saw the holy city, the new Jerusalem, coming down out of heaven from God, prepared as a bride adorned for her husband.

3 And I heard a great voice from the throne, saying: Behold the tabernacle of God with men: and he will dwell with them. And they shall be his people: and God himself with them shall be their God.

4 [2] And God shall wipe away all tears from their eyes: and death shall be no more. Nor mourning, nor crying, nor sorrow shall be any more: for the former things are passed away.

5 And he that sat on the throne, said: [3] Behold, I make all things new. And he said to me: Write. For these words are most faithful and true.

6 And he said to me: It is done. I am Alpha and Omega: the Beginning and the End. To him that thirsteth, I will give of the fountain of the water of life, freely.

7 He that shall overcome shall possess these things. And I will be his God: and he shall be my son.

8 But the fearful and unbelieving and the abominable and murderers and whoremongers and sorcerers and idolaters and all liars, they shall have their portion in the pool burning with fire and brimstone, which is the second death.

9 And there came one of the seven angels, who had the vials full of the seven last plagues, and spoke with me, saying: Come and I will shew thee the bride, the wife of the Lamb.

10 And he took me up in spirit to a great and high mountain: and he shewed me the holy city Jerusalem, coming down out of heaven from God,

11 Having the glory of God. And the light thereof was like to a precious stone, even as crystal.

12 And it had a wall great and high, having twelve gates, and in the gates twelve angels, and names written thereon, which are the names of the twelve tribes of the children of Israel.

13 On the east, three gates: and on the north, three gates: and on the south, three gates: and on the west, three gates.

14 And the wall of the city had twelve foundations: and in them, the twelve names of the twelve apostles of the Lamb.

15 And he that spoke with me had a measure of a reed of gold, to measure the city and the gates thereof and the wall.

16 And the city lieth in a foursquare: and the length thereof is as great as the breadth. And he measured the city with the golden reed for twelve thousand furlongs: and the length and the height and the breadth thereof are equal.

17 And he measured the wall thereof, an hundred forty-four cubits, the measure of a man, which is of an angel.

18 And the building of the wall thereof was of jasper stone: but the city itself pure gold, like to clear glass.

19 And the foundations of the wall of the city were adorned with all manner of precious stones. The first foundation was jasper: the second, sapphire: the third, a chalcedony: the fourth, an emerald:

20 The fifth, sardonyx: the sixth, sardius: the seventh, chrysolite: the eighth, beryl: the ninth, a topaz: the tenth, a chrysoprasus: the eleventh, a jacinth: the twelfth, an amethyst.

21 And the twelve gates are twelve pearls, one to each: and every several gate was of one several pearl. And the street of the city was pure gold, as it were, transparent glass.

22 And I saw no temple therein. For the Lord God Almighty is the temple thereof, and the Lamb.

23 [4] And the city hath no need of the sun, nor of the moon, to shine in it. For the glory of God hath enlightened it: and the Lamb is the lamp thereof.

24 And the nations shall walk in the light of it: and the kings of the earth shall bring their glory and honour into it.

25 [5] And the gates thereof shall not be shut by day: for there shall be no night there.

26 And they shall bring the glory and honour of the nations into it.

27 There shall not enter into it any thing defiled or that worketh abomination or maketh a lie: but they that are written in the book of life of the Lamb.

CHAPTER 22

The water and tree of life. The conclusion.

AND he shewed me a river of water of life, clear as crystal, proceeding from the throne of God and of the Lamb.

2 In the midst of the street thereof, and on both sides of the river, *was* the tree of life, bearing twelve fruits, yielding its fruits every month: and the leaves of the tree were for the healing of the nations.

3 And there shall be no curse any more: but the throne of God and of the Lamb shall be in it. And his servants shall serve him.

4 And they shall see his face: and his name shall be on their foreheads.

5 [1] And night shall be no more. And they shall not need the light of the lamp, nor the light of the sun, because the Lord God shall enlighten them. And they shall reign for ever and ever.

6 And he said to me: These words are most faithful and true. And the Lord God of the spirits of the prophets sent his angel to shew his servant the things which must be done shortly.

7 And: Behold I come quickly. Blessed is he that keepeth the words of the prophecy of this book.

8 And I, John, who have heard and seen these things. And, after I had heard and seen, I fell down to adore before the feet of the angel who shewed me these things.

9 And he said to me: See thou do it not. For I am thy fellow servant, and of thy brethren the prophets and of them that keep the words of the prophecy of this book. Adore God.

10 And he saith to me: Seal not the words of the prophecy of this book. For the time is at hand.

11 He that hurteth, let him hurt still:

[4] Isai. 60, 19. [5] Isai. 60, 11. CHAP. 22. [1] Isai. 60, 20.

Ver. 17. *The measure of a man.* That is, *According to the measure of men, and used by the angel.* This seems to be the true meaning of these words.

CHAP. 22. Ver. 10. *For the time is at hand.* That is, when compared to eternity, all time and temporal things vanish and are but of short duration. As to the time when the chief predictions should come to pass, we have no certainty, as appears by the different opinions, both of the ancient fathers and late interpreters. Many think that most things set down from the fourth chapter to the end will not be fulfilled till a little time before the end of the world. Others are of opinion that a great part of them, and particularly the fall of the wicked Babylon, happened at the destruction of paganism, by the destruction of heathen Rome and its persecuting heathen emperors. In fine, others think that St. John's design was in a mystical way, by metaphors and allegories, to represent the attempts and persecutions of the wicked against the servants of God, the punishments that should in a short time fall upon Babylon, that is, upon all the wicked in general: the eternal happiness and reward, which God had reserved for his pious inhabitants of Jerusalem, that is, for his faithful servants, after their short trials and the tribulations of this mortal life. In the mean time, we meet with many profitable instructions and admonitions, which we may easily enough understand: but we have no certainty, when we apply these predictions to particular events: for as St. Jerome takes notice, the Apocalypse has as many mysteries as words, or rather mysteries in every word.

Ver. 11. *Let him hurt still.* It is not an exhortation, or license to go on in sin; but an intimation, that, how far soever the wicked may proceed, their progress shall quickly end, and then they must expect to meet with proportionable punishments.

and he that is filthy, let him be filthy still: and he that is just, let him be justified still: and he that is holy, let him be sanctified still.

12 Behold, I come quickly: and my reward is with me, to render to every man according to his works.

13 [2] I am Alpha and Omega, the First and the Last, the Beginning and the End.

14 Blessed are they that wash their robes in the blood of the Lamb: that they may have a right to the tree of life and may enter in by the gates into the city.

15 Without are dogs and sorcerers and unchaste and murderers and servers of idols and every one that loveth and maketh a lie.

16 I, Jesus, have sent my angel, to testify to you these things in the

[2] Isai. 41, 4; 44, 6; 48, 12; Apoc. 1, 8; 21, 6.
[3] Isai. 55, 1.

churches. I am the root and stock of David, the bright and morning star.

17 And the spirit and the bride say: Come. And he that heareth, let him say: Come. And he that thirsteth, let him come. [3] And he that will, let him take the water of life, freely.

18 For I testify to every one that heareth the words of the prophecy of this book: If any man shall add to these things, God shall add unto him the plagues written in this book.

19 And if any man shall take away from the words of the book of this prophecy, God shall take away his part out of the book of life, and out of the holy city, and from these things that are written in this book.

20 He that giveth testimony of these things, saith: Surely, I come quickly: Amen. Come, Lord Jesus.

21 The grace of our Lord Jesus Christ be with you all. Amen.

THE END OF THE NEW TESTAMENT.